WHO WAS WHO WHO ON SCREEN

WHO WAS WHO ON SCREEN

EVELYN MACK TRUITT

65754

R. R. BOWKER COMPANY

A Xerox Education Company
New York & London 1974

Published by R. R. Bowker Co. (A Xerox Education Company)
1180 Avenue of the Americas, New York, N.Y. 10036

Library of Congress Cataloging in Publication Data

Truitt, Evelyn Mack, 1931-
   Who was who on screen.

   Bibliography: p.
   1. Moving-picture actors and actresses—Biography.
I. Title.
PN1998.A2T73   791.43′028′0922 [B]   74-4325
ISBN 0-8352-0719-6

This book is dedicated to all my friends,
and especially to my boss, who "tolerated"
me during this literary effort.

PREFACE

This book is a collection of facts—over a million or so of them — unobtainable from any other single source. It covers over 6,000 screen personalities, primarily American, British, and French, who died between the years 1920 and 1971. To gather the information contained within these pages, the researcher, movie buff, or member of the audience would normally have to consult 25 or more sources, many of them almost inaccessible, and then resolve the problem of almost as much conflicting data.

Who Was Who on Screen is concerned with the players, not only stars but less familiar supporting names. Also listed are persons who appeared on screen but are better known for their achievements in other fields: athlete Jim Thorpe, newscaster Edward R. Murrow, and author James MacArthur, for example. Animal performers are not forgotten, and the efforts of Rin Tin Tin (Sr. and Jr.), Trigger, and others are recognized. Because screen appearances are what this book is all about, directors, producers, and other behind-the-scene luminaries are included only if they also appeared in front of the camera.

For ease of reference, performers are listed alphabetically. Each entry is comprised of a brief biographical sketch, including birth, death, and marriage information, together with a *complete* list of screen credits if available, rather than the summary or highlighted version found in most reference works.

To assure accuracy, all reference sources have been cross-checked and vital records and living sources consulted whenever possible. Today it is impossible for two active members of the Screen Actors Guild to have the same name, but this was not the case years ago. Without the kind assistance of Mrs. Frances Delmar, widow of Victor Daniels (Chief Thundercloud), and Mrs. Anne Bauer, widow of Scott T. Williams (the other Chief Thundercloud), it would not have been possible to accurately credit each actor. Harry Houdini was actually born on March 24, 1874 according to his biographer Milbourne Christopher. However, perhaps to give him the security of American citizenship, Houdini's parents told him he was born April 6, 1874 in Appleton, Wisconsin, and the latter date and place are indicated in practically all reference sources.

Also clarified is the confusion arising from a single film being released two or more times, often under different titles. For example, in 1949 a film was made in Britain under the title "Mad Little Island," renamed "Whiskey Galore," and released in the United States as "Tight Little Island." The British then made and released a totally different "Mad Little Island" in 1958. Even the most painstaking research, however, has left some information open to question. For example, for Pearl White there remains the enigma of birth dates of 1889, 1893, or 1897 and for Sophie Tucker alternate birth places of Russia or Boston. In such instances where the conflicting information could not be resolved, all the data and their sources are mentioned. Any data supplementing or correcting the information herein is welcome and should be submitted to me via the publisher.

For consistency, *Film Daily* has been used for all release dates, thus avoiding the discrepancy of East Coast vs. West Coast and foreign opening dates. And, because all early films were short in length — anywhere from one to four reels — only after 1920 are shorts distinguished from features. For purposes of this book a short is defined as any film less than five reels and a feature as five reels or more.

In sum, the purpose of this book is to provide you, the researcher, movie buff, or member of the audience, facts at your fingertips — completely and accurately.

I wish to thank first, Carol Cullen, my dear friend, neighbor, research assistant, and now expert on motion picture history; the Academy of Motion Pictures Arts & Sciences Library (DeWitt Bodeen, Mildred Simpson, Bonnie Rothbart); Mrs. Scott T. Williams Bauer; Darlene Blix; Margaret Breckenridge; Lois Burson; Don Canady; Cathy Conti; Mrs. Victor Daniels (Mrs. Frances Delmar Daniels); Brenda Forbes; Suzanne Goodwin; Abel Green; Michael P. Kelly; Elaine Langwell; Bobby Lopez; Chris Swan Lopez; Janet Louks; Larry Edmunds Book Shop, Inc.; Pat McDonald; William Schaefer; Jan Stevenson; Katherine Stinson; Bob Swanson; Diane Tilgren; Zoe Voigtsberg Truitt; Bill Wallace; Frances Walrabenstein; Maurine Westerson; and finally, my dear friend, Charles Pollack, who convinced me to get this project from the hobby stage to reference book status.

E.M.T.

ABBE, CHARLES S.
Born: 1860. Died: June 16, 1932, Darien, Conn.(blood poisoning). Screen and stage actor.

Appeared in: 1915 Niobe. 1921 Cappy Ricks; The Conquest of Canaan. 1922 Back Home and Broke. 1923 Homeward Bound. 1924 West of the Water Tower.

ABBOTT, AL
Born: 1884. Died: Sept. 4, 1962, Reseda, Calif.(heart attack). Screen and vaudeville actor.

Appeared in: 1929 Small Town's Ramblers (short).

ABBOTT, FRANK
Born: 1879. Died: 1957, Los Angeles, Calif. Screen actor. Entered films during early silents.

Appeared in: 1925 The Wild Bull's Lair.

ABBOTT, JAMES FRANCIS
Born: 1873. Died: Jan. 19, 1954, North Hollywood, Calif. Screen actor.

ABEL, ALBERT
Born: 1865, Germany. Died: Dec. 12, 1937, Berlin, Germany. Screen actor known as "The Lewis Stone of German pictures."

Appeared in: 1937 Boxes on the Ear.

ABURTO, ARMANDO
Born: 1910, Mexico. Died: July 1, 1955, Mexico City, Mexico. Screen and stage actor.

ACCORD, ART
Born: 1890, Stillwater, Minn. Died: Jan. 4, 1931, Chihuahua, Mexico (suicide-poison). Screen actor. Entered films in 1912. Divorced from actresses Edythe Sterling and Louise Lorraine.

Appeared in: 1914 The Squaw Man. 1915 A Man Afraid of His Wardrobe. 1920 The Moon Riders (serial). 1921 The White Horseman (serial); Winners of the West (serial). 1922 In the Days of Buffalo Bill (serial). 1923 The Oregon Trail (serial). 1924 Fighting for Justice; Looped for Life. 1925 The Scrappin' Kid; The Call of Courage; Three in Exile; The Circus Cyclone; Pals; Triple Action; The Wild Girl. 1926 Lazy Lightning; The Man from the West; The Ridin' Rascal; Rustler's Ranch; The Set-Up; The Silent Guardian; Sky High Corral; The Terror; Western Pluck. 1927 Hard Fists; Loco Luck; Set Free; Spurs and Saddles; The Western Rover. 1928 Two Gun O'Brien. 1929 The Arizona Kid; Bullets and Justice; Fighters of the Saddle; An Oklahoma Cowboy; The White Outlaw; Wyoming Tornado.

ACKERMAN, WALTER
Born: 1881. Died: Dec. 12, 1938, Hollywood, Calif. Screen actor. Entered films in 1907.

Appeared in: 1925 Rugged Water. 1926 Man of the Forest. 1927 Aflame in the Sky; Back to God's Country. 1929 Bride of the Desert.

ACUFF, EDDIE
Born: 1908, Caruthersville, Mo. Died: Dec. 17, 1956, Hollywood, Calif.(heart attack). Screen and stage actor.

Appeared in: 1935 I Found Stella Parish; Shipmates Forever; Miss Pacific Fleet. 1936 The Petrified Forest; The Black Legion; Crash Donovan; Boulder Dam; The Law in Her Hands; Jail Break; The Case of the Velvet Claws; The Golden Arrow; The Walking Dead. 1937 Talent Scout; The Go-Getter; The Outer Gate; They Won't Forget; The Singing Marine; Love Is On the Air; Without Warning; The Missing Witness; Hollywood Hotel; Back in Circulation; What Price Vengeance; Laughing at Trouble; Guns of the Pecos; Behind Prison Bars. 1938 Four Daughters; Smashing the Rackets; Law of the Underworld; She Loved a Fireman; Ladies in Distress; Rhythm of the Saddle; The Invisible Menace. 1939 The Mysterious Miss X; Rough Riders' Roundup; Two Bright Boys; Cowboy Quarterback; Meet Doctor Christian; Backfire; Lawyer Woman. 1940 Shooting High; Cafe Hostess; One Night in the Tropics; The Boys from Syracuse; Texas Rangers Ride Again; Blondie Goes Latin; The Great American Broadcast; The People vs. Dr. Kildare; Here Comes Happiness; Rags to Riches; Blondie for Victory; Hellzapoppin. 1942 Dr. Gillespie's New Assistant; Pardon My Sarong; Mr. District Attorney in the Carter Case; The Traitor Within; The Lady is Willing; Dr. Kildare's Victory; Mississippi Gambler; Girl Trouble; War against Mrs. Hadley; Army Surgeon. 1943 He Hired the Boss; Headin' for God's Country; Guadalcanal Diary. 1944 Carolina Blues; South of Dixie; Weekend Pass; In the Meantime, Darling; It Happened Tomorrow. 1945 Sergeant Mike; The Hidden Eye; She Gets Her Man; Don Juan Quilligan; Diamond Horseshoe; Honeymoon Ahead; Her Lucky Night; Leave It to Blondie; Shadow of Terror; Jungle Captive. 1946 The Notorious Lone Wolf; Flying Serpent; Wake up and Dream; Night Train to Memphis. 1947 Bandits of Dark Canyon; Blondie's Holiday; Buck Privates Come Home; Bells of San Angelo; Helldorado; Blondie's Big Moment; Swing the Western Way; Blondie in the Dough; Slippy McGee. 1948 Blondie's Big Deal; Blondie's Reward.

ADAIR, JACK
Born: 1894. Died: Sept. 22, 1940, Hollywood, Calif. Screen actor.

Appeared in: 1935 Peter Ibbetson. 1936 Lady Be Careful. 1937 52nd Street; Manhattan Merry-Go-Round.

ADAIR, JEAN
Born: 1873. Died: May 11, 1953, New York, N.Y. Screen, stage, and vaudeville actress.

Appeared in: 1922 In the Name of the Law. 1933 Advice to the Lovelorn. 1944 Arsenic and Old Lace. 1946 Something in the Wind. 1947 Living in a Big Way.

ADAIR, JOHN
Born: 1885. Died: Jan. 22, 1952, New York. Screen, stage, radio, and television actor.

Appeared in: 1936 Muss 'Em Up. 1940 The Ramparts We Watch.

ADAIR, ROBERT
Born: Jan. 3, 1900, San Francisco, Calif. Died: Aug. 10, 1954, London, England. Screen, stage, television, and vaudeville actor.

Appeared in: 1925 Raffles. 1930 Journey's End. 1933 King of the Jungle; The Kiss Before the Mirror. 1935 Where Sinners Meet; Limehouse Blues. 1935 The Crusades; The Last Outpost; Peter Ibbetson; The Girl Who Came Back. 1937 The Prince and the Pauper. 1950 Silk Noose. 1953 Norman Conquest. 1955 Eight O'Clock Walk.

ADAMS, EDITH
Born: 1879. Died: Jan. 10, 1957, New York, N.Y. Screen and stage actress.

ADAMS, ERNEST S.
Born: 1885. Died: Nov. 26, 1947, Hollywood, Calif. Screen and stage actor.

Appeared in: 1919 A Regular Girl. 1924 Curlytop; Hutch of the U.S.A.; The Beloved Brute. 1925 The Best People; The Pony Express; Where the Worst Begins. 1926 Hair Trigger Baxter; The Jazz Girl; Pals in Paradise; The Valley of Bravery; The Black Bird. 1927 Jewels of Desire; The Main Event; Men of Daring; The Gay Defender; Nevada; Melting Millions (serial). 1928 So This is Love; Stool Pigeon; What a Night; A Woman's Way; Tenth Avenue. 1929 One Splendid Hour; The Saturday Night Kid. 1930 The Fighting Legion; Shadow Ranch; The Storm; For the Defense. 1931 The Gang Buster; The Tip Off. 1932 Panama Flo; The Big Broadcast; Hold 'Em Jail. 1933 West of Singapore; Breed of the Border; Secrets of Hollywood. 1934 Here Comes the Groom; We're Not Dressing. 1935 Men of the Hour; The Perfect Clue. 1936 Three on the Trail; Hopalong Cassidy Returns. 1937 San Quentin; Hopalong Rides Again; Stars over Arizona; Colorado Kid; Two Gun Law. 1938 The Purple Vigilantes; The Painted Trail. 1939 Trigger Pals. 1940 The Man with Nine Lives. 1941 The Invisible Ghost. 1942 The Pride of the Yankees; Cactus Makes Perfect (short). 1947 The Perils of Pauline; The Pretender; Buck Privates Come Home.

ADAMS, HOWARD
Born: 1909. Died: Sept. 29, 1936, Chicago, Ill.(plane crash). Screen actor, film director, and radio announcer.

ADAMS, KATHRYN
Born: 1894. Died: Feb. 17, 1959, Hollywood, Calif. Screen actress.

Appeared in: 1920 The Forbidden Woman; The Best of Luck. 1921 The Silver Car. 1922 The Man from Downing Street. 1924 Borrowed Husbands. 1925 Pampered Youth. 1931 The Squaw Man. 1939 Fifth Avenue Girl. 1940 Argentine Nights; If I Had My Way; Ski Patrol; Black Diamonds. 1941 The Invisible Woman; Bachelor Daddy; Meet the Chump; Unfinished Business; Saboteur.

ADAMS, NICK (Nicholas Aloysius Adamshock)
Born: July 10, 1932, Nanticoke, Pa. Died: Feb. 5, 1968, Beverly Hills, Calif.(drug overdose). Screen and television actor. Nominated for Academy Award as Best Supporting Actor in 1963 for Twilight of Honor.

Appeared in: 1952 Somebody Loves Me. 1955 Rebel without a Cause; Strange Lady in Town; Picnic; The Jagged Edge; Mr. Roberts. 1956 Our Miss Brooks; The Last Wagon; A Strange Adventure; Frankenstein Meets the Giant Devil Fish. 1957 Fury at Showdown. 1958 No Time for Sergeants; Teacher's Pet; Sing, Boy, Sing. 1959 The FBI Story; Pillow Talk. 1962 The Interns; Hell Is for Heroes. 1963 Twilight of Honor; The Hook; A Girl Named Tamiko. 1964 The Young Lovers. 1965 Die, Monster, Die; The House at the End of the World; Young Dillinger. 1966 Frankenstein Conquers the World; Don't Worry, We'll Think of a Title. 1968 Fever Heat; Mission Mars.

ADLON, LOUIS
Died: Mar. 31, 1947, Los Angeles, Calif.(heart attack). Screen actor.

Appeared in: 1938 Dramatic School. 1939 Confessions of a Nazi Spy. 1940 Mystery Sea Raider. 1945 Counter-Attack.

ADOREE, RENEE (Renee LaFonte)
Born: Sept. 30, 1898, Lille, France. Died: Oct. 5, 1933, Tujunga, Calif.(tuberculosis). Screen actress and circus performer.

Appeared in: 1921 Made in Heaven. 1922 Daydreams; Monte Cristo; Honor First; Mixed Faces; A Self-Made Man; West of Chicago. 1923 The Eternal Struggle; The Six-Fifty. 1924 The Bandolero; Defying the Law; A Man's Mate; Women Who Give. 1925 The Big Parade; Exchange of Wives; Excuse Me; Parisian Nights; Man and Maid. 1926 Tin Gods; La Boheme; Blarney; The Exquisite Sinner; The Flaming Forest; The Black Bird. 1927 Mr. Wu; On Ze Boulevard; The Show; Back to God's Country; Heaven on Earth. 1928 Forbidden Hours; The Cossacks; Show People; A Certain Young Man; The Mating Call; The Michigan Kid; The Spieler. 1929 The Pagan; His Glorious Night; Tide of Empire. 1930 The Spoiler; The Singer of Seville; Redemption; Call of the Flesh.

AFRIQUE (Alexander Witkin)
Born: 1907, South Africa. Died: Dec. 17, 1961, London, England. Screen and stage actor, vocalist, and impersonator.

Appeared in: 1937 Let's Make a Night of It.

AGAR, JANE
Born: 1889. Died: June 10, 1948, Lakewood, Ohio. Screen and stage actress.

Appeared in silents.

AGUGLIA, MIMI
Born: 1885, Italy. Died: July 31, 1970, Woodland Hills, Calif. Screen and stage actress.

Appeared in: 1924 The Last Man on Earth. 1933 El Eltimo Varon Sobre la Tierra; Su Ultimo Amor. 1934 Tres Amores. 1937 The Lady Escapes. 1945 A Bell for Adano. 1947 Carnival in Costa Rica; The Outlaw. 1948 Cry of the City. 1949 That Midnight Kiss. 1950 Black Hand; Deported; The Man Who Cheated Himself; Right Cross. 1951 Cuban Fireball. 1952 When in Rome. 1955 The Rose Tattoo. 1957 The Brothers Rico.

AGUIRRE, MANUEL B.
Born: 1907, Mexico. Died: Dec. 3, 1957, Mexico City, Mexico. Screen actor.

AHEARNE, TOM
Born: 1906, Boston, Mass. Died: Jan. 5, 1969, New York, N.Y. (influenza). Screen, stage, and television actor.

Appeared in: 1949 Project X; The Window. 1950 Cry Murder. 1951 Mister Universe. 1968 Three in the Attic.

AHERNE, PATRICK
Born: 1901, Ireland. Died: Sept. 30, 1970, Hollywood, Calif.(cancer). Screen, stage, and television actor.

Appeared in British films prior to 1933: City of Play; Oh, What a Duchess; Bindle; A Daughter in Revolt; Silver Lining; Huntingtower; Auld Lang Syne; Virginia's Husband; Carry On; The Game Chicken; Come into My Parlor. 1936 Trouble Ahead. Entered U.S. films in 1946.

Appeared in: 1947 Green Dolphin Street. 1948 The Paradine Case. 1952 Bwana Devil. 1953 Botany Bay; Rogue's March; The Royal African Rifles. 1956 The Court Jester.

AHLM, PHILIP E.
Born: 1905. Died: July 5, 1954, Hollywood, Calif.(shot) Screen actor.

AINLEY, HENRY H.
Born: Aug. 21, 1879, Morley, England. Died: Oct. 31, 1945, London, England. Screen and stage actor. Father of actor Richard Ainley (dec. 1967).

Appeared in: 1914 Bachelor's Love Story; She Stoops to Conquer. 1915 The Prisoner of Zenda; Sweet Lavender; Rupert of Hentzau; The Outrage. 1916 Iris; Sowing the Wind. 1917 The Manxman. 1919 Quinney. 1923 The Royal Oak. 1924 Sally Bishop. 1932 The First Mrs. Fraser. 1933 The Good Companions. 1936 As You Like It.

AINLEY, RICHARD (aka RICHARD RIDDLE)
Born: Dec. 22, 1910, Stanmore, Middlesex, England. Died: May 18, 1967, London, England. Screen, stage, and radio actor. Son of actor Henry Ainley (dec. 1945). Occasionally used the name of Richard Riddle on stage.

Appeared in: 1936 As You Like It. 1939 The Frog; A Stolen Life. 1940 Lady With Red Hair. 1941 Singapore Woman; Bullets for O'Hara; The Smiling Ghost; Shining Victory. 1942 White Cargo. 1943 Three Hearts for Julie; I Dood It; Above Suspicion. 1949 Passage to Hong Kong. Other British films: Our Fighting Navy; The Gang Show.

AINSLEY, NORMAN
Born: May 4, 1881, Edinburgh, Scotland. Died: Jan. 23, 1948, Hollywood, Calif. Screen and stage actor.

Appeared in: 1930 Scotland Yard. 1933 International House, Horseplay. 1934 The Notorious Sophie Lang. 1936 Too Many Parents; Modern Times; Drawing Roomers; Tale of Two Cities; Lost Horizon; Sworn Enemy; Libeled Lady; Captains Courageous. 1937 Shall We Dance; The Shadow Strikes. 1940 Adventure in Diamonds. 1943 The Good Fellows. 1944 Man in Half Moon Street. 1945 Kitty.

AINSWORTH, SIDNEY (aka SYDNEY AINSWORTH)
Born: 1872, England. Died: May 1922, Madison, Wisc. Screen and stage actor. Entered films in 1909.

Appeared in: 1915 The White Sister. 1916 The Strange Case of Mary Page (serial). 1919 A Man and His Money; The Crimson

Gardenia; Heartsease; The Girl from Outside. 1920 Madame X. 1921 Boys Will Be Boys; Hold Your Horses; The Invisible Power; A Poor Relation; Doubling for Romeo. 1922 Mr. Barnes of New York.

AITKEN, FRANK "SPOTTSWORTH"
Born: 1869. Died: Feb. 26, 1933, Los Angeles, Calif. Screen and stage actor.

Appeared in: 1911 The Battle. 1915 Birth of a Nation. 1919 Captain Kidd, Jr.; The White Heather; Hay Foot, Straw Foot; Her Kingdom of Dreams. 1920 Nomads of the North. 1921 At the End of the World; Beyond; Reputation; The Unknown Wife. 1922 A Dangerous Game; Man of Courage; Manslaughter; Monte Cristo; One Wonderful Night; The Price of Youth; The Snowshoe Trail; The Trap; The Young Rajah. 1923 Around the World in 18 Days (serial); The Love Pirate; Merry-Go-Round; Six Days. 1924 The Fire Patrol; Lure of the Yukon; Gerald Cranston's Lady; Triumph; Those Who Dare. 1925 The Eagle; The Coast Patrol; Accused; The Goose Woman. 1926 The Power of the Weak; The Two-Gun Man. 1927 God's Great Wilderness; Roaring Fires.

AKED, MURIEL
Born: Nov. 9, 1887, Bingley, Yorkshire, England. Died: Mar. 23, 1955, Settle, Yorkshire, England. Screen and stage actress. Appeared in British silents approx. 1920.

Appeared in: 1930 Bed and Breakfast; The Middle Watch. 1931 Goodnight Vienna; One Magic Night; Indiscretions of Eve; A Sister to Assist 'Er. 1932 The Mayor's Nest; Rome Express. 1933 The Good Companions; Friday the Thirteenth; The Night of the Party; No Funny Business; Trouble. 1934 Autumn Crocus. 1935 Evensong; Josser on the Farm. 1936 Public Nuisance No. 1; Fame; Royal Eagle; Can You Hear Me; Mother, Don't Rush Me. 1937 Mr. Stringfellow Says No. 1938 A Girl Must Live; A Sister to Assist 'Er (and 1931 version). 1941 Cottage to Let. 1942 Continental Express. 1944 2,000 Women. 1945 The Life and Death of Colonel Blimp. 1946 The Wicked Lady. 1947 The Years Between. 1948 So Evil My Love; Just William's Luck; It's Hard to be Good. 1950 The Blue Lamp; The Happiest Days of Your Life. 1951 Another Shore; The Wonder Kid. 1953 Gilbert and Sullivan. 1954 Adventure for Two (aka Demi Paradise). Other British films: They Knew Mr. Knight; Flesh and Blood; What the Butler Saw; Paris by Night; William Goes to Town.

AKERS, HENRY CARL "HANK"
Born: 1908. Died: Aug. 22, 1967, Hollywood, Fla. Screen actor and stand-in for Johnny Weismuller.

ALADDIN (Aladdin Abdullah Achmed Anthony Pallante)
Born: 1913, New York. Died: June 9, 1970, Van Nuys, Calif. (heart disease). Screen, radio, television actor, and comic singer.

ALBERNI, LUIS
Born: 1887, Spain. Died: Dec. 23, 1962, Hollywood, Calif. Screen and stage actor.

Appeared in: 1921 Little Italy. 1922 The Man from Beyond. 1923 The Bright Shawl; The Valley of Lost Souls. 1930 The Santa Fe Trail. 1931 Men in Her Life; Side Show; Svengali; The Mad Genius; The Last Flight; I Like Your Nerve; Sweepstakes; Children of Dreams. 1932 Girl in the Tonneau; Woman in Room 13; The Cohens and the Kellys in Hollywood; Working Wives; Hypnotized; Guilty or Not Guilty; Crooner; The Kid from Spain; Manhattan Parade; Week-End Marriage; Cock of the Air; Big Stampede; A Parisian Romance; High Pressure. 1933 The Last Trail; Topaze; Child of Manhattan; Men Must Fight; I Love that Man; The Sphinx; When Ladies Meet; Trick for Trick; California Trial; The Man From Monterey; Above the Clouds. 1934 The Black Cat; The Captain Hates the Sea; When Strangers Meet; Goodbye Love; La Ciudad de Carton; Count of Monte Cristo; La Buenaventura; I Believed in You; Glamour; One Night of Love. 1935 Love Me Forever; Bad Boy; Roberta; The Gilded Lily; Goin' to Town; The Winning Ticket; Let's Live Tonight; In Caliente; The Gay Deception; Music is Magic; Metropolitan; Public Opinion; Manhattan Moon. 1936 Colleen; Anthony Adverse; Dancing Pirate; Ticket to Paradise; Follow Your Heart; Hat's Off. 1937 Sing and Be Happy; Two Wise Maids; Manhattan Merry-Go-Round; When You're in Love; Under Suspicion; The King and the Chorus Girl; The Great Garrick; Easy Living; Hitting a New High; Madame X. 1938 I'll Give a Million; Love on Toast. 1939 The Great Man Votes; Naughty but Nice; The Housekeeper's Daughter. 1940 Enemy Agent; Public Deb No. 1; Scatterbrain; Santa Fe Trail. 1941 They Met in Argentina; The Lady Eve; They Met in Bombay; Road to Zanzibar; San Antonio Rose; World Premier; Babes on Broadway; That Hamilton Woman. 1942 Mexican Spitfire's Elephant; Oblig-

ing Young Lady; Two Weeks to Live. 1943 Here Comes Kelly; Submarine Base; Nearly Eighteen; Here Comes Elmer; Harvest Melody; My Son, the Hero. 1944 When the Lights Go on Again; In Society; Men on Her Mind; Voice in the Wind; Machine Gun Mama. 1945 A Bell for Adano. 1946 In Fast Company. 1950 Captain Carey, U.S.A.; When Willie Comes Marching Home. 1952 What Price Glory.

ALBERS, HANS
Born: 1892, Hamburg, Germany. Died: July 24, 1960, Munich, Germany. Screen, stage, vaudeville and circus actor.

Appeared in: 1929 Rasputin. 1930 Der Blaue Engel (The Blue Angel); Die Nacht Gehoert Uns (The Night Belongs to Us). 1931 Bomben Auf Monte Carlo (Monte Carlo Madness); Der Draufganger (The Daredevil); Der Sieger (The Victor); Drei Tage Liebe (Three Days of Love). 1932 Der Weisse Damon; F.P. 1 Antwortet Nicht; Liebe Ist Lieb (Love is Love); Koenigin der Unterwelt. 1933 Heut Kommts Drauf An; Quick, Koenig der Clowns; Ein Gewisser Herr Gran; Fluchtlinge. 1934 Gold. 1935 Peer Gynt; Variete; Henker, Frauen und Soldaten (Hangmen, Women and Soldiers—U.S. 1940). 1936 Casanova. 1938 Sergeant Berry. 1939 Zwei Lustige Abenteurer (Two Merry Adventures). 1941 Carl Peters. 1943 Baron Munchausen. 1950 City of Torment. 1953 The White Hell of Pitz Palu. 1955 Der Letzte Mann (The Last Laugh). Other German film: Wasser fur Canitoga.

ALBERTSON, FRANK
Born: Feb. 2, 1909, Fergus Falls, Minn. Died: Feb. 29, 1964, Santa Monica, Calif. Screen, stage and television actor. Entered films in 1922.

Appeared in: 1928 Prep and Pep; The Farmer's Daughter. 1929 Salute; Words and Music; Blue Skies; Happy Days. 1930 Son of the Gods; The Big Party; Born Reckless; Men without Women; So This Is London; Wild Company; Just Imagine; Spring Is Here. 1931 The Connecticut Yankee; The Brat; The Tiger's Son; Big Business Girl; Old Greatheart; Traveling Husbands. 1932 Lost Special (serial); The Cohens and the Kellys in Hollywood; Way Back Home; Huddle. 1933 King for a Night; Ann Carver's Profession; Dangerous Crossroads; Midshipman Jack; Ever in My Heart; Racing Youth; Impossible Lover; Air Mail; Billion Dollar Scandal; The Cohens and the Kellys in Trouble; Rainbow Over Broadway. 1934 The Last Gentleman; The Life of Vergie Winters; Bachelor of Arts; Hollywood Hoodlum; Enter Madame. 1935 Doubting Thomas; Alice Adams; Ah, Wilderness; Personal Maid's Secret; East of Java; Kind Lady; Waterfront Lady. 1936 The Farmer in the Dell; Fury; The Plainsman. 1937 Navy Blue and Gold. 1938 Hold That Kiss; Spring Madness; The Shining Hour; Mother Carey's Chickens; Fugitives for a Night; Room Service. 1939 Bachelor Mother. 1940 Framed; Dr. Christian Meets the Women; The Ghost Comes Home; When the Daltons Rode; Behind the News. 1941 Man-Made Monster; Louisiana Purchase; Ellery Queen's Penthouse Mystery; Citadel of Crime; Flying Cadets; Father Steps Out; City Limits; Burma Convoy. 1942 Wake Island; Underground Agent; Shepherd of the Ozarks; The Man From Headquarters; Junior G-Men of the Air (serial); City of Silent Men. 1943 Keep 'Em Slugging; Here Comes Elmer; O, My Darling Clementine; Mystery Broadcast. 1944 And the Angels Sing; I Love a Soldier; Rosie the Riveter. 1945 Arson Squad; How Do You Do?. 1946 They Made Me a Killer; Gay Blades; It's A Wonderful Life; Ginger. 1947 Killer Dill; The Hucksters. 1948 Shed No Tears. 1956 Nightfall. 1957 The Enemy Below. 1958 The Last Hurrah. 1960 Psycho. 1961 Girl on the Run. 1962 Don't Knock the Twist. 1963 Johnny Cool; Bye Bye Birdie.

ALBRIGHT, BOB "OKLAHOMA"
Born: 1884. Died: Apr. 30, 1971, Hollywood, Calif.(heart attack). Screen, stage, vaudeville actor and orchestra leader.

Appeared in: 1929 Oklahoma Bob Albright and His Rodeo Do Flappers (short).

ALDEA, MERCEDES
Born: Spain. Died: Oct. 28, 1954, Sabadell, Spain (killed when struck by airplane propeller while filming What Never Dies). Screen actress.

ALDEN, BETTY
Born: 1898. Died: Apr. 1948, Beverly Hills, Calif. Screen and stage actress.

Appeared in: 1930 Lightnin'. 1934 The Fountain. 1935 The Nut Farm.

ALDEN, MARY (Mary Maguire Alden)
Born: 1883, New Orleans, La. Died: July 2, 1946, Woodland Hills, Calif. Screen and stage actress.

Appeared in: 1915 Birth of a Nation. 1916 Hell-to-Pay; Austin. 1919 The Unpardonable Sin. 1920 Milestone; Honest Hutch. 1921 The Old Nest; Snowblind; Trust Your Wife; Parted Curtains; The Witching Hour. 1922 Man with Two Mothers; A Woman's Woman; The Bond Boy; The Hidden Woman; Notoriety. 1923 Pleasure Mad; The Eagle's Feather; The Empty Cradle; Has the World Gone Mad!; The Steadfast Heart; The Tents of Allah. 1924 Babbitt; A Fool's Awakening; Painted People; The Beloved Brute; When a Girl Loves; Soiled. 1925 Faint Perfume; The Happy Warrior; Siege; Under the Rouge; The Plastic Age; The Unwritten Law. 1926 April Fool; Brown of Harvard; The Earth Woman; Lovely Mary. 1927 The Potters; The Joy Girl; Twin Flappers. 1928 Ladies of the Mob; The Cossacks; Fools for Luck; Sawdust Paradise; Someone to Love. 1929 Girl Overboard. 1932 Hell's House; Strange Interlude.

ALDERSON, ERVILLE
Born: 1883. Died: Aug. 4, 1957, Glendale, Calif. Screen actor.

Appeared in: 1921 The Good-Bad Wife. 1923 The Exciters; The White Rose. 1924 America; Isn't Life Wonderful. 1925 Sally of the Sawdust. 1926 The White Black Sheep. 1927 The Fortune Hunter; The Girl from Chicago; The Heart of Maryland; The Price of Honor; Salvation Jane. 1928 A Thief in the Dark; Fazil; Fleetwing. 1929 Speakeasy. 1930 The Bad Man; Guilty?; Redemption; The Lash; The Dawn Trail. 1931 Too Many Cooks; Arrowsmith; Shanghaied Love. 1932 Alias the Doctor; Cabin in the Cotton; They Call It Sin; I Am a Fugitive from a Chain Gang. 1933 To the Last Man. 1934 Lazy River; The Scarlet Empress. 1935 Square Shooter; The County Chairman; Woman Wanted; Pursuit; Public Opinion; The Virginia Judge; Seven Keys to Baldpate. 1936 Educating Father; Career Woman; Jungle Princess. 1937 The Mighty Treve; Small Town Boy. 1939 Jesse James; Mr. Smith Goes to Washington; Romance of the Redwoods; Andy Hardy Gets Spring Fever; The Hardys Ride High; Outside These Walls; Nancy Drew, Trouble Shooter; Vitaphone short. 1940 Santa Fe Trail. 1941 Sergeant York; Bad Men of Missouri; Parachute Battalion. 1942 The Commandos Strike at Dawn; My Favorite Blonde; The Postman Didn't Ring; The Loves of Edgar Allan Poe; You Can't Escape Forever; Careful; Soft Shoulders. 1943 First Comes Courage. 1945 Along Came Jones. 1947 Smash-Up; The Story of a Woman. 1952 Something to Live For.

ALDRIDGE, ALFRED
Born: 1876, New Orleans, La. Died: May 4, 1934, Hollywood, Calif. Screen and stage actor.

Appeared in: 1921 It Can Be Done.

ALEXANDER, BEN (Nicholas Benton Alexander)
Born: May 26, 1911, Goldfield, Nev. Died: June, 1969, Westchester, Calif.(natural causes). Screen, television actor, radio emcee, and announcer.

Appeared in: 1916 Each Pearl a Tear (first picture at age 4). 1918 Hearts of the World. 1919 The Turn in the Road; The White Heather. 1921 The Heart Line. 1922 In the Name of the Law. 1923 Penrod and Sam; Boy of Mine; Jealous Husbands. 1924 A Self-Made Failure. 1925 Pampered Youth; Flaming Love; The Shining Adventure; Frivolous Sal. 1926 Scotty of the Scouts (serial); The Highbinders. 1927 Fighting for Fame (serial). 1930 All Quiet on the Western Front. 1931 A Wise Child; Many a Slip; Are These Our Children?; Mystery Ship; Suicide Fleet. 1932 The Strange Love of Molly Louvain; Tom Brown of Culver; The Vanishing Frontier; High Pressure. 1933 What Price Innocence?; This Day and Age; Stage Mother. 1934 Once to Every Woman; The Most Precious Thing in Life; The Life of Vergie Winters. 1935 Reckless Roads; Splendor; Grand Old Girl; Annapolis Farewell; Born to Gamble. 1936 Hearts in Bondage. 1937 Red Lights Ahead; The Outer Gate; Behind Prison Bars; Western Gold. 1938 The Spy Ring; Mr. Doodle Kicks Off. 1939 Convicts' Code. 1940 The Leather Pushers. 1954 Dragnet. 1957 Pay the Devil; Man in the Shadow.

ALEXANDER, CLAIRE
Born: 1898. Died: Nov. 16, 1927, Alhambra, Calif.(double pneumonia). One of the first Mack Sennett bathing beauties and was in early Keystone films.

Appeared in: 1920 The Fatal Sign (serial).

ALEXANDER, EDWARD
Born: 1888. Died: Aug. 15, 1964, Dearborn, Ohio (heart attack). Screen actor and film producer. Entered films in 1910.
Appeared in: 1915 Curse of the Black Pearl. 1917 Chosen Prince (aka The Friendship of David and Jonathan).

ALEXANDER, FRANK "FATTY"
Born: 1879. Died: Sept. 8, 1937, North Hollywood, Calif. Screen actor. Entered films in 1913 with Keystone.

Appeared in: 1923 Cyclone Jones. 1925 SOS Perils of the Sea. 1926 Oh, What a Night!. 1927 Play Safe.

ALEXANDER, JOHN
Born: 1865. Died: Apr. 5, 1951, Ontario, Calif. Screen and stage actor. In recent years a stand-in for Guy Kibbee and Donald Meek. (Not to be confused with John Alexander born in 1897.)

ALEXANDER, ROSS
Born: July 27, 1907, Brooklyn, N.Y. Died: Jan. 2, 1937, Los Angeles, Calif.(suicide—gun). Screen and stage actor. Married to actress Anna Nagel (dec. 1966).

Appeared in: 1932 The Wiser Sex. 1934 Flirtation Walk; Gentlemen Are Born; Loudspeaker Lowdown; Social Register. 1935 A Midsummer Night's Dream; Captain Blood; We're in the Money; Shipmates Forever; Going Highbrow; Maybe It's Love. 1936 Brides Are Like That; I Married a Doctor; Boulder Dam; China Clipper; Hot Money; Here Comes Carter! 1937 Ready, Willing, and Able.

ALEXANDER, SARA
Born: 1839. Died: Dec. 24, 1926, New York, N.Y. Screen and stage actress.

ALGARO, GABRIEL
Born: 1888. Died: Oct. 1951, Sargozza, Spain. Screen and stage actor and film director.

ALGIER, SIDNEY H.
Born: Dec. 5, 1889, Shamokin, Pa. Died: Apr. 24, 1945, West Los Angeles, Calif.(heart attack). Screen, stage, vaudeville, burlesque actor, film director, and screenwriter. Entered films as an actor in 1915.

Appeared in: 1922 The Dangerous Age. 1923 The Wanters. 1924 Husbands and Lovers; Why Men Leave Home. 1925 Fine Clothes. 1926 The Gay Deceiver; Memory Lane. 1927 Lovers.

ALIPPI, ELIAS
Died: May 4, 1942, Buenos Aires, Argentina. Screen actor.

Appeared in: 1939 Viento Norte (North Wind); Cadetes de San Martin. 1940 Asi es la Vida (Such Is Life). 1942 Viejo Hucha.

ALLBEURY, DAISY
Born: 1885. Died: Oct. 1961, London, England. Screen film extra.

ALLEBORN, AL
Born: 1892. Died: June 14, 1968, Hollywood, Calif.(leukemia). Retired studio executive and former assistant director who entered films as a screen stuntman.

ALLEN, ARTHUR B.
Born: 1881. Died: Aug. 25, 1947, New York, N.Y. Screen, stage actor, and radio emcee.

Appeared in: 1937 Ebb Tide. 1940 Our Town; Rangers of Fortune.

ALLEN, DOROTHY
Born: 1896. Died: Sept. 30, 1970, N.Y. Screen and stage actress.

Appeared in: 1921 Beyond Price; The Power Within; Dynamite Allen. 1922 The Broken Silence; Free Air. 1923 If Winter Comes. 1924 Second Youth; The Hoosier Schoolmaster. 1925 Pearl of Love; School for Wives.

ALLEN, ETHAN
Born: 1882. Died: Aug. 21, 1940, Hollywood, Calif. Screen, stage actor, film director, and screenwriter.

Appeared in: 1930 The Border Legion. 1931 The Flood. 1939 Trigger Pals.

ALLEN, FRED (John Florence Sullivan)
Born: May 31, 1894, Cambridge, Mass. Died: Mar. 17, 1956, New York, N.Y.(heart attack). Screen, stage, vaudeville actor, columnist, radio emcee, and film director. Billed in vaudeville as "Fred St. James," "Freddie James, World's Worst Juggler" and "Paul Huckle, European Entertainer." In 1927 was part of emcee team "Allen & York."

Appeared in: 1929 Fred Allen's Prize Playettes (short). 1920 The Still Alarm (short). 1935 Thanks a Million. 1938 Sally, Irene and Mary. 1940 Love Thy Neighbor. 1945 It's in the Bag (aka The Fifth Chair). 1952 We're Not Married; O. Henry's Full House.

ALLEN, GRACIE (Grace Ethel Cecile Rosale Allen)
Born: July 26, 1906, San Francisco, Calif. Died: Aug. 28, 1964, Los Angeles, Calif.(heart attack). Screen, vaudeville, radio, and television actress. Married to actor George Burns and was half of comedy team "Burns & Allen." She was known as "the smartest dumbbell in the history of show business."

Appeared with Burns in: 1929 Lamb Chops (short). 1930 Pulling a Bone (short); Fit to Be Tied (short). 1931 Burns & Allen (short); The Antique Shop (short); Once over Lightly (short); One Hundred Percent Service (short). 1932 The Big Broadcast of 1932; Oh, My Operation (short); The Babbling Book (short); Hollywood on Parade #2 (short). 1933 International House; College Humor; Walking the Baby (short); Let's Dance (short). 1934 Six of a Kind; Many Happy Returns; We're Not Dressing; College Rhythm. 1935 Love in Bloom; Here Comes Cookie; The Big Broadcast of 1936. 1936 College Holiday; The Big Broadcast of 1937. 1937 A Damsel in Distress. 1938 College Swing. 1939 Honolulu. 1944 Hollywood on Parade. 1954 Hollywood Grows Up (film clips); Hollywood Fathers (film clips). Appeared without Burns in: 1939 Gracie Allen Murder Case. 1941 Mr. and Mrs. North. 1944 Two Girls and a Sailor.

ALLEN, JOE
Born: 1888. Died: Jan. 31, 1955, Hollywood, Calif. Screen actor.

ALLEN, JOSEPH, JR.
Born: Mar. 30, 1918, Boston, Mass. Died: Nov. 9, 1962, Patchogue, N.Y. Screen, stage, and television actor. Son of actor Joseph Allen, Sr.(dec. 1952).

Appeared in: 1936 Motor Madness. 1939 Lucky Night; Our Leading Citizen. 1942 Who Is Hope Schuyler?; Death of Champion; Right to the Heart; It Happened in Flatbush; The Night before the Divorce. 1946 Dangerous Money. 1947 I Cover Big Town; Road to the Big House. 1948 The Time of Your Life.

ALLEN, JOSEPH, SR.
Born: 1872. Died: Sept. 9, 1952, Newton, Mass. Screen and stage actor. Father of actor Joseph Allen, Jr.(dec. 1962).

Appeared in: 1912 Essaney films. 1929 Seven Keys to Baldpate.

ALLEN, LESTER
Born: 1891, England. Died: Nov. 6, 1949, Hollywood, Calif.(struck by auto). Screen, stage, vaudeville, minstrel, burlesque, circus actor, and film director.

Appeared in: 1930 Leave It to Lester. 1932-33 Paramount shorts. 1943 The Heat's On. 1945 The Great Flamario; The Dolly Sisters. 1946 The Dark Mirror. 1948 Crime on Their Hands (short); The Pirate; That Lady in Ermine. 1949 Ma and Pa Kettle.

ALLEN, MAUDE (Maude Allen Giannone)
Died: Nov. 7, 1956, Washington. Screen and stage actress.

Appeared in: 1930 La Grande Mare (The Big Pond). 1931 The Smiling Lieutenant. 1935 The Cowboy Millionaire; It's in the Air; Whispering Smith Speaks. 1936 The Captain's Kid. 1937 Secret Valley. 1938 Painted Desert. 1939 The Women. 1940 Black Diamonds. 1942 Juke Box Jennie; I Married an Angel. Other French film: Modern Cinderella.

ALLEN, PHYLLIS
Born: 1861. Died: Mar. 26, 1938, Los Angeles, Calif. Screen and vaudeville actress.

Appeared in: 1914 Caught in a Cabaret (reissued as The Jazz Waiter); The Property Man; The Rounders; Dough and Dynamite (reissued as The Doughnut Designers); Gentlemen of Nerve (reissued as Some Nerve); Fatty's Jonah Day; Getting Acquainted. 1915 Giddy, Gay and Ticklish (reissued as A Gay Lothario); Gussle's Wayward Path; Fickle Fatty's Fall; A Submarine Pirate; A Movie Star; The Judge.

ALLEN, SAM
Born 1861, Md. Died: Sept. 13, 1934, Los Angeles, Calif. Screen and stage actor. Entered films with Biograph in 1910.

Appeared in: 1921 The Conflict. 1922 Forget-Me-Not; The Son of the West; Confidence. 1923 Are You a Failure?; The Virginian. 1925 Timber Wolf; Bashful Buccaneer; Midnight Limited. 1926 The Call of the Klondike; Man Rustlin'; The Sea Beast. 1927 Blackjack; Death Valley; Mother; Woman's Law. 1928 Burning Bridges. 1930 The Sea Wolf. 1934 The Last Round-Up.

ALLENBY, THOMAS
Born: 1861, Australia. Died: Dec. 19, 1933, Hollywood, Calif. Screen actor.

ALLERTON, LITTLE HELEN (aka HELEN KILDUFF and HELEN SCHWEISTHAL)
Born: 1888. Died: Nov. 4, 1959, Golf, Ill. Screen, stage, and vaudeville actress. Appeared in vaudeville as part of "May & Kilduff" team. Entered films with Essanay and Selig Studios in Chicago and appeared in films from 1910 to 1916.

ALLGOOD, SARA
Born: Oct. 31, 1883, Dublin, Ireland. Died: Sept. 13, 1950, Woodland Hills, Calif.(heart attack). Screen and stage actress.

Appeared in: 1929 Blackmail (British film debut). 1930 Juno and the Paycock. 1934 The Bride of the Lake. 1935 The Passing of the Third Floor Back; Riders to the Sea. 1936 It's Love Again. 1937 Storm in a Teacup. 1938 Kathleen. 1939 On the Night of the Fire. 1940 The Fugitive. 1941 That Hamilton Woman; How Green Was My Valley; Dr. Jekyll and Mr. Hyde; Lydia. 1942 The War against Mrs. Hadley; Roxie Hart; This above All; It Happened in Flatbush; Life Begins at 8:30. 1943 City without Men. 1944 The Lodger; Between Two Worlds; Jane Eyre; Keys of the Kingdom. 1945 The Strange Affair of Uncle Harry. 1946 Cluny Brown; Kitty; The Spiral Staircase. 1947 Mother Wore Tights; The Fabulous Dorseys; Ivy; Mourning Becomes Electra; My Wild Irish Rose. 1948 One Touch of Venus; The Man from Texas; The Girl from Manhattan; The Accused. 1949 Challenge to Lassie. 1950 Sierra; Cheaper by the Dozen.

ALLISON, STEVE
Born: 1916. Died: Mar. 6, 1969, Hollywood, Calif.(lung cancer). Screen actor, radio emcee, and singer.

Appeared in: 1957 The Burglar.

ALLISTER, CLAUD (Claud Palmer)
Born: Oct. 3, 1893, London, England. Died: July 26, 1970, Santa Barbara, Calif. Screen and stage actor. Entered films in 1929.

Appeared in: 1929 The Trial of Mary Dugan; Bulldog Drummond; Three Live Ghosts; Charming Sinners. 1930 Monte Carlo; The Floradora Girl; The Czar of Broadway; Slightly Scarlet; In the Next Room; Such Men Are Dangerous; Murder Will Out; Ladies Love Brutes. 1931 Captain Applejack; Reaching for the Moon; Meet the Wife; Papa Loves Mama; I Like Your Nerve; Roughhouse Rhythm; Platinum Blonde. 1932 Two White Arms; Diamond Cut Diamond; Blame the Woman; The Return of Raffles; On the Loose (short); The Unexpected Father. 1933 The Private Life of Henry VIII; Private Wives. 1934 The Lady Is Willing; The Private Life of Don Juan; Those Were the Days; The Return of Bulldog Drummond. 1935 The Dark Angel; Three Live Ghosts (and 1929 version). 1936 Dracula's Daughter; Yellowstone; Lady Luck. 1937 Bulldog Drummond at Bay; Danger—Love at Work; Radio Parade of 1937; The Awful Truth. 1938 Let's Make a Night of It; Men Are Such Fools; Storm over Bengal; Kentucky Moonshine; The Blonde Cheat. 1939 Arrest Bulldog Drummond; Captain Fury. 1940 Lillian Russell. 1941 Charley's Aunt; The Reluctant Dragon; A Yank in the RAF; Confirm or Deny. 1943 Forever and a Day. 1944 Kiss the Bride Goodbye; Hundred Pound Widow. 1945 Don Chicago. 1946 Gaiety George. 1948 Quartet. 1949 Ichabod and Mr. Toad. 1951 Hong Kong. 1953 Kiss Me, Kate; Down among the Sheltering Palms. Other British films: First Gentleman; Friendly Island.

ALLYN, LILLY (Elizabeth A. Tatu)
Born: 1866. Died: May 5, 1944, Philadelphia, Pa. Screen, stage, vaudeville, and light opera actress.

ALMAR THE CLOWN. See Albert A. Marx

ALONSO, JULIO
Born: 1906. Died: Feb. 9, 1955, Hollywood, Calif. Screen actor. Brother of actor Gilbert Roland.

ALTHOFF, CHARLES R.
Born: 1890. Died: Oct. 14, 1962, Irvington, N.J. Screen, vaudeville, and radio actor.

ALTHOUSE, EARL F.
Born: 1893. Died: Feb. 6, 1971, Gladwyne, Pa. Screen cowboy actor. Entered films with Lubin Studios.

ALVARADO, DON (Jose Paige)
Born: Nov. 4, 1900, Albuquerque, N.M. Died: Mar. 31, 1967, Los Angeles, Calif.(cancer). Screen and television actor. Also known professionally as Don Page.

Appeared in: 1925 The Pleasure Buyers; Satan in Sables; The Wife Who Wasn't Wanted. 1926 A Hero of the Big Snows; The Night Cry; His Jazz Bride. 1927 Loves of Carmen; Breakfast at

Sunrise; Drums of Love; The Monkey Talks. 1928 The Battle of the Sexes; No Other Woman; The Scarlet Lady; Driftwood. 1929 Rio Rita; The Apache; The Bridge of San Luis Rey. 1930 Free and Easy; The Bad One; Forever Yours. 1931 Beau Ideal; Captain Thunder; Reputation. 1932 The Bachelor's Affair; La Cucaracha; Lady With a Past; The King Murder. 1933 Under Secret Orders; Contraband; Black Beauty; Morning Glory. 1934 Demon for Trouble; No Sleep on the Deep; Once to Every Bachelor. 1935 The Devil Is a Woman; Red Wagon; I Live for Love; Sweet Adeline. 1936 Rosa de Francia; Federal Agent; Rio Grande Romance; Put on the Spot; Rose of the Rancho; Spy 77. 1937 Nobody's Baby; The Lady Escapes; Love under Fire. 1938 Rose of the Rio Grande. 1939 Cafe Society. 1940 One Night in the Tropics. 1949 The Big Steal.

AMARANTE, ESTEVAO
Born: 1890. Died: Jan. 1952, Oporto, Portugal. Screen and stage actor. During 1930's did first talkies in Portugese language for Paramount in Paris.

AMAYA, CARMEN
Born: 1913. Died: Nov. 19, 1963, Bagur, Spain (kidney ailment). Screen, stage actress, and flamenco dancer.

Appeared in: 1944 Follow the Boys; Knickerbocker Holiday. 1945 See My Lawyer (with her dancing company). 1964 Los Torantos.

AMBLER, JOSS
Born: 1900, England. Died: 1959. Screen actor.

Appeared in: 1938 The Citadel. 1939 Trouble Brewing; Come on George. 1940 Contraband. 1941 Break the News; The Black Sheep of Whitehall. 1942 Flying Fortress. 1943 Jeannie; Courageous Mr. Penn. 1944 A Canterbury Tale; The Agitator. 1945 The Silver Fleet; The Halfway House. 1947 The Years Between. 1949 Mine Own Executioner. 1956 The Long Arm. Other British films: Candles at Nine; Here Comes the Sun; The Bitter Bit.

AMES, ADRIENNE
Born: Aug. 3, 1909, Fort Worth, Tex. Died: May 31, 1947, New York, N.Y.(cancer). Screen and stage actress, and radio commentator. Divorced from actor Bruce Cabot.(dec. 1972).

Appeared in: 1931 Girls About Town; Twenty-Four Hours; The Road to Reno. 1932 Husband's Holiday; Two Kinds of Women; Merrily We Go to Hell; Sinners in the Sun. 1933 Broadway Bad; The Death Kiss; From Hell to Heaven; A Bedtime Story; Disgraced; The Avenger. 1934 You're Telling Me; George White's Scandals. 1935 Abdul the Damned; Black Sheep; Gigolette; Woman Wanted; Harmony Lane; Ladies Love Danger. 1938 Slander House; City Girl; Fugitives for a Night. 1939 Zero Hour; Panama Patrol.

AMES, GERALD
Born: 1881. Died: July 4, 1933, London, England (accident—fall). Screen and stage actor.

AMES, HARRY
Born: 1893. Died: Aug. 11, 1969, Hollywood, Calif. Screen and stage actor.

AMES, JIMMY
Born: 1915. Died: Aug. 14, 1965, Hollywood, Calif.(heart attack). Screen and television actor.

Appeared in: 1946 Whistle Stop. 1949 The Lucky Stiff.

AMES, ROBERT
Born: Mar. 23, 1898, Hartford, Conn. Died: Nov. 27, 1931, New York, N.Y.(bladder hemorrhage). Screen and stage actor. Entered films in 1925.

Appeared in: 1925 Without Mercy; The Wedding Song. 1926 Three Faces East; The Crown of Lies. 1929 Voice of the City; Marianne; Rich People; Black Waters; Nix on Dames; The Trespasser. 1930 Holiday; Madonna of the Streets; Double Cross Roads; Not Damaged; A Lady to Love; War Nurse. 1931 Rebound; Millie; Behind Office Doors; Smart Woman; Rich Man's Folly. 1932 The Slippery Pearls (short).

AMORES, ADELINA
Born: 1883, Spain. Died: Mar. 10, 1958, Madrid, Spain. Screen and stage actress.

AMUARRIZ, RAUL CANCIO
Born: 1911, Spain. Died: Oct. 23, 1961, Madrid, Spain. Screen and stage actor who appeared in more than 100 Spanish films.

ANALLA, ISABEL
Born: 1920. Died: Jan. 17, 1958, San Francisco, Calif.(cancer). Screen and television actress.

Appeared in: 1957 Pal Joey; Kiss Them for Me. 1958 Vertigo.

ANDERSON, CLAIRE
Born: 1896, Detroit, Mich. Died: Mar. 23, 1964, Venice, Calif. Screen actress. Was one of the original Mack Sennett beauties.

Appeared in: 1916 Cinders of Love; The Lion and the Girl; Bath Tub Perils; She Loved a Sailor. 1917 A Clever Dummy; The Late Lamented; The Hidden Spring. 1920 The Palace of Darkened Windows. 1921 The Road Demon; When We Were Twenty-One; Who Am I; The Servant in the House. 1922 The Yellow Stain. 1923 The Clean-Up. 1925 The Meddler.

ANDERSON, GENE
Born: 1931, London, England. Died: May 5, 1965, London, England (cerebral hemorrhage). Screen, stage, and television actress.

Appeared in: 1955 The Intruder. 1956 Double Cross. 1957 The Long Haul; Battle Hell (aka Their Greatest Glory and Yangtse Incident). 1960 Shakedown. 1962 The Day the Earth Caught Fire. 1963 The Break. Other British films: Background; Laughing in the Sunshine.

ANDERSON, GEORGE
Born: 1891. Died: Aug. 28, 1948, Los Angeles, Calif. Screen and stage actor.

Appeared in: 1937 Under Suspicion. 1938 Born to Be Wild. 1939 Our Neighbors, the Carters; King of Chinatown; The Lady's from Kentucky; Union Pacific; A Woman Is the Judge. 1940 Santa Fe Marshal; Hidden Gold; The Secret Seven. 1942 The Palm Beach Story. 1944 Wilson; Murder, My Sweet. 1945 Mildred Pierce; Nob Hill.

ANDERSON, GILBERT M. "BRONCHO BILLY" (Max Aronson)
Born: Mar. 21, 1882, Little Rock, Ark. Died: Jan. 20, 1971, South Pasadena, Calif. Screen, stage, vaudeville, television actor, film director, and screenwriter. In 1907 he co-founded Essanay Film Manufacturing Co. In 1958 he won Special Academy Award for his pioneer contribution to the film industry. He appeared in "Broncho Billy"series, beginning in 1908 with The Bandit Makes Good; "Snakeville Comedy"series, beginning in 1911; and "Alkali Ike" series, beginning in 1912.

Appeared in: 1902 The Messenger Boy's Mistake (film debut). 1903 The Great Train Robbery. 1907 An Awful Skate. 1908 The Bandit Makes Good. 1909 The Heart of a Cowboy; The Indian Trailer; A Western Maid; The Ranchman's Rival; The Spanish Girl; His Reformation; Judgment; The Best Man Wins; A Tale of the West; The Black Sheep; A Mexican's Gratitude. 1910 Away Out West; The Cowboy and the Squaw; The Cowpuncher's Ward; The Flower of the Ranch; The Forest Ranger; The Mistaken Bandit; The Outlaw's Sacrifice; The Ranch Girl's Legacy; The Ranchman's Feud; The Sheriff's Sacrifice; The Bandit's Wife; Western Chivalry; Take Me Out to the Ball Game; The Bad Man's Last Deed; The Unknown Claim; Trailed by the West; The Desperado; Under Western Skies; The Dumb Half Breed's Defense; The Deputy's Love Affair; The Millionaire and the Girl; An Indian Girl's Love; The Pony Express Rider; The Tout's Remembrance; Patricia of the Plains; The Bearded Bandit; A Cowboy's Mother-in-Law; Pals of the Range; The Silent Message; A Westerner's Way; The Marked Trail; A Western Woman's Way; A Cowboy's Vindication; The Tenderfoot Messenger; A Gambler of the West; The Bad Man's Christmas; Broncho Billy's Redemption. 1911 The Girl from the Triple X; Last Round-Up; The Cowboy Coward; When Love and Honor Called; A Girl of the West; The Border Ranger; The Two Reformations; The Bad Man's Downfall; On the Desert's Edge; The Romance of Bar O; The Faithful Indian; A Thwarted Vengeance; Across the Plains; Carmenita the Faithful; The Sheriff's Chum; The Indian Maiden's Lesson; The Puncher's New Love; The Lucky Card; The Infant at Snakeville; The Tribe's Penalty; The Sheriff's Brother; The Hidden Mine; The Corporation and the Ranch Girl; The Count and the Cowboy; The Outlaw and the Child; Broncho Billy's Adventure. 1912 Broncho Billy's Outwitted; The Outlaw's Sacrifice; The Shotgun Ranchman; The Tomboy on Bar Z; The Ranch Girl's Trail; The Mother of the Ranch; An Indian Friendship; Cutting California Redwoods; Broncho Billy's Heart; The Dance at Silver Gulch; Broncho Billy's Mexican Wife; The Boss of the Katy Mine; Western Girls; Broncho Billy's Promise; The Prospector; The Sheriff's Luck; The Sheriff's Inheritance; The Reward for Broncho Billy; The Smuggler's Daughter; Alkali Ike Plays the Devil; Alkali Ike Stung!; Alkali Ike's Boarding House; Alkali Ike's Pants; Love on Tough

Luck Ranch; Alkali Ike's Close Shave; Alkali Ike's Motorcycle. 1913 Oath; Alkali Ike's Misfortunes; Alkali Ike's in Jayville; Alkali Ike's Homecoming; Alkali Ike's Auto; Broncho Billy and the Maid; Broncho Billy and the Outlaw's Mother; Broncho Billy's Gun Play; The Sheriff's Child; The Making of Broncho Billy; The Sheriff's Story; Broncho Billy's Last Deed; Broncho Billy's Ward; Broncho Billy and the Squatter's Daughter; Broncho Billy and the Step-Sisters; Broncho Billy's Sister; Broncho Billy's Gratefulness; Broncho Billy's Way; The Sheriff's Honeymoon; Broncho Billy's Secret; Broncho Billy's First Arrest; Broncho Billy's Squareness; Broncho Billy's Christmas Deed; The Three Gamblers. 1914 The Treachery of Broncho Billy's Pal; Broncho Billy and the Rattler; Broncho Billy's True Love; Broncho Billy's Close Call; Broncho Billy Gun-Man; Broncho Billy's Sermon; Broncho Billy's Leap; Broncho Billy's Cunning; Broncho Billy's Duty; Broncho Billy's Jealousy; Broncho Billy and the Mine Shark; Broncho Billy Outlaw; Red Riding Hood of the Hills; Broncho Billy's Punishment; Broncho Billy and the Sheriff; The Redemption of Broncho Billy; Snakeville's New Doctor; Broncho Billy Guardian; Broncho Billy and the Bad Man; Broncho Billy and the Settler's Daughter; Broncho Billy and the Red Man; The Calling of Jim Barton; The Interference of Broncho Billy; Broncho Billy's Bible; Broncho Billy and the Sister; The Good-for-Nothing; Broncho Billy and the Claim Jumpers; Broncho Billy and the Escaped Bandit. 1915 Broncho Billy and the Land Grabber; Broncho Billy and the Lumber King; Broncho Billy and the Posse; Broncho Billy Evens Matters; Broncho Billy's Love Affair; Broncho Billy Well Repaid; Broncho Billy's Marriage; Broncho Billy and the False Note; Broncho Billy and the Vigilante; Broncho Billy's Parents; Broncho Billy's Protege; Broncho Billy's Sentence; Broncho Billy's Teachings; Broncho Billy and the Baby; Broncho Billy Begins Life Anew; Broncho Billy Sheepman; Broncho Billy's Brother; Broncho Billy's Greaser Deputy; Broncho's Surrender; Broncho Billy's Word of Honor; Broncho Billy's Vengeance; Broncho Billy's Cowardly Brother; Broncho Billy Steps In. 1918 Shootin' Mad. 1965 The Bounty Killer.

ANDERSON, JAMES
Born: 1872. Died: Mar. 22, 1953, Glasgow, Scotland (burns received in fire). Screen, stage, and radio actor.

Appeared in: 1925 The Freshman. 1926 Butterflies in the Rain; The College Boob; Flying High. 1928 Fleetwing. 1929 Welcome Danger. 1930 The Runaway Bride. 1949 Whiskey Galore (aka Tight Little Island-U.S. & aka Mad Little Island).

ANDERSON, JAMES
Born: 1921. Died: Sept. 14, 1969, Billings, Mont. Screen actor. Entered films in 1951.

Appeared in: 1951 Hunt the Man Down; Along the Great Divide; Five. 1952 The Last Musketeer; Duel at Silver Creek; Ruby Gentry. 1953 China Venture; The Great Jesse James Raid; Flight to Tangier. 1954 Drums Across the River; Dragnet; Riot in Cell Block 11. 1955 The Violent Men; The Marauders; Seven Angry Men. 1956 Fury at Gunsight Pass; Running Target; The Rawhide Years. 1957 The Big Land. 1958 I Married a Monster from Outer Space; The Thing That Couldn't Die. 1962 To Kill a Mocking Bird; The Connection; Pressure Point. 1963 The Brig. 1969 Little Big Man; Cotton Comes to Harlem; Take the Money and Run; A Man Called Gannon; Young Billy Young.

ANDRE, GWILI
Born: 1908, Copenhagen, Denmark. Died: Feb. 5, 1959, Venice, Calif.(apartment fire). Screen actress.

Appeared in: 1932 The Roar of the Dragon; Secrets of the French Police. 1933 No Other Woman. 1937 The Girl Said No; Meet the Boy Friend. 1941 A Woman's Face. 1942 The Public Be Damned; The Falcon's Brother.

ANDREWS, LAVERNE
Born: July 6, 1915 Minneapolis, Minn. Died: May 8, 1967, West Los Angeles, Calif.(cancer). Screen, radio, television actress, and vaudeville singer. One of the "Andrew Sisters" trio.

Appeared in: 1940 Argentine Nights. 1941 Buck Privates; In the Navy; Hold that Ghost; Private Buckaroo. 1942 What's Cookin'?; Give Out, Sisters. 1943 How's About It?; Always a Bridesmaid. 1944 Swingtime Johnny; Moonlight and Cactus; Follow the Boys; Hollywood Canteen. 1945 Her Lucky Night. 1946 Make Mine Music. 1947 Road to Rio. 1948 Melody Time.

ANDREWS, LOIS (Lorraine Gourley)
Born: Mar. 24, 1924, Huntington Park, Calif. Died: Apr. 1968, Encino, Calif.(lung cancer). Screen and stage actress. Divorced from entertainer George Jessel.

Appeared in: 1943 Dixie Dugan; Roger Touhy, Gangster. 1949 Rustlers. 1950 The Desert Hawk. 1951 Meet Me after the Show.

ANDREWS, ORVILLE
Born: Nebr. Died: Mar. 29, 1968, Hartford, Conn. Screen, television actor, and radio comedy singer.

ANDREWS, STANLEY
Born: 1892. Died: June 23, 1969, Los Angeles, Calif. Screen and television actor.

Appeared in: 1935 All the King's Horses; Private Worlds; People Will Talk; The Crusades; Nevada; Wanderer of the Wasteland; Drift Fence; Hold 'Em Yale; Escape from Devil's Island; The Big Broadcast of 1936. 1936 Wild Brian Kent; Desire; In His Steps; Happy Go Lucky. 1937 John Meade's Woman; High, Wide and Handsome; The Devil's Playground; The Man Who Found Himself; Nancy Steele Is Missing. 1938 The Buccaneer; Cocoanut Grove; Spawn of the North; The Mysterious Rider; When G-Men Step in; Blondie; Adventure in Sahara; Alexander's Ragtime Band; I'll Give a Million; Kentucky; The Lone Ranger (serial); Stablemates. 1939 Mr. Smith Goes to Washington; Homicide Bureau; Beau Geste; Union Pacific; Geronimo. 1940 The Blue Bird; Little Old New York; Brigham Young—Frontiersman; Kit Carson. 1941 Play Girl; Meet John Doe; Strange Alibi; Mr. and Mrs. North; Wild Geese Calling; Time Out for Rhythm. 1942 North to the Klondike; The Major and the Minor; Canal Zone; My Gal Sal; The Postman Didn't Ring; Ten Gentlemen from West Point. 1943 Crash Dive; 1944 Murder, My Sweet; Tucson Raiders; Princess and the Pirate. 1946 The Virginian. 1947 Michigan Kid. 1948 The Paleface; Northwest Stampede. 1949 Blondie's Big Deal; Brothers in the Saddle; Man from Colorado; Trail of the Yukon; The Last Bandit; The Valiant Hombre; Brimstone; Tough Assignment. 1950 Across the Badlands; Arizona Cowboy; Blonde Dynamite; Mule Train; The Nevadan; Outcast of Black Mesa; Salt Lake Raiders; Short Grass; Streets of Ghost Town; Trigger, Jr.; Two Flags West; Tyrant of the Sea; Under Mexicali Stars; West of Wyoming. 1951 Al Jennings of Oklahoma; Saddle Legion; Utah Wagon Train; Vengeance Valley. 1952 Fargo; Kansas Territory; The Man from Black Hills; Montana Belle; Talk about a Stranger; Thundering Caravans; Waco. 1953 Appointment in Honduras; Dangerous Crossing. 1954 Dawn at Socorro; Southwest Passage; The Steel Cage. 1955 Treasure of Ruby Hills. 1956 Frontier Gambler.

ANGELI, PIER (Anna Maria Pierangeli)
Born: June 19, 1932, Sardinia, Italy. Died: Sept. 10, 1971, Beverly Hills, Calif.(overdose of drugs). Screen, stage, and television actress. Twin sister of actress Marisa Pavan. Divorced from singer/actor Vic Damone.

Appeared in: 1951 Teresa; The Light Touch. 1952 The Devil Makes Three; Tomorrow Is Too Late. 1953 The Story of Three Loves (aka Equilibrium); Sombrero. 1954 Flame and the Flesh. 1955 The Silver Chalice. 1956 Port Afrique; Somebody up There Likes Me. 1957 The Vintage. 1958 Merry Andrew. 1960 S.O.S. Pacific; The Angry Silence. 1962 White Slave Ship. 1963 Sodom and Gomorrah. 1964 M.M.M. 83. 1965 The Battle of the Bulge. 1966 Spy in Your Eye. 1967 King of Africa. 1968 Every Bastard a King.

ANGELO, JEAN
Born: 1888. Died: Nov. 26, 1933, Paris, France. Screen and stage actor.

Appeared in: 1928 Une Java. 1929 Nana; La Vierge Folle. 1930 The Strange Case of District Attorney M. 1932 Atlantide L'.

ANGOLD, EDIT (Edit Goldstandt)
Born: 1895, Berlin, Germany. Died: Oct. 4, 1971, Los Angeles, Calif. Screen, stage, radio, and television actress.

Appeared in: 1944 Tomorrow the World! (stage and film versions). 1946 Suspense. 1949 Ringside; Tough Assignment. 1950 The White Tower; Molly (aka The Goldbergs, film and radio versions). 1952 Woman in the Dark. 1953 Murder without Tears. 1956 The Birds and the Bees. 1957 Bernardine. 1959 The Blue Angel. 1967 The Ambushers.

ANKRUM, MORRIS
Born: Aug. 27, 1904, Danville, Ill. Died: Sept. 2, 1964, Pasadena, Calif.(trichinosis). Screen, stage actor, and film director.

Appeared in: 1940 Buck Benny Rides Again; Knights of the Range; The Showdown; Three Men from Texas; Light of the Western Stars; Cherokee Strip. 1941 I Wake up Screaming; This Woman Is Mine; The Roundup; In Old Colorado; Border Vigilantes; Wide Open Town; Doomed Caravan; Pirates on Horseback; Road Agent; The Bandit Trail. 1942 Tales of Manhattan; Roxie Hart; Ride 'Em

Cowboy!; Ten Gentlemen from West Point; The Loves of Edgar Allen Poe; The Omaha Trail; Time to Kill; Tennessee Johnson. 1943 Let's Face It; Reunion in France; Swing Fever; Dixie Dugan; The Heavenly Body. 1944 Marriage Is a Private Affair; Barbary Coast Gent; Meet the People; Rationing; Gentle Annie; The Thin Man Goes Home. 1945 The Hidden Eye. 1946 The Harvey Girls; Courage of Lassie; Little Mr. Jim; Cockeyed Miracle; Lady in the Lake; The Mighty McGurk. 1947 Undercover Maisie; Cynthia; Good News; Desire Me; High Wall; Sea of Grass. 1948 Joan of Arc; For the Love of Mary; Fighting Back; Bad Men of Tombstone. 1949 We Were Strangers; Colorado Territory; Slattery's Hurricane. 1950 Borderline; Chain Lightning; The Damned Don't Cry; Redhead and the Cowboy; Rocketship XM; In a lonely Place; Short Grass; Southside 1-000. 1951 Tomorrow Is Another Day; My Favorite Spy; Fighting Coast Guard; Along the Great Divide; The Lion Hunters; Flight to Mars. 1952 The Raiders; The Man Behind the Gun; Hiawatha; Mutiny; Red Planet Mars; Son of Ali Baba; Fort Osage. 1953 Arena; Devil's Canyon; The Moonlighter; Invaders from Mars; Fort Vengeance; Sky Commando; Mexican Manhunt. 1954 Vera Cruz; Southwest Passage; Apache; The Three Young Texans; Taza, Son of Cochise; Silver Lode; Drums Across the River; The Steel Cage; Cattle Queen of Montana; Two Guns and a Badge; The Outlaw Stallion; The Saracen Blade. 1955 Chief Crazy Horse; The Eternal Sea; The Silver Star; Tennessee's Partner; No Man's Woman; Crashout; Jupiter's Darling; Abbott and Costello Meet the Mummy; Jujin Yukiotoko (Half Human). 1956 Fury at Gunsight Pass; Quincannon, Frontier Scout; Earth vs. The Flying Saucers; Death of a Scoundrel; Walk the Proud Land; When Gangland Strikes. 1957 Omar Khayyam; Hell's Crossroads; Drango; Zombies of Mora-Tau; Kronos; The Giant Claw; Beginning of the End. 1958 Badman's Country; From the Earth to the Moon; Twilight for the Gods; Young and Wild; The Saga of Hemp Brown; Frontier Gun; How to Make a Monster; Giant from the Unknown. 1961 The Most Dangerous Man Alive.

ANSELMI, ROSINA
Born: 1880, Italy. Died: May 23, 1965, Cantania, Sicily. Screen and stage actress.

Appeared in: 1935 The Rich Uncle; L'Eredita dello Zio; L'Aria del Continente (Continental Atmosphere-U.S. 1939); Milizia Territoriale. 1937 El Feroce Saladino; Signora Fortuna (Lady Luck); Gat Ci Cova; Lasciate Ogni Speranza. 1939 El Marchese De Rivolito (The Marquis of Rivolito); L'Ha Fatto Una Signora (A Woman Did It); Re di Danari (Money King). 1940 El Paraninfo (The Matchmaker).

ANSON, A. E.
Born: 1879, England. Died: June 25, 1936, Monrovia, Calif. Screen and stage actor.

Appeared in: 1931 Arrowsmith; The Road to Singapore.

ANSON, LAURA
Born: 1892. Died: July 15, 1968, Woodland Hills, Calif. Screen actress. Married to film actor Philo McCullough. She was a leading lady of Roscoe "Fatty" Arbuckle.

Appeared in: 1921 The Easy Road; Crazy to Marry; The Little Clown. 1922 Bluebeard, Jr.; If You Believe It, It's So; The Great Alone. 1923 Flames of Passion; Skid Proof; The Call of the Canyon; The Silent Partner; The Way of the Transgressor.

ANTRIM, HARRY
Born: 1895, Chicago, Ill. Died: Jan. 18, 1967, Hollywood, Calif. (heart attack). Screen, stage, television, and vaudeville actor.

Appeared in: 1947 Miracle on 34th Street (film debut). 1948 The Luck of the Irish; Larceny; Let's Live a Little; Words and Music; Act of Violence. 1949 Free for All; Johnny Allegro; Thelma Jordan; Intruder in the Dust; Prison Warden; The Heiress; Chicago Deadline; Ma and Pa Kettle. 1950 Devil's Doorway; I'll Get By; Outside the Wall; No Man of Her Own; Side Street; There's A Girl in My Heart. 1951 Appointment with Danger; Night into Morning; Meet Me after the Show; Tomorrow Is Another Day; Follow the Sun; Mr. Belvedere Rings the Bell; I'll See You in My Dreams. 1952 The Lion and the Horse; Mutiny. 1954 The Bounty Hunter. 1955 A Lawless Street. 1956 The Solid Gold Cadillac. 1958 Teacher's Pet. 1959 Gunmen from Laredo.

AOKI, TSURU
Born: 1893. Died: Nov. 1961, Tokyo, Japan (acute peritonitis). Screen and stage actress. Married to actor Sessue Hayakawa. (dec. 1973).

Appeared in: 1914 The Typhoon. 1916 Alien Souls. 1920 The Breath of the Gods. 1921 Black Roses. 1922 Night Life in Hollywood; Five Days to Live. 1924 The Danger Line. 1960 Hell to Eternity.

APFEL, OSCAR C.
Born: Cleveland, Ohio. Died: Mar. 24, 1938, Hollywood, Calif. (heart attack). Screen and stage actor, film and stage director, and stage producer. Entered films with Edison and Reliance in 1911.

Appeared in: 1922 Ten Nights in a Bar Room; Auction of Souls; The Man Who Paid; The Wolf's Fangs. 1923 A Man's Man; In Search of a Thrill; The Social Code. 1924 The Heart Bandit; Trail of the Law. 1925 Borrowed Finery; The Thoroughbred; The Sporting Chance. 1926 Perils of the Coast Guard; Somebody's Mother; The Call of the Klondike; The Last Alarm; Midnight Limited; Race Wild. 1927 When Seconds Count; Cheaters; Code of the Cow Country. 1928 The Valley of Hunted Men; The Heart of Broadway; Romance of the Underworld. 1929 Marianne; Not Quite Decent; True Heaven; Halfway to Heaven; Smiling Irish Eyes; Hurdy Gurdy. 1930 The Texan; Misbehaving Ladies; The Spoilers; Virtuous Sin; The Right to Love; Man Trouble; Abraham Lincoln. 1931 Men in Her Life; Huckleberry Finn; Five-Star Final; Finger Points; Wicked; Big Business Girl; The Maltese Falcon; Sidewalks of New York; The Bargain; Sooky; Inspiration. 1932 State's Attorney; High Pressure; Woman from Monte Carlo; Hot Saturday; Shopworn; East Side; Cardigan's Last Case; The Silent Voice; Business and Pleasure; Woman in Room 13; You Said a Mouthful; Heart of New York; It's Tough To Be Famous; Old Greatheart; The World and the Flesh; Alias the Doctor; When a Fellow Needs a Friend; Two against the World; Mad Masquerade; Sporting Widow; Way Back Home; The Man Who Played God; Make Me a Star; Hell's Highway; False Faces; Madame Racketeer. 1933 Pick Up; Story of Temple Drake; Tomorrow at Seven; Emergency Call; One Man's Journey; Before Dawn; Ladies Must Love; Only Yesterday; The Bowery; The World Changes; Hold the Press. 1934 Fifteen Wives; The Old-Fashioned Way; Take the Stand; I Am a Thief; Romance in Manhattan; Beloved; Madame Spy; The House of Rothschild; Are We Civilized?; White Lies; Whirlpool. 1935 Border Town; Two Faces; Death Flies East; The Nut Farm; Mary Jane's Pa; The Man on the Flying Trapeze; Cappy Ricks Returns; O'Shaughnessey's Boy; His Night Out; Another Face; The Fire Trap. 1936 Murder at Glen Athol; Sutter's Gold; Bridge of Sighs; Every Saturday Night; The Criminal Within; Hearts in Bondage; Bulldog Edition; And Sudden Death; Hollywood Boulevard; We Who Are About to Die; The Plot Thickens; Crack-Up. 1937 Fifty Roads to Town; The Soldier and the Lady; Conquest; Shadows of the Orient; History Is Made at Night; Trouble in Morocco; Jim Hanvey—Detective; The Toast of New York.

APPEL, ANNA
Born: 1888. Died Nov. 19, 1963, New York, N.Y. Screen, stage, and television actress.

Appeared in: 1926 Broken Hearts. 1932 The Heart of New York; Symphony of Six Million; Faithless. 1937 Green Fields; The Singing Blacksmith.

APPLEGARTH, JONAS
Born: 1920. Died: July 23, 1965, Bashaw, Alberta, Canada (auto accident). Screen actor.

Appeared in: 1954 Saskatchewan. 1955 Battle Cry. 1959 The Sheriff of Fractured Jaw.

APPLEGATE, HAZEL
Born: 1886. Died: Oct. 30, 1959, Chicago, Ill. Screen actress. Entered films in Chicago with Essaney.

AQUISTAPACE, JEAN
Born: 1882, France. Died: Oct. 20, 1952, Nice, France. Screen actor and opera singer. Appeared in a number of French films.

ARBENZ, ARABELLA
Born: 1945. Died: Oct. 5, 1965, Bogota, Columbia (suicide—gun). Screen actress.

Appeared in: A Pure Soul (played dual lead role, in Mexico and N.Y., in the experimental film).

ARBUCKLE, MACKLYN
Born: July 9, 1866, San Antonio, Tex. Died: Apr. 1, 1931, Waddington, N.Y. Screen and stage actor.

Appeared in: 1915 The County Chairman. 1922 The Prodigal Judge; Squire Phin; Welcome to Our City; Mr. Potter of Texas; Mr. Bingle; The Young Diana. 1923 Broadway Broke. 1924 Yolanda; Janice Meredith. 1925 That Old Gang of Mine; Lure of the Track; The Thoroughbred. 1926 The Gilded Highway.

ARBUCKLE, ROSCOE "FATTY"
Born: May 24, 1887, San Jose, Calif. Died: June 29, 1933, New York, N.Y.(heart attack). Screen, stage, vaudeville, and burlesque actor, film director, and film producer. Directed under name of William Goodrich. Married to actress Addie McPhail.

Appeared in: 1913 The Gangsters (film debut); Passions, He Had Three; Help! Help!, Hydrophobia!; The Waiters' Picnic; A Bandit; For the Love of Mabel; The Telltale Light; A Noise from the Deep; Love and Courage; The Riot; Mabel's New Hero; Fatty's Day Off; Mabel's Dramatic Career (reissued as Her Dramatic Debut); The Gypsy Queen; The Faithful Taxicab; Mother's Boy; A Quiet Little Wedding; Fatty at San Diego; Fatty Joins the Force; The Woman Haters; Fatty's Flirtation; He Would a Hunting Go. 1914 A Misplaced Foot; The Under Sheriff; A Flirt's Mistake; In the Clutches of a Gang; Rebecca's Wedding Day; A Film Johnnie; Tango Tangles; His Favorite Pastime; A Rural Demon; Barnyard Flirtations; Chicken Chaser; A Suspended Ordeal; The Water Dog; The Alarm; The Knock-out (reissued as The Pugilist); Our Country Cousin; Fatty and the Heiress; Fatty's Finish; The Sky Pirate; Caught in a Flue; The Baggage Smasher; Those Happy Days; That Minstrel Man; Those Country Kids; Fatty's Gift; The Masquerade; A Brand New Hero; The Rounders; Fatty's Debut (reissued as Fatty Butts In); Fatty Again (reissued as Fatty the Fourflusher); Killing Horace; Their Ups and Downs; Zip, the Dodger; Lovers Post Office; An Incompetent Hero; Fatty's Jonah Day; Fatty's Wine Party; The Sea Nymphs (reissued as His Diving Beauty); Leading Lizzie Astray; Among the Mourners; Shotguns That Kick; Tillie's Punctured Romance; Fatty's Magic Pants (reissued as Fatty's Suitless Day); Fatty and Minnie-He-Haw. 1915 Mabel and Fatty's Wash Day; Rum and Wall Paper; Mabel and Fatty's Simple Life; Fatty and Mabel at the San Diego Exposition; Mabel, Fatty and the Law (reissued as Fatty's Spooning Day); Fatty's New Role; Colored Villainy; Fatty and Mabel's Married Life; Fatty's Reckless Fling; Fatty's Chance Acquaintance; Love in Armor; That Little Band of Gold (reissued as For Better or Worse); Fatty's Faithful Fido; When Love Took Wings; Mabel and Fatty Viewing the World's Fair at San Francisco; Miss Fatty's Seaside Lovers; The Little Teacher; Fatty's Plucky Pup; Fatty's Tin Type Tangle; Fickle Fatty's Fall; The Village Scandal; Fatty and the Broadway Stars. 1916 Fatty and Mabel Adrift; He Did and Didn't (working title: Love and Lobsters); The Bright Lights (working title: The Lure of Broadway); His Wife's Mistakes; The Other Man; The Waiter's Ball; A Creampuff Romance (working titles: His Alibi; A Reckless Romance). 1916 Rebecca's Wedding Day. 1917 The Butcher Boy; Rough House; His Wedding Night; Fatty at Coney Island; Oh! Doctor!; Out West. 1918 The Bell Boy; Goodnight Nurse; Moonshine; The Cook. 1919 A Desert Hero; Backstage; A Country Hero; The Garage. 1920 Life of the Party; The Roundup. 1921 Dollar a Year Man; Gasoline Gus; Traveling Salesman; Brewster's Millions; Crazy to Marry; The Fast Freight. 1923 Hollywood. Also appeared in: 1960 When Comedy Was King (documentary). 1961 Days of Thrills and Laughter (documentary).

ARCHER, ANNE
Born: 1912. Died: Aug. 5, 1959, Los Angeles, Calif. Screen actress.

ARCHINBAUD, GEORGE
Born: May 7, 1890, Paris, France. Died: Feb. 20, 1959, Beverly Hills, Calif.(heart attack). Screen, stage actor, film and television director, and film producer.

ARDELL, JOHN E.
Born: 1881. Died: Apr. 26, 1949, Hollywood, Calif.(monoxide gas). Screen actor.

ARDEN, EDDIE
Born: 1908. Died: June 23, 1952, Hollywood, Calif.(heart attack). Screen and stage actor.

ARDEN, VICTOR
Born: 1893, Ill. Died: July 30, 1962, New York, N.Y. Screen actor, orchestra leader, musician, and radio performer.

ARENAS, MIGUEL
Born: 1902, Alicante, Spain. Died: Nov. 3, 1965, Mexico City, Mexico (heart attack). Screen and stage actor.

Appeared in: 1933 In Fraganti. 1936 Mas Alla de la Muerta. 1937 El Misterio del Rostro Palido. 1938 No Basta ser Madre (Motherhood Is Not Enough); Abnegacion. 1939 Un Domingo en la Tarde (On a Sunday Afternoon); Maria. 1940 Herencia Macabra (A Macabre Legacy); Vivire Otra Vez (I Shall Live Again); El Conde de Monte Cristo. 1944 La Dama de las Camelias. 1951 Toast to Love.

ARLEDGE, JOHN (Johnson Lundy Arledge)
Born: Mar. 12, 1906, Crockett, Tex. Died: May 15, 1947. Screen, stage, and vaudeville actor.

Appeared in: 1930 The King of Jazz. 1931 Young Sinners; Daddy Long Legs; Heartbreak; Spider. 1932 Careless Lady; Huddle; Week Ends Only. 1933 Jimmy and Sally. 1934 Olsen's Big Moment; Flirtation Walk. 1935 Devil Dogs of the Air; Mary Jane's Pa; Old Man Rhythm; Shipmates Forever. 1936 We're Only Human; You May Be Next; Two in Revolt; Murder on a Bridle Path; Don't Turn 'Em Loose; The Big Game. 1937 Saturday's Heroes; County Fair; The Big City. 1938 Prison Nurse; Numbered Woman; Campus Confessions. 1939 Twelve Crowded Hours; Gone with the Wind; You Can't Cheat an Honest Man; 6,000 Enemies. 1940 The Grapes of Wrath; All Women Have Secrets; Strange Cargo; Ski Patrol; Flight Angels; City of Conquest. 1941 Cheers for Miss Bishop. 1947 I Wonder Who's Kissing Her Now.

ARLISS, FLORENCE
Died: Mar. 11, 1950, London, England. Screen actress. Married to actor George Arliss (dec. 1946).

Appeared in: 1921 The Devil; Disraeli. 1929 Disraeli (and 1921 version). 1932 The Millionaire. 1933 The King's Vacation. 1934 The House of Rothschild.

ARLISS, GEORGE
Born: Apr. 10, 1868, London, England. Died: Feb. 5, 1946, London, England (bronchial trouble). Screen and stage actor. Married to actress Florence Arliss (dec. 1950). Won Academy Award for Best Actor in Disraeli, 1929; also nominated Best Actor in The Green Goddess, 1930.

Appeared in: 1921 The Devil; Disraeli. 1922 Man Who Played God. 1923 The Green Goddess; The Ruling Passion. 1924 $20 a Week. 1929 Disraeli (and 1921 version). 1930 The Green Goddess (and 1923 version); Old English. 1931 The Millionaire; Alexander Hamilton. 1932 Man Who Played God (and 1922 version); A Successful Calamity. 1933 The Working Man; A King's Vacation; Voltaire; The Adopted Father. 1934 The House of Rothschild; The Last Gentleman. 1935 Cardinal Richelieu; Mr. Hobo; Transatlantic Tunnel; East Meets West; Iron Duke. 1936 Man of Affairs. 1937 Dr. Syn.

ARMAND, TEDDY V. (Edwin C. Winscott)
Born: 1874. Died: July 12, 1947, Los Angeles, Calif. Screen and stage actor.

ARMENDARIZ, PEDRO
Born: May 9, 1912, Mexico City, Mexico. Died: June 18, 1963, Los Angeles, Calif.(suicide—gun and cancer). Screen and stage actor. Father of screen actor Pedro Armendariz, Jr.

Appeared in: 1936 Rosario. 1937 Jalisco Nuca Pierde (Jalisco Never Loses). 1938 Mi Candidato (My Candidate). 1939 El Indio, La China Hilaria. 1940 Los Olvidados de Dios (Those Forgotten by God); La Reina del Rio (The Queen of the River). 1941 Isle of Passion (aka Passion Island-U.S. 1943). 1943 Maria Candeleria (U.S. 1944); Guadalajara; The Life of Simon Bolivar. 1944 Tierra de Passiones. 1945 Flor Sylvestre. 1947 The Fugitive; Juan Charrasqueado. 1948 The Pearl; Three Godfathers; Fort Apache; Maclovia. 1949 La Masquereda; Tulsa; We Were Strangers; Enamorada. 1950 The Torch. 1951 Elly y Yo. 1952 Lucretia Borgia. 1954 Border River; Lovers of Toledo; El Bruto; Both Sides of the Law. 1955 The Littlest Outlaw; Diane. 1956 Viva Revolution; Sins of the Borgios; The Conqueror. 1957 The Big Boodle (aka A Night in Havana); Stowaway Girl; Manuela. 1958 Conqueror of the Desert. 1959 The Little Savage; The Wonderful Country. 1960 Soldiers of Pancho Villa. 1961 Beyond All Limits (aka Flowers of Mayo); La Cucaracha; Francis of Assisi. 1962 La Bandida (The Bandit). 1963 My Son, the Hero (aka The Titans); Captain Sinbad. 1964 From Russia with Love.

ARMETTA, HENRY
Born: July 4, 1888, Palermo, Italy. Died: Oct. 21, 1945, San Diego, Calif.(heart attack). Screen, stage, and television actor.

Appeared in: 1928 The Silent Command. 1928 Street Angel. 1929 Lady of the Pavements; In Old Arizona; Homesick; Love, Live and Laugh; Jazz Heaven. 1930 A Lady to Love; The Climax; The Little Accident; Lovin' the Ladies; Romance; Sins of the Children; Die Sehnsuht Jeder Frau. 1931 Strangers May Kiss; A Tailor Made Man; Five and Ten; Hush Money; The Unholy Garden; Speak Easily. 1932 Scarface; Arsene Lupin; The Passionate Plumber; The Doomed Battalion; Impossible Lover; Tiger Shark; Weekends Only; Penalty of Fame; Central Park; Cauliflower Alley; Steady Company; Huddle; They Just Had to Get Married; Prosperity; Farewell to Arms; Uptown New York; Okay, America; Men of America. 1932-33 Universal shorts; 1933 Fra Diavolo (The Devil's Brother); The Cohens and the Kellys in Trouble; Her First Mate; Too Much Harmony; Laughing at Life; Deception; What! No Beer?; So This Is Africa; Don't Bet on Love. 1934 Cat and the Fiddle; Cross Country Cruise; One Night of Love; Viva Villa!; Poor Rich; Hide-Out; Embarrassing Moments; Gift of Gab; Two Heads on a Pillow; Wake up and Dream; Imitation of Life; The Merry Widow; The Man Who Reclaimed His Head; Kiss and Make Up; Cheating Cheaters; Romance in the Rain; Let's Talk It Over; Universal shorts; 1935 Straight from the Heart; Vanessa, Her Love Story; Night Life of the Gods; After Office Hours; I've Been Around; Dinky; Princess Ohara; Unknown Woman; Three Kids and a Queen; The Show Goes On; Magnificent Obsession; Manhattan Moon. 1936 Let's Sing Again; The Crime of Dr. Forbes; Poor Little Rich Girl; The Magnificent Brute; Two in a Crowd. 1937 Top of the Town; Make a Wish; Manhattan Merry-Go-Round; Seventh Heaven. 1938 Everybody Sing; Speed to Burn; Road Demon; Submarine Patrol. 1939 Fisherman's Wharf; The Lady and the Mob; My Pop; Winner Take All; I Stole a Million; The Outsider; Dust Be My Destiny; The Escape. 1940 Three Cheers for the Irish; We Who Are Young; You're Not So Tough; The Man Who Talked Too Much. 1941 Caught in the Act; The Big Store; Slick Chick; Stage Door Canteen; Good Luck, Mr. Yates. 1943 Thank Your Lucky Stars. 1944 Allergic to Love; The Ghost Catchers. 1945 Penthouse Rhythm; A Bell for Adano; Col. Effingham's Raid; Anchors Aweigh.

ARMITAGE, WALTER W.
Born: 1907, South Africa. Died: Feb. 22, 1953, New York, N.Y. Screen, stage actor, playwright, and screenwriter.

Appeared in: 1931 The Love Habit. 1934 Bombay Mail; Where Sinners Meet; British Agent.

ARMSTRONG, CLYDE
Born: 1879. Died: Sept. 30, 1937, N.Y. Screen, stage, and vaudeville actor.

ARMSTRONG, LOUIS "SATCHMO" (Daniel Louis Armstrong)
Born: July 4, 1900, New Orleans, La. Died: July 6, 1971, Queens, N.Y. Screen, stage, television actor, and jazz trumpeter. Winner of Down Beat Hall of Fame Award in 1952.

Appeared in: 1930 Ex-Flame. 1932 Paramount shorts. 1936 Pennies from Heaven. 1937 Artists and Models; Every Day's a Holiday. 1938 Going Places; Doctor Rhythm. 1940 The Philadelphia Story. 1943 Cabin in the Sky. 1944 Jam Session; Atlantic City. 1945 Pillow to Post. 1947 New Orleans. 1948 A Song Is Born. 1951 Glory Alley; The Strip; Here Comes the Groom. 1954 The Glenn Miller Story. 1957 The Five Pennies; The Beat Generation. 1960 Jazz on a Summer's Day. 1961 Paris Blues. 1965 When the Boys Meet the Girls; Girl Crazy. 1966 A Man Called Adam. 1969 Hello, Dolly.

ARMSTRONG, WILL H.
Born: 1869. Died: July 28, 1943, Hollywood, Calif. Screen and vaudeville actor.

Appeared in: 1927 Clancy's Kosher Wedding; A Boy of the Streets.

ARNA, LISSY
Born: Germany. Died: Jan. 22, 1964, Berlin, Germany (cancer). Screen and television actress. Entered films in German silents and entered U.S. films in 1930.

Appeared in: 1929 The Prince of Rogues. 1930 Der Tanz Geht Weiter (Those Who Dance). 1931 Beyond Victory. 1932 Der Ungetreue Eckehart. 1933 Theodor Koerner. 1937 Die Schwebende Jungfrau. Other German films: The Yellow Flag; Mountains in Flames.

ARNAUD, YVONNE
Born: Dec. 20, 1892, Bordeaux, France. Died: Sept. 20, 1958, London, England. Screen, stage, television actress, and pianist.

Appeared in: 1930 Canaries Sometimes Sing (British film and stage versions); On Approval (British film and stage versions). 1933 A Cuckoo in the Nest. 1935 Princess Charming; Lady in Danger. 1936 Improper Duchess; Stormy Weather; Gay Adventure. 1940 Neutral Port. 1942 Tomorrow We Live. 1943 At Dawn We Die. 1947 Woman to Woman; The Ghosts of Berkeley Square. 1958 My Uncle. Other British silents: Desire; The Temptress.

ARNHEIM, GUS
Born: 1899. Died: Jan. 19, 1955, Beverly Hills, Calif. (heart attack). Screen, television actor, bandleader, and songwriter. Wrote "Sweet and Lovely."

Appeared with his orchestra in: 1928 Gus Arnheim and His Am-

bassadors (short); Gus Arnheim and His Cocoanut Grove Orchestra (short). 1929 Broadway; Half Marriage; Street Girl; Gus Arnheim and His Ambassador Hotel Orchestra (short). 1934 Gift of Gab. 1937 Paramount short.

ARNOLD, EDWARD
Born: Feb. 18, 1890. Died: Apr. 26, 1956, Encino, Calif.(cerebral hemorrhage). Screen, stage, and television actor. Father of actor Edward Arnold, Jr. Entered films in 1915 with Essanay.

Appeared in: 1916 The Primitive Strain. 1927 Sunrise—a Song of Two Humans. 1932 Man of the Nile; Rasputin and the Empress; The White Sister; Afraid to Talk; Okay America; Three on a Match. 1933 Whistling in the Dark; I'm No Angel; Gennie Gerhardt; The Barbarian; Her Bodyguard; Secret of the Blue Room; Roman Scandals. 1934 The President Vanishes; Unknown Blonde; Thirty Day Princess; Madame Spy; Million Dollar Ransom; Hide-Out; Sadie McKee; Wednesday's Child. 1935 Remember Last Night?; Biography of a Bachelor Girl; The Glass Key; Diamond Jim; Cardinal Richelieu. 1936 Meet Nero Wolf; Sutter's Gold; Crime and Punishment; Come and Get It. 1937 The Toast of New York; Easy Living; Blossoms on Broadway; John Meade's Woman. 1938 The Crowd Roars; You Can't Take It with You. 1939 Idiot's Delight; Mr. Smith Goes to Washington; Let Freedom Ring; Man About Town. 1940 Slightly Honorable; Johnny Apollo; The Earl of Chicago; Lillian Russell. 1941 Unholy Partners; All That Money Can Buy; Meet John Doe; The Penalty; The Lady from Cheyenne; Johnny Eager; Nothing but the Truth; Design for Scandal. 1942 The War against Mrs. Hadley; Eyes in the Night. 1943 The Youngest Profession. 1944 Kismet; Mrs Parkington; Standing Room Only; Janie; Main Street after Dark. 1945 The Hidden Eye; Weekend at the Waldorf. 1946 Janie Gets Married; Ziegfeld Follies; Three Wise Fools; No Leave, No Love; My Brother Talks to Horses; The Mighty McGurk. 1947 Dear Ruth; The Hucksters. 1948 Three Daring Daughters; The Big City; Wallflower. 1949 John Loves Mary; Command Decision; Big Jack; Take Me out to the Ball Game; Honest John (Horner); Feudin' Rhythm; Dear Wife. 1950 Annie Get Your Gun; The Yellow Cab Man; The Skipper Surprised His Wife. 1951 Dear Brat. 1952 Belles on Their Toes; The Devil and Daniel Webster (reissue and retitle of All That Money Can Buy - 1941). 1953 Man of Conflict; Money From Home; City That Never Sleeps. 1954 Living It Up. 1956 Miami Expose; The Huston Story; The Ambassador's Daughter.

ARNOLD, MABEL
Born: 1889. Died: Jan. 7, 1964, Hollywood, Calif. Screen actress.

ARNOLD, PHIL
Born: 1909, Hackensack, N.J. Died: May 9, 1968, Van Nuys, Calif. Screen, stage, television, and vaudeville actor.

Appeared in: 1939 King of the Turf. 1941 Sis Hopkins. 1942 Men of San Quentin. 1947 Buffalo Bill Rides Again. 1949 I Cheated the Law. 1951 G.I. Jane; Yes Sir, Mr. Bones; Kentucky Jubilee. 1953 The Jazz Singer. 1954 The Big Chase; Money From Home; A Star Is Born. 1955 It's Always Fair Weather; The Court Martial of Billy Mitchell; Illegal. 1957 Jet Pilot; My Gun Is Quick. 1958 Damn Yankees. 1960 Studs Lonigan. 1962 The Errand Boy. 1963 The Three Stooges Go around the World in a Daze. 1964 Robin and the Seven Hoods; Three Nuts in Search of a Bolt. 1967 The Cool Ones; Good Times. 1968 Skiddo.

ARNOLD, SETH
Born: 1885, London, England. Died: Jan. 3, 1955, New York, N.Y. Screen, stage actor, and stage director.

Appeared in: 1949 Lost Boundaries.

ARNOLD, WILLIAM R.
Born: 1883. Died: July 20, 1940, Hollywood, Calif.(streptococcus infection). Screen, stage, and vaudeville actor.

Appeared in: 1931 Oh! Oh! Cleopatra (short); Gun Smoke; The Vice Squad; Rich Man's Folly. 1932 The Crowd Roars. 1934 In Love with Life. 1937 Four Days' Wonder. 1938 The Overland Express. 1940 Edison, The Man; The Great Dictator.

ARRAS, HARRY
Born: 1882. Died: Jan. 28, 1942, Hollywood, Calif.(heart attack). Screen actor. Entered films approximately 1918.

Appeared in: 1922 Blind Circumstances. 1942 Escape from Crime.

ARTEMAL, TALAT
Born: 1902, Turkey. Died: Aug. 1957, Bolu, Turkey (heart attack). Screen and stage actor.

ARTHUR, JOHNNY (John Williams)
Born: 1883, Scottsdale, Pa. Died: Dec. 31, 1951, Woodland Hills, Calif. Screen and stage actor. Appeared in silent "Christie" comedies.

Appeared in: 1923 The Unknown Purple. 1924 Mlle. Midnight; Daring Love. 1925 The Monster. 1928 On Trial. 1929 The Desert Song; The Gamblers; Show of Shows; Divorce Made Easy; Lover's Delight; Adam's Eve; The Aviator; Stimulation (short). 1930 Cheer up and Smile; Personality; She Couldn't Say No; Scrappily Married; Down with Husbands; Paper Hanging (short); Bridal Night (short). 1931 Penrod and Sam, Going Wild; It's a Wise Child. 1933 Convention City; Easy Millions. 1934 Twenty Million Sweethearts; Many Happy Returns; Hell in Heaven. 1935 Traveling Saleslady; Doubting Thomas; The Ghost Walks; All American Toothache (short); It's in the Air; The Bride Comes Home; Crime and Punishment; Too Tough to Kill. 1936 Freshmen Love; Murder of Dr. Harrigan; The King Steps Out; Stage Struck. 1937 The Hit Parade; Exiled to Shanghai; Pick a Star; Make a Wish; Blossoms on Broadway; It Had to Happen Out West; Something to Sing About. 1938 Danger on the Air. 1940 Road to Singapore. 1941 Mountain Moonlight. 1942 Shepherd of the Ozarks. 1943 The Nazty Nuisance; The Masked Marvel (serial).

ARTHUR, JULIA
Born: 1869, Hamilton, Ontario, Canada. Died: Mar. 28, 1950, Boston, Mass. Screen and stage actress.

Appeared in: 1918 The Common Cause; The Woman the Germans Shot.

ARVIDSON, LINDA
Died: July 26, 1949, New York, N.Y. Screen, stage actress, and author. First wife of film producer David Wark Griffith (dec. 1948).

Appeared in: 1908 When Knighthood Was in Flower; When Knights Were Bold. 1909 Edgar Allan Poe; The Cricket on the Hearth; Lines of White on a Sullen Sea. 1910 The Unchanging Sea; Fisher Folks. 1911 Enoch Arden.

ASH, SAMUEL HOWARD
Born: 1884. Died: Oct. 20, 1951, Hollywood, Calif. Screen and stage actor.

Appeared in: 1929 Unmasked. 1933 Girl without a Room. 1934 Kiss and Make Up. 1935 Four Hours to Kill; Paris in the Spring. 1936 A Man Betrayed. 1939 Some Like It Hot. 1943 The Dancing Master; The Heat's On. 1949 Oh, You Beautiful Doll.

ASHE, WARREN
Born: New York. Died: Sept. 19, 1947, Madison, Conn.(auto accident). Screen, stage, and radio actor.

Appeared in: 1940 Military Academy. 1941 The Face Behind the Mask; Naval Academy, Harmon of Michigan. 1942 Smith of Minnesota. 1943 What's Buzzin' Cousin?; Destroyer. 1947 Monsieur Verdoux.

ASHER, MAX
Born: 1880. Died: Apr. 15, 1957, Hollywood, Calif. Screen actor. 1913-14 appeared in a series of "Joker" comedies.

Appeared in: 1913 Mike and Jake at the Beach; The Cheese Special. 1915 P. A. Powers' Comedies; Lady Baffles and Detective Duck. 1921 Rip Van Winkle; The Silver Car. 1922 The Ladder Jinx. 1923 The Courtship of Miles Standish. 1924 Trigger Finger; The Shooting of Dan McGrew. 1925 Heir-Loons; The Snob Buster. 1926 Beyond the Rockies; The Carnival Girl; The Call of the Wilderness; What Happened to Jane (series); We're in the Navy Now. 1927 Avenging Fangs; Galloping Fury; Painting the Town; She's My Baby; Lost at the Front. 1928 Burning up Broadway. 1929 Show Boat; Kid's Clever. 1930 Trigger Tricks; Sweethearts on Parade. 1931 Bag O' Tricks; Talking Picture Epics (shorts). 1933 The Perils of Pauline (serial). 1934 Little Man, What Now?.

ASHLEY, BEULAH
Died: July 6, 1965, Hollywood, Calif. Screen actress.

ASHTON, DORRIT
Born: 1873. Died: July 25, 1936, Los Angeles, Calif. Screen, stage, and vaudeville actress. Entered films in 1915 with American Films. Married to actor Charles Newton (dec. 1926).

ASHTON, SYLVIA
Born: 1880. Died: Nov. 17, 1940, Los Angeles, Calif. Screen and stage actress.

Appeared in: 1917 The Nick of Time Baby; Her Fame and Shame; Secrets of a Beauty. 1919 The Lottery Man; Men, Women and Money; Don't Change Your Husband. 1920 Jenny Be Good; Conrad in Quest of His Youth. 1921 The Blushing Bride; Garments of Truth; Her Sturdy Oak; Hold Your Horses; The Love Charm; Sham; The Love Special; A Prince There Was. 1922 Manslaughter; Is Matrimony a Failure?; For the Defense; Borderland; Saturday Night; Our Leading Citizen; A Daughter of Luxury; Youth to Youth; While Satan Sleeps. 1923 Desire; The White Flower; Souls for Sale. 1924 Greed. 1926 Dancing Days. 1927 Cheating Cheaters; Red Signals; Woman's Wares. 1928 Bachelor's Paradise; The Head Man; The Leopard Lady; Ladies' Night in a Turkish Bath; Queen Kelly; The Barker; The Crash.

ASHTON, VERA
Died: Apr. 28, 1965, Hollywood, Calif. Screen actress. Doubled for Viola Dana in silent films and also appeared in talkies.

ASKAM, EARL
Born: 1899. Died: Apr. 3, 1940, Los Angeles, Calif.(heart attack). Screen and stage actor.

Appeared in: 1930 Madam Satan. 1936 Empty Saddles; Trail Dust. 1938 Pride of the West. 1940 Northwest Mounted Police.

ASQUITH, ANTHONY
Born: 1902, London, England. Died: Feb. 20, 1968, London, England. Screen actor, film director, and screenwriter. Son of first Earl of Oxford, British W.W.I. Prime Minister. Doubled in blonde wig for Phyliss Neilson Terry in: 1926 Boadicea.

ASTANGOV, MIKHAIL
Born: 1901, Russia. Died: Apr. 21, 1965, Moscow, Russia. Screen and stage actor. Winner of three Stalin Awards.

Appeared in: 1937 Prisoners. 1949 The First Front. 1950 The Victors and the Vanquished. 1953 Sadko (re-released as The Magic Voyalte of Sinbad); Maximba.

ASTOR, JUNIE
Born: 1918, France. Died: Aug. 23, 1967, Avalon, France (auto accident). Screen actress.

Appeared in: 1937 The Lower Depths; Club Des Femmes (Girls' Club). 1939 Entente Cordiale. 1940 Il Carnevale di Venezia (The Carnival of Venice). 1948 L'Eternel Retour (The Eternal Return).

ATCHLEY, HOOPER
Born: 1887, Tenn. Died: Nov. 16, 1943, Hollywood, Calif.(shot himself). Screen and stage actor.

Appeared in: 1929 Love at First Sight. 1930 The Santa Fe Trail. 1931 Millie; Men in Her Life; The Secret Witness; Branded Men; Sundown Trail; Clearing the Range; Arizona Terror. 1932 Hell's House. 1933 The Sphinx; Gambling Ship; Big Time or Bust; Gun Justice; Speed Wings. 1935 Hot Money (short); Behind the Green Lights. 1936 The Return of Jimmy Valentine; Hearts in Bondage; Navy Born. 1937 A Day At the Races; Portia on Trial. 1938 The Old Barn Dance; Cipher Bureau; Hunted Men; Mr. Wong, Detective. 1939 Chicken Wagon Family; East Side of Heaven. 1940 The Gay Caballero. 1941 In the Navy. 1942 Are Husbands Necessary?; Rings on Her Fingers; In Old California; Fingers at the Window.

ATES, ROSCOE
Born: Jan. 20, 1892. Died: Mar. 1, 1962, Hollywood, Calif.(lung cancer). Screen, stage, vaudeville, and television actor. Married to actress Barbara Ray (dec. 1955).

Appeared in: 1929 South Sea Rose. 1930 The Lone Star Ranger; Billy the Kid; The Big House; Caught Short; Love in the Rough; City Girl. 1931 The Great Lover; Cimarron; A Free Soul; The Champ; Politics; Too Many Cooks; Cracked Nuts. 1932 Freaks; Ladies of the Jury; Rainbow Trail; The Optimist; Roadhouse Murder; Young Bride; Deported; The Big Shot; Come on Danger; Hold 'Em Jail. 1933 Renegades of the West; What! No Beer?; Lucky Devils; The Scarlet River; Past of Mary Holmes; Cheyenne Kid; Golden Harvest; Alice in Wonderland. 1934 Woman in the Dark; She Made Her Bed; Merry Wives of Reno. 1935 The People's Enemy; a Vitaphone short. 1936 God's Country and the Woman. 1937 Universal and Columbia shorts. 1938 Riders of the Black Hills; Wild Bill Hickok (serial). 1939 Three Texas Steers; Gone With the Wind. 1940 Rancho Grande; A Cowboy from Sundown; Untamed; Captain Caution; Chad Hannah. 1941 I'll Sell My Life; Mountain Moonlight; Bad Men of Missouri; Robin Hood of the Pecos; One Foot in Heaven; Reg'lar Fellers. 1942 Palm Beach Story; Affairs of Mimi Valentine. 1946 Colorado Serenade; Down Missouri Way; Driftin' River; Stars over Texas. 1947 Wild

Country; West to Glory; Range Beyond the Blue. 1948 Black Hills; Inner Sanctum; Tumbleweed Trail. 1949 Thunder in the Pines. 1950 Hills of Oklahoma; Father's Wild Game. 1951 Honeychile. 1952 The Blazing Forest. 1953 The Stranger Wore a Gun; Those Redheads from Seattle. 1955 Lucy Gallant; Abbott and Costello Meet the Keystone Kops. 1956 The Birds and the Bees; Come Next Spring. 1957 The Big Caper; Short Cut to Hell. 1961 The Silent Call; The Errand Boy.

ATKINS, ALFRED
Born: 1900. Died: June 1941, London, England.(air raid). Screen and stage actor.

ATKINSON, EVELYN
Born: 1900. Died: Dec. 16, 1954, Seattle, Wash. Screen and stage actress.

Appeared in: 1926 The Boy Friend.

ATKINSON, FRANK
Born: Mar. 19, 1893, Blackpool, England. Died: Feb. 23, 1963, Pinner, England. Screen, stage, vaudeville, television actor, circus performer, and screenwriter.

Appeared in: 1931 Ladies' Man; Along Came Youth; Ambassador Bill. 1932 The Woman in Room 13; The Man from Yesterday; Devil's Lottery; Sherlock Holmes. 1933 Sailor's Luck; Pleasure Cruise; Cavalcade. 1934 The Great Defender. 1937 The Woman Alone. 1938 I've Got a Horse. 1947 The Green Cockatoo. 1953 Terror on a Train. 1954 Track the Man Down. 1955 The Green Buddha. 1956 Shadow of Fear. 1957 Wicked as They Come; Just My Luck; The Cat Girl. 1958 At the Stroke of Nine; Three Men in a Boat; High Flight. 1960 Left, Right and Center. 1961 The Kitchen.

ATWELL, ROY
Born: 1880, Syracuse, N.Y. Died: Jan. 6, 1962, New York. Screen, stage, vaudeville, and radio actor.

Appeared in: 1922 The Heart Specialist; South of Suva; Red Hot Romance; Grand Larceny; Don't Get Personal. 1923 Souls for Sale. 1926 The Outsider. 1933 A Universal short, Strike Me Pink. 1936 The Harvester. 1937 Varsity Show; Behind the Mike. 1942 The Fleet's In. 1956 People Are Funny; Gentleman Joe Palooka.

ATWILL, LIONEL
Born: Mar. 1, 1885, Croydon, England. Died: Apr. 22, 1946, Pacific Palisades, Calif.(pneumonia). Screen and stage actor.

Appeared in: 1919 The Marriage Price. 1921 The Highest Bidder; Indiscretion. 1932 Silent Witness; Mystery of the Wax Museum; Dr. X. 1933 Solitaire Man; The Sphinx; Song of Songs; Secret of the Blue Room; Vampire Bat: Secret of Madame Blanche; Murders in the Zoo. 1934 Beggars in Ermine; Nana; The Firebird; Age of Innocence; One More River; Stamboul Quest. 1935 The Devil Is a Woman; Mark of the Vampire; Captain Blood; Murder Man; The Man Who Reclaimed His Head; Rendezvous; Lives of a Bengal Lancer. 1936 Lady of Secrets; 'Til We Meet Again; Absolute Quiet; High Command. 1937 Last Train from Madrid; The Road Back; Lancer Spy; The Wrong Road; The Great Gerrick. 1938 The Three Comrades; The Great Waltz. 1939 The Mad Empress; The Sun Never Sets; The Gorilla; The Hound of the Baskervilles; The Three Musketeers; Son of Frankenstein; Mr. Moto Takes a Vacation; Balalaika; The Secret of Dr. Kildare. 1940 Johnny Apollo; Boom Town; Charlie Chan's Murder Cruise; The Girl in 313; The Great Profile; Charlie Chan in Panama. 1941 Man-Made Monster. 1942 Strange Case of Dr. X; Cairo; Night Monster; Junior G-Men of the Air (serial); Pardon My Sarong; The Mad Doctor of Market Street; The Ghost of Frankenstein; To Be or Not To Be. 1943 Sherlock Holmes and the Secret Weapon; Captain America (serial); Frankenstein Meets the Wolf Man. 1944 Raiders of Ghost City (serial); Secrets of Scotland Yard; Lady in the Death House. 1945 House of Dracula; Fog Island; Crime, Inc.; The House of Frankenstein. 1946 Lost City of the Jungle (serial); Genius At Work. 1953 Return of Captain America (re-issued serial).

AUBREY, WILL
Born: 1894, Lithuania. Died: Jan. 3, 1958, San Francisco, Calif. Screen, vaudeville actor, and radio emcee. Entered films in 1927 and appeared in Vitaphone shorts.

Appeared in: 1934 The Thin Man. 1936 After the Thin Man.

AUBURN, JOY. See Alyce McCormick

AUDRAN, EDMOND
Born: 1919. Died: July 1951, Lyons, France (injuries from auto accident). Screen actor, dancer, and choreographer.

Appeared in: 1948 The Red Shoes. 1951 Tales of Hoffman.

AUER, ANNA. See Mrs. Willis Baker

AUER, MISCHA (Mischa Ounskowski)
Born: Nov. 17, 1905, St. Petersburg, Russia. Died: Mar. 5, 1967, Rome, Italy (heart attack). Screen, stage, and television actor.

Appeared in: 1928 Something Always Happens (film debut). 1929 Marquis Preferred. 1930 Just Imagine; The Benson Murder Case; Inside the Lines; Paramount on Parade. 1931 This Unholy Garden; Delicious; Women Love Once; The Yellow Ticket. 1932 Rasputin and the Empress; No Greater Love; The Midnight Patrol; Scarlet Dawn. 1933 Infernal Machine; Dangerously Yours; Sucker Money; Corruption; Tarzan, the Fearless; After Tonight; Cradle Song; Girl without a Room; Woman Condemned. 1934 Crosby Case; Wharf Angel; Bulldog Drummond Strikes Back; Stamboul Quest. 1935 Lives of a Bengal Lancer; I Dream Too Much; The Crusaders; Clive of India; Mystery Woman; Murder in the Fleet. 1936 We're Only Human; The House of a Thousand Candles; One Rainy Afternoon; The Gay Desperado; Sons O' Guns; The Princess Comes Across; My Man Godfrey; Winterset; That Girl from Paris; Tough Guy. 1937 Three Smart Girls; We Have Our Moments; Top of the Town; One Hundred Men and a Girl; Prescription for Romance; Pick a Star; Marry the Girl; Merry-Go-Round of 1938; Vogues of 1938. 1938 It's All Yours; Rage of Paris; Service De Luxe; Little Tough Guys in Society; Sweethearts; You Can't Take It with You. 1939 East Side of Heaven; Unexpected Father; Destry Rides Again. 1940 Seven Sinners; Trail of the Vigilantes; Alias the Deacon; Sandy Is a Lady; Margie; Spring Parade; Public Deb No. 1. 1941 Moonlight in Hawaii; Sing Another Chorus; Cracked Nuts; Flame of New Orleans; Hold That Ghost; Hellzapoppin'. 1942 Don't Get Personal. 1943 Twin Beds; Around the World. 1944 Up in Mabel's Room; Lady in the Dark. 1945 A Royal Scandal; Czarina; And Then There Were None; Brewster's Millions. 1946 She Wrote the Book; Sentimental Journey. 1947 For You I Die. 1948 Sofia. 1952 Fame and the Devil; Song of Paris; The Sky Is Red. 1953 Confidential Report; Bachelor of Paris. 1957 The Monte Carlo Story. 1958 Foxiest Girl in Paris; Mam'zelle Pigalle; That Naughty Girl. 1960 A Pied, a Cheval et un Sputnik (A Dog, a Mouse and a Sputnik); School for Love. 1962 We Joined the Navy; Mr. Arkadin. 1963 Ladies First; Dynamite Girl (Fr.). 1966 Arriverderci, Baby!; The Christmas That Almost Wasn't.

AUERBACH, ARTHUR
Born: 1903, N.Y. Died: Oct. 3, 1957, Van Nuys, Calif.(heart attack). Screen, stage, television, and radio actor.

Appeared in: 1937 an MGM short.

AUGUST, EDWIN (Edwin August Philip Von der Butz)
Born: 1883. Died: Mar. 4, 1964, Hollywood, Calif. Screen, stage actor, film director, and author. Entered films in 1908 with Biograph.

Appeared in: 1910 The Fugitive; Simple Charity; Winning Back His Love; His Daughter; Madame Rex. 1911 A Tale of the Wilderness; A Blot of the 'Scutcheon. 1912 The Girl and Her Trust; The Lesser Evil; The Old Actor; The School Teacher and the Waif; The Sands of Dee. 1918 The Lion's Claw (serial). 1921 The Idol of the North. 1922 The Blonde Vampire. 1925 Scandal Sheet. 1929 Side Street. 1930 Romance of the West. 1942 Over My Dead Body.

AULT, MARIE (Marie Cragg)
Born: Sept. 2, 1870, Wigan, England. Died: May 9, 1951, London, England. Screen and stage actress. Entered films approximately 1923.

Appeared in: 1923 Paddy-the-Next-Best-Thing. 1924 Woman to Woman. 1925 The Rat. 1926 The Lodger. 1927 Mademoiselle from Armentieres; The Triumph of the Rat. 1928 Madame Pompadour; Dawn; Roses of Picardy. 1929 Fanny Hawthorne; Kitty. 1930 Down Stream; Third Time Lucky. 1931 The Speckled Band; Hobson's Choice. 1933 Little Fella; Money for Speed; Daughters of Today. 1941 Major Barbara. 1943 We Dive at Dawn. 1945 Love on the Dole. 1946 I See a Dark Stranger. 1949 Madness of the Heart. 1951 Cheer the Brave. Other British films prior to 1933: Class and No Class; Wee McGregor's Sweetheart; A Prince of Lovers; Every Mother's Son; Monkey's Paw; Starlit Garden; The Colleen Bawn; Hindle Wakes; The Silver Lining; Return of the Rat; Contraband Love; Peace and Quiet.

AUSTIN, ALBERT
Born: 1882. Died: Aug. 17, 1953, North Hollywood, Calif.
Screen actor, film director, and screenwriter. Entered films in
1910.

Appeared in: 1921 The Kid; My Boy. 1922 Trouble. 1923 A
Prince of a King. 1925 Keep Smiling.

AUSTIN, JERE
Born: 1876. Died: Nov. 12, 1927, Hollywood, Calif.(cancer).
Screen actor.

Appeared in: 1914 The School for Scandal. 1927 King of Kings.

AUSTIN, JOHANNA (Anna R. Austin)
Born: 1853. Died: June 1, 1944, Hollywood, Calif. Screen actress. Appeared in early Edison Co. films.

AUSTIN, STEPHEN E.
Born: 1891. Died: May 12, 1955, Dallas, Tex.(heart attack).
Screen and radio actor.

AVOLO, ROSALIE. See Rosalie Avolo Wincott

AYE, MARION
Born: 1906. Died: July 21, 1951, Hollywood, Calif.(suicide—
poison). Screen and stage actress.

Appeared in: 1921 Montana Bill; The Vengeance Trail. 1923
The Meanest Man in the World; The Eternal Three. 1924 The
Last Man on Earth; The Roughneck. 1926 Irene.

AYLMER, DAVID
Born: 1933. Died: July 20, 1964, London, England (suicide).
Screen, stage, and television actor. Son of actor Felix Aylmer.

Appeared in: 1957 Battle Hell (aka Their Greatest Glory; Yangtse Incident). 1959 Gideon of Scotland Yard (aka Gideon's Day).
1960 The Man Who Wouldn't Talk.

AYRES, AGNES (Agnes Hinkle)
Born: Sept. 4, 1898, Carbondale, Ill. Died: Dec. 25, 1940, Los
Angeles, Calif.(cerebral hemorrhage). Screen, stage, radio, and
vaudeville actress.

Appeared in: 1920 The Furnace; Held by the Enemy; Go and Get
It. 1921 Affairs of Anatole; Forbidden Fruit; The Sheik; Cappy
Ricks; The Love Special; Too Much Speed. 1922 Clarence; The
Ordeal; The Lane That Had No Turning; Bought and Paid for;
Borderland; A Daughter of Luxury. 1923 The Ten Command-
ments; Tess of the Storm Country; Racing Hearts; The Heart
Raider; Hollywood; The Marriage Maker. 1924 The Story With-
out a Name; When a Girl Loves; Bluff; Don't Call It Love; The
Guilty One; Worldly Goods. 1925 Tomorrow's Love; Morals for
Men; The Awful Truth. 1926 The Son of the Sheik; Her Market
Value. 1928 The Lady of Victory; Into the Night. 1929 Bye, Bye,
Buddy; The Donovan Affair; Broken Hearted; Eve's Love Letters.

AYRES, ROBERT
Born: 1914, Michigan. Died: Nov. 5, 1968, Hemel Hempstead,
England (heart attack). Screen, stage, and television actor.

Appeared in: 1949 They Were Not Divided. 1951 The Black
Widow; To Have and to Hold. 1952 Cosh Boy. 1953 Affair In
Monte Carlo; A Night without Stars; The Slasher. 1954 A Prize
of Gold; River Beat. 1955 Contraband Spain; It's Never Too
Late. 1956 The Baby and the Battleship; Depraved. 1957 The
Story of Esther Costello; The Cat Girl; Operation Murder. 1958
A Night to Remember. 1959 First Man into Space; John Paul
Jones; Time Lock. 1962 The Road to Hong Kong. 1963 The
Sicilians. 1968 Battle Beneath the Earth; The Loves of Isadora.

BACCALONI, SALVATORE
Born: 1900, Rome, Italy. Died: Dec. 31, 1969, New York, N.Y.
Screen actor and operatic comedian.

Appeared in: 1956 Full of Life (film debut). 1958 Rock-A-Bye
Baby; Merry Andrew. 1961 Operation Bottleneck; Fanny. 1962
The Pigeon That Took Rome.

BACH. See Charles Pasquier

BACH, MRS. RUDI
Died: Apr. 11, 1960, Buffalo, N.Y. Screen and stage actress.

BACKUS, GEORGE
Born: 1858. Died: May 22, 1939, Merrick, N.Y. Screen, stage
actor, and playwright.

Appeared in: 1921 The Price of Possession. 1923 The Exciters.
1924 Her Own Free Will; The Warrens of Virginia.

BACON, BESSIE (Bessie Bacon Allen)
Born: 1886. Died: Dec. 7, 1952, Los Angeles, Calif. Screen
actress and writer.

BACON, DAVID
Born: 1914. Died: Sept. 13, 1943, Hollywood, Calif.(stab wounds).
Screen actor.

Appeared in: 1942 Ten Gentlemen from West Point. 1943 The
Masked Marvel (serial); Crash Dive; Gals Inc.

BACON, FAITH
Born: 1909. Died: Sept. 26, 1956, Chicago, Ill.("suicide-jump
from window"). Screen and vaudeville actress.

Appeared in: 1938 Prison Train.

BACON, FRANK
Born: 1864, Marysville, Calif. Died: July 21, 1922, Chicago,
Ill.(heart attack). Screen and stage actor.

Appeared in: 1915 The Silent Voice.

BACON, IRVING
Born: Sept. 6, 1893, St. Joseph, Mo. Died: Feb. 5, 1965, Hollywood, Calif. Screen, stage, and television actor. Entered films
in 1913 with Mack Sennett.

Appeared in: 1927 California or Bust. 1928 Head Man; The
Good-Bye Kiss. 1929 Half Way to Heaven; Side Street; "Dane &
Arthur" series; "Louise Fazenda" series; Two Sisters; The
Saturday Night Kid. 1930 Street of Chance. 1931 Alias the Bad
Man; Branded Men. 1932 Union Depot; No One Man; This Is the
Night; Gentleman for a Day; Central Park; File 113; Million
Dollar Legs. 1933 He Learned About Women; Hello, Everybody!;
Private Detective 62; Big Executive. 1934 Shadows of Sing
Sing; You Belong to Me; Hat, Coat and Glove; Ready for Love; The
Pursuit of Happiness; Lone Cowboy; Miss Fane's Baby Is Stolen;
Six of a Kind; It Happened One Night; The Hell Cat; No Ransom.
1935 West of the Pecos; Powder Smoke Range; Here Comes
Cookie; Private Worlds; Goin' to Town; The Glass Key; The Vir-
ginia Judge; Ship Cafe; Two-Fisted; It's a Small World; Diamond
Jim; Manhattan Moon; Bright Leaves; Millions in the Air. 1936
Petticoat Fever; Earthworm Tractors; Drift Fence; Hollywood
Boulevard; Lady Be Careful; Murder with Pictures; Wives Never
Know; Valiant Is the Word for Carrie; Hopalong Cassidy Returns;
It's a Great Life; Big Town Girl; Three Cheers for Love; The
Big Broadcast of 1937. 1937 Let's Make a Million; Interns Can't
Take Money; Exclusive; Seventh Heaven; Arizona Mahoney; Big
City; Marry the Girl; It's Love I'm After. 1938 The Big Broad-
cast of 1938; The Texans; There Goes My Heart; The Cowboy and
the Lady; You Can't Take It with You; Midnight Intruder; Exposed;
The First Hundred Years; The Chaser; Tip-Off Girls; Sing, You
Sinners; Spawn of the North; Kentucky Moonshine; The Amazing
Dr. Clitterhouse; The Sisters. 1939 Too Busy to Work; Holly-
wood Slaves; Tailspin; Lucky Night; Second Fiddle; Hollywood
Cavalcade; Gone with the Wind; I Stole a Million; Blondie Takes
a Vacation; Rio; Blondie Brings up Baby; The Gracie Allen
Murder Case; The Oklahoma Kid; Torchy Runs for Mayor. 1940
Indianapolis Speedway; Heaven with a Barbed Wire Fence; The
Grapes of Wrath; The Man Who Wouldn't Talk; Young People; Dr.
Ehrlich's Magic Bullet; Blondie On a Budget; Manhattan Heart-
beat; The Return of Frank James; Gold Rush Maisie; The Howards
of Virginia; Dreaming Out Loud; Blondie Has Servant Trouble;
Michael Shayne, Private Detective; Star Dust; You Can't Fool
Your Wife; Blondie Plays Cupid. 1941 Blondie Goes Latin; She
Couldn't Say No; Western Union; Ride on, Vaquero; Caught in
the Draft; Accent on Love; Too Many Blondes; Moon over Her
Shoulder; It Started with Eve; Never Give a Sucker an Even
Break; Blondie in Society; Remember the Day; Meet John Doe;
A Girl, a Guy and a Gob; Great Guns; Henry Aldrich for Presi-
dent; Cadet Girl; Tobacco Road. 1942 The Bashful Bachelor;
Pardon My Sarong; Through Different Eyes; Juke Girl; Young
America; Give Out, Sister; Between Us Girls; Get Hep to Love;
Blondie for Victory; Holiday Inn; Footlight Serenade. 1943
Shadow of a Doubt; Johnny Come Lately; Hers to Hold; Follow
the Band; King of the Cowboys; Two Weeks to Live; Happy Go
Lucky; So's Your Uncle; The Good Fellows; In Old Oklahoma;
Action in the North Atlantic; The Desperados; Stranger in Town;
Dixie Dugan. 1944 Weekend Pass; Chip Off the Old Block; Her
Primitive Man; Since You Went Away; Heavenly Days; Pin Up
Girl; Wing and a Prayer. 1945 Under Western Skies; Roughly
Speaking; Patrick the Great; Out of This World; Guest Wife; Hitch-
hike to Happiness. 1946 Night Train to Memphis; One Way to
Love; Wake up and Dream. 1947 My Brother Talks to Horses;
Saddle Pals; Monsieur Verdoux; The Bachelor and the Bobby-
Soxer. 1948 Albuquerque; Moonrise; Adventures in Silverado;
State of the Union; The Velvet Touch; Good Sam; Rocky; Family

Honeymoon. 1949 Night unto Night; John Loves Mary; The Green Promise; The Big Cat; Dynamite; It's a Great Feeling; Man-handled; Woman in Hiding. 1950 Wabash Avenue; Born to Be Bad; Emergency Wedding; Dear Wife; Sons of New Mexico. 1951 Honeychile; Cause for Alarm; Katie Did It; Desert of Lost Men. 1952 O. Henry's Full House; Room for One More. 1953 Fort Ti; Devil's Canyon; Kansas Pacific; Sweethearts on Parade. 1954 Ma and Pa Kettle at Home; Black Horse Canyon; Duffy of San Quentin; A Star Is Born; The Glenn Miller Story. 1955 Run for Cover; At Gunpoint. 1956 Hidden Guns; The Dakota Incident. 1958 Ambush at Cimarron Pass; Fort Massacre.

BACON, LLOYD
Born: Jan. 16, 1890, San Jose, Calif. Died: Nov. 15, 1955, Burbank, Calif.(cerebral hemorrhage). Screen, stage, vaude-ville actor, and film director. Entered films with Essanay Co.

Appeared in: 1917 A Dark Room Secret. 1918 Lloyd Hamilton Comedies. 1919 Triangle Comedies. 1921 The Great Profit; Hands Off; Hearts and Masks; The Road Demon. 1922 Smudge.

BACUS, LUCIA. See Lucia Segar

BAER, MAX
Born: 1909. Died: Nov. 21, 1959, Hollywood, Calif.(heart attack). Screen, stage, radio, and vaudeville actor and former heavyweight boxing champion of the world. Divorced from actress Dorothy Dunbar.

Appeared in: 1933 The Prizefighter and the Lady. 1942 The Navy Comes Through. 1943 Ladies' Day; Buckskin Frontier. 1944 The Iron Road. 1949 Africa Screams; Bride for Sale. 1950 Riding High. 1951 Skipalong Rosenbloom. 1956 The Harder They Fall. 1957 Utah Blaine. 1958 Once upon a Horse; Over She Goes.

BAER, THAIS
Born: 1929. Died: Sept. 8, 1930, Painted Desert, Ariz. Fourteen-month-old baby girl making fourth screen appearance when she died during filming of Painted Desert.

Appeared in: 1931 Painted Desert.

BAGGETT, LYNNE
Born: 1928. Died: Mar. 22, 1960, Hollywood, Calif.(overdose of barbiturates). Screen actress. Divorced from film producer Sam Spiegel.

Appeared in: 1941 Manpower. 1944 The Adventures of Mark Twain; Hollywood Canteen. 1946 The Time of Their Lives. 1950 D.O.A; Flame and the Arrow. 1951 The Mob.

BAGGOT, KING
Born: 1874, St. Louis, Mo. Died: July 11, 1948, Los Angeles, Calif.(stroke). Screen, stage actor, film director, and screen-writer. Entered films in 1910 as an actor.

Appeared in: 1911 The Scarlet Letter. 1912 Lady Audley's Secret. 1913 Dr. Jekyll and Mr. Hyde; Ivanhoe. 1915 The Corsi-can Brothers. 1916 Lovely Mary. 1918 The Eagle's Eye (serial). 1920 Dwelling Place of Light; The Cheater; The Hawk's Trail (serial). 1921 Moonlight Follies; Snowy Baker; The Shadow of Lightning Ridge; The Fighting Breed; The Butterfly Girl; The Girl in the Taxi. 1922 Going Straight. 1923 His Last Race; The Thrill Chaser. 1925 Tumbleweeds. 1926 Lovely Mary. 1927 The Notorious Lady. 1930 Once a Gentleman; The Czar of Broad-way. 1931 Scareheads; Sweepstakes. 1932 Fame Street. 1934 Beloved. 1935 It Happened in New York; Father Brown, Detective; Mississippi; Chinatown Squad; She Gets Her Man. 1941 Come Live with Me. 1945 Abbott and Costello in Hollywood.

BAGLEY, SAM (Samuel Borken)
Born: 1903. Died: July 3, 1968, Hollywood, Calif.(heart ailment). Screen actor. Entered films approx. 1930.

Appeared in: 1955 The Lieutenant Wore Skirts.

BAGNI, JOHN
Born: 1911. Died: Feb. 13, 1954, Hollywood, Calif.(heart attack). Screen and stage actor, screen, radio, and television writer.

Appeared in: 1942 Bombay Clipper. 1943 Mug Town. 1945 A Bell for Adano. 1946 The Phantom Thief. 1947 The Pretender. 1950 Captain China.

BAILEY, ALBERT
Born: 1891. Died: July 31, 1952, Hollywood, Calif.(suicide—gun). Western screen actor and trainer of film horses.

BAILEY, EDWARD LORENZ
Born: 1883. Died: Oct. 16, 1951, Lima, Ohio. Screen and stage actor.

BAILEY, EDWIN B.
Born: 1873. Died: July 22, 1950, Santa Monica, Calif. Screen, stage, and vaudeville actor. Married to actress Grace Lock-wood (dec. 1955).

BAILEY, FRANKIE (Frankie Walters)
Born: 1859, New Orleans, La. Died: July 8, 1953, Los Angeles, Calif. Screen, stage, and burlesque actress. Known around the turn of the century as "The Girl with the Million Dollar Legs." Entered films in 1922.

Appeared in: 1923 The Famous Mrs. Fair. 1925 Flower of Night; Thank You. 1926 The Crown of Lies.

BAILEY, WILLIAM (William Norton Bailey)
Born: 1886. Died: Nov. 8, 1962, Hollywood, Calif. Screen actor and film director.

Appeared in: 1913 The Snare. 1918 The Eagle's Eye (serial). 1920 The Phantom Foe (serial). 1921 The Yellow Arm (serial). 1923 Is Money Everything?; Three O'Clock in the Morning. 1924 The Cyclone Rider; The Desert Hawk; The Uninvited Guest; Against All Odds; The Flaming Forties; Gold Heels; Winner Take All. 1925 Big Pal; My Neighbor's Wife; Bustin' Thru; The Desert Flower; Fighting Youth; Lazybones; Top Hand; You're Fired. 1926 House without a Key (serial); Queen O'Diamonds; Ranson's Folly; The Stolen Ranch; Fighting Jack; Lightning Bill; Lash of the Law. 1927 Melting Millions (serial); Wild Beauty; High School Hero; The Fighting Three. 1928 Waterfront; The Flyin' Cowboy; The Lone Patrol; Burning Bridges; Hit of the Show; Man in the Rough; The Stronger Will; The Way of the Strong. 1929 The Aviator. 1930 Back Pay; Today. 1932 The Midnight Patrol. 1933 The Lone Avenger. 1934 Search for Beauty. 1935 George White's Scandals; Thunder Mountain; One Hour Late. 1936 Charlie Chan's Secret. 1949 Brand of Fear; Across the Rio Grande. 1950 Lightning Guns.

BAINES, BEULAH
Born: 1905. Died: Aug. 1930, Banning, Calif. Screen and stage actress.

Appeared in: 1921 The Charm School.

BAINTER, FAY
Born: Dec. 7, 1891, Los Angeles, Calif. Died: Apr. 16, 1968, Los Angeles, Calif. Screen, stage, and television actress. In 1938 won Academy Award for Best Supporting Actress in Jezebel and was nominated for Best Actress in White Banners—did not win. A change in the Academy Awards nominating and voting rules was made because of confusion of her two nominations in 1938.

Appeared in: 1934 This Side of Heaven (film debut). 1937 The Soldier and the Lady; Make Way for Tomorrow; Quality Street. 1938 Mother Carey's Chickens; Jezebel; White Banners; The Arkansas Traveler; The Shining Hour. 1939 Daughters Coura-geous; The Lady and the Mob; Yes, My Darling Daughter; Our Neighbors, the Carters. 1940 A Bill of Divorcement; Our Town; Young Tom Edison; Maryland. 1941 Babes on Broadway; Love Crazy. 1942 Journey for Margaret; Mrs. Wiggs of the Cabbage Patch; The War against Mrs. Hadley; Woman of the Year. 1943 Cry Havoc; The Human Comedy; Salute to the Marines; Present-ing Lily Mars; The Heavenly Body. 1944 Three Is a Family; Dark Waters. 1945 State Fair. 1946 The Virginian; The Kid from Brooklyn. 1947 The Secret Life of Walter Mitty; Deep Valley. 1948 June Bride; Give My Regards to Broadway. 1951 Close to My Heart. 1953 The President's Lady. 1962 The Chil-dren's Hour; Bon Voyage.

BAIRD, CORA
Born: 1913. Died: Dec. 7, 1967, New York, N.Y. Screen, stage, and television actress. Partner in puppet team of "Bill and Cora Baird."

BAIRD, LEAH
Born: approx. 1891. Died: Oct. 3, 1971, Hollywood, Calif. (anemia). Screen, stage actress, screenwriter, and film pro-ducer. Entered films with Vitagraph in New York.

Appeared in: 1912 Stenographers Wanted; Chumps. 1913 Ivan-hoe. 1914 Neptune's Daughter. 1915 Tried for His Own Murder. 1917 A Sunset. 1918 Wolves of Kultur (serial). 1921 The Heart Line. 1922 Don't Doubt Your Wife; When the Devil Drives; The Bride's Confession; When Husband's Deceive. 1923 Destroying

Angel; Is Divorce a Failure?; The Miracle Makers. 1924 The Law Demands; The Radio Flyer. 1925 The Unnamed Woman. 1942 Lady Gangster.

BAKER, MRS. ANNA WILLIS (Anna Auer)
Born: 1860. Died: Apr. 2, 1944, Fort Lee, N.J. Screen and stage actress.

BAKER, ART
Born: 1898, New York, N.Y. Died: Aug. 26, 1966, Los Angeles, Calif.(heart attack). Screen, radio, and television actor.

Appeared in: 1944 Once upon a Time. 1945 Spellbound. 1946 Abie's Irish Rose. 1947 The Beginning of the End; Dark Delusion; Daisy Kenyon; The Farmer's Daughter. 1948 Silver River; A Southern Yankee; Walk a Crooked Mile; The Decision of Christopher Blake; State of the Union; The Walls of Jericho. 1949 Easy Living; Take One False Step; Any Number Can Play; Night Unto Night; Massacre River; Cover Up; Impact; Task Force. 1950 The Underworld Story; Hot Rod. 1951 Cause for Alarm; Only the Valiant. 1954 Living It Up. 1955 Artists and Models. 1960 Twelve Hours to Kill. 1962 Swingin' Along. 1965 Young Dillinger. 1966 The Wild Angels.

BAKER, BELLE
Born: 1895, New York, N.Y. Died: Apr. 29, 1957, Los Angeles, Calif.(heart attack). Screen, stage, vaudeville, and television actress.

Appeared in: 1929 Song of Love. 1944 Atlantic City.

BAKER, EDDIE (Edward King)
Born: Nov. 17, 1897, Davis, W. Va. Died: Feb. 4, 1968, Hollywood, Calif. Screen actor. Entered films as a prop boy with Biograph in 1914. Was one of the original Keystone Kops.

Appeared in early "Joker" comedies and later in "Gale Henry" comedies, Hal Roach pictures and Christie shorts.
Appeared in: 1924 Hold Your Breath. 1929 All at Sea. 1931 Come Clean (short); City Lights; Monkey Business. 1933 In the following shorts: Beauty and the Bus; Kickin' the Crown Around; Sons of the Desert. 1934 Elmer and Elsie; Them Thar Hills (short); Babes in Toyland (aka The March of the Wooden Soldiers). 1950 Revenge Is Sweet (reissue and retitle of Babes in Toyland-1934). 1955 Land of Fury. 1965 Ship of Fools.

BAKER, ELSIE
Born: 1893, Chicago, Ill. Died: Aug. 16, 1971, Hollywood, Calif. (heart attack). Screen, stage, vaudeville, radio, and television actress. Made stage debut at age of ten months.

Appeared in: 1952 No Room for the Groom.

BAKER, FLOYD
Born: 1906. Died: Mar. 17, 1943, Hollywood, Calif. Screen actor.

BAKER, LEE
Born: 1876, Ovid, Mich. Died: Feb. 24, 1948, Los Angeles, Calif. Screen and stage actor.

Appeared in: 1923 The Fighting Blade. 1925 Soul Fire. 1947 Mourning Becomes Electra.

BAKER, PHIL
Born: Aug. 24, 1898, Philadelphia, Pa. Died: Dec. 1, 1963, Copenhagen, Denmark. Screen, stage, radio, and vaudeville actor. Appeared in vaudeville with Ben Bernie as part of "Bernie & Baker" team.

Appeared in: 1929 A Bad Boy from a Good Family (short); In Spain (short). 1934 Gift of Gab. 1938 The Goldwyn Follies; Start Cheering. 1943 The Gang's All Here. 1944 Take It or Leave It.

BALDRA, CHARLES M.
Born: 1899, Albany, Ore. Died: May 14, 1949, Hollywood, Calif. (his car hit by train). Screen and stage actor. Entered films in 1920.

Appeared in: 1936 The Law-less Nineties.

BALDWIN, GEORGE
Died: Feb. 28, 1923, Manila, Philippine Islands (poisoned). Screen and vaudeville actor.

BALDWIN, KITTY
Born: 1853. Died: June 27, 1934, Buffalo, N.Y. Screen and stage actress.

BALFOUR, LORNA
Born: 1913, England. Died: Mar. 2, 1932, Hollywood, Calif. (complications following surgery). Screen and stage actress.

Appeared in: 1931 Merely Mary Ann.

BALIN, MIREILLE
Born: 1911, France. Died: Nov. 8, 1968, Paris, France. Screen actress.

Appeared in: 1933 Don Quixote. 1936 Pepe Le Moko. 1938 Gueurde d'Amour. 1940 The Kiss of Fire.

BALL, SUZAN (Susan)
Born: Feb. 3, 1933, Buffalo, N.Y. Died: Aug. 5, 1955, Beverly Hills, Calif.(cancer). Screen actress. Married to actor Richard Long. Injured her right knee while filming East of Sumatra in 1952; injury developed into cancer.

Appeared in: 1952 Untamed Frontier (film debut); Yankee Buccaneer. 1953 East of Sumatra; City beneath the Sea. 1954 War Arrow. 1955 Chief Crazy Horse.

BALLANTINE, E. J.
Born: 1888, Edinburgh, Scotland. Died: Oct. 20, 1968, London, England. Screen and stage actor.

Appeared in: 1943 The Moon Is Down. 1944 Tampico.

BALLANTYNE, NELL
Died: Feb. 19, 1959, Glasgow, Scotland. Screen, stage, and radio actress.

Appeared in: 1954 Scotch on the Rocks. 1958 Rockets Galore. 1959 The Bridal Path.

BALLIN, MRS. MABEL
Born: 1885. Died: July 24, 1958, Santa Monica, Calif. Screen actress.

Appeared in: 1921 East Lynne; Pagan Love; Jane Eyre; The Journey's End. 1922 Other Women's Clothes; Married People. 1923 Vanity Fair; Souls for Sale. 1925 Barriers Burned Away; Beauty and the Bad Man; Code of the West; Riders of the Purple Sage; The Shining Adventure.

BALLOU, MARION
Born: 1871. Died: Mar. 25, 1939, Hollywood, Calif. Screen and stage actress.

Appeared in: 1930 Night Work; The Big Pond. 1933 Little Women; Cradle Song. 1935 David Copperfield; The Melody Lingers On. 1936 Camille. 1937 Portia on Trial.

BAMATTRE, MARTHA
Born: 1892. Died: July 12, 1970, Glendale, Calif. Screen and stage actress. Entered films in 1927.

Appeared in: 1951 An American in Paris. 1955 To Catch a Thief.

BANCROFT, CHARLES (Fred Bently)
Born: 1911. Died: May 17, 1969, Woodland Hills, Calif.(cancer). Screen actor. Entered films approx. 1930.

BANCROFT, GEORGE
Born: Sept. 30, 1882, Philadelphia, Pa. Died: Oct. 2, 1956, Santa Monica, Calif. Screen and stage actor. Father of actress Ann Bancroft.

Appeared in: 1921 The Journey's End. 1922 Driven; The Prodigal Judge. 1924 The Deadwood Coach; Teeth. 1925 The Pony Express; Code of the West; The Rainbow Trail; The Splendid Road. 1926 Old Ironsides; The Enchanted Hill; The Runaway; Sea Horses. 1927 White Gold; Underworld; The Rough Riders; Tell It to Sweeney; Too Many Crooks. 1928 The Dragnet; The Docks of New York; The Showdown. 1929 The Wolf of Wall Street; Thunderbolt. 1930 The Mighty; Ladies Love Brutes; Derelict; Paramount on Parade. 1931 Scandal Sheet; Rich Man's Folly; The Skin Game. 1932 The World and the Flesh; Lady and Gent. 1933 Blood Money; Hello, Everybody!; A Lady's Profession; Under the Tonto Rim; Sunset Pass; Mama Loves Papa; This Day and Age; Turn Back the Clock; Love, Honor and Oh, Baby!; Tillie and Gus. 1934 Elmer and Elsie; Miss Fane's Baby Is Stolen; Journal of a Crime; Many Happy Returns; Merry Widow; She Loves Me Not; The Cat's Paw; Ladies Should Listen; College Rhythm. 1936 Mr. Deeds Goes to Town; Hell Ship Morgan; Wedding Present. 1937 John Meade's Woman; Racketeers in Exile. 1938 A Doctor's Diary; Submarine Patrol; Angels with Dirty Faces. 1939 Stagecoach; Each Dawn I Die; Rulers of the Sea; Espionage Agent. 1940 Green Hell; When the Daltons Rode; North West Mounted Police; Little Men; Young Tom Edison. 1941 Texas; The Bugle Sounds. 1943 Whistling in Dixie; Syncopation.

BANDO, TSUMASABURO
Born: 1898, Japan. Died: July 7, 1953, Kyoto, Japan(cerebral hemorrhage). Screen and Kabuki actor. Entered films approx. 1923.

BANKHEAD, TALLULAH
Born: Jan. 31, 1902, Huntsville, Ala. Died: Dec. 12, 1968, New York, N.Y.(double pneumonia). Screen, stage, radio, and television actress. Divorced from actor John Emery (dec. 1964).

Appeared in: 1918 Thirty a Week. 1931 Tarnished Lady; The Cheat; My Sin. 1932 Thunder Below; The Devil and the Deep; Faithless; Make Me a Star (guest without billing). 1943 Stage Door Canteen. 1944 Lifeboat. 1945 A Royal Scandal. 1953 Main Street to Broadway. 1961 The Big Show. 1965 Die! Die! My Darling!. 1966 The Daydreamer (voice only).

BANKS, LESLIE
Born: June 9, 1890, Liverpool, England. Died: Apr. 21, 1952, London, England. Screen, stage actor, stage director, and stage producer.

Appeared in: 1932 The Most Dangerous Game (film debut) (aka The Hounds of Zaroff). 1933 Strange Evidence; The Fire Raisers; Night of the Party; Red Ensign. 1934 I Am Suzanne. 1935 The Man Who Knew Too Much; Sanders of the River; Transatlantic Tunnel. 1936 The Three Maxims; Debt of Honor. 1937 Fire over England; Farewell Again; Wings of the Morning. 1938 The Drum; Troopship. 1939 Jamaica Inn. 1940 21 Days Together; Neutral Port; The Door with Seven Locks; Haunted Honeymoon. 1941 Cottage to Let. 1942 Ships with Wings; The Big Blockade; Went the Day Well?; They Came in Khaki. 1944 Forty-Eight Hours; Henry V (U.S. 1946). 1950 Mrs. Fitzherbert; Madeleine; Your Witness (aka Eye Witness). 1952 The Small Back Room. 1958 Henry V (reissue of 1944 film).

BANKS, MONTY (aka MONTAGUE BANKS; real name Mario Bianchi)
Born: 1897, Casene, Italy. Died: Jan. 7, 1950, Arona, Italy(heart attack). Screen and stage actor, film director, and film producer. Married to actress Gracie Fields. Divorced from screen actress Gladys Frazin (dec. 1939). Appeared in a number of Mack Sennett films.

Appeared in: 1921 "Monte Banks" series. 1924 Racing Luck. 1925 Keep Smiling. 1926 Atta Boy. 1927 Flying Luck; Horse Shoes; Play Safe. 1928 A Perfect Gentleman. 1929 Week-End Wives; Honeymoon Abroad. 1930 Atlantic. 1932 My Wife's Family; Kiss Me Sergeant; Hold 'Em Jail; Old Soldiers Never Die; Money for Nothing; Not So Quiet on the Western Front. 1933 Heads We Go; You Made Me Love You; The Charming Deceiver; Leave It to Me. 1935 So You Won't Talk; Church Mouse; No Limit. 1936 Olympic Honeymoon. 1941 Blood and Sand. 1945 A Bell for Adano. 1961 Days of Thrills and Laughter (documentary).

BANNISTER, HARRY
Born: 1889, Holland, Mich. Died: Feb. 26, 1961, N.Y. Screen, stage, and television actor. Divorced from actress Ann Harding.

Appeared in: 1921 The Porcelain Lamp. 1929 Her Private Affair. 1930 The Girl of the Golden West. 1931 Suicide Fleet; Husband's Holiday. 1961 Girl on the Run.

BARA, THEDA (Theodosia Goodman)
Born: 1890, Cincinnati, Ohio. Died: Apr. 7, 1955, Los Angeles, Calif.(cancer). Screen and stage actress. Also appeared under the name of Theodosia DeCoppett. Married to director Charles J. Brabin.

Appeared in: 1915 The Two Orphans (film debut); The Clemenceau Case; The Stain; A Fool There Was; Sin; Carmen. 1916 Romeo and Juliet; Destruction; The Light; Gold and the Woman; The Serpent; Eternal Sappho; East Lynne; Her Double Life. 1917 Cleopatra; Madame DuBarry; Under Two Flags; Camille; Heart and Soul; The Tiger Woman. 1918 Salome; When a Woman Sins; The Forbidden Path; The She Devil; Rose of the Blood. 1919 Kathleen Mavourneen; La Belle Russe. 1921 The Prince of Silence; Her Greatest Love. 1923 The Hunchback of Notre Dame. 1925 The Unchastened Woman. 1926 Madame Mystery; The Dancer of Paris.

BARBANELL, FRED
Born: 1931. Died: Sept. 11, 1959, Hollywood, Calif.(following surgery). Screen and television actor.

BARBIER, GEORGE W.
Born: 1865, Philadelphia, Pa. Died: July 19, 1945, Los Angeles, Calif.(heart attack). Screen and stage actor.

Appeared in: 1924 Monsieur Beaucaire. 1930 The Big Pond; The Sap from Syracuse. 1931 The Smiling Lieutenant; 24 Hours; Girls about Town; Touchdown. 1932 Skyscraper Souls; Evenings for Sale; No Man of Her Own; No One Man; Strangers in Love; The Broken Wing; One Hour with You; The Strange Case of Clara Deane; Million Dollar Legs; Madame Racketeer; The Phantom President; The Big Broadcast. 1933 Hello, Everybody!; Mama Loves Papa; Sunset Pass; Under the Tonto Rim; This Day and Age; Tillie and Gus; Turn Back the Clock; A Lady's Profession; Love, Honor and Oh, Baby!. 1934 Miss Fane's Baby Is Stolen; Many Happy Returns; Ladies Should Listen; She Loves Me Not; College Rhythm; Elmer and Elsie; The Notorious Sophie Lang; Journal of a Crime; The Merry Widow. 1935 McFadden's Flats; Hold 'Em Yale; The Crusades; Here Comes Cookie; Millions in the Air; Life Begins at 40; Broadway Gondolier; Old Man Rhythm; The Cat's Paw. 1936 The Milky Way; Preview Murder Mystery; Wife vs. Secretary; The Princess Comes Across; Spendthrift; Early to Bed; Three Married Men. 1937 On the Avenue; Waikiki Wedding; Hotel Haywire; It's Love I'm After; A Girl with Ideas. 1938 Tarzan's Revenge; Little Miss Broadway; My Lucky Star; Hold That Coed; Straight, Place and Show; Thanks for Everything; Hold That Kiss; Sweethearts; The Adventures of Marco Polo. 1939 Wife, Husband and Friend; SOS Tidal Wave; News Is Made at Night; Smuggled Cargo; Remember?. 1940 Village Barn Dance; The Return of Frank James; 1941 Repent at Leisure; The Man Who Came to Dinner; Million Dollar Baby; Marry the Boss's Daughter; Weekend in Havana. 1942 The Magnificent Dope; Thunder Birds; Song of the Islands; Yankee Doodle Dandy. 1943 Hello, Frisco, Hello. 1944 Weekend Pass. 1945 Blonde Ransom; Her Lucky Night.

BARD, MARIA (aka MIGO BARD)
Born: 1901, Germany. Died: Apr. 1944, Germany. Screen and stage actress.

Appeared in German films: 1932 Mansch Ohne Namen (Man without a Name). 1933 Berlin-Alexanderplatz. 1938 Liebe im Gleitflug (Love in Stunt Flying). Also in Emperor of America.

BARKER, BRADLEY
Born: 1883. Died: Sept. 29, 1951, New York, N.Y. Screen, radio actor, film producer, and animal imitator (original screen voice of Leo the Metro lion).

Appeared in: 1919 Erstwhile Susan. 1920 The Master Mind. 1921 Coincidence; Devotion; God's Crucible. 1922 Insinuation; The Secrets of Paris. 1923 Adam and Eva; The Fair Cheat; The Fighting Blade; The Leavenworth Case; Twenty-One. 1924 The Man without a Heart; Playthings of Desire; Into the Net (serial). 1925 The Crackerjack; The Early Bird; Ermine and Rhinestones; The Live Wire; The Police Patrol. 1926 The Brown Derby; Rainbow Riley. 1927 Combat; His Rise to Fame; The Potters; Rubber Heels. 1928 The Ape; Inspiration.

BARKER, REGINALD
Born: 1886, Bothwell, Scotland. Died: Feb. 23, 1945, Los Angeles, Calif.(heart attack). Screen, stage actor, film, and stage director. Entered films as an actor in 1913.

BARLOW, REGINALD
Born: 1867, Mass. Died: July 6, 1943, Hollywood, Calif. Screen, stage, and minstrel actor. Entered films temporarily in 1916 and permanently in 1931. Married to screen actress

Appeared in: 1925 Clothes Make the Pirate. 1932 The Washington Masquerade; Age of Consent; If I Had a Million; Night Court; World and the Flesh; Wet Parade; Blessed Event; I Am a Fugitive from a Chain Gang; Sinners in the Sun; Mata Hari; This Reckless Age; Alias the Doctor; Afraid to Talk; Horse Feathers. 1933 His Private Secretary; The Big Cage; Grand Slam; Flying Down to Rio. 1934 You Can't Buy Everything; Romance in Manhattan; Half a Sinner. 1935 Cardinal Richelieu; Strangers All; The Bride of Frankenstein; Mutiny Ahead. 1936 Little Lord Fauntleroy; The Last of the Mohicans; O'Malley of the Mounted; Lloyds of London. 1937 It Happened Out West. 1939 The Witness Vanishes. 1940 The Courageous Dr. Christian.

BARNELL, NORA ELY
Born: 1882. Died: July 10, 1933, Los Angeles, Calif.(cerebral hemorrhage). Screen actress and casting director. Entered films as an actress with Thomas Ince.

BARNES, BARRY K.
Born: 1906, England. Died: Jan. 12, 1965, London, England.
Screen and stage actor.

Appeared in: 1938 The Return of the Scarlet Pimpernel; This
Man Is News; The Ware Case. 1939 Prison without Bars. 1940
The Midas Touch; Spies of the Air. 1941 The Girl in the News.
1946 Dancing with Crime; Bedelia.

BARNES, EDNA REMING
Born: 1883. Died: Mar. 7, 1935, Los Angeles, Calif.(cancer).
Screen character actress.

BARNES, FRANK (Richard Allen)
Died: Nov. 1, 1940, Bronx, N.Y. Screen and stage actor.
Entered films prior to 1917.

Appeared in: 1927 The General.

BARNES, GEORGE
Born: 1890. Died: Nov. 18, 1949, Hollywood, Calif.(cancer).
Screen and stage actor.

Appeared in: 1903 The Great Train Robbery.

BARNES, JUSTUS D.
Born: 1862. Died: Feb. 6, 1946, Weedsport, N.Y. Screen and
stage actor.

Appeared in: 1915 The Country Girl.

BARNES, T. ROY
Born: Aug. 11, 1880, Lincolnshire, England. Died: Mar. 30,
1937, Hollywood, Calif. Screen, stage, and vaudeville actor.
Appeared in vaudeville with his wife, Bessie Crawford, in an
act billed as "Package of Smiles."

Appeared in: 1920 Scratch My Back; So Long Letty. 1921 See
My Lawyer; Exit the Vamp; Her Face Value; A Kiss in Time.
1922 The Old Homestead; Is Matrimony a Failure?; Don't Get
Personal; Too Much Wife. 1923 Adam and Eva; The Go-Getter;
Hollywood; Souls for Sale. 1924 The Great White Way; Butterfly;
Reckless Romance; Young Ideas. 1925 Seven Chances; The
Crowded Hour; The Price of Pleasure; The Re-Creation of
Brian Kent. 1926 Dangerous Friends; Ladies of Leisure; A
Regular Scout; The Unknown Cavalier. 1927 Body and Soul;
Chicago; Smile, Brother, Smile; Tender Hour. 1928 A Blonde
for a Night; The Gate Crasher. 1929 Sally; Dangerous Curves.
1930 Wide Open; Caught Short. 1931 Alpha; Women of All Na-
tions. Prior to 1933 the following shorts: How's My Baby; His
Error; Carnival Revue. 1934 Kansas City Princess; It's a Gift.
1935 Village Tale; The Virginia Judge; Doubting Thomas.

BARNES, V. L.
Born: 1870. Died: Aug. 9, 1949, Los Angeles, Calif. Screen
actor.

Appeared in: 1921 Cold Steel. 1924 Crossed Trails. 1925
Peggy of the Secret Service. 1926 The Fighting Cheat.

BARNETT, CHESTER A.
Born: 1885. Died: Sept. 22, 1947, Jefferson City, Mo.(pneumonia).
Screen and stage actor.

Appeared in: 1912 The Girl in the Next Room. 1913 Where
Charity Begins. 1916 La Boheme. 1919 The Wishing Ring.

BARNETT, GRIFF
Born: 1885. Died: Jan. 12, 1958, Hollywood, Calif.(heart condition
and pneumonia). Screen actor.

Appeared in: 1946 To Each His Own. 1947 Possessed; Gunfighters; Cass Timberlane; Wild Harvest; Daisy Kenyon.
1948 Fighting Father Dunne; Fury at Furnace Creek; The Walls
of Jericho; Tap Roots; For the Love of Mary; Apartment for
Peggy. 1949 Criss Cross; The Doolins of Oklahoma; Mother Is
a Freshman; Pinky. 1950 Customs Agent; No Man of Her Own;
Peggy; Sierra. 1951 Cattle Drive; Passage West; Two of a
Kind; When I Grow Up. 1952 Scandal Sheet; The Sellout. 1953
Angel Face.

BAROUX, LUCIEN
Born: 1889, Toulouse, France. Died: May 21, 1968, Toulouse,
France. Screen and stage actor.

Appeared in: 1931 Un Soir de Rafle (Night Raid). 1933 Levy and
Co; Le Petit Ecart. 1935 Charlemagne; Ces Messieurs do la
Sante. 1936 Bacara. 1937 Le Mioche; Les Mysteres de Paris;
L'Enfant de Troupe. 1938 Forty Little Mothers. 1939 Champs
Elysees; Behind the Facade. 1943 Fire in the Straw. 1944 32

Rue de Montmartre; Moulin Rouge. 1952 The French Way;
Father's Dilemma. 1953 Naughty Martine. 1958 Lovers and
Thieves. 1963 Le Diable et les Dix Commandments (The Devil
and the Ten Commandments).

BARR, JEANNE
Born: 1932. Died: Aug. 10, 1967, New York, N.Y. Screen,
stage, and television actress.

Appeared in: 1960 The Fugitive Kind. 1962 Long Day's Journey
into Night. 1964 Lilith.

BARRAT, ROBERT
Born: July 10, 1891, New York, N.Y. Died: Jan. 7, 1970, Hollywood, Calif. Screen, stage, and television actor.

Appeared in: 1933 Baby Face; Major of Hell; The Picture
Snatcher; The Silk Express; Heroes for Sale; The Kennel Murder
Case; Wild Boys of the Road; Lily Turner; Captured; King of the
Jungle; I Loved a Woman; The Secrets of the Blue Room; From
Headquarters; Ann Carver's Profession. 1934 Dark Hazard;
Massacre; Wonder Bar; Fog Over Frisco; Friends of Mr.
Sweeney; Dames; Here Comes the Navy; A Very Honorable Guy;
Midnight Alibi; Hi, Nelli; Gambling Lady; Upper World; The
Dragon Murder Case; Housewife; Return of the Terror; Big-
Hearted Herbert; The St. Louis Kid; I Sell Anything; The Fire-
bird. 1935 Devil Dogs of the Air; Captain Blood; Moonlight on
the Prairie; While the Patient Slept; Bordertown; The Florentine
Dagger; Stranded; Dr. Socrates; Village Tale; Special Agent;
Dressed to Thrill; The Murder Man; I Am a Thief. 1936 The
Last of the Mohicans; Exclusive Story; The Country Doctor; I
Married a Doctor; Sons O'Guns; Draegerman Courage; Charge
of the Light Brigade; God's Country and the Woman; The Black
Legion; Trail of the Lonesome Pine; Trailin' West; Mary of
Scotland. 1937 Mountain Justice; Life of Emile Zola; Confessions;
Love Is on the Air; The Barrier. 1938 Bad Man of Brimstone;
Penetentiary; The Texans; Charlie Chan in Honolulu; Breaking
the Ice; Shadows over Shanghai; The Buccaneer; Forbidden
Valley. 1939 Colorado Sunset; Allegheny Uprising; Conspiracy;
Bad Lands; The Cisco Kid and the Lady; Return of the Cisco Kid;
Man of Conquest; Heritage of the Desert; Union Pacific. 1940
The Man from Dakota; Northwest Passage; Laddie; Go West;
Captain Caution; Fugitive from a Prison Camp. 1941 Parachute
Battalion; Riders of the Purple Sage; They Met in Argentina.
1942 The Girl from Alaska; American Empire; Fall In. 1943
Johnny Come Lately; The Bomber's Moon; They Came to Blow
up America; A Stranger in Town; Dr. Paul Joseph Goebbels.
1944 The Adventures of Mark Twain; Enemy of Women. 1945
They Were Expendable (he portrayed General Douglas Mac-
Arthur as he did in American Guerilla in the Philippines-1950);
Road to Utopia; Grissly's Millions; Dakota; The Great John L;
Strangler of the Swamp; San Antonio; Wanderer of the Waste-
land. 1946 The Magnificent Doll; Dangerous Millions; Sunset
Pass; Just before Dawn; The Time of Their Lives. 1947 Sea
of Grass; Fabulous Texan; Road to Rio. 1948 Joan of Arc; I
Love Trouble; Relentless; Bad Men of Tombstone. 1949 Riders
of the Range; The Lone Wolf and His Lady; Canadian Pacific;
Song of India; The Doolins of Oklahoma. 1950 An American
Guerilla in the Philippines; Baron of Arizona; Davy Crockett,
Indian Scout; The Kid from Texas; Double Crossbones. 1951
Darling, How Could You?; Distant Drums; Flight to Mars; The
Pride of Maryland. 1952 Denver and the Rio Grande; Son of
Ali Baba. 1953 Cow Country. 1955 Tall Man Riding.

BARRETT, CHARLES C.
Born: 1871. Died: Feb. 11, 1929, Baltimore, Md. Screen,
stage, vaudeville, and burlesque actor.

BARRETT, IVY RICE
Born: 1898. Died: Nov. 8, 1962, Hollywood, Calif. Screen and
stage actress. In Sennett films as a bathing beauty from 1915 to
1920.

BARRETT, JANE
Born: May 7, 1923, Highgate, London, England. Died: July 20,
1969, England. Screen, stage, radio, and television actress.

Appeared in: 1938 The Citadel (film debut). 1945 The Captive
Heart. 1948 Eureka Stockade. 1950 Massacre Hill. 1952 Time,
Gentlemen, Please. 1953 The Sword and the Rose. Other British
films: Bond of Fear; Colonel Bogey.

BARRI, MARIO
Died: Nov. 21, 1963, Manila, Philippine Islands. Screen actor
and film producer.

Appeared in: 1956 Huk. 1961 The Steel Claw. 1962 Out of the
Tiger's Mouth; Samar. 1964 A Yank in Viet-Nam.

BARRIER, EDGAR
Born: 1902, New York, N.Y. Died: 1964. Screen and stage actor.

Appeared in: 1940 Escape; Comrade X. 1941 The Penalty; They Dare Not Love. 1942 Eagle Squadron; Danger in the Pacific; Arabian Nights; Journey into Fear. 1943 We've Never Been Licked; Flesh and Fantasy; Phantom of the Opera. 1944 The Cobra Woman; Secrets of Scotland Yard. 1945 Nob Hill; A Game of Death (U.S. 1946); Song of Mexico. 1946 Cornered; Tarzan and the Leopard Woman. 1948 Adventures in Silverado; Rocky; To the Ends of the Earth; Port Said; Macbeth; Rogues' Regiment. 1949 The Secret of St. Ives. 1950 Last of the Buccaneers; The Squared Circle; Cyrano de Bergerac. 1951 The Whip Hand; Hurricane Island. 1953 Count the Hours; The Stand at Apache River; Destination Gobi; The Prince of Pirates; Eyes of the Jungle; The Golden Blade. 1954 The Saracen Blade; Princess of the Nile. 1956 Rumble on the Docks. 1957 The Giant Claw. 1959 Juke Box Rhythm. 1961 On the Double; Snow White and the Three Stooges; Pirates of Tortuga. 1963 Irma la Douce.

BARRINGTON, HERBERT (Herbert Barrington Hollingsworth)
Born: 1872. Died: Oct. 26, 1933, Tarrytown, N.Y. Screen and stage actor. Entered films in Yonkers, N.Y. with Pilot Films.

BARRISCALE, BESSIE
Born: 1884. Died: June 30, 1965, Kentfield, Calif. Screen, stage, and vaudeville actress.

Appeared in: 1914 The Rose of the Rancho. 1916 Home, Plain Jane; Not My Sister. 1917 Wooden Shoes. 1919 A Trick of Fate. 1921 The Broken Gate; The Breaking Point. 1923 Girl of the Golden West. 1928 Show Folks. 1933 Above the Clouds. 1934 Beloved; 1935 The Man Who Reclaimed His Head.

BARRON, FREDERICK C.
Born: 1888, Melbourne, Australia. Died: Oct. 9, 1955; Central Islip, N.Y. Screen, stage, and television actor. Entered films in U.S. in 1898.

BARROWS, JAMES O.
Born: 1853. Died: Dec. 7, 1925, Hollywood, Calif.(heart attack). Screen and stage actor.

Appeared in: 1921 Silent Years. 1922 Pawned; The Pride of Palomar; When Love Comes; The Call of Home; Hurricane's Gal; White Shoulders. 1923 The Old Fool; Cause for Divorce; Shadows of the North; Stephen Steps Out. 1924 Her Night of Romance; The Tomboy; The Gaiety Girl; The Signal Tower; Young Ideas. 1925 The Goose Woman; Daddy's Gone A-Hunting; The Price of Pleasure. 1926 The Sea Beast.

BARRY, ROBERT
Born: 1901. Died: Mar. 21, 1931, Santa Monica, Calif.(auto accident injuries). Screen actor.

BARRY, TOM (Hal Donahue)
Born: 1884. Died: Nov. 7, 1931, Hollywood, Calif.(heart trouble). Screen, stage, vaudeville actor, playwright, screenwriter, and newspaperman. Appeared in one film: 1931 The Cisco Kid.

BARRY, VIOLA
Born: 1894. Died: Apr. 2, 1964, Hollywood, Calif. Screen, stage actress, screenwriter, stage producer, and stage director.

Appeared in: 1913 The Mothering Heart. 1920 Sea Wolf.

BARRYE, EMILY
Born: 1896. Died: Dec. 15, 1957, Hollywood, Calif. Screen actress. Entered films in 1915 with Universal.

Appeared In: 1924 Fast and Fearless. 1925 The Bloodhound; Border Intrigue; Fast Fightin'. 1926 The Bonanza Buckaroo; Speedy Spurs; Volcano. 1927 King of Kings. 1929 The Godless Girl.

BARRYMORE, DIANA (Diana Blanche Barrymore Blythe)
Born: Mar. 3, 1921, New York, N.Y. Died: Jan. 25, 1960, New York, N.Y.(natural causes). Screen, stage actress, and author. Daughter of actor John Barrymore (dec. 1942) and Blanche Oelrichs who wrote under the pen name of Michael Strange. Regarding family, see John Barrymore.

Appeared in: 1941 Manpower. 1942 Eagle Squadron; Between Us Girls; Nightmare. 1943 Fired Wife; Frontier Badman; When Ladies Fly. 1944 The Ghost Catchers; Ladies Courageous; The Adventures of Mark Twain; Hollywood Canteen. 1950 D.O.A; Flame and the Arrow. 1951 The Mob.

BARRYMORE, ETHEL (Ethel Blythe)
Born: Aug. 15, 1879, Philadelphia, Pa. Died: June 18, 1959, Beverly Hills, Calif.(heart condition). Screen, stage, and television actress. Regarding family, see John Barrymore. In 1944 won Academy Award for Best Supporting Actress in None but the Lonely Heart. Nominated in 1946 for Academy Award for Best Supporting Actress in The Spiral Staircase. In 1949 nominated for Academy Award for Best Supporting Actress in Pinky.

Appeared in: 1914 The Nightingale (film debut). 1915 The Final Judgement. 1916 Kiss of Hate. 1917 The Awakening of Helen Ritchie; The Lifted Veil; The Call of Her People; The White Raven; The American Widow. 1918 Our Mrs. McChesney; The Whirlpool. 1919 The Divorcee. 1932 Rasputin and the Empress. 1933 All at Sea (short). 1935 Peter Ibbetson. 1944 None but the Lonely Heart. 1946 The Spiral Staircase. 1947 Night Song; Moss Rose; The Farmer's Daughter. 1948 Portrait of Jenny; The Paradine Case; Moonrise. 1949 Pinky; The Great Sinner; That Midnight Kiss; The Red Danube. 1951 Kind Lady; The Secret of Convict Lake; Daphne, the Virgin of the Golden Laurels (narr.). 1952 Deadline U.S.A; Just for You, It's a Big Country. 1953 The Story of Three Loves; Main Street to Broadway. 1954 Young at Heart. 1957 Johnny Trouble.

BARRYMORE, JOHN (John Blythe)
Born: Feb. 15, 1882, Philadelphia, Pa. Died: May 29, 1942, Los Angeles, Calif. Screen and stage actor. Son of actor Maurice Barrymore (dec. 1905) and actress Georgia Drew (dec.). Brother of actor Lionel Barrymore (dec. 1954) and actress Ethel Barrymore (dec. 1959); father of actress Diana Barrymore (dec. 1960) and actor John Drew Barrymore, Jr. Divorced from actress Dolores Costello.

Appeared in: 1908 The Boys of Company B. 1914 The Man from Mexico; An American Citizen. 1915 The Dictator; Incorrigible Dukane; Are You a Mason?. 1916 The Lost Bridegroom; The Red Widow. 1917 Raffles; The Empress. 1918 On the Quiet; Here Comes the Bride. 1919 Test of Honor. 1920 Dr. Jekyll and Mr. Hyde. 1921 The Lotus Eaters. 1922 Sherlock Holmes. 1924 Beau Brummel. 1926 The Sea Beast; When a Man Loves; Don Juan; The Beloved Rogue. 1928 Tempest. 1929 The Show of Shows; Eternal Love; General Crack. 1930 Moby Dick; The Man from Blankley's; Handsome Gigolo, Poor Gigolo. 1931 Svengali; The Mad Genius. 1932 Arsene Lupin; Rasputin and the Empress; A Bill of Divorcement; Grand Hotel; State's Attorney. 1933 Dinner at Eight; Counsellor at Law; Reunion in Vienna; Topaze; Night Flight. 1934 Long Lost Father; Twentieth Century. 1936 Romeo and Juliet. 1937 Maytime, True Confession; Night Club Scandal; Bulldog Drummond Comes Back; Bulldog Drummond's Revenge. 1938 Bulldog Drummond's Peril; Romance in the Dark; Spawn of the North; Marie Antoinette; Hold That Co-Ed. 1939 The Great Man Votes; Jesse James; Midnight. 1940 The Great Profile. 1941 Invisible Woman; Playmates; World Premiere.

BARRYMORE, LIONEL (Lionel Blythe)
Born: Apr. 28, 1878, Philadelphia, Pa. Died: Nov. 15, 1954, Van Nuys, Calif.(heart attack). Screen, stage, radio, vaudeville actor, film producer, and screenwriter. Acted from wheelchair from 1940 due to the effects of arthritis and hip injury. Regarding family, see John Barrymore. Won Academy Award in 1931 for Best Actor in A Free Soul.

Appeared in: 1908 The Paris Hat. 1911 Fighting Blood; The Battle. 1912 Friends; The One She Loved; The Musketeers of Pig Alley; Gold and Glitter; My Baby; The Informer; The New York Hat; My Hero; Oil and Water; The Burglar's Dilemma; A Cry for Help; The God within; Fate; An Adventure in the Autumn Woods. 1913 The Sheriff's Baby; The Perfidy of Mary; A Misunderstood Boy; The Wanderer; The House of Darkness; Just Gold; The Yaqui Cur; The Ranchero's Revenge; A Timely Interception; Death's Marathon; Judith of Bethulia. 1915 The Exploits of Elaine; The Romance of Elaine; The Yellow Streak. 1916 The Brand of Cowardice; The Quitter. 1917 His Father's Son. 1918 The Yellow Ticket. 1920 The Copperhead; The Master Mind. 1921 Jim the Penman; The Devil's Garden; The Great Adventure. 1922 The Face in the Fog; Unseeing Eyes. 1924 I Am the Man; America; Wedding Women. 1925 The Little Colonel; The Wrongdoers; Wildfire; The Iron Man; Fifty-Fifty; The Girl Who Wouldn't Work; Children of the Whirlwind. 1926 The Bells; The Splendid Road; The Barrier; The Temptress; Brooding Eyes; The Lucky Lady; Paris at Midnight. 1927 Love; The Show; The Thirteenth Hour; Body and Soul; Women Love Diamonds. 1928 The River Woman; Drums of Love; Sadie Thompson; Alias Jimmy Valentine; The Lion and the Mouse; Road House; Decameron Nights; West of Zanzibar. 1929 Stark

Mad; The Mysterious Island; The Hollywood Revue of 1929. 1930 Free and Easy. 1931 A Free Soul; Guilty Hands; The Yellow Ticket (and 1918 version). 1932 Mata Hari; Broken Lullaby; Grand Hotel; Rasputin and the Empress; Arsene Lupin; Washington Masquerade; The Man I Killed. 1933 Sweepings; One Man's Journey; Christopher Bean; Should Ladies Behave?; Reunion in Vienna; Dinner at Eight; The Stranger's Return; Night Flight; Looking Forward. 1934 Treasure Island; This Side of Heaven; The Girl from Missouri; Carolina. 1935 Mark of the Vampire; David Copperfield; The Return of Peter Grimm; Ah, Wilderness!; Public Hero Number One; The Little Colonel. 1936 The Devil Doll; The Gorgeous Hussy; The Road to Glory; The Voice of Bugle Ann; Camille. 1937 A Family Affair; Saratoga; Captains Courageous; Navy Blue and Gold. 1938 Young Doctor Kildare; You Can't Take It with You; A Yank at Oxford; Test Pilot. 1939 Let Freedom Ring; Calling Dr. Kildare; Secret of Dr. Kildare; On Borrowed Time. 1940 Dr. Kildare Goes Home; Dr. Kildare's Strange Case; Dr. Kildare's Crisis. 1941 The Bad Man; The Penalty; The People vs. Dr. Kildare; Lady Be Good; Dr. Kildare's Victory; Dr. Kildare's Wedding Day; Invisible Women. 1942 Dr. Gillespie's New Assistant; Calling Dr. Gillespie; Tennessee Johnson. 1943 Dr. Gillespie's Criminal Case; Thousands Cheer; A Guy Named Joe. 1944 Three Men in White; Since You Went Away; Dragon Seed (narr.); Between Two Women. 1945 Valley of Decision. 1946 Duel in the Sun; It's a Wonderful Life; The Secret Heart; Three Wise Fools. 1947 Dark Delusion; Cynthia. 1948 Key Largo. 1949 Down to the Sea in Ships; Malaya; Some of the Best (documentary). 1950 Right Cross. 1951 Bannerline. 1952 Lone Star. 1953 Main Street to Broadway. 1964 Big Parade of Comedy (documentary).

BARTELL, RICHARD
Born: 1898. Died: July 22, 1967, Woodland Hills, Calif.(cancer). Screen and stage actor.

Appeared in: 1941 Design for Scandal. 1942 My Sister Eileen; Sabotage Squad. 1951 Abbott and Costello Meet the Invisible Man; The Enforcer. 1953 The Vanquished.

BARTELS, LOUIS JOHN
Born: 1895, Bunker Hill, Ill. Died: Mar. 4, 1932, Hollywood, Calif.(stomach disorder). Screen and stage actor.

Appeared in: 1927 Broadway Nights; Dance Magic. 1929 The Canary Murder Case; Nothing but the Truth. 1930 The Florodora Girl; The Cohens and the Kellys in Africa; Sin Takes a Holiday. 1931-32 Pathe shorts. 1931 The Prodigal. 1932 The Big Shot.

BARTER, TEDDY
Born: 1889. Died: Oct. 10, 1939, Hollywood, Calif.(auto crash). Screen actor and stage manager.

BARTHELMESS, RICHARD
Born: May 9, 1897, New York, N.Y. Died: Aug. 17, 1963, South Hampton, N.Y.(cancer). Screen actor and film producer. Son of stage actress Carolina Harris (dec. 1958). Won Special Academy Award in 1927 for The Patent Leather Kid.

Appeared in: 1916 War Brides. 1917 The Seven Swans; Bab's Burglar; The Eternal Sin. 1918 Hit-the-Trail-Haliday; Rich Man, Poor Man. 1919 The Girl Who Stayed Home; Three Men and a Girl; I'll Get Him Yet; Scarlet Blossoms; Boots; The Hope Chest; Peppy Poppy. 1920 The Love Flower; Way down East; The Idol Dancer. 1921 Experience; Tol'able David. 1922 The Seventh Day; Sonny; The Bond Boy; Just a Song at Twilight. 1923 The Bright Shawl; Fury; Twenty-One; The Fighting Blade. 1924 The Enchanted Cottage; Classmates. 1925 Soul Fire; Shore Leave; The Beautiful City; New Toys. 1926 Ransom's Folly; Just Suppose; The White Black Sheep; The Amateur Gentleman. 1927 The Drop Kick; The Patent Leather Kid. 1928 Wheel of Chance; Out of the Ruins; Scarlet Seas; Little Shepherd of Kingdom Come; The Noose. 1929 Weary River; Drag; Young Nowheres; The Show of Shows; Adios. 1930 The Dawn Patrol; Son of the Gods. 1931 The Lash; The Last Flight; The Finger Points. 1932 The Cabin in the Cotton; Alias the Doctor; Cock of the Air; The Slippery Pearls (short). 1933 Central Airport; Heroes for Sale. 1934 Massacre; A Modern Hero; Midnight Alibi. 1935 Four Hours to Kill. 1936 Spy of Napoleon. 1939 Only Angels Have Wings. 1940 The Man Who Talks Too Much. 1942 The Mayor of 44th Street; The Spoilers. 1963 The Great Chase (film strip); Hallelujah the Hills (film clip from Way Down East).

BARTHOLOMEW, AGNES
Born: Scotland. Died: Sept. 10, 1955, Glasgow, Scotland. Screen and stage actress. Married to actor Holmes Herbert (dec. 1956).

Appeared in: 1955 A Man Called Peter.

BARTLETT, CLIFFORD
Born: 1903, England. Died: Dec. 1936, London, England. Screen and stage actor.

BARTON, JAMES
Born: Nov. 1, 1890, Gloucester, N.J. Died: Feb. 19, 1962, Mineola, N.Y.(heart attack). Screen, vaudeville, and burlesque actor.

Appeared in: 1923 Why Women Re-Marry. 1930 The Underdog (short). 1935 Captain Hurricane; His Family Tree. 1938 Universal short. 1941 The Shepherd of the Hills. 1944 Lifeboat. 1948 The Time of Your Life; Yellow Sky. 1950 Daughter of Rosie O'Grady; Wabash Avenue. 1951 Here Comes the Groom; The Scarf; Golden Girl. 1956 The Naked Hills; 1957 Quantez. 1961 The Misfits.

BARTON, JOE
Born: 1883. Died: July 5, 1937, Los Angeles, Calif.(following surgery). Screen actor. Entered films approx. 1930.

Appeared in: 1933 Lone Cowboy. 1935 McFadden's Flats.

BARTOSCH, CHESTER
Born: 1899. Died: Oct. 31, 1967, San Diego, Calif.(heart ailment). Screen and television actor.

BARTY, JACK
Born: 1889, London, England. Died: Jan. 1943, Streatham, London, England. Screen, stage, and vaudeville actor, screenwriter, and film producer. Appeared in British and U.S. films.

Appeared in: 1934 the following shorts: Maid in Hollywood; Babes in the Goods, Oliver the Eighth.

BARZELL, WOLFE
Born: 1897, Poland. Died: Feb. 14, 1969, off Acapulco, Mexico (heart attack). Screen and stage actor.

Appeared in: 1957 Street of Sinners. 1959 The Blue Angel; Frankenstein's Daughter. 1961 Homicidal; Atlantis, The Lost Continent. 1962 The Scarface Mob. 1963 Love with the Proper Stranger.

BASCH, FELIX
Born: 1889. Died: May 17, 1944, Los Angeles, Calif. Screen actor, film producer, and film director.

Appeared in: 1942 Destination Unknown; Desperate Journey; Once upon a Honeymoon; Pacific Rendezvous; Enemy Agents Meet Ellery Queen. 1943 Hitler-Dead or Alive; Mission to Moscow; The Falcon in Danger; Bomber's Moon; Hostages; The Cross of Lorraine; Chitnicks; Desert Song. 1944 Woman in Bondage; Uncertain Glory.

BASKETT, JAMES
Born: 1904, Indianapolis, Ind. Died: Sept. 9, 1948, Los Angeles, Calif.(heart ailment). Negro screen, stage, and radio actor. Won a Special Academy Award for his performance as Uncle Remus in Song of the South, 1946.

BASSERMANN, ALBERT
Born: Sept. 7, 1865, Mannheim, Germany. Died: May 15, 1952, Zurich, Switzerland(heart attack). Screen and stage actor. Married to actress Else Bassermann-Schiff (dec. 1961). Nominated for Academy Award in 1940 for Best Supporting Actor in Foreign Correspondent.

Appeared in: 1931 Vorunter Suchung (Inquest). 1932 1914: The Last Days before the War. 1933 Kadetten. 1934 Ein Gewisser Herr Gran; Alraune. 1938 Letzte Liebe (Last Love). 1939 Le Famille Lefrancois (Heroes of the Marne). 1940 The Story of Dr. Ehrlich's Magic Bullet; Foreign Correspondent; A Dispatch from Reuters; Moon over Burma; This Man Reuter; Knute Rockne, All American; Escape. 1941 The Shanghai Gesture; The Great Awakening; New Wine; A Woman's Face. 1942 The Moon and Sixpence; Invisible Agent; Once upon a Honeymoon; Fly by Night; Desperate Journey. 1943 Good Luck, Mr. Yates; Passport to Heaven; Reunion in France. 1944 Madame Curie; Since You Went Away. 1945 Rhapsody in Blue. 1946 Strange Holiday; The Searching Wind. 1947 Private Affairs of Bel Ami; Escape Me Never. 1948 The Red Shoes.

BASSERMANN-SCHIFF, ELSE
Born: Jan. 14, 1878, Leipzig, E. Germany. Died: May 30, 1961, Baden-Baden, W. Germany. Screen, stage actress, author, and playwright. Married to actor Albert Bassermann (dec. 1952).

Appeared in: 1938 Letzte Liebe (Last Love). 1940 Escape. 1941 Captain of Koepenich. 1942 Desperate Journey. 1944 Madame Curie.

BASSETT, TONY (Albert Anthony Bassett)
Born: 1885. Died: Aug. 4, 1955, Hollywood, Calif. Screen and vaudeville actor.

BATEMAN, VICTORY
Born: 1866. Died: Mar. 2, 1926, Los Angeles, Calif.(bronchial asthma). Screen and stage actress. Entered films approx. 1920.

Appeared in: 1921 The Idle Rich; Keeping up with Lizzie; A Trip to Paradise. 1922 Captain Fly-By-Night; A Girl's Desire; If I Were Queen. 1923 Can a Woman Love Twice?; The Eternal Three; Human Wreckage. 1924 Tess of the D'Urbervilles; The Turmoil.

BATES, BARBARA
Born: Aug. 6, 1925, Denver, Colo. Died: Mar. 18, 1969, Denver, Colo. Screen actress.

Appeared in: 1945 Salome, Where She Danced; This Love of Ours. 1946 A Night in Paradise; Strange Holiday. 1947 The Fabulous Joe. 1948 June Bride. 1949 The House across the Street; One Last Fling; The Inspector General. 1950 All about Eve; Quicksand; Cheaper by the Dozen. 1951 The Secret of Convict Lake; I'd Climb the Highest Mountain; Let's Make It Legal. 1952 Belles on Their Toes; The Outcasts of Poker Flat. 1953 All Ashore; The Caddy. 1954 Rhapsody. 1956 House of Secrets. 1957 Town on Trial; Triple Deception. 1958 Campbell's Kingdom; Apache Territory.

BATES, BLANCHE
Born: 1873, Portland, Oreg. Died: Dec. 25, 1941, San Francisco, Calif.(following stroke). Screen and stage actress.

Appeared in: 1914 The Seats of the Mighty. 1918 The Border Legion.

BATES, FLORENCE (Florence Rabe)
Born: Apr. 15, 1888, San Antonio, Tex. Died: Jan. 31, 1954, Burbank, Calif.(heart attack). Screen, stage, television actress, and attorney.

Appeared in: 1937 The Man in Blue. 1940 Rebecca; Calling All Husbands; Son of Monte Cristo; Kitty Foyle. 1941 Road Show; Love Crazy; The Chocolate Soldier; Strange Alibi; The Devil and Miss Jones. 1942 The Tuttles of Tahiti; The Moon and Sixpence; My Heart Belongs to Daddy; The Mexican Spitfire at Sea; We Were Dancing. 1943 Slightly Dangerous; His Butler's Sister; They Got Me Covered; Mister Big; Heaven Can Wait; Mr. Lucky; Whistle Stop at Eaton Falls. 1944 Since You Went Away; The Mask of Dimitrios; Kismet; The Belle of the Yukon; The Racket Man. 1945 Saratoga Trunk; Tahiti Nights; Tonight and Every Night; San Antonio; Out of This World. 1946 Claudia and David; Cluny Brown; The Diary of a Chambermaid; Whistle Stop; The Time, the Place and the Girl. 1947 The Brasher Doubloon; Love and Learn; Desire Me; The Secret Life of Walter Mitty; The High Window. 1948 Texas, Brooklyn and Heaven; Winter Meeting; The Inside Story; River Lady; My Dear Secretary; Portrait of Jennie. 1949 A Letter to Three Wives; I Remember Mama; The Judge Steps Out; The Girl from Jones Beach; On the Town. 1950 Belle of Old Mexico; County Fair. 1951 The Second Woman; Lullaby of Broadway; The Tall Target; Havana Rose; Father Takes the Air. 1952 San Francisco Story; Les Miserables. 1953 Paris Model; Main Street to Broadway.

BATES, GRANVILLE
Born: 1882, Chicago, Ill. Died: July 8, 1940, Hollywood, Calif. (heart attack). Screen and stage actor.

Appeared in: 1929 Jealousy. 1930 The Sap from Syracuse. 1934 The Smiling Lieutenant; Midnight; Warner Bros, newspaper shorts; 1935 Woman Wanted; Pursuit; O'Shaughnessey's Boy. 1936 Here Comes Trouble; Poppy; Chatterbox; 13 Hours by Air; The Plainsman; The Captain's Kid; Times Square Playboy; Sing Me a Love Song; Beloved Enemy; Under Suspicion. 1937 When's Your Birthday?; Let's Get Married; It Happened in Hollywood; Green Light; They Won't Forget; The Perfect Specimen; Larceny on the Air; Nancy Steel Is Missing; Waikiki Wedding; Wells Fargo; Mountain Justice; Back in Circulation. 1938 The Jury's Secret; Youth Takes a Fling; Mr. Chump; Go Chase Yourself; The Affairs of Annabel; A Man to Remember; Next Time I Marry; Gold Is Where You Find It; Romance on the Run; Cowboy from Brooklyn; Garden of the Moon; Hard to Get. 1939 The Great Man Votes; Blackwell's Island; Twelve Crowded Hours; Naughty but Nice; Pride of the Blue Grass; Our Neigh-

bors, the Carters; Fast and Furious; Internationally Yours; Sweepstakes Winner; Of Mice and Men; Charlie McCarthy, Detective; Indianapolis Speedway; Jesse James. 1940 Millionaire Playboy; Thou Shalt Not Kill; My Favorite Wife; The Mortal Storm; Private Affairs; Men against the Sky; Flowing Gold; Brother Orchid.

BATES, LESLIE A. (aka LES BATES)
Born: 1877. Died: Aug. 8, 1930, Hollywood, Calif.(auto accident). Screen actor.

Appeared in: 1921 A Broken Doll. 1922 Belle of Alaska; Big Stakes; Deserted at the Altar; My Dad; Strength of the Pines. 1923 Blood Test; Vanity Fair. 1924 Martyr Sex; Shackles of Fear. 1925 Once in a Lifetime; Triple Action. 1926 Beyond All Odds; Blue Blazes; In Search of a Hero; Lure of the West; The Texas Streak; While London Sleeps. 1927 Irish Hearts. 1928 Buck Privates; The Glorious Trail. 1930 The Fighting Legion; Mountain Justice.

BATTIER, ROBERT
Born: 1887. Died: Dec. 16, 1946, Hollywood, Calif. Screen actor.

Appeared in: 1937 Love and Hisses.

BATTY, ARCHIBALD
Born: 1887. Died: Nov. 24, 1961, Budleigh, Salterton, England. Screen, stage actor, and playwright.

Appeared in: 1938 I See Ice; The Drum. 1939 Four Feathers. Other British film: The Tontine.

BAUM, MRS. H. WILLIAM
Born: 1882. Died: Mar. 9, 1970, Farmingdale, N.Y. Screen and radio actress. Was the model for the U.S. Liberty 25-cent piece.

Appeared in: 1915 Birth of a Nation.

BAUR, HARRY
Born: 1881, France. Died: Apr. 1943, Paris, France. Screen, stage, and radio actor.

Appeared in: 1913 Shylock. 1923 La Voyante. 1932 David Golder. 1933 Poil de Carotte; Les Trois Mousquetaires; The Red Head. 1934 Golgotha. 1935 Moscow Nights; Le Cap Perdu; Les Mirables; Crime et Chatiment (Crime and Punishment); Celle Vielle Canaille; Taras Bulba. 1936 I Stand Condemned. 1936 The Golem; The Life and Loves of Beethoven; Le Juif Polonaise. 1938 Un Carnet de Bal, Dark Eyes; Rothchild; The Rebel Son; Moscow Nights; Rasputin. 1939 A Man and His Wife. 1941 Volpone; Hatred; The Mad Empress.

BAXTER, JAMES C. "JIMMY"
Born: 1923. Died: Apr. 20, 1969, Dallas, Tex. Screen actor and singer.

Appeared in: 1935 The Dark Angel.

BAXTER, LORA
Born: 1908. Died: June 16, 1955, New York, N.Y. Screen, stage, vaudeville, television actress, and screenwriter.

BAXTER, WARNER
Born: Mar. 29, 1891, Columbus, Ohio. Died: May 7, 1951, Beverly Hills, Calif. Screen and stage actor. Married to actress Winifred Bryson. Won Academy Award for Best Actor in 1929 for In Old Arizona.

Appeared in: 1914 Her Own Money. 1918 All Woman. 1919 Lombardi, Ltd; 1921 Cheated Hearts; First Love; The Love Charm; Sheltered Daughters. 1922 If I Were Queen; The Girl in His Room; A Girl's Desire; The Ninety and Nine; Her Own Money (and 1914 version). 1923 Blow Your Own Horn; In Search of a Thrill; St. Elmo. 1924 Alimony; Christine of the Hungry Heart; The Female; The Garden of Weeds; His Forgotten Wife; Those Who Dance. 1925 The Golden Bed; The Air Mail; The Awful Truth; The Best People; Rugged Water; A Son of His Father; Welcome Home. 1926 Mannequin; Miss Brewster's Millions; Mismates; Aloma of the South Seas; The Great Gatsby; The Runaway. 1927 The Telephone Girl; The Coward; Drums of the Desert; Singed. 1928 Danger Street; Three Sinners; Ramona; Craig's Wife; The Tragedy of Youth; A Woman's Way. 1929 Linda; Far Call; Thru Different Eyes; Behind That Curtain; Romance of the Rio Grande; In Old Arizona; West of Zanzibar; Happy Days. 1930 The Arizona Kid; Such Men Are Dangerous; Renegades. 1931 The Cisco Kid; Squaw Man; Doctor's Wives; Their Mad Moment; Daddy Long Legs;

Surrender. 1932 Six Hours to Live; Man about Town; The Slippery Pearls (short); Amateur Daddy. 1933 Paddy, the Next Best Thing; Forty-Second Street; Dangerously Yours; I Loved You Wednesday; Penthouse. 1935 Stand up and Cheer; Broadway Bill; As Husbands Go; Such Women Are Dangerous; Grand Canary; Hell in the Heavens. 1935 Under the Pampas Moon, One More Spring; King of Burlesque. 1936 The Prisoner of Shark's Island; Road to Glory; To Mary, with Love; White Hunter; Robin Hood of El Dorado. 1937 Slave Ship; Vogues of 1938; Wife, Doctor and Nurse. 1938 Kidnapped; I'll Give a Million. 1939 Wife, Husband and Friend; Barricade; The Return of the Cisco Kid. 1940 Earthbound. 1941 Adam Had Four Sons. 1943 Crime Doctor; Crime Doctor's Strangest Case. 1944 Lady in the Dark; Shadows in the Night. 1945 The Crime Doctor's Courage; The Crime Doctor's Warning. 1946 Just before Dawn; The Crime Doctor's Man Hunt; The Razor's Edge; Smoky. 1947 The Millerson Case; The Crime Doctor's Gamble. 1948 A Gentleman from Nowhere. 1949 Prison Warden; The Devil's Henchman; The Crime Doctor's Diary. 1950 State Penitentiary.

BAY, TOM (aka TOMMY BAY)
Born: 1901. Died: Oct. 13, 1933, Burbank, Calif.(shooting). Screen actor.

Appeared in: 1922 The Better Man Wins. 1926 The Dead Line; The Devil's Gulch; The Fighting Boob; The Valley of Bravery. 1927 Drifting On; Tearin' into Trouble; White Pebbles. 1928 Desperate Courage; Devil's Tower; Lightnin' Shot; Mystery Valley; Painted Trail; Trail Riders; Trailin' Back. 1929 The Oklahoma Kid; Pioneers of the West; Code of the West; Fighters of the Saddle; The Fighting Terror; The Lone Horseman. 1930 The Parting of the Trails.

BAYER, CHARLES W.
Born: 1893. Died: Nov. 28, 1953, Hollywood, Calif.(cancer). Screen actor. Entered films with Vitagraph.

BEAL, FRANK
Born: 1864. Died: Dec. 20, 1934, Hollywood, Calif. Screen actor and film director. Married to actress Louise Lester (dec. 1952) and father of actor/director Scott Beal (dec. 1973).

Appeared in: 1922 A Question of Honor. 1923 Playing It Wild; Soft Boiled; When Odds Are Even. 1924 The Arizona Express; The Cyclone Rider; Hook and Ladder; The Lone Chance. 1925 The Best Bad Man; The Golden Strain; Marriage in Transit. 1926 Man Four Square. 1927 The Final Extra; Galloping Fury; The Stolen Bride. 1928 The Danger Rider; Women Who Dare. 1929 Broken Barriers; The Big Diamond Robbery; Senor Americano. 1930 Wide Open. 1931 Everything's Rosie (short); Cimarron.

BEAL, ROYAL
Born: 1900. Died: May 20, 1969, Keene, N.H.(cancer). Screen, stage, and television actor.

Appeared in: 1949 Lost Boundaries. 1951 Death of a Salesman. 1953 The Joe Lewis Story. 1959 Anatomy of a Murder.

BEAMISH, FRANK
Born: 1881, Memphis, Tenn. Died: Oct. 3, 1921, New York, N.Y. Screen and stage actor.

Appeared in: 1922 The Blonde Vampire; The Faithless Sex.

BEATTY, CLYDE R.
Born: June 10, 1903, Chillicothe, Ohio. Died: July 19, 1965, Ventura, Calif.(cancer). Screen actor, circus performer, animal trainer, and circus owner.

Appeared in: 1933 The Big Cage. 1934 The Lost Jungle (serial). 1936 Darkest Africa (serial). 1937 Paramount short. 1949 Africa Screams. 1954 Ring of Fear.

BEATTY, GEORGE
Born: Sept. 5, 1895, Steubenville, Ohio. Died: Aug. 6, 1971, Hollywood, Calif.(stroke). Screen, stage, vaudeville, radio actor, screenwriter, and radio writer.

Appeared in 1943 Hi' Ya, Sailor; Crazy Horse. 1944 Johnny Doesn't Live Here.

BEATTY, MAY
Born: 1881, Christ Church, New Zealand. Died: Apr. 1, 1945, Covina, Calif. Screen and stage actress. Married to stage actor William Lauri (dec.).

Appeared in: 1930 The Benson Murder Case; The Boudoir Diplomat. 1931 Ex-Flame. 1934 Horse Play. 1935 Night

Life of the Gods; Becky Sharp; Mad Love; Here Comes the Band; The Girl Who Came Back; Bonnie Scotland. 1936. Little Lord Fauntleroy; Show Boat; Private Number; Lloyds of London. 1937 Four Days' Wonder; She Loved a Fireman. 1938 If I Were King. 1939 The Women; Eternally Yours; We Are Not Alone; Adventures of Sherlock Holmes; Union Pacific. 1940 Pride and Prejudice; My Son, My Son. 1943 Forever and a Day.

BEAUBIEN, JULIEN (Julien A. Dolenzai)
Born: 1896. Died: Oct. 18, 1947, Long Branch, N.J. Screen and stage actress.

Appeared in: 1919 The Winning Stroke; Checkers. 1923 Main Street.

BEAUMONT, DIANA MURIEL
Born: May 8, 1909, London, England. Died: June 21, 1964, London, England. Screen and stage actress.

Appeared in: 1927 Adam's Apple (film debut). 1930 Alibi. 1934 Autumn Crocus; A Real Bloke. 1936 While London Sleeps; Birds of a Feather. 1937 Mannequin. 1939 Black Limelight; Murder in Soho; Old Mother Riley. 1940 Let George Do It. 1941 Hi Gang!. 1942 Let the People Sing. 1944 Out of Chaos. 1952 Stolen Face. 1953 Murder on Monday. 1959 I Was Monty's Double (aka Hell, Heaven or Hoboken). Other British films: The Secret Voice; Screen Struck; Millions Like Us; The Old Man; A Lucky Sweep; Cutie.

BEAUMONT, HARRY
Born: Feb. 10, 1888, Abilene, Kan. Died: Dec. 22, 1966, Santa Monica, Calif. Screen actor, film director, and screenwriter.

Appeared in: 1914 The Active Life of the Dailies (serial).

BEAUMONT, LUCY
Born: May 18, 1873, Bristol, England. Died: Apr. 24, 1937, New York, N.Y. Screen, stage, and radio actress.

Appeared in: 1923 Ashes of Vengeance; Enemies of Children; Lucretia Lombard; Cupid's Fireman. 1924 The Family Secret; The Last of the Duanes; Good Bad Boy. 1925 The Man without a Country. The Trouble with Wives. 1926 The Greater Glory; The Old Soak; The Fighting Failure; Men of the Night; Torrent. 1927 The Beloved Rogue; Closed Gates; The Love Wager; Resurrection; Hook and Ladder No. 9; Stranded; Savage Passions. 1928 Stool Pigeon; The Crowd; A Bit of Heaven; Branded Man; The Little Yellow House; Outcast Souls; Comrades. 1929 The Greyhound Limited; Knights Out (short); One Splendid Hour; The Ridin' Demon; Hard Boiled Rose; The Girl in the Show; Sonny Boy. 1931 A Free Soul; Caught Plastered; Get Rich Quick Wallingford. 1932 Union Depot; Three Wise Girls; Cheaters at Play; Midnight Lady; Movie Crazy; Thrill of Youth. 1934 His Double Life. 1935 False Pretenses; Temptation. 1936 The Devil Doll. 1937 The Maid of Salem.

BEAUMONT, VERTEE
Born: 1889. Died: June 27, 1934, Hollywood, Calif.(heart disease). Screen, stage, and vaudeville actress. Married to stage actor Jack Arnold (dec.) with whom she teamed in vaudeville as "Beaumont and Arnold."

BEAVERS, LOUISE
Born: 1898, Cincinnati, Ohio. Died: Oct. 26, 1962, Hollywood, Calif.(heart attack). Negro screen, television, and minstrel actress. Entered films in 1924.

Appeared in: 1927 Uncle Tom's Cabin. 1929 The Glad Rag Doll, Gold Diggers of Broadway; Barnum Was Right; Coquette; Nix on Dames; Wall Street. 1930 Back Pay; Wide Open; She Couldn't Say No, Safety in Numbers. 1931 Party Husbands; Reckless Living; Sundown Trail; Annabell's Affairs; Six Cylinder Love; Good Sport; Up for Murder; Girls about Town. 1932 Ladies of the Big House; Old Man Minick; The Expert; Freaks; Night World; Street of Women; What Price Hollywood; Unashamed; Young America; Divorce in the Family; Wild Girl; Too Busy to Work; It's Tough to Be Famous; We Humans; Jubilo. 1933 Girl Missing; What Price Innocence; Her Bodyguard; Bombshell; Her Splendid Folly; Notorious but Nice; Pick Up; She Done Him Wrong; A Shriek in the Night. 1934 In the Money; Glamour; I Believed in You; I Give My Love; Merry Wives of Reno; A Modern Hero; Registered Nurse; Imitation of Life; I've Got Your Number; Bedside; The Merry Frinks; Cheaters; Hat, Coat and Glove; Dr. Monica. 1935 West of the Pecos; Annapolis Farewell. 1936 Bullets or Ballots; General Spanky; Wives Never Know; Rainbow on the River. 1937 Make Way for Tomorrow; Wings over Honolulu; Love in a Bungalow; The Last Gangster. 1938 Scandal Sheet; Peck's Bad Boy with the Circus; The Headleys at Home;

Life Goes On; Brother Rat; Reckless Living. 1939 The Lady's from Kentucky; Reform School; Made for Each Other. 1940 I Want a Divorce; Women without Names; Parole Fixer; No Time for Comedy. 1941 Shadow of the Thin Man; The Vanishing Virginian; Sign of the Wolf; Belle Starr; Virginia. 1942 Holiday Inn; Reap the Wild Wind; The Big Street; Seven Sweethearts (aka Tulip Time); Tennessee Johnson. 1943 Good Morning, Judge; DuBarry Was a Lady; All by Myself; There's Something about a Soldier; Jack London; Top Man. 1944 South of Dixie; Dixie Jamboree; Follow the Boys; Barbary Coast Gent. 1945 Delightfully Dangerous. 1946 Lover Come Back; Young Widow. 1947 Banjo. 1948 Mr. Blandings Builds His Dream House; For the Love of Mary; Good Sam. 1949 Tell It to the Judge. 1950 My Blue Heaven; Girls' School; The Jackie Robinson Story. 1952 Colorado Sundown; I Dream of Jeannie; Never Wave at a WAC. 1956 Goodbye, My Lady; You Can't Run Away from It; Teenage Rebel. 1957 Tammy and the Bachelor. 1958 The Goddess. 1959 Uncle Tom's Cabin (re-release of 1927 film). 1960 The Facts of Life; All the Fine Young Cannibals.

BEBAN, GEORGE

Born: 1873, San Francisco, Calif. Died: Oct. 5, 1928, Los Angeles, Calif.(fall from horse). Screen, stage, vaudeville, minstrel actor, screenwriter, and film director.

Appeared in: 1915 The Alien. 1916 Pasquale. 1917 Lost in Transit. 1921 One Man in a Million. 1922 The Sign of the Rose. 1924 The Greatest Love of All. 1926 The Loves of Ricardo. 1928 The Loves of Ricardo (and 1926 version).

BECHTEL, WILLIAM A. "BILLY"

Born: 1867, Germany. Died: Oct. 27, 1930, Hollywood, Calif. Screen and stage actor. Entered films approx. 1907.

Appeared in: Early Sennett films. 1921 Idle Hands. 1924 Meddling Women. 1929 Spite Marriage; Jazz Age. 1930 The Social Lion; Die Sehnsucht jeder Frau.

BECK, DANNY

Born: 1904. Died: Nov. 8, 1959, Hollywood, Calif. Screen actor.

Appeared in: 1941 Birth of the Blues. 1957 Man of a Thousand Faces.

BECK, NELSON C.

Born: 1887. Died: Mar. 3, 1952, Hollywood, Calif.(overdose of sleeping pills). Screen actor.

BECKETT, SCOTTY (Scott Hastings Beckett)

Born: Oct. 4, 1929, Oakland, Calif. Died: May 10, 1968, Los Angeles, Calif. Screen actor. Was in Roach "Our Gang" films during early 1930s at age of three.

Appeared in: 1934 Gallant Lady; Stand up and Cheer; I Am Suzanne; Sailor Made Widow; Whom the Gods Destroy; George White's Scandals. 1935 Dante's Inferno; Pursuit; I Dream Too Much. 1936 Anthony Adverse; Charge of the Light Brigade; The Case against Mrs. Ames. 1937 Life Begins with Love; Conquest. 1938 Marie Antoinette; Listen, Darling; You're Only Young Twice; The Devil's Party; Four's a Crowd; Marie Walewska; Bad Man from Brimstone. 1939 The Flying Irishman; Mickey the Kid; Our Neighbors, the Carters; The Escape; Days of Jesse James; Blind Alley. 1940 Street of Memories; Gold Rush Maisie; My Favorite Wife; The Blue Bird; My Son, My Son. 1941 Aloma of the South Seas; Father's Son; The Vanishing Virginian; Kings Row. 1942 Between Us Girls; It Happened in Flatbush. 1943 Good Luck, Mr. Yates; The Youngest Profession. 1944 Ali Baba and the Forty Thieves; The Climax. 1945 Junior Miss; Circumstantial Evidence. 1946 The Jolson Story; My Reputation; White Tie and Tails; Her Adventurous Night. 1947 Cynthia; Dangerous Years. 1948 Michael O'Halloran; A Date with Judy. 1950 Battleground; Nancy Goes to Rio; The Happy Years; Louisa. 1951 Corky of Gasoline Alley. 1952 Savage Triangle. 1953 Hot News. 1956 Three for Jamie Dawn.

BECKWITH, REGINALD

Born: 1908, York, England. Died: June 26, 1965, Bourne End, England. Screen, stage, television actor, stage director, and playwright.

Appeared in: 1940 Freedom Radio (film debut). 1941 Voice in the Night. 1946 This Man Is Mine. 1948 My Brother's Keeper. 1949 Scott of the Antarctic. 1951 Mr. Drake's Duck; Circle of Danger. 1952 Whispering Smith vs. Scotland Yard; Another Man's Poison. 1953 Penny Princess; The Million Pound Note (aka Man with a Million); Genevieve; The Titfield Thunderbolt;

Fast and Loose. 1954 Lease of Life; Dance Little Lady; The Runaway Bus. 1955 Innocents in Paris. 1957 Law and Disorder; Light Fingers; Lucky Jim; Men of Sherwood Forest (U.S. 1956); These Dangerous Years (aka Dangerous Youth-U.S. 1958); Break in the Circle; Carry on Admiral (aka The Ship Was Loaded-U.S. 1959). 1958 Night of the Demon (aka Curse of the Demon); The Horse's Mouth; The Captain's Table (U.S. 1960); Up the Creek; Mad Little Island. 1960 The 39 Steps; Expresso Bongo; Next to No Time. 1961 Double Bunk; Dentist in the Chair; Five Golden Hours. 1962 Doctor in Love; The Day the Earth Caught Fire; Night of the Eagle (aka Burn, Witch, Burn); Just for Fun; Mr. Hobbs Takes a Vacation; There Was a Crooked Man; The Password Is Courage (U.S. 1963). 1963 Doctor in Distress; Get with It; The V.I.P.'s; Lancelot and Guinevere (aka The Sword of Lancelot). 1964 A Shot in the Dark; Never Put It in Writing. 1965 Mister Moses. Other British films: The Intelligence Man (aka Spylarks); Yank in Ermine; Charley Moon; March Hare; Navy Lark.

BECKWITH, ROGER. See Wilhelm Von Bricken

BEDOYA, ALFONSO

Born: 1904, Vicam, Sonora, Mexico. Died: Dec. 15, 1957, Mexico City, Mexico. Screen actor.

Appeared in: 1948 The Treasure of Sierra Madre (Hollywood film debut); Angel of the Amazon; The Pearl; Angel in Exile. 1949 Border Incident; Streets of Laredo. 1950 Fortunes of Captain Blood; The Black Rose. 1951 The Man in the Saddle. 1952 California Conquest; Stronghold. 1953 Sombrero; The Stranger Wore a Gun. 1954 Ricochet Romance; Border River; The Black Pirates; Both Sides of the Law. 1955 Ten Wanted Men. 1958 The Big Country.

BEECHER, ADA

Born: 1862. Died: Mar. 30, 1935, Hollywood, Calif. Screen actress.

BEECHER, JANET (J. B. Meysenburg)

Born: 1884, Jefferson City, Mo. Died: Aug. 6, 1955, Washington, Conn. Screen and stage actress.

Appeared in: 1933 Gallant Lady. 1934 The Last Gentleman; The Mighty Barnum; The President Vanishes; Once a Gentleman. 1935 Let's Live Tonight; Village Tale; The Dark Angel; So Red the Rose. 1936 Love before Breakfast; I'd Give My Life; The Longest Night. 1937 The Good Old Soak; The Thirteenth Chair; Between Two Women; Big City; My Dear Miss Aldrich; Beg, Borrow or Steal; Rosalie. 1938 Judge Hardy's Children; Yellow Jack; Woman against Woman; Say It in French. 1939 The Story of Vernon and Irene Castle; I Was a Convict; Man of Conquest; Career; Laugh It Off. 1940 Slightly Honorable; The Gay Caballero; All This and Heaven Too; Bitter Sweet; The Mark of Zorro. 1941 The Man Who Lost Himself; The Lady Eve; A Very Young Lady; West Point Widow; The Parson of Panamint; For Beauty's Sake. 1942 Hi, Neighbor; Silver Queen; Reap the Wild Wind; Men of Texas. 1943 Mrs. Wiggs of the Cabbage Patch; Henry Gets Glamour.

BEECROFT, VICTOR R.

Born: 1887, London, England. Died: Mar. 25, 1958, Newport News, Va. Screen, stage, television, and radio actor.

Appeared in: 1915 A Dawn of Tomorrow.

BEERY, NOAH, SR.

Born: Jan. 17, 1884, Kansas City, Mo. Died: Apr. 1, 1946, Los Angeles, Calif.(heart attack). Screen and stage actor. Brother of actor Wallace Beery (dec. 1949) and father of actor Noah Beery, Jr.

Appeared in: 1918 The Mormon Maid. 1919 The Red Lantern; In Mizzoura; The Woman Next Door; Louisiana. 1920 The Sea Wolf; The Mark of Zorro; The Fighting Shepherdess; Go and Get It; Dinty. 1921 Beach of Dreams; Bits of Life; The Call of the North; Lotus Blossom; Bob Hampton of Placer. 1922 I Am the Law; The Heart Specialist; The Lying Truth; Omar the Tentmaker; Good Men and True; Flesh and Blood; Belle of Alaska; Ebb Tide; The Crossroads of New York; The Power of Love; Youth to Youth; Tillie; Wild Honey. 1923 The Spoilers; Wandering Daughters; When Law Comes to Hades; Dangerous Trails; The Call of the Canyon; The Destroying Angel; Stephen Steps Out; Stormswept; To the Last Man; Forbidden Lover; His Last Race; Main Street; Hollywood; Quicksands; The Spider and the Rose; Soul of the Beast; Tipped Off. 1924 The Heritage of the Desert; North of 36; The Female; The Fighting Coward; Lily of the Dust; Wanderer of the Wasteland; Welcome Stranger. 1925 The Coming of Amos; East of Suez; Lord Jim; The Thundering Herd; Contraband; The Light of Western Stars; Old Shoes; The Spaniard; Wild Horse Mesa; The Vanishing American. 1926 Beau Geste; The Crown of Lies; Padlocked; Paradise; The Enchanted Hill. 1927 The Rough Riders; The Dove; Evening Clothes; The Love Mart. 1928 Two Lovers; Beau Sabreaur; Hellship Bronson. 1929 False Feathers; Noah's Ark; Passion Song; Linda; Careers; Two O'Clock in the Morning; The Isle of Lost Ships; Four Feathers; Love in the Desert; The Show of Shows; The Godless Girl; Glorifying the American Girl. 1930 Bright Lights; Murder Will Out; Sin Flood; Song of the Flame; The Way of All Men; Under a Texas Moon; Golden Dawn; Big Boy; El Dorado; Isle of Escape; Feet First; The Love Trader; Renegades; Tol'able David; Oh, Sailor, Behave!; Mammy. 1931 Honeymoon Lane; Lost Men; Millionaire; In Line of Duty; Soldiers Plaything; Homicide Squad; Shanghai Love; Riders of the Purple Sage. 1932 Stranger in Town; The Stoker; No Living Witness; Big Stampede; Long Loop Laramie; The Drifter; The Kid from Spain; Out of Singapore; Heroes of the West (serial). 1933 The Flaming Signal; Cornered; Man of the Forest; Easy Millions; Sunset Pass; She Done Him Wrong; To the Last Man (and 1923 version); Laughing at Life; The Woman I Stole. 1934 David Harum; Kentucky Kernels; Madame Spy; Happy Landing; The Trail Beyond; Caravan; Mystery Liner; Cockeyed Cavalier; The Thundering Herd (and 1925 version). 1935 Sweet Adeline. 1936 King of the Damned; The Crimson Circle; The Marriage of Corbal. 1937 Our Fighting Navy; Strangers on a Honeymoon; Zorro Rides Again (serial). 1938 Bad Man of Brimstone; The Girl of the Golden West; Panamints Bad Man. 1939 Mexicali Rose; Prisoner of Corbal; Mutiny on the Blackhawk. 1940 A Little Bit of Heaven; The Tulsa Kid; Pioneers of the West; Grandpa Goes to Town; Adventures of Red Ryder (serial). 1941 A Missouri Outlaw. 1942 Isle of Missing Men; Tennessee Johnson. 1943 Clancy Street Boys; Salute to the Marines. 1944 Block Busters; Barbary Coast Gent; The Million Dollar Kid; Gentle Annie; The Honest Thief. 1945 This Man's Navy; Sing Me a Song of Texas.

BEERY, WALLACE
Born: Apr. 1, 1885, Kansas City, Mo. Died: Apr. 15, 1949, Los Angeles, Calif.(heart attack). Screen, stage, circus actor, and film director. Entered films with Essanay in 1913. Brother of actor Noah Beery, Sr. (dec. 1946). Divorced from actress Gloria Swanson. Won a foreign award for Viva Villa! in 1934 and Academy Award for Best Actor in the Champ in 1931.

Appeared in: 1914 "Sweedie" series. 1916 A Dash of Courage; Teddy at the Throttle. 1917 Cactus Nell. 1919 The Unpardonable Sin; The Love Burglar; The Life Line; Victory. 1920 Behind the Door; Virgin of Stamboul; The Mollycoddle. 1921 The Four Horsemen of the Apocalypse; The Last of the Mohicans; A Tale of Two Worlds; The Golden Snare; The Last Trail; The Rookie's Return. 1922 Only a Shop Girl; The Sagebrush Trail; Hurricane's Gal; Robin Hood; Wild Honey; I Am the Law; The Man from Hell's River; The Rosary; Trouble. 1923 The Three Ages; Patsy; Ashes of Vengeance; White Tiger; The Spanish Dancer; Richard the Lion-Hearted; Drifting; The Eternal Struggle; Bavu; The Flame of Life; The Drums of Jeopardy; Stormswept. 1924 The Signal Tower; The Red Lily; Another Man's Wife; Dynamite Smith; Madonna of the Streets; The Sea Hawk; Unseen Hands. 1925 The Lost World; The Wanderer; Rugged Water; Adventure; The Devil's Cargo; The Great Divide; The Pony Express; So Big; Coming Through; The Night Club; In the Name of Love; Let Women Alone. 1926 Old Ironsides; Behind the Front; We're in the Navy Now; Volcano. 1927 We're in the Air Now; Fireman, Save My Child; Casey at the Bat. 1928 The Big Killing; Partners in Crime; Wife Savers; Beggars of Life. 1929 Stairs of Sand; River of Romance; Chinatown Nights. 1930 The Big House; Min and Bill; Way for a Sailor; A Lady's Morals; Billy the Kid; Derelict; Soul Kiss. 1931 The Champ; Jenny Lind; The Secret Six; Hell Divers; Stolen Jools (short). 1932 Grand Hotel; Flesh; The Slippery Pearls (short). 1933 Viva Villa!; The Mighty Barnum. 1935 China Seas; West Point of the Air; O'Shaughnessy's Boy; Ah, Wilderness!. 1936 A Message to Garcia; Old Hutch. 1937 Slave Ship; Good Old Soak. 1938 Stablemates; Bad Man from Brimstone; Port of Seven Seas. 1939 Stand up and Fight; Thunder Afloat; Sergeant Madden. 1940 Two Gun Cupid; Wyoming; The Man from Dakota; Twenty-Mule Team. 1941 Barnacle Bill; The Bugle Sounds; The Bad Man. 1942 Jackass Mail. 1943 Salute to the Marines. 1944 Barbary Coast Gent; Rationing; Gold Town; The Honest Thief; Airship Squadron. 1945 This Man's Navy. 1946 The Mighty McGurk; Bad Bascomb. 1948 A Date with Judy; Alias a Gentleman. 1949 Big Jack. 1960 When Comedy Was King (documentary). 1964 Big Parade of Comedy (documentary).

BEGGS, MALCOLM LEE
Born: 1907. Died: Dec. 10, 1956, Chicago, Ill.(beaten to death). Screen, stage, television actor, and stage director.

Appeared in: 1952 It Grows on Trees; Love Island. 1953 Botany Bay; Houdini. 1958 Edge of Fury.

BEGLEY, ED
Born: Mar. 25, 1901, Hartford, Conn. Died: Apr. 28, 1970, Hollywood, Calif.(heart attack). Screen, stage, radio, and television actor. Won Academy Award in 1962 for Best Supporting Actor in Sweet Bird of Youth.

Appeared in: 1947 Boomerang; The Web; The Roosevelt Story (narr.); Big Town. 1948 Sorry, Wrong Number; Sitting Pretty; Deep Waters; The Street with No Name. 1949 It Happens Every Spring; The Great Gatsby; Tulsa. 1950 Stars in My Crown; Saddle Tramp; Dark City; Backfire; Wyoming Mail; Convicted. 1951 The Lady from Texas; You're In the Navy Now (aka U.S.S. Teakettle); On Dangerous Ground. 1952 Boots Malone; Lone Star; Deadline U.S.A; The Turning Point; What Price Glory. 1956 Patterns. 1957 Twelve Angry Men. 1959 Odds against Tomorrow. 1961 The Green Helmet. 1962 Sweet Bird of Youth. 1964 The Unsinkable Molly Brown. 1966 The Oscar. 1967 The Warning Shot; Billion Dollar Brain. 1968 Firecreek; A Time to Sing; Hang 'Em High; Wild in the Streets. 1969 Secrets of the Pirates' Inn; The Violent Enemy.

BEHRENS, FREDERICK
Born: 1854. Died: Jan. 5, 1938, Los Angeles, Calif. Screen and stage actor.

BEHRLE, FRED
Born: 1891, San Diego, Calif. Died: May 20, 1941, San Fernando Valley, Calif.(heart attack). Screen actor. Entered films with Vitagraph Co.

Appeared in: 1923 The Midnight Alarm. 1927 Through Thick and Thin. 1929 Big News. 1941 Texas.

BELASCO, GENEVIEVE
Born: 1871, London, England. Died: Nov. 17, 1956, New York, N.Y. Screen, stage, and radio actress.

Appeared in: 1923 Ten Commandments. 1924 The Sainted Devil.

BELCHER, ALICE
Born: 1880. Died: May 9, 1939, Hollywood, Calif. Screen and stage actress.

Appeared in: 1922 Second Hand Rose. 1926 Mistaken Orders; Pals First. 1927 Blondes by Choice. 1928 The Cowboy Kid.

BELGADO, MARIA
Born: 1906. Died: June 24, 1969, Hollywood, Calif. Screen actress. Entered films approx. 1932.

BELL, DIANA
Born: Queensland, Australia. Died: Oct. 30, 1965, Melbourne, Australia. Screen, stage, and television actress.

BELL, GASTON
Born: 1877, Boston, Mass. Died: Dec. 11, 1963, Woodstock, N.Y. Screen and stage actor. Appeared in silents.

BELL, GENEVIEVE
Died: Oct. 3, 1951, Los Angeles, Calif.(after surgery). Screen actress. Entered films in silents.

Appeared in: 1952 Phone Call from a Stranger.

BELL, HANK (Henry Bell)
Born: 1892. Died: Feb. 4, 1950, Hollywood, Calif.(heart attack). Screen actor.

Appeared in: 1923 Don Quickshot of the Rio Grande. 1925 The Pony Express; Gold and Grit. 1926 Double Daring; The Terror; Twin Triggers; Ace of Action; The Scrappin' Kid. 1927 Code of the Cow Country; Between Dangers. 1928 Saddle Mates. 1929 The Fighting Terror; The Last Roundup; 'Neath Western Skies. 1930 Trails of Peril, Abraham Lincoln. 1935 Westward Ho. 1936 Disorder in Court (short); The Trail of the Lonesome Pine. 1939 Geronimo. 1942 Valley of the Sun. 1945 Flame of Barbary Coast.

BELL, MONTA
Born: Feb. 5, 1891, Washington, D.C. Died: Feb. 4, 1958, Hollywood, Calif. Screen, stage actor, screenwriter, film producer,

and film director. Divorced from screen actress Betty Lawford (dec. 1960).

Appeared in: 1923 The Pilgrim.

BELL, RALPH W.
Born: 1883. Died: July 14, 1936, San Francisco, Calif.(pneumonia). Screen, stage actor, and stage director.

Appeared in: 1930 Clancy in Wall Street; Cock o' the Walk. 1931 Connecticut Yankee.

BELL, REX
Born: Oct. 16, 1905, Chicago, Ill. Died: July 4, 1962, Las Vegas, Nev.(coronary occlusion). Screen actor. Married to actress Clara Bow (dec. 1965) and was Lieutenant Governor of Nevada from 1954 to 1962.

Appeared in: 1928 Wild West Romance; The Girl-Shy Cowboy; The Cowboy Kid. 1929 Taking a Chance; Joy Street; Pleasure Crazed; Salute; They Had to See Paris; Happy Days. 1930 Courage; True to the Navy; Harmony at Home; Lightnin'. 1932 Forgotten Women; Law of the Sea; From Broadway to Cheyenne; The Man from Arizona; Arm of the Law; Crashin' Broadway; Diamond Trail; Lucky Larrigan; The Fighting Texans. 1935 Fighting Pioneers; Fun Fire; Saddle Acres. 1936 Too Much Beef; The Idaho Kid; West of Nevada; Men of the Plains; Stormy Trails. 1942 Tombstone, The Town Too Tough to Die; Dawn on the Great Divide. 1952 Lone Star.

BELL, RUTH
Born: 1907. Died: June 17, 1933, Los Angeles, Calif.(suicide—poison). Screen actress.

BELLEW, COSMO KYRLE
Born: 1886. Died: Jan. 25, 1948, Hollywood, Calif. Screen and stage actor.

Appeared in: 1904 A Gentleman of France. 1926 Summer Bachelors. 1927 The Magic Flame. 1928 Black Butterflies; Midnight Life; Hit of the Show. 1929 The Devil's Apple Tree; Strange Cargo; Disraeli. 1930 Lummox. 1931 The Lady Who Dared. 1934 Beloved; Norah O'Neill.

BELMAR, HENRY
Born: 1849. Died: Jan. 12, 1931, New Castle, Pa. Screen, stage actor, playwright, and stage producer. Appeared in silents. Married to screen actress Laurel Love (dec.-year unknown).

BELMONT, JOE A.
Born: 1860. Died: Mar. 28, 1930, Toledo, Ohio. Screen actor double, and circus acrobat. Not to be confused with screen actor Joseph Belmont.

BELMONT, MICHAEL
Born: 1915. Died: Nov. 9, 1941, Beverly Hills, Calif.(injuries—fall from horse). Screen actor.

BELMORE, BERTHA
Born: Dec. 22, 1882, Manchester, England. Died: Dec. 14, 1953, Barcelona, Spain. Screen and stage actress.

Appeared in: 1934 Going Gay; Are You a Mason?; Over the Garden Wall. 1935 Give Her a Ring; So You Won't Talk; You Never Can Tell; In the Soup. 1936 Broken Blossoms. 1937 Let's Make a Night of It. 1938 Over She Goes. 1939 Discoveries; The Midas Touch; Yes, Madam. 1941 She Couldn't Say No; Pirates of the Seven Seas.

BELMORE, DAISY (Daisy Garstin)
Born: 1874, London, England. Died: Dec. 12, 1954, New York, N.Y.(heart attack). Screen and stage actress. Entered films with Famous Players in N.Y. in 1912.

Appeared in: 1928 We Americans. 1930 Seven Days' Leave; Alias French Gertie; Scarlet Pages; All Quiet on the Western Front; Way for a Sailor. 1931 Fifty Million Frenchmen; My Past; Born to Love.

BELMORE, LIONEL
Born: 1867, England. Died: Jan. 30, 1953, Woodland Hills, Calif. Screen and stage actor.

Appeared in: 1920 Jes' Call Me Jim; Madame X. 1921 Courage; A Shocking Night; Guile of Women; Moonlight Follies; Two Minutes to Go; The Sting of the Lash. 1922 Oliver Twist; The Barnstormer; The Galloping Kid; Iron to Gold; Head over Heels; Enter Madame; The Kentucky Derby; Kindred of the Dust; The World's Champion; Peg o' My Heart. 1923 Within the Law;

Jazzmania; Forgive and Forget; Red Lights; Quicksands; Railroaded. 1924 A Boy of Flanders; A Lady of Quality; The Sea Hawk; Try and Get It; A Fool's Awakening; The Man Who Fights Alone; Racing Luck; The Silent Watcher. 1925 Madame Behave; Without Mercy; Eve's Secret; Never the Twain Shall Meet; The Storm Breaker. 1926 Bardelys the Magnificent; The Return of Peter Grimm; The Black Bird; The Checkered Flag; Shipwrecked; Stop, Look, and Listen. 1927 The Student Prince in Old Heidelberg; Sorrell and Son; Roaring Fires; Winners of the Wilderness; The Sunset Derby; The Demi-Bride; The Dice Woman; The King of Kings; The Tender Hour; Wide Open. 1928 The Play Girl; Rose Marie; The Circus Kid; The Matinee Idol; The Wife's Relations; The Good-Bye Kiss; Heart Trouble. 1929 The Redeeming Sin; The Love Parade; The Yellowback; The Unholy Night; Evidence; From Headquarters; Stark Mad. 1930 Love Comes Along; The Rogue Song; Hell's Island; Monte Carlo; Sweet Kitty Bellairs; The Boudoir Diplomat; Queen of Scandal; Playing Around; One Heavenly Night; Captain of the Guard. 1931 Ten Nights in a Barroom; Shanghai Love; Frankenstein; Alexander Hamilton. 1932 So Big; Vanity Fair; Police Court, Malay Nights. 1933 The Vampire Bat; Oliver Twist (and 1922 version); The Constant Wife; Warrior's Husband. 1934 Cleopatra; The Count of Monte Cristo; Caravan; I Am Suzanne; Jane Eyre. 1935 Red Morning; Dressed to Kill; Forced Landing; Vanessa, Her Love Story; Hitch Hike Lady; Bonnie Scotland; Cardinal Richeli u; Clive of India. 1936 Little Lord Fauntleroy; The Last of the M - hicans; Mary of Scotland. 1937 It's Love I'm After; Maid of Salem; The Prince and the Pauper; The Toast of New York. 1939 Tower of London; Son of Frankenstein. 1940 My Son, My Son; Diamond Frontier.

BELTRI, RICARDO
Born: 1899, Mexico. Died: June 1962, Mexico City, Mexico. Mexican screen and stage actor. Appeared in silents.

BENADERET, BEA
Born: Apr. 4, 1906, New York, N.Y. Died: Oct. 13, 1968, Los Angeles, Calif.(cancer). Screen, stage, television, and radio actress.

Appeared in: 1962 Tender Is the Night.

BEN-ARI, RAIKIN
Born: 1904, Russia. Died: Jan. 2, 1968, Moscow, Russia. Screen, stage actor, and stage director.

Appeared in: 1959 Gangster Story.

BENASSI, MEMO
Born: 1886, Italy. Died: Feb. 24, 1957, Bologna, Italy. Screen and stage actor.

Appeared in: 1936 La Signora di Tutti. 1937 Signora Paradiso. 1939 Scipio Africanus. 1948 Rossini.

BENCHLEY, ROBERT
Born: Sept. 15, 1889, Worcester, Mass. Died: Nov. 21, 1945, New York, N.Y.(cerebral hemorrhage). Screen, radio actor, writer, critic, and film director. Won Academy Award for his short, How to Sleep, in 1936.

Appeared in: 1928 The Sex Life of the Polyp. 1932 Sport Parade. 1933 Headline Shooter; Dancing Lady. 1934 Rafter Romance; Treasurer's Report (short); Social Register. 1935 China Seas; How to Sleep (short). 1936 An MGM short; Piccadilly Jim. 1937 Live, Love and Learn; Broadway Melody of 1938 (short); a Columbia short; an MGM short. 1938 an MGM short. 1940 Hired Wife; Foreign Correspondent. 1941 Nice Girl?; The Reluctant Dragon; You'll Never Get Rich; Three Girls about Town; Bedtime Story. 1942 Take a Letter, Darling; The Major and the Minor; I Married a Witch. 1943 Flesh and Fantasy (narr.), Young and Willing; The Song of Russia; The Sky's the Limit. 1944 Her Primitive Man; The National Barn Dance; See Here, Private Hargrove; Practically Yours; Janie. 1945 Pan-Americana; It's in the Bag; Weekend at the Waldorf; Kiss and Tell; Duffy's Tavern; Stork Club; The Road to Utopia. 1946 The Bride Wore Boots; Snafu; Janie Gets Married; Blue Skies. 1964 Big Parade of Comedy (documentary).

BENDER, RUSSELL
Born: 1910. Died: Aug. 16, 1969, Hollywood, Calif. Screen and television actor.

Appeared in: 1956 It Conquered the World. 1957 The Amazing Colossal Man; Badlands of Montana; Dragstrip Girl; Invasion of the Saucer Men; The Joker Is Wild; Motorcycle Gang. 1958 Hot Rod Gang; I Bury the Living; War of the Colossal Beast; Suicide Battalion. 1959 Ghost of Dragstrip Hollow; Compulsion;

No Name on the Bullet. 1960 Vice Raid. 1961 Anatomy of a Psycho; The Purple Hills. 1962 A Gathering of Eagles; Air Patrol; Panic in the Year Zero!. 1964 The Strangler. 1965 The Satan Bug. 1967 Devil's Angels. 1968 Maryjane; The Young Animals; Born Wild.

BENDIX, WILLIAM
Born: Jan. 14, 1906, New York, N.Y. Died: Dec. 14, 1964, Los Angeles, Calif.(lobar pneumonia and complications). Screen, stage, television, and radio actor.

Appeared in: 1941 Woman of the Year (film debut). 1942 Brooklyn Orchid; Wake Island; The Glass Key; Star Spangled Rhythm; Who Done It?. 1943 The McGuerins from Brooklyn; Guadalcanal Diary; China; The Crystal Ball; Taxi, Mister; Hostages. 1944 Lifeboat; The Hairy Ape; Abroad with Two Yanks; Greenwich Village; Skirmish on the Home Front (short). 1945 It's in the Bag; Don Juan Quilligan; A Bell for Adano. 1946 The Blue Dahlia; Two Years before the Mast; Sentimental Journey; The Dark Corner; White Tie and Tails. 1947 Blaze of Noon; The Web; I'll Be Yours; Calcutta; Where There's Life; Variety Girl. 1948 Race Street; The Babe Ruth Story; The Time of Your Life. 1949 Life of Riley; Streets of Laredo; Cover Up; The Big Steal; Connecticut Yankee in King Arthur's Court. 1950 Johnny Holiday; The Gambling House; Kill the Umpire. 1951 Submarine Command; Detective Story. 1952 Macao; Blackbeard the Pirate; A Girl in Every Port. 1954 Dangerous Mission. 1955 Crash Out. 1956 Battle Stations. 1958 The Deep Six. 1959 Idle on Parade; The Rough and the Smooth. 1961 Portrait of a Sinner. 1962 Boys' Night Out. 1963 The Young and the Brave; For Love or Money. 1964 Law of the Lawless; The Phony American; Invitation to a Hanging. 1965 Young Fury; Johnny Nobody.

BENELL, JOHN THOMAS
Born: 1915. Died: Aug. 12, 1940, Beverly Hills, Calif. Screen and stage actor.

BENGE, WILSON
Born: 1875, Greenwich, London, England. Died: July 1, 1955, Hollywood, Calif. Screen, stage actor, and stage producer.

Appeared in: 1922 Robin Hood. 1923 Ten Commandments. 1925 Alias Mary Flynn; The Road to Yesterday. 1926 A Trip to Chinatown; The Midnight Message. 1927 King of Kings; Fast and Furious; The Lone Eagle. 1928 Anybody Here Seen Kelly?; A Gentleman Preferred; Freedom of the Press; That's My Daddy. 1929 A Most Immoral Lady; Bulldog Drummond; Untamed; Cynara; This Thing Called Love. 1930 Raffles; Her Wedding Night; Charley's Aunt; The Bat Whispers. 1931 Men in Her Life. 1933 Big Executive; By Appointment Only. 1934 Twin Husbands. 1935 Cardinal Richelieu; The Ghost Walks; False Pretenses. 1936 Dancing Feet; Murder at Glen Athol. 1937 The Shadow Strikes; Mr. Boggs Steps Out. 1938 Trade Winds.

BENNETT, BARBARA
Born: 1911. Died: Aug. 8, 1958, Montreal, Canada(heart attack). Screen and stage actress. Sister of actresses Constance Bennett (dec. 1965) and Joan Bennett and daughter of actor Richard Bennett (dec. 1944). Divorced from singer Morton Downey. Married to actor Addison "Jack" Randall (dec. 1945).

Appeared in: 1927 Black Jack. 1929 Syncopation; Mother's Boy. 1930 Love among the Millionaires.

BENNETT, BELLE
Born: 1891, Milaca, Minn. Died: Nov. 4, 1932, Los Angeles, Calif. Screen, stage, and vaudeville actress.
Appeared in: 1916 Sweet Kitty Bellairs. 1917 Fuel of Life.

1918 A Soul in Trust. 1920 The Courage of Marge O'Doone. 1922 Flesh and Spirit; Robin Hood; Your Best Friend. 1924 In Hollywood with Potash and Perlmutter. 1925 Stella Dallas; Playing with Souls; East Lynne; His Supreme Moment; If Marriage Fails. 1926 The Lily; Reckless Lady; Fourth Commandment; The Amateur Gentleman. 1927 Wild Geese; Mother; Way of all Flesh. 1928 The Devil's Skipper; The Devil's Trademark; The Sporting Age; Mother Machree; Battle of the Sexes; The Power of Silence. 1929 The Iron Mask; Molly and Me; My Lady's Past; Big Money; Fashions in Love. 1930 Their Own Desire; Courage; Recaptured Love; Night Work; One Romantic Night; The Woman Who Was Forgotten. 1932 The Big Shot.

BENNETT, CHARLES
Died: July 1925, New York, N.Y.(hemorrhage). Screen actor and scenery designer.

BENNETT, CHARLES J.
Born: 1891. Died: Feb. 15, 1943, Hollywood, Calif. Screen actor.

Appeared in: 1914 Tillie's Punctured Romance. 1919 The Adventures of Ruth (serial). 1922 The Top of New York. 1924 America.

BENNETT, CONSTANCE
Born: Oct. 22, 1905, New York, N.Y. Died: July 24, 1965, Ft. Dix, N.J.(cerebral hemorrhage). Screen, stage actress, and film producer. Daughter of actor Richard Bennett (dec. 1944), sister of actresses Barbara (dec. 1958) and Joan Bennett.

Appeared in: 1922 Reckless Youth; What's Wrong with Women? Evidence. 1924 Cytherea; The Forbidden Way; Into the Net. 1925 My Wife and I; Sally, Irene and Mary; The Pinch Hitter; Code of the West; The Goose Hangs High; The Goose Woman; My Son; Wandering Fires. 1926 Should a Woman Tell; Married. 1929 This Thing Called Love. 1930 Three Faces East; Common Clay; Rich People; Sin Takes a Holiday; Son of the Gods. 1931 The Common Law; The Easiest Way; Born to Love; Bought. 1932 What Price Hollywood; Lady with a Past; Two against the World; Rockabye. 1933 Our Betters; Bed of Roses; After Tonight. 1934 The Affairs of Cellini; Moulin Rouge; Outcast Lady. 1935 After Office Hours. 1936 Everything Is Thunder; Ladies in Love. 1937 Topper. 1938 Merrily We Live; Service de Luxe; Topper Takes a Trip. 1939 Tail Spin. 1940 Escape to Glory (aka Submarine Zone). 1941 Two-Faced Woman; Law of the Tropics; Wild Bill Hickok Rides. 1942 Sin Town; Madame Spy. 1945 Madame Pimpernel; Paris Underground. 1946 Centennial Summer. 1947 The Unsuspected. 1948 Smart Woman; Blonde Ice. 1949 Angel on the Amazon. 1951 As Young as You Feel. 1954 It Should Happen to You. 1966 Madame X.

BENNETT, ENID
Born: Jan. 2, 1895, Australia. Died: May 14, 1969, Malibu, Calif.(heart attack). Screen and stage actress. Entered films in 1917.

Appeared in: 1917 Princess in the Dark. 1918 The Biggest Show on Earth; The Vamp; Fuss and Feathers. 1919 The Haunted Bedroom; Stepping Out. 1920 The Woman and the Suitcase; Hairpins. 1921 Her Husband's Friend; Keeping up with Lizzie; Silk Hosiery. 1922 Robin Hood; The Bootlegger's Daughter; Scandalous Tongues. 1923 The Bad Man; The Courtship of Miles Standish; Strangers of the Night; Your Friend and Mine. 1924 The Sea Hawk; The Red Lily; A Fool's Awakening. 1926 A Woman's Heart. 1927 The Wrong Mr. Wright. 1929 Good Medicine. 1931 Skippy; Waterloo Bridge; Sooky. 1939 Meet Dr. Christian; Intermezzo: A Love Story. 1940 Strike up the Band.

BENNETT, JOE (Joseph Bennett Aldert)
Born: 1889, Charleston, S.C. Died: Aug. 31, 1967, Amityville, N.Y. Screen, vaudeville, minstrel actor, and dancer. Appeared in vaudeville as part of "The Dark Clouds" team with Edward Richards and later in a vaudeville act billed as "The Georgia Trio," both blackface acts.

BENNETT, JOSEPH
Born: 1896, Los Angeles, Calif. Died: Dec. 4, 1931, Hollywood, Calif. Screen actor. Entered films in 1917.

Appeared in: 1921 Love Never Dies; The Night Horsemen; A Daughter of the Law; The Home Stretch. 1922 Elope If You Must. 1924 Barbara Frietchie; The Breed of the Border; Trigger Finger; Flashing Spurs. 1925 Cold Nerve. 1926 The Sign of the Claw; The Man in the Shadow. 1927 God's Great Wilderness; Shooting Straight; Men of Daring; Straight Shootin', Wolf's Trail; Three Miles Up; Somewhere in Sonora; The Valley of Hell. 1928 The Shepherd of the Hills; Vultures of the Sea (serial); Won in the Clouds. 1929 The Lariet Kid. 1930 After the Fog.

BENNETT, LEE
Born: 1911. Died: Oct. 10, 1954, Chicago, Ill. Screen, radio actor, singer, and orchestra leader.

Appeared in: 1937 Hold 'Em Navy. 1947 Spirit of West Point. 1950 At War with the Army. 1951 The Dakota Kid; Three Desperate Men.

BENNETT, MICKEY
Born: 1915, Victoria, B.C., Canada. Died: Sept. 6, 1950, Hollywood, Calif.(heart attack). Screen actor and assistant film director.

Appeared in: 1922 The Man Who Played God; Reported Missing. 1923 Big Brother; The Empty Cradle; The Last Moment; Loyal Wives; Marriage Morals. 1924 The New School Teacher; Second

Youth. 1926 Big Pal; The Cohens and the Kellys; Grabbing Grabbers (short); It's the Old Army Game; There Ain't No Santa Claus (short); Honesty—The Best Policy. 1927 A Boy of the Streets; Babe Comes Home; Slaves of Beauty. 1928 Tillie's Punctured Romance; United States Smith; The Vanishing West (serial); The Head of the Family. 1929 The Dummy; Footlights and Fools; The Ghost Talks. 1930 Strictly Modern; Swing High; Father's Son. 1931 Big Business Girl. 1932 Laughter in Hell. 1933 The Mayor of Hell.

BENNETT, RAY
Born: 1895. Died: Dec. 17, 1957, Hollywood, Calif.(heart attack). Screen actor.

Appeared in: 1942 The Spoilers. 1948 Canon City; Northwest Stampede. 1949 Song of Surrender; Rimfire; Ma and Pa Kettle; The Dalton Gang. 1951 Apache Drums. 1952 The Man from Black Hills; Waco. 1953 The Redhead from Wyoming; The Great Sioux Uprising. 1956 The Wrong Man. 1957 African Manhunt.

BENNETT, RED (William Houghton)
Born: 1873. Died: May 10, 1941, Hollywood, Calif. Screen actor.

BENNETT, RICHARD
Born: May 21, 1873, Deacon's Mills, Cass County, Ind. Died: Oct. 22, 1944, Los Angeles, Calif.(heart attack). Screen, stage, and vaudeville actor. Father of actresses Constance (dec. 1965), Barbara (dec. 1958) and Joan Bennett.

Appeared in: 1915 Damaged Goods. 1923 The Eternal City. 1924 Youth for Sale. 1925 Lying Wives. 1928 The Home Towners. 1931 Five and Ten; Arrowsmith; Bought. 1932 No Greater Love; Strange Justice; This Reckless Age; If I Had a Million; Madame Racketeer. 1933 The Woman Accused; The Song of Songs; Big Executive. 1934 Nana. 1935 This Woman Is Mine. 1942 Journey into Fear; The Magnificent Ambersons.

BENNETT, SAM
Born: 1887. Died: Aug. 25, 1937, Hollywood, Calif. Screen and stage actor.

BENNETT, WILDA
Born: 1894. Died: Dec. 20, 1967, Winnemucca, Nev. Screen and stage actress.

Appeared in: 1939 What a Life. 1940 Those Were the Days.

BENNISON, ANDREW
Born: 1887. Died: Jan. 7, 1942, Oxnard, Calif. Screen, stage actor, screenwriter, and film director.

BENNISON, LOUIS
Born: 1884. Died: June 9, 1929, New York, N.Y.(suicide—gun). Screen actor and playwright.

Appeared in: 1921 Lavender and Old Lace.

BENSON, JOHN WILLIAM
Born: 1862. Died: July 12, 1926, New York, N.Y. (complications of diseases). Screen, stage, and vaudeville actor.

BENSON, JULIETTE V. P.
Born: 1875. Died: Dec. 22, 1962, Hollywood, Calif. Screen actress. Entered films approx. 1933.

BENSON, SANDFORD
Born: 1914. Died: Feb. 4, 1935, Hollywood, Calif.(injuries from auto accident). Screen and stage actor.

BENTLEY, ROBERT
Born: 1895. Died: Apr. 19, 1958, Benton Harbor, Mich. Screen, stage, and radio actor. Appeared in early D. W. Griffith films.

Appeared in: 1921 The Power Within. 1923 None So Blind. 1924 The New School Teacher.

BERANGERE, MME.
Born: France. Died: Nov. 1928, Paris, France. Screen actress.

BEREGI, OSCAR, SR.
Born: 1875, Hungary. Died: Oct. 18, 1965, Hollywood, Calif. Hungarian screen and stage actor. Father of actor Oscar Beregi, Jr.

Appeared in: 1926 Butterflies in the Rain; The Love Thief; The Flaming Forest. 1927 Camille; Moon of Israel. 1933 A Key Balvany (A Blue Idol). 1934 Iza Neni; Rakoczi Indulo.

BERESFORD, HARRY
Born: 1864, London, England. Died: Oct. 4, 1944, Los Angeles, Calif. Screen, stage actor, screenwriter, and novelist.

Appeared in: 1926 The Quarterback. 1931 Charlie Chan Carries On; Sob Sister; Heaven on Earth; Sooky; Finn and Hattie; Scandal Sheet; Up Pops the Devil; The Secret Call. 1932 Ambition; High Pressure; Scandal for Sale; So Big; Strange Love of Molly Louvain; Prosperity; Dr. X; The Match King; Dance Team; Forgotten Commandments; The Sign of the Cross. 1933 Murders in the Zoo; The Mind Reader; I Cover the Waterfront; Dinner at Eight; Night Flight; Bureau of Missing Persons; Ever in My Heart; College Coach. 1934 Friends of Mr. Sweeney; Cleopatra; The Little Minister; Fashions of 1934; The Merry Frinks. 1935 Seven Keys to Baldpate; Anna Karenina; David Copperfield; A Dog of Flanders; I'll Love You Always; Page Miss Glory; I Found Stella Parrish. 1936 Klondike Annie; Follow the Fleet; Grand Jury; Postal Inspector; In His Steps. 1937 The Prince and the Pauper; The Go-Getter; She's No Lady; She Asked for It; They Won't Forget. 1944 The Sign of the Cross (revised version of 1932 film).

BERG, GERTRUDE
Born: Oct. 3, 1900, New York, N.Y. Died: Sept. 14, 1966, N.Y. (heart ailment). Screen, stage, television, radio actress, author, and screenwriter.

Appeared in: 1951 Molly. 1953 Main Street to Broadway.

BERGER, NICOLE
Born: 1934, France. Died: Apr. 1967, Rougen, France (following auto accident). Screen, stage, and television actress.

Appeared in: 1955 The Game of Love. 1956 Bold Adventure. 1957 Julietta. 1958 He Who Must Die; Premier May (The First Day of May). 1959 Filles de la Niut (Girls of the Night). 1960 Siege of Hell Street (aka The Siege of Sidney Street); The Chasers (aka Les Diagueurs [The Dredgers]). 1962 La Denonciation (The Denunciation); Love Is my Profession; Shoot the Piano Player. 1963 The Girl from Flanders. 1967 The Story of a Three-Day Pass.

BERGERE, RAMONA
Born: 1902. Died: Apr. 26, 1941, Glendale, Calif. Screen actress.

BERGERE, VALERIE
Born: Feb. 2, 1875, Alsace-Lorraine, France. Died: Sept. 16, 1938, Hollywood, Calif. Screen, stage, and vaudeville actress.

Appeared in: 1937 The Singing Marine; It's Love I'm After.

BERGMAN, HENRY
Born: 1870, San Francisco, Calif. Died: Oct. 22, 1946, Hollywood, Calif.(heart attack). Screen actor, circus and opera performer, screenwriter, and assistant film director. Entered films with Pathe-Lehrman in 1913.

Appeared in: 1915 His New Job; A Night Out; The Champion; In the Park; The Jitney Elopement; The Tramp; By the Sea; Work; A Woman; The Bank; Shanghaied; A Night in the Show. 1916 Carmen; Police; Triple Trouble; The Floorwalker; The Fireman; The Vagabond; One A.M.; The Count; The Pawnshop; Behind the Screen; The Rink. 1917 Easy Street; The Cure; The Immigrant; The Adventurer. 1918 A Dog's Life; The Bond; Shoulder Arms. 1919 Sunnyside; A Day's Pleasure. 1920 The Idle Class. 1921 The Kid. 1922 Pay Day. 1923 The Pilgrim; A Woman of Paris. 1925 The Gold Rush. 1928 The Circus. 1931 City Lights. 1936 Modern Times. 1940 The Great Dictator.

BERISTAIN, LEOPOLDO
Born: 1883, Mexico. Died: Jan. 5, 1948, Tijuana, Mexico(diabetes). Screen actor.

Appeared in: 1939 Mexico Lindo.

BERISTAIN, LUIS
Born: 1918, Mexico. Died: Apr. 1, 1962, Mexico City, Mexico (heart attack). Screen and television actor.

Appeared in: 1955 This Strange Passion. 1967 The Exterminating Angel.

BERKELEY, ARTHUR
Born: 1896. Died: July 29, 1962, Hollywood, Calif. Screen actor.

Appeared in: 1957 Teenage Monster.

BERKELEY, REGINALD
Born: 1882, London, England. Died: Mar. 20, 1936, Hollywood, Calif. Screen actor, screenwriter, and author.

BERKES, JOHN PATRICK
Born: 1897. Died: July 5, 1951, Hollywood, Calif. Screen and stage actor.

Appeared in: 1947 The Corpse Came C.O.D., The Egg and I. 1948 Romance on the High Seas. 1949 My Dream is Yours. 1950 Branded. 1951 Journey into Light; The Big Carnival.

BERLE, SANDRA
Born: 1877. Died: May 31, 1954, New York, N.Y.(cerebral hemorrhage). Screen and television actress. An occasional extra at Biograph Studios in youth. Mother of actor Milton Berle and often in his various acts.

BERLINER, MARTIN
Born: 1896, Germany. Died: Jan. 26, 1966, Berlin, Germany (heart attack). Screen, stage, and television actor.

Appeared in: 1964 Three Penny Opera.

BERN, PAUL (Paul Levy)
Born: 1889, Wandabeck, Germany. Died: Sept. 4, 1932, Beverly Hills, Calif.(suicide—gun). Screen, stage actor, film producer, film director, and screenwriter. Married to actress Jean Harlow (dec. 1937).

BERNARD, AL
Born: 1888. Died: Mar. 6, 1949, New York, N.Y. Screen, television, radio, vaudeville, minstrel actor, singer, author, and songwriter.

BERNARD, BARNEY
Born: Aug. 17, 1877, Rochester, N.Y. Died: Mar. 21, 1924, New York, N.Y.(bronchial pneumonia). Screen, stage, and vaudeville actor. He and Alexander Carr created the roles of Potash and Perlmutter on stage.

They appeared in: 1933 Potash and Perlmutter.

BERNARD, DOROTHY
Born: 1890. Died: Dec. 14, 1955, Hollywood, Calif.(heart attack). Screen and stage actress.

Appeared in: 1909 The Cricket on the Hearth, "Jonsey" series. 1910 Fate's Turning. 1911 The Failure; Sunshine through the Dark; A Tale of the Wilderness; A Sister's Love; A Blot on the 'Scutcheon; The Root of Evil. 1912 The Girl and Her Trust; The Female of the Species; A Siren of Impulse; The Goddess of Sagebrush Gulch, His Lesson; Heaven Avenges. 1916 A Man of Sorrow. 1918 Little Women; Les Miserables. 1921 The Wild Goose.

BERNARD, HARRY
Born: 1878. Died: Nov. 4, 1940, Hollywood, Calif. Screen and vaudeville actor. Appeared in Keystone films in 1915.

Appeared in: 1915 Crossed Love and Swords; Dirty Work in a Laundry; The Battle of Ambrose and Walrus; Our Daredevil Chief. 1928 Two Tars (short). 1929 the following shorts: Liberty; Wedding Again; That's My Wife; Men O'War; A Perfect Day. 1930 the following shorts: Night Owls; Blotto; Another Fine Mess. 1931 Laughing Gravy (short). 1932 Any Old Port (short). 1933 the following shorts: Sneak Easily; Maids a la Mode; Bargain of the Century. 1934 Sons of the Desert; Three Chumps Ahead (short); The Live Ghosts (short). 1935 Top Flat (short). 1936 The Bohemian Girl; Our Relations; On the Wrong Trek (short). 1937 New Faces of 1937.

BERNARD, IVOR
Born: June 13, 1887, London, England. Died: June 30, 1953. Screen and stage actor.

Appeared in: 1931 The Skin Game; Sally in Our Alley. 1932 The Good Companions. 1933 Illegal; Sleeping Car; Waltz Time; The Crime of Blossoms; The Wandering Jew. 1934 Princess Charming. 1935 Death at Broadcasting House; The Roof; Mr. Hobo; Behind the Mask. 1936 Double Exposure; Foreign Affairs; The House of the Spaniard; Secret Lives; Farewell to Cinderella. 1937 What a Man; Victoria the Great; Storm in a Teacup; The Mill on the Floss. 1938 Pygmalion. 1941 Stars Look down; The Saint's Vacation. 1944 Hotel Reserve (aka Epitaph for a Spy); Escape to Danger; Undercover. 1945 The Silver Fleet. 1946 Great Day; The Wicked Day; Caesar and Cleopatra. 1947 Appointment with Crime; Princess Fitz; Great Expectations; So Well Remembered; Murder in Reserve. 1948 Dulcimer Street. 1949 Don't Take it to Heart; Queen of Spades. 1950

Madeline; Mrs. Fitzherbert. 1951 Oliver Twist; Sin of Esther Waters. 1952 Time, Gentlemen, Please. 1953 Malta Story; Sea Devils. 1954 Beat the Devil. Other British films: London Belongs to Me; Paper Orchid; 999.

BERNARD, LOIS
Born: 1898. Died: Apr. 25, 1945, Los Angeles, Calif.(suicide—jumped). Screen actress. Wife of screen actor Joseph Bernard.

BERNARD, PAUL
Born: France. Died: May 1958, Paris, France. Screen and stage actor.

Appeared in: 1936 Pension Mimosas. 1947 Panic. 1948 Les Maudits (The Damned); Un Ami Viendra Ce Soir (A Friend Will Come Tonight). 1954 Caroline Cherie. 1956 Les Dames du Bois du Boulogne (Women of the Bois du Boulogne)

BERNARD, PETER
Born: 1888, U.S. Died: Dec. 22, 1960, Huddersfield, England. Screen, vaudeville actor, vocalist, and songwriter.

BERNARD, SAM
Born: 1889. Died: July 5, 1950, Hollywood, Calif. Screen and stage actor.

Appeared in: 1931 Wanted by the Police; Prison Train. 1941 Tumbledown Ranch in Arizona. 1942 Let's Get Tough; Today I Hang; Smart Alecks; Baby Face Morgan; Ice Capades Revue. 1943 The Crime Smashers. 1945 Thoroughbreds. 1948 The Vicious Circle; When My Baby Smiles at Me.

BERNARD, SAM (aka SAMUEL BARNET)
Born: 1863, Birmingham, England. Died: May 16, 1927, on board ship in the Atlantic ("apoplexy"). Screen, stage, and vaudeville actor. Entered films with Triangle Film Corp. in 1915. Appeared in vaudeville under name of Samuel Barnet.

Appeared in: 1915 Fatty and the Broadway Stars. 1916 Because He Loved Her; The Great Pearl Tangle.

BERNES, MARK
Born: 1912, Russia. Died: Aug. 25, 1969, Moscow, Russia. Screen, television actor, and singer.

Appeared in: 1943 Diary of a Nazi. 1944 Two Soldiers. 1945 The Ural Front. 1946 The Turning Point. 1952 Taras Shevchenko. 1953 Maximka. 1955 The Boys from Leningrad; The Frigid Sea. 1957 School of Courage.

BERNHARDT, SARAH (Rosalie Bernard)
Born: Oct. 22, 1844, Paris, France. Died: Mar. 26, 1923, Paris, France(uremic poisoning and weak heart). Screen, stage, and vaudeville actress.

Appeared in: 1900 Hamlet (title role). 1910 La Dame aux Camelias (Camille-U.S. 1912); Queen Elizabeth. 1915 Jeanne Dore. 1917 Mothers of France. 1931 Stars of Yesterday (short-film clips).

BERNIE, BEN (Benjamin Anzelvitz)
Born: 1891, Bayonne, N.J. Died: Oct. 20, 1943, Hollywood, Calif. Screen, vaudeville, radio actor, and bandleader.

Appeared in: 1930 Ben Bernie and His Orchestra (short). 1934 Shoot the Works. 1935 Stolen Harmony. 1937 Wake Up and Live; Love and Hisses.

BERNIVICI, COUNT (aka BERNAVICI and BERNI VICI)
Born: 1884. Died: July 12, 1966, Hollywood, Calif. Screen and vaudeville actor.

BERRY, ALINE
Born: 1905. Died: Apr. 3, 1967, Hollywood, Calif.(heart attack). Screen, stage, and radio actress.

Appeared in: 1925 Soul Fire.

BERRY, ARTHUR NELSON
Born: 1887. Died: June 12, 1945, Hollywood, Calif. Screen and vaudeville actor. Married to screen actress Elizabeth Berry with whom he appeared in vaudeville.

BERRY, JULES (Jules Peaufichet)
Born: 1883, France. Died: Apr. 25, 1951, Paris, France(heart ailment). Screen and stage actor.

Appeared in: 1929 Crossroads; Le Four Se Leve. 1940 Daybreak. 1942 Les Visiteurs du Soir. 1944 32 Rue de Montmartre. 1947 Etoile Sans Lumiere (Star without a Light); The Devil's Own Envoy;

La Symphonie Fantastique. 1954 Dreams of Love. 1964 The Crime of Monsieur Lange.

BERTRAND, MARY
Died: May 12, 1955, Woodland Hills, Calif. Screen actress. Appeared in silents.

BESSENT, MARIE
Born: 1898. Died: Oct. 12, 1947, Los Angeles, Calif. Screen, stage, and vaudeville actress. Also double for actress Mabel Normand.

BESSERER, EUGENIE
Born: 1870. Died: May 30, 1934, Los Angeles, Calif. Screen and stage actress. Entered films in 1910.

Appeared in: 1912 The Count of Monte Cristo. 1919 Scarlet Days; The Greatest Question. 1920 The Fighting Shepherdess. 1921 Molly O; The Sin of Martha Queed; The Light in the Clearing; The Breaking Point; Good Women; What Happened to Rosa?. 1922 The Hands of Nara; June Madness; The Rosary; Penrod; The Stranger's Banquet. 1923 Anna Christie; Her Reputation; Enemies of Children; The Rendezvous; The Lonely Road. 1924 Bread; The Price She Paid. 1925 A Fool and His Money; Friendly Enemies; Bright Lights; The Circle; Confessions of a Queen; The Coast of Folly; Wandering Footsteps. 1926 The Millionaire Policeman; The Skyrocket. 1927 The Jazz Singer; When a Man Loves; Flesh and the Devil; The Fire Brigade; Captain Salvation; Slightly Used; Wandering Girls. 1928 The Yellow Lily; Two Lovers; Drums of Love; Lilac Time. 1929 Seven Faces; The Bridge of San Luis Rey; A Lady of Chance; Madame X; Fast Company; Illusion; Thunderbolt; Mister Antonio; Speedway; Whispering Winds. 1930 In Gay Madrid; A Royal Romance. 1933 To the Last Man.

BEST, DOLLY
Born: 1899. Died: Oct. 6, 1968, Los Angeles, Calif. Screen and stage actress. Appeared in silents.

BEST, WILLIE (aka "SLEEP 'N EAT")
Born: 1916, Miss. Died: Feb. 27, 1962, Hollywood, Calif. (cancer). Screen and television actor.

Appeared in: 1932 The Monster Walks. 1934 Little Miss Marker; Kentucky Kernels; several RKO shorts. 1935 West of the Pecos; Murder on a Honeymoon; The Nitwits; The Arizonian; Hot Tip; The Littlest Rebel. 1936 Murder on the Bridle Path; The Bride Walks Out; Mummu's Boys; Racing Lady; Make Way for a Lady; Thank you, Jeeves!; General Spanky; Two in Revolt; Down the Stretch. 1937 Meet the Misses; Breezing Home; The Lady Fights Back; Super Sleuth; Saturday's Heroes. 1938 Vivacious Lady; Gold Is Where You Find It; Merrily We Live; Goodbye Broadway; Blondie; Youth Takes a Fling. 1939 Nancy Drew, Trouble Shooter; The Covered Trailer; At the Circus. 1940 Money and the Woman; Who Killed Aunt Maggie?; I Take This Woman; The Ghost Breakers. 1941 Road Show; High Sierra; The Lady from Cheyenne; Nothing but the Truth; Flight from Destiny; Scattergood Baines; Highway West; The Smiling Ghost. 1942 Juke Girl; Whispering Ghosts; Busses Road; The Hidden Hand; Scattergood Survives a Murder; The Body Disappears; A Haunting We Will Go. 1943 Cabin in the Sky; Thank Your Lucky Stars; The Kansan; Cinderella Swings It. 1944 Adventures of Mark Twain; Home in Indiana; The Girl Who Dared. 1945 Hold that Blonde; Pillow to Post. 1946 The Bride Wore Boots; Red Dragon; The Face of Marble; Dangerous Money. 1947 The Red Stallion; Suddenly It's Spring. 1948 The Smart Woman; Half Past Midnight; The Shanghai Chest. 1949 Jiggs and Maggie in Jackpot Jitters; The Hidden Hand. 1951 South of Caliente.

BETTS, WILLIAM E.
Born: 1856. Died: Apr. 6, 1929, New York, N.Y. (pneumonia and heart disease). Screen and stage actor.

Appeared in: 1924 A Sainted Devil.

BETZ, MATTHEW
Born: 1881, St. Louis, Mo. Died: Jan. 26, 1938, Los Angeles, Calif. Screen, stage, and vaudeville actor.

Appeared in: 1921 Salvation Nell; Burn 'Em Up Barnes; The Single Track. 1922 My Old Kentucky Home; Boomerang Bill. 1923 The Self-Made Wife; Let's Go; Sawdust; Luck. 1924 Those Who Dance; The Heart Bandit; Love's Whirlpool; The Lighthouse by the Sea; The Only Woman; The Siren of Seville. 1925 The Way of a Girl; My Lady's Lips; The White Desert; The Unholy Three; Lights of Old Broadway; White Fang. 1926 The Flame of the Yukon; The Exquisite Sinner; Oh, What a

Nurse!; The Little Irish Girl; Shipwrecked. 1927 The Patent Leather Kid; Broadway after Midnight. 1928 The Wedding March; Sins of the Fathers; The Big City; Shepherd of the Hills; The Terror; The Crimson City; Telling the World. 1929 Girls Gone Wild; Fugitives; The Girl in the Glass Case. 1930 The Big House; Shooting Straight; The Squealer; See America Thirst; Her Man. 1931 Salvation Nell (and 1921 version); Side Show. 1932 The Fighting Marshal; Alias Mary Smith; Dynamite Denny; From Broadway to Cheyenne; Speed Madness; Gold. 1933 Western Code; Via Pony Express; The Big Chance; Silent Men; Under Secret Orders; State Trooper; The Whirlwind; Tarzan the Fearless; I Have Lived. 1934 Fighting Rookie; The Woman Who Dared; Countess of Monte Cristo; The House of Rothschild. 1935 Men of the Night; Mississippi; On Probation; Let 'Em Have It; The Tin Man (short); Reckless Roads; Mutiny Ahead; The Girl Who Came Back. 1936 Just My Luck; The Last Assignment; Racing Blood; Florida Special. 1937 Outcast. 1938 Fury Below.

BEVAN, BILLY (William Bevan Harris)
Born: Sept. 29, 1897, Orange, Australia. Died: 1957. Screen, stage, and opera actor. Appeared in Sennett films/shorts from approx. 1919 to 1929.

Appeared in the following (shorts, unless otherwise noted): 1920 Let 'er Go; The Quack Doctor; It's a Boy; My Goodness; Love, Honor and Behave (feature); A Fireside Brewer. 1921 A Small Town Idol (feature); Be Reasonable; By Heck; Astray from the Steerage. 1922 The Duck Hunter; On Patrol; Oh, Daddy; Gymnasium Jim; Ma and Pa; When Summer Comes; The Crossroads of New York. 1923 Nip and Tuck; Sinbad the Sailor; The Extra Girl. 1924 One Spooky Night; Wall Street Blues; Lizzies of the Field; Wandering Waistlines; The Cannon Ball Express; The White Sin. 1925 Honeymoon Hardships; Giddap; The Lion's Whiskers; Butter Fingers; Skinners in Silk; Super-Hooper-Dyne Lizzies; Sneezing Beezers; The Iron Nag; Over There-Abouts; From Rags to Britches. 1926 Whispering Whiskers; Trimmed in Gold; Circus Today; Wandering Willies; Hayfoot, Strawfoot; Fight Night; Muscle Bound Music; Ice Cold Cocos; A Sea Dog's Tale; Hubby's Quiet Little Game; Masked Mamas; Hoboken to Hollywood; The Divorce Dodger; Flirty Four-Flushers. 1927 Should Sleepwalkers Marry?; Peaches and Plumbers; A Small Town Princess; The Bull Fighter; Cured in the Excitement; The Golf Nut; Gold Digger of Weepah; Easy Pickings. 1928 The Beach Club; The Best Man; The Bicycle Flirt; His Unlucky Night; Caught in the Kitchen ("Tired Businessman's" series); Motorboat Mamas; Motoring Mamas; Hubby's Latest Alibi; Hubby's Weekend Trip; The Lion's Roar; His New Steno; Riley the Cop. 1929 Calling Hubby's Bluff; Button My Back; Foolish Husbands; Pink Pajamas; Don't Get Jealous. The following are features unless so noted: 1929 High Voltage; Sky Hawk. 1930 Journey's End; For the Love O' Lil; Temptation; Peacock Alley. 1931 Transatlantic. 1932 Sky Devils; Spot on the Rug; Honeymoon Beach; The Silent Witness; Vanity Fair; Payment Deferred. Honey-moon Beach (short). 1933 Alice in Wonderland; Looking Forward; Midnight Club; Too Much Harmony; A Study in Scarlet, Cavalcade; Luxury Liner; Peg O' My Heart; The Way to Love. 1934 The Lost Patrol; Shock; Caravan; Limehouse Blues. 1935 Mystery Woman; Black Sheep; The Last Outpost; A Tale of Two Cities. 1936 The Song and Dance Man; Lloyds of London; Private Number; Dracula's Daughter; Piccadilly Jim; God's Country and the Woman. 1937 Slave Ship; Another Dawn; The Sheik Steps Out; The Wrong Road. 1938 Girls of the Golden West; Shadows over Shanghai. 1939 Captain Fury; Let Freedom Ring; Grand Jury Secrets; We Are Not Alone. 1940 Earl of Chicago; The Long Voyage Home; Tin Pan Alley. 1941 Shining Victory; Dr. Jekyll and Mr. Hyde; Confirm or Deny. 1942 The Man Who Wouldn't Die; London Blackout Murders; Counter Espionage. 1943 Forever and a Day; Young and Willing. 1944 The Lodger; National Velvet; The Invisible Man's Revenge; South of Dixie. 1945 The Picture of Dorian Gray; Tonight and Every Night. 1946 Cluny Brown; Devotion; Terror by Night. 1947 Moss Rose; It Had to be You; Swordsman. 1948 The Black Arrow; Let's Live a Little. 1949 The Secret of St. Ives; The Secret Garden. 1950 Rogues of Sherwood Forest; Fortunes of Captain Blood. 1960 When Comedy Was King (documentary). 1963 Thirty Years of Fun (documentary).

BEVANS, CLEM
Born: 1880, Cozaddle, Ohio. Died: Aug. 11, 1963, Woodland Hills, Calif. Screen, stage, television, and vaudeville actor.

Appeared in: 1935 Way Down East (film debut). 1936 Rhythm on the Range. 1937 Riding on Air; Big City; Idol of the Crowds. 1938 Of Human Hearts; Young Fugitives; Comet over Broadway; Tom Sawyer, Detective; Hold That Coed. 1939 Ambush; Zenobia; Hell's Kitchen; Night Work; Thunder Afloat; Main

Street Lawyer; The Cowboy Quarterback. 1940 Abe Lincoln in Illinois; Go West; Young Tom Edison; 20 Mule Team; Half a Sinner; The Captain Is a Lady; Untamed; Girl from God's Country; Calling All Husbands; Granney Get Your Gun. 1941 Sergeant York; She Couldn't Say No; Midnight Angel; The Parson of Panamint; The Smiling Ghost. 1942 Tombstone, The Town Too Tough to Die; The Forest Rangers; Captains of the Clouds; Mrs. Wiggs of the Cabbage Patch; Saboteur. 1943 The Human Comedy; The Kansan; Lady Bodyguard; Happy Go Lucky; The Woman of the Town. 1944 Night Club Girl. 1945 Grissly's Millions; Captain Eddie. 1946 Wake Up and Dream; Gallant Bess; The Yearling. 1947 The Yankee Fakir; The Millerson Case; Mourning Becomes Electra. 1948 Texas, Brooklyn and Heaven; Highway 13; Portrait of Jenny; Paleface; The Relentless. 1949 Loaded Pistols; Big Jack; Streets of Laredo; Rim of the Canyon; The Gal Who Took the West; Deputy Marshal; Moonrise; Tell It to the Judge. 1950 Joe Palooka Meets Humphrey; Harvey. 1951 Gold Raiders; Silver City Bonanza; Man in the Saddle. 1952 Captive of Billy the Kid; Hangman's Knot. 1953 The Stranger Wore a Gun. 1954 Boy from Oklahoma. 1955 Ten Wanted Men; The Kentuckian. 1956 Davy Crockett and the River Pirates.

BEVANS, LIONEL
Born: 1884. Died: Feb. 17, 1965, Los Angeles, Calif. Screen, stage actor, and stage director.

BEVANS, PHILIPPA
Born: 1913, London, England. Died: May 10, 1968, New York, N.Y. Screen, stage, and television actress.

Appeared in: 1962 The Notorious Landlady. 1964 The World of Henry Orient. 1966 The Group.

BIANCHI, GEORGIO
Born: 1904. Died: Feb. 9, 1968, Rome, Italy. Screen actor, film director, and film producer.

Appeared in: 1932 Il Miracolo di Sant' Antonio.

BIAS, CHESTER
Born: 1917. Died: Mar. 1, 1954, Woodland Hills, Calif. Screen actor.

BIBY, EDWARD
Born: 1885. Died: Oct. 3, 1952, Los Angeles, Calif. Screen actor.

Appeared in: 1947 The Strange Woman.

BICKEL, GEORGE L.
Born: 1863, Saginaw, Mich. Died: June 5, 1941, Los Angeles, Calif. Screen, stage, circus, and vaudeville actor. Entered films approx. 1915 with Edison Feature Film Co.

Appeared in: 1929 Beneath the Law (short); In Holland (short). 1930 Soup to Nuts; Maybe It's Love; Recaptured Love. 1931 One Heavenly Night. 1932 The Man I Killed.

BICKFORD, CHARLES
Born: Jan. 1, 1889, Cambridge, Mass. Died: Nov. 9, 1967, Los Angeles, Calif.(emphysema). Screen, stage, television, and burlesque actor. Nominated for Academy Award for Best Supporting Actor in 1943 for Song of Bernadette; in 1947 for The Farmer's Daughter; and 1948 for Johnny Belinda.

Appeared in: 1929 Dynamite (film debut); South Sea Rose; Hell's Heroes. 1930 Anna Christie; The Sea Bat; The Passion Flower. 1931 The Squaw Man; East of Borneo; The Pagan Lady; River End; Men in Her Life. 1932 Ambition; Scandal for Sale; Vanity Street; The Last Man; Thunder below; Devil and the Deep; Panama Flo. 1933 No Other Woman; Song of the Eagle; This Day and Age; White Woman. 1934 Little Miss Marker; A Wicked Woman. 1935 Under Pressure; A Notorious Gentleman; The Farmer Takes a Wife; East of Java; Red Wagon; The Littlest Rebel. 1936 Rose of the Rancho; The Plainsman; Pride of the Marines. 1937 High, Wide and Handsome; Thunder Trail; Night Club Scandal; Daughter of Shanghai. 1938 Gangs of New York; Valley of the Giants; The Storm. 1939 Stand Up and Fight; Street of Missing Men; Mutiny in the Big House; Romance of the Redwoods; Our Leading Citizens; One Hour to Live; Of Mice and Men. 1940 Thou Shalt Not Kill; Girl from God's Country; South to Karango; Queen of the Yukon. 1941 Burma Convoy; Riders of Death Valley (serial). 1942 Reap the Wild Wind; Tarzan's New Adventure. 1943 The Song of Bernadette; Mr. Lucky. 1944 Wing and a Prayer. 1945 Fallen Angel; Captain Eddie. 1946 Duel in the Sun. 1947 The Farmer's Daughter; The Woman on the Beach; Brute Force. 1948 The Babe Ruth Story; Johnny Belinda; Four Faces West; Command Decision. 1949 Guilty of

Treason; Roseanna McCoy; Whirlpool. 1950 Branded; Riding High. 1951 Elopement; Jim Thorpe All-American. 1952 The Raging Tide; Man of Bronze. 1953 The Last Posse. 1954 A Star is Born. 1955 Prince of Players; Not as a Stranger; The Court-Martial of Billy Mitchell. 1956 You Can't Run Away from It. 1957 Mister Cory. 1958 The Big Country. 1960 The Unforgiven. 1962 Days of Wine and Roses. 1966 A Big Hand for the Little Lady.

BIEGEL, ERWIN
Born: 1896. Died: May 24, 1954, Berlin, Germany (heart ailment). German screen and stage actor.

Appeared in: 1938 Wenn Du eine Schwiegermutter hast (When You Have a Mother-in-Law). 1949 Palace Scandal. 1952 The Berliner. 1959 Das Tanzende Herz (The Dancing Heart).

BILDT, PAUL
Born: 1885, Germany. Died: Mar. 16, 1957, Berlin, Germany. German screen and stage actor.

Appeared in: 1927 Slums of Berlin. 1933 The Rebel. 1935 Schwarzer Jaeger Johanna; Die Toerichte Jungfrau. 1939 Der Schritt vom Were (The False Step). 1940 The Dreyfus Case. 1948 Razzia. 1949 Somewhere in Berlin; The Affair Blum. 1950 Our Daily Bread. 1956 As Long as You're Near Me; Anastasia; The Last Czar's Daughter. 1958 International Counterfeiters. 1959 Himmel Ohne Sterne (Sky without Stars).

BILLINGS, ELMO
Born: 1913. Died: Feb. 6, 1964, Los Angeles, Calif.(stroke). Screen actor. Freckle-faced urchin of early "Our Gang" comedies.

Appeared in: 1925 Locked Doors; The Midnight Flyer. 1927 Tumbling River.

BILLINGS, GEORGE A.
Born: 1871. Died: Apr. 15, 1934, West Los Angeles, Calif. Screen and stage actor.

Appeared in: 1924 Barbara Frietchie; Abraham Lincoln. 1925 The Man without a Country. 1926 Hands Up!; The Greater Glory. 1929 Woman to Woman. 1930 Night Work; The Third Alarm; Traffic (short); "Folly Comedies" second series. 1933 King for a Night. 1934 As the Earth Turns; The Pursuit of Happiness. 1935 The Gilded Lily.

BING, GUS (aka GEORGE BINGHAM)
Born: 1893. Died: Aug. 4, 1967, Los Angeles, Calif.(leukemia). Screen, stage, vaudeville, and burlesque actor. Brother of screen actor Herman Bing (dec. 1947).

BING, HERMAN
Born: Mar. 30, 1889, Germany. Died: Jan. 9, 1947, Los Angeles, Calif.(suicide—gun). Screen, opera actor, and film producer. Brother of screen actor Gus Bing (dec. 1967).

Appeared in: 1929 A Song of Kentucky; Married in Hollywood. 1930 Show Girl in Hollywood; The Three Sisters; Menschen Hinter Gettern. 1931 The Great Lover; The Guardsman; Women Love Once. 1932 Silver Dollar; Hypnotized; Jewel Robbery; Flesh. 1933 The Nuisance; Dinner at Eight; The Bowery; My Lips Betray; Fits in a Fiddle (short); Footlight Parade; The Great Jasper; The College Coach. 1934 The Hide-Out; Embarrassing Moments; Love Time; The Crimson Romance; When Strangers Meet; The Mighty Barnum; Mandalay; Melody in Spring; The Merry Widow; Manhattan Love Song; I'll Tell the World; The Black Cat; Twentieth Century. 1935 Night Is Young; It Happened in New York; Thunder in the Night; Hands across the Table; Great Hotel Murder; Redheads on Parade; Call of the Wild; The Florentine Dagger; Don't Bet on Blondes; Calm Yourself; In Caliente; Every Night at Eight; His Family Tree; Three Kids and a Queen; Fighting Youth; A Thousand Dollars a Minute; The Misses Stooge (short). 1936 Laughing Irish Eyes; The Music Goes 'Round; Tango; Come Closer Folks; Rose Marie; The Great Ziegfeld; Three Wise Guys; Human Cargo; Dimples; The King Steps Out; Adventure in Manhattan; Champagne Waltz. 1937 Maytime; Beg, Borrow or Steal; Every Day's a Holiday. 1938 Paradise for Three; Vacation from Love; The Great Waltz; Sweethearts; Bluebeard's Eighth Wife; Four's a Crowd. 1940 Bitter Sweet. 1942 The Devil with Hitler. 1945 Where Do We Go from Here?. 1946 Rendezvous 24; Night and Day.

BINGHAM, GEORGE. See Gus Bing

BISHOP, CHESTER
Born: 1858. Died: May 23, 1937, Los Angeles, Calif. Screen and stage actor.

Appeared in: 1923 Lights Out. 1924 Missing Daughters.

BISHOP, RICHARD
Born: 1898. Died: May 28, 1956, Sharon, Conn. Screen, stage, radio, and television actor.

Appeared in: 1942 Native Land. 1948 Call Northside 777. 1951 Teresa. 1955 The Long Gray Line.

BISHOP, STARK, JR.
Born: 1932. Died: Jul. 9, 1945, Hollywood, Calif. Screen actor 13 yrs. old.

BISHOP, WILLIAM
Born: Jul. 16, 1917, Oak Park, Ill. Died: Oct. 3, 1959, Malibu, Calif.(cancer). Screen, stage, television, and radio actor.

Appeared in: 1943 A Guy Named Joe. 1946 Pillow to Post. 1947 Romance of Rosy Ridge; Song of the Thin Man; Devil Ship. 1948 Thunderhoof; Untamed Breed; Coroner Creek; Adventures in Silverado; Port Said; Black Eagle. 1949 Walking Hills; Anna Lucasta. 1950 The Tougher They Come; Harriet Craig; Killer That Stalked New York. 1951 Lorna Doone; The Texas Ranger; The Frogmen; Basketball Fix. 1952 Cripple Creek; Breakdown; The Raiders; The Redhead from Wyoming. 1953 Gun Belt. 1954 Overland Pacific. 1955 Top Gun; Wyoming Renegades. 1956 The White Squaw; The Boss. 1957 The Phantom Stagecoach; Short Cut to Hell. 1959 The Oregon Trail.

BJORNE, HUGO
Born: 1886, Sweden. Died: Feb. 14, 1966, Stockholm, Sweden. Screen, stage, radio, and television actor.

Appeared in: 1912 Lojen och Tarar (film debut). 1938 Karl Fredrik Reigns; Sun over Sweden; Frun Tillhanda (Servant Girl). 1944 Himlaspelet. 1947 Torment. 1948 Crime and Punishment.

BLACK, MAURICE
Born: Warsaw, Poland. Died: Jan. 18, 1938, Hollywood, Calif. Screen and stage actor. Entered films approx. 1923.

Appeared in: 1928 Marked Money. 1929 Broadway Babies; Dark Streets; The Carnation Kid. 1930 Numbered Men; Little Caesar; Playing Around; The Street of Chance; Live and Learn; Brothers; The Sea God; Framed; The Runaway Bride. 1931 Front Page; Oh! Oh! Cleopatra (short); Women Go on Forever; Smart Money; Sob Sister; While Paris Sleeps. 1932 High Pressure; Dancers in the Dark; The Strange Love of Molly Louvain; Scarlet Dawn. 1933 The Cohens and the Kellys in Trouble; Grand Slam; A Shriek in the Night; I Cover the Waterfront; Flying down to Rio; Ship of Wanted Men; Murder on the Campus. 1934 Sixteen Fathoms Deep; Twin Husbands; Wake Up and Dream; West of the Pecos; Down to Their Last Yacht. 1935 The Crusades; Bonnie Scotland; Stars over Broadway. 1936 Laughing Irish Eyes. 1937 Three Legionnaires; The Californian; Adventure's End.

BLACKFORD, MARY
Born: 1914, Philadelphia, Pa. Died: Sept. 24, 1937, Santa Monica, Calif.(results of auto accident). Screen actress.

Appeared in: 1933 The Sweetheart of Sigma Chi.

BLACKMORE, E. WILLARD
Born: 1870. Died: Nov. 20, 1949, East St. Louis, Mo. Screen and stage actor. Aided Thomas A. Edison in making the first talking film.

BLACKWELL, CARLYLE
Born: 1888, Troy, Pa. Died: June 17, 1955, Miami, Fla. Screen, stage, film and stage producer. Entered films in 1909 with Vitagraph. Father of screen actor Carlyle Blackwell, Jr.

Appeared in: 1909 Uncle Tom's Cabin. 1910 A Dixie Mother. 1912 A Bell of Penance. 1913 Perils of the Sea. 1914 Such a Little Queen; The Spitfire; The Key to Yesterday. 1916 A Woman's Way. 1917 The Burglar. 1918 His Royal Highness; The Road to France. 1920 The Restless Sex. 1922 Sherlock Holmes; The Virgin Queen. 1923 Bulldog Drummond. 1924 The Beloved Vagabond. 1926 She. 1929 The Wrecker. 1930 The Crooked Bullet.

BLACKWOOD, BONNIE
Born: 1909. Died: Feb. 18, 1949, Burbank, Calif. Screen and stage actress.

BLACKWOOD, DIANA
Died: March 1961, London, England. Screen, stage, and television actress.

BLAGOI, GEORGE
Born: 1898, Russia. Died: June 23, 1971, Hollywood, Calif. Screen actor. Married to actress Tina Blagoi.

Appeared in: 1926 Into Her Kingdom. 1928 Four Sons.

BLAISELL, CHARLES "BIG BILL"
Born: 1874. Died: May 10, 1930, Hollywood, Calif. Screen and vaudeville actor. Appeared in early Christie Comedies.

BLAKE, MADGE
Born: 1900. Died: Feb. 19, 1969, Pasadena, Calif.(heart attack). Screen and television actress.

Appeared in: 1950 Between Midnight and Dawn; A Life of Her Own. 1951 The Prowler; Queen for a Day; An American in Paris. 1952 Singin' in the Rain; Something for the Birds. 1954 Rhapsody; The Long, Long Trailer; Fireman, Save My Child!. 1956 Please Murder Me; Glory. 1962 Sergeants Three. 1966 Batman. 1967 Follow Me, Boys!.

BLAKE, PAUL
Died: Jan. 28, 1960, London, England. Screen and stage actor.

Appeared in: 1937 Cafe Colette. 1940 The Lilac Domino.

BLAKECLOCK, ALBAN
Died: Dec. 6, 1966, London, England. Screen, stage, radio, and television actor.

Appeared in: 1952 Murder in the Cathedral.

BLAKENEY, OLIVE
Born: Aug. 21, 1903, Newport, Ky. Died: Prior to 1972. Screen and stage actress. Married to actor Bernard Nedell (dec. 1972). Entered films in England in 1934.

Appeared in: 1934 Mr. What's His Name (film debut); Give Her a Ring; Butter and Egg Man. 1935 Come Out of the Pantry; Excuse My Glove. 1936 Don't Get Me Wrong; Two's Company; The Three Maxinis. 1937 Gangway. 1941 That Uncertain Feeling. 1942 Henry and Dizzy; Henry Aldrich, Editor; Random Harvest. 1943 Henry Aldrich Gets Glamour; Henry Aldrich Swings It. 1944 Henry Aldrich Plays Cupid; Henry Aldrich's Little Secret; Henry Aldrich, Boy Scout; The Ghost Catchers; Experiment Perilous. 1945 Dakota; Leave Her to Heaven. 1946 Sentimental Journey; The Strange Woman. 1947 Time out of Mind 1948 Sealed Verdict. 1954 Roogie's Bump. 1957 The Green-Eyed Blonde; Three Brave Men.

BLANCHAR, PIERRE
Born: 1893, Philippeville, Algeria. Died: Nov. 21, 1963, Paris, France. Screen and stage actor.

Appeared in: 1923 Jocelyn. 1929 La Marche Nuptiale. 1930 The Chess Player. 1931 L'Atlantide. 1932 La Courtourierre de Luneville. 1934 Le Diable en Bouteille. 1934 Crime et Chatiment (Crime and Punishment). 1937 The Late Mattia Pascal; L'Affaire du Courrier de Lyon (U.S. 1938); Mademoisell Docteur. 1935 Celle Vielle Canaille. 1938 Un Carnet de Bal; The Volga Boatman. 1940 Two Women. 1942 Poncarral. 1944 La Dame de Pique. 1946 La Symphonie Pastorals (U.S. 1948). 1948 They Are Not Angels; Street of Shadows. 1958 Riff Raff Girls (U.S. 1962) (aka Rififi for Girls and Rififi among the Women). 1963 Magnificent Sinner.

BLANCHARD, MARI
Born: 1927. Died: May 10, 1970, Woodland Hills, Calif.(cancer). Screen and television actress.

Appeared in: 1951 On the Riviera; Ten Tall Men; No Questions Asked; The Unknown Man; The Overland Telegraph. 1952 The Brigand; Assignment—Paris; Back at the Front. 1953 Abbott and Costello Go to Mars; The Veils of Bagdad. 1954 Destry; Rails into Laramie; Black Horse Canyon. 1955 The Return of Jack Slade; Son of Sinbad; The Crooked Web. 1956 Stagecoach to Fury; The Cruel Tower. 1957 Jungle Heat; She Devil. 1958 Machete; No Place to Land. 1962 Don't Knock the Twist. 1963 Twice Told Tales; McLintock.

BLAND, JOYCE
Born: 1906, England. Died: Aug. 24, 1963, Bournemouth, England. Screen and stage actress.

Appeared in: 1932 Magic Night. 1936 Spy of Napoleon (U.S. 1939). 1937 Dreaming Lips. 1938 Sixty Glorious Years; The Citadel.

BLANDICK, CLARA
Born: 1881, aboard American ship in harbor of Hong Kong, China. Died: Apr. 15, 1962, Hollywood, Calif.(suicide). Screen and stage actress. Entered films in 1929.

Appeared in: 1929 Men Are Like That; Poor Aubrey. 1930 Wise Girls; Burning Up; The Girl Said No; Sins of the Children; Romance; Last of the Duanes; Tom Sawyer. 1931 Once a Sinner; The Easiest Way; Dance Fools, Dance; Inspiration; Drums of Jeopardy; Daybreak; It's a Wise Child; Laughing Sinners; I Take This Woman; Bought; Murder at Midnight; Huckleberry Finn; New Adventures of Get-Rich-Quick Wallingford; Possessed. 1932 Shopworn; The Strange Case of Clara Deane; The Pet Parade; Life Begins; Two against the World; The Expert; Three on a Match; Rockabye. 1933 Bitter Tea of General Yen; Child of Manhattan; The Mind Reader; Three-Cornered Moon; One Sunday Afternoon; Turn Back the Clock; Charlie Chan's Greatest Case; Ever in My Heart. 1934 The President Vanishes; Broadway Bill; Jealousy; Beloved; As the Earth Turns; Harold Teen; The Show-Off; The Girl from Missouri; Sisters under the Skin; Fugitive Lady. 1935 The Winning Ticket; Straight from the Heart; Princess O'Hara; Party Wire. 1936 Transient Lady; The Trail of the Lonesome Pine; Anthony Adverse; The Case of the Velvet Claws; Hearts Divided; The Gorgeous Hussy; In His Steps; Make Way For a Lady. 1937 A Star Is Born; Wings Over Honolulu; The Road Back; The League of Frightened Men; Small Town Boy; You Can't Have Everything; Her Husband's Secretary. 1938 My Old Kentucky Home; Tom Sawyer, Detective; Professor Beware; Swing, Sister, Swing; Crime Ring. 1939 Drums along the Mohawk; Swanee River; I Was a Convict; Adventures of Huckleberry Finn; The Wizard of Oz; The Star Maker. 1940 Alice in Movieland; Tomboy; Anne of Windy Poplars; Dreaming Out Loud; Youth Will Be Served; Northwest Mounted Police. 1941 The Big Store; Enemy Within; Private Nurse; One Foot in Heaven; It Started with Eve; The Nurse's Secret; The Wagons Roll at Night. 1942 Lady in a Jam; Gentleman Jim; Rings on Her Fingers. 1943 Heaven Can Wait; DuBarry Was a Lady; Dixie. 1944 Shadow of Suspicion; Can't Help Singing. 1945 Frontier Gal. 1946 She Wolf of London; Pillow of Death; People Are Funny; Claudia and David; So Goes My Love; A Stolen Life. 1947 Philo Vance Returns; Life with Father. 1948 Bride Goes Wild. 1949 Mr. Soft Touch; Roots in the Soil. 1950 Love that Brute; Key to the City.

BLANKMAN, GEORGE
Born: 1877. Died: Mar. 13, 1925, Los Angeles, Calif. Screen actor.

Appeared in: 1925 Don Q.

BLATCHFORD, WILLIAM
Born: 1886, Pittsburgh, Pa. Died: Dec. 30, 1936, Los Angeles, Calif. Screen and stage actor.

Appeared in: 1934 The Old Fashioned Way.

BLEDSOE, JULES
Born: 1899. Died: Jul. 14, 1943, Hollywood, Calif. Negro screen, stage actor, and singer.

Appeared in: 1929 Show Boat. 1942 Drums of the Congo.

BLEIBTREAU, HEDWIG
Born: 1868, Austria. Died: Jan. 24, 1958, Vienna, Austria. Screen and stage actor.

Appeared in: 1933 Ein Maedel der Strasse. 1937 Das Maedchen Irene. 1939 Hotel Sacher. 1940 Waldrausch (Forest Fever); Maria Ilona; Wiener Geschichten (Vienna Tales). 1950 The Third Man.

BLICK, NEWTON
Born: 1899, Bristol, England. Died: Oct. 1965, Dublin, Ireland. Screen, stage, and television actor.

Appeared in: 1955 Court Martial (aka Carrington V.C.). 1957 The Third Key; Town on Trial; Gypsy and the Gentleman; The Gentle Touch; Barnacle Bill. 1962 Term of Trial; Flame in the Streets; Bachelor of Hearts. 1964 Ring of Treason (aka Ring of Spies). 1965 Lord Jim.

BLINN, BENJAMIN F.
Born: 1872. Died: Apr. 28, 1941, Hollywood, Calif. Screen and stage actor.

Appeared in: 1923 Danger. 1925 Quicker'n Lightnin'.

BLINN, GENEVIEVE (Genevieve Namary)
Born: St. John, New Brunswick, Canada. Died: July 20, 1956, Ross, Calif. Screen and stage actress. Worked in almost all of Theda Bara's films.

Appeared in: 1921 Queen of Sheba; Crazy to Marry; Don't Tell Everything; The Witching Hour. 1922 If I Were Queen; The Call of Home. 1924 Abraham Lincoln. 1930 Common Clay.

BLINN, HOLBROOK
Born: 1872, San Francisco, Calif. Died: June 24, 1928, Crotan, N.Y.(fall from horse). Screen, stage actor, and film producer.

Appeared in: 1915 The Boss; McTeague; The Butterfly on the Wheel. 1916 The Weakness of Man; Husband and Wife. 1921 Power. 1923 The Bad Man; Rosita. 1924 Janice Meredith; Yolanda. 1925 Zander the Great; The New Commandment. 1926 The Unfair Sex. 1927 The Masked Woman; The Telephone Girl.

BLOOMFIELD, DEREK
Born: 1920. Died: July 23, 1964, Brittany, France. Screen, stage, television actor, and playwright. Entered films in 1932.

BLORE, ERIC
Born: Dec. 23, 1887, London, England. Died: Mar. 2, 1959, Hollywood, Calif.(heart attack). Screen, stage actor, and songwriter.

Appeared in: 1926 The Great Gatsby. 1930 Laughter. 1931 My Sin; Tarnished Lady. 1933 Flying Down to Rio. 1934 Gay Divorcee (stage and film versions); Limehouse Blues. 1935 Follies Bergere; The Good Fairy; Diamond Jim; The Casino Murder Case; I Live My Life; Top Hat; I Dream Too Much; Old Man Rhythm; To Beat the Band; Seven Keys to Baldpate; Glitter; Behold My Wife. 1936 Two in the Dark; The Ex-Mrs. Bradford; Swing Time; Smartest Girl in Town; Sons O' Guns; Picadilly Jim. 1937 The Soldier and the Lady; Quality Street; Shall We Dance?; Breakfast for Two; Hitting a New High; It's Love I'm After; Michael Strogoff. 1938 The Joy of Living; Swiss Miss; A Desperate Adventure. 1939 $1,000 a Touchdown; Island of Lost Men; A Gentleman's Gentleman. 1940 The Man Who Wouldn't Talk; The Lone Wolf Meets a Lady; The Boys from Syracuse; Earl of Puddlestone; South of Suez. 1941 Road to Zanzibar; The Lone Wolf Keeps a Date; The Lady Eve; The Lone Wolf Takes a Chance; Red Head; New York Town; Lady Scarface; Three Girls about Town; Confirm or Deny; The Shanghai Gesture; Sullivan's Travels; Secrets of the Lone Wolf. 1942 The Moon and Sixpence; Counter Espionage. 1943 Forever and a Day; Submarine Base; Holy Matrimony; One Dangerous Night; Passport to Suez; The Sky's the Limit; Happy Go Lucky. 1944 San Diego; I Love You. 1945 Penthouse Rhythm; Easy to Look At; Men in Her Diary. 1946 Kitty; The Notorious Lone Wolf; Abie's Irish Rose; Two Sisters from Boston. 1947 Winter Wonderland; The Lone Wolf in London; The Lone Wolf in Mexico; Love Happy. 1948 Romance on the High Seas. 1949 Adventures of Ichabod and Mr. Toad (voice). 1950 Fancy Pants. 1952 Babes From Bagdad. 1955 Bowery to Bagdad.

BLUE, MONTE
Born: Jan. 11, 1890, Indianapolis, Ind. Died: Feb. 18, 1963, Milwaukee, Wis.(coronary attack). Screen actor, screenwriter, and circus performer. Entered films as a screenwriter and stuntman with Griffith.

Appeared in: 1915 Birth of a Nation; Intolerance. 1918 Till I Come Back to You. 1919 In Mizzoura; Every Woman; Pettigrew's Girl. 1920 Jucklins; Something to Think About. 1921 Moonlight and Honeysuckle; The Affairs of Anatole; A Broken Doll; A Perfect Crime; The Kentuckians. 1922 Orphans of the Storm; Peacock Alley; My Old Kentucky Home. 1923 Loving Lies; Defying Destiny; Main Street; Lucretia Lombard; Brass; The Tents of Allah; The Purple Highway; Loving Lies. 1924 Being Respectable; Revelation; The Lover of Camille; The Marriage Circle; Daddies; The Dark Swan; Daughters of Pleasure; Her Marriage Vow; How to Educate a Wife; Mademoiselle Midnight. 1925 Kiss Me Again; Red Hot Tires; Hogan's Alley; The Limited Mail; Recompense. 1926 Across the Pacific; So This Is Paris; The Man Upstairs; Other Women's Husbands. 1927 Bitter Apples; The Black Diamond Express; Brass Knuckles; The Brute; The Bush Leaguer; Wolf's Clothing; One-Round Hogan. 1928 Across the Atlantic; White Shadows of the South Seas. 1929 Tiger Rose; Conquest; From Headquarters; The Greyhound Limited; No Defense; Skin Deep; The Show of Shows. 1930 Isle of Escape; Those Who Dance. 1931 The Flood. 1932 The Stoker; The Valley of Adventure. 1933 The Nectors; Her Forgotten Past; The Intruder; Officer 13. 1934 The Last Round-Up; Come On Marines!; The Thundering Herd; Student Tour; Wagon Wheels; College Rhythm. 1935 Hot off the Press; Trails of the Wild; Nevada; G-Men; Lives of a Bengal Lancer;

Wanderer of the Wasteland; On Probation. 1936 Undersea Kingdom; Treachery Rides the Range; Mary of Scotland; Song of the Gringo; Desert Gold. 1937 The Outcasts of Poker Flat; Rootin' Tootin' Rhythm; Thunder Trail; Souls at Sea; High, Wide and Handsome. 1938 Hawk of the Wilderness; Spawn of the North; Big Broadcast of 1938; The Mysterious Rider; Illegal Traffic; Wild Bill Hickok; Born to the West; Rebellious Daughters; Cocoanut Grove. 1939 Dodge City; Geronimo; Frontier Pony Express; Days of Jesse James; Juarez; Port of Hats; Our Leading Citizen. 1940 A Little Bit of Heaven; Mystery Sea Rider; Young Bill Hickok; Texas Rangers Ride Again. 1941 The Great Train Robbery; Arkansas Judge; Law of the Timber; Scattergood Pulls the Strings; New York Town; Sunset in Wyoming; Bad Man of Deadwood. 1942 The Palm Beach Story; The Road to Morocco; North to the Klondike; Secret Enemies; Across the Pacific; Panama Hattie. 1943 Truck Busters; Edge of Darkness; Northern Pursuit; Mission to Moscow; Thank Your Lucky Stars; Secret Enemies; Thousands Cheer. 1944 The Mask of Dimitrios; The Conspirators; Passage to Marseille; The Adventure of Mark Twain. 1945 San Antonio. 1946 Cinderella Jones; Shadow of a Woman; Two Sisters from Boston; Easy to Wed. 1947 Bells of San Fernando; Life with Father; Speed to Spare; That Way with Women; Cheyenne; Possessed; My Wild Irish Rose. 1948 Silver River; Two Guys from Texas; Key Largo; Johnny Belinda. 1949 The Younger Brothers; Ranger of Cherokee Strip; Flaxy Martin; Homicide; South of St. Louis. 1950 Dallas; This Side of the Law; The Tomahawk Trail; The Blonde Bandit; Backfire; Montana; The Iroquois Trail. 1951 Warpath; Snake River Desperadoes; Three Desperate Men; Gold Raiders; The Sea Harvest. 1952 Rose of Cimarron; Hangman's Knot. 1953 The Last Posse. 1954 Apache.

BLUM, MAX
Born: 1874. Died: Jan. 10, 1944, Hollywood, Calif. Screen actor.

BLUM, SAMMY
Born: 1889, New York, N.Y. Died: June 1, 1945, Hollywood, Calif.(heart attack). Screen and stage actor. Entered films in 1905.

Appeared in: 1925 Galloping Jinx. 1926 The Winning of Barbara Worth; Black Paradise; Siberia. 1927 Smile, Brother, Smile; The Wheel of Destiny. 1929 Rio Rita; The Delightful Rogue; The Prince of Hearts. 1930 More Sinned against Than Usual (short); The Grand Parade; Party Girl. 1931 Iron Man. 1932 Night World.

BOARDMAN, VIRGINIA TRUE
Born: 1889. Died: June 10, 1971, Hollywood, Calif. Screen and stage actress. Entered films in 1911 with Selig Studios in Chicago. Appeared on stage as "Virginia Eames." Married to screen actor True Boardman (dec. 1918).

Appeared in: 1922 The Village Blacksmith; Where Is My Wandering Boy Tonight?; A Blind Bargain; Penrod; The Third Alarm. 1923 The Town Scandal; The Barefoot Boy; The Gunfighter; Pioneer Trails; Three Jumps Ahead; The Mailman; Michael O'Halloran. 1924 Girl of the Limberlost; The Tomboy. 1925 The Home Maker; The Red Rider. 1926 The Test of Donald Norton. 1927 Down the Stretch; King of the Jungle (serial); Speedy Smith. 1929 The Lady Lies. 1933 One Year Later. 1934 The Road to Ruin. 1934 "Baby Burlesque" series (shorts). 1936 The Fugitive Sheriff.

BOETIGER, JULIA
Born: 1852. Died: Oct. 28, 1938, Los Angeles, Calif. Screen actress.

BOGART, HUMPHREY (Humphrey DeForest Bogart)
Born: Dec. 25, 1899, New York, N.Y. Died: Jan. 14, 1957, Los Angeles, Calif.(cancer). Screen and stage actor. Married to actress Lauren Bacall. Divorced from actresses Helen Menken (dec. 1966), Mary Phillips and Mayo Method (dec. 1951). Nominated for Academy Award in 1942 for Best Actor in Casablanca. Won Academy Award in 1952 for Best Actor in The African Queen. Nominated for Academy Award in 1954 for Best Actor in The Caine Mutiny.

Appeared in: 1930 A Devil With Women (film debut); Broadway's Like That (short); Up the River. 1931 Body and Soul; Bad Sister; Women of all Nations; A Holy Terror. 1932 Love Affair; Big City Blues; Three on a Match. 1934 Midnight. 1935 Black Fury. 1936 The Petrified Forest (stage and film versions); Two against the World; Bullets or Ballots; China Clipper; Isle of Fury. 1937 The Great O'Malley; Black Legion; San Quentin; Marked Woman; Kid Galahad; Dead End; Stand-In. 1938 Swing Your Lady; Men Are Such Fools; Crime School; The Amazing

Dr. Clitterhouse; Racket Busters; Angels with Dirty Faces. 1939 King of the Underworld; You Can't Get Away with Murder; Dark Victory; The Oklahoma Kid; The Return of Dr. X; The Roaring Twenties; Invisible Stripes; Arizona Kid. 1940 Virginia City; It All Came True; Brother Orchid; They Drive by Night. 1941 High Sierra; The Wagons Roll at Night; The Maltese Falcon. 1942 All Through the Night; The Big Shot; Across the Pacific; Casablanca; In This Our Life (unbilled). 1943 Action in the North Atlantic; Thank Your Lucky Stars; Sahara. 1944 Passage to Marseille. 1945 Conflict; To Have and Have Not; Hollywood Victory Canteen (short). 1946 The Big Sleep; Two Guys from Milwaukee (unbilled). 1947 The Two Mrs. Carrolls; Dead Reckoning; Dark Passage; Always Together. 1948 The Treasure of Sierra Madre; Key Largo. 1949 Knock on Any Door; Tokyo Joe. 1950 Chain Lightning; In a Lonely Place. 1951 The Enforcer; Sirocco; Saving Bond (short); The African Queen. 1952 Road to Bali (film clip); Deadline-U.S.A. 1953 Battle Circus. 1954 Beat the Devil; The Caine Mutiny; Sabrina; The Barefoot Countessa; Love Lottery (unbilled). 1955 We're No Angels; The Desperate Hours; The Left Hand of God. 1956 The Harder They Fall.

BOHNEN, ROMAN
Born: Nov. 24, 1894, St. Paul, Minn. Died: Feb. 24, 1949, Hollywood, Calif.(heart attack). Screen and stage actor.

Appeared in: 1937 52nd Street; Vogues of 1938. 1939 Of Mice and Men. 1940 The Living Dead. 1941 They Dare Not Love; The Bugle Sounds; Appointment for Love; So Ends Our Night. 1942 Young America; The Hard Way; Grand Central Murder; Affairs of Jimmy Valentine. 1943 Edge of Darkness; Mission to Moscow; The Mask of Dimitrios; The Song of Bernadette. 1944 The Hitler Gang; None but the Lonely Heart; The Hairy Ape. 1945 A Bell for Adano; Counter-Attack. 1946 Deadline at Dawn; The Hoodlum Saint; Mr. Ace; The Strange Love of Martha Ivers; Miss Susie Slagle's; Two Years Before the Mast; California; The Best Years of Our Lives. 1947 Brute Force; For You I Die; Winter Wonderland; Song of Love. 1948 Arch of Triumph; Joan of Arc; Open Street; The Night Has a Thousand Eyes. 1949 Kazan; Mr. Soft Touch.

BOLAND, EDDIE
Born: 1883, San Francisco, Calif. Died: Feb. 3, 1935, Santa Monica, Calif.(heart attack). Screen actor. Entered films in 1913.

Appeared in: 1922 Oliver Twist. 1923 Within the Law; Long Live the King. 1924 Little Robinson Crusoe. 1926 Hard Boiled; Unknown Dangers; A Gentleman Roughneck. 1927 Sunrise; The Kid Brother. 1928 Manhattan Knights; Shorts prior to 1929 Nobody's Business; Nothing Matters and Who's My Wife?. 1929 Last Performance. 1930 Wings of Adventure; City Girl. 1931 The Miracle Woman. 1932 Vanity Street. 1933 I Have Lived.

BOLAND, MARY
Born: Jan. 28, 1880, Philadelphia, Pa. Died: June 23, 1965, New York, N.Y. Screen, stage, and television actress.

Appeared in: 1916 The Edge of the Abyss (film debut); The Stepping Stone. 1918 His Temporary Wife. 1931 Personal Maid; Secrets of a Secretary. 1932 If I Had a Million; The Night of June Thirteen; Trouble in Paradise; Evening for Sale; Night after Night. 1933 Mama Loves Papa; Three-Cornered Moon; The Solitaire Man. 1934 Six of a Kind; Stingaree; Down to Their Last Yacht; Four Frightened People; Melody in Spring; Here Comes the Groom; The Pursuit of Happiness. 1935 People Will Talk; Two for Tonight; The Big Broadcast of 1936; Ruggles of Red Gap. 1936 Wives Never Know; Early to Bed; College Holiday; A Son Comes Home. 1937 Marry the Girl; There Goes the Groom; Mama Runs Wild; Danger-Love at Work. 1938 Little Tough Guys in Society; Artists and Models Abroad. 1939 The Magnificent Fraud; The Women; Boy Trouble; Night Work. 1940 He Married His Wife; The Hit Parade of 1941; One Night in the Tropics; New Moon; Pride and Prejudice. 1944 Nothing but Trouble; In Our Time. 1945 The Right to Live; They Shall Have Faith. 1948 Julia Misbehaves. 1950 Guilty Bystander.

BOLDER, ROBERT "BOBBIE"
Born: 1859, London, England. Died: Dec. 10, 1937, Beverly Hills, Calif. Screen and stage actor.

Appeared in: 1919 Strictly Confidential. 1921 The Fighting Lover; The Silent Call; Black Beauty; The House that Jazz Built; The Marriage of William Ash; Beyond the Rocks; The Lane that Had No Turning. 1923 Grumpy; The Christian; The Love Piker. 1924 Abraham Lincoln; Captain Blood; What Three Men Wanted; Vanity's Price; The Sea Hawk. 1925 Raffles; The Amateur Cracksman; Stella Maris; The Handsome Brute; Blue Blood. 1926 Butterflies in the Rain. 1927 The Wise Wife; Woman's Wares; Tarzan and the Golden Lion. 1929 The Tip Off. 1930 Grumpy (and 1923 version); Lady of Scandal; Charlie's Aunt. 1931 Get-Rich-Quick Wallingford; The Miracle Woman; East Lynne.

BOLES, JOHN
Born: Oct. 1895, Greenville, Tex. Died: Feb. 27, 1969, San Angelo, Tex.(heart attack). Screen and stage actor. During W.W. I he was a U.S. spy in Germany, Bulgaria and Turkey.

Appeared in: 1925 So This Is Marriage; Excuse Me. 1927 The Love of Sunya. 1928 Shepherd of the Hills; Bride of the Colorado; What Holds Men?; We Americans; Fazil; The Water Hole; Virgin Lips; Man-Made Woman. 1929 The Desert Song; The Last Warning; Rio Rita; Scandal; Romance of the Underworld; She Goes to War. 1930 Song of the West; Captain of the Guard; Queen of Scandal; King of Jazz; One Heavenly Night. 1931 Seed; Good Sport; Resurrection; Frankenstein. 1932 Careless Lady; Back Street; Six Hours to Live. 1933 Hollywood on Parade (short); Child of Manhattan; My Lips Betray; Only Yesterday; Beloved. 1934 I Believed in You; Age of Innocence; Bottoms Up; Stand Up and Cheer; Life of Vergie Winters; The White Parade; Music in the Air; Wild Gold. 1935 Orchids to You; Curly Top; Readheads on Parade; The Littlest Rebel; Masquerade (aka Escapade). 1936 Rose of the Rancho; A Message to Garcia; Craig's Wife. 1937 As Good as Married; Stella Dallas; Fight for Your Lady. 1938 Romance in the Dark; She Married an Artist; Sinners in Paradise. 1942 Road to Happiness; Between Us Girls. 1943 Thousands Cheer. 1952 Babes in Bagdad.

BOLEY, MAY
Born: Washington, D.C. Died: Jan. 7, 1963, Hollywood, Calif. (cancer). Screen and stage actress.

Appeared in: 1928 The Wagon Show. 1929 Dangerous Curves; Dance of Life, Beneath the Law (short); Hail the Princess; Woman from Hell. 1930 Lillies of the Field; Moby Dick; Children of Pleasure. 1931 Going Wild. 1932 A Woman Commands; The Expert. 1933 Advice to the Lovelorn. 1935 The Informer. 1936 Without Orders. 1937 Ready; Willing and Able; Tovarich. 1938 Reckless Living; Cowboy from Brooklyn; Prison Farm. 1939 Persons in Hiding; Death of a Champion; Undercover Doctor; The Women.

BONANOVA, FORTUNIO
Born: Jan. 13, 1893, Palma de Mallorca, Spain. Died: Apr. 2, 1969, Woodland Hills, Calif.(cerebral hemorrhage). Screen, stage, opera, television actor, and playwright.

Appeared in: 1924 Don Juan (Spain film debut). 1932 Careless Lady; A Successful Calamity. 1936 El Desaparecido; Podoroso Caballer. 1938 Tropic Holiday; Romance in the Dark; Bulldog Drummond in Africa. 1939 La Immaculada. 1940 I Was an Adventuress; Down Argentine Way. 1941 They Met in Argentina; Moon over Miami; A Yank in the R.A.F., Two Latins from Manhattan; Mr. and Mrs. North; Obliging Young Lady; Citizen Kane; That Night in Rio; Blood and Sand. 1942 Sing Your Worries Away; Girl Trouble; Larceny, Inc.; The Black Swan. 1943 The Sultan's Daughter; For Whom the Bell Tolls; Five Graves to Cairo. 1944 Double Indemnity; My Best Gal; Ali Baba and the Forty Thieves; Falcon in Mexico; Mrs. Parkington; Brazil; Going My Way. 1945 Where Do We Go from Here?; A Bell for Adano; Hit the Hay; Man Alive; The Red Dragon. 1946 Monsieur Beaucaire. 1947 Rose of Santa Rosa; Fiesta; The Fugitive. 1948 Bad Men of Tombstone; Angel on the Amazon; Romance on the High Seas; Adventures of Don Juan. 1949 Whirlpool. 1950 Nancy Goes to Rio; September Affair. 1951 Havana Rose. 1953 So This Is Love; Conquest of Cochise; Second Chance; Thunder Bay; The Moon Is Blue. 1955 New York Confidential; Kiss Me Deadly. 1956 Jaguar. 1957 An Affair to Remember. 1958 The Saga of Hemp Brown. 1959 Thunder in the Sun. 1963 The Running Man. 1967 The Million Dollar Collar.

BOND, JACK (Alfred Welch)
Born: 1899. Died: Apr. 29, 1952, Hollywood, Calif. Screen and stage actor.

BOND, WARD
Born: Apr. 9, 1903, Denver, Colo. Died: Nov. 5, 1960, Dallas, Tex.(heart attack). Screen, stage, and television actor. Entered films in 1928 while attending U.S.C.

Appeared in: 1929 Salute (film debut); Words and Music. 1930 Born Reckless; The Big Trail. 1932 High Speed; White Eagle; Rackety Rax; Hello Trouble; Virtue. 1933 Obey the Law; The Sundown Rider; Heroes for Sale; Wild Boys of the Road; When Strangers Marry; The Wrecker; Whirlpool; Unknown Valley; Police Car 17. 1934 Straightaway; The Most Precious Thing; Tall Timber; The Fighting Code; The Voice in the Night; A Man's Game; The Crime of Helen Stanley; Girl in Danger; The Human Side; Kid Millions; Against the Law; The Poor Rich; The Frontier Marshal; It Happened One Night; The Defense Rests; The Fighting Ranger; Here Comes the Groom. 1935 Western Courage; Men of the Night; Justice of the Range; Too Tough to Kill; Devil Dogs of the Air; The Crimson Trail; She Gets Her Man; His Night Out; Black Fury; Fighting Shadows; Guard that Girl; Murder in the Fleet; Headline Woman; Waterfront Lady; The Informer. 1936 Cattle Thief; Pride of the Marines; Avenging Waters; Muss 'Em Up; The Bride Walks Out; Second Wife; Without Orders; Crash Donovan; Conflict; They Met in a Taxi; The Man Who Lived Twice; The Legion of Terror; The Leathernecks Have Landed. 1937 The Wildcatter; A Fight to the Finish; You Only Live Once; Dead End; Park Avenue Logger; The Devil's Playground; 23½ Hours' Leave; Night Key; Escape by Night. 1938 Hawaii Calls; Born to be Wild; Flight into Nowhere; Reformatory; Gun Law; The Law West of Tombstone; Professor Beware; Mr. Moto's Gamble; Submarine Patrol; Prison Break; Numbered Woman; Over the Wall; The Amazing Dr. Clitterhouse. 1939 They Made Me a Criminal; Made for Each Other; Dodge City; Waterfront; Gone with the Wind; Trouble in Sundown; The Return of the Cisco Kid; Frontier Marshal (and 1934 version); The Girl from Mexico; The Kid from Kokomo; The Oklahoma Kid; Drums along the Mohawk; Dust Be My Destiny; Young Mr. Lincoln. 1940 Heaven with a Barbed Wire Fence; Virginia City; The Cisco Kid and the Lady; The Grapes of Wrath; Little Old New York; Santa Fe Trail; Buck Benny Rides Again; The Mortal Storm; Kit Carson; The Long Voyage Home. 1941 The Shepherd of the Hills; A Man Betrayed; Sergeant York; Manpower; Doctors Don't Tell; Swamp Water; Wild Bill Hickok Rides; Tobacco Road; The Maltese Falcon. 1942 In This Our Life; The Falcon Takes Over; Gentleman Jim; Sin Town; Ten Gentlemen from West Point. 1943 Slightly Dangerous; They Came to Blow up America; Cowboy Commandos; Hello, Frisco, Hello; Hitler, Dead or Alive; A Guy Named Joe. 1944 Home in Indiana; The Sullivans; Tall in the Saddle. 1945 Dakota; They Were Expendable. 1946 Canyon Passage; My Darling Clementine; It's a Wonderful Life. 1947 The Fugitive; Unconquered. 1948 Fort Apache; The Time of Your Life; Joan of Arc; Tap Roots; Three Godfathers. 1950 Riding High; Wagonmaster; Singing Guns; Kiss Tomorrow Goodbye; Dodge City; Great Missouri Raid. 1951 Operation Pacific; Only the Valiant; On Dangerous Ground. 1952 The Quiet Man; Hellgate; Thunderbirds. 1953 Blowing Wild; The Moonlighter; Hondo. 1954 Gypsy Colt; The Bob Mathias Story; Johnny Guitar. 1955 Mr. Roberts; A Man Alone; The Long, Gray Line. 1956 The Searchers; Dakota Incident; Pillars of the Sky. 1957 Halliday Brand; The Wings of Eagles. 1958 China Doll. 1959 Rio Bravo; Alias Jesse James.

BONDHILL, GERTRUDE (Gertrude Schafer)
Born: 1880. Died: Sept. 15, 1960, Chicago, Ill. Screen, stage, and radio actress. Appeared in early silents made at Essanay Studios in Chicago.

BONIFACE, SYMONA
Born: 1894. Died: Sept. 2, 1950, Woodland Hills, Calif. Screen, stage actor, stage producer, and playwright.

Appeared in: 1932 Strictly Unreliable (short). 1936 Girls Dormitory. 1940 the following shorts: A-Plumbing We Will Go; No Census No Feeling. 1941 the following shorts: All the World's a Stooge; An Ache in Every Stake; In the Sweet Pie and Pie. 1943 Spook Louder (short). 1945 Micro Phonies (short). 1946 G. I. Wanna Go Home (short). 1947 Half-Wits Holiday (short). 1950 Pirates of High Seas (serial). 1951 The Pest Man Wins (short-stock footage). 1955 Bedlam in Paradise (short-stock footage). 1956 Scheming Schemers (short-stock footage). 1958 Pies and Guys (short-stock footage).

BONIFANT, CARMEN
Born: 1890, Mexico. Died: Aug. 1, 1957, Mexico City, Mexico. Screen actress.

BONILLAS, MYRNA
Born: 1890. Died: Nov. 13, 1959, Hollywood, Calif.(heart attack). Screen actress.

Appeared in: 1922 Shackles of Gold; A Stage Romance. 1923 The Custard Cup. 1927 The Claw; The Gingham Girl. 1930 Lummox; Asi es la Vida.

BONN, FRANK
Born: 1873. Died: Mar. 4, 1944, Los Angeles, Calif. Screen actor. Appeared in silents.

Appeared in: 1926 Old Ironsides.

BONN, WALTER
    Born: 1889. Died: Sept. 8, 1953, Hollywood, Calif. Screen and
    stage actor.

    Appeared in: 1938 International Crime; Cipher Bureau.

BONNARD, MARIO
    Born: 1889, Italy. Died: Mar. 22, 1965, Rome, Italy.(heart attack).
    Screen actor, film director, and screenwriter. One of Italy's top
    matinee idols. Entered films as actor and director in 1909.

BONNER, ISABEL
    Born: 1908. Died: Jul. 1, 1955, Los Angeles, Calif.(brain
    hemorrhage). Screen, stage, television, and radio actress.

    Appeared in: 1955 The Shrike.

BONUCCI, ALBERTO
    Born: 1919, Italy. Died: Apr. 7, 1969, Rome, Italy.(heart attack).
    Screen actor and film director.

    Appeared in: 1954 Fugitive in Trieste. 1956 The Magnificent
    Seven (Japan). 1961 Neapolitan Carousel; Blood and Roses. 1963
    Love and Larceny. 1966 The Little Nuns. 1967 The Taming of
    the Shrew. Other Italian films: The Tenor from Oklahoma; Walter
    and His Cousins.

BOOKER, HARRY
    Born: 1850. Died: June 28, 1924, San Diego, Calif. Screen and
    vaudeville actor, and film director. Played in vaudeville as
    part of "Canfield and Booker" team. Entered films with Mack
    Sennett in Keystone comedies.

    Appeared in: 1915 The Great Vacuum Robbery; Her Painted
    Hero; A Game Old Knight. 1916 The Feathered Nest (working
    title Girl Guardian. Reissued 1920 as Only a Farmer's Daugh-
    ter); Her Marble Heart; The Judge; His Hereafter (working
    title Murray's Mix-Up); Maid Mad (working title The Fortune
    Teller); A Love Riot; Pills or Peril; Bombs. 1917 Maggie's First
    False Step; Her Fame and Shame; Her Torpedoed Love; She
    Needed a Doctor; His Uncle Dudley. 1921 Skirts. 1922 The Hotten-
    tot.

BOOT, GLADYS
    Born: 1890. Died: Oct. 16, 1964, London, England. Screen,
    stage, and television actress.

    Appeared in: 1949 The Blue Lagoon. 1956 Murder Reported.
    1957 Gypsy and the Gentleman. 1958 Harry Black and the
    Tiger. 1960 Virgin Island.

BOOTH, HELEN
    Died: Feb. 5, 1971, England. Screen, stage, and television
    actress.

    Appeared in: 1967 The Family Way.

BOOTH, NESDON
    Born: 1919. Died: Mar. 25, 1964, Hollywood, Calif.(heart
    attack). Screen and television actor.

    Appeared in: 1955 Pete Kelly's Blues. 1957 Reform School
    Girl; The Shadow on the Window; Funny Face. 1958 Cattle
    Empire; Escape from Red Rock. 1960 Let No Man Write My
    Epitaph. 1962 Gun Street.

BORDAS, EMILIA F.
    Born: 1874, Spain. Died: 1958, Madrid, Spain. Spanish
    screen and stage actress.

BORDEN, EDDIE
    Born: 1888, Deer Lodge, Tenn. Died: Jul. 1, 1955, Hollywood,
    Calif. Screen, stage, and vaudeville actor. Entered films in
    1921.

    Appeared in: 1922 Back Home and Broke. 1925 Bad Boy (short).
    1926 Hold Everything (short); Battling Butler. 1927 The Show
    Girl; One Chance in a Million. 1928 The Dove. 1930 The
    Rampant Age; Rough Romance. 1932 Breach of Promise. 1933
    Jungle Bride. 1935 The Devil Is a Woman. 1936 Early to
    Bed; Conflict. 1938 Give Me a Sailor. 1939 The Day the Bookies
    Wept. 1940 A Chump at Oxford; Secrets of a Model.

BORDEN, OLIVE
    Born: July 14, 1907, Richmond, Va. Died: Oct. 1, 1947, Los
    Angeles, Calif.(stomach ailment). Screen actress. Entered
    films with Sennett as a Sennett bathing beauty in 1922, and was
    one of the twelve Wampas Baby Stars of 1925.

    Appeared in: 1925 Dressmaker from Paris; The Happy Warrior;
The Overland Limited. 1926 Three Bad Men; Fig Leaves; Yel-
low Fingers; The Country Beyond; My Own Pal; The Yankee
Senor. 1926 Monkey Talks; The Joy Girl; Come to My House;
Pajamas; The Secret Studio. 1928 The Albany Night Boat;
Sinners in Love; Gang War; Stool Pigeon; Virgin Lips. 1929
The Eternal Woman; Love in the Desert; Half Marriage; Dance
Hall. 1930 Wedding Rings; The Social Lion; Hello Sister. 1933
Hotel Variety.

BORDONI, IRENE
    Born: 1895, Ajaccio, Corsica. Died: Mar. 19, 1953, New York,
    N.Y. Screen, stage, radio, and vaudeville actress.

    Appeared in: 1929 Paris (film debut); The Show of Shows.
    1936 A Vitaphone short. 1942 Louisiana Purchase (stage and film
    versions).

BORELLI, LYDA
    Born: 1888, Genoa, Italy. Died: June 2, 1958, Rome, Italy.
    Screen and stage actress.

    Appeared in: 1913 Ma l' Amore Mio non Muore (My Love
    Never Dies); Memorie Dell 'Altro. 1914 La Donna Nuda. 1915
    Il Bosco Dacr; Fior di Male; Rapsodia Sat Anica; Marica Nu-
    ziale (Wedding March). 1916 La Falena; Malombra; Madame
    Tallian. 1917 Carnevalesca (Carnival); Il Dramma di una
    Notte; La Storia dei Tredici. Other Italian film: Vergine Folle
    (Foolish Virgin).

BOREO, EMIL
    Born: 1885. Died: July 27, 1951, New York, N.Y. Screen,
    stage, and vaudeville actor.

    Appeared in: 1938 The Lady Vanishes. 1947 Carnegie Hall.

BORGATO, AGOSTINO
    Born: 1871, Venice, Italy. Died: Mar. 14, 1939, Hollywood,
    Calif.(heart attack). Screen actor. Entered films in 1913.

    Appeared in: 1925 The Street of Forgotten Men. 1926 The Love
    Thief. 1927 Magic Flame; Kiss in a Taxi; Helen of Troy; Hula;
    Fashions for Women; Horse Shoes. 1928 A Perfect Gentleman.
    1929 Romance of the Rio Grande; She Goes to War; Hot for
    Paris. 1930 Behind the Make-Up; Redemption. 1931 The
    Maltese Falcon; Transgression. 1932 Bird of Paradise.

BORGSTROM, HILDA
    Born: 1871, Sweden. Died: Jan. 2, 1953, Stockholm, Sweden.
    Screen and stage actress.

    Appeared in: 1912 En Sommarsaga (film debut). 1939 Du Fria,
    Du Gamla (Thou Old, Tho Free); Familjen Andersson (The An-
    derson Family). 1962 Night Is My Future (aka Musih I Morku—
    Music in the Night).

BOROS, FERIKE
    Born: 1880, Nagvarad, Hungary. Died: Jan. 16, 1951, Holly-
    wood, Calif. Screen, stage actress, and playwright.

    Appeared in: 1930 Born Reckless; Little Caesar; Ladies Love
    Brutes. 1931 Bought; Gentlemen's Fate; Svengali. 1932 The
    World and the Flesh; Huddle. 1933 Humanity; Rafter Romance.
    1934 Eight Girls in a Boat; The Fountain. 1935 Symphony of
    Living. 1937 Make Way for Tomorrow. 1939 Love Affair;
    Stronger than Desire; Bachelor Mother; Fifth Avenue Girl; Dust
    Be My Destiny; Rio; The Light That Failed. 1940 Argentine
    Nights; Three Cheers for the Irish; La Conga Nights; Girl from
    God's Country; Christmas in July. 1941 Sleepers West; Caught
    in the Draft; Private Nurse. 1942 Once upon a Honeymoon; The
    Pied Piper; The Talk of the Town. 1943 Margin for Error;
    Princess O'Rourke. 1944 The Doughgirls. 1945 This Love of
    Ours; A Tree Grows in Brooklyn. 1946 Specter of the Rose.

BORZAGE, FRANK
    Born: Apr. 23, 1893, Salt Lake City, Utah. Died: June 19, 1962,
    Hollywood, Calif.(cancer). Screen, stage actor, and film
    director.

    Appeared in: 1915 American Beauty Comedy production. 1916
    That Gal of Burke's; Immediate Lee. 1922 Hair Trigger Casey
    (re-release and retitle of Immediate Lee 1916 film).

BOSTON, NELROY BUCK
    Born: 1911. Died: Feb. 28, 1962, Van Nuys, Calif.(auto acci-
    dent). Screen and stage actor. Entered films approx. 1940.

BOSWELL, MARTHA
    Born: 1905. Died: July 2, 1958, Peekskill, N.Y. Screen, stage,
    radio actress, and singer. Was one of the three singing Boswell
    Sisters.

Appeared in: 1932 The Big Broadcast; Universal shorts; a Paramount short. 1934 Radio Star. 1937 a Paramount short.

BOSWORTH, HOBART
Born: Aug. 11, 1867, Marietta, Ohio. Died: Dec. 30, 1943, Glendale, Calif.(pneumonia). Screen, stage actor, film producer, director, and screenwriter. Formed Bosworth Film Company approx. 1913.

Appeared in: 1908 The Roman. 1909 The Sultan's Power. 1912 The Count of Monte Cristo. 1913 Sea Wolf. 1914 The Country Mouse; Odessy of the North. 1916 Joan the Woman; Oliver Twist. 1917 The Little American. 1919 The Border Legion. 1920 Behind the Door. 1921 The Foolish Matrons; The Brute Master; Below the Surface; His Own Law; A Thousand to One; Blind Hearts; The Cup of Life. 1922 The Sea Lion; White Hands; The Stranger's Banquet. 1923 Man Alone; The Common Law; The Eternal Three; Little Church Around the Corner; In the Place of the King; Vanity Fair; The Man Life Passed By; Rupert of Hentzau; Souls for Sale. 1924 Captain January; Bread; The Silent Watcher; Name the Man; Hearts of Oak; Nellie, the Beautiful Cloak Model; Sundown; Through the Dark; The Woman on the Jury. 1925 The Big Parade; Zander the Great; My Son; Chickie; The Half-Way Girl; Winds of Chance; The Golden Strain; If I Marry Again. 1926 Steel Preferred; The Nervous Wreck; Spangles; The Far Cry. 1927 The Blood Ship; Annie Laurie; My Best Girl; The Chinese Parrot; Three Hours. 1928 Annapolis; Hangman's House; After the Storm; Freckles; The Sawdust Paradise; The Smart Set; A Man of Peach (short). 1929 The Show of Shows; Hurricane; King of the Mountain; A Woman of Affairs; Eternal Love; General Crack. 1930 Just Imagine; The Office Wife; Sit Tight; The Third Alarm; DuBarry, Woman of Passion; The Devil's Holiday; Mammy; Abraham Lincoln; A Man of Peace. 1931 Dirigible; Shipmates; This Modern Age; Fanny Foley Herself; Bad Timber. 1932 Carnival Boat; No Greater Love; Phantom Express; The Miracle Man; County Fair. 1933 Divine Love; Last of the Mohicans; Lady for a Day. 1934 Music in the Air; Whom the Gods Destroy. 1935 The Crusades; Keeper of the Bees; Steamboat Round the Bend. 1937 Portia on Trial. 1938 The Secret of Treasure Island (serial); Wolves of the Sea. 1941 One Foot in Heaven; Law of the Tropics. 1942 Sin Town; I Was Framed; Bullet Scars.

BOTELER, WADE
Born: 1891, Santa Ana, Calif. Died: May 7, 1943, Hollywood, Calif.(heart attack). Screen, stage actor, and screenwriter.

Appeared in: 1919 Twenty-Three and Half Hours' Leave; An Old Fashioned Boy. 1921 Blind Hearts; One Man in a Million; Stranger than Fiction; Ducks and Drakes; Fifty Candles; The Home Stretch. 1922 At the Sign of the Jack O'Lantern; Second Hand Rose; Ridin' Wild; Afraid to Fight; The Lying Truth; The Woman's Side; Deserted at the Altar; While Satan Sleeps; Through a Glass Window; The Unfoldment; Don't Shoot; The Great Night. 1923 Going Up; A Man of Action; The Ghost Patrol; Around the World in 18 Days (serial); Alias the Night Wind (serial). 1924 Through the Dark; The Whipping Boss; Never Say Die; The Phantom Horseman. 1925 Capital Punishment; Introduce Me; Seven Keys to Baldpate; Marriage in Transit; Winds of Chance; Havoc; Jimmie's Millions; The Last Edition. 1926 Hold That Lion; That's My Baby. 1927 Let It Rain; High School Hero; Soft Cushions. 1928 Let 'Er Go Gallaher; Sporting Goods; Warming Up; Just Married; A Woman Against the World; The Toilers; The Baby Cyclone; Top Sergeant Mulligan; The Crash. 1929 Close Harmony; Big News; The Leatherneck; The Godless Girl. 1930 Navy Blues; The Devil's Holiday; Soldiers and Women; Way of All Men; College Lovers; Top Speed; Derelict. 1931 Painted Desert; Beyond Victory; Kick In; Silence; Twenty-Four Hours; Bad Company; Penrod and Sam; The Way Back Home; Local Boy Makes Good. 1932 Night Mayor; Painted Woman; Speed Madness; Manhattan Tower; Central Park; Death Kiss; The Man Who Played God. 1933 End of the Trail; Come on Danger; She Done Him Wrong; Speed Demon; Humanity; This Day and Age; College Humor; Unknown Valley; King for a Night. 1934 Melody in Spring; A Man's Game; Among the Missing; Belle of the Nineties; The Richest Girl in the World; The Crosby Case; Operator 13, Fugitive Lady. 1935 Love in Bloom; Goin' to Town; Baby Face Harrington; O'Shaughnessey's Boy; Black Fury; The Goose and the Gander; Headline Woman; The Three Musketeers; Cheers of the Crowd; Freckles; Melody Trail; Streamline Express. 1936 Whipsaw; Riff Raff; Exclusive Story; The Return of Jimmy Valentine; The President's Mystery; The Country Gentleman; Here Comes Trouble; Charlie Chan at the Circus; Human Cargo; The Bride Walks Out; Alibi for Murder; Poppy. 1937 The Great Hospital Mystery; The Frame-Up; A Fight to a Finish; The Mandarin Mystery; You Only Live Once; 52nd Street; Dead Yesterday; Find

the Witness; Jim Hanvey—Detective; Dangerous Holiday; Youth on Parole; It Can't Last Forever; Borrowing Trouble. 1938 The Marines Are Here; Little Miss Roughneck; In Old Chicago; Peck's Bad Boy with the Circus; Spawn of the North; Valley of the Giants; Billy the Kid Returns. 1939 Southward Ho!; Sabotage; The Man from Down Under; Days of Jesse James; Everything's on Ice; Missing Daughters; The Mysterious Miss X; Thunder Afloat; Ambush; Chicken Wagon Family. 1940 Double Alibi; Torrid Zone; Gaucho Serenade; Three Faces West; Castle on the Hudson; Young Buffalo Bill; Hot Steel; The Leather Pushers; The Howards of Virginia; Under Texas Skies; Till We Meet Again; My Little Chickadee; Three Cheers for the Irish. 1941 Where Did You Get That Girl?; A-Hunting We Will Go; Shanghai Alibi; It Started with Eve; The Single Hills; Kathleen; The Kid from Kansas; The Body Disappears. 1942 Blue, White and Perfect; Bombay Clipper; Ride 'Em Cowboy; I Was Framed; Escape from Crime; Moonlight in Havana; Mississippi Gambler; Gentleman Jim. 1943 It Ain't Hay; Hi, Buddy; The Good Fellows; Find the Blackmailer; Hit the Ice; Eyes of the Underworld. 1944 The Last Ride.

BOTHWELL, JOHN F.
Born: 1921. Died: Mar. 1967, Long Branch, N.J. Screen actor. "Freckles" in "Our Gang" comedies.

BOUCHER, VICTOR
Born: France. Died: Feb. 1942, France. Screen and stage actor.

Appeared in: 1931 La Douceur D'Aimer. 1942 Nine Bachelors.

BOUCOT, LOUIS
Born: 1889. Died: Mar. 30, 1949, Paris, France. Screen and stage actor.

BOURKE, FAN
Born: 1886, Brooklyn, N.Y. Died: Mar. 9, 1959, Norwalk, Conn. Screen, stage, vaudeville actress, and screenwriter. Entered films in 1915.

Appeared in: 1930 Lummox.

BOURVIL (Andre Raimbourg)
Born: 1913, Normandy, France. Died: Sept. 23, 1970, Paris, France. Screen, stage, and radio actor.

Appeared in: 1945 La Ferme due Pendu. 1946 Pas si Bete. 1947 Blanc Comme Neige. 1948 Le Coeur Sur la Maine. 1949 Miguette et Sa Mere. 1950 Le Rosier de Madame Husson. 1951 Garou-Garou au le Passe - Murail - le; Seul dans Paris; Miquette; Mr. Peek-A-Boo. 1952 The Prise. 1953 Le Trois Mousquetaires (The Three Musketeers U.S. 1954). 1954 Le Cadet Rousselle; Poisson d'avril. 1955 Les Hussards. 1956 La Traversee de Paris (The Crossing of Paris - aka Four Bags Full - U.S. 1957). 1957 Le Chanteur de Mexico. 1959 The Mirror Has Two Faces. 1960 Crazy for Love. 1962 Tout l'or du Monde; The Longest Day; La Jument Verte (The Green Mare). 1963 Les Culottes Roughes (The Red Pants); Les Bonnes Causes (The Good Causes); Heaven Sent. 1964 La Cuisine au Beurre (Cooking with Butter); Don't Tempt the Devil. 1965 The Secret Agents; Thank Heaven for Small Favors; My Wife's Husband. 1966 La Grande Vadrouille (The Big Spree); The Dirty Game; The Sucker. 1967 Don't Look Now. 1968 Le Verveau (The Brain). 1969 Monte Carlo or Bust; Those Daring Young Men in Their Jaunty Jalopies. Other French films: The Atlantic Wall; The Christmas Tree; Le Corniaud (The Dumbbell).

BOW, CLARA
Born: Aug. 25, 1905, Brooklyn, N.Y. Died: Sept. 27, 1965, Los Angeles, Calif.(heart attack). Screen actress. Married to Rex Bell, former actor and Lt. Gov. of Nevada (dec. 1962). She was known as the "It" Girl.

Appeared in: 1922 Beyond the Rainbow. 1923 Down to the Sea in Ships; The Daring Years; Maytime. 1924 Black Oxen; Black Lightning; Grit; Daughters of Pleasure; Helen's Babies; Poisoned Paradise; Empty Hearts; This Woman; Wine. 1925 Free to Love; Keeper of the Bees; The Plastic Age; Kiss Me Again; The Scarlet West; Capital Punishment; The Primrose Path; My Lady of Whims; Eve's Lover; The Adventurous Sex; The Best Bad Man; The Ancient Mariner; Lawful Cheaters; My Lady's Lips; Parisian Love. 1926 Dancing Mothers; Kid Boots; Fascinating Youth; Mantrap; Two Can Play; The Runaway; The Shadow of the Law. 1927 Hula; Rough House Rosie; Get Your Man; Children of Divorce; It; Wings. 1928 Red Hair; The Fleet's In; Three Week Ends; Ladies of the Mob. 1929 Dangerous Curves; The Saturday Night Kid; The Wild Party. 1930 Love among the Millionaires; Paramount on Parade; True to the Navy; Her Wedding Night. 1931 Kick In; No Limit. 1932 Call Her Savage. 1933 Hoopla.

BOWERS, JOHN
    Born: Dec. 25, 1899, Garrett, Ind. Died: Nov. 17, 1936, Santa
Monica, Calif.(drowned). Screen and stage actor. Entered
films in 1916. Divorced from actress Marguerite de la
Motte (dec. 1950).

    Appeared in: 1916 Hulda from Holland; Madame X. 1919 Sis
Hopkins; Through the Wrong Door; Strictly Confidential. 1921
Roads of Destiny; The Silent Call; The Sky Pilot; The Ace of
Hearts; Bits of Life; Godless Men; The Night Rose; An Unwilling
Hero; The Poverty of Riches. 1922 Quincy Adams Sawyer;
Affinities; South of Suva; The Bonded Woman; The Golden Gift.
1923 Lorna Doone; The Woman of Bronze; Desire; The Barefoot
Boy; What a Wife Learned; Crinoline and Romance; The De-
stroying Angel; Divorce; Richard, The Lion-Hearted. 1924
When a Man's a Man; Code of the Wilderness; The White Sin;
Those Who Dare; Empty Hearts; So Big. 1925 Confessions of
a Queen; Chickie; Flattery; Daughters Who Pay; Off the Highway;
The People vs. Nancy Preston. 1926 Pals in Paradise; The Dan-
ger Girl; Whispering Smith; Hearts and Fists; Rocking Moon;
Laddie. 1927 The Dice Woman; For Ladies Only; Ragtime; The
Heart of the Yukon; Heroes in Blue; The Opening Night; Three
Hours; Jewels of Desire. 1929 Skin Deep; Say It with Songs.
1931 Mounted Fury.

BOWERS, LYLE
    Born: 1896. Died: Mar. 8, 1943, Hollywood, Calif. Screen actor.
Entered films approx. 1923.

BOWES, MAJOR EDWARD
    Born: 1874, San Francisco, Calif. Died: June 13, 1946, Rumson,
N.J. Screen, radio actor, and composer. Married to actress
Margaret Illington (dec. 1934). Began radio career in 1925 and
originated Major Bowes Amateur Radio Hour in 1934.

    Appeared in: 1936 Amateur Parade (short); Amateur Theatre
of the Air (short). Other shorts he appeared in are as follows:
Musical Varieties; Variety Review; Radio Revels; Stars of
Tomorrow; Harmony Broadcast and Melody Maker.

BOWMAN, PALMER
    Born: 1883. Died: Sept. 25, 1933, Chicago, Ill.(heart disease).
Screen, stage, vaudeville actor, film director, and screenwriter.

    Appeared in early Selíg and Essanay Company productions.

BOYCE, JACK
    Born: 1885. Died: Dec. 13, 1923, New York, N.Y. Screen and
stage actor.

BOYD, BLANCHE "DEEDEE"
    Born: 1889. Died: Apr. 14, 1959, Laguna Beach, Calif.(heart
attack). Screen and stage actress.

BOYD, WILLIAM "STAGE"
    Born: 1890. Died: Mar. 20, 1935, Hollywood, Calif.(liver ailment).
Not to be confused with William "Hopalong Cassady" Boyd (dec.
1972). Screen, stage actor, and circus rider.

    Appeared in: 1930 The Locked Door; The Benson Murder Case;
The Spoilers; Derelict. 1931 Gun Smoke; City Streets; Murder
by the Clock; The Road to Reno. 1932 The False Madonna;
State's Attorney. 1933 The House on 56th Street; Oliver Twist;
The Chief. 1934 Transatlantic Merry-Go-Round.

BOYNE, SUNNY
    Born: 1883, Boston, Mass. Died: Aug. 27, 1966, Van Nuys, Calif.
Screen actress and dancer.

    Appeared in: 1941 All That Money Can Buy. 1950 Born to be
Bad. 1952 The Devil and Daniel Webster (re-issue & retitle of
All That Money Can Buy, 1941). 1958 King Creole.

BOZO, LITTLE. See Little Bozo

BRACE, NORMAN C.
    Born: 1892. Died: June 20, 1954, New York, N.Y. Screen, stage
actor, film and stage director. Appeared in early films.

BRACEY, SIDNEY
    Born: 1877, Melbourne, Australia. Died: Aug. 5, 1942, Holly-
wood, Calif. Screen and stage actor. Entered films in 1910.

    Appeared in: 1914 Zudora (The Twenty Million Dollar Mystery)
(serial). 1920 The Invisible Ray (serial). 1921 An Amateur
Devil; The Outside Woman; Passion Fruit; Crazy to Marry;
The March Hare; Morals. 1922 Manslaughter; The Dictator;
The Radio King (serial); Is Matrimony a Failure?; Midnight;
One Wonderful Night. 1923 Merry-Go-Round; Nobody's Bride;
The Wild Party; The Social Buccaneer (serial); Ruggles of Red
Gap. 1924 Being Respectable; By Divine Right; Her Night of
Romance; So This Is Marriage?; Why Men Leave Home. 1925
Her Market Value; The Merry Widow; Wandering Footsteps; A
Slave of Fashion. 1926 A Man Four-Square; The Mystery Club;
The Black Bird; My Official Wife; You Never Know Women. 1927
Birds of Prey; Painting the Town; The Thirteenth Juror; The
Woman on Trial. 1928 Show People; Haunted House; The Camera-
man; Queen Kelly; The Wedding March; Win That Girl; Home
James; Man-Made Women. 1929 His Captive Woman; Sioux
Blood; The Bishop Murder Case. 1930 Second Floor Mystery;
Anybody's Woman; Outside the Law; Free Love; Monte Carlo;
Redemption. 1931 The Avenger; Parlor, Bedroom and Bath;
Lion and the Lamb; A Dangerous Affair; Subway Express;
Shanghaied Love; The Deceiver. 1932 The Monster Walks; The
Greeks Had a Word for Them; Tangled Destinies; No More
Orchids; Little Orphan Annie. 1933 The Intruder; Corruption;
Broken Dreams. 1934 The Poor Rich; The Ninth Guest. 1935
Anna Karenina. 1936 Magnificent Obsession; Sutter's Gold; Isle
of Fury; Preview Murder Mystery. 1938 Mr. Chump; Dawn
Patrol; The Baroness and the Butler; Merrily We Live; My Bill.
1939 On Trial; Smashing the Money Ring; Everybody's Hobby;
Sweepstakes Winner. 1940 My Love Came Back; Devil's Island;
Tugboat Annie Sails Again. 1941 Bullets for O'Hara; Shadows
on the Stairs. 1942 The Gay Sisters.

BRACY, CLARA T.
    Born: 1847. Died: Feb. 22, 1941, Los Angeles, Calif. Screen
and stage actress. Made early films with Kinemacolor and later
Biograph.

    Appeared in: 1909 Eloping with Auntie, The Awakening. 1910
Three Sisters; A Decree of Destiny. 1924 Her Night of Romance.

BRADBURY, JAMES, SR.
    Born: Oct. 12, 1857, Old Town, Me. Died: Oct. 12, 1940, Clifton,
Staten Island, N.Y. Screen and stage actor. Father of screen actor
James Bradbury, Jr.

    Appeared in: 1924 Manhattan. 1926 Fascinating Youth; The High
Flyer. 1927 The Blood Ship: The Fair Co-Ed; Babe Comes
Home; The Circus Ace; Romantic Rogue; The Racing Fool.
1928 Skinner's Big Idea; Blockade; Waterfront; Scarlet Seas;
Hot Heels; The Leopard Lady; Walking Back; Midnight Mad-
ness. 1929 Tide of the Empire; Woman from Hell. 1930 The
Matrimonial Bed; Tol'able David; Abraham Lincoln. 1934 The
Silver Streak.

BRADFORD, CHARLES AVERY
    Born: 1873. Died: July 23, 1926, Hollywood, Calif.("possible
suicide"). Screen actor.

BRADFORD, MARSHALL
    Born: 1896. Died: Jan. 11, 1971, Hollywood, Calif.(heart attack).
Screen, stage, and television actor.

    Appeared in: 1949 Western Renegades. 1950 Texas Dynamo.
1951 Ghost Chasers; Night Riders of Montana; Colorado Ambush.
1952 Hellgate. 1954 Yukon Vengeance. 1957 I Was a Teenage
Frankenstein. 1958 Teenage Caveman.

BRADLEY, BENJAMIN R.
    Born: 1898. Died: Sept. 29, 1950, St. Louis, Mo.(heart disease
and complications). Screen actor and magician. Appeared in
silents.

BRADLEY, HARRY C.
    Born: Apr. 15, 1869, San Francisco, Calif. Died: Oct. 18, 1947,
Hollywood, Calif.(heart attack). Screen and stage actor.

    Appeared in: 1933 I Love That Man; This Day and Age; I Have
Lived. 1934 It Happened One Night; Heat Lighning; The Merry
Frinks; The Last Gentleman; City Limits; White Lies. 1935
Love in Bloom; Private Worlds; Way Down East. 1936 It Had
to Happen; Three of a Kind; Gold Diggers of 1937. 1937 New
Faces of 1937; Trouble at Midnight. 1938 Women Are Like
That; The Little Adventuress. 1939 When Tomorrow Comes.
1940 Slightly Tempted. 1941 The Big Store. 1942 Busses Roar;
Hi, Neighbor; Got Hep to Love; Mrs. Wiggs of the Cabbage Patch.
1944 Henry Aldrich's Little Secret; Make Your Own Bed.

BRADLEY, LOVYSS
    Born: 1906. Died: June 21, 1969, Woodland Hills, Calif.(cancer).
Screen and television actress.

    Appeared in: 1950 Outrage. 1951 Golden Girl; The Blue Veil.
1968 Up Tight.

BRADY, ALICE

Born: Nov. 2, 1892, New York, N.Y. Died: Oct. 28, 1939, New York, N.Y.(cancer). Screen and stage actress. Won Academy Award for Best Supporting Actress in 1938 for In Old Chicago.

Appeared in: 1915 The Boss. 1916 La Boheme; Bought and Paid For; The Gilded Cage. 1917 Betsy Ross. 1918 Woman and Wife. 1919 A Dark Lantern. 1920 Fear Market; The New York Idea. 1921 Out of the Chorus; Little Italy; The Land of Hope; The Dawn of the East; Hush Money. 1922 Anna Ascends; Missing Millions. 1923 Leopardess; Snow Bride. 1933 When Ladies Meet; Beauty for Sale; Broadway to Hollywood; Stage Mother; Should Ladies Behave?. 1934 Miss Fane's Baby is Stolen; The Gay Divorcee; False Faces. 1935 Gold Diggers of 1935; Let 'Em Have It; Lady Tubbs; Metropolitan. 1936 The Harvester; My Man Godfrey; Go West, Young Man; Mind Your Own Business. 1937 Three Smart Girls; One Hundred Men and a Girl; Mama Steps Out; Call It a Day; Mr. Dodd Takes the Air; Merry-Go-Round of 1938. 1938 In Old Chicago; Joy of Living; Goodbye Broadway. 1939 Senobia; Young Mr. Lincoln.

BRADY, EDWARD J.

Born: 1888, New York, N.Y. Died: Mar. 31, 1942, Hollywood, Calif.(heart attack). Screen, stage, and vaudeville actor.

Appeared in: 1915 Who Pays?; Neal of the Navy (serial). 1919 The Great Radium Mystery (serial). 1921 The Rough Diamond; The Silent Call; Cheated Love; The Kiss. 1922 The Old Homestead; The Pride of Palomar; Over the Border; The Siren Call; Boy Crazy; If You Believe It, It's So; A Question of Honor. 1923 To the Last Man; The Broken Wing; Racing Hearts; The Trail of the Lonesome Pine; The Eternal Struggle. 1924 The Dancing Cheat; The Fighting American; The Rose of Paris; The Price She Paid; Stolen Secrets; Fool's Highway. 1925 Marry Me; The Thundering Herd; A Child of the Prairie; Flower of Night. 1926 Three Faces East; Whispering Canyon. 1927 The Rose of Kildare; Hoof Marks; Lost at the Front; King of Kings; Clancy's Kosher Wedding. 1928 Harold Teen; The Noose; Do Your Duty; The Code of the Scarlet; The Bushranger; Dressed to Kill. 1929 The Delightful Rogue; Alibi. 1930 The Texan; City Girl; Cameo Kirby. 1931 The Squaw Man; The Sin of Madelon Claudet; Shanghaied Love; The Conquering Horde. 1932 Union Depot; The Night Club Lady. 1933 The Lone Avenger; Son of Kong. 1934 Redhead; In a Pig's Eye (short). 1935 It's a Small World. 1938 Blockade.

BRAGA, EURICO

Born: 1894, Rio De Janeiro, Brazil. Died: Nov. 19, 1962, Lisbon, Portugal(cancer). Screen, stage actor, and columnist.

BRAHAM, HARRY

Born: 1874, Longdon, England. Died: Sept. 21, 1923, Staten Island, N.Y. Screen and stage actor. Appeared in Griffith films.

BRAHAM, HORACE

Born: 1893. Died: Sept. 7, 1955, New York, N.Y. Screen, stage, radio, and television actor.

Appeared in: 1922 The Prodigal Judge. 1923 Sinner or Saint.

BRAHAM, LIONEL

Born: 1879, England. Died: Oct. 6, 1947, Hollywood, Calif. (heart attack). Screen and stage actor.

Appeared in: 1916 Diane the Huntress. 1925 I'll Show You the Town. 1926 Skinner's Dress Suit; Don Juan. 1927 Night Life; Out All Night. 1936 As You Like It. 1937 Personal Property; The Prince and the Pauper; Wee Willie Winkle. 1938 A Christmas Carol. 1939 The Little Princess. 1948 Macbeth.

BRAITHWAITE, DAME LILIAN

Born: 1871. Died: Sept. 17, 1948, London, England(heart attack). Screen and stage actress.

BRANDON, DOLORES

Born: 1917. Died: Aug. 9, 1959, Hollywood, Calif. Screen and vaudeville actress.

BRANDON, FLORENCE

Born: 1879. Died: Oct. 11, 1961, London, England. Screen and stage actress. Appeared in silents.

BRANDT, LOUISE

Born: 1877. Died: July 13, 1959, San Diego, Calif. Screen actress.

BRAVO, JAMIE

Born: 1932. Died: Feb. 2, 1970, Zacatecas, Mexico(auto accident). Matador and screen actor.

Appeared in: 1965 Love Has Many Faces.

BRAWN, JOHN P.

Born: 1869, New York, N.Y. Died: June 16, 1943, New York, N.Y. Screen and stage actor.

BRAY, JOHN F.

Born: 1906. Died: May 3, 1955, Gladewater, Tex. Screen actor.

Appeared in: 1948 Paleface. 1949 Mr. Belvedere Goes to College. 1951 Here Comes the Groom. 1952 Viva Zapata!

BREAMER, SYLVIA

Born: 1903. Died: June 7, 1943, New York, N.Y. Screen actress.

Appeared in: 1918 Missing. 1921 The Devil; Not Guilty; Doubling for Romeo; The Roof Tree; A Poor Relation. 1922 Wolf Law; Money to Burn; The Man Who Married His Own Wife; The Man with Two Mothers; The Man Unconquerable; Calvert's Valley; The Face Between; Money to Burn; Sherlock Brown. 1923 Bavu; The First Degree; Flaming Youth; The Barefoot Boy; Her Temporary Husband; The Girl of the Golden West; Thundergate. 1924 Lilies of the Field; The Woman on the Jury; Reckless Romance; Robes of Sin. 1925 Too Much Youth; Women and Gold. 1926 Up in Mabel's Room; Lightning Reporter. 1936 Too Many Parents.

BRECHER, EGON

Born: Feb. 16, 1885, Czechoslovakia. Died: Aug. 12, 1946, Hollywood, Calif.(heart attack). Screen and stage actor, and stage director.

Appeared in: 1929 The Royal Box. 1933 To the Last Man. 1934 As the Earth Turns; No Greater Glory; Many Happy Returns; The Black Cat; Now and Forever. 1935 Black Fury; The Florentine Dagger; Here's to Romance; Charlie Chan's Secret. 1936 Boulder Dam; Till We Meet Again; Sins of Man; Ladies in Love; The White Angel; Stolen Holiday; Alibi for Murder. 1937 The Black Legion; Heidi; I Met Him in Paris; Love under Fire; Thin Ice. 1938 I'll Give a Million; Suez; Cocoanut Grove; You and Me; Spawn of the North; The Spy Ring; Invisible Enemy. 1939 Devil's Island; The Three Musketeers; Nurse Edith Cavell; Judge Hardy and Son; Juarez; Angels Wash Their Faces. 1940 Four Sons; The Man I Married; I Was an Adventuress. 1941 Kings Row; They Dare Not Love; Underground; Manpower. 1942 Isle of Missing Men; Berlin Correspondent. 1944 The Hairy Ape; U-Boat Prisoner. 1945 A Royal Scandal; White Pongo. 1946 The Wife of Monte Cristo; OSS; So Dark the Night.

BREEN, HURLEY "RED"

Born: 1913. Died: Sept. 8, 1963, Hollywood, Calif. Screen actor and boxer. Double for James Cagney.

Appeared in: 1952 Boots Malone.

BREEN, MARGARET

Died: Dec. 5, 1960, Santa Monica, Calif. Screen, stage, and vaudeville actress. Was part of the "Breen Family" vaudeville act.

Appeared in: 1930 Heads Up.

BREESE, EDMUND

Born: June 18, 1871, Brooklyn, N.Y. Died: Apr. 6, 1936, New York, N.Y. (peritonitis). Screen, stage actor, and playwright. Entered films in 1914.

Appeared in: 1915 The Song of the Wage Slave. 1916 The Spell of the Yukon. 1921 Burn 'Em up Barnes. 1922 Beyond the Rainbow; Sure-Fire Flint; The Curse of Drink. 1923 Luck; The Little Red Schoolhouse; You are Guilty; Bright Lights of Broadway; The Fair Cheat; Jacqueline of Blazing Barriers; Marriage Morals; Three O'Clock in the Morning. 1924 The Early Bird; The Shooting of Dan McGrew; Damaged Hearts; Restless Wives; Playthings of Desire; The Sixth Commandment; The Speed Spook; Those Who Judge. 1925 The Police Patrol; Wildfire; The Live Wire. 1926 Stepping Along; Woman Handled; The Brown Derby; The Highbinders. 1927 Paradise for Two; Back to Liberty; Home Made. 1928 Finders Keepers; Burning Daylight; Perfect Crime; The Wright Idea; On Trial; The Haunted House. 1929 Sonny Boy; Fancy Baggage; Conquest; Girls Gone Wild; From Headquarters; The Gamblers; The Hottentot; Girl Overboard; In the Headlines. 1930 Hold Everything; The Sea

Bat; Rough Waters; Top Speed; Bright Lights; Tol'able David;
All Quiet on the Western Front; Kismet; The Czar of Broadway;
Playboy of Paris. 1931 Playthings of Hollywood; Oh! Oh! Cleo-
patra (short); Public Defender; Wicked; Chinatown after Dark;
Mother's Millions; Millie; The Last Parade; Defender's of the
Law; Young Sinners; The Good Bad Girl; The Painted Desert;
Platinum Blonde; Morals for Women; Bad Girl. 1932 Cross
Examination; The Hatchet Man; Mata Hari; Police Court; The
Reckoning; Love Bound; Drifting Souls; Alias Mary Smith; Cabin
in the Cotton; Golden West; Madame Butterfly; The Match King.
1933 Women Won't Tell; Billion Dollar Scandal; International
House; Laughing at Life; Man of Sentiment; Ladies Must Love;
Duck Soup; Above the Clouds. 1934 Come on Marines; Beloved;
Treasure Island; Broadway Bill; The Dancing Man; Lost in the
Stratosphere. 1935 The Marriage Bargain.

BRENDEL, EL (Elmer G. Brendel)
Born: Mar. 25, 1890, Philadelphia, Pa. Died: Apr. 9, 1964,
Hollywood, Calif.(heart attack). Screen, stage, vaudeville,
and television actor. Married to Sophie Flo Bert with whom he
appeared in vaudeville. Entered films in 1926.

Appeared in: 1926 The Campus Flirt; You Never Know Women.
1927 Ten Modern Commandments; Too Many Crooks; Wings;
Arizona Bound; Rolled Stockings. 1929 The Cock-Eyed World;
Sunny-Side Up; Frozen Justice; Hot for Paris; Beau Night
(short). 1930 Happy Days; The Big Trail; The Golden Calf;
Just Imagine; New Movietone Follies of 1930. 1931 Mr. Lemon
of Orange; Spider; Delicious; Women of All Nations; Six Cylinder
Love. 1932 West of Broadway; Disorderly Conduct; Handle
with Care. 1933 Hot Pepper; My Lips Betray; The Last Trail.
1934 The Meanest Gal in Town; Olsen's Big Moment. 1935
Broadway Brevities (short) and a Vitaphone short. 1936
Career Woman; God's Country and the Woman. 1937 The Holy
Terror; Blonde Trouble. 1938 Happy Landing; Little Miss
Broadway; Valley of Giants. 1939 Code of the Streets; House
of Fear; Risky Business; Spirit of Culver; Call of a Messenger.
1940 If I Had My Way; Captain Caution; Gallant Sons. 1944 I'm
From Arkansas; Machine Gun Mama; Defective Detective
(short); Mopey Dope (short). 1945 Pistol Packin' Nitwits (short),
Snoopy Service (short). 1949 The Beautiful Blonde from Bashful
Bend. 1953 Paris Model. 1956 The She-Creature.

BRENDLIN, ANDRE
Born: 1911, France. Died: Oct. 6, 1934, Marne, France
(drowned). Screen actor.

BRENEMAN, TOM
Born: 1902. Died: Apr. 28, 1948, Encino, Calif. Screen actor
and radio emcee of "Breakfast in Hollywood."

Appeared in: 1946 Breakfast in Hollywood.

BRENNAN, ROBERT
Born: 1892. Died: Apr. 17, 1940, Los Angeles, Calif. Screen
and stage actor. Entered films during silents.

BRENON, HERBERT
Born: Jan. 13, 1880, Dublin, Ireland. Died: June 21, 1958, Los
Angeles, Calif. Screen, stage, vaudeville actor, film director,
film producer, and screenwriter. Married to Helen Oberg (dec.)
with whom he appeared in vaudeville.

Appeared in: 1913 Ivanhoe. 1915 The Two Orphans.

BREON, EDMUND (E. McLaverty)
Born: Dec. 12, 1882, Hamilton, Scotland. Died: 1951. Screen
and stage actor.

Appeared in: 1930 The Dawn Patrol; On Approval. 1931 I Like
Your Nerve; Chances; The Love Habit; Uneasy Virtue; Born to
Love. 1932 Wedding Rehearsal; Leap Year. 1933 Waltz Time;
Three Men in a Boat. 1934 The Scarlet Pimpernel. 1934 No
Funny Business; The Private Life of Don Juan. 1935 The Divine
Spark; She Shall Have Music (U.S. 1937). 1936 Love in Exile.
1937 Strangers on Honeymoon; Keep Fit; Premiere. 1938 The
Return of the Scarlet Pimpernel; A Yank at Oxford; Dangerous
Medicine; Many Tanks, Mr. Atkins; French Leave; Almost a
Honeymoon; Bees and Honey; Crackerjax. 1939 Goodbye Mr.
Chips. 1940 The Outsider; One Night in Paris. 1941 It Happened
to One Man. 1944 The Murder in Thornton Square; Casanova
Brown; Man in Half Moon Street; Hour before the Dawn; Our
Hearts Were Young and Gay; Gaslight. 1945 The Corn is Green;
Woman in the Window. 1946 Devotion; Six Gun Man; Outlaw of
the Plains; Dressed to Kill; Sherlock Holmes and the Secret
Code. 1947 The Imperfect Lady. 1948 Forever Amber; Hills
of Home. 1949 Challenge to Lassie; Enchantment. 1951 Sons
of the Musketeers. 1952 At Sword's Point. Other British films:
Women Who Pay; Laughter in Court; Owd Bob.

BRERTON, TYRONE
Born: 1894. Died: Apr. 25, 1939, Hollywood, Calif. Screen
actor.

Appeared in: 1925 Secrets of the Night. 1928 The Canyon of
Adventure.

BRESSART, FELIX
Born: 1880, Eydtkuhnen, Germany. Died: Mar. 17, 1949, Los
Angeles, Calif.(leukemia). Screen and stage actor.

Appeared in: 1931 Die Drei von ver Tankstelle; Der Wahre
Jakob, Das Alte Lied; Nie Wieder Liebe (No More Love); Eine
Freundin so Goldig wie Du. 1932 Der Schrecken der Garnison;
Hirsekorn Greift Ein; Der Herr Buerovorsteher. 1933 Hol-
sapfel Weiss Alles; Drei Tage Mittelarrest; Der Sohn der
Weissen Berg. 1934 Der Glueckszylinder. 1935 Und Wer
Kuesst Mich?. 1939 Swanee River; Ninotchka; Three Smart
Girls Grow Up; Bridal Suite. 1940 Third Finger, Left Hand;
The Shop around the Corner; Edison the Man; Bitter Sweet; It
All Came True; Comrade X. 1941 Married Bachelor; Kathleen;
Mr. and Mrs. North; Blossoms in the Dust; Ziegfeld Girl; Es-
cape. 1942 Iceland; Crossroads; To Be or Not to Be. 1943
Song of Russia; Three Hearts for Julia; Above Suspicion. 1944
The Seventh Cross; Greenwich Village; Secrets in the Dark;
Blonde Fever. 1945 Dangerous Partners; Without Love. 1946
I've Always Loved You; Ding Dong Williams; The Thrill of
Brazil; Her Sister's Secret. 1947 Concerto. 1948 A Song Is
Born; Portrait of Jennie. 1949 Take One False Step; My
Friend Irma.

BREWER, MONTE
Born: 1934. Died: Apr. 21, 1942, Hollywood, Calif.(stomach ailment). Eight-year-old screen actor and radio singer.

Appeared in: 1941 Mr. Dynamite.

BRIAN, DONALD
Born: 1871, St. Johns, Newfoundland. Died: Dec. 22, 1948,
Greatneck, N.Y. Screen, stage actor, and singer. Married to
actress Virginia O'Brien.

Appeared in: 1915 The Voice in the Fog. 1916 The Smugglers.
1929 America's Foremost Musical Comedy Star (short). 1930
My Mistake (short). 1931 Squaring the Triangle (short).

BRIANT, GEORGE HAMILTON
Born: 1922. Died: Oct. 22, 1946, near San Antonio, Tex.(died
during filming of Blaze at Noon in air accident). Screen actor
and stunt flyer.

Appeared in: 1947 Blaze at Noon.

BRICE, BETTY
Born: 1896. Died: Feb. 15, 1935, Van Nuys, Calif. Screen and
stage actress.

Appeared in: 1921 The Spenders. 1922 The Green Temptation;
Heart's Haven. 1924 Beau Brummell.

BRICE, FANNY (Fanny Borach)
Born: Oct. 29, 1891, New York, N.Y. Died: May 29, 1951,
Beverly Hills, Calif.(cerebral hemorrhage). Screen, stage,
radio, vaudeville, and burlesque actress. Divorced from Nick
Arnstein and producer Billy Rose (dec. 1966).

Appeared in: 1928 My Man (film debut). 1929 The Man From
Blankleys'. 1930 Be Yourself. 1936 The Great Ziegfeld. 1938
Everybody Sing. 1944 Ziegfeld Follies.

BRICKER, BETTY
Born: 1890. Died: Feb. 15, 1954, Hollywood, Calif. Screen
actress. Entered films approx. 1914.

BRICKERT, CARLTON
Born: 1891. Died: Dec. 23, 1943, New York, N.Y. Screen, stage,
and radio actor.

Appeared in: 1921 The Rider of the King Log. 1923 You Are
Guilty.

BRIGGS, HARLAN
Born: 1880. Died: Jan. 26, 1952, Woodland Hills, Calif.(stroke).
Screen and stage actor.

Appeared in: 1936 Dodsworth; Mad Holiday; Happy-Go-Lucky;
Easy Money. 1937 A Family Affair; Easy Living; Live, Love and
Learn; Beg, Borrow or Steal; Riding on Air; Exclusive. 1938
That's My Story; Reckless Living; The Missing Guest; Dynamite
Delaney; One Wild Night; You and Me; Meet the Girls; Quick

Money; Trouble at Midnight; Having a Wonderful Time; A Man to Remember. 1939 Calling Dr. Kildare; Tell Me No Tales; Flight at Midnight; The Mysterious Miss X; The Wizard of Oz; Mr. Smith Goes to Washington; Maisie; Blondie Takes a Vacation. 1940 Abe Lincoln in Illinois; Young as You Feel; The Man Who Wouldn't Talk; The Bank Dick; My Little Chickadee; Charlie Chan's Murder Cruise. 1941 Among the Living; One Foot in Heaven. 1942 Lady Bodyguard; The Remarkable Andrew; The Vanishing Virginian. 1943 Tennessee Johnson. 1945 State Fair. 1946 A Stolen Life. 1947 Cynthia. 1948 A Double Life. 1949 Rusty Saves a Life. 1952 Carrie.

BRIGGS, MATT
Born: 1883. Died: June 10, 1962, Seattle, Wash. Screen and stage actor.

Appeared in: 1933 Advice to the Lovelorn. 1934 Hips, Hips, Hooray; Born to Be Bad. 1943 The Ox-Bow Incident; The Dancing Master; Meanest Man in the World. 1944 Roger Touhy, Gangster; Coney Island; Buffalo Bill. 1948 The Babe Ruth Story.

BRIGGS, OSCAR
Born: 1877, Wisc. Died: Jan. 17, 1928, Hollywood, Calif. (paralysis-stroke). Screen, stage, and vaudeville actor.

BRINDMOUR, GEORGE
Born: 1870. Died: July 21, 1941, Los Angeles, Calif. Screen and vaudeville actor. Married to Helen Hilliard with whom he appeared in vaudeville. He was known as the "Handcuff King."

BRINKMAN, ERNEST
Born: 1872. Died: Dec. 28, 1938, Los Angeles, Calif. Screen, stage, and vaudeville actor. Married to Mary Steele with whom he appeared in vaudeville in an act billed as "Brinkman and the Steele Sisters."

BRISCOE, LOTTIE
Born: 1881. Died: Mar. 19, 1950, New York, N.Y. Screen, stage, and radio actress.

Appeared in: 1914 The Beloved Adventurer (serial).

BRISSON, CARL (Carl Brisson Petersen)
Born: Dec. 24, 1893, Copenhagen, Denmark. Died: Sept. 24, 1958, Copenhagen, Denmark (jaundice). Screen, stage actor, and singer.

Appeared in: 1917 De Mysteske Fodspor. 1928 The Ring; Hjartats Triumf. 1929 The Manxman; The American Prisoner. 1930 Song of Soho; Knowing Men; Two Hearts in Waltz Time. 1933 Prince of Arcadia. 1934 Murder at the Vanities. 1935 All the King's Horses; Ship Cafe.

BRISTER, ROBERT S.
Born: 1889. Died: Mar. 2, 1945, Hollywood, Calif. Screen, stage, and radio actor.

Appeared in: 1937 Night Club Scandal. 1938 Dangerous to Know.

BRITTON, MILT (Milton Levy)
Born: 1894, Winston-Salem, N.C. Died: Apr. 29, 1948, New York, N.Y. (heart attack). Screen, stage, vaudeville actor, and bandleader. His band was known as "America's Craziest Orchestra"; "The Brown Derby Band" and "The Mad Musical Maniacs."

Appeared in: 1933 Moonlight and Pretzels. 1935 Sweet Music. 1937 A Vitaphone short. 1945 Riding High.

BROCKWELL, GLADYS
Born: 1894, Brooklyn, N.Y. Died: July 2, 1929, Hollywood, Calif. (peritonitis as result of auto accident injuries). Screen and stage actress.

Appeared in: 1916 Sins of the Parent. 1918 The Devil's Wheel. 1921 The Sage Hen. 1922 Paid Back; Double Stakes; Oliver Twist. 1923 The Drug Traffic; Penrod and Sam; The Darling of New York; His Last Race; The Hunchback of Notre Dame. 1924 So Big; The Foolish Virgin; Unmarried Wives. 1925 The Ancient Mariner; Chickie; Stella Maris; The Necessary Evil; The Reckless Sex; The Splendid Road. 1926 The Carnival Girl; Spangles; Her Sacrifice; The Skyrocket; Twinkletoes; The Last Frontier. 1927 Seventh Heaven; The Satin Woman; The Country Doctor; Long Pants; Man, Woman and Sin. 1928 The Law and the Man; My Home Town; Lights of New York; Home Towners; Woman Disputed; Hollywood Bound. 1929 From Headquarters; Hard-Boiled Rose; The Hottentot; The Argyle Case; The Drake Case.

BRODERICK, HELEN
Born: 1891, Philadelphia, Pa. Died: Sept. 25, 1959, Beverly Hills, Calif. Screen, stage, vaudeville, and radio actress. Mother of film actor Broderick Crawford.

Appeared in: 1924 High Speed. 1926 The Mystery Club. 1930 Nile Green (short); For Art's Sake (short). 1931 Fifty Million Frenchmen; The Spirits of 76th Street (short); Court Plastered (short). 1932 Cold Turkey (short). 1935 Top Hat; To Beat the Band. 1936 Love on a Bet; Murder on the Bridle Path; The Bride Walks Out; Swing Time; Smartest Girl in Town. 1937 We're on the Jury; Meet the Missus; The Life of the Party. 1938 She's Got Everything; Radio City Revels; The Rage of Paris; The Road to Reno; Service Deluxe. 1939 Stand Up and Fight; Honeymoon in Bali; Naughty but Nice. 1940 The Captain Is a Lady; No, No, Nanette. 1941 Virginia; Father Takes a Wife; Nice Girl. 1942 Are Husbands Necessary?. 1943 Stage Door Canteen. 1944 Her Primitive Man; Three Is a Family; Chip Off the Old Block. 1945 Love, Honor and Goodbye. 1946 Because of Him.

BRODIE, BUSTER
Born: 1886. Died: Apr. 9, 1948, Hollywood, Calif. (heart attack). Screen, stage, and vaudeville actor. Entered films approx. 1926.

Appeared in: 1927 All Aboard.

BRODY, ANN (Ann Brody Goldstein)
Born: Aug. 29, 1884, Poland. Died: July 16, 1944, New York, N.Y. Screen and stage actress. Entered films with Vitagraph Co. in 1912.

Appeared in: 1921 Shams of Society. 1923 Lost in a Big City. 1924 A Sainted Devil. 1925 The Manicure Girl; Red Love. 1926 Too Much Money. 1927 Alias the Lone Wolf; Clancy's Kosher Wedding; Jake the Plumber; Heroes in Blue. 1928 Turn Back the Hours; My Man. 1929 Times Square; So This Is College; The Case of Lena Smith; The Wolf Song; Alpine Tale; The Man from Blankley's. 1930 Fall Guy; A Royal Romance; Playing Around. 1931 Oh! Oh! Cleopatra (short); Drums of Jeopardy. 1932 The Drifter; Lawyer Man; Heart of New York. 1933 High Gear; Bloody Money. 1934 Money Means Nothing.

BROMBERG, J. EDWARD
Born: Dec. 25, 1903, Temesvar, Hungary. Died: Dec. 6, 1951, London, England (natural causes). Screen and stage actor.

Appeared in: 1936 Under Two Flags; Reunion; Stowaway; Sins of Man; The Crime of Dr. Forbes; Girls' Dormitory; Star for a Night; Ladies in Love. 1937 Fair Warning; That I May Live; Seventh Heaven; Charlie Chan on Broadway; Second Honeymoon. 1938 Mr. Moto Takes a Chance; The Baroness and the Butler; One Wild Night; Four Men and a Prayer; Sally, Irene and Mary; Rebecca of Sunnybrook Farm; I'll Give a Million; Suez. 1939 Wife, Husband and Friend; Hollywood Cavalcade; Jesse James; The Mark of Zorro. 1941 Hurricane Smith; Midnight Angel; Dance Hall. 1942 Life Begins at 8:30; Invisible Agent; Pacific Blackout; Reunion in France; Tennessee Johnson; The Devil Pays Off; Halfway to Shanghai. 1943 Sons of Dracula; Lady of Burlesque; Phantom of the Opera. 1944 Chip Off the Old Block; A Voice in the Wind. 1945 Salome, Where She Danced; The Missing Corpse; Easy to Look At; Pillow of Death. 1946 Tangier; The Walls Came Tumbling Down; Cloak and Dagger. 1947 Queen of the Amazon. 1948 Arch of Triumph; A Song is Born. 1949 I Shot Jesse James. 1950 Guilty Bystander.

BRONSON, BETTY
Born: Nov. 17, 1906, Trenton, N.J. Died: Oct. 19, 1971, Pasadena, Calif. Screen, stage, and television actress.

Appeared in: 1922 Anna Ascends. 1923 Java Head. 1925 Are Parents People?; Not So Long Ago; The Golden Princess; Peter Pan. 1926 The Cat's Pajamas; Everybody's Acting; A Kiss for Cinderella; Paradise; Ben Hur. 1927 Brass Knuckles; Paradise for Two; Open Range; Ritzy. 1928 The Singing Fool; The Companionate Marriage. 1929 Bellamy Trial; Sonny Boy; One Stolen Night. 1930 The Medicine Man; A Modern Sappho; The Locked Door. 1931 Lover Come Back; Ben Hur (sound of 1926 film version). 1932 The Midnight Patrol. 1937 The Yodelin' Kid from Pine Ridge. 1961 Pocketful of Miracles. 1964 The Naked Kiss. 1968 Blackbeard's Ghost. 1971 Evel Knievel.

BROOKE, CLAUDE
Born: 1853, Died: Dec. 14, 1933, Leonia, N.J. Screen and stage actress.

Appeared in: 1922 Silver Wings. 1923 Does It Pay?. 1924 Pied Piper Malone; Classmates. 1926 Great Gatsby; Sorrows of Satan; God Save Me Twenty Cents.

BROOKE, CLIFFORD
Born: 1872, England. Died: Dec. 28, 1951, Santa Monica, Calif. (injuries sustained after struck by auto). Screen and stage actor. Entered films approx. 1939.

Appeared in: 1941 A Woman's Face. 1944 Wilson. 1945 Hangover Square; Molly and Me; The Suspect. 1946 Three Strangers; Black Beauty. 1948 The Woman in White. 1951 The First Legion.

BROOKE, MRS. MYRA
Born: 1865. Died: Feb. 9, 1944, Amityville, N.Y. Screen and stage actress.

BROOKE, TYLER (Victor Huge de Biere)
Born: 1891, New York, N.Y. Died: Mar. 2, 1943, North Hollywood, Calif.(suicide-carbon monoxide poisoning). Screen and stage actor.

Appeared in: 1927 Rich, But Honest; Stage Madness; The Cradle Snatchers. 1928 Fazil; None But the Brave. 1929 Dynamite; eight Van Bibber Fox comedies. 1930 Playboy of Paris; Madame Satan; The Furies; The Divorcee; Monte Carlo; Lilies of the Field. 1931 The Magnificent Lie; Oh! Oh! Cleopatra (short); A Dangerous Affair. 1932 Love Me Tonight. 1933 Hallelujah, I'm a Bum; Child of Manhattan; Morning Glory. 1934 Blind Date; Belle of the Nineties; Imitation of Life. 1935 Call of the Wild; Reckless; Times Square Lady; Here Comes the Band. 1936 The Poor Little Rich Girl; To Mary—With Love; Two in a Crowd. 1937 This Is My Affair; You Can't Have Everything. 1938 Bluebeard's Eighth Wife; In Old Chicago; Alexander's Ragtime Band. 1940 Tin Pan Alley; Little Old New York; One Night in the Tropics. 1942 Lucky Legs; I Married an Angel; The McGuerins from Brooklyn.

BROOK-JONES, ELWYN
Born: Dec. 11, 1911, Borneo. Died: Sept. 4, 1962, Reading, England. Screen, stage, and television actor.

Appeared in: 1940 Dangerous Moonlight (aka Suicide Squadron, U.S. 1942). 1942 Tomorrow We Live. 1946 Odd Man Out. 1948 The Three Weird Sisters; It's Hard to be Good. 1949 Queen of Spades. 1950 Good Time Girl; Dear Mr. Prohack; Wonder Kid. 1951 Life in Her Hands; Lucky Nick Cain (aka I'll Get You for This); Judgement Deferred. 1954 Beau Brummel. 1955 Assignment—Redhead. 1959 Room 43 (aka Passport to Shame). 1961 The Pure Hell of St. Trinians. Other British films: Pimpernel Smith; Night Invader; Nursing Service.

BROOKS, ALAN (Irving Hayward)
Born: 1888. Died: Sept. 1936, Saranac, N.Y. Screen and vaudeville actor, stage and vaudeville producer.

Appeared in: 1926 Red Dice; Young April; Pals in Paradise. 1927 King of Kings; Home Struck; Ladies Beware; Shanghaied; South Sea Love. 1929 Mr. Intruder (short); The Hole in the Wall. 1932-33 in Paramount shorts. 1937 The League of Frightened Men.

BROOKS, HANK
Died: Dec. 3, 1925, Los Angeles, Calif. Screen actor. Entered films with Sennett in 1915.

BROOKS, JESS LEE
Born: 1894. Died: Dec. 13, 1944, Hollywood, Calif.(heart attack). Negro screen and stage actor.

Appeared in: 1941 Sullivan's Travels. 1942 Drums of the Congo; Jungle Siren. 1945 Wilson; The Lost Weekend.

BROOKS, PAULINE
Born: 1913. Died: June 7, 1967, Glendale, Calif.(cancer). Screen and stage actress.

Appeared in: 1933 Beauty for Sale. 1934 Student Tour. 1935 Age of Indiscretion; Make a Million; Alibi Ike.

BROOKS, RANDY
Born: 1918. Died: Mar. 21, 1967, Springvale, Me.(result of smoke inhalation). Band leader, trumpeter, and screen actor. Not to be confused with screen actor with same name. In 1945 Randy Brooks & Orchestra appeared in a Columbia short.

BROPHY, EDWARD
Born: Feb. 27, 1895, New York, N.Y. Died: May 30, 1960, Los Angeles, Calif. Screen actor. Entered films in 1919.

Appeared in: 1920 Yes or No (film debut). 1927 West Point. 1929 The Cameraman. 1930 Our Blushing Brides; Free and Easy; Those Three French Girls; Paid; Doughboys; Remote Control. 1931 Parlor, Bedroom and Bath; A Dangerous Affair; A Free Soul; The Champ. 1932 Speak Easily; Freaks; Flesh; The Big Shot. 1933 What, No Beer?; Broadway to Hollywood. 1934 Hide-Out; Death on the Diamond; Evelyn Prentice; I'll Fix It; The Thin Man; Paris Interlude. 1935 I Live My Life; A $1,000 a Minute; Naughty Marietta; The Whole Town's Talking; Shadow of Doubt; Mad Love; China Seas; People Will Talk; She Gets Her Man; Remember Last Night?; Show Them No Mercy. 1936 Mr. Cinderella; The Soldier and the Lady; Strike Me Pink; Woman Trap; The Case against Mrs. Ames; Spendthrift; Wedding Present; All American Chump; Kelly the Second; Here Comes Trouble; Career Woman; Great Guy. 1937 Hideaway Girl; Michael Strogoff; The Great Gambini; Blossoms on Broadway; Varsity Show; Jim Hanvey—Detective; The Hit Parade; Oh, Doctor!; The Last Gangster; The Girl Said No; The River of Missing Men; Trapped by G-Men. 1938 A Slight Case of Murder; Romance on the Run; Come On, Leathernecks!; Gambling Ship; Hold That Kiss; Vacation from Love; Passport Husband; Pardon Our Nerve; Golddiggers in Paris. 1939 You Can't Cheat an Honest Man; For Love or Money; Society Lawyer; The Kid from Kokomo; Golden Boy; The Amazing Mr. Williams; Kid Nightingale. 1940 The Big Guy; Dance, Girl, Dance, Sandy Gets Her Man, Calling Philo Vance; Alias the Deacon; Golden Gloves; The Great Profile. 1941 Sleepers West; A Dangerous Game; The Invisible Woman; Dumbo (voice); Thieves Fall Out; Nine Lives Are Not Enough; Steel against the Sky; The Bride Came C.O.D.; Buy Me That Town; The Gay Falcon. 1942 Broadway; Lady Bodyguard; Air Force; Madame Spy; One Exciting Night; Destroyer; Larceny, Inc.; All Through the Night. 1944 It Happened Tomorrow; A Night of Adventure; The Thin Man Goes Home; Cover Girl. 1945 I'll Remember April; Wonder Man; See My Lawyer; The Falcon in San Francisco; Penthouse Rhythm. 1946 Swing Parade of 1946; Girl on the Spot; Falcon's Adventure; Sweetheart of Sigma Chi. 1947 It Happened on Fifth Avenue. 1949 Arson, Inc. 1951 Pier 23; Danger Zone; Roaring City. 1956 Bundle of Joy. 1958 The Last Hurrah.

BROSIG, EGON
Born: 1890, Germany. Died: May 23, 1961, Berlin, Germany. Screen, stage, and radio actor. Appeared in the following German films: The Old and the Young King; The Strange Adventures of Mr. Fridolin; The Cold Heart; The Subject.

BROUGH, MARY
Born: Apr. 16, 1863, London, England. Died: Sept. 30, 1934, London, England(heart trouble). Screen and stage actress.

Appeared in: 1930 On Approval; Tons of Money; Plunder; One Embarrassing Night; Rookery Nook. 1931 A Night Like This. 1932 Thark, Turkey Time. Other British films prior to 1933: A Sister to Assist 'Er; His Grace Gives Notice; Mr. Pickwick; Lily of the Valley. 1933 Cuckoo in the Nest. 1934 A Cup of Kindness.

BROWER, OTTO
Born: Dec. 2, 1895, Grand Rapids, Mich. Died: Jan. 25, 1946, Hollywood, Calif.(heart failure). Screen actor and film director.

Appeared in: 1922 On the High Seas. 1923 All the Brothers Were Valiant.

BROWN, BLY
Born: 1898. Died: Dec. 19, 1950, Los Angeles, Calif. Screen and stage actress.

BROWN, CHARLES D.
Born: July 1, 1887, Council Bluffs, Iowa. Died: Nov. 25, 1948, Hollywood, Calif.(heart ailment). Screen and stage actor.

Appeared in: 1921 The Man of Stone; The Way of a Maid. 1929 The Dance of Life; Dangerous Curves. 1931 The Road to Reno; Twenty-four Hours; Murder by the Clock; Touchdown. 1933 The Woman I Stole. 1934 It Happened One Night. 1936 Golddiggers of 1937. 1937 Thoroughbreds Don't Cry. 1938 Island in the Sky; Mr. Moto's Gamble; Speed to Burn; Inside Story; Up the River; Exposed; Algiers; Duke of West Point; Shopworn Angel; The Crowd Roars; Barefoot Boy; Five of a Kind. 1939 Tell No Tells; Mr. Moto in Danger Island; Charlie Chan in Reno; Hotel for Women; Kid Nightingale; Smashing the Money Ring; Ice Follies of 1939; Little Accident; Disbarred. 1940 Brother Orchid; Pier 13, The Santa Fe Trail; The Grapes of Wrath; He Married His Wife; Sailor's Lady. 1941 Tall, Dark and Handsome; Reaching for the Sun; International Lady. 1942 Fingers at the Window; Roxie Hart; Sweater Girl. 1943 A Lady Takes a Chance. 1944 Up in Arms; The Fighting Seabees; The Contender; Jam Session; Secret Command. 1945 Having a Wonderful

Crime; Don Juan Quilligan; Apology for Murder; Sunbonnet Sue. 1946 Wake Up and Dream; The Killers; The Last Crooked Mile; The Big Sleep; Night Editor; The Strange Loves of Martha Ivers. 1947 Smash-Up; The Story of a Woman; Merton of the Movies; The Senator Was Indiscreet. 1948 A Miracle Can Happen; In This Corner. 1949 Follow Me Quietly. 1951 Sealed Cargo.

BROWN, MELVILLE
Born: 1888, Portland, Oreg. Died: Jan. 31, 1938, Hollywood, Calif.(heart attack). Screen, stage, vaudeville actor, film, stage director, and screenwriter. Entered films in 1916.

BROWN, RAYMOND (Ray A. Brown)
Born: Aug. 16, 1880, Champaign, Ill. Died: July 30, 1939, Los Angeles, Calif. Screen and stage actor. Entered films in 1929.

Appeared in: 1933 My Woman. 1934 Jealousy; I'll Fix It; Blind Date; Whom the Gods Destroy; White Lies; Successful Failure; Mystery Liner. 1935 Million Dollar Baby; Baby Face Harrington; The Flame Within; Dr. Socrates; Moonlight on the Prairie. 1936 The Story of Louis Pasteur; Laughing Irish Eyes; Comin' Round the Mountain; Down the Stretch; The Magnificent Brute; Career Woman. 1937 The Holy Terror; Two Wise Maids; We Have Our Moments; Parole Rackets; Back in Circulation. 1939 They Made Me a Criminal; King of the Underworld; The Family Next Door.

BROWN, RONALD C.
Born: 1911. Died: Oct. 27, 1962, Hollywood, Calif. Screen actor and dancer. Entered films approx. 1937.

BROWN, RUSS
Born: May 30, 1892, Philadelphia, Pa. Died: Oct. 19, 1964, Englewood, N.J. Screen, stage, and vaudeville actor. Divorced from screen actress Gertrude Whitaker. Appeared in vaudeville in an act with Bert Wheeler and later with Gertrude Whitaker in an act billed as "Brown & Whitaker." 1928 "Brown & Whitaker" appeared in the following shorts: A Laugh or Two; In the Park. Brown later appeared in: 1933 Moulin Rouge; My Woman. 1934 The Love Captive; Let's Talk It Over. 1958 South Pacific; Damn Yankees. 1959 Anatomy of a Murder; It Happened to Jane. 1962 Advise and Consent. 1963 The Cardinal.

BROWN, WALLY
Born: Oct. 9, 1904, Malden, Mass. Died: Nov. 13, 1961, Los Angeles, Calif. Screen, vaudeville, radio, and television actor. Was part of comedy team of "Brown and Carney" in films.

Appeared in: 1943 Petticoat Larceny; Mexican Spitfire's Blessed Event; The Seventh Victim; Gangway for Tomorrow; Around the World. 1944 The Girl in the Case. 1946 From This Day Forward; Notorious; Vacation in Reno. 1948 Family Honeymoon. 1949 Come to the Stable. 1951 As Young as You Feel. 1954 The High and the Mighty. 1956 The Wild Dakotas. 1957 Untamed Youth; The Joker is Wild. 1958 The Wink of an Eye; The Left-Handed Gun. 1959 Westbound; Holiday for Lovers. 1961 The Absent Minded Professor. Brown and Carney films: 1943 The Adventures of a Rookie (their film debut together) and Rookies in Burma. 1944 Girl Rush; Seven Days Ashore; Step Lively. 1945 Radio Stars on Parade; Zombies on Broadway. 1946 Genius at Work.

BROWNE, EARLE
Born: 1872. Died: Nov. 28, 1944, Hollywood, Calif. Screen and stage actor.

Appeared in: 1922 Sherlock Holmes. 1926 Sparrows. 1927 Love of Sunya. 1929 The Iron Mask; The Locked Door; Taming of the Shrew. 1930 DuBarry, Woman of Passion. 1932 Mr. Robinson Crusoe.

BROWNE, IRENE
Born: 1893, London, England. Died: July 24, 1965, London, England(cancer). Screen and stage actress.

Appeared in: 1929 The Letter. 1933 Cavalcade; Berkeley Square; My Lips Betray; Peg O'My Heart; Christopher Strong. 1936 The Amateur Gentleman. 1938 Pygmalion. 1941 The Prime Minister. 1948 Meet Me at Dawn; The Red Shoes. 1949 Quartet. 1950 Madeleine. 1951 I'll Never Forget You (aka Man of Two Worlds and The House on the Square). 1957 All at Sea; Barnacle Bill. 1958 Rooney. 1962 Immoral Charge (aka Serious Charge and A Touch of Hell). 1963 The Wrong Arm of the Law.

BROWNING, WILLIAM E.
Died: Dec. 21, 1930, Middle Village, N.Y. Screen, stage, and radio actor.

Appeared in: 1929 Applause; plus numerous shorts.

BRUCE, BEVERLY
Died: July, 1925, Bryn Mawr, Calif. Screen, stage, and vaudeville actress.

Appeared in: 1920 Empty Arms.

BRUCE, NIGEL
Born: Feb. 4, 1895, Ensenada, Mexico. Died: Oct. 8, 1953, Santa Monica, Calif.(heart attack). Screen, stage, and radio actor. Married to actress Violet Campbell (dec. 1970). Best known for his long film and radio portrayal as Dr. Watson in Sherlock Holmes series.

Appeared in: 1929 Red Aces. 1931 The Squeaker; The Calendar; Escape; Birds of Prey. 1932 Lord Camber's Ladies; The Midshipmaid. 1934 Channel Crossing; I Was a Spy; Stand Up and Cheer; Coming Out Party; Murder in Trinidad; The Lady is Willing; Springtime for Henry; Treasure Island. 1935 Jalna; She; The Man Who Broke the Bank at Monte Carlo; The Scarlet Pimpernel; Becky Sharp. 1936 Follow Your Heart; Make Way for a Lady; The Man I Marry; The Trail of the Lonesome Pine; The Charge of the Light Brigade; The White Angel; Under Two Flags. 1937 Thunder in the City; The Last of Mrs. Cheyney. 1938 The Baroness and the Butler; Kidnapped; Suez. 1939 Adventures of Sherlock Holmes; Hound of the Baskervilles; The Rains Came. 1940 Adventures in Diamonds; Lillian Russell; A Dispatch from Reuters; Hudson's Bay; The Blue Bird; Rebecca; Susan and God. 1941 Play Girl; Free and Easy; The Chocolate Soldier; This Woman is Mine; Suspicion. 1942 Roxie Hart; Eagle Squadron; Sherlock Holmes and the Voice of Terror; Journey for Margaret; Sherlock Holmes and the Secret Weapon; This Above All. 1943 Sherlock Holmes in Washington; Forever and a Day; Sherlock Holmes Faces Death; Crazy House; Lassie, Come Home. 1944 The Scarlet Claw; The Pearl of Death; Follow the Boys; Spider Woman; Gypsy Wildcat; Frenchman's Creek. 1945 Son of Lassie; The House of Fear; The Corn is Green; Pursuit to Algiers; The Woman in Green. 1946 Terror by Night; Dressed to Kill; Two Mrs. Carrolls. 1947 Exile. 1948 Julia Misbehaves. 1950 Vendetta. 1951 Hong Kong; B'wana Devil; Limelight. 1954 World for Ransom.

BRUCE, PAUL
Died: May 2, 1971, Hollywood, Calif.(heart attack). Screen, stage, and television actor.

Appeared in: 1967 Born Losers.

BRUCE, TONIE EDGAR. See Edgar-Bruce, Toni

BRUNDAGE, BERTHA
Born: 1860. Died: May 7, 1939, Long Beach, Calif. Screen actress.

BRUNETTE, FRITZI
Born: 1890. Died: Sept. 28, 1943, Hollywood, Calif. Screen and stage actress.

Appeared in: 1919 The Woman Thou Gavest Me. 1920 The Devil to Pay. 1921 The Butterfly Girl; Sure Fire; The Man from Lost River; Tiger True; Discontented Wives; A Wife's Awakening. 1922 Give Me My Son; Bells of San Juan; The Boss of Camp 4; While Satan Sleeps; The Crusader; The Other Side. 1923 The Footlight Ranger; Cause for Divorce. 1925 Camille of the Barbary Coast; The Pace that Thrills. 1928 Driftwood.

BRYAN, ARTHUR Q.
Born: 1899. Died: Nov. 30, 1959, Hollywood, Calif. Screen, television, and radio actor.

Appeared in: 1932 The Big Shop; Fast Life; The Mummy. 1933 20,000 Years in Sing Sing; Tonight is Ours; Gabriel over the White House; The Silk Empress; Mayor of Hell; Private Detective 62; College Coach. 1934 House of Rothschild; Two Alone; Fog over Frisco; The Notorious Sophie Lang; The Man with Two Faces; That's Gratitude!; The President Vanishes; Marie Gallante. 1935 Secret Brides; The Casino Murder Case; Shadow of a Doubt; The Whole Town's Talking; Oil for the Lamps of China; Murder in the Fleet. 1936 Prisoner of Shark Island. 1940 Millionaire Playboy. 1941 Devil Bat. 1943 Swing Out the Blues. 1944 I'm from Arkansas. 1946 Dark Horse. 1949 Samson and Delilah. 1954 Broken Lance. 1955 Hell's Outpost. 1956 The Lieutenant Wore Skirts.

BRYAN, JACKSON "JACK" LEE
Born: 1909. Died: Sept. 14, 1964, Hollywood, Calif.(following surgery). Screen, stage, and television actor.

BRYANT, CHARLES
Born: 1879, England. Died: Aug. 7, 1948, Mt. Kisco, N.Y.
Screen and stage actor, film director, and stage producer.
Divorced from screen actress Alla Nazimova (dec. 1945).

Appeared in: 1918 Eye for Eye; Revelation. 1919 The Brat;
Out of the Fog; The Red Lantern. 1920 Stronger than Death;
The Heart of a Child.

BRYANT, NANA
Born: 1888, Cincinnati, Ohio. Died: Dec. 24, 1955, Hollywood,
Calif. Screen, stage, and television actress.

Appeared in: 1935 Guard that Girl (film debut); Crime and
Punishment; Unknown Woman; One Way Ticket; A Feather in
Her Hat. 1936 Lady of Secrets; The Blackmailer; The Lone
Wolf Returns; You May Be Next; The King Steps Out; The Man
Who Lived Twice; Theodora Goes Wild; Pennies from Heaven;
Meet Nero Wolf; Panic on the Air. 1937 Let's Get Married;
The League of Frightened Men; The Devil is Driving; Counsel
for Crime. 1938 Man Proof; Midnight Intruder; Mad about
Music; The Adventures of Tom Sawyer; Sinners in Paradise;
Swing, Swing, Swing; Give Me a Sailor; Always in Trouble; Out
West with the Hardys; Peck's Bad Boy with the Circus. 1939
Espionage Agent; Streets of Missing Men; Parents on Trial; Our
Neighbor, The Carters. 1940 Brother Rat and the Baby; If I Had
My Way; A Little Bit of Heaven; Father is a Prince. 1941 Thieves
Fall Out; Nice Girl?; One Foot in Heaven; Public Enemies; The
Corsican Brothers. 1942 Youth on Parade; Thunder Birds; Calling
Dr. Gillespie; Get Hep to Love; The Reluctant Dragon (voice);
Madam Spy. 1943 The West Side Kid; Hangmen Also Die; Get
Going; The Song of Bernadette; Princess O'Rourke. 1944 The
Adventures of Mark Twain; Take It or Leave It; Bathing Beauty;
Jungle Woman; Marriage Is A Private Affair. 1945 Black Mar-
ket Babies; Weekend at the Waldorf; Brewster's Millions. 1946
The Virginian; The Runaround. 1947 The Perfect Marriage;
Millie's Daughter; Big Town; The Big Fix; Possessed; Her
Husband's Affair; The Hal Roach Comedy Carnival; The Unsus-
pected; The Fabulous Joe. 1948 Stage Struck; The Eyes of Texas;
Lady at Midnight; Dangerous Years; Return of October; Inner
Sanctum. 1949 Hideout; State Department File 649; Ladies of
the Chorus; The Lady Gambles. 1950 The Blonde Bandit; Modern
Marriage; Harvey. 1951 Follow the Sun; Bright Victory; Only the
Valiant. 1954 About Mrs. Leslie; The Outcast; Geraldine. 1955
The Private War of Major Benson.

BUCHANAN, JACK
Born: Apr. 2, 1891, Glasgow, Scotland. Died: Oct. 20, 1957, London, England (spinal arthritis). Screen, stage and television actor,
screenwriter, stage director, and film producer and director.

Appeared in: 1925 Bulldog Drummond's Third Round; Happy Land-
ing. 1927 Toni. 1928 Confetti. 1929 Paris; The Show of Shows;
Bulldog Drummond. 1930 The Glee Quartette (short); Monte
Carlo. 1931 Good Night Vienna; A Man of Mayfair. 1932 Yes,
Mr. Brown; Magic Night. 1933 Brewster's Millions; That's a
Good Girl. 1934 That Girl. 1935 Come Out of the Pantry.
1936 Sons O'Guns; When Knights Were Bold. 1937 Smash and
Grab; This'll Make You Whistle. 1938 The Sky's the Limit.
1939 The Gang's All Here; The Middle Watch; Alias the Bulldog.
1940 Larceny Street. 1941 Break the News; Penny Serenade.
1942 When Knights Were Bold. 1953 The Band Wagon. 1955
Josephine and Men; Les Carnets du Major Thompson. 1957
As Long as They're Happy; The French Are a Funny Race.

BUCK, ELIZABETH
Born: 1912. Died: Mar. 31, 1934, Van Nuys, Calif.(hit by auto).
Screen dancer.

BUCK, FORD (Ford Lee Washington)
Died: Jan. 31, 1955, New York, N.Y. Negro screen, stage, and
radio comedian.

BUCK, FRANK
Born: Mar. 17, 1888, Gainesville, Tex. Died: March 25, 1950,
Houston, Tex.(lung ailment). Screen, circus actor, film director,
and producer.
Appeared in: 1932 Bring 'Em Back Alive. 1934 Wild Cargo.
1935 Fang and Claw. 1937 Jungle Menace (serial). 1943 Jacare.
1949 Africa Screams.

BUCK, INEZ
Born: 1890, Oetrichs, S.D. Died: Sept. 6, 1957, Oakland, Calif.
Screen and stage actress. Entered films in silents with Lubin
Studios.

BUCKLEY, FLOYD
Born: 1874. Died: Nov. 14, 1956, New York, N.Y.(heart attack).
Screen, stage, vaudeville and radio actor, film producer, direc-
tor, and stuntman. Appeared in the following serials: 1914 Ex-
ploits of Elaine. 1916 Pearl of the Army. 1917 The Fatal Ring;
Patria; The Seven Pearls. 1918 The House of Hate. 1919 The
Fatal Fortune; The Master Mystery.

BUCKLEY, JOSEPH
Born: 1875. Died: Dec. 2, 1930, Van Nuys, Calif. Screen
actor.

BUCQUET, HAROLD S.
Born: 1891, England. Died: Feb. 13, 1946, Hollywood, Calif.
Screen actor and film director. Entered films as an extra.

BULGAKOV, LEO
Born: Mar. 22, 1889, Moscow, Russia. Died: July 20, 1948,
Binghamton, N.Y. Screen, stage actor, stage director, film
producer, and director.

Appeared in: 1943 This Land Is Mine; For Whom the Bell Tolls.
1944 Song of Russia; And Now Tomorrow.

BUMP, EDMOND
Born: 1877. Died: Nov. 6, 1938, Hollywood, Calif. Screen
and stage actor.

BUMPAS, H.W. "BOB"
Born: 1911. Died: Dec. 9, 1959, Gulf of Mexico (airline crash).
Screen, stage, television actor, screenwriter, and radio writer.

Appeared in: 1951 The Big Carnival.

BUNCE. ALAN
Born: 1903, Westfield, N.J. Died: Apr. 27, 1965, New York,
N.Y. Screen, stage, radio, and television actor.

Appeared in: 1930 She's My Weakness. 1959 The Last Mile. 1960
Sunrise at Campobello. 1961 Homicidal.

BUNKER, RALPH
Born: 1889, Boston, Mass. Died: Apr. 28, 1966, New York, N.Y.
(stroke). Screen and stage actor.

Appeared in: 1921 Scrambled Wives. 1922 That Woman. 1924
Another Scandal. 1936 The Ghost Goes West. 1947 The Hucksters.

BUNNY, GEORGE
Born: 1870, New York, N.Y. Died: Apr. 16, 1952, Hollywood,
Calif.(heart attack). Screen and stage actor. Brother of screen
actor John Bunny (dec. 1915).

Appeared in: 1921 "If Only" Jim; Danger Ahead. 1922 The Super
Sex. 1925 The Dark Angel; The Lost World; Enticement; Lights
of Old Broadway. 1926 Thrilling Youth. 1927 Tender Hour; Laddie Be Good. 1928 Breed of the Sunsets; Heroes in Blue; The
Love Mart. 1929 The Man and the Moment; The Locked Door.

BUNSTON, HERBERT
Born: 1874. Died: Feb. 27, 1935, Los Angeles, Calif.(heart
attack). Screen and stage actor.

Appeared in: 1929 The Last of Mrs. Cheyney. 1930 The Lady
of Scandal. 1931 Always Good-Bye; Once a Lady.
1932 Charlie Chan's Chance; File No. 113. 1933 Trick for
Trick. 1934 Long Lost Father; Doctor Monica; The Richest
Girl in the World; The Little Minister. 1935 A Shot in the
Dark; Cardinal Richelieu; After Office Hours; Clive of India.

BURANI, MICHELETTE
Born: 1882, Paris, France. Died: Oct. 27, 1957, Eastchester,
N.Y. Screen, stage, opera, radio, and television actress.

Appeared in: 1926 Aloma of the South Seas. 1935 Enter Madame;
The Gilded Lily. 1936 Give Us This Night. 1938 Fools for Scandal; Everybody Sing.

BURBANK, GOLDIE
Born: 1880. Died: Mar. 1, 1954, Toledo, Ohio. Screen and
vaudeville actress. Appeared in vaudeville as part of "Melville
Sisters" and later as part of "Sutherland Sisters" acts. Was in
films from 1910 to 1913.

BURCH, BETTY EVANS

Born: 1888. Died: May 30, 1956, Pasadena, Calif. Screen actress.

BURCH, JOHN

Born: Aug. 17, 1896, Chicago, Ill. Died: July 29, 1969, Honolulu, H.I. Screen actor, film and television director.

Appeared in: 1925 White Fang. 1947 Great Expectations.

BURGESS, HELEN

Born: 1918. Died: Apr. 7, 1937, Beverly Hills, Calif.(lobar pneumonia). Screen and stage actress.

Appeared in: 1936 The Plainsman. 1937 A Doctor's Diary; King of Gamblers; A Night of Mystery.

BURIAN, VLASTA

Born: 1891. Died: Feb. 5, 1962, Prague, Czechoslovakia. Screen and stage actor. Barred from appearing in public for ten years after W.W. II for allegedly collaborating with Nazis.

Appeared in: 1931 Versuchen Sie Meine Schwester. 1932 Der Falsche Feldmarschall. 1934 Der Adjutant Seiner Hoheit. 1937 The Inspector General.

BURKE, BILLIE (Mary William Ethelberg Appleton Burke)

Born: Aug. 7, 1885, Washington, D.C. Died: May 14, 1970, Los Angeles, Calif. Screen and stage actress. Married to stage producer Flo Ziegfeld (dec. 1932).

Appeared in: 1915 Peggy. 1916 Gloria's Romance (serial). 1917 The Land of Promise. 1918 Eve's Daughter; Let's Get a Divorce; In Pursuit of Polly; The Make-Believe Wife. 1919 Good Gracious, Annabelle; The Misleading Widow; Sadie Love. 1921 The Education of Elizabeth; Frisky Mrs. Johnson. 1930 Ranch House Blues. 1932 A Bill of Divorcement. 1933 Dinner at Eight; Only Yesterday; Christopher Strong. 1934 Forsaking All Others; Finishing School; We're Rich Again; Where Sinners Meet. 1935 Becky Sharp; Only Eight Hours; Society Doctor; After Office Hours; Doubting Thomas; She Couldn't Take It; Splendor; A Feather in Her Hat. 1936 Craig's Wife; My American Wife; Piccadilly Jim; The Great Ziegfeld. 1937 Topper; Navy Blue and Gold; The Bride Wore Red; Parnell. 1938 Merrily We Live; Everybody Sing; The Young in Heart. 1939 The Wizard of Oz; Topper Takes a Trip; Bridal Suite; Remember?; Eternally Yours; Zenobia. 1940 The Captain Is a Lady; The Ghost Comes Home; And One Was Beautiful; Irene; Dulcy; Hullabaloo. 1941 Topper Returns; The Man Who Came to Dinner; Wild Man of Borneo; One Night in Lisbon. 1942 In This Our Life; They All Kissed the Bride; Girl Trouble; What's Cooking?. 1943 Hi Diddle Diddle; So's Your Uncle; Gildersleeve on Broadway; You're a Lucky Fellow, Mr. Smith. 1944 Laramie Trail. 1945 Swing Out, Sister; The Cheaters. 1946 Breakfast in Hollywood; The Bachelor Daughter. 1949 The Barkleys of Broadway. 1950 Father of the Bride; Three Husbands; The Boy from Indiana; And Baby Makes Three. 1951 Father's Little Dividend; Darling, How Could You. 1953 Small Town Girl. 1959 The Young Philadelphians. 1960 Sgt. Rutledge; Pepe.

BURKE, JAMES

Born: New York, N.Y. Died: May 28, 1968, Los Angeles, Calif. Married to screen actress Elinor Durkin (dec. year unknown). and they appeared in vaudeville together in an act billed as "Burke and Durkin," and they made a short in 1929 A Tete-a-Tete in Songs.

He appeared in: 1932 Hollywood Handicap. 1933 Torch Singer; A Lady's Profession; Girl in 419; College Humor; To the Last Man; Lady Killer. 1934 Little Miss Marker; Wharf Angel; City Limits; Treasure Island; Scarlet Empress; Love Time; The Lemon Drop Kid; Lady by Choice; Six of a Kind; It's a Gift; It Happened One Night. 1935 The Case of the Missing Man; Ruggles of Red Gap; Mystery Man; Mississippi; Dinky; Call of the Wild; Make a Million; Here Comes Cookie; Affairs of Susan; Coronado; Frisco Waterfront; Man on the Flying Trapeze; Welcome Home; Broadway Gondolier; So Red the Rose. 1936 Rhythm on the Range; 36 Hours to Kill; Can This Be Dixie; Song and Dance Man; Dancing Feet; The Leathernecks Have Landed; Klondike Annie; Forgotten Faces; Old Dutch; The Great Guy. 1937 Champagne Waltz; Laughing at Trouble; Dead End; High, Wide and Handsome; The Perfect Specimen; Life Begins with Love. 1938 The Mad Miss Manton; Dawn Patrol; The Joy of Living; Flight into Nowhere; Affairs of Annabel; Men with Wings; Orphans of the Street; Little Orphan Annie. 1939 I'm from Missouri; The Saint Strikes Back; Within the Law; On Borrowed Time; Beau Geste; At the Circus; Fast and Furious. 1940 The Way of all Flesh; No Time for Comedy; The Cisco Kid and the Lady; Double Alibi; Charlie Chan's Murder Cruise; Buck Benny Rides Again; Opened by Mistake; The Saint Takes Over; The Golden Fleecing; Little Nellie Kelly; Ellery Queen; Master

Detective. 1941 The Maltese Falcon; Pot O' Gold; Ellery Queen's Penthouse Mystery; Ellery Queen and the Perfect Crime; Ellery Queen and the Murder Ring; Reaching for the Sun; Million Dollar Baby. 1942 It Happened in Flatbush; Enemy Agents Against Ellery Queen; Army Surgeon; All Through the Night. 1943 A Night to Remember; Riding High; No Place for a Lady; Dixie. 1945 Anchors Aweigh; The Horn Blows at Midnight; I Love a Bandleader; Shady Lady; How Do You Do. 1946 Two Years Before the Mast; Bowery Bombshell; The Virginian. 1947 The Gashouse Kids in Hollywood; California; Easy Come, Easy Go; Philo Vance's Gamble; Body and Soul; Down to Earth; Nightmare Alley; Blaze of Noon. 1948 The Timber Trail; Night Wind; June Bride. 1949 Shamrock Hill. 1950 Mrs. O'Malley and Mr. Malone; Copper Canyon. 1951 Raton Pass; The Last Outpost. 1952 Denver and Rio Grande; Lone Star. 1953 Arrowhead. 1954 Lucky Me. 1955 You're Never Too Young. 1957 Public Pigeon No. 1; The Unholy Wife. 1962 Geronimo. 1965 The Hallelujah Trail.

BURKE, THOMAS F.

Died: Mar. 25, 1941, Los Angeles, Calif. Screen actor.

Appeared in: 1932 Carmen. 1938 Kathleen; Father O'Flynn.

BURLANDO, CLAUDE

Born: 1918. Died: Sept. 25, 1938, Hollywood, Calif.(traffic injuries). Screen actor and extra.

BURNABY, DAVY

Born: Apr. 7, 1881, Buckland, Herts, England. Died: Apr. 18, 1949, Angmering, Sussex, England. Screen, stage, radio actor, and songwriter.

Appeared in: 1930 The Co-Optimists. 1933 Three Men in a Boat; A Shot in the Dark; Strike It Rich; Cleaning Up; On the Air; The Wishbone; Just My Luck. 1935 How's Chances?; Are You a Mason?; Dandy Dick. 1935 Boys Will be Boys; Radio Parade of 1935. 1937 Feather Your Nest; The Song of the Road (U.S. 1940); Talking Feet. 1938 Kicking the Moon Around. 1939 Many Tanks, Mr. Atkins; Prisoner of Corbal. Other British films: The Song of the Forge; Leave It to Me; Second Best Bed; Calling All Stars.

BURNE, NANCY

Born: 1913, England. Died: Mar. 25, 1954, Maidstone, England. Screen, stage, and vaudeville actress.

Appeared in: 1934 Dandy Dick; Norah O'Neale; Song at Eventide; Irish Hearts. 1935 It Happened in Paris. 1936 Knights for a Day; Royal Eagle. 1937 Thunder in the City; When the Poppies Bloom Again. 1938 John Halifax; Gentleman; Flying Fifty-Five.

BURNETTE, "SMILEY" (Lester Alvin Burnett)

Born: Mar. 18, 1911, Summum, Ill. Died: Feb. 16, 1967, Los Angeles, Calif.(leukemia). Screen, television, radio actor, and songwriter. Entered films in 1934. Appeared in Roy Rogers, Gene Autry and Charles Starrett (as Durango Kid) series.

Appeared in: 1934 In Old Santa Fe; Mountain Mystery (serial). 1935 Tumbling Tumbleweeds; Waterfront Lady; Melody Trail; Sagebrush Troubadour; The Singing Vagabond; Hitch Hike Lady; Rex and Rinty; Streamline Express; Harmony Lane; Red River Valley; Phantom Empire (serial). 1936 Doughnuts and Society; Hearts in Bondage; Oh, Susannah; Ride, Ranger, Ride; Round up Time in Texas; Comin' 'Round the Mountain; The Singing Cowboy; Guns and Guitars; A Man Betrayed; The Border Patrolman. 1937 The Old Corral; The Big Show; Springtime in the Rockies; Larceny on the Air; Dick Tracy (serial); Git Along Little Dogies; Rootin' Tootin' Rhythm; Yodelin' Kid from Pine Ridge; Meet the Boy Friend; Public Cowboy No. 1, Manhattan Merry-Go-Round; Boots and Saddles. 1938 Prairie Moon; The Old Barn Dance; Hollywood Stadium Mystery; Under Western Stars; Gold Mine in the Sky; Man from Music Mountain; Billy the Kid Returns; Rhythm of the Saddle; Western Jamboree. 1939 Home on the Prairie; Blue Mountain Skies; Mountain Rhythm; Colorado Sunset; In Old Monterey; Rovin' Tumbleweeds; South of the Border; Mexicali, Rose. 1940 Rancho Grande; Men with Steel Faces; Gaucho Serenade; Carolina Moon; Ride, Tenderfoot, Ride. 1941 Ridin' on a Rainbow; Back in the Saddle; The Singing Hills; Sunset in Wyoming; Under Fiesta Stars; Down Mexico Way; Sierra Sue. 1942 Cowboy Serenade; Heart of the Rio Grande; Home in Wyoming; Stardust on the Sage; Call of the Canyon; Bells of Capistrano; Heart of the Golden West. 1943 Beyond the Last Frontier; Idaho; King of the Cowboys; Silver Spurs. 1944 Beneath Western Skies; The Laramie Trail; Call of the Rockies; Code of the Prairie; Pride of the Plains; Bordertown Trail; Firebrands of Arizona. 1946 The Desert Horseman; The Fighting Frontiersman; The Galloping Thunder; Gunning for Vengeance; Land Rush; Roaring Rangers; Two-Fisted Stranger; Hunting West. 1947 The Lone Hand Texan;

Terror Trail; West of Dodge City; Law of the Canyon; Prairie Raiders; Riders of the Lone Star; South of Chisholm Trail. 1948 Buckaroo from Powder River; Last Days of Boot Hill; Phantom Valley; Six-Gun Law; West of Sonora; Whirlwind Raiders; Trail to Laredo. 1949 Quick on the Trigger; Laramie; Eldorado Pass; Desert Vigilante; Challenge of the Range; Horsemen of the Sierras; Blazing Trail; South of Death Valley; Bandits of El Dorado; Renegades of the Sage. 1950 Outcast of Black Mesa; Texas Dynamo; Trail of the Rustlers; Streets of Ghost Town; Across the Badlands; Raiders of Tomahawk Creek; Lightning Guns; Frontier Outpost. 1951 Whirlwind; Riding the Outlaw Trail; Prairie Roundup; Snake River Desperadoes; Fort Savage Raider; Bonanza Town; Cyclone Fury; The Kid from Amarillo; Pecos River. 1952 Smoky Canyon; The Hawk of Wild River; The Kid from Broken Gun; The Rough, Tough West; Junction City; Laramie Mountains. 1953 Winning of the West; Goldtown Ghost Riders; On Top of Old Smoky, Pack Train, Saginaw Trail.

BURNEY, HAL (Harold Burmeister)
Born: 1900. Died: Nov. 11, 1933, Eureka, Calif. Screen, stage, vaudeville, and radio actor.

BURNS, BOB "BAZOOKA"
Born: Aug. 2, 1893, Van Buren, Ark. Died: Feb. 2, 1956, San Fernando Valley, Calif. Screen, vaudeville, radio, and carnival actor. Known as "The Arkansas Philosopher."

Appeared in: 1931 Quick Millions. 1935 The Singing Vagabond; The Courageous Avenger; Restless Knights (short). 1936 Rhythm on the Range; Guns and Guitars. 1937 The Big Broadcast of 1937; Waikiki Wedding; Wells Fargo; Mountain Music. 1938 The Arkansas Traveler; Tropic Holiday; Radio City Revels. 1939 Our Leading Citizen; I'm From Missouri. 1940 Alias the Deacon; Comin' Round the Mountain; Prairie Schooner. 1942 The Hillbilly Deacon. 1944 Belle of the Yukon.

BURNS, DAVID
Born: June 22, 1901, New York, N.Y. Died: Mar. 12, 1971, Philadelphia, Pa.(heart attack). Screen, stage, and television actor.

Appeared in: 1954 Knock on Wood; Deep in My Heart. 1960 Let's Make Love.

BURNS, HARRY
Born: 1885. Died: July 9, 1948, Santa Monica, Calif.(heart attack). Screen, stage, and vaudeville actor.

Appeared in: 1935 A Vitaphone short. 1936 Hot Money. 1937 Two Wise Maids. 1939 Kid Nightingale. 1940 North West Mounted Police. 1941 Redhead. 1942 Tortilla Flat; What's the Matador (short).

BURNS, HARRY
Born: 1884. Died: Jan. 9, 1939, Los Angeles, Calif.(heart attack). Screen actor and film director. Married to screen actress Dorothy Vernon and father of screen actor Bobby Vernon (dec. 1939).

BURNS, IRVING
Born: 1914. Died: Sept. 21, 1968, Hollywood, Calif.(heart attack). Screen actor.

BURNS, LULU. See Lulu Burns Jenks

BURNS, NAT (Nat Burden Haines)
Born: 1887, Philadelphia, Pa. Died: Nov. 8, 1962, New York, N.Y. Screen, stage, and television actor.

BURNS, PAUL E.
Born: Jan. 26, 1881. Died: May 17, 1967, Van Nuys, Calif. (heart attack). Screen and television actor.

Appeared in: 1930 Framed; Hell Harbor. 1932 Renegades. 1939 Return of the Cisco Kid; Rose of Washington Square; Jesse James. 1940 Little Orvie; New Moon; Chad Hanna; Seventeen. 1941 Men of Timberland; Belle Starr; Swamp Water. 1942 Mystery of Marie Roget; Timber; The Mummy's Tomb. 1943 Dixie Dugan; Crash Dive; The Ox-Bow Incident; The Meanest Man in the World. 1944 Dragon Seed; Barbary Coast Gent; Seventh Cross. 1945 State Fair; Fallen Angel. 1946 Mysterious Intruder; Night Editor; Devil's Mask; Gallant Journey; Sing While You Dance; Shadowed; My Pal Trigger. 1947 Desperate; Framed (and 1930 version); Smoky River Serenade; Exposed; Blind Sport. 1948 Relentless; Hollow Triumph. 1949 Johnny Allegro; Look for the Silver Lining; I Married A Communist; Arctic Manhunt; Cover Up; Hideout; Lust For Gold. 1950 Montana;

Father Makes Good; It's a Small World; Sunset in the West; Tarnished; The Woman on Pier 13; 1951 The Big Gusher; Frenchie; Santa Fe; Storm Warning. 1952 Son of Paleface; Sound Off. 1956 Fury at Gunsight Pass. 1958 Gunman's Walk. 1959 Face of a Fugitive. 1960 Guns of the Timberland. 1961 A Pocketful of Miracles.

BURNS, ROBERT PATRICK
Born: 1929. Died: June 8, 1955, Los Angeles, Calif. Screen actor.

Appeared in: 1930-1935 "Our Gang" comedies.

BURROUGHS, ERIC
Died: Aug. 1960, New York. Screen and stage actor.

Appeared in: 1959 Odds Against Tomorrow.

BURT, FREDERIC
Born: Feb. 12, 1876, Onarga, Ill. Died: Oct. 2, 1943, Twenty-nine Palms, Calif. Screen and stage actor. Entered films in 1930. Married to screen actress Helen Ware (dec. 1939).

Appeared in: 1930 The Shadow of the Law; The Eyes of the World; Outside the Law. 1931 Cimarron; The Yellow Ticket; The Cisco Kid; The Royal Bed; Up For Murder.

BURT, WILLIAM P. (William Presley Burt)
Born: Feb. 11, 1873, St. Peter, Minn. Died: Feb. 23, 1955, Denver, Colo. Screen, stage, minstrel, circus actor, film director, radio, and screenwriter. Entered films with the Thanhouser Picture Co. in 1915.

Appeared in: 1920 Pirate Gold (serial). 1927 King of Kings. 1928 The Leopard Lady; Night of Mystery. 1930 Girl of the Port; Danger Lights; Midnight Mystery; Rogue of the Rio Grande. 1931 Sally of the Subway; Cimarron. 1933 Her Splendid Folly.

BURTON, CHARLOTTE
Born: 1882. Died: Mar. 28, 1942, Los Angeles, Calif.(heart attack). Screen actress.

Appeared in: 1913 Trapped in a Forest Fire. 1915 The Diamond from the Sky (serial); A Man's Way. 1916 The Sequel to the Diamond from the Sky (serial).

BURTON, CLARENCE
Born: May 10, 1882, Fort Lyons, Mo. Died: Dec. 2, 1933, Hollywood, Calif.(heart attack). Screen and stage actor. Entered films in 1912.

Appeared in: 1921 Miss Lulu Bett; Forbidden Fruit; Crazy to Marry; Fool's Paradise; High Gear Jeffrey; The Lost Romance; The Love Special. 1922 Manslaughter; The Ordeal; The Beautiful and Damned; The Crimson Challenge; One Glorious Day; The Law and the Woman; A Daughter of Luxury; Her Husband's Trademark; Her Own Money; The Impossible Mrs. Bellew; The Man Unconquerable. 1923 The Ten Commandments; Adam's Rib; Mr. Billings Spends His Dime; Sixty Cents an Hour; Garrison's Finish; Hollywood; Nobody's Money; Salomy Jane; The Satin Girl. 1924 The Navigator; No More Women; Bluff; The Guilty One; The Mine with the Iron Door. 1925 The Coming of Amos; Flyin' Thru; The Wedding Song; The Million Dollar Handicap; The Road to Yesterday; Savages of the Sea. 1926 The Danger Girl; The Nervous Wreck; Red Dice; Three Faces East; Shipwrecked; The Warning Signal. 1927 King of Kings; The Angel of Broadway; Chicago; The Fighting Eagle; The Yankee Clipper; A Harp in Hock; Rubber Tires. 1928 Stool Pigeon; Submarine; Square Crooks; Midnight Madness; Stand and Deliver. 1929 Godless Girl; Barnum Was Right; The Love Racket; Dynamite. 1930 The Unholy Three; Love Trader; Only Saps Work. 1932 The Sign of the Cross. 1944 The Sign of the Cross (revised version of 1932 film).

BURTON, FREDERICK
Born: Oct. 20, 1871, Indianapolis, Ind. Died: Oct. 23, 1957, Woodland Hills, Calif. Screen, stage, and opera actor.

Appeared in: 1919 Anne of Green Gables. 1920 Yes or No; Heliotrope. 1921 Bits of Life; If Women Only Knew; The Education of Elizabeth. 1922 The Man She Brought Back; Anna Ascends; Back Home and Broke. 1923 Broadway Broke; The Fighting Blade. 1924 The Rejected Woman. 1925 Back to Life. 1927 Running Wild. 1930 The Big Trail. 1931 Sweepstakes; Secret Service; An American Tragedy. 1932 Woman From Monte Carlo; Fireman Save My Child; Alias the Doctor; Mata Hari; The Wet Parade; State's Attorney; Okay America; One Way Passage; Too Busy to Work. 1933 No Other Woman; Broadway Baby; The Working Man; Golden Harvest; Counsellor-at-Law. 1934 Love Birds;

Belle of the Nineties; Flirtation Walk. 1935 Transient Lady; Mc-Fadden's Flats; Shipmates Forever. 1936 The Calling of Dan Matthews; Theodora Goes Wild; Everybody's Old Man; Mummy's Boys; The Voice of Bugle Ann. 1937 The Man in Blue; Love is News; Nancy Steele Is Missing; The Duke Comes Back. 1938 Air Devil; Saint in New York; My Lucky Star; Kentucky. 1939 Hollywood Cavalcade; Old Maid; Mr. Smith Goes to Washington; Confessions of a Nazi Spy. 1940 The Man from Dakota; Go West Brigham Young. 1941 Bowery Boys; Washington Melodrama. 1942 Silver Queen; Babes on Broadway; Gentleman After Dark. 1944 Town Went Wild.

BURTON, GEORGE H.
Born: 1900. Died: Dec. 8, 1955, Los Angeles, Calif.(heart attack). Bird Trainer, screen, stage, and television actor.

Appeared in: 1935 Ruggles of Red Gap. 1947 Bill and Coo.

BURTON, NED
Born: Approx. 1850. Died: Dec. 11, 1922, New York, N.Y. Screen, stage, and vaudeville actor.

Appeared in: 1921 Jim the Penman. 1922 Back Home and Broke.

BURTON, WILLIAM H.
Born: 1845. Died: Mar. 15, 1926, New York, N.Y. Screen and stage actor.

Appeared in: 1923 Radio Mania. 1924 Born Rich. 1925 Makers of Men.

BUSCAGLIONE, FRED
Born: 1921, Italy. Died: Feb. 3, 1960, Rome, Italy (auto accident). Screen, stage actor, singer, and composer.

Appeared in: I Ragazzi del Juke Box (The Jukebox Boys); A Qualcuno Piace Fred (Someone Likes Fred).

BUSCH, MAE
Born: Jan. 20, 1891, Melbourne, Australia. Died: Apr. 19, 1946, Woodland Hills, Calif. Screen, stage, and vaudeville actress. Entered films with Mack Sennett.

Appeared in: 1915 A One Night Stand; Settled at the Seaside; The Rent Jumpers; A Rascal of Wolfish Ways (reissued as A Polished Villain); The Best of Enemies; A Favorite Fool. 1916 The Worst of Friends; Because He Loved Her; Better Late Than Never (working title Getting Married); Wife and Auto Trouble; A Bath House Blunder; Sisters of Eve. 1919 The Grim Game. 1920 The Devil's Passkey. 1921 The Love Charm; A Parisian Scandal. 1922 Foolish Wives; Brothers under the Skin; Her Own Money; Only a Shop Girl; Pardon My Nerve! 1923 The Christian; Souls for Sale. 1924 Broken Barriers; Bread; Married Flirts; Nellie, the Beautiful Cloak Model; The Shooting of Dan McGrew; Name the Man; A Woman Who Sinned; The Triflers. 1925 Camille of the Barbary Coast; The Unholy Three; Frivolous Sal; Time, the Comedian. 1926 Nutcracker; Fools of Fashion; The Miracle of Life. 1927 San Francisco Nights; Tongues of Scandal; The Truthful Sex; Love 'Em and Weep (short); Husband Hunters; Perch of the Devil. 1928 Fazil; The Beauty Shoppers; Sisters of Eve; Black Butterflies; While the City Sleeps. 1929 Alibi; Unaccustomed as We Are (short); A Man's Man. 1930 Young Desire. 1931 Chickens Come Home (short); Defenders of the Law; Wicked; Come Clean (short). 1932 Their First Mistake (short); Without Honor; Man Called Back; Doctor X; Heart Punch; Scarlet Dawn; Rider of Death Valley; Racing Strain. 1933 Women Won't Tell; Blondie Won't Tell; Blondie Johnson; Sucker Money; Lilly Turner; Cheating Blondes; Secrets of Hollywood; Picture Brides; Dance, Girl Dance (short); Sons of the Desert. 1934 Going Bye Bye (short); The Live Ghost (short); Beloved; The Road to Ruin; I Like it that Way; Oliver the Eighth (short) Them Thar Hills (short). 1935 Tit for Tat (short); The Fixer Uppers (short); Affair of Susan; Stranded. 1936 The Bohemian Girl. 1937 Daughter of Shanghai. 1938 Prison Farm; Nancy Drew Detective. 1940 Women without Names. 1942 Hello, Annapolis; The Mad Monster. 1945 Stork Club; Masquerade in Mexico.

BUSH, GEORGE
Born: 1858, Janesville, Wis. Died: Nov. 23, 1937, Culver City, Calif. Screen actor.

Appeared in: 1938 The Adventures of Tom Sawyer.

BUSHMAN, FRANCIS X. (Francis Xavier Bushman)
Born: Jan. 10, 1883, Baltimore, Md. Died: Aug. 23, 1966, Pacific Palisades, Calif.(heart attack due to fall). Screen, stage,

radio, and television actor. Father of screen actor Francis Bushman, Jr. Divorced from screen actress Beverly Bayne. Entered films with Essannay.

Appeared in: 1911 Last Year (film debut). 1912 When Soul Meets Soul; The Magic Wand; A Good Catch. 1913 The Spy's Defeat. 1914 One Wonderful Night; Blood Will Tell; Under Royal Patronage. 1915 Graustark; The Return of Richard Neal; The Silent Voice. 1916 The Great Secret; Romeo and Juliet. 1917 Red, White and Blue Blood. 1918 Social Quicksands. 1921 Smiling All the Way. 1922 According to Hoyle; Making the Grade. 1923 Modern Marriage. 1924 Marriage Circle. 1925 The Masked Bride. 1926 Ben Hur; The Marriage Clause. 1927 The Lady in Ermine; The Thirteenth Juror. 1928 The Grip of the Yukon; Man Higher Up; Midnight Life; Say It with Sables; The Charge of the Gauchos. 1930 The Call of the Circus; The Dude Wrangler; Once a Gentleman. 1931 Spell of the Circus (serial); Ben Hur (re-release of 1926 film). 1933 The Three Musketeers (serial). 1936 Hollywood Boulevard. 1937 Dick Tracy (serial). 1944 Wilson. 1951 David and Bathsheba. 1952 Apache Country. 1954 Sabrina. 1957 The Story of Mankind. 1960 Twelve to the Moon. 1962 The Phantom Planet. 1965 Peer Gent. 1966 The Ghost in the Invisible Bikini.

BUSLEY, JESSIE
Born: 1869, Albany, N.Y. Died: Apr. 20, 1950, New York, N.Y. Screen and stage actress.

Appeared in: 1930 Seeing Off Service (short); Home Made (short). 1931 Personal Maid. 1938 Brother Rat. 1939 King of the Underworld. 1940 It All Came True; Brother Rat and a Baby; Escape to Glory.

BUSQUETS, JOAQUIN
Born: 1875, Mexico. Died: Dec. 4, 1942, Mexico City, Mexico. Screen, radio actor, and radio producer. Entered films in Mexican silents.

Appeared in: 1934 La Sangre Manda; Enemigos. 1935 Tierra, Amor y Dolor. 1936 La Mujer del Puerto. 1937 El Misterio del Rostro Palido; La Gran Cruz (The Heavy Cross).

BUSSEY, HANK
Born: 1891. Died: Jan. 14, 1971, Hollywood, Calif. Screen, stage, and vaudeville actor. Member of vaudeville team of "Bussey & Case."

BUTCHER, ERNEST
Born: 1885. Died: June 8, 1965, London, England. Screen, stage, and radio actor.

Appeared in: 1942 Variety Jubilee. 1943 The Tawny Pipit (U.S. 1947). 1948 The Years Between; My Brother Jonathan (U.S. 1949). 1951 Highly Dangerous. 1953 Terror on a Train; Background.

BUTI, CARLO
Born: 1902. Died: Nov. 16, 1963, Florence, Italy. Screen actor and singer.

Appeared in: 1938 I due Gemelli (The Twins). 1939 Per Vomini Soli (For Men Only).

BUTLER, EDDIE
Born: 1888. Died: May 31, 1944, Hollywood, Calif. Screen actor.

BUTLER, FRANK
Born: Dec. 28, 1890, Oxford, England. Died: June 10, 1967, Hollywood, Calif. Screen, stage actor, and screenwriter.

Appeared in: The "In-Law" series. 1921 The Sheik; The Great Moment. 1922 A Tailor-Made Man; Beyond the Rocks; My American Wife. 1923 The Self-Made Wife; The Tiger's Claw; Bluebeard's Eighth Wife; The Call of the Wild. 1924 The King of the Wild Horses. 1925 Tol'able Romeo (short); Compromise; Satan in Sables. 1926 Made for Love; The Passionate Quest; The Fighting Buckaroo; Thirty Below Zero.

BUTLER, JAMES "JIMMY"
Born: 1921. Died: Feb. 18, 1945, France.(killed in action, W. W. II). Screen actor. One of the original "Dead End Kids."

Appeared in: 1933 Only Yesterday; Beloved. 1934 No Greater Glory; Romance in Manhattan; Mrs. Wiggs of the Cabbage Patch; Manhattan Melodrama. 1934 I'll Fix It. 1935 When a Man's a Man; Laddie; Dinky; The Dark Angel. 1937 Battle of Greed; Stella Dallas; County Fair. 1937 Wells Fargo. 1938 Boys Town. 1939 The Escape; Nurse Edith Cavell; Winter Carnival. 1940 Military Academy. 1941 Naval Academy. 1942 Tough as They Come.

BUTLER, LOUISE (Estelle Louise Fiske)
Died: Dec. 8, 1958, Chicago, Ill. Screen and stage actress.

BUTLER, WILLIAM J.
Born: 1860. Died: Jan. 27, 1927, Staten Island, N.Y. Screen and stage actor.

Appeared in: 1917 The Great Secret (serial).

BUTTERFIELD, HERBERT
Born: 1896. Died: May 2, 1957, Los Angeles, Calif. Screen and television actor.

Appeared in: 1950 Never Fear; The Young Lovers. 1951 House on Telegraph Hill. 1953 A Blueprint for Murder. 1954 Shield for Murder.

BUTTERWORTH, CHARLES
Born: July 26, 1896, South Bend, Ind. Died: June 14, 1946, Los Angeles, Calif.(auto accident). Screen, stage, vaudeville, and radio actor.

Appeared in: 1930 Life of the Party (film debut); Illicit. 1931 Side Show; The Bargain; The Mad Genius. 1932 Beauty and the Boss; Love Me Tonight; The Slippery Pearls (short); Manhattan Parade. 1933 The Nuisance; Penthouse; My Weakness. 1934 The Cat and the Fiddle; Hollywood Party; Student Tour; Forsaking All Others; Bulldog Drummond Strikes Back; Ruggles of Red Gap. 1935 The Night Is Young; Baby Face Harrington; Orchids to You. 1936 The Magnificent Obsession; The Moon's Our Home; Half Angel; We Went to College; Rainbow on the River. 1937 Swing High, Swing Low; Every Day's a Holiday. 1938 Thanks for the Memory. 1940 Second Chorus; The Boys from Syracuse. 1941 Bonde Inspiration; Sis Hopkins; Road Show. 1942 Love Me Tonight; Night in New Orleans, Give Out, Sisters; What's Cooking?. 1943 Always a Bridesmaid; The Sultan's Daughter; This Is the Army. 1944 Bermuda Mystery; Follow the Boys; Dixie Jamboree.

BUTTERWORTH, WALTER T.
Born: 1893. Died: Mar. 10, 1962, Hollywood, Calif. Screen, stage, and vaudeville actor.

BUZZI, PIETRO
Died: Feb. 16, 1921, Los Angeles, Calif. Screen and opera actor. Entered films approx. 1910.

BYFORD, ROY
Born: 1873. Died: Jan. 31, 1939, London, England. Screen and stage actor.

Appeared in: 1922 The Spanish Jade; Love's Boomerang.

BYINGTON, SPRING
Born: Oct. 17, 1893, Colorado Springs, Colo. Died: Sept. 7, 1971, Hollywood, Calif. Screen, stage, radio, and television actress.
Appeared in "Jones Family" series from 1936-40.
Appeared in: 1931 Papa's Slay Ride (short). 1933 Little Women. 1935 Mutiny on the Bounty; The Werewolf of London; Love Me Forever; Orchids to You; Way Down East; Ah, Wilderness; Broadway Hostess; The Great Impersonation. 1936 The Charge of the Light Brigade; Every Saturday Night; Educating Father; Back to Nature; The Voice of Bugle Ann; Palm Springs; Stage Struck; The Girl on the Front Page; Dodsworth; Theodora Goes Wild. 1937 Green Light; Penrod and Sam; Off to the Races; Big Business; Hot Water; Borrowing Trouble; Hotel Haywire; The Road Back; It's Love I'm After; Clarence; A Family Affair. 1938 You Can't Take It with You; Love on a Budget; A Trip to Paris; Safety in Numbers; The Buccaneer; Penrod and His Twin Brother; Jezebel; Down on the Farm; The Adventures of Tom Sawyer. 1939 Everybody's Baby; The Jones Family in Hollywood; Quick Millions; The Story of Alexander Graham Bell; Chicken Wagon Family; Too Busy to Work; Jones Family at the Grand Canyon. 1940 A Child Is Born; The Bluebird; On Their Own; My Love Came Back; Lucky Partners; Laddie; Young As You Feel; The Ghost Comes Home. 1941 Arkansas Judge; Meet John Doe; The Devil and Miss Jones; When Ladies Meet; Ellery Queen and the Perfect Crime; The Vanishing Virginian. 1942 Roxie Hart; Once Upon a Thursday; The War Against Mrs. Hadley; Rings on Her Fingers; The Affairs of Martha. 1943 Heaven Can Wait; Presenting Lily Mars; The Heavenly Body. 1944 I'll Be Seeing You; Thrill of a Romance; Captain Eddie; Salty O'Rourke; The Enchanted Cottage; A Letter for Evie. 1946 Dragonwyck; Meet Me on Broadway; Little Mr. Jim; Faithful in My Fashion; My Brother Talks to Horses. 1947 Living in a Big Way; Singapore; It Had to Be You; Cynthia; The Rich Full Life. 1948 B. F.'s Daughter. 1949 The Big Wheel; In the Good Old Summertime. 1950 Please Believe Me; Devil's Doorway; Louisa; Walk Softly, Stranger; The Skipper Surprised

His Wife; The Reformer and the Redhead (voice only). 1951 Angels in the Outfield; Bannerline; According to Mrs. Hoyle. 1952 No Room for the Groom; Because You're Mine. 1954 The Rocket Man. 1960 Please Don't Eat the Daisies.

BYLES, BOBBY
Born: 1931. Died: Aug. 26, 1969, Hollywood, Calif.(heart attack). Screen and television actor.

Appeared in: 1958 Onionhead. 1964 War is Hell.

BYRD, RALPH
Born: Apr. 22, 1909, Dayton, Ohio. Died: Aug. 18, 1952, Tarzana, Calif.(heart attack). Screen and television actor. Starred as Dick Tracy in film and TV series.

Appeared in: 1936 Hell-Ship Morgan; Border Caballero; Swing Time. 1937 S.O.S. Coast Guard (serial); Motor Madness; The Trigger Trio; Paid to Dance; Blake of Scotland Yard (serial); Dick Tracy (serial); Criminals of the Air. 1938 Down in "Arkansaw"; Born to be Wild; Army Girl; Dick Tracy Returns (serial). 1939 Mickey, the Kid; Dick Tracy's G-Men (serial); Fighting Thoroughbreds; S.O.S. Tidal Wave. 1940 Misbehaving Husbands; The Howards of Virginia; Drums of the Desert; The Golden Fleecing; The Son of Monte Cristo; Dark Streets of Cairo; North West Mounted Police. 1941 Dick Tracy vs. Crime, Inc. (serial); The Penalty; Desperate Cargo; A Yank in the RAF. 1942 Broadway Big Shot; Jungle Book; Careful, Soft Shoulders; Time to Kill; Moontide; Duke of the Navy; Ten Gentlemen from West Point; Manila Calling. 1943 They Came to Blow Up America; Guadalcanal Diary. 1944 Tampico. 1947 The Vigilante (serial); Dick Tracy's Dilemma; Dick Tracy Meets Gruesome; Stallion Road, Mark of the Claw. 1948 Jungle Goddess; Thunder in the Pines; Canon City; Stage Struck; The Argyle Secrets. 1950 Radar Secret Service. 1951 The Redhead and the Cowboy. 1952 Dick Tracy vs. The Phantom Empire (serial).

BYRENS, MYER
Born: 1840. Died: June 29, 1933, Los Angeles, Calif. Screen and stage actor.

BYRNES, MRS. NANCY ROSENBLUTH
Born: 1915. Died: June 15, 1962, Union, N.J. Screen actress and singer.

BYRON, ARTHUR
Born: Apr. 3, 1872, Brooklyn, N.Y. Died: July 17, 1943, Hollywood, Calif. Screen and stage actor.

Appeared in: 1929 A Family Affair (short). 1932 Twenty Thousand Years in Sing Sing; The Mummy; Fast Life. 1933 Gabriel over the White House; Tonight Is Ours; Silk Express; Mayor of Hell; Private Detective 62, College Coach. 1934 The Man with Two Faces; Marie Galante; Two Alone; Notorious Sophie Lang; The House of Rothschild; The President Vanishes; Stand Up and Cheer; The Secret Bride; Fog over Frisco. 1935 The Whole Town's Talking; Shadows of Doubt; The Casino Murder Case; Murder in the Fleet; Oil for the Lamps of China. 1936 The Prisoner of Shark Island.

BYRON, PAUL
Born: 1891. Died: May 12, 1959, San Diego, Calif. Screen and stage actor. Entered films with Universal in 1915.

BYRON, ROYAL JAMES
Born: 1887. Died: Mar. 4, 1943, Trenton, N.J. Screen, stage, and vaudeville actor. Entered films with Vitagraph.

Appeared in: 1926 The Palm Beach Girl. 1930 Unmasked.

BYSTROM, WALTER E.
Born: 1894. Died: Sept. 13, 1969, San Diego, Calif. Screen actor. Entered films as an extra before joining Sennett as a Keystone Kop.

CABANNE, WILLIAM CHRISTY
Born: 1888, St. Louis, Mo. Died: Oct. 15, 1950, Philadelphia, Pa. (heart attack). Film director, screen, stage actor, and screenwriter. Appeared in early Griffith films.

Appeared in: 1912 Under Burning Skies; The Punishment. 1913 Judith of Bethulia.

CADELL, JEAN
Born: Sept. 13, 1884, Edinburgh, Scotland. Died: Sept. 1967, London, England. Screen, stage, and television actress.

Appeared in: 1919 Man Who Stayed at Home (film debut). 1930 The Loves of Robert Burns. 1933 Fires of Fate. 1934 Little

Friend. 1935 David Copperfield. 1937 Love from a Stranger; Whom the Gods Love; South Riding. 1938 Pygmalion. 1940 Quiet Wedding. 1942 Young Mr. Pitt. 1943 Dear Octopus. 1947 I Know Where I'm Going. 1948 Jazzy. 1949 That Dangerous Age (aka If This Be Sin - U.S. 1950); Whiskey Galore (aka Tight Little Island-U.S. & aka Mad Little Island). 1950 Madeleine. 1951 Reluctant Widow; No Place for Jennifer; Obsessed; The Late Edwina Black. 1952 Marry Me. 1953 Meet Mr. Lucifer. 1956 Rockets Galore. 1957 The Surgeon's Knife; The Little Hut. 1958 Mad Little Island. 1960 A Taste of Money. 1961 Upstairs and Downstairs. 1962 Immoral Charge (aka Serious Charge and A Touch of Hell). Other British films: Case of Lady Brooke; I Want to Get Married.

CAHILL, LILLY
Born: 1886. Died: July 20, 1955, San Antonio, Tex. Screen, stage, and television actress. Married to screen actor Blandon Tynan (dec. 1967).

Appeared in: 1910 The Fugitive. 1931 My Sin.

CAHILL, MARIE
Born: 1874, Brooklyn, N.Y. Died: Aug. 23, 1933, N.Y.(heart trouble). Screen, stage, and vaudeville actress.

Appeared in: 1915 Judy Forgot. 1917 Gladys' Day Dreams and three two-reel comedies.

CAHILL, THOMAS M.
Born: 1889, Chillicothe, Ohio. Died: Apr. 3, 1953, near Washington, D.C. Screen, stage, and television actor, and newspaper reporter.

Appeared in government-made short documentary films.

CAHOON, MILLIAN BENEDICT
Born: 1860. Died: Jan. 28, 1951, Darien, Conn. Screen and stage actor.

CAIN, ROBERT
Born: 1887. Died: Apr. 27, 1954, New York, N.Y. Screen, stage, television, and radio actor.

Appeared in: 1916 My Lady Incog. 1918 He Comes Up Smiling. 1919 In Mizzoura, Male and Female. 1921 The Witching Hour; Man-Woman-Marriage. 1922 The Impossible Mrs. Bellew; The Crossroads of New York; Burning Sands; Reported Missing. 1923 Children of Jazz; Hollywood; Drums of Fate; Racing Hearts; The Tiger's Claw. 1924 Three Weeks; Conductor 1492; Soiled; The Rose of Paris. 1925 The Everlasting Whisper; The Golden Bed; When the Door Opened; Every Man's Wife; Wing's of Youth. 1926 The Danger of Paris; Too Much Money; The Wilderness Woman. 1927 Husband Hunters; Rich Men's Sons.

CAINE, GEORGIA
Born: 1876, San Francisco, Calif. Died: Apr. 4, 1964, Hollywood, Calif. Screen and stage actress.

Appeared in: 1930 Good Intentions; Night Work. 1933 The Cradle Song. 1934 Call It Luck; Love Theme; I Am Suzanne; Once to Every Woman; Count of Monte Cristo; The Crusades; The White Angel. 1935 Hooray for Love. 1936 One Rainy Afternoon; Sing Me a Love Song; Navy Born. 1937 Time Out for Romance; It's Love I'm After; Bill Cracks Down; The Affairs of Cappy Ricks. 1938 Women Are Like That; His Exciting Night. 1939 Dodge City; Juarez; No Place to Go; Honeymoon in Bali; Tower of London. 1940 Remember the Night; Babes for Sale; Nobody's Children; The Lone Wolf Meets a Lady; Christmas in July. 1941 The Nurse's Secret; The Great Lie; Ridin' on a Rainbow; Hurry, Charlie, Hurry. 1942 Hello, Annapolis; The Wife Takes a Flyer; Are Husbands Necessary?. 1944 The Miracle of Morgan's Creek; Hail the Conquering Hero. 1947 Mad Wednesday; A Double Life. 1948 Give My Regards to Broadway; Unfaithfully Yours. 1949 The Beautiful Blonde from Bashful Bend.

CAIRNES, SALLY
Born: 1920. Died: Feb. 9, 1965, Hollywood, Calif. Screen actress and singer.

CAITS, JOSEPH
Born: 1889. Died: Mar. 9, 1957, New York, N.Y. Screen, stage, and vaudeville actor. Appeared in vaudeville with his brother Louis, in an act billed as "The Caits Brothers."

Appeared in: 1937 Hollywood Cowboy; Youth on Parole. 1938 A Slight Case of Murder; Reformatory. 1939 Lady and the Mob; Babes in Arms. 1940 Brother Orchid.

CALDER, KING
Born: 1900. Died: June 28, 1964, Los Angeles, Calif.(heart attack). Screen, stage, and television actor.

Appeared in: 1956 Timetable; On the Threshold of Space; The Rains of Ranchipur. 1958 Hong Kong Confidential; Mardi Gras. 1960 Three Came to Kill. 1961 Everything's Ducky. 1964 Ready for the People.

CALDWELL, ORVILLE R.
Born: 1896, Oakland, Calif. Died: Sept. 24, 1967, Santa Rosa, Calif. Screen and stage actor.

Appeared in: 1923 The French Doll; The Lonely Road; The Six-Fity; The Scarlet Lily. 1924 Daughters of the Night. 1925 Sackcloth and Scarlet. 1926 The Wives of the Prophet; Flame of the Argentine. 1927 The Harvester; Judgment of the Hills. 1928 The Patsy; The Little Yellow House. 1938 Just around the Corner; The Last Warning.

CALHERN, LOUIS (Carl Henry Vogt)
Born: 1895, Brooklyn, N.Y. Died: May 12, 1956, Tokyo, Japan (heart attack). Screen, stage, vaudeville, and burlesque actor. Divorced from screen actresses Ilka Chase; Julia Hoyt (dec. 1955); Natalie Schaefer and Marianne Stewart.

Appeared in: 1921 The Blot; Too Wise Wives; What's Worth While?. 1922 Woman, Wake Up!. 1923 The Last Moment. 1931 Stolen Heaven; Road to Singapore; Larceny Lane; Blonde Crazy; 1932 Okay, America; They Call It Sin; Night After Night; Afraid to Talk. 1933 Strictly Personal; 20,000 Years In Sing Sing; Frisco Jenny; The Woman Accused; Diplomaniacs; The World Gone Mad; Duck Soup. 1934 The Affairs of Cellini; The Count of Monte Cristo; The Man with Two Faces. 1935 The Arizonian; The Last Days of Pompeii; Woman Wanted; Sweet Adeline. 1936 The Gorgeous Hussy. 1937 Her Husband Lies; The Life of Emile Zola. 1938 Fast Company. 1939 Juarez; 5th Avenue Girl; Charlie McCarthy, Detective. 1940 I Take This Woman; Dr. Erlich's Magic Bullet. 1943 Up in Arms; Nobody's Darling; Heaven Can Wait. 1944 The Bridge of San Luis Rey. 1946 Notorious. 1948 Arch of Triumph. 1949 The Red Danube; The Red Pony. 1950 Annie Get Your Gun; The Asphalt Jungle; Two Weeks with Love; Devil's Doorway; A Life of Her Own; Nancy Goes to Rio. 1951 The Man with a Cloak; The Magnificent Yankee (stage and film versions). 1952 The Invitation; The Washington Story; We're Not Married; The Prisoner of Zenda. 1953 Julius Caesar; Confidentially Connie; Remains to Be Seen; Main Street to Broadway; Latin Lovers. 1954 Executive Suite; The Student Prince; Men of the Fighting Lady; Betrayed; Athena; Rhapsody. 1955 High Society; The Blackboard Jungle; The Prodigal. 1956 Forever, Darling; The Teahouse of the August Moon.

CALHOUN, ALICE
Born: Nov. 24, 1904, Cleveland, Ohio. Died: June 3, 1966, Los Angeles, Calif.(cancer). Screen actress. Entered films with Vitagraph in N.Y.

Appeared in: 1921 The Charming Deceiver; Closed Doors; Peggy Puts It Over; Princess Jones. 1922 Angel of Crooked Street; Girl in His Room; The Little Minister; Matrimonial Web; The Rainbow; A Girl's Desire; Little Wildcat; Blue Blood. 1923 The Man from Brodney; The Man Next Door; The Midnight Alarm; One Stolen Night; Masters of Men; Pioneer Trails. 1924 Between Friends; Code of the Wilderness; Flowing Gold. 1925 Pampered Youth; The Other Woman's Story; The Part Time Wife; The Everlasting Whisper; The Happy Warrior; The Man on the Box. 1926 Flying High; Hero of the Big Snows; The Power of the Weak; Kentucky Handicap; Tentacles of the North. 1927 The Down Grade; Savage Passions; The Trunk Mystery; Hidden Aces; In the First Degree; Isle of Forgotten Women; 1929 Bride of the Desert.

CALLAHAN, BILLY
Born: 1911. Died: Feb. 21, 1964, Queens, N.Y.(heart attack). Screen and vaudeville actress. Appeared in vaudeville with Louise Brooks in an act billed as "Brooks & Callahan." Doubled for Thelma Todd.

CALLAHAN, CHARLES S. "CHUCK"
Born: 1891. Died: Nov. 12, 1964, New York, N.Y. Screen, stage, radio, television and vaudeville actor. Brother of actor Bobby Callahan (dec. 1938), with whom he appeared in vaudeville in an act billed as "Bob & Chuck Callahan."

Appeared in: 1937 Grips, Grunts and Groans (short).

CALLAHAN, ROBERT "BOBBY"
Born: 1896. Died: May 15, 1938, West Los Angeles, Calif. Screen and vaudeville actor. Brother of actor Chuck Callahan

(dec. 1964) with whom he appeared in vaudeville in an act billed as "Bob & Chuck Callahan."

Appeared in: 1929 The Champion Golfer (short). 1930 Wild Company. 1934 Men in Black (short). 1937 Battle of Greed.

CALLIS, DAVID
Born: 1888. Died: Sept. 10, 1934, Los Angeles, Calif. Screen and stage actor.

Appeared in: 1929 The Sin Sister; What's Your Racket?

CALTHROP, DONALD
Born: Apr. 11, 1888, England. Died: Aug. 1940, England (heart attack). Screen and stage actor.

Appeared in: 1918 The Gay Lord Quex (film debut). 1919 Nelson. 1927 Shooting Star. 1929 The Flying Squad. 1930 Two Worlds; Loose Ends; Elstree Calling; Blackmail; Atlantic. 1931 Murder; Love Storm; The Bells; Money for Nothing; Many Waters. 1932 The Ghost Trail; Almost a Honeymoon; Rome Express; Fires of Fate. 1933 F.P.1; Orders is Orders; I Was a Spy; Early to Bed. 1934 Friday the Thirteenth; Red Ensign; Sorrell and Son; It's a Cop. 1935 The Phantom Light; The Clairvoyant; The Divine Spark; Scrooge. 1936 Broken Blossoms; The Man Who Lived Again. 1937 Dreaming Lips; Fire over England; Love from a Stranger. 1940 Major Barbara; Let George Do It.

CALVERT, CATHERINE (Catherine Cassidy)
Born: 1891, Baltimore, Md. Died: Jan. 18, 1971, Uniondale, N.Y. Screen and stage actress.

Appeared in: 1918 A Romance of the Underworld. 1919 Fires of Faith; The Career of Catherine Bush. 1920 Dead Men Tell No Tales. 1921 The Heart of Maryland; Moral Fibre; You Find It Everywhere. 1922 That Woman.

CALVERT, ELISHA H.
Born: June 27, 1873, Alexandria, Va. Died: Oct. 5, 1941, Hollywood, Calif. Screen, stage, vaudeville actor, film director, and film producer.

Appeared in: 1911 The Love Test (film debut). 1923 The Silent Partner. 1924 Bluff; The Only Woman; Why Men Leave Home; Inez from Hollywood. 1925 Havoc; Sally; East of Suez; The Talker. 1926 Ella Cinders; The Girl from Montmarte. 1927 Melting Millions (serial); The First Auto; Lonesome Ladies; The Wizard; Rookies. 1928 Moran of the Marines; The Man without a Face (serial); The Legion of the Condemned; Let 'Er Go Gallagher; Why Sailors Go Wrong; Prop and Pep. 1929 The Greene Murder Case; Darkened Rooms; The Mighty; The Virginian; Dark Street; The Studio Murder Mystery; The Canary Murder Case; Fast Company; The Love Parade; Thunderbolt. 1930 Half Shot at Sunrise; Behind the Makeup; The Benson Murder Case; The Border Legion; The Kibitzer; Ladies Love Brutes; A Man from Wyoming; Men Are Like That; Only the Brave; The Widow from Chicago; The Social Lion; Peacock Alley. 1932 Beyond Victory; Horse Feathers. 1933 Wild Horse Mesa; The Mysterious Rider; Duck Soup. 1934 Here Comes the Groom. 1936 The Glory Trail.

CAMELIA, MURIEL
Born: 1913. Died: Nov. 15, 1925, Miami, Fla. (motor bus accident). Screen and stage actress.

Appeared in D. W. Griffith Productions.

CAMERON, BRUCE (Paul Brachard, Jr.)
Born: 1910. Died: Apr. 10, 1959, Los Angeles, Calif. Screen actor and circus acrobat.

CAMERON, DONALD
Born: 1889. Died: July 11, 1955, West Cornwall, Conn. Screen and stage actor.

Appeared in: 1921 The Education of Elizabeth.

CAMERON, GENE
Died: Nov. 16, 1928, Yuma, Ariz. Screen actor.

Appeared in: 1922 The Sign of the Rose. 1923 An Old Sweetheart of Mine. 1924 Circe, The Enchantress. 1925 Excuse Me. 1926 The Midnight Kiss. 1927 Chain Lightning; The Gay Retreat.

CAMP, SHEPPARD
Born: 1882, West Point, Ga. Died: Nov. 20, 1929, Hollywood, Calif. (injuries from fall). Screen and stage actor.

Appeared in: 1929 The Greene Murder Case. 1930 Playing Around; Song of the Flame.

CAMPBELL, ALAN
Born: 1905. Died: June 14, 1963, West Hollywood, Calif. Screen, stage actor, and screenwriter. Married to writer Dorothy Parker.

CAMPBELL, COLIN
Born: 1883, Falkirk, Scotland. Died: Mar. 27, 1966, Woodland Hills, Calif. Screen and stage actor. Entered films in 1915.

Appeared in: 1915 Tillie's Tomato Surprise. 1921 Where Lights Are Low; The Girl from Nowhere; The Man of Stone; Black Roses; The First Born; The Lure of Jade; The Swamp. 1922 Cardigan; Two Kinds of Women; The World's a Stage. 1923 Bucking the Barrier; The Buster; The Grail; Three Who Paid. 1924 Pagan Passions; The Bowery Bishop. 1925 The White Monkey. 1930 Big Boy; The Road to Singapore; Unwanted; The Gay Diplomat. 1931 The Deceiver. 1933 Alice in Wonderland. 1934 Eight Girls in a Boat. 1941 San Francisco Docks. 1942 Life Begins at 8:30; Mrs. Miniver; This Above All; The War against Mrs. Hadley. 1944 The Lodger. 1945 The Fatal Witness; Scotland Yard Investigator. 1947 Moss Rose; The Wife of Monte Cristo; Exposed; The Two Mrs. Carrolls. 1948 Texas; Brooklyn and Heaven. 1949 The Fan; Mr. Belvedere Goes to College; Adventures of Icabod and Mr. Toad (voice). 1955 Abbott and Costello Meet the Keystone Kops. 1954 Sabrina. 1960 The Lost World. 1963 The Three Stooges Go Around the World in a Daze. 1964 Saturday Night Out. 1966 McGuire, Go Home!; The Leather Boys.

CAMPBELL, FRANK
Born: 1847. Died: Apr. 30, 1934, Hollywood, Calif. Screen and stage actor.

Appeared in: 1929 Frozen River.

CAMPBELL, MARGARET
Born: 1873. Died: June 27, 1939, Los Angeles, Calif. ("murdered-hammer attack"; son confessed to crime). Screen actress. Divorced from screen actor Josef Swickard (dec. 1940).

Appeared in: 1921 Lying Lips, Eden and Return, The Girl in the Taxi. 1922 Don't Shoot; Confidence; The Top O' the Morning. 1923 The Clean Up; Legally Dead; His Mystery Girl. 1924 The Dangerous Blonde; The Fast Worker. 1925 Home Maker. 1926 The Better Man; Monte Carlo; The Lady from Hell. 1927 Children of Divorce; Wages of Conscience. 1929 One Hysterical Night. 1930 Take the Heir.

CAMPBELL, MRS. PATRICK (Beatrice Stella Tanner)
Born: Feb. 1865, Kensington, London, England. Died: Apr. 10, 1940, Pau, France. Screen and stage actress.

Appeared in: 1930 The Dancers (film debut), 1934 Riptide; Outcast Lady; One More River. 1935 Pygmalion, Crime and Punishment.

CAMPBELL, VIOLET (Violet Shelton)
Born: 1893. Died: Jan. 1970, London, England. Screen and stage actress. Married to screen actor Nigel Bruce (dec. 1953).

Her only picture: 1941 Suspicion.

CAMPEAU, FRANK
Born: 1864, Detroit, Mich. Died: Nov. 5, 1943, Woodland Hills, Calif. Screen and stage actor.

Appeared in: 1915 Jordan In a Hard Road. 1917 Reaching for the Moon; Man from Painted Post. 1918 Bound in Morocco; Light of the Western Stars; Headin' South; Arizona. 1919 Cheating Cheaters; The Knickerbocker Buckaroo; His Majesty the American. 1920 The Life of the Party. 1921 The Kid; The Killer; For Those We Love. 1922 The Sin of Martha Queed; The Crimson Challenge; Just Tony; The Lane That Had No Turning; The Yosemite Trail; The Trap; Skin Deep. 1923 Isle of Lost Ships; To the Last Man; Modern Matrimony; North of Hudson Bay; Quicksands; The Spider and the Rose; Three Who Paid. 1924 Hoodman Blind; Those Who Dance; The Alaskan, Not a Drum Was Heard. 1925 Battling Bunyon; Heir-Looms; Coming Through; The Man from Red Gulch; The Saddle Hawk; The Pleasure Buyers; Manhattan Madness; The Golden Cocoon. 1926 The Three Bad Men; The Frontier Trail; No Man's Gold; Sea Horses; Whispering Wires. 1927 The First Auto; Let it Rain; The Heart of the Yukon. 1928 Across the Border (short); The Candy Kid. 1929 In Old Arizona; In the Headlines; Sea Fury; Points West; The Gamblers; Frozen River; Say It with Songs. 1930 Hideout; The Last of the Duanes; Abraham Lincoln; Captain Thunder; The People Versus (short); Lightnin'; Trifles (short); Danger (short). 1931 Fighting Caravans; Soldier's Plaything; Lasco of the Rio Grande. 1932 Girl of the Rio; White Eagle; The Dove. 1933 Smoky. 1935 Hopalong Cassidy. 1936 Everyman's Law; Empty Saddles. 1937 Black Aces. 1938 Border Wolves; The Painted Trail.

CANTOR, CHARLES
Born: 1898. Died: Sept. 11, 1966, Hollywood, Calif.(heart attack). Screen, stage, and radio actor. Brother of screen actor Nat Cantor (dec. 1956).

Appeared in: 1952 Stop; You're Killing Me.

CANTOR, EDDIE (Edward Israel Iskowitz)
Born: Jan. 31, 1892, New York, N.Y. Died: Oct. 10, 1964, Beverly Hills, Calif.(heart attack). Screen, stage, vaudeville, burlesque, radio, television actor, and screenwriter. Received a Special Academy Award in 1956 for distinguished service to the film industry.

Appeared in: 1926 Kid Boots (film debut). 1927 Special Delivery; Follies. 1929 Glorifying the American Girl. 1930 Whoopie; Paramount shorts. 1931 Palmy Days. 1932 The Kid from Spain. 1933 Roman Scandals. 1934 Kid Millions. 1936 Strike Me Pink. 1937 Ali Baba Goes to Town. 1940 Forty Little Mothers. 1943 Thank Your Lucky Stars. 1944 Hollywood Canteen; Show Business. 1945 Rhapsody in Blue. 1948 If You Knew Susie. 1952 The Story of Will Rogers.

CANTOR, HERMAN
Born: 1896. Died: Oct. 12, 1953, Jersey City, N.J. Screen actor.

Appeared in: 1948 Trouble Makers.

CANTOR, NAT
Born: 1897. Died: Mar. 15, 1956, Queens, N.Y. Screen, stage, vaudeville, burlesque, radio, and television actor. Brother of screen actor Charles Cantor (dec. 1966).

CANTWAY, FRED R.
Born: 1883. Died: Mar. 12, 1939, Hollywood, Calif. Screen and stage actor.

CAPRICE, JUNE
Born: 1899. Died: Nov. 9, 1936, Los Angeles, Calif. Screen actress. Married to screen actor/director Harry Millarde (dec.-date unknown).

Appeared in: 1916 Caprice of the Mountains. 1917 A Modern Cinderella. 1918 The Heart of Romance. 1921 Rogues and Romance.

CARD, KATHRYN
Born: 1893. Died: Mar. 1, 1964, Costa Mesa, Calif.(heart attack). Screen, stage, radio, and television actress.

Appeared in: 1945 Kiss and Tell. 1946 It Shouldn't Happen to a Dog; Undercurrent. 1947 The Hucksters; Born to Kill; That Hagen Girl. 1948 Three Daring Daughters; The Sainted Sisters. 1949 The Dark Past; A Kiss for Corliss; Mother Is a Freshman. 1950 Harriet Craig; The Skipper Surprised His Wife. 1951 Never Trust a Gambler. 1952 Paula; The Girl in White; You for Me; The Model and the Marriage Broker; The Pride of St. Louis. 1953 Remains to Be Seen; It Happens Every Thursday. 1955 Daddy Long Legs. 1956 Hollywood or Bust; The Birds and the Bees. 1958 Home Before Dark; Good Day for a Hanging. 1960 Because They're Young. 1962 Walk on the Wild Side. 1964 The Unsinkable Molly Brown.

CARDWELL, ALBERT C. (James Cardwell)
Born: 1921, Camden, N.J. Died: Feb. 4, 1954, Hollywood, Calif. (suicide-gun). Screen actor.

Appeared in: 1944 The Sullivans; Sweet and Low Down. 1945 The Shanghai Cobra; Voice of the Whistler. 1946 Fear; A Walk in the Sun; Behind the Mask; The Missing Lady. 1947 Devil on Wheels. 1948 Harpoon; He Walked by Night. 1949 Daughter of the Jungle; Down Dakota Way; San Antone Ambush; Tokyo Joe; And Baby Makes Three. 1950 Arizona Cowboy.

CARELL, ANNETTE
Died: Oct. 20, 1967, London, England. Screen, stage, and television actress. Appeared in U.S., British and German films.

Appeared in: 1953 Martin Luther. 1962 The Tell-Tale Heart. 1967 Our Mothers House.

CARETTE (Julien Carette)
Born: Dec. 23, 1897, France. Died: July 20, 1966, Paris, France (burns). Screen and stage actor.

Appeared in: 1932 L'affaire est dans le Sac; L'amour a L'Americaine; Les Gaites de l'Escadron. 1933 Adieu les Beaux Jorurs; Le Billet de Mille; Georges et Georgette; Je te Confie ma Femme; Gonzague; Moi et l'Imperatrice; Ganster Malgre; Le Greluchon Delicat. 1934 Quadrille d'amour; La Marraine; Paris-Camargue;

Marinella. 1935 Fanfare d'amour; Et Moi j' te Dis Qu' elle t'a Fait d' L'oeil; Fernand le Noceur; Dora Nelson; Les Soeurs Hortensias; Une Nuit de Noce. 1936 Mon Coeur t'appelle; Adventure a Paris; Les Rois du Sport. 1937 Gribouille; La vie Est Belle; 27 Reu de la Paix; La Grand Illusion. 1938 Cafe de Paris; Entree des Artistes; La Marseillaise; La Bete Humaine; La Route Enchantee; L'accroche-coeur. 1939 Le Monde Tremblera; Sixieme Etage; Tempete sur Paris; Menaces; La Famille Duraton; Je Chante; Battements de Coeur; Derriere la Facade; La Regle du Jeu; Le Recif de Corail. 1940 24 Heures de Perm; Soyez le Bienvenus. 1941 Parade en Sept Nuits; Fromont Jeune et Risler Aine. 1942 Fou d'amour; Une Etoile au Soleil; Croisteres Siderales, Lettres d'amour; Monsieur des Lourdines. 1943 Coup de Tete; Adieu Leonard; Service de Nuit; Bonsoir Mesdames, Bonsoir Mess Messieurs; Le bal des Passants. 1944 L'enquete sur le 58; Le Merle Blanc. 1945 Impasse; Sylvie et le Fantome. 1946 Les Portes de la Nuit; Histoire de Chanter; Monsieur Ludovic; L'ampir Autor de la Maison; Le Chateau de la Derniere Chance. 1947 La Mannequin Assassine; La Fleur de l'age. 1948 Une si Jolie Petite Plage. 1949 Branquigno!; Amedee; Premieres Armes; Le 84 Prend des Vacances; La Marie du Port; Occupe-toi d'Armelie; Ronde de Nuit; Oh, Amelia. 1950 Sans Laisser d'Addressee; L'auberge Rouge (The Red Inn - U.S. 1954). 1951 Pour l'amour du Ciel Ovvero E' piu Facile Che un Cammello; Rome-Paris-Rome Ovvero Signori in Carrozza!. 1952 Drole de Noce; Agence Matrimoniale. 1953 Au Diable la Vertue; La Fete a Henriette; Gli Unomini che Mascalzoni; Le bon Dieu sans Confession. 1954 Chateaux en Espagne; Sur le Banc; Pas de Coup dur Par Johnny; La Mome Pigalle; Si Paris Nous Etait Conte; Ces Sacrees Vacances; Elena et les Hommes. 1956 Coup dur Chez les Mous; Je Reviendrai a Kandara; Paris-Palace-Hotel. 1957 Crime et Chatiment. 1959 The Mirror Has Two Faces. 1961 Rules of the Game. 1962 La Jument Verte (The Green Mare). Other French film: A Nous la Liberte.

CAREW, ARTHUR EDMUND (aka ARTHUR EDMUND CAREWE)
Born: 1894, Trebeizond, Armenia. Died: Apr. 23, 1937, Santa

Appeared in: 1920 Rio Grande. 1921 Bar Nothin'; Her Mad Bargain; The Easy Road; Sham; The Mad Marriage. 1922 The Ghost Breaker; His Wife's Husband; My Old Kentucky Home; The Prodigal Judge. 1923 Trilby; Refuge; Daddy. 1924 The Long of Love; Sandra; The Price of a Party. 1925 Phantom of the Opera; The Only Thing; The Boomerang; A Lover's Oath. 1926 The Torrent; The Silent Lover; Diplomacy; Volcano. 1927 Uncle Tom's Cabin; A Man's Past; The Cat and the Canary; The Claw. 1930 The Matrimonial Bed; Sweet Kitty Bellairs; The Life of the Party. 1931 God's Gift to Women; The Gay Diplomat. 1932 Doctor X. 1933 The Mystery of the Wax Museum. 1935 Thunder in the Night. 1936 Charlie Chan's Secret. 1959 Uncle Tom's Cabin (re-release of 1927 film).

CAREW, JAMES
Born: Feb. 5, 1876, Goshen, Ind. Died: Apr. 4, 1938, London, England. Screen, stage, and radio actor. Entered films in England in 1915. Married to screen actress Ellen Terry (dec. 1928).

Appeared in: 1919 Twelve: Ten. 1930 The Lady of the Lake. 1931 Brother Alfred. 1933 You Made Me Love You. 1934 Freedom of the Seas; Mayfair Girl. 1935 Come Out of the Pantry; Mystery of Mary Celeste; Transatlantic Tunnel; The Improper Duchess. 1936 Living Dangerously. 1937 Thunder in the City, Spy of Napoleon; David Livingstone; Wings Over Africa; Strange Experiment; Murder at Madame Tussauds; Murder in the Stalls; Knight Without Armor; Racketeer Rhythm; Jericho. 1938 Dark Sands.

CAREW, ORA (Ora Whytock)
Born: 1893, Salt Lake City, Utah. Died: Oct. 26, 1955, Los Angeles, Calif. Screen, stage, and vaudeville actress. Entered films with Sennett in 1915.

Appeared in: 1915 Saved by the Wireless; The Martyrs of the Alamo. 1916 A La Cabaret; Dollars and Sense (working title The Twins); Love Comet; Wings and Wheels. 1917 Her Circus Knight (working title The Circus Girl); Oriental Love; Skidding Hearts. 1918 Too Many Millions; Go West Young Man. 1919 The Terror of the Range (serial); Loot; Under Suspicion. 1920 The Peddler of Lies. 1921 The Big Town Roundup; Little Fool; Ladyfingers; Alias Ladyfingers; A Voice in the Dark; After Your Own Heart. 1922 Sherlock Brown; Beyond the Crossroads; The Girl from Rocky Point; Smiles Are Trumps; Smudge. 1924 Paying the Limit; Getting Her Man; Three Days to Live; Waterfront Wolves; The Torrent. 1925 Cold Fury.

CAREWE, EDWIN (Jay J. Fox)
Born: Mar. 5, 1883, Gainesville, Tex. Died: Jan. 22, 1940, Los Angeles, Calif.(heart attack). Screen, stage actor, film, stage di-

rector, and film producer. Entered films as an actor with Lubin Company in 1910. Father of screen actress Rita Carewe (dec. 1955).

Appeared in: 1916 The Snow Bird.

CAREWE, RITA (Violette Carewe and aka RITA MASON)
Born: 1908. Died: Oct. 22, 1955, Torrance, Calif. Screen actress. Daughter of screen actor/director Edwin Carewe (dec. 1940).

Appeared in: 1925 Joanna. 1926 High Steppers. 1928 Revenge; Ramona; The Stronger Will. 1930 Radio Kisses (short).

CAREY, HARRY
Born: Jan. 16, 1878, New York, N.Y. Died: Sept. 21, 1947, Brentwood, Calif.(coronary thrombosis). Screen, stage actor, and playwright. Father of screen actor Harry Carey, Jr.

Appeared in: 1912 An Unseen Enemy; The Musketeers of Pig Alley; In the Aisles of the Wild; Friends; Heredity; The Informer; The Unwelcome Guest; An Adventure in the Autumn Woods. 1913 Love in an Apartment Hotel; Broken Ways; The Sheriff's Baby; The Ranchero's Revenge; The Left Handed Man; The Hero of Little Italy; Olaf—An Atom; Judith of Bethulia. 1915 Graft (serial). 1917 Straight Shooting. 1919 The Outcasts of Poker Flat; The Blind Husband. 1921 Freeze-Out; Hearts Up; If Only Jim; Sundown Slim; The Wallop; West Is West; The Fox; Desperate Trails. 1922 Man to Man; Good Men and True; Kickback. 1923 Canyon of the Fools; Crashin' Thru; Desert Driven; Miracle Baby; 1924 The Lightning Rider; The Night Hawk; The Man from Texas; Tiger Thompson; Roaring Rails; The Flaming Forties. 1925 Beyond the Border; Soft Shoes; The Texas Trail; Silent Sanderson; Bad Lands; The Prairie Pirate; The Man from Red Gulch; Wanderer. 1926 The Frontier Trail; Satan Town; Driftin' Thru; The Seventh Bandit. 1927 Slide, Kelly, Slide; A Little Journey. 1928 Trail of '98; The Border Patrol; Burning Bridges. 1931 Cavalier of the West; Trader Horn; Bad Company; The Vanishing Legion (serial); Across the Line; Double Sixes; Horsehoofs; The Hurricane Rider; Border Devils. 1932 Without Honor; Law and Order; The Devil Horse (serial); Last of the Mohicans (serial); Night Rider. 1933 Man of the Forest; Sunset Pass. 1934 Thundering Herd. 1935 Rustler's Paradise; Powdersmoke Range; Barbary Coast; The Last of the Clintons; Wild Mustang; The Last Outpost; Wagon Trail. 1936 The Last Outlaw; The Prisoner of Shark Island; Little Miss Nobody; Sutter's Gold; Valiant Is the Word for Carrie; The Accusing Finger; The Three Mesquiteers; The Man Behind the Mask; Ghost Town. 1937 Kid Galahad; Born Reckless; Souls at Sea; Border Cafe; Annapolis Salute; Danger Patrol; Aces Wild. 1938 The Port of Missing Girls; You and Me; King of Alcatraz; Sky Giant; The Law West of Tombstone; Gateway. 1939 Burn 'Em Up O'Connor; Mr. Smith Goes to Washington; Street of Missing Men; Inside Information; Code of the Streets. 1940 They Knew What They Wanted; My Son Is Guilty; Outside the 3-Mile Limit; Beyond Tomorrow. 1941 Shepherd of the Hills; Sundown; Among the Living; Parachute Battalion. 1942 The Spoilers. 1943 Air Force; Happy Land. 1944 The Great Moment. 1945 China's Little Devils. 1946 Duel in the Sun. 1947 Sea of Grass; The Angel and the Badman. 1948 So Dear to My Heart; Red River.

CARLE, RICHARD (Charles Nicholas Carleton)
Born: July 7, 1871, Somerville, Mass. Died: June 28, 1941, North Hollywood, Calif.(heart attack). Screen, stage actor, and playwright.

Appeared in: 1925 Zander the Great; The Mad Marriage; The Coming of Amos; 1926 Eve's Leaves; 1927 Soft Cushions; The Understanding Heart; Stranded (short). 1928 Fleet's In; While the City Sleeps; Habeus Corpus (short); Sunny California (short); The Worrier (short). 1928 It Can Be Done; Madam X; His Glorious Night. 1930 Brothers; The Grand Parade; A Lady to Love; Free and Easy. 1931 Flying High. 1932 One Hour with You; Fireman, Save My Child!; Night of June 13th; Other shorts prior to 1933: Rich Uncles; Hold the Babies; Some Babies. 1933 Private Jones; Man Hunt; Diplomaniacs; Morning Glory; Ladies Must Love; Golden Harvest. 1934 Hollywood Party (short); The Witching Hour; Wake Up and Dream; Caravan; Beloved; Last Round Up; Old Fashioned Way; Harold Teen; George White Scandals; Such Women Are Dangerous; Sing and Like It; Affairs of a Gentleman. 1935 Life Returns; Home on the Range; The Ghost Walks; When a Man's a Man; The Gay Deception; Love in Bloom; Here Comes Cookie; The Bride Comes Home; Night Life of the Gods; Baby Face Harrington; Moonlight on the Prairie; Dangerous. 1936 Little Red Schoolhouse; Easy to Take; The Man I Marry; College Holiday; The Trail of the Lonesome Pine; Love before Breakfast; Nevada; Anything Goes; The Case against Mrs. Ames; Drift Fence; Spendthrift; The Texas Rangers; The Arizona Raiders; Let's Sing Again; One Rainy Afternoon; Three of a Kind. 1937 She's Danger-

ous; Top of the Town; She Asked for It; Outcast; Arizona Mahoney; True Confession; The Man in Blue; Love in a Bungalow; Racketeers in Exile; It's All Yours; I'll Take Romance; Rhythm in the Clouds; 45 Fathers. 1939 Persons in Hiding; It's a Wonderful World; Undercover Doctor; Maisie; Nonotchka; Remember?. 1940 Ma, He's Making Eyes at Me; Parole Fixer; Lillian Russell; The Great McGinty; Comin' 'Round the Mountain; One Night in the Tropics; Seven Sinners; The Golden Fleecing; The Ghost Comes Home. 1941 A Dangerous Game; That Uncertain Feeling; Buy Me That Town; Moonlight in Hawaii; New Wine; The Devil and Miss Jones; My Life with Caroline; Million Dollar Baby.

CARLETON, GEORGE
Born: 1885. Died: Sept. 23, 1950, Hollywood, Calif.(heart attack). Screen and stage actor.

Appeared in: 1942 Just Off Broadway; The Great Gildersleeve; Over My Dead Body. 1944 And Now Tomorrow. 1945 A Tree Grows in Brooklyn. 1949 Prince of the Plains.

CARLETON, LLOYD B.
Born: 1872. Died: Aug. 8, 1933, N.Y. Screen, stage actor, and film director.

Appeared in: 1927 Tongues of Scandal.

CARLETON, WILLIAM P.
Born: 1873. Died: Apr. 6, 1947, Hollywood, Calif.(injuries from auto accident). Screen and stage actor. Entered films in silents.

Appeared in: 1921 A Wife's Awakening; Behind Masks; Good Women; Morals; The Inside of the Cup; Straight from Paris; What No Man Knows. 1922 Bobbed Hair; The Danger Point; Our Leading Citizen; The Law and the Woman; The Worldly Madonna; Domestic Relations. 1923 Homeward Bound; Sinner or Saint; The Truth about Wives; The Tie That Binds. 1924 Half-a-Dollar Bill. 1932 Charlie Chan's Chance. 1933 Girl without a Room; Ann Vickers. 1935 The Perfect Clue. 1936 The Bohemian Girl; The Border Patrolman. 1938 La Zandunga.

CARLETON, WILL C.
Born: 1871. Died: Sept. 21, 1941, Los Angeles, Calif. Screen and stage actor, and screenwriter. Appeared in silents.

CARLIE, EDWARD
Born: 1878. Died: Nov. 25, 1938, Hollywood, Calif.(heart attack). Screen and vaudeville actor.

Appeared in: 1924 Racing Luck. 1939 I'm from Missouri (died while dancing during filming).

CARLISLE, ALEXANDRA (Alexandra Swift)
Born: Jan. 15, 1886, Yorkshire, England. Died: Apr. 21, 1936, New York, N.Y. Screen and stage actress.

Appeared in: 1934 Half a Sinner.

CARLYLE, HELEN
Born: 1893. Died: June 30, 1933, Hollywood, Calif.("complications of ailments"). Screen and stage actress.

Appeared in: 1932 Forgotten Commandments.

CARLYLE, RICHARD
Born: May 21, 1879, Guelph, Ontario, Canada. Died: June 12, 1942, San Fernando, Calif. Screen and stage actor. Married to stage actress Mirza Marston. Entered films in 1913.

Appeared in: 1920 The Copperhead. 1921 The Inside of the Cup; Out of the Chorus; Ten Nights in a Bar Room. 1922 Women Men Marry; Back Home and Broke. 1923 Haldane of the Secrete Service. 1927 Shootin' Irons. 1928 Brotherly Love; Lingerie. 1929 Taking a Chance; The Valiant; Children of the Ritz; The Girl in the Show; It Can Be Done; In Old California; Hearts in Dixie. 1930 Guilty?; Mountain Justice; Playing Around; Tol'able David; Hideout; The Girl of the Golden West; Kismet. 1931 West of Broadway; Oh! Oh! Cleopatra (short); Quick Trigger Lee. 1932 Saddle Buster; Unholy Love. 1933 Midnight Club. 1935 When a Man's a Man; Sons of Steel; Public Opinion; Happiness C.O.D.

CARMI, MARIA
Born: 1880, Germany. Died: Aug. 1957, Myrtle Beach, S.C. Screen actress. Appeared in early UFA productions.

CARMINATI, TULLIO (Count Tullio Carminati de Brambilla)
Born: Zara, Dalmatia, Italy. Died: Feb. 26, 1971, Rome, Italy (stroke). Screen and stage actor.

Appeared in: 1926 The Bat; The Duchess of Buffalo. 1927 Stage Madness; Honeymoon Hate. 1928 Three Sinners. 1933 Gallant

Lady. 1934 Moulin Rouge; One Night of Love. 1935 Let's Live Tonight; Paris in Spring. 1936 The Three Maxims; The Wedding March; London Melody; Sunset in Vienna; La Marcia Nuzialf. 1938 Girl in the Street; The Show Goes On. 1940 Safari; Suicide Legion. 1949 The Golden Madonna. 1952 Beauty and the Devil. 1953 Roman Holiday; The Secret Conclave. 1956 War and Peace. 1960 A Breath of Scandal. 1961 El Cid. 1962 Swordsman of Siena; Hemingway's Adventures of a Young Man. 1963 The Cardinal.

CARNEY, DON "UNCLE DON" (Howard Rice)
Born: 1897. Died: Jan. 14, 1954, Miami, Fla.(heart trouble). Screen, stage, radio, and vaudeville actor. Appeared in films briefly prior to 1928.

CARNEY, GEORGE
Born: Nov. 21, 1887, Bristol, England. Died: 1947. Screen, stage, and vaudeville actor.

Appeared in: 1933 Say It with Flowers (U.S. 1934), Lest We Forget. 1934 Music Hall; Hyde Park. 1935 A Real Broke; The Small Man; City of Beautiful Nonsense. 1936 Land without Music. 1937 Dreaming Lips; Father Steps Out. 1938 Forbidden Music. 1940 The Stars Look Down. 1941 Convoy; Love on the Dole (U.S. 1945); The Common Touch. 1942 Lady in Distress. 1943 In Which We Serve. 1944 The Tawny Pipit (U.S. 1947). 1945 Waterloo; The Agitator (U.S. 1949); I Know Where I'm Going. 1950 Good Time Girl. 1951 The Little Ballerina. Other British films: Easy Riches; Paid in Error; Lancashire Luck; No Use Lying; The Root of All Evil.

CAROL, MARTINE (Marie-Louise de Mourer aka MARYSE MOURER)
Born: 1921, France. Died: Feb. 6, 1967, Monte Carlo (heart attack). Screen, stage, and radio actress. Known on stage as Catherine Arley and appeared in "Caroline" film series as Carol Martine.

Appeared in: 1943 La femme aux Loups. 1944 The Wolf Farm. 1945 Bifur III; L'extravagante Mission; Trente et Quarante. 1946 En Estes-Vous Bien Sur?. 1947 La Fleur de l'age o L'ile des Enfants Perdus; Voyage. 1948 Les Souvenirs ne Sont pas a Vendre. 1949 Les Amants de Verone (Lovers of Verone U.S. 1954); Je N'aime que Toi. 1950 Une Nuit de Noces; Mefiez-vou des Blondes; Caroline Cherie (U.S. 1954); Nous Irons a Paris. 1951 El Deseo y el Amor; Nana (U.S. 1957). 1952 Adorable Creature (U.S. 1956); A Night with Caroline; Les Belles de Nuit (Beauties of the Night U.S. 1954). 1953 Un Caprice de Caroline Cherie; Lucrece Borgia; Destinees Destini di Donne; The Bed (U.S. 1955). 1954 Secrets d'Alcove; Il Letto Della Pompadour; La Spiaggia (The Beach); Madam DuBarry. 1956 Le Carnet du Major Thompson; Defendo il Mio Amour (Defend My Love-U.S. 1959); Around the World in 80 Days; Austerlitz. 1957 La Passager Clandestin; The French Are a Funny Race (U.S. 1958); Action of the Tiger. 1958 Sins of the Borgias; The Foxiest Girl in Paris (aka Nathalie). 1959 Ten Seconds to Hell. 1960 The Sins of Lola Montes. 1961 La Francoise et l'Amour (Love and the Frenchwoman). 1962 Money, Money, Money. 1966 Hell is Empty.

CARPENTER, GLORIA
Born: 1927. Died: Sept. 11, 1958, Hollywood, Calif. Screen actress.

CARPENTER, HORACE B.
Born: 1875. Died: May 21, 1945, Hollywood, Calif.(heart attack). Screen, stage actor, and screenwriter. Entered films with Famous Players-Lasky Co.

Appeared in: 1914 The Virginian. 1923 King's Creek Law. 1924 Headin' Through; The Silent Stranger; Travelin' Fast. 1928 Texas Tommy. 1929 False Feathers; Riders of the Rio Grande; West of the Rockies; Bride of the Desert. 1930 South of Sonora. 1937 Range Defenders. 1944 Belle of the Yukon.

CARPENTER, PAUL
Born: 1921, Montreal, Canada. Died: June 12, 1964, London, England. Screen, television actor, and singer with Ted Heath's band.

Appeared in: 1946 School for Secrets. 1948 Uneasy Terms. 1953 Heat Wave; Albert RN. 1954 Duel in the Jungle; Chance Meeting (aka The Young Lovers); Paid to Kill; The Unholy Four; Black Glove; Night People. 1955 The Sea Shall Not Have Them; Break to Freedom. 1956 Scotland Yard Dragnet; Fire Maidens from Outer Space; The Iron Petticoat; No Road Back. 1957 The Hypnotist. 1958 Black Ice. 1959 Intent to Kill. 1960 Murder Reported; I Aim at the Stars. 1963 Jet Storm; Dr. Crippen; Call Me Bwana. Other film: Les Espions (The Spies).

CARR, ALEXANDER
Born: 1878, Rumni, Russia. Died: Sept. 19, 1946, Los Angeles, Calif. Screen, stage, burlesque, and circus actor. He was "Perlmutter" in the Potash and Perlmutter series on both screen and film.

Appeared in: 1923 Potash and Perlmutter. 1924 In Hollywood with Potash and Perlmutter. 1926 Partners Again; The Beautiful Cheat; April Fool. 1929 The End of the World (short). 1932 Uptown New York; No Greater Love; Hypnotized; Pathe comedies. 1933 The Death Kiss; Constant Woman; Her Splendid Folly; Out All Night. 1934 I Hate Women. 1940 Christmas in July.

CARR, GEORGIA
Born: 1925. Died: July 4, 1971, Los Angeles, Calif.(stroke). Negro singer and screen, stage, television actress. Sang with bands during 1950s and early 1960s.

Appeared in: 1957 Will Success Spoil Rock Hunter?.

CARR, GERALDINE
Born: 1917. Died: Sept. 2, 1954, near Hollywood, Calif.(auto accident). Screen and television actress.

Appeared in: 1950 The Great Jewel Robbery; The Company She Keeps. 1952 The Sniper.

CARR, JANE (Rita Brunstrom)
Born: 1909, England. Died: 1957. Screen and stage actress.

Appeared in: 1932 Let Me Explain, Dear. 1933 Orders Is Orders; Dick Turpin; Keep It Quiet. 1934 Those Were the Days; The Outcast; The Night Club Queen; The Church Mouse; Intermezzo; A Taxi to Paradise. 1935 The Triumph of Sherlock Holmes. 1936 The Interrupted Honeymoon; It's You I Want. 1937 Millions; Lilac Domino; Melody and Romance; Captain's Orders; Little Miss Somebody; Lord Edgware Dies; The Lady from Lisbon. 1948 It's Not Cricket. 1953 Terror Street. 1954 36 Hours; The Saints Girl Friday.

CARR, NAT
Born: Aug. 12, 1886, Russia. Died: July 6, 1944, Hollywood, Calif. Screen, stage, vaudeville, burlesque actor, and screenwriter.

Appeared in: 1923 Little Johnny Jones. 1925 His People. 1926 The Cohens and the Kellys; Private Izzy Murphy; Millionaires; Kosher Kitty Kelly; April Fool; Her Big Night; The Mystery Club; Watch Your Wife. 1927 The Jazz Singer; The Love Thrill; Popular Comedian (short). 1929 Madonna of the Sleeping Cars; Wall Street; "Ginsburg" series including One Gun Ginsburg; Gunboat Ginsburg and General Ginsburg. 1930 Red Heads; The Talk of Hollywood; plus the following shorts: Traffic; Two Plus Fours. 1931 Fifty Million Frenchmen; His People; plus the following shorts: Night Class; Campus Champs; Open House; Humanette. 1932 Union Depot; High Pressure. 1933 Big Time or Bust. 1934 Hey Nanny Nanny (short). 1936 Next Time We Love. 1937 Portia on Trial. 1938 Comet Over Broadway; Torchy Gets Her Man. 1939 On Trial; Everybody's Hobby; Torchy Plays with Dynamite. 1940 King of the Lumberjacks; Granny Get Your Gun.

CARR, PERCY
Born: 1865, England. Died: Nov. 22, 1926, Saranac Lake, N.Y. Screen and stage actor.

Appeared in: 1922 One Exciting Night. 1923 The Ragged Edge.

CARR, SADE (Sade Latham)
Born: 1889, London, England. Died: Nov. 17, 1940, Carmel, Calif. Screen and stage actress. Appeared in early Essaney films.

CARR, WILLIAM
Born: 1867. Died: Feb. 13, 1937, Los Angeles, Calif. Screen Actor and film director. Entered films as an actor with Lubin Company in 1907.

Appeared in: 1921 Get-Rich-Quick Wallingford.

CARRE, BARTLETT A.
Born: July 10, 1897, Melrose, Mass. Died: Apr. 26, 1971, Hollywood, Calif.(respiratory ailment). Screen actor, stuntman, assistant film production manager.

Appeared in: 1924 Behind Two Guns. 1925 Flying Hoofs.

CARRICO, CHARLES
Born: 1888. Died: Jan. 18, 1967, Desert Hot Springs, Calif. Screen actor. Appeared in films during the 1920s.

CARRIGAN, THOMAS J.
Born: 1886. Died: Oct. 2, 1941, Lapeer, Mich.(cerebral hemorrhage). Screen and stage actor. Entered films during experimen-

tal days with Powers in New York and later with Selig. Divorced from stage actress Mabel Taliaferro.

Appeared in: 1911 Cinderella. 1919 Checkers. 1921 Room and Board. 1923 Crooked Alley; Salomy Jane; You Can't Fool Your Wife. 1925 The Making of O'Malley. 1927 Wings. 1932 The Big Broadcast.

CARRILO, LEO
Born: Aug. 6, 1881, Los Angeles, Calif. Died: Sept. 10, 1961, Santa Monica, Calif.(cancer). Screen, stage, and vaudeville actor.

Appeared in: 1927 the following shorts: Italian Humorist; At the Ballgame. 1928 The Dove; plus the following shorts: The Hell Gate of Soissons; The Foreigner. 1929 Mister Antonio. 1931 Lasca of the Rio Grande; Homicide Squad; Guilty Generation; Hell Bound. 1932 Lost Men; Broken Wing; Second Fiddle; Cauliflower Alley; Girl of the Rio. 1933 Parachute Jumper; City Streets; Deception; Men Are Such Fools; Moonlight and Pretzels; Obey the Law; Racetrack; Before Morning. 1934 The Barretts of Wimpole Street; Band Plays On; Four Frightened People; The Gay Bride; Manhattan Melodrama; Viva Villa. 1935 If You Could Only Cook; In Caliente; Love Me Forever; The Winning Ticket. 1936 The Gay Desperado; La Fiesta de Santa Barbara (short); It Had to Happen; Moonlight Murder. 1937 The Barrier; History Is Made at Night; Hotel Haywire; I Promise to Pay; Manhattan Merry-Go-Round; 52nd Street. 1938 Arizona Wildcat; Blockade; Flirting with Fate; Girl of the Golden West; Little Miss Roughneck; Too Hot to Handle; City Streets. 1939 The Girl and the Gambler; Society Lawyer; Chicken Wagon Family; Rio; Fisherman's Wharf. 1940 Twenty-Mule Team; One Night in the Tropics; Wyoming; Captain Caution; Bad Man of Wyoming; Lillian Russell. 1941 Horror Island; Riders of Death Valley (serial); Tight Shoes; The Kid from Kansas; Road Agent; Barnacle Bill. 1942 What's Cooking?; Unseen Enemy; Escape from Hong Kong; Men of Texas; Top Sergeant; Danger in the Pacific; Timber; Sin Town; American Empire. 1943 Crazy House; Screen Snapshot #5 (short); Frontier Badmen; Larceny with Music; Follow the Band; Phantom of the Opera. 1944 Babes on Swing Street; Bowery to Broadway; The Ghost Catchers; Gypsy Wildcat; Merrily We Sing; Moonlight and Cactus. 1945 Crime, Inc.; Mexicana; Under Western Skies. 1947 The Fugitive. 1948 The Valiant Hombre. 1949 The Gay Amigo; The Daring Caballero; Satan's Cradle. 1950 The Girl from San Lorenzo; Pancho Villa Returns. 1964 Big Parade of Comedy (documentary).

CARRINGTON, EVELYN
Born: 1876. Died: Nov. 21, 1942, Hollywood, Calif. Screen and stage actress.

Appeared in: 1920 In Search of a Sinner. 1921 Salvation Nell. 1937 Living on Love.

CARRINGTON, HELEN
Born: 1895. Died: Oct. 22, 1963, Morristown, N.J. Screen and stage actress.

Appeared in: 1930 Heads Up; Queen High (film and stage versions).

CARROLL, NANCY (Ann Veronica La Hiff)
Born: Nov. 19, 1906, New York, N.Y. Died: Aug. 6, 1965, New York, N.Y.(natural causes). Screen, stage, and television actress.

Appeared in: 1927 Ladies Must Dress (film debut). 1928 Chicken a la King; Abie's Irish Rose; Easy Come, Easy Go; The Water Hole; Manhattan Cocktail. 1929 The Shopworn Angel; The Wolf of Wall Street; The Sin Sister; Close Harmony; The Dance of Life; Illusion; Sweetie. 1930 Dangerous Paradise; The Devil's Holiday; Honey; Paramount on Parade; Follow Thru; Laughter; Two against Death; 1931 Revolt; Stolen Heaven; Personal Maid; The Night Angel. 1932 The Man I Killed; Broken Lullaby; Wayward; Scarlet Dawn; Hot Saturday; Under Cover Man. 1933 I Love That Man; Child of Manhattan; The Woman Accused; The Kiss Before the Mirror. 1934 Transatlantic Merry-Go-Round; Jealousy; Springtime for Henry; Broken Melody. 1935 I'll Love You Always; After the Dance; Atlantic Adventure. 1938 There Goes My Heart; That Certain Age.

CARROLL, WILLIAM A.
Born: 1876. Died: Jan. 26, 1928, Glendale, Calif.(cancer). Screen and stage actor. Entered films with Selig and Vitagraph.

Appeared in: 1912 Black Sheep. 1919 Bill Henry; Trail of the Octopus (serial). 1920 The Branded Four (serial); The Screaming Shadow (serial). 1921 Fifty Candles. 1922 A Motion to Adjourn; Confidence; Chain Lightning; Remembrance; Yellow Men and Gold; Gas, Oil and Water. 1924 North of 36; Women First; Alimony; Wanderer of the Wasteland; K—The Unknown; Stolen Secrets; Sporting Youth. 1925 The Unwritten Law; The Ancient Highway;

I'll Show You the Town. 1926 Born to the West; College Days; Joselyn's Wife; The Fighting Edge. 1927 Snowbound; Beauty Shoppers.

CARRON, GEORGE
Born: 1930, Canada. Died: Apr. 23, 1970, Montreal, Canada (heart attack). Screen, stage, television, and radio actor.

Appeared in the following Canadian films: Footsteps in the Snow; Entre la mer et l'eau Douce.

CARRUTHERS, BRUCE C.
Born: 1901, Bedeque, Prince Edward Island, Canada. Died: Jan. 1954, Woodland Hills, Calif. Screen actor and film technical advisor.

CARSON, JACK
Born: Oct. 27, 1910, Carmen, Canada. Died: Jan. 2, 1963, Encino, Calif.(cancer). Screen, stage, television, and vaudeville actor. Married to screen actress Lola Albright.

Appeared in: 1937 Stage Door (film debut); Stand-In; You Only Live Once; Too Many Wives; Music for Madame; It Could Happen to You; High Flyers; The Toast of New York; Reported Missing; The Saint in New York. 1938 Vivacious Lady; Mr. Doodle Kicks Off; Crashing Hollywood; Bringing Up Baby; She's Got Everything; Night Spot; Go Chase Yourself; Law of the Underworld; This Marriage Business; Maids Night Out; Having a Wonderful Time; Carefree; Everybody's Doing It; Quick Money. 1939 Destry Rides Again; The Kid from Texas; Mr. Smith Goes to Washington; Legion of Lost Flyers; The Escape; The Honeymoon's Over. 1940 The Girl in 313; I Take This Woman; Shooting High; Young As You Feel; Enemy Agent; Parole Fixer; Typhoon; Alias the Deacon; Queen of the Mob; Sandy Gets Her Man; Love Thy Neighbor; Lucky Partners. 1941 Mr. and Mrs. Smith; Love Crazy; The Bride Came C.O.D.; Navy Blues; Blues in the Night; The Strawberry Blonde. 1942 Larceny, Inc.; Wings for the Eagle; Gentleman Jim; The Hard Way; The Male Animal. 1943 Thank Your Lucky Stars; Princess O'Rourke. 1944 The Doughgirls; Make Your Own Bed; Hollywood Canteen; Shine on Harvest Moon; Arsenic and Old Lace; Road to Glory (short). 1945 Mildred Pierce; Roughly Speaking. 1946 The Time, the Place and the Girl; One More Tomorrow; Two Guys from Milwaukee. 1947 Love and Learn; Royal Flush. 1948 Two Guys from Texas; April Showers; Romance on the High Seas; 1949 John Loves Mary; My Dream Is Yours. 1950 Bright Leaf; The Good Humor Man. 1951 Mister Universe; The Groom Wore Spurs. 1953 Dangerous When Wet. 1954 Red Garters; Phffft; A Star Is Born. 1955 Ain't Misbehaving. 1956 The Bottom of the Bottle; Magnificent Roughnecks. 1957 The Tattered Dress; The Tarnished Angels. 1958 Rally 'Round the Flag, Boys!; Cat On a Hot Tin Roof. 1960 The Bramble Bush; Circus of Horrors. 1961 The Big Bankroll; King of the Roaring 20's. 1962 Sammy the Way-Out Seal.

CARSON, JAMES B.
Born: 1885. Died: Nov. 18, 1958, Los Angeles, Calif. Screen, stage, and vaudeville actor.

Appeared in: 1930 Everything Happens to Me (short). 1933 Moonlight and Pretzels. 1935 Harmony Lane; Coronado. 1938 Secrets of an Actress; Crime School; The Girl Downstairs. 1939 The Gracie Allen Murder Case; Disputed Passage.

CARTER, CHARLES CALVERT
Born: 1859. Died: Aug. 29, 1932, Long Beach, Calif.(heart ailment). Screen actor. Entered films in 1912.

Appeared in: 1921 The Smart Set; Lying Lips. 1923 The Bolted Door; Slave of Desire. 1924 Abraham Lincoln. 1929 Broadway Fever.

CARTER, FRANK
Died: May 9, 1920, Grantville, Md. Screen actor.

Appeared in: 1922 Foolish Lives.

CARTER, MRS. LESLIE (Caroline Louise Dudley)
Born: June 10, 1862, Lexington, Ky. Died: Nov. 12, 1937, Los Angeles, Calif.(heart disease). Screen, stage, and vaudeville actress.

Appeared in: 1915 The Heart of Maryland (film and stage versions), Du Barry (film and stage versions). 1934 The Vanishing Pioneer. 1935 Rocky Mountain Mystery.

CARTER, LOUISE
Born: 1875, Denison, Iowa. Died: Nov. 10, 1957, Hollywood, Calif. Screen and stage actress, and playwright.

Appeared in: 1924 The Truth about Women. 1925 The Lost Chord;

Scandal Street; The Substitute Wife; 1926 Striving for Fortune; In Borrowed Plumes. 1932 Broken Lullaby; The Strange Case of Clara Deane; Madame Butterfly; Week-End Marriage; Two against the World; Blondie of the Follies; The Last Mile; Tess of the Storm Country. 1933 Jennie Gerhardt; This Day and Age; Pilgrimage; East of Fifth Avenue; Beauty for Sale; The Right to Romance; The Money's Paw. 1934 Beloved; You're Telling Me; Ready for Love. 1935 Straight from the Heart; The Mystery of Edwin Drood; Paddy O'Day; Reckless Roads. 1936 Rose of the Rancho. 1938 Inside Story. 1939 Nancy Drew and the Hidden Staircase.

CARTER, MONTE
Born: 1886, San Francisco, Calif. Died: Nov. 14, 1950, San Francisco, Calif. Screen, stage, burlesque, vaudeville actor; film director, and stage director.

Appeared in: 1928 Midnight Life. 1929 Melody Lane. 1931 The Vice Squad. 1934 Redhead. 1935 Make a Million; Confidential. 1936 Give Us This Night. 1937 Million Dollar Racket.

CARTIER, INEZ GIBSON
Born: 1918. Died: Aug. 4, 1970, Hollywood, Calif. Screen actress and film stunt pilot.

CARUSO, ENRICO
Born: Feb. 25, 1873, Naples, Italy. Died: Aug. 2, 1921, Naples, Italy (peritonitis). Opera singer and screen actor.

Appeared in: 1917 Webb Singing Pictures. 1918 My Cousin; The Splendid Romance (not released).

CARVER, KATHRYN (aka KATHRYN HILL)
Born: 1906, New York, N.Y. Died: July 17, 1947, Elmhurst, N.Y. (gastric ulcer). Screen actress. Appeared under both names. Divorced from screen actor Adolphe Menjou (dec. 1963).

Appeared in: 1925 When Love Grows Cold. 1926 The Wanderer; The Yankee Senor. 1927 Beware of Widows; Service for Ladies; Serenade. 1928 His Private Life; Outcast. 1929 No Defense.

CARVER, LOUISE (Louise Spilger Murray)
Born: June 9, 1869, Davenport, Iowa. Died: Jan. 18, 1956, Hollywood, Calif. Screen, stage, opera, and vaudeville actress. Appeared in Mack Sennett silent films. Married to screen actor Tom Murray (dec. 1935).

Appeared in: 1923 The Extra Girl; Main Street; Scaramouche. 1924 The Breed of the Border. 1926 Shameful Behavior?. 1927 Blondes by Choice; Backstage; The Fortune Hunter. 1929 The Redeeming Sin; The Sap; Must We Marry?; Tonight at Twelve; Wolves of the City. 1930 Back Pay; The Man from Blankley's; Big Trail. 1931 Side Show. 1932 The Monkey's Paw. 1933 Hallelujah, I'm a Bum. 1935 Every Night at Eight. 1937 Dizzy Doctors (short). 1941 Some More of Samoa (short).

CARVER, LYNN (Virginia Reid Sampson)
Born: Sept. 13, 1909. Died: Aug. 12, 1955, New York, N.Y. Screen, stage, and television actress.

Appeared in: 1935 Strangers All; Roberta; Old Man Rhythm; To Beat the Band. 1937 Maytime; The Bride Wore Red; Madame X. 1938 Young Dr. Kildare; Everybody Sing; A Christmas Carol. 1939 Huckleberry Finn; Calling Dr. Kildare; Within the Law. 1940 Sporting Blood; A Door Will Open; Broadway Melody of 1940; Dulcy; Bitter Sweet. 1941 Mr. District Attorney in the Carter Case; County Fair; Blood and Sand; Charley's Aunt. 1942 Man from Cheyenne; Yokel Boy; Sunset on the Desert. 1942 Tennessee Johnson. 1944 Law of the Valley. 1945 Flame of the West. 1946 Drifting Along. 1948 Crossed Trails. 1953 One Came Home.

CASADESUS, MATHILDE
Born: May 15, 1921, Paris, France. Died: Aug. 30, 1965, Minorca Island, Spain (heart attack). Screen and stage actress.

Appeared in: 1943 La Boite aux Reves. 1945 Le Part de L'ombre. 1946 L'ediota. 1948 Marlene. 1949 Au Royaume des Cieux; Branguignol. 1950 Boniface Sonnambule. 1951 Le Plaisir. 1953 La Dame aux Camelias. 1955 Gerviase (U.S. 1957). 1956 Ce soir les Jupons Volent. 1962 Love Is My Profession. 1963 Five Miles to Midnight. Other French film: L'Air de Paris.

CASALEGGIO, GIOVANNI
Born: 1880, Italy. Died: Nov. 11, 1955, Turin, Italy. Italian screen actor and film director.

Appeared in: 1913-1914 Cabiria.

CASE, PAUL
Born: 1895. Died: March 29, 1933, Los Angeles, Calif.(injuries from fall from horse). Screen actor.

CASEY, DOLORES (Margaret Dolores Katherine Casey)
Born: 1917, New York, N.Y. Died: May 11, 1945, Hollywood, Calif. Screen actress.

Appeared in: 1936 Big Brown Eyes. 1937 Artists and Models Abroad. 1938 Cocoanut Grove; Doctor Rhythm.

CASEY, KENNETH
Born: 1899, N.Y. Died: Aug. 10, 1965, Newburg, N.Y.(heart condition). Screen actor and songwriter.

Appeared in: 1911 Vitagraph films. 1935 MGM short.

CASEY, STUART F.
Born: 1896, London, England. Died: Jan. 23, 1948, Saratoga, N.Y. Screen and stage actor.

Appeared in: 1935 Reckless; The Age of Indiscretion; Captain Blood.

CASH, WILLIAM F.
Born: approx. 1880. Died: April 15, 1963, New York, N.Y.(stroke). Screen and stage actor.

CASS, GUY (Caster Abney Gay, Jr.)
Born: 1921. Died: Sept. 28, 1959, near Hollywood, Calif.(auto accident). Screen actor.

CASS, MAURICE
Born: Oct. 12, 1884, Vilna, Lithuania. Died: June 8, 1954, Hollywood, Calif.(heart attack). Screen, stage actor, and playwright.

Appeared in: 1923 experimental picture (sound-on-film) by Dr. Lee De Forest, exhibited at Rivoli Theatre in N.Y. 1930 Wife vs. Secretary. 1935 Two for Tonight; Millions in the Air; Whispering Smith Speaks. 1936 Professional Soldier; Everybody's Old Man; Pepper; Charlie Chan at the Opera; Give Us This Night; Champagne Waltz. 1937 Maytime; Women of Glamour; This Is My Affair; The Lady Escapes; She Had to Eat; Thin Ice; Wife, Doctor and Nurse; Danger—Love at Work, Life Begins in College; Ali Baba Goes to Town; Big Town Girl; Exiled to Shanghai. 1938 Making the Headlines; The Lone Wolf in Paris; Gangs of New York; Walking Down Broadway; The Baroness and the Butler; When Were You Born?; Josette; Sunset Trail; Gold Diggers in Paris; A Desperate Adventure; Exposed; Breaking the Ice. 1939 Second Fiddle; Mr. Smith Goes to Washington. 1940 Florian. 1941 Chocolate Soldier; Charley's Aunt; Blood and Sand. 1942 My Heart Belongs to Daddy. 1943 Mission to Moscow. 1944 Up in Arms; Mrs. Parkington. 1945 Easy to Look At; Hit the Hay; Paris Underground; Her Lucky Night; Wonder Man. 1946 The Notorious Lone Wolf; Angel on My Shoulder; Catman of Paris; Spook Busters. 1947 High Conquest; Spoilers of the North. 1948 Song of My Heart. 1949 Once More My Darling. 1952 We're Not Married.

CASSEL, SID
Born: 1897, Leeds, England. Died: Jan. 17. 1960. Hollywood. Calif. Screen, stage, and television actor.

CASSIDY, BILL (William E. Cassidy)
Born: 1876. Died: April 6, 1943, Cincinnati, Ohio. Screen and stage actor.

Appeared in: 1915 Birth of a Nation. 1916 Intolerance.

CASSIDY, ED (Edward Cassidy)
Born: 1893. Died: Jan. 1968, Woodland Hills, Calif. Screen actor.

Appeared in: 1935 Toll of the Desert; Commodore. 1937 Come on, Cowboys. 1938 Frontier Town; The Purple Vigilantes; Man from Music Mountain; Cassidy of Bar 20; Rawhide; The Mexicali Kid; Starlight Over Texas 1939 Wild Horse Canyon; Silver on the Sage; Mountain Rhythm; Desperate Trails; Cowboy from Texas. 1940 Riders of Pasco Basin; Ragtime Cowboy Joe. 1941 Wide Open Town; Robbers of the Range; Wyoming Wildcat; The Gang's All Here. 1942 House of Errors; The Mad Monster; Pirates of the Prairie. 1943 Cowboy in the Clouds; The Avenging Rider. 1944 Boss of Rawhide; Brand of the Devil; Frontier Outlaws; Fuzzy Settles Down; The Great Mike; The Pinto Bandit; Saddle Leather; Rustlers' Hideout; Trigger Law; Tucson Raiders. 1945 Along the Navajo Trail; Arson Squad; Corpus Christi Bandits; The Gangster's Den; Sheriff of Cimarron; Stagecoach Outlaws; Sunset in Eldorado; Three in the Saddle. 1946 Alias Billy the Kid; Ambush Trail; Days of Buffalo Bill; Trigger Fingers; The El Paso Kid; The Navajo Kid; Prairie Badmen; Roaring Rangers; Roll on Texas Moon; Sun Valley Cyclone. 1947 Homesteaders of Paradise Valley; Oregon Trail Scouts; Son of Zorro (serial); Valley of Fear; Stagecoach to Denver; Buffalo Bill Rides Again; Border Feud. 1948 The Bold Frontiersman; Desperadoes of Dodge City. 1949 Roughshod. 1950 Fence Riders; Trail of Robin Hood; Buckaroo Sheriff of Texas. 1951 Million Dollar Pursuit. 1952 Desperadoes Outpost; Black Hills Ambush; Night Raiders; And Now Tomorrow; Talk about a Stranger. 1956 The First Traveling Saleslady.

CASSON, SIR LEWIS
Born: 1876. Died: May 16, 1969, London, England. Screen, stage, television actor, and stage producer and stage director.

Appeared in: 1930 Escape. 1936 Rhodes; Calling the Tune. 1937 Victoria the Great. 1938 South Riding; Sixty Glorious Years; 1949 Shake Hands with the Devil. 1951 Men of the Sea.

CASTIGLIONI, IPHIGENE
Born: 1901. Died: July 30, 1963, Hollywood, Calif. Screen, stage, and television actress.

Appeared in: 1935 Story of Louis Pasteur. 1937 Life of Emile Zola; Maytime. 1953 Greatest Show on Earth. 1954 Rear Window. 1955 Conquest of Space. 1957 Funny Face; Wild Is the Wind; Valerie. 1962 Rome Adventure; Comancheros.

CASTLE, DON
Born: Sept. 29, 1917, Beaumont, Tex. Died: May 26, 1966, Hollywood, Calif.(overdose of medication). Screen actor.

Appeared in: 1938 Love Finds Andy Hardy (film debut); Rich Man, Poor Girl; Out West with the Hardys. 1939 These Glamour Girls; 1940 I Take This Woman. 1941 Power Dive; World Premiere. 1942 Tombstone, the Town Too Tough to Die. 1947 The Invisible Wall; The Guilty; High Tide; Roses Are Red. 1948 Perilous Waters; I Wouldn't Be in Your Shoes; Strike It Rich; Who Killed "Doc" Robbin?. 1949 Stampede. 1950 Motor Patrol. 1957 The Big Land; Gunfight at the O.K. Corral.

CASTLE, IRENE (Irene Foote)
Born: 1893, New Rochelle, N.Y. Died: Jan. 25, 1969, Eureka Springs, Ark. Screen actress and dancer. Married to actor, dancing partner Vernon Castle (dec. 1919).

Appeared in: 1915 The Whirl of Life. 1917 Patria (serial). 1918 The Hillcrest Mystery. 1919 The Firing Line; The Invisible Bond. 1921 The Broadway Bride. 1922 French Heels; No Trespassing; Slim Shoulders. 1924 Broadway after Dark.

CASTLE, LILLIAN
Born: 1865. Died: April 24, 1959, Los Angeles, Calif. Screen and vaudeville actress.

Appeared in: 1935 Confidential.

CASTLE, NICK
Born: March 21, 1910, Brooklyn, N.Y. Died: Aug. 18, 1968, Los Angeles, Calif.(heart attack). Screen and vaudeville dancer, and film and TV dance director.

Appeared in: 1955 Artists and Models.

CASTRO, STEVEN
Born: 1864. Died: Nov. 19, 1952, Hollywood, Calif. Screen cowboy actor and rodeo rider.

CATLETT, WALTER
Born: Feb. 4, 1889, San Francisco, Calif. Died: Nov. 14, 1960, Woodland Hills, Calif.(stroke). Screen, stage, opera, vaudeville actor, and screenwriter.

Appeared in: 1924 Second Youth. 1926 Summer Bachelors. 1929 Married in Hollywood; Why Leave Home?; The Gay Nineties. 1930 The Floradora Girl; Let's Go Places; Happy Days; The Big Party; The Golden Calf; Aunts in the Pants. 1931 Front Page; Cock of the Air; Platinum Blonde; Yellow; Palmy Days; Gold Fish Bowl; The Maker of Men. 1932 The Expert; It's Tough to Be Famous; Big City Blues; The Penalty of Fame; Sky Devils; Back Street; Rain; Free, White and 21; Rockabye; Okay America; Sport Parade. 1933 Private Jones; Only Yesterday; Mama Loves Papa; Arizona to Broadway. 1934 Unknown Blonde; The Captain Hates the Sea; Olsen's Big Moment; Lightning Strikes Twice. 1935 Every Night at Eight; A Tale of Two Cities; Affair of Susan. 1936 I Loved a Soldier; Mr. Deeds Goes to Town; We Went to College; Follow Your Heart; Sing Me a Love Song; Cain and Mable; Banjo on My Knee. 1937 Four Days' Wonder; On the Avenue; Love Is News; Wake Up and Live; Love Under Fire; Danger— Love at Work; Varsity Show; Every Day's a Holiday; Come Up Smiling. 1938 Bringing Up Baby; Going Places. 1939 Kid Nightingale; Exile Express; Zaza. 1940 Pop Always Pays; Remedy for

Riches; Comin' 'Round the Mountain; Spring Parade; Half a Sinner; Pinocchio (voice); Li'l Abner; The Quarterback. 1941 You're the One; Honeymoon for Three; Horror Island; It Started with Eve; Wild Man of Borneo; Million Dollar Baby; Hello Sucker; Manpower; Mad Men of Missouri; Unfinished Business; Steel Against the Sky; Wild Bill Hickok Rides. 1942 Star Spangled Rhythm; My Gal Sal; Maisie Get Her Man; Yankee Doodle Dandy; Give Out Sisters; Heart of the Golden West; Between Us Girls. 1943 West Side Kid; Hit Parade of 1943; How's About It?; Cowboy in Manhattan; Get Going; They Got Me Covered; Fired Wife; His Butler's Sister. 1944 Her Primitive Man; Pardon My Rhythm; The Ghost Catchers; Hat Check Honey; Up in Arms; Lady, Let's Dance!; Three Is a Family; Hi, Beautiful; My Gal Loves Music; Lake Placid Serenade. 1945 The Man Who Walked Alone; I Love a Bandleader. 1946 Riverboat Rhythm; Slightly Scandalous. 1947 I'll Be Yours. 1948 Mr. Reckless: Are You With It?; The Boy with Green Hair. 1949 Henry, the Rainmaker; Look for the Silver Lining; Dancing in the Dark; The Inspector General; Leave It to Henry. 1949 Father Makes Good. 1950 Father's Wild Game. 1951 Father Takes the Air; Honeychile; Here Comes the Groom. 1956 The Gay Nineties; Davy Crockett and the River Pirates; Friendly Persuasion. 1957 Beau James.

CAULKINS, RUFUS
Died: July 15, 1935, Los Angeles, Calif.(auto accident). Screen actor.

CAVANAUGH, HOBART
Born: 1887, Virginia City, Nev. Died: April 27, 1950, Woodland Hills, Calif. Screen, stage, and vaudeville actor.

Appeared in: 1928 San Francisco Nights. 1929 Sympathy (short). 1930 The Poor Fish (short); The Headache Man (short). 1932 Close Friends (short). 1933 Footlight Parade; Picture Snatcher; Death Watch; Study in Scarlet; Gold Diggers of 1933; Goodbye Again; Mary Stevens, M.D.; The Mayor of Hell; Private Detective 62; Kennel Murder Case; From Headquarters; Broadway Thru a Keyhole; Lilly Turner; Havana Widows; Convention City; Headline Shooter; No Marriage Ties; The Devil's Mate; My Woman; I Cover the Waterfront. 1934 Wonder Bar; Mandalay; The Firebird; Dark Hazard; I Sell Everything; Madame Du Barry; I Am a Thief; St. Louis Kid; Housewife; A Lost Lady; Fashions of 1934; Kansas City Princess; Moulin Rouge; Hi Nellie; Easy to Love; I've Got Your Number; Harold Teen; Jimmy the Gent; Merry Wives of Reno; The Key; A Very Honorable Guy; A Modern Hero; Now I'll Tell. 1935 Wings in the Dark; While the Patient Slept; Captain Blood; Broadway Breveties (short); Don't Bet on Blondes; We're in the Money; Border Town; Broadway Gondolier; Page Miss Glory; Dr. Socrates; A Midsummer Night's Dream; I Live for Love. 1936 The Lady Consents; Love Letters of a Star; Colleen; Love Begins at Twenty; Two against the World; Hearts Divided; Sing Me a Love Song; Cain and Mabel; Here Comes Carter; The Golden Arrow; Stage Struck; Wife vs. Secretary. 1937 The Great O'Malley; Three Smart Girls; Mysterious Crossing; The Mighty Treve; Night Key; Girl Overboard; Love in a Bungalow; Reported Missing. 1938 That's My Story; Cowboy from Brooklyn; Orphans of the Street. 1939 Zenobia; Career; Tell No Tales; Chicken Wagon Family; Reno; That's Right, You're Wrong; The Covered Trailer; The Honeymoon's Over; Adventures of Jane Arden; Rose of Washington Square. 1940 You Can't Fool Your Wife; A Child Is Born; I Stole a Million; Shooting High; An Angel from Texas; Street of Memories; Stage to Chino; Public Deb. No. 1; The Great Plane Robbery; Santa Fe Trail; Charter Pilot; Love, Honor and Oh-Baby!; The Ghost Comes Home; Hired Wife. 1941 Horror Island; Meet the Chump; Thieves Fall Out; Land of the Open Range; I Wanted Wings. 1942 A Tragedy at Mid-Night; Jackass Mail; Whistling in Dixie; Stand by for Action; My Favorite Spy; The Magnificent Dope. 1943 Skylark; Dangerous Blondes; The Meanest Man in the World; The Kansan; Gildersleeve on Broadway; Man from Down Under. 1944 Louisiana Hayride; Sweet Rosie O'Grady; Jack London; Kismet. 1945 House of Fear; Roughly Speaking; Don Juan Quilligan; I'll Remember April; Lady on a Train. 1946 Cinderella Jones; The Spider Woman Strikes Back; Faithful in My Fashion; Black Angel; Little Iodine; Margie. 1947 Driftwood. 1948 Best Man Wins; You Gotta Stay Happy; Up on Central Park; The Inside Story. 1949 A Letter to Three Wives. 1950 Stella.

CAVANNA, ELISE
Born: 1902. Died: May 12, 1963, Hollywood, Calif.(cancer). Screen, stage actress, author, and painter.

Appeared in: 1926 Love 'Em and Leave 'Em. 1931 A Melon-Drama (short). 1933 The Barber Shop; The Pharmacist. 1934 You're Telling Me. 1938 I Met My Love Again; Everybody Sing. 1946 Ziegfeld Follies.

CAVEN, ALLAN
Born: Mar. 25, 1880, Concord, Calif. Died: Jan. 19, 1941, Hollywood, Calif. Screen and stage actor. Entered films in 1919.

Appeared in: 1921 The Primal Law. 1923 When Odds are Even. 1927 London After Midnight; Shanghai Bound. 1928 The Terrible People (serial); The Man Who Laughs. 1929 Leave It to Gerry; The Million Dollar Collar. 1934 Opened by Mistake (short). 1935 Thicker Than Water (short). 1936 Rebellion. 1937 Old Louisiana; Nation Aflame. 1938 I Am a Criminal.

CAVENDER, GLEN W.
Born: 1884. Died: Feb. 9, 1962, Hollywood, Calif. Screen actor and film director. One of the original Keystone Kops; and appeared in numerous Sennett films.

Appeared in: 1915 Fickle Fatty's Fall; A Submarine Pirate. 1916 Fatty and Mable Adrift; Because He Loved Her; The Village Blacksmith; The Surf Girl. 1917 A Dog Catcher's Love; The Pawnbroker's Heart. 1921 Hearts of Youth; The Primal Law; Skirts; Little Miss Hawkshaw; Straight from the Shoulder; What Love Will Do. 1922 Iron to Gold. 1923 Main Street. 1925 Keep Smiling; Manhattan Madness. 1927 The General. 1929 Ships of the Night.

CAVENDISH, DAVID
Born: 1891. Died: Oct. 8, 1960, Hollywood, Calif. (heart attack). Screen and stage actor.

Appeared in: 1942 Random Harvest.

CAWTHORN, JOSEPH
Born: March 29, 1868, N.Y. Died: Jan. 21, 1949, Beverly Hills, Calif. (stroke). Married to screen actress Queenie Vass (dec. 1960). Screen and stage actor.

Appeared in: 1927 Very Confidential; Two Girls Wanted; The Secret Studio. 1928 Silk Legs; Hold 'Em Yale. 1929 Street Girl; Jazz Heaven; Dance Hall; The Taming of the Shrew; Speakeasy. 1930 Dixiana; The Princess and the Plumber. 1931 Kiki; The Runaround; Peach O'Reno; A Tailor Made Man. 1932 White Zombie; Love Me Tonight; They Call It Sin. 1933 Whistling in the Dark; Blondie Johnson; Grand Slam; Men Are Such Fools; Made on Broadway; Best of Enemies; Broken Dreams; Radio short. 1934 Housewife; Young and Beautiful; The Human Side; Lazy River; The Last Gentleman; Twenty Million Sweethearts; Glamour; Music in the Air; The Cat and the Fiddle. 1935 Adeline; Maybe It's Love; Go into Your Dance; Sweet Music; Page Miss Glory; Bright Lights; Harmony Lane; Gold Diggers of 1935; Naughty Marietta; Smart Girl. 1936 Freshman Love; Hot Money; The Great Ziegfeld; One Rainy Afternoon; Brides are Like That; Crime Over London. 1940 Lillian Russell; Scatterbrain. 1941 So Ends the Night. 1942 The Postman Didn't Ring.

CAZENUVE, PAUL
Born: France. Died: June 22, 1925, Hollywood, Calif. Screen, stage actor, and film director.

Appeared in: 1921 Big Town Ideas; The Queen of Sheba. 1923 Six Days; The French Doll.

CECCARELLI, VINCENZO
Born: 1889. Died: Aug. 8, 1969, Los Angeles, Calif. Screen actor and singer.

CECIL, EDWARD
Born: Sept. 1888, San Francisco, Calif. Died: Dec. 13, 1940, Los Angeles, Calif. Screen, stage, and vaudeville actor.

Appeared in: 1921 Big Game; The Greater Claim; Parted Curtains; There Are No Villains; The Off-Shore Pirate. 1922 The Guttersnipe; The Love Gambler; My Wild Irish Rose; The Top of New York. 1923 The Scarlet Car. 1924 Wolves of the North (serial); The Sword of Valor. 1925 The Phantom of the Opera; Hidden Loot; Secrets of the Night; What Happened to Jones?. 1926 Vanishing Millions (serial); The Crown of Lies; The Stolen Ranch; The Smoke Eaters. 1927 Woman's Law; Hoof Marks; Cheaters; The Desert of the Lost. 1928 Jazzland; The Sky Rider; Saddle Mates; A Midnight Adventure. 1929 Silent Sentinel; The Black Book (serial). 1930 Guilty?; Lotus Lady. 1931 Resurrection.

CECIL, MARY
Born: 1885, N.Y. Died: Dec. 21, 1940, New York, N.Y. (pneumonia). Screen, stage, and radio actress.

Appeared in: 1939 The Women (stage and film versions).

CELESTE, OLGA
Born: 1887, Sweden. Died: Aug. 31, 1969, Burbank, Calif. (heart attack after treatment for pneumonia). Screen, circus, vaudeville actress, and animal trainer.

CELLIER, FRANK
Born: Feb. 23, 1884, Surbiton, Surrey, England. Died: Sept. 27, 1948, London, England. Screen and stage actor.

Appeared in: 1931 Tin Gods; Her Reputations. 1933 Soldiers of the King; The Golden Cage; The Fire Raisers; Colonel Blood. 1934 The Woman in Command. 1935 Loves of a Dictator; Lorna Doone; The 39 Steps; Mister Hobo; The Passing of the Third Floor Back. 1936 Rhodes; Nine Days a Queen; The Man Who Lived Again; Tudor Rose; O.H.M.S. (You're in the Army Now—U.S. 1937). 1937 Non-Stop New York; Take My Tip; Kate Plus Ten; Action for Slander. 1938 Sixty Glorious Years; The Ware Case (U.S. 1939); A Royal Divorce. 1939 The Midas Touch. 1940 Queen of Destiny; Quiet Wedding (U.S. 1942). 1941 Queen of Crime; Love on the Dole (U.S. 1945). 1942 The Big Blockade; Ship with Wings. 1944 Give Us the Moon. 1946 Quiet Week-End (U.S. 1948); The Magic Bow. 1948 The Blind Goddess. 1949 Easy Money.

CESANA, RENZO
Born: 1907. Died: Nov. 8, 1970, Hollywood, Calif. (lung cancer). Screen and television actor.

Appeared in: 1950 A Lady without a Passport; Stromboli. 1951 Mark of the Renegade; Try and Get Me. 1952 California Conquest. 1959 For the First Time; The Naked Maja. 1960 Fast and Sexy. 1961 Francis of Assisi.

CESAR, M.
Died: Sept. 1921. Screen actor.

CHABRIER, MARCEL
Born: 1888, France. Died: Aug. 18, 1946, Piedmont, Canada (drowned). Screen, stage, radio actor, and painter.

Appeared in: 1943 Le Pere Chopin.

CHADWICK, HELENE
Born: Nov. 25, 1897, Chadwick, N.Y. Died: Sept. 4, 1940, Los Angeles, Calif. (injuries from fall). Screen and stage actress. Entered films in 1916.

Appeared in: 1919 Heartsease. 1920 Scratch My Back; Cupid; The Cowpuncher, Long Arm of Mannister, The Cup of Fury. 1921 The Sin Flood; From the Ground Up; Godless Men; The Old Nest; Dangerous Curve Ahead; Made in Heaven. 1922 Yellow Men and Gold; Glorious Fool; Dust Flower; Brothers under the Skin. 1923 Quicksands; Gimme. 1924 Her Own Free Will; Reno; The Border Legion; Her Dark Swan; Love of Women; The Masked Dancer; The Naked Truth; Trouping with Ellen; Why Men Leave Home. 1925 Re-Creation of Brian Kent; The Woman Hater. 1926 Dancing Days; Hard Boiled; The Golden Cocoon; Pleasures of the Rich; The Still Alarm. 1927 The Rose of Kildare; The Bachelor's Baby; Stage Kisses; Stolen Pleasures. 1928 Modern Mothers; Say It with Sables; Women Who Dare. 1929 Father and Son; Confessions of a Wife. 1930 Men Are Like That. 1931 Hell Bound. 1935 Mary Burns, Fugitive.

CHALIAPIN, FEODOR
Born: Feb. 13, 1873, Kazan-Kazan, Russia. Died: April 12, 1938, Paris, France (anemia brought on by kidney ailment). Screen, opera, and vaudeville actor. Most celebrated Russian bassos. Father of screen actor Feodor Chaliapin, Jr.

Appeared in: 1933 Don Quixote.

CHALMERS, THOMAS
Born: Oct. 20, 1890, New York, N.Y. Died: June 12, 1966, Greenwich, Conn. Screen, opera, television, radio actor, film director, and producer of industrial and documentary films.

Appeared in: 1923 Puritan Passions. 1927 Blind Alleys. 1938 The Rivers (narr.), 1961 Romanoff and Juliet. 1963 All the Way Home. 1964 The Outrage.

CHALZEL, LEO
Born: 1901. Died: July 16, 1953, Westport, Conn. (heart ailment). Screen, stage, vaudeville, and television actor.

Appeared in: 1934 Men in White; Come on Marines.

CHAMBERLIN, FRANK
Born: 1870. Died: Aug. 29, 1935, Los Angeles, Calif. Cowboy screen actor and songwriter.

CHAMBERS, J. WHEATON
Born: 1888. Died: Jan. 31, 1958, Hollywood, Calif. Screen and stage actor. Entered films in 1929.

Appeared in: 1942 Reap the Wild Wind; Even as I.O.U. (short); The Wife Takes a Flyer; They All Kissed the Bride. 1943 This Land

Is Mine. 1944 The Falcon out West; Tall in the Saddle. 1945 The Clock; That's the Spirit; Marshal of Laredo. 1946 People Are Funny. 1949 Deputy Marshal; Not Wanted; Mississippi Rhythm. 1950 Baron of Arizona; Between Midnight and Dawn. 1951 The Prowler; The Well; The Cimarron Kid; The Day the Earth Stood Still. 1952 Wagons West; Slaves of Babylon. 1954 The Big Chase. 1956 The Peacemaker.

CHAMBERS, MARGARET
Died: Oct. 6, 1965, Hollywood, Calif. Screen actress.

Appeared in: 1929 Woman to Woman.

CHAMBERS, MARIE
Born: 1889. Died: March 21, 1933, Paris, France. Screen and stage actress.

Appeared in: 1925 That Royal Girl.

CHAN, MRS. PON Y.
Born: 1870. Died: April 1, 1958, Hollywood, Calif. Screen character actress.

CHANCE, ANNA
Born: Oct. 25, 1884, Oxford, Md. Died: Sept. 11, 1943, Hollywood, Calif. Screen, stage, and vaudeville actress. Married to screen actor Charles Grapewin (dec. 1956). Entered films in 1929.

Appeared in all Charley Grapewin comedies for Christie, which included in 1929 the following: Jed's Vacation; Ladies Choice; That Red Headed Hussy. Prior to 1930 was in The Wanderlust (short).

CHANDLER, ANNA
Born: 1887. Died: July 10, 1957, El Sereno, Calif. Screen, vaudeville actress, and singer.

Appeared in: 1928 Popular Songs (short). 1932 The Big Broadcast.

CHANDLER, HELEN
Born: Feb. 1, 1906, Charleston, S.C. Died: Apr. 30, 1965, Hollywood, Calif.(following surgery). Screen and stage actress. Divorced from screen actor Branwell Fletcher and writer Cyril Hume.

Appeared in: 1927 The Joy Girl; The Music Master. 1929 Salute; Mother's Boy; The Sky Hawk. 1930 Outward Bound; Rough Romance; Mother's Cry. 1931 Fanny Foley Herself; Daybreak; Salvation Nell; The Last Flight; A House Divided; Dracula. 1932 Cock of the Air; Vanity Street; Behind Jury Doors. 1933 Goodbye Again; Alimony Madness; Dance Hall Hostess; The Worst Woman in Paris?; Christopher Strong. 1934 Long Lost Father; Lover Divine; Midnight Alibi; Unfinished Symphony. 1935 Radio Parade of 1935; It's a Bet. 1938 Mr. Boggs Steps Out.

CHANDLER, JAMES ROBERT
Born: 1860. Died: Mar. 17, 1950, East Islip, N.Y. Screen and stage actor.

Appeared in: 1921 Home Stuff. 1925 Hurricane Horseman. 1927 Hawk of the Hills (serial). 1928 Quick Triggers. 1929 Hawk of the Hills (re-release of 1927 serial as a feature film).

CHANDLER, JEFF (Ira Grossel)
Born: Dec. 1918, Brooklyn, N.Y. Died: June 17, 1961, Culver City, Calif.(blood poisoning following surgery). Screen, stage, and radio actor.

Appeared in: 1947 Johnny O'Clock; The Invisible Wall; The Roses Are Red. 1949 Sword in the Desert; Mr. Belvedere Goes to College; Abandoned. 1950 Deported; Two Flags West; Broken Arrow. 1951 The Iron Man; The Bird of Paradise; Flame of Araby; Smuggler's Island. 1952 The Battle at Apache Pass; Red Ball Express; Yankee Buccaneer; Meet Danny Wilson (unbilled); Because of You. 1953 East of Sumatra; The Great Sioux Uprising; War Arrows. 1954 The Sign of the Pagan; Taza; Son of Coshise (unbilled); Yankee Pasha. 1955 Foxfire; Female on the Beach; The Spoilers. 1956 Away All Boats; Pillars of the Sky; Toy Tiger. 1957 Jeanne Eagles; The Tattered Dress; Drango; Pay the Devil. 1958 The Lady Takes a Flyer; Raw Wind in Eden. 1959 Ten Seconds to Hell; Stranger in My Arms; The Jayhawkers; Thunder in the Sun. 1960 The Plunderers. 1961 Mad Dog Coll; Return to Peyton Place. 1962 Merrill's Marauders.

CHANEY, LON, SR.
Born: Apr. 1, 1883, Colorado Springs, Colo. Died: Aug. 26, 1930, Los Angeles, Calif. Screen, stage actor, film director, screenwriter, and stage producer. Father of screen actor Lon Chaney, Jr.(dec. 1973).

Appeared in: 1914 Where the Forest Ends. 1915 The Chimney's Street; The Oyster Dredger; The Stool Pidgeon. 1917 Fires of Rebellion; Triumph. 1918 That Devil "Bateese"; Riddle Gawn; Kaiser, the Beast of Berlin. 1919 Paid In Advance; The Rap; The Unholy Three; The Miracle Man; False Faces; Victory; The Wolf Breed; The Wicked Darling. 1920 Nomads of the North; Treasure Island; Daredevil Jack. 1921 The Penalty; Outside the Law; The Ace of Hearts; Bit of Life; For Those We Love; The Night Rose. 1922 The Trap; Quincy Adams Sawyer; Shadows; A Blind Bargain; Flesh and Blood; Voices of the City; The Light in the Dark; Oliver Twist. 1923 The Hunchback of Notre Dame; The Shock; All the Brothers Were Valiant; While Paris Sleeps. 1924 He Who Gets Slapped; The Next Corner. 1925 The Phantom of the Opera; The Tower of Lies; The Monster; The Unholy Three (also 1919 and 1930 versions). 1926 The Black Bird; The Road to Mandalay; Tell It to the Marines. 1937 Mr. Wu; The Unknown; Mockery; London After Midnight. 1928 The Big City; Laugh, Clown, Laugh; While The City Sleeps; West of Zanzibar. 1929 The Thunder; Where East Is East. 1930 The Unholy Three (also 1919 and 1925 versions).

CHANEY, NORMAN "CHUBBY"
Born: Jan. 18, 1918, Baltimore, Md. Died: May 30, 1936, Baltimore, Md. (glandular trouble). Screen actor. Entered the "Our Gang" series in 1926 and appeared in part of Joe Cobb until he outgrew his assignment in 1934.

CHAPLIN, CHARLES, JR.
Born: 1925, Beverly Hills, Calif. Died: March 20, 1968, Hollywood, Calif.(blood clot). Screen, stage, and television actor. Son of screen actor Charles Chaplin and screen actress Lita Grey Chaplin.

Appeared in: 1952 Limelight. 1954 Follow the Hunter; Fangs of the Wild. 1958 High School Confidential. 1959 Night of the Quarter Moon; The Beat Generation; Girls Town; The Big Operator.

CHAPLIN, SYDNEY
Born: Mar. 17, 1885, Capetown, South Africa. Died: Apr. 16, 1956, Nice, France. Screen, stage actor, and film producer. Half brother of screen actor Charles Chaplin. Entered films with Sennett.

Appeared in: 1914 Fatty's Wine Party; Tillie's Punctured Romance; Gussle, the Golfer (in which he appeared as "Gussle" in the series). 1915 Hushing the Scandal (reissued as Friendly Enemies); A Steel Rolling Mill; The United States Army in San Francisco; Giddy, Gay and Ticklish (aka A Gay Lothario); That Springtime Feeling; Gussle's Day of Rest; Gussle's Wayward Path; Gussle Rivals Jonah; Gussle's Backward Way; Gussle Tied to Trouble; A Lover's Lost Control (aka Looking Them Over); A Submarine Pirate. 1918 Shoulder Arms; A Dog's Life. 1921 King, Queen, Joker. 1922 Pay Day. 1923 Her Temporary Husband; The Rendezvous; The Pilgrim. 1924 The Perfect Flapper; Galloping Fish. 1925 The Man on the Box; Charley's Aunt. 1926 Oh, What a Nurse; The Better 'Ole. 1927 The Missing Link. 1928 A Little Bit of Fluff; The Fortune Hunter. 1963 Thirty Years of Fun (documentary).

CHAPMAN, BLANCHE
Born: 1851, Covington, Ky. Died: June 7, 1941, Rutherford, N.J. Screen, stage, and radio actress. Appeared in silents and talking films.

CHAPMAN, EDYTHE
Born: Oct. 8, 1863, Rochester, N.Y. Died: Oct. 15, 1948, Glendale, Calif. Screen and stage actress. Married to screen actor James Neill (dec. 1931).

Appeared in: 1917 The Little American; The Evil Eye. 1919 Everywoman. 1920 Huckleberry Finn; Double Dyed Deceiver. 1921 Alias Ladyfingers; Ladyfingers; Bits of Life; The Night Rose; Bunty Pulls the Strings; Dangerous Curves Ahead; Just Out of College; One Wild Week; A Tale of Two Worlds; A Wife's Awakening. 1922 Manslaughter; Beyond the Rocks; Her Husband's Trademark; Youth to Youth; My American Wife; North of the Rio Grande; The Sleepwalker; Saturday Night; Tailor-Made Man. 1923 The Ten Commandments; Divorce; The Miracle Makers; The Girl I Loved; Hollywood. 1924 Chastity; Broken Barriers; Worldly Goods; The Breaking Point; Daughters of Pleasure; The Shadow of the East; The Wise Virgin. 1925 Lightnin'; Soul Mates; Classified; Havoc; The Pride of the Force; Daddy's Gone A'Hunting; In the Name of Love; Lazybones; Learning to Love. 1926 Faithful Wives; The Runaway; Three Faces East; One Minute to Play. 1927 King of Kings; American Beauty; The Student Prince in Old Heildelberg; The Crystal Cup; Naughty but Nice; Man Crazy. 1928 Happiness Ahead; Shepherd of the Hills; The Count of Ten; Love Hungry;

Three Week Ends; The Little Yellow House; Sally's Shoulders. 1929 Twin Beds; Synthetic Sin; The Idle Rich. 1930 Double Cross Roads; Take the Heir; Navy Blues; Up the River; Man Trouble.

CHAPMAN, THOMAS H. (Maj. Gen.)
Born: 1896. Died: June 7, 1969, Boerne, Tex. Screen actor and pilot.

Appeared in: 1927 Wings (flew the plane in Buddy Rogers' role).

CHARLESWORTH, JOHN
Born: 1935, England. Died: Apr. 2, 1960, Birmingham, England. (suicide). Screen, stage, and television actor.

Appeared in: 1951 Scrooge; Tom Brown's Schooldays. 1952 The Magic Box. 1954 The Horse's Mouth; John of the Fair. 1956 A Question of Adultery (U.S. 1959); Blonde Sinner (aka Yield to the Night). 1957 Yangtse Incident; Battle Hill. 1959 Blue Peter; The Angry Silence (U.S. 1960); The Man Upstairs.

CHARSKY, BORIS
Born: May 28, 1893, Petrograd, Russia. Died: June 1, 1956, Hollywood, Calif. Screen and stage actor.

Appeared in: 1928 The Red Dance. 1929 Captain Lash.

CHARTERS, SPENCER
Born: 1875, Ducannon, Pa. Died: Jan. 25, 1943, Hollywood, Calif. (suicide-pills and carbon monoxide). Screen and stage actor.

Appeared in: 1923 Little Old New York. 1924 Janice Meredith. 1930 Whoopee (film and stage versions). 1931 Lonely Wives; The Front Page; Traveling Husbands; Palmy Days; The Bat Whispers. 1932 Movie Crazy; Central Park; Hold 'Em Jail; The Match King; The Tenderfoot; Jewell Robbery; The Crooked Circle. 1933 20,000 Years in Sing Sing; Broadway Bad; So This Is Africa; Gambling Ship; Female; The Kennel Murder Case. 1934 The Firebird; Wake Up and Dream; The St. Louis Kid; It's a Gift; Million Dollar Ransom; Blind Date; Wonder Bar; Pursuit of Happiness; Fashions of 1934; The Circus Clown; Hips, Hips Hooray; Half a Sinner; Loud Speaker. 1935 $1000 a Minute; Alibi Ike; Murder on a Honeymoon; In Person; The Nut Farm; The Ghost Walks; The Raven; Welcome Home; Don't Bet on Blondes; The Goose and the Gander; Whispering Smith Speaks. 1936 F-Man; Colleen; Postal Inspector; The Farmer in the Dell; The Lady from Nowhere; Love on a Bet; Murder on the Bridle Path; Career Woman; Banjo on My Knee; Preview Murder Mystery; The Moon's Our Home; 'Til We Meet Again; Spendthrift; Don't Get Personal; The Mine with the Iron Door; Mr. Deeds Goes to Town; The Harvester; All American Chump; Libeled Lady; Fugitive in the Sky. 1937 Dangerous Number; Wells Fargo; The Mighty Treve; Girl Loves Boy; Venus Makes Trouble; The Prisoner of Zenda; Behind the Mike; The Hurricane; Four Days' Wonder; Back in Circulation; Fifty Roads to Town; Wife, Doctor and Nurse; Danger—Love at Work; Big Town Girl; Checkers; Pick a Star; Mountain Music; Mr. Boggs Steps Out. 1938 The Joy of Living; Forbidden Valley; Mr. Chump; The Texans; Five of a Kind; In Old Chicago; One Wild Night; Three Blind Mice; Inside Story; Professor Beware; Breaking the Ice; The Road to Reno; Lady Behave; Crime School. 1939 Woman Doctor; I'm from Missouri; Women in the Wind; Young Mr. Lincoln; Second Fiddle; Drums Across the Mohawk; Yes, My Darling Daughter; Topper Takes a Trip; The Covered Trailer; The Flying Irishman; In Name Only; They Made Her a Spy; Two Thoroughbreds; The Hunchback of Notre Dame; Exile Express; They Asked for It; The Under-Pup; Unexpected Father; Jesse James. 1940 Friendly Neighbors; Maryland; The Refuge; Remember the Night; He Married His Wife; Our Town; Alias the Deacon; The Girl from God's Country; The Golden Fleecing; Meet the Missus; Blondie Plays Cupid; Santa Fe Trail. 1941 Moon over Miami; Tobacco Road; Petticoat Politics; High Sierra; So Ends Our Night; She Couldn't Say No; The Lady from Cheyenne; Mr. District Attorney in the Carter Case; Midnight Angel; Look Who's Laughing; Man at Large; The Singing Hill. 1942 The Remarkable Andrew; Born to the Heart; The Night Before the Divorce; The Postman Didn't Ring; The Affairs of Jimmy Valentine; Scattergood Survives a Murder; Juke Girl; Pacific Blackout.

CHASE, ARLINE
Born: 1900. Died: Apr. 19, 1926, Sierra Madre, Calif. (tuberculosis). Screen, vaudeville actress, and dancer. Was a Mack Sennett bathing beauty.

CHASE, CHARLEY (Charles Parrott)
Born: Oct. 20, 1893, Baltimore, Md. Died: June 20, 1940, Hollywood, Calif. (heart attack). Screen and vaudeville actor. Under name of Charles Parrott he was a film producer, director, and screenwriter. Brother of screen actor James Parrott (dec. 1939). Entered films in 1912.

Appeared in: 1914 Our Country Cousin; The Knock-Out (reissued as The Pugilist); Mabel's New Job; The Masquerader; Her Last Chance; His New Profession (reissued as The Good-for-Nothing); The Rounders; Dough and Dynamite (reissued as The Doughnut Designer); Gentlemen of Nerve (reissued as Some Nerve); Cursed by His Beauty; Tillie's Punctured Romance. 1915 Love in Armor; Only a Farmer's Daughter; Hash House Mashers; Settled at the Seaside; Love, Loot and Crash; A Versatile Villain; His Father's Footsteps; The Rent Jumpers; The Hunt. 1917 Her Torpedoed Love; Chased Into Love. 1918 Hello Trouble (short). 1919 Ship Ahoy (short). 1920 Kids is Kids (short). 1923 Long Live the King. 1925 Appeared in the following shorts: The Rat's Knuckles; Hello Baby; Fighting Fluid; The Family Entrance; Bad Boy; Is Marriage the Bunk; Big Red Riding Hood; Looking for Sally; What Price Goofy; Isn't Life Terrible; Innocent Husbands; No Father to Guide Him; Hard Boiled; The Caretaker's Daughter; The Uneasy Three; His Wooden Wedding. 1927 The Call of the Cuckoo (short). 1929 Modern Love; You Can't Buy Love; appeared in the following shorts Snappy Sneezer; Leaping Love; Stepping Out; The Big Squawk; Crazy Fight; The Real McCoy. 1930 Appeared in the following shorts: 50 Million Husbands; Fast Work. 1931 Appeared in the following shorts: Great Gobs; Whispering Whoopee; All Tied Up. 1932 Nature in the Wrong (short). 1934 The Sons of the Desert. 1935 MGM shorts. 1936 Neighborhood House; On the Wrong Tek (short); Kelly the Second. 1939 Mutiny on the Body (short). 1957 The Golden Age of Comedy (documentary). 1960 When Comedy Was King (documentary). 1961 Days of Thrills and Laughter (documentary). 1963 Thirty Years of Fun (documentary). 1965 Laurel & Hardy's Laughing 20's (documentary). 1968 The Further Perils of Laurel & Hardy (documentary).

CHASE, COLIN
Born: 1886. Died: Apr. 24, 1937, Los Angeles, Calif. (paralysis attack). Screen and stage actor.

Appeared in: 1923 Bucking the Barrier; Snowdrift. 1924 The Iron Horse. 1926 Silver Fingers. 1927 King of Kings. 1929 The Air Legion; Big News; The Godless Girl. 1930 Renegades; The Lone Star Ranger. 1935 The Cyclone Ranger; The Vanishing Riders.

CHATTERTON, RUTH
Born: Dec. 24, 1893, New York, N.Y. Died: Nov. 24, 1961, Norwalk, Conn. Screen, stage actress, film producer, and novelist. Married to stage actor Barry Thomson (dec. 1960). Divorced from screen actors Ralph Forbes (dec. 1951) and George Brent.

Appeared in: 1928 Sons of the Fathers (film debut). 1929 The Doctor's Secret; Madame X; Charming Sinners; The Dummy; The High Road. 1930 The Laughing Lady; Sarah and Son; The Right to Love; Paramount on Parade; The Lady of Scandal; Anybody's Woman. 1931 Once a Lady; Unfaithful; Magnificent Lie. 1932 The Rich are Always with Us; Tomorrow and Tomorrow; The Crash. 1933 Frisco Jenny; Female; Lilly Turner. 1934 Journal of a Crime. 1936 Dodsworth; Girl's Dormitory; The Lady of Secrets. 1938 The Rat; A Royal Divorce.

CHATTERTON, THOMAS
Born: Feb. 12, 1881, Geneva, N.Y. Died: Aug. 17, 1952, Hollywood, Calif. Screen and stage actor. Was in Kay-Bee productions in 1915.

Appeared in: 1916 The Secret of the Submarine. 1921 The Price of Silence. 1937 A Fight to the Finish; Sandflow. 1938 Under Western Stars. 1939 Arizona Legion. 1947 Smash-Up, the Story of a Woman. 1949 Gun Law Justice; Highway 13.

CHATTON, SYDNEY
Born: 1918, Bolton, England. Died: Oct. 6, 1966, Berkeley, Calif. (coronary). Screen, stage, radio, and television actor. Known as "the man of 1,000 voices."

Appeared in: 1938 The Rangers Roundup. 1958 Once Upon a Horse.

CHAUTARD, EMILE
Born: 1881, Paris, France. Died: Apr. 24, 1934, Westwood, Calif. (organic trouble). Screen, stage actor, and film director. Entered films in Paris, in 1907.

Appeared in: 1926 Bardley's The Magnificent; The Flaming Forest; My Official Wife; Broken Hearts of Hollywood; Paris at Midnight. 1927 Blonde or Brunette; Now We're in the Air; Seventh Heaven; Upstage; Whispering Sage. 1928 Love Mart; Lilac Time; Out of the Ruins; Caught in the Fog; The Olympic Hero; Adoration; The Noose; His Tiger Lady. 1929 Times Square; Marianne; South Sea Rose; Tiger Rose; The House of Horrors. 1930 Just Like Heaven; Morocco; A Man from Wyoming; Estrellados (Spanish version of Free and Easy); Contre-

Enquete; L'Enigmatique Monsieur Parkes. 1931 Le Petit Cafe; Road to Reno. 1932 Cock of the Air; Blonde Venus; Man from Yesterday; Shanghai Express. 1933 California Trail; The Devil's in Love; Design for Living. 1934 Man of Two Worlds.

CHAUVEL, CHARLES E.
Born: 1897. Died: Nov. 11, 1959, Sydney, Australia. Screen actor, screenwriter, film producer, and film director. Worked as an extra in Hal Roach comedies during the 1920s.

CHEIREL, JEANNE (Jeanne Leriche)
Born: 1868, France. Died: Nov. 2, 1934, Paris, France. Screen and stage actress.

CHEKHOV, MICHAEL
Born: Aug. 29, 1891, Leningrad, Russia. Died: Sept. 30, 1955, Beverly Hills, Calif. Screen, stage actor, film and stage director. Nephew of author Anton Chekhov.

Appeared in: 1944 In Our Time; Song of Russia. 1945 Spellbound. 1946 Specter of the Rose. 1947 Cross My Heart. 1948 Arch of Truimph. 1952 Holiday for Sinners; The Invitation. 1954 Rhapsody.

CHERKASSOV, NIKOLAI
Born: 1903, Russia. Died: 1966. Screen actor.

Appeared in: 1937 Baltic Deputy, Peter the First. 1938 Ski Battalion. 1939 Friends; Captain Grant's Children; The Man with the Gun; Alexander Nevsky; Lenin in 1918; The Conquests of Peter The Great. 1941 General Suvorov. 1942 Ivan the Terrible Part I (U.S. 1947); In the Name of Life. 1948 Spring. 1949 The First Front. 1950 Ivan Pavlov. 1951 Mussorgsky. 1954 Rimsky Korsakov. 1959 Ivan the Terrible Part II.

CHERRYMAN, REX
Born: 1898. Died: Aug. 10, 1928, Harve, France (septic poisoning) Screen and stage actor.

Appeared in: 1920 Madame Peacock. 1921 Camille. 1923 The Sunshine Trail.

CHESNEY, ARTHUR
Born: 1882, England. Died: Aug. 27, 1949, London, England. Screen and stage actor. Brother of screen actor Edmund Gwenn (dec. 1959). Divorced from screen actress Estelle Winwood.

Appeared in: 1931 French Leave. 1933 Fires of Fate. 1934 Sensation; Sorrell and Son. 1936 O.H.M.S. (aka You're in the Army Now-U.S. 1937). 1938 Girl in the Street.

CHESTER, ALMA
Born: 1871. Died: Jan. 22, 1953, Woodland Hills, Calif. Screen and stage actress.

Appeared in 1931 Beloved Bachelor. 1934 Dude Ranger.

CHESTER, BROCK
Born: 1947. Died: Apr. 29, 1971. Screen actor.

CHIEF JACK
Born: 1877. Died: Jan. 9, 1943, Los Angeles, Calif. Screen and vaudeville actor.

CHIEF JOHN BIG TREE (Isaac Johnny John)
Born: 1865. Died: July 1967, Onondaga Reservation, N.Y. Screen actor. Posed for artist James Fraser for the profile which became the famous Indian head nickel.

Appeared in: 1922 The Primitive Lover. 1923 The Huntress. 1924 The Iron Horse. 1925 The Red Rider. 1926 The Desert's Toll; The Frontier Trail; Ranson's Folly. 1927 Painted Ponies; Winners of the Wilderness; The Frontiersman; Spoilers of the West. 1928 Wyoming. 1929 The Overland Telegraph; Sioux Blood. 1937 Hills of Old Wyoming. 1939 Stagecoach; Susannah of the Mounties; Drums Along the Mohawk. 1940 Brigham Young, Frontiersman; Hudson's Bay. 1941 Western Union; Las Vegas Nights. 1947 Unconquered. 1949 She Wore a Yellow Ribbon. 1950 Devil's Doorway.

CHIEF MANY TREATIES (William Hazlett)
Born: 1875. Died: Feb. 29, 1948, Hollywood, Calif.(heart attack). Screen actor and rodeo performer.

CHIEF NIPO STRONGHEART (Nee-hah-pouw Tah-che-num)
Born: May 15, 1891, Wakima (Indian reservation), Wash. Died: Dec. 30, 1966, Woodland Hills, Calif. Screen and stage actor. Entered films with Lubin Co. in 1905.

Appeared in: 1925 Braveheart; The Road to Yesterday. 1926 The Last Frontier. 1947 Canyon Passage; Black Passage; Black Gold. 1950 The Outriders; Young Daniel Boone. 1951 The Painted Hills; Across the Wide Missouri; Westward the Women. 1952 Lone Star; Pony Soldier. 1953 Charge at Feather River; Take the High Ground. 1954 Rose Marie. 1955 Fox Fire; Seven Cities of Gold. 1960 Ten Who Dared. 1963 Savage Sam.

CHIEF THUNDERCLOUD (Victor Daniels)
Born: Apr. 12, 1889, Muskogee, Okla. Died: Nov. 30, 1955, Ventura, Calif.(cancer). Screen and radio actor, singer, and rodeo performer. Married to screen singer/dancer Frances Delmar. Entered films as a stuntman in 1929.

Appeared in: 1935 Rustler's Paradise; The Farmer Takes a Wife. 1936 Ramona; Silly Billies; The Plainsman. 1937 Renfrew of the Royal Mounted. 1938 The Lone Ranger (serial); The Great Adventures of Wild Bill Hickok (serial); Flaming Frontier (serial). 1939 Geronimo; Union Pacific; The Lone Ranger Rides Again (serial). 1940 Young Buffalo Bill; Hi-Yo Silver; Typhoon; Wyoming; Northwest Mounted Police; Hudson's Bay; Murder on the Yukon. 1941 Western Union; Silver Stallion. 1942 My Gal Sal; Shut My Big Mouth; King of the Stallions. 1944 The Falcon Out West; Black Arrow (serial); Fighting Seabees; Buffalo Bill; "The Trail Blazers" series, two of which are: Sonora Stage-Coach; An Outlaw Trail. 1946 Romance of the West; Badman's Territory. 1947 Senator Was Indiscreet; Unconquered. 1948 Blazing Across the Pecos; Renegade Girl. 1949 Ambush; Call of the Forest. 1950 Colt .45; Ticket to Tomahawk; The Traveling Saleswoman; Davy Crockett—Indian Scout; I Killed Geronimo. 1951 Santa Fe. 1952 Buffalo Bill in Tomahawk Territory; The Half-Breed.

CHIEF THUNDERCLOUD (Scott T. Williams)
Born: Dec. 20, 1898, Cedar, Mich. Died: Jan. 31, 1967, Chicago, Ill. Was great, great, great grandson of Chief Pontiac of the Ottawa Tribe. Screen and radio actor. Portrayed "Tonto" on early Lone Ranger radio program and appeared in numerous western films during the 1930s but should not be confused with Victor Daniels also known as "Chief Thundercloud."

CHILDERS, NAOMI
Born: 1893. Died: May 9, 1964, Hollywood, Calif. Screen actress.

Appeared in: 1915 Anselo Lee. 1919 Lord and Lady Algy. 1920 Earthbound. 1921 Hold Your Horses; Courage. 1922 Mr. Barnes of New York. 1923 Success. 1924 Restless Wives; Virtuous Liars. 1934 White Heat.

CHILDS, MONROE (J. Monroe Rothschild)
Born: 1891. Died: Nov. 7, 1963, Santa Monica, Calif. Screen and stage actor.

CHIRELLO, GEORGE "SHORTY"
Born: 1897. Died: Feb. 9, 1963, Honolulu, Hawaii. Screen actor. Formerly Orsen Wells' cook and chauffeur.

Appeared in: 1948 Macbeth.

CHITTISON, HERMAN
Died: Mar. 8, 1967, Cleveland, Ohio. Screen, radio actor, and jazz pianist.

Appeared in: French film Pepe Le Moko.

CHIVVIS, CHIC
Born: 1884. Died: Oct. 26, 1963, Hollywood, Calif. Screen actor and stuntman. Entered films during silents.

CHRISTIAN, JOHN
Born: 1884. Died: Aug. 29, 1950, Hollywood, Calif. Screen and stage actor.

CHRISTIANS, MADY
Born: 1900, Vienna, Austria. Died: Oct. 28, 1951, Norwalk, Conn. (cerebral hemorrhage). Screen, stage, and radio actress. Appeared in U.S., Austrian, German, French and British films.

Appeared in: 1926 The Waltz Dream. 1929 Slums of Berlin; The Runaway Princess. 1930 Because I Love You; The Burning Heart. 1932 Leutnant Warst Du Einst bei den Husaren; Der Schwartze Husar (The Black Hussars). 1933 One Year Later; Die Frau von der Man Spricht; Friederike; Das Schicksal der Renate Langen (The Fate of the Renata Lancer). 1934 Wicked Woman; Heart Song. 1935 Escapade; Ship Cafe; Ich Und die

Kaiserin. 1936 Come and Get It. 1937 Seventh Heaven; Heidi; Salon Dora Green (House of Dora Green); The Woman I Love. 1943 Tender Comrade. 1944 Address Unknown. 1948 All My Sons; Letter from an Unknown Woman. Other European films: Cinderella; Glass of Water; Finances of the Archduke; Queen Louise; Duel; Priscilla's Fortnight; Meet My Sister; Dich-halder Gelieb; Mon Amour.

CHRISTIANS, RUDOLPH
Born: 1869. Died: Feb. 7, 1921, Pasadena, Calif.(pneumonia). Screen actor.

Appeared in: 1922 Foolish Wives.

CHRISTY, BILL
Born: 1925. Died: Feb. 25, 1946, Los Angeles, Calif.(form of paralysis). Screen and radio actor.

Appeared in: 1944 Song of the Open Road.

CHRISTY, IVAN
Born: 1888. Died: May 9, 1949, Burbank, Calif.(heart attack). Screen actor.

Appeared in: 1921 Rainbow. 1922 Island Wives; The Madness of Love. 1926 Man of the Forest. 1927 Nevada; The Mysterious Rider. 1929 Seven Footprints to Satan. 1930 Son of the Gods.

CHRISTY, KEN
Born: 1895. Died: July 23, 1962, Hollywood, Calif. Screen, stage, vaudeville, radio, and television actor.

Appeared in: 1941 Burma Convoy; Harmon of Michigan. 1942 The Big Shop; Manilla Calling; Just Off Broadway; Top Sergeant. 1943 He Hired the Boss; Secrets of the Underworld; Gildersleeve's Bad Day; Hit the Ice. 1944 Wilson; The Big Noise. 1948 Scudda Hoo! Scudda Hay! 1949 The Devil's Henchman; Trapped. 1950 No Way out; Cheaper by the Dozen. 1951 Call Me Mister. 1952 The Model and the Marriage Broker. 1955 My Sister Eileen; Inside Detroit. 1956 Blackjack Ketchum; Desperado; The Were-wolf. 1957 Fury at Showdown; Outlaw's Son; Utah Blaine; Escape from San Quentin.

CHURCHILL, BERTON
Born: 1876, Toronto, Canada. Died: Oct. 10, 1940, New York, N.Y.(uremic poisoning). Screen and stage actor.

Appeared in: 1923 Six Cylinder Love. 1924 Tongues of Flame. 1929 Nothing But the Truth. 1930 Five Minutes from the Station (short). 1931 Secrets of a Secretary; Air Eagles; A Husband's Holiday. 1932 The Rich Are Always with Us; Cabin in the Cotton; The Dark Horse; Taxi!; Impatient Maiden; Two Seconds; Week Ends Only; Crooked Circle; Silver Dollar; Big Stampede; Okay America; Laughter in Hell; Washington Parade; Fast Companions; Afraid to Talk; It's Tough to Be Famous; The Mouthpiece; The Wet Parade; The Information Kid; Faith; If I Had a Million; Common Ground; Forgotten Million; American Madness; False Faces; Scandal for Sale; I Am a Fugitive from a Chain Gang; Madame Butterfly. 1933 Ladies Must Love; From Hell to Heaven; Employees' Entrance; The Mysterious Rider; Billion Dollar Scandal; Elmer the Great; Private Jones; Her First Mate; Only Yesterday; The Little Giant; Heroes for Sale; The Big Brain; Golden Harvest; Master of Men; The Avenger; Doctor Bull; College Coach; So This Is Africa. 1934 The Girl Is Mine; King of the Ritz; Dizzy Dames; Life Is Worth Living; Men of Steel; Men in White; If I was Rich; Alias the Deacon; Bachelor of Arts; Dames; Take the Stand; Kid Millions; Lillies of Broad-way; Friends of Mr. Sweeney; Hi, Nellie; Babbitt; The Menace; Half a Sinner; Let's Be Ritzy; Judge Priest; Frontier Marshall; Helldorado; Sing Sing Nights; Red Head; Strictly Dynamite; Bachelor Bait; Murder in the Private Car. 1935 The County Chairman; $10 Raise; Steamboat 'Round the Bend; A Night at the Ritz; Page Miss Glory; I Live for Love; Vagabond Lady; The Rainmakers; Colorado; Speed Devils; The Spanish Cape Mystery. 1936 Colleen; You May Be Next; Three of a Kind; Dimples; Under Your Spell; Bunker Bean; Racing Lady; Parole; The Dark Hour. 1937 You Can't Beat Love; Quick Money; Parnell; The Singing Marine; He Couldn't Say No; Wild and Wooly; Racing Lady; Public Wedding; Sing and Be Happy. 1938 Wide Open Faces; Meet the Mayor; In Old Chicago; Four Men and a Prayer; Kentucky Moon-shine; The Cowboy and the Lady; Ladies in Distress; Down in "Arkansaw"; Danger on the Air; Sweethearts. 1939 Daughters Courageous; Should Husbands Work?; Angels Wash Their Faces; Hero for a Day; On Your Toes; Stagecoach. 1940 Brother Rat and a Baby; I'm Nobody's Sweetheart Now; Saturday's Children; Twenty-Mule Team; Turnabout; Cross-Country Romance; The Way of All Flesh; Public Deb. No. 1.

CIANELLI, ALMA
Born: 1892. Died: June 23, 1968, Villa San Pietro, Italy (stroke). Screen and stage actress. Wife of screen actor Eduardo Cianelli (dec. 1969).

CIANELLI, EDUARDO
Born: 1887, Naples, Italy. Died: Oct. 8, 1969, Rome, Italy (cancer). Screen, stage, opera, television actor, and playwright. Married to screen actress Alma Cianelli (dec. 1968).

Appeared in: 1933 Reunion in Vienna. 1935 The Scoundrel. 1936 Winterset (film and stage versions). 1937 Criminal Lawyer; The Marked Woman; Super Sleuth; Hitting a New High; The League of Frightened Men; On Such a Night; Girl from Scotland Yard. 1938 Law of the Underworld; Blind Alibi. 1939 Angels Wash Their Faces; Society Lawyer; Risky Business; Bulldog Drummond's Bride; Gunga Din. 1940 Forgotten Girls; Outside the Three-Mile Limit; Strange Cargo; Zanzibar; Foreign Correspondent; Kitty Foyle; The Mummy's Hand; Mysterious Dr. Satan (serial). 1941 Ellery Queen's Penthouse Mystery; They Met in Bombay; I Was a Pris-oner on Devil's Island; Paris Calling; Sky Raiders (serial). 1942 Dr. Broadway; You Can't Escape Me Forever; Cairo. 1943 Flight from Freedom; The Constant Nymph; They Got Me Covered; For Whom the Bell Tolls. 1944 The Mask of Dimitrios; Storm over Lisbon; The Conspirators; Passage to Marseille. 1945 A Bell for Adano; Incendiary Blonde; Dillinger. 1946 The Wife of Monte Cristo; The Crime Doctor's Warning; Joe Palooka, Champ; Heart-beat; Perilous Holiday. 1947 Seven Keys to Baldpate; The Lost Moment; Crime Doctor's Gamble; Miracles Can Happen; I Love Trouble; California. 1948 On Our Merry Way; To the Victor; Rose of Santa Rosa; The Creeper. 1950 Rapture. 1951 The Peo-ple against O'Hara; Fugitive Lady. 1953 Volcano. 1954 The City Stands Trial; Voice of Silence. 1955 The Stranger's Hand; Mambo; Helen of Troy. 1957 Love Slaves of the Amazon. 1958 Houseboat; Attila; The Monster from Green Hell. 1962 Forty Pounds of Trouble. 1964 The Visit. 1966 Dr. Satan's Robot. 1968 The Brotherhood. 1969 Mackenna's Gold; The Secret of Santa Vit-toria; Boot Hill.

CLAIRE, GERTRUDE
Born: 1852. Died: Apr. 28, 1928, Los Angeles, Calif. Screen and stage actress.

Appeared in: 1919 Stepping Out; Widow by Proxy. 1920 The Cradle of Courage. 1921 The Fox; Hail the Woman; Greater Than Love; Things Men Do; The Sin of Martha Queed; The Invisible Power; Society Secrets. 1922 The Crusader; Human Hearts; Forget-Me-Not; The Adventures of Robinson Crusoe (serial); Environment; The Super-Sex; Ridin' Wild; Oliver Twist. 1923 Itching Palms; Double Dealing. 1924 Daughters of Today; The Heart Bandit; Wine of Youth; Ladies to Board. 1925 The Wedding Song; Romance Road; The Goose Hangs High; Her Sister from Paris; His Majesty, Bunker Bean; The Storm Breaker; Tumbleweeds. 1926 The Little Irish Girl; Out of the West. 1927 We're all Gamblers; Married Alive. 1928 Red Head.

CLARANCE, ARTHUR
Born: 1883. Died: Oct. 26, 1956, Newcastle, England. Screen, stage, vaudeville, and television actor.

CLARE, MARY
Born: July 17, 1894, London, England. Died: Aug. 30, 1970, Lon-don, England. Screen and stage actress.

Appeared in: 1924 Becket. 1927 The Prince of Lovers. 1931 Hiddle Wakes. 1932 Many Waters. 1933 The Constant Nymph; Say It with Flowers; Jew Seuss. 1935 Lorna Doone; The Clair-voyant; The Passing of the Third Floor Back; The Guv'nor; Mr. Hobo. 1937 Young and Innocent; The Mill on the Floss (U.S. 1939); The Rat; Our Royal Heritage; The Challenger (U.S. 1939). 1938 The Citadel; Climbing High; The Lady Vanishes. 1939 A Girl Must Live (U.S. 1942); There Ain't No Justice. 1940 Old Bill and Son; Mrs. Pym of Scotland Yard; The Fugitive. 1942 Next of Kin; The Night has Eyes. 1944 The Hundred-Pound Window. 1947 The Patient Vanishes. 1948 Oliver Twist (U.S. 1951); The Three Weird Sisters. 1949 My Brother Jonathan; Portrait of Claire. 1950 The Black Rose; Mrs. Fitzherbert. 1953 Moulin Rouge; My Heart Goes Crazy (aka London Town); Penny Princess. 1954 The Beggar's Opera. 1955 Mambo. 1959 The Price of Silence.

CLARENCE, O.B. (Oliver B. Clarence)
Born: Mar. 25, 1870, London, England. Died: 1955. Screen and stage actor.

Appeared in: 1915 Liberty Hall. 1930 East Meets West. 1931 The Man From Chicago; Keepers of Youth. 1932 Perfect Under-standing (U.S. 1933); The Flag Lieutenant; Magic Night; Feathered Serpent (aka The Menace); Goodnight Vienna. 1934 The Scarlet

Pimpernel (U.S. 1935); Nell Gwyn; Heart Song; Friday the 13th; The Great Defender. 1935 A Shot in the Dark. 1936 Doomed Cargo; East Meets West; Seven Sinners. 1937 The Return of the Scarlet Pimpernel (U.S. 1938); The Mill on the Floss. 1938 Pygmalion; Calling All Crooks; Stolen Life; It's in the Air; Me and My Pal; Black Eyes; Jamaica Inn. Other British films prior to 1939: Jack's The Boy; The Only Girl; Turkey Time; Private Secretary; His Grace Gives; D'ye Ken John Peel; Squibbs; King of Paris; Dandy Dick; Help Yourself; I Adore You; Silver Spoon; Soldiers of the King; All In; Falling for You; All the Winners; Song at Eventide; Birthday; The Belles; King of Hearts; Captain Bill; The Cardinal. Later British film: Front Line Kids. 1940 Penn of Pennsylvania; Saloon Bar. 1941 Major Barbara; Inspector Hornleigh Goes to It. 1944 On Approval (U.S. 1945). 1946 Great Expectations (U.S. 1947); Caesar and Cleopatra. 1947 The Magic Bow; Uncle Silas; Meet Me at Dawn; School for Secrets. 1948 The Calendar. 1949 No Room at the Inn; A Place of One's Own. 1951 The Inheritance. 1954 Top Secret (aka Mr. Potts Goes to Moscow).

CLARENS, HENRY F.
Born: 1860. Died: Dec. 19, 1928, New York, N.Y. Screen and stage actor.

CLARK, ANDREW J. "ANDY"
Born: Mar. 1903, New York, N.Y. Died: Nov. 16, 1960, New Rochelle, N.Y. Screen, stage, and vaudeville actor. Entered films with Edison in 1914 and starred in "Andy" series.

Appeared in: 1914 The Adventures of Andy Clark. 1925 The Sporting Chance. 1926 The Shamrock Handicap. 1927 One Round Hogan; Wings. 1928 Beggar's of Life. 1929 Rio Rita; The Man I Love. 1930 Hit the Deck.

CLARK, BOBBY (Robert Edwin Clark)
Born: June 16, 1888, Springfield, Ohio. Died: Feb. 12, 1960, New York, N.Y.(heart attack). Screen, stage, vaudeville, minstrel, circus, and burlesque actor. Was part of "Clark & McCullough" team.

Together they appeared in the following shorts: 1928 Clark and McCullough in the Interview; Clark and McCullough in the Honor System. 1929 The Bath Between; The Diplomats; Waltzing Around; In Holland; Belle of Samoa; Beneath the Law; The Medicine Men; Music Fiends; Knights Out; All Steamed Up; Hired and Fired; Detectives Wanted. 1931 False Roomers; Chesterfield Celebrities; A Melon-Drama; Scratch as Catch Can. 1932 The Iceman's Ball; The Millionaire Cat; Jitters the Butler. 1933 Hokus Focus; The Druggist's Dilemma; The Gay Nighties; Fits in a Fiddle; Kickin' the Crown Around; Snug in the Jug. 1934 Hey, Nanny Nanny; In the Devil's Doghouse; Bedlam of Beards; Love and Hisses; Odor in the Court; Everything's Ducky; In a Pig's Eye. 1935 Flying Down to Zero; Alibi Bye Bye. 1938 Clark appeared without McCullough in The Goldwyn Follies (feature).

CLARK, CHARLES DOW
Born: 1870. Died: Mar. 26, 1959, N.Y. Screen and stage actor.

Appeared in: 1924 The Confidence Man. 1925 Old Home Week. 1930 The Bat Whispers. 1932 Ladies of the Jury; The Half-Naked Truth.

CLARK, CLIFF
Born: 1893. Died: Feb. 8, 1953, Hollywood, Calif.(heart attack). Screen, vaudeville, and television actor.

Appeared in: 1937 Mountain Music. 1938 Mr. Moto's Gamble; Time Out for Murder; The Patient in Room 18; While New York Sleeps; Inside Story; Kentucky; Cocoanut Grove. 1939 They Made Me a Criminal; Within the Law; Honolulu; It's a Wonderful World; Miracles for Sale; Fast and Furious; Joe and Ethel Turp Call on the President; Young Mr. Lincoln; Missing Evidence; Dust Be My Destiny. 1940 Slightly Honorable; Grapes of Wrath; Double Alibi; Black Diamonds; Honeymoon Deferred; Three Cheers for the Irish; Cross Country Romance; Stranger on the Third Floor; Wagon Train. 1941 Law of the Tropics; Nine Lives Are Not Enough; Strange Alibi; Washington Melodrama; Manpower; Golden Hoofs; The Wagons Roll at Night. 1942 Kid Glove Killer; Babes on Broadway; Jail House Blues; Fingers at the Window; Monkey; Who Is Hope Schuyler?; Secret Enemies; Henry Aldrich, Editor; The Falcon's Brother; Army Surgeon; The Mummy's Tomb; Taxi, Mister? 1943 Ladies' Day; The Falcon Strikes Back; The Falcon in Danger. 1944 Barbary Coast Gent; The Falcon Out West; In the Meantime, Darling; The Missing Juror. 1947 Bury Me Dead; Buck Private Come Home. 1948 Deep Waters; Trouble Makers. 1949 Flaming Fury; Home of the Brave; Homicide; Powder River Rustlers; The Stratton Story; Post Office Investigator. 1950 Try and Get It; Vigilante Hideout;

The Man; The Cariboo Trail; Gunfighter. 1951 Joe Palooka in the Triple Cross; Operation Pacific; Saddle Legion; The Second Woman; Cavalry Scout; Warpath. 1952 High Noon; The Pride of St. Louis; The Sniper.

CLARK, EDDIE (Edward Clark)
Born: 1879. Died: Nov. 18, 1954, Hollywood, Calif.(heart attack). Screen, stage, television actor, and playwright.

Appeared in: 1926 Millionaires; Broken Hearts of Hollywood; Private Izzy Murphy. 1927 Finger Prints; The Gay Old Bird; Sally in Our Alley; Hills of Kentucky. 1928 Marriage by Contract. 1929 Unmasked; Silks and Saddles. 1930 Bitter Friends (short); Carnival Revue (short). 1949 Abandoned; Amazon Quest; Oh, You Beautiful Doll. 1950 Dancing in the Dark; Pretty Girl; A Ticket to Tomahawk. 1951 Little Egypt; Bedtime for Bonzo; Branded; Million Dollar Pursuit; Mr. Belvedere Rings the Bell; Savage Drums; Rhubarb. 1952 Thundering Caravans. 1953 Flame of Calcutta; It Happens Every Thursday; Topeka; Money from Home. 1954 Hell's Outpost. 1955 Crashout.

CLARK, ETHEL (Ethel Schneider)
Born: 1916. Died: Feb. 18, 1964, Hollywood, Calif. Screen, vaudeville, and television actress.

Appeared in: 1938 The Headleys at Home.

CLARK, FRED (Frederic Leonard Clark)
Born: Mar. 9, 1914, Lincoln, Calif. Died: Dec. 5, 1968, Santa Monica, Calif.(liver ailment). Screen, stage, television, and radio actor. Divorced from screen actress Benay Venuta.

Appeared in: 1947 Ride the Pink Horse; The Unsuspected. 1948 Fury at Furnace Creek; Mr. Peabody and the Mermaid; Cry of the Night; Hazard; Two Guys from Texas. 1949 The Younger Brothers; Task Force; Alias Nick Beal; The Lady Takes a Sailor; White Heat; Flamingo Road. 1950 The Eagle and the Hawk; Return of the Frontiersman; The Jackpot; Mrs. O'Malley and Mr. Malone; Sunset Boulevard; Dynamite Pass; Treasure Island. 1951 The Lemon Drop Kid; Hollywood Story; Meet Me after the Show; A Place in the Sun. 1952 Three for Bedroom C; Dreamboat. 1953 The Stars Are Singing; How to Marry a Millionaire; Here Comes the Girls; The Caddy. 1954 Living It Up. 1955 How to Be Very, Very Popular; The Court-Martial of Billy Mitchell; Daddy Long Legs; Abbott and Costello Meet the Keystone Kops. 1956 The Solid Gold Cadillac; Miracle in the Rain; The Birds and the Bees; Back from Eternity. 1957 The Fuzzy Pink Nightgown; Joe Butterfly; Don't Go Near the Water. 1958 Mardi Gras; Auntie Mame. 1959 The Mating Game; It Started with a Kiss. 1960 The Passionate Thief; Bells are Ringing; Visit to a Small Planet. 1962 Hemingway's Adventures of a Young Man; Boys' Night Out; Zotz! 1963 Move Over, Darling. 1964 John Goldfarb, Please Come Home. 1965 Sergeant Deadhead; When the Boys Meet the Girls; Dr. Goldfoot and the Bikini Machine; The Curse of the Mummy's Tomb. 1967 War Italian Style. 1968 The Horse in the Gray Flannel Suit; Skidoo. 1969 Eve.

CLARK, HARVEY (aka HARVEY CLARKE)
Born: 1886, Boston, Mass. Died: July 19, 1938, Hollywood, Calif.(heart attack). Screen, stage, and vaudeville actor. Entered films with New York Motion Picture Co. in 1916.

Appeared in: 1921 The Kiss; High Gear Jeffrey; Payment Guaranteed; The Servant in the House; Her Face Value. 1922 Don't Shoot; Alias Julius Caesar; The Gray Dawn; Mixed Faces; Money to Burn; Elope If You Must; The Men of Zanzibar; Thelma; The Woman He Loved; Shattered Idols. 1923 In the Palace of the King; The Man Who Won; Brass; Second Hand Love. 1924 Secrets; He Who Gets Slapped; The Man Who Came Back; The Roughnecks. 1925 Havoc; The Arizona Romeo; Blue Blood; The Man Without a Country; Marriage in Transit. 1926 Black Paradise; The Frontier Trail; The Flying Horseman; The Dixie Merchant; Midnight Lovers; The Cowboy and the Countess; The Silver Treasure; The Palace of Pleasure. 1927 Rose of Golden West; Get Your Man; Putting Pants on Phillip (short); The Magic Flame; Camille; In Old Kentucky; McFadden's Flats; The Understanding Heart. 1928 A Woman Against the World; Tragedy of Youth; Ladies Night in a Turkish Bath; Floating College; The Toilers; Beautiful But Dumb; The Head Man; The Night Bird; The Olympic Hero. 1929 His Lucky Day; The Rainbow; Seven Keys to Baldpate. 1930 Main Trouble; Going Wild; Anybody's Woman; Up the River; What a Man. 1931 Millie; The Deceiver; Cracked Nuts. 1932 The Big Shot; Red Headed Woman; Down to Earth. 1933 Strictly Personal; West of Singapore; I Love that Man; A Shriek in the Night; Alice in Wonderland; Picture Brides. 1934 Charlie Chan's Courage; Peck's Bad Boy; Countess of Monte Cristo. 1936 Three Godfathers; Grand Jury; Sitting on the Moon; Empty Saddles. 1937

History Is Made at Night; Dance, Charlie Dance; Dangerous Holiday; It's Love I'm After; Blonde Trouble; Partners of the Plains. 1938 Mother Carey's Chickens; Spawn of the North.

CLARK, JOHN J.
Born: 1877. Died: Apr. 13, 1947, Hollywood, Calif. Screen, stage actor, film director, and stage producer. Entered films with Kalem in 1907.

Appeared in: 1927 Pajamas. 1928 Love and Learn. 1929 Howdy, Broadway.

CLARK, JOHNNY
Born: Aug. 10, 1916, Hampton, Iowa. Died: July 3, 1967, Hollywood, Calif.(heart attack). Screen, stage, television actor, and composer.

Appeared in: 1941 Las Vegas Nights. 1943 Jive Junction. 1944 Hey Rookie; Weekend Pass; The Sultan's Daughter; Irish Eyes Are Smiling. 1947 The Locket.

CLARK, LES
Born: 1907. Died: Mar. 24, 1959, London, England(heart attack). Screen and vaudeville actor.

Appeared in: 1950 When Willie Comes Marching Home. 1954 The Country Girl; White Christmas.

CLARK, MARGUERITE
Born: Feb. 22, 1887, Avondale, Ohio. Died: Sept. 25, 1940, New York, N.Y.(pneumonia as a result of a cerebral hemorrhage). Screen and stage actress. Entered films with Famous Players.

Appeared in: 1914 Wildflower (film debut); The Crucible; The Pretty Sister of Jose; Gretna Green. 1915 Still Waters; The Prince and the Pauper; The Goose Girl; Morals of Marcus. 1916 Molly Make-Believe; Little Lady Eileen; Miss George Washington; Silks and Satins; Out of the Drifts. 1917 The Seven Sisters; The Amazons; The Seven Swans; Snow White. 1918 Out of a Clear Sky; Rich Man, Poor Man; Uncle Tom's Cabin. 1919 Mrs. Wiggs of the Cabbage Patch; Girls, Come Out of the Kitchen; Widow by Proxy; Luck in Pawn; Three Men and a Girl; Prunella. 1920 All-of-a-Sudden Peggy. 1921 Scrambled Wives.

CLARK, PAUL
Born: 1927. Died: May 20, 1960, Santa Barbara, Calif.(auto accident). Screen, stage, and television actor.

Appeared in: 1938 Boy Meets Girl.

CLARK, WALLIS
Born: Mar. 2, 1889, Essex, England. Died: Feb. 14, 1961. Screen actor.

Appeared in: 1932 Hell's House; The Final Edition; Alias the Doctor; Shopworn; Attorney for the Defense; Okay America; My Pal the King; The Night Mayor. 1933 Double Harness; The World Gone Mad; Bureau of Missing Persons; Ever in My Heart; Police Car 17; Lady for a Day; Luxury Liner; They Just Had to Get Married; The Working Man; The Kiss before the Mirror; The World Changes. 1934 Beloved; Massacre; A Woman's Man; I've Got Your Number; It Happened One Night; The Life of Vergie Winters; I'll Fix It. 1935 It Happened in New York; Chinatown Squad; Mutiny on the Bounty. 1936 The Unguarded Hour; Parole; Missing Girls; Come Closer Folks; Great Guy; Easy Money. 1937 The Last of Mrs. Cheyney; I Promise to Pay; Gib Business; She Had to Eat; Woman in Distress; River of Missing Men. 1938 The Higgins Family. 1939 Main Street Lawyer; Allegheny Uprising; I Stole a Million; Smuggled Cargo. 1940 The Big Guy. 1941 Penny Serenade; Murder by Invitation. 1942 The Remarkable Andrew; Gentleman Jim. 1944 Uncertain Glory. 1949 Free for All. 1951 Criminal Lawyer.

CLARKE, DOWNING GEORGE
Born: Birmingham, England. Died: Aug. 1930, New Haven, Conn. Screen and stage actor.

Appeared in: 1921 The Ghost in the Garret; Know Your Men. 1922 When Knighthood Was in Flower. 1923 Human Wreckage. 1924 Sandra; America; Monsieur Beaucaire. 1925 The Fool. 1932 Okay America; Here's George.

CLARKE-SMITH, D. A. (Douglas A. Clarke-Smith)
Born: 1888, Montrose, Scotland. Died: Mar. 12, 1959, Withyham, Sussex, England. Screen, stage, and television actor.

Appeared in: 1930 Atlantic. 1932 Michael and Mary; The Good Companions. 1933 I Was a Spy; Waltz Time; Friday, the Thirteenth; The Man with a Million; Mayfair Girl; Skipper of the Osprey; The Ghoul. 1934 Passing Shadows; Flat Number 3;

Criminal at Large; Warn London. 1935 Lorna Doone. 1936 Sabotage. 1939 The Flying Fifty-Five. 1947 Frieda. 1951 Quo Vadis. 1953 The Pickwick Papers; The Sword and the Rose. 1955 The Man Who Never Was. 1956 The Baby and the Battleship.

CLAUDIUS, DANE
Born: 1874. Died: Apr. 26, 1946, Los Angeles, Calif. Screen, stage, and vaudeville actor. Entered films approx. 1930.

CLAYTON, ETHEL
Born: 1884, Champaign, Ill. Died: June 11, 1966, Oxnard, Calif. Screen and stage actress. Entered films in 1909. Divorced from screen actor Ian Keith (dec. 1969).

Appeared in: 1912 Her Own Money. 1914 Mazie Puts One Over; The Fortune Hunter. 1915 The College Widow; The Great Divide. 1916 A Woman's Way. 1919 Pettigrew's Girl; The Woman Next Door; Men, Women and Money; A Sporting Chance; Maggie Pepper. 1921 Sham; City Sparrow; Price of Possession; Sins of Rosanne; Wealth; Beyond. 1922 The Cradle; Exit the Vamp; For the Defense; Her Own Money (and 1912); If I Were Queen; 1923 Can A Woman Love Twice; The Remittance Woman. 1925 Lightnin'; The Mansion of Aching Hearts; Wings of Youth. 1926 The Bar-C Mystery (serial and feature film); His New York Wife; Risky Business; Sunny Side Up. 1927 The Princess on Broadway; The Princess from Hoboken. 1928 Mother Machree. 1930 The Call of the Circus; Hit the Deck. 1932 Thrill of Youth; The All-American; Hotel Continental; Crooked Circle. 1933 Private Jones; Secrets. 1937 Artists and Models. 1938 The Buccaneer; Cocoanut Grove. 1939 Ambush.

CLAYTON, HAZEL. See Mrs. Mack Hilliard

CLAYTON, LOU
Born: 1887. Died: Sept. 12, 1950, Santa Monica, Calif.(cancer). Screen and vaudeville actor. Was part of "Clayton & Durante" vaudeville team.

Appeared in: 1930 Roadhouse Nights.

CLEARY, LEO THOMAS
Born: 1895. Died: Apr. 11, 1955, Hollywood, Calif.(uremic poisoning). Screen and radio actor.

Appeared in: 1940 You Can't Fool Your Wife. 1949 The Red Menace. 1950 Bells of Coronado; State Penitentiary; Johnny Holiday. 1952 The Price of St. Louis. 1954 The Human Jungle.

CLEGG, VALCE V.
Born: 1888. Died: July 29, 1947, Hollywood, Calif. Screen and stage actor.

Appeared in: 1926 Lucky Spurs.

CLEMENT, CLAY
Born: 1888, Greentree, Ky. Died: Oct. 20, 1956, Watertown, N.Y. Screen, stage, and television actor. Entered films approx. 1914.

Appeared in: 1930 Curses (short); Keeping Company (short). 1932 Washington Merry-Go-Round; False Faces; Evenings for Sale. 1933 Tonight Is Ours; Past of Mary Holmes; Second Hand Wife; Hold Me Tight; Bureau of Missing Persons; Son of a Sailor; The World Changes. 1934 I've Got Your Number; Journal of a Crime; Let's Be Ritzy; The Personality Kid. 1935 Sweet Music; Murder in the Clouds; Don't Bet on Blondes; Dinky; Chinatown Squad; Streamline Express; Confidential; Whipsaw. 1936 The Leavenworth Case; The Leathernecks Have Landed; Heart in Bondage; It Had to Happen; Let's Sing Again; Two against the World; Nobody's Fool. 1937 Bad Guy; Rosalie. 1938 A Trip to Paris; Arson Gang Busters; Numbered Woman. 1939 Each Dawn I Die; Disbarred; Off the Record. 1940 Passport to Alcatraz; I'm Still Alive.

CLEMENT, DONALD
Born: 1941, Wantagh, N.Y. Died: July 28, 1970, New York, N.Y. (electrocuted). Screen and stage actor.

Appeared in: 1970 Tell Me That You Love Me, Junie Moon.

CLEMONS, JAMES K.
Born: 1883. Died: June 5, 1950, Hollywood, Calif. Screen and stage actor.

CLERGET, PAUL
Born: 1867, France. Died: Dec. 4, 1935, Paris, France. Screen and stage actor.

Appeared in: 1918 Woman. 1920 My Lady's Garter.

CLEVELAND, GEORGE
Born: 1883, Sydney, Nova Scotia. Died: July 15, 1957, Burbank, Calif.(heart attack). Screen, stage, vaudeville, television actor, film producer, and film director.

Appeared in: 1934 Mystery Line; Blue Steel; City Limits; Monte Carlo Nights; The Man from Utah; Star Packer; School for Girls. 1935 Make a Million; His Night Out;The Keeper of the Bees; The Spanish Cape Mystery; Forced Landing. 1936 I Conquer the Sea; Revolt of the Zombies; North of Nome; Don't Get Personal; Rio Grande Romance; Brilliant Marriage; Put on the Spot. 1937 Paradise Express; The River of Missing Men; Boy of the Streets; Swing It, Professor; The Adventure's End. 1938 Rose of the Rio Grande; Romance of the Limberlost; Under the Big Top; Ghost Town Riders; The Port of Missing Girls. 1939 Home on the Prairie; Streets of New York; Wolf Call; Stunt Pilot; Mutiny in the Big House; Overland Mail. 1940 Midnight Limited; Tomboy; The Haunted House; Queen of the Yukon; The Ol' Swimmin' Hole; Pioneers of the West; Hi-Yo-Silver!; One Man's Law; Blazing Six Shooters; West of Abilene; Chasing Trouble; Konga; The Wild Stallion; The Ape. 1941 A Girl, a Guy and a Gob; All That Money Can Buy; Nevada City; Sunset in Wyoming; Two in a Taxi; Obliging Young Lady; Here Is a Man; Man at Large; Look Who's Laughing; Playmates. 1942 The Big Street; Call Out the Marines; Seven Miles from Alcatraz; Valley of the Sun; The Spoilers; My Favorite Spy; The Falcon Takes Over; The Mexican Spitfire's Elephant; Army Surgeon;The Traitor Within; Valley of the Giants; Powder Town; Highway by Night. 1943 Cowboy in Manhattan; Woman of the Town; Johnny Come Lately; Ladies Day; The Man from Music Mountain. 1944 It Happened Tomorrow; Abroad with Two Yanks; Alaska; Yellow Rose of Texas; Home in Indiana; Can't Help Singing; My Best Gal; When the Lights Go on Again; My Pal Wolf. 1945 Song of the Sarong; It's in the Bag; Dakota; Senorita from the West; She Wouldn't Say Yes; Pillow of Death; Sunbonnet Sue; Her Highness and the Bellboy. 1946 Little Giant; Wake up and Dream; The Runaround; Angel on My Shoulder; Step by Step; Wild Beauty; Courage of Lassie; The Show-off. 1947 Mother Wore Tights; I Wonder Who's Kissing Her Now; The Wistful Widow of Wagon Gap; Easy Come, Easy Go; My Wild Irish Rose. 1948 Alburquerque; Fury at Furnace Creek; Miraculous Journey; The Plunderers; A Date with Judy. 1949 Kazan; Miss Grant Takes Richmond; Home in San Antone; Rimfire. 1950 Boy from Indiana; Please Believe Me; Trigger, Jr.; Frenchie. 1951 Flaming Feather; Fort Defiance. 1952 Cripple Creek; Carson City; Wac from Walla Walla; The Devil and Daniel Webster (reissue and retitle of All That Money Can Buy, 1941). 1953 San Antone; Affair with a Stranger; Walking My Baby Back Home. 1954 Outlaw's Daughter; Fireman Save My Child; Racing Blood; Untamed Heiress.

CLIFF, LADDIE (Laddie Perry)
Born: Sept. 3, 1891, Briston, England. Died: Dec. 8, 1937, London, England. Screen, stage actor, and stage producer.

Appeared in: 1930 The Co-Optimists; 1933 Sleeping Car; Happy.

CLIFFE, H. COOPER
Born: 1862, Oxford, England. Died: May 1, 1939, New York, N.Y.(pneumonia). Screen, stage, and radio actor.

Appeared in: 1921 The Woman God Changed; Love's Redemption. 1922 Missing Millions. 1923 His Children's Children. 1924 Monsieur Beaucaire.

CLIFFORD, JACK (Virgil James Montani)
Born: 1880. Died: Nov. 10, 1956, New York, N.Y. Screen, stage actor, and boxer. Divorced from screen actress Evelyn Nesbit Thaw (dec. 1967).

Appeared in: 1926 Sweet Adeline. 1931 Skippy. 1933 One Sunday Afternoon; One Track Minds (short). 1934 The Poor Rich. 1935 One Way Ticket. 1936 King of the Pecos; The Gallant Defender; Dimples; Timothy's Quest. 1937 Racketeers in Exile; High, Wide and Handsome; Midnight Madonna. 1938 Colorado Trail. 1940 Murder on the Yukon Flight. 1941 Beyond the Sacramento; The Bandit Trail. 1944 The Old Texas Trail. 1945 Honeymoon Ahead; Rockin' in the Rockies. 1946 Canyon Passage.

CLIFFORD, KATHLEEN
Born: Charlottesville, Va. Died: Jan. 11, 1962, Hollywood, Calif. Screen, stage, and vaudeville actress.

Appeared in: 1917 Who Is "Number One"? (serial). 1920 When the Clouds Roll By. 1921 Cold Steel. 1922 Kick In. 1923 Richard, the Lion-Hearted. 1924 No More Women. 1925 The Love Gamble; Sporting Life. 1928 Excess Baggage.

CLIFFORN, WILLIAM
Born: 1877. Died: Dec. 23, 1941, Los Angeles, Calif. Screen and stage actor.

Appeared in: 1921 The Mask; Sowing the Wind; Parted Curtains. 1923 Ashes of Vengeance. 1924 Stepping Lively. 1927 Out of the Past; Three Miles Up.

CLIFT, MONTGOMERY
Born: Oct. 17, 1920, Omaha, Neb. Died: July 23, 1966, New York, N.Y.(heart attack). Screen and stage actor. Nominated for Academy Award for Best Actor in The Search (1948) and A Place in the Sun (1951). Nominated for Academy Award for Best Supporting Actor in From Here to Eternity (1953) and Judgment at Nuremberg (1961).

Appeared in: 1948 Red River; The Search. 1949 The Heiress. 1950 The Big Lift. 1951 A Place in the Sun. 1953 I Confess; From Here to Eternity. 1954 Indiscretion of an American Wife. 1957 Raintree County. 1958 The Young Lions; Lonelyhearts. 1960 Suddenly Last Summer; Wild River. 1961 The Misfits; Judgment at Nuremberg. 1962 Freud. 1966 The Defector.

CLIFTON, ELMER
Born: 1893, Chicago, Ill. Died: Oct. 15, 1949, Los Angeles, Calif.(cerebral hemorrhage). Screen, stage actor and film producer, film director, and screenwriter.

Appeared in: 1915 Birth of a Nation. 1916 Intolerance. 1919 The Fall of Babylon.

CLIFTON, HERBERT
Born: 1884, London, England. Died: Sept. 26, 1947, Hollywood, Calif.(after major operation). Screen and stage actor.

Appeared in: 1935 False Pretenses. 1937 High Flyers; She's Got Everything. 1947 Ivy.

CLINE, EDDIE (Edward Francis Cline)
Born: Nov. 7, 1892, Kenosha, Wisc. Died: May 22, 1961, Hollywood, Calif. Screen actor, film director, and screenwriter. Entered films as an actor with Keystone in 1913.

Appeared in: 1921 The Haunted House.

CLIVE, COLIN (Clive Greig)
Born: Jan. 9, 1898, St. Malo, France. Died: June 25, 1937, Los Angeles, Calif.(pulmonary and intestinal ailment). Screen and stage actor.

Appeared in: 1930 Journey's End; The Stronger Sex. 1931 Frankenstein. 1932 Lily Christine. 1933 Christopher Strong; Looking Forward. 1934 Jane Eyre; The Key; One More River. 1935 Bride of Frankenstein; Clive of India; The Hands of Orlac; The Right to Live; The Widow from Monte Carlo; The Girl from 10th Avenue; Mad Love; The Man Who Broke the Bank at Monte Carlo. 1937 History is Made at Night; The Woman I Love.

CLIVE, E. E. (Edward E. Clive)
Born: 1898, Monmouthshire, Wales. Died: June 6, 1940, North Hollywood, Calif.(heart attack). Screen, stage actor, film producer, and film director. Appeared as "Tenny" in the Bulldog Drummond series, 1937-1939.

Appeared in: 1933 The Invisible Man. 1934 The Poor Rich; Tin Pants; Bulldog Drummond Strikes Back; Charlie Chan in London; One More River; Long Lost Father; Riptide; Service; Bulldog Drummond. 1935 Atlantic Adventure; Father Brown, Detective; Sylvia Scarlett; The Widow from Monte Carlo; The Mystery of Edwin Drood; The Bride of Frankenstein; Remember Last Night?; We're in the Money; Stars over Broadway; A Tale of Two Cities; Captain Blood. 1936 Little Lord Fauntleroy; Love before Breakfast; Dracula's Daughter; The Unguarded Hour; Trouble for Two; Piccadilly Jim; All American Chump; Libeled Lady; Tarzan Escapes; Camille; The Golden Arrow; Isle of Fury; Charge of the Light Brigade; Cain and Mabel; Palm Springs; Ticket to Paradise; Lloyds of London; The Dark Hour. 1937 They Wanted to Marry; Maid of Salem; Bulldog Drummond Escapes; Bulldog Drummond Comes Back; Bulldog Drummond's Revenge; Ready, Willing and Able; On the Avenue; Love under Fire; Danger—Love at Work; Personal Property; Night Must Fall; The Emperor's Candlesticks; Live, Love and Learn; Beg, Borrow or Steal. 1938 Bulldog Drummond's Peril; Bulldog Drummond in Africa; Arsene Lupin Returns; The First Hundred Years; The Last Warning; Kidnapped; Gateway; Submarine Patrol. 1939 Arrest Bulldog Drummond; The Little Princess; I'm from Missouri; Bulldog Drummond's Secret Police; Bulldog Drummond's Bride; Man about Town; Hound of the Baskervilles; Rose of Washington Square; Adventures of Sherlock Holmes; The Honeymoon's Over; Bachelor Mother; Mr. and Mrs. Bulldog Drummond; Raffles. 1940 Foreign Correspondent; Pride and Prejudice; Earl of Chicago; Congo Maisie.

CLIVE, HENRY (Henry Clive O'Hara)
Born: Oct. 3, 1883, Melbourne, Australia. Died: Dec. 12, 1960, Hollywood, Calif.(lung cancer). Screen, stage, vaudeville actor, commercial artist, and magician.

Appeared in: 1917 The Fighting Odds. 1921 Heedless Moths; The Oath. 1923 Obey the Law.

CLOSE, IVY
Born: 1890. Died: Dec. 4, 1968, Goring, England. Screen actress. Entered films with Britain's Hepworth Co. Mother of British film director Ronald Neame.

Appeared in: 1920 La Roue. 1929 The Jolly Peasant.

CLOUZOT, VERA
Died: Dec. 15, 1960, Paris, France(possible heart attack). Screen actress. Married to French film director Henri Georges Clouzot.

Appeared in: 1955 Diabolique. 1956 Wages of Fear. 1957 Les Espions.

CLOVELLY, CECIL
Born: 1891, England. Died: Apr. 25, 1965, New York, N.Y. Screen, stage actor, and film director.

Appeared in: 1930 The Forest Ring. 1950 So Young, So Bad. 1951 Two Gals and a Guy.

CLUNES, ALEX
Born: 1913, London, England. Died: Mar. 13, 1970, London, England (lung ailment). Screen, stage actor, stage producer, and stage director.

Appeared in: 1940 Convoy. 1941 Saloon Bar. 1953 Melba. 1955 Quentin Durward. 1956 Richard III. 1962 Tomorrow at Ten (U.S. 1964).

CLUTE, CHESTER L.
Born: 1891. Died: Apr. 5, 1956, Woodland Hills, Calif.(heart attack). Screen actor.

Appeared in: 1930 The Jay Walker (short). 1931 The Antique Shop (short). 1932 The Babbling Book (short). 1933 Walking the Baby (short). 1937 Dance, Charlie, Dance; The Great Garrick; He Couldn't Say No; Navy Blues; The Wrong Road; Exclusive; There Goes My Girl; Living on Love. 1938 Change of Heart; Touchdown Army; Pardon Our Nerve; Comet over Broadway; Annabel Takes a Tour; Service DeLuxe; Mr. Chump. 1939 I Was a Convict; Dancing Coed; Laugh It Off; Too Busy to Work; East Side of Heaven. 1940 The Doctor Takes a Wife; Hired Wife; Millionaires in Prison; Dance, Girl, Dance; Too Many Girls; Love Thy Neighbor. 1941 Footlight Fever; She Couldn't Say No; Hold Back the Dawn; Sun Valley Serenade; Scattergood Meets Broadway; Niagara Falls; The Perfect Snob; The Man Who Came to Dinner. 1942 Larceny, Inc.; The Wife Takes a Flyer; Yankee Doodle Dandy; Just Off Broadway; The Forest Rangers; My Favorite Spy; George Washington Slept Here; Star Spangled Rhythm. 1943 Chatterbox; The Desperadoes; Someone to Remember; The Good Fellows; So's Your Uncle; Here Comes Elmer; Crazy House. 1944 Arsenic and Old Lace; Nothing but the Truth; Bermuda Mystery; Hat Check Honey; Rationing; San Diego, I Love You; The Reckless Age; Johnny Doesn't Live Here Anymore. 1945 She Gets Her Man; She Went to the Races; Guest Wife; The Man Who Walked Alone; Anchors Aweigh; Arson Squad; Blonde Ransom; Mildred Pierce; Earl Carroll Vanities. 1946 Angel on My Shoulder; Cinderella Jones; One Exciting Week; Spook Busters. 1947 Hit Parade of 1947; Web of Danger; Joe Palooka in the Knockout; The Crimson Key; Something in the Wind. 1948 Mary Lou; Winner Take All; The Strange Mrs. Crane; Train to Alcatraz; Jiggs and Maggie in Court; Blondie's Reward. 1949 Master Minds; Square Dance Jubilee; Ringside; Blondie's Big Deal. 1950 Lucky Losers; Joe Palooka in Humphrey Takes a Chance; Mary Ryan, Detective. 1951 Kentucky Jubilee; Stop That Cab. 1952 Colorado Sundown.

CLYDE, ANDY
Born: Mar. 25, 1892, Blairgowrie, Scotland. Died: May 18, 1967, Los Angeles, Calif. Brother of screen actor David Clyde (dec. 1945) and screen actress Jean Clyde (dec. 1962). Married to actress Elsie Maud Tarron, one time Mack Sennett bathing beauty. Screen and television actor. Appeared in numerous westerns including several Hopalong Cassidy series films.

Appeared in: 1926 A Sea Dog's Tale (short). 1928 Branded Man; The Goodbye Kiss; Blindfold (short). 1929 Should a Girl Marry?; Ships of the Night; Midnight Daddies; the following shorts: Bulls and Bears; The Lunkhead; The Golfers; Hollywood Star; Clancy at the Bat; The New Half Back; Uppercut O'Brien. 1930 the following shorts: Scotch; Sugar Plum Papa; Match Play; Fat Wives for Thin; Campus Crushes; The Chumps; Goodbye Legs; Hello Television; Average Husband; Vacation Loves; plus Educational shorts. 1931 the following shorts: Speed; Taxi Troubles; Half Holiday. 1932 Million Dollar Legs, plus the following shorts: Shopping with Wife; Heavens! My Husband; Speed in the Gay Nineties; The Boudoir Butler; Alaska Love; Her Royal Shyness; The Giddy Age; Sunkissed Sweeties; For the Love of Ludwig; A Fool about Women; Boy Oh Boy! 1933 Artist's Muddles (short); Feeling Rosy (short). 1934 The Little Minister, plus the following shorts: Frozen Assets; The Super Snooper; Hello Prosperity; Half-Baked Relations. 1935 McFadden's Flats; The Village Tale; Annie Oakley; a Columbia short. 1936 Yellow Dust; Straight from the Shoulder; Two in a Crowd; Red Lights Ahead; a Columbia short. 1937 The Barrier, a Columbia short. 1938 Columbia shorts. 1939 It's a Wonderful World; Bad Lands. 1940 Cherokee Strip; Three Men from Texas; Abe Lincoln in Illinois; Hopalong Cassidy. 1941 Doomed Caravan; In Old Colorado; Pirates on Horseback; Men of Action; Wide Open Town; Riders of the Timberline; Twilight on the Trail; Stick to Your Guns; Secrets of the Wasteland; Outlaws of the Desert. 1943 Undercover Man; Lost Canyon; This above All. 1943 Border Patrol; Leather Burners; Hoppy Serves a Writ; Missing Men; False Colors; Bar 20; Sunset Riders. 1944 Texas Masquerade; Riders of the Deadline; Lumberjack; Forty Thieves; Mystery Man. 1945 Roughly Speaking; Son of the Prairie; A Miner Affair (short); Spook to Me (short). 1946 The Devil's Playground; Fool's Gold; Dangerous Venture; The Green Years; That Texas Jamboree; Throw a Saddle on a Star; The Plainsman and the Lady; The Blonde Stayed On (short). 1947 Unexpected Guest; The Marauders; Hoppy's Holiday. 1948 Strange Gamble; The Dead Don't Dream; Silent Conflict; False Paradise. 1949 Crashing Thru; Riders of the Dusk; Shadows of the West; Haunted Trails; Range Land. 1950 Gunslingers; Silver Raiders; Fence Riders; Arizona Territory; Outlaws of Texas; Cherokee Uprising. 1951 Abilene Trail. 1955 Caroline Cannonball; The Road to Denver. 1960 When Comedy Was King (documentary). 1963 Thirty Years of Fun (documentary); The Sound of Laughter (documentary).

CLYDE, DAVID
Born: 1855. Died: May 17, 1945, San Fernando Valley, Calif. Screen actor. Married to screen actress Fay Holden. Brother of actor Andy Clyde (dec. 1967) and screen actress Jean Clyde (dec. 1962).

Appeared in: 1935 Cardinal Richelieu; Hard Rock Harrigan; The Man on the Flying Trapeze; Bonnie Scotland. 1936 Suzy. 1937 Fury and the Woman; Another Dawn; Love under Fire. 1938 Bulldog Drummond's Peril; Kidnapped. 1939 Arrest Bulldog Drummond; Bulldog Drummond's Secret Police; Death of a Champion; Captain Fury; Ruler of the Sea. 1941 Smilin' Through; The Feminine Touch; H. M. Pulham, Esq. 1942 Nightmare; Random Harvest; Mrs. Miniver; The Gay Sisters; Now, Voyager; Eagle Squadron. 1944 The Lodger; The Scarlet Claw. 1945 The Lost Weekend; Molly and Me; Love Letters; Molly, Bless Her; The House of Fear.

CLYDE, JEAN
Born: 1889. Died: July, 1962, Helensburgh, Scotland. Sister of screen actors Andy (dec. 1967) and David Clyde (dec. 1945). Screen actress.

CLYMER, BETH
Born: 1887. Died: Jan. 14, 1952, Woodland Hills, Calif.(heart attack). Screen actress.

COBB, IRVIN S.
Born: June 23, 1876, Paducah, Ky. Died: Mar. 11, 1944, New York, N.Y. Screen, radio actor, humorist, playwright, novelist, screenwriter, and newspaperman.

Appeared in: 1921 Pardon My French; Peck's Bad Boy. 1922 The Five Dollar Baby. 1924 The Great White Way. 1927 Turkish Delight. 1934 Judge Priest, a series of MGM shorts. 1935 Steamboat 'Round the Bend. 1936 Everybody's Old Man; Pepper. 1938 Hawaii Calls; The Arkansas Traveler; The Young in Heart.

COBURN, CHARLES DOUVILLE
Born: June 19, 1877, Savannah, Ga. Died: Aug. 30, 1961, N.Y. (heart ailment). Screen, stage, radio, television actor, stage producer, and stage director. Won Academy Award for Best Sup-

porting Actor in 1943 for The More the Merrier and was nominated for Best Supporting Actor in 1941 for The Devil and Miss Jones and in 1946 for The Green Years. Married to stage actress Ivah Wills (dec. 1937).

Appeared in: 1933 Boss Tweed. 1935 The People's Enemy. 1938 Idiot's Delight; Bachelor Mother; The Story of Alexander Graham Bell; Stanley and Livingstone; Made for Each Other; In Name Only. 1940 Road to Singapore; Edison the Man; The Captain Is a Lady; Three Faces West; Florian; Refugee. 1941 The Devil and Miss Jones; H.M. Pulham, Esq.; The Lady Eve; Our Wife; Unexpected Uncle; King's Row. 1942 In This Our Life; George Washington Slept Here. 1943 The More the Merrier; The Constant Nymph; Heaven Can Wait; Princess O'Rourke; My Kingdom for a Cook. 1944 Since You Went Away; Knickerbocker Holiday; Wilson; The Impatient Years; Together Again. 1945 A Royal Scandal; Colonel Effingham's Raid; Shady Lady; Over 21, Rhapsody in Blue. 1946 The Green Years; Man of the Hour. 1947 Lured; Personal Column. 1948 B.F.'s Daughter; Green Grass of Wyoming; Rose of Singapore; The Paradine Case. 1949 The Doctor and the Girl; Everybody Does It; The Gal Who Took the West; Impact; Yes Sir, That's My Baby. 1950 Louisa; Mr. Music; Peggy. 1951 The Highwayman; Oh Money, Money. 1952 Monkey Business; Has Anybody Seen My Gal?; Alma Mater. 1953 Gentlemen Prefer Blondes; Trouble along the Way. 1954 The Rocket Man; The Long Wait. 1955 How to Be Very, Very Popular. 1956 Around the World in 80 Days; The Power and the Prize. 1957 How to Murder a Rich Uncle; Town on Trial; The Story of Mankind; Uncle George. 1959 The Remarkable Mr. Pennypacker; Stranger in My Arms; John Paul Jones. 1960 Pepe.

COCHRAN, STEVE (Robert A. Cochran)
Born: May 25, 1917, Eureka, Calif. Died: June 15, 1965, Pacific Ocean, off coast of Guatemala (acute infectious edema which caused swelling in a lung). Screen and stage actor. Divorced from singer Fay McKenzie.

Appeared in: 1945 Boston Blackie Booked on Suspicion; Boston Blackie's Rendezvous; The Gay Senorita; Wonder Man. 1946 The Kid from Brooklyn; The Best Years of Our Lives; The Chase. 1947 Copacabana. 1948 A Song Is Born. 1949 White Heat. 1950 The Big Stickup; The West Point Story; The Damned Don't Cry; Storm Warning; Dallas; Highway 301. 1951 Raton Pass; The Tanks Are Coming; Jim Thorpe—All American; Inside the Walls of Folsom Prison; Tomorrow Is Another Day. 1952 The Lion and the Horse; Operation Secret. 1953 The Desert Song; She's Back on Broadway; Back to God's Country; Shark River. 1954 The Carnival Story; Private Hell 36. 1956 Come Next Spring; Slander. 1957 The Weapon. 1958 I, Mobster; Quantrill's Raiders. 1959 The Beat Generation; The Big Operator. 1961 The Deadly Companions. 1962 Il Grito (The Outcry). 1963 Of Love and Desire. 1965 Tell Me in Sunlight; Mozambique.

COCHRANE, FRANK
Born: Oct. 28, 1882, Durham, England. Died: 1962, London, England. Screen, stage, and radio actor.

Appeared in: 1930 The Yellow Mask. 1934 Chu-Chin-Chow. 1935 McGlusky the Sea Rover. 1936 The Tenth Man. 1937 Bulldog Drummond at Bay; Jericho; Ticket of Leave Man; What a Man. 1938 Dark Sands; Queer Cargo. 1953 Ali Baba Nights.

COCKELBERG, LOUIS J.
Born: 1880. Died: July 7, 1962, Hollywood, Calif. Screen actor.

CODEE, ANN
Born: 1890, Belgium. Died: May 18, 1961, Hollywood, Calif.(heart attack). Screen, television, and vaudeville actress. Married to screen actor Frank Orth (dec. 1962). Appeared in vaudeville with her husband in an act billed "Codee & Orth," and they appeared together (1929-31) under the same billing in the following shorts: 1929 A Bird in the Hand, Zwie Und Fierzigste Strasse; Stranded in Paris; Music Hath Charms; Meine Frau (Meet the Wife). 1930 Taking Ways; Imagine My Embarrassment. 1931 On the Job; Sleepy Head; Dumb Luck; The Bitter Half.

Appeared in: 1935 Under the Pampus Moon. 1936 Hi, Gaucho; Brilliant Marriage. 1937 Expensive Husbands. 1940 Drums of the Desert; Captain Caution; Arise My Love. 1941 Come Live with Me; Charlie Chan in Rio. 1942 Army Surgeon. 1943 Paris after Dark; Tonight We Raid Calais; Old Acquaintance. 1944 Bathing Beauty. 1945 Hangover Square; This Love of Ours; Tonight and Every Night; The Clock; Her Highness and the Bellboy. 1946 Holiday in Mexico; Kitty; It's Great to Be Young; So Dark the Night. 1947 Unfinished Dance; The Other Love. 1948 Rose of Santa Rosa. 1949 That Midnight Kiss. 1950 Under My Skin; When Willie Comes Marching Home. 1951 Mr. Imperium; The Lady Pays Off; On the Riviera. 1952 What Price Glory. 1953

Kiss Me, Kate; Dangerous When Wet; War of the Worlds. 1954 So This Is Paris. 1955 Daddy Long Legs; Interrupted Melody. 1958 Kings Go Forth. 1960 Can-Can.

CODY, BILL, SR. (William Frederick Cody, Sr.)
Born: 1891. Died: Jan. 24, 1948, Santa Monica, Calif. Screen actor and rodeo performer. Father of screen actor Bill Cody, Jr.

Appeared in: 1924 Border Justice. 1925 Cold Nerve; Dangerous Odds; Riders of Mystery; The Fighting Sheriff; The Fighting Smile; Love on the Rio Grande; Moccasins. 1926 The Galloping Cowboy; King of the Saddle. 1927 Laddie Be Good; The Arizona Whirlwind; Born to Battle; Gold from Weepah. 1928 Price of Fear. 1929 Wolves of the City; Slim Fingers; Eyes of the Underworld; Tip Off. 1931 Under Texas Skies; Dugan of the Bad Lands; The Montana Kid; Oklahoma Jim. 1932 Texas Pioneers; Ghost City; Law of the North; Mason of the Mounted; Land of Wanted Men. 1934 Frontier Days. 1935 The Cyclone Ranger; The Texas Rambler; The Vanishing Riders; Six-Gun Justice; Lawless Border. 1936 Outlaws of the Range; Blazing Justice. 1938 Girl of the Golden West. 1939 The Fighting Cowboy; The Fighting Gringo. 1948 Joan of Arc.

CODY, HARRY (Van Doak Covington)
Born: 1896. Died: Oct. 22, 1956, Hollywood, Calif. Screen and stage actor.

Appeared in: 1951 Callaway Went Thataway; People against O'Hara. 1952 Singin' in the Rain. 1954 The Vanquished.

CODY, LEW
Born: Feb. 22, 1887, Waterville, Me. Died: May 31, 1934, Beverly Hills, Calif.(heart disease). Screen, stage, vaudeville actor, and film producer. Married to screen actress Mabel Norman (dec. 1930).

Appeared in: 1915 A Branded Soul; Comrade John. 1917 Treasure of the Sea. 1918 The Demon; For Husbands Only; The Mating. 1919 Don't Change Your Husband; The Life Line; Our Better Selves. 1920 The Beloved Chester. 1921 Sign of the Door. 1922 Dangerous Pastime; The Secrets of Paris; The Valley of Silent Men. 1923 Within the Law; Rupert of Hentzau; Jacqueline of Blazing Barriers; Lawful Larceny; Souls for Sale. 1924 Reno; Husbands and Lovers; Defying the Law; Nellie, the Beautiful Cloak Model; Revelation; The Woman on the Jury; The Shooting of Dan McGrew; Three Women. 1925 The Tower of Lies; Man and Maid; Exchange of Wives; His Secretary; Slave of Fashion; So This Is Marriage?; Time, the Comedian. 1926 The Gay Deceiver; Monte Carlo. 1927 On Ze Boulevard; Adam and Evil; The Demi-Bride; Tea for Three. 1928 Beau Broadway; Wickedness Preferred; The Baby Cyclone. 1929 A Single Man. 1930 What a Widow. 1931 Dishonored; Stout Hearts and Willing Hands; Not Exactly Gentlemen; Common Law; Three Girls Lost; X Marks the Spot; Beyond Victory; Sweepstakes; Woman of Experience; Meet the Wife; Sporting Blood; Divorce among Friends. 1932 The Tenderfoot; 70,00 Witnesses; The Crusader; Madison Square Gardens; Unwritten Law; Undercover Man; File 113; A Parisian Romance. 1933 I Love That Man; Wine, Women and Song; By Appointment Only; Sitting Pretty. 1934 Private Scandal; Shoot the Works.

COEDEL, LUCIEN
Born: 1905. Died: Oct. 1947, France (fell from train). Screen actor.

Appeared in: 1946 Resistance: Releton d'Execution; Carmen. 1947 The Bellman. 1948 The Idiot; Portrait of Innocence. 1949 Strangers in the House; Counter Investigation.

COFFER, JACK
Born: 1939. Died: Feb. 18, 1967, Encino, Calif.(results of auto accident). Screen actor and stuntman.

COFFEY, JOHN
Born: 1909. Died: Mar. 25, 1944, Hollywood, Calif. Screen actor.

COFFIN, HANK
Born: 1904, Lakeport, Calif. Died: Sept. 17, 1966, Los Angeles, Calif. Screen, television actor, and stunt flyer.

Appeared in: 1930 Dawn Patrol; Hell's Angels.

COGAN, FANNY HAY
Born: 1866, Philadelphia, Pa. Died: May 18, 1929, N.Y.(heart disease). Screen, stage, and opera actress. Often called "the mother of the movies."

COGDELL, JOSEPHINE
Born: 1901. Died: May 2, 1969, N.Y. Screen actress and ballet dancer. Appeared as a Mack Sennett bathing beauty.

COGHLAN, KATHERINE
Born: 1889. Died: Sept. 21, 1965, Hollywood, Calif.(cancer). Screen actress (film extra 1919-20). Mother of screen actor Junior Coghlan.

COGHLAN, ROSE
Born: 1850, Peterborough, England. Died: Apr. 2, 1932, Harrison, N.Y.(cerebral hemorrhage). Screen and stage actress.

Appeared in: 1912 As You Like It. 1915 The Sporting Duchess. 1922 The Secrets of Paris; Beyond the Rainbow. 1923 Under the Red Rose. 1932 Hot Saturday. 1933 Jennie Gerhardt.

COGLEY, NICHOLAS "NICK" (Nicholas P.J. Cogley)
Born: 1869, N.Y. Died: May 20, 1936, Santa Monica, Calif. (following operation). Screen, stage actor, and film director. Entered films with Selig.

Appeared in: 1913 Mabel's Heroes; Mother's Boy. 1915 Peanuts and Bullets; A Lucky Leap; Saved by the Wireless. 1916 Dizzy Heights and Daring Hearts; Hearts and Sparks; A La Cabaret; Dollars and Sense (sometimes referred to as The Twins). 1917 Her Circus Knight (sometimes referred to as The Circus Girl); Oriental Love. 1919 Toby's Bow. 1920 Jes' Call Me Jim. 1921 Beating the Game; Boys Will Be Boys; Guile of Women; The Old Nest; An Unwilling Hero. 1922 The Marriage Chance; One Clear Call; Restless Souls. 1923 Crinoline and Romance; Desire. 1924 Abraham Lincoln. 1927 The Missing Link; The Heart of Maryland; In Old Kentucky; Hey! Hey! Cowboy. 1928 Abie's Irish Rose. 1930 Ranch House Blues; The Cohens and the Kellys in Africa. 1933 Cross Fire.

COHAN, GEORGE M.
Born: July 4, 1878, Providence, R.I. Died: Nov. 3, 1942, New York, N.Y.(cancer). Screen, stage, vaudeville, radio actor, songwriter, stage producer, screenwriter, and playwright. Appeared in vaudeville as "The Cohen Mirthmakers."

Appeared in: 1917 Seven Keys to Baldpate; Broadway Jones. 1918 Hit-the-Trail-Haliday. 1932 The Phantom President. 1934 Gambling.

COLBURN, CARRIE
Born: 1859. Died: May 23, 1932, New York, N.Y. Screen and stage actress.

COLCORD, MABEL
Born: 1872, San Francisco, Calif. Died: June 6, 1952, Los Angeles, Calif. Screen and stage actress.

Appeared in: 1933 Little Women. 1934 Sadie McKee. 1935 David Copperfield; Reckless. 1936 The Law in Her Hands; Three Married Men. 1937 The Great O'Malley. 1938 Out West with the Hardys; The Cowboy and the Lady. 1939 The Women.

COLE, FRED
Born: 1901. Died: Sept. 20, 1964, Hollywood, Calif. Screen actor.

Appeared in: 1924 The Dangerous Blonde. 1925 Daring Days; Secrets of the Night; Two-Fisted Jones.

COLE, LESTER
Born: 1900. Died: May 4, 1962, New York, N.Y. Screen, stage actor, and singer.

Appeared in: 1929 Desert Song; Painted Faces. 1930 Love at First Sight.

COLE, NAT "KING" (Nathaniel Adams Coles)
Born: Mar. 17, 1919, Montgomery, Ala. Died: Feb. 15, 1965, Santa Monica, Calif.(lung cancer). Negro screen, television actor, singer, and composer.

Appeared in: 1945 See My Lawyer. 1949 Make Believe Ballroom. 1953 The Blue Gardenia; Small Town Girl. 1955 Kiss Me Deadly. 1957 Istanbul; China Gate. 1958 St. Louis Blues. 1959 The Night of the Quarter Moon. 1965 Cat Ballou.

COLEAN, CHUCK
Born: 1908. Died: Jan. 8, 1971, Hollywood, Calif.(cancer). Screen actor, extra, stuntman, and assistant film director.

COLEMAN, CHARLES
Born: Dec. 22, 1885, Sydney, Australia. Died: Mar. 8, 1951, Woodland Hills, Calif.(stroke). Screen, stage, and television actor. Acted in butler roles mainly.

Appeared in: 1923 Big Dan; Second Hand Love. 1924 That French Lady; The Vagabond Trail. 1926 Sand. 1928 Good Morning, Judge; That's My Daddy. 1930 What a Man; Lawful Larceny; Once a Gentleman. 1931 Beyond Victory; Bachelor Apartment. 1932 The Heart of New York; Play Girl; Merrily We Go to Hell; Winner Take All; Jewel Robbery. 1933 Diplomaniacs; Midnight Club; Gallant Lady; Sailor Be Good. 1934 Born to Be Bad; The Merry Frinks; Housewife; Million Dollar Ransom; Down to Their Last Yacht. 1935 Becky Sharp; The Goose and the Gander; His Family Tree. 1936 Colleen, Her Masters Voice; Don't Get Personal; Everybody's Old Man; The Poor Little Rich Girl; Mummy's Boys; Walking on Air; Lloyds of London. 1937 Love Is News; Too Many Wives; There Goes My Girl; Fight for Your Lady; Three Smart Girls. 1938 Alexander's Ragtime Band; Little Miss Broadway; Gateway; The Rage of Paris; That Certain Age; Little Orphan Annie. 1939 Mexican Spitfire; You Can't Cheat an Honest Man; First Love. 1940 Mexican Spitfire Out West. 1941 Buck Privates; Free and Easy; It Started with Eve. 1942 Almost Married; Twin Beds; Miss Annie Rooney; Between Us Girls; Highways by Night; Arabian Nights; Design for Scandal. 1943 Air Raid Wardens; It Ain't Hay; It Comes up Love; Pittsburgh. 1944 Frenchman's Creek; In Society; The Whistler. 1945 The Picture of Dorian Gray; Missing Corpse; Stork Club; Diamond Horseshoe. 1946 Kitty; Cluny Brown; In High Gear; Magnificent Rogue; The Runaround; Never Say Goodbye; Ziegfeld Follies. 1947 Pilgrim Lady; The Imperfect Lady. 1948 Trouble Makers. 1949 My Friend Irma.

COLEMAN, CLAUDIA
Born: 1889, Atlanta, Ga. Died: Aug. 17, 1938, Hollywood, Calif. Screen, stage, and vaudeville actress.

Appeared in: 1927 Putting It On (short). 1933 I Cover the Waterfront; Warrior's Husband; Son of the Border; Frisco Jenny; Let's Live Tonight. 1934 Big Hearted Herbert. 1935 Frisco Kid. 1936 King of Burlesque; Little Miss Nobody; The Country Beyond; Lady from Nowhere; Under Your Spell; Navy Born. 1938 Penrod and His Twin Brother; Test Pilot; Keep Smiling.

COLEMAN, EMIL
Born: 1893, Russia. Died: Jan. 26, 1965, New York, N.Y.(kidney infection). Bandleader and screen actor.

Appeared in: 1935 Melody Masters (short). 1945 Nob Hill.

COLEMAN, THOMAS
Born: 1897. Died: Jan. 28, 1959, Hollywood, Calif. Screen and television actor. Stand-in and double for Ben Alexander on tv's Dragnet.

COLEMAN, WARREN R.
Born: 1901. Died: Jan. 13, 1968, Martha's Vineyard, Mass. Negro screen, stage, television, radio actor, film director, stage director, film producer and stage producer. Played "Kingfish" on Amos 'n Andy tv show.

COLES, RUSSELL
Born: 1909. Died: Sept. 26, 1960, Hollywood, Calif.(heart attack). Screen actor. Lou Costello's double for three years during 1940s.

COLL, OWEN G.
Born: 1879. Died: Feb. 7, 1960, L.I., N.Y. Screen, stage, and television actor.

COLLEANO, BONAR (Bonar Sullivan)
Born: Mar. 14, 1924, New York, N.Y. Died: Aug. 17, 1958, Birkenhead, England (auto accident). Screen, stage, vaudeville, and circus actor. Member of the Colleano circus family.

Appeared in: 1945 Way to the Stars (film debut). 1946 Wanted for Murder; A Matter of Life and Death; Johnny in the Clouds; While the Sun Shines (U.S. 1950). 1948 One Night with You. 1949 Give Us This Day (aka Salt and the Devil); Sleeping Car to Trieste. 1950 Good Time Girl; Stars in Your Eyes. 1951 Pool of London. 1952 A Tale of Five Women; Eight Iron Men. 1954 The Flame and the Flesh. 1955 The Sea Shall Not Have Them. 1956 Joe Macbeth. 1957 Zarak; Interpol; Fire Down Below; Pickup Alley. 1958 Tank Force; No Time to Die; The Man Inside. Other British films: Rescue; Once a Jolly Swagman; Dance Hall; Escape by Night.

COLLIER, CONSTANCE (Laura Constance Hardie)
Born: Jan. 22, 1878, Winsor Berks, England. Died: Apr. 25, 1955, New York, N.Y. Screen, stage, radio actress, stage producer, director, and playwright.

Appeared in: 1915 Intolerance (film debut). 1916 The Code of Marcia Gray; Macbeth. 1920 Bleak House. 1933 Our Betters; Dinner at Eight. 1935 Peter Ibbetson; Shadow of Doubt. 1936 The Bohemian Girl; Professional Soldier; Girls' Dormitory; Little Lord Fauntleroy. 1937 Thunder in the City; Wee Willie Winkie; She Got What She Wanted; Stage Door; A Damsel in Distress. 1939 Zaza. 1940 Susan and God; Half a Sinner. 1945 Weekend at the Waldorf. 1946 Kitty; Monsieur Beaucaire; Dark Corner. 1947 The Perils of Pauline. 1948 An Ideal Husband; Rope; The Girl from Manhattan. 1950 Whirlpool.

COLLIER, WILLIAM, SR.
Born: Nov. 12, 1866, New York, N.Y. Died: Jan. 13, 1944, Beverly Hills, Calif.(pneumonia). Screen, stage actor, film dialog director, and playwright. Father of screen actor William Collier, Jr.

Appeared in: 1915 Fatty and the Broadway Stars. 1916 Better Late Than Never (working title Getting Married); Plain Jane; Wife and Auto Trouble. 1920 The Servant Question. 1930 Happy Days; High Society Blues; Free and Easy; She's My Weakness; Up the River; Harmony at Home. 1931 Mr. Lemon of Orange; The Seas Beneath; The Brat; Six Cylinder Love; Annabel's Affairs. 1932 After Tomorrow; Hot Saturday; Washington Masquerade; Madison Square Garden; Stepping Sisters. 1934 A Successful Failure; All of Me; The Crosby Case; Cheaters. 1935 The Murder Man; Annapolis Farewell; The Bride Comes Home. 1936 Love on a Bet; Give Us This Night; Valiant Is the Word for Carrie; Cain and Mabel. 1938 Josette; Thanks for the Memory; Say It in French. 1939 I'm from Missouri; Invitation to Happiness; Television Spy; Disputed Passage; Persons in Hiding. 1940 A Miracle on Main Street. 1941 The Hard-Boiled Canary; There's Magic in Music.

COLLINS, EDDIE (Edward Bernard Collins)
Born: 1884. Died: Sept. 2, 1940, Arcadia, Calif.(heart attack). Screen and stage actor.

Appeared in: 1938 In Old Chicago (film debut); Penrod and His Twin Brother; Sally, Irene and Mary; Kentucky Moonshine; Alexander's Ragtime Band; Little Miss Broadway; Always in Trouble; Up the River; Charlie Chan in Honolulu. 1939 Charlie Chan in Reno; News Is Made at Night; Stop, Look and Love; Quick Millions; Drums along the Mohawk; Young Mr. Lincoln; Hollywood Cavalcade. 1940 The Blue Bird; The Return of Frank James.

COLLINS, G. (George Pat Collins)
Born: Dec. 16, 1895, Brooklyn, N.Y. Died: Aug. 5, 1959, Los Angeles, Calif.(cancer). Screen, stage, and television actor.

Appeared in: 1928 The Racket. 1929 Half Marriage. 1930 All Quiet on the Western Front; Manslaughter; Be Yourself!; Big Money; Only Saps Work. 1931 The Vice Squad. 1932 Central Park; Hold 'Em Jail. 1933 20,000 Years in Sing Sing; Parachute Jumper; Girl Missing; Picture Snatcher; The Silk Express; Heroes for Sale; Fog. 1934 Keep 'Em Rolling; The Crime Doctor; The Big Shakedown; A Very Honorable Guy; The Personality Kid. 1935 Black Fury; Alibi Ike; West Point of the Air; Baby Face Harrington; West of the Pecos; Mr. Dynamite. 1949 Flaming Fury; I Married a Communist; White Heat. 1950 The Woman on Pier 13. 1955 Betrayed Women; The Big Tip-Off; The Naked Street; Night Freight. 1956 Yaqui Drums.

COLLINS, JOSE
Born: 1887. Died: Dec. 6, 1958, London, England. Screen, stage, and vaudeville actress.

Appeared in: 1916 The Light That Failed.

COLLINS, MONTE F., JR. (Monte Francis Collins, Jr.)
Born: Dec. 3, 1898, New York, N.Y. Died: June 1, 1951, North Hollywood, Calif.(heart attack). Screen, stage, vaudeville actor, film producer, director, and screenwriter.

Appeared in: 1920 Forty Five Minutes from Broadway (film debut as an extra). 1921 Old Swimmin' Hole; Nineteen and Phyllis; The Cup of Life; The Man from Lost River; Midnight Bell; My Best Girl. 1922 My Wife's Relations (short); At the Sign of the Jack O'Lantern; The Man with Two Mothers; Come on Over. 1923 Big Dan; Long Live the King; Our Hospitality; The Old Fool. 1924 Men; A Boy of Flanders; Pride of Sunshine Alley; Tiger Love. 1925 All around Frying Pan; That Man Jack!; Cold Nerve; The Desert Flower; Tumbleweeds; plus a series of Fox short

comedies. 1926 The Loves of Ricardo; The Cowboy and the Countess. 1927 King of Kings; Painting the Town. 1928 Arizona Wildcat. 1929 Why Bring That Up?; The Talkies; Romance Deluxe, plus the following two shorts: The Madhouse and Ticklish Business. 1930 the following shorts: Hail the Princess; Peace and Harmony; How's My Baby; His Error; French Kisses. 1931 Peach O'Reno. 1932 Girl Crazy, plus the following shorts: Show Business; Anybody's Goat; It's a Cinch; Keep Laughing; Hollywood Handicap; Hollywood Runaround. 1933 The Gay Nighties (short). 1934 the following shorts: Woman Haters; Love and Hisses; In a Pig's Eye; Hey Nanny Nanny. 1935 The Mystery Man; Flying Down to Zero (short). 1936 Columbia shorts. 1937 Hollywood Round-Up; Columbia shorts. 1938 Columbia shorts; Wild Bill Hickok (serial); The Missing Link (short). 1939 Moochin' through Georgia; The Gracie Allen Murder Case. 1940 Buck Benny Rides Again. 1941 She's Oil Mine (short); Kathleen. 1942 Cactus Makes Perfect (short).

COLLINS, RAY
Born: 1890, Sacramento, Calif. Died: July 11, 1965, Santa Monica, Calif.(emphysema). Screen, stage, television, radio, and vaudeville actor.

Appeared in: 1940 The Grapes of Wrath. 1941 Citizen Kane. 1942 The Magnificent Ambersons; Highways by Night; Commandos Strike at Dawn; The Big Street; The Navy Comes Through. 1943 The Crime Doctor; The Human Comedy; Slightly Dangerous; Salute to the Marines; Whistling in Brooklyn. 1944 Eve of St. Mark; See Here, Private Hargrove; Barbary Coast Gent; The Seventh Cross; The Hitler Gang; Can't Help Singing. 1945 Roughly Speaking; The Hidden Eye; Leave Her to Heaven; Miss Susie Slagle's. 1946 Badman's Territory; Boys' Ranch; Crack-Up; Return of Monte Carlo; The Best Years of Our Lives; Two Years before the Mast; Night in Paradise; Up Goes Maisie; Three Wise Fools. 1947 The Red Stallion; The Bachelor and the Bobby-Soxer; The Senator Was Indiscreet; The Swordsman. 1948 Homecoming; Good Sam; For the Love of Mary; The Man from Colorado; A Double Life. 1949 Red Stallion in the Rockies; Hideout; Francis; The Fountainhead; The Heiress; It Happens Every Spring; Free for All; Command Decision. 1950 Kill the Umpire!; Paid in Full; The Reformer and the Redhead; Summer Stock. 1951 Ma and Pa Kettle Back on the Farm; I Want You; You're in the Navy Now (aka U.S.S. Teakettle); Reunion in Reno; The Racket; Vengeance Valley. 1952 The Invitation; Young Man with Ideas; Dreamboat. 1953 Ma and Pa Kettle at the Fair; Ma and Pa Kettle on Vacation; The Desert Song; Column South; The Kid from Left Field; Bad for Each Other. 1954 Rose Marie; Athena. 1955 The Desperate Hours; Texas Lady. 1956 Never Say Goodbye; The Solid Gold Cadillac. 1957 Spoilers of the Forest. 1958 Touch of Evil. 1961 I'll Give My Life.

COLLINS, RUSSELL
Born: Oct. 11, 1897. Died: Nov. 14, 1965, West Hollywood, Calif. (heart attack). Screen, stage, and television actor.

Appeared in: 1948 Close-Up. 1949 The Walking Hills; Shockproof. 1953 Destination Gobi; Miss Sadie Thompson; Niagara. 1955 Canyon Crossroads; The Last Frontier; Bad Day at Black Rock; Soldier of Fortune. 1957 Raintree County; The Enemy Below. 1958 The Matchmaker; God's Little Acre. 1959 The Rabbit Trap. 1964 Fail Safe; Those Calloways. 1965 When the Boys Meet the Girls.

COLLINS, S. D. J.
Born: 1907. Died: Dec. 28, 1947, Leavenworth, Kan.(heart ailment). Screen and circus actor.

Appeared in: 1935 A Night at the Opera.

COLLUM, JOHN
Born: 1926. Died: Aug. 28, 1962, Hollywood, Calif. Screen actor.

Appeared in: 1940 Tom Brown's School Days.

COLLYER, JUNE (Dorothea Heermance)
Born: Aug. 19, 1907. Died: Mar. 16, 1968, Los Angeles, Calif. (bronchial pneumonia). Screen, stage, and television actress. Married to screen actor Stuart Erwin (dec. 1967).

Appeared in: 1927 East Side, West Side (film debut). 1928 Me, Gangster; Four Sons; Hangman's House; Woman Wise. 1929 Red Wine; Let's Make Whoopee; Not Quite Decent; Illusion; River of Romance; The Love Doctor; The Pleasant Sin. 1930 Extravagance; Charley's Aunt; A Man from Wyoming; Sweet Kitty Bellairs; Toast of the Legion; Three Sisters; Beyond Victory. 1931 Damaged Love; The Brat; Honeymoon Lane; Kiss Me Again; Drums of

Jeopardy; Alexander Hamilton; Dude Ranch. 1933 Revenge at Monte Carlo; Before Midnight. 1934 Cheaters; Lost in the Stratosphere. 1935 The Ghost Walks; Murder by Television.

COLMAN, RONALD
Born: Feb. 9, 1891, Richmond-Sunney, England. Died: May 19, 1958, Santa Barbara, Calif.(lung infection). Screen, stage, television, and radio actor. Divorced from screen actress Victoria Maud (aka Thelma Ray) and married to screen actress Benita Hume (dec. 1967). Won Academy Award for Best Actor in A Double Life (1947).

Appeared in: 1919 The Toilers; The Snow in the Desert (serial); Anna the Adventuress. 1920 The Black Spider. 1921 Handcuffs or Kisses. 1923 The White Sister; The Eternal City. 1924 Romola; $20 a Week; Heart Trouble; Her Night of Romance; Tarnish. 1925 The Sporting Venus; Stella Dallas; The Dark Angel; His Supreme Moment; Her Sister from Paris; Lady Windermere's Fan; A Thief in Paradise. 1926 Beau Geste; Kiki; The Winning of Barbara Worth. 1927 The Magic Flame; The Night of Love. 1928 Two Lovers. 1929 The Rescue; Condemned; I Have Been Faithful; Bulldog Drummond. 1930 Raffles; The Devil to Pay. 1931 Arrowsmith; The Unholy Garden. 1932 Cynara. 1933 The Masquerader. 1934 Bulldog Drummond Strikes Back. 1935 Clive of India; The Man Who Broke the Bank at Monte Carlo; A Tale of Two Cities. 1936 Under Two Flags. 1937 Lost Horizon; The Prisoner of Zenda. 1938 If I Were King. 1939 The Light that Failed. 1940 Lucky Partners. 1941 My Life with Caroline. 1942 Random Harvest; Talk of the Town. 1944 Kismet. 1947. A Double Life; The Late George Apley. 1950 Champagne for Caesar. 1956 Around the World in 80 Days. 1957 The Story of Mankind.

COLUMBO, RUSS (Ruggerio de Rudolpho Columbo)
Born: Jan. 14, 1908, Philadelphia, Pa. Died: Sept. 2, 1934, Hollywood, Calif.(accidentally shot). Screen, radio actor, singer, and songwriter.

Appeared in: 1929 Wolf Song; The Street Girl; Dynamite; The Wonders of Women. 1931 Hellbound. 1933 Broadway Thru a Keyhole. 1934 Moulin Rouge; Wake Up and Dream.

COLVIG, VANCE D. "PINTO"
Born: 1892, Jacksonville, Oreg. Died: Oct. 3, 1967, Woodland Hills, Calif. Screen, stage actor, and songwriter. Known as the "Dean of Hollywood Voice Men." Entered films with Sennett in 1923. He created the voices for "Goofy," "Pluto," and "Grumpy" in Snow White and the Seven Dwarfs (1937) and was the voice of "Bozo the Clown" on Capitol Records.

COMANCHE, LAURENCE "TEX"
Born: 1908. Died: Oct. 10, 1932, Hollywood, Calif.("suicide or accident—gun shot wounds"). Screen actor and Indian film extra.

COMANT, MATHILDA
Born: 1888, France. Died: June 22, 1938, Hollywood, Calif. Screen and stage actress.

Appeared in: 1935 Ceiling Zero. 1936 Anthony Adverse.

COMBER, BOBBIE (Edmund Comber)
Born: Jan. 8, 1890, Bury St. Edmunds, England. Died: Apr. 1942, Wales (heart attack). Screen, stage, revues, and radio actor.

Appeared in: 1930 Lilies of the Field. 1933 Sleeping Car. Other British films: Don't Rush Me; Brother Alfred; Here Comes Susie; Ace of Spades.

COMINGORE, DOROTHY
Born: 1918. Died: Dec. 30, 1971, Stonington, Conn. Screen and stage actress.

Appeared in: 1939 Mr. Smith Goes to Washington. 1941 Citizen Kane. 1944 The Hairy Ape. 1949 Any Number Can Play. 1952 The Big Night.

COMPTON, BETTY
Born: 1907, Isle of Wight. Died: July 12, 1944, N.Y. Screen, stage actress, singer, and dancer. Divorced from James J. Walker, former Mayor of New York.

Appeared in: 1930 The Legacy (short). 1934 a British International film.

COMPTON, FRANCIS
Born: 1885, San Francisco, Calif. Died: Sept. 17, 1964, Noroton, Conn. Screen actor.

Appeared in: 1958 Witness for the Prosecution.

CONDE, JOHNNY
Born: 1895. Died: Dec. 5, 1960, Hollywood, Calif.(heart attack). Screen actor.

CONE, MIKE "ZETS"
Born: 1910. Died: Jan. 4, 1969, North Miami Beach, Fla.(cancer). Screen, television actor, and musician.

CONKLIN, CHARLES "HEINIE"
Born: 1880. Died: July 30, 1959, Hollywood, Calif. Screen actor.

Appeared in: 1923 The Day of Faith. 1924 The Cyclone Rider; Find Your Man; George Washington, Jr.; Troubles of a Bride. 1925 Below the Line; A Fool and His Money; Hogan's Alley; Clash of the Wolves; Red Hot Tires; Seven Sinners. 1926 The Fighting Edge; Hardboiled; The Man Upstairs; More Pay—Less Work; Whispering Wires; Fig Leaves; Honesty—the Best Policy; The Night Cry; The Sap. 1927 Beware of Widows; Ham and Eggs at the Front; Cheaters; Drums of the Desert; Silk Stockings. 1928 The Air Circus; Beau Broadway; Feel My Pulse; A Horseman of the Plains; A Trick of Hearts. 1929 The Show of Shows; Side Street; Tiger Rose. 1930 Ducking Duty (short); All Quiet on the Western Front. 1932 Trailing the Killer. 1933 Riders of Destiny. 1935 Girl from 10th Avenue. 1936 Wedding Present. 1938 Little Miss Broadway. 1939 Hollywood Cavalcade. 1940 Dr. Christian Meets the Women. 1942 Even as I.O.U. (short). 1943 Three Little Twerps (short). 1944 Lost in a Harem. 1945 Song of the Prairie. 1947 The Perils of Pauline. 1950 Joe Palooka in Humphrey Takes a Chance; County Fair. 1955 Abbott and Costello Meet the Keystone Kops.

CONKLIN, CHESTER
Born: Jan. 11, 1888, Oskaloosa, Iowa. Died: Oct. 11, 1971, Woodland Hills, Calif. Screen, stage, vaudeville, and circus actor. Entered films in 1913 with Majestic and later appeared in several Keystone Kop comedies.

Appeared in: 1913 Ambrose-Walrus Series. 1914 Making a Living (reissued as A Busted Johnny); Mabel's Strange Predicament; Between Showers; Tango Tangles; Mabel at the Wheel (reissued as His Daredevil); Twenty Minutes of Love; Caught in a Cabaret (reissued as The Jazz Waiter); Mabel's Busy Day; Mabel's New Job; The Face on the Barroom Floor (reissued as The Ham Artist); Those Love Pangs; The Love Thief; Dough and Dynamite (reissued as The Doughnut Designers); Gentlemen of Nerve (reissued as Some Nerve); Curses! They Remarked; How Heroes Are Made; His Taking Ways; A Colored Girl's Love; Wild West Love. 1915 Hushing the Scandal (reissued as Friendly Enemies); Hash House Mashers; Love, Speed and Thrills; The Home Breakers (reissued as Other People's Wives); Caught in a Park; A Bird's a Bird; A One Night Stand; Hearts and Planets; Ambrose's Sour Grapes; Droppington's Devilish; Dream; Droppington's Family Tree; A Hash House Fraud; Do-Re-Me-Fa; The Cannon Ball (reissued as The Dynamiter); When Ambrose Dared Walrus; The Battle of Ambrose and Walrus; Saved By the Wireless; The Best of Enemies. 1916 Dizzy Heights and Daring Hearts; Cinders of Love; Bucking Society; His First False Step; A Tugboat Romeo. 1917 The Pullman Bride; Dodging His Doom; A Clever Dummy; The Pawnbroker's Heart. 1919 Uncle Tom's Cabin. 1920 "Sunshine" comedies; Chicken a la Cabaret. 1921 Skirts. 1923 Anna Christie; Desire; Souls for Sale; Tea with a Kick. 1924 Galloping Fish; Another Man's Wife; The Fire Patrol; North of Nevada; Greed. 1925-26 12 "Blue Ribbon" comedies (shorts). 1925 A Woman of the World; Battling Bunyon; The Great Love; The Masked Bride; Where Was I?; The Winding Stair; The Great Jewel Robbery; My Neighbor's Wife; One Year to Live; The Phantom of the Opera; The Pleasure Buyers; Under the Rouge; The Gold Rush. 1926-27 series of shorts for Tennek Film Corp. 1926 The Wilderness Woman; A Social Celebrity; Say It Again; We're in the Navy Now; Behind the Front; The Duchess of Buffalo; Fascinating Youth; The Lady of the Harem; The Nervous Wreck; Midnight Lovers. 1927 Cabaret; Rubber Heels; Kiss in a Taxi; Tell It to Sweeney; McFadden's Flats. 1928 Two Flaming Youths; Fools for Luck; Gentlemen Prefer Blondes; Tillie's Punctured Romance; Varsity; The Big Noise; Trick of Hearts; The Haunted House; Feel My Pulse; Horseman of the Plains; Beau Broadway. 1929 Marquis Preferred; The House of Horror; Stairs of Sand; The Studio Murder Mystery; Sunset Pass; The Virginian; Shanghai Rose; Show of Shows; Taxi Thirteen; Fast Company, plus several Hal Roach shorts. 1930 Swing High; The Master Sweeper (short); The Love Trader. 1930-31 six shorts for Paramount. 1931 The New Yorker; Her Majesty, Love; Stout Hearts and Willing Hands. 1933 Hallelujah, I'm a Bum. 1935 a Vitaphone short. 1936 Call of the Prairie; Modern Times; The Preview Murder Mystery. 1937 Hotel Haywire; Forlorn River. 1938 Flatfoot Stooges (short); Every Day's a Holiday. 1939 Zenobia; Hollywood Cavalcade. 1940 The Great Dictator;

Li'l Abner. 1941 Goodnight Sweetheart; Harmon of Michigan; Dutiful But Dumb (short). 1942 Sons of the Pioneers. 1943 Three Little Twerps (short); Phony Express (short). 1944 Adventures of Mark Twain; Knickerbocker Holiday; Sunday Dinner for a Soldier; Hail the Conquering Hero. 1945 Micro Phonies (short); Abbott and Costello in Hollywood. 1946 Little Giant. 1947 Perils of Pauline; Springtime in the Sierras. 1949 Jiggs and Maggie in Jackpot Jitters; The Beautiful Blonde from Bashful Bend; The Golden Stallion. 1950 Joe Palooka in Humphrey Takes a Chance. 1955 Apache Woman; Beast with a Million Eyes. 1948 Rock-a-Bye Baby. 1960 When Comedy Was King (documentary). 1962 Paradise Alley. 1966 A Big Hand for the Little Lady.

CONKLIN, WILLIAM
Born: Brooklyn, N.Y. Died: Mar. 21, 1935, Hollywood, Calif. (paralytic stroke). Screen, stage actor, and film producer. Entered films in 1915.

Appeared in: 1915 Neal of the Navy (serial). 1917 Law of the Land. 1919 Hay Foot, Straw Foot; Red Hot Dollars. 1920 The Woman in the Suitcase; Hairpins. 1921 Beau Revel; Blind Hearts; The Lure of Youth; The Other Woman. 1922 Iron to Gold; The Unfoldment; Up and Going; When Husbands Deceive; The Woman He Married. 1923 Daytime Wives; The Darlings of New York; The Lone Star Ranger; The Lonely Road; The Man Alone; The Meanest Man in the World; Three Who Paid. 1924 The Goldfish; Never Say Die; Stolen Secrets. 1925 Counsel for the Defense; Fifth Avenue Models; A Gentleman Roughneck; The Man without a Country; Ports of Call; The Rag Man; Winds of Chance. 1926 Faithful Wives; Old Ironsides; Sweet Rosie O'Grady. 1927 Outlaws of Red River; Rose of the Golden West; Tumbling River. 1928 Life's Crossroads. 1929 The Divine Lady; Shanghai Rose.

CONLEY, LIGE
Born: 1899. Died: Dec. 11, 1937, Hollywood, Calif.(hit by auto). Screen actor. Entered films in silents with Sennett.

Appeared in: 1928 The Charge of the Gauchos.

CONLIN, JIMMY (aka JIMMY CONLON)
Born: Oct. 14, 1884, Camden, N.J. Died: May 7, 1962, Encino, Calif. Screen, stage, vaudeville, and television actor. Married to actress Myrtle Glass with whom he appeared in vaudeville as "Conlin & Glass."

Appeared in: 1928 Sharps and Flats (film debut); Lights of New York. 1933 20,000 Years in Sing Sing; College Humor. 1934 Now I'll Tell; Cross Country Cruise; City Limits. 1935 The Bride Comes Home. 1936 And Sudden Death; Rose Bowl. 1937 Find the Witness; The Bad Man Who Found Himself; The Adventurous Blonde. 1938 Crashing Hollywood; Torchy Blane in Panama; Broadway Musketeers; Cocoanut Grove. 1939 $1000 a Touchdown; No Place to Go. 1940 Calling Philo Vance; Second Chorus; The Great McGinty. 1941 Ridin' on a Rainbow; Sullivan's Travels. 1942 The Remarkable Andrew; The Forest Rangers; The Palm Beach Story; The Man in the Trunk. 1943 Hitler's Madness; Petticoat Larceny; Jitterbugs; Taxi, Mister?. 1944 Lost in a Harem; Town Went Wild; Hail the Conquering Hero; Summer Storm; Army Wives; Ali Baba and the Forty Thieves; Miracle of Morgan's Creek. 1945 Bring on the Girls; Don Juan Quilligan; An Angel Comes to Brooklyn; Fallen Angel; Picture of Dorian Gray. 1946 Whistle Stop. 1947 Mad Wednesday; It's a Joke, Son; Dick Tracy's Dilemma; Rolling Home; Seven Keys to Baldpate; The Hucksters; Mourning Becomes Electra. 1949 Prejudice; Knock on Any Door; Tulsa. 1950 Operation Haylift; Sideshow; The Great Rupert. 1953 It Happens Every Thursday. 1959 Anatomy of a Murder; The 30 Foot Bride of Candy Rock.

CONNELLY, BOBBY
Born: 1909. Died: July 5, 1922, Lynbrook, N.Y.(enlarged heart and bronchitis). Screen and vaudeville actor. Entered films at age of three for Kalem in 1912.

Appeared in: 1913 Love's Sunset. 1916 A Prince in a Pawnshop. 1917 Intrigue. 1918 A Youthful Affair; The Seal of Silence. 1919 The Unpardonable Sin. 1920 Humoresque. 1921 The Old Oaken Bucket. 1922 A Wide-Open Town; Wildness of Youth.

CONNELLY, EDWARD J.
Born, 1855, New York. Died: Nov. 21, 1928, Hollywood, Calif. (influenza). Screen and stage actor.

Appeared in: 1914 The Good Little Devil (film debut). 1917 The Great Secret (serial). 1920 Shore Acres; The Willow Tree. 1921 The Four Horsemen of the Apocalypse; Camille; The Conquering Power; The Conflict. 1922 Quincy Adams Sawyer; Kisses; Love in the Dark; Seeing's Believing; Red Hot Romance; The Prisoner of Zenda; Turn to the Right; Trifling Women. 1923 Desire; Where

the Pavement Ends; Slave of Desire; Her Fatal Millions. Scaramouche. 1924 The Beauty Prize; The Goldfish; Revelation; Sinners in Silk; So This Is Marriage; A Fool's Awakening. 1925 Sun-Up; The Only Thing; The Denial; The Unholy Three; The Merry Widow. 1926 The Gay Deceiver; Bardely's, The Magnificent; Brown of Harvard; The Torrent. 1927 Lovers?; Winners of the Wilderness; The Show; The Student Prince. 1928 Brotherly Love; Across to Singapore; Forbidden Hours; The Mysterious Lady. 1929 The Desert Rider.

CONNELLY, ERWIN
Born: 1873. Died: Feb. 12, 1931, Los Angeles, Calif.(auto accident injuries). Screen, stage, and vaudeville actor. Married to screen actress Jane Connelly (dec. 1925) and together they appeared in vaudeville.

Appeared in: 1922 The Man from Beyond. 1924 Sherlock, Jr. 1925 Beggar on Horseback; Marry Me; Seven Chances; When Husbands Flirt. 1926 The Blind Goddess; The Crown of Lies; The Danger Girl; The Fire Brigade; Kiki; Shipwrecked; The Son of the Sheik; The Winning of Barbara Worth. 1927 Cheating Cheaters; Rubber Tires.

CONNELLY, JANE
Died: Oct. 25, 1925, Los Angeles: Calif.(result of a nervous breakdown). Screen and vaudeville actress. Married to screen actor Erwin Connelly (dec. 1931) and together they appeared in vaudeville.

Appeared in: 1922 The Man from Beyond. 1924 Sherlock, Jr.

CONNOLLY, WALTER
Born: Apr. 8, 1887, Cincinnati, Ohio. Died: May 28, 1940, Beverly Hills, Calif.(stroke). Screen and stage actor.

Appeared in: 1930 Many Happy Returns (short). 1932 Washington Merry-Go-Round; Plainsclothes Man; No More Orchids; Man against Woman. 1933 Lady for a Day; Master of Men; East of Fifth Avenue; A Man's Castle; Paddy the Next Best Thing; The Bitter Tea of General Yen. 1934 Eight Girls in a Boat; It Happened One Night; Twentieth Century; Whom the Gods Destroy; Broadway Bill; Lady by Choice; White Lies; Once to Every Woman; Servants' Entrance; Captain Hates the Sea; Many Happy Returns. 1935 So Red the Rose; She Couldn't Take It; Father Brown, Detective; One Way Ticket. 1936 Soak the Rich; The Music Goes 'Round; The King Steps Out; Libeled Lady. 1937 The Good Earth; Nancy Steele Is Missing; Let's Get Married; The League of Frightened Men; First Lady; Nothing Sacred. 1938 Start Cheering; Penitentiary; Four's a Crowd; Too Hot to Handle. 1939 The Girl Downstairs; Those High Gray Walls; Good Girls Go to Paris; Bridal Suite; Coast Guard; The Adventures of Huckleberry Finn; Fifth Avenue Girl; The Great Victor Herbert.

CONNOR, EDRIC
Born: 1915, Mayaro, Trinidad. Died: Oct. 16, 1968, London, England (stroke). Screen, stage, radio, television actor, singer, author, and film producer. Entered films in 1952.

Appeared in: 1952 Cry, the Beloved Country. 1954 West of Zanzibar. 1956 Moby Dick. 1957 Fire Down Below. 1958 The Roots of Heaven; The Vikings. 1959 Beasts of Marseilles. 1960 Virgin Island. 1961 King of Kings. 1963 Four for Texas. 1968 Nobody Runs Forever; Only When I Larf.

CONNOR, EDWARD
Died: May 14, 1932, New York, N.Y. Screen and stage actor. Entered films with Edison in 1913.

Appeared in: 1921 Anne of Little Smoky.

CONRAD, EDDIE
Born: 1891. Died: Apr. 1941, Los Angeles, Calif. Screen, stage, and vaudeville actor.

Appeared in: 1927 Broadway's Favorite Comedian (short). 1929 Blaze O'Glory. 1935 Duel in Oil (short); Every Night at Eight; I Live for Love; Stars over Broadway; The Melody Lingers on. 1936 Big Brown Eyes; Hot Money. 1938 Happy Landing; Romance in the Dark; Always Goodbye; I'll Give a Million; Gateway; Just around the Corner; Topper Takes a Trip. 1940 Saps at Sea; I Was an Adventuress; Foreign Correspondent; Lucky Partners; Down Argentine Way; Chad Hanna; Behind the News. 1941 You're the One; That Night in Rio; West Point Widow; Hurry, Charlie, Hurry; Angels with Broken Wings.

CONROY, FRANK
Born: Oct. 14, 1890, Derby, England. Died: Feb. 24, 1964, Paramus, N.J.(heart ailment). Screen, stage, and television actor.

Appeared in: 1930 The Royal Family of Broadway. 1931 Bad Company; Possessed; Hell Divers. 1932 Manhattan Parade; West of Broadway; Grand Hotel; Disorderly Conduct. 1933 Midnight Mary; Night Flight; Ann Carver's Profession; Ace of Aces; The Kennel Murder Case. 1934 Little Miss Marker; Keep 'Em Rolling; The Crime Doctor; The White Parade; The Little Minister; Frontier Marshal; Such Women Are Dangerous; The Cat and the Fiddle. 1935 Call of the Wild; Last Days of Pompeii; Show Them No Mercy; Charlie Chan in Egypt; West Point of the Air; I Live My Life. 1936 The White Angel; Stolen Holiday; Meet Nero Wolfe; Nobody's Fool; The Georgeous Hussy; Charlie Chan at the Opera. 1937 Love Is News; Wells Fargo; That I May Live; Nancy Steele Is Missing; Big Business; This Is My Affair; The Emperor's Candlesticks; The Last Gangster; Music for Madame. 1941 This Woman Is Mine. 1942 Adventures of Martin Eden; Crossroads; The Loves of Edgar Allen Poe. 1943 The Ox-Bow Incident; Crash Dive; Lady of Burlesque. 1947 That Hagen Girl. 1948 Sealed Verdict; Rogues' Regiment; Naked City; All My Sons; The Snake Pit; For the Love of Mary. 1949 The Threat. 1951 The Day the Earth Stood Still; Lightning Strikes Twice. 1959 The Last Mile; Compulsion; The Young Philadelphians. 1960 The Bramble Bus.

CONROY, THOM
Born: 1911. Died: Nov. 16, 1971, Hollywood, Calif.(heart attack). Screen and stage actor.

Appeared in: 1955 Man with the Gun. 1961 The Young Savages.

CONSTANT, MAX
Born: France. Died: May, 1943, Mojave Desert (died during flying test for Air Force). Screen actor.

Appeared in: 1923 Trilby.

CONTI, ALBERT (Albert De Conti Cadassamare)
Born: Jan. 29, 1887, Trieste, Austria. Died: Jan. 18, 1967, Hollywood, Calif.(stroke). Screen actor. Entered films in 1922.

Appeared in: 1923 Merry-Go-Round (film debut). 1925 The Merry Widow; Eagle. 1926 The Blonde Saint; Old Loves and New; Watch Your Wife. 1927 Slipping Wives (short); Camille; The Chinese Parrot; The Devil Dancer; South Sea Love. 1928 Love Me and the World Is Mine; Stocks and Blondes; Plastered in Paris; Legion of the Condemned; Magnificent Flirt; Dry Martini; Alex the Great; Show People; Tempest. 1929 Making the Grade; The Exalted Flapper; Jazz Heaven; Captain Lash; Lady of the Pavements; Saturday's Children; He Loved the Ladies. 1930 Such Men Are Dangerous; Oh, For a Man!; The Melody Man; One Romantic Night; Morocco; Sea Legs; Madame Satan; Average Husband; Monte Carlo; Our Blushing Brides. 1931 This Modern Age; Reputation; Gang Busters; Strangers May Kiss; Just a Gigolo; Heartbreak. 1932 Shopworn; Doomed Battalion; As You Desire Me; Night Club Lady; Freaks; Lady with a Past; Second Fiddle. 1933 Gigolettes of Paris; Topaze; Men Are Such Fools; Love Is Dangerous; Love Is Like That; Shanghai Madness; Torch Singer. 1934 Love Time; Beloved; Elmer and Elsie. 1935 The Night Is Young; Hands Across the Table; Mills of the Gods; Symphony of Living; Diamond Jim; The Crusades; Here's to Romance. 1936 Fatal Lady; Hollywood Boulevard; One in a Million; Collegiate. 1937 Dangerously Yours; Cafe Metropole. 1938 Always Goodbye; Gateway; Suez. 1942 My Gal Sal.

CONWAY, JACK
Born: Ireland. Died: May, 1951, Forest Hills, N.Y. Screen and vaudeville actor. Appeared in early Paramount pictures.

CONWAY, JACK
Born: July 17, 1887, Graceville, Minn. Died: Oct. 11, 1952, Pacific Palisades, Calif. Screen, stage actor, and film director.

Appeared in: 1909 Her Indian Hero. 1914 The Old Arm Chair. 1919 Restless Souls.

CONWAY, JOSEPH
Born: Approx. 1889, Philadelphia, Pa. Died: Feb. 28, 1959, Philadelphia, Pa. Screen actor and circus owner. Appeared in early silents made in Philadelphia.

CONWAY, TOM (Thomas Charles Sanders)
Born: 1904, St. Petersburg, Russia. Died: Apr. 22, 1967, Culver City, Calif.(liver ailment). Screen, television, and radio actor. Brother of screen actor George Sanders (dec. 1972).

Appeared in: 1940 Sky Murder. 1941 The People vs. Dr. Kildare; Tarzan's Secret Treasure; Mr. and Mrs. North; The Trial of Mary Dugan; Free and Easy; The Bad Man; Lady Be Good. 1942 Mrs. Miniver; Grand Central Murder; Rio Rita; The Falcon's Brother; The Cat People. 1943 The Falcon in Danger; The Falcon and the Co-Eds; The Seventh Victim; The Falcon Strikes Back; I Walked with a Zombie; One Exciting Night. 1944 The Falcon in Mexico; The Falcon Out West; A Night of Adventure; The Falcon in Hollywood. 1945 Two O'Clock Courage; The Falcon in San Francisco; One Exciting Month. 1946 Criminal Court; The Falcon's Adventure; The Falcon's Alibi; Whistle Stop; Runaway Daughters. 1947 Repeat Performance; Fun on a Weekend; Lost Honeymoon. 1948 One Touch of Venus; 13 Lead Soldiers; The Challenge; Repeat Performance; Bungalow 13; Checkered Coat. 1949 I Cheated the Law. 1950 The Great Plane Robbery. 1951 Painting the Clouds with Sunshine; The Bride of the Gorilla; Triple Cross. 1952 Confidence Girl. 1953 Tarzan and the She-Devil; Peter Pan (voice only); Park Plaza 505, Paris Model; Norman Conquest. 1954 Three Stops to Murder; Prince Valiant. 1955 Barbados Quest. 1956 The Last Man to Hang; Operation Murder; Breakaway; Death of a Scoundrel; The She-Creature; Murder on Approval. 1957 Voodoo Woman. 1959 The Atomic Submarine; Rocket to the Moon. 1960 12 to the Moon. 1961 One Hundred and One Dalmatians (voice only). 1964 What a Way to Go.

COOK, AL
Born: 1882. Died: July 6, 1935, Santa Monica, Calif. Screen actor.

Appeared in: 1916 Fighting Blood. 1927 The Telephone Girl. 1929 As You Like It; Meet the Quince; Love's Labor Found; They Shall Not Pass Out; Eventually, but Not Now; The Captain of the Roll. 1930 The Sleeping Cutie; Lost and Foundered; Old Vamps for New; The Setting Son; The Dear Slayer; Cash and Merry; Land of the Sky Blue Daughters.

COOK, DONALD
Born: Sept. 26, 1901, Portland, Oreg. Died: Oct. 1, 1961, New Haven, Conn.(heart attack). Screen, stage, television, radio and vaudeville actor.

Appeared in: 1930 Roseland (short). 1931 Eastside; The Silent Voice; Mad Genius; The Unfaithful; Party Husband; Side Show; The Public Enemy. 1932 Heart of New York; New Morals for Old; The Conquerors; So Big; Washington Merry-Go-Round; The Man Who Played God; The Trial of Vivienne Ware; The Unfaithful; The Penguin Pool Murder; Safe in Hell. 1933 Frisco Jenny; Kiss before the Mirror; Jennie Gerhardt; The Circus Queen Murder; Private Jones; Baby Face; The World Changes; The Woman I Stole; Brief Moment. 1934 The Lost Lady; Fury of the Jungle; Fog; The Ninth Guest; Jealousy; The Most Precious Thing in Life; Whirlpool; Viva Villa. 1935 The Night Is Young; Ladies Love Danger; Behind the Evidence; Fugitive Lady; Gigolette; Confidential; The Casino Murder Case; Here Comes the Band; Motive for Revenge; Murder in the Fleet; The Spanish Cape Mystery. 1936 Ring around the Moon; Girl from Mandalay; Can This Be Dixie?; Ellis Island; The Calling of Dan Matthews; The Leavenworth Case; Showboat. 1937 Circus Girl; Two Wise Maids; Beware of Ladies. 1944 Bowery to Broadway; Murder in the Blue Room; Patrick the Great. 1945 Blonde Ransom; Here Come the Co-Eds. 1950 Our Very Own.

COOK, KEN
Born: 1914. Died: Dec. 28, 1963, Hollywood, Calif.(heart attack). Screen and stage actor.

COOK, MARY
Died: May 27, 1944, Hollywood, Calif. Screen actress, singer, and dancer. Divorced from screen actor Elisha Cook, Jr.

Appeared in: 1942 Ride 'Em Cowboy.

COOK, ROSS
Born: 1898. Died: Jan. 2, 1930. Screen pilot.

Appeared in: 1930 Hell's Angels.

COOK, WARREN
Born: 1879. Died: May 2, 1939, New York, N.Y. Screen and stage actor.

Appeared in: 1920 My Lady's Garter; Lady Rose's Daughter. 1921 Conceit; The Fighter; The Girl from Nowhere; Is Life Worth Living?; The Last Door; The Man of Stone; Suspicious Wives; Worlds Apart. 1922 John Smith; Slim Shoulders. 1923 The Broken Violin; Dark Secrets; Fog Bound; The Silent Command. 1924 His Darker Self; The Truth about Women. 1925 Shore Leave; The Knockout; Wild, Wild Susan. 1926 Lew Tyler's Wives. 1927 The Lunatic at Large.

COOKE, STEPHEN BEACH
Born: 1898. Died: Sept. 16, 1948, Cooperstown, N.Y. Screen and stage actor.

COOKSEY, CURTIS
Born: 1892. Died: Apr. 19, 1962, Hollywood, Calif.(suicide—cancer). Screen and stage actor.

Appeared in: 1920 The Silver Horde. 1922 A Virgin's Sacrifice. 1932 The Misleading Lady. 1952 Because You're Mine; The Girl in White; Young Man with Ideas; Scaramouche. 1953 Taxi. 1956 Storm Center; Death of a Scoundrel.

COOLEY, CHARLES (Charles Cali)
Born: 1903, Cleveland, Ohio. Died: Nov. 15, 1960, Hollywood, Calif.(rare blood disease). Screen, television, and vaudeville actor.

Appeared in: 1951 The Lemon Drop Kid. 1952 Son of Paleface, Sound Off.

COOLEY, FRANK L.
Born: 1870, Natchez, Miss. Died: July 6, 1941, Hollywood, Calif. Screen, stage actor, and film director. Entered films with Keystone Company in 1912.

Appeared in: 1926 First Year; More Pay—Less Work. 1927 Wanted—A Coward. 1928 Honor Bound.

COOLEY, JAMES R.
Born: 1880. Died: Nov. 15, 1948, Hollywood, Calif. Screen and stage actor.

Appeared in: 1917 A Tale of Two Nations. 1924 The Song of Love.

COOLEY, SPADE (Donnell C. Cooley)
Born: 1910, Grand, Okla. Died: Nov. 23, 1969, Oakland, Calif.(heart attack). Bandleader, screen and television actor.

Appeared in: 1943 Chatterbox; The Silent Bandit. 1944 The Singing Sheriff. 1945 Rockin' in the Rockies; Outlaws of the Rockies. 1946 Texas Panhandle. 1947 Vacation Days. 1949 Square Dance Jubilee; The Kid from Gower Gulch; Border Outlaw; I Shot Billy the Kid. 1951 Casa Manana.

COOLIDGE, PHILIP
Born: Aug. 25, 1908, Concord, Mass. Died: May 23, 1967, Hollywood, Calif.(cancer). Screen, stage, and television actor.

Appeared in: 1947 Boomerang. 1956 The Shark Fighters. 1957 Slander. 1958 I Want to Live! 1959 The Tingler; It Happened to Jane; The Mating Game; North by Northwest. 1960 Because They're Young; The Bramble Bush; Inherit the Wind. 1964 Hamlet. 1965 The Greatest Story Ever Told. 1966 The Russians Are Coming, The Russians Are Coming. 1968 Never a Dull Moment.

COOPER, ASHLEY
Born: 1882, Australia. Died: Jan. 3, 1952, New York, N.Y. Screen, stage, and vaudeville actor.

Appeared in: 1921 Partners of the Tide; Shadows of Conscience. 1922 Gay and Devilish; The Hands of Nara; The Son of the Wolf; Tillie. 1923 Desert Driven; Robin Hood, Jr. 1924 The Torrent. 1926 Paradise.

COOPER, CLAUDE
Born: 1881. Died: July 20, 1932, Laurelton, N.Y.(heart attack). Screen, stage actor, and film director.

Appeared in: 1915 The Country Girl. 1921 A Heart to Let; The Plaything of Broadway. 1924 Daughters of the Night. 1931 The Struggle.

COOPER, GARY (Frank James Cooper)
Born: May 7, 1901, Helena, Mont. Died: May 13, 1961, Hollywood, Calif.(cancer). Screen, television actor, and film producer. Made one television special. Married to screen actress Veronica Balfe who acted under the name of Sandra Shaw. Won Academy Award for Best Actor in 1941 for Sergeant York and in 1952 for High Noon. Nominated for Academy Award in 1943 for Best Actor in For Whom the Bell Tolls.

Appeared in: 1925 The Lucky Horseshoe; The Vanishing American; The Eagle; The Enchanted Hill; Watch Your Wife; Tricks. 1926 Three Pals; Lightning Justice; The Winning of Barbara

Worth. 1927 Arizona Bound; Nevada; The Last Outlaw; Wings; Children of Divorce; It. 1928 Beau Sabreur; The Legion of the Condemned; Doomsday; The First Kiss; Lilac Time; Half a Bride. 1929 Shopworn Angel; Wolf Song; The Betrayal; The Virginian. 1930 Only the Brave; Paramount on Parade; The Texan; Seven Days' Leave; A Man from Wyoming; The Spoilers; Morocco. 1931 Fighting Caravans; City Streets; I Take This Woman; His Woman. 1932 The Devil and the Deep; Make Me a Star; If I Had a Million; A Farewell to Arms. 1933 Today We Live; One Sunday Afternoon; Design for Living; Alice in Wonderland; The Eagle and the Hawk. 1934 Operator 13; Now and Forever. 1935 The Wedding Night; Lives of a Bengal Lancer; Peter Ibbetson. 1936 Desire; Mr. Deeds Goes to Town; The General Died at Dawn; Hollywood Boulevard; The Plainsman. 1937 Souls at Sea. 1938 The Adventures of Marco Polo; Bluebeard's Eighth Wife; The Cowboy and the Lady. 1939 Beau Geste; The Real Glory. 1940 The Westerner; Northwest Mounted Police. 1941 Meet John Doe; Sergeant York; Ball of Fire. 1942 The Pride of the Yankees. 1943 For Whom the Bell Tolls. 1944 The Story of Dr. Wassell; Casanova Brown. 1945 Along Came Jones; Saratoga Trunk. 1946 Cloak and Dagger. 1947 Unconquered; Variety Girl. 1948 Good Sam. 1949 The Fountainhead; It's a Great Feeling; Task Force. 1950 Bright Leaf; Dallas. 1951 You're in the Navy Now (aka U.S.S. Teakettle); Starlift; It's a Big Country; Distant Drums. 1952 High Noon; Springfield Rifle. 1953 Return to Paradise; Blowing Wild. 1954 Garden of Evil; Vera Cruz. 1955 The Court-Martial of Billy Mitchell. 1956 Friendly Persuasion. 1957 Love in the Afternoon. 1958 Ten North Frederick; Man of the West. 1959 The Hanging Tree; They Came to Cordura; The Wreck of the Mary Deare; Alias Jesse James. 1961 The Naked Edge.

COOPER, GEORGIA (aka GEORGIE COOPER)
Born: 1882. Died: Sept. 3, 1968, Hollywood, Calif. Screen and stage actress.

Appeared in: 1928 The Question of Today (short). 1937 Four Days' Wonder; Hollywood Hotel.

COOPER, GLADYS DAME
Born: Dec. 18, 1888, England. Died: Nov. 17, 1971, Henley-on-Thames, England (pneumonia). Screen, stage, television actress, and author. Was made a Dame Commander of the Order of the British Empire in 1967. Won Academy Award for Best Supporting Actress in 1942 for Now, Voyager. Married to screen actor Philip Merivale (dec. 1946).

Appeared in: 1917 Masks and Faces. 1921 Headin' North. 1923 The Bohemian Girl. 1935 The Iron Duke. 1938 The Eleventh Commandment; Bonnie Prince Charlie. 1940 Kitty Foyle; Rebecca. 1941 That Hamilton Woman (aka Lady Hamilton); The Gay Falcon; The Black Cat. 1942 This above All; Eagle Squadron; Now, Voyager. 1943 The Song of Bernadette; Forever and a Day; Mr. Lucky; Princess O'Rourke. 1944 The White Cliffs of Dover; Mrs. Parkington. 1945 The Valley of Decision; Love Letters. 1946 The Green Years; Mr. Griggs Returns; The Cockeyed Miracle. 1947 Green Dolphin Street; The Bishop's Wife; Beware of Pity. 1948 The Pirate; Homecoming. 1949 Madame Bovary; The Secret Garden. 1951 Thunder on the Hill. 1952 At Sword's Point (aka Sons of the Musketeers). 1955 The Man Who Loved Redheads. 1958 Separate Tables. 1962 A Passage to India. 1963 The List of Adrian Messenger. 1964 My Fair Lady; The Chalk Garden. 1967 The Happiest Millionaire. 1969 A Nice Girl Like Me.

COOPER, HARRY
Born: 1882. Died: Aug. 28, 1957, Hollywood, Calif. Screen, vaudeville actor, stuntman and double. Appeared in vaudeville with his wife in an act billed "Cooper & Valli." Entered films as a stunt man with Vitagraph.

Appeared in: 1953 The Caddy.

COOPER, TEX
Born: 1877. Died: Mar. 29, 1951, Hollywood, Calif. Screen actor. Entered films in 1916.

Appeared in: 1921 The Man Worthwhile.

COOTE, BERT
Born: 1868, England. Died: Sept. 1, 1938, London, England. Screen and stage actor.

COPELAND, NICHOLAS W. "NICK"
Born: 1895. Died: Aug. 17, 1940, Los Angeles, Calif. Screen, stage, vaudeville actor, and screenwriter.

Appeared in: 1934 Manhattan Love Song; The Hell Cat. 1935 Murder in the Clouds. 1936 Man Hunt; Neighborhood House; The Legion of Terror. 1937 Midnight Madonna. 1938 The Main Event.

CORBETT, BEN "BENNY"
Born: 1892, Hudson, Ill. Died: May 19, 1961, Hollywood, Calif. Screen actor. Entered films approx. 1915. Doubled for actors William Duncan and Antonio Moreno.

Appeared in: 1919 Lightning Bryce (serial). 1921 Black Sheep. 1922 The Heart of a Texan; The Kingfisher's Roost; Lure of Gold; Rangeland; South of Northern Lights; West of the Pecos. 1923 Don Quickshot of the Rio Grande; The Red Warning. 1924 The Man from Wyoming; The Phantom Horseman; The Riddle Rider (serial). 1925 The Circus Cyclone; Daring Days; The Outlaw's Daughter. 1926 Law of the Snow Country; Shadows of Chinatown; Without Orders. 1927 The Border Cavalier; The Man from Hardpan; Somewhere in Sonora; One Glorious Scrap. 1928 The Black Ace; The Boss of Rustler's Roost; The Bronc Stomper; The Fearless Rider; A Made-to-Order Hero; Put 'Em Up; Quick Triggers; Arizona Cyclone; The Mystery Rider (serial). 1929 Forty-Five Calibre War; The Royal Rider. 1930 Bar-L Ranch; Beau Bandit; The Lonesome Trail; Phantom of the Desert; Ridin' Law; Romance of the West; Westward Bound. 1934 The Last Round-Up; Girl Trouble. 1936 Empty Saddles. 1937 Texas Trail. 1938 Gold Mine in the Sky. 1939 Racketeers of the Range. 1950 County Fair. 1953 The Charge at Feather River.

CORBETT, JAMES J.
Born: 1867. Died: Feb. 18, 1933, Bayside, N.Y.(cancer of liver). Heavyweight boxing champion, screen, stage, and vaudeville actor. Divorced from stage actress Olive Lake.

Appeared in: 1894 Corbett and Peter Courteney made the first fight film for Edison. 1919 The Midnight Man (serial). 1922 The Beauty Shop. 1924 Broadway After Dark. 1929 Happy Days; James J. Corbett & Neil O'Brien (short). 1930 At the Round Table (short). 1942 Gentleman Jim (film clips). 1968 The Legendary Champions (documentary).

CORBETT, LEONORA
Born: June 28, 1908, London, England. Died: July 29, 1960, Vleuten, Holland. Screen, stage actress, and film producer.

Appeared in: 1934 The Constant Nymph; Wild Boy; Friday the 13th. 1935 Heart's Desire. 1936 Living Dangerously. 1937 Farewell Again; Night Alone. 1938 Troopship. 1940 Under Your Hat.

CORBIN, VIRGINIA LEE
Born: Dec. 5, 1910, Prescott, Ariz. Died: June 5, 1942, Winfield, Ill.(heart disease). Screen and stage actress.

Appeared in: 1917 Aladdin and the Wonderful Lamp; Jack and the Beanstalk. 1923 Enemies of Children. 1924 Broken Laws; The Chorus Lady; The City That Never Sleeps; Sinners in Silk; Wine of Youth. 1925 The Cloud Rider; The Handsome Brute; Headlines; Lillies of the Streets; North Star; Three Keys. 1926 The Honeymoon Express; Hands Up!; Ladies at Play; The Whole Town's Talking. 1927 Driven from Home; No Place to Go; The Perfect Sap; Play Safe. 1928 Bare Knees; The Head of the Family; Jazzland; The Little Snob. 1929 Footlights and Fools; Knee High. 1931 Morals for Women; X Marks the Spot.

CORDER, LEETA
Born: 1890. Died: Aug. 10, 1956, New York, N.Y.(cancer). Screen, stage, opera, and radio actress.

CORDING, HARRY
Born: Apr. 29, 1894, New York, N.Y. Died: 1954. Screen actor. Entered films in 1921.

Appeared in: 1925 The Knockout. 1927 Black Jack. 1928 Daredevil's Reward; The Patriot; Sins of the Fathers. 1929 The Rescue; The Squall; The Isle of Lost Ships; Christina. 1930 Captain of the Guard; Rough Romance; Bride of the Regiment. 1931 The Right of Way; The Conquering Horde; Honor of the Family. 1932 File No. 113; The World and the Flesh; Forgotten Commandments; Cabin in the Cotton. 1933 Captured; To the Last Man. 1934 The Black Cat. 1935 The Crusades; Peter Ibbetson; Captain Blood. 1936 Road Gang; Sutter's Gold; The White Angel; Daniel Boone. 1937 The Prince and the Pauper. 1938 Crime School; The Adventures of Robin Hood; Valley of the Giants; Painted Desert. 1939 Each Dawn I Die. 1940 Passport to Alcatraz; The Great Plane Robbery; Trail of the Vigilantes. 1941 The Lady from Cheyenne; Mutiny in the Arctic. 1942 Arabian Nights; Yukon Patrol; Ride 'Em Cowboy. 1943 Sherlock Holmes and the Secret Weapon. 1944 Ali Baba and the Forty Thieves; Gypsy Wildcat; Mrs. Parkington; Lost in a Harem. 1945 The House of Fear; Sudan; San Antonio. 1946 Dressed to Kill. 1947 The Marauders. 1948 A Woman's Vengeance; That Lady in Ermine. 1949 The Fighting O'Flynn; Bad Men of Tombstone; Secret of St. Ives. 1950 For-

tunes of Captain Blood; Last of the Buccaneers. 1951 Mask of the Avenger; Santa Fe. 1952 The Big Trees; Against All Flags; Brave Warrior; Cripple Creek; Night Stage to Galveston. 1953 Treasure of the Golden Condor; Abbott and Costello Meet Dr. Jekyll and Mr. Hyde. 1954 Man in the Attic; Demetrius and the Gladiators; Killer Leopard; Jungle Gents.

CORDY, HENRY (Henry Korn)
Born: 1908. Died: Nov. 27, 1965, New York, N.Y.(heart ailment). Screen actor and opera performer.

Appeared in: 1941 The Great American Broadcast; Unfinished Business.

CORDY, RAYMOND (Raymond Cordiaux)
Born: 1898, France. Died: 1956. Screen actor.

Appeared in: 1931 Le Million; A Nous la Liberte. 1933 La Quatorze Juillet. 1934 Le Dernier Milliardaire. 1937 Ignace. 1938 The Slipper Episode; They Were Five. 1942 Les Inconnus dans la Maison. 1946 Le Silence Est d'Or. 1947 Retour a l'Aube (She Returned at Dawn); Man About Town. 1949 Le Beaute de Diable (Beauty and the Devil - U.S. 1952). 1954 A Nous la Liberte (re-release of 1931 film). 1955 Les Grandes Maneuvers (The Grand Maneuver - U.S. 1956). 1958 The Girl in the Bikini. 1960 Sin and Desire (aka L'e Pave-The Wreck).

COREY, WENDELL
Born: Mar. 20, 1914, Dracut, Mass. Died: Nov. 9, 1968, Woodland Hills, Calif.(liver ailment). Screen, stage, and television actor.

Appeared in: 1947 Desert Fury (film debut); I Walk Alone. 1948 Man-Eater of Kumaon; The Search; Sorry, Wrong Number; The Accused. 1949 Holiday Affair; Thelma Jordan; Any Number Can Play. 1950 No Sad Songs for Me; Harriet Craig; The Great Missouri Raid; The Furies; There's a Girl in My Heart. 1951 The Wild Blue Yonder; Rich, Young and Pretty. 1952 My Man and I; The Wild North; Carbine Williams. 1953 Jamaica Run. 1954 Fireman Save My Child; Rear Window; Laughing Anne; Hell's Half Acre. 1955 The Big Knife. 1956 The Killer Is Loose; The Bold and the Brave; The Rack; The Rainmaker. 1957 Loving You. 1958 The Light in the Forest. 1959 Giant Leeches; Alias Jesse James. 1964 Blood on the Arrow. 1965 Broken Sabre. 1966 Waco; Picture Mommy Dead; Agent for H.A.R.M. 1967 Cyborg 2087; Red Tomahawk. 1968 Buckskin. 1969 Young Billy Young.

CORNER, JAMES W.
Born: 1919. Died: Dec. 2, 1944, Germany (killed in action). Screen and stage actor.

Appeared in: 1939 Winter Carnival; What a Life.

CORNER, SALLY
Born: 1894. Died: Mar. 5, 1959, Hollywood, Calif.(heart attack). Screen and stage actress.

Appeared in: 1949 Abandoned Woman; Once More, My Darling. 1950 Two Flags West. 1953 The Robe. 1954 A Man Called Peter. 1957 The True Story of Jesse James.

CORRIGAN, CHARLES
Born: 1894. Died: Apr. 4, 1966, New York, N.Y. Screen and stage actor.

Appeared in: 1939 The Roaring 20's.

CORRIGAN, EMMETT
Born: 1867, Amsterdam; Holland. Died: Oct. 29, 1932, Los Angeles, Calif. Screen and stage actor.

Appeared in: 1923 The Rendezvous. 1924 The Turmoil. 1928 The Lion and the Mouse. 1930 Soldiers and Women. 1931 An American Tragedy; Corsair. 1932 The Beast of the City; The World and the Flesh; The Night Mayor; Man against Woman; Silver Dollar. 1933 The Bitter Tea of General Yen.

CORRIGAN, JAMES
Born: 1871. Died: Feb. 28, 1929, Los Angeles, Calif. Screen and stage actor.

Appeared in: 1921 Brewster's Millions; Lavender and Old Lace; Peck's Bad Boy; The Sky Pilot. 1922 A Front Page Story. 1923 April Showers; Divorce; Her Reputation. 1924 The Law Forbids; The Man from Wyoming; The White Sin. 1925 Durand of the Bad Lands; A Slave of Fashion. 1926 The Auction Block. 1927 Johnny Get Your Hair Cut.

CORRIGAN, LLOYD
Born: Oct. 16, 1900, San Francisco, Calif. Died: Nov. 5, 1969, Woodland Hills, Calif. Screen, television actor, film director, and screenwriter. Entered films as an actor approx. 1925 and then turned to writing and directing for the screen. Wrote and directed as early as 1926. Son of screen actress Lillian Elliott (dec. 1959).

Appeared in: 1925 The Splendid Crime. 1939 The Great Commandment. 1940 Queen of the Mob; Sporting Blood; Captain Caution; Return of Frank James; Dark Streets of Cairo; Lady in Question; High School; Young Tom Edison; Two Girls on Broadway; Public Deb No. 1; The Ghost Breakers. 1941 Whistling in the Dark; Kathleen; Confessions of Boston Blackie; A Girl, a Guy and a Gob; Men of Boys Town. 1942 Tennessee Johnson; London Blackout Murders; Bombay Clipper; North of the Klondike; Treat 'Em Rough; The Great Man's Lady; The Wife Takes a Flyer; The Mystery of Marie Roget; Maisie Gets Her Man; Lucky Jordan; Man Trap. 1943 Captive Wild Woman; Stage Door Canteen; Nobody's Darling; Desert Mystery; Hitler's Children; Secrets of the Underworld; King of the Cowboys; Song of Nevada. 1944 Passport to Adventure; Rosie the Riveter; Gambler's Choice; Goodnight, Sweetheart; Reckless Age; Lights of Old Santa Fe; Thin Man Goes Home; Since You Went Away. 1945 Bring on the Girls; Boston Blackie Booked on Suspicion; The Fighting Guardsman; Lake Placid Serenade; Crime Doctor's Courage. 1946 She-Wolf of London; The Bandit of Sherwood Forest; Two Smart People; Lady Luck; The Chase; Alias Mr. Twilight. 1947 Stallion Road; Blaze of Noon; Shadowed; Ghost Goes Wild. 1948 Adventures of Cassanova; Mr. Reckless; The Bride Goes Wild; A Date with Judy; Strike It Rich; Homicide for Three; The Big Clock; Return of October. 1949 Home in San Antone; Blondie Hits the Jackpot; Dancing in the Dark; Girl from Jones Beach. 1950 Father Is a Bachelor; And Baby Makes Three; When Willie Comes Marching Home; My Friend Irma Goes West. 1951 Her First Romance; The Last Outpost; Sierra Passage; Ghost Chasers; New Mexico; Cyrano de Bergerac. 1952 Son of Paleface; Rainbow 'Round My Shoulder; Sound Off. 1953 The Stars Are Singing; Marry Me Again. 1954 Return from the Sea; The Bowery Boys Meet the Monsters. 1955 Paris Follies of 1956. 1956 Hidden Guns. 1962 The Manchurian Candidate. 1963 It's a Mad, Mad, Mad, Mad World.

CORTEZ, LEON
Born: 1898, England. Died: Dec. 31, 1970, Brighton, England. Screen, television, radio, and vaudeville actor.

Appeared in: 1944 Can't Help Singing. 1963 I Could Go on Singing.

CORTHELL, HERBERT
Born: 1875, Boston, Mass. Died: Jan. 23, 1947, Hollywood, Calif. Screen and stage actor.

Appeared in: 1924 Classmates; Second Youth. 1933 The Cohens and the Kellys in Trouble; Only Yesterday; Lone Cowboy. 1934 Bombay Mail; There Ain't No Justice; Let's Talk It Over; Uncertain Lady. 1935 The Fire Trap. 1936 The Story of Louis Pasteur; Dancing Feet. 1937 Renfrew of the Royal Mounted; Man in Blue; Blazing Barriers. 1938 Sing You Sinners. 1939 Fifth Avenue Girl; Career; House of Fear; Espionage. 1942 Duke of the Navy.

CORY, ROBERT
Born: 1883. Died: Nov. 9, 1955, Hollywood, Calif.(cancer). Screen and stage actor. Entered films approx. 1925.

COSGRAVE, LUKE
Born: Aug. 6, 1862, Ballaghdreen, County Mayo, Ireland. Died: June 28, 1949, Woodland Hills, Calif. Screen and stage actor. Entered films in 1923.

Appeared in: 1923 Hollywood; The Light That Failed. 1924 The Border Legion; Code of the Sea; Flaming Barriers; Merton of the Movies. 1925 Contraband; Durand of the Bad Lands; Welcome Home. 1926 Rocking Moon; Sir Lumberjack. 1927 Jewels of Desire. 1928 Gentlemen Prefer Blondes; The Mating Call; The Red Mark. 1929 The Duke Steps Out. 1930 Men on Call; Lightin'. 1931 Not Exactly Gentlemen; The Squaw Man. 1932 Sinners in the Sun. 1940 Comin' 'Round the Mountain.

COSGROVE, ROBERT
Born: 1900. Died: Sept. 1960, Saranac Lake, N.Y.(tuberculosis—heart attack). Screen actor.

COSSAEUS, SOPHIE
Born: 1893, Wiesbaden, Germany. Died: Sept. 23, 1965, Frankfurt-Main, Germany. Screen, stage, television, radio actress, and dancer.

COSSAR, JOHN HAY
Born: 1865, London, England. Died: Apr. 28, 1935, Hollywood, Calif. Screen, stage, and vaudeville actor.

Appeared in: 1921 Hearts and Masks; Made in Heaven; The Night Rose; The Poverty of Riches; That Something. 1922 Doubling for Romeo; Grand Larceny; Thorns and Orange Blossoms; Watch Your Step; When Husbands Deceive. 1923 The Steel Trail (serial); Fools and Riches; The Hunchback of Notre Dame. 1924 The Fast Express (serial); The Great Diamond Mystery. 1926 The Sap. 1927 Melting Millions (serial); Web of Fate; Woman's Law. 1929 The Fire Detective (serial).

COSSART, ERNEST
Born: Sept. 24, 1876, Cheltenham, England. Died: Jan. 21, 1951, New York, N.Y. Screen and stage actor.

Appeared in: 1916 The Strange Case of Mary Page (serial). 1935 The Scoundrel; Accent on Youth; Two for Tonight. 1936 Desire; Big Broadcast of 1937; Palm Springs; My American Wife; Murder with Pictures; Champagne Waltz; The Great Ziegfeld. 1937 Three Smart Girls; Top of the Town; As Good as Married; The Lady Fights Back; Angel. 1938 A Letter of Introduction. 1939 Zaza; Tower of London; The Light That Failed; Lady of the Tropics; The Magnificent Fraud; Three Smart Girls Grow Up; Never Say Die. 1940 A Bill of Divorcement; Kitty Foyle; Tom Brown's School Days. 1941 Kings Row; Charley's Aunt; One Foot in Heaven; Skylark. 1944 Knickerbocker Holiday; Casanova Brown. 1945 The Girl of the Limberlost; Love Letters; Tonight and Every Night. 1946 Cluny Brown; The Jolson Story. 1947 Love from a Stranger. 1949 John Loves Mary.

COSTA, SEBASTIANO
Born: 1876. Died: July 18, 1935, New Rochelle, N.Y.(heart attack). Screen actor.

COSTE, MAURICE R.
Born: 1875. Died: Mar. 22, 1963, Chatham, Ontario, Canada. Screen and stage actor.

COSTELLO, DON
Born: 1901. Died: Oct. 24, 1945, Hollywood, Calif. Screen and stage actor.

Appeared in: 1939 Another Thin Man. 1940 Joe and Ethel Turp Call on the President; One Crowded Night. 1941 Sleepers West; Ride on Vaquero; I'll Wait for You; Here Comes Mr. Jordan; Unholy Partners; Whistling in the Dark. 1942 Johnny Eager; Joe Smith, American; A-Haunting We Will Go; Just Off Broadway. 1943 A Night to Remember; Truck Busters; Air Raid Wardens; Crime Doctor; A Lady Takes a Chance. 1944 The Whistler. 1945 Incendiary Blonde; Here Come the Co-Eds. 1946 The Blue Dahlia.

COSTELLO, HELENE
Born: June 21, 1903, New York, N.Y. Died: Jan. 26, 1957, Los Angeles, Calif.(pneumonia, tuberculosis and narcotics). Screen and stage actress. Entered films with Vitagraph in 1912. Was a Wampus Baby Star of the 1920s. Sister of screen actress Dolores Costello and daughter of screen actor Maurice Costello (dec. 1950). Divorced from screen actor Lovell Sherman (dec. 1934).

Appeared in: 1925 The Man on the Box; Bobbed Hair; Ranger of the Big Pines. 1926 Wet Paint; Don Juan; The Honeymoon Express; The Love Toy; Millionaires; While London Sleeps. 1927 In Old Kentucky; Good Time Charley; Heart of Maryland; The Broncho Twister; Finger Prints. 1928 Burning Up Broadway; Comrades; The Circus Kid; The Midnight Taxi; Fortune Hunter; Lights of New York; Husbands for Rent; Phantom of the Turf. 1929 Broken Barriers; The Fatal Warning (serial); When Dreams Come True; Show of Shows. 1935 Riffraff.

COSTELLO, LOU (Louis Francis Cristillo)
Born: Mar. 6, 1906, Paterson, N.J. Died: Mar. 3, 1959, Los Angeles, Calif.(heart attack). Screen, stage, burlesque, vaudeville, and radio actor. Was part of comedy team of Abbott & Costello.

Together they appeared in: 1940 One Night in the Tropics. 1941 Buck Privates; In the Navy; Hold That Ghost; Keep 'Em Flying. 1942 Ride 'Em Cowboy; Rio Rita; Hold Your Horses; Who Done It?; Pardon My Sarong. 1943 It Ain't Hay; Hit the Ice. 1944 Lost in a Harem; In Society. 1945 Here Comes the Co-Eds; The Naughty Nineties; Abbott and Costello in Hollywood. 1946 Little Giant; The Time of Their Lives. 1947 Buck Privates Come Home; The Wistful Widow of Wagon Gap. 1948 The Noose Hangs High; Abbott and Costello Meet Frankenstein; Mexican Hayride. 1949 Abbott and Costello Meet the Killer, Boris Karlof; Africa Screams. 1950 Abbott and Costello in the Foreign Legion. 1951 Abbott and Costello Meet the Invisible Man; Comin' Round the Mountain. 1952 Jack and the Beanstalk; Lost in Alaska; Abbott and Costello Meet Captain Kidd; News of the Day (MGM short [newsreel] for promotion of U.S. Bonds). 1953 Abbott and Costello Go to Mars; Abbott and Costello Meet Dr. Jekyll and Mr. Hyde. 1954 Hollywood Grows Up (short). 1955 Abbott and Costello Meet the Keystone Kops; Abbott and Costello Meet the Mummy. 1956 Dance with Me, Henry. 1959 The 30-Foot Bride of Candy Rock (Costello appeared without Abbott). 1964 Big Parade of Comedy (documentary). 1965 The World of Abbott and Costello (documentary).

COSTELLO, MAURICE
Born: 1877, Pittsburgh, Pa. Died: Oct. 30, 1950, Hollywood, Calif.(heart ailment). Screen, stage, and vaudeville actor. Entered films with Edison in 1905. Divorced from stage actress Ruth Reeves. Father of screen actresses Dolores and Helene (dec. 1957) Costello.

Appeared in: 1910 The New Stenographer. 1911 A Tale of Two Cities. 1912 The Night before Christmas; As You Like It. 1914 Mr. Barnes of New York. 1915 The Man Who Couldn't Beat God; Tried for His Own Murder. 1916 The Crown Prince's Double; The Crimson Stain Mystery (serial). 1918 Cap'n Abe's Niece. 1919 The Cambric Mask. 1920 Human Collateral. 1921 Conceit. 1922 Determination. 1923 None So Blind; Glimpses of the Moon; Fog Bound; Man and Wife. 1924 Virtuous Liars; Love of Women; Let No Man Put Asunder; The Story without a Name; Week-End Husbands; The Law and the Lady; Heart of Alaska; Roulette. 1925 The Mad Marriage. 1926 Wives of the Prophet; The Last Alarm. 1927 Johnny Get Your Hair Cut; The Shamrock and the Rose; Camille; Spider Webs; Wolves of the Air. 1928 The Wagon Show; Eagle of the Night (serial); Black Feather. 1936 Hollywood Boulevard. 1940 A Little Bit of Heaven. 1941 Lady from Louisiana.

COSTELLO, WILLIAM A.
Born: 1898. Died: Oct. 9, 1971, San Jose, Calif. Screen, radio actor, musician, and singer. Voice of "Popeye the Sailor Man."

Appeared in: 1927 King of Kings. 1930 Border Romance. 1935 Melody Trail. 1938 The Port of Missing Girls; Wanted by the Police. 1939 Balalaika.

COTTO DEL VALLE, LUIS
Born: 1913. Died: Mar. 1971, Mexico City, Mexico. Screen and stage actor.

COTTON, BILLY (William Edward Cotton)
Born: 1900, England. Died: Mar. 25, 1969, London, England (heart attack). Bandleader, screen, radio, and television actor.

Appeared in: 1921 The Old Nest.

COTTON, FRED AYRES
Born: 1907, Hastings, Neb. Died: Jan. 29, 1964, New York, N.Y. Screen and stage actor.

Appeared in: 1944 Winged Victory (stage and screen versions).

COTTON, LUCY (Lucy Cotton Magraw)
Born: 1891. Died: Dec. 12, 1948, Miami Beach, Fla.("overdose of sleeping pills—suicide"). Screen and stage actress.

Appeared in: 1910 The Fugitive. 1921 The Devil; Whispering Shadows; The Man Who.

COUNTESS DUCELLA
Born: Buffalo, N.Y. Died: Nov. 28, 1921, Los Angeles, Calif. Screen actress.

COURT, ALFRED C.
Born: 1886, Australia. Died: Dec. 31, 1953, Hollywood, Calif. Screen and stage actor.

COURTENAY, WILLIAM
Born: 1875, Worcester, Mass. Died: Apr. 20, 1933, Rye, N.Y. (severe cold and heart weakness). Screen and stage actor. Married to stage actress Virginia Harned (dec. 1946).

Appeared in: 1894 Miss Jerry. 1917 Kick In. 1929 Evidence; The Show of Shows; The Sacred Flame. 1930 The Way of All Men; Three Faces East.

COURTLEIGH, WILLIAM, JR.
Born: 1869, Guelph, Ontario, Canada. Died: 1930. Screen actor.

Appeared in: 1915 Neal of the Navy. 1916 Out of the Drifts; Susie Snowflake; Eyes of Youth. 1920 Madame X. 1922 Handle with Care; Ashes; Any Night; Midnight.

COURTNEY, OSCAR W.
Born: 1877. Died: June 13, 1962, Chicago, Ill. Screen and vaudeville actor. Entered films with Essanay in 1912.

COURTRIGHT, CLYDE
Born: 1885. Died: Oct. 6, 1967, Santa Cruz, Calif. Screen actor. Stand-in for Gary Cooper and Charles Bickford.

COURTRIGHT, WILLIAM "UNCLE BILLY"
Born: Mar. 10, 1848, New Milford, Ill. Died: Mar. 6, 1933, Ione, Calif. Screen, stage, and minstrel actor. Entered films in 1910.

Appeared in: 1920 Peaceful Valley. 1921 The Rookie's Return; The Speed Girl; Extravagance; R.S.V.P.; The Lure of Youth; The Millionaire. 1922 At the Sign of the Jack O'Lantern; The Deuce of Spades; A Man of Action; The Sunset Trail; The Man under Cover. 1923 The Girl I Loved; Bell Boy 13. 1924 The Heart Buster; George Washington, Jr. 1925 Are Parents People?; Some Pun'kins; Thank You; The Trouble With Wives; All around Frying Pan. 1926 For Wives Only; The Grand Duchess and the Waiter; Atta Boy; The Two Gun Man; A Regular Scout; The Tough Guy; Lone Hand Saunders; Hands Across the Border. 1927 Don Mike; Arizona Nights; Jesse James; My Best Girl; Silver Comes Thru; The Poor Nut. 1928 The Pioneer Scout; Kit Carson; Sunset Legion.

COWL, JANE
Born: 1887, Boston, Mass. Died: June 22, 1950, Santa Monica, Calif.(cancer). Screen, stage actress, and playwright.

Appeared in: 1915 The Garden of Lies. 1917 The Spreading Dawn. 1943 Stage Door Canteen. 1949 Once More, My Darling, Come Be My Love. 1950 No Man of Her Own; The Secret Fury. 1951 Payment on Demand.

COWLES, JULES
Born: 1878, Farmington, Conn. Died: May 22, 1943, Hollywood, Calif. Screen actor.

Appeared in: 1921 The Idol of the North, Tangled Trails; God's Crucible. 1922 The Bootleggers. 1923 Lost in a Big City; The Ne'er-Do-Well. 1924 The Love Bandit; High Speed. 1925 Seven Chances; The Lost World; Lord Jim. 1926 Man Rustlin'; Money to Burn; The Scarlet Letter; The Ace of Clubs. 1927 The Road to Romance. 1928 Bringing up Father; Dog Law; Why Sailors Go Wrong; Terror; Isle of Lost Men; Thundergod. 1929 Sal of Singapore; The Leatherneck. 1930 His First Command; One Hysterical Night. 1931 Heaven on Earth. 1933 Cross Fire; The Fighting Parson. 1934 The Scarlet Letter; The Pursuit of Happiness. 1935 Barbary Coast; Mississippi. 1943 Air Raid Wardens.

COXEN, EDWARD ALBERT
Born: 1884. Died: Nov. 21, 1954, Hollywood, Calif. Screen and stage actor.

Appeared in: 1921 Desperate Trails; No Man's Woman. 1922 Nine Points of the Law; The Stranger of the Hills; The Veiled Woman. 1923 A Man's Man; Scaramouche; Temporary Marriage; Our Hospitality; The Flying Dutchman; Foolish Mothers. 1924 Flashing Spurs; Singer Jim McKee; One Glorious Night. 1925 Cold Nerve; The Man without a Country. 1926 The Man in the Shadow. 1927 The Web of Fate; Galloping Fury; God's Great Wilderness. 1930 The Spoilers. 1933 Gun Justice. 1934 Wheels of Destiny; Smoking Guns.

COYAN, BETTY
Born: 1901. Died: Feb. 10, 1935, Council Bluffs, Iowa. Screen actress. Entered films approx. 1921.

COYLE, WALTER V.
Born: 1888. Died: Aug. 3, 1948, Freeport, N.Y. Screen and stage actor.

CRADDOCK. CLAUDIA
Born: 1889. Died: Dec. 17, 1945, Hollywood, Calif. Screen actress.

Appeared in: 1933 A Lady's Profession.

CRAIG, ALEC
Born: 1885, Scotland. Died: June 25, 1945, Glendale, Calif. Screen and stage actor.

Appeared in: 1934 The Little Minister. 1935 Old Homestead; Vanessa, Her Love Story; Sweepstakes Annie. 1936 Winterset; Mary of Scotland (film and stage versions). 1937 That Girl from Paris; Hideaway; The Man Who Found Himself; The Woman I Love; China Passage; There Goes My Girl; Super Sleuth; She's Got Everything. 1938 Crashing Hollywood; Wise Girl; Double

Danger; Vivacious Lady. 1939 Confessions of a Nazi Spy; Ruler of the Seas; Night Work; They Made Her a Spy. 1940 Abe Lincoln in Illinois; Phantom Raiders; Tom Brown's School Days; Golden Gloves; Stranger on the Third Floor. 1941 Shining Victory; A Date with the Falcon. 1942 Random Harvest; The Night before the Divorce; Cat People; Wrecking Crew. 1943 Action in the North Atlantic; Tennessee Johnson; Appointment in Berlin; Holy Matrimony; Lassie Come Home; Northern Pursuit. 1944 Spider Woman; Calling Dr. Death. 1945 Serenade for Murder. 1946 Three Strangers; Kitty.

CRAIG, FRANCES B.
Born: Approx. 1869. Died: July 22, 1925, Los Angeles, Calif. Screen and stage actress.

CRAIG, GODFREY
Born: 1915. Died: May 26, 1941, Los Angeles, Calif. Screen actor. Appeared in "Our Gang" comedies.

CRAIG, NELL
Born: 1891. Died: Jan. 5, 1965, Hollywood, Calif. Screen and stage actress. Entered films in 1913. Appeared in Essanay films in 1914.

Appeared in: 1915 The Return of Richard Neal; In the Palace of the King; The Primitive Strain. 1921 The Queen of Sheba. 1922 The Flirt; Remembrance. 1923 The Abysmal Brute. 1924 A Boy of Flanders; Abraham Lincoln. 1931 Cimarron; Consolation Marriage. 1936 Palm Springs. 1939 Calling Dr. Kildare; Secret of Dr. Kildare. 1940 Dr. Kildare's Strange Case; Dr. Kildare's Crisis. 1941 Dr. Kildare's Wedding Day; Dr. Kildare's Victory; The People vs. Dr. Kildare. 1942 Calling Dr. Gillespie; Dr. Gillespie's New Assistant. 1944 Between Two Women; Three Men in White. 1945 Out of This World. 1946 Our Hearts Were Growing Up. 1947 Dark Delusion.

CRAIG, RICHY, JR.
Born: 1902. Died: Nov. 28, 1933, New York, N.Y. Screen, stage, vaudeville, and radio actor.

Appeared in: 1932-33 "Vitaphone Big Star" comedies and "Big V" comedies.

CRAMER, EDD
Born: 1924. Died: Dec. 21, 1963, New York, N.Y. Screen, stage, and television actor.

Appeared in: 1954 On the Waterfront.

CRAMER, SUSANNE
Born: 1938, Germany. Died: Jan. 7, 1969, Hollywood, Calif. (pneumonia). Screen and television actress. Appeared in U.S., German, and French films.

Appeared in: 1957 Every Second Counts. 1958 Wie ein Sturmwind (Tempestuous Love). 1959 Vacanzie a Lzchia (Holiday Island). 1964 Bedtime Story.

CRANE, DIXIE
Born: 1888. Died: Nov. 18, 1936, Hollywood, Calif. Screen and vaudeville actress. Appeared with her husband Henry Johnson in a vaudeville act billed as "Johnson and Crane." She appeared in early Lasky films.

CRANE, ETHEL G.
Died: Oct. 1930, San Bernardino, Calif. (suicide—poison). Screen actress.

CRANE, MAE
Born: 1925. Died: Apr. 15, 1969, Port Washington, N.Y. (lung ailment). Screen, stage, radio, and television actress.

Appeared in: 1967 The Producers. 1968 For Love of Ivy; No Way to Treat a Lady.

CRANE, RICHARD O.
Born: 1918. Died: Mar. 9, 1969, San Fernando Valley, Calif. (heart attack). Screen and television actor.

Appeared in: 1940 Susan and God. 1941 In the Navy; Keep 'Em Flying. 1942 This Time for Keeps. 1943 Someone to Remember; Happy Land. 1944 Wing and a Prayer; None Shall Escape. 1945 Captain Eddie. 1946 Johnny Comes Flying Home; Behind Green Lights. 1948 Angel on the Amazon; Arthur Takes Over; Waterfront at Midnight; Campus Honeymoon; Triple Threat. 1949 Dynamite. 1950 A Lady without a Passport. 1951 The Last Outpost; Mysterious Island (serial); Man in the Saddle. 1952 Thundering Caravans; Leadville Gunslinger. 1953 Winning of the West; The Neanderthal Man; The Woman They Almost Lynched. 1955 No

Man's Woman; The Eternal Sea. 1957 Bailout at 43,000. 1958 The Deep Six. 1959 Battle Flame; The Alligator People. 1960 Thirteen Fighting Men. 1961 Boy Who Caught a Crook. 1962 The Devil's Partner. 1963 House of the Damned. 1964 Surf Party.

CRANE, WARD
Born: 1891, Albany, N.Y. Died: July 21, 1928, Saranac Lake, N.Y. (pneumonia). Screen actor.

Appeared in: 1921 Heedless Moths. 1922 Broadway Rose; French Heels; No Trespassing; Destiny's Isle. 1923 Enemies of Children; Pleasure Mad; The Famous Mrs. Fair; Within the Law; The Meanest Man in the World. 1924 Sherlock, Jr.; Empty Hands; Bread; Gambling Wives. 1925 How Baxter Butted In; The Crimson Runner; The Mad Whirl; The Million Dollar Handicap; Classified; Borrowed Finery; The Phantom of the Opera; Peacock Feathers. 1926 Boy Friend; Risky Business; Upstage; That Model from Paris; The Blind Goddess; The Flaming Frontier; The Sporting Lover; Under Western Skies. 1927 The Lady in Ermine; The Auctioneer; Beauty Shoppers; The Rush Hour; Down the Stretch. 1928 Honeymoon Flats.

CRANE, WILLIAM H.
Born: 1892. Died: Jan. 22, 1957, Scranton, Pa. Screen and stage actor.

CRANE, WILLIAM H.
Born: 1845, Leicester, Mass. Died: Mar. 7, 1928, Hollywood, Calif. ("general breakdown"). Screen and stage actor.

CRAVAT, NOEL
Born: 1910. Died: Feb. 20, 1960, Hollywood, Calif. (after surgery). Screen actor.

Appeared in: 1943 G-Men vs. the Black Dragon (serial). 1948 The Iron Curtain. 1953 South Sea Woman; The 5,000 Fingers of Dr. T.

CRAVEN, FRANK
Born: 1875, Boston, Mass. Died: Sept. 1, 1945, Beverly Hills, Calif. (heart ailment). Screen, stage actor, film director, playwright, and screenwriter.

Appeared in: 1928 We Americans. 1929 The Very Idea. 1933 State Fair. 1934 That's Gratitude; He Was Her Man; Let's Talk It Over; City Limits; Funny Thing Called Love. 1935 Barbary Coast; Car 99; Vagabond Lady. 1936 Small Town Girl; The Harvester. 1937 Penrod and Sam; Blossoms on Broadway; You're Only Young Once. 1938 Penrod and His Twin Brother. 1939 Our Neighbors, the Carters; Miracles for Sale. 1940 Dreaming Out Loud; City for Conquest; Our Town. 1941 The Lady from Cheyenne; The Richest Man in Town. 1942 In This Our Life; Pittsburgh; Girl Trouble; Through Different Eyes. 1943 Son of Dracula; Harrigan's Kid; Jack London; The Human Comedy; Keeper of the Flame. 1944 Destiny; My Best Gal; They Shall Have Faith. 1945 The Right to Live; Colonel Effingham's Raid.

CRAWFORD, ANNE (Imelda Crawford)
Born: Nov. 22, 1920, Haifa, Israel. Died: Oct. 17, 1956, London, England. Screen, stage, and television actress.

Appeared in: 1942 They Flew Alone (film debut); The Peterville Diamond; The Dark Tower. 1943 The Hundred Pound Window; Millions Like Us. 1944 Two Thousand Women. 1946 They Were Sisters; Cameron. 1947 Bedelia; Master of Bankdam (U.S. 1949); Caravan. 1948 Daughter of Darkness; It's Hard to Be Good (U.S. 1950). 1949 Blind Goddess. 1950 Mr. Know-All; Bonaventure. 1951 Tony Draws a Horse; Trio; Thunder on the Hill. 1952 Street Corner. 1954 Knights of the Round Table; Both Sides of the Law; Mad about Men.

CRAWFORD, BESSIE
Born: 1882. Died: Nov. 11, 1943, Hollywood, Calif. (heart attack). Screen, stage, and vaudeville actress. Married to screen actor T. Roy Barnes (dec. 1937). Appeared with her husband in a standard vaudeville act billed as "Barnes & Crawford."

CRAWFORD, HOWARD M. (Howard Mariam Crawford)
Born: 1914. Died: Nov. 24, 1969, London, England (overdose of sleeping pills). Screen, stage, radio, and television actor.

Appeared in: 1950 The Hasty Heart. 1952 The Man in the White Suit; Where's Charley? 1955 West of Zanzibar. 1956 His Excellency. 1957 Reach for the Sky; The Silken Affair. 1960 Othello. 1962 Lawrence of Arabia. 1965 The Face of Fu Manchu. 1968 The Vengeance of Fu Manchu.

CREAMER, CHARLES
Born: 1894. Died: July 22, 1971, Hollywood, Calif. (heart attack).
Screen actor, extra, and stand-in for Walter Brennan.

CREGAR, LAIRD
Born: 1917, Philadelphia, Pa. Died: Dec. 9, 1944, Los Angeles,
Calif. (heart attack). Screen and stage actor.

Appeared in: 1940 Granny Get Your Gun; Oh Johnny, How You
Can Love; Hudson's Bay. 1941 Blood and Sand; Charley's Aunt;
I Wake up Screaming. 1942 Rings on Her Fingers; This Gun for
Hire; Joan of Paris; Black Swan; Ten Gentlemen from West
Point. 1943 Heaven Can Wait; Holy Matrimony; Hello, Frisco,
Hello. 1944 The Lodger. 1945 Hangover Square.

CREHAN, JOSEPH
Born: July 12, 1886, Baltimore, Md. Died: Apr. 15, 1966, Hollywood, Calif. Screen, stage, and television actor.

Appeared in: 1931 Stolen Heaven. 1933 Hold the Press. 1934
Against the Law; Jimmy the Gent; Identity Parade; Before Mid-
night; The Line-Up; The Hell Cat. 1935 Go into Your Dance;
Black Fury; The Traveling Saleslady; Bright Lights; The Case
of the Lucky Legs; Shipmates Forever; Man of Iron; The Payoff;
Oil for the Lamps of China; Stranded; Page Miss Glory; Front
Page Woman; Alibi Ike; Special Agent; Dinky; Frisco Kid. 1936
Brides Are Like That; The Singing Kid; Bengal Tiger; Murder of
Dr. Harrigan; Road Gang; God's Country and the Woman; King of
Hockey; Smart Blonde; Gold Diggers of 1937; Here Comes Carter;
Murder by an Aristocrat; Boulder Dam; The Law in Her Hands;
Jail Break; Anthony Adverse; Bullets or Ballots; Earthworm
Tractors; China Clipper; Cain and Mabel; Down the Stretch;
Trailin' West. 1937 Draegerman Courage; Don't Pull Your
Punches; Kid Galahad; Her Husband's Secretary; Once a Doctor;
Midnight Court; Talent Scout; This Is My Affair;
Born Reckless; There Goes My Girl; Midnight Madonna; The
Wrong Road; The Duke Comes Back; Mama Runs Wild; Here's
Flash Casey; Guns of the Pecos; Girls Can Play; Outlaws of the
Orient; The Case of the Stuttering Bishop. 1938 Midnight In-
truder; The Goldwyn Follies; Happy Landing; Alexander's Rag-
time Band; The Arkansas Traveler; Illegal Traffic; Billy the Kid
Returns; Night Spot; Four's a Crowd; Crime Takes a Holiday;
Woman against Woman; The Kid Comes Back. 1939 Navy Secrets;
Star Maker; Society Lawyer; Tell No Tales; Maisie; Babes in
Arms; Hollywood Cavalcade; Behind Prison Gates; Private Detec-
tive; Geronimo; The Roaring Twenties; The Return of Dr. X;
Whispering Enemies; You Can't Get Away with Murder; Pride
of the Navy; Stanley and Livingstone; Union Pacific. 1940 Emer-
gency Squad; Music in My Heart; The Secret Seven; The House
across the Bay; City for Conquest; Gaucho Serenade; Brother
Orchid. 1941 Andy Hardy's Private Secretary; Nine Lives Are Not
Enough; Doctors Don't Tell; Texas; The Case of the Black Parrot;
Washington Melodrama; Scattergood Baines; Manpower; Love
Crazy; Here Comes Happiness; Nevada City. 1942 Treat 'Em
Rough; The Courtship of Andy Hardy; Cadets on Parade; Larceny,
Inc.; To the Shores of Tripoli; Murder in the Big House; Men of
Texas; Hello, Annapolis; Girl Trouble; You Can't Escape Forever;
Gentleman Jim. 1943 Old Acquaintance; Eyes of the Underworld;
Mystery Broadcast; Hit the Ice; Mission to Moscow; Hands Across
the Border; The Desert Song. 1944 When the Lights Go on Again;
Roger Touhy, Gangster; Phantom Lady; The Navy Way; Shine on
Harvest Moon; The Adventures of Mark Twain; Black Magic; One
Mysterious Night. 1945 The Missing Juror; The Chicago Kid; I
Love a Mystery; Brewster's Millions; Man Alive; Dick Tracy;
Youth on Trial; Captain Tugboat Annie. 1946 A Guy Could Change;
Girl on the Spot; The Big Sleep; Deadline at Dawn; Dick Tracy
vs. Cueball; The Shadow Returns; O.S.S.; Phantom Thief; Behind
the Mask; Night Train to Memphis; The Falcon's Adventure; Dan-
gerous Money; The Virginian. 1947 The Trespasser; Philo
Vance's Gamble; The Foxes of Harrow; Louisiana; Dick Tracy
Meets Gruesome; Night Time in Nevada. 1948 Triple Threat;
The Enchanted Valley; The Hunted; April Showers; Silver River;
Adventures in Silverado; Homicide for Three; The Countess of
Monte Cristo; Street Corner; Bad Men of Tombstone; Sundown at
Santa Fe; The Story of Life. 1949 Red Desert; The Last Bandit;
The Duke of Chicago; Prejudice; Alias the Champ; Ringside; Ali-
mony; State Department File 649; Amazon Quest. 1950 The Ari-
zona Cowboy; Square Dance Katy; The Tougher They Come;
Triple Trouble. 1951 Pride of Maryland; Roadblock; Hometown
Story. 1952 Deadline U.S.A. 1953 Crazylegs. 1954 Highway
Dragnet.

CREWS, KAY C.
Born: 1901. Died: Nov. 29, 1959, San Antonio, Texas. Screen,
stage, and vaudeville actress. Appeared in silent films.

CREWS, LAURA HOPE
Born: 1880, San Francisco, Calif. Died: Nov. 13, 1942, New York,
N.Y. Screen and stage actress.

Appeared in: 1929 Charming Sinners. 1932 Rockabye; New Morals
for Old. 1933 Out All Night; The Silver Cord; I Love You Wednesday; Blind Adventure; If I Were Free; Female; Ever in My Heart.
1934 Rafter Romance; Age of Innocence. 1935 Behold My Wife;
The Flame Within; Lightning Strikes Twice; Escapade; The Melody Lingers On. 1936 Her Master's Voice (film and stage versions); Camille. 1937 The Road Back; Confession; Angel. 1938
Dr. Rhythm; The Sisters; Thanks for the Memory. 1939 Idiot's
Delight; Gone with the Wind; Remember?; Reno; The Rains Came;
Starmaker. 1940 The Lady with Red Hair; The Bluebird; I'm No-
body's Sweetheart Now; Girl from Avenue A. 1941 The Man Who
Came to Dinner; The Flame of New Orleans. 1942 One Foot in
Heaven.

CRINLEY, WILLIAM A.
Died: Jan. 1, 1927, Hollywood, Calif. (following operation). Screen
actor and film director.

Appeared in: 1921 Big Town Round-Up.

CRISMAN, ARLINE C.
Died: May 10, 1956, Hollywood, Calif. Screen actress.

CROCKETT, CHARLES B.
Born: 1872, Md. Died: June 12, 1934, Los Angeles, Calif. Screen
and stage actor.

Appeared in: 1924 Sundown; The Millionaire Cowboy. 1925 The
Dressmaker from Paris; The Vanishing American; Daddy's Gone
A-Hunting; Winds of Chance. 1926 Into Her Kingdom. 1927 The
Princess from Hoboken; Arizona Bound; The Gingham Girl. 1930
Abraham Lincoln; Ex-Flame. 1931 Guilty Hands.

CROMWELL, RICHARD (Roy Radabaugh)
Born: Jan. 8, 1910, Los Angeles, Calif. Died: Oct. 11, 1960,
Hollywood, Calif. Screen and stage actor.

Appeared in: 1930 Tol'able David (film debut); King of Jazz. 1931
Fifty Fathoms Deep; Shanghaied Love; Are These Our Children?;
Maker of Men. 1932 Strange Love of Molly Louvain; The Age of
Consent; Emma; Tom Brown of Culver; That's My Boy.
1933 This Day and Age; Above the Clouds; Hoopla. 1934
Among the Missing; When Strangers Meet; The Most Precious
Thing in Life; Name the Woman; Carolina. 1935 Lives of a Bengal
Lancer; McFadden's Flats; Unknown Woman. 1936 Poppy. 1937
Our Fighting Navy; The Road Back; The Wrong Road. 1938 Jez-
ebel; Come on, Leathernecks; Storm over Bengal. 1939 Young
Mr. Lincoln; Torpedoed. 1940 Enemy Agent; The Villian Still
Pursued Her; Village Barn Dance. 1941 Riot Squad; Parachute
Battalion. 1942 Baby Face Morgan. 1943 The Crime Doctor.
1948 Bungalow 13.

CROSBY, MARSHAL
Born: 1883, Australia. Died: Jan. 3, 1954, Port Macquarie,
N.S.W., Australia (heart attack). Screen, stage, radio, and vaude-
ville actor.

Appeared in: 1946 The Overlanders. 1947 Pacific Adventure.
1952 Kangaroo. Other Australian film: Eureka Stockade.

CROSMAN, HENRIETTA
Born: 1861, Wheeling, W. Va. Died: Oct. 31, 1944, Pelham Manor,
N.Y. Screen and stage actress.

Appeared in: 1915 How Molly Made Good. 1923 Broadway Broke.
1925 Wandering Fires. 1930 The Roy Family of Broadway.
1933 Pilgrimage. 1934 Among the Missing; Carolina; Three on a
Honeymoon; Such Women Are Dangerous; Menace; The Curtain
Falls. 1935 Elinor Norton; The Right to Live; The Dark Angel.
1936 Hitchhike to Heaven; Charlie Chan's Secret; The Moon's Our
Home; Girl of the Ozarks; Follow Your Heart. 1937 Personal
Property.

CROSS, ALFRED FRANCIS
Born: 1891. Died: Jan. 28, 1938, San Diego, Calif. (heart attack).
Screen, stage actor, and stage director. Entered films approx.
1920.

Appeared in: 1931 Smart Woman.

CROSSLEY, SID (aka SYD CROSSLEY)
Born: Nov. 18, 1885, London, England. Died: Nov., 1960, Troon,
England. Screen actor in both U.S. and British films, and music
hall comedian.

Appeared in: 1925 Keep Smiling, North Star. 1926 The Golden

Web; The Unknown Soldier; One Hour Married. 1927 Ain't Love Funny?; Jewels of Desire; Romantic Rogue; Play Safe; The Blood Ship; The Gorilla. 1928 A Perfect Gentleman; That Certain Thing; Fangs of the Wild; The Circus Kid; The Cowboy Kid; Into No Man's Land. 1929 The Younger Generation; Atlantic; Hate Ship; Just for a Song; The Fatal Warning (serial). 1930 Suspense; The Middle Watch; Man from Chicago; All of a Tremble; Flying Fool; Never Trouble Trouble. 1931 Men Like These; Tonight's the Night. 1932 For the Love of Mike; Letting in the Sunshine; Leave It to Me. 1933 The Medicine Man; Excess Baggage; The Umbrella; Meet My Sister; You Made Me Love You; The Bermondsey Kid. 1934 Those Were the Days; Over the Garden Wall; Night Club Queen; Give Me a Ring; Gay Love; It's a Bet; Eighteen Minutes; Dandy Dick; Radio Parade of 1935. 1935 Me and Marlborough; Royal Cavalcade; Jimmy Boy; Honeymoon for Three; The Deputy Drummer; Music Hath Charms; Another Spot of Bother; Cheer Up; The Ghost Goes West; One Good Turn; Public Nuisance No. 1; Queen of Hearts; Man Behind the Mask; Royal Romance. 1936 Two's Company; Everything Is Rhythm. 1937 Man in the Mirror; Silver Blaze; Sensation; The Gang Show; Old Mother Riley. 1938 Young and Innocent (aka The Girl Was Young); We're Going to Be Rich; The Return of Carol; Everything Happens to Me; His Lordship Goes to Press; Peter's Pence; Save a Little Sunshine; Penny Paradise. Other British films: Romantic Rhythm; Paybox Adventure; Boys Will Be Girls; Sporting Love; Keep Your Seats, Please; Cotton Queen; The Limping Man; Ghosts Alive; Full Steam Ahead; Feather Your Nest; Double Alibi; Lucky Jade; Pearls Bring Tears; Racketeer Rhythm; Dark Stairway; Sweet Devil; Little Dolly Daydream; Open House; He Was Her Man.

CROUCH, WORTH
Born: 1917. Died: Feb. 6, 1943, Calabasas, Calif. Screen actor and stuntman.

Appeared in: 1943 We've Never Been Licked (died on location during filming).

CROWELL, BURT (Walter J. Crowley)
Born: 1873. Died: Mar. 26, 1946, Chicago, Ill. Screen, stage, and vaudeville actor. Appeared in vaudeville with his wife Ann as "Crowell & Gardner."

CRUME, CAMILLA
Born: 1874. Died: Mar. 20, 1952, Norwalk, Conn. Screen, stage, and radio actress. Appeared in early films made at Vitaphone Studios, Brooklyn, N.Y.

CRUSTER, AUD (Cruster Aud Olsen)
Born: 1889. Died: May 18, 1938, Moline, Ill. Screen and vaudeville actor.

Appeared in: 1926 Kid Boots.

CRUTE, SALLY (Sally C. Kirby)
Born: 1886. Died: Aug. 12, 1971, Miami, Fla. Screen actress.

Appeared in: 1915 While the Tide Was Rising. 1916 Helen of the Chorus. 1921 It Isn't Being Done This Season; Perjury. 1923 Broadway Broke; His Children's Children; The Tents of Allah. 1925 The Half-Way Girl; A Little Girl in a Big City; Ermine and Rhinestones.

CRUZE, JAMES (Jens Cruz Bosen)
Born: Mar. 27, 1894, Ogden, Utah. Died: Aug. 3, 1942, Los Angeles, Calif. Screen, stage, vaudeville actor, film director, producer, and screenwriter. Divorced from screen actresses Margarite Snow (dec. 1958) and Betty Compson.

Appeared in: 1912 Lucille. 1914 The Million Dollar Mystery (serial); Joseph in the Land of Egypt; Zudora—the Twenty Million Dollar Mystery (serial).

CRUZE, MAE
Born: 1891. Died: Aug. 16, 1965, Hollywood, Calif. Screen actress. Entered films in silents.

Appeared in: 1964 Mary Poppins.

CULLINGTON, MARGARET
Born: 1891. Died: July 18, 1925, Hollywood, Calif. Screen actress. Appeared in early "Christie" comedies.

Appeared in: 1921 The Son of Wallingford; The Mad Marriage. 1923 Wolves of the Border. 1924 Excitement; The Breathless Moment; That Wild West.

CUMMING, RUTH
Born: 1904. Died: Aug. 11, 1967, New York, N.Y. Screen, stage, and opera actress.

CUMMINGS, FRANCES
Died: Aug. 12, 1923, New York, N.Y.(cancer). Screen and stage actress. Appeared in early Lupin Film Company and Famous Players productions.

CUMMINGS, IRVING, SR.
Born: Oct. 9, 1888, New York, N.Y. Died: Apr. 18, 1959, Hollywood, Calif.(heart attack). Screen, stage actor, and film director. Entered films as an actor in 1909.

Appeared in: 1914 The Million Dollar Mystery (serial). 1915 The Diamond from the Sky (serial). 1919 Men, Women and Money; Everywoman. 1921 The Saphead. 1925 As Man Desires. 1936 Girl's Dormitory. 1941 The Devil and Mrs. Jones.

CUMMINGS, RICHARD H.
Born: 1858. Died: Dec. 25, 1938, Los Angeles, Calif. Screen, stage, vaudeville, and minstrel actor. Entered films with Tannhauser Co. in 1912.

Appeared in: 1915 Birth of a Nation. 1921 Red Courage; The Bride's Play; Partners of Fate; No Woman Knows; The Tomboy. 1922 Great Alone; The Top O' the Morning; Wolf Law. 1923 Thundergate; Itching Palms. 1925 Thank You. 1926 The Galloping Cowboy. 1930 The Social Lion.

CUMMINGS, VICKI
Born: 1919, Northhampton, Mass. Died: Nov. 30, 1969, New York, N.Y. Screen, stage, and television actress.

Appeared in: 1951 I Can Get It for You Wholesale. 1962 The Time and the Touch.

CUNARD, GRACE
Born: 1894, Paris, France. Died: Jan. 19, 1967, Woodland Hills, Calif.(cancer). Screen and stage actress. Married to screen actor Jack Shannon (dec. 1968).

Appeared in: 1914 Lucille Love; Girl of Mystery (serial). 1915 The Broken Coin (serial); The Campbells Are Coming. 1916 The Adventures of Peg O' the Ring (serial); Purple Mask (serial). 1918 The Silent Mystery (serial). 1919 Elmo, The Mighty (serial). 1922 The Girl in the Taxi; The Heart of Lincoln. 1924 The Last Man on Earth; Emblems of Love. 1925 The Kiss Barrier; Outwitted. 1926 Fighting with Buffalo Bill (serial); The Winking Idol (serial); Exclusive Rights. 1927 The Return of Riddle Rider (serial); Blake of Scotland Yard (serial); The Denver Dude. 1928 The Masked Angel (serial); Haunted Island (serial); The Price of Fear. 1929 Untamed; The Ace of Scotland Yard (serial; released in two versions—silent and sound). 1930 A Lady Surrenders; Little Accident. 1931 Ex-Bad Boy; Resurrection. 1933 Ladies They Talk About. 1936 The Rest Cure.

CUNNINGHAM, ALOYSIUS
Died: July 27, 1936, Pottsville, Pa.(heart attack). Screen and stage actor.

CUNNINGHAM, GEORGE
Born: 1904. Died: May 1, 1962, Los Angeles, Calif. Screen actor and dancer.

Appeared in: 1929 Broadway Melody (film debut); The Hollywood Revue of 1929; Our Modern Maidens; Thunder.

CUNNINGHAM, ZAMAH
Born: 1893. Died: June 2, 1967, New York, N.Y. Screen, stage, vaudeville, and television actress. Entered films with Griffith.

Appeared in: 1948 Dream Girl. 1950 Key to the City. 1953 Here Come the Girls. 1965 Baby, the Rain Must Fall.

CURRAN, THOMAS A.
Born: 1880. Died: Jan. 24, 1941, Hollywood, Calif.(pneumonia). Screen and stage actor.

Appeared in: 1928 The Black Pearl. 1929 Object Alimony; Anne against the World; Ships of the Night; Two Sisters; Must We Marry?; Trial of Mary Dugan; Wolf of Wall Street; The Phantom in the House. 1930 Morocco; The Kibitzer; Worldly Goods. 1931 Dishonored; Mother and Son; Forgotten Women; The Ghost City. 1932 Dance Team; Charlie Chan's Chance; Lost Squadron; Lady with a Past. 1935 The Cowboy Millionaire. 1940 Her First Romance.

CURRIE, FINLAY
Born: Jan. 20, 1878, Edinburgh, Scotland. Died: May 9, 1968, Gerrards Cross, England. Screen, stage, minstrel, and television actor. Married to stage actress Maude Courtney (dec. 1959).

Appeared in: 1932 The Case of the Frightened Lady. 1933 Rome Express; The Good Companions; Orders Is Orders. 1934 Criminal at Large; Princess Charming. 1937 Glamorous Night. 1938 The Edge of the World. 1941 49th Parallel (aka The Invaders-U.S. 1942). 1942 The Bells Go Down. 1944 Warn That Man; Thunder Rock. 1947 Great Expectations; I Know Where I'm Going; Trojan Brothers. 1948 So Evil My Love. 1949 Sleeping Car to Triest; Mr. Perrin and Mr. Traill; My Daughter Joy; My Brother Jonathan; Edward, My Son. 1950 The Mudlark; Sanitorium; The Black Rose; Treasure Island; Trio. 1951 Operation X; Quo Vadis; People Will Talk; History of Mr. Polly. 1952 Bonnie Prince Charlie; Ivanhoe; Kangaroo; Walk East on Beacon; Stars and Stripes Forever. 1953 Rob Roy, The Highland Rogue; Treasure of the Golden Condor. 1954 Deadly Game; Beau Brummel; The End of the Road (U.S. 1957). 1955 Captain Lightfoot; Footsteps in the Fog. 1956 Make Me an Offer; Third Party Risk; Around the World in 80 Days. 1957 The King's Rhapsody; Saint Joan; Abandon Ship; Zarak; The Little Hut. 1958 Dangerous Exile; The Naked Earth; Campbell's Kingdom. 1959 The Tempest; Ben Hur; Solomon and Sheba. 1960 The Angel Wore Red; The Adventures of Huckleberry Finn; Kidnapped. 1961 Francis of Assisi; Hand in Hand; Five Golden Hours. 1962 Lisa; Joseph and His Brethren; The Inspector. 1963 Billy Liar; Three Lives of Thomasina; Corridors of Blood; The Cracksman. 1964 The Fall of the Roman Empire; Who Was Maddox?. 1965 Battle of the Villa Fiorita; Bunny Lake Is Missing; The Amorous Mr. Pawn.

CURRIER, FRANK
Born: 1857, Norwich, Conn. Died: Apr. 22, 1928, Hollywood, Calif. (blood poisoning). Screen and stage actor.

Appeared in: 1919 Her Kingdom of Dreams; Should Women Tell? 1921 Clay Dollars; The Rookie's Return; Smiling All the Way; The Lotus Eater; Man Who; A Message from Mars; Without Limit. 1922 The Woman Who Fooled Herself; Why Announce Your Marriage?; The Lights of New York; Reckless Youth; My Old Kentucky Home; The Snitching Hour. 1923 The Tents of Allah; Children of Jazz; The Fog; The Victor; The Go-Getter; The Darling of New York, Desire; Stephen Steps Out. 1924 The Red Lily; Being Respectable; The Family Secret; The Heart Buster; The Sea Hawk; The Rose of Paris; Revelation; The Story without a Name; The Trouble Shooter. 1925 Graustark; Lights of Old Broadway; The White Desert; The Great Love; Too Many Kisses. 1926 The Big Parade; Ben Hur; La Boheme; Men of Steel; The First Year; Tell It to the Marines; The Exquisite Sinner. 1927 Annie Laurie; The Callahans and the Murphys; Rookies; California; The Enemy; Winners of the Wilderness; Foreign Devils. 1928 Across to Singapore; Easy Come, Easy Go; Telling the World; Riders of the Dark.

CURTIS, ALAN (Harry Ueberroth)
Born: July 24, 1909, Chicago, Ill. Died: Feb. 1, 1953, New York, N.Y. (kidney operation). Screen actor. Divorced from screen actresses Ilona Massey and Betty Sundmark (dec. 1959).

Appeared in: 1936 The Smartest Girl in Town; Winterset; Walking on Air. 1937 Between Two Women; Bad Gun; China Passage; Don't Tell the Wife. 1938 Mannequin; Yellow Jack; Shopworn Angel; Duke of West Point. 1939 Good Girls Go to Paris; Sergeant Madden; Burn 'Em up O'Connor; Hollywood Cavalcade. 1940 Four Sons. 1941 Come Live with Me; New Wine; High Sierra; We Go Fast; Buck Privates; The Great Awakening. 1942 Remember Pearl Harbor. 1943 Crazy House; Two Tickets to London; Hitler's Madman; Gung Ho!. 1944 Destiny; Phantom Lady; The Invisible Man's Revenge; Follow the Boys. 1945 Frisco Sal; Shady Lady; The Naughty Nineties; See My Lawyer; The Daltons Ride Again. 1946 Inside Job. 1947 Flight to Nowhere; Renegade Girl; Philo Vance's Secret Mission; Philo Vance's Gamble. 1948 Enchanted Valley. 1949 Captain Sorocco; Pirates of Capri; Apache Chief. 1950 The Masked Pirate.

CURTIS, BEATRICE (Beatrice White)
Born: 1901. Died: Mar. 26, 1963, Los Angeles, Calif. Screen and vaudeville actress. Divorced from screen actor Harry Fox (dec. 1959) with whom she appeared in vaudeville; together they made the following two shorts: 1929 The Fox and the Bee. 1930 The Play Boy. She appeared without Fox in: 1937 Paid to Dance.

CURTIS, DICK
Born: May 11, 1902, Newport, Ky. Died: Jan. 3, 1952, Hollywood, Calif. Screen and stage actor.

Appeared in: 1918 The Unpardonable Sin (film debut as an extra). 1930 Shooting Straight. 1932 Girl Crazy. 1933 King Kong. 1934 Wilderness Mail; Racing Luck; Burning Gold; Silver Streak; Mutiny Ahead. 1935 Code of the Mounted; Fighting Trooper; Lion's Den; Northern Frontier. 1936 The Wildcat Trooper. 1937 Paid to Dance; The Shadow. 1938 Penitentiary; Women in Prison;

The Main Event; Adventure in Sahara; Rawhide. 1939 West of Santa Fe; Spoilers of the Range; Western Caravans; Taming of the West; Behind Prison Gates; Riders of Black River; The Man They Could Not Hang; Outpost of the Mounties; The Stranger from Texas; plus the following shorts: Three Little Sew and Sews; We Want Money; Oily to Bed—Oily to Rise. 1940 Blazing Six-Shooters; Bullets for Rustlers; Pioneers of the Frontier; Two-Fisted Rangers; Texas Stagecoach; Three Men from Texas; Ragtime Cowboy Joe; Men without Souls; My Son Is Guilty. 1941 The Roundup; Billy the Kid; Across the Sierras; Mystery Ship; I Was a Prisoner on Devil's Island. 1942 Two Yanks in Trinidad; Arizona Cyclone; Men of San Quentin; City of Silent Men; The Power of God; Jackass Mail. 1943 Pardon My Gun; Jack London; Salute to the Marines; Cowboy in the Clouds. 1944 Spook Town; Crash Goes the Hash (short). 1945 Wagon Wheels Westward; Song of the Prairie; Singing Guns; Hidden Trails; Shotgun Rider. 1946 California Gold Rush; Traffic in Crime; Song of Arizona; Abilene Town; Santa Fe Uprising; The Three Troubledoers (short). 1947 Wyoming. 1949 Navajo Trail Raiders. 1950 Covered Wagon Raid; The Vanishing Westerner. 1951 Lorna Doone; Rawhide; Whirlwind; Government Agents vs. Phantom Legion (serial), plus the following shorts: Three Arabian Nuts; Don't Throw That Knife. 1952 Rose of Cimarron; My Six Convicts.

CURTIS, JACK
Died: Mar. 16, 1956, Hollywood, Calif. Screen actor.

Appeared in: 1916 Lydia Gilmore. 1921 The Big Punch; Steelheart; The Torrent; Beach of Dreams; Flowers of the North; An Unwilling Hero; The Servant in the House; The Sea Lion. 1922 Caught Bluffing; The Long Chance; The Silent Vow; Two Kinds of Women; Western Speed; His Back to the Wall; The Stranger's Banquet. 1923 Reno; The Spoilers; Quicksands; Times Have Changed; Canyon of the Fools; Dangerous Trails; The Day of Faith; Masters of Men; Soft Boiled. 1924 Captain Blood; Fighter's Paradise. 1925 Greed; Baree, Son of Kazan; The Shadow on the Wall; Free and Equal; The Wedding Song. 1926 The Texas Streak; Through Thick and Thin; Hearts and Fists. 1927 Brass Knuckles; Jaws of Steel; Wolf's Clothing. 1929 The Love Racket; Scarlet Seas; The Phantom in the House; The Show of Shows. 1930 Moby Dick; Under a Texas Moon; Mammy; The Love Trader; The Dawn Trail; Hold Everything. 1935 Westward Ho.

CURTIS, SPENCER M.
Born: 1856. Died: July 13, 1921, Long Beach, Calif. Screen and stage actor.

CURTIZ, MICHAEL (Mihaly Kertesz)
Born: Dec. 24, 1888, Budapest, Hungary. Died: Apr. 11, 1962, Hollywood, Calif. Screen, stage actor, film director, film producer, and screenwriter.

CUSCADEN, SARAH D.
Born: 1873. Died: Oct. 18, 1954, Hollywood, Calif. Screen actress.

CUTELLI, COUNT GAETANO
Died: July 16, 1944, Seattle, Wash. Screen actor. Voice of many animal characters in cartoon comedy films.

CYBULSKI, ZBIGNIEW
Born: 1927, Poland. Died: Jan. 8, 1967, Wroclaw, Breslau, Poland (accidental fall). Screen and stage actor.

Appeared in: 1954 A Generation. 1958 Ashes and Diamonds (U.S. 1961). 1959 The Eighth Day of the Week. 1962 La Poupee (He, She or It). 1963 Milczenie (Silence); Love at Twenty. 1964 Att Alska (To Love). 1965 Manuscript Found in Saragossa. 1966 Salto.

DA CUNHA, JOSE
Born: 1889, Portugal. Died: Sept. 25, 1956, Lisbon, Portugal. Screen, stage actor, and stage manager.

DADE, FRANCES
Born: Feb. 14, 1910, Philadelphia, Pa. Died: Jan. 21, 1968, Philadelphia, Pa. Screen and stage actress.

Appeared in: 1930 Grumpy; Raffles; He Knew Women. 1931 Dracula; Mother's Millions; Daughter of the Dragon; Range Law; Seed. 1932 Pleasure; Big Town.

DAI, LIN
Born: 1931, China. Died: July 17, 1964, Hong Kong, China ("accident?"). Screen actress. Chinese actress who entered films approximately 1950.

Appeared in: 1964 The Last Woman of Shang.

DAIX, DAISY (Denis Cariveac)
Born: 1930, Belgium. Died: Aug. 16, 1950, suburbs of Asnieres, France (auto accident). Screen and stage actress.

DALBY, AMY
Born: Approx. 1888, England. Died: 1969. Screen actress.

Appeared in: 1946 The Wicked Lady. 1959 The Man Upstairs. 1962 The Lamp in Assassin Mews. 1963 The Haunting. 1964 Topkapi. 1965 The Secret of My Success. 1966 Who Killed the Cat?; The Spy with a Cold Nose.

DALE, CHARLES (Charles Marks)
Born: 1881, New York, N.Y. Died: Nov. 16, 1971, Teaneck, N.J. Screen, vaudeville, and television actor. Partner of Joseph Smith in vaudeville team of "Smith and Dale." Was the "Dr. Kronkhite" of the team. The team was originally called "Charlie Marks (Dale) and Joe Seltzer (Smith)" but they changed it to just "Smith and Dale."

Appeared in: 1931 Manhattan Parade. 1932 The Heart of New York. 1951 Two Tickets to Broadway.

DALE, DOROTHY
Born: 1883. Died: May 13, 1957, Hollywood, Calif.(fire). Screen actress and stand in for Mabel Normand. Her husband, Dr. Jacob Hyman (dec. 1944), had at one time been a partner with Harry Houdini in an act billed as the "Houdini Brothers."

Appeared in: 1923 The Ten Commandments. The makeup with which she painted herself bronze for role of an Egyptian girl caused severe facial scars and she then went into retirement.

DALE, DOROTHY
Born: 1925. Died: Aug. 1, 1937 (heart ailment). Child screen and stage actress. Appeared in shorts.

DALE, ESTHER
Born: 1886, Beaufort, S.C. Died: July 23, 1961, Hollywood, Calif. Screen and stage actress. Married to producer/ writer Arthur Beckhard.

Appeared in: 1934 Crime without Passion(film debut). 1935 The Great Impersonation; I Dream Too Much; Curly Top; In Old Kentucky; Private Worlds; The Wedding Night. 1936 Lady of Secrets; Fury; The Magnificent Brute; The Case against Mrs. Ames; Timothy's Quest; Hollywood Boulevard; The Farmer in the Dell. 1937 Wild Money; On Such a Night; Of Human Hearts; The Awful Truth; Damaged Goods; Dead End; Easy Living; Outcast. 1938 Condemned Women; Girls on Probation; Prison Farm; Stolen Heaven; 6,000 Enemies. 1939 Made for Each Other; Broadway Serenade; Big Town Czar; Tell No Tales; Blackmail; Swanee River; The Women. 1940 Convicted Woman; Village Barn Dance; And One Was Beautiful; Opened by Mistake; Women without Names; Untamed; Laddie; Blondie Has Servant Trouble; A Child is Born; Love Thy Neighbor; Arise, My Love; The Mortal Storm. 1941 Mr. and Mrs. Smith; There's Magic in Music; Aloma of the South Seas; Unfinished Business; All-American Co-ed; Dangerously They Live; Back Street. 1942 Blondie Goes to College; Ten Gentlemen from West Point; Wrecking Crew. 1943 The Amazing Mrs. Holiday; Swing Your Partner; Murder in Times Square; North Star; Old Acquaintance. 1945 Behind City Lights; Bedside Manner; On Stage, Everybody. 1946 A Stolen Life; Margie; My Reputation; Smoky. 1947 The Egg and I; The Unfinished Dance. 1948 A Song Is Born. 1949 Holiday Affair; Ma and Pa Kettle. 1950 No Man of Her Own; Surrender; Walk Softly, Stranger. 1951 Too Young to Kiss. 1952 Ma and Pa Kettle at the Fair; Monkey Business. 1955 Ma and Pa Kettle at Waikiki; Betrayed Women. 1957 The Oklahoman.

DALE, PEGGY (Margaret Dale Dudley).
Born: Dec. 25, 1903, New York, N.Y. Died: June 6, 1967, Hollywood, Calif.(suicide—pills). Screen actress.

Appeared in: 1929 Desert Song.

DALL, JOHN (John Dall Thompson)
Born: 1918. Died: Jan. 15, 1971, Beverly Hills, Calif.(heart attack). Screen, stage, and television actor. Nominated for Academy Award for Best Supporting Actor in 1946 for The Corn Is Green.

Appeared in: 1939 For the Love of Mary. 1946 The Corn Is Green. 1947 Something in the Wind. 1948 The Rope; Another Part of the Forest. 1949 Deadly Is the Female. 1950 Gun Crazy; The Man Who Cheated Himself. 1960 Spartacus. 1961 Atlantis, the Lost Continent.

DALROY, HARRY "RUBE"
Born: 1879. Died: Mar. 8, 1954, Hollywood, Calif. Western screen actor. Known as the "Mayor of Gower Gulch."

Appeared in: 1923 Stormy Seas.

DALTON, IRENE
Born: 1901. Died: Aug. 15, 1934, Chicago, Ill. Screen and stage actress. Divorced from screen actor Lloyd Hamilton (dec. 1935).

Appeared in: 1922 "Christie" comedies. 1923 Bluebeard's Eighth Wife; Children of Jazz.

DALY, ARNOLD
Born: Oct. 4, 1875, Brooklyn, N.Y. Died: Jan. 13, 1927 New York, N.Y.(burned to death). Screen, stage, and vaudeville actor.

Appeared in: 1915 The Exploits of Elaine (serial); The Romance of Elaine (serial). 1916 The New Exploits of Elaine (serial). 1924 For Another Woman. 1926 In Borrowed Plumes.

DALY, JAMES L.
Born: 1852. Died: Nov. 10, 1933, Philadelphia, Pa.(heart trouble). Screen and stage actor. Married to screen actress Clara Lamber (dec. 1921). Appeared in silents.

DALY, MARK
Born: Aug. 23, 1887, Edinburgh, Scotland. Died: 1957. Screen, stage, vaudeville, and radio actor who appeared mostly in British films.

Appeared in: 1930 The Third String. 1931 The Beggar Student. 1933 Private Life of Henry VIII; Up for the Derby; A Cuckoo in the Nest; Dosshouse; Say It with Flowers. 1934 That's My Uncle; Floodtide; Music Hall. 1935 Bypass to Happiness; The Small Man; The Man Who Could Work Miracles; The Ghost Goes West. 1936 Lilac Time; Shipmates; Southern Roses. 1937 Knight without Armor; Command Performance; Wings of the Morning; The Captain's Table; Good Morning, Boys; The Taming of the Shrew; Captain's Orders; Break the News; Follow the Star; Lassie from Lancashire; Q Planes. 1939 Ten Days in Paris. 1942 Next of Kin; The Big Blockade. 1949 Bonnie Prince Charlie. 1951 Naughty Arlette. 1954 Lease of Life. 1956 The Dynamiters. 1957 Rock around the World; The Gentle Touch; You Pay Your Money; The Shiralee. 1958 The Tommy Steele Story. Other British films; East Lynn on the Western Front; Farmers Wife.

DALY, PAT (Gordon C. Munger).
Born: 1891. Died: Nov. 19, 1947, Detroit, Mich. Screen, stage, minstrel, vaudeville, and radio actor.

Appeared in vaudeville with his wife, Genevieve, in an act billed as "Pat and Genevieve Daly."
Appeared in: 1938 A Slight Case of Murder.

D'AMBRICOURT, ADRIENNE
Born: 1888, France. Died: Dec. 6, 1957, Hollywood, Calif.(heart attack). Screen and stage actress.

Appeared in: 1924 Wages of Virtue; The Humming Bird. 1926 God Gave Me Twenty Cents. 1929 Footlights and Fools; The Trial of Mary Dugan. 1930 L'Enigmatique Monsieur Parkes (Mysterious Mr. Parkes); The Bad One; What a Widow!. 1931 Svengali; This Modern Age; Transgression; The Men in Her Life. 1933 Eagle and the Hawk; Disgraced!; Design for Living; Gallant Lady. 1934 Marie Galante; Caravan; The Cat and the Fiddle; The Way to Love. 1935 It Happened in New York; Goin' to Town; Peter Ibbetson. 1936 Valiant Is the Word for Carrie. 1937 Seventh Heaven; Mama Steps Out. 1938 Artists and Models Abroad. 1939 Bulldog Drummond's Bride; Pack up Your Troubles; Charlie Chan in City in Darkness; Nurse Edith Cavell; The Story of Vernon and Irene Castle. 1942 The Pied Piper. 1945 Paris Underground; Saratoga Trunk. 1952 Bal Tabarin.

DAMPIER, CLAUDE (Claude Cowan).
Born: 1885. Died: Jan. 1, 1955, London, England (pneumonia). English screen, stage, and radio actor.

Appeared in: 1935 So You Won't Talk; White Lilac; Boys will Be Boys; King of the Castle; No Monkey Business; She Shall Have Music; Public Nuisance No. 1; Radio Parade of 1935. 1936 She Knew What She Wanted; All In; Such Is Life; Sing as You Swing; Wanted. 1937 Mr. Strungfellow Says No. 1939 Riding High. 1944 Don't Take It to Heart (U.S. 1949). 1954 Meet Mr. Malcolm.

DANDRIDGE, DOROTHY
Born: 1923, Cleveland, Ohio. Died: Sept. 8, 1965, West Hollywood, Calif.(drug overdose). Negro screen and stage actress.

Received Academy Award nomination in 1954 for Best Actress in Carmen Jones.

Appeared in: 1937 A Day at the Races. 1941 Lady from Louisiana; Sundown; Sun Valley Serenade; Bahama Passage. 1942 Drums of the Congo. 1943 Hit Parade of 1943. 1944 Since You Went Away; Atlantic City. 1945 Pillow to Post. 1951 Tarzan's Peril; Jungle Queen; Harlem Globetrotters. 1953 Bright Road; Remains to Be Seen. 1954 Carmen Jones. 1957 The Happy Road; Island in the Sun. 1958 The Decks Ran Red. 1959 Porgy and Bess; Tamango. 1960 Moment of Danger. 1962 Malaga.

DANDY, JESS (Jesse A. Danzig)
Born: 1871, Rochester, N.Y. Died: Apr. 15, 1923, Brookline, Mass.(septicemia). Screen and stage actor.

Appeared in early Keystone films.

DANE, KARL
Born: Oct. 12, 1886, Copenhagen, Denmark. Died: Apr. 15, 1934, Los Angeles, Calif.(suicide—gun). Screen and stage actor.

Appeared in: 1925 The Big Parade; His Secretary; Lights of Old Broadway; The Everlasting Whisper. 1926 Bardely's, The Magnificent; The Son of the Shiek; The Scarlet Letter; Monte Carlo; War Paint. 1927 The Red Mill; Rookies; Slide, Kelly, Slide. 1928 The Trail of 98; Show People; The Enemy; Alias Jimmy Valentine; Circus Rookies; Detectives; Baby Mine; Brotherly Love. 1929 Speedway; The Hollywood Revue of 1929; All at Sea; China Bound; The Duke Steps Out; The Voice of the Storm. 1930 The Big House; Navy Blues; Montana Moon; Free and Easy; Numbered Men; Billy the Kid. 1933 A Paramount Short; Whispering Shadow. 1964 Big Parade of Comedy (documentary). 1967 Show People (reissue of 1928 film).

DANEGGER, THEODOR
Born: 1891. Died: Oct. 11, 1959, Vienna, Austria. Screen, stage, and opera actor.

Appeared in: 1935 Ehestreik. 1936 The Royal Waltz; Weiberregiment. 1940 Drei Vater um Anna (Three Fathers for Anna).

DANERI, JULIE
Born: 1914, Mexico. Died: Aug. 28, 1957, Mexico City, Mexico. Mexican screen and stage actor.

DANIELL, HENRY
Born: Mar. 5, 1894, London, England. Died: Oct. 31, 1963, Santa Monica, Calif. Screen and stage actor.

Appeared in: 1929 Jealousy (film debut); The Awful Truth. 1930 Last of the Lone Wolf. 1934 The Path of Glory. 1936 The Unguarded Hour; Camille. 1937 Under Cover of Night; The Thirteenth Chair; The Firefly; Madame X. 1938 Holiday; Marie Antoinette. 1939 We Are Not Alone; Private Lives of Elizabeth and Essex. 1940 The Sea Hawk; The Great Dictator; The Philadelphia Story; All This, and Heaven Too. 1941 A Woman's Face; Dressed to Kill; Four Jacks and a Jill; The Feminine Touch. 1942 Sherlock Holmes and the Voice of Terror; Reunion; Castle in the Desert; The Great Impersonation; Nightmare. 1943 Mission to Moscow; Sherlock Holmes in Washington; Watch on the Rhine. 1944 Jane Eyre; The Suspect. 1945 Captain Kidd; Hotel Berlin; The Woman in Green; The Body Snatcher. 1946 The Bandit of Sherwood Forest. 1947 Song of Love; The Exile. 1948 Siren of Atlantis; Wake of the Red Witch. 1949 Secret of St. Ives. 1950 Buccaneer's Girl. 1954 The Egyptian. 1955 The Prodigal; Diane. 1956 The Man in the Gray Flannel Suit; Lust for Life. 1957 The Story of Mankind; Les Girls; The Sun Also Rises; Mr. Cory; Witness for the Prosecution. 1958 From the Earth to the Moon. 1959 The Four Skulls of Jonathan Drake. 1961 The Comancheros; Voyage to the Bottom of the Sea. 1962 Five Weeks in a Balloon; The Notorious Landlady; The Chapman Report; Madison Avenue. 1964 My Fair Lady.

DANIELS, BEBE (Virginia Daniels)
Born: Jan. 14, 1901, Dallas, Tex. Died: Mar. 16, 1971, London, England (cerebral hemorrhage). Screen, stage, radio, television actress, and stage producer. Entered films at age seven. Married to screen actor Ben Lyon.

Appeared in: 1908 A Common Enemy (film debut). 1916-1917 "Lonesome Luke" series. 1919 Everywoman; Male and Female; Captain Kidd's Kids. 1920 Sick Abed; Why Change Your Wife; The Dancin' Fool; Feet of Clay. 1921 The Affairs of Anatol; Ducks and Drakes; Oh, Lady, Lady; She Couldn't Help It; You Never Can Tell; The March Hare; One Wild Week; Speed Girl; Two Weeks with Pay. 1922 Nice People; The Game Chicken; Nancy from Nowhere; North of the Rio Grande; Pink Gods; Singed Wings. 1923 The Exciters; Glimpses of the Moon; His

Children's Children; The World's Applause. 1924 Sinners in Heaven; Dangerous Money; The Heritage of the Desert; Monsieur Beaucaire; Daring Youth; Argentine Love; Unguarded Women. 1925 Wild, Wild Susan; The Manicure Girl; Miss Bluebeard; The Crowded Hour; Lovers in Quarantine. 1926 The Splendid Crime; Stranded in Paris; The Campus Flirt; Mrs. Brewster's Millions; The Palm Beach Girl; Volcano. 1927 She's a Sheik; Swim, Girl, Swim; Senorita; A Kiss in a Taxi. 1928 Feel My Pulse; The Fifty-Fifty Girl; What a Night!; Hot News; Take Me Home. 1929 Rio Rita. 1930 Love Comes Along; Alias French Gertie; Dixiana; Lawful Larceny. 1931 Reaching for the Moon; My Past; The Maltese Falcon; Honor of the Family. 1932 Silver Dollar; The Slippery Pearls (short); Radio Girl (short). 1933 Hollywood on Parade (short); Forty-Second Street; Cocktail Hour; Counsellor-at-Law. 1934 The Song You Gave Me; Registered Nurse. 1935 Music Is Magic; The Return of Carol Deane (U.S. 1939). 1936 A Southern Maid. 1938 Not Wanted on a Voyage. 1940 Hi, Gang!. 1953 Life with the Lyons. 1955 The Lyons in Paris.

DANIELS, FRANK
Born: 1860, Dayton, Ohio. Died: Jan. 12, 1935, West Palm Beach, Fla. Screen and stage actor. Entered films with Vitagraph in 1915.

Appeared in: 1915 Crooky Scruggs.

DANIELS, VICTOR. See Chief Thundercloud.

DANIELS, WALTER
Born: 1875. Died: Mar. 30, 1928, Los Angeles, Calif. Screen and vaudeville actor. Appeared in vaudeville with his wife, Mina Daniels.

Appeared in: 1927 The Dove. 1928 Stolen Love; Rough Ridin' Red. 1929 The Jazz Age; The Vagabond Cub.

DANILO, DON. See Elmer Dewey.

DANIS, IDA
Born: France. Died: Apr. 9, 1921, Nice, France (consumption). Screen actress.

Appeared in: 1921 La Roue.

DANTE (Harry A. Jansen)
Born: 1884. Died: June 15, 1955, near Northridge, Calif.(heart attack). Screen, stage, vaudeville, burlesque, circus, radio, and television actor. Billed as "Dante, King of Magicians."

Appeared in: 1942 A-Haunting We Will Go. 1954 The Golden Coach.

D'ARCY, ROY (Roy F. Guisti)
Born: Feb. 10, 1894, San Francisco, Calif. Died: Nov. 15, 1969, Redlands, Calif. Screen, stage, and vaudeville actor.

Appeared in: 1925 The Merry Widow; Graustark; The Masked Bride; Pretty Ladies. 1926 Beverly of Graustark; La Boheme; The Temptress; Bardely's, The Magnificent; The Gay Deceiver; Monte Carlo. 1927 On Ze Boulevard; Lovers?; Winners of the Wilderness; Buttons; Valencia; The Road to Romance; Adam and Evil; Frisco Sally Levy. 1928 Beyond the Sierras; Riders of the Dark; Beware of Blondes; Domestic Meddlers; The Actress; Forbidden Hours. 1929 A Woman of Affairs; Stolen Kisses; The Last Warning; Girls Gone Wild; Woman from Hell; The Black Watch. 1930 Romance. 1931 Masquerade (short). 1932 Gay Buckaroo; File 113; Discarded Lovers; From Broadway to Cheyenne; Sherlock Holmes; Lovebound. 1933 Flying Down to Rio. 1934 Orient Express. 1935 Outlawed Guns; Kentucky Blue Streak. 1936 Revolt of the Zombies; Hollywood Boulevard; Captain Calamity. 1939 Chasing Danger.

DARE, DORRIS (Dorris Prince)
Born: 1899. Died: Aug. 16, 1927, Los Angeles, Calif. Screen and stage actress.

Appeared in: 1919 The Mystery of 13 (serial). 1923 Tango Cavalier. 1925 Fightin' Odds.

DARE, VIRGINIA
Died: July 8, 1962, Hollywood, Calif. Screen, stage, and television actress. Entered films in early 1920s.

DARIEN, FRANK, JR.
Born: New Orleans, La. Died: Oct. 20, 1955, Hollywood, Calif. Screen and stage actor. Entered films approx. 1912.

Appeared in: 1914 D. W. Griffith productions; 1915 "Mack Sennett'' comedies; 1931 Cimarron; Bad Girl; Big Business Girl; June Moon. 1932 The Miracle Man; Prosperity; The Big Shot; Okay America. 1933 Hello, Everybody!; Professional Sweetheart; Big Executive; From Headquarters. 1934 Marie Galante; Fashions of 1934; Journal of a Crime. 1935 Behind the Evidence; The Perfect Clue; The Little Colonel; Here Comes Cookie. 1936 Brides Are Like That. 1937 Jim Hanvey, Detective; The River of Missing Men; Trapped by G-Men. 1938 Cassidy of Bar 20; Western Jamboree; Love Finds Andy Hardy; Long Shot; Prison Break. 1939 At the Circus; Sabotage; Maisie. 1940 The Grapes of Wrath; Arizona. 1942 The Gay Sisters; Hello, Frisco, Hello. 1943 Get Hep to Love. 1945 Abbott and Costello in Hollywood; Kiss and Tell; The Clock; Counter-Attack. 1946 Claudia and David; The Fabulous Suzanne; Bad Bascomb. 1947 Woman on the Beach; Magic Town. 1948 Belle Starr's Daughter. 1950 The Flying Saucer.

DARCLOUD, BEULAH (Beulah T. Filson).
Died: Jan. 2, 1946, Thermolite, Calif. Screen actress. Entered films with D. W. Griffith in 1912.

Appeared in: 1922 The Crimson Challenge.

DARK, CHRISTOPHER
Died: Oct. 8, 1971, Hollywood, Calif.(heart attack). Screen, stage, and television actor.

Appeared in: 1953 Raiders of the Seven Seas; The Steel Lady. 1954 Suddenly. 1955 Diane. 1956 World without End; Johnny Concho. 1957 The Halliday Brand; Baby Face Nelson. 1958 Day of the Bad Man; Wild Heritage. 1959 The Rabbit Trap. 1960 Platinum High School. 1965 None But the Brave. 1968 The Private Navy of Sgt. O'Farrell.

DARLING, IDA
Born: 1875. Died: June 5, 1936, Hollywood, Calif. Screen and stage actress.

Appeared in: 1914 The Nightingale. 1921 Society Snobs; Nobody; Wedding Bells. 1922 Destiny's Isle; The Ruling Passion. 1923 The Exciters. 1924 Meddling Women. 1925 The Sky Raider; Heart of a Sire. 1926 Irene; Stranded in Paris. 1927 Singed. 1928 The House of Scandal; A Woman against the World. 1929 Love in the Desert. 1930 Lummox. 1935 The Girl Who Came Back.

DARMOND, GRACE
Born: 1898, Toronto, Canada. Died: Oct. 8, 1963, Los Angeles, Calif.(lung ailment). Screen and stage actress.

Appeared in: 1916 The Shielding Shadow (serial). 1920 Below the Surface; The Hawk's Trail (serial). 1921 The Hope Diamond Mystery (serial); The Beautiful Gambler; See My Lawyer; White and Unmarried. 1922 A Dangerous Adventure (serial and feature film); Handle with Care; The Song of Life; I Can Explain. 1923 The Midnight Guest; Gold Madness; Daytime Wives. 1924 Alimony; The Gaiety Girl; Discontented Husbands. 1925 Flattery; Where the Worst Begins; The Great Jewel Robbery. 1926 Honesty—The Best Policy; Her Big Adventure; The Marriage Clause; The Night Patrol; Midnight Thieves; Her Man O'War. 1927 Wide Open; Hour of Reckoning; Wages of Conscience.

DARNELL, LINDA
Born: Oct. 16, 1921, Dallas, Tex. Died: Apr. 12, 1965, Chicago, Ill.(fire burns). Screen, stage, and television actress.

Appeared in: 1939 Hotel for Women; Daytime Wife. 1940 Star Dust; Mark of Zorro; Brigham Young—Frontiersman; Chad Hanna. 1941 Blood and Sand; Rise and Shine. 1942 The Loves of Edgar Allan Poe. 1943 City without Men; The Song of Bernadette. 1944 Buffalo Bill; It Happened Tomorrow; Summer Storm; Sweet and Low Down. 1945 Hangover Square; All-Star Bond Rally (short); Fallen Angel; The Great John L; Strange Confession. 1946 My Darling Clementine; Centennial Summer; Anna and the King of Siam. 1947 Forever Amber. 1948 Unfaithfully Yours; The Walls of Jericho; A Letter to Three Wives. 1949 Slattery's Hurricane; Everybody Does It. 1950 No Way Out; Two Flags West. 1951 The 13th Letter; The Guy Who Came Back; The Lady Pays Off. 1952 Island of Desire; Blackbeard the Pirate; Night without Sleep. 1953 Second Chance. 1954 This Is My Love. 1956 Dakota Incident; Angels of Darkness. 1957 Zero Hour. 1965 Boeing Boeing; Black Spurs.

DARNOLD, BLAINE A.
Born: 1886. Died: Mar. 11, 1926, Kansas City, Mo.(pneumonia). Screen, stage, and vaudeville actor.

DARRELL, J. STEVAN
Born: 1905. Died: Aug. 14, 1970, Hollywood, Calif. Screen, stage, radio, and television actor.

DARVI, BELLA (Báyla Wegier)
Born: Oct. 23, 1928, Sosnowiec, Poland. Died: Sept. 1971, Monte Carlo, Monaco (suicide—gas). Screen and television actress.

Appeared in: 1954 Hell and High Water; The Egyptian. 1955 The Racers; Je Suis un Sentimental. 1959 Sinners of Paris. 1965 Lipstick.

DARWELL, JANE (Patti Woodward)
Born: Oct. 15, 1880, Palmyra, Mo. Died: Aug. 1967, Woodland Hills, Calif.(heart attack). Screen, stage, and television actress. Won Academy Award for Best Supporting Actress in The Grapes of Wrath (1940)

Appeared in: 1914 Rose of the Rancho (film debut); The Only Son; Brewster Millions; The Master Mind. 1930 Tom Sawyer. 1931 Huckleberry Finn; Fighting Caravans. 1932 Ladies of the Big House; Hot Saturday; Back Street; No One Man. 1933 Jennie Gerhardt; Air Hostess; Women Won't Tell; One Sunday Afternoon; Design for Living; Emergency Call; Before Dawn; Only Yesterday; He Couldn't Take It; Bondage; Child of Manhattan; Murders in the Zoo; Roman Scandals. 1934 Wonder Bar; Fashions of 1934; Jimmy the Gent; Embarrassing Moments; Heat Lightning; Gentlemen Are Born; Blind Date; Once to Every Woman; The Most Precious Thing in Life; Happiness Ahead; The Scarlet Empress; The White Parade; Bright Eyes; Change of Heart; Let's Talk It Over; Desirable; Wake up and Dream; The Firebird; David Harum; Journal of a Crime; Million Dollar Ransom; One Night of Love. 1935 Tomorrow's Youth; Beauty's Daughter; One More Spring; Life Begins at Forty; Curly Top; McFadden's Flats; Paddy O'Day; Navy Wife; Metropolitan. 1936 We're Only Human; Captain January; The Country Doctor; Little Miss Nobody; The First Baby; Private Number; The Poor Little Rich Girl; White Fang; Star for a Night; Ramona; Craig's Wife. 1937 The Great Hospital Mystery; Love Is News; Dead Yesterday; Nancy Steele Is Missing; Fifty Roads to Town; Slave Ship; Wife, Doctor and Nurse; Dangerously Yours; The Singing Marine; Laughing at Trouble. 1938 Five of a Kind; Change of Heart (and 1934 version); Battle of Broadway; Three Blind Mice; Time Out for Murder; Inside Story; Up the River; The Jury's Secret. 1939 Jesse James; Unexpected Father; The Zero Hour; Grand Jury Secrets; The Rains Came; Gone with the Wind; 20,000 Men a Year. 1940 The Grapes of Wrath; Brigham Young—Frontiersman; A Miracle on Main Street; Youth Will Be Served; Chad Hanna; Untamed. 1941 Here Is a Man; All That Money Can Buy; Private Nurse; Small Town Deb. 1942 On the Sunny Side; Highways by Night; The Great Gildersleeve; All through the Night; Battle of Midway (documentary); The Loves of Edgar Allan Poe; It Happened in Flatbush; Young America; Men of Texas. 1943 Gildersleeve's Bad Day; The Ox-Bow Incident; Tender Comrade; Stagedoor Canteen; Government Girl. 1944 She's a Sweetheart; Music in Manhattan; Double Indemnity; The Impatient Years; Reckless Age; Sunday Dinner for a Soldier. 1945 Captain Tugboat Annie. 1946 My Darling Clementine; A Yank in London; Three Wise Fools; Dark Horse. 1947 The Red Stallion; Keeper of the Bees. 1948 The Time of Your Life; Train to Alcatraz; Three Godfathers. 1949 Red Canyon. 1950 Red-Wood Forest Trail; Surrender; Three Husbands; The Second Face; Father's Wild Game; Wagonmaster; Caged; The Daughter of Rosie O'Grady. 1951 Fourteen Hours; Excuse My Dust; Journey into Light; The Lemon Drop Kid. 1952 We're Not Married; The Devil and Daniel Webster (reissue and retitle of All That Money Can Buy, 1941). 1953 It Happens Every Thursday; The Sun Shines Bright; Affair with a Stranger; The Bigamist. 1955 Hit the Deck; A Life at Stake. 1956 There's Always Tomorrow; Girls in Prison. 1958 The Last Hurrah. 1959 Hound-Dog Man. 1964 Mary Poppins.

DASHIELL, WILLARD
Born: 1867. Died: Apr. 19, 1943, Holyoke, Mass. Screen, stage, vaudeville actor, playwright, and lawyer. Entered films during silents.

Appeared in: 1931 The Cheat. 1934 War is a Racket.

DA SILVA, HENRY
Born: 1881, Lisbon, Portugal. Died: June 6, 1947, Los Angeles, Calif. Actor.

DASTAGIR, "SABU". See Sabu

DATE, KESHAVRAO
Born: 1939, India. Died: Sept. 13, 1971, Bombay, India. Screen and stage actor.

DAUBE, HARDA (Belle Daube)
Born: 1888, Northampton, England. Died: May 25, 1959, Hollywood, Calif. Screen and stage actress.

DAVENPORT, ANN
Died: Jan. 28, 1968, Hollywood, Calif. Screen actress. See Harry Davenport for family information.

DAVENPORT, HARRY
Born: Jan. 19, 1866, New York, N.Y. Died: Aug. 9, 1949, Los Angeles, Calif.(heart attack). Screen, stage actor, and film director. Married to screen actress Phyllis Rankin (dec. 1934) and father of screen actor Arthur Rankin (dec. 1947) and screen actresses Ann (dec. 1968), Kate (dec. 1954) and Dorothy Davenport Reid (widow of screen actor Wallace Reid). Entered films in 1912.

Appeared in: 1930 Her Unborn Child. 1931 My Sin. 1932 His Woman. 1933 Get That Venus. 1934 Three Cheers for Love. 1935 The Scoundrel. 1936 Three Men on a Horse; The Case of the Black Cat; King of Hockey. 1937 Fly-Away Baby; The Life of Emile Zola; Under Cover of Night; Her Husband's Secretary; White Bondage; They Won't Forget; Mr. Dodd Takes the Air; First Lady; The Perfect Specimen; Paradise Express; As Good as Married; Armored Car; Wells Fargo; Fit for a King. 1938 Gold Is Where You Find It; Saleslady; The Sisters; Long Shot; The First Hundred Years; The Cowboy and the Lady; Reckless Living; The Rage of Paris; Tailspin; Young Fugitives; You Can't Take It with You; The Higgins Family; Orphans of the Street. 1939 Made for Each Other; My Wife's Relatives; Should Husbands Work?; The Covered Trailer; Money to Burn; Exile Express; Death of a Champion; The Story of Alexander Graham Bell; Juarez; Gone with the Wind; The Hunchback of Notre Dame. 1940 The Story of Dr. Ehrlich's Magic Bullet; Granny Get Your Gun; Too Many Husbands; Grandpa Goes to Town; Earl of Puddlestone; Lucky Partners; I Want a Divorce; All This and Heaven Too; Foreign Correspondent. 1941 That Uncertain Feeling; I Wanted Wings; Hurricane Smith; The Bride Came C.O.D.; One Foot in Heaven; Kings Row. 1942 Son of Fury; Larceny, Inc.; Ten Gentlemen from West Point; Tales of Manhattan. 1943 Headin' for God's Country; We've Never Been Licked; Riding High; The Ox-Bow Incident; Shantytown; The Amazing Mrs. Holliday; Gangway for Tomorrow; Government Girl; Jack London; Princess O'Rourke. 1944 Meet Me in St. Louis; The Impatient Years; The Thin Man Goes Home; Kismet. 1945 Music for Millions; The Enchanted Forest; Too Young to Know; This Love of Ours; She Wouldn't Say Yes. 1947 Courage of Lassie; Blue Sierra; A Boy, a Girl and a Dog; Faithful in My Fashion; Three Wise Fools; GI War Brides; Lady Luck; Claudia and David; Pardon My Past; Adventure. 1947 The Farmer's Daughter; That Hagen Girl; Stallion Road; Keeper of the Bees; Sport of Kings; The Fabulous Texan; The Bachelor and the Bobbysoxer. 1948 Three Daring Daughters; The Man from Texas; For the Love of Mary; That Lady in Ermine; The Decision of Christopher Blake. 1949 Down to the Sea in Ships; Little Women; Tell It to the Judge; That Forsyte Woman. 1950 Riding High (and 1943 version).

DAVENPORT, HARRY J.
Born: 1858. Died: Feb. 20, 1949, Glendale, Calif.(complication of diseases). Screen actor. Married to screen actress Milla Davenport (dec. 1936).

DAVENPORT, KATE
Born: 1896. Died: Dec. 7, 1954, Hollywood, Calif. Screen actress. Daughter of screen actor Harry Davenport (dec. 1949). See Harry Davenport for family information.

Appeared in: 1921 Sentimental Tommy.

DAVENPORT, KENNETH
Born: 1879. Died: Nov. 10, 1941, Los Angeles, Calif.(heart attack). Screen and stage actor.

Appeared in: 1921 The Nut.

DAVENPORT, MILLA
Born: 1871, Sicily, Italy. Died: May 17, 1936, Los Angeles, Calif. Screen, stage, vaudeville, and burlesque actress. Married to screen actor Harry J. Davenport (dec. 1949). Entered films approx. 1911.

Appeared in: 1919 Daddy Long Legs; In Mizzoura. 1920 Stronger Than Death; The Forbidden Woman; You Never Can Tell. 1921 Rip Van Winkle; Why Trust Your Husband; The Girl from God's Country; The Man from Lost River; Patsy. 1922 The Worldly Madonna; The Man Who Waited. 1923 The Christian; Dulcy. 1924 Daddies; The Red Lily; The Shooting of Dan McGrew; The Right of the Strongest. 1925 Wild West (serial); Dangerous Innocence. 1926 Crossed Signals; The Road to Glory. 1927 Hey!

Hey! Cowboy; King of Kings. 1928 Sins of the Fathers; The Danger Rider. 1929 The Girl from Woolworth's. 1932 Merrily We Go To Hell. 1934 In Love with Life. 1935 The Wedding Night; Here Comes Cookie.

DAVID, WILLIAM
Born: 1882, Vicksburg, Miss. Died: Apr. 10, 1965, East Islip, N.Y. Screen and stage actor.

Appeared in: 1922 Outcast; Received Payment. 1923 Fog Bound.

DAVIDSON, BING
Born: 1939. Died: July 18, 1965, San Francisco, Calif.(fall from hotel window). Screen actor. Also in films as James B. Davidson.

DAVIDSON, DORE
Born: 1850. Died: Mar. 7, 1930 (complication of diseases). Screen, stage actor, stage producer, and playwright.

Appeared in: 1920 Humoresque. 1922 The Rosary; Your Best Friend; The Good Provider; The Light in the Dark. 1923 Broadway Broke; The Purple Highway; Success; None So Blind. 1924 The Great White Way; Welcome Stranger; Grit. 1925 The Royal Girl. 1927 The Music Master; East Side, West Side.

DAVIDSON, J. B. See Bing Davidson

DAVIDSON, MAX
Born: 1875, Berlin, Germany. Died: Sept. 4, 1950, Woodland Hills, Calif. Screen and stage actor. Entered films in 1913.

Appeared in: 1915 Love in Armor. 1916 The Village Vampire (working title The Great Leap). 1921 The Idle Rich; No Woman Knows. 1922 Remembrance; The Right That Failed; Second Hand Rose. 1923 The Extra Girl; The Rendezvous; The Ghost Patrol; The Darling of New York. 1924 Fool's Highway; Untamed Youth; Hold Your Breath. 1925 Old Clothes; Hogan's Alley; The Rag Man; Justice of the Far North. 1926 Into Her Kingdom; Sunshine of Paradise Alley; The Johnstown Flood. 1927 Hotel Imperial; Pleasure Before Business; Cheaters; Hats Off (short); The Call of the Cuckoo (short). 1929 So This Is College; Hurdy Gurdy (short); shorts prior to 1930 Pass the Gravy; Dumb Daddies; Blow by Blow; Should Women Drive. 1931 Oh! Oh! Cleopatra (short). 1932 Docks of San Francisco; Daring Danger. 1933 The Cohens and the Kellys in Trouble; Hokus Focus (short); The World Gone Wrong. 1936 Roamin' Wild. 1937 The Girl Said No. 1940 No Census No Feeling (short). 1942 The Great Commandment. 1965 Laurel and Hardy's Laughing 20's (documentary).

DAVIDSON, WILLIAM B.
Born: June 16, 1888, Dobbs Ferry, N.Y. Died: Sept. 28, 1947, Santa Monica, Calif.(following an operation). Screen and stage actor. Entered films with Vitagraph in 1914.

Appeared in: 1917 White Raven; The Call of Her People; Modern Cinderella. 1921 Nobody; Conceit; The Girl from Nowhere. 1922 Destiny's Isle. 1923 Salomy Jane; Adam and Eve. 1924 The Storm Daughter. 1925 Hearts and Spurs; Ports of Call; Women and Gold; Recompense. 1927 The Cradle Snatchers; The Lash (short); Gentleman of Paris; The Last Trail; Love Makes 'Em Wild. 1928 Sharp Tools (short); Good Morning, Judge; The Gaucho. 1929 Queen of the Night Clubs; Ain't It the Truth (short); The Carnation Kid; Woman Trap; Painted Faces. 1930 Sunny; A Man from Wyoming; Hell's Angels; Playboy of Paris; Captain Applejack; The Silver Horde; Hook, Line and Sinker; Oh, For a Man!; The Costello Case; Men Are Like That; For the Defense; How I Play Golf; The Feathered Serpent; Blaze O'Glory; Scarlet Face; Letters (short). 1931 No Limit; The Secret Call; Vice Squad; Graft. 1932 The Menace; The 13th Guest; Her Mad Night; Guilty or Not Guilty; Sky Devils; Scarface. 1932 Guilty as Hell; The Animal Kingdom. 1933 Dangerously Yours; Hello, Everybody!; The Intruder; I'm No Angel; Sitting Pretty; Meet the Baron; Lady Killer; Torch Singer; Billion Dollar Scandal. 1934 The Big Shakedown; Housewife; Circus Clown; Friends of Mr. Sweeney; Dragon Murder Case; The Lemon Drop Kid; St. Louis Kid; Massacre; Fog over Frisco; Laughing Boy; The Secret Bride. 1935 Sweet Music; Bordertown; Devil Dogs of the Air; A Night at the Ritz; Oil for the Lamps of China; Special Agent; Dangerous; Go into Your Dance; In Caliente; The Crusades; Woman Wanted; Show Them No Mercy; Bright Lights. 1936 Road Gang; The Singing Kid; Murder by an Aristocrat; The Big Noise; Earthworm Tractors; Gold Diggers of 1937; Mind Your Own Business. 1937 Easy Living; Behind the Mike; Marked Woman; Midnight Court; Ever Since Eve; Marry the Girl; Sergeant Murphy; Hollywood Hotel; Let Them Live; The Road Back; The Affairs of Cappy Ricks; Paradise Isle; Something to Sing About; It Happened in Hollywood. 1938 The Jury's Secret; Cocoanut Grove; Mr. Doddle Kicks Off; Blockade; Cowboy from Brooklyn; Illegal Traffic; On Trial; Indianapolis Speedway; Private Detective; Hidden Power; Each Dawn I Die; Smashing the Money Ring; The Honeymoon's Over; They Made Me a Criminal; On the Record; Dust Be My Destiny; Honeymoon in Bali. 1940 Tin Pan Alley; Three Cheers for the Irish; Florian; Lillian Russell; Half a Sinner; My Love Came Back; The Girl in 313; Sailor's Lady; Maryland; Hired Wife; Seven Sinners; A Night at Earl Carroll's; Sandy Gets Her Man; My Little Chicadee. 1941 San Francisco Docks; In the Navy; The Lady from Cheyenne; Thieves Fall Out; Hold That Ghost; Highway West; Three Sons O' Guns; Keep 'Em Flying; Sun Valley Serenade. 1942 In This Our Life; Juke Girl; The Magnificent Dope; Over My Dead Body; The Male Animal; Larceny, Inc; Affairs of Jimmy Valentine; Careful, Soft Shoulders. 1943 Mission to Moscow; Calaboose; Truck Busters; Murder on the Waterfront; The Good Fellows; Slick Chick. 1944 Greenwich Village; The Imposter; In Society; Shine on Harvest Moon; Song of Nevada. 1945 Blonde Ransom; The Man Who Walked Alone; Tell It to the Judge; Circumstantial Evidence; See My Lawyer. 1946 The Cat Creeps; Ding Dong Williams; The Plainsman and the Lady; The Notorious Lone Wolf. 1947 Dick Tracey's Dilemma; That's My Man; That Hagen Girl; My Wild Irish Rose; Farmer's Daughter.

DAVIDT, MICHAEL
Born: 1877. Died: Mar. 15, 1944, Hollywood, Calif. Screen actor.

DAVIES, BETTY ANN
Born: Dec. 24, 1910, London, England. Died: May 14, 1955, Manchester, England.(following appendectomy). Screen and stage actress. Entered films in 1934.

Appeared in: 1934 Chick. 1935 Tropical Trouble. 1938 Mountains of Mourne. 1940 Kipps. 1941 Death at a Broadcast; I Bet. 1948 Escape. 1949 It Always Rains on Sunday; The History of Mr. Polly; One Woman's Story. 1950 Sanitarium; The Blue Lamp. 1951 The Woman with No Name; Trio. 1952 Cosh Boy (aka The Slasher, U.S. 1953). 1953 Tonight at 8:30 (aka Fumed Oak); Outcast of the Island; Grand National Night. 1954 Blackout. 1955 Alias John Preston; Wicked Wife; The Belles of St. Trinian's. Other British films: Joy Ride; Play up the Band; She Knew What She Wanted; Radio Lover; Youthful Folly; Merry Comes to Town; Under a Cloud; Silver Top; The Passionate Friends; Meet Me Tonight; Murder by Proxy; To the Public Danger.

DAVIES, DAVID
Died: May 1920, Chicago, Ill. Screen, stage, and vaudeville actor.

DAVIES, GEORGE
Born: 1891. Died: Mar. 1960, Edinburgh, Scotland. Screen, stage, radio, and television actor.

DAVIES, MARION
Born: Jan. 3, 1898. Died: Sept. 22, 1961, Hollywood, Calif.(cancer). Screen actress.

Appeared in: 1917 Runaway Romany (film debut). 1918 Cecilia of the Pink Roses. 1919 The Cinema Murder; The Dark Star; The Belle of New York. 1920 The Restless Sex; April Folly. 1921 Enchantment; Buried Treasure. 1922 The Bride's Play; Beauty Worth; When Knighthood Was in Flower; The Young Diana; Daughter of Luxury. 1923 Little Old New York; Adam and Eva. 1924 Janice Meredith; Yolanda. 1925 Lights of Old Broadway; Zander the Great. 1926 Beverly of Graustark. 1927 Quality Street; The Fair Co-ed; The Red Mill; Tillie the Toiler. 1928 The Cardboard Lover; The Patsy; Show People. 1929 The Hollywood Revue of 1929; Marianne; The Gay Nineties. 1930 Not So Dumb; The Floradora Girl. 1931 It's a Wise Child; Five and Ten; Bachelor Father. 1932 Polly of the Circus; Blondie of the Follies; The Dark Horse. 1933 Peg O' My Heart. 1934 Operator Thirteen; Going Hollywood. 1935 Page Miss Glory. 1936 Hearts Divided; Cain and Mabel. 1937 Ever Since Eve. 1964 Big Parade of Comedy (documentary). 1967 Show People (reissue of 1928 film).

DAVIS, ANNA
Born: 1890. Died: May 5, 1945, Hollywood, Calif. Screen actress.

DAVIS, BOB "ALABAM"
Born: 1910. Died: Sept. 22, 1971, Hollywood, Calif.(heart attack). Screen actor and sometime stand-in for Franchot Tone.

DAVIS, BOYD
Born: June 19, 1885, Santa Rosa, Calif. Died: Jan. 25, 1963, Hollywood, Calif. Screen and stage actor. Entered films in 1925.

Appeared in: 1932 Smiling Faces. 1941 You'll Never Get Rich; Two Latins from Manhattan. 1942 Hello, Annapolis; Harvard Here I Come; Star Spangled Rhythm. 1943 The Ghost Ship. 1945 Captain Eddie; Youth on Trial; Col. Effingham's Raid. 1946 Terror by Night; The Unknown. 1947 The Senator Was Indiscreet. 1948 The Wreck of the Hesperus; A Foreign Affair. 1949 Samson and Delilah; Ma and Pa Kettle. 1950 Girl's School. 1952 At Sword's Point.

DAVIS, DANNY
Born: 1929. Died: Feb. 10, 1970, N.Y.(struck by a car). Screen and stage actor, comedian/comedy writer.

DAVIS, EDWARDS
Born: 1871, Santa Clara, Calif. Died: May 16, 1936, Hollywood, Calif. Screen, stage, and vaudeville actor.

Appeared in: 1920 The Invisible Ray (serial). 1921 The Right Way; Shams of Society; The Plaything of Broadway; The Silver Lining. 1924 Tainted Money; The Sea Hawk; Good Bad Boy; Hook and Ladder; The Woman on the Jury; On the Stroke of Three; The Only Woman; The Price She Paid; Stolen Secrets. 1925 The Best People; Flattery; Joanna; The Splendid Road; Part Time Wife; Not So Long Ago; Her Husband's Secret; The Charmer; Contraband; A Fool and His Money; My Neighbor's Wife. 1926 The Amateur Gentleman; High Steppers; Tramp, Tramp, Tramp; Butterflies in the Rain. 1927 A Hero on Horseback; The Life of Riley; A Reno Divorce; Face Value; Marriage; Singed; Winds of the Pampas. 1928 The Sporting Age; Happiness Ahead; The Power of the Press. 1929 A Song of Kentucky. 1930 The Love Racket; Love in the Rough; Madam Satan; Madonna of the Streets. 1933 Hello, Everybody!.

DAVIS, GEORGE
Born: 1889, Amsterdam, Holland. Died: Apr. 19, 1965, Woodland Hills, Calif.(cancer). Screen and vaudeville actor. Appeared in U.S., French, German, English and Italian films.

Appeared in: 1924 Sherlock, Jr.; He Who Gets Slapped. 1926 Into Her Kingdom. 1927 The Magic Flame. 1928 The Circus; The Wagon Show; The Awakening; the following shorts: Going Places; Leaping Luck; Who's Lyin'. 1929 4 Devils; Broadway; The Kiss; Devil May Care. 1930 Men of the North; A Lady to Love; Not So Dumb; Die Sennsucht Jeder Frau; Le Petit Cafe; Le Spectre Vert (The Unholy Night). 1931 Parlor, Bedroom and Bath; Laugh and Get Rich; Strangers May Kiss; Private Lives. 1932 Arsene Lupin; The Man from Yesterday; Broken Lullaby; Love Me Tonight; Under-cover Man. 1934 The Black Cat. 1935 The Good Fairy. 1937 History Is Made at Night; I Met Him in Paris; Thin Ice; Charlie Chan at Monte Carlo; Conquest; You Can't Have Everything. 1938 The Baroness and the Butler; Always Goodbye; Hunted Men. 1939 Topper Takes a Trip; Bulldog Drummond's Bride; Everything Happens at Night; Charlie Chan in City in Darkness. 1940 Chad Hanna. 1945 See My Lawyer. 1951 On the Riviera; Secrets of Monte Carlo; The Lady Says No. 1953 Gentlemen Prefer Blondes. Other foreign films: Louis the Fox (English, French, German and Italian versions); The Little Cafe and The Queen's Husband (both French versions).

DAVIS, HARRY
Born: 1874. Died: Apr. 4, 1929, New York, N.Y.(heart disease). Screen and stage actor.

Appeared in: 1925 Old Clothes. 1926 Devil's Dice; Unknown Treasures; Whispering Canyon; Dangerous Friends; Lightning Reporter. 1927 The Blood Ship; Burning Gold. 1928 Runaway Girls; Crashing Through.

DAVIS, JAMES GUNNIS
Born: 1874, Sunderland, England. Died: Mar. 23, 1937, Los Angeles, Calif. Screen and stage actor. Entered films in 1912.

Appeared in: 1921 A Certain Rich Man; The Secret of the Hills. 1922 The Gray Dawn. 1923 The Midnight Alarm; Refuge; Jealous Husbands; Chastity. 1924 The Trouble Shooter. 1925 Lord Jim; Winds of Chance; His Lucky Horseshoe. 1927 Twinkle Toes; The Notorious Lady. 1928 Lilac Time. 1930 Headin' North. 1931 A Melon Drama (short); East Lynne; Charlie Chan Carries On. 1934 One More River. 1935 The Bride of Frankenstein.

DAVIS, JOAN
Born: June 29, 1907, St. Paul, Minn. Died: May 23, 1961, Palm Springs, Calif.(heart attack). Screen, radio, and television actress. Mother of screen actress Beverly Wills (dec. 1963).

Appeared in: 1935 Way Up Thar (short); Millions in the Air.
1937 The Holy Terror; On the Avenue; Time Out for Romance;
The Great Hospital Mystery; Life Begins in College; Wake Up
and Live; Thin Ice; Sing and Be Happy; Angel's Holiday; Love
and Hisses; Nancy Steele Is Missing; You Can't Have Everything.
1938 Sally, Irene and Mary; Josette; My Lucky Star; Just around
the Corner; Hold That Co-Ed. 1939 Day-Time Wife; Tail Spin;
Too Busy to Work. 1940 Free, Blonde and 21; Manhattan Heartbeat; Sailor's Lady. 1941 Sun Valley Serenade; For Beauty's
Sake; Two Latins from Manhattan; Hold That Ghost. 1942 Sweetheart of the Fleet; Yokel Boy. 1943 He's My Guy; Two Senoritas
from Chicago; Around the World. 1944 Beautiful but Broke; Kansas City Kitty; Show Business. 1945 She Gets Her Man; George
White's Scandals. 1946 She Wrote the Book. 1948 If You Knew
Susie. 1949 Make Mine Laughs. 1950 Love That Brute; Traveling Saleswoman. 1951 The Groom Wore Spurs. 1952 Harem
Girl. 1963 The Sound of Laughter (documentary).

DAVIS, MILDRED
Born: Jan. 1, 1900, Brooklyn, N.Y. Died: Aug. 18, 1969, Santa
Monica, Calif.(heart attack). Screen actress. Married to screen
actor Harold Lloyd (dec. 1971) and mother of screen actor Harold
Lloyd, Jr. (dec. 1971).

Appeared in: 1916 Marriage a la Carte. 1919 His Royal Slyness;
From Hand to Mouth. 1921 Among Those Present; Sailor-Made
Man. 1922 Grandma's Boy; Doctor Jack. 1923 Condemned; Safety
Last; Temporary Marriage. 1927 Too Many Crooks.

DAVIS, OWEN JR.
Born: 1907, New York, N.Y. Died: May 21, 1949, Long Island
South, N.Y.(drowned—accident). Screen, stage, and radio actor.
Son of writer Owen Davis.

Appeared in: 1929 They Had to See Paris. 1930 Good Intentions;
All Quiet on the Western Front. 1936 Bunker Bean; Murder on the
Bridle Path; Special Investigator; Grand Jury; The Plot Thickens.
1937 It Could Happen to You; The Woman I Love. 1938 Touch-
down Army. 1939 These Glamour Girls. 1940 Thou Shalt Not
Kill; Knute Rockne—All American; Henry Goes to Arizona.

DAW, EVELYN
Born: 1912, Geddes, S.D. Died: Nov. 29, 1970, San Diego, Calif.
Screen, stage, and opera actress.

Appeared in: 1937 Something to Sing About. 1938 Panamint's Bad
Man.

DAWN, ISABEL
Born: Oct. 20, 1905, Evansville, Ind. Died: June 29, 1966, Woodland Hills, Calif.(pulmonary infection). Screen, stage actress,
and screenwriter.

DAWSON, DORICE (Doris Dawson)
Born: Apr. 16, 1909, Goldfield, Nev. Died: Nov. 14, 1950, Riverside, Calif. Screen actress.

Appeared in: 1927 Gold from Weepah; The Arizona Night. 1928
Kentucky Courage; The Little Shepherd of Kingdom Come; The
Little Wildcat; Do Your Duty; Heart Trouble. 1929 Naughty Baby;
Hot Stuff; Children of the Ritz; Broadway Scandals; His Captive
Woman. 1935 The Silver Streak. 1950 Sunset Boulevard.

DAWSON, FRANK
Born: 1870. Died: Oct. 11, 1953, Hollywood, Calif. Screen actor.

Appeared in: 1934 Double Door. 1935 My Marriage; The Last
Outpost; Broadway Hostess. 1936 Private Number; Ladies in
Love. 1937 A Day at the Races. 1938 Four Men and a Prayer;
I'll Give a Million. 1939 Adventures of Sherlock Holmes; Beau
Geste; Cafe Society. 1940 The Blue Bird. 1941 Scotland Yard.
1942 They All Kissed the Bride. 1943 What a Woman; Crash
Dive. 1944 Bermuda Mystery; Woman in the Window. 1945 Wil-
son.

DAY, DULCIE
Born: 1911. Died: Dec. 1, 1954, Woodland Hills, Calif. Screen
actress and singer.

DAY, EDITH
Born: 1896, Minneapolis, Minn. Died: May 1, 1971, London, England. Screen and stage actress.

Appeared in: 1918 The Grain of Dust; A Romance of the Air.

DAY, MARIE L.
Born: 1855, Troy, N.Y. Died: Nov. 7, 1939, Cleveland, Ohio
(pneumonia). Screen and stage actress.

Appeared in: 1922 Timothy's Quest. 1923 The Ragged Edge.
1938 Mother Cary's Chickens.

DAZE, MERCEDES
Born: 1892. Died: Mar. 18, 1945, Los Angeles, Calif. Screen
and stage actress.

DEAGAN, CHARLES
Born: 1880. Died: July 19, 1932, New York, N.Y.(heart failure).
Screen, vaudeville, and radio actor.

Appeared in vaudeville as part of "Charles and Madeline Dunbar"
team.

DE ALBA, CARLOS
Born: 1925. Died: Oct. 1960, Mexico City, Mexico (after brain
surgery). Mexican screen and television actor.

DEAN, BARNEY
Born: 1904, Russia. Died: Aug. 31, 1954, Santa Monica, Calif.
(cancer). Screen, vaudeville actor, and screenwriter. Appeared
in vaudeville with Sid Tarradasch as the "Dean Bros."

Appeared in: 1938 Thanks for the Memory.

DEAN, FABIAN (Gibilaro)
Born: 1930. Died: Jan. 15, 1971, Hollywood, Calif. Screen and
television actor.

Appeared in: 1962 Fallguy. 1967 The Ride to Hangman's Tree.
1969 The Computer Wore Tennis Shoes.

DEAN, JAMES (James Byron)
Born: Feb. 8, 1931, Marion, Ind. Died: Sept. 30, 1955 near Paso
Robles, Calif.(auto accident). Screen, stage, and television actor.

Appeared in: 1951 Fixed Bayonets; Sailor Beware. 1952 Has Anybody Seen My Girl. 1954 East of Eden. 1955 Rebel Without a
Cause. 1956 Giant.

DEAN, JULIA
Born: May 12, 1878, St. Paul, Minn. Died: Oct. 17, 1952, Hollywood, Calif. Screen and stage actress.

Appeared in: 1915 How Molly Made Good; Judge Not. 1916 Matri-
mony. 1917 Rasputin; The Black Monk. 1942 The Cat People.
1944 Experiment Perilous; The Curse of the Cat People. 1946
Do You Love Me?; O.S.S. 1947 Magic Town; Nightmare Alley;
Out of the Blue. 1948 The Emperor Waltz. 1949 Easy Living;
Rimfire; Red Desert; Ringside; Treasure of Monte Cristo; Grand
Canyon. 1950 Girl's School. 1951 People Will Talk; Elopement.
1952 You for Me.

DEAN, MAN MOUNTAIN (Frank S. Leavitt)
Born: 1890. Died: May 29, 1953, Norcross, Ga. Screen actor and
wrestler.

Appeared in: 1933 Private Life of Henry VIII (doubled for Charles
Laughton). 1935 Reckless; We're in the Money. 1937 Three Legionaires; Big City. 1938 The Gladiator. 1960 Surprise Package.

DEAN, MAY
Died: Sept. 1, 1937, N.Y. Screen and stage actress.

Appeared in: 1923 Riders of the Range. 1935 Mississippi.

DEAN, NELSON (Nelson S. Whipple)
Born: 1882. Died: Dec. 19, 1923, Detroit, Mich.(apoplexy).
Screen and stage actor.

DEAN, RALPH
Born: 1868. Died: Sept. 15, 1923, New York, N.Y. Screen, stage
actor, and film director.

DEAN, ROSE
Born: 1892. Died: Oct. 6, 1952, Hollywood, Calif. Screen actress.

DEAN, RUBY
Born: 1887. Died: Feb. 23, 1935, Cleveland, Ohio. Screen and
vaudeville actress.

DE ANDA, AGUSTIN
Born: 1935, Mexico. Died: May 29, 1960, Mexico (murdered).
Mexican screen actor. Son of screen actor/producer Raoul de
Anda. Entered films in 1952 with his father in a series of "Charro
Negro" pictures.

DEARLY, MAX
Born: 1874, France. Died: June 2, 1943, Paris, France. Screen and stage actor.

Appeared in: 1934 Madame Bovary. 1935 Le Dernier Milliardaire. 1936 Les Miserables. 1940 Claudine. 1941 They Met on Skis. 1942 Nine Bachelors.

DEASE, BOBBY (Robert C. McCahan)
Born: 1899. Died: Feb. 22, 1958, Reading, Pa. Screen actor.

Appeared in: 1939 Some Like It Hot. 1940 Dancing Co-Ed.

DE AUBRY, DIANE (Diane Rubini)
Born: 1890, Sault St. Marie, Mich. Died: May 24, 1969, Los Angeles, Calif.(heart attack). Screen, stage, and vaudeville actress. Entered films with Biograph and World Films.

DE BECKER, HAROLD
Born: 1889. Died: July 23, 1947, Hollywood, Calif. Screen, stage, and radio actor. Brother of screen actress Marie de Becker (dec. 1946).

Appeared in: 1942 Sherlock Holmes and the Secret Weapon; Eagle Squadron; This above All.

DE BECKER, MARIE
Born: 1881. Died: Mar. 23, 1946, Hollywood, Calif.(heart attack). Screen and stage actress. Sister of screen actor Harold De Becker (dec. 1947).

Appeared in: 1942 Mrs. Miniver; Random Harvest. 1944 None But the Lonely Heart. 1946 Devotion.

DE BRAY, HAROLD
Born: 1874. Died: Oct. 31, 1932, Los Angeles, Calif.(heart disease). Screen actor.

DE BRAY, HENRI
Born: 1889. Died: Apr. 5, 1965, Nottingham, England. Screen, stage, television actor, and dancer.

DE BRAY, YVONNE
Born: 1889, France. Died: Feb. 1, 1954, Paris, France (heart ailment). Screen and stage actress.

Appeared in: 1944 The Eternal Return. 1949 Gigi; Les Parents Terribles (aka The Storm Within, U.S. 1950). 1950 Olivia. 1952 Nous Sommes Tous Les Assassins. 1954 Caroline Cherie.

DE BRULIER, NIGEL
Born: 1878, England. Died: 1948. Screen actor.

Appeared in: 1915 Ghost. 1916 Intolerance. 1919 The Mystery of 13 (serial); Sahara. 1920 Virgin of Stamboul. 1921 Cold Steel; The Devil Within; The Four Horsemen of the Apocalypse; His Pajama Girl; That Something; The Three Musketeers; Without Benefit of Clergy. 1922 A Doll's House; Omar the Tentmaker. 1923 Salome; The Eleventh Hour; The Hunchback of Notre Dame; Rupert of Hentzau; St. Elmo. 1924 A Boy of Flanders; Mademoiselle Midnight; Three Weeks; Wild Oranges. 1925 The Ancient Mariner; A Regular Fellow. 1926 Ben-Hur; Don Juan; The Greater Glory; Yellow Fingers. 1927 The Beloved Rogue; Patent Leather Kid; Soft Cushions; Surrender; Wings. 1928 The Divine Sinner; The Gaucho; Loves of an Actress; Me, Gangster; Two Lovers. 1929 Noah's Ark; The Iron Mask; Thru Different Eyes; The Wheel of Life. 1930 Golden Dawn; The Green Goddess; Moby Dick; Redemption. 1931 Song of India. 1932 Miss Pinkerton; Rasputin and the Empress. 1933 I'm No Angel; Life in the Raw. 1935 Charlie Chan in Egypt; The Three Musketeers (and 1921 version). 1936 Half Angel; Down to the Sea; Mary of Scotland; The Garden of Allah; The White Legion. 1937 The Californians. 1939 The Hound of the Baskervilles; Mutiny in the Big House; The Man in the Iron Mask; The Mad Empress. 1940 Viva Cisco Kid; One Million B.C.; Heaven With a Barbed Wire Fence. 1941 For Beauty's Sake; Adventure of Captain Marvel (serial). 1943 Tonight We Raid Calais.

DEBUCOURT, JEAN
Born: 1894, France. Died: Mar. 1958, Paris, France. Screen and stage actor.

Appeared in: 1922 Le Petit Chose. 1933 Mistigri. 1934 L'Agonie des Aigles. 1936 Le Prince Jean. 1937 Mayerling; The Life and Loves of Beethoven. 1940 Mayerling to Sarajevo. 1943 Douce. 1946 Le Diable au Corps. 1948 The Eagle Has Two Heads; The Idiot; Not Guilty. 1949 Man to Men; Monsieur Vincent. 1949 Woman Who Dared; Devil in the Flesh; Love Story; Occupe-Toi D'Amelie. 1950 Tainted. 1951 The Secret of Mayerling; Nana (U.S. 1957). 1953 Justice Is Done; Fanfan La Tulipe (Fanfan the Tulip); Seven

Deadly Sins. 1954 Desperate Decision; The Golden Coach. 1956 The Doctors; La Lumiere d'en Face (The Light across Street). 1958 Inspector Maigret. 1959 Miracle of Saint Therese.

DE CASALIS, JEANNE (De Casalis de Pury)
Born: May 22, 1897, Basutoland, South Africa. Died: Aug. 19, 1966, London, England. Screen, stage, radio actress, and playwright.

Appeared in: 1932 Nine Till Six. 1933 Radio Parade; The Feather Bed; Mixed Doubles. 1934 Nell Gwyn. 1941 Cottage to Let. 1942 Those Kids from Town. 1944 Medal for the General. 1945 They Met in the Dark. 1946 This Man is Mine. 1948 Woman Hater. Other British films: The Arcadians (silent); Turners of Prospect Road; Twenty Questions Murder Mystery.

DE CASTREJON, BLANCE
Born: 1916, Mexico. Died: Dec. 26, 1969, Mexico City, Mexico. Mexican and U.S. screen and stage actress.

Appeared in: 1963 Signs of the Zodiac.

DECKER, JOHN
Born: 1895, San Francisco, Calif. Died: June 7, 1947, Hollywood, Calif. Artist/painter employed to do stand-in painting for actors playing role of artists. Was a pal of numerous famous Hollywood film personalities.

DE COPPETT, THEODOSIA. See Theda Bara

DE CORDOBA, PEDRO
Born: Sept. 28, 1881, New York, N.Y. Died: Sept. 17, 1950, Sunland, Calif.(heart attack). Screen, stage, and radio actor.

Appeared in: 1915 Carmen. 1916 Maria Rosa. 1917 Runaway Romany. 1919 The New Moon. 1920 The World and His Wife; Barbary Sheep. 1921 The Inner Chamber. 1922 The Young Diana; Just a Song at Twilight; When Knighthood Was in Flower. 1923 The Enemies of Women; The Purple Highway. 1924 The Bandolero; The Desert Sheik. 1925 The New Commandment. 1933 Through the Centuries. 1935 The Crusades; Captain Blood; Professional Soldier. 1936 Ramona; Rose of the Rancho; Moonlight Murder; Trouble for Two; The Devil Doll; His Brother's Wife; Anthony Adverse; The Garden of Allah. 1937 Maid of Salem; Damaged Goods; Girl Loves Boy. 1938 International Settlement; Keep Smiling; Heart of the North; Storm Over Bengal. 1939 Chasing Danger; The Light That Failed; Juarez; Winner Take All; Man of Conquest; Law of the Pampas; Range War; Charlie Chan in City in Darkness. 1940 My Favorite Wife; South of Pago-Pago; Earthbound; The Mark of Zorro; Devil's Island; Before I Hang; The Sea Hawk; The Ghost Breakers. 1941 Romance of the Rio Grande; Phantom Submarine; Blood and Sand; The Corsican Brothers; Aloma of the South Seas. 1942 Saboteur; The Son of Fury; Shut My Big Mouth. 1943 Tarzan Triumphs; The Song of Bernadette; Background to Danger; For Whom the Bell Tolls. 1944 The Falcon in Mexico; Uncertain Glory; Tahiti Nights. 1945 Club Havana; Keys of the Kingdom; San Antonio; In Old New Mexico; Picture of Dorian Gray. 1946 Cuban Pete; A Scandal in Paris; Swamp Fire. 1947 The Beast with Five Fingers; Carnival in Costa Rica; Robin Hood of Monterey. 1948 Time of Your Life; Mexican Hayride. 1949 Omoo Omoo the Shark God; The Daring Caballero; Daughter of the West; Samson and Delilah. 1950 Comanche Territory; The Lawless; When the Redskins Rode. 1951 Crisis.

DE COSTA, MORRIS (Morris Miller).
Born: 1890. Died: Oct. 6, 1957, Phoenixville, Pa. Screen and vaudeville actor, and xylophonist. Appeared in silents.

DECTREAUX, EVELYN
Born: 1902. Died: Aug. 28, 1952, Santa Monica, Calif. Screen actress.

DEE, FREDDIE (Freddie De Piano)
Born: 1924. Died: Apr. 27, 1958, Hollywood, Calif. Screen actor.

DEELEY, J. BERNARD "BEN"
Born: 1878. Died: Sept. 23, 1924, Hollywood, Calif.(pneumonia). Screen, stage, and vaudeville actor. Divorced from screen actress Barbara La Marr (dec. 1925) with whom he had appeared in vaudeville.

Appeared in: 1919 Victory. 1921 Kazan; Molly O; Sowing the Wind. 1922 The Crossroads of New York. 1923 The Acquittal; Lights Out. 1924 Passions Pathway; Winner Take All; The Cycle Rider. 1925 Never the Twain Shall Meet.

DEERING, JOHN
Born: 1905. Died: Jan. 28, 1959, Hollywood, Calif.(cerebral hemorrhage). Screen, radio, and television actor.

Appeared in: 1932 Forgotten Commandments.

DE FOREST, HAL (Aloysius J. De Sylva)
Born: 1862. Died: Feb. 16, 1938, New York, N.Y.(heart attack). Screen, stage actor, and stage director.

Appeared in one film only: 1916 Daughter of the Gods.

DE GRASSE, JOSEPH
Born: 1873, Bathurst, New Brunswick, Canada. Died: May 25, 1940, Eagle Rock, Calif.(heart attack). Brother of screen actor Sam De Grasse (dec. 1953). Screen, stage actor, screenwriter, screen director, and newspaperman. Entered films in 1910 as an actor.

Appeared in: 1924 So Big. 1928 The Cowboy Kid.

DE GRASSE, SAM
Born: 1875, Bathurst, New Brunswick, Canada. Died: Nov. 29, 1953, Hollywood, Calif.(heart attack). Screen actor. Brother of screen actor/director Joseph De Grasse (dec. 1940). Entered films in 1912.

Appeared in: 1916 Birth of a Nation. 1917 Wild and Wooly. 1919 Sis Hopkins; Blind Husbands. 1920 The Devil's Pass Key. 1921 Courage; A Wife's Awakening; The Cheater Reformed. 1922 Robin Hood; Forsaking All Others. 1923 Circus Days; A Prince of a King; Slippy McGee; The Spoilers; Tiger Rose; The Courtship of Miles Standish; The Dancer of the Nile; In the Palace of the King. 1924 Painted People; The Virgin; Pagan Passions; A Self-Made Failure. 1925 One Year to Live; Sun-Up; Sally, Irene and Mary. 1926 Mike; Love's Blindness; The Black Pirate; Her Second Chance; Broken Hearts of Hollywood; The Eagle of the Sea. 1927 King of Kings; Captain Salvation; The Country Doctor; The Fighting Eagle; The Last Performance; When a Man Loves; The Wreck of the Hesperus. 1928 Dog Law; The Racket; The Man Who Laughs; Honor Bound; Our Dancing Daughters; The Farmer's Daughter. 1929 Silks and Saddles; Last Performance; Wall Street; 1930 Captain of the Guard.

DE KEREKJARTO, DUCI
Born: 1901. Died: Jan. 3, 1962, Hollywood, Calif.(heart attack). Concert violinist and screen actor.

Appeared in prior to 1933: Meto Movietone short. 1951 Rich, Young, and Pretty.

DEKKER, ALBERT
Born: Dec. 20, 1904, Brooklyn, N.Y. Died: May 5, 1968, Hollywood, Calif.("accidental death" per coroner). Screen, stage, and television actor. Served in California Legislature 1944 to 1946 as the Democratic Assemblyman of 57th District.

Appeared in: 1937 The Great Garrick. 1938 Marie Antoinette; The Last Warning; She Married an Artist; The Lone Wolf in Paris; Extortion. 1939 Paris Honeymoon; Never Say Die; Hotel Imperial; The Great Commandment; Beau Geste; The Man in the Iron Mask. 1940 Rangers of Fortune; Seven Sinners; Dr. Cyclops; Strange Cargo. 1941 You're the One; Blonde Inspiration; Reaching for the Sun; Buy Me That Town; Honky Tonk; Among the Living. 1942 The Lady Has Plans; Yokel Boy; The Forest Rangers; Night in New Orleans; Wake Island; Once upon a Honeymoon; Star Spangled Rhythm. 1943 The Woman of the Town; In Old Oklahoma; Buckskin Frontier; The Kansan. 1944 Experiment Perilous; The Hitler Gang (narr.). 1945 Incendiary Blonde; Salome, Where She Danced; Hold That Blonde. 1946 Suspense; The French Key; Two Years before the Mast; The Killers. 1947 California; Slave Girl; The Fabulous Texan; The Pretender; Gentleman's Agreement; Wyoming; Cass Timberlane. 1948 Fury at Furnace Creek; Lulu Belle. 1949 Bride of Vengeance; Tarzan's Magic Fountain; Search for Danger. 1950 Destination Murder; The Kid from Texas; The Furies. 1951 As Young as You Feel. 1952 Wait 'til the Sun Shines, Nellie. 1954 The Silver Chalice. 1955 East of Eden; Kiss Me Deadly; Illegal. 1957 She Devil. 1958 Machete. 1959 The Sound and the Fury; These Thousand Hills; Middle of the Night; The Wonderful Country; Suddenly, Last Summer. 1967 Come Spy with Me. 1968 Ganmora the Invincible. 1969 The Wild Bunch.

DE KOCK, HUBERT
Born: 1863. Died: Nov. 25, 1941, Montrose, Calif. Screen, stage, and vaudeville actor.

DELAMARE, GIL
Born: France. Died: June 1966, near Paris, France. Screen actor and stuntman.

Appeared in: 1955 One Step to Eternity. 1960 Amazing Mr. Callaghan.

DE LA MOTHE, LEON
Born: 1880. Died: June 12, 1943, Woodland Hills, Calif. Screen actor and film director.

Appeared in: 1919 The Red Glove (serial). 1924 The Desert Hawk. 1925 Ridin' Wild; Northern Code. 1926 Desperate Chance; Cyclone Bob. 1928 Trailin' Back; Painted Trail; Trail Riders.

DE LA MOTTE, MARGURIETE
Born: June 22, 1902, Duluth, Minn. Died: Mar. 10, 1950, San Francisco, Calif.(cerebral thrombosis). Screen actress. Entered films in 1919. Married to screen actor John Bowers (dec. 1936).

Appeared in: 1919 Arizona. 1920 Mark of Zorro. 1921 The Three Musketeers; The Nut; Ten Dollar Raise. 1922 The Jilt; Shadows; Shattered Idols; Fools of Fortune. 1923 Desire; The Famous Mrs. Fair; What a Wife Learned; Just Like a Woman; Richard the Lion-Hearted; Scars of Jealousy; A Man of Action; Wandering Daughters. 1924 The Beloved Brute; The Clean Heart; Behold This Woman; When a Man's a Man; Those Who Dare; East of Broadway; In Love with Love; Gerald Cranston's Lady. 1925 The People vs. Nancy Preston; Off the Highway; Cheaper to Marry; Flattery; Daughters Who Pay; Children of the Whirlwind; The Girl Who Wouldn't Work. 1926 The Unknown Soldier; Red Dice; Fifth Avenue; Hearts and Fists; The Last Frontier; Meet the Prince; Pals in Paradise. 1927 Broadway Madness; Held by the Law; Ragtime; The Kid Sister; His Final Extra. 1929 Montmartre Rose; The Iron Mask. 1930 Shadow Ranch. 1934 A Woman's Man. 1942 Reg'lar Fellers.

DE LANDA, JUAN
Born: 1894, Motrico, Spain. Died: Feb. 18, 1968, Mortrico, Spain. Screen and opera actor.

Appeared in: 1935 Se ha Fugado un Preso. 1938 The Penitentiary. 1947 The King's Jester. 1952 Brief Rapture. 1953 Devotion. 1954 Beat the Devil.

DELANEY, CHARLES
Born: Aug. 1892, New York, N.Y. Died: Aug. 31, 1959, Hollywood, Calif. Screen, stage, vaudeville, and television actor.

Appeared in: 1922 Solomon in Society. 1923 The Devil's Partner. 1924 Emblems of Love; Those Who Dance; Barbara Frietchie. 1925 Accused; Sporting Life; Enemies of Youth. 1926 College Days; The Jade Cup; The Night Watch; Flaming Fury; Satan Town; The Sky Pirate; The Silent Power. 1927 The Main Event; Frisco Sally Levy; The Thirteenth Hour; Husband Hunters; Mountains of Manhattan; Lovelorn; The Silent Avenger; The Tired Business Man. 1928 Women Who Dare; The Cohens and the Kellys in Paris; Branded Man; After the Storm; The Air Circus; Home, James; The Show Girl; Stool Pigeon; The Adventurer; Do Your Duty; The River Woman; Outcast Souls. 1929 The Faker; Hard to Get; Girl from Woolworth's; The Clean-Up; Broadway Babies. 1930 The Man Hunter; Lonesome Trail; Kathleen Mavoureen; Around the Corner; Millie; Air Police; Playthings of Hollywood; Hell Bent for Frisco. 1932 Big Timber; Hearts of Humanity; Midnight Morals. 1933 Officer 13; Elmer the Great; Corruption; The Important Witness. 1934 Fighting Trooper; Big Time or Bust. 1935 What Price Crime?; Captured in Chinatown; Trails of the Wild. 1936 The Millionaire Kid; Below the Deadline. 1937 Bank Alarm; The Gold Racket. 1945 Blonde Ransom. 1950 Kansas Raiders. 1952 The Half-Breed. 1953 Winning of the West. 1959 Running Target. 1960 The Beatniks.

DELANEY, JERE A.
Born: 1888. Died: Jan. 2, 1954, Forest Hills, N.Y. Screen and stage actor.

Appeared in: 1928 Lights of New York. 1929 Rubeville. 1954 On the Waterfront.

DELANEY, MAUREEN
Born: 1888, Kilkenny, Ireland. Died: Mar. 27, 1961, London, England. Screen and stage actress.

Appeared in: 1935 His Family Tree. 1947 Odd Man Out. 1948 Captain Boycott. 1949 Under Capricorn; Saints and Sinners. 1954 The Holly and the Ivy. 1956 Jacqueline. 1957 The Rising of the Moon; The Scamp; The Story of Esther Costello; The Third Key. 1959 The Doctor's Dilemma; Tread Softly, Stranger.

DE LANGE, EDDIE
Born: 1904, Long Island City, N.Y. Died: July 16, 1949, Hollywood, Calif. Orchestra leader, screen actor, stuntman, and composer. Stunted for Reginald Denny whom he resembled.

Appeared in: 1930 Half Shot at Sunrise.

DELANO, GWEN
Born: 1882. Died: Nov. 20, 1954, Hollywood, Calif. Screen, stage, radio, and television actress. Appeared in silents.

DE LA VEGA, ALFREDO GOMEZ
Born: 1897, Mexico. Died: Jan. 15, 1958, Mexico City, Mexico. Screen and stage actor.

DE LAY, MEL
Born: 1900. Died: May 3, 1947, Saugus, Calif.(heart attack—collapsed on location). Screen actor and film director. Entered films as an actor in 1923.

DE LEON, ARISTIDES
Born: 1904. Died: July 23, 1954, New York, N.Y. Screen, stage, radio, and television actor.

DE LIGUORO, RINA
Born: 1893, Italy. Died: Apr. 1966, Rome, Italy. Screen actress.

Appeared in: 1923 Messalina. 1928 The Mystic Mirror. 1929 Loves of Casanova. 1930 Romance. 1963 The Leopard.

DELINSKY, VICTOR A.
Born: 1883. Died: May 8, 1951, Hollywood, Calif.(injuries from auto accident). Screen actor and stand-in for Adolphe Menjou.

Appeared in: 1927 King of Kings.

DELL, DOROTHY (Dorothy Goff)
Born: Jan. 30, 1915, Hattiesburg, Miss. Died: June 8, 1934, Pasadena, Calif.(auto accident). Screen and stage actress.

Appeared in: 1934 Wharf Angel; Little Miss Marker; Shoot the Works.

DEL MAR, CLAIRE (Clare Eloise Mohr)
Born: 1901. Died: Jan. 10, 1959, Carmel, Calif.(murdered). Screen actress.

Appeared in: 1921 The Four Horsemen of the Apocalypse. 1927 The Jazz Singer. 1928 The Wedding March.

DELMAR, EDDIE (Robert Frandsen)
Born: 1886. Died: Mar. 2, 1944, Hollywood, Calif. Screen actor.

DEL VALLE, LUIS COTTO. See Luis Cotto del Valle.

DE MARCO, TONY
Born: 1898, Buffalo, N.Y. Died: Nov. 14, 1965, Palm Beach, Fla. (cerebral hemorrhage). Screen actor and dancer.

Appeared in: 1938 The Shining Hour. 1943 The Gang's All Here. 1944 Greenwich Village.

DEMAREST, RUBIN
Born: 1886. Died: Sept. 20, 1962, Hollywood, Calif.(cerebral hemorrhage). Screen and television actor. Brother of screen actor William Demarest.

Appeared in: 1939 The Gracie Allen Murder Case. 1941 A Girl, a Guy and a Gob.

DE MARNEY, TERRENCE
Born: 1909. Died: May 25, 1971, London, England (accidental subway fall). Screen, stage, radio, television actor, and stage director. Brother of screen actor Derrick DeMarney.

Appeared in: 1936 The Mystery of the Marie Celeste. 1938 I Killed the Count. 1946 Dual Alibi. 1949 No Way Back; Uneasy Terms. 1955 The Silver Chalice; Target Zero; Desert Sands. 1956 23 Paces to Baker Street. 1957 Pharaoh's Curse; My Gun Is Quick. 1959 The Wreck of the Mary Deare. 1960 The Secret of the Purple Reef. 1961 On theDouble. 1962 Confessions of an Opium Eater. 1965 Die, Monster, Die. 1966 Death Is a Woman. 1968 The Strange Affair; Separation. 1969 All Neat in Black Stockings.

DE MILLE, CECIL B.
Born: Aug. 12, 1881, Ashfield, Mass. Died: Jan. 21, 1959, Los Angeles, Calif.(heart disease). Film producer, director, screen, stage, radio actor, and playwright. Brother of film director/producer William C. De Mille (dec. 1955).

Appeared in: 1925 Hollywood. 1930 Free and Easy. 1931 The Squaw Man. 1942 Star Spangled Rhythm. 1947 Variety Girl. 1950 Sunset Boulevard.

DE MILLE, WILLIAM C.
Born: July 25, 1878, Washington, D.C. Died: Mar. 8, 1955, Playa Del Rey, Calif. Playwright, screenwriter, film producer, director, and one-time screen actor. Brother of film director/producer Cecil B. De Mille (dec. 1959).

DEMPSEY, CLIFFORD
Born: 1865. Died: Sept. 4, 1938, Atlantic Highlands, N.J. Screen and stage actor.

Appeared in: 1929 Salute; The Ghost Talks; Knights Out (short); Happy Days; The Valiant. 1930 Only Saps Work; Soup to Nuts. 1931 Too Many Cooks; Everything's Rosie. 1932 Guilty as Hell.

DEMPSEY, THOMAS
Born: 1862. Died: Oct. 7, 1947, Hollywood, Calif. Screen, stage, and vaudeville actor. Entered films during early 1920s and played for a number of years in Sennett comedies.

Appeared in: 1927 The Bush Leaguer. 1934 Elmer and Elsie.

DENNIS, RUSSELL
Born: 1916. Died: May 29, 1964, N.Y.(heart attack). Screen actor and physician.

Appeared in: 1951 Bright Victory.

DENNY, REGINALD (Reginald Leigh Daymore)
Born: Nov. 20, 1891, Richmond, Surrey, England. Died: June 16, 1967, Surrey, England.(stroke). Screen, stage actor, and screenwriter. Entered films in England in 1914. Starred in 24 "Leather Pusher" series (shorts) from 1922 to 1924.

Appeared in: 1920 49 East. 1921 Footlights; Disraeli; The Iron Trail; Tropical Love; Paying the Piper; The Prince of Possession. 1922 The Kentucky Derby; Sherlock Holmes, plus the following "Leather Pusher" shorts: Let's Go; Round Two; Payment Through the Nose; A Fool and His Money; The Taming of the Shrew; Whipsawed, plus the following "New Leather Pusher" series shorts: Young King Cole; He Raised Kane; Chichasha Bone Crusher; When Kane Met Abel. 1923 The Abysmal Brute; The Thrill Chaser, plus the following "New Leather Pusher" series shorts: Strike Father, Strike Son; Joan of Newark; The Wandering Two; The Widower's Mite; Don Coyote; Something for Nothing; Columbia the Gem and the Ocean; Barnaby's Grudge; That Kid from Madrid; He Loops to Conquer. 1924 Sporting Youth; Captain Fearless; The Fast Worker; The Reckless Age; Oh, Doctor!, plus the following "New Leather Pusher" series shorts: Girls Will be Girls; A Tough Tenderfoot; Swing Bad the Sailor; Big Boy Blue. 1925 Where Was I?; California Straight Ahead; I'll Show You the Town; Skinner's Dress Suit. 1926 Take It from Me; Rolling Home; What Happened to Jones?. 1927 The Cheerful Fraud; On Your Toes; Out All Night; Fast and Furious; Jaws of Steel. 1928 The Night Bird; That's My Daddy; Good Morning, Judge. 1929 Clear the Decks; His Lucky Day; Red Hot Speed. 1930 Madam Satan; What a Man!; Embarrassing Moments; Those Three French Girls; Oh, for a Man!; One Hysterical Night; A Lady's Morals. 1931 Private Lives; Kiki; Parlor, Bedroom and Bath; Stepping Out. 1932 Strange Justice. 1933 The Iron Master; The Barbarian; Only Yesterday; The Big Bluff. 1934 Fog; Of Human Bondage; The Richest Girl in the World; The World Moves On; Dancing Man; One More River; We're Rich Again; The Lost Patrol; The Little Minister. 1935 Lottery Lover; No More Ladies; Vagabond Lady; Anna Karenina; Here's to Romance; Midnight Phantom; Remember Last Night?; The Lady in Scarlet. 1936 The Rest Cure; The Preview Murder Mystery; Romeo and Juliet; It Couldn't Have Happened; Two in a Crowd; More Than a Secretary; Penthouse Party. 1937 Join the Marines; Bulldog Drummond Escapes; The Great Gambini; Let's Get Married; Bulldog Drummond Comes Back; Bulldog Drummond's Revenge; Beg, Borrow or Steal; Women of Glamour; Jungle Menace (serial). 1938 Bulldog Drummond's Peril; Bulldog Drummond in Africa; Blockade; Four Men and a Prayer; Everybody's Baby. 1939 Bulldog Drummond's Bride; Bulldog Drummond's Secret Police; Arrest Bulldog Drummond. 1940 Spring Parade; Seven Sinners; Rebecca. 1941 One Night in Lisbon; Appointment for Love; International Squadron. 1942 Eyes in the Night; Sherlock Holmes and the Voice of Terror; Thunder Birds; Over My Dead Body; Captains of the Clouds. 1943 The Ghost Ship; The Crime Doctor's Strangest Case. 1944 Song of the Open Road. 1945 Love Letters. 1946 Tangier; The Locket. 1947 Escape Me Never; My Favorite Brunette; The Macomber Affair; Christmas Eve; The Secret Life of Walter Mitty. 1948 Mr. Blandings Builds

His Dream House. 1950 The Iroquois Trail. 1953 Abbott and Costello Meet Dr. Jekyll and Mr. Hyde; Fort Vengeance; Hindu (aka Sadaka U.S. 1955). 1954 Bengal Brigade; The Snow Creature; World for Ransom. 1955 Escape to Burma. 1956 Around the World in 80 Days. 1957 Street of Sinners. 1959 Fort Vengeance. 1964 Advance to the Rear. 1965 Cat Ballou. 1966 Assault on a Queen; Batman.

DENT, VERNON
Born: 1900, San Jose, Calif. Died: Nov. 5, 1963, Hollywood, Calif. Screen actor and screenwriter. Appeared in early Mann comedies, Mack Sennett and Educational comedies.

Appeared in: 1921 Hail the Woman. 1923 The Extra Girl; Soul of the Beast. 1925 Remember When?. 1926 A Sea Dog's Tale; Flirty Four-Flushers. 1927 His First Flame. 1928 Golf Widows. 1929 Ticklish Business; The Talkies. 1930 Johnny's Week End; Midnight Daddies. 1931 Passport to Paradise; Fainting Lover; Educational shorts. 1932 Million Dollar Legs; The Big Flash; The Iceman's Ball (short); Hollywood Handicap (short). 1933 Hooks and Jabs; On Ice. 1934 You're Telling Me, plus the following shorts: Circus Hoodoo; Petting Preferred. 1936 Slippery Silks (short). 1937 The Shadow, plus the following shorts: Dizzy Doctors; Back to the Woods. 1938 Thanks for the Memory; Reformatory, plus the following shorts: See My Lawyer; Wee Wee Monsieur; Tassels in the Air; Mutts to You. 1939 Beasts of Berlin, plus the following shorts: Three Little Sew and Sews; A-Ducking They Did Go; Yes, We Have No Bonanza. 1940 the following shorts: From Nurse to Worse; Nutty but Nice; No Census, No Feeling; How High Is Up. 1941 the following shorts: In the Sweet Pie and Pie; So Long, Mr. Chumps; Dutiful but Dumb; I'll Never Heil Again; An Ache in Every Stake. 1942 House of Errors, plus the following shorts: Loco Boy Makes Good; Cactus Makes Perfect; Even As I.O.U. 1943 Blitz on the Fritz (short); Back from the Front (short). 1944 the following shorts: Crash Goes the Hash; Busy Buddies; Idle Roomers; No Dough, Boys. 1945 Rockin' in the Rockies; See My Lawyer, plus the following shorts: Three Pests in a Mess; Booby Dupes; Idiots Deluxe. 1946 A Bird in the Hand (short); Beer Barrel Polecats. 1947 Half-Wits Holiday (short); Out West (short). 1948 the following shorts: Squareheads of the Round Table; Heavenly Daze; Mummy's Dummies. 1949 Make Believe Ballroom; Malice in the Palace (short). 1950 Punchy Cowpunchers (short). 1951 Bonanza Town, plus the following shorts: Three Arabian Nuts; The Pest Man Wins; Scrambled Brains. 1952 Gents in a Jam (short). 1953 Booty and the Best (short). 1955 Bedlam in Paradise (short). 1956 Hot Stuff (short). 1957 Gun A-Poppin' (short). 1960 When Comedy Was King (documentary). 1963 Thirty Years of Fun (documentary).

DENTON, CRAHAN
Born: 1914. Died: Dec. 4, 1966, Piedmont, Calif.(heart attack). Screen, stage, and television actor.

Appeared in: 1959 Great St. Louis Robbery. 1961 The Parent Trap; The Young One. 1962 To Kill a Mockingbird; Birdman of Alcatraz. 1963 Captain Newman, M.D.; Hud. 1965 Bus Riley's Back in Town.

DEPP, HARRY
Born: 1886. Died: Mar. 31, 1957, Hollywood, Calif. Screen actor.

Appeared in: 1922 Quincy Adams Sawyer. 1923 His Last Race; Nobody's Money. 1924 Inez from Hollywood. 1926 When the Wife's Away. 1937 Bill Cracks Down; Swing It, Professor. 1938 Pals of the Saddle. 1941 Blues in the Night. 1942 Priorities on Parade; The Magnificent Dope.

DEPPE, HANS
Born: 1898, Berlin, Germany. Died: Sept. 23, 1969, West Berlin, Germany (diabetes). Screen, stage, television actor, and film director.

Appeared in: 1933 Ein Tuer geht Auf. 1934 Der Stern von Valencia. 1935 Der Schimmelreiter (The Rider of the White Horse). 1952 The Berliner.

DE PUTTI, LYA
Born: 1901, Budapest, Hungary. Died: Nov. 27, 1931, New York, N.Y.(pneumonia after operation). Screen, stage, and vaudeville actor. Entered films in 1921 and appeared in German, British, and U.S. films.

Appeared in: 1921 The Hidden Tombstone. 1925 The Phantom; Variety. 1926 God Gave Me Twenty Cents; The Sorrow's of Satan; The Prince of Tempters. 1927 The Heart Thief. 1928 Midnight Rose; Jealousy: Buck Privates; The Scarlet Lady. 1929 The Informer.

DE RAVENNE, RAYMOND
Born: 1904. Died: Oct. 14, 1950, Hollywood, Calif.(heart attack). Screen actor.

DERBA, MIMI (Hermina Perez de Leon).
Born: 1894, Mexico. Died: July 1953, Mexico City, Mexico (lung trouble). Screen and stage actress.

Appeared in: 1935 Martin Garatuza. 1936 So Juana Ines de La Cruz. 1938 Abnegacion. 1945 Flor Sylvestre.

DE ROCHE, CHARLES
Born: 1880, France. Died: Feb. 2, 1952, Paris, France. Screen, stage actor, and stage producer.

Appeared in: 1923 Hollywood; The Law of the Lawless; The Ten Commandments; The Cheat; The Marriage Maker. 1924 Love and Glory; Shadows of Paris; The White Moth. 1925 Madame Sans Gene.

DE ROSAS, ENRIQUE
Died: Jan. 20, 1948, near Buenos Aires, Argentina. Argentine screen, stage, circus, and radio actor.

Appeared in: 1937 Sandflow.

DERWENT, CLARENCE
Born: 1884, London, England. Died: Aug. 6, 1959, New York, N.Y. Screen, stage actor, and film director.

Appeared in: 1931 The Night Angel. 1939 Stanley and Livingston; The Story of Vernon and Irene Castle. 1940 British Intelligence. 1958 Uncle Vanya (stage and film versions).

DES AUTELS, VAN
Born: 1911. Died: Sept. 2, 1968, Los Angeles, Calif. Screen, radio, and television actor.

Appeared in: 1953 The Robe; How to Marry a Millionaire. 1955 Inside Detroit; The Crooked Web.

DE SEGUROLA, ANDREAS (Count Andreas Perello de Segurola)
Born: 1875, Madrid, Spain. Died: Jan. 23, 1953, Barcelona, Spain. Screen, stage, and opera actor.

Appeared in: 1927 The Love of Sunya. 1928 The Red Dance; Glorious Betsy; My Man; Bringing up Father; The Cardboard Lover. 1929 Behind Closed Doors; Careers; General Crack. 1930 Mamba; The Man from Blankleys; Son O' My Heart. 1933 Cascarrabia; Su Eltimo Amor; El Principe Gondolero. 1934 La Ciudad de Carton; Granaderos del Amore; Dos Mas Uno Dos; One Night of Love; We're Rich Again. 1935 Public Opinion.

DESFIS, ANGELO
Born: 1888. Died: July 28, 1950, Hollywood, Calif. Screen and stage actor. Appeared in silents and talkies.

DE SILVA, FRANK
Born: 1890, India. Died: Mar. 20, 1968, New York, N.Y. Screen, stage, and television actor.

DESLYS, GABY
Born: Marseilles, France. Died: Feb. 11, 1920, Paris, France. Screen and stage actor.

Appeared in: 1915 Her Triumph. 1918 Infatuation.

DESMOND, ETHEL
Born: 1874. Died: Feb. 5, 1949, San Bernardino, Calif. Screen, stage, and vaudeville actress.

DESMOND, LUCILLE
Born: 1894. Died: Nov. 20, 1936, Los Angeles, Calif. Screen actress.

DESMOND, WILLIAM
Born: 1878, Dublin, Ireland. Died: Nov. 3, 1949, Los Angeles, Calif.(heart attack). Screen, stage, and vaudeville actor. Married to screen actress Mary McIvor (dec. 1941).

Appeared in: 1915 Peggy (film debut). 1916 Not My Sister; The Captive God. 1917 Paws of the Bear. 1918 An Honest Man; The Sudden Gentleman; Society for Sale; The Pretender; Deuce Duncan. 1920 The Prince and Betty; The Man from Make Believe; Twin Beds. 1921 The Child Thou Gavest Me; Dangerous Toys; Women Men Love; Don't Leave Your Husband; The Parish Priest; Fighting Mad. 1922 Perils of the Yukon; Night Life in Hollywood. 1923 The Extra Girl; McGuire of the Mounted; Shadows of the North; Beast of Paradise (serial); The Phantom Fortune (serial); Around the World in 18 Days (serial). 1924 The Breathless Moment; The Riddle Rider (serial); Big Timber; The Sunset Trail; Measure of a Man. 1925 Barriers of the Law; Duped; Outwitted; Straight Through; The Meddler; Ace of Spades (serial); Blood and Steel; The Burning Trail; Ridin' Pretty. 1926 The Winking Idol (serial); Strings of Steel (serial). 1927 The Return of the Riddle Rider (serial); Red Clay; Tongues of Scandal. 1928 The Vanishing Rider (serial); The Mystery Rider (serial); The Devil's Trade-Mark. 1929 No Defense. 1931 Hell Bent for Frisco. 1932 Scarlet Week-End; Heroes of the West (serial). 1933 Flying Fury; Rustlers Round-Up; Laughing at Life; The Phantom of the Air (serial); Mr. Broadway; Fargo Express; Strawberry Roan. 1935 Rustler's of Red Gap; Roaring West (serial); Courage of the North; Powder-smoke Range. 1936 Arizona Days; Nevada; Song of the Saddle; Cavalry; Hollywood Boulevard; Song of the Gringo; Headin' for the Rio Grande. 1940 A Little Bit of Heaven. 1945 The Naughty Nineties.

DESMONDE, JERRY
Born: July 20, 1908, Middlesbrough, England. Died: Feb. 11, 1967, London, England. Screen, stage, and television actor.

Appeared in: 1946 London Town. 1948 Cardboard Cavalier. 1954 Malta Story. 1955 Trouble in Store. 1956 The Angel Who Pawned Her Harp. 1957 A King in New York. 1959 Follow a Star. 1963 Carry on Regardless; Stolen Hours; A Stitch in Time. 1965 The Early Bird. Other British films: Alf's Baby; Man of the Moment; Up in the World; Rainsbottom Rides Again; The Beauty Jungle.

DE STAFINI, HELEN
Born: 1880. Died: Jan. 8, 1938, Hollywood, Calif. Screen and stage actress. Married to screen actor Joseph de Stafini.

DESTE, LULI (Luli Kollsman and Luli Hohenberg)
Born: 1902, Vienna, Austria. Died: July 7, 1951, New York, N.Y. Screen and stage actress, and author.

Appeared in: 1937 Thunder over the City; Thank You, Madame. 1938 She Married an Artist. 1940 Ski Patrol; South to Karanga. 1941 The Case of the Black Parrot.

DE TELLIER, MARIETTE
Born: 1891, France. Died: Dec. 11, 1957, Cincinnati, Ohio. Screen actress. Appeared in silents.

DEUTSCH, ERNST
Born: 1891, Germany. Died: Mar. 22, 1969, Berlin, Germany. Screen and stage actor.

Appeared in: 1939 Nurse Edith Cavell. 1940 The Man I Married. 1941 So Ends Our Night. 1950 The Third Man.

DE VALDEZ, CARLOS J.
Born: Mar. 19, 1894, Arica, Peru. Died: Oct. 30, 1939, Encino, Calif. Screen and stage actor.

Appeared in: 1934 Little Man, What Now?. 1935 Bonnie Scotland; Robin Hood of Eldorado. 1936 Men in Exile; Littlest Diplomat. 1937 Conquest; Drums of Destiny; Lancer Spy. 1938 Blockade; Romance in the Dark; Girl from Mexico; Suez; The Girl and the Gambler; The Llano Kid. 1940 British Intelligence.

DEVAULL, WILLIAM P.
Born: 1871. Died: June 4, 1945, Hollywood, Calif. Screen and vaudeville actor.

Appeared in: 1915 Birth of a Nation. 1921 Hole in the Wall. 1922 White Shoulders. 1923 Around the World in 18 Days (serial); Kentucky Days; Tea with a Kick. 1925 Lights of Old Broadway. 1927 In the First Degree.

DEVERE, ARTHUR
Born: 1883. Died: Sept. 23, 1961, Brussels, Belgium. Screen, stage, and vaudeville actor.

Appeared in: 1936 La Kermesse Heroique. 1939 The End of a Day. 1945 Goupi Mains-Rouges (It Happened at the Inn). Other French films: Un de la Legion; Midnight Circuit.

DEVERE, FRANCESCA "FRISCO"
Born: 1891. Died: Sept. 11, 1952, Port Townsend, Wash. (heart attack). Screen and stage actress. Appeared in Keystone comedies and Mack Sennett Productions.

DEVEREAUX, JACK
Born: 1882. Died: Jan. 19, 1958, New York, N.Y. Screen and stage actor. Married to stage actress Louise Drew (dec. 1954). Father of stage actor John Drew Devereaux.

Appeared in: 1922 Superstition.

DE VERNON, FRANK
Born: 1845. Died: Oct. 19, 1923, New York, N.Y. Screen and stage actor.

Appeared in: 1921 The Black Panther's Cub; The Man Worth While. 1923 Under the Red Robe. 1924 Cain and Mabel; Yolande.

DEVOE, BERT
Born: 1884. Died: Jan. 17, 1930, Steelton, Pa. (cancer). Screen and vaudeville actor. Toured in vaudeville with Lew Worth. Appeared in early Mack Sennett comedies.

Appeared in: 1924 Shackles of Fear.

DEWEY, EARL S.
Born: June 2, 1881, Manhattan, Kans. Died: Feb. 5, 1950, Hollywood, Calif. Screen, stage, and vaudeville actor. Married to Billie Rogers with whom he appeared in vaudeville. Appeared in "Pathe Folly" comedies, first series.

Appeared in: 1929 Fancy That (short); So This Is Marriage (short). 1940 Howards of Virginia; Arizona. 1942 I Married an Angel; This Gun for Hire; Between Us Girls. 1943 Shadow of a Doubt. 1944 Adventures of Mark Twain. 1945 Rogues Gallery; Captain Eddie; George White's Scandals; Blonde Ransom. 1950 All the King's Men.

DEWEY, ELMER
Born: 1884. Died: Oct. 28, 1954, Hollywood, Calif. (heart attack). Screen actor. Also appeared under name of Don Danilo.

Appeared in: 1921 Bring Him In; Girls Don't Gamble. 1922 Taking Chances. 1926 Shadows of Chinatown; The Escape. 1927 Million Dollar Mystery.

DEWHURST, WILLIAM
Born: 1888. Died: Oct. 26, 1937, London, England (heart failure). Screen and stage actor.

Appeared in: 1937 A Woman Alone; Victoria the Great; Non-Stop New York; Dark Journey; Bulldog Drummond at Bay; Dinner at the Ritz. 1938 Sailing Along. 1939 Sabotage. 1940 21 Days Together.

DEXTER, ELLIOTT
Born: 1870, Galveston, Tex. Died: June 23, 1941, Amityville, N.Y. Screen and vaudeville actor. Divorced from screen actress Marie Doro (dec. 1956).

Appeared in: 1915 The Masqueraders. 1916 The Heart of Nora Flynn; The Lash; Diplomacy. 1917 A Romance of the Redwoods; Castles for Two; The Rise of Jennie Cushing. 1918 Woman and Wife. 1919 Don't Change Your Husband; For Better, For Worse; The Squaw Man; Maggie Pepper; We Can't Have Everything. 1920 Behold My Wife; Something to Think About. 1921 The Witching Hour; Forever; The Affairs of Anatol; Don't Tell Everything. 1922 Grand Larceny; Enter Madam; The Hands of Nara. 1923 Adam's Rib; Mary of the Movies; Only 38; Souls for Sale; Broadway Gold; The Common Law; Flaming Youth; An Old Sweetheart of Mine. 1924 The Fast Set; Age of Innocence; By Divine Right; For Woman's Favor; The Triflers; The Spitfire. 1925 Capital Punishment; The Verdict; Wasted Lives. 1926 Stella Maris.

DICKEY, PAUL
Born: May 12, 1885, Chicago, Ill. Died: Jan. 8, 1933, N.Y. (heart disease). Screen, stage actor, and screenwriter, playwright, and stage director.

Appeared in: 1922 Robin Hood.

DICKINSON, HOMER
Born: 1890. Died: June 6, 1959, Hollywood, Calif. Screen, stage, and vaudeville actor. Appeared in vaudeville from 1914 to 1926 with his wife, Florence Tempest, and her sister in an act billed as "Sunshine & Tempest."

Appeared in: 1928 Broadway's Smart Musical Comedy Star (short).

DICKSON, GLORIA (Thais Dickerson)
Born: Aug. 13, 1916, Pocatello, Idaho. Died: Apr. 10, 1945, Hollywood, Calif. (asphyxiation from fire). Screen and stage actress.

Appeared in: 1936 They Won't Forget (film debut). 1938 Gold Diggers in Paris; Secrets of an Actress; Racket Busters; Heart of the North. 1939 Private Detective; No Place to Go; Cowboy Quarterback; On Your Toes; Waterfront; They Made Me a Criminal. 1940 I Want a Divorce; King of the Lumberjacks; Tear Gas Squad; This Thing Called Love. 1941 The Big Boss; Mercy Island. 1942 Affairs of Jimmy Valentine. 1943 The

Crime Doctor's Strangest Case; Power of the Press; Lady of Burlesque. 1944 Crime Doctor; Rationing.

DICKSON, LYDIA
Born: 1878. Died: Apr. 2, 1928, Hollywood, Calif. Screen and stage comedienne/actress.

Appeared in: 1928 Don't Marry; Square Crooks.

DIDWAY, ERNEST
Born: 1872. Died: Jan. 3, 1939, Los Angeles, Calif. Screen and stage actor. Entered films approx. 1932.

DIEHL, KARL LUDWIG
Born: 1897, Germany. Died: Mar. 1958, Oberbayern, West Germany. Screen and stage actor.

Appeared in: 1931 Rosenmontag; Liebeswalzer. 1932 Koenigin der Unterwelt; Zirkus Leben. 1933 Ein Maedel der Strasse. 1934 Die Freundin Eines Grossen Mannes; Schuss in Morgengrauen; Ien Mann Will Nach Deutschland. 1935 Aschermittwoch (Ash Wednesday). 1936 Spy 77; Der Hoehere Befehl; Ein Liebesroman im Hause Hasburg; Die Ganze Welt Dreht Sich um Liebe. 1937 Ein Idealer Gatte; Episode. 1938 Seine Tochter 1st der Peter (His Daughter Is Peter); Es geht um mein Leben (My Life Is at Stake). 1939 Der Schritt vom Wege (The False Step); Ein Hoffnungsloser Fall. 1957 Des Teufeis General (The Devil's General). 1958 The Story of Vickie.

DIESEL, GUSTAV
Born: 1900, Austria. Died: Mar. 20, 1948, Vienna, Austria. Screen and stage actor.

Appeared in: 1929 That Murder in Berlin; Die Drein um Edith. 1930 Die Weisse Holle von Piz Palu (The White Hell of Pitz Palu); Menschen hinter Gettern. 1931 The Living Corpse; Mother Love; Comrades of 1918. 1932 Leutnant Warst Du Einst bei den Husaren; Teilnehmer Antwortet Nicht. 1934 Roman Einer Nacht. 1935 Alles um Eine Frau. 1937 Gilgi Eine Von Uns. 1938 Der Tiger von Eschnapur (The Indian Tomb). 1939 Die Gruene Hoelle (The Green Hell); Die Wiesse Majestat (The White Majesty); Amore sulle Alpi. 1940 Schatten der Vergangeheit (Shadows of the Past).

DIGGES, DUDLEY
Born: 1879, Dublin, Ireland. Died: Oct. 24, 1947, New York, N.Y.(stroke). Screen, stage actor and screen dialogue director.

Appeared in: 1929 Condemned. 1930 Outward Bound. 1931 Upper Underworld; The Maltese Falcon; The Ruling Voice; Alexander Hamilton; Devotion; Honorable Mr. Wong. 1932 The Hatchet Man; The Strange Case of Clara Deane; Roar of the Dragon; The First Year; Tess of the Storm Country. 1933 The King's Vacation; The Mayor of Hell; Silk Express; The Narrow Corner; Emperor Jones; Before Dawn; The Invisible Man. 1934 Fury of the Jungle; Caravan; The World Moves On; Massacre; What Every Woman Knows. 1935 I Am a Thief; A Notorious Gentleman; Mutiny on the Bounty; China Seas; The Bishop Misbehaves. 1936 Three Live Ghosts; The Voice of Bugle Ann; The Unguarded Hour; The General Died at Dawn; Valiant Is the Word for Carrie. 1937 Love Is News. 1939 The Light That Failed. 1940 The Fight for Life; Raffles. 1942 Son of Fury. 1946 The Searching Wind.

DI GOLCONDA, LIGIA
Born: 1884. Died: 1942, Mexico City, Mexico. Mexican screen actor.

DILLARD, BURT
Born: 1909. Died: June 19, 1960, Ruidoso Downs, N.M.(heart attack). Screen actor, stuntman, and horse trainer.

Appeared in: 1935 Rainbow Valley.

DILLIGIL, AVNI
Born: 1909, Turkey. Died: June, 1971, Ankara, Turkey (heart attack). Screen and stage actor.

DILLON, DICK (Kenneth Bowstead)
Born: 1896. Died: 1961, Boston, Mass. Screen and vaudeville actor. Known in vaudeville as part of "Dean & Dillon" act with Bob Dean.

Appeared in: 1914 Perils of Pauline (serial).

DILLON, EDWARD "EDDIE"
Born: 1880, N.Y. Died: July 11, 1933, Hollywood, Calif.(heart attack). Screen, stage actor, and film director.

Appeared in: 1908 The Feud and the Turkey; The Reckoning; After Many Years; The Welcome Burglar; The Salvation Army Lass. 1909 As the Bells Rang Out; The Sorrows of the Unfaithful; Examination Day at School; Muggsy Becomes a Hero; The Fugitive; His Sister-in-Law. 1910 Fisher Folks. 1911 The Miser's Heart;

Sunshine through the Dark. 1912 The Spirit Awakened. 1913 Love in an Apartment Hotel; An Indian's Loyalty; Judith of Bethulia. 1915 Faithful to the Finish. 1926 The Skyrocket. 1928 Lilac Time. 1929 The Broadway Melody; Hot for Paris. 1930 Caught Short. 1931 Sob Sister. 1932 The Trial of Vivienne Ware; Sherlock Holmes.

DILLON, GEORGE "TIM"
Born: 1888. Died: Oct. 22, 1965, Burbank, Calif. Screen actor.

Appeared in: 1951 The Mudlark.

DILLON, JOHN
Born: 1876. Died: Dec. 29, 1937, Los Angeles, Calif.(pneumonia). Screen and stage actor.

Appeared in: 1921 The Family Closet. 1922 For His Sake. 1924 Stepping Lively; Tiger Thompson. 1925 Midnight Molly. 1928 Bitter Sweets. 1929 In Old Arizona. 1931 The Cisco Kid.

DILLON, JOHN FRANCIS
Born: 1887, New York, N.Y. Died: Apr. 4, 1934, Beverly Hills, Calif.(heart attack). Screen, stage actor, and film director. Married to screen actress Edith Hallor (dec. 1971).

Appeared in: 1921 The Journey's End. 1922 Without Compromise. 1923 Double Dealing. 1926 The Test of Donald Norton. 1927 Smile, Brother, Smile.

DILLON, JOHN WEBB
Born: 1877. Died: Dec. 20, 1949, Hollywood, Calif. Screen and stage actor.

Appeared in: 1916 Romeo and Juliet. 1920 Trailed by Three (serial). 1921 Jane Eyre; The Inner Chamber; The Mountain Woman; Perjury. 1922 Speed (serial); Married People; The Mohican's Daughter. 1923 The Exiles; No Mother to Guide Her. 1924 Rip Roarin' Roberts. 1925 The Air Mail; The Vanishing American; The Devil's Cargo; The Phantom Express. 1926 The Seventh Bandit; House without a Key (serial); Snowed In (serial). 1927 A Bowery Cinderella; Wolf's Clothing. 1928 Dry Martini. 1929 The Black Book (serial). 1930 Girl of the Port; In the Next Room. 1933 The Diamond Trail. 1934 Carolina.

DILLON, MRS. STELLA
Born: 1878. Died: Apr. 28, 1934, Los Angeles, Calif. Screen actress.

DILLON, THOMAS P. "TOM"
Born: 1896. Died: Sept. 15, 1962, Hollywood, Calif. Screen, stage, circus, and vaudeville actor.

Appeared in: 1944 Going My Way; Whistling in Brooklyn; Thin Man Goes Home. 1945 Captain Eddie. 1946 The Virginian; Black Beauty. 1948 My Girl Lisa. 1949 Saints and Sinners. 1950 Woman on the Run. 1956 The Search for Bridey Murphy; The Oklahoma Woman. 1963 Night Tide.

DILSON, JOHN H.
Born: 1893. Died: June 1, 1944, Ventura, Calif. Screen and stage actor.

Appeared in: 1935 Twin Triplets (short); Cheers of the Crowd; Every Night at Eight; The Girl Who Came Back. 1936 The Case of the Velvet Claws. 1939 At the Circus; Lady of the Tropics; When Tomorrow Comes; Women in the Wind; Fixer Dugan; Forgotten Women; Racketeers of the Range; A Woman Is the Judge; The Man with Nine Lives. 1940 Girls under 21. 1941 Father's Son; Man Made Monster; Naval Academy. 1942 They All Kissed the Bride; You Can't Escape Forever. 1943 Lady Bodyguard.

DIMON, MRS. FLORENCE IRENE. See Florence Irene Fitzgerald.

DINEHART, ALAN
Born: Oct. 3, 1889, Missoula, Mont. Died: July 17, 1944, Hollywood, Calif. Screen, stage, vaudeville actor, and playwright.

Appeared in: 1931 Sob Sister; Girls about Town; Good Sport; The Brat; Wicked. 1932 The Trial of Vivienne Ware; Disorderly Conduct; Street of Women; Bachelor's Affairs; Almost Married; Week Ends Only; Penalty of Fame; Silver Dollar; Washington Merry-Go-Round; Rackety Rax; Devil Is Driving; Okay America; Lawyer Man. 1933 Sweepings; As the Devil Commands; Supernatural; Her Bodyguard; The Sin of Nora Moran; A Study in Scarlet; No Marriage Ties; Bureau of Missing Persons; I Have Lived; Dance, Girl, Dance; The World Changes. 1934 Cross Country Cruise; The Crosby Case; The Love Captive; A Very Honorable Guy; Jimmy the Gent; Baby, Take a Bow; Fury of the Jungle; The Cat's Paw. 1935 Dante's Inferno; Lottery Lover; $10 Raise; In Old Kentucky; Redheads on Parade; Thanks a Million; Your Uncle

Dudley; The Pay-Off. 1936 It Had to Happen; Everybody's Old Man; The Country Beyond; Human Cargo; The Crime of Dr. Forbes; Charlie Chan at the Race Track; Star for a Night; King of the Royal Mounted; Reunion; Parole; Born to Dance. 1937 Fifty Roads to Town; King of the Turf; Step Lively, Jeeves!; Woman Wise; Midnight Taxi; This Is My Affair; Dangerously Yours; Danger—Love at Work; Ali Baba Goes to Town; Big Town Girl. 1938 Love on a Budget; Rebecca of Sunnybrook Farm; Up the River; The First Hundred Years. 1939 Hotel for Women; Fast and Loose; House of Fear; Two Bright Boys; Second Fiddle; Everything Happens at Night. 1940 Slightly Honorable. 1942 Girl Trouble. 1943 The Heat's On; Sweet Rosie O'Grady; Fired Wife; What a Woman. 1944 Johnny Doesn't Live Here Anymore; Moon over Las Vegas; The Whistler; Oh, What a Night; Seven Days Ashore; Minstrel Man; A Wave, a Wac and a Marine.

DINGLE, CHARLES W.
Born: Dec. 28, 1887, Wabash, Ind. Died: Jan. 19, 1956, Worchester, Mass. Screen, stage, radio, and television actor.

Appeared in: 1939 One Third of a Nation. 1941 Unholy Partners; The Little Foxes; Johnny Eager. 1942 Calling Dr. Gillespie; Are Husbands Necessary?; Tennessee Johnson; Somewhere I'll Find You; George Washington Slept Here; The Talk of the Town. 1943 Someone to Remember; She's for Me; Edge of Darkness; Lady of Burlesque. 1944 Home in Indiana; National Barn Dance; Practically Yours; The Song of Bernadette; Together Again. 1945 A Medal for Benny; Guest Wife; Here Come the Co-Eds; Three's a Crowd; A Song to Remember. 1946 Cinderella Jones; Sister Kenny; Centennial Summer; Three Wise Fools; Wife of Monte Cristo. 1946 The Beast with Five Fingers; Duel in the Sun. 1947 My Favorite Brunette; Welcome Stranger; The Romance of Rosy Ridge. 1948 If You Knew Susie; State of the Union; A Southern Yankee; The World and His Wife. 1949 Big Jack. 1952 Never Wave at a Wac. 1953 Call Me Madam; President's Lady; Half a Hero. 1955 The Court-Martial of Billy Mitchell.

DIONNE, EMELIE
Born: May 28, 1934, Callander, Ontario, Canada. Died: Aug. 6, 1954 (epileptic seizure). One of Dionne quintuplets. Screen actress. Surviving quintuplets are: Annette Dionne Allard; Yvonne Dionne; Cecile Dionne Langlois.

Appeared in: 1936 Reunion; The Country Doctor; Going on Two (short), Pathe shorts. 1938 Five of a Kind; Quintupland (short).

DIONNE, MARIE
Born: May 28, 1934, Callander, Ontario, Canada. Died: Feb. 27, 1970. One of Dionne quintuplets. Screen actress.

Appeared in: 1936 Reunion; The Country Doctor; Going on Two (short) Pathe shorts. 1938 Five of a Kind; Quintupland (short).

DIX, MAE
Born: 1895, Lake Ann, Mich. Died: Oct. 21, 1958, Los Angeles, Calif.(burns in apartment fire). Screen, stage, burlesque, and vaudeville actress. Entered films as an extra with Biograph in 1913.

DIX, RICHARD (Ernest Carlton Brimmer)
Born: Aug. 8, 1894, St. Paul, Minn. Died: Sept. 20, 1949, Los Angeles, Calif.(heart trouble). Screen and stage actor. Nominated for Academy Award in 1931 for Best Actor in Cimarron.

Appeared in: 1921 The Sin Flood; The Old Nest; All Fair in Love; Not Guilty; The Poverty of Riches; Dangerous Curve Ahead. 1922 Yellow Men and Gold; The Glorious Fool; Bonded Women; Wall Flower; Fools First. 1923 Quicksands; Racing Hearts; The Woman with Four Faces; The Christian; The Call of the Canyon; The Ten Commandments; Souls for Sale; To the Last Man. 1924 Manhattan; Sinners in Heaven; Icebound; Iron Horse; The Stranger; Unguarded Women. 1925 The Vanishing American; Too Many Kisses; The Shock Punch; The Lucky Devil; A Man Must Live; Men and Women; The Lady Who Lied. 1926 Womanhandled; The Quarterback; Let's Get Married; Fascinating Youth; Say It Again. 1927 Paradise for Two; Knock-Out Reilly; Manpower; Shanghai Bound; Quicksands (and 1923 version); The Gay Defender. 1928 Sporting Goods; Easy Come, Easy Go; Warming Up; Moran of the Marines. 1929 Nothing but the Truth; The Wheel of Life; The Love Doctor; Redskin; Seven Keys to Baldpate. 1930 Lovin' the Ladies; Shooting Straight. 1931 Cimarron; The Public Defender; Donovan's Kid; Secret Service. 1932 The Slippery Pearls (short); The Lost Squadron; Roar of the Dragon; Hell's Highway; The Conquerors; Liberty Road. 1933 No Marriage Ties; The Great Jasper; Day of Reckoning; The Aces of Aces. 1934 Stingaree; West of the Pecos; His Greatest Gamble; I Won a Medal. 1935 Trans-Atlantic Tunnel; The Arizonian. 1936 Yellow Dust; Special Investigator; Devil's Squadron. 1937 Once a Hero;

The Devil's Playground; The Devil Is Driving; It Happened in Hollywood. 1938 Blind Alibi; Sky Giant. 1939 Man of Conquest; Twelve Crowded Hours; Here I Am a Stranger. 1940 The Marines Fly High; Men against The Sky; Cherokee Strip. 1941 The Roundup; Badlands of Dakota. 1942 American Empire; Tombstone, the Town Too Tough to Die. 1943 The Iron Road; Buckskin Frontier; Top Man; The Kansan; Eyes of the Underworld; The Ghost Ship. 1944 The Whistler. 1946 The Voice of the Whistler; The Mysterious Intruder; The Secret of the Whistler. 1947 The 13th Hour. 1949 The Fountainhead.

DIXEY, HENRY E.
Born: 1859, Boston, Mass. Died: Feb. 25, 1943, Atlantic City, N.J.(struck by bus). Screen and stage actor. Signed with Universal in 1915.

DIXON, CHARLOTTE L.
Died: 1970, West Palm Beach, Fla. Screen actress.

Appeared in:1915 Birth of a Nation.

DIXON, HENRY
Born: 1871. Died: May 3, 1943, Hollywood, Calif. Screen, vaudeville actor, and burlesque producer.

DIXON, LEE
Born: Jan. 22, 1914, Brooklyn, N.Y. Died: Jan. 8, 1953, New York, N.Y. Screen, stage, and vaudeville actor.

Appeared in: 1936 Gold Diggers of 1937. 1937 Ready, Willing and Able; The Singing Marine; Variety Show. 1947 Angel and the Badman.

DOBBINS, EARL E.
Born: 1911. Died: Feb. 9, 1949, Los Angeles, Calif.(result of knife wound). Screen actor and stuntman.

DOCKSON, EVELYN
Born: 1888. Died: May 20, 1952, Burbank, Calif.(cancer). Screen and vaudeville actress.

Appeared in: 1943 Let's Face It.

DODD, MRS. ELAN E.
Born: 1868. Died: Mar. 12, 1935, Brooklyn, N.Y. Screen actress. Entered films with Vitaphone.

DODD, JIMMIE
Born: 1910, Cincinnati, Ohio. Died: Nov. 10, 1964, Honolulu, Hawaii. Screen, television actor, and songwriter.

Appeared in: 1940 Those Were the Days; Law and Order. 1941 The Richest Man in Town. 1942 Snuffy Smith; Hillbilly Blitzkrieg; Yard Bird; Flying Tigers. 1943 Shadows on the Sage; Riders of the Rio Grande. 1944 Hi, Beautiful!; Moon over Las Vegas; Twilight on the Prairie. 1945 Penthouse Rhythm; The Crimson Canary; China's Little Devils; Men in Her Diary. 1947 Rolling Home; Buck Privates Come Home; The Tender Years; Song of My Heart. 1948 The Noose Hangs High; Daredevils of the Clouds; You Gotta Stay Happy. 1949 Flaming Fury; Post Office Investigator; Incident. 1950 Singing Guns. 1951 Al Jennings of Oklahoma; The Second Woman; G. I. Jane. 1952 The Winning Team; The Lusty Men.

DODD, REV. NEAL
Born: Sept. 6, 1878, Port Madison, Iowa. Died: May 26, 1966, Los Angeles, Calif. Screen actor, film director, and religious advisor. Known as the "Padre of Hollywood." Entered films in 1920.

Appeared in: 1924 The Only Woman. 1926 Lost at Sea. 1932 Merrily We Go to Hell. 1934 It Happened One Night; You Belong to Me. 1939 Mr. Smith Goes to Washington. 1947 The Secret Life of Walter Mitty. 1948 Sorry, Wrong Number. 1951 Here Comes the Groom.

DODDS, CHUCK
Born: 1936. Died: Oct. 1, 1967, Hollywood, Calif.(leukemia). Screen actor and night club singer.

DODDS, JACK
Born: 1927. Died: June 2, 1962, Hollywood, Calif.(cancer). Screen, stage, television actor, and dancer.

Appeared in: 1962 State Fair.

DOLENZ, GEORGE
Born: Jan. 5, 1908, Trieste, Italy. Died: Feb. 8, 1963, Hollywood, Calif.(heart attack). Screen, stage, and television actor.

Appeared in: 1941 The Unexpected Uncle (film debut); Faculty Row. 1943 Fired Wife; The Strange Death of Adolf Hitler; She's for Me; Moonlight in Vermont; Calling Dr. Death; Young Ideas. 1944 In Society; The Climax; Enter Arsene Lupin; Bowery to Broadway. 1945 Song of the Sarong; Easy to Look At. 1946 Idea Girl; A Night in Paradise; Girl on the Spot. 1947 Song of Schererazade. 1950 Vendetta. 1952 My Cousin Rachel. 1953 Thunder Bay; Scared Stiff; Wings of the Hawk. 1954 The Last Time I Saw Paris; Sign of the Pagan. 1955 The Racers; A Bullet for Joey; The Purple Mask. 1957 Sad Sack. 1959 Timbuktu. 1961 Look in Any Window. 1962 The Four Horsemen of the Apocalypse.

DOLLY, JENNY (Janszieka Deutsch)
Born: Oct. 25, 1892, Hungary. Died: June 1, 1941, Hollywood, Calif.(suicide—hanging). Screen, stage, and vaudeville actress. She and her twin sister Rosie Dolly (dec. 1970), were known as the famous dancing "Dolly Sisters." Divorced from screen actor Harry Fox (dec. 1959).

Appeared in: 1918 The Million Dollar Dollies.

DOLLY, LADY
Born: 1876. Died: Sept. 5, 1953, Hollywood, Calif. Screen actress (midget performer). Was also a stand-in for child actors.

DOLLY, ROSIE (Roszicka Deutsch)
Born: Oct. 15, 1892, Hungary. Died: Feb. 1, 1970, New York, N.Y. (heart failure). Screen, stage, and vaudeville actress. She and her twin sister Jenny Dolly (dec. 1941) were known as the famous dancing "Dolly Sisters."

Appeared in: 1918 The Million Dollar Dollies.

DOMINGUEZ, BEATRICE
Died: Mar. 1921, Los Angeles, Calif.(after operation complications). Screen actress.

Appeared in: 1920 The Moon Riders (serial). 1921 The White Horseman (serial); The Fire Cat; The Four Horsemen of the Apocalypse.

DONAHUE, JACK (John J. Donahue)
Born: 1892. Died: Oct. 1, 1930, New York, N.Y.(heart disease). Stage, burlesque, vaudeville actor, stage producer, and playwright.

Appeared in vaudeville with his wife in a team billed "Donahue & Stewart."

DONAT, ROBERT
Born: Mar. 18, 1905, Manchester, England. Died: June 9, 1958, London, England (respiratory ailment, asthma). Screen, stage actor, and film director. Won Academy Award for Best Actor in Goodbye, Mr. Chips (1939).

Appeared in: 1932 Men of Tomorrow (film debut); That Night in London; Cash. 1933 The Private Life of Henry VIII. 1934 The Count of Monte Cristo; For Love or Money. 1935 The 39 Steps. 1936 The Ghost Goes West. 1937 Knight without Armor. 1938 The Citadel. 1939 Goodbye, Mr. Chips. 1942 The Young Mr. Pitt. 1943 The Adventures of Tartu. 1945 Perfect Stranger; Vacation from Marriage. 1947 Captain Boycott. 1950 The Winslow Boy. 1952 The Magic Box. 1955 Lease of Life; The Cure for Love. 1959 Inn of the Sixth Happiness.

DONATH, LUDWIG
Born: 1900, Vienna, Austria. Died: Sept. 29, 1967, New York, N.Y.(leukemia). Screen, stage, and television actor.

Appeared in: 1942 Ellery Queen; Lady from Chungking. 1943 Hangmen Also Die; The Strange Death of Adolf Hitler; Hostages. 1944 The Seventh Cross; The Hitler Gang; Tampico. 1945 The Story of Dr. Wassell; The Master Race; Counter-Attack. 1946 Blondie Knows Best; Gilda; The Jolson Story; The Devil's Mask; Prison Ship; Renegades; Return of Monte Cristo. 1947 Cigarette Girl; Assignment to Treasury. 1948 Sealed Verdict; To the Ends of the Earth. 1949 The Fighting O'Flynn; The Great Sinner; There's a Girl in My Heart; The Lovable Cheat. 1950 The Killer That Stalked New York; Mystery Submarine; Jolson Sings Again. 1951 Journey into Light; Sirocco; The Great Caruso. 1952 My Pal Gus. 1953 Sins of Jezebel; The Veils of Bagdad. 1966 Torn Curtain; Death Trap.

DONER, MAURICE
Born: 1905. Died: Feb. 21, 1971, Hollywood, Calif. Screen, stage, and television actor.

Appeared in: 1949 Flame of Youth. 1952 Assignment—Paris. 1956 Congo Crossing. 1966 Torn Curtain.

DONER, ROSE
Born: 1905. Died: Aug. 15, 1926, New York, N.Y.(following operation for appendicitis). Screen, stage, vaudeville actress, and dancer. Appeared in vaudeville with her brother and sister, Ted and Kitty Doner.

DONLAN, JAMES
Born: 1889. Died: June 7, 1938, Hollywood, Calif.(heart attack). Screen and stage actor.

Appeared in: 1929 Wise Girls; Big News. 1930 Night Work; The Bishop Murder Case; Beau Bandit; Remote Control; Sins of the Children. 1931 Good Bad Girl. 1932 Back Street. 1933 They Just Had to Get Married; College Humor; Design for Living; The Avenger. 1934 A Very Honorable Guy; The Cat's Paw; Now I'll Tell; Hi, Nellie!; Belle of the Nineties. 1935 Under Pressure; The Daring Young Man; The Whole Town's Talking; Traveling Saleslady; The Case of the Curious Bride; We're Only Human. 1936 The Plot Thickens; Crash Donovan; Murder on the Bridle Path. 1937 This Is My Affair; It Happened in Hollywood. 1938 Professor Beware.

DONLIN, MIKE
Born: May 30, 1877, Peoria, Ill. Died: Sept. 2, 1933, Los Angeles, Calif. Screen, stage, vaudeville actor, and baseball player.

Appeared in: 1923 Woman Proof; Railroaded; The Unknown Purple. 1924 Oh, Doctor; Flaming Barriers; Hit and Run; The Trouble Shooter. 1925 Raffles; Fifth Avenue Models; The Unnamed Woman. 1926 The Sea Beast; Her Second Chance; Ella Cinders; The Fighting Marine (serial and feature film). 1927 The General; Slide, Kelly, Slide. 1928 Riley the Cop; Beggars of Life; Warming Up. 1929 Below the Deadline; Thunderbolt; Noisy Neighbors. 1930 Born Reckless; Hot Curves. 1931 Arrowsmith; Iron Man; The Tip Off. 1933 Air Hostess; High Gear.

DONNELLY, JAMES
Born: 1865, Boston, Mass. Died: Apr. 13, 1937, Hollywood, Calif. Screen and stage actor.

Appeared in: 1916 The Snow Cure; Bubbles of Trouble. 1917 She Needed a Doctor. 1921 Black Beauty. 1922 A Girl's Desire.

DONNELLY, LEO
Born: 1878. Died: Aug. 21, 1935, Atlantic City, N.J. Screen, stage, and vaudeville actor.

Appeared in: 1923 Potash and Perlmutter. 1930 Roadhouse Nights; Stepping Out (short); The Music Racket (short).

DONOHUE, JOSEPH
Born: 1884. Died: Oct. 25, 1921, Brooklyn, N.Y. Screen and vaudeville actor.

Appeared in: 1917 Within the Law. 1920 Over the Hill. 1924 $20.00 a Week.

DOOLEY, BILLY
Born: Feb. 8, 1893, Chicago, Ill. Died: Aug. 4, 1938, Hollywood, Calif.(heart attack). Screen, stage, and vaudeville actor. Entered films with Al Christie.

Appeared in: 1926-28 Christie shorts. Other shorts prior to 1933 include: The Dizzy Diver; Happy Heels and early "Goofy Gob" series. 1936 Anything Goes. 1938 Call of the Yukon; The Marines Are Here.

DOOLEY, JOHNNY (John D. Dool)
Born: 1887, Glasgow, Scotland. Died: June 7, 1928, Yonkers, N.Y.(intestinal trouble). Screen, stage, and vaudeville actor.

Appeared in: 1921 Skinning Skinners. 1922 When Knighthood Was in Flower. 1924 Yolanda. 1927 East Side, West Side.

DOONAN, PATRIC
Born: 1927. Died: Mar. 10, 1958, London, England (suicide—gas). Screen and stage actor.

Appeared in: 1948 Once a Jolly Swagman. 1950 The Blue Lamp. 1951 Blackout; Calling Bulldog Drummond; The Lavender Hill Mob. 1952 High Treason; Island Rescue (aka Appointment with Venus); The Man in the White Suit. 1953 Project M-7; Glory at Sea (aka Gift Horse); The Gentle Gunman. 1954 Crest of the Wave; Paratrooper; What Every Woman Wants; Seagulls over Sorrento. 1956 The Cockleshell Heroes. 1957 John and Julie.

DORALDINA
Born: 1888. Died: Feb. 13, 1936, Los Angeles, Calif.(heart attack). Screen actress and stage dancer.

Appeared in: 1918 The Naulahka. 1921 Passion Fruit; Woman Untamed.

DORETY, CHARLES R.
Born: May 20, 1898, San Francisco, Calif. Died: Apr. 2, 1957, Hollywood, Calif. Screen, circus, vaudeville actor, film director, and film producer.

Appeared in: 1934 Men in Black (short); Three Little Pigskins (short). 1935 Uncivil Warriors (short). 1936 Ants in the Pantry (short); Movie Maniacs (short).

DORIAN, CHARLES
Born: 1893. Died: Oct. 21, 1942, Albuquerque, N.M.(heart attack). Screen, vaudeville actor, and assistant film director. Entered films in 1917.

DORLEAC, FRANCOISE
Born: 1941, France. Died: June 26, 1967, Nice, France (auto accident). Screen actress.

Appeared in: 1957 Mensonges. 1958 The Door Slams. 1959 Les Loups Dans la Berbaries. 1960 Ce Soir ou Jamis; Les Portes Claquent. 1961 Le Jeu de la Verite; A D'Autres Amours; La Gamberge; Tout L'Or de Monde; Payroll. 1962 The Girl with the Golden Eyes; Arsene Lupin Contra Arsene Lupin (Arsene Lupin against Arsene Lupin). 1964 La Peau Douce (The Soft Skin); L'Homme de Rio (That Man from Rio). 1965 La Chasse a L'Homme (Manhunt); Genghis Khan; Where the Spies Are. 1966 Cul-de-Sac. 1967 Billion Dollar Brain. 1968 The Young Girls of Rochefort.

DORO, MARIE (Marie K. Steward)
Born: 1882, Duncannon, Pa. Died: Oct. 9, 1956, New York, N.Y. (heart ailment). Screen and stage actress. Divorced from screen actor Elliott Dexter (dec. 1941).

Appeared in: 1915 The Morals of Marcus (film debut); The White Pearl. 1916 The Heart of Nora Flynn; Oliver Twist (stage and film versions); Diplomacy; The Wood Nymph. 1917 Lost and Won; Castles for Two. 1919 The Mysterious Princess; Twelve Ten. 1920 Maid of Mystery. 1922 The Stronger Passion.

DORSAY, EDMUND
Born: 1897. Died: June 12, 1959, New York, N.Y. Screen, stage, vaudeville, and television actor. Appeared in silents.

D'ORSAY, LAWRENCE
Born: 1860, England. Died: Sept. 13, 1931, London, England. Screen and stage actor.

Appeared in: 1918 Ruggles of Red Gap. 1922 The Bond Boy. 1923 His Children's Children. 1924 The Side Show of Life. 1925 Miss Bluebeard. 1926 The Sorrows of Satan.

DORSCH, KAETHE
Born: Dec. 29, 1889, Nurenburg, Germany. Died: Dec. 1957, Vienna, Austria. Screen and stage actress.

Appeared in: 1931 Krei Tage Liebe (Three Days of Love); Die Lindenwirtin Vom Rhein. 1938 Ein Frau Ohne Bedeutung. 1940 Mutterliebe (Mother Love). 1952 Singende Engel (Singing Angel). Other German film: Yvette.

DORSEY, JIMMY (James Francis Dorsey)
Born: 1904, Shenandoah, Pa. Died: June 12, 1957, New York, N.Y. (cancer). Bandleader and screen actor. Brother of bandleader and screen actor Tommy Dorsey (dec. 1956).

Appeared in: 1940 Paramount short. 1942 The Fleet's In. 1943 I Dood It. 1944 Lost in a Harem; Four Jills in a Jeep; Hollywood Canteen. 1947 The Fabulous Dorseys. 1949 Make Believe Ballroom.

DORSEY, TOMMY (Thomas Francis Dorsey)
Born: 1905, Mahanoy Plane, Pa. Died: Nov. 26, 1956, Greenwich, Conn.(choked while asleep). Bandleader and screen actor. Brother of bandleader and screen actor Jimmy Dorsey (dec. 1957).

Appeared in: 1941 Las Vegas Nights. 1942 Ship Ahoy. 1943 Du Barry Was a Lady; Presenting Lily Mars; Girl Crazy; I Dood It. 1944 Broadway Rhythm. 1947 The Fabulous Dorseys. 1948 A Song Is Born.

DOTY, WESTON and WINSTON
Born: 1915. Died: Jan. 2, 1934, Calif.(both drowned in flood). Twin screen actors.

Appeared in: 1925 Peter Pan; and four "Our Gang" comedies.

DOUCET, M. PAUL
Born: 1886, France. Died: Oct. 10, 1928, N.Y.(septic poisoning). Screen and stage actor.

Appeared in: 1921 Tropical Love. 1922 Polly of the Follies. 1923 The Leavenworth Case. 1924 America. 1925 Heart of a Siren; The Little French Girl. 1927 The Broadway Drifter.

DOUGHERTY, VIRGIL JACK
Born: 1895. Died: May 16, 1938, Hollywood, Calif.(suicide—carbon monoxide). Screen actor. Married to screen actress Barbara Lamar (dec. 1925).

Appeared in: 1921 The Greater Claim. 1922 Impulse; Second Hand Rose; Chain Lightning. 1923 Money! Money! Money!. 1924 Girl of the Limberlost. 1925 The Burning Trail; The Meddler. 1926 The Runaway Express. 1927 Arizona Bound; Special Delivery; Down the Stretch; The Lure of the Night Club. 1928 Gypsy of the North; Into No Man's Land. 1929 The Body Punch. 1936 Yodelin' Kid from Pine Ridge.

DOUGLAS, BYRON
Born: 1865. Died: Apr. 21, 1935, New York, N.Y. Screen and stage actor.

Appeared in: 1920 Held by the Enemy. 1921 Dynamite Allan; Know Your Man; Beyond Price. 1923 Under the Red Robe; The Silent Command; The Net. 1924 It Is the Law. 1925 That Devil Quemado; Two-Fisted Jones; Marriage in Transit. 1927 The Perfect Sap; The Coward; Dead Man's Curve; Ladies Beware; Red Clay. 1928 Man, Woman and Wife. 1929 Born to the Saddle; The Drake Case. 1931 Secret Service.

DOUGLAS, DON (Douglas Kinleyside)
Born: 1905, New York or London, England. Died: Dec. 31, 1945, Los Angeles, Calif.(complications after emergency appendectomy). Screen, stage, and opera actor.

Appeared in: 1929 Great Gabbo; Tonight at Twelve. 1930 Ranch House Blues. 1932 Love in High Gear. 1933 He Couldn't Take It. 1934 A Woman's Man; Tomorrow's Children; Men in White. 1937 Headin' East. 1938 Law of the Texan; Alexanders Ragtime Band; Orphans of the Street; Fast Company; The Crowd Roars; The Gladiator; Convicted; Smashing the Rackets. 1939 Fast and Loose; Within the Law; Zero Hour; The House of Fear; Fugitive at Large; Manhattan Shakedown; Sabotage; On Dress Parade; The Mysterious Miss X; Wings of the Navy. 1940 A Fugitive from Justice; Calling Philo Vance; Gallant Sons; Deadwood Dick (serial); Charlie Chan in Panama; I Love You Again. 1941 Flight Command; Sleepers West; Dead Men Tell; Murder among Friends; The Great Swindle; The Get-Away; Hold Back the Dawn; Night of January 16th; Mercy Island; Melody Lane;. Cheers for Miss Bishop; Whistling in the Dark. 1942 On the Sunny Side; Tales of Manhattan; Now, Voyager; Little Tokyo, U.S.A.; Juke Box Jenny; A Daring Young Man. 1943 The Meanest Man in the World; He's My Guy; Wintertime; Appointment in Berlin; Action in the North Atlantic; Behind the Rising Sun; The More the Merrier; The Crystal Ball. 1944 The Falcon Out West; Heavenly Days; Murder, My Sweet; Show Business; Tall in the Saddle. 1945 Grissly's Millions; A Royal Scandal; Tarzan and the Amazons; Tokyo Rose; Club Havana. 1946 The Strange Mr. Gregory; The Truth about Women; Gilda.

DOUGLAS, KENT. See Douglass Montgomery.

DOUGLAS, PAUL
Born: Apr. 11, 1907, Philadelphia, Pa. Died: Sept. 11, 1959, Hollywood, Calif.(heart attack). Screen, stage, television, and radio actor. Married to screen actress Jan Sterling; divorced from screen actress Virginia Field.

Appeared in: 1948 A Letter to Three Wives (film debut). 1949 It Happens Every Spring; Everybody Does It; Twelve O'Clock High. 1950 Panic in the Streets; The Big Lift; Love That Brute. 1951 Angels in the Outfield; Fourteen Hours; The Guy Who Came Back; Rhubarb (unbilled). 1952 We're Not Married; When in Rome; Clash by Night; Never Wave at a WAC. 1953 Forever Female. 1954 High and Dry; Executive Suite; Green Fire. 1956 Joe Macbeth; Solid Gold Cadillac; The Gamma People; The Leather Saint. 1957 This Could Be the Night; Beau James. 1959 The Mating Game.

DOUGLAS, WALLY. See Walter Froes.

DOVEY, ALICE
Born: 1885, England. Died: Jan. 11, 1969, Tarzana, Calif. Screen and stage actress. Entered films with Famous Players-Lasky in 1915. Married to stage actor/playwright Jack Hazzard.

DOVZHENKO, ALEXANDER (aka ALEXANDER DOVJHENKO)
Born: 1894. Died: 1956. Screen actor, film director, film producer, and screenwriter.

Appeared in: 1929 Arsenal. 1930 Earth. 1932 Ivan. 1935 Aerograd. 1947 Life in Blossom.

DOWLINING, CONSTANCE
Born: 1920, New York, N.Y. Died: Oct. 28, 1969, Los Angeles, Calif.(cardiac arrest). Screen and stage actress.

Appeared in: 1944 Knickerbocker Holiday; Up in Arms. 1946 The Black Angel; Blackie and the Law; The Well-Groomed Bride. 1947 Blind Spot. 1948 The Flame. 1950 Her Wonderful Lie; Mad about Opera. 1951 Stormbound. 1952 A Voice in Your Heart; Miss Italy. 1953 Duel without Honor. 1954 Gog. 1955 Othello.

DOWLING, JOAN
Born: Jan. 1928, England. Died: Mar. 31, 1954, London, England ("found dead in gas-filled room"). Screen and stage actress. Married to screen actor Harry Fowler.

Appeared in: 1946 Hue and Cry (film debut—U.S. 1950). 1948 No Room at the Inn. 1949 Landfall (U.S. 1953). 1950 Bond Street; For Them That Trespass. 1951 Pool of London; Murder without Crime. 1952 Train of Events; The Magic Box. 1953 Twilight Women (aka Woman of Twilight); Affair in Monte Carlo.

DOWLING, JOSEPH J.
Born: 1848. Died: July 10, 1928, Hollywood, Calif. Screen actor. Achieved fame as the "Miracle Man."

Appeared in: 1915 The Coward. 1919 The Miracle Man. 1920 The Kentucky Colonel. 1921 Fightin' Mad; The Lure of Egypt; The Spenders; The Other Woman; The Beautiful Liar; Breaking Point; The Sin of Martha Queed; A Certain Rich Man; The Grim Comedian; His Nibs; Little Lord Fauntleroy. 1922 If You Believe It, It's So; The Infidel; Quincy Adams Sawyer; The Girl Who Ran Wild; Half Breed; The Pride of Palomar; One Clear Call; The Trail of the Axe; The Danger Point. 1923 The Christian; A Man's Man; The Spider and the Rose; Dollar Devils; Tiger Rose; The Courtship of Miles Standish; Enemies of Children; The Girl Who Came Back. 1924 Those Who Dare; One Night in Rome; The Gaiety Girl; Tess of the D'Urbervilles; Untamed Youth; Her Night of Romance; The Law Forbids; Unseen Hands; Women Who Give; Free and Equal (reissue and retitle of The Coward, 1915). 1925 Lorraine of the Lions; Confessions of a Queen; Lord Jim; The Golden Princess; Flower of Night; New Lives for Old. 1926 The Rainmaker; The Little Irish Girl; Why Girls Go Back Home; Two Gun Man.

DOWNES, OLIN
Born: 1886. Died: Aug. 22, 1955, New York, N.Y.(heart attack). Screen actor and writer.

Appeared in: 1947 Carnegie Hall. 1948 First Opera Film Festival (narr.).

DOWNING, WALTER
Born: 1874. Died: Dec. 21, 1937, Hollywood, Calif. Screen actor. Entered films in 1915.

Appeared in: 1924 Pied Piper Malone.

DOWSEY, ROSE WALKER. See Rose Walker.

DOYLE, BUDDY
Born: 1901. Died: Nov. 9, 1939, New York, N.Y.(appendix operation). Screen and stage actor.

Appeared in: 1927 Take in the Sun (short); Georginia (short). 1929 At a Talkie Studio (short). 1936 The Great Ziegfeld.

DOYLE, LEN
Born: 1893. Died: Dec. 6, 1959, Port Jervis, N.Y. Screen, stage, radio and television actor, stage director, and stage producer.

Appeared in: 1962 Dead to the World.

DOYLE, REGINA
Born: 1907. Died: Sept. 30, 1931, Hollywood, Calif.(auto accident). Screen actress.

DRAINIE, JOHN
Born: 1916. Died: Oct. 30, 1966, Toronto, Ontario, Canada (cancer). Screen, television, and radio actor.

Appeared in: 1963 the Incredible Journey.

DRAKE, JOSEPHINE S.
Died: Jan. 7, 1929, New York, N.Y.(pneumonia). Screen and stage actress.

Appeared in: 1926 The Song and Dance Man; A Social Celebrity; The Palm Beach Girl.

DRAKE, STEVE (Dale Laurence Fink)
Born: 1923. Died: Dec. 19, 1948, Burbank, Calif.(auto accident). Screen actor.

DRANEM
Born: 1869, France. Died: Oct. 13, 1935, Paris, France. Screen and stage actor.

Appeared in: 1932 Il est Charmant (He Is Coming); Miche. 1935 Soir de Reveillon.

DRAYTON, ALFRED (Alfred Varick)
Born: Nov. 1, 1881, Brighton, England. Died: Apr. 25, 1949, London, England. Screen and stage actor.

Appeared in: 1925 A Scandal in Bohemia. 1931 The Calendar; Lord Babs. 1933 Friday the 13th; The Little Damozel. 1934 Jack Ahoy; Red Ensign; It's a Boy. 1935 Loves of a Dictator; Oh! Daddy; First a Girl; Radio Parade of 1935. 1936 The Crimson Circle. 1938 So This Is London (U.S. 1940). 1939 Aren't Men Beasts. 1940 A Spot of Bother. 1942 The Big Blockade. 1944 They Knew Mr. Knight; Don't Take It to Heart (U.S. 1949); The Halfway House. 1947 Nicholas Nickleby. 1948 Things Happen at Night. Other British film: Falling for You.

DRESSER, LOUISE (Louise Kerlin)
Born: Oct. 5, 1882, Evansville, Ind. Died: Apr. 24, 1965, Woodland Hills, Calif.(intestinal obstruction). Screen, stage, and vaudeville actress. Divorced from screen actor Jack Norworth (dec. 1959) and later married screen actor/singer Jack Gardner (dec. 1950). During the first presentation of the Academy Awards she received a citation of merit.

Appeared in: 1922 Enter Madame; Burning Sands; The Glory of Clementina. 1923 The Fog; Prodigal Daughters; Ruggles of Red Gap; Salomy Jane; Woman Proof; To the Ladies. 1924 The City That Never Sleeps; Cheap Kisses; What Shall I Do?; The Next Corner. 1925 The Eagle; The Goose Woman; Enticement; Percy. 1926 The Blind Goddess; Padlocked; Everybody's Acting; Gigolo; Broken Hearts of Hollywood; Fifth Avenue. 1927 The Third Degree; The White Flannels; Mr. Wu. 1928 The Air Circus; A Ship Comes in; The Garden of Eden; Mother Knows Best. 1929 The Madonna of Avenue A; Not Quite Decent. 1930 This Mad World; Mammy; Lightnin'; The Three Sisters. 1931 Caught. 1932 Stepping Sisters. 1933 Doctor Bull; Song of the Eagle; Cradle Song; State Fair. 1934 Hollywood on Parade (short); Servants Entrance; Girl of the Limberlost; David Harum; The Scarlet Empress; The World Moves On. 1935 The County Chairman. 1937 Maid of Salem.

DRESSLER, MARIE (Leila Koerber)
Born: Nov. 9, 1869, Coburg, Canada. Died: July 28, 1934, Santa Barbara, Calif.(cancer). Screen, stage, vaudeville, and circus actress. Won Academy Award for Best Actress in 1930 for Min and Bill.

Appeared in: 1914 Tillie's Punctured Romance (film debut). 1915 Tillie's Tomato Surprise; Tillie's Nightmare. 1917 The Scrublady. 1918 The Red Cross Nurse; The Agonies of Agnes. 1927 The Callahans and the Murphys; Breakfast at Sunrise; The Joy Girl. 1928 Bringing up Father; The Patsy. 1929 The Divine Lady; The Vagabond Lovers; The Hollywood Revue of 1929; Road Show. 1930 Chasing Rainbows; One Romantic Night; Let Us Be Gay; Derelict; Voice of Hollywood (short); Anna Christie; Caught Short; The Swan; March of Time; Call of the Flesh; The Girl Said No; Min and Bill. 1931 Reducing; Politics. 1932 Emma; Prosperity. 1933 Tugboat Annie; Dinner at Eight; Singer of Seville; Christopher Bean. 1964 Big Parade of Comedy (documentary).

DREW, MRS. SIDNEY (Lucille McVey)
Born: 1890. Died: Nov. 3, 1925, Hollywood, Calif. Screen, stage actress, film producer, and screenwriter. She also appeared under her real name, Lucille McVey, and as Jane Morrow. Was second wife of screen actor Sidney Drew (dec. 1919) and appeared with him in a series of comedies between 1915 and 1919.

Appeared in: 1915 The Story of a Glove; Miss Sticky-Moufie-Kiss; A Safe Investment. 1916 At the Count of Ten; Childhood's Happy Days. 1917 Cave Man's Buff; His Perfect Day; The Pest; Blackmail; Her Obsession; Reliable Henry; Locked Out; High Cost of Living; Awakening of Helen Minor; Putting It over on Henry; Handy Henry; One of the Family; Safety First; Her Lesson; Nothing to Wear; Her Anniversaries; Tootsie; The Hypochondriac; The Matchmakers; Lest We Forget; Mr. Parker, Hero; Henry's Ancestors; His Ear for Music; Her Economic Independence; Her First Game; The Patriot; Music Hath Charms; Rubbing It In; His Curiosity; The Joy of Friends!; His Double Life; The Dentist; Hist! Spies; Twelve Good Hens and True; His Deadly Calm; Rebellion of Mr. Minor; A Close Resemblance; As Others See Us; Too Much Henry; Wages No Object; The Spirit of Merry Christmas; The Unmarried Look; Shadowing Henry. 1918 A Youthful Affair; Duplicity. 1919 Romance and Rings; Once a Mason; A Sisterly Scheme; Bunkered; The Amateur Liar; Harold and the Saxons.

DREYFUSS, MICHAEL
Born: 1928. Died: Mar. 30, 1960, New York, N.Y. Screen, stage, television, radio actor, and television director.

Appeared in: 1956 Patterns.

DRISCOLL, BOBBY (Robert Driscoll)
Born: Mar. 3, 1937, Cedar Rapids, Iowa. Died: Jan. 1968, New York, N.Y.(occlusive coronary arteriosclerosis—hardening of the arteries). Screen actor. Won a juvenile Academy Award in 1947 for So Dear to My Heart and in 1949 for The Window.

Appeared in: 1943 Lost Angel (film debut). 1944 The Sullivans; Sunday Dinner for a Soldier. 1945 Big Bonanza; From This Day Forward; Identity Unknown. 1946 Miss Susie Slagle's; O.S.S.; So Goes My Love. 1947 So Dear to My Heart. 1948 Song of the South; If You Knew Susie; Melody Time. 1949 The Window. 1950 Treasure Island. 1951 When I Grow Up. 1952 The Happy Time. 1953 Peter Pan (voice). 1955 Scarlet Coat. 1958 Party Chasers.

DRISCOLL, SAM W.
Born: 1868. Died: Dec. 13, 1956, Hollywood, Calif. Screen actor and musician.

Appeared in: 1935 Mutiny on the Bounty.

DRUMIER, JACK
Born: 1869. Died: Apr. 22, 1929, Clearwater, Fla.(pneumonia). Screen, stage, and vaudeville actor.

Appeared in: 1921 You Find It Everywhere; The Girl from Porcupine. 1922 The Broken Silence; The Splendid Lie; Shadows of the Sea. 1924 Emblems of Love. 1925 The Pinch Hitter; Enemies of Youth.

DU BOIS, JEAN
Born: 1888, Sumatra, West Indonesia. Died: Oct. 28, 1957, Denver, Colo.(cancer). Screen actor. Entered films as a cameraman in 1925.

DUCHESS OLGA (Eva Liminana)
Born: 1899, Mexico. Died: Oct. 1953, Mexico City, Mexico. Screen actress, film producer, and screenwriter. Divorced from Argentinian screen actor Jose Bohr. Appeared in Spanish language films made in both U.S. and Mexico.

DUCHIN, EDDY
Born: Apr. 1, 1909, Cambridge, Mass. Died: Feb. 9, 1951, New York, N.Y.(leukemia). Pianist, bandleader, and screen actor.

Appeared in: 1932 Mr. Broadway. 1935 Coronado. 1937 Hit Parade.

DUDLAH, DAVID (David Wiliford Kelly)
Born: 1892. Died: Feb. 26, 1947, Memphis, Tenn. Screen and carnival actor.

DUDLEY, ROBERT Y.
Born: Sept. 13, 1875, Cincinnati, Ohio. Died: Nov. 12, 1955, San Clemente, Calif. Screen and stage actor. Entered films in 1920. Founder of the "Troupers Club of Hollywood."

Appeared in: 1921 The Traveling Salesman. 1922 Making a Man; The Ninety and Nine. 1923 Sixty Cents an Hour; The Tiger's Claw; The Day of Faith; Nobody's Bride. 1924 Flapper Wives; On the Stroke of Three. 1926 The Marriage Clause. 1927 Broadway Madness; The Lure of the Night Club. 1928 Skinner's Big Idea; On Trial; Fools for Luck; Baby Cyclone; The Night Flyer. 1929 Mysterious Island; Big News; Shanghai Rose. 1930 Wide Open. 1932 Three Wise Girls. 1937 The Toast of New York. 1941 All That Money Can Buy. 1942 Palm Beach Story; Tennessee Johnson. 1944 It Happened Tomorrow. 1945 Col. Effingham's Raid. 1947 Magic Town. 1949 Portrait of Jennie. 1952 The Devil and Daniel Webster (reissue and retitle of All That Money Can Buy, 1941).

DUEL, PETER (Peter Deuel)
Born: 1940, Rochester, N.Y. Died: Dec. 31, 1971, Hollywood, Calif.(gunshot—suicide?). Screen and television actor. Brother of screen actor Geoffrey Deuel.

Appeared in: 1969 Generation.

DUFFY, HENRY
Born: 1890, Chicago, Ill. Died: Nov. 18, 1961, Hollywood, Calif. (cancer). Screen, stage actor, and stage producer.

DUFFY, JACK
Born: Sept. 4, 1882, Pawtucket, R.I. Died: July 23, 1939, Hollywood, Calif. Screen, stage, vaudeville actor, and make-up artist.

Appeared in: 1924 The Brass Bowl; Reckless Romance. 1925 Madame Behave; Stop Flirting. 1926 Ella Cinders. 1927 No Control. 1928 Harold Teen. 1929 Loose Change (short); Hot Scotch (short); Divorce Made Easy; Sally. 1930 The Skin Game (short). 1931 Heaven on Earth. 1933 Alice in Wonderland. 1935 Here Comes Cookie. 1936 Wild Brian.

DUFKIN, SAM
Born: 1891. Died: Feb. 19, 1952, Hollywood, Calif. Screen actor.

Appeared in Mack Sennett's silent films.

DUFRAINE, ROSA
Born: 1901. Died: Apr. 29, 1935, Duarte, Calif. Screen actress.

DUGAN, MARIE. See Marie Engle

DUGAN, TOM (Thomas J. Dugan)
Born: 1889, Dublin, Ireland. Died: Mar. 6, 1955, Redlands, Calif. (auto accident). Screen, stage, and vaudeville actor.

Appeared in: 1926 Early to Wed. 1927 By Whose Hand?; Swell Head; My Friend from India; The Kid Sister; The Small Bachelor. 1928 Soft Living; Shadows of the Night; The Barker; Broadway Daddies; Sharp Shooters; Dressed to Kill; Melody of Love; Midnight Taxi; Lights of New York. 1929 Broadway Babies; Drag; The Drake Case; The Million Dollar Collar; Kid Gloves; Sonny Boy; Hearts in Exile. 1930 They Learned about Women; The Bad One; Bright Lights; Night Work; The Medicine Man; She Who Gets Slapped; Surprise. 1931 Woman Hungry; Star Witness; The Hot Heiress. 1932 Big Timber; Dr. X; Big City Blues; Pride of the Legion; Blessed Event. 1933 Grand Slam; Skyway; Trick for Trick; The Sweetheart of Sigma Chi; Don't Bet on Love. 1934 Palooka; A Woman's Man; No More Women; The Circus Clown; Let's Talk It Over; Girl O' My Dreams; The President Vanishes. 1935 The Gilded Lady; One New York Night; Chinatown Squad; The Case of the Missing Man; Affair of Susan; Princess O'Hara; Three Kids and a Queen; Murder in the Fleet. 1936 The Calling of Dan Matthews; Pennies from Heaven; Wife vs. Secretary; Neighborhood House; Mister Cinderella. 1937 Nobody's Baby; Pick a Star; True Confession; She Had to Eat. 1938 Sing You Sinners; There's That Woman Again; Four Daughters. 1939 The Lone Wolf Spy Hunt; I'm from Missouri; Mystery of the White Room; The Lady and the Mob; House of Fear; Missing Evidence; $1000 a Touchdown; Laugh It Off; The Housekeeper's Daughter. 1940 Too Many Husbands; The Farmer's Daughter; The Fighting 69th; Isle of Destiny; The Ghost Breakers; Cross Country Romance; Half a Sinner; So You Won't Talk; A Little Bit of Heaven; Star Dust. 1941 Where Did You Get That Girl?; Ellery Queen's Penthouse Mystery; The Monster and the Girl; You're the One; A Dangerous Game; Tight Shoes; The Richest Man in Town; We Go Fast; Ellery Queen and the Murder Ring; The Bugle Sounds; Texas. 1942 Yokel Boy; A Haunting We Will Go; To Be or Not to Be; Yankee Doodle Dandy; Moontide; Meet the Stewarts; Star Spangled Rhythm. 1943 Bataan; Johnny Come Lately. 1944 Bermuda Mystery; Gambler's Choice; In Society; Greenwich Village; Hi, Beautiful!; Home in Indiana; Moon over Las Vegas; Swingtime Johnny; Ghost Catchers; Up in Arms. 1945 Don Juan Quilligan; Eadie Was a Lady; Earl Carroll Vanities; See My Lawyer; The Kid Sister; The Man Who Walked Alone; Tell It to a Star; Trail of Kit Carson; Her Highness and the Bellboy. 1946 Bringing up Father; Hoodlum Saint; Johnny Comes Flying Home; The Shadow Returns; Accomplice; It Shouldn't Happen to a Dog. 1947 The Fabulous Dorseys; The Pilgrim Lady; Good News; The Senator Was Indiscreet. 1948 Half Past Midnight; Texas, Brooklyn and Heaven. 1949 Take Me Out to the Ball Game. 1951 Painting the Clouds with Sunshine; The Lemon Drop Kid. 1952 Belle of New York. 1955 Crashout. 1968 The Further Perils of Laurel and Hardy (documentary).

DUGGAN, TOM
Born: 1915, Chicago, Ill. Died: May 29, 1969, Los Angeles, Calif.(auto accident injuries). Screen, radio, television actor, and newscaster.

Appeared in: 1950 You Can't Fool an Irishman. 1957 Hear Me Good!. 1958 Andy Hardy Comes Home; Frankenstein—1970. 1959 But Not for Me; Born Reckless. 1960 Tarzan the Magnificent. 1961 Blueprint for Robbery; Gorgo.

DULAC, ARTHUR
Born: 1910, France. Died: Sept. 18, 1962, Hollywood, Calif. (coronary thrombosis). Screen actor.

Appeared in: 1953 Little Boy Lost.

DUMKE, RALPH
Born: 1900. Died: Jan. 4, 1964, Sherman Oaks, Calif. Screen, stage, radio, and vaudeville actor.

Appeared in: 1949 All the King's Men. 1950 Where Danger Lives; Mystery Street; The Breaking Point; The Fireball. 1951 When I Grow Up; The Mob; The Law and the Lady. 1952 The San Francisco Story; Boots Malone; Carbine Williams; We're Not Married; Holiday for Sinners; Hurricane Smith. 1953 Lili; Hannah Lee; Mississippi Gambler; Massacre Canyon; The President's Lady. 1954 She Couldn't Say No; Alaska Seas; They Rode West; Rails into Laramie. 1955 Daddy Long Legs; Artists and Models; Violent Saturday; Hell's Island; They Came from Another World. 1956 Francis in the Haunted House; Forever Darling; When Gangland Strikes; Invasion of the Body Snatchers; Solid Gold Cadillac. 1957 The Buster Keaton Story; Loving You. 1960 Wake Me When It's Over. 1961 All in a Night's Work.

DUMONT, MARGARET
Born: 1889. Died: Mar. 6, 1965, Los Angeles, Calif.(heart attack). Screen, stage, and television actress. Won Screen Actor Guild award for A Day at the Races, 1937.

Appeared in: 1929 The Cocoanuts. 1930 Animal Crackers. 1931 Girl Habit. 1933 Duck Soup. 1934 Gridiron Flash; Fifteen Wives; Kentucky Kernels. 1935 A Night at the Opera; Orchids to You; Rendezvous. 1936 Song and Dance Man; Anything Goes. 1937 A Day at the Races; The Life of the Party; High Flyers; Youth on Parole; Wise Girl. 1938 Dramatic School. 1939 At the Circus. 1941 The Big Store; Never Give a Sucker an Even Break; For Beauty's Sake. 1942 Born to Sing; Sing Your Worries Away; Rhythm Parade; About Face. 1943 The Dancing Masters. 1944 Bathing Beauty; Seven Days Ashore; Up in Arms. 1945 The Horn Blows at Midnight; Diamond Horseshoe; Sunset in El Dorado. 1946 The Little Giant; Susie Steps Out. 1952 Three for Bedroom C. 1953 Stop, You're Killing Me. 1956 Shake, Rattle and Rock. 1958 Auntie Mame. 1962 Zotz!. 1964 What a Way to Go.

DUNBAR, DAVID
Born: Sept. 14, 1893, West Maitland, N.S.W., Australia. Died: Nov. 7, 1953, Woodland Hills, Calif. Screen actor.

Appeared in: 1924 Trail Dust; The Fortieth Door (serial and feature); Leatherstocking (serial); North of 36. 1925 The Bloodhound; Fair Play; The Cowboy Musketeer; Ridin' the Wind; Galloping Vengeance; A Man of Nerve. 1926 The Galloping Cowboy; The Non-Stop Flight; Beyond the Rockies. 1927 King of Kings; The Boy Rider; The Broncho Buster; Gold from Weepah; The Arizona Whirlwind; The Fighting Hombre. 1929 Plunging Hoofs. 1930 The Return of Dr. Fu Manchu. 1938 Kidnapped.

DUNBAR, HELEN
Born: 1868. Died: Aug. 28, 1933, Los Angeles, Calif. Screen, stage, and vaudeville actress.

Appeared in: 1915 Graustark. 1917 The Great Secret (serial). 1920 Behold My Wife. 1921 Her Winning Way; The House That Jazz Built; Sham; The Great Moment; Sacred and Profane Love; The Little Clown. 1922 Beyond the Rocks; The Impossible Mrs. Bellew; The World's Champion; A Homespun Vamp; The Law and the Woman; Man of Courage; Thirty Days. 1923 Hollywood; The Call of the Canyon; The Cheat. 1924 Changing Husbands; This Woman; The Fighting Coward; Three Weeks. 1925 Siege; The Reckless Sex; Rose of the World; Compromise; The Man without a Conscience; The Woman Hater; His Majesty, Bunker Bean; Lady Windermere's Fan; New Lives for Old; She Wolves. 1926 Meet the Prince; Stranded in Paris; His Jazz Bride; Fine Manners; The Man Upstairs.

DUNCAN, BOB
Born: Dec. 7, 1904, Topeka, Kans. Died: Mar. 13, 1967, North Hollywood, Calif.(suicide—gun). Screen actor and television director.

Appeared in: 1944 End of the Road. 1945 Weekend at the Waldorf. 1949 The Fighting Redhead. 1950 Law of the Panhandle. 1953 The Marshal's Daughter. 1957 The Parson and the Outlaw.

DUNCAN, EDITH JOHNSON. See Edith Johnson

DUNCAN, ROSETTA
Born: 1900, Los Angeles, Calif. Died: Dec. 4, 1959, Acero, Ill. (auto accident injuries). Screen, stage, and vaudeville actress. Sister of Vivian Duncan and Evelyn Duncan (dec. 1972). Entered films in 1926.

Appeared in: 1927 Two Flaming Youths; Topsy and Eva. 1929 It's a Great Life. 1935 Broadway Brevities (short).

DUNCAN, WILLIAM A.
Born: 1880. Died: Feb. 8, 1961, Hollywood, Calif. Screen, stage actor, and film director. Entered films in 1910. Married to screen actress Edith Johnson with whom he appeared in film serials.

Appeared in: 1917 Vengeance and the Woman (serial); The Fight Trail (serial). 1918 A Fight for Millions (serial). 1919 Man of Might (serial); Smashing Barriers (serial); Perils of Thunder Mountain (serial). 1920 The Silent Avenger (serial). 1921 Fighting Fate (serial); Where Men Are Men; Steelheart. 1922 No Defense; The Silent Vow; When Danger Smiles; The Fighting Guide. 1923 The Steel Trail (serial); Smashing Barriers (1919 serial re-released as feature film); Playing It Wild. 1924 The Fast Express (serial); Wolves of the North (serial).

DUNCAN, WILLIAM CARY
Born: Feb. 6, 1874, North Brookfield, Mass. Died: Nov. 12, 1945, North Brookfield, Mass.(heart ailment). Screen actor, playwright, author, screenwriter, and lyricist. Entered films with Famous Players in 1929.

Appeared in: 1935 Nevada. 1936 Three on the Trail. 1937 Hopalong Rides Again; Thunder Trail. 1938 Bar 20 Justice; The Frontiersman. 1939 Law of the Pampas. 1940 The Farmer's Daughter. 1941 Texas Rangers Ride Again.

DUNDEE, JIMMY
Born: 1901. Died: Nov. 20, 1953, Woodland Hills, Calif.(leukemia). Screen actor, stuntman, boxer, and auto racer.

Appeared in: 1938 The Buccaneer. 1944 Hail the Conquering Hero. 1948 Whispering Smith. 1949 My Friend Irma. 1950 My Friend Irma Goes West; At War with the Army. 1951 Sailor Beware.

DUNN, EDWARD F. "EDDIE"
Born: 1896. Died: May 5, 1951, Hollywood, Calif. Screen actor.

Appeared in: 1928 The Fleet's In. 1929 The Saturday Night Kid. 1930 Headin' North; True to the Navy; The Land of Missing Men; Another Fine Mess (short). 1931 The Gang Buster; A Melon-Drama (short); False Roomers (short); The Pajama Party (short). 1932 The Big Broadcast. 1933 Me and My Pal (short); The Midnight Patrol (short); Asleep in the Feet (short). 1935 Car 99; Here Comes Cookie; The Bride Comes Home; Powder Smoke Range. 1936 The Big Broadcast of 1937; The Preview Murder Mystery. 1938 The Sky Parade; The Bride Walks Out; Rascals; Give Me a Sailor. 1939 Let Freedom Ring; Hollywood Cavalcade; Three Smart Girls Grow Up; Tail Spin. 1940 On Their Own; The Great Profile; Mexican Spitfire Out West; The Great Dictator; One Night in the Tropics. 1941 In the Navy; The Saint in Palm Springs; A Date with the Falcon. 1942 Mississippi Gambler; The Falcon's Brother; Invisible Agent; Ride 'Em Cowboy; Mexican Spitfire at Sea. 1943 Hit the Ice; The Falcon in Danger; Hello, Frisco, Hello; Dixie Dugan. 1944 Bermuda Mystery; Dead Man's Eyes; Henry Aldrich's Little Secret; Army Wives; Nothing but Trouble; Lost in a Harem. 1945 Frontier Gal; Wonder Man; George White's Scandals; State Fair; See My Lawyer; Here Come the Co-Eds. 1946 Centennial Summer; Bowery Bombshell. 1947 Buck Privates Come Home; The Flame. 1948 Call Northside 777; Lightning in the Forest; Big Punch; Homicide for Three; Checkered Coat. 1949 Incident; I Shot Jesse James; Mother Is a Freshman. 1950 Mary Ryan, Detective; Lonely Hearts; Bandits; Whirlpool. 1951 Buckaroo Sheriff of Texas.

DUNN, EMMA
Born: 1875, Cheshire, England. Died: Dec. 14, 1966, Los Angeles, Calif. Screen and stage actress. Entered films in 1919.

Appeared in: 1920 Old Lady 31. 1924 Pied Piper Malone. 1929 Side Street. 1930 The Texan; Broken Dishes; Manslaughter. 1931 Too Young to Marry; Big Business Girl; The Prodigal; Compromised; Bad Company; Morals for Women; Bad Sister; This Modern Age; The Guilty Generation. 1932 We Three; Wet Parade; The Man I Killed; The Cohens and the Kellys in Hollywood; Hell's House; Letty Lynton; It's Tough to Be Famous; Blessed Event; Broken Lullaby; Under Eighteen. 1933 Grand Slam; Hard to Handle; Man of Sentiment; Elmer, the Great; Private Jones; It's Great to Be Alive; Walls of Gold. 1934 Dark Hazard; The Quitter; Doctor Monica. 1935 This Is the Life; George White's Scandals of 1935; The Glass Key; Keeper of the Bees; The Little Big Shop; Ladies Crave Excitement; Another Face; Seven Keys to Baldpate; The Crusades. 1936 The Harvester; Second Wife; Mr. Deeds Goes to Town. 1937 When You're in Love; The Emperor's Candlesticks; Madame X; The Hideaway; Varsity Show; Circus Girl. 1938 The Cowboy from Brooklyn; Thanks for the Memory; The Cowboy and the Lady; Lord Jeff; Three Loves Has Nancy; Duke of West Point; Young Dr. Kildare. 1939 Calling Dr. Kildare; The Secret of Dr. Kildare; Hero for a Day; The Llano Kid; Son of Frankenstein; Each Dawn I Die. 1940 High School; Little Orvie; Dr. Kildare's Strange Case; Dr. Kildare Goes Home; You Can't Fool Your Wife; Half a Sinner; One Crowded Night; Dance, Girl, Dance; Yesterday's Heroes; The Great Dictator. 1941 The Penalty; Scattergood Baines; Scattergood Pulls the Strings; Scattergood Meets Broadway; Mr. and Mrs. Smith; Dr. Kildare's Wedding Day; Ladies in Retirement; Rise and Shine. 1942 The Postman Didn't Ring; The Talk of the Town; Babes on Broadway; When Johnny Comes Marching Home; I Married a Witch. 1943 Hoosier Holiday; Minesweeper; The Cross of Lorraine. 1944 The Bridge of San Luis Rey; It Happened Tomorrow; Are These Our Parents?; My Buddy. 1945 The Horn Blows at Midnight. 1946 The Hoodlum Saint; Night Train from Memphis. 1947 Life with Father; Mourning Becomes Electra. 1948 Woman in White.

DUNN, J. MALCOLM
Born: England. Died: Oct. 10, 1946, Long Island, N.Y. Screen, stage, and radio actor.
Appeared in: 1920 Dr. Jekyll and Mr. Hyde. 1921 The Magic Cup; Dawn of the East. 1926 Sandy. 1930 The Sap from Syracuse; Absent Minded (short).

DUNN, JACK (John Edward Powell Dunn)
Born: Mar. 28, 1917, Turnbridge Wells, England. Died: July 16, 1938, Los Angeles, Calif.(tularemia). Ice skater and screen actor. Won male figure skating title at 1936 Olympic Games.

DUNN, JAMES (James Howard Dunn)
Born: Nov. 2, 1905, New York, N.Y. Died: Sept. 1967, Santa Monica, Calif. Screen, stage, and television actor. Won Academy Award for Best Supporting Actor in A Tree Grows in Brooklyn, 1945.

Appeared in: 1931 Bad Girl; Over the Hill; Sob Sister. 1932 Society Girl; Handle with Care; Dance Team; Walking Down Broadway. 1933 Jimmy and Sally; Sailor's Luck; Hello Sister; Hold Me Tight; Arizona to Broadway; Take a Chance; The Girl in 419. 1934 Hold That Girl; Change of Heart; Baby Takes a Bow; Have a Heart; She Learned about Sailors; 365 Nights in Hollywood; Bright Eyes; Stand up and Cheer. 1935 George White's Scandals of 1935; The Daring Young Man; Welcome Home; The Pay-Off; Bad Boy. 1936 Don't Get Personal; Hearts in Bondage; Come Closer Folks; Two-Fisted Gentlemen. 1937 Mysterious Crossing; We Have Our Moments; Living on Love; Venus Makes Trouble. 1938 Shadows over Shanghai. 1939 Pride of the Navy. 1940 Son of the Navy; Mercy Plane; A Fugitive from Justice; Hold That Woman. 1942 The Living Ghost. 1943 The Ghost and the Guest; Government Girl. 1944 Leave It to the Irish. 1945 The Caribbean Mystery; A Tree Grows in Brooklyn. 1946 That Brennan Girl. 1947 Killer McCoy. 1948 Texas, Brooklyn and Heaven. 1950 The Golden Gloves Story. 1951 A Wonderful Life. 1960 The Bramble Bush. 1962 Hemingway's Adventures of a Young Man. 1966 The Oscar.

DUNN, JOHN J.
Born: 1906, Binghamton, N.Y. Died: Apr. 2, 1938, Bluefield, W.V. (pneumonia). Screen, stage, and radio actor.
Appeared in: 1917 The Seven Pearls (serial).

DUNN, ROBERT "BOBBY"
Born: 1891, Milwaukee, Wis. Died: Mar. 24, 1939, Hollywood, Calif.(heart attack). Screen actor.

DUNN, REV. ROBERT H.
Born: 1896. Died: Feb. 11, 1960, Portsmouth, N.H. Screen actor and clergyman.

Appeared in: 1949 Lost Boundaries. 1951 The Whistle at Eaton Falls. 1952 Walk East on Beacon.

Appeared in: 1920 "Mirthquake" comedies. 1921 Skirts. 1926 The Thrill Hunter; When the Wife's Away. 1928 The Upland Rider. 1929 The Wagon Master; Captain Cowboy; 'Neath Western Skies; Code of the West; The Racketeer; Riders of the Storm; The Royal Rider. 1930 Half Pint Polly (short); Call of the Desert; Canyon Hawks; Trails of Peril; The Parting of the Trails; Parade of the West; The Canyon of Missing Men; The Cry Baby (short). 1933 Me and My Pal (short). 1934 Them Thar Hills (short). 1935 Tit for Tat (short); The Fixer-Uppers (short). 1936 The Bohemian Girl; Our Relations.

DUNNE, CHARLES
Died: Sept. 16, 1951, "Heartbreak Ridge," Korea (killed in action). Screen actor.

DUNROBIN, LIONEL CLAUDE
Born: 1875. Died: Aug. 15, 1950, Hollywood, Calif.(suicide). Screen actor.

DUNSKUS, ERICH
Born: 1890, Germany. Died: Nov. 25, 1967, Hagen, West Germany. Screen, stage, and television actor.

Appeared in: 1940 Gluck auf den Lande (Rural Happiness). 1950 Girls behind Bars. 1954 A Prize of Gold.

DUNSMUIR, ALEXANDER
Born: 1877, Scotland. Died: July 30, 1938, Los Angeles, Calif. (auto crash injuries). Screen actor.

DUNTON, HELEN
Died: Nov. 1920, San Francisco, Calif.(suicide). Screen actress.

DUPREE, MINNIE
Born: 1873, San Francisco, Calif. Died: May 23, 1947, New York, N.Y. Screen and stage actress.

Appeared in: 1929 Night Club. 1938 The Young in Heart. 1940 Anne of Windy Poplars.

DURAN, VAL
Born: 1896. Died: Feb. 1, 1937, Los Angeles, Calif.(influenza). Screen actor.

Appeared in: 1936 The General Died at Dawn. 1937 Join the Marines; The Lost Horizon.

DURAND, EDOUARD
Born: 1871, France. Died: July 31, 1926, Port Chester, N.Y. (stroke). Screen and stage actor.

Appeared in: 1922 Anna Ascends. 1923 Potash and Perlmutter. 1924 The Lone Wolf. 1925 The King on Main Street; The Sky Raider.

DURIEUX, TILLA (Ottilie Godeffroy)
Born: 1881, Vienna, Austria. Died: Feb. 21, 1971, Berlin, Germany (after operation necessitated by fall). Screen, stage, and television actress.

Appeared in: 1957 The Last Bridge.

DURKIN, ELEANOR
Died: prior to 1968. Screen and vaudeville actress. Married to actor James Burke (dec. 1968) and appeared with him in vaudeville in an act billed as "Burke and Durkin."

They appeared in: 1929 A Tete-A-Tete in Songs (short).

DURKIN, JAMES PETER
Born: 1879. Died: Mar. 12, 1934, Los Angeles, Calif. Screen and stage actor.

Appeared in: 1930 Derelict; Shadow of the Law. 1934 Uncertain Lady; Wild Girl; Nice Women; Alexander Hamilton; Vice Squad; Gun Smoke; Conquering Horde; Heat Lightning.

DURKIN, JUNIOR (Trent Junior Durkin)
Born: 1915, New York, N.Y. Died: May 4, 1935, near San Diego, Calif.(auto accident). Screen and stage actor.

Appeared in: 1930 Fame (film debut); Tom Sawyer; Santa Fe Trail; Recaptured Love; The Law Rides West. 1931 The Conquering Horde; Huckleberry Finn. 1932 Hell's House. 1933 Manhunt. 1934 Little Men; Big Hearted Herbert.

DURNING, BERNARD J.
Born: 1893. Died: Aug. 29, 1923, New York, N.Y.(typhoid).

Screen actor and film director. Married to screen actress Shirley Mason.

Appeared in: 1921 Devil Within; Seeds of Vengeance.

DURST, EDWARD
Born: 1917. Died: Mar. 10, 1945, Hollywood, Calif. Screen and stage actor.

Appeared in: 1944 Days of Glory.

DURYEA, DAN
Born: Jan. 23, 1907, White Plains, N.Y. Died: June 7, 1968, Los Angeles, Calif.(cancer). Screen, stage, and television actor. Father of screen actor Peter Duryea.

Appeared in: 1941 The Little Foxes; Ball of Fire. 1942 Pride of the Yankees; That Other Woman. 1943 Sahara. 1944 Woman in the Window; Ministry of Fear; Main Street after Dark; Mrs. Parkington; None but the Lonely Heart; The Man from Frisco. 1945 Scarlet Street; Lady on a Train; Along Came Jones; The Great Flamarion; Valley of Decision. 1946 White Tie and Tails; Black Angel. 1948 Larceny; Another Part of the Forest; Black Bart; River Lady. 1949 Criss Cross; Manhandled; Too Late for Tears; Johnny Stool-Pigeon. 1950 One Way Street; Winchester 73; The Underworld Story. 1951 Al Jennings of Oklahoma; Chicago Calling. 1953 Thunder Bay; Sky Commando; Terror Street. 1954 Ride Clear of Diablo; World for Ransom; Rails into Laramie; This Is My Love; Silver Lode. 1955 The Marauders; Foxfire. 1956 Battle Hymn; Storm Fear. 1957 The Burglar; Slaughter on Tenth Avenue; Night Passage. 1958 Kathy O'. 1960 Platinum High School; Rich, Young and Deadly. 1962 Six Black Horses. 1964 He Rides Tall; Taggart; Walk a Tightrope. 1965 Flight of the Phoenix; The Faceless Men; The Bounty Killer. 1966 Incident at Phantom Hill. 1967 The Hills Run Red; A River of Dollars. 1968 Five Golden Dragons; The Bamboo Saucer.

DURYEA, GEORGE. See Tom Keene

DUSBURY, ELSPETH
Born: 1912, India. Died: Mar. 10, 1967, London, England. Screen, stage and television actress. Entered films in 1960.

Appeared in: 1960 Make Mine Mink.

DUSE, ELEANORA
Born: 1858, Vigerano, Italy. Died: Apr. 23, 1924, Pittsburgh, Pa. Screen and stage actress.

Appeared in: 1916 Cenere. 1927 Madre.

DYALL, FRANKLIN
Born: Feb. 3, 1874, Liverpool, England. Died: May 8, 1950, Worthing, England. Screen, stage, radio actor, and stage producer. Father of British screen actor Valentine Dyall.

Appeared in: 1929 Atlantic (film debut). 1930 Alibi. 1931 A Night in Montmarte; A Safe Affair; Creeping Shadows. 1932 Men of Steel; The Ringer; The Limping Man; First Division. 1933 The Private Life of Henry VIII; Called Back; Case of Gabriel Perry; No Satan. 1935 The Iron Duke. 1939 All at Sea. 1940 Conquest of the Air. 1944 The Yellow Canary. 1952 Bonnie Prince Charlie.

DYER, BOB (James Robert Dyer).
Born: 1900. Died: Nov. 19, 1965, Hollywood, Calif. Entered films approx. 1930. Screen actor.

DYER, JOHN E.
Born: 1884. Died: Oct. 11, 1951, Detroit, Mich. Screen and vaudeville actor.

EAGAN, EVELYN
Born: 1908. Died: July 17, 1946, Hollywood, Calif. Screen actress.

EAGELS, JEANNE
Born: 1894. Died: Oct. 3, 1929, New York, N.Y. Screen and stage actress.

Appeared in: 1916 The World and the Woman. 1917 Under False Colors. 1927 Man, Woman and Sin. 1929 The Letter; Jealousy.

EAGER, JOHNNEY (John Tanner)
Born: 1930. Died: Sept. 8, 1963, Hollywood, Calif. Screen, stage, and television actor.

Appeared in: 1963 Four for Texas.

EAMES, CLARE
Born: 1896, Hartford, Conn. Died: Nov. 8, 1930, London, England. Screen and stage actress.

Appeared in: 1924 Dorothy Vernon of Haddon Hall. 1929 The Three Passions.

EARL, CATHERINE V.
Born: 1886. Died: Aug. 14, 1946, Hollywood, Calif.(heart attack). Screen and stage actress.

EARL, KATHLEEN
Born: 1913. Died: May 21, 1954, Hollywood, Calif. Screen and stage actress.

EARLCOTT, GLADYS
Died: May 18, 1939, Los Angeles, Calif. Screen and stage actress.

EARLE, BLANCHE "BONNIE"
Born: 1883. Died: Jan. 22, 1952, Woodland Hills, Calif.(heart attack). Screen actress. Married to silent film director William P. S. Earle.

Appeared in: 1915 Battle Cry of Peace. 1917 Within the Law.

EARLE, DOROTHY
Died: 1958. Screen actress. Married to screen actor Gabby Hayes (dec. 1969).

Appeared in: 1927 Out of the Night; Pioneers of the West.

EARLY, MARGOT
Died: Jan. 1936, Hollywood, Calif.(auto crash). Screen actress.

Appeared in: 1934 Operator 13. 1935 Naughty Marietta.

EARLY, PEARL M.
Born: 1879, Wooster, Ohio. Died: June 17, 1960, Oceanside, Calif. Screen and vaudeville actress. Toured in vaudeville with her husband John Early in an act billed as "Early & Laight."

Appeared in: 1942 My Favorite Blonde.

EAST, ED
Born: 1896, Bloomington, Ind. Died: Jan. 18, 1952, New York, N.Y.(heart attack). Screen, stage, vaudeville, radio actor, and pianist. Appeared in vaudeville with Ralph Dumke.

Appeared in: 1937 Educational short. 1938 Universal short. 1949 Jackpot Jitters. 1951 Stop That Cab.

EATON, JAY
Born: 1900. Died: Feb. 5, 1970, Hollywood, Calif.(heart attack). Screen actor. Entered films in 1919.

Appeared in: 1921 Where Lights Are Low. 1928 Lady Be Good; Man-Made Woman; The Noose; Three-Ring Marriage. 1929 Synthetic Sin. 1933 The Cocktail Hour. 1934 The Affairs of Cellini. 1935 A Night at the Opera.

EATON, MARY
Born: 1901, Norfolk, Va. Died: Oct. 10, 1948, Hollywood, Calif. (heart attack). Screen and stage actress. Married to screen actor Eddie Lawton.

Appeared in: 1923 His Children's Children. 1924 Broadway after Dark. 1929 The Cocoanuts; Glorifying the American Girl.

EBERT, BERNIE
Born: 1915. Died: Jan. 13, 1969, Hollywood, Calif.(heart attack). Screen, stage, television actor and television producer, director.

EBURNE, MAUDE
Born: 1875. Died: Oct. 15, 1960, Hollywood, Calif. Screen and stage actress.

Appeared in: 1931 Lonely Wives; Bought; The Man in Possession; Larceny Lane; Blonde Crazy; The Bat Whispers; The Guardsman; Her Majesty; Love; Indiscreet. 1932 Under Eighteen; Panama Flo; Polly of the Circus; The Passionate Plumber; Woman from Monte Carlo; The Trial of Vivienne Ware; First Year; Stranger in Town; This Reckless Age. 1933 Vampire Bat; Ladies They Talk About; Ladies Must Love; Robbers' Roost; Shanghai Madness; The Warrior's Husband; My Lips Betray; Big Executive; East of Fifth Avenue; Havana Widows. 1934 Fog; When Strangers Meet; Here Comes the Navy; Return of the Terror; Lazy River; Love Birds. 1935 Maybe It's Love; Happiness C.O.D., Ruggles of Red Gap; Party Wire; Don't Bet on Blondes. 1936 Doughnuts and Society; Reunion; Man Hunt; The Leavenworth Case; Poppy; Valiant Is the Word for Carrie. 1937 Champagne Waltz; When's

Your Birthday?; Hollywood Cowboy; Fight for Your Lady; Live, Love and Learn; Paradise Express. 1938 Riders of the Black Hills. 1939 Exile Empress; My Wife's Relatives; Mountain Rhythm; Meet Dr. Christian; Sabotage; The Covered Trailer. 1940 Courageous Dr. Christian; Dr. Christian Meets the Women; Remedy for Riches; The Border Legion. 1941 Melody for Three; West Point Widow; Among the Living; You Belong to Me. 1942 Henry and Dizzy; To Be or Not to Be; Almost Married; Henry Aldrich, Editor; The Boogie Men Will Get You. 1943 Lady Bodyguard. 1944 Henry Aldrich Plays Cupid; The Princess and the Pirate; Rosie the Riveter; The Suspect; Goodnight, Sweetheart; The Town Went Wild; Bowery to Broadway; I'm from Arkansas. 1945 Man from Oklahoma; Hitchhike to Happiness; Leave It to Blondie. 1947 Mother Wore Tights. 1948 The Plunderers. 1949 Arson, Inc. 1951 Prince of Peace.

ECCLES, JANE
Born: 1896. Died: July 1966, London, England. Screen, stage, and television actress.

Appeared in: 1959 Look Back in Anger.

ECKERLEIN, JOHN E.
Born: 1884, N.Y. Died: Sept. 9, 1926, New York, N.Y. Screen and vaudeville actor.

Appeared in: 1923 Little Old New York.

ECKHARDT, OLIVER J.
Born: 1873. Died: Sept. 15, 1952, Hollywood, Calif. Screen actor.

Appeared in: 1925 Sporting Life. 1927 The Last Trail. 1928 The Cavalier. 1930 The Lone Star Ranger.

ECKLUND, CAROL
Born: 1934. Died: Nov. 4, 1939 (burns). Five-year-old screen actress.

EDDY, MRS. AUGUSTA ROSSNER
Born: 1860. Died: Sept. 21, 1925, New York, N.Y. Screen and stage actress.

EDDY, DOROTHY
Born: 1907. Died: June 10, 1959, Brooklyn, N.Y. Screen and vaudeville actress. One of the "Four Eddy Sisters," of vaudeville and film fame.

EDDY, NELSON
Born: June 29, 1901, Providence, R.I. Died: Mar. 6, 1967, Miami, Fla.(stroke). Screen, radio, television, and opera actor.
Appeared in: 1933 Broadway to Hollywood; Dancing Lady. 1934 Student Tour. 1935 Naughty Marietta. 1936 Rose Marie. 1937 Maytime; Rosalie. 1938 The Girl of the Golden West; Sweethearts. 1939 Let Freedom Ring; Balalaika. 1940 Bitter Sweet; New Moon. 1941 The Chocolate Soldier. 1942 I Married an Angel. 1943 The Phantom of the Opera. 1944 Knickerbocker Holiday. 1946 Never Say Goodbye; Nobody Lives Forever; Willy, The Operatic Whale (voice only); Make Mine Music (voice only). 1947 End of the Rainbow; Northwest Outpost.

EDESON, ROBERT
Born: 1868, New Orleans, La. Died: Mar. 24, 1931, Hollywood, Calif.(heart attack). Screen and stage actor. Divorced from screen actress Mary Newcomb (dec. 1967).

Appeared in: 1914 Where the Trail Divides. 1915 How Molly Made Good. 1916 The Light That Failed. 1921 Extravagance. 1922 Any Night; The Prisoner of Zenda; Sure-Fire Flint; 1923 The Spoilers; Has the World Gone Mad; Luck; The Silent Partner; Souls for Sale; The Ten Commandments; The Tie That Binds; To the Last Man; You Are Guilty. 1924 Feet of Clay; The Bedroom Window; Don't Call It Love; Mademoiselle Midnight; Men; Missing Daughters; Thy Name Is Woman; Triumph; Welcome Stranger. 1925 Blood and Steel, Braveheart; The Danger Signal; Go Straight; The Golden Bed; Hell's Highroad; Keep Smiling; Locked Doors; Men and Women; The Prairie Pirate; The Rag Man; The Scarlet West. 1926 The Blue Eagle; The Clinging Vine; Eve's Leaves; Her Man O'War; The Volga Boatman; Whispering Smith. 1927 King of Kings; Altars of Desire; The Heart Thief; His Dog; The Night Bride; The Rejuvenation of Aunt Mary. 1928 Tenth Avenue; Marriage by Contract; Chicago; The Home Towners; The Man Higher Up; The Power of the Press; Beware of Blondes; A Ship Comes In; Walking Back. 1929 George Washington Cohen; Marianne; The Little Wildcat; The Doctor's Secret; A Most Immoral Lady; Romance of the Rio Grande; Dynamite. 1930 Danger Lights; Big Money; The Lash; Little Johnny Jones; Way of All Men; Cameo Kirby; Pardon My Gun; Swing High; A Devil with Women. 1931 Aloha.

EDGAR-BRUCE, TONI
Born: June 4, 1892, London, England. Died: Mar. 28, 1966, Chertsey, England. Screen, stage, and radio actress.

Appeared in: 1931 The Battle of Gallipoli. 1932 Blame the Woman. 1933 Leave It to Me; As Good As New; The Private Life of Henry VIII. 1934 The Broken Melody. 1936 Captain Bill; Boys Will Be Girls; Mr. What's His Name; Scruffy. 1938 Falling for You; The Citadel. 1943 Spitfire. 1955 Four Against Fate. Other British films: Somewhere on Leave, Heaven Is 'Round the Corner.

EDLER, CHARLES
Born: 1877. Died: Mar. 29, 1942, Santa Monica, Calif. Screen and stage actor.

Appeared in: 1921 The Magnificent Brute; That Girl Montana. 1922 The Sign of the Rose.

EDMAN, GOESTA
Born: 1887, Sweden. Died: Jan. 12, 1938, Stockholm, Sweden. Screen and stage actress.

Appeared in: 1926 Faust. 1928 Heart of a Clown; Discord; A Husband by Proxy. 1930 The Last Night; For Her Sake. 1931 Brokiga Blad. 1933 Charles XII. 1934 Kaera Slaekten. 1935 Swedenhielms; The Noble Prize Winner. 1937 Intermezzo.

EDWARDS, ALAN
Born: June 3, 1900, New York, N.Y. Died: May 8, 1954, Los Angeles, Calif. Screen and stage actor. Entered films with Edison Co. in 1912. Married to screen actress Nita Pike (dec. 1954).

Appeared in: 1921 A Virgin Paradise. 1933 The White Sister; Clear All Wires; Looking Forward; Stage Mother; Life in the Raw. 1934 The Show Off; The Frontier Marshall; Hold That Girl. 1935 If You Could Only Cook; Women Must Dress. 1936 Ring around the Moon; Forgotten Faces; Make Way for a Lady. 1937 Forty Naughty Girls. 1939 South of the Border. 1941 Mr. District Attorney. 1945 Thoroughbreds; Junior Miss. 1946 Mr. Ace.

EDWARDS, CLIFF "UKELELE IKE"
Born: June 14, 1895, Hannibal, Mo. Died: July 17, 1971, Hollywood, Calif. Screen, stage, vaudeville actor, and singer. Divorced from singer Irene Wiley and screen actress Nancy Dover.

Appeared in: 1929 The Hollywood Revue of 1929; So This Is College?; Marianne; What Price Glory?. 1930 Montana Moon; Way Out West; Romeo in Pajamas; Those Three French Girls; Good News; Forward March; The Lullaby; Dough Boys; Lord Byron of Broadway; War Babies. 1931 Parlor, Bedroom and Bath; The Great Lover; The Sin of Madelon Claudet; Dance, Fools, Dance!; Stepping Out; The Prodigal; Shipmates; Sidewalks of New York; Laughing Sinners; Hell Divers. 1932 Young Bride; The Big Shot; Fast Life; Love Starved. 1933 Flying Devils; Take a Chance; MGM short. 1934 George White's Scandals. 1935 George White's 1935 Scandals; Red Salute. 1936 The Man I Marry. 1937 They Gave Him a Gun; Between Two Women; Saratoga; Bad Guy; The Women Men Marry; MGM short. 1938 The Girl of the Golden West; The Bad Man of Brimstone; The Little Adventuress. 1939 Maisie; Smuggled Cargo; Gone with the Wind. 1940 High School; His Girl Friday; Pinocchio (voice of Jiminy Cricket); Millionaires in Prison; Flowing Gold; Friendly Neighbors. 1941 The Monster and the Girl; She Couldn't Say No; Power Dive; Knockout; International Squadron; Thunder Over the Prairie; Prairie Stranger. 1942 West of Tombstone; Sundown Jim; Lawless Plainsmen; Riders of the Northland; Bad Men of the Hills; Seven Miles to Alcatraz; Pirates of the Prairie; Overland to Deadwood; American Empire; Bandit Ranger. 1943 Fighting Frontier; The Falcon Strikes Back; Salute for Three; The Avenging Rider. 1947 Fun and Fancy Free (voice). 1965 The Man from Button Willow (voice).

EDWARDS, EDNA PARK
Born: 1895, Pittsburgh, Pa. Died: June 5, 1967, Burbank, Calif. Screen, stage, vaudeville actress, and radio writer.

EDWARDS, ELEANOR
Born: 1883, N.Y. Died: Oct. 22, 1968, Los Angeles, Calif. Screen and stage actress. Entered films in 1922. Married to screen actor Snitz Edwards (dec. 1937).

EDWARDS, GUS (Gus Simon)
Born: Aug. 18, 1881, Germany. Died: Nov. 7, 1945, Los Angeles, Calif. Screen, stage, vaudeville, radio actor, songwriter, and film producer.

Appeared in: 1929 The Hollywood Revue of 1929. 1932 Screen Songs (short). 1933 Screen Songs (short); Mr. Broadway.

EDWARDS, HENRY
Born: Sept. 18, 1882, Weston-Super-Mare, England. Died: Nov. 2, 1952, Chobham, England. Screen, stage actor, film director, and stage producer.

Appeared in: 1911 Clancarty. 1915 The Man Who Stayed at Home; A Welsh Singer; Lost and Won. 1916 Far from the Maddening Crowd. 1917 Merely Mrs. Stubbs. 1918 Broken Threads; The Refugee; Dick Carson Wins Through; Tares; Nearer My God to Thee; Hepworth; The Hanging Judge; The Touch of the Child; Toward the Light; "Edwards" series. 1919 His Dearest Possession; The City of Beautiful Nonsense; The Kinsman; Possession. 1920 Aylwin; John Forest Finds Himself; A Temporary Vagabond. 1921 The Bargain. 1922 The Amazing Quest of Ernest Bliss; Simple Simon; Tit for Tat. 1923 Boden's Boy; The Naked Man. 1924 World of Wonderful Reality; The Lunatic at Large; Lily of the Alley. 1926 The Flag Lieutenant; The Fake; Further Adventures of the Flag Lieutenant. 1927 Fear. 1928 Three Kings; Ringing the Charges. 1931 Call of the Sea. 1932 The Barton Mystery. 1933 General John Regan. 1934 The Man Who Changed His Name; Are You a Mason?. 1935 Scrooge. 1937 High Treason; Juggernaut. 1946 Green for Danger. 1947 The Magic Bow. 1948 Take My Life; Long Belongs to Me. 1949 Woman Hater. 1950 The Verger; Madeleine; The Golden Salamander; Dear Mr. Prohack; Trio. 1951 The Lady with a Lamp; The Lucky Mascot; The Rossiter Case; Oliver Twist. 1952 The Long Memory. 1953 Double Confession. Other British films: The Joker; The Girl in the Night; Stranglehold; Brother Alfred.

EDWARDS, JAMES
Born: 1912, Ind. Died: Jan. 4, 1970, San Diego, Calif.(heart attack). Negro screen, stage, and television actor.

Appeared in: 1949 Man Handled; The Set-Up; Home of the Brave. 1951 The Steel Helmet; Bright Victory. 1952 The Member of the Wedding. 1953 The Joe Louis Story. 1954 The Caine Mutiny. 1955 African Manhunt; Seven Angry Men; The Phoenix City Story.

EDWARDS, MATTIE
Born: 1886. Died: June 26, 1944, Los Angeles, Calif. Screen actress. Entered films approx. 1924.

Appeared in: 1936 Give Us This Night.

EDWARDS, NEELY (Cornelius Limbach)
Born: Sept. 16, 1889, Delphos, Ohio. Died: July 10, 1965, Woodland Hills, Calif. Screen, stage, and vaudeville actor. Married to screen actress Margarita Snow (dec. 1958). Was half of hoofer-comedy team known as "The Hall Room Boys."

Appeared in: 1921 Brewster's Millions; The Little Clown. 1922 The Green Temptation. 1925 I'll Show You the Town. 1926 Footloose Widows; Made for Love. 1927 The Princess on Broadway. 1928 Excess Baggage; Sunny California (short). 1929 Dynamite; Gold Diggers of Broadway; Show Boat. 1930 Scarlet Pages,plus the following shorts: Her Relatives; The Window Cleaners; The Milky Way. 1931 The Hangover (short). 1932 the following shorts: Junior; The Weekend. 1933 Diplomaniacs; Love, Honor, and Oh, Baby!

EDWARDS, SARAH
Born: 1883. Died: Jan. 7, 1965, Hollywood, Calif. Screen, stage, and vaudeville actress.

Appeared in: 1929 Glorifying the American Girl. 1935 Ruggles of Red Gap; The World Accuses; Welcome Home; The Dark Angel; Two-Fisted. 1936 The Golden Arrow; Earthworm Tractors; Palm Springs; Early to Bed. 1937 We're on the Jury; It's Love I'm After;Hollywood Hotel. 1938 Touchdown Army; Women Are Like That. 1939 Boy Trouble; Meet Doctor Christian; The Shop around the Corner. 1940 Young People; Strike up the Band; Mr. District Attorney. 1941 Meet John Doe; Sunset in Wyoming; All That Money Can Buy. 1942 Rings on Her Fingers; Dudes are Pretty People; The Forest Rangers; Scattergood Survives a Murder. 1943 Dixie Dugan; Calaboose. 1944 Storm over Lisbon; The Big Noise; Where Are Your Children?. 1945 Abbot and Costello in Hollywood; Saratoga Trunk. 1946 It's a Wonderful Life. 1947 The Bishop's Wife. 1950 Petty Girl; The Fuller Brush Girl; The Glass Menagerie. 1951 Honeychile. 1952 The Devil and Daniel Webster (reissue and retitle of All That Money Can Buy, 1941).

EDWARDS, SNITZ
Born: 1862, Hungary. Died: May 1, 1937, Los Angeles, Calif. (arthritis). Screen and stage actor. Entered films in 1920. Married to screen actress Eleanor Edwards (dec. 1968).

Appeared in: 1920 The City of Masks. 1921 The Charm School; Cheated Love; Ladies Must Live; The Love Special; No Woman Knows. 1922 The Ghost Breaker; The Gray Dawn; Human Hearts; June Madness; Love Is an Awful Thing; Rags to Riches; Red Hot Romance. 1923 Children of Jazz; Hollywood; The Huntress; Modern Matrimony; Rosita; Souls for Sale; Tea with a Kick. 1924 The Thief of Bagdad; Hill Billy; In Fast Company; Inez from Hollywood; Passion's Pathway; Tarnish; Tiger Love; The Tornado, A Woman Who Sinned. 1925 Seven Chances; Heir-Loons; A Lover's Oath; Old Shoes; The Phantom of the Opera; The White Desert. 1926 Battling Butler; April Fool; The Clinging Vine; The Cruise of the Jasper B; The Lady of the Harem; The Sea Wolf; Volcano; The Wanderer. 1927 Red Mill; College; Night Life. 1929 A Dangerous Woman; The Mysterious Island; The Phantom of the Opera (and 1925 version). 1931 Right of Way; Sit Tight; Public Enemy.

EDWARDS, TED (M. E. Barrell)
Born: 1883. Died: Sept. 29, 1945, Los Angeles, Calif. Screen and vaudeville actor. In Mack Sennett comedies and an original Keystone Kop.

Appeared in: 1924 Fires of Youth.

EDWARDS, VIRGINIA
Died: Mar. 7, 1964, Hollywood, Calif. Screen, stage actor, playwright, and drama coach.

Appeared in: 1932 Silver Dollar.

EGAN, MISHKA
Born: 1891. Died: Feb. 15, 1964, Hollywood, Calif. Screen and vaudeville actor.

EGGENTON, JOSEPH
Born: 1870. Died: June 3, 1946, Hollywood, Calif. Screen and stage actor.

Appeared in: 1940 The Doctor Takes a Wife; You'll Find Out.

EINSTEIN, HARRY. See Parkyakarkus

EKSTROM, MARTA
Born: 1899, Sweden. Died: Jan. 26, 1952, Stockholm, Sweden. Screen and stage actress.

Appeared in: 1938 John Ericsson Victor of Hampton Roads. 1949 Katrina.

ELBA, MARTA
Born: 1920, Cuba. Died: Apr. 19, 1954, Mexico City, Mexico (cancer). Screen, stage actress, and newspaper columnist.

ELDER, DOTTIE
Born: 1929. Died: Nov. 28, 1965, Hollywood, Calif.(heart attack). Screen and television actress.

ELDER, RICHARD LT. COL.
Born: 1911. Died: Oct. 4, 1963, Fort Huachuca, Ariz.(heart attack). Screen and radio actor.

ELDRIDGE, ANNA MAE
Born: 1894. Died: Apr. 17, 1950, Van Nuys, Calif. Screen actress.

Appeared in silents.

ELDRIDGE, CHARLES E.
Born: 1854. Died: Oct. 29, 1922 (cancer). Screen and stage actor.
Appeared in: 1918 Sporting Life. 1921 Ashamed of Parents; Made in Heaven. 1922 No Trespassing. 1925 Hearts and Spurs.

ELDRIDGE, JOHN
Born: Aug. 30, 1904, San Francisco, Calif. Died: Sept. 23, 1961, Laguna Beach, Calif.(heart attack). Screen, stage, and television actor.

Appeared in: 1934 Flirtation Walk; The Man with Two Faces. 1935 Dangerous; Dr. Socrates; The Goose and the Gander; The Girl from Tenth Avenue; Snowed Under; Man of Iron; Oil for the Lamps of China; The Woman in Red; The White Cockatoo. 1936 The Murder of Dr. Harrigan; Follow Your Heart; His Brother's Wife; Murder by an Aristocrat. 1937 Fair Warning; Charlie Chan at the Olympics; The Go-Getter; The Holy Terror; Mr. Dodd Takes the Air; Mysterious Crossing; One Mile from Heaven; Sh! the Octopus. 1938 Blind Alibi; Women Are Like That; Persons in Hiding. 1939 King of Underworld; Private Detective; Television Spy; Undercover Doctor. 1940 Always a Bride; The Devil's Pipeline; Dr. Kildare's Strange Case; The Marines Fly High; Son of Roaring Dan. 1941 Flight from Destiny; The Black Cat; Blossoms in the Dust; High Sierra; Horror Island; Mr. District Attorney in the Carter Case. 1942 Madame Spy; The Mad Doctor of Market Street. 1944 Beautiful but Broke; Bermuda Mystery; Song of Nevada. 1945 Bad Men of the Border; Dangerous Passage; Eve Knew Her Apples; Dangerous Partners. 1946 Swing Parade of 1946; Dark Alibi; Passkey to Danger; Little Miss Big; Temptation; Circumstantial Evidence; The French Key; I Ring Doorbells; Live Wires; There Goes Maisie. 1947 Backlash; Seven Were Saved; Second Chance; The Fabulous Joe; 1948 Angels' Alley; California's Gold; Jinx Money; Whispering Smith. 1949 The Sickle or the Cross; Sky Dragon; Square Dance Jubilee; Stampede; Top of the Morning. 1950 Champagne for Caesar; Lonely Hearts Bandits; Rustlers on Horseback; Unmashed. 1951 All That I Have; Insurance Investigator; Rhythm Inn; Street Bandits. 1953 Loophole. 1955 Toughest Man Alive. 1956 The First Traveling Saleslady. 1958 I Married a Monster from Outer Space. 1960 Freckles. 1961 Five Guns to Tombstone.

ELINOR, CARLI D.
Born: Sept. 21, 1890, Bucharest, Rumania. Died: Oct. 20, 1958, Hollywood, Calif.(heart attack). Screen actor and musician. Appeared in silents.

ELIZONDO, JOAQUIN
Born: 1896. Died: June 15, 1952, Hollywood, Calif. Screen actor and dancer. Formerly Mae Murray's Dancing partner.

ELLINGFORD, WILLIAM
Born: 1863. Died: May 20, 1936, Los Angeles, Calif. Screen and stage actor.

Appeared in: 1927 Hands Off.

ELLIOTT, DICK
Born: 1886. Died: Dec. 22, 1961, Hollywood, Calif. Screen, stage, and television actor.

Appeared in: 1934 We're Rich Again. 1935 Annie Oakley; It Happened in New York. 1936 Brilliant Marriage; Her Master's Voice; Neighborhood House. 1937 China Passage; Quick Money; The Outcasts of Poker Flat. 1938 Campus Confessions; Penitentiary; Under Western Stars. 1939 Frontiers of '49; Nancy Drew and the Hidden Staircase; Let Us Live; The Story of Alexander Graham Bell; Boy Trouble; Mr. Smith Goes to Washington; Sudden Money. 1940 Behind the News; Flight Angels; Florian; L'il Abner; One Man's Law. 1941 The Pittsburgh Kid; Top Sgt. Mulligan; Up in the Air; Sunset in Wyoming. 1942 The Man from Headquarters; Scattergood Survives a Murder; Sweetheart of the Fleet. 1943 Wintertime; After Midnight with Boston Blackie; Laugh Your Eyes Away. 1944 Adventures of Mark Twain; Silent Partners; Girl in the Case; Henry Aldrich Plays Cupid; Hi Beautiful; Whispering Footsteps; Goin' to Town; When Strangers Marry. 1945 Adventures of Kitty O'Day; The Clock; Gangs of the Waterfront; Christmas in Connecticut. 1946 Partners in Time; Rainbow over Texas; That Texas Jamboree; Hot Cargo; High School Hero; Dangerous Money; Ginger; Her Sister's Secret. 1947 For the Love of Rusty; Heading for Heaven. 1948 Main Street Kid; The Dude Goes West; Homicide for Three; Slippy McGee. 1949 Feudin' Rhythm; Night Unto Night; Rose of the Yukon; Trail of the Yukon. 1950 Across the Badlands; A Modern Marriage; Rock Island Trail; Western Pacific Agent. 1951 Fort Defiance; Honeychile. 1952 High Noon; Montana Belle. 1954 Witness to Murder. 1957 Don't Knock the Rock; The Joker Is Wild; New Day at Sundown; Up in Smoke. 1958 In the Money.

ELLIOTT, GERTRUDE (Gertrude Dermott)
Born: 1874, Rockland, Me. Died: Dec. 24, 1950, Kent, England. Screen and stage actress. Sister of screen actress Maxine Elliott (dec. 1940).

Appeared in: 1915 Hamlet.

ELLIOTT, GORDON. See William ''Wild Bill'' Elliott

ELLIOTT, LESTER
Born: 1888. Died: Nov. 9, 1954, Van Nuys, Calif.(heart attack). Screen and stage actor.

ELLIOTT, LILLIAN
Born: 1875. Died: Jan. 15, 1959, Hollywood, Calif.(stroke). Screen and stage actress. Mother of screen actor Lloyd Corrigan (dec. 1969).

Appeared in: 1921 Lavender and Old Lace; Too Much Married. 1924 The Chorus Lady; One Glorious Night. 1925 Old Clothes; Proud Flesh; Sally, Irene and Mary. 1926 The City; The Family Upstairs; Partners Again. 1927 Ankles Preferred; King of Kings. 1930 Her Wedding Night; Liliom; The Swellhead. 1931

The Single Sin. 1932 The Man I Killed; Polly of the Circus. 1934 Trumpet Blows; Palsie Walsie (short). 1938 The Jury's Secret; Wanted by the Police. 1939 Tough Kid. 1942 Road to Happiness. 1965 Laurel and Hardy's Laughing 20's (documentary).

ELLIOTT, MAXINE (Jessica Dermott)
Born: Feb. 5, 1873, Rockland, Me. Died: Mar. 5, 1940, Juan Les Pins, France (heart ailment). Stage and screen actress. Sister of screen actress Gertrude Elliott (dec. 1950). Divorced from stage actor Nat Goodwin.

Appeared in: 1917 Fighting Odds. 1919 The Eternal Magdalene.

ELLIOTT, ROBERT
Born: Ireland. Died: 1951. Screen actor.

Appeared in: 1919 Checkers. 1921 Lonely Heart; Money Maniac; A Virgin Paradise. 1922 The Broken Silence; Fair Lady; A Pasteboard Crown; Without Fear. 1923 Man Wife. 1928 Happiness Ahead; Light of New York; Obey Your Husband; Romance of the Underworld. 1929 The Lone Wolf's Daughter; Protection; Thunderbolt. 1930 Captain Thunder; The Divorcee; The Doorway to Hell; Hide-out; Kathleen Mavoureen; Men of the North; Sweet Mama. 1931 The Finger Points; The Maltese Falcon; The Star Witness; Five Star Final; Murder at Midnight; The Midnight Patrol; White Eagle; Madison Square Garden; The Phantom of Crestwood; Rose of the Rio Grande; Conquering Horde; The Montana Kid; Secret Menace; Mother and Son; Oklahoma Jim. 1932 Galloping Thru; Riders of the Desert; Call Her Savage; Broadway to Cheyenne; Two-Fisted Justice; Single-Handed Sanders; Week Ends Only; Texas Pioneers. 1933 Self Defense; Crime of the Century; Return of Casey Jones; Heroes for Sale; Lady Killer. 1934 Girl of the Limberlost; Transatlantic Merry-Go-Round; Gambling Lady; Woman Who Dared; Twin Husbands. 1935 The World Accuses; Black Sheep; Times Square Lady; Port of Lost Dreams; Circumstantial Evidence. 1936 I'd Give My Life. 1938 Trade Winds. 1939 The Roaring Twenties; I Stole a Million; Mickey the Kid; Gone with the Wind; The Saint Strikes Back. 1940 Half a Sinner. 1945 Captain Tugboat Annie. 1946 The Devil's Playground.

ELLIOTT, WILLIAM ''WILD BILL'' (Gordon Elliott)
Born: 1904, Pattonsburg, Mo. Died: Nov. 26, 1965, Las Vegas, Nev.(cancer). Screen, stage, and television actor.

Appeared in: 1927 The Private Life of Helen of Troy. 1928 Valley of Hunted Men; The Arizona Wildcat; Beyond London's Lights. 1929 Passion Song; Restless Youth; Broadway Scandals; Napoleon, Jr. 1930 The Great Divide. 1933 Gold Diggers of 1933. 1934 Registered Nurse; Wonder Bar. 1935 The Traveling Saleslady; Devil Dogs of the Air; The Woman in Red; The Girl from 10th Avenue; The Goose and the Gander; Moonlight on the Prairie; Man of Iron; Gold Diggers of 1935. 1936 The Murder of Dr. Harrigan; Murder by an Aristocrat; Down the Stretch; The Case of the Velvet Claws; Trailin' West; Polo Joe; The Case of the Black Cat. 1937 Melody for Two; Midnight Court; Fugitive in the Sky; Guns of the Pecos; Speed to Spare; Love Takes Flight; Wife, Doctor and Nurse; Swing it, Professor; Boots and Saddles; Boy of the Streets. 1938 The Great Adventures of Wild Bill Hickok (serial); In Early Arizona; The Devil's Party; Lady in the Morgue. 1939 The Taming of the West; Lone Star Pioneers; The Law Comes to Texas; Overland with Kit Carson (serial); Frontiers of '49. 1940 Man from Tumbleweed; Prairie Schooners; The Return of Wild Bill; Pioneers of the Frontier. 1941 Return of Daniel Boone; Where Did You Get That Girl?; Roaring Frontiers; Beyond the Sacramento; The Wildcat of Tucson; North from the Lone Star; Hands across the Rockies; Across the Sierras; The Lone Star Vigilantes; The Son of Davy Crockett; King of Dodge City. 1942 Valley of Vanishing Men (serial); Bullets for Bandits; Vengeance of the West: The Devil's Trail; North of the Rockies; Prairie Gunsmoke. 1943 Calling Wild Bill Elliott; Bordertown Gun Fighters; The Man from Thunder River; Wagon Tracks West; Death Valley Manhunt. 1944 Marshall of Reno; Hidden Valley Outlaws; Cheyenne Wildcat; Vigilantes of Dodge City; Mojave Firebrand; Sheriff of Las Vegas; Tucson Raiders; Overland Mail Robbery; The San Antonio Kid. 1945 The Great Stagecoach Robbery; Lone Texas Ranger; Phantom of the Plains; Bells of Rosarita; Colorado Pioneers; Marshal of Laredo; Wagon Wheels Westward. 1946 Sun Valley Cyclone; Sheriff of Redwood Valley; Conquest of Cheyenne; California Gold Rush; In Old Sacramento; The Plainsman and the Lady. 1947 Wyoming; The Fabulous Texan. 1948 The Gallant Legion; In Old Los Angeles. 1949 The Last Bandit; Hellfire. 1950 The Savage Horde; The Showdown. 1952 The Maverick; The Longhorn; Waco; Vengeance Trail; Kansas Territory; Fargo. 1953 The Homesteaders; Revel City; Vigilante

Terror; Topeka. 1954 Bitter Creek; The Forty-Niners. 1955 Dial Red O; Sudden Danger. 1956 Calling Homicide. 1957 Footsteps in the Night; Chain of Evidence.

ELLIS, DIANE
Born: Dec. 20, 1909, Los Angeles, Calif. Died: Dec. 16, 1930, Madras, India. Screen actress.

Appeared in: 1927 Paid to Love; The Cradle Snatchers; Chain Lightning; Is Zat So?; Hook and Ladder No. 9. 1928 Happiness Ahead. 1929 The Leatherneck; High Voltage. 1930 Laughter.

ELLIS, EDWARD
Born: 1871, Coldwater, Mich. Died: July 26, 1952, Hollywood, Calif. Screen and stage actor.

Appeared in: 1921 The Frontier of the Stars. 1932 I Am a Fugitive from a Chain Gang. 1933 Girl Missing; From Headquarters; Without Glory; After Tonight; Strictly Personal. 1934 Madame Spy; Hi, Nellie; The Ninth Guest; The Last Gentleman; Trumpet Blows; The President Vanishes; The Thin Man. 1935 The Return of Peter Grimm; Wanderer of the Wasteland; Village Tale; Transient Lady; The Black Sheep. 1936 Chatterbox; The Lady Consents; Winterset; Fury; The Texas Rangers. 1937 Maid of Salem; Midnight Madonna; Let Them Live; The Man in Blue. 1938 Little Miss Broadway; A Man to Remember. 1939 Man of Conquest; Main Street Lawyer; Career; Three Sons; Remember. 1942 A Man Betrayed; Steel against the Sky. 1942 The Omaha Trail.

ELLIS, EVELYN
Born: 1894. Died: June 5, 1958, Saranac Lake, N.Y.(heart ailment). Screen, stage, and television actress.

Appeared in: 1948 The Lady from Shanghai. 1953 The Joe Louis Story. 1955 Interrupted Melody.

ELLIS, PATRICIA (Patricia Gene O'Brien)
Born: May 20, 1916, Birmingham, Mich. Died: Mar. 26, 1970, Kansas City, Mo. Screen and stage actress. She was a Wampus Baby Star.

Appeared in: 1932 Three on a Match; Central Park. 1933 Forty-Second Street; Hollywood on Parade (short); Picture Snatcher; Elmer the Great; The King's Vacation; The Narrow Corner; Convention City; The World Changes. 1934 Harold Teen; Melody for Two; St. Louis Kid; Easy to Love; Big Hearted Herbert; The Circus Clown; Here Comes the Groom; Let's Be Ritzy; Affairs of a Gentleman. 1935 While the Patient Slept; Bright Lights; The Case of the Lucky Legs; The Pay Off; A Night at the Ritz; Stranded; Hold 'Em Yale. 1936 Sing Me a Love Song; Freshman Love; Snowed Under; Boulder Dam; Love Begins at Twenty; Down the Stretch; Postal Inspector. 1937 Venus Makes Trouble; Step Lively, Jeeves!, Rhythm in the Clouds; Paradise for Two; Melody for Two. 1938 The Lady in the Morgue; Blockheads; Romance on the Run; The Gaiety Girls. 1939 Back Door to Heaven; Fugitives at Large.

ELLIS, ROBERT
Born: June 27, 1892, Brooklyn, N.Y. Died: May 19, 1935, Hollywood, Calif. Screen, stage actor, and film director. Married to screen actress Vera Reynolds (dec. 1962).

Appeared in: 1919 Louisiana; Upstairs and Down. 1921 Handcuffs or Kisses; Ladies Must Live. 1922 The Woman Who Fooled Herself; Anna Ascends; Hurricane's Gal; The Dangerous Little Demon; Wild Honey; The Infidel; Love's Masquerade. 1923 The Wild Party; The Wanters; Dark Secrets; The Flame of Life; Mark of the Beast. 1924 A Cafe in Cairo; For Sale; The Law Forbids; On Probation; Lover's Lane; Silk Stocking Gal. 1925 Forbidden Cargo; Lady Robinhood; Northern Code; Capital Punishment; Defend Yourself; The Part Time Wife; Speed. 1926 S.O.S. Perils of the Sea; Brooding Eyes; The Girl from Montmartre; Devil's Dice; Ladies of Leisure; Whispering Canyon. 1927 The Lure of the Night Club; Ragtime. 1928 Varsity; Freedom of the Press; Law and the Man; The Law's Lash; Marry the Girl. 1929 Restless Youth; Tonight at Twelve; The Love Trap; Broadway. 1930 The Squealer; Undertow; What Men Want. 1931 The Last Parade; The Good Bad Girl; Murder at Midnight; Aloha; Caught Cheating; The Fighting Sheriff; Dancing Dynamite; Is There Justice?; The Devil Plays; Mounted Fury. 1932 American Madness; The Last Man; White Eagle; The Deadline; One Man Law; Behind Stone Walls; Fighting Fools; Phantom Express; Daring Danger; Last Man; From Broadway to Cheyenne; White Eagle; All American; The Penal Code; Women Won't Tell; Come on Danger?; A Man's Land; Slightly Married. 1933 Officer 13; Speed Demon; Reform Girl; Constant Woman; Treason; Soldiers of the Storm; Thrill Hunter;

The Sphinx; Police Call; The Important Witness; Only Yesterday; Notorious but Nice. 1934 I've Got Your Number; Dancing Man; Madame Spy; Girl of the Limberlost.

ELLSLER, EFFIE
Born: 1855, Philadelphia, Pa. Died: Oct. 9, 1942, Hollywood, Calif.(heart attack). Screen and stage actress.

Appeared in: 1926 Old Ironsides. 1927 Honeymoon Hate. 1928 The Actress. 1929 Woman Trap. 1930 Song O' My Heart; The Lady of Scandal. 1931 The Front Page; Up Pops the Devil; Daddy Long Legs. 1933 Doctor Bull; Second Hand Wife; The Girl in 419, The Chief. 1934 Hold that Girl. 1935 The Whole Town's Talking; Black Fury; We're Only Human. 1936 Drift Fence.

ELLSWORTH, JACK HERSCHEL
Born: 1911. Died: Aug. 19, 1949, Hollywood, Calif. Screen actor.

ELMAN, HARRY "ZIGGY"
Born: May 26, 1914, Philadelphia, Pa. Died: June 25, 1968, Van Nuys, Calif. Bandleader, musician, screen actor, and composer.

Appeared in: 1955 The Benny Goodman Story.

ELMER, BILLY (William E. Johns)
Born: 1870. Died: Feb. 24, 1945, Hollywood, Calif. Screen, stage, and vaudeville actor.

Appeared in: 1914 The Virginian. 1921 The Foolish Age; The Road Demon. 1922 The Bootlegger's Daughter; Pawned. 1923 In Search of a Thrill. 1924 Battling Mason; The Whipping Boss.

ELTINGE, JULIAN (Bill Dalton)
Born: 1883, Butte, Mont. Died: Mar. 7, 1941, New York, N.Y. (cerebral hemorrhage). Screen, stage, and vaudeville actor.

Appeared in: 1915 How Molly Made Good. 1917 The Countess Charming; The Clever Mrs. Carfax. 1918 Over the Rhine; Widows Might; War Relief. 1922 The Isle of Love. 1925 Madame Behave. 1940 If I Had My Way.

ELVIDGE, JUNE
Born: 1893. Died: May 1, 1965, Eatontown, N.J. Screen, stage, and vaudeville actress.

Appeared in: 1915 The Lure of a Woman. 1916 La Boheme. 1919 The Poison Pen. 1921 Fine Feathers. 1922 Beauty's Worth; Beyond the Rocks; Forsaking All Others; The Impossible Mrs. Bellew; The Man Who Saw Tomorrow; The Power of a Lie; Quincy Adams Sawyer; Thelma; The Woman Conquers. 1923 The Eleventh Hour; The Prisoner; Temptation. 1924 Chalk Marks; Pagan Passions; Painted People; The Right of the Strongest; The Torrent.

ELY, HARRY R.
Born: 1883. Died: July 15, 1951, Hollywood, Calif. Silent screen actor.

EMERICK, BESSE
Born: 1875, Rochester, Ind. Died: Dec. 13, 1939, Boston, Mass. Screen actress.

Appeared in: 1917 The Black Stork. 1922 Welcome to Our City.

EMERSON, HOPE
Born: Oct. 29, 1897, Hawarden, Iowa. Died: Apr. 25, 1960, Hollywood, Calif.(liver ailment). Screen, stage, television, and radio actress. Nominated for Academy Award for Best Supporting Actress in Caged (1950).

Appeared in: 1932 Smiling Faces. 1948 Cry of the City; That Wonderful Urge. 1949 House of Strangers; Adam's Rib; Dancing in the Dark; Roseanne McCoy; Thieves' Highway. 1950 Caged; Copper Canyon; Double Crossbones. 1951 Belle Le Grande. 1952 Westward the Women. 1953 Lady Wants Mink; Champ for a Day; A Perilous Journey. 1954 Casanova's Big Night. 1955 Untamed. 1956 The Day They Gave Babies Away. 1957 Guns of Fort Petticoat; All Mine to Give. 1958 Rock-A-Bye Baby.

EMERSON, JOHN
Born: May 29, 1874, Sandusky, Ohio. Died: Mar. 7, 1956, Pasadena, Calif. Screen, stage actor, playwright, screenwriter, film, stage producer, and film director. Married to authoress Anita Loos.

Appeared in: 1914 The Conspiracy; Bachelor's Romance. 1915 The Failure; Ghosts. 1916 The Flying Torpedo.

EMERTON, ROY
Born: 1892, Canada. Died: 1944. Screen actor.

Appeared in: 1932 The Sign of Four. 1934 The Lash; The Triumph of Sherlock Holmes. 1935 Lorna Doone; Java Head. 1936 Everything Is Thunder; Nine Days a Queen. 1937 The Silent Barrier; Big Fella; The Last Adventurers. 1938 Doctor Syn; Drums; Convict 99; Q Planes; Home from Home. 1940 Haunted Honeymoon; The Thief of Bagdad; Busman's Honeymoon. 1941 Frightened Lady. 1943 The Young Mr. Pitt; The Man in Grey. 1944 Henry V (U.S. 1946). 1958 Henry V (re-release of 1944 film).

EMERY, MRS. EDWARD. See Isabel Waldron

EMERY, GILBERT
Born: 1882. Died: Dec. 31, 1934, Los Angeles, Calif. Screen and stage actor. Entered films in 1924.

EMERY, GILBERT (Arthur MacArthur)
Born: 1875, Naples, N.Y. Died: Oct. 26, 1945. Screen, stage actor, and screenwriter. Entered films in 1920.

Appeared in: 1921 Cousin Kate. 1929 Behind That Curtain; Sky Hawk. 1930 Sarah and Son; Prince of Diamonds; Let Us Be Gay; A Lady's Morals; Soul Kiss. 1931 A Royal Bed; Scandal Sheet; The Lady Refuses; Ladies' Man; Party Husband; Upper Underworld; Rich Man's Folly; The Ruling Voice. 1932 Man Called Back; A Farewell to Arms. 1933 Gallant Lady. 1934 Coming Out Party; All of Me; The House of Rothschild; Where Sinners Meet; One More River; Now and Forever; Grand Canary; I Believed in You; Whom the Gods Destroy. 1935 Clive of India; Man Who Reclaimed His Head; Night Life of the Gods; Let's Live Tonight; Cardinal Richelieu; Goin' to Town; Reckless Roads; Ladies Crave Excitement; Harmony Lane; Without Regret; Peter Ibbetson; Magnificent Obsession. 1936 Wife vs. Secretary; Dracula's Daughter; Bullets or Ballots; The Girl on the Front Page; Little Lord Fauntleroy. 1937 The Life of Emile Zola; Double or Nothing; Souls at Sea. 1938 Making the Headlines; The House of Mystery; The Buccaneer; Lord Jeff; A Man to Remember; Storm over Bengal; Always Goodbye. 1939 The Saint Strikes Back; Juarez; The Lady's from Kentucky; Nurse Edith Cavell. 1940 Raffles; The House of the Seven Gables; Anne of Windy Poplars; The Rivers End; South of Suez. 1941 That Hamilton Woman; Rage in Heaven; Adam Had Four Sons; Scotland Yard; A Woman's Face; Singapore Woman; New Wine; Sundown. 1942 The Remarkable Andrew; Escape from Hong Kong; The Loves of Edgar Allan Poe. 1944 The Return of the Vampire; Between Worlds. 1945 The Brighton Strangler.

EMERY, JOHN
Born: 1905, New York, N.Y. Died: Nov. 16, 1964, New York, N.Y. Screen, stage, and television actor. Divorced from screen actress Tallulah Bankhead (dec. 1968).

Appeared in: 1937 The Road Back. 1941 Here Comes Mr. Jordan; The Corsican Brothers. 1942 Two Yanks in Trinidad; Ship Ahoy; Eyes in the Night; George Washington Slept Here. 1943 Assignment in Brittany. 1944 Mademoiselle Fifi. 1945 Spellbound; Blood on the Sun; The Spanish Main. 1947 The Voice of the Turtle. 1948 Joan of Arc; The Woman in White; The Gay Intruders; Let's Live Again. 1950 Dakota Lil; Rocket Ship X-M; Frenchie; Double Crossbones. 1951 Joe Palooka in the Triple Cross. 1954 The Mad Magician. 1955 A Lawless Street. 1956 Forever Darling; The Girl Can't Help It. 1957 Kronos. 1958 Ten North Frederick. 1964 Youngblood Hawke.

EMMET, KATHERINE
Died: June 6, 1960, N.Y. Screen, stage, and radio actress.

Appeared in: 1921 Orphans of the Storm; Paying the Piper. 1929 Hole in the Wall.

EMMETT, FERN
Born: 1896. Died: Sept. 3, 1946, Hollywood, Calif. Screen and stage actress.

Appeared in: 1930 Bar L Ranch; Ridin' Law; The Land of Missing Men; Romance of the West; Second Honeymoon; Westbound. 1932 the following shorts: Anybody's Goat; Bridge Wives; Mother's Holiday. 1933 East of Fifth Avenue; The Vampire Bat; Hello Everybody; The Trail Drive. 1934 City Limits. 1935 Behind the Green Lights; Motive for Revenge; Smart Girl; Melody Trail. 1936 The Trail of the Lonesome Pine; The Harvester; M'Liss. 1937 Paradise Express; Come On, Cowboy; Dangerous Holiday. 1938 Scandal Sheet; Hunted Men; Overland Stage Raiders. 1939 Made for Each Other; The Rains Came; They Shall Have Music; Disputed Passage; In Love Only. 1940 Star Dust. 1941 All That Money Can Buy; Scattergood Baines; Love Crazy. 1942 Broadway; In Old California; Careful, Soft Shoulders. 1944 Together Again; Can't Help Singing; San Diego I Love You. 1945 A Song to Remember. 1946 Pillow of Death. 1952 The Devil and Daniel Webster (retitle and reissue of All That Money Can Buy, 1941).

EMMONS, LOUISE
Born: 1852. Died: Mar. 6, 1935, Hollywood, Calif. Screen actress. Entered films in 1909.

Appeared in: 1931 Heaven on Earth.

EMPEY, ARTHUR GUY
Born: 1884. Died: Feb. 22, 1963, Wadsworth, Kan. Screen actor, author, screenwriter, film director, and film producer (president of Guy Empey Pictures Corp.).

Appeared in: 1918 Over the Top. 1919 The Undercurrent. 1921 Millionaire for a Day.

ENFIELD, HUGH. See Craig Reynolds

ENGEL, ALEXANDER
Born: 1902. Died: Sept. 1968, Saarbruecken, Germany. Screen, stage, and television actor.

Appeared in: 1934 Eines Prinzen Junge Liebe. 1936 Einer zu viel an Bord. 1952 The Merry Wives of Windsor. 1958 A Time to Love and a Time to Die. 1959 Taiga. 1962 Hamlet.

ENGLE, BILLY
Born: 1889. Died: Nov. 28, 1966, Hollywood, Calif.(heart attack). Screen and burlesque actor. Entered films in 1919 and appeared in Christie comedies during the 1920s.

Appeared in: 1926 Red Hot Leather. 1927 The Cat and the Canary; The Western Whirlwind. 1935 Uncivil Warriors (short); Big Broadcast of 1936; It's a Gift. 1936 Wedding Present. 1940 Our Neighbors—the Carters. 1947 The Wistful Widow of Wagon Gap.

ENGLE, MARIE
Born: 1902. Died: Mar. 23, 1971, Hollywood, Calif.(stroke). Screen and vaudeville actress. Married to screen actor Tom Dugan (dec. 1955) and they appeared in vaudeville in an act billed as "Dugan & Engle."

ENGLISCH, LUCIE
Born: 1897, Germany. Died: Oct. 1965, Erlangen, Germany (liver ailment). Screen actress.

Appeared in: 1931 Das Rheinlandmaedel; Zwei Menschen. 1932 Der Ungetreue Eckehart; Mein Leopold; Reserve Hat Ruh; Rendez-Vous; Die Graefin von Monte Christo (The Countess of Monte Cristo); Der Schrecken der Garnison; Dienst 1st Dienst; Hurra! Ein Junge!; Schubert's Fruehlingstraum; Keine Feier Ohne Meyer. 1933 Drei Tage Mittelarrest; Das Lockende Ziel. 1934 Annemarie, Die Braut der Kompanie; Heimat am Rhein. 1935 Meine Frau; Die Schuetzenkoenigin; Die Kalte Mamsell; Gretl Zieht das Grosse Los; Die Unschuld vom Lande; Der Unbekannte Gast (The Unknown Guest). 1936 Der Mutige Seefahrer. 1937 Ein Falscher Fuffziger; The Postillon of Lonjumeau. 1938 Der Lachende Dritte; Die Landstreicher (The Hoboes). 1939 Kleines Bezirksgericht (Little Country Court); Dingehort mein Herz (My Heart Belongs to Thee); Solo per Danne; Der Kampf mit dem Dralhen (The Fight with the Dragon). 1940 Our Little Wife; Walzerlange (Waltz Melodies).

ENNIS, SKINNAY
Born: 1907. Died: June 2, 1963, Los Angeles, Calif.(suffocation). Bandleader, radio, and screen actor.

Appeared in: 1938 College Swing.

ENRIGHT, FLORENCE
Died: Apr. 3, 1961, Hollywood, Calif. Screen, stage actress, and drama coach. Entered films in 1931.

Appeared in: 1931 Women Love Once; Street Scene; Possessed. 1932 Nice Women. 1934 Six of a Kind; Gift of Gab.

ENTWISTLE, HAROLD (Charles H. Entwistle)
Born: Sept. 5, 1865, London, England. Died: Apr. 1, 1944, Hollywood, Calif. Screen, stage actor, and film director. Entered films in 1910.

Appeared in: 1932 Two against the World. 1933 Our Betters; She Done Him Wrong. 1934 The Journal of a Crime. 1935 Vanessa, Her Love Story; Paris in Spring; Mutiny on the Bounty; The Perfect Gentleman; Two Sinners. 1936 The Suicide Club.

ENTWISTLE, PEG (Lillian Millicent Entwistle)
Born: 1908, London, England. Died: Sept. 18, 1932, Hollywood, Calif.(suicide—leap off "Hollywoodland" sign). Screen and stage actress.

Appeared in: 1932 Thirteen Women.

ERICKSON, KNUTE
Born: 1871, Norrkoping, Sweden. Died: Jan. 1, 1946, Los Angeles, Calif. Screen, stage, radio, and television actor. Entered films in 1920.

Appeared in: 1921 The Conflict; Gasoline Gus. 1922 They Like 'Em Rough. 1924 Fair Week. 1925 The Commandment; Johnny Get Your Hair Cut. 1928 The Fourflusher; Scarlet Seas; Waterfront. 1929 The Squall; Twin Beds; Illusion. 1930 The Spoilers. 1933 The Bitter Tea of General Yen.

ERMELLI, CLAUDIO (Ettore Foa)
Born: 1892, Turin, Italy. Died: Oct. 29, 1964, Rome, Italy. Screen and stage actor. Entered films in 1932.

Appeared in: 1949 The Golden Madonna. 1953 Roman Holiday. 1957 A Farewell to Arms. 1960 It Started in Naples.

ERROL, LEON
Born: July 3, 1881, Sydney, Australia. Died: Oct. 12, 1951, Los Angeles, Calif.(heart attack). Screen, stage, and vaudeville actor. Entered films in 1924. Was Lord Epping in the "Mexican Spitfire" features of the early 1940s.

Appeared in: 1924 Yolanda. 1925 Sally; Clothes Make the Pirate. 1927 The Lunatic at Large. 1930 Only Saps Work; Let's Merge (short); Paramount on Parade; Queen of Scandal; One Heavenly Night. 1931 Finn and Hattie; Her Majesty, Love. 1933 Alice in Wonderland. 1934 We're Not Dressing; The Captain Hates the Sea; Hold Your Temper; Perfectly Mismated (short); The Notorious Sophie Lang. 1935 Princess O'Hara; Coronado; Vitaphone shorts. 1936 RKO shorts and Columbia shorts. 1937 Make a Wish; RKO shorts. 1938 RKO shorts. 1939 The Girl from Mexico; Career; Dancing Co-Ed; Mexican Spitfire. 1940 Pop Always Pays; Mexican Spitfire Out West; The Golden Fleecing. 1941 Six Lessons from Madame La Zonga; Where Did You Get That Girl?; Hurry, Charlie, Hurry; Mexican Spitfire's Baby; Never Give a Sucker an Even Break; Melody Lane. 1942 Moonlight in Hawaii; Mexican Spitfire at Sea; Mexican Spitfire Sees a Ghost; Mexican Spitfire's Elephant. 1943 Strictly in the Groove; Follow the Band; Mexican Spitfire's Blessed Event; Gals, Inc.; Higher and Higher; Cross Your Fingers; Cowboy in Manhattan; Cocktails for Two. 1944 Hat Check Honey; The Invisible Man's Revenge; Slightly Terrific; Babes on Swing Street; Twilight on the Prairie. 1945 She Gets Her Man; Beware of Redheads (short); Panamericana; Under Western Skies; Mama Loves Papa; What a Blonde. 1946 Riverboat Rhythm; Joe Palooka, Champ; Maid Trouble (short); Oh, Professor, Behave (short); Gentleman Joe Palooka. 1947 Joe Palooka in the Knockout. 1948 Joe Palooka in the Big Fight; Joe Palooka in the Counterpunch; Make Mine Laughs. 1950 Joe Palooka in Humphrey Takes a Chance; Joe Palooka Meets Humphrey. 1951 Footlight Varieties.

ERSKINE, WALLACE
Born: 1862, England. Died: Jan. 6, 1943, Massapequa, L.I., N.Y. Screen and stage actor.

Appeared in: 1921 Perjury. 1923 The Ragged Edge.

ERWIN, JUNE
Born: 1918. Died: Dec. 28, 1965, Carmichael, Calif. Screen actress. Appeared in "Our Gang" comedies.

ERWIN, ROY (LeRoy Franklin Erwin)
Born: 1925. Died: June 18, 1958, Rosarito Beach, Baja, Calif. (heart attack). Screen, television actor, and television writer.

ERWIN, STUART
Born: Feb. 14, 1902, Squaw Valley, Calif. Died: Dec. 21, 1967, Beverly Hills, Calif.(heart attack). Screen, stage, and television actor. Married to screen actress June Collyer (dec. 1968).

Appeared in: 1928 Mother Knows Best (film debut). 1929 Happy Days; The Exalted Flapper; New Year's Eve; Dangerous Curves; This Thing Called Love; Cockeyed World; Speakeasy; Hold Your Man; Sweetie; The Sophomore; The Trespasser; Thru Different Eyes. 1930 Men without Women; Young Eagles; Dangerous Nan McGrew; Love among the Millionaires; Playboy of Paris; Only Saps Work; Along Came Youth; Paramount on Parade; Maybe It's Love. 1931 No Limit; Up Pops the Devil; Dude Ranch; Working Girls; The Magnificent Lie. 1932 Two Kinds of Women; Make Me a Star; The Big Broadcast; Hollywood on Parade (short); The Misleading Lady; Strangers in Love. 1933 The Crime of the Century; He Learned about Women; Face in the Sky; International House; Under the Tonto Rim; Stranger's Return; Day of Reckoning; Going Hollywood; Before Dawn; Make Me a Star; Hold Your

Man. 1934 Palooka; Viva Villa!; The Band Plays On; Chained; Bachelor Bait; The Party's Over; Have a Heart. 1935 Ceiling Zero; After Office Hours; Three Men on a Horse. 1936 Exclusive Story; Pigskin Parade; Absolute Quiet; Women Are Trouble; All American Chump. 1937 Dance, Charlie, Dance; Slim; Second Honeymoon; Checkers; Small Town Boy; I'll Take Romance. 1938 Three Blind Mice; Passport Husband; Mr. Boggs Steps Out. 1939 Hollywood Cavalcade; The Honeymoon's Over; Back Door to Heaven; It Could Happen to You. 1940 Our Town; When the Daltons Rode; A Little Bit of Heaven; Sandy Gets Her Man. 1941 The Bride Came C.O.D.; Cracked Nuts. 1942 Drums of the Congo; Adventures of Martin Eden; Blondie for Victory; Through Different Eyes. 1943 He Hired the Boss. 1944 The Great Mike. 1945 Pillow to Post. 1947 Killer Dill; Heaven Only Knows; Heading for Heaven. 1948 Strike It Rich. 1950 Father Is a Bachelor. 1953 Mainstreet to Broadway. 1960 For the Love of Mike; When Comedy was King (documentary). 1963 Son of Flubber. 1964 The Misadventures of Merlin Jones.

ESSER, PETER
Born: 1896, Germany. Died: June 23, 1970, Dusseldorf, Germany. Screen and stage actor.

Appeared in: 1960 King in Shadow.

ESTEE, ADELYN
Born: 1871. Died: June 3, 1941, Los Angeles, Calif. Screen, vaudeville, and opera actress.

ESTUDILLO, LEO B.
Born: 1900, San Diego, Calif. Died: Sept. 21, 1957, San Francisco, Calif. Screen actor and trick rider.

ETHIER, ALPHONSE
Born: 1875, Springville, Utah. Died: Jan. 4, 1943, Hollywood, Calif. Screen and stage actor.

Appeared in: 1910 Thelma. 1921 A Message from Mars; The Frontier of the Stars. 1924 The Moral Sinner; The Alaskan; The Lone Wolf. 1925 Contraband; The Midnight Flyer; Gold and the Girl; The People vs. Nancy Preston. 1926 Breed of the Sea; The Lone Wolf Returns. 1927 Cheaters; Alias the Lone Wolf; The Fighting Eagle. 1928 Say It with Sables; Shadows of the Night. 1929 The Donovan Affair; In Old Arizona; Hardboiled; Smoke Bellew. 1930 The Storm; His First Command; Lightnin'; The Big Trail. 1931 Fair Warning; Transgression; Honor of the Family. 1932 Rebecca of Sunnybrook Farm; Law and Order; Wild Girl; The Match King. 1933 Men of America; Ex-Lady; Baby Face. 1934 Voice in the Night; British Agent; No More Women. 1935 Secret of the Chateau; Red Morning; The Crusades. 1936 Boss Rider of Gun Creek. 1938 The Baroness and the Butler; Sunset Trail.

EVANS, CECILIA
Born: 1902. Died: Nov. 11, 1960, San Rafael, Calif. Screen and stage actress. Entered films with Sennett.

Appeared in: 1924 Worldly Goods. 1925 Blue Blood; The Goose Hangs High; Heir-Loons; The Talker. 1926 The Family Upstairs; Whispering Wires. 1927 Prince of Headwaiters.

EVANS, CHARLES EVAN
Born: 1857, Rochester, N.Y. Died: Apr. 16, 1945, Santa Monica, Calif. Screen, stage actor, and stage producer. Married to screen actress Helena Phillips Evans (dec. 1955).

Appeared in: 1929 The Greene Murder Case; Disraeli; Happy Days. 1932 The Man Who Played God; The Expert. 1933 The King's Vacation; The Working Man. 1934 Peck's Bad Boy; The House of Rothschild. 1935 Clive of India; Cardinal Richelieu.

EVANS, DOUGLAS "DOUG"
Born: 1904, Va. Died: Mar. 25, 1968, Hollywood, Calif. Screen, stage, and radio actor.

Appeared in: 1947 The Crimson Key. 1949 Powder River Rustlers; The Golden Stallion; Hideout. 1950 No Sad Songs for Me; North of the Great Divide; At War with the Army; Rustlers on Horseback; Champagne for Caesar; Lucky Losers. 1951 Sky High; Horsie; Leave It to the Marines; Let's Go Navy. 1952 Actors and Sin. 1953 City of Bad Men. 1954 The Eddie Cantor Story. 1956 The Birds and the Bees. 1957 Short Cut to Hell; The Female Animal. 1962 The Errand Boy. 1965 The Family Jewels. 1966 The Oscar.

EVANS, EDITH
Born: 1894. Died: Oct. 12, 1962, Madison, N.J. Screen actress.

Appeared in silents. Not to be confused with Dame Edith Evans, English actress.

EVANS, EVAN
Born: 1901, Birkenhead, England. Died: Jan. 3, 1954, New York, N.Y.(heart ailment). Opera singer and screen actor. Appeared during the 1930s in film/musical shorts.

Appeared in: 1941 How Green Was My Valley.

EVANS, HELENA PHILLIPS
Born: 1875. Died: July 24, 1955, Santa Monica, Calif.(heart attack). Screen and stage actress. She appeared as both Helena Phillips and Helena Evans. Married to screen actor Charles E. Evans (dec. 1945).

Appeared in: 1921 My Lady's Latchkey. 1929 The Greene Murder Case. 1932 Two Seconds; Life Begins. 1933 The King's Vacation; Voltaire; Design for Living. 1934 Elmer and Elsie; I'll Fix It; Kiss and Make Up. 1935 College Scandal. 1938 My Bill. 1939 6,000 Enemies.

EVANS, HERBERT
Born: Apr. 16, 1883, London, England. Died: Feb. 10, 1952, San Gabriel, Calif. Screen and stage actor. Entered films in 1914.

Appeared in: 1927 The Devil Dancer. 1928 Speedy; Beyond London Lights; The Naughty Duchess. 1930 Way for a Sailor. 1933 Reunion in Vienna; Secrets; One Year Later; Brief Moment. 1935 The Glass Key; Peter Ibbetson. 1936 And Sudden Death. 1937 High Flyers. 1938 Everybody's Doing It; Dawn Patrol; Gangster's Boy. 1939 Susannah of the Mounties; The Rains Came; The Kid from Kokomo; Man about Town. 1940 The Blue Bird. 1941 Man Hunt. 1944 Abroad with Two Yanks; Her Primitive Man. 1945 The Corn Is Green. 1946 Pardon My Past; Bringing up Father; Kitty. 1949 Sky Liner; The Great Sinner.

EVANS, JACK
Born: 1893. Died: Mar. 14, 1950, Hollywood, Calif.(heart attack). Screen actor.

Appeared in: 1922 The Hidden Woman.

EVANS, NANCY
Died: July 29, 1963, Los Angeles, Calif.(cancer). Screen and stage actress. Married to actor/agent Jack Stuart-Fife.

Appeared in: 1945 Weekend at the Waldorf. 1946 My Reputation. 1947 Life with Father. 1956 The Peacemaker.

EVANS, PAULINE
Born: 1917. Died: Jan. 22, 1952, Calexico, Calif. Screen actress.

EVANS, RENEE
Born: 1908. Died: Dec. 22, 1971, Hollywood, Calif.(heart condition). Screen, stage actress, and dancer. Married to stage actor John Alban and mother of stage actress Diane Alban.

Appeared in: 1933 42nd Street.

EVANS, REX
Born: 1903, England. Died: Apr. 3, 1969, Glendale, Calif. Screen and stage actor.

Appeared in: 1933 Along Came Sally. 1936 Camille. 1937 The Prince and the Pauper; The Wrong Road. 1939 Zaza. 1940 The Philadelphia Story; Adventure in Diamonds. 1941 A Woman's Face; The Shanghai Gesture. 1943 Frankenstein Meets the Wolf Man. 1944 Higher and Higher; The Thin Man Goes Home. 1946 Till the Clouds Roll By. 1947 Dangerous Millions. 1952 Captain Pirate. 1953 Loose in London; Jamaica Run. 1954 Knock on Wood; A Star Is Born; It Should Happen to You. 1956 The Birds and the Bees. 1957 Merry Andrew. 1958 The Matchmaker. 1961 On the Double.

EVELYN, JUDITH (J. E. Allen)
Born: 1913. Died: May 7, 1967, New York, N.Y.(cancer). Screen, stage, television, and radio actress.

Appeared in: 1951 The Thirteenth Letter. 1954 The Egyptian; Rear Window. 1955 Female on the Beach. 1956 Hilda Crane; Giant. 1958 The Brothers Karamazov; Twilight for the Gods. 1959 The Tingler.

EVELYNNE, MAY
Born: 1856. Died: Apr. 3, 1943, Los Angeles, Calif. Screen and stage actress.

EVEREST, BARBARA
Born: June 9, 1890, London, England. Died: Feb. 9, 1968, London, England. Screen, stage, television, and radio actress.

Appeared in: 1931 Lily Christine. 1932 When London Sleeps; The Lodger; There Goes the Bride; The World, The Flesh and the Devil. 1933 The Umbrella; Love's Old Sweet Song; The Wandering Jew. 1934 Passing Shadows; The Warren Case. 1935 The Passing of the Third Floor Back; Scrooge; The Phantom Fiend. 1936 Love in Exile; Man behind the Mask. 1937 When Thief Meets Thief; Jump for Glory; Old Mother Riley. 1940 He Found a Star. 1942 Commandoes Strike at Dawn. 1943 Mission to Moscow; The Phantom of the Opera. 1944 Jane Eyre; The Uninvited; Gaslight. 1945 The Fatal Witness; The Valley of Decision. 1946 Wanted for Murder. 1947 The Patient Vanishes; Frieda. 1949 Madeleine. 1951 Tony Draws a Horse; Children of Chance. 1958 The Safecracker. 1961 Upstairs and Downstairs. 1964 Nurse of Wheels; These Are the Damned.

EVERS, ERNEST P.
Born: 1874. Died: July 22, 1945, Hollywood, Calif. Screen and stage actor. Entered films approx. 1915.

EVERTON, PAUL
Born: 1869. Died: Feb. 26, 1948, Woodland Hills, Calif.(heart attack). Screen and stage actor.

Appeared in: 1918 The Eagle's Eye (serial). 1921 Cappy Ricks; City of Silent Men; The Conquest of Canaan; Proxies; The Silver Lining. 1923 The Little Red Schoolhouse. 1925 That Royle Girl. 1937 They Won't Forget; The Life of Emile Zola; The Great Garrick. 1938 Reformatory; Touchdown Army; Midnight Intruder; The Beloved Brat; Merrily We Live; Outside the Law; Orphans of the Street; Gun Law; Strange Case of Dr. Meade. 1939 Topper Takes a Trip; Stand up and Fight; Whispering Enemies; Trapped in the Sky; Maisie; Joe and Ethel Turp Call on the President; The Great Man Votes. 1940 Mexican Spitfire Out West; Prairie Law. 1942 Tennessee Johnson. 1945 Leave Her to Heaven.

EYSOLDT, GERTRUD
Born: 1871, Germany. Died: Jan. 6, 1955, Ohlstadt, West Germany. Screen, stage actress, and stage director.

Appeared in: 1953 Keepers of the Night.

EYTHE, WILLIAM
Born: Apr. 7, 1918, Mars, Pa. Died: Jan. 26, 1957, Los Angeles, Calif.(acute hepatitis). Screen, stage, radio, television actor, stage producer, and stage director.

Appeared in: 1943 The Ox-Bow Incident (film debut); The Song of Bernadette. 1944 The Eve of St. Mark; Wilson; A Wing and a Prayer. 1945 Czarina; The House on 92nd Street; A Royal Scandal; Colonel Effingham's Raid. 1946 Centennial Summer; Man of the Hour. 1948 Meet Me at Dawn; Mr. Reckless. 1949 Special Agent. 1950 Customs Agent.

FABRE, SATURNIN
Born: 1884, France. Died: Oct. 24, 1961, Paris, France. Screen and stage actor.

Appeared in: 1932 Paris-Beguin. 1936 Les Petits. 1937 Pepe le Moko (U.S. 1941). 1938 Generals without Buttons. 1940 The Mayor's Dilemma. 1942 Nine Bachelors; The Pasha's Wives. 1948 Un Ami Viendra Ce Soir (A Friend Will Come Tonight). 1950 Gates of the Night; The Scandals of Clochemerle; Ignace. 1951 Miquette. 1952 The French Way (U.S. 1959); 1955 Holiday for Henrietta. 1962 The Most Wanted Man in the World.

FABREGAS, VIRGINIA
Born: 1870, Vautepec, Morelos, Mexico. Died: Nov. 17, 1950, Mexico City, Mexico. Screen and stage actress. Made Spanish language films in Hollywood in 1919 and 1937-38.

Appeared in: 1934 La Sangre Manda. 1938 Abnegacion.

FABRIZI, MARIO
Born: 1925. Died: Apr. 5, 1963, London, England. Screen, stage, and television actor.

Appeared in: 1961 Postman's Knock. 1962 On the Beat; Operation Snatch; Ring-A-Ding Rhythm!. 1963 The Punch and Judy Man.

FADDEN, GENEVIEVE
Born: Oakdale, Calif. Died: Mar. 28, 1959, Santa Monica, Calif. Screen, stage, and vaudeville actress. Married to screen actor Tom Fadden.

FAHRNEY, MILTON H.
Born: 1871. Died: Mar. 27, 1941, Culver City, Calif.(heart attack). Screen, stage actor, and film director. Entered films in 1907.

Appeared in: 1924 Not Built for Runnin'; Yankee Speed. 1926 Chasing Trouble. 1927 In the First Degree. 1929 Untamed.

FAIN, JOHN
Born: 1915, Jonesville, La. Died: Jan. 9, 1970, Malibu, Calif.(hit by car). Screen actor.

Appeared in: 1963 Beach Party. 1964 Pajama Party.

FAIRBANKS, DOUGLAS, SR.
Born: May 23, 1883, Denver, Colo. Died: Dec. 12, 1939, Santa Monica, Calif.(heart attack). Screen, stage actor, and film director. Won Photoplay 1922 Medal of Honor for Robin Hood. Divorced from screen actress Mary Pickford. Father of screen actor Douglas Fairbanks, Jr.

Appeared in: 1915 The Lamb (film debut); His Picture in the Papers; Double Trouble. 1916 Reggie Mixes In; The Americano; The Matrimaniac; Manhattan Madness; The Good Bad Man; Flirting with Fate; Half Breed; American Aristocracy; The Habit of Happiness. 1917 In Again, out Again; Wild and Wooly; Down to Earth; The Man from Painted Post; Reaching for the Moon. 1918 Headin' South; Mr. Fix-It; Say! Young Fellow; War Relief; Bound in Morocco; He Comes up Smiling; Arizona. 1919 Knickerbocker Buckaroo; His Majesty the American; Modern Musketeers. 1920 Where the Clouds Roll By; The Mollycoddle; The Mark of Zorro. 1921 The Nut; The Three Musketeers. 1922 Robin Hood. 1924 The Thief of Bagdad. 1925 Don Q. 1926 The Black Pirate. 1927 The Gaucho; Show People. 1929 The Iron Mask; Taming of the Shrew. 1931 Reaching for the Moon (and 1917 version); Around the World in Eighty Minutes. 1932 Mr. Robinson Crusoe. 1934 The Private Life of Don Juan. 1961 Days of Thrills and Laughter (documentary). 1963 The Great Chase (documentary). 1973 Sky High (documentary).

FAIRBROTHER, SYDNEY
Born: July 31, 1872, England. Died: Jan. 4, 1941, London, England. Screen and stage actress.

Appeared in: 1916 Iron Justice. 1926 Nell Gwyn. 1928 Confetti. 1931 The Third String; Murder on the Second Floor; Bindle. 1932 The Second Mrs. Phipps; Lucky Ladies; Insult: Excess Baggage. 1933 Chu Chin Chow. 1934 The Crucifix. 1935 Brewster's Millions; The Private Secretary. 1936 The Last Journey. 1937 King Solomon's Mines; Dreaming Lips; Paradise for Two. 1938 Little Dolly Daydream; The Gaiety Girls.

FAIRE, VIRGINIA BROWN (Virginia Labuna)
Born: 1899, Brooklyn, N.Y. Died: Sept. 8, 1948, Hollywood, Calif. Screen and stage actress. Entered films in 1918. Married to screen actor Dick Durham.

Appeared in: 1921 Without Benefit of Clergy; Fightin' Mad. 1922 Omar the Tentmaker; Monte Cristo. 1923 Vengeance of the Deep; Stormswept; The Cricket on the Hearth; Thundergate; Shadows of the North. 1924 The Lightning Rider; Peter Pan; The Air Hawk; Romance Ranch; Welcome Stranger. 1925 His People; Friendly Enemies; The Calgary Stampede; The Thoroughbred; Recompense. 1926 The Temptress; Frenzied Flames; The Wolf Hunters; Desert Valley; Broadway Billy; Chip of the Flying U; The Mile-a-Minute Man; Racing Romance; Wings of the Storm. 1927 The Devil's Masterpiece; Tracked by the Police; Hazardous Valley; White Flannels; Gun Gospel; Pleasure before Business. 1928 The Chorus Kid; Queen of the Chorus; The House of Shame; The Body Punch; Danger Patrol; The Canyon of Adventure; A Race for Life; Undressed. 1929 The Donovan Affair; The Devil's Chaplain; Handcuffed; Burning the Wind; Untamed Justice. 1930 Murder on the Roof; Trails of Peril; The Lonesome Trail; Breed of the West. 1934 West of the Divide.

FAIRFAX, JAMES
Born: 1897, England. Died: May 8, 1961, Papeete, Tahiti (heart attack). Screen, television, and vaudeville actor.

Appeared in: 1948 The Challenge. 1949 Mrs. Mike. 1950 Tyrant of the Sea; Customs Agent; Fortunes of Captain Blood. 1952 Last Train from Bombay. 1953 White Goddess; Abbott and Costello Meet Dr. Jekyll & Mr. Hyde. 1962 Mutiny on the Bounty (died while filming).

FAIRMAN, AUSTIN
Born: 1892, London, England. Died: Mar. 26, 1964, Dedham, Mass. Screen, stage, radio actor, and playwright.

Appeared in: 1930 Her Hired Husband. 1931 The Grand Dame (short). 1938 Bulldog Drummond's Peril. 1940 British Intelligence.

FALCONETTI, RENEE
Born: 1901, France. Died: Dec. 12, 1946, Buenos Aires, Argentina. Screen and stage actress.

FALLON, CHARLES (Charles von Der Belin)
Born: 1885, Antwerp, Belgium. Died: Mar. 11, 1936, Hollywood, Calif.(heart attack). Screen, stage actor, film producer, and film director.

Appeared in: 1935 The Man Who Broke the Bank at Monte Carlo. 1936 Next Time We Love.

FANNING, FRANK B.
Born: 1880. Died: Mar. 3, 1934, Los Angeles, Calif. Screen and stage actor. Appeared in: 1922 The Masked Avenger. 1930 Guilty.

FARFAN, MARIAN
Born: 1913. Died: Apr. 3, 1965, Hollywood, Calif. Screen actress.

FARFARIELLO (Edward Migliaccio)
Born: 1881, Salerno, Italy. Died: Mar. 28, 1946, N.Y. Screen, vaudeville, and radio actor. Appeared in several Hollywood shorts.

FARLEY, JAMES LEE "JIM"
Born: Jan. 8, 1882, Waldron, Ark. Died: Oct. 12, 1947, Pacoima, Calif. Screen and stage actor.

Appeared in: 1919 Nugget Nell. 1921 That Something; The Devil Within; Bar Nothin'; The One-Man Trail; Bucking the Line. 1922 Gleam O'Dawn; Travelin' On; When Danger Smiles; Boy Crazy; Little Wildcat; My Wild Irish Rose. 1923 Trifling with Honor; The Woman with Four Faces; Wild Bill Hickok. 1924 The City That Never Sleeps. 1925 A Son of His Father. 1926 The Lodge in the Wilderness. 1927 King of Kings; The Tired Business Man; The General. 1928 The Racket; Shady Lady; The Grip of the Yukon; Mad Hour; The Perfect Crime; A Woman against the World. 1929 Weary River; In Old Arizona; Hunted; The Voice of the City; The Dance of Life; The Godless Girl; Courtin' Wildcats; Dynamite. 1930 Lucky Larkin; Danger Lights. 1931 Fighting Caravans; Three Rogues. 1932 Scandal for Sale. 1934 Here Comes the Groom. 1935 Hold 'Em Yale; Down to Their Last Yacht; Midnight Phantom; Westward Ho. 1936 High Treason; Captain January; Dancing Pirate; Song of the Saddle; The Bride Walks Out. 1937 Mannequin; City of Havens; The Californian. 1938 Quick Money. 1939 Dodge City; I stole a Million; The Forgotten Woman. 1940 East Side Kids. 1941 World Premiere; Badlands of Dakota; Among the Living; All That Money Can Buy. 1942 This Gun for Hire; Quiet Please, Murder; The Silver Bullet; You Can't Escape Forever. 1943 What a Man!. 1944 Hail the Conquering Hero; San Fernando Valley; The Adventures of Mark Twain; Gambler's Choice. 1952 The Devil and Daniel Webster (retitle and reissue of All that Money Can Buy, 1941).

FARMER, FRANCES
Born: Sept. 19, 1914, Seattle, Wash. Died: Aug. 1, 1970, Indianapolis, Ind.(cancer). Screen, stage, and television actress. Divorced from screen actor Leif Erickson.

Appeared in: 1936 Come and Get It (film debut); Too Many Parents; Border Flight; Rhythm on the Range. 1937 Ebb Tide; The Toast of New York; Exclusive. 1938 Ride a Crooked Mile. 1940 South of Pago Pago; Flowing Gold. 1941 Badlands of Dakota; World Premiere; Among the Living. 1942 Son of Fury. 1958 The Party Crashers.

FARNUM, DUSTIN
Born: 1874, Hampton Beach, Maine. Died: July 3, 1929, New York, N.Y.(kidney trouble). Screen, stage, and vaudeville actor. Brother of screen actor William Farnum (dec. 1953).

Appeared in: 1913 The Squaw Man. 1915 Cameo Kirby; Captain Courtesy; The Gentlemen from Indiana. 1916 The Iron Strain; David Garrick; Davy Crockett. 1917 The Scarlet Pimpernel; The Spy; North of 53. 1918 Light of the Western Stars. 1919 A Man's Fight; A Man in the Open; The Corsican Brothers. 1920 Big Happiness. 1921 The Primal Law; The Devil Within; Call of the North. 1922 Strange Idols; Iron to Gold; The Yosemite Trail; While Justice Waits; The Trail of the Axe; Oathbound; Three Who Paid. 1923 The Virginian; Bucking the Barrier; The Buster; The Grail; The Man Who Won. 1924 Kentucky Days; My Man. 1926 The Flaming Frontier.

FARNUM, FRANKLYN
Born: 1876, Boston, Mass. Died: July 4, 1961, Hollywood, Calif.(cancer). Screen and stage actor. Entered films in 1917.

Appeared in: 1920 Vanishing Trails (serial). 1921 The Fighting Stranger; The Hunger of the Blood; The White Masks; The Struggle; The Last Chance; The Raiders. 1922 Cross Roads; Gold Grabbers; Angel Citizens; Gun Shy; Texas; Smiling Jim; So This Is Arizona; When East Comes West; Trail's End; The Firebrand. 1923 The Man Getter; It Happened out West; Wolves of the Border. 1924 A Desperate Adventure; Two Fisted Tenderfoot; Battling Brewster; Calibre 45; Baffled; Courage; Crossed Trails; Western Vengeance. 1925 Border Intrigue; The Drug Store Cowboy; The Gambling Fool; The Bandit Tamer; Double-Barreled Justice; Rough Going; Two Gun Sap. 1930 Beyond the Rio Grande; Beyond the Law. 1931 Hell's Valley; Not Exactly Gentlemen; Three Rogues; Leftover Ladies; Oklahoma Jim. 1932 Human Targets; Mark of the Spur; Honor of the Bad Man. 1934 Frontier Days; Honor of the Range. 1935 Hopalong Cassidy; The Crusades; The Ghost Riders; Powdersmoke Range. 1936 Frontier Justice; Preview Murder Mystery. 1938 Prison Train. 1944 Saddle Leather Law. 1948 Assigned to Danger. 1950 Destination Murder; Sunset Boulevard. 1952 My Pal Gus. 1958 King Creole; Rock-a-Bye Baby.

FARNUM, WILLIAM
Born: July 4, 1876, Boston, Mass. Died: June 5, 1953, Los Angeles, Calif.(cancer). Screen and stage actor. Brother of screen actor Dustin Farnum (dec. 1929).

Appeared in: 1913 The Redemption of David Corson. 1914 The Spoilers (small part in 1942 remake); The Sign of the Cross. 1915 The Plunderer; The Nigger. 1916 A Man of Sorrow. 1917 A Tale of Two Cities; The Heart of a Lion; The Conqueror. 1918 Les Miserables; Rough and Ready. 1919 The Last of the Duanes; The Man Hunter; The Lone Star Ranger. 1920 The Adventurer; Drag Harlan; If I Were King. 1921 His Greatest Sacrifice; The Scuttlers; Perjury. 1922 A Stage Romance; Shackles of Gold; Without Compromise; Moonshine Valley. 1923 The Gun Fighter; Brass Commandments. 1924 The Man Who Fights Alone. 1927 Ben Hur. 1930 If I Were King (and 1920 version): Du Barry, Woman of Passion. 1931 The Painted Desert; Oh! Oh! Cleopatra (short); Ten Nights in a Bar Room; A Connecticut Yankee; Pagan Lady. 1932 The Drifter; Mr. Robinson Crusoe; Law of the Sea; Wide Open Spaces (short). 1933 Supernatural; Marriage on Approval; Another Language; Flaming Guns. 1934 Cleopatra; Brand of Hate; Happy Landing; The Count of Monte Cristo; School for Girls; Good Dame; The Scarlet Letter; Are We Civilized?; The Silver Streak. 1935 The Crusades; The Eagles' Brood; Powdersmoke Range; Custer's Last Stand (serial); Between Men. 1936 The Last Assignment; The Clutching Hand (serial). 1937 Git along Little Dogies; Public Cowboy No. 1; Maid of Salem. 1938 Santa Fe Stampede; If I Were King (and 1920 and 1930 versions); Shine on Harvest Moon. 1939 Mexicali Rose; Colorado Sunset; Rovin' Tumbleweeds; South of the Border. 1940 Convicted Woman; Hi-Yo Silver; Kit Carson. 1941 Cheers for Miss Bishop; A Woman's Face; Gangs of Sonora; The Corsican Brothers; Last of the Duanes. 1942 The Lone Star Ranger; Today I Hang; The Silver Bullet; Deep in the Heart of Texas; The Boss of Hangtown Mesa; American Empire; The Spoilers (and 1914 version); Tennessee Johnson. 1943 Frontier Badmen; Hangmen Also Die. 1944 The Mummy's Curse. 1945 Captain Kidd. 1946 God's Country. 1947 Perils of Pauline; Rolling Home. 1948 My Dog Shep. 1949 Bride of Vengeance; Daughter of the West. 1950 The Undersea Kingdom (serial). 1951 Samson and Delilah. 1952 Jack and the Beanstalk; Lone Star.

FARQUHARSON, ROBERT
Born: 1878. Died: Jan. 11, 1966, Ticiono, Switzerland. Screen, stage, and radio actor.

Appeared in: 1931 Captivation. 1933 The Man They Couldn't Arrest.

FARR, FRANKIE (Frankie Farinacci)
Born: 1903, Albany, N.Y. Died: Mar. 20, 1953, Tulsa, Okla. Screen actor.

Appeared in: 1936 The Great Ziegfeld. 1939 Gone with the Wind.

FARR, PATRICIA
Born: 1915. Died: Feb. 23, 1948, Burbank, Calif. Screen actress.

Appeared in: 1931 The Secret Call; Silence. 1933 I Loved You Wednesday; My Weakness. 1934 I Am Suzanne; Stand up and Cheer; Tailspin Tommy (serial). 1935 Orchids to You; Helldorado. 1936 Three of a Kind; Speed to Spare. 1937 Criminals of the Air; All American Sweetheart. 1938 Lady Behave; Trade Winds. 1941 Mr. and Mrs. Smith; West Point Story.

FARRAR, GERALDINE
Born: 1882. Died: Mar. 11, 1967, Conn. Opera and screen actress.

Appeared in: 1915 Carmen. 1916 Temptation; Maria Rosa. 1917 The Devil Stone; Joan, the Woman; The Woman God Forgot. 1918 The Hell Cat; The Turn of the Wheel. 1919 The World and Its Women; The Stranger Vow; Flame of the Desert; Shadows. 1920 The Woman and the Puppet. 1921 Riddle Woman.

FARRAR, MARGARET
Born: 1901. Died: Aug. 9, 1925, Los Angeles, Calif.(suicide— poison). Screen actress.

FARRELL, CHARLES "SKIP" (Charles Farrell Fielder)
Born: 1919. Died: May 8, 1962, Hollywood, Calif.(heart attack). Screen, radio, television actor, and singer. Not to be confused with U.S. actor born in 1902 nor Irish actor born in 1905.

Appeared in: 1950 Night and the City. 1957 Morning Call. 1958 The Strange Case of Dr. Manning. 1959 The Sheriff of Fractured Jaw. 1960 Hidden Homicide. 1963 The Girl Hunters.

FARRELL, GLENDA
Born: June 30, 1904, Enid, Okla. Died: May 1, 1971, New York, N.Y. Screen, stage, and television actress. Starred in several "Torchy Blane" series films. Won 1963 Emmy Award for Best Supporting Actress in Ben Casey tv show.

Appeared in: 1929 Lucky Boy. 1930 Little Caesar; The Lucky Break (short). 1932 Life Begins (film and stage versions), I Am a Fugitive from a Chain Gang; The Match King; Three on a Match; Scandal for Sale; Night Nurse. 1933 The Mayor of Hell; Central Airport; The Keyhold; Girl Missing; Mary Stevens, M.D.; Bureau of Missing Persons; Gambling Ship; Lady for a Day; Man's Castle; Havana Widows; Grand Slam; The Mystery of the Wax Museum. 1934 The Big Shakedown; Dark Hazard; The Personality Kid; Hi, Nellie!; Merry Wives of Reno; Kansas City Princess; I've Got Your Number; Heat Lightning. 1935 Go into Your Dance; In Caliente; Traveling Saleslady; Gold Diggers of 1935; We're in the Money; Little Big Shot; Miss Pacific Fleet; The Secret Bride. 1936 Snowed Under; The Law in Her Hands; Smart Blonde; Here Comes Carter!; Gold Diggers of 1937; High Tension; Nobody's Fool. 1937 Dance, Charlie, Dance; Fly Away Baby; The Adventurous Blonde; Hollywood Hotel; Breakfast for Two; You Live and Learn. 1938 Stolen Heaven; Prison Break; The Road to Reno; Exposed; Blondes at Work; Torchy Gets Her Man. 1939 Torchy Blane in Chinatown; Torchy Runs for Mayor. 1941 Johnny Eager. 1942 A Night for Crime; The Talk of the Town; Twin Beds. 1943 Klondike Kate; City without Men. 1944 Ever since Venus. 1947 Heading for Heaven. 1948 I Love Trouble; Mary Lou; Lulu Belle. 1952 Apache War Smoke. 1953 Girls in the Night. 1954 Secret of the Incas; Susan Slept Here. 1955 The Girl in the Red Velvet Swing. 1959 Middle of the Night. 1964 The Disorderly Orderly; Kissin' Cousins. 1968 Dead Heat. 1969 Tiger by the Tail.

FARRELL, JOHN W.
Born: 1885. Died: July 8, 1953, Brooklyn, N.Y. Screen, stage, vaudeville, and television actor. Appeared in vaudeville with his wife Josephine Saxton in an act billed as "Saxton & Farrell."

Appeared in: 1949 Portrait of Jenny.

FARRELL, VESSIE
Born: 1890. Died: Sept. 30, 1935, Los Angeles, Calif. Screen and stage actress.

Appeared in: 1935 The Healer.

FARRINGTON, ADELE
Born: 1867. Died: Dec. 19, 1936, Los Angeles, Calif. Screen, stage, and vaudeville actress. Divorced from screen actor Hobart Bosworth (dec. 1943).

Appeared in: 1914 The Country Mouse. 1921 Black Beauty; The Charm School; The Child Thou Gavest Me; A Connecticut Yankee at King Arthur's Court; Her Mad Bargain; The Spenders. 1922 The Bachelor Daddy; Bobbed Hair; The Cradle; Little Wildcat; The Ordeal; A Question of Honor. 1923 Bag and Baggage; A Gentleman of Leisure; The Man Next Door; One Stolen Night; The Scarlet Lily. 1924 Along Came Ruth. 1926 The Shadow of the Law; The Traffic Cop.

FARRINGTON, FRANK
Born: 1874. Died: May 27, 1924, Los Angeles, Calif. Screen actor.

Appeared in: 1914 The Million Dollar Mystery (serial); Zudora—

The Twenty Million Dollar Mystery (serial). 1923 The Clean Up; The Courtship of Miles Standish. 1924 The Man Who Fights Alone.

FAUST, MARTIN J.
Born: Jan. 16, 1886, Poughkeepsie, N.Y. Died: July 20, 1943, Los Angeles, Calif. Screen and stage actor. Entered films in 1908.

Appeared in: 1910 A Winters Tale. 1921 Hell Bound. 1923 Big Brother; Under the Red Robe; The Silent Command; The Tents of Allah. 1924 I Am the Man; Yolanda. 1925 North Star. 1927 Chain Lightning; Spider Webs. 1928 Hello Cheyenne. 1929 Caress. 1934 Six of a Kind. 1943 The North Star (and 1925 version); This Is the Army. 1944 Ali Baba and the Forty Thieves.

FAVERSHAM, WILLIAM
Born: Feb. 12, 1868, London, England. Died: Apr. 7, 1940, Bay Shore, N.Y.(coronary embolism). Screen and stage actor.

Appeared in: 1919 The Silver King. 1920 The Man Who Lost Himself; The Sin That Was His. 1924 The Sixth Commandment. 1934 Lady by Choice. 1935 Becky Sharp; Secret of the Chateau; Mystery Woman. 1937 Arizona Days.

FAWCETT, GEORGE D.
Born: Aug. 25, 1860, Alexandria, Va. Died: June 6, 1939, Nantucket Island, Mass.(heart ailment). Screen and stage actor. Married to screen actress Percy Haswell (dec. 1945) who also appeared in films as Mrs. George Fawcett.

Appeared in: 1915 The Majesty of the Law (film debut). 1917 Panthea; The Cinderella Man. 1918 The Great Love; Hearts of the World. 1919 The Girl Who Stayed at Home; The Hope Chest; A Romance of Happy Valley; I'll Get Him Yet; Nobody Home; Turning the Tables; Scarlet Days; The Greatest Question. 1920 Two Weeks; The Branded Women; Little Miss Rebellion. 1921 Burn 'Em up Barnes; Chivalrous Charley; Hush Money; Lessons in Love; Little Italy; Nobody; Paying the Piper; Sentimental Tommy; Such a Little Queen; The Way of a Maid. 1922 Beyond the Rainbow; The Curse of Drink; Destiny's Isle; Ebb Tide; His Wife's Husband; Isle of Doubt; John Smith; Manslaughter; The Old Homestead; Polly of the Follies. 1923 Salomy Jane; The Drums of Fate; His Children's Children; Hollywood; Java Head; Just Like a Woman; Mr. Billinds Spends His Dime; Only 38; The Woman with Four Faces. 1924 West of the Water Tower; The Bedroom Window; The Breaking Point; Broken Barriers; Code of the Sea; Her Love Story; In Every Woman's Life; A Lost Lady; Pied Piper Malone; Tess of the D'Urbervilles; Triumph. 1925 The Merry Widow; The Circle; The Fighting Cub; Go Straight; The Home Maker; Joanna; The Mad Whirl; 9 3/5 Seconds; Peacock Feathers; The Price of Pleasure; Some Pun'kins; Souls for Sables; The Sporting Venus; Thank You; Up the Ladder; The Verdict; The Sporting Chance. 1926 The Flaming Frontier; Flesh and the Devil; Man of the Forest; Men of Steel; Out of the Storm; The Son of the Sheik; There You Are; Two Can Play; Under Western Skies. 1927 Captain Salvation; Duty's Reward; The Enemy; Hard-Boiled Haggerty; The Little Firebrand; Love; Painting the Town; The Private Life of Helen of Troy; Rich Men's Sons; Riding to Fame; See You in Jail; Snowbound; Spring Fever; Tillie the Toiler; The Valley of the Giants. 1928 Prowlers of the Sea; Tempest; The Wedding March. 1929 Little Wildcat; Fancy Baggage; His Captive Woman; Tide of Empire; Lady of the Pavements; Innocents of Paris; Four Feathers; The Gamblers; Wonder of Women; Hot for Paris; The Great Divide; Hearts in Exile; Men Are Like That; The Prince of Hearts. 1930 Once a Gentleman; Ladies of Leisure; Wild Company; Swing High; Hello Sister; The Bad One. 1931 Drums of Jeopardy; Woman of Experience; Personal Maid.

FAWCETT, JAMES
Born: 1905. Died: June 9, 1942, San Fernando Valley, Calif. (auto accident). Film stuntman and vaudeville acrobat.

FAY, FRANK
Born: Nov. 17, 1894, San Francisco, Calif. Died: Sept. 25, 1961, Santa Monica, Calif. Screen, stage, vaudeville, radio actor, and stage producer. Divorced from screen actress Barbara Stanwyck.

Appeared in: 1929 Show of Shows (film debut). 1930 The Matrimonial Bed; Under a Texas Moon. 1931 Bright Lights; God's Gift to Women; Stout Hearts and Willing Hands. 1932 The Slippery Pearls (short); Fool's Advice. 1935 Stars over Broadway. 1937 Nothing Sacred. 1938 Meet the Mayor. 1940 I Want a Divorce; They Knew What They Wanted; A WAC in His Life. 1943 Spotlight Scandals. 1951 Love Nest; When Worlds Collide; Stage from Blue River.

FAY, JACK
Born: 1903. Died: Nov. 15, 1928, Los Angeles, Calif. (after effects dut to injuries from explosion at Fox Studios while filming What Price Glory, 1926). Screen actor.

FAY, WILLIAM GEORGE
Born: Nov. 12, 1872, Dublin, Ireland. Died: Oct. 27, 1947, London, England. Screen, stage actor, film producer, and stage producer. Was co-founder of Abbey Theatre, Dublin.

Appeared in: 1918 Doing Her Bit (film debut). 1933 The Blarney Stone. 1934 General John Regan. 1935 Dark World. 1936 The Show Goes On; Storm in a Teacup. 1937 Kathleen Mavourneen; My Last Curtain. 1938 My Irish Molly. 1941 Spellbound. 1947 Odd Man Out; The Patient Vanishes.

FAYE, JULIA
Born: Sept. 24, 1896, Richmond, Va. Died: Apr. 6, 1966, Santa Monica, Calif.(cancer). Screen actress. Entered films in 1916.

Appeared in: 1916 His Auto Ruination; His Last Laugh; A Lover's Might. 1919 Stepping Out; Male and Female; Don't Change Your Husband. 1920 The Life of the Party. 1921 Affairs of Anatol; Fool's Paradise; Forbidden Fruit; The Great Moment; The Snob. 1922 Manslaughter; Nice People; Saturday Night. 1923 The Ten Commandments; Adam's Rib; Hollywood; Nobody's Money. 1924 Feet of Clay; Changing Husbands; Don't Call It Love; Triumph. 1925 The Golden Bed; Hell's Highroad; The Road to Yesterday. 1926 Volga Boatman; Corporal Kate; Meet the Prince; Bachelor Brides. 1927 King of Kings; The Yankee Clipper; His Dog; The Main Event; The Fighting Eagle. 1928 Chicago; Turkish Delight. 1929 The Godless Girl; Dynamite. 1930 Not So Dumb. 1933 Only Yesterday. 1936 'Til We Meet Again. 1938 You and Me. 1939 Union Pacific. 1940 North West Mounted Police. 1943 So Proudly We Hail!. 1946 The Californian. 1949 Red, Hot and Blue; A Connecticut Yankee in King Arthur's Court. 1950 Copper Canyon. 1951 Samson and Delilah. 1952 The Greatest Show on Earth. 1956 The Ten Commandments (and 1923 version). 1958 Buccaneer.

FAYLAUER, ADOLPH
Born: 1884. Died: Jan. 11, 1961, Los Angeles, Calif.(heart attack). Screen actor.

Appeared in: 1929 The Dream Melody.

FAZENDA, LOUISE
Born: June 17, 1889, Lafayette, Ind. Died: Apr. 17, 1962, Beverly Hills, Calif.(cerebral hemorrhage). Screen and vaudeville actress. Married to film producer Hal Wallis.

Appeared in: 1913 The Cheese Special; Mike and Jake at the Beach. 1915 The Great Vacuum Robbery; Wilful Ambrose; Ambrose's Fury; Ambrose's Lofty Perch; A Bear Affair; Crossed Love and Swords; A Versatile Villain; A Hash House Fraud; Fatty's Tin Type Tangle; A Game Old Knight. 1916 His Hereafter (working title Murray's Mix-Up); The Judge; A Love Riot; Her Marble Heart; The Feathered Nest; Maid Mad (working title The Fortune Teller); Bombs. 1917 The Summer Girls; Maggie's First False Step; Her Fame and Shame; Her Torpedoed Love; The Betrayal of Maggie; His Precious Life. 1920 Down on the Farm. 1922 Quincy Adams Sawyer; The Beauty Shop. 1923 Beautiful and Damned; Main Street; The Fog; The Gold Diggers; Mary of the Movies; The Old Fool; The Spider and the Rose; The Spoilers; Tea with a Kick; The Wanters. 1924 Abraham Lincoln; Being Respectable; Galloping Fish; The Lighthouse by the Sea; Listen, Lester; This Woman; True As Steel. 1925 Bobbed Hair; A Broadway Butterfly; Cheaper to Marry; Compromise; Declassee; Grounds for Divorce; Hogan's Alley; The Love Hour; The Night Club; The Price of Pleasure. 1926 The Bat; Footloose Widows; Loose Ankles; Ladies at Play; The Lady of the Harem; Millionaires; Miss Nobody; The Old Soak; The Passionate Quest. 1927 The Cradle Snatchers; Babs Comes Home; Finger Prints; The Gay Old Bird; The Red Mill; A Sailor's Sweetheart; Simple Sis; A Texas Steer. 1928 The Terror; Tillie's Punctured Romance; Domestic Troubles; Five and Ten-Cent Annie; Heart to Heart; Outcast; Pay As You Enter; Riley the Cop; Vamping Venus. 1929 The Desert Song; Hot Stuff; The House of Horror; On with the Show; Noah's Ark; Stark Mad; Hard to Get; The Show of Shows. 1930 No, No, Nanette; Rain or Shine; Gold Diggers of Broadway; Viennese Nights; Loose Ankles (and 1926 version); Leathernecking; Wide Open; Bride of the Regiment; Broadway Hoofer; High Society Blues; Spring Is Here. 1931 Gun Smoke; Cuban Love Song; Mad Parade; Newly Rich. 1932 The Slippery Pearls (short); Forbidden Adventure; Racing Youth; Unwritten Law; Once in a Lifetime. 1933 Alice in Wonderland; Universal shorts. 1934 Wonder Bar; Caravan; Mountain Music. 1935 Bad Boy; The Casino Murder Case; The Winning Ticket; Broadway Gondolier; The

Widow from Monte Carlo. 1936 Doughnuts and Society; Colleen; I Married a Doctor. 1937 Ready, Willing and Able; Ever Since Eve; First Lady; The Road Back; Merry-Go-Round of 1938. 1938 Swing Your Lady. 1939 Down on the Farm (and 1920 version); The Old Maid.

FEALY, MAUDE
Born: 1881. Died: Nov. 9, 1971, Woodland Hills, Calif. Screen and stage actress. Reportedly appeared in roles in every De-Mille picture after the advent of sound movies, including the producer's last The Ten Commandments (1956).

Appeared in: 1931 Laugh and Get Rich. 1938 The Buccaneer. 1956 The Ten Commandments.

FEILER, HERTA
Born: 1916. Died: Nov. 4, 1970, Munich, Germany. Screen actress.

Appeared in: 1939 Manner Mussen so Sein (Men Are That Way).

FELDARY, ERIC
Born: 1920, Budapest, Hungary. Died: Feb. 25, 1968, Los Angeles, Calif.(fire burns). Screen and stage actor.

Appeared in: 1941 Hold Back the Dawn. 1943 Hostages; For Whom the Bell Tolls. 1944 The Master Race; U-Boat Prisoner. 1948 I, Jane Doe; 16 Fathoms Deep. 1951 Sealed Cargo. 1954 The Iron Glove. 1956 Magnificent Roughnecks.

FELDMAN, EDYTHE A.
Born: 1913. Died: Feb. 29, 1971, Miami Beach, Fla. Screen, stage, and television actress.

Appeared in: 1969 Midnight Cowboy.

FELIPE, ALFREDO
Born: 1931. Died: 1958, Lisbon, Portugal. Screen and radio actor. Known as the Portuguese "Fernandel."

FELIX, GEORGE
Born: 1866. Died: May 12, 1949, New York, N.Y. Screen, stage, and vaudeville actor. Married to actress Lydia Berry (dec.) with whom he appeared in vaudeville.

Appeared in: 1916 Haystacks and Steeples.

FELLOWES, ROCKLIFFE
Born: 1885, Ottawa, Canada. Died: Jan. 30, 1950, Los Angeles, Calif.(heart attack). Screen and stage actor.

Appeared in: 1917 The Easiest Way. 1918 Friendly Husbands. 1920 In Search of a Sinner; Yes or No. 1921 Bits of Life; The Price of Possession. 1922 Island Wives; The Stranger's Banquet. 1923 Boy of Mine; Penrod and Sam; The Remittance Woman; The Spoilers; Trifling with Honor. 1924 The Border Legion; The Signal Tower; The Garden of Weeds; Borrowed Husbands; Cornered; Flapper Wives; Missing Daughters. 1925 The Golden Princess; Rose of the World; East of Suez; Declassee; Without Mercy; Counsel for the Defense. 1926 Syncopating Sue; Honesty—the Best Policy; The Road to Glory; Rocking Moon; Silence. 1927 The Understanding Heart; Third Degree; The Crystal Cup; The Taxi Dancer; The Satan Woman. 1929 The Charlatan. 1930 Outside the Law. 1931 Vice Squad; Monkey Business. 1932 Hotel Continental; Huddle; Renegades of the West; All American; Lawyer Man; 20,000 Years in Sing Sing; Ladies of the Big House. 1933 Rusty Rides Again; The Phantom Broadcast. 1934 Back Page.

FELLS, GEORGE (George Flevitsky)
Born: 1902. Died: May 10, 1960, N.Y. Screen, stage, radio actor, and screen writer.

FELTON, HAPPY (Francis J. Felton, Jr.)
Born: 1908. Died: Oct. 21, 1964, New York, N.Y. Screen, stage, television, vaudeville, and circus actor. Was part of "Adele Jason & The Boys" vaudeville act.

Appeared in: 1943 Swing Shift Maisie; Whistling in Brooklyn; A Guy Named Joe.

FELTON, VERNA
Born: July 20, 1890, Salinas, Calif. Died: Dec. 14, 1966, North Hollywood, Calif.(stroke). Screen, stage, television and radio actress. Married to screen actor Lee Millar (dec. 1941).

Appeared in: 1940 If I Had My Way. 1941 Dumbo (voice only). 1946 She Wrote the Book. 1949 Cinderella (voice only). 1950 Bucaneer's Girl; The Gunfighter. 1951 Alice in Wonderland; Little Egypt; New Mexico. 1952 Belles on Their Toes; Don't Bother to Knock. 1955 Picnic; The Lady and the Tramp (voice only). 1957 The Oklahoman; Taming Sutton's Gal. 1959 Sleeping Beauty (voice only). 1960 Guns of the Timberland. 1965 The Man from Button Willow. 1967 Jungle Book (voice only).

FENIMORE, FORD (Ford Fenimore Hoft)
Died: Apr. 20, 1941, El Paso, Tex. Screen and stage actor. Appeared in early Griffith films.

FENTON, FRANK (Frank Fenton-Morgan)
Born: Apr. 9, 1906, Hartford, Conn. Died: July 24, 1957, Los Angeles, Calif. Screen, stage, television actor, and screenwriter.

Appeared in: 1942 The Navy Comes Through. 1943 Claudia; Lady of Burlesque. 1944 Buffalo Bill; The Big Noise; Secret Command. 1945 Destiny; Hold That Blonde; This Man's Navy. 1946 If I'm Lucky; It's a Wonderful Life; Magic Town. 1947 Hit Parade of 1947. 1948 Red River; Mexican Hayride; Hazard; Relentless. 1949 The Clay Pigeon; The Doolins of Oklahoma; The Golden Stallion; Joe Palooka in the Big Fight; Ranger of Cherokee Strip; Rustlers. 1950 Modern Marriage; Sideshow; Trigger, Jr.; Tripoli; Rogue River; Wyoming Mail; The Lawless. 1951 The Man with a Cloak; Silver City. 1953 Eyes of the Jungle; Island in the Sky; Vicki. 1956 Emergency Hospital; Fury at Gunsight Pass; The Naked Hills. 1957 Hell Bound.

FENTON, LUCILLE
Born: approx. 1916. Died: Oct. 17, 1966, London, England. Screen and stage actress.

Appeared in: 1948 Citizen Saint.

FENTON, MABEL
Born: 1868, Van Buren County, Mich. Died: Apr. 19, 1931, Hollywood, Calif. Screen, stage, vaudeville, and burlesque actress.

Appeared in: 1915 How Molly Made Good.

FENTON, MARK
Born: 1870. Died: July 29, 1925, Los Angeles, Calif.(surgery complications after auto accident). Screen actor.

Appeared in: 1915 The Black Box (serial). 1916 The Adventures of Peg O' the Ring (serial). 1919 The Mystery of 13. 1920 Behold My Wife. 1921 The Conquering Power; The Four Horsemen of the Apocalypse; Life's Darn Funny; The Unknown; The Wallop. 1922 Headin' West; Little Eva Ascends; Too Much Business; The Village Blacksmith; The Yellow Stain. 1923 Alias the Night Wind; Speed King. 1924 American Manners; The Battling Fool; Black Lightning; A Fool's Awakening; Name the Man; The Passing of Wolf MacLean; The Spirit of the U.S.A. 1925 Brand of Cowardice; The Storm Breaker.

FENWICK, IRENE (Irene Frizzel)
Born: 1887, Chicago, Ill. Died: Dec. 24, 1936, Beverly Hills, Calif. Screen and stage actress. Married to screen actor Lionel Barrymore (dec. 1954).

Appeared in: 1916 A Coney Island Princess.

FEODOROFF, LEO
Born: 1867, Odessa, Russia. Died: Nov. 23, 1949, Long Beach, N.Y.(auto accident injuries). Screen, stage, and opera actor.

Appeared in: 1926 God Gave Me Twenty Cents. 1927 The Music Master. 1928 Laugh, Clown, Laugh.

FERGUSON, CASSON
Born: 1894. Died: Feb. 12, 1929, Culver City, Calif.(pneumonia). Screen and stage actor. Entered films with Selig.

Appeared in: 1919 Flame of the Desert. 1920 Madame X. 1921 At the End of the World; Bunty Pulls the Strings; The Unknown Wife; A Virginia Courtship; What's a Wife Worth?. 1922 Manslaughter; Borderland; The Law and the Woman; Over the Border; The Truthful Liar. 1923 Grumpy; Drums of Fate; A Gentleman of Leisure; Her Reputation. 1925 Cobra; The Road to Yesterday; The Wedding Song. 1926 For Alimony Only; Forbidden Waters. 1927 King of Kings. 1928 Tenth Avenue.

FERGUSON, ELSIE
Born: 1883, N.Y. Died: Nov. 15, 1961, New London, Conn. Screen and stage actress. Divorced from screen actor Frederick Worlock (dec. 1973).

Appeared in: 1917 Barbary Sheep (film debut); The Rise of Jennie Cushing. 1918 Rose of the World; Song of Songs; The Lie; Heart of the Wilds; A Doll's House; The Danger Mark; Under the Greenwood Tree. 1919 A Society Exile; His Parisian Wife; The Marriage Price; Eyes of the Soul; The Witness for the Defense;

The Avalanche. 1920 His House in Order. 1921 Forever; Lady Rose's Daughter; Sacred and Profane Love; Footlights. 1922 Outcast. 1924 Broadway after Dark. 1930 Scarlet Pages.

FERGUSON, GEORGE S.
Born: 1884. Died: Apr. 24, 1944, Hollywood, Calif. Screen and stage actor. Appeared in silents.

FERGUSON, HILDA (Hildegarde Gibbons)
Born: 1903. Died: Sept. 3, 1933, N.Y.(heart disease). Screen actress and show girl. Appeared in Sennett films.

FERGUSON, WILLIAM J.
Born: 1845. Died: May 4, 1930, Pikesville, Md. Screen and stage actor. He was last surviving member of cast that played in Our American Cousin, the night President Lincoln was assassinated.

Appeared in: 1920 Passers By. 1921 Dream Street. 1922 John Smith; To Have and to Hold; Kindred of the Dust; Peacock Alley; The World's Champion; The Yosemite Trail.

FERN, FRITZIE
Born: Sept. 19, 1901, Akron, Ohio. Died: Sept. 10, 1932, Hollywood, Calif. Screen and stage actress.

Appeared in: 1929 It Can Be Done; Clear the Decks; The Charlatan.

FERNANDEL (Fernand Joseph Desire Contandin)
Born: May 8, 1903, Marseilles, France. Died: Feb. 26, 1971, Paris, France.(lung cancer). Screen actor and singer.

Appeared in: 1930 Black and White (film debut). 1931 Le Rosier de Madame Husson. 1932 Angele (U.S. 1934); Francois Her; Les Bois du Sport; Paris-Beguin. 1933 He. 1935 L'Ordonnance (The Orderly). 1936 Francois Premier; La Porteuse de Pain. 1937 Regain (aka Harvest—U.S. 1939); Le Schountz; Un Carnet de Bal. 1939 Fric-Frac; Paris Honeymoon; Heartbeat. 1940 La Fille de Puisatier. 1946 The Well Digger's Daughter. 1947 Francis the First; Nais. 1950 Ignace; Hoboes in Paradise. 1952 Little World of Don Camillo (U.S. 1953, first of the Don Camillo series); Forbidden Fruit (U.S. 1959); Three Sinners; Topaz; The Cupboard Was Bare. 1953 Ali Baba. 1954 The Red Inn; The French Touch. 1955 The Sheep Has Five Legs. 1956 The Return of Don Camillo; Around the World in 80 Days; The Wild Oat. 1957 Pantaloons; Fernandel the Dressmaker; Three Feet in a Bed. 1958 Paris Holiday; Senechal the Magnificent; The Man in the Raincoat. 1959 The Law Is the Law; The Virtuous Bigamist. 1960 The Big Chief; The Easiest Profession; Croesus; Virgin Man. 1961 The Cow and I. 1962 The Most Wanted Man in the World. 1963 La Cúisine au Beurre (Cooking with Butter); Le Voyage a Biarritz (The Trip to Biarritz); The Devil and the Ten Commandments. 1964 Cherchez L'Idole (Find the Idol). 1965 My Wife's Husband. 1966 Your Money or My Life; Le Voyage du Pere. 1967 L'Homme a la Buick.

FERNANDES, BERTA LUISA
Born: 1935, Spain. Died: 1954, near Lisbon, Portugal (injuries from auto accident). Screen and stage actress. Appeared in Spanish and Portuguese films.

FERNANDES, NASCIMENTO
Born: approx. 1880, Portugal. Died: late 1955 or early 1956, Lisbon, Portugal. Screen, stage actor, and film producer.

FERNANDEZ, BIJOU
Born: 1877. Died: Nov. 7, 1961, N.Y. Screen and stage actor.

Appeared in: 1925 New Toys. 1926 Just Suppose.

FERNANDEZ, RAMON S.
Born: 1922, Mexico. Died: Sept. 22, 1962, Mexico City, Mexico (heart attack). Screen actor. Appeared in approx. 200 Mexican films.

FERRAND, EULA PEARL
Died: July 17, 1970, Visalia, Calif. Screen actress.

FERRIS, DILLON J.
Born: 1914. Died: Apr. 25, 1951, Pittsburgh, Pa. Screen and stage actor.

FETHERSTON, EDDIE (aka EDDIE FEATHERSTONE)
Died: June 12, 1965, Yucca Valley, Calif.(heart attack). Screen, stage, vaudeville, and television actor.

Appeared in: 1925 The Flame Fighter (serial). 1926 Remember; Old Ironsides. 1930 True to the Navy; Worldly Goods. 1932

Movie Crazy. 1933 Cheating Blondes. 1935 The Lost City (serial). 1937 The Shadow (short). 1938 The Lone Wolf in Paris; Women in Prison; Who Killed Gail Preston?; Violent Is the World for Curly (short). 1939 Homicide Bureau. 1947 Second Chance.

FEUSIER, NORMAN
Born: 1885. Died: Dec. 27, 1945, Hollywood, Calif. Screen and stage actor.

Appeared in: 1933 The Diamond Trail.

FIDLER, BEN
Born: 1867. Died: Oct. 19, 1932, Los Angeles, Calif. Screen actor.

FIELD, GLADYS (Gladys O'Brien)
Born: San Francisco, Calif. Died: Aug. 1920, Mount Vernon, N.Y. (childbirth). Screen actress. Appeared in early Essanay films.

FIELD, NORMAN
Born: 1879. Died: Sept. 11, 1956, Hollywood, Calif. Screen and stage actor.

Appeared in: 1950 Destination Big House; Mister 880. 1951 Street Bandits. 1952 The Invitation; The Greatest Show on Earth. 1953 The Twonky; Crazylegs. 1954 Tobor the Great.

FIELD, SID (Sidney Arthur Field)
Born: Apr. 1, 1904, Birmingham, England. Died: Feb. 3, 1950, Surrey, England (heart attack). Screen, stage, and vaudeville actor.

Appeared in: 1938 That's the Ticket. 1946 London Town. 1948 Cardboard Cavalier.

FIELDING, EDWARD
Born: 1885, N.Y. Died: Jan. 10, 1945, Beverly Hills, Calif.(heart attack). Screen and stage actor.

Appeared in: 1930 the following shorts: Grounds for Murder; Seeing Things; The Pest of Honor. 1939 Intermezzo, a Love Story. 1940 The House across the Bay; The Invisible Man Returns; All This and Heaven Too; Down Argentine Way; South of Suez; Kitty Foyle; Rebecca. 1941 So Ends Our Night; In the Navy; Hold Back the Dawn; Badlands of Dakota; Scotland Yard; Parachute Battalion; Belle Starr. 1942 In This Our Life; Beyond the Blue Horizon; Star-Spangled Rhythm; Pride of the Yankees; The Major and the Minor; Pacific Rendezvous; Ten Gentlemen from West Point. 1943 Mr. Lucky; What a Woman; Song of Bernadette. 1944 See Here, Private Hargrove; My Pal Wolf; The Man in Half Moon Street; Belle of the Yukon; Lady in the Dark; Dead Man's Eyes; Wilson. 1945 A Medal for Benny; The Beautiful Cheat; Guest Wife.

FIELDING, MARJORIE
Born: 1892, England. Died: 1956. Screen and stage actress.

Appeared in: 1940 Quiet Wedding (film and stage versions). 1943 Jeannie. 1944 The Yellow Canary. 1945 Adventure for Two (aka Demi Paradise). 1946 Quiet Weekend (U.S. 1948). 1949 Spring in Park Lane; Easy Money; Fame Is the Spur; Portrait of Clare (U.S. 1951). 1950 Conspirator; The Amazing Mr. Beecham (aka Chiltern Hundreds); The Franchise Affair (U.S. 1952). 1951 The Lavender Hill Mob; The Mudlark; Circle of Danger. 1952 The Magic Box. 1953 The Story of Mandy (aka Crash of Silence); Project M7. 1954 Rob Roy; The Highland Rogue; A Woman's Angle.

FIELDING, MINNIE (Minnie Flynn)
Born: 1871. Died: July 22, 1936. Screen, stage, and vaudeville actress. Appeared in early Biograph pictures.

FIELDING, ROMAINE
Born: 1882. Died: Dec. 16, 1927, Hollywood, Calif.(clot on brain due to infected tooth). Screen, stage actor, film director, and film producer.

Appeared in: 1921 The Man Worth While; The Rich Slave. 1927 Gun Gospel; Rose of the Golden West; Ten Modern Commandments. 1928 The Noose; The Shepherd of the Hills.

FIELDS, BENNY (Benjamin Geisenfeld)
Born: 1894, Milwaukee, Wisc. Died: Aug. 16, 1959, New York, N.Y.(heart attack). Screen, minstrel, and vaudeville actor. Married to actress Blossom Seeley, his one time vaudeville partner.

Appeared in: 1933 Mr. Broadway. 1936 The Big Broadcast of 1937. 1944 Minstrel Man.

FIELDS, JOHN
Born: 1876. Died: Nov. 8, 1938, Los Angeles, Calif. Screen and stage actor.

FIELDS, LEW (Lewis Maurice Fields)
Born: 1867, N.Y. Died: July 20, 1941, Beverly Hills, Calif. Screen, stage, vaudeville, burlesque, and minstrel actor. Was partner in comedy team of "Weber and Fields." See Joe Weber for films they appeared in.

He appeared in the following without Weber: 1930 "23 Skidoo" (short); The Duel (short); 1936 an RKO short.

FIELDS, STANLEY (Walter L. Agnew)
Born: 1880, Allegheny, Pa. Died: Apr. 23, 1941, Los Angeles, Calif.(heart attack). Screen, stage, and vaudeville actor.

Appeared in: 1930 See America Thirst; Hook, Line and Sinker; Mammy; The Border Legion; Ladies Love Brutes; The Street of Chance; Manslaughter; Cimarron; Little Caesar; City Streets; The Dove; Traveling Husbands; Her Man. 1931 A Holy Terror; Riders of the Purple Sage; Skyline; Cracked Nuts. 1932 Two Kinds of Women; Destry Rides Again; Girl of the Rio Grande; Painted Woman; Hell's Highway; Rackety Rax; The Mouthpiece; Sherlock Holmes; The Kid from Spain; Way Back Home; Girl Crazy. 1933 Constant Woman; Destination Unknown; Island of Lost Souls; Terror Abroad; He Couldn't Take It. 1934 Name the Woman; Rocky Rhodes; Palooka; Sing and Like It; Strictly Dynamite; Many Happy Returns; Kid Millions. 1935 Life Returns; Helldorado; Baby Face Harrington; Mutiny on the Bounty; The Daring Young Man. 1935 It Had to Happen; O'Malley of the Mounted; The Mine with the Iron Door; Showboat; The Gay Desperado; The Devil Is a Sissy; Ticket to Paradise. 1937 Way out West; Maid of Salem; Souls at Sea; Wells Fargo; Three Legionaires; The Hit Parade; The Sheik Steps Out; All over Town; Counsel for Crime; The Toast of New York; Wife, Doctor and Nurse; Danger—Love at Work; Ali Baba Goes to Town; Midnight Court. 1938 Wide Open Faces; Panamint's Bad Men; The Adventures of Marco Polo; Algiers; Flirting With Fate; Painted Desert; Straight, Place and Show. 1939 Fugitive at Large; Pack up Your Troubles; Exile Express; Chasing Danger; Hell's Kitchen; Blackwell's Island; The Kid from Kokomo. 1940 Viva Cisco Kid; The Great Plane Robbery; New Moon; King of the Lumberjacks. 1941 Where Did You Get That Girl?; I'll Sell My Life; The Lady from Cheyenne.

FIELDS, W. C. (Claude William Dukenfield)
Born: Feb. 20, 1879, Philadelphia, Pa. Died: Dec. 25, 1946, Pasadena, Calif.(dropsy and other ailments). Screen, stage, vaudeville, circus actor, and screenwriter. Sometimes wrote under name of Otis Criblecoblis.

Appeared in: 1915 Pool Sharks (film debut). 1924 Janice Meredith. 1925 Sally of the Sawdust. 1926 So's Your Old Man; That Royle Girl; It's the Old Army Game. 1927 Two Flaming Youths; The Potters; Running Wild. 1928 Tillie's Punctured Romance; Fools for Luck. 1930 The Golf Specialist. 1931 Her Majesty Love. 1932 If I Had a Million; The Dentist (short); Million Dollar Legs. 1933 International House; Hollywood on Parade (short); Tillie and Gus; Alice in Wonderland; The Fatal Glass of Beer (short); The Pharmacist (short); The Barber Shop (short). 1934 Six of a Kind; You're Telling Me; Old-Fashioned Way; Mrs. Wiggs of the Cabbage Patch; It's a Gift. 1935 Mississippi; David Copperfield; The Man on the Flying Trapeze. 1936 Poppy. 1938 Big Broadcast of 1938. 1939 You Can't Cheat an Honest Man. 1940 My Little Chickadee; The Bank Dick. 1941 Never Give a Sucker an Even Break. 1942 Tales of Manhattan. 1944 Follow the Boys; Song of the Open Road; Sensations of 1945. 1964 Big Parade of Comedy (documentary). 1966 W.C. Fields Comedy Festival (documentary).

FILLMORE, NELLIE
Born: 1864. Died: June 20, 1942, Winthrop, Mass. Screen, stage, vaudeville, and radio actress.

FINCH, FLORA
Born: 1869, England. Died: Jan. 4, 1940, Los Angeles, Calif. (streptococcus infection). Screen, stage, vaudeville actress, and film producer. She made 260 shorts with actor John Bunny between 1910 and 1915. They were billed as Mr. and Mrs. Bunny and/or Mr. and Mrs. Brown and fans referred to these shorts as "Bunnygraphs," "Bunnyfinches," and "Bunnyfinchgraphs." A few of these "Bunnygraphs," etc. shorts, in which she appeared during 1910-1914, are as follows: 1910 The New Stenographer. 1911 The Subdoing of Mrs. Nag; Her Crowning Glory. 1912 A Cure for Pokeritis; Leap Year Proposals. 1914 Love's Old Dream and Polishing Up.

Other films appeared in: 1908 Mrs. Jones Entertains. 1909 Jones and the Lady Book Agent. 1914 The New Secretary. 1915 The Starring of Flora Finchurch. 1917 War Prides. 1921 Lessons in Love; Orphans of the Storm. 1922 Man Wanted; Orphan Sally; When Knighthood Was in Flower. 1923 Luck. 1924 Monsieur Beaucaire; Roulette. 1925 The Adventurous Sex; The Early Bird; His Buddy's Wife; The Live Wire; Lover's Island; Men and Women; The Wrongdoers. 1926 The Brown Derby, Fifth Avenue; A Kiss for Cinderella; Oh, Baby. 1927 The Cat and the Canary; Captain Salvation; Quality Street; Rose of the Golden West. 1928 The Wife's Relations; The Haunted House; Five and Ten-Cent Annie. 1929 The Faker; Come across. 1930 Sweet Kitty Bellairs. 1931 I Take This Woman. 1934 The Scarlet Letter. 1926 Showboat; Way out West; Postal Inspector. 1939 The Women.

FINDLAY, RUTH
Born: 1904, N.Y. Died: July 13, 1949, New York, N.Y. Screen and stage actress.

Appeared in: 1937 Heroes of the Alamo. 1939 The Women.

FINDLEY, THOMAS BRUCE
Born: 1874, Guelph, Ontario, Canada. Died: May 29, 1941, Aylmer, Quebec, Can. Screen and stage actor.

Appeared in: 1920 Heliotrope. 1921 Buried Treasure. 1923 Little Old New York. 1924 Yolanda. 1925 Lucky Devil. 1926 Let's Get Married.

FINK, EMMA
Born: 1910, Guanajuato, Mexico. Died: June 13, 1966, Mexico City, Mexico (cancer). Screen and stage actress.

FINLAY, ROBERT "BOB" (Robert Finlay Bush)
Born: 1888, New Haven, Conn. Died: Apr. 2, 1929, Prescott, Ariz. Screen and vaudeville actor.

Appeared in: 1917 The Winning Punch.

FINLAYSON, HENDERSON (James Henderson Finlayson)
Born: Aug. 27, 1887, Falkirk, Scotland. Died: Oct. 9, 1953, Los Angeles, Calif.(heart attack). Screen, stage, and television actor. Was in early Keystone Kop comedies.

Appeared in: 1921 Home Talent; A Small Town Idol. 1922 The Crossroads of New York. 1923 Hollywood. 1925 Welcome Home. 1927 No Man's Law plus the following shorts: With Love and Hisses; Love 'Em and Weep; Do Detectives Think?, Flying Elephants; Sugar Daddies; The Call of the Cuckoo; The Second Hundred Years. 1928 Show Girl; Lady Be Good; Ladies Night in a Turkish Bath; Bachelor's Paradise. 1929 Two Weeks Off; Hard to Get; Wall Street; plus the following shorts: Liberty Big Business; Men O'War; The Hoosegow. 1930 Young Eagles; Flight Commander; For the Defense; The Dawn Patrol. plus the following shorts: Night Owls; Another Fine Mess. 1931 Pardon Us; Chickens Come Home; Our Wife; Stout Hearts and Willing Hands; Big Business; plus the following shorts: One Good Turn; False Roomers; A Melon-Drama; Scratch as Catch Can; Oh! Oh! Cleopatra. 1932 Thunder Below; Pack up Your Troubles; plus the following shorts: The Chimp; The Iceman's Ball; The Millionaire Cat; Jitters the Butler. 1933 Me and My Pal; Fra Diavola (The Devil's Brother); The Girl in Possession; Dick Turpin; plus the following shorts: Hokus Focus; The Druggist's Dilemma; The Gay Nighties. 1935 Treasure Blues (photo only); Thicker Than Water; Bonnie Scotland. 1936 The Bohemian Girl; Our Relations; Way out West. 1937 All over Town; Pick a Star. 1938 Blockheads. 1939 The Great Victor Herbert; Hollywood Cavalcade; The Flying Deuces. 1940 A Chump at Oxford; Saps at Sea. 1942 To Be or Not to Be. 1943 Yanks Ahoy. 1947 Perils of Pauline; Thunder in the Valley (aka Bob, Son of Battle). 1948 Grand Canyon Trail. 1949 Down Memory Lane. 1951 Royal Wedding. 1955 Soldier of Fortune. 1960 When Comedy Was King (documentary). 1964 Big Parade of Comedy (documentary). 1965 Laurel and Hardy's Laughing 20's (documentary). 1968 The Further Perils of Laurel and Hardy (documentary).

FINN, SAM
Born: 1893. Died: Dec. 14, 1958, Hollywood, Calif.(undergoing brain surgery). Screen actor and extra for 30 years.

FINNEGAN, WALTER
Born: 1873. Died: May 30, 1943, Hollywood, Calif. Screen actor.

FINNERTY, LOUIS
Born: 1883, N.J. Died: Aug. 4, 1937, Los Angeles, Calif.(intestinal obstruction). Screen and vaudeville actor.

Appeared in: 1937 Saratoga.

FIORENZA, ALFREDO
Born: 1868, Italy. Died: Feb. 24, 1931, Hollywood, Calif.
Screen and stage actor. Entered films approx. 1924.

FIO RITO, TED (Ted Fiorito)
Born: Dec. 20, 1900, Newark, N.J. Died: July 22, 1971, Scottsdale,
Ariz.(heart attack). Screen, radio actor, bandleader, and song
writer.

Appeared in: 1934 Twenty Million Sweethearts (with his orchestra). 1943 Silver Skates.

FISCHMAN, DAVID
Born: 1910. Died: Jan. 24, 1958, Los Angeles, Calif. Screen actor.

FISHER, ALFRED
Born: 1849, England. Died: Aug. 26, 1933, Glendale, Calif.
Screen, stage actor, and stage director. Entered films in 1918.

Appeared in: 1919 Third Degree. 1923 Burning Words; Railroaded. 1924 The Breathless Moment; The Fighting American;
The Storm Daughter. 1925 The Home Maker. 1926 Atta Boy; The
Country Beyond. 1927 Broadway Madness; Driven from Home.
1928 Fangs of Fate; A Million for Love; Romance of a Rogue.

FISHER, GEORGE B.
Born: 1894. Died: Aug. 13, 1960, Los Angeles, Calif. Screen and
stage actor.

Appeared in: 1913 The Man Who Went Out. 1916 Civilization. 1917
Environment. 1921 Bare Knuckles; Beach of Dreams; Colorado
Pluck; Hearts of Youth; Moonlight Follies; A Parisian Scandal;
Sure Fire. 1922 Domestic Relations; Don't Shoot; The Trail of
the Axe. 1923 Divorce. 1924 The Bowery Bishop; Excitement.
1925 After Marriage; Justice of the Far North. 1929 Apartment
Hunting (short). 1949 Joe Palooka in the Big Fight. 1950 Cham-
pagne for Caesar. 1951 Hard, Fast and Beautiful.

FISHER, MAGGIE (Maggie Holoway Fisher)
Born: 1854, England. Died: Nov. 3, 1938, Glendale, Calif.
Screen and stage actress.

FISHER, SALLY
Born: 1881. Died: June 8, 1950, Twenty-nine Palms, Calif.(heart
attack). Screen, stage, and vaudeville actress.

FISHER, WILLIAM
Born: 1868. Died: July 4, 1933, Hollywood, Calif.(heart attack).
Screen actor and acrobat.

Appeared in: 1922 The Broken Silence. 1925 The Keeper of the
Bees.

FISHER, WILLIAM G.
Born: 1883. Died: Oct. 4, 1949, Hollywood, Calif. Screen actor.

FITZGERALD, BARRY (William Joseph Shields)
Born: Mar. 10, 1888, Dublin, Ireland. Died: Jan. 4, 1961, Dublin,
Ireland. Screen and stage actor. Won Academy Award for Best
Supporting Actor in Going My Way (1944). Brother of screen
actor Arthur Shields (dec. 1970).

Appeared in: 1930 Juno and the Paycock. 1937 Ebb Tide;
Plough and the Stars. 1938 Bringing up Baby; Dawn Pa-
trol; Four Men and a Prayer; Marie Antoinette. 1939 Pacific
Liner; Saint Strikes Back; Full Confessions. 1940 The Long Voy-
age Home. 1941 The Sea Wolf; San Francisco Docks; Tarzan's
Secret Treasure; How Green Was My Valley. 1943 Amazing Mrs.
Halliday; Corvette K-225; Two Tickets to London. 1944 None but
the Lonely Heart; I Love a Soldier; Going My Way. 1945 Stork
Club; Duffy's Tavern; Incendiary Blonde; And Then There Were
None; Forever Yours; The Bells of St. Mary's. 1946 California;
Two Years before the Mast. 1947 Welcome Stranger; Easy Come,
Easy Go; Variety Girl. 1948 Naked City; The Sainted Sisters;
Miss Tatlock's Millions. 1949 Top O' the Morning; Story of Sea-
biscuit. 1950 Union Station. 1951 Silver City. 1952 The Quiet
Man. 1954 Happy Ever After; Tonight's the Night. 1956 The Ca-
tered Affair. 1958 Rooney. 1959 Broth of a Boy.

FITZGERALD, CISSY
Born: 1874, England. Died: May 5, 1941, Ovingdean, England.
Screen and stage actress. Entered films in a 50-foot film taken
at the studio where Edison was attempting to perfect a motion
picture camera.

Appeared in: 1914 The Win(k)some Widow. 1924 Babbitt; Cornered; Daring Love; Flowing Gold; Lilies of the Field; Vanity's
Price; A Woman Who Sinned. 1925 If Marriage Fails; I'll Show You
the Town; Steppin' Out. 1926 The Crown of Lies; The Danger Girl;

Flames; Her Big Night; The High Flyer; The Love Thief; Red-
heads Preferred. 1927 The Arizona Wildcat; Beauty Shoppers;
Fire and Steel; Matinee Ladies; McFadden's Flats; Two Flaming
Youths; Women Love Diamonds; Women's Wares. 1928 No Babies
Wanted; Ladies of the Night Club; Laugh, Clown, Laugh. 1929
Seven Footprints to Satan; The Diplomat (short); His Lucky Day;
The Painted Angel; Social Sinners (short). 1931 Transgression.
1933 The Masquerade; Only Yesterday. 1935 Strictly Legal.

FITZGERALD, EDWARD P.
Born: 1883. Died: May 1, 1942, Buffalo, N.Y. Screen and vaudeville actor. In vaudeville he was part of an act known as "Fitzgerald and Quigley" and later as "Fitzgerald and Madison."
Appeared in Mack Sennett comedies during 1920s.

FITZGERALD, FLORENCE IRENE
Born: 1890. Died: Jan. 31, 1962, Hartford, Conn. Screen actress.

FITZMAURICE, GEORGE
Born: Feb. 13, 1895, Paris, France. Died: June 13, 1940, Los
Angeles, Calif.(streptococcus). Screen actor, film director, and
screenwriter.

Appeared in: 1919 The Avalanche.

FITZMAURICE, MICHAEL T. (Michael Fitzmaurice-Kelly)
Born: Apr. 28, 1908, Chicago, Ill. Died: Aug. 31, 1967, New York,
N.Y. Screen, stage, radio, and television actor.

Appeared in: 1936 The House of a Thousand Candles; The Plough
and the Stars. 1937 Reported Missing. 1951 Fourteen Hours.

FITZROY, EMILY
Born: 1861, London, England. Died: Mar. 3, 1954, Gardena,
Calif.(stroke). Screen and stage actress.

Appeared in: 1920 Way Down East. 1921 Straight Is the Way;
Jane Eyre; Out of the Chorus; Wife against Wife. 1922 The
Splendid Lie; Fascination; Find the Woman; No Trespassing. 1923
Fury; Driven; Jealous Husbands; Strangers of the Night; The Pur-
ple Highway. 1924 His Hour; Secrets; The Whispered Name; Girl
of the Limberlost; Her Night of Romance; Love's Wilderness;
The Red Lily; The Man Who Came Back; Untamed Youth. 1925
Are Parents People?; Lazybones; Bobbee Hair; Outwitted; Zan-
der the Great; Thunder Mountain; The Denial; The Lady; Learn-
ing to Love; The Winding Stair; Never the Twain Shall Meet; The
Spaniard. 1926 The Bat; Bardley's, the Magnificent; Marriage
License?; What Happened to Jones; Hard Boiled; Don Juan;
High Steppers. 1927 Love; The Cheerful Fraud; Orchids and Er-
mine; Married Alive; Mockery; The Sea Tiger; Once and For-
ever; One Increasing Purpose. 1928 The Trail of '98; Foreign
Devils; Gentlemen Prefer Blondes; Love Me and the World Is
Mine; No Babies Wanted. 1929 The Bridge of San Luis Rey; The
Case of Lena Smith; Show Boat; Flirting Widow; Man from
Blankley's; She's My Weakness; Song O' My Heart; New Moon.
1931 Misbehaving Ladies; Aren't We All; The Green Spot Mystery;
It's a Wise Child; Unfaithful. 1932 High Society; Lucky Ladies.
1933 Dick Turpin. 1934 Don Quixote; Man with Two Faces; Two
Heads on a Pillow; The Captain Hates the Sea. 1935 China Seas.
1936 The Bold Caballero. 1938 The Frontiersman. 1940 Vigil
in the Night. 1943 Forever and a Day.

FLAGSTAD, KIRSTEN
Born: 1895. Died: Dec. 9, 1962, Oslo, Norway. Screen and opera
actress.

Appeared in: 1938 The Big Broadcast of 1938.

FLAHERTY, PAT J., SR.
Born: Mar. 8, 1903, Washington, D.C. Died: Dec. 2, 1970, N.Y.
(heart attack). Screen actor, film technician, and former ball-
player.

Appeared in: 1934 Come on Marines; Twentieth Century; Baby,
Take a Bow; Brand of Hate. 1935 Secret of the Chateau; Chinatown Squad; One Way Ticket. 1936 Mutiny on the Bounty; My Man
Godfrey; Hearts in Bondage; Pigskin Parade; Flying Hostess.
1937 Woman Wise; Navy Blue and Gold; On Again, off Again; A
Day at the Races; A Star Is Born; Hold 'Em Navy. 1938 Holly-
wood Stadium Mystery; Always in Trouble; She Loved a Fireman;
Telephone Operator; The Main Event. 1939 Legion of Lost Fly-
ers; Only Angels Have Wings. 1940 A Miracle on Main Street;
My Son, My Son; Midnight Limited; Black Diamonds; Flight Com-
mand. 1941 Sergeant York; Meet John Doe; Affectionately Yours;
Highway West. 1942 Gentleman Jim; Who Is Hope Schuyler?; It
Happened in Flatbush; Yankee Doodle Dandy. 1943 Hit the Ice.
1946 It Shouldn't Happen to a Dog; Home Sweet Homicide; Best
Years of Our Lives. 1947 The Bachelor and the Bobby-Soxer.

1948 Give My Regards to Broadway; The Noose Hangs High; The Babe Ruth Story; The Cobra Strikes. 1950 The Jackie Robinson Story; The Good Humor Man; Blondie's Hero. 1952 Hoodlum Empire; The Winning Team; Blackbeard the Pirate. 1955 The Desperate Hours.

FLANAGAN, BUD (Robert Winthrop)
Born: 1896, England. Died: Oct. 20, 1968, London, England. Screen, stage actor, and song writer. Appeared with Chesney Allen as part of comedy team "Flanagan & Allen" and also appeared in "Crazy Gang" films and stage presentations. Crazy Gang films included: 1937 OK for Sound. 1938 Alf's Button Afloat. 1939 The Frozen Limits. 1940 Gasbags. 1954 Life Is a Circus. Other film: 1958 Dunkirk (with Flanagan and Allen).

FLANAGAN, BUD. See Dennis O'Keefe

FLANAGAN, EDWARD J.
Born: 1880, St. Louis, Mo. Died: Aug. 18, 1925, Los Angeles, Calif.(peritonitis). Screen, stage, and vaudeville actor. Was on screen and in vaudeville as "Flanagan & Edwards" and also worked separately.

Appeared in: 1921 Don't Call Me Little Girl; Hunch.

FLANAGAN, REBECCA
Born: 1876. Died: Jan. 30, 1938, Hollywood, Calif. Screen and stage actress. Entered films approx. 1928. Married to screen actor D. J. Flanagan.

FLATEAU, GEORGES
Born: 1882, France. Died: Feb. 13, 1953, Paris, France. Screen, stage, radio, and television actor.

Appeared in: 1939 Katia.

FLEISCHMANN, HARRY
Born: 1899. Died: Nov. 28, 1943, Bakersfield, Calif.(heart attack). Screen actor.

Appeared in: 1937 She Asked for It. 1939 Ambush. 1942 Crossroads. 1943 Stand by for Action.

FLEMING, ALICE
Born: 1882. Died: Dec. 6, 1952, New York, N.Y. Screen, stage, and radio actress.

Appeared in: 1921 The Conquest of Canaan; His Greatest Sacrifice. 1941 Playmates. 1942 Who Done It? 1944 Storm over Lisbon; Vigilantes of Dodge City; Marshal of Reno. 1945 Affairs of Susan; It's a Pleasure.

FLEMING, ERIC
Born: 1926, Santa Paula, Calif. Died: Sept. 28, 1966, Tingo Maria area, Peru (drowned). Screen, stage, and television actor.

Appeared in: 1955 Conquest of Space. 1957 Fright. 1958 Queen of Outer Space. 1959 Curse of the Undead. 1966 The Glass Bottom Boat.

FLEMING, IAN
Born: Sept. 10, 1888, Melbourne, Australia. Died: Jan. 1, 1969, London, England. Screen, stage, and television actor. Not to be confused with deceased writer. Was Dr. Watson in English version of Sherlock Holmes series of films in 1930s with Arthur Wonter as Holmes.

Appeared in: 1929 The Ware Case. 1931 Sherlock Holmes' Fatal Hour. 1932 The Missing Rembrandt. 1935 The Triumph of Sherlock Holmes. 1936 The Crouching Beast. 1937 When Thief Meets Thief; Silver Blaze. 1940 The Lion Has Wings. 1941 Hatter's Castle (U.S. 1948). 1947 Captain Boycott. 1949 Quartet. 1950 Appointment with Crime; Woman in Question (aka Five Angles on Murder—U.S. 1953). 1953 Norman Conquest; Murder Will Out. 1958 High Flight. 1960 Too Hot to Handle (aka Playgirl after Dark, U.S. 1962); The Man with the Green Carnation (aka The Green Carnation and The Trials of Oscar Wilde); Bluebeards Ten Honeymoons. 1964 No, My Darling Daughter. 1965 Return of Mr. Moto. Other British films: The Briggs Family; George in Civvy Street.

FLETCHER, LAWRENCE M.
Born: 1902. Died: Feb. 11, 1970, Bridgeport, Conn. Screen, stage, and television actor.

Appeared in: 1956 The Search for Bridey Murphy.

FLEU, DORRIS BELL
Born: 1922. Died: Sept. 12, 1955, Bryn Mawr, Pa. Screen actress and singer with bands of Bunny Berrigan, Harry James and Woody Herman.

FLICK, PAT C.
Born: 1899. Died: Nov. 1, 1955, Hollywood, Calif.(cancer). Screen, stage, radio actor, and screenwriter.

Appeared in: 1935 Stars over Broadway. 1937 The Black Legion. 1938 Little Tough Guy; The Missing Guest.

FLIEGEL, MRS. ERNIE
Born: Minneapolis, Minn. Died: June 25, 1966, Minneapolis, Minn. Screen and vaudeville actress. In vaudeville appeared as part of the "Albee Sisters" act.

Appeared in: 1937 Turn off the Moon.

FLINT, HAZEL
Born: 1893. Died: Aug. 18, 1959, Hollywood, Calif. Screen and stage actress.

Appeared in: 1922 The Bootleggers. 1927 Modern Daughters.

FLINT, HELEN
Born: 1898. Died: Sept. 9, 1967, Washington, D.C.(auto injuries). Screen and stage actress.

Appeared in: 1920 Uncle Sam of Freedom Ridge. 1930 Married (short). 1934 The Ninth Guest; Broadway Bill; Midnight; Manhattan Love Song; Handy Andy. 1935 While the Patient Slept; Doubting Thomas; Ah, Wilderness. 1936 Riff Raff; Fury; Give Me Your Heart; Early to Bed; Little Lord Fauntleroy. 1937 Step Lively, Jeeves!; Married before Breakfast; Blonde Trouble; Sea Devils; The Black Legion. 1942 Time to Kill.

FLINT, JOSEPH W.
Born: 1893. Died: May 5, 1933, Los Angeles, Calif.(suicide—gunshot wounds). Screen actor.

FLIPPEN, JAY C.
Born: 1898, Little Rock, Ark. Died: Feb. 3, 1971, Hollywood, Calif.(aneurysm). Screen, stage, minstrel, vaudeville, radio, and television actor.

Appeared in: 1928 The Ham What Am (short). 1934 Marie Galante; Million Dollar Ransom. 1947 Brute Force; Intrigue. 1948 The Twisted Road. 1949 A Woman's Secret; Down to the Sea in Ships; Oh, You Beauiful Doll; They Live by Night. 1950 Buccaneer's Girl; The Yellow Cab Man; Love That Brute; Winchester "73"; Two Flags West. 1951 The Lemon Drop Kid; Flying Leathernecks; The People against O'Hara; The Lady from Texas; The Model and the Marriage Broker. 1952 The Las Vegas Story; Bend of the River; Woman of the North Country. 1953 Thunder Bay; Devil's Canyón; East of Sumatra. 1954 The Wild One; Carnival Story. 1955 Six Bridges to Cross; The Far Country; Man without a Star; It's Always Fair Weather; Kismet; Oklahoma!; Strategic Air Command. 1956 The Killing; The Seventh Cavalry; The King and Four Queens. 1957 The Restless Breed; The Halliday Brand; Hot Summer Night; Public Pigion No. 1; Night Passage; Run of the Arrow; The Midnight Story; Jet Pilot; The Deerslayer; Lure of the Swamp. 1958 Escape from Red Rock; From Hell to Texas (aka Manhunt). 1960 Wild River; Studs Lonigan; The Plunderers. 1962 Six-Gun Law; How the West Was Won. 1964 Looking for Love. 1965 Cat Ballou. 1967 The Spirit Is Willing. 1968 Fire Creek; The Hellfighters. 1969 Hello, Dolly!.

FLIPPER (Mitzi, the Dolphin)
Died: June 25, 1971, Grassy Key, Fla.(heart attack). Approx. 22 years old. Screen and television acting dolphin.

Appeared in: 1963 Flipper.

FLORATH, ALBERT
Born: 1889, Germany. Died: Mar. 10, 1957, Gailsdorf-Nordwuertemberg, West Germany. Screen, stage actor, and film producer.

Appeared in: 1933 Berlin-Alexanderplatz. 1939 Speil in Sommerwind (Play in the Summer Breezes); Der Biberpelz (The Beaver Coat). 1940 Hurra! Ich bin Papa (Hurrah! I'm a Papa).

FLOWERTON, CONSUELO
Born: 1900. Died: Dec. 21, 1965, New York, N.Y. Screen, stage, television actress, and singer. Mother of screen actress Nina Foch.

Appeared in: 1921 Camille. 1924 The Sixth Commandment.

FLYNN, ERROL
Born: June 20, 1909, Hobart, Tasmania. Died: Oct. 14, 1959, Vancouver, B.C., Canada (heart attack). Screen, stage, television actor, screenwriter, and author. Married to screen actress Patrice Wymore. Divorced from screen actresses Lili Damita and Nora Eddington. Father of screen actor Sean Flynn.

Appeared in: 1934 Murder at Monte Carlo; In the Wake of the Bounty (documentary). 1935 The Case of the Curious Bride; Don't Bet on Blondes; Captain Blood; I Found Stella Parish. 1936 Charge of the Light Brigade; Private Party on Catalina (short). 1937 Green Light; Prince and the Pauper; Another Dawn; The Perfect Specimen. 1938 Four's a Crowd; The Sisters; Dawn Patrol; Adventures of Robin Hood. 1939 Dodge City; The Private Lives of Elizabeth and Essex. 1940 Santa Fe Trail; The Sea Hawk; Virginia City. 1941 They Died with Their Boots On; Dive Bomber; Footsteps in the Dark. 1942 Desperate Journey; Gentleman Jim. 1943 Edge of Darkness; Northern Pursuit; Thank Your Lucky Stars. 1944 Uncertain Glory. 1945 Objective, Burma!; San Antonio. 1946 Never Say Goodbye. 1947 Cry Wolf; Escape Me Never. 1948 Silver River; The Adventures of Don Juan. 1949 That Forsyte Woman. 1950 Rocky Mountain; Montana; Hello, God (U.S. 1958); Kim. 1951 The Adventures of Captain Fabian. 1952 Against All Flags; Mara Maru. 1953 The Master of Ballantrae. 1954 Crossed Swords. 1955 The Dark Avenger; The Warriors. 1956 King's Rhapsody; Let's Make Up (aka Lilacs in the Spring). 1957 Instanbul; The Sun Also Rises; The Big Boodle. 1958 Too Much, Too Soon; Roots of Heaven. 1959 Cuban Rebel Girls.

FLYNN, HAZEL E.
Born: Mar. 31, 1899, Chicago, Ill. Died: May 15, 1964, Santa Monica, Calif.(heart ailment). Screen extra actress, drama editor, and newspaper film columnist. Appeared in early Essanay films.

FOLEY, JOSEPH F.
Born: 1910, Alpena, Mich. Died: July 22, 1955, Holyoke, Mass. (heart attack). Screen, stage, and television actor.

Appeared in: 1951 The Whistle at Eaton Falls.

FOLEY, RED (Clyde Julian Foley)
Born: 1910, Bluelick, Ky. Died: Sept. 19, 1968, Fort Wayne, Ind. (acute pulmonary adema). Singer and screen, television, and radio actor.

FONSS, OLAF
Born: 1882, Denmark. Died: Nov. 4, 1949, Copenhagen, Denmark (heart ailment). Screen and stage actor. Appeared in German and Danish films from 1911 to 1929.

Appeared in: Ich Lebe fur Dich (I Live for You).

FOO, WING
Born: 1910. Died: Dec. 9, 1953, Los Angeles, Calif.(heart attack). Screen and television actor.

Appeared in: 1941 Out of the Fog. 1944 The Purple Heart. 1945 Hotel Berlin; God Is My Co-Pilot; Blood on the Sun; Wonder Man.

FOOK, MONTE (Yuk Mong)
Born: 1908. Died: Mar. 27, 1933, Los Angeles, Calif.(gunshot wound). Screen actor.

FORAN, ARTHUR F.
Born: 1912. Died: Jan. 30, 1967, Queens, N.Y. Screen and stage actor.

FORBES, MARY ELIZABETH
Born: 1880, Rochester, N.Y. Died: Aug. 20, 1964, Los Angeles, Calif.(heart attack). Screen and stage actress. She was one of the original models for artists Charles Dana Gibson and Harrison Fisher. Not to be confused with British born actress, Mary Forbes.

Appeared in: 1913 Prisoner of Zenda. 1914 Zudora—The Twenty Million Dollar Mystery (serial). 1921 The Child Thou Gavest Me. 1923 The Ten Commandments.

FORBES, RALPH (Ralph Taylor)
Born: Sept. 30, 1896, London, England. Died: Mar. 31, 1951, New York, N.Y. Screen and stage actor. Married to screen actress Dora Sayers and divorced from screen actresses Ruth Chatterton (dec. 1961) and Heather Angel. Son of screen actress Mary Forbes and brother of screen actress Brenda Forbes. Appeared in early British films, a few prior to 1921 are: Reveille; Brown Sugar. 1921 The Fifth Form at St. Dominics. Entered U.S. films in 1926.

Appeared in: 1926 Beau Geste. 1927 The Enemy; Mr. Wu. 1928 The Actress; Dog of War; The Masks of the Devil; The Latest from Paris; The Trail of '98; Under the Black Eagle; The Whip. 1929 Restless Youth; The High Road. 1930 The Lady of Scandal; Mamba; The Green Goddess; Inside the Lines; Her Wedding Night; The Devil's Battalion; Lilies of the Field. 1931 Beau Ideal; Bachelor Father. 1932 Thunder Below; Christopher Strong; Smilin' Through. 1933 False Front; Pleasure Cruise; Phantom Broadcast; The Avenger; The Solitaire Man. 1934 The Barretts of Wimpole Street; Shock; Bombay Mail; Outcast Lady; The Mystery of Mr. X; Riptide; Twentieth Century; The Fountain. 1935 Strange Wives; Enchanted April; Rescue Squad; Age of Indiscretion; Streamline Express; The Goose and the Gander; The Three Musketeers. 1936 Romeo and Juliet; Piccadilly Jim; Mary of Scotland; Daniel Boone; Love Letters of a Star. 1937 The Last of Mrs. Cheyney; The Thirteenth Chair; Make a Wish; Stage Door. 1938 Women Are Like That; Annabel Takes a Tour; Kidnapped; If I Were King; Women against the World; Convicts at Large. 1939 The Hound of the Baskervilles; The Magnificent Fraud; Private Lives of Elizabeth and Essex; Tower of London. 1940 Calling Philo Vance; Curtain Call. 1944 Frenchman's Creek; Adventure in Diamonds.

FORBES-ROBERTSON, SIR JOHNSTON
Born: 1853, London, England. Died: Nov. 6, 1937, St. Margaret's Bay, England. Screen and stage actor.

Appeared in: 1915 Hamlet. 1917 The Passing of the Third Floor Back.

FORCE, FLOYD CHARLES
Born: 1876. Died: June 9, 1947, Hollywood, Calif. Screen actor. Was one of the original Keystone Kops.

Appeared in: 1921 Cupid's Brand. 1922 The Infidel; The Game Chicken; The Lone Rider. 1923 The Love Pirate. 1924 Turned Up; Surging Seas. 1926 Hearts and Spangles. 1927 The Heart of Maryland.

FORD, DAISY
Born: 1906. Died: Dec. 14, 1959, Hollywood, Calif. Screen, stage, and vaudeville actress.

FORD, FRANCIS (Francis O'Feeney)
Born: Aug. 15, 1882, Portland, Maine. Died: Sept. 5, 1953, Los Angeles, Calif. Screen, stage actor, screenwriter, film director, and producer. Entered films as an actor with Edison and then went to Vitagraph and directed and acted. Brother of film director John Ford (dec. 1973).

Appeared in: 1914 Lucille Love; Girl of Mystery (serial). 1915 The Broken Coin (serial). 1916 The Adventures of Peg O' the Ring (serial); The Purple Mask (serial). 1918 The Silent Mystery (serial). 1919 The Mystery of 13 (serial). 1921 The Great Reward (serial); Action; The Lady from Longacre; The Stampede. 1922 Another Man's Boots; The Boss of Camp 4; The Heart of Lincoln; So This Is Arizona; Storm Girl; They're Off; The Village Blacksmith; Thundering Hoofs. 1923 Mine to Keep; Haunted Valley (serial); Three Jumps Ahead. 1924 Western Feuds; Lash of the Whip; The Measure of a Man; Rodeo Mixup; Hearts of Oak; In the Days of the Covered Wagon; The Diamond Bandit. 1925 "Scar" Hanan; The Fighting Heart; The Red Rider; The Four from Nowhere; Ridin' Thunder; The Taming of the West; Soft Shoes; The Sign of the Cactus; A Roaring Adventure. 1926 Speed Cop. 1927 The Devil's Saddle; Upstream; The Wreck of the Hesperus; The Cruise of the Hellion; The Heart of Maryland; Men of Daring; One Glorious Scrap; Uncle Tom's Cabin. 1928 The Branded Sombrero; Sisters of Eve; The Chinatown Mystery (serial); Four-Footed Ranger. 1929 The Black Watch; The Drake Case; The Lariat Kid. 1930 Mounted Stranger; Kathleen Mavoureen; Song of the Caballero; Sons of the Saddle; The Indians are Coming (serial silent and sound versions); The Jade Box (serial silent and sound versions). 1931 The Sea Beneath. 1932 The Last Ride; Tangled Fortunes; Airmail. 1933 Pilgrimage; Charlie Chan's Greatest Case; Life in the Raw; Man from Monterey; Gun Justice. 1934 Cheaters; Murder in Trinidad; Judge Priest. 1935 Goin' to Town; This Is the Life; The Informer; The Arizonian; Steamboat 'Round the Bend; Charlie Chan's Secret; Paddy O'Day. 1936 The Prisoner of Shark Island; Gentle Julia; Charlie Chan at the Circus; Sins of Man; Educating Father. 1937 Slave Ship; Checkers. 1938 In Old Chicago; Kentucky Moonshine; The Texans. 1939 Stagecoach; Young Mr. Lincoln; Drums along the Mohawk; Bad Lands; Geronimo. 1940 Viva Cisco Kid; Lucky Cisco Kid; South of Pago Pago; Diamond Frontier. 1941 Tobacco Road; Last of the Duanes. 1942 The Loves of Edgar Allan Poe; Outlaws of Pine Ridge; The Man Who Wouldn't Die. 1943 Girls in Chains; The Ox-Bow Incident. 1944 The Climax; The Big Noise; Bowery Champs. 1945 Gilda; A Stolen Life; Gallant Journey;

Hangover Square. 1946 Renegades; Accomplice; My Darling, Clementine; Wake up and Dream. 1947 Bandits of Dark Canyon; Driftwood; High Tide. 1948 The Timber Trail; Eyes of Texas; The Plunderers. 1949 The Far Frontier; Frontier Investigator; San Antone Ambush. 1950 Father Makes Good; Wagonmaster. 1952 The Quiet Man; Toughest Man in Arizona. 1953 The Sun Shines Bright; The Marshal's Daughter.

FORD, HARRISON
Born: Mar. 16, 1894, Kansas City, Mo. Died: Dec. 2, 1957, Woodland Hills, Calif. Screen and stage actor.

Appeared in: 1916 The Mysterious Mrs. M. 1918 The Cruise of the Make-Believe; A Pair of Silk Stockings; Such a Little Pirate. 1919 The Lottery Man; The Veiled Adventure; Hawthorne of the U.S.A.; The Third Kiss. 1921 The Passion Flower; Wedding Bells; A Heart to Let; Love's Redemption; Wonderful Thing. 1922 Smilin' Through; Find the Woman; The Primitive Lover; When Love Comes; The Old Homestead; Foolish Wives; Her Gilded Cage; Shadows. 1923 Little Old New York; Vanity Fair; Bright Lights of Broadway; Maytime. 1924 Janice Meredith; The Average Woman; A Fool's Awakening; The Price of a Party; Three Miles Out. 1925 Proud Flesh; The Wheel; Lovers in Quarantine; The Mad Marriage; The Marriage Whirl; Zander the Great. 1926 Up in Mabel's Room; That Royal Girl; Almost a Lady; The Song and Dance Man; Hell's 400; Sandy; The Nervous Wreck. 1927 The Rejuvenation of Aunt Mary; No Control; The Girl in the Pullman; The Night Bride; Rubber Tires. 1928 Let 'Er Go Gallagher; A Woman against the World; Golf Widows; Just Married; The Rush Hour; Three Week Ends. 1929 Her Husband's Women; The Flattering Word (short). 1932 Love in High Gear. prior to 1933 Advice to Husbands (short).

FORD, MARTY
Born: 1900. Died: Nov. 12, 1954, Hollywood, Calif. Screen and stage actor.

FORD, WALLACE
Born: Feb. 12, 1899, England. Died: June 11, 1966, Woodland Hills, Calif.(heart ailment). Screen and stage actor.

Appeared in: 1930 Swellhead; Absent Minded (short); Fore (short). 1931 Possessed; X Marks the Spot. 1932 Wet Parade; Hypnotized; Freaks; City Sentinel; Are You Listening?; Skyscraper Souls; Prosperity; Central Park; Beast of the City. 1933 Employees' Entrance; The Big Cage; She Had to Say Yes; Goodbye Again; Headline Shooter; Night of Terror; My Woman; East of Fifth Avenue; Three-Cornered Moon. 1934 A Woman's Man; Money Means Nothing; The Lost Patrol; Men in White; I Hate Women. 1935 The Nut Farm; The Informer; Another Face; Swell Head (and 1930 version); The Whole Town's Talking; In Spite of Danger; Men of the Hour; She Couldn't Take It; The Mysterious Mr. Wong; One Frightened Night; Mary Burns Fugitive; The Man Who Reclaimed His Head; Sanders of the River; Get That Man. 1936 Two in the Dark; Absolute Quiet; A Son Comes Home; The Rogues' Tavern; O.H.M.S. (You're in the Army Now, U.S. 1937). 1937 Swing It, Sailor; Jericho; Exiled to Shanghai. 1938 Dark Sands; He Loves an Actress. 1939 Back Door to Heaven. 1940 The Mummy's Hand; Scatterbrain; Two Girls on Broadway; Isle of Destiny; Love, Honor and Oh Baby!; Give Us Wings. 1941 A Man Betrayed; The Roar of the Press; Murder by Invitation; Blues in the Night. 1942 All through the Night; Inside the Law; Scattergood Survives a Murder; Seven Days' Leave; The Mummy's Tomb. 1943 The Ape Man; Shadow of a Doubt; The Marines Come Through; The Cross of Lorraine. 1944 Secret Command; Machine Gun Mama. 1945 On Stage Everybody; Spellbound; Blood on the Sun; They Were Expendable; The Great John L. 1946 Lover Come Back; Crack-Up; Black Angel; Rendezvous with Annie; A Guy Could Change; The Green Years. 1947 Magic Town; T-Men; Dead Reckoning. 1948 Coroner Creek; The Man from Texas; Shed No Tears; Embraceable You; Belle Starr's Daughter. 1949 Red Stallion in the Rockies; The Set-Up. 1950 The Furies; Dakota Lil; The Breaking Point; Harvey. 1951 Warpath; Painting the Clouds with Sunshine; He Ran All the Way. 1952 Flesh and Fury; Rodeo. 1953 The Great Jesse James Raid; The Nebraskan. 1954 Destry; She Couldn't Say No; The Boy from Oklahoma; Three Ring Circus. 1955 The Man from Laramie; The Spoilers; Lucy Gallant; Wichita; A Lawless Street. 1956 The Maverick Queen; Johnny Concho; Thunder over Arizona; Stagecoach to Fury; The First Texan; The Rainmaker. 1958 The Last Hurrah; Twilight for the Gods; The Matchmaker. 1959 Warlock. 1961 Tess of the Storm Country. 1965 A Patch of Blue.

FORMBY, GEORGE
Born: May 26, 1904, Wigan, Lancashire, England. Died: Mar. 6, 1961, Preston, Lancashire, England. Screen, vaudeville, television actor, and song writer. Voted among first ten money mak-

ing stars in British productions in Motion Picture Herald—Fame Poll, 1942 and 1945. Son of British Music Hall star George Formby.

Appeared in: 1933 Boots Boots (film debut). 1934 On the Dole. 1935 No Limit. 1936 Keep Your Seats, Please. 1937 Feather Your Nest; Keep Fit. 1938 I See Ice; It's in the Air (U.S. 1940). 1939 Trouble Brewing; Come on, George. 1940 Let George Do It. 1941 Spare a Copper; Turned out Nice Again; South American George. 1942 Much Too Shy. 1943 Get Cracking; Bell-Bottom George. 1944 He Snoops to Conquer. 1945 I Didn't Do It. 1946 George in Civvy Street. Other British film: Remember the Unicorn.

FORREST, ALAN (Allan Forest Fisher)
Born: Sept. 1, 1889, Brooklyn, N.Y. Died: July 25, 1941, Detroit, Mich. Screen and stage actor.

Appeared in: 1919 Rosemary Climbs the Heights. 1921 Cheated Love; Forgotten Woman; The Hole in the Wall; The Invisible Fear; The Man from Lost River; They Shall Pay; What Women Will Do. 1922 The Heart Specialist; Lights of the Desert; The New Teacher; Seeing's Believing; Tillie; Very Truly Yours. 1923 Long Live the King; Crinoline and Romance; Her Fatal Millions; The Man between; A Noise in Newboro; Wandering Daughters. 1924 Don't Doubt Your Husband; In Love with Love; The Siren of Seville; Captain Blood; Dorothy Vernon of Haddon Hall. 1925 The Dressmaker from Paris; The Great Divide; Old Clothes; Pampered Youth; Rose of the World. 1926 The Carnival Girl; Fifth Avenue; Partners Again; The Phantom Bullet; The Prince of Pilsen; Summer Bachelors; Two Can Play. 1927 Ankles Preferred; The Lovelorn. 1928 Black Feather; The Desert Bride; Riding for Fame; Sally of the Scandals; The Wild West Show. 1929 The Winged Horseman. 1930 Dangerous Nan McGrew.

FORREST, BELFORD
Born: 1878. Died: May 1, 1938, Hollywood, Calif. Screen actor and playwright. One of the first comics signed by Hal Roach in silent bathing beauty days.

FORSYTHE, MIMI (Marie G. Armstrong)
Born: 1922. Died: Aug. 17, 1952, Hollywood, Calif. Screen actress.

FORTE, JOE (Josef Forte)
Born: 1896. Died: Feb. 22, 1967, Hollywood, Calif.(heart attack). Screen, radio, and television actor.

Appeared in: 1938 Pals of the Saddle. 1946 The Crimson Ghost (serial). 1949 Riders in the Sky. 1950 County Fair. 1952 Assignment Paris. 1953 Three Sailors and a Girl. 1955 Cell 2455, Death Row. 1956 Fury at Gunsight Pass; He Laughed Last; The Buster Keaton Story. 1957 Short Cut to Hell. 1958 Return to Warbow. 1961 Homicidal.

FORTIER, HERBERT
Born: 1867, Toronto, Canada. Died: Feb. 16, 1949, Philadelphia, Pa. Screen and stage actor.

Appeared in: 1921 Beyond; Children of the Night; A Connecticut Yankee at King Arthur's Court; Garments of Truth; The Shark Master; Whatever She Wants. 1922 The Black Bag; Dusk to Dawn; Little Wildcat; Midnight. 1923 Clean-Up; Legally Dead; Railroaded; Slander the Woman. 1924 Ridgeway of Montana; The Western Wallop; The Whispered Name.

FORTUNE, WALLACE
Born: 1884. Died: Jan. 12, 1926, New York, N.Y.(typhoid, pneumonia). Screen actor and stage director.

FOSHAY, HAROLD A.
Born: 1884. Died: Feb. 23, 1953, Charleston, S.C. Screen actor, film producer, and film director.

Appeared in: 1921 The Devil's Confession; The Shadow. 1922 Why Not Marry?. 1923 The Fair Cheat. 1924 Youth for Sale. 1926 The Brown Derby. 1936 To Mary with Love.

FOSTER, DONALD
Born: 1889. Died: Dec. 22, 1969, Hollywood, Calif. Screen, stage, and television actor.

Appeared in: 1959 The Al Capone Story; Horse Soldiers. 1960 Please Don't Eat the Daisies. 1961 All in a Night's Work.

FOSTER, PRESTON
Born: Aug. 24, 1900, Ocean City, N.J. Died: July 14, 1970, La Jolla, Calif. Screen, stage, opera, and television actor.

Appeared in: 1929 Nothing but the Truth. 1930 Follow the Leader; Heads Up. 1932 The Last Mile; Life Begins; Doctor X; Two Seconds; I Am a Fugitive from a Chain Gang; The All-American; You Said a Mouthful. 1933 Elmer the Great; Danger Crossroads; Corruption; The Man Who Dared; Hoopla; Devil's Mate; Ladies They Talk About; Sensation Hunters. 1934 Wharf Angel; Sleepers East; Heat Lightning; The Band Plays On. 1935 A Night at the Biltmore Bowl (short); People's Enemy; The Arizonian; Strangers All; Annie Oakley; The Last Days of Pompeii; The Informer. 1936 Muss 'Em Up; We Who Are about to Die; Love before Breakfast; We're Only Human; The Plough and the Stars. 1937 Sea Devils; The Outcasts of Poker Flat; You Can't Beat Love; The Westland Case; First Lady. 1938 Everybody's Doing It; Double Danger; Submarine Patrol; Up the River; The Lady in the Morgue; The Storm; The Last Warning; Army Girl; White Banners. 1939 Geronimo; Street of Missing Men; Chasing Danger; 20,000 Men a Year; Society Smugglers; News Is Made at Night; Missing Evidence. 1940 Moon over Burma; Cafe Hostess; North West Mounted Police. 1941 The Roundup; Unfinished Business. 1942 Secret Agent of Japan; Night in New Orleans; Little Tokyo, USA; American Empire; A Gentleman after Dark; Thunder Birds. 1943 Guadalcanal Diary; My Friend Flicka. 1944 The Bermuda Mystery; Roger Touhy, Gangster. 1946 Valley of Decision; The Last Gangster; Twice Blessed; Thunderhead, Son of Flicka; Abbott and Costello in Hollywood. 1946 The Harvey Girls; Tangiers; Inside Job; Strange Triangle; Blonde from Brooklyn. 1947 Ramrod; King of Wild Horses. 1948 Green Grass of Wyoming; The Hunted; Thunderhoof. 1949 I Shot Jesse James; The Big Cat. 1950 The Tougher They Come. 1951 The Big Gusher; 3 Desperate Men; Tomahawk; The Big Night. 1952 Face to Face; Montana Territory; Kansas City Confidential. 1953 I, the Jury; Law and Order. 1957 Destination 60,000. 1964 The Man from Galveston; The Time Travelers; Advance to the Rear. 1967 You've Got to Be Smart. 1968 Chubasco.

FOSTER, RUDOLPH
Born: 1884. Died: 1968. Screen actor.

FOUGERS, PIERRE
Born: France. Died: Nov. 28, 1922, Paris, France (accidentally shot himself). Screen actor.

FOUGEZ, ANNA
Born: 1895, Italy. Died: Sept. 1966, Santa Marinella, Italy. Italian screen, stage actress, and singer. Entered films in 1920.

FOULGER, BYRON
Born: 1900. Died: Apr. 4, 1970, Hollywood, Calif.(heart condition). Screen and television actor.

Appeared in: 1937 The Prisoner of Zenda; Larceny on the Air; The Duke Comes Back; A Day at the Races. 1938 Born to Be Wild; Tenth Avenue Kid; Tarnished Angel; I Am a Criminal; It's All in Your Mind. 1939 At the Circus; Exile Express; The Man They Could Not Hang; Mutiny on the Blackhawk; Television Spy; The Girl from Rio; Fools of Desire; In Name Only; Union Pacific. 1940 Edison, the Man; Heroes of the Saddle; The Man with Nine Lives; Ellery Queen, Master Detective; Arizona; Sky Murder. 1941 Sullivan's Travels; Man-Made Monster; The Gay Vagabond; Ridin' on a Rainbow; Sweetheart of the Campus; Mystery Ship; Dude Cowboy. 1942 The Panther's Claw; The Tuttles of Tahiti; Harvard, Here I Come; Quiet Please, Murder; Stand by for Action; Man from Headquarters. 1943 The Human Comedy; So Proudly We Hail!; Sweet Rosie O'Grady; The Adventures of a Rookie; In Old Oklahoma; Hi Diddle Diddle; Hoppy Serves a Writ; Hangmen Also Die; Enemy of Women; The Power of God; Dixie Dugan; Coney Island; Silver Spurs; Black Raven. 1944 Since You Went Away; Summer Storm; The Whistler; Roger Touhy, Gangster; Dark Mountain; Henry Aldrich's Little Secret; Ministry of Fear; Marriage Is a Private Affair; Swing in the Saddle; Beautiful but Broke. 1945 The Hidden Eye; Let's Go Steady; Circumstantial Evidence; The Adventures of Kitty O'Day; Brewster's Millions; Arson Squad; The Blonde from Brooklyn; It's in the Bag. 1946 Snafu; Sensation Hunters; Sentimental Journey; The French Key; Dick Tracy vs. Cueball; 'Til the Clouds Roll By; The Plainsman and the Lady. 1947 The Michigan Kid; Lady Be Good; Hard-Boiled Mahoney; Adventures of Don Coyote; The Bells of San Fernando; Too Many Winners; The Red Hornet; The Chinese Ring; Stallion Road. 1948 Arch of Triumph; The Hunted; Return of October; Out of the Storm; I Surrender Dear. 1949 Arson, Inc.; Dancing in the Dark: I Shot Jesse James; The Inspector General; The Dalton Gang; Red Desert; Satan's Cradle. 1950 Champagne for Caesar; The Girl from San Lorenzo; The Return of Jesse James; Experiment Alcatraz; Salt Lake Raiders. 1951 Footlight Varieties; A Millionaire for Christy; FBI Girl; Gasoline Alley; The Sea Hornet; Lightning Strikes Twice; Home Town Story.

1952 Cripple Creek; My Six Convicts; Apache Country; The Steel Fist. 1953 The Magnetic Monster; Bandits of the West; Cruisin' Down the River; Confidentially Connie; Paris Model. 1956 You Can't Run Away from It. 1957 The River's Edge; Dino; Sierra Stranger; Gun Battle at Monterey; Up in Smoke; The Buckskin Lady; New Day at Sundown. 1958 The Long, Hot Summer; Going Steady. 1959 King of the Wild Stallions. 1960 Ma Barker's Killer Brood; Twelve Hours to Kill. 1962 The Devil's Partner. 1967 The Gnome-Mobile. 1969 There Was a Crooked Man.

FOWLER, ART
Born: 1902. Died: Apr. 4, 1953, Suffern, N.Y. Screen, radio, and television actor.

FOWLER, BRENDA
Born: 1883, Los Angeles, Calif. Died: Oct. 27, 1942, Los Angeles, Calif. Screen, stage actress, and playwright. Entered films with Kalem and Rex productions.

Appeared in: 1923 Money! Money! Money!. 1934 The World Moves On; Judge Priest. 1935 The Ruggles of Red Gap. 1936 The Case against Mrs. Ames; Second Wife. 1938 The Cowboy and the Lady. 1939 Stage Coach; Dust Be My Destiny. 1940 Comin' 'Round the Mountain.

FOX, FRANKLYN
Born: 1894, England. Died: Nov. 2, 1967, Wantagh, N.Y.(heart attack). Screen, stage, radio, and television actor.

Appeared in: 1957 High Tide at Noon. 1959 First Man into Space.

FOX, HARRY (Arthur Carringford)
Born: 1882, Pomona, Calif. Died: July 20, 1959, Woodland Hills, Calif. Screen, stage, and vaudeville actor. Married to screen actress Evelyn Brent. Divorced from actresses Yancsi (Jenny) Dolly, of the famed "Dolly Sisters" (dec. 1941) and Beatrice Curtis (dec. 1936). He appeared in vaudeville with his wife at the time, Beatrice Curtis, and together they made two film shorts.

He appeared in: 1916 Beatrice Fairfax (serial). 1928 The Lemon (short). 1929 Harry Fox and His Six American Beauties (short); The Fox and the Bee (short with Beatrice Curtis). 1930 The Play Boy (short with Beatrice Curtis); The Lucky Break. 1931 Fifty Million Frenchmen. 1934 Love Time; 365 Nights in Hollywood.

FOX, SIDNEY (aka SYDNEY FOX)
Born: Dec. 10, 1910, New York, N.Y. Died: Nov. 14, 1942, Beverly Hills, Calif. Screen and stage actress. Entered films in 1931 as a Wampus Baby.

Appeared in: 1931 Strictly Dishonorable; Bad Sister; Six Cylinder Love. 1932 Afraid to Talk; The Cohens and the Kellys in Hollywood; Mouthpiece; Once in a Lifetime; Nice Women; Murders in the Rue Morgue. 1933 Don Quixote. 1934 Down to Their Last Yacht; Midnight; School for Girls.

FOY, EDDIE (Edward Fitzgerald)
Born: 1854. Died: Feb. 16, 1928, Kansas City, Mo. Screen, stage, and vaudeville actor. Head of vaudeville team "Seven Foys" which included actor Eddie Foy, Jr. Widower three times by stage actresses Rose Howland (of the Howland Sisters), Lola Sefton and Madeline Morondo (who was the mother of his seven children).

Appeared in: 1915 A Favorite Fool. 1928 Foys for Joys (short).

FOYER, EDDIE
Born: 1883. Died: June 15, 1934, Los Angeles, Calif. Screen and vaudeville actor.

Appeared in: 1930 Big House.

FRALICK, FREDDIE
Born: June 4, 1888, Detroit, Mich. Died: May 13, 1958, Hollywood, Calif. Screen, stage, and vaudeville actor. Entered films with Biograph in 1912 and remained in silents until 1917.

FRANCE, CHARLES V.
Born: June 30, 1868, Bradford, England. Died: Apr. 13, 1949, Gerrards Cross, England. Screen and stage actor.

Appeared in: 1930 The Skin Game (film debut). 1931 These Charming People; Black Coffee; A Night Like This. 1934 Chu Chin Chow; Lord Edgware Dies. 1935 Scrooge; Tudor Rose. 1936 Secret Agent; Broken Blossoms; Crime over London. 1937 Victoria the Great. 1938 A Yank at Oxford; Strange Borders; If I Were King; The Ware Case. 1939 Ten Days in Paris. 1940 Night Train to Munich. 1941 Missing Ten Days; Breach of

Promise. 1942 Went the Day Well?. 1943 Queen Victoria; The Yellow Canary. 1944 The Half-Way House; 48 Hours.

FRANCIS, ALEC B.
Born: Suffolk, England. Died: July 6, 1934, Hollywood, Calif.(following an emergency operation). Screen and stage actor. Entered films in 1911.

Appeared in: 1915 Lola. 1919 Flame of the Desert; Heartsease; Lord and Lady Algy. 1920 The Man Who Had Everything; The Paliser Case. 1921 What's a Wife Worth?; Godless Men; A Voice in the Dark; The Great Moment; A Virginia Courtship; Courage. 1922 Smilin' Through; The Man Who Saw Tomorrow; Beyond the Rocks; North of the Rio Grande; The Forgotten Law. 1923 Three Wise Fools; Hollywood; Little Church Around the Corner; Children of Jazz; Is Divorce a Failure?; The Last Hour; The Eternal Three; The Spider and the Rose; The Drivin' Fool; Lucretia Lombard; Mary of the Movies; A Gentleman of Leusure; The Gold Diggers; His Last Race. 1924 A Fool's Awakening; Do It Now; Soiled; Listen Lester; The Tenth Woman; The Human Terror; Half-a-Dollar Bill. 1925 The Bridge of Sighs; Charley's Aunt; Thank You; The Coast of Folly; Champion of Lost Causes; A Thief in Paradise; The Mad Whirl; Thunder Mountain; The Circle; Rose of the World; Capital Punishment; The Reckless Sex; Waking up the Town; Wandering Footsteps; Where the Worst Begins; Man and Maid; Outwitted. 1926 Tramp, Tramp, Tramp; The Return of Peter Grimm; Forever After; Pals First; Three Bad Men; High Steppers; Faithful Wives; The Yankee Senor; Transcontinental Limited. 1927 The Music Master; Camille; Sally in Our Alley; The Tender Hour. 1928 The Lion and the Mouse; The Terror; The Little Snob; Companionate Marriage; Broadway Daddies; Life's Mockery; The Shepherd of the Hills. 1929 Evidence; The Sacred Flame; Evangeline; Murder Will Out; The Mississippi Gambler. 1930 The Bishop Murder Case; Feet First; The Case of Sgt. Grischa; Captain Apple Jack; Outward Bound. 1931 Arrowsmith; Oh! Oh! Cleopatra (short). 1932 .45 Calibre Echo; No Greater Love; The Last Man; The Last Mile; Alias Mary Smith; Mata Hari. 1933 Oliver Twist; Looking Forward; His Private Secretary; Alice in Wonderland. 1934 Mystery of Mr. X; I'll Tell the World; Outcast Lady.

FRANCIS, KAY (Katherine Edwina Gibbs)
Born: Jan. 13, 1903, Oklahoma City, Okla. Died: Aug. 26, 1968, New York, N.Y.(cancer). Screen, stage actress, and film producer.

Appeared in: 1929 Dangerous Curves; Honest Finder; The Marriage Playground; The Illusion; Gentlemen of the Press; The Cocoanuts. 1930 Behind the Makeup; The Children; Paramount on Parade; A Notorious Affair; Raffles; Let's Go Native; For the Defense; The Virtuous Sin; Passion Flower; The Street of Chance. 1931 The Vice Squad; Transgression; Guilty Hands; Scandal Sheet; Ladies Man; Girls about Town; 24 Hours. 1932 The False Madonna; House of Scandal; Strangers in Love; Man Wanted; Jewel Robbery; Street of Women; One Way Passage; Trouble in Paradise; Cynara. 1933 The Keyhole; The House on 56th Street; Mary Stevens, M.D.; Storm at Daybreak; I Loved a Woman. 1934 Mandalay; Wonder Bar; Dr. Monica; British Agent. 1935 Living on Velvet; The Goose and the Gander; Stranded; I Found Stella Parish. 1936 The White Angel; Give Me Your Heart; Stolen Holiday; One Hour of Romance. 1937 Another Dawn; Confession; First Lady; Unlawful. 1938 Secrets of an Actress; My Bill; Women Are Like That; Comet over Broadway. 1939 In Name Only; King of the Underworld; Women in the Wind. 1940 It's a Date; Little Men; When the Daltons Rode. 1941 The Man Who Lost Himself; Charley's Aunt; The Feminine Touch; Play Girl. 1942 Always in My Heart; Between Us Girls. 1944 Four Jills in a Jeep; Hours Between. 1945 Divorce; Allotment Wives, Inc. 1946 Wife Wanted.

FRANCIS, OLIN
Born: Sept. 13, 1892, Mooreville, Miss. Died: June 30, 1952, Hollywood, Calif. Screen and stage actor.

Appeared in: 1921 A Knight of the West. 1922 Fighting Devil; The Jungle Goddess (serial). 1924 Rarin' to Go; Walloping Wallace. 1925 Let's Go Gallagher. 1926 Call of the Klondike; Sea Beast. 1927 Win That Girl; The Kid Brother; Cross Breed; Flying U Ranch. 1928 The Devil's Trademark; Stormy Waters; Free Lips. 1930 Kismet. 1931 Adios; Homicide Squad; Lariat and Sixshooters; Suicide Fleet. 1932 Tex Takes a Holiday; A Woman Commands; .45 Calibre Echo; The Drifter. 1935 Hard Rock Harrigan. 1936 I Conquer the Sea; O'Malley of the Mounted. 1938 Two-Gun Justice; Overland Stage Raiders. 1939 Captain Fury. 1940 Kit Carson.

FRANCIS, ROBERT
Born: Feb. 26, 1930, Glendale, Calif. Died: July 31, 1955, Burbank, Calif.(plane crash). Screen actor.

Appeared in: 1954 The Caine Mutiny (film debut); They Rode West. 1955 The Long Gray Line; The Bamboo Prison.

FRANCISCO, BETTY
Born: 1900, Little Rock, Ark. Died: Nov. 25, 1950, El Cerito, Calif.(heart attack). Screen and stage actress.

Appeared in: 1921 Greater Than Love; A Guilty Conscience; Riding with Death; Straight from Paris. 1922 Across the Continent; Her Night of Nights. 1923 Ashes of Vengeance; Crinoline and Romance; The Darling of New York; Double Dealing; Flaming Youth; The Love Piker; Maytime; Noise in Newboro; The Old Fool; Poor Men's Wives. 1924 Big Timber; East of Broadway; Gambling Wives; How to Educate a Wife; On Probation. 1925 Faint Perfume; Fair Play; Fifth Avenue Models; Jimmie's Millions; Private Affairs; Seven Keys to Baldpate; Wasted Lives. 1926 Don Juan's Three Nights; The Lily; Man Bait; The Phantom of the Forest. 1927 The Gingham Girl; A Boy of the Streets; The Gay Retreat; Uneasy Payments; Too Many Crooks. 1928 Broadway Daddies; You Can't Beat the Law; Queen of the Chorus. 1929 Smiling Irish Eyes; Broadway; The Spirit of Youth. 1930 The Lotus Lady; Street of Chance; Madam Satan; The Widow from Chicago. 1931 Charlie Chan Carries On; Good Sport. 1932 Mystery Ranch.

FRANEY, WILLIAM "BILLY"
Born: 1885, Chicago, Ill. Died: Dec. 9, 1940, Hollywood, Calif. (influenza). Screen actor and film producer. Entered films in 1915.

Appeared in: 1915 Hubby's Cure. 1917 One Damp Day. 1918 An Honest Man. 1921 A Knight of the West. 1922 Quincy Adams Sawyer; A Western Demon. 1923 The Town Scandal; Tea with a Kick. 1924 Mile-a-Minute Morgan; North of Alaska; Border Women. 1925 Manhattan Madness; S.O.S. Perils of the Sea; The Great Sensation; The Fear Fighter; Kit Carson over the Great Divide. 1926 Senor Daredevil; King of the Saddle; The King of the Turf; A Desperate Moment; Code of the Northwest; Danger Quest; Moran of the Mounted; The Dead Line; The Dangerous Dude. 1927 Aflame in the Sky; The Royal American; The Racing Fool; She's a Sheik; King of the Herd; Out All Night; The Lost Limited; Red Signals. 1928 Five and Ten-Cent Annie; Under the Tonto Rim; The Glorious Trail; Romance of a Rogue; The Canyon of Adventure. 1929 The Broadway Hoofer; Anne against the World; The Royal Rider; Cheyenne. 1930 The Heroic Lover. 1932 The Millionaire Cat (short); The Iceman's Ball (short). 1933 Somewhere in Sonora; Kickin' the Crown Around (short). 1934 No More Women. 1935 Restless Knights (short). 1937 Quick Money; Maid's Night Out; The Marriage Business; Joy of Living; Having a Wonderful Time. 1938 RKO short.

FRANK, WILLIAM
Born: 1880. Died: Dec. 23, 1925, Hollywood, Calif.(Bright's disease). Screen and stage actor.

Appeared in: Roach comedies. 1925 The Last Edition.

FRANKAU, RONALD
Born: Feb. 1894. Died: 1951. British screen, stage, and radio actor.

Appeared in: 1929 On with the Show. 1931 The Skin Game. 1935 Radio Parade of 1935. 1939 His Brother's Keeper. 1946 Double Alibi. 1947 The Ghosts of Berkley Square. Other British films: Potiphar's Wife; Let's Love and Laugh; The Calendar; The Other Mrs. Phipps; International Revue; Talking Hands.

FRANKEL, FRANCHON
Born: 1874. Died: Aug. 12, 1937, Hollywood, Calif. Screen and stage actress.

Appeared in: 1927 Jake the Plumber; Sensation Seekers. 1928 Desperate Courage. 1930 Pick 'Em Young (short).

FRANKLIN, IRENE
Born: 1884 or 1876, St. Louis, Mo. Died: June 16, 1941, Englewood, N.J.(cerebral hemorrhage). Screen, stage, radio, vaudeville actress, and singer.

Appeared in: 1929 The American Comedienne (short); Those Were the Days (short). 1934 Change of Heart; A Very Honorable Guy; Registered Nurse; The Women in His Life; Lazy River; The President Vanishes; Strictly Dynamite; Down to Their Last Yacht. 1935 Ladies Crave Excitement; Affairs of Susan; Death Flies East. 1936 Whipsaw; The Song and Dance Man; Timothy's Quest; Fatal

Lady; Wanted: Jane Turner; Along Came Love. 1937 Midnight Madonna; Married before Breakfast; Blazing Barriers; Saratoga. 1938 Rebellious Daughters; Flirting with Fate. 1939 Fixer Dugan.

FRANKLIN, RUPERT
Born: 1862. Died: Jan. 14, 1939, Los Angeles, Calif. Screen actor.

Appeared in: 1925 The Prairie Wife.

FRANKLIN, SIDNEY
Born: 1870. Died: Mar. 18, 1931, Hollywood, Calif. Screen and stage actor.

Appeared in: 1921 Playing with Fire; The Three Musketeers. 1922 Welcome Children; The Vermillion Pencil; The Guttersnipe; Call of Home; Dusk to Dawn. 1923 The Love Trap; Fashion Row. 1924 A Boy of Flanders; In Hollywood with Potash and Perlmutter. 1925 One of the Bravest; The Texas Trail; His People. 1926 Block Signal; Rose of the Tenements; Somebody's Mother. 1927 Fighting Failure; King of Kings; Colleen. 1928 Wheel of Chance. 1930 Lummox; Puttin' on the Ritz. 1932 The Kid from Spain.

FRANKS, DENNIS
Born: 1902. Died: Oct. 1967, Dublin, Ireland (heart attack). Screen and stage actor.

FRAWLEY, WILLIAM
Born: Feb. 26, 1887, Burlington, Iowa. Died: Mar. 3, 1966, Los Angeles, Calif.(heart attack). Screen, stage, vaudeville, and television actor.

Appeared in: 1929 Turkey for Two (short) (film debut); Fancy That (short). 1931 Surrender. 1933 Hell and High Water; Moonlight and Pretzels. 1934 Bolero; The Witching Hour; Shoot the Works; Here Is My Heart; The Lemon Drop Kid; The Crime Doctor; Miss Fane's Baby Is Stolen. 1935 Ship Cafe; Alibi Ike; Welcome Home; Harmony Lane; Car 99; Hold 'Em Yale; College Scandal. 1936 Strike Me Pink; Desire; The Princess Comes Along; F Man; Rose Bowl; Three Cheers for Love; Three Married Men; The General Died at Dawn. 1937 Blossoms on Broadway; Something to Sing About; High, Wide and Handsome; Double or Nothing. 1938 Mad about Music; Professor Beware; Sons of the Legion; Touchdown Army; Crime Takes a Holiday. 1939 Persons in Hiding; St. Louis Blues; Ambush; Huckleberry Finn; Rose of Washington Square; Ex-Champ; Grand Jury Secrets; Stop, Look and Love; Night Work. 1940 The Farmer's Daughter; Opened by Mistake; Those Were the Days; Untamed; Golden Gloves; Rhythm on the River; The Quarterback; Sandy Gets Her Man; One Night in the Tropics. 1941 The Bride Came C.O.D.; Public Enemies; Six Lessons from Madame La Zonga; Dancing on a Dime; Footsteps in the Dark; Cracked Nuts; Blondie in Society. 1942 Treat 'Em Rough; Roxie Hart; It Happened in Flatbush; Give Out, Sisters; Moonlight in Havana; Wildcat; Gentleman Jim. 1943 Larceny with Music; We've Never Been Licked; Whistling in Brooklyn. 1944 The Fighting Seabees; Going My Way; Minstrel Man; Lake Placid Serenade. 1945 Flame of Barbary Coast; Lady on a Train; Hitchhike to Happiness. 1946 The Ziegfeld Follies; Rendezvous with Annie; The Inner Circle; The Crime Doctor's Manhunt; The Virginian. 1947 Mother Wore Tights; Miracle on 34th Street; My Wild Irish Rose; I Wonder Who's Kissing Her Now; Monsieur Verdoux; Down to Earth; The Hit Parade of 1947; Blondie's Anniversary. 1948 The Babe Ruth Story; Good Sam; Texas, Brooklyn and Heaven; Joe Palooka in Winner Take All; Chicken Every Sunday; The Girl from Manhattan. 1949 Home in San Antone; The Lady Takes a Sailor; East Side, West Side; The Lone Wolf and His Lady. 1950 Kiss Tomorrow Goodbye; Pretty Baby; Blondie's Hero; Kill the Umpire. 1951 The Lemon Drop Kid (and 1934 version); Abbott and Costello Meet the Invisible Man; Rhubarb. 1952 Rancho Notorious. 1962 Safe at Home!

FRAZER, ALEX
Born: 1900. Died: July 30, 1958, Hollywood, Calif.(heart attack). Screen, stage, and radio actor.

Appeared in: 1949 The Blonde Bandit; The Cowboy and the Indians; Secret of St. Ives. 1953 Gentlemen Prefer Blondes; Loose in London; War of the Worlds. 1956 Bigger than Life; The Boss.

FRAZER, ROBERT W.
Born: June 29, 1891, Worcester, Mass. Died: Aug. 17, 1944, Los Angeles, Calif. Screen and stage actor.

Appeared in: 1912 Robin Hood. 1916 The Feast of Life. 1921 Love, Hate and a Woman; Without Limit. 1922 The Faithless Sex; Fascination; How Women Love; My Friend the Devil; Partners of the Sunset; When the Desert Calls. 1923 As a Man Lives; A Chapter in Her Life; Jazzmania; The Love Piker. 1924 Women Who

Give; Men; After the Ball; Bread; Broken Barriers; The Foolish Virgin; When a Man's a Man; The Mine with the Iron Door; Traffic in Hearts. 1925 Splendid Road; Keeper of the Bees; The Charmer; The Scarlet West; The Golden Strain; The Love Gamble; Miss Bluebeard; The Other Woman's Story; Why Women Love; The White Desert. 1926 The City; Dame Chance; Desert Gold; The Isle of Retribution; Secret Orders; Sin Cargo; The Speeding Venus. 1927 Back to God's Country; One Hour to Love; The Silent Hero; Wanted a Coward. 1928 Out of the Ruins; The Little Snob; The Scarlet Dove; Burning up Broadway; City of Purple Dreams; Black Butterflies. 1929 The Woman I Love; Frozen Justice; Sioux Blood; Careers; The Drake Case. 1930 Beyond the Law. 1931 Ten Nights in a Barroom; Mystery Trooper (serial); Two-Gun Caballero. 1932 Rainbow Trail; Saddle Buster; Discarded Lovers; Arm of the Law; King Murder; White Zombie; The Crooked Circle. 1933 Vampire Bat; Justice Takes a Holiday; Notorious But Nice; The Fighting Parson; Found Alive. 1934 Guilty Parents; Monte Carlo Nights; Fifteen Wives; Love Past Thirty; The Trail Beyond; Counsel for the Defense; Fight Trooper; One in a Million. 1935 The Fighting Pilot; Death from a Distance; Ladies Crave Excitement; Never Too Late; The World Accuses; Circumstantial Evidence; Public Opinion. 1936 Garden of Allah; Murder at Glen Athol; Below the Deadline; Gambling Souls; The Rest Cure; It Couldn't Have Happened; Easy Money. 1937 Black Aces; Left Handed Law. 1938 On the Great White Trail; Religious Racketeer; Cipher Bureau. 1939 Navy Secrets; Six-Gun Rhythm; Juarez and Maximilian; Mystic Circle Murder; Danger of the Tong; Crashing Thru. 1940 One Man's Law. 1941 Pals of the Pecos; Law of the Wilds; Roar of the Press; Gangs of Sonora; Gunman from Bodie. 1942 Black Dragons; Riders of the West; Dawn of the Great Divide; A Night for Crime. 1943 Daredevils of the West; The Stranger from Pecos; Wagon Tracks West. 1944 Lawmen; Partners of the Trail; Forty Thieves.

FRAZIER, H. C.
Born: 1894. Died: Aug. 2, 1949, Hollywood, Calif. Screen actor and stand-in.

FRAZIN, GLADYS
Born: 1901. Died: Mar. 9, 1939, New York, N.Y.(suicide—jumped from apartment window). Screen and stage actress. Divorced from screen actor Monte Banks (dec. 1950).

Appeared in: 1924 Let Not Man Put Asunder. 1927 The Winning Oar. 1928 Inspiration.

FREDERICK, PAULINE (Pauline Libbey)
Born: Aug. 12, 1884, Boston, Mass. Died: Sept. 19, 1938, Los Angeles, Calif.(asthma). Screen and stage actress. Divorced from screen actor Willard Mack (dec. 1934).

Appeared in: 1915 The Eternal City (film debut); Bella Donna; Zaza; Sold; Lydia Gilmore. 1916 The Moment Before; The Woman in the Case; Her Honor, the Governor; Audrey. 1917 The Slave Island; Sleeping Fires. 1918 Her Final Reckoning; Fedora; La Tosca; Resurrection; Mrs. Dane's Defense. 1919 Out of the Shadow; One Week of Life; The Peace of the Roaring River; Bonds of Love; Paid in Full. 1920 Paliser Case; Madame X. 1921 Slave of Vanity; Roads of Destiny; Mistress of Shenstone; Salvage; The Sting of the Lash; The Lure of Jade. 1922 Two Kinds of Women; The Woman Breed; The Glory of Clementine. 1924 Three Women; Fast Set; Smouldering Fires; Let Not Man Put Asunder; Married Flirts. 1925 The Lady. 1926 Devil's Island; Her Honor, the Governor (and 1916 version); Josselyn's Wife. 1927 Mumsie; The Nest. 1928 Woman from Moscow; On Trial. 1929 The Sacred Flame; Evidence. 1931 This Modern Age. 1932 Wayward; The Phantom of Crestwood. 1933 Self-Defense. 1934 Social Register. 1935 My Marriage. 1936 Ramona. 1937 Thank You, Mr. Moto. 1938 The Buccaneer.

FREDERICKS, CHARLES
Born: 1920. Died: May 14, 1970, Sherman Oaks, Calif.(heart attack). Screen, stage, radio, and television actor.

Appeared in: 1954 Thunder Pass. 1955 Night Freight; Tarzan's Hidden Jungle. 1957 Hell Canyon. 1961 Lad: A Dog. 1962 Tender Is the Night; The Cabinet of Caligari. 1963 To Kill a Mockingbird. 1964 A House Is Not a Home.

FREEMAN, AL
Born: 1884. Died: Mar. 22, 1956, Los Angeles, Calif. Screen actor. Father of screen actor Al Freeman, Jr.

FREEMAN, HOWARD
Born: Dec. 9, 1899, Helena, Mont. Died: Dec. 11, 1967, New York, N.Y. Screen, stage, and television actor.

Appeared in: 1943 Pilot No. 5; Margin for Error; Girl Crazy;

Whistling in Brooklyn; Lost Angel; Air Raid Wardens; Slightly Dangerous; Hitler's Hangman. 1944 Carolina Blues; Dancing in Manhattan; Meet Miss Bobby-Socks; Meet the People; Once upon a Time; Rationing; Secret Command; The Unwritten Code. 1945 I'll Tell the World; Mexicana; This Love of Ours; That Night with You; You Came Along; Where Do We Go from Here?; A Song to Remember. 1946 House of Horrors; Inside Job; Night and Day; So Goes My Love; Abilene Town; Susie Steps Out; Sweet Guy; Monsieur Beaucaire; The Blue Dahlia. 1947 California; Cigarette Girl; Cross My Heart; My Brother Talks to Horses; That Way with Women; Cass Timberland; Magic Town; Long Night; Perfect Marriage. 1948 Summer Holiday; The Time of Your Life; Cry of the City; Arthur Takes Over; Give My Regards to Broadway; Letter from an Unknown Woman; Up in Central Park; Girl from Manhattan; The Snake Pit; If You Knew Suzie. 1949 Take One False Step. 1950 Perfect Strangers. 1951 Double Dynamite. 1952 Scaramouche; The Turning Point; Million Dollar Mermaid. 1953 No Time for Sergeants; Remains to Be Seen; Raiders of the Seven Seas. 1965 Dear Brigitte. Foreign films: We Are All Gamblers; Carriage Trade; Monsieur Et Madame.

FREEMAN, MAURICE
Born: 1872. Died: Mar. 26, 1953, Bayshore, N.Y. Screen, stage, and vaudeville actor. Was in vaudeville with his wife, Nadine Winston, in an act billed as "Tony and the Stork." Entered films in 1915.

Appeared in: 1923 Stephen Steps Out. 1937 Strangers on a Honeymoon.

FREEMAN-MITFORD, RUPERT
Born: 1895. Died: Aug. 7, 1939, London, England. Screen actor.

Appeared in: 1939 Goodbye, Mr. Chips.

FREIL, EDWARD
Born: 1878. Died: July 30, 1938, Los Angeles, Calif. Screen, vaudeville, circus actor, and film stuntman.

FRENCH, CHARLES K. (Charles E. Krauss)
Born: 1860, Columbus, Ohio. Died: Aug. 2, 1952, Hollywood, Calif. (heart attack). Screen, stage, minstrel actor, and film director. Entered films in 1908.

Appeared in: 1909 A True Indian's Heart. 1915 The Coward. 1920 Stronger Than Death. 1921 Bare Knuckles; Hands Off; The Last Trail; The Night Horsemen; The Road Demon; Beyond. 1922 The Bearcat; Her Own Money; If You Believe It, It's So; Mixed Faces; The Unfoldment; West of Chicago; The Woman He Loved; The Yosemite Trail; Moran of the Lady Letty; Smudge; The Truthful Liar; White Shoulders. 1923 The Extra Girl; The Abysmal Brute; Grumpy; The Lonely Road; A Woman of Paris; Alias the Night Wind; Blinky; Gentle Julia; Hell's Hole; Man's Size; The Ramblin' Kid. 1924 Abraham Lincoln; The Torrent; Free and Equal (reissue and retitle of The Coward—1915); Oh, You Tony; Pride of Sunshine Alley; The Sawdust Trail; Being Respectable. 1925 The Girl of Gold; The Saddle Hawk; Let 'Er Buck; Speed Mad; The Texas Trail; Too Much Youth; The Way of a Girl. 1926 War Paint; The Flaming Frontier; Frenzied Flames; Hands Up!; The Hollywood Reporter; The Rainmaker; Oh, What a Night!; The Runaway Express; Under Western Skies; The Winning Wallop. 1927 Good as Gold; The Adventurous Soul; Cross Breed; The Cruise of the Hellion; The Down Grade; Fast and Furious; Man, Woman and Sin; The Meddlin' Stranger; One Chance in a Million; Ride 'Em High. 1928 Big Hop; The Charge of the Gauchos; The Cowboy Cavalier; The Flying Buckaroo; Riding for Fame. 1929 King of the Rodeo; The Last Warning. 1930 Overland Bound. 1933 Crossfire. 1935 When a Man Sees Red; The Crimson Trail.

FRENCH, GEORGE B.
Born: Apr. 14, 1883, Storm Lake, Iowa. Died: June 9, 1961, Hollywood, Calif. (heart attack). Screen and stage actor.

Appeared in: 1918 Tarzan of the Apes. 1921 His Pajama Girl. 1924 Reckless Romance; Wandering Husbands. 1925 Bashful Buccaneer; Flying Thru; The Snob Buster. 1926 Cupid's Knockout. 1927 Grinning Guns; Horse Shoes; The Lost Limited; One Gloriour Scrap. 1928 Sawdust Paradise; Won in the Clouds; The Black Pearl. prior to 1929 "Christie" comedies. 1930 Street of Chance. 1935 Hoi Polloi (short).

FREY, NATHANIEL
Born: 1913, N.Y. Died: Nov. 7, 1970, New York, N.Y. (cancer). Screen, stage, and television actor.

Appeared in: 1957 Kiss Them for Me. 1958 Damn Yankees (film and stage versions). 1968 What's So Bad about Feeling Good?.

FRIEDMANN, SHRAGA
Born: 1923, Warsaw, Poland. Died: July, 1970, Tel Aviv, Israel (heart attack). Israeli screen and stage actor. Married to screen actress Shoshannah Ravid.

Appeared in: 1965 Sallah. 1966 Judith.

FRIGANZA, TRIXIE (Delia O'Callahan)
Born: Nov. 29, 1870, Grenola, Kan. Died: Feb. 27, 1955, Flintridge, Calif. (arthritis). Screen, stage, and vaudeville actress. Sister of screen actress Therese Thompson (dec. 1936).

Appeared in: 1923 Mind over Motor. 1925 The Charmer; The Road to Yesterday; Proud Flesh; Borrowed Finery; The Coming of Amos. 1926 Almost a Lady; Monte Carlo; The Whole Town's Talking. 1927 A Racing Romeo. 1928 Thanks for the Buggy Ride; Gentlemen Prefer Blondes. 1929 My Bag o'Trix (short). 1930 Free and Easy; Strong and Willing (short). Other shorts prior to 1933: Motor Maniac; The March of Time. 1933 Myrt and Marge. 1935 Wanderer of the Wasteland. 1940 If I Had My Way.

FRINTON, FREDDIE (Freddie Hargate)
Born: 1912, England. Died: Oct. 16, 1968, Poole, England. Screen, vaudeville, television actor, and comedian.

Appeared in: 1960 Make Mine Mink.

FRISCH, LORE
Born: 1925, Germany. Died: July 1962, East Berlin, Germany (suicide). German screen and television actress.

Appeared in: Csar and Carpenter; My Wife Makes Music.

FRISCO, JOE (Lewis Joseph)
Born: 1890, Rock Island, Ill. Died: Feb. 16, 1958, Hollywood, Calif. Screen, stage, and vaudeville actor.

Appeared in: 1930 the following shorts: The Benefit; The Song Plugger; The Happy Hottentots; The Border Patrol. 1931 The Gorilla. 1933 Mr. Broadway. 1938 Western Jamboree. 1944 Atlantic City. 1945 Shady Lady. 1947 That's My Man. 1950 Riding High. 1957 Sweet Smell of Success.

FRITH, THOMAS PRESTON
Born: 1883. Died: Jan. 9, 1945, North Hollywood, Calif. Screen cowboy actor. Entered films approx. 1918.

FROES, WALTER J. (aka WALLY DOUGLAS)
Born: 1922. Died: May 10, 1958, Los Angeles, Calif. Screen and radio actor. Known on radio as "Froggie Froes." Worked with Fred Waring and appeared in numerous film shorts.

Appeared in: 1940 Spies of the Air. 1941 Break the News; Chinese Den.

FRYE, DWIGHT
Born: 1899, Salina, Kan. Died: Nov. 9, 1943, Los Angeles, Calif. (heart attack). Screen and stage actor.

Appeared in: 1931 Man to Man; The Maltese Falcon; Dracula; The Black Camel; Frankenstein. 1932 Attorney for the Defense. 1933 Strange Adventure; Western Code; The Vampire Bat; The Circus Queen Murder. 1935 The Crime of Dr. Crespi; The Great Impersonation; Atlantic Adventure; Bride of Frankenstein. 1936 Florida Special; Alibi for Murder. 1937 The Man Who Found Himself; Something to Sing About; Beware of Ladies; The Shadow. 1938 The Invisible Enemy; The Night Hawk; Fast Company; Adventure in Sahara. 1939 Conspiracy. 1940 Gangs of Chicago; Phantom Raiders. 1941 Mystery Ship; Son of Monte Cristo. 1942 Prisoner of Japan. 1943 Frankenstein Meets the Wolf Man; Dead Men Walk; Drums of Fu Manchu; Submarine Alert.

FULLER, CLEM
Born: 1909. Died: May 24, 1961, Hollywood, Calif. (cancer). Screen, television actor, and stuntman. Entered films approx. 1931.

Appeared in: 1949 Gun Runner; Shadows of the West. 1950 The Sundowners; High Lonesome. 1951 The Cave of the Outlaws. 1953 Gunsmoke; The Great Sioux Uprising. 1959 They Came to Cordura.

FULLER, IRENE. See Mary Lygo (Not to be confused with actress listed below)

FULLER, IRENE
Born: 1898. Died: Mar. 20, 1945, Hollywood, Calif. Screen actress. Appeared in silents.

FULLER, LESLIE

Born: 1889, Margate, England. Died: Apr. 24, 1948, Margate, England. Screen, stage, and radio actress.

Appeared in: 1931 Kiss Me, Sergeant; Not So Quiet on the Western Front. 1932 The Stoker. 1933 The Pride of the Force; Hawleys of the High Street. 1935 Doctor's Orders; Strictly Illegal. 1936 Captain Bill. 1937 Darling You. 1940 Two Smart Men; The Middle Watch. 1942 Front Line Kids. Other British films: The Outcast; Poor Old Bill; Old Soldiers Never Die; Tonight's the Night; Bill's Legacy; Old Spanish Customers; The Last Coupon; Laughing Time; Why Sailors Leave Home; Political Party; Lost in the Legion; One Good Turn; Big Hearted Bill.

FULLER, MARGARET

Born: 1905. Died: Jan. 6, 1952, Whittier, Calif. Screen, stage, and radio actress. Married to screen actor Robert Griffin.

FULTON, MAUDE

Born: May 14, 1881, Eldorado, Kan. Died: Nov. 9, 1950, Los Angeles, Calif. Screen, stage, vaudeville actress, playwright, screenwriter, and author.

Appeared in: 1927 The Gingham Girl, Silk Legs. 1928 Bare Knees. 1929 Nix on Dames. 1933 The Cohens and the Kellys in Trouble.

FUQUA, CHARLES

Born: 1911. Died: Dec. 21, 1971, New Haven, Conn. Negro screen actor and singer. A member of the original "Ink Spots" quartet.

FYFFE, WILL

Born: 1884. Died: Dec. 14, 1947, St. Andrews, Scotland (fall from hotel window). Screen, stage, and vaudeville actor.

Appeared in: 1934 Happy. 1936 Annie Laurie; Love in Exile. 1937 Cotton Queen; Said O'Reilly to McNap. 1938 To the Victor. 1939 Rulers of the Sea; The Mind of Mr. Reeder. 1940 They Came by Night; For Freedom; Missing People; Neutral Port. 1941 The Prime Minister. 1944 Heaven Is 'Round the Corner. 1946 Rolling Home. 1948 The Brothers. Other British films: King of Hearts; Owd Bob; Debt of Honor; Men of Yesterday; Well Done, Henry; Spring Handicap; Give Me the Stars.

GABLE, CLARK (Clark William Gable)

Born: Feb. 1, 1901, Cadiz, Ohio. Died: Nov. 17, 1960, Los Angeles, Calif.(heart attack). Screen and stage actor. Won Academy Award in 1934 for Best Actor in It Happened One Night. Received Academy Award nominations for Best Actor in 1935 for Mutiny on the Bounty and in 1939 for Gone with the Wind. Married to screen actress Carole Lombard (dec. 1942).

Appeared in: 1924 White Man; Forbidden Paradise. 1925 The Merry Widow; Declassee; The Plastic Age; North Star. 1930 The Painted Desert. 1931 Night Nurse; The Easiest Way; The Secret Six; The Finger Points; Laughing Sinners; A Free Soul; Sporting Blood; Dance, Fools, Dance; Possessed; Hell Divers; Susan Lennox, Her Rise and Fall. 1932 Polly of the Circus; Strange Interlude; Red Dust; No Man of Her Own. 1933 The White Sister; Hold Your Man; Night Flight; Dancing Lady. 1934 It Happened One Night; Men in White; Manhattan Melodrama; Chained; Forsaking All Others; Hollywood on Parade (short). 1935 After Office Hours; Call of the Wild; China Seas; Mutiny on the Bounty; Riffraff. 1936 Wife vs. Secretary; San Francisco; Cain and Mabel; Love on the Run. 1937 Parnell; Saratoga. 1938 Test Pilot; Too Hot to Handle. 1939 Idiot's Delight; Gone with the Wind. 1940 Strange Cargo; Boom Town; Comrade X. 1941 They Met in Bombay; Honky Tonk. 1942 Somewhere I'll Find You. 1943 Aerial Gunner; Wings Up (narr.); Hollywood in Uniform (short). 1944 Combat America (documentary). 1945 Adventure. 1947 The Hucksters. 1948 Command Decision; Homecoming. 1949 Any Number Can Play. 1950 Key to the City; To Please a Lady; Pygmy Island. 1951 Across the Wide Missouri; Callaway Went Thataway. 1952 Lone Star. 1953 Never Let Me Go; Mogambo. 1954 Betrayed. 1955 Soldier of Fortune; The Tall Men. 1957 Band of Angels; The King and Four Queens. 1958 Run Silent, Run Deep; Teacher's Pet. 1959 But Not for Me. 1960 It Started in Naples. 1961 The Misfits. 1964 The Big Parade of Comedy (documentary).

GABY, FRANK

Born: 1896. Died: Feb. 12, 1945, St. Louis, Mo.(suicide-hanging). Screen, stage, and vaudeville actor.
Appeared in: 1927 The Tout (short). 1941 Mr. Dynamite.

GAILING, GRETCHEN

Born: 1918. Died: June 17, 1961, Hollywood, Calif. Screen actress.

GALE, MRS. MARGUERITE H.

Born: 1885. Died: Aug. 20, 1948, Amsterdam, N.Y. Screen and stage actress. Appeared in films between 1914 and 1918.

Appeared in: 1915 The Missing Link; How Molly Made Good. 1916 The Yellow Menace (serial).

GALLAGHER, GLEN B.

Born: 1909. Died: Mar. 31, 1960, Hollywood, Calif.(heart attack). Screen actor and cameraman.

GALLAGHER, "SKEETS" (Richard Gallagher)

Born: July 28, 1891, Terre Haute, Ind. Died: May 22, 1955, Santa Monica, Calif.(heart attack). Screen, stage, and vaudeville actor.

Appeared in: 1923 The Daring Years. 1927 The Potters; For the Love of Mike; New York. 1928 The Racket; Three-Ring Marriage; Alex the Great; Stocks and Blondes. 1929 Close Harmony; Fast Company; Dance of Life; Pointed Heels. 1930 Paramount on Parade; Honey; The Social Lion; Let's Go Native; Her Wedding Night; Love among Millionaires. 1931 It Pays to Advertise; Possessed; Up Pops the Devil; Road to Reno. 1932 The Night Club Lady; The Unwritten Law; Merrily We Go to Hell; Trial of Vivenne Ware; Bird of Paradise; The Phantom of Crestwood; The Conquerors; The Sport Parade; Universal shorts; Hollywood on Parade (short). 1933 Easy Millions; The Past of Mary Holmes; Too Much Harmony; Reform Girl; Alice in Wonderland; Universal shorts. 1934 Riptide; The Meanest Girl in Town; Bachelor Bait; In the Money; Women Unafraid; The Crosby Case. 1935 Lightning Strikes Twice; The Perfect Clue. 1936 Polo Joe; Yours for the Asking; The Man I Marry; Hats Off. 1937 Espionage. 1938 Danger in the Air. 1939 Idiot's Delight. 1941 Zis Boom Bah; Citadel of Crime. 1942 Brother Orchid. 1949 The Duke of Chicago. 1952 Three for Bedroom C.

GALLARDO, LUIS ROJAS

Born: Chile. Died: Mar. 5, 1957, Santiago, Chile. Screen, stage, radio actor, and writer.

GALVANI, DINO (aka DINO GALVANONI)

Born: Oct. 27, 1890, Milan, Italy. Died: Sept. 14, 1960, London, England. Screen, stage, radio, and television actor.

Appeared in: 1926 Paradise. 1927 Toni. 1928 Adam's Apple; Adventurous Youth. 1929 The Vagabond Queen. 1930 Atlantic; Life's a Stage; Nightbirds. 1931 The Chance of a Night Time; In a Monastery Garden; The Missing Rembrandt; Black Coffee. 1932 Those We Love. 1933 The Silver Greyhound; Heads We Go; No Funny Business. 1935 Princess Charming; Midnight Menace. 1936 Secret Agent. 1937 Mr. Satan; The Viper; George Bizet; Special Edition; Vengeance of Kali. 1938 Who's Your Lady Friend; Last Barricades; Four Feathers. 1942 It's That Man Again. 1949 Sleeping Car to Trieste. 1951 Fugitive Lady; Paul Temple's Triumph; Three Steps North. 1954 Father Brown (aka The Detective); Always a Bride. 1957 Checkpoint; Second Fiddle. 1960 Bluebeard's Ten Honeymoons; Breakout (aka Danger Within). Other British films: Lady in Danger; Don't Rush Me; Bad Blood; Ball at the Savoy; Cafe Colette; Port of Call; Cross My Heart; Vienna Sunset; Faithful.

GAMBLE, FRED

Born: 1869. Died: Feb. 17, 1939, Hollywood, Calif. Screen, stage, and vaudeville actor. Billed in vaudeville as part of "Queen City Four" team. Entered films in 1906.

Appeared in: 1915 Oh, Daddy. 1920 The Screaming Shadow (serial). 1921 Love Never Dies; Passing Thru. 1922 Boy Crazy; The Firebrand. 1923 The Virginian. 1924 The Tornado; Black Oxen. 1925 Tumbleweeds. 1926 Chasing Trouble; Born to Battle. 1927 Laddie Be Good; The Red Mill. 1928 Painted Post.

GAMBLE, RALPH

Born: 1902. Died: Mar. 11, 1966, Hollywood, Calif. Screen and vaudeville actor.

Appeared in: 1953 Mister Scoutmaster. 1955 Sudden Danger. 1958 In the Money; Unwed Mother.

GAN, CHESTER

Born: 1909. Died: June 30, 1959, San Francisco, Calif. Screen and television actor.

Appeared in: 1936 Klondike Annie; Drift Fence; Sea Spoilers. 1937 West of Shanghai; The Good Earth. 1938 Shadows of Shanghai. 1939 Mystery of Mr. Wong; Blackwell's Island; King of Chinatown. 1940 'Til We Meet Again; Victory. 1941 The Maltese Falcon; Man Made Monster; The Get-Away; Burma Convoy. 1942 Flying Tigers; Moontide; China Girl; Across the Pacific. 1943 Crash Dive. 1955 Blood Alley.

GANNON, JOHN "JACK"
Born: 1903. Died: Nov. 8, 1969, Hollywood, Calif.(respiratory failure). Screen actor and stuntman.

GANTVOORT, HERMAN L.
Born: 1887. Died: Sept. 17, 1937, N.Y. Screen, stage actor, and screenwriter.

GANZHORN, JOHN W. (aka JACK GANSHORN)
Born: 1881. Died: Sept. 19, 1956, Hollywood, Calif. Screen actor.

Appeared in: 1922 Thorobred. 1924 The Iron Horse. 1925 Fightin' Odds. 1927 Hawk of the Hills (serial). 1928 The Apache Raider; The Valley of Hunted Men. 1929 Hawk of the Hills (feature of 1927 serial).

GARAT, HENRI
Born: Apr. 3, 1902, Paris, France. Died: Aug. 13, 1959, Toulon, France. Screen and stage actor.

Appeared in: 1932 Congress Dances; Il est Charmant (He Is Charming); La Fille et le Garcon (The Girl and the Boy); Le Roi des Resquilleurs. 1933 Adorable. 1935 Soir de Revillon. 1937 Amphytrion. 1938 Advocate D'Amour. Other French films: The Fair Dream; The Charm School; Her Highness' Command.

GARCIA, HENRY
Born: 1904. Died: Nov. 3, 1970, San Antonio, Tex. Screen, stage actor, musician, screenwriter, and film technician.

GARCIA, HUMBERTO RODRIGUEZ
Born: 1915, Mexico. Died: June 21, 1960, Mexico City, Mexico. Screen and stage actor.

GARDEL, CARLOS
Born: Uruguay. Died: June 24, 1935, Colombia, South America (plane crash). Screen, stage actor, and singer. Appeared in a series of pictures made by Paramount for Spanish market.

Appeared in: 1933 Esperame; Melodia de Arrabal. 1934 Cuesta Abajo; El Tango en Broadway. 1935 Tango-Bar; El Dia que me Quieras (The Day You Love Me).

GARDEN, MARY
Born: Feb. 20, 1874, Aberdeen, Scotland. Died: Jan. 3, 1967, Aberdeen, Scotland. Screen and opera actress.

Appeared in: 1918 The Splendid Sinner; Thais.

GARDINER, PATRICK
Born: 1926. Died: Sept. 30, 1970, Dublin, Ireland(heart attack). Screen, stage, and radio actor. Appeared in Irish films.

GARDNER, CYRIL
Born: May 30, 1898, Paris, France. Died: Dec. 30, 1942, Hollywood, Calif.(heart attack). Screen actor, film director, and film editor. Appeared on the screen at the age of 13.

GARDNER, ED
Born: 1901, Astoria, N.Y. Died: Aug. 17, 1963, Los Angeles, Calif.(liver ailment). Screen, stage, radio actor, stage director, stage producer, film producer, and writer for radio. Divorced from screen actress Shirley Booth.

Appeared in: 1945 Duffy's Tavern, a film take-off of his famous radio program of the same name.

GARDNER, GEORGE
Born: 1868. Died: May 12, 1929, East Islip, N.Y. Screen and stage actor.

GARDNER, HELEN LOUISE
Died: Nov. 20, 1968, Orlando, Fla. Screen actress and film producer. She was the first film star to form her own picture company, Helen Gardner Picture Corporation (1912).

Appeared in: 1911 Vanity Fair. 1912 Cleopatra; A Princess of Bagdad. 1913 A Sister to Carmen. 1922 Devil's Angel. 1924 Sandra. 1930 Monte Carlo.

GARDNER, HUNTER
Born: 1899. Died: Jan. 16, 1952, Hollywood, Calif.(suicide-slashed wrists). Screen and stage actor.

Appeared in: 1934 Gambling.

GARDNER, JACK
Born: 1876. Died: Dec. 29, 1929, Glendale, Calif.(heart disease). Screen, stage, and vaudeville actor. In vaudeville he had several partners namely, Jeanette Lowery, Al Lloyd, Marie Hartman and Edna Leedom.

Appeared in: 1917 Gift O' Gab. 1922 Wonders of the Sea; Youth to Youth. 1923 Hollywood; Wild Bill Hickok; To the Ladies. 1924 Bluff. 1927 Wild Geese; Blondes by Choice. 1929 Scarlet Seas; The Girl from Woolworth's.

GARDNER, JACK
Born: 1915. Died: Oct. 20, 1955, near Camarillo, Calif. Screen, television, radio actor, and newscaster.

Appeared in: 1938 Cocoanut Grove. 1942 The Glass Key; The Pride of the Yankees. 1943 Adventures of Smilin' Jack (serial). 1944 Three Russian Girls; It Happened Tomorrow.

GARDNER, PETER
Born: 1898. Died: Nov. 13, 1953, Studio City, Calif. Screen and stage actor. Entered films approx. 1918.

GARFIELD, JOHN (Jules Garfinkle)
Born: Mar. 4, 1913, New York, N.Y. Died: May 21, 1952, New York, N.Y.(heart attack). Screen and stage actor. Father of screen actor John Garfield, Jr.

Appeared in: 1933 Footlight Parade. 1938 Four Daughters. 1939 Blackwell's Island; They Made Me a Criminal; Dust Be My Destiny; Daughters Courageous; Juarez; Four Wives. 1940 Saturday's Children; Castle on the Hudson; East of the River; Flowing Gold. 1941 The Sea Wolf; Out of the Fog; Dangerously They Live. 1942 Tortilla Flat. 1943 The Fallen Sparrow; Air Force; Thank Your Lucky Stars. 1944 Between Two Worlds; Destination Tokyo; Hollywood Canteen. 1945 Pride of the Marines. 1946 Nobody Lives Forever; Humoresque; The Postman Always Rings Twice. 1947 Body and Soul; Gentleman's Agreement. 1948 Force of Evil. 1949 We Were Strangers. 1950 The Breaking Point; Under My Skin; Difficult Years (narr.). 1952 He Ran All the Way.

GARGAN, EDWARD
Born: 1902. Died: Feb. 19, 1964, New York, N.Y. Screen and stage actor. Brother of screen actor William Gargan.

Appeared in: 1933 The Girl in 419, Gambling Ship; Three-Cornered Moon. 1934 Behold My Wife; Registered Nurse; Belle of the Nineties; The Lemon Drop Kid; Wild Gold; David Harum; Twentieth Century. 1935 Port of Lost Dreams; Hold 'Em Yale; The Gilded Lily; Here Comes Cookie; Hands across the Table; The Bride Comes Home; Behind the Green Lights; We're in the Money; False Pretenses. 1936 Anything Goes; Roaming Lady; Ceiling Zero; Stage Struck; Dangerous Waters; My Man Godfrey; Nobody's Fool; Two in a Crowd; Hearts in Bondage; Grand Jury; Wives Never Know; Great Guy. 1937 You Can't Buy Luck; We're on the Jury; High, Wide and Handsome; Jim Hanvey, Detective; Wake up and Live; The Go-Getter; A Girl with Ideas; Danger Patrol. 1938 That's My Story; The Devil's Party; The Texans; While New York Sleeps; Straight, Place and Show; Up the River; Thanks for the Memory; Annabel Takes a Tour; Crime School. 1939 Honolulu; The Saint Strikes Back; Yes, My Darling Daughter; For Love or Money; Lucky Night; Fixer Dugan; Night Work; They All Come Out; Pack up Your Troubles; 20,000 Men a Year. 1940 Three Cheers for the Irish; Road to Singapore; Wolf of New York; Brother Rat and a Baby; Spring Parade; Girl from God's Country; Queen of the Mob; Street of Memories; We're in the Army Now; Go West. 1941 Meet the Chump; San Francisco Docks; The Lone Wolf Keeps a Date; Bowery Boys; Tight Shoes; Tillie the Toiler; Here Comes Happiness; Thieves Fall Out; A Date with the Falcon; Dr. Kildare's Victory; Niagara Falls. 1942 Fly by Night; The Falcon's Brother; Over My Dead Body; The Falcon Takes Over; Meet the Stewarts; They All Kissed the Bride; A-Haunting We Will Go; Miss Annie Rooney; Between Us Girls. 1943 The Falcon Strikes Back; The Falcon in Danger; The Falcon and the Co-eds; Prairie Chickens; Princess O'Rourke; My Kingdom for a Cook; Taxi, Mister; Hit the Ice. 1944 The Falcon out West; Detective Kitty Kelly; San Fernando Valley. 1945 Follow That Woman; Her Highness and the Bellboy; Sporting Chance; The Bullfighters; Diamond Horseshoe; High Powered; Wonder Man; The Beautiful Cheat; Earl Carroll Vanities; Sing Your Way Home; Life with

Blondie; See My Lawyer; The Naughty Nineties. 1946 Behind the Mask; Cinderella Jones; The Dark Horse; The Inner Circle; Gay Blades; Little Giant. 1947 Linda Be Good; That's My Girl; Saddle Pals; Web of Danger; Little Miss Broadway; Exposed. 1948 Scudda Hoo! Scudda Hay!; The Dude Goes West; Strike It Rich; Campus Honeymoon; Miss Annie Rooney (reissue of 1942 film); Argyle Secrets; Waterfront at Midnight. 1949 Hold That Baby; Red Light; Dynamite; Love Happy. 1950 Belle of Old Mexico; Triple Trouble; Square Dance Katy; Gallant Bess; Hit Parade of 1951. 1951 Bedtime for Bonzo; Abbott and Costello Meet the Invisible Man; Cuban Fireball.

GARLAND, JUDY (Frances Gumm)
Born: June 10, 1922, Grand Rapids, Mich. Died: June 22, 1969, London, England(accidental overdose of drugs). Screen, stage, vaudeville, and television actress. She and her sisters appeared in vaudeville in an act billed as the "Gumm Sisters." Won Academy's "Special" Award in 1939 for The Wizard of Oz. Nominated for Academy Award in 1961 for Best Supporting Actress in Judgement at Nuremberg. Divorced from composer David Rose, film director Vincent Minnelli, producer Sid Luft and screen actor Mark Herron. Mother of screen actress/singer Liza Minnelli.

Appeared in: 1935 Every Sunday (short). 1936 Pigskin Parade. 1937 Thoroughbreds Don't Cry; Broadway Melody of 1938. 1938 Everybody Sing; Listen, Darling; Love Finds Andy Hardy. 1939 Babes in Arms; The Wizard of Oz. 1940 Strike Up the Band; Little Nellie Kelly; Andy Hardy Meets a Debutante. 1941 Life Begins for Andy Hardy; Ziegfeld Girl; Babes on Broadway. 1942 For Me and My Gal. 1943 Girl Crazy; Presenting Lily Mars; Thousands Cheer. 1944 Meet Me in St. Louis. 1945 The Clock. 1946 Ziegfeld Follies; The Harvey Girls; Till the Clouds Roll By. 1948 The Pirate; Words and Music; Easter Parade. 1949 In the Good Old Summertime. 1950 Summer Stock. 1954 A Star Is Born. 1960 Pepe (voice only). 1961 Judgement at Nuremberg. 1962 Gay Purr-Ee (voice only). 1963 A Child Is Waiting; I Could Go on Singing.

GARLY, EDWARD H.
Died: Nov. 25, 1938, Hollywood, Calif. Screen, vaudeville, and minstrel actor.

GARON, PAULINE (Marie Pauline Garon)
Born: Sept. 9, 1901, Montreal, Canada. Died: Aug. 30, 1965. Screen and stage actress. Divorced from screen actor Lowell Sherman (dec. 1934).

Appeared in: 1921 The Power Within. 1922 Sonny; Reported Missing. 1923 Adam's Rib; The Marriage Market; The Man from Glengarry; You Can't Fool Your Wife; Children of Dust; Forgive and Forget. 1924 The Average Woman; The Turmoil; Wine of Youth; Pal O'Mine; The Painted Flapper; The Spitfire. 1925 Satan in Sables; Compromise; Fighting Youth; Flaming Waters; The Love Gamble; Speed; The Great Sensation; Passionate Youth; Rose of the World; Where Was I?; The Splendid Road. 1926 Christine of the Big Tops. 1927 The Princess on Broadway; The College Hero; Eager Lips; Temptations of a Shop Girl; Love of Sunya; Naughty; Driven from Home; Ladies at Ease. 1928 The Candy Kid; Girl He Didn't Buy; The Heart of Broadway; The Devil's Cage; Dugan of the Dugouts; Riley of the Rainbow Division. 1929 The Gamblers; Must We Marry?; In the Headlines; Show of Shows. 1930 The Thoroughbred; Le Spectre Vert; the following shorts: Lovers Delight; Jack White Talking Pictures; Letters. 1933 One Year Later; Phantom Broadcast; By Appointment Only; Lost in the Stratosphere. 1935 The White Cockatoo; Becky Sharp. 1937 Her Husband's Secretary.

GARR, EDDIE
Born: 1900. Died: Sept. 3, 1956, Burbank, Calif.(heart ailment). Screen and stage actor.

Appeared in: 1933 Obey the Law; a Universal short. 1949 Ladies of the Chorus. 1951 Varieties on Parade.

GARRICK, RICHARD T.
Born: 1879. Died: Aug. 21, 1962, Hollywood, Calif. Screen actor.

Appeared in: 1947 Boomerang. 1948 Green Grass of Wyoming. 1951 A Streetcar Named Desire. 1952 Viva Zapata; Dream Boat; O. Henry's Full House; Something for the Birds; Stars and Stripes Forever. 1953 Call Me Madam; Law and Order. 1954 Desiree; Riding Shotgun. 1955 High Society; A Man Called Peter; Violent Saturday. 1956 Hilda Crane; The Mountain.

GARRISON, MICHAEL
Born: 1923. Died: Aug. 17, 1966, Bel Air, Calif.(skull fracture-fall). Screen, stage actor, film producer, and television executive producer. Entered films approx. 1947.

GARTH, OTIS
Born: 1901. Died: Dec. 21, 1955, Hollywood, Calif. Screen and television actor.

Appeared in: 1953 Mister Scoutmaster.

GARZA, EVA
Born: 1917, Mexico. Died: Nov. 1, 1966, Tucson, Ariz.(pneumonia). Screen actress and singer.

GATES, BERT
Born: 1883. Died: Dec. 18, 1952, Aberdeen, Scotland. Screen actor. He gave "talking films" to audiences, standing behind the screen with his wife and speaking the various parts.

GAUGE, ALEXANDER
Born: 1914, England. Died: Sept. 1960, Woking Surrey, England. Screen, stage, and television actor.

Appeared in: 1949 The Interrupted Journey (film debut, U.S. 1951). 1952 Murder in the Cathedral; Pickwick Papers (U.S. 1953). 1953 Martin Luther; Penny Princess. 1954 Dance, Little Lady (U.S. 1955); Fast and Loose. 1955 Will Any Gentleman?; The Square Ring; Cross Up (aka Tiger by the Tail). 1956 The Iron Petticoat; Shadow of Fear (aka Before I Wake). 1957 A Novel Affair (aka Passionate Stranger); Two Grooms for a Bride. 1963 Les Canilles (The Ruffians).

GAULT, MILDRED
Born: 1905. Died: Sept. 15, 1938, Los Angeles, Calif. Screen actress and film dancer.

GAUNTIER, GENE (Genevieve Gauntier Liggett)
Born: approx. 1880. Died: Dec. 18, 1966, Cuernavaca, Mexico. Screen actress, screenwriter, and film producer.

Appeared in: 1908 Days of 61 (aka The Blue and the Gray). 1910 The Kalem Girl. 1912 From the Manger to the Cross.

GAWTHORNE, PETER
Born: Sept. 1, 1884, Queen's County, Ireland. Died: Mar. 17, 1962, London, England. Screen and stage actor.

Appeared in: 1929 Behind That Curtain; Sunny Side Up; His Glorious Night. 1930 Those Three French Girls; Temple Tower. 1931 Charlie Chan Carries On; The Man Who Came Back. 1932 The Flag Lieutenant; Jack's the Boy. 1933 Lodger; Perfect Understanding; Night and Day; The Blarney Kiss; Prince of Arcadia; A Cuckoo in the Nest. 1934 Something Always Happens; Grand Prix. 1935 Dirty Work; Phantom Fiend; The Iron Duke. 1936 Wolf's Clothing; A Woman Alone; The Amazing Quest; East Meets West; Everybody Dance. 1937 Gangway. 1938 Convict 99; Alf's Button Afloat. 1939 Ask a Policeman. 1942 Much Too Shy; Mister V. 1949 The Case of Charles Peace. 1951 Soho Conspiracy. 1954 Five Days.

GAXTON, WILLIAM (Arturo Gaxiola)
Born: Dec. 2, 1893, San Francisco, Calif. Died: Feb. 2, 1963, New York, N.Y. Screen, stage, and vaudeville actor.

Appeared in: 1926 Stepping Along; It's the Old Army Game. 1931 Fifty Million Frenchmen. 1932 Silent Partners (short). 1934 Their Big Moment. 1942 Something to Shout About. 1943 The Heat's On; Best Foot Forward. 1944 Tropicana. 1945 Diamond Horseshoe.

GAY, FRED
Born: 1882. Died: June 11, 1955, Long Beach, Calif. Screen actor.

GAY, MAISIE
Born: 1883, England. Died: Sept. 14, 1945, London, England. British screen and stage actress.

GAY, RAMON (Ramon Gaytan)
Born: 1917. Died: June 1960, Mexico City, Mexico. Screen and stage actor.

Appeared in: 1953 Eugenia Grandet. 1962 La Estrella Vacia (The Empty Star).

GAYE, ALBIE
Died: Nov. 26, 1965, Chicago, Ill. Screen, stage, television actress, and singer.

Appeared in: 1953 The Miami Story. 1956 The Vagabond King.

GEARY, BUD
Born: 1899. Died: Feb. 22, 1946, Hollywood, Calif.(injuries sustained in motor crash). Screen actor.

Appeared in: 1921 Everyman's Price. 1922 Four Hearts. 1932 High Flyers. 1936 The Trail of the Lonesome Pine. 1940 Adventures of Red Ryder; Saps at Sea. 1941 Great Guns; King of the Texas Rangers. 1942 A-Haunting We Will Go. 1944 Sheriff of Las Vegas; Haunted Harbor; Song of the Open Road. 1946 Smoky.

GEBUEHR, OTTO
Born: 1877, Germany. Died: Mar. 13, 1954, Wiesbaden, West Germany. Screen and stage actor who greatly resembled Frederick the Great. Entered films in 1920.

Appeared in: 1922 Fredericus Rex. 1929 Waterloo. 1931 Das Floetenkonzert von Sanssouci (A Flute Concert at Sanssouci). 1932 Barberina; Die Taenzerin Von Sans-Souci. 1935 Der Choral von Leuthen. 1937 Pretty Miss Schragg. 1938 Nanon. 1939 Fridericus. 1940 Leidenschaft (Passion). 1950 City of Torment. 1952 The Devil Makes Three. 1954 Angelika. 1956 Circus Cirl. Other German films: Dr. Holl; Die Luege; Fritz and Friederike; Das Ewige Spiel.

GEE, GEORGE
Born: 1895, England. Died: Oct. 17, 1959, Coventry, England. Screen and stage actor.

Appeared in: 1931 Week-End Wives; Let's Love and Laugh. 1932 Leave It to Me. 1933 Cleaning Up; Strike It Rich.

GEHRMAN, MRS. LUCY
Died: May 8, 1954, New York, N.Y. Yiddish screen and stage actress.

Appeared in: 1950 God, Man and Devil.

GEIGER, HERMANN
Born: 1913. Died: Aug. 25, 1966, near Sitten, West Germany. (plane crash). Screen actor and pilot.

GELDERT, CLARENCE
Born: June 9, 1867, St. John, B.C., Canada. Died: May 13, 1935, Calabasas, Calif.(heart attack). Screen, stage actor, and film director. Entered films with D. W. Griffith in 1915.

Appeared in: 1917 Joan the Woman. 1921 All Souls Eve; The Great Moment; The Hell Diggers; The House That Jazz Built; The Lost Romance; The Witching Hour. 1922 Rent Free. 1923 A Woman of Paris; Adam's Rib; Richard the Lion-Hearted; Wasted Lives. 1924 Behind the Curtain; The Fighting American; Love's Whirlpool; North of 36; The Whipping Boss; Oh, Doctor. 1925 The Bandit's Baby; My Neighbor's Wife. 1926 The Flaming Forest; Boy Friend; Hands across the Border; Racing Blood; Young April. 1927 Dress Parade; One Man Game. 1929 Overland Telegraph; Square Shoulders; Sioux Blood; The Ghost Talks; Unholy Night; Thirteenth Chair. 1930 The Bishop Murder Case. 1931 Guilty Hands; Cuban Love Song; Daddy Long Legs. 1932 The Stoker; White Eagle; Emma. 1933 Jungle Bride; Lucky Dog; Telephone Trail; Revenge at Monte Carlo; Dance Hall Hostess; Rusty Rides Alone; Marriage on Approval; Lone Adventure. 1934 In Love with Life; Man Trailer. 1935 Mississippi. 1936 Go Get-'Em Haines.

GEMORA, CHARLIE
Born: 1903, Philippine Islands. Died: Aug. 19, 1961, Hollywood, Calif.(heart attack). Screen actor.

Appeared in: 1928 The Circus Kid. 1933 King Kong (was the gorilla). 1938 Swiss Miss. 1939 At the Circus; The Gorilla. 1948 Beauty and the Beast. 1953 War of the Worlds; White Witch Doctor. 1961 One-Eyed Jacks.

GENDRON, PIERRE
Born: Mar. 4, 1896, Toledo, Ohio. Died: Nov. 27, 1956, Hollywood, Calif. Screen, stage actor, and screenwriter.

Appeared in: 1921 The Bashful Suitor. 1922 The Man Who Played God; The Young Painter. 1923 Broadway Broke; Does It Pay?; Outlaws of the Sea. 1924 The Dangerous Flirt; The City That Never Sleeps; Just off Broadway; The Lover of Camille;

Three Women. 1925 The Scarlet Honeymoon. 1927 The Enchanted Island. 1928 What Price Beauty.

GENTLE, ALICE
Born: 1889, Chatsworth, Ill. Died: Feb. 28, 1958, Oakland, Calif. Screen, stage, and opera actress.

Appeared in: 1930 The Golden Dawn (film debut); Song of the Flame; A Scene from Carmen (short).

GEORGE, GLADYS (Gladys Clare)
Born: Sept. 13, 1900, Hatton, Maine. Died: Dec. 8, 1954, Los Angeles, Calif.(brain hemorrhage). Screen and stage actress.

Appeared in: 1920 Red Hot Dollars; Home Spun Folks. 1921 The Easy Road; Chickens; The House That Jazz Built. 1934 Straight Is the Way. 1936 Valiant Is the Word for Carrie. 1937 They Gave Him a Gun; Madame X. 1938 Love Is A Headache; Marie Antoinette. 1939 The Roaring Twenties; Here I Am a Stranger; I'm from Missouri. 1940 A Child Is Born; The Way of All Flesh; The House across the Bay. 1941 The Lady from Cheyenne; The Maltese Falcon; Hit the Road. 1942 The Hard Way. 1943 Nobody's Darling; The Crystal Ball. 1944 Minstrel Man; Christmas Holiday. 1945 Steppin' in Society. 1946 The Best Years of Our Lives. 1947 Millie's Daughter. 1948 Alias a Gentleman. 1949 Flamingo Road. 1950 The Undercover Girl; Bright Leaf. 1951 Detective Story; He Ran All the Way; Lullaby of Broadway; Silver City. 1953 It Happens Every Thursday.

GEORGE, GRACE
Born: Dec. 25, 1879, New York, N.Y. Died: May 19, 1961, New York, N.Y. Screen, stage actress, and stage director.

Appeared in one film only. 1943 Johnny Come Lately.

GEORGE, HEINRICH
Born: 1893, Germany. Died: Sept. 27, 1946, Russia (Soviet internment camp). German screen and stage actor.

Appeared in: 1927 Metropolis. 1928 Bondage; Armored Vault. 1929 The Whirl of Life; The Wrath of the Seas; Theatre; Wasted Love. 1931 Der Mann der den Mord Beging (The Man Who Committed the Murder); Berlin-Alexanderplatz (U.S. 1933). 1932 Der Andere; 1914: The Last Days before the War. 1934 Unsere Fahne Flattert Uns Voran. 1935 Hermine und die Sieben Aufrechten; Das Maedchen Johanna. 1936 Reifende Jugend; Stuetzen der Gesellschaft; Wenn der Hahn Kraeht. 1937 Promise Me Nothing. 1938 Ball im Metropol; Unternehmen Michael (The Private's Job); Magda. 1939 Der Biberpelz (The Beaver Coat); Frau Sylvelin. 1940 The Dreyfus Case.

GEORGE, MURIEL
Born: Aug. 29, 1883, London, England. Died: Oct. 22, 1965, England. Screen, stage, and television actress.

Appeared in: 1932 His Lordship. 1933 Yes, Mr. Brown. 1934 Nell Gwyn; Something Always Happens; My Song for You. 1935 Old Faithful; French Salad; Limelight; Whom the Gods Love; Not So Dusty. 1936 Busman's Holiday. 1937 Merry Comes to Town; The Man without a Home; Doctor Syn; Lancaster Luck; Cracker Jack. 1938 A Sister to Assist 'Er. 1939 Pack up Your Troubles. 1940 Quiet Wedding. 1941 The Voice in the Night. 1943 Alibi; Went the Day Well; The Bells Go Down; Dean Octopus; Rookery Nook; Knight of the Garter. 1944 Place of One's Own; 48 Hours; I'll Be Your Sweetheart. 1945 Vacation from Marriage. 1947 The Years Between. 1950 Perfect Strangers; The Dancing Years; Last Holiday. 1955 Simon and Laura. Other British films: Freedom Radio; Cottage to Let.

GEORGE, VOYA (Voya George Djordjevich)
Born: 1895. Died: May 8, 1951, New York, N.Y. Screen actor.

Appeared in: 1928 The Legion of the Condemned.

GERAGHTY, CARMELITA
Born: 1901, Rushville, Ind. Died: June 7, 1966, New York, N.Y. Screen actress.

Appeared in: 1923 Bag and Baggage; Jealous Husbands. 1924 Black Oxen; Discontented Husbands; Geared to Go; High Speed; Through the Dark. 1925 Passionate Youth; Brand of Cowardice; Cyclone Cavalier; The Mysterious Stranger; Under the Rouge. 1926 My Lady of Whims; The Great Gatsby; The Canyon of Light; The Flying Mail; Josselyn's Wife; The Lily. 1927 The Last Trail; My Best Girl; The Slaver; The Small Bachelor; Venus of Venice; What Every Girl Should Know. 1928 The Goodbye Kiss. 1929 Object Alimony; Paris Bound; South of Panama; The Mississippi Gambler; This Thing Called Love. 1930 After the Fog; What Men Want; Men without Law; Rogue of the Rio Grande;

Fighting Through. 1931 Fifty Million Frenchmen; The Devil Plays; Millie; Texas Ranger; Night Life in Reno. 1932 Prestige; Forgotten Women; Escapade. 1933 Malay Nights; Flaming Signal. 1935 Manhattan Butterfly.

GERALD, JIM (Jacques Guenod)
Born: 1889, France. Died: 1958. Screen and stage actor. Entered films approx. 1911.

Appeared in: 1927 An Italian Straw Hat. 1931 La Chant au Marin; La Nuit est a Nous (The Night Is Ours); The Horse Ate the Hat. 1934 The Constant Nymph. 1936 The Robber Symphony. 1937 Bulldog Drummond at Bay. 1939 French without Tears. 1943 The Last Will of Dr. Mabuse. 1945 Boule de Suif. 1951 The Lady from Boston; Pardon My French; Adventures of Captain Fabian. 1952 The Crimson Curtain. 1953 Moulin Rouge. 1954 Father Brown (aka The Detective); The Barefoot Contessa; The Moment of Truth. 1956 Foreign Intrigue. 1957 Eric Frac en Dentelles. 1959 Le Vente se Leve (The Wind Rises-aka Time Bomb, U.S. 1961).

GERARD, JOSEPH SMITH
Born: 1871. Died: Aug. 20, 1949, Woodland Hills, Calif. Screen actor.

GERARD, TEDDIE (Teresa Cabre)
Born: 1890, Buenos Aires, Argentina. Died: Aug. 31, 1942, London, England. Screen, stage actress, and dancer.

Appeared in: 1922 Cave Girl; Seventh Day.

GERRARD, GENE (Eugene O'Sullivan)
Born: Aug. 31, 1892, Clapham, London, England. Died: June 1971, Sidmouth, Devon, England. Screen, stage actor, film director, and playwright. Entered films with Hepworth Co. in 1912.

Appeared in: 1930 Let's Love and Laugh. 1932 Out of the Blue; My Wife's Family; Lucky Girl; Bridegroom for Two; Her Radio Romeo. 1933 Leave It to Me; Let Me Explain, Dear. 1935 No Monkey Business; It's a Bet. 1936 Mister Hobo. 1937 Wake up Famous.

GERSON, EVA
Born: 1903. Died: Sept. 5, 1959, New York, N.Y. Screen, stage, and television actress.

Appeared in: 1957 Street of Sinners. 1959 North by Northwest; Middle of the Night; The Last Angry Man.

GERSON, PAUL
Born: 1871. Died: June 5, 1957, Hollywood, Calif. Screen, stage actor, and film director.

Appeared in: 1923 The Cricket on the Hearth.

GERSTLE, FRANK "FRANKIE"
Born: 1917. Died: Feb. 23, 1970, Los Angeles, Calif.(cancer). Screen and television actor.

Appeared in: 1951 I Was a Communist for the FBI; Blue Veil; You Never Can Tell; Strictly Dishonorable. 1953 The Glory Brigade; Killers from Space; The Magnetic Monster; Vicki. 1955 I Cover the Underworld; Slightly Scarlet; Tight Spot. 1956 Autumn Leaves; Between Heaven and Hell; The Proud Ones. 1957 Top Secret Affair; The River's Edge; Under Fire. 1958 Ambush at Cimarron Pass. 1959 Vice Raid; The Wasp Woman; The Four Skulls of Jonathan Drake; Inside the Mafia; I, Mobster; Submarine Seahawk. 1962 13 West Street. 1963 Shock Corridor. 1964 The Atomic Brain; The Quick Gun; Monstrosity. 1965 Young Dillinger. 1966 The Wild Angels; The Silencers.

GEST, INNA
Born: 1922. Died: Jan. 1, 1965, San Francisco, Calif.(hepatitis). Screen actress.

Appeared in: 1940 The Ghost Creeps.

GHIO, NINO
Born: 1887. Died: Jan. 15, 1956, Culver City, Calif. Screen actor and opera singer.

GIACOMINO (Giuseppe Cireni)
Born: 1884. Died: 1956, Milan, Italy. Screen actor and circus clown. Was a stand-in for Charles Chaplin in several films.

GIBBONS, ROSE
Born: 1886. Died: Aug. 13, 1964, Oakland, Calif. Screen and stage actress.

GIBSON, "HOOT" EDWARD
Born: Aug. 6, 1892, Tememah, Neb. Died: Aug. 23, 1962, Woodland Hills, Calif.(cancer). Screen, vaudeville, circus, and rodeo actor. Married to singer Dorothy Dunstan and divorced from screen actresses Helen Johnson and Sally Eilers.

Appeared in: 1915 The Hazards of Helen. 1917 Straight Shooting. 1919 The Cactus Kid. 1921 Action; Red Courage; The Fire Eater; Sure Fire. 1922 Step on It; Headin' West; Trimmed; Ridin' Wild; The Galloping Kid; The Loaded Door; The Lone Hand; The Bearcat; The Denver Dude. 1923 Dead Game; Double Dealing; The Gentleman from Arizona; Out of Luck; Kindled Courage; The Ramblin' Kid; Shootin' for Love; Single Handed; The Thrill Chaser; Blinky. 1924 Hit and Run; Ride for Your Life; The Sawdust Trail; Hook and Ladder; Broadway or Bust; Forty Horse Hawkins; The Ridin' Kid from Powder River. 1925 Taming the West; Spook Ranch; The Saddle Hawk; The Hurricane Kid; Let 'Er Buck; The Calgary Stampede; Arizona Sweepstake. 1926 The Buckaroo Kid; Chip of the Flying U; The Flaming Frontier; The Man in the Saddle; The Phantom Bullet; The Texas Streak. 1927 Rawhide Kid; Galloping Fury; Straight Shootin'; A Hero on Horseback; Hey, Hey, Cowboy; Painted Ponies; The Prairie King; The Hawaiian Serenaders (short); The Silent Rider. 1928 Clearing the Trail; The Danger Rider; The Flying Cowboy; Ridin' for Fame; A Trick of Heart; The Wild West Show. 1929 Smilin' Guns; King of the Rodeo; The Lariat Kid; Burning the Wind; Winged Horseman; Courtin' Wildcats; Points West; The Long, Long Trail. 1930 Roaring Ranch; Spurs; Trigger Tricks; Trailin' Trouble; The Mounted Stranger; The Concentratin' Kid. 1931 Clearing the Range; Wild Horse; Hard Hombre. 1932 The Boiling Point; Spirit of the West; Gay Buckaroo; Local Bad Man; A Man's Land. 1933 Cowboy Counsellor; The Dude Bandit; The Fighting Parson; Boots of Destiny. 1935 Sunset Range; Powdersmoke Range; Rainbow's End. 1936 The Last Outlaw; The Riding Avenger; Swifty; Frontier Justice; Feud of the West; Cavalcade of the West. 1937 The Painted Stallion (serial). 1940 The Trail Blazers. 1943 The Law Rides Again; Death Valley Rangers; Blazing Guns; Wild Horse Stampede. 1944 Marked Trails; The Outlaw Trail; Sonora Stagecoach; Trigger Law; Arizona Whirlwind; The Utah Kid; Westward Bound. 1948 Flight to Nowhere. 1953 The Marshal's Daughter. 1959 The Horse Soldiers. 1961 Ocean's Eleven.

GIBSON, JAMES
Born: 1866. Died: Oct. 13, 1938, Los Angeles, Calif. Screen and vaudeville actor.

Appeared in: 1924 The Right of the Strongest. 1925 Greed. 1926 Glenister of the Mounted. 1930 The Social Lion; Arizona Kid.

GIGLI, BENIAMINO
Born: 1890, Italy. Died: Nov. 30, 1957, Rome, Italy. Opera singer and screen actor. Was seen in both U.S. and Italian films.

Appeared in: 1927 in the following shorts: Scenes from "Cavalleria Rusticana"; Quartet from "Rigoletto"; Bergere Legere; Scenes from "Lucia Di Lammermoor"; Scenes from "La Gioconda." 1928 The Pearl Fishers (short). 1937 Forever Yours; Ave Maria. 1938 Solo per To (Only for Me). 1939 Dingehort mein Herz (My Heart Belongs to Thee). 1940 Du Bist mein Gluck (Thou Art My Joy); Legittima Difesa (Self Defense). 1942 Pagliacci. 1950 Night Taxi. 1951 Soho Conspiracy. 1953 Singing Taxi Driver.

GILBERT, BILLY (William V. Campbell)
Born: 1891. Died: Apr. 29, 1961, Hollywood, Calif. Not to be confused with "sneezing" comedian with same name (dec. 1971). Screen, stage, and vaudeville actor. Entered films in 1928.

GILBERT, BILLY
Born: Sept. 12, 1894, Louisville, Ky. Died: Sept. 23, 1971, North Hollywood, Calif.(stroke). Screen, stage, vaudeville, minstrel, television actor, and stage producer. Married to stage actress Lolly McKenzie.

Appeared in: 1916 Bubbles of Trouble. 1929 Noisy Neighbors; The Woman Tamer (short). 1930 The Beauties (short); The Doctor's Wife (short). 1931 Chinatown after Dark, plus the following shorts: One Good Turn; A Melon-Drama; Catch as Catch Can; The Pajama Party. 1932 Pack up Your Troubles; Million Dollar Legs; "The Taxi Boys" series, plus the following shorts: County Hospital; Their First Mistake; The Music Box; The Chimp; Strictly Unreliable; Seal Skins; On the Loose; Red Noses. 1933 This Day and Age, plus the following shorts: Towed in a Hole; Sneak Easily; Asleep in the Feet; Maids a la Mode; Bargain of the Century; One Track Minds. 1934 Happy Landing; Peck's Bad Boy; Sons of the Desert (voice); Cockeyed Cavaliers, plus the following shorts: Them Thar Hills; Men in

Black; Soup and Fish. 1935 A Night at the Opera, plus the following shorts: His Bridal Sweet; Pardon My Scotch; Just Another Murder; Hail Brother. 1936 Dangerous Waters; Sutter's Gold; Three of a Kind; The Bride Walks Out; Grand Jury; The Big Game; Night Waitress; Early to Bed; Kelly the Second; The Brain Busters (short). 1937 We're on the Jury; Sea Devils; The Man Who Found Himself; The Outcasts of Poker Flat; China Passage; Music for Madame; The Toast of New York; The Life of the Party; On the Avenue; Espionage; Broadway Melody of 1938; Rosalie; One Hundred Men and a Girl; Captains Courageous; The Firefly; Maytime; Fight for Your Lady. 1938 She's Got Everything; My Lucky Star; The Girl Downstairs; Maid's Night Out; The Joy of Living; Breaking the Ice; Mr. Doodle Kicks Off; Peck's Bad Boy with the Circus; Army Girl; Block Heads; Snow White and the Seven Dwarfs (voice of Sneezy); Angels with Dirty Faces; Happy Landing. 1939 Forged Passport; The Under-Pup; Rio; Destry Rides Again; The Star Maker. 1940 His Girl Friday; Women in War; Scatterbrain; Sing, Dance, Plenty Hot; Safari; A Night at Earl Carroll's; Sandy Is a Lady; A Little Bit of Heaven; Seven Sinners; Queen of the Mob; Cross Country Romance; The Villain Still Pursued Her; No, No, Nanette; The Great Dictator; Tin Pan Alley. 1941 Reaching for the Sun; One Night in Lisbon; Angels with Broken Wings; Model Wife; New Wine; Week-End in Havana; Our City. 1942 Sleepytime Gal; Arabian Nights; Valley of the Sun; Song of the Islands; Mr. Wise Guy. 1943 Shantytown; Crazy House; Spotlight Scandals; Stage Door Canteen; Always a Bride's Maid. 1944 Three of a Kind; Crazy Knights; Ghost Crazy; Three's a Family; Ever since Venus. 1945 Anchors Aweigh; Trouble Chasers. 1947 Fun and Fancy Free (voice). 1948 The Kissing Bandit. 1949 Bride of Vengeance; Mickey and the Giant Killer (voice). 1953 Down among the Sheltering Palms. 1962 Paradise Valley; Five Weeks in a Balloon. 1963 The Sound of Laughter (documentary).

GILBERT, JOE
Born: 1903. Died: May 26, 1959, Hollywood, Calif. Screen actor. Entered films in 1923.

GILBERT, JOHN (John Pringle)
Born: July 10, 1897, Logan, Utah. Died: Jan. 9, 1936, Los Angeles, Calif.(heart attack). Screen, stage actor, screenwriter, film producer, and film director. Divorced from screen actresses Olivia Burwell, Leatrice Joy, Ina Claire and Virginia Bruce. Son of screen actor/extra John Pringle (dec. 1929).

Appeared in: 1915 The Mother Instinct. 1916 Hell's Hinges. 1917 Princess of the Dark; The Devil Dodger; Apostle of Vengeance; Golden Rule Kate. 1919 Heart of the Hills; Should a Woman Tell; Busher; Widow by Proxy. 1920 White Circle; The Great Redeemer. 1921 Ladies in Love; Ladies Must Live; The Servant in the House; The Bait; Love's Penalty; Shame. 1922 The Love Gambler; Arabian Love; The Yellow Stain; Gleam O'Dawn; The Count of Monte Cristo; Calbert's Valley; Honor First. 1923 Madness of Youth; California Romance; Truxton King; Cameo Kirby; The Exiles; St. Elmo; While Paris Sleeps. 1924 Romance Ranch; The Wolf Man; Just Off Broadway; The Lone Chance; The Snob; His Hour; Married Flirts; A Man's Mate; He Who Gets Slapped. 1925 The Big Parade; The Merry Widow; The Wife of the Centaur. 1926 La Boheme; Bardely's, The Magnificent. 1927 Flesh and the Devil; Twelve Miles Out; Love; The Show; Man, Woman and Sin. 1928 The Cossacks; Show People; Four Walls; Masks of the Devil. 1929 A Woman of Affairs; Desert Nights; His Glorious Night; Hollywood Revue of 1929; A Man's Mate. 1930 Redemption; Way for a Sailor. 1931 Phantom of Paris; Gentleman's Fate. 1932 Big Parade; West of Broadway; Downstairs. 1933 Queen Christina; Fast Workers. 1934 The Captain Hates the Sea. 1967 Show People (reissue of 1928 film).

GILBERT, MAUDE
Died: July 7, 1953, Laguna Beach, Calif. Screen and stage actress.

GILBERT, OH GRAN. See Gilbert Oh Gran

GILL, BASIL
Born: 1877, England. Died: Apr. 23, 1955, Hove, England. Screen and stage actor.

Appeared in: 1930 High Treason. 1931 Should a Doctor Tell. 1935 The Devine Spark; The Wandering Jew. 1936 Rembrandt; His Lordship. 1937 Knight without Armor; Man of Affairs. 1938 St. Martin's Lane; The Citadel. 1940 Sidewalks of London.

GILLETT, ELMA
Born: 1874. Died: July 23, 1941, Hollywood, Calif. Screen and stage actress.

GILLETTE, WILLIAM
Born: 1856, Hartford, Conn. Died: Apr. 29, 1937, Hartford, Conn.(pulmonary hemorrhage). Screen, stage actor, and playwright.

Appeared in: 1916 Sherlock Holmes.

GILLIE, JEAN
Born: 1915, England. Died: Feb. 19, 1949, London, England. Screen and stage actress.

Appeared in: 1935 School for Stars. 1936 While Parents Sleep. 1937 This'll Make You Whistle; The Live Wire; Sweet Devil. 1939 What Would You Do, Chums?; The Middle Watch. 1940 Tillie of Bloomsbury; Sailors Don't Care. 1943 The Gentle Sex. 1944 Flight from Folly; Tawney Pipit (U.S. 1947). 1945 The Spider. 1947 The Macomber Affair; Decoy. Other British films: Playtime in Mayfair; The Girl in the Taxi.

GILLINGWATER, CLAUDE
Born: Aug. 2, 1870, Lauseanna, Mo. Died: Oct. 31, 1939, Beverly Hills, Calif.(suicide-gunshot). Screen and stage actor.

Appeared in: 1921 Little Lord Fauntleroy (film debut). 1922 My Boy; The Dust Flower; Fools First; Remembrance; The Stranger's Banquet. 1923 Alice Adams; Three Wise Fools; Dulcy; A Chapter in Her Life; The Christian; Crinoline and Romance; Souls for Sale; Tiger Rose. 1924 Daddies; How to Educate a Wife; Idle Tongues; Madonna of the Streets. 1925 Cheaper to Marry; Seven Sinners; A Thief in Paradise; Wages for Wives; We Moderns; Winds of Chance. 1926 For Wives Only; Into Her Kingdom; That's My Baby. 1927 Barbed Wire; Fast and Furious; The Gorilla; Husbands for Rent; Naughty but Nice. 1928 Little Shepherd of Kingdom Come; Oh, Kay; Women They Talk About; Remember. 1929 Stark Mad; Stolen Kisses; A Dangerous Woman; Smiling Irish Eyes; Glad Rag Doll. 1930 The Flirting Widow; The Great Divide; Toast of the Legion; Dumbbells in Ermine; So Long Letty. 1931 Illicit; The Conquering Horde; Kiss Me Again; Gold Dust Gertie; Daddy Long Legs; Compromised; Oh! Oh! Cleopatra (short). 1932 Tess of the Storm Country. 1933 Skyway; Ace of Aces; Ann Carver's Profession; Before Midnight; The Avenger. 1934 In Love with Life; Back Page; Green Eyes; Broadway Bill; The Captain Hates the Sea; You Can't Buy Everything; The Show-Off; The Unknown Blonde; City Limits. 1935 Mississippi; Baby Face Harrington; Calm Yourself; A Tale of Two Cities; The Woman in Red. 1936 Florida Special; Counterfeit; The Prisoner of Shark Island; The Poor Little Rich Girl; Can This Be Dixie?; Ticket to Paradise; Wives Never Know. 1937 Top of the Town; Conquest. 1938 Little Miss Broadway; Just around the Corner; There Goes My Heart; A Yank at Oxford. 1939 Cafe Society.

GILLIS, WILLIAM S.
Died: Apr. 24, 1946, Los Angeles, Calif. Screen actor. Entered films approx. 1906.

Appeared in: 1920 Ruth of the Rockies (serial).

GILMORE, LOWELL
Died: Feb. 1, 1960, Hollywood, Calif. Screen actor.

Appeared in: 1944 Days of Glory. 1945 Johnny Angel; The Picture of Dorian Gray. 1946 Step by Step; Strange Conquest. 1947 The Arnelo Affair; Calcutta. 1948 The Prince of Thieves; Black Arrow; Walk a Crooked Mile; Dream Girl. 1949 The Secret Garden; Sword in the Desert. 1950 Fortunes of Captain Blood; Tripoli; King Solomon's Mines; Rogues of Sherwood Forest. 1951 Roadblock; Hong Kong; Darling, How Could You?; The Highwayman. 1952 The Plymouth Adventure; Androcles and the Lion; Lone Star. 1953 Francis Covers the Big Town. 1954 Day of Triumph; Saskatchewan. 1955 The Sea Chase; Ma and Pa Kettle at Waikiki. 1956 Comanche.

GILPIN, CHARLES S.
Born: 1879. Died: May 6, 1930, Eldredge Park, N.J. Screen, stage actor, and playwright.

Appeared in: 1926 Ten Nights in a Barroom.

GINIVA, JOHN "ALASKA JACK"
Born: 1868. Died: Feb. 22, 1936, Hollywood, Calif. Screen and vaudeville actor.

GINN, WELLS WATSON
Born: 1891, Bellefontaine, Ohio. Died: Apr. 15, 1959, Cincinnati, Ohio. Screen, stage, radio, vaudeville actor, and film director.

Appeared in and directed early Cosmopolitan Co. films in New York.

GIRADOT, ETIENNE

Born: 1856, London, England. Died: Nov. 10, 1939, Hollywood, Calif. Screen and stage actor. Entered films with Vitagraph Co. in Brooklyn (1912).

Appeared in: 1912 The Violin of Monsieur. 1933 The Kennell Murder Case; Blood Money; Advice to the Lovelorn. 1934 Twentieth Century (stage and film versions); Fashions of 1934; Mandalay; Return of the Terror; Little Man, What Now?; The Dragon Murder Case; The Fire Brand. 1935 Grand Old Girl; The Whole Town's Talking; Clive of India; Chasing Yesterday; Hooray for Love; In Old Kentucky; Curly Top; The Bishop Misbehaves; I Live My Life; Metropolitan. 1936 The Garden Murder Case; The Devil Is a Sissy; The Longest Night; Go West, Young Man; College Holiday; The Music Goes 'Round; Half Angel; Hearts Divided. 1937 Wake up and Live; Danger—Love at Work; The Road Back; The Great Garrick; Breakfast for Two. 1938 Port of Seven Seas; Arizona Wildcat; Professor Beware; There Goes My Heart. 1939 Little Accident; The Hunchback of Notre Dame; The Story of Vernon and Irene Castle; Fast and Loose; Exile Express; For Love or Money; Hawaiian Nights. 1940 Isle of Destiny.

GISH, DOROTHY (Dorothy de Guiche)

Born: Mar. 11, 1898, Dayton, Ohio. Died: June 4, 1968, Rapallo, Italy (bronchial pneumonia). Screen and stage actress. Entered films in 1912. Sister of screen actress Lillian Gish. Divorced from screen actor James Rennie (dec. 1965).

Appeared in: 1912 The New York Hat; The Burglar's Dilemma; An Unseen Enemy. 1913 The Perfidy of Mary; Her Mother's Oath; Judith of Bethulia. 1915 Out of Bondage; Jordan Is a Hard Road; In Old Heidelberg. 1916 Little Meena's Romance; Betty of Graystone. 1918 Battling Jane; The Hun Within; Hearts of the World. 1919 The Hope Chest; Mr. Boots; Peppy Polly; Nobody Home; Turning the Tables; I'll Get Him Yet; Nugget Nell. 1920 Remodeling Her Husband; Mary Ellen Comes to Town. 1921 Flying Pat; Ghost in the Garret; Little Miss Rebellion; Oh, Jo!. 1922 The Country Flapper; Orphans of the Storm. 1923 Out of Luck; Fury; The Bright Shawl. 1924 Romola. 1925 Night Life in New York, Clothes Make the Pirate; The Beautiful City. 1926 Nell Gwyn; London. 1927 Madame Pompadour; Tip Toes. 1936 Wanted Men. 1944 Our Hearts Were Young and Gay. 1946 Centennial Summer. 1951 The Whistle at Eaton Falls; Mornings at Seven. 1963 The Cardinal. 1964 The Chalk Garden.

GLADMAN, ANNABELLE

Born: 1899. Died: Jan. 15, 1948, Hollywood, Calif. Screen actress.

GLAGOLIN, BORIS S.

Born: 1878, Russia. Died: Dec. 12, 1948, Hollywood, Calif. Screen, stage actor, and stage director.

GLASER, VAUGHAN

Born: 1872. Died: Nov. 23, 1958, Van Nuys, Calif. Screen and stage actor.

Appeared in: 1939 What a Life; Rulers of the Sea. 1940 Those Were the Days. 1941 Adventure in Washington; Henry Aldrich for President. 1942 Saboteur; Henry and Dizzy; My Favorite Spy. 1944 Arsenic and Old Lace.

GLASS, GASTON

Born: Dec. 31, 1898, Paris, France. Died: Nov. 11, 1965, Santa Monica, Calif. Screen, stage actor, assistant film director, and television production manager. Married to screen actress "Bo-Peep" Karlin (dec. 1969).

Appeared in: 1919 Open Your Eyes. 1920 Humoresque; The World and His Wife. 1921 God's Crucible; Her Winning Way; The Lost Battalion; There Are No Villains. 1922 I Am the Law; Glass Houses; The Kingdom Within; Little Miss Smiles; Monte Cristo; Rich Men's Wives; The Song of Life. 1923 The Hero; Gimme; The Spider and the Rose; Mothers-in-Law; Daughters of the Rich. 1924 I Am the Man; After the Ball. 1925 The Bad Lands; The Danger Signal; Fair Play; Flying Fool; The Mad Marriage; Parisian Nights; The Prince of Success; Pursued; The Scarlet West; Three Keys; The Verdict. 1926 Broken Homes; The Call of the Klondike; Exclusive Rights; Her Sacrifice; The Jazz Girl; Midnight Limited; The Road to Broadway; The Romance of a Million Dollars; Subway Sadie; Sweet Sadie; Sweet Daddies; Tentacles of the North; Wives at Auction. 1927 Better Days; Compassion; False Morals; The Gorilla; The Love Wager; The Show Girl; Sinews of Steel. 1928 The Red Mark; Name the Woman; A Gentleman Preferred; Innocent Love; My Home Town; Obey Your Husband; The Wife's Relations. 1929 Broken Barriers; Untamed Justice; Behind Closed Doors; Geraldine; The Faker; Tiger Rose. 1930 Just Like Heaven; She Got What She Wanted;

The South Sea Pearl (short). 1931 The Bad Man; The Big Trail (both French versions). 1934 LeGong (narr.). 1935 Sylvia Scarlett. 1936 The Princess Comes Across; Desire; Gambling with Souls; Sutter's Gold; Mary of Scotland. 1937 Death in the Air; Espionage.

GLASSMIRE, AUGUSTIN J. "GUS"

Born: 1879. Died: July 23, 1946, Hollywood, Calif. Screen and stage actor. Entered films in 1932.

Appeared in: 1939 Our Leading Citizen. 1942 My Gal Sal; Saboteur; The Big Shot; Syncopation. 1944 Wilson. 1945 Fallen Angel; Scarlet Street; Enchanted Cottage; Col. Effingham's Raid; The Bullfighters.

GLAUM, LOUISE

Born: 1900, Baltimore, Md. Died: Nov. 25, 1970, Los Angeles, Calif.(pneumonia). Screen and stage actress. Appeared in Mack Sennett comedies.

Appeared in: 1915 The Lure of Woman; The Iron Strain. 1916 The Aryan; Honor Thy Name; Return of Draw Egan; Home; Hell's Hinges. 1919 The Poppy Girl's Husband; Sahara; The Lone Wolf's Daughter. 1920 Sex. 1921 I Am Guilty; The Leopard Woman; Love; Greater Than Love. 1925 Fifty-Fifty.

GLAZER, EVE F.

Born: 1903. Died: June 29, 1960, Hollywood, Calif.(cancer). Screen actress.

GLEASON, FRED

Born: 1854. Died: June 9, 1933, New York, N.Y. Screen and stage actor.

GLEASON, JAMES "JIMMY"

Born: May 23, 1886, New York, N.Y. Died: Apr. 12, 1959, Woodland Hills, Calif.(asthma). Screen, stage actor, and screenwriter. Nominated for Academy Award in 1941 for Best Supporting Actor in Here Comes Mr. Jordan. Married to screen actress Lucille Gleason (dec. 1947). Father of screen actor Russell Gleason (dec. 1945).

Appeared in: 1922 Polly of the Follies. 1928 The Count of Ten. 1929 Garden of Eatin'; Fairways and Foul; The Shannons of Broadway; The Broadway Melody; The Flying Fool; High Voltage; His First Command. 1930 Oh, Yeah!; Free Soul; Puttin' on the Ritz; Dumbbells in Ermine; The Matrimonial Bed; Big Money; Don't Believe It; No Brakes; The Swellhead; What a Widow!; Her Man. 1931 The Big Gamble; Sweepstakes; It's a Wise Child; Beyond Victory; Suicide Fleet. 1932 Information Kid; Blondie of the Follies; Lady and Gent; The Crooked Circle; The Penguin Pool Murder; The All American; The Devil Is Driving; Fast Companions. 1933 Hoopla; Billion Dollar Scandal; Clear All Wires. 1934 Pie for Two; Murder on the Blackboard; The Meanest Gal in Town; Search for Beauty; Orders Is Orders. 1935 Murder on a Honeymoon; Hot Tip; West Point of the Air; Helldorado. 1936 Murder on the Bridle Path; The Ex- Mrs. Bradford; Don't Turn 'Em Loose; The Big Game; The Plot Thickens; Yours for the Asking; We're Only Human. 1937 Forty Naughty Girls; Manhattan Merry-Go-Round. 1938 Army Girl; The Higgins Family; Dawn over Ireland; Goodbye Broadway. 1939 On Your Toes; My Wife's Relatives; Should Husbands Work?; The Covered Trailer. 1940 Money to Burn; Grandpa Goes to Town; Earl of Puddlestone. 1941 Meet John Doe; Here Comes Mr. Jordan; Tanks a Million; Nine Lives Are Not Enough; Affectionately Yours; A Date with the Falcon; Babes on Broadway. 1942 Tramp, Tramp, Tramp; Hay Foot; My Gal Sal; The Falcon Takes Over; Footlight Serenade; Tales of Manhattan; Manila Calling; All through the Night. 1943 A Guy Named Joe; Crash Dive. 1944 Keys of the Kingdom; Arsenic and Old Lace; Once Upon a Time; This Man's Navy. 1945 A Tree Grows in Brooklyn; Captain Eddie; The Clock. 1946 Lady Luck; Home Sweet Homicide; The Well-Groomed Bride; The Hoodlum Saint. 1947 Down to Earth; Tycoon; The Homestretch; The Tenderfoot; The Bishop's Wife. 1948 When My Baby Smiles at Me; The Return of October; Smart Woman; The Dude Goes West. 1949 The Life of Riley; Bad Boy; Take One False Step; Miss Grant Takes Richmond. 1950 The Jackpot; Joe Palooka in the Squared Circle; Key to the City; Riding High; Two Flags West; The Yellow Cab Man. 1951 Two Gals and a Guy; Come Fill the Cup; Joe Palooka in the Triple Cross; I'll See You in My Dreams. 1952 The Story of Will Rogers; What Price Glory; We're Not Married. 1953 Forever Female. 1954 Hollywood Thrillmakers; Suddenly. 1955 The Night of the Hunter; The Girl Rush. 1956 Star in the Dust. 1957 Spring Reunion; The Female Animal; Loving You; Money, Women and Guns; Man in the Shadow. 1958 Once Upon a Horse; Man or Gun; Rock-a-Bye Baby; The Last Hurrah.

GLEASON, LUCILLE (Lucille Webster)
Born: Feb. 6, 1888, Pasadena, Calif. Died: May 13, 1947, Brentwood, Calif.(heart attack). Screen and stage actress. Ran for California Assembly in 1944 but was defeated. Wife of screen actor James Gleason (dec. 1959) and mother of screen actor Russell Gleason (dec. 1945).

Appeared in: 1929 Garden of Eatin'; Fairways and Foul; The Shannons of Broadway; Pathe "Golden Rooster" comedies. 1930 Don't Believe It. 1931 Pagan Lady; Girls about Town. 1932 A Hockey Hick (short); Girl of the Rio; Nice Women. 1933 Don't Bet on Love; The Solitaire Man; Love, Honor and Oh, Baby!. 1934 Woman Afraid; Successful Failure; Beloved; I Like It That Way. 1936 Klondike Annie; Rhythm on the Range; The Ex-Mrs. Bradford. 1937 Red Light Ahead; Navy Blues; First Lady. 1938 The Beloved Brat; The Nurse from Brooklyn; The Higgins Family. 1939 My Wife's Relatives; Should Husbands Work?; The Covered Trailer. 1940 Money to Burn; Grandpa Goes to Town; Earl of Puddlestone; Lucky Partners. 1941 The Gay Falcon. 1943 Stage Door Canteen. 1945 The Clock; Don't Fence Me In.

GLEASON, RUSSELL
Born: Feb. 6, 1908, Portland, Oreg. Died: Dec. 26, 1945, New York, N.Y.(fall from hotel window). Screen actor. Son of screen actor James Gleason (dec. 1959) and screen actress Lucille Gleason (dec. 1947).

Appeared in: 1929 The Flying Fool; The Shady Lady; The Sophomore; Strange Cargo; Seven Faces. 1930 Officer O'Brien; All Quiet on the Western Front; Sisters. 1931 Beyond Victory; Laugh and Get Rich; Homicide Squad. 1932 Always Kickin' (sports short); The Strange Case of Clara Deane; Nice Women; Off His Base (sports short); A Hockey Hick (sports short). 1933 Private Jones. 1934 I Can't Escape. 1935 Hot Tip. 1936 Hitchhike to Heaven. 1937 Off to the Races; Big Business; Hot Water; Borrowing Trouble. 1938 Fury Below; The Higgins Family; Down on the Farm; Love on a Budget; A Trip to Paris; Safety in Numbers. 1939 My Wife's Relatives; News Is Made at Night; Should Husbands Work; The Covered Trailer; Here I Am a Stranger. 1940 Money to Burn; Young as You Feel; Grandpa Goes to Town; Earl of Puddlestone; Yesterday's Heroes. 1941 Unexpected Uncle. 1942 Dudes Are Pretty People; Fingers at the Window. 1943 Salute to the Marines. 1944 Adventures of Mark Twain.

GLECKLER, ROBERT P.
Born: Jan. 11, 1890, Pierre, S.D. Died: Feb. 26, 1939, Los Angeles, Calif.(uremic poisoning). Screen and stage actor. Entered films in 1928.

Appeared in: 1928 The Dove. 1929 Mother's Boy. 1930 The Sea God; Big Money. 1931 Night Nurse; Defenders of the Law; She Went for a Tramp; Finger Points. 1933 Take a Chance. 1934 Now I'll Tell; The Defense Rests; Million Dollar Ransom; The Personality Kid. 1935 Great Hotel Murder; The Perfect Clue; The Daring Young Man; The Farmer Takes a Wife; Dante's Inferno; Mr. Dynamite; It Happened in New York; The Case of the Curious Bride; The Glass Key; Headline Woman; Here Comes the Band; Whipsaw; Show Them No Mercy. 1936 Absolute Quiet; Sworn Enemy; Love Begins at Twenty; Forgotten Faces; Yours for the Asking; I'd Give My Life; The Girl on the Front Page; North of Nome; Great Guy. 1937 Pick a Star; King of Gamblers; Bulldog Drummond's Revenge; Hot Water; The Man Who Cried Wolf. 1938 Rascals; Alexander's Ragtime Band; Gangs of New York; Gun Law; Little Miss Broadway. 1939 They Made Me a Criminal; Stand up and Fight.

GLENDINNING, ERNEST
Born: 1884, Ulverston, England. Died: May 17, 1936, South Coventry, Conn. Screen and stage actor.

Appeared in: 1922 When Knighthood Was in Flower. 1930 Grounds for Murder (short).

GLENDON, JONATHAN FRANK
Born: 1887. Died: Mar. 17, 1937, Hollywood, Calif. Screen and stage actor.

Appeared in: 1917 The Third Judgement. 1918 The Wooing of Princess Pat; A Woman in the Web (serial). 1920 Mid-Channel. 1921 Forgotten Woman; Hush; A Tale of Two Worlds; What Do Men Want?. 1922 Belle of Alaska; Kissed; More to Be Pitied Than Scorned; Night Life in Hollywood; Yankee Doodle, Jr. 1923 Just Like a Woman; Rip Tide; Shattered Faith; South Sea Love. 1925 Lights of Old Broadway; Private Affairs; Tricks. 1926 Upstage. 1927 Cross Breed; Compassion. 1930 Border Romance. 1933 Sucker Money; Strange People; Gun Law; Her Splendid Folly. 1936 King of the Pecos; Border Caballero.

GLENN, ROY, SR.
Born: 1915, Pittsburg, Kan. Died: Mar. 12, 1971, Los Angeles, Calif.(heart attack). Negro screen, stage, and television actor.

Appeared in: 1970 The Great White Hope.

GLOECKNER-KRAMER, PEPI
Born: 1874, Austria. Died: 1954, Vienna, Austria. Screen and stage actress.

Appeared in: 1939 Verliebte Herzen (Hearts in Love).

GLORI, ENRICO
Born: 1901, Naples, Italy. Died: Apr. 22, 1966, Rome, Italy. Screen and stage actor.

Appeared in: 1936 Il Fu Mattia Pascal. 1937 Les Perles de la Couronne (Pearls of the Crown). 1948 Man of the Sea; The Spirit and the Flesh. 1949 Lost in the Dark. 1953 Stranger on the Prowl. 1961 La Dolce Vita. 1963 Romolo e Remo (Romulus and Remus aka Duel of the Titans).

GLYNNE, MARY
Born: Jan. 25, 1898, Penarth, Wales. Died: Sept. 22, 1954, London, England. Screen, stage, and television actress.

Appeared in: 1919 The Cry of Justice. 1920 The Hundredth Chance. 1921 The Call of Youth; Appearances; The Bonnie Brier Bush; The Mystery Road; Dangerous Lies; The Princess of New York. 1932 The Good Companions (U.S. 1933); Inquest. 1933 The Lost Chord; Flat No. 3. 1934 The Outcast; Emil and the Detectives. 1935 Scrooge. 1936 Finale. 1937 The Heirloom Mystery. 1938 Emil.

GOBBLE, HARRY A. "HANK"
Born: 1923. Died: May 19, 1961, Hollywood, Calif. Screen actor and stuntman.

Appeared in: 1961 The Deadly Companions.

GODFREY, PETER
Born: Oct. 16, 1899, London, England. Died: Mar. 4, 1970, Hollywood, Calif. Screen, stage, vaudeville actor, screen, stage director, and playwright. Married to screen actress Renee Haal (dec. 1966) with whom he appeared briefly in vaudeville.

Appeared in: 1938 Blockade. 1940 Raffles; The Earl of Chicago; Edison the Man. 1941 Dr. Jekyll and Mr. Hyde. 1947 The Two Mrs. Carrolls.

GODFREY, RENEE HAAL
Born: 1920. Died: May 2, 1964 (cancer). Screen and vaudeville actress. Married to screen actor/director Peter Godfrey (dec. 1970) with whom she appeared briefly in vaudeville. She was "Miss New York" in the 1937 Miss America contest. Entered films in 1941.

Appeared in: 1945 Bedside Manner. 1946 Terror by Night. 1960 Inherit the Wind.

GODFREY, SAMUEL T.
Born: Oct. 5, 1891, Brooklyn, N.Y. Died: Apr. 18, 1935, Los Angeles, Calif.(brain tumor). Screen, stage actor, playwright, dialog screenwriter, and stage director.

Appeared in: 1932 Washington Merry-Go-Round. 1933 Frisco Jenny; I Loved a Woman; Parole Girl; After Tonight; Blondie Johnson. 1934 Beggars in Ermine; The Love Captive. 1935 Love in Bloom; Private Worlds.

GOLD, JIMMY
Born: 1886, Glasgow, Scotland. Died: Oct. 7, 1967, London, England. Screen and stage actor. Appeared with Charlie Naughton as a comedy team and they made several "Crazy Gang" films and stage presentations.

Appeared in the following "Crazy Gang" films: 1937 OK for Sound. 1938 Alf's Button Afloat. 1939 The Frozen Limits. 1940 Gasbags. 1954 Life Is a Circus.

GOLDENBERG, SAMUEL
Born: 1886. Died: Oct. 31, 1945, Brooklyn, N.Y.(heart attack). Screen and stage actor.

Appeared in: 1935 Shir Hashirim. 1943 Mission to Moscow; Fallen Sparrow.

GOLDNER, CHARLES
Born: 1900, Austria. Died: Apr. 15, 1955, London, England. Screen and stage actor.

Appeared in: 1940 Room for Two (U.S. 1944). 1947 Brighton Rock. 1948 One Night With You; Third Time Lucky (U.S. 1950). 1949 Give Us This Day (aka Salt and the Devil); Black Magic; Dear Mr. Prohack. 1950 Shadow of the Eagle (U.S. 1955); Bond Street; The Laughing Lady; The Rocking Horse Winner. 1951 No Orchids for Miss Blandish; I'll Get You for This (aka Lucky Nick Cain). 1952 Encore; Secret People. 1953 The Master of Ballantrae; The Captain's Paradise. 1954 Always a Bride; Duel in the Jungle; Flame and the Flesh; The Golden Mask; Mr. Potts Goes to Moscow (aka Top Secret). 1955 The End of the Affair; The Racers.

GOLDSTEIN, BECKY
Born: 1887. Died: May, 1971, London, England. Screen and stage actress.

GOLUBEFF, GREGORY
Died: Feb. 11, 1958, Hollywood, Calif. Screen actor and musician.

Appeared in: 1934 Bolero.

GOMEZ, AUGUSTINE "AUGIE" WHITECLOUD
Born: 1891. Died: Jan. 1, 1966, Hollywood, Calif. Screen, stage, and vaudeville actor.

Appeared in: 1948 Old Los Angeles.

GOMEZ, RALPH
Born: 1897. Died: Apr. 18, 1954, Hollywood, Calif.(cancer). Screen actor and stuntman. Entered films approx. 1924.

GOMEZ, THOMAS
Born: July 10, 1905, Long Island, N.Y. Died: June 18, 1971, Santa Monica, Calif. Screen, stage, and television actor.

Appeared in: 1942 Sherlock Holmes and the Voice of Terror (film debut); Arabian Nights; Pittsburgh; Who Done It?. 1943 White Savage; Corvette K-225; Frontier Badman; Crazy House. 1944 The Climax; Phantom Lady; Dead Man's Eyes; Follow the Boys; In Society; Bowery to Broadway; Can't Help Singing. 1945 Patrick the Great; I'll Tell the World; The Daltons Ride Again; Frisco Sal. 1946 A Night in Paradise; Swell Guy; The Dark Mirror. 1947 Singapore; Ride the Pink Horse; Captain from Castile; Johnny O'Clock. 1948 Casbah; Angel in Exile; Key Largo; Force of Evil. 1949 Come to the Stable; Sorrowful Jones; That Midnight Kiss; I Married a Communist. 1950 Kim; The Woman on Pier 13; Toast of New Orleans; The Eagle and the Hawk; The Furies; Dynamite Pass. 1951 Anne of the Indies; The Harlem Globetrotters; The Sellout. 1952 The Merry Widow; Pony Soldier; Macao. 1953 Sombrero. 1954 The Gambler from Natchez; The Adventures of Haji Baba. 1955 The Looters; The Magnificent Matador; Las Vegas Shakedown; Night Freight. 1956 Trapeze; The Conqueror. 1959 John Paul Jones; But Not for Me. 1961 Summer and Smoke. 1968 Stay Away, Joe!. 1969 Beneath the Planet of the Apes.

GONDI, HARRY
Born: 1900, Germany. Died: Nov. 1968, Hamburg, Germany. Screen, stage, and radio actor.

GONZALEZ, GILBERTO
Born: 1906, Mexico. Died: Mar. 21, 1954, Palenque, Chiapas, Mexico(heart attack). Screen actor.

Appeared in: 1933 Vica Villa. 1940 Amor con Amor (Love for Love). 1948 The Pearl. 1952 Stronghold. 1955 The Littlest Outlaw.

GONZALEZ, MARIO TECERO
Born: 1919, Mexico. Died: Aug. 28, 1957 Mexico City, Mexico. Screen and stage actor.

GONZALO, MARIA EDUARDA
Born: 1929, Portugal. Died: Jan. 24, 1955, Lisbon, Portugal (tuberculosis). Screen and stage actress.

GOOD, KIP
Born: 1919. Died: May 1, 1964, Gadsden, Ala. Screen, stage actor, and stage director.

Appeared in: 1943 Stage Door Canteen.

GOODE, JACK (Irwin Thomas Whittridge)
Born: 1908, Columbus, Ohio. Died: June 24, 1971, New York, N.Y.(acute infectious hepatitis). Screen, stage, and television actor. Married to stage dancer/actress Renalda Green.

Appeared in: 1933 Flying Down to Rio. 1935 Top Hat. 1936 Swing Time.

GOODRICH, AMY
Born: 1889. Died: July 1939, Hollywood, Calif. Screen actress. Married to screen actor Hal Price.

GOODRICH, CHARLES W.
Born: 1861. Died: Mar. 20, 1931, Norwalk, Conn. Screen and stage actor.

Appeared in: 1926 Show Off (film and stage versions).

GOODRICH, LOUIS (L. G. Abbott Anderson)
Born: 1865, Sandhurst, England. Died: Jan. 31, 1945, London, England. Screen, stage actor, and playwright.

Appeared in: 1931 Sherlock Holmes' Fatal Hour. 1932 The Flag Lieutenant. 1933 The Thirteenth Candle; Night of the Party. Other British films: 9:45; Mr. What's His Name; Egg and Butter Man; Fair Exchange; The Captain's Table.

GOODWIN, BILL
Born: July 28, 1910, San Francisco, Calif. Died: May 9, 1958, Palm Springs, Calif.(heart attack). Screen, radio, and television actor. Married to screen actress Phillippa Hilber.

Appeared in: 1940 Let's Make Music. 1941 Blondie in Society. 1942 Wake Island. 1943 Riding High; So Proudly We Hail; No Time for Love. 1944 Bathing Beauty. 1945 River Gang; Incendiary Blonde; Spellbound; The Stork Club. 1946 House of Horrors; Earl Carroll Sketchbook; To Each His Own; The Jolson Story. 1947 Hit Parade of 1947; Heaven Only Knows. 1948 Mickey; So This Is New York. 1949 It's a Great Feeling; The Life of Riley. 1950 Tea for Two; Jolson Sings Again. 1952 The First Time. 1954 The Atomic Kid; Lucky Me. 1956 The Opposite Sex; Bundle of Joy. 1958 The Big Beat; Going Steady.

GOODWIN, NAT
Born: 1857, Boston, Mass. Died: Jan. 31, 1920, New York. Screen actor.

Appeared in: 1912 Oliver Twist. 1915 The Master Hand.

GOODWIN, RUBY BERKLEY
Died: May 31, 1961, Hollywood, Calif. Screen, television actress, and author.

Appeared in: 1955 The View from Pompey's Head. 1956 Strange Intruder. 1959 The Alligator People. 1961 Wild in the Country.

GOODWINS, ERCELL WOODS. See Ercell Woods.

GOODWINS, LESLIE
Born: Sept. 17, 1899, London, England. Died: Jan. 8, 1969, Hollywood, Calif.(pneumonia). Screen actor, film director, and screenwriter. Appeared in silent Christie comedies.

GORCEY, BERNARD
Born: 1888, Switzerland. Died: Sept. 11, 1955, Hollywood, Calif. (auto accident). Screen and stage actor. Father of screen actors Leo (dec. 1969) and David Gorcey.

Appeared in: 1928 Abie's Irish Rose. 1940 The Great Dictator. 1941 Out of the Fog. 1942 Joan of Paris. 1943 The Unknown Guest. 1946 Mr. Hex; In High Gear; Spook Busters; Bowery Bombshell; The French Key; In Fast Company. 1947 Bowery Buckaroos; Hard Boiled Mahoney; News Hounds. 1948 Angels' Alley; No Minor Vices; Jinx Money; Trouble Makers. 1949 Fighting Fools; Angels in Disguise; Hold That Baby; Master Minds. 1950 Blonde Dynamite; Lucky Losers; Blues Busters; Triple Trouble. 1951 Ghost Chasers; Crazy over Horses; Bowery Battalion; Let's Go Navy; Pickup; Win, Place and Show. 1952 Here Come the Marines; Feudin' Fools; No Holds Barred; Hold That Line; Tell It to the Marines. 1953 Jalopy; Loose in London; Clipped Wings; Private Eyes. 1954 Paris Playboys; Jungle Gents; The Bowery Boys Meet the Monsters. 1955 Bowery to Bagdad; High Society; Jail Busters; Spy Chasers. 1956 Dig That Uranium.

GORCEY, LEO B.
Born: June 3, 1915, New York, N.Y. Died: June 2, 1969, Oakland, Calif. Screen and stage actor. Son of screen actor Bernard Gorcey (dec. 1955) and brother of screen actor David Gorcey. One of the original "Dead End Kids."

Appeared in: 1937 Dead End (film and stage versions); Portia on Trial. 1938 Mannequin; Crime School; Angels with Dirty Faces. 1939 Hell's Kitchen; Angels Wash Their Faces; Battle of City Hall; They Made Me a Criminal; Dress Parade. 1940 That Gang of Mine; Boys of the City; Gallant Sons; Junior G-Men (serial); Angels with Broken Wings; Invisible Stripes. 1941 Flying Wild;

Pride of the Bowery; Road to Zanzibar; Out of the Fog; Spooks Run Wild; Bowery Blitzkrieg; Down in San Diego; Sea Raiders (serial). 1942 Mr. Wise Guy; Sunday Punch; Let's Get Tough; Smart Alecks; 'Neath Brooklyn Bridge; Maisie Gets Her Man; Born to Sing; Jr. G-Men of the Air (serial). 1943 Clancy Street Boys; Destroyer; Mr. Muggs Steps Out. 1944 Block Busters; Follow the Leader; Million Dollar Kid; Bowery Champs. 1945 One Exciting Night; Docks of New York; Mr. Muggs Rides Again; Come out Fighting; Midnight Manhunt. 1946 In Fast Company; Mr. Hex; Bowery Bombshell; Spook Busters; Live Wires. 1947 Hard Boiled Mahoney; News Hounds; Pride of Broadway; Bowery Buckaroos. 1948 So This Is New York; Jinx Money; Trouble Makers; Angel's Alley; Smugglers Cove. 1949 Hold That Baby; Angels in Disguise; Master Minds; Fighting Fools. 1950 Blonde Dynamite; Blues Busters; Triple Trouble; Lucky Losers. 1951 Win, Place and Show; Ghost Chasers; Bowery Battalion; Crazy over Horses; Let's Go Navy. 1952 Hold That Line; Here Come the Marines; Feudin' Fools; No Holds Barred; Tell It to the Marines. 1953 Jalopy; Loose in London; Clipped Wings; Private Eyes. 1954 The Bowery Boys Meet the Monsters; Paris Playboys; Jungle Gents. 1955 Bowery to Bagdad; High Society; Spy Chasers; Jail Busters. 1956 Crashing Las Vegas; Dig That Uranium. 1957 Spook Chasers; Hold That Hypnotist; Looking for Danger; Up in Smoke. 1958 In the Money. 1963 It's a Mad, Mad, Mad, Mad World. 1969 The Phynx.

GORDON, A. GEORGE
Born: 1882. Died: Dec. 27, 1953, Chicago, Ill.(heart ailment). Screen, stage actor, and stage producer. Appeared in silents with Selig Poliscop Corp.

GORDON, C. HENRY (Henry Racke)
Born: June 17, 1883, New York, N.Y. Died: Dec. 3, 1940, Los Angeles, Calif.(result of leg amputation). Screen and stage actor. Entered films in 1911.

Appeared in: 1930 A Devil with Women; Renegades. 1931 The Black Camel; Honor of the Family; Young As You Feel; Woman of Experience; Charlie Chan Carries On; Once a Sinner; Hush Money. 1932 State's Attorney; The Strange Love of Molly Louvain; Washington Masquerade; Miss Pinkerton; Jewel Robbery; Roar of the Dragon; Kongo; Hell's Highway; Thirteen Women; Scarlet Dawn; Rasputin and the Empress; Doomed Battalion; Scarface; Mata Hari; Gay Caballero; The Crooked Circle. 1933 Whistling in the Dark; Secret of Madame Blanche; Clear All Wires; Made on Broadway; Gabriel over the White House; Storm at Daybreak; Night Flight; Turn Back the Clock; Penthouse; Stage Mother; The Chief; The Devil's in Love; Broadway Thru a Keyhole; Advice to the Lovelorn; The Women in His Life. 1934 Straight Is the Way; Fugitive Lovers; This Side of Heaven; Hide-Out; Stamboul Quest; Death on a Diamond; Men in White; Lazy River. 1935 Lives of a Bengal Lancer; The Great Hotel Murder; Pursuit; The Crusades; The Big Broadcast of 1936. 1936 Professional Soldier; Under Two Flags; Hollywood Boulevard; The Big Game; Love Letters of a Star; Charge of the Light Brigade. 1937 Charlie Chan of the Olympics; Trouble in Morocco; The River of Missing Men; Trapped by G-Men; Sophie Lang Goes West; Stand-In; Conquest. 1938 Yellow Jack; Tarzan's Revenge; The Black Doll; Sharpshooters; The Long Shot; Adventure in Sahara; Invisible Enemy. 1939 Heritage of the Desert; Man of Conquest; Charlie Chan in City in Darkness; The Return of the Cisco Kid; Trapped in the Sky. 1940 Passport to Alcatraz; Kit Carson; Charlie Chan at the Wax Museum.

GORDON, EDWARD R.
Born: 1886. Died: Nov. 10, 1938, Hollywood, Calif. Screen actor and film director.
Appeared in: 1927 Gun-Hand Garrison; Ridin' Luck; Wild Born.

GORDON, G. SWAYNE
Born: 1880. Died: June 23, 1949, New York, N.Y. Screen, stage, radio, and vaudeville actor. Appeared in vaudeville with his wife, Spain Thorne.

GORDON, GAVIN
Born: 1901, Chicora, Miss. Died: Nov. 18, 1970, London, England. (coronary thrombosis). Screen, stage actor, vocalist, and composer.

Appeared in: 1929 Chasing Through Europe; All Steamed Up (short); Knights Out (short). 1930 His First Command; Romance; The Silver Horde; The Great Meadow; The Medicine Man. 1931 Secret Service; Shipmates. 1932 Two against the World; The Phantom of Crestwood; American Madness; Man against Woman. 1933 The Bitter Tea of General Yen; Black Beauty; Female; Hard to Handle; Mystery of the Wax Museum. 1934 Lone Cowboy; The Scarlet Empress; Happiness Ahead; Wake up and Dream. 1935

Red Hot Tires; Grand Old Girl; Women Must Dress; Bordertown; Stranded; Page Miss Glory; The Bride of Frankenstein; Love Me Forever. 1936 The Leavenworth Case; Ticket to Paradise; As You Like It. 1937 The Toast of New York; Windjammer; They Gave Him a Gun. 1938 I See Ice. 1941 I Killed That Man; Gangs, Inc.; The Lone Star Vigilantes; Paper Bullets; Murder by Invitation; Mr. Celebrity. 1946 Centennial Summer. 1947 Philo Vance's Gamble; Three on a Ticket. 1954 Knock on Wood; There's No Business Like Show Business; White Christmas. 1956 The Vagabond King; Pardners. 1957 Johnny Tremain; Chicago Confidential. 1958 The Matchmaker. 1959 The Bat. 1961 Pocketful of Miracles.

GORDON, GLORIA
Died: Nov. 23, 1962, Hollywood, Calif. Screen and television actress. Mother of screen actor Gale Gordon.

Appeared in: 1926 Dancing Days; Exclusive Rights. 1949 My Friend Irma. 1953 Beneath the 12 Mile Reef; Titanic. 1955 A Man Called Peter.

GORDON, HAROLD
Born: 1919. Died: Jan. 19, 1959, New York, N.Y. Screen, stage, opera, and television actor.

Appeared in: 1952 Viva Zapata; The Jazz Singer; The Iron Mistress. 1954 Bengal Brigade. 1955 East of Eden; Yellowneck.

GORDON, HARRIS
Born: 1887. Died: Apr. 2, 1947, Burbank, Calif.(heart attack). Screen and stage actor.

Appeared in: 1921 Live and Let Live. 1922 Burning Sands; Out of the Silent North; The Woman Who Walked Alone; A Wonderful Wife. 1923 Hollywood. 1924 The Dawn of a Tomorrow. 1925 Easy Going Gordon; Let Women Alone; Romance and Rustlers; Too Much Youth. 1934 Our Daily Bread.

GORDON, HUNTLY
Born: 1897, Montreal, Quebec, Canada. Died: Dec. 7, 1956, Hollywood, Calif.(heart attack). Screen and radio actor.

Appeared in: 1918 Our Mrs. McChesney. 1921 Chivalrous Charley; Enchantment; The Girl from Nowhere; Society Snobs; Tropical Love; At the Stage Door. 1922 Beyond the Rainbow; His Wife's Husband; Man Wanted; Reckless Youth; What Fools Men Are; What's Wrong with the Women?; When the Desert Calls; Why Announce Your Marriage?. 1923 Bluebeard's Eighth Wife; The Famous Mrs. Fair; Chastity; Cordelia the Magnificent; Male Wanted; Pleasure Mad; The Wanters; Her Fatal Millions; The Social Code; Your Friend and Mine. 1924 The Enemy Sex; Shadows of Paris; True as Steel; Wine; Darling Love; Married Flirts. 1925 Golden Cocoon; The Love Hour; The Great Divide; Never the Twain Shall Meet; My Wife and I; The Wife Who Wasn't Wanted. 1926 Gilded Butterfly; Her Second Chance; Silken Shackles; Lost at Sea; Other Women's Husbands; The Golden Web. 1927 The Sensation Seekers; The Truthful Sex; One Increasing Purpose; Don't Tell the Wife. 1928 Outcast; Sinners in Love; A Certain Young Man; Name the Women; Their Hour; Our Dancing Daughters; Sally's Shoulder; Gypsy of the North. 1929 The Marriage Playground; Melody Lane; Scandal. 1930 Anybody's Woman; Fox Movietone Follies of 1930. 1932 Phantom Express; Night World; From Broadway to Cheyenne; The King Murder; Red Haired Alibi; Speed Madness; The All American; Race Track; Sally of the Subway. 1933 Midnight Warning; Sailor Be Good; Secrets; Justice Takes a Holiday; The World Gone Mad; Corruption; Only Yesterday. 1934 The Dancing Man; Their Big Moment; Embarrassing Moments; Bombay Mail. 1935 The Spanish Cape Mystery; It Happened in New York; Front Page Woman; Circumstantial Evidence. 1936 Daniel Boone; Yours for the Asking. 1937 China Passage; Stage Door; Idol of the Crowds; Portia on Trial. 1938 Gangster's Boy. 1939 Mr. Wong in Chinatown. 1940 Phantom of Chinatown.

GORDON, JAMES
Born: 1881, Pittsburgh, Pa. Died: May 12, 1941, Hollywood, Calif.(operation complications). Screen and stage actor. Married to screen actress Mabel Van Buren (dec. 1947).

Appeared in: 1921 The Bait; The Man from Lost River; The Old Swimmin' Hole; Sunset Jones; Trailin'. 1922 Man's Size; The Game Chicken; The Love Gambler; Nancy from Nowhere; On the High Seas; Self-Made Man. 1923 Defying Destiny; Grail. 1924 The Courageous Coward; Hearts of Oak; The Iron Horse; The Man Who Came Back; Wanderer of the Wasteland; The White Sin. 1925 Beauty and the Bad Man; Tumbleweeds. 1926 The Buckaroo Kid; Devil's Dice; Flying High; The Ice Flood; Miss Nobody; Rose of the Tenements; The Social Highwayman. 1927 Babe Comes Home; Publicity Madness; Tongues of Scandal;

The War Horse; The Wolf's Fangs; Cancelled Debts; Wanted a Coward. 1928 The Escape. 1929 Masked Emotions. 1931 The Bachelor Father; The Front Page.

GORDON, JULIA SWAYNE
Born: 1879, Hollywood, Calif. Died: May 28, 1933, Los Angeles, Calif. Screen and stage actress.

Appeared in: 1910 Twelfth Night. 1911 Lady Godiva; Tale of Two Cities. 1912 The Troublesome Stepdaughters; Cardinal Wolsey; Stenographers Wanted. 1913 Beau Brummel. 1914 Two Women. 1921 Behind Masks; Burn 'Em up Barnes; Handcuffs or Kisses; Love, Hate and a Woman; The Passionate Pilgrim; Shams of Society; The Silver Lining; Why Girls Leave Home. 1922 The Darling of the Rich; How Women Love; My Old Kentucky Home; The Road to Arcady; Till We Meet Again; What's Wrong with the Women?; When Desert Calls; Wildness of Youth; Women Men Marry. 1923 Scaramouche; Dark Secrets; The Tie That Binds; You Can't Fool Your Wife. 1925 Lights of Old Broadway; Not So Long Ago; The Wheel. 1926 Bride of the Storm; Diplomacy; Early to Wed; The Far Cry. 1927 Children of Divorce; Heaven on Earth; Wings; It; King of Kings. 1928 Hearts of Men; Road House; The Scarlet Dove; The Smart Set; 13 Washington Square; Three Week Ends. 1929 The Eternal Woman; The Younger Generation; The Divine Lady; The Girl in the Glass Cage; The Viking; Is Everybody Happy?; Gold Diggers of Broadway; Scandal. 1930 The Dude Wrangler; Today; Dumbbells in Ermine; For the Love O' Lil. 1931 Misbehaving Ladies; Primrose Path; Drums of Jeopardy; Captain Applejack. 1932 Secrets of the French Police; The Golden West; Broken Lullaby; False Madonna. 1933 Hello, Everybody!.

GORDON, MARY
Born: 1882, Scotland. Died: Aug. 23, 1963, Pasadena, Calif. Screen and radio actress. Played housekeeper for Sherlock Holmes in films and radio, 1939-1946.

Appeared in: 1925 The People vs. Nancy Preston; Tessie, The Home Maker. 1926 Black Paradise. 1927 Clancy's Kosher Wedding; Naughty Nanette. 1928 The Old Code. 1929 Dynamite; The Saturday Night Kid. 1930 Dance with Me. 1931 Black Camel; Subway Express. 1932 The Texas Cyclone; Almost Married; Pack up Your Troubles. 1934 Beloved; The Little Minister. 1935 Mutiny on the Bounty; Vanessa, Her Love Story; Bonnie Scotland; The Bride of Frankenstein; The Irish in Us; Waterfront Lady. 1936 Yellowstone; Way Out West; Laughing Irish Eyes; Forgotten Faces; Mary of Scotland; Stage Struck; Great Guy. 1937 The Great O'Malley; The Plough and the Stars; Meet the Boy Friend; Double Wedding; Pick a Star; A Damsel in Distress. 1938 City Streets; Lady Behave; Kidnapped. 1939 Tail Spin; She Married a Cop; Parents on Trial; Rulers of the Sea; Hound of the Baskervilles; Adventures of Sherlock Holmes; Captain Fury. 1940 Tear Gas Squad; Joe and Ethel Turp Call on the President; The Last Alarm; I Take This Oath; Queen of the Mob; When the Daltons Rode; No, No, Nanette; Nobody's Children; My Son, My Son; Marshal of Mesa City. 1941 Pot O' Gold; Flight from Destiny; Appointment for Love; Riot Squad; The Invisible Man; Borrowed Hero; Bombay; Clipper; Meet the Stewarts; Dr. Broadway; Fly by Night; It Happened in Flatbush; Boss of Big Town; The Mummy's Tomb; Sherlock Holmes and the Voice of Terror; Sherlock Holmes and the Secret Weapon. 1943 Half Way to Shanghai; Sarong Girl; Sherlock Holmes Faces Death; Keep 'Em Sluggin'; Two Tickets to London; Here Comes Kelly. 1944 Follow the Leader; Hat Check Honey; Hollywood Canteen; Whispering Footsteps; The Spider Woman; The Racket Man; Smart Guy; The Hour before the Dawn; Pearl of Death; The Last Ride. 1945 Divorce; See My Lawyer; Captain Eddie; The Woman in Green; Strange Confession; The Body Snatcher; Kitty. 1946 The Dark Horse; In Fast Company; Sing While You Dance; The Hoodlum Saint; Little Giant; Sentimental Journey. 1947 Exposed; The Invisible Wall. 1948 Highway 13, The Strange Mrs. Crane; Angels' Alley. 1949 Deputy Marshal; Shamrock Hill; Haunted Trails. 1950 West of Wyoming.

GORDON, NORA
Born: 1894, England. Died: May 11, 1970, London, England. Screen and television actress.

Appeared in: 1949 The Fallen Idol. 1950 Woman in Question (aka Five Angles On Murder, U.S. 1953). 1951 Blackmailed; Night Was Our Friend. 1954 A Woman's Angle. 1955 The Glass Tomb. 1959 Horrors of the Black Museum. 1964 Carry on Spying.

GORDON, PETER
Born: 1888. Died: May 25, 1943, Los Angeles, Calif. Screen, vaudeville actor, and acrobat. Entered films in 1916. Appeared in Vitagraph shorts with Larry Lemon.

Appeared in: 1934 The Live Ghost (short). 1935 Tit for Tat (short).

GORDON, RICHARD H.
Born: 1893, Philadelphia, Pa. Died: Sept. 20, 1956, Hollywood, Calif.(after operation). Screen and television actor. Entered films in 1918. Was president of Screen Actors Guild.

Appeared in: 1925 Romance Road; The Flame Fighter (serial). 1929 Synthetic Sin; Words and Music. 1947 13 Rue Madeleine. 1951 St. Benny the Dip. 1956 The Birds and the Bees.

GORDON, ROBERT (Robert Gordon Duncan)
Born: 1895, Kan. Died: Oct. 26, 1971, Victorville, Calif. Screen actor. Entered films in 1917.

Appeared in: 1917 Tom Sawyer. 1918 Huck and Tom; Missing. 1921 If Women Only Knew. 1922 The Super Sex; The Rosary. 1923 The Greatest Menace; The Mysterious Witness; Main Street. 1924 The Night Message; The Wildcat; Borrowed Husbands. 1925 Danger Signal; Night Ship; On the Threshold; Shattered Lives. 1926 Hearts and Spangles; King of the Pack.

GORDON, VERA
Born: June 11, 1886, Russia. Died: May 8, 1948, Beverly Hills, Calif. Screen, stage, and vaudeville actress. Entered films in 1919.

Appeared in: 1920 Humoresque; North Wind's Malice. 1921 The Greatest Love. 1922 The Good Provider; Your Best Friend. 1923 Potash and Perlmutter. 1924 In Hollywood with Potash and Perlmutter. 1926 Cohens and Kellys; Millionaires; Sweet Daddies; Private Izzy Murphy; Kosher Kitty Kelly. 1928 The Cohens and the Kellys in Paris; Four Walls. 1929 The Cohens and the Kellys in Atlantic City. 1930 Madam Satan; The Cohens and the Kellys in Scotland; The Cohens and the Kellys in Africa. 1931 Fifty Million Frenchmen. 1934 When Strangers Meet. 1937 Michael O'Halloran. 1938 You and Me. 1942 The Living Ghost; The Big Street. 1946 Abie's Irish Rose.

GORE, ROSA
Born: 1867. Died: Feb. 4, 1941, Hollywood, Calif. Screen, stage, and vaudeville actress. Appeared in vaudeville with her husband in an act billed as "Crimmins and Gore." Entered films with Pathe in 1912.

Appeared in: 1921 Colorado; The Mistress of Shenstone. 1922 A Dangerous Game. 1923 The Town Scandal; Vanity Fair. 1924 Half-A-Dollar Bill; Hold Your Breath; Madonna of the Streets. 1925 The Million Dollar Handicap; Seven Days; Three Weeks in Paris. 1926 The Adorable Deceiver; Lovey Mary. 1927 The Man from Hardpan; Play Safe; The Prairie King; The Royal American; Stranded. 1928 Anybody Here Seen Kelly?; The Head Man; That's My Daddy. 1929 Blue Skies.

GORGEOUS GEORGE (George Raymond Wagner)
Born: 1915. Died: Dec. 25, 1963, Los Angeles, Calif.(heart attack). Wrestler and television, screen actor.

GORMAN, ERIC
Born: 1886. Died: Nov. 24, 1971, Dublin, Ireland. Screen, stage, and television actor.

Appeared in: 1949 Saints and Sinners. 1952 The Quiet Man. 1957 The Rising of the Moon (aka The Majesty of the Law).

GORMAN, TOM
Born: 1908. Died: Oct. 2, 1971, Flushing, N.Y.(pulmonary embolism). Screen, stage, television actor, and gag writer.

Appeared in: 1957 Edge of the City; 12 Angry Men.

GORSS, SAUL M.
Born: 1908. Died: Sept. 10, 1966, Los Angeles, Calif.(heart attack). Screen actor and stuntman. Entered films in 1933.

Appeared in: 1940 Flowing Gold. 1955 Unchained. 1956 Yaqui Drums. 1958 Legion of the Doomed; Bullwhip. 1966 Murderer's Row.

GOSFIELD, MAURICE
Born: 1913. Died: Oct. 19, 1964, Saranac Lake, N.Y. Screen, stage, television, and radio actor.

Appeared in: 1947 Kiss of Death. 1948 The Naked City. 1961 Teenage Millionaire. 1963 The Thrill of It All.

GOTTSCHALK, FERDINAND
Born: 1869, London, England. Died: Nov. 10, 1944, London, England. Screen and stage actor.

Appeared in: 1923 Zaza. 1930 Many Happy Returns (short). 1931 Tonight or Never. 1932 Without Honor; Land of the Wanted Men; Doomed Battalion; The Sign of the Cross; Grand Hotel. 1933 Parole Girl; Ex-Lady; Ann Vickers; Gold Diggers of 1933; Berkeley Square; Grand Slam; Goodbye Again; Girl Missing; Warrior's Husband; She Had to Say Yes; Female; Midnight Club. 1934 Madame Du Barry; The Notorious Sophie Lang; King Kelly of the U.S.A.; I Sell Anything; One Exciting Adventure; Nana; Bombay Mail; Horse Play; The Witching Hours; Long Lost Father; Gambling Lady; Upper World; Sing Sing Nights. 1935 Secret of the Chateau; I Am a Thief; The Man Who Reclaimed His Head; Folies Bergere; Night Life of the Gods; Clive of India; Les Miserables; Break of Hearts; Vagabond Lady; Here Comes the Band; The Gay Deception; The Man Who Broke the Bank at Monte Carlo; The Melody Lingers On; Peter Ibbetson. 1936 Bunker Bean; The White Legion; The Garden of Allah; The Man I Marry; That Girl from Paris; Along Came Love. 1937 The Crime Nobody Saw; Cafe Metropole; Ali Baba Goes to Town; I'll Take Romance. 1938 The Adventures of Marco Polo; Romance in the Dark; Stolen Heaven; Josette. 1944 The Sign of the Cross (revised version of 1932 film).

GOUGH, JOHN
Born: Sept. 22, 1897, Boston, Mass. Died: June 30, 1968, Hollywood, Calif.(cancer). Screen and stage actor. Entered films in 1916.

Appeared in: 1921 The Girl in the Taxi. 1922 Gleam O'Dawn; Up and at 'Em. 1924 Silk Stocking Sal. 1925 Alias Mary Flynn; Border Justice; High and Handsome; Three Wise Crooks; Midnight Molly; When Love Grows Cold; Broadway Lady; Smooth as Satin. 1926 Secret Orders; A Poor Girl's Romance; Flaming Waters. 1927 The Gorilla; Ain't Love Funny?; Hook and Ladder No. 9; Judgment of the Hills. 1928 The Street of Sin; The Circus Kid; The Haunted House; Air Legion. 1930 Sarah and Son. 1935 Two for Tonight.

GOULD, MYRTLE
Born: 1880. Died: Feb. 25, 1941, Los Angeles, Calif. Screen and stage actress. Appeared in silents until 1918.

GOULD, VIOLET
Born: 1884. Died: Mar. 29, 1962, England. Screen and television actress.

GOVI, GILBERTO
Born: 1885, Italy. Died: 1966, Genoa, Italy(following pneumonia). Screen, stage, and television actor.

GOWERS, SULKY
Died: Mar. 1970, London, England. Screen, television, and cabaret actor.

GOWLAND, GIBSON
Born: Jan. 4, 1872, Spennymoor, England. Died: Sept. 9, 1951, London, England. Screen actor.

Appeared in: 1914 Birth of a Nation. 1919 Blind Husbands; The Fighting Shepherdess. 1921 Ladies Must Live. 1923 Shifting Sands. 1924 Greed; The Border Legion; Love and Glory; The Red Lily. 1925 The Phantom of the Opera; The Prairie Wife. 1926 College Days; Don Juan; The Outsider. 1927 The Broken Gate; The Land Beyond the Law; The First Auto; Topsy and Eva; Isle of Forgotten Women; The Night of Love; The Tired Business Man. 1928 Rose Marie. 1929 The Mysterious Island. 1930 The Sea Bat; Hell Harbor; Phantom of the Opera (and 1925 version). 1932 Land of the Wanted Men; Without Honor; Doomed Battalion. 1933 S.O.S. Iceberg. 1934 The Private Life of Don Juan; The Secret of the Loch. 1936 The Mystery of the Marie Celeste. 1937 Cotton Queen; The Phantom Ship. 1938 The Revenge of General Ling.

GOWMAN, MILTON J.
Born: 1907. Died: Aug. 17, 1952, Los Angeles, Calif. Screen actor.

GRACE, CHARITY
Born: 1879. Died: Nov. 28, 1965, St. Louis, Mo.(cancer). Screen, stage, opera, and television actress.

GRACE, DINAH (Ilse Schmidt)
Born: Germany. Died: May 12, 1963, Hamburg, Germany(cancer). Screen actress and dancer. Married to screen actor Willy Fritsch.

GRAETZ, PAUL
Born: 1890. Died: Feb. 17, 1937, Hollywood, Calif. Screen actor.

Appeared in: 1923 Monna Vanna. 1931 Wien Du Stadt der Lieder (Vienna City of Song). 1933 Jew Suess. 1934 Blossom Time. 1935 Alias Bulldog Drummond; Mimi; Car of Dreams; Bulldog Jack. 1936 Mr. Cohen Takes a Walk; Red Wagon; Hot Money; Bengal Tiger; Isle of Fury. 1937 Heart's Desire; April Romance. 1939 The Fight for Matterhorn.

GRAF, PETER
Born: 1872. Died: Oct. 20, 1951, New York, N.Y. Screen, stage, and radio actor. Appeared in Yiddish films.

GRAFF, WILTON
Born: 1903. Died: Jan. 13, 1969, Pacific Palisades, Calif. Screen and stage actor.

Appeared in: 1945 Pillow of Death; Strange Confession; An Angel Comes to Brooklyn; Earl Carroll Vanities; Gangs of the Waterfront; A Royal Scandal. 1946 Avalanche; Just before Dawn; The Unknown; The Phantom Thief; Traffic in Crime; Valley of the Zombies. 1947 High Conquest; Shadowed; The Corpse Came C.O.D.; Bulldog Drummond Strikes Back; A Double Life; Gentleman's Agreement; Key Witness; The Web. 1948 The Wreck of the Hesperus; Return of the Whistler; Gallant Blade; Another Part of the Forest. 1949 Take Me out to the Ball Game; Once More, My Darling; Caught; Blondie's Big Deal; And Baby Makes Three; Reign of Terror; The Dark Past. 1950 Rogues of Sherwood Forest; Fortunes of Captain Blood; The West Point Story; Mother Didn't Tell Me; Girls School. 1951 Mark of the Avenger; My True Story. 1952 Fearless Fagan; Springfield Rifle; Operation Secret; Million Dollar Mermaid; Something for the Birds; Young Man with Ideas. 1953 Lili; The I Don't Care Girl; Scandal at Scourie; Miss Sadie Thompson; So This Is Love. 1954 King Richard and the Crusaders; A Star Is Born. 1955 The Sea Chase; The Benny Goodman Story. 1956 Lust for Life. 1959 Compulsion. 1961 Return to Peyton Place; Sail a Crooked Ship; Bloodlust.

GRAHAM, CHARLIE
Born: 1897. Died: Oct. 9, 1943, Los Angeles, Calif. Screen actor.

Appeared in: 1919 The Master Mystery (serial). 1921 The Mountain Woman; On the High Card. 1922 Cardigan; Dawn of Revenge; The Headless Horseman; The Love Nest; White Hell. 1925 The Making of O'Malley. 1926 The Untamed Lady. 1929 Frozen Justice.

GRAHAM, FRANK
Born: 1915. Died: Sept. 2, 1950, Hollywood, Calif.(possible suicide). Radio announcer and narrator of many films. Known as "man with thousand voices."

Appeared in: 1945 The Three Caballeros.

GRAHAM, JULIA ANN
Born: 1915. Died: July 15, 1935, Los Angeles, Calif.(suicide—gunshot). Screen actress.

Appeared in: 1935 Love in Bloom.

GRAHAM, MORLAND (aka GRAHAM MORELAND)
Born: Aug. 8, 1891, Glasgow, Scotland. Died: Apr. 8, 1949, London, England(heart attack). Screen and stage actor.

Appeared in: 1935 Moscow Nights; The Scarlet Pimpernel. 1936 I Stand Condemned; Where's Sally?. 1939 Jamaica Inn. 1940 Old Bill and Son; Night Train. 1941 This England; The Voice in the Night; The Ghost Train. 1942 The Big Blockade; Ships with Wings; The Tower of Terror. 1944 The Shipbuilders; Henry V (U.S. 1946). 1946 The Gay Intruders. 1947 The Upturned Glass; The Brothers. 1948 Bonnie Prince Charlie; Showtime. 1949 Whiskey Galore (aka Tight Little Island and aka Mad Little Island). 1958 Henry V (re-release of 1944 film). Other British films: Full Speed Ahead; Gaiety George.

GRAHAM, RONALD
Born: 1912, Hamilton, Scotland. Died: July 4, 1950, New York, N.Y. Screen, stage, radio, and television actor.

Appeared in: 1935 Old Man Rhythm. 1944 Ladies of Washington.

GRAHAME, BERT (R.A.S. Stanford)
Born: 1892. Died: Mar. 23, 1971, England. Screen, stage, and vaudeville actor. Appeared in silents.

GRAINGER, WILLIAM F.(aka WILLIAM F. GRANGER)
Born: 1854. Died: Dec. 23, 1938, Hollywood, Calif. Screen and stage actor.

Appeared in: 1930 The Other Tomorrow.

GRAMATICA, EMMA
Born: 1875, Fidenza, Parma, Italy. Died: Nov. 1965, Ostia, Italy. Screen, stage, and television actress. Entered films in 1931.

Appeared in: 1932 La Vecchia Signora. 1935 Il Delitto di Mastrovanni. 1936 La Damigela di Bard; Il Fu Mattia Pascal. 1937 Marcella; Napoli d'Altri Tempi. 1938 Jeanne d'Ore; Il Destino; Quella (That One); La Vedova (The Widow). 1951 Miracle in Milan. Other Italian film: La Fortuna Di Zanze.

GRAN, ALBERT
Born: 1862. Died: Dec. 16, 1932, Los Angeles, Calif.(auto accident injuries). Screen actor.

Appeared in: 1916 Out of the Drifts. 1924 Her Night of Romance; Tarnish. 1925 Graustark. 1926 Beverly of Graustark; Early to Wed; Honesty—the Best Policy; More Pay—Less Work. 1927 Seventh Heaven; Breakfast at Sunrise; Children of Divorce; Hula; Love Makes 'Em Wild; Soft Cushions. 1928 We Americans; The Blue Danube; Dry Martini; Four Sons; Mother Knows Best; The Whip. 1929 The Gold Diggers of Broadway; Geraldine; The Glad Rag Doll; Our Modern Maidens; Show of Shows; Tanned Legs. 1930 Little Accident; Follow Thru; The Kibitzer; The Man from Blankley's; Sweethearts and Wives. 1931 Kiss Me Again; The Brat. 1932 Fast Life. 1933 Employees' Entrance.

GRANACH, ALEXANDER
Born: 1891, Poland. Died: Mar. 14, 1945, New York, N.Y. Screen and stage actor.

Appeared in: 1925 Lazybones. 1928 Warning Shadows. 1929 Nosferatu the Vampire. 1931 Danton. 1932 Der Raub der Mona Lisa; 1914: The Last Days before the War; Kameradschaft (Comradship). 1936 Der Kampf; Gypsies. 1939 Ninotchka. 1941 So Ends Our Night; A Man Betrayed. 1942 Joan of Paris; Wrecking Crew; Half Way to Shanghai. 1943 For Whom the Bell Tolls; Hangmen Also Die; Three Russian Girls. 1944 The Hitler Gang; Seventh Cross. 1945 Voice in the Wind.

GRANBY, JOSEPH
Born: 1885. Died: Sept. 22, 1965, Hollywood, Calif.(cerebral hemorrhage). Screen, stage, radio, and television actor.

Appeared in: 1916 Jealousy. 1944 Kismet. 1945 The Great Flamarion; The Phantom Speaks. 1949 Amazon Quest. 1950 Redwood Forest Trail; Where the Sidewalk Ends. 1952 Viva Zapata. 1956 Written on the Wind.

GRANDAIS, SUSANNE
Born: France. Died: Aug. 1920 (auto accident). French screen actress. Was called the "Mary Pickford of France."

GRANGER, ELSA G.
Born: 1904, Australia. Died: Feb. 8, 1955, New York, N.Y. Screen and stage actress. Appeared in Australian silent films; later appeared in U.S. films.

GRANT, EARL
Born: 1931. Died: June 10, 1970, near Lordsburg, N.M.(auto accident). Negro screen, television actor, and musician.

Appeared in: 1959 Imitation of Life; Juke Box Rhythm. 1962 Tender Is the Night.

GRANT, LAWRENCE
Born: 1870, England. Died: Feb. 19, 1952, Santa Barbara, Calif. Screen and stage actor.

Appeared in: 1918 To Hell with the Kaiser (film debut). 1921 Extravagance; The Great Impersonation. 1924 His Hour; Abraham Lincoln; Happiness. 1926 The Duchess of Buffalo; The Grand Duchess and the Waiter. 1927 A Gentleman of Paris; Service for Ladies; Serenade. 1928 Doomsday; Hold 'Em Yale; Red Hair; The Woman from Moscow; Something Always Happens. 1929 The Canary Murder Case; The Case of Lena Smith; The Rainbow; The Exalted Flapper; Is Everybody Happy?; Bulldog Drummond. 1930 Safety in Numbers; Boudoir Diplomat; The Cat Creeps; Oh, Sailor, Behave!. 1931 Daughter of the Dragon; Command Performance; The Squaw Man; Their Mad Moment; The Unholy Garden. 1932 Man about Town; Speak Easily; Divorce in the Family; Jewel Robbery; Faithless; The Mask of Fu Manchu; Grand Hotel; Shanghai Express. 1933 Clear All Wires; Queen

Christina; Looking Forward. 1934 The Count of Monte Cristo; By Candlelight; Nana; I'll Tell the World. 1935 The Man Who Reclaimed His Head; Werewolf of London; A Feather in Her Hat; Vanessa, Her Love Story; The Devil Is a Woman; The Dark Angel; Three Kids and a Queen; A Tale of Two Cities. 1936 Little Lord Fauntleroy; The House of a Thousand Candles; Mary of Scotland. 1937 Under the Red Robe; The Prisoner of Zenda. 1938 Service de Luxe; Bluebeard's Eighth Wife; The Young in Heart. 1939 Son of Frankenstein; Wife, Husband and Friend; Rulers of the Sea. 1940 The Son of Monte Cristo; Women in War. 1941 Dr. Jekyll and Mr. Hyde. 1942 S.O.S. Coast Guard; The Living Ghost. 1945 Confidential Agent.

GRANT, SYDNEY
Born: 1873. Died: July 12, 1953, Santa Monica, Calif. Screen and stage actor.

Appeared in: 1915 Jane.

GRANVILLE, LOUISE
Born: 1896. Died: Dec. 22, 1969, Hollywood, Calif.("Hong Kong" flu). Screen actress.

Appeared in: 1915 The Scrapper. 1918 Vitagraph shorts.

GRAPEWIN, CHARLES "CHARLIE"
Born: Dec. 20, 1875, Xenia, Ohio. Died: Feb. 2, 1956, Corona, Calif. Screen, stage, vaudeville actor, playwright, composer, and author. Married to screen actress Anna Chance (dec. 1943).

Appeared in: 1929 The Shannons of Broadway (film debut). Starred in comedy series for Christie which included the following shorts: Jed's Vacation; Ladies Choice; That Red Headed Hussy. 1930 Only Saps Work. 1931 Millionaire; Gold Dust Gertie. 1932 Hell's House; Big Timer; Disorderly Conduct; The Woman in Room 13; Lady and Gent; Wild Horse Mesa; The Night of June 13th. 1933 Hello, Everybody!; Kiss before the Mirror; Lady of the Night; Heroes for Sale; Wild Boys of the Road; Midnight Mary; Beauty for Sale; Pilgrimage; Don't Bet on Love; Torch Singer; Hell and High Water. 1934 Return of the Terror; Caravan; Two Alone; Anne of Green Gables; Judge Priest; She Made Her Bed; The President Vanishes; The Quitter; The Loud Speaker. 1935 Superspeed; One Frightened Night; In Spite of Danger; Party Wire; Shanghai; Alice Adams; King Solomon of Broadway; Rendezvous; Ah, Wilderness; Eight Bells. 1936 The Petrified Forest; The Voice of Bugle Ann; Small Town Girl; Libeled Lady; Sinner Take All; Without Orders. 1937 The Good Earth; A Family Affair; Captains Courageous; Between Two Women; Bad Guy; Big City; Broadway Melody of 1938. 1938 Bad Man of Brimstone; Of Human Hearts; Girl of the Golden West; Three Comrades; Three Loves Has Nancy; Listen, Darling; Artists and Models Abroad. 1939 Sudden Money; I Am Not Afraid; The Man Who Dared; Hero for a Day; Sabotage; Dust Be My Destiny; Stand up and Fight; Burn 'Em up O'Connor; The Wizard of Oz. 1940 The Grapes of Wrath; Johnny Apollo; Earthbound; Rhythm on the River; Ellery Queen, Master Detective. 1941 Ellery Queen's Penthouse Mystery; Ellery Queen and the Perfect Crime; Ellery Queen and the Murder Ring; Texas Rangers Ride Again; Tobacco Road. 1942 Enemy Agents Meet Ellery Queen; They Died with Their Boots On. 1943 Crash Dive. 1944 Follow the Boys; The Impatient Years; Atlantic City. 1947 The Gunfighter. 1948 The Enchanted Valley. 1949 Sand. 1951 When I Grow Up.

GRASSBY, MRS. GERARD A.
Born: 1877. Died: Apr. 6, 1962, Hollywood, Calif. Screen actress.

GRAVET, FERNAND (aka FERNAND GRAVEY)
Born: Dec. 25, 1904, Belgium. Died: Nov. 2, 1970, Paris, France. Screen and stage actor.

Appeared in: 1932 Coiffeur Pour Dames; Tu Seras Duchesse. 1933 Easy to Bed; Bitter Sweet. 1934 The Queen's Affair. 1937 The King and the Chorus Girl. 1938 Fools for Scandal; The Great Waltz; La Dernier Tournant; The Lie of Nina Petrovna. 1941 Compliments of Mr. Iflow. 1942 Four Flights to Love. 1946 Symphonie d'Amour. 1948 Foolish Husbands. 1951 La Ronde. 1953 Short Head. 1955 Too Young to Love. 1957 Royal Affairs. in Versailles. 1958 Mitsou. 1959 Time Running Out. 1966 How to Steal a Million. 1968 Guns for San Sebastian. 1969 The Mad Woman of Chaillot. Other foreign film: The Widow's Bed.

GRAY, GENE
Born: 1899. Died: Feb. 10, 1950, Hollywood, Calif. Screen actor. Known as "Silver King of the Cowboys" because of the rich silver trappings on his horse.

GRAY, GEORGE G.
Born: 1894. Died: Sept. 1967, Asheville, N.C.(stroke). Screen actor, stuntman, and film director. Appeared in early Sennett films and was a Keystone Kop.

Appeared in: 1934 Woman Haters (short). 1935 Uncivil Warriors (short). 1937 Goofs and Saddles (short).

GRAY, GILDA
Born: Oct. 24, 1901, Krakow, Poland. Died: Dec. 22, 1959, Hollywood, Calif.(heart attack). Screen, stage, and vaudeville actress.

Appeared in: 1923 Lawful Larceny. 1926 Aloma of the South Seas. 1927 The Devil Dancer; Cabaret. 1929 Piccadilly. 1936 Rose Marie.

GRAY, GLEN
Born: 1900, Roanoke, Ill. Died: Aug. 23, 1963, Plymouth, Mass. Orchestra leader, musician, and screen actor. Leader of the "Casa Loma Orchestra."

Appeared in: 1941 Time Out for Rhythm. 1943 Gals, Inc. 1944 Jam Session.

GRAY, JACK
Born: 1880. Died: Apr. 13, 1956, Woodland Hills, Calif. Screen actor.

Appeared in: 1933 Fugitive Lovers.

GRAY, JEAN
Born: 1902. Died: Sept. 23, 1953, Beverly Hills, Calif. Screen actress.

GRAY, LAWRENCE
Born: July 27, 1898, San Francisco, Calif. Died: Feb. 2, 1970, Mexico City, Mexico. Screen and stage actor.

Appeared in: 1925 Are Parents People?; Coast of Folly; The Dressmaker from Paris; Stage Struck. 1926 The American Venus; Everybody's Acting; Kid Boots; Love 'Em and Leave 'Em; The Palm Beach Girl; The Untamed Lady. 1927 After Midnight; Ankles Preferred; The Callahans and the Murphys; Convoy; Ladies Must Dress; Pajamas; The Telephone Girl. 1928 Diamond Handcuffs; Domestic Meddlers; Love Hungry; Marriage by Contract; Oh, Kay; The Patsy; Shadows of the Night. 1929 It's a Great Life; Marianne; The Rainbow; The Sin Sister; Trent's Last Case. 1930 Children of Pleasure; The Florodora Girl; Spring Is Here; Sunny; Temptation. 1931 Going Wild; Man of the World; Mother's Millions. 1933 Golden Harvest. 1934 Here Comes the Groom. 1935 Dizzy Dames; Danger Ahead; The Old Homestead. 1936 Timber War; In Paris A.W.O.L.

GRAY, LINDA
Born: 1913. Died: Sept. 4, 1963, Hollywood, Calif. Screen actress.

Appeared in: 1938 Shadow over Shanghai. 1952 The Pickwick Papers (U.S. 1953). 1958 In between Age.

GREEN, DENIS
Born: Apr. 11, 1905, London, England. Died: Nov. 6, 1954, New York, N.Y.(heart ailment). Screen, stage actor, and screenwriter, and writer for television and radio.

Appeared in: 1939 The Witness Vanishes; The Hound of the Baskervilles. 1940 Northwest Passage; Men against the Sky. 1941 They Met in Bombay; Yank in the RAF; Scotland Yard; Dr. Jekyll and Mr. Hyde. 1942 This above All. 1944 Frenchman's Creek. 1947 Lone Wolf in London. 1949 Mighty Joe Young.

GREEN, DOROTHY
Born: 1892. Died: Nov. 16, 1963, New York, N.Y. Screen actress.

Appeared in: 1916 A Parisian Romance. 1917 Patria (serial). 1918 The Grouch. 1919 The American Way; Forest Rivals; Her Mother's Secret; The Dark Star. 1920 The Good Bad Wife.

GREEN, FRED E.
Born: 1890. Died: Aug. 1940, near San Mateo, Calif.(auto accident injuries). Screen actor.

Appeared in: 1927 Topsy and Eva.

GREEN, HARRY (Harry Blitzer)
Born: Apr. 1, 1892, New York, N.Y. Died: May 31, 1958, London, England. Screen, stage, vaudeville, television actor, and magician.

Appeared in: 1929 Close Harmony; Why Bring That Up?; The Man I Love. 1930 The Kibitzer; Paramount on Parade; Be Yourself; Honey; True to the Navy; Light of Western Stars; The Spoilers; Sea Legs; No Limit. 1933 Marry Me; This Day and Age; Too Much Harmony; Hollywood on Parade (short). 1934 Coming out Party; Wild Gold; Love Time; Bottoms Up; She Learned About Sailors; A Woman's Man; Born to Be Bad. 1937 The Cisco Kid and the Lady. 1940 Star Dust. 1956 Joe Macbeth. 1957 A King in New York. 1960 Next to No Time.

GREEN, KENNETH
Born: 1908. Died: Feb. 24, 1969, Hollywood, Calif(heart attack). Screen actor. Appeared in "Our Gang" series.

Appeared in: 1922 Penrod.

GREEN, MITZI
Born: Oct. 22, 1920, New York, N.Y. Died: May 24, 1969, Huntington Harbour, Calif.(cancer). Screen and stage actress.

Appeared in: 1929 Marriage Playground. 1930 Honey; Paramount on Parade; Love among the Millionaires; Santa Fe Trail; Tom Sawyer. 1931 Finn and Hattie; Skippy; Dude Ranch; Forbidden Adventure; Newly Rich; Huckleberry Finn. 1932 Girl Crazy; Little Orphan Annie; The Slippery Pearls (short). 1934 Transatlantic Merry-Go-Round. 1940 Walk with Music. 1952 Lost in Alaska; Bloodhounds of Broadway.

GREEN, SUE
Born: 1902. Died: Aug. 12, 1939, Hollywood, Calif. Screen actress.

Appeared in: 1931-1939 Hal Roach shorts.

GREENE, HARRISON
Born: 1884. Died: Sept. 28, 1945, Hollywood, Calif. Screen, stage, and television actor.

Appeared in: 1933 International House; The Vampire Bat; Riot Squad; Murder on the Campus. 1934 Manhattan Love Song; Kentucky Kernels. 1935 Alibi Bye Bye (short). 1936 Ants in the Pantry (short); The Singing Cowboy; Ticket to Paradise; The Gentleman from Louisiana; The Sea Spoilers. 1937 Gripes, Grunts and Groans (short); Midnight Court; Range Defenders; A Bride for Henry; Mr. Boggs Steps Out. 1938 Born to Be Wild. 1939 Career; Dust Be My Destiny; New Frontier; The Honeymoon's Over. 1940 You Can't Fool Your Wife. 1941 Arkansas Judge. 1942 Blondie for Victory. 1944 Between Two Women.

GREENE, WILLIAM
Born: 1927, Ga. Died: Mar. 12, 1970, Cleveland Heights, Ohio. (heart attack). Screen, stage, television actor, and stage director.

Appeared in: 1955 The Shrike. 1957 Slaughter on Tenth Avenue. 1958 Orders to Kill. 1959 Never Steal Anything Small. 1962 Lolita.

GREENLEAF, RAYMOND
Born: 1892. Died: 1963. Screen actor.

Appeared in: 1948 Deep Waters; For the Love of Mary. 1949 Pinky; Slattery's Hurricane; A Kiss in the Dark; East Side, West Side; All the King's Men. 1950 A Ticket to Tomahawk; David Harding, Counterspy; Harriet Craig; On the Isle of Samoa; Storm Warning; No Sad Songs for Me. 1951 The Family Secret; FBI Girl; Pier 23; Al Jennings of Oklahoma; Secret of Convict Lake; A Millionaire for Christy; Ten Tall Men. 1952 Paula; She's Working Her Way through College; Deadline U.S.A.; Washington Story. 1953 Powder River; The Last Posse; Three Sailors and a Girl; The Bandits of Corsica; South Sea Woman; Angel Face. 1954 Living It Up. 1955 Violent Saturday; Son of Sinbad; Headline Hunters; Texas Lady. 1956 When Gangland Strikes; Never Say Goodbye; Over-Exposed; You Can't Run Away from It; Three Violent People. 1957 Monkey on My Back; The Vampire; The Night the World Exploded. 1958 The Buccaneer. 1959 The Story on Page One. 1960 From the Terrace. 1961 Wild in the Country. 1962 Bird Man of Alcatraz.

GREENSTREET, SYDNEY
Born: Dec. 27, 1879, Sandwich, Kent, England. Died: Jan. 19, 1954, Los Angeles, Calif.(natural causes). Screen and stage actor. Received Academy Award nomination in 1941 for Best Supporting Actor in The Maltese Falcon.

Appeared in: 1941 The Maltese Falcon (film debut). They Died with Their Boots On. 1942 Across the Pacific; Casablanca. 1943 Background to Danger. 1944 Hollywood Canteen; Passage to Marseille; Between Two Worlds; The Conspirators; The Mask of Dimitrios; One Man's Secret. 1945 Conflict; Christmas in Connecticut; Pillow to Post. 1946 Devotion; The Verdict; Three Strangers. 1947 That Way with Women; The Hucksters. 1948 Ruthless; The Velvet Touch; The Woman in White. 1949 Flamingo Road; East of the Rising Sun; It's a Great Feeling. 1950 Malaya.

GREENWOOD, ETHEL
Born: 1898. Died: Dec. 8, 1970, Hollywood, Calif.(heart attack). Screen and television actress.

GREER, JULIAN
Born: 1871, London, England. Died: Apr. 15, 1928, N.Y. Screen, stage, and vaudeville actor.

Appeared in: 1921 The Passion Flower. 1922 Sunshine Harbor.

GREET, CLARE
Born: June 14, 1871, England. Died: Feb. 14, 1939, London, England. Screen and stage actress.

Appeared in: 1927 The Ring. 1929 The Manxman. 1931 Should a Doctor Tell? 1932 The Sign of the Four; White Face. 1933 Lord Camber's Ladies; Channel Crossing. 1934 Little Friend. 1935 Escape Me Never; The Man Who Knew Too Much. 1936 The Royal Eagle; Murder in the Red Barn; Romance and Riches (U.S. 1937). 1938 St. Martin's Lane; Emil. 1939 Jamaica Inn. 1940 Sidewalks of London. Other British films: Lord Babs; Many Waters.

GREGG, EVERLY
Died: June 9, 1959, Beaconfield, England. Screen, stage, and television actress.

Appeared in: 1933 Private Life of Henry VIII (film debut). 1935 The Scoundrel. 1936 The Ghost Goes West. 1937 Thunder in the City. 1938 Pygmalion; Piccadilly Incident (aka They Met at Midnight). 1940 Spies in the Air. 1941 Major Barbara. 1942 In Which We Serve. 1944 Uncensored. 1946 Great Expectations; Brief Encounter. 1947 This Happy Breed. 1950 Madeleine; Women in Question (aka Five Angles on Murder U. S. 1953). 1952 Franchise Affair; Stolen Face. 1954 Genevieve; Father Brown (aka The Detective U. S. 1955); Adventure for Two (aka Demi-Paradise). 1956 The Man Who Never Was; Brothers in Law. 1957 Carry on Admiral (aka The Ship Was Loaded U.S. 1959). 1959 Room at the Top. Other British-French films: First of the Few; Conversational Piece; Official Secret; I Met a Dark Stranger; Gaiety George.

GREGOR, NORA
Born: Gorizia, Italy. Died: Jan. 20, 1949, Santiago, Chile. Screen and stage actress.

Appeared in: 1930 Olympia. 1931 Und das 1st die Hauptsache (That's All That Matters). 1932 But the Flesh Is Weak. 1933 Was Frauen Traeumen (What Women Dream). 1950 The Rules of the Game.

GREGORY, BOBBY
Born: 1900. Died: May 13, 1971, Nashville, Tenn. Screen actor, bandleader, song writer, and rodeo performer. His band was called "The Cactus Cowboys."

GREGORY, DORA
Born: 1873, England. Died: Mar. 5, 1954, London, England. Screen, stage, radio, and vaudeville actress. Appeared in: 1931 The Skin Game. 1937 The Dominant Sex; Star of the Circus. 1942 In Which We Serve.

GREGORY, EDNA (Edna Steinberg)
Born: Jan. 25, 1905, Winnipeg, Canada. Died: July 3, 1965, Los Angeles, Calif. Screen and stage actress. Appeared in early Educational Comedies and in Christie films.

Appeared in: 1921 Short Skirts. 1922 Defying the Law. 1923 Devil's Door Yard; In the Palace of the King; The Law Rustlers; Prepared to Die. 1924 The Folly of Vanity. 1925 The Calgary Stampede; Cold Nerve; Sporting Life; The Desert Flower. 1926 The Better Man; Doubling with Danger; One Man Trail; Red Hot Leather. 1927 Blazing Days; Down the Stretch; Grinning Guns; Men of Daring; Romantic Rogue; The Rose of Kildare; Rough and Ready; The Western Rover. 1929 The Great Garbo.

GREGORY, WILLIAM H.
Died: Dec. 24, 1926, Los Angeles, Calif. Screen and stage actor.

Appeared in: 1927 Sensation Seekers.

GREIG, ROBERT
Born: Dec. 27, 1880, Melbourne, Australia. Died: June 27, 1958, Hollywood, Calif. Screen and stage actor.

Appeared in: 1930 Animal Crackers; Paramount on Parade. 1931 Tonight or Never. 1932 Trouble in Paradise; Jitters the Butler (short); Stepping Sisters; Beauty and the Boss; Man Wanted; The Cohens and the Kellys in Hollywood; The Tenderfoot; Merrily We Go to Hell; Jewel Robbery; Horse Feathers; Love Me Tonight. 1933 Pleasure Cruise; It's Great to Be Alive; Peg O' My Heart; They Just Had to Get Married; Dangerously Yours; Men Must Fight; The Mind Reader. 1934 Easy to Love; One More River; The Love Captive; Cockeyed Cavaliers. 1935 Clive of India; Follies Bergere; Woman Wanted; The Bishop Misbehaves; The Gay Deception; I Love for Love. 1936 Three Live Ghosts; Rose Marie; The Unguarded Hour; Small Town Girl; Trouble for Two; The Devil Doll; Witch of Timbuctu; Suicide Club; Right in Your Lap; Theodora Goes Wild; Lloyds of London; Stowaway; Easy to Take; Michael O'Halloran. 1937 Easy Living; My Dear Miss Aldrich. 1938 Lady Behave; Midnight Intruder; The Adventures of Marco Polo; Algiers. 1939 Drums along the Mohawk; It Could Happen to You; Way Down South. 1940 Hudson Bay; No Time for Comedy. 1941 The Lady Eve; Moon Over Miami; Sullivan's Travels. 1942 The Moon and Sixpence; I Married a Witch; Palm Beach Story. 1944 The Great Moment; Summer Storm. 1945 Hollywood and Vine; The Cheaters; Earl Carroll Vanities; Nob Hill; The Picture of Dorian Gray; Love, Honor and Goodbye. 1948 Unfaithfully Yours. 1949 Bride of Vengeance.

GREY, GLORIA
Born: 1909. Died: Nov. 22, 1947, Hollywood, Calif. Screen, stage, and vaudeville actress. Was a Wampus Baby Star in 1924.

Appeared in: 1922 The Great Alone (film debut). 1923 Bag and Baggage; The Supreme Test. 1924 Girl of the Limberlost; Dante's Inferno; The House of Youth; Little Robinson Crusoe; The Millionaire Cowboy; No Gun Man; The Spirit of the U.S.A. 1925 Heartless Husbands; The Snob Buster. 1926 The Boaster; The Ghetto Shamrock; The Hidden Way; The Night Watch; Officer Jim; Thrilling Youth; Unknown Dangers. 1927 The Broncho Buster; Range Courage; Blake of Scotland Yard (serial). 1928 The Thrill Seekers; The Cloud Dodger; The Hound of Silver Creek; Put 'Em Up. 1929 Married in Hollywood.

GREY, JANE
Born: 1883, Middleburg, Vt. Died: Nov. 9, 1944, N.Y. Screen and stage actress. Signed by Triangle Films in 1914.

Appeared in: 1914 The Little Gray Lady. 1923 The Governor's Lady. 1927 The Love Wager.

GREY, JERRY (Gerald J. Grey)
Born: 1910. Died: June 7, 1954, San Antonio, Tex.(heart attack). Screen, stage, and television dancer.

GREY, MADELINE
Born: 1887. Died: Aug. 16, 1950, Los Angeles, Calif. Screen and stage actress.

Appeared in: 1929 Nothing but the Truth.

GRIBBON, EDWARD T. "EDDIE"
Born: Jan. 3, 1890, New York, N.Y. Died: Sept. 29, 1965, North Hollywood, Calif. Screen, stage, and vaudeville actor. Brother of screen actor Harry Gribbon (dec. 1961). Entered films with Mack Sennett in 1916.

Appeared in: 1921 Home Talent; Molly O; Playing with Fire; A Small Town Idol. 1922 Alias Julius Caesar; The Crossroads of New York; Tailor-Made Man; The Village Blacksmith; Captain Fly-by-Night. 1923 The Victor; Crossed Wires; Double Dealing; The Fourth Musketeer. 1924 Hoodman Blind; After the Ball; East of Broadway; Jack O'Clubs; The Border Legion. 1925 Seven Days; Code of the West; Just a Woman; Limited Mail; Mansion of Aching Hearts. 1926 Bachelor Brides; The Bat; Desert Gold; The Flaming Frontier; The Flying Mail; Man Bait; There You Are; Under Western Skies. 1927 Tell It to the Marines; The Callahans and the Murphys; Cheating Cheaters; Convoy; Night Life; Streets of Shanghai. 1928 United States Smith; Bachelor's Paradise; Buck Privates; Gang War; Nameless Men; Stop That Man. 1929 Two Weeks Off; Twin Beds; Honeymoon; Two Men and a Maid; Fancy Baggage; From Headquarters. 1930 Good Intentions; Lottery Bride; They Learned about Women; Born Reckless; Dames Ahoy; Song of the West. 1931 Mr. Lemon of Orange; Not Exactly Gentlemen. 1933 Hidden Gold. 1934 Search for Beauty; I Can't Escape; Everything's Ducky (short). 1935 The Cyclone Ranger; Rip Roaring Riley; Flying Down to Zero (short). 1936 Love on a Bet; The

Millionaire Kid; I Cover Chinatown. 1937 The Big Shot; You Can't Buy Luck; Gangway. 1938 Maid's Night Out. 1940 The Great Dictator; The Leather Pushers. 1946 Joe Palooka, Champ; Mr. Hex; Gentleman Joe Palooka. 1947 Joe Palooka in the Knockout. 1948 Fighting Mad; Winner Take All. 1949 Joe Palooka in the Big Fight; Fighting Fools; Joe Palooka in the Counterpunch. 1950 Joe Palooka Meets Humphrey; Joe Palooka in Humphrey Takes a Chance; Triple Trouble; Joe Palooka in Triple Cross; Joe Palooka in the Squared Circle.

GRIBBON, HARRY
Born: 1886, New York, N.Y. Died: July 28, 1961, Los Angeles, Calif. Screen, stage, and vaudeville actor. Brother of screen actor Eddie Gribbon (dec. 1965). Entered films with Sennett.

Appeared in: 1915 Colored Villainy; Mabel, Fatty and the Law; Ye Olden Grafter; Ambrose's Sour Grapes; A Janitor's Wife's Temptation. 1916 The Worst of Enemies; Perils of the Park; Love Will Conquer; His Auto Ruination; A Dash of Courage; His Wild Oats; A Lover's Might (working title The Fire Chief); The Great Pearl Tangle. 1917 Stars and Bars; Pinched in the Finish; Two Crooks (working title A Noble Crook). 1922 Self-Made Man. 1923 The Extra Girl. 1924 The Tomboy. 1927 Knockout Reilly. 1928 The Cameraman; Shakedown; Rose Marie; Smart Set; Show People; Chinatown Charlie. 1929 Tide of Empire; Honeymoon; On with the Show; The Mysterious Island; Midnight Daddies; The Lunkhead; The Golfers; A Hollywood Star; Clancy at the Bat; The New Halfback; Uppercut O'Brien. 1930 So Long Letty; Song of the West; Sugar Plum Papa; Swell People; Big Hearted; The Lottery Bride. 1931 The Gorilla. 1932 Ride Him, Cowboy; You Said a Mouthful; Ladies They Talk About. 1932-33 "Whoopee" comedies and Mack Sennett "Featurettes." 1933 Baby Face; Snug in the Jug (short). 1936 Sleepless Hollow (short). 1944 Arsenic and Old Lace (stage and film versions). 1963 The Sound of Laughter (documentary).

GRIFFELL, JOSE MARTINEZ
Born: 1905, Mexico. Died: Nov. 14, 1955, Mexico City, Mexico. Screen and stage actor.

GRIFFIN, CARLTON ELLIOTT
Born: 1893. Died: July 23, 1940, Hollywood, Calif.(heart attack). Screen and vaudeville actor. Appeared in vaudeville with Grace Gordon in an act billed as "Magic Glasses." Divorced from vaudeville actress Pauline Saxon. Entered films with Lubin Co.

Appeared in: 1921 At the Stage Door. 1922 Shackles of Gold. 1924 Girl Shy; The Painted Flapper. 1925 The Great Jewel Robbery. 1926 Her Big Adventure; The Imposter; Tramp, Tramp, Tramp. 1934 Maid in Hollywood (short). 1935 Slightly Static (short).

GRIFFIN, CHARLES
Born: 1888. Died: Aug. 17, 1956, Hollywood, Calif. Screen actor.

GRIFFIN, FRANK L.
Born: 1889. Died: Mar. 17, 1953, Hollywood, Calif.(heart attack). Screen actor, screenwriter, film director, and film producer. Entered films as an actor with Lubin Co. in 1906.

GRIFFIN, MARGARET FULLER. See Margaret Fuller

GRIFFITH, DAVID WARK
Born: Jan. 22, 1875, La Grange, Ky. Died: July 23, 1948, Los Angeles, Calif.(stroke). Screen, stage actor, screenwriter, playwright, and film director. Divorced from screen actresses Evelyn Marjorie Baldwin and Linda Arvidson (dec. 1948).

Appeared in: 1907 Rescued from an Eagle's Nest. 1908 At the Crossroads of Life. 1922 When Knighthood Was in Flower.

GRIFFITH, GORDON
Born: July 4, 1907, Chicago, Ill. Died: Oct. 12, 1958, Hollywood, Calif.(heart attack). Entered films as a child actor in 1913 and later became a film director.

Appeared in: 1914 Chicken Chaser; Caught in a Cabaret (reissued as The Jazz Waiter). 1920 Huckleberry Finn; Son of Tarzan (serial). 1921 That Something. 1922 Catch My Smoke; More to Be Pitied Than Scorned; Penrod; The Village Blacksmith. 1923 Jungle Trail of the Son of Tarzan (reduced version of 1920 serial Son of Tarzan); Main Street. 1924 The Street of Tears. 1925 Little Annie Rooney. 1926 The Cat's Pajamas. 1928 The Branded Man. 1935 The Crusades.

GRIFFITH, MRS. LINDA. See Linda Arvidson

GRIFFITH, RAYMOND
Born: Jan. 23, 1890, Boston, Mass. Died: Nov. 25, 1957, Hollywood, Calif. Screen actor, film director, producer, and screenwriter. Entered films with Vitagraph in 1914.

Appeared in: 1917 The Surf Girl; The Scoundrel's Tale; A Royal Rogue. 1922 Crossroads of New York; Minnie; Fools First. 1923 Eternal Three; The Day of Faith; Going Up; Red Lights; Souls for Sale; White Tiger. 1924 Poisoned Paradise; Changing Husbands; The Dawn of a Tomorrow; Lily of the Dust; Nellie, the Beautiful Cloak Model; Never Say Die; Open All Night; The Yankee Consul. 1925 The Night Club; Forty Winks; Paths to Paradise; A Regular Fellow; Fine Clothes; Miss Bluebeard; When Winter Went. 1928 Wet Paint; Hands Up; You'd Be Surprised. 1927 Wedding Bill$; Time to Love. 1929 Trent's Last Case; The Sleeping Porch. 1930 All Quiet on the Western Front.

GRIFFITH, WILLIAM M.
Born: 1897. Died: July 21, 1960, Hollywood, Calif.(heart attack). Screen and stage actor.

Appeared in: 1937 Time out for Romance. 1949 Everybody Does It; Range Land. 1955 Devil Goddess.

GRIGGS, JOHN
Born: 1909. Died: Feb. 25, 1967, Englewood, N.Y. Screen, stage, and radio actor.

Appeared in: 1937 Annapolis Salute.

GRISEL, LOUIS R.
Born: 1848, New Castle, Del. Died: Nov. 19, 1928, Fort Lee, N.J. Screen and stage actor.

Appeared in: 1921 The Black Panther's Cub; Jane Eyre.

GROONEY, ERNEST G.
Died: Jan. 20, 1946, Hollywood, Calif. Screen actor and film music director.

GROSS, WILLIAM J.
Born: 1837. Died: Apr. 12, 1924, Brooklyn, N.Y. Screen, stage, and vaudeville actor.

Appeared in: 1918 Prunelia. 1921 Rainbow; Ashamed of Parents.

GROSSMITH, GEORGE
Born: May 11, 1875, London, England. Died: June 6, 1935, London, England. Screen, stage actor, stage producer, and playwright. Brother of screen actor Lawrence Grossmith (dec. 1944).

Appeared in: 1930 Women Everywhere (film debut); Are You There?; Those Three French Girls. 1931 Reserved for Ladies. 1932 Wedding Rehearsal; The Girl from Maxim's (U.S. 1936). 1933 L'Homme a l'Hispano (The Man in the Hispano-Suiza). 1934 Princess Charming. 1940 Les Amoureux.

GROSSMITH, LAWRENCE
Born: Mar. 29, 1877, London, England. Died: Feb. 21, 1944, Woodland Hills, Calif. Screen and stage actor. Brother of screen actor George Grossmith (dec. 1935).

Appeared in: 1933 Cash; Counsel's Opinion; Tiger Bay. 1934 The Private Life of Don Juan; Catherine the Great; Rolling in Money; Contraband. 1937 Men Are Not Gods; Make Up; Silver Blaze. 1939 Captain Fury; I'm from Missouri. 1941 Larceny Street. 1944 Gaslight. Other British films: Girl in the Taxi; Smash and Grab.

GROWER, RUSSELL GORDON
Died: Feb. 21, 1958, Ontario, Calif.(shot by bandit). Screen actor.

GRUENDGENS, GUSTAF (aka GUSTAF GRUNDGENS)
Born: 1900, Dusseldorf, Germany. Died: Oct. 7, 1963, Manila, Philippine Islands(internal hemorrhage). Screen, stage actor, and film director.

Appeared in: 1930 Hocuspocus; Brand in der Opera (Fire in the Opera House - U.S. 1932). 1931 Danton. 1932 Der Raub der Mona Lisa; Luise, Koenigin von Preussen; Yorck; Teilnehmer Antwortet Nicht; Die Graefin von Monte Chisto (The Countess of Monte Christo). 1933 La Voce del Sangue; M; Die Schonen Tage van Aranjuez. 1934 Die Finanzen des Grossherzogs; Schwarzer Jager Johanna; Terra; So Endete Eine Liebe; Das Erbe in Pretoria (U.S. 1936). 1935 Hundred Days; Das Madchen Johanna; Pygmalion. 1936 Ein Glas Wasser; Liebelei. 1938 Ein Frau Ohne Bedeutung; Liebe im Gleitflug (Love in Stunt Flying). 1963 Faust.

GUARD, KIT (Christen Klitgaard)
Born: May 5, 1894, Hals, Denmark. Died: July 18, 1961, Hollywood, Calif. Screen and stage actor. Entered films in 1922.

Appeared in: 1925 The "Go-Getters" series of shorts including: The Sleeping Cutie; Ain't Love Grand; The Way of a Maid. The "Pacemaker" series of shorts including: Welcome Granger; He Who Gets Rapped; Merton of the Goofies; The Great Decide; The Fast Male; The Covered Flagon; Madame Sans Gin; Three Bases East; The Merry Kiddo; What Price Gloria?; Don CooCoo; Miss Me Again. 1926 One Minute to Play; plus the "Bill Grimm's Progress" series of shorts including: The Lady of Lyons, N.Y.; The Fight That Failed; Where There's a Bill; The Last of His Face; When a Man's a Fan; The Midnight Son; Bruisers and Losers; Little Miss Bluffit; Ladies Prefer Brunettes; Assorted Nuts; Blisters under the Skin; The Knight before Christmas. 1927 Her Father Said No; In a Moment of Temptation plus the "Beauty Parlor" series of shorts including: Beloved Rouge; Boys Will be Girls; Chin He Lived to Lift; Fresh Hair Fiends; Helene of Troy, N.Y.; New Faces for Old; Last Nose of Summers; Peter's Pan; She Troupes to Conquer; Toupay or Not Toupay. 1928 Lingerie; Legionnaires in Paris; Beau Broadway; Dead Man's Curve; Shamrock Alley(short). 1930 Big Money; Night Work; The Racketeer. 1931 Defenders of the Law; The Unholy Garden; Sky Raiders. 1932 Two-Fisted Justice; County Fair; Flames; The Last Man; The Fighting Champ; Tom Brown of Culver; The Racing Strain. 1933 Carnival Lady; Corruption; One Year Later; Riot Squad; Sucker Money. 1935 Kid Courageous; Reckless Roads; Rip Roaring Riley. 1937 Shadows of the Orient. 1938 Code of the Rangers; You and Me; Frontier Scout; Heroes of the Hills; Prison Train. 1939 Six-Gun Rhythm; El Diablo Rides; The Flying Deuces. 1943 It Ain't Hay. 1947 Johnny O'Clock; The Perils of Pauline. 1951 Fort Defiance; Abbott and Costello Meet the Invisible Man. 1956 Around the World in 80 Days.

GUDGEON, BERTRAND C.
Died: Oct. 22, 1948, North Bergen, N.J. Screen actor and stuntman. Entered films in 1908.

Appeared in: 1914 The Exploits of Elaine (serial); The Perils of Pauline (serial). 1916 The Iron Claw (serial).

GUENSTEQ, F.F.
Born: 1862. Died: Mar. 28, 1936, Glendale, Calif. Screen and stage actor. Entered films approx. 1916.

GUHL, GEORGE
Died: June 27, 1943, Los Angeles, Calif. Screen, vaudeville, and burlesque actor. Was in vaudeville in an act billed as "The Guhl Bros." and later, with another partner, in an act billed as "Adams & Guhl."

Appeared in: 1936 The Case against Mrs. Ames; Sing Me a Love Song. 1937 The Adventurous Blonde; Fly Away Baby; Night Club Scandal. 1938 Torchy Gets Her Man; Gold Mine in the Sky. 1939 Torchy Runs for Mayor; I Am Not Afraid; What a Life; Dust Be My Destiny; Nancy Drew in the Hidden Staircase. 1940 Buck Benny Rides Again; She Couldn't Say No. 1941 The Great Train Robbery; Murder by Invitation. 1942 Hidden Hand; Scattergood Survives a Murder. 1944 Crime by Night.

GUILFOYLE, PAUL
Born: July 14, 1902, Jersey City, N.J. Died: 1961. Screen and stage actor.

Appeared in: 1935 The Crime of Dr. Crespi; Special Agent. 1936 Roaming Lady; Two-Fisted Gentleman; Wanted: Jane Turner; Winterset. 1937 Behind the Headlines; Danger Patrol; Fight for Your Lady; Flight from Glory; Hideaway; Soldier and the Lady; Super Sleuth; You Can't Buy Luck; The Woman I Love; You Can't Beat Love. 1938 Crashing Hollywood; The Mad Miss Manton; Law of the Underworld; Double Danger; Blind Alibi; Fugitives for a Night; I'm from the City; The Law West of Tombstone; The Marriage Business; Quick Money; The Saint in New York; Sky Giant; Tarnished Angel. 1939 Heritage of the Desert; News Is Made at Night; Pacific Liner; Boy Slaves; One Hour to Live; Our Leading Citizen; Sabotage; Society Lawyer. 1940 Remember the Night; The Saint Takes Over; Brother Orchid; Millionaires in Prison; One Crowded Night; Thou Shalt Not Kill; East of the River; Wildcat Bus; Grapes of Wrath. 1941 The Saint in Palm Springs. 1942 The Man Who Returned to Life; Time to Kill; Who Is Hope Schuyler? 1943 Petticoat Larceny; The North Star; Three Russian Girls; White Savage; It Happened Tomorrow; Mark of the Whistler; The Seventh Cross. 1944 The Master Race; Thou Shalt Not Kill. 1945 The Missing Corpse; Why Girls Leave Home. 1946 Sweetheart of Sigma Chi; The Virginian. 1947 Second Chance; The Millerson Case; Roses Are Red. 1948 The Hunted. 1949 There's a Girl in My Heart; Trouble Preferred; Follow Me Quietly; Mighty

Joe Young; The Judge; I Married a Communist; Miss Mink of 1949; White Heat. 1950 Bomba and the Hidden City; Davy Crockett, Indian Scout; The Woman on Pier 13, Messenger of Peace. 1951 When I Grow Up. 1952 Actors and Sin; Confidence Girl; Japanese War Bride. 1953 Julius Caesar; Torch Song. 1954 Apache; Golden Idol. 1955 Chief Crazy Horse; Valley of Fury; A Life at Stake. 1960 The Boy and the Pirates.

GUINAN, TEXAS (Mary Louise Cecelle Guinan)
Died: Nov. 5, 1933, Vancouver, B.C. Canada(infection of intestines). Screen, stage, vaudeville actress, and club hostess.

Appeared in: 1918 The Gun Woman. 1919 Little Miss Deputy. 1921 I Am the Woman; The Stampede. 1929 Queen of the Night Clubs; Glorifying the American Girl. 1933 Broadway Thru a Keyhole.

GUITRY, SACHA
Born: Feb. 21, 1885, St. Petersburg, Russia. Died: July 24, 1957, Paris, France. Screen, stage actor, playwright, film producer, director, and screenwriter.

Appeared in: 1915 Ceux de Chez Nous. 1932 Les Deux Couverts. 1936 Pasteur. 1937 Les Perles de la Couronne (Pearls of the Crown). 1938 Quadrille; The Story of a Cheat. 1939 Champs Elysees; Indiscretions. 1942 Nine Bachelors. 1943 Donne-Moi tes Yeux. 1948 En Scene (Private Life of an Actor); Mlle Desire. 1949 Le Comedien. 1951 Deburau. 1954 Versailles (aka Royal Affairs in Versailles—U.S. 1957).

GUITTY, MADELEINE
Born: 1871. Died: Apr. 12, 1936, Paris, France. Screen, stage actress, and song writer.

Appeared in: 1925 Madame Sans-Gene. 1932 Ilest Charmant. 1934 Le Roi des Champs Elysees. 1935 Les As Du Turf; Avel l'Assurance; Cette Veille Canaille; Sans Famille. 1936 La Porteuse de Pain; Ciboulette. Other French film: Bacarolle.

GURIE, SIGRID (Sigrid Gurie Haukelid)
Born: 1911, Brooklyn, N.Y. Died: Aug. 14, 1969, Mexico City, Mexico (embolism). Screen actress.

Appeared in: 1938 The Adventures of Marco Polo (film debut); Algiers. 1939 Forgotten Woman. 1940 Rio; Three Faces West; The Refugee; Dark Streets of Cairo. 1943 The Private Life of Dr. Joseph Goebbels (apparently never released). 1944 Enemy of Women; A Voice in the Wind. 1948 Sofia; Sword of the Avenger.

GURNEY, EDMUND
Born: 1852. Died: Jan. 14, 1925, N.Y. Screen and stage actor.

Appeared in: 1921 Tol'able David.

GUTHRIE, CHARLES W.
Born: 1871. Died: June 30, 1939, Washington, D.C. Screen and stage actor.

GWENN, EDMUND
Born: Sept. 26, 1875, Glamorgan, Wales. Died: Sept. 6, 1959, Woodland Hills, Calif. Screen and stage actor. Won Academy Award for Best Supporting Actor in 1947 for The Miracle of 34th Street.

Appeared in: 1916 The Real Thing at Last. 1920 The Skin Game. 1930 The Skin Game (U.S. 1932 and 1920 version). 1931 How She Lied to Her Husband; Money for Nothing; Hindle Wakes; Smithy. 1932 Condemned to Death; Frail Woman; Tell Me Tonight; Good Companions; Early to Bed (U.S. 1936); Cash. 1934 I Was a Spy; Channel Crossing; Friday the 13th; Passing Shadows; Marooned; For Love or Money; Spring in the Air; Father and Son; Warn London!. 1935 Sylvia Scarlet; The Bishop Misbehaves; Waltzes from Vienna (aka Strauss' Great Waltz); Java Head. 1936 The Walking Dead; Anthony Adverse; Country Bumpkin (aka All American Chump); Laburum Grove (U.S. 1941—film and stage versions); Mad Holiday. 1937 Parnell. 1938 South Riding; A Yank at Oxford; Penny Paradise; Tell Me Tonight. 1939 An Englishman's Home. 1940 The Earl of Chicago; Mad Men of Europe; The Doctor Takes a Wife; Pride and Prejudice; Foreign Correspondent. 1941 Scotland Yard; Cheers for Miss Bishop; The Devil and Miss Jones; Charley's Aunt; One Night in Lisbon. 1942 A Yank at Eton. 1943 The Meanest Man in the World; Forever and a Day; Lassie Come Home. 1944 Between Two Worlds. 1945 Keys to the Kingdom; Bewitched; Dangerous Partners; She Went to the Races. 1946 Of Human Bondage; Undercurrent. 1947 The Miracle of 34th Street; Thunder in the Valley; Life with Father; Green Dolphin Street. 1948 Apartment for Peggy; Hills of Home. 1949 Challenge to Lassie. 1950 A Woman of Distinction; Louisa; Pretty Baby; Mister 880; For Heaven's Sake.

1951 Peking Express. 1952 Sally and St. Anne; Bonzo Goes to College; Les Miserables; Something for the Birds. 1953 Mr. Scoutmaster; The Bigamist. 1954 Them; The Student Prince. 1955 The Trouble with Harry; It's a Dog's Life. 1958 Calabuch.

GYPSY GOULD. See Vivian Vaughn

HAAGEN, AL H.
Born: 1871. Died: Mar. 8, 1953, Los Angeles, Calif. Screen, stage, vaudeville, and minstrel actor.

HAAL, RENEE. See Renee Haal Godfrey

HAAS, HUGO
Born: Feb. 19, 1902, Brno, Czechoslovakia. Died: Dec. 1968, Vienna, Austria. Screen actor, film and stage director, film producer, and screenwriter.

Appeared in: 1940 Skeleton on Horseback. 1944 Summer Storm; Days of Glory; Mrs. Parkington; The Princess and the Pirate; Strange Affair. 1945 Jealousy; A Bell for Adano; Dakota; What Next, Corporal Hargrove?. 1946 Holiday in Mexico; Two Smart People. 1947 Northwest Outpost; The Foxes of Harrow; Fiesta; The Private Affairs of Bel Ami; Merton of the Movies. 1948 My Girl Tisa; Casbah; For the Love of Mary. 1949 The Fighting Kentuckian. 1950 King Solomon's Mines; Vendetta. 1951 Pickup; Girl on the Bridge. 1952 Strange Fascination. 1953 One Girl's Confession; The Neighbor's Wife. 1954 Bait; The Other Woman. 1955 Hold Back Tomorrow; Tender Trap. 1956 Edge of Hell. 1957 Hit and Run; Lizzie. 1959 Born to Be Loved.

HACK, HERMAN
Born: 1899. Died: Oct. 19, 1967, Hollywood, Calif.(heart attack). Screen actor.

HACKATHORNE, GEORGE
Born: Feb. 13, 1896, Pendleton, Ore. Died: June 25, 1940, Los Angeles, Calif. Screen, stage, and vaudeville actor.

Appeared in: 1918 The Heart of Humanity. 1920 To Please One Woman. 1921 What Do Men Want?; The Little Minister; The Light in the Clearing; High Heels; The Sin of Martha Queed; The Last of the Mohicans. 1922 Human Hearts; The Village Blacksmith; The Gray Dawn; Notoriety; The Worldly Madonna. 1923 Merry-Go-Round; The Human Wreckage. 1924 The Turmoil; When a Man's a Man; Judgment of the Storm; Surging Seas. 1925 Night Life in New York; Capital Punishment; Wandering Fires; The Lady; His Masters Voice. 1926 The Highbinders. 1927 Cheaters; Paying the Price. 1928 Shepherd of the Hills; Sally Shoulders. 1929 Tip Off; The Squall. 1930 Lonesome Trail; Beyond the Law; Hideout. 1933 Self Defense; Flaming Guns. 1936 I Cover Chinatown; The Magnificent Obsession. 1939 Gone with the Wind.

HACKER, MARIA
Born: 1904, Germany. Died: Feb. 20, 1963, Sherman Oaks, Calif. Screen actress. Wife of screen actor/tenor Lauritz Melchior.

HACKETT, FLORENCE
Born: 1882. Died: Aug. 21, 1954, New York, N.Y. Screen and stage actress. Mother of screen actors Ramond (dec. 1958) and Albert Hackett.

Appeared in: 1914 The Beloved Adventurer (serial). 1915 Siren of Corsica.

HACKETT, HAL
Born: 1923. Died: Dec. 4, 1967, New York, N.Y. Screen, stage, radio, and television actor.

Appeared in: 1946 The Show Off. 1947 Love Laughs at Andy Hardy. 1948 Campus Honeymoon; Summer Holiday.

HACKETT, JAMES K.
Born: Sept. 6, 1869, Wolf Island, Ontario, Canada. Died: Nov. 8, 1926, Paris, France (cirrhosis of the liver). Screen and stage actor. Entered films with Famous Players in 1912.

Appeared in: 1913 The Prisoner of Zenda.

HACKETT, KARL
Born: 1893. Died: Oct. 24, 1948, Los Angeles, Calif. Screen actor.

Appeared in: 1936 Down to the Sea; Happy Go Lucky. 1937 The Gold Racket; Sing, Cowboy, Sing; Tex Rides with the Boy Scouts; Texas Trail; Colorado Kid. 1938 Paroled to Die; Phantom Ranger; Down in Arkansaw; The Rangers Roundup; Starlight over Texas; Where the Buffalo Roam; Frontier Town. 1940 Yukon

Flight; Take Me Back to Oklahoma; Chip of the Flying U. 1941 Outlaws of the Rio Grande. 1942 Sons of the Pioneers; Pirates of the Prairie; Jesse James, Jr.; Billy the Kid's Smoking Guns; Phantom Killer; Outlaws of Boulder Pass. 1943 The Avenging Rider; Fugitive of the Plains; Bordertown Gunfighters; The Renegade; Lost Canyon. 1944 Tucson Raiders; Wolves of the Range; Sonora Stagecoach; Westward Bound; Mojave Firebrand; Arizona Whirlwind; Oath of Vengeance; Thundering Gunslinger; The Pinto Bandit; Brand of the Devil. 1945 Lightning Raiders; His Brother's Ghost; Rustlers of the Badlands; Prairie Rustlers. 1946 Ghost of Hidden Valley; Gentlemen with Guns; Terrors on Horseback; Outlaw of the Plains; Gunman's Code. 1947 The Michigan Kid; Frontier Fighters; Raiders of Red Rock; Code of the Plains.

HACKETT, RAYMOND
Born: July 15, 1902, New York, N.Y. Died: June 9, 1958, Hollywood, Calif. Screen and stage actor. Married to screen actress Blanche Sweet. Son of screen actress Florence Hackett (dec. 1954) and brother of screen actor Albert Hackett.

Appeared in: 1918 The Cruise of the Make-Believe. 1922 The Country Flapper. 1927 The Love of Sunya. 1928 Faithless Lover. 1929 Girl in the Show; The Trial of Mary Dugan; Madam X; Footlights and Fools. 1930 Let Us Be Gay; Our Blushing Brides; The Sea Wolf; Numbered Men; On Your Back; The Cat Creeps; Not So Dumb. 1931 Seed.

HADDON, PETER (Peter Tildsley)
Born: 1898, England. Died: Sept. 7, 1962, England. Screen, stage actor, and author.

Appeared in: 1935 Death at the Broadcasting House; The Silent Passenger; No Monkey Business; Don't Rush Me; Publis Nuisance No. 1. 1936 The Beloved Vagabond; The House of the Spaniard; The Secret of Stamboul. 1937 Kate Plus Ten; Over the Moon. 1949 Helter Skelter. 1954 The Second Mrs. Tanqueray.

HAEFELI, CHARLES "JOCKEY"
Born: 1889. Died: Feb. 12, 1955, Hollywood, Calif. Screen actor.

Appeared in: 1921 Four Horseman of the Apocalypse. 1923 The Hunchback of Notre Dame. 1935 Les Miserables.

HAGEN, CHARLES F.
Born: 1872. Died: June 13, 1958, Hollywood, Calif. Screen and stage actor. Entered films with Griffith.

Appeared in: 1950 All about Eve.

HAGEN, MARGARETHE
Born: 1890, Germany. Died: Dec. 14, 1966, Gruenwald, Germany. Screen and stage actress.

Appeared in: Uncle Filsner; Kohlhiesel's Daughter; In Those Days; Beloved Liar; Fireworks; Her 106th Birthday.

HAGER, CLYDE
Born: 1887. Died: May 21, 1944, Harrisburg, Pa.(heart attack). Screen, stage, vaudeville actor, and song writer.

Appeared in: 1930 Railroad Follies (short). 1936 Strike Me Pink.

HAGGARD, STEPHEN
Born: 1912, England. Died: Feb. 1943, Middle East (during war). Screen, stage actor, and author.

Appeared in: 1939 Jamaica Inn. 1940 Mozart. 1943 The Young Mr. Pitt.

HAHN, SALLY
Born: 1908. Died: June 2, 1933, Los Angeles, Calif. Screen actress.

HAIG, RAYMOND V.
Born: 1917. Died: Sept. 17, 1963, Chicago, Ill.(auto accident). Screen and vaudeville actor. Appeared in vaudeville in an act billed as "Haig & Haig" and the team made Paramount shorts.

HAINE, HORACE J.
Born: 1868, Detroit, Mich. Died: Sept. 26, 1940, New York, N.Y. Screen, stage, opera actor, and stage producer.

Appeared in: 1916 The Other Man; The Moonshiners. 1924 The Fifth Horseman.

HAINES, RHEA
Born: 1895. Died: Mar. 12, 1964, Los Angeles, Calif. Screen actress.

Appeared in: 1919 Scarlet Days. 1920 Mary Ellen Comes to Town; Always Audacious; Master Stroke; Girls Don't Gamble. 1921 Smiling All the Way; Uncharterd Seas.

HAINES, ROBERT T.
Born: 1870, Muncie, Ind. Died: May 6, 1943, N.Y. Screen, stage, vaudeville, radio actor, stage producer, director, and playwright.

Appeared in: 1912 The Capitol. 1921 The Victim; God's Crucible. 1923 Does It Pay?; The Governor's Lady. 1924 The Lone Wolf. 1926 Lew Tyler's Wives. 1928 How to Handle Women; The First Kiss; Ladies of the Mob; The Noose. 1928 Ten Minutes (short). 1929 Careers; Dynamite; The Girl in the Glass Cage; The Shannons of Broadway. 1930 Guilty?. 1934 These Thirty Years. 1935 Gigolette.

HALE, ALAN, SR. (Rufas Alan McKanan)
Born: Feb. 10, 1892, Washington, D.C. Died Jan. 22, 1950, Hollywood, Calif.(liver ailment—virus infection). Screen, stage actor, film director, writer, and singer. Entered films with Lubin Film Co. in Philadelphia in 1911. Father of screen actor Alan Hale. Married to former screen actress Gretchen Hartman.

Appeared in: 1911 The Cowboy and the Lady (film debut). 1914 Cricket on the Hearth. 1915 Jane Eyre; Under Two Flags; Dora; an untitled short. 1916 Pudd'n Head Wilson. 1917 The Price She Paid. 1921 A Voice in the Dark; A Wise Fool; The Four Horsemen of the Apocalypse; The Barbarian; The Fox; The Great Impersonation; Over the Wire. 1922 One Glorious Day; Robin Hood; A Doll's House; Dictator; Shirley of the Circus; The Trap. 1923 The Covered Wagon; Hollywood; Cameo Kirby; The Eleventh Hour; Long Live the King; Main Street; Quicksands. 1924 Troubles of a Bride; Black Oxen; Code of the Wilderness; For Another Woman; Girls Men Forget; One Night in Rome. 1925 Rolling Stones; Braveheart; The Crimson Runner; Dick Turpin; Flattery; The Scarlet Honeymoon; The Wedding Song. 1926 Forbidden Waters; Hearts and Fists; Risky Business; The Sporting Lover. 1927 Rubber Tires; Vanity; The Wreck of the Hesperus. 1928 The Leopard Lady; Skyscraper; The Cop; Power; Oh, Kay!. 1929 Sal of Singapore; The Spieler; The Leatherneck; A Bachelor's Secret; Red Hot Rhythm; The Sap; Sailor's Holiday. 1930 She Got What She Wanted. 1931 Up and at 'Em; Aloha; The Night Angel; Susan Lennox, Her Rise and Fall; Sea Ghost; The Sin of Madelon Claudet; Rebound; So Big; The Match King; Union Depot; Rebecca of Sunnybrook Farm; Gentlemen for a Day. 1933 Picture Brides; What Price Decency?; Eleventh Commandment; Destination Unknown. 1934 It Happened One Night; Imitation of Life; Of Human Bondage; Little Man, What Now?; Great Expectations; The Lost Patrol; Miss Fane's Baby Is Stolen; The Little Minister; Fog over Frisco; The Scarlet Letter; Babbitt; There's Always Tomorrow; Broadway Bill. 1935 Grand Old Girl; Last Days of Pompeii; Another Face; The Good Fairy; The Crusades. 1936 Jump for Glory; Two in the Dark; A Message to Garcia; The Country Beyond; Parole!; Yellowstone; Our Relations; God's Country and the Woman. 1937 When Thief Meets Thief; High, Wide and Handsome; Thin Ice; Music for Madame; The Prince and the Pauper; Stella Dallas. 1938 Valley of the Giants; The Adventures of Marco Polo; The Adventures of Robin Hood; Algiers; Four Men and a Prayer; Listen, Darling; The Sisters. 1939 Pacific Liner; Dust Be My Destiny; On Your Toes; The Private Lives of Elizabeth and Essex; Dodge City; Man in the Iron Mask. 1940 The Sea Hawk; Three Cheers for the Irish; Green Hell; Virginia City; The Fighting 69th; They Drive by Night; Santa Fe Trail; Tugboat Annie Sails Again. 1941 The Great Mr. Nobody; Strawberry Blonde; Manpower; The Smiling Ghost; Thieves Fall Out; Footsteps in the Dark. 1942 Desperate Journey; Captains of the Clouds; Juke Girl; Gentlemen Jim. 1943 Action in the North Atlantic; This Is the Army; Thank Your Lucky Stars; Destination Tokyo. 1944 The Adventures of Mark Twain; Make Your Own Bed; Janie; Hollywood Canteen; Strangers in Our Midst. 1945 Roughly Speaking; Hotel Berlin; God Is My Co-Pilot; Escape in the Desert. 1946 Perilous Holiday; The Time, the Place and the Girl; The Man I Love; Night and Day. 1947 My Wild Irish Rose; Cheyenne; That Way with Women; Pursued. 1948 The Adventures of Don Juan; My Girl Tisa; Whiplash. 1949 South of St. Louis; The Younger Brothers; The House across the Street; Always Leave Them Laughing; The Inspector General. 1940 Rogues of Sherwood Forest; Stars in My Crown; Colt .45.

HALE, BARNABY
Born: 1927. Died: Nov. 5, 1964, Los Angeles, Calif.(following surgery). Screen, stage, and television actor.

HALE, CREIGHTON (Patrick Fitzgerald)
Born: May 1882, Cork, Ireland. Died: Aug. 9, 1965, South Pasadena, Calif. Screen actor.

Appeared in: 1915 The New Exploits of Elaine (serial); The Romance of Elaine (serial). 1916 The Iron Claw (serial). 1917 The Seven Pearls (serial). 1919 The Thirteenth Chair. 1920 The Idol Dancer; Way Down East. 1921 Forbidden Love; Orphans of the Storm. 1922 Fascination; Her Majesty. 1923 Broken Hearts of Broadway; Mary of the Movies; Tea with a Kick; Three Wise Fools; Trilby. 1924 How to Educate a Wife; The Mine with the Iron Door; Name the Man; Riders Up; This Woman; Wine of Youth; The Marriage Circle. 1925 The Bridge of Sighs; The Circle; Exchange of Wives; Seven Days; The Shadow on the Wall; Time, the Comedian; Wages for Wives. 1926 Beverly of Graustark; The Midnight Message; Oh, Baby; A Poor Girl's Romance; Speeding Through. 1927 Annie Laurie; The Cat and the Canary; Thumbs Down. 1928 The House of Shame; Sisters of Eve; Rose Marie. 1929 Seven Footprints to Satan; Reilly of the Rainbow Division. 1930 Holiday; The Great Divide. 1931 Grief Street. 1932 Prestige; Shop Angel; Stage Whispers. 1933 The Masquerader. 1934 Sensation Hunters; What's Your Racket?. 1935 Death from a Distance. 1936 The Millionaire Kid; Hollywood Boulevard. 1939 Nancy Drew and the Hidden Staircase; Return of Dr. X. 1940 Calling Philo Vance. 1941 The Bride Came C.O.D. 1942 Bullet Scars; Larceny, Inc.; Murder in the Big House; Gorilla Man. 1943 Watch on the Rhine; The Mysterious Doctor; Action in the North Atlantic. 1944 The Adventures of Mark Twain; Crime by Night. 1947 That Way with Women; The Two Mrs. Carrolls; Perils of Pauline. 1949 Beyond the Forest.

HALE, JONATHAN
Born: 1891. Died: Feb. 28, 1966, Woodland Halls, Calif.(suicide—gun). Screen actor.

Appeared in: 1934 Lightning Strikes Twice (film debut). 1935 Navy Wife; Alice Adams; The Voice of Bugle Ann; A Night at the Opera. 1936 Charlie Chan's Secret; Fury; The Devil Is a Sissy; Too Many Parents; The Case against Mrs. Ames; Educating Father; Charlie Chan at the Race Track; 36 Hours to Kill; Flying Hostess; Happy Go Lucky; Three Live Ghosts. 1937 She's Dangerous; Charlie Chan at the Olympics; League of the Frightened Men; Big Time Girl; You Only Live Once; Man of the People; Saratoga; Midnight Madonna; Outcast; John Meade's Woman; Madame X; This Is My Affair; Mysterious Crossing; Racketeers in Exile; Danger—Love at Work; Exiled to Shanghai. 1938 Blondie; The First Hundred Years; Bringing up Baby; Arsene Lupin Returns; Judge Hardy's Children; Yellow Jack; Boys Town; Road Demon; There's That Woman Again; Her Jungle Love; Duke of West Point; Wives under Suspicion; A Letter of Introduction; Over the Wall; Saint in New York; Fugitives for a Night; Breaking the Ice; Tarnished Angel; Gangs of New York; Scandal Sheet. 1939 Thunder Afloat; The Saint Strikes Back; In Name Only; Blondie Meets the Boss; Fugitive at Large; Blondie Brings up Baby; The Amazing Mr. Williams; The Story of Alexander Graham Bell; Barricade; In Old Monterey; Stand up and Fight; Wings of the Navy; Tail Spin. 1940 The Big Guy; The Saint's Double Trouble; The Saint Takes Over; Private Affairs; We Who Are Young; Blondie Has Servant Trouble; Dulcy; Melody and Moonlight; Blondie Plays Cupid; Johnny Apollo. 1941 Blondie Goes Latin; Flight from Destiny; Ringside Maisie; The Pittsburgh Kid; Blondie in Society; The Saint in Palm Springs; The Great Swindle; Strange Alibi; The Bugle Sounds. 1942 Joe Smith, American; Blondie Goes to College; Lone Star Ranger; Miss Annie Rooney; Calling Dr. Gillespie; Flight Lieutenant; Blondie's Blessed Event; Blondie for Victory. 1943 Hangmen Also Die; Jack London; Mission 36; The Amazing Mrs. Holliday; Sweet Rosie O'Grady. 1944 This Is the Life; The Black Parachute; Since You Went Away; Hollywood Canteen; Dead Man's Eyes; My Buddy; And Now Tomorrow; The End of the Road. 1945 The Phantom Speaks; Dakota; Man Alive; G.I. Honeymoon; Life with Blondie; Allotment Wives. 1946 Angel on My Shoulder; Blondie Knows Best; Blondie's Lucky Day; The Cat Creeps; Easy to Wed; Riverboat Rhythm; The Walls Came Tumbling Down; The Strange Mr. Gregory; Gay Blades; Wife Wanted. 1947 The Beginning or the End; The Ghost Goes Wild; Rolling Home; The Vigilantes Return; Her Husband's Affair; High Wall. 1948 Michael O'Halloran; King of the Gamblers; Silver River; Johnny Belinda; Call Northside 777; Rocky. 1949 Rose of the Yukon; Stampede; The Judge; State Department File 649. 1950 Federal Agent at Large; Three Husbands; Short Grass; Triple Trouble. 1951 Insurance Investigator; On the Sunny Side of the Street; Strangers on a Train; Let's Go Navy!; Rodeo King and the Senorita; Rhythm Inn. 1952 Steel Trap; My Pal Gus; Son of Paleface; Scandal Sheet. 1953 A Blueprint for Murder; Kansas Pacific; Taxi. 1954 Duffy of San Quentin; Riot in Cell Block 11. 1955 The Night Holds Terror; A Man Called Peter. 1956 Jaguar; The Opposite Sex.

HALE, LOUISE CLOSSER
Born: Oct. 13, 1872, Chicago. Ill. Died: July 26, 1933, Los Angeles, Calif.(following an accident). Screen, stage actress, and playwright.

Appeared in: 1929 The Hole in the Wall; Paris. 1930 Dangerous Nan McGrew; Big Boy; The Princess and the Plumber. 1931 Captain Applejack; Born to Love; Rebound; Devotion; Daddy Long Legs; Platinum Blonde. 1932 Sky Bride; Faithless; No More Orchids; The Son-Daughter; Rebecca of Sunnybrook Farm; Movie Crazy; Rasputin and the Empress; The Shanghai Express; The Man Who Played God; New Morals for Old; Letty Lynton. 1933 The White Sister; Today We Live; The Barbarian; Storm at Daybreak; Another Language; Dinner at Eight.

HALE, ROBERT
Born: 1874, Devonshire, England. Died: Apr. 18, 1940, Maidenhead, Berkshire, England. Screen and stage actor.

Appeared in: 1935 Strauss' Great Waltz. 1936 It's Love Again. 1937 Storm in a Teacup.

HALE, ROBERTSON
Born: 1891, England. Died: 1967. Screen and stage actor.

HALE, SONNIE (John Robert Hale-Munro)
Born: May 1, 1902, London, England. Died: June 9, 1959, London, England. Screen, stage actor, film director, and playwright.

Appeared in: 1932 Tell Me Tonight (film debut); Happy Ever After. 1933 Be Mine Tonight. 1934 Wild Boy; Friday the 13th; My Heart Is Calling; First a Girl; Are You a Mason?. 1935 Evergreen. 1936 It's Love Again; My Song for You. 1938 The Gaunt Stranger; Sailing Along. 1944 Fiddler's Three. 1946 London Town. Other British film: Let's Be Famous.

HALL, ALEXANDER
Born: 1894, Boston, Mass. Died: July 30, 1968, San Francisco, Calif.(stroke). Screen, stage actor, and film director.

Appeared in: 1927 Million Dollar Mystery (serial—film debut).

HALL, ALFRED HENRY
Born: 1880. Died: Apr. 21, 1943, Hollywood, Calif.(heart attack). Screen and stage actor.

Appeared in: 1942 Scattergood Survives a Murder; The Old Homestead.

HALL, CHARLES D. "CHARLIE"
Born: Aug. 18, 1899, Birmingham, England. Died: Dec. 7, 1959, North Hollywood, Calif. Screen, stage actor, and film art director. Entered films as an actor in 1923.

Appeared in: 1927 Battle of the Century; Love 'em and Weep (short). 1928 Must We Marry?; Crooks Can't Win, plus the following shorts: You're Darn Tootin'; Two Tars; Leave 'em Laughing. 1929 Why Bring That Up?, plus the following shorts: They Go Boom; Wrong Again; That's My Wife; Double Whoopee; Berth Marks; Men O'War; Bacon Grabbers; Angora Love. 1930 Below Zero (short). 1931 Pardon Us, plus the following shorts: The Pajama Party; Laughing Gravy; Scratch as Catch Can; Come Clean; War Mamas. 1932 the following shorts: Any Old Port; The Music Box; Strictly Unreliable; Show Business; The Soilers. 1933 the following shorts: Sneak Easily; Maids a la Mode; One Tract Minds; Beauty and the Bus; Backs to Nature; Air Fright; Twice Two; Me and My Pal; Busy Bodies; Kickin' the Crown around; Fits in a Fiddle. 1934 Cockeyed Cavaliers; Sons of the Desert; Kentucky Kernels, plus the following shorts: Them Thar Hills; The Live Ghost; Babes in the Goods; Soup and Fish; One Horse Farmers; Opened by Mistake; Maid in Hollywood. 1935 the following shorts: Treasure Blues; Sing, Sister, Sing; Twin Triplest; Hot Money; All American Toothache; Tit for Tat; Thicker Than Water. 1936 Pick a Star. 1940 One Night in the Tropics; A Chump at Oxford; Saps at Sea; You Can't Fool Your Wife. 1941 Top Sergeant Mulligan. 1944 In Society. 1945 Hangover Square; Mama Loves Papa. 1951 The Vicious Years. 1968 The Further Perils of Laurel and Hardy (documentary).

HALL, DOROTHY
Born: 1906. Died: Feb. 3, 1953, New York, N.Y. Screen and stage actress.

Appeared in: 1927 Back to Liberty; The Broadway Drifter; The Winning Oar. 1929 Nothing but the Truth; The Laughing Lady. 1930 Home Made (short).

HALL, GABRIELLE
Died: Jan. 1, 1967, El Cajon, Calif. Screen and television actress. Entered films during silents.

HALL, GEORGE M.
Born: 1890, Sweden. Died: Apr. 24, 1930, Saranac Lake, N.Y. Screen and stage actor.

Appeared in: 1926 West of Broadway.

HALL, GERALDINE
Born: 1905. Died: Sept. 18, 1970, Woodland Hills, Calif. Screen and stage actress. Married to screen actor Porter Hall (dec. 1953).

Appeared in: 1936 More Than a Secretary. 1951 The Big Carnival. 1952 The Captive City. 1954 Secret of the Incas. 1955 Five against the House. 1956 Over-Exposed; The Proud and the Profane.

HALL, HENRY LEONARD
Died: Dec. 11, 1954, Woodland Hills, Calif. Screen and stage actor.

Appeared in: 1933 Story of Temple Drake (film debut); Sagebrush Trail. 1934 Our Daily Bread; The Dude Ranger. 1935 Mary Burns, Fugitive. 1936 Jailbreak. 1937 County Fair; Yodelin' Kid from Pine Ridge. 1938 Block-Heads. 1940 Blazing Six Shooter; Prairie Law; The Haunted House; The Ape; Chip of the Flying U. 1941 The Lone Star Vigilantes. 1942 Murder in the Big House; Stagecoach Buckaroo; Boss of Hangtown Mesa; The Old Homestead; Butch Minds the Baby; Queen of Broadway. 1943 Girls in Chains. 1945 San Antonio; Jade Mask. 1946 Flying Serpent. 1947 The Beginning of the End. 1948 Panhandle. 1949 Cover Up.

HALL, JAMES
Born: Oct. 22, 1900, Dallas, Tex. Died: June 7, 1940, Jersey City, N.J.(liver ailment). Screen and stage actor.

Appeared in: 1923 The Man Alone. 1926 The Campus Flirt; Stranded in Paris. 1927 Hotel Imperial; Love's Greatest Mistake; Ritzy; Swim, Girl, Swim; Senorita; Silk Legs; Rolled Stockings. 1928 Just Married; The Fifty-Fifty Girl; The Fleet's In; Four Sons. 1929 The Saturday Night Kid; The Canary Murder Case; Smiling Irish Eyes; The Case of Lena Smith; This Is Heaven. 1930 Hell's Angels; Dangerous Nan McGrew; Maybe It's Love; Let's Go Native; Paramount on Parade; The Third Alarm. 1931 Mother's Millions; Sporting Chance; Millie; Man to Man; Lightning Flyer; The Good Bad Girl; Divorce Among Friends. 1932 Manhattan Tower.

HALL, JOHN (Michael Braughal)
Born: 1878. Died: Apr. 25, 1936, Los Angeles, Calif. Screen actor.

Appeared in: 1927 Men of Daring. 1928 The Wild West Show.

HALL, JUANITA
Born: 1902. Died: Feb. 28, 1968, Keyport, N.J.(diabetes). Screen and stage actress.

Appeared in: 1949 Miracle in Harlem. 1958 South Pacific. 1961 Flower Drum Song.

HALL, KATHRYN. See Kathryn Carver

HALL, NELSON L.
Born: 1881. Died: July 28, 1944, Philadelphia, Pa. Screen actor and acrobat stuntman.

HALL, PORTER
Born: 1888, Cincinnati, Ohio. Died: Oct. 6, 1953, Los Angeles, Calif.(heart attack). Screen and stage actor. Won Screen Actors Guild Award for Best Supporting Actor in 1936 for The Plainsman. Married to screen actress Geraldine Hall (dec. 1970).

Appeared in: 1934 The Thin Man (film debut); Murder in the Private Car. 1935 The Case of the Lucky Legs. 1936 The Story of Louis Pasteur; The Petrified Forest; The General Died at Dawn; Satan Met a Lady; Too Many Parents; Princess Comes Across; And Sudden Death; Snowed Under; The Plainsman. 1937 Let's Make a Million; Bulldog Drummond Escapes; Souls at Sea; Wells Fargo; Wild Money; Hotel Haywire; Make Way for Tomorrow; King of Gamblers; This Way, Please; True Confession. 1938 Scandal Street; Stolen Heaven; Dangerous to Know; Prison Farm; King of Alcatraz; The Arkansas Traveler; Men with Wings; Tom Sawyer, Detective; Bulldog Drummond's Peril. 1939 Grand Jury Secrets; They Shall Have Music; Mr. Smith Goes to Washington. 1940 Arizona; The Dark Command; Trail of the Vigilantes; His Girl Friday. 1941 The Parson of Panamint; Sullivan's Travels; Mr. and Mrs. North. 1942 The Remarkable Andrew; Butch Minds the Baby. 1943 A Stranger in Town; The Desperadoes; Woman of the Town. 1944 Standing Room Only; Double Indemnity; The Miracle of Morgan's Creek; Mark of the Whistler; Going My Way; The Great Moment. 1945 Murder, He Says; Kiss and Tell; Blood on the Sun; Weekend at the Waldorf; Bring on the Girls. 1947 Singapore; Miracle on 34th Street; Mad Wednesday. 1948 Unconquered; That Wonderful Urge. 1949 You Gotta Stay Happy; Beautiful Blonde From Bashful Bend; Chicken Every Sunday; Intruder in the Dust. 1951 The Big Carnival. 1952 The Half Breed; Carbine Williams; Holiday for Sinners. 1953 Pony Express; Vice Squad. 1954 Return to Treasure Island.

HALL, THURSTON
Born: 1883, Boston, Mass. Died: Feb. 20, 1958, Beverly Hills, Calif.(heart attack). Screen, stage, television, vaudeville actor, and stage producer. Entered films in 1915.

Appeared in: 1917 Cleopatra. 1918 We Can't Have Everything. 1921 Idle Hands; The Iron Trail; Mother Eternal. 1922 Fair Lady; Wildness of Youth. 1930 Absent Minded (short). 1935 Hooray for Love; Metropolitan; Guard That Girl; Crime and Punishment; The Girl Friend; Too Tough to Live; Black Room; After the Dance; Love Me Forever; Public Menace; One Way Ticket; Case of the Missing Man; A Feather in Her Hat. 1936 Pride of the Marines; Roaming Lady; Two-Fisted Gentleman; Lady from Nowhere; The Lone Wolf Returns; Don't Gamble with Love; The Man Who Lived Twice; Killer at Large; Theodora Goes Wild; Devil's Squadron; The King Steps Out; Trapped by Television; Shakedown; Three Wise Guys. 1937 I Promise to Pay; Women of Glamour; Parole Racket; It Can't Last Forever; Counsel for Crime; Murder in Greenwich Village; We Have Our Moments; Oh, Doctor; Don't Tell the Wife. 1938 No Time to Marry; There's Always a Woman; Little Miss Roughneck; Campus Confessions; The Affairs of Annabel; Professor Beware; Women Are Like That; The Amazing Dr. Clitterhouse; Hard to Get; Fast Company; Going Places; Extortion; Squadron of Honor; Main Event. 1939 You Can't Cheat an Honest Man; First Love; Stagecoach; Ex-Champ; Our Neighbors, the Carters; Mutiny on the Blackhawk; Hawaiian Nights; Million Dollar Legs; The Star Maker; Each Dawn I Die; Jeepers Creepers; Money to Burn; The Day the Bookies Wept; Dancing Coed. 1940 The Great McGinty; Sued for Libel; The Blue Bird; Blondie on a Budget; In Old Missouri; Alias the Deacon; Millionaires in Prison; The Lone Wolf Meets a Lady; City for Conquest; Friendly Neighbors; The Golden Fleecing. 1941 The Great Lie; The Lone Wolf Takes a Chance; Repent at Leisure; Tuxedo Junction; The Invisible Woman; Flight from Destiny; The Lone Wolf Keeps a Date; Where Did You Get That Girl?; Washington Melodrama; She Knew All the Answers; Accent on Love; Design for Scandal; Midnight Angel; Remember That Day; In the Navy; Hold That Ghost. 1942 The Night before the Divorce; Sleepytime Gal; Rings on her Fingers; The Great Man's Lady; Shepherd of the Ozarks; Call of the Canyon; Hello, Annapolis; Counter Espionage; The Hard Way; The Great Gildersleeve; Pacific Blackout. 1943 Sherlock Holmes in Washington; Hoosier Holiday; Here Comes Elmer; He Hired the Boss; The Youngest Profession; This Land Is Mine; I Dood It. 1944 Adventures of Mark Twain; Good Night, Sweetheart; Something for the Boys; Song of Nevada; Wilson; Cover Girl; The Great Moment; In Society; Ever since Venus. 1945 Brewster's Millions; Bring on the Girls; The Blonde from Brooklyn; Don Juan Quilligan; Col. Effingham's Raid; Lady on a Train; The Gay Senorita; Thrill of a Romance; Song of the Prairie; West of the Pecos. 1946 Dangerous Business; One More Tomorrow; She Wrote the Book; Three Little Girls in Blue; Two Sisters from Boston; Without Reservations. 1947 The Secret Life of Walter Mitty; Black Gold; The Unfinished Dance; It Had to Be You; The Farmer's Daughter; Welcome Stranger; Mourning Becomes Electra; Son of Rusty. 1948 King of Gamblers; Up in Central Park; Miraculous Journey. 1949 Stagecoach Kid; Manhattan Angel; Rim of the Canyon; Rusty Saves a Life; Square Dance Jubilee; Tell It to the Judge; Blondie's Secret. 1950 Bright Leaf; Bandit Queen; Belle of Old Mexico; Chain Gang; Federal Agent at Large; Girls' School; One Too Many. 1951 Belle Le Grand; Texas Carnival; Whirlwind. 1952 Carson City; One Big Affair; Night Stage to Galveston; Skirts Ahoy!; The Wac from Walla Walla. 1957 Affair in Reno.

HALLARD, C. M.
Born: 1866, England. Died: Apr. 1942, Surrey, England. Screen and stage actor. Entered films in 1917.

Appeared in: 1930 Two Worlds. 1931 Almost a Honeymoon; The W Plan; The Battle of Gallipoli. 1935 Jubilee Cavalcade; Moscow Nights; King of the Damned. 1936 Jack of All Trades. 1937 The Live Wire; The Sky's the Limit.

HALL-DAVIS, LILIAN
Died: Oct. 25, 1933, London, England (suicide—gas). Screen actress.

Appeared in: 1929 White Sheik. 1930 The Farmer's Wife. 1933 Volga Volga.

HALLET, AGNES
Born: 1880. Died: Nov. 19, 1954, Hollywood, Calif. Screen actress.

HALLETT, ALBERT
Born: 1870. Died: Apr. 3, 1935, Hollywood, Calif. Screen and stage actor.

Appeared in: 1924 The Passing of Wolf McLean. 1925 The Gold Hunters. 1926 The Haunted Range; Midnight Faces.

HALLIDAY, GARDNER
Born: 1910. Died: Sept. 6, 1966, Hollywood, Calif.(suicide due to cancer). Screen and stage actor. Entered films in 1946.

HALLIDAY, JOHN
Born: Sept. 14, 1880, Brooklyn, N.Y. Died: Oct. 17, 1947, Honolulu, Hawaii (heart ailment). Screen and stage actor.

Appeared in: 1920 The Woman Gives. 1929 East Side Sadie. 1930 Father's Sons; Recaptured Love; Scarlet Pages. 1931 Smart Woman; Consolation Marriage; The Ruling Voice; Millie; Once a Sinner; Captain Applejack; Fifty Million Frenchmen; The Spy; Transatlantic. 1932 Men of Chance; Man Called Back; The Impatient Maiden; The Age of Consent; Weekends Only; Bird of Paradise. 1933 Perfect Understanding; Terror Abroad; Bed of Roses; The House on 56th Street; The Woman Accused. 1934 Return of the Terror; Housewife; A Woman's Man; Happiness Ahead; Registered Nurse; The Witching Hour; Desirable; Finishing School. 1935 Mystery Woman; The Dark Angel; The Melody Lingers On; Peter Ibbetson. 1936 Desire; Fatal Lady; Three Cheers for Love; Hollywood Boulevard. 1938 Arsen Lupin Returns; Blockade; That Certain Age. 1939 The Light That Failed; Hotel for Women; Intermezzo: A Love Story. 1940 The Philadelphia Story. 1941 Lydia; Escape to Glory.

HALLIGAN, WILLIAM
Born: Mar. 29, 1884. Died: Jan. 28, 1957, Woodland Hills, Calif. Screen, stage actor, and screen writer.

Appeared in: 1919 The Wonder Man (film debut). 1929 Somewhere in Jersey (short). 1930 Follow the Leader; At Your Service (short); The Darling Brute (short). 1931 The Public Defender. 1932 Lady and Gent; The Crooner; Blessed Event; Babykins (short). 1940 You Can't Fool Your Wife; Hired Wife; 'Til We Meet Again; Boom Town; Third Finger, Left Hand. 1941 Gangs Incorporated. 1942 Life Begins at Eight-Thirty; Moontide; Lucky Jordan; The Powers Girl. 1943 He's My Guy; Coney Island; Dixie; The Leopard Man; Mission to Moscow. 1944 Show Business; Minstrel Man; Great Mike; The Hairy Ape. 1945 Within These Walls; The Spider; Dick Tracy. 1946 If I'm Lucky; Til' the Clouds Roll By. 1947 The Shocking Miss Pilgrim.

HALLOR, EDITH
Born: 1896, Washington, D.C. Died: May 21, 1971, Newport Beach, Calif. Screen and stage actress. Married to screen actor/film director John Francis Dillon (dec. 1934).

Appeared in: 1921 The Inside of the Cup; Just outside the Door. 1922 Human Hearts. 1944 Wilson. 1945 A Tree Grows in Brooklyn.

HALLOR, RAY
Born: Jan. 14, 1900, Washington, D.C. Died: Apr. 16, 1944, near Palm Springs, Calif.(auto crash). Screen and stage actor.

Appeared in: 1923 The Courtship of Miles Standish; The Dangerous Maid. 1924 The Circus Cowboy; Izez from Hollywood. 1925 The Last Edition; Learning to Love; Sally; The Storm Breaker. 1926 The High Flyer; It Must Be Love; Red Dice. 1927 The Trail of '98; Driven from Home; Man Crazy; Quarantined Rivals; Tongues of Scandal. 1928 The Haunted Ship; The Avenging Shadow; Black Butterflies; The Black Pearl; Green Grass Widows; Manhattan Knights; Nameless Men; Tropical Nights. 1929 Thundergod; Circumstantial Evidence; Fast Life; In Old California; Noisy Neighbors. 1930 The Truth about Youth.

HALLS, ETHEL MAY
Born: 1882. Died: Sept. 16, 1967, Hollywood, Calif. Screen, stage, and television actress. Entered films with Biograph.

Appeared in: 1939 Our Leading Citizen. 1940 Thou Shalt Not Kill. 1951 Katie Did It.

HALTON, CHARLES
Born: 1876. Died: Apr. 16, 1959, Los Angeles, Calif.(hepatitis). Screen and stage actor.

Appeared in: 1931 The Strange Case (short). 1936 Sing Me a Love Song; Dodsworth; Golddiggers of 1937; Stolen Holiday; Come and Get It; More Than a Secretary. 1937 The Black Legion; Penrod and Sam; Ready, Willing and Able; Talent Scout; Pick a Star; The Prisoner of Zenda; Woman Chases Man; Dead End; Blossoms on Broadway; Partners in Crime. 1938 Trouble at Midnight; Penitentiary; Bluebeard's Eighth Wife; Penrod and His Twin Brother; Penrod's Double Trouble; Stolen Heaven; The Saint in New York; Room Service; I'll Give a Million; I Am the Law; A Man to Remember. 1939 News Is Made at Night; Swanee River; They Made Her a Spy; Reno; Indianapolis Speedway; Charlie Chan at Treasure Island; I'm from Missouri; Juarez; Ex-Champ; They Asked For It; Young Mr. Lincoln; Dodge City; Jesse James; Federal Manhunt. 1940 They Drive by Night; The Shop Across the Corner; The Story of Dr. Ehrlich's Magic Bullet; Gangs of Chicago; Young People; Stranger on the Third Floor; The Doctor Takes a Wife; Tugboat Annie Sails Again; Calling All Husbands; Behind the News; Dr. Cyclops; 20 Mule Team; Lillian Russell; The Westerner. 1941 Mr. District Attorney; Mr. and Mrs. Smith; Meet the Chump; A Very Young Lady; Million Dollar Baby; I Was a Prisoner on Devil's Island; Dance Hall; The Smiling Ghost; Three Sons O' Guns; Look Who's Laughing; Unholy Partners; H. M. Pulham, Esq.; Tobacco Road; The Body Disappears. 1942 To Be or Not to Be; Juke Box Jenny; Whispering Ghosts; Priorities on Parade; Across the Pacific; You Can't Escape Forever; Henry Aldrich, Editor; That Other Woman; The Spoilers; In Old California; My Sister Eileen; Captains of the Clouds. 1943 My Kingdom for a Cook; Jitterbugs; Lady Bodyguard; The Private Life of Dr. Paul Joseph Goebbels. 1944 Rationing; Address Unknown; Enemy of Women; The Town Went Wild; Shadows in the Night; Wilson; Up in Arms. 1945 One Exciting Night; She Went to the Races; A Tree Grows in Brooklyn; The Fighting Guardsman; Rhapsody in Blue; Midnight Manhunt; Mama Loves Papa. 1946 Singin' in the Corn; Because of Him; Three Little Girls in Blue; The Best Years of Our Lives. 1947 The Ghost Goes Wild. 1948 Three Godfathers. 1949 The Sickle or the Cross; The Daring Caballero; Hideout. 1950 Stella; Traveling Saleswoman; When Willie Comes Marching Home; Sabotage. 1951 Gasoline Alley. 1952 Carrie. 1953 The Moonlighter; A Slight Case of Larceny. 1956 Friendly Persuasion.

HAMER, FRED B.
Born: 1873. Died: Dec. 30, 1953, Los Angeles, Calif. Screen, stage actor, and film director. Appeared in silents approx. 1910.

HAMID, SWEENEY
Born: approx. 1898, Morocco. Died: Mar. 25, 1968, Baltimore, Md.(lung cancer). Screen, circus, vaudeville actor, and acrobat.

HAMILTON, GEORGE W. "SPIKE"
Born: 1901. Died: Mar. 31, 1957, New York, N.Y. Orchestra leader, song writer, and screen actor.

HAMILTON, GORDON GEORGE
Born: Coytesville, N.J. Died: Jan. 16, 1939, Fort Lee, N.J. (heart attack). Screen and stage actor.

Appeared in: 1914 The Perils of Pauline (serial).

HAMILTON, HALE
Born: Feb. 28, 1880, Ft. Madison, Iowa. Died: May 19, 1942, Los Angeles, Calif.(cerebral hemorrhage). Screen and stage actor. Married to screen actress Grace LaRue (dec. 1956).

Appeared in: 1915 Her Painted Hero. 1918 The Winning of Beatrice. 1919 That's Good. 1923 His Children's Children. 1925 The Manicure Girl. 1926 The Great Gatsby; The Greater Glory; Summer Bachelors; Tin Gods. 1929 Listen, Lady. 1927 Girl in the Rain; The Telephone Girl. 1930 Common Clay; Good Intentions. 1931 Never the Twain Shall Meet; A Tailor-Made Man; Beau Ideal; Dance, Fools, Dance; Drums of Jeopardy; Rebound; The Great Lover; Strangers May Kiss; New Adventures of Get-Rich-Quick Wallingford; Cuban Love Song; The Champ; Paid; Susan Lennox, Her Rise and Fall; Murder at Midnight; Oh! Oh! Cleopatra (short). 1932 A Fool's Advice; Love Affair; Life Begins; Two against the World; Those We Love; Call Her Savage; Most Dangerous Game; Three on a Match; Manhattan Tower; Grand Hotel; The Woman in Room 13; A Successful Calamity. 1933 Employees' Entrance; Billion Dollar Scandal; Reform Girl; Parole Girl; Black Beauty; Strange People; One Man's Journey; Sitting Pretty. 1934 City Park; Big-Hearted Herbert; When Strangers Meet; The Marines Are Coming; Curtain at Eight; The Quitter; Twin Husbands; Heartburn (short); Doctor Monica; The Girl from Missouri. 1935 I Live My Life; After Office Hours;

Grand Old Girl; The Nitwits; Hold 'Em Yale; The Woman in Red; Let 'Em Have It; Calm Yourself; Three Kids and a Queen. 1938 The Adventures of Marco Polo; Meet the Mayor.

HAMILTON, JOHN
Born: 1887. Died: Oct. 15, 1958, Hollywood, Calif.(heart condition). Screen, stage, vaudeville, and television actor.

Appeared in: 1926 Rainbow Riley. 1930 White Cargo; Dangerous Nan McGrew; Heads Up. 1936 Two in a Crowd; The Legion of Terror; A Man Betrayed. 1937 Two Wise Maids; Seventh Heaven; This Is My Affair; Night Club Scandal; Bad Guy; Criminals of the Air. 1938 I Stand Accused; Mr. Moto's Gamble; Over the Wall; Dr. Rhythm; Mr. Wong, Detective. 1939 Rose of Washington Square. 1940 Johnny Apollo; The Great Plane Robbery. 1942 Always in My Heart; To the Shores of Tripoli; In This Our Life; The Big Shot. 1944 The Girl Who Dared; Sheriff of Las Vegas; Meet Miss Bobby Socks; I'm from Arkansas; Crazy Knights. 1945 The Great Flamarion; Army Wives; Circumstantial Evidence. 1946 Wife Wanted; Johnny Comes Flying Home; Home on the Range; Dangerous Business. 1947 Violence; The Beginning or the End. 1948 Song of My Heart. 1949 Law of the Golden West; The Wyoming Bandit; Sheriff of Wichita; Alias the Champ; Bandit King of Texas; Canadian Pacific; The Judge; Pioneer Marshal. 1950 Her Wonderful Lie; Bells of Coronado; Davy Crockett, Indian Scout; The Missourians. 1951 Million Dollar Pursuit. 1952 The Pace That Thrills. 1953 Donovan's Brain; Iron Mountain Trail; Marshal of Cedar Rock. 1954 On the Waterfront; Sitting Bull. 1957 Chicago Confidential. 1958 Outcasts of the City.

HAMILTON, JOHN F.
Born: 1894. Died: July 11, 1967, Paramus, N.J. Screen, stage, vaudeville, and television actor.

Appeared in: 1927 The Masked Menace (serial). 1939 Allegheny Uprising. 1940 The Saint's Double Trouble; Gold Rush Maisie. 1949 The Undercover Man; Prison Warden. 1950 Body Hold; Military Academy.

HAMILTON, KAREN SUE
Born: 1946. Died: Sept. 3, 1969, Hollywood, Calif.(suicide). Screen and television actress.

HAMILTON, LAUREL L.
Died: Dec. 15, 1955, Hollywood, Calif. Screen, stage, and vaudeville actress. Appeared in Sennett comedies.

HAMILTON, LLOYD
Born: Aug. 19, 1891, Oakland, Calif. Died: Jan. 19, 1935, Hollywood, Calif.(following operation for a stomach disorder). Screen, stage actor, screenwriter, and film director. Entered films with Lubin Co. in 1914. Was "Ham" in "Ham and Bud" comedy series (1914-1917). Appeared in "Sunshine" comedies (1918) and in "Mermaid" comedies (1921-1922). Divorced from screen actresses Ethel Floyd and Irene Dalton (dec. 1934).

Appeared in: 1914 Ham, The Piano Mover (short). 1915 Ham at the Garbage Gentlemen's Ball (short). 1923 Hollywood. 1924 His Darker Self; A Self-Made Failure. 1925 the following shorts: Hooked; Half a Hero; King Cotton; Waiting; The Movies; Framed. 1929 The Show of Shows; Tanned Legs; Black Waters. 1931 Are You There? 1932-1933 Universal shorts.

HAMLER, JOHN E.
Born: 1891. Died: Dec. 2, 1969, N.Y. Screen actor, and song and dance man.

HAMLIN, WILLIAM H.
Born: 1885. Died: Sept. 27, 1951, Los Angeles, Calif. Screen actor and stage director. Appeared in silents with Vitagraph.

HAMMERSTEIN, ELAINE
Born: 1897, Philadelphia, Pa. Died: Aug. 13, 1948, near Tijuana, Mexico (auto crash). Screen and stage actress. Daughter of producer Arthur Hammerstein.

Appeared in: 1917 The Argyle Case; The Mad Lover. 1920 Greater Than Fame. 1921 The Daughter Pays; The Miracle of Manhattan; Pleasure Seekers; Poor, Dear Margaret Kirby; The Girl from Nowhere; Remorseless Love; Way of a Maid; Handcuffs and Kisses. 1922 Evidence; Reckless Youth; Why Announce Your Marriage?; Under Oath; One Week of Love. 1923 Souls for Sale; Broadway Gold; Rupert of Hentzau. 1924 Daring Love; The Drums of Jeopardy; The Foolish Virgin; The Midnight Express; One Glorious Night. 1925 The Unwritten Law; After Business Hours; Every Man's Wife; Paint and Powder; Parisian Nights; S.O.S. Perils of the Sea. 1926 The Checkered Flag; Ladies of Leisure.

HAMPDEN, WALTER (Walter Hempden Daughterty)
Born: June 30, 1879, Brooklyn, N.Y. Died: June 11, 1955, Hollywood, Calif.(stroke). Screen, stage, and television actor.

Appeared in: 1915 The Dragon's Claw. 1940 Northwest Mounted Police; The Hunchback of Notre Dame; All This, and Heaven Too. 1941 They Died with Their Boots On. 1942 Reap the Wild Wind. 1944 The Adventures of Mark Twain. 1950 All about Eve. 1951 The First Legion. 1952 Five Fingers. 1953 Treasure of the Golden Condor; Sombrero. 1954 Sabrina. 1955 The Prodigal; Strange Lady in Town; The Silver Chalice. 1956 The Vagabond King.

HAMPER, GENEVIEVE
Born: 1889. Died: Feb. 13, 1971, N.Y. Screen and stage actress. Married to screen actor John Alexander and widow of stage actor Robert Mantell.

Appeared in: 1916 A Wife's Sacrifice. 1923 Under the Red Robe.

HAMPTON, FAITH
Born: 1909. Died: Apr. 1, 1949, Hollywood, Calif.(suffocation due to fire). Screen actress. Entered films during silents.

HAMPTON, LOUISE
Born: 1881, Stockport, England. Died: Feb. 11, 1954, London, England (bronchial trouble). Screen and stage actress.

Appeared in: 1932 Nine Till Six (film debut). 1938 His Lordship Goes to Press. 1939 Goodbye Mr. Chips; The Middle Watch. 1940 Hell's Cargo; Haunted Honeymoon. 1943 The Saint Meets the Tiger. 1946 Bedelia. 1952 Story of Robin Hood and His Merry Men. 1953 Background (aka Edge of Divorce). 1954 The Horse's Mouth. Other British films: The House of Mr. Arrow; That's Just the Way It Was; Ministry of Information films.

HANCOCK, TONY (Anthony Hancock)
Born: May 12, 1924, Birmingham, England. Died: June 25, 1968, Sydney, Australia (overdose of sleeping tablets). Screen actor.

Appeared in: 1955 Orders Is Orders. 1961 Call Me Genius; The Rebel. 1963 The Punch and Judy Man. 1965 Those Magnificent Men in Their Flying Machines. 1966 The Wrong Box.

HANDLEY, TOMMY
Born: 1902, England. Died: Jan. 9, 1949, London, England (cerebral hemorrhage). Screen, radio, and vaudeville actor.

Appeared in: 1930 Elstree Calling. 1938 Two Men in a Box. 1942 It's That Man Again. 1943 Time Flies. 1946 Tom Tom Topia (short).

HANEY, CAROL
Born: 1934. Died: May 5, 1964, Saddle River, N.J.(pneumonia—diabetes). Screen, television actress, and dancer/choreographer.

Appeared in: 1953 Kiss Me, Kate. 1956 Invitation to the Dance. 1957 Pajama Game (film and stage versions).

HANLEY, JIMMY
Born: Oct. 22, 1918, Norwich, Norfolk, England. Died: Jan. 13, 1970, England. Screen, circus, radio, television actor, and writer.

Appeared in: 1933 Red Wagon (film debut, U.S. 1935). 1934 Little Friend. 1935 Boys Will Be Boys; Born for Glory; Transatlantic Tunnel; Brown on Revolution. 1937 Night Ride. 1938 Coming of Age; Housemaster. 1939 There Ain't No Justice. 1940 Gaslight 1942 Salute John Citizen. 1944 For You Alone; Henry V (U.S. 1946). 1945 Acacia Avenue; The Way Ahead. 1946 The Captive Heart. 1947 Murder in Reverse; Master of Bankdam (U.S. 1949). 1948 It Always Rains on Sunday; Holiday Camp. 1949 Facts of Love; It's Hard to Be Good. 1949 to 1952 The "Huggetts" series (including Here Come the Huggetts). 1950 The Blue Lamp. 1951 The Galloping Major. 1952 Angel Street. 1954 The Black Rider. 1956 Satellite in the Sky; The Deep Blue Sea. 1958 Henry V (reissue of 1944 film). Other British films: Forever England; Cotton Queen; Landslide; Kiss the Bride Goodbye; Don't Ever Leave Me; Boys in Brown; Gentle Sex; The Crowthers of Bankdam.

HANLEY, MICHAEL E.
Born: 1858. Died: June 18, 1942, Fort Wayne, Ind.(suicide—gun). Screen actor, film director, and film producer.

HANLEY, WILLIAM B., JR.
Born: 1900. Died: Oct. 2, 1959, Hollywood, Calif.(heart attack). Screen and stage actor. Married to screen actress Madge Kennedy

HANNEFORD, EDWIN POODLES
Born: 1892, Barnsby, Yorkshire, England. Died: Dec. 9, 1967, Kattskill Bay, N.Y. Screen, circus and television actor, and trick horseback rider.

Appeared in: 1928 The Circus Kid. 1935 Our Little Girl; Educational short. 1951 The Golden Horde; When I Grow Up. 1952 Springfield Rifle.

HANOFER, FRANK
Born: 1897, Hungary. Died: Dec. 16, 1955, Newhall, Calif. Screen actor and stuntman.

HANSEN, HANS
Born: 1886, Germany. Died: June 18, 1962, New York, N.Y. Screen and stage actor.

Appeared in: 1945 The House on 92nd Street.

HANSEN, JUANITA
Born: 1897, Des Moines; Iowa. Died: Sept. 26, 1961, Hollywood, Calif.(heart attack). Screen and stage actress. Was a Mack Sennett bathing beauty.

Appeared in: 1916 His Pride and Shame; Secret of the Submarine (serial). 1917 Glory; A Royal Rogue; Dangers of a Bride; Whose Baby?; A Clever Dummy. 1918 The Brass Bullet (serial). 1919 A Midnight Romance. 1920 The Lost City (serial); The Phantom Foe (serial). 1921 The Yellow Arm (serial). 1922 The Broadway Madonna. 1923 Girl from the West; The Jungle Princess.

HANSON, EINER (aka EINER HANSEN)
Born: June 15, 1899, Stockholm, Sweden. Died: June 3, 1927, Santa Monica, Calif.(auto accident). Screen actor.

Appeared in: 1926 Her Big Night; Into Her Kingdom. 1927 The Lady in Ermine; The Masked Woman; Barbed Wire; Children of Divorce; Fashions for Women; Woman on Trial.

HANSON, LARS
Born: 1887, Sweden. Died: Apr. 8, 1965, Stockholm, Sweden. Screen and stage actor who appeared in U.S. & Swedish films.

Appeared in: 1913 Ingeborg Holm. 1916 Dolken. 1919 Erotikon. 1924 The Atonement of Gosta Berling. 1926 The Scarlet Letter; The Flesh and the Devil. 1927 Captain Salvation; Buttons. 1928 The Divine Woman; The Wind; The Legend of Gosta Berling. 1929 The Informer; In Dalarna and Jerusalem; Homecoming. 1936 Paa Solsidan. 1964 One Minute to Hell (aka Gates of Hell). 1967 491.

HARBAUGH, CARL
Born: 1886. Died: Feb. 26, 1960, Hollywood, Calif. Screen actor, screenwriter, and film director.

Appeared in: 1915 Carmen. 1923 Jazzmania; Lost and Found on a South Sea Island; The Silent Command. 1927 College. 1933 The Devil's Brother. 1955 The Tall Men. 1956 The Revolt of Mamie Stover.

HARBEN, HUBERT
Born: July 12, 1878, London, England. Died: Aug. 24, 1941, London, England. Screen and stage actor.

Appeared in: 1931 The Battle of Gallipoli. 1933 Fires of Fate. 1934 The Secret of the Loch. 1935 Scrooge. 1936 Living Dangerously; Dish on Our Rights; For Valour. 1937 Victoria the Great. 1940 Suicide Legion; Mozart.

HARBOROUGH, WILLIAM
Born: 1899. Died: Oct. 1924, Yuma, Ariz.(drowned during filming of a western movie). Screen actor and stuntman.

HARDING, GILBERT
Born: June 5, 1907, Hereford, England. Died: Nov. 16, 1960, London, England. Screen and television actor.

Appeared in: 1956 Simon and Laura. 1957 An Alligator Named Daisy; As Long As They're Happy. 1960 Expresso Bongo.

HARDING, LYN (David Llewellyn Harding)
Born: Oct. 12, 1867, Newport, Wales. Died: Dec. 26, 1952, London, England. Screen and stage actor.

Appeared in: 1920 The Barton Mystery. 1922 When Knighthood Was in Flower. 1924 Yolanda. 1930 Sleeping Partners. 1931 The Speckled Band. 1934 The Man Who Changed His Name; The Lash; The Constant Nymph; Wild Boy. 1935 The Triumph of Sherlock Holmes; Escape Me Never; An Old Spanish Custom (aka The Invaders). 1936 Spy of Napoleon (U.S. 1939); The Man Who Lived Again. 1937 Fire over England; Knight without Armor; Les

Perles de la Couronne (Pearls of the Crown); Silver Blaze; The Mutiny of the Elsinore. 1939 Goodbye Mr. Chips. 1940 Missing People. 1941 The Prime Minister.

HARDTMUTH, PAUL

Born: 1889, Germany. Died: Feb. 5, 1962, London, England (fall from 2nd floor of apartment building). Screen and television actor.

Appeared in: 1949 The Lost People. 1951 Highly Dangerous; The Wonder Kid. 1953 Desperate Moment; Shadow Man. 1955 Assignment Redhead; The Atomic Man. 1956 The Gamma People. 1957 The Curse of Frankenstein. 1961 Doctor Blood's Coffin; The Guns of Navarone.

HARDWICKE, SIR CEDRIC (Cecil Webster Hardwicke)

Born: Feb. 19, 1893, Stourbridge, England. Died: Aug. 6, 1964, New York, N.Y.(lung ailment). Screen, stage, television actor, film director, and film producer. Father of screen actor Edward Hardwicke.

Appeared in: 1931 Dreyfus (film debut). 1933 Rose Express; The Ghoul. 1934 Orders Is Orders; The Lady Is Willing; Nell Gwyn; King of Paris; Jew Seuss. 1935 Becky Sharp; Les Miserables; Bella Donna. 1936 Things to Come; Nine Days a Queen; Peg of Old Drury; Tudor Rose. 1937 The Green Light; King Solomon's Mines. 1939 On Borrowed Time; Stanley and Livingstone; The Hunchback of Notre Dame. 1940 The Invisible Man Returns; Tom Brown's School Days; The Howards of Virginia; Victory. 1941 Suspicion; Sundown; Laburnum Grove. 1942 Valley of the Sun; The Ghost of Frankenstein; Invisible Agent; Commandos Strike at Dawn. 1943 The Moon Is Down; Forever and a Day; The Cross of Lorraine. 1944 The Lodger; Wilson; The Keys of the Kingdom; Wing and a Prayer. 1945 The Picture of Dorian Gray. 1946 Mrs. Loring's Secret; Sentimental Journey; Tragic Symphony; Beware of Pity. 1947 The Imperfect Lady; Ivy; Song of My Heart; Lured; Nicholas Nickleby; Tycoon; A Woman's Vengeance. 1948 Personal Column; I Remember Mama; Rope. 1949 Now Barabbas Was a Robber; A Connecticut Yankee in King Arthur's Court. 1950 The White Tower; The Winslow Boy. 1951 Mr. Imperium; The Desert Fox. 1952 The Green Glove; Caribbean. 1953 Salome; Botany Bay; The War of the Worlds (narr.). 1954 Bait (prologue). 1955 Diane; Helen of Troy. 1956 The Vagabond King; The Power and the Prize; The Ten Commandments; Around the World in 80 Days; Richard III; Gaby. 1957 The Story of Mankind; Baby Face Nelson. 1962 Five Weeks in a Balloon. 1964 The Pumpkin Eater; The Magic Fountain.

HARDY, OLIVER (Oliver Norvell Hardy)

Born: Jan. 18, 1892, Atlanta, Ga. Died: Aug. 7, 1957, North Hollywood, Calif.(paralytic stroke). Screen, stage, minstrel actor, and film director. Was partner in comedy team of "Laurel and Hardy." See Stan Laurel for films they appeared in together.

Appeared in the following films without Laurel: 1913 Outwitting Dad (film debut). 1915 "Pokes and Jabbs" series; The Paperhanger's Helper; Spaghetti a la Mode; Charley's Aunt; Artists and Models; The Tramps; Mother's Child. 1916 Back Stage; The Hero; The Millionaire; Dough Nuts; The Scholar; The Try Out; Ups and Downs; This Way out; Chickens; Frenzied Finance; Busted Hearts. 1916-18 "Plump and Runt" series. 1917 He Winked and Won. 1918 The Villain; The Artist; King Solomon; The Chief Cook; Lucky Dog. 1920 The "Fly Cop" series. 1921 The Sawmill; Scars and Stripes; Kid Speed. 1922 Fortune's Mask; Little Wildcat. 1923 The Three Ages; Be Your Age; One Stolen Night. 1924 The Girl in the Limousine. 1925 The Wizard of Oz. 1926 Stop, Look and Listen; The Gentle Cyclone. 1927 No Man's Law. 1939 Zenobia; Elephants Never Forget. 1949 The Fighting Kentuckian; Riding High.

HARDY, SAM

Born: 1883, New Haven, Conn. Died: Oct. 16, 1935, Los Angeles, Calif.(intestinal problems). Screen, stage actor, and screenwriter. Entered films in 1917.

Appeared in: 1917 The Savage. 1918 A Woman's Experience. 1921 Get-Rich-Quick Wallingford. 1923 Little Old New York; Mighty Lak a Rose. 1925 The Half-Way Girl; When Love Grows Cold. 1926 Bluebeard's Seven Wives; The Great Deception; The Prince of Tempters; The Savage; Great Deception. 1927 High Hat; The Perfect Sap; Orchids and Ermine; Broadway Nights; The Life of Riley; A Texas Steer. 1928 Burning up Broadway; Turn Back the Hours; The Big Noise; Diamond Handcuffs; The Butter and Egg Man; The Night Bird; Outcast; Give and Take. 1929 The Rainbow Man; On with the Show; Big News; Acquitted; Mexicali Rose; A Man's Man; Fast Company. 1930 Burning up; True to the Navy; Reno; Song of the West; The Floradora Girl; Borrowed Wives. 1931 The Millionaire; June Moon; Annabelle's

Affairs; The Magnificent Lie; The Miracle Woman; Peach O'Reno. 1932 The Dark Horse; Make Me a Star; The Phantom of Crestwood. 1933 Face in the Sky; King Kong; Goldie Gets Along; Three-Cornered Moon; The Big Brain; One Sunday Afternoon; Ann Vickers. 1934 Curtain at Eight; Little Miss Marker; I Give My Love; The Gay Bride; Transatlantic Merry-Go-Round; Night Alarm; Along Came Sally. 1935 Hooray for Love; Break of Hearts; Powdersmoke Range.

HARE, F. LUMSDEN

Born: Oct. 17, 1874, Cashel, Ireland. Died: Aug. 28, 1964, Hollywood, Calif. Screen, stage actor, and stage director. Entered films in 1916.

Appeared in: 1919 The Avalanche. 1921 The Education of Elizabeth. 1922 Sherlock Holmes. 1923 On the Banks of the Wabash. 1924 Second Youth. 1925 One Way Street. 1929 Fugitives; The Black Watch; Girls Gone Wild; Salute; The Sky Hawk. 1930 Crazy That Way; So This Is London; Scotland Yard. 1931 Under Suspicion; Always Goodbye; Svengali; Charlie Chan Carries On; The Road to Singapore; Arrowsmith. 1932 The Silent Witness; The Crusader. 1933 International House; College Humor. 1934 The World Moves On; Outcast Lady; His Double Life; Man of Two Worlds; The Little Minister; The House of Rothschild; Black Moon. 1935 Lady Tubbs; The Great Impersonation; Professional Soldier; Clive of India; Follies Bergere; Lives of a Bengal Lancer; The Crusades; Cardinal Richelieu; She; Freckles; The Three Musketeers; The Bishop Misbehaves. 1936 The Charge of the Light Brigade; Under Two Flags; Lloyds of London; The Princess Comes Across; The Last of the Mohicans. 1937 The Last of Mrs. Cheyney; The Life of Emile Zola; Life Begins with Love. 1940 Northwest Passage; Rebecca; A Dispatch from Reuters. 1941 Shadows on the Stairs; Dr. Jekyll and Mr. Hyde; The Blonde from Singapore; Suspicion; Passage from Hong Kong; Hudson's Bay. 1942 London Blackout Murders; The Gorilla Man. 1943 Mission to Moscow; Holy Matrimony; Jack London; Forever and a Day. 1944 Passport to Destiny; The Canterville Ghost; The Lodger. 1945 The Keys of the Kingdom; Love Letters; Valley of Decision. 1946 Three Strangers. 1947 Private Affairs of Bel Ami; The Swordsman; The Exile. 1948 Mr. Peabody and the Mermaid; Hills of Rome. 1949 That Forsythe Woman; Fighting O'Flynn; Challenge to Lassie. 1950 Fortunes of Captain Blood. 1951 David and Bathsheba; The Lady and the Bandit; The Desert Fox. 1952 And Now Tomorrow; Diplomatic Courier; My Cousin Rachel. 1953 Julius Caesar; Young Bess. 1957 Johnny Tremain. 1959 Count Your Blessings; The Oregon Trail; The Four Skulls of Jonathan Drake.

HARKER, GORDON

Born: Aug. 7, 1885, London, England. Died: Mar. 2, 1967, London, England. Screen, stage, and radio actor.

Appeared in: 1927 The Ring (film debut); The Crooked Billet. 1929 The Wrecker. 1930 The Farmer's Wife; Escape. 1931 The W Plan; The Calendar. 1932 Condemned to Death; The Ringer; Whiteface; Love on Wheels; Rome Express. 1933 The Man They Couldn't Arrest; The Luck Number; Britannia of Billingsgate; Friday the Thirteenth. 1934 My Old Dutch; Road-House; Dirty Work; Criminal at Large; Squibs. 1935 The Lad; Admirals All; Wolf's Clothing; The Phantom Light; Boys Will Be Boys; Hyde Park Corner. 1936 The Amateur Gentleman; Two's Company; Millions; Beauty and the Barge. 1937 The Frog. 1938 The Return of the Frog; Blondes for Danger; No Parking; Lightning Conductor. 1939 Inspector Hornleigh. 1941 Inspector Hornleigh Goes to It; Saloon Bar; Once a Crook. 1943 Warn That Man. 1945 Acacia Avenue. 1948 Things Happen at Night. 1949 Facts of Love. 1950 The Taming of Dorothy; Her Favorite Husband; The Second Mate. 1952 Derby Day. 1955 Four against Fate. 1958 Small Hotel. 1960 Left, Right and Center. Other British films: Taxi for Two; Elstree Calling; The Squeaker; The Stronger Sex; Third Time Lucky; The Sport of Kings; Jack O'Lantern; Out of the Clouds.

HARKINS, DIXIE

Born: 1906. Died: Sept. 1, 1963, Jacksonville, Fla. Screen actress.

Appeared in: 1925 Sally, Irene and Mary. 1926 The Temptress. 1927 Resurrection.

HARLAN, KENNETH

Born: July 26, 1895, Boston, Mass. Died: Mar. 6, 1967, Sacramento, Calif.(aneurysm). Screen, stage, and vaudeville actor.

Appeared in: 1917 Betsy's Burglar (film debut); The Flame of the Yukon; Cheerful Givers. 1919 The Hoodlum. 1920 The Penalty; Dangerous Business. 1921 The Barricade; Dawn of the East;

Finders Keepers; Mama's Affair; Lessons in Love; Nobody; Woman's Place. 1922 The Beautiful and Damned; The Toll of the Sea; I Am the Law; Polly of the Follies; The Married Flapper; The World's a Stage; Received Payment; The Primitive Lover; Thorns and Orange Blossoms. 1923 The Virginian; The Broken Wing; April Showers; East Side, West Side; The Girl Who Came Back; Little Church Around the Corner; A Man's Man; Temporary Marriage. 1924 Butterfly; For Another Woman; White Man; Soiled; Two Shall Be Born; The Virgin; The Man without a Heart; On the Stroke of Three; Poisoned Paradise. 1925 Bobbed Hair; The Marriage Whirl; Learning to Love; The Crowded Hour; Drusilla with a Million; The Golden Strain; Ranger of the Big Pines; Re-Creation of Brian Kent. 1926 The Sap; King of the Turf; The Ice Flood; The Fighting Edge; Twinkletoes. 1927 Easy Pickings; Cheating Cheaters; Streets of Shanghai; Stage Kisses. 1928 Willful Youth; United States Smith; Midnight Rose; Code of the Air; Man, Woman and Wife. 1930 Under Montana Skies; Paradise Island. 1931 Air Police; Danger Island (serial); Finger Prints (serial); Women Men Marry. 1932 Widow in Scarlet. 1935 Cappy Ricks Returns; Wanderer of the Wasteland. 1936 Man Hunt; The Walking Dead; Song of the Saddle; The Case of the Velvet Claws; Public Enemy's Wife; China Clipper; Movie Maniacs (short); San Francisco; They Met in a Taxi; Trail Dust; Flying Hostess. 1937 Hideaway Girl; Marked Woman; Wine, Women and Horses; The Shadow Strikes; Renfrew of the Royal Mounted; Paradise Isle; The Mysterious Pilot (serial); Penrod and Sam; Gunsmoke Ranch; Something to Shout about. 1938 Duke of West Point; The Saleslady; Under Western Stars; Blondes at Work; The Little Adventuress; Accidents Will Happen; Pride of the West; Law of the Texan; Sunset Trail; The Headleys at Home; Held for Ransom. 1939 Range War; On Trial; Port of Hate. 1940 Slightly Honorable; Santa Fe Marshal; Murder in the Air; A Little Bit of Heaven; Prairie Schooners. 1941 Pride of the Bowery; Paper Bullets; Dangerous Lady; Secret Evidence; Desperate Cargo; Wide Open Town. 1942 Black Dragon; Fighting Bill Fargo; Klondike Fury; Foreign Agent; The Corpse Vanishes; The Phantom Killer; Deep in the Heart of Texas. 1943 You Can't Beat the Law; Hitler—Dead or Alive; Wild Horse Stampede; The Law Rides Again; Melody Parade; The Underdog.

HARLAN, MACEY
Born: New York, N.Y. Died: June 17, 1923, Saranac Lake, N.Y. Screen and stage actor.

Appeared in: 1920 The Woman and the Puppet. 1921 The Conquest of Canaan; The Plaything of Broadway; Shams of Society; You Find It Everywhere. 1922 Always the Woman; Beyond the Rainbow; The Face in the Fog; Fair Lady; When Knighthood Was in Flower; Without Fear. 1923 Broadway Broke; The Tents of Allah; Bella Donna.

HARLAN, OTIS
Born: Dec. 29, 1865, Zanesville, Ohio. Died: Jan. 20, 1940, Martinsville, Ind.(stroke). Screen, stage, and vaudeville actor.

Appeared in: 1921 Diamonds Adrift; The Foolish Age; The Girl in the Taxi; Keeping up with Lizzie. 1922 The Eternal Flame; Gay and Devilish; Is Matrimony a Failure?; The Ladder Jinx; Right That Failed; Two Kinds of Women; The Understudy; Up and at 'Em; Without Compromise; The World's a Stage. 1923 The Barefoot Boy; The Brass Bottle; Main Street; The Near Lady; Pioneer Trails; The Spider and the Rose; Truxton King; The Victor. 1924 Abraham Lincoln; Captain Blood; The Clean Heart; The Code of the Wilderness; George Washington, Jr.; The Lullaby; Mademoiselle Midnight; One Law for the Woman; Welcome Stranger; The White Sin; Oh, Doctor!. 1925 The Redeeming Sin; Lightnin'; What Happened to Jones?; The Dixie Handicap; Dollar Down; Fine Clothes; How Baxter Butted In; The Limited Mail; 9 3/5 Seconds; The Perfect Clown; Thunder Mountain; Where Was I?. 1926 The Cheerful Fraud; The Midnight Message; The Prince of Pilsen; Three Bad Men; The Unknown Cavalier; Winning the Futurity; The Whole Town's Talking. 1927 Don't Tell the Wife; Down the Stretch; Galloping Fury; The Silent Rider; Silk Stockings; The Student Prince. 1928 Shepherd of the Hills; The Speed Classic; Grip of the Yukon; Good Morning Judge. 1929 Silks and Saddles; Show Boat; Clear the Decks; Broadway; Girl Overboard; His Lucky Day; Barnum Was Right; The Mississippi Gambler. 1930 Take the Heir; Parade of the West; Captain of the Guard; The King of Jazz; Loose Ankles; Dames Ahoy; Embarrassing Moments; Mountain Justice; Parade of the West. 1931 Man to Man; Millie; The Grand Parade; Ex-Rooster; Air Eagles. 1932 Racing Youth; The Big Shot; No Living Witness; Ride Him, Cowboy; That's My Boy; Rider of Death Valley; Pardners; The Hawk. 1933 Women Won't Tell; Telegraph Trail; Laughing at Life; The Sin of Nora Morgan; Marriage on Approval. 1934 I Can't Escape; King Kelly of the U.S.A; The Old-Fashioned Way; Let's Talk It Over; Married in Haste. 1935

Life Returns; Chinatown Squad; Western Frontier; Hitchhike Lady; Diamond Jim; A Midsummer Night's Dream; The Hoosier Schoolmaster. 1936 Can This Be Dixie?. 1937 Western Gold; Snow White and the Seven Dwarfs (voice of "Happy"). 1938 Mr. Boggs Steps Out; Outlaws of Sonora; The Texans.

HARLOW, JEAN (Harlean Carpenter)
Born: Mar. 3, 1911, Kansas City, Mo. Died: June 7, 1937, Los Angeles, Calif.(uremic poisoning). Screen actress. Divorced from screen actor/producer Paul Bern (dec. 1932).

Appeared in: 1928 Moran of the Marines; a Hal Roach short. 1929 The Saturday Night Kid; The Love Parade; Close Harmony; Double Whoopee (short); Bacon Grabbers (short); Liberty (short); The Unkissed Man (short); Weak but Willing (short). 1939 Hell's Angels; New York Nights. 1931 The Secret Six; The Iron Man; The Public Enemy; Goldie; Platinum Blonde; City Lights. 1932 Three Wise Girls; The Beast of the City; Red Headed Woman; City Sentinel; Red Dust. 1933 Hold Your Man; Dinner at Eight; Bombshell. 1934 The Girl from Missouri; Reckless. 1935 China Seas; Riffraff. 1936 Wife vs. Secretary; Libeled Lady; The Man in Possession; Suzy. 1937 Personal Property; Saratoga. 1964 Big Parade of Comedy (documentary). 1968 The Further Perils of Laurel and Hardy (documentary); The Queen (documentary).

HARMER, LILLIAN
Born: 1886. Died: May 15, 1946, Hollywood, Calif. Screen and stage actress.

Appeared in: 1931 She-Wolf; Huckleberry Finn; Smart Woman. 1932 New Morals for Old; Guilty as Hell; No Man of Her Own. 1933 Alice in Wonderland; Jennie Gerhardt; A Shriek in the Night. 1934 Forsaking All Others; Lady by Choice. 1935 Three Kids and a Queen; Romance in Manhattan; Public Hero No. 1; Riffraff. 1936 Don't Get Personal; Little Miss Nobody; Dancing Feet; Fugitive in the Sky; The Great O'Malley; Rainbow on the River.

HARMON, PAT
Born: 1888. Died: Nov. 26, 1958, Riverside, Calif. Screen actor and double for actor Wallace Beery.

Appeared in: 1922 The Firebrand; The Kentucky Derby. 1923 Ruth of the Range (serial); The Eternal Struggle; The Midnight Guest. 1924 American Manners; The Back Trail; The Battling Fool; Behind the Curtain; The Martyr Sex; The Midnight Express; Ridgeway of Montana; The Sawdust Trail; Surging Seas. 1925 Barriers Burned Away; A Fight to the Finish; Fighting Youth; The Freshman; The Lure of the Wild; S.O.S. Perils of the Sea. 1926 The Barrier; Breed of the Sea; College Days; The Cowboy Cop; The Dixie Flyer; The Fighting Edge; Josselyn's Wife; The Phantom Bullet; Sin Cargo; The Unknown Cavalier; Winning the Futurity. 1927 The Bachelor's Baby; The Haunted Ship; Hazardous Valley; Lightning; Snowbound; The Warning. 1928 The Broken Mask; Court-Martial; Homesick; The Sideshow; Waterfront. 1929 Dark Streets; Sal of Singapore; Sunset Pass; Berth Marks (short). 1930 Hell's Angels. 1931 The Gang Buster. 1944 Teen Age. 1953 The Freshman.

HARRIGAN, WILLIAM
Born: Mar. 27, 1894, New York, N.Y. Died: Feb. 1, 1966, New York, N.Y.(following surgery). Screen and stage actor.

Appeared in: 1927 Cabaret. 1929 Nix on Dames. 1930 On the Level; Born Reckless. 1933 Pick Up; The Girl in 419; Disgraced; The Invisible Man. 1935 G-Men; Stranded; Silk Hat Kid; His Family Tree; The Melody Lingers On; Whipsaw. 1936 Frankie and Johnnie. 1937 Over the Goal; Federal Bullets; Exiled to Shanghai. 1938 Hawaii Calls. 1939 Back Door to Heaven. 1947 Desert Fury. 1948 Citizen Saint. 1951 Flying Leathernecks. 1952 Steel Town. 1953 Francis Covers the Big Town. 1954 Roogie's Bump. 1957 Street of Sinners.

HARRIS, AVERELL
Died: Sept. 25, 1966, New York, N.Y. Screen and stage actor.

Appeared in: 1929 Her New Chauffeur (short). 1931 Secrets of a Secretary; His Woman.

HARRIS, ELSIE
Born: 1892. Died: May 17, 1953, Hollywood, Calif. Screen actress.

HARRIS, JOSEPH
Born: 1870. Died: June 11, 1953, Hollywood, Calif. Screen and stage actor.

Appeared in: 1915 Oh, Daddy. 1921 Freeze-Out; Red Courage; Sure Fire; The Wallop. 1922 The Bearcat; For Big Stakes; Pardon My Nerve; The Loaded Door. 1923 Canyon of the Fools; Crashin' Thru.

HARRIS, MILDRED
Born: Nov. 29, 1901, Cheyenne, Wyo. Died: July 20, 1944, Los Angeles, Calif.(pneumonia after surgery). Screen, stage, burlesque, and vaudeville actress. Entered films at the age of nine. Divorced from screen actor Charles Chaplin.

Appeared in: 1917 Price of a Good Time. 1918 For Husbands Only; Borrowed Clothes. 1921 Old Dad; Habit; A Prince There Was; Fool's Paradise. 1922 The First Woman. 1923 The Fog; The Daring Years. 1924 One Law for the Women; Unmarried Wives; By Divine Right; The Desert Hawk; In Fast Company; The Shadow of the East; Soiled; Stepping Lively; Traffic in Hearts. 1925 Flaming Love; My Neighbor's Wife; Beyond the Border; The Dressmaker from Paris; Easy Money; Super Speed; The Unknown Lover; The Fighting Cub; Frivolous Sal; Iron Man; A Man of Iron; Private Affairs. 1926 The Cruise of the Jasper B; Dangerous Traffic; The Isle of Retribution; The Mystery Club; The Self Starter; The Wolf Hunters. 1927 The Adventurous Soul; Burning Gold; The Girl from Rio; Husband Hunters; One Hour of Love; Out of the Past; Rose of the Bowery; She's My Baby; The Show Girl; The Swell-Head; Wandering Girls; Wolves of the Air. 1928 Lingerie; Melody of Love; Heart of a Follies Girl; Power of the Press; Hearts of Men; Last Lap; The Speed Classic. 1929 Side Street; Sea Fury. 1930 No, No Nanette; Ranch House Blues; The Melody Man. 1931 Night Nurse. 1935 Lady Tubbs; Never Too Late. 1936 Movie Maniacs (short). 1944 Here Comes the Waves.

HARRIS, WADSWORTH
Born: 1865, Calais, Maine. Died: Dec. 1942, Los Angeles, Calif. Screen and stage actor.

Appeared in: 1920 The Dragon's Net (serial). 1921 Rich Girl, Poor Girl. 1922 The Call of Home.

HARRISON, CAREY (Capt. Carey Harrison Reppeteau)
Born: 1890. Died: Mar. 25, 1957, Los Angeles, Calif. Screen actor.

Appeared in: 1929 Married in Hollywood. 1936 Pepper. 1938 The Buccaneer.

HARRON, BOBBY (Robert Harron)
Died: Sept. 6, 1920, New York, N.Y.(gunshot—accident). Screen actor. Brother of screen actress Tish Harron (dec. 1920) and screen actor John Harron (dec. 1939).

Appeared in: 1909 Sweet Revenge. 1910 Ramona; In the Season of Buds. 1911 Enoch Arden, Part I; The White Rose of the Wilds; The Last Drop of Water; Bobby, the Coward; The Unveiling; Billy's Strategem. 1912 Fate's Interception; A Pueblo Legend; The Sands of Dee; An Unseen Enemy; Home Folks; Friends; So Near, Yet So Far; The Musketeers of Pig Alley; Brutality; The New York Hat; The Massacre; My Hero; Oil and Water; The Burglar's Dilemma; A Cry for Help; Fate; The Tender Hearted Boy; Man's Genesis. 1913 Judith of Bethulia; Love in an Apartment Hotel; Broken Ways; The Sheriff's Baby; A Misunderstood Boy; The Little Tease; His Mother's Son; The Yaqui Cur; A Timely Interception; Death's Marathon; Her Mother's Oath; The Reformers; The Battle of Elderberry Gulch; In Prehistoric Days. 1914 Home Sweet Home. 1915 Birth of a Nation; The Escape. 1916 Intolerance; The Wild Girl of the Sierras; The Marriage of Molly O; Fighting Blood. 1917 The Bad Boy; The Great Love. 1918 Hearts of the World. 1919 The Greatest Thing in Life; A Romance of Happy Valley; The Mother and the Law; The Girl Who Stayed at Home; True Heart Susie. 1920 Everybody's Sweetheart; The Greatest Question. 1921 Coincidence; Darling Mine; The Rebel of Kitty Beale.

HARRON, JOHN
Born: Mar. 31, 1903, N.Y. Died: Nov. 24, 1939, Seattle, Wash. Screen actor. Married to screen actress Betty Egan. Brother of screen actor Bobby Harron (dec. 1920) and screen actress Tessie Harron (dec. 1920).

Appeared in: 1921 Through the Back Door (film debut); The Grim Comedian; The Fox. 1922 The Five Dollar Baby; Love in the Dark; Penrod; The Ragged Heiress. 1923 Dulcy; The Gold Diggers; The Supreme Test; The Westbound Limited. 1924 Behind the Curtain; The Fire Patrol; The Painted Flapper; What Shall I Do?. 1925 Learning to Love; Old Shoes; Below the Line; My Wife and I; Satan in Sables; The Wife Who Wasn't Wanted; The Woman Hater. 1926 Bride of the Storm; The Boy Friend; The False Alarm; The Gilded Highway; Hell-Bent for Heaven; The Little Irish Girl; The Night Cry; Rose of the Tenements. 1927 Once and Forever; Silk Stockings; Closed Gates; Love Makes 'Em Wild; Naughty; Night Life. 1928 Finders Keepers; Green Grass Widows; Their Hour. 1929 Man in Hobbles; Street Girl. 1930 The Czar of Broadway; Big Boy. 1931 Laugh and Get Rich;

The Last of the Tongs. 1932 White Zombie; Beauty Parlor. 1933 Sister to Judas; Midnight Warning. 1934 Stolen Sweets; City Park; Murder in the Private Car. 1935 Symphony of Living. 1937 That Girl from Paris; Without Warning; The Missing Witness; Talent Scout. 1938 Torchy Gets Her Man; A Slight Case of Murder; Torchy Blane in Panama; The Invisible Menace. 1939 Secret Service of the Air; The Cowboy Quarterback; Indianapolis Speedway.

HARRON, TESSIE
Died: 1920, N.Y.(Spanish influenza). Screen actress. Sister of screen actors Bobby (dec. 1920) and John Harron (dec. 1939).

HART, ALBERT
Born: 1874, Liverpool, England. Died: Jan. 10, 1940, Hollywood, Calif. Screen and stage actor.

Appeared in: 1921 Cotton and Cattle; A Cowboy Ace; Diane of Star Hollow; Flowing Gold; Out of the Clouds; Doubling for Romeo; The Range Pirate; Rustlers of the Night; The Trail to Red Dog; The White Masks. 1922 Angel Citizens; Cross Roads; The Girl Who Ran Wild; Gold Grabbers; So This Is Arizona; Trail's End; The Hidden Woman. 1923 Can a Woman Love Twice; Spawn of the Desert; Crooked Alley; Kindled Courage; Shadows of the North; The Sunshine Trail. 1924 The Breathless Moment; Excitement. 1925 The Pony Express; The Man without a Country. 1926 Blind Trail; Forlorn River; The Outlaw Express. 1927 The Fire Fighters (serial); The Ridin' Rowdy; The Devil's Twin; Blake of Scotland Yard (serial); The Long Loop of the Pecos; The Man from Hardpan; The Mysterious Rider. 1928 The Ballyhoo Buster; The Boss of Rustler's Roost; Mother Knows Best; Honor Bound. 1929 Making the Grade; .45 Calibre War; The Diamond Master (serial). 1931 An American Tragedy. 1933 Big Executive. 1934 Home on the Range.

HART, BILLY (William Lenhart)
Born: 1864. Died: June 18, 1942, Los Angeles, Calif. Screen, stage, burlesque, and vaudeville actor. Appeared in vaudeville as part of "Billy and Marie Hart" team.

HART, JAMES T.
Born: 1868. Died: Aug. 12, 1926, Los Angeles, Calif.(stroke). Screen actor.

HART, NEAL (Cornelius A. Hart, Jr.)
Born: 1879, Richmond, N.Y. Died: Apr. 2, 1949, Woodland Hills, Calif. Screen actor and film director. Entered films in 1914.

Appeared in: 1916 Liberty, A Daughter of the USA (serial). 1919 The Wolf and His Mate (serial). 1921 South of Northern Lights; Danger Valley; Tangled Trails; Black Sheep; God's Gold. 1922 The Kingfisher's Roost; Rangeland; Lure of Gold; The Heart of a Texan; Butterfly Range; Table Top Ranch; West of the Pecos. 1923 The Secret of the Pueblo; Below the Rio Grande; The Devil's Bowl; Salty Saunders; The Fighting Strain; The Forbidden Range. 1924 The Left Hand Brand; Tucker's Top Hand; Branded a Thief; Lawless Men; Safe Guarded; The Valley of Vanishing Men. 1925 The Verdict of the Desert. 1927 Scarlet Brand(serial). 1930 Trigger Tricks. 1931 Wild Horse. 1932 Law and Order. 1939 The Renegade Ranger.

HART, RICHARD
Born: 1916, Providence, R.I. Died: Jan. 2, 1951, New York, N.Y. (heart attack). Screen, stage, and television actor.

Appeared in: 1947 Desire Me; Green Dolphin Street. 1948 B. F.'s Daughter. 1949 The Black Book; Reign of Terror.

HART, TEDDY
Born: 1897. Died: Feb. 17, 1971, Los Angeles, Calif. Screen, stage, and television actor. Brother of lyricist Lorenz Hart (dec.). Won Screen Actors Guild Award for Best Supporting Actor in 1936 for Three Men on a Horse.

Appeared in: 1932 Million Dollar Legs. 1933 Diplomaniacs. 1936 Three Men on a Horse (film and stage versions); After the Thin Man. 1937 Ready, Willing and Able; That Man's Here Again; Hotel Haywire; Marry the Girl; Talent Scout; The Footloose Heiress. 1941 You're the One. 1942 My Favorite Spy. 1946 Lady Luck. 1951 Ma and Pa Kettle Back on the Farm; The Fat Man. 1952 Ma and Pa Kettle at the Fair; A Girl in Every Port. 1953 Ma and Pa Kettle on Vacation. 1955 Ma and Pa Kettle at Waikiki. 1965 Mickey One.

HART, WILLIAM S. (William Surrey Hart)
Born: Dec. 6, 1862, Newburgh, N.Y. Died: June 23, 1946, Los Angeles, Calif.(stroke). Screen, stage actor, writer, and film director.

Appeared in: 1913 The Fugitive. 1914 His Hour of Manhood; The Bargain; Jim Cameron's Wife; The Passing of Two-Gun Hicks; The Scourge of the Desert. 1915 On the Night Stage; Pinto Ben; The Grudge; In the Sagebrush Country; The Man from Nowhere; Bad Buck of Santa Ynez; The Sheriff's Streak of Yellow; Mr. Silent Haskins; The Taking of Luke McVane; The Ruse; Cash Parrish's Pal; The Conversion of Frosty Blake; The Rough Neck; Keno Bates; Liar; The Disciple; The Darkening Trail; A Knight of the Trail; The Tool of Providence; Grit; The Golden Claw; Between Men. 1916 The Last Act; Hell's Hinges; The Primal Lure; The Aryan; The Sheriff; The Captive God; The Apostle of Vengeance; The Patriot; The Dawn Maker; The Return of Draw Egan; The Devil's Double; Truthful Tolliver. 1917 The Gun Fighter; Square Deal Man; The Desert Man; Wolf Diary; The Cold Deck; The Narrow Trail; The Silent Man; The Last Ace. 1918 Wolves of the Rail; Blue Blazes Rawden; Tiger Man; Shark Monroe; Riddle Gawne; The Border Wireless; Branding Broadway; The Toll Gate; Selfish Yates; War Relief; John Petticoats. 1919 Breed of Men; The Poppy Girl's Husband; The Money Corral; Square Deal Sanderson; Wagon Tracks. 1920 Sand!; The Toll Gate; The Cradle of Courage; The Testing Block. 1921 O'Malley of the Mounted; The Whistle; Three Word Brand; White Oak. 1922 The Covered Wagon; Travelin' On. 1923 Wild Bill Hickock; Hollywood; The Spoilers. 1924 Singer Jim McKee; Grit (and 1915 version). 1925 Tumbleweeds. 1928 Show People. 1939 Tumbleweeds (also appeared in 1925 version and did the prologue for the 1939 version). 1943 One Foot in Heaven; The Silent Man (1917 footage). 1963 The Great Chase (documentary).

HART, WILLIAM V. "POP"
Born: 1867. Died: Oct. 1925, New York, N.Y. Screen and vaudeville actor.

HARTE, BETTY (Daisy Mae Light)
Born: 1883. Died: Jan. 3, 1965, Sunland, Calif. Screen actress.

Appeared in: 1908 The Roman. 1914 The Pride of Jennico. 1922 Eternal Peace.

HARTFORD, DAVID
Born: Jan. 11, 1876, Ontonian, Mich. Died: Oct. 29, 1932, Hollywood, Calif.(heart attack). Screen, stage actor, film, stage director, and film and stage producer.

Appeared in: 1926 Dame Chance. 1930 Rough Romance.

HARTLEY, CHARLES
Born: 1852. Died: Oct. 13, 1930, Fort Lee, N.J.(complication of diseases). Screen and stage actor.

Appeared in: 1919 Prunella. 1921 The Conquest of Canaan.

HARTMAN, AGNES A.
Born: 1860, Sweden. Died: Dec. 22, 1932, Los Angeles, Calif. Screen actress. Mother of screen actress Gretchen Hartman.

HARTMAN, GRACE (Grace Barrett)
Born: 1907. Died: Aug. 8, 1955, Van Nuys, Calif.(cancer). Screen, stage, and television actress. Divorced from screen actor Paul Hartman.

Appeared in: 1937 45 Fathers. 1941 Sunny. 1944 Higher and Higher.

HARTMAN, JONATHAN WILLIAM "POP"
Born: 1872, Louisville, Ky. Died: Oct. 19, 1965, Tampa, Fla. Screen, stage, and vaudeville actor.

HARVEY, DON C.
Born: 1912. Died: Apr. 24, 1963, Hollywood, Calif.(heart attack). Screen, stage, radio, and television actor.

Appeared in: 1949 Angels in Disguise; The Mutineers; Rimfire; Son of a Badman. 1950 Chain Gang; Forbidden Jungle; The Fighting Stallion; Trail of the Rustlers; The Girl from San Lorenzo; Gunmen of Abilene; Hoedown; Joe Palooka in the Triple Cross; The Lost Volcano. 1951 Night Riders of Montana; Fort Worth; Northwest Territory; According to Mrs. Hoyle; Hurricane Island. 1952 The Old West; Prince of Pirates; A Yank in Indo-China. 1954 Golden Idol; Pushover; Violent Men. 1955 Apache Ambush; Wyoming Renegades; Creature with the Atom Brain; Women's Prison. 1956 Flagpole Sitters (short); Blackjack Ketchum Desperado; Blazing the Overland Trail (serial); Jubal; Picnic; The Werewolf. 1957 Beginning of the End; No Time to Be Young. 1958 Buchanan Rides Alone. 1959 Gunmen from Laredo. 1962 The Wild Westerners. 1963 It's a Mad, Mad, Mad, Mad World.

HARVEY, FORRESTER
Born: 1880, County Cork, Ireland. Died: Dec. 14, 1945, Laguna Beach, Calif.(stroke). Screen and stage actor.

Appeared in: 1929 The White Sheik. 1931 Devotion; A Tailor-Made Man; The Man in Possession; Guilty Hands. 1932 Smilin' Through; Red Dust; Kongo; Young Onion (short); Tarzan the Ape Man; Shanghai Express; Sky Devils; But the Flesh Is Weak; The Wet Parade; Mystery Ranch. 1933 Destination Unknown; The Eagle and the Hawk; Midnight Club; The Invisible Man. 1934 The Painted Veil; Menace; Limelight Blues; Great Expectations; Forsaking All Others; The Mystery of Mr. X; Tarzan and His Mate; Man of Two Worlds; Broadway Bill. 1935 The Best Man Wins; The Woman in Red; Captain Blood; Vagabond Lady; The Perfect Gentleman; Jalna; Gilded Lily; Right to Live; Mystery of Edwin Drood. 1936 Love before Breakfast; Petticoat Fever; Lloyds of London; White Hunter. 1937 Personal Property; Thoroughbreds Don't Cry; The Prince and the Pauper; The Man Who Cried Wolf. 1938 Bulldog Drummond in Africa. 1939 Bulldog Drummond's Secret Police; The Lady's from Kentucky; The Witness Vanishes. 1940 The Invisible Man Returns; A Chump at Oxford; Tom Brown's School Days. 1941 Free and Easy; The Wolf Man; Dr. Jekyll and Mr. Hyde. 1942 Mrs. Miniver; This above All. 1944 The Lodger; None but the Lonely Heart; Secrets of Scotland Yard. 1945 Scotland Yard Investigator; Devotion (and 1931 version).

HARVEY, HANK (Herman Heacker)
Died: Dec. 4, 1929, Culver City, Calif. Screen actor.

HARVEY, JOHN "JACK"
Born: 1881. Died: Nov. 10, 1954, Hollywood, Calif.(natural causes). Screen cowboy actor.

HARVEY, LILIAN (Lilian Muriel Helen Harvey)
Born: Jan. 19, 1907, Horsey, England. Died: July 27, 1968, Antibes, France. Screen actress. Entered films in German pictures prior to 1925. German films prior to 1925: The Crowd Entertains Itself; Road from Paradise.

Appeared in: 1925 Die Liebschaften der Hella von Gilsa (The Love Story from the Hella von Gilsa). 1927 Vater Werden 1st Nicht Schwer (It's Easy to Become a Father) (U.S. 1929); Eheferien; Die Tolle Lola. 1928 The Love Commandment. 1929 Wenn du Einmal Dien Herz Verschenkst. 1930 Hokus Pokus (aka Temporary Wife); Liebeswalzer (The Love Waltz); Murder for Sale. 1931 Princesse a Vos Ordres; Nie Wieder Liebe (No More Love); Ihre Holeit Befiehlt; Die Drei von Der Tankstelle (Three from the Gasoline Station). 1932 Zwei Herzes und ein Schlag (Two Hearts Beat As One); Le Congre's S'Amuse (The Congress Dances); Ein Blonder Tram (A Blonde Dream); Happy Ever After. Other German films prior to 1933 Du Solst Nicht Stehlen (You Should Not Steal); Adieu Mascotte; Ich und Die Kaiserin. 1933 My Weakness; My Lips Betray; Quick; Koenig der Clows. 1934 I Am Suzanne; Heart Song. 1935 Schwarze Rosen (Black Rose); Mein ist Die Rache; Leidenschaft; The Only Girl; Prinzessin Trulala (Princess Trulala); Let's Live Tonight; Invitation to the Waltz. 1936 Liebe Und Trompetenblasen; Gluckskinder (Lucky Children). 1937 Fanny Elssler; Untitled Dance. 1938 Capriccio; Castelli in Aria; Sieben Ohrfeigen (Seven Slaps). 1939 Frau ein Seuer; Serenade Eternelle; La Fille et le Garcon. 1940 Schubert's Serenade. 1950 Herrliche Zeiten (Wonderful Times). 1951 Miquette and Her Mother. 1956 Serenade. 1958 Das Gab's Nur Einmal (It Only Happened Once). 1960 Das Kommt Nicht Wieder (It Won't Happen Again).

HARVEY, LOTTIE
Born: 1890. Died: Aug. 2, 1948, Hollywood, Calif. Screen actress.

HARVEY, PAUL
Born: 1884, Ill. Died: Dec. 14, 1955, Hollywood, Calif.(coronary thrombosis). Screen and stage actor. Entered films with Selig Film Co. in 1917.

Appeared in: 1929 The Awful Truth. 1930 Strong Arm (short). 1932 The Wiser Sex. 1933 Advice to the Lovelorn. 1934 Hat, Coat and Glove; Handy Andy; Kid Millions; She Was a Lady; A Wicked Woman; The President Vanishes; Looking for Trouble; The House of Rothschild; The Affairs of Cellini; Born to Be Bad; Broadway Bill; Charlie Chan's Courage. 1935 Alibi Ike; Thanks a Million; The Whole Town's Talking; I'll Love You Always; Four Hours to Kill; Goin' to Town. 1936 August Week-End; Postal Inspector; Rose of the Rancho; The Return of Sophie Lang; The Plainsman; Mind Your Own Business; The Petrified Forest; The Walking Dead; Three Men on a Horse; The Witness Chair; Private Number; Yellowstone. 1937 The Black Legion; Michael Strogoff;

On Again—off Again; High Flyers; The Devil Is Driving; Big City; My Dear Miss Aldrich; 23—1/2 Hours' Leave; The Soldier and the Lady. 1938 A Slight Case of Murder; If I Were King; Love on a Budget; Rebecca of Sunnybrook Farm; I'll Give a Million; Charlie Chan in Honolulu; There's That Woman Again; Algiers; The Higgins Family; The Sisters. 1939 Never Say Die; The Gorilla; News Is Made at Night; Stanley and Livingston; Mr. Moto in Danger Island; High School; The Forgotten Woman; They Shall Have Music; Meet Dr. Christian. 1940 Brother Rat and a Baby; The Marines Fly High; Typhoon; Manhattan Heartbeat; Maryland; Behind the News; Arizona. 1941 Ride on, Vaquero; Out of the Fog; Puddin' Head; Law of the Tropics; Great Guns; You Belong to Me; Three Girls about Town; Remember the Night; Mr. District Attorney in the Carter Case; High Sierra; You're in the Army Now. 1942 A Tragedy at Midnight; The Man Who Wouldn't Die; Moonlight Masquerade; Heart of the Golden West; You Can't Escape Forever. 1943 The Man from Music Mountain; Mystery Broadcast. 1944 Four Jills in a Jeep; Henry Aldrich Plays Cupid; The Thoroughbreds; Jamboree; In the Meantime, Darling. 1945 Don't Fence Me In; Spellbound; Mama Loves Papa; The Chicago Kid; The Horn Blows at Midnight; Swingin' on a Rainbow; The Southerner; Swingin' on Broadway; State Fair; Pillow to Post. 1946 Gay Blades; They Made Me a Killer; Up Goes Maisie; In Fast Company; Blondie's Lucky Day; I've Always Loved You; The Bamboo Blonde; Helldorado; Early to Wed. 1947 The Beginning or the End; Out of the Blue; High Barbaree; Danger Street; When a Girl's Beautiful; The Late George Apley; Wyoming. 1948 Waterfront at Midnight; Lightnin' in the Forest; Give My Regards to Broadway; Blondie's Reward; Family Honeymoon; Smuggler's Cove; Speed to Spare; Call Northside 777. 1949 Take One False Step; The Fountainhead; The Girl from Jones Beach; Down to the Sea in Ships; The Duke of Chicago; Family Honeymoon; John Loves Mary; Make Believe Ballroom; Mr. Belvedere Goes to College. 1950 The Lawless; Father of the Bride; The Milkman; Side Street; The Skipper Surprised His Wife; Three Little Words; A Ticket to Tomahawk; Unmasked; Riding High; The Yellow Cab Man; Stella. 1951 The Tall Target; Let's Go, Navy!; Father's Little Dividend; Excuse My Dust; The Flying Missile; Thunder in God's Country; Up Front. 1952 The First Time; Has Anybody Seen My Gal?; Dreamboat; April in Paris; Here Come the Nelsons. 1953 Calamity Jane; Remains to Be Seen. 1954 Sabrina. 1955 Three for the Show; High Society.

HASKIN, CHARLES W.
Born: 1868. Died: June 10, 1927, New York, N.Y. Screen, stage actor, and stage manager.

HASSELL, GEORGE
Born: May 4, 1881, Birmingham, England. Died: Feb. 17, 1937, Chatsworth, Calif.(heart attack). Screen and stage actor.

Appeared in: 1915 Old Dutch. 1926 La Boheme. 1930 Where There's A Will (short). 1935 Night Life of the Gods; The Flame Within; Becky Sharp; Dressed to Thrill; Captain Blood. 1936 Petticoat Fever; The King Steps Out; Girl's Dormitory; White Hunter. 1937 Woman Wise.

HASTINGS, VICTORIA
Died: May 24, 1934, Hollywood, Calif.(heart ailment). Screen actress. Married to British screen actor Trevor Bland-Addinsell.

HASWELL, PERCY
Born: 1871. Died: June 14, 1945, Nantucket, Mass. Screen and stage actress. She appeared as Mrs. George Fawcett and as Percy Haswell. Married to screen actor George Fawcett (dec. 1939).

Appeared in: 1929 Innocents of Paris; River of Romance.

HATHAWAY, JEAN
Born: 1876. Died: Aug. 23, 1938, Los Angeles, Calif. Screen actress.

Appeared in: 1914 The Master Key (serial). 1916 The Purple Mask (serial). 1921 Short Skirts. 1922 Boy Crazy.

HATHAWAY, LILIAN
Born: 1876, Liverpool, England. Died: Jan. 12, 1954, Englewood Cliffs, N.J. Screen and stage actress.

HATHAWAY, RHODY
Born: 1869. Died: Feb. 18, 1944, Hollywood, Calif. Screen actor. Appeared in American Film Co. productions in 1908.

Appeared in: 1924 Not a Drum Was Heard. 1925 A Daughter of the Sioux. 1926 Bigger Than Barnum's; The Phantom of the Forest. 1928 Into the Night; The Old Code.

HATTON, FRANCES
Born: 1888. Died: Oct. 1971, Palmdale, Calif. Screen and stage actress. Married to screen actor Raymond Hatton (dec. Oct. 1971); she died one week prior to his death.

Appeared in: 1921 The Mother Heart; Straight from the Shoulder; The Rowdy. 1922 At the Sign of the Jack O'Lantern. 1923 Java Head; The Grail; The Day of Faith. 1925 Confessions of a Queen.

HATTON, RAYMOND (Raymond William Hatton)
Born: July 7, 1892, Red Oak, Iowa. Died: Oct. 21, 1971, Palmdale, Calif.(heart attack). Screen, stage, and television actor. Entered films with Kalem in 1911. Married to screen actress Frances Hatton (dec. Oct. 1971); she died less than one week prior to his death.

Appeared in: 1916 Oliver Twist. 1917 Woman God Forgot; Joan the Woman; The Little American. 1918 The Whispering Chorus; We Can't Have Everything; The Source. 1919 You're Fired; The Love Burglar; Male and Female; Everywoman. 1920 The Dancin' Fool; Jes' Call Me Jim. 1921 The Ace of Hearts; The Affairs of Anatol; Bunty Pulls the Strings; The Concert; Peck's Bad Boy; Salvage; All's Fair in Love; Pilgrims of the Night. 1922 Doubling for Romeo; Ebb Tide; Head over Heels; Pink Gods; To Have and to Hold; Manslaughter; The Hottentot; His Back against the Wall; At Bay. 1923 The Barefoot Boy; Java Head; The Virginian; Trimmed in Scarlet; The Tie That Binds; Three Wise Fools; A Man of Action; Big Brother; Enemies of Children; The Hunchback of Notre Dame. 1924 True As Steel; Triumph; The Mine with the Iron Door; Cornered; The Fighting American; Half-a-Dollar Bill. 1925 Adventure; Contraband; In the Name of Love; The Devil's Cargo; A Son of His Father; The Thundering Herd; The Top of the World; Tomorrow's Love; Lord Jim. 1926 Behind the Front; Born to the West; Silence; Forlorn River; We're in the Navy Now. 1927 Fashions for Women; Fireman Save My Child; Now We're in the Air. 1928 The Big Killing; Wife Savers; Partners in Crime. 1929 The Office Scandal; Trent's Last Case; When Caesar Ran a Newspaper (short); Dear Vivien; Christie Talking Plays; Hell's Heroes; Christie shorts. 1930 The Silver Horde; Rogue of the Rio Grande; Murder on the Roof; Her Unborn Child; Midnight Mystery; The Road to Paradise; Pineapples; The Mighty. 1931 The Squaw Man; Honeymoon Lane; The Lion and the Lamb; Arrowsmith; The Challenge; Woman Hungry. 1932 Law and Order; Polly of the Circus; The Fourth Horseman; Uptown New York; Exposed; The Crooked Circle; Vanity Street; Malay Nights; Stranger in Town; Drifting Souls; Vanishing Frontier; Alias Mary Smith; Long Loop Laramie; Divorce a la Mode (short). 1933 State Trooper; Under the Tonto Rim; Alice in Wonderland; Lady Killer; Penthouse; Day of Reckoning; Tom's in Town; Terror Trail; Cornered; Hidden Gold; The Big Cage. 1934 The Defense Rests; Women in His Life; Lazy River; Once to Every Bachelor; Fifteen Wives; The Thundering Herd; Straight Is the Way; Wagon Wheels. 1935 Times Square Lady; Murder in the Fleet; Calm Yourself; Rustlers of Red Gap (serial); Nevada; Wanderer of the Wasteland; Red Morning; G-Men; The Daring Young Man; Steamboat 'Round the Bend; Stormy. 1936 Exclusive Story; Women Are Trouble; Mad Holiday; Laughing Irish Eyes; Desert Gold; Timothy's Quest; The Vigilantes Are Coming (serial); The Arizona Raiders; Yellowstone; Jungle Jim (serial). 1937 Marked Woman; Fly Away Baby; The Adventurous Blonde; Love Is on the Air; The Missing Witness; Roaring Timber; Public Wedding; Over the Goal. 1938 He Couldn't Say No; Come Rangers; Love Finds Andy Hardy; The Texans; Touchdown Army; Tom Sawyer, Detective; Over the Wall. 1939 I'm from Missouri; Ambush; Undercover Doctor; Rough Riders' Roundup; Frontier Pony Express; Paris Honeymoon; New Frontier; Wyoming Outlaw; Wall Street Cowboy; Kansas Terrors; The Cowboys from Texas; Six Thousand Enemies; Career. 1940 Heroes of the Saddle; Pioneers of the West; Covered Wagon Days; Rocky Mountain Rangers; Oklahoma Renegades; Queen of the Mob; Kit Carson. 1941 Arizona Bound; Gunman from Bodie; Forbidden Trails. 1942 Ghost Town Law; Cadets on Parade; Girl from Alaska; Down Texas Way; Riders of the West; Dawn on the Great Divide; Below the Border; West of the Law. 1943 The Texas Kid; Outlaws of Stampede Pass; Six-Gun Gospel; Stranger from Pecos; The Ghost Rider. 1944 Raiders of the Border; Rough Riders; Partners of the Trail; West of the Rio Grande; Land of the Outlaws; Tall in the Saddle; Range Law; Ghost Guns; The Law Men. 1945 Law of the Valley; Flame of the West; Sunbonnet Sue; Frontier Feud; Gun Smoke; The Lost Trail; Northwest Trail; Rhythm Roundup; Stranger from Santa Fe. 1946 Fool's Gold; Drifting Along; Under Arizona Skies; The Haunted Mine; Border Bandits; Shadows on the Range; Raiders of the South; The Gentleman from Texas; Silver Range; Trigger Fingers. 1947 Trailing Danger; Land of the Lawless; Rolling Home; Valley of Fear; Black Gold; The Law Comes to Gunsight; Code of the Saddle; Prairie Express; Gun Talk; Unconquered. 1948 Crossed Trails; Triggerman; Overland Trails; Frontier Agent; Back Trail. 1949 Sheriff of Medicine Bow; Gunning for Trouble; Hidden Danger; The Fighting Ranger. 1950 Operation Haylift; County Fair; West of the Brazos; Marshal of Heldorado; Crooked River; Colorado Ranger; Fast on the Draw; Hostile Country. 1951 Skipalong Rosenbloom; Kentucky Jubilee. 1952 The Golden Hawk. 1953 Cow Country. 1954 Thunder Pass. 1955 The Twinkle in God's Eye; Treasure of Ruby Hills. 1956 Dig That Uranium; Shake, Rattle and Rock; Flesh and the Spur; Girls in Prison. 1957 Pawnee; Invasion of the Saucer Men; Motorcycle Gang. 1959 Alaska Passage. 1964 The Quick Gun. 1965 Requiem for a Gunfighter. 1967 In Cold Blood.

HATTON, RICHARD "DICK"
Born: 1891. Died: July 9, 1931, Los Angeles, Calif.(traffic accident). Screen actor and film director.

Appeared in: 1922 Four Hearts; Fearless Dick; Hellhounds of the West. 1923 In the West; The Seventh Sheriff; Unblazed Trail; Blood Test; The Golden Flame; Playing Double; Ridin' Thru. 1924 Come on, Cowboys; Western Fate; The Whirlwind Ranger; Rip Snorter; Horse Sense; Sagebrush Gospel; Trouble Trail; Two-Fisted Justice. 1925 Sell 'Em Cowboy; "Scar" Hanan; The Cactus Cure; My Pal; Range Justice; Ridin' Easy; The Secret of Black Canyon; Warrior Gap; A Western Engagement; Where Romance Rides. 1926 He-Man's Country; In Broncho Land; Roaring Bill Atwood; Temporary Sheriff. 1927 The Action Graver; Saddle Jumpers; Speeding Hoofs; Western Courage. 1928 The Boss of Rustler's Roost. 1930 Romance of the Week.

HATTON, RONDO
Born: 1895. Died: Feb. 2, 1946, Beverly Hills, Calif.(heart attack). Screen actor.

Appeared in: 1930 Hell Harbor. 1938 In Old Chicago. 1943 The Ox-Bow Incident. 1944 Pearl of Death. 1945 Jungle Captive. 1946 House of Horrors; The Brute Man; Spider Woman Strikes Back. 1947 Joan Bedford Is Missing; The Creeper.

HAUPT, ULLRICH
Born: Aug. 8, 1887, Prussia. Died: Aug. 5, 1931, near Santa Maria, Calif.(hunting accident). Screen, stage actor, stage director, stage producer, and screenwriter. Entered films at old Essanay Studios in Chicago and after that appeared in Hollywood films in 1927.

Appeared in: 1928 Captain Swagger; The Tempest. 1929 Wonder of Women; The Far Call; Frozen Justice; The Iron Mask; Madame X; The Greene Murder Case. 1930 A Royal Romance; The Bad One; DuBarry, Woman of Passion; Morocco; The Rogue Song. 1931 The Man Who Came Back; The Unholy Garden.

HAVEL, JOE
Born: 1869. Died: Jan. 27, 1932, Los Angeles, Calif. Screen and vaudeville actor. Entered films in 1920.

HAVER, PHYLLIS
Born: Jan. 16, 1899, Douglas, Kans. Died: Nov. 19, 1960, Falls Village, Conn.(suicide). Screen actress. Was a Mack Sennett bathing beauty and appeared in many Keystone comedies.

Appeared in: 1917 The Sultan's Wife. 1921 A Small Town Idol; Home Talent. 1923 The Temple of Venus; The Balloonatics; The Bolted Door; The Christian; The Common Law. 1924 The Perfect Flapper; The Breath of Scandal; The Fighting Coward; The Foolish Virgin; Lilies of the Field; The Midnight Express; One Glorious Night; Singer Jim McKee; Single Wives; The Snob; So Big. 1925 After Business Hours; A Fight to the Finish; The Golden Princess; Her Husband's Secret; I Want My Man; New Brooms; Rugged Water. 1926 What Price Glory; Up in Mabel's Room; The Nervous Wreck; The Caveman; Don Juan; Fig Leaves; Hard Boiled; Other Women's Husbands; Three Bad Men. 1927 The Way of All Flesh; No Control; The Little Adventuress; The Rejuvenation of Aunt Mary; The Wise Wife; The Fighting Eagle; Your Wife and Mine; Nobody's Widow. 1928 Tenth Avenue; The Battle of the Sexes; Chicago. 1929 Sal of Singapore; The Shady Lady; The Office Scandal; Thunder; Hell's Kitchen. 1963 30 Years of Fun (documentary).

HAVIER, JOSE ALEX
Born: 1909. Died: Dec. 18, 1945, Hollywood, Calif.(self-inflicted bullet wound). Screen actor.

Appeared in: 1943 Bataan. 1945 Back to Bataan; They Were Expendable.

HAVILAND, RENA
Born: 1878. Died: Feb. 20, 1954, Woodland Hills, Calif. Screen, stage, and vaudeville actress. Entered films in 1911.

HAWKE, ROHN OLIN
Born: 1924. Died: Feb. 15, 1967, Albuquerque, N.M.(self-inflicted gunshot). Screen actor, disc jocky, and writer. Appeared in films during late 1940s.

HAWKINS, "PUNY"
Died: Mar. 30, 1947, Wichita, Kans.(heart attack). Screen, stage, and radio actor. Appeared in silent films.

HAWKS, CHARLES MONROE
Born: 1874. Died: Dec. 15, 1951, Los Angeles, Calif. Screen actor. Appeared in silents.

HAWLEY, ALLEN BURTON
Born: 1895. Died: Sept. 1925, Troy, N.Y. Screen actor. Entered films approx. 1915. Divorced from screen actress Wanda Hawley.

HAWLEY, DUDLEY
Born: 1879, England. Died: Mar. 29, 1941, New York, N.Y.(coronary thrombosis). Screen and stage actor.

Appeared in: 1917 An American Widow. 1930 Young Man of Manhattan.

HAWTREY, ANTHONY
Born: 1909. Died: Oct. 18, 1954, London, England (heart attack). Screen and stage actor.

Appeared in: 1949 The Affairs of a Rogue.

HAY, MARY
Died: June 4, 1957, Inverness, Calif. Screen and stage actress. Former Ziegfeld Follies star. Divorced from screen actor Richard Barthelmess (dec. 1963).

Appeared in: 1920 Way Down East. 1925 New Toys.

HAY, WILLIAM "WILL"
Born: 1888, Stockton-on-Tees, England. Died: Apr. 18, 1949, London, England. Screen, stage, vaudeville, radio actor, and author.

Appeared in: 1934 Those Were the Days (film debut). 1935 Radio Parade of 1935; Dandy Dick; Boys Will Be Boys. 1936 Good Morning, Boys. 1938 Oh! Mr. Porter; Convict 99; Hey! Hey! U.S.A. 1939 Old Bones of the River. 1940 Ask a Policeman. 1941 Where's That Fire; The Black Sheep of Whitehall. 1942 The Goose Steps Out; Big Blockade; The Ghost of St. Michael's. 1944 My Learned Friend. Other British films: Where There's a Will; Sinbad the Sailor.

HAYDEN, HARRY
Born: 1882. Died: July 24, 1955, Los Angeles, Calif. Screen, stage, and television actor.

Appeared in: 1936 I Married a Doctor; Two against the World; Public Enemy's Wife; The Case of the Black Cat; God's Country and the Woman; The Man I Marry; Killer at Large; College Holiday. 1937 The Black Legion; Melody for Two; John Meade's Woman; Ever since Eve; Love Is on the Air. 1938 Double Danger; Saleslady; Four Men and a Prayer; I'll Give a Million; Hold That Co-ed; Kentucky. 1939 Mr. Smith Goes to Washington; Wife, Husband and Friend; Rose of Washington Square; Frontier Marshal; The Rains Came; Here I Am a Stranger; The Honeymoon's Over; The Cisco Kid and the Lady; Barricade; Swanee River; Hidden Power; Flight at Midnight; At the Circus. 1940 He Married His Wife; Lillian Russell; Yesterday's Heroes; You're Not So Tough; Christmas in July; Saps at Sea. 1941 Sleepers West; Hold That Ghost; A Man Betrayed; The Parson of Panamint; The Night of January 16th; Remember the Day. 1942 Rings on Her Fingers; Whispering Ghost; Mississippi Gambler; Tales of Manhattan; The Palm Beach Story; War against Mrs. Hadley; Joan of Ozark; Springtime in the Rockies; Get Hep to Love. 1943 Hello, Frisco, Hello; Meanest Man in the World; Submarine Alert. 1944 Barbary Coast Gent; Hail the Conquering Hero; The Big Noise; Weird Woman; Up in Mable's Room; The Great Moment. 1945 Colonel Effingham's Raid; Boston Blackie's Rendezvous; Where Do We Go from Here; Guest Wife. 1946 The Blue Dahlia; The Virginian; If I'm Lucky; Two Sisters from Boston; The Killers; Til' the Clouds Roll By. 1947 The Unfinished Dance; Key Witness; My Brother Talks to Horses; Merton of the Movies. 1948 Every Girl Should Be Married; Good Sam. 1949 The Judge Steps Out; Beautiful Blonde from Bashful Bend; Bad Men of Tombstone; Deadly Is the Female; Joe Palooka in the Big Fight; The Lone Wolf and His

Lady; Prison Warden; Abbott and Costello Meet the Killer, Boris Karloff. 1950 Intruder in the Dust; Traveling Saleswoman; Union Station. 1951 Double Dynamite; Pier 23; Street Bandits; Angels in the Outfield. 1952 Army Bound; Carrie; O'Henry's Full House; When in Rome. 1953 The Last Posse; Money from Home.

HAYDEN, MARGARET. See Margaret Hayden Rorke

HAYE, HELEN
Born: Aug. 28, 1874, Assam, India. Died: Sept. 1, 1957, London, England. Screen and stage actress.

Appeared in: 1930 Atlantic. 1931 The Skin Game; Congress Dances. 1932 Monte Carlo Madness; Her First Affair. 1933 It's a Boy; 39 Steps (U.S. 1935); This Week of Grace; Loves of a Dictator (U.S. 1935); Elizabeth of England. 1936 Everybody Dance; Girl in the Taxi; The Interrupted Honeymoon. 1937 Wings of the Morning; A Girl Must Live; Spy in Black; St. Martin's Lane. 1939 U-Boat 29. 1940 Sidewalks of London. 1941 The Frightened Lady; Kipps. 1943 Dear Octopus. 1945 Randolph Family. 1946 Madonna of the Seven Moons. 1948 Man of Evil; Mine Own Executioner; Anna Karenina. 1949 A Place of One's Own. 1950 Mrs. Fitzherbert; Third Time Lucky; Conspirator. 1954 Hobson's Choice. 1955 Front Page Story. 1956 Richard III. 1957 Gypsy and the Gentleman; Action of the Tiger. 1959 Teenage Bad Girl(aka My Teenage Daughter). Other British films: The Man in Grey; Fanny by Gaslight.

HAYES, CARRIE
Born: 1878. Died: Dec. 22, 1954, Philadelphia, Pa. Screen and stage actress. Appeared in silent films.

HAYES, CATHERINE
Born: 1886. Died: Jan. 4, 1941, Los Angeles, Calif. Screen, stage, and vaudeville actress.

Appeared in: 1933 Zoo in Budapest; Warrior's Husband.

HAYES, FRANK
Born: 1875. Died: Dec. 28, 1923, Hollywood, Calif.(pneumonia). Screen, stage, and vaudeville actor.

Appeared in: 1915 Colored Villainy; Mabel, Fatty and the Law (re-issued Fatty's Spooning Day); Stolen Magic. 1916 Fatty and Mabel Adrift; Fido's Fate; A Bath House Blunder; Her Marble Heart; Madcap Ambrose. 1917 His Uncle Dudley. 1918 A Hoosier Romance. 1921 The Killer; The Lure of Egypt; The Man of the Forest; Mysterious Rider. 1922 Golden Dreams; Heart's Haven; The Old Homestead; When Romance Rides. 1923 Double Dealing; Souls in Bondage; Vanity Fair. 1924 Greed.

HAYES, GEORGE "GABBY"
Born: May 7, 1885, Wellesville, N.Y. Died: Feb. 9, 1969, Burbank, Calif.(heart ailment). Screen, stage, and television actor. Appeared in both Hopalong Cassidy film series and Roy Rogers film series. Married to screen actress Dorothy Earle (dec. 1958).

Appeared in: 1929 The Rainbow Man (film debut); Smiling Irish Eyes. 1930 For the Defense. 1931 Rose of the Rio Grande; God's Country and the Man; Cavalier of the West; Nevada Buckaroo; Big Business Girl. 1932 Dragnet Patrol; Border Devils; Night Rider; Riders of the Desert; The Man from Hell's Edges; From Broadway to Cheyenne; Klondike; Texas Buddies; The Boiling Point; The Fighting Champ; Without Honor; Love Me Tonight; The Slippery Pearls (short). 1933 Wild Horse Mesa; Sagebrush Trail; Self Defense; Trailing North; Return of Casey Jones; Skyway; Gallant Fool; The Ranger's Code; Galloping Romeo; The Fugitive; The Phantom Broadcast; The Sphinx; Crashing Broadway; Breed of the Border; Fighting Texans; Devil's Mate; Riders of Destiny. 1934 In Old Santa Fe; Brand of Hate; Monte Carlo Nights; The Man from Utah; The Star Packer; West of the Divide; The Lucky Texan; Beggars in Ermine; Mystery Liner; Blue Steel; Randy Rides Along; City Limits; The Lost Jungle (serial); 'Neath Arizona Skies. 1935 Justice of the Range; Smokey Smith; The Throwback; $1,000 a Minute; Tumbling Tumbleweeds; Texas Terror; Lawless Frontier; Death Flies East; Rainbow Valley; The Hoosier School-Master; Honeymoon Limited; Headline Woman; Ladies Crave Excitement; Thunder Mountain; Hopalong Cassidy; The Eagle's Brood; Bar 20 Rides Again; Mister Hobo; Hitch Hike Lady; The Lost City (serial); Welcome Home. 1936 Call of the Prairie; Three on a Trail; The Lawless Nineties; Glory Parade; Hearts in Bondage; I Married a Doctor; Mr. Deeds Goes to Town; Heart of the West; Swifty; The Texas Rangers; Valiant Is the Word for Carrie; Hopalong Cassidy Returns; The Plainsman; Trail Dust. 1937 Borderland; Hills of Old Wyoming; Mountain Music; North of the Rio Grande; Rustler's Valley; Hopalong Rides Again; Texas Trail. 1938 Forbidden Music; Gold Is Where You Find It; Hearts of Arizona; Bar 20 Justice; Pride of the West; In

Old Mexico; Sunset Trail; The Frontiersman; Emil. 1939 Man of Conquest; Let Freedom Ring; Southward Ho!; In Old Caliente; In Old Monterey; Wall Street Cowboy; The Arizona Kid; Saga of Death Valley; Silver on the Sage; Days of Jesse James; Renegade Trail; Fighting Thoroughbreds. 1940 Wagons Westward; The Dark Command; Young Buffalo Bill; The Carson City Kid; The Ranger and the Lady; Colorado; Young Bill Hickok; Melody Ranch; The Border Legion. 1941 Robin Hood of the Pecos; In Old Cheyenne; Sheriff of Tombstone; Nevada City; Jesse James at Bay; Bad Man of Deadwood; Red River Valley; The Voice in the Night; Frightened Lady. 1942 South of Santa Fe; Sunset on the Desert; Romance of the Range; Man of Cheyenne; Sons of the Pioneers; Sunset Serenade; Heart of the Golden West; Ridin' Down the Canyon. 1943 Calling Wild Bill Elliott; Bordertown Gunfighters; Wagon Tracks West; The Man from Thunder River; Death Valley Manhunt; In Old Oklahoma. 1944 Tucson Raiders; Leave It to the Irish; Mojave Firebrand; Tall in the Saddle; Lights of Old Santa Fe; Hidden Valley Outlaws; Marshal of Reno. 1945 Utah; The Big Bonanza; The Man from Oklahoma; Sunset in Eldorado; Don't Fence Me In; Out California Way; Bells of Rosarita; Along the Navajo Trail. 1946 My Pal Trigger; Home in Oklahoma; Badman's Territory; Song of Arizona; Rainbow over Texas; Roll on Texas Moon; Under Nevada Skies. 1947 Helldorado; Trail Street; Bells of San Angelo; Wyoming; The Trespasser; Great Expectations. 1948 Albuquerque; Slippy McGee; The Untamed Breed; Return of the Bad Men. 1949 Susanna Pass; Golden Stallion; Bells of Coronado; Trigger, Jr.; El Paso. 1950 The Cariboo Trail; Twilight in the Sierras. 1951 Pals of the Golden West.

HAYES, SIDNEY
Born: 1865. Died: May 2, 1940, Beverly Hills, Calif. Screen, stage, and vaudeville actor. Appeared in vaudeville in an act billed as "Hayes & Hayes."

HAYES, WILLIAM
Born: 1887. Died: July 13, 1937, Hollywood, Calif.(heart attack). Screen actor.

Appeared in: 1921 Get-Rich-Quick Wallingford. 1924 Flashing Spurs. 1925 A Gentleman Roughneck; Lena Rivers. 1926 Ace of Action; Cupid's Knockout; Hollywood Reporter. 1930 Terry of the Times (serial).

HAYLE, GRACE
Born: 1889. Died: Mar. 20, 1963, Los Angeles, Calif. Screen actress.

Appeared in: 1934 Twenty Million Sweethearts. 1937 Tovarich. 1939 Death of a Champion; Forgotten Woman; The Starmaker; Lady of the Tropics. 1940 Our Neighbors, the Carters; The Great Dictator. 1942 Madame Spy; Just Off Broadway; Crossroads; I Married an Angel. 1943 Let's Face It. 1952 Don't Bother to Knock. 1953 Houdini; Money from Home.

HAYNES, ARTHUR
Born: 1914. Died: Nov. 19, 1966, London, England (heart attack). Screen, vaudeville, radio, and television actor.

Appeared in: 1964 Strange Bedfellows. Other British film: Doctor in Clover.

HAYNES, DANIEL L.
Died: July 23, 1954, Kingston, N.Y. Negro screen and stage actor, and clergyman.

Appeared in: 1929 Hallelujah (first all Negro film). 1932 The Last Mile. 1935 So Red the Rose; Escape from Devil's Island. 1936 The Invisible Ray.

HAYWORTH, VINTON J.
Born: 1906. Died: May 21, 1970, Van Nuys, Calif.(heart attack). Screen, stage, radio, and television actor.

Appeared in: 1956 The Girl He Left Behind; The Great Man. 1961 Police Dog Story.

HAZELL, HY (Hyacinth Hazel O'Higgins)
Born: 1920. Died: May 10, 1970, London, England. Screen and stage actress.

Appeared in: 1946 Meet Me at Dawn (U.S. 1948). 1949 Paper Orchid; Celia. 1950 The Lady Craved Excitement. 1952 Franchise Affair; The Night Won't Talk. 1954 The Yellow Balloon. 1956 Up in the World; Anastasia. 1957 The Key Man; Light Fingers. 1958 The Whole Truth.

HAZELTON, JOSEPH
Born: 1853. Died: Oct. 8, 1936, Hollywood, Calif. Screen and stage actor.

Appeared in: 1921 False Kisses; "If Only" Jim; The Little Minister. 1922 Oliver Twist. 1937 Mountain Justice.

HEALY, DAN
Born: 1889. Died: Sept. 1, 1969, Jackson Heights, N.Y. Screen and stage actor, and song and dance man. Married to singer/ screen actress Helen Kane (dec. 1966).

Appeared in: 1929 The Laughing Lady; Glorifying the American Girl. 1931 The Unfair Sex (short).

HEALY, TED
Born: Oct. 1, 1896, Houston, Tex. Died: Dec. 21, 1937, Los Angeles, Calif.(heart attack). Screen, stage, radio, and vaudeville actor. Billed in vaudeville as "Ted Healy and His Racketeers" and "Ted Healy and His Stooges."

Appeared in: 1930 Soup to Nuts. 1932 Meet the Baron. 1933 Stage Mother; Bombshell; Dancing Lady (short). 1934 Myrt and Marge; Fugitive Lovers; Hollywood Party; Death on the Diamond; The Band Plays On; Lazy River; Operation 13; Paris Interlude (short). 1935 The Winning Ticket; The Casino Murder Case; Reckless; Murder in the Fleet; Mad Love; Here Comes the Bank; It's in the Air. 1936 Speed; San Francisco; The Longest Night; Mad Holiday; Sing, Baby, Sing. 1937 Man of the People; Hollywood Hotel; Good Old Soak. 1938 Love Is a Headache.

HEARN, SAM
Born: 1889, New York, N.Y. Died: Oct. 28, 1964, Los Angeles, Calif.(heart attack). Screen, stage, radio, and television actor. Best known for his role of "Schlepperman" on Jack Benny's radio and television programs.

Appeared in: 1936 Florida Special; The Big Broadcast of 1937. 1942 The Man in the Trunk. 1949 Inspector General. 1953 The I Don't Care Girl. 1958 Once upon a Horse.

HEATH, TED
Born: 1902, Wadsworth, London, England. Died: Nov. 18, 1969, Virginia Water, England. Band leader, screen and radio actor.

Appeared in: 1960 Jazz Boat. 1961 It's a Wonderful World.

HEATHERLEY, CLIFFORD (Clifford Lamb)
Born: Oct. 8, 1888, Preston, Lancashire, England. Died: Sept. 15, 1937, London, England. Screen and stage actor.

Appeared in: 1929 The Constant Nymph. 1930 Glamour. 1931 Brother Alfred; Help Yourself; Good Night Vienna; The Love Habit. 1932 One Magic Night; Indiscretions of Eve; After the Ball; Happy Ever After; Fires of Fate; Discord. 1933 Cash; Catherine the Great; Bitter Sweet. 1934 The Private Life of Don Juan. 1935 Church Mouse; Abdul the Damned. Other British film: The Sea Urchin.

HECHT, TED (Theodore Hekt)
Born: 1908, New York, N.Y. Died: June 24, 1969, Los Angeles, Calif. Screen, stage, and television actor.

Appeared in: 1942 Time to Kill (film debut); Manila Calling. 1943 So Proudly We Hail; Corregidor; Rookies in Burma. 1944 Dragon Seed; End of the Road. 1945 Three's a Crowd; Counterattack; The Lost Weekend. 1946 The Fighting Guardsman. 1947 Tarzan and the Huntress; Spoilers of the North; The Gangster. 1948 Man-Eater of Kumaon. 1949 Apache Chief; Bad Men of Tombstone; Song of India. 1950 Tall Timber; Blue Grass of Kentucky; Killer Shark; Sideshow; Abbott and Costello in the Foreign Legion. 1953 Desert Legion. 1955 Abbott and Costello Meet the Mummy.

HEFLIN, VAN (Emmet Evan Heflin)
Born: Dec. 13, 1910, Walters, Okla. Died: July 23, 1971, Hollywood, Calif.(heart attack). Screen, stage, and television actor. Won Academy Award in 1941 for Best Supporting Actor in Johnny Eager. Divorced from screen actress Frances Neal.

Appeared in: 1936 A Woman Rebels (film debut). 1937 The Outcasts of Poker Flat; Flight from Glory; Annapolis Salute; Saturday's Heroes; Salute to Romance. 1939 Back Door to Heaven. 1940 Santa Fe Trail. 1941 The Feminine Touch; H. M. Pulham, Esq.; Johnny Eager. 1942 Kid Glove Killer; Grand Central Murder; Seven Sweethearts; Tennessee Johnson. 1943 Presenting Lily Mars. 1946 The Strange Love of Martha Ivers; Til' the Clouds Roll By. 1947 Green Dolphin Street; Possessed. 1948 B. F.'s Daughter; Act of Violence; The Three Musketeers; Tap Roots; Secret Land (narr.). 1949 East Side, West Side; Madame Bovary. 1951 The Prowler; Weekend with Father; Tomahawk. 1952 My Son, John. 1953 Shane; Wings of the Hawk. 1954 The Golden Mask; Tanganyika; The Raid; Woman's World; Black Widow. 1955 Battle Cry; Count Three and Pray. 1956 Patterns.

1957 3:10 to Yuma. 1958 Gunman's Walk. 1959 Tempest; They Came to Cordura. 1960 Five Branded Women; Under Ten Flags. 1961 Il Relitto (The Wastrel, aka To Be a Man—U.S. 1963). 1963 Cry of Battle. 1965 The Greatest Story Ever Told; Once a Thief. 1966 Stagecoach. 1968 Each Man for Himself. 1969 The Trackers; The Man Outside; The Big Bounce. 1970 Airport. 1972 Revengers.

HEGGIE, O. P.
Born: Sept. 17, 1879, Angaston, South Australia. Died: Feb. 7, 1936, Los Angeles, Calif.(pneumonia). Screen and stage actor.

Appeared in: 1928 The Actress. 1929 The Letter; The Mysterious Dr. Fu Manchu; The Mighty; The Wheel of Life. 1930 Broken Dishes; Playboy of Paris; Sunny; The Vagabond King; Return of Dr. Fu Manchu; The Bad Man; One Romantic Night. 1931 The Women Between; Too Young to Marry; Devotion; East Lynne. 1932 Smilin' Through. 1933 The King's Vacation; Zoo in Budapest. 1934 Anne of Green Gables; Count of Monte Cristo; Peck's Bad Boy; Midnight. 1935 Chasing Yesterday; Dog of Flanders; Return of Frankenstein; Ginger; Bride of Frankenstein. 1936 Prisoner of Shark Island.

HEIDEMANN, PAUL "PAULCHEN"
Born: 1886, Cologne, Germany. Died: June 20, 1968, Berlin, Germany. Screen and stage actor.

Appeared in: 1931 Der Hampelmann (The Jumping Jack); Khre Hoheit Befiehlt. 1932 Kyritz-Pyritz; Schoen 1st die Manoeverzeit; Pension Schoeller; Wenn die Soldaten. 1934 Die Mutter der Kompagnie; Ja, Treu 1st die Soldatenliebel; Wie Man Maenner Fesselt; Abel Mit der Mundharmonika; Liebe in Uniform. 1935 Drie von der Kavallerie; Der Schuechterme Felix; Der Tolle Bomberg. 1936 Der Vetter aus Dingsda; Die Ganze Welt Dreht Sich um Liebe; 1st Mein Mann Nich Fabelhaft; Der Junge Graf. 1937 Freuhling im Wien; Hilde Petersen; Postlagernd; Der Unwiderst Ehliche (The Irresistable Man). 1938 Der Lachdoktor (The Laugh Doctor). 1940 Peter, Paul and Nanette.

HELTON, PERCY
Born: 1894, N.Y. Died: Sept. 11, 1971, Hollywood, Calif. Screen, stage, and television actor.

Appeared in: 1922 Silver Wings. 1947 Miracle on 34th Street. 1948 Hazard; Call Northside 777; Let's Live Again; Chicken Every Sunday; That Wonderful Urge; Larceny, Inc. 1949 Thieves' Highway; The Crooked Way; Criss Cross; The Set-Up; My Friend Irma; Abbott and Costello Meet the Killer, Boris Karloff. 1950 Harbor of Missing Men; Copper Canyon; Wabash Avenue; The Sun Sets at Dawn; Cyrano de Bergerac; Under Mexicali Skies; Fancy Pants; Tyrant of the Sea. 1951 Chain of Circumstance; The Barefoot Mailman. 1952 A Girl in Every Port; The Belle of New York; I Dream of Jeanie. 1953 Down Laredo Way; Call Me Madam; The Robe; How to Marry a Millionaire; Wicked Woman; The Stooge; Scared Stiff; Ambush at Tomahawk Gap. 1954 20,000 Leagues under the Sea; A Star Is Born; About Mrs. Leslie; White Christmas. 1955 Kiss Me Deadly; Crashout; No Man's Woman; Jail Busters. 1956 Fury at Gunsight Pass; Terror at Midnight; Shake, Rattle and Rock. 1957 The Phantom Stagecoach; Spook Chasers; Looking for Danger. 1958 Rally 'Round the Flag, Boys!. 1962 The Music Man; Ride the High Country. 1963 Four for Texas; The Wheeler Dealers. 1965 Hush, Hush, Sweet Charlotte; Zebra in the Kitchen; The Sons of Katie Elder. 1966 Don't Worry, We'll Think of a Title. 1968 Head; Funny Girl. 1969 Butch Cassidy and the Sundance Kid.

HEMSLEY, ESTELLE
Born: May 5, 1887, Boston, Mass. Died: Nov. 4, 1968, Los Angeles, Calif. Screen, stage, radio, and television actress.

Appeared in: 1950 Harvey (film and stage versions). 1957 Edge of the City. 1959 Green Mansions. 1960 Take a Giant Step; The Leech Woman. 1963 America, America. 1965 Baby, The Rain Must Fall.

HENDEE, HAROLD F.
Born: 1879. Died: June 24, 1966, New York, N.Y. Screen and stage actor. Appeared in films during the 1920s.

HENDERSON, DEL (George Delbert Henderson)
Born: July 5, 1883, St. Thomas, Ontario, Canada. Died: Dec. 2, 1956, Hollywood, Calif. Screen, stage actor, and film director. Entered films as a director with D. W. Griffith in 1909 and later turned to acting. Also directed several Mack Sennett films. Married to screen actress Florence Lee (dec. 1962).

Appeared in: 1909 Lines of White on the Sullen Sea. 1910 The Purgation; That Chink at Golden Gulch; When a Man Loves. 1911 Teaching Dad to Like Her; In the Days of '49; The Crooked Road; The Last Drop of Water; The Making of a Man; A String of Pearls; Comrades. 1913 The Battle of Elderberry Gulch. 1916 Intolerance. 1926 The Clinging Vine. 1927 Getting Gertie's Garter. 1928 Wrong Again (short); Riley the Cop; The Patsy; The Crowd; Power of the Press; Three-Ring Marriage; Show People. 1930 The Laurel and Hardy Murder Case; The Richest Man in the World; Hit the Deck; Sins of the Children. 1931 The Champ; Playthings of Hollywood; Newly Rich. 1933 Too Much Harmony; I Have Lived; From Hell to Heaven; The Big Brain; Rainbow over Broadway. 1934 Lone Cowboy; The Notorious Sophie Lang; The Lemon Drop Kid; The Marines Are Coming; Mrs. Wiggs of the Cabbage Patch; It's a Gift; Search for Beauty; Bolero; You're Telling Me; The Old Fashioned Way; Bottoms Up. 1935 Ruggles of Red Gap; Slightly Statics (short); Here Comes Cookie; Diamond Jim; The Mystery Man; Fighting Youth; Hot Tip; Hitch Hike Lady; The Daring Young Man; Black Sheep; This Is the Life. 1936 Our Relations; Poppy. 1937 Artists and Models; Make Way for Tomorrow. 1938 Rebellious Daughters; Goodbye Broadway. 1939 Frontier Marshal. 1940 Little Orvie; You Can't Fool Your Wife; If I Had My Way. 1944 Nothing but Trouble. 1945 Wilson. 1965 Laurel and Hardy's Laughing 20's (documentary).

HENDERSON, GEORGE A.
Born: New York, N.Y. Died: Nov. 28, 1923, San Francisco, Calif. (stroke). Screen, stage, and vaudeville actor.

Appeared in: 1923 The Fog.

HENDERSON, LUCIUS
Born: 1848. Died: Feb. 18, 1947, N.Y. Screen, stage, vaudeville actor, film director, and film producer.

Appeared in: 1923 Toilers of the Sea. 1925 A Man Must Live; The New Commandment. 1926 The Great Deception; White Mice.

HENDERSON, TALBOT V.
Born: 1879. Died: May 24, 1946, Los Angeles, Calif. Screen and stage actor.

Appeared in: 1929 The Bachelors' Club.

HENDERSON-BLAND, ROBERT
Born: England. Died: Aug. 18, 1941, London, England. British screen and stage actor.

Appeared in: From Manger to Cross.

HENDRICKS, BEN, SR.
Born: 1862, Buffalo, N.Y. Died: Apr. 30, 1930, Hollywood, Calif. Screen, stage, and vaudeville actor. Father of screen actor Ben Hendricks, Jr. (dec. 1938).

Appeared in: 1923 Big Dan. 1924 The City That Never Sleeps. 1925 Greater Than a Crown; Tides of Passion; Welcome Home. 1926 Satan Town. 1930 Black Waters.

HENDRICKS, BEN, JR.
Born: Nov. 2, 1893, New York, N.Y. Died: Aug. 15, 1938, Los Angeles, Calif. Screen actor. Made film debut in 1911. Son of screen actor Ben Hendricks, Sr.(dec. 1930).

Appeared in: 1921 The Land of Hope; Room and Board. 1922 The Headless Horseman; Free Air. 1923 The Broad Road; The Old Fool; Marriage Morals. 1924 Cyclone Rider; Just off Broadway; Against All Odds; The Man Who Played Square. 1926 Take It from Me; The Fighting Buckaroo; One Minute to Play; Rolling Home; Skinner's Dress Suit; What Happened to Jones?. 1927 Barbed Wire; Birds of Prey; A Racing Romeo. 1928 My Friend from India; Waterfront. 1929 Footlights and Fools; The Great Divide; Twin Beds; Synthetic Sin; The Wild Party. 1930 Men without Women; The Furies; The Girl of the Golden West; Ladies Love Brutes; Road to Paradise; Sunny. 1931 The Public Enemy. 1932 Rain; Pack up Your Troubles; Fireman Save My Child; The Kid from Spain; Fast Life; The Woman from Monte Carlo. 1933 Out All Night; The Important Witness; After Tonight. 1934 The Big Shakedown; We're Not Dressing; Blind Date. 1935 Northern Frontier; O'Shaughnessy's Boy. 1936 Draegerman Courage; North of Nome. 1937 Slim; Roaring Timber. 1938 Sergeant Murphy; Born to Be Wild.

HENDRICKS, LOUIS
Born: Buffalo, N.Y. Died: Dec. 18, 1923 (long illness). Screen and stage actor.

Appeared in: 1921 The Conquest of Canaan; The Sign on the Door. 1923 The Custard Cup.

HENIE, SONJA
Born: Apr. 8, 1912, Oslo, Norway. Died: Oct. 12, 1969, in air near Oslo (leukemia). Screen, television actress, and Olympic skating star.

Appeared in: 1936 One in a Million (film debut). 1937 Thin Ice. 1938 Happy Landing; My Lucky Star. 1939 Second Fiddle; Everything Happens at Night. 1941 Sun Valley Serenade. 1942 Iceland. 1943 Wintertime. 1945 It's a Pleasure. 1948 The Countess of Monte Cristo. 1961 Hello, London.

HENLEY, HOBART
Born: Nov. 23, 1891, Louisville, Ky. Died: May 22, 1964, Los Angeles, Calif. Screen, stage actor, film director, and film producer. Appeared in one-reelers produced in New York during early days of pictures.

Appeared in: 1915 Graft.

HENNECKE, CLARENCE R.
Born: Sept. 16, 1894, Omaha, Nebr. Died: Aug. 28, 1969, Santa Monica, Calif. Screen, vaudeville, television actor, film director, and screenwriter. Entered films as a stuntman with Vitagraph. Appeared in Keystone Kop comedies.

Appeared in: 1950 Joe Palooka in Humphrey Takes a Chance.

HENNESSEY, DAVID
Born: 1852. Died: Mar. 24, 1926, Chicago, Ill. Screen and stage actor.

HENNINGS, JOHN
Died: Nov. 8, 1933, St. Joseph, Mo.(suicide—gun shot). Screen and stage actor.

Appeared in: 1930 The Poor Millionaire.

HENRY, FRANK THOMAS PATRICK
Born: 1894. Died: Oct. 3, 1963, Hollywood, Calif. Screen and vaudeville actor.

HENRY, JAY
Born: July 14, 1910, New York, N.Y. Died: Dec. 23, 1951, White Plains, N.Y. Screen actor.

Appeared in: 1934 We're Not Dressing.

HENRY, JOHN
Born: 1882. Died: Aug. 12, 1958, Winthrop, Mass. Screen and vaudeville actor.

Appeared in: 1924 Poison; Those Who Judge; Yankee Speed.

HENSON, LESLIE
Born: Aug. 3, 1891, London, England. Died: Dec. 2, 1957, England. Screen and stage actor.

Appeared in: 1931 Tons of Money; A Warm Corner (U.S. 1934); The Sport of Kings (U.S. 1933); It's A Boy (U.S. 1933); The Girl from Maxims. 1935 Oh Daddy. 1943 The Demi-Paradise. 1956 Home and Away. Other British films: Alf's Button; Broken Bottles (both silents).

HEPBURN, BARTON
Born: Feb. 28, 1906, Minneapolis, Minn. Died: Oct. 10, 1955, Hollywood, Calif. Screen and stage actor. Entered films in 1928.

Appeared in: 1929 Dynamite. 1930 Painted Faces. 1943 Hi Diddle Diddle. 1944 The Bridge of San Luis Rey. 1945 A Song for Miss Julie.

HERBERT, HANS
Born: 1875. Died: June 21, 1957, Hollywood, Calif. Screen. stage, and television actor.

Appeared in: 1943 The Phantom of the Opera. 1944 Mr. Skeffington. 1950 Under My Skin.

HERBERT, HELEN
Born: 1873. Died: Oct. 27, 1946, Hollywood, Calif. Screen and stage actress. Entered films approx. 1924.

HERBERT, HENRY J.
Born: England. Died: Feb. 20, 1947, Flushing, N.Y. Screen and stage actor.

Appeared in: 1921 Suspicious Wives. 1923 The Day of Faith. 1924 Daughters of Today; Week-End Husbands; So Big; Stolen Secrets; Captain Blood. 1925 The Range Terror. 1926 The Blue Streak; The Mystery Club. 1927 The Girl from Rio; Whispering Smith Rides (serial); One Chance in a Million. 1928 Laddie Be Good; Look-Out Girl. 1930 Their Own Desire.

HERBERT, HOLMES E. (Edward Sanger)
Born: July 3, 1882, Mansfield Notts, England. Died: Dec. 26, 1956, Hollywood, Calif. Screen, stage, circus, and minstrel actor.

Appeared in: 1918 The Doll's House. 1919 The White Heather. 1920 Black Is White; His House in Order; My Lady's Garter; The Right to Love; Lady Rose's Daughter. 1921 The Inner Chamber; The Family Closet; The Wild Goose; Heedless Moths; Her Lord and Master. 1922 Any Wife; A Woman's Woman; Divorce Coupons; Evidence; A Stage Romance; Moonshine Valley. 1923 Toilers of the Sea. 1924 Love's Wilderness; The Enchanted Cottage; Another Scandal; Sinners in Heaven; Her Own Free Will. 1925 Daddy's Gone A'Hunting; A Woman of the World; Wreckage; Up the Ladder; Wildfire. 1926 The Honeymoon Express; The Wanderer; The Passionate Quest; Josselyn's Wife. 1927 The Fire Brigade; East Side, West Side; Lovers?; Mr. Wu; The Heart of Salome; One Increasing Purpose; The Silver Slave; When a Man Loves; Slaves of Beauty; The Gay Retreat; The Nest. 1928 The Terror; On Trial; Gentlemen Prefer Blondes; The Sporting Age; Their Hour; Through the Breakers. 1929 Madame X; The Charlatan; Careers; The Careless Age; Her Private Life; The Kiss; The Thirteenth Chair; Untamed; Say It with Songs. 1930 The Ship from Shanghai. 1931 Chances; Broadminded; Daughter of Fu Manchu; The Hot Heiress; The Single Sin; Daughter of the Dragon. 1932 Dr. Jekyll and Mr. Hyde; Shop Angel; Central Park; Miss Pinkerton. 1933 Mystery of the Wax Museum; Sister of Judas; The Invisible Man. 1934 Beloved; The House of Rothschild; Count of Monte Cristo; The Curtain Falls; One in a Million; Pursuit of Happiness. 1935 Captain Blood; Cardinal Richelieu; Mark of the Vampire; Sons of Steel; Accent on Youth. 1936 The Country Beyond; 15 Maiden Lane; Lloyds of London; Brilliant Marriage; The Gentleman from Louisiana. 1937 Slave Ship; The Girl Said No; Here's Flash Casey; The Prince and the Pauper; Love under Fire; Lancer Spy; The Thirteenth Chair (and 1929 version); House of Secrets. 1938 The Adventures of Robin Hood; The Buccaneer; Mystery of Mr. Wong; Say It in French; The Black Doll. 1939 Juarez; Trapped in the Sky; The Little Princess; Hidden Power; Stanley and Livingstone; Adventures of Sherlock Holmes; Everything Happens at Night; We Are Not Alone; Wolf Call; Bad Boy. 1940 South of Suez; British Intelligence. 1941 Man Hunt; International Squadron. 1942 This above All; Invisible Agent; The Undying Monster; The Ghost of Frankenstein; Sherlock Holmes and the Secret Weapon. 1943 Corvette K-225; Two Tickets to London; Sherlock Holmes in Washington. 1944 The Uninvited; Our Hearts Were Young and Gay; Pearl of Death; The Bermuda Mystery; Enter Arsene Lupin; Calling Dr. Death. 1945 Jealousy; The House of Fear; The Mummy's Curse; Confidential Agent. 1946 Three Strangers; The Verdict; Sherlock Holmes and the Secret Code (aka Dressed to Kill). 1947 This Time for Keeps; Over the Santa Fe Trail; Singapore; Bulldog Drummond Strikes Back; Bulldog Drummond at Bay; The Swordsman. 1948 Johnny Belinda; Wreck of the Hesperus; Jungle Jim. 1949 Barbary Pirate; Post Office Investigator. 1950 The Iroquois Trail. 1951 David and Bathsheba; Anne of the Indies; Law and the Lady. 1952 At Sword's Point; The Brigand.

HERBERT, HUGH
Born: Aug. 10, 1887, Binghamton, N.Y. Died: Mar. 13, 1952, North Hollywood, Calif.(heart attack). Brother of screen actor Thomas Herbert (dec. 1946). Screen, stage, vaudeville, television actor, playwright, and screenwriter.

Appeared in: 1927 Realization (short); Solomon's Children (short). 1928 The Lemon (short); On the Air (short); The Prediction (short); Husbands for Rent; Caught in the Fog. 1930 Danger Lights; Hook, Line and Sinker; Mind Your Own Business; Sin Ship. 1931 Laugh and Get Rich; Traveling Husbands; Friends and Lovers. 1932 The Lost Squadron; Faithless; Million Dollar Legs. 1933 Strictly Personal; Diplomaniacs; Goodbye Again; Bureau of Missing Persons; Footlight Parade; College Coach; From Headquarters; She Had to Say Yes; Convention City; Goldie Gets Along. 1934 Fashions of 1934; Easy to Love; Dames; Kansas City Princess; Wonder Bar; Harold Teen; Merry Wives of Reno; Fog over Frisco; The Merry Frinks. 1935 The Traveling Saleslady; Gold Diggers of 1935; A Midsummer Night's Dream; We're in the Money; Miss Pacific Fleet; To Beat the Band; Sweet Adeline. 1936 Colleen; Love Begins at 20; Sing Me a Love Song; One Rainy Afternoon; We Went to College. 1937 That Man's Here Again; The Singing Marine; Marry the Girl; The Perfect Specimen; Sh! The Octopus; Hollywood Hotel; Top of the Town. 1938 Men Are Such Fools; Gold Diggers in Paris; Four's a Crowd; The Great Waltz. 1939 Eternally Yours; The Little Accident; The Family Next Door; The Lady's from Kentucky. 1940 La Conga Nights; Private Affairs; Slightly Tempted; A Little Bit of Heaven; The Villain Still Pursued Her; The Hit Parade of 1941. 1941 Hellzapoppin!; Cracked Nuts; Meet the Chump; The Black Cat; Hello Sucker; Badlands of Dakota; Nobody's Fool. 1942 Mrs.

Wiggs of the Cabbage Patch; There's One Born Every Minute; Don't Get Personal; You're Killing Me. 1943 Stage Door Canteen. 1944 Kismet; Beauty for Sale; Ever since Venus; Music for Millions. 1946 One Way to Love; Carnegie Hall; The Mayor's Husband (short); When the Wife's Away (short). 1947 Blondie in the Dough. 1948 A Miracle Can Happen; So This is New York; A Song Is Born; Girl from Manhattan; On Our Merry Way. 1949 Beautiful Blonde from Bashful Bend. 1951 Havana Rose.

HERBERT, LEW
Born: 1903. Died: July 30, 1968, Pittsburgh, Pa. Screen, stage, and television actor.

Appeared in: 1950 Young Man with a Horn. 1963 Love with a Proper Stranger.

HERBERT, THOMAS F.
Born: Nov. 25, 1888, New York, N.Y. Died: Apr. 3, 1946, Los Angeles, Calif. Screen, stage, and vaudeville actor. Brother of screen actor Hugh Herbert (dec. 1952).

Appeared in: 1931 Traveling Husbands. 1933 Bed of Roses. 1934 Belle of the Nineties. 1937 Topper; Banjo on My Knee; Think Fast; Mr. Moto; Stars over Arizona. 1938 Professor Beware.

HERLEIN, LILLIAN
Born: approx. 1895. Died: Apr. 13, 1971, New York, N.Y. Screen, stage, vaudeville, radio, and television actress.

Appeared in: 1922 Solomon in Society.

HERMAN, JILL KRAFT
Born: 1931, N.Y. Died: June 25, 1970, Chicago, Ill.(cancer). Screen, stage, and television actress.

Appeared in: 1951 Goodbye, My Fancy.

HERMAN, MILTON C.
Born: 1896. Died: Jan. 21, 1951, Astoria, N.Y.(coronary thrombosis). Screen, radio, and television actor.

HERNANDEZ, ALBERT
Born: 1899, Mexico. Died: Jan. 2, 1948, Los Angeles, Calif.(after a fall). Screen actor. Appeared in silent films.

HERNANDEZ, JUAN G. "JUANO"
Born: 1896, San Juan, Puerto Rico. Died: July 17, 1970, San Juan, Puerto Rico (cerebral hemorrhage). Negro screen, stage, and circus actor.

Appeared in: 1949 Intruder in the Dust; The Accused. 1950 Stars in My Crown; The Breaking Point; Young Man with a Horn. 1955 Kiss Me Deadly; The Trial. 1956 Ransom. 1957 Something of Value. 1958 The Roots; St. Louis Blues; Machete; The Mark of the Hawk. 1960 Sergeant Rutledge. 1961 The Sins of Rachel Cade; Two Loves. 1962 Hemingway's Adventures of a Young Man. 1965 The Pawnbroker. 1969 The Reivers; The Extraordinary Seaman.

HERRNFELD, ANTON
Born: 1865. Died: Oct. 1929, Berlin, Germany. Yiddish screen and stage actor.

HERSHOLT, JEAN
Born: July 12, 1886, Copenhagen, Denmark. Died: June 2, 1956, Beverly Hills, Calif.(cancer). Screen, stage, and radio actor. Won Special Academy Award for his work for the Motion Picture Relief Fund in 1939 and won Special Award for Dancing in the Dark (1949).

Appeared in: 1915 Don Quixote. 1916 Princess Virtue. 1921 The Four Horsemen of the Apocalypse; A Certain Rich Man; The Man of the Forest; The Servant in the House. 1922 Tess of the Storm Country; Golden Dreams; The Gray Dawn; Heart's Haven; The Stranger's Banquet; When Romance Rides. 1923 Jazzmania; Quicksands; Red Lights. 1924 Cheap Kisses; The Goldfish; Her Night of Romance; Sinners in Silk; Torment; The Woman on the Jury; Greed. 1925 Dangerous Innocence; Don Q; Fifth Avenue Models; So Big; If Marriage Fails; Stella Dallas; A Woman's Faith. 1926 Flames; The Greater Glory; It Must Be Love; My Old Dutch; The Old Soak. 1927 The Student Prince in Old Heidelberg; The Wrong Mr. Wright. 1928 Alias the Deacon; The Battle of the Sexes; Give and Take; Jazz Mad; The Secret Hour; 13 Washington Square; Abie's Irish Rose. 1929 The Girl on the Barge; Modern Love; The Younger Generation; You Can't Buy Love. 1930 The Case of Sergeant Grischa; The Cat Creeps; The Climax; Hell Harbor; Mamba; A Soldier's Plaything; The Third Alarm; Viennese Nights; The Rise of Helga. 1931 Transatlantic; Susan Lennox, Her Rise and Fall; Sin of Madelon Claudet; Daybreak; Soldier's Plaything; Phantom of Paris; Private Lives;

Lullaby. 1932 Emma; Grand Hotel; Hearts of Humanity; The Mask of Fu Manchu; Beast of the City; Are You Listening?; Night Court; New Morals for Old; Skyscraper Souls; Unashamed; Justice for Sale; Flesh. 1933 The Crime of the Century; Song of the Eagle; Dinner at Eight; Christopher Bean. 1934 Men in White; The Painted Veil; The Cat and the Fiddle; The Fountain. 1935 Mark of the Vampire; Murder in the Fleet; Break of Hearts. 1936 Tough Guy; His Brother's Wife; The Country Doctor; Sins of Man; Reunion; One in a Million; The Old Soak. 1937 Seventh Heaven; Heidi. 1938 Happy Landing; Alexander's Ragtime Band; I'll Give a Million; Five of a Kind. 1939 Mr. Moto in Danger Island; Meet Dr. Christian. 1940 The Courageous Dr. Christian; Dr. Christian Meets the Women; Remedy for Riches. 1941 They Met Again; Melody for Three. 1943 Stage Door Canteen. 1949 Dancing in the Dark. 1955 Run for Cover.

HERTEL, ADOLPH R.
Born: 1878. Died: Mar. 16, 1958, Hollywood, Calif. Screen actor and film director.

HESLOP, CHARLES
Born: June 8, 1883, Thames Ditton, Surrey, England. Died: Apr. 13, 1966, London, England. Screen, stage, and vaudeville actor.

Appeared in: 1931 Hobson's Choice. 1932 Sunshine Susie. 1933 This Is the Life. 1934 Waltzes from Vienna. 1936 Charing Cross Road. 1938 The Man with 100 Faces; Crackerjack. 1939 The Lambeth Walk. 1942 Flying Fortress. 1951 The Late Edwina Black. 1959 Follow a Star (U.S. 1961). 1962 A Pair of Briefs (U.S. 1964). Other British film: The Second Mate.

HESSE, BARON WILLIAM
Born: 1885, Russia. Died: Apr. 4, 1936, West Coast, U.S.(following amputation of leg; also diabetes). Screen actor.

Appeared in: 1929 Prisoners.

HEYBURN, WELDON
Born: Sept. 19, 1904, Selma, Ala. Died: May 18, 1951, Los Angeles, Calif. Screen and stage actor. His film career was hampered due to his resemblance to actor Clark Gable. Divorced from screen actress Greta Nissen.

Appeared in: 1932 Careless Lady; Chandu the Magician; Call Her Savage; The Gay Caballero; The Silent Witness. 1933 West of Singapore. 1934 Hired Wife. 1935 Convention Girl. 1936 Speed. 1937 Git Along Little Dogies; Sea Racketeers; Atlantic Flight; The Thirteenth Man. 1938 Saleslady; Crime School; The Mysterious Rider; Dynamite Delaney. 1939 Fugitive at Large; Panama Patrol; Should a Girl Marry?. 1940 The Trail Blazers. 1941 Flight from Destiny; Redhead; Criminals Within; Jungle Man. 1942 Code of the Outlaw; Rock River Renegades; Murder in the Fun House. 1943 Death Valley Manhunt; Bordertown Trails; Code of the Prairie; Westward Bound; Yellow Rose of Texas. 1944 The Chinese Cat. 1946 Frontier Gun Law.

HEYDT, LOUIS JEAN
Born: Apr. 17, 1905, Montclair, N.J. Died: Jan. 29, 1960, Boston, Mass. Screen, stage, and television actor. Entered films in 1937.

Appeared in: 1937 Make Way for Tomorrow. 1938 Test Pilot; I Am the Law. 1939 Charlie Chan at Treasure Island; Let Freedom Ring; They Made Her a Spy; Reno; Gone with the Wind; They Made Me a Criminal; Each Dawn I Die. 1940 A Child Is Born; The Man Who Talked Too Much; Pier 13; Let's Make Music; Abe Lincoln in Illinois; Dr. Ehrlich's Magic Bullet; The Great McGinty; Joe and Ethel Turp Call on the President. 1941 Sleepers West; Dive Bomber; Power Dive; Midnight Angel. 1942 Ten Gentlemen from West Point; Manila Calling; Tortilla Flat; Triumph over Pain; Commandos Strike at Dawn; Pacific Blackout; Captains of the Clouds. 1943 Mission to Moscow; Stage Door Canteen; Gung Ho. 1944 The Great Moment; See Here, Private Hargrove; Her Primitive Man; Thirty Seconds over Tokyo. 1945 Betrayal from the East; Our Vines Have Tender Grapes; Zombies on Broadway; They Were Expendable. 1946 The Big Sleep; The Hoodlum Saint; Gentleman Joe Palooka. 1947 I Cover Big Town; Spoilers of the North. 1948 California's Golden Beginning; Bad Men of Tombstone. 1949 Make Believe Ballroom; Come to the Stable; The Kid from Cleveland. 1950 The Great Missouri Raid; The Furies; Paid in Full. 1951 Raton Pass; Rawhide; Criminal Lawyer; Roadblock; Drums in the Deep South; Warpath; Two of a Kind; Sailor Beware. 1952 The Old West; Models, Inc. 1953 The Vanquished; Island in the Sky. 1954 Boy from Oklahoma. 1955 The Eternal Sea; Ten Wanted Men; No Man's Woman. 1956 Stranger at My Door; Wetbacks. 1957 Badge of Marshal Brennan; Raiders of Old California; The Wings of Eagles. 1958 The Man Who Died Twice. 1959 Inside the Mafia.

HEYES, HERBERT
Born: Aug. 3, 1889, Vader, Wash. Died: May 30, 1958, North Hollywood, Calif. Screen and stage actor. Entered films in 1916.

Appeared in: 1916 Under Two Flags; The Vixen. 1917 The Tiger Woman. 1918 The Heart of the Sunset; Salome; The Lesson. 1919 The Adventures of Ruth (serial). 1920 Ruth of the Rockies (serial). 1921 The Queen of Sheba; The Blushing Bride; The Dangerous Moment; Dr. Jim; Wolves of the North; Ever since Eve. 1922 Shattered Dreams. 1923 One Stolen Night. 1924 It Is the Law. 1942 Destination Unknown; Tennessee Johnson. 1943 Calling Wild Bill Elliott; Campus Rhythm; Death Valley Manhunt; Mission to Moscow; It Ain't Hay. 1944 Detective Kitty O'Day; Outlaws of Santa Fe; Million Dollar Kid; Mr. Winkle Goes to War. 1945 Wilson. 1947 Miracle on 34th Street. 1948 T-Men; The Cobra Strikes; Behind Locked Doors. 1950 Kiss Tomorrow Goodbye; Tripoli; Union Station. 1951 Bedtime for Bonzo; Only the Valiant; A Place in the Sun; Three Guys Named Mike. 1952 Park Row; Carbine Williams; Ruby Gentry; Something to Live For. 1953 Man of Conflict; Let's Do It Again. 1955 The Court-Martial of Billy Mitchell; The Far Horizons; Love Is a Many Splendored Thing; New York Confidential; The Seven Little Foys; Sincerely Yours.

HIBBARD, EDNA
Born: 1895, Calif. Died: Dec. 26, 1942, New York, N.Y. Screen, stage, and vaudeville actress.

Appeared in: 1922 Island Wives. 1930 An Ill Wind (short).

HIBBERT, GEOFFREY
Born: June 2, 1922, Hull, Yorkshire, England. Died: Feb. 3, 1969, Epsom, England (heart attack). Screen, stage, and television actor.

Appeared in: 1941 Love on the Dole (film and stage versions). 1942 The Common Touch; Next of Kin; In Which We Serve. 1943 The Shipbuilders. 1952 Secret People. 1953 Hundred Hour Hunt. 1955 Break to Freedom; Cocktails in the Kitchen (aka For Better, For Worse). 1957 The End of the Line. 1958 Orders to Kill. 1959 Crash Drive. 1962 Live Now, Pay Later. 1963 The Great Van Robbery.

HICKEY, HOWARD L.
Born: 1897. Died: Mar. 25, 1942, San Fernando, Calif. Screen actor and horse trainer.

HICKMAN, ALFRED D.
Born: Feb. 25, 1873, England. Died: Apr. 9, 1931, Hollywood, Calif.(cerebral hemorrhage). Screen and stage actor.

Appeared in: 1914 The Master Key (serial). 1917 Fall of The Romanoffs. 1919 The Mad Woman; Here Comes the Bride. 1924 The Enchanted Cottage. 1929 The Rescue. 1930 The Last of the Lone Wolf. 1931 Phantom of Paris; A Woman of Experience.

HICKMAN, HOWARD C.
Born: Feb. 9, 1880, Columbia, Mo. Died: Dec. 31, 1949, Los Angeles, Calif.(heart attack). Screen, stage actor, and film director.

Appeared in: 1913 Rancho (film debut). 1916 Matrimony; Civilization. 1928 Alias Jimmy Valentine. 1930 Hello Sister; Brothers; The Broadway Hoofer; His First Command. 1931 Civilization (reissue of 1916 version). 1933 The Right to Romance. 1934 Madame DuBarry; Jimmy the Gent; Mystery Liner; Sisters under the Skin; Here Comes the Navy. 1935 Bright Lights; Rendezvous; It's In the Air. 1936 Too Many Parents; Hell-Ship Morgan; Fury; We Who Are about to Die; Wild Brian Kent; Career Woman; Happy Go Lucky; Two against the World; Crack-Up; August Weekend; Fifteen Maiden Lane. 1937 Charlie Chan at the Olympics; Artists and Models; The Lady Escapes; One Mile from Heaven; Western Gold; Borrowing Trouble; Join the Marines; Jim Hanvey, Detective; The Crime Nobody Saw; One Hundred Men and a Girl. 1938 Start Cheering; Flight into Nowhere; Juvenile Court; Rascals; Everybody's Baby; Numbered Woman; Come on, Leathernecks; I Stand Accused; Young Dr. Kildare. 1939 Convicts Code; Wife, Husband and Friend; Kansas Terrors; Good Girls Go to Paris; Espionage Agent; Little Accident; Gone with the Wind; The Return of Dr. X; Kid from Texas. 1940 The Man from Dakota; Strike up the Band; Gangs of Chicago; Girls of the Road; The Secret Seven; Slightly Honorable; It All Came True; Bullet Code. 1941 Cheers for Miss Bishop; Washington Melodrama; Scattergood Pulls the Strings; Hurricane Smith; Sign of the Wolf; Nine Lives Are Not Enough; Belle Starr; Doctors Don't Tell; Tuxedo Junction; Bowery Boy; Golden Hoofs; Robbers of the Range; Blossoms in the Dust; Hold That Ghost. 1942 I Was Framed; Tarzan's New York Adventure. 1943 Watch on the Rhine; Three Hearts for Julie. 1944 Follow the Boys.

HICKOK, RODNEY
Born: 1892. Died: Mar. 9, 1942, Los Angeles, Calif. Screen and stage actor.

Appeared in: 1921 Father Tom. 1924 The Bandolero. 1928 The Rawhide Kid.

HICKS, BERT
Born: 1920. Died: Jan. 8, 1965, Pacoima, Calif. Screen actor. Father of former screen actress Dolores Hart.

Appeared in: 1952 O'Henry's Full House.

HICKS, RUSSELL (Edward Russell Hicks)
Born: June 4, 1895, Baltimore, Md. Died: June 1, 1957, Hollywood, Calif.(heart attack). Screen, stage, television actor, and film director.

Appeared in: 1928 Happiness Ahead. 1933 Enlighten Thy Daughter; Before Morning. 1934 Happiness Ahead (and 1928 version); The Firebird; The St. Louis Kid; Murder in the Clouds; Gentlemen Are Born; The Case of the Howling Dog; Babbitt. 1935 Sweet Music; While the Patient Slept; Living on Velvet; The Woman in Red; Lady Tubbs; Thunder in the Night; $1,000 a Minute; Devil Dogs of the Air; Cardinal Richelieu; Honeymoon Limited; Charlie Chan in Shanghai; Ladies Love Danger. 1936 Two in the Dark; Follow the Fleet; Special Investigator; Grand Jury; We Who Are about to Die; Ticket to Paradise; Bunker Bean; Woman Trap; Laughing Irish Eyes; Hearts in Bondage; 15 Maiden Lane; The Sea Spoilers. 1937 Secret Valley; Midnight Taxi; Espionage; Pick a Star; 23 1/2 Hour's Leave; Girl Overboard; The Westland Case; On Again, Off Again; The Toast of New York; The Big Shot; Fit for a King; Criminals of the Air. 1938 In Old Chicago; Kidnapped; Little Miss Broadway; Gateway; Hold That Co-Ed; Kentucky; Fugitives for a Night; Big Broadcast of 1938. 1939 The Real Glory; Hollywood Cavalcade; Our Leading Citizen; Hotel for Women; Boy Trouble; The Three Musketeers; The Story of Alexander Graham Bell; The Honeymoon's Over; Swanee River; Stanley and Livingstone; I Was a Convict; Joe and Ethel Turp Call on the President; Honolulu; East Side of Heaven. 1940 The Mortal Storm; Earthbound; The Big Guy; The Blue Bird; Virginia City; Johnny Apollo; Enemy Agent; Sporting Blood; The Return of Frank James; East of the River; Seven Sinners; A Night at Earl Carroll's; The Bank Dick; No, No, Nanette; Love Thy Neighbor. 1941 The Big Store; Western Union; The Great Lie; The Arkansas Judge; A Man Betrayed; Man-Made Monster; Ellery Queen's Penthouse Mystery; Here Comes Happiness; Blood and Sand; The Parson of Panamint; Buy Me That Town; Hold That Ghost; The Little Foxes; Doctors Don't Tell; Public Enemies; Midnight Angel; Dangerous Game; Great Guns. 1942 We Were Dancing; To the Shores of Tripoli; Butch Minds the Baby; Joe Smith, American; Fingers at the Window; Tarzan's New York Adventure; Tennessee Johnson; Pacific Rendezvous; Blondie for Victory; Wings for the Eagle; Ride 'Em Cowboy. 1943 Follow the Band; Strictly in the Groove; Harrigan's Kid; King of the Cowboys; Air Raid Wardens; The Woman of the Town; His Butler's Sister; Hitler—Dead or Alive. 1944 Hat Check Honey; Janie; Louisiana Hayride; Port of Forty Thieves; Blind Fools. 1945 Apology for Murder; The Valley of Decision; Flame of the Barbary Coast; A Game of Death; A Guy, a Gal and a Pal; The Hidden Eye; Scarlet Street; She Gets Her Man. 1946 Swing Parade of 1946, The Bandit of Sherwood Forest; Gay Blades; A Close Call for Boston Blackie; Dark Alibi; GI War Brides; The Plainsman and the Lady; The Bachelor's Daughters. 1947 The Pilgrim Lady; Exposed; Fun on a Weekend; Sea of Grass; Louisiana; Web of Danger; Buck Privates Come Home. 1948 The Hunted; Assigned to Danger; The Black Arrow; The Gallant Legion; Race Street; The Velvet Touch; The Shanghai Chest; My Dear Secretary; The Plunderers; The Return of October; Maggie and Jiggs in Court; The Noose Hangs High. 1949 Samson and Delilah; I Cheated the Law; Barbary Pirate; Manhattan Angel. 1950 Blue Grass of Kentucky; The Flying Saucer; Unmasked; Square Dance Katy; Halls of Montezuma; The Big Hangover. 1951 Bowery Battalion; As You Were; Overland Telegraph; Kentucky Jubilee; All That I Have. 1952 The Maverick; Old Oklahoma Plains; Mr. Walkie Talkie. 1953 Man of Conflict. 1956 Seventh Cavalry.

HICKS, SIR SEYMOUR
Born: Jan. 30, 1871, St. Heliers, Jersey, England. Died: Apr. 6, 1949, Hampshire, England. Screen, stage actor, playwright, stage manager, and film producer. Married to screen actress Ellaline Terriss (Lady Hicks) (dec. 1971).

Appeared in: 1922 Always Tell Your Wife. 1926 Sleeping Partners (U.S. 1930). 1931 The Love Habit. 1932 Money for Nothing. 1934 The Secret of the Loch; Mr. What's His Name. 1935 Scrooge; Vintage Wine. 1939 The Lambeth Walk; Young Man's Fancy (U.S. 1943). 1940 Pastor Hall; Busman's Honeymoon;

Haunted Honeymoon. 1948 Silent Dust (U.S. 1950). 1949 Fame Is the Spur. Other British films: Glamour; The Catch of the Season and the following two silents: Bluebell in Fairyland; It's You I Want.

HIERS, WALTER
Born: July 18, 1893, Cordele, Ga. Died: Feb. 27, 1933, Los Angeles, Calif.(pneumonia). Screen and stage actor. Entered films as an extra in 1915 with Griffith at Biograph.

Appeared in: 1919 It Pays to Advertise; Leave It to Susan; Why Smith Left Home. 1920 Hunting Trouble. 1921 Sham; A Kiss in Time; Her Sturdy Oak; The Speed Girl; The Snob; Two Weeks with Pay. 1922 The Ghost Breaker; Bought and Paid For; Her Gilded Cage; Is Matrimony a Failure?. 1923 Mr. Billing Spends His Dime; Sixty Cents an Hour; Hollywood. 1924 Fair Week; Along Came Ruth; Christine of the Hungry Heart; The Triflers; Hold Your Breath; The Virgin; Flaming Barriers; plus Educational shorts: 1925 Excuse Me, plus the following shorts: Good Spirits; A Rarin' Romeo; Tender Feet; Oh, Bridget; Off His Beat; Hot Doggies. 1926 Hold That Lion. 1927 Beware of Widows; A Racing Romeo; Naughty; Hot Lemonade (short); Blondes by Choice; The Girl from Gay Paree; The Wrong Mr. Wright; The First Night; Husband Hunters; Night Life. 1928 A Woman against the World. 1931 Private Scandal; Oh! Oh! Cleopatra (short). 1932 Dancers in the Dark; 70,000 Witnesses.

HIGBY, WILBUR
Born: 1866. Died: Dec. 1, 1934, Hollywood, Calif.(heart attack). Screen and stage actor. Entered films in 1913. Married to stage actress Carolyn Higby.

Appeared in: 1919 Nugget Nell. 1921 Miracles of the Jungle (serial); Desert Blossoms; Live Wires; Play Square; Girls Don't Gamble. 1922 Do and Dare; My Dad; The Ladder Jinx. 1923 The Love Trap; Richard the Lion-Hearted. 1924 The Flaming Forties. 1925 Lights of Old Broadway; Confessions of a Queen. 1926 The Border Whirlwind. 1927 God's Great Wilderness. 1934 Hat, Coat and Glove.

HILDERBRAND, LO
Born: 1894. Died: Sept. 11, 1936, Los Angeles, Calif.(heart attack). Screen cowboy actor.

HILFORDE, MARY (Mary Griggs)
Born: 1853, Carbondale, Pa. Died: Dec. 12, 1927, Amityville, N.Y. Screen and stage actress.

HILL, ARTHUR
Born: 1875. Died: Apr. 9, 1932, Hollywood, Calif.(heart attack). Screen and stage actor.

HILL, BEN A.
Born: 1894. Died: Nov. 30, 1969, Dallas, Tex. Screen actor.

Appeared in: 1921 On the High Card; The Border Raiders.

HILL, DUDLEY S.
Born: 1881. Died: Jan. 7, 1960, Wilkesboro, N.C. Screen and stage actor. Entered films in 1913.

HILL, CAPT. GEORGE
Born: 1872. Died: Mar. 2, 1945, Hollywood, Calif. Screen actor and stand-in for Nigel Bruce and Harry Lauder.

HILL, RAYMOND
Born: 1891. Died: Apr. 16, 1941, Hollywood, Calif. Screen and radio actor.

HILL, THELMA (Thelma Hillerman)
Born: Dec. 12, 1906, Emporia, Kans. Died: May 11, 1938, Culver City, Calif. Screen actress. Entered films with Sennett in 1927 and was a Mack Sennett bathing girl.

Appeared in: 1927 The Fair Co-ed. 1928 The Chorus Kid; Hearts of Men; Crooks Can't Win; The Play Girl. 1929 the following shorts: The Bride's Relations; The Lunkhead; The Golfers. 1930 Two Plus Fours (short). 1931 The Miracle Woman.

HILLIARD, ERNEST
Born: Feb. 1, 1890, New York, N.Y. Died: Sept. 3, 1947, Santa Monica, Calif.(heart attack). Screen and stage actor. Entered films in 1912.

Appeared in: 1921 Annabel Lee; Tropical Love; The Matrimonial Web. 1922 Evidence; The Ruling Passion; Married People; Who Are My Parents?; Silver Sings. 1923 Love's Old Sweet Song; Man and Wife; Modern Marriage. 1924 Galloping Hoofs (serial);

The Recoil; Trouping with Ellen. 1925 Broadway Lady. 1926 The Fighting Failure; Forest Havoc; White Mice; The Frontier Trail; The High Flyer. 1927 Broadway after Midnight; The Wheel of Destiny; Wide Open; A Bowery Cinderella; Let It Rain; Compassion; The Scorcher; The Dancing Fool; The Silent Hero; Smile, Brother, Smile; The Midnight Watch; Modern Daughters. 1928 Divine Sinners; The Matinee Idol; Dugan of the Dugouts; Lady Raffles; Out with the Tide; The Big Hop; A Midnight Adventure; Burning up Broadway; Devil Dogs; The Noose; Sinners in Love. 1929 Red Wine; When Dreams Come True; The Big Diamond Robbery; Red Hot Rhythm; Dynamite; Say It with Songs; Weary River; Wall Street; Awful Truth. 1930 Broadway Hoofer. 1931 Second Honeymoon; Drums of Jeopardy; Mother and Son; Good Sport; Millie. 1934 The Witching Hour; Flirting with Danger. 1935 Smart Girl; Racing Luck. 1936 Boss Rider of Gun Creek; The Sea Spoilers. 1937 Life of the Party. 1942 The Magnificent Dope; Random Harvest. 1944 The Soul of a Monster. 1946 Deadline for Murder.

HILLIARD, HARRY S.
Died: Apr. 21, 1966, St. Petersburg, Fla.(complications after fall) Screen and stage actor.

Appeared in: 1916 Romeo and Juliet.

HILLIARD, MRS. MACK (Hazel Clayton)
Born: 1886. Died: Mar. 8, 1963, Forest Hills, N.Y. Screen and stage actress. Entered films during silents with original Fox Films Co. in Fort Lee, N.J. Appeared professionally as Mrs. Mack Hilliard.

HILLIAS, MARGARET "PEG"
Died: Mar. 18, 1960, Kansas City, Mo. Screen, stage, television, and radio actress.

Appeared in: 1951 A Streetcar Named Desire. 1957 Peyton Place; The Wayward Girl.

HINDS, SAMUEL S.
Born: Apr. 4, 1875, Brooklyn, N.Y. Died: Oct. 13, 1948, Pasadena, Calif. Screen, stage actor, and attorney.

Appeared in: 1932 If I Had a Million. 1933 The World Changes; The House on 56th Street; Convention City; Women in His Life; The Crime of the Century; Gabriel over the White House; The Nuisance; Day of Reckoning; Lady for a Day; Bed of Roses; Berkeley Square; The Deluge; Little Women; One Man's Journey; Penthouse; Hold the Press; This Day and Age; Son of a Sailor. 1935 The Big Shakedown; Manhattan Melodrama; Operator 13; A Wicked Woman; The Most Precious Thing in Life; Evelyn Prentice; He Was Her Man; Massacre; Crime Doctor; Straightaway; The Defense Rests; Have a Heart; A Lost Lady; Men in White; The Ninth Guest; No Greater Glory; West of the Pecos; Sisters under the Skin; Hat, Coat and Glove; Fog. 1935 Bordertown; Devil Dogs of the Air; Black Fury; Wings in the Dark; Sequoia; Strangers All; She; In Person; Mills of the Gods; Behind the Evidence; Dr. Socrates; Rhumba; Private Worlds; College Scandal; Accent on Youth; Annapolis Farewell; The Big Broadcast of 1936; Two Fisted; Millions in the Air; Shadow of Doubt; Rendezvous; The Raven; Living on Velvet. 1936 I Loved a Soldier; The Longest Night; Timothy's Quest; Woman Trap; The Trail of the Lonesome Pine; Border Flight; Fatal Lady; Rhythm on the Range; Sworn Enemy; His Brother's Wife; Love Letters of a Star. 1937 She's Dangerous; The Black Legion; Top of the Town; The Mighty Treve; Night Key; Wings over Honolulu; The Road Back; A Girl with Ideas; Prescription for Romance; Double or Nothing; Navy, Blue and Gold; Stage Door. 1938 Forbidden Valley; Young Dr. Kildare; Personal Secretary; The Jury's Secret; The Devil's Party; Wives under Suspicion; The Rage of Paris; The Road to Reno; The Storm; Swing That Cheer; Secrets of a Nurse; Test Pilot; You Can't Take It with You; Double Danger. 1939 Calling Dr. Kildare; Ex-Champ; Hawaiian Night; The Under-Pup; Newsboys' Home; Within the Law; Charlie McCarthy, Detective; Career; Tropic Fury; Rio; First Love; Hero for a Day; You're a Sweetheart; Pirates of the Skies; Destry Rides Again; No Greater Glory; One Hour to Live; The Secret of Dr. Kildare. 1940 It's a Date; Dr. Kildare's Strange Case; Ski Patrol; Boys from Syracuse; I'm Nobody's Sweetheart Now; Dr. Kildare Goes Home; Spring Parade; Seven Sinners; Trail of the Vigilantes; Zanzibar. 1941 Man-Made Monster; Buck Privates; Tight Shoes; Dr. Kildare's Wedding Day; Unfinished Business; Badlands of Dakota; Mob Town; Road Agent; Back Street; The Lady from Cheyenne; Adventure in Washington; The Shepherd of the Hills; Blossoms in the Dust. 1942 Frisco Lil; Ride 'Em Cowboy; Jail House Blues; Pittsburgh; Don Winslow of the Navy (serial); The Strange Case of Dr. Rx; The Spoilers; Kid Glove Killer; Grand Central Murder; Lady in a Jam; Pardon My Sarong. 1943 Mr. Big; No-

torious Gentleman; Top Man; Fired Wife; Larceny with Music; Great Alaskan Mystery (serial); Weird Woman; Murder in the Blue Room; Son of Dracula; Strangers in Our Midst; It Ain't Hay; Good Morning Judge; Follow the Band; Hi, Buddy; We've Never Been Licked; Hers to Hold; Keep 'Em Slugging; He's My Guy. 1944 Sing a Jingle; Follow the Boys; Ladies Courageous; South of Dixie; The Singing Sheriff; Cobra Woman; A Chip off the Old Block; Jungle Woman. 1945 Frisco Sal; Swing out, Sister; I'll Remember April; Secret Agent X-9 (serial); Men in Her Diary; Lady on a Train; The Strange Affair of Uncle Harry; Weekend at the Waldorf; Scarlet Street; Escape in the Desert. 1946 It's a Wonderful Life; White Tie and Tails; Blonde Alibi; Strange Conquest; Little Miss Big; Danger Woman; Inside Job; Notorious Gentlemen; The Runaround. 1947 The Egg and I; Time out of Mind; In Self Defense; Slave Girl. 1948 Perilous Waters; The Return of October; Call Northside 777; The Boy with the Green Hair. 1949 The Bribe.

HINES, ADRIAN R.
Born: 1903. Died: Mar. 6, 1946, San Antonio, Tex. Screen actor, extra, and circus animal trainer.

HINES, HARRY
Born: 1889. Died: May 3, 1967, Hollywood, Calif.(emphysema). Screen, burlesque, and vaudeville actor.

Appeared in: 1950 One Too Many. 1951 Mr. Belvedere Rings the Bell. 1952 Boots Malone; Talk about a Stranger. 1953 Last of the Pony Riders; City of Bad Men; Houdini. 1954 The Raid. 1956 The Kettles in the Ozarks. 1965 Cincinnati Kid. 1966 Texas across the River.

HINES, JOHNNY
Born: July 25, 1897, Golden, Colo. Died: Oct. 24, 1970, Los Angeles, Calif.(heart attack). Screen and stage actor. Entered films in 1915. Brother of screen actor Samuel E. Hines (dec. 1939).

Appeared in: 1920 "Torchy" series of shorts. 1921 Burn 'Em up Barnes. 1922 Sure-Fire Flint. 1923 Little Johnny Jones; Luck. 1924 The Speed Spook; Conductor 1492. 1925 The Crackerjack; The Early Bird; The Live Wire. 1926 The Brown Derby; Stepping Along; Rainbow Riley. 1927 All Aboard; Home Made; White Pants Willie. 1928 Chinatown Charlie; The Wright Idea. 1929 Alias Jimmy Valentine. 1930 Johnny's Week End (short). 1931 Runaround. 1932 Whistling in the Dark. 1933 The Girl in 419; Her Bodyguard. 1935 Society Doctor. 1938 Too Hot to Handle.

HINES, SAMUEL E.
Born: 1881. Died: Nov. 17, 1939, Los Angeles, Calif. Screen and stage actor. Brother of screen actor Johnny Hines (dec. 1970).

Appeared in: 1925 The Lost Chord; Shore Leave. 1933 The Road Is Open (short). 1934 He Was Her Man.

HINTON, ED
Born: 1928. Died: Oct. 12, 1958, Catalina Island, Calif.(airplane accident). Screen actor.

Appeared in: 1948 Harpoon. 1952 The Lion and the Horse; Hellgate; Leadville Slinger. 1953 Three Sailors and a Girl. 1954 Alaska Seas; River of No Return. 1955 Devil Goddess; Jungle Moon Men; Seminole Uprising. 1956 Julie; Walk the Proud Land. 1957 The 27th Day; Under Fire; The Dalton Girls. 1958 Cry Terror; The Decks Ran Red; Escape from Red Rock; Fort Bowie. 1959 Gidget.

HIPPE, LEW
Born: 1880. Died: July 19, 1952, Hollywood, Calif.(following operation for lung ailment). Screen actor for Mack Sennett.

HIRST, ALAN
Born: 1931. Died: Jan. 16, 1937, Hollywood, Calif. Six-year-old screen actor.

HITCHCOCK, RAYMOND
Born: 1870, Auburn, N.Y. Died: Nov. 24, 1929, Beverly Hills, Calif.(heart trouble). Screen, stage, and vaudeville actor. Married to screen actress Flora Zabelle (dec. 1968).

Appeared in: 1915 My Valet; Stolen Magic; The Village Scandal. 1922 The Beauty Shop. 1924 Broadway after Dark. 1926 Redheads Preferred; Everybody's Acting. 1927 The Money Talks; Upstream; The Tired Business Man. 1929 An Evening at Home with Hitchy (short).

HIX, DON (Don T. Hicks)
Died: Dec. 31, 1964, Hollywood, Calif. Screen, stage, and radio actor. Entered films with Universal in 1914.

Appeared in: 1959 Diary of a High School Bride.

HOAGLAND, HARLAND
Born: 1896. Died: Jan. 9, 1971, Hollywood, Calif.(cancer). Screen and stage actor. Entered films in 1921.

HOBBES, HALLIWELL
Born: Nov. 16, 1877, Stratford-on-Avon, England. Died: Feb. 20, 1962, Santa Monica, Calif.(heart attack). Screen and stage actor.

Appeared in: 1929 Lucky in Love; Jealousy. 1930 Grumpy; Charley's Aunt; Scotland Yard. 1931 The Right of Way; The Bachelor Father; Five and Ten; Platinum Blonde; The Sins of Madelon Claudet; The Woman Between. 1932 The Menace; The Devil's Lottery; Man about Town; Week Ends Only; Love Affair; Six Hours to Live; Dr. Jekyll and Mr. Hyde; Lovers Courageous; Forbidden; Payment Deferred. 1933 Lady of the Night; Looking Forward; Midnight Mary; Should Ladies Behave?; A Study in Scarlet; Captured; Lady for a Day; The Masquerader. 1934 I Am Suzanne; All Men Are Enemies; Mandalay; The Key; Riptide; Double Door; Bulldog Drummond Strikes Back; Madame DuBarry; British Agent. 1935 Follies Bergere; Cardinal Richelieu; The Right to Live; Millions in the Air; Jalna; Charlie Chan in Shanghai; Father Brown, Detective. 1936 The Story of Louis Pasteur; Here Comes Trouble; Dracula's Daughter; Love Letters of a Star; The White Angel; Hearts Divided; Give Me Your Heart; Spendthrift; Whipsaw. 1937 Maid of Salem; The Prince and the Pauper; Varsity Show; Fit for a King. 1938 You Can't Take It with You; The Jury's Secret; Service DeLuxe; Bulldog Drummond's Peril; Storm over Bengal; Kidnapped. 1939 The Light That Failed; Pacific Liner; The Hardy's Ride High; Naughty but Nice; Nurse Edith Cavell; Tell No Tales; Remember?. 1940 The Sea Hawk; The Earl of Chicago; Third Finger, Left Hand. 1941 That Hamilton Woman; Here Comes Mr. Jordan. 1942 To Be or Not to Be; The War against Mrs. Hadley; Journey for Margaret; The Undying Monster; Son of Fury. 1943 Sherlock Holmes Faces Death; Forever and a Day. 1944 The Invisible Man's Revenge; Gaslight; Mr. Skeffington; Casanova Brown. 1946 Canyon Passage. 1947 If Winter Comes. 1948 You Gotta Stay Happy; Black Arrow. 1949 That Forsyte Woman. 1956 Miracle in the Rain.

HOCK, RICHARD
Born: 1933. Died: July 13, 1961, Santa Monica, Calif.(burned in auto accident). Screen actor and stuntman. Married to stunt woman Margo Hock.

HODD, JOSEPH B., SR.
Born: 1896. Died: June 26, 1965, Philadelphia, Pa. Screen actor and stuntman. Entered films in 1927.

HODGEMAN, THOMAS
Born: 1875. Died: Apr. 24, 1931, Los Angeles, Calif. Screen, stage actor, and stage manager.

HODGES, WILLIAM CULLEN
Born: 1876, Newbury Township, Ohio. Died: July 28, 1961, Chardon, Ohio. Screen and stage actor.

HODGINS, EARL
Born: 1899. Died: Apr. 14, 1964, Hollywood, Calif.(heart attack). Screen, stage, and television actor.

Appeared in: 1934 The Circus Clown. 1935 The Cyclone Ranger; The Texas Rambler; Paradise Canyon; Harmony Lane. 1936 The Singing Cowboy; Guns and Guitars; Ticket to Paradise; Border Caballero; Aces and Eights. 1937 Borderland; Hills of Old Wyoming; Partners of the Plains; I Cover the War; Range Defenders; All over Town; A Law Man Is Born; Round-up Time in Texas; Heroes of the Alamo; Headin' East; Nation Aflame. 1938 The Old Barn Dance; The Purple Vigilantes; Call the Mesquiteers; The Rangers Roundup; Long Shot; Pride of the West; Lawless Valley; Barefoot Boy. 1939 Home on the Prairie; Almost a Gentleman; Panama Lady; The Day the Bookies Wept. 1940 Santa Fe Marshal; Men against the Sky; The Range Busters; Under Texas Skies; Law and Order; The Bad Man from Red Butte. 1941 Scattergood Pulls the Strings; Riding the Wind; Sierra Sue; Keep 'em Flying. 1942 The Bashful Bachelor; Deep in the Heart of Texas; Scattergood Survives a Murder; The Power of God; Inside the Law. 1943 False Colors; Tenting Tonight on the Old Camp Ground; The Old Chisholm Trail; The Avenging Rider; Hi! Ya, Chum; Colt Comrades; Bar 20; Lone Star Trail; Hoppy Serves a Writ. 1944 Riders of the Deadline; Hidden Valley Outlaws;

Firebrands of Arizona; San Antonio Kid; Sensations of 1945. 1945 The Southerner; Bedside Manner; GI Honeymoon; The Topeka Terror; Under Western Skies. 1946 The Bachelor's Daughters; Crime of the Century; The Devil's Playground; Live Wires; Fool's Gold; Unexpected Guest; Accomplice; Valley of the Zombies. 1947 The Marauders; Oregon Trail Scouts; Vigilantes of Boomtown; Rustler's Roundup; The Return of Rin-Tin-Tin. 1948 The Main Street Kid; Silent Conflict; Old Los Angeles; Let's Live Again. 1949 Henry, the Rainmaker; Sheriff of Wichita; Jiggs and Maggie in Jackpot Jitters; Slightly French. 1950 The Savage Horde; Square Dance Katy. 1953 Thunder over the Plains; The Great Jesse James Raid. 1954 Bitter Creek; The Forty-Niners. 1957 The D.I.; Up in Smoke. 1958 The Missouri Traveler. 1962 Saintly Sinners.

HODGINS, LESLIE
Born: 1885. Died: Sept. 1927, St. Louis, Mo. Screen actor and singer.

HODIAK, JOHN
Born: Apr. 16, 1914, Pittsburgh, Pa. Died: Oct. 19, 1955, Tarzana, Calif.(coronary thrombosis). Screen, stage, radio, and television actor. Divorced from screen actress Anne Baxter.

Appeared in: 1943 A Stranger in Town (film debut); I Dood It; Song of Russia; Swing Shift Maisie. 1944 Lifeboat; Marriage Is a Private Affair; Maisie Goes to Reno; Sunday Dinner for a Soldier; You Can't Do That to Me. 1945 A Bell for Adano. 1946 Ziegfeld Follies; The Harvey Girls; Somewhere in the Night; Two Smart People. 1947 The Arnelo Affair; Love from a Stranger; Desert Fury. 1948 Homecoming; Command Decision. 1949 Ambush; The Bribe. 1950 A Lady without a Passport; Malaya; Battleground; The Miniver Story. 1951 Night into Morning; People against O'Hara; Across the Wide Missouri. 1952 Battle Zone; The Sellout. 1953 Conquest of Cochise; Ambush at Tomahawk; Mission over Korea. 1954 Dragonfly Squadron. 1955 Trial. 1956 On the Threshold of Space.

HODSTON, LELAND (aka LEYLAND HODSTON)
Born: England. Died: Mar. 16, 1949, Hollywood, Calif.(heart attack). Screen and stage actor.

Appeared in: 1930 The Case of Sergeant Grisha. 1932 Under Cover Man; Ladies of the Jury. 1933 The Eagle and the Hawk. 1935 Perfect Gentleman; Feather in Her Hat. 1936 Beloved Enemy; Trouble for Two. 1937 The Adventurous Blonde. 1938 The Buccaneer. 1939 Susannah of the Mounties; Eternally Yours; The Witness Vanishes; Mr. Moto's Last Warning. 1940 He Married His Wife; My Son, My Son; Murder over New York. 1941 The Case of the Black Parrot; Scotland Yard; International Lady. 1942 To Be or Not to Be; The Ghost of Frankenstein; Secret Agent of Japan; The Strange Case of Dr. Rx; Escape from Hong Kong; Sherlock Holmes and the Voice of Terror; Just off Broadway. 1944 Enter Arsene Lupin. 1945 Hangover Square; Molly and Me. 1946 Three Strangers; Terror by Night; Rendezvous 24; Black Beauty; Bedlam. 1947 Thunder in the Valley. 1948 Kiss the Blood off My Hands; A Woman's Vengeance. 1949 That Forsyte Woman.

HOEFLICH, LUCIE
Born: 1883, Germany. Died: Oct. 9, 1956, Berlin, Germany (heart attack). Screen and stage actress.

Appeared in: 1936 1914: The Last Days before the War. 1959 Himmel Ohne Sterne (Sky without Stars).

HOEY, DENNIS (Samuel David Hyams)
Born: Mar. 30, 1893, England. Died: July 25, 1960, Palm Beach, Fla. Screen and stage actor. Entered films in 1931. Played character of "Inspector Lestrade" in Basil Rathbone's Sherlock Holmes series from 1939 to 1945.

Appeared in: 1931 The Battle of Gallipoli. 1932 The Good Companions. 1933 The Maid of the Mountains; I Spy; Lily of Killarney; Love in Morocco. 1934 Jew Seuss; Chu Chin Chow; Faust; The Bride in the Lake. 1935 The Wandering Jew; Brewster's Millions; Maria Martin. 1936 Murder in the Red Barn. 1937 Uncivilized; Phantom Ship. 1941 How Green Was My Valley. 1942 Son of Fury; This above All; Cairo; Sherlock Holmes and the Secret Weapon. 1943 Frankenstein Meets the Wolf Man; They Came to Blow up America; Forever and a Day; Sherlock Holmes Faces Death; Bomber's Moon. 1944 National Velvet; Keys of the Kingdom; Uncertain Glory; The Pearl of Death; The Spider Woman. 1945 House of Fear; A Thousand and One Nights. 1946 Roll on Texas Moon; She-Wolf of London; Tarzan and the Leopard Woman; The Strange Woman; Kitty; Terror by Night; Anna and the King of Siam. 1947 The Crimson Key; Second Chance; Golden Earrings; The Foxes of Harrow; Christmas Eve; Where There's Life; If Winter Comes. 1948 Ruthless; Badmen of Tombstone; Wake of the Red Witch. 1949 The Secret Garden. 1950 Joan of Arc; The Kid from Texas. 1951 David and Bathsheba. 1952 Caribbean. 1953 Ali Baba Nights.

HOEY, GEORGE J.
Born: 1885. Died: Feb. 17, 1955, Hollywood, Calif. Screen actor.

HOFER, CHRIS (Martin Christopher Hofer)
Born: 1920, N.Y. Died: Feb. 11, 1964, Rome, Italy (auto accident). Screen, stage, and television actor.

Appeared in: 1959 Londra Chiama Polo Nord (London Calling North Pole aka The House of Intrigue).

HOFFE, MONCKTON
Born: Dec. 26, 1880, Connemara, Ireland. Died: Nov. 4, 1951, London, England. Screen, stage actor, playwright, and screenwriter.

Appeared in: 1951 Lady with a Lamp.

HOFFMAN, EBERHARD
Born: 1883. Died: June 16, 1957, Denville, N.Y. Screen actor. Appeared in silents.

HOFFMAN, GERTRUDE (Gertrude Anderson)
Born: 1898, Montreal, Canada. Died: June 3, 1955, Washington, D.C. Screen and stage actress.

HOFFMAN, GERTRUDE W.
Born: May 17, 1871, Heidelberg, Germany. Died: Oct. 21, 1966, Hollywood, Calif. (heart attack). Screen, vaudeville actress, and dancer. Mother of screen actor Max Hoffman, Jr. (dec. 1945).

Appeared in: 1933 Hell and High Water; Before Dawn. 1935 Les Miserables. 1936 A Son Comes Home; The Gentleman from Louisiana. 1938 Cassidy of Bar 20. 1940 The Ape; Untamed; Foreign Correspondent. 1941 Lydia. 1942 I Married an Angel; Tish; Commandos Strike at Dawn; A Wife Takes a Flier. 1943 The Moon Is Down; A Guy Named Joe; The Heavenly Body; What a Woman. 1949 Thelma Jordan.

HOFFMAN, HERMINE H.
Born: 1921. Died: Dec. 7, 1971, Broomall, Pa. Screen, stage, and circus actress.

Appeared in: 1945 See My Lawyer.

HOFFMAN, HOWARD R.
Born: 1893. Died: June 26, 1969, Hollywood, Calif. (heart attack). Screen, stage, vaudeville, radio, and television actor.

Appeared in: 1958 Macabre; The Littlest Hobo. 1959 House on Haunted Hill.

HOFFMAN, MAX, JR.
Born: Dec. 13, 1902, Norfolk, Va. Died: Mar. 31, 1945, New York, N.Y. Screen, stage, and vaudeville actor. Son of dancer/screen actress Gertrude W. Hoffman (dec. 1966). Divorced from screen actress Helen Kane (dec. 1966).

Appeared in: 1936 Draegerman's Courage (film debut); King of Hockey. 1937 Counterfeit Lady; Rootin' Tootin' Rhythm; Swing it, Sailor; Sergeant Murphy; San Quentin. 1938 Sky Giant; Accidents Will Happen; The Great Waltz; Kidnapped; Little Orphan Annie. 1939 Ambush; Wings of Victory; Topper Takes a Trip; Hell's Kitchen; Confessions of a Nazi Spy; Kid Nightingale; Dust Be My Destiny. 1940 Brother Orchid; Lady from Hell; Virginia City; It All Came True; Castle on the Hudson. 1942 Man from Headquarters; Black Dragons.

HOGAN, PAT
Born: 1931. Died: Nov. 22, 1966, Hollywood, Calif. (cancer). Screen actor.

Appeared in: 1951 Fixed Bayonets. 1952 Luke of the Wilderness; Return of Gilbert and Sullivan. 1953 Arrowhead; Back to God's County; Gun Fury; Overland Pacific; Pony Express. 1954 Sign of the Pagan. 1955 Davy Crockett, King of the Wild Frontier; Kiss of Fire; Smoke Signal. 1956 The Last Frontier; Pillars of the Sky; Secret of Treasure Mountain; 7th Cavalry.

HOGAN, "SOCIETY KID" (Salvatore de Lorenzo)
Born: 1899. Died: Apr. 10, 1962, Chicago, Ill. Screen actor.

Appeared in: 1951 Lemon Drop Kid. 1953 Money from Home.

HOLDEN, HARRY MOORE
Born: 1868. Died: Feb. 4, 1944, Woodland Hills, Calif. Screen and stage actor.

Appeared in: 1927 The Gay Defender; The Yankee Clipper; Winds of the Pampas; Show Boat. 1930 Code of Honor.

HOLDEN, VIOLA (Viola Martinelli)
Died: Aug. 23, 1967, Saratoga, N.Y. (heart attack). Screen and stage actress.

Appeared in: 1948 Mexican Hayride. 1952 Sailor Beware.

HOLDEN, WILLIAM
Born: May 22, 1872, Rochester, N.Y. Died: Mar. 2, 1932, Hollywood, Calif. (heart attack). Screen and stage actor. Do not confuse with actor born in 1918.

Appeared in: 1928 Roadhouse (film debut); The First Kiss; Three Week Ends. 1929 Weary River; The Trespasser; Dynamite; His Captive Woman; Fast Life. 1930 Not So Dumb; Numbered Men; Framed; Holiday; What a Widow; Three Faces East. 1931 The Man Who Came Back; Charlie Chan Carries On; Six Cylinder Love; Dance, Fool, Dance.

HOLLAND, MIRIAM
Born: 1917. Died: Sept. 24, 1948, Hollywood, Calif. Screen actress.

HOLLAND, RALPH
Born: 1888. Died: Dec. 7, 1939, Los Angeles, Calif. Screen and stage actor. Entered films approx. 1927.

HOLLES, ANTONY
Born: Jan. 17, 1901, London, England. Died: 1950. Screen and stage actor.

Appeared in: 1931 Hotel Splendid (film debut). 1932 Reunion; The Lodger; The Missing Rembrandt. 1933 Cash; Loyalties; Britannia of Billingsgate; That's A Good Girl. 1934 Borrowed Clothes. 1935 Brewster's Millions; The Phantom Fiend. 1936 Things to Come; Public Nuisance No. 1; Doomed Cargo; Seven Sinners. 1937 The Tenth Man; Dark Journey; Mademoisell Docteur; Glamorous Night; Talk of the Devil; The Gaiety Girls. 1938 This'll Make You Whistle; Action for Slander; Let's Make a Night of It. 1939 They Drive by Night. 1941 Neutral Port; Missing Ten Days; Larceny Street. 1943 Warn That Man. 1944 Old Mother Riley Overseas; English without Tears; Canterbury Tale. 1945 They Met in the Dark; It's in the Bag; Battle for Music. 1946 Caesar and Cleopatra; Carnival. 1946 The Magic Bow. 1948 Jassy. 1949 Bonnie Prince Charlie. 1950 The Rocking Horse Winner. Other British films: Smash and Grab; Ten Days in Paris; Lady from Lisbon; Thursday's Child; Sensation; Up with the Lark; Give Me the Stars; Lisbon Story.

HOLLIDAY, FRANK, JR.
Born: 1913. Died: Aug. 3, 1948, Hollywood, Calif. (suicide—hanging). Screen and radio actor.

HOLLIDAY, JUDY
Born: June 21, 1923, New York, N.Y. Died: June 7, 1965, New York, N.Y. (cancer). Screen and stage actress. Won Academy Award in 1951 for Best Actress in Born Yesterday.

Appeared in: 1944 Greenwich Village; Something for the Boys; Winged Victory. 1949 Adam's Rib. 1951 Born Yesterday. 1952 The Marrying Kind. 1954 Phffft; It Should Happen to You. 1956 The Solid Gold Cadillac; Full of Life. 1960 Bells Are Ringing.

HOLLIDAY, MARJORIE (Marjorie St. Angel)
Born: 1920. Died: June 16, 1969, Hollywood, Calif. (brain hemorrhage). Screen actress.

HOLLINGSHEAD, GORDON
Born: Jan. 8, 1892, Garfield, N.J. Died: July 8, 1952, Balboa, Calif. Screen actor and film director. Entered films as an actor in 1914.

HOLLINGSWORTH, ALFRED
Born: 1874. Died: June 20, 1926, Glendale, Calif. Screen and stage actor.

Appeared in: 1916 Hell's Hinges. 1919 Leave It to Susan. 1921 The Infamous Miss Revell. 1922 The Bearcat; Trimmed. 1924 Marry in Haste. 1925 The Mystery Box (serial).

HOLLINGSWORTH, HARRY
Born: Sept. 3, 1888, Los Angeles, Calif. Died: Nov. 5, 1947, Los Angeles, Calif. Screen, stage, vaudeville, and radio actor. Married to Nan Crawford with whom he appeared in vaudeville in act billed as "Hollingsworth & Crawford."

Appeared in: 1916 The Tarantula. 1929 Bedtime (short with "Hollingsworth & Crawford"). 1936 Sing Me a Love Song. 1942 My Favorite Blonde.

HOLMAN, HARRY
Born: 1874. Died: May 2, 1947, Hollywood, Calif.(heart attack). Screen, stage, and vaudeville actor.

Appeared: 1929 Hard Boiled Hampton (short). 1930 Give Me Action (short). The Big Deal (short). 1933 Lucky Dog; Devil's Mate; One Year Later; My Woman; East of Fifth Avenue; Circus Queen Murder; Roman Scandals. 1934 It Happened One Night. 1935 Calling All Cars; Traveling Saleslady; In Caliente; Welcome Home; Cheers of the Crowd; Here Comes Cookie. 1936 Gentle Julia; The Criminal Within; Hitch Hike to Heaven. 1937 Nation Aflame. 1938 Western Jamboree. 1939 I Was a Convict. 1940 Slightly Tempted. 1941 Meet John Doe. 1942 Inside the Law; Seven Days' Leave. 1943 Shadows on the Sage. 1944 Swing Hostess.

HOLMES, BEN
Born: 1890, Richmond, Va. Died: Dec. 2, 1943, Hollywood, Calif. Screen, stage actor, film and stage director.

Appeared in: 1932 The Expert.

HOLMES, BURTON
Born: Jan. 8, 1870, Chicago, Ill. Died: July 22, 1958, Hollywood, Calif. Screen actor and film producer. Pioneer of travel films and shorts. Made first travel films in Italy (1897) and first travel films in Hawaii (1898).

Appeared in: 1922 Around the World with Burton Holmes. 1924 Glorious Switzerland. 1925 Teak Logging with Elephants; Tyrolean Perspectives; Under Cuban Skies; The Salt of Amping; A Cabaret of Old Japan; The Garden of the East. 1926 So This Is Florida. 1927 Closeups of China. 1928 Happy Hawaii. 1929 Motoring Thru Spain; Siam, the Land of Chang. 1930 France; Germany; London; Mediterranean Cruise; Venice.

HOLMES, HELEN
Born: 1892, Chicago, Ill. Died: July 8, 1950, Burbank, Calif. (heart attack). Screen actress. Entered films with Sennett in 1912.

Appeared in: 1914 The Hazards of Helen (serial). 1915 The Girl and the Game (serial). 1916 A Lass of the Lumberlands (serial). 1917 The Lost Express (serial); The Railroad Raiders (serial). 1919 The Fatal Fortune (serial). 1920 The Tiger Band (serial). 1921 A Crook's Romance. 1922 Ghost City; Hills of Missing Men; The Lone Hand. 1923 Stormy Seas; One Million in Jewels. 1924 Battling Brewster (serial); The Riddle Rider (serial); Fighting Fury; Forty Horse Hawkins. 1925 Blood and Steel; Barriers of the Law; The Sign of the Cactus; Webs of Steel; Duped; Outwitted; The Train Wreckers. 1926 Mistaken Orders; Crossed Signals; Peril of the Rail; The Lost Express; The Open Switch. 1936 Poppy. 1937 The Californian. 1941 Dude Cowboy.

HOLMES, PHILLIPS
Born: July 22, 1909, Grand Rapids, Mich. Died: Aug. 12, 1942, near Armstrong, Ontario, Canada (air collision of an RCAF Plane). Screen and stage actor. Son of screen actor Taylor Holmes (dec. 1959) and brother of screen actor Ralph Holmes (dec. 1945).

Appeared in: 1928 Varsity (film debut); His Private Life. 1929 The Wild Party; Stairs of Sand; Pointed Heels; The Return of Sherlock Holmes. 1930 The Dancers; Man to Man; Grumpy; Her Man; The Devil's Holiday; Only the Brave; Paramount on Parade. 1931 An American Tragedy; Stolen Heaven; Confessions of a Co-ed; The Criminal Code. 1932 Justice for Sale; Rockabye; The Man I Killed; Broken Lullaby; Two Kinds of Women; 70,000 Witnesses; Night Court. 1933 Dinner at Eight; Penthouse; Storm at Daybreak; Beauty for Sale; The Secret of Madame Blanche; Men Must Fight; Looking Forward; Stage Mother; The Big Brain; State Fair. 1934 Great Expectations; Nana; Million Dollar Ransom; Caravan; Private Scandal. 1935 No Ransom; Ten Minute Alibi; The Divine Spark. 1936 The House of a Thousand Candles; Chatterbox; General Spanky. 1937 The Dominant Sex. 1939 Housemaster.

HOLMES, RALPH
Born: May 20, 1889, Detroit, Mich. Died: Nov. 1945, New York, N.Y.(natural causes). Screen, stage actor, and editor. Son of screen actor Taylor Holmes (dec. 1959) and brother of screen actor Phillips Holmes (dec. 1942).

HOLMES, STUART
Born: Mar. 10, 1887, Chicago, Ill. Died: Dec. 29, 1971, Hollywood, Calif.(ruptured abdominal aortic aneurism). Screen, stage, and vaudeville actor.

Appeared in: 1914 Life's Shop Window. 1916 A Daughter of the Gods. 1917 The Scarlet Letter. 1919 The New Moon; The Other Man's Wife. 1920 The Evil Eye (serial); Trailed by Three (serial). 1921 The Four Horsemen of the Apocalypse; No Woman Knows; All's Fair in Love; Passion Fruit. 1922 The Prisoner of Zenda; Her Husband's Trademark; Paid Back; The Stranger's Banquet; Under Two Flags. 1923 Daughters of the Rich; The Rip-Tide; Tea with a Kick; Hollywood; The Scarlet Lily; Tipped Off; Temporary Marriage; The Unknown Purple. 1924 Tess of the D'Urbervilles; The Age of Innocence; Between Friends; Vanity's Price; The Beloved Brute; Three Weeks; In Every Woman's Life; On Time; The Siren of Seville. 1925 North Star; Fighting Cub; Three Keys; Friendly Enemies; Heir-Loons; The Primrose Path; The Salvation Hunters; Steele of the Royal Mounted; A Fool and His Money; Paint and Powder. 1926 Devil's Island; Good and Naughty; The Hurricane; The Midnight Message; Broken Hearts of Hollywood; Beyond the Trail; The Shadow of the Law; Everybody's Acting; My Official Wife. 1927 When a Man Loves; Your Wife and Mine; Polly of the Movies. 1928 The Man Who Laughs; Beware of Married Men; Burning Daylight; Danger Trail; Devil Dogs; The Cavalier; The Hawk's Nest. 1929 The Heroic Lover. 1930 Captain of the Guard. 1931 War Mamas (short). 1932 My Pal the King; The Millionaire Cat (short); Jitters the Butler (short). 1934 Are We Civilized?; Belle of the Nineties. 1936 Murder by an Aristocrat; Earthworm Tractors; The Case of the Velvet Claws; Trailin' West. 1937 Her Husband's Secretary. 1939 On Trial. 1940 British Intelligence; Devil's Island. 1944 Last Ride; The Adventures of Mark Twain. 1945 Shady Lady. 1947 Moss Rose. 1948 A Letter to Three Wives. 1953 Remains to Be Seen. 1955 The Cobweb. 1956 The Birds and the Bees. 1962 The Man Who Shot Liberty Valance.

HOLMES, TAYLOR
Born: 1872, Newark, N.J. Died: Sept. 30, 1959, Hollywood, Calif. Screen, stage, vaudeville, and television actor. Married to screen actress Edna Phillips (dec. 1952). Father of screen actors Phillips (dec. 1942) and Ralph Holmes (dec. 1945).

Appeared in: 1917 Efficiency Edgar's Courtship. 1918 Ruggles of Red Gap. 1924 Twenty Dollars a Week. 1925 The Crimson Runner; The Verdict; Borrowed Finery; Her Market Value. 1927 One Hour of Love. 1929 the following shorts: He Did His Best; He Loved the Ladies. 1930 Dad Knows Best (short). 1931 An American Tragedy. 1933 Before Morning; Dinner at Eight. 1934 Nana. 1936 The Crime of Dr. Forbes; The First Baby; Make Way for a Lady. 1947 Kiss of Death; Nightmare Alley; The Egg and I; Time out of Mind; In Self Defense; Boomerang; Great Expectations. 1948 Smart Woman; Let's Love Again; The Plunderers; Act of Violence; That Wonderful Urge; Joan of Arc. 1949 Woman in Hiding; Joe Palooka in the Big Fight; Mr. Belvedere Goes to College; Once More My Darling. 1950 Bright Leaf; Caged; Copper Canyon; Double Deal; Father of the Bride; Quicksand. 1951 Drums in the Deep South; The First Legion; Rhubarb; Two Tickets to Broadway. 1952 Woman in the North Country; Beware My Lovely; Hold That Line; Hoodlum Empire; Ride the Man Down. 1953 Gentlemen Prefer Blondes. 1954 The Outcast; Tobor the Great; Untamed Heiress. 1955 The Fighting Chance; Hell's Outpost. 1956 The Maverick Queen; The Peace Maker. 1958 Wink of an Eye.

HOLMES, WENDELL
Born: 1915. Died: Apr. 26, 1962, Paris, France. Screen, stage, and television actor.

Appeared in: 1949 Lost Boundaries. 1958 Young and Wild. 1959 Edge of Eternity; Good Day for a Hanging. 1960 Because They're Young; Elmer Gantry.

HOLMES, WILLIAM J.
Born: 1877. Died: Dec. 1, 1946, Hollywood, Calif. Screen, stage, vaudeville actor, playwright, and stage producer.

Appeared in: 1930 Once a Gentleman.

HOLT, JACK (John Charles Holt)
Born: May 31, 1888, Winchester, Va. Died: Jan. 18, 1951, Los Angeles, Calif.(heart attack). Screen, stage, and vaudeville actor. Father of screen actor Tim Holt (dec. 1973). Entered films as a stuntman in 1913.

Appeared in: 1914 A Cigarette—That's All. 1916 The Dumb Girl of Portici; Joan the Woman; Liberty, a Daughter of the U.S.A. (serial). 1917 The Little American. 1918 The Claw; The Road through the Dark. 1919 The Woman Thou Gavest Me; Victory; Cheating Cheaters; A Midnight Romance; A Sporting Chance; The Life Line. 1920 Held by the Enemy; The Best of Luck; Midsummer Madness. 1921 After the Show; All Souls Eve; The Call of the North; Ducks and Drakes; The Grim Comedian; The Lost Romance; The Mask. 1922 Bought and Paid For; North of the

Rio Grande; While Satan Sleeps; The Man Unconquerable; Making a Man; On the High Seas. 1923 The Cheat; A Gentleman of Leisure; Nobody's Money; The Tiger's Claw; Hollywood; The Marriage Maker. 1924 Wanderer of the Wasteland; Empty Hands; The Lone Wolf; Don't Call It Love; North of 36. 1925 The Thundering Herd; The Light of Western Stars; The Ancient Highway; Evil's Secret; Wild Horse Mesa. 1926 The Enchanted Hill; Born to the West; Forlorn River; The Blind Goddess; Man of the Forest; Sea Horses. 1927 The Mysterious Rider; The Tigress; The Warning. 1928 Submarine; The Vanishing Pioneer; The Water Hole; Avalanche; Court-Martial; The Smart Set. 1929 The Donovan Affair; Father and Son; Flight; Sunset Pass. 1930 Vengeance; The Border Legion; Hell's Island; The Squealer. 1931 The Dangerous Affair; The Last Parade; Fifty Fathoms Deep; Subway Express; Dirigible; White Shoulders; Maker of Men. 1932 The Last Man; The Plain Clothes Man; Behind the Mask; War Correspondent; Man against Woman; This Sporting Age. 1933 Fever; The Forgotten Man; Tampico; When Strangers Marry; The Woman I Stole; The Wrecker; Master of Men; The Whirlpool; End of the Trail. 1934 The Defense Rests; Black Moon; I'll Fix It. 1935 The Best Man Wins; Unwelcome Stranger; The Awakening of Jim Burke; Storm over the Andes; The Littlest Rebel; Curly Top. 1936 Dangerous Waters; Crash Donovan; San Francisco; North of Nome; End of the Trail (and 1933 version). 1937 Trouble in Morocco; Roaring Timber; The River of Missing Men; Trapped by G-Men; Under Suspicion; Outlaws of the Orient. 1938 Making the Headlines; Flight into Nowhere; Crime Takes a Holiday; Reformatory; Outside the Law; House of Mystery. 1939 Trapped in the Sky; Hidden Power; Fugitive at Large; Whispering Enemies. 1940 Outside the 3-Mile Limit; Passport to Alcatraz; Fugitive from a Prison Camp; The Great Plane Robbery; Laddie; Alien Sabotage. 1941 The Great Swindle; Holt of the Secret Service (serial). 1942 Thunder Birds; Northwest Rangers; The Cap People. 1945 There Goes Kelly; They Were Expendable. 1946 The Chase; My Pal Trigger. 1947 Renegade Girl; Wild Frontier. 1948 Strawberry Roan; Arizona Ranger; The Gallant Legion; Loaded Pistols; Treasure of Sierra Madre; Flight to Nowhere. 1949 Brimstone; The Last Bandit; Loaded Pistols; Red Desert; Task Force. 1950 Return of the Frontiersman; Trail of Robin Hood. 1951 Across the Wide Missouri.

HOLZWORTH, FRED
Died: Feb. 1, 1970, Cleveland, Ohio. Screen and stage actor.

HOMANS, ROBERT E.
Born: 1875, Malden, Mass. Died: July 28, 1947, Los Angeles, Calif.(heart attack). Screen and stage actor.

Appeared in: 1923 Legally Dead. 1924 The Breathless Moment; Dark Stairways. 1925 Border Justice. 1926 Fighting with Buffalo Bill (serial); The Silent Power; College Days. 1927 The Fightin' Comeback; The Bandit Buster (serial); Ride 'em High; Fast and Furious; Range Courage; The Galloping Gobs; The Princess from Hoboken; Heroes of the Night; Mountains of Manhattan; The Silent Avenger. 1928 The Masked Angel; Pals in Peril; Obey Your Husband; Blindfold. 1929 Burning the Wind; The Isle of Lost Ships; Smiling Irish Eyes; Fury of the Wild. 1930 The Concentratin' Kid; Son of the Gods; Spurs; Trigger Tricks; The Thoroughbred. 1931 The Black Camel; Silence. 1932 Pack up Your Troubles; Young America; Madame Racketeer. 1933 From Headquarters; She Done Him Wrong. 1936 Here Comes Trouble; Laughing Irish Eyes; The President's Mystery; Easy Money; It Couldn't Have Happened; Bridge of Sighs; Below the Deadline. 1937 The Plough and the Stars; Penrod and Sam; Don't Pull Your Punches; Dance, Charlie, Dance; Forlorn River; Jim Hanvey, Detective. 1938 The Kid Comes Back; Penrod and His Twin Brother; Over the Wall; Little Miss Thoroughbred; The Amazing Dr. Clitterhouse; Heart of the North; Gold Is Where You Find It; Hollywood Stadium Mystery; Gold Mine in the Sky; The Night Hawk; Hunted Men. 1939 Hell's Kitchen; Young Mr. Lincoln; Inside Information; Smuggled Cargo; The Old Maid; Ruler of the Sea; Five Came Back; King of the Turf. 1940 West of Carson City; East of the River; The Grapes of Wrath; Lillian Russell. 1941 Out of the Fog. 1942 Fingers at the Window; For Me and My Gal; It Happened in Flatbush; Lady in a Jam; The Sombrero Kid; X Marks the Spot; Night Monster. 1943 Happy Go Lucky; You Can't Beat the Law; Shantytown; Frontier Badmen; It Ain't Hay. 1944 Pin Up Girl; It Happened Tomorrow; Nothing but Trouble; Jack London; The Whistler; The Merry Monahans; Cover Girl. 1945 Rogues' Gallery; River Gang; Beyond the Pecos; A Medal for Benny; Come Out Fighting; Captain Eddie; Scarlet Clue. 1946 Earl Carroll Sketchbook.

HONDA, FRANK
Born: 1884, Japan. Died: Feb. 3, 1924, N.Y. Screen actor.
Appeared in: 1921 Dawn of the East; Wedding Bells. 1923 Lawful Larceny.

HONN, ELDON
Born: 1890. Died: Aug. 11, 1927, San Diego, Calif.(died in parachute fall). Screen actor and motorcycle stuntman.

HOOD, TOM
Born: 1919. Died: Dec. 8, 1950, Hollywood, Calif.(murdered). Screen actor.

HOOPII, SOL (Sol Hoopii Kaaiai)
Born: 1905, Hawaii. Died: Nov. 16, 1953, Seattle, Wash. Screen actor and musician.

HOPE, DIANA
Born: 1872, England. Died: Nov. 20, 1942, Hollywood, Calif. (heart attack). Screen, stage and vaudeville actress.

Appeared in: 1930 The Man from Blankley's.

HOPE, VIDA
Born: 1918, England. Died: Dec. 23, 1963, Chelmsford, England (auto accident). Screen, stage actress, and stage director.

Appeared in: 1944 English without Tears. 1945 Johnny in the Clouds. 1947 Nicholas Nickleby. 1948 It Always Rains on Sunday. 1950 Woman in Question (aka Five Angles on Murder—U.S. 1953); While the Sun Shines; For Them That Trespass. 1951 Cheer the Brave; Green Grow the Rushes; The Man in the White Suit (U.S. 1952); Interrupted Journey. 1953 The Long Memory; Double Confession; Twilight Women (aka Women of Twilight); Hundred Hour Hunt. 1954 Lease of Life. 1958 Prescription for Murder (aka Rx Murder; Prescription Murder); Family Doctor. 1961 Roadhouse Girl.

HOPKINS, BOB
Born: 1918. Died: Oct. 5, 1962, Hollywood, Calif.(acute leukemia). Screen, stage, and television actor.

Appeared in: 1945 On Stage Everybody. 1949 The Lucky Stiff. 1953 The Kid from Left Field. 1956 Autumn Leaves; Flight to Hong Kong. 1962 The Errand Boy; Saintly Sinners. 1963 Papa's Delicate Condition.

HOPPER, DE WOLF (William DeWolf Hopper)
Born: Mar. 30, 1858, New York, N.Y. Died: Sept. 23, 1935, Kansas City, Mo. Screen and stage actor. Married to stage actress Lillian Glaser (dec. 1969) and divorced from screen actresses Edna Wallace (dec. 1959) and Elda Furry (known professionally as Hedda Hopper) (dec. 1966) and father of screen actor William Hopper (dec. 1970).

Appeared in: 1915 Don Quixote. 1916 Casey at the Bat; Macbeth; A Rough Knight; Wings and Wheels; The Girl and the Mummy; Puppets; Sunshine Dad. 1930 For Two Cents (short); At the Round Table (short). 1935 The Return of Dr. X.

HOPPER, EDNA WALLACE
Born: 1874, San Francisco, Calif. Died: Dec. 14, 1959, N.Y. Screen and stage actress. Filmed her own face-lifting operation. Divorced from actor DeWolf Hopper (dec. 1935).

HOPPER, HEDDA (Elda Furry)
Born: June 2, 1890, Hallisdaysburg, Pa. Died: Feb. 1, 1966, Los Angeles, Calif.(pneumonia). Screen, stage, radio and television actress, and columnist. Divorced from screen actor DeWolf Hopper (dec. 1935) and mother of screen actor William Hopper (dec. 1970).

Appeared in: 1916 Battle of Hearts (film debut). 1917 Seven Keys to Baldpate; Her Excellency, the Governor; The Food Gamblers; Nearly Married. 1918 By Right of Purchase. 1919 Virtuous Wives. 1920 The New York Idea; The Man Who Lost Himself. 1921 Heedless Moths; Conceit. 1922 Women Men Marry; What's Wrong with Women?; Sherlock Holmes. 1923 Has the World Gone Mad?; Reno. 1924 Happiness; Free Love; Miami; Another Scandal; Gambling Wives; The Snob; Sinners in Silk; Why Men Leave Home. 1925 Declassee; Raffles, the Amateur Cracksman; Zander the Great; Borrowed Finery; Dangerous Innocence; Her Market Value; The Teaser. 1926 Mona Lisa (short); Don Juan; The Caveman; Obey the Law; The Silver Treasure; Pleasures of the Rich; Dance Madness; Fools of Fashion; Lew Tyler's Wives; Skinner's Dress Suit. 1927 Wings; Children of Divorce; Adam and Evil;

Black Tears; One Woman to Another; Matinee Ladies; The Cruel Truth; Orchids and Ermine; Venus of Venice; The Drop Kick; A Reno Divorce. 1928 Diamond Handcuffs; Companionate Marriage; The Chorus Kid; The Whip Woman; Giving In (short); Runaway Girls; Green Grass Widows; Harold Teen; The Port of Missing Girls; Undressed; Love and Learn. 1929 The Racketeer; Girls Gone Wild; Hurricane; His Glorious Night; The Last of Mrs. Cheyney; A Song of Kentucky. 1930 Our Blushing Brides; High Society Blues; Divorcee; Such Men Are Dangerous; Holiday; War Nurse; Let Us Be Gay; Murder Will Out. 1931 Shipmates; The Easiest Way; Up for Murder; The Prodigal; Men Call It Love; Strangers May Kiss; A Tailor-Made Man; Rebound; Mystery Train; Flying High; Good Sport; Common Law. 1932 West of Broadway; Happy Landing; Night World; Speak Easily; Skyscraper Souls; The Unwritten Law; Downstairs; As You Desire Me; The Man Who Played God; The Slippery Pearls (short). 1933 The Barbarian; Pilgrimage; Beauty for Sale; Men Must Fight. 1934 Bombay Mail; Let's Be Ritzy; Little Man, What Now?; No Ransom. 1935 I Live My Life; Society Fever; One Frightened Night; Lady Tubbs; Three Kids and a Queen; Alice Adams. 1936 Dracula's Daughter; Doughnuts and Society; Bunker Bean; Dark Hour. 1937 You Can't Buy Luck; Topper; Dangerous Holiday; Artists and Models; Nothing Sacred; Vogues of 1938. 1938 Tarzan's Revenge; Dangerous to Know; Thanks for the Memory; Maid's Night Out. 1939 The Women; What a Life; Laugh It Off; Midnight; That's Right—You're Wrong. 1940 Queen of the Mob; Cross Country Romance. 1941 Life with Henry; I Wanted Wings. 1942 Reap the Wild Wind. 1946 Breakfast in Hollywood. 1950 Sunset Boulevard. 1960 Pepe. 1964 The Patsy. 1966 The Oscar.

HOPPER, WILLIAM (William DeWolf Hopper)
Born: Jan. 26, 1915, New York, N.Y. Died: Mar. 6, 1970, Palm Springs, Calif.(pneumonia). Screen, stage, and television actor. Entered films in 1937. Son of screen actress Hedda Hopper (dec. 1966) and screen actor DeWolf Hopper (dec. 1935).

Appeared in: 1937 The Adventurous Blonde; Footloose Heiress; Over the Goal; Love Is on the Air; Public Wedding; Women Are Like That. 1938 Mystery House; Daredevil Drivers. 1939 The Old Maid; Pride of the Bluegrass; Nancy Drew and the Hidden Staircase; The Cowboy Quarterback. 1940 Knute Rockne—All American; The Fighting Sixty-Ninth; Tear Gas Squad; Flight Angels; Ladies Must Live. 1941 The Maltese Falcon; The Bride Came C.O.D.; Flight from Destiny; Bullets for O'Hara; Here Comes Happiness. 1942 Lady Gangster. 1943 The Mysterious Doctor; Murder on the Waterfront. 1954 The High and the Mighty; Track of the Cat; Sitting Bull; This Is My Love. 1955 Conquest of Space; Rebel without a Cause; Robber's Roost; One Desire. 1956 The Bad Seed; Goodbye, My Lady; The First Texan. 1957 The Deadly Mantis; Slim Carter; 20,000,000 Miles to Earth. 1970 Myra Breckenridge.

HOPTON, RUSSELL
Born: Feb. 18, 1900, New York, N.Y. Died: Apr. 7, 1945, North Hollywood, Calif. Screen, stage actor, and film director.

Appeared in: 1926 Ella Cinders. 1930 College Lovers; The Pay Off (short); Call of the Flesh; Min and Bill; Remote Control. 1931 Dance, Fools, Dance; Street Scene; Miracle Woman; Reckless Living; Arrowsmith; Twenty Grand; Blonde Crazy; Dance Team; The Criminal Code; Star Witness; Falling Star; Law and Order. 1932 Man Who Played God; The Drifter; Discarded Lovers; Big Timber; Night World; The Famous Ferguson Case; Radio Patrol; Back Street; Fast Companions; Air Mail; Tom Brown of Culver; Once in a Life Time. 1933 Successful Failure; I Sell Anything; Take the Stand; Destination Unknown; Desirable; Elmer the Great; The Little Giant; Lady Killer; One Year Later; Secret of the Blue Room; I'm No Angel. 1934 Good Dame; Men in White; Curtain at Eight; Half a Sinner; He Was Her Man; Born to Be Bad; School for Girls. 1935 Circus Shadows; Valley of Wanted Men; Time Square Lady; Northern Frontier; G-Men; Wings in the Dark; The World Accuses; Death from a Distance; False Pretenses; Star of Midnight; Headline Woman; Cheers of the Crowd; Frisco Waterfront; Car 99. 1936 The Last Outlaw; We Who Are about to Die; Below the Deadline; Rose of the Rancho. 1937 Beware of Ladies; Angel's Holiday; One Mile from Heaven; Idol of the Crowds. 1938 Crime Takes a Holiday. 1939 Made for Each Other; The Saint Strikes Back; Torture Ship; Mutiny in the Big House; Renegade Trail. 1944 A Night of Adventure. 1945 Zombies on Broadway; West of the Pecos.

HORAN, JAMES
Born: 1908. Died: May 4, 1967, Hollywood, Calif.(cancer). Screen and television actor.

HORNBROOK, CHARLES "GUS"
Born: 1874. Died: May 8, 1937, Los Angeles, Calif.(pneumonia). Screen and vaudeville actor.

HORNE, DAVID
Born: July 14, 1898, Blacome, Sussex, England. Died: Mar. 15, 1970, London, England. Screen, stage actor, and playwright.

Appeared in: 1933 General John Regan. 1934 Spitfire. 1936 The Mill on the Floss; It's Love Again; Seven Sinners; Doomed Cargo; The Interrupted Honeymoon. 1937 The House of the Spaniard; Farewell Again; The Wrecker; Four Dark Hours; The First and the Last. 1940 Twenty-One Days Together. 1941 Inspector Hornleigh Goes to It. 1942 Wings and the Woman; The Avengers; The First of the Few. 1943 Adventure in Blackmail. 1944 The Yellow Canary. 1945 The Seventh Veil; The Rake's Progress. 1946 The Man Within; They Were Sisters; Notorious Gentleman; The Man from Morocco; The Wicked Lady. 1947 The Magic Bow; Caravan. 1948 The Smugglers; Showtime. 1949 It's Hard to Be Good; Easy Money; Once upon a Dream; Saraband. 1950 Madeleine. 1953 Spaceways; Martin Luther. 1954 Beau Brummell. 1955 Three Cases of Murder, The Intruder. 1956 Lust for Life. 1957 The Prince and the Showgirl. 1958 The Safecracker. 1959 The Devil's Disciple; The Sheriff of Fractured Jaw. 1961 Goodbye Again. 1964 Nurse of Wheels. 1968 A Flea in Her Ear. Other British films: Chamber of Horrors; Men of Two Worlds; Gaiety George; Five Pound Note; Policewoman; Wedding Gift; Spring Song.

HORTON, BENJAMIN
Born: 1872. Died: Aug. 9, 1952, Hollywood, Calif. Screen actor.

HORTON, EDWARD EVERETT
Born: Mar. 18, 1886, Brooklyn, N.Y. Died: Sept. 29, 1970, Encino, Calif.(cancer). Screen, stage, television actor, and stage producer.

Appeared in: 1922 A Front Page Story; The Ladder Jinx; Too Much Business. 1923 Ruggles of Red Gap; To the Ladies. 1924 Helen's Babies; Flapper Wives; The Man Who Fights Alone; Try and Get It. 1925 The Beggar on Horseback; Marry Me; The Business of Love. 1926 The Whole Town's Talking; La Boheme; The Nut Cracker; Poker Faces. 1927 Taxi! Taxi!. 1928 The Terror; Miss Information (short). 1929 Sonny Boy; The Hottentot; The Sap; The Victor; The Aviator; and the following shorts: Good Medicine; The Right Bed; Trusting Wives; Prince Babby. 1930 Take the Heir; Toast of the Legion; Wide Open; Holiday; Once a Gentleman. 1931 Kiss Me Again; Reaching for the Moon; Smart Money; The Front Page; Lonely Wives; Six Cylinder Love; Age for Love; Smart Woman. 1932 But the Flesh Is Weak; Thieves and Lovers; Roar of the Dragon; Trouble in Paradise. 1933 A Bedtime Story; The Way to Love; Design for Living; Alice in Wonderland; It's a Boy. 1934 The Poor Rich; Uncertain Lady; Easy to Love; Smarty; The Merry Widow; Kiss and Make Up; Ladies Should Listen; Sing and Like It; Success at Any Price; The Woman in Command; The Gay Divorcee. 1935 The Night Is Young; Biography of a Bachelor Girl; All the King's Horses; The Devil Is a Woman; Ten Dollar Raise; Little Big Shot; Going Highbrow; Top Hat; The Private Secretary; His Night Out; Your Uncle Dudley; In Caliente; Caprice Espagnol. 1936 Her Master's Voice; The Singing Kid; Hearts Divided; Nobody's Fool; The Man in the Mirror. 1937 Lost Horizon; Let's Make a Million; Angel; Wild Money; The King and the Chorus Girl; The Perfect Specimen; The Great Garrick; Oh, Doctor; Shall We Dance; Hitting a New High; Danger—Love at Work. 1938 College Swing; Bluebeard's Eighth Wife; Holiday; Little Tough Guy in Society. 1939 That's Right—You're Wrong; Paris Honeymoon. 1941 You're the One; Sunny; Week-End for Three; Here Comes Mr. Jordan; The Body Disappears; Ziegfeld Girl; Sandy Steps Out; Bachelor Daddy. 1942 I Married an Angel; The Magnificent Dope; Springtime in the Rockies. 1943 Forever and a Day; Thank Your Lucky Stars; The Gang's All Here. 1944 Summer Storm; Brazil; San Diego; I Love You; The Town Went Wild; The Amazing Mr. Forrest; Arsenic and Old Lace; Her Primitive Man. 1945 Strange Confession; Lady on a Train; Steppin' in Society. 1946 Cinderella Jones; Faithful in My Fashion; Earl Carroll Sketchbook. 1947 The Ghost Goes Wild; Down to Earth; Her Husband's Affairs. 1948 All My Sons. 1957 The Story of Mankind. 1961 Pocketful of Miracles. 1963 It's a Mad, Mad, Mad, Mad World. 1964 Sex and the Single Girl. 1967 The Perils of Pauline. 1969 2,000 Years Later. 1970 Cold Turkey.

HORWITZ, JOSEPH
Born: 1858. Died: Oct. 26, 1922, Mt. Clemens, Mich.(uremic poisoning). Screen actor.

HOSTETTER, ROY
Born: 1885. Died: Sept. 22, 1951, near Carlsbad, Calif.(auto accident). Screen actor.

HOTALING, ARTHUR D. (Arthur Douglas Hotaling)
Born: 1872. Died: July 13, 1938, enroute to San Pedro from Palm Springs, Calif.(heart attack). Screen actor and film director.

Appeared in: 1925 Kit Carson over the Great Divide. 1927 Better Days; King of the Herd. 1928 The Little Wild Girl; Old Age Handicap.

HOUDINI, HARRY (Erik aka Ehrich Weisz and Henry Weiss)
Born: Mar. 24, 1874, Hungary. (Numerous publications indicate date of birth as Feb. 29, 1876, however, correct date explained as follows: "Perhaps to give Ehrich the security of American citizenship, she (his mother) told him that he, like his younger brother Theo, had been born in Appleton. The date she said was Apr. 6, 1874. That became his 'adopted birthday' ")[1]. Died: Oct. 31, 1926, Detroit, Mich.(following appendectomy). Magician, screen, stage, vaudeville actor, and film producer. Entered films in 1918.

Appeared in: 1918 The Master Mystery (serial). 1919 The Grim Game. 1920 Terror Island. 1921 The Soul of Bronz. 1922 The Man from Beyond. 1923 Haldane of the Secret Service. 1961 Days of Thrills and Laughter (documentary).

HOUGHTON, ALICE
Born: 1888. Died: May 12, 1944, Los Angeles, Calif. Screen actress.

HOUSE, BILLY
Born: 1890. Died: Sept. 23, 1961, Hollywood, Calif.(heart attack). Screen, stage, and vaudeville actor.

Appeared in: 1931 Smart Money; God's Gift to Women. 1932-33 Paramount shorts. 1937 Merry-Go-Round of 1938. 1945 Thrill of a Romance. 1946 Bedlam; The Strangers. 1947 The Egg and I; Trail Street. 1950 Rogues of Sherwood Forest; Where Danger Lives. 1951 People Will Talk; Santa Fe. 1952 Aladdin and His Lamp; Outlaw Women. 1955 Imitation of Life.

HOUSE, JACK
Born: 1887. Died: Nov. 20, 1963, Hollywood, Calif. Screen actor and stuntman. Doubled for Rudolf Valentino and Fred Thomas.

Appeared in: 1924 The Smoking Trail. 1925 Fightin' Odds.

HOUSEMAN, ARTHUR (aka ARTHUR HOUSMAN)
Born: 1890, New York, N.Y. Died: Apr. 7, 1942, Los Angeles, Calif.(pneumonia). Screen and stage actor.

Appeared in: 1921 The Fighter; The Way of a Maid; Clay Dollars; Room and Board; Worlds Apart; Is Life Worth Living?. 1922 The Snitching Hour; Man Wanted; Destiny's Isle; Love's Masquerade; Shadows of the Sea; Why Announce Your Marriage?; The Prophet's Paradise. 1923 Male Wanted; Under the Red Robe; Wife in Name Only. 1924 Manhandled; Nellie, the Beautiful Cloak Model. 1925 A Man Must Live; Braveheart; The Necessary Evil; Thunder Mountain; The Coast of Folly; The Desert's Price; Night Life of New York. 1926 The Bat; Early to Wed; Whispering Wires; The Midnight Kiss. 1927 Bertha, the Sewing Machine Girl; Publicity Madness; The Spotlight; Sunrise; Rough House Rosie; Love Makes 'Em Wild. 1928 The Singing Fool; Partners in Crime; Fools for Luck; Sins of the Fathers. 1929 Side Street; Queen of the Night Clubs; Fast Company; Times Square; Broadway; The Song of Love. 1930 Girl of the Golden West; The Squealer; Officer O'Brien; Feet First. 1931 Bachelor Girl; Five and Ten; Night Life in Reno; Anybody's Blonde; Caught Plastered. 1932 Movie Crazy; No More Orchids; Afraid to Talk; Scram! (short); Any Old Port (short). 1933 She Done Him Wrong; The Intruder; Her Bodyguard; The Way to Love; Sing, Sinner, Sing. 1934 Mrs. Wiggs of the Cabbage Patch; The Live Ghost (short); Here Is My Heart; Babes in the Goods (short); Done in Oil (short); Punch Drunks (short). 1935 Hold 'Em Yale; Riffraff; The Fixer Upper (short); Paris in the Spring; Here Comes Cookie; Diamond Jim; The Fire Trap; Treasure Blues (short); Sing, Sister, Sing (short). 1936 Our Relations; Wives Never Know; Racing Blood; With Love and Kisses. 1937 Step Lively; Jeeves!. 1939 Navy Secrets. 1940 Go West.

1. From Houdini: The Untold Story by Milbourne Christopher, c1969 by Milbourne Christopher. With permission of the publisher, Thomas Y. Crowell Company, Inc.

HOUSTON, CISCO
Born: 1919. Died: Apr. 23, 1961, San Bernardino, Calif. Screen actor, folk singer, and song writer. Appeared in western films.

HOUSTON, GEORGE
Born: 1900, Hampton, N.J. Died: Nov. 12, 1944, Los Angeles, Calif.(heart ailment). Screen, stage, and opera actor.

Appeared in: 1935 The Melody Lingers On (film debut). 1936 Let's Sing Again; Captain Calamity. 1937 Hurricane; Conquest; Wallaby Jim of the Islands. 1938 Frontier Scout; The Great Waltz. 1940 Laughing at Danger; The Howards of Virginia. 1941 The Lone Rider in Ghost Town; The Lone Rider Ambushed; The Lone Rider Fights Back. 1942 The Lone Rider in Border Roundup; The Lone Rider in Cheyenne.

HOVICK, ROSE LOUISE. See Gypsy Rose Lee

HOWARD, ART
Born: 1892. Died: May 28, 1963, Hollywood, Calif.(coronary thrombosis). Screen and stage actor.

HOWARD, BERT
Born: 1873. Died: Oct. 27, 1958, Hollywood, Calif. Screen and stage actor.

HOWARD, BOOTH
Born: 1889. Died: Oct. 4, 1936, Los Angeles, Calif.(hit by auto). Screen and stage actor.

Appeared in: 1933 My Woman; Hot Pepper; Trick for Treat; The Avenger. 1934 Mystery Liner; Midnight Alibi. 1935 Smart Girl; Every Night at Eight; Mary Burns, Fugitive; Show Them No Mercy. 1936 The Robin Hood of El Dorado; Charlie Chan at the Circus; Undersea Kingdom (serial).

HOWARD, DAVID H.
Born: 1860, N.Y. Died: Dec. 9, 1944, Woodland Hills, Calif. Screen and stage actor.

HOWARD, EDDY
Born: 1909, Ill. Died: May 23, 1963, Palm Desert, Calif.(cerebral hemorrhage). Bandleader, song writer, and screen actor.

HOWARD, ERNEST (Ernest Ladd)
Born: 1875. Died: Nov. 8, 1940, Brooklyn, N.Y. Screen and stage actor. Appeared in silent films.

HOWARD, ESTHER
Born: 1893. Died: Mar. 8, 1965, Hollywood, Calif.(heart attack). Screen and stage actress.

Appeared in: 1930 the following shorts: Twixt Love and Duty; Ship Ahoy; The Woman Tamer; Who's the Boss; The Victim. 1931 Wicked; The Vice Squad. 1932 Ladies of the Big House; The Cohens and the Kellys in Hollywood; Merrily We Go to Hell; Winner Take All; Rackerty Rax. 1933 Below the Sea; Second Hand Wife; The Iron Master. 1935 Straight from the Heart; Ready for Love; The Misses Stooge (short). 1936 Klondike Annie; M'Liss. 1937 Rhythm in the Clouds. 1938 Scandal Street; Swing, Sister, Swing. 1939 Broadway Serenade. 1940 The Great McGinty. 1941 Sullivan's Travels. 1942 The Palm Beach Story. 1944 Murder, My Sweet; Hail the Conquering Hero; The Big Noise; The Miracle of Morgan's Creek. 1945 The Great Flamarion; Detour; A Letter for Evie. 1946 The Falcon's Alibi; Dick Tracy vs. Cueball. 1947 Born to Kill. 1949 Champion; The Lady Gambles; The Beautiful Blonde from Bashful Bend; Hellfire; Homicide. 1951 All That I Have.

HOWARD, EUGENE (Eugene Levkowitz)
Born: 1881, Germany. Died: Aug. 1, 1965, New York, N.Y. Screen, stage, vaudeville, and radio actor. Brother of screen actor Willie Howard (dec. 1949); together they appeared in vaudeville as "Eugene and Willie Howard" and in 1927-29 the team appeared in the following shorts: 1927 A Theatrical Managers Office; Between the Acts of the Opera; Pals. 1929 The Music Makers; My People.

HOWARD, FLORENCE
Born: 1888. Died: Aug. 11, 1954, Hollywood, Calif.(heart attack). Screen and stage actress.

HOWARD, GERTRUDE
Born: Oct. 13, 1892, Hot Springs, Ark. Died: Sept. 30, 1934, Los Angeles, Calif. Negro screen and stage actress. Entered films in 1914.

Appeared in: 1925 The Circus Cyclone. 1927 River of Romance; Easy Pickings; South Sea Love; Uncle Tom's Cabin. 1928 On Your Toes. 1929 Hearts in Dixie; His Captive Woman; Synthetic Sin; Mississippi Gambler; Show Boat. 1930 Guilty; Conspiracy. 1931 Father's Son; The Prodigal. 1932 Strangers in Love; The Wet Parade. 1933 I'm No Angel. 1934 Peck's Bad Boy. 1959 Uncle Tom's Cabin (rerelease of 1927 film).

HOWARD, JEROME "CURLY"
Born: 1906, Brooklyn, N.Y. Died: Jan. 19, 1952, San Gabriel, Calif. Screen, stage, and vaudeville actor. One of the original "Three Stooges" of stage and screen. Brother of screen actors Samuel "Shemp" (dec. 1955) and Moe Howard.

Appeared in: 1933 Turn Back the Clock; Meet the Baron; Dancing Lady. 1934 Fugitive Lovers; Hollywood Party; Gift of Gab; The Captain Hates the Sea and the following shorts: Woman Haters; Men in Black; Punch Drunks and Three Little Pigskins. 1935 the following shorts: Horse Collars; Restless Knights; Pop Goes the Easel; Uncivil Warriors; Pardon My Scotch; Hoi Polloi; Three Little Beers; Screen Snapshots #6. 1936 the following shorts: Ants in the Pantry; Movie Maniacs; Half-Shot Shooters; Disorder in the Court; A Pain in the Pullman; False Alarms; Whoops I'm an Indian; Slippery Silks. 1937 the following shorts: Grips, Grunts, and Groans; Dizzy Doctors; Three Dumb Clucks; Goofs and Saddles; Back to the Woods; Cash and Carry; Playing the Ponies; The Sitter-Downers. 1938 Start Cheering, plus the following shorts: Termites of 1938; Wee Wee Monsieur; Tassels in the Air; Healthy, Wealthy and Dumb; Three Missing Links; Violent Is the Word for Curly; Mutts to You; Flat Foot Stooges. 1939 the following shorts: Three Little Sew and Sews; We Want Our Mummy; A-Ducking They Did Go; Yes We Have no Bonanza; Saved by the Belle; Calling All Curs; Oily to Bed—Oily to Rise; Three Sappy People. 1940 the following shorts: You Natzy Spy; Rockin' Through the Rockies; A-Plumbing We Will Go; From Nurse to Worse; Nutty But Nice; How High Is Up; No Census No Feeling; Cuckoo Cavaliers; Boobs in Arms. 1941 Time Out for Rhythm, plus the following shorts: So Long, Mr. Chumps; Dutiful But Dumb; All the World's a Stooge; I'll Never Heil Again; An Ache in Every Stake; In the Sweet Pie and Pie; Some More of Samoa. 1942 My Sister Eileen, plus the following shorts: Loco Boy Makes Good; Cactus Makes Perfect; What's the Matador; Matri-Phony; Three Smart Saps; Even as I.O.U.; Sock-a-Bye Baby. 1943 the following shorts: They Came to Conga; Dizzy Detectives; Spook Louder; Back from the Front; Three Little Twerps; Higher Than a Kite; I Can Hardly Wait; Dizzy Pilots; Phony Express; A Gem of a Jam. 1944 Ghost Crazy, plus the following shorts: Crash Goes the Hash; Busy Buddies; The Yoke's on Me; Idle Roomers; Gents without Cents; No Dough, Boys. 1947 the following shorts: Rockin' in the Rockies; Three Pests in a Mess; Booby Dupes; Idiots Deluxe; If a Body Meets a Body; Micro Phonies. 1947 Hold That Lion (short).

HOWARD, KATHLEEN
Born: 1879, Canada. Died: Apr. 15, 1956, Hollywood, Calif. Screen and opera actress, and magazine editor.

Appeared in: 1934 Once to Every Bachelor; Death Takes a Holiday; It's a Gift; You're Telling Me; One More River. 1935 The Man on the Flying Trapeze. 1936 Stolen Holiday. 1939 Little Accident; First Love. 1940 Young People; Mystery Sea Raider; One Night in the Tropics; Five Little Peppers in Trouble. 1941 Miss Polly; Blossoms in the Dust; A Girl, a Guy and a Gob; Sweetheart of the Campus. 1941 Ball of Fire. 1942 The Mad Marindales; You Were Never Lovelier; Lady in a Jam. 1943 Crash Dive; My Kingdom for a Cook; Swing Out the Blues. 1944 Laura; Reckless Age. 1945 Sadie Was a Lady; Shady Lady; Snafu. 1946 Centennial Summer; Miss Susie Slagle's; Dangerous Woman; The Mysterious Intruder. 1947 The Late George Apley; Take a Letter, Darling; Cynthia; Curley. 1948 The Bride Goes Wild; Cry of the City. 1950 Born to Be Bad; Petty Girl.

HOWARD, LESLIE (Leslie Stainer)
Born: Apr. 24, 1893, London, England. Died: June 2, 1943, Bay of Biscay (air crash). Screen, stage actor, film director and film producer. Received Academy Award nominations for Best Actor in 1933 for Berkeley Square and in 1938 for Pygmalion.

Appeared in: 1930 Outward Bound (film debut). 1931 Devotion; Five and Ten; Never the Twain Shall Meet. 1932 Smilin' Through; Reserved for Ladies; The Animal Kingdom. 1933 Secrets; Berkeley Square; Captured. 1934 British Agent; The Lady Is Willing; Of Human Bondage; Hollywood on Parade (short). 1935 The Scarlet Pimpernel. 1936 The Petrified Forest; Romeo and Juliet. 1937 It's Love I'm After; Stand-In. 1938 Pygmalion. 1939 Intermezzo, a Love Story; Gone with the Wind. 1941 Pimpernel Smith; 49th Parallel (aka The Invaders—U.S. 1942). 1942 From Four Corners; The First of the Few; Mr. V. 1943 Spitfire.

HOWARD, MAY
Born: 1870. Died: Feb. 1, 1935, Hollywood, Calif. (heart attack). Screen, stage, burlesque, and vaudeville actress.

HOWARD, PETER "PETE THE HERMIT"
Born: June 26, 1878, Knocklong, Ireland. Died: Mar. 14, 1969, Los Angeles, Calif. (brain hemorrhage). Screen actor.

Appeared in: 1923 Souls in Bondage. 1964 Three Nuts in Search of a Bolt.

HOWARD, RUTH
Born: 1894. Died: Dec. 28, 1944, Los Angeles, Calif. Screen and vaudeville actress. Member of the "Ross & Howard" vaudeville team.

Appeared in: 1933 My Woman.

HOWARD, SAMUEL "SHEMP"
Born: Mar. 17, 1900, New York, N.Y. Died: Nov. 22, 1955, Hollywood, Calif. (coronary occlusion). Screen, stage, and vaudeville actor. Brother of screen actors Jerome "Curly" (dec. 1952) and Moe Howard. Appeared in vaudeville with Ted Healy in an act billed as "Ted Healy and His Stooges" and that same act (also referred to as "Ted Healy and His Racketeers") appeared in 1930 Soup to Nuts (film debut). He became a member of the "Three Stooges" team of screen fame upon the retirement of his brother "Curly" in 1947.

Appeared in: 1934—1936 numerous Vitaphone shorts; 1937 Hollywood Round-Up; Headin' East. 1938 Columbia short; 1940 Millionaires in Prison; The Leather Pushers; Give Us Wings; The Bank Dick. 1941 Meet the Chump; Buck Privates; The Invisible Woman; Six Lessons from Madame La Zonga; Mr. Dynamite; In the Navy; Tight Shoes; San Antonio Rose; Hold That Ghost; Hit the Road; Too Many Blondes; Hellzapoppin. 1942 The Strange Case of Dr. Rx; Butch Minds the Baby; Mississippi Gambler; Private Buckaroo; Pittsburgh; Arabian Nights. 1943 It Ain't Hay; Keep 'Em Sluggin; How's about It?; Strictly in the Groove; Crazy House. 1944 Three of a Kind; Moonlight and Cactus; Strange Affair. 1945 Rockin' in the Rockies. 1946 Blondie Knows Best; Dangerous Business; The Gentleman Misbehaves; One Exciting Week; Swing Parade of 1946, plus the following shorts: Beer Barrel Polecats; A Bird in the Head; Uncivil Warbirds; Monkey Businessmen; The Three Troubledoers; Three Loan Wolves; G.I. Wanno Go Home; Rhythm and Weep; Three Little Pirates. 1947 the following shorts: Half-Wits Holiday; Fright Night; Out West; Hold That Lion; Brideless Groom; Sing a Song of Six Pants; All Gummed Up. 1948 the following shorts: Shivering Sherlocks; Pardon My Clutch; Squareheads of the Round Table; Fiddlers Three; Heavenly Daze; Hot Scots; I'm a Monkey's Uncle; Mummy's Dummies; Crime on Their Hands. 1949 Africa Screams, plus the following shorts: The Ghost Talks; Who Done It?; Hocus Pokus; Fuelin' Around; Malice in the Palace; Vagabond Loafers; Dunked in the Deep. 1950 Punch Cowpunchers; Hugs and Mugs; Dopey Dicks; Love at First Bite; Self Made Maids; Three Hams on Rye; Studio Stoops; Slap Happy Sleuths; A Snitch in Time. 1951 Gold Raiders, plus the following shorts: Three Arabian Nuts; Baby Sisters' Jitters; Don't Throw that Knife; Scrambled Brains; Merry Mavericks; The Tooth Will Out; Hula La-La; The Pest Man Wins. 1952 the following shorts: A Missed Fortune; Listen Judge; Corny Casanovas; He Cooked His Goose; Gents in a Jam; Three Dark Horses; Cuckoo in a Choo Choo. 1953 the following shorts: Spooks; Up in Daisy's Penthouse; Booty and the Beast; Tricky Dicks; Pardon My Backfire; Rip, Sew and Stitch; Goof on the Roof; Bubble Trouble. 1954 the following shorts: Income Tax Sappy; Musty Musketeers; Pals and Gals; Knutzy Knights; Shot in the Frontier; Scotched in Scotland.

HOWARD, SYDNEY
Born: 1885, England. Died: June 12, 1946, London, England. Screen and stage actor.

Appeared in: 1929 Splinters (film debut). 1930 French Leave. 1931 Almost a Divorce; Tilly of Bloomsbury. 1932 The Mayor's Nest; Up for the Derby. 1933 Up for the Cup; It's a King. 1934 Transatlantic Merry-Go-Round; Splinters in the Navy; Girls, Please; What a Man. 1936 Night of the Garter; Chick. 1939 Shipyard Sally. 1940 Tilly of Bloomsbury (and 1931 version). 1941 Once a Crook. 1942 When We Are Married. 1945 Flight from Folly.

HOWARD, TOM
Born: 1886, County Tyrone, Ireland. Died: Feb. 27, 1955, Long Branch, N.J. Screen, stage, vaudeville, burlesque, radio, and television actor.

Appeared in: 1930 Rain or Shine. 1932 the following shorts: The Mouse Trapper; The Acid Test; The Vest With a Tale, plus several Paramount shorts. 1933 the following shorts: A Drug on the Market; The Great Hokum Mystery; plus several Paramount shorts. 1934 the following shorts: Static; The Big Meow; A Good Scout. 1935 the following shorts: Easy Money; An Ear for Music; Grooms in Gloom; Time Out; The Magic Word; Stylish Stouts; He's a Prince. 1936 Where Is Wall Street.

HOWARD, WILLIAM
Born: 1884. Died: Jan. 23, 1944, Hollywood, Calif. Screen and stage actor.

Appeared in: 1935 Diamond Jim. 1936 Come and Get It.

HOWARD, WILLIE (William Levkowitz)
Born: 1887, Germany. Died: Jan. 14, 1949, New York, N.Y. Screen, stage, vaudeville, and radio actor. Brother of screen actor Eugene Howard (dec. 1965) and together they appeared in vaudeville as "Eugene and Willie Howard" and in 1927-29 they made shorts as a team. He later appeared in vaudeville with Al Kelly.

Appeared in: 1927 the following shorts: A Theatrical Managers Office; Between the Acts of the Opera; Pals. 1929 the following shorts: The Music Makers; My People. 1930 The Thirteenth Prisoner (aka The Thirteenth Hour). 1935 Millions in the Air. 1936 Rose of the Rancho. 1937 Broadway Melody of 1938. 1937-38 starred in a series of Educational shorts.

HOWLAND, JOBYNA
Born: 1881, Indianapolis, Ind. Died: June 7, 1936, Los Angeles, Calif.(heart attack). Screen and stage actress. Sister of screen actor Olin Howlin (Howland) (dec. 1959).

Appeared in: 1919 The Way of a Woman. 1924 Second Youth. 1930 A Lady's Morals; Soul Kiss; Honey; Dixiana; Hook, Line and Sinker; The Cuckoos; The Virtuous Sin. 1932 Big City Blues; Silver Dollar; Once in a Lifetime; Rockabye; Stepping Sisters. 1933 Topaze; Story of Temple Drake; Cohens and Kellys in Trouble. 1935 Ye Old Saw Mill (short).

HOWLIN, OLIN (aka OLIN HOWLAND)
Born: Feb. 10, 1896, Denver, Colo. Died: Sept. 20, 1959, Hollywood, Calif. Screen, stage, and vaudeville actor. Brother of screen actress Jobyna Howland (dec. 1936).

Appeared in: 1918 Independence B'Gosh. 1924 The Great White Way; Janice Meredith. 1925 Zander the Great. 1931 Over the Hill. 1932 Cheaters at Play; So Big. 1933 Blondie Johnson. 1934 Treasure Island; Wagon Wheels. 1935 Behold My Wife; The Case of the Curious Bride; The Case of the Lucky Legs; Follies Bergere. 1936 The Widow from Monte Carlo; Man Hunt; Satan Met a Lady; Road Gang; I Married a Doctor; Boulder Dam; The Big Noise; The Case of the Velvet Claws; Earthworm Tractors; Country Gentlemen; Love Letters of a Star; The Longest Night; Gold Diggers of 1937. 1937 Mountain Music; Marry the Girl; Wife, Doctor and Nurse; Nothing Sacred; Men in Exile. 1938 Mad Miss Manton; Swing Your Lady; The Adventures of Tom Sawyer; Girl of the Golden West; Sweethearts; Kentucky Moonshine; Little Tough Gun; Brother Rat. 1939 Blondie Brings Up Baby; Return of Dr. X; Days of Jesse James; Zenobia; Gone with the Wind; Disbarred; Boy Slaves; Made for Each Other; One Hour to Live. 1940 Comin' Round the Mountain; Young People; Chad Hanna. 1941 Shepherd of the Hills; Buy Me That Town; One Foot in Heaven; Ellery Queen and the Murder Ring; The Great Lie; Belle Starr. 1942 Almost Married; Henry and Dizzy; Dr. Broadway; When Johnny Comes Marching Home; The Man Who Wouldn't Die; Home in Wyoming; This Gun for Hire; You Can't Escape Forever; Orchestra Wives. 1943 Lady Bodyguard; Young and Willing; Secrets of the Underground; A Stranger in Town; The Good Fellows; Jack London; The Falcon and the Co-eds. 1944 A Strange Lady in Town; Sing, Neighbor, Sing; Bermuda Mystery; Can't Help Singing; I'll Be Seeing You; The Man from Frisco; The Town Went Wild; Twilight on the Prairie; Goodnight, Sweetheart; Bermuda; In the Meantime, Darling; Nothing but Trouble. 1945 Sheriff of Cimarron Gap; Captain Eddie; Her Lucky Night; Colonel Effingham's Raid; Dakota; Fallen Angel; Senorita from the West; Santa Fe Saddlemates. 1946 Home Sweet Homicide; Crime Doctor's Man Hunt; Secrets of the Underworld. 1947 The Angel and the Badman; The Wistful Widow of Wagon Gap; Apache Rose; For the Love of Rusty; The Tenderfoot. 1948 The Dude Goes West; Return of the Whistler; My Dog Rusty; The Paleface; The Last of the Wild Horses; Station West; Bad Men of Tombstone. 1949 Massacre River; Grand Canyon; Leave It to Henry; Little Women. 1950 Father Makes Good; Rock Island Trail; A Ticket to Tomahawk; Stage to Tucson. 1951 Fighting Coast Guard; Santa Fe. 1952 The Fabulous Senorita; Gobs and Gals. 1954 Them. 1958 The Blob.

HOXIE, JACK
Born: Jan. 24, 1890, Okla. Died: Mar. 28, 1965, Keyes, Okla. Screen actor. Entered films in 1918.

Appeared in: 1919 Lightning Bryce (serial). 1920 Thunderbolt Jack (serial). 1921 The Broken Spur; Sparks of Flint; Hills of Hate; Cupid's Brand; Dead or Alive; Cyclone Bliss; Devil Dog Dawson; The Sheriff of Hope Eternal; Man from Nowhere. 1922 The Marshal of Moneymind; Two Fisted Jefferson; Barb-Wire; The Crow's Nest; Back Fire; The Desert's Crucible; Riders of the Law; A Desert Bridegroom. 1923 The Double O; Desert Rider; The Forbidden Trail; Don Quickshot of the Rio Grande; Wolf's Tracks; Men in the Raw; Where Is the West?; Galloping Thru; The Red Warning. 1924 Ridgeway of Montana; Fighting Fury; The Western Wallop; The Back Trail; Daring Chances; The Man from Wyoming; The Phantom Horseman; The Galloping Ace. 1925 The White Outlaw; A Roaring Adventure; Bustin' Thru; Don Daredevil; The Sign of the Cactus; Flying Hoofs; Hidden Loot; Two Fisted Jones; The Red Rider; Ridin' Thunder. 1926 The Last Frontier; The Border Sheriff; The Fighting Peacemaker; Red Hot Leather; The Wild Horse Stampede; The Demon; Looking for Trouble; Six Shootin' Romance. 1927 Men of Daring; The Fighting Three; Rough and Ready; The Western Whirlwind; Grinning Guns; The Rambling Ranger; Heroes of the Wild (serial). 1929 Forbidden Trail. 1932 The Phantom Express; Gold. 1933 Law and Lawless; Via Pony Express; Gun Law; Trouble Buster; Outlaw Justice.

HOYT, ARTHUR
Born: 1874, Georgetown, Colo. Died: Jan. 4, 1953, Woodland Hills, Calif. Screen, stage actor, and stage director. Entered films in 1916.

Appeared in: 1920 Nurse Marjorie. 1921 The Foolish Age; The Four Horsemen of the Apocalypse; Camille; Don't Neglect Your Wife; Red Courage. 1922 Restless Souls; The Top of New York; Is Matrimony a Failure?; Kissed; Love Is an Awful Thing; The Understudy; Little Wildcat; The Stranger's Banquet; Too Much Wife. 1923 The Love Piker; An Old Sweetheart of Mine; To the Ladies; The White Flower; Souls for Sale. 1924 Bluff; Do It Now; Sundown; When a Man's a Man; Her Marriage Vow; The Dangerous Blonde; Daring Youth. 1925 The Lost World; Any Woman; Eve's Lover; The Sporting Venus; The Coming of Amos; Head Winds; Private Affairs. 1926 For Wives Only; The Crown of Lies; The Danger Girl; Monte Carlo; Eve's Leaves; Dangerous Friends; Up in Mabel's Room; Footloose Widows; The Gilded Butterfly; The Midnight Sun. 1927 An Affair of the Follies; Husband for Rent; The Rejuvenation of Aunt Mary; A Texas Steer; The Love Thrill; The Mysterious Rider; Shanghai Bound; Ten Modern Commandments; Tillie the Toiler. 1928 Just Married; My Man; Home James. 1929 The Wheel of Life; Stolen Kisses; Protection; Her Private Affair. 1930 Peacock Alley; Extravagance; The Life of the Party; Dumbbells in Ermine; Night Work; On Your Back; Going Wild; The Boss's Orders (short); Seven Days' Leave. 1931 The Criminal Code; Inspiration; The Flood; Gold Dust Gertie; Young Sinners; Side Show; Palmy Days; Peach O'Reno; Bought. 1932 Impatient Maiden; Love in High Gear; American Madness; The Devil and the Deep; Dynamite Ranch; Madame Racketeer; Make Me a Star; The Crusader; Washington Merry-Go-Round; Red Haired Alibi; Vanity Street; Call Her Savage; All American. 1933 Dangerously Yours; The Eleventh Commandment; Shriek in the Night; Pleasure Cruise; Shanghai Madness; Darling Daughters; Cohens and Kellys in Trouble; Only Yesterday; Laughing at Life; Goldie Gets Along; Emergency Call; His Private Secretary; Sing, Sinner, Sing; 20,000 Years in Sing Sing. 1934 The Meanest Girl in Town; In the Money; The Notorious Sophie Lang; Kansas City Princess; Wake up and Dream; When Strangers Meet; Babbitt; It Happened One Night; The Crosby Case; Uncertain Lady; Springtime for Henry; Unknown Blonde; Let's Try Again. 1935 Men of Action; No Ransom; A Night at the Ritz; Chinatown Squad; The Raven; Welcome Home; $1,000 a Minute; One Hour Late; Murder on a Honeymoon. 1936 Lady Luck; Magnificent Obsession; Mr. Deeds Goes to Town; The Poor Little Rich Girl; M'Liss; Walking on Air; Early to Bed. 1937 Four Day's Wonder; Join the Marines; Paradise Express; The Westland Case; The Wrong Road; A Star Is Born; It's All Yours; Ever since Eve; Love Takes Flight; She's No Lady. 1938 The Black Doll; The Devil's Party; Start Cheering; The Cowboy and the Lady; The Sisters; You and Me; Girls on Probation. 1939 It Could Happen to You; Should Husbands Work?; Made for Each Other; East Side of Heaven. 1940 I Take This Oath; The Great McGinty. 1944 Hail the Conquering Hero. 1947 Mad Wednesday; My Favorite Brunette; Brute Force.

HOYT, CLEGG
Born: 1911. Died: Oct. 6, 1967, Hollywood, Calif.(complications following stroke). Screen and television actor.

Appeared in: 1956 Fighting Trouble; Santiago. 1957 Damn Citizen; The Restless Breed; The True Story of Jesse James. 1958 Gun Fever. 1961 The Young Savages. 1962 Incident in an Alley; Pressure Point; 13 West Street.

HOYT, JULIA
Born: 1897. Died: Oct. 31, 1955, New York, N.Y. Screen and stage actress. Entered films in 1921.

Appeared in: 1921 The Wonderful Thing. 1925 The Man Who Found Himself.

HUBER, HAROLD
Born: 1910. Died: Sept. 29, 1959, New York, N.Y. Screen, stage, radio, television actor, and radio and television writer.

Appeared in: 1932 Central Park; The Match King. 1933 Central Airport; Girl Missing; Mary Stevens, M.D.; Mayor of Hell; Midnight Mary; The Silk Express; The Life of Jimmy Dolan; The Bowery; Police Car; Frisco Jenny; 20,000 Years in Sing Sing; Parachute Jumper; Ladies They Talk About. 1934 Hi, Nellie; He Was Her Man; The Merry Frinks; No More Women; A Very Honorable Guy; The Crosby Case; The Line-Up; The Thin Man; The Defense Rests; Hide-Out. 1935 Naughty Marietta; Mad Love; Pursuit; G-Men. 1936 We're Only Human; The Gay Desperado; Muss'Em Up; Klondike Annie; Women Are Trouble; San Francisco; The Devil Is a Sissy; Kelly the Second. 1937 The Good Earth; Trouble in Morocco; Midnight Taxi; Angel's Holiday; Charlie Chan on Broadway; Love under Fire; Charlie Chan at Monte Carlo; You Can't Beat Love; Outlaws of the Orient. 1938 International Settlement; Mr. Moto's Gamble; A Trip to Paris; Mysterious Mr. Moto; Passport Husband; While New York Sleeps; The Adventures of Marco Polo; A Slight Case of Murder; Going Places; Gangs of New York; Little Tough Guys in Society. 1939 Charlie Chan in City in Darkness; King of the Turf; Chasing Danger; Main Street Lawyer; You Can't Get Away with Murder; Charlie McCarthy, Detective; Beau Geste; 6,000 Enemies; The Lady and the Mob. 1940 The Ghost Comes Home; Kit Carson; Dance, Girls, Dance. 1941 A Man Betrayed; Country Fair; Down Mexico Way; Charlie Chan in Rio. 1942 Pardon My Stripes; Sleepytime Gal; A Gentleman After Dark; Little Tokyo, U.S.A.; Lady from Chungking; Manila Calling. 1943 Crime Doctor. 1950 My Friend Irma Goes West; Let's Dance.

HUBER, MRS. JUANITA "BILLIE"
Born: 1905. Died: May 22, 1965, Camden, N.J. Screen actress and dancer. Entered films in early 1930s.

HUBERT, GEORGE
Born: 1881. Died: May 8, 1963, Hollywood, Calif. Screen, stage, and vaudeville actor. Entered films in 1917.

Appeared in: 1956 Foreign Intrigue.

HUDD, WALTER
Born: Feb. 20, 1898, London, England. Died: Jan. 20, 1963, London, England. Screen, stage, television actor, and playwright.

Appeared in: 1935 Moscow Nights (film debut). 1936 Rembrandt; I Stand Condemned. 1937 Elephant Boy. 1938 Housemaster. 1939 Black Limelight. 1940 The Outsider; Dr. O'Dowd; Major Barbara. 1941 Dead Man's Shoes. 1944 Uncensored. 1946 I Live in Grosvenor Square (aka A Yank in London). 1947 I Know Where I'm Going; Love Story (aka A Lady Surrenders). 1948 Escape. 1949 Paper Orchid. 1952 Cosh Boy (aka The Slasher—U.S. 1953); The Importance of Being Earnest; Landfall. 1955 The Good Die Young. 1956 Satellite in the Sky; The Last Man to Hang. 1957 Loser Takes All; Cast a Dark Shadow; Reach for the Sky. 1959 The Man Upstairs; The Two Headed Spy; Look Back in Anger. 1960 Sink the Bismarck. 1961 Two Way Stretch. 1962 Life for Ruth. 1963 It's All Happening; The Punch and Judy Man. 1964 The Dream Maker. Other British films: Further up the Creek; The Navy Lark.

HUDMAN, WESLEY
Born: 1916. Died: Feb. 29, 1964, Williams, Ariz. (murdered). Screen and television actor.

Appeared in: 1949 Satan's Cradle. 1950 Battle of Rogue River; The Girl from San Lorenzo. 1951 Fort Defiance. 1952 Leadville Gunslinger; Black Hills Ambush. 1953 Pack Train. 1954 Masterson of Kansas. 1956 The Lonely Man; Blackjack Ketchum, Desperado. 1958 The Sheepman.

HUDSON, LARRY
Born: 1920. Died: Jan. 8, 1961, Hollywood, Calif. (suicide). Screen and television actor.

Appeared in: 1952 Smoky Canyon. 1953 The Redhead from Wyoming. 1956 Jubal; Solid Gold Cadillac. 1959 Tank Commandos.

HUESTIS, RUSSELL
Born: 1894. Died: Dec. 1, 1964, Seattle, Wash. (heart attack). Screen actor.

HUFF, FORREST
Born: 1876. Died: Aug. 21, 1947, New York, N.Y. Screen, stage, and opera actor.

Appeared in: 1927 The Love of Sunya.

HUGHES, CHARISSA
Died: June 13, 1963, Hollywood, Calif. Screen actress.

HUGHES, GARETH
Born: Aug. 23, 1894, Llanelly, Wales. Died: Oct. 1, 1965, Woodland Hills, Calif. Screen and stage actor. Entered films in 1919.

Appeared in: 1919 Mrs. Wiggs and the Cabbage Patch; Eyes of Youth. 1921 Sentimental Tommy; The Hunch; Garments of Truth; Indiscretion; Life's Darn Funny; The Lure of Youth. 1922 Don't Write Letters; Little Eva Ascends; Forget-Me-Not. 1923 The Christian; The Spanish Dancer; The Enemies of Women; Kick In; Penrod and Sam. 1924 The Sunset Trail; Shadows of Paris. 1925 The Midnight Girl. 1926 Men of the Night. 1927 The Whirlwind of Youth; The Auctioneer; Broadway after Midnight; Heroes in Blue; Better Days; Eyes of the Totem; In the First Degree. 1928 The Sky Rider; Old Age Handicap; Better Days; Comrades; Top Sergeant Mulligan. 1929 Silent Sentinel; Mister Antonio; Broken Hearted.

HUGHES, LLOYD
Born: Oct. 21, 1897, Bisbee, Ariz. Died: June 6, 1958, Los Angeles, Calif. Screen actor.

Appeared in: 1915 Turn of a Road. 1919 Dangerous Hours; The Haunted Bedroom. 1920 Below the Surface; Home Spun Folks. 1921 Love Never Dies; Beau Revel; Mother O'Mine. 1922 Hail the Woman; Tess of the Storm Country. 1923 Scars of Jealousy; The Old Fool; Are You a Failure?; Her Reputation; Children of Dust; The Huntress. 1924 The Sea Hawk; The Heritage of the Desert; Untamed Youth; Judgment of the Storm; Welcome Stranger; In Every Woman's Life; The Whipping Boss. 1925 Declassee; The Dixie Handicap; The Desert Flower; The Half-Way Girl; If I Marry Again; The Lost World; Sally; Scarlet Saint. 1926 Pals First; Valencia; Ella Cinders; Irene; Loose Angles; Forever After; High Steppers; Ladies at Play. 1927 No Place to Go; American Beauty; The Stolen Bride; An Affair of the Follies; Too Many Crooks. 1928 Heart to Heart; Sailors' Wives; Three-Ring Marriage. 1929 Where East Is East; Acquitted; The Mysterious Island. 1930 The Runaway Bride; Sweethearts on Parade; Love Comes Along; Hello Sister; Big Boy; Moby Dick; Hell Bound; Extravagance. 1931 Drums of Jeopardy; Sky Raiders; Unwanted; Air Eagles; The Deceiver; Private Scandal. 1932 The Miracle Man; Heart Punch. 1935 Reckless Roads; Midnight Phantom; Skybound; Society Fever; Rip Roaring Riley; Honeymoon Limited; Harmony Lane. 1936 Night Cargo; Little Red School House; Kelly of the Secret Service. 1937 A Man Betrayed. 1938 Numbered Woman; Clipped Wings; I Demand Payment. 1939 Romance of the Redwoods. 1940 Vengeance of the Deep.

HUGHES, THOMAS ARTHUR
Born: 1887. Died: Nov. 25, 1953, Los Angeles, Calif. Screen actor. Resemblance to Sir Winston Churchill brought historical roles. Also played in many westerns.

HULBERT, CLAUDE (Claude Noel Hulbert)
Born: Dec. 25, 1900, London, England. Died: Jan. 22, 1964, Sydney; Australia. Screen, stage, radio actor, and screenwriter.

Appeared in: 1931 A Night Like This. 1932 Thark; Let Me Explain, Dear; Hullo Radio; King of the Ritz. 1933 Their Night Out; Radio Parade; Heads We Go; The Song You Gave Me; Love at Second Sight; The Girl in Possession. 1934 Bulldog Jack. 1935 Alias Bulldog Drummond. 1936 The Vulture; Ship's Concert; Hail and Farewell; The Interrupted Honeymoon; It Isn't Cricket. 1937 His Lordship Regrets. 1938 Many Thanks, Mr. Atkins. 1942 The Ghost of St. Michael's. 1943 The Dummy Talks; Sailors Three; My Learned Friend. 1946 London Town. 1947 The Ghosts of Berkeley Square. 1953 My Heart Goes Crazy (aka London Town). 1955 Fun at St. Fanny's.

HULL, JOSEPHINE (Josephine Sherwood)
Born: 1884, Newton, Mass. Died: Mar. 12, 1957, New York, N.Y. (cerebral hemorrhage). Screen, stage, radio, television actress,

and stage director. Won Academy Award in 1950 for Best Supporting Actress in Harvey.

Appeared in: 1929 The Bishop's Candlestick (short). 1932 After Tomorrow; Careless Lady. 1944 Arsenic and Old Lace (film and stage versions). 1950 Harvey (film and stage versions). 1951 The Lady from Texas.

HUME, BENITA
Born: Oct. 14, 1906, London, England. Died: Nov. 1, 1967, Egerton, England. Screen, stage, radio, and television actress. Widow of screen actor Ronald Coleman (dec. 1958) and later married to screen actor George Sanders (dec. 1972).

Appeared in: 1928 South Sea Bubble. 1929 The Wrecker; High Treason. 1930 The Lady of the Lake. 1931 Jaws of Hell; The Flying Fool. 1932 Reserved for Ladies; Men of Steel; Women Who Play; Diamond Cut Diamond (aka Blame the Women). 1933 Gambling Ship; Lord Camber's Ladies; The Worst Woman in Paris?; Only Yesterday; Looking Forward; Clear All Wires; Jew Suess. 1934 The Private Life of Don Juan. 1935 The Divine Spark; The Gay Deception. 1936 The Garden Murder Case; Moonlight Murder; Suzy; Tarzan Escapes; Rainbow on the River. 1937 The Last of Mrs. Cheyney. 1938 Peck's Bad Boy with the Circus. Other British films: The Happy Ending; Second to None; The Constant Nymph (all silents).

HUMMELL, MARY ROCKWELL
Born: 1889. Died: Feb. 16, 1946, Hollywood, Calif. Screen actress. Entered films approx. 1916.

HUMPHREY, BESSIE
Born: Boston, Mass. Died: Mar. 8, 1933, Hollywood, Calif. Screen and stage actress.

HUMPHREYS, CECIL
Born: July 21, 1883, Cheltenham, England. Died: Nov. 6, 1947, New York, N.Y. Screen and stage actor. Entered films in 1916.

Appeared in: 1922 The Glorious Adventure. 1925 Irish Luck. 1931 7 Park Lane. 1932 The Old Man; It's a King; Dick Turpin. 1934 Gay Lord Strathpeffer; The Silver Spoon; No, No, Doctor; The Unfinished Symphony. 1935 Koenigsmark. 1936 Fair Exchange; Accused; Reasonable Doubt. 1939 Wuthering Heights. 1946 The Razor's Edge. 1947 Desire Me. 1948 A Woman's Vengeance.

HUN, HADI
Born: 1900, Turkey. Died: Dec. 1969, Istanbul, Turkey (heart attack). Screen and stage actor.

HUNT, JAY
Born: 1857, Pa. Died: Nov. 18, 1932, Los Angeles, Calif. Screen and stage actor.

Appeared in: 1923 Hunchback of Notre Dame. 1924 After a Million; Yankee Speed. 1925 Counsel for the Defense; Lightnin'. 1926 A Man Four-Square; Three Bad Men; The Gentle Cyclone; The Golden Web; Men of the Night; My Own Pal; Out of the Storm; One Minute to Play. 1927 The Harvester; The Overland Stage; Captain Salvation; Better Days. 1930 The Poor Millionaire. 1931 The Sky Spider.

HUNT, MARTITA
Born: 1900, Argentina. Died: June 13, 1969, London, England. Screen and stage actress.

Appeared in: 1932 Reserved for Ladies. 1933 I Was a Spy. 1934 Friday the 13th; Mr. What's His Name; Wild Justice. 1935 First a Girl. 1936 When Knights Were Bold; Nine Days a Queen; The Interrupted Honeymoon. 1957 The Mill on the Floss (U.S. 1939); Farewell Again. 1938 Strange Boarders; Troopship. 1939 Trouble Brewing; Young Man's Fancy (U.S. 1943); Prison without Bars; A Girl Must Live. 1942 The Strangler; When Knights Were Bold; Wings and the Woman. 1943 The Man in Grey (U.S. 1945). 1945 The Seventh Survivor. 1946 The Wicked Lady. 1947 The Ghosts of Berkeley Square; Great Expectations. 1948 So Evil My Love; My Sister and I; Anna Karenina. 1949 Lady Windermere's Fan. 1951 The Little Ballerina. 1952 Treasure Hunt; Folly to Be Wise; The Story of Robin Hood. 1953 Melba; Tonight at 8:30; It Started in Paradise. 1956 Anastasia; Three Men in a Boat (U.S. 1958); King's Rhapsody. 1957 Les Espions; Paradise Lagoon (aka The Admirable Crichton). 1958 Bonjour Tristesse; Me and the Colonel; Dangerous Exile. 1960 The Brides of Dracula; Song without End. 1962 The Wonderful World of the Brothers Grimm; I Like Money. 1964 Becket; The Unsinkable Molly Brown. 1965 Bunny Lake Is Missing. 1968 The Long Day's Dying. 1969 The Best House in Town.

HUNTER, GLENN
Born: 1897, Highland, N.Y. Died: Dec. 30, 1945, New York, N.Y. Screen, stage, and vaudeville actor.

Appeared in: 1921 The Case of Becky. 1922 The Country Flapper; The Cradle Buster; Smilin' Through. 1923 Puritan Passions; Second Fiddle; Youthful Cheaters; The Scarecrow. 1924 Grit; The Silent Watcher; Merton of the Movies; West of the Water Tower. 1925 The Little Giant; His Buddy's Wife. 1926 The Pinch Hitter; The Broadway Boob; The Romance of a Million Dollars; The Little Giant.

HUNTER, JACKIE
Born: 1901, Canada. Died: Nov. 21, 1951, London, England. Screen, stage, vaudeville, and radio actor.

HUNTER, JEFFREY (Henry Herman McKinnies)
Born: Nov. 23, 1926, New Orleans, La. Died: May 27, 1969, Van Nuys, Calif.(injuries from fall). Screen, stage, and television actor. Married to screen actress Emily McLaughlin and divorced from screen actress Barbara Rush.

Appeared in: 1951 Call Me Mister; The Frogman; Take Care of My Little Girl; Fourteen Hours. 1952 Red Skies of Montana (aka Smoke Jumpers); Belles on Their Toes; Lure of the Wilderness; Dreamboat. 1953 Sailor of the King. 1954 Three Young Texans; Princess of the Nile. 1955 Seven Angry Men; White Feather; Seven Cities of Gold. 1956 The Proud Ones; A Kiss before Dying; The Great Locomotive Chase; Four Girls in Town; The Searchers. 1957 The True Story of Jesse James; The Way to the Gold; No Down Payment; Gun for a Coward. 1958 The Last Hurrah; In Love and War; Count Five and Die; Mardi Gras. 1960 Key Witness; Hell to Eternity; Sergeant Rutledge. 1961 Man-Trap; King of Kings. 1962 The Longest Day; No Man Is an Island. 1964 The Man from Galveston; Gold for the Caesars. 1965 Vendetta; Brainstorm; The Woman Who Wouldn't Die. 1967 A Witch without a Broom; The Christmas Kid; A Guide for the Married Man. 1968 The Private Navy of Sgt. O'Farrell; Custer of the West; Sexy Susan at the King's Court; Joe, Find a Place to Die. 1969 The Hostess Also Has a County.

HUNTER, RICHARD
Born: 1875. Died: Dec. 22, 1962, Santa Monica, Calif. Cowboy screen actor.

HUNTLEY, FRED (aka FRED HUNTLEY)
Born: 1862. Died: Nov. 1, 1931, Hollywood, Calif.(heart attack). Screen and stage actor.

Appeared in: 1918 Heart of Wetona. 1919 Heart o' the Hills; Everywoman. 1921 Brewster's Millions; Bronze Bell; Face of the World; Gasoline Gus; A Prince There Was; A Wise Fool; Little Minister; What Every Woman Knows. 1922 Crimson Challenge; Man with Two Mothers; Borderland; North of the Rio Grande; To Have and to Hold; While the City Sleeps. 1923 Peg O' My Heart; Law of the Lawless; Where the North Begins; To the Last Man; Call of the Canyon; Go Getter. 1924 The Age of Innocence; Thundering Hoofs. 1927 King of Kings.

HURST, BRANDON
Born: Nov. 30, 1866, London, England. Died: July 1947, Hollywood, Calif. Screen and stage actor.

Appeared in: 1923 The Hunchback of Notre Dame; World's Applause; Legally Dead. 1924 He Who Gets Slapped; Thief of Bagdad; Silent Watcher; Cytherea; Lover of Camille; One Night in Rome. 1925 Lightnin' Lady. 1926 Amateur Gentleman; Grand Duchess and the Waiter; Secret Orders; Lady of the Harem; Volcano; Enchanted Hill; Made for Love; Paris at Midnight; Rainmaker; Shamrock Handicap. 1927 Seventh Heaven; High School Hero; Love; King of Kings; Annie Laurie. 1928 Man Who Laughs; Interference; News Parade. 1929 Voice of the Storm; Her Private Life; Greene Murder Case; Wolf of Wall Street. 1930 High Society Blues; Eyes of the World. 1931 A Connecticut Yankee; Right of Way; Young As You Feel; Murder at Midnight. 1932 Down to Earth; White Zombies; Sherlock Holmes; Murders in the Rue Morgue; Scarface; Midnight Lady. 1934 Sequoia; Bombay Mail; Lost Patrol; Little Minister; House of Rothschild. 1935 The Great Impersonation; While the Patient Slept; Bright Eyes; Red Morning; Bonnie Scotland; Woman in Red. 1936 The Plough and the Stars; The Moon's Our Home; Mary of Scotland. 1937 Maid of Salem; Wee Willie Winkle. 1938 Four Men and a Prayer; Suez. 1939 Stanley and Livingstone. 1940 The Blue Bird; If I Had My Way; Rhythm on the River. 1941 Sign of the Wolf. 1942 Mad Martindales; The Remarkable Andrew; The Pied Piper; Road to Happiness. 1943 Dixie; Frankenstein Meets the Wolf Man. 1944 The Princess and the Pirate; The Man in Half Moon Street. 1945 The Corn Is Green; House of Frankenstein.

HURST, PAUL

Born: 1888, Tulare County, Calif. Died: Feb. 27, 1953, Hollywood, Calif.(suicide). Screen, stage actor, film director, and screenwriter. Appeared in Monte Hale western series.

Appeared in: 1926 The High Hand; The Outlaw Express. 1927 Buttons; The Valley of Giants; The Red Raiders; The Devil's Saddle; The Man from Hardpan; The Overland Stage. 1928 The Cossacks. 1929 Tide of Empire; The California Mail; The Lawless Legion; The Rainbow; Sailor's Holiday. 1930 The Swellhead; Mountain Justice; The Runaway Bride; Hot Curves; Shadow of the Law; Paradise Island; Borrowed Wives; The Third Alarm; Oh, Yeah?; The Racketeer; His First Command; Officer O'Brien; Lucky Larkin. 1931 The Single Sin; The Secret Six; The Kick In; The Public Defender; Sweepstakes; Bad Company; Terror by Night; The Secret Witness. 1932 Panama Flow; The 13th Guest; Hold 'Em Jail; The Big Stampede; My Pal the King. 1933 Island of Lost Souls; Men Are Such Fools; Hold Your Man; Saturday's Millions; Women in His Life; Scarlet River; Terror Abroad; The Sphinx; Tugboat Annie; Day of Reckoning. 1934 The Big Race; Among the Missing; Take the Stand; Sequoia; The Line-Up; Midnight Alibi; There Ain't No Justice (short). 1935 Tomorrow's Youth; Star of Midnight; The Case of the Curious Bride; Mississippi; Shadow of Doubt; Public Hero No. 1; Calm Yourself; Wilderness Mail; The Gay Deception; Riffraff. 1936 The Blackmailer; It Had to Happen; To Mary with Love; I'd Give My Life; The Gay Desperado; We Who Are about to Die; North of Nome; Robin Hood of El Dorado. 1937 Trouble in Morocco; You Can't Beat Love; Super Sleuth; Fifty Roads to Town; Wake up and Live; Angel's Holiday; This Is My Affair; Slave Ship; Wife, Doctor and Nurse; Danger—Love at Work; Ali Baba Goes to Town; Second Honeymoon; Small Town Boy; She's No Lady; The Lady Fights Back. 1938 In Old Chicago; Rebecca of Sunnybrook Farm; Island in the Sky; Alexander's Ragtime Band; Josette; My Lucky Star; Hold That Co-ed; Thanks for Everything; No Time to Marry; Prison Break; The Last Express; Secrets of a Nurse. 1939 Broadway Serenade; Cafe Society; Topper Takes a Trip; It Could Happen to You; Each Dawn I Die; Remember?; The Kid from Kokomo; Quick Millions; Bad Lands; On Your Toes; Gone with the Wind. 1940 Edison the Man; Torrid Zone; They Drive by Night; South of Karango; The Westerner; Heaven with a Barbed Wire Fence; Tugboat Annie Sails Again; Star Dust; Men against the Sky. 1941 The Parson of Panamint; This Woman Is Mine; Tall, Dark and Handsome; The Great Mr. Nobody; Ellery Queen and the Murder Ring; Bowery Boy; Petticoat Politics; Virginia; Caught in a Draft. 1942 Pardon My Stripes; Sundown Jim; Night in New Orleans; Dudes Are Pretty People. 1943 The Ox-Bow Incident; Hi'Ya, Chum; Young and Willing; Jack London; The Sky's the Limit; Coney Island; Calaboose. 1944 The Ghost That Walks Alone; Greenwich Village; Barbary Coast Gent; Something for the Boys; Girl Rush; Summer Storm. 1945 One Exciting Night; Nob Hill; The Big Show-Off; Dakota; The Dolly Sisters; Penthouse Rhythm; Midnight Manhunt; Scared Stiff; Steppin' in Society. 1946 In Old Sacramento; The Virginian; The Plainsman and the Lady; Murder in the Music Hall. 1947 The Angel and the Badman; Death Valley; Under Colorado Skies. 1948 The Arizona Ranger; California Firebrand; Heart of Virginia; Son of God's Country; Gun Smugglers; Yellow Sky; A Miracle Can Happen; Old Los Angeles; Madonna of the Desert. 1949 Law of the Golden West; Outcasts of the Trail; Prince of the Plains; Ranger of Cherokee Strip; San Antone Ambush; South of Rio. 1950 The Missourians; The Old Frontier; Pioneer Marshal; The Vanishing Westerner. 1951 Million Dollar Pursuit. 1952 Big Jim McLain; Toughest Man in Arizona. 1953 The Sun Shines Bright; Pine Bluff.

HUSSY, JIMMY

Born: 1891. Died: Nov. 20, 1930, Woodcliff, N.J.(stomach trouble and tuberculosis). Screen, stage, and vaudeville actor. Appeared in early Vitaphone shorts.

HUSTON, WALTER

Born: Apr. 6, 1884, Toronto, Canada. Died: Apr. 7, 1950, Beverly Hills, Calif.(aneurism). Screen, stage, and vaudeville actor. Nominated for Academy Award for Best Actor in 1936 for Dodsworth and Best Supporting Actor in 1942 for Yankee Doodle Dandy. Won for Best Supporting Actor in 1948 for The Treasure of the Sierra Madre. Father of film director John Huston. Married to screen actress Nan Sutherland (dec. 1973).

Appeared in: 1929 Gentlemen of the Press (film debut); The Lady Lies; The Bishop's Candlesticks (short); The Carnival Man (short); Two Americans (short); The Virginian. 1930 The Bad Man; Abraham Lincoln; The Virtuous Sin. 1931 The Criminal Code; The Star Witness; The Ruling Voice; Upper Underworld. 1932 A Woman from Monte Carlo; A House Divided; Law and Order; The Beast of the City; The Wet Parade; American Madness; Rain; Night Court; Kongo. 1933 The Prizefighter and the

Lady; Hell Below; Gabriel over the White House; Ann Vickers; Storm at Daybreak. 1934 Keep 'Em Rolling. 1935 Rhodes. 1936 Transatlantic Tunnel; Dodsworth. 1938 Of Human Hearts. 1939 The Light That Failed. 1941 All That Money Can Buy; Swamp Water; Maltese Falcon; The Shanghai Gesture. 1942 Our Russian Front (narr. Russian war relief documentary); Always in My Heart; Yankee Doodle Dandy; Prelude to War (narr. U.S. War Dept. documentary); In This Our Life. 1943 Armored Attack (documentary); Edge of Darkness; The Outlaw (released nationally 1950); Mission to Moscow; The North Star; Safeguarding Military Information (Army training film documentary). 1944 Dragon Seed. 1945 And Then There Were None. 1946 Dragonwyck; Duel in the Sun. 1947 Let There Be Light (Signal Corps film). 1948 Summer Holiday; The Treasure of the Sierra Madre. 1949 The Great Sinner. 1950 The Furies. 1952 The Devil and Daniel Webster (reissue and retitle of All That Money Can Buy, 1941).

HUTCHINSON, CANON CHARLES

Born: 1887, England. Died: Apr. 22, 1969, Brighton, England. Actor Canon Charles Hutchinson is not to be confused with American actor and director "Lightning Hutch" (Charles Hutchinson). Canon Charles Hutchinson was former president of the Actors Church Union.

HUTH, HAROLD

Born: 1892, Huddersfield, Yorkshire, England. Died: Oct. 26, 1967, London, England. Screen, stage actor, film director, and film producer.

Appeared in: 1929 The Triumph of the Scarlet Pimpernel; The Silver King. 1930 Guilty. 1931 Jaws of Hell; The Outsider. 1932 Aren't We All?; The First Mrs. Fraser; Sally Bishop; Rome Express. 1933 The Ghoul; The Camels Are Coming. 1951 Blackmailed. Other British films: One of the Best; Hours of Loneliness; Bracelets; Down River; A Honeymoon Adventure.

HUTTON, LEONA

Born: 1892. Died: Apr. 1, 1949, Toledo, Ohio (overdose of sleeping pills). Appeared in silent films from 1913 to 1924. Screen and stage actress.

HUXHAN, KENDRICK

Born: 1892. Died: July 24, 1967, Hollywood, Calif.(heart attack). Screen and stage actor.

Appeared in: 1961 Pirates of Tortuga. 1967 Games.

HYAMS, JOHN

Born: 1877, Syracuse, N.Y. Died: Dec. 9, 1940, Hollywood, Calif. Screen, stage, vaudeville, and minstrel actor. Appeared in vaudeville with his wife screen actress Leila McIntyre (dec. 1953). Father of former screen actress Leila Hyams.

Appeared in: 1927 Life of an Actress; All in Fun (short). 1929 Broadway Scandals. 1930 Cameo Kirby; Swell People; Mind Your Business; Give Me Action; Some Babies. 1934 The Mighty Barnum. 1935 Murder in the Fleet; In Caliente; The Virginia Judge. 1936 And Sudden Death. 1937 Pick a Star; A Day at the Races. 1939 The Housekeeper's Daughter.

HYATT, CLAYTON

Died: July 1932, Windsor, Ontario, Canada (suicide—hanging). Screen actor.

HYATT, HERMAN

Born: 1906, Russia. Died: Jan. 24, 1968, Baltimore, Md. Screen and burlesque actor.

HYLAN, DONALD

Born: 1899. Died: June 20, 1968, New York, N.Y.(heart attack). Screen, stage, and television actor. Appeared in silent films.

HYLAND, AUGUSTIN ALLEN

Born: 1905. Died: Feb. 8, 1963, Hollywood, Calif. Screen actor and stand-in for James Cagney.

HYLTON, RICHARD

Born: 1921. Died: May 12, 1962, San Francisco, Calif.(heart attack). Screen, stage, and television actor.

Appeared in: 1949 Lost Boundaries. 1950 Halls of Montezuma. 1951 Secret of Convict Lake; Fixed Bayonets!. 1952 The Pride of St. Louis.

HYMACK, MR. See Quinton McPherson

HYMER, WARREN
Born: Feb. 25, 1906, New York, N.Y. Died: Mar. 25, 1948, Los Angeles, Calif. Screen and stage actor. Son of screen actress Elinor Kent (dec. 1957). Divorced from screen actress Virginia Meyer.

Appeared in: 1929 The Far Call; The Girl from Havana; Speakeasy; Frozen Justice; Fox Movietone Follies of 1929. 1930 Born Reckless; Lone Star Ranger; Oh, For a Man!; Men without Women; Sinner's Holiday; Up the River; Men on Call. 1931 The Spider; Seas Beneath; Goldie; The Unholy Garden; Charlie Chan Carries On. 1932 Hold 'Em Jail; One Way Passage; The Night Mayor; Madison Square Garden; Love Is a Racket. 1933 20,000 Years in Sing Sing; I Love That Man; Midnight Mary; Her First Mate; King for a Night; My Woman; In the Money; The Billion Dollar Scandal; Mysterious Rider; A Lady's Profession. 1934 George White's Scandals; The Crosby Case; Belle of the Nineties; Little Miss Marker; The Cat's Paw; She Loves Me Not; Young and Beautiful; One Is Guilty; Woman Unafraid; Kid Millions. 1935 Hold 'Em Yale; The Gilded Lily; The Case of the Curious Bride; The Daring Young Man; Silk Hat Kid; She Gets Her Man; Confidential; Show Them No Mercy; Navy Wife; Hitch Hike Lady; Straight from the Heart; Our Little Girl; Beauty's Daughter; Hong Kong Nights. 1936 Tango; Desert Justice; The Widow from Monte Carlo; The Leavenworth Case; Laughing Irish Eyes; Everybody's Old Man; 36 Hours to Kill; Mr. Deeds Goes to Town; San Francisco; Rhythm on the Range; Nobody's Fool; Love Letters of a Star. 1937 You Only Live Once; Join the Marines; Navy Blues; Meet the Boy Friend; Sea Racketeers; We Have Our Moments; Wake up and Live; Ali Baba Goes to Town; Married before Breakfast; Bad Guy; Tainted Money; She's Dangerous. 1938 Lady Behave; Arson Gang Busters; Joy of Living; Gateway; Submarine Patrol; Thanks for Everything; Bluebeard's Eighth Wife; You and Me. 1939 The Lady and the Mob; Coast Guard; Destry Rides Again; Boy Friend; Calling All Marines; Charlie McCarthy, Detective; Mr. Moto in Danger Island. 1940 I Can't Give You Anything but Love, Baby; Love, Honor and Oh-Baby!. 1941 Meet John Doe; Buy Me That Town; Birth of the Blues; Skylark. 1942 Mr. Wise Guy; So's Your Aunt Emma; Henry and Dizzy; Dr. Broadway; Girl's Town; Baby Face Morgan; She's in the Army; One Thrilling Night; Phantom Killer; Police Bullets; Jail House Blues; Meet the Mob; Lure of the Islands. 1943 Danger! Women at Work; Hitler—Dead or Alive; Gangway for Tomorrow. 1944 Since You Went Away; Three Is a Family. 1946 Gentleman Joe Palooka; Joe Palooka, Champ.

HYNES, JOHN E.
Born: 1853. Died: Apr. 12, 1931, Long Island, N.Y. Screen and stage actor.

HYTTEN, OLAF
Born: 1888, Scotland. Died: Mar. 11, 1955, Los Angeles, Calif. (heart attack). Screen actor.

Appeared in: 1924 It Is the Law. 1925 The Salvation Hunters; Chu Chin Chow. 1928 Old Age Handicap. 1929 Kitty. 1930 Grumpy; Playboy of Paris. 1933 Daughter of the Dragon. 1933 Berkeley Square. 1934 Mystery Liner; Jane Eyre; Money Means Nothing; Glamour. 1935 Becky Sharp; The Dark Angel; Two Sinners; The Last Outpost; Bonnie Scotland. 1936 The House of a Thousand Candles; The Last of the Mohicans; White Hunter. 1937 The Good Earth; California Straight Ahead; I Cover the War; Dangerous Holiday; First Lady. 1938 The Lone Wolf in Paris; Adventures of Robin Hood; Blonde Cheat; Youth Takes a Fling. 1939 Andy Hardy Gets Spring Fever; Rulers of the Sea; Allegheny Uprising; Our Leading Citizen. 1940 Our Neighbors, the Carters. 1941 Washington Melodrama; All the World's a Stooge (short); That Hamilton Woman. 1942 The Black Swan; Sherlock Holmes; Spy Ship; Sherlock Holmes and the Voice of Terror; The Ghost of Frankenstein; To Be or Not to Be; Bedtime Story; Destination Unknown; The Great Commandment. 1943 Sherlock Holmes Faces Death. 1944 The Lodger. 1945 My Name is Julia Ross; The Brighton Strangler; Christmas in Connecticut. 1946 The Notorious Lone Wolf; Three Strangers; Black Beauty. 1947 That Way with Women. 1953 Perils of the Jungle.

ILLING, PETER
Born: 1899, Vienna, Austria. Died: Oct. 29, 1966, London, England. Screen, stage, television, and radio actor. Was the voice of Winston Churchill on BBC European radio programs.

Appeared in: 1946 The End of the River. 1948 Eureka Stockade. 1949 Against the Wind. 1950 State Secret; Massacre Hill; Operation X. 1951 Lucky Nick Cain (aka I'll Get You for This); Children of Chance; The Great Manhunt; Traveler's Joy. 1952 Outcast of the Islands. 1953 Affair in Monte Carlo; Heat Wave; Never Let Me Go. 1954 Flame and the Flesh;

West of Zanzibar; A Race for Life; A Woman's Angle. 1955 Bhowani Junction; Svengali; Innocents in Paris; Chance Meeting (aka The Young Lovers). 1956 That Lady; Loser Takes All. 1957 Zarak; Fire Down Below; Pickup Alley; A Farewell to Arms; As Long as They're Happy; Interpol; Man in the Shadow; Manuela; Miracle in Soho; Pursuit of the Graf Spee; Stowaway Girl. 1958 I Accuse!; Campbell's Kingdom. 1959 The Wreck of the Mary Deare; The Angry Hills; Whirlpool. 1960 The Electronic Monster (aka Escapement); Bluebeard's Ten Honeymoons; Sands of the Desert; The Twenty-fifth Hour. 1961 The Secret Partner; Village of Daughters. 1962 Malaga; The Happy Thieves. 1963 Nine Hours to Rama; The V.I.P.'s; Jet Storm. 1964 The Secret Door. 1966 A Man Could Get Killed.

ILLINGTON, MARGARET
Born: 1881, Bloomington, Ill. Died: Mar. 11, 1934, Miami Beach, Fla. Screen and stage actress. Married to radio and screen actor Major Bowes (dec. 1946).

Appeared in: 1917 The Inner Shrine (film debut); Sacrifice.

IMBODEN, HAZEL (Hazel Bourne)
Born: Washburn, Ill. Died: Oct. 8, 1956, Kansas City, Mo. Screen and stage actress. Married to screen actor David Imboden. Entered films in 1914.

IMHOF, ROGER
Born: Apr. 15, 1875, Rock Island, Ill. Died: Apr. 15, 1958, Hollywood, Calif. Screen, stage, circus, and vaudeville actor. Was in vaudeville with his wife Marcelle Coreine. Appeared in most of Will Rogers pictures.

Appeared in: 1930 Rural Hospital (short). 1933 Paddy, The Next Best Thing; Charlie Chan's Greatest Case; Hoopla. 1934 David Harum; Wild Gold; Judge Priest; Handy Andy; Ever since Eve; Grand Canary; Music in the Air; Under Pressure. 1935 One More Spring; Life Begins at Forty; The Farmer Takes a Wife; George White's 1935 Scandals; Steamboat 'Round the Bend. 1936 Riff Raff; Three Godfathers; San Francisco; A Son Comes Home; In His Steps; North of Nome. 1937 There Goes the Groom; Every Day's a Holiday. 1939 Young Mr. Lincoln; They Shall Have Music; Everything Happens at Night; Drums along the Mohawk. 1940 Abe Lincoln in Illinois; The Grapes of Wrath; Little Old New York; The Way of All Flesh; I Was an Adventuress. 1941 Mystery Ship; Man Hunt. 1942 It Happened in Flatbush; Tennessee Johnson; This Gun for Hire. 1944 Casanova in Burlesque; Home in Indiana; Adventures of Mark Twain. 1945 Wilson.

INCE, ETHEL. See Ethel Kent

INCE, JOHN E. (John Edward Ince)
Born: 1877, New York, N.Y. Died: Apr. 10, 1947, Hollywood, Calif.(pneumonia). Screen, stage actor, film director, and film producer. Brother of screen actors Thomas (dec. 1924) and Ralph Ince (dec. 1937). Entered films in 1913 in various capacities.

Appeared in: 1918 Madame Sphinx. 1921 The Hole in the Wall. 1922 Hate. 1927 The Hour of Reckoning. 1930 Alias French Gertie; Hot Curves; Little Caesar; Moby Dick. 1931 Children of Dreams. 1932 Human Targets; Passport to Paradise; No Living Witness; Afraid to Talk. 1933 The Penal Code; One Year Later; Thrill Hunter. 1935 Circle of Death; Circus Shadows; Men of Action; Behind the Green Lights; In Old Kentucky. 1936 Night Cargo; Way Out West; The Speed Reporter; Don't Turn 'em Loose. 1939 Mr. Smith Goes to Washington. 1941 Mr. Celebrity. 1942 Code of the Outlaw; The Miracle Kid; The Panther's Claw; Prison Girls; Broadway Big Shot; Pride of the Yankees. 1943 Man of Courage; What a Man!. 1944 Wilson. 1945 The Lost Trail. 1947 The Last Frontier Uprising. 1948 The Paradine Case.

INCE, RALPH WALDO
Born: 1887, Boston, Mass. Died: Apr. 10, 1937, London, England(auto accident). Screen, stage actor, film director, and screenwriter. Brother of screen actors Thomas (dec. 1924) and John Ince (dec. 1947). Entered films in 1905 as a director.

Appeared in: 1906 "Historical" series on Lincoln for Vitagraph. 1920 Land of Opportunity. 1921 The Highest Law; Wet Gold. 1926 The Sea Wolf; Bigger Than Barnum's; The Better Way; Breed of the Sea; Yellow Fingers. 1927 Not for Publication; Shanghaied. 1928 Chicago after Midnight; The Singapore Mutiny. 1929 Wall Street. 1930 Numbered Men; The Big Fight; Little Caesar. 1931 A Gentleman's Fate; Hell Bound; The Star Witness; Big Gamble; Law and Order; The Dove; Exposed. 1932 The Lost Squadron; Men of Chance; Girl of the Rio; The Mouthpiece; State's Attorney; The Tenderfoot; Guilty as Hell; The Pride of the Legion; Law of the Sea; Gorilla Ship; Malay Nights; Men of America;

Lucky Devils; The Hatchet Man; County Fair. 1933 Havana Widows; No Escape; The Big Payoff. 1935 So You Won't Talk. 1937 The Perfect Crime.

INCE, THOMAS H.
Born: 1882. Died: Nov. 20, 1924, Beverly Hills, Calif.(heart failure). Screen, stage actor, film director, producer, and screenwriter. Entered films in 1911. Brother of screen actors John (dec. 1947) and Ralph Ince (dec. 1937).

INCLAN, MIGUEL
Born: 1900, Mexico. Died: July 25, 1956, Tijuana, Mexico. Screen actor.

Appeared in: 1943 Creo en Dios. 1947 The Fugitive. 1948 Fort Apache. 1952 Indian Uprising; The Young and the Damned. 1955 Bandido; Seven Cities of Gold.

INDRISANO, JOHN "JOHNNY"
Born: 1906, Boston, Mass. Died: July 9, 1968, San Fernando Valley, Calif.(apparent suicide-hanging). Screen actor and boxer.

Appeared in: 1935 The Winning Ticket; She Gets Her Man; Two Fisted. 1936 Laughing Irish Eyes. 1937 Every Day's a Holiday. 1941 Ringside Maisie. 1944 Lost in a Harem. 1945 The Naughty Nineties. 1948 In This Corner; Lulu Belle; Trouble Makers. 1949 Joe Palooka in the Counterpunch; The Lady Gambles. 1950 The Yellow Cab Man. 1951 Pier 23; Callaway Went Thataway. 1952 Glory Alley; No Holds Barred. 1957 Chicago Confidential. 1958 Hot Spell. 1960 The Purple Gang. 1961 Blueprint for Robbery. 1962 Who's Got the Action? 1964 A House is Not a Home.

INFANTE, PEDRO
Born: 1918, Mexico. Died: Apr. 15, 1957, Merida, Yucatan (airplane crash). Mexican screen, radio actor, and singer.

INGERSOLL, WILLIAM
Born: 1860. Died: May 7, 1936, Los Angeles, Calif.(acute indigestion). Screen and stage actor.

Appeared in: 1920 Partners of the Night. 1931 The Cheat. 1935 Mary Burns, Fugitive; Whipsaw. 1936 Half Angel.

INGRAHAM, LLOYD
Born: Rochelle, Ill. Died: Apr. 4, 1956, Woodland Hills, Calif. (pneumonia). Screen, stage actor, and film and stage director. Entered films in 1912.

Appeared in: 1922 A Front Page Story. 1923 Scaramouche. 1924 The Chorus Lady. 1929 Untamed; Night Parade; The Rainbow Man. 1930 So Long Letty; Montana Moon; The Spoilers; Last of the Duanes; A Lady to Love; Wide Open. 1931 The Lady Who Dared. 1932 Texas Gun Fighter; The Crusader; Get That Girl; Sinister Hands; The Widow in Scarlet. 1933 I Love That Man; The World Gone Mad; Midnight Warning; Officer 13; Cornered; Revenge at Monte Carlo; Silent Men. 1934 Sixteen Fathoms Deep; In Love with Life; Lost Jungle; The Dude Rancher; The Curtain Falls. 1935 The World Accuses; Northern Frontier; Rainbow Valley; Circumstantial Evidence; The Cowboy Millionaire; Headline Woman; Sons of Steel; On Probation; Rider of the Law; Between Men. 1936 Ghost Patrol; Empty Saddles; The Lonely Trail; Timber Way; Frontier Justice; Captain Calamity; Rogue of the Range; Burning Gold; Hearts in Bondage; Too Much Beef; Everyman's Law; Go Get 'em, Haines!; Conflict; Stormy Trails. 1937 Park Avenue Logger; Battle of Greed; Riders of the Dawn. 1938 Painted Desert; Man from Music Mountain; Reformatory; Gun Packer. 1940 Marshal of Mesa City; 20 Mule Team; Bad Man from Red Butte; Colorado; My Little Chicadee. 1941 Dude Cowboy; Never Give a Sucker an Even Break. 1942 Stagecoach Buckaroo; Boss of Big Town. 1943 Blazing Guns; The Mystery of the 13th Guest. 1944 Partners of the Trail; Range Law; West of the Rio Grande; The Merry Monahans. 1945 Frontier Gal; Frontier Feud; Lawless Empire; The Man Who Walked Alone; Springtime in Texas. 1946 The Caravan Trail. 1950 The Savage Horde.

INGRAM, JACK
Born: 1903. Died: Feb. 20, 1969, Canoga Park, Calif.(heart attack). Screen actor.

Appeared in: 1936 Rebellion; The Lonely Trail; With Love and Kisses. 1937 Public Cowboy No. 1; Zorro Rides Again (serial); Headline Crasher. 1938 Code of the Rangers; Wild Horse Rodeo; Outlaws of Sonora; Riders of the Black Hills; Dick Tracy Returns (serial); Frontier Scout. 1939 The Night Riders; Home on the Prairie; Blue Montana Skies; Wyoming Outlaw; Colorado Sunset; New Frontier; Wall Street Cowboy; Sage of Death Valley; Rovin' Tumbleweeds; Down the Wyoming Trail. 1940 Ghost Valley Raiders; Under Texas Skies; Young Bill Hickock; The

Green Archer (serial). 1941 South of Panama; King of the Texas Rangers (serial); Sheriff of Tombstone; Nevada City; The Gang's All Here; Prairie Pioneers; Law of the Wolf; The Lone Rider Ambushed. 1942 The Man from Cheyenne; Tomorrow We Live; Billy the Kid Trapped. 1943 The Mysterious Rider; Fugitive of the Plains; Lone Star Trail; Border Buckaroos; Riders of the Rio Grande; Silver Raiders. 1945 Bandits of the Badlands; Devil Riders; Enemy of the Law; Flame of the West; The Jade Mask; Out of Vengeance; Outlaw Roundup; Saddle Serenade; Sheriff of Cimarron; Stranger from Santa Fe; Frontier Gal. 1946 Frontier Fugitives; Moon over Montana; West of the Alamo. 1947 Pioneer Justice; Slave Girl; South of the Chisholm Trail; Ghost Town Renegades. 1948 Strawberry Roan; Whirlwind Raiders; Racing Luck. 1949 Son of a Badman; Law of the West; Roaring Westward; Desert Vigilante. 1950 The Texan Meets Calamity Jane; Short Grass; Bandit Queen; Sierra; Sideshow; Streets of Ghost Town. 1951 Fort Dodge Stampede. 1952 The Battle of Apache Pass; Fargo. 1953 Cow Country; Son of the Renegade. 1955 Man without a Star; Five Guns West. 1957 Utah Blaine. 1959 Zorro Rides Again.

INGRAM, REX (Rex Fitchcock).
Born: 1892, Dublin, Ireland. Died: July 21, 1950, North Hollywood, Calif. (Not to be confused with Negro actor who died Sept. 19, 1969.) Screen and stage actor, film director, producer, and screenwriter. Married to screen actress Alice Terry.

Appeared in: 1913 The Artists Madonna.

INGRAM, REX
Born: Oct. 20, 1895, Cairo, Ill. Died: Sept. 19, 1969, Los Angeles, Calif.(heart attack). Negro screen, stage, and television actor.

Appeared in: 1918 Tarzan of the Apes; Salome. 1923 Scaramouche; The Ten Commandments. 1926 The Big Parade. 1927 King of Kings. 1929 Hearts in Dixie; The Four Feathers. 1932 Sign of the Cross. 1933 King Kong; The Emperor Jones; Love in Morocco. 1935 Captain Blood. 1936 Green Pastures. 1939 Adventures of Huckleberry Finn. 1940 The Thief of Bagdad. 1942 The Talk of the Town. 1943 Fired Wife; Sahara; Cabin in the Sky. 1944 Dark Waters. 1945 A Thousand and One Nights. 1948 Moonrise. 1950 King Solomon's Mines. 1955 Tarzan's Hidden Jungle; Desire in the Dust. 1956 The Ten Commandments (and 1923 version); Congo Crossing. 1957 Hell on Devil's Island. 1958 God's Little Acre; Anna Lucasta. 1959 Escort West; Watusi. 1960 Elmer Gantry. 1964 Your Cheatin' Heart. 1967 Hurry Sundown; Journey to Shiloh; How to Succeed in Business without Really Trying.

INGRAM, WILLIAM D.
Born: 1857. Died: Feb. 2, 1926, New York, N.Y. Screen and stage actor.

IRELAND, ANTHONY
Born: Feb. 5, 1902, Peru. Died: Dec. 4, 1957, London, England. Screen, stage, and television actor.

Appeared in: 1931 These Charming People. 1932 The Water Gypsies. 1933 Called Back. 1936 The Three Maxims; Juggernaut. 1937 When Thief Meets Thief; Twin Faces; Sweet Devil; Sweet Racket. 1942 The Prime Minister. 1952 Gambler and the Lady. 1953 Spaceways. 1958 I Accuse!

IRGAT, CAHIT
Born: 1916, Luleburgaz, Turkey. Died: June 1971, Sisli, Turkey (lung cancer). Screen, stage actor, poet, and writer.

Appeared in: Yil maz Ali (film debut).

IRVING, GEORGE
Born: 1874, New York. Died: Sept. 11, 1961, Hollywood, Calif. (heart attack). Screen, stage actor, and film director. Entered films in 1913.

Appeared in: 1924 Wanderer of the Wasteland; The Man Who Fights Alone; North of 36; For Sale; Madonna of the Streets. 1925 The Goose Hangs High; The Air Mail; The Golden Princess; Wild Horse Mesa; Her Market Value. 1926 Desert Gold; The City; His Jazz Bride; The Midnight Kiss; The Eagle of the Sea; Fangs of Justice; Three Bad Men; Risky Business; The King of the Turf. 1927 The Broncho Twister; Home Struck; Two Flaming Youths; Man Power; Drums of the Desert; One Increasing Purpose; Shanghai Bound; Wings. 1928 Modern Mothers; The Port of Missing Girls; Craig's Wife; Feel My Pulse; Honor Bound; Partners in Crime; The Wright Idea; Runaway Girls. 1929 The Godless Girl; The Dance of Life; Thunderbolt; Paris Bound; Coquette; The Last Performance. 1930 Son of the Gods; The

Divorcee; Puttin' on the Ritz; Shadow of the Law; The Poor Millionaires; Conspiracy; Maybe It's Love; Only Saps Work; Free Love; Young Eagles; Young Desire. 1931 Dishonored; Hush Money; The Naughty Flirt; The American Tragedy; Cisco Kid; Hot Heiress; Five and Ten; A Free Soul; Resurrection; Graft; Confessions of a Co-Ed; The Runaround; Shipmates; Girls Demand Excitement; The Star Witness; Touchdown; Wicked. 1932 Merrily We Go to Hell; Vanishing Frontier; Thrill of Youth; Guilty or Not Guilty; All-American; Broken Lullaby; Lady with a Past; Ladies of the Big House. 1933 Island of Lost Souls; The Worst Woman in Paris; Humanity; One Year Later; Son of a Sailor. 1934 The World Moves On; Bright Eyes; Here Comes the Navy; George White's Scandals; Manhattan Love Song; Once to Every Bachelor; You're Telling Me. 1935 Beauty's Daughter; Society Fever; Dangerous; Death Flies East; Age of Indiscretion; A Notorious Gentleman; Under the Pampas Moon; A Night at the Opera. 1936 Captain January; Charlie Chan at the Race Track; Hearts Divided; Hearts in Bondage; Hats Off; It Had to Happen; Nobody's Fool; Private Number; Sutter's Gold; The Sea Spoilers; Navy Born. 1937 Border Cafe; China Passage; The Mandarin Mystery; Don't Tell the Wife; The Big Shot; High Flyers; The Life of the Party; The Man Who Found Himself; Meet the Missus; Saturday's Heroes; She's Got Everything; There Goes the Groom; The Toast of New York; Too Many Wives; We're on the Jury; You Can't Buy Luck. 1938 Blind Alibi; Condemned Women; Crashing Hollywood; Crime Ring; Bringing up Baby; Go Chase Yourself; The Law West of Tombstone; Maid's Night Out; Mother Carey's Chickens; Mr. Doodle Kicks Off; Smashing the Rackets; This Marriage Business. 1939 Wife, Husband and Friend; The Hardy's Ride High; Dust Be My Destiny; Hotel for Women; Streets of New York. 1940 Knute Rockne—All American; A Child Is Born; Florian; Johnny Apollo; New Moon; Yesterday's Heroes. 1941 Bullets for O'Hara; Golden Hoofs; She Couldn't Say No; Out of the Fog; The Vanishing Virginian. 1942 The Great Man's Lady; Spy Ship. 1943 Hangmen Also Die; Son of Dracula. 1944 The Impostor; Christmas Holiday; Lady in the Death House. 1947 Magic Town.

IRVING, PAUL
Born: 1877, Boston, Mass. Died: May 8, 1959, Hollywood, Calif. Screen and stage actor.

Appeared in: 1932 Bill of Divorcement. 1933 The Silver Cord. 1934 Count of Monte Cristo. 1936 The Great Ziegfeld; Gold Diggers of 1937. 1937 On the Avenue; Hollywood Hotel. 1938 Battle of Broadway; Gold Diggers of 1939. 1939 Balalaika.

IRVING, WILLIAM J.
Born: 1893. Died: Dec. 25, 1943, Los Angeles, Calif. Screen and vaudeville actor.

Appeared in: 1923 Gentle Julia; The Love Trap. 1924 Love Letters. 1925 Pampered Youth. 1927 She's My Baby; Ham and Eggs at the Front. 1928 Coney Island; Beautiful but Dumb; The Singapore Mutiny; Nothing to Wear; Red Hair. 1929 From Headquarters; Hearts in Exile. 1930 All Quiet on the Western Front; Song of the Caballero; On the Border; Rough Waters; plus the following shorts: The Body Slam; Won to Lose; Surprise; Ginsberg of Newberg; Skin Game. 1931 Her Majesty, Love; Manhattan Parade. 1933 Diplomaniacs. 1934 Orient Express; Melody in Spring; Three Little Big Skins (short). 1935 Air Hawks; The Big Broadcast of 1936; Restless Knights (short); Hoi Polloi (short). 1937 The Shadow. 1938 Convicted.

IRWIN, BOYD
Born: Mar. 12, 1880, Brighton, England. Died: Jan. 22, 1957, Woodland Hills, Calif. Screen and stage actor.

Appeared in: 1921 The Three Musketeers. 1922 The Long Chance. 1923 Ashes of Vengeance; Enemies of Children. 1924 Captain Blood. 1932 The Man from Yesterday. 1934 What Every Woman Knows; Pursuit of Happiness. 1935 Cardinal Richelieu; The Crusades; The Werewolf of London. 1936 Dangerous Intrigue; The Blackmailer; Killer at Large; Devil's Squadron; Meet Nero Wolfe. 1937 Prisoner of Zenda. 1939 Man in the Iron Mask; Sky Patrol. 1940 The Invisible Killer; Drums of the Desert. 1941 Mr. and Mrs. North; Secret Evidence; City of Missing Girls; The Great Swindle; Passage from Hong Kong. 1942 Joe Smith, American; True to the Army; The Major and the Minor; Random Harvest; Foreign Agent. 1943 Thank Your Lucky Stars; Chatterbox. 1944 Frenchman's Creek; The Lodger; Double Indemnity; Our Hearts Were Young and Gay; The Story of Dr. Wassell. 1945 Molly and Me. 1946 Rendezvous 29; Dragonwyck; Tomorrow Is Forever; Devotion; The Time of Their Lives. 1947 A Double Life; King of the Bandits. 1948 Docks of New Orleans; Campus Honeymoon.

IRWIN, CHARLES W.
Born: 1888, Ireland. Died: Jan. 12, 1969, Woodland Hills, Calif.(cancer). Screen, stage actor, and screenwriter.

Appeared in: 1928 The Debonair Humorist (short). 1930 The King of Jazz; Blind Adventure. 1933 Looking Forward; Hell Below; Kickin' the Crown Around (short). 1934 The Mystery of Mr. X. 1935 The Gilded Lily; Whipsaw. 1936 The White Angel. 1937 Another Dawn; The League of Frightened Men. 1938 Kidnapped; Lord Jeff. 1937 Susannah of the Mounties; The Light That Failed; Man about Town. 1940 The Man I Married. 1941 International Squadron. 1942 To Be or Not To Be; Desperate Journey; Great Impersonation; Mrs. Miniver; Yankee Doodle Dandy; The Black Swan. 1943 No Time for Love; The Gorilla Man. 1944 Sing, Neighbor, Sing; Nothing but Trouble. 1945 Hangover Square. 1947 The Foxes of Harrow; Thunder in the Valley; My Wild Irish Rose. 1949 Bomba on Panther Island; Challenge to Lassie. 1950 Montana. 1951 Mystery Junction. 1952 Captain Pirate; A Tale of Five Women. 1953 Charge of the Lancers; Fort Vengeance; The Caddy; Son of the Renegade. 1954 The Iron Glove. 1956 The King and I; The Court Jester. 1959 The Sheriff of Fractured Jaw.

IRWIN, MAY
Born: 1862, Whitby, Ontario, Canada. Died: Oct. 22, 1958, New York, N.Y. Screen and stage actress.

Appeared in: 1896 The Kiss (Edison—One of the most famous of the early films showing the kissing scene from the stage play The Widow Jones.) 1914 Mrs. Black is Back.

ISAACS, ISADORE "IKE"
Born: 1901. Died: Mar. 18, 1957, Culver City, Calif. Screen actor and stand-in. Entered films approx. 1932.

ISBERT, JOSE
Born: 1884, Spain. Died: Nov. 28, 1966, Madrid, Spain(heart ailment). Screen and stage actor.

Appeared in Spanish films: Ramon and Dalila; Broken Lives; The Whole Truth; The Dancer and the Laborer; Welcome, Mr. Marshall; Manolo the Policeman; Calabuch; An Afternoon of Bulls; El Verdugo. 1961 The Man Who Wagged His Tail. 1965 El Ver (The Executioner) (aka Not on Your Life).

IVAN, ROSALIND
Born: 1884, England. Died: Apr. 6, 1959, New York, N.Y. Screen and stage actress.

Appeared in: 1944 The Suspect. 1945 The Corn Is Green; Scarlet Street; Pillow of Death; Pursuit to Algiers. 1946 The Verdict; Three Strangers; That Brennan Girl; Alias Mr. Twilight. 1947 Ivy. 1948 Johnny Belinda. 1953 The Robe. 1954 Elephant Walk.

IVES, DOUGLAS
Died: Mar. 6, 1969, London, England. Screen and stage actor.

Appeared in: 1954 What Every Woman Wants. 1955 Doctor in the House; Innocents in Paris; Room in the House. 1956 The Big Chance. 1957 Man in the Shadow; Miracle in Soho. 1962 Just for Fun. 1964 Sing and Swing.

JACK, T. C.
Born: 1882. Died: Oct. 4, 1954, Hollywood, Calif.(heart attack). Screen actor. Entered films approx. 1914.

Appeared in: 1925 Daring Days.

JACKIE, WILLIAM "BILL"
Born: 1890. Died: Sept. 19, 1954, San Francisco, Calif.(heart attack). Screen actor. Entered films during silents.

Appeared in: 1937 Don't Tell the Wife.

JACKSON, ANDREW, IV
Born: 1887. Died: May 23, 1953, Los Angeles, Calif. Screen actor. Great grandson of President Andrew Jackson.

Appeared in: 1953 The President's Lady.

JACKSON, ETHEL. See Ethel Kent

JACKSON, ETHEL SHANNON. See Ethel Shannon

JACKSON, THOMAS
Born: 1886, New York, N.Y. Died: Sept. 8, 1967, Hollywood, Calif.(heart attack). Screen, stage, and television actor.

Appeared in: 1929 Broadway (stage and film versions). 1930 Little Caesar; Good News; The Fall Guy; Double Cross Roads; For the Defense. 1931 Lawless Woman; Sweepstakes; Twenty-four Hours; Women Go on Forever; Reckless Living. 1932 Afraid to Talk; Big City Blues; Escapade; Unashamed; Doctor X; Strange Justice. 1933 Terror Abroad; The Avenger; Parachute Jumper; The Mystery of the Wax Museum; From Hell to Heaven; Strictly Personal. 1934 Myrt and Marge; Manhattan Melodrama; The Personality Kid; Melody in Spring. 1935 Carnival; Call of the Wild; Gold Diggers of 1935; The Case of the Curious Bride; Fugitive in the Sky; The Irish in Us; George White's 1935 Scandals. 1936 Preview Murder Mystery; A Son Comes Home; Hollywood Boulevard; It Had to Happen; Little Miss Nobody; Grand Jury; A Man Betrayed; The Magnificent Brute. 1937 Beware of Ladies; Dangerous Holiday; Outcast; The Westland Case; Fugitive in the Sky; She's No Lady. 1938 International Crime; I Stand Accused; Crime Takes a Holiday; The Lady in the Morgue; Torchy Gets Her Man. 1938-39 appeared in "Torchy Blaine" and "Nancy Drew" series. 1940 Free, Blonde and 21; A Fugitive from Justice; Millionaires in Prison; Golden Gloves; Girl from God's Country. 1941 Law of the Tropics. 1944 Woman in the Window; "Thin Man" series. 1945 Circumstantial Evidence; Why Girls Leave Home; How Do You Do; Shady Lady; The Hidden Eye. 1946 Valley of the Zombies; The Face of Marble; The Big Sleep. 1947 The Guilty; Dead Reckoning; The Guilt of Janet Ames. 1948 Here Comes Trouble. 1949 The Great John L. 1952 Stars and Stripes Forever; Phone Call from a Stranger. 1953 Meet Me at the Fair. 1958 Attack of the 50 Foot Woman. 1965 Synanon.

JACKSON, WARREN
Born: 1893. Died: May 10, 1950, Hollywood, Calif.(auto accident). Screen and television actor.

Appeared in: 1937 Hollywood Round-Up. 1938 Call the Mesquiteers. 1949 Oh, You Beautiful Doll. 1950 Montana; Square Dance Katy.

JACOBS, ANGELA
Born: 1893, Sioux City, Iowa. Died: Feb. 7, 1951, Detroit, Mich. (heart attack). Screen, stage, and vaudeville actress.

Appeared in: 1933 Counsellor-at-Law (stage and film versions).

JAHR, ADOLF
Born: 1894. Died: Apr. 19, 1964, Stockholm, Sweden. Screen, stage, and opera actor. Known as the "Swedish Douglas Fairbanks."

Appeared in: 1924 Den Gamia Herrgarden (The Old Manor). 1934 Petterson and Bendel. 1937 Adolf Armstrong. 1940 Kryss med Albertin (Cruise in the Albertina). 1944 Homsoborna.

JAMES, ALF P.
Born: 1865, Australia. Died: Oct. 9, 1946, Hollywood, Calif. Screen, stage, and vaudeville actor. Was in vaudeville with his wife in an act billed as "James and Pryor."

Appeared in: 1931 Everything's Rosie; Heaven on Earth. 1933 Thrill Hunter; Hokus Focas (short). 1934 Six of a Kind; Elmer and Elsie; Cockeyed Cavaliers.

JAMES, CLIFTON
Born: 1898. Died: May 8, 1963, Worthing, England. Screen actor and author. Impersonated Marshall Montgomery so well was trained as Marshall Montgomery to "hoodwink" the Germans during W.W. II. Wrote a book, I Was Monty's Double.

Appeared in: 1957 The Strange One. 1959 I Was Monty's Double; The Last Mile. 1960 Experiment in Terror. 1961 Something Wild. 1962 David and Lisa. 1964 Black Like Me. 1967 The Happening; The Caper of the Golden Bulls. 1968 Will Penny.

JAMES, EDDIE
Born: 1880. Died: Dec. 22, 1944, New York. Screen, stage actor, and assistant film director.

Appeared in: 1925 Lucky Devil. 1926 Wild Oaks Lane.

JAMES, GLADDEN
Born: 1892, Zanesville, Ohio. Died: August 28, 1948, Hollywood, Calif.(leukemia). Screen and stage actor.

Appeared in: 1917 The Mystery of the Double Cross (serial). 1919 The Heart of the Wetona. 1920 Yes or No. 1921 His Brother's Keeper; Bucking the Tiger; Wise Husbands; The Silver Lining; Footfalls. 1922 Channing of the Northwest; The Faithless Sex. 1923 The Broken Violin; The Woman with Four Faces; A Clouded Name. 1924 Marry in Haste. 1925 Alias Mary Flynn; The Wedding Song. 1926 Tex. 1927 The Temptations of a Shop Girl. 1928 Sweet Sixteen; Adorable Cheat; Driftin' Sands; The Hound of Silver Creek; The Look Out Girl; The Girl He Didn't Buy. 1929 The Peacock Fan; His Captive Woman; The Girl from Woolworth's; Weary River. 1930 Paradise Island. 1931 Bad Company. 1933 Lucky

Devils. 1936 The Case against Mrs. Ames; The Princess Comes Across. 1942 For Me and My Gal; The Postman Didn't Ring; Tennessee Johnson.

JAMES, HORACE D.
Born: 1853, Baltimore, Md. Died: Oct. 16, 1925, Orange, N.J. Screen and stage actor.

Appeared in: 1921 Get-Rich-Quick Wallingford (stage and film versions). 1922 A Woman's Woman. 1923 Adam and Eve.

JAMES, JOHN
Died: May 20, 1960, New York. Screen and stage actor.

Appeared in: 1942 Flying Tigers. 1943 Gung Ho!. 1944 Sign of the Cross. 1945 Bedside Manner; This Man's Navy; Saddle Pals. 1946 Our Hearts Were Growing Up. 1949 Gun Law Justice; The Valiant Hombre. 1953 Topeka.

JAMES, WALTER
Born: 1886, Tenn. Died: June 27, 1946, Gardena, Calif.(heart attack). Screen and stage actor.

Appeared in: 1922 Fair Lady; The Secrets of Paris. 1924 Two Shall Be Born. 1925 Little Annie Rooney; The Everlasting Whisper; The Monster. 1926 The Seventh Bandit; Battling Butler; Glenister of the Mounted. 1927 The Blood Ship; Patent Leather Kid; The Irresistible Lover; The Kid Brother. 1928 The Wright Idea; The Big Killing; Me, Gangster. 1930 Shadow of the Law. 1931 Street Scene.

JAMESON, HOUSE
Born: 1903. Died: Apr. 23, 1971, Danbury, Conn. Screen, stage, radio, and television actor. Noted for his radio and television portrayals of the father in The Aldrich Family.

Appeared in: 1948 The Naked City. 1965 Mirage. 1968 The Swimmer.

JAMIN, GEORGES
Born: 1907. Died: Feb. 23, 1971, Hemptinne, Belgium. Screen, stage, and television actor.

Appeared in: 1931 Occupe-toi d'Amelia (film debut). 1939 Bouquets from Nicholas.

JAMISON, WILLIAM "BUD"
Born: 1894, Vallejo, Calif. Died: Sept. 30, 1944, Hollywood, Calif. Screen, stage, and vaudeville actor.

Appeared in: 1917 Lonesome Luke. 1924 Troubles of a Bride; Dante's Inferno; Darwin Was Right; The Cyclone Rider. 1927 Jake the Plumber; Closed Gates; Ladies Beware; His First Flame; Play Safe; Texas Steer; Wolves of the Air. 1928 Buck Privates; The Chaser; Heart Trouble. 1930 The Grand Parade; Traffic. 1931 "Folly Comedies" second series of shorts including: Help Wanted Female; Gossipy Plumber; Parents Wanted. 1932 Hurry Call; Make Me a Star, plus the following shorts: In the Devil's Doghouse; In a Pig's Eye; Men in Black; Woman Haters; Three Little Pigskins. 1935 the following shorts: Flying Down to Zero; Alibi Bye Bye; All American Toothache; Uncivil Warriors; Hoi Polloi; Three Little Beers. 1936 Ticket to Paradise; plus the following shorts: Movie Maniacs; On the Wrong Trek; A Pain in the Pullman; Ants in the Pantry; Whoops I'm an Indian. 1937 Melody of the Plains; Back to the Woods (short); Dizzy Doctors (short). 1938 See My Lawyer, plus the following shorts: Termites of 1938; Wee Wee Monsieur; Tassels in the Air; Healthy, Wealthy and Dumb; Violent Is the Word for Curly; Mutts to You. 1939 Topper Takes a Trip; Mooching Through Georgia, plus the following shorts: Three Little Sew and Sews; A-Ducking We Will Go; We Want Our Mummy; Three Sappy People. 1940 Li'l Abner; Slightly Honorable; Captain Caution; A-Plumbing We Will Go (short). 1941 Wild Bill Hickock Rides, plus the following shorts: I'll Never Heil Again; Dutiful but Dumb; All the World's a Stooge; An Ache in Every Stake. 1942 You Can't Escape Forever; Her Cardboard Lover, plus the following shorts: Sock-a-Bye Baby; Loco Boy Makes Good; Even as I.O.U. 1943 True to Life; Blitz on the Fritz, plus the following shorts: Dizzy Detectives; Back from the Front; Three Little Twerps; I Can Hardly Wait; Phony Express; A Gem in a Jam. 1944 Lost in a Harem; Crash Goes the Hash (short). 1945 Nob Hill.

JANIS, ELSIE (Elsie Bierbower).
Born: Mar. 16, 1889, Ohio. Died: Feb. 26, 1956, Beverly Hills, Calif. Screen, stage and vaudeville actor, composer, author, and screenwriter.

Appeared in: 1915 The Caprices of Kitty; Betty in Search of a

Thrill; Nearly a Lady. 1919 A Regular Girl. 1920 Everybody's Sweetheart. 1927 Behind the Lines (short). 1940 Women in War; also several short subjects.

JANNINGS, EMIL
Born: July 26, 1886, Brooklyn, N.Y. Died: Jan. 3, 1950, Austria (cancer). Screen and stage actor. Entered films in 1915. Won Academy Award for Best Actor in 1927-28 for his two roles in The Way of All Flesh and The Last Command. Was the first actor ever to receive an Academy Award.

Appeared in: 1917 Passion. 1918 Madame DuBarry. 1920 Passion (and 1917 version). 1921 Deception; All for a Woman; Vendetta. 1922 The Loves of Pharoah. 1923 Othello; Peter the Great. 1925 Quo Vadis; The Last Laugh; Variety. 1926 Faust; The Three Way Works. 1927 Tartuffe; Husband or Lovers; The Way of All Flesh. 1928 The Street of Sin; The Patriot; Fortune's Fool; The Last Command; Power; Sins of the Fathers. 1929 Betrayal; Fighting the White Slave Traffic. 1930 The Blue Angel; Liebling der Gotter; (Darling of the Gods). 1932 Stuerme der Leidenschaft (Storms of Passion); The Tempest. 1933 Der Grosse Tenor (The Great Tenor). 1934 Der Schwarze Walfisch. 1935 Der Alte und der Junge Konig. 1936 Traumulus. 1937 The Ruler. 1938 Der Zerbrochene Krug (The Broken Jug). 1941 Ohm Kruger (German propaganda film).

JANS, HARRY
Born: 1900. Died: Feb. 4, 1962, Hollywood, Calif. (heart attack). Screen, stage, and vaudeville actor. Was in vaudeville team of "Jans & Whalen."

Appeared in: 1929 Two Good Boys Gone Wrong (short). 1936 Special Investigator; Two in Revolt; The Last Outlaw; Grand Jury; Don't Turn 'Em Loose; Smartest Girl in Town; Racing Lady; Charlie Chan at the Race Track; Murder on a Bridal Path. 1937 Don't Tell the Wife; That Girl from Paris.

JANSEN, HARRY A. See Dante

JANSON, VICTOR
Born: 1885, Germany. Died: July, 1960, Berlin. Screen actor and film director.

Appeared in: 1929 At the Edge of the World. 1932 1914: The Last Days Before the War. 1939 Nanu; Sie Kennen Korff noch Nicht (So You Don't Know Korff Yet?). 1950 Marriage of Figaro. 1952 Prince of Pappenheim. 1953 Hit Parade. 1954 Anne of Tharau.

JARRETT, ARTHUR L. "ART"
Born: Feb. 5, 1888, Marysville, Calif. Died: June 12, 1960, New York, N.Y. Screen, stage, television actor, and song writer. Father of Art Jarrett, singer/orchestra leader and brother of screen actor Dan Jarrett (dec. 1938).

Appeared in: 1932-33 Universal "Radio Star Reels." 1933 Ace of Aces; Dancing Lady; Sitting Pretty; Let's Fall in Love. 1934 Riptide; Hollywood Party. 1937 an Educational short. 1939 Trigger Pals. 1950 The Tattooed Stranger.

JARRETT, DAN
Born: 1894. Died: Mar. 13, 1938, Hollywood, Calif. (heart ailment). Screen, stage actor, screenwriter, and playwright. Brother of screen actor Arthur Jarrett (dec. 1960).

Appeared in: 1922 Sunshine Harbor. 1935 The Cowboy Millionaire.

JARVIS, AL
Born: 1910, Winnipeg, Canada. Died: May 6, 1970, Newport Beach, Calif. (heart attack). Screen, radio, and television actor.

Appeared in: 1953 The Twonky. 1962 The Phantom Planet.

JARVIS, JEAN
Born: 1903. Died: Mar. 16, 1933, Hollywood, Calif. Screen actress/showgirl.

Appeared in: 1925 Fear-bound. 1926 The Little Giant.

JARVIS, LAURA E.
Born: 1866. Died: Mar. 9, 1933, near Downey, Calif. (injuries received from hit and run driver). Screen actress.

JARVIS, ROBERT C.
Born: 1892. Died: Nov. 13, 1971, Bloomsbury, N.J. Screen, stage actor, and stage director. Appeared in "Torchy Blane" series with Glenda Farrell.

Appeared in: 1930 Putting It On (short). 1933 Gold Diggers of 1933. 1938 Torchy Gets Her Man. 1939 Torchy Blane Runs for Mayor; Torchy Blane in Chinatown.

JARVIS, SYDNEY (aka SIDNEY JARVIS)
Born: 1881, New York, N.Y. Died: June 6, 1939, Hollywood, Calif. Screen, stage, and vaudeville actor. Entered films in 1914.

Appeared in: 1927 Casey at the Bat; The Prairie King. 1928 Circus Rookies; The Upland Rider; The Wagon Show. 1929 The Unholy Night; Footlights and Fools. 1930 Kismet. 1932 Movie Crazy. 1934 The Count of Monte Cristo; Hey Nanny Nanny (short).

JAUDENES, JOSE ALVARES "LEPE"
Born: 1891. Spain. Died: July, 1967, Madrid, Spain. Screen actor. Entered films in 1935.

Appeared in: Nine Letters to Bertha.

JAVOR, PAL (Paul Javor)
Born: Jan. 31, 1902, Arad, Hungary. Died: Aug. 14, 1959, Budapest, Hungary. Screen and stage actor.

Appeared in: 1933 A Key Balvany. 1934 Iza Neni (Aunt Isa); My Wife; The Miss; Rakoczi Indulo. 1935 Huszarszerelem; Koeszoenoem Hogy Elgazolt; Igloi Diakok; Elnoek Kisasszony; A Csunya Lany. 1936 The New Squire; Nem Elhetek Muzsikaszo Nelkuel; Az uj Foeldesur. 1937 Salary, 200 a Month; Naszut Felaron; Fizessen Nagysag; Viki; A Ferfi Mind Oeruelt (All Men Are Crazy); Toprini Nasz (Wedding in Toprin). 1938 Pusztai Szel (Beauty of the Pusta); Torockoi Menyasszony (Torockoi Bride); Ill-es Szobaban (In Room 111); Mother Love; Noszty Flue Este Toth Marival; Maga Lesz a Ferjem (You Will Be My Husband); Marika; Ket Fogoly (Two Prisoners). 1939 Fekete Gyemantok (Black Diamonds). 1940 Uz Bence. 1949 Carmela. 1951 The Great Caruso; Assignment—Paris.

JAY, ERNEST
Born: 1894. Died: 1957. Screen and stage actor.

Appeared in: 1934 Tiger Bay. 1935 The Iron Duke. 1936 Broken Blossoms. 1937 O.H.M.S. (aka You're in the Army Now). 1938 I See Ice. 1944 Don't Take It to Heart. 1947 Vice Versa. 1948 Blanche Fury. 1949 The History of Mr. Polly; Edward My Son. 1952 I Believe in You (U.S. 1953); Franchise Affair; Secret Flight. 1953 The Sword and the Rose. 1954 Mr. Potts Goes to Moscow (aka Top Secret). 1955 Who Done It? 1956 The Curse of Frankenstein (U.S. 1957).

JEAYES, ALLAN
Born: Jan. 19, 1885, London, England. Died: Sept. 20, 1963, London, England (heart attack). Screen, stage actor, playwright, and author.

Appeared in: 1922 Hound of the Baskervilles. 1930 The Hate Ship. 1931 The Ghost Train. 1932 High Treason; The Impassive Footman; Woman in Chains. 1933 All the Winners; Paris Plane; The Song of the Plough; Colonel Blood; Dick Turpin; Purse Strings. 1934 Red Ensign; The Camels Are Coming; Catherine the Great; The Scarlet Pimpernel. 1935 Elizabeth of England; King of the Damned; Sanders of the River. 1936 Doomed Cargo; His Lordship; Rembrandt; Things to Come; Seven Sinners. 1937 Elephant Boy; Knight without Armour; Action for Slander; The Squeaker; The Return of the Scarlet Pimpernel; Forever Yours; Man of Affairs; Murder on Diamond Row. 1939 The Four Feathers. 1940 The Thief of Bagdad. 1941 The Stars Look Down; Convoy; Proud Valley. 1942 Mister V. 1943 At Dawn We Die. 1945 Vacation from Marriage. 1946 Dead of Night; The Man Within. 1947 The Green Cockatoo. 1948 An Ideal Husband; The Smugglers; Blanche Fury. 1949 Saraband. 1950 Waterfront; Perfect Strangers; The Hidden Room. Other British films: The Ship Builder; Pimpernel Smith; Unity Is Strength; Obsession.

JEFFERS, JOHN S.
Born: 1874. Died: Jan. 3, 1939, Long Beach, N.Y. Screen and stage actor. Entered films with Bison Company.

JEFFERS, WILLIAM L.
Born: 1898. Died: Apr. 18, 1959, Hollywood, Calif. Screen and stage actor. Appeared in silents.

JEFFERSON, HILTON W.
Born: 1902. Died: Nov. 14, 1968, Sydenham, N.Y. Negro screen actor and musician.

Appeared in: 1943 Stormy Weather.

JEFFERSON, THOMAS
  Born: 1859. Died: Apr. 2, 1932, Hollywood, Calif. Screen and stage actor. Entered films with D. W. Griffith in 1909.

  Appeared in: 1913 Judith of Bethulia. 1915 Sable Lorcha; The Fortune Hunter. 1916 The Beloved Liar. 1918 A Hoosier Romance; Tarzan of the Apes. 1919 Sis Hopkins; The Spenders. 1921 Rip Van Winkle; The Idle Rich; My Lady's Latchkey; Straight from Paris. 1922 Beauty's Worth; A Tailor Made Man; The Son of the Wolf; Good Men and True; Vermillion Pencil. 1925 Thoroughbred. 1927 Paid to Love. 1928 The Fortune Hunter (and 1915 version); Soft Living. 1929 On with the Show. 1930 Double Cross Roads; Just Like Heaven; Lightnin'. 1931 Ten Nights in a Bar Room. 1932 Forbidden.

JEFFREY, MICHAEL
  Born: 1895. Died: Sept. 30, 1960, Hollywood, Calif.(heart attack). Screen, stage, and television actor.

  Appeared in: 1937 Dangerous Holiday; Mr. Boggs Steps Out. 1956 Man in the Gray Flannel Suit.

JEFFREYS, ELLIS
  Born: May 17, 1877, Ceylon. Died: Jan. 21, 1943, Surrey, England. Screen and stage actress.

  Appeared in: 1931 The Perfect Alibi. 1934 Lilies of the Field. 1935 While Parents Sleep; Limelight. 1936 Eliza Comes to Stay.

JENKINS, ELIZABETH
  Born: 1879. Died: Jan. 18, 1965, Caldwell, N.Y. Screen and stage actress. Appeared in silent films.

JENKS, FRANK
  Born: 1902, Des Moines, Iowa. Died: May 13, 1962, Hollywood, Calif.(cancer). Screen and television actor.

  Appeared in: 1933 College Humor. 1936 Farmer in the Dell; The Smartest Girl in Town; Follow the Fleet; The Witness Chair; The Last Outlaw; Walking on Air; Don't Turn 'Em Loose; We Who Are about to Die; That Girl from Paris; The Big Broadcast of 1937. 1937 When's Your Birthday?; There Goes my Girl; Saturday's Heroes; Angel's Holiday; One Hundred Men and a Girl; The Westland Case; You're a Sweetheart; Prescription for Romance. 1938 Love is a Headache; Goodbye Broadway; Reckless Living; The Lady in the Morgue; The Devil's Party; A Letter of Introduction; Youth Takes a Fling; The Storm; Strange Faces; The Last Warning. 1939 Society Smugglers; Big Town Czar; S.O.S. Tidal Wave; First Love; You Can't Cheat an Honest Man; The Under-Pup. 1940 Melody and Moonlight; Three Cheers for the Irish; A Little Bit of Heaven; His Girl Friday. 1941 Tall, Dark and Handsome; Dancing on a Dime; Scattergood Meets Broadway; Back Street; Flame of New Orleans. 1942 Maisie Gets Her Man; The Navy Comes Through; Manhattan Maisie; Syncopation; Two Yanks in Trinidad; Seven Miles from Alcatraz. 1943 Hi Ya, Sailor; Shantytown; Corregidor; Thousands Cheer; His Butler's Sister; Gildersleeve's Bad Day; So's Your Uncle. 1944 Take It or Leave It; Dixie Jamboree; This Is the Life; Shake Hands with Murder; Ladies Courageous; Rosie the Riveter; Follow the Boys; Two Girls and a Sailor; Three Little Sisters; The Falcon in Hollywood; The Impatient Years; Strange Affair; Rogue's Gallery; Roger Touhy-Gangster. 1945 The Kid Sister; The Missing Corpse; Zombies on Broadway; The Phantom of 42nd Street; Christmas in Connecticut; Bedside Manner; G. I. Honeymoon; Steppin' in Society. 1946 Blondie's Lucky Day; That Brennan Girl; White Tie and Tails; One Way to Love. 1947 Philo Vance's Gamble; That's My Girl; Kilroy Was Here; Philo Vance's Secret Mission. 1948 Blonde Savage; Family Honeymoon; Mary Lou; Winner Take All. 1949 Blondie's Reward; Shep Comes Home. 1950 Motor Patrol; Blondie's Hero; To Please a Lady; Woman on the Run; The Petty Girl; Mother Didn't Tell Me; Joe Palooka in the Squared Circle. 1951 Silver City Bonanza; The Scarf; Let's Go Navy; Bowery Battalion; Utah Wagon Train; Pecos River. 1952 Mr. Walkie-Talkie. 1953 White Lightning. 1954 Highway Dragnet. 1955 Artists and Models; Sudden Danger. 1956 The She-Creature; The Houston Story; Shake, Rattle and Rock. 1957 The Amazing Colossal Man.

JENKS, LULU BURNS
  Born: 1870. Died: Apr. 15, 1939, Los Angeles, Calif. Screen actress.

JENNINGS, AL
  Born: 1864, Va. Died: Dec. 26, 1961, Tarzana, Calif. Screen actor and author. Onetime real "badman" of the Old West—convicted train robber, cattle thief and gunman.

  Appeared in: 1918 The Lady of the Dugout. 1924 Fighting Fury; The Sea Hawk. 1926 The Demon; The Ridin' Rascal. 1927 Loco Luck. 1930 The Land of Missing Men.

JENNINGS, DE WITT
  Born: June 21, 1879, Cameron, Mo. Died: Mar. 1, 1937, Hollywood, Calif. Screen and stage actor. Entered films in 1920.

  Appeared in: 1921 Lady Fingers; The Invisible Power; Alias Lady Fingers; Beating the Game; There Are No Villains; Three Sevens; The Poverty of Riches; The Greater Claim; The Golden Snare; From the Ground Up. 1922 The Face Between; Mixed Faces; Flesh and Blood; Sherlock Brown; The Right That Failed. 1923 Circus Days; Out of Luck; Within the Law; Blinky. 1924 Name the Man; Hit and Run; Along Came Ruth; By Divine Right; The Silent Watcher; The Heart Bandit; The Deadwood Coach; The Desert Outlaw; The Enemy Sex; The Gaiety Girl; Merton of the Movies. 1925 Go Straight; Don't; The Mystic; The Splendid Road; The Re-Creation of Brian Kent. 1926 Chip of the Flying U; The Passionate Quest; The Ice Flood; Exit Smiling; While London Sleeps; The Fire Brigade. 1927 McFadden's Flats; The Great Mail Robbery; Home Made; Two Arabian Knights. 1928 The Night Flyer; Marry the Girl; The Air Mail Pilot; The Crash. 1929 Through Different Eyes; Fox Movietown Follies of 1929; Seven Keys to Baldpate; Alibi; The Trial of Mary Dugan; The Valiant; Seven Footprints to Satan; Red Hot Speed. 1930 The New Racket (short); The Big House; Scarlet Pages; Outside the Law; The Bat Whispers; Min and Bill; In the Next Room; Captain of the Guard; Those Who Dance; Night Ride; The Big Trail. 1931 The Criminal Code; Primrose Path; Secret Six; The Squaw Man; Full of Notions; Salvation Nell; Caught Plastered; A Dangerous Affair; The Deceiver; Arrowsmith. 1932 Dancers in the Dark; Midnight Morals; Movie Crazy; Tess of the Storm Country; Central Park; The Match King; Silver Dollar. 1933 Mystery of the Wax Museum; Strictly Personal; Ladies They Talk About; A Lady's Profession; Reform Girl; One Year Later; Police Car 17. 1934 Death on the Diamond; The Fighting Rookie; A Man's Game; Take the Stand; A Wicked Woman; The President Vanishes; Massacre; Little Man, What Now? 1935 Secret of the Chateau; The Daring Young Man; A Dog of Flanders; Murder on a Honeymoon; The Village Tale; Mary Jane's Pa; Mutiny on the Bounty. 1936 Sins of Man; The Crime of Dr. Forbes; Kelly the Second; We Who Are about to Die; The Accusing Finger. 1937 That I May Live; Nancy Steele is Missing; This is My Affair; Slave Ship; Fifty Roads to Town.

JEROME, EDWIN
  Born: 1884. Died: Sept. 10, 1959, Pasadena, Calif.(following surgery). Screen, stage, radio, and television actor.

  Appeared in: 1930 Grounds for Murder (short). 1945 The House on Ninety-Second Street. 1957 The Three Faces of Eve; The Tattered Dress. 1959 The Man Who Understood Women.

JEROME, PETER
  Born: 1893. Died: July 9, 1967, Tucson, Ariz. Screen, stage, television actor, playwright, and novelist.

JERROLD, MARY (Mary Allen)
  Born: Dec. 4, 1877. Died: Mar. 3, 1955, London, England. Screen, stage, and television actress. Entered films in 1931.

  Appeared in: 1931 The "W" Plan; Alibi. 1932 The Last Coupon; The Blind Spot; Perfect Understanding. 1934 Friday the 13th; The Lash; The Great Defender. 1935 Doctor's Orders; Price of Wisdom; Fighting Stock; Jack of All Trades; Transatlantic Tunnel. 1941 The Man at the Gate. 1944 The Way Ahead. 1947 The Magic Bow. 1948 The Queen of Spades. 1949 Mr. Perrin and Mr. Traill; Woman Hater. 1950 Bond Street. 1951 She Shall Have Murder. 1952 Top of the Form; Marry Me. 1953 Tonight at 8:30 (aka Ways and Means).

JESKE, GEORGE
  Born: 1891. Died: Oct. 28, 1951, Hollywood, Calif. Screen actor and film director. One of the original seven Keystone Kops.

  Appeared in: 1927 Heart of the Yukon.

JESSEL, PATRICIA
  Born: 1920, Hong Kong, British Crown Colony. Died: June 10, 1968, London, England.(heart attack). Screen, stage, and television actress.

  Appeared in: 1951 Quo Vadis. 1958 The Flesh Is Weak. 1959 The Man Upstairs. 1960 Model for Murder. 1961 City of the Dead. 1964 They All Died Laughing (aka A Jolly Bad Fellow). 1966 A Funny Thing Happened on the Way to the Forum.

JETT, SHELDON
Born: 1901. Died: Feb. 1, 1960, New York. Screen and television actor.

Appeared in: 1942 The Pride of the Yankees. 1944 Hollywood Canteen. 1945 Yolanda and the Thief. 1947 Body and Soul. 1951 The Lady and the Bandit. 1953 The Robe. 1961 King of Kings.

JIMINEZ, SOLEDAD
Born: Feb. 28, 1874, Santander, Spain. Died: Oct. 17, 1966, Hollywood, Calif.(stroke). Screen actress.

Appeared in: 1929 In Old Arizona; The Cock-Eyed World; Romance of the Rio Grande. 1930 The Texan; Billy the Kid; A Devil with Women; The Arizona Kid. 1931 Captain Thunder. 1932 Broken Wing. Spanish versions of films prior to 1933: Resurrection; Cat and the Canary; Ten Cents a Dance. 1935 Bordertown; Rumba; The Cyclone Ranger; Under the Pampas Moon; In Caliente. 1936 Robin Hood of El Dorado; The Traitor. 1937 Man of the People; Kid Galahad. 1938 Forbidden Valley; California Frontier. 1939 Return of the Cisco Kid; The Kid from Rio. 1945 South of the Rio Grande. 1946 Bad Men of the Border. 1947 Carnival in Costa Rica. 1948 Black Bart. 1949 Red Light.

JOBY, HANS
Born: 1884. Died: Apr. 30, 1943, Los Angeles, Calif. Screen, stage, and opera actor.

Appeared in: 1929 The Prince of Hearts. 1930 Hell's Angels. 1931 Suicide Fleet. 1936 Sons O' Guns. 1937 I Met Him in Paris. 1939 Thunder Afloat; Beasts of Berlin.

JOHANNSEN, CARY
Born: 1939. Died: Aug. 28, 1966, San Quentin Prison, Calif. (suicide). Screen, stage actor, and writer. Appeared in a documentary film dealing with the Farm Labor Program for the Department of Corrections while in prison.

JOHNSON, A. EMORY
Born: 1894. Died: Apr. 18, 1960, San Mateo, Calif.(burns from fire). Screen actor, screen director, producer, and screenwriter.

Appeared in: 1917 The Gray Ghost (serial); A Kentucky Cinderella. 1920 Prisoners of Love. 1921 The Sea Lion. 1922 Don't Doubt Your Wife; In the Name of the Law; Always the Woman.

JOHNSON, CHIC (Harold Ogden Johnson)
Born: Mar. 5, 1891 or 1895, Chicago, Ill. Died: Feb. 1962, Las Vegas, Nev.(kidney ailment). Screen, stage, vaudeville, and television actor. Was partner in comedy team of "Olsen & Johnson." For films they appeared in, see Ole Olsen.

JOHNSON, EDITH
Died: Sept. 6, 1969, Los Angeles, Calif.(injuries from fall). Screen actress. Married to screen actor William Duncan (dec. 1961). She appeared with him in silent serials.

Appeared in: 1918 A Fight for Millions (serial). 1919 Man of Might (serial); Smashing Barriers (serial). 1920 The Silent Avenger (serial). 1921 No Defense; Where Men Are Men; Steelheart; Fighting Fate (serial). 1922 The Fighting Guide; When Danger Smiles; The Silent Vow. 1923 The Steel Trail (serial); Smashing Barriers (re-release of 1919 serial as a feature film); Playing It Wild. 1924 The Fast Express (serial); Wolves of the North (serial).

JOHNSON, EDWARD
Born: 1862. Died: Feb. 7, 1925, San Jose, Calif. Screen actor.

Appeared in: 1919 The Egg Crate Wallop. 1923 The Hunchback of Notre Dame.

JOHNSON, JAY
Born: 1928. Died: June 13, 1954, San Fernando Valley, Calif. (motorcycle accident). Screen actor and vocalist with Stan Kenton orchestra.

Appeared in: 1955 A Star Is Born.

JOHNSON, KATIE (Katherine Johnson)
Born: 1878, England. Died: May 4, 1957, Elham, England. Screen and stage actress. Voted the best British actress in 1955 for her performance in The Lady Killers.

Appeared in: 1936 Dusty Ermine; Laburnum Grove; Hail and Farewell; On a Dark Stairway; Farewell Again; Sunset in Vienna; The Rat; The Last Adventurers. 1941 The Voice in the Night; Hellzapoppin. 1943 Jeannie. 1947 The Years Between. 1948 Meet Me

at Dawn. 1950 Sideshow. 1952 The Old West. 1953 I Believe in You. 1955 The Lady Killers. 1956 How to Murder a Rich Uncle (U.S. 1957). 1960 Studs Lonigan.

JOHNSON, LORIMER GEORGE
Born: 1859. Died: Feb. 20, 1941, Hollywood, Calif. Screen, stage actor, and film director.

Appeared in: 1922 The Stranger's Banquet. 1923 Scaramouche; The Cricket on the Hearth; Ruth of the Range (serial). 1924 A Fool's Awakening; The Shadow of the East; Dante's Inferno. 1925 Enticement; The Top of the World; Never Too Late. 1926 Modern Youth. 1928 Midnight Rose; Tarzan, The Mighty (serial). 1930 Madam Satan; Ex-Flame.

JOHNSON, RITA
Born: Aug. 13, 1913, Worcester, Mass. Died: Oct. 31, 1965, Los Angeles, Calif.(brain hemorrhage). Screen actress.

Appeared in: 1931 The Spy. 1937 London by Night; My Dear Miss Aldrich. 1938 Man Proof; A Letter of Introduction; Rich Man, Poor Girl; Smashing the Rackets. 1939 Stronger Than Desire; Honolulu; Within the Law; 6,000 Enemies; They All Come Out; Nick Carter, Master Detective; The Girl Downstairs; Broadway Serenade. 1940 Congo Maisie; The Golden Fleecing; Forty Little Mothers; Edison the Man. 1941 Here Comes Mr. Jordan; Appointment for Love. 1942 The Major and the Minor. 1943 My Friend Flicka. 1944 Thunderhead, Son of Flicka. 1945 The Affairs of Susan; The Naughty Nineties. 1946 The Perfect Marriage; Pardon My Past. 1947 They Won't Believe Me; The Michigan Kid. 1948 Sleep My Love; The Big Clock; The Innocent Affair; Family Honeymoon. 1950 The Second Face. 1954 Susan Slept Here. 1956 Emergency Hospital. 1957 The Day They Gave Babies Away; All Mine to Give.

JOHNSON, WILLIAM
Born: 1916. Died: Mar. 6, 1957, Flemington, N.J.(heart attack). Screen, stage, television actor, and singer.

Appeared in: 1945 Keep Your Powder Dry; It's a Pleasure.

JOHNSTON, JOHN W.
Born: 1876, Ireland. Died: Aug. 1, 1946, Hollywood, Calif. Screen and stage actor.

Appeared in: 1914 The Virginian; Where the Trail Divides. 1915 Runaway June (serial). 1921 The Kentuckians; Mother Eternal. 1922 The Ruling Passion; The Valley of Silent Men; Channing of the Northwest; Partners of the Sunset. 1923 Backbone; Unseeing Eyes. 1925 The Greatest Love of All; Winds of Chance. 1926 Desert Valley; The New Klondike. 1927 Flying Luck; The Black Diamond Express. 1928 Driftwood; Take Me Home; The Sawdust Paradise.

JOHNSTON, JOHNNY
Born: 1869. Died: Jan. 4, 1931, Hollywood, Calif.(heart disease). Screen and vaudeville actor. Was half of vaudeville team of "Hardy and Johnston."

JOHNSTON, OLIVER
Born: 1888. Died: Dec. 22, 1966, London, England. Screen, stage, and television actor.

Appeared in: 1955 Room in the House. 1957 The Hypnotist; A King in New York. 1958 Indiscreet. 1959 Web of Evidence. 1960 Kidnapped; A Touch of Larceny. 1961 Make Mine a Double (aka The Night We Dropped a Clanger); Francis of Assisi. 1962 Island of Love (aka Not on Your Life); Waltz of the Toreadors. 1963 Doctor Crippen; The Fast Lady; The Three Lives of Thomasina; Cleopatra. 1965 You Must Be Joking; Tomb of Ligeia. 1967 Countess from Hong Kong. Other British film: The Curse of the Golem.

JOLSON, AL (Asa Yoelson)
Born: May 26, 1886, St. Petersburg, Russia. Died: Oct. 23, 1950, San Francisco, Calif.(heart attack). Screen, stage, vaudeville, radio actor, and singer. Married to screen actress Erle Galbraith. Divorced from Henrietta Keller and screen actresses Ruby Keeler, Alma Osborne (aka Ethel Delmar).

Appeared in: 1926 Vitaphone short. 1927 The Jazz Singer. 1928 The Singing Fool. 1929 Say It with Songs; New York Nights; Sonny Boy; Lucky Boy. 1930 Mammy; Big Boy. 1933 Hallelujah, I'm a Bum; Wonder Bar. 1935 Go into Your Dance. 1936 The Singing Kid; Sons O' Guns; The New Yorker. 1938 Alexander's Ragtime Band. 1939 Rose of Washington Square; Swanee River; Hollywood Cavalcade. 1945 Rhapsody in Blue; Burlesque. 1946 The Jolson Story (voice). 1949 Jolson Sings Again (voice).

JONES, BUCK (Charles Frederick Gebhart)
Born: Dec. 4, 1889, Vincennes, Ind. Died: Nov. 30, 1942, Boston, Mass.(burned in fire). Screen actor, film director, and circus performer.

Appeared in: 1917 Blood Will Tell. 1918 Riders of the Purple Sage. 1920 The Last Straw. 1921 Big Punch; Get Your Man; Just Pals; One Man Trail; Sunset Sprague; Two Moons; Straight from the Shoulder; To a Finish; Riding with Death. 1922 Western Speed; The Fast Mail; Trooper O'Neil; Riding Speed; Rough Shod; Chain Lightning; Pardon My Nerve; Bar Nothin'; West of Chicago; The Boss of Camp 4, Bells of San Juan. 1923 Footlight Ranger; The Eleventh Hour; Hell's Hole; Second Hand Love; Skid Proof; Snowdrift; Big Dan; Cupid's Fireman. 1924 Western Luck; Against All Odds; The Vagabond Trail; Not a Drum Was Heard; The Circus Cowboy; The Desert Outlaw; Winner Take All. 1925 Arizona Romeo; Gold and the Girl; The Trail Rider; Hearts and Spurs; The Man Who Played Square; The Timber Wolf; Lazybones; Durand of the Bad Lands; The Desert's Price; Good as Gold. 1926 The Fighting Buckaroo; 30 Below Zero; The Cowboy and the Countess; The Gentle Cyclone; A Man Four Square. 1927 The Flying Horseman; War Horse; Hills of Peril; Whispering Sage. 1928 The Branded Sombrero; The Big Hop; Blood Will Tell (and 1917 version). 1930 Stranger from Arizona; The Lone Rider; Shadow Ranch; Men without Law. 1931 Border Law; Branded; Range Feud; Ridin' for Justice; Desert Vengeance; The Avenger; The Texas Ranger; Fugitive Sheriff; South of the Rio Grande; Sundown Trail. 1932 Deadline; Born to Trouble; High Speed; One Man Law; Hello Trouble; McKenna of the Mounted; White Eagle; Riders of Death Valley; Reckless Romance. 1933 California Trail; Unknown Valley; Treason; The Forbidden Trail; Thrill Hunter; Gordon of Ghost City (serial); The Sundown Rider; Child of Manhattan; Fighting Sheriff. 1934 Dawn Trail; The Fighting Code; The Fighting Rangers; The Man Trailer; Rocky Rhodes; When a Man Sees Red; The Red Rider (serial); Texas Ranger. 1935 The Crimson Trail; Stone of Silver Creek; The Roaring West (serial); Border Brigands; Outlawed Guns; The Throwback; The Ivory-Handled Gun; Square Shooter. 1936 The Boss of Gun Creek; The Phantom Rider (serial); Sunset of Power; Silver Spurs; For the Service; The Cowboy and the Kid; Empty Saddles; Ride 'em, Cowboy! 1937 Sandflow; Law for Tombstone; The Left-Handed Law; Smoke Tree Range; Black Aces; Hollywood Round-Up; Headin' East; Boss of Lonely Valley; Pony Express. 1938 The Overland Express; Sudden Bill Dorn; California Frontier; Law of the Texan; Stranger from Arizona. 1939 Unmarried. 1940 Wagons Westward. 1941 Riders of Death Valley (serial); White Eagle (serial); Arizona Bound; The Gunman from Bodie; Forbidden Trails. 1942 Ghost Town Law; Down Texas Way; Riders of the West; West of the Law; Below the Border; Down on the Great Divide.

JONES, CHARLES. See Buck Jones

JONES, CURTIS ASHY "CURT"
Born: 1873. Died: Dec. 1956, Winchester, Ill. Screen, vaudeville actor, and stuntman.

JONES, ELIZABETH "TINY"
Died: Mar. 22, 1952, Hollywood, Calif. Screen actress. Entered films during silents.

Appeared in: 1930 The Man from Blankley's. 1939 Drums along the Mohawk.

JONES, FUZZY Q. See Al "Fuzzy" St. John

JONES, GORDON
Born: Apr. 5, 1911, Alden, Iowa. Died: June 20, 1963, Tarzana, Calif.(heart attack). Screen and television actor.

Appeared in: 1930 Beau Bandit. 1935 Let 'Em Have It; Red Salute. 1936 Strike Me Pink; The Devil's Squadron; Walking on Air; Don't Turn 'Em Loose; We Who Are about to Die; Night Waitress. 1937 They Wanted to Marry; Sea Devils; China Passage; There Goes My Girl; The Big Shot; Fight for Your Lady. 1938 Quick Money; Long Shot; Night Spot; Rich Man, Poor Girl; I Stand Accused; Out West with the Hardys. 1939 Disputed Passage; Pride of the Navy; Big Town Czar. 1940 The Green Hornet (serial); I Take This Oath; The Doctor Takes a Wife; Girl from Havana. 1941 Up in the Air; Among the Living; The Blonde from Singapore; You Belong to Me; The Feminine Touch. 1942 To the Shores of Tripoli; True to the Army; They All Kissed the Bride; My Sister Eileen; Flying Tigers; Highways by Night. 1947 The Secret Life of Walter Mitty; The Wistful Widow of Wagon Gap. 1948 A Foreign Affair; The Untamed Breed; The Black Eagle; Sons of Adventure. 1949 Easy Living; Dear Wife; Mr. Soft Touch; Black Midnight; Tokyo Joe. 1950 Belle of Old Mexico; Sunset in

the West; Trigger, Jr.; Bodyhold; The Palomino; North of the Great Divide; Arizona Cowboy. 1951 Spoilers of the Plains; Corky of Gasoline Alley; Heart of the Rockies; Yellow Fin. 1952 Sound Off; The Winning Team; Wagon Team; Gobs and Gals. 1953 Island in the Sky; The Woman They almost Lynched. 1954 The Outlaw Stallion. 1955 Treasure of Ruby Hills; Smoke Signals. 1957 The Monster That Challenged the World; Spring Reunion; Shoot-Out at Medicine Bend. 1958 Live Fast, Die Young; The Perfect Furlough. 1959 Battle of the Coral Sea; Battle Flame. 1960 The Rise and Fall of Legs Diamond. 1961 Everything's Ducky. 1963 McLintock!

JONES, JOHNNY (Charles Edward Peil, Jr.)
Born: 1908. Died: Nov. 7, 1962, San Andreas, Calif. Screen actor. Appeared as a child actor during silents as Johnny Jones and later as Edward Peil, Jr. See Edward Peil, Jr for later films.

Appeared in: 1920 Edgar and the Teacher's Pet; Edgar's Little Saw. 1921 The Old Nest. 1922 Night Life in Hollywood.

JONES, MORGAN
Born: 1879. Died: Sept. 21, 1951, New York, N.Y. Screen actor.

Appeared in: 1903 The Great Train Robbery. 1928 Mark of the Frog (serial).

JONES, NORMAN
Born: 1928. Died: Mar. 26, 1963, London, England. Screen and television actor.

JONES, PAUL MEREDITH
Born: 1897, Bristol, Tenn. Died: Dec. 30, 1966, North Hollywood, Calif.(heart attack). Screen actor, extra, film producer, and screenwriter.

Appeared in: 1916 Intolerance.

JONES, R. D.
Died: 1925.(drowned while shooting rapids in canoe for the film Ancient Highway). Screen actor and stuntman.

JONES, ROZENE K.
Born: 1890. Died: July 8, 1964, Hollywood, Calif.(heart attack). Screen and stage actor. Entered films approx. 1940.

JONES, SPIKE (Lindley Armstrong Jones).
Born: Dec. 14, 1911, Long Beach, Calif. Died: May 1, 1965, Beverly Hills, Calif.(emphysema). Screen, radio actor, and bandleader.

Appeared in: 1943 Thank Your Lucky Stars. 1944 Meet the People. 1945 Bring on the Girls. 1946 Breakfast in Hollywood. 1947 Variety Girl; Ladies' Man. 1954 Fireman Save My Child.

JONES, STANLEY "STAN D."
Born: 1914. Died: Dec. 13, 1963, Los Angeles, Calif. Screen, television actor, and song writer.

Appeared in: 1950 Rio Grande. 1952 The Last Musketeer. 1956 The Great Locomotive Chase; The Rainmaker. 1959 The Horse Soldiers. 1960 Ten Who Dared. 1964 Invitation to a Gunfighter.

JONES, T. C. (Thomas Craig Jones)
Born: 1921. Died: Sept. 25, 1971, Duarte, Calif.(cancer). Femme impersonator and screen, stage, television, and night club actor.

Appeared in: 1963 Promises, Promises. 1964 Three Nuts in Search of a Bolt. 1967 The President's Analyst. 1968 Head; The Name of the Game Is Kill!.

JONES, WALLACE
Born: 1883, London, England. Died: Oct. 7, 1936, Los Angeles, Calif. Screen actor.

Appeared in: 1925 Red Love.

JORDAN, MARIAN (Marian Driscoll)
Born: Apr. 15, 1897, Peoria, Ill. Died: Apr. 7, 1961, Encino, Calif. (cancer). Screen, stage, radio and vaudeville actress. Married to Jim Jordan and the two of them teamed as "Fibber McGee & Molly"—famous radio program.

They appeared in the following films: 1938 This Way, Please (their film debut). 1941 Look Who's Laughing. 1942 Here We Go Again. 1944 Heavenly Days.

JORDAN, ROBERT "BOBBY"
Born: 1923. Died: Sept. 10, 1965, Los Angeles, Calif.(liver ailment). Screen and stage actor.

Appeared in: 1933 a Universal short. 1937 Dead End (stage and film versions). 1938 A Slight Case of Murder; My Bill; Crime School; Angels with Dirty Faces; Reformatory. 1939 Dust Be My Destiny; On Dress Parade; They Made Me a Criminal; Off the Record; Hell's Kitchen; Angel's Wash Their Faces. 1940 Young Tom Edison; Boys of the City; That Gang of Mine; You're Not So Tough; Give Us Wings; Military Academy. 1941 Bride of the Bowery; Flying Wild; Bowery Blitzkrieg; Spooks Run Wild. 1942 Mr. Wise Guy; Let's Get Tough; Smart Alecks; 'Neath Brooklyn Bridges. 1943 Clancy Street Boys; Keep 'Em Slugging; Adventures of the Flying Cadets (serial); Kid Dynamite; Ghosts on the Loose. 1944 Bowery Champs. 1946 Bowery Bombshell; In Fast Company; Mr. Hex; Spook Busters; Live Wires. 1947 Hard-Boiled Mahoney; News Hounds; Bowery Buckaroos. 1949 Treasure of Monte Cristo. 1956 The Man Is Armed.

JORGE, PAUL
Born: 1849, France. Died: Jan. 1929, France. Screen actor.

Appeared in: 1926 Les Miserables. 1929 La Passion de Jeanne d'Arc.

JOUVET, LOUIS
Born: 1888, France. Died: Aug. 16, 1951, Paris, France.(heart attack). Screen, stage actor, and film and stage producer.

Appeared in: 1932 Topaze. 1933 Dr. Knock. 1936 Carnival in Flanders; La Kermesse Heroique. 1937 Un Carpet de Bal; The Lower Depths; Mademoiselle Docteur; Life Dances On; Ramuntcho. 1938 Hotel de Nord; La Fin du Jour; L'Alibi. 1939 Bizarre, Bizarre; The Curtain Rises; The End of a Day; Marseillaise. 1940 La Charrette Fantome; Schubert's Serenade. 1941 Compliments of Mr. Iflow. 1943 The Heart of a Nation. 1945 De Drame Shanghai (The Shanghai Drama); The Barge-Keeper's Daughter. 1946 Sirocco; Le Revenant (A Lover's Return). 1947 Quai des Orfeures; Volpone. 1948 Jenny Lamour; Return to Life; Confessions of a Rogue. Street of Shadows. 1949 Retour a la Vie. 1950 Between Eleven and Midnight; Dr. Knock (and 1933 version). 1951 Miquette; Lady Paname; Un Histoire d'Amour. 1953 Ramuntcho.

JOY, NICHOLAS
Born: 1884, Paris, France. Died: Mar. 16, 1964, Philadelphia, Pa. Screen, stage, and television actor.

Appeared in: 1947 Daisy Kenyon; Dishonored Lady; A Gentleman's Agreement; If Winter Comes. 1948 The Fuller Brush Man; Joan of Arc; Larceny; The Iron Curtain. 1949 The Great Gatsby; Bride of Vengeance; The Sun Comes Up; Abbott and Costello Meet the Killer, Boris Karloff; Song of Surrender. 1950 And Baby Makes Three. 1951 Native Son; Here Comes the Groom; The Man with a Cloak. 1953 Affair with a Stranger. 1957 Desk Set.

JOYCE, ALICE
Born: Oct. 1, 1890, Kansas City, Mo. Died: Oct. 9, 1955, Hollywood, Calif.(heart ailment). Screen actress. Entered films with Kalem in 1909. Divorced from screen actor Tom Moore (dec. 1955).

Appeared in: 1910 Engineer's Sweetheart. 1912 A Bell of Penance. 1913 Nina of the Theatre. 1914 The Brand; The Vampire's Trail; The School for Scandal; The Mystery of the Sleeping Death. 1915 Battle Cry of Peace. 1917 Womanhood; Within the Law; The Courage of Silence. 1918 A Woman between Friends; Cap'n Abe's Niece; Captains' Captain. 1919 The Cambric Mask; The Third Degree; The Lion and the Mouse. 1920 The Sporting Duchess. 1921 Vice of Fools; The Scarab Ring; Cousin Kate; Her Lord and Master; The Inner Chamber. 1923 The Green Goddess. 1924 Passionate Adventurer; White Man. 1925 Stella Dallas; The Little French Girl; Headlines; Daddy's Gone A-Hunting; The Home Maker. 1926 Beau Geste; So's Your Old Man; Dancing Mothers; The Ace of Cads; Mannequin. 1927 Sorrell and Son. 1928 13 Washington Square; The Noose. 1929 The Squall. 1930 The Green Goddess (and 1923 version); Song O'My Heart; He Knew Women; The Midnight Mystery. 1931/32 Paramount Screen Songs (shorts).

JOYCE, MARTIN
Born: 1915. Died: Jan. 2, 1937, Los Angeles, Calif.(injuries received in auto accident). Screen actor.

JOYCE, PEGGY HOPKINS (Margaret Upton)
Born: 1893, Norfolk, Va. Died: June 12, 1957, New York, N.Y. Screen and stage actress.

Appeared in: 1926 Skyrocket. 1933 International House.

JUANO. See Juan G. Hernandez

JULIAN, ALEXANDER
Born: 1893. Died: May 18, 1945, Hollywood, Calif. Screen actor.

JULIAN, RUPERT
Born: Jan. 25, 1889, Auckland, New Zealand. Died: Dec. 27, 1943, Hollywood, Calif.(stroke). Screen, stage actor, film director, and screenwriter.

Appeared in: 1914 The Merchant of Venice. 1915 The Dumb Girl of Portici. 1916 The Bugler of Algiers. 1917 A Kentucky Cinderella. 1918 Kaiser, The Beast of Berlin.

JUNE, MILDRED
Born: 1906. Died: June 19, 1940, Hollywood, Calif. Screen actress. Entered films in 1920.

Appeared in: 1922 Ma and Pa; The Crossroads of New York; The Rosary; Rich Men's Wives. 1923 Crinoline and Romance; Fashionable Fakers; The Greatest Menace. 1924 Troubles of a Bride; Hook and Ladder. 1927 The Snarl of Hate; When Seconds Count.

JUUL, RALPH
Born: 1888. Died: Nov. 5, 1955, Chicago, Ill. Screen, stage, and radio actor.

KAART, HANS
Born: 1924. Died: June 1963, Amsterdam, Holland (following ear surgery). Screen actor and operatic singer. Appeared in German and Dutch films.

KAHANAMOKU, DUKE P.
Born: Aug. 24, 1890, Honolulu, Hawaii. Died: Jan. 22, 1968, Honolulu, Hawaii (heart attack). Screen actor and Olympic swimming champion.

Appeared in: 1925 Adventure; Lord Jim. 1926 Old Ironsides. 1927 Isle of Sunken Gold. 1928 Woman Wise. 1929 The Rescue. 1930 Girl of the Port; Isle of Escape. 1948 Wake of the Red Witch. 1955 Mr. Roberts.

KAHN, RICHARD C.
Born: 1897. Died: Jan. 28, 1960, Hollywood, Calif.(heart attack). Screen actor, film director, and film producer. Entered films as an actor in silents.

KAHN, WILLIAM "SMITTY"
Born: 1882. Died: May 14, 1959, Hollywood, Calif. Screen and television actor.

Appeared in: 1951 Girl on the Bridge. 1956 Edge of Hell.

KALICH, BERTHA
Born: 1875, Lemberg, Poland. Died: Apr. 18, 1939, New York, N.Y. Screen and stage actress.

Appeared in: 1914 Marta of the Lowlands. 1916 Slander; Ambition.

KALIONZES, JANET (Janet Manson)
Born: 1922. Died: Aug. 10, 1961, New York, N.Y. Screen and television actress.

Appeared in: 1948 A Double Life.

KALIZ, ARMAND
Born: Oct. 23, 1892, Paris, France. Died: Feb. 1, 1941, Beverly Hills, Calif.(heart attack). Screen, stage, vaudeville actor, and screenwriter.

Appeared in: 1919 A Temperamental Wife. 1926 The Temptress; Yellow Fingers; The Belle of Broadway; The Better Way. 1927 The Stolen Bride; Fast and Furious; Say It with Diamonds; Temptations of a Shop Girl; Wandering Girls. 1928 The Love Mart; The Devil's Cage; Lingerie; That's My Daddy; The Wife's Relations; A Woman's Way. 1929 The Marriage Playground; Twin Beds; The Aviator; Gold Diggers of Broadway; Noah's Ark. 1930 L'Enigmatique Monsieur Parkes (The Mysterious Mr. Parkes); Little Caesar; The Eternal Triangle (short). 1931 Honeymoon Lane. 1932 Three Wise Girls. 1933 Secret Sinners; Design for Living; Flying Down to Rio. 1934 Caravan; George White's Scandals. 1935 Diamond Jim; Here's to Romance. 1936 Desire. 1937 Cafe Metropole; The King and the Chorus Girl. 1938 Algiers; A Trip to Paris; Josette; I'll Give a Million; Gold Diggers in Paris; Vacation from Love. 1939 Off the Record; Topper Takes a Trip; Midnight. 1940 Down Arentine Way. 1941 Skylark.

KALKHURST, ERIC
Born: 1902. Died: Oct. 13, 1957, Washington, D.C. Screen and stage actor. Entered films in 1922.

Appeared in: 1930 The Virtuous Sin. 1931 Unfaithful.

KALSER, ERWIN
Born: 1883, Germany. Died: Mar. 26, 1958, Berlin, Germany. Screen and stage actor.

Appeared in: 1930 Rasputin: The Holy Devil. 1931 The Last Company; Thirteen Men and a Girl. 1933 Hertha's Erwachen. 1941 Submarine Zone (aka Escape to Glory); Kings Row; Dressed to Kill. 1942 Berlin Correspondent. 1943 Watch on the Rhine; Underground. 1944 Address Unknown; Strange Affair; U-Boat Prisoner. 1945 Hotel Berlin. 1952 The Girl in White. 1953 Stalag 17.

KAMENZKY, ELIEZER
Born: 1889, Russia. Died: 1957, Lisbon, Portugal. Screen and stage actor.

KAMIYAMA, SOJIN
Born: 1884, Japan. Died: July 28, 1954, Tokyo, Japan. Screen actor. Appeared in U.S. films from approx. 1929 to 1931 and then appeared in Japanese films.

Appeared in: 1924 The Thief of Bagdad. 1925 East of Suez. 1926 The Bat. 1928 Chinese Parrot.

KAMMER, KLAUS
Born: 1929, Hannover, Germany. Died: May 9, 1964, Berlin, Germany (suicide—carbon monoxide). Screen, stage, and television actor.

Appeared in: 1959 Kriegsgericht (Court Martial).

KANE, BLANCHE
Born: 1889. Died: Aug. 24, 1937, Hollywood, Calif. Screen and stage actress.

KANE, EDDIE
Born: 1888. Died: Apr. 30, 1969, Hollywood, Calif.(heart attack). Screen and television actor.

Appeared in: 1928 Lights of New York. 1929 Why Bring That Up?; The Broadway Melody; Street Girl; Times Square; Illusion. 1930 The Cohens and the Kellys in Africa; The Doorway to Hell; The Squealer; Puttin' on the Ritz; Framed; The Kibitzer. 1931 My Past; Stolen Jools (short); Dirigible; Public Enemy; Smart Money; Goldie; Son of Rajah; Ex Bad Boy; Bought; Susan Lennox, Her Rise and Fall; Forbidden; Peach O'Reno; Forgotten Women. 1932 Stepping Sisters; Once in a Lifetime; Love Is a Racket; The Slippery Pearls (short). 1933 Dangerous Crossroads; Thrill Hunter; The Mummy. 1935 Million Dollar Baby; Hooray for Love. 1936 an RKO short. 1937 Melody for Two; All over Town; Manhattan Merry-Go-Round; Hollywood Round-up; Mr. Boggs Steps Out; Small Town Boy; Pick a Star. 1938 Swiss Miss; The Gladiator; You Can't Take It with You; Give Me a Sailor; an RKO short. 1939 Some Like It Hot; Missing Daughters. 1940 Music in My Heart. 1943 Mission to Moscow. 1944 Jam Session; Two Girls and a Sailor; Up in Arms; Minstrel Man; The Hairy Ape; Dark Mountains. 1945 Man from Oklahoma. 1948 Mexican Hayride. 1949 Jiggs and Maggie in Jackpot Jitters.

KANE, GAIL (Abigail Kane)
Born: 1885. Died: Feb. 17, 1966, Augusta, Maine. Screen and stage actress.

Appeared in: 1916 Paying the Price. 1917 Souls in Pawn. 1921 A Good Woman; Idle Hands; Wise Husbands. 1923 The White Sisters. 1927 Convoy.

KANE, HELEN "BABE"
Born: Aug. 4, 1908, New York, N.Y. Died: Sept. 26, 1966, Jackson Heights, N.Y.(chest cancer). Screen, stage, vaudeville, and television actress.

Appeared in: 1929 Nothing but the Truth; Sweetie; Pointed Hills. 1930 Dangerous Nan McGrew; Paramount on Parade; Heads Up. 1932 The Dentist (short); The Spot on the Rug (short). 1933 The Pharmacist (short). 1934 Counsel on the Fence.

KANE, JOHN J. "JOHNNY"
Died: Mar. 15, 1969, N.Y. Screen, stage, radio, and television actor.

Appeared in: 1951 Man with My Face. 1959 The FBI Story. 1964 Fail Safe.

KANE, LIDA
Died: Oct. 7, 1955, New York, N.Y. Screen, stage, radio, and television actress.

Appeared in: 1930 Follow the Leader. 1931 Secrets of a Secretary.

KANE, WHITFORD
Born: 1881, Ireland. Died: Dec. 17, 1956, New York, N.Y. Screen and stage actor.

Appeared in: 1934 Hideout. 1944 The Adventures of Mark Twain. 1947 The Ghost and Mrs. Muir. 1948 The Walls of Jericho. 1949 The Judge Steps Out.

KARLIN, BO-PEEP
Died: Feb. 25, 1969, Hollywood, Calif. Screen and television actress. Married to screen actor Gaston Glass (dec. 1965).

Appeared in: 1929 Happy Days. 1930 Just Imagine. 1963 Bye Bye Birdie.

KARLOFF, BORIS (William Henry Pratt)
Born: Nov. 23, 1887, London, England. Died: Feb. 2, 1969, London, England.(respiratory ailment). Screen, stage, radio, and television actor.

Appeared in: 1919 His Majesty the American; Prince and Betty. 1920 The Deadlier Sex; The Courage of Marge O'Doone; The Last of the Mohicans. 1921 Without Benefit of Clergy; The Hope Diamond Mystery; Cheated Hearts; The Cave Girl. 1922 The Man from Downing Street; The Infidel; The Altar Stairs; Omar the Tentmaker. 1923 Woman Conquers; The Prisoner. 1924 Dynamite Dan. 1925 Parisian Nights; Forbidden Cargo; The Prairie Wife; Lady Robinhood; Never the Twain Shall Meet. 1926 The Bells; The Greater Glory; Her Honor, the Governor; The Nicklehopper; Eagle of the Sea; Old Ironsides; Flames; The Golden Web; Flaming Fury; Man in the Saddle. 1927 The Meddlin' Stranger; The Phantom Buster; Tarzan and the Golden Lion; Soft Cushions; Two Arabian Knights; Let It Rain; The Princess from Hoboken. 1928 The Love Mart; Vultures of the Sea (serial). 1929 The Fatal Warning (serial); Little Wild Girl; The Phantom of the North; Two Sisters; Devil's Chaplain; King of the Kongo (serial); The Unholy Night; Behind That Curtain; Burning the Wind. 1930 The Sea Bat; The Bad One; The Utah Kid; Mother's Cry; The Scar on the Nation; Assorted Nuts (short). 1931 King of the Wild (serial); The Criminal Code; Cracked Nuts (short); Smart Money; The Public Defender; I Like Your Nerve; Five Star Final; The Mad Genius; Frankenstein; Young Donovan's Kid; The Guilty Generation; The Yellow Ticket; Graft; Tonight or Never. 1932 Business and Pleasure; Behind the Mask; The Cohens and the Kellys in Hollywood; The Mummy; Night World; The Old Dark House; The Mask of Fu Manchu; Alias the Doctor; The Miracle Man; Scarface. 1933 The Man Who Dared; The Ghoul. 1934 The House of Rothschild; The Lost Patrol; The Black Cat; Gift of Gab. 1935 The Raven; The Black Room; Mysterious Mr. Wong; The Bride of Frankenstein. 1936 The Walking Dead; The Invisible Ray; Charlie Chan at the Opera; The Man Who Changed His Mind (U.S.—The Man Who Lived Again). 1937 Juggernaut; Night Key; Without Warning; West of Shanghai; War Lord. 1938 Mr. Wong, Detective; The Invisible Menace. 1939 The Man They Could Not Hang; Mr. Wong in Chinatown; Son of Frankenstein; Tower of London; The Mystery of Mr. Wong. 1940 British Intelligence; The Man with Nine Lives; Devil's Island; Doomed to Die; The Ape; You'll Find Out; Before I Hang; The Fatal Hour; Black Friday. 1941 Behind the Door; The Devil Commands. 1942 The Boogie Man Will Get You. 1944 The Climax; House of Dracula; House of Frankenstein; Isle of the Dead; The Body Snatchers. 1946 Bedlam. 1947 The Secret Life of Walter Mitty; Lured; Dick Tracy Meets Gruesome; Unconquered. 1948 Tap Roots. 1949 Abbott and Costello Meet the Killer, Boris Karloff. 1951 The Strange Door; Emperor's Nightingale (narr.). 1952 The Black Castle. 1953 Abbott and Costello Meet Dr. Jekyll and Mr. Hyde; The Monster of the Island; The Hindu (aka Sabaka—U.S. 1955). 1957 Voodoo Island; The Juggler of Our Lady. 1958 The Haunted Strangler; Frankenstein—1970. 1961 Days of Thrills and Laughter (documentary). 1963 The Raven (and 1935 version); The Terror; Corridors of Blood. 1964 A Comedy of Terrors; Black Sabbath; Bikini Beach; Today's Teen (short-narr.); Scarlet Friday. 1965 Die, Monster, Die! 1966 The Daydreamer (narr.); Ghost in the Invisible Bikini; The Venetian Affair; Monster of Terror; The House at the End of the World. 1965 The Corpse Collector; Mad Monster Party; Mondo Balordo (narr.); The Sorcerers. 1968 The Curse of the Crimson Altar; Targets.

KARLSTADT, LIESL
Born: 1893, Germany. Died: Aug. 1, 1960, Garmisch-Partenkirchen, Germany (stroke). Screen, stage actress, singer, and dancer.

Appeared in: 1934 Mit dir Durch Dick und Duenn. 1937 Kirschen in Nachbars Garten. 1958 Wir Wunderkinder (We Amazing Children, aka Aren't We Wonderful-U.S. 1959). Other German film: Feuerwerk.

KARNS, ROSCOE
Born: Sept. 7, 1893, San Bernardino, Calif. Died: Feb. 6, 1970, Los Angeles, Calif. Screen, stage, and television actor.

Appeared in: 1921 The Man Turner; Too Much Married. 1922 Afraid to Fight; Conquering the Woman; Her Own Money; The Trouper. 1923 Other Man's Daughters. 1924 Bluff; The Foolish Virgin; The Midnight Express. 1925 Headlines; The Overland Limited; Dollar Down. 1927 The Jazz Singer; Ritzy; Ten Modern Commandments. 1928 Win That Girl; Warming Up; The Desert Bride; Object—Alimony; Moran of the Marines; Beggars of Life; Something Always Happens; Jazz Mad; Beau Sabreau. 1929 This Thing Called Love; New York Nights. 1930 Safety in Numbers; Troopers Three; New York Lights; Man Trouble; The Costello Case; Little Accident. 1931 The Gorilla; Dirigible; Laughing Sinners; Leftover Ladies; Many a Slip. 1932 Ladies of the Big House; Lawyer Man; Night after Night; Roadhouse Murder; Week-End Marriage; Two against the World; The Crooked Circle; I Am a Fugitive from a Chain Gang; One Way Passage; If I Had a Million; Under Cover Man; The Stowaway; Pleasure; Rockabye. 1933 Gambling Ship; One Sunday Afternoon; Alice in Wonderland; Today We Live; A Lady's Profession; 20,000 Years in Sing Sing. 1934 Twentieth Century; Search for Beauty; The Women in His Life; Shoot the Works; Come on Marines; Elmer and Elsie; It Happened One Night; I Sell Anything. 1935 Red Hot Tires; Stolen Harmony: Four Hours to Kill; Wings in the Dark; Two-Fisted; Alibi Ike; Front Page Woman. 1936 Woman Trap; Border Flight; Three Cheers for Love; Three Married Men; Cain and Mabel. 1937 Murder Goes to College; A Night of Mystery; On Such a Night; Clarence; Partners in Crime. 1938 Scandal Sheet; Dangerous to Know; Tip-Off Girls; You and Me; Thanks for the Memory. 1939 King of Chinatown; Everything's on Ice; That's Right—You're Wrong; Dancing Co-ed. 1940 Double Alibi; His Girl Friday; Saturday's Children; They Drive by Night; Ladies Must Live; Meet the Missus. 1941 Petticoat Politics; Footsteps in the Dark; The Gay Vagabond. 1942 The Road to Happiness; A Tragedy at Midnight; Yokel Boy; You Can't Escape Forever; Woman of the Year. 1943 Stage Door Canteen; My Son, the Hero; His Butler's Sister; Old Acquaintance. 1944 The Navy Way; Hi, Good Lookin'; Minstrel Man. 1946 I Ring Doorbells; One Way to Love; The Kid from Brooklyn; Avalanche; It's a Wonderful Life; Down Missouri Way. 1947 That's My Man; Vigilantes of Boomtown; Will Tomorrow Ever Come. 1948 The Devil's Cargo; The Inside Story; Speed to Spare; Texas, Brooklyn and Heaven. 1958 Onionhead. 1964 Man's Favorite Sport?

KARRINGTON, FRANK
Born: Mar. 9, 1858. Died: Mar. 5, 1936, Cornwall, N.Y. Screen and stage actor.

KATCH, KURT (Isser Kac)
Born: Jan. 28, 1896, Grodno, Poland. Died: Aug. 14, 1958, Los Angeles, Calif.(during cancer surgery). Screen and stage actor.

Appeared in: 1938 Tkies Khaf (The Vow). 1941 Men at Large. 1942 The Wife Takes a Flyer; Berlin Correspondent; Counter Espionage; They Came to Blow up America; Edge of Darkness; Quiet Please, Murder; Secret Agent of Japan. 1943 Background to Danger; Mission to Moscow; Watch on the Rhine. 1944 Ali Baba and the Forty Thieves; The Purple Heart; The Mask of Dimitrios; Make Your Own Bed; The Conspirators; The Seventh Cross. 1945 The Mummy's Curse; Salome, Where She Danced. 1946 Angel on My Shoulder; Rendezvous 24. 1947 Song of Love; Strange Journey. 1954 The Secret of the Incas; The Adventures of Hajji Baba. 1955 Abbott and Costello Meet the Mummy. 1956 Hot Cars. 1957 The Girl in the Kremlin; The Pharaoh's Curse. 1958 The Young Lions; The Beast of Budapest.

KAY, HENRY
Born: 1911. Died: Dec. 9, 1968, London, England. Screen and television actor.

KAYE, PHIL
Born: 1912. Died: Nov. 28, 1959, New York, N.Y. Screen, stage, vaudeville actor, and singer.

Appeared in: 1950 The Asphalt Jungle. 1951 The Red Badge of Courage.

KAYE, SPARKY (Philip Kaplan)
Born: 1906, New York, N.Y. Died: Aug. 23, 1971, Las Vegas, Nev.(heart attack). Screen, stage, burlesque, and night club actor.

Appeared in: 1937 Firefly. 1960 Ocean's 11.

KEAN, RICHARD
Born: 1892. Died: Dec. 30, 1959, Laguna Beach, Calif.(heart attack). Screen and stage actor.

Appeared in: 1949 The Beautiful Blonde from Bashful Bend. 1950 Storm over Wyoming. 1952 The Story of Will Rogers. 1956 The Court Jester.

KEANE, DORIS
Born: 1885, Mich. Died: Nov. 25, 1945, New York, N.Y. Screen and stage actress. Divorced from screen actor Basil Sydney (dec. 1968).

Appeared in: 1920 Romance (film and stage versions); Kismit.

KEARNS, ALLEN B.
Born: 1895. Died: Apr. 20, 1956, Albany, N.Y. Screen, stage, and television actor.

Appeared in: 1929 Tanned Legs; The Very Idea. 1930 Lovin' the Ladies; Purely an Accident (short).

KEARNS, JOSEPH
Born: 1907, Salt Lake City, Utah. Died: Feb. 17, 1962, Los Angeles, Calif. Screen, television, and radio actor. Played Mr. Wilson on Dennis the Menace TV show.

Appeared in: 1951 Hard, Fast and Beautiful. 1955 Daddy-Long Legs. 1956 Our Miss Brooks; Storm Center. 1958 The Gift of Love. 1959 Anatomy of Murder.

KEATAN, A. HARRY
Born: 1896. Died: June 18, 1966, Hollywood, Calif.(heart attack). Screen actor, film producer, director, and screenwriter. A comic in two-reelers during silent days.

KEATING, FRED
Born: Mar. 27, 1902, New York, N.Y. Died: June 29, 1961, N.Y. (heart attack). Screen, stage, vaudeville, circus actor, and writer.

Appeared in: 1929 Illusions (short). 1934 The Captain Hates the Sea. 1935 The Nitwit; To Beat the Band; Shanghai; I Live My Life. 1936 13 Hours by Air; The Devil on Horseback. 1937 Melody for Two; When's Your Birthday?. 1938 Dr. Rhythm; Prison Train. 1939 Eternally Yours; Society Smugglers. 1940 Tin Pan Alley.

KEATING, LARRY
Born: 1896, St. Paul, Minn. Died: Aug. 26, 1963, Hollywood, Calif.(leukemia). Screen, radio, and television actor.

Appeared in: 1945 Song of the Sarong. 1949 Whirlpool. 1950 Mister 880; Right Cross; My Blue Heaven; Three Secrets; Mother Didn't Tell Me; Stella. 1951 The Mating Season; Francis Goes to the Races; Follow the Sun; Bright Victory; Too Young to Kiss; Bannerline; The Light Touch; Come Fill the Cup; When Worlds Collide. 1952 Carson City; About Face; Monkey Business; Something for the Birds; Above and Beyond. 1953 Inferno; She's Back on Broadway; Give a Girl a Break; A Lion Is in the Streets. 1954 Gypsy Colt. 1955 Daddy Long Legs. 1956 The Eddie Duchin Story; The Best Things in Life Are Free. 1957 The Wayward Bus; The Buster Keaton Story; Stopover Tokyo. 1960 Who Was That Lady? 1962 Boys' Night Out; Be Careful How You Wish (aka The Incredible Mr. Limpet—U.S. 1964).

KEATON, BUSTER, JR. (Joseph Keaton, Jr.)
Born: Oct. 4, 1895, Piqua, Kan. Died: Feb. 1, 1966, Woodland Hills, Calif.(lung cancer). Screen, stage, vaudeville, television actor, screenwriter, and film director. Son of screen actor Joseph Keaton, Sr. (dec. 1946) and screen actress Myra Keaton (dec. 1955). Divorced from actress Natalie Talmadge (dec. 1969) and father of screen actor Robert Talmadge. After his divorce from Miss Talmadge, she had her son's name legally changed from Keaton to Talmadge. Appeared in vaudeville with his parents in an act billed as "The Three Keatons."

Appeared in: 1917 The Butcher Boy (film debut); The Rough House; His Wedding Night; Fatty at Coney Island; Oh, Doctor!; A Country Hero; A Reckless Romeo. 1918 The Bell Boy; Goodnight Nurse; Moonshine; The Cook; Out West. 1919 A Desert Hero; The Hayseed; Back Stage. 1920 The Saphead, plus the following shorts: The Garage, One Week; Convict 13; The Scarecrow; Neighbors. 1921 the following shorts; The Haunted House; Hard Luck; The Goat; The Electric House (incomplete first version, destroyed); The Playhouse; The Boat; The Paleface; The High Sign. 1922 the following shorts: Cops; My Wife's Relations; The Blacksmith; The Frozen North; Daydreams; The Electric House (second version). 1923 The

Three Ages; Our Hospitality, plus the following shorts: Balloon-atics; The Love Nest. 1924 Sherlock, Jr.; Navigator. 1925 Seven Chances; Go West. 1926 Battling Butler; The General. 1927 College. 1928 Steamboat Bill, Jr.; The Cameraman. 1929 Spite Marriage; Hollywood Review of 1929. 1930 Free and Easy; The Big Shot; Dough Boys. 1931 Sidewalks of New York. 1932 Speak Easily; Parlor, Bedroom and Bath; The Passionate Plumber; The Slippery Pearls (short). 1933 What, No Beer? 1934 Le Roi Des Champs-Elysees (The Champ of the Champs Elysees); Educational shorts and in British and Continental films. 1935 The Invaders, plus the following shorts: Allez Ooop; The Gold Ghost; Palooka from Paducah; Tars and Strips; Hayseed Romance; E-Flat Man; Timid Young Man; One Run Elmer. 1936 Three Men on a Horse, plus the following shorts: The Chemist; Three on a Limb; Grand Slam Opera; Blue Blazes; Mixed Magic; La Fiesta de Santa Barbara. 1937 Ditto; Jail Bait; Love Nest on Wheels. 1938 Hollywood Handicap; Streamlined Swing; Life in Sometown U.S.A. 1939 Hollywood Cavalcade; The Jones Family in Hollywood; The Jones Family in Quick Millions; Nothing but Pleasure; Mooching through Georgia (short). 1940 Lil' Abner; The Villian Still Pursued Her, plus the following shorts: Pardon My Berth Marks; The Spook Speaks; Taming of the Snood. 1941 the following shorts: So You Won't Squawk; His Ex Marks the Spot; She's Oil Mine; General Nuisance. 1943 Forever and a Day. 1944 San Diego, I Love You; Two Girls and a Sailor; Bathing Beauty. 1945 That's the Spirit; That Night with You. 1946 El Moderno Barba Azul; God's Country. 1948 Un Duel a Mort. 1949 A Southern Yankee; You're My Everything; In the Good Old Summertime; The Loveable Cheat; Neptune's Daughter. 1950 Sunset Boulevard. 1952 Limelight. 1953 The Awakening; Paradise for Buster (never released commercially). 1956 Around the World in 80 Days. 1960 The Adventures of Huckleberry Finn; When Comedy Was King (documentary). 1962 Ten Girls Ago. 1963 It's a Mad, Mad, Mad, Mad World; The Triumph of Lester Snapwell; The Great Chase (documentary); 30 Years of Fun (documentary); The Sound of Laughter (documentary). 1965 Sergeant Deadhead; Beach Blanket Bingo; The Railrodder; How to Stuff a Wild Bikini; Marines e un General; Seven Chances; Film. 1966 A Funny Thing Happened on the Way to the Forum; The Scribee. 1967 War Italian Style.

KEATON, JOSEPH, SR.
Born: 1867. Died: Jan. 13, 1946, Hollywood, Calif. Screen, vaudeville and burlesque actor. Appeared in vaudeville as "The Three Keatons" and also with magician Harry Houdini. Married to screen actress Myra Keaton (dec. 1955) and father of screen actor Buster Keaton (dec. 1966).

Appeared in: 1918 Out West; The Bell Boy. 1920 Convict 13. 1921 The Electric House (incomplete first version, destroyed). 1922 The Electric House (second version). 1923 Our Hospitality. 1924 Sherlock, Jr. 1927 The General. 1935 Palooka from Paducah (short).

KEATON, MYRA
Died: 1955. Screen and vaudeville actress. Married to screen actor Joseph Keaton, Sr. (dec. 1946) and mother of screen actor Buster Keaton, Jr. (dec. 1966). Appeared in vaudeville with husband and son in act billed as "The Three Keatons."

Appeared in: 1920 Convict 13. 1921 The Electric House (incomplete first version, destroyed). 1922 The Electric House (second version). 1935 Palooka from Paducah (short).

KEENAN, FRANCES
Born: 1886, Boston, Mass. Died: Feb. 28, 1950, Los Angeles, Calif. Screen actress. Daughter of screen actor Frank Keenan (dec. 1929).

KEENAN, FRANK
Born: 1859, Dubuque, Iowa. Died: Feb. 24, 1929, Hollywood, Calif.(pneumonia). Screen, stage, and vaudeville actor. Father of screen actress Frances Keenan (dec. 1950).

Appeared in: 1915 The Coward. 1916 Honor Thy Name; The Thoroughbred. 1918 More Trouble; The Bells. 1922 Hearts Aflame; Lorna Doone. 1923 Brass; Scars of Jealousy. 1924 Women Who Give. 1925 The Dixie Handicap; My Lady's Lips; When the Door Opened; East Lynne. 1926 The Gilded Butterfly.

KEENE, TOM (George Duryea aka RICHARD POWERS)
Born: Dec. 20, 1898, Rochester, N.Y. Died: Aug. 4, 1963, Woodland Hills, Calif. Screen, stage actor, and cowboy.

Appeared in: 1928 Marked Money. 1929 The Godless Girl; Honky Tonk; Thunder; Tide of Empire; In Old California. 1930 Night Work; Radio Kisses (short); The Dude Wrangler; Tol'able David; Beau Bandit; Pardon My Gun. 1931 Freighters of Destiny; Sun-

down Trail. 1932 Partners; Ghost Valley; Saddle Buster; Beyond the Rockies. 1933 Renegades of the West; Come on Danger; Scarlet River; Cheyenne Kid; Strictly Business; Crossfire; Son of the Border; Sunset Pass. 1934 Our Daily Bread. 1935 Hong Kong Nights. 1936 Timothy's Quest; Drift Fence; Desert Gold; The Glory Trail; Rebellion. 1937 The Law Commands; Where Trails Divide; Battle of Greed; Old Louisiana; Drums of Destiny. 1938 Under Strange Flags; The Painted Trail. 1941 Wanderers of the West; Riding the Sunset Trail. The Driftin' Kid; Dynamite Cargo. 1942 Arizona Roundup; Where the Trail Ends. 1944 Up in Arms. 1945 The Enchanted Cottage; Girls of the Big House. 1946 San Quentin. 1948 If You Knew Susie. 1950 Desperadoes of the West (serial); Trail of Robin Hood. 1952 Red Planet Mars. 1958 Once upon a Horse. 1959 Plan 9 from Outer Space.

KEITH, IAN (Keith Ross)
Born: Feb. 27, 1899, Boston, Mass. Died: Mar. 26, 1960, New York, N.Y. Screen and stage actor. Married to screen actress Ethel Clayton (dec. 1966).

Appeared in: 1924 Christine of the Hungry Heart; Love's Wilderness; Manhandled; Her Love Story. 1925 Enticement; My Son; The Tower of Lies; The Talker. 1926 The Lily; The Prince of Tempters; The Truthful Sex; Greater Glory. 1927 Convoy; Two Arabian Knights; A Man's Past; The Love of Sunya; What Every Girl Should Know. 1928 The Street of Illusion; Look-Out Girl. 1929 Prisoners; Light Fingers; The Divine Lady. 1930 Abraham Lincoln; The Great Divide; The Big Trail; Prince of Diamonds; The Boudoir Diplomat. 1931 A Tailor Made Man; The Phantom of Paris; The Deceiver; Sin Ship; Susan Lennox, Her Rise and Fall. 1932 The Sign of the Cross. 1933 Queen Christina. 1934 Dangerous Corner; Cleopatra. 1935 The Crusades; The Three Musketeers. 1936 Preview Murder Mystery; Don't Gamble with Love; Mary of Scotland; The Wife Legion. 1938 The Buccaneer; Comet over Broadway. 1940 All This, and Heaven Too; The Sea Hawk. 1942 Remember Pearl Harbor; The Pay-Off. 1943 Five Graves to Cairo; The Sundown Kid; Wild Horse Stampede; That Nazty Nuisance; Bordertown Gun Fighters; Corregidor; I Escaped from the Gestapo; Here Comes Kelly. 1944 Casanova in Burlesque; Arizona Whirlwind; The Cowboy from Lonesome River; Chinese Cat; Bowery Champs; The Sign of the Cross (revised version of 1932 film). 1945 The Spanish Main; Identity Unknown; Phantom of the Plains; Captain Kidd; China's Little Devils. 1946 Fog Island; Northwest Trail; She Gets Her Man; Song of Old Wyoming; Under Western Skies; Valley of the Zombies; Mr. Hex; Dick Tracy vs. Cueball. 1947 Dick Tracy's Dilemma; Border Feud; Nightmare Alley; The Strange Woman. 1948 The Three Musketeers (and 1935 version). 1954 The Black Shield of Falworth. 1955 Prince of Players; New York Confidential; It Came from beneath the Sea; Duel on the Mississippi. 1956 The Ten Commandments.

KEITH, JAMES
Born: 1902. Died: Dec. 27, 1970, Pasadena, Calif.(heart attack). Screen and stage actor.

KEITH, ROBERT
Born: Feb. 10, 1898, Fowler, Ind. Died: Dec. 22, 1966, Los Angeles, Calif. Screen, stage, and television actor. Father of screen actor Brian Keith.

Appeared in: 1924 The Other Kind of Love. 1930 Just Imagine. 1931 Bad Company. 1939 Spirit of Culver. 1947 Boomerang; Kiss of Death. 1949 My Foolish Heart. 1950 Branded; Woman on the Run; The Reformer and the Redhead; Edge of Doom. 1951 Fourteen Hours; Here Comes the Groom; I Want You. 1952 Just across the Street; Somebody Loves Me. 1953 Small Town Girl; Battle Circus; Devil's Canyon. 1954 The Wild One; Drum Beat; Young at Heart. 1955 Underwater!; Guys and Dolls; Love Me or Leave Me. 1956 Ransom; Written on the Wind; Between Heaven and Hell. 1957 Men in War; My Man Godfrey. 1958 The Lineup; The Tempest. 1959 They Came to Cordura; Orazi et Curiazzi. 1960 Cimarron. 1961 Posse from Hell.

KELLER, GERTRUDE
Born: 1881. Died: July 12, 1951, Hollywood, Calif. Screen and stage actress. Appeared in silent films.

KELLER, NELL CLARK
Born: 1876. Died: Sept. 2, 1965, Tacoma, Wash. Screen and stage actress.

Appeared in: 1922 Ten Nights in a Bar Room. 1924 The Virgin. 1925 Lightnin'.

KELLOGG, CONELIA
Born: 1877. Died: Feb. 21, 1934, Los Angeles, Calif. Screen actress and fashion model.

Appeared in: 1928 Lingerie.

KELLY, DOROTHY HELEN
Born: 1918. Died: Nov. 28, 1969, La Jolla, Calif.(burned to death). Screen actress. Entered films during the 1940s.

KELLY, MRS. FANNIE
Born: 1876. Died: Jan. 27, 1925, Hollywood, Calif. Screen and vaudeville actress. Appeared in vaudeville with her husband in an act billed as "Pat and Fannie Kelly." Entered films with Sennett approx. 1922.

KELLY, GREGORY
Born: 1891. Died: July 9, 1927, New York, N.Y.(heart attack). Screen, stage, and vaudeville actor. Married to screen actress Ruth Gordon who later married writer Garson Kanin.

Appeared in: 1924 Manhattan. 1926 The Show-Off.

KELLY, JAMES
Born: 1915. Died: May 5, 1964, Hollywood, Calif (heart ailment). Screen and vaudeville actor. Appeared in vaudeville as "Tiny" (340 lbs).

KELLY, JOHN T.
Born: 1852, South Boston, Mass. Died: Jan. 16, 1922, New York, N.Y.(Bright's disease). Screen, stage, vaudeville actor, song and dance man, and song writer. Divorced from actress Florence Moore Eques with whom he appeared in a vaudeville sketch billed as "A Game of Con." He also appeared in vaudeville with Thomas J. Ryan in an act billed as "Kelly & Ryan" and later appeared with Dan Mason in an act billed as "Kelly & Mason."

KELLY, KITTY
Born: 1902, New York, N.Y. Died: June 29, 1968, Hollywood, Calif.(cancer). Screen and stage actress.

Appeared in: 1925 A Kiss in the Dark 1930 The Head Man (short). 1931 Behind Office Doors; White Shoulders; Bachelor Apartment; La Nuit est a Nous (The Night Is Ours). 1932 Men of Chance; Ladies of the Jury; Girl Crazy. 1933 The Girl in 419; Too Much Harmony. 1934 All of Me; A Woman's Man; The Lemon Drop Kid. 1935 The Farmer Takes a Wife. 1937 Blossoms on Broadway; Heart's Desire. 1938 Men with Wings. 1939 Grand Jury Secrets; All Women Have Secrets; The Mutiny of the Elsinore; Geronimo. 1940 Women without Names. 1941 The Mad Doctor. 1942 The Lady Is Willing. 1943 So Proudly We Hail. 1958 The Lost Missile.

KELLY, LEW
Born: 1879, St Louis, Mo. Died: June 10, 1944, Los Angeles, Calif Screen, stage, vaudeville, and burlesque actor.

Appeared in: 1929 Barnum Was Right. 1930 The Woman Racket. 1931 Heaven on Earth. 1932 Scandal for Sale; The Miracle Man; Pack up Your Troubles. 1933 State Trooper; Strange People; Laughter in Hell. 1934 What's Your Racket?; Six of a Kind; Old Fashioned Way. 1935 The Nitwits; Diamond Jim; The Man on the Flying Trapeze; Circumstantial Evidence; Death from a Distance; Public Opinion. 1936 Three of a Kind; Wild Brian Kent; Rainbow on the River; The Man I Marry. 1937 Paradise Express; All over Town; Forlorn River; Western Gold; Some Blondes Are Dangerous 1938 Born to Be Wild; Man from Music Mountain; The Overland Express; Lawless Valley; Flirting with Fate; Painted Desert. 1939 Tough Kid. 1943 Lady of Burlesque; Taxi, Mister.

KELLY, MARY "BUBBLES"
Born: 1895, Chicago, Ill. Died: June 7, 1941, Hollywood, Calif. Screen, stage, radio, and vaudeville actress.

Appeared in: 1937 Universal short. 1940 Love Thy Neighbor 1941 Model Wife.

KELLY, NELL
Born: 1910, Memphis, Tenn. Died: Dec. 16, 1939, New York, N.Y. (diabetes). Screen, stage, and vaudeville actress.

Appeared in: 1928 College Swing. 1935 the following shorts: Rhythm of Paree; Sorority Blues; Perfect Thirty-Sixes. 1936 Thanks, Mr. Cupid (short).

KELLY, PAUL (Paul Michael Kelly)
Born: Aug. 9, 1899, Brooklyn, N.Y. Died: Nov. 6, 1956, Los Angeles, Calif.(heart attack). Screen, stage, and television actor. Married to screen actress Claire Owen and was widower of stage actress Dorothy MacKaye (dec. 1940). Served two years for manslaughter of Miss MacKaye's first husband, stage actor Ray Raymond.

Appeared in: 1911 Vitagraph pictures. 1915 The "Jarr Family" series. 1918 Fit to Fight (U.S. government information film). 1919 Ann of Green Gables. 1920 Uncle Sam of Freedom Ridge 1921 The Old Oaken Bucket; The Great Adventure 1926 The New Klondike. 1927 Special Delivery; Slide, Kelly, Slide. 1932 Girl from Calgary. 1933 Broadway Thru a Keyhole. 1934 The Love Captive; The President Vanishes; Blind Date; Death on the Diamond; Side Streets; School for Girls. 1935 When a Man's a Man; Star of Midnight; Public Hero No. 1; Silk Hat Kid; My Marriage; Speed Devils. 1936 Here Comes Trouble; Song and Dance Man; The Country Beyond; Women Are Trouble; Murder with Pictures; The Accusing Finger; It's a Great Life. 1937 Join the Marines; Fit for a King; Parole Racket; Navy Blue and Gold; The Frame Up; It Happened Out West. 1938 Island in the Sky; Nurse from Brooklyn; The Devil's Party; The Missing Guest; Torchy Blane in Panama; Juvenile Court; Adventure in Sahara. 1939 Forged Passport; The Flying Irishman; 6,000 Enemies; Within the Law; The Roaring Twenties. 1940 Girls under 21; Invisible Stripes; Queen of the Mob; The Howards of Virginia; Flight Command; Wyoming 1941 Ziegfeld Girl; I'll Wait for You; Parachute Battalion; Mystery Ship; Mr. and Mrs. North. 1942 Call Out the Marines; Tarzan's New York Adventure; Tough As They Come; Not a Ladies' Man; Flying Tigers; The Secret Code (serial); Gang Busters (serial). 1943 The Man from Music Mountain. 1944 The Story of Dr. Wassell; That's My Baby; Dead Man's Eyes; Faces in the Fog. 1945 Grissly's Millions; China's Little Devils; San Antonio; Allotment Wives. 1946 The Cat Creeps; Strange Impersonation; Strange Journey; Deadline for Murder; The Glass Alibi. 1947 Fear in the Night; Wyoming; Adventures of the North; Crossfire. 1949 Thelma Jordan; Guilty of Treason. 1950 Side Street; There's a Girl in My Heart; The Secret Fury; Frenchie; Treason. 1951 Shep of the Painted Hills. 1952 Springfield Rifle. 1953 Split Second; Gunsmoke. 1954 Duffy of San Quentin; The High and the Mighty; Johnny Dark; Steel Cage. 1955 Narcotic Squad; The Square Jungle. 1956 Storm Center. 1957 Bailout at 43,000.

KELLY, WALTER C.
Born: Oct. 29, 1873, Mineville, N.Y. Died: Jan. 6, 1939, Philadelphia, Pa.(result of head injury). Screen, stage, vaudeville actor, and screenwriter.

Appeared in: 1931 Seas Beneath. 1935 McFadden's Flats; The Virginia Judge. 1936 Laughing Irish Eyes.

KELLY, WILLIAM J.
Born: approx. 1875, Boston, Mass. Died: May 17, 1949, New York, N.Y.(heart attack). Screen and stage actor.

Appeared in: 1924 Lily of the Dust. 1925 Parisian Nights; Proud Flesh. 1926 Her Second Chance. 1933 Below the Sea; The Woman Accused. 1934 Spook Louder (short); Six of a Kind.

KELSEY, FRED A.
Born: Aug. 20, 1884, Sandusky, Ohio. Died: Sept. 2, 1961, Hollywood, Calif. Screen actor. Entered films in 1909.

Appeared in: 1921 Four Horsemen of the Apocalypse (played four roles); The Match-Breaker; There Are No Villains; Puppets of Fate. 1922 The Song of Life; Captain Fly-by-Night; Manslaughter; One Clear Call; South of Suva; Deserted at the Altar; Don't Shoot 1923 The Eleventh Hour; Lovebound; Bag and Baggage; The Bishop of the Ozarks; Souls for Sale; Lights Out. 1924 Stepping Lively; The Yankee Consul; Madonna on the Streets. 1925 Excuse Me; Seven Sinners; Smooth As Satin; Seven Keys to Baldpate; Paths to Paradise; Friendly Enemies; Youth and Adventure. 1926 Atta Boy; The Social Highwayman; That's My Baby; Doubling with Danger; The Third Degree. 1927 Held by the Law; Thirteenth Juror; Thirteenth Hour; The Gorilla; Soft Cushions. 1928 Ladies' Night in a Turkish Bath; Harold Teen; A Midnight Adventure; Tenderloin; The Wright Idea; On Trial. 1929 The Donovan Affair; The Faker; The Fall of Eve; The Last Warning; Naughty Baby; Smiling Irish Eyes. 1930 Murder on the Roof; She Got What She Wanted; Men without Law; The Laurel and Hardy Murder Case (short); Only Saps Work; The Big Jewel Case; Going Wild; Wide Open; Scarlet Pages. 1931 The Falling Star; Subway Express; Young Donovan's Kid. 1932 Discarded Lovers; Love in High Gear; Guilty As Hell; Red Haired Alibi; The Iceman's Ball (short). 1933 Girl Missing; School for Girls. 1934 Young and Beautiful; Shadows of Sing Sing; Beloved; The Crime Doctor. 1935 Horse Collars (short); Hot Money (short); One Frightened Night; Danger Ahead; Public Menace; Hot Off the Press; Sagebrush Troubadour; Carnival; Death Flies East; Diamond Jim; Lightning Strikes Twice. 1936 At Sea Ashore (short). 1937 All over Town; Super Sleuth; That I May Live; Time Out for Romance; A Damsel in Distress. 1939

Rough Riders' Round-Up; Too Busy to Work. 1940 The Lone Wolf Keeps a Date. 1942 Counter Espionage; Gentleman Jim; Murder in the Big House; X Marks the Spot. 1943 Murder on the Waterfront; True to Life; One Dangerous Night. 1944 Adventures of Mark Twain; Crime by Night; The Great Mystic; Busy Buddies (short). 1945 Come Out Fighting; How Do You Do?; If a Body Meets a Body (short). 1946 Bringing up Father; Strange Mr. Gregory; Monkey Businessmen (short). 1948 Jiggs and Maggie in Court; The Noose Hangs High. 1952 Hans Christian Andersen; O. Henry's Full House. 1953 Murder without Tears. 1954 Racing Blood.

KELTON, PERT

Born: 1907, Great Falls, Mont. Died: Oct. 30, 1968, Westwood, N.Y.(stroke). Screen, stage, vaudeville, television, and radio actress. Married to screen actor Ralph Bell.

Appeared in:1929 Sally. 1930 Hot Curves. 1933 Wine, Women and Song; Bed of Roses; The Bowery. 1934 Pursued; The Meanest Gal in Town; Sing and Like It; Bachelor Bait. 1935 Lightning Strikes Twice; Hooray for Love; Annie Oakley; Mary Burns, Fugitive. 1936 Sitting on the Moon; Kelly the Second; Cain and Mabel; Pan Handlers (short). 1937 Women of Glamour; The Hit Parade; Meet the Boy Friend; Laughing at Trouble. 1938 Slander House; Whispering Enemies; Rhythm of the Saddle. 1962 The Music Man (film and stage versions). 1965 Love and Kisses. 1969 Billy Bright.

KEMBLE-COOPER, VIOLET

Born: 1886, London, England. Died: Aug. 17, 1961, Hollywood, Calif (Parkinson's disease—stroke). Screen and stage actress.

Appeared in: 1933 Our Betters. 1934 The Fountain. 1935 David Copperfield; Vanessa, Her Love Story; Cardinal Richelieu. 1936 Romeo and Juliet; The Invisible Ray.

KEMP, EVERETT

Born: 1874, Shelbyville, Ill. Died: Oct. 1, 1958, Kansas City, Mo.(heart attack). Screen, stage, radio, and television actor. Appeared in shorts with Mr. and Mrs. Sidney Drew (1915-1919).

KEMP, HAL

Born: 1904. Died: Dec. 21, 1940, Madera, Calif.(pneumonia after auto injuries). Orchestra leader and screen actor.

Appeared in: 1938 Radio City Revels.

KEMP, PAUL

Born: May 20, 1899, Godesburg, Germany. Died: Aug. 13, 1953, Godesberg, West Germany. Screen and stage actor.

Appeared in: 1931 Die Blonde Nachtigall; Die Grosse Sehnsucht; Lumpenball; Dolly Macht Karriere. 1932 Gitta Entdeckt Ihr Herz; Sehnsucht 202 (Longing 202); Mein Herz Ruft Nach Dir. 1933 Ein Lied fur Dich (A Song for You); Der Fluchtling aus Chikago (U.S. 1936). 1934 Die Verkaufte Braut; Roman Einer Nacht; Mit dir Durch Dink und Duenn; Czardasfuerstin (The Czardas Duchess— U.S. 1935); Charley's Tante (Charlie's Aunt, film and stage versions); Prinzessin Turandot. 1935 Amphytrion; Les Dieux s'Amusent; Das Lied vom Glueck (The Song of Happiness). 1936 Das Schloss im Sueden; Der Schuechterne Casanova; Heisses Blut; Der Mutige Seefahrer; Boccaccio. 1937 Glueckskinder; Die Schwebende Jungfrau. 1938 Capriccio; Ihr Leibhusar; The Charm of la Boheme; Aus den Wolken Kommt das Glueck (Luck Comes from the Clouds). 1939 Dingehort Mein Herz (My Heart Belongs to Thee); Blumen aus Nizza (Flowers from Nice); Solo per Danne. 1940 Das Leichte Madchen. 1941 Immer nur Du. 1942 Ein Windstoss. 1944 Fahrt ins Abenteurer. 1947 Triumph der Liebe; Das Singende Haus. 1948 Das Himmlische Walzer; Lysistrata. 1949 Lambert Fuhlt Sich Bedroht. 1950 Kein Engel; Der Mann der Sich Selber Sucht; Madchen mit Beztehunger; Die Nacht Ohne Sunde; Die Dritte von Rechts. 1951 Die Mitternachtsvenus; Engel im Abendlkleid; Mutter sein Dagegen Sehr. 1952 In Muchen Steht ein Hofbrauhaus; Die Diebin von Bagdad; Konigin der Arena. 1953 Salto Mortale; Liebeskrieg nach Noten; Gluk Muss Man Haben. 1960 The Threepenny Opera.

KEMPER, CHARLES

Born: 1901. Died: May 12, 1950, Burbank, Calif.(auto crash injuries). Screen, stage, minstrel, vaudeville, and radio actor.

Appeared in: 1929 Beach Babies; Haunted; His Operation; Wednesday at the Ritz. 1945 The Southerner. 1946 Gallant Journey; Scarlet Street; Sister Kenny. 1947 The Shocking Miss Pilgrim; Gunfighters; That Hagen Girl. 1948 Fighting Father Dunne; Fury at Furnace Creek; Yellow Sky. 1949 Adventure in Baltimore; The Doolins of Oklahoma; Belle Star's Daughter; Intruder in the Dust.

1950 A Ticket to Tomahawk; Mr. Music; Stars in My Crown; Mad with Much Heart; California Passage; The Nevadan; Wagonmaster; Where Danger Lives. 1951 On Dangerous Ground.

KENDALL, CY

Born: Mar. 10, 1898, St. Louis, Mo. Died: July 22, 1953, Woodland Hills, Calif. Screen, stage, and radio actor.

Appeared in: 1936 Man Hunt; Hot Money; Dancing Feet; King of the Pecos; Bulldog Edition; The Lonely Trail; Women Are Trouble; Sworn Enemy; Sea Spoilers; Dancing Pirate. 1937 Once a Doctor; White Bondage; They Won't Forget; Without Warning; Angel's Holiday; Borrowing Trouble; Meet the Boy Firend; The Shadow Strikes. 1938 Crime School; Valley of the Giants; The Night Hawks; Hollywood Hotel; The Invisible Menace; Hawaii Calls. 1939 Stand up and Fight; Twelve Crowded Hours; Fugitive at Large; Angels Wash Their Faces; Calling All Marines; Pacific Liner. 1940 The House across the Bay; The Saint Takes Over; Prairie Law; The Fargo Kid; Men without Souls; Andy Hardy Meets a Debutante; Youth Will Be Served; 'Til We Meet Again. 1941 Billy the Kid; Midnight Angel; Johnny Eager; Robin Hood of the Pecos; Ride, Kelly, Ride; Mystery Ship. 1942 Fly by Night; Road to Morocco; Tarzan's New York Adventure; The Wife Takes a Flyer; Silver Queen. 1943 A Lady Takes a Chance; After Midnight with Boston Blackie; Laura; Outlaw Trail; Roger Touhy, Gangster; A Wave, a Wac and a Marine; Whispering Footsteps; Crime by Night; Girl Rush; The Last Ride; Dancing in Manhattan; Lady in the Death House; The Whistler. 1945 Scarlet Street; She Gets Her Man; Docks of New York; The Cisco Kid Returns; Wilson; Tahiti Nights; The Tiger Woman; Shadow of Terror; Power of the Whistler; A Thousand and One Nights. 1946 Blonde for a Day; The Glass Alibi; The Invisible Informer. 1947 The Farmer's Daughter; Sinbad the Sailor; In Self Defense. 1948 In This Corner; Fighting Mad; Sword of the Avenger; Perilous Waters. 1949 Secret Agent X-9 (serial).

KENDALL, HENRY

Born: May 28, 1898, London, England. Died: June 9, 1962, France (heart attack). Screen, stage actor, stage producer, and song writer. Entered films in 1930.

Appeared in: 1930 The House Opposite. 1931 The Flying Fool; French Leave. 1932 King of the Ritz; Counsel's Opinion; East of Shanghai; Why Saps Leave Home; Timbuctoo; This Week of Grace; Rich and Strange; The Innocents of Chicago. 1933 The Man Who Won. 1934 Death at Broadcasting House. 1935 Twelve Good Men; Death on the Set; The Three Witnesses. 1936 Amazing Quest (aka Romance and Riches—U.S. 1937). 1939 School for Husbands. 1943 The Butler's Dilemma. 1945 Acacia Avenue. 1949 Facts of Love. 1952 The Voice of Merrill. 1953 Murder Will Out. 1957 An Alligator Named Daisy. Other British films: A Rich Young Man; A Wife or Two; Side Street Angel; It's Not Cricket; Compulsory Wife; Take a Chance.

KENDALL, KAY

Born: 1926, Hull, Yorkshire, England. Died: Sept. 6, 1959, London, England (leukemia). Screen and stage actress. Married to screen actor Rex Harrison.

Appeared in: 1946 Caesar and Cleopatra; The London Town. 1952 Wings of Danger. 1953 Curtain Up; Shadow Man; My Heart Goes Crazy. 1954 Genevieve; Lady Godiva Rides Again. 1955 The Constant Husband; A Doctor in the House; The Square Ring; Quentin Durward. 1956 Simon and Laura; Abdullah's Harem. 1957 Les Girls. 1958 The Reluctant Debutante. 1960 Once More, with Feeling. Other British film: Meet Mr. Lucifer.

KENDRICK, BRIAN

Born: 1930. Died: Mar. 11, 1970, Ruislip, England (heart attack). Screen, television, and radio actor.

KENNEDY, CHARLES RANN

Born: 1871, England. Died: Feb. 16, 1950, Westwood, Calif. Screen, stage actor, and playwright.

Appeared in: 1923 Little Old New York. 1934 Crime without Passion.

KENNEDY, EDGAR

Born: Apr. 26, 1890, Monterey, Calif. Died: Nov. 9, 1948, Woodland Hills, Calif.(throat cancer). Screen, stage, and vaudeville actor. Married to actress Patricia Allwyn, with whom he appeared in vaudeville acts. Was one of the original Keystone Kops. Was star of "Mr. Average Man" series from 1929 to 1934.

Appeared in: 1912 Hoffmeyer's Legacy. 1914 The Star Boarder; Twenty Minutes of Love; Caught in a Cabaret (reissued as The Jazz Waiter); The Knock-out (reissued as The Pugilist); Our

Country Cousin; The Noise of Bombs; Getting Acquainted; Tillie's Punctured Romance. 1915 Fatty's Tin Type Tangle; A Game Old Knight; The Great Vacuum Robbery. 1916 His Hereafter (working title Murry's Mix-up); His Bitter Pill; Madcap Ambrose; Bombs; The Scoundrel's Tale; Ambrose's Cup of Woe; Bucking Society. 1917 Her Fame and Shame; Oriental Love; Her Torpedoed Love. 1918 She Loved Him Plenty. 1922 The Leather Pushers. 1924 The Night Message. 1925 Golden Princess; His People; Proud Heart. 1926 Better 'Ole; My Old Dutch; Oh! What a Nurse! 1927 Wedding Bill$; The Wrong Mr. Wright. 1928 The Chinese Parrot; plus the following shorts: The Finishing Touch; Leave 'Em Laughing; Should Married Men Go Home; Two Tars. 1929 The Gay Old Bird; Going Crooked; They Had to See Paris; Trent's Last Case; "Mr. Average Man" series, plus the following shorts: Bacon Grabbers; Unaccustomed as We Are; Hurdy-Gurdy; Dad's Day; A Perfect Day; Angora Love. 1930 "Mr. Average Man" series; Night Owls (short). 1931 "Mr. Average Man" series; Midnight Patrol; Bad Company. 1932 "Mr. Average Man" series; Carnival Boat; Hold 'Em Jail; The Penguin Pool Murder; Little Orphan Annie. 1933 "Mr. Average Man" series; Scarlet River; Crossfire; Professional Sweetheart; Son of the Border; Duck Soup; Tillie and Gus; Kickin' the Crown Around (short— seen in stock footage). 1934 "Mr. Average Man" series; Flirting With Danger; All of Me; Heat Lightning; Murder on the Blackboard; The Silver Streak; We're Rich Again; Kid Millions; Twentieth Century; Money Means Nothing; Gridiron Flash; King Kelly of the USA; The Marines Are Coming. 1935 Living on Velvet; Woman Wanted; The Cowboy Millionaire; Little Big Shot; In Person; A Thousand Dollars a Minute; The Bride Comes Home; Rendezvous at Midnight; A Night at the Biltmore Bowl (short). 1936 San Francisco; The Return of Jimmy Valentine; Small Town Girl; Mad Holiday; Fatal Lady; Yours for the Asking; Three Men on a Horse; Robin Hood of El Dorado, plus "Edgar Kennedy" comedies (shorts). 1937 When's Your Birthday?; Super Sleuth; A Star Is Born; Double Wedding; True Confession; Hollywood Hotel. 1938 The Black Doll; Scandal Street; Hey! Hey! U.S.A.; Peck's Bad Boy with the Circus. 1939 It's a Wonderful World; Little Accident; Everything's on Ice; Charlie McCarthy, Detective; Laugh It Off. 1940 Sandy Is a Lady; Dr. Christian Meets the Women; The Quarterback; Margie; Who Killed Aunt Maggie?; Remedy for Riches; Sandy Gets Her Man; Li'l Abner. 1941 The Bride Wore Crutches; Public Enemies; Blondie in Society. 1942 Snuffy Smith, Yard Bird; Pardon My Stripes; In Old California; Hillbilly Blitzkrieg. 1943 The Falcon Strikes Back; Cosmo Jones-Crime Smasher; Air Raid Wardens; Hitler's Madman; The Girl from Monterey; Crazy House. 1944 It Happened Tomorrow; The Great Alaskan Mystery (serial). 1945 Anchors Aweigh; Captain Tugboat Annie; The Big Beef (short); Mother-in-Law's Day (short). 1946 Trouble or Nothing (short). 1947 Heaven Only Knows; Sin of Harold Diddlebock (aka Mad Wednesday-U.S. 1951). 1948 Variety Time; Unfaithfully Yours. 1949 My Dream Is Yours. 1960 When Comedy Was King (documentary). 1963 The Sound of Laughter (documentary). 1965 Laurel and Hardy's Laughing '20's (documentary). 1968 The Further Perils of Laurel and Hardy (documentary).

KENNEDY, FREDERICK O.
Born: 1910. Died: Dec. 5, 1958, Natchitoches, La.(killed while filming The Horse Soldiers). Screen actor and stuntman.

Appeared in: 1949 She Wore a Yellow Ribbon. 1950 Rio Grande. 1953 The Charge at Feather River. 1959 The Horse Soldiers

KENNEDY, JOHN F.
Died: Nov. 6, 1960, Hollywood, Calif. Screen actor. Appeared in "Keystone Kop" comedies.

KENNEDY, JOSEPH C.
Born: 1890, Canada. Died: May 4, 1949, Halifax, Canada. Screen and stage actor. Appeared in Canadian Bioscope Co. films.

KENNEDY, JOYCE
Born: 1898, London, England. Died: Mar. 12, 1943, London, England (pneumonia). Screen and stage actress.

Appeared in: 1931 Bracelets. 1932 The Man from Chicago. 1933 Say It with Music. 1934 Return of Bulldog Drummond; Dangerous Ground. 1935 Seven Sinners; Twelve Good Men; Black Mask; Debt of Honour. 1936 Doomed Cargo; Hail and Farewell; Big Fella.

KENNEDY, MERNA (Maude Kahler)
Born: Sept. 7, 1908, Kankakee, Ill. Died: Dec. 20, 1944, Los Angeles, Calif.(heart attack). Screen and stage actress. Divorced from dance director Busby Berkeley.

Appeared in: 1928 The Circus. 1929 Broadway; Barnum Was Right; Skinner Steps Out. 1930 The Rampant Age; Worldly Goods;

Midnight Special; Embarassing Moments; The King of Jazz. 1931 Stepping Out. 1932 The Gay Buckaroo; Ghost Valley; The All American; Laughter in Hell; Red Haired Alibi; Reputation; Lady with a Past. 1933 Come on Tarzan; Big Chance; Easy Millions; Emergency Call; Don't Bet on Love; Arizona to Broadway; Police Call; Son of a Sailor. 1934 Wonder Bar; I Like It That Way.

KENNEDY, TOM
Born: 1884, New York, N.Y. Died: Oct. 6, 1965, Woodland Hills, Calif.(bone cancer). Screen and television actor. Entered films in 1915.

Appeared in: 1916 The Village Blacksmith; Hearts and Sparks; Ambrose's Rapid Rise. 1917 Nick of Time Baby. 1921 Serenade; Skirts. 1922 The Flirt; If You Believe It, It's So; Afraid to Fight; The Flaming Hour; Our Leading Citizen. 1923 Scaramouche; With Naked Fists. 1924 Loving Lies; Madonna of the Streets. 1925 The Knockout; As Man Desires; The Best Bad Man; High and Handsome; The Fearless Lover. 1926 Behind the Front; Mantrap; Better 'Ole; Sir Lumberjack; We're in the Navy Now; The Yankee Senor; Born to the West; Man of the Forest. 1927 Fireman Save My Child; Silver Valley; The Mysterious Rider; One Round Hogan; Alias the Deacon. 1928 Hold 'Em Yale; The Cop; Tillie's Punctured Romance; Love over Night; Marked Money; None but the Brave; Wife Savers. 1929 The Glad Rag Doll; Post Mortems; Big News; The Cohens and the Kellys in Atlantic City; The Shannons of Broadway; Liberty (short). 1930 See America Thirst; The Big House; Fall Guy. 1931 It Pays to Advertise; Caught; The Gang Busters; Monkey Business. 1932 Pack up Your Troubles; The Devil Is Driving. 1933 Blondie Johnson; Man of the Forest; She Done Him Wrong; an RKO short. 1934 Odor in the Court (short); Hollywood Party; Strictly Dynamite; Down to Their Last Yacht; In the Devil's Doghouse (short). 1935 Bright Lights; Alibi Bye Bye (short); a Columbia short. 1936 Poppy; Hollywood Boulevard; Smart Blonde; an RKO short. 1937 Fly Away Baby; Marry the Girl; The Adventurous Blonde; He Couldn't Say No; Behind the Headlines; The Big Shot; Forty Naughty Girls; Living on Love; Married before Breakfast; Armored Car; Swing It, Sailor; She Had to Eat; The Case of the Stuttering Blonde; Columbia short. 1938 Making the Headlines; Torchy Blane in Panama; Pardon Our Nerve; Long Shot; Crime Ring; Go Chase Yourself; Wise Girl; Crashing Hollywood; House of Mystery; Blondes at Work; Torchy Gets Her Man. 1939 Torchy Blane in Chinatown; Torchy Runs for Mayor; Covered Trailer; Society Lawyer; Torchy Plays with Dynamite; The Day the Bookies Wept. 1940 Flowing Gold; Remember the Night; Millionaire Playboy; Curtain Call; Pop Always Pays; Mexican Spitfire Out West; An Angel from Texas; Sporting Blood. 1941 The Great Swindle; Angels with Broken Wings; The Officer and the Lady; Sailors on Leave. 1942 Pardon My Stripes; Wildcat. 1943 Ladies' Day; Dixie; Here Comes Elmer; My Darling Clementine; Petticoat Larceny; Hit Parade of 1943; Stage Door Canteen. 1944 Rosie the Riveter; Princess and the Pirate; And the Angels Sing; Moonlight and Cactus. 1945 The Man Who Walked Alone. 1946 Voice of the Whistler; Bringing up Father. 1947 The Burning Cross; The Case of the Baby Sister; The Pretender. 1948 The Devil's Cargo; Jinx Money; The Paleface; Thunder in the Pines. 1949 Jackpot Jitters; Square Dance Jubilee; The Mutineers. 1950 Border Rangers. 1951 Havana Rose; Let's Go Navy. 1952 Invasion U.S.A. 1953 Gold Fever. 1963 It's a Mad, Mad, Mad, Mad World. 1968 The Further Perils of Laurel and Hardy (documentary).

KENNETH, HARRY D.
Born: 1854. Died: Jan. 18, 1929, Newark, N.J.(brain hemorrhage). Screen, stage, and vaudeville actor. Appeared in early Essanay films.

KENNEY, JACK
Born: 1888. Died: May 26, 1964, Hollywood, Calif. Screen actor.

Appeared in: 1929 Not Quite Decent; Beauty and Bullets. 1938 a Columbia short. 1944 Atlantic City. 1952 Cattle Town. 1955 The Country Girl. 1957 The Tin Star; Chicago Confidentiai. 1958 Hong Kong Confidential; Toughest Gun in Tombstone. 1959 Inside the Mafia; Invisible Invaders. 1960 Vice Raid; When the Clock Strikes; Cage of Evil; Three Came to Kill; Walking Target. 1961 The Gambler Wore a Gun; Gun Fight.

KENNY, LEOLA (aka LEE KENNY)
Born: 1892. Died: Oct. 17, 1956, Hollywood, Calif. Screen and stage actress.

Appeared in: 1930 Just Imagine.

KENT, ARNOLD (Lido Manetti)
Born: Jan. 21, 1899, Florence, Italy. Died: Sept. 29, 1928, Los Angeles, Calif.(auto accident). Screen actor.

Appeared in: 1927 The Woman on Trial; Hula; The World at Her Feet. 1928 Beau Sabreur; Easy Come, Easy Go; The Woman Disputed; The Showdown.

KENT, CRAUFORD
Born: 1881, London, England. Died: May 14, 1953, Los Angeles, Calif. Screen actor. Entered films in 1915.

Appeared in: 1917 Thais. 1918 The Song of Songs. 1919 Good Gracious Annabelle. 1920 Other Men's Shoes. 1921 Silas Marner; Jane Eyre; The Plaything of Broadway. 1922 Shadows of the Sea; The Hidden Woman; Shirley of the Circus; Other Women's Clothes. 1923 The Eagle's Feather; Mothers-in-Law; Self Made Wife; The Abysmal Brute. 1924 Daddies; Flowing Gold; Lover's Lane; Virtue's Revolt; The Painted Flapper; The Guilty One; Lilies of the Field; Turned Up. 1925 Easy Money; The Pride of the Force; The Midshipman; Seven Keys to Baldpate; Man and Maid. 1926 Fifth Avenue; Out of the Storm; College Days; Morganson's Finish; The Outsider; The Winning Wallop; That Model from Paris. 1927 The Missing Link; Pirates of the Sky; His Dog; Little Mickey Grogan; See You in Jail; Mother. 1928 The Foreign Legion; Blindfold; Man, Woman and Wife; Into No Man's Land; Bitter Sweets; Manhattan Knights; Out with the Tide; Wallflowers; The Olympic Hero; Queen of the Chorus; Show Folks. 1929 The Charlatan; Seven Keys to Baldpate (and 1925 version); The Wolf of Wall Street; Come Across; The Ace of Scotland Yard (serial); Careers. 1930 Ladies Love Brutes; In the Next Room; Sweethearts and Wives; The Second Floor Mystery; The Devil to Pay; Three Faces East; The Unholy Three. 1931 Grief Street; Body and Soul; Transatlantic; Delicious; The Feathered Serpent; Women Men Marry; His Last Performance; Goldberg; Oh! Oh! Cleopatra (short). 1932 Sinister Hands; The 13th Guest; File 113; The Menace; Murder at Dawn; The Fighting Gentleman; Western Limited; Sally of the Subway; The Purchase Price. 1933 Sailor Be Good; The Eagle and the Hawk; Only Yesterday; Humanity. 1934 The Lost Jungle; The House of Rothschild; Little Miss Marker. 1935 Vanessa, Her Love Story; Mutiny on the Bounty. 1936 Hitchhike to Heaven; Down the Stretch; Magnificent Obsession; Daniel Boone; O'Malley of the Mounted; It Couldn't Have Happened. 1937 Navy Spy. 1938 Love, Honor and Behave; Service de Luxe. 1939 I Was a Convict; We Are Not Alone. 1940 Foreign Correspondent; South of Suez. 1941 Shining Victory; International Squadron. 1943 The Constant Nymph; Mysterious Doctor. 1944 The Black Parachute. 1945 The Fatal Witness. 1946 Kitty. 1950 Tea for Two.

KENT, DOUGLASS. See Douglass Montgomery

KENT, ELINOR
Died: Sept. 15, 1957, Hollywood, Calif. Screen actress. Mother of screen actor Warren Hymer (dec. 1948). Married to stage actor/playwright John B. Hymer (dec.).

KENT, ETHEL (Ethel Jackson)
Born: 1884, New York, N.Y. Died: July 27, 1952, Hollywood, Calif. (cerebral hemorrhage). Screen actress. Entered films in 1911. Married to screen actor/director John Ince (dec. 1947).

Appeared in: 1950 Buccaneer's Girl.

KENT, GERALD (Gerald MacIntosh Johnston)
Born: Canada. Died: Nov. 5, 1944, Germany (German prison camp). Screen and stage actor. Appeared in British film: Four Corners.

KENT, KENETH
Born: 1892. Died: Nov. 17, 1963, London, England. Screen, stage, opera, television actor, and playwright.

Appeared in: 1940 Night Train. 1942 Suicide Squad. Other British films: St. Helena; Napoleon Couldn't Do It.

KENT, MARSHA (Marjorie Kent)
Born: 1919. Died: Mar. 1971, Huntington, N.Y. Screen actress and ballerina.

Appeared in: 1936 The Great Ziegfeld. 1937 Prisoner of Zenda; The Bride Wore Red. 1938 The Great Waltz. 1939 The Wizard of Oz; Gone with the Wind.

KENT, WILLIAM T.
Born: 1886. Died: Oct. 5, 1945, N.Y. Screen, stage, vaudeville, burlesque, and circus actor.

Appeared in: 1922 When Knighthood Was in Flower. 1930 The King of Jazz. 1933 Saturday's Millions. 1934 Scarlet Letter.

KEPPENS, EMILE
Born: France. Died: Oct. 1926, France. Screen actor.

KERN, JAMES V.
Born: Sept. 22, 1909, New York, N.Y. Died: Nov. 9, 1966, Encino, Calif.(pneumonia). Screen actor, film and television director, screenwriter, composer, and member of "Yacht Club Boys" singers on stage, radio and screen.

KERR, FREDERICK (Frederick Keen)
Born: Oct. 11, 1858, London, England. Died: May 3, 1933, London, England. Screen and stage actor.

Appeared in: 1927 The Honour of the Family (U.S. 1931). 1929 Raffles. 1930 The Devil to Pay; The Lady of Scandal. 1931 Born to Love; Frankenstein; Waterloo Bridge; Always Good-Bye. 1932 The Midshipmaid; The Man from Toronto; Lovers Courageous; Beauty and the Boss; But the Flesh Is Weak.

KERR, JANE
Born: 1871 or 1891. Died: Nov. 19, 1954, Compton, Calif. Screen, stage, vaudeville, and television actress.

Appeared in: 1934 Broadway Bill. 1935 Les Miserables. 1936 The Garden of Allah.

KERRICK, THOMAS
Died: Apr. 27, 1927. Screen actor.

Appeared in: 1923 Men in the Raw.

KERRIGAN, J. WARREN (George Warren Kerrigan)
Born: July 25, 1889, Louisville, Ky. Died: June 9, 1947, Balboa, Calif.(bronchial pneumonia). Screen, stage actor, and film producer.

Appeared in: 1909 Hand of Uncle Sam. 1912 Strangers at Coyote; For the Flag. 1913 The Wishing Seat. 1914 Samson. 1915 The Adventures of Terrence O'Rourke. 1916 Landon's Legacy. 1918 A Man's Man. 1919 A White Man's Chance. 1920 Thirty Thousand Dollars. 1921 Coast of Opportunity; House of Whispers. 1923 The Man from Brodney's; The Girl of the Golden West; Hollywood; Mary of the Movies; Thundering Dawn; The Covered Wagon. 1924 Captain Blood.

KERRIGAN, JOSEPH M.
Born: Dec. 16, 1887, Dublin, Ireland. Died: Apr. 29, 1964, Hollywood, Calif. Screen and stage actor.

Appeared in: 1923 Little Old New York. 1924 Captain Blood. 1929 Lucky in Love. 1930 Song O' My Heart; New Movietone Follies of 1930; Under Suspicion; Lightnin'. 1931 Don't Bet on Women; Merely Mary Ann; The Black Camel. 1932 The Rainbow Trail; Careless Lady; Rockabye. 1933 Air Hostess; Lone Cowboy; A Study in Scarlet; Paddy, the Next Best Thing. 1934 The Fountain; Happiness Ahead; The Lost Patrol; A Modern Hero; The Key; Gentlemen Are Born; Treasure Island. 1935 A Feather in Her Hat; Mystery of Edwin Drood; Werewolf of London; The Informer; Hot Tip; Barbary Coast. 1936 Timothy's Quest; Spendthrift; The General Died at Dawn; Colleen; The Prisoner of Shark Island; Lloyds of London; Laughing Irish Eyes; Hearts in Bondage; Special Investigator. 1937 The Plough and the Stars; Lets Make a Million; The Barrier; London by Night. 1938 Vacation from Love; Ride a Crooked Mile; Little Orphan Annie; The Great Man Votes; Boy Slaves. 1939 The Flying Irishman; Sorority House; The Kid from Texas; Two Thoroughbreds; Two Bright Boys; 6,000 Enemies; Gone with the Wind; The Zero Hour; Sabotage; Union Pacific; The Witness Vanishes. 1940 Congo Maisie; Young Tom Edison; The Long Voyage Home; Three Cheers for the Irish; The Sea Hawk; No Time for Comedy; Curtain Call; One Crowded Night; Untamed. 1941 Adventure in Washington; Appointment for Love; The Wolf Man. 1942 Captains of the Clouds; The Vanishing Virginian. 1943 None but the Lonely Heart; Mr. Lucky; Action in the North Atlantic; The American Romance. 1944 The Fighting Seabees; Wilson. 1945 The Great John L; Big Bonanza; Tarzan and the Amazons; The Crime Doctor's Warning; The Spanish Main. 1946 Abie's Irish Rose; Black Beauty; She Went to the Races. 1948 Call Northside 777; The Luck of the Irish. 1949 Mrs. Mike; Fighting O'Flynn. 1951 Sealed Cargo; Two of a Kind. 1952 The Wild North; Park Row; My Cousin Rachel. 1953 The Silver Whip. 1954 20,000 Leagues under the Sea. 1955 It's a Dog's Life. 1956 The Fastest Gun Alive.

KERRY, NORMAN (Arnold Kaiser)
Born: June 16, 1889, Rochester, N.Y. Died: Jan. 12, 1956, Hollywood, Calif. Screen and stage actor.

Appeared in: 1916 Manhattan Madness (film Debut); The Black Butterfly. 1918 The Rose of Paradise. 1919 The Dark Star; Soldiers of Fortune. 1921 Get-Rich-Quick Wallingford; Buried Treasure; The Wild Goose; Little Italy; Proxies. 1922 Brothers under the Skin; Three Live Ghosts; Find the Woman; The Man from Home; 'Til We Meet Again. 1923 Merry-Go-Round; The Hunchback of Notre Dame; The Spoilers; The Acquittal; Is Money Everything?; The Satin Girl; The Thrill Chaser. 1924 Cytherea; Butterfly; Between Friends; Daring Youth; The Shadow of the East; True As Steel; Tarnish. 1925 Fifth Avenue Models; The Price of Pleasure; Lorraine of the Lions; The Phantom of the Opera. 1926 The Love Thief; Mlle. Modiste; The Barrier; Under Western Skies. 1927 The Unknown; Annie Laurie; Body and Soul; The Claw; The Irresistible Lover. 1928 Man, Woman and Wife; The Foreign Legion; Love Me and the World Is Mine; The Woman from Moscow; Affairs of Hannerl. 1929 The Bondsman; Trial Marriage; The Prince of Hearts; The Woman I Love. 1930 Phantom of the Opera (and 1925 version). 1931 Ex-Flame; Bachelor Apartments; Air Eagles. 1941 Tanks a Million.

KEY, KATHLEEN
Born: 1906, Buffalo, N.Y. Died: Dec. 22, 1954, Woodland Hills, Calif. Screen actress.

Appeared in: 1921 The Four Horsemen of the Apocalypse; The Rookie's Return. 1922 Bells of San Juan; Where Is My Wandering Boy Tonight?; West of Chicago. 1923 Beautiful and Damned; Hell's Hole; The Rendezvous; Reno; The Man from Brodney's; North of Hudson Bay. 1924 The Sea Hawk; The Trouble Shooter; Revelation. 1925 A Lover's Oath; The Midshipman. 1926 Ben Hur; College Days; Money Talks; The Desert's Toll; Under Western Skies; The Flaming Frontier. 1927 Hey! Hey! Cowboy; Irish Hearts. 1928 Golf Widows. 1929 The Phantom of the North. 1931 Ben Hur (sound version).

KEYS, NELSON
Born: 1887. Died: Apr. 26, 1939, London, England (heart attack). Screen and stage actor. Entered films approx. 1927.

Appeared in: 1927 Madame Pompadour. 1929 The Scarlet Devil; The Triumph of the Scarlet Pimpernel. 1936 The Last Journey.

KIBBEE, GUY
Born: Mar. 6, 1886, El Paso, Tex. Died: May 24, 1956, East Islip, N.Y.(Parkinson's disease). Screen and stage actor. Married to former stage actress Lois Kibbee.

Appeared in: 1931 Man of the World; Stolen Heaven; Laughing Sinners; Happy Landing; Side Show; New Adventures of Get-Rich-Quick Wallingford; Flying High; Blonde Crazy; Larceny Lane; City Streets. 1932 Crooner; Scarlet Dawn; Taxi; Fireman Save My Child; Mouthpiece; Weekend Marriage; Union Depot; High Pressure; Play Girl; Central Park; The Conquerors; The Crowd Roars; Rain; Gentleman for a Day; Two Seconds; Big City Blues; Man Wanted; The Dark Horse; Strange Love of Molly Louvain; So Big; Winner Take All. 1933 They Just Had to Get Married; 42nd Street; Lilly Turner; The Silk Express; Girl Missing; The Life of Jimmy Dolan; Gold Diggers of 1933; Footlight Parade; Lady for a Day; The World Changes; Havana Widows; Convention City. 1934 Easy to Love; Dames; Harold Teen; Big Hearted Herbert; Merry Wives of Reno; The Merry Frinks; Wonder Bar; Babbitt. 1935 While the Patient Slept; Mary Jane's Pa; Don't Bet on Blondes; Crashing Society; Going Highbrow; I Live for Love; Captain Blood. 1936 Three Men on a Horse; Little Lord Fauntleroy; Captain January; I Married a Doctor; The Big Noise; Earthworm Tractors; M'Liss; The Captain's Kid. 1937 Mamma Steps Out; Don't Tell the Wife; Riding on Air; The Big Shot; Jim Hanvey, Detective; Mountain Justice. 1938 Bad Man of Brimstone; Of Human Hearts; Three Comrades; Rich Man, Poor Girl; Three Loves Has Nancy; Joy of Living. 1939 It's a Wonderful World; Bad Little Angel; Let Freedom Ring; Mr. Smith Goes to Washington; Babes in Arms. 1940 Our Town; Henry Goes Arizona; Street of Memories. 1941 Scattergood Baines; Scattergood Pulls the Strings; Scattergood Meets Broadway; It Started with Eve; Design for Scandal. 1940 Chad Hanna. 1942 Scattergood Rides High; This Time for Keeps; Sunday Punch; Miss Annie Rooney; Tish; Whistling in Dixie; Scattergood Survives a Murder. 1943 Cinderella Swings It; Girl Crazy; White Savage; The Power of the Press. 1944 Dixie Jamboree. 1945 The Horn Blows at Midnight; White Pongo. 1946 Singing on the Trail; Cowboy Blues; Gentleman Joe Palooka; Lone Star Moonlight. 1947 Over the Santa Fe Trail; The Red Stallion; The Romance of Rosy Ridge. 1948 Fort Apache; Three Godfathers.

KIDD, KATHLEEN
Born: 1899, England. Died: Feb. 23, 1961, Toronto, Canada. Screen, stage, radio, and television actress.

Appeared in: 1926 What Price Glory.

KIDDER, HUGH
Born: 1880. Died: June 3, 1952, Hollywood, Calif. Screen, stage, and radio actor.

Appeared in: 1933 His Private Secretary.

KIEPURA, JAN
Born: May 16, 1902, Warsaw, Poland. Died: Aug. 15, 1966, Harrison, N.Y.(heart ailment). Screen, stage, and opera actor.

Appeared in: 1931 Ein Lied fur Dich (A Song for You-U.S. 1933). 1932 Die Singende Stadt (U.S. 1935). 1933 Das Lied Ein Nach; Mein Herz Ruft Nach Dir; Farewell to Love; Be Mine Tonight. 1934 Ich Liebe Alles Frauen; My Song Goes Round the World. 1935 My Heart Is Calling; My Son for You. 1936 Zauber der Boheme (The Charm of La Boheme-U.S. 1938); Give Us This Night. 1937 Thank You Madame. 1949 La Vie de Boheme. 1950 Her Wonderful Lie.

KILBRIDE, PERCY
Born: July 16, 1888, San Francisco, Calif. Died: Dec. 11, 1964, Los Angeles, Calif.(brain injury due to auto accident). Screen and stage actor.

Appeared in: 1933 White Woman. 1936 Soak the Rich. 1942 Keeper of the Flame. 1943 George Washington Slept Here; Crazy House; The Woman of the Town. 1944 The Adventures of Mark Twain; Guest in the House; Knickerbocker Holiday. 1945 She Wouldn't Say Yes; State Fair; Fallen Angel. 1946 The Well-Groomed Bride. 1947 The Egg and I; Riffraff; Welcome Stranger. 1948 Black Bart; Feudin', Fussin' and A-Fightin'; You Were Meant for Me; You Gotta Stay Happy. 1949 Mr. Soft Touch; The Sun Comes Up; Free for All; Ma and Pa Kettle. 1950 Ma and Pa Kettle Go to Town; Riding High. 1951 Ma and Pa Kettle Back on the Farm. 1952 Ma and Pa Kettle at the Fair. 1953 Ma and Pa Kettle on Vacation; Ma and Pa Kettle Hit the Road. 1954 Ma and Pa Kettle at Home. 1955 Ma and Pa Kettle at Waikiki.

KILBRIDE, RICHARD D.
Born: 1919. Died: June 20, 1967, Cambridge, Mass. Screen, stage, and television actor.

Appeared in: 1965 The Playground.

KILDUFF, HELEN. See Helen Allerton

KILGALLEN, DOROTHY
Born: July 3, 1913, Chicago, Ill. Died: Nov. 8, 1965, N.Y. Radio, television, screen actress, and columnist.

Appeared in: 1936 Sinner Take All.

KILPACK, BENNETT
Born: 1883, England. Died: Aug. 17, 1962, Santa Monica, Calif. Screen, stage, and radio actor. Star of Mr. Keen, Tracer of Lost Persons on radio.

Appeared in: 1932 Way Back Home.

KIMBALL, EDWARD M.
Born: June 26, 1859, Keokuk, Iowa. Died: Jan. 4, 1938, Hollywood, Calif. Screen and stage actor. Father of screen actress Clara Kimball Young (dec. 1960). Entered films with Solax Studio in 1910; at Vitagraph 1911-14; and World's films 1914-16.

Appeared in: 1915 Lola. 1917 Magda; The Marionettes. 1920 Mid-Channel. 1921 An Unwilling Hero; Charge It; Boys Will Be Boys. 1922 The Masquerader; Yankee Doodle, Jr.; Omar the Tentmaker. 1923 The Woman of Bronze; The Cheat; Trilby; The Remittance Woman. 1924 Passion's Pathway. 1925 I'll Show You the Town.

KING, ANITA
Born: 1889. Died: June 10, 1963, Hollywood, Calif.(heart attack). Screen and stage actress.

Appeared in: 1914 The Virginian. 1915 Snobs.

KING, CHARLES
Born: Oct. 31, 1894, New York, N.Y. Died: Jan. 11, 1944, London, England (pneumonia). Screen, stage, and vaudeville actor.

Appeared in: 1929 Broadway Melody (film debut); Road Show; Hollywood Revue of 1929; Orange Blossom Time; Climbing the Golden Stairs. 1930 The Girl in the Show; Chasing Rainbows; Remote Control. 1935 The Singing Vagabond; Tumbling Tumbleweeds. 1936 The Lawless Nineties; Guns and Guitars. 1937 Rootin' Tootin' Rhythm; The Trusted Outlaw; A Lawman Is Born; Ridin' the Lone Trail. 1938 Thunder in the Desert.

KING, CHARLES L., SR.
Born: 1899. Died: May 7, 1957, Hollywood, Calif. Screen actor. Father of screen actor Charles L. King, Jr.

Appeared in: 1921 A Motion to Adjourn; Singing River. 1922 The Black Bag; Price of Youth. 1923 Merry-Go-Round. 1925 Hearts of the West; Triple Action. 1926 What Happened to Jane (serial). 1927 Range Courage. 1928 You Can't Beat the Law; Sisters of Eve. 1929 Slim Fingers. 1930 Dawn Trail; Fighting Through; Oklahoma Cyclone; Beyond the Law. 1931 Oh, Sailor, Behave!; Branded Men; Range Law. 1932 Gay Buckaroo; A Man's Land; The Fighting Champ; Ghost City; Honor of the Mounted. 1933 The Fighting Parson; Crashing Broadway; Son of the Border; The Lone Avenger; Strawberry Roan; Young Blood; Outlaw Justice. 1934 Mystery Ranch; Men in Black. 1935 Northern Frontier; Outlawed Guns; The Ivory-Handled Gun; His Fighting Blood; Mississippi; Red Blood of Courage. 1936 Just My Luck; O'Malley of the Mounted; Headin' for the Rio Grande; Sunset of Power; Desert Phantom; Sundown Saunders; Men of the Plains; Last of the Warrens; Idaho Kid. 1937 Trouble in Texas; Sing, Cowboy, Sing; Tex Rides with the Boy Scouts; Headline Crasher; Island Captives; Black Aces; Riders of the Rockies; The Red Rope; The Mystery of the Hooded Horsemen; The Trusted Outlaw; Hittin' the Trail. 1938 Starlight over Texas; Where the Buffalo Roam; Gun Packer; Frontier Town; Song and Bullets; Phantom Ranger; Man's Country. 1939 Wild Horse Canyon; Song of the Buckaroo; Zorro's Fighting Legion (serial); Rollin' Westward; Mutiny in the Big House; Down the Wyoming Trail; Oklahoma Frontier. 1940 Son of the Navy; West of Carson City; Wild Horse Range. 1941 Billy the Kid's Fighting Pals; Outlaws of the Rio Grande; The Roar of the Press; The Lone Ranger in Ghost Town; Texas Marshal; Gunman from Bodie; Borrowed Hero; Billy the Kid Wanted; Billy the Kid's Roundup; The Lone Ranger Fights Back. 1942 Riders of the West; Law and Order; Pirates of the Prairie. 1943 Ghost Rider; Two-Fisted Justice; The Rangers Take Over; The Stranger from Pecos; Border Buckaroos; Riders of the Rio Grande. 1946 The Caravan Trail.

KING, CLAUDE (Claude Ewart King)

Born: Jan. 15, 1879, Northhampton, England. Died: Sept. 18, 1941, Los Angeles, Calif. Screen, stage actor, and stage director.

Appeared in: 1920 Judy of Rogue's Harbor. 1921 The Scarab Ring; Why Girls Leave Home. 1923 Bella Donna; Six Days. 1925 The Making of O'Malley; Irish Luck; The Unguarded Hour; The Knockout. 1926 Paradise; The Silent Lover. 1927 Mr. Wu; Becky; Singed; London after Midnight. 1928 Red Hair; A Night of Mystery; Love and Learn; Outcast; Oh, Kay!; Warming Up; Sporting Goods. 1929 Strange Cargo; Nobody's Children; Madame X; Behind That Curtain; The Black Watch; Blue Skies; The Mysterious Dr. Fu Manchu. 1930 Son of the Gods; In Gay Madrid; Second Floor Mystery; Love among the Millionaires; Prince of Diamonds; One Night at Susie's; Follow Thru. 1931 Rango; The Reckless Hour; Women Love Once; Transatlantic; Devotion; Once a Lady; Heartbreak; Arrowsmith; Born to Love. 1932 Behind the Mask; He Learned about Women; Sherlock Holmes; Shanghai Express. 1933 The Big Brain; Charlie Chan's Greatest Case; White Woman. 1934 The Moonstone; Stolen Sweets; The World Moves On; Two Heads on a Pillow; Long Lost Father; Murder in Trinidad. 1935 The Great Impersonation; The Right to Live; The Gilded Lily; Smart Girl; The Last Outpost; Circumstantial Evidence; A Thousand Dollars a Minute; Bonnie Scotland. 1936 The Leathernecks Have Landed; Shanghai Gesture; Three on a Trail; The Last of the Mohicans; Beloved Enemy; It Couldn't Have Happened; Happy Go Lucky. 1937 Lover under Fire; Lancer Spy. 1938 Four Men and a Prayer; Booloo. 1939 Within the Law. 1940 New Moon.

KING, DENNIS (aka DENNIS PRATT and DENNY PRATT)

Born: Nov. 2, 1897, Warwickshire, Coventry, England. Died: May 21, 1971, New York, N.Y.(heart condition). Screen and stage actor. Married to stage actress Edith Wright (dec.).

Appeared in: 1919 Monsieur Beaucaire (film debut). 1930 The Vagabond King; Paramount on Parade. 1931 Fra Diavolo (The Devil's Brother). 1937 Between Two Worlds. 1959 The Miracle. 1969 The One with the Fuzz; Some Kind of a Nut.

KING, EMMETT C.

Born: 1866, Griffin, Ga. Died: Apr. 21, 1953, Woodland Hills, Calif. Screen, stage, and radio actor.

Appeared in: 1921 Fightin' Mad; Flower of the North; Lying Lips; Three Sevens; Eden and Return; The Mistress of Shenstone; Little Lord Fauntleroy; The Silver Car. 1922 The Adventures of Robinson Crusoe (serial); The Beautiful and Damned; The Call of Home; The Kentucky Derby; Human Hearts; Manslaughter. 1923 Don Quickshot of the Rio Grande; The Flame of Life; The Acquittal; Trifling with Honor; The Near Lady; The Day of Faith. 1924 Barbara Fritchie; Captain January; T.N.T.; The Air Hawk; Dark Stairways; The Fighting American. 1925 The Man without a Country; The Devil's Cargo; Counsel for the Defense; Peacock Feathers; Pampered Youth; The Overland Limited. 1926 The Arizona Sweepstakes; The Man in the Saddle. 1928 Laugh, Clown,

Laugh; God of Mankind; Midnight Madness. 1929 When Dreams Come True; On Trial; Noisy Neighbors; Shopworn Angel. 1930 Reno; Africa Speaks; The Right of Way. 1931 Three Who Loved; Public Defender. 1932 Mata Hari; Westward Passage. 1937 The Prisoner of Zenda.

KING, EUGENE W.

Died: Nov. 1950, Hollywood, Calif. Screen actor.

Appeared in: 1937 Bill Cracks Down. 1951 The Great Caruso.

KING, JACK

Born: 1883. Died: Oct. 8, 1943, New York, N.Y.(stroke). Screen, vaudeville actor, and song writer. Married to actress Rhea King who appeared with him in vaudeville in a song-dance-patter act.

Appeared in: 1930 Madam Satan; Harmonizing Songs (short).

KING, WILL

Born: 1886. Died: Jan. 22, 1958, San Francisco, Calif. Screen, stage, vaudeville actor, playwright, and stage producer. Married to actress Claire Starr who appeared in vaudeville with him.

Appeared in: 1929 The Fatal Forceps; Weak but Willing.

KINGDON, DOROTHY

Born: 1894. Died: Mar. 31, 1939, Los Angeles, Calif. Screen and stage actress.

Appeared in: 1925 The Iron Man; A Man of Iron; The Lost Chord.

KINGSFORD, ALISON

Born: 1899. Died: June 10, 1950, North Hollywood, Calif. Screen actress. Married to screen actor Walter Kingsford (dec. 1958).

KINGSFORD, WALTER

Born: Sept. 20, 1882, Redhill, England. Died: Feb. 7, 1958, North Hollywood, Calif.(heart attack). Screen and stage actor. Married to screen actress Alison Kingsford (dec. 1950).

Appeared in: 1934 Pursuit of Happiness; The President Vanishes. 1935 The Mystery of Edwin Drood; The White Cockatoo; Naughty Marietta; Shanghai; I Found Stella Parish; The Melody Lingers On; Frankie and Johnnie. 1936 The Story of Louis Pasteur; Hearts Divided; Stolen Holiday; Professional Soldier; The Invisible Ray; Little Lord Fauntleroy; Trouble for Two; Mad Holiday; Meet Nero Wolfe; The Music Goes 'Round. 1937 Maytime; Captains Courageous; My Dear Miss Aldrich; Bulldog Drummond Escapes; Double or Nothing; The Life of Emile Zola; The League of Frightened Men; The Devil Is Driving; I'll Take Romance; It Could Happen to You. 1938 Paradise for Three; A Yank at Oxford; The Toy Wife; Lord Jeff; There's Always a Woman; Algiers; The Young in Heart; Carefree; If I Were Young; Say It in French; The Lone Wolf in Paris; Young Dr. Kildare. 1939 Juarez; Smashing the Spy Ring; Calling Dr. Kildare; Man in the Iron Mask; Miracles for Sale; The Witness Vanishes; The Secret of Dr. Kildare; Dancing Co-ed. 1940 Star Dust; Lucky Partners; A Dispatch from Reuters; Kitty Foyle; Dr. Kildare Goes Home; Dr. Kildare's Crisis; Adventure in Diamonds; Dr. Kildare's Strange Case. 1941 The Devil and Miss Jones; The Lone Wolf Takes a Chance; The People vs. Dr. Kildare; Hit the Road; Ellery Queen and the Perfect Crime; Dr. Kildare's Wedding Day; Unholy Partners; Dr. Kildare's Victory; The Corsican Brothers. 1942 Fly by Night; Fingers at the Window; My Favorite Blonde; Calling Dr. Gillespie; Dr. Gillespie's New Assistant; The Loves of Edgar Allan Poe. 1943 Flight for Freedom; Forever and a Day; Bomber's Moon; Dr. Gillespie's Criminal Case; Hi Diddle Diddle; Mr. Lucky. 1944 Secrets of Scotland Yard; Three Men in White; The Hitler Gang; Mr. Skeffington; Ghost Catchers; Between Two Women. 1948 The Black Arrow; The Velvet Touch. 1949 Slattery's Hurricane. 1950 Experiment Alcatraz. 1951 My Forbidden Past; The Desert Fox; Tarzan's Peril; Two Dollar Bettor. 1952 The Brigand; Confidence Girl. 1953 Loose in London; Walking My Baby Back Home; The Pathfinder. 1956 The Search for Bridey Murphy; Around the World in 80 Days. 1958 Merry Andrew.

KINGSTON, THOMAS

Born: 1902. Died: Jan. 27, 1959, Hollywood, Calif.(heart attack). Screen and television stand-in.

KINGSTON, WINIFRED

Born: 1895. Died: Feb. 3, 1967, La Jolla, Calif. Screen actress. Married to screen actor Dustin Farnum (dec. 1929).

Appeared in: 1914 The Squaw Man; Son of Erin; Where the Trail Divides. 1916 David Garrick. 1917 The Scarlet Pimpernel. 1919 The Corsican Brothers. 1921 Beyond. 1922 The Trail of the Axe. 1929 The Virginian.

KINNELL, MURRAY
Born: 1889, London, England. Died: Aug. 11, 1954, Santa Barbara, Calif. Screen and stage actor.

Appeared in: 1930 Old English (film debut); The Princess and the Plumber. 1931 Reckless Living; The Secret Six; The Public Enemy; The Black Camel; The Guilty Generation; Honor of the Family; The Deceiver. 1932 Grand Hotel; Under Eighteen; The Beast of the City; The Man Who Played God; The Menace; The Mouthpiece; The Purchase Price; The Painted Woman; Secrets of the French Police. 1933 Zoo in Budapest; Voltaire; From Headquarters; I Loved a Woman; Ann Vickers; The Avenger. 1934 I Am Suzanne; Such Women Are Dangerous; The House of Rothschild; Affairs of a Gentleman; Hat, Coat and Glove; Murder in Trinidad; Charlie Chan's Courage; Charlie Chan in London; Anne of Green Gables. 1935 Charlie Chan in Paris; Cardinal Richelieu; Mad Love; Kind Lady; The Silver Streak; The Great Impersonation; The Last Days of Pompeii; The Three Musketeers; Fighting Youth. 1936 The Witness Chair; Mary of Scotland; The Big Game; Make Way for a Lady; One Rainy Afternoon; Lloyds of London; Fifteen Maiden Lane. 1937 Four Days' Wonder; Outcast; Think Fast, Mr. Moto; Damaged Lives.

KINSELLA, KATHLEEN (Kathleen Freeland)
Born: 1878, Liverpool, England. Died: Mar. 25, 1961, Washington. Screen and stage actress. Appeared in silents for Biograph.

KIPPEN, MANART
Died: Oct. 12, 1947, Claremore, Okla.(auto accident injuries). Screen, stage, and radio actor.

Appeared in: 1941 Flight from Destiny. 1942 The Wife Takes a Flyer; Jungle Siren. 1943 Mission to Moscow; The Song of Bernadette. 1944 Three Russian Girls. 1945 Mildred Pierce; Roughly Speaking; Flame of Barbary Coast.

KIRBY, DAVID D.
Born: 1880. Died: Apr. 4, 1954, Hollywood, Calif. Screen actor.

Appeared in: 1921 The Ranger and the Law. 1923 Danger Ahead; The Mailman; In the Palace of the King. 1924 Darwin Was Right; Spirit of the U.S.A.; The Man Who Came Back; Nellie, the Beautiful Cloak Model; The Dangerous Coward; Life's Greatest Game; The Man Who Played Square; Lightning Romance; The Mask of Lopez. 1925 Easy Money; Ridin' the Wind; Youth's Gamble; The Last Edition; Lawful Cheaters; The Snob Buster. 1926 Danger Quest; The King of the Turf; The Fighting Edge; The Dangerous Dude; The Night Owl. 1927 The Royal American; The Shield of Honor; The Sunset Derby; The Silent Avenger. 1928 Burning Bridges; The Upland Rider.

KIRK, FAY B. (Fay Baker)
Born: 1894. Died: Nov. 13, 1954, New York, N.Y.(heart attack). Screen, stage, and vaudeville actress.

Appeared in: 1946 Notorious. 1950 Chain Lightning. 1951 The House on Telegraph Hill.

KIRKLAND, HARDEE
Born: approx. 1864, England. Died: Feb. 20, 1929. Screen, stage, and vaudeville actor.

Appeared in: 1918 Sporting Life. 1919 The Peace of Roaring River. 1921 The Ace of Hearts; Ladies Must Live; From the Ground Up; A Perfect Crime; Roads of Destiny; The Lure of Jade. 1922 Sherlock Brown; Honor First; Youth to Youth; Without Compromise; They Like 'Em Rough; The Face Between; Very Truly Yours. 1923 Woman-Proof; Are You a Failure?; The Mailman; Quicksands; Hell's Hole; While Paris Sleeps. 1924 The Great Diamond Mystery. 1925 The Shadow on the Wall; Private Affairs; The Arizona Romeo.

KIRKLAND, MURIEL
Born: Aug. 19, 1903, Yonkers, N.Y. Died: Sept. 25, 1971, New York, N.Y.(emphysema and complications). Screen, stage, radio, and television actress. Married to screen actor Staats Cotsworth.

Appeared in: 1933 Fast Workers; Hold Your Man; Cocktail Hour; To the Last Man; Secret of the Blue Room. 1934 Nana; Little Man, What Now?; The White Parade.

KIRKWOOD, GERTRUDE. See Gertrude Robinson

KIRKWOOD, JACK
Born: 1895, Scotland. Died: Aug. 2, 1964, Las Vegas, Nev.(heart attack). Screen, stage, vaudeville, burlesque, radio, and television actor.

Appeared in: 1949 Chicken Every Sunday. 1950 Father Makes Good; Joe Palooka in Humphrey Takes a Chance; Never a Dull Moment; Fancy Pants.

KIRKWOOD, JAMES
Born: Feb. 22, 1883, Grand Rapids, Mich. Died: Aug. 21, 1963, Woodland Hills, Calif. Screen and stage actor. Divorced from screen actresses Gertrude Robinson (dec. 1962), Beatrice Power and Lila Lee (dec. 1973).

Appeared in: 1909 The Road to the Heart; The Message; Was Justice Served?; The Renunciation; The Seventh Day; A Convict's Sacrifice; The Indian Runner's Romance; The Better Way; Pippa Passes; The Death Disc; 1776, or the Hessian Renegades; Through the Breakers; A Corner in Wheat; The Redman's View; The Rocky Road; The Honor of His Family; The Last Deal; The Renovations; The Mended Lute; Comato the Sioux. 1910 The Final Settlement; A Victim of Jealousy; The Modern Prodigal; Winning Back His Love. 1914 The Eagle's Mate; Home Sweet Home. 1920 Luck of the Irish; Heart of a Fool; Man, Woman and Marriage; The Branding Iron. 1921 The Sin Flood; The Great Impersonation; Bob Hampton of Placer; A Wise Fool. 1922 The Man from Home; Ebb Tide; Pink Gods; Under Two Flags. 1923 The Eagle's Feather; Ponjola; Human Wreckage; You Are Guilty. 1924 Wandering Husbands; Another Man's Wife; Broken Barriers; Circe, the Enchantress; The Painted Flapper; Discontented Husbands; Gerald Cranston's Lady; Love's Whirlpool. 1925 Lover's Island; Secrets of the Night; The Top of the World; The Police Patrol. 1926 That Royle Girl; Butterflies in the Rain; The Reckless Lady; The Wise Guy. 1927 Million Dollar Mystery. 1928 Someone to Love. 1929 Hearts in Exile; Black Waters; The Time, the Place and the Girl. 1930 Devil's Holiday; Worldly Goods; The Spoilers. 1931 A Holy Terror; Over the Hill; Young Sinners. 1932 Cheaters at Play; Charlie Chan's Chance; Lena Rivers; Careless Lady; She Wanted a Millionaire; The Rainbow Trail; My Pal, the King. 1934 Hired Wife. 1941 The Lady from Cheyenne; No Hands on the Clock. 1947 Driftwood. 1948 The Untamed Breed. 1949 The Doolins of Oklahoma; Red Stallion in the Rockies. 1950 The Nevadan; Fancy Pants; Stage to Tucson. 1951 Man in the Saddle. 1952 I Dream of Jeanie. 1953 The Last Posse. 1954 Passion. 1956 The Search for Bridey Murphy.

KIRKWOOD-HACKETT, EVA
Born: 1877, England. Died: Feb. 8, 1968, Dublin, Ireland. Screen actress and singer.

KITZMILLER, JOHN
Born: 1913, Battlecreek, Mich. Died: Feb. 23, 1965, Rome, Italy (cirrhosis of the liver). Negro screen actor. Received Cannes Film Festival Best Acting Award in 1957 for Dolina Mira.

Appeared in: 1946 Paisa; To Live in Peace. 1948 Senza Pieta (Without Pity-U.S. 1950). 1951 Lieutenant Craig—Missing. 1957 Dolina Mira; The Naked Earth. 1960 The Island Sinner. 1963 Doctor No. 1965 Luci del Varieta (Variety Lights); Uncle Tom's Cabin. Other Italian films: Tombolo; Music Hall Lights.

KLEIN, AL
Born: 1885, New York, N.Y. Died: Sept. 5, 1951, Los Angeles, Calif.(cancer). Screen, stage, and vaudeville actor. Part of vaudeville team of "The Klein Bros."

Appeared in: 1928 Jest Moments (short). 1932 Opportunity Night (short); Gold Digging Gentlemen (short). 1933 Broadway Bad; One Year Later. 1934 That's Gratitude; Million Dollar Ransom; 365 Nights in Hollywood. 1949 Oh, You Beautiful Doll.

KLEINAU, WILLY A.
Born: Germany. Died: Oct. 23, 1957, Berlin-Nuernberg Hwy.; Germany (auto accident). Screen and stage actor.

Appeared in: 1958 Der Hauptmann von Koepenick (The Captain from Koepenick); Wie Ein Sturmwind (Tempestuous Love). Other German film: Mein Bruder Josua.

KLEIN-ROGGE, RUDOLF
Born: 1889, Germany. Died: 1955. Screen actor.

Appeared in: 1921 Der Mude Tod. 1922 Dr. Mabuse (U.S. 1927). 1924 Siegfried; Between Worlds. 1926 Metropolis. 1927 Peter the Pirate. 1928 Kriemhild's Revenge; Spione (Spies). 1929 Loves of Casanova; Forbidden Love. 1932 The Testament of Dr. Mabuse. 1935 Zwischen Himmel und Erde (Between Heaven and Earth). 1936 Die Frauen vom Tannhof; Grenzfeuer. 1937 Truxa. 1943 The Last Will of Dr. Mabuse.

KNABB, HARRY G.
Born: 1891. Died: Dec. 17, 1955, Cincinnati, Ohio (heart attack). Screen and stage actor. Appeared in silent films.

KNAGGS, SKELTON
Born: 1913. Died: Apr. 30, 1955, Los Angeles, Calif. Screen actor.

Appeared in: 1943 The Ghost Ship. 1945 None but the Lonely Heart; Island of the Dead; House of Dracula. 1946 Terror by Night; A Scandal in Paris; Dick Tracy vs. Cueball. 1947 Dick Tracy and Gruesome. 1949 Master Minds. 1952 Blackbeard the Pirate. 1953 Rogue's March. 1955 Moonfleet.

KNIGHT, PERCIVAL
Born: approx. 1873. Died: Nov. 27, 1923, Switzerland (tuberculosis). Screen and stage actor.

Appeared in: 1922 Sherlock Holmes.

KNOTT, CLARA
Born: 1882. Died: Nov. 11, 1926, Hollywood, Calif. Screen and stage actress.

Appeared in: 1920 Old Lady 31.

KNOX, HUGH (Hugo B. Koch)
Died: Sept. 9, 1926, Seattle, Wash. Screen, stage actor, film and stage director.

KOBS, ALFRED
Born: 1881. Died: Oct. 20, 1929, Los Angeles, Calif.(tuberculosis). Screen actor.

KOERBER, HILDE
Born: 1906, Germany. Died: June 1, 1969, Berlin, Germany. Screen and stage actress.

Appeared in: 1936 Maria Die Magd (Maria, the Maiden). 1938 The Kreutzer Sonata. 1948 Morituri. 1956 Hot Harvest. 1959 The Third Sex. 1961 The Girl of the Moors. Other German films: The Ruler; The Great King.

KOHLER, FRED, SR.
Born: Apr. 20, 1889, Kansas City, Mo. Died: Oct. 28, 1938, Los Angeles, Calif.(heart attack). Screen, stage, and vaudeville actor. Father of screen actor Fred Kohler, Jr.

Appeared in: 1911 Code of Honor (film debut). 1919 The Tiger's Trail (serial); Soldiers of Fortune. 1921 Cyclone Bliss; The Stampede; Thunder Island; A Daughter of the Law; Partners of the Tide. 1922 The Son of the Wolf; His Back against the Wall; Trimmed; The Scrapper; Without Compromise; Yellow Men and Gold. 1923 Anna Christie; Three Who Paid; The Eleventh Hour; The Flame of Life; Thru the Flames; Hell's Hole; The Red Warning; Shadows of the North. 1924 North of Hudson Bay; The Iron Horse; Abraham Lincoln; Fighting Fury. 1925 Dick Turpin; Winds of Chance; The Prairie Pirate; The Thundering Herd; Riders of the Purple Sage. 1926 The Country Beyond; The Ice Flood; Old Ironsides; Danger Quest. 1927 Shootin' Irons; The Way of All Flesh; The City Gone Wild; Underworld; The Blood Ship; The Gay Defender; Open Range; Loves of Carmen; The Devil's Masterpiece; The Rough Riders. 1928 The Spieler; Chinatown Charlie; The Vanishing Pioneer; The Dragnet; The Showdown; Forgotten Faces. 1929 Tide of Empire; Sal of Singapore; Say It with Songs; The Leatherneck; The Quitter; Broadway Babies; The Case of Lena Smith; The Dummy; River of Romance; Stairs of Sand; Thunderbolt. 1930 The Light of Western Stars; Roadhouse Nights; Hell's Heroes; Under a Texas Moon; The Steel Highway. 1931 The Lash; Fighting Caravans; Right of Way; Woman Hungry; Other Men's Women; Soldiers Plaything; Corsair; X Marks the Spot. 1932 Carnival Boat; Call Her Savage; Wild Horse Mesa; Rider of Death Valley; The Texas Bad Man. 1933 Constant Woman; The Fiddlin' Buckaroo; Under the Tonto Rim; The Deluge; Ship of Wanted Men; The Fourth Horseman. 1934 The Man from Hell; Last Round Up; Honor of the Range; Little Man; What Now? 1935 The Pecos Kid; Outlawed Guns; Border Brigand; Men of Action; The Trail's End; Toll of the Desert; Mississippi; Times Square Lady; West of the Pecos; Wilderness Mail; Goin' to Town; Hard Rock Harrigan; Stormy; The Frisco Kid; Horse Collars (short). 1936 Dangerous Intrigue; I Loved a Soldier; For the Service; Heart of the West; The Accusing Finger; Texas Ranger; The Plainsman. 1937 Arizona Mahoney; Daughter of Shanghai. 1938 Forbidden Valley; Gangs of New York; Painted Desert; Billy the Kid Returns; The Buccaneer; Blockade; Pure in Mind; Lawless Valley.

KOHLMAR, LEE
Born: 1878, Nuremberg, Germany. Died: May 15, 1946, Hollywood, Calif.(heart attack). Screen and stage actor.

Appeared in: 1920 The Flaming Disc (serial). 1921 High Heels; Orphans of the Storm. 1922 Breaking Home Ties. 1923 Potash

and Perlmutter. 1930 Caught Short; Children of Pleasure; The Thirteenth Prisoner (short); The Richest Man in the World; Sins of the Children; The Kibitzer; The Melody Man; Personality. 1932 Jewel Robbery; Scarlet Dawn; The Strange Case of Clara Deane; The Tenderfoot; Silver Dollar. 1933 She Done Him Wrong; I Love That Man; Forgotten; Roman Scandals; Son of Kong. 1934 When Strangers Meet; The House of Rothschild; Twentieth Century; Shoot the Works. 1935 One More Spring; The Girl Friend; McFadden's Flats; Love in Bloom; Four Hours to Kill; Here Comes Cookie; Break of Hearts; Death from a Distance. 1936 A Son Comes Home. 1941 The Big Store.

KOLB, CLARENCE
Born: 1875. Died: Nov. 25, 1964, Los Angeles, Calif.(stroke). Screen, vaudeville and television actor. Partner in vaudeville team of "Kolb and Dill" who appeared in film comedies in 1916 and 1917. In 1917 they appeared in Glory.

Appeared in: 1937 The Toast of New York; Portia on Trial; Wells Fargo. 1938 Gold Is Where You Find It; Merrily We Live; Give Me a Sailor; Carefree; The Law West of Tombstone. 1939 The Great Man Votes; It Could Happen to You; Honolulu; Society Lawyer; Five Little Peppers; I Was a Convict; Good Girls Go to Paris; Beware, Spooks!; Amazing Mr. Williams; Our Leading Citizen. 1940 The Five Little Peppers at Home; His Girl Friday; The Man Who Talked Too Much; No Time for Comedy; Tugboat Annie Sails Again; Michael Shayne, Private Detective. 1941 You're in the Army Now; Caught in the Draft; Nothing but the Truth; Bedtime Story; Night of January 16th; Hellzapoppin; Blossoms in the Dust. 1942 True to Life; The Falcon in Danger; The Ship's the Limit. 1944 Standing Room Only; Irish Eyes Are Smiling; Something for the Boys; Three Is a Family. 1945 Road to Alcatraz; What a Blonde. 1946 The Kid from Brooklyn; White Tie and Tails. 1947 The Pilgrim Lady; Fun on a Weekend; Christmas Eve; The Lost Honeymoon; The Fabulous Joe; Shadowed; The High Cost of Living. 1948 Blondie in the Dough. 1949 Impact; Adam's Rib. 1952 The Rose Bowl Story. 1956 Glory; Shake, Rattle and Rock. 1957 Man of a Thousand Faces.

KOLKER, HENRY
Born: 1874, Germany. Died: July 15, 1947, Los Angeles, Calif. (injured in fall). Screen, stage actor, stage, film director, and writer.

Appeared in: 1915 How Molly Made Good. 1916 Gloria's Romance. 1921 Disraeli; Bucking the Tiger; The Fighter; Who Am I? 1923 The Leopardess; The Snow Bride; The Purple Highway. 1925 Any Woman; Sally, Irene and Mary. 1926 Hell's 400; The Palace of Pleasure; Winning the Futurity; Wet Paint. 1927 Kiss in a Taxi; Rough House Rosie. 1928 Don't Marry; The Charge of the Gauchos; Midnight Rose; Soft Living. 1929 The Valiant; Pleasure Crazed; Coquette; Love, Live and Laugh. 1930 The Bad One; East Is West; Way of All Men; Good Intentions; DuBarry, Woman of Passion. 1931 Don't Bet on Women; The Spy; Indiscreet; I Like Your Nerve. 1932 Washington Masquerade; The Devil and the Deep; The First Year; The Crash; Faithless; Jewel Robbery; Invincible. 1933 Gigolettes of Paris; Baby Face; The Keyhole; The Narrow Corner; Bureau of Missing Persons; A Bedtime Story; Golden Harvest; The Power and the Glory; Blood Money; I Loved a Woman; Meet the Baron; Notorious but Nice; Love, Honor and Oh, Baby! 1934 Name the Woman; Madame DuBarry; Blind Date; Imitation of Life; Exciting Adventure; The Band Plays On; A Lost Lady; Love Time; Million Dollar Ransom; Lady by Choice; Sing Sing Nights; Massacre; Wonder Bar; Sisters under the Skin; The Hell Cat; Whom the Gods Destroy; Journal of a Crime; Success at Any Price; She Loves Me Not; The Girl from Missouri; Now and Forever. 1935 One New York Night; Only Eight Hours; The Black Room Mystery; Ladies Love Danger; Times Square Lady; Red Hot Tires; The Case of the Curious Bride; Shipmates Forever; Charlie Chan in Paris; Diamond Jim; Three Kids and a Queen; Society Doctor; Mad Love; Here Comes the Band; Red Salute; The Mystery Man; Honeymoon Limited; My Marriage; The Ghost Walks; The Florentine Dagger; Last Days of Pompeii; Frisco Waterfront. 1936 Collegiate; Bullets or Ballots; Romeo and Juliet; Sitting on the Moon; In His Steps; Great Guy; The Man Who Lived Twice; Theodora Goes Wild. 1937 They Wanted to Marry; Holiday; Under Cover of Night; Conquest; Thoroughbreds Don't Cry; Green Light; Once a Doctor; Without Warning; Maid of Salem; Let Them Live; The Devil Is Driving. 1938 The Invisible Menace; The Adventures of Marco Polo; The Cowboy and the Lady; Safety in Numbers; Too Hot to Handle. 1939 Let Us Live; Hidden Power; Parents on Trial; Should Husbands Work?; Main Street Lawyer; The Real Glory; Here I Am a Stranger; Union Pacific. 1940 Grand Ole Opry; Money and the Woman. 1941 The Parson of Panamint; The Man Who Lost Himself; The Great Swindle; A

Woman's Face; Sing for Your Supper; Las Vegas Nights. 1942 Reunion. 1943 Sarong Girl. 1944 Bluebeard. 1947 Monsieur Verdoux.

KOLOSSY, ERIKA
Born: Hungary. Died: Aug. 14, 1963, New York, N.Y.(leukemia). Screen, opera actress, and singer.

KOOY, PETE
Died: Apr. 20, 1963, Hollywood, Calif. Screen actor.

Appeared in: 1957 Death in Small Doses.

KOPPENS, EMILE. See Emile Keppens

KORFF, ARNOLD
Born: 1871. Died: June 2, 1944, New York, N.Y.(heart ailment). Screen, stage, and radio actor.

Appeared in: 1929 Dancing Vienna. 1930 Doughboys; Monsieur Le Fox; The Royal Family at Broadway; Men of the North; Olympia; The Jazz King. 1931 An American Tragedy; Ambassador Bill; The Unholy Garden. 1932 Scarlet Dawn; Evenings for Sale; Secrets of the French Police. 1934 Black Moon. 1935 Shanghai; All the Kings Horses; Wings in the Dark; Paris in Spring. 1936 Magnificent Obsession.

KORTNER, FRITZ
Born: May 12, 1892, Vienna, Austria. Died: July 22, 1970, Munich, Germany (leukemia). Screen actor, stage director, and writer.

Appeared in: 1926 Backstairs. 1927 Beethoven; Warning Shadows. 1928 Maria Stuart; Primanerliebe; Dame Care; The Hands of Orlac; Mata Hari; The Red Dancer; Pandora's Box. 1929 The Life of Beethoven; A Scandal in Paris; Three Loves; The Spy of Madame de Pompadour. 1930 Caught in Berlin's Underworld; The Last Night; Murderer Dimitri Karamasoff; Danton. 1931 The Dreyfus Case. 1932 Der Andere. 1934 Chu Chin Chow; Evensong. 1935 Abdul the Damned. 1936 The Crouching Beast. 1940 The Dreyfus Case (and 1931 version). 1943 The Strange Death of Adolf Hitler. 1945 The Hitler Gang. 1946 Somewhere in the Night; The Wife of Monte Cristo. 1947 The Brasher Doubloon; The High Window; The Razor's Edge. 1945 The Vicious Circle; Berlin Express. 1951 The Last Illusion. 1953 Ali Baba Nights.

KOSHETZ, NINA
Born: 1892, Russia. Died: May 14, 1965, Santa Ana, Calif. Screen actress and singer. Mother of screen actress Marina Koshetz.

Appeared in: 1938 Algiers. 1944 Our Hearts Were Young and Gay. 1946 The Chase. 1950 It's a Small World. 1952 Captain Pirate. 1956 Hot Blood.

KOSLOFF, THEODORE
Born: Russia. Died: Nov. 22, 1956, Los Angeles, Calif. Screen actor and ballet dancer.

Appeared in: 1917 The Woman God Forgot. 1920 Why Change Your Wife; The City of Masks. 1921 The Affairs of Anatol; Fool's Paradise; Forbidden Fruit. 1922 The Green Temptation; To Have and to Hold; The Dictator; The Lane That Had No Turning; The Law of the Lawless. 1924 Triumph; Don't Call It Love; Feet of Clay. 1925 Beggar on Horseback; The Golden Bed; New Lives for Old. 1926 The Volga Boatman. 1927 King of Kings; The Little Adventuress. 1928 Woman Wise. 1930 Sunny; Madam Satan.

KOVACS, ERNIE
Born: Jan. 23, 1919, Trenton, N.J. Died: Jan. 12, 1962, Beverly Hills, Calif.(auto accident). Screen, stage, and television actor. Married to screen actress Edie Adams.

Appeared in: 1957 Operation Mad Ball (film debut). 1958 Bell, Book and Candle; Showdown at Ulcer Gulch (a commercial short for Saturday Evening Post). 1959 It Happened to Jane. 1960 Our Man in Havana; Strangers When We Meet; Wake Me When It's Over; North to Alaska; Pepe. 1961 Sail a Crooked Ship; Cry for Happy; Five Golden Hours.

KOWAL, MITCHELL (aka MITCHELL KOWAL)
Born: 1916. Died: May 1, 1971, near Fuernitz, Austria (train wreck). Screen actor. Appeared in U.S., Italian and Polish films.

Appeared in: 1953 Violated. 1955 The Big Bluff; Abbott and Costello Meet the Mummy. 1959 John Paul Jones. 1963 55 Days at Peking. 1965 Jada Goscie Jada (Guests Are Coming-U.S. 1967). 1969 Francesco Bertazzoli; Investigator.

KRAMER, WRIGHT
Born: 1870. Died: Nov. 14, 1941, Hollywood, Calif. Screen, stage, and vaudeville actor.

Appeared in: 1938 The Gladiator; Professor Beware. 1939 Mr. Smith Goes to Washington; Good Girls Go to Paris; It Could Happen to You. 1940 Anne of Windy Poplars; Before I Hang; Dark Streets of Cairo.

KRAUSS, CHARLES
Born: France. Died: Oct. 1926. Screen actor and film producer.

KRAUSS, WERNER
Born: 1884, Gestungshausen, Germany. Died: Oct. 20, 1959, Vienna, Austria. Screen actor.

Appeared in: 1919 The Cabinet of Dr. Caligari. 1921 All for a Woman; Shattered. 1923 Othello. 1924 Waxworks. 1925 The Student of Prague. 1926 Secrets of a Soul; The Three Way Works; Shattered (and 1921 version). 1927 Streets of Sorrow; Tartuffe. 1928 Jealousy; Unwelcome Children; The Man Who Cheated Life; Midsummer Night's Dream; Decameron Nights. 1929 Three Wax Men; The Jolly Peasant; Nana; Royal Scandal; The Treasure; Looping the Loop; Fighting the White Slave Traffic. 1932 Mensch Ohne Namen (The Man without a Name); Yorck. 1934 Crown of Thorns. 1937 Vienna Burgtheater. 1939 Robert Koch. 1940 Jew Suess (German propaganda film).

KRIEGER, LEE
Born: 1919. Died: Dec. 22, 1967, Van Nuys, Calif. Screen, stage, and television actor.

Appeared in: 1961 Bachelor in Paradise. 1962 Period of Adjustment; Convicts Four; The Horizontal Lieutenant. 1967 The Reluctant Astronaut.

KROHNER, SARAH
Born: 1883. Died: June 9, 1959, Brooklyn, N.Y. Screen, stage, and radio actress. Appeared in Yiddish films.

Appeared in: 1939 Molly. 1951 Mirele Efros.

KRUEGER, BUM (Willy Krueger)
Born: 1906, Germany. Died: Mar. 15, 1971, West Berlin, Germany (heart attack). Screen, stage, and television actor.

Appeared in: 1959 The Eighth Day of the Week. Other German films: Film without Title; The Gentleman from the Other Star; The Devil's General.

KRUGER, ALMA
Born: 1868, Pittsburgh, Pa. Died: Apr. 5, 1960, Seattle, Wash. Screen, stage, and radio actress. Her best known role in films was as Mollie Bird, head nurse, in Metro's "Dr. Kildare" series.

Appeared in: 1936 These Three; Craig's Wife; Love Letters of a Star. 1937 Breezing Home; The Mighty Treve; The Man in Blue; One Hundred Men and a Girl; Vogues of 1938. 1938 The Toy Wife; Marie Antoinette; The Great Waltz; Mother Carey's Chickens; Tarnished Angel; Four's a Crowd. 1939 The Secret of Dr. Kildare; Made for Each Other; Balalaika; Calling Dr. Kildare. 1940 His Girl Friday; Dr. Kildare's Strange Case; Dr. Kildare's Crisis; Dr. Kildare Goes Home; Anne of Windy Poplars; You'll Find Out. 1941 Blonde Inspiration; Trial of Mary Dugan; Puddin' Head; The People vs. Dr. Kildare; Dr. Kildare's Wedding Day; Dr. Kildare's Victory. 1942 Saboteur; Calling Dr. Gillespie; Dr. Gillespie's New Assistant; That Other Woman. 1943 Dr. Gillespie's Criminal Case. 1944 Three Men in White; Our Hearts Were Young and Gay; Babes on Swing Street. 1945 The Crime Doctor's Warning; A Royal Scandal; Between Two Women. 1946 Do You Love Me?. 1947 Forever Amber; Dark Delusion; Fun On a Weekend.

KRUGER, FRED H.
Born: 1913. Died: Dec. 5, 1961, Hollywood, Calif.(cerebral hemorrhage). Screen and television actor.

Appeared in: 1958 Girls on the Loose.

KRUGER, HAROLD "STUBBY"
Born: 1897, Honolulu, Hawaii. Died: Oct. 7, 1965, Hollywood, Calif.(heart attack). Screen stuntman and swimmer. Doubled for Douglas Fairbanks in the Black Pirate (1926) and Spencer Tracy in The Old Man and the Sea (1958).

Appeared in: Paramount shorts, Grantland Rice Sportlight for Pathe; 1926 Beloved Rogue. 1955 Mister Roberts.

KRUMSCHMIDT, EBERHARD
Born: 1905. Died: June 3, 1956, New York, N.Y. Screen, stage, radio, television actor, and stage director.

Appeared in: 1946 Notorious.

KRUPP, VERA (Vera Hosenfeldt)
Born: 1910, Germany. Died: Oct. 16, 1967, Los Angeles, Calif. German screen actress.

KULKAVICH, BOMBER. See Henry Kulky

KULKY, HENRY "HANK"
Born: Aug. 11, 1911, Hastings-on-the-Hudson, N.Y. Died: Feb. 12, 1965, Oceanside, Calif.(heart attack). Screen, television actor, and professional wrestler known as "Bomber Kulkavich."

Appeared in: 1947 A Likely Story. 1948 Call Northside 777. 1949 Tarzan's Magic Fountain; Bandits of El Dorado. 1950 Wabash Avenue; South Sea Sinner; Bodyhold; Jiggs and Maggie Out West. 1951 The Guy Who Came Back; The Love Nest; The Kid from Amarillo; Fixed Bayonets. 1952 The World in His Arms; Gobs and Gals; No Holds Barred; Target Hong Kong; My Wife's Best Friend; Red Skies of Montana; What Price Glory. 1953 The Robe; The 5,000 Fingers of Dr. T.; Down Among the Sheltering Palms; The Glory Brigade; The Charge at Feather River. 1954 A Star Is Born; Fireman Save My Child; Yukon Vengeance; Hell and High Water; Tobor the Great; The Steel Cage. 1955 Prince of Players; New York Confidential; Abbott and Costello Meet the Keystone Kops; Illegal. 1957 Sierra Stranger. 1959 Up Periscope; The Gunfight at Dodge City. 1960 Guns of the Timberland. 1964 A Global Affair.

KUN, MAGDA
Born: 1911, Hungary. Died: Nov. 7, 1945, London, England. Screen and stage actress.

Appeared in: 1933 Filleres Gyoers. 1934 Und Es Leuchtet die Puszta. 1935 Dance Band. 1938 Busuini Nem Jo (Don't Worry); Majd a Zsuzsi.

KUNDE, AL
Born: 1888. Died: Aug. 10, 1952, Los Angeles, Calif.(cancer). Screen actor. Formerly a boxer known as "Al Krieger."

KUNDE, ANNE
Born: 1896. Died: June 14, 1960, Hollywood, Calif. Screen actress.

Appeared in: 1959 Li'l Abner. 1961 One-Eye Jacks.

KUNKEL, GEORGE
Born: 1867. Died: Nov. 8, 1937, Hollywood, Calif.(heart attack). Screen actor.

Appeared in: 1919 Leave It to Susan. 1921 An Unwilling Hero; Where Men Are Men.

KUPCINET, KARYN
Born: Mar. 6, 1941. Died: Nov. 28, 1963, West Los Angeles, Calif. (murdered). Screen, stage, and television actress.

Appeared in: 1961 The Ladies' Man.

KUZNETZOFF, ADIA
Born: 1890, Russia. Died: Aug. 10, 1954, Port Washington, N.Y. Screen, television actor, and gypsy singer.

Appeared in: 1930 A Russian Rhapsody. 1935 a Universal short. 1937 Madame X. 1938 Swiss Miss. 1939 Devil's Island. 1941 Second Chorus; The Wolf Man. 1942 My Sister Eileen. 1944 Lost in a Harem.

LACKAYE, WILTON
Born: 1862, London County, Va. Died: Aug. 22, 1932, New York (heart attack). Screen and stage actor. Appeared in "World" productions in 1915.

Appeared in: 1921 God's Crucible. 1922 What's Wrong with Women?. 1924 For Woman's Favor; The Lone Wolf. 1925 The Sky Raider.

LACKTEEN, FRANK
Born: Aug. 29, 1894, Kubber-Ilias, Asia Minor. Died: July 8, 1968, Woodland Hills, Calif.(cerebral and respiratory illness). Screen actor.

Appeared in: 1916 Less Than Dust; The Yellow Menace (serial). 1921 The Avenging Arrow (serial). 1922 White Eagle (serial). 1924 The Virgin; The Fortieth Door (serial). 1925 The Pony Ex-

press, plus the following serials: The Green Archer; Idaho; Sunken Silver. 1926 Desert Gold; The Last Frontier; The Unknown Cavalier; House without a Key (serial). 1927 Melting Millions (serial); Hawk of the Hills (serial). 1928 The Warning; Court Martial; Prowlers of the Sea; Mark of the Frog (serial). 1929 The Black Book (serial); The Fire Detective (serial); Hawk of the Hills (feature of 1927 serial). 1931 Law of the Tong; Hell's Valley, Cracked Nuts. 1932 Texas Pioneer; Jungle Mystery (serial). 1933 Nagana; Rustler's Roundup; Tarzan the Fearless (serial and feature film). 1934 The Perils of Pauline (serial). 1935 Escape from Devil's Island. 1936 Under Two Flags; Mummy's Boys; Isle of Fury. 1937 I Cover the War; The Mysterious Pilot (serial). 1939 The Girl and the Gambler; Juarez; The Kansas Terrors. 1940 Stagecoach War; The Girl from Havana; Moon over Burma. 1941 The Sea Wolf; South of Tahiti; Jungle Girl (serial). 1942 Bombs over Burma. 1943 Chetniks; Frontier Badmen. 1944 Moonlight and Cactus. 1945 Frontier Gal. 1946 A Bird in the Hand (short). 1947 Oregon Trail Scouts; Singin' in the Corn. 1948 Man-Eater of Kumoan. 1949 The Cowboy and the Indians; Amazon Quest; Daughter of the Jungle; Son of the Badman; The Mysterious Desperado; Malice in the Palace (short). 1951 Flaming Feather. 1953 King of the Khyber Rifles; Northern Patrol. 1954 The Bounty Killer. 1955 Devil Goddess; Of Cash and Hash (short). 1956 Flesh and the Spur. 1959 The Atomic Submarine. 1960 Three Came to Kill. 1962 The Underwater City. 1965 Requiem of a Gunfighter.

LADD, ALAN
Born: Sept. 3, 1913, Hot Springs, Ark. Died: Jan. 29, 1964, Palm Springs, Calif.(accidental death). Screen, television, and radio actor. Married to former screen actress Sue Carol and father of screen actor David Ladd.

Appeared in: 1932 Once in a Lifetime. 1936 Pigskin Parade. 1937 Last Train from Madrid; Souls at Sea; Hold 'Em Navy. 1938 Born to the West; The Goldwyn Follies; Freshman Year; Come on Leathernecks. 1939 Green Hornet; Rulers of the Sea; Beasts of Berlin. 1940 Light of Western Stars; In Old Missouri; Meet the Missus; Captain Caution; Her First Romance; Gangs of Chicago; Howards of Virginia; Those Were the Days; Wildcat Bus. 1941 The Reluctant Dragon; Paper Bullets; Citizen Kane; Great Guns; Cadet Girl; Petticoat Politics; The Black Cat. 1942 This Gun for Hire; Joan of Paris; The Glass Key; Star Spangled Rhythm; Lucky Jordan. 1943 China; Hollywood Uniform (short). 1944 And Now Tomorrow; Skirmish on the Home Front (short); Salty O'Rourke. 1945 Duffy's Tavern; Hollywood Victory; Caravan. 1946 Two Years before the Mast; Blue Dahlia; O.S.S. 1947 Wild Harvest; Variety Girl; Calcutta; My Favorite Brunette. 1948 Saigon; Beyond Glory; Whispering Smith. 1949 Great Gatsby; Chicago Deadline; Eyes of Hollywood (short). 1950 Captain Carey, U.S.A. Branded; Quantrell's Raiders. 1951 Appointment with Danger; Red Mountain. 1952 The Iron Mistress. 1953 Shane; Thunder in the East; Botany Bay; Desert Legion. 1954 Hell below Zero; Paratrooper; Saskatchewan; The Black Knight; Drum Beat; The Red Beret. 1955 The McConnell Story; The Long Gray Line; Hell on Frisco Bay. 1956 Santiago. 1957 The Big Land; Boy on a Dolphin. 1958 The Deep Six; The Proud Rebel; The Badlanders. 1959 The Man in the Net. 1960 Guns of the Timberland; One Foot in Hell. 1961 Duel of Champions; Orazio. 1963 13 West Street. 1964 The Carpetbaggers.

LADMIRAL, NICOLE
Born: 1931, France. Died: Apr. 1958, Paris, France (fell or jumped under subway train?). Screen and stage actress.

Appeared in: 1954 The Diary of a Country Priest.

LAEMMLE, CARL, SR.
Born: Jan. 17, 1867, Laupheim, Germany. Died: Sept. 24, 1939, Beverly Hills, Calif.(heart attack). Film producer and screen actor.

Appeared in: 1929 Show Boat (gave a short speech in an 18-minute prologue.

LAFAYETTE, RUBY
Born: 1845. Died: Apr. 3, 1935, Bell, Calif. Screen and stage actress. Married to stage actor John Curran (dec. 1918). Entered films approx. 1917.

Appeared in: 1918 My Mother. 1919 The Miracle Man; Toby's Bow. 1922 Borderland; Catch My Smoke; The Power of a Lie. 1923 The Day of Faith; Hollywood. 1924 Idle Tongues; The Phantom Horseman. 1925 The Coming of Amos; The Wedding Song; Tomorrow's Love. 1926 Butterflies in the Rain. 1928 Mother O' Mine; Marriage By Contract. 1930 Not So Dumb.

LA FLEUR, JOY
Born: 1914, Canada. Died: Nov. 6, 1957, Los Angeles, Calif. Screen, stage, radio, and television actress.

Appeared in: 1948 Whispering City. 1956 D-Day the Sixth of June.

LAHR, BERT (Irving Lahrheim)
Born: Aug. 13, 1895, New York, N.Y. Died: Dec. 4, 1967, New York, N.Y.(internal hemorrhage). Screen, stage, television, vaudeville, and burlesque actor.

Appeared in: 1929 Faint Heart (short). 1931 Flying High. 1933 Mr. Broadway. 1934 Hizzoner (short). 1936 Gold Bricks (short). 1937 Merry-Go-Round of 1938; Love and Hisses. 1938 Josette; Just around the Corner. 1939 Wizard of Oz; Zaza. 1940 DuBarry Was a Lady. 1942 Sing Your Worries Away; Ship Ahoy. 1944 Meet the People. 1949 Always Leave Them Laughing. 1951 Mr. Universe. 1954 Rose Marie. 1955 The Second Greatest Sex. 1962 Ten Girls Ago. 1963 The Sound of Laughter (documentary). 1964 Big Parade of Comedy (documentary). 1965 The Fantasticks. 1968 The Night They Raided Minskey's.

LAHTINEN, WARNER H. "DUKE"
Born: 1910. Died: Dec. 12, 1968, Minneapolis, Minn. Screen and stage actor.

LAIDLAW, ETHAN
Born: Nov. 25, 1899, Butte, Mont. Died: May 25, 1963. Screen actor. Entered films in 1923.

Appeared in: 1925 The Wyoming Wildcat; No Man's Law; Crack O'Dawn; Makers of Men. 1926 Born to Battle; Is That Nice?; Racing Romance; Out of the West; Dangerous Traffic; The Masquerade Bandit; Wild to Go. 1927 The Sonora Kid; Wolf's Clothing; When Danger Calls; Breed of Courage; The Silent Rider; Thunderbolt's Tracks. 1928 The Big Killing; Bitter Sweets; Rough Ridin' Red; Danger Patrol; The Riding Renegade. 1929 Big Diamond Robbery; Laughing at Death; The Little Savage; Outlawed; Bride of the Desert. 1930 Pardon My Gun. 1931 A Melon Drama (short); Monkey Business. 1935 Powdersmoke Range. 1936 Silly Billies; Yellow Dust; Special Investigator; Two in Revolt; The Sea Spoilers; Mummy's Boys. 1937 Goofs and Saddler (short). 1938 Rhythm of the Saddle; I'm from the City; Border G-Man. 1939 Home on the Prairie; Night Riders; Cowboys from Texas; Western Caravans; Three Texas Steers. 1940 The Marines Fly High; Son of Roaring Dan; The Tulsa Kid; Wagon Train; Stage to Chino; Law and Order. 1941 Law of the Range; The Lone Star Vigilantes. 1942 Stagecoach Express. 1943 Riding through Nevada; Border Buckaroos; The Desperadoes; Fugitive from Sonora. 1944 Marshal of Gunsmoke; Oklahoma Raiders. 1945 Lawless Empire; Blazing the Western Trail. 1947 Rustler's Round-up; Singin' in the Corn. 1948 Six-Gun Law; Buckaroo from Powder River; Joan of Arc. 1950 The Great Missouri Raid; Traveling Saleswoman. 1951 Flaming Feather. 1952 Montana Territory. 1953 Powder River.

LAIR, GRACE (Grace Gaylor)
Died: Jan. 5, 1955, Cleveland, Ohio. Screen, stage actress, and singer. Was the original "Coca-Cola Girl" in Coca Cola's advertising.

LAKE, ALICE
Born: Brooklyn, N.Y. Died: Nov. 15, 1967, Paradise, Calif.(heart attack). Screen actress.

Appeared in: 1912 Her Picture Idol. 1916 The Moonshiners; The Waiter's Ball; A Creampuff Romance (sometimes referred to as His Alibi). 1917 Her Nature Dance; The Butcher Boy; His Wedding Night; Oh, Doctor; Come Through. 1918 Out West; Coney Island; Goodnight, Nurse; Moonshine; The Cook. 1919 A Desert Hero; Backstage; A Country Hero; The Garage. 1920 Shore Acres; Should a Woman Talk?. 1921 Body and Soul; The Greater Claim; Uncharted Seas; A Hole in the Wall; Over the Wire; The Infamous Miss Revell. 1922 The Golden Gift; Hate; Kisses; Environment; I Am the Law; More to Be Pitied Than Scorned. 1923 The Spider and the Rose; Red Lights; Broken Hearts of Broadway; The Unknown Purple; The Marriage Market; Modern Matrimony; Souls for Sale; Nobody's Bride. 1924 The Dancing Cheat; The Law and the Lady; The Virgin. 1925 Broken Homes; The Hurricane; The Wives of the Prophet. 1927 The Angel of Broadway; Roaring Fires; The Haunted Ship; Spider Webs. 1928 Obey Your Husband; Women Men Like; Runaway Girls. 1929 Untamed Justice; Circumstantial Evidence; Twin Beds; Frozen Justice. 1930 Dining Out (short); I'll Fix It (short); Young Desire. 1931 Wicked. 1933 Skyward. 1934 Wharf Angel; Glamour.

LAKE, FRANK
Born: 1849. Died: Apr. 19, 1936, Los Angeles, Calif. Screen actor.

Appeared in: 1930 The Rogue Song.

LAKE, HARRY
Born: 1885. Died: Mar. 4, 1947, Chicago, Ill. Screen actor.

LAKE, JOHN (John W. Laycock)
Born: 1904, Leesburg, Va. Died: June 28, 1960, Saranac Lake, N.Y. (tuberculosis). Screen and radio actor.

LA MARR, BARBARA (Reatha Watson)
Born: July 28, 1896. Died: Jan. 30, 1925, Altadena, Calif. (over dieting). Screen, stage actress, and cabaret artist.

Appeared in: 1921 Desperate Trails; The Nut; Cinderella of the Hills; The Three Musketeers. 1922 Trifling Women; The Prisoner of Zenda; Quincy Adams Sawyer; Arabian Love; Domestic Relations. 1923 The Eternal Struggle; Strangers of the Night; The Eternal City; The Brass Bottle; The Hero; St. Elmo; Mary of the Movies; Poor Men's Wives. 1924 The Name Is Woman; The White Moth; The Shooting of Dan McGrew; My Husband's Wives; Sandra; The White Monkey.

LAMBERT, CLARA
Died: 1921. Screen actress. Married to screen actor James L. Daly (dec. 1933).

LAMBERTI, PROFESSOR (Michael Lamberti)
Died: Mar. 13, 1950, Hollywood, Calif. Screen, stage, and vaudeville actor.

Appeared in: 1945 Tonight and Every Night. 1946 The Gay Intruders. 1947 Linda Be Good.

LA MONT, HARRY (Alfred Gilbert)
Born: June 17, 1887, New York, N.Y. Died: May 8, 1957, Venice, Calif. Screen, stage, vaudeville, and radio actor.

Appeared in: 1915 A Tale of Two Cities (film debut). 1920 Fazil. 1922 Blood and Sand; Peaceful Peters. 1923 Robin Hood, Jr. 1928 Two Lovers; Mysterious Lady. 1942 The Black Swan; China Girl. 1947 San Antonio.

LAMONT, JACK (Jack Capitola)
Born: 1893. Died: Feb. 28, 1956, Cleveland, Ohio (heart attack). Screen, stage, and burlesque actor. Appeared in silents and was in several "Keystone Kop" comedies.

LAMY, DOUGLAS N. See John Mitchell

LANCASTER, ANN
Born: 1920. Died: Oct. 31, 1970, London, England. Screen, stage, television, and radio actress.

Appeared in: 1954 Angels One Five. 1967 Three Bites of the Apple; Fathom.

LANDAU, DAVID
Born: 1878. Died: Sept. 20, 1935, Hollywood, Calif. Screen and stage actor.

Appeared in: 1931 Street Scene; Arrowsmith. 1932 I Am a Fugitive from a Chain Gang; Union Depot; Taxi; This Reckless Age; 70,000 Witnesses; Under Cover Man; Polly of the Circus; It's Tough to Be Famous; Amateur Daddy; Roadhouse Murder; The Purchase Price; Horse Feathers; Air Mail; False Faces; Under Cover Man; Lawyer Man. 1933 Heritage of the Desert; She Done Him Wrong; The Crime of the Century; One Man's Journey; Gabriel over the White House; The Nuisance; No Marriage Ties; They Just Had to Get Married. 1934 As the Earth Turns; Judge Priest; Bedside; Wharf Angel; The Man with Two Faces; Death on the Diamond.

LANDI, ELISSA
Born: Dec. 6, 1904, Venice, Italy. Died: Oct. 31, 1948, Kingston, N.Y.(cancer). Screen, stage, radio actress, and novelist.

Appeared in: 1926 London. 1928 Bolibar. 1929 The Betrayal; Underground. 1930 Knowing Men. 1931 Parisian; The Price of Things; The Inseparables; Sin; Children of Chance; Body and Soul; Always Goodbye; Wicked; The Yellow Tickets. 1932 The Devil's Lottery; The Woman in Room 13; A Passport to Hell; The Sign of the Cross. 1933 The Masquerader; The Warrior's Husband; I Loved You Wednesday. 1934 By Candlelight; Man of Two Worlds; The Count of Monte Cristo; The Great Flirtation; Sisters under the Skin. 1935 Enter Madam. 1936 The Amateur Gentleman;

Mad Holiday; After the Thin Man. 1937 The Thirteenth Chair. 1943 Corregidor. 1944 The Sign of the Cross (revised version of 1932 film).

LANDIS, CAROLE (Frances Ridste)
Born: Jan. 1, 1919, Fairchild, Wis. Died: July 5, 1948, Brentwood Heights, Calif.(suicide). Screen and stage actress. The screen's original "sweater girl."

Appeared in: 1937 A Day at the Races; The Emperor's Candlesticks; Broadway Melody of 1938; Varsity Show; Adventurous Blonde; Hollywood Hotel; A Star is Born. 1938 Golddiggers in Paris; Four's a Crowd; Blondes at Work; Boy Meets Girl; Men are Such Fools; Over the Wall; When Were You Born?. 1939 Daredevil's of the Red Circle (serial); Three Texas Steers; Cowboys from Texas. 1940 Mystery Sea Raider; One Million, B.C.; Turnabout. 1941 I Wake up Screaming; Topper Returns; Dance Hall; Hot Spot; Cadet Girl; Road Show; Moon over Miami. 1942 A Gentleman at Heart; The Power's Girl; My Gal Sal; Orchestra Wives; It Happened in Flatbush; Manila Calling. 1943 Screen Snapshot #2 (short); Wintertime. 1944 Secret Command; Four Jills in a Jeep. 1945 Having a Wonderful Crime; Behind Green Lights. 1946 It Shouldn't Happen to a Dog; A Scandal in Paris. 1947 Out of the Blue. 1948 The Brass Monkey; Noose (aka The Silk Noose—U.S. 1950). 1951 The Lucky Mascot.

LANDRETH, GERTRUDE GRIFFITH
Born: 1897, New York, N.Y. Died: Nov. 25, 1969, Palo Alto, Calif. Screen and vaudeville actress. Appeared in silent films and was in several "Keystone" comedies. She founded the Hollywood Studio Club, a home for aspiring actresses.

LANE, DOROTHY
Born: 1905. Died: Oct. 7, 1923, New York, N.Y.(heart disease). Screen actress and dancer.

LANE, HARRY
Born: 1910. Died: July 1960, London, England. Screen, stage, and television actor.

Appeared in: 1950 Appointment with Crime. 1951 Old Mother Riley's Jungle Treasure; Operation X. 1954 Fire over Africa. 1960 Too Hot to Handle (aka Playgirl after Dark—U.S. 1962).

LANE, LUPINO "NIPPER" (Henry George Lupino)
Born: June 16, 1892, London, England. Died: Nov. 10, 1959, London, England. Screen, stage actor, playwright, and director. Brother of screen actor Wallace Lupino (dec. 1961).

Appeared in: 1922 The Broker; The Reporter. 1923 A Friendly Husband. 1924 Isn't Life Wonderful?. 1925 The Fighting Dude (short). 1927 Monty of the Mounted. 1929 Show of Shows; The Love Parade; "Educational—Lupino Lane" comedies among them being: Ship Mates; Buying a Gun; Fireproof; Purely Circumstantial; Only Me; Evolution of the Dance. 1930 Bride of the Regiment; Golden Dawn; Yellow Mask; The Love Parade. 1931-32 appeared in British films. 1935 The Deputy Drummer. 1939 Me and My Gal (aka The Lambeth Walk).

LANE, PAT
Born: 1900. Died: July 4, 1953, Beverly Hills, Calif.(heart attack). Screen and vaudeville actress.

LANE, WALLACE. See Wallace Lupino

LANG, HAROLD
Born: 1923, England. Died: Nov. 16, 1970, Cairo, Egypt. Screen, stage, and television actor.

Appeared in: 1952 Cloudburst; Franchise Affair; Wings of Danger; The Spider and the Fly. 1953 The Long Memory; Terror Street. 1954 The Saint's Girl Friday; Blackout. 1956 The Creeping Unknown. 1957 Men of Sherwood Forest. 1958 The Flesh Is Weak. 1961 It's a Wonderful World. 1962 Paranoiac (U.S. 1963).

LANG, HARRY
Born: 1895. Died: Aug. 3, 1953, Hollywood, Calif.(heart attack). Screen, radio, television, and vaudeville actor. Part of vaudeville teams "Lang & Haley" and "Lang & O'Neill."

Appeared in: 1929 Who's Who (short). 1951 Soldiers Three.

LANG, HOWARD
Born: 1876. Died: Jan. 26, 1941, Hollywood, Calif. Screen and stage actor.

Appeared in: 1922 Peacock Alley. 1933 This Day and Age; Cradle Song. 1934 The Witching Hour; Born to Be Bad. 1935 Bar 20 Rides Again; Mystery Woman. 1936 Call of the Prairie. 1937 Navy Spy; Here's Flash Casey; The Prisoner of Zenda.

LANG, MATHESON
Born: May 15, 1879, Montreal, Canada. Died: Apr. 11, 1948, Bridgeton, Barbados. Screen, stage actor, and playwright. Entered films in 1916.

Appeared in: 1921 Merchant of Venice; The Carnival; Mr. Wu. 1922 Dick Turpin's Ride to York. 1923 The Wandering Jew. 1925 Beyond the Veil; The Chinese Bungalow. 1926 Island of Despair. 1929 The Triumph of the Scarlet Pimpernel; The Scarlet Devil. 1930 The Chinese Bungalow (and 1925 version). 1931 The Carnival (and 1921 version). 1934 Channel Crossing; Little Friend; The Great Defender. 1935 Drake of England; Elizabeth of England. 1936 The Cardinal; other British films: White Slippers; The Kings Highway; The Guns of Loos; The Blue Peter; The Passing of the Third Floor Back; The School for Scandal; The Bad Man; The Purple Mask; The Ware Case.

LANG, PETER
Born: 1867. Died: Aug. 20, 1932, New York (heart attack). Screen and stage actor.

Appeared in: 1913 Peter's Pledge (serial). 1924 Dangerous Money.

LANGDON, HARRY
Born: June 15, 1884, Council Bluffs, Iowa. Died: Dec. 22, 1944, Los Angeles, Calif.(cerebral hemorrhage). Screen, stage, vaudeville actor, film director, producer, and screenwriter.

Appeared in: 1918 The Mastery Mystery. 1924 Picking Peaches; plus the following shorts: The Luck O' the Foolish; Smile Please; Feet of Mud; All Night Long; Shanghaied Lovers; Flickering Youth; The Cat's Meow; His New Mamma; The First Hundred Years; The Hanson Cabman. 1925 the following shorts: The Sea Squawk; Boobs in the Woods; His Marriage Vow; Plain Clothes; Remember When?; Lucky Stars; Horace Greely, Jr.; There He Goes; The White Wing's Bride. 1926 Ella Cinders; The Strong Man; Tramp Tramp Tramp; plus the following shorts: Saturday Afternoon; Fiddlesticks; The Soldier Man. 1927 Long Pants; Three's a Crowd; His First Flame. 1928 The Chaser; Heart Trouble; There He Goes. 1929 the following shorts: Hotter Than Hot; The Fighting Parson; The Sky Boy; Skirt Shy. 1930 See America Thirst; The Head Guy; The Shrimp; The King; The Big Kick. 1931 Soldier's Plaything. 1932-33 appeared in "Mermaid" comedies, among them being: Tired Feet; The Big Flash; The Hitch Hiker. 1933 My Weakness; Hallelujah, I'm a Bum, plus the following shorts: Tied for Life; Hooks and Jabs; Marriage Humor; The Stage Hand; Leave It to Dad; On Ice; Pop's Pal; A Roaming Romeo. 1934 Shivers; Trimmed in Furs; Goodness! a Ghost; Circus Hoodoo; No Sleep on the Deep; Petting Preferred. 1935 Atlantic Adventure; plus the following shorts: His Bridal Sweet; The Leather Necker; His Marriage Mixup; I Don't Remember, and Columbia shorts. 1938 Block Heads; There Goes My Heart; He Loved an Actress; plus the following shorts: A Doggone Mixup; Sue My Lawyer. 1939 Zenobia; Elephants Never Forget. 1940 A Chump at Oxford; Saps at Sea; Cold Turkey; Misbehaving Husbands. 1941 Road Show; All-American Coed; Double Trouble. 1942 House of Errors, plus the following shorts: What Makes Lizzie Dizzy?; Tire Man, Spare My Tires; Carry Harry; Piano Mooner. 1943 Spotlights Scandals; plus the following shorts: A Blitz on the Fritz; Here Comes Mr. Zerk. 1944 the following shorts: Hot Rhythm; To Heir Is Human; Defective Detectives; Block Busters; Money Dope. 1945 Swingin' on a Rainbow, plus the following shorts: Snooper Service; Pistol Packin' Nitwits. 1961 Days of Thrills and Laughter (documentary). 1963 Thirty Years of Fun (documentary); The Sound of Laughter (documentary).

LANGDON, LILLIAN
Born: New Jersey. Died: Feb. 8, 1943, Santa Monica, Calif. Screen and stage actress.

Appeared in: 1921 The Swamp; What's a Wife Worth?; The Mother Heart. 1922 Another Man's Shoes; Kissed; Lights of the Desert; The Glorious Fool; The Stranger's Banquet; Fools of Fortune; Too Much Wife. 1923 The Prisoner; Going Up; Nobody's Bride; Crossed Wires; The Footlight Ranger; The Wanters. 1924 Daring Youth; Circe the Enchantress. 1925 Cobra; Raffles; The Amateur Cracksman; After Business Hours; The Wall Street Whiz; The Thoroughbred; Joanna; Enticement. 1926 The Millionaire Policeman; The Blonde Saint; Pleasures of the Rich; Fifth Avenue. 1927 What Every Girl Should Know; Compassion. 1928 The Cheer Leader.

LANGFORD, MARTHA
Died: Apr. 21, 1935, Syracuse, N.Y. Screen and stage actress.

LANGFORD, WILLIAM
Born: 1920, Montreal, Canada. Died: July 20, 1955, New York, N.Y. Screen, stage, and television actor.

Appeared in Swedish film: The True and the False.

LANGLEY, HERBERT
Born: 1888. Died: Oct. 1967. Screen actor and opera baritone.

Appeared in: 1925 Chu Chin Chow.

LANGTRY, LILLIE (Emilie Charlotte Le Breton)
Born: Oct. 13, 1853, Isle of Jersey, Great Britain. Died: Feb. 12, 1929, Monaco (heart attack). Screen, stage actress, and author. Entered films with Famous Players in 1913.

Appeared in: 1913 His Neighbor's Wife.

LANI, MARIA
Born: 1906, Warsaw, Poland. Died: Mar. 11, 1954, Paris, France. Screen, stage actress, and writer. Appeared in French silents.

LANPHIER, FAYE
Born: 1906. Died: June 21, 1959, Oakland, Calif.(pneumonia). Screen actress. She was "Miss America" of 1925.

LANSING, RUTH DOUGLAS
Born: 1881. Died: Aug. 19, 1931, Hollywood, Calif.(toxic poisoning). Screen and stage actress.

LANZA, MARIO (Alfred Arnold Cocozza)
Born: Jan. 31, 1921 or 1925, Philadelphia, Pa. Died: Oct. 7, 1959, Rome, Italy (heart attack). Screen, television actor, and opera performer.

Appeared in: 1944 Winged Victory (appeared as an extra while in the service). 1949 That Midnight Kiss. 1950 Toast of New Orleans. 1951 The Great Caruso. 1952 Because You're Mine. 1954 The Student Prince (voice). 1956 Serenade. 1958 Seven Hills of Rome. 1959 For the First Time.

LA RENO, RICHARD "DICK"
Born: Oct. 31, 1873, County Limerick, Ireland. Died: July 26, 1945, Hollywood, Calif. Screen and stage actor.

Appeared in: 1914 The Squaw Man. 1915 Cameo Kirby. 1917 The Gray Ghost (serial). 1921 A Daughter of the Law. 1922 One-Eighth Apache; Out of the Silent North; Trimmed. 1923 Playing It Wild; Times Have Changed; Single Handed. 1924 Oh, You Tony!; Crashin' Through; Ridin' Mad; Waterfront Wolves; Three Days to Live. 1925 Flashing Steeds; Drug Store Cowboy. 1926 The High Hand; Buffalo Bill on the U.P. Trail; Sea Horses. 1927 The Long Loop on the Pecos; The Border Cavalier; Gold from Weepah; The Silent Rider. 1928 The Apache Raider.

LARIMORE, EARLE
Born: 1899, Portland, Ore. Died: Oct. 22, 1947, New York, N.Y. Screen, stage, and radio actor.

Appeared in: 1922 Inspection. 1926 The Kickoff.

LARKIN, JOHN
Born: 1874. Died: Mar. 19, 1936, Los Angeles, Calif.(pneumonia). Negro screen actor.

Appeared in: 1931 Smart Money; Man to Man; The Prodigal; Sporting Blood. 1932 Wet Parade; The Tenderfoot; Stranger in Town. 1933 Black Beauty; Day of Reckoning; The Great Jasper. 1934 The Witching Hour. 1935 Mississippi; A Notorious Gentleman. 1936 Frankie and Johnnie; Hearts Divided; Green Pastures.

LARKIN, JOHN
Born: 1912, Oakland, Calif. Died: Jan. 29, 1965, Studio City, Calif.(heart attack). Screen, radio, and television actor. Not to be confused with John Larkin, Negro actor (dec. 1936) nor stage actor (dec. 1929).

Appeared in: 1950 Farewell to Yesterday. 1964 Seven Days in May; Those Calloways. 1965 The Satan Bug.

LA ROCQUE, ROD (Roderick la Rocque de la Rour)
Born: Nov. 29, 1898, Chicago, Ill. Died: Oct. 15, 1969, Beverly Hills, Calif. Screen, stage actor, and radio producer. Married to screen actress Vilma Banky.

Appeared in: 1917 Efficiency Edgar's Courtship. 1918 The Venus Model. 1920 Stolen Kiss. 1921 Paying the Piper; Suspicious Wives. 1922 What's Wrong with the Women?; Notoriety; The Challenge; Slim Shoulders; A Woman's Woman. 1923 The Ten Commandments; Zaza; Jazzmania; The French Doll. 1924 Tri-

umph; Feet of Clay; Forbidden Paradise; A Society Scandal; Code of the Sea; Don't Call it Love; Phantom Justice. 1925 The Coming of Amos; Braveheart; The Golden Bed; Night Life of New York; Wild, Wild Susan. 1926 Hold 'Em Yale; Stand and Deliver; Captain Swagger; Love Pirate; Love over Night. 1929 The Man and the Moment; The One Woman Idea; Our Modern Maidens; The Locked Door; Our Dancing Daughter; The Delightful Rogue; Forbidden Paradise. 1930 One Romantic Night; Let Us Be Gay; Beau Bandit. 1931 The Yellow Ticket. 1933 S.O.S. Iceberg. 1935 Mystery Woman; Frisco Waterfront. 1936 The Preview Murder Mystery; Till We Meet Again; Hi, Gaucho!; The Dragnet. 1937 The Shadow Strikes. 1938 International Crime; Taming the Wild. 1939 The Hunchback of Notre Dame. 1940 Beyond Tomorrow; Dr. Christian Meets the Women; Dark Streets of Cairo. 1941 Meet John Doe.

LARQUEY, PIERRE
Born: 1884, France. Died: Apr. 17, 1962, Paris, France. Screen actor.

Appeared in: 1935 Topaze. 1936 Second Bureau. 1937 Dr. Knock. 1939 A Man and His Wife; Mademoiselle ma Mere; The Citadel of Silence. 1940 The Mayor's Dilemma; Two Women. 1944 Moulin Rouge. 1945 Des Dames aux Chapeaux Verts (The Ladies in the Great Hats). 1946 Jericho. 1947 The Murderer Lives at Number 21; The Blue Veil. 1948 Le Corbeau (The Raven); Jenny Lamour; Portrait of Innocence. 1950 Sylvie and the Phantom. 1951 Face to the Wind. 1952 A Simple Case of Money; Topaze (and 1935 version). 1955 Diabolique. 1958 Witches of Salem.

LARSON, LORLEE
Born: 1935. Died: Oct. 4, 1954, Los Angeles, Calif. Screen and radio actress.

LA RUE, FRANK H.
Died: Sept. 26, 1960, Hollywood, Calif. Screen, stage, and vaudeville actor.

Appeared in: 1931 Sidewalks of New York. 1932 Once in a Life Time. 1933 Strange People; Flying Devils; Thrill Hunter. 1934 The Fighting Ranger. 1935 When a Man Sees Red; Motive for Revenge; The Girl Who Came Back; The Singing Vagabond. 1937 Bar-Z Bad Men; Gun Lords of Stirrup Basin; A Lawman Is Born; It Happened Out West; Boothill Brigade; Public Cowboy No. 1; Colorado Kid. 1938 Song and Bullets; Lightning Carson Rides Again; I Demand Payment; Outlaws of Sonora; Overland Stage Raiders; Knight of the Plains; Frontier Scout. 1939 In Old Montana; Down the Wyoming Trail; Port of Hate; Roll Wagons Roll; Code of the Fearless; Song of the Buckaroo; Trigger Pals. 1940 Frontier Crusader; The Durango Kid; Arizona Frontier; Westbound Stage; Land of the Six Guns; The Range Busters; Riders of Pasco Basin; Return of Wild Bill; Fugitive from a Prison Camp; The Durango Kid. 1941 Beyond the Sacramento; Gunman from Bodie; Robbers of the Range; Prairie Stranger; Hands across the Rockies; A Missouri Outlaw. 1943 Robin Hood of the Range; Saddles and Sagebrush. 1944 Ghost Guns; The Last Horseman; Saddle Leather Law; West of the Rio Grande. 1945 Blazing the Western Trail; Devil Riders; Frontier Feud; The Lost Trail. 1946 Border Bandits; The Fighting Frontiersman; Frontier Gun Law; The Gentleman from Texas; Gunning for Vengeance; The Haunted Mine; Silver Range; Under Arizona Skies. 1947 Prairie Raiders; South of Chisholm Trail; Cheyenne Takes Over; Gun Talk. 1948 Song of the Drifter; Frontier Agent. 1949 Sheriff of Medicine Bow.

LA RUE, GRACE
Born: 1881. Died: Mar. 12, 1956, Burlingame, Calif. Screen, stage, and vaudeville actress. Married to screen actor Hale Hamilton (dec. 1942).

Appeared in: 1919 That's Good (she used the name of Stella Gray and received no billing for that film). 1929 The International Star of Songs (short). 1933 She Done Him Wrong. 1940 If I Had My Way.

LA RUE, JEAN (Eugene Marcus Bailey)
Born: 1901. Died: June 1956, San Antonio, Texas. Screen actor.

Appeared in: 1923 Where the Pavement Ends. 1928 Tracy, the Outlaw.

LASCOE, HENRY
Born: 1914. Died: Sept. 1, 1964, Hollywood, Calif.(heart attack). Screen, stage, and television actor.

Appeared in: 1951 The Man with My Face.

LATELL, LYLE (Lyle Zeiem)
Born: Apr. 9, 1905, Elma, Iowa. Died: Oct. 24, 1967, Hollywood, Calif.(heart attack). Married to screen actress Mary Foy (one of the Seven Little Foys). Screen and television actor. Appeared in the "Boston Blackie" series, during the 1940s.

Appeared in: 1941 Texas; Great Guns; In the Navy. 1942 The Wife Takes a Flyer; The Night before the Divorce. 1944 One Mysterious Night. 1945 Hold That Blonde; Dick Tracy vs. Cueball. 1947 Dick Tracy's Dilemma; Dick Tracy and Gruesome; Buck Privates Come Home. 1948 The Noose Hangs High. 1949 Sky Dragon. 1955 The Girl Rush.

LATHROP, DONALD
Born: 1888, England. Died: July 15, 1940, London, England (heart ailment). Screen and stage actor.

Appeared in: 1937 Love from a Stranger; Fire over England.

LAUDER, SIR HARRY
Born: Aug. 4, 1870, Portobello, Scotland. Died: Feb. 25, 1950, Lenarkshire, Scotland (kidney ailment). Screen and stage actor.

Appeared in: 1927 Huntingtower. 1929 Happy Days. 1933 Auld Lang Syne. 1936 The End of the Road. 1940 Song of the Road.

LAUGHTON, CHARLES
Born: July 1, 1899, Scarborough, England. Died: Dec. 15, 1962, Los Angeles, Calif.(cancer). Screen, stage actor, film and stage director. Married to screen actress Elsa Lanchester. Won Academy Award in 1933 for Best Actor for Private Life of Henry VIII.

Appeared in: 1928 Bluebattles. 1929 Piccadilly. 1930 Wolves (aka Wanted Men); Comets; Down Under; Daydreams. 1931 Devil and the Deep; Payment Deferred; The Old Dark House. 1932 The Sign of the Cross; If I Had a Million. 1933 Island of Lost Souls; White Woman; The Private Life of Henry VIII. 1934 The Barretts of Wimpole Street. 1935 Les Miserables; Ruggles of Red Gap; Mutiny on the Bounty; Frankie and Johnny (short). 1936 Rembrandt; Wanted Men. 1937 Vessel of Wrath; I Claudius. 1938 St. Martin's Lane; The Beachcomber. 1939 A Miracle Can Happen; Jamaica Inn; The Hunchback of Notre Dame; Sidewalks of London. 1940 They Knew What They Wanted. 1941 It Started with Eve. 1942 The Tuttles of Tahiti; Tales of Manhattan; Stand by for Action. 1943 Forever and a Day; This Land Is Mine. 1944 The Canterville Ghost; The Suspect; The Man from Down Under; The Sign of the Cross (revised version of 1932 film). 1945 Captain Kidd. 1946 Because of Him. 1947 The Queen's Necklace. 1948 The Paradine Case; Arch of Triumph; Girl from Manhattan; The Big Clock. 1949 The Bribe; Man on the Eiffel Tower. 1951 The Strange Door; The Blue Veil. 1952 O' Henry's Full House; Abbott and Costello Meet Captain Kidd; "News of the Day" (newsreel). 1953 Young Bess; Salome. 1954 Hobson's Choice. 1957 Witness for the Prosecution. 1960 Spartacus; Under Ten Flags. 1962 Advise and Consent.

LAUGHTON, EDWARD "EDDIE"
Born: 1903, Sheffield, England. Died: Mar. 21, 1952, Hollywood, Calif.(pneumonia). Screen and vaudeville actor.

Appeared in: 1938 Highway Patrol; Convicted; Smashing the Spy Ring. 1939 The Lone Wolf Spy Hunt; My Son Is a Criminal; Flying G-Men (serial); North of Shanghai; Romance of the Redwood; Scandal Sheet; Outside These Walls; Mandrake the Magician; Beware Spooks; Those High Grey Walls; The Amazing Mr. Williams; Cafe Hostell; Bullets for Rustlers. 1940 Blazing Six Shooters; Texas Stagecoach; Men without Souls; The Doctor Takes a Wife; Girls of the Road. 1941 Outlaws of the Panhandle; I Was a Prisoner on Devil's Island; Mystery Ship. 1942 Canal Zone; Lawless Plainsmen; Submarine Raider; Honolulu Lu; Sabotage Squad; The Boogie Man Will Get You; Atlantic Convoy. 1944 The Girl in the Case. 1945 The Lost Weekend. 1947 The Shocking Miss Pilgrim. 1949 Chicken Every Sunday.

LAUNDERS, PERC
Born: 1905. Died: Oct. 2, 1952, Hollywood, Calif. Screen actor and studio musician.

Appeared in: 1944 The Falcon Out West. 1945 The Stork Club. 1949 Abandoned Woman. 1950 For Heaven's Sake.

LAUREL, STAN
Born: June 16, 1890, Ulverston, England. Died: Feb. 23, 1965, Santa Monica, Calif.(heart attack). Won Academy Award in 1933 for The Music Box (short). Was partner in comedy team of "Laurel and Hardy" with Oliver Hardy (dec. 1957).

Appeared in: 1917 Nuts in May; The Evolution of Fashion. 1918 Hoot Mon; Hickory Hiram; Whose Zoo; Huns and Hyphens; Just Rambling Along; No Place Like Jail; Bears and Bad Men; Frauds and Frenzies; Do You Love Your Wife?; Lucky Dog. 1919 Mixed Nuts; Scars and Stripes; When Knights Were Cold. 1920 the following shorts: Under Two Jags; Wild Bill Hiccup; Rupert of Hee-Haw (aka Coleslaw); The Spoilers; Oranges and Lemons. 1921 The Rent Collector (short). 1922 the following shorts: The Pest; The Egg. 1923 the following shorts: The Noon Whistle; White Wings; Pick and Shovel; Kill and Cure; Gas and Air; Mud and Sand; The Handy Man; Short Orders; A Man about Town; The Whole Truth; Scorching Sands; Save the Ship; Roughest Africa; Frozen Hearts; Mother's Joy. 1924 the following shorts: Smithy; Zeb vs. Paprika; Postage Due; Near Dublin; Brothers under the Chin; Short Kilts. 1924 the following shorts: Monsieur Don't Care; Mandam Mix-Up; West of Hot Dog. 1925 the following shorts: Somewhere in Wrong; Dr. Pycle and Mr. Pryde; Pie-Eyed; The Snow Hawk; Navy Blues Days; Twins; The Sleuth; Half a Man; Cowboys Cry for It. 1926 Atta Boy; On the Front Page. Appeared with Oliver Hardy in the following shorts: 1926 Putting Pants on Phillip; Get 'Em Young; Slipping Wives. 1927 the following shorts: With Love and Hisses; Sailors Beware; Forty-Five Minutes from Hollywood; Do Detectives Think?; Flying Elephants; Sugar Daddies; Call of the Cuckoo; The Rap; Duck Soup; Eve's Love Letters; Love 'Em and Weep; Why Girls Love Sailors; Should Tall Men Marry?; Hats Off; The Battle of the Century; The Second Hundred Years; Let George Do It; The Way of All Pants. 1928 the following shorts: Leave 'Em Laughing; From Soup to Nuts; You're Darn Tootin'; Their Purple Moment; Should Married Men Go Home?; Habeas Corpus; Two Tars; We Faw Down; The Finishing Touch; Early to Bed. 1929 Hollywood Revue of 1929; following shorts: Liberty; Unaccustomed as We Are; Double Whoopee; Big Business; Men O'War; A Perfect Day; Angora Love; Bacon Grabbers; They Go Boom; The Goosegow; Berth Marks; Wrong Again; That's My Wife. 1930 The Rogue Song; plus the following shorts: Night Owls; Blotto; Be Big; Hay Wire; Brats; Below Zero; The Laurel and Hardy Murder Case; Another Fine Mess; Hog Wild (aka Aerial Antics). 1931 Pardon Us; plus the following shorts: Chickens Come Home; Our Wife; Laughing Gravy; Come Clean; One Good Turn; Helpmates; Beau Hunks (aka Beau Chumps); Slippery Pearls. 1932 Pack up Your Troubles; plus following shorts: Any Old Port; The Music Box; The Chip; County Hospital; Scram; Their First Mistake. 1933 Fra Diavolo (The Devil's Brother); plus following shorts: Busy Bodies; Towed in a Hole; Twice Two; Me and My Pal; The Midnight Patrol; Wild Roses; Dirty Work. 1934 Sons of the Desert; Babes in Toyland; Hollywood Party of 1934; plus following shorts: Going Bye-Bye; Oliver the Eighth; Them Thar Hills; The Live Ghost. 1935 Bonnie Scotland; plus following shorts: Tit for Tat; The Fixer-Uppers; Thicker Than Water. 1936 The Bohemian Girl; Our Relations; plus following shorts: On the Wrong Trek. 1937 Way Out West; Pick a Star. 1938 Swiss Miss; Blockheads. 1939 The Flying Deuces. 1940 A Chump at Oxford; Saps at Sea. 1941 Great Guns; 1942 A-Haunting We Will Go. 1943 Air Raid Wardens; Jitterbugs; The Dancing Masters; Tree in a Test Tube (Government short). 1944 The Big Noise; Nothing but Trouble. 1945 The Bullfighters. 1951 Atoll K (aka Escapade—England 1952; aka Utopia 1954; aka Robincrusoeland—France 1952). 1957 Big Parade of Comedy (documentary). 1960 When Comedy Was King (documentary). 1961 Days of Thrills and Laughter (documentary). 1963 30 Years of Fun (documentary). 1964 Big Parade of Comedy (documentary). 1967 The Crazy World of Laurel and Hardy (documentary); Further Peril's of Laurel and Hardy (documentary).

LAURENZ, JOHN
Born: 1909. Died: Nov. 7, 1958, Brooklyn, N.Y. Screen actor and singer.

Appeared in: 1946 A Walk in the Sun. 1947 Apache Rose. 1948 Tarzan and the Mermaids. 1950 Border Outlaws; Federal Agent at Large.

LAURIER, JAY (Jay Chapman)
Born: May 31, 1879, Birmingham, England. Died: Apr. 1969, Durban, South Africa. Screen, stage, and vaudeville actor.

Appeared in: 1932 Hobson's Choice; Pajamas Preferred. 1933 Waltz Time; I'll Stick to You; Black Tulip.

LA VERNE, LUCILLE
Born: Nov. 8, 1872, Nashville, Tenn. Died: May 4, 1945, Culver City, Calif. Screen and stage actress. Her voice was that of the Queen and the Wicked Witch in Walt Disney's Snow White (1937)

Appeared in: 1917 Polly of the Circus. 1922 Orphans of the Storm. 1923 The White Rose; Zaza. 1924 America; His Darker Self. 1925 Sun Up. 1928 The Last Moment. 1930 Abraham Lincoln; Sinner's Holiday; Little Caesar. 1931 The Great Meadow; Union Depot; An American Tragedy; Twenty-four Hours; The Unholy Garden. 1932 Hearts of Humanity; Breach of Promise; Alias the Doctor; She Wanted a Millionaire; When Paris Sleeps. 1933 Wild Horse Mesa; The Last Trail; Strange Adventure; Pilgrimage. 1934 Kentucky Kernels; The Mighty Barnum; Beloved; School for Girls. 1935 A Tale of Two Cities. 1937 Snow White (voice).

LA VERNIE, LAURA (Laura Anderson)
Born: Mar. 2, 1853, Jefferson City, Mo. Died: Sept. 18, 1939, Los Angeles, Calif. Screen and stage actress. Entered films in 1909.

Appeared in: 1925 Who's Your Friend. 1930 Devil's Holiday; Lummox. 1931 Kiki.

LAW, DONALD
Born: 1920. Died: Feb. 26, 1959, Meadville, Pa. Screen actor.

Appeared in "Our Gang" comedies.

LAW, WALTER
Born: 1876. Died: Aug. 8, 1940, Hollywood, Calif. Screen, stage, and vaudeville actor.

Appeared in: 1918 A Perfect Lady. 1920 If I Were King. 1922 Forgotten Law; Great Alone. 1923 Flying Dutchman. 1924 Janice Meredith. 1925 Clothes Make the Pirate. 1930 Whoopee.

LAWES, LEWIS E.
Born: 1884. Died: Apr. 23, 1947, Garrison, N.Y.(cerebral hemorrhage). Had been warden of Sing Sing prison for 20 years. Film, radio actor, and writer.

Appeared in prologue of San Quentin (1946)

LAWFORD, BETTY
Born: 1910, England. Died: Nov. 20, 1960, N.Y. Screen, stage, and television actress. Cousin of screen actor Peter Lawford.

Appeared in: 1925 The Night Club. 1929 Gentlemen of the Press; Return of Sherlock Holmes; Lucky in Love. 1930 Old English. 1931 Secrets of a Secretary. 1933 Berkeley Square; Gallant Lady. 1934 Let's Be Ritzy; The Human Side. 1936 Love before Breakfast; Stolen Holiday. 1937 Criminal Lawyer. 1943 Stage Door Canteen. 1947 The Devil Thumbs a Ride.

LAWFORD, LT. GEN. SIR SYDNEY
Born: 1866. Died: Feb. 15, 1953, Hollywood, Calif. Screen actor. Father of screen actor Peter Lawford.

LAWRENCE, EDDY
Born: San Francisco, Calif. Died: Dec. 5, 1931, San Diego, Calif. (suicide—gas). Screen and stage actor.

Appeared in: 1925 The Knockout.

LAWRENCE, FLORENCE
Born: 1888. Died: Dec. 27, 1938, Beverly Hills, Calif.(suicide—ant paste). Screen actress. Was known as the "Biograph Girl" and the "Imp Girl." Entered films with Vitagraph in 1907.

Appeared in: 1908 A Calamitous Elopement; The Girl and the Outlaw; Betrayed by a Hand Print; Behind the Scenes; Where the Breakers Roar; The Heart of Oyama; A Smoked Husband; The Devil; The Barbarian, Ingomar; The Vaquero's Vow; The Planter's Wife; The Zulu's Heart; Romance of a Jewess; The Call of the Wild; Mr. Jones at the Ball; Concealing a Burglar; Taming of the Shrew; The Ingrate; A Woman's Way; The Song of the Shirt; Mr. Jones Entertains; An Awful Moment; The Christmas Burglars; Mr. Jones Has a Card Party; The Salvation Army Lass; Romeo and Juliet. 1909 Redemption; "Jonesy Picture" series; Mrs. Jones Entertains; The Mended Lute; The Slave; The Brahma Diamond; Resurrection; The Jones Have Amateur Theatricals; His Wife's Mother; The Deception; The Lure of the Gown; Lady Helen's Escapade; Jones and His New Neighbor; The Winning Coat; The Road to the Heart; Confidence; The Note in the Shoe; Eloping with Auntie; Her First Biscuits; The Peach Basket Hat; The Necklace; The Way of Man; Mrs. Jones' Lover; The Cardinal's Conspiracy; The Slave; Mr. Jones' Burglar. 1910 The Angel of the Studio. 1911 Flo's Discipline; Her Two Sons; A Good Turn. 1912 In Swift Waters. 1914 A Singular Cynic. 1922 The Unfoldment. 1923 Satin Girl. 1924 Gambling Wives.

LAWRENCE, GERTRUDE (Gertrude Klasen and Alexandre Dagmar Lawrence Klasen)
Born: July 4, 1898 or 1902, London, England. Died: Sept. 6, 1952, New York, N.Y.(liver ailment—infectious hepatitis). Screen, stage actress, and dancer.

Appeared in: 1929 The Battle of Paris (film debut). 1932 Aren't We All; Lord Camber's Ladies. 1933 No Funny Business. 1935 Mimi. 1936 Rembrandt. 1937 Men Are Not Gods. 1950 The Glass Menagerie.

LAWRENCE, LILLIAN
Born: 1870, Alexander, W. Va. Died: May 7, 1926, Beverly Hills, Calif. Screen and stage actress.

Appeared in: 1921 Making the Grade; A Parisian Scandal. 1922 A Girl's Desire; The Eternal Flame; East Is West; White Shoulders. 1923 The Common Law; Fashionable Fakers; Three Ages; Crinoline and Romance; The Voice from the Minaret. 1924 Christine of the Hungry Heart. 1925 Graustark. 1926 Stella Maris. 1927 Sensation Seekers.

LAWRENCE, WILLIAM E. "BABE"
Born: 1896, Los Angeles, Calif. Died: Nov. 28, 1947, Hollywood, Calif. Screen and stage actor.

Appeared in: 1915 Birth of a Nation. 1920 Bride 13 (serial). 1921 Get Your Man; The Kiss; The Snob; Fightin' Mad; Morals; Ducks and Drakes. 1922 They Like 'Em Rough; Blood and Sand; Forget-Me-Not; A Front Page Story; The Love Gambler. 1923 Blinky; Cameo Kirby; The Thrill Chaser. 1924 The Law Forbids; The Reckless Age; The Whispered Name. 1926 A Man Four-Square; Hard Boiled. 1930 The Costello Case. 1931 Hell Bound.

LAWSON, HELEN MITCHELL MOROSCO. See Helen Mitchell

LAWSON, WILFRID
Born: Jan. 14, 1900, Bradford, Yorkshire, England. Died: Oct. 10, 1966, London, England (heart attack). Screen, stage, and television actor.

Appeared in: 1935 Turn of the Tide (film debut). 1936 Ladies in Love; White Hunter. 1937 The Terror. 1938 Bank Holiday; Pygmalion; Yellow Sands; The Gaunt Stranger; Stolen Life. 1939 Pastor Hall; Allegheny Uprising. 1940 The Long Voyage Home. 1941 It Happened to One Man; Jeannie (U.S. 1943). 1942 Hard Steel; Danny Boy (U.S. 1946). 1943 The Night Has Eyes. 1944 The Great Mr. Handel; Fanny by Gaslight. 1948 Man of Evil. 1949 The Turners of Prospect Road. 1955 The Prisoner. 1956 Make Me an Offer; War and Peace. 1957 An Alligator Named Daisy; Miracle in Soho. 1958 Hell Drivers; Tread Softly Stranger. 1959 Room at the Top. 1960 Expresso Bongo. 1961 The Naked Edge; Postman's Knock. 1963 Tom Jones. 1966 The Wrong Box; Other British films: Gentleman of Venture; Thursday's Child; Salute the Soldier.

LAWTON, FRANK
Born: Sept. 30, 1904, London, England. Died: June 10, 1969, London, England. Screen and stage actor.

Appeared in: 1930 Birds of Prey; The Outsider; The Skin Game; Young Woodley. 1931 The Perfect Alibi. 1932 Michael and Mary; After Office Hours. 1933 Heads We Go; Cavalcade; Friday, the 13th; The Charming Deceiver. 1934 Voice in the Night; One More River. 1935 David Copperfield; Bar-20 Rides Again. 1936 The Invisible Ray; The Devil Doll. 1937 The Mill on the Floss. 1939 The Four Just Men. 1940 Ministry of Information; The Secret Four. 1942 Went the Day Well?. 1944 48 Hours. 1948 The Winslow Boy (U.S. 1950). 1953 Rough Shoot. 1957 The Rising of the Moon. 1958 A Night to Remember. 1959 Gideon of Scotland Yard (aka Gideon's Day). 1963 The Queen's Guards.

LAWTON, THAIS
Born: 1881, Louisville, Ky. Died: Dec. 18, 1956, N.Y. Screen and stage actress.

Appeared in: 1915 The Battle Cry for Peace.

LAY, IRVING T.
Died: Mar. 1932, Seneca Falls, N.Y.(suicide—gas poisoning). Screen actor.

LEASE, REX
Born: Feb. 11, 1901, Central City, W. Va. Died: Jan. 3, 1966, Hollywood, Calif. Screen actor. Entered films as an extra.

Appeared in: 1924 A Woman Who Sinned; Chalk Marks. 1925 Before Midnight; The Last Edition; Easy Money. 1926 The Timid Terror; Mystery Pilot (serial); The Last Alarm; Race Wild; Somebody's Mother. 1927 Clancy's Kosher Wedding; Moulders of Men; Heroes of the Night; The Cancelled Debt; The College Hero; Not for Publication; The Outlaw Dog. 1928 The Law of the Range; Last Lap; Riders of the Dark; Broadway Daddies; The Candy Kid; Red Riders of Canada; The Speed Classic; Phantom of the Turf; Making the Varsity; Queen of the Chorus. 1929 Stolen Love; The

Younger Generation; Two Sisters; When Dreams Come True; Girls Who Dare. 1930 Borrowed Wives; The Utah Kid; Wings of Adventure; Troopers 3; Sunny Skies; Hot Curves; So This Is Mexico. 1931 In Old Cheyenne; Why Marry; Chinatown after Dark; Monster Walks; Is There Justice; Sign of the Wolf (serial). 1932 The Lone Trail; Midnight Morals; Cannonball Express. 1934 Inside Information. 1935 Fighting Caballero; The Ghost Rider; The Man from Gun Town; Cowboy and the Bandit; Pals of the Range; Rough Riding Ranger; Cyclone of the Saddle. 1936 Fast Bullets; Lightnin' Bill Carson; Roarin' Guns; Cavalcade of the West; Aces and Eight; The Clutching Hand (serial); The Man from Gun Town; Gentleman Jim McGee. 1937 The Silver Trail; Heroes of the Alamo; The Freedom; Swing it Sailor; The Mysterious Pilot (serial). 1938 Fury Below; Code of the Rangers; Desert Patrol. 1939 South of the Border. 1940 Rancho Grande; Under Texas Skies; Lone Star Raiders; A Chump at Oxford. 1941 Outlaws of the Rio Grande; The Phantom Cowboy; Death Valley Outlaws; Pals of the Range; Sierra Sue; Outlaws of the Cherokee Trail. 1942 Arizona Terrors; The Silver Bullet; The Cyclone Kid; Tomorrow We Live; The Boss of Hangtown Mesa. 1943 Haunted Ranch; Tenting on the Old Camp Ground; Dead Man's Gulch. 1944 Firebrands of Arizona; Bordertown Trail; The Cowboy and the Senorita. 1945 Texas Ranger; The Naughty Nineties; Santa Fe Saddlemates; Frontier Gal; Flame of Barbary Coast. 1946 Days of Buffalo Bill; Sun Valley Cyclone; The Time of Their Lives. 1947 Helldorado; Slave Girl; The Wistful Widow of Wagon Gap; Buck Privates Come Home. 1948 Out of the Storm. 1949 Ma and Pa Kettle. 1950 Singing Guns; Bells of Coronado; Code of the Silver Sage; Curtain Call at Cactus Creek; Covered Wagon Raiders; Hills of Oklahoma; Frisco Tornado. 1952 Ma and Pa Kettle at the Fair; Lone Star; Abbott and Costello Meet Captain Kidd. 1953 Ride, Vaquero!; Money from Home; Abbott and Costello Go to Mars. 1956 On the Threshold of Space.

LEAVITT, DOUGLAS "ABE"
Born: 1883. Died: Mar. 3, 1960, Levittown, Pa. Screen, burlesque, and vaudeville actor. Was part of vaudeville team of "Leavitt & Lockwood."

Appeared in: 1942 You Were Never Lovelier; Smith of Minnesota. 1943 Reveille with Beverly; Murder in Times Square; Two Senoritas from Chicago.

LE BEAU, STEPHANIE
Died: June 5, 1967, New York, N.Y. Screen, stage, and television actress.

LEBEDEFF, IVAN
Born: June 18, 1899, Uspoliai, Lithuania. Died: Mar. 31, 1953, Hollywood, Calif.(heart attack). Screen actor, screenwriter, and author. Appeared in French, German, U.S. films, etc. Married to screen actress Vera Engels.

Appeared in: 1922 King Frederick (German film debut). 1924 The Lucky Death; The Soul of an Artist; 600,000 Francs per Month; The Charming Prince. 1925 Burned Fingers. 1926 The Sorrows of Satan. 1927 The Loves of Sunya; The Angel of Broadway; The Forbidden Woman. 1928 Let 'Er Go Gallagher; Walking Back. 1929 Sin Town; The Veiled Woman; The Cuckoos; The Midnight Mystery; The Conspiracy; Half-Shot at Sunrise. 1931 The Bachelor Apartment; The Lady Refuses; Deceit; Woman Pursued; The Gay Diplomat. 1932 Unholy Love; Hollywood Handicap (short); Hollywood on Parade (short). 1933 Bombshell; Made on Broadway; Laughing at Life; Sweepings. 1934 Kansas City Princess; Merry Widow; The Merry Frinks; Moulin Rouge. 1935 China Seas; Sweepstakes Annie; Goin' to Town. 1936 Pepper; The Golden Arrow; Love on the Run. 1937 Fair Warning; History is Made at Night; Atlantic Flight; Mama Steps Out; Conquest; Angel. 1938 Straight, Place and Show; Wise Girl. 1939 Trapped in the Sky; The Mystery of Mr. Wong; Hotel for Women; You Can't Cheat an Honest Man. 1940 Passport to Alcatraz; Public Deb No. 1. 1941 The Shanghai Gesture; Blue, White, and Perfect. 1942 Lure of the Islands; Foreign Agent. 1943 Mission to Moscow; Around the World. 1944 Oh, What a Night!; Are These Our Parents?. 1945 Rhapsody in Blue; They Are Guilty. 1952 The Snow of Kilimanjaro; California Conquest.

LE BOZOKY, BARBARA
Born: 1892. Died: Nov. 28, 1937, Hollywood, Calif. Screen and stage actress.

LE BRANDT, GERTRUDE N.
Born: 1863. Died: Aug. 28, 1955, Hollywood, Calif. Screen and stage actress.

Appeared in: 1921 Mama's Affair.

LE BRUN, MINON
Born: 1888. Died: Sept. 20, 1941, Los Angeles, Calif. Screen actress. Divorced from screen actor Cullen Landis.

LEDERER, GRETCHEN
Born: 1891. Died: Dec. 20, 1955, Anaheim, Calif. Screen actress. Appeared in films between 1910 and 1920. Divorced from screen actor Otto Lederer.

Appeared in: 1917 A Kentucky Cinderella.

LEDNER, DAVID
Born: 1900. Died: Dec. 17, 1957, Hollysood, Calif.(heart attack). Screen actor and stand-in. Entered films in 1941.

Appeared in: 1958 The Buccaneer (stand-in).

LEDUC, CLAUDINE (Sadi Lindsay)
Born: Paris, France. Died: Feb. 15, 1969, New York, N.Y. Screen, stage, television, radio actress, and writer.

Appeared in: 1943 Once upon a Honeymoon; The Song of Bernadette.

LEE, ALLEN
Born: 1875. Died: Feb. 5, 1951, New York, N.Y. Screen and stage actor.

LEE, AURIOL
Born: London, England. Died: July 2, 1941, Hutchinson, Kans.(auto accident). Screen, stage actress, stage producer, and stage director.

Appeared in: 1941 Suspicion (only film).

LEE, BELINDA
Born: June 15, 1935, Devon, England. Died: Mar. 13, 1961, San Bernardino, Calif.(auto accident). Screen, stage, and television actress.

Appeared in: 1950 Eye Witness. 1954 Blackout (aka Murder by Proxy); Runaway Bus. 1955 Man of the Moment; The Bells of St. Trinian's; Footsteps in the Fog. 1957 Miracle in Soho; The Gentle Touch (aka Feminine Touch). 1958 The Secret Place; Dangerous Exile. 1959 Elephant Gun. 1960 Goddess of Love; Le Notti Di Lucrezia Borgia (The Nights of Lucretia Borgia); The Chasers (aka Les Dragueurs—The Dredgers). 1961 She Walks by Night; Aphrodite; Die Wahrheit Uber Rosemarie (The Truth about Rosemarie). 1962 Messalina; Joseph and His Brethren; Constantine and the Cross. 1963 Long Night at 43 (aka It Happened in '43); The Devil's Choice. 1964 Love the Italian Way. Other foreign films: Eyewitness; Marie des Iles; Visa Pour Caracas; Ce Corps Tant Desire; I Magliari; Katja.

LEE, BESSIE
Born: 1904. Died: Nov. 1931, Hollywood, Calif.(cerebral hemorrhage). Screen actress.

LEE, CANADA
Born: 1907. Died: May 9, 1952, New York, N.Y.(heart attack). Screen, stage, radio, television actor, and orchestra leader.

Appeared in: 1944 Lifeboat. 1947 Body and Soul; The Roosevelt Story (narr.). 1949 Lost Boundaries. 1952 Cry, the Beloved Country. 1955 Othello.

LEE, CHARLES T.
Born: 1882. Died: Mar. 14, 1927, Los Angeles, Calif.(heart trouble). Screen actor.

LEE, DIXIE (Wilma Wyatt)
Born: Nov. 4, 1911, Harriman, Tenn. Died: Nov. 1, 1952, Holmby Hills, Calif.(cancer). Screen and stage actress. Married to screen actor/singer Bing Crosby. Mother of screen actors Gary, Phillip, Dennis and Lindsay Crosby.

Appeared in: 1924 Not for Sale. 1929 Fox Movietone Follies of 1929; Knights Out (short); Why Leave Home?. 1930 Happy Days; Cheer up and Smile; The Big Party; Let's Go Places; Harmony at Home. 1931 No Limit; Night Life in Reno. 1934 Manhattan Love Song. 1935 Love in Bloom; Redheads on Parade.

LEE, DUKE R.
Born: 1881, Va. Died: Apr. 1, 1959, Los Angeles, Calif. Screen, stage, and vaudeville actor. Entered films in 1918.

Appeared in: 1918 Lure of the Circus. 1921 Trailin'; "If Only" Jim. 1922 In the Days of Buffalo Bill (serial); Don't Shoot; Just Tony; Tracked to Earth. 1923 Mile-a-Minute Romeo; In the Days of Daniel Boone (serial). 1924 The Gaiety Girl; Fighting Fury;

The Western Wallop. 1925 The Red Rider; Don Dare Devil; Flying Hoofs; The Call of Courage; The White Outlaw. 1926 Tony Runs Wild; The Canyon of Light; Sky High Corral; The Man in the Saddle; Man of the Forest; Rustlers' Ranch. 1927 Galloping Fury; The Terror of Bar X; The Circus Ace; Lands of the Lawless; Outlaws of Red River. 1928 Crashing Through; Clearing the Trail; Son of the Golden West; The Big Hop; The Heart of Broadway. 1929 .45 Calibre War. 1930 The Concentratin' Kid. 1948 Fort Apache.

LEE, EARL
Born: 1886. Died: June 2, 1955, Redwood City, Calif. Screen and stage actor.

Appeared in: 1951 Five. 1952 Assignment—Paris; The Story of Will Rogers; Tropical Heat Wave. 1954 Geraldine.

LEE, ETTA
Born: 1906. Died: Oct. 27, 1956, Eureka, Calif. Screen actress.

Appeared in: 1921 The Sheik; A Tale of Two Worlds. 1922 The Toll of the Sea. 1923 The Untameable; The Remittance Woman. 1924 The Thief of Bagdad. 1925 A Thief in Paradise; The Trouble with Wives; Recompense. 1927 Camille; The Chinese Parrot. 1928 Out with the Tide. 1933 International House.

LEE, FLORENCE
Born: 1888. Died: Sept. 1, 1962, Hollywood, Calif. Screen and stage actress. Married to screen actor Del Henderson (dec. 1956).

Appeared in: 1922 The Top O' the Morning; The Trouper. 1923 Blood Test; Mary of the Movies. 1924 Jack O' Clubs; Virtue's Revolt; Way of a Man (serial and feature). 1925 Luck and Sand; Across the Deadline; Speed Mad. 1926 The High Hand; Man Rustlin'. 1928 The Bronc Stomper; The Little Buckaroo. 1929 Illusion of Love. 1931 City Lights.

LEE, GYPSY ROSE (Rose Louise Hovick)
Born: Jan. 9, 1914, Seattle, Wash. Died: Apr. 26, 1970, Los Angeles, Calif.(cancer). Screen, stage, burlesque, radio, vaudeville actress, and author. Sister of screen actress June Havoc.

Appeared in: 1936 The Ziegfeld Follies of 1936. 1937 You Can't Have Everything; Ali Baba Goes to Town. 1938 Sally, Irene and Mary; The Battle of Broadway. 1939 My Lucky Star. 1943 Stage Door Canteen. 1944 Belle of the Yukon. 1945 Doll Face. 1952 Babes in Bagdad. 1958 Wind across the Everglades; The Screaming Mimi. 1963 The Stripper. 1966 The Trouble with Angels.

LEE, HARRY (William Henry Lee)
Born: June 1, 1872, Richmond, Va. Died: Dec. 8, 1932, Hollywood, Calif.(suicide—jump). Screen and stage actor.

Appeared in: 1921 Bucking the Tiger. 1922 Channing of the Northwest; Boomerang Bill; The Man She Brought Back. 1924 Monsieur Beaucaire. 1925 The Wrongdoers. 1926 Men of Steel. 1929 Gentlemen of the Press; Sunny Skies.

LEE, JENNIE
Born: 1850. Died: Aug. 4, 1925, Hollywood, Calif. Screen, stage, and vaudeville actress.

Appeared in: 1913 His Mother's Son; Her Mother's Oath. 1915 Birth of a Nation. 1921 The Big Punch; One Man in a Million. 1923 North of Hudson Bay. 1924 Young Ideas; Hearts of Oak.

LEE, JOHN D.
Born: 1898. Died: Dec. 12, 1965, Los Angeles, Calif.(heart attack). Screen, radio, vaudeville, and television actor.

Appeared in: 1964 Dr. Crippen.

LEE, LILA DEAN
Born: 1890. Died: Nov. 3, 1959, West Covina, Calif. Screen actress. Do not confuse with screen actress Lila Lee, (dec. 1973).

LEE, MARGO
Died: Oct. 8, 1951, Los Angeles, Calif. Screen, radio, and television actress.

Appeared in: 1950 So Young, So Bad.

LEE, ROSE. See Rose Lee McQuoid

LEE, SAMMY
Born: 1890. Died: Mar. 30, 1968, Woodland Hills, Calif. Screen, stage actor, and dance director.

Appeared in: 1939 The Gracie Allen Murder Case.

LEFAUR, ANDRE (Andre Lefaurichon)
Born: 1879, France. Died: Dec. 4, 1952, Paris, France. Screen and stage actor.

Appeared in: 1932 Le Bal. 1939 With a Smile. 1941 The King. 1942 Nine Bachelors. 1944 32 Rue de Montmartre.

LE FEUVRE, PHILIP
Born: 1871. Died: Aug. 23, 1939, Arcadia, Calif. Screen and stage actor.

LEGAL, ERNEST
Born: 1881, Germany. Died: June 29, 1955, Berlin, Germany. Screen, stage actor, playwright, and stage director.

Appeared in: 1938 Kater Lampe. 1939 Das Unsterbliche Herz (The Immortal Heart). 1950 Marriage of Figaro. Other German film: Heaven is Never Brought Out.

LEGNEUR, CHARLES
Born: 1892. Died: Feb. 14, 1956, Hollywood, Calif.(heart attack). Screen actor.

LEHR, LEW
Born: May 14, 1895, Philadelphia, Pa. Died: Mar. 6, 1950, Brookline, Mass. Screen, stage, vaudeville, radio actor, screenwriter, and film producer. Married to actress Anna Leonhardt, professionally known as Nancy Belle, with whom he toured in vaudeville. Well known for his comedy newsreel commentary, "Monkeys is the Angriest People."

Appeared in prior to 1936: Looking Back (voice); Tintypes (comm.); Adventures of a Newsreel Cameraman (comm.); Magic Carpet; Newsettes; Lew Lehr's Unnatural History. 1937 Borneo (narr.).

LEHRER, GEORGE J.
Born: 1889. Died: Aug. 25, 1966, Cleveland, Ohio. Screen, stage actor, and stage director. Known for his Abraham Lincoln impersonations.

LEHRMAN, HENRY
Born: Mar. 30, 1886, Vienna, Austria. Died: Nov. 7, 1946, Hollywood, Calif.(heart attack). Screen actor, film producer, film director, and screenwriter. Entered films with Griffith in 1910. Founded L-KO productions ("Lehrman-Knockout" comedies) in 1914.

Appeared in: 1910 As the Bells Rang Out; The Iconoclast; Her Sacrifice. 1912 A Beast at Bay. 1914 Making a Living (later reissued as A Bustled Johnny); Kid Auto Races at Venice.

LEIBER, FRITZ
Born: Jan. 31, 1882, Chicago, Ill. Died: Oct. 14, 1949, Pacific Palisades, Calif.(heart attack). Screen and stage actor.

Appeared in: 1917 Cleopatra. 1920 If I Were King. 1921 Queen of Sheba. 1935 A Tale of Two Cities. 1936 Sins of Man; Under Two Flags; Down to the Sea; Camille; The Story of Louis Pasteur; Anthony Adverse; Hearts in Bondage. 1937 Champagne Waltz; The Prince and the Pauper; The Great Garrick. 1938 The Jury's Secret; Flight into Nowhere; Gateway; If I Were King (and 1920 version). 1939 Nurse Edith Cavell; They Made Her a Spy; Pack up Your Troubles; The Hunchback of Notre Dame. 1940 Lady with Red Hair; The Way of All Flesh; All This and Heaven Too; The Sea Hawk. 1941 Aloma of the South Seas. 1942 Crossroads. 1943 The Desert Song; First Comes Courage; Phantom of the Opera. 1944 The Impostor; Cry of the Werewolf; Bride of the Vampire. 1945 The Cisco Kid Returns; This Love of Ours; The Spanish Main; Son of Lassie. 1946 A Scandal in Paris; Strange Journey; Humoresque; Angel on my Shoulder. 1947 High Conquest; Bells of San Angelo; The Web; Monsieur Verdoux; Dangerous Venture. 1948 Adventures of Casanova; To the Ends of the Earth; Inner Sanctum; Another Part of the Forest. 1949 Bagdad; Bride of Vengeance; Samson and Delilah; Song of India; Devil's Doorway.

LEIGH, FRANK
Born: London, England. Died: May 9, 1948, Hollywood, Calif. Screen and stage actor. Entered films in England in 1912.

Appeared in: 1918 Fedora. 1919 Lord and Lady Algy. 1920 Nurse Marjorie; Cup of Fury; Dangerous Days; One Hour before Dawn. 1921 Bob Hampton of Placer; The Light in the Clearing; Pilgrims of the Night. 1922 Golden Dreams; Domestic Relations; Out of the Silent North. 1923 Ashes of Vengeance; Truxton King; The Gentleman from America; North of Hudson Bay; Rosita; The Lonely Road. 1924 The Hill Billy; The Breath of Scandal; The Reckless Age; Flames of Desire; Hutch of the U.S.A.; Honor among Men.

1925 Contraband; The Winding Stair; His Majesty Bunker Bean; American Pluck; As Man Desires. 1926 The Adorable Deceiver; Flame of the Argentine; The Flaming Forest; The Lady of the Harem; The Imposter; Secret Orders. 1927 Soft Cushions; The Tigress; Somewhere in Sonora. 1928 A Night of Mystery; King Cowboy; Prowlers of the Sea. 1929 Below the Deadline; Love in the Desert; Montmartre Rose; Thirteenth Chair; Captain's Wife. 1930 The Lotus Lady. 1931 The Woman from Monte Carlo; Ten Nights in a Barroom.

LEIGH, VIVIEN (Vivian Mary Hartley)
Born: Nov. 5, 1913, Darjeeling, India. Died: July 8, 1967, London, England (natural causes). Screen and stage actress. Divorced from screen actor Sir Laurence Olivier. Won Academy Award for Best Actress in 1939 for Gone with the Wind and again in 1951 for A Streetcar Named Desire.

Appeared in: 1934 Things Are Looking Up (film debut); Village Squire. 1935 Gentleman's Agreement; Look up and Laugh. 1937 Fire over England; Dark Journey; Storm in a Teacup. 1938 St. Martin's Lane (aka Sidewalks of London—U.S. 1940); Twenty-one Days Together (aka First and Last—U.S. 1940); A Yank at Oxford. 1939 Gone with the Wind. 1940 Waterloo Bridge. 1941 That Hamilton Woman. 1945 Caesar and Cleopatra (U.S. 1946). 1948 Anna Karenina. 1951 A Streetcar Named Desire. 1955 The Deep Blue Sea. 1961 The Roman Spring of Mrs. Stone. 1965 Ship of Fools.

LEIGHTON, LILLIAN
Born: 1874, Auroville, Wis. Died: Mar. 19, 1956, Woodland Hills, Calif. Screen, stage, and vaudeville actress.

Appeared in: 1911 The Two Orphans; Cinderella. 1912 Katzenjammer Kids. 1913 "Sweeney" series. 1921 Crazy to Marry; The Lost Romance; Peck's Bad Boy; Love Never Dies; The Barbarian; The Girl from God's Country; Under the Lash. 1922 Is Matrimony a Failure?; The Lane That Had No Turning; Rent Free; Red Hot Romance; Saturday Night; Tillie. 1923 The Call of the Canyon; Hollywood; Only 38; Crinoline and Romance; Ruggles of Red Gap; Wasted Lives; The Eternal Three. 1924 The Bedroom Window; $50,000 Reward; Code of the Sea; Phantom Justice. 1925 Code of the West; Go Straight; In the Name of Love; Parisian Love; Tumbleweeds; The Thundering Herd; Contraband. 1926 The False Alarm; Sandy; The Torrent. 1927 California; The Fair Co-Ed; The Frontiersman; By Whose Hand?; The Golden Yukon; Lovers?. 1930 Feet First; The Grand Parade; The Last Dance. 1931 Subway Express; Sweepstakes. 1933 The Sphinx. 1935 Whipsaw.

LE MAIRE, GEORGE
Born: 1884, Fort Worth, Tex. Died: Jan. 20, 1930, New York, N.Y. (heart attack). Screen, stage, vaudeville actor, and film producer. Appeared in vaudeville with his brother William and later as partner in "Conroy and Le Maire" vaudeville team. Brother of screen actor William Le Maire (dec. 1933).

Appeared in: 1928 The Circus Kid. 1929 seventeen "George Le Maire" shorts.

LE MAIRE, WILLIAM
Born: Dec. 21, 1892, Fort Worth, Tex. Died: Nov. 11, 1933, Los Angeles, Calif.(heart ailment). Screen, vaudeville, and radio actor. Brother of screen actor George Le Maire (dec. 1930). Appeared in vaudeville with his brother George and later with Ed Gallagher. Entered films in 1928.

Appeared in: 1928 The Circus Kid. 1930 The Light of Western Stars; Only the Brave; Whoopee; Common Clay. 1931 The Painted Desert. 1932 Cabin in the Cotton; I Am a Fugitive from a Chain Gang. 1933 20,000 Years in Sing Sing; Captured.

LE MANS, MARCEL
Born: 1897, Antwerp, Belgium. Died: Jan. 9, 1946, Lyons, N.J. Screen and stage actor. Flying ace of Lafayette Escadrille in W.W. I. Entered films with Pathe in 1924.

LE MOYNE, CHARLES (Charles J. Lemon)
Born: 1880. Died: Sept. 13, 1956, Hollywood, Calif. Screen and stage actor.

Appeared in: 1921 Colorado; The Fox; The Freeze Out; The Wallop. 1922 Headin' West; The Kick Back; Rough Shod; Good Men and True; Man to Man. 1923 Canyon of the Fools; Desert Driven; Brass Commandments; Crashin' Thru. 1925 Riders of the Purple Sage.

LEMUELS, WILLIAM E.
Born: 1891. Died: Feb. 21, 1953, Los Angeles, Calif. Screen, stage, and vaudeville actor. Appeared in vaudeville with James Barton and they made several short subjects.

Appeared in: 1935 His Family Tree.

LENGLEN, SUZANNE
Born: 1899, France. Died: July 4, 1938, Paris, France (pernicious anemia). Screen actress and tennis champion. Appeared in film shorts.

LENI, PAUL
Born: July 8, 1885, Stuttgart, Germany. Died: 1929, Hollywood, Calif. Screen, stage actor, and film director.

LENIHAN, WINIFRED
Born: 1899, Brooklyn, N.Y. Died: July 27, 1964, Sea Cliff, N.Y. Screen, stage, radio actress, and radio director.

Appeared in: 1949 Jigsaw.

LENOIR, PASS
Born: 1874. Died: June 12, 1946, Hollywood, Calif.(heart attack). Screen, stage actor, and circus and minstrel gymnast.

LENROW, BERNARD "BERNIE"
Born: 1903. Died: Oct. 9, 1963, Englewood, N.J. Screen, stage, television, and radio actor.

Appeared in: 1957 The Violators.

LEON, CONNIE
Born: 1880. Died: May 10, 1955, Hollywood, Calif. Screen actress.

Appeared in: 1935 Clive of India. 1939 The Little Princess. 1941 Singapore Woman. 1942 Bombs over Burma; Mrs. Miniver; This above All; Thunder Birds. 1944 And Now Tomorrow. 1945 Love Letters; Hangover Square. 1946 Anna and the King of Siam; That Brennan Girl; Of Human Bondage; Three Strangers.

LEON, VALERIANO
Born: 1892, Spain. Died: Dec. 1955 or Jan. 1956 in Madrid, Spain. Screen and stage actor.

LEONARD, ARCHIE
Born: 1917. Died: Feb. 7, 1959, Des Moines, Iowa (heart attack). Screen, stage, radio actor, television director, and writer.

Appeared in: 1949 Mrs. Mike.

LEONARD, EDDIE
Born: 1870, Richmond, Va. Died: July 29, 1941, New York, N.Y. Minstrel and screen actor.

Appeared in: 1929 Melody Lane. 1940 If I Had My Way.

LEONARD, GUS (Gustav Lerond)
Born: 1856, Marseilles, France. Died: Mar. 27, 1939, Los Angeles, Calif. Screen, stage, and vaudeville actor. Entered films in 1915.

Appeared in: 1917 The Lonesome Luke. 1921 Two Minutes to Go. 1922 The Deuce of Spades; The Barnstormer; Watch Your Step. 1923 The Girl I Loved; Second Hand Love; Her Reputation; Times Have Changed. 1928 Coney Island. 1932 Babes in Toyland; When a Feller Needs a Friend. 1937 Maytime. 1950 Revenge is Sweet (reissue of 1932 version of Babes in Toyland).

LEONARD, JAMES
Born: 1868. Died: July 4, 1930, Glendale, Calif. Screen, vaudeville, and burlesque actor. Was partner in vaudeville team of "Jim and Sadie Leonard."

Appeared in: 1927 All Aboard. 1928 The Cheer Leader.

LEONARD, MURRAY
Born: 1898. Died: Nov. 6, 1970, Sherman Oaks, Calif.(heart attack). Screen, stage, burlesque, and vaudeville actor.

Appeared in: 1944 Lost in a Harem; In Society. 1945 Thousand and One Nights. 1955 Bring Your Smile Along.

LEONARD, ROBERT Z.
Born: Oct. 7, 1889, Chicago, Ill. Died: Aug. 27, 1968, Beverly Hills, Calif.(aneurysm). Screen, stage, opera actor, film producer, film director, and screenwriter. Entered films as an actor with Selig in 1907. Married to screen actress Gertrude Olmstead. Divorced from screen actress Mae Murray (dec. 1965).

Appeared in: 1910 The Courtship of Miles Standish. 1913 Robinson Crusoe. 1914 The Primeval Test; The Master Key (serial). 1945 Abbott and Costello in Hollywood.

LEONARDO, HARRY (H. L. Gottsacker)
Born: 1903. Died: Nov. 23, 1964, New York, N.Y.(heart ailment). Screen and vaudeville actor. Was partner in vaudeville team of "Ward Hall & Leonardo."

LE PAUL, PAUL (Paul Braden)
Born: 1901. Died: June 8, 1958, St. Louis, Mo. Screen, stage actor, magician, and author.

Appeared in: 1939 Eternally Yours.

LE SAINT, EDWARD J.
Born: 1871. Died: Sept. 10, 1940, Hollywood, Calif. Screen, stage actor, film director, and screenwriter. Entered films in 1912.

Appeared in: 1923 Mary of the Movies. 1929 The Talk of Hollywood. 1930 The Dawn Trail; For the Defense. 1931 The Last Parade. 1932 The Night of June 13th; The Last Man; Central Park; The Cohens and the Kellys in Trouble; Tomorrow at Seven; The Wrecker; Horse Feathers. 1933 No More Orchids; Thrill Hunter; Torch Singer; Broken Dreams. 1934 George White's Scandals; The Lemon Drop Kid; The Frontier Marshal; Once to Every Woman; The Old Fashioned Way. 1935 In Spite of Danger; Fighting Shadows; Public Opinion; Thunder Mountain. 1936 The Trail of the Lonesome Pine; The Witness Chair; We Who Are about to Die; The Case against Mrs. Ames; The Cowboy Star; The Gallant Defender; The Legion of Terror; End of the Trail; Bulldog Edition; College Holiday; Disorder in the Court (short). 1937 Counterfeit Lady; The Gold Racket; A Day at the Races. 1938 College Swing; My Lucky Star. 1939 Jesse James; Arizona Legion; The Stranger from Texas.

LE SAINT, STELLA R.
Born: 1881. Died: Sept. 21, 1948, Malibu, Calif. Screen actress.

Appeared in: 1926 The Three Bad Men. 1936 Ants in the Pantry (short).

LESLIE, GENE (Leslie Eugene Halverson)
Born: 1904. Died: Feb. 20, 1953, Los Angeles, Calif. Screen actor, dancer, and ice skater.

Appeared in: 1945 The Bells of St. Mary's; The Spanish Main; Ten Cents a Dance; Twice Blessed. 1946 The Gay Senorita; Holiday in Mexico; People Are Funny. 1948 Duel in the Sun.

L'ESTELLE, ELEANOR SCOTT
Born: 1880. Died: Apr. 25, 1962, Los Angeles, Calif. Screen actress.

LESTER, LOUISE
Born: 1867. Died: Nov. 18, 1952, Hollywood, Calif. Screen and stage actress. Married to screen actor/director Frank Beal (dec. 1934) and mother of screen actor Scott Beal (dec. 1973). Entered films with the Flying A Co. in Santa Barbara.

Appeared in: "Calamity Ann" series beginning in 1912. 1923 Her Reputation. 1924 The Desert Hawk. 1925 Galloping On.

L'ESTRANGE, DICK (Gunther von Strensch)
Born: Dec. 27, 1889, Asheville, N.C. Died: Nov. 19, 1963, Burbank, Calif. Screen, opera, vaudeville actor, and film director. Appeared in early Sennett films and was one of the original Keystone Kops.

Appeared in: 1919 The Squaw Man. 1927 Blazing Days; The Border Cavalier; The Silent Rider; Desert Dust; One Glorious Scrap. 1928 Arizona Cyclone; Made-to-Order Hero; Thunder Riders; Quick Triggers.

LE SUEUR, HAL
Born: 1904. Died: May 3, 1963, Los Angeles, Calif.(ruptured appendix). Screen actor. Brother of screen actress Joan Crawford.

LETONDAL, HENRI
Born: 1902, France. Died: Feb. 14, 1955, Burbank, Calif.(heart attack). Screen actor.

Appeared in: 1946 The Razor's Edge. 1948 Apartment for Peggy. 1949 Come to the Stable; Madame Bovary; Mother Is a Freshman. 1950 Please Believe Me. 1951 Across the Wide Missouri; Kind Lady; On the Riviera; Royal Wedding; Ten Tall Men. 1952 The Big Sky; Monkey Business; What Price Glory. 1953 Dangerous When Wet; Desert Legion; South Sea Woman; Gentlemen Prefer Blondes; Little Boy Lost. 1954 The Gambler from Natchez. 1955 A Bullet for Joey.

LEVANCE, CAL (Charles Waite)
Died: Sept. 6, 1951, Toronto, Canada. Screen, stage, and vaudeville actor.

LEVELLE, ESTELLE
Born: 1896. Died: Jan. 6, 1960, Chicago, Ill. Screen, stage actress, dancer, and singer.

LEVIN, LUCY
Born: 1907, Russia. Died: Sept. 4, 1939, New York, N.Y. Screen and stage actor. Appeared in Yiddish films.

LE VINESS, CARL
Born: 1885. Died: Oct. 15, 1964, Hollywood, Calif.(pneumonia). Screen actor and film director.

Appeared in: 1929 Twin Beds. 1935 Slightly Static (short).

LEVY, SYLVAN
Born: 1906. Died: Oct. 30, 1962, New York. Screen, stage, and vaudeville actor.

Appeared in: 1929 The Cocoanuts.

LEWIS, CATHY
Born: 1918. Died: Nov. 20, 1968, Hollywood Hills, Calif.(cancer). Screen, stage, television, radio actress and singer.

Appeared in: 1941 Double Trouble. 1942 The Kid Glove Killer. 1949 My Friend Irma; The Story of Molly X. 1950 My Friend Irma Goes West. 1958 Party Crashers. 1961 The Devil at 4 O'Clock.

LEWIS, DOROTHY W.
Born: 1871. Died: June 16, 1952, Hollywood, Calif. Screen actress.

LEWIS, ELLIOTT. See Frankie Remlye

LEWIS, GORDON
Died: Mar. 17, 1933, Tucson, Ariz.(suicide—gun). Screen actor.

LEWIS, HARRY
Born: 1886. Died: Nov. 18, 1950, Hollywood, Calif. Screen and stage actor.

Appeared in: 1926 God Save Me Twenty Cents. 1942 Always in My Heart; Busses Roar. 1944 The Last Ride; Winged Victory. 1946 Her Kind of Man. 1947 The Unsuspected. 1948 Key Largo. 1949 Bomba on Panther Island; Deadly is the Female; Joe Palooka in the Counterpunch. 1950 Gun Crazy. 1951 The Fat Man.

LEWIS, IDA
Born: 1871, New York. Died: Apr. 21, 1935, Hollywood, Calif. Screen, stage, and vaudeville actress. Entered films with Horsley Co.

Appeared in: 1918 The Bells. 1923 A Man's Man. 1925 Some Pun'kins. 1926 Sweet Adeline. 1928 Law of Fear. 1932 Sinners in the Sun.

LEWIS, JAMES H. "DADDY"
Died: Nov. 3, 1928, Pawtucket, R.I. Screen and stage actor.

Appeared in: 1923 The Broken Violin.

LEWIS, JOE
Born: 1898. Died: Oct. 9, 1938, Corning, Calif. Film actor and stunt flyer. Not to be confused with famous prize-fighter with same name.

LEWIS, MARY (Mary Kidd)
Born: 1900, Hot Springs, Ark. Died: Dec. 31, 1941, New York. Screen, stage actress, and opera star. Entered films in 1920 and appeared in early Christie comedies.

Appeared in: 1927 Way Down South (short).

LEWIS, MEADE LUX
Born: 1906. Died: June 6, 1964, Minneapolis, Minn.(auto accident). Screen actor and jazz pianist.

Appeared in: 1947 New Orleans.

LEWIS, MITCHELL J.
Born: June 26, 1880, Syracuse, New York. Died: Aug. 24, 1956, Woodland Hills, Calif. Screen and stage actor. Entered films in 1914 with Thanhauser.

Appeared in: 1914 The Million Dollar Mystery (serial). 1917 The Barrier; The Bar Sinister. 1918 The Sign Invisible; Safe for Democracy. 1921 At the End of the World. 1922 The Siren Call; Salome; The Marriage Chance; On the High Seas; The Woman Conquers. 1923 The Destroying Angel; The Little Girl Next Door; The Miracle Makers; The Spoilers; Gold Madness; Her Accidental Husband; A Prince of a King; Rupert of Hentzau. 1924 The Mine with the Iron Door; Half-a-Dollar Bill; The Red Lily; Three Weeks. 1925 Frivolous Sal; The Crimson Runner; The Mystic; Tracked in the Snow Country; Flaming Love. 1926 The Eagle of the Sea; Ben Hur; The Last Frontier; Miss Nobody; Old Ironsides; The Sea Wolf; Tell It to the Marines; Wild Oats Lane; Typhoon Love. 1927 Hard-Boiled Hagerty; Back to God's Country. 1928 Tenderloin; The Way of the Strong; Beau Sabreur; The Docks of New York; The Hawk's Nest; Out with the Tide; The Speed Classic; The Death Ship (short). 1929 The Bridge of San Luis Rey; Madame X; The Leatherneck; Linda; The Black Watch; One Stolen Night. 1930 The Cuckoos; Beau Bandit; See America Thirst; The Bad One; Girl of the Port; Mammy. 1931 Never the Twain Shall Meet; The Squaw Man; Oh! Oh! Cleopatra (short); Song of India; Ben Hur (sound of 1926 version). 1932 World and the Flesh; New Morals for Old; McKenna of the Mounted; Kongo. 1933 Secret of Madame Blanche; Ann Vickers. 1934 Count of Monte Cristo. 1935 Red Morning; The Best Man Wins; A Tale of Two Cities. 1936 Sutter's Gold; The Dancing Pirate; Mummy's Boys; The Bohemian Girl. 1937 Mama Steps Out; Espionage; Waikiki Wedding. 1938 Mysterious Mr. Moto. 1940 Go West. 1941 Meet John Doe; The Big Store; I'll Wait for You; Billy the Kid. 1942 Cairo; Rio Rita. 1944 Lost in a Harem. 1946 Courage of Lassie. 1951 Man with a Cloak. 1952 Talk about a Stranger. 1953 All the Brothers Were Valiant; The Sun Shines Bright.

LEWIS, RALPH
Born: 1872, Englewood, Ill. Died: Dec. 1937, Los Angeles, Calif. Screen and stage actor. Entered films with Reliance-Majestic in 1912.

Appeared in: 1915 The Birth of a Nation. 1919 Eyes of Youth. 1921 The Conquering Power; Man-Woman-Marriage; A Private Scandal; Salvage; Outside the Law; Prisoners of Love; Sowing the Wind. 1922 Broad Daylight; Environment; The Five Dollar Baby; Flesh and Blood; The Third Alarm; In the Name of the Law; The Sin Flood. 1923 Blow Your Own Horn; Desire; The Fog; Manhattan; Vengeance of the Deep; The Westbound Limited; Tea With a Kick. 1924 Dante's Inferno; East of Broadway; The Man Who Came Back; In Every Woman's Life; Untamed Youth. 1925 Heir-Looms; The Last Edition; The Million Dollar Handicap; The Bridge of Sighs; Who Cares; The Recreation of Brian Kent; The Overland Limited; One of the Bravest. 1926 Bigger Than Barnum's; The Lady from Hell; The Silent Power; The Block Signal; The False Alarm; Fascinating Youth; The Shadow of the Law. 1927 Casey Jones; Held by the Law; Outcast Souls. 1929 The Girl in the Glass Cage. 1930 Abraham Lincoln; The Bad One; The Fourth Alarm. 1933 Sucker Money; Riot Squad. 1934 Mystery Liner. 1935 The Lost City; Behind the Green Light.

LEWIS, RICHARD
Born: 1869. Died: Apr. 30, 1935, Los Angeles, Calif. Screen actor.

Appeared in: 1924 Yankee Speed. 1926 Stick to Your Story.

LEWIS, SAM
Born: 1878. Died: Apr. 28, 1963, Hollywood, Calif.(heart ailment). Screen actor and extra.

LEWIS, SHELDON
Born: 1869, Philadelphia, Pa. Died: May 7, 1958, San Gabriel, Calif. Screen and stage actor. Married to screen actress Virginia Pearson (dec. 1958).

Appeared in: 1914 The Exploits of Elaine (serial). 1916 The Iron Claw (serial); Dr. Jekyll and Mr. Hyde. 1917 The Hidden Hand (serial). 1918 Wolves of Kultur (serial). 1919 The Bishop's Emeralds. 1922 Orphans of the Storm; When the Desert Calls. 1923 The Darling of New York; The Little Red Schoolhouse; Jacqueline of Blazing Barriers. 1924 The Enemy Sex; Honor among Men; In Fast Company; Missing Daughters; Those Who Dare; The Dangerous Flirt. 1925 Top of the World; Bashful Buccaneer; Fighting the Flames; Kit Carson over the Great Divide; Super Speed; Lure of the Track; Accused; Defend Yourself; The Mysterious Stranger; New Lives for Old; Silent Sanderson; The Sporting Chance. 1926 Bride of the Storm; Lightning Hutch (serial); Vanishing Millions (serial); Beyond the Trail; Buffalo Bill on the U.P. Trail; Exclusive Rights; A Desperate Moment; The Sky Pirate; Senor Daredevil; The Self Starter; The Gilded Highway; Moran of the Mounted; Don Juan; The Two-Gun Man; The Red Ki-

mono. 1927 Burning Gold; Hazardous Valley; Life of an Actress; The Cruise of the Hellion; Driven from Home; The Ladybird; The Love Wager; The Overland Stage. 1928 The Sky Rider; The Chorus Kid; The Code of the Scarlet; Marlie the Killer; The Little Wild Girl; The River Woman; Turn Back the Hours; Top Sergeant Mulligan. 1929 Untamed Justice; Seven Footprints to Satan; Black Magic. 1930 Firebrand Jordan; Terry of the Times (serial released in two versions; silent and sound); Danger Man. 1932 The Monster Walks; Tex Takes a Holiday. 1933 Tombstone Canyon. 1934 Gun Justice. 1936 The Cattle Thief.

LEWIS, TED (Theodore Leopold Friedman)
Born: June 6, 1891, Circleville, Ohio. Died: Aug. 25, 1971, New York, N.Y.(heart attack). Screen, stage, vaudeville actor, and bandleader. Entered films in 1929.

Appeared in: 1929 Is Everybody Happy?. 1929 Show of Shows. 1935 Here Comes the Band. 1937 Manhattan Merry-Go-Round. 1941 Hold That Ghost. 1943 Follow the Boys; Is Everybody Happy? (and 1929 version).

LEWIS, TOM
Born: 1864, St. John, New Brunswick, Canada. Died: Oct. 19, 1927, New York (cancer). Screen, stage, circus, and minstrel actor.

Appeared in: 1920 Passers By. 1921 Enchantment. 1923 Adam and Eva; The Go-Getter; Marriage Morals. 1924 The Great White Way. 1927 The Callahans and the Murphys. 1928 Steamboat Bill, Jr.

LEWIS, VERA
Born: New York, N.Y. Died: Feb. 8, 1956, Los Angeles, Calif. Screen and stage actress. Entered films in 1914.

Appeared in: 1914 Intolerance. 1919 The Mother and the Law. 1920 Nurse Marjorie. 1922 The Glorious Fool; Nancy from Nowhere. 1923 Peg O'My Heart; Long Live the King; Brass; Desire; The Marriage Market. 1924 Broadway after Dark; The Dark Swan; How to Educate a Wife; Cornered; In Every Woman's Life. 1925 Enticement; Eve's Secret; Stella Dallas; The Only Thing; Who Cares. 1926 Ella Cinders; The Gilded Butterfly; Take it from the Pack; Take it from Me; The Lily; The Passionate Quest. 1927 Thumbs Down; Resurrection; The Broken Gate; The Small Bachelor; What Happened to Father. 1928 The Home Towners; Ramona; Satan and the Woman. 1929 The Iron Mask. 1930 Wide Open. 1931 Command Performance; Night Nurse. 1933 Hold Your Man. 1935 Never Too Late; The Man on the Flying Trapeze; Way Down East; Paddy O'Day. 1936 Missing Girls; Dancing Pirate. 1938 Four Daughters; Nancy Drew, Detective; Comet over Broadway. 1939 Naughty but Nice; Sweepstakes Winner; Nancy Drew and the Hidden Staircase; Mr. Smith Goes to Washington; Women in the Wind; On Trial; Hell's Kitchen; Roaring Twenties; Four Wives; Return of Dr. X. 1940 Granny Get Your Gun; A Night at Earl Carroll's; The Courageous Dr. Christian. 1941 Nine Lives Are Not Enough; She Couldn't Say No; Four Mothers; Here Comes Happiness. 1942 Lady Gangster; Busses Roar; Moon Tide; The Hard Way. 1945 Hollywood and Vine; Rhythm on the Range; The Suspect. 1946 The Cat Creeps; Spook Busters; The Time, the Place and the Girl. 1947 It's a Joke, Son.

LEYSSAC, PAUL
Born: Denmark. Died: Aug. 20, 1946, Copenhagen, Denmark. Screen, stage, and radio actor.

Appeared in: 1937 Victoria the Great; Head over Heels. 1941 Paris Calling.

LICHO, EDGAR ADOLPH
Born: 1876, Russia. Died: Oct. 11, 1944, Hollywood, Calif. Screen and stage actor.

Appeared in: 1930 Menschen hinter Gettern. 1944 White Cliff's of Dover; Seventh Cross; Days of Glory.

LIEB, HERMAN
Born: 1873, Chicago, Ill. Died: Mar. 9, 1966, Tucson, Ariz. Screen, stage, and vaudeville actor.

Appeared in: 1936 The Chestnut.

LIEBERMAN, JACOB
Born: 1879. Died: Feb. 16, 1956, Philadelphia, Pa. Screen and stage actor.

LIEBMANN, HANS H.
Born: 1895. Died: Jan. 24, 1960, Hannacroix, N.Y. Screen, vaudeville, television actor, and dancer. With his wife Lois, was known in vaudeville as part of team of "Harold & Lola."

Appeared in: 1945 Pan-Americana. 1948 Variety Time.

LIEVEN, ALBERT
Born: June 23, 1906, Hohenstein, Prussia. Died: Dec. 22, 1971, near London, England. Screen, stage, television, and opera actor. Divorced from screen actresses Tatiana Lieven, Petra Peters, Valerie White and Susan Shaw.

Appeared in: 1935 Krach um Iolanthe; Die Vom Niederrhein (Lower Rhine Folks); Fraeulein Liselott; Hermine und Die Sieben Aufrechten. 1936 Reifende Jugend; Gluecksspilze. 1938 Ein Frau Ohne Bedeutung; Kater Lampe. 1940 Jeannie; Night Train to Munich. 1941 Convoy. 1942 The Young Mr. Pitt; Big Blockade (war documentary). 1943 The Yellow Canary. 1944 English without Tears. 1945 The Life and Death of Colonel Blimp. 1946 The Seventh Veil; Beware of Pity. 1947 Frieda. 1949 Sleeping Car to Trieste; Her Man Gilbey. 1951 Hotel Sahara. 1953 Desperate Moment. 1957 Des Teufels General (The Devil's General); Loser Takes All. 1958 Der Fischer Von Heiligensee (The Fisherman from Heiligensee (aka The Big Barrier). 1959 Subway in the Sky; The House of Intrigue; Londra Chiama Polo Nord (London Calling North Pole). 1960 Conspiracy of Hearts. 1961 Foxhole in Cairo; The Guns of Navarone; Brainwashed. 1963 The Victors; Mystery Submarine. 1965 City of Terror; Coast of Skeletons. 1966 Traitor's Gate. Other British films: Yellow Daffodils; Wolf Pack; Secret City; Ride the High Wind.

LIGERO, MIGUEL
Born: 1898, Spain. Died: Feb. 20, 1968, Madrid, Spain. Screen, stage, and television actor.

Appeared in: 1927 Frivolina (film debut). 1938 Nobleza Baturra (Rustic Chivalry); La Verbena de la Paloma; Morena Clara; Hamelin. 1939 La Vida Bohemia. 1940 Rumbo al Cairo (Bound for Cairo).

LIGETY, LOUIS
Born: 1881, Hungary. Died: Nov. 27, 1928, Los Angeles, Calif. (results of auto accident). Screen actor.

LIGHTNER, WINNIE
Born: Sept. 17, 1901, Greenport, N.Y. Died: Mar. 5, 1971, Sherman Oaks, Calif.(heart attack). Screen, stage, and vaudeville actress.

Appeared in: 1928 The Song-a-Minute Girl(short); Broadway Favorite (short). 1929 Show of Shows; Gold Diggers of Broadway. 1930 She Couldn't Say No; Hold Everything; Life of the Party. 1931 Sit Tight; Why Change Your Husband?; Side Show; Gold Dust Gertie. 1932 Play Girl; Eight to Five; Manhattan Parade; The Slippery Pearls (short). 1933 She Had to Say Yes; Dancing Lady. 1934 I'll Fix It.

LIGON, GROVER (aka GROVER LIGGON)
Born: 1885. Died: Mar. 4, 1965, Hollywood, Calif. Screen actor and stuntman. Entered films with Biograph.

Appeared in: 1913 Sennett films and was one of the first Keystone Kops. 1917 A Maiden's Trust. 1929 The Million Dollar Collar. 1931 Father's Son.

LILLARD, CHARLOTTE
Born: 1844. Died: Mar. 4, 1946, Hollywood, Calif. Screen and stage actress. Entered films with Edison and Vitagraph Companies.

Appeared in: 1935 Mary Burns, Fugitive; The Great Impersonation. 1936 The Garden of Allah. 1938 Kentucky; Marie Antoinette.

LINCOLN, ELMO (Otto Elmo Linkenhelt).
Born: 1889. Died: June 27, 1952, Hollywood, Calif.(heart attack). Screen actor and circus performer. He was the original "Tarzan" of silent pictures.

Appeared in: 1914 Birth of a Nation. 1916 Intolerance. 1918 Tarzan of the Apes; Romance of Tarzan. 1919 Elmo the Mighty (serial); The Greatest Thing in Life; Lafayette, We Come. 1920 Elmo, the Fearless (serial); The Flaming Disc (serial); Under Crimson Skies. 1921 The Adventures of Tarzan (serial—recut and re-released with sound effects in 1928). 1922 Quincy Adams Sawyer. 1923 Fashion Row; Rupert of Hentzau; The Rendezvous. 1925 All around Frying Pan. 1926 Whom Shall I Marry? 1934 The Hunchback of Notre Dame. 1949 Tarzan's Magic Fountain. 1951 The Hollywood Story; The Iron Man. 1952 Carrie.

LINDENBURN, HENRY
Born: 1874. Died: Mar. 28, 1952, Cincinnati, Ohio. Screen actor and riverboat captain.

Appeared in: 1939 Gone with the Wind (piloted steamer in the film).

LINDER, ALFRED
Died: July 6, 1957, Hollywood, Calif. Screen, stage actor, and stage director.

Appeared in: 1945 The House on 92nd Street. 1947 13 Rue Madeline; The Brasher Doubloon. 1948 Canon City. 1949 I Was a Male War Bride. 1950 Guilty of Treason. 1952 Diplomatic Courier. 1957 The Invisible Boy; The Girl in the Kremlin.

LINDER, MAX (Gabriel Leviell)
Born: 1883, France. Died: 1925. Screen, stage actor, screenwriter, and film director.

Appeared in: 1917 Max Wants a Divorce; Max Comes Across. 1921 Be My Wife; Seven Years Bad Luck. 1922 The Three Must-Get-Theres; Au Secours! (never released).

LINDO, OLGA
Born: 1899, London, England. Died: May 7, 1968, London, England. Screen, stage, and television actress.

Appeared in: 1932 The Shadow Between; The Case of Gabriel Perry. 1935 The Last Journey; Widow's Island. 1941 The Stars Look Down. 1942 When We Are Married. 1946 Bedelia. 1947 The Adventure. 1950 The Hidden Room. 1949 Train of Events. 1954 An Inspector Calls; Raising a Riot (U.S. 1957). 1956 Blonde Sinner (aka Yield to the Night). 1957 Woman in a Dressing Gown. 1958 Twelve Desperate Hours. 1959 Sapphire. 1963 Dr. Crippen.

LINDSAY, HOWARD
Born: Mar. 29, 1889, Waterford, N.Y. Died: Feb. 11, 1968, New York, N.Y. Screen, stage, vaudeville and burlesque actor, playwright, stage director, and stage producer. Appeared in silent films.

LINDSAY, LEX
Born: 1901. Died: Apr. 24, 1971, Pa.(stroke). Screen and stage actor.

Appeared in: 1931 Sob Sister.

LINDSEY, EMILY
Born: 1887. Died: Mar. 3, 1944, Los Angeles, Calif. Screen, stage, opera, vaudeville actress, and singer.

LINGHAM, THOMAS J.
Born: Apr. 7, 1874, Indianapolis, Ind. Died: Feb. 19, 1950, Woodland Hills, Calif. Screen and stage actor. Entered films in 1913.

Appeared in: 1916 Lass of the Lumberlands (serial). 1917 The Railroad Raiders (serial); The Lost Express (serial). 1918 The Lion's Claw (serial). 1919 The Adventures of Ruth (serial); The Red Glove (serial). 1920 Ruth of the Rockies (serial); The Vanishing Dagger (serial). 1921 My Lady Friends; The Fire Eater. 1922 The Crow's Nest. 1923 The Forbidden Trail; Desert Driven; Desert Rider; Eyes of the Forest; The Lone Star Ranger; Itching Palms. 1924 The Lightning Rider; Western Luck. 1925 Don Dare Devil; Riders of Mystery; Where Was I?; Heartless Husbands; Across the Deadline. 1926 The Set-Up; The Border Sheriff; Sky High Corral; Davy Crockett at the Alamo. 1927 The Bandit's Son; Tom's Gang; Splitting the Breeze; The Desert Pirate; Daring Dude; Sitting Bull at the Spirit Lake Massacre. 1928 The Bandit Cowboy; Fangs of the Wild; Orphan of the Sage; The Trail of Courage; Young Whirlwind; The Rawhide Kid; The Bantam Cowboy; Into the Night; Man in the Rough; Son of the Golden West. 1929 The Cowboy and the Outlaw; The Fatal Warning; The Amazing Vagabond; The Freckles Rascal; Pals of the Prairie; Two Sisters; The Invaders.

LINK, WILLIAM
Born: 1867. Died: Apr. 17, 1937, Hollywood, Calif. Screen and stage actor.

LINK, WILLIAM E.
Born: 1897. Died: Dec. 13, 1949, Hollywood, Calif. Screen and stage actor.

LINLEY, BETTY
Born: 1890, England. Died: May 9, 1951, New York, N.Y. Screen and stage actress.

Appeared in: 1949 The Heiress (film and stage version).

LIPSON, MELBA
Born: 1901. Died: July 1, 1953, Hollywood, Calif. Screen actress.

LISTER, FRANCIS
Born: Apr. 2, 1899, London, England. Died: Oct. 28, 1951, London, England. Screen and stage actor.

Appeared in: 1930 Atlantic (film debut); Mystery at the Villa Rose. 1931 Uneasy Virtue. 1932 Jack's the Boy. 1933 Hawleys of High Street; Counsel's Opinion; Up to the Neck; Night and Day. 1935 Clive of India; Cardinal Richelieu; Mutiny on the Bounty; Les Miserables. 1936 Living Dangerously. 1937 Sensation. 1938 The Return of the Scarlet Pimpernel. 1939 Murder in Soho. 1944 Henry V (U.S. 1946). 1945 The Wicked Lady. 1949 Christopher Columbus. 1951 Home to Danger. 1958 Henry V (reissue of 1944 film).

LITTLE, BILLY (Billy Rhodes)
Born: 1895. Died: July 24, 1967, Hollywood, Calif.(stroke). Midget screen and stage actor.

Appeared in: 1926 Oh Baby. 1929 The Flaming Youth (short); The Head of the Family (short); The Side Show. 1930 Swing High; No Questions Asked (short); prior to 1933 Some Babies (short); The Bigger They Are (short). 1934 Men in Black. 1938 The Terror of Tiny Town. 1939 The Wizard of Oz. 1967 Mondo Hollywood.

LITTLE BOZO (John F. Pizzo)
Born: 1907. Died: May 9, 1952, Los Angeles, Calif.(heart ailment). Screen actor and circus performer.

Appeared in: 1927 White Pants Willie. 1932 Sign of the Cross; Freaks. 1939 At the Circus.

LITTLE, JAMES F.
Born: 1907. Died: Oct. 12, 1969, Miami, Fla.(cancer). Screen, stage, and television actor.

Appeared in: 1953 Taxi.

LITTLE, LITTLE JACK (John Leonard)
Born: 1901, England. Died: Apr. 9, 1956, Hollywood, Calif.(possible suicide). Screen, radio, vaudeville actor, bandleader, song writer, singer.

Appeared in: 1932-33 Universal's "Radio Star Reels." 1934 a Vitaphone short; a Paramount short. 1936 a Vitaphone short.

LITTLEFIELD, LUCIEN
Born: Aug. 16, 1895, San Antonio, Tex. Died: June 4, 1960, Hollywood, Calif. Screen actor and screenwriter. Entered films in 1913.

Appeared in: 1921 The Little Clown; The Hell Diggers; The Sheik; Too Much Speed; Crazy to Marry. 1922 Her Husband's Trademark; Rent Free; Tillie; To Have and to Hold; Across the Continent; Our Leading Citizen; Manslaughter; The Siren Call. 1923 The French Doll; The Tiger's Claw; Three Wise Fools; In the Palace of the King; The Rendezvous; Mr. Billings Spends His Dime. 1924 Babbitt; The Deadwood Coach; Gold Heels; True as Steel; Gerald Cranston's Lady; Name the Man; The Painted Lady; Teeth; A Woman Who Sinned; Never Say Die. 1925 Tumbleweeds; Charley's Aunt; Gold and the Girl; The Rainbow Trail; Soul Mates. 1926 The Torrent; Bachelor Brides; Brooding Eyes; Take It from Me; Tony Runs Wild; Twinkletoes. 1927 The Small Bachelor; My Best Girl; The Cat and the Canary; Cheating Cheaters; Taxi!, Taxi!; Uncle Tom's Cabin; A Texas Steer. 1928 Heart to Heart; The Head Man; Do Your Duty; Mother Knows Best; Harold Teen; A Ship Comes In. 1929 Seven Keys to Baldpate; Drag; The Girl in the Glass Cage; Saturday's Children; Making the Grade; This Is Heaven; Clear the Decks; The Man in Hobble's; Dark Streets. 1930 Tom Sawyer; Clancy in Wall Street; She's My Weakness; No, No, Nanette; Captain of the Guard; The Great Divide; High Society Blues, also starred in "The Potter" series of shorts, including the following: Getting a Raise; At Home; Done in Oil; Pa Gets a Vacation; Big Money; Out for Game; His Big Ambition. 1931 Misbehaving Ladies; It Pays to Advertise; Reducing; Scandal Sheet; Young as You Feel. 1932 High Pressure; Broken Lullaby; Strangers in Love; Shopworn; Strangers of the Evening; Miss Pinkerton; Downstairs; Speed Madness; Pride of the Legion; That's My Boy; Evenings for Sale; If I Had a Million, a Paramount short. 1933 The Bitter Tea of General Yen; Dirty Work; Sailor's Luck; Sweepings; Skyway; Rainbow over Broadway; Alice in Wonderland; The Big Brain; Professional Sweetheart; Chance at Heaven; East of Fifth Avenue, a Paramount short. 1934 When Strangers Meet; Love Time; Sons of the Desert; Thirty Day Princess; Kiss and Make Up; Mandalay; Gridiron Flash. 1935 Ruggles of Red Gap; Sweepstake Annie; The Man on

the Flying Trapeze; One Frightened Night; The Murder Man; She Gets Her Man; The Return of Peter Grimm; I Dream Too Much; Cappy Ricks Returns; Magnificent Obsession. 1936 Rose Marie; Early to Bed; The Moon's Our Home; Let's Sing Again. 1937 Hotel Haywire; Wild Money; Partners in Crime; High, Wide and Handsome; Souls at Sea; Bull Dog Drummond's Revenge; Wells Fargo. 1938 Wide Open Faces; Born to the West; Scandal Street; Hollywood Stadium Mystery; The Night Hawk; The Gladiator. 1939 Mystery Plane; Sky Pirate; Tumbleweeds; Unmarried; What a Life!; Sabotage; Jeepers Creepers. 1940 Money to Burn; Those Were the Days; The Great American Broadcast. 1941 Murder among Friends; Henry Aldrich for President; Man at Large; The Little Foxes; Mr. and Mrs. North. 1942 Hillbilly Blitzkrieg; Castle in the Desert; The Great Man's Lady; Bells of Capistrano; Whistling in Dixie. 1943 Henry Aldrich Haunts a House; Johnny Come Lately. 1944 Lady, Let's Dance; When the Lights Go on Again; Lights of Old Santa Fe; Casanova in Burlesque; Goodnight, Sweetheart; Cowboy and the Senorita; One Body Too Many. 1945 The Caribbean Mystery; Detour; Scared Stiff. 1946 Rendezvous with Annie; That Brennan Girl. 1947 The Hal Roach Comedy; The Fabulous Joe; Sweet Genevieve. 1948 Lightnin' in the Forest; Jinx Money; Badmen of Tombstone. 1949 Susanna Pass. 1952 At Sword's Point. 1953 Roar of the Crowd. 1954 Casanova's Big Night. 1955 Sudden Danger. 1957 Bop Girl. 1958 Wink of an Eye. 1959 Uncle Tom's Cabin (reissue of 1927 film).

LIVESEY, JACK
Born: 1901, England. Died: Oct. 12, 1961, Burbank, Calif. Screen, stage, and television actor.

Appeared in: 1933 The Wandering Jew. 1935 The Passing of the Third Floor Back. 1936 Rembrandt. 1938 Penny Paradise. 1939 Old Bones of the River. 1940 Old Bill and Son. 1947 The First Gentleman. 1949 The Affairs of a Rogue. 1950 Mystery at the Burlesque. 1951 Paul Temple's Triumph. 1962 The Notorious Landlady; That Touch of Mink.

LIVESEY, SAM
Born: Oct. 14, 1873, Flintshire, England. Died: Nov. 7, 1936, London, England (following surgery). Screen and stage actor.

Appeared in: 1922 Foolish Monte Carlo. 1930 Young Woodley. 1931 Hound of the Baskervilles; The Dreyfus Case; Jealousy; The Girl in the Night; The Wickham Mystery; Many Waters; Bill the Conqueror. 1932 Insult; The Flag Lieutenant. 1933 Private Life of Henry VIII; Jew Suess; The Man Who Won; The Wonderful Story; The Shadow; Commissionaire. 1934 The Great Defender. 1935 Elizabeth of England; Turn of the Tide; Variety; Drake of England. 1936 Rembrandt. 1937 Wings of the Morning.

LLOYD, AL
Born: 1884. Died: July 10, 1964, Hollywood, Calif.(heart attack). Screen and vaudeville actor. Appeared as partner in vaudeville team of "Aveling & Lloyd."

LLOYD, CHARLES M.
Born: 1870. Died: Dec. 4, 1948, Hollywood, Calif.(heart attack). Screen, stage, and vaudeville actor. Entered films with Mack Sennett.

LLOYD, DORIS
Born: 1900, Liverpool, England. Died: May 21, 1968, Santa Barbara, Calif.("strained"heart). Screen and stage actress.

Appeared in: 1925 The Lady (film debut); The Man from Red Gulch. 1926 The Black Bird; Exit Smiling; The Midnight Kiss; Black Paradise. 1927 Is Zat So?; The Auctioneer; Two Girls Wanted; Lonesome Ladies; The Bronco Twister; Rich but Honest. 1928 Come to My House; Trail of '98. 1929 The Careless Age; The Drake Case. 1930 Disraeli; Sarah and Son; Reno; Old English; Way for a Sailor; Charley's Aunt. 1931 The Bachelor Father; Once a Lady; Waterloo Bridge; Bought; Transgression; Devotion. 1932 Back Street; Tarzan the Ape Man. 1933 Oliver Twist; Always a Lady; Robbers' Roost; Looking Forward; Peg O'My Heart; A Study in Scarlet; Voltaire; Secrets. 1934 Glamour; Sisters under the Skin; She Was a Lady; One Exciting Adventure; Tarzan and His Mate; Dangerous Corner; Kiss and Make Up; British Agent. 1935 Clive of India; Straight from the Heart; Kind Lady; The Perfect Gentlemen; The Woman in Red; Motive for Revenge; Chasing Yesterday; Becky Sharp; A Shot in the Dark; Peter Ibbetson; A Feather in Her Hat. 1936 Don't Get Personal; Too Many Parents; Mary of Scotland; Brilliant Marriage. 1937 The Plough and the Stars; Tovarich. 1938 The Black Doll; Alcatraz Island. 1939 I'm from Missouri; The Under-Pup; Barricade; First Love; The Private Lives of Elizabeth and Essex; The Old Maid; The Spellbinder. 1940 The Great Plane Robbery; Till We Meet Again; The Letter; Vigil in the Night. 1941 Keep 'Em Flying; The Great Lie; Shining Victory. 1942 Night Monster; This above All; Journey for Margaret; Ghost of Frankenstein. 1943 Mission to Moscow; Forever and a Day; The Constant Nymph; Eyes of the Underworld. 1944 The Invisible Man's Revenge; Frenchman's Creek; Follow the Boys; The Conspirators; Phantom Lady; The Lodger. 1945 Allotment Wives; Molly and Me; Scotland Yard Investigates; My Name is Julia Ross. 1946 Devotion (and 1931 version); G. I. War Brides; Holiday in Mexico; Of Human Bondage; Tarzan and the Leopard Woman; To Each His Own; Three Strangers. 1947 The Secret Life of Walter Mitty. 1948 Sign of the Ram. 1950 Tyrant of the Sea. 1951 The Son of Dr. Jekyll; Kind Lady. 1953 Young Bess. 1955 A Man Called Peter. 1956 The Swan. 1960 Midnight Lace; The Time Machine. 1962 The Notorious Landlady. 1965 Sound of Music. 1967 Rosie.

LLOYD, FRANK
Born: Feb. 1889, Glasgow, Scotland. Died: Aug. 10, 1960, Santa Monica, Calif. Screen, stage actor, film director, producer and screenwriter. Won Academy Awards for Best Director for his The Divine Lady 1928-29 and Cavalcade, 1932-33. Entered films as an actor in 1910, and then a writer and director.

Appeared in: 1914 The Test. 1915 The Black Box (serial); Damon and Pythias.

LLOYD, FREDERICK W.
Born: Jan. 15, 1880, London, England. Died: Nov. 24, 1949, Hove, England. Screen, stage, and radio actor.

Appeared in: 1930 Balaclava (film debut). 1931 The Battle of Gallipoli. 1932 Sleepless Nights; Up for the Derby. 1933 The Crime at Blossoms; The Song You Gave Me; Mixed Doubles. 1935 Blossom Time. 1936 Everything Is Thunder; Hound of the Baskervilles; Tell England; Radio Pirates; The Beggar Student. 1937 April Romance; The Perfect Lady; The Great Gay Road; No Escape; Mademoiselle Docteur; Jubilee; Heidelburg; First and Last; Denham; Lieut. Darling; Weddings Are Wonderful. 1940 Twenty-one Days Together. 1951 Oliver Twist. Other British films: Arms and the Man; The W Plan; Temporary Widow.

LLOYD, GLADYS
Born: 1896, Yonkers, N.Y. Died: June 6, 1971, Culver City, Calif.(stroke). Screen and stage actress. Divorced from screen actor Edward G. Robinson (dec. 1973). Mother of screen actor Edward G. Robinson, Jr. Played roles as an extra in many films with Robinson.

Appeared in: 1931 Smart Money; Five Star Final. 1932 The Hatchet Man; Two Seconds.

LLOYD, HAROLD
Born: Apr. 20, 1893, Burchard, Nebr. Died: Mar. 8, 1971, Beverly Hills, Calif.(cancer). Screen, stage actor, film producer, director, and screenwriter. Married to screen actress Mildred Davis (dec. 1969). Father of screen actor Harold Lloyd, Jr.(dec. 1971). Appeared in "Lonesome Luke" series. In 1952 received Special Academy Award as "Master Comedian and Good Citizen."

Appeared in: 1914 From Italy's Shore; Curses! They Remarked. 1915 Once Every Ten Minutes; Spit Ball Sadie; Soaking the Clothes; Pressing the Suit; Terribly Stuck Up; A Mixup for Mazie; Some Baby; Fresh from the Farm; Giving Them Fits; Bughouse Bell Hops; Tinkering with Trouble; Great While It Lasted; Ragtime Snap Shots; A Fozzle at a Tea Party; Ruses, Rhymes, Roughnecks; Peculiar Patients Pranks; Social Gangster; Just Nuts; A One Night Stand; "Phunphilms" series. 1916 Luke Leans to the Literary; Luke Lugs Luggage; Luke Rolls in Luxury; Luke the Candy Cut-Up; Luke Foils the Villain; Luke and Rural Roughnecks; Luke Pipes the Pippins; Lonesome Luke; Circus King; Skylight Sleep; Luke's Double; Them Was the Happy Days; Trouble Enough; Luke and the Bomb Throwers; Reckless Wrestlers; Luke's Late Lunches; Ice; Luke Laughs Out; An Awful Romance; Luke's Fatal Fliver; Luke's Washful Waiting; Luke Rides Roughshod; Unfriendly Fruit; Luke, Crystal Gazer; A Matrimonial Mixup; Luke's Lost Lamb; Braver Than the Bravest; Luke Does the Midway; Caught in a Jam; Luke Joins the Navy; Busting the Beanery; Luke and the Mermaids; Jailed; Luke's Speedy Club Life; Luke and the Bang-Tails; Luke Laughs Last; Luke's Society Mix-Up. 1916 Luke, the Chauffeur; Luke's Preparedness Preparation; Luke's Newsie Knockout; Luke, Gladiator; Luke, Patient Provider; Luke's Movie Muddle; Luke's Fireworks Fizzle; Luke Locates the Loot; Luke's Shattered Sleep; Marriage a la Carte. 1917 Luke's Last Liberty; Luke's Busy Days; Drama's Dreadful Deal; Luke's Trolley Trouble; Lonesome Luke, Lawyer; Luke Wins Ye Ladye Faire; Lonesome Luke's Lively Rifle; Lonesome Luke on Tin Can Alley; Lonesome Luke's Lively Life; Lonesome Luke's Honeymoon; Lonesome Luke, Plumber; Stop! Luke! Listen!; Lonesome Luke, Messenger; Lonesome Luke, Mechanic;

Lonesome Luke's Wild Women; Over the Fence; Lonesome Luke Loses Patients; Pinched; By the Sad Sea Waves; Birds of a Feather; Bliss; Lonesome Luke from London to Laramie; Rainbow Island; Love, Laughs and Lather; The Flirt; Clubs Are Trump; All Aboard; We Never Sleep; Bashful; The Tip; Step Lively; Move On. 1918 The Big Idea; The Lamb; Hit Him Again; Beat It; A Gasoline Wedding; Look Pleasant Please; Here Comes the Girls; Let's Go; On the Jump; Follow the Crowd; Pipe the Whiskers; It's a Wild Life; Hey There; Kicked Out; The Non-Stop Kid; Two-Gun Gussie; Fireman Save My Child; The City Slicker; Sic 'Em Towser; Somewhere in Turkey; Are Crooks Dishonest?; An Ozark Romance; Kicking the Germ Out of Germany; That's Him; Too Scrambled; Swing Your Partner; Why Pick on Me?; Nothing But Trouble; Hear 'Em Rave; Take a Chance; She Loses Me; Bride and Groom; Bees in His Bonnet; She Loves Me Not. 1919 Wanted—$5,000; Going! Going! Going!; Ask Father; On the Fire; I'm on My Way; Look Out Below; The Dutiful Dub; Next Aisle Over; A Sammy in Siberia; Just Dropped In; Crack Your Heels; Ring up the Curtain; Young Mr. Jazz; Si, Senor; Before Breakfast; The Marathon; Back to the Woods; Pistols for Breakfast; The Rajah; Swat the Crook; Off the Trolley; Spring Fever; Billy Blazes, Esq.; Just Neighbors; At the Stage Door; Never Touched Me; A Jazzed Honeymoon; Count Your Change; Chop Suey & Co.; Heap Big Chief; Don't Shove; Be My Wife; He Leads, Others Follow; Soft Money; Count the Votes; Pay Your Dues; Bumping into Broadway; Captain Kidd's Kids; From Hand to Mouth; His Royal Slyness. 1920 the following shorts: Haunted Spooks; An Eastern Westerner; High and Dizzy; Get out and Get Under; Number, Please. 1921 Among Those Present; I Do; A Sailor-Made Man, plus the following shorts: Now or Never; Never Weaken. 1922 Grandma's Boy; Doctor Jack. 1923 Safety Last; Why Worry?. 1924 Girl Shy; Hot Water. 1925 The Freshman. 1926 For Heaven's Sake. 1927 The Kid Brother. 1928 Speedy. 1929 Welcome Danger. 1930 Feet First. 1931 Stout Hearts and Willing Hands. 1932 Movie Crazy. 1934 The Cat's Paw. 1936 The Milky Way. 1938 Professor Beware. 1947 Mad Wednesday (aka The Sin of Harold Diddlebock). 1957 The Golden Age of Comedy (documentary). 1962 Harold Lloyd's World of Comedy (documentary). 1964 Funny Side of Life.

LLOYD, HAROLD, JR. "DUKE"
Born: 1931. Died: June 9, 1971, North Hollywood, Calif. Screen, television actor, and singer. Son of screen actor Harold Lloyd, Sr. (dec. 1971) and screen actress Mildred Davis (dec. 1969).

Appeared in: 1949 Our Very Own (film debut). 1955 Yank in Ermine. 1958 Frankenstein's Daughter. 1959 Girls Town. 1960 Platinum High School. 1965 Mutiny in Outer Space.

LLOYD, ROLLO
Born: Mar. 22, 1883, Akron, Ohio. Died: July 24, 1938, Los Angeles, Calif. Screen, stage actor, screenwriter, stage and film director.

Appeared in: 1932 Okay America; Laughter in Hell; Prestige. 1933 Destination Unknown; Today We Live; Carnival Lady; Strictly Personal; Out All Night. 1934 Private Scandal; Madame Spy; The Party's Over; Whom the Gods Destroy. 1935 Lives of a Bengal Lancer; His Night Out; Mad Love; Barbary Coast; Hot Tip; The Mystery Man; Murder on a Honeymoon; The Man Who Reclaimed His Head. 1936 Come and Get It; Professional Soldier; Magnificent Obsession; Yellowstone; The Man I Marry; Love Letters of a Star; I Conquer the Sea; The White Legion; Hell-Ship Morgan; Anthony Adverse; The Devil Doll; Straight from the Shoulder. 1937 Four Days Wonder; Armored Car; The Westland Case; Seventh Heaven; Women Men Marry. 1938 Arsene Lupin Returns; The Lady in the Morgue; Goodbye Broadway.

LOBACK, MARVIN
Born: 1896. Died: Aug. 18, 1938, Hollywood, Calif. Screen and stage actor.

Appeared in: 1921 Hands Off. 1935 Uncivil Warriors (short).

LOCHER, FELIX
Born: 1882. Died: Mar. 13, 1969, Hollywood, Calif. Screen and television actor. Father of screen actor Jon Hall.

Appeared in: 1957 Hell Ship Mutiny. 1958 Curse of the Faceless Man; Desert Hell. 1959 Frankenstein's Daughter; Thunder in the Sun. 1962 The Firebrand. 1963 California.

LOCKHART, GENE
Born: July 18, 1891, London, Ontario, Canada. Died: Apr. 1, 1957, Santa Monica, Calif.(coronary thrombosis). Screen, stage, television, vaudeville, radio actor, song writer, stage director, stage producer, and radio writer. Father of screen actress June Lockhart. Wrote the song "The World is Waiting for the Sunrise."

Appeared in: 1934 By Your Leave. 1935 I've Been Around; Captain Hurricane; Star of Midnight; Thunder in the Night; Storm over the Andes; Crime and Punishment. 1936 Brides Are Like That; Times Square Playboy; Earthworm Tractors; The First Baby; Career Woman; The Garden Murder Case; The Gorgeous Hussy; The Devil Is a Sissy; Wedding Present; Mind Your Own Business; Come Closer, Folks!. 1937 Mama Steps Out; Too Many Wives; The Sheik Steps Out; Something to Sing About; Make Way for Tomorrow. 1938 Of Human Hearts; Listen, Darling; A Christmas Carol; Sweethearts; Penrod's Double Trouble; Men Are Such Fools; Blondie; Sinners in Paradise; Algiers; Meet the Girls. 1939 Blackmail; I'm from Missouri; Hotel Imperial; Our Leading Citizen; Geronimo; Tell No Tales; Bridal Suite; The Story of Alexander Graham Bell. 1940 Edison the Man; Dr. Kildare Goes Home; We Who Are Young; South of Pago Pago; A Dispatch from Reuter's; His Girl Friday; Abe Lincoln in Illinois. 1941 Keeping Company; Meet John Doe; The Sea Wolf; Billy the Kid; All That Money Can Buy; One Foot in Heaven; They Died with Their Boots On; Steel against the Sky; International Lady. 1942 Juke Girl; The Gay Sisters; You Can't Escape Forever. 1943 Forever and a Day; Hangmen Also Die; Mission to Moscow; The Desert Song; Madame Curie; Find the Blackmailer; Northern Pursuit. 1944 Going My Way; The White Cliffs of Dover; Action in Arabia; The Man from Frisco. 1945 The House on 92nd Street; That's the Spirit; Leave Her to Heaven. 1946 A Scandal in Paris; Meet Me on Broadway; She-Wolf of London; The Strange Woman. 1947 Miracle on 34th Street; The Shocking Miss Pilgrim; The Foxes of Harrow; Cynthia; Honeymoon; Her Husband's Affairs. 1948 Joan of Arc; Inside Story; That Wonderful Urge; Apartment for Peggy; I, Jane Doe. 1949 The Inspector General; Down to the Sea in Ships; Madame Bovary; Red Light. 1950 The Big Hangover; Riding High. 1951 Rhubarb; I'd Climb the Highest Mountain; Seeds of Destruction. 1951 The Lady from Texas. 1952 Face to Face; Hoodlum Empire; Bonzo Goes to College; Androcles and the Lion; Apache War Smoke; A Girl in Every Port; The Devil and Daniel Webster (reissue and retitle of All That Money Can Buy, 1941). 1953 Francis Covers the Big Town; Down among the Sheltering Palms; Confidentially Connie; The Lady Wants Mink. 1954 World for Ransom. 1955 The Vanishing American. 1956 The Man in the Gray Flannel Suit; Carousel. 1957 Jeanne Eagles.

LOCKHART, TIM
Born: 1930, Columbus, Ga. Died: Mar. 26, 1963, Louisville, Ky. (heart attack). Screen, stage, radio, and television actor.

LOCKLEAR, OMAR
Born: Oct. 28, 1891, Fort Worth, Tex. Died: Aug. 2, 1920, Los Angeles, Calif. (airplane accident). Screen actor/stunt flyer in films. Died during filming of The Skywayman.

Appeared in: 1919 Cassidy of the Air Lanes. 1920 The Great Air Robbery; The Skywayman.

LOCKWOOD, KING
Born: 1898. Died: Feb. 23, 1971, Hollywood, Calif. (stroke). Screen and television actor.

Appeared in: 1956 The Man in the Gray Flannel Suit.

LOEB, PHILIP
Born: 1894. Died: Sept. 1, 1955, New York, N.Y. Screen, stage, and television actor.

Appeared in: 1938 Room Service. 1948 A Double Life. 1951 Molly.

LOEDEL, ADI
Born: 1937, Germany. Died: June 2, 1955, Hamburg, Germany (suicide—hanging). Screen, stage, radio, and television actor.

Appeared in: 1950 Lockende Gefahr. Other German film: Kinder, Mutter und ein General.

LOESSER, FRANK
Born: June 29, 1910, New York, N.Y. Died: July 28, 1969, New York, N.Y. (lung cancer). Composer, screenwriter, and screen actor.

Appeared in: 1949 Red, Hot and Blue.

LOFF, JEANETTE (Jeanette Lov)
Born: Oct. 9, 1906, Orofino, Idaho. Died: Aug. 4, 1942, Los Angeles, Calif. (ammonia poisoning). Screen and stage actress.

Appeared in: 1927 My Friend from India. 1928 The Black Ace; Man-Made Woman; Hold 'Em Yale; Love over Night; Annapolis; Geraldine; The Man without a Face (serial). 1929 The Racketeer;

.45 Calibre War; The Sophomore. 1930 The Boudoir Diplomat; Fighting Through; Party Girl; The King of Jazz. 1935 Million Dollar Baby; St. Louis Woman.

LOFTUS, CECILIA "CISSIE"
Born: 1876, Glasgow, Scotland. Died: July 12, 1943, New York, N.Y. (heart attack). Screen, stage, and vaudeville actress.

Appeared in: 1913 Lady of Quality. 1929 Famous Impersonations (short). 1931 Doctor's Wives; Young Sinners; East Lynn. 1935 Once in a Blue Moon. 1939 On Dress Parade; The Old Maid. 1940 It's a Date; The Bluebird; Lucky Partners. 1941 The Black Cat.

LOFTUS, WILLIAM C.
Born: 1862. Died: Mar. 11, 1931, Hollywood, Calif. (hit by auto). Screen actor.

LOGAN, ELLA
Born: Mar. 6, 1913, Glasgow, Scotland. Died: May 1, 1969, San Mateo, Calif. Screen, stage, vaudeville actress, and vocalist.

Appeared in: 1936 Flying Hostess. 1937 Top of the Town; Woman Chases Man; 52nd Street. 1938 The Goldwyn Follies.

LOGAN, STANLEY
Born: June 12, 1885, Earlsfield, England. Died: Jan. 30, 1953, New York. Screen, stage actor, stage producer, film producer, director, and screenwriter.

Appeared in: 1939 We Are Not Alone. 1940 My Son, My Son; Women in War; South of Suez. 1941 Submarine Zone (aka Escape to Glory); Singapore Woman. 1942 Counter Espionage; Nightmare. 1943 Two Tickets to London. 1945 Wilson. 1946 Three Strangers; Home Sweet Homicide. 1949 Double Crossbones; Sword in the Desert. 1950 Young Daniel Boone. 1951 Pride of Maryland. 1952 The Prisoner of Zenda; Five Fingers; With a Song in My Heart.

LOHMAN, ZALLA
Born: 1906, Yugoslavia. Died: July 17, 1967, Hollywood, Calif. Screen actress. Appeared in silent films.

LOMAS, HERBERT
Born: 1887, Burnley, England. Died: Apr. 11, 1961, Devonshire, England. Screen, stage, and television actor.

Appeared in: 1932 The Missing Rembrandt; The Sign of Four. 1935 Java Head; The Phantom Light. 1936 The Ghost Goes West. 1937 Knight without Armour; Fire over London. 1938 South Riding. 1939 Ask a Policeman; Jamaica Inn; Calling Dr. Kildare. 1940 Over the Moon. 1941 The Ghost Train. 1942 The Young Mr. Pitt. 1943 Courageous Mr. Penn. 1945 I Know Where I'm Going; They Met in the Dark. 1948 The Smugglers; Bonnie Prince Charlie (U.S. 1952). 1949 The Guinea Pig. 1952 The Magic Box. 1953 The Net. Other British films: Inquest; South American George; Master of Bankdom; Welcome Mr. Washington.

LOMAS, JACK M.
Born: 1911. Died: May 13, 1959, Hollywood, Calif. Screen actor.

Appeared in: 1952 April in Paris. 1957 Copper Sky; The Night Runner; The Shadow on the Window. 1955 Seven Angry Men. 1956 That Certain Feeling. 1958 Cattle Empire.

LOMBARD, CAROLE (Jane Peters)
Born: Oct. 6, 1909, Fort Wayne, Ind. Died: Jan. 16, 1942, near Las Vegas (air crash). Screen actress. Married to screen actor Clark Gable (dec. 1960).

Appeared in: 1921 The Perfect Crime. 1925 Marriage in Transit; Hearts and Spurs; Durand of the Bad Lands. 1928 Power; Me, Gangster; Show Folks; Ned McCobb's Daughter; Divine Sinner. 1929 Big News; The Racketeer; Dynamite; High Voltage; Parachute. 1930 Fast and Loose; Safety in Numbers; The Arizona Kid; It Pays to Advertise. 1931 Man of the World. 1932 Ladies' Man; No Man of Her Own; Up Pops the Devil; I Take This Woman; Sinners in the Sun; No More Orchids; Virtue; No One Man. 1933 White Woman; The Match King; Supernatural; From Hell to Heaven; Brief Moment; Billion Dollar Scandal; The Eagle and the Hawk. 1934 Bolero; The Gay Bride; Now and Forever; 20th Century; We're Not Dressing; Lady by Choice. 1935 Hands across the Table; Rumba. 1936 My Man Godfrey; Love before Breakfast; The Princess Comes Across. 1937 Swing High, Swing Low; Nothing Sacred; True Confession. 1938 Fools for Scandal. 1939 Made for Each Other; In Name Only; Vigil in the Night. 1940 They Knew What They Wanted. 1941 Mr. and Mrs. Smith; To Be or Not To Be. 1964 Big Parade of Comedy (documentary).

LOMBARDO, CARMEN
Born: 1904. Died: Apr. 17, 1971, North Miami, Fla.(cancer). Musician (saxophonist), song writer, and screen actor. Brother of bandleader Guy Lombardo.

Appeared in: 1934 Many Happy Returns.

LONDON, JACK
Born: 1905, British Guiana. Died: May 31, 1966, London, England. Film actor and pianist.

Appeared in British film: Bones of the River.

LONDON, TOM (Leonard Clapham)
Born: Aug. 24, 1893, Louisville, Ky. Died: Dec. 5, 1963, North Hollywood, Calif. Screen and television actor.

Appeared in: 1903 The Great Train Robbery. 1924 The Loser's End. 1925 The Demon Rider; Ranchers and Rascals; Three in Exile; Winds of Chance. 1926 Snowed In (serial); Chasing Trouble; Code of the Northwest; The Grey Devil; West of the Rainbow's End; Dangerous Traffic. 1927 Return of the Riddle Rider (serial); King of Kings; Border Blackbirds; The Devil's Twin; The Long Loop of the Pecos. 1928 The Mystery Rider (serial); The Yellow Cameo (serial); The Apache Raider; The Boss of Rustler's Roost; The Bronc Stomper; Put 'Em Up; Yellow Contraband; The Price of Fear. 1929 Lawless Region; The Devil's Twin; Hell's Heroes; The Harvest of Hate; Untamed Justice; The Border Wildcat. 1930 Troopers Three; The Third Alarm; Romance of the West; Firebrand Jordan; The Woman Racket; The Storm; All Quiet on the Western Front; Borrowed Wives. 1931 Under Texas Skies; Westbound; Air Police; Two Gun Man; Trails of the Golden West; Range Law; The Arizona Terror; Lightnin' Smith Returns; Secret Six; Hell Divers; River's End; East of Borneo; The Men in Her Life; Dishonored. 1932 Night Rider; Gold; Beyond the Rockies; The Boiling Point; Trailing the Killer; Without Honors; Freaks; Dr. Jekyll and Mr. Hyde. 1933 Iron Master; Outlaw Justice; The Fugitive; Sunset Pass; One Year Later. 1934 Mystery Ranch; Outlaw's Highway; Fighting Hero; Burn 'Em up Barnes. 1935 Tumbling Tumbleweeds; The Miracle Rider (serial); Toll of the Desert; Courage of the North; Sagebrush Troubadour; Just My Luck; The Last of the Clintons; Hong Kong Nights; Skull and Crown; Gun Play. 1936 The Lawless Nineties; Guns and Guitars; O'Malley of the Mounted; The Border Patrolman; Heroes of the Range. 1937 Bar-Z Bad Men; Law of the Range; Roaring Timber; Springtime in the Rockies; Western Gold. 1938 Prairie Moon; Pioneer Trail; Six Shootin' Sheriff; Phantom Ranger; Outlaws of Sonora; Riders of the Black Hills; Santa Fe Stampede; Sunset Trail. 1939 Rollin' Westward; The Renegade Ranger; Southward Ho!; The Night Riders; Mountain Rhythm; Roll, Wagons, Roll; Song of the Buckaroo. 1940 Westbound Stage; Shooting High; Ghost Valley Raiders; Hi-Yo, Silver; Covered Wagon Days; Wild Horse Range; Stage to Chino; Trailing Double Trouble; The Kid from Santa Fe; Lone Star Raiders. 1941 Dude Cowboy; Robbers of the Range; Land of the Open Range; Romance of the Rio Grande; Pals of the Pecos; Twilight on the Trail; Stick to Your Guns; Fugitive Valley. 1942 West of Tombstone; Stardust on the Sage; Down Texas Way; Arizona Terrors; Ghost Town Law; Sons of the Pioneers; American Empire. 1943 Tenting Tonight on the Old Camp Ground; The Renegade; Wild Horse Stampede; Daredevils of the West; Hail to the Rangers; Shadows on the Sage; Wagon Tracks West; Fighting Frontier. 1944 Yellow Rose of Texas; Sheriff of Sundown; Code of the Prairie; The Cheyenne; Beneath Western Skies; The San Antonio Kid; Hidden Valley Outlaws; Vigilantes of Dodge City; Stagecoach to Monterey; Firebrands of Arizona; The Cheyenne Wildcat; Faces in the Fog; Three Little Sisters; Thoroughbreds. 1945 Colorado Pioneers; Three's a Crowd; Don't Fence Me In; Sunset in Eldorado; Corpus Christi Bandits; Wagon Wheels Westward; Marshal of Laredo; The Cherokee Flash; Oregon Trail; Trail of Kit Carson; Rough Riders of Cheyenne; The Topeka Terror; Sheriff of Cimarron; Grissly's Millions; Earl Carroll Vanities; Behind City Lights. 1946 Sheriff of Redwood Valley; Days of Buffalo Bill; Crime of the Century; Out California Way; California Gold Rush; The Undercover Woman; Alias Billy the Kid; Roll on Texas Moon; Rio Grande Raiders; The Invisible Informer; Man from Rainbow Valley; Red River Renegades; Murder in the Music Hall; Passkey to Danger. 1947 Last Frontier Uprising; Homesteaders of Paradise Valley; Santa Fe Uprising; Saddle Pals; Wyoming; Marshal of Cripple Creek; Rustlers of Devil's Canyon; Thunder Gap Outlaws; Along the Oregon Trail; The Wind Frontier; Shootin' Irons; Under Colorado Skies; Code of the Plains. 1948 Mark of the Lash; Marshal of Amarillo. 1949 Brand of Fear; Sand; Red Desert; Riders of the Sky; Frontier Investigator; South of Rio; San Antone Ambush. 1950 The Old Frontier; Code of the Pony Express; The Blazing Sun. 1951 The Secret of Convict Lake; Hills of Utah; Rough Riders of Durango. 1952 The Old West; High Noon; Trail Guide; Blue Canadian Rockies; Apache Country. 1953 Pack Train; The Marshal's Daughter. 1958 The Lone Texan.

LONERGAN, LESTER
Born: 1869. Died: Aug. 13, 1931, Lynn, Mass. Screen, stage actor, film director, and stage producer. Entered films with Thanhauser Co. Father of screen actor Lester Lonergan, Jr.(dec. 1959).

Appeared in: 1929 Seven Faces.

LONERGAN, LESTER, JR.
Born: 1894. Died: Dec. 23, 1959, New York, N.Y. Screen, stage, vaudeville, television actor, and stage director. Son of screen actor Lester Lonergan (dec. 1931).

Appeared in: 1947 Boomerang.

LONG, FREDERIC
Born: 1857. Died: Oct. 18, 1941, Hollywood, Calif. Screen, stage, and vaudeville actor.

Appeared in: 1929 The Lost Patrol.

LONG, JACK
Died: Aug. 7, 1938, Los Angeles, Calif.(motorcycle accident). Screen actor and stuntman.

Appeared in: 1933 Police Car. 1934 Speed Wings.

LONG, MELVYN HARRY
Born: 1895. Died: Nov. 14, 1940, Los Angeles, Calif.(stroke). Screen, stage, and vaudeville actor.

Appeared in: 1940 Queen of the Yukon. 1941 Meet John Doe.

LONG, WALTER
Born: Mar. 5, 1879, Milford, N.H. Died: July 4, 1952, Los Angeles, Calif.(heart attack). Screen, stage actor, and film director. Entered films in 1909.

Appeared in: 1915 The Birth of a Nation. 1916 Intolerance. 1917 The Evil Eye; The Little America. 1918 The Queen of the Sea. 1919 The Mother and the Law; Scarlet Days. 1920 What Women Love; The Fighting Shepherdess; Go and Get It. 1921 The Fire Cat; The Sheik; Tiger True; A Giant of His Race; White and Unmarried. 1922 Moran of the Lady Letty; The Dictator; Blood and Sand; Across the Continent; The Beautiful and Damned; My American Wife; Omar the Tentmaker; To Have and to Hold; South of Suva; Shadows. 1923 Kick In; The Broken Wing; Desire; The Call of the Wild; His Great Chance; Little Church around the Corner; The Isle of Lost Ships; Quicksands; The Shock; A Shot in the Night; The Huntress; The Last Hour. 1924 Daring Love; The Ridin' Kid from Powder River; Yankee Madness; Wine; White Man; Missing Daughters. 1925 Soul-Fire; Raffles; The Amateur Cracksman; The Verdict; Bobbed Hair; The Lady; The Reckless Sex; The Road to Yesterday; The Shock Punch. 1926 Eve's Leaves; Red Dice; Steel Preferred; The Highbinders; West of Broadway. 1927 White Pants Willie; Back to God's Country; The Yankee Clipper; Jewels of Desire; Jim the Conqueror. 1928 Gang War; Me, Gangster; Forbidden Grass; Thundergod. 1929 Black Cargoes of the South Seas; The Black Watch. 1930 Beau Bandit; Conspiracy; Moby Dick; The Steel Highway. 1931 Sea Devils; The Maltese Falcon; Other Men's Women; Souls of the Slums; Pardon Us. 1932 Dragnet Patrol; Escapade; Any Old Port. 1933 Women Won't Tell. 1934 The Live Ghost; Going Bye Bye (short); Six of a Kind; Operator 13; Lightning Strikes Twice. 1935 Naughty Marietta. 1936 Drift Fence; The Glory Trail; The Bold Caballero. 1937 Pick a Star; North of the Rio Grande. 1938 The Painted Trail; Bar 20 Justice; Six-Shootin' Sheriff; Man's Country. 1939 Wild Horse Canyon. 1941 Silver Stallion; City of Missing Girls. 1950 Wabash Avenue.

LOOS, THEODOR
Born: 1883, Germany. Died: June 27, 1954, Stuttgart, West Germany. German screen and stage actor.

Appeared in: 1925 Siegfried. 1926 Manon Lescaut. 1927 Mr. Metropolis. 1928 Kriemhild's Revenge. 1929 The Weavers. 1931 Die Grosse Sehnsucht; In Geheimdienst (In the Employ of the Secret Service). 1932 Der Fall des Oberst Redl; 1914: The Last Days before the War; Ich Geh' aus und Du Bleibst da; Yorck. 1933 Halzapfel Weiss Alles; Tod Ueber Schanghai. 1934 Die Blonde Christl; Trenck. 1956 Circus Girl (U.S.).

LOPEZ, CARLOS (Carlos Chaflan Lopez y Valles)
Born: Nov. 4, 1887, Durango, Mexico. Died: Feb. 13, 1942, Tapachula, Mexico.(drowned). Screen and stage actor.

Appeared in: 1925 El Qguila y el Nopal. 1933 Sobre las Olas; Una Vida por Otra. 1934 El Compadre Mendoza; El Escandalo; Clemencia; La Sangre Manda; Quien mato a Eva. 1935 Hu Hijo; Chucho El Roto; Oro y Plata; Silencio Subline; Mujeres sin Alma; Martin Garatuza; Corazon Bandolero; Cruz Diablo; Juarez y Maximiliano; El Tesora de Pancho Villa; Monja u Casada; Virgen y Martir; Payada de la vida. 1936 Vamanos Con Pancho Villa; El Baul Macabro (The Big Trunk); Alla en el Rancho Grande (Three on the Big Ranch); Cielito Lindo. 1938 Ave sin Rumbo (Wandering Bird); Rancho Grande. 1939 El Inio.

LOPEZ, TONY
Born: 1902, Mexico. Died: Sept. 23, 1949, Hollywood, Calif. Screen actor.

LORCH, THEODORE A.
Born: 1873, Springfield, Ill. Died: Nov. 12, 1947, Hollywood, Calif. Screen, stage, and vaudeville actor.

Appeared in: 1921 Gasoline Gus. 1923 Shell Shocked Sammy. 1924 The Sea Hawk; Westbound. 1925 Heir-Loons; Once in a Lifetime; Where the Worst Begins; Manhattan Madness; The Man on the Box. 1926 Across the Pacific; Unknown Dangers; The Better 'Ole. 1927 Black Jack; Ginsberg the Great; King of Kings; Sailor Izzy Murphy; Tracked by the Police. 1928 The Canyon of Adventure; Grip of the Yukon. 1929 Show Boat; The Royal Rider; Wild Blood; Spite Marriage. 1930 The Runaway Bride, plus the following shorts: An Ill Wind; The Border Patrol; More Sinned against Than Usual. 1933 Black Beauty; The Whirlwind. 1935 Rustler's Paradise; Hold 'Em Yale. 1936 Romance Rides the Range; Rebellion.

LORD, MARION
Born: 1883. Died: May 25, 1942, Hollywood, Calif. Screen and stage actress.

Appeared in: 1929 Broadway. 1930 Queen of Scandal. 1931 One Heavenly Night.

LORD, PAULINE
Born: 1890, Hanford, Calif. Died: Oct. 11, 1950, Alamogordo, N.M.(heart trouble). Screen and stage actress.

Appeared in: 1934 Mrs. Wiggs of the Cabbage Patch. 1935 A Feather in Her Hat.

LORNE, MARION (M. L. MacDougal)
Born: 1888, Pa. Died: May 9, 1968, New York, N.Y.(heart attack). Screen, stage, and television actress.

Appeared in: 1951 Strangers on a Train. 1955 The Girl Rush. 1957 The Graduate.

LORRAINE, OSCAR
Born: 1878. Died: May 10, 1955, Hollywood, Calif. Screen and vaudeville actor. Appeared as partner in vaudeville team of "Lorraine & Starr."

LORRE, PETER
Born: June 26, 1904, Rosenberg, Hungary. Died: Mar. 23, 1964, Hollywood, Calif.(stroke). Screen, stage, and television actor.

Appeared in: 1928 Pioniere in Inoplastadt; Springs Awakening. 1931 Thirteen Trunks of Mr. O.F.; White Demon; De Haute A Bas; The Man Who Knew Too Much. 1932 F.P.I. Antwortet Nicht. 1933 "M"; What Women Dream. 1935 Mad Love (aka The Hands of Orlac); Crime and Punishment. 1936 The Hidden Power; The Secret Agent; Crack-Up. 1937 Nancy Steele is Missing; Think Fast Mr. Moto; Lancer Spy; Thank You Mr. Moto. 1938 Mr. Moto Takes a Chance; Mr. Moto's Gamble; Mysterious Mr. Moto; I'll Give a Million. 1939 Mr. Moto Takes a Vacation; Mr. Moto's Last Warning; Mr. Moto in Danger Island; Confessions of a Nazi Spy. 1940 Strange Cargo; I Was an Adventuress; Island of Doomed Men; The Stranger on the Third Floor; You'll Find Out. 1941 The Face behind the Mask; Mr. District Attorney; They Met in Bombay; The Maltese Falcon. 1942 All through the Night; Invisible Agent; The Boogie Man Will Get You; Casablanca; In This Our Life. 1943 The Constant Nymph; Background to Danger; The Cross of Lorraine. 1944 Passage to Marseille; The Mask of Dimitrios; The Conspirators; Arsenic and Old Lace; Hollywood Canteen. 1945 Hotel Berlin; Confidential Agent. 1946 Three Strangers; The Verdict; The Black Angel; The Chase; The Beast with Five Fingers. 1947 My Favorite Brunette. 1948 Casbah. 1949 Rope of Sand. 1950 Quicksand. 1951 Die Verlorne (German); Double Confession. 1954 Beat the Devil; 20,000 Leagues under the Sea. 1956 Congo Crossing; Meet Me in Las Vegas; Around the World in 80 Days. 1957 The Buster Keaton Story; The Story of Mankind; The Sad Sack; Silk Stockings. 1958 Hell Ship Mutiny. 1959 The Big Circus. 1960 Scene of Mystery. 1961 Voyage to the Bottom of the Sea. 1962 Five Weeks in a Balloon; Tales of Terror. 1963 The Raven; The Comedy of Terrors. 1964 Muscle Beach Party; The Patsy. 1966 Torn Curtain.

LOSEE, FRANK
Born: 1856. Died: Nov. 14, 1937, Yonkers, N.Y.(pulmonary embolism). Screen and stage actor.

Appeared in: 1915 The Masqueraders; The Old Homestead. 1916 Ashes of Embers; Hulda from Holland. 1917 The Valentine Girl. 1918 La Tasca; Uncle Tom's Cabin; The Song of Songs; In Pursuit of Polly. 1919 His Parisian Wife; Here Comes the Bride. 1920 Lady Rose's Daughter. 1921 Dangerous Toys; Orphans of the Storm; Such a Little Queen; Disraeli. 1922 False Fronts; The Man She Brought Back; Man Wanted; The Seventh Day; Missing Millions. 1923 As a Man Lives. 1924 The Speed Spook; Unguarded Women. 1935 Four Hours to Kill; Annapolis Farewell.

LOTHAR, HANNS
Born: Hanover, Germany. Died: Mar. 11, 1967, Hamburg, Germany (heart attack). Screen, stage, and television actor.

Appeared in: 1959 Buddenbrooks. 1961 One, Two, Three. 1964 Schloss Gripholm (The Gripholm Castle).

LOTINGA, ERNEST (aka DAN ROY)
Born: 1895, Sunderland, England. Died: 1951. Screen and vaudeville actor.

Appeared in: 1928 The Raw Recruit. 1931 P.C. Josser. 1932 Josser on the River; Josser Joins the Navy. 1933 Josser in the Army. 1936 Love up the Polex.

LOUDEN, THOMAS
Born: 1874. Died: Mar. 15, 1948, Hollywood, Calif.(stroke). Screen and stage actor.

Appeared in: 1938 Kidnapped; Prison Break. 1939 Our Leading Citizen. 1940 Safari. 1942 Are Husbands Necessary. 1945 The Corn Is Green; Dangerous Partners. 1946 Tomorrow Is Forever.

LOUIS, WILLARD
Born: 1886. Died: July 22, 1926, Glendale, Calif.(Typhoid fever and pneumonia). Screen and stage actor.

Appeared in: 1920 Going Some; Madame X. 1921 Moonlight and Honeysuckle; Roads of Destiny. 1922 The Man Unconquerable; Robin Hood; Too Much Wife; Only a Shop Girl. 1923 Vanity Fair; McGuire of the Mounted; Daddies; The French Doll; The Marriage Market. 1924 Beau Brummell; Babbitt; The Lover of Camille; Three Women; Pal O' Mine; A Lady of Quality; The Age of Innocence; Broadway after Dark; Don't Doubt Your Husband; Her Marriage Vow. 1925 A Broadway Butterfly; Eve's Lover; Kiss Me Again; Three Weeks in Paris; The Man without a Conscience; His Secretary; Hogan's Alley; The Limited Mail; The Love Hour. 1926 Mlle. Modiste; Don Juan; The Honeymoon Express; The Love Toy; The Shamrock Handicap; The Passionate Quest. 1928 A Certain Young Man.

LOUISE, ANITA (Anita Louise Fremault)
Born: Jan. 9, 1915, New York, N.Y. Died: Apr. 25, 1970, West Los Angeles, Calif.(massive stroke). Screen, stage, and television actress.

Appeared in: 1920 The Sixth Commandment (film debut at age 5). 1927 The Music Master; The Life of Franz Schubert (short). 1929 Wonder of Women; Square Shoulders; The Marriage Playground. 1930 The Floradora Girl; What a Man!; Just Like Heaven; The Third Alarm. 1931 The Great Meadow; Heaven on Earth; Everything's Rosie; Millie; Madame Julie; Marriage Interlude; Fraternity House; Are These Our Children?; The Woman Between. 1932 Pack up Your Troubles; Phantom of Crestwood; Duck Soup. 1933 Little Women; Our Betters. 1934 The Most Precious Thing in Life; Are We Civilized; Madame du Barry; The Firebrand; Cross Streets; Bachelor of Arts; I Give My Love; Judge Priest. 1935 Here's to Romance; Personal Maid's Secret; Midsummer Night's Dream; Lady Tubbs; The Story of Louis Pasteur. 1936 Anthony Adverse; Brides Are Like That. 1937 The Go Getter; That Certain Woman; Green Light; Call It a Day; First Lady; Tovarich. 1938 Going Places; Marie Antoinette; My Bill; The Sisters. 1939 These Glamour Girls; Reno; The Little Princess; The Gorilla; Main Street Lawyer; Hero for a Day; The Personality Kid. 1940 Glamour for Sale; Wagons Westward; The Villain Still Pursued Her. 1941 Harmon of Michigan; Two in a Taxi; The Phantom Submarine. 1943 Dangerous Blondes. 1944 Nine Girls; Casanova Brown. 1945 Love Letters; The Fighting Guardsman. 1946 The Bandit of Sherwood Forest; The Devil's Mask; The Swan Song; Shadowed; Personality Kid. 1947 Bulldog Drummond at Bay; Blondie's Holiday; Blondie's Big Moment. 1952 Retreat, Hell!

LOVE, LAURA
Died: Date-unknown. Screen actress. Married to screen actor Henry Belmar (dec. 1931).

LOVE, MONTAGU (aka MONTAGUE LOVE)
Born: 1877, Portsmouth, England. Died: May 17, 1943, Beverly Hills, Calif. Screen, stage, and vaudeville actor.

Appeared in: 1916 A Woman's Way; Bought and Paid For. 1917 Rasputin; The Black Monk. 1919 The Gilded Cage. 1920 The World and His Wife. 1921 The Case of Becky; The Wrong Woman; Forever; Love's Redemption; Shams of Society. 1922 What's Wrong with the Women?; The Beauty Shop; The Darling of the Rich; The Secrets of Paris. 1923 The Eternal City; The Leopardess. 1924 Restless Wives; Week End Husbands; Roulette; Who's Cheating?; Love of Women; A Son of the Sahara; Sinners in Heaven. 1925 The Mad Marriage; The Ancient Highway; The Desert's Price. 1926 Hands Up!; Don Juan; Brooding Eyes; The Son of the Sheik; The Social Highwayman; The Silent Lover; Out of the Storm. 1927 The Night of Love; Good Time Charley; The Haunted Ship; King of Kings; Jesse James; One Hour of Love; Rose of the Golden West; The Tender Hour. 1928 The Haunted House; The Devil's Skipper; The Hawk's Nest; The Wind; The Noose; Character Studies (short). 1929 The Divine Lady; Her Private Life; A Most Immoral Lady; Synthetic Sin; The Mysterious Island; Charming Sinners; Midstream; Bulldog Drummond; The Last Warning; Silks and Saddles; The Voice Within. 1930 Back Pay; A Notorious Affair; Double Cross Roads; Reno; Inside the Lines; Outward Bound; Love Comes Along; The Cat Creeps; Kismit; The Furies. 1931 Alexander Hamilton; Lion and the Lamb. 1932 Stowaway; The Fighting Tornado; Vanity Fair; The Silver Lining; Midnight Lady; The Broadway Tornado; Love Bond; Dream Mother; The Engineer's Daughter; Out of Singapore. 1933 His Double Life. 1934 The Menace; Limehouse Blues. 1935 Clive of India; The Crusades; The Man Who Broke the Bank at Monte Carlo. 1936 The Country Doctor; Sing, Baby, Sing; Reunion; Lloyds of London; One in a Million; Sutter's Gold; The White Angel; Hi Gaucho; Champagne Charlie. 1937 The Prince and the Pauper; The Life of Emile Zola; Tovarich; Parnell; London by Night; The Prisoner of Zenda; Adventure's End; A Damsel in Distress. 1938 The Buccaneer; The Adventures of Robin Hood; Professor Beware; If I Were King; Kidnapped. 1939 Gunga Din; Ruler of the Seas; Man in the Iron Mask; Juarez; We Are Not Alone. 1940 Son of Monte Cristo; Northwest Passage; A Dispatch from Reuter's; The Lone Wolf Strikes; Private Affairs; Hudson's Bay; Dr. Ehrlich's Magic Bullet; Northwest Mounted Police; All This and Heaven Too; The Mark of Zorro; The Sea Hawk. 1941 The Devil and Miss Jones; Shining Victory; Lady for a Night. 1942 Devotion; Tennessee Johnson; The Remarkable Andrew; Sherlock Holmes and the Voice of Terror. 1943 Forever and a Day; Constant Nymph; Holy Matrimony.

LOVE, ROBERT
Born: 1914. Died: July 8, 1948, Hollywood, Calif.(suicide—leap). Screen actor.

Appeared in: 1945 Counterattack; Blonde from Brooklyn.

LOVEJOY, FRANK
Born: Mar. 28, 1914, New York, N.Y. Died: Oct. 2, 1962, New York, N.Y.(heart attack). Screen, stage, radio, and television actor.

Appeared in: 1948 Black Bart. 1949 Home of the Brave. 1950 Three Secrets; Breakthrough; South Sea Sinner; In a Lonely Place. 1951 Force of Arms; I Was a Communist for the FBI; Goodbye, My Fancy; Starlift; I'll See You in My Dreams; Try and Get Me. 1952 Retreat, Hell!; The Winning Team. 1953 The Hitch Hiker; House of Wax; The System; She's Back on Broadway; The Charge at Feather River. 1954 Beachhead; Men of the Fighting Lady. 1955 The Americano; Strategic Air Command; Mad at the World; Top of the World; Finger Man; The Crooked Web; Shack Out on 101. 1956 Julie; Country Husband. 1957 Three Brave Men. 1958 Cole Younger, Gunfighter.

LOVELL, RAYMOND
Born: Apr. 13, 1900, Montreal, Canada. Died: Oct. 2, 1953, London, England. British screen and stage actor, and stage director.

Appeared in: 1933 Love, Life and Laughter. 1934 The Third Clue; Warn London. 1935 King of the Damned; Case of Gabriel Perry; Someday; Crime Unlimited; Jailbreak. 1936 Gypsy Melody; Fair Exchange; Secret Lives. 1937 Mademoiselle Docteur; Glamorous Night; Murder Tomorrow; Behind Your Back. 1938 Q Planes. 1940 Blackout; Contraband. 1941 49th Parallel (aka The Invaders-U.S. 1942). 1942 The Young Mr. Pitt; Alibi. 1943 Warn That Man. 1944 Candlelight in Algeria; Uncensored. 1945 The Way Ahead. 1946 Caesar and Cleopatra; Hotel Reserve; The Man in Grey. 1948 So Evil, My Love; Three Weird Sisters. 1949 Easy Money; Blind Goddess; Quartet; Once upon a Dream; My Brother's Keeper. 1950 Madness of the Heart; Appointment with Crime. 1951 The Bad Lord Byron; Naughty Arlette; The Mudlark. 1952 Time Gentlemen Please; The Pickwick Papers (U.S. 1953). 1953 The Steel Key. Other British films: The Common Touch; The Goose Steps Out; Night Boat to Dublin; 999; Green Days and Blue Days; Calendar; But Not in Vain; Fools Rush In.

LOW, JACK
Born: 1898. Died: Feb. 21, 1958, Hollywood, Calif. Screen and television actor. Entered films approx. 1930.

Appeared in: 1956 The Proud Ones.

LOWE, EDMUND
Born: Mar. 3, 1892, San Jose, Calif. Died: Apr. 21, 1971, Woodland Hills, Calif.(lung ailment). Screen, stage, and television actor. Married to screen actress Lilyan Tashman (dec. 1934) and later married and divorced actresses Rita Kaufman and Ester Miller.

Appeared in: 1917 The Spreading Dawn. 1918 Vive La France. 1919 Eyes of Youth. 1921 The Devil; My Lady's Latchkey. 1922 Living Lies; Peacock Alley. 1923 The Silent Command; The White Flower; In the Palace of the King; Wife in Name Only. 1924 Barbara Frietchie; Honor among Men; The Brass Bowl; Nellie, The Beautiful Cloak Model. 1925 The Winding Stair; Soul Mates; The Kiss Barrier; Marriage in Transit; Greater Than a Crown; East Lynne; Ports of Call; The Fool; Champion of Lost Causes; East of Suez. 1926 What Price Glory; Black Paradise; Soul Mates; The Palace of Pleasure; Siberia. 1927 Is Zat So?; Publicity Madness; Baloo; One Increasing Purpose; The Wizard. 1928 Happiness Ahead; Dressed to Kill; Outcast. 1929 Cock Eyed World; Making the Grade; In Old Arizona; This Thing Called Love; Thru Different Eyes. 1930 Good Intentions; Born Reckless; The Painted Angel; The Bad One; Happy Days; Men on Call; More Than a Kiss; Scotland Yard; Part Time Wife; The Squealer; The Shepper - Newfounder. 1931 Women of All Nations; The Spider; The Cisco Kid; Don't Bet on Women; Transatlantic. 1932 Attorney for the Defense; Guilty As Hell; The Misleading Lady; American Madness; Chandu, the Magician; The Devil Is Driving; The Slippery Pearls (short). 1933 Hot Pepper; I Love That Man; Her Bodyguard; Dinner at Eight. 1934 Let's Fall in Love; No More Women; Bombay Mail; Gift of Gab. 1935 Under Pressure; The Great Hotel Murder; Black Sheep; Mr. Dynamite; The Best Man Wins; Thunder in the Night; King Solomon of Broadway; The Great Impersonation. 1936 The Grand Exit; The Wrecker; The Garden Murder Case; Mad Holiday; Doomed Cargo; The Girl on the Front Page; Seven Sinners. 1937 Under Cover of Night; Espionage; The Squeakers; Every Day's a Holiday; Murder on Diamond Row. 1938 Secrets of a Nurse. 1939 The Witness Vanishes; Our Neighbors, the Carters; Newsboys' Home. 1940 The Crooked Road; Honeymoon Deferred; I Love You Again; Men against the Sky; Wolf of New York. 1941 Double Date; Flying Cadets. 1942 Call Out the Marines; Klondike Fury. 1943 Dangerous Blonde; Oh, What a Night!; Murder in Times Square. 1944 The Girl in the Case. 1945 Dillinger; The Enchanted Forest; The Great Mystic. 1946 The Strange Mr. Gregory. 1948 Good Sam. 1956 Around the World in 80 Days. 1957 The Wings of Eagles. 1958 The Last Hurrah. 1959 Plunderers of Painted Flats. 1960 Heller in Pink Tights.

LOWE, JAMES B.
Born: 1880. Died: May 18, 1963, Hollywood, Calif. Screen and stage actor.

Appeared in: 1925 The Demon Rider. 1926 Blue Blazes. 1927 Uncle Tom's Cabin. 1959 Uncle Tom's Cabin (reissue of 1927 film).

LOWELL, DOROTHY
Born: 1916. Died: July 1, 1944, New York. Screen and radio actress. Entered films approx. 1936.

LOWELL, HELEN (Helen Lowell Robb)
Born: June 2, 1866, New York, N.Y. Died: June 28, 1937, Hollywood, Calif. Screen and stage actress.

Appeared in: 1923 Love's Old Sweet Song. 1924 Three Days to Live; Isn't Life Wonderful?. 1934 Midnight Alibi; Side Street; The Dragon Murder Case; Madame du Barry; The Merry Frinks; Big Hearted Herbert; The Case of the Howling Dog. 1935 Maybe It's Love; Transient Lady; Devil Dogs of the Air; Page Miss Glory; The Goose and the Gander; Dr. Socrates; Living on Velvet; Party Wire. 1936 Strike Me Pink; Snowed Under; I'd Give My Life; Valiant Is the Word for Carrie; Wild Brian Kent. 1937 Four Days Wonder; Racketeers in Exile; The Party Getter; High, Wide and Handsome.

LOWELL, JOAN (aka HELEN TRASK)
Born: 1900. Died: Nov. 7, 1967, Brasilia, Brazil. Screen, stage actress, and author.

Appeared in: 1924 Loving Lies. 1925 Cold Nerve. 1934 Adventure Girl.

LOWELL, JOHN (John L. Russell)
Died: Sept. 19, 1937, Los Angeles, Calif. Screen actor and film director.

Appeared in: 1922 Ten Nights in a Barroom. 1923 Lost in a Big City. 1924 Floodgates. 1925 Red Love. 1926 The Big Show. 1928 Silent Trail; Headin' Westward. 1929 Bad Men's Money; Captain Cowboy; Fighters of the Saddle.

LOWERY, ROBERT (Robert Lowery Hanks)
Born: 1914, Kansas City, Mo. Died: Dec. 26, 1971, Hollywood, Calif.(heart attack). Screen, stage, television actor, and singer. Divorced from screen actresses Vivian Wilcox; Rusty Farrell and Jean Parker.

Appeared in: 1937 Wake up and Live; Life Begins in College. 1938 Passport Husband; Submarine Patrol. 1939 Young Mr. Lincoln; Charlie Chan in Reno; Hollywood Cavalcade; Drums along the Mohawk; Mr. Moto in Danger Island; Tail Spin. 1940 City of Chance; Free, Blonde and Twenty-One; Shooting High; Star Dust; Charlie Chan's Murder Cruise; Four Sons; Maryland; The Mark of Zorro; Murder over New York. 1941 Private Nurse; Ride On, Vaquero!; Cadet Girl; Great Guns. 1942 Who Is Hope Schuyler?; She's in the Army; Criminal Investigator; Lure of the Islands; Rhythm Parade; Dawn on the Great Divide. 1943 The Immortal Sergeant; Tarzan's Desert Mystery; So's Your Uncle; The North Star; Campus Rhythm; Revenge of the Zombies. 1944 The Navy Way; Hot Rhythm; Dark Mountain; Dangerous Passage; The Mummy's Ghost; Mystery of the River Boat (serial); A Scream in the Dark. 1945 Thunderbolt; Homesick Angel; Road to Alcatraz; Fashion Model; High Powered; Prison Ship; The Monster and the Ape. 1946 Sensation Hunters; They Made Me a Killer; House of Horrors; God's Country; Lady Chaser; The Gas House Kids. 1947 Big Town; Danger Street; I Cover Big Town; Killer at Large; Queen of the Amazons; Jungle Flight. 1948 Death Valley; Mary Lou; Heart of Virginia; Highway 13. 1949 Shep Comes Home; Arson, Inc.; The Dalton Gang; Batman and Robin (serial); New Adventures of Batman (serial); Call of the Forest. 1950 Gunfire; Border Rangers; Western Pacific Agent; Train to Tombstone; Everybody's Dancing. 1951 Crosswinds. 1953 Jalopy; Cow Country; The Homesteaders. 1955 Lay That Rifle Down. 1956 Two Gun Lady. 1957 The Parson and the Outlaw. 1960 The Rise and Fall of Legs Diamond. 1962 When the Girls Take Over; Deadly Duo; Young Guns of Texas. 1963 McLintock!. 1964 Stage to Thunder Rock. 1965 A Zebra in the Kitchen. 1966 Johnny Reno; Waco; Pride of Virginia. 1967 The Adventures of Batman and Robin; The Undertaker and His Pals; The Ballad of Josie.

LOWRY, RUDD
Born: 1892. Died: Dec. 15, 1965, New York, N.Y. Screen, stage, and television actor.

LUBITSCH, ERNST
Born: Jan. 28, 1892, Berlin, Germany. Died: Nov. 30, 1947, Los Angeles, Calif.(heart attack). Screen, stage actor, film producer, film director, and screenwriter. Entered films in 1913.

Appeared in: 1921 One Arabian Night. 1922 The Loves of Pharoah. 1923 Souls for Sale. 1933 Mr. Broadway.

LUCAN, ARTHUR (Arthur Towle)
Born: 1887, England. Died: May 17, 1954, Hull, England. Screen, stage, and vaudeville actor. Appeared in vaudeville as part of "Lucan & McShane" team. Married to screen actress Kitty McShane (dec. 1964). Voted among first ten money making stars in British motion pictures in 1942.

Appeared in: ("Old Mother Riley" series, Lucan played the mother and his wife played the daughter.) 1937 Old Mother Riley. 1938 Old Mother Riley in Paris. 1939 Old Mother Riley, M.P. 1944 Old Mother Riley Overseas. 1945 Old Mother Riley Joins Up; Old Mother Riley's Circus. 1946 Old Mother Riley at Home; My Son, the Vampire; Old Mother Riley in Business. 1947 Old Mother Riley, Detective; Old Mother Riley in Society. 1948 Old Mother Riley's Ghosts. 1949 Old Mother Riley's New Venture. 1950 Old Mother Riley, Headmistress. 1951 Old Mother Riley's Jungle Treasure. 1952 Old Mother Riley Meets the Vampire.

LUCAS, JIMMY
Born: 1888. Died: Feb. 21, 1949, Hollywood, Calif.(heart attack). Screen, vaudeville actor, and song writer.

Appeared in: 1942 My Heart Belongs to Daddy; Saboteur. 1943 Strictly in the Groove.

LUCAS, WILFRED
Born: 1871, Ontario, Canada. Died: Dec. 13, 1940, Los Angeles, Calif. Screen, stage actor, film director, and screenwriter. Entered films with Biograph Co. in 1907.

Appeared in: 1908 The Barbarian; Ingomar. 1909 1776, or the Hessian Renegades. 1910 Fisher Folks; The Lonedale Operator; Winning Back His Love; His Trust; His Trust Fulfilled; Heart Beats of Long Ago; The Diamond Star. 1911 Was He a Coward?; The Spanish Gypsy; His Mother's Scarf; The New Dress; Enoch Arden, Part I and Part II; The Primal Call; The White Rose of the Wild; The Indian Brother; The Thief and the Girl; The Rose of Kentucky; The Sorrowful Example; Swords and Hearts; The Old Confectioner's Mistake; Dan and Dandy; Italian Blood; A Woman Scorned; The Miser's Heart; The Failure; As in a Looking Glass; A Terrible Discovery; The Transformation of Mike; Billy's Strategem. 1912 Under Burning Skies; Fate's Interception; Just Like a Woman; When Kings Were the Law; Man's Genesis; A Pueblo Legend; The Massacre; The Girl and Her Trust. 1913 Cohen's Outing 1916 Acquitted; The Wild Girl of the Sierras; Hell-to-Pay Austin. 1919 The Westerners. 1921 The Beautiful Liar; The Breaking Point; The Fighting Breed; The Better Man; Through the Back Door; The Shadow of Lightning Ridge. 1922 The Kentucky Derby; Barriers of Folly; Flesh and Blood; Across the Dead-Line; Paid Back; The Barnstormer; Heroes of the Street. 1923 Can a Woman Love Twice?; Jazzmania; Trilby; The Girl of the Golden West; The Greatest Menace; Innocence; Why Women Remarry. 1924 The Fatal Mistake; Daughters of Pleasure; Racing for Life; Women First; Cornered; The Valley of Hate; The Price She Paid; Dorothy Vernon of Haddon Hall; A Fight for Honor; Lightning Romance; The Fighting Sap; Girls Men Forget; North of Nevada; Passion's Pathway; On Probation; The Mask of Lopez. 1925 Easy Money; How Baxter Butted In; The Snob Buster; The Bad Lands; Youth's Gamble; Cyclone Cavalier; A Broadway Butterfly; The Wife Who Wasn't Wanted; Was It Bigamy?; Riders of the Purple Sage; The Man without a Country. 1926 Her Sacrifice. 1927 The Nest; Burnt Fingers. 1930 One Good Deed (short); Hello Sister; Madame Satan; The Arizona Kid; Those Who Dance; Cock of the Walk; Just Imagine. 1931 The Age for Love; House of Mystery ("Shadow" detective series); The Phantom; Convicted; Homicide Squad; His Woman; Caught; Politics; Pardon Us; Le Petit Cafe; Dishonored; Young Donovan's Kid; Are These Our Children?; Thirty Days; Men Call It Love; Rich Man's Folly; Millie. 1932 Cross Examination; Midnight Patrol; The Tenderfoot; The Unwritten Law. 1933 Sister to Judas; Lucky Larrigan; The Intruder; Fra Diavolo (The Devil's Brother); Phantom Thunderbolt; The Big Cage; The Sphinx; Day of Reckoning; I Cover the Waterfront; Notorious but Nice; Breed of the Border; Racetrack; Strange People. 1934 Count of Monte Cristo; The Moth; Sweden, Land of Vikings (narr.). 1936 Modern Times; Chatterbox; Mary of Scotland; We Who Are about to Die. 1937 Mile a Minute Love; Criminal Lawyer. 1938 Crime Afloat; The Baroness and the Butler. 1939 Zenobia. 1940 A Chump at Oxford; Ragtime Cowboy Joe; Triple Justice; Brother Orchid. 1941 The Sea Wolf.

LUCHAIRE, CORINNE
Born: 1921. Died: Jan. 22, 1950, Paris, France. French screen and stage actress.

Appeared in English and French versions of: 1939 Prison with Bars; The Affair Lafont (Conflict). 1944 Three Hours.

LUGOSI, BELA
Born: Oct. 20, 1882, Lugos, Hungary. Died: Aug. 16, 1956, Hollywood, Calif.(heart attack). Screen and stage actor. Entered films in Budapest in 1915 and in German films between 1919-20.

Appeared in: 1919-20 Sklaven Fremder Willens; Der Tanz Auf Dem Vulken; The Last of the Mohicans; Die Frau Im Delphin. 1923 The Silent Command. 1924 The Rejected Woman; The Daughters Who Pay. 1925 The Midnight Girl. 1929 Prisoners; The Thirteenth Chair; The Veiled Woman. 1930 Renegades; Wild Company; Such Men Are Dangerous; Oh, for a Man!; Viennese Nights. 1931 50 Million Frenchmen; Women of All Nations; Dracula; The Black Camel; Broadminded. 1932 Murders in the Rue Morgue; White Zombie; Chandu the Magician; The Phantom Creeps (serial); The Yellow Phantom (serial). 1933 The Whispering Shadow (serial); Island of Lost Souls; The Death Kiss; International House; Night of Terror. 1934 Return of Chandu (serial); The Black Cat; The Gift of Gab. 1935 Best Man Wins; Mysterious **Mr.** Wong; Mandrake the Magician (serial). 1936 Shadow of

Chinatown (serial); The Invisible Ray; Dracula's Daughter; Postal Inspector. 1937 Phantom Ship; Blake of Scotland Yard (serial). 1938 Killer Rats. 1939 The Phantom Creeps; Son of Frankenstein; Ninotchka; The Gorilla. 1940 The Human Monster; The Saint's Double Trouble; Black Friday; You'll Find Out; Fantasia (voice only). 1941 Devil Bat; The Wolf Man; The Invisible Ghost; Spooks Run Wild. 1942 Black Dragons; The Corpse Vanishes; Night Monster; The Ghost of Frankenstein; Bowery at Midnight; Phantom Killer. 1943 The Ape Man; Ghosts on the Loose; Eyes of the Underworld; Frankenstein Meets the Wolf Man. 1944 Return of the Vampire; Voodoo Man; Return of the Ape Man; One Body Too Many. 1945 Zombies on Broadway; The Body Snatcher. 1946 Genius at Work; My Son, the Vampire. 1947 Scared to Death. 1948 Abbott and Costello Meet Frankenstein. 1949 Master Minds. 1952 Bela Lugosi Meets the Brooklyn Gorilla; Old Mother Riley Meets the Vampire (aka Vampire over London). 1956 He Lived to Kill; Bride of the Monster; The Black Sheep; The Shadow Creeps. 1959 Plan 9 from Outer Space. 1965 The World of Abbott and Costello (film clips).

LUKAS, PAUL (Paul Lukacs)
Born: May 26, 1895, Budapest, Hungary. Died: Aug. 15, 1971, Tangier, Morocco (heart attack). Screen, stage, and television actor. Appeared in both stage and screen versions of Watch on the Rhine, receiving New York Drama League award for stage role and the Academy Award in 1943 for Best Actor in the film version.

Appeared in: Samson and Delilah (German film debut). 1928 Loves of an Actress; Three Sinners; The Woman from Moscow; Hot News; Two Lovers; Manhattan Cocktail; The Night Watch. 1929 Illusion; The Wolf of Wall Street; Half Way to Heaven; The Shopworn Angel. 1930 Behind the Make Up; The Benson Murder Case; The Devil's Holiday; Slightly Scarlet; Young Eagles; Grumpy; Anybody's Woman; The Right to Love. 1931 Beloved Bachelor; Women Love Once; Unfaithful; City Streets; Working Girls; Strictly Dishonorable; The Vice Squad. 1932 No One Man; Tomorrow and Tomorrow; Downstairs; Burnt Offering; Rockabye; A Passport to Hell; Thunder Below. 1933 Grand Slam; The Kiss Before the Mirror; Captured!; Sing, Sinner, Sing; The Secret of the Blue Room; Little Women. 1934 By Candlelight; Nagana; The Countess of Monte Cristo; Glamour; Affairs of a Gentleman; I Give My Love; Gift of Gab; The Fountain. 1935 The Casino Murder Case; Father Brown, Detective; The Three Musketeers; I Found Stella Parrish; Age of Indiscretion. 1936 Dodsworth; Ladies in Love. 1937 Espionage; Dinner at the Ritz; Mutiny on the Elsinore (U.S. 1939). 1938 The Lady Vanishes; Dangerous Secrets; Rebellious Daughters. 1939 Confessions of a Nazi Spy; Captain Fury. 1940 The Ghost Breakers; Strange Cargo; A Window in London. 1941 The Monster and the Girl; The Chinese Den; They Dare Not Love. 1942 Lady in Distress. 1943 Watch on the Rhine; Hostage. 1944 Uncertain Glory; Address Unknown; One Man's Secret; Experiment Perilous. 1946 Deadline at Dawn; Temptation. 1947 Whispering City. 1948 Berlin Express. 1950 Kim. 1954 20,000 Leagues under the Sea. 1956 The Chinese Bungalow. 1957 Under Fire. 1958 The Roots of Heaven. 1960 Scent of Mystery. 1962 The Four Horsemen of the Apocalypse; Tender Is the Night. 1963 55 Days at Peking; Fun in Acapulco. 1965 Lord Jim. 1968 Sol Madrid.

LUKIN, MRS. CECIL E. SCHULTZ. See Cecil E. Schultz

LULLI, FOLCO
Born: 1912, Italy. Died: May 24, 1970, Rome, Italy (heart attack). Screen actor.

Appeared in: 1948 Tragic Hunt. 1949 The Bandit; Flight into France. 1950 Senza Pieta (Without Pity). 1951 No Peace among the Olive Trees. 1953 Times Gone By (aka A Question of Property). 1955 Maddalena. 1956 Wages of Fear; Air of Paris. 1959 Oeil Pour Oeil (An Eye for an Eye); Companions; Sign of the Gladiator; Londra Chiama Polo Nord (London Calling North Pole aka The House of Intrigue); La Grande Speranza (The Great Hope aka Torpedo Zone). 1960 Esther and the King; Under Ten Flags; Always Victorious; The Island Sinner. 1961 Neapolitan Carousel; La Grande Guerra (The Great War). 1962 Dulcinea; La Regina Dei Tartare (The Queen of the Tartars aka The Huns); The Tartars; La Guerra Continua (The War Continues, aka Warriors Five). 1963 Gli Invasori (The Invaders, aka Erik, the Conqueror); Lafayette; Rice Girl; I Compagne (The Organizer, aka The Strikers). 1964 Parias de la Gloire (Pariahs of Glory). 1965 Luci del Varieta (Variety Lights). 1966 Marco the Magnificent. 1967 All the Other Girls Do!.

LUND, GUS A.
Born: 1896. Died: June 5, 1951, Los Angeles, Calif. Screen, stage, and television actor.

LUPINO, STANLEY
Born: June 17, 1895, London, England. Died: June 10, 1942, London, England. Screen, stage actor, screenwriter, playwright, and stage producer. Father of screen actress Ida Lupino. Entered films in England in 1931.

Appeared in: 1931 Love Lies. 1932 The Love Race; King of the Ritz. 1933 Sleepless Nights. 1934 Happy; You Made Me Love You. 1935 Honeymoon for Three. 1936 Cheer Up. 1937 Sporting Love. 1938 Side by Side. 1939 Hold My Hand; Lucky to Me.

LUPINO, WALLACE (aka WALLACE LANE)
Born: Jan. 23, 1898, Edinburgh, Scotland. Died: Oct. 11, 1961, Ashford, England. Screen and stage actor. Brother of screen actor Lupino Lane (dec. 1959).

Appeared in: Educational shorts 1923 to 1933. 1929 Buying a Gun (short). 1933 The Maid of the Mountains. 1935 The Student's Romance. 1936 The Man Who Could Work Miracles (U.S. 1937); Old Spanish Customers; Pajamas Preferred. 1939 Me and My Gal (aka The Lambeth Walk).

LUTHER, JOHNNY
Born: 1909. Died: July 31, 1960, San Pedro, Calif.(drowned in boating accident). Screen actor.

LUTHER, LESTER
Born: 1888. Died: Jan. 19, 1962, Hollywood, Calif.(stroke). Screen, stage, and radio actor.

Appeared in: 1949 The Red Menace.

LUTTRINGER, ALFONSE "AL"
Born: 1879, San Francisco, Calif. Died: June 9, 1953, Hollywood, Calif. Screen and stage actor.

LYGO, MARY (Irene Goodall aka Irene "Rene" Fuller)
Died: June 1, 1927, Los Angeles, Calif.(suicide—poison). Screen and vaudeville actress. Appeared professionally under both names.

LYMAN, ABE
Born: 1897. Died: Oct. 23, 1957, Los Angeles, Calif. Screen, radio actor, bandleader and song writer.

Appeared in: 1933 a Vitaphone short; Mr. Broadway; Broadway Thru a Keyhole.

LYNCH, FRANK J.
Died: Dec. 4, 1932, Springfield, Mass.(air crash burns). Screen actor, stunt flyer, and exhibitionist.

LYNCH, FRANK T.
Born: 1869. Died: Dec. 18, 1933, New York, N.Y.(heart attack). Screen, stage actor, ball player, and stage manager.

LYNDON, ALICE
Born: 1874. Died: July 9, 1949, Woodland Hills, Calif. Screen and vaudeville actress. Entered films with Sennett in 1914.

LYNN, DIANA (Dolores Loehr aka Dolly Loehr)
Born: Oct. 7, 1926, Los Angeles, Calif. Died: Dec. 18, 1971, Los Angeles, Calif.(brain hemorrhage). Screen, stage actress, and pianist.

Appeared in: 1939 They Shall Have Music. 1941 There's Magic in Music. 1942 The Major and the Minor; Star-Spangled Rhythm. 1943 Henry Aldrich Gets Glamour. 1944 The Miracle of Morgan's Creek; Henry Aldrich Plays Cupid; And the Angels Sing; Our Hearts Were Young and Gay. 1945 Out of This World; Duffy's Tavern. 1946 Our Hearts Were Growing Up; The Bride Wore Boots. 1947 Variety Girl; Easy Come, Easy Go. 1948 Ruthless; Texas, Brooklyn and Heaven; Every Girl Should Be Married. 1949 My Friend Irma. 1950 Paid in Full; Rogues of Sherwood Forest; My Friend Irma Goes West; Peggy. 1951 Bedtime for Bonzo; Take Care of My Little Girl; The People against O'Hara. 1952 Meet Me at the Fair. 1953 Plunder of the Sun. 1954 Track of the Cat. 1955 An Annapolis Story; You're Never Too Young; The Kentuckian.

LYNN, EMMETT
Born: Feb. 14, 1897, Muscatine, Iowa. Died: Oct. 20, 1958, Hollywood, Calif.(heart attack). Screen, stage, vaudeville, radio, and burlesque actor. Entered films with Biograph in 1913.

Appeared in: 1913 The Imp. 1940 Grandpa Goes to Town; Scatterbrain; Wagon Train; The Fargo Kid. 1941 Along the Rio Grande; Robbers of the Range; Thunder over the Ozarks; Puddin' Head. 1942 Frisco Lil; Baby Face Morgan; Stagecoach Express; In Old

California; Road Agent; The Spoilers; City of Silent Men; Tomorrow We Live; Outlaws of Pine Ridge; Westward Ho!; Queen of Broadway. 1943 Carson City Cyclone; The Law Rides Again; Girls in Chains; Sundown Kid; Dead Man's Gulch. 1944 Good Night, Sweetheart; Outlaws of Santa Fe; Frontier Outlaws; Return of the Rangers; Cowboy Canteen; When the Lights Go on Again; The Laramie Trail; Johnny Doesn't Live Here Any More; The Town Went Wild; Swing Hostess; Bluebeard. 1945 Song of Old Wyoming; Shadow of Terror; Hollywood and Vine; The Big Show-Off; The Cisco Kid Returns. 1946 The Caravan Trail; Romance of the West; Throw a Saddle on a Star; Man from Rainbow Valley; The Fighting Frontiersmen; Stagecoach to Denver; Conquest of Cheyenne; Landrush; Santa Fe Uprising. 1947 Code of the West; Oregon Trail Scouts; Rustlers of Devil's Canyon. 1948 Relentless; West of Sonora; Grand Canyon Trail; Here Comes Trouble. 1949 Roll, Thunder, Roll; Cowboy and the Prizefighter; Ride, Ryder, Ride; The Fighting Redhead. 1951 Badman's Gold; Best of the Badmen; The Scarf. 1952 Desert Pursuit; Lone Star; Monkey Business; Oklahoma Annie; Skirts Ahoy!; Apache War Smoke; Sky Full of Moon. 1953 Pickup on South Street; The Robe; The Homesteaders; Northern Patrol. 1954 Ring of Fear; Living It Up; Bait. 1955 A Man Called Peter.

LYNN, HASTINGS
Born: 1879. Died: June 30, 1932, Elstree, England (liver ailment). Screen actor.

LYNN, NATALIE
Died: Dec. 3, 1964, Isleworth, England. Screen, stage, radio, and television actress.

Appeared in: 1960 For Members Only (aka The Nudist Story).

LYNN, RALPH
Born: 1881, Manchester, England. Died: Aug. 8, 1962, London, England. Screen and stage actor.

Appeared in: 1930 Plunder. 1931 Tons of Money; The Chance of a Night Time. 1932 A Night Like This; Thark; Mischief; Just My Luck; Turkey Time. 1933 A Cuckoo in the Nest; Up to the Neck. 1934 A Cup of Kindness. 1935 Fishing Stock; Dirty Work. 1936 Foreign Affairs. 1937 For Valour; In the Soup.

LYNN, ROBERT
Born: 1897. Died: Dec. 18, 1969, Los Angeles, Calif. Screen actor.

Appeared in: 1951 The Barefoot Mailman. 1958 The Return of Dracula; Good Morning Miss Dove.

LYNN, SHARON E. (D'Auvergne Sharon Lindsay)
Born: 1904, Weatherford, Tex. Died: May 26, 1963, Hollywood, Calif. Screen, stage actress, and song writer. Entered films as an extra.

Appeared in: 1927 Aflame in the Sky; Clancy's Kosher Wedding; Jake the Plumber; The Cherokee Kid; Tom's Gang; The Coward. 1928 Red Wine; Give and Take; None but the Brave; Son of the Golden West. 1929 Fox Movietone Follies of 1929; Speakeasy; Sunny Side Up; Hollywood Night; The One Woman Idea; Trail of the Horse Thieves. 1930 Crazy That Way; Lightnin'; Up the River; Happy Days; Let's Go Places; Wild Company; Man Trouble. 1931 Men on Call; Too Many Cooks; Fallen Star. 1932 Discarded Lovers; The Big Broadcast. 1933 Big Executive. 1935 Enter Madame; Go into Your Dance. 1937 Way Out West. 1941 West Point Widow.

LYNN, WILLIAM H.
Born: 1889. Died: Jan. 5, 1952, New York, N.Y. Screen, stage, vaudeville, radio, and television actor.

Appeared in: 1951 Mr. Belvedere Rings the Bell; Harvey; Katie Did It. 1952 Outcasts of Poker Flat. 1953 The Twonky.

LYON, FRANK
Born: 1901, Bridgeport, Conn. Died: Jan. 6, 1961, Gardner, Mass. Screen and stage actor.

Appeared in: 1930 The Big Pond. 1932 Lovers Courageous. 1936 After the Thin Man. 1937 Parnell; Night Must Fall; Conquest. 1938 I Met My Love Again; Dramatic School; Invisible Enemy; The Road to Reno. 1943 Paris after Dark.

LYONS, CANDY
Born: 1945. Died: June 19, 1966, aboard an Atlantic liner. Screen actress.

Appeared in: 1963 Palm Springs Holiday.

LYONS, FRECKLES (Francis Lunakiaki Lyons)
Born: 1909. Died: Sept. 1, 1960, Honolulu, Hawaii. Screen, stage actor, musician, and singer.

LYONS, FRED (Fred F. Leyva)
Died: Mar. 16, 1921 (auto accident). Screen actor.

LYTELL, BERT
Born: Feb. 24, 1885, New York, N.Y. Died: Sept. 28, 1954, New York, N.Y. (following surgery). Screen, stage, radio, television, vaudeville actor, and film director. Married to stage actress Grace Mencken; divorced from screen actress Claire Windsor (dec. 1972); and brother of screen actor Wilfred Lytell (dec. 1954). Entered films in 1917.

Appeared in: 1917 The Lone Wolf. 1918 The Trail to Yesterday. 1919 Easy to Make Money. 1920 Alias Jimmy Valentine. 1921 A Message from Mars; Misleading Lady; Price of Redemption; The Man Who; A Trip to Paradise; The Idle Rich; Ladyfingers; Alias Ladyfingers. 1922 The Face Between; The Right That Failed; Sherlock Brown; To Have and to Hold. 1923 Kick In; Rupert of Hentzau; The Eternal City; The Meanest Man in the World. 1924 Born Rich; A Son of the Sahara; Sandra. 1925 Lady Windermere's Fan; Steele of the Royal Mounted; The Boomerang; Eve's Lover; Never the Twain Shall Meet; Ship of Souls; Sporting Life. 1926 That Model from Paris; The Lone Wolf Returns; The Gilded Butterfly; Obey the Law. 1927 Alias the Lone Wolf; The First Night; Women's Wares. 1928 On Trial. 1929 The Lone Wolf's Daughter. 1930 The Last of the Lone Wolf; Brothers (stage and film versions). 1931 The Single Sin; Stolen Jools (short). 1943 Stage Door Canteen.

LYTELL, WILFRED
Born: 1892. Died: Sept. 10, 1954, Salem, N.Y. Screen, stage, radio, and television actor. Brother of screen actor Bert Lytell (dec. 1954).

Appeared in: 1916 The Combat. 1918 Our Mrs. McChesney. 1920 Heliotrope. 1921 Know Your Men; The Kentuckians. 1922 The Man Who Paid; The Wolf's Fangs. 1923 The Fair Cheat; The Leavenworth Case. 1924 Trail of the Law; The Wardens of Virginia. 1926 Bluebeard's Seven Wives.

MAC ARTHUR, CHARLES
Born: Nov. 5, 1895, Scranton, Pa. Died: Apr. 21, 1956, New York (internal hemorrhage). Screenwriter, film director, film producer, playwright, and screen actor. Married to screen actress Helen Hayes and father of screen actor James Mac Arthur.

Appeared in: 1934 Crime without Passion. 1935 The Scoundrel.

MAC BRIDE, DONALD. See Donald McBride

MACCHIA, JOHN
Born: 1932. Died: July 30, 1967, Los Angeles, Calif. (stroke). Screen actor.

Appeared in: 1963 The Nutty Professor. 1964 The Disorderly; Beach Party. 1966 Three on a Couch.

MAC COLL, JAMES A.
Born: 1912. Died: Apr. 18, 1956, New York, N.Y. Screen, stage, television actor, and playwright.

Appeared in: 1954 This Is the Army (stage and film versions).

MAC DERMOTT, JOHN W. "JACK"
Born: Sept. 9, 1892, Green River, Wyo. Died: July 22, 1946, Los Angeles, Calif. Screen, stage actor, screenwriter, and film director. Entered films in 1913.

Appeared in: 1923 Mary of the Movies.

MAC DONALD, DONALD
Born: Mar. 13, 1898, Denison, Tex. Died: Dec. 9, 1959, New York, N.Y. Screen, stage, television, and radio actor. Married to stage actress Ruth Hammond.

Appeared in: 1955 The Kentuckian. 1956 The Brass Legend; Great Day in the Morning.

MAC DONALD, EDMUND
Born: 1911. Died: Sept. 1951, Los Angeles, Calif. Screen and radio actor.

Appeared in: 1933 Enlighten Thy Daughter. 1938 Prison Break. 1939 I Stole a Million. 1940 Sailor's Lady; Black Friday; The Gay Caballero. 1941 Great Guns; The Bride Wore Crutches; Texas. 1942 Whispering Ghosts; To the Shores of Tripoli; The Strange Case of Dr. Rx; Flying Tigers; Heart of the Golden West; Madame

Spy; Who Done It?. 1943 Hangmen Also Die; Sherlock Holmes in Washington; Hi Ya Chum; Corvette K-225. 1944 Sailor's Holiday. 1945 The Lady Confesses; Detour; Hold That Blonde. 1946 They Made Me a Killer. 1947 Shoot to Kill; Blondie's Anniversary. 1948 That Lady in Ermine; Black Eagle. 1949 Red Canyon.

MAC DONALD, J. FARRELL
Born: June 6, 1875, Waterbury, Conn. Died: Aug. 2, 1952, Hollywood, Calif. Screen, stage actor, film director, and opera singer. Was in Imp Productions in 1911.

Appeared in: 1915 The Heart of Maryland. 1921 Little Miss Hawkshaw; Bucking the Line; Riding with Death; Trailin'; Sky High; Action; Desperate Youth; The Freeze Out; The Wallop. 1922 The Ghost Breaker; The Bachelor Daddy; The Bonded Woman; Manslaughter; Tracks; Come On Over; The Young Rajah; Over the Border. 1923 Drifting; Quicksands; The Age of Desire; Fashionable Fakers; Racing Hearts; While Paris Sleeps. 1924 Western Luck; The Brass Bowl; The Iron Horse; Fair Week; Mademoiselle Midnight; The Signal Tower; The Storm Daughter. 1925 Gerald Cranston's Lady; The Scarlet Honeymoon; The Fighting Heart; Lightnin'; Thank You; The Lucky Horseshoe; Kentucky Pride; Let Women Alone. 1926 The First Year; A Trip to Chinatown; The Dixie Merchant; The Shamrock Handicap; The Family Upstairs; The Country Beyond; Three Bad Men. 1927 Bertha the Sewing Machine Girl; Love Makes 'Em Wild; Ankles Preferred; The Cradle Snatchers; Rich but Honest; Colleen; Paid to Love; Sunrise; East Side, West Side. 1928 The Cohens and the Kellys in Paris; Bringing up Father; Abie's Irish Rose; Riley the Cop; None but the Brave. 1929 In Old Arizona; Masked Emotion; Masquerade; Strong Boy; Four Devils; South Sea Rose. 1930 Broken Dishes; The Truth about Youth; Song O' My Heart; Born Reckless; The Painted Angel; The Steel Highway; Men without Women; Happy Days; The Girl of the Golden West. 1931 The Easiest Way; The Millionaire; Woman Hungry; The Maltese Falcon; Other Men's Women; The Squaw Man; Too Young to Marry; The Brat; Sporting Blood; The Spirit of Notre Dame; Touchdown; The Painted Desert; River's End. 1932 Under Eighteen; Discarded Lovers; Hotel Continental; Probation; The Phantom Express; Week-End Marriage; The 13th Guest; 70,000 Witnesses; The Vanishing Frontier; Hearts of Humanity; This Sporting Age; The Pride of the Legion; No Man of Her Own; Me and My Gal; Steady Company; The Racing Strain; Scandal for Sale. 1933 The Iron Master; Heritage of the Desert; Under Secret Orders; The Working Man; Peg O' My Heart; Laughing at Life; The Power and the Glory; I Loved a Woman; Murder on the Campus. 1934 Myrt and Marge; Man of Two Worlds; The Crime Doctor; Romance in Manhattan; Once to Every Woman; The Cat's Paw; The Crosby Case; Beggar's Holiday. 1935 Swell Head; Maybe It's Love; Danger Ahead; Square Shooter; The Whole Town's Talking; Northern Frontier; Star of Midnight; The Best Man Wins; The Healer; Let 'Em Have It; Our Little Girl; The Irish in Us; Front Page Woman; Stormy; Fighting Youth; Waterfront Lady. 1936 Hitchhike Lady; Florida Special; Riff Raff; Exclusive Story; Showboat. 1937 The Game That Kills; Courage of the West; Shadows of the Orient; Maid of Salem; Mysterious Crossing; The Silent Barrier; Roaring Timber; The Hit Parade; Slave Ship; County Fair; Slim; Topper; My Dear Miss Aldrich. 1938 My Old Kentucky Home; Numbered Woman; Gang Bullets; State Police; Little Orphan Annie; White Banners; Come on Rangers; The Crowd Roars; Submarine Patrol; Flying Fists; There Goes My Heart. 1939 Susannah of the Mounties; Mickey the Kid; Conspiracy; The Gentleman from Arizona; Zenobia; Coast Guard; East Side of Heaven. 1940 Knights of the Range; The Dark Command; Light of the Western Stars; Prairie Law; I Take This Oath; The Last Alarm; Untamed; Stagecoach War; Friendly Neighbors. 1941 Meet John Doe; The Great Lie; In Old Cheyenne; Riders of the Timberline; Law of the Timber; Broadway Limited. 1942 One Thrilling Night; Phantom Killer; Bowery at Midnight; Little Tokyo, U.S.A.; Snuffy Smith, Yardbird; The Living Ghost; Captains of the Clouds. 1943 The Ape Man; Clancy Street Boys; True to Life; Tiger Fangs. 1944 The Miracle of Morgan's Creek; Texas Masquerade; The Great Moment; Follow the Boys; Shadow of Suspicion. 1945 The Woman Who Came Back; A Tree Grows in Brooklyn; Nob Hill; Johnny Angel; Pillow of Death. 1946 Smoky; My Darling Clementine; Joe Palooka; Champ. 1947 Thunder in the Valley; Web of Danger; Keeper of the Bees. 1948 Whispering Smith; Panhandle; Fury at Furnace Creek; Walls of Jericho; Belle Star's Daughter. 1949 She Comes Home; Streets of San Francisco; Beautiful Blonde from Bashful Bend; Fighting Man of the Plains; The Dalton Gang; Law of the Barbary Coast. 1950 Dakota Lil; Hostile Country; Woman on the Run. 1951 Elopement; Mr. Belvedere Rings the Bell.

MAC DONALD, JAMES W.
Born: 1899. Died: Aug. 31, 1962, Santa Cruz, Calif. Screen and stage actor.

Appeared in: 1949 Cinderella (voice only).

MAC DONALD, JEANETTE
Born: June 18, 1906, Philadelphia, Pa. Died: Jan. 14, 1965, Houston, Tex.(heart attack). Married to screen actor Gene Raymond. Screen, stage, television, radio actress, and opera singer.

Appeared in: 1929 The Love Parade (film debut). 1930 The Vagabond King; The Lottery Bride; Let's Go Native; Monte Carlo; Oh, for a Man!. 1931 Don't Bet on Women; Annabelle's Affairs (aka The Affairs of Annabelle). 1932 One Hour with You; Love Me Tonight. 1934 The Merry Widow; The Cat and the Fiddle. 1935 Naughty Marietta. 1936 Rose Marie; San Francisco. 1937 Maytime; The Firefly. 1938 The Girl of the Golden West; Sweethearts. 1939 Broadway Serenade. 1940 New Moon; Bitter Sweet. 1941 Smilin' Through. 1942 I Married an Angel; Cairo. 1944 Follow the Boys. 1948 Three Daring Daughters; The Birds and the Bees. 1949 The Sun Comes Up. 1951 Miquette.

MAC DONALD, KATHERINE
Born: 1894. Died: June 4, 1956, Santa Barbara, Calif. Screen actress and film producer.

Appeared in: 1918 Headin' South; Riddle Gawne. 1919 The Woman Thou Gavest Me; The Squaw Man. 1920 Curtain; The Beauty Market. 1921 The Beautiful Liar; My Lady's Latchkey; Passion's Playground; Stranger Than Fiction; Trust Your Wife. 1922 Domestic Relations; Her Social Value; Heroes and Husbands; The Infidel; The Woman Conquers; The Woman's Side; White Shoulders. 1923 The Lonely Road; Money, Money, Money; Refuge; Chastity; The Scarlet Lily. 1925 The Unnamed Woman. 1926 Old Loves and New.

MAC DONALD, RAY. See Ray McDonald

MAC DOUGALL, ALLAN R.
Born: 1894, Scotland. Died: July 19, 1956, Paris, France. Screen, stage actor, author, and editor.

Appeared in: 1936 Soak the Rich.

MAC DOWELL, MELBOURNE
Born: 1857, South River, N.J. Died: Feb. 18, 1941, Decoto, Calif.(blood clot on the brain). Screen and stage actor.

Appeared in: 1920 Nomads of the North. 1921 Diamonds Adrift; The March Hare; The Golden Snare; Outside the Law. 1922 Beyond the Crossroads; The Bootlegger's Daughter; Confidence; The Infidel; The Flaming Hour; Forsaking All Others. 1923 The Ghost Patrol; The Love Pirate; A Million to Burn; Richard the Lion-Hearted. 1924 Virtue's Revolt; Geared to Go. 1925 Bandits of the Air; Savages of the Sea; Sky's the Limit; The Cloud Rider; Fighting Courage; Speed Mad. 1926 The Outlaw Express; Behind the Front; The Rainmaker; The Winning Wallop; Stick to Your Story; What Happened to Jones; The City. 1927 Code of the Cow Country; Driven from Home. 1928 Feel My Pulse; The Old Code.

MAC FADDEN, GERTRUDE "MICKEY"
Born: 1900. Died: June 3, 1967, Hollywood, Calif. Screen, stage, and vaudeville actress. Appeared with her sister, Florence, in vaudeville and films as the "Mac Fadden Sisters."

MAC FARLANE, BRUCE
Born: 1910. Died: Nov. 25, 1967, Hollywood, Calif. Screen, stage, and television actor. Son of opera singer Alice Gentle.

Appeared in: 1938 Come on, Leathernecks; Come on, Rangers.

MAC FARLANE, GEORGE
Born: 1877. Died: Feb. 22, 1932, Hollywood, Calif.(auto accident). Screen, stage, and vaudeville actor.

Appeared in: 1929 Frozen Justice; Nix on Dames; South Sea Rose; Wall Street; Happy Days. 1930 Cameo Kirby; Double Cross Roads; Painted Angel; Half Shot at Sunrise; Up the River. 1931 Rich Man's Folly. 1932 Union Depot; Taxi; Fireman, Save My Child; The Heart of New York.

MAC GREGOR, HARMAN
Born: 1878, New York, N.Y. Died: Dec. 5, 1948, Marblehead, Mass. Screen and stage actor.

Appeared in: 1923 Cause for Divorce; Slave of Desire; Vengeance of the Deep. 1924 The Dancing Cheat.

MAC GREGOR, MALCOLM. See Malcolm McGregor

MAC INTOSH, LOUISE
Born: 1865. Died: Nov. 1, 1933, Beverly Hills, Calif. Screen and stage actress.

Appeared in: 1930 Up the River.

MACK, ANDREW
Born: Boston, Mass. Died: May 21, 1931, Bayside, N.Y. Screen, stage actor, and singer.

Appeared in: 1914 The Ragged Earl. 1926 Bluebeard's Seven Wives.

MACK, ARTHUR
Born: 1877. Died: June 19, 1942, Jamaica Plain, Mass.("gas poisoning suffered in Flanders during W.W.I"). Screen and stage actor.

Appeared in: 1929 The Return of Sherlock Holmes.

MACK, BILL "BILLY"
Died: Jan. 27, 1961, New York, N.Y.(stroke). Screen and vaudeville actor. Was part of vaudeville acts of "Reigel & Mack" and later as "Rickard & Mack."

Appeared in: 1926 The Black Bird. 1944 A Wave, a Wac and a Marine.

MACK, CHARLES (Charles McGaughey)
Born: 1878. Died: Nov. 29, 1956, Hollywood, Calif. Screen, stage actor, and film producer. Entered films in 1919.

Appeared in: 1925 The Lost Chord; Silent Pal; The White Monkey. 1927 The Trunk Mystery.

MACK, CHARLES E. (Charles E. Sellers)
Born: Nov. 22, 1887, White Cloud, Kans. Died: Jan. 11, 1934 near Mesa, Ariz.(auto accident). Screen, stage, vaudeville, radio actor, and minstrel. He was the Mack in "Moran and Mack" comedy team, usually referred to as the "Two Black Crows."

Films he appeared in as part of team are: 1927 Two Flaming Youths. 1929 Why Bring That Up. 1930 Anybody's War (previous title was Two Black Crows in the A.E.F.). 1932 Hypnotized. 1932-33 appeared in "Moran and Mack" shorts for Educational: Two Black Crows in Africa; As the Crows Fly. Note: Anybody's War and a few other shorts were without George Moran as the Moran in the act. Moran left the team after Why Bring That Up, but returned to do Hypnotized and a few shorts.

MACK, CHARLES EMMETT
Born: 1900, Scranton, Pa. Died: Mar. 17, 1927, Riverside, Calif. (auto accident). Screen and vaudeville actor. Entered films as a property man with Griffith in 1917.

Appeared in: 1921 Dream Street. 1922 One Exciting Night. 1923 Driven; The Daring Years; The White Rose. 1924 America; The Sixth Commandment; Youth for Sale. 1925 Down upon the Suwanee River; Bad Company; A Woman of the World; The White Monkey. 1926 The Devil's Circus; The Unknown Soldier. 1927 The First Auto; The Rough Riders; Old San Francisco.

MACK, DICK
Born: 1854. Died: Feb. 4, 1920, San Francisco, Calif. Screen, stage, and vaudeville actor.

MACK, FRANCES
Born: 1907. Died: Sept. 26, 1967, Hollywood, Calif. Screen and stage actress. Entered films approx. 1945. Married to screen actor and costumer Alexis Davidoff.

MACK, HUGHIE (Hugh McGowan)
Born: 1884, Brooklyn, N.Y. Died: Oct. 13, 1927, Santa Monica, Calif.(heart disease). Screen actor.

Appeared in: 1913 John Tobin's Sweetheart; Roughing the Cub. 1914 The Win(k)some Widow; The New Secretary. 1922 Trifling Women. 1923 Going Up; Reno. 1924 The Riddle Rider (serial); Greed. 1925 A Woman's Faith; The Merry Widow. 1926 Mare Nostrum. 1927 The Arizona Whirlwind; Where Trails Begin. 1928 Four Sons; The Wedding March.

MACK, JAMES "BUCK"
Died: Sept. 19, 1959, Los Angeles, Calif. Screen, stage, and vaudeville actor. Not to be confused with actor James T. Mack. Was member of vaudeville dance team of "Miller & Mack."

MACK, JAMES T.
Born: 1871, Chicago, Ill. Died: Aug. 12, 1948, Hollywood, Calif. Screen and stage actor.

Appeared in: 1926 The Cruise of the Jasper B; Sin Cargo; Fools of Fashion. 1927 Wild Geese; The First Night; Husband Hunters; Women's Wares; Swim, Girl, Swim. 1928 The Home Towners. 1929 Ain't It the Truth (short); Queen of the Night Clubs. 1930 Anna Christie; Hello Sister. 1932 Arsene Lupin. 1933 One Year Later. 1934 I Hate Women; In Love with Life. 1935 Mary Burns, Fugitive.

MACK, JOSEPH P."JOE"
Born: May 4, 1878, Rome, Italy. Died: Apr. 8, 1946, Hollywood, Calif. Screen and vaudeville actor.

Appeared in: 1903 Great Train Robbery. 1918 Wild Honey. 1920 Wonder Man. 1927 Cross Breed. 1928 Finders Keepers; Man from Headquarters; Driftwood. 1936 A Woman Rebels.

MACK, ROSE
Born: 1866. Died: Oct. 1927, New York, N.Y. Screen, stage, and vaudeville actor.

MACK, WILBUR
Born: Binghamton, N.Y. Died: Mar. 13, 1964, Hollywood, Calif. Screen, stage, vaudeville actor, and long time film extra. Married to screen actress Gertrude Purdy with whom he appeared in vaudeville in the team of "Mack & Purdy." Divorced from actress Nella Walker with whom he appeared in vaudeville in the team of "Mack & Walker."

Appeared in: 1925 Gold and Grit. 1926 The Hidden Way. 1927 The Love of Paquita; Shooting Straight; Straight Shootin'. 1928 The Avenging Shadow; Quick Triggers; The Crimson Canyon; The Body Punch. 1929 Honky Tonk; The Argyle Case; Slim Fingers; Beauty and Bullets; and "Mack & Purdy" appeared in An Everyday Occurance (short). 1930 Remove Control; The Girl Said No; Up the River; Woman Racket; Sweethearts on Parade; The Czar of Broadway; Scarlet Pages; The Stand Up (short). 1931 Annabelle's Affairs. 1934 The Loud Speaker. 1935 Redheads on Parade; Million Dollar Baby; A Night at the Opera. 1936 The Crime Patrol. 1937 Larceny on the Air; Atlantic Flight; A Day at the Races. 1938 Law of the Texan. 1939 Tough Kid. 1940 Doomed to Die; That Gang of Mine; Half a Sinner. 1943 Dixie. 1944 Atlantic City. 1948 Stage Struck. 1951 According to Mrs. Hoyle. 1957 Up in Smoke.

MACK, WILLARD
Born: 1873, Morrisburg, Ontario, Canada. Died: Nov. 18, 1934, Brentwood Heights (Los Angeles), Calif. Screen, stage actor, film director, screenwriter, and playwright. Divorced from screen actresses Pauline Fredericks (dec. 1938) and Marjorie Rambeau (dec. 1970).

Appeared in: 1916 Aloha Oe. 1923 Your Friend and Mine. 1929 The Voice of the City. 1933 What Price Innocence; Broadway to Hollywood.

MACK, WILLIAM B.
Born: 1872. Died: Sept. 13, 1955, Islip, N.Y. Screen and stage actor.

Appeared in: 1920 Heliotrope. 1922 Missing Millions. 1923 Backbone; The Steadfast Heart. 1926 The Song and Dance Man; The American Venus.

MACKAY, CHARLES
Born: 1867. Died: Nov. 19, 1935, Englewood, N.J. Screen and stage actor. Entered films with Edison.

Appeared in: 1921 Diane of Star Hollow; Ten Nights in a Bar Room; Peggy Puts It Over; The Matrimonial Web. 1922 The Inner Man; The Man She Brought Back; Without Fear. 1923 Lost in a Big City.

MACKAY, EDWARD J.
Born: 1874. Died: Dec. 26, 1948, Elizabeth, N.J. Screen, stage actor, film producer, and film director. Appeared in early silents.

MAC KAYE, NORMAN. See Norman McKay

MAC KENNA, KATE
Born: 1878. Died: June 14, 1957, Hollywood, Calif. Screen and television actress.

Appeared in: 1935 The Bride Comes Home. 1941 So Ends Our Night. 1942 The Wife Takes a Flyer; Fly by Night. 1951 Lemon Drop Kid. 1956 Bus Stop.

MAC KENNA, KENNETH (Leo Mielziner)
Born: Aug. 19, 1899, Canterbury, N.H. Died: Jan. 15, 1962, Hollywood, Calif.(cancer). Screen, stage actor, film director, story editor, stage director, and stage producer. Entered films with Paramount Astoria Studios in 1925.

Appeared in: 1925 A Kiss in the Dark; Miss Bluebeard. 1926 The American Venus. 1927 The Lunatic at Large. 1929 Pleasure Crazed; South Sea Rose. 1930 Crazy That Way; Men without Women; Temple Tower; The Three Sisters; Man Trouble; Sin Takes a Holiday; Virtuous Sin. 1931 The Man Who Came Back. 1932 Those We Love. 1960 High Time. 1961 Judgement at Nuremberg. 1962 13 West Street.

MACKENZIE, MARY
Born: 1922. Died: Sept. 20, 1966, London, England (auto accident). Screen, stage, and television actress.

Appeared in: 1952 Scotland Yard Inspector; Stolen Face. 1953 The Long Memory. 1954 Duel in the Jungle; Track the Man Down; Trouble in the Glen. 1956 Blonde Sinner (aka Yield to the Light). 1958 A Question of Adultery.

MACKIE, BERT (Robert James Mackie)
Born: 1893. Died: July 23, 1967, Hollywood, Calif. Screen actor.

MACKIN, WILLIAM
Born: 1883. Died: Sept. 9, 1928, Los Angeles, Calif. Screen actor.

MAC LANE, BARTON
Born: Dec. 25, 1900, Columbia, S.C. Died: Jan. 1, 1969, Santa Monica, Calif.(double pneumonia). Screen, stage, and television actor.

Appeared in: 1926 The Quarterback (film debut). 1929 The Cocoanuts. 1933 Men of the Forest; Big Executive; The Torch Singer; To the Last Man; Tillie and Gus; Hell and High Water; Let's Dance (short). 1934 The Last Round-Up; The Thundering Herd; Lone Cowboy. 1935 Black Fury; Go into Your Dance; The G-Men; Case of the Curious Bride; Stranded; Page Miss Glory; Dr. Socrates; I Found Stella Parish; Frisco Kid; The Case of the Lucky Legs; Man of Iron; Ceiling Zero. 1936 The Walking Dead; Times Square Playboy; Jail Break; Bullets or Ballots; Bengal Tiger; Smart Blonde; God's Country and the Woman. 1937 Draegerman Courage; You Only Live Once; Don't Pull Your Punches; San Quentin; The Prince and the Pauper; Fly Away Baby; Ever since Eve; Wine, Woman and Horses; The Adventurous Blonde; Born Reckless. 1938 The Kid Comes Back; Blondes at Work; Torchy Gets Her Man; Gold Is Where You Find It; You and Me; Prison Break; The Storm. 1939 Big Town Czar; Torchy Blane in Chinatown; I Was a Convict; Stand up and Fight; Torchy Runs for Mayor; Mutiny in the Big House. 1940 Men without Souls; The Secret Seven; Gangs of Chicago; Melody Ranch. 1941 Manpower; Barnacle Bill; Wild Geese Calling; Hit the Road; Come Live with Me; Western Union; Dr. Jekyll and Mr. Hyde; The Maltese Falcon; High Sierra. 1942 The Big Street; Highways by Night; All through the Night. 1943 The Underdog; The Crime Doctor's Strangest Case; Man of Courage; Bombardier; Song of Texas. 1944 The Cry of the Werewolf; The Mummy's Ghost; Nobonga; Marine Raiders; Secret Command; Gentle Annie. 1945 Treasure of Fear; The Spanish Main; Scared Stiff; Tarzan and the Amazons. 1946 Santa Fe Uprising; Mysterious Intruder; San Quentin. 1947 Tarzan and the Huntress; Jungle Flight; Cheyenne. 1948 Silver River; The Dude Goes West; The Walls of Jericho; Angel in Exile; Relentless; Unknown Island; The Treasure of the Sierra Madre. 1949 Red Light. 1950 Kiss Tomorrow Goodbye; Rookie Fireman; The Bandit Queen; Let's Dance. 1951 Best of the Badmen; Drums in the Deep South. 1952 The Half Breed; Thunderbirds; Bugles in the Afternoon. 1953 Kansas Pacific; Cow Country; Jack Slade; Sea of Lost Ships; Captain Scarface. 1954 Rails into Laramie; Jubilee Trail; The Glenn Miller Story. 1955 The Last of the Desperados; Hell's Outpost; Treasure of Ruby Hills; The Silver Star; Foxfire; Jail Busters. 1956 The Man Is Armed; Three Violent People; The Naked Gun; Jaguar; Backlash; Wetbacks. 1957 Sierra Stranger; Naked in the Sun; The Storm Rider; Hell's Crossroads. 1958 Girl in the Woods; Frontier Gun; The Geisha Boy. 1960 Noose for a Gunman; Gunfighters of Abilene. 1961 Pocketful of Miracles. 1964 Law of the Lawless. 1965 The Rounders; Town Tamer. 1968 Arizona Bushwackers; Buckskin.

MACLAREN, IVOR
Born: 1904, Wimbleton, England. Died: Oct. 30, 1962, London, England. Screen, television actor, and film director.

Appeared in: 1933 Aunt Sally. 1934 Evergreen; Princess Charming; Friday the 13th; The Woman in Command; Along Came Sally. 1935 Radio Parade of 1935.

MAC LEAN, DOUGLAS
Born: Jan. 14, 1890 or 1897?, Philadelphia, Pa. Died: July 9, 1967, Beverly Hills, Calif.(stroke). Screen, stage actor, film producer, and screenwriter.

Appeared in: 1917 Souls in Pawn. 1918 Johanna Enlists; The Hun Within; Fuss and Feathers; Mirandy Smiles. 1919 Captain Kidd, Jr.; As Ye Sow; The Home Breaker; Twenty-Three and One-Half Hours' Leave. 1920 Let's Be Fashionable; Mark's Ankle; The Jailbird. 1921 Chickens; The Home Stretch; One a Minute; Passing Thru; The Rookie's Return. 1922 The Hottentot. 1923 The Sunshine Trail; Going Up; Bell Boy 13; A Man of Action; Mary of the Movies. 1924 Never Say Die; The Yankee Consul. 1925 Introduce Me; Seven Keys to Baldpate. 1926 That's My Baby; Hold That Lion. 1927 Soft Cushions; Let It Rain. 1929 The Carnation Kid; Divorce Made Easy.

MAC LEAN, REZIN D.
Born: 1859. Died: June 27, 1948, Hollywood, Calif. Screen and stage actor.

Appeared in: 1921 Don't Neglect Your Wife. 1923 Bag and Baggage; The Bishop of the Ozarks. 1933 Cradle Song.

MAC LEOD, KENNETH
Born: 1895. Died: Dec. 6, 1963, Hollywood, Calif. Screen actor.

MAC MILLIAN, VIOLET
Born: 1887. Died: Dec. 28, 1953, Grand Rapids, Mich. Screen and stage actress.

Appeared in: 1915 Mrs. Plumb's Pudding. 1920 The Mystery Mind (serial).

MACOWAN, NORMAN
Born: Jan. 2, 1877, St. Andrews, Scotland. Died: Dec. 29, 1961. Screen actor.

Appeared in: 1951 Valley of the Eagles. 1953 Laxdale Hall. 1955 Footsteps in the Fog. 1956 X the Unknown. 1957 Action of the Tiger. 1958 Tread Softly Stranger (U.S. 1959). 1959 The Boy and the Bridge. 1960 Kidnapped; Battle of the Sexes. 1961 Horror Hotel (U.S. 1963, aka City of the Dead).

MAC PHERSON, JEANIE
Born: Boston, Mass. Died: Aug. 26, 1946, Hollywood, Calif. Screen, stage actress, screenwriter, and film director.

Appeared in: 1908 The Vaquero's Vow; Mr. Jones at the Ball; Mrs. Jones Entertains. 1909 The Death Disc; A Corner in Wheat. 1910 Winning Back His Love; Heart Beats of Long Ago; The Last Drop of Water; Enoch Arden, Part I; Fisher Folks. 1913 Carmen. 1923 Hollywood. 1939 Land of Liberty (narr.).

MAC QUARRIE, MURDOCK
Born: 1878, San Francisco, Calif. Died: Aug. 22, 1942, Los Angeles, Calif. Screen, stage actor, and film director. Entered films with Biograph in 1902.

Appeared in: 1921 Cheated Hearts; Sure Fire. 1922 If I Were Queen; The Unfoldment; The Hidden Woman. 1923 Ashes of Vengeance; Canyon of the Fools. 1924 The Only Woman. 1925 A Gentleman Roughneck. 1926 Going the Limit; Hair Trigger Baxter; The High Hand; The Jazz Girl. 1927 Black Jack; The Long Loop on the Pecos. 1928 The Man from Hardpan; The Apache Raider. 1929 A .45 Calibre War. 1930 Captain of the Guard. 1932 Dr. Jekyll and Mr. Hyde. 1933 Cross Fire. 1934 Return of Chandu. 1935 Stone of Silver Creek. 1938 Blockage.

MACRAE, DUNCAN (aka DUNCAN MC RAE)
Born: 1905, Glasgow, Scotland. Died: Mar. 23, 1967, Glasgow, Scotland. Screen, stage, and television actor. Married to screen actress Gertrude McCoy (dec. 1967).

Appeared in: 1947 The Brothers. 1952 Woman in Question (aka Five Angles on Murder—U.S. 1953). 1953 You're Only Young Twice. 1954 The Little Kidnappers. 1956 Wee Geordie. 1958 Mad Little Island. 1959 The Bridal Path. 1960 Kidnapped; Tunes of Glory; Our Man in Havana. 1961 Greyfriars' Bobby. 1963 Girl in the Headlines. 1964 Model Murder Case; A Jolly Bad Fellow (aka They All Died Laughing). 1968 30 Is a Dangerous Age; Cynthia.

MAC SARIN, KENNETH (Max Kenneth Sarin)
Born: 1912. Died: Jan. 17, 1967, New York, N.Y.(cancer). Screen and stage actor.

MACY, CARLETON
Born: 1861. Died: Oct. 18, 1946, Bay Shore, N.Y. Screen, stage, and vaudeville actor. Was in vaudeville with his wife Maude Hall in an act billed as "Magpie and the Jay" and later was with Al Lydell in an act billed as "Two Old Cronies."

Appeared in: 1929 Seven Keys to Baldpate.

MACY, JACK
Born: 1886. Died: July 2, 1956, Wyom.(heart attack). Screen, stage, and television actor.

Appeared in: 1955 Untamed.

MADEIRA, HUMBERTO
Born: 1921, Portugal. Died: July 15, 1971, Lisbon, Portugal (cancer). Screen and stage actor.

Appeared in:1956 Lisbon.

MADISON, CLEO
Born: 1883. Died: Mar. 11, 1964, Burbank, Calif.(heart attack). Screen actress.

Appeared in: 1913 The Heart of a Cracksman; The Trey O' Hearts (serial). 1915 Damon and Pythias. 1916 The Severed Hand. 1919 The Great Radium Mystery (serial). 1921 Ladies Must Live; The Lure of Youth. 1922 The Dangerous Age; A Woman's Woman. 1923 Gold Madness; Souls in Bondage. 1924 The Roughneck; The Lullaby; True as Steel; Discontented Husbands; Unseen Hands.

MADISON, HARRY
Born: 1877. Died: July 8, 1936, Los Angeles, Calif.(throat ailment). Screen, stage, and vaudeville actor. Was part of vaudeville team of "Bailey & Madison" and later "Thurber & Madison."

Appeared in: 1920 King of the Circus (serial).

MAE, JIMSEY (Charlotte Rawley)
Born: 1894. Died: Apr. 10, 1968, Jackson, Oreg. Screen actress.

Appeared in: 1915 Damaged Goods.

MAERTENS, WILLY
Born: 1893, Germany. Died: Nov. 28, 1967, Hamburg, Germany. Screen, stage, television actor, and stage director.

MAGEE, HARRIETT
Born: 1878. Died: Apr. 19, 1954, Los Angeles, Calif. Screen actress. Appeared in silent films.

MAGRILL, GEORGE
Born: Jan. 5, 1900, New York, N.Y. Died: May 31, 1952, Los Angeles, Calif. Screen, stage actor, and stuntman. Entered films in 1921.

Appeared in: 1922 Rose of the Sea. 1924 Fast and Fearless; North of Nevada; The Mask of Lopez; Stolen Secrets. 1925 Lord Jim; Vanishing American; Wild Horse Mesa; Duped; The Fighting Smile. 1926 The Enchanted Hill. 1927 The Desert of the Lost; The Ballyhoo Buster; Roarin' Broncs; Hawk of the Hills (serial); Ride 'Em High; The Cyclone Cowboy. 1928 Blockage; Vultures of the Sea (serial); The Count of Ten. 1929 Hawk of the Hills (feature of 1927 serial). 1937 Outcast; Midnight Madonna. 1938 Born to Be Wild; Give Me a Sailor. 1939 The Flying Irishman. 1941 Meet Boston Blackie. 1947 Pirates of Monterey. 1950 When Willie Comes Marching Home. 1952 At Sword's Point.

MAGUIRE, CHARLES J.
Born: 1882. Died: July 22, 1939, North Hollywood, Calif. Screen, stage, and circus actor. Married to stage actress Janet Sully.

MAGUIRE, TOM "LITTLE TOM MAGUIRE"
Born: Sept. 7, 1869, Milford, Conn. Died: June 21, 1934, North Hollywood, Calif.(blood clot on the heart). Screen and stage actor.

Appeared in: 1921 Star Dust. 1922 The Bond Boy. 1926 The Savage; Then Came the Woman. 1927 One Increasing Purpose; Shanghai Bound; Colleen. 1928 Cameraman; The Sawdust Paradise. 1930 City Girl.

MAGYARI, IMRE
Born: 1894, Hungary. Died: June 1940. Hungarian screen, stage actor, and gypsy band leader.

MAHAN, VIVIAN L.
Born: 1902. Died: Oct. 13, 1933, Los Angeles, Calif.(suicide). Screen actress and film extra. Married to screen actor Harry Bayfield.

MAHER, WALTER "WALLY"
Born: 1908. Died: Dec. 27, 1951, Los Angeles, Calif. Screen, radio, and television actor.

Appeared in: 1935 Murder in the Fleet. 1937 23½ Hours' Leave; Submarine D-1; Hollywood Hotel. 1945 Strange Holiday. 1949 Johnny Stool Pigeon. 1950 Mystery Street; The Reformer and the Redhead; Right Cross; The Story of Molly X.

MAIGNE, CHARLES M.
Born: 1879, Va. Died: Nov. 23, 1929, San Francisco, Calif. (pneumonia). Screen actor, film director, and screenwriter.

MAILES, CHARLES HILL
Born: May 25, 1870, Halifax, Nova Scotia, Canada. Died: Feb. 17, 1937, Los Angeles, Calif. Screen and stage actor.

Appeared in: 1909 At the Altar. 1911 A Woman Scorned; The Miser's Heart; A Terrible Discovery; A Tale of the Wilderness; A Blot on the 'Scutcheon. 1912 The Girl and Her Trust; Just Like a Woman; A Beast at Bay; Home Folks; Lena and the Geese; Man's Genesis; The Sands of Dee; The Narrow Road; Iola's Promise; A Change of Spirit; Friends; So Near, Yet So Far; The Painted Lady; The Unwelcome Guest; The New York Hat; An Adventure in the Autumn Woods. 1913 A Welcome Intruder; The Hero of Little Italy; A Misunderstood Boy; The House of Darkness; Olaf—an Atom; Her Mother's Oath; The Coming of Angelo; The Reformers; The Battle of Elderberry Gulch; Judith of Bethulia. 1918 The Brass Bullet (serial). 1919 Red Hot Dollars. 1920 Treasure Island; Go and Get It. 1921 Chickens; The Home Stretch; Courage; The Ten Dollar Raise; Uncharted Seas. 1922 The Bond Boy; The Man from Downing Street; The Lying Truth. 1923 Held to Answer; East Side-West Side; Soft Boiled; Crashin' Thru; The Town Scandal; Michael O'Halloran. 1924 Thundering Hoofs; The Lighthouse by the Sea; Fine Your Man; Name the Man; When a Man's a Man. 1925 The Midnight Flyer; The Fighting Demon; The Crimson Runner; The Overland Limited; Free to Love; Playing with Souls. 1926 Old Ironsides; The Combat; The Blue Streak; The Social Highwayman; Exclusive Rights; The Man in the Saddle; The Frontier Trail; Hearts and Fists; The Better Man. 1927 Bitter Apples; Play Safe; Man Power; Ain't Love Funny?; The City Gone Wild; The College Widow; Somewhere in Sonora. 1928 What a Night!; Give and Take; The Charge of the Gauchos; Drums of Love; Queen of the Chorus. 1929 The Bellamy Trial; The Faker; The Carnation Kid; One Stolen Night; Phantom City. 1930 Mother's Cry; Lilies of the Field. 1931 The Unholy Garden. 1932 No More Orchids. 1933 Women Won't Tell.

MAINES, DON
Born: 1869. Died: Jan. 2, 1934, Los Angeles, Calif.(heart trouble). Screen actor.

Appeared in: 1922 The Man Who Waited.

MAISON, EDNA
Born: 1893. Died: Jan. 11, 1946, Hollywood, Calif. Screen actress and opera singer. Entered films in 1911.

MAJERONI, MARIO
Born: 1870. Died: Nov. 18, 1931, New York, N.Y. Screen and stage actor.

Appeared in: 1920 Partners of the Night. 1921 The Face in the Fog; The Valley of Silent Men; Destiny's Isle. 1923 The Enemies of Women; The Snow Bride; The Steadfast Heart. 1924 Argentine Love; The Humming Bird; Her Love Story. 1925 Share and Share Alike; The Little French Girl; The Substitute Wife; The King on Main Street. 1927 Rubber Heels.

MAJOR, SAM COLLIER
Died: July 31, 1955, Houston, Tex. Screen, stage actor and stage director. Father of screen actress Colleen Moore.

MAKEHAM, ELIOT
Born: Dec. 22, 1882, London, England. Died: Feb. 8, 1956, London, England. Screen and stage actor.

Appeared in: 1932 Rome Express. 1933 I Was a Spy; Britannia of Billingsgate; Orders Is Orders; The Lost Chord; I Lived with You; Friday the 13th; Little Napoleon. 1935 Lorna Doone; Two Hearts in Harmony; Unfinished Symphony; Peg of Old Drury; The Clairvoyant. 1936 Hands Off; East Meets West; A Star Fell from Heaven; Calling the Tune; The Last Journey. 1937 Head over Heels in Love; The Mill on the Floss; Dark Journey; Farewell Again; Storm in a Teacup; It's in the Air; The Beachcomber; Nursemaid Who Got Lost; Good Old Days; The Citadel; Four Just Men; Darts Are Trumps; Coming of Age; Troopship. 1939 Inspector Hornleigh. 1940 The Secret Four;

Saloon Bar; Night Train to Munich; Haunted Honeymoon; Busman's Honeymoon; Pastor Hall. 1941 Spare a Copper; John Smith Wakes Up. 1942 Wings and the Woman; The Common Touch. 1945 Vacation from Marriage; The Halfway House. 1947 Frieda. 1948 Jassy. 1949 Daybreak; A Canterbury Tale. 1950 The Miniver Story; Mystery at the Burlesque; The Verger. 1951 Scrooge; Children of Chance; The Scarlet Thread; Trio. 1952 Sailor Beware; Crimson Pirate. 1953 Decameron Nights; The Fake. 1954 Always a Bride; The Weak and the Wicked; Million Pound Note (aka Man with a Million). Other British film: Stryker of the Yard.

MALA, RAY "MALA"
Born: 1906 near Candle, Alaska. Died: Sept. 23, 1952, Hollywood, Calif.(heart attack). Screen actor.

Appeared in: 1932 Igloo. 1933 Eskimo. 1935 The Last of the Pagans. 1936 Jungle Princess; Robinson Crusoe of Clipper Island. 1938 Call of the Yukon; Hawk of the Wilderness (serial). 1939 Mutiny on the Blackhawk; Coast Guard; Desperate Trails. 1940 Zanzibar; Green Hell; Girl from God's Country; The Devil's Pipeline. 1942 The Tuttles of Tahiti. 1952 Red Snow.

MALAN, WILLIAM
Born: 1868. Died: Feb. 13, 1941, Hollywood, Calif. Screen and stage actor. Appeared in early Sennett films.

Appeared in: 1923 Slow as Lightning. 1924 Flashing Spurs. 1926 The College Boob; Red Hot Leather; One Punch O'Day. 1927 The Broncho Buster; Men of Daring; The Fighting Three; A One Man Game; The Overland Stage; Three Miles Up. 1929 The Border Wildcat.

MALATESTA, FRED
Born: Apr. 18, 1889, Naples, Italy. Died: Apr. 8, 1952, Burbank, Calif.(following surgery). Screen actor and film director. Entered films in 1915.

Appeared in: 1919 The Terror of the Range (serial). 1921 The Mask; All Dolled Up; Little Lord Fauntleroy. 1922 White Shoulders; The Woman He Loved. 1923 The Girl Who Came Back; Refuge; The Man Between. 1924 The Lullaby; Broadway or Bust; Honor among Men; The Reckless Age; Forbidden Paradise; The Night Hawk. 1925 Without Mercy. 1926 Bardely's the Magnificent. 1928 The Gate Crasher; The Wagon Show. 1929 The Peacock Fan. 1930 Wings of Adventure. 1932 A Farewell to Arms. 1933 Picture Brides; What's Your Racket. 1935 The Crusades; A Night at the Opera. 1938 The Black Doll.

MALCOLM, REGINALD
Born: 1884, Nottingham, England. Died: Jan. 20, 1966, Ottawa, Canada. Screen, stage, and radio actor.

MALLESON, MILES
Born: May 25, 1888, Croydon, England. Died: Mar. 15, 1969, London, England. Screen, stage, television actor, playwright, and screenwriter.

Appeared in: 1931 Frail Women. 1932 The Sign of Four; The Mayor's Nest. 1933 Summer Lightning; Bitter Sweet; The Queen's Affaire. 1934 Nell Gwyn. 1936 Nine Days a Queen. 1937 Knight without Armour. 1938 Sixty Glorious Years. 1940 The Thief of Bagdad. 1941 Major Barbara. 1942 Unpublished Story; Wings and the Woman. 1945 Dead of Night. 1948 Queen of Spades; Saraband. 1949 Treasure Hunt; Woman Hater; One Night with You. 1950 Mr. Lord Say No!; The Perfect Woman; The Golden Salamander; Kind Hearts and Coronets; While the Sun Shines; Stagefright. 1951 Train of Events; Scrooge. 1952 The Magic Box; The Man in the White Suit. 1953 Trent's Last Case; The Captain's Paradise; The Importance of Being Earnest; The Assassin. 1954 A Woman's Angle; Folly to Be Wise. 1955 King's Rhapsody. 1956 Private's Progress; The Man Who Never Was; Wee Geordie. 1957 The Admirable Crichton (aka Paradise Lagoon); Brothers-in-Law; Horror of Dracula; Barnacle Bill. 1958 Your Past Is Showing; The Silken Affair; Three Men in a Boat; Bachelor of Hearts (U.S. 1962). 1959 I'm All Right Jack (U.S. 1960); Gideon of Scotland Yard; Happy Is the Bride; The Hound of the Baskervilles. 1960 Man in a Cocked Hat; The Captain's Table; Kidnapped; The Bride of Dracula; The Day They Robbed the Bank of England. 1961 Double Bunk. 1962 Postman's Knock; Peeping Tom; The Phantom of the Opera; Go to Blazes. 1963 Heavens Above!; The Hellfire Club. 1964 Murder Ahoy; Circus World; They All Died Laughing; First Men in the Moon. 1965 The Brain; You Must Be Joking.

MALLORY, PATRICIA "BOOTS"
Born: 1913, New Orleans, La. Died: Dec. 1, 1958, Santa Monica, Calif.(chronic throat ailment). Screen and stage actress. Married to screen actor Herbert Marshall (dec. 1966).

Appeared in: 1932 Handle with Care. 1933 Humanity; Hello Sister!; Carnival Lady; Hollywood on Parade (short). 1935 Sing Sing Nights; Powdersmoke Range. 1937 Here's Flash Casey.

MALLOY, JOHN J. (aka JOHN J. MALLOR).
Born: 1898, Dover, Del. Died: Feb. 9, 1968, Los Angeles, Calif. (heart attack). Screen actor, singer, and artist. Appeared in silents.

MALO, GINA (Janet Flynn)
Born: June 1, 1909, Cincinnati, Ohio. Died: Nov. 30, 1963, New York, N.Y. Screen and stage actress.

Appeared in: 1932 In a Monastery Garden; Good-night Vienna; One Magic Night; King of the Ritz. 1933 Waltz Time; Strike It Rich; Lily of Killarney. 1934 The Private Life of Don Juan. 1936 My Song for You; Where There's a Will; Jack of All Trades; 1937 The Gang Show. 1938 Over She Goes. 1939 The Gentle People. 1940 Door with Seven Locks. 1941 Chamber of Horrors.

MALONE, DUDLEY FIELD
Born: 1882. Died: Oct. 5, 1950, Culver City, Calif.(heart attack). Screen actor. He was Asst. Secretary of State for Woodrow Wilson.

Appeared in: 1943 Mission to Moscow (played role of Churchill, whom he resembled).

MALONE, FLORENCE
Died: Mar. 4, 1956, Lyons, N.Y. Screen, stage, radio, and television actress.

Appeared in: 1916 The Yellow Menace (serial).

MALONE, MOLLY
Born: Denver, Colo. Died: Feb. 15, 1952, Hollywood, Calif. Screen, vaudeville, and radio actress. Entered films in 1919. Appeared in Christie comedies.

Appeared in: 1920 It's a Great Life. 1921 Just out of College; Bucking the Line; Made in Heaven; Not Guilty; A Poor Relation; An Unwilling Hero; The Old Nest; Sure Fire; Red Courage. 1922 Blaze Away; Trail of Hate; Across the Dead-Line; The Freshie. 1923 Little Johnny Jones. 1924 Westbound. 1925 Battling Bunyon; The Knockout Kid. 1926 The Bandit Buster; Bad Man's Bluff; Rawhide. 1927 Daring Deeds; The Golden Stallion (serial).

MALONE, PAT
Died: Oct. 5, 1963, New York, N.Y. Screen, stage, and television actor. Appeared in films prior to 1941.

MALONEY, LEO D.
Born: 1888. Died: Nov. 2, 1929, New York, N.Y.(heart disease). Screen actor, film director, and film producer.

Appeared in: 1914 Hazards of Helen (serial). 1915 The Girl and the Game. 1916 The Lumberlands (serial). 1920 The Fatal Sign (serial). 1921 No Man's Woman; The Wolverine. 1922 Ghost City; Nine Points of the Law; The Western Musketeer. 1923 King's Creek Law; The Rum Runners. 1924 Built for Running; Headin' Through; Payable on Demand; Riding Double; Huntin' Trouble; The Perfect Alibi; Not Built for Runnin'; The Loser's End. 1925 Across the Deadline; The Blood Bond; Flash O' Lightning; Ranchers and Rascals; Luck and Sand; The Shield of Silence; Win, Lose or Draw; The Trouble Buster.

MALTBY, HENRY F.
Born: Nov. 25, 1880, Ceres, South Africa. Died: Oct. 25, 1963, London, England. Screen, stage actor, playwright, and screenwriter.

Appeared in: 1933 Facing the Music; Home Sweet Home; I Spy; The Political Party. 1934 Those Were the Days; Freedom of the Seas; Lost in the Legion; Girls Will Be Boys; Falling in Love; The Morals of Marcus; Emil and the Detectives; Josser on the Farm. 1935 The Right Age to Marry; Vanity; Jack of All Trades; King of the Castle; Calling the Tune; Secret Agent. 1936 Fame; Where There's a Will; Tudor Rose; Everything Is Thunder; Not So Dusty; To Catch a Thief; Busman's Holiday; Heirloom Mystery; Everything in Life; Sing As We Swing; Wake up Famous; Take My Tip; OK for Sound; Trouble Ahead. 1937 Pearls Bring Tears; Hurry for Darts; The Live Wire; Young and Innocent; The Sky's the Limit; Ow'd Bob; A Yank at Oxford; What a Man. 1938 Pygmalion; Everything Happens to Me; Good Old Days; On the Road; His Lordship Goes to Press; The Gang's All Here; The Girl Was Young; To the Victor. 1940 Under Your Hat. 1944 Great Mr. Handel; Canterbury Tale. 1945 The Trojan Brothers. 1946 Caesar and Cleopatra.

MANDEL, FRANCES WAKEFIELD
Born: 1891. Died: Mar. 26, 1943, Batavia, N.Y. Screen actress. Posed for a number of James Montgomery Flagg's W.W. I posters.

MANDER, MILES (Lionel Mander)
Born: Nov. 14, 1888, Wolverhampton, England. Died: Feb. 8, 1946, Hollywood, Calif.(heart attack). Screen actor, film director, film producer, and screenwriter.

Appeared in: 1929 The Physician; The Doctor's Women; The First Born. 1930 Loose Ends; Murder. 1931 The Missing Rembrandt; Jaws of Hell. 1932 Lily Christine; That Night in London. 1933 Bitter Sweet; The Private Life of Henry VIII; Loyalties. 1934 The Queen's Affair; The Four Masked Men; The Battle; Don Quixote. 1935 Here's to Romance; The Three Musketeers. 1936 Lloyd's of London. 1937 Slave Ship; Wake up and Live; Youth on Parole. 1938 Kidnapped; Suez; The Mad Miss Manton. 1939 Stanley and Livingstone; Man in the Iron Mask; Little Princess; The Three Musketeers (and 1935 version); Wuthering Heights; Tower of London. 1940 Road to Singapore; Primrose Path; The House of Seven Gables; Babies for Sale; Captain Caution; South of Suez. 1941 Shadows on the Stairs; Dr. Kildare's Wedding Day; That Hamilton Woman. 1942 Fingers at the Window; Fly by Night; A Tragedy at Midnight; To Be or Not to Be; Tarzan's New York Adventure; Journey for Margaret; The War against Mrs. Hadley; Apache Trail; This above All. 1943 Assignment in Brittany; Secrets of the Underground; Guadalcanal Diary; Five Graves to Cairo; The Phantom of the Opera. 1944 Enter Arsene Lupin; Four Jills in a Jeep; The Pearl of Death; The Return of the Vampire; The Scarlet Claw. 1945 Confidential Agent; The Picture of Dorian Gray; Brighton Strangler; Weekend at the Waldorf. 1946 The Crime Doctor's Warnings; The Bandit of Sherwood Forest; The Walls Came Tumbling Down. 1947 The Imperfect Lady.

MANDY, JERRY
Born: 1893. Died: May 1, 1945, Hollywood, Calif.(heart attack). Screen, stage, and vaudeville actor.

Appeared in: 1925 North Star. 1927 The Gay Defender; Underworld. 1928 Hold 'Em Yale!; Love and Learn. 1929 The Sap; Love, Live and Laugh. 1930 The Doorway to Hell. 1931 Girls Demand Excitement. 1933 Strange People; Sailor's Luck. 1935 It's a Gift; The Bride Who Comes Home; McFadden's Flats. 1936 King of Burlesque; Spendthrift. 1938 Hawaii Calls. 1939 Naughty but Nice. 1940 The Ghost Creeps.

MANJEAN, TEDDY
Born: 1901. Died: Sept. 9, 1964, Hollywood, Calif. Screen actor and stuntman.

MANLEY, DAVE
Born: 1883. Died: May 1943, Calif. Screen and vaudeville actor.

Appeared in: 1931 The Struggle

MANN, HANK (David W. Lieberman)
Born: 1887, New York, N.Y. Died: Nov. 25, 1971, South Pasadena, Calif. Screen actor and film director. Entered films in 1912.

Appeared in: 1914 In the Clutches of a Gang; Mabel's Strange Predicament; Caught in a Cabaret (reissued as The Jazz Waiter); The Knock-Out (reissued as The Pugilist); Mabel's Married Life (reissued as The Squarehead). 1915 L-KO comedies. 1916 Fox Film Co. productions; A Modern Enoch Arden; The Village Blacksmith; His Bread and Butter; Hearts and Sparks. 1920 Arrow Film shorts. 1922 Quincy Adams Sawyer. 1923 Hollywood; Lights Out; Tea with a Kick; Don't Marry for Money; The Near Lady; A Noise in Newboro; The Wanters. 1924 The Man Who Played Square; A Woman Who Sinned; Empty Hands; Rivers Up. 1925 The Arizona Romeo; The Sporting Venus. 1926-27 Tennek Film Corp. shorts. 1926 Wings of the Storm; The Skyrocket; The Boob; The Flying Horseman. 1927 The Patent Leather Kid; Broadway after Midnight; When Danger Calls; Paid to Love; Smile, Brother, Smile; The Scorcher; Lady Bird. 1928 Fazil; The Garden of Eden. 1929 Morgan's Last Raid; The Donovan Affair; Fall of Eve; Spite Marriage. 1930 The Arizona Kid; Sinners' Holiday; The Dawn Trail. 1931 City Lights; Annabelle's Affairs; Stout Hearts and Willing Hands. 1932 Ridin' for Justice; Strange Love of Molly Louvain; Million Dollar Legs. 1933 The Big Chance; Smoky. 1934 Fugitive Road; Men in Black (short). 1935 a Vitaphone short; The Devil Is a Woman; The Big Broadcast of 1936. 1936 Call of the Prairie; Modern Times; Reunion; Preview Murder Mystery. 1937 Goofs and Saddles (short). 1938 Stranger from Arizona. 1939 Hollywood Cavalcade. 1940 The Great Dictator. 1941 Bullets for O'Hara. 1942 Bullet Scars. 1943 The Mysterious Doctor; The Dancing Masters. 1944 Crime by Night. 1947 The Perils of Pauline. 1949 Jackpot Jitters. 1950 Joe Palooka in Humphrey Takes a Chance. 1953 The Caddy. 1954 Living It Up. 1955 Abbott and Costello Meet the Keystone Kops; Abbott and Costello Meet the Mummy. 1956 Pardners. 1957 Man of a Thousand Faces. 1958 Rock-a-Bye Baby. 1959 Daddy-O.

MANN, LOUIS
Born: Apr. 20, 1865, New York, N.Y. Died: Feb. 15, 1931, New York, N.Y. Screen, stage actor, and playwright.

Appeared in: 1929 Father's Day. 1930 The March of Time; The Richest Man in the World; Sins of the Children.

MANN, NED H.
Born: 1893, Redkey, Ind. Died: July 1, 1967, La Jolla, Calif. Screen actor and special effects director. Entered films as an actor in 1930 and then became technical director, etc.

MANN, STANLEY
Born: 1884. Died: Aug. 10, 1953, Los Angeles, Calif. Screen actor. Entered films during silents.

Appeared in: 1953 The Robe.

MANNERING, LEWIN
Born: 1879, Poland. Died: June 7, 1932, London, England. Screen and stage actor.

MANNES, FLORENCE V.
Born: 1896. Died: Oct. 30, 1964, Hollywood, Calif.(heart attack). Screen actress. Entered films as a bit player and extra approx. 1924.

MANNING, AILEEN
Born: 1886, Denver, Colo. Died: Mar. 25, 1946, Hollywood, Calif. Screen actress.

Appeared in: 1921 Home Stuff. 1922 The Power of Love; A Tailor Made Man; Rags to Riches; Mixed Faces; Beauty's Worth. 1923 Main Street; Nobody's Money. 1924 The House of Youth; Lovers' Lane; The Snob; Her Marriage Vow. 1925 The Bridge of Sighs; Enticement; Under the Rouge; Thank You. 1926 Stella Maris; The Whole Town's Talking; The Boy Friend. 1927 Uncle Tom's Cabin; Man, Woman and Sin. 1928 Heart to Heart; The Olympic Hero; Home James. 1929 "Great Events" series. 1930 Wedding Rings; The Third Alarm. 1931 Huckleberry Finn. 1959 Uncle Tom's Cabin (re-release of 1927 film).

MANNING, JOSEPH
Died: July 31, 1946, Hollywood, Calif.(heart attack). Screen and stage actor.

Appeared in: 1920 The Screaming Shadow (serial).

MANNING, MARY LEE
Died: Dec. 7, 1937, Hollywood, Calif. Screen actress.

MANNING, TOM
Born: 1880. Died: Oct. 10, 1936, Hollywood, Calif. Screen and stage actor.

Appeared in: 1936 The Singing Kid.

MANSFIELD, JAYNE (Jayne Palmer)
Born: Apr. 19, 1932, Bryn Mawr, Pa. Died: June 29, 1967, New Orleans, La.(auto accident). Screen and stage actress. Divorced from screen actor/former Mr. Universe, Mickey Hargitay and mother of screen actress Jayne Marie Hargitay.

Appeared in: 1955 Underwater; Pete Kelly's Blues; Illegal. 1956 The Girl Can't Help It; The Female Jungle; Hell on Frisco Bay. 1957 Will Success Spoil Rock Hunter?; The Wayward Bus; Kiss Them for Me; The Burglar. 1958 The Sheriff of Fractured Jaw. 1960 It Takes a Thief (aka The Challenge—U.S. 1962); Too Hot to Handle (aka Play Girl After Dark—U.S. 1962). 1961 The George Raft Story. 1962 It Happened in Athens. 1963 Promises! Promises!; Heimweh Nach St. Paul; When Strangers Meet; The Bernde and the Psychiatrist. 1964 Panic Button. 1965 The Loved One; Country Music. 1966 Dog Eat Dog; Las Vegas Hillbillies; The Fat Spy; Primitive Love. 1967 Spree; A Guide for the Married Man. 1968 Single Room Furnished.

MANSFIELD, JOHN
Born: 1919. Died: Sept. 18, 1956, Hollywood, Calif.(heart attack). Screen actor.

Appeared in: 1948 Man-Eater of Kumaon. 1951 F.B.I. Girl; Savage Drums; Silver City; Warpath. 1952 Denver and Rio Grande. 1953 Pony Express; Prisoners of the Casbah. 1954 The Naked Jungle. 1956 The Boss.

MANSFIELD, MARTHA (Martha Ehrlich)
Born: 1900, Mansfield, Ohio. Died: Nov. 20, 1923, San Antonio, Tex.(burns). Screen and stage actress. Died while filming The Warrens of Virginia, when her dress was accidentally ignited.

Appeared in: 1918 Broadway Bill. 1920 Civilian Clothes; Dr. Jekyll and Mr. Hyde. 1921 The Man of Stone; Gilded Lies; The Last Door; Women Men Love; His Brother's Keeper. 1922 Queen of the Moulin Rouge; Till We Meet Again. 1923 Youthful Cheaters; Fog Bound; Is Money Everything?; The Leavenworth Case; Potash and Perlmutter; The Little Red Schoolhouse; The Silent Command; The Woman in Chains. 1924 The Warrens of Virginia.

MANSO, JUANITA
Born: 1873, Spain. Died: Feb. 25, 1957, Madrid, Spain. Screen and stage actress.

MANSON, ISABEL MERSON
Born: 1884. Died: May 19, 1952, New York, N.Y. Screen and stage actress.

MANTELL, ROBERT BRUCE
Born: 1854, Ayrshire, Scotland. Died: June 27, 1928, Atlantic Highlands, N.J.("effects of a breakdown"). Screen and stage actor.

Appeared in: 1915 The Blindness of Devotion. 1916 The Green Eyed Monster; A Wife's Sacrifice. 1923 Under the Red Robe.

MANTZ, PAUL (Albert Paul Mantz)
Born: 1904, Redwood City, Calif. Died: July 8, 1965, Buttercup Valley, Calif.(Ariz. border plane crash). Screen actor and aerial stuntman. Died in plane crash while filming Flight of the Phoenix.

Appeared in: 1930 Airmail; Hell's Angels. 1938 Men with Wings; Test Pilot. 1949 Twelve O'Clock High. 1951 Flying Leathernecks. 1957 The Spirit of St. Louis. 1963 It's a Mad, Mad, Mad, Mad World. 1965 The Flight of the Phoenix.

MANX, KATE
Born: 1930. Died: Nov. 15, 1964, Torrance, Calif.(suicide—pills). Screen and television actress.

Appeared in: 1960 Private Property. 1962 Hero's Island.

MAPLE, AUDREY
Born: 1899. Died: Apr. 18, 1971, N.Y. Screen, stage, and vaudeville actress.

Appeared in: 1934 Enlighten Thy Daughter.

MARCH, HAL
Born: 1920, San Francisco, Calif. Died: Jan. 19, 1970, Los Angeles, Calif.(pneumonia—lung cancer). Screen, stage, radio, television, burlesque, and vaudeville actor.

Appeared in: 1939 The Gracie Allen Murder Case. 1950 Ma and Pa Kettle Go to Town; Outrage. 1953 Combat; The Eddie Cantor Story. 1954 Yankee Pasha; The Atomic Kid. 1955 It's Always Fair Weather; My Sister Eileen. 1957 Here Me Good. 1964 Send Me No Flowers. 1967 A Guide for the Married Man.

MARCHAT, JEAN
Born: 1902, France. Died: Oct., 1966, Paris, France (following surgery). Screen, stage actor, and stage director.

Appeared in: 1946 Stormy Waters. 1961 Tomorrow Is My Turn. 1962 The Most Wanted Man in the World. 1964 Ladies of the Park; Les Dames du Bois du Boulogne (Woman of the Bois du Boulogne).

MARCUS, JAMES A.
Born: Jan. 21, 1868, New York, N.Y. Died: Oct. 15, 1937, Hollywood, Calif.(heart attack). Screen and stage actor. Entered films in 1915.

Appeared in: 1921 Little Lord Fauntleroy; Serenade. 1922 Broken Chains; Oliver Twist; Come on Over; The Stranger's Banquet. 1923 Scaramouche; Vanity Fair; Quicksands. 1924 The Iron Horse; Beau Brummell. 1925 The Eagle; The Goose Hangs High; All around Frying Pan; Lightnin'; Dick Turpin; The Fighting Heart; The Isle of Hope. 1926 The Lily; The Scarlet Letter; The Eagle of the Sea; Hell-Bent for Heaven; Siberia; The Traffic Cop; The Texas Streak. 1927 Captain Salvation; The Bachelor's Baby; The Meddlin' Stranger; Beauty Shoppers;

King of Kings; Life of an Actress; Marriage. 1928 Revenge; Sadie Thompson; The Border Patrol; Isle of Lost Men; The Broken Mask; Buck Privates. 1929 Evangeline; In Old Arizona; Whispering Winds; In Holland (short). 1930 Back Pay; Captain of the Guard; Billy the Kid; Liliom; The Texan. 1931 Fighting Caravans; Arrowsmith. 1932 Hell's House. 1933 The Lone Avenger; Strawberry Roan. 1934 Wagon Wheels; Honor of the Range. 1936 The Lonely Trail.

MARCUSE, THEODORE
Born: 1920. Died: Nov. 29, 1967, Los Angeles, Calif.(auto accident). Screen, stage, and television actor.

Appeared in: 1961 Operation Eichmann; The Two Little Bears. 1962 For Love or Money; Hitler. 1964 A Tiger Walks. 1965 The Cincinnati Kid. 1966 The Glass Bottom Boat; Sands of Beersheba; Last of Secret Agents. 1967 Picasso Summer. 1968 The Wicked Dreams of Paula Schultz.

MARGETSON, ARTHUR
Born: 1897, England. Died: Aug. 12, 1951, London, England. Screen and stage actor.

Appeared in: 1931 Other People's Sins. 1933 His Grace Gives Notice. 1934 The Great Defender; Little Friend. 1935 The Divine Spark; Music Hath Charms; I Give My Heart. 1936 Wanted Men. 1937 Broken Blossoms; Juggernaut; Pagliacci (aka A Clown Must Laugh); Action for Slander. 1938 The Loves of Madame DuBarry. 1940 Return to Yesterday. 1941 Larceny Street. 1942 Commandos Strike at Dawn. 1943 Random Harvest. 1944 Sherlock Holmes Faces Death.

MARGOLIS, CHARLES "DOC"
Born: 1874. Died: Sept. 22, 1926, Glendale, Calif. Screen actor.

Appeared in: 1925 The Merry Widow.

MARGULIES, VIRGINIA M.
Born: 1916. Died: Feb. 16, 1969, Hollywood, Calif. Screen actress. Daughter of screen actor Edward Peil (dec. 1958).

MARGULIS, CHARLES "CHARLIE"
Born: 1903. Died: Apr. 24, 1967, Little Falls, Minn. Screen, television actor, and trumpeter.

Appeared in: 1930 King of Jazz.

MARINOFF, FARIA
Born: 1890, Russia. Died: Nov. 17, 1971, Englewood, N.J. Screen and stage actress.

Appeared in: 1915 McTeague. 1917 The Rise of Jennie Cushing.

MARION, EDNA (Edna Hannam).
Born: Dec. 12, 1908, Chicago, Ill. Died: Dec. 2, 1957, Hollywood, Calif. Screen, stage, and vaudeville actress. Appeared in Charlie Chase and Edna Marion comedies.

Appeared in: 1925 The Desert's Price, plus the following shorts: Her Daily Dozen; My Baby Doll; Powdered Chickens; Putting on Airs; Puzzled by Crosswords; Dangerous Peach. 1926 The Call of the Wilderness; Readin' Ritin' Rithmetic; The Still Alarm. 1927 For Ladies Only; Flying Elephants (short); Sugar Daddies (short). 1928 From Soup to Nuts (short); Should Married Men Go Home?. 1929 Skinner Steps Out. 1930 Romance of the West; Today.

MARION, GEORGE F., SR.
Born: July 16, 1860, San Francisco, Calif. Died: Nov. 30, 1945, Carmel, Calif.(heart attack). Screen, stage actor, and stage director. Father of screenwriter George F. Marion, Jr. Entered films in 1914.

Appeared in: 1921 Go Straight. 1922 Gun Shy. 1923 Anna Christie; The Girl I Loved; A Million to Burn. 1924 Bringin' Home the Bacon. 1925 On the Go; Clothes Make the Pirate; Straight Through; Tumbleweeds; The White Monkey. 1926 The Highbinders; Rolling Home; The Wise Guy. 1927 King of Kings; A Texas Steer; Loco Luck; Skedaddle Gold. 1929 Evangeline. 1930 Anna Christie (and 1923 version); The Bishop Murder Case; The Pay Off; The Sea Bat; A Lady's Morals; Hook, Line and Sinker; The Big House. 1931 Man to Man; Laughing Sinners; Safe in Hell. 1932 Six Hours to Live. 1933 Her First Mate. 1935 Port of Lost Dreams; Rocky Mountain Mystery; Death from a Distance; Metropolitan.

MARION, SID
Born: 1900. Died: June 29, 1965, Hollywood, Calif.(heart attack). Screen and stage actor.

Appeared in: 1936 Magnificent Obsession. 1937 an RKO-Radio short. 1943 Lady of Burlesque. 1949 Oh, You Beautiful Doll; Jiggs and Maggie in Jackpot Jitters. 1950 Love That Brute; Trial without Jury; Woman from Headquarters. 1953 Call Me Madam.

MARLE, ARNOLD (aka A. MARLE)
Born: 1888, England. Died: Feb. 21, 1970, London, England. Screen, stage, and television actor.

Appeared in: 1942 One of Our Aircraft Is Missing. 1945 Mr. Emmanuel. 1949 The Girl in the Painting (aka Portrait from Life); The Glass Mountain. 1952 Kisenga, Man of Africa (aka Men of Two Worlds). 1955 The Case of the Red Monkey; Cross Channel; The Green Buddha. 1957 The Abominable Snowman; The Break in the Circle; Davy. 1959 The Man Who Died Twice. 1961 The Snake Woman.

MARLO, MARY
Born: 1898. Died: Feb. 25, 1960, Hollywood, Calif.(heart attack). Screen, stage, radio, and television actress.

Appeared in: 1955 The Second Greatest Sex.

MARLOWE, ANTHONY
Born: 1910. Died: June 29, 1962, Detroit, Mich. Screen actor and opera tenor.

Appeared in: 1941 Flame of New Orleans. 1942 The Great Commandment. 1944 Mrs. Parkington. 1953 Saadia. 1955 Doctor in the House; Room in the House.

MARLOWE, FRANK
Born: 1904. Died: Mar. 30, 1964, Hollywood, Calif.(heart attack). Screen and television actor.

Appeared in: 1934 Now I'll Tell. 1935 The Glass Key. 1944 Murder in the Blue Room. 1950 Barricade; Triple Trouble. 1952 The Winning Team; My Pal Gus. 1954 The Long Wait. 1955 The Square Jungle; Lucy Gallant; The Americano. 1956 The Man with the Golden Arm. 1957 Rockabilly Baby; Chicago Confidential. 1958 Escape from Red Rock; The Lone Texan.

MARR, WILLIAM (William Dobie)
Born: 1897. Died: May 15, 1960, N.Y. Screen and stage actor.

Appeared in: 1926 Men of Steel.

MARRIOTT, MOORE (George Thomas Moore-Marriott)
Born: 1885, West Drayton, England. Died: 1949. Screen and stage actor.

Appeared in: 1926 Passion Island. 1929 Widecombe Fair. 1931 The Lyons Mail. 1932 The Water Gypsies. 1933 Hawleys of High Street; Money for Speed; The Man Who Won. 1935 Elizabeth of England; Turn of the Tide. 1936 When Knights Were Bold; Nell Gwyn; Peg of Old Drury; Strange Cargo; Wednesday's Luck; Quests of Mr. Bliss; Gay Old Dog; Accused; As You Like It. 1937 Dreaming Lips. 1938 To the Victor; Windbag the Sailor; Oh! Mr. Porter; Old Bones of the River; Ask a Policeman; Where's That Fire; Convict 99. 1939 A Girl Must Live; The Frozen Limits. 1940 Gasbags; Cheer, Boys, Cheer; Band Wagon; Charlie's Aunt. 1941 I Thank You; Hi Gang; Back Room Boys. 1944 Time Flies. 1946 Green for Danger. 1949 A Place of One's Own; The Agitator; The History of Mr. Polly (U.S. 1951); High Jinks in Society. Other British films: Hills of Donegal; A Political Party; A Moorland Tragedy; Root of All Evil; Green Fingers.

MARRIOTT, SANDEE
Born: 1902. Died: June 7, 1962, Hollywood, Calif. Screen actor.

Appeared in: 1956 Hilda Crane.

MARSDEN, MARY. See Mary Marsden Young

MARSH, CHARLES L. "CHARLEY"
Died: Mar. 7, 1953, Hollywood, Calif. Screen and vaudeville actor.

Appeared in: 1944 Atlantic City. 1945 Christmas in Connecticut; Out of This World; Too Young to Know. 1947 My Wild Irish Rose.

MARSH, MAE (Mary Warne Marsh)
Born: Nov. 9, 1895, Madrid, N. M. Died: Feb. 13, 1968, Hermosa Beach, Calif.(heart attack). Screen actress. Mother of prominent Beverly Hills attorney Brewster Arms and sister of screen actress Marguerite Marsh (dec.) She won the George Eastman Award in 1957 naming her one of five leading actresses of the silent era. Was known as Samuel Goldwyn's original "Goldwyn Girl."

Appeared in: 1912 Man's Genesis; The Lesser Evil; The New York Hats; One Is Business, the Other Crime; Lena and the Geese; The Sands of Dee; Brutality; An Adventure in the Autumn Woods. 1913 Judith of Bethulia; The Telephone Girl and the Lady; Love in an Apartment Hotel; The Perfidy of Mary; The Little Tease; The Wanderer; His Mother's Son; The Reformers; The Battle of Elderberry Gulch; In Prehistoric Days. 1914 Home Sweet Home; The Avenging Conscience. 1915 The Birth of a Nation. 1916 Intolerance; The Wild Girl; A Child of the Paris Street; The Wharf Rat; Hoodoo Ann; The Marriage of Molly-O. 1917 Cinderella Man; Polly and the Circus; Brute Force. 1918 The Beloved Traitor; All Woman; The Face in the Dark. 1919 Spotlight Sadie; The Mother and the Law. 1921 Little 'Fraid Lady; Nobody's Kid. 1922 Flames of Passion; Till We Meet Again. 1923 The White Rose; Paddy-the-Next-Best-Thing. 1924 A Woman's Secret; Daddies. 1925 The Rat; Rides of Passion. 1928 Racing Through. 1931 Over the Hill. 1932 That's My Boy; Rebecca of Sunnybrook Farm. 1933 Alice in Wonderland. 1934 Little Man, What Now?; Bachelor of Arts. 1935 Black Fury. 1936 Hollywood Boulevard. 1940 The Man Who Wouldn't Talk; Young People. 1941 Great Guns; Blue, White and Perfect. 1942 Tales of Manhattan. 1943 Dixie Dugan. 1944 In the Meantime, Darling; Jane Eyre. 1945 A Tree Grows in Brooklyn. 1948 Apartment for Peggy; Three Godfathers; Deep Waters; The Snakepit. 1949 The Fighting Kentuckian; Impact. 1950 When Willie Comes Marching Home; The Gunfighter. 1952 Night without Sleep; The Sun Shines Bright. 1953 The Robe; Blueprint for Murder. 1955 The Tall Men; Hell on Frisco Bay; Prince of Players. 1956 Julie; While the City Sleeps. 1957 The Wings of Eagles. 1958 Cry Terror. 1960 Sergeant Rutledge; From the Terrace. 1961 Two Rode Together. 1968 Arabella.

MARSH, MARGUERITE (Margaret Marsh)
Died: mid-1920s, Los Angeles, Calif. Screen actress. Sister of screen actress Mae Marsh (dec. 1968).

Appeared in: 1912 The Mender of the Nets. 1921 The Idol of the North; Oh Mary Be Careful; Women Men Love. 1922 Boomerang Bill; Face to Face; Iron to Gold.

MARSH, RISLEY HALSEY
Born: 1927. Died: Jan. 14, 1965, Newark, N.J. Screen and stage actor.

MARSHAL, ALAN
Born: Jan. 29, 1909, Sydney, Australia. Died: July 9, 1961, Chicago, Ill. Screen and stage actor.

Appeared in: 1936 After the Thin Man; The Garden of Allah. 1937 Conquest; Night Must Fall; Parnell; The Robbery Symphony. 1938 Dramatic School; I Met My Love Again; Invisible Enemy; The Road to Reno. 1939 The Adventures of Sherlock Holmes; Exile Express; Four Girls in White; The Hunchback of Notre Dame. 1940 He Stayed for Breakfast; The Howards of Virginia; Irene; Married and in Love. 1941 Lydia; Tom, Dick and Harry. 1944 Bride by Mistake; The White Cliffs of Dover. 1949 The Barkleys of Broadway. 1956 The Opposite Sex. 1958 House on Haunted Hill. 1959 Day of the Outlaw.

MARSHALL, BOYD
Born: 1885, Ohio. Died: Nov. 9, 1950, Jackson Heights, N.Y. Screen and stage actor.

Appeared in: 1916 King Lear.

MARSHALL, HERBERT
Born: May 23, 1890, London, England. Died: Jan. 22, 1966, Beverly Hills, Calif.(heart attack). Screen, stage, radio, television actor, and writer. Divorced from English stage actress Sarah Best and screen actress "Boots" Mallory (dec. 1958). Father of stage actress Sarah Best Marshall.

Appeared in: 1927 Mumsie. 1929 The Letter. 1930 Murder. 1931 The Calendar; Secrets of a Secretary. 1932 Michael and Mary; Evenings for Sale; Blonde Venus; Trouble in Paris. 1933 White Woman; Clear All Wires; The Solitaire Man; Faithful Heart. 1934 I Was a Spy; Four Frightened People; Outcast Lady; The Painted Veil; Riptide. 1935 If You Could Only Cook; Morning, Noon and Night (U.S. 1937); The Good Fairy; The Flame Within; Accent on Youth; The Dark Angel. 1936 Crack-Up; The Lady Consents; A Woman Rebels; Make Way for a Lady; Till We Meet Again; Forgotten Faces; Girls Dormitory. 1937 Fight for Your Lady; Angel; Breakfast for Two. 1938 Marie Antoinette; Mad about Music; Always Goodbye; Woman against Woman. 1939 Zaza. 1940 A Bill of Divorcement; Foreign Correspondent; The Letter. 1941 The Little Foxes; Adventure in Washington; When Ladies Meet; Kathleen. 1942 The Moon and Sixpence; Portrait of a Rebel. 1943 Flight for Freedom; Forever and a Day; Young Ideas. 1944 Andy Hardy's Blonde Trouble. 1945 The Unseen; The Enchanted Cottage. 1946 The Razor's Edge; Duel in the Sun; Crack-Up. 1947 High Wall; Ivy. 1949 The Secret Garden. 1950 Underworld Story. 1951 Anne of the Indies. 1952 Captain Black Jack. 1953 Angel Face. 1954 Riders to the Stars; Gog; The Black Shield of Falworth. 1955 The Virgin Queen. 1956 Portrait in Smoke. 1957 The Weapon; Wicked As They Come. 1958 Stage Struck; The Fly. 1960 Midnight Lace; College Confidential. 1961 Fever in the Blood. 1962 Five Weeks in a Balloon. 1963 The List of Adrian Messenger; The Caretakers. 1965 The Third Day.

MARSHALL, OSWALD
Born: 1875, Newcastle-on-Tyne, England. Died: Apr. 19, 1954, New York, N.Y. Screen and stage actor.

MARSHALL, TULLY (William Phillips)
Born: Apr. 13, 1864, Nevada City, Calif. Died: Mar. 10, 1943, Encino, Calif.(heart and lung ailment). Screen and stage actor. Entered films in 1915.

Appeared in: 1916 Oliver Twist; Intolerance; Joan the Woman. 1917 Countess Charming. 1918 We Can't Have Everything; Too Many Millions. 1919 Cheating Cheaters; The Girl Who Stayed Home; The Crimson Gardenia; The Fall of Babylon; Her Kingdom of Dreams; The Life Line; The Lottery Man; Hawthorne of the U.S.A; Everywoman. 1920 The Slim Princess; Double Speed; The Dancin' Fool. 1921 The Cup of Life; Hail the Woman; Silent Years; What Happened to Rosa?. 1922 Any Night; Good Men and True; Is Matrimony a Failure?; The Super-Sex; Without Compromise; The Village Blacksmith; The Beautiful and Damned; Deserted at the Altar; Fools of Fortune; The Ladder Jinx; The Lying Truth; Only a Shop Girl; Penrod; The Marriage Chance; Too Much Business. 1923 The Hunchback of Notre Dame; Let's Go; The Barefoot Boy; Broken Hearts of Broadway; Temporary Marriage; Thundergate; The Covered Wagon; The Brass Bottle; The Dangerous Maid; Dangerous Trails; Defying Destiny; Fools and Riches; His Last Race; The Law and the Lawless; Ponjola; Richard, the Lion-Hearted; Her Temporary Husband. 1924 He Who Gets Slapped; Hold Your Breath; Pagan Passions; Passion's Pathway; Along Came Ruth; For Sale; The Stranger; The Right of the Strongest; The Ridin' Kid from Powder River; Reckless Romance. 1925 The Merry Widow; Clothes Make the Pirate; Anything Once; The Half-Way Girl; The Pace That Thrills; Smouldering Fires; The Talker. 1926 Her Big Night; Torrent; Twinkletoes; Old Loves and New. 1927 Beware of Widows; The Gorilla; The Cat and the Canary; Jim the Conqueror. 1928 Drums of Love; The Mad Hour; The Perfect Crime; Queen Kelly; Trail of '98; Alias Jimmy Valentine. 1929 Redskin; The Show of Shows; Thunderbolt; Tiger Rose; Conquest; The Bridge of San Luis Rey; The Mysterious Dr. Fu Manchu; Skin Deep. 1930 Murder Will Out; The Big Trail; Numbered Men; One Night at Susie's; Burning Up; Mammy; She Couldn't Say No; Under a Texas Moon; Common Clay; Redemption; Dancing Sweeties; Tom Sawyer. 1931 Fighting Caravans; The Unholy Garden; The Millionaire; The Virtous Husband; Mr. Wong; City Sentinels. 1932 City Streets; The Beast of the City; Night Court; Scandal for Sale; Strangers of the Evening; Two-Fisted Law; Exposure; Klondike; Cabin in the Cotton; Afraid to Talk; Hurricane Express (serial); Arsene Lupin; The Hatchet Man; Scarface; Red Dust; Grand Hotel; The Man I Killed. 1933 Laughing at Life; Corruption; Night of Terror. 1934 Massacre; Murder on the Blackboard. 1935 Black Fury; A Tale of Two Cities; Diamond Jim. 1937 California Straight Ahead; Souls at Sea; She Asked for It; Hold 'Em Navy; Stand In; Behind Prison Bars. 1938 Mr. Boggs Steps Out; Making the Headlines; A Yank at Oxford; Arsene Lupin Returns; College Swing; Hold That Kiss; House of Mystery. 1939 Blue Montana Skies; The Kid from Texas. 1940 Invisible Stripes; Brigham Young, Frontiersman; Youth Will Be Served; Go West; Chad Hanna. 1941 Ball of Fire; For Beauty's Sake. 1942 This Gun for Hire; Moontide; Ten Gentlemen from West Point. 1943 Behind Prison Walls; Hitler's Madman.

MARSHALOV, BORIS
Born: 1902, Russia. Died: Oct. 16, 1967, New York, N.Y. Screen and stage actor.

Appeared in: 1964 Pie in the Sky.

MARSON, AILEEN
Born: 1913, England. Died: May 5, 1939, London, England (child birth). Screen and stage actress.

Appeared in: 1934 Lucky Loser; Way to Youth; My Song for You; Roadhouse; Passing Shadows; The Green Pack; Ten Minute Alibi; Jubilee Cavalcade. 1935 Honeymoon for Three; The Black Mask; Living Dangerously. 1936 Waves of Desire; Someone at the Door. 1937 Four Dark Hours; Spring Handicap; The Tenth Man.

MARSTINI, ROSITA
Born: 1894. Died: Apr. 24, 1948, Hollywood, Calif. Screen actress.

Appeared in: 1917 Tale of Two Cities. 1921 The Outside Woman; The Primal Law; Serenade. 1922 Enter Madame. 1924 Shadows of Paris; The Lover of Camille. 1925 The Big Parade; The Redeeming Sin; Proud Flesh. 1926 Flame of the Argentine. 1928 We Americans; No Other Woman. 1929 Hot for Paris. 1933 I Cover the Water. 1934 In Love with Life.

MARSTON, ANN
Born: 1939. Died: Mar. 6, 1971, Detroit, Mich.(stroke caused by vascular complications of diabetes). Screen actress (starlet at age 9). Was "Miss Michigan" of the 1960 Miss America Pageant.

MARSTON, JOHN
Born: 1890. Died: Sept. 2, 1962, New York, N.Y. Screen and stage actor.

Appeared in: 1932 Cabin in the Cotton; Three on a Match; Silver Dollar; Love Is a Racket; Skyscraper Souls; Scarlet Dawn. 1933 Son of a Sailor; Good Dame; All of Me; Hell and High Water; Heroes for Sale; Lady Killer; Mary Stevens, M.D.; Mayor of Hell; Son of Kong. 1934 The Pursuit of Happiness. 1937 History Is Made at Night. 1939 Union Pacific. 1950 Broken Arrow.

MARTIN, CHRIS-PIN
Born: 1894, Tucson, Ariz. Died: June, 1953, Montebello, Calif. (heart attack). Screen actor.

Appeared in: 1929 In Old Arizona. 1931 The Squaw Man; The Cisco Kid. 1932 South of Santa Fe; Girl Crazy; The Stoker; The Painted Woman. 1933 Outlaw Justice; California Trail. 1934 Four Frightened People. 1935 Bordertown; Under the Pampas Moon. 1936 The Gay Desperado; The Bold Cabalero. 1938 Flirting with Fate; Tropic Holiday; The Texans. 1939 Stagecoach; The Return of the Cisco Kid; The Girl and the Gambler; Fighting Fringo; Frontier Marshal; The Llano Kid. 1940 Down Argentine Way; The Cisco Kid and the Lady; Charlie Chan in Panama; Viva Cisco Kid; Lucky Cisco Kid; The Gay Caballero; The Mark of Zorro. 1941 Romance of the Rio Grande; Ride on Vaquero; The Bad Man; Week-End in Havana. 1942 Undercover Man; Tombstone, the Town Too Tough to Die; American Empire. 1943 The Sultan's Daughter; The Ox-Bow Incident. 1944 Ali Baba and the Forty Thieves; Tampico. 1945 Along Came Jones; San Antonio. 1946 Suspense; Gallant Journey. 1947 King of the Bandits; Robin Hood of Monterey; The Fugitive. 1948 Belle Starr's Daughter; The Return of Wildfire; Mexican Hayride. 1949 Rimfire; The Beautiful Blonde from Bashful Bend. 1950 Arizona Cowboy. 1951 The Lady from Texas; A Millionaire for Christy. 1952 Ride the Man Down.

MARTIN, EDIE
Born: 1880. Died: Feb. 23, 1964, London, England. Screen, stage, and vaudeville actress.

Appeared in: 1937 Farewell Again; Under the Red Robe. 1938 Troopship. 1949 The History of Mr. Polly; A Place of One's Own. 1951 Oliver Twist; The Lavender Hill Mob. 1952 The Man in the White Suit; Time, Gentlemen, Please. 1953 The Titfield Thunderbolt. 1954 Lease of Life; Adventure for Two (aka Demi Paradise). 1955 Room in the House. 1956 The Ladykillers. 1957 As Long As They're Happy. 1959 Teenage Bad Girl (aka My Teenage Daughter); The End of the Road; Too Many Crooks. 1961 A Weekend with Lulu. Other British film: Sparrows Can't Sing.

MARTIN, FRANK WELLS
Born: 1880. Died: Aug. 9, 1941, Los Angeles, Calif. Screen actor and film director.

MARTIN, JOHN E.
Born: 1865. Died: Nov. 22, 1933, New York. Screen and stage actor.

MARTIN, LEWIS H.
Died: Feb. 21, 1969, Los Angeles, Calif.(heart attack). Screen, stage, and television actor.

Appeared in: 1950 Experiment Alcatraz. 1951 The Big Carnival; Drums in the Deep South; Operation Pacific; Three Guys Named Mike. 1952 Red Planet Mars; The Wild North. 1953 Arrowhead; The Caddy; Houdini; No Escape; Pony Express; The War of the Worlds. 1954 Cry Vengeance; Knock on Wood; Men of the Fighting Lady; Witness to Murder. 1955 Las Vegas Shakedown; The Man Who Knew Too Much; Night Nurse. 1956 The Court Jester; These Wilder Years. 1957 The Quiet Gun; Rockabilly Baby; Slander. 1958 Crash Landing. 1963 Diary of a Madman.

MARTIN, OWEN
Born: 1889. Died: May 4, 1960, Saranac Lake, N.Y. Screen and stage actor.

Appeared in: 1957 The Pajama Game.

MARTIN, TONY
Died: Feb. 1932, N.Y. Screen actor. Not to be confused with singer/actor. Appeared in shorts as half of "Nick and Tony" comedy team.

MARTINDEL, EDWARD B.
Born: July 8, 1876, Hamilton, Ohio. Died: May 4, 1955, Woodland Hills, Calif.(heart attack). Screen, stage, and vaudeville actor. Entered films in 1917.

Appeared in: 1921 The Call of the North; Ducks and Drakes; Greater Than Love; Short Skirts; Hail the Woman. 1922 The Dangerous Little Demon; Nice People; Clarence; Little Eva Ascends; The Ordeal; A Daughter of Luxury; The Glory of Clementina; Manslaughter; Midnight. 1923 The White Flower; Lovebound; The Day of Faith. 1924 Love's Whirlpool. 1925 The Dixie Handicap; The Sporting Venus; Compromise; Lady Windermere's Fan; Scandal Proof; The Man with a Country. 1926 The Duchess of Buffalo; The Dixie; You'd Be Surprised; Everybody's Acting; Tony Runs Wild; Somebody's Mother. 1927 Lovers?; In Old Kentucky; Children of Divorce; Fashions for Women; Lonesome Ladies; Taxi! Taxi!; Venus of Venice. 1928 The Singing Fool; On Trial; Companionate Marriage; We Americans; The Desert Bride; The Garden of Eden. 1929 The Devil's Apple Tree; Footlights and Fools; Why Be Good?; The Desert Song; Modern Love; Hard-boiled Rose; The Phantom of the Opera; The Aviator. 1930 Second Choice; Mamba; Song of the West; Golden Dawn; Rain or Shine; Check and Double Check; Song O' My Heart. 1931 Divorce among Friends; High Stakes; Woman Pursued; The Gay Diplomat. 1932 American Madness; False Faces; Afraid to Talk. 1933 By Appointment Only. 1934 Two Heads on a Pillow. 1935 Champagne for Breakfast; The Girl Who Came Back.

MARTINEZ, CONCHITA
Born: 1912, Mexico. Died: May, 1960, Mexico City, Mexico (heart attack). Screen, stage, radio actress, and singer.

MARTINEZ, EDUARDO L.
Born: 1900, Mexico. Died: Oct. 31, 1968, San Antonio, Tex. Screen actor and orchestra leader.

MARTYN, PETER
Born: 1928, England. Died: Feb. 16, 1955, London, England. Screen, stage, and television actor.

Appeared in: 1952 Folly to Be Wise. 1954 Orders Are Orders; You Know What Sailors Are.

MARX, ALBERT A.
Born: 1892. Died: Feb. 18, 1960, Houston, Tex. Screen, radio actor, and clown. Known professionally as "Almar the Clown." Appeared in film shorts.

MARX, "CHICO" (Leonard Marx)
Born: Mar. 22, 1891, New York, N.Y. Died: Oct. 11, 1961, Hollywood, Calif.(heart attack). Screen, stage, vaudeville, and television actor. Member of Marx Bros. comedy team. For films the Marx Bros. appeared in see Harpo Marx listing.

Appeared in: 1933 Hollywood on Parade (Chico only-short).

MARX, "HARPO" (Adolph—later changed to Arthur Marx)
Born: Nov. 23, 1893, New York, N.Y. Died: Sept. 28, 1964, Los Angeles, Calif.(heart surgery). Screen, stage, vaudeville, television actor, and author. Was member of Marx Bros. comedy team. Brothers remaining are: Groucho, Gummo and Zeppo. Unless otherwise stated, all films shown were for the Marx Bros. team.

Appeared in: 1925 Too Many Kisses (Harpo only). 1929 The Cocoanuts. 1930 Animal Crackers. 1931 Monkey Business. 1932 Horse Feathers; Hollywood on Parade (short). 1933 Duck Soup. 1935 A Night at the Opera. 1936 La Fiesta de Santa Barbara (short). 1937 A Day at the Races. 1938 Room Service. 1939 At the Circus. 1940 Go West. 1941 The Big Store. 1943 Screen Snapshots (short); Stage Door Canteen. 1944 Hollywood Canteen (Harpo only). 1945 All-Star Bond Rally (Harpo only—short). 1946 A Night in Casablanca. 1949 Love Happy. 1957 The Story of Mankind. 1958 Showdown at Ulcer Gulch. 1964 Big Parade of Comedy (documentary).

MARX, MAX
Died: 1925, Universal City, Calif.(killed when rope snapped during shooting of Strings of Steel). Screen actor and stuntman.

Appeared in: 1926 Strings of Steel (serial).

MASKELL, VIRGINIA
Born: Feb. 27, 1936, Shepherd's Bush, London, England. Died: Jan. 25, 1968, Stoke Mandeville, England (exposure and overdose of drugs). Screen, stage, and television actress.

Appeared in: 1958 Our Virgin Island (film debut—U.S. 1960). 1959 The Man Upstairs; Jet Storm; Suspect; Happy Is the Bride; Carve Her Name with Pride. 1960 Doctor in Love (U.S. 1962). 1961 The Risk. 1962 Only Two Can Play; The Wild and the Living (aka Young and Willing—U.S. 1963). 1968 Interlude.

MASON, DAN (Dan Grassman)
Born: 1853. Died: July 6, 1929, Baersville, N.Y. Screen and stage actor. Created the role of Skipper in the "Toonerville Trolley" series. Entered films approx. 1912.

Appeared in: 1918 The Yellow Ticket. 1921 Why Girls Leave Home; "Toonerville Trolley" series of shorts including: Boos-Em-Friends; Skipper's Scheme; Skipper's Treasure Garden; Toonerville Tactics; Skipper Has His Fling. 1922 Iron to Gold; Is Matrimony a Failure. 1924 A Self-Made Failure; Conductor 1492; Darwin Was Right; The Plunderer; Idle Tongues. 1925 Sally; Seven Sinners; The Wall Street Whiz; American Pluck; Thunder Mountain; Wages for Wives. 1926 A Desperate Moment; The Fire Brigade; Stepping Along; Hearts and Fists; Forbidden Waters; Rainbow Riley; Hard Boiled. 1927 The Chinese Parrot; A Hero on Horseback; The Price of Honor; Out All Night.

MASON, ELLIOTT
Born: 1897. Died: 1949. Screen and stage actress.

Appeared in: 1936 The Ghost Goes West; Jailbreak; Born That Way; First and the Last; O'wd Bob; Break the News. 1938 The Ware Case; Marigold; The Citadel. 1939 Black Limelight. 1940 21 Days Together. 1941 The Ghost of St. Michael's; Turned Out Nice Again. 1943 The Gentler Sex. 1944 On Approval. 1945 Vacation from Marriage. 1946 The Captive Heart. 1949 The Agitator.

MASON, EVELYN M.
Born: 1892. Died: Oct. 29, 1926, Los Angeles, Calif.(following surgery for ptomaine poisoning). Negro screen actress.

MASON, JAMES
Born: 1890, Paris, France. Died: Nov. 7, 1959, Hollywood, Calif. (heart attack). Screen actor. Do not confuse with British actor with same name.

Appeared in: 1914 The Squaw Man. 1918 Knickerbocker Buckaroo. 1921 The Silent Call; Godless Men; The Sage Hen; Two Weeks with Pay; Mysterious Rider. 1922 The Fast Mail; Lights of the Desert; The Old Homestead. 1923 Why Worry?; Scars of Jealousy; Mile-a-Minute Romeo; The Footlight Ranger. 1924 The Flaming Forties; The Heritage of the Desert; Wanderer of the Wasteland; The Plunderer. 1925 Beggar on Horseback; Rugged Water; Barriers Burned Away; Dashing Thru; Old Clothes; Under the Rouge. 1926 Bred in Old Kentucky; For Heaven's Sake; Ladies of Leisure; The Phantom of the Forest; Whispering Smith; Whispering Canyon; The Unknown Cavalier; The Night Owl. 1927 King of Kings; Let It Rain; Alias the Lone Wolf; Back to God's Country; Dead Man's Curve. 1928 Chicago after Midnight; Race for Life; The Big Killing; Across to Singapore; A Thief in the Dark; The Singapore Mutiny; The Speed Classic. 1929 The Phantom City; The Long Long Trail. 1930 The Concentratin' Kid; Last of the Duanes. 1931 The Painted Desert; Caught; Border Love. 1932 Texas Gun Fighter. 1933 Renegades of the West; Drum Taps; The Story of Temple Drake; Sunset Pass. 1934 The Dude Ranger; The Last Round-Up. 1935 Hopalong Cassidy. 1936 Call of the Prairie; The Plainsman. 1939 The Renegade Stranger; I Met a Murderer.

MASON, LeROY
Born: 1903, Larimore, N. Dak. Died: Oct. 13, 1947, Los Angeles, Calif.(heart attack). Screen actor. Entered films with the old William Fox studios.

Appeared in: 1926 The Arizona Streak; Born to Battle; Flying High; Tom and His Pals. 1927 Closed Gates. 1928 The Law's Lash; Hit of the Show; Revenge; The Viking; The Avenging Shadow; Golden Shackles. 1929 Bride of the Desert. 1930 The Climax; See America Thirst; The Danger Man; The Woman Who Was Forgotten. 1933 The Phantom of the Air (serial); Smoky. 1934 Redhead; Are We Civilized?; The Dude Ranger; When a Man Sees Red. 1935 The Mystery Man; Rainbow Valley. 1936 The Border Patrolman. 1937 California Straight Ahead; Yodelin' Kid from Pine Ridge; Western Gold; The Painted Stallion (serial); It Happened Out West; Jungle Menace (serial). 1938 The Spy Ring; The Painted Trail; Gold Mine in the Sky; Heroes of the Hills; Rhythm of the Saddle; Santa Fe Stampede; Topa Topa. 1939 West of Santa Fe; Wyoming Outlaw; Mexicali Rose; New Frontier; Fighting Gringo; Sky Patrol; Saved by the Belle (short). 1940 Rocky Mountain Rangers; The Range Busters; Triple Justice; Ghost Valley Raiders; Killers of the Wild. 1941 Silver Stallion; Across the Sierras; Robbers of the Range; The Apache Kid; The Perfect Snob; Great Guns. 1942 Time to Kill; It Happened in Flatbush; Six-Gun Gold; Sundown Jim; The Man Who Wouldn't Die; The Silver Bullet. 1943 Chetniks; Blazing Guns; Hands across the Border. 1944 Beneath Western Skies; Firebrands of Arizona; Hidden Valley Outlaws; The Rockies; Call of the South Seas; None Shall Escape; The Silver City Kid; Marshal of Reno; The Mojave Firebrand; Outlaws of Santa Fe; The San Antonio Kid; Song of Nevada; Stagecoach of Monterey; Tuscon Raiders; Vigilantes of Dodge City. 1945 Home on the Range. 1946 Heldorado; My Pal Trigger; Daughter of Don Q. (serial); Night Train to Memphis; Red River Renegades; Under Nevada Skies; Valley of the Zombies; Murder in the Music Hall; The Tiger Woman (serial). 1947 Apache Rose; Along the Oregon Trail; Under Colorado Skies; Bandits of Dark Canyon. 1948 California Firebrand; The Gay Ranchero.

MASON, LOUIS
Born: 1888, Danville, Ky. Died: Nov. 12, 1959, Hollywood, Calif. Screen, stage, and radio actor. Entered films in 1933.

Appeared in: 1934 Kentucky Kernels; Spitfire; This Man Is Mine; Judge Priest. 1935 Mary Jane's Pa; In Person. 1936 Girl of the Ozarks; M'Liss; Banjo on My Knee. 1937 Marry the Girl; Trouble at Midnight. 1939 Stagecoach. 1940 Gold Rush Maisie; The Return of Frank James. 1941 The Sea Wolf. 1942 Whistling in Dixie. 1943 What's Buzzin' Cousin. 1944 Broadway Rhythm. 1945 Grissly's Missions; Hit the Hay. 1946 Somewhere in the Night; Decoy. 1947 Sport of Kings. 1949 I Cheated the Law.

MASON, REGINALD
Born: 1882, San Francisco, Calif. Died: July 10, 1962, Hermosa Beach, Calif. Screen and stage actor.

Appeared in: 1920 Two Weeks. 1921 The Highest Bidder. 1932 Life Begins. 1933 A Bedtime Story; Emergency Call; Topaze; Shanghai Madness; Brief Moment; The Big Brain; Baby Face; Mary Stevens, M.D.; Kiss before the Mirror. 1934 Call It Luck; Charlie Chan's Courage; You Can't Buy Everything. 1936 Suzy.

MASON, SULLY P.
Born: 1906. Died: Nov. 27, 1970, Los Angeles, Calif.(cerebral hemorrhage). Screen, television actor, saxophonist, and vocalist.

Appeared in: 1939 That's Right, You're Wrong. 1940 You'll Find Out. 1941 Playmates. 1943 Around the World.

MASON, WILLIAM C. "SMILING BILLY"
Born: 1888. Died: Jan. 24, 1941, Orange, N.J. Screen, stage, and vaudeville actor.

Appeared in: 1913 Essanay films. 1916 Dizzy Heights and Daring Hearts; Cinders of Love; A Dash of Courage. 1922 a series of short comedies.

MASSINGHAM, RICHARD
Born: 1898, England. Died: 1953. Screen actor, film director, and film producer. British doctor who gave up medical career to make propaganda movies for England during World War II.

MASTERS, DARYL
Born: 1913. Died: May 24, 1961, Toronto, Canada. Screen and television actor.

Appeared in: 1958 Wolf Dog; Flaming Frontier.

MASTERS, RUTH
Born: 1899. Died: Sept. 22, 1969, Stamford, Conn. Screen, stage, and television actress.

Appeared in: 1961 Bridge to the Sun.

MATA, MIGUEL P.
Born: 1914, Spain. Died: Feb. 1956, Madrid, Spain (auto accident). Screen, stage, and radio actor.

MATEOS, HECTOR
Born: 1901, Mexico. Died: Feb. 13, 1957, Mexico City, Mexico. Screen actor.

MATHER, AUBREY
Born: Dec. 17, 1885, Minchinhampton, England. Died: Jan. 16, 1958, London, England. Screen and stage actor.

Appeared in: 1909 Brewster's Millions (film debut). 1919 Luck of the Navy. 1931 Young Woodley; The Impassive Footman. 1932 Love on the Spot; Aren't We All?; Tell Me Tonight; Woman in Chains. 1933 Red Wagon; Be Mine Tonight. 1934 The Lash; The Admiral's Secret; The Man Who Changed His Name. 1935 The Silent Passenger. 1936 When Knights Were Bold; Ball in Savoy; As You Like It; The Man in the Mirror; A Woman Alone; Chick; Underneath the Arches. 1937 Night Must Fall; Life Begins With Love. 1938 Jamaica Inn. 1940 No, No, Nanette. 1941 Rage in Heaven. 1942 The Wife Takes a Flyer; Careful, Soft Shoulders; The Undying Monster; The Great Impersonation; Random Harvest; Ball of Fire. 1943 Hello, Frisco, Hello; Forever and a Day; Heaven Can Wait. 1944 Jane Eyre; The Lodger; The Song of Bernadette. 1945 Wilson; National Velvet; Keys of the Kingdom; The House of Fear. 1947 The Mighty McGurk; Temptation; It Happened in Brooklyn; For the Love of Rusty; The Hucksters. 1948 Julia Misbehaves. 1949 That Forsyte Woman; Adventures of Don Juan; Everybody Does It; The Secret Garden; Secret of St. Ives. 1950 Joan of Arc. 1953 The Importance of Being Earnest. 1954 Cash on Delivery; The Golden Mask.

MATHER, JACK
Born: 1908. Died: Aug. 15, 1966, Wauconda, Ill.(heart attack). Screen, radio, and television actor.

Appeared in: 1952 Dream Boat. 1954 River of No Return; Broken Lance. 1955 How to Be Very, Very Popular; The View from Pompey's Head (aka Secret Interlude). 1956 The Man in the Gray Flannel Suit; The Revolt of Mamie Stover. 1957 My Man Godfrey. 1958 The Bravados. 1959 This Earth Is Mine.

MATHEWS, GEORGE H.
Born: 1877. Died: June 7, 1952, Woodland Hills, Calif. Screen and stage actor.

MATHOT, LEON
Born: 1896, France. Died: Mar. 6, 1968, Paris, France. Screen actor and film director. Entered films in 1914.

Appeared in: 1928 A Daughter of Israel. 1929 Apassionata.

MATIESEN, OTTO
Born: 1873, Copenhagen, Denmark. Died: Feb. 20, 1932, Safford, Ariz. Screen and stage actor.

Appeared in: 1922 Bells of San Juan; Money to Burn. 1923 Scaramouche; Alias the Night Wind; Boston Blackie; Vanity Fair; The Dangerous Maid. 1924 The Dawn of Tomorrow; Captain Blood; The Folly of Vanity; Revelation. 1925 The Happy Warrior; Morals for Men; Parisian Love; Sackcloth and Scarlet; The Salvation Hunters. 1926 Bride of the Storm; The Silver Treasure; The Beloved Rogue; Christine of the Big Tops; While London Sleeps; Whispering Wires; Yellow Fingers. 1927 The Road to Romance; Too Many Crooks; Surrender. 1928 The Desert Bride; The Last Moment; The Woman from Moscow; The Scarlet Lady. 1929 Strange Cargo; Prisoners; General Crack; Behind Closed Doors; The Show of Shows; Golden Dawn; Last of the Lone Wolf; Conspiracy. 1931 Beau Ideal; Man of the Sky; Soldier's Plaything; The Maltese Falcon.

MATTERSTOCK, ALBERT
Born: 1912. Died: June 30, 1960, Hamburg, West Germany. Screen actor.

Appeared in: 1937 Stimme des Blutes (Blood Bond). 1939 Ziel den Wolken (Goal in the Clouds); Solo per Danne. 1940 Our Little Wife.

MATTHEWS, A. E. (Alfred Edward Matthews) "MATTY"
Born: Nov. 22, 1869, Bridlington, England. Died: July 24, 1960, Bushey Heath, England. Screen, stage, and television actor.

Appeared in: 1937 Men Are Not Gods. 1940 Quiet Wedding. 1942 Mister V. 1943 The Life and Death of Colonel Blimp; The Great Mr. Handel. 1945 They Came to a City. 1948 Just William's Luck. 1949 The Chiltern Hundreds (stage and film versions); Piccadilly Incident; The Forbidden Street. 1950 Amazing Mr. Beecham. 1951 The Galloping Major; Laughter in Paradise; Mister Drake's Duck. 1952 The Magic Box; Castle in the Air; Made in Heaven. 1953 Penny Princess; Landfall; Something Money Can't Buy; The Passionate Sentry. 1954 Man with a Million; Tonight's the Night; The Million Pound Note. 1956 Three Men in a Boat (U.S. 1959); Around the World in 80 Days; Loser Takes All. 1957 Carry on Admiral (aka The Ship Was Loaded—U.S. 1959); Doctor at Large. 1960 Inn for Trouble.

MATTHEWS, BEATRICE
Born: 1890. Died: Nov. 10, 1942, Hollywood, Calif. Screen actress.

MATTHEWS, JEAN D.
Died: Jan. 20, 1961, Dallas, Tex. Screen and stage actress. Appeared in films prior to 1918.

MATTHISON, EDITH WYNNE
Born: 1875, England. Died: Sept. 23, 1955, Los Angeles, Calif. Screen and stage actress. Entered films with Lasky Co. in 1915.

MATTIOLI, RAF
Born: 1936, Naples, Italy. Died: Oct. 12, 1960, Rome, Italy (heart attack). Screen actor.

Appeared in: 1958 Guendalina. 1959 Vacanzie a Izchia (Holiday Island). 1960 Where the Hot Wind Blows (aka La Legge—The Law). 1961 Violent Summer. Other Italian films: First Love; Young Husbands; Tunisi Top Secret; Le Baccanti.

MATTOX, MARTHA
Born: 1879, Natchez, Miss. Died: May 2, 1933, Sidney, N.Y. (heart ailment). Screen and stage actress. Entered films in 1913.

Appeared in: 1920 Huckleberry Finn. 1921 The Conflict; The Son of Wallingford. 1922 Restless Souls; Rich Men's Wives; The Top O' the Morning; Beauty's Worth; The Angel of Crooked Street; The Game Chicken; The Hands of Nara; The Married Flapper. 1923 The Hero; Three Wise Fools; Bavu; Hearts Aflame; Look Your Best; Penrod and Sam; Maytime; Times Have Changed; Woman-Proof. 1924 The Family Secret. 1925 Dangerous Innocence; East Lynne; Heir-Loons; I'll Show You the Town; The Keeper of the Bees; The Home Maker; Oh, Doctor!; The Man in Blue; Inflation; With This Ring. 1926 Lonely Mary; Torrent; Christine of the Big Tops; Forest Havoc; The Nut-Cracker; The Rainmaker; Shameful Behavior?; The Waning Sex; The Warning Signal; The Yankee Senor. 1927 The Cat and the Canary; The Devil Dancer; Finger Prints; Her Wild Oat; Snowbound; The 13th Juror. 1928 Love Me and the World Is Mine; A Bit of Heaven; Fools for Luck; The Little Shepherd of Kingdom Come; The Naughty Duchess; The Singapore Mutiny; Kentucky Courage. 1929 The Big Diamond Robbery; Montmartre Rose. 1930 Night Work; Extravagance; The Love Racket. 1931 Misbehaving Ladies; Born to Love; Dangerous Affair; Thirty Days; Murder by the Clock. 1932 Murder at Dawn; The Silver Lining; The Monster Walks; Careless Lady; So Big; No Greater Love; Heroes of the West (serial); Dynamite Ranch; Torchy Raises the Auntie (short). 1933 Haunted Gold; Bitter Tea of General Yen.

MATTRAW, SCOTT
Born: Oct. 19, 1885, Evans Mills, N.Y. Died: Nov. 9, 1946, Hollywood, Calif. Screen, stage, and minstrel actor.

Appeared in: 1924 The Thief of Bagdad (film debut). 1927 The Return of the Riddle Rider (serial); One Glorious Scrap. 1928 Haunted Island (serial); A Made-to-Order Hero; Quick Triggers; Two Lovers. 1929 Captain Cowboy. 1934 Babes in Toyland. 1938 In Old Chicago. 1950 Revenge Is Sweet (reissue of 1934 version of Babes in Toyland).

MAUDE, CYRIL
Born: Apr. 24, 1862, London, England. Died: Feb. 20, 1951, Torquay, England. Screen and stage actor.

Appeared in: 1915 Peer Gynt. 1930 Grumpy. 1931 These Charming People. 1932 Counsel's Opinion. 1933 Orders Is Orders. 1950 While the Sun Shines.

MAURUS, GERDA
Born: 1909, Germany. Died: Aug. 1968, Dusseldorf, Germany. Screen and stage actress.

Appeared in: 1928 Spione (Spies). 1931 By Rocket to the Moon. 1933 Tod Ueber Schanghai. 1939 Prinzessin Sissy.

MAXAM, LOUELLA MODIE
Born: 1896. Died: Sept. 4, 1970, Burbank, Calif. Screen actress.

Appeared in: 1916 A Movie Star; An Oily Scoundrel; Bucking Society; His Bitter Pill; His Lying Heart; Ambrose's Rapid Rise.

MAXEY, PAUL
Born: 1908, Wheaton, Ill. Died: June 3, 1963, Pasadena, Calif. (heart attack). Screen, stage, and television actor.

Appeared in: 1941 Father Steps Out; I'll Sell My Life; City Limits; Let's Go Collegiate. 1946 Till the Clouds Roll By; Below the Deadline; Personality Kid. 1947 Millie's Daughter; 1948 Winter Meeting; The Noose Hangs High. 1949 Mississippi Rhythm; Bride for Sale; Sky Dragon; Fighting Fools; South of St. Louis. 1950 The Reformer and the Redhead; The Return of Jesse James. 1951 Casa Manana; Abbott and Costello Meet the Invisible Man. 1952 The Narrow Margin; Kid Monk Baroni; Here Come the Marines; Singing in the Rain; With a Song in My Heart; Stars and Stripes Forever; Dream Boat. 1953 The Stranger Wore a Gun. 1954 Black Tuesday. 1957 High Tide at Noon. 1958 Showdown at Boot Hill. 1961 20,000 Eyes.

MAXTED, STANLEY
Born: 1900, England. Died: May 10, 1963, London, England. Screen, stage, television, and radio actor.

Appeared in: 1953 Never Let Me Go. 1954 The Final Test. 1955 I Am a Camera. 1956 The Weapon. 1957 Fiend without a Face. 1958 Across the Bridge; Campbell's Kingdom. 1960 Female Friends (aka The Strange Awakening).

MAXWELL, EDWIN
Born: 1886, Dublin, Ireland. Died: Aug. 1948, Falmouth, Mass. (cerebral hemorrhage). Screen, stage actor, stage director, and associate film director.

Appeared in: 1929 The Taming of the Shrew. 1930 All Quiet on the Western Front; Top Speed; The Gorilla; Du Barry, Woman of Passion. 1931 Kiki; Inspiration; Daybreak; Daddy Long Legs; Men of the Sky; Yellow Ticket; Ambassador Bill. 1932 Two Kinds of Women; Shopworn; Scarface; American Madness; Those We Love; Six Hours to Live; You Said a Mouthful; The Girl from Calgary; Grand Hotel; The Cohens and the Kellys in Hollywood; Blessed Event. 1933 The Mystery of the Wax Museum; Tonight Is Ours; State Trooper; Fog; The Mayor of Hell; Heroes for Sale; Dinner at Eight; Gambling Ship; Duck Soup; Emergency Call; The Woman I Stole; Night of Terror; Police Car 17; Big Time or Bust. 1934 The Dancing Man; Cleopatra; Gift of Gab; Happiness C.O.D.; Miss Fane's Baby Is Stolen; The Ninth Guest; Mystery Liner; Burn 'Em up Barnes (feature and serial); The Cat's Paw. 1935 Men of Action; The Devil is a Woman; All the King's Horses; Great God Gold; Motive for Revenge; The Crusades; Thanks a Million; G Men. 1936 The Plainsman; Dangerous Waters; Big Brown Eyes; Panic on the Air; Fury; Come and Get It. 1937 Love Is News; Night Key; The Road Back; Slave Ship; Love Takes Flight; A Man Betrayed. 1938 Romance on the Run. 1939 Young Mr. Lincoln; Drums along the Mohawk; Way Down South; Ninotchka. 1940 The Shop around the Corner; The Blue Bird; New Moon; His Girl Friday; Kit Carson; Brigham Young—Frontiersman. 1941 The Devil and Miss Jones; Ride On, Vaquero!; Midnight Angel. 1942 I Live on Danger; Ten Gentlemen from West Point. 1943 Holy Matrimony; Behind Prison Walls; Mr. Big; The Great Moment; Since You Went Away; Waterfront; Wilson. 1945 Mama Loves Papa. 1946 Swamp Fire; The Jolson Story. 1947 Second Chance; The Gangster. 1948 The Vicious Circle. 1949 Ride, Ryder, Ride!; The Set Up; Follow Me Quietly; Thieves' Highway; Law of the Barbary Coast; Side Street.

MAY, EDNA
Born: 1879, Syracuse, N.Y. Died: Jan. 1, 1948, Lausanne, Switzerland. (heart attack). Screen and stage actress. Entered films with Vitagraph in 1916.

Appeared in: 1916 Salvation Joan.

MAY, JAMES
Born: 1857, England. Died: Aug. 25, 1941, Los Angeles, Calif. Screen actor and double for W. C. Fields.

MAY, SAMUEL RODERICK
Born: 1910, Lamont, Iowa. Died: Aug. 9, 1963, Lebanon, Mo. Screen, stage, and radio actor.

MAYALL, HERSHELL
Born: 1863. Died: June 10, 1941, Detroit, Mich. (cerebral hemorrhage). Screen, stage, and radio actor.

Appeared in: 1917 Cleopatra. 1919 The Money Corporal. 1920 Daredevil Jack (serial). 1921 The Beautiful Gambler; The Blushing Bride; Three Word Brand; To a Finish; The Queen of Sheba; Straight from the Shoulder. 1922 Arabian Love; The Yellow Stain; Thirty Days; Smiles Are Trumps; Extra! Extra!; Calvert's Valley; Oath-Bound. 1923 The Isle of Lost Ships; Itching Palms; Money! Money! Money!; Wild Bill Hickok. 1924 Alimony. 1925 After Marriage. 1929 Great Power. 1930 Fast and Loose; The Royal Family of Broadway. 1931 His Women; plus the following shorts: The Antique Shop; Second Childhood; Revenge Is Sweet. 1934 War Is a Racket.

MAYER, PAUL M.
Born: 1914. Died: June 1968, Tuscon, Ariz.(traffic accident). Screen and television actor, and commentator.

MAYFIELD, CLEO
Born: 1897. Died: Nov. 8, 1954, New York, N.Y. Screen, stage, and vaudeville actress.

Appeared in: 1930 MGM shorts.

MAYHEW, KATE
Born: 1853. Died: June 16, 1944, New York, N.Y. Screen and stage actress.

Appeared in: 1916 Hazel Kirke. 1924 Tongues of Flame.

MAYNARD, CLAIRE (Marie McCarthy)
Born: 1912, Brooklyn, N.Y. Died: July 1941, New York, N.Y. (suicide—gas). Screen and stage actress.

Appeared in: 1931 Over the Hill; Good Sport.

MAYNARD, KERMIT
Born: Sept. 20, 1902, Mission, Tex. or Vevey, Ind. Died: Jan. 16, 1971, Hollywood, Calif.(heart attack). Screen and circus actor. Once doubled for actors George O'Brien, Victor McLaglen, Warner Baxter and Edmund Lowe. Brother of screen actor Ken Maynard (dec. 1973).

Appeared in: 1933 Drum Taps; Outlaw Justice. 1934 The Fighting Trooper; Sandy of the Mounted. 1935 Northern Frontier; Code of the Mounted; The Red Blood of Courage; Wilderness Mail; His Fighting Blood; Trails of the Wild. 1936 Timber War; Song of the Trail; Phantom Patrol; Wildcat Trooper; Wild Horse Roundup; Valley of Terror; Whistling Bullets; The Fighting Texan. 1937 Galloping Dynamite; Roaring Six-Guns. 1938 Wild Bill Hickok (serial); Western Jamboree. 1939 The Night Riders; Colorado Sunset. 1940 The Showdown; The Range Busters; Pony Post. 1941 Billy the Kid; The Man from Montana; Sierra Sue; Blazing Frontier. 1942 Rock River Renegades. 1943 The Mysterious Rider; Fugitive of the Plains; Beyond the Last Frontier. 1944 The Drifter; Gunsmoke Mesa; Frontier Outlaws; Thundering Gunslingers; Brand of the Devil. 1945 Devil Riders; Enemy of the Law; Fighting Bill Carson; Gangsters; Stagecoach Outlaws; Wild Horse Phantom. 1946 Oath of Vengeance; Ambush Trail; Galloping Thunder; Prairie Badmen; Prairie Rustlers; Under Arizona Skies; Stars over Texas; Terror on Horseback. 1947 Buckaroo from Powder River; Ridin' down the Trail; Raiders of Red Rock; Frontier Fighters; Panhandle Trail. 1948 Tumbleweed Trail; 'Neath Canadian Skies. 1949 Massacre River; Range Land. 1950 Law of the Panhandle; Silver Raiders. 1951 Three Desperate Men; Fort Dodge Stampede; Golden Girl. 1956 Flesh and the Spur. 1958 Once upon a Horse. 1960 Noose for a Gunman.

MAYNE, ERIC
Born: 1866, Dublin, Ireland. Died: Feb. 10, 1947, Hollywood, Calif. Screen and stage actor.

Appeared in: 1921 Garments of Truth; Little Miss Hawkshaw; The Silver Car; The Conquering Power. 1922 Suzanne; Doctor Jack; My American Wife; Turn to the Right; Pawned; Shattered Dreams. 1923 The Last Hour; Prodigal Daughters; Refuge; A Prince of a King; Cameo Kirby; The Christian; Human Wreckage; Her Reputation; Drums of Jeopardy. 1924 Behind the Curtain; Black Oxen; His Forgotten Wife; The Goldfish; Gerald Cranston's Lady; Never Say Die; The Yankee Consul; The Extra Girl. 1926 The Black Bird; Money to Burn; Beyond the Trail; Hearts and Spangles; Midnight Limited; Transcontinental Limited; Barriers Burned Away. 1927 Married Alive; Driven from Home. 1928 The Canyon of Adventure; Hangman's House. 1931 The Easiest Way; East Lynne. 1932 Rackety Rax. 1933 Duck's Soup. 1935 All the King's Horses. 1936 Ticket to Paradise.

MAYO, ALBERT
Born: 1887. Died: May 20, 1933, Los Angeles, Calif.(heart attack). Screen and stage actor.

MAYO, ARCHIE
Born: 1898, New York, N.Y. Died: Dec. 4, 1968, Guadalajara, Mexico. Screen actor, film director, and screenwriter. Entered films as an extra.

MAYO, FRANK
Born: 1886, New York. Died: July 9, 1963, Laguna Beach, Calif. (heart attack). Screen, stage, vaudeville actor, and film director. Entered films with World Film Co. of New Jersey approx. 1913.

Appeared in: 1915 The Red Circle (serial). 1918 The Interloper. 1919 The Brute Breaker; Mary Regan. 1921 The Blazing Trail; Colorado; Honor Bound; Magnificent Brute; The Marriage Pit; Tiger True; Dr. Jim; Go Straight; The Fighting Lover; The Shark Master. 1922 Afraid to Fight; Across the Dead-Line; Man Who Married His Own Wife; Out of the Silent North; Tracked to Earth; Wolf Law; The Flaming Hour; The Altar Stairs; Caught Bluffing. 1923 The Bolted Door; The First Degree; Souls for Sale; Six Days. 1924 Is Love Everything?; The Perfect Flapper; The Price She Paid; The Shadow of the East; The Plunderer; The Triflers; The Woman on the Jury; Wild Oranges. 1925 If I Marry Again; Passionate Youth; Barriers Burned Away; The Necessary Evil; The Unknown Lover; Women and Gold. 1926 Lew Tyler's Wives; Then Came the Woman. 1930 Doughboys; Big Shot. 1931 Alias the Bad Man; Range Law; Chinatown after Dark. 1932 The Last Ride; Hell's Headquarters. 1935 One Hour Late. 1936 Hollywood Boulevard; Desert Gold; Burning Gold; Magnificent Obsession. 1939 Confessions of a Nazi Spy; Nancy Drew and the Hidden Staircase. 1940 British Intelligence; Torrid Zone; Flowing Gold. 1941 The Gorilla Man; She Couldn't Say No; The Wagons Roll at Night. 1942 Lady Gangster; The Male Animal; Gentleman Jim. 1943 Murder on the Waterfront; Mysterious Doctor. 1944 Adventures of Mark Twain; The Last Ride (and 1932 version). 1945 The Great Mystic. 1946 The Devil's Mask; The Strange Mr. Gregory. 1947 Her Husband's Affair; Buck Privates Come Home.

MAYO, GEORGE
Born: 1891. Died: Dec. 21, 1950, Hollywood, Calif.(heart ailment). Screen, stage, and vaudeville actor.

Appeared in: 1930 A Perfect Match (short). 1934 A Woman's Man.

MAYO, HARRY A. (Ray Sampson)
Born: Mar. 11, 1898, Helena, Mont. Died: Jan. 6, 1964, Woodland Hills, Calif.(heart illness). Screen actor.

Appeared in: 1914 A Birth of a Nation (film debut).

MAYO, JOSEPH ANTHONY
Born: 1930. Died: Nov. 12, 1966, Hollywood, Calif.(heart attack). Screen and stage actor.

MAYOR, AGUSTIN G.
Born: 1935. Died: Nov. 19, 1968, Woodside, N.Y. Screen, stage, television actor, dancer, and at one time a matador in Spain.

Appeared in: 1962 Requiem for a Heavyweight. 1964 The Horror of Party Beach.

MC ATEE, BEN
Born: 1903. Died: Dec. 3, 1961, Hollywood, Calif. Screen, stage, vaudeville, television, and minstrel actor.

MC ATEE, CLYDE
Born: 1880. Died: Feb. 20, 1947, Woodland Hills, Calif. Screen actor.

Appeared in: 1925 Percy. 1926 Crossed Signals.

MC BRIDE, CARL
Born: 1894, Sioux City, Iowa. Died: Dec. 17, 1937, Los Angeles, Calif. Screen, vaudeville actor, and film director. Appeared in Charles B. Dillingham productions on screen.

MC BRIDE, DONALD (aka DONALD MACBRIDE)
Born: 1889, Brooklyn, N.Y. Died: June 21, 1957, Los Angeles, Calif. Screen, stage, television and, vaudeville actor. Appeared in films at old Vitagraph studio in Brooklyn approx. 1913.

Appeared in: 1932 Misleading Lady. 1933 Get That Venus. 1936 The Chemist. 1938 Room Service (film and stage versions); Annabel Takes a Tour. 1939 The Great Man Votes; Twelve Crowded Hours; The Girl and the Gambler; The Flying Irishman; The Story of Vernon and Irene Castle; The Girl from Mexico; The Gracie Allen Murder Case; Blondie Takes a Vacation; The Amazing Mr. Williams; Charlie Chan at Treasure Island. 1940 The Saint's Double Trouble; Northwest Passage; Murder over New York; Michael Shayne, Private Detective; Curtain Call; My favorite Wife; Hit Parade of 1941. 1941 The Invisible Woman; Footlight Fever; Topper Returns; High Sierra; Love Crazy; Here Comes Mr. Jordan; You'll Never Get Rich; Rise and Shine; You're in the Navy Now; Louisiana Purchase. 1942 Two Yanks in Trinidad; Juke Girl; The Mexican Spitfire Sees a Ghost; The Glass Key; My Sister Eileen. 1943 A Night to Remember; They Got Me Covered; Best Foot Forward; Lady Bodyguard; A Stranger in Town. 1944 The Doughgirls; The Thin Man Goes Home. 1945 Penthouse Rhythm; Hold That Blonde; Out of This World; Girl on the Spot; She Gets Her Man; Abbott and Costello in Hollywood; Doll Face. 1946 Blonde Alibi; Little Giant; The Killers; The Time of Their Lives; The Dark Horse; The Brute Man. 1947 Beat the Band; The

Old Gray Mayor; Joe Palooka in the Knockout; Hal Roach Comedy Carnival; Good News; Buck Privates Come Home; The Egg and I; The Fabulous Joe. 1948 Campus Sleuth; Jinx Money; Smart Politics. 1949 The Story of Seabiscuit; Challenge to Lassie. 1950 Joe Palooka Meets Humphrey; Holiday Rhythm. 1951 Cuban Fireball; Bowery Battalion; Texas Carnival; Sailor Beware. 1952 Gobs and Gals. 1953 The Stooge. 1955 The Seven Year Itch.

MC CABE, HARRY
Born: 1881. Died: Feb. 11, 1925, Los Angeles, Calif. Screen actor.

Appeared in: 1922 A Western Thoroughbred. 1924 The No-Gun Man.

MC CABE, MAY
Born: 1873. Died: June 22, 1949, New York, N.Y. Screen and stage actor. Appeared in silents. Married to stage actor Jack Mc Cabe (dec. 1967) and mother of stage actor Clyde North.

MC CALL, WILLIAM
Born: May 19, 1879, Delavan, Ill. Died: Jan. 10, 1938, Hollywood, Calif. Screen, stage, and television actor. Was billed in vaudeville as "McCall Trio."

Appeared in: 1919 Smashing Barriers (serial). 1921 Fighting Fate (serial); Flower of the North; Where Men Are Men; It Can Be Done. 1922 Across the Border; The Angel of Crooked Street; Fortune's Mask; The Fighting Guide; The Little Minister; Rounding up the Law; When Danger Smiles. 1923 Smashing Barriers. 1924 Sell 'Em Cowboy; The Back Trail; Daring Chances; The Phantom Horseman. 1925 His Marriage Vow; The Red Rider; Ridin' Thunder. 1930 The Lonesome Trail; Under Texas Skies; Trailin' Trouble.

MC CANN, CHARLES ANDREW
Died: Sept. 1927, Paris, France. Screen actor and musician.

Appeared in: 1917 The Tiger Woman (film debut).

MC CARROLL, FRANK
Died: Mar. 9, 1954, Burbank, Calif.(accidental fall at home). Screen actor, stuntman, and rodeo rider.

Appeared in: 1949 Brand of Fear; Lawless Code; Renegades of the Sage. 1950 Fence Riders; Gunslingers; Over the Border.

MC CARTHY, MYLES (aka MILES MC CARTHY)
Born: Toronto, Canada. Died: Sept. 27, 1928, Hollywood, Calif. (heart attack). Screen, stage, and vaudeville actor.

Appeared in: 1922 Smiles Are Trumps. 1923 Dollar Devils; The Day of Faith. 1924 Captain Blood; Abraham Lincoln; Oh, You Tony!. 1925 Tricks; The Lady. 1926 The Heart of a Coward. 1927 The Racing Fool.

MC CARTHY, PAT (Patricia Cook)
Born: 1911. Died: Jan. 25, 1943, New York. Screen, stage actress, and dancer.

MC CLAIN, BILLY (William C. McClain)
Born: 1857. Died: Jan. 28, 1950, near Los Angeles, Calif.(trailer fire). Screen actor and minstrel.

Appeared in: 1935 The Virginia Judge. 1936 Dimples.

MC CLAY, CLYDE
Born: 1895. Died: June 30, 1939, Hollywood, Calif.(accident on location filming In Old Monterey—crushed by army tank). Screen actor and extra.

Appeared in: 1939 In Old Monterey

MC CLELLAN, HURD
Died: Apr. 20, 1933, Los Angeles, Calif.(accidental gunshot while filming). Screen actor and stuntman.

MC CLOSKEY, ELIZABETH H.
Born: 1870. Died: Jan. 8, 1942, Hollywood, Calif. Screen and stage actor. Entered films approx. 1920.

MC CLUNG, BOBBY
Born: 1921. Died: Jan. 27, 1945, Columbia, S. C.(pneumonia). Screen, stage, and vaudeville actor. Appeared in many "Dead End Kids" movies.

Appeared in: 1937 Two Wise Maids; Paradise Express; The Toast of New York.

MC CLURE, BUD
Born: 1886. Died: Nov. 2, 1942, North Hollywood, Calif. Screen actor and cowboy.

MC CLURE, IRENE
Died: Sept. 4, 1928, Bakersfield, Calif.(injuries from auto accident). Screen actress.

MC COMAS, CARROLL
Born: 1886, Albuquerque, N. Mex. Died: Nov. 9, 1962, New York. Screen stage, vaudeville, television actress, singer, and dancer.

Appeared in: 1953 Jamaica Run. 1955 Chicago Syndicate.

MC COMAS, GLENN
Born: 1900. Died: June 10, 1959, Los Angeles, Calif. Screen actor.

MC COMAS, LILA
Born: 1906. Died: June 13, 1936, Los Angeles, Calif.(auto accident). Screen actress.

MC CONNELL, LULU
Born: 1882, Kansas City, Mo. Died: Oct. 9, 1962, Hollywood, Calif.(cancer). Screen, stage, vaudeville, and radio actress. Married to screen actor Grant Simpson (dec. 1932).

Appeared in: 1936 Stage Struck.

MC CONNELL, MOLLY
Born: Dec. 10, 1920, Los Angeles, Calif. Screen and stage actress.

Appeared in: 1915 Who Pays?. 1921 Black Beauty; Hearts and Masks; The Home Stretch.

MC CORMACK, BILLIE (Blance E. Burke)
Died: Feb. 1, 1935, Santa Monica, Calif. Screen actress.

MC CORMACK, JOHN
Born: June 14, 1884, Athlone, Ireland. Died: Sept. 16, 1945, Dublin, Ireland. Screen actor, radio, and opera tenor.

Appeared in: 1930 Song O' My Heart. 1937 Wings of the Morning.

MC CORMACK, WILLIAM M.
Born: 1891. Died: Aug. 19, 1953, Hollywood, Calif.(heart attack). Screen actor.

Appeared in: 1921 Red Courage; The Robe. 1922 Robin Hood. 1923 Danger; Good Men and Bad. 1924 Abraham Lincoln. 1925 Fangs of Fate; Reckless Courage; The Secret of Black Canyon; Flashing Steeds; Vic Dyson Pays. 1926 The Desperate Game. 1927 The Long Loop on the Pecos; Arizona Nights; Whispering Smith Rides (serial). 1928 The Apache Raider; A Son of the Desert. 1929 Romance of the Rio Grande; Born to the Saddle; Riders of the Rio Grande. 1936 Trail of the Lonesome Pine; Tundra. 1953 Salome; The Robe (and 1921 version).

MC CORMICK, ALYCE (aka JOY AUBURN)
Died: Jan. 7, 1932, Hollywood, Calif.(pneumonia). Screen and stage actress.

Appeared in: 1928 Mother Knows Best. 1930 Reno. 1931 Spirit of Notre Dame; Frankenstein; Bad Girl. 1939 The Mysterious Mr. X.

MC CORMICK, F. J. (Peter Judge)
Born: 1891. Died: Apr. 24, 1947, Dublin, Ireland. Screen and stage actor.

Appeared in: 1937 The Plough and the Stars. 1947 Odd Man Out; Hungry Hill.

MC CORMICK, MYRON
Born: Feb. 8, 1908, Albany, Ind. Died: July 30, 1962, New York, N.Y.(cancer). Screen, stage, radio, and television actor.

Appeared in: 1937 Winterset. 1939 One Third of a Nation. 1940 The Fight for Life. 1943 China Girl. 1949 Jigsaw; Jolson Sings Again; Gun Moll. 1955 Three for the Show; Not As a Stranger. 1958 No Time for Sergeants. 1959 The Man Who Understood Women. 1961 The Hustler. 1962 The Haircut (short); A Public Affair.

MC COY, GERTRUDE
Died: July 17, 1967, Atlanta, Ga. Screen actress. Entered films as and extra and appeared in early Edison Co. films. Made films in U.S., England, Germany and South America. Married to screen actor Duncan McRae (dec. 1967).

Appeared in: 1912 Every Rose Has Its Stem (short). 1918 The Blue Bird. 1921 Out of the Darkness. 1928 On the Stroke of 12. 1931 The Working Girl. 1932 The Silent Witness.

MC COY, HARRY
Born: 1894. Died: Sept. 1, 1937, Hollywood, Calif.(heart attack). Screen, radio actor, film director, and song writer. Was a Keystone Cop and appeared in "Joker" comedies.

Also appeared in: 1913 Mike and Jake at the Beach; The Cheese Special (short). 1914 Mabel's Strange Predicament; Caught in a Cabaret; Mabel at the Wheel; Mabel's Busy Day; Mabel's Married Life; The Masquerader; Getting Acquainted. 1915 One Night Stand; For Better—But Worse; A Human Hound's Triumph; Those Bitter Sweets; Merely a Married Man; Saved by Wireless; The Village Scandal. 1916 His Last Laugh; The Great Pear Tangle; Love Will Conquer; Perils of the Park; A Movie Star; Cinders of Love; His Auto Ruination; Bubbles of Trouble; She Loved a Sailor. 1921 Skirts; plus "Hallroom Boys" comedies. 1924 The Fatal Mistake. 1925 Dashing Thru; Heads Up; Heir-Loons. 1938 Hearts of Men.

MC COY, KID. See Norman Selby

MC CRACKEN, JOAN
Born: 1923. Died: Nov. 1, 1961, New York, N.Y.(heart condition). Screen, stage actress, and dancer.

Appeared in: 1944 Hollywood Canteen. 1947 Good News.

MC CULLOUGH, PAUL
Born: 1884, Springfield, Ohio. Died: Mar. 25, 1936, Boston, Mass.(suicide). Screen, stage, vaudeville, minstrel actor, and circus performer. Was partner in comedy team of "Clark and McCullough." For films he appeared in see Bobby Clark.

MC CUTCHEON, WALLACE
Born: 1881. Died: Jan. 27, 1928, Los Angeles, Calif.(shot himself). Screen, stage actor, and film director. Divorced from screen actress Pearl White (dec. 1938).

Appeared in: 1919 A Virtuous Vamp; The Black Secret (serial). 1920 The Phantom Foe (serial).

MC DANIEL, GEORGE
Born: 1886. Died: Aug. 20, 1944, Hollywood, Calif. Screen and stage actor.

Appeared in: 1915 The Girl and the Game (serial). 1921 Silent Years. 1922 The Scrapper. 1923 The Barefoot Boy. 1926 Burning Words. 1927 The Iron Hearts.

MC DANIEL, HATTIE
Born: 1895, Wichita, Kans. Died: Oct. 26, 1952, San Fernando Valley, Calif. Negro screen, radio, vaudeville, and television actress, and singer. Won Academy Award in 1939 for Best Supporting Actress in Gone with the Wind.

Appeared in: 1932 The Golden West; Blonde Venus; Hypnotized; Washington Masquerade. 1933 I'm No Angel; The Story of Temple Drake. 1934 Operator 13; Little Men; Judge Priest; Lost in the Stratosphere; Babbitt; Imitation of Life. 1935 Music Is Magic; China Seas; Another Face; Alice Adams; The Little Colonel; The Travelling Saleslady. 1936 Gentle Julia; The First Baby; High Tension; Star for a Night; Can This Be Dixie?; Reunion; Showboat; Postal Inspector; Hearts Divided; The Bride Walks Out; Big Time Vaudeville Reels (shorts); Valiant Is the Word for Carrie; Next Time We Love; Libeled Lady; High Treason; The Singing Kid. 1937 Don't Tell the Wife; Racing Lady; The Crime Nobody Saw; True Confession; Saratoga; Over the Goal; 45 Fathers; Nothing Sacred; Merry-Go-Round of 1938; The Wildcatter. 1938 Battle of Broadway; Everybody's Baby; Shopworn Angel; The Shining Hour; The Mad Miss Manton. 1939 Gone with the Wind; Zenobia. 1940 Maryland. 1941 Affectionately Yours; The Great Lie; They Died with Their Boots On. 1942 The Male Animal; In This Our Life; George Washington Slept Here; Reap the Wild Wind. 1943 Thank Your Lucky Stars; Johnny Come Lately. 1944 Since You Went Away; Janie; Three Is a Family. 1945 Hi, Beautiful. 1946 Margie; Never Say Goodbye; Janie Gets Married. 1947 Song of the South; The Flame. 1948 Mr. Blandings Builds His Dream House; Mickey. 1949 Family Honeymoon; The Big Wheel.

MC DERMOTT, MARC
Born: 1881, England. Died: Jan. 5, 1929, Glendale, Calif.(gall bladder surgery). Screen and stage actor.

Appeared in: 1911 Aida. 1912 What Happened to Mary (serial). 1914 The Man Who Disappeared (serial). 1916 Ranson's Folly. 1917 Intrigue. 1919 New Moon. 1920 While New York Sleeps.

1921 Blind Wives; Amazing Lovers; Footlights. 1922 The Lights of New York; The Spanish Jade. 1923 Hoodman Blind; Lucretia Lombard; The Satin Girl. 1924 Dorothy Vernon of Haddon Hall; In Every Woman's Life; The Sea Hawk; This Woman; Three Miles Out; He Who Gets Slapped. 1925 The Lady; The Goose Woman; Siege; Graustark. 1926 Flesh and the Devil; Kiki; The Temptress; The Love Thief; The Lucky Lady. 1927 California; Man, Woman, and Sin; The Taxi Driver; The Road to Romance; Resurrection. 1928 The Whip; The Yellow Lily; Under the Black Eagle; Glorious Betsy.

MC DONALD, CHARLES B.
Born: May 26, 1886, Springfield, Mass. Died: Dec. 29, 1964, Hollywood, Fla. Screen, stage, vaudeville actor, journalist, and film executive. Entered films with Essanay in the early 1900s.

Appeared in: 1914 Michael Strogoff. 1921 Salvation Neil. 1925 Irish Luck.

MC DONALD, FRANCIS J.
Born: Aug. 22, 1891, Bowling Green, Ky. Died: Sept. 18, 1968, Hollywood, Calif. Screen and stage actor.

Appeared in: 1918 The Gun Woman. 1920 Nomads of the North. 1921 The Call of the North; The Golden Snare; Puppets of Fate; Hearts and Masks. 1922 Captain Fly-by-Night; The Man Who Married His Own Wife; The Woman Conquers; Trooper O'Neil; Monte Cristo. 1923 Mary of the Movies; South Sea Love; Going Up; Trilby; The Buster; Look Your Best. 1924 The Arizona Express; East of Broadway; Racing Luck; So This Is Marriage. 1925 Anything Once; Bobbed Hair; Go Straight; The Hunted Woman; My Lady of Whims; Satin in Sables; Northern Code. 1926 Battling Butler; The Yankee Senor; The Desert's Toll; Puppets; The Temptress; The Palace of Pleasure. 1927 The Notorious Lady; The Valley of Hell; Outlaws of Red River; The Wreck. 1928 The Dragnet; Legion of the Condemned; A Girl in Every Port. 1929 The Carnation Kid; Girl Overboard. 1930 Brothers; Dangerous Paradise; Safety in Numbers; The Runaway Bride; Burning Up; Morocco. 1931 The Lawyer's Secret; In Line of Duty; The Gang Buster. 1932 Honor of the Mounted; Texas Buddies; The Devil Is Driving; Trailing the Killer; Woman from Monte Carlo. 1933 Broadway Bad; Terror Trail; Kickin' the Crown Around. 1934 Voice in the Night; Girl in Danger; Straightaway; The Trumpet Blows; The Line-Up; Burn 'Em up Barnes (feature film and serial). 1935 Mississippi; Marriage Bargain; Star of Midnight; Red Morning; Ladies Crave Excitement. 1936 Robin Hood of El Dorado; The Prisoner of Shark Island; Under Two Flags; Big Brown Eyes; The Plainsman; Mummy's Boys. 1937 The Devil's Playground; Parole Racket; Born Reckless; Love under Fire; Every Day's a Holiday. 1938 Gun Law; If I Were King. 1939 Range War; Union Pacific; The Bad Lands; The Light That Failed. 1940 One Night in the Tropics; The Carson City Kid; The Sea Hawk; Northwest Mounted Police; Green Hell; The Devil's Pipeline. 1941 The Sea Wolf; Men of Timberland; The Kid from Kansas. 1942 The Girl from Alaska. 1943 Buckskin Frontier; Bar 20; The Kansan. 1944 Texas Masquerade; Cheyenne Wildcat; Lumberjack; Mystery Man; Border Town; Zoro's Black Whip (serial). 1945 The Great Stagecoach Robbery; South of the Rio Grande; Strange Confessions; Corpus Christi Bandits. 1945 Bad Men of the Border; Canyon Passage; The Catman of Paris; Invisible Informer; Tangier; My Pal Trigger; Roll on Texas Moon; Night Train to Memphis; The Magnificent Doll. 1947 Duel in the Sun; Saddle Pals; Dangerous Venture; Spoilers of the North; The Perils of Pauline. 1948 Bold Frontiersman; The Paleface; Panhandle; Desert Passage; Bandits of Corsica. 1949 Son of God's Country; Brothers in the Saddle; Daughter of the Jungle; Rose of the Yukon; Son of the Badman; Apache Chief; Samson and Delilah; Strange Gamble; Rim of the Canyon; Abandoned; Powder River Rustlers. 1950 California Passage. 1952 The Raiders; Rancho Notorious; Red Mountain; Fort Osage. 1954 Three Hours to Kill; The Bandits of Corsica. 1955 Ten Wanted Men. 1956 Thunder over Arizona; The Ten Commandments. 1957 Last Stagecoach West; Duel at Apache Wells; Pawnee. 1958 Saga of Hemp Brown; Fort Massacre. 1959 The Big Fisherman.

MC DONALD, JAMES
Born: 1886. Died: Dec. 26, 1952, Los Angeles, Calif. Screen actor and trick rider.

MC DONALD, JOSEPH
Born: 1861. Died: Oct. 24, 1935, Redondo Beach, Calif.(drowned). Screen actor.

MC DONALD, MARIE (Marie Frye)
Born: 1923, Burgin, Ky. Died: Oct. 21, 1965, Hidden Hills, Calif. (accidental drug overdose). Screen, stage actress, and singer. Known as "The Body." Entered films in 1941.

Appeared in: 1941 It Started with Eve; You're Telling Me. 1942 Pardon My Sarong; Lucky Jordan. 1943 Tornado; Riding High. 1944 I Love a Soldier; Standing Room Only; Guest in the House; A Scream in the Dark. 1945 It's a Pleasure; Getting Gertie's Garter. 1946 Swell Guy. 1947 Living in a Big Way. 1949 Tell It to the Judge. 1950 Once a Thief; Hit Parade of 1951. 1958 The Geisha Boy. 1963 Promises, Promises.

MC DONALD, RAY
Born: 1924, Boston, Mass. Died: 1959. Screen, stage, and vaudeville actor.

Appeared in: 1941 Down in San Diego; Life Begins for Andy Hardy; Babes on Broadway. 1942 Born to Sing. 1943 Presenting Lily Mars. 1946 Till the Clouds Roll By. 1947 Good News. 1949 Shamrock Hill. 1950 There's a Girl in My Heart. 1953 All Ashore.

MC DONOUGH, MICHAEL
Born: 1876. Died: Aug. 8, 1956, Hollywood, Calif. Screen actor.

MC DOWELL, CLAIRE
Born: Nov. 2, 1877, New York, N.Y. Died: Oct. 23, 1966, Woodland Hills, Calif. Screen and stage actress. Entered films with American Biograph Co. in 1910.

Appeared in: 1919 Heart O' the Hills. 1920 Something to Think About; Midsummer Madness; The Woman in the Suitcase. 1921 Love Never Dies; Prisoners of Love; Wealth; Chickens; What Every Woman Knows; Mother O'Mine. 1922 The Gray Dawn; Heart's Haven; In the Name of the Law; The Lying Truth; Penrod; Quincy Adams Sawyer; Nice People; Rent Free; The Ragged Heiress. 1923 The Westbound Limited; Ponjola; Michael O'Halloran; Ashes of Vengeance; Enemies of Children; Human Wreckage; Circus Days. 1924 Black Oxen; A Fight for Honor; Judgement of the Storm; Leave It to Gerry; Secrets; Thy Name Is Woman; Those Who Date. 1925 The Big Parade; One of the Bravest; The Reckless Sex; Walking up the Town; The Town of Lies; Dollar Down; The Midnight Flyer. 1926 Ben Hur; The Show-Off; The Devil's Circus; The Dixie Merchant; The Flaming Forest; The Shamrock Handicap; The Unknown Soldier. 1927 Almost Human; The Auctioneer; The Black Diamond Express; The Taxi Dancer; Winds of the Pampas; Cheaters; A Little Journey; The Shield of Honor; Tillie the Toiler. 1928 The Viking; Don't Marry; Marriage by Contract; The Tragedy of Youth. 1929 Silks and Saddles; Whispering Winds; The Quitter; When Dreams Come True; Four Devils. 1930 The Big House; Mothers Cry; Redemption; Wild Company; Young Desire; The Second Floor Mystery; Brothers. 1931 An American Tragedy. 1932 Manhattan Parade; It's Tough to Be Famous; Strange Love of Molly Louvain; Phantom Express; Rebecca of Sunnybrook Farm. 1933 Cornered; Two Heads on a Pillow; Central Airport; The Working Man; Paddy, the Next Best Thing; Wild Boys of the Road; By Appointment Only. 1936 August Weekend. 1937 Two-Fisted Sheriff; High, Wide and Handsome. 1939 Honolulu. 1944 Are These Our Parents?; Men on Her Mind; Teen Age.

MC DOWELL, NELSON
Born: Aug. 18, 1875, Greenville, Mo. Died: Nov. 3, 1947, Hollywood, Calif.(suicide—gun). Screen actor. Entered films with American Biograph in 1910.

Appeared in: 1916 Wheels of Destiny. 1921 The Silent Call; Home Stuff; Shadows of Conscience; The Last of the Mohicans. 1922 The Phantom Bullet; Whispering Smith; Blind Trail; Crossed Signals; Lightning Reporter; The Outlaw Express; The Frontier Trail; The Valley of Bravery. 1927 Uncle Tom's Cabin; The Claw; Code of the Range; Hands Off; Border Blackbirds; The Bugle Call; The Great Mail Robbery. 1928 Heart Trouble; The Vanishing Rider (serial); The Little Shepherd of Kingdom Come; Kit Carson; Kentucky Courage. 1929 Wild Blood; Born to the Saddle; Grit Wins. 1930 Billy the Kid. 1933 Oliver Twist. 1934 Wheels of Destiny (and 1916 version). 1935 Wilderness Mail. 1936 The Desert Phantom; Feud of the West; Girls of the Ozark. 1938 College Swing. 1959 Uncle Tom's Cabin (reissue of 1927 film).

MC ELROY, JACK
Born: 1914. Died: Mar. 2, 1959, Santa Monica, Calif.(lung cancer). Screen, radio, and television actor.

Appeared in: 1956 Hollywood or Bust.

MC EVOY, ERNEST SIMON
Born: 1894. Died: Apr. 14, 1953, Hollywood, Calif. Screen and stage actor.

MC EWAN, ISABELLE
Born: 1897, Scotland. Died: Feb. 19, 1963, Vancouver, B C., Canada. Screen, stage, and radio actress.

MC FADDEN, CHARLES I.
Born: 1888. Died: Aug. 14, 1942. Screen actor and film producer. Entered films approx. 1917.

MC GAUGH, WILBUR
Born: 1895. Died: Jan. 31, 1965, Hollywood, Calif.(heart attack). Screen actor and film director. Entered films in 1911.

Appeared in: 1921 The Broken Spur; Dead or Alive; Devil Dog Dawson; Cupid's Brand; The Sheriff of Hope Eternal. 1922 One Eighth Apache; Peaceful Peters. 1923 At Devil's Gorge; The Law Rustlers; The Devil's Dooryard. 1924 Days of '49 (serial); California in '49 (feature of Days of '49 serial); Bringin' Home the Bacon; Ridin' Mad; Cupid's Rustler. 1925 The Cactus Cure; Whistling Jim; The Fugitive. 1926 Bad Man's Bluff. 1929 The Sky Skidder.

MC GIVENEY, OWEN
Born: 1884. Died: July 31, 1967, Woodland Hills, Calif. Screen, stage, and vaudeville actor.

Appeared in: 1948 If Winter Comes. 1951 Show Boat. 1952 Scaramouche; Pat and Mike; Plymouth Adventure. 1953 The Maze. 1954 Brigadoon. 1955 The King's Thief. 1958 Hong Kong Confidential; In the Money. 1961 Snow White and the Three Stooges. 1964 My Fair Lady.

MC GLYNN, FRANK
Born: 1867, San Francisco, Calif. Died: May 17, 1951, Newburgh, N.Y. Screen and stage actor. Played Abraham Lincoln in many films. Appeared in Edison Stock Company films in 1907.

Appeared in: 1916 Gloria's Romance (serial). 1924 America. 1927 Judgement of the Hills. 1930 Min and Bill; Good News; Jazz Cinderella. 1931 The Secret Six; Huckleberry Finn; Riders of the Purple Sage. 1932 The Silent Partners (short); No Man of Her Own. 1933 Unknown Valley; Charlie Chan's Greatest Case; Frisco Jenny; Face in the Sky. 1934 Massacre; Little Miss Marker; Kentucky Kernels; Search for Beauty; Are We Civilized?; Lost in the Stratosphere. 1935 Follies Bergere; It's a Small World; Roaring West (serial); Outlawed Guns; The Littlest Rebel; Custer's Last Stand (serial); Captain Blood; Hopalong Cassidy. 1936 The Prisoner of Shark Island; King of the Royal Mounted; Career Woman; Hearts in Bondage; Parole; The Last of the Mohicans; North of Nome; The Plainsman; For the Service; The Trail of the Lonesome Pine. 1937 Wild West Days (serial); Western Gold; Wells Fargo; Silent Barriers; Sing and Be Happy. 1938 Sudden Bill Dorn; Kentucky Moonshine. 1939 The Honeymoon's Over; Union Pacific; The Mad Empress. 1940 Hi-Yo Silver; Boom Town. 1941 A Girl, a Guy and a Gob; Marry the Boss's Daughter; Three Girls in Town. 1944 Delinquent Daughters. 1945 Rogues' Gallery. 1947 Hollywood Barn Dance.

MC GOWAN, JOHN P.
Born: Feb., 1880, Terowie, South Australia. Died: Mar. 26, 1952, Hollywood, Calif. Screen, stage actor, film director, film producer, and screenwriter. Entered films as an actor with Kalem in 1909.

Appeared in: 1912 From the Manger to the Cross. 1915 Hazards of Helen (serial). 1917 The Railroad Raiders (serial). 1921 Do or Die (serial); Discontented Wives; Cold Steel; A Crook's Romance; The White Horseman (serial); King of the Circus (serial). 1922 Hills of Missing Men; Reckless Chances; The Ruse of the Rattler. 1923 The Whipping Boss; One Million in Jewels; Stormy Seas. 1924 Crossed Trails; A Two Fisted Tenderfoot. 1925 Barriers of the Law; Border Intrigue; Crack O'Dawn; Duped; The Fear Fighter; Makers of Men; Outwitted; Blood and Steel; The Fighting Sheriff. 1926 Danger Quest; Moran of the Mounted; The Patent Leather Kid; Red Blood; Senor Daredevil; The Ace of Clubs; The Lost Express. 1927 Arizona Nights; Gun Gospel; The Lost Limited; Red Signals; The Red Raiders; The Slaver; The Royal American; Tarzan and the Golden Lion. 1928 The Black Ace; Arizona Days; The Code of the Scarlet; Devil Dogs; Devil's Tower; Dugan of the Dugouts; Headin' Westward; Law of the Mounted; Lighting Shot; The Old Code; On the Divide; Ships of the Night; Silent Trail; Texas Tommy; The Two Outlaws; West of Sante Fe; Painted Trail; Chinatown Mystery (serial); Senor Americano. 1929 The Phantom Raider; The Invaders; Fighting Terror; Arizona Days; Bad Man's Money; The Clean Up; Below the Deadline; The Lawless Legion; Captain Cowboy; On the Divide; The Silent Trail; The Last Roundup; West of Santa Fe; The Lone Horseman; Oklahoma Kid; The Golden Bridle; Ships of the Night; Plunging Hoofs; Riders of the Rio Grande; 'Neath Western Skies. 1930 Cowboy and the Outlaw; Pioneers of the West; Canyon of Missing Men; Covered Wagon Trails; O'Malley Rides Alone;

Breezy Bill; Near the Rainbow's End. 1931 Riders of the North. 1932 Hurricane Express. 1933 Somewhere in Arizona; When a Man Rides Alone. 1934 No More Women; Wagon Wheels; Fighting Hero. 1935 Mississippi; Border Brigands; Bar 20 Rides Again. 1936 Stampede; Guns and Guitars; The Three Musquiteers; Secret Patrol; Ride 'Em Cowboy. 1937 Fury and the Woman; Slave Ship. 1938 The Buccaneer; Hunted Men. 1939 In Old Montana; Code of the Fearless; Calling All Marines; Stagecoach.

MC GOWAN, OLIVER F.
Born: 1907. Died: Aug. 23, 1971, Hollywood, Calif. Screen, stage, radio, and television actor.

Appeared in: 1958 Screaming Mimi. 1967 Banning.

MC GRAIL, WALTER B.
Born: 1899, Brooklyn, N.Y. Died: Mar. 19, 1970. Screen and stage actor.

Appeared in: 1916 The Scarlet Runner (serial). 1917 Within the Law. 1919 The Black Secret (serial). 1921 Playthings of Destiny; The Invisible Fear; The Breaking Point; Her Mad Bargain; Pilgrims of the Night. 1922 The Cradle; The Kentucky Derby; Suzanna; The Top of New York. 1923 The Bad Man; The Eleventh Hour; Flaming Youth; Is Divorce a Failure?; Nobody's Money; Lights Out; Where the North Begins. 1924 A Son of the Sahara; Gerald Cranston's Lady; Is Love Everything?; Unguarded Women. 1925 Havoc; The Dancers; The Mad Marriage; Champion of Lost Causes; Adventure; A Son of His Father; When the Door Opened; The Teaser; Her Husband's Secret; The Scarlet West. 1926 Across the Pacific; The City; The Combat; Forbidden Waters; Marriage License?; Prisoners of the Storm. 1927 The Secret Studio; American Beauty; Man Crazy. 1928 The Play Girl; Stop That Man; Midnight Madness; Blockade; The Old Code. 1929 One Splendid Hour; Confessions of a Wife; Hey Rube!; The Veiled Woman; River of Romance. 1930 Soldiers and Women; The Lone Star Ranger; Men without Women; Women Everywhere; Last of the Duanes; River's End; Anybody's War; The Pay-Off; Part Time Wife. 1931 The Seas Beneath; Murder by the Clock; Night Nurse. 1932 Night Beat; Under Eighteen; McKenna of the Mounted; Exposed. 1933 State Trooper; Robbers' Roost; Sing, Sinner, Sing!; Police Call. 1935 All the King's Horses; Sunset Range; Men of the Night. 1937 The Shadow Strikes. 1938 Held for Ransom. 1939 Stagecoach; Calling All Marines; The Sun Never Sets. 1940 My Little Chickadee. 1942 Billy the Kid Trapped; Riders of the West.

MC GRATH, FRANK
Born: 1903. Died: May 13, 1967, Beverly Hills, Calif.(heart attack). Screen and television actor. Entered films as a stuntman.

Appeared in: 1942 Sundown Jim. 1945 They Were Expendable. 1949 She Wore a Yellow Ribbon. 1953 Ride, Vaquero. 1957 Hell Bound; The Tin Star. 1965 The Sword of Ali Baba. 1967 The Last Challenge; Tammy and the Millionaire; Gunfight in Abilene; The Last Wagon; The Reluctant Astronaut. 1968 The Shakiest Gun in the West.

MC GREGOR, MALCOLM (aka MALCOLM MAC GREGOR)
Born: Oct. 13, 1892, Newark, N.J. Died: Apr. 29, 1945, Los Angeles, Calif.(burns). Screen actor.

Appeared in: 1922 The Prisoner of Zenda; Broken Chains. 1923 The Untamable; All the Brothers Were Valiant; The Dancer of the Nile; Can a Woman Love Twice?; A Noise in Newboro; The Social Code; You Can't Get Away It. 1924 Smouldering Fires; The House of Youth; The Bedroom Window; Idle Tongues. 1925 Headlines; Alias Mary Flynn; The Circle; The Happy Warrior; Flaming Waters; The Girl of Gold; Infatuation; Lady of the Night; The Overland Limited; The Vanishing American. 1926 The Silent Flyer (serial); Don Juan's Three Nights; It Must Be Love; The Gay Deceiver; Money to Burn. 1927 A Million Bid; The Girl from Gay Paree; The Kid Sister; The Ladybird; Matinee Ladies; The Wreck; The Price of Honor. 1928 Buck Privates; Freedom of the Press; Lingerie; The Port of Missing Girls; Tropical Nights; Stormy Waters. 1929 The Girl on the Barge; Whispering Winds. 1930 Murder Will Out. 1935 Happiness C.O.D.

MC GREGOR, PARKE (Parke Cushnie)
Born: 1907. Died: Dec. 5, 1962, Hollywood, Calif.(heart attack). Screen actor and singer.

MC GUINN, JOSEPH FORD "JOE"
Born: Jan. 21, 1904, Brooklyn, N.Y. Died: Sept. 22, 1971, Hollywood, Calif.(heart attack). Screen and stage actor.

Appeared in: 1942 The Glass Key; Flight Lieutenant; In Old California; Two Yanks in Trinidad; The Cyclone Kid. 1945 Three's a Crowd. 1953 Prince of Pirates. 1957 Chicago Confidential; Three Brave Men. 1958 Ten North Frederick; Showdown at Boot Hill. 1959 The Story on Page One. 1961 The Gambler Wore a Gun. 1962 The Wild Westerners.

MCGUIRE, BENJAMIN
Born: 1875. Died: Apr. 10, 1925, New York, N.Y.(heart failure). Screen actor. Appeared in Famous Players productions.

MC GUIRE, TOM
Born: 1874. Died: May 6, 1954, Hollywood, Calif. Screen and stage actor.

Appeared in: 1921 The Girl in the Taxi; R.S.V.P.; See My Lawyer; Stranger Than Fiction. 1922 Afraid to Fight; The Five Dollar Baby; A Front Page Story; The Ladder Jinx; The Married Flapper. 1923 April Showers; A Million to Burn; The Scarlet Car; The Self-Made Wife; Single Handed; The Spoilers; The Victor. 1924 Captain Blood; Dark Stairways; Her Man; The Reckless Age. 1925 Fighting Fate; Red Hot Tires; We Moderns. 1926 The Better 'Ole; My Own Pal. 1927 Babe Comes Home; Colleen; The Missing Link; Pleasure before Business; Shanghai Bound. 1928 Lights of New York; A Thief in the Dark; The Sawdust Paradise; Steamboat Bill, Jr. 1930 Voice of the City. 1931 Politics; Oh! Oh! Cleopatra (short). 1932 No Greater Love. 1933 She Done Him Wrong.

MC GURK, BOB
Born: 1907. Died: May 30, 1959, Los Angeles, Calif. Screen actor.

MC HUGH, CATHERINE
Born: 1869. Died: June 28, 1944, Hollywood, Calif. Screen actress. Mother of screen actors Matt (dec. 1971) and Frank McHugh.

MC HUGH, CHARLES PATRICK
Born: Philadelphia, Pa. Died: Oct. 22, 1931, Los Angeles, Calif. (heart attack). Screen and stage actor.

Appeared in: 1921 Be My Wife; A Shocking Night; Smiling All the Way. 1922 The Beautiful and Damned. 1923 Cupid's Fireman; The Eagle's Feather; The Girl of the Golden West. 1924 The Trouble Shooter. 1925 Brand of Cowardice; Lights of Old Broadway; Smilin' at Trouble. 1926 The Golden Cocoon; Her Honor the Governor; The Prince of Broadway; The Sporting Lover; The Waning Sex. 1927 Finnegan's Ball; The Princess from Hoboken. 1928 Phantom of the Range. 1929 Smiling Irish Eyes; The Quitter.

MC HUGH, JIMMY
Born: July 10, 1894, Boston, Mass. Died: May 23, 1969, Beverly Hills, Calif.(heart attack). Song writer and screen actor.

Appeared in: 1957 The Helen Morgan Story.

MC HUGH, MATT (Mathew O. McHugh)
Born: 1894, Connellsville, Pa. Died: Feb. 22, 1971, Northridge, Calif.(heart attack). Screen, stage, and vaudeville actor. Entered films with Mack Sennett. Brother of screen actor Frank McHugh. Son of screen actress Catherine McHugh (dec. 1944).

Appeared in: 1931 Street Scene (screen and stage versions); Reckless Living. 1932 Paramount shorts, RKO shorts; Freaks; The Wet Parade; Afraid to Talk. 1933 Paramount shorts; The Last Trail; The Man Who Dared; Jimmy and Sally; Devil's Brother; Night of Terror. 1934 She Loves Me Not; Sandy McKee; Judge Priest; Wake up and Dream. 1935 Wings in the Dark; Lost in the Stratosphere; Murder on a Honeymoon; The Good Fairy; Enter Madame; Mr. Dynamite; Diamond Jim; The Glass Key; Ladies Crave Excitement; Barbary Coast. 1936 Two in a Crowd; The Big Broadcast of 1937. 1937 Navy Blue and Gold. 1938 No Time to Marry; Tropic Holiday. 1939 Federal Man Hunt; Jones Family in Hollywood; The Excape; At the Circus. 1940 Yesterday's Heroes. 1942 It Happened in Flatbush; The Man in the Trunk; Girl Trouble. 1943 Flight for Freedom; The West Side Kid. 1944 My Buddy; Home in Indiana. 1945 Salome, Where She Danced; The Bells of St. Mary's; How Do You Do?. 1946 Deadline for Murder; Dark Corner; Vacation in Reno. 1947 The Trouble with Women. 1948 Pardon My Clutch (short). 1949 Duke of Chicago. 1950 Bodyhold; Return of the Frontiersman. 1955 Wham-Bam-Slam.

MC ILLWAIN, WILLIAM A.
Born: 1863. Died: May 27, 1933, Los Angeles, Calif.(heart attack). Screen and stage actor.

Appeared in: 1924 Abraham Lincoln. 1925 Passionate Youth; Reckless Courage.

MC INTOSH, BURR
Born: Aug. 21, 1862, Wellsville, Ohio. Died: Apr. 28, 1942, Hollywood, Calif.(heart attack). Screen, stage, radio actor, screenwriter, and writer for radio. Entered films in 1913.

Appeared in: 1915 Adventures of Wallingford. 1920 Way Down East. 1923 Driven; The Exciters; On the Banks of the Wabash. 1924 The Average Woman; Lend Me Your Husband; Reckless Wives; The Spitfire; Virtuous Liars. 1925 Camille of the Barbary Coast; Enemies of Youth; The Pearl of Love; The Green Archer (serial). 1926 The Buckaroo Kid; Dangerous Friends; Lightning Reporter; The Wilderness Woman. 1927 The Golden Stallion (serial); A Hero for the Night; Breakfast at Sunrise; Fire and Steel; Framed; Hazardous Valley; Naughty but Nice; Once and Forever; See You in Jail; Silk Stockings; Taxi! Taxi!; The Yankee Clipper; Non Support (short). 1928 Across the Atlantic; The Adorable Cheat; The Grip of the Yukon; Me, Gangster; The Racket; That Certain Thing; Lilac Time; The Four Flusher; Sailor's Wives. 1929 The Last Warning; Fancy Baggage; Skinner Steps Out. 1930 The Rogue Song. 1933 The Sweetheart of Signa Chi. 1934 The Richest Girl in the World.

MC INTYRE, FRANK
Born: 1878. Died: June 8, 1949, Ann Arbor, Mich. Screen, stage and radio actor.

Appeared in: 1917 The Traveling Salesman. 1918 Too Fat to Fight.

MC INTYRE, LEILA
Born: 1882. Died: Jan. 9, 1953, Los Angeles, Calif. Screen, stage, and vaudeville actress. She appeared in vaudeville with her husband, actor John Hyams (dec. 1940), in an act called "Hyams & McIntyre." Mother of screen actress Leila Hyams. Her married name was Leila Hyams, but do not confuse her with her daughter by the same name (Leila Hyams) who was born on May 1, 1905.

Appeared in: 1927 All in Fun (Hyams & McIntyre short). 1929 Hurricane. 1930 On the Level; Swell People; All for Mabel. 1933 Marriage on Approval. 1935 Murder in the Fleet. 1936 The Prisoner of Shark Island. 1937 Pick a Star; Live, Love and Learn; Topper. 1939 The Housekeeper's Daughter; Three Smart Girls Grow Up; Zenobia.

MC IVOR, MARY
Born: 1901. Died: Feb. 28, 1941, Hollywood, Calif.(heart attack). Screen and vaudeville actress. Married to screen actor William Desmond (dec. 1949).

Appeared in: 1925 The Burning Trail.

MC KAY, GEORGE W. (George Reuben)
Born: 1880, Minsk, Russia. Died: Dec. 3, 1945, Hollywood, Calif. Screen, stage, and vaudeville actor. Married to actress Ottie Ardine with whom he appeared in vaudeville; prior to that he teamed with Johnny Cantwell in vaudeville acts.

Appeared in: 1929 Back from Abroad (McKay & Ardine short). 1930 Sixteen Sweeties. 1935 The Case of the Missing Man. 1936 Don't Gamble with Love; You May Be Next; Superspeed; Shakedown; Killer at Large; End of the Trail; One Way Ticket; Pride of the Marines; Counterfeit; The Final Hour; Two Fisted Gentleman; Come Closer, Folks. 1937 A Fight to the Finish. Frame-up; Right Guy; Counterfeit Lady; Woman in Distress; The Devil's Playground; It's All Yours; Murder in Greenwich Village; Racketeers in Exile. 1938 There's Always a Woman; Highway Patrol; Convicted; Duke of West Point; Illegal Traffic. 1939 King of the Turf; Babes in Arms. 1940 The Big Guy. 1941 The Face behind the Mask. 1942 Canal Zone; Sabotage Zone; The Boogie Man Will Get You. 1943 Murder in Times Square. 1944 Going My Way.

MC KAY, NORMAN
Born: 1906. Died: Apr. 24, 1968, New York, N.Y. Screen, stage, radio and television actor.

Appeared in: 1947 Untamed Fury; Kiss of Death. 1948 Call Northside 777. 1951 The Frogmen; USS Teakettle (aka You're in the Navy Now.) 1953 Niagara. 1961 The Hoodlum Priest.

MC KEE, BUCK
Born: 1865, Claremore, Okla. Died: Mar. 1, 1944, Roseville, Calif. Screen actor.

MC KEE, DONALD M.
Born: 1899. Died: June 27, 1968, Chebeague Island, Maine. Screen, stage, and television actor.

Appeared in: 1951 The Whistle at Eaton Falls. 1958 The Goddess.

MC KEE, TOM
Born: 1917. Died: June 20, 1960, Burbank, Calif.(accidental fall). Screen, radio, and television actor.

Appeared in: 1955 The Court Martial of Billy Mitchell. 1956 The Search for Bridey Murphy. 1957 Fury at Showdown; The River's Edge; Under Fire; Valerie. 1960 Three Came to Kill; Vice Raid.

MC KEEN, LAWRENCE D., JR. "SNOOKUMS"
Born: 1925. Died: Apr. 2, 1933, Los Angeles, Calif.(blood poisoning). Screen actor. Made his film debut as "Baby Snookums" at age of 18 months. By the time he was four he had his own series.

Appeared in: 1926 The Newlyweds and Their Baby (series).

MC KELVIE, HAROLD
Born: 1910. Died: June, 1937, Los Angeles, Calif. Screen actor and stuntman.

MC KENNA, HENRY T.
Born: 1894, Brooklyn, N.Y. Died: June 17, 1958, Hollywood, Calif.(heart attack). Screen actor.

MC KENZIE, ALEXANDER
Born: 1886. Died: Jan. 1966, Glasgow, Scotland. Screen actor and song writer.

Appeared in: 1954 High and Dry. 1958 Mad Little Island. 1959 The Bridal Path. 1960 The Battle of the Sexes. 1961 Greyfriars' Bobby. Other film: The Maggie.

MC KENZIE, EVA B.
Born: 1889. Died: Sept. 15, 1967, Hollywood, Calif. Screen actor. Entered films in 1915.

Appeared in: 1931 Virtuous Husband.

MC KENZIE, ROBERT B.
Born: Sept. 22, 1883, Bellymania, Ireland. Died: July 8, 1949, R.I.(heart attack). Screen and stage actor. Entered films in 1915.

Appeared in: 1921 A Knight of the West. 1922 Fightin' Devil; The Sheriff of Sun-Dog; A Western Demon. 1923 The Devil's Dooryard; Don Quickshort of the Rio Grande; The Gentleman from America; Single Handed; Where Is This West?; In the West. 1924 The Covered Trail; The Desert Hawk; The Whirlwind Ranger. 1925 Fifth Avenue Models. 1926 A Six Shootin' Romance; Bad Man's Bluff; The Fighting Peacemaker. 1927 One Glorious Scrap; Red Signals; Set Free. 1929 The White Outlaw. 1930 Shadow Ranch. 1931 Cimarron. 1933 Tillie and Gus; Beauty and the Bus (short). 1934 You're Telling Me; Opened by Mistake (short); Little Minister. 1935 Stone of Silver Creek; A Shot in the Dark; The Bride Comes Home; Hoi Polloi (short). 1936 Love before Breakfast; Comin' Round the Mountain; Rebellion. 1937 Sing Cowboy Sing; Hideaway; Stars over Arizona. 1939 They Asked for It; Blondie Takes a Vacation; Death of a Champion. 1940 Dreaming Out Loud; Buried Alive; Triple Justice. 1941 Citadel of Crime; Death Valley Outlaws. 1942 In Old California; The Sombrero Kid. 1943 Jive Junction. 1944 Texas Masquerade; Three of a Kind; Tall in the Saddle. 1946 Duel in the Sun; Romance of the West; Colorado Serenade.

MC KIM, ROBERT
Born: 1887, San Francisco, Calif. Died: June 2, 1927, Hollywood, Calif.(cerebral hemorrhage). Screen and vaudeville actor.

Appeared in: 1915 The Edge of the Abyss; The Disciple. 1916 The Primal Lure; The Stepping Stone; The Return of Draw Egan. 1919 Wagon Tracks; Her Kingdom of Dreams. 1920 The Mark of Zorro; Riders of the Dawn; The Silver Horde. 1921 A Certain Rich Man; The Lure of Egypt; The Man of the Forest; Mysterious Rider; The Spenders. 1922 The Gray Dawn; Heart's Haven; Monte Cristo; White Hands; Without Compromise. 1923 All the Brothers Were Valiant; Dead Game; His Last Race; Hollywood; Human Wreckage; Maytime; Mr. Billings Spends His Dime; The Spider and the Rose; The Spoilers; Strangers of the Night; Thundergate. 1924 Flaming Barriers; The Galloping Ace; Mademoiselle Midnight; Ride for Your Life; The Torrent; When a Girl Loves. 1925 North of Nome; The Police Patrol; Spook Ranch. 1926 The Bat; The Dead Line; Kentucky Handicap; The Pay Off; A Regular Scout; The Strong Man; Tex; The Tough Guy; The Wolf Hunters. 1927 A Flame in the Sky; The Denver Dude; The Show Girl; The Thrill Seekers.

MC KINNEL, NORMAN
Born: 1870, England. Died: Mar. 29, 1932, London, England (heart disease). Screen, stage actor, and stage director.

Appeared in: 1931 Sherlock Holmes Fatal Hour. 1933 White Face; Criminal at Large.

MC KINNEY, NINA MAE
Born: 1909, New York, N.Y. Died: 1968. Negro screen actress.

Appeared in: 1929 Hallelujah. 1931 Safe in Hell. 1935 Sanders of the River; Reckless. 1939 Pocomania. 1944 Dark Waters; Together Again. 1946 Night Train to Memphis. 1947 Danger Street. 1949 Pinky.

MC LAGLEN, VICTOR
Born: Dec. 11, 1886, Tunbridge Wells, Kent, England. Died: Nov. 7, 1959, Newport Beach, Calif.(heart attack). Screen, stage, and vaudeville actor. Won Academy Award for Best Actor in 1935 for The Informer. Nominated for Academy Award for Best Supporting Actor in 1952 for The Quiet Man.

Appeared in: 1920 The Call of the Road. 1922 The Glorious Adventure. 1924 The Beloved Brute. 1925 The Hunted Woman; Percy; The Fighting Heart; The Unholy Three; Winds of Chance. 1926 Beau Geste; What Price Glory; Men of Steel; The Isle of Retribution. 1927 Loves of Carmen. 1928 Mother Machree; A Girl in Every Port; Hangman's House; The River Pirate. 1929 Captain Lash; Strong Boy; King of the Khyber Rifles; The Cock Eyed World; The Black Watch; Sez You—Sez Me; Hot for Paris. 1930 Happy Days; On the Level; A Devil with Women; Wings of Adventures. 1931 Not Exactly Gentlemen; Dishonored; Women of All Nations; Wicked; Annabelle's Affairs. 1932 Guilty as Hell; Devil's Lottery; While Paris Sleeps; The Slippery Pearls (short); The Gay Caballero; Rackety Rax. 1933 Hot Pepper; Laughing at Life; Dick Turpin. 1934 The Lost Patrol; No More Women; Wharf Angel; Murder at the Vanities; The Captain Hates the Sea. 1935 Under Pressure; Great Hotel Murder; The Informer; Professional Soldier. 1936 Under Two Flags; Mary of Scotland; Klondike Annie; The Magnificent Brute. 1937 Sea Devils; Nancy Steele Is Missing; Wee Willie Winkle; This Is My Affair. 1938 We're Going to Be Rich; The Devil's Party; Battle of Broadway. 1939 Gunga Din; Pacific Liner; Rio; Let Freedom Ring; Black Watch; Captain Fury; Ex-Champ; Full Confession. 1940 The Big Guy; Diamond Frontier; South of Pago Pago. 1941 Broadway Limited. 1942 Call Out the Marines; Powder Town; China Girl. 1943 Forever and a Day. 1944 Tampico; The Princess and the Pirate. 1945 Rough, Tough and Ready; Roger Touhy, Gangster; Love, Honor and Goodbye. 1946 Whistle Stop. 1947 Michigan Kid; Foxes of Harrow; Calendar Girl. 1948 Fort Apache. 1949 She Wore a Yellow Ribbon. 1950 Rio Grande. 1952 The Quiet Man. 1953 Fair Wind to Java. 1954 Prince Valiant; Trouble in the Glen. 1955 Many Rivers to Cross; Bengazi; Lady Godiva; City of Shadows. 1956 Around the World in 80 Days. 1957 The Abductors. 1959 Sea Fury.

MC LEOD, BARBARA (Barbara Fielding)
Born: 1908. Died: May 26, 1940, Van Nuys, Calif.(suicide—gun). Screen actress.

MC LEOD, HELEN
Born: 1924. Died: Apr. 20, 1964, Bakersfield, Calif.(cancer). Screen actress.

MC MAHON, HORACE (aka HORACE MAC MAHON)
Born: 1907, South Norwalk, Conn. Died: Aug. 17, 1971, Norwalk, Conn.(heart ailment). Screen, stage, vaudeville, radio, and television actor. Married to screen actress Louise Campbell.

Appeared in: 1937 Navy Blues; The Wrong Road; Exclusive; A Girl with Ideas; They Gave Him a Gun; Double Wedding; Kid Galahad. 1938 King of the Newsboys; When G-Men Step In; Fast Company; Ladies in Distress; Tenth Avenue Kid; Secrets of a Nurse; Broadway Musketeers; Pride of the Navy; Alexander's Ragtime Band; Gangs of New York. 1939 Sergeant Madden; The Gracie Allen Murder Case; Rose of Washington Square; I Was a Convict; Federal Man-Hunt; Laugh It Off; Big Town Czar; For Love or Money; She Married a Cop; Quick Millions; Sabotage. 1940 The Marines Fly High; Dr. Kildare's Strange Case; I Can't Give You Anything but Love, Baby; Gangs of Chicago; Millionaires in Prison; Oh Johnny, How You Can Love!; We Who Are Young; The Leather Pushers; Melody Ranch; Dr. Kildare's Crisis. 1941 Come Live with Me; Rookies on Parade; The Bride Wore Crutches; Lady Scarface; Buy Me That Town; Birth of the Blues; The Stork Pays Off. 1942 Jail House Blues. 1944 Roger Touhy, Gangster; Timber Queen. 1945 Lady Gangster. 1948 Smart Woman; Fighting Mad; Waterfront at Midnight; The Return of October. 1951 Detective Story (film and stage versions). 1953 Abbott and Costello Go to Mars; Man in the Dark; Fast Company; Champ for a Day. 1954 Duffy of San Quentin; Susan Slept Here. 1955 The

Blackboard Jungle; My Sister Eileen; Texas Lady. 1957 The Delicate Delinquent; Beau James. 1959 Never Steal Anything Small. 1966 The Swinger. 1968 The Detective.

MC MILLAN, WALTER KENNETH
Born: 1917. Died: Jan., 1945 (killed in action in Philippine invasion W.W. II). Screen and stage actor. Was a member of Hal Roach's "Our Gang."

MC NAMARA, EDWARD C.
Born: 1884, Paterson, N.J. Died: Nov. 9, 1944, on train near Boston, Mass.(heart attack). Screen and stage actor, and opera tenor.

Appeared in: 1929 Lucky in Love. 1932 I Am a Fugitive from a Chain Gang. 1933 20,000 Years in Sing Sing. 1937 Great Guy; Girl Overboard; The League of Frightened Men. 1941 Strawberry Blonde; The Devil and Miss Jones. 1943 Johnny Come Lately; Margin of Error. 1944 Arsenic and Old Lace.

MC NAMARA, TED
Born: Australia. Died: Feb. 3, 1928, Ventura, Calif.(pneumonia). Screen and vaudeville actor.

Appeared in: 1925 Shore Leave. 1926 What Price Glory. 1927 Chain Lightning; Colleen; The Gay Retreat; The Monkey Talks; Rich but Honest; Upstream. 1928 The Gateway of the Moon; Mother Machree; Why Sailor's Go Wrong.

MC NAMARA, THOMAS J.
Died: May 21, 1953, Brooklyn, N.Y. Screen and vaudeville actor.

MC NAMEE, DONALD
Born: 1897. Died: July 17, 1940, Hollywood, Calif.(skull fracture). Screen and stage actor.

Appeared in: 1928 Fashion Madness. 1929 The Great Garbo.

MC NAUGHTON, GUS (August le Clerq)
Born: 1884, London, England. Died: Dec., 1969, Castor, England. Screen, stage, and vaudeville actor.

Appeared in: 1930 Murder. 1931 Children of Chance. 1932 Lucky Girl; Maid of the Mountains; His Wife's Mother; The Last Coupon; Double Trouble; Radio Parade. 1933 His Night Out; Their Night Out; Leave It to Me; Heads We Go; The Love Nest; The Charming Deceiver. 1934 Luck of the Navy; Spring in the Air; Seeing Is Believing. 1935 The Thirty-Nine Steps; Jubilee; Music Hath Charms. 1936 Storm in a Tea Cup (U.S. 1938); Not So Dusty; Busman's Holiday; Must Get Married; Strange Adventures of Mr. Smith; Southern Roses. 1937 Action for Slander; Keep Your Seats Please. 1938 The Divorce of Lady X; South Riding; St. Martin's Lane; We're Going to Be Rich. 1939 Clouds over Europe; Trouble Brewing. 1940 Sidewalks of London. 1941 Jeannie. 1942 Much Too Shy. 1943 Courageous Mr. Penn. 1946 Here Comes the Sun. 1949 A Place of One's Own.

MC NAUGHTON, HARRY
Born: 1897, England. Died: Feb. 26, 1967, Amityville, N.Y. Screen, stage, and radio actor.

Appeared in: 1921 Wet Gold (short). 1930 the following shorts: All Stuck Up; Sixteen Sweeties; The Fight; Office Steps; Her Hired Husband; Seeing Off Service; Tom Thumbs Down. 1956 The Vagabond King.

MC NEAR, HOWARD
Born: 1905. Died: Jan. 3, 1969, San Fernando Valley, Calif. Screen, radio, and television actor. Played Doc Adams on radio's Gunsmoke.

Appeared in: 1954 Drums across the River. 1956 You Can't Run Away from It; Bundle of Joy. 1957 Public Pigeon No. 1; Affair in Reno. 1958 Bell, Book and Candle; Good Day for a Hanging. 1959 Anatomy of a Murder; The Big Circus. 1961 Bachelor Flat; Blue Hawaii; Voyage to the Bottom of the Sea. 1962 Follow That Dream; The Errand Boy. 1963 Irma La Douce; The Wheeler Dealers. 1964 Kiss Me, Stupid!. 1965 My Blood Runs Cold; Love and Kisses. 1966 The Fortune Cookie.

MC PETERS, TAYLOR
Born: 1900. Died: Apr. 16, 1962, Hollywood, Calif.(heart attack). Screen actor.

MC PHAIL, DOUGLAS
Born: Apr. 16, 1910, Los Angeles, Calif. Died: Dec. 7, 1944, Los Angeles, Calif.(effects of poison). Screen, stage actor, and singer. Divorced from screen actress Betty Jaynes.

Appeared in: 1936 Born to Dance. 1937 Maytime. 1938 Sweethearts; Toy Wife; Test Pilot. 1939 Babes in Arms; Honolulu. 1940 Little Nellie Kelly; Broadway Melody of 1940. 1942 Born to Sing.

MC PHERSON, QUINTON (aka MR. HYMACK)
Born: 1871, England. Died: Jan. 1940, London, England. Screen, stage, and vaudeville actor.

Appeared in: 1936 First and Last; The Amazing Quest; Rembrandt; Storm in a Teacup; The Ghost Goes West; The Tenth Man; Follow the Sun; Beloved Vagabond; Annie Laurie; Land without Music; Captain's Orders; Murder in the Old Barn. 1937 Talk of the Devil; Dangerous Medicine; No Park. 1938 Forbidden Music.

MC QUARY, CHARLES S.
Born: 1908. Died: Feb. 9, 1970, Hollywood, Calif.(stroke). Screen, television actor, stand-in for Buddy Ebsen in television, and double for Smiley Burnett in films.

MC QUOID, ROSE LEE (aka ROSE LEE)
Born: 1887. Died: May 4, 1962, Hollywood, Calif. Screen actress. Entered films approx. 1912.

Appeared in: 1930 Just Imagine.

MC RAE, BRUCE
Born: Jan. 18, 1867, India. Died: May 7, 1927, City Island, N.Y. (heart trouble). Screen and stage actor.

Appeared in: 1916 Hazel Kirke. 1919 A Star Overnight. 1922 The World's a Stage.

MC SHANE, KITTY
Born: 1898. Died: Mar. 24, 1964, London, England. Screen, stage, and vaudeville actress. Appeared in vaudeville as part of "Lucan & McShane." Married to screen actor Arthur Lucan (dec. 1954). For the "Old Mother Riley" series, Lucan played the role of mother and his wife played the daughter.

Appeared in: 1937 Old Mother Riley. 1938 Old Mother Riley in Paris. 1939 Old Mother Riley, M.P. 1944 Old Mother Riley Overseas. 1945 Old Mother Riley Joins Up; Old Mother Riley's Circus. 1946 Old Mother Riley at Home; My Son, the Vampire; Old Mother Riley in Business. 1947 Old Mother Riley, Detective; Old Mother Riley in Society. 1948 Old Mother Riley's Ghosts. 1949 Old Mother Riley's New Venture. 1950 Old Mother Riley, Headmistress. 1951 Old Mother Riley's Jungle Treasure. 1952 Old Mother Riley Meets the Vampire.

MC TAGGART, JAMES
Born: 1911. Died: May 29, 1949, Beverly Hills, Calif.(swimming pool accident). Screen actor.

MC TURK, JOE
Born: 1899. Died: July 19, 1961, Hollywood, Calif.(heart attack). Screen, stage, and television actor.

Appeared in: 1953 Money from Home. 1955 Guys and Dolls. 1956 Man with the Golden Arm. 1961 Pocketful of Miracles.

MC VEY, LUCILLE. See Mrs. Sidney Drew

MC VICKER, JULIUS
Born: 1876. Died: Mar. 11, 1940, Beverly Hills, Calif. Screen and stage actor.

Appeared in: 1932 The Phantom President.

MC WADE, EDWARD
Died: May 1943, Hollywood, Calif. Screen actor.

Appeared in: 1921 Wing Toy. 1922 The Stranger's Banquet. 1923 The Town Scandal. 1925 The Monster. 1932 Big City Blues; The Big Shot; Two Seconds; Six Hours to Live; Lawyer Man. 1933 Murders in the Zoo. 1934 I'll Tell the World; Journal of a Crime; The Notorious Sophie Lang; A Lady Lost. 1935 Murder in the Clouds; Oil for the Lamps of China; Stranded; Frisco Kid; The Girl from Tenth Avenue; Red Salute; Dr. Socrates. 1936 The Calling of Dan Matthews; The Big Noise; The Man I Marry; Reunion. 1937 Let's Get Married; They Won't Forget; The Women Men Marry. 1938 White Banners; Garden of the Moon; Comet over Broadway; The Patient in Room 18. 1939 They Asked for It; Indianapolis Speedway; The Magnificent Fraud. 1940 Our Neighbors the Carters; Hot Steel; The Return of Frank James; Chad Hanna. 1941 The Big Store. 1942 The Hard Way; You Can't Escape Forever; Lady in a Jam. 1943 Crash Dive. 1944 Arsenic and Old Lace.

MC WADE, ROBERT
Born: 1882, Buffalo, N.Y. Died: Jan. 20, 1938, Culver City, Calif. (heart attack). Screen and stage actor.

Appeared in: 1924 Second Youth. 1925 New Brooms. 1928 The Home Towners. 1930 Night Work; Good Intentions; Feet First; The Pay Off; Sins of the Children. 1931 Cimarron; Too Many Cooks; Kept Husbands; Skyline; It's a Wise Child. 1932 Grand Hotel; The First Year; Ladies of the Jury; Madame Racketeer; Back Street; The Match King; Movie Crazy; The Phantom of Crestwood; Once in a Lifetime. 1933 I Loved a Woman; The Prizefighter and the Lady; Journal of a Crime; Heroes for Sale; The Solitaire Man; Fog; The Kennel Murder Case; A Lost Lady; Employee's Entrance; Big City Blues; High Spot; Two Seconds; Hard to Handle; Ladies They Talk About; 42nd Street; Pick Up; The Big Cage. 1934 Countess of Monte Cristo; Let's Be Ritzy; No Ransom; Operator 13; Cross Country Cruise; Hold That Girl; Thirty-Day Princess; Midnight Alibi; The Dragon Murder Case; The Lemon Drop Kid; College Rhythm; The President Vanishes. 1935 The County Chairman; Society Doctor; Here Comes the Band; Straight from the Heart; Diamond Jim; His Night Out; Mary Jane's Pa; The Healer; Cappy Ricks Returns; Frisco Kid. 1936 Next Time We Love; The Big Noise; Anything Goes; Early to Bed; Moonlight Murder; Old Hutch; High Tension; 15 Maiden Lane; Bunker Bean. 1937 Benefits Forgot; We're on the Jury; California Straight Ahead; The Good Old Soak; This Is My Affair; Mountain Justice; On Such a Night; Under Cover of Night. 1938 Gold Is Where You Find It; Of Human Hearts.

MC WATTERS, ARTHUR J.
Born: 1871. Died: July 16, 1963, Freeport, N.Y. Screen, stage, and vaudeville actor. Appeared in vaudeville with his wife, Grace Tyson, as "McWatters and Tyson." Appeared in early George Burns and Gracie Allen Films.

MEADE, BILL
Died: 1941 (fell from horse onto his sword during filming of They Died with Their Boots On). Screen actor.

MEAKIN, CHARLES
Born: 1880. Died: Jan. 17, 1961, Hollywood, Calif. Screen and stage actor.

Appeared in: 1921 Maid of the West. 1922 Penrod. 1926 Lightning Bill; The Marriage Clause; Upstage. 1927 Ladies at Ease.

MEAKIN, RUTH
Born: 1879. Died: Nov. 3, 1939, Los Angeles, Calif. Screen and stage actress.

MEARS, BENJAMIN S.
Born: 1872. Died: Jan. 27, 1952, Cliffside, N.J. Screen, stage, and vaudeville actor.

MEARS, MARION
Born: 1899. Died: Jan. 26, 1970, Hollywood, Calif. Screen and stage actress. Stand-in for Margaret Lindsay, Hilary Brooks and Natalie Schaefer.

MEECH, EDWARD "MONTANA" (Edward Raymond Meech)
Died: Mar. 2, 1952, Findlay, Ohio. Screen, radio, and circus actor. Appeared in silents riding horses and performed riding feats.

MEEHAN, JOHN
Born: May 8, 1890, Lindsay, Ontario, Canada. Died: Nov. 12, 1954, Woodland Hills, Calif. Screen, stage actor, playwright, stage director, screenwriter, and film director.

MEEK, DONALD
Born: July 14, 1880, Glasgow, Scotland. Died: Nov. 18, 1946, Los Angeles, Calif. Screen and stage actor.

Appeared in: 1923 Six Cylinder Love. 1929 The Hole in the Wall. 1930 The Love Kiss. 1931 The Girl Habit; Personal Maid. 1932-33 "S.S. Van Dine" series. 1932 The Babbling Brook(short). 1933 Love, Honor and Oh, Baby!; College Coach. 1934 Hi, Nellie; Bedside; Mrs. Wiggs of the Cabbage Patch; Murder at the Vanities; The Merry Widow; The Last Gentleman; The Defense Rests; The Captain Hates the Sea; Romance in Manhattan. 1935 Biography of a Bachelor Girl; Peter Ibbetson; Happiness C.O.D.; The Whole Town's Talking; The Informer; Only Eight Hours; Village Tale; The Return of Peter Grimm; Old Man Rhythm; The Gilded Lily; Accent on Youth; The Bride Comes Home; Society Doctor; Mark of the Vampire; Baby Face Harrington; Kind Lady; Barbary Coast; She Couldn't Take It; Captain Blood; China Seas; Top Hat. 1936 Everybody's Old Man; And So They Were Married; Pennies from Heaven; One Rainy Afternoon; Three Wise Guys; Old Hutch; Love on the Run; Three Married Men; Two in a Crowd. 1937 Double Wedding; Maid of Salem; Artists and Models; Parnell; Three Legionnaires; Behind the Headlines; The Toast of New York; Make a Wish; Breakfast for Two; You're a Sweetheart. 1938 Double Danger; Having a Wonderful Time; The Adventures of Tom Sawyer; Goodbye Broadway; Little Miss Broadway; Hold That Coed; You Can't Take It with You. 1939 Hollywood Cavalcade; Jesse James; Young Mr. Lincoln; The Housekeeper's Daughter; Blondie Takes a Vacation; Nick Carter—Master Detective; Stagecoach. 1940 Hullabaloo; Oh Johnny, How You Can Love; Dr. Ehrlich's Magic Bullet; The Man from Dakota; Turnabout; Star Dust; Phantom Raiders; The Return of Frank James; Third Finger, Left Hand; Sky Murder; The Ghost Comes Home; My Little Chickadee. 1941 Blonde Inspiration; Come Live with Me; Rise and Shine; Babes on Broadway; A Woman's Face; Wild Man of Borneo; Barnacle Bill; The Feminine Touch. 1942 Tortilla Flat; Maisie Gets Her Man; Seven Sweethearts; The Omaha Trail; Keeper of the Flame. 1943 Air Raid Wardens; They Got Me Covered; Du Barry Was a Lady; Lost Angel; The Honest Thief. 1944 Rationing; Two Girls and a Sailor; Bathing Beauty; Barbary Coast Gent; Maisie Goes to Reno; Thin Man Goes Home. 1945 Colonel Effingham's Raid; State Fair. 1946 Because of Him; Janie Gets Married; Affairs of Geraldine. 1947 The Hal Roach Comedy Carnival; The Fabulous Joe; Magic Town.

MEEKER, ALFRED
Born: 1901. Died: June 6, 1942, Los Angeles, Calif.(heart attack). Screen and stage actor.

MEEKER, GEORGE
Born: Mar. 5, 1904 or 1888?, Brooklyn, N.Y. Died: 1963. Screen and stage actor.

Appeared in: 1928 Four Sons; The Girl Shy Cowboy; Chicken a la King; The Escape; A Thief in the Dark. 1932 Emma; Fireman Save My Child; Fool's Advice; The Famous Ferguson Case; The Misleading Lady; The First Year; Vanity Street; Tess of the Storm Country; The Match King; Back Street; Afraid to Talk; Blessed Event; Strictly Dishonorable. 1933 Sweepings; Pick Up; Song of the Eagle; The Life of Jimmy Dolan; Double Harness; A Chance at Heaven; Night of Terror; Only Yesterday; King for a Night. 1934 Dark Hazard; Hips, Hips, Horray; Hi, Nellie!; I Believed in You; Ever since Eve; Melody in Spring; Little Man, What Now?; Uncertain Lady; Broadway Bill; Paris Interlude; The Dragon Murder Case; Richest Girl in the World; Against the Law; Bachelor of Arts. 1935 The Wedding Night; Murder on a Honeymoon; The Rainmakers; Oil for the Lamps of China; Welcome Home; Remember Last Night; Manhattan Butterfly. 1936 Don't Get Personal; Gentle Julia; The Country Doctor; Tango; In Paris A.W.O.L.; Neighborhood House; Walking on Air; Wedding Present; Career Woman. 1937 Beware of Ladies; History Is Made at Night; On Again, off Again; Escape by Night; The Westland Case. 1938 Tarzan's Revenge; Marie Antoinette; Danger on the Air; Slander House; Meet the Mayor; Long Shot; Four's a Crowd. 1939 Rough Riders' Roundup; The Lady and the Mob; Undercover Doctor; Stunt Pilot; The Roaring Twenties; Everything's on Ice; Swanee River; Gone with the Wind. 1940 A Night at Earl Carroll's; Michael Shayne, Private Detective; Yesterday's Heroes. 1941 High Sierra; The Singing Hill; Mountain Music; Marry the Boss's Daughter; You're in the Army Now. 1942 Larceny, Inc.; Murder in the Big House; Wings for the Eagle; Spy Ship; The Busses Roar; Secret Enemies; You Can't Escape Forever; Casablanca. 1943 The Ox-Bow Incident. 1944 Take It Big; Seven Doors to Death; Dead Man's Eyes; The Port of Forty Thieves; I Accuse My Parents; Song of Nevada; Silent Partner; Up in Arms. 1945 Big Show-Off; Black Market Babies; Blonde Ransom; Come Out Fighting; Crime, Inc.; Docks of New York; A Guy, a Gal and a Pal; Mr. Muggs Rides Again; Northwest Trail. 1946 Angel on My Shoulder; Below the Deadline; Home in Oklahoma; Murder is My Business; The Red Dragon; The People's Choice. 1947 Apache Rose; Smash-Up; The Story of a Woman; Case of the Baby-Sitter; Her Sister's Secret. 1948 The Dude Goes West; The Gay Ranchero; King of the Gamblers; The Denver Kid. 1949 Omoo-Omoo, The Shark God; Sky Liner; The Crime Doctor's Diary; Ranger of Cherokee Strip. 1950 Twilight of the Sierras. 1951 Spoilers of the Plains; Wells Fargo Gunmaster.

MEHRMANN, HELEN ALICE
Died: Sept. 25, 1934, Oakland, Calif. Screen and stage actress.

Appeared in: 1929 The Shannons on Broadway.

MEIGHAM, MARGARET
Died: Sept. 29, 1961, Chatsworth, Calif. Screen actress. Entered films approx. 1930.

MEIGHAN, THOMAS
Born: Apr. 9, 1879, Pittsburgh, Pa. Died: July 8, 1936, Great Neck, N.Y. Screen and stage actor.

Appeared in: 1915 The Secret Sin; Kindling. 1916 Pudd'nhead Wilson; The Sowers; The Trail of the Lonesome Pine. 1917 The Land of Promise; The Mysterious Miss Terry. 1918 M'Liss; Out of a Clear Sky; Heart of the Wilds; Her Moment. 1919 Male and Female; The Miracle Man. 1920 Conrad in Quest of His Youth; Why Change Your Wife?; Civilian Clothes. 1921 The Easy Road; City of Silent Men; The Frontier of the Stars; White and Unmarried; A Prince There Was; The Conquest of Canaan; Cappy Ricks. 1922 The Bachelor Daddy; Our Leading Citizen; Back Home and Broke; If You Believe It, It's So; The Man Who Saw Tomorrow; Manslaughter; Hollywood. 1923 The Ne'er-Do-Well; Homeward Bound; Woman Proof. 1924 Pied Piper Malone; Tongues of Flame; The Confidence Man; The Alaskan. 1925 Irish Luck; The Man Who Found Himself; Old Home Week; Coming Through. 1926 Tin Gods; The New Klondike; The Canadian; Fascinating Youth. 1927 We're All Gamblers; The City Gone Wild; Blind Alleys. 1928 The Racket; The Mating Call. 1929 The Argyle Case. 1931 Young Sinners; Skyline. 1932 Madison Square Gardens; Cheaters at Play. 1934 Peck's Bad Boy.

MEISTER, OTTO L.
Born: 1869. Died: July 10, 1944, Milwaukee, Wis. Screen, stage, and medicine show actor.

Appeared in: 1914 Droppington's Family Tree.

MELACHRINO, GEORGE
Born: 1909. Died: June 18, 1965, London, England. Orchestra leader, screen, and television actor.

MELESH, ALEX (Alexander Melesher)
Born: Oct. 21, 1890, Kiev, Russia. Died: Mar. 5, 1949, Hollywood, Calif. Screen and stage actor.

Appeared in: 1928 His Private Life; The Adventurer. 1929 Charming Sinners. 1932 The Big Broadcast. 1933 Girl without a Room. 1938 Golden Boy; Artists and Models Abroad. 1939 Paris Honeymoon; On Your Toes. 1940 Beyond Tomorrow. 1942 Once upon a Honeymoon. 1943 A Lady Takes a Chance. 1948 The Fuller Brush Man.

MELFORD, GEORGE
Born: Rochester, N.Y. Died: Apr. 25, 1961, Hollywood, Calif. (heart attack). Screen, stage actor, and film director. Married to screen actress Louise Melford (dec. 1942). Entered films as an actor with Kalem.

Appeared in: 1933 The Cowboy Counselor; Officer 13. 1939 Ambush; Rulers of the Sea. 1940 My Little Chickadee; Safari; Brigham Young, Frontiersman. 1941 Robbers of the Range; Flying Cadets. 1942 That Other Woman; Lone Star Ranger. 1943 Dixie Dugan. 1944 The Miracle of Morgan's Creek; Hail the Conquering Hero. 1945 Col. Effingham's Raid; Diamond Horseshoe; A Tree Grows in Brooklyn. 1946 Strange Triangle. 1948 Call Northside 777. 1953 A Blueprint for Murder; City of Bad Men; President's Lady; The Robe. 1954 The Egyptian; There's No Business Like Show Business; Woman's World. 1955 Prince of Players. 1956 The Ten Commandments. 1960 Bluebeard's Ten Honeymoons.

MELFORD, LOUISE
Born: 1880. Died: Nov. 15, 1942, North Hollywood, Calif. Screen and stage actress. Married to screen actor, film director George Melford (dec. 1961).

MELGAREJO, JESUS
Born: 1876, Mexico. Died: Dec. 29, 1941, Mexico City, Mexico. Screen and stage actor.

MELLER, HARRO
Born: 1907. Died: Dec. 26, 1963, New York, N.Y. Screen actor and playwright.

Appeared in: 1945 The House on 92nd Street; Counter-Attack. 1946 A Night in Casablanca. 1947 Jewels of Brandenburg.

MELLER, RAQUEL
Born: 1888, Madrid, Spain. Died: July 26, 1962, Barcelona, Spain. Screen actress and singer. Appeared in U.S. films during the 1920s.

Appeared in: 1928 Carmen; La Veneosa; Violette Imperiale (The Imperial Violet). 1929 The Oppressed. 1935 La Viletera. Other foreign films: The Promised Land; The White Gypsy.

MELLISH, FULLER, JR.
Born: 1895. Died: Feb. 8, 1930, Forest Hills, N.Y.(cerebral hemorrhage). Screen and stage actor. Son of stage actor Fuller Mellish, Sr.(dec. 1936) and stage actress Mrs. Fuller Mellish, Sr.(dec. 1950). Married to screen actress Olive Reeves-Smith (dec. 1972).

Appeared in: 1921 Diane of Star Hollow; The Land of Hope; The Scarab Ring; The Single Track. 1923 Sinner or Saint. 1924 Two Shall Be Born. 1929 Applause. 1930 Sarah and Son. 1934 Crime without Passion.

MELTON, FRANK
Born: Dec. 6, 1907, Pineapple, Ala. Died: Mar. 19, 1951, Hollywood, Calif.(heart attack). Screen actor.

Appeared in: 1933 Cavalcade; State Fair; Mr. Skitch; Ace of Aces. 1934 The White Parade; 365 Nights in Hollywood; Stand up and Cheer; David Harum; Handy Andy; Judge Priest; The World Moves On. 1935 The County Chairman; $10 Raise; The Daring Young Man; Welcome Home. 1936 The Return of Jimmy Valentine; The Glory Trail; They Met in a Taxi. 1937 Outcast; Too Many Wives; The Affairs of Cappy Ricks; Damaged Goods; Wild and Wooly; Trouble at Midnight. 1938 Riders of the Black Hills; Freshman Year; Marriage Forbidden. 1939 Big Town Czar; Cat and the Canary. 1940 Second Chorus. 1941 Pot O' Gold; Tanks a Million. 1942 The Loves of Edgar Allan Poe; To the Shores of Tripoli; Wrecking Crew. 1945 It's a Pleasure. 1946 Do You Love Me?.

MELTON, JAMES
Born: Jan. 2, 1905, Moultrie, Ga. Died: Apr. 21, 1961, New York, N.Y.(pneumonia). Screen, stage, radio, and opera star.

Appeared in: 1934 Song Hit Stories (short). 1935 Stars Over Broadway. 1936 Sing Me a Love Song. 1937 Melody for Two. 1945 Ziegfeld Follies.

MELVILLE, ROSE
Born: Jan. 30, 1873, Terre Haute, Ind. Died: Oct. 8, 1946. Screen, stage, and vaudeville actress. Married to screen actor Frank Minzey (dec. 1949). They appeared in early Biograph and Keystone films and later in shorts produced by Fox, Goldwyn, etc.

Appeared in: 1916 She Came, She Saw, She Conquered; Leap Year Wooing.

MENARD, MICHAEL M.
Born: 1898. Died: Apr. 27, 1949, Los Angeles, Calif. Screen actor.

MENDEL, JULES
Born: 1875. Died: Mar. 17, 1938, Los Angeles, Calif. Screen and stage actor.

MENDELSSOHN, ELEONORA
Born: 1900. Died: Jan. 24, 1951, New York, N.Y.(suicide—pills). Screen and stage actress.

Appeared in: 1950 The Black Hand.

MENDES, JOHN PRINCE
Born: 1919. Died: Sept. 30, 1955, New York, N.Y. Screen, stage, television actor, and magician.

Appeared in: 1943 This Is Your Army (stage and film versions).

MENDOZA, HARRY
Born: 1905. Died: Feb. 15, 1970, Houston, Tex.(heart ailment). Screen actor and magician.

MENHART, ALFRED
Born: 1899, Germany. Died: Nov. 14, 1955, Munich, Germany (following surgery). Screen actor.

Appeared in: The Major and the Steers.

MENJOU, ADOLPHE
Born: Feb. 18, 1890, Pittsburgh, Pa. Died: Oct. 29, 1963, Beverly Hills, Calif.(chronic hepatitis). Screen, stage, and television actor. Divorced from screen actress Kathryn Carver (dec. 1947).

Appeared in: 1916 Blue Envelope. 1917 The Amazons; The Valentine Girl; The Moth. 1921 The Sheik; Courage; The Three Musketeers; Queenie; Through the Back Door; Kiss; The Faith Healer. 1922 Clarence; The Eternal Flame; The Fast Mail; Head over Heels; Is Matrimony a Failure?; Pink Gods; Singed Wings. 1923 A Woman of Paris; Rupert of Hentzau; The World's Applause; The Spanish Dancer; Bella Donna. 1924 Broadway after Dark; Broken Barriers; The Fast Set; The Marriage Circle; For Sale; Forbid-

den Paradise; The Marriage Cheat; Open All Night; Shadows of Paris; Sinners in Silk. 1925 Are Parents People?; The King on Main Street; A Kiss in the Dark; Lost—a Wife; The Swan. 1926 The Grand Duchess and the Waiter; The Sorrows of Satan; A Social Celebrity; The Ace of Cads; Fascinating Youth. 1927 Blonde or Brunette; Service for Ladies; Serenade; A Gentleman of Paris; Evening Clothes. 1928 His Private Life; The Tiger Lady; A Night of Mystery. 1929 Marquis Preferred; Fashions in Love; Bachelor Girl; The Kiss (and 1921 version). 1930 Morocco; New Moon; Mon Gosse de Pere; L'Enigmatique Monsieur Parkes. 1931 Easiest Way; Men Call It Love; The Great Lover; The Front Page; Friends and Lovers; The Marriage Interlude; The Parisian. 1932 Prestige; The Man from Yesterday; Two White Arms; Bachelor's Affair; Forbidden; A Farewell to Arms; The Night Club Lady; Blame the Woman. 1933 Convention City; Morning Glory; The Circus Queen Murder; The Worst Woman in Paris?. 1934 The Trumpet Blows; Little Miss Marker; Journal of a Crime; Easy to Love; The Great Flirtation; The Human Side; The Mighty Barnum. 1935 Broadway Gondolier; Gold Diggers of 1935. 1936 The Milky Way; Wives Never Know; One in a Million; Sing, Baby, Sing!. 1937 One Hundred Men and a Girl; A Star Is Born; Stage Door; Cafe Metropole. 1938 The Goldwyn Follies; Thanks for Everything; Letter of Introduction. 1939 Golden Boy; That's Right, You're Wrong; The Housekeeper's Daughter; King of the Turf. 1940 A Bill of Divorcement; Turnabout. 1941 Road Show; Father Takes a Wife. 1942 Roxie Hart; Syncopation; You Were Never Lovlier. 1943 Sweet Rosie O'Grady; Hi Diddle Diddle. 1944 Step Lively. 1945 Man Alive. 1946 The Bachelor's Daughter; Heartbeat. 1947 I'll Be Yours; Mr. District Attorney; The Hucksters. 1948 State of the Union. 1949 My Dream Is Yours; Dancing in the Dark. 1950 To Please a Lady. 1951 Across the Wide Missouri; The Tall Target. 1952 The Sniper. 1953 Man on a Tightrope. 1955 Timberjack. 1956 Bundle of Joy; Ambassador's Daughter. 1957 The Fuzzy Pink Nightgown; Paths of Glory. 1958 I Married a Woman. 1960 Pollyanna.

MENKEN, HELEN
Born: 1902, New York. Died: Mar. 27, 1966, New York, N.Y. (heart attack). Screen, stage, and radio actress.

Appeared in: 1943 Stage Door Canteen.

MENKEN, MARIE
Born: 1909. Died: Dec. 1970, Brooklyn, N.Y. Screen actress.

MERA, EDITH
Born: France. Died: Feb. 24, 1935, Paris, France.(anthrax). Screen and stage actress. Had appeared in French and U.S. films.

Appeared in: 1931 Le Culte de Beaute; Un Soire de Rafle. 1932 Miche. 1933 Les Trois Mousquetaires (The Three Musketeers). 1935 Criez-Le Sur les Toits (Shout It from the Housetops). 1937 Grandeur et Decadence.

MERCER, BERYL
Born: 1882, Seville, Spain. Died: July 28, 1939, Santa Monica, Calif. Screen and stage actress.

Appeared in: 1922 Broken Chains. 1923 Christian. 1928 We Americans. 1929 Mother's Boy; Three Live Ghosts. 1930 In Gay Madrid; All Quiet on the Western Front; Dumbells in Ermine; Common Clay; The Matrimonial Bed; Outward Bound; Seven Days Leave. 1931 East Lynne; The Public Enemy; Inspiration; Always Goodbye; Merely Mary Ann; The Miracle Woman; The Man in Possession; Are These Our Children?; Sky Spider. 1932 The Devil's Lottery; Forgotten Women; Lovers Courageous; Lena Rivers; Young America; No Greater Love; Unholy Love; Smilin' Through; Six Hours to Live; Midnight Morals. 1933 Cavalcade; Berkeley Square; Her Splendid Folly; Broken Dreams; Blind Adventure; Supernatural. 1934 Change of Heart; The Little Minister; Jane Eyre; Richest Girl in the World. 1935 Age of Indiscretion; My Marriage; Hitch Hike Lady; Magnificent Obsession; Three Live Ghosts (and 1929 version). 1936 Forbidden Heaven. 1937 Call It a Day; Night Must Fall. 1939 Hound of the Baskervilles; The Little Princess; A Woman Is the Judge.

MEREDITH, CHARLES
Born: 1894, Knoxville, Pa. Died: Nov. 28, 1964, Los Angeles, Calif. Screen, stage, and television actor.

Appeared in: 1919 Luck in Pawn. 1920 Simple Souls. 1921 The Beautiful Liar; Beyond; The Cave Girl; The Foolish Matrons; Hail the Woman; That Something. 1922 The Cradle; Woman, Wake up!. 1924 In Hollywood with Potash and Perlmutter. 1947 Daisy Kenyon. 1948 The Boy with the Green Hair; A Foreign Affair; The Miracle of the Bells; For the Love of Mary. 1949 Tokyo Joe; Francis; The Lady Takes a Sailor. 1950 Perfect Strangers; The Sun Sets at Dawn; Counterspy Meets Scotland Yard. 1951 Al Jennings of Oklahoma; Along the Great Divide; Submarine Command. 1952 The Big Trees; Cattle Town. 1953 So This Is Love. 1956 The Lone Ranger; The Birds and the Bees. 1957 Chicago Confidential. 1958 The Buccaneer. 1960 Twelve Hours to Kill. 1962 Be Careful How You Wish (U.S. 1964); The Incredible Mr. Limpet. 1964 The Quick Gun.

MEREDITH, CHEERIO
Born: 1890. Died: Dec. 25, 1964, Woodland Hills, Calif. Screen and television actress.

Appeared in: 1958 The Case against Brooklyn; I Married a Woman. 1959 The Legend of Tom Dooley. 1962 The Wonderful World of the Brothers Grimm; The Three Stooges in Orbit.

MEREDYTH, BESS (Helen MacGlashan)
Born: Buffalo, N.Y. Died: July 6, 1969, Woodland Hills, Calif. Screen actress and screenwriter. Entered films as an extra with Biograph in 1911.

MERIVALE, PHILIP
Born: Nov. 2, 1880, Rehutia, Manickpur, India. Died: Mar. 1946, Los Angeles, Calif.(heart ailment). Screen and stage actor. Married to screen actress Gladys Cooper (dec. 1971). Entered films during silents.

Appeared in: 1933 I Loved You Wednesday. 1935 The Passing of the Third Floor Back. 1936 Give Us This Night. 1941 Midnight Angel; Rage in Heaven; Mr. and Mrs. Smith; Lady for a Night. 1942 Crossroads; This above All; Pacific Blackout. 1943 This Land Is Mine. 1944 Lost Angel; Nothing but Trouble; The Hour before Dawn. 1945 Adventure; Tonight and Every Night. 1946 Sister Kenny; The Stranger.

MERRILL, FRANK
Born: 1894. Died: Feb. 12, 1966, Hollywood, Calif. Screen actor. Fifth actor to play Tarzan.

Appeared in: 1921 The Adventures of Tarzan (serial). 1924 Battling Mason; A Fighting Heart; Reckless Speed. 1925 Dashing Thru; A Gentleman Roughneck; Savages of the Sea; Shackled Lightning; Speed Madness. 1926 Cupid's Knockout; The Fighting Doctor; The Hollywood Reporter; Unknown Dangers. 1928 The Little Wild Girl. 1929 Below the Deadline; Tarzan the Tiger (serial).

MERRILL, LOUIS
Born: 1911. Died: Apr. 7, 1963, Hollywood, Calif. Screen and television actor.

Appeared in: 1939 Tropic Fury. 1940 Kit Carson. 1948 The Lady from Shanghai. 1953 Charge of the Lancers; The Hindu (aka Sabaka—U.S. 1955). 1955 The Crooked Web. 1957 The Giant Claw. 1961 The Devil at 4 O'Clock.

MERTON, COLLETTE (Collette Helene Mazzoletti)
Born: Mar. 7, 1907, New Orleans, La. Died: July 24, 1968, Hollywood, Calif. Screen actress. Appeared in three of the "Collegians" series prior to 1929.

Appeared in: 1929 Clear the Decks; Walking Back; Why Be Good; King of the Campus; The Godless Girl.

MERTON, JOHN (John Merton La Varre)
Born: 1901. Died: Sept. 19, 1959, Los Angeles, Calif.(heart attack). Screen and stage actor.

Appeared in: 1934 Sons of the Desert. 1935 The Eagle's Brood; Bar 20 Rides Again. 1936 Call of the Prairie; Aces and Eights; The Three Mesquiteers. 1937 Drums of Destiny; Range Defenders; Colorado Kid; Federal Bullets. 1938 Female Fugitive; Two Gun Justice; Where the Buffalo Roam; Gang Bullets; Knight of the Plains; Dick Tracy Returns (serial). 1939 Code of the Fearless. 1940 Hi-Yo Silver; Covered Wagon Days; The Trail Blazers; Lone Star Raider; Frontier Crusader; Queen of the Yukon. 1942 Billy the Kid's Smoking Guns; Law and Order. 1943 Frontier Marshal in Prairie Pals; Mysterious Rider. 1944 Girl Rush. 1947 Jack Armstrong (serial); Brick Bradford (serial). 1949 Riders of the Dusk; Thieves Highway; Western Renegades. 1950 Arizona Territory; Bandit Queen; Border Rangers; Fence Riders; West of Wyoming. 1951 Gold Raiders; Man from Sonora.

MESSENGER, BUDDY (Melvin Joe Messenger)
Born: Oct. 26, 1909, San Francisco, Calif. Died: Oct. 25, 1965, Hollywood, Calif. Screen and stage actor.

Appeared in: 1917 Aladdin and His Wonderful Lamp. 1921 The Old Nest. 1922 The Flirt; A Front Page Story; Shadows; When Love Comes. 1923 The Abysmal Brute; Penrod and Sam; Trifling

with Honor. 1924 The Whispered Name; Young Ideas. Buddy Messenger Comedies (shorts) including: All for a Girl; Breaking into the Movies; The Homing Birds. 1928 Undressed. 1929 A Lady of Chance; Hot Stuff. 1930 Cheer up and Smile. 1935 All American Toothache (short). 1936 College Holiday.

MESSITER, ERIC
Born: 1892. Died: Sept. 13, 1960, London, England (heart attack). Screen and stage actor.

Appeared in: 1950 Kind Hearts and Coronets. 1951 The Mudlark; Other British films: The Banbury Nose; A Hundred Years Old.

MESTEL, JACOB
Born: 1884, Poland. Died: Aug. 5, 1958, New York, N.Y. Screen, stage, television actor, stage director, and screenwriter.

Appeared in: 1933 The Wandering Jew. 1939 Mirele Efros. 1949 A Vilna Legend.

METAXA, GEORGES
Born: Sept. 11, 1899, Bucharest, Romania. Died: Dec. 8, 1950, Monroe, La. Screen and stage actor.

Appeared in: 1931 Secrets of a Secretary. 1936 Swing Time. 1940 Submarine Base; The Doctor Takes a Wife. 1942 Paris Calling. 1943 Hi Diddle Diddle. 1944 The Mask of Dimitrios. 1945 Scotland Yard Investigator.

METCALF, EARL
Born: 1889, Newport, Ky. Died: Jan. 1928, Burbank, Calif.(flying accident—fell from plane). Screen and stage actor. Entered films with Vitagraph.

Appeared in: 1915 The Insurrection. 1916 Perils of Our Girl Reporters (serial). 1921 Eden and Return; Mother Eternal; What Woman Will Do. 1922 White Eagle (serial); The New Teacher; While Justice Waits; Back to Yellow Jacket; The Great Night; Ignorance; The Power of a Lie. 1923 The Lone Wagon; Skid Proof; Look Your Best. 1924 The Courageous Coward; Fair Week; The Valley of Hate; The Silent Accuser; Silk Stocking Sal; Surging Seas. 1925 The Man without a Country; Ship of Souls; Kit Carson over the Great Divide. 1926 Atta Boy; Love's Blindness; The Midnight Message; The Midnight Sun; The Mystery Club; Partners Again; Buffalo Bill on the U.P. Trail; The Call of the Klondike; The High Flyer; Remember; Sin Cargo. 1927 King of Kings; Night Life; Daring Deeds; The Devil's Saddle; The Notorious Lady. 1928 The Air Mail Pilot; Eagle of the Night (serial).

METCALFE, JAMES S.
Born: 1901. Died: Apr. 2, 1960, Northridge, Calif.(heart attack). Screen and stage actor.

Appeared in: 1942 The Hard Way; Who Is Hope Schuyler?; A Gentleman at Heart.

METHOT, MAYO
Born: 1904, Portland, Oreg. Died: June 9, 1951, Portland, Oreg. Screen and stage actress. Divorced from screen actor Humphrey Bogart (dec. 1957).

Appeared in: 1930 Taxi Talks(short). 1931 Corsair; Squaring the Triangle (short). 1932 The Night Club Lady; Virtue; Vanity Street; Afraid to Talk. 1933 The Mind Reader; Lilly Turner; Counsellor-at-Law. 1934 Jimmy the Gent; Goodbye Love; Harold Teen; Side Streets; Registered Nurse. 1935 Mills of the Gods; The Case of the Curious Bride; Dr. Socrates. 1936 Mr. Deeds Goes to Town; The Case against Mrs. Ames. 1937 Marked Woman. 1938 Women in Prison; The Sisters; Numbered Woman. 1939 Unexpected Father; A Woman Is the Judge; Should a Girl Marry?. 1940 Brother Rat and a Baby.

METZ, ALBERT
Born: 1886. Died: Aug. 20, 1940, North Hollywood, Calif. Screen and stage actor.

METZ, OTTO
Born: 1891. Died: Feb. 1, 1949, Hollywood, Calif. Screen, vaudeville actor, and stunt flyer.

METZETTI, VICTOR
Born: 1895. Died: Aug. 21, 1949, Los Angeles, Calif.(pneumonia). Screen, circus actor, and stuntman.

Appeared in: 1922 Putting It Over. 1924 Stepping Lively. 1927 Bulldog Pluck. 1950 The Border Outlaws.

MEYER, HYMAN "HY"
Born: 1875, San Francisco, Calif. Died: Oct. 7, 1945, Hollywood, Calif. Screen and vaudeville actor.

Appeared in: 1929 The Saturday Night Kid. 1934 Judge Priest.

MICHAEL, GERTRUDE
Born: June 1, 1911, Talladega, Ala. Died: Dec. 31, 1964, Beverly Hills, Calif. Screen, stage, and television actress. She was heroine of "Sophie Lang" series.

Appeared in: 1932 Wayward; Unashamed. 1933 A Bedtime Story; Night of Terror; Ann Vickers; Sailor Be Good; Cradle Song; I'm No Angel. 1934 She Was a Lady; Murder on the Blackboard; Notorious Sophie Lang; Murder at the Vanities; Menace; George White's Scandals; I Believed in You; Search for Beauty; Hold That Girl; Bolero; Cleopatra; The Witching Hour. 1935 Father Brown, Detective; It Happened in New York; Four Hours to Kill; The Last Outpost; Protegees. 1936 Woman Trap; The Return of Sophie Lang; Make Way for a Lady; Second Wife; 'Til We Meet Again. 1937 Sins of the Fathers; Mr. Dodd Takes the Air; Sophie Lang Goes West; Just Like a Woman. 1939 Hidden Power. 1940 The Farmer's Daughter; The Hidden Menace; I Can't Give You Anything but Love, Baby; Parole Fixer; Slightly Tempted. 1942 Prisoner of Japan. 1943 Behind Prison Walls; Where Are Your Children?; Women in Bondage. 1944 Faces in the Fog. 1945 Three's a Crowd; Club Havana; Allotment Wives. 1948 That Wonderful Urge. 1949 Flamingo Road. 1950 Caged. 1951 Darling, How Could You?. 1952 Bugles in the Afternoon. 1953 No Escape. 1955 Women's Prison. 1961 The Outsider. 1962 Twist All Night.

MICHAELS, SULLY
Born: 1917. Died: Jan. 4, 1966, New York, N. Y. Screen, stage, and television actor.

Appeared in: 1959 The Last Mile.

MICHELENA, BEATRICE (Beatriz Michelena)
Born: 1890. Died: Oct. 10, 1942, San Francisco, Calif. Screen and stage actress. Entered films in 1913. Sister of screen actress Vera Michelena (dec. 1961).

Appeared in: 1914 Salomy Jane. 1915 Mignon.

MICHELENA, VERA
Born: 1884. Died: Aug. 26, 1961, Bayside, N. Y. Screen, stage, and vaudeville actress. Sister of screen actress Beatrice Michelena (dec. 1942).

MIDDLETON, CHARLES B.
Born: Oct. 3, 1879, Elizabethtown, Ky. Died: Apr. 22, 1949, Los Angeles, Calif. Screen, stage, circus, and vaudeville actor. Entered films in 1927. Best remembered as "Ming the Merciless" in the "Flash Gordon" serials. Married to screen actress Leora Spellman (dec. 1945) with whom he appeared in vaudeville as "Middleton & Spellmeyer."

Appeared in: 1928 A Man of Peace (short); The Farmer's Daughter. 1929 Bellamy Trail; The Far Call; Welcome Danger. 1930 Beau Bandit; Way Out West; The Frame (short); Christmas Knight (short); East Is West; More Sinned against Than Usual (short). 1931 An American Tragedy; Beau Hunks (short); Full of Notions; Ships of Hate; Caught Plastered; Miracle Woman; Palmy Days; Alexander Hamilton. 1932 The Sign of the Cross; High Pressure; The Hatchet Man; Manhattan Parade; Strange Love of Molly Louvain; Pack Up Your Troubles; Hell's Highway; Silver Dollar; Rockabye; Breach of Promise; Mystery Ranch; Kongo. 1933 Pickup; Destination Unknown; Tomorrow at Seven; Sunset Pass; Disgraced; This Day and Age; Big Executive; White Woman; Duck Soup. 1934 When Strangers Meet; Lone Cowboy; Last Round Up; Murder at the Vanities; Behold My Wife; Massacre; David Harum; Mrs. Wiggs of the Cabbage Patch. 1935 Special Agent; The Fixer-Uppers; Steamboat 'Round the Bend; County Chairman; Hopalong Cassidy; Square Shooter; In Spite of Danger; Red Morning; The Virginia Judge. 1936 Texas Rangers; Space Soldiers; Sunset of Power; Road Gang; The Trail of the Lonesome Pine; Flash Gordon (serial); Showboat; Empty Saddles; Song of the Saddle; Jail Break; A Son Comes Home; Career Woman. 1937 Two-Gun Law; We're on the Jury; Hollywood Cowboy; Yodelin' Kid from Pine Ridge. 1938 Flash Gordon's Trip to Mars (serial: also titled Mars Attacks the World); Flaming Frontiers (serial); Dick Tracy Returns (serial); Outside the Law; Kentucky. 1939 Captain Fury; Blackmail; Daredevils of the Red Circle (serial); Wyoming Outlaws; Slave Ship; Cowboys from Texas; Way down South; $1,000 a Touchdown; Jesse James; The Flying Deuces; The Oklahoma Kid. 1940 Thou Shalt Not Kill; Charlie Chan's Murder Cruise; Virginia City; Flash Gordon Conquers the Universe (serial); Chad Hanna; Abe Lincoln

in Illinois; The Grapes of Wrath; Shooting High; Santa Fe; Island of Doomed Men. 1941 Western Union; Wild Geese Calling; Belle Starr; Wild Bill Hickok Rides; Jungle Man. 1942 The Mystery of Marie Roget; Men of San Quentin. 1943 The Black Raven; Two Weeks to Live. 1944 The Sign of the Cross (revised version of 1932 film); The Town Went Wild. 1945 Our Vines Have Tender Grapes; Hollywood and Vine; Captain Kidd; How Do You Do. 1946 Spook Busters; Strangler of the Swamp. 1947 The Pretender. 1948 Station West; Jiggs and Maggie in Court. 1949 The Last Bandit; The Black Arrow.

MIDDLETON, JOSEPHINE
Born: 1883. Died: Apr. 8, 1971, England. Screen, stage, and vaudeville actress.

Appeared in: 1947 A Lady Surrenders. 1950 Five Angles on Murder (aka Woman in Question-British 1953). 1951 The Browning Version. 1956 Shadow of Fear (aka Before I Wake).

MIDDLETON, LEORA. See Leora Spellman

MIDGLEY, FLORENCE
Born: 1890. Died: Nov. 16, 1949, Hollywood, Calif. Screen and stage actress. Entered films in 1918.

Appeared in: 1921 The Great Impersonation; Partners of the Tide. 1926 Memory Lane. 1928 Sadie Thompson; Burning Bridges. 1929 The Three Outcasts; Painted Faces.

MIDGLEY, RICHARD A.
Born: 1910. Died: Nov. 30, 1956, New York, N.Y. Screen and stage actor.

MILAM, PAULINE
Born: 1912. Died: May 2, 1965, Hollywood, Calif. Screen, vaudeville actress, and dancer. Was a "Goldwyn Girl."

MILASH, ROBERT E. (aka ROBERT E. MILASCH)
Born: 1885, New York, N.Y. Died: Nov. 14, 1954, Woodland Hills, Calif.(uremic poisoning). Screen and stage actor. Entered films with Edison Co.

Appeared in: 1903 The Great Train Robbery. 1921 Black Beauty. 1922 Confidence; The Prodigal Judge; Catch My Smoke. 1924 Abraham Lincoln; The Right of the Strongest; Captain Blood. 1925 Thank You. 1927 Grinning Guns; Men of Daring; A Hero for a Night. 1928 The Little Shepherd of Kingdom Come; The Upland Rider. 1930 Dangerous Nan McGrew. 1936 Give Us This Night.

MILCREST, HOWARD
Born: 1892. Died: Dec. 1920, Huachuca Mountains, Ariz.(fall from horse). Screen actor. Entered films with Griffith approx. 1910.

MILES, ARTHUR K.
Born: 1899. Died: Nov. 6, 1955, Hollywood, Calif. Screen actor.

Appeared in: 1939 The Gorilla. 1942 The Spoilers. 1944 Gentle Annie. 1945 Paris Underground. 1946 Night in Paradise.

MILES, LOTTA (Florence Court)
Born: 1899. Died: July 25, 1937, Los Angeles, Calif.(heart ailment). Screen and stage actress.

Appeared in: 1935 Waterfront Lady.

MILJAN, JOHN
Born: Nov. 9, 1893, Lead City, S.D. Died: Jan. 24, 1960, Hollywood, Calif. Screen and stage actor.

Appeared in: 1923 Love Letters (film debut). 1924 The Painted Lady; Romance Ranch; The Lone Wolf; On the Stroke of Three; Empty Hearts; The Lone Chance. 1925 The Unnamed Woman; Silent Sanderson; Sackcloth and Scarlet; Morals for Men; The Overland Limited; The Phantom of the Opera; Sealed Lips; Wreckage; The Unchastened Woman. 1926 The Devil's Circus; Flaming Waters; Almost a Lady; Footloose Widows; My Official Wife; The Amateur Gentleman; Brooding Eyes; Devil's Island; Race Wild; Unknown Treasures. 1927 The Yankee Clipper; Old San Francisco; Wolf's Clothing; The Ladybird; What Happened to Father?; A Sailor's Sweetheart; The Desired Woman; Sailor Izzy Murphy; The Silver Slave; The Clown; Stranded; The Final Extra; Framed; Lovers?; Paying the Price; Quarantined Rivals; Rough House Rosie; The Satin Woman; The Slaver. 1928 Lady Be Good; Husbands for Rent; The Beast (short); The Crimson City; The Little Snob; Glorious Betsy; Tenderloin; Land of the Silver Fox; Women They Talk About; The Terror; The Home Towners; His Night Out (short); Devil-May-Care. 1929 Untamed; The Desert Song; Hard-boiled Rose; Hunted; Stark Mad; The Unholy Night; Queen of the

Night Club; Speedway; Voice of the City; The Eternal Woman; Times Square; Fashions in Love; Innocents in Paris; Gossip (short). 1930 Lights and Shadows; Remote Control; Not So Dumb; Free and Easy; Our Blushing Brides; The Sea Bat; The Woman Racket; Showgirl in Hollywood; The Unholy Three. 1931 Inspiration; The Iron Man; The Secret Six; A Gentleman's Fate; Son of India; Rise of Helga; The Green Meadow; War Nurse; Politics; Hell Divers; Susan Lennox, Her Rise and Fall; Possessed; Paid. 1932 Emma; Sky Devils; West of Broadway; Beast of the City; Arsen Lupin; The Wet Parade; Are You Listening?; Justice for Sale; Grand Hotel; The Rich Are Always with Us; Unashamed; Flesh; Night Court; Prosperity; The Kid from Spain. 1933 What! No Beer?; Whistling in the Dark; The Sin of Nora Moran; The Nuisance; King for a Night; Blind Adventure; The Way to Love; The Mad Game. 1934 Young and Beautiful; The Poor Rich; Madame Spy; Whirlpool; The Line-Up; The Belle of the Nineties; Unknown Blonde; Twin Husbands. 1935 Tomorrow's Youth; Mississippi; Charlie Chan in Paris; Under the Pampas Moon; The Ghost Walks; Three Kids and a Queen. 1936 Murder at Glen Athol; Sutter's Gold; The Criminal Within; Private Number; The Gentleman from Louisiana; North of Nome; The Plainsman. 1937 Arizona Mahoney. 1938 Man-Proof; If I Were King; Pardon Our Nerve; Border G-Man; Ride a Crooked Mile. 1939 Juarez; The Oklahoma Kid; Torchy Runs for Mayor; Fast and Furious. 1940 Emergency Squad; Women without Names; Queen of the Mob; New Moon; Young Bill Hickok. 1941 Texas Rangers Ride Again; Forced Landing; The Cowboy and the Blonde; The Deadly Game; Riot Squad; Double Cross. 1942 The Big Street; True to the Army; Scattergood Survives a Murder; Boss of the Big Town; Criminal Investigator. 1943 Bombadier; Submarine Alert; The Fallen Sparrow. 1944 Bride by Mistake; I Accuse My Parents; The Merry Monahans. 1945 It's in the Bag. 1946 The Last Crooked Mile; The Killers; White Tie and Tails; Gallant Man. 1947 Unconquered; Sinbad, the Sailor; Queen of the Amazons; In Self Defense; The Flame; That's My Man; Quest of Willie Hunter. 1948 Perilous Waters. 1949 Adventure in Baltimore; Mrs. Mike; Stampede; Samson and Delilah. 1950 Mule Train. 1951 M. 1952 The Savage; Bonzo Goes to College. 1955 Pirates of Tripoli; Run for Cover. 1956 The Ten Commandments; The Wild Dakotas. 1957 Apache Warrior. 1958 The Lone Ranger and the Lost City of Gold.

MILLAR, LEE
Born: 1888. Died: Dec. 24, 1941, Glendale, Calif.(heart attack). Screen, stage, and radio actor. Voice of Pluto in Walt Disney cartoons. Married to screen actress Verna Felton (dec. 1966).

MILLARD, HARRY W. (Harry Millard Williams)
Born: 1928. Died: Sept. 2, 1969, New York, N.Y.(cancer). Screen, stage, television actor, and film producer.

Appeared in: 1959 The Last Mile.

MILLARDE, HARRY
Died: Prior to 1936. Screen actor and film director. Married to screen actress June Caprice (dec. 1936).

Appeared in: 1915 Don Caesar de Bazan.

MILLER, ALICE MOORE. See Alice Moore

MILLER, ASHLEY
Born: 1867. Died: Nov. 19, 1949, New York, N.Y. Screen, stage actor, and stage director. Appeared in early films.

MILLER, CHARLES B.
Born: 1891. Died: June 5, 1955, Hollywood, Calif.(shot). Screen actor.

Appeared in: 1939 The Night of Nights. 1940 Phantom of Chinatown. 1941 Caught in the Act. 1942 South of Santa Fe; Raiders of the Range; The Phantom Plainsman; Joan of Ozark; They All Kissed the Bride. 1943 Days of Old Cheyenne. 1944 Black Hills Express. 1945 Wilson; House of Frankenstein; Honeymoon Ahead; The Caribbean Mystery. 1946 Rendezvous 24-F; Rustler's Round-Up; Gunman's Code. 1947 I'll Be Yours. 1948 Mexican Hayride.

MILLER, EDWARD G. "GEORGE"
Born: 1883. Died: Dec. 1, 1948, Los Angeles, Calif. Screen actor. Appeared in most of D. W. Griffith's early films.

MILLER, FLOURNOY E.
Born: 1887, Nashville, Tenn. Died: June 6, 1971, Hollywood, Calif.(coronary failure). Negro screen, stage, vaudeville actor, script writer for television, playwright, and stage producer. Partner in vaudeville team of "Miller and Lyles."

Appeared in: 1943 Stormy Weather. 1951 Yes Sir, Mr. Bones.

MILLER, GLENN (Alton Glenn Miller)
Born: Mar. 1, 1904, Clarinda, Iowa. Died: Dec. 15, 1944, Europe (plane crash). Bandleader, composer, and screen actor.

Appeared in: 1942 Orchestra Wives; Sun Valley Serenade.

MILLER, HUGH J.
Born: 1902. Died: May 11, 1956, Los Angeles, Calif. Screen actor. Father of screen actress Barbara Heller.

Appeared in: 1927 Blind Alleys. 1935 The Divine Spark; I Give My Heart. 1937 The Dominant Sex; Victoria the Great; Bulldog Drummond at Bay. 1938 The Rat; The Return of the Scarlet Pimpernel; The Loves of Madame Du Barry.

MILLER, JACK
Born: 1888. Died: Sept. 25, 1928, San Diego, Calif.(intestinal trouble). Screen and stage actor.

Appeared in: 1930 Hell's Angels.

MILLER, JACK "SHORTY"
Born: 1895. Died: Feb. 28, 1941, Burbank, Calif.(heart attack). Screen cowboy actor.

MILLER, JUANITA
Born: 1880. Died: Apr. 1970, Oakland, Calif. Poet and screen actress. Appeared in films during early 1920s. Daughter of poet Joaquin Miller (dec. 1913). "Her second marriage in April, 1921, began with the bride in a corpse-like state in a funeral setting. The groom kissed her and she awoke. There followed a naturalistic ritual involving the sacrifice of a goat and a demonstration of Miss Miller's cooking prowess."

MILLER, LOU (aka LU MILLER)
Born: 1906. Died: May 2, 1941, Hollywood, Calif. Screen actress. Married to screen actor William Ruhl.

Appeared in: 1938 Hunted Men.

MILLER, MARILYN (Marilyn or Mary Ellen Reynolds)
Born: Sept. 1, 1898, Evansville, Ind. Died: Apr. 7, 1936, New York, N.Y.(toxic poisoning). Screen and stage actress. Divorced from screen actor Jack Pickford (dec. 1933).

Appeared in: 1929 Sally. 1930 Sunny. 1931 Her Majesty, Love.

MILLER, MARTIN (Rudolph Muller)
Born: 1899, Czechoslovakia. Died: Aug. 26, 1969, Austria (heart attack). Screen, stage, and television actor.

Appeared in: 1940 Squadron Leader X. 1943 The Adventures of Tartu. 1946 Frenzy. 1949 Her Man Gilbey; Sands of Iwo Jima. 1951 The Huggetts Abroad. 1952 Encore; Where's Charley. 1953 Front Page Story (U.S. 1955). 1954 Cash on Delivery; You Know What Sailors Are. 1956 The Baby and the Battleship; The Gamma People. 1957 An Alligator Named Daisy. 1959 The Beasts of Marseilles (aka The Seven Thunders). 1960 Libel; Exodus; Expresso Bongo; The Private Lives of Adam and Eve; Thirteen Ghosts. 1962 55 Days at Peking; Peeping Tom; The Phantom of the Opera. 1963 The V.I.P.'s. 1964 Children of the Damned; The Pink Panther. 1965 Up Jumped a Swagman.

MILLER, MAX (Thomas Sargent)
Born: 1895, England. Died: May 7, 1963, Brighton, England. Screen, circus, and vaudeville actor. Known as "The Cheeky Chappie."

Appeared in: 1932 The Good Companions. 1933 Friday the 13th; Channel Crossing. 1934 Princess Charming. 1935 They Are Looking Up; Get Off My Foot. 1936 Educated Evans. 1940 Hoots Mon. 1943 Asking for Trouble.

MILLER, MORRIS
Died: Oct. 6, 1957, Phoenixville, Pa. Screen and vaudeville actor.

Appeared in: 1958 The Deep Six; Stakeout on Dope Street.

MILLER, RANGER BILL
Born: 1878. Died: Nov. 12, 1939, Los Angeles, Calif. Screen actor. Adopted son of Buffalo Bill.

Appeared in: 1923 The Web of the Law. 1924 A Pair of Hellions. 1925 Heartbound.

MILLER, THOMAS
Born: 1872. Died: Dec. 6, 1942, Los Angeles, Calif. Screen and stage actor.

Appeared in: 1934 The Old Fashioned Way.

MILLER, WALTER C.
Born: Mar. 9, 1892, Dayton, Ohio. Died: Mar. 30, 1940, Los Angeles, Calif. Screen, stage, and vaudeville actor.

Appeared in: 1912 The Musketeers of Pig Alley; Oil and Water; Two Daughters of Eve; So Near, Yet So Far; A Feud in the Kentucky Hills; Brutality; An Adventure in the Autumn Woods. 1913 Love in an Apartment Hotel; The Perfidy of Mary; His Mother's Son; Death's Marathon; The Wanderer; The Mothering Heart; The Coming of Angelo. 1916 The Marble Heart. 1917 Miss Robinson Crusoe; The Slacker. 1919 A Girl at Bay. 1920 The Stealers. 1921 The Shadow; Luxury. 1922 Beyond the Rainbow; The Bootleggers; 'Til We Meet Again; The Woman Who Believed; Unconquered Woman. 1923 The Tie That Binds; Unseeing Eyes. 1924 Men, Women and Money; Those Who Judge; Playthings of Desire. 1925 Sunken Silver (serial); Play Ball (serial); The Green Archer (serial); The Sky Raider. 1926 House without a Key (serial); The Fighting Marine (serial and feature film); Snowed In (serial); The Unfair Sex. 1927 Hawk of the Hills (serial); Melting Millions (serial). 1928 Police Reporter (serial); The Man without a Face (serial); The Mysterious Airman (serial); The Terrible People (serial); Manhattan Knights. 1929 The Black Book (serial); King of the Kongo (serial) (released in silent and sound versions); Queen of the Northwoods (serial); Hawk of the Hills (feature of 1927 serial). 1930 Lone Defender (serial); On the Border; The Utah Kid; Rogue of the Rio Grande; King of the Wild (serial); Rough Waters. 1931 The Galloping Ghost (serial); Swanee River; Street Scene; Hell's Valley; Sky Raiders; Hurricane Horseman. 1932 Three Wise Girls; Manhattan Parade; The Famous Ferguson Case; Ridin' for Justice; Ghost City; Face on the Barroom Floor; Heart Punch. 1933 Sin of a Sailor; Parachute Jumper; Maisie; Behind Jury Doors; Gordon of Ghost City (serial). 1934 Rocky Rhodes; Fighting Trooper; Gun Justice; Pirate Treasure (serial); The Vanishing Shadow (serial); The Red Rider (serial); Smoking Guns. 1935 Alias Mary Down; Gun Valley; Valley of Wanted Men; Call Her Savage (serial); Rustlers of Red Dog (serial); The Roaring West (serial); Stormy. 1936 Heart of the West; Desert Gold; The Fugitive Sheriff; Ghost Patrol; Without Orders; Night Waitress. 1937 Draegerman Courage; Boss of Lonely Valley; Midnight Court; Slim; Border Cafe; Flight from Glory; Saturday's Heroes; Danger Patrol; Wild West Days (serial). 1938 Wild Horse Rodeo; The Secret of Treasure Island (serial); Blind Alibi; Crime Ring; Lawless Valley; Come on Leathernecks; Down in "Arkansaw"; Smashing the Rackets. 1939 Dick Tracy's 6-Men (serial); Home on the Prairie. 1940 Bullet Code; Grandpa Goes to Town; Three Cheers for the Irish.

MILLICAN, JAMES
Born: 1910, Pallisades, N.Y. Died: Nov. 24, 1955, Los Angeles, Calif. Screen actor.

Appeared in: 1932 The Sign of the Cross. 1933 Mills of the Gods. 1938 Who Killed Gail Preston?. 1942 The Remarkable Andrew; Star Spangled Rhythm. 1943 So Proudly We Hail!. 1944 The Story of Dr. Wassell; The Sign of the Cross (revised version of 1932 film). 1945 Bring on the Girls; Tokyo Rose; The Affairs of Susan; Love Letters. 1946 The Tender Years; The Trouble with Women; Stepchild; Rendezvous with Annie. 1948 Mr. Reckless; Hazard; Let's Live Again; Disaster; Man from Colorado; Return of Wildfire; Last of the Wild Horses; Rogue's Regiment; In This Corner. 1949 Command Decision; The Dalton Gang; Fighting Man of the Plains; The Gal Who Took the West; Grand Canyon; Rimfire. 1950 Beyond the Purple Hills; The Devil's Doorway; Gunfighter; Military Academy with That 10th Ave. Gang; Mister 880; Winchester "73". 1951 Al Jennings of Oklahoma; Calvary Scout; Fourteen Hours; The Great Missouri Raid; I Was a Communist for the FBI; Missing Women; Rawhide; Warpath. 1952 Bugles in the Afternoon; Carson City; Diplomatic Courier; High Noon; Scandal Sheet; Springfield Rifle; The Winning Team. 1953 Cow Country; Gun Belt; Silver Whip; Torpedo Alley; A Lion in the Streets. 1954 Crazylegs; Dawn at Socorro; Jubilee Trail; The Long Wait; The Outcast; Riding Shotgun. 1955 Las Vegas Shakedown; Top Gun; The Vanishing American; Strategic Air Command; The Man from Laramie; Big Tip Off; Chief Crazy Horse; I Died One Thousand Times. 1956 Red Sundown.

MILLMAN, WILLIAM (William L'Estrange Millman)
Born: 1883. Died: July 19, 1937, Hollywood, Calif. Screen and stage actor.

Appeared in: 1935 The Lost City; Motive for Revenge. 1937 Silent Barriers.

MILLS, GUY (Louis Miller)
Born: 1898. Died: Oct. 15, 1962, Chichester, England. Screen and stage actor. Appeared in films mostly doubling for stars in riding sequences.

MILLS, JOSEPH S. (Joseph Stapleton Mills)
Born: 1875. Died: Oct. 19, 1935 (heart attack). Screen and stage actor.

Appeared in: 1924 Abraham Lincoln; Love's Whirlpool. 1934 Men in Black (short).

MILLS, THOMAS R.
Born: 1878. Died: Nov. 29, 1953, Woodland Hills, Calif. Screen, stage, and radio actor.

Appeared in: 1916 The Scarlet Runner (serial). 1924 The Guilty One; The Star Dust Trail; A Man's Mate; The Wolf Man. 1925 The Kiss Barrier; Tides of Passion; The Arizona Romeo. 1926 The Gilded Highway. 1934 Great Expectations. 1935 Les Miserables. 1937 It's Love I'm After. 1938 an MGM short.

MILTERN, JOHN
Born: 1870. Died: Jan. 15, 1937, Los Angeles, Calif.(hit by auto). Screen and stage actor.

Appeared in: 1920 On with the Dance. 1921 Experience; The Kentuckians. 1922 Manslaughter; The Hands of Nara; Kick In; Love's Boomerang; The Man Who Saw Tomorrow; Three Live Ghosts; The Man from Home. 1923 The Ne'er-Do-Well. 1924 Tongues of Flame. 1925 Coming Through. 1926 Fine Manners. 1927 East Side, West Side; The Love of Sunya. 1935 Diamond Jim; The Dark Angel. 1936 Give Us This Night; Everybody's Old Man; Sins of Man; Ring around the Moon; Murder on the Bridle Path; Parole. 1937 The Lost Horizon.

MILTON, GEORGES (Georges Michaud)
Born: 1888, France. Died: Oct. 16, 1970, Nice, France. Screen and stage actor.

Appeared in: 1932 Le Roi des Resquilleurs (King of the Gate Crashers). 1933 Nu Comme un Ver (Naked As a Worm). 1944 The Queen and the Cardinal.

MILTON, HARRY
Born: June 26, 1900, London, England. Died: Mar. 8, 1965, London, England. Screen, stage actor, and assistant director.

Appeared in: 1932 The King's Cup; King of the Ritz. 1933 To Brighton with Gladys.

MILTON, LOUETTE
Born: 1907. Died: Oct. 29, 1930, Wyo. Screen and stage actress.

Appeared in: 1930 Bride of the Regiment.

MINCIOTTI, ESTHER
Born: 1888, Italy. Died: Apr. 15, 1962, New York, N.Y. Screen, stage, and television actress. Married to screen actor Silvio Minciotti (dec. 1961).

Appeared in: 1949 House of Strangers; Shockproof; The Undercover Man. 1951 Strictly Dishonorable. 1955 Marty. 1956 Full of Life. 1957 The Wrong Man.

MINCIOTTI, SILVIO
Born: 1883, Italy. Died: May 2, 1961, Elmhurst, N.Y. Screen and stage actor. Married to screen actress Esther Minciotti (dec. 1962).

Appeared in: 1949 House of Strangers. 1950 Deported. 1951 Strictly Dishonorable; The Great Caruso; Up Front; Fourteen Hours. 1952 Clash by Night. 1953 Francis Covers the Big Town. 1955 Marty; Kiss Me Deadly. 1956 Serenade; Full of Life. 1957 The Wrong Man.

MINER, DANIEL
Born: 1880. Died: June 24, 1938, Hollywood, Calif. Screen and stage actor. Entered films approx. 1914.

MINEVITCH, BORRAH
Born: approx. 1904, Kief, Russia. Died: June 25, 1955, Paris, France. Screen actor, television producer, and musician.

Appeared in: 1934 a Vitaphone short (with his "Harmonica Rascals"). 1936 One in a Million. 1937 Love under Fire. 1938 Rascals. 1942 Always in My Heart. 1952 Jour de Fete.

MINNER, KATHRYN
Born: 1892. Died: May 26, 1969, Van Nuys, Calif.(heart attack). Screen, stage, and television actress.

Appeared in: 1968 The Love Bug; Blackbeard's Ghost.

MINOR, ROY
Born: 1905. Died: Mar. 28, 1935, Los Angeles, Calif.(heart attack). Screen actor and stunt flyer.

Appeared in: 1930 Hell's Angels.

MINTER, W. F.
Born: 1892. Died: July 13, 1937, Los Angeles, Calif. Screen actor. Entered films approx. 1922.

MINZEY, FRANK
Born: 1879. Died: Nov. 12, 1949, Lake George, N.Y. Screen, stage, and vaudeville actor. Appeared in early Biograph and Keystone films. Later in shorts produced by Fox, Goldwyn, etc. Married to screen actress Rose Melville (dec. 1946).

Appeared in: 1916 Leap Year Wooing.

MIRANDA, CARMEN (Maria Da Carmo Miranda da Cunha)
Born: Feb. 9, 1904, Marco Canavezes, Portugal. Died: Aug. 5, 1955, Beverly Hills, Calif.(heart attack). Screen and television actress.

Appeared in: 1934-38 Alo, Alo, Brazil; Estudiantes; Alo, Alo, Carnaval; Banana La Terra. 1940 Down Argentine Way. 1941 That Night in Rio; Weekend in Havana. 1942 Springtime in the Rockies. 1943 The Gang's All Here. 1944 Four Jills in a Jeep; Greenwich Village; Something for the Boys. 1945 Doll Face; Hollywood on Parade (short). 1946 If I'm Lucky; Come Back to Me. 1947 Copacabana. 1948 A Date with Judy. 1950 Nancy Goes to Rio. 1953 Scared Stiff.

MIROSLAVA (Miroslava Stern)
Born: 1930, Czechoslovakia. Died: Mar. 10, 1955, Mexico City, Mexico (suicide—poison). Screen and stage actress.

Appeared in: 1946 Cinco Nostras de Mujer. 1947 Nocturno de Amor; A Volar Joven; Juane Charrasqueado. 1948 Secreto Entre Mujeres; Adventures of Casanova. 1949 La Casa Chica; La Posesion. 1951 The Brave Bulls; Elly y Yo; Carcel de Mujeres; El de Los Siete Vicios; Trotocalles. 1952 Los Tres Perfectas Casadas; The Bullfighter and the Lady; La Bestia Magnifica. 1953 Reportaje. 1954 La Visita Que no Toco el Timbre; Escuella de Vagabundos. 1955 Stranger on Horseback; Ensayo de un Crimen.

MISHIMA, YUKIO
Born: Japan. Died: Nov. 25, 1971, Tokyo, Japan.(hara-kiri). Screen actor, film director, film producer; screenwriter, and novelist. The film Yukoku (1966) was destroyed at widow's request because the movie/novel which he wrote, starred in and directed featured a hero who committed hara-kiri also.

MITCHELL, BRUCE
Born: Nov. 16, 1883, Freeport, Ill. Died: Sept. 26, 1952, Hollywood, Calif.(anemia). Screen actor, film director, and screenwriter. Entered films as a director in 1912.

Appeared in: 1934 Burn 'Em up Barnes. 1935 Four Hours to Kill. 1936 Half Angel. 1937 Paradise Express. 1938 Bar 20 Justice; Pride of the West. 1939 Riders of the Frontier.

MITCHELL, CHARLES
Born: 1884. Died: Dec. 14, 1929, Hollywood, Calif.(suicide). Screen actor.

MITCHELL, GRANT
Born: June 17, 1874, Columbus, Ohio. Died: May 1, 1957, Los Angeles, Calif. Screen and stage actor.

Appeared in: 1923 Radio Mania. 1931 Man to Man; The Star Witness; a DeForest Phonofilm short. 1932 M.A.R.S.; Three on a Match; Big City Blues; The Famous Ferguson Case; Week-End Marriage; No Man of Her Own; 20,000 Years in Sing Sing; A Successful Calamity. 1933 Central Airport; Lily Turner; Heroes for Sale; I Love That Man; Tomorrow at Seven; Dinner at Eight; Stranger's Return; Dancing Lady; Saturday's Millions; King for a Night; Wild Boys of the Road; Convention City; Our Betters. 1934 The Poor Rich; The Show-Off; We're Rich Again; The Gridiron Flash; Twenty Million Sweethearts; The Secret Bride; Shadows of Sing Sing; The Cat's Paw; The Case of the Howling Dog; 365 Nights in Hollywood; One Exciting Adventure. 1935 One More Spring; Traveling Saleslady; Gold Diggers of 1935; Straight from the Heart; Broadway Gondolier; Men without Names; A Midsummer Night's Dream; In Person; Seven Keys to Baldpate; It's in the Air. 1936 Next Time We Love; The Garden Murder Case; Moonlight Murder; Picadilly Jim; The Devil Is a Sissy; Her Master's Voice; My American Wife; The Ex-Mrs. Bradford; Parole!; 1937 The Life of Emile Zola; Hollywood Hotel; Music for Madame;

The Last Gangster; First Lady; Lady Behave. 1938 The Headleys at Home; Women Are Like That; Peck's Bad Boy at the Circus; Reformatory; Youth Takes a Fling; That Certain Age. 1939 6,000 Enemies; On Borrowed Time; Mr. Smith Goes to Washington; Juarez; The Secret of Dr. Kildare; Hell's Kitchen. 1940 It All Came True; The Grapes of Wrath; My Love Came Back; Edison the Man; New Moon; We Who Are Young; Father Is a Prince. 1941 Tobacco Road; The Bride Wore Crutches; Nothing but the Truth; Skylark; One Foot in Heaven; Footsteps in the Dark; The Penalty; The Feminine Touch; The Man Who Came to Dinner; The Great Lie. 1942 Larceny, Inc.; Meet the Stewarts; My Sister Eileen; The Gay Sisters; Cairo; Orchestra Wives. 1943 The Amazing Mrs. Holiday; The Gold Tower; Dixie; All by Myself. 1944 Laura; See Here, Private Hargrove; The Impatient Years; And Now Tomorrow; When the Lights Go on Again; Arsenic and Old Lace; Step Lively. 1945 Crime, Inc.; A Medal for Benny; Bring on the Girls; Colonel Effingham's Raid; Bedside Manner; Guest Wife; Leave Her to Heaven; Conflict. 1946 Cinderella Jones; Easy to Wed. 1947 The Corpse Came C.O.D.; It Happened on Fifth Avenue; Blondie's Anniversary; Blondie's Holiday; Honeymoon. 1948 Who Killed "Doc" Robbin?.

MITCHELL, HELEN (Helen McRuer)
Died: June 25, 1945, Los Angeles, Calif. Screen, stage actress, and playwright. Divorced from producer Oliver Morosco and married to screen actor Robert Sterling Lawson.

Appeared in: 1929 Unmasked.

MITCHELL, HOWARD
Born: 1888. Died: Oct. 9, 1958, Hollywood, Calif. Screen actor and film director.

Appeared in: 1914 The Beloved Adventurer (serial). 1915 The Road of Strife (serial). 1927 A Bowery Cinderella. 1938 Hunted Men; Tom Sawyer, Detective; Prison Farm. 1940 Queen of the Mob. 1941 The Mad Doctor. 1949 Abandoned.

MITCHELL, JAMES IRVING
Born: 1891. Died: Aug. 3, 1969, Hollywood, Calif.(heart attack). Screen, stage, and television actor. Do not confuse with actor Irving Mitchell born in 1920.

MITCHELL, JOHN (Douglas N. Lamy)
Born: 1919. Died: Jan. 19, 1951, New York, N.Y.(suicide-gun). Screen and radio actor. Known in films as John Mitchell and on radio as Douglas Drake.

Appeared in: 1944 Mr. Skeffington. 1945 Pillow to Post. 1952 Navajo.

MITCHELL, JULIEN
Born: Nov. 13, 1888, Glossop, Derbyshire, England. Died: 1954. Screen and stage actor.

Appeared in: 1935 The Last Journey (film debut). 1937 It's in the Air (U.S. 1940). 1938 The Drum. 1940 Vigil in the Night; The Sea Hawk. 1944 Hotel Reserve. 1946 Bedelia. 1948 Bonnie Prince Charlie. 1951 The Magnet; The Galloping Major; Chance of a Lifetime. 1954 Hobson's Choice. Other British films: The Frog; Double Exposure; Goose Steps Out; Rhythm Serenade.

MITCHELL, MARY RUTH
Born: 1906. Died: May 21, 1941, Los Angeles, Calif. Screen actress.

MITCHELL, MILLARD
Born: 1900, Havana, Cuba. Died: Oct. 12, 1953, Santa Monica, Calif.(lung cancer). Screen and stage actor.

Appeared in: 1941 Mr. and Mrs. North (film debut). 1942 The Mayor of 44th Street; Grand Central Murder; Get Hep to Love; Little Tokyo; Big Street. 1943 Slightly Dangerous. 1946 Swell Guy. 1947 Kiss of Death. 1948 A Double Life; A Foreign Affair. 1949 Twelve O'Clock High; Everybody Does It; Thieves' Highway. 1950 The Gunfighter; Mr. 880, Winchester "73"; Convicted. 1951 Strictly Dishonorable; You're in the Navy Now (aka U.S.S. Teakettle). 1952 My Six Convicts; Singin' in the Rain. 1953 The Naked Spur; Here Come the Girls.

MITCHELL, NORMA
Born: Boston, Mass. Died: May 29, 1967, Essex, Conn. Screen, stage actress, and playwright.

Appeared in: 1933 The Woman Accused. 1934 Melody in Spring. 1940 Susan and God.

MITCHELL, RHEA "GINGER"
Born: 1905. Died: Sept. 16, 1957, Los Angeles, Calif.(found strangled). Screen actress.

Appeared in: 1915 On the Night Stage. 1916 The Sequel to the Diamond from the Sky (serial). 1918 Honor's Cross. 1919 The Money Corporal. 1920 The Hawk's Trail.

MITCHELL, THOMAS
Born: 1895, Elizabeth, N.J. Died: Dec. 17, 1962, Beverly Hills, Calif.(cancer). Screen, stage, television actor, stage producer, stage director, playwright, and screenwriter. Won Academy Award in 1939 for Best Supporting Actor in Stagecoach.

Appeared in: 1934 Cloudy with Showers. 1936 Craig's Wife; Theodora Goes Wild. Adventure in Manhattan. 1937 Man of the People; When You're in Love; Lost Horizon; I Promise to Pay; Make Way for Tomorrow; The Hurricane. 1938 Love, Honor and Behave; Trade Winds. 1939 Stagecoach; Only Angels Have Wings; Mr. Smith Goes to Washington; The Hunchback of Notre Dame; Gone with the Wind. 1940 Three Cheers for the Irish; Our Town; The Long Voyage Home; Angels over Broadway; Swiss Family Robinson. 1941 Flight from Destiny; Out of the Fog. 1942 Joan of Paris; Song of the Islands; This above All; Moontide; Tales of Manhattan; The Black Swan. 1943 The Outlaw; Bataan; Flesh and Fantasy; The Immortal Sargent. 1944 The Sullivans; Wilson; Buffalo Bill; The Keys of the Kingdom; Dark Waters. 1945 Within These Walls; Captain Eddie; Adventure. 1946 It's a Wonderful Life; Three Wise Fools; The Dark Mirror. 1947 High Barbaree; The Romance of Rosy Ridge; Silver River. 1949 Alias Nick Beal; The Big Wheel. 1951 Journey into Light. 1953 High Noon. 1953 Tumbleweed. 1954 Destry; Secret of the Incas. 1956 While the City Sleeps. 1958 Handle with Care. 1961 By Love Possessed; Pocketful of Miracles.

MITTELL, LYN DONALDSON
Born: 1892. Died: Mar. 2, 1966, Los Angeles, Calif. Screen and radio actress.

MIX, TOM
Born: Jan. 6, 1880, El Paso, Tex. Died: Oct. 12, 1940, Florence, Ariz.(auto accident). Screen, vaudeville, circus, and rodeo actor. Married to circus aerialist Mabel Ward.

Appeared in: 1910 The Feud; The Ranch Life in the Great Southwest. 1911 Back to the Primitive. 1911-1913 Sagebrush Tom; Mr. Haywood Producer. 1913 Child of the Prairie; The Escape of Tom Dolan. 1914 Chip of the Flying U. 1916 The Drifter. 1917 Twisted Trails; The Hearts of Texas, Ryan; Durand of the Badlands. 1918 Western Blood; Fame and Fortune; Treat 'Em Rough; Ace High; Cupid's Round-Up; The Rainbow Trail; Six-Shooter Andy. 1919 Rough Riding Romance; Fighting for Gold; The Daredevils; The Wilderness Trail; Coming of the Law. 1920 The Untamed. 1921 The Rough Diamond; Hands Off; Prairie Trails; The Queen of Sheba; A Ridin' Romeo; The Road Demon; The Texan; Big Town Round-Up; The Night Horsemen; After Your Own Heart; Trailin!. 1922 Up and Going; Sky High; For Big Stakes; The Fighting Streak; Chasing the Moon; Do and Dare; Just Tony; Tom Mix in Arabia; Arabia; Catch My Smoke. 1923 The Lone Star Ranger; Romance Land; Softboiled; Stepping Fast; Three Jumps Ahead; Mile-a-Minute Romeo. 1924 Oh, You Tony; North of Hudson Bay; A Golden Thought; The Last of the Duanes; Ladies to Board; Teeth; Eyes of the Forest; The Trouble Shooter; The Heart Buster; The Foreman of Bar Z Ranch. 1925 Everlasting Whisper; The Lucky Horseshoe; Law and the Outlaw; The Best Bad Man; Riders of the Purple Sage; The Rainbow Trail; Dick Turpin; The Deadwood Coach; A Child of the Prairie. 1926 The Great K and a Train Robbery; The Yankee Senor; No Man's Gold; Hardboiled; The Canyon of Light; My Own Pal; Tony Runs Wild. 1927 Tumbling River; The Circus Ace; The Last Trail; Silver Valley; Outlaws of Red River; The Broncho Twister. 1928 Painted Post; King Cowboy; Hello Cheyenne; A Horseman of the Plains; Arizona Wildcat; Son of the Golden West; Daredevil's Reward. 1929 Drifter; Outlawed. 1930 Under a Texas Moon. 1931 The Dude Ranch; Six Cylinder Love; The Galloping Ghost (serial). 1932 The Fourth Horseman; Destry Rides Again; My Pal, the King; Texas Bad Man; Rider of Death Valley. 1933 Flaming Guns; Hidden Gold; Terror Trail; Rustler's Roundup. 1935 The Miracle Rider. 1943 Daredevils of the West (serial).

MIZOGHUCHI, KENJI
Born: 1898, Japan. Died: 1956. Screen actor and film director.

Appeared in: 1925 A Paper Doll's Whisper of Spring. 1932 The Gorge between Love and Hate. 1939 The Story of the Last Chrysanthemums. 1940 Woman of Osaka. 1942 The Forty-Nine Ronin. 1952 The Live of O'Haru.

M'KIN, ROBERT. See Robert McKim

MODIE, LOUELLA. See Louella Modie Maxam

MOFFAT, MARGARET
Born: 1892, England. Died: Feb. 19, 1942, Los Angeles, Calif. (pneumonia). Screen actress.

Appeared in: 1934 Just Smith. 1937 Farewell Again. 1938 Troopship. 1939 U-Boat 29. 1940 Song of the Road. 1941 Ringside Maisie. 1942 My Gal Sal.

MOFFATT, GRAHAM
Born: 1919, London, England. Died: July 2, 1965, Bath, England. Screen and television actor.

Appeared in: 1934 A Cup of Kindness. 1936 Where There's a Will; To the Victor (U.S. 1938); Oh! Mr. Porter; Windbag the Sailor; Convict 99; Old Bones of the River (U.S. 1939); Ask a Policeman (U.S. 1939); Where's That Fire. 1937 Gangway. 1938 Dr. Syn. 1941 I Thank you. 1945 I Know Where I'm Going (U.S. 1947). 1950 The Second Mate. 1959 Inn for Trouble. 1963 Eighty Thousand Suspects.

MOHAN, EARL
Died: Oct. 15, 1928, Los Angeles, Calif. Screen actor.

Appeared in: 1927 Love Makes 'Em Wild.

MOHR, GERALD
Born: June 11, 1914, New York, N.Y. Died: Nov. 10, 1968, Stockholm, Sweden. Screen, stage, radio, and television actor. He was on the "Lone Wolf" series, both radio and screen, and was Philip Marlowe, radio private eye.

Appeared in: 1941 We Go Fast; Jungle Girl (serial); The Monster and the Girl. 1942 The Lady Has Plans. 1943 Murder in Times Square; King of the Cowboys; Lady of Burlesque; One Dangerous Night; The Desert Song. 1946 The Notorious Lone Wolf; Gilda; A Guy Could Change; The Catman of Paris; Passkey to Danger; Invisible Informer; The Truth about Murder; Dangerous Business; The Magnificent Rogue. 1947 Lone Wolf in Mexico; Heaven Only Knows; The Lone Wolf in London. 1948 Two Guys from Texas. 1949 The Blonde Bandit. 1950 Undercover Girl; Hunt the Man Down. 1951 Sirocco; Ten Tall Men; Detective Story. 1952 The Sniper; The Ring; Son of Ali Baba; The Duel at Silver Creek; Invasion U.S.A. 1953 Raiders of the Seven Seas; Money from Home; The Eddie Cantor Story. 1954 Dragonfly Squadron. 1957 The Buckskin Lady. 1958 Terror in the Haunted House. 1959 Guns, Girls and Gangsters; A Date with Death. 1960 This Rebel Breed; The Angry Red Planet. 1968 Funny Girl.

MOISSI, ALEXANDER
Born: 1880, Trieste, Italy. Died: Apr. 1935, Vienna, Austria (pneumonia). Screen and stage actor.

Appeared in: 1929 The Royal Box. 1936 Lorenzino de Medici.

MOJA, HELLA
Born: 1898, Germany. Died: Feb., 1937, Berlin, Germany. Screen actress and screenwriter. Entered films approx. 1916.

Appeared in: 1929 U-Boat 9.

MOLONEY, JOHN
Born: 1911. Died: July 14, 1969, Los Angeles, Calif. Screen actor, emcee, and singer.

Appeared in: 1962 Gypsy.

MONCRIES, EDWARD (aka EDWARD MONCRIEF)
Born: 1859. Died: Mar. 22, 1938, Hollywood, Calif.(heart attack). Screen, stage actor, and stage manager. Appeared in many Charles Chaplin films.

Appeared in: 1921 Western Hearts. 1923 The Girl I Loved.

MONG, WILLIAM V.
Born: 1875, Clambersbury, Pa. Died: Dec. 10, 1940, Studio City, Calif. Screen, stage, and vaudeville actor. Entered films in 1910.

Appeared in: 1910 The Connecticut Yankee. 1916 The Severed Hand. 1921 Connecticut Yankee at King Arthur's Court; Sowing the Wind; Shame; The Ten Dollar Raise; The Winding Trail; Ladies Must Live; Pilgrims of the Night; Playthings of Destiny. 1922 Fool There Was; Shattered Idols; The Woman He Loved; Monte Cristo. 1923 All the Brothers Were Valiant; Drifting; In the Palace of the King; Lost and Found; Wandering Daughters; Penrod and Sam. 1924 Thy Name Is Woman; Flapper Wives; Why

Men Leave Home; Welcome Stranger; What Shall I Do?. 1925 Alias Mary Flynn; Excuse Me; Fine Clothes; Under the Rouge; The Unwritten Law; Barriers Burned Away; Off the Highway; Oh, Doctor!; The People vs. Nancy Preston; The Shadow on the Wall; Speed. 1926 The Old Soak; What Price Glory; Brooding Eyes; Fifth Avenue; The Shadow of the Law; The Silent Lover; Steel Preferred; The Strong Man. 1927 Alias the Lone Wolf; The Clown; The Magic Garden; Taxi! Taxi!; The Price of Honor; Too Many Crooks. 1928 The Broken Mask; The Haunted House; Code of the Air; The Devil's Trademark; No Babies Wanted; Ransom; Telling the World; White Flame. 1929 Should a Girl Marry?; Dark Skies; The House of Horror; Seven Footprints to Satan; Noah's Ark. 1930 The Girl Said No; In Gay Madrid; Murder on the Roof; Double Cross Roads; The Big Trail. 1931 The Flood; Gun Smoke; Bad Company; A Dangerous Affair. 1932 Cross Examination; By Whose Hands?; Fighting Fool; Widow in Scarlet; Dynamite Denny; The Sign of the Cross; No More Orchids. 1933 Women Won't Tell; Strange Adventure; The Vampire Bat; The 11th Commandment; Fighting for Justice; Silent Men; Her Forgotten Past; The Mayor of Hell; The Narrow Corner; I Loved a Woman. 1934 Dark Hazard; Massacre; Treasure Island. 1935 The County Chairman; The Hoosier Schoolmaster; The Last Days of Pompeii; Whispering Smith Speaks. 1936 Dancing Pirate; The Last of the Mohicans; The Dark Hour. 1937 Stand-In. 1938 Painted Desert. 1944 The Sign of the Cross (revised version of 1932 film).

MONROE, MARILYN (Norma Jeane Baker)
Born: June 1, 1926, Los Angeles, Calif. Died: Aug. 5, 1962, Brentwood, Calif. (suicide?). Screen actress. Divorced from professional baseball player Joe DiMaggio and playwright Arthur Miller.

Appeared in: 1948 Dangerous Years (film debut). 1949 Love Happy; Ladies of the Chorus. 1950 A Ticket to Tomahawk; All about Eve; Asphalt Jungle; Right Cross; The Fire Ball. 1951 Let's Make It Legal; Love Nest; As Young as You Feel; Hometown Story. 1952 Don't Bother to Knock; We're Not Married; Clash by Night; Monkey Business; O. Henry's Full House. 1953 Gentlemen Prefer Blondes; How to Marry a Millionaire; Niagara. 1954 River of No Return; There's No Business Like Show Business. 1955 The Seven Year Itch. 1956 Bus Stop. 1957 The Prince and the Showgirl. 1959 Some Like It Hot. 1960 Let's Make Love. 1961 The Misfits. 1963 Marilyn (film clips documentary).

MONTAGUE, EDNA WOODRUFF. See Edna Woodruff

MONTAGUE, RITA
Born: 1884. Died: May 5, 1962, Hollywood, Calif. Screen, stage actress, and playwright. Married to stage actor Frederick Montague (dec.).

MONTANA, BULL (Lugia Montagna)
Born: May 16, 1887, Vogliera, Italy. Died: Jan. 24, 1950, Los Angeles, Calif. (coronary thrombosis). Screen actor, wrestler, and fighter. Entered films in 1918.

Appeared in: 1919 Victory; Brass Buttons; The Unpardonable Sin. 1920 Treasure Island; Go and Get It. 1921 The Four Horsemen of the Apocalypse; Crazy to Marry; The Foolish Age; One Wild Week. 1922 Gay and Devilish; The Three Must-Get-There's; The Timber Queen (serial). 1923 Breaking into Society; Hollywood; Held to Answer; Jealous Husbands. 1924 The Fire Patrol; Painted People. 1925 Bashful Buccaneer; Dick Turpin; The Gold Hunters; Manhattan Madness; Secrets of the Night; The Lost World. 1926 Vanishing Millions (serial); The Skyrocket; The Son of the Sheik; Stop, Look and Listen. 1928 How to Handle Women; Good Morning Judge. 1929 The Show of Shows; Tiger Rose. 1935 an Educational short. 1937 Big City. 1943 Good Morning Judge.

MONTEIRO, PILAR
Born: 1886, Portugal. Died: Dec. 1962, Lisbon, Portugal. Screen actress. Appeared in films during 1920s and 1930s.

MONTEZ, MARIA (Maria de Santo Silas)
Born: June 6, 1918, Barahona, Dominican Republic. Died: Sept. 7, 1951, France (heart failure or drowning?). Screen and stage actress. Married to screen actor Jean Pierre Aumont.

Appeared in: 1941 Boss of Bullion City; The Invisible Woman; That Night in Rio; Raiders of the Desert; Moonlight in Hawaii; South of Tahiti; Lucky Devils. 1942 Bombay Clipper; The Mystery of Marie Roget; Arabian Nights. 1943 White Savage. 1944 Ali Baba and the Forty Thieves; Follow the Boys; Cobra Woman; Gypsy Wildcat; Bowery to Broadway. 1945 Sudan. 1946 Tangier. 1947 Pirates of Monterey; The Exile; Song of Scheherazade. 1948 The Siren of Atlantis. 1951 Wicked City; The Pirates Revenge. 1952 The Thief of Venice. Italian film: Sensuality.

MONTGOMERY, DOUGLAS (Robert Douglass Montgomery, aka KENT DOUGLAS)
Born: Oct. 29, 1908, Los Angeles, Calif. Died: July 23, 1966, Ridgefield, Conn. Screen, stage, and television actor. Appeared in films as Douglass Montgomery and Kent Douglas.

Appeared in: 1931 Waterloo Bridge; Five and Ten; Paid; Daybreak. 1932 A House Divided. 1933 Little Women. 1934 Music in the Air; Little Man, What Now?; Eight Girls in a Boat. 1935 The Mystery of Edwin Drood; Lady Tubbs; Harmony Lane; Tropical Trouble. 1936 Everything Is Thunder. 1937 Life Begins with Love; Counsel for Crime. 1939 The Cat and the Canary. 1945 Johnny in the Clouds; The Way to the Stars. 1947 Woman to Woman. 1948 Forbidden. 1952 When in Rome.

MONTGOMERY, JACK
Born: 1892. Died: Jan. 21, 1962, Hollywood, Calif. (cancer). Screen actor and stuntman. Entered films during early silents. Father of "Baby Peggy," silent film moppet.

Appeared in: 1955 Run for Cover.

MONTIEL, NELLY
Born: Mexico. Died: Sept. 14, 1951, near Acapulco, Mexico (auto accident). Screen actress.

MONTROSE, BELLE
Born: 1886. Died: Oct. 25, 1964, Hollywood, Calif. (heart attack). Screen, vaudeville, and television actress. Mother of screen actor Steve Allen. Appeared in vaudeville as part of team "Allen & Montrose."

Appeared in: 1961 The Absent-Minded Professor.

MONTT, CHRISTINA
Born: 1897, Chili. Died: Apr. 22, 1969, Hollywood, Calif. (coronary failure). Screen actress.

Appeared in: 1924 The Sea Hawk. 1927 Rose of the Golden West. 1930 Alma de Gaucho.

MOODY, RALPH
Born: Nov. 5, 1887, St. Louis, Mo. Died: Sept. 16, 1971, Burbank, Calif. (heart attack). Screen, stage, radio, television, and circus actor. Entered films in 1944.

Appeared in: 1948 Man-Eater of Kumaon. 1949 Square Dance Jubilee. 1951 Red Mountain. 1952 Affair in Trinidad; Road to Bali. 1953 Seminole; Column South; Tumbleweed. 1955 Many Rivers to Cross; Strange Lady in Town; Rage at Dawn; The Far Horizons; I Died a Thousand Times. 1956 The Last Hunt; The Steel Jungle; Toward the Unknown; Reprisal!. 1957 The Monster That Challenged the World; Pawnee. 1958 Going Steady; The Lone Ranger and the Lost City of Gold. 1959 The Legend of Tom Dooley; The Big Fisherman. 1960 The Story of Ruth. 1961 Homicidal; The Outsider.

MOOERS, DE SACIA
Born: 1888, Allesandro, Mojave Desert, Calif. Died: Jan. 11, 1960, Hollywood, Calif. Screen and stage actress.

Appeared in: 1904 The Great Train Robbery. 1922 The Blonde Vampire; The Challenge. 1923 Potash and Perlmutter. 1924 The Average Woman; It Is the Law; Restless Wives. 1925 Any Woman. 1926 Forbidden Waters. 1927 Tongues of Scandal; Lonesome Ladies; By Whose Hand?; Back to Liberty. 1928 Broadway Daddies; Confessions of a Wife. 1929 Shanghai Rose; Just Off Broadway. 1930 The Arizona Kid.

MOON, GEORGE
Born: 1886, Australia. Died: June 4, 1961, London, England. Screen and stage actor.

Appeared in: 1957 Davy; An Alligator Named Daisy; Carry on Admiral (aka The Ship Was Loaded—U.S. 1959).

MOORE, ALICE (Alice Moore Miller)
Born: 1916. Died: May 7, 1960, Washington, D.C. Screen actress. Daughter of screen actor Tom Moore (dec. 1955) and screen actress Alice Joyce (dec. 1955). Niece of screen actors Matt (dec. 1960) and Owen Moore (dec. 1939).

Appeared in: 1934 Babes in Toyland. 1950 Revenge Is Sweet (reissue of 1934 film Babes in Toyland).

MOORE, DEL
Born: 1917. Died: Aug. 30, 1970, Encino, Calif. (heart attack). Screen, stage, and television actor.

Appeared in: 1961 The Last Time I Saw Archie. 1962 The Errand

Boy; Stagecoach to Dancer's Rock. 1963 The Nutty Professor. 1964 The Patsy; The Disorderly Orderly. 1967 The Big Mouth. 1968 The Catalina Caper.

MOORE, EULABELLE
Born: 1903. Died: Nov. 30, 1964, New York, N.Y. Screen, stage, and television actress.

Appeared in: 1964 The Horror of Party Beach.

MOORE, EVA
Born: Feb. 9, 1870, Brighton, Sussex, England. Died: Apr. 27, 1955. Screen and stage actress.

Appeared in: 1925 Chu Chin Chow. 1931 Brown Sugar. 1932 The Old Dark House; The Flesh Is Weak. 1933 I Was a Spy. 1934 Just Smith; Jew Suess; Cup of Kindness. 1935 Vintage Wine. 1939 Old Iron. 1940 A Star Comes Home. 1941 Wasn't It Odd?. 1942 It Happened in September. 1945 Scotland Yard Investigates. 1946 The Bandit of Sherwood Forest; Of Human Bondage. Other British films: Blind Justice; Annie Leave the Room; Little Stranger.

MOORE, FLORENCE
Born: 1886, Philadelphia, Pa. Died: Mar. 9, 1935, Darby, Pa. (operation complications). Screen and stage actress. Sister of screen actor Frank F. Moore (dec. 1924).

Appeared in: 1924 Broadway after Dark. 1928 Broadway Comedienne (short); Soldier Composer (short).

MOORE, FRANK F.
Died: May 28, 1924, Los Angeles, Calif. Screen, stage, and vaudeville actor. Brother of screen actress Florence Moore (dec. 1935)

MOORE, GRACE
Born: Dec. 5, 1901, Jellico, Tenn. Died: Jan. 26, 1947, Copenhagen, Denmark (plane crash). Screen, stage, and opera actress.

Appeared in: 1930 A Lady's Morals; New Moon; Soul Kiss. 1934 One Night of Love. 1935 Love Me Forever. 1936 The King Steps Out. 1937 When You're in Love; I'll Take Romance. 1940 Louise.

MOORE, HARRY R. "TIM"
Born: 1888, Rock Island, Ill. Died: Dec. 13, 1958, Los Angeles, Calif. Screen, radio, and television actor. Was Kingfish of Amos 'n Andy radio series.

MOORE, IDA
Born: 1883. Died: Sept. 1964. Screen actress.

Appeared in: 1925 The Merry Widow; Thank You. 1944 Riders of the Santa Fe; The Ghost Walks Alone; She's a Soldier Too. 1945 Rough, Tough and Ready; Her Lucky Night; Girls of the Big House. 1946 To Each His Own; Cross My Heart. 1947 The Egg and I; Easy Come, Easy Go; It's a Joke, Son. 1948 Good Sam; Johnny Belinda; Money Madness; Rusty Leads the Way. 1949 Manhattan Angel; Ma and Pa Kettle; Leave It to Henry; Hold That Baby; Paid in Full. 1950 Harvey; Backfire; Mr. Music; Mother Didn't Tell Me. 1951 The Lemon Drop Kid; Comin' 'Round the Mountain; Leave It to the Marines; Honeychile. 1952 Scandal Sheet; Rainbow 'Round My Shoulders. 1953 Scandal at Scourie. 1954 The Country Girl. 1955 Ma and Pa Kettle at Waikiki. 1957 The Desk Set. 1958 Rock-a-Bye Baby.

MOORE, MATT
Born: Jan. 1888, County Meath, Ireland. Died: Jan. 21, 1960, Hollywood, Calif. Screen actor. See Alice Moore for family information.

Appeared in: 1913 Traffic in Souls. 1914 A Singular Cynic. 1917 Pride of the Clan. 1919 The Unpardonable Sin; Sahara; A Regular Girl. 1920 Everybody's Sweetheart; Don't Ever Marry; Hairpins. 1921 A Man's Home; The Miracle of Manhattan; The Passionate Pilgrim; Straight Is the Way. 1922 Back Pay; Minnie; Sisters; The Storm; The Jilt. 1923 White Tiger; Strangers of the Night; Drifting. 1924 Fools in the Dark; Another Man's Wife; The Breaking Point; A Lost Lady; The Narrow Street; A Self-Made Failure; No More Women; The Wise Virgin. 1925 How Baxter Butted In; Grounds for Divorce; His Majesty, Bunker Bean; Three Weeks in Paris; The Unholy Three; Where the Worst Begins; The Way of a Girl. 1926 His Jazz Bride; The First Year; The Caveman; Three Weeks in Paris; Early to Wed; The Mystery Club; Summer Bachelors; Diplomacy. 1927 Married Alive; Tillie the Toiler. 1928 Dry Martini; Beware of Blondes; Phyllis of the Follies. 1929 Coquette; Side Street. 1930 The Squealer; Call of the West. 1931 Penrod and Sam; The Front Page; Married in Haste; Consolation Marriage. 1932 Rain; Cock of the Air. 1933 The Deluge. 1934 All Men Are Enemies; Such Women Are Dangerous. 1936 Anything Goes; Absolute Quiet. 1939 Bad Boy; Range War.

1941 My Life with Caroline. 1942 Mokey. 1943 Happy Land. 1944 Wilson. 1945 Spellbound. 1946 The Hoodlum Saint. 1948 Good Sam. 1949 That Forsyte Woman. 1950 The Big Hangover. 1952 Plymouth Adventure; Invitation. 1954 Seven Brides for Seven Brothers. 1956 The Birds and the Bees; Pardners. 1957 An Affair to Remember. 1958 I Bury the Living.

MOORE, MONETTE
Born: 1912. Died: Oct. 21, 1962, Anaheim, Calif.(heart attack). Screen and stage actress.

Appeared in: 1951 Yes Sir, Mr. Bones.

MOORE, OWEN
Born: Dec. 12, 1886, County Meath, Ireland. Died: June 9, 1939, Beverly Hills, Calif. Screen, stage actor, and film producer. Signed with Biograph in 1908. Divorced from screen actress Mary Pickford. Married to screen actress Kathryn Perry. See Alice Moore for family information.

Appeared in: 1908 In a Lonely Villa; In Old Kentucky; The Honor of Thieves; The Salvation Army Lass. 1909 The Cricket on the Hearth; The Winning Coat; A Baby's Shoe; The Violin Maker of Cremona; The Mended Lute; Pippa Passes; 1776, or the Hessian Renegades; Leather Stocking; A Change of Heart; His Lost Love; The Expiation; The Restoration; The Light That Came; The Open Gate; The Dancing Girl of Butte; Her Terrible Ordeal; The Last Deal; The Iconoclast. 1911 Flo's Dicipline; The Courting of Mary. 1912 Swift Waters. 1913 Caprice. 1914 Battle of the Sexes. 1915 Mistress Nell; Pretty Mrs. Smith; Nearly a Lady; The Little Teacher (reissued as A Small Town Bully). 1916 A Coney Island Princess; Betty of Graystone; Little Meera's Romance; Under Cover. 1917 The Little Boy Scout; The Silent Partner; A Girl Like That. 1919 Crimson Gardenia. 1920 Piccadilly Jim; Poor Simp. 1921 A Divorce of Convenience; The Chicken in the Case. 1922 Oh, Mabel Behave; Reported Missing; Love Is an Awful Thing. 1923 Hollywood; Modern Matrimony; Her Temporary Husband; The Silent Partner. 1924 Thundergate; Torment; East of Broadway. 1925 The Parasite; Go Straight; Married?; Camille of the Barbary Coast; Code of the West. 1926 False Pride; The Skyrocket; The Black Bird; Money Talks; The Road to Mandalay. 1927 The Red Mill; The Taxi Dancer; Women Love Diamonds; Becky; Tea for Three. 1928 The Actress; Husbands for Rent. 1929 High Voltage; Stolen Love; Side Street. 1930 Outside the Law; What a Widow!; Extravagance. 1931 Hush Money. 1932 Cannonball Express; As You Desire Me. 1933 She Done Him Wrong; Man of Sentiment. 1937 A Star Is Born.

MOORE, RUTH HART
Died: May 2, 1952, New York, N.Y. Screen, stage, and vaudeville actress.

Appeared in: 1913 Judith of Bethulia. 1928 The Companionate Marriage.

MOORE, SCOTT
Born: 1889. Died: Dec. 18, 1967, Miami Beach, Fla. Screen actor.

Appeared in: 1931 The Struggle.

MOORE, TOM
Born: 1885, County Weath, Ireland. Died: Feb. 12, 1955, Santa Monica, Calif.(cancer). Screen, stage, vaudeville, and television actor. Entered films with the Kalem Company. Married to actress Eleanor Merry. Divorced from film actresses Alice Joyce (dec. 1955) and Renee Adoree (dec. 1933). See Alice Moore for family information.

Appeared in: 1913 Nine of the Theatre. 1914 The Brand; Vampire's Trail; The Mystery of the Sleeping Death. 1916 Who's Guilty. 1917 The Cinderella Man; The Primrose Ring. 1918 Thirty a Week; The Kingdom of Youth. 1919 Lord and Lady Algy; Toby's Bow; City of Comrades; Heartease; Dub; A Man and His Money; One of the Finest. 1920 Great Accident; Officer 666; Stop Thief. 1921 Dangerous Money; Made in Heaven; Hold Your Horses; Beating the Game; From the Ground Up. 1922 Over the Border; Mr. Barnes of New York; The Cowboy and the Lady; Pawned. 1923 Rouged Lips; Big Brother; Marriage Morals; Harbor Lights; Mary of the Movies. 1924 One Night in Rome; Manhandled; The Isle of Vanishing Men; Dangerous Money. 1925 Adventure; The Trouble with Wives; On Thin Ice; Pretty Ladies; Under the Rough. 1926 Kiss for Cinderella; The Clinging Vine; Good and Naughty; Syncopating Sue; The Song and Dance Man. 1927 The Love Thrill; The Wise Wife; Cabaret; The Siren. 1928 Anybody Here Seen Kelly?. 1929 The Yellowback; His Last Haul; Side Street. 1930 The Costello Case; The Woman Racket. 1931 The Last Parade. 1932 Cannonball Express; Vanishing Men.

1933 Men Are Such Fools; Neighbors' Wives; Mr. Broadway. 1934 Bombay Mail. 1936 Trouble for Two; Reunion. 1946 Behind Green Lights. 1947 Moss Rose; Forever Amber. 1948 Scudda Hoo! Scudda Hay!. 1949 The Fighting O'Flynn. 1950 The Redhead and the Cowboy.

MOORE, VICTOR
Born: Feb. 24, 1876, Hammonton, N.J. Died: July, 1962, Long Island, N.Y.(heart attack). Screen, stage, and vaudeville actor. Entered films in 1915.

Appeared in: 1915 Chimmie Fadden; Chimmie Fadden Out West; Snobs. 1916 The Clown; The Race; The Best Man. 1917 Bungalowing; Commuting; Moving; Flivering; Home Defense. 1925 The Man Who Found Himself; prior to 1930 appeared in 41 Lever Co. shorts. 1930 Heads Up; Dangerous Nan McGrew. 1932-33 appeared in Vitaphone shorts. 1934 Romance in the Rain; Gift of Gab. 1936 Swing Time; Gold Diggers of 1937. 1937 We're on the Jury; Meet the Missus; The Life of the Party; She's Got Everything; Make Way for Tomorrow. 1938 Radio City Revels; This Marriage Business. 1941 Louisiana Purchase. 1942 Star Spangled Rhythm. 1943 True to Life; Riding High; The Heat's On. 1944 Carolina Blues. 1945 Duffy's Tavern; It's in the Bag. 1946 Ziegfeld Follies. 1947 It Happened on Fifth Avenue. 1948 A Miracle Can Happen. 1949 A Kiss in the Dark. 1952 We're Not Married. 1955 The Seven Year Itch.

MOORE, VIN
Born: 1878, Mayville, N.Y. Died: Dec. 5, 1949, Hollywood, Calif. Screen, stage actor, film director, and screenwriter.

Appeared in: 1916 By Stork Delivery. 1926 Lazy Lightning; The Man from the West.

MOORHOUSE, BERT
Born: 1895. Died: Jan. 26, 1954, Hollywood, Calif.(suicide—gun). Screen actor.

Appeared in: 1928 Rough Ridin' Red. 1929 Hey Rube!; The Woman I Love; The Delightful Rogue; The Girl from Woolworths. 1930 Conspiracy; Pay Off. 1950 Sunset Boulevard; The Big Hangover; Duchess of Idaho.

MORALES, "ESY" ISHMAEL
Born: 1917, Puerto Rico. Died: Nov. 2, 1950, New York, N.Y. (heart attack). Screen actor and orchestra leader.

Appeared in: 1945 Film Vodvil (short with his Copacabana Orchestra). 1949 Criss Cross.

MORAN, GEORGE (George Searcy)
Born: 1882, Elwood, Kan. Died: Aug. 1, 1949, Oakland, Calif. (stroke). Screen, stage, vaudeville, minstrel, and radio actor. He was the Moran in Moran in "Moran & Mack" comedy team, usually referred to as the "Two Black Crows," however, he did not appear in several shorts and films as he was replaced by Bert Swor, but did return to the team for Hypnotized and later shorts.

Appeared in, as part of team: 1927 Two Flaming Youths. 1929 Why Bring That Up. 1932 Hypnotized. 1932-33 "Moran & Mack" short comedies for Educational, Two Black Crows in Africa; As the Crows Fly. 1940 My Little Chickadee; The Bank Dick.

MORAN, LEE
Born: June 23, 1890, Chicago, Ill. Died: Apr. 24, 1961, Woodland Hills, Calif.(heart attack). Screen and stage actor. Entered films in 1909. Was part of comedy team of "Lyons and Moran" in Christie comedies beginning in 1914. The team appeared in Christie shorts from 1914 to 1920, among their shorts are the following: 1915 When the Mummy Cried for Help; Wanted, a Leading Woman; Eddie's Little Love Affair. 1917 War Bridegrooms.

He also appeared in: 1921 A Shocking Night; Fixed by George; Once a Plumber. 1924 The Fast Worker; Gambling Wives; Daring Youth; The Tomboy; Listen, Lester. 1925 After Business Hours; Fifth Avenue Models; Where Was I?; Tessie; My Lady of Whims; Jimmie's Millions. 1926 Her Big Night; Syncopating Sue; The Little Irish Girl; Take It from Me. 1927 Fast and Furious; The Rose of Kildare; The Irresistible Lover; Spring Fever; The Thrill Seekers; Wolf's Clothing. 1928 The Actress; Ladies of the Night Club; Outcast; Look-Out Girl; The Racket; Taxi 13; Thanks for the Buggy Ride; A Woman against the World; Show Girl. 1929 On with the Show; The Aviator; Children of the Ritz; Dance Hall; Glad Rag Doll; Gold Diggers of Broadway; Madonna of Avenue A; No Defense; The Show of Shows; Hearts in Exile. 1930 Golden Dawn; Hide Out; Mammy; Pardon My Gun; Sweet Mama. 1931 A Soldiers' Plaything; Caught Plastered. 1932 Stowaway; Exposure; Racetrack; The Fighting Gentleman. Uptown New York; The Death Kiss. 1933 Sister of Judas; Grand Slam; The 11th Com-

mandment; Goldie Gets Along; High Gear; Sitting Pretty. 1934 Circus Clown. 1935 Circumstantial Evidence; Honeymoon Limited. 1936 The Calling of Dan Matthews.

MORAN, MANOLO
Born: 1904, Madrid, Spain. Died: Apr. 27, 1967, Alicante, Spain. Screen actor. Won the Spanish Oscar in 1958 for his role in Viva la Imposible (Long Live the Impossible).

Appeared in: 1949 Don Quixote de la Mancha. 1958 Viva la Imposible (Long Live the Impossible). Other Spanish films: Angels of the Wheel; Manolo, Guardia Urbana (Manolo, Traffic Cop).

MORAN, PAT
Born: 1901. Died: Aug. 9, 1965, Woodland Hills, Calif. Screen, stage actor, and stuntman. Married to screen actress Patsy Moran (dec. 1968).

Appeared in: 1949 Trouble Makers.

MORAN, PATSY
Born: 1905. Died: Dec. 10, 1968, Hollywood, Calif. Screen and stage actress. Married to screen actor/stuntman Pat Moran (dec. 1965).

Appeared in: 1938 Topa Topa; Blockheads. 1940 Cowboy from Sundown; The Golden Trail. 1942 Foreign Agent. 1945 Come Out Fighting; Trouble Chasers.

MORAN, POLLY (Pauline Theresa Moran)
Born: June 28, 1883, Chicago, Ill. Died: Jan. 25, 1952, Los Angeles, Calif.(heart ailment). Screen, stage, vaudeville, and radio actress. Entered films as a Mack Sennett bathing beauty in 1915.

Appeared in: 1915 Their Social Splash; Those College Girls (reissued as His Better Half); A Favorite Fool; Her Painted Hero; The Hunt. 1916 The Village Blacksmith; By Stork Alone; A Bath House Blunder; His Wild Oats; Madcap Ambrose; Pills of Peril; Vampire Ambrose; Love Will Conquer; Because He Loved Her. 1917 Her Fame and Shame; His Naughty Thought; Cactus Nell; She Needed a Doctor; His Uncle Dudley; Roping Her Romeo. 1921 The Affairs of Anatol; Two Weeks with Pay; Skirts. 1923 Luck. 1927 The Callahans and the Murphys; London after Midnight; Buttons; The Thirteenth Hour. 1928 The Enemy; Rose Marie; The Divine Woman; Bringing up Father; Telling the World; Show People; Beyond the Sierras; Shadows of the Night; While the City Sleeps; Movie Chatterbox (short). 1929 The Unholy Night; Honeymoon; China Bound; Dangerous Females; Hollywood Revue of 1929; Hot for Paris; So This Is College; Speedway. 1930 Remote Control; Way for a Sailor; Way Out West; The Girl Said No; Chasing Rainbows; Caught Short; Paid. 1931 Guilty Hands; Reducing; Politics; It's a Wise Child. 1932 The Passionate Plumber; Prosperity; The Slippery Pearls (short). 1933 Alice in Wonderland. 1934 Hollywood Party; Down to Their Last Yacht. 1936 Columbia shorts. 1937 Two Wise Maids. 1938 Ladies in Distress. 1939 Ambush 1940 Tom Brown's School Days; Meet the Missus. 1941 Petticoat Politics. 1949 Adam's Rib. 1950 The Yellow Cab Man. 1964 Big Parade of Comedy (documentary).

MORANTE, JOSEPH
Born: 1853. Died: Apr. 13, 1940, Hollywood, Calif. Screen actor.

MORDANT, EDWIN
Born: 1868. Died: Feb. 15, 1942, Hollywood, Calif. Screen and stage actor. Married to screen actress Grace Atwell Mordant (dec, 1952).

Appeared in: 1915 Seven Sisters; The Prince and the Pauper. 1934 I'll Tell the World. 1937 County Fair. 1938 Outlaws of Sonora; Shadows over Shanghai.

MORDANT, GRACE (Grace Atwell)
Born: 1872. Died: Nov. 2, 1952, Hollywood, Calif. Screen and stage actress. Married to screen actor Edwin Mordant (dec, 1942).

MORENCY, ROBERT "BUSTER"
Born: 1932. Died: Mar. 30, 1937, Regina, Saskatchewan, Canada (leukemia). Five-year-old screen actor.

MORENO, ANTONIO
Born: Sept. 26, 1888, Madrid, Spain. Died: Feb. 15, 1967, Beverly Hills, Calif. Screen actor.

Appeared in: 1912 Two Daughters of Eve; So Near, Yet So Far; Voice of the Million. 1913 Judith of Bethulia. 1914 In the Latin Quarter. 1915 The Island of Regeneration. 1916 The Tarantula; Kennedy Square. 1917 The Magnificent Meddler; Aladdin from

Broadway. 1918 The House of Hate (serial); The Iron Test (serial); The House of a Thousand Candles. 1919 Perils of Thunder Mountain (serial). 1920 The Invisible Hand (serial); The Veiled Mystery (serial). 1921 Three Sevens; The Secret of the Hills. 1922 Guilty Conscience. 1923 The Exciters; The Trail of the Lonesome Pine; The Spanish Dancer; My American Wife; Look Your Best; Lost and Found. 1924 The Story without a Name; The Border Legion; Bluff; Flaming Barriers; Riger Love. 1925 Learning to Love; Her Husband's Secret; One Year to Live. 1926 Mare Nostrum; The Temptress; Beverly of Graustark; Love's Blindness; The Flaming Forest. 1927 It; Venus of Venice; Madame Pompadour; Come to My House. 1928 The Midnight Taxi; Adoration; The Air Legion; The Whip Woman; Nameless Men. 1929 Careers; Synthetic Sin; Romance of the Rio Grande. 1930 One Mad Kiss; Rough Romance; The Benson Murder Case; The Cat Creeps; Those Who Dance; Desire of Aguilas Frente al Sol (Eagles across the Sun); Wide Open Spaces. 1933 Primavera en Otono; El Precio de un Beso. 1934 La Cuidad de Carton. 1935 Senora Casada Necesita Marido (My Second Wife); Storm over the Andes; Rosa de Francia; Asegure a su Mujer (Insure Your Wife); He Trusted His Wife. 1936 The Bohemian Girl; Rose of the Rancho. 1938 Rose of the Rio Grande. 1939 Ambush. 1940 Seven Sinners. 1941 They Met in Argentina; Two Latins from Manhattan; The Kid from Kansas. 1942 Undercover Man; Valley of the Sun; Fiesta. 1944 Tampico. 1945 The Spanish Main. 1946 Notorious. 1947 Captain from Castile. 1949 Lust for Gold. 1950 Crisis; Dallas; Saddle Tramp. 1951 Mark of the Renegade. 1952 Untamed Frontier. 1953 Wings of the Hawk; Thunder Bay. 1954 Saskatchewan; Creature from the Black Lagoon. 1956 The Searchers. 1958 El Senore Faron y la Cleopatra (Mr. Pharoah and Cleopatra).

MORENO, DARIO
Born: Apr. 3, 1921, Smirne, Turkey. Died: Dec. 1968, Istanbul, Turkey. Screen, stage actor, and singer.

Appeared in: 1951 Pas de Vacances pour Monsieur. 1952 Le Salire de la Peur; Rires de Paris; Deux de l'Escadrille; La Mome Vert-de-Gris. 1953 Les Femmes s'en Balancent; Quai des Blondes. 1954 Le Mouton a Cinq Patles. 1956 Pardonnez-nous nos Offenses. 1957 Le feu aux Poudres. 1958 Incognito; Oh! Que Mambo. 1959 Oeil pour Oeil (Eye for an Eye); Wages of Fear; The Prisoner. 1960 Come Dance with Me; The Female (aka A Woman Like Satan); Toucher pas aux Blondes; Nathalie Agent Secrets. 1961 The Revolt of the Slaves. 1962 Candide. 1966 Hotel Paradiso.

MORENO, MARGUERITE
Born: 1871, France. Died: July 14, 1948, France. Screen and stage actress.

Appeared in: 1937 Amphytrion; Les Perles de la Couronne (Pearls of the Crown). 1949 Chips Are Down. Other French film: La Sexe Faible.

MORENO, PACO
Born: 1886. Died: Oct. 15, 1941, Beverly Hills, Calif. Screen and stage actor.

Appeared in: 1935 The Devil Is a Woman; Storm over the Andes. 1939 Papa Soltero (Bachelor Father).

MORENO, THOMAS "SKY BALL"
Born: 1895. Died: Oct. 25, 1938, West Los Angeles, Calif. Screen actor and stuntman.

MOREY, HARRY T.
Born: 1873, Mich. Died: Jan. 25, 1936, Brooklyn, N.Y.(abcessed lung). Screen, stage, and opera actor. Entered films with Vitagraph.

Appeared in: 1911 The Deerslayer. 1914 My Official Wife. 1916 Salvation Joan. 1917 Within the Law; The Courage of Silence. 1918 Forgotten Faces. 1921 A Man's Home. 1922 Beyond the Rainbow; Wildness of Youth; The Curse of Drink. 1923 The Green Goddess; The Empty Cradle; Marriage Morals; Where the Pavement Ends. 1924 Captain January; The Painted Lady; The Roughneck. 1925 Camille of the Barbary Coast; The Adventurous Sex; Heart of a Siren; Headlines; Barriers Burned Away. 1926 Aloma of the South Seas. 1927 Twin Flappers. 1928 Return of Sherlock Holmes; Under the Tonto Rim.

MOREY, HENRY A.
Born: 1848. Died: Jan. 8, 1929, Astoria, N.Y.(heart trouble). Screen and stage actor.

Appeared in: 1921 Inside of the Cup.

MORGAN, FRANK (Frank Wupperman)
Born: July 1, 1890, New York, N.Y. Died: Sept. 18, 1949, Beverly Hills, Calif. Screen, stage, vaudeville, and radio actor. Brother of screen actor Ralph Morgan (dec. 1956).

Appeared in: 1917 Modern Cinderella; Baby Mine. 1924 Born Rich; Manhandled. 1925 The Crowded Hour; The Man Who Found Himself; Scarlet Saint. 1927 Love's Greatest Mistake. 1930 Dangerous Nan McGrew; Queen High; Fast and Loose; Laughter. 1932 Secrets of the French Police; The Half-Naked Truth. 1933 Luxury Liner; Reunion in Vienna; The Nuisance; Bombshell; Best of Enemies; When Ladies Meet; Broadway to Hollywood; The Billion Dollar Scandal; Sailor's Luck; Kiss before the Mirror; Hallelujah, I'm a Bum. 1934 The Cat and the Fiddle; The Affairs of Celini; There's Always Tomorrow; By Your Leave; Success at Any Price; Sisters under the Skin; Lost Lady. 1935 Naughty Marietta; The Good Fairy; Escapade; I Live My Life; The Perfect Gentleman; Enchanted April. 1936 Dancing Pirate; Trouble for Two; Piccadilly Jim; Dimples; The Great Ziegfeld. 1937 The Last of Mrs. Cheyney; The Emperor's Candlesticks; Saratoga; Beg, Borrow or Steal; Rosalie. 1938 Paradise for Three; Port of Seven Seas; Sweethearts; The Crowd Roars. 1939 Broadway Serenade; The Wizard of Oz; Balalaika. 1940 The Shop around the Corner; Henry Goes Arizona; Broadway Melody of 1940; The Ghost Comes Home; The Mortal Storm; Boom Town; Hullabaloo. 1941 Keeping Company; Washington Melodrama; Wild Man of Borneo; Honky Tonk; The Vanishing Virginian. 1942 Tortilla Flat; White Cargo; Night Monster. 1943 A Stranger in Town; The Human Comedy; Thousands Cheer. 1944 The White Cliffs of Dover; Casanova Brown; Dear Barbara; The Miracle of Morgan's Creek; Hail the Conquering Hero. 1945 Yolanda and the Thief. 1946 Courage of Lassie; The Great Morgan; Mr. Griggs Returns; Pardon My Past; Lady Luck; The Cockeyed Miracle. 1947 Green Dolphin Street. 1948 The Three Musketeers; Summer Holiday. 1949 Any Number Can Play; The Stratton Story; The Great Sinner. 1950 Key to the City.

MORGAN, GENE (Eugene Schwartzkopf)
Born: 1892, Montgomery, Ala. Died: Aug. 13, 1940, Santa Monica, Calif.(heart attack). Screen, stage, vaudeville actor, and orchestra leader. Appeared in Pathe "Folly" comedies, and in early Hal Roach silent films.

Appeared in: 1926 Kid Boots. 1930 The Boss; Rogue of the Rio Grande; Orders; "Railroad" (shorts). 1932 Night World; Blonde Venus. 1933 "Railroad" (shorts); Elmer the Great; Song of the Eagle; Jennie Gerhardt. 1935 Men of the Hour; Bright Lights; If You Could Only Cook. 1936 Lady from Nowhere; Come Closer, Folks; The Music Goes 'Round; You May Be Next; Mr. Deeds Goes to Town; Devil's Squadron; Meet Nero Wolfe; Shakedown; Alibi for Murder; End of the Trail; Panic on the Air; Counterfeit. 1937 Counterfeit Lady; Woman in Distress; Speed to Spare; Parole Racket; Counsel for Crime; Murder in Greenwich Village; All American Sweetheart; Make Way for Tomorrow. 1938 Start Cheering; There's Always a Woman; The Main Event; When G-Men Step In; Who Killed Gail Preston?. 1939 Captain Fury; Mr. Smith Goes to Washington; Federal Man-Hunt; Homicide Bureau; The Housekeeper's Daughter; Columbia shorts. 1940 Girl from God's Country; Saps at Sea. 1941 Meet John Doe.

MORGAN, HELEN
Born: 1900, Danville, Ill. Died: Oct. 9, 1941, Chicago, Ill.(kidney and liver ailments). Screen, stage actress, and club entertainer.

Appeared in: 1929 Applause (film debut); Glorifying the American Girl; Show Boat. 1930 Roadhouse Nights. 1932 Gigolo Racket (short). 1934 Marie Galante; The Lemon Drop Kid; You Belong to Me. 1935 Go into Your Dance; Sweet Music; Frankie and Johnnie. 1936 Showboat (and 1929 version).

MORGAN, MARGO (Margaret Rockwood)
Born: 1897. Died: May 16, 1962, Hollywood, Calif. Screen actress and singer.

MORGAN, PAUL
Born: Germany. Died: Jan. 1939 (congestion of the lungs). Screen and stage actor.

Appeared in: 1930 Why Cry at Parting?; Menschen Hinter Geitern; Zwei Hertzen in Drei-Viertel Takt. 1931 Wien Du Stadt der Lieder (Vienna City of Song); Das Kabinett des Dr. Larifari. 1932 Theaternaechte von Bath; Liebeskommando. 1933 Holzapfel Weiss Alles.

MORGAN, RALPH (Ralph Kuhner Wupperman)
Born: July 6, 1883, New York, N.Y. Died: June 11, 1956, N.Y. Screen and stage actor. Married to screen actress Grace Arnold

(dec. 1948). Father of screen actress Claudia Morgan and brother of screen actor Frank Morgan (dec. 1949).

Appeared in: 1930 Excuse the Pardon (short). 1931 Honor among Lovers. 1932 Charlie Chan's Chance; Dance Team; Rasputin and the Empress; Strange Interlude; Cheaters at Play; Disorderly Conduct; The Devil's Lottery; The Son-Daughter. 1933 The Power and the Glory; Shanghai Madness; Humanity; Trick for Trick, The Mad Game; Walls of Gold; Doctor Bull; The Kennel Murder Case. 1934 Transatlantic Merry-Go-Round; Their Big Moment; Hell in the Heavens; Orient Express; She Was a Lady; Stand up and Cheer; No Greater Glory; Girl of the Limberlost; The Last Gentleman; Little Men; The Cat and the Fiddle. 1935 Condemned to Live; I've Been Around; Star of Midnight; Unwelcome Stranger; Calm Yourself. 1936 Anthony Adverse; Magnificent Obsession; Yellowstone; Muss 'Em Up; The Ex-Mrs. Bradford; Little Miss Nobody; Human Cargo; Speed; General Spanky; Crack Up. 1937 The Man in Blue; The Life of Emile Zola; Exclusive; Wells Fargo; Behind Prison Bars. 1938 Love Is a Headache; Out West with the Hardys; Wives under Suspicion; Army Girl; Orphans of the Street; Mother Carey's Chickens; Barefoot Boy; Shadow over Shanghai; Mannequin; That's My Story. 1939 Off the Record; Fast and Loose; Man of Conquest; Smuggled Cargo; Way Down South; Trapped in the Sky; The Lone Spy Hunt; Geronimo. 1940 Forty Little Mothers; I'm Still Alive; Wagons Westward. 1941 The Mad Doctor; Adventure in Washington; Dick Tracy vs. Crime, Inc. (serial). 1942 Close Call for Ellery Queen; Klondike Fury; Night Monster; The Traitor Within; Gang Busters (serial). 1943 Stage Door Canteen; Jack London; Hitler's Madman. 1944 Trocadero; Double Furlough; I'll Be Seeing You; The Monster Maker; Weird Woman; The Imposter; The Great Alaskan Mystery (serial); Enemy of Women. 1945 Black Market Babies; This Love of Ours; Hollywood and Vine; Monster and the Ape (serial). 1947 The Last Round-Up; Song of the Thin Man; Mr. District Attorney. 1948 Sleep My Love; The Sword of the Avenger; The Creeper. 1950 Blue Grass of Kentucky. 1951 Heart of the Rockies. 1952 Dick Tracy vs. the Phantom Empire (serial). 1953 Gold Fever.

MORGAN, RUSS
Born: 1904, Scranton, Pa. Died: Aug. 7, 1969, Las Vegas, Nev. (cerebral hemorrhage). Bandleader, song writer, and screen actor. Wrote hit songs "Your Nobody Till Somebody Loves You," "Somebody New Is Taking My Place" and "Does Your Heart Beat for Me?".

Appeared in: 1951 Disc Jockey. 1956 The Great Man; Mister Cory. 1958 The Big Beat.

MORIARTY, JOANNE
Born: 1939. Died: Mar. 2, 1964, Hollywood, Calif. (suicide—pills). Screen actress.

Appeared in: 1964 Bedtime Story.

MORIYA, SHIZU
Born: 1911, Japan. Died: Mar. 12, 1961, N.Y. Screen, stage, and television actor.

MORLAY, GABY (Blanche Fumoleau)
Born: 1897. Died: July 4, 1964, Nice, France. Screen and stage actress.

Appeared in: 1913 La Sandale Rouge. 1929 Les Nouveau Messieurs (The New Gentlemen). 1934 Le Scandale. 1935 Jeanne. 1936 Le Bonheur. 1938 Derriere La Facade; The Kreutzer Sonata. 1939 Entente Cordiale. 1940 Life of Giuseppe Verdi; The Living Corpse. 1941 The King. 1942 Le Voile Bleu (The Blue Veil—U.S. 1947). 1944 32 Rue de Montmartre. 1948 Gigi (U.S. 1950); Le Revenant (A Lover's Return); Mlle. Desiree. 1951 Le Plaisir (House of Pleasure—U.S. 1953); Anna. 1952 Father's Dilemma; A Simple Case of Money. 1954 The Mask. 1955 Mitsou (U.S. 1958). 1957 Royal Affairs in Versailles. 1958 Ramuntcho. Other French films: The Most Dangerous Sin; Crime and Punishment; Accusee; Levez-Vous; Les Amants Terribles; Entente Cordiale; Sa Majeste M.Dupont; L'Amour d'Une Femme; Paris-New York.

MORLEY, ROBERT JAMES
Born: 1892. Died: Aug. 30, 1952, Hollywood, Calif. Screen actor.

MORNE, MARYLAND
Born: 1900. Died: July 28, 1935, Hollywood, Calif. Screen actress.

MORPHY, LEWIS H. (Lewis Harris Morphy)
Born: 1904. Died: Nov. 7, 1958, Hollywood, Calif. (suicide). Screen actor, stuntman, and rodeo performer.

MORRELL, GEORGE
Born: 1873. Died: Apr. 28, 1955, Hollywood, Calif. Screen and stage actor.

Appeared in: 1921 The Heart of the North. 1929 Silent Sentinel.

MORRIS, ? (married name: Mrs. Harold (Buddy) Kusell)
Born: 1903. Died: May 13, 1971, Buffalo, N.Y. Screen, stage, radio, and vaudeville actress. See William Morris for family information.

MORRIS, ADRIAN
Born: 1903, Mt. Vernon, N.Y. Died: Nov. 30, 1941, Los Angeles, Calif. Screen, stage, and vaudeville actor. See William Morris for family information.

Appeared in: 1929 Fast Life; The Jazz Age. 1931 The Age for Love. 1932 Me and My Gal. 1933 Trick for Trick; Bureau of Missing Persons; Wild Boys on the Road. 1934 The Big Shakedown; Let's Be Ritzy; The Pursuit of Happiness. 1935 Age of Indiscretion; One Frightened Night; Powder Smoke Range; Dr. Socrates. 1936 The Petrified Forest; Poppy; My American Wife; Rose Bowl. 1937 Her Husband Lies; The Woman I Love; There Goes the Groom; Every Day's a Holiday. 1938 You and Me; If I Were King; Angels with Dirty Faces. 1939 Return of the Cisco Kid; 6,000 Enemies; Wall Street Cowboy; Gone with the Wind. 1940 Florian; The Grapes of Wrath.

MORRIS, CHESTER (John Chester Brooks Morris)
Born: Feb. 16, 1901, New York, N.Y. Died: Sept. 11, 1970, New Hope, Pa.(overdose of barbiturates). Screen, stage, vaudeville, radio, and television actor. Entered films at age of 9 in 1910. Best known as film and television's "Boston Blackie." See William Morris for family information.

Appeared in: 1929 Alibi; Fast Life; Woman Trap; The Show of Shows. 1930 Playing Around; The Big House; The Divorcee; The Case of Sergeant Grischa; She Couldn't Say No; Second Choice. 1931 Bat Whispers; Corsair. 1932 Cock of the Air; The Miracle Man; Breach of Promise; Sinners in the Sun; Red Headed Woman. 1933 Blondie Johnson; The Infernal Machine; Kid Gloves; Tomorrow at Seven; Golden Harvest; King for a Night. 1934 The Gay Bride; Let's Talk It Over; Embarassing Moments; Gift of Gab. 1935 Princess O'Hara; Public Hero No. 1; Society Doctor; Pursuit; I've Been Around; Frankie and Johnnie. 1936 Three Godfathers; Moonlight Murder; They Met in a Taxi; Counterfeit. 1937 I Promise to Pay; The Devil's Playground; Flight to Glory. 1938 Law of the Underworld; Sky Giant; Smashing the Rackets. 1939 Blind Alley; Pacific Liner; Five Came Back; Thunder Afloat. 1940 The Marines Fly High; Wagons Westward; The Girl from God's Country. 1941 Meet Boston Blackie; Confessions of Boston Blackie; No Hands on the Clock; The Phantom Thief. 1942 Canal Zone; I Live on Danger; The Wrecking Crew; Boston Blackie Goes to Hollywood. 1943 High Explosive; Aerial Gunner; After Midnight with Boston Blackie; Tornado; Thunderbolt; The Chance of a Lifetime. 1944 Dark Mountain; One Mysterious Night; Gambler's Choice; Derelick Ship; Secret Command; The Awakening of Jim Burke; Double Exposure; Men of the Deep. 1945 The Blonde from Brooklyn; One Way to Love; Rough, Tough and Ready; Boston Blackie Booked on Suspicion; Boston Blackie's Rendezvous. 1946 Boston Blackie and the Law; A Close Call for Boston Blackie; Phantom Thief. 1947 Blind Spot. 1948 Trapped by Boston Blackie. 1949 Boston Blackie's Chinese Venture. 1955 Unchained. 1956 The She-Creature. 1964 Big Parade of Comedy (documentary).

MORRIS, CLARA
Born: 1897, Omaha, Neb. Died: 1925. Screen actress.

Appeared in: 1921 My Lady Friends. 1925 Where Romance Rides.

MORRIS, DIANA
Born: 1907. Died: Feb. 19, 1961, Hollywood, Calif.(throat cancer). Screen and stage actress. Was one of the original Wampus Baby stars.

MORRIS, GORDON
Born: 1899. Died: Apr. 7, 1940, Hollywood, Calif. Screen, stage actor, and screenwriter. See William Morris for family information.

MORRIS, MARY
Born: 1896, Mass. Died: Jan. 16, 1970, N.Y. Screen and stage actress. Do not confuse with Mary Morris born in 1915.

Appeared in: 1934 Double Door. 1937 Victoria the Great.

MORRIS, PHILIP (Francis Charles Philip Morris)
Born: Jan. 20, 1893, Duluth, Minn. Died: Dec. 18, 1949, Los Angeles, Calif. Screen and stage actor.

Appeared in: 1934 Home on the Range. 1935 Seven Keys to Baldpate. 1936 Desert Gold. 1937 Super Sleuth. 1946 Cluny Brown; Home Sweet Homicide. 1947 Buckaroo from Powder River. 1948 Whirlwind Raiders. 1949 The Flying Saucer.

MORRIS, WAYNE (Bert de Wayne Morris)
Born: Feb. 17, 1914, Los Angeles, Calif. Died: Sept. 14, 1959, Pacific Ocean, aboard aircraft carrier (heart attack). Screen, stage, and television actor.

Appeared in: 1936 China Clipper (film debut); King of Hockey; Here Comes Carter; Polo Joe; Smart Blonde. 1937 Don't Pull Your Punches; Kid Galahad; Submarine D-1; Once a Doctor. 1938 Love, Honor and Behave; Men Are Such Fools; Valley of the Giants; The Kid Comes Back; Brother Rat. 1939 The Kid from Kokomo; Return of Dr. X. 1940 Brother Rat and a Baby; An Angel from Texas; Double Alibi; Ladies Must Live; The Quarterback; Gambling on the High Seas; Flight Angels. 1941 Three Sons O'Guns; I Wanted Wings; Bad Men of Missouri; The Smiling Ghost. 1947 Deep Valley; The Voice of the Turtle. 1948 The Big Punch; The Time of Your Life. 1949 A Kiss in the Dark; The Younger Brothers; John Loves Mary; The House across the Street; Task Force. 1950 Johnny One Eye; The Tougher They Come; Stage to Tucson. 1951 Sierra Passage; The Big Gusher; Yellow Fin. 1952 The Bushwhackers; Desert Pursuit; Arctic Flight. 1953 The Fighting Lawman; The Marksman; The Star of Texas. 1954 Riding Shotgun; The Desperado; Two Guns and a Badge; Port of Hell. 1955 Lord of the Jungle; The Master Plan; The Green Buddha; Cross Channel; The Lonesome Trail. 1956 The Dynamiters. 1957 Plunder Road. 1958 Paths of Glory.

MORRIS, WILLIAM
Born: 1861. Died: Jan. 11, 1936, Los Angeles, Calif.(heart attack). Screen and stage actor. Married to screen actress Etta Hawkins Morris (dec. 1945) and father of screen actors Chester (dec. 1970), Adrian (dec. 1941) and Gordon Morris (dec. 1940) and screen actress Mrs. Harold Kusell (Morris) (dec. 1971).

Appeared in: 1930 Brothers; The Convict's Code. 1931 The Gang Buster; Behind Office Doors. 1932 The Washington Masquerade.

MORRISON, ARTHUR
Born: 1880, St. Louis, Mo. Died: Feb. 20, 1950, Los Angeles, Calif. Screen, stage, and vaudeville actor. Entered films with World Films in 1917.

Appeared in: 1921 The Light in the Clearing; The Sage Hen; Singing River; The Roof Tree. 1922 The Men of Zanzibar; Strength of the Pines. 1923 The Gunfighter; In the West; The Sting of the Scorpion. 1925 Cold Nerve; Riders of the Purple Sage. 1926 Lazy Lightning; Riding Romance; Tony Runs Wild; Silver Fingers. 1927 The Silent Rider; Grinning Guns; King of the Jungle (serial). 1928 Willful Youth. 1929 Slim Fingers.

MORRISON, CHIT
Died: prior to 1970 (fall from horse). Screen actor and animal trainer. Married to screen actress Anna Marie Morrison (dec. 1972).

Appeared in: 1921 The Duke of Chimney Butte. 1922 Hair Trigger Casey.

MORRISSEY, BETTY (aka BETTY MORRISEY)
Born: N.Y. Died: Apr. 20, 1944, New York, N.Y. Screen actress.

Appeared in: 1923 A Woman of Paris. 1924 What Shall I Do?; The Fast Worker; Virtue's Revolt; Traffic in Hearts; Turned Up. 1925 Lady of the Night; The Gold Rush; Skinner's Dress Suit; The Desert Demon. 1928 The Circus.

MORRISSEY, WILL
Born: 1885. Died: Dec. 16, 1957, Santa Barbara, Calif. Screen, vaudeville actor, stage producer, song writer, and playwright. Billed in vaudeville with Midgie Miller in an act billed as "Morrissey and Miller." Together they appeared in the following shorts: 1927 The Morrissey and Miller Vitaphone Revue. 1928 The Morrissey and Miller Night Club.

MORROW, DORETTA (Doretta Marano)
Born: 1927, Brooklyn, N.Y. Died: Feb. 28, 1968, London, England. (cancer). Screen, stage, television actress, and singer. Cousin of singer Vic Damone.

Appeared in: 1952 Because You're Mine.

MORROW, JANE. See Mrs. Sidney Drew

MORSE, LEE
Born: 1904. Died: Dec. 16, 1954, Rochester, N.Y. Screen, vaudeville, radio actress, singer and composer.

Appeared in: 1930 The Music Racket (short).

MORSE, ROBIN
Born: 1915. Died: Dec. 11, 1958, Hollywood, Calif.(heart attack). Screen and television actor.

Appeared in: 1953 The Great Jesse James Raid. 1955 Marty; Abbot and Costello Meet the Mummy. 1956 The Boss; He Laughed Last. 1957 Pal Joey; Sabu and the Magic Ring.

MORTIMER, CHARLES
Born: 1885. Died: May, 1964, London, England. Screen and stage actor.

Appeared in: 1933 You Made Me Love You. 1934 The Return of Bulldog Drummond. 1935 The Triumph of Sherlock Holmes; Someone at the Door; Rhodes; Mister Hobo. 1939 Poison Pen; Aren't Men Beasts; Things Are Looking Up; Living Dangerously. 1955 Dial Nine Nine Nine (aka The Way Out). 1957 Counterfeit Plan.

MORTIMER, EDMUND
Born: 1875. Died: May 21, 1944, Hollywood, Calif. Screen actor, film director, and screenwriter.

Appeared in: 1937 It's Love I'm After.

MORTIMER, HENRY (John O. D. Rennie)
Born: 1875. Died: Aug. 20, 1952, Whitby, Ontario, Canada. Screen and stage actor. Entered films during silents.

Appeared in: 1930 La Grande Mare.

MORTON, JAMES C.
Born: 1884, Helena, Mont. Died: Oct. 24, 1942, Reseda, Calif. Screen, stage, and vaudeville actor.

Appeared in: 1930 Follow the Leader. 1932 Pack up Your Troubles, plus the following shorts: Alum and Eve; The Soilers. 1933 The Midnight Patrol; The Devil's Brother, plus the following shorts: Me and My Pal; Hokus Focus; Snug in the Jug; Sneak Easily. 1934 One Horse Farmers (short); Maid in Hollywood (short). 1935 the following shorts: Tit for Tat; The Fixeruppers; Pardon My Scotch; The Misses Stooge; Hoi Polloi. 1936 The Bohemian Girl; Our Relations; Way Out West, plus the following shorts: Hill Tillies; Ants in the Pantry; Disorder in the Court; A Pain in the Pullman. 1937 Two Wise Maids; Rhythm in the Clouds; Public Cowboy #1; Mama Runs Wild, plus the following shorts: Dizzy Doctors; The Sitter-Downers. 1938 Topper Takes a Trip, plus the following shorts: Healthy, Wealthy and Dumb; Three Missing Links. 1939 We Want Our Mummy (short); Three Little Sew and Sews (short). 1940 Earl of Puddlestone; My Little Chickadee; an RKO short. 1941 Never Give a Sucker an Even Break; Lady from Louisiana; Wild Geese Calling; Bashful but Dumb (short). 1942 Yokel Boy; The Boogie Man Will Get You.

MORTON, MAXINE. See Katherine West

MOSCOVITCH, MAURICE
Born: Nov. 23, 1871, Odessa, Russia. Died: June 18, 1940, Los Angeles, Calif.(following operation). Screen and stage actor.

Appeared in: 1936 Winterset. 1937 Lancer Spy; Make Way for Tomorrow. 1938 Gateway; Suez. 1939 Everything Happens at Night; Susanna of the Mountains; Love Affair; In Name Only; Rio. 1940 Dance, Girl, Dance; South to Karanga; The Great Dictator. 1942 The Great Commandment.

MOSER, HANS (Jean Juliet)
Born: 1880, Austria. Died: June 19, 1964, Vienna, Austria (cancer). Screen actor.

Appeared in: 1930 Liebling der Gotter; (Darling of the Gods). 1931 Der Grosse Tenor. 1932 His Majesty; King Ballyhoo; Causa Kaiser (The Kaiser Case); Man Braucht Kein Geld. 1933 Madame Wuenscht Keine Kinder. 1935 Polenblut (Polish Blood); Der Himmel auf Erden; Winternachtstraum. 1936 Frasquite; Karneval und Liebe; Die Fahrt in Die Jugend. 1937 The World's in Love; Masquerade in Vienna; Endstation; Schabernack; Das Gaesschen zum Paradies; Vienna Burgtheater. 1938 Eva, das Fabriksmaedel; Solo per To (Only for Thee); Die Glueclichste Ehe von Wien (Happiest Married Couple in Vienna); Wir Sind von K u K Infantrie-Regiment. 1939 Alles Fuer Veronika; Kleines Bezirksgericht (Little Country Court); Fasching in Wien; Hohe Schule

(College); Familie Schimek; Das Ekel (The Grouch). 1940 Wal-zerlange (Waltz Melodies); Wiener Geschichten (Vienna Tales); Opernball (Opera Ball). 1950 State Secret. 1951 The Great Man-hunt; Vienna Blood. 1953 Der Onkel aus Amerika (Uncle from America). 1955 Congress Dances. 1962 Der Flendermaus.

MOSJOUKINE, IVAN
Born: 1889. Died: Jan. 18, 1939, Paris, France. Franco-Russian screen actor.

Appeared in: 1911 The Defense of Sevastopol. 1922 Satan Tri-umphant; Tempest. 1923 Shadows That Mass. 1926 Michael Strogoff. 1927 Surrender; The Living Dead Man; Edmund Kean; Prince among Lovers; The Loves of Casanova (U.S. 1929); Sur-render. 1929 The President; The White Devil (U.S. 1931). 1936 Nitchevo. Other French film: Sergeant X.

MOSKVIN, IVAN M.
Born: 1874, Russia. Died: Feb. 16, 1946, Moscow, Russia. Screen and stage actor.

Appeared in: 1927 Polikushka. 1928 The Station Master. 1933 An Hour with Tchekhof. Other Russian film: Death of a Govern-ment Clerk.

MOSLEY, FRED (Frederick Charles Mosley)
Born: 1854. Died: Mar. 9, 1972, Staten Island, N.Y. Screen and stage actor.

MOULAN, FRANK
Born: 1876. Died: May 13, 1939, New York, N.Y. Screen and opera actor.

Appeared in: 1927 Oh, How I Love My Little Bed (short). 1937 The Girl Said No.

MOULDER, WALTER C.
Born: 1933. Died: July 1, 1967, New York, N.Y.(heart attack). Screen, stage, and television actor.

Appeared in: 1959 North by Northwest; That Kind of Woman.

MOVAR, DUNJA
Born: 1940, Germany. Died: Mar. 30, 1963, Goettingen, Germany. (suicide—sleeping pills). Screen, stage, and television actress. Received Federal Youth Film Award in 1959 for The Angel That Pawned a Harp.

Appeared in: 1959 The Angel That Pawned a Harp. 1962 Hamlet.

MOWBRAY, ALAN
Born: Aug. 18, 1896, London, England. Died: Mar. 25, 1969, Hollywood, Calif.(heart attack). Screen, stage, television actor, and playwright.

Appeared in: 1931 Guilty Hands; Honor of the Family; God's Gift to Women; Alexander Hamilton; The Man in Possession; Leftover Ladies. 1932 The Silent Witness; Lovers Courageous; Man about Town; Winner Take All; Jewel Robbery; Two against the World; The Man Called Back; Nice Women; Hotel Continental; The World and the Flesh; The Man from Yesterday; Sherlock Holmes. 1933 Our Betters; Her Secret; Peg O' My Heart; A Study in Scarlet; Voltaire; Berkeley Square; Midnight Club; The World Changes; Roman Scandals. 1934 One More River; Embarrassing Moments; Long Lost Father; Where Sinners Meet; The Girl from Missouri; Charlie Chan in London; The House of Rothschild; Cheaters; Lit-tle Man, What Now?. 1935 Lady Tubbs; Night Life of the Gods; Becky Sharp; The Gay Deception; In Person; She Couldn't Take It. 1936 Rose Marie; Muss 'Em Up; Mary of Scotland; Rainbow on the River; Desire; Give Us This Night; The Case against Mrs. Ames; Fatal Lady; My Man Godfrey; Ladies in Love. 1937 Four Days' Wonder; As Good As Married; Topper; Stand-In; On Such a Night; Music for Madame; On the Avenue; The King and the Chorus Girl; Marry the Girl; Hollywood Hotel; Vogues of 1938. 1938 Mer-rily We Live; There Goes My Heart. 1939 Never Say Die; Way Down South; The Llano Kid; Topper Takes a Trip. 1940 Music in My Heart; Curtain Call; The Villain Still Pursued Her; The Boys from Syracuse; Scatterbrain; The Quarterback. 1941 Ice-Capades; The Perfect Snob; That Hamilton Woman; That Uncertain Feeling; Footlight Fever; The Cowboy and the Blonde; I Woke up Scream-ing; Moon over Her Shoulder. 1942 Yokel Boy; So This Is Wash-ington; Panama Hattie; The Mad Martindales; A Yank at Eton; Isle of Missing Men; The Devil with Hitler; We Were Dancing; The Powers Girl. 1943 Stage Door Canteen; His Butler's Sister; Holy Matrimony; Slightly Dangerous; Screen Snapshots No. 8 (short). 1944 Ever since Venus; The Dough Girls; My Gal Loves Music. 1945 Tell It to a Star; The Phantom of 42nd Street; Earl Carroll Vanities; Men in Her Diary; Where Do We Go from Here?; Sun-bonnet Sue; Bring on the Girls. 1946 Terror by Night; My Darling

Clementine; Idea Girl. 1947 Captain from Castile; Lured; Merton of the Movies; Pilgrim Lady. 1948 My Dear Secretary; An Inno-cent Affair; Every Girl Should Be Married; Main Street Kid; Prince of Thieves. 1949 Abbott and Costello Meet the Killer, Boris Karloff; The Lone Wolf and His Lady; You're My Every-thing; The Lovable Cheat. 1950 The Jackpot; Wagonmaster. 1951 Crosswinds; The Lady and the Bandit; Dick Turpin's Ride. 1952 Just across the Street; Blackbeard the Pirate. 1953 An-drocles and the Lion. 1954 Ma and Pa Kettle at Home; The Steel Cage. 1955 The King's Thief. 1956 Around the World in 80 Days; The Man Who Knew Too Much; The King and I. 1962 A Ma-jority of One.

MOWER, JACK
Born: 1890, Honolulu, Hawaii. Died: Jan. 6, 1965, Hollywood, Calif. Screen, stage, and vaudeville actor.

Appeared in: 1920 The Third Eye (serial); The Tiger Band (ser-ial). 1921 The Beautiful Gambler; Cotton and Cattle; Danger Ahead; Silent Years; The Trail to Red Dog; A Cowboy Ace; Flow-ing Gold; Out of the Clouds; The Range Pirate; Riding with Death; The Rowdy; Rustlers of the Night; Short Skirts. 1922 Manslaugh-ter; The Crimson Challenge; The Golden Gallows; Saturday Night; When Husbands Deceive. 1923 The Last Hour; Pure Grit; The Shock; In the Days of Daniel Boone (serial). 1924 Robes of Sin; Ten Scars Make a Man (serial). 1925 Cyclone Cavalier; Kit Car-son over the Great Divide; Perils of the Wind (serial); The Rat-tler. 1926 False Friends; Her Own Story; Officer 444 (serial); The Ghetto Shamrock; The Radio Detective (serial); Sky High Corral; Melodies; The Lost Express. 1927 Trail of the Tiger (serial); Uncle Tom's Cabin; Pretty Clothes; Face Value. 1928 The Water Hole; Sailor's Wives; The Air Patrol; Sinners' Parade. 1929 Anne against the World; Ships of the Night. 1930 Ridin' Law; The Woman Who Was Forgotten. 1932 Midnight Patrol; Phantom Express; Lone Trail. 1933 Come on Tarzan; Law and the Lawless; King of the Arena; Fiddlin' Buckaroo. 1935 Revenge Rider. 1936 Hollywood Boulevard. 1937 White Bondage; Love Is on the Air; Without Warning; The Missing Witness. 1938 Penrod and His Twin Brother; Crime School; Hard to Get; Comet over Broadway; Tarzan and the Green Goddess; The Invisible Menace. 1939 Code of the Secret Service; Smashing the Money Ring; Everybody's Hobby; Confessions of a Nazi Spy; The Return of Dr. X; Private Detectives. 1940 Always a Bride; British Intelligence; King of the Lumberjacks; Torrid Zone; Tugboat Annie Sails Again. 1941 The Bride Came C.O.D.; Bullets for O'Hara; The Wagons Roll at Night. 1942 Murder in the Big House; Spy Ship. 1943 Mysterious Doctor. 1944 Adventures of Mark Twain; The Last Ride. 1946 Dangerous Business. 1947 That Way with Women; Shadows over Chinatown. 1948 Fighting Mad. 1949 Angels in Dis-guise. 1950 County Fair. 1959 Uncle Tom's Cabin (reissue of 1927 version).

MOZART, GEORGE
Born: Feb. 15, 1864, Yarmouth, England. Died: Dec. 10, 1947, London, England. Screen and stage actor.

Appeared in: 1936 The Song of Freedom. 1938 Pygmalion. Other British films: Mystery of the Mary Celeste; Breakers Ahead; Medicine Man; Stand up and Sing.

MUDIE, LEONARD (Leonard Mudie Cheetham)
Born: Apr. 11, 1884, England. Died: Apr. 14, 1965, Hollywood, Calif.(heart ailment). Screen and stage actor.

Appeared in: 1921 A Message from Mars. 1922 Through the Storm. 1932 The Mummy. 1933 Voltaire. 1934 The Mystery of Mr. X; The House of Rothschild; Cleopatra. 1935 Clive of India; Cardinal Richelieu; Becky Sharp; Rendezvous; Captain Blood; The Great Impersonator. 1936 Magnificent Obsession; Anthony Ad-verse; Mary of Scotland; His Brother's Wife; Lloyds of London. 1937 The King and the Chorus Girl; They Won't Forget; The League of Frightened Men; London by Night; Lancer Spy. 1938 The Jury's Secret; Adventures of Robin Hood; Kidnapped; Suez; When Were You Born?. 1939 Tropic Fury; Arrest Bulldog Drummond; Don't Gamble with Strangers; Dark Victory; Mutiny on the Black Hawk; Man about Town. 1940 Congo Maisie; Charlie Chan's Murder Cruise; South of Suez; Devil's Island; British In-telligence. 1941 Shining Victory; The Nurse's Secret. 1942 Ber-lin Correspondent; Random Harvest. 1943 Appointment in Berlin. 1944 Winged Victory; Dragon Seed. 1945 Divorce; My Name Is Julia Ross; The Corn Is Green. 1946 Don't Gamble with Strang-ers. 1947 Private Affairs of Bel Ami; Bulldog Drummond at Bay. 1948 The Checkered Coat; Song of My Heart. 1951 Bomba and the Elephant Stempede. 1952 Bomba and the Jungle Girl; Af-rican Treasure. 1953 Safari Drums; The Magnetic Monster; Perils of the Jungle. 1954 Killer Leopard; Golden Idol. 1955

Lord of the Jungle. 1956 Autumn Leaves. 1957 The Story of Mankind. 1959 Timbuktu; The Big Fisherman. 1965 The Greatest Story Ever Told.

MUELLER, WOLFGANG (aka WOLFGANG MULLER)
Born: 1923, Berlin, Germany. Died: Apr. 26, 1960, Lostallo, Switzerland (plane crash). Screen and stage actor.

Appeared in: 1958 Wir Wunderkinder (narr.) (We Amazing Children—aka Aren't We Wonderful—U.S. 1959). 1960 Das Wirthaus im Spessart (Restaurant in the Spessart—aka The Spessart Inn—U.S. 1961).

MUIR, HELEN
Born: 1864. Died: Dec. 2, 1934, Los Angeles, Calif. Screen and stage actress. Entered films with Griffith in 1915.

Appeared in: 1919 Strictly Confidential. 1921 Live and Let Live; The Mistress of Shenstone.

MULCASTER, G. H.
Born: 1891, London, England. Died: Jan. 19, 1964, England. Screen and stage actor.

Appeared in: 1940 Pack up Your Troubles; Sailor Don't Care. 1941 This Man Is Dangerous. 1942 Let the People Sing; Asking for Trouble. 1943 The Dummy Talks; My Learned Friend. 1945 For You Alone. 1946 Under New Management. 1949 Spring in Park Lane; That Dangerous Age (aka If This Be Sin—U.S. 1950); Under Capricorn. 1951 The Naked Heart. 1955 Contraband Spain—U.S. 1958). 1957 Lady of Vengeance.

MULGREW, THOMAS G.
Born: 1889. Died: Dec. 3, 1954, Providence, R.I. Screen, stage, and vaudeville actor. Appeared in early films with Eastern Film Co.

MULHAUSER, JAMES
Born: Oct. 31, 1890. Brooklyn, N.Y. Died: June 15, 1939, Beverly Hills, Calif. Screen, stage actor, and screenwriter. Entered films in 1918.

Appeared in: 1928 The Head Man. 1929 China Bound. 1932 Slim Summerville Comedies.

MULLE, IDA
Born: approx. 1864. Died: Aug. 9, 1934, New York, N.Y.(complications from fall). Screen and stage actress.

MULLER, RENATE (aka RENATE MUELLER)
Born: 1907, Germany. Died: Oct. 7, 1937, Berlin, Germany. Appeared in German and British films.

Appeared in: 1930 Liebe im Ring; Liebling der Gotter (Darling of the Gods). 1931 Der Grosse Tenor; Das Floetenkonzert von Sanssouci. 1932 Der Kleine Seitensprung; Office Girl; Die Blumenfrau von Lindenau (Flower Lady of Lindenau); Herzblut. 1933 Der Sohn der Weissen Berge; Wenn die Liebe Mode Macht; Saison in Kairo. 1934 Wie Sag' Iche's Meinem Mann?; Waltz Time in Vienna. 1935 Viktor und Viktoria. 1936 The Private Life of Louis XIV; Liebesleute. 1937 Togger; For Her Country's Sake.

MUNDIN, HERBERT
Born: Aug. 21, 1898, England. Died: Mar. 4, 1939, Van Nuys, Calif.(auto accident). Screen and stage actor.

Appeared in: 1932 Life Begins; One Way Passage; The Silent Witness; Almost Married; The Devil's Lottery; The Trial of Vivienne Ware; Bachelor's Affairs; Chandu, the Magician; Sherlock Holmes; Love Me Tonight. 1933 Dangerously Yours; Cavalcade; Pleasure Cruise; Adorable; It's Great to Be Alive; Arizona to Broadway; The Devil's in Love; Shanghai Madness; Hoopla. 1934 Bottoms Up; Call It Luck; Such Women Are Dangerous; Orient Express; Springtime for Harry; All Men Are Enemies; Hell in Heavens; Love Time; Ever since Eve. 1935 Mutiny on the Bounty; Black Sheep; The Perfect Gentlemen; The Widow from Monte Carlo; Ladies Love Danger; King of Burlesque; David Copperfield. 1936 Charlie Chan's Secret; A Message to Garcia; Under Two Flags; Tarzan Escapes; Champagne Charlie. 1937 Another Dawn; You Can't Beat Love; Angel. 1938 The Adventures of Robin Hood; Lord Jeff; Invisible Enemy; Exposed. 1939 Society Lawyer.

MUNI, PAUL (Muni Weisenfreund)
Born: Sept. 22, 1895, Austria or Poland. Died: Aug. 25, 1967, Montecito, Calif.(heart trouble). Screen, stage, vaudeville, and burlesque actor. Won Academy Award in 1936 for Best Actor in The Story of Louis Pasteur.

Appeared in: 1929 The Valiant (film debut); Seven Faces. 1932 I Am a Fugitive from a Chain Gang; Scarface. 1933 The World Changes. 1934 Hi, Nellie. 1935 Bordertown; Dr. Socrates; Black Fury. 1936 The Story of Louis Pasteur. 1937 The Good Earth; The Life of Emile Zola; The Woman I Love. 1938 For Auld Lang Syne (short); Rasputin. 1939 Juarez.

MUNIER, FERDINAND
Born: Dec. 3, 1889, San Diego, Calif. or Boston, Mass.? Died: May 27, 1945, Hollywood, Calif.(heart attack). Screen, stage, radio, and vaudeville actor.

Appeared in: 1923 The Broken Wing. 1931 Ambassador Bill. 1932 Stepping Sister; After Tomorrow. 1933 The Woman I Stole; Queen Christina; The Bowery; Kickin' the Crown Around (short). 1934 The Barretts of Wimpole Street; Love and Hisses (short); Babes in Toyland; The Merry Widow; Count of Monte Christo. 1935 Roberta; Clive of India; The Gilded Lily; China Seas; His Family Tree; Follies Bergere; Page Miss Glory; Hands across the Table; Harmony Lane; Two Sinners; Top Flat (short). 1936 One Rainy Afternoon; The White Legion; Can This Be Dixie?; The Bold Caballero; The White Angel. 1937 Tovarich; Damaged Goods. 1938 Marriage Forbidden; The Great Waltz; Going Places. 1939 Midnight; Everything Happens at Night. 1941 Model Wife. 1942 Invisible Agent; Commandos Strike at Dawn; Tennessee Johnson. 1943 Claudia. 1945 Diamond Horseshoe. 1950 Revenge Is Sweet (reissue of Babes in Toyland, 1934 film).

MUNIZ, JUAN DE DIOS
Born: 1906. Died: Oct. 1951, Madrid, Spain. Screen and stage actor. Dubbed Spanish voice of Spencer Tracy.

MUNSHIN, JULES
Born: 1915, New York, N.Y. Died: Feb. 19, 1970, N.Y.(heart attack). Screen and stage actor.

Appeared in: 1948 Easter Parade. 1949 On the Town; Take Me Out to the Ball Game; That Midnight Kiss. 1954 Monte Carlo Baby. 1957 Silk Stockings; Ten Thousand Bedrooms. 1964 Wild and Wonderful. 1967 Monkeys, Go Home!.

MUNSON, ONA (Ona Wolcott)
Born: June 16, 1903, Portland, Oreg. Died: Feb. 11, 1955, New York, N.Y.(suicide—sleeping pills). Screen, stage, vaudeville, and radio actress. Received Academy Award nomination in 1939 for Best Supporting Actress in Gone with the Wind.

Appeared in: 1928 Head of the Family. 1931 Going Wild; The Hot Heiress; The Collegiate Model (short); Broadminded; Five Star Final. 1938 His Exciting Night. 1939 Gone with the Wind; Legion of Lost Flyers. 1940 The Big Guy; Wagons Westward; Scandal Sheet. 1941 Lady from Louisiana; Wild Geese Calling; The Shanghai Gesture. 1942 Drums of the Congo. 1943 Idaho. 1945 Dakota; The Cheaters. 1946 The Magnificent Rogue. 1947 The Red House.

MURA, CORRINE (Corinna Wall)
Born: 1910. Died: Aug. 1, 1965, Mexico City, Mexico (cancer). Screen, stage, radio actress, and singer.

Appeared in: 1942 Call Out the Marines. 1943 Casablanca. 1944 Passage to Marseille. 1945 The Gay Senorita. 1947 Honeymoon.

MURPHY, ADA
Born: 1888. Died: Aug. 25, 1961, Encino, Calif. Screen actress. Entered films in 1915.

MURPHY, AUDIE
Born: June 20, 1924, Kingston, Tex. Died: May 21, 1971, near Roanoke, Va.(plane crash). Screen, television actor, and author. Most decorated hero of W.W. II. Divorced from screen actress Wanda Hendrix.

Appeared in: 1948 Beyond Glory (film debut); Texas, Brooklyn and Heaven. 1949 Bad Boy. 1950 Sierra; The Kid from Texas; Kansas Raiders. 1951 The Cimarron Kid; The Red Badge of Courage. 1952 Duel at Silver Creek. 1953 Gunsmoke; Column South; Tumbleweed. 1954 Ride Clear of Diablo; Drums across the River; Destry. 1955 To Hell and Back. 1956 World in My Corner; Walk the Proud Land. 1957 Guns of Fort Petticoat; Joe Butterfly; Night Passage. 1958 Ride a Crooked Trail; The Gun Runner; The Quiet American. 1959 No Name on the Bullet; Cast a Long Shadow; The Wild and the Innocent. 1960 Hell Bent for Leather; The Unforgiven; Seven Ways from Sundown. 1961 Posse from Hell; The Battle at Bloody Beach. 1962 Six Black Horses. 1963 Showdown; Gunfight at Comanche Creek. 1964 The Quick Gun; Bullet for a Badman; Apache Rifles; War Is Hell (narr.).

1965 Arizona Raiders. 1966 Gunpoint; The Texican. 1967 Forty Guns to Apache Pass; Trunk to Cairo. 1969 A Time for Dying (cameo).

MURPHY, CHARLES B.
Born: 1884. Died: June 11, 1942, Bakersfield, Calif.(accident on location of Lost Canyon). Screen actor.

Appeared in: 1921 The Man of the Forest; The Rowdy; The Man Tamer. 1922 Golden Dreams; The Gray Dawn. 1923 Single Handed; Red Lights. 1937 County Fair. 1938 The Road to Reno. 1942 Lost Canyon.

MURPHY, JOHN DALY
Born: 1873, Ireland. Died: Nov. 20, 1934, New York, N.Y.(heart attack). Screen and stage actor.

Appeared in: 1918 Our Mrs. McChesney. 1921 Thunderclap. 1922 Polly of the Follies. 1923 The Truth about Wives; You Can't Fool Your Wife. 1924 Icebound.

MURPHY, JOSEPH J.
Born: 1877. Died: July 31, 1961, San Jose, Calif. Screen actor. One of the original Keystone Kops. Also portrayed "Andy Gump" on the screen.

MURPHY, ROBERT "BOB"
Born: 1889. Died: Aug. 6, 1948, Santa Monica, Calif.(pneumonia). Screen and vaudeville actor.

Appeared in: 1935 Broadway Gondolier. 1936 The Case against Mrs. Ames; Hideaway Girl; Two in a Crowd. 1937 Nancy Steele Is Missing; Portia on Trial; You're a Sweetheart. 1938 Girl of the Golden West; In Old Chicago. 1944 Shine on Harvest Moon.

MURRAY, CHARLIE (Charles Murray)
Born: June 22, 1872, Laurel, Ind. Died: July 29, 1941, Hollywood, Calif.(pneumonia). Screen, stage, and vaudeville actor. Entered films with Biograph Co. in 1912. He was Murray of the vaudeville team "Murray & Mack." Mack was Oliver Trumbull (dec. 1934). In the Keystone comedies, Murray was the Hogan characterization; and in later years, he was the Kelly of "The Cohens and the Kellys" series.

Appeared in: 1914 The Passing of Izzy; A Fatal Flirtation; Her Friend the Bandit; Love and Bullets (reissued as The Trouble Mender); Soldiers of Misfortune; The Great Toe Mystery; She's a Cook (reissued as The Bungling Burglars); The Masquerader; The Anglers; Stout Heart but Weak Knees; Cursed by His Beauty; His Talented Wife; The Noise of Bombs; His Halted Career; The Plumber; Tillie's Punctured Romance; Hogan's Annual Spree; His Second Childhood; The Fatal Bumping; Mabel's Married Life; A Missing Bride; A Gambling Rube. 1915 Hogan's Wild Cats; Hogan's Mussy Job; Hogan the Porter; Hogan's Romance Upset; Hogan's Aristocratic Dream; Hogan Out West; From Patches to Plenty; The Beauty Bunglers; Their Social Splash; Those College Girls; A Game Old Knight; Her Painted Hero; The Great Vacuum Robbery; Only a Farmer's Daughter. 1916 His Hereafter; Fido's Fate; The Judge; A Love Riot; Her Marble Heart; Pills of Peril; The Feathered Nest (aka Girl Guardian); Maid Mad; Bombs. 1917 Maggie's First False Step; Her Fame and Shame; The Betrayal of Maggie; His Precious Life; A Bedroom Blunder. 1918 Watch Your Neighbor. 1921 A Small Town Idol; Home Talent. 1922 The Crossroads of New York. 1923 Luck; Bright Lights of Broadway. 1924 Empty Hearts; Lilies of the Field; The Girl in the Limousine; The Fire Patrol; The Mine with the Iron Door; Fool's Highway; Painted People; Sundown. 1925 My Son; Who Cares; Classified; Fighting the Flames; White Fang; Paint and Powder; Percy; Why Women Love; The Wizard of Oz. 1926 The Cohens and the Kellys; Irene; The Boob; Mismates; Subway Sadie; Her Second Chance; Mike; Paradise; The Reckless Lady; Steel Preferred; The Silent Lover; Sweet Daddies. 1927 McFadden's Flats; The Gorilla; The Life of Riley; Lost at the Front; The Poor Nut; The Masked Woman. 1928 The Head Man; Flying Romeos; The Cohens and the Kellys in Paris; Do Your Duty; Vamping Venus. 1930 Clancy in Wall Street; Around the Corner; Cohens and the Kellys in Scotland; The King of Jazz; The Duke of Dublin; His Honor the Mayor; The Cohens and the Kellys in Africa; 10 Universal shorts. 1931 Caught Cheating. 1932 The Cohens and the Kellys in Hollywood. Hypnotized. 1933 The Cohens and the Kellys in Trouble. 1936 Dangerous Waters. 1937 Circus Girl. 1938 Breaking the Ice.

MURRAY, DAVID MITCHELL
Born: 1853. Died: Oct. 20, 1923, Long Island, N.Y. Screen and stage actor.

Appeared in: 1924 The Silent Watcher.

MURRAY, EDGAR
Born: 1865. Died: Oct. 31, 1932, Hollywood, Calif.(complication of diseases). Screen actor.

MURRAY, EDGAR
Born: 1892. Died: Oct. 16, 1959, Hollywood, Calif.(heart attack). Screen actor. Married to stage actress Nadia Popkova. Entered films with Vitagraph.

MURRAY, ELIZABETH M.
Born: 1871. Died: Mar. 27, 1946, Philadelphia, Pa. Screen, stage, and vaudeville actress.

Appeared in: 1923 Little Old New York. 1929 Lucky in Love. 1931 The Bachelor Father.

MURRAY, J. HAROLD
Born: Feb. 17, 1891, South Berwick, Maine. Died: Dec. 11, 1940, Killingworth, Conn. Screen, stage, and vaudeville actor.

Appeared in: 1929 Married in Hollywood. 1930 Cameo Kirby; Happy Days; Women Everywhere. 1937 Universal and RKO shorts.

MURRAY, JACK (John W. B. Murray)
Died: May 1, 1941, Bronx, N.Y. Screen, stage, vaudeville, burlesque, and radio actor.

MURRAY, JAMES
Born: Feb. 9, 1901, New York, N.Y. Died: July 11, 1936, New York, N.Y.(drowned in Hudson River). Screen and stage actor.

Appeared in: 1922 When Knighthood Was in Flower. 1923 The Pilgrims. 1927 In Old Kentucky; The Last Outlaw; The Lovelorn; Stark Love; Rough House Rosie. 1928 The Crowd; Rose Marie; The Big City. 1929 The Little Wildcat; The Shakedown; Thunder; Shanghai Lady. 1930 Hide-Out; The Rampant Age. 1931 Kick In; In Line of Duty; Bright Lights. 1932 The Reckoning; Bachelor Mother. 1933 Air Hostess; Heroes for Sale; Frisco Jenny; High Gear; Central Airport; Baby Face; Peerless. 1935 $20 a Week; Skull and Crown; Ship Cafe.

MURRAY, JEAN
Born: Sydney, Nova Scotia, Canada. Died: Oct. 5, 1966, Winnipeg, Canada. Screen, stage, and radio actress.

MURRAY, JOHN T.
Born: 1886, Australia. Died: Feb. 12, 1957, Woodland Hills, Calif. (stroke). Screen and vaudeville actor. Married to screen actress Vivian Oakland (dec. 1958). They appeared in vaudeville as "John T. Murray and Vivian Oakland" and also made several shorts together during 1929-30.

Appeared in: 1924 Madonna of the Streets. 1925 Joanna; Sally; Stop Flirting; Winds of Chance. 1926 High Steppers; Bardely's the Magnificent. 1927 Finger Prints; The Gay Old Bird. 1928 Fazil. 1929 Sonny Boy; Honky Tonk, plus the following shorts billed as "John T. Murray and Vivian Oakland": Satires; The Hall of Injustice. 1930 Personality; Night Work and the following shorts with his wife: Who Pays; The Servant Problems. 1931 Charlie Chan Carries On; Young as You Feel; Alexander Hamilton. 1932 Man Called Back; Vanity Comedies shorts. 1933 Keyhold Kati-e (short). 1934 Air Maniacs (short); Love Birds. 1935 Great God Gold. 1936 Here Comes Carter. 1937 The Lost Horizon; Ever since Eve; True Confession; Girl Loves Boy; Sweetheart of the Navy. 1938 Gang Bullets; Violent Is the Word for Curly (short). 1939 The Hardys Ride High; Andy Hardy Gets Spring Fever.

MURRAY, JULIAN "BUD"
Born: Nov. 21, 1888, New York, N.Y. Died: Nov. 1, 1952, West Los Angeles, Calif.(cerebral hemorrhage). Screen actor, stage dance director, and film dance director.

MURRAY, LOLA
Born: 1914. Died: Nov. 11, 1961, Shrewsbury, N.J. Screen actress.

MURRAY, MAE (Marie Adrienne Koenig)
Born: Apr. 10, 1890, Portsmouth, Va. Died: Mar. 23, 1965, Woodland Hills, Calif.(heart condition). Screen, stage actress, and dancer. Divorced from screen actor/film director Robert Z. Leonard (dec. 1968).

Appeared in: 1916 To Have and To Hold (film debut); Honor Thy Name; Sweet Kitty Bellairs; The Dream Girl. 1918 Modern Love; Her Body in Bond. 1919 The Bride's Awakening; What Am I Bid; The Delicious Little Devil; Blind Husbands. 1920 On with the

Dance; The Right to Love; The Mormon Maid. 1921 The Gilded Lily; Idols of Clay. 1922 Fascination; Peacock Alley; Broadway Rose. 1923 The French Doll; Jazzmania; Fashion Row. 1924 Madamoiselle Midnight; Married Flirts; Circe, the Enchantress. 1925 The Masked Bride; The Merry Widow. 1927 Valencia; Alters of Desire. 1928 Show People. 1930 Peacock Alley (and 1922 version). 1931 Bachelor Apartment; High Stakes.

MURRAY, MARION
Born: 1885. Died: Nov. 11, 1951, New York, N.Y. Screen actress. Entered films during silents. Married to screen actor Jed Prouty (dec. 1956).

Appeared in: 1942 Paris Calling. 1948 The Pirate.

MURRAY, THOMAS
Born: 1902. Died: Nov. 20, 1961, Hollywood, Calif.(heart attack). Screen actor.

MURRAY, TOM
Born: 1875. Died: Aug. 27, 1935, Hollywood, Calif. Screen, vaudeville, and radio actor.

Appeared in: 1922 French Hells; The Ladder Jinx; Too Much Business. 1923 The Pilgrim; The Meanest Man in the World. 1925 The Business of Love; The Gold Rush. 1926 Private Izzy Murphy; Tramp, Tramp, Tramp; Into Her Kingdom.

MURRAY, "UNCLE". See Murray Parker

MURRAY-HILL, PETER
Born: Apr. 20, 1908, Bushy Heath, Herts, England. Died: 1957. Screen and stage actor. Divorced from screen actress Phillis Calvert.

Appeared in: 1935 Mr. Reeder in Room 13 (film debut). 1938 A Yank at Oxford. 1939 The Outsider. 1940 Jane Steps Out. 1941 The Ghost Train. 1944 Madonna of the Seven Moons. 1945 They Were Sisters. 1954 House of the Arrow.

MURROW, EDWARD R.
Born: Apr. 25, 1908, Greensboro, N.C. Died: Apr. 27, 1965, Pawling, N.Y. Radio, television, and screen actor.

Appeared in: 1943 Siege of Leningrad (narr.). 1956 Around the World in 80 Days. 1958 Satchmo the Great (narr.). 1960 Sink the Bismarck.

MURTH, FLORENCE
Born: 1902. Died: Mar. 29, 1934, Los Angeles, Calif. Screen actress. Appeared in early Sennett and Christie comedies.

Appeared in: 1922 Thundering Hoofs.

MUSIDORA (Jeanne Roques)
Born: 1889, France. Died: Dec. 1957, Paris, France. Screen, stage actress, and film director. Became celebrated for her work in two 12-episode serials, Les Vampires and Judex.

MUSSELMAN, JOHNSON J.
Born: 1890. Died: Apr. 8, 1958, Louisville, Ky. Magician and screen and vaudeville actor. Known as "Aska the Magician."

MUSSEY, FRANCINE
Born: France. Died: Mar. 26, 1933, Paris, France (suicide—poison). Screen actress.

Appeared in: 1932 La ronde des Heures.

MUSSON, BENNET
Born: 1866. Died: Feb. 17, 1946, Amityville, N.Y. Screen and stage actor.

Appeared in: 1921 White Oak.

MUZQUIZ, CARLOS
Born: 1906, Mexico. Died: Feb., 1960, Mexico City, Mexico. Screen actor. Known as "Compadre Muzquiz."

Appeared in: 1950 Hidden River. 1951 My Outlaw Brother. 1955 A Life in the Balance. 1957 The Sun Also Rises; The Black Scorpion.

MYERS, HARRY
Born: 1886, Philadelphia, Pa. or New Haven, Conn.? Died: Dec. 26, 1938, Los Angeles, Calif.(pneumonia). Screen and stage actor. Married to screen actress Rosemary Theby.

Appeared in: 1908 The Guerrilla. 1909 Her First Biscuits; "The Jonesy Pictures". 1911 Her Two Sons. 1916 Housekeeping (first Myers and Thelby film in series made from 1916 to April 1917). 1919 The Masked Rider (serial). 1920 Peaceful Valley. 1921 A Connecticut Yankee in King Arthur's Court; On the High Card; The March Hare; Nobody's Fool; Oh, Mary Be Careful; R.S.V.P. 1922 The Beautiful and Damned; The Adventures of Robinson Crusoe (serial); Boy Crazy; Handle with Care; Kisses; Turn to the Right; Top O' the Morning; When the Lad Comes Home. 1923 The Bad Man; Stephen Steps Out; Brass; Brass Bottle; Little Johnny Jones; The Printer's Devil; The Common Law; Main Street. 1924 Behold This Woman; Daddies; Listen, Lester; Reckless Romance; The Marriage Circle; Tarnish. 1925 Grounds for Divorce; She Wolves; Zander the Great. 1926 Exit Smiling; Up in Mabel's Room; The Beautiful Cheat; Monte Carlo; Nut Cracker. 1927 Getting Gertie's Garter; The Girl in the Pullman; The Bachelor's Baby; The First Night. 1928 The Dove; The Street of Illusion; Dream of Love. 1929 The Clean Up; Montmartre Rose; Wonder of Women. 1931 City Lights; Meet the Wife. 1932 The Savage Girl. 1933 Police Call; The Important Witness; Strange Adventure. 1935 Mississippi. 1936 Hollywood Boulevard. 1937 Dangerous Lives.

MYERS, ROBERT FRANCIS
Born: 1925. Died: July 18, 1962, Hollywood, Calif.(murdered—stabbed). Screen, stage actor, and cab driver.

NAGEL, ANNE (Ann Dolan)
Born: Sept. 30, 1912, Boston, Mass. Died: July 6, 1966, Los Angeles, Calif.(cancer). Screen and stage actress.

Appeared in: 1933 I Loved You Wednesday (film debut); College Humor. 1934 Stand up and Cheer. 1936 Hot Money; China Clipper; King of Hockey; Here Comes Carter; Love Begins at Twenty. 1937 Guns of the Pecos; The Case of the Stuttering Bishop; Footloose Heiress; Three Legionnaires; The Hoosier Schoolboy; A Bride for Henry; Escape by Night; The Adventurous Blonde; She Loved a Fireman. 1938 Saleslady; Under the Big Top; Gang Bullets; Mystery House. 1939 Convict's Code; Unexpected Father; Call a Messenger; Legion of Lost Flyers; Should a Girl Marry? 1940 Black Friday; Ma, He's Making Eyes at Me; Winners of the West (serial); Hot Steel; My Little Chickadee; Argentine Nights; Diamond Frontier; The Green Hornet (serial); The Green Hornet Strikes Again (serial). 1941 Road Agent; The Invisible Woman; Meet the Chump; Man-Made Monster; Mutiny in the Arctic; Don Winslow of the Navy (serial); Sealed Lips; Never Give a Sucker an Even Break. 1942 The Mad Doctor of Market St; Dawn Express; Nazi Spy Ring; Stagecoach Buckaroo; The Secret Code (serial). 1943 Women in Bondage. 1946 Murder in the Music Hall; Traffic in Crime. 1947 Blondie's Holiday; The Trap; The Spirit of West Point. 1948 Don't Trust Your Husband. 1949 Prejudice.

NAGEL, CONRAD
Born: Mar. 16, 1897, Keokuk, Iowa. Died: Feb. 24, 1970, New York, N.Y. Screen, stage, radio, television actor, and film director. In 1940 he received a Special Academy Award Oscar for his work on the Motion Picture Relief Fund.

Appeared in: 1918 Little Women. 1920 The Fighting Chance; Midsummer Madness. 1921 What Every Woman Knows; The Lost Romance; A Fool's Paradise; Sacred and Profane Love. 1922 The Impossible Mrs. Bellew; Nice People; Hate; The Ordeal; Saturday Night; Singed Wings. 1923 The Rendezvous; Lawful Larceny; Bella Donna; Grumpy. 1924 Three Weeks; Tess of the D'Urbervilles; The Snob; Married Flirts; Name the Man; The Rejected Woman; Sinners in Silk; So This Is Marriage. 1925 Sun-Up; The Only Thing; Cheaper to Marry; Pretty Ladies; Lights of Old Broadway; Excuse Me. 1926 The Waning Sex; Tin Hats; The Exquisite Sinner; Memory Lane; Dance Madness; There You Are. 1927 Quality Street; The Hypnotist; Slightly Used; The Jazz Singer; Heaven on Earth; The Girl from Chicago; If I Were Single; London after Midnight. 1928 The Mysterious Lady; Glorious Betsy; Caught in the Fog; The Terror; Tenderloin; Diamond Handcuffs; The Michigan Kid; State Street Sadie; The Divine Woman. 1929 Dynamite; Red Wine; The Idle Rich; Kid Gloves; The Kiss; Thirteenth Chair; The Sacred Flame; Hollywood Revue of 1929; The Redeeming Sin. 1930 Redemption; The Ship from Shanghai; Numbered Men; Second Wife; DuBarry, Woman of Passion; One Romantic Night; A Lady Surrenders; Free Love; The Divorcee; Today. 1931 The Right of Way; East Lynne; Bad Sister; The Reckless Hour; Son of India; Three Who Loved; Hell Divers; The Pagan Lady. 1932 The Man Called Back; Divorce in the Family; Kongo; Fast Life. 1933 The Constant Woman; Ann Vickers. 1934 Dangerous Corner; Marines Are Coming. 1935 One Hour Late; Death Flies East; One New York Night. 1936 Wedding Present; Yellow Cargo; Girl from Mandalay. 1937 Navy Spy; The Gold Racket. 1939 The Mad Express. 1940 I Want a Divorce; One Million B.C. (narr.). 1944 They Shall Have Faith; Dangerous Money (narr.). 1945 The Adventures of Rusty; Forever Yours. 1947 The Vicious

Circle. 1948 Stage Struck; The Woman in Brown. 1949 Dynamite. 1955 All That Heaven Allows. 1957 Hidden Fear. 1959 Stranger in My Arms; The Man Who Understood Women.

NAIDOO, BOBBY
Born: 1927, South Africa. Died: July 6, 1967, London, England. Screen, stage, and television actor.

Appeared in: 1962 Nine Hours to Rama.

NALDI, NITA (Anita Donna Dooley)
Born: Apr. 1, 1899, New York, N.Y. Died: Feb. 17, 1961, New York, N.Y. Screen, stage, and television actress.

Appeared in: 1920 Dr. Jekyll and Mr. Hyde. 1921 Experience, A Divorce of Convenience; The Last Door. 1922 Blood and Sand; Anna Ascends; Channing of the Northwest; The Man from Beyond; The Snitching Hour; Reported Missing. 1923 The Glimpses of the Moon; Lawful Larceny; The Ten Commandments; You Can't Fool Your Wife; Hollywood. 1924 A Sainted Devil; The Breaking Point; Don't Call It Love. 1925 Clothes Make the Pirate; Cobra; The Lady Who Lied; The Marriage Whirl. 1926 The Unfair Sex; The Miracle of Life. 1928 What Price Beauty?

NAMU
Died: July 1966, Seattle, Wash.(drowned). Screen whale actor. The first killer whale to become a film star.

Appeared in: 1966 Namu, the Killer Whale.

NARES, OWEN
Born: Aug. 11, 1888, Maiden Erlegh, England. Died: July 30, 1943, Brecon, Wales. Screen and stage actor. Entered films in 1913.

Appeared in: 1914 Dandy Donovan. 1918 God Bless the Red, White and Blue. 1923 Indian Love Lyrics; Young Lochinvar. 1927 The Sorrows of Satan. 1928 Milestones. 1930 Loose Ends. 1931 Frail Women; Aren't We All (U.S. 1932); The Middle Watch. 1932 The Impassive Footman (aka Woman in Chains); The Woman Decides; The Love Contract; There Goes the Bride; Sunshine Susie; Where Is This Lady?; Discord; Office Girl. 1934 The Private Life of Don Juan. 1935 I Give My Heart. 1937 The Show Goes On. 1938 The Loves of Madame DuBarry. 1941 The Prime Minister.

NARVAEZ, SARA
Born: Nicaragua. Died: Dec. 1935, Mexico City, Mexico. Screen, stage, vaudeville, and radio actress.

NASH, EUGENIA
Born: 1866. Died: Apr. 8, 1937, Culver City, Calif. Screen actress. Mother of screen actor Ted Healy (dec. 1937).

NASH, FLORENCE
Born: 1888, Troy, N.Y. Died: Apr. 2, 1950, Los Angeles, Calif. Screen, stage, and vaudeville actress. Sister of screen actress Mary Nash (dec. 1966).

Appeared in: 1939 The Women.

NASH, GEORGE FREDERICK
Born: 1873. Died: Dec. 31, 1944, Amityville, N.Y. Screen and stage actor. Married to stage actress Julia Hay (dec. 1937).

Appeared in: 1922 The Face in the Fog; The Valley of Silent Men; When Knighthood Was in Flower. 1923 Under the Red Robe. 1924 The Confidence Man; Janice Meredith. 1925 A Man Must Live. 1926 The Great Gatsby; The Song and Dance Man. 1933 Oliver Twist; Fighting Texans; Phantom Broadcast. 1934 Sixteen Fathoms Deep; Mystery Liner; Blue Steel; City Limits.

NASH, MARY
Born: Aug. 15, 1885, Troy, N.Y. Died: 1966. Screen and stage actress. Sister of screen actress Florence Nash (dec. 1950).

Appeared in: 1934 Uncertain Lady (film debut). 1935 College Scandal. 1936 Come and Get It. 1937 The King and the Chorus Girl; Easy Living; Wells Fargo; Heidi. 1939 The Little Princess; The Rains Came. 1940 Charlie Chan in Panama; Sailor's Lady; Gold Rush Maisie; The Philadelphia Story. 1941 Men of Boys Town. 1942 Calling Dr. Gillespie. 1943 The Human Comedy. 1944 Cobra Woman; The Lady and the Monster; In the Meantime, Darling. 1945 Yolanda and the Thief. 1946 Monsieur Beaucaire; Swell Guy; 'Til the Clouds Roll By.

NATHEAUX, LOUIS
Born: 1898, Pine Bluff, Ark. Died: Aug. 23, 1942, Los Angeles, Calif. Screen actor.

Appeared in: 1921 Passing Thru. 1922 The Super Sex. 1924 The Fast Set. 1926 Man Bait; Risky Business; Sunny Side Up. 1927 The Country Doctor; Dress Parade; Harp in Hock; Fighting Love; King of Kings; My Friend from India; Turkish Delight. 1928 Stand and Deliver; Midnight Madness; A Ship Comes In; Tenth Avenue; The Cop; Four Walls; Stool Pigeons; Ned McCobb's Daughter. 1929 Broadway Babies; Weary River; Why Be Good?; Girls Gone Wild; Mexicali Rose. 1930 Madame Satan; Big Money; The Big House; The Squealer; Lightnin'; This Mad World; Murder on the Roof. 1931 Secret Six; Bad Girl; Transatlantic; Young as You Feel; Reckless Living; Street Scene. 1932 Behind the Mask. 1933 Gambling Ship. 1935 Freckles; Slightly Static (short); Hot Money (short). 1936 Murder on the Roof; Modern Times; Captain Calamity; Yours for the Asking; Go Get-'Em Haines. 1937 Missing Witnesses.

NATRO, JIMMY
Born: 1908. Died: Jan. 31, 1946, Los Angeles, Calif. Screen actor.

NAVARRO, CARLOS
Born: Feb. 24, 1922, Mexico. Died: Feb. 13, 1969, Mexico City, Mexico. Screen and television actor.

Appeared in: 1956 The Brave One. 1962 La Estrella Vacia (The Empty Star). Other Mexican film: Dona Perfecta.

NAVARRO, JESUS GARCIA
Born: 1913, Mexico. Died: Sept. 1960, Mexico City, Mexico (heart attack). Screen and stage actor. Appeared in approx. 90 Mexican films.

Appeared in: 1952 The Young and the Damned.

NAZIMOVA, ALLA
Born: May 22, 1879, Yalta, Crimea, Russia. Died: July 13, 1945, Los Angeles, Calif.(coronary thrombosis). Screen, stage actress, film producer, and screenwriter. Divorced from screen actor Charles Bryant (dec. 1948).

Appeared in: 1916 War Brides (film debut). 1918 Revelation, Eye for Eye; Toys of Fate. 1919 The Red Lantern; The Brat; Out of the Fog. 1920 Stronger Than Death; Billions; Heart of a Child. 1921 Madame Peacock; Camille. 1922 A Doll's House. 1923 Salome. 1924 The Madonna of the Streets. 1925 My Son; The Redeeming Sin. 1940 Escape. 1941 Blood and Sand. 1943 Song of Bernadette. 1944 Since You Went Away; In Our Time; The Bridge of San Luis Rey.

NEAL, FRANK
Born: 1917. Died: May 8, 1955, Astoria, N.Y.(auto accident). Negro screen actor and dancer.

Appeared in: 1943 Stormy Weather. 1955 Three in the Round (short).

NEDELL, ALICE BLAKENEY
Died: Oct. 21, 1959, Hollywood, Calif. Screen, stage, and television actress. Married to screen actor Bernard Nedell (dec. 1972).

NEGRETE, JORGE
Born: 1911, Mexico. Died: Dec. 5, 1953, Los Angeles, Calif. (cirrhosis of liver). Mexican screen, stage, and singer/actor.

Appeared in: 1938 La Madrina del Diablo (The Devil's Godmother). 1939 Perjura; El Cemetario de las Aquilas (The Eagles' Cemetery); Juntos Pero No Revueltos (United but Not Mixed). 1943 Silk, Blood and Sun; Ay Jalisco No te Rajes; Asi Se Quiere En Jalisco. 1944 Tierra de Pasiones.

NEILAN, MARSHALL
Born: 1891, San Bernardino, Calif. Died: Oct. 26, 1958, Woodland Hills, Calif.(cancer). Screen actor, film director, film producer, and screenwriter. Appeared in Ruth Roland films. Divorced from actress Blanche Sweet.

Appeared in: 1912 The Stranger at Coyote. 1913 Judith of Bethulia. 1915 Madam Butterfly. 1916 The Crisis. 1923 Broadway Gold; Souls for Sale. 1957 A Face in the Crowd.

NEILL, JAMES
Born: 1861, Savannah, Ga. Died: Mar. 16, 1931, Glendale, Calif. (heart trouble). Screen and stage actor. Married to screen actress Edythe Chapman (dec. 1948).

Appeared in: 1917 The Bottle Imp. 1919 Men, Women and Money; Everywoman. 1920 The Paliser Case. 1921 Bits of Life; Dangerous Curve Ahead; A Voice in the Dark. 1922 Dusk to Dawn; The Heart Specialist; Her Husband's Trademark; Our Leading

Citizen; Saturday Night; Manslaughter. 1923 The Thrill Chaser; Ten Commandments; The Lonely Road; Nobody's Money; Salomy Jane; Scars of Jealousy; The World's Applause. 1924 A Man's Mate. 1925 Any Woman; The Crimson Runner; New Brooms; Thank You. 1926 A Desperate Moment. 1927 King of Kings. 1928 The Border Patrol; Love Hungry; Three-Ring Marriage. 1929 Idle Rich. 1930 Shooting Straight; Only the Brave. 1931 Man to Man.

NEILL, RICHARD R.
Born: 1876, Philadelphia, Pa. Died: Apr. 8, 1970, Woodland Hills, Calif. Screen and stage actor.

Appeared in: 1914 The Active Life of Dolly of the Dailies (serial). 1919 The Great Gamble (serial). 1920 The Whirlwind (serial). 1922 Go Get 'Em Hutch (serial); Jan of the Big Snows. 1923 A Clouded Name; Sinner or Saint. 1924 Trail of the Law; The Heritage of the Desert; Wanderer of the Wasteland; The Fighting Coward. 1925 Tumbleweeds; Peggy of the Secret Service; Percy. 1926 Born to the West; Whispering Smith; Satan Town. 1927 Bulldog Pluck; Galloping Thunder; Code of the Cow Country; The Fightin' Comeback; King of Kings; Somewhere in Sonora; The Trunk Mystery. 1928 Beyond the Sierras; The Law's Lash; The Desert of the Lost; The Bushranger.

NEILSEN-TERRY, DENNIS
Born: 1895. Died: July 12, 1932, Bulawayo, South Africa (double pneumonia). Screen, stage actor, stage producer, and stage manager. Son of screen actor Fred Terry (dec, 1933) and stage actress Julia Neilsen.

NELL, MRS. LOUISE M.
Born: 1884. Died: Nov. 1, 1944, Los Angeles, Calif.(killed—bus). Screen and stage actress.

NELSON, ANNE
Born: 1911. Died: July 6, 1948, Torrance, Calif. Screen actress.

NELSON, EDDIE "SUNKIST"
Born: 1894. Died: Dec. 5, 1940, Hollywood, Calif.(heart attack). Screen and vaudeville actor.

Appeared in: 1928 Stop and Go (short).

NELSON, HAROLD
Died: Jan. 26, 1937, Los Angeles, Calif.(pneumonia). Screen actor.

Appeared in: 1928 Sisters of Eve.

NELSON, LOTTIE
Born: 1875. Died: May 8, 1966, Hollywood, Calif.(stroke). Screen actress. Appeared in silents.

NESBIT, EVELYN. See Evelyn Nesbit Thaw

NESS, OLE M.
Born: 1888. Died: July 19, 1953, North Hollywood, Calif. Screen actor.

Appeared in: 1928 Chicago after Midnight; The Price of Fear; Skinner's Big Idea; Danger Street; Hit of the Show. 1929 Jazz Heaven; Hardboiled. 1931 The Sin of Madelon Claudet. 1933 Dawn to Dawn. 1935 The Last Days of Pompeii.

NESTELL, BILL
Born: 1895. Died: Oct. 18, 1966, Bishop, Calif.(stroke-heart attack). Screen actor.

Appeared in: 1926 Sir Lumberjack. 1928 Cheyenne Trails; Texas Flash; The Thrill Chaser; When the Law Rides. 1929 The Trail of the Horse Thieves. 1930 The Fighting Legion; The Man from Nowhere.

NEU, OSCAR F.
Born: June 22, 1886, Buffalo, N.Y. Died: Aug. 26, 1957, Crestwood, N.Y. Screen, vaudeville actor, and film director. Neu toured in vaudeville with comedian Al Wilson. Appeared in silents from 1911 to 1912.

NEUSSER, ERIC
Born: 1902. Died: Aug. 30, 1957, Vienna, Austria.(heart attack). Screen actor and film producer. Appeared in German films.

NEVARO (Otto Willkomm)
Born: 1887. Died: Nov. 13, 1941, Milwaukee, Wisc. Screen actor and acrobat. Was part of acrobatic act billed as "Mareena, Nevaro and Mareena."

NEWALL, GUY
Born: 1885, England. Died: Feb. 25, 1937, London, England. Screen, stage actor, and film director. Entered films with London Film Co. in 1912.

Appeared in: 1918 Comradeship. 1919 The Garden of Resurrection. 1920 The Lure of Croning Water; The Duke's Son. 1922 Beauty and the Beast; Boy Woodburn. 1923 The Starlit Garden. 1927 The Ghost Train. 1930 The Eternal Feminine; The Marriage Bond. 1937 Grand Finale; Merry Comes to Town. Other British film: Rodney Steps In.

NEWBERRY, HAZZARD P.
Born: 1907. Died: May 27, 1952, Chicago, Ill. Screen and stage actor. Entered films approx. 1935.

NEWBURG, FRANK
Born: 1886. Died: Nov. 11, 1969, Woodland Hills, Calif. Screen and vaudeville actor. Entered films approx. 1912.

Appeared in: 1924 Abraham Lincoln. 1925 The Sign of the Cactus; The Home Maker; Smouldering Fires; Lorraine of the Lions. 1927 Fire and Steel. 1928 The Singapore Mutiny.

NEWCOMB, MARY
Born: 1894, North Adams, Mass. Died: Jan. 1967, Dorchester, England. Screen and stage actress. Divorced from screen actor Robert Edeson (dec. 1931).

Appeared in: 1921 The Passionate Pilgrim. 1932 Frail Women; Women Who Play.

NEWCOMBE, JESSAMINE
Born: London, England. Died: Mar. 15, 1961, Hollywood, Calif. Screen, stage, and radio actress.

NEWELL, WILLIAM "BILLY"
Born: 1894. Died: Feb. 21, 1967, Hollywood, Calif. Screen, stage, vaudeville, and television actor.

Appeared in: 1935 Riffraff. 1936 The Voice of Bugle Ann; Libeled Lady; Navy Born; Bulldog Edition; Sitting on the Moon; The Mandarin Mystery; Happy Go Lucky; A Man Betrayed. 1937 Larceny on the Air; Beware of Ladies; Bill Cracks down; Rhythm in the Clouds; Dangerous Holiday. 1938 Ride a Crooked Mile; Mr. Smith Goes to Washington. 1940 The Invisible Killer; Slightly Tempted; Mysterious Doctor Satan (serial); Fugitive from Justice; Hold That Woman. 1941 Caught in the Act; The Bride Came C.O.D.; Miss Polly. 1942 Keeper of the Flame; A Tragedy at Midnight; Who Is Hope Schuyler?; Get Hep to Love; Orchestra Wives; Priorities on Parade. 1944 Sing a Jingle; Kansas City Kitty. 1945 Captain Eddie; Her Lucky Night; Out of the Depths; Stork Club; The Dolly Sisters. 1946 Girl on the Spot. 1947 Key Witness; The Second Chance. 1948 Song of My Heart. 1949 The Lone Wolf and His Lady. 1950 Traveling Saleswoman. 1955 Our Miss Brooks. 1957 Short Cut to Hell. 1958 Tank Force; The Missouri Traveler. 1959 High Flight; The Man Inside. 1960 Who Was That Lady?; The High-Powered Rifle.

NEWHALL, MAYO
Born: 1890. Died: Dec. 11, 1958, Burbank, Calif. Screen actor.

Appeared in: 1944 Meet Me in St. Louis. 1945 Yolanda and the Thief; Her Highness and the Bellboy. 1946 Of Human Bondage. 1948 That Lady in Ermine.

NEWLAND, ANNA DEWEY
Born: 1881. Died: June 24, 1967, Hollywood, Calif. Screen actress, model, and author.

NEWMAN, ALFRED
Born: Mar. 17, 1901, New Haven, Conn. Died: Feb. 17, 1970, Los Angeles, Calif.(emphysema and complications). Composer, conductor, and screen actor.

Appeared in: 1939 They Shall Have Music.

NEWMAN, JOHN K.
Born: 1864. Died: Mar. 2, 1927, New York, N.Y. Screen and stage actor.

Appeared in: 1924 Greatest Love of All.

NEWMAN, NELL
Born: 1881. Died: Aug. 1931, Hollywood, Calif.(pneumonia). Screen actress.

NEWTON, CHARLES
Died: 1926. Screen and stage actor. Married to screen actress Dorrit Ashton (dec. 1936).

Appeared in: 1920 The Moon Riders (serial). 1921 Red Courage; Sure Fire; Action; High Gear Jeffrey; Colorado. 1922 The Loaded Door; Western Speed. 1923 Danger; In the Palace of the King. 1924 The Iron Horse; $50,000 Reward; Vanity's Price. 1925 Riders of the Purple Sage. 1926 Yellow Fingers; Western Pluck.

NEWTON, ROBERT
Born: June 1, 1905, Shaftesbury, Dorset, England. Died: Mar. 25, 1956, Beverly Hills, Calif.(heart attack). Screen, stage, and television actor. Voted one of top ten British moneymaking stars in Motion Picture Herald - Fame Poll, 1947-51.

Appeared in: 1937 Fire over England (film debut); Dark Journey; Farewell Again; The Squealer; Murder on Diamond Row. 1938 The Beachcomber; Vessel of Wrath; Yellow Sands; Troopship. 1939 Jamaica Inn; Dead Men Are Dangerous; 21 Days Together. 1940 Hell's Cargo; Haunted Honeymoon. 1941 Hatter's Castle; Major Barbara. 1942 Wings and the Woman; They Flew Alone. 1944 Gaslight; Henry V (U.S. 1946). 1947 Odd Man Out; The Deep End; This Happy Breed; The Green Cockatoo. 1948 Kiss the Blood off My Hands. 1949 Snowbound; Temptation Harbor. 1950 The Hidden Room (aka Obsession); Treasure Island. 1951 Oliver Twist; Soldiers Three; Tom Brown's School Days. 1952 Blackbeard the Pirate; Les Miserables; Waterfront Women; Angel Street. 1953 The Desert Rats; Androcles and the Lion. 1954 The High and the Mighty. 1955 Long John Silver; The Beachcomber. 1956 Around the World in 80 Days. 1958 Henry V (reissue of 1944 film). Other British films: London Life; Night Boat to Dublin.

NEWTON, THEODORE
Born: 1905, Lawrenceville, N.Y. Died: Feb. 23, 1963, Hollywood, Calif.(cancer). Screen, stage, and television actor.

Appeared in: 1933 The House on 56th Street; The Working Man; Voltaire; From Headquarters; Ace of Aces; The World Changes; The Sphinx. 1934 Gambling; Blind Date; Heat Lightning; Upperworld; Now I'll Tell; A Modern Hero; Let's Try Again. 1935 Jalna. 1945 The Hidden Eye; What Next, Corporal Hargrove? 1946 Two Years before the Mast; Miss Susie Slagle's. 1956 The Come On; The Proud and the Profane; Friendly Persuasion; Somebody up There Likes Me. 1959 The Story on Page One (U.S. 1960). 1963 Dime with a Halo.

NIBLO, FRED, SR. (Federico Nobile)
Born: Jan. 6, 1874, York, Neb. Died: Nov. 11, 1948, New Orleans, La.(pneumonia). Screen, stage, vaudeville actor, film and stage director, and stage producer. Father of screenwriter Fred Niblo, Jr. Married to screen actress Enid Bennett (dec. 1969).

Appeared in: 1930 Free and Easy. 1940 I'm Still Alive; Ellery Queen, Master Detective. 1941 Life with Henry.

NICHOLS, ERNEST LORING "RED"
Born: May 8, 1905, Ogden, Utah. Died: June 28, 1965, Las Vegas, Nev.(heart attack). Screen, television, radio actor, and bandleader.

Appeared in: 1929 Red Nichols and His Five Pennies (short). 1935 Melody Masters (short). 1936 Red Nichols and His World Famous Pennies (short).

NICHOLS, GEORGE, SR.
Born: 1865. Died: Sept. 20, 1927, Hollywood, Calif. Screen actor and film director. Father of screen actor/director George Nichols, Jr.(dec. 1939).

Appeared in: 1910 The Usurer. 1919 The Turn in the Road. 1920 The Greatest Question. 1921 The Fox; Live and Let Live; Shame; The Queen of Sheba; Molly O.; Oliver Twist, Jr. 1922 The Barnstormer; Don't Get Personal; Suzanna; The Pride of Palomar; The Flirt; One Glorious Day. 1923 Children of Dust; The Country Kid; Let's Go; The Miracle Makers; The Ghost Patrol; The Extra Girl; Don't Marry for Money. 1924 The Midnight Express; Secrets; The Beautiful Sinner; Daughters of Today; Geared to Go; The Red Lily; The Slanderers; East of Broadway; The Silent Stranger; The Silent Watcher. 1925 The Goose Woman; Capital Punishment; The Eagle; Proud Flesh; His Majesty, Bunker Bean; The Light of Western Stars. 1926 Bachelor Brides; Broken Hearts of Hollywood; The Timid Terror; Sea Horses; Senor Daredevil; Flames; Gigolo; Miss Nobody; Rolling Home. 1927 Ritzy; White Gold; White Flannels; Finger Prints. 1928 The Wedding March.

NICHOLS, GEORGE, JR.
Born: May 5, 1897, San Francisco, Calif. Died: Nov. 13, 1939, Los Angeles, Calif.(auto accident). Screen actor and film director. Son of screen actor/director George Nichols, Sr. (dec. 1927).

Appeared as a child actor in early Biograph films.

NICHOLS, MARGARET
Born: 1900. Died: Mar. 17, 1941, Los Angeles, Calif.(pneumonia). Screen actress. Married to film producer Hal Roach.

NICHOLS, MARJORIE J.
Died: Sept. 26, 1970, N.Y. Screen, stage, and television actress.

Appeared in: 1959 North by Northwest. 1961 Splendor in the Grass.

NICHOLS, NELLIE V.
Born: 1885. Died: July 16, 1971, Los Angeles, Calif. Screen and vaudeville actress.

Appeared in: 1930 Playing Around (film debut). 1931 Women Go on Forever. 1937 Manhattan Merry-Go-Round.

NICHOLSON, PAUL
Born: 1877, Orange, N.J. Died: Feb. 2, 1935, Santa Monica, Calif.(influenza). Screen, stage, and vaudeville actor. Appeared in vaudeville as part of the "Mimic Four" act. Entered films with American Motoscope and Biograph Co. in 1897.

Appeared in: 1921 The Woman God Changed. 1924 Married Flirts. 1925 As Man Desires; Chickie; I Want My Man; Joanna. 1926 Bachelor Brides; The Johnstown Flood; The Nervous Wreck; Up in Mabel's Room. 1927 The Broncho Twister; The Brute; Bertha the Sewing Machine Girl. 1928 The Smart Set; Port of Missing Girls. 1929 Not Quite Decent. 1930 Fox Movietone Follies of 1930. 1931 Oh! Oh! Cleopatra (short); Man to Man; Silence. 1932 Scandal for Sale. 1934 Two Alone.

NICKOLS, WALTER
Born: 1853. Died: Dec. 25, 1927, New York, N.Y.(heart trouble). Screen and stage actor.

NICOL, JOSEPH E.
Born: 1856. Died: June 1, 1926, Bernardsville, N.J. Screen, stage actor, and musical director.

NIEMEYER, JOSEPH H.
Born: 1887. Died: Sept. 27, 1965, Santa Monica, Calif. Screen, vaudeville actor, and dancer.

NIGHT, HARRY A. "HANK"
Born: 1847. Died: Apr. 24, 1930, Hollywood, Calif. Screen actor. Abraham Lincoln impersonator.

NILE, FLORIAN MARTINEZ
Born: 1936, Spain. Died: Jan. 8, 1959, Madrid, Spain. Screen actor.

NIXON, CLINT (Clinton James Hecht)
Born: 1906. Died: Oct. 22, 1937, Hollywood, Calif. Screen actor.

NOA, JULIAN
Born: 1879. Died: Nov. 26, 1958, New York, N.Y. Screen, stage, radio, and television actor.

Appeared in: 1956 Pacific Destiny.

NOBLES, MILTON
Born: 1844, Cincinnati, Ohio, or Almont, Mich.? Died: June 14, 1924, Brooklyn, N.Y.(heart trouble). Screen, stage, and vaudeville actor. Father of stage actor Milton Nobles, Jr.(dec. 1925). Married to actress Dollie Woolwine and together they appeared in vaudeville in an act billed as "Dolly and Milton Nobles."

Appeared in: 1924 America.

NOLAN, MARY (Mary Imogene Robertson)
Born: Dec. 18, 1905, Louisville, Ky. Died: Oct. 31, 1948, Los Angeles, Calif. Screen and stage actress. She used numerous names: Imogene "Bubbles" Wilson while with Ziegfeld; Mary Robertson while film star in Germany; Imogene Robertson, also while in Germany; and Mary Nolan in American pictures.

Appeared in: 1927 Sorrell and Son. 1928 Armored Vault; Silks and Saddles; The Foreign Legion; Uneasy Money; Good Morning Judge. 1929 Charming Sinners; Desert Nights; Eleven Who Were Loyal; Shanghai Lady; West of Zanzibar. 1930 Outside the Law;

Undertow; Young Desire. 1931 Enemies of the Law; X Marks the Spot. 1932 The Big Shot; File 113; Docks of San Francisco; Midnight Patrol. Foreign films prior to 1930: The Viennese Lover; The Woman God Forgot.

NOMIS, LEO

Born: Iowa. Died: Feb. 5, 1932, Los Angeles, Calif.(plane crash while filming Sky Bride). Film stunt flyer.

Appeared in: 1926 California Straight Ahead. 1930 Hell's Angels. 1932 The Lost Squadron; The Crowd Roars; Sky Bride.

NOON, PAISLEY

Born: 1897, Los Angeles, Calif. Died: Mar. 27, 1932, Hollywood, Calif.(appendicitis). Screen and stage actor. Entered films approx. 1927.

Appeared in: 1932 Night World.

NOONAN, PATRICK

Born: Jan. 9, 1887, Dublin, Ireland. Died: May 19, 1962, Wokinham, England. Screen and stage actor.

Appeared in: 1930 Arms and the Man. 1934 The Bride of the Lake. 1936 Ourselves Alone; A Woman Alone. 1937 The Mutiny of the Elsinor; 1938 Kathleen. 1940 Over the Moon. 1947 Captain Boycott. 1948 Anna Karenina. Other British film: Dr. O'Dowd.

NOONAN, TOMMY (Tommy Noon)

Born: Apr. 29, 1922, Bellingham, Wash. Died: Apr. 24, 1968, Woodland Hills, Calif.(brain tumor). Screen, stage, burlesque actor, film producer, and screenwriter. Part of film comedy team "Noonan and Marshall." Half-brother of screen actor John Ireland.

Appeared in: 1945 George White's Scandals (film debut). 1946 Ding Dong Williams; The Truth about Murder; The Bamboo Blonde. 1947 The Big Fix. 1948 Jungle Patrol; Open Secret. 1949 I Shot Jesse James; I Cheated the Law. 1950 The Return of Jesse James; Holiday Rhythm. 1951 Starlift (with Marshall); F.B.I. Girl. 1953 Gentlemen Prefer Blondes. 1954 A Star Is Born. 1955 How to Be Very, Very Popular; Violent Saturday. 1956 The Ambassador's Daughter; Bundle of Joy; The Best Things in Life Are Free. 1957 The Girl Most Likely. 1959 The Rookie (with Marshall). 1961 Double Trouble. 1962 Swingin' Along (with Marshall). 1963 Promises! Promises! 1964 Three Nuts in Search of a Bolt.

NORCROSS, FRANK

Born: 1856. Died: Sept. 13, 1926, Glendale, Calif. Screen and stage actor.

Appeared in: 1921 All Dolled Up; Garments of Truth. 1922 The Challenge. 1924 The Flaming Forties. 1925 The Man from Red Gulch. 1926 The Escape; King of the Pack.

NORDEN, CLIFF

Born: 1923. Died: Sept. 23, 1949, Hollywood, Calif.(suicide-pills). Screen actor.

NORDSTROM, CLARENCE

Born: 1893. Died: Dec. 1, 1968, East Orange, N.J. Screen and stage actor.

Appeared in: 1922 The Lights of New York. 1930 Ship Ahoy (short). 1932 The Crooner. 1933 Gold Diggers of 1933; 42nd Street.

NORIEGA, MANOLO

Born: 1880, Mexico. Died: Aug. 1961, Mexico City, Mexico. Screen actor, film director, and screenwriter. Appeared in films as an actor since approx. 1935.

Appeared in: 1935 Los Muertos Hablan (The Dead Speak). 1936 Malditas Sean las Mujeres; Asi es la Mujer. 1937 El Misterio del Rostro Palida; El Baul Macabro (The Macabre Trunk). 1938 Ave Sin Rumbo (Wandering Bird); El Traidor; Huapango; Rancho Grande. 1939 Ojos Tapatios; Estrellita (Starlet); Odio (Hate); Vivire Otra Vez (I Shall Live Again).

NORMAN, GERTRUDE

Born: 1848, London, England. Died: July 20, 1943, Hollywood, Calif. Screen and stage actress.

Appeared in: 1914 The Unwelcome Mrs. Hatch. 1919 Widow by Proxy; Strictly Confidential. 1921 Partners of the Tide; Little Italy; A Voice in the Dark; Beach of Dreams. 1922 The Game

Chicken. 1924 The Age of Innocence; The Right of the Strongest. 1927 King of Kings. 1929 The Greene Murder Case. 1933 Cradle Song. 1934 The Trumpet Blows.

NORMAN, JOSEPHINE (Josephine Arrich)

Born: Nov. 12, 1904, Vienna, Austria. Died: Jan. 24, 1951, Roslyn, N.Y. Screen actress. Entered films in 1925. Married to screen actor Herbert Rawlins (dec. 1947).

Appeared in: 1924 Ramshackle House. 1925 The Road to Yesterday. 1926 Fifth Avenue; Prince of Pilsen. 1927 King of Kings; Wreck of the Hesperus; The Forbidden Woman. 1928 Chicago; Into No Man's Land.

NORMAND, MABEL

Born: Nov. 10, 1894, Boston, Mass. Died: Feb. 23, 1930, Monrovia, Calif.(tuberculosis). Screen, stage actress, and film director. Married to screen actor Lew Cody (dec. 1934).

Appeared in: 1911 The Unveiling; The Eternal Mother; The Squaw's Love; Her Awakening; Saved from Herself; The Subduing of Mrs. Nag. 1912 Race for a Life; The Mender of the Nets; The Water Nymph; Pedro's Dilemma; Ambitious Butler; The Grocery Clerk's Romance; Mabel's Lovers; The Deacon's Trouble; A Temperamental Husband; A Desperate Lover; A Family Mixup; Mabel's Adventures; Mabel's Stratagem; The New Neighbor; Stolen Glory; The Flirting Husband; Cohen at Coney Island; At It Again; The Rivals; Mr. Fix-It; Brown's Seance; A Midnight Elopement; The Duel. 1913 Teddy Telzlaff and Earl Cooper; Speed Kings; Love Sickness at Sea; Cohen Saves the Flag; Fatty's Flirtation; Zuzu, the Band Leader; The Cure That Failed; For Lizzie's Sake; The Battle of Who Run; Mabel's Heroes; A Tangled Affair; A Doctored Affair; The Rural Third Degree; Foiling Fickle Father; At Twelve O'Clock; Her New Beau; Hide and Seek; The Ragtime Band; (reissued as The Jazz Band); Mabel's Awful Mistake (reissued as Her Deceitful Lover); The Foreman of the Jury; The Hansom Driver; The Waiter's Picnic; The Telltale Light; Love and Courage; A Muddy Romance (Reissued as Muddled in Mud); The Gusher; Saving Mabel's Dad; The Champion; The Mistaken Masher; Just Brown's Luck; Heinze's Resurrection; The Professor's Daughter; A Red Hot Romance; The Sleuths at the Floral Parade; A Strong Revenge; The Rube and the Baron; The Chief's Predicament; Those Good Old Days; Father's Choice; A Little Hero; Hubby's Job; Barney Oldfield's Race for a Life; The Speed Queen; For the Love of Mabel; A Noise from the Deep; Professor Bean's Removal; The Riot; Mabel's New Hero; The Gypsy Queen; The Faithful Taxicab; Baby Day; Mabel's Dramatic Career; (reissued as Her Dramatic Debut); The Bowling Match. 1914 A Misplaced Foot; Mabel's Stormy Love Affair; Mabel's Bare Escape; Love and Gasoline; Mabel at the Wheel; Mabel's Nerve; The Fatal Mallet; Mabel's Busy Day; Mabel's New Job; Those Country Kids; Mabel's Blunder; Hello, Mabel; Lovers Post Office; How Heroes Are Made; Fatty's Wine Party; Getting Acquainted; A Missing Bride; Between Showers; A Glimpse of Los Angeles; Won in a Closet; Mabel's Strange Predicament; Back at It Again; Caught in a Cabaret; The Alarm; Her Friend the Bandit; Mabel's Married Life (reissued as The Squarehead); Mabel's Latest Prank (reissued as Touch of Rheumatism); Gentlemen of Nerve (reissued as Some Nerve); His Trysting Place; Fatty's Jonah Day; The Sea Nymphs (reissued as His Diving Beauty); Tillie's Punctured Romance; A Gambling Rube. 1915 Rum and Wallpaper; Mabel and Fatty's Simple Life; Mabel, Fatty and the Law (reissued as Fatty's Spooning Day); That Little Band of Gold (reissued as For Better or Worse); Wished on Mabel; Mabel's Wilful Way; Mabel Lost and Won; My Valet; Stolen Magic; Mabel and Fatty's Wash Day; Fatty and Mabel at the San Diego Exposition; Fatty's and Mabel's Married Life; His Luckless Love; Their Social Splash; Mabel and Fatty Viewing the World's Fair at San Francisco; The Little Teacher (reissued as A Small Town Bully). 1916 Fatty and Mabel Adrift; The Bright Lights (The Lure of Broadway); He Did and He Didn't (Love and Lobsters). 1918 Back to the Woods; The Venus Model; The Floor Below; Mickey; Peck's Bad Girl. 1919 Sis Hopkins; Sis; Upstairs. 1920 The Slim Princess. 1921 Mooly O'; What Happened to Rose? 1922 Head over Heels; Oh, Mabel Behave. 1923 Suzanna; The Extra Girl. 1960 When Comedy Was King (documentary). 1961 Days of Thrills and Laughter (documentary).

NORRIS, WILLIAM

Born: 1872, New York, N.Y. Died: Mar. 20, 1929, West Bronxville, N.Y. Screen and stage actor.

Appeared in: 1922 When Knighthood Was in Flower. 1923 The Go-

Getter; The Love Piker; Maytime; Adam and Eve; The Eternal Three. 1924 My Man. 1925 Never the Twain Shall Meet. 1927 The Joy Girl.

NORTH, BOB (Harold Young)
Born: 1881. Died: Mar. 18, 1936, Hollywood, Calif.("suicide-inhaled gas"). Screen actor.

NORTH, JOSEPH B.
Born: 1874, England. Died: Jan. 8, 1945, Woodland Hills, Calif. Screen and stage actor.

Appeared in: 1924 Stolen Secrets; The Whispered Name. 1930 Ex-Flame. 1934 Ladies Should Listen. 1935 Paris Spring; Without Regret.

NORTH, WILFRID
Born: 1853, London, England. Died: June 3, 1935, Hollywood, Calif. Screen actor and film director. Joined Vitagraph as a director in 1915.

Appeared in: 1921 A Millionaire for a Day; The Son of Wallingford. 1923 The Huntress; The Love Brand; The Driven' Fool. 1924 The Beloved Brute; A Man's Mate; Captain Blood. 1925 The Happy Warrior; On Thin Ice. 1926 The Belle of Broadway; Hell Bent for Heaven; Peril of the Rail. 1927 Tongues of Scandal; The Bush Leaguer; Tracked by the Police. 1928 The Terrible People (serial); The Four-Flusher; Captain Careless. 1929 Girl Overboard; The Trial of Mary Dugan. 1930 The Dude Wrangler. 1932 Unashamed.

NORTON, BARRY (Alfredo Biraben)
Born: June 16, 1905, Buenos Aires, Argentina. Died: Aug. 24, 1956, Hollywood, Calif.(heart attack). Screen actor.

Appeared in: 1926 The Lily; What Price Glory; The Canyon of Light. 1927 The Wizard; The Heart of Salome; Ankles Preferred; Sunrise. 1928 Fleetwing; Mother Knows Best; Legion of the Condemned; Sins of the Fathers. 1929 The Exalted Flapper; Four Devils. 1930 The Benson Murder Case (Spanish version); Slightly Scarlet (French and Spanish versions). 1933 Dishonored; Cascarrabias; The Cocktail Hour; Only Yesterday; Lady for a Day. 1934 Nana; Unknown Blonde; Grand Canary; The World Moves On. 1935 Storm over the Andes. 1936 The Criminal Within; Murder at Glen Athol; Captain Calamity; El Diablo Del Mar; Asi es la Mujer. 1937 History Is Made at Night; I'll Take Romance; Timberesque. 1938 The Buccaneer; El Trovador de la Radio (Radio Troubador); El Traidor; El Pasado Acusa (The Accusing Past). 1939 Should Husbands Work?; Papa Soltero (Bachelor Father). 1946 Devil Monster. 1956 Around the World in 80 Days.

NORTON, CECIL A.
Born: 1895. Died: Nov. 30, 1955, Hollywood, Calif. Screen, stage actor, and television writer. Entered films approx. 1915.

NORTON, ELDA
Born: 1891. Died: Apr. 22, 1947, Hollywood, Calif. Screen and stage actress.

NORTON, FLETCHER
Born: 1877. Died: Oct. 3, 1941, Los Angeles, Calif. Screen and stage actor.

Appeared in: 1926 The Cowboy and the Countess; Davy Crockett at the Fall of the Alamo; Exclusive Rights. 1928 Dream of Love. 1930 Sweethearts and Wives; The Big House; Let's Go Places; Men of the North. 1931 The Phantom of Paris; The Secret Six; The Star Witness. 1932 Is My Face Red. 1933 Sucker Money; The Bowery. 1934 The Private Scandal. 1935 Call of the Wild.

NORTON, HENRY FIELD
Born: 1899. Died: Aug. 10, 1945, Hollywood, Calif.(following operation). Screen actor and singer. One of the founders of the Screen Extras Guild.

NORTON, JACK (Mortimer J. Naughton)
Born: 1889, Brooklyn, N.Y. Died: Oct. 15, 1958, Saranac Lake, N.Y.(respiratory ailment). Screen, stage, and vaudeville actor. Played the drunk in more than 200 films; in real life never took a drink. Married to screen actress Lucille Norton (dec. 1959) with whom he appeared in vaudeville.

Appeared in: 1934 Counsel on De Fence (short); Sweet Music; Woman Haters (short); Cockeyed Cavaliers. 1935 Bordertown; Ship Cafe; Calling All Cars; Stolen Harmony; Don't Bet on Blondes; His Night Out. 1936 Too Many Parents. 1937 Marked Woman; Meet the Missus; Pick a Star; an RKO short; A Day at the Races. 1938 Meet the Girls; Thanks for the Memory. 1939 Grand Jury Secrets; Joe and Ethel Turp Call on the President. 1940 The Farmer's Daughter; Opened by Mistake; A Night at Earl Carroll's; The Bank Dick. 1941 Louisiana Purchase; Road Show. 1942 The Fleet's In; The Spoilers; The Palm Beach Story; Moonlight Havana; Dr. Renault's Secret; Brooklyn Orchid; Tennessee Johnson. 1943 Taxi, Mister; Lady Bodyguard; Prairie Chicken; It Ain't Hay. 1944 The Chinese Cat; Hail the Conquering Hero; The Big Noise; Ghost Catchers. 1945 Wonder Man; Fashion Model; Flame of the Barbary Coast; A Guy, a Gal, a Pal; Captain Tugboat Annie; Strange Confession; Man Alive; Hold That Blonde; Her Highness and the Bellboy; The Scarlet Clue; The Naughty Nineties. 1946 Blue Skies; No Leave, No Love; The Kid from Brooklyn; The Sin of Harold Diddlebock (aka Mad Wednesday); Shadows over China; Corpus Delecti; The Strange Mr. Gregory; Bringing up Father; Rendezvous 24; Rhythm and Weep (short). 1947 Linda, Be Good. 1948 Variety Time.

NORTON, LUCILLE
Born: 1894. Died: June 17, 1959, Beverly Hills, Calif. Screen, stage, and vaudeville actress. Was in vaudeville as one of the "Haley Sisters" and later teamed in vaudeville with husband, screen actor Jack Norton (dec. 1958).

NORWORTH, JACK
Born: Jan. 5, 1879, Philadelphia, Pa. Died: Sept. 1, 1959, Laguna Beach, Calif. Screen, stage, vaudeville, minstrel, radio, television actor, and song writer. Divorced from stage actress Nora Bayes (dec. 1928), and screen actresses Dorothy Adelphi Norworth and Louise Dresser (dec. 1965). Entered films in 1928. Appeared in "Nagger" series shorts with Mrs. Dorothy Norworth during 1930-33.

Appeared in: 1929 Queen of the Night Clubs, plus the following shorts: Song and Things; Odds and Ends. 1930 the following two shorts: Song and Things and Odds and Ends. 1930 the following "Nagger" series shorts: The Naggers; The Naggers at Breakfast; The Naggers Go South. 1931 The Nagger's Day of Rest; The Naggers Go Rooting; The Naggers Go Camping; The Naggers at the Dentist's; The Naggers in the Subway. 1932 The Naggers at the Ringside; The Naggers Go Shopping; The Naggers at the Races; The Naggers' Housewarming. 1942 Shine on Harvest Moon. 1945 The Southerner.

NORWORTH, NED
Born: 1889. Died: Feb. 12, 1940, New York, N.Y.(after fall and brain operation). Screen and vaudeville actor. Appeared in vaudeville with his first wife, actress Josephine Bennett, in an act billed as "Ned Norworth and Co."

NOTARI, GUIDO
Born: 1894, Italy. Died: Jan. 21, 1957, Rome, Italy. Screen and radio actor.

Appeared in: 1947 Before Him All Rome Trembled. 1956 Helen of Troy.

NOVARRO, RAMON (Ramon Samaniegoes)
Born: Feb. 6, 1899, Durango, Mexico. Died: Oct. 31, 1968, Hollywood, Calif.(murdered). Screen, television actor, screen-writer, and film director.

Appeared in: 1919 The Goat (film debut). 1921 A Small Town Idol. 1922 The Prisoner of Zenda; Trifling Women; Mr. Barnes of New York. 1923 Scaramouche; Where the Pavement Ends. 1924 The Arab; The Red Lily; Thy Name Is Woman. 1925 The Midshipman; A Lover's Oath. 1926 Ben Hur. 1927 The Student Prince; The Road to Romance; Lovers? 1928 A Certain Young Man; Forbidden Hours; Across to Singapore. 1929 The Flying Fleet; The Pagan; Devil May Care. 1930 In Gay Madrid; The Singer of Seville; Call of the Flesh. 1931 Son of India; Ben Hur (re-release of 1926 version in sound); Daybreak. 1932 Mata Hari; Son-Daughter; Huddle. 1933 The Barbarian. 1934 The Cat and the Fiddle; Laughing Boy. 1935 The Night Is Young. 1937 The Sheik Steps Out. 1938 La Comedie de Bonheur; A Desperate Adventure; As You Are. 1942 La Virgen Que Forjo una Patria. 1949 We Were Strangers; The Big Steal. 1950 The Outriders; Crisis. 1960 Heller in Pink Tights.

NOVELLO, IVOR (Ivor Novello Davies)
Born: Jan. 15, 1893, Cardiff, Wales. Died: Mar. 6, 1951, London, England (coronary thrombosis). Screen, stage actor, screen-writer, playwright, and composer. Wrote song "Keep the Home-Fires Burning."

Appeared in: 1921 Carnival. 1923 The White Rose; The Bohemian Girl; The Man without Desire. 1925 The Rat. 1927 The Return of the Rat; Triumph of the Rat; Downhill. 1928 When Boys Leave

Home; The Vortex; South Sea Bubble; The Case of Jonathan Drew; Phantom Fiend. 1929 The Constant Nymph. 1931 Once a Lady. 1932 A Symphony in Two Flats; The Lodger; Call of the Flesh. 1933 Love and Let Love; Sleeping Car. 1934 Autumn Crocus; I Lived with You. 1935 The Phantom Fiend (and 1928 version).

NOVIS, DONALD
Born: Mar. 3, 1907, Hastings, England. Died: July 23, 1966, Norwalk, Calif. Screen, stage, radio actor, and singer.

Appeared in: 1929 New York Nights; Irish Fantasy (short). 1930 Monte Carlo. 1931 The Pajama Party (short). 1932 The Singing Plumber (short); One Hour with You; The Big Broadcast; "Mack Sennett Star" series. 1933 The Singing Boxer (short); a Vitaphone short. 1934 an RKO short. 1935 Paramount shorts. 1944 Slightly Terrific. 1950 Mr. Universe.

NOWELL, WEDGEWOOD
Born: 1878, Portsmouth, N.H. Died: June 17, 1957, Philadelphia, Pa. Screen, stage actor, and stage producer. Entered films in 1915.

Appeared in: 1916 The Deserter. 1921 813; Devotion; The Match-Breaker. 1922 The Eternal Flame; Enter Madame; Ashes; A Doll's House; The Song of Life; Heroes of the Street; Thelma. 1923 The Westbound Limited; A Wife's Romance; Adam's Rib; Don't Marry for Money; Jealous Husbands. 1936 To Mary, with Love; Stolen Holiday. 1937 The Big Show. 1940 Calling Philo Vance.

NOYES, JOSEPH
Born: 1869. Died: Apr. 17, 1936, Los Angeles, Calif. (hit by auto). Screen actor.

NUEMANN, CHARLES
Born: 1873. Died: July 16, 1927, Glendale, Calif. Screen actor.

NUGENT, J. C.
Born: Apr. 6, 1875, Niles, Ohio. Died: Apr. 21, 1947, New York, N.Y. (coronary thrombosis). Screen, stage actor, playwright, screenwriter, and film director. Father of screen actor Elliott Nugent.

Appeared in: 1929 Wise Girls; Navy Blues. 1930 They Learned About Women; Love in the Rough; Remote Control; The Big House. 1931 The Millionaire; Many a Slip; Virtuous Husbands. 1935 Love in Bloom; Men without Names. 1937 A Star Is Born; Stand-In; This Is My Affair; Life Begins in College. 1938 It's All Yours; Midnight Intruder; Give Me a Sailor.

OAKLAND, VIVIEN (Vivian Anderson)
Born: 1895. Died: Aug. 1, 1958, Hollywood, Calif. Screen, stage, and vaudeville actress. Married to screen actor John T. Murray (dec. 1957). They appeared in vaudeville as "John T. Murray and Vivian Oakland," and also made several shorts together during 1929-30.

Appeared in: 1924 Madonna of the Streets. 1925 The Teaser; The Rainbow Trail. 1926 Tony Runs Wild; Redheads Preferred; Tell 'Em Nothing (short). 1927 Love 'Em and Weep (short); Wedding Bills; Uncle Tom's Cabin. 1929 The Man in Hobbles; The Time, the Place and the Girl; The Crazy Nut; In the Headlines; "Educational Mermaid" shorts, plus the following shorts billed as "John T. Murray and Vivian Oakland": Satires; The Hall of Injustice. 1930 The Floradora Girl; Personality; Back Pay; A Lady Surrenders; The Matrimonial Bed; plus the following shorts: Oh, Sailor Behave!; Below Zero; Big Hearted; Let Me Explain; Vanity; A Mother of Ethics; and the following two with her husband: Who Pays and The Servant Problems. 1931 Gold Dust Gertie. 1932 A House Divided; Cock of the Air; The Tenderfoot; Scram! (short). 1933 They Just Had to Get Married; Neighbors' Wives; Only Yesterday. 1934 The Defense Rests; Money Means Nothing. 1935 Rendezvous at Midnight; Star of Midnight. 1936 Lady Luck; The Bride Walks Out. 1937 Way Out West; Mile a Minute Love. 1938 Double Danger; Crime Afloat; Slander House; Rebellious Daughters; RKO shorts. 1939 RKO shorts. 1940 On Their Own. 1942 The Man in the Trunk. 1943 Laugh Your Blues Away. 1944 The Girl Who Dared. 1945 Utah; The Man Who Walked Alone. 1950 Bunco Squad. 1959 Uncle Tom's Cabin (re-release of 1927 film). 1965 Laurel and Hardy's Laughing 20's (documentary).

OAKLAND, WILL
Born: 1883. Died: May 15, 1956, Bloomfield, N.J. Screen, radio, vaudeville, minstrel actor, and singer.

Appeared in: 1927 While We Danced Till Dawn; Dreamy Melody (both shorts).

OAKLEY, FLORENCE
Born: 1891. Died: Sept. 25, 1956, Hollywood, Calif. Screen actress.

Appeared in: 1929 A Most Immoral Lady.

OAKMAN, WHEELER
Born: 1890, Va. Died: Mar. 19, 1949, Van Nuys, Calif. Screen and stage actor.

Appeared in: 1913 The Long Ago. 1914 The Spoilers. 1916 The Ne'er Do-Well. 1920 The Virgin of Stamboul. 1921 Peck's Bad Boy; Outside the Law; Penny of Top Hill Trail. 1922 The Half Breed; The Son of the Wolf. 1923 Slippery McGee; The Love Trap; Mine to Keep; Other Men's Daughters. 1925 Lilies of the Street; The Pace That Thrills. 1926 In Borrowed Plumes; Fangs of Justice; Outside the Law (revised version of 1921 film). 1927 Out All Night; Hey! Hey! Cowboy; Heroes of the Night. 1929 Top Sergeant Mulligan; Lights of New York; The Broken Mask; Masked Angel; The Power of the Press; What a Night; While the City Sleeps; Black Feather; Danger Patrol; The Good-Bye Kiss; The Heart of Broadway. 1929 The Show of Shows; The Hurricane; The Girl from Woolworth's; On with the Show; Devil's Chaplain; Handcuffed; Morgan's Last Raid; The Donovan Affair; Father and Son; Shanghai Lady; The Shakedown. 1930 Little Johnny Jones; On Your Back; The Big Fight; The Costello Case; Roaring Ranch. 1931 The Good Bad Girl; The Lawless Woman; First Aid; Sky Raiders. 1932 Texas Cyclone; Two-Fisted Law; Riding Tornado; Gorilla Ship; Beauty Parlor; The Heart Punch; The Boiling Point; Guilty or Not Guilty; Devil on Deck. 1933 Revenge at Monte Carlo; Sundown Rider; Rusty Rides Alone; Silent Men; Hold the Press; Man of Action; Western Code; Speed Demon; End of the Trail; Soldiers of the Storm. 1934 Lost Jungle; Frontier Days; In Old Santa Fe; Murder in the Clouds; One Is Guilty. 1935 Code of the Mounted; Death from a Distance; Annapolis Farewell; Trails of the Wild; The Man from Guntown; Square Shooter; Motive for Revenge; Headline Woman. 1936 Timber War; Song of the Trail; Roarin' Guns; Gambling with Souls; Darkest Africa (serial); Aces and Eights; Ghost Patrol. 1937 Death in the Air; Bank Alarm. 1938 Code of the Rangers; Mars Attacks the World. 1939 In Old Montana; Torture Ship; Mutiny in the Big House. 1940 Men with Steel Faces. 1941 Meet the Mob. 1942 Double Trouble; Bowery at Midnight; So's Your Aunt Emma. 1943 Ghosts on the Loose; The Girl from Monterey; What a Man!; The Ape Man; Kid Dynamite; Fighting Buckaroo; Saddles and Sagebrush. 1944 Riding West; Sundown Valley; Three of a Kind; Bowery Champs. 1945 Rough Ridin' Justice; Trouble Chasers; Brenda Starr, Reporter (serial).

OBECK, FRED
Born: 1881. Died: Jan. 31, 1929, Hollywood, Calif. (heart trouble). Screen actor.

Appeared in: 1927 The Patent Leather Kid; Wanted a Coward. 1928 Vamping Venus; Oh, Kay!.

OBER, KIRT
Born: 1875. Died: June 1, 1939, Huntington Beach, Calif. (heart attack). Screen, stage, vaudeville actor, and jockey.

OBER, ROBERT
Born: 1882, St. Louis, Mo. Died: Dec. 7, 1950, New York, N.Y. Screen, stage actor, and film director. Married to screen actress Mabel Taliaferro.

Appeared in: 1922 The Young Rajah. 1925 Souls for Sables; Time, the Comedian; The Big Parade; Introduce Me; The Mystic; Morals for Man. 1926 Butterflies in the Rain; Fools of Fashion; The Whole Town's Talking; The Checkered Flag. 1927 King of Kings; A Reno Divorce; The Little Adventuress; Held by the Law. 1928 Across the Atlantic; Black Butterflies; A Regular Business Man (short). 1929 The Idle Rich; In the Headlines; Four in a Flat (short). 1930 The Woman Racket.

OBERLE, FLORENCE
Born: 1870. Died: July 10, 1943, Hollywood, Calif. Screen and stage actress.

Appeared in: 1921 R.S.V.P. 1922 Smudge; The Barnstormer.

O'BRIEN, DAVID "DAVE" (David Barclay)
Born: May 13, 1912, Big Spring, Tex. Died: Nov. 8, 1969, Catalina Island, Calif. (heart attack). Screen actor, film director, television director, screenwriter, and television writer.

Appeared in: 1933 College Humor; Jennie Gerhardt. 1934 Little Colonel. 1935 Welcome Home. 1936 The Black Coin (serial). 1937 Million Dollar Racket; Victory. 1938 Frontier Scout; Where the Buffalo Roam; Man's Country. 1939 Song of the Buckaroo;

Driftin' Westward, Water Rustlers; Rollin' Westward; Mutiny in the Big House; New Frontier; Daughter of the Tong. Joined the "Renfrew of the Royal Mounted" series which included: Crashing Thru and Fighting Mad. 1940 other "Renfrew" films include: Danger Ahead; Yukon Flight; Murder on the Yukon; Sky Bandits; other 1940 films are: The Cowboy from Sundown; Boys of the City; Queen of the Yukon; That Gang of Mine; Murder on the Yukon; A Fugitive from Justice; Gun Code; The Kid from Santa Fe; Hold That Woman!; East Side Kids; Son of the Navy; The Ghost Creeps. 1941 Flying Wild; Texas Marshal; Murder by Invitation; Buzzy and the Phantom Pinto; The Deadly Game; Gunman from Bodie; Spooks Run Wild; Double Trouble; Billy the Kid Wanted. 1942 Down Texas Way; Prisoner of Japan; Billy the Kid's Smoking Guns: King of the Stallions; Bowery at Midnight; The Yanks Are Coming; Captain Midnight (serial); 'Neath Brooklyn Bridge; Devil Bat; plus seven Pete Smith shorts. 1943 Texas Ranger; The Rangers Take Over; Border Buckaroo. 1944 Trail of Terror; Gunsmoke Mesa; Return of the Rangers; Boss of Rawhide; Outlaw Roundup; Guns of the Law; The Pinto Bandit; Spook Town Dead or Alive; The Whispering Skull; Gangsters of the Frontier. 1945 The Man Who Walked Alone; Enemy of the Law; Flaming Bullets; Three in the Saddle; Marked for Murder; Tahiti Nights; The Phantom of 42nd St. 1946 Frontier Fugitives. 1947 Thundercap Outlaws; Shootin' Irons. 1953 Kiss Me Kate. 1954 Tennessee Champ. 1956 The Desperadoes Are in Town. 1964 Big Parade of Comedy (documentary).

O'BRIEN, DONNELL
Died: July 27, 1970, New York, N.Y. Screen, stage, vaudeville, and television singer/actor.

Appeared in: 1954 On the Waterfront. 1959 The Last Angry Man; That Kind of Woman. 1960 Butterfield 8. 1961 The Hustler. 1965 The Pawnbroker.

O'BRIEN, EUGENE
Born: Nov. 14, 1882, Boulder, Col. Died: Apr. 29, 1966, Los Angeles, Calif.(bronchial pneumonia). Screen and stage actor.

Appeared in: 1916 The Chaperon; Return of Eve; Poor Little Peppina. 1917 Poppy; Brown of Harvard; Rebecca of Sunnybrook Farm. 1918 The Safety Curtain; A Romance of the Underworld; Under the Greenwood Tree. 1919 Come out of the Kitchen; The Perfect Lover; By Right of Purchase; Fires of Faith. 1920 The Thief. 1921 Worlds Apart; Gilded Lies; Wonderful Chance; Broadway and Home; The Last Door; Is Life Worth Living?; Clay Dollars. 1922 Chivalrous Charley; Channing of the Northwest; John Smith; The Prophet's Paradise. 1923 The Voice from a Minaret; Souls for Sale. 1924 The Only Woman; Secrets. 1925 Graustark; Siege; Dangerous Innocence; Flaming Love; Frivolous Sal; Simon the Jester; Souls for Sables. 1926 Fine Manners; Flames. 1927 The Romantic Age. 1928 Faithless Lover.

O'BRIEN, "SHOTS" (Charles Brennan)
Born: 1895. Died: Mar. 29, 1961, Los Angeles, Calif.(heart attack). Screen, stage, circus, and vaudeville actor.

O'BRIEN, TOM (Thomas O'Brien)
Born: July 25, 1891, San Diego, Calif. Died: June 9, 1947, Los Angeles, Calif. Screen, stage, and vaudeville actor. Entered films in 1913.

Appeared in: 1921 Scrap Iron; The Devil Within. 1925 The Big Parade; White Fang; Crack O'Dawn; So This Is Marriage. 1926 The Runaway Express; Tin Hats; The Flaming Forest; Poker Faces; The Winner; Take It from Me. 1927 The Bugle Call; The Fire Brigade; The Frontiersman; San Francisco Nights; The Private Life of Helen of Troy; Rookies; Twelve Miles Out; Winners of the Wilderness. 1928 That's My Daddy; Anybody Seen Kelly?; The Last Warning; The Chorus Kid; Outcast Souls. 1929 Dark Skies; Dance Hall; The Peacock Fan; Hurricane; Smiling Irish Eyes; The Flying Fool; His Lucky Day; It Can Be Done; Untamed; Broadway Scandals; Last Warning. 1930 Call of the West; Moby Dick; The Midnight Special. 1931 The Stowaway; Scared Stiff; Sailor Maid Love; Trapped; Hell Bent for Frisco; Yesterday in Santa Fe; The Hawk; Pudge. 1932 Unexpected Father; Phantom Express; The Night Mayor. 1933 Lucky Dog. 1934 Woman Condemned.

O'BYRNE, PATSY
Born: 1886, Kan. Died: Apr. 18, 1968, Woodland Hills, Calif. Screen actress. Entered films with Mack Sennett and appeared in "Charlie Chase" comedies.

Appeared in: 1920 Paris. 1926 My Old Dutch; A Sea Dog's Tale. 1928 Outcast. 1929 South Sea Rose; Condemned; Barnum Was

Right. 1930 Loose Ankles. 1932 Nice Women. 1933 Doctor Bull; Alice in Wonderland. 1935 It's a Gift. 1940 You Can't Fool Your Wife; Saps at Sea.

O'CONNELL, HUGH
Born: Aug. 4, 1898, New York, N.Y. Died: Jan. 19, 1943, Hollywood, Calif.(heart attack). Screen and stage actor.

Appeared in: 1929 the following shorts: The Familiar Face; Dead or Alive; The Interview; The Ninety-Ninth Amendment. 1930 The Head Man (short); Find the Woman (short). 1931 The Smiling Lieutenant; Secrets of a Secretary; Personal Maid. 1931 Hello Sucker (short). 1933 Cheating Cheaters; Broadway Through a Keyhole. 1934 Gift of Gab. 1935 The Good Fairy; The Man Who Reclaimed His Head; It Happened in New York; Chinatown Squad; Diamond Jim; She Gets Her Man; Manhattan Moon. 1937 Ready, Willing and Able; Fly Away Baby; That Certain Woman; Marry the Girl; The Perfect Specimen. 1938 Swing Your Lady; Accidents Will Happen; Penrod's Double Trouble; Torchy Blane in Panama; Women Are Like That; Mystery House. 1940 My Favorite Wife; Lucky Partners. 1941 The Mad Doctor; My Life with Caroline.

O'CONNOR, FRANK
Born: Apr. 11, 1888, N.Y. Died: Nov. 22, 1959, Hollywood, Calif. Screen, stage actor, screenwriter, and film director.

Appeared in: 1932 Handle with Care. 1933 Son of Kong; Kickin' the Crown Around (short). 1934 As Husbands Go. 1935 False Pretenses. 1937 Night Club Scandal. 1938 The Purple Vigilantes; Riders of the Black Hills. 1939 Boy Slaves. 1940 Adventure in Diamonds; Our Neighbors, the Carters. 1941 Man-Made Monster. 1947 Shoot to Kill. 1950 County Fair; The Tougher They Come.

O'CONNOR, HARRY M.
Born: 1873, Chicago, Ill. Died: July 10, 1971, Woodland Hills, Calif.(pneumonia). Screen, stage, and vaudeville actor. Entered films approx. 1910.

Appeared in: 1921 Stranger Than Fiction. 1925 Flashing Steeds. 1926 Red Hot Hoofs. 1927 Cyclone of the Range. 1928 When the Law Rides. 1929 The Trail of the Horse Thieves; Come and Get It. 1930 Half Pint Polly (short).

O'CONNOR, JOHN
Born: 1874. Died: Sept. 10, 1941, Santa Monica, Calif. Screen and stage actor.

Appeared in: 1921 The Barricade.

O'CONNOR, KATHLEEN
Born: 1897. Died: June 25, 1957, Hollywood, Calif. Screen actress. Entered films with Mack Sennett.

Appeared in: 1919 The Lion Man (serial); The Midnight Man (serial). 1921 Life's Darn Funny; Sunset Jones. 1922 The Married Flapper; The Trouper; Come on Over; The Old Homestead. 1923 Wild Bill Hickok. 1924 Dark Stairways.

O'CONNOR, KATHRYN
Born: 1894, Cortland, N.Y. Died: Nov. 16, 1965, Albuquerque, N.M. Screen and stage actress.

O'CONNOR, LOUIS J.
Born: 1880, Providence, R.I. Died: Aug. 9, 1959, Los Angeles, Calif. Screen and stage actor.

Appeared in: 1921 Diane of Star Hollow. 1922 Watch Your Step; Don't Shoot. 1923 The Call of the Hills; Souls for Sale. 1924 Four Sons; Rarin' To Go; Sporting Youth. 1925 Gold and Grit; The Night Ship; Thundering Through; Heartless Husbands. 1926 The Silent Guardian; Out of the West; Midnight Limited. 1929 The Tip-Off.

O'CONNOR, ROBERT EMMETT
Born: 1885, Milwaukee, Wisc. Died: Sept. 4, 1962, Hollywood, Calif.(burns). Screen actor.

Appeared in: 1926 Tin Gods. 1928 The Noose; Dressed to Kill; Four Walls; Freedom of the Press; The Singing Fool. 1929 The Isle of Lost Ships; Smiling Irish Eyes. 1930 Up the River; Alias French Gertie; The Big House; Shooting Straight; Our Blushing Brides; In the Next Room; Framed. 1931 Man to Man; Paid; The Single Sin; The Public Enemy; Three Who Loved; Reckless Living; Fanny Foley Herself. 1932 Two Kinds of Women; Big Timber; Night World; The Dark Horse; Blonde Venus; The Kid from Spain; American Madness. 1933 Lady of the Night; Don't Bet on Love; Frisco Jenny; The Great Jasper; Picture Snatcher; The Big Brain; Midnight Mary; Lady for a Day; Penthouse. 1934 Return of the Terror; White Lies; The Big Shakedown; Bottoms Up. 1935 Waterfront Lady; The Whole Town's Talking; The Mysterious Mr. Wong; Star of Midnight; Stolen Harmony; Let 'Em Have It; Diamond Jim; A Night at the Opera. 1936 We Who Are about to Die; Desire; The Lone Wolf Returns; Little Lord Fauntleroy; Sing Me a Love Song; At Sea Ashore (short). 1937 The Frame up; Super Sleuth; Park Avenue Logger; The Crime Nobody Saw; Girl Overboard; The River of Missing Men; Trapped by G-Men; Boy of the Streets; Wells Fargo. 1938 Trade Winds. 1939 Streets of New York; Joe and Ethel Turp Call on the President. 1940 Double Alibi; Hot Steel; A Fugitive from Justice; No Time for Comedy. 1941 Tight Shoes. 1943 Air Raid Wardens; Whistling in Brooklyn. 1944 Gentle Annie; Nothing but Trouble. 1946 Boys' Ranch.

O'CONNOR, UNA
Born: Oct. 23, 1880, Belfast, Ireland. Died: Feb. 4, 1959, New York, N.Y. Screen and stage actress.

Appeared in: 1929 Dark Red Roses (film debut). 1930 Murder; To Oblige a Lady; Timbuctoo. 1933 Cavalcade; The Invisible Man; Mary Stevens, M.D.; Pleasure Cruise. 1934 The Poor Rich; Horse Play; Orient Express; All Men Are Enemies; The Barretts of Wimpole Street; Stingaree; Chained. 1935 David Cooperfield; The Informer; The Bride of Frankenstein; Thunder in the Night; The Perfect Gentleman; Father Brown, Detective. 1936 Rose Marie; The Plough and the Stars; Little Lord Fauntleroy; Lloyds of London; Suzy. 1937 Call It a Day; Personal Property. 1938 The Adventures of Robin Hood; The Return of the Frog. 1939 We Are Not Alone; All Women Have Secrets. 1940 It All Came True; Lillian Russell; The Sea Hawk; He Stayed for Breakfast. 1941 Kisses for Breakfast; Strawberry Blonde; Her First Beau; Three Girls about Town; How Green Was My Valley. 1942 Always in My Heart; My Favorite Spy; Random Harvest. 1943 This Land Is Mine; Forever and a Day; Holy Matrimony; Government Girl. 1944 The Canterville Ghost; My Pal Wolf. 1945 Christmas in Connecticut; The Bells of St. Mary's; Whispering Walls. 1946 Cluny Brown; Of Human Bondage; Child of Divorce; Unexpected Guest; The Return of Monte Cristo; Banjo. 1947 Lost Honeymoon; Ivy; The Corpse Came C.O.D. 1948 Fighting Father Dunne; Adventures of Don Juan. 1957 Witness for the Prosecution.

O'DAY, PEGGY (Peggy Reis)
Born: 1900. Died: Nov. 26, 1964, Santa Monica, Calif. Screen actress and stuntwoman.

Appeared in: 1922 Thundering Hoofs; The Storm Girl; Angel Citizens; They're Off; Trail's End. 1923 The Fighting Skipper (serial); The Man Getter. 1924 Ace of the Law; Battlin' Buckaroo; Crashin' Through; Shootin' Square; Travelin' Fast. 1925 Peggy of the Secret Service; The Four from Nowhere; Red Blood and Blue; Riders of the Sand Storm; Sporting West; Whistling Jim. 1927 Hoof Marks. 1928 The Clean-Up Man.

O'DEA, JIMMY
Born: 1899, England. Died: Jan. 7, 1965, Dublin, Ireland. Screen, vaudeville, radio, and television actor.

Appeared in: 1939 Ireland's Border Line. 1957 The Rising of the Moon. 1959 Darby O'Gill and the Little People. 1965 Jimmy Nobody.

O'DEA, JOSEPH
Born: 1903, Ireland. Died: Mar. 1, 1968, Dublin, Ireland. Screen, stage, and radio actor.

Appeared in: 1952 The Quiet Man. 1957 The Rising of the Moon.

O'DELL, DIGGER (John H. Brown)
Born: 1904. Died: May 16, 1957, Hollywood, Calif.(heart attack). Screen, stage, radio, and television actor.

O'DELL, SEYMOUR H.
Born: 1863, Ireland. Died: Apr. 3, 1937, Los Angeles, Calif. Screen, stage, and radio actor.

ODELL, "SHORTY" (Solomon Schwartz)
Born: approx. 1874. Died: Nov. 11, 1924, New York, N.Y. Screen actor.

ODEMAR, FRITZ
Born: 1890, Germany. Died: June 3, 1955, Munich, Germany. Screen actor.

Appeared in: 1932 Das Lied ist Aus; Der Raub der Mona Lisa; Liebeskommando. 1941 The Last Days before the War. 1933 Ich Will Nicht Wissen Wer Du Bist; Hertha's Erwachen; M; Eine Tur

geht Auf; Salon Dora Green; Stern von Valencia; Ein gewisser herr Gran; Ein Unsichtbarer geht durch die Stadt; Schloss im Suden; Viktor and Viktoria (U.S. 1935). 1934 Der Doppelganger; Fraulein; Frau; Heute abend bei mir; Ein Walzer for Dich; Charlesy Tante; Furst Woronzeff; Englische Heirat; Peer Gynt; Ein Toller Einfall; Roman Einer Nacht; Schuss im Morgengrauen; Eine Frau wie Du. 1935 Der alte und der Junge Konig; Der Gefangene des Konigs; Lady Windemere's Fan; Ich Sing Mich in Dein Herz Hinein: Gruen ist die Heide; Herr Kobin Geht auf Abenteurer (Mr. Kobin Seeks Adventure). 1936 Der junge Graf; Familie Schimek; Zwichen Zwei Herzen (Between Two Hearts); Knock-Out. 1938 Gross Reinemachen (General Housecleaning); Ein Teufelskerl (A Devil of a Fellow); Famile Schimek; Der Arme Millionar (The Poor Millionaire).

O'DONNELL, CATHY (Ann Steely)
Born: July 6, 1925, Siluria, Ala. Died: Apr. 11, 1970, Los Angeles, Calif. Screen and stage actress.

Appeared in: 1946 The Best Years of Our Lives (film debut). 1947 Bury Me Dead. 1948 They Live by Night (aka The Twisted Road); Your Red Wagon; The Amazing Mr. X. 1950 Side Street; The Miniver Story. 1951 Never Trust a Gambler; Detective Story. 1954 The Woman's Angle. 1955 Eight O'Clock Walk; The Man from Laramie; Mad at the World. 1957 The Deerslayer; The Story of Mankind. 1959 Ben Hur; Terror in the Haunted House (aka My World Dies Screaming).

O'DONNELL, CHARLES H.
Born: 1886. Died: Sept. 10, 1962, Pompano Beach, Fla. Screen and vaudeville actor.

Appeared in vaudeville team of "Lane and O'Donnell" and later "O'Donnell and Blair."

O'DUNN, IRVIN
Born: 1904. Died: Jan. 1, 1933, New York, N.Y.(accidental fall). Screen, vaudeville actor, and magician. Appeared in vaudeville team as part of "O'Dunn and O'Day."

OFFENBACH, JOSEPH
Born: 1905, Germany. Died: Oct. 15, 1971, Darmstadt, West Germany (heart attack). Screen, stage, and television actor.

Appeared in: 1959 Mon Petit (aka Monpti). 1961 Girl of the Moors. 1963 Willy.

OFFERMAN, GEORGE, SR.
Born: 1880. Died: Mar. 5, 1938, Hollywood, Calif. Screen, stage, and vaudeville actor. Appeared in vaudeville in an act billed as "The Original Singing Nut" and later in an act with his wife. Father of screen actor George Offerman, Jr. (dec. 1963). Married to screen actress Marie Offerman (dec. 1950).

Appeared in: 1929 Girl on the Barge. 1933 The Mayor of Hell.

OFFERMAN, GEORGE, JR.
Born: Mar. 14, 1917, Chicago, Ill. Died: Jan. 14, 1963, New York, N.Y. Screen and stage actor. Son of screen actor George Offerman, Sr.(dec. 1938) and screen actress Marie Offerman (dec. 1950).

Appeared in: 1927 The Broadway Drifter. 1929 The Girl on the Barge. 1933 Mayor of Hell. 1934 The House of Rothschild. 1935 Grand Old Girl; Jalna; Black Fury; Old Grey Mayor (short). 1936 Chatterbox; Wedding Present. 1937 Midnight Court; Night Club Scandal. 1938 Scandal Sheet; Crime Street; Three Comrades. 1939 Dust Be My Destiny; They Asked for It; Calling Dr. Kildare. 1940 Prison Camp. 1942 Whispering Ghosts; War against Mrs. Hadley; Saboteur. 1943 Action in the North Atlantic. 1944 The Sullivans; See Here, Private Hargrove. 1945 Out of the Depths. 1946 A Walk in the Sun. 1949 A Letter to Three Wives. 1951 People Will Talk; Purple Heart Diary. 1952 With a Song in My Heart.

OFFERMAN, MARIE
Born: 1894. Died: May 14, 1950, Hollywood, Calif. Screen, stage, and vaudeville actress. Wife of screen actor George Offerman, Sr. (dec. 1938), with whom she appeared in vaudeville, and mother of screen actor George Offerman, Jr. (dec. 1963).

O'HARA, FISKE
Born: 1878. Died: Aug. 2, 1945, Hollywood, Calif. Screen, stage, radio, and vaudeville actor.

Appeared in: 1933 Paddy the Next Best Thing. 1934 Change of Heart.

OHARDIENO, ROGER
Born: 1919. Died: July 14, 1959, New York, N.Y. Negro screen and stage dancer.

Appeared in: 1943 Stormy Weather.

OH GRAN GILBERT (Justo Masso)
Born: 1886, Spain. Died: Sept. 12, 1971, Barcelona, Spain. Screen and stage actor.

Appeared in: 1965 Broken Toys.

OJEDA, JESUS "CHUCHO"
Born: 1892, Mexico. Died: Nov. 1943, Mexico City, Mexico (heart attack). Screen and stage actor.

O'KEEFE, ARTHUR J.
Born: 1874. Died: Mar. 29, 1959, Hollywood, Calif. Screen stuntman and vaudeville actor. Entered films approx. 1915.

O'KEEFE, DENNIS (Edward Vanes Flanagan, Jr.)
Born: Mar. 28, 1908, Fort Madison, Iowa. Died: Aug. 31, 1968, Santa Monica, Calif.(cancer). Screen, stage, vaudeville, television actor, film director, and screenwriter. Entered films as a stuntman and extra and appeared as Bud Flanagan until approx. 1936 and then used the name of Dennis O'Keefe. Wrote screen scripts under his pen name, Jonathan Ricks.

Appeared in: 1931 Reaching for the Moon; Cimarron. 1932 I Am A Fugitive from a Chain Gang; Two against the World; Cabin in the Cotton; Central Park; Night after Night. 1933 Girl Missing; Hello, Everybody!; The Eagle and the Hawk; From Hell to Heaven; Gold Diggers of 1933; Too Much Harmony; Duck Soup; I'm No Angel; The House on 56th Street; Torch Singer; Lady Killer. 1934 Jimmy the Gent; Upperworld; Wonder Bar; Smarty; Registered Nurse; Fog over Frisco; Man with Two Faces; Lady by Choice; Madame Du Barry; College Rhythm; Imitation of Life; Transatlantic Merry-Go-Round; Everything's Ducky (short). 1935 Gold Diggers of 1935; Devil Dogs of the Air; Rumba; Mississippi; Let 'Em Have It; Doubting Thomas; Every Night at Eight; The Daring Young Man; Anna Karenina; Personal Maid's Secret; It's in the Air; Shipmates Forever; Broadway Hostess; A Night at the Biltmore Bowl (short). 1936 Born to Dance; Anything Goes; Hats Off; Mr. Deeds Goes to Town; 13 Hours by Air; Love before Breakfast; Great Guy; Libeled Lady; Theodora Goes Wild; The Accusing Finger; Sworn Enemy; And So They Were Married; Nobody's Fool; Rhythm on the Range; Yours for the Asking; The Plainsman; Burning Gold. 1937 When's Your Birthday?; Top of the Town; Married before Breakfast; Parole Racket; Swing High, Swing Low; Captains Courageous; A Star Is Born; Riding on Air; The Girl from Scotland Yard; Easy Living; Saratoga; The Firefly; Blazing Barriers. 1938 Bad Man of Brimstone; Hold That Kiss; The Chaser; Vacation from Love. 1939 Unexpected Father; Burn 'Em up O'Connor; The Kid from Texas; That's Right—You're Wrong. 1940 Alias the Deacon; La Conga Nights; I'm Nobody's Sweetheart Now; Pop Always Pays; You'll Find Out; The Girl from Havana; Arise, My Love. 1941 Topper Returns; Bowery Boy; Mr. District Attorney; Broadway Limited; Lady Scarface; Weekend for Three. 1942 Affairs of Jimmy Valentine; Moonlight Masquerade. 1943 Hangmen Also Die; Good Morning Judge; Tahiti Honey; The Leopard Man; Hi Diddle Diddle. 1944 The Fighting Seabees; Up in Mabel's Room; Abroad with Two Yanks; The Story of Dr. Wassell; Sensations of 1945. 1945 The Affairs of Susan; Doll Face; Brewster's Millions; Earl Carroll Vanities; Getting Gertie's Garter. 1946 Her Adventurous Night; Come Back to Me. 1947 T-Men; Dishonored Lady; Mister District Attorney (and 1941 version). 1948 Raw Deal; Siren of Atlantis; Walk a Crooked Mile. 1949 Cover Up; The Great Dan Patch; Abandoned. 1950 The Eagle and the Hawk; Woman on the Run; The Company She Keeps. 1951 Passage West; Follow the Sun. 1952 One Big Affair; Everything I Have Is Yours. 1953 The Lady Wants Mink; The Fake. 1954 Diamond Wizard; Drums of Tahiti. 1955 Angela; Chicago Syndicate; Las Vegas Shakedown. 1956 Inside Detroit. 1957 Dragon Wells Massacre; Lady of Vengeance. 1958 Graft and Corruption. 1961 All Hands on Deck.

OLAND, WARNER
Born: Oct. 3, 1880, Umea, Sweden. Died: Aug. 5, 1938, Stockholm, Sweden (bronchial pneumonia). Screen, stage actor, and stage producer. Star of Charlie Chan series. Married to screen actress Edith Shearn (dec. 1968).

Appeared in: 1909 Jewels of the Madonna (film debut). 1916 The Eternal Question. 1917 The Fatal Ring (serial); Patria (serial). 1918 The Niulahka; The Yellow Ticket. 1919 The Lightning Raider; The Avalanche; Witness for the Defense. 1920 The Phantom Foe; The Third Eye. 1921 Hurricane Hutch; The Yellow Arm. 1922 East Is West; The Pride of Palomar. 1923 His Chil-

dren's Children. 1924 One Night in Rome; Curlytop; The Fighting American; So This Is Marriage. 1925 Don Q.; Flower of Night; Riders of the Purple Sage; The Winding Stair. 1926 Infatuation; The Mystery Club; Tell It to the Marines; Twinkletoes; Don Juan; Man of the Forest; The Marriage Clause. 1927 The Jazz Singer; Good Time Charley; A Million Bid; Old San Francisco; Sailor Izzy Murphy; What Happened to Father; When a Man Loves. 1928 Wheels of Chance; Stand and Deliver; The Scarlet Lady; Dream of Love. 1929 The Faker; Chinatown Nights; The Mysterious Dr. Fu Manchu; The Studio Murder Case. 1930 The Mighty; Dangerous Paradise; Paramount on Parade; Return of Dr. Fu Manchu; The Vagabond King. 1931 Drums of Jeopardy; Dishonored; The Black Camel; Daughter of the Dragon; The Big Gamble; Charlie Chan Carries On. 1932 Charlie Chan's Chance; A Passport to Hell; The Son-Daughter; Shanghai Express. 1933 Charlie Chan's Greatest Case; As Husband's Go; Before Dawn. 1934 Mandalay; Bulldog Drummond Strikes Back; Charlie Chan's Courage; Charlie Chan in London; The Painted Veil. 1935 Charlie Chan in Paris; Charlie Chan in Egypt; Werewolf of London; Shanghai; Charlie Chan in Shanghai; Charlie Chan's Secret. 1936 Charlie Chan at the Circus; Charlie Chan at the Race Track; Charlie Chan at the Opera. 1937 Charlie Chan on Broadway; Charlie Chan at the Olympics; Charlie Chan at Monte Carlo. 1961 Days of Thrills and Laughter (documentary).

OLCOTT, SIDNEY (John S. Alcott)
Born: 1873, Toronto, Canada. Died: Dec. 16, 1949, Hollywood, Calif. Screen and stage actor, and film and stage director. Entered films with Biograph and joined Kalen studios as an actor and director in 1907.

OLDFIELD, BARNEY (Berna Eli)
Born: Jan. 29, 1878, near York Township, Fulton County, Ohio. Died: Oct. 4, 1946 (cerebral hemorrhage). Screen, circus actor, and sportsman (racer).

Appeared in: 1913 Barney Oldfield's Race for a Life. 1925 The Speed Demon. 1927 The First Auto.

OLDHAM, DEREK (John Stephens Oldham)
Born: 1893, Accrington Lanes, England. Died: Mar. 20, 1968, England. Screen, stage, and opera actor.

Appeared in: 1934 The Broken Rosary. 1935 Charing Cross Road. 1958 Dangerous Exile.

OLGA, DUCHESS. See Duchess Olga

OLIN, BOB
Born: 1908. Died: Dec. 16, 1956, New York, N.Y. Screen, radio actor, and pro boxer.

OLIVER, EDNA MAY (Edna May Cox Nutter)
Born: Nov. 9, 1883, Mass. Died: Nov. 9, 1942, Hollywood, Calif. (intestinal disorder). Screen, stage, and radio actress. Entered films with Famous Players in 1923.

Appeared in: 1923 Three O'Clock in the Morning; Wife in Name Only. 1924 Icebound; Manhattan; Restless Wives. 1925 Lucky Devil; Lovers in Quarantine; The Lady Who Lied. 1926 Let's Get Married; The American Venus. 1929 The Saturday Night Kid. 1930 Half Shot at Sunrise; Hook, Line and Sinker. 1931 Laugh and Get Rich; Fanny Foley Herself; Cracked Nuts; Newly Rich; Cimarron. 1932 Ladies of the Jury; The Penguin Pool Murder; The Conquerors; Hold 'Em Jail; Lost Squadron; March of a Nation. 1933 The Great Jasper; Only Yesterday; Hell Bent for Election; Whoopee Cruise; Little Women; It's Great to Be Alive; Alice in Wonderland; Ann Vickers; Meet the Baron; Strawberry Roan. 1934 The Last Gentleman; Murder on the Blackboard; The Poor Rich; We're Rich Again. 1935 David Copperfield; A Tale of Two Cities; No More Ladies; Murder on a Honeymoon.

OLIVER, GUY
Born: 1875, Chicago, Ill. Died: Sept. 1, 1932, Hollywood, Calif. Screen and vaudeville actor. Entered films in 1908.

Appeared in: 1912 Robin Hood. 1919 Secret Service; The Lottery Man; Hawthorne of the U.S.A. 1921 City of Silent Men; Fool's Paradise; The Little Minister; Moonlight and Honeysuckle; A Prince There Was; Too Much Speed; A Virginia Courtship; What Every Woman Knows. 1922 Across the Continent; The Cowboy and the Lady; A Homespun Vamp; Manslaughter; Our Leading Citizen; Pink Gods; The World's Champion. 1923 The Covered Wagon; To the Last Man; The Cheat; Hollywood; Mr. Billings Spends His Dime; Ruggles of Red Gap; Sixty Cents an Hour; The Woman with Four Faces. 1924 The Bedroom Window; The Dawn of a Tomorrow; North of '36. 1925 The Air Mail; The Vanishing

American; A Woman of the World. 1926 The Eagle of the Sea; Man of the Forest; Old Ironsides. 1927 Arizona Bound; Drums of the Desert; The Mysterious Rider; Nevada; Open Range; Shootin' Irons. 1928 Avalanche; The Vanishing Pioneer; Three Week Ends; Beggars of Life; Hot News; The Docks of New York; Easy Come, Easy Go; Half a Bride; Love and Learn. 1929 Texas Tommy; Far Western Trails; Fighting Terror; Stairs of Sand; The Studio Murder Case; Sunset Pass; Woman Trap; Half Way to Heaven. 1930 Playboy of Paris; The Devil's Holiday; The Kibitzer; The Light of Western Stars; Only the Brave. 1931 Gun Smoke; Skippy; Dude Ranch; Up Pops the Devil; I Take This Woman; Caught; Huckleberry Finn; The Beloved Bachelor; Rich Man's Folly; Sooky.

OLIVER, TED
Born: 1895. Died: June 30, 1957, Los Angeles, Calif. Screen actor.

Appeared in: 1925 Daring Days; Triple Action. 1926 The Fighting Peacemaker. 1934 We're Not Dressing. 1936 Klondike Annie; The Return of Sophie Lang; Border Flight; Yellow Dust. 1937 The Frame-Up; Trapped. 1938 She Loved a Fireman. 1939 Geronimo.

OLIVER, VIC (Viktor Oliver Samek)
Born: July 8, 1898, Vienna, Austria. Died: Aug. 15, 1964, Johannesburg, South Africa. Screen and stage actor. Divorced from screen actress Sarah Churchill.

Appeared in: 1937 Rhythm in the Air. 1940 Room for Two. 1941 He Found a Star; Hi, Gang. 1944 Give Us the Moon. 1945 I'll Be Your Sweetheart. Other British films: Who's Your Lady Friend?; Meet Mr. Penny; Around the Town.

OLIVETTE, MARIE
Born: 1892. Died: Mar. 15, 1959, New York, N.Y.(burns from fire accident). Screen and stage actress.

OLIVETTE, NINA
Born: 1908. Died: Feb. 21, 1971, N.Y.(heart attack). Screen, stage, and vaudeville actress. Married to screen actor Harry Stockwell and mother of screen actors Dean and Guy Stockwell.

Appeared in: 1930 Queen High.

OLSEN, GEORGE
Born: 1893. Died: Mar. 18, 1971, Paramus, N.J. Bandleader, screen, stage actor, and recording artist.

Appeared with his orchestra in: 1930 Happy Days.

OLSEN, IRENE
Born: 1902. Died: Apr. 1931, Brooklyn, N.Y. Screen, stage, and vaudeville actress.

OLSEN, MORONI
Born: 1889, Ogden, Utah. Died: Nov. 22, 1954, Los Angeles, Calif.(natural causes). Screen and stage actor.

Appeared in: 1935 The Three Musketeers (film debut); Annie Oakley; Seven Keys to Baldpate. 1936 The Farmer in the Dell; Air Force; Two in the Dark; We're Only Human; Yellow Dust; The Witness Chair; Two in Revolt; M'Liss; Mary of Scotland; Grand Jury; Mummy's Boys. 1937 The Plough and the Stars; Adventure's End; Manhattan Merry-Go-Round. 1938 Gold Is Where You Find It; Kidnapped; Submarine Patrol; Kentucky. 1939 Homicide Bureau; Code of the Secret Service; Susannah of the Mounties; Allegheny Uprising; Dust Be My Destiny; That's Right—You're Wrong; Barricade; Rose of Washington Square; The Three Musketeers (and 1935 version). 1940 Invisible Stripes; Brother Rat and a Baby; East of the River; Virginia City; Santa Fe Trail; If I Had My Way; Brigham Young, Frontiersman. 1940 Life with Father; Dive Bomber; Three Sons O' Guns; One Foot in Heaven; Dangerously They Live. 1942 Mrs. Wiggs of the Cabbage Patch; Reunion; Sundown Jim; My Favorite Spy; The Glass Key; Nazi Spy. 1943 Mission to Moscow; The Song of Bernadette; Air Force; Reunion in France. 1944 Ali Baba and the Forty Thieves; Roger Toughy, Gangster; Cobra Woman; Buffalo Bill. 1945 Pride of the Marines; Weekend at the Waldorf; Mildred Pierce; Don't Fence Me In; Behind City Lights. 1946 A Night in Paradise; Boys' Ranch; Notorious; The Strange Woman; The Walls Came Tumbling Down. 1947 The Beginning or the End?; The Long Night; That Hagen Girl; Possessed; High Wall; Life with Father; Black Gold. 1948 Up in Central Park; Call Northside 777. 1949 The Fountainhead; Samson and Delilah; Command Decision; Task Force. 1950 Father of the Bride. 1951 Father's Little Dividend; Submarine Command; Payment on Demand; No Questions Asked.

1952 The Lone Star; Washington Story; At Sword's Point. 1953 Marry Me Again; So This Is Love. 1954 The Long, Long Trailer; Sign of the Pagan.

OLSEN, OLE (John Sigvard Olsen)
Born: 1892, Peru, Ind. Died: Jan. 26, 1963, Albuquerque, N.M. (kidney ailment). Screen, stage, vaudeville, and television actor. Brother of screen actor Stephen Olsen (dec. 1946). Was partner in comedy team of "Olsen & Johnson" in both vaudeville and on screen.

The films they appeared in are: 1930 Oh, Sailor Behave! (film debut). 1931 Fifty Million Frenchmen; Gold Dust Gertie. 1932 Hollywood on Parade (short). 1934 Holly on Parade (short). 1937 Country Gentlemen; All over Town. 1941 Hellzapoppin (film and stage versions). 1943 Crazy House. 1944 Ghost Catchers. 1945 See My Lawyer.

OLSEN, STEPHEN
Born: 1900. Died: Dec. 14, 1946, Van Nuys, Calif.(sinus infection). Screen and vaudeville actor. Entered films approx. 1941. Brother of Ole Olsen (dec. 1963). He was member of vaudeville team of "Olsen & Alexandria."

OLVERA, ERNESTO HILL (Hermengildo Olvera Gonzalez)
Born: 1937, Mexico. Died: Mar. 1967, Guadaljara, Mexico (heart attack). Screen actor and organist.

Appeared in one film: Crimen en tus Manos.

O'MADIGAN, ISABEL
Born: 1872. Died: Jan. 23, 1951, Los Angeles, Calif. Screen and stage actress.

Appeared in: 1932 Smiling Faces. 1947 The Egg and I. 1949 Ma and Pa Kettle.

O'MALLEY, JOHN
Born: 1904. Died: Feb. 27, 1945, Malibu Beach, Calif.(auto crash). Screen and stage actor.

Appeared in: 1945 A Sporting Chance (film debut).

O'MALLEY, JOHN P.
Born: 1916, Australia. Died: Aug. 26, 1959, Hollywood, Calif. (heart attack). Screen and television actor.

Appeared in: 1951 Kind Lady. 1952 Julius Caesar. 1953 The Desert Rats. 1955 The Scarlet Coat. 1956 Diane; The Court Jester. 1957 The Invisible Boy.

O'MALLEY, PAT (Patrick H. O'Malley, Jr.)
Born: Sept. 3, 1892, Forest City, Pa. Died: May 21, 1966, Van Nuys, Calif. Screen, vaudeville, and television actor. Entered films with Edison.

Appeared in: 1911 The Papered Door. 1919 The Red Glove (serial). 1920 The Blooming Angel; Go and Get It. 1922 Brothers under the Skin. 1923 The Man from Brodney's; Wandering Daughters; The Eternal Struggle. 1924 Worldly Goods; Happiness; The Fighting American; Bread. 1925 The Teaser; Tomorrow's Love; Proud Flesh; The White Desert. 1926 Spangles; The Midnight Sun. 1929 Alibi; The Man I Love. 1930 The Fall Guy; Mothers Cry; Average Husband (short); The People Versus (short). 1931 Night Life in Reno; Sky Spider; Homicide Squad; Anybody's Blonde. 1932 The Reckoning; High Speed; American Madness; Exposure; Those We Love; Klondike; Speed Madness; The Penal Code. 1933 Frisco Jenny; Mystery of the Wax Museum; One Year Later; Sing, Sinner, Sing; Sundown Rider; Man of Sentiment; Parachute Jumper; I Love That Man; Laughing at Life; The Whirlwind; Riot Squad. 1934 Love Past Thirty; Crime Doctor; Girl in Danger. 1935 Man on the Flying Trapeze; The Perfect Clue; Heir to Trouble; Behind the Evidence; Men of the Hour; Lady Tubbs; Wanderer of the Wasteland. 1936 Hollywood Boulevard; Beloved Enemy. 1937 Mysterious Crossing. 1939 Wolf Call; Stunt Pilot; Romance of the Redwoods; Frontier Marshal; Dust Be My Destiny. 1940 Shooting High; Rocky Mountain Rangers; The Night of Nights; Captain Caution; A Little Bit of Heaven. 1941 Pals of the Pecos; Law of the Range; Reg'lar Fellers; Paris Calling; Double Dates; Meet Boston Blackie. 1942 Two Yanks in Trinidad; Over My Dead Body; Cairo; The Glass Key. 1943 Lassie Come Home; Deep in the Heart of Texas; Thumbs Up; Through Different Eyes. 1944 Sailor's Holiday; Adventures of Mark Twain. 1948 Blazing across the Pecos. 1949 Boston Blackie's Chinese Venture; The Rugged O'Riordans; Icabod and Mr. Toad (voice). 1950 Mule Train. 1951 Alice in Wonderland; Kid from Broken Gun; Kind Lady. 1954 The Wild One. 1956 Invasion of the Body Snatchers; Black-jack Ketchum; Desperado. 1957 Four Boys and a Gun. 1958 The Long Hot Summer.

1961 Blueprint for Robbery. 1962 The Cabinet of Caligari. 1964 A House Is Not a Home; Hey There, It's Yogi Bear (voice). 1967 Gunn.

O'MALLEY, THOMAS E.
Born: 1856, Boston, Mass. Died: May 5, 1926, Brooklyn, N.Y. (complications of disease). Screen and stage actor.

Appeared in: 1921 Cappy Ricks; Rainbow. 1924 His Darker Self.

O'MOORE, BARRY. See Herbert A. Yost

O'NEAL, WILLIAM J.
Born: 1898. Died: May 23, 1961, Hollywood, Calif. Screen, stage, television actor, and singer.

O'NEIL, NANCE
Born: 1875, Oakland, Calif. Died: Feb. 7, 1965, Englewood, N.J. Screen and stage actress.

Appeared in: 1915 The Kreutzer Sonata. 1917 The Fall of the Romanoffs; Hedda Gabler; Greed. 1919 The Mad Woman. 1929 His Glorious Night. 1930 The Rogue Song; The Floradora Girl; The Lady of Scandal; The Singer of Seville; Ladies of Leisure; The Eyes of the World; Call of the Flesh. 1931 The Good Bad Girl; Cimarron; Their Mad Moment; A Woman of Experience; Transgression; Secret Service; Resurrection; The Royal Bed. 1932 False Faces; Okay, America. 1935 Jack Ahoy; Brewster's Millions.

O'NEIL, SALLY (aka SALLY O'NEILL) (Virginia Louise Noonan)
Born: Oct. 23, 1910, Bayonne, N.J. Died: June 18, 1968, Galesburg, Ill.(internal bleeding). Screen and stage actress.

Appeared in: 1925 Sally, Irene and Mary. 1926 The Battling Butler; Mike; The Auction Block; Don't. 1927 Frisco Sally Levy; The Callahans and the Murphys; Slide, Kelly, Slide; Becky; The Lovelorn. 1928 The Mad Hour; The Battle of the Sexes; Bachelor's Paradise; The Floating College. 1929 Show of Shows; Mysterious Island; The Sophomore; Hardboiled; Broadway Fever; The Girl on the Barge; On with the Show; Broadway Scandals; Jazz Heaven. 1930 Hold Everything; Girl of the Port; Sisters; Kathleen Mavourneen. 1931 Salvation Nell; Murder by the Clock; The Brat. 1933 Ladies Must Love; By Appointment Only. 1934 Sixteen Fathoms Deep. 1935 Convention Girl. 1936 Too Tough to Kill. 1938 Kathleen.

O'NEILL, HENRY
Born: Aug. 10, 1891, Orange, N.J. Died: May 18, 1961, Hollywood, Calif. Screen and stage actor.

Appeared in: 1933 Strong Arm (film debut); I Loved a Woman; The World Changes; The Kennel Murder Case; Ever in My Heart; Footlight Parade; The House on 56th Street; From Headquarters; Lady Killer. 1934 The Key; Murder in the Clouds; Bedside; Wonder Bar; Twenty Million Sweethearts; Madame Du Barry; The Big Shakedown; Massacre; Fashions of 1934; Journal of a Crime; I've Got Your Number; Fog over Frisco; The Upperworld; Side Streets; The Personality Kid; The Man with Two Faces; Big-Hearted Herbert; Gentlemen Are Born; Flirtation Walk; Now I'll Tell; Midnight; Midnight Alibi. 1935 The Man Who Reclaimed His Head; The Secret Bride; While the Patient Slept; Great Hotel Murder; Bordertown; The Florentine Dagger; Oil for the Lamps of China; Stranded; We're in the Money; Dinky; Dr. Socrates; Special Agent; Bright Lights; The Case of the Lucky Legs; Alias Mary Down; The Story of Louis Pasteur; Black Fury; Sweet Music; Living on Velvet. 1936 Anthony Adverse; Road Gang; The Golden Arrow; Bullets or Ballots; The White Angel; Freshman Love; The Walking Dead; Boulder Dam; The Big Noise; Two against the World; Rainbow on the River. 1937 Draegerman Courage; The Great O'Malley; Green Light; Marked Woman; The Go Getter; The Life of Emile Zola; The Singing Marine; Mr. Dodd Takes the Air; First Lady; The Great Garrick; Submarine D-1; Wells Fargo. 1938 Brother Rat; Jezebel; White Banners; The Amazing Dr. Clitterhouse; Racket Busters; Yellow Jack; The Chaser; Girls on Probation; Gold Is Where You Find It. 1939 Torchy Blane in Chinatown; Wings of the Navy; Confessions of a Nazi Spy; Juarez; Lucky Night; The Man Who Dared; Angels Wash Their Faces; Everybody's Hobby; Four Wives; Dodge City. 1940 Invisible Stripes; A Child Is Born; Calling Philo Vance; The Story of Dr. Ehrlich's Magic Bullet; Castle on the Hudson; The Fighting 69th; 'Til We Meet Again; Money and the Woman; Santa Fe Trail; They Drive by Night. 1941 Johnny Eager; The Bugle Sounds; Men of Boys Town; The Get-Away; Blossoms in the Dust; Whistling in the Dark; Down in San Diego; Honky Tonk; Shadow of the Thin Man; The Trial of Mary Dugan; Billy the Kid. 1942 Born to Sing; Stand by for Action; Tortilla Flat; White Cargo; This Time for Keeps. 1943 The

Human Comedy; Air Raid Wardens; Dr. Gillespie's Criminal Case; Girl Crazy; Whistling in Brooklyn; Lost Angel; The Heavenly Body; A Guy Named Joe; Best Foot Forward. 1944 The Honest Thief; Airship Squadron No. 4; Rationing; Two Girls and a Sailor; Barbary Coast Gent; Nothing but Trouble. 1945 Keep Your Powder Dry; Anchors Aweigh; This Man's Navy; Dangerous Partners. 1946 The Hoodlum Saint; Bad Bascombe; The Virginian; The Green Years; Three Wise Fools; Little Mr. Jim. 1947 This Time for Keeps; The Beginning or the End. 1948 Leather Gloves; Return of October. 1949 Alias Nick Beal; Holiday Affair; The Reckless Moment; You're My Everything; Strange Bargain. 1950 No Man of Her Own; The Milkman; Convicted; The Flying Missile. 1951 Family Secret; The Second Woman; People against O'Hara. 1952 Scandal Sheet; Scarlet Angel. 1953 The Sun Shines Bright. 1955 Untamed. 1957 The Wings of Eagles.

O'NEILL, JACK
Born: 1883. Died: Aug. 20, 1957, Hollywood, Calif. Screen actor and film director. Entered films with Lubin in 1905. Was a stand-in for Percy Kilbride.

O'NEILL, JAMES
Born: 1849, Kilkenny, Ireland. Died: Oct. 8, 1938, Hollywood, Calif. Screen and vaudeville actor.

Appeared in: 1913 The Count of Monte Cristo.

O'NEILL, MARIE (Marie Allgood)
Born: 1885, Ireland. Died: 1952. Screen and stage actress. Sister of screen actress Sara Allgood (dec. 1950).

Appeared in: 1930 Juno and the Paycock. 1934 Sing As We Go. 1935 Peg of Old Drury; Come out of the Pantry. 1936 Ourselves Alone. 1937 Glamorous Night; Farewell Again; Bulldog Drummond at Bay; River of Unrest. 1938 St. Martin's Lane; Penny Paradise; Troopship. 1940 Dr. O'Dowd; Sidewalks of London. 1941 You Will Remember; Love on the Dole; Those Kids from Town. 1943 Courageous Mr. Penn. 1945 Love on the Dole (and 1941 version). 1946 Gaiety George. 1947 Murder in Reverse. 1948 Showtime; Piccadilly Incident. 1949 Saints and Sinners. 1950 Someone at the Door. 1952 Treasure Hunt. 1953 The Horse's Mouth.

O'NEILL, MICKEY (Clarence J. H. Dion)
Born: 1903. Died: May 14, 1932, Atascadero, Calif.(auto accident). Screen actor, film director, and screenwriter.

O'NEILL, PEGGY
Born: 1924. Died: Apr. 13, 1945, Beverly Hills, Calif.(suicide—sleeping tablets). Screen actress.

Appeared in: 1944 Song of the Open Road. 1945 It's a Pleasure.

O'NEILL, ROBERT A. Born: 1911. Died: Oct. 8, 1951, Hollywood, Calif. Screen actor.

Appeared in: 1951 The Raging Tide; Drums in the Deep South.

ORDE, BERYL
Born: 1912, England. Died: Sept. 10, 1966, London, England. Screen, stage, and radio actress.

Appeared in: 1935 Radio Parade of 1935.

ORELLANA, CARLOS
Born: 1901, Mexico. Died: Feb. 1960, Mexico City, Mexico (heart attack). Screen actor.

Appeared in: 1935 La Llorona. 1937 Corazon No te Enganes (Don't Fool Thyself, Heart). 1938 No Basta Ser Madre (Motherhood Is Not Enough). 1939 El Hotel de Los Chiflados; El Capitan Aventurero (The Adventurous Captain). 1940 La Cancion del Milagro (The Miracle Song); En un Burro Tres Baturros (Three Rustics on One Donkey). 1943 The Life of Simon Bolivar. 1944 Tierra de Pasiones.

ORLIK, IVAN A. "VANYA"
Born: 1898, Russia. Died: July 4, 1953, Alexandria, Va. Screen actor and dancer. Appeared in German and U.S. films.

ORMAN, FELIX (Gus Abraham)
Born: 1884. Died: Jan. 1933, Nashville, Tenn. Screen actor.

Appeared in: 1922 The Glorious Adventure.

ORONA, VICENTE, JR.
Born: 1931, Mexico. Died: Mar. 11, 1961, Mexico City, Mexico (heart attack). Screen and television actor.

Appeared in: 1934 A Cafe in Cairo. 1935 Cruz Diablo. 1936

Mater Nostra. 1938 Abnegacion; Guadalupe la Chinaca; A la Orilla de un Palmar (At the Edge of a Palm Grove). 1940 Luna Criolla (Creole Moon).

O'ROURKE, BREFNI (aka BREFNI O'RORKE)
Born: June 26, 1889, Dublin, Ireland. Died: Nov. 11, 1946. Screen and stage actor.

Appeared in: 1941 The Ghost of St. Michael's; Hatter's Castle (U.S. 1948). 1942 Wings and the Woman. 1943 The Lamp Still Burns; Tomorrow We Live; Tawney Pipitt (U.S. 1947). 1944 Don't Take It to Heart. 1945 I See a Dark Stranger; Love on the Dole. 1946 Waltz Time; Vacation from Marriage; They Were Sisters. 1947 Murder in Reverse; The Patient Vanishes. Other British films: Unpublished Story; Twilight Hour; Perfect Strangers; Rake's Progress.

O'ROURKE, THOMAS
Born: 1872. Died: Oct. 16, 1958, Queens, N.Y. Screen actor. Appeared in films between 1910-1940.

O'ROURKE, TIM
Born: 1933. Died: Nov. 17, 1962, Hollywood, Calif.(auto accident). Screen actor.

ORRACA, JUAN
Born: 1911, Mexico. Died: Aug. 2, 1956, Mexico City, Mexico (heart attack). Screen and stage actor.

ORTES, ARMAND F.
Born: 1880. Died: Nov. 20, 1948, San Francisco, Calif. Screen and stage actor. Appeared in early silents.

ORTH, FRANK
Born: Feb. 21, 1880, Philadelphia, Pa. Died: Mar. 17, 1962, Hollywood, Calif. Married to screen actress Ann Codee (dec. 1961). Screen, stage, vaudeville, and television actor. Appeared in vaudeville with his wife in an act billed as "Codee and Orth." In 1928 he made first foreign language shorts in sound for Warner Bros.

Appeared in: 1929-31 the following shorts with his wife, billed as "Codee and Orth": 1929 A Bird in the Hand; Zwie Und Fierzigste Strasse; Stranded in Paris; Music Hath Charms; Meine Frau (Meet the Wife). 1930 Taking Ways; Imagine My Embarrassment. 1931 On the Job; Sleepy Head; Dumb Luck; The Bitter Half. Without Codee in the following shorts: 1930 The Salesman; The Victim. 1931 The Painter. Other films: 1935 Unwelcome Stranger. 1936 Hot Money; Polo Joe; Two against the World. 1937 The Footloose Heiress; The Patient in Room 18. 1939 Burn 'Em up O'Connor; Broadway Serenade; Fast and Furious; Nancy Drew and the Hidden Staircase; The Secret of Dr. Kildare; At the Circus. 1940 Dr. Kildare's Strange Case; La Conga Nights; Pier No. 13; Gold Rush Maisie; Let's Make Music; Dr. Kildare's Crisis; Michael Shayne, Private Detective; Father Is A Prince; His Girl Friday; Boom Town; 'Til We Meet Again. 1941 The Great American Broadcast; The People vs. Dr. Kildare; Dr. Kildare's Wedding Day; Dr. Kildare's Victory; Blue, White and Perfect; Come Live with Me; Strawberry Blonde. 1942 I Wake up Screaming; Right to the Heart; The Magnificent Dope; Footlight Serenade; Little Tokyo; Tales of Manhattan; Orchestra Wives; Springtime in the Rockies; Dr. Gillespie's New Assistant; Over My Dead Body; To the Shores of Tripoli; My Gal Sal; Rings on Her Fingers. 1943 Sweet Rosie O'Grady; Hello, Frisco, Hello; Coney Island; The Ox-Bow Incident. 1944 Caroline Blues; Storm over Lisbon; Greenwich Village; Buffalo Bill; Summer Storm; Wilson; The Impatient Years. 1945 She Went to the Races; Tell It to a Star; Pillow to Post; Colonel Effingham's Raid; The Lost Weekend; Doll Face; Nob Hill; The Dolly Sisters. 1944 Blondie's Lucky Day; It's Great to Be Young; The Strange Love of Martha Ivers; Murder in the Music Hall; The Well Groomed Bride. 1947 Born to Speed; The Guilt of Janet Ames; Heartaches; Gas House Kids in Hollywood; Mother Wore Tights; It Had to Be You. 1948 So This Is New York; Fury at Furnace Creek; The Girl from Manhattan. 1949 Red Light; Blondie's Secret; Make Believe Ballroom. 1950 The Great Rupert; Father of the Bride; Cheaper by the Dozen; Petty Girl. 1951 Double Dynamite. 1952 Something to Live For. 1953 Houdini; Here Come the Girls.

ORTIN, LEOPOLDO "CHATO"
Born: 1893, Mexico. Died: Aug. 1953, enroute to Acapulco, Mexico (heart attack). Screen and stage actor.

Appeared in: 1939 Alla en el Rancho Chico (Out on the Little Ranch); El Muerto Murio (The Dead Man Died). 1940 Caballo a Caballo (Horse for Horse).

ORTIZ, THULA
Born: 1894. Died: July 30, 1961, New York, N.Y. Screen, stage, and television actress.

OSBORN, LYN
Born: 1923. Died: Aug. 30, 1958, Los Angeles, Calif.(following brain surgery). Screen and television actor.

Appeared in: 1957 The Amazing Colossal Man; Invasion of the Saucer Men. 1958 Torpedo Run. 1959 Arson for Hire; The Cosmic Man.

OSBORNE, JEFFERSON (J. W. Schroeder)
Born: 1871, Bay City, Mich. Died: June 11, 1932, Hondo, Calif. (stroke). Screen and stage actor. Entered films in 1912.

OSBORNE, LENNIE "BUD"
Born: July 20, 1881, Knox County, Tex. Died: Feb. 2, 1964, Hollywood, Calif. Screen and television actor. Entered films with Thomas Ince Co. in 1915.

Appeared in: 1921 The Raiders; The Struggle. 1922 White Eagle (serial); Barriers of Folly. 1923 The Prairie Mystery. 1924 Way of a Man (serial); Cyclone Buddy; The Loser's End; Not Built for Runnin'; The Silent Stranger. 1925 Fighting Ranger (serial); Across the Deadline; Flash O'Lightning; The Knockout Kid; Ranchers and Rascals; The Trouble Buster; Win, Lose or Draw. 1926 Blind Trail; Hi Jacking Rustlers; Law of the Snow Country; Lawless Trails; Looking for Trouble; The Outlaw Express; Three Bad Men; Without Orders. 1927 The Long Loop on the Pecos; A One Man Game; Riders of the West; Don Desperado; Two-Gun of the Tumbleweed; Border Blackbirds; Sky High Saunders; Cactus Trails; The Devil's Twin; King of the Herd. 1928 The Bronc Stomper; The Mystery Rider (serial and feature film); The Vanishing Rider (serial); Cheyenne Trails; The Danger Rider; Forbidden Trails; On the Divide; Secrets of the Range; Texas Flash; Texas Tommy; The Thrill Chaser; Yellow Contraband. 1929 The Cowboy and the Outlaw; West of the Rockies; Bad Man's Money; Days of Daring; The Fighting Terror; The Lariat Kid; The Law of the Mounted; On the Divide; The Last Round-Up; West of Santa Fe; The Invaders. 1930 Half Pint Polly; The Indians Are Coming (serial); Canyon of Missing Men; O'Malley Rides Alone; Call of the Desert; Western Honor; Code of the West; Breezy Bill; The Utah Kid. 1931 Red Fork Range. 1932 Mark of the Spur. 1933 When a Man Rides Alone; The Diamond Trail; Flaming Guns; Deadwood Pass; Rustler's Roundup. 1934 Riding Through. 1935 Outlaw Deputy; The Crimson Trail. 1936 Roamin' Wild; Treachery Rides the Range; Song of the Saddle; Heroes of the Range; Headin' for the Rio Grande. 1937 Guns of the Pecos; The Californian; Western Gold; Boots and Saddles. 1938 Man's Country; The Prairie Moon; The Painted Trail; The Mexicali Kid; The Overland Express. 1939 Racketeers of the Range; Legion of the Lawless; New Frontier; Across the Plains. 1940 Pioneer Days; Land of Six-Guns; West of Abilene; Lone Star Raiders. 1941 The Phantom Cowboy; Outlaws of the Panhandle; The Medico of Painted Springs; Riding the Wind; Robbers of the Range; The Return of Daniel Boone; The Bandit Trail. 1942 'Neath Brooklyn Bridge; The Spoilers; Riders of the West. 1943 Robin Hood of the Range; Stranger from Pecos; The Carson City Cyclone; Haunted Ranch; Rangers Take Over; The Avenging Rider; Cowboy Commandos; The Ghost Rider. 1944 Sonora Stagecoach; Song of the Range; Adventures of Mark Twain; Law Men; Range Law; Valley of Vengeance; Outlaw Trail; Marked Trails; Trigger Law; Laramie Trail; Outlaw Roundup; Dead or Alive. 1945 Prairie Rustlers; Three in the Saddle; The Cisco Kid Returns; Fighting Bill Carson; The Navajo Kid; Flaming Bullets; The Cherokee Flash; His Brother's Ghost. 1946 Thundertown; Six-Gun Man; Border Bandits; Overland Riders; Outlaw of the Plains; Landrush; Desert Horseman. 1947 Six-Gun Serenade; Thundergap Outlaws; Trailing Danger; Code of the Saddle; Bowery Buckaroos. 1948 Six-Gun Law; Song of the Drifter; Blood on the Moon; Indian Agent; Crossed Trails; Courtin' Trouble. 1949 Frontier Revenge; Gunning for Justice; The Gay Amigo. 1950 Six-Gun Mesa; Cow Town; The Cowboy and the Prizefighter; Hostile Country; Arizona Territory; Border Rangers; Over the Border; West of the Brazos; Colorado Ranger; Fast on the Draw; Marshal of Heldorado; The Crooked River. 1951 Nevada Badmen; Valley of Fire; Whistling Hills. 1952 Texas City. 1954 The Lawless Rider. 1958 Escape from Red Rock.

OSCAR, HENRY (Henry Wale)
Born: July 14, 1891, London, England. Died: Dec. 28, 1969, London, England. Screen, stage, and television actor.

Appeared in: 1932 After Dark (film debut). 1933 I Was a Spy. 1935 Transatlantic Tunnel. 1936 Love in Exile; Doomed Cargo;

The Man Who Knew Too Much; Seven Sinners; Me and Marlboro; Case of Gabriel Perry; Spy of Napoleon (U.S. 1939). 1937 Fire over England; Dark Journey; The Return of the Scarlet Pimpernel; The Academy Decides; The Terror; No Exit; Who Killed John Savage?; Sensation. 1938 Black Limelight; Luck of the Navy; Four Feathers; Father O'Flynn. 1939 The Saint in London. 1940 Spies of the Air; The Fugitive; Hell's Cargo. 1941 Hatter's Castle. 1942 The Avengers. 1943 Squadron Leader X; Courageous Mr. Penn. 1947 They Made Me a Fugitive; The Upturned Glass. 1948 The Greed of William Hart; Bonnie Prince Charlie; Hatter's Castle (re-release of 1941). 1950 Mrs. Fitzherbert; The Black Rose; Prelude to Fame. 1953 Martin Luther; Knights of the Round Table. 1954 Beau Brummell. 1955 Private's Progress. 1956 Postmark for Danger. 1957 The Little Hut. 1960 The Brides of Dracula; Oscar Wilde. 1961 Foxhole in Cairo; Mein Kampf (My Crimes). 1963 Lawrence of Arabia. 1964 The Long Ships; Murder Ahoy. Other British films: On the Night of the Fire; Flying Squad; Four Cases of Murder; Men at Work; Beyond This Place; The Secret Man; City in the Sea; Atlantic Ferry; Seventh Survivor; A Day Will Dawn; Crimes of Burke and Hare; Idol of Paris.

O'SHEA, JACK "BLACKJACK" (Jack Rellfaord)
Born: 1906, San Francisco, Calif. Died: Oct. 2, 1967, Paradise, Calif.(heart attack). Screen and television actor.

Appeared in: 1942 Sons of the Pioneers. 1944 The San Antonio Kid. 1946 Rio Grande Raiders. 1947 Law of the Lash; Wyoming. 1949 Ride, Ryder, Ride.

O'SHEA, OSCAR
Born: 1882. Died: Apr. 6, 1960, Hollywood, Calif. Screen actor.

Appeared in: 1937 Captains Courageous; Rosalie; Big City; Mannequin. 1938 Man Proof; The Main Event; King of the Newsboys; International Crime; Stablemates; The Shining Hour; Numbered Woman; Racket Busters; Youth Takes a Fling. 1939 Lucky Night; King of the Turf; Big Town Czar; Missing Evidence; Invitation to Happiness; The Star Maker; Tell No Tales; S.O.S, Tidal Wave; She Married a Cop; Those High Grey Walls; Of Mice and Men; The Night of Nights. 1940 Zanzibar; The Singing Dude; 20 Mule Team; You Can't Fool Your Wife; Wildcat Bus; Stranger on the Third Floor; Pier 13; Always a Bride. 1941 The Strawberry Blonde; Ringside Maisie; The Phantom Submarine; Sleepers West; The Officer and the Lady; Harmon of Michigan; Mutiny in the Arctic. 1942 The Bashful Bachelor; I Was Framed; The Postman Didn't Ring; Just Off Broadway; Halfway to Shanghai; Henry Aldrich, Editor. 1943 Two Weeks to Live; Good Morning Judge; Two Tickets to London; Corvette K-225. 1944 Her Primitive Man; The Mummy's Ghost. 1945 Bewitched. 1946 Personality Kid. 1947 Sport of Kings; My Wild Irish Rose. 1948 The Senorita from the West; One Sunday Afternoon.

O'SULLIVAN, ANTHONY "TONY"
Died: July 5, 1920, Bronx, N.Y. Screen actor. Entered films with Biograph and later with Mack Sennett. Appeared in some "Jonsey" comedies, including Mrs. Jones Entertains (1909).

Appeared in: 1908 The Red Girl; The Pirate's Gold. 1909 'Tis An Ill Wind That Blows No Good; What Drink Did; A Convict's Sacrifice; A Strange Meeting; Getting Even; In the Watches of the Night; Her Terrible Ordeal; The Honor of His Family. 1910 The Newlyweds; The Final Settlement.

O'SULLIVAN, MICHAEL
Born: 1934, Phoenix, Ariz. Died: July 24, 1971, San Francisco, Calif. Screen and stage actor.

Appeared in: 1967 You're a Big Boy Now.

OTT, FREDERICK P.
Born: 1860. Died: Oct. 24, 1936, West Orange, N.J. He was the first person to be photographed in the motion picture experiments of Thomas A. Edison; was a member of Edison's scientific staff and not an actor.

Appeared in: 1893 Sneeze.

OTTIANO, RAFAELA
Born: Mar. 4, 1894, Venice, Italy. Died: Aug. 18, 1942, Boston, Mass. Screen, stage, and radio actress.

Appeared in: 1924 The Law and the Lady. 1932 As You Desire Me; Grand Hotel; Washington Masquerade. 1933 Her Man; She Done Him Wrong; Bondage; Ann Vickers; Female. 1934 Mandalay; A Lost Lady; The Last Gentleman; All Men Are Enemies; Great Expectations. 1935 The Florentine Dagger; Lottery Lover; Curly Top; One Frightened Night; Remember Last Night?; Enchanted April. 1936 That Girl from Paris; Riffraff;

Anthony Adverse; The Devil Doll; Mad Holiday; We're Only Human. 1937 Maytime; Seventh Heaven; The League of Frightened Men. 1938 I'll Give a Million; Suez. 1939 Paris Honeymoon. 1940 The Long Voyage Home; Victory. 1941 Topper Returns. 1942 The Adventures of Martin Eden.

OTTO, HENRY
Born: 1878. Died: Aug. 3, 1952, Hollywood, Calif. Screen actor and film director.

Appeared in: 1926 The Outlaw Express. 1929 The Quitter; The Iron Mask. 1930 A Matter of Ethics (short); One Hysterical Night.

OUSPENSKAYA, MARIA
Born: July 29, 1876, Tula, Russia. Died: Dec. 3, 1949, Los Angeles, Calif.(burns). Screen and stage actress.

Appeared in: 1936 Dodsworth (film debut—screen and stage versions). 1937 Conquest (aka Marie Walewska). 1939 Love Affair; The Rains Came; Judge Hardy and Son. 1940 Dr. Ehrlich's Magic Bullet; Waterloo Bridge; The Man I Married; Beyond Tomorrow; Dance, Girl, Dance; The Mortal Storm. 1941 The Wolf Man; King's Row; The Shanghai Gesture. 1942 The Mystery of Marie Roget. 1943 Frankenstein Meets the Wolf Man. 1944 Destiny. 1945 Tarzan and the Amazons. 1946 I've Always Loved You. 1947 Wyoming. 1949 A Kiss in the Dark.

OVERMAN, JACK
Born: 1916. Died: Jan. 4, 1950, Hollywood, Calif.(heart attack). Screen actor.

Appeared in: 1947 Johnny Angel; Honeymoon Ahead; The Naughty Nineties. 1946 The Runaround. 1947 Brute Force; The Brasher Doubloon. 1948 Force of Evil; T-Men; The Noose Hangs High. 1949 Flaxy Martin; The Lone Wolf and His Lady; Prison Warden. 1950 The Good Humor Man. 1957 Jet Pilot.

OVERMAN, LYNNE
Born: Sept. 19, 1887, Maryville, Mo. Died: Feb. 19, 1943, Santa Monica, Calif.(heart attack). Screen, stage, minstrel, and vaudeville actor.

Appeared in: 1930 Horseshoes; Five Minutes from the Station (both shorts). 1934 Little Miss Marker; The Great Flirtation; She Loves Me Not; Midnight; Broadway Bill; You Belong to Me. 1935 Paris in Spring; Rhumba; Men without Names; Two for Tonight; Enter Madame. 1936 Collegiate; Poppy; Yours for the Asking; Three Married Men; Jungle Princess. 1937 Wild Money; Nobody's Baby; Don't Tell the Wife; Murder Goes to College; Hotel Haywire; Blonde Trouble; Night Club Scandal; True Confession; Partners in Crime. 1938 Big Broadcast of 1938; Her Jungle Love; Hunted Man; Spawn of the North; Sons of the Legion; Men with Wings; Ride a Crooked Mile. 1939 Persons in Hiding; Death of a Champion; Union Pacific. 1940 Safari; Northwest Mounted Police; Typhoon; Edison the Man. 1941 Aloma of the South Seas; Caught in the Draft; There's Magic in Music; The Hard-Boiled Canary; New York Town. 1942 Reap the Wild Wind; The Forest Rangers; Star Spangled Rhythm; Roxie Hart; Silver Queen. 1943 Dixie; The Desert Song.

OVERTON, FRANK
Born: 1918. Died: Apr. 24, 1967, Pacific Palisades, Calif. (heart attack). Screen, stage, and television actor.

Appeared in: 1950 No Way Out. 1957 The True Story of Jesse James. 1958 Desire under the Elms; Lonelyhearts. 1959 The Last Mile. 1960 Wild River; The Dark at the Top of the Stairs; Khovanschina. 1961 Posse from Hell; Claudelle Inglish. 1962 To Kill a Mockingbird. 1964 Fail Safe.

OWEN, CATHERINE DALE
Born: July 28, 1903, Louisville, Ky. Died: Sept. 7, 1965, New York, N.Y. Screen and stage actress.

Appeared in: 1927 Forbidden Woman. 1929 His Glorious Night. 1930 The Rogue Song; Born Reckless; Today; Such Men Are Dangerous; Strictly Unconventional. 1931 The Circle; Behind Office Doors; In Defense of the Law.

OWEN, GARRY
Born: Dec. 18, 1902, Brookhaven, Miss. Died: June 1, 1951, Los Angeles, Calif.(heart attack). Screen, stage, and vaudeville actor.

Appeared in: 1933 Son of a Sailor; Hold Your Man; Child of Manhattan; Stage Mother; The Prizefighter and the Lady; Havana Widows; Bombay Mail. 1934 Little Miss Marker; No Ransom; The Thin Man. 1935 Hold 'Em Yale; Top Flat (short). 1936 Ceiling Zero; The Case of the Black Cat; King of Hockey; The Return of

Sophie Lang. 1937 Racketeers in Exile; San Quentin; True Confession. 1938 Call of the Yukon; Heart of the North. 1940 Grandpa Goes to Town. 1941 Meet John Doe; The Wagons Roll at Night. 1942 Yankee Doodle Dandy; Pride of the Yankees. 1944 Arsenic and Old Lace; Nothing but Trouble. 1945 Abbott and Costello in Hollywood; Fallen Woman; Mildred Pierce; Anchors Aweigh. 1946 The Tiger Woman; Crime of the Century; The Killers; Dark Mirror; Swell Guy. 1947 The Flame. 1949 I Cheated the Law. 1950 The Admiral Was a Lady; The Flying Missile; The Milkman.

OWEN, SEENA
Born: 1896, Spokane, Wash. Died: Aug. 15, 1966, Hollywood, Calif. Screen, stage actress, and screenwriter.

Appeared in: 1915 The Lamb. 1916 Intolerance. 1918 Branding Broadway. 1919 Victory; The Sheriff's Son; A Man and His Money; The Life Line. 1921 The Cheater Reformed; Lavender and Old Lace; The Woman God Changed. 1922 Back Pay; The Face in the Fog; Sisters; At the Cross Roads. 1923 The Go Getter; The Leavenworth Case; Unseeing Eyes. 1924 For Woman's Favor; I Am the Man. 1925 Faint Perfume; The Hunted Woman. 1926 Shipwrecked; The Flame of the Yukon. 1928 His Last Haul; Man-Made Woman; Queen Kelly; Sinners in Love; The Blue Danube; The Rush Hour. 1929 The Marriage Playground.

OWENS, PEGGY
Born: 1905. Died: May 27, 1931 (heart failure). Screen wild west rider.

OWENS, WILLIAM
Born: 1863, N.Y. Died: Aug. 20, 1926, Chicago, Ill. Screen and stage actor.

OWSLEY, MONROE
Born: 1901, Atlanta, Ga. Died: June 7, 1937, Belmont, Calif. (heart attack). Screen and stage actor.

Appeared in: 1928 The First Kiss. 1930 Free Love; Holiday (screen and stage versions). 1931 Ten Cents a Dance; Honor among Lovers; Indiscreet; This Modern Age. 1932 Hat Check Girl; Call Her Savage. 1933 The Keyhole; Ex-Lady; Brief Moment. 1934 She Was a Lady; Little Man, What Now?; Wild Gold; Twin Husbands. 1935 Goin' to Town; Behold My Wife; Rumba; Remember Last Night?. 1936 Private Number; Yellowstone; Hideaway Girl. 1937 The Hit Parade.

OYSHER, MOISHE
Born: 1907, Lipkon, Bessarabia, Russia. Died: Nov. 27, 1958, New Rochelle, N.Y. Screen, stage, radio actor, composer, and cantor.

Appeared in: 1938 The Singing Blacksmith. 1940 Overture to Glory. 1956 Singing in the Dark (also composed words and music).

PACE, MAX
Born: 1906. Died: Aug. 3, 1942, Hollywood, Calif. (suicide-gun). Screen actor.

PACKARD, CLAYTON L.
Born: 1888. Died: Sept. 6, 1931, San Diego, Calif. (complications following surgery). Screen and stage actor.

Appeared in: 1927 King of Kings.

PACKER, NETTA
Born: 1897. Died: Nov. 7, 1962, Hollywood, Calif. Screen actor.

Appeared in: 1938 Condemned Woman. 1942 Enemy Agents Meet Ellery Queen; Powder Town. 1948 Good Sam. 1959 It Started with a Kiss.

PADEREWSKI, IGNACE JAN
Born: 1860. Died: June 2, 1941. Former Polish prime minister and classical pianist.

Appeared in: 1937 Moonlight Sonata.

PADILLA, EMA
Born: 1900, Mexico City, Mexico. Died: July 2, 1966, Mexico City, Mexico (diabetes). Screen actress.

Appeared in: 1916 La Luz.

PAGE, DON. See Don Alvarado

PAGE, LUCILLE (Lucille Berdell)
Born: 1871. Died: Dec. 31, 1964, Hollywood, Calif. Screen, stage, and vaudeville actress. Married to actor Art Wellington and they appeared in vaudeville as "Berdell and Wellington."

Appeared in: 1935 and 1937 Educational shorts.

PAIA, JOHN
Born: 1908, Hawaii. Died: Oct. 24, 1954, Los Angeles, Calif. Screen actor.

PAIGE, MABEL
Born: 1880, New York, N.Y. Died: Feb. 8, 1954, Van Nuys, Calif. Screen and stage actress. Entered films during silents.

Appeared in: 1942 Lucky Jordan, My Heart Belongs to Daddy; Girl's Town. 1943 Young and Willing; True to Life; Happy Go Lucky; Star Spangled Rhythm; The Crystal Ball; The Good Fellows; The Prodigal's Mother. 1944 Someone to Remember; National Barn Dance; Fun Time; Can't Help Singing; You Can't Return Love. 1945 Kitty; She Wouldn't Say Yes; Out of This World; Dangerous Partners; Murder, He Says. 1946 Behind Green Lights; Nocturne. 1947 Johnny O'Clock; Her Husband's Affairs; Beat the Band. 1948 If You Knew Susie; Johnny Belinda; Hollow Triumph; The Mating of Millie; Half Past Midnight; Canon City. 1949 Roseanna McCoy. 1950 The Petty Girl; Edge of Doom. 1952 The Sniper. 1953 Houdini.

PAIVA, NESTOR
Born: June 30, 1905, Fresno, Calif. Died: Sept. 9, 1966, Sherman Oaks, Calif. Screen, stage, television, and radio actor. Entered films in 1937.

Appeared in: 1938 Ride a Crooked Mile; Prison Trail. 1939 Beau Geste; Bachelor Mother; The Magnificent Fraud. 1940 Dark Streets of Cairo; The Primrose Path; Northwest Mounted Police; Arise, My Love; The Marines Fly High. 1941 Hold Back the Dawn; The Kid from Kansas; Tall, Dark and Handsome; Johnny Eager; Hold That Ghost. 1942 Fly by Night; The Girl from Alaska; Broadway; Timber; Reap the Wild Wind; Road to Morocco; The Hard Way; Flying Tigers. 1943 Rhythm of the Islands; The Dancing Masters; The Desert Song; The Crystal Ball; Song of Bernadette; Pittsburgh. 1944 The Falcon in Mexico; The Purple Heart. 1945 Along the Navajo Trail; A Medal for Benny; The Southerner; Salome, Where She Danced; Nob Hill; Fear; A Thousand and One Nights. 1946 Badman's Territory; Sensation Hunters; The Last Crooked Mile; Road to Utopia; Humoresque. 1947 Ramrod; Carnival in Costa Rica; Shoot to Kill; A Likely Story; Robin Hood of Monterey; Lone Wolf in Mexico; Road to Rio. 1948 Mr. Reckless; Adventures of Casanova; Mr. Blandings Builds His Dream House; The Paleface; Angels' Alley. 1949 Bride of Vengeance; Alias Nick Beal; Oh, You Beautiful Doll; The Inspector General; Mighty Joe Young; Follow Me Quietly. 1950 Joan of Arc; Young Man with a Horn. 1951 Flame of Stamboul; The Great Caruso; Millionaire for Christy; The Lady Pays Off; Double Dynamite; Jim Thorpe—All American. 1952 The Fabulous Senorita; South Pacific Trail; Phone Call from a Stranger; Five Fingers; Mara Maru. 1953 The Bandits of Corsica; The Killer Cop; Call Me Madam; Prisoners of the Casbah, Killer Ape. 1954 The Cowboy; Jivaro; Casanova's Big Night; Thunder Pass; The Desperado; Four Guns to the Border; The Creature from the Black Lagoon. 1955 New York Confidential; Revenge of the Creature; Tarantula; Hell on Frisco Bay. 1956 The Mole People; Ride the High Iron; Scandal, Incorporated; Comanche. 1957 Guns of Fort Petticoat; 10,000 Bedrooms; Les Girls. 1958 The Deep Six; The Lady Takes a Flyer; Outcasts of the City; The Left-Handed Gun; The Case against Brooklyn. 1959 Pier 5, Havana; The Nine Lives of Elfego Baca. 1960 Vice Raid; The Purple Gang; Can-Can. 1961 Frontier Uprising. 1962 The Three Stooges in Orbit; Girls! Girls! Girls!; The Four Horsemen of the Apocalypse; The Martians; The Wild Westerners. 1963 California. 1964 Madmen of Mandoras. 1966 Jesse James Meets Frankenstein's Daughter. 1967 The Spirit Is Willing.

PALLANTE, ALADDIN. See Aladdin

PALLETTE, EUGENE
Born: July 8, 1889, Winfield, Kan. Died: Sept. 3, 1954, Los Angeles, Calif. Screen and stage actor.

Appeared in: 1913 Intolerance. 1919 Fair and Warmer. 1920 Parlor, Bedroom and Bath; Alias Jimmy Valentine. 1921 Fine Feathers; The Three Musketeers. 1922 Two Kinds of Women; Without Compromise. 1923 Hell's Hole; A Man's Man; To the Last Man; North of Hudson Bay. 1924 The Cyclone Rider; The Wolf Man; Wandering Husbands. 1925 The Light of Western Stars; Without Mercy. 1926 Desert Valley; The Fighting Edge; Mantrap; Rocking Moon; Whispering Canyon; Whispering Smith. 1927 Chicago; Moulders of Men; plus 12 Roach shorts including: Sugar Daddies;

The Second Hundred Years; Battle of the Century. 1928 The Good-Bye Kiss; Lights of New York; His Private Life; How's Your Stock? (short); Out of the Ruins; The Red Mark. 1929 The Canary Murder Case; The Dummy; The Greene Murder Case; The Love Parade; The Studio Murder Mystery; The Virginian; Pointed Heels. 1930 The Benson Murder Case; The Border Legion; Men Are Like That; Slightly Scarlet; Let's Go Native; The Santa Fe Trail; Follow Thru; The Sea God; Paramount on Parade; The Kibitzer; Sea Legs; Playboy of Paris. 1931 Fighting Caravans; Gun Smoke; Dude Ranch; The Adventures of Huckleberry Finn; It Pays to Advertise; Girls about Town. 1932 Tom Brown of Culver; Shanghai Express; Off His Base (short); Thunder Below; Strangers of the Evening; The Night Mayor; Wild Girl; The Half-Naked Truth; A Hocky Hick (short), Dancers in the Dark; Phantom Fame; Pig Boat; Slippery Pearls (short). 1933 Made on Broadway; Hell Below; Storm at Daybreak; Shanghai Madness; Mr. Skitch; The Kennel Murder Case; From Headquarters. 1934 Cross Country Cruise; I've Got Your Number; Strictly Dynamite; Friends of Mr. Sweeney; The Dragon Murder Case; Caravan; One Exciting Adventure. 1935 Bordertown; All the King's Horses; Baby Face Harrington; Black Sheep; Steamboat 'Round the Bend. 1936 Easy to Take; The Ghost Goes West; The Golden Arrow; My Man Godfrey; The Luckiest Girl in the World; Stowaway. 1937 Clarence; The Crime Nobody Saw; Topper; She Had to Eat; One Hundred Men and a Girl; Song of the City. 1938 The Adventures of Robin Hood; There Goes My Heart. 1939 Wife, Husband and Friend; First Love. 1940 It's a Date; Sandy Is a Lady; Young Tom Edison; A Little Bit of Heaven; He Stayed for Breakfast; The Mark of Zorro. 1941 Ride, Kelly, Ride; The Bride Came C.O.D., World Premiere; The Lady Eve; Unfinished Business; Appointment for Love; Swamp Water. 1942 Are Husbands Necessary?; Almost Married; The Forest Rangers; Silver Queen; Lady in a Jam; The Big Street; Tales of Manhattan; The Male Animal. 1943 Slightly Dangerous; It Ain't Hay; The Kansan; Heaven Can Wait; The Gang's All Here. 1944 Laramie Trail; Pin-Up Girl; Sensations of 1945; Step Lively; In the Meantime, Darling; Lake Placid Serenade; Heavenly Days; Manhattan Serenade. 1945 The Cheaters. 1946 In Old Sacramento; Suspense. 1948 Silver River.

PALMER, EFFIE

Died: Aug. 19, 1942, New York, N.Y. Screen, stage and radio actress.

Appeared in: 1931 Huckleberry Finn. 1932 Way Back Home (film and radio versions).

PALMESE, ROSE MARIE

Born: 1871. Died: Mar. 21, 1953, Altadena, Calif. Screen actress.

PANGBORN, FRANKLIN

Born: 1894, Newark, N.J. Died: July 20, 1958, Santa Monica, Calif. Screen, stage, and television actor.

Appeared in: 1926 Exit Smiling. 1927 The Girl in the Pullman; The Cradle Snatchers; Finger Prints; Getting Gertie's Garter; The Night Bride; The Rejuvenation of Aunt Mary. 1928 On Trial; Blonde for a Night; My Friend from India. 1929 The Sap; The Crazy Nut; Watch Out; Lady of the Pavements. 1930 Cheer up and Smile; Her Man; A Lady Surrenders; Not So Dumb; plus the following shorts: The Doctor's Wife; Reno or Bust; Poor Aubrey; The Chumps; Who's the Boss?. 1931 A Woman of Experience. 1932 A Fool's Advice, plus the following shorts: Torchy Turns the Trick; Torchy's Nightcap; Torchy's Vocation; What Price Taxi?; The Candid Camera; Torchy Rolls His Own. 1933 Design for Living; Flying Down to Rio; International House; Headline Woman; The Important Witness; Only Yesterday; Professional Sweetheart; plus the following shorts: Torchy's Kitty Coup; Wild Poses, and Universal shorts. 1934 Imitation of Life; King Kelly of the U.S.A., College Rhythm; Manhattan Love Song; Many Happy Returns; Strictly Dynamite; That's Gratitude; Tomorrow's Children; Unknown Blonde; Young and Beautiful; Cockeyed Cavaliers; Stand up and Cheer. 1935 Eight Bells; Headline Woman; A Thousand Dollars a Minute; She Couldn't Take It; Tomorrow's Youth; Ye Old Saw Mill (short). 1936 Don't Gamble with Love; Doughnuts and Society; Hats Off; The Luckiest Girl in the World; Mr. Deeds Goes to Town; The Mandarin Mystery; My Man Godfrey; Tango; To Mary with Love. 1937 Danger, Love at Work; Dangerous Number; High Hat; Easy Living; The Lady Escapes; Dangerous Holiday; The Life of the Party; Living on Love; She's Dangerous; She Had to Eat; Stage Door; A Star Is Born; Step Lively, Jeeves; Swing High, Swing Low; Thrill of a Lifetime; Turn off the Moon; Vivacious Lady; All over Town; When Love Is Young; Hotel Haywire; It Happened in Hollywood. 1938 Love on Toast; Mad about Music; Rebecca of Sunnybrook Farm; She Married an Artist; Meet the Mayor; Four's a Crowd; Topper Takes a Trip; Three Blind Mice; Always Goodbye; Just around the Corner; The Joy of Living; Carefree; Bluebeard's Eighth Wife; Dr. Rhythm. 1939 Broadway Serenade; Fifth

Avenue Girl; The Girl Downstairs. 1940 The Bank Dick; Public Deb No. 1; Spring Parade; Turnabout; The Villain Still Pursued Her; The Hit Parade of 1941; Christmas in July. 1941 Bachelor Daddy; A Girl, a Guy and a Gob; The Flame of New Orleans; Mr. District Attorney in the Carter Case; Neve Give a Sucker an Even Break; Obliging Young Lady; Sandy Steps Out; Sullivan's Travels; Tillie the Toiler; Week-End for Three; Where Did You Get That Girl?. 1942 Call Out the Marines; George Washington Slept Here; Moonlight Masquerade; The Palm Beach Story; Now Voyager; What's Cooking?. 1943 His Butler's Sister; Crazy House; Holy Matrimony; Reveille with Beverly; Two Weeks to Live; Stage Door Canteen; Strictly in the Groove; Honeymoon Lodge; Slick Chick. 1944 The Great Moment; My Best Gal; Reckless Age; Hail the Conquering Hero. 1945 Hollywood and Vine; The Horn Blows at Midnight; See My Lawyer; You Came Along; Tell It to a Star. 1946 Two Guys from Milwaukee; Lover Come Back. 1947 I'll Be Yours; Calendar Girl; Mad Wednesday. 1948 Romance on the High Seas. 1949 My Dream Is Yours; Down Memory Lane. 1950 Her Wonderful Lie. 1957 Oh, Men!, Oh, Women!; The Story of Mankind.

PANNACI, CHARLES

Born: 1904. Died: Mar. 1927, Long Branch, N.J.(pneumonia). Screen actor.

PANZER, PAUL

Born: approx. 1867. Died: Apr. 11, 1937, New York, N.Y.(heart trouble). Screen, stage, and circus actor. Do not confuse with actor Paul W. Panzer (dec. 1958).

PANZER, PAUL WOLFGANG (Paul Panzerbeiter)

Born: 1872, Wurtzberg, Bavaria. Died: Aug. 16, 1958, Hollywood, Calif. Screen and stage actor. Entered films with Vitagraph.

Appeared in: 1904 Stolen by Gypsies (film debut). 1908 Romeo and Juliet. 1913 The Cheapest Way. 1914 The Perils of Pauline (serial); Exploits of Elaine (serial). 1917 Jimmy Dale; Alias the Grey Seal (serial). 1918 The House of Hate (serial). 1919 The Masked Rider. 1920 The Mystery Mind (serial). 1922 The Bootleggers; The Mohican's Daughter; When Knighthood Was in Flower. 1923 The Enemies of Women; Big Brother; Unseeing Eyes; Jacqueline of Blazing Barriers; Mighty Lak' a Rose; Under the Red Robe. 1924 A Son of the Sahara; Wages of Virtue; Monsieur Beaucaire; Week-End Husbands. 1925 Thunder Mountain; Too Many Kisses; The Fool; The Shock Punch; The Best Bad Man; East Lynne; Greater Than a Crown; The Mad Marriage. 1926 The Ancient Mariner; Siberia; The Johnstown Flood; Black Paradise; The Dixie Merchant; The High Flyer; 30 Below Zero. 1927 Sally in Our Alley; Hawk of the Hills (serial); The Girl from Chicago; Wolf's Clothing; Brass Knuckles. 1928 Glorious Betsy; Rinty of the Desert; The Candy Kid; City of Purple Dreams; George Washington Cohen. 1929 Hawk of the Hills (feature of 1927 serial); Redskin; The Black Book (serial). 1930 Der Tanz Geht Weiter. 1931 The Montana Kid; First Aid; Cavalier of the West. 1933 A Bedtime Story. 1934 Bolero. 1939 Beasts of Berlin. 1942 Casablanca. 1943 Action in the North Atlantic. 1944 The Adventures of Mark Twain. 1945 Hotel Berlin; Roughly Speaking. 1947 The Perils of Pauline.

PAPE, EDWARD LIONEL

Born: 1867. Died: Oct. 24, 1944, Woodland Hills, Calif. Screen and stage actor.

Appeared in: 1921 Nobody. 1935 The Man Who Broke the Bank at Monte Carlo. 1936 Mary of Scotland; The White Legion; Beloved Enemy. 1937 The King and the Chorus Girl; The Prince and the Pauper; Wee Willie Winkie; Angel. 1938 Big Broadcast of 1938; Outside of Paradise; Bluebeard's Eighth Wife; Booloo; The Young in Heart. 1939 Love Affair; Rulers of the Sea; Midnight; Fifth Avenue Girl; Drums along the Mohawk. 1940 Raffles; Tin Pan Alley; Zanzibar; The Philadelphia Story; Congo Maisie; The Long Voyage Home; Arise My Love. 1941 Hudson's Bay; Scotland Yard; Charley's Aunt; How Green Was My Valley. 1942 Almost Married.

PARDAVE, JOAQUIN

Born: 1901, Guanajuato, Mexico. Died: July 20, 1955, Mexico City, Mexico. Screen actor, film director, and composer.

Appeared in: 1938 La Zandunga; Los Millones de Chaflan; Cancion del Alma (Song of the Soul); Tierra Brava; Mi Candidato (My Candidato); Bajo el Cielo de Mexico (Beneath the Sky of Mexico); El Senor Alcade (The Mayor); 1939 La Tia de las Muchachas (The Girls' Aunt). 1940 Caballo a Caballo (Horse for Horse); Luna Criolla (Creole Moon); En un Burro Tres Gaturros (Three Rustics on One Donkey); Vivire Otra Vez (I Shall Live Again). 1943 Guadalajara.

PARDAVE, JOSE
Born: 1902, Mexico. Died: May 26, 1970, Mexico City, Mexico. Screen actor.

PARERA, GRACE MOORE. See Grace Moore

PARK, CUSTER B.
Born: 1900. Died: Sept. 25, 1955, Hollywood, Calif. Screen actor and stuntman. Entered films approx. 1927.

Appeared in: 1939 Gone with the Wind. 1954 Vera Cruz.

PARKE, MACDONALD
Born: 1892. Died: July, 1960, London, England. Screen, stage, and television actor.

Appeared in: 1940 Shipyard Sally. 1944 Candlelight in Algeria. 1951 No Orchids for Miss Blandish. 1952 A Tale of Five Women; Babes in Bagdad. 1953 The Paris Express; Penny Princess. 1955 The Good Die Young; Summertime. 1957 Beyond Mombasa. 1959 The Mouse That Roared; I Was Monty's Double (aka Hell, Heaven or Hoboken). 1960 The Battle of the Sexes; A Touch of Larceny.

PARKE, WILLIAM, SR.
Born: 1873. Died: July 28, 1941, New York, N.Y.(heart attack). Screen, stage actor, and film and stage director.

Appeared in: 1922 Tailor-Made Man. 1923 The Hunchback of Notre Dame.

PARKER, BARNETT
Died: Aug. 1941, Los Angeles, Calif. Screen and stage actor.

Appeared in: 1936 The President's Mystery; We Who Are about to Die; Born to Dance. 1937 Personal Property; Dangerous Number; The Last of Mrs. Cheyney; Espionage; Live, Love and Learn; Married before Breakfast; The Emperor's Candlesticks; Broadway Melody of 1938; Double Wedding; Navy Blue and Gold; Wake up and Live. 1938 Love Is a Headache; Hold That Kiss; Marie Antoinette; Listen Darling; The Girl Downstairs; Sally, Irene and Mary; Ready, Willing and Able. 1939 Babes in Arms; At the Circus. 1940 He Married His Wife; La Conga Nights; Hit Parade of 1941; Love Thy Neighbor; One Night in the Tropics. 1941 Tall, Dark and Handsome; A Man Betrayed; The Reluctant Dragon. 1942 New Wine.

PARKER, CECIL (Cecil Schwabe)
Born: Sept. 3, 1897, Hastings, Sussex, England. Died: Apr. 21, 1971, Brighton, England. Screen, stage, and television actor.

Appeared in: 1928 Woman in White. 1933 The Silver Spoon; A Cuckoo in the Nest. 1935 Dirty Work. 1936 The Man Who Lived Again. 1937 Storm in a Teacup; Dark Journey; Bank Holiday. 1938 The Lady Vanishes; Housemaster; The Citadel. 1941 The Saint's Vacation; The Stars Look Down. 1942 Ships with Wings; Suicide Squadron. 1946 Caesar and Cleopatra. 1947 Captain Boycott; The First Gentleman; The Magic Bow; Hungry Hill. 1949 The Weaker Sex; Under Capricorn; The Affairs of a Rogue; The Woman in the Hall; Dear Mr. Prohack; Quartet. 1950 The Amazing Mr. Beecham (aka Chiltern Hundreds). 1951 Tony Draws a Horse. 1952 The Man in the White Suit; The Magic Box. 1953 I Believe in You. 1954 Isn't Life Wonderful?; The Detective (aka Father Brown). 1955 The Constant Husband; Cocktails in the Kitchen (aka For Better, For Worse). 1956 The Court Jester; His Excellency; It's Great to Be Young; Ladykillers; 23 Paces to Baker Street. 1957 True As a Turtle; Paradise Lagoon (aka The Admirable Crichton). 1958 A Tale of Two Cities; Indiscreet. 1959 Happy Is the Bride; The Wreck of the Mary Deare; I Was Monty's Double (aka Hell, Heaven or Hoboken); The Navy Lark. 1960 Swiss Family Robinson; A French Mistress; Under Ten Flags. 1961 The Pure Hell of St. Trinian's; On the Fiddle; Make Mine a Double (aka The Night We Dropped a Clanger). 1962 Petticoat Pirates; Follow That Horse!; The Iron Maiden (aka The Swingin' Maiden—U.S. 1964). 1964 The Comedy Man; Guns at Batasi; Carry on, Jack; The Brain. 1965 A Study in Terror; The Amorous Adventures of Moll Flanders; Operation Snafu; Heavens Above!. 1966 Lady L; A Man Could Get Killed. 1967 Psycho Circus. 1968 The Amorous Mr. Pawn. 1969 Oh, What a Lovely War.

PARKER, FRANK "PINKY"
Born: 1891. Died: June 13, 1962, Hollywood, Calif.(heart attack). Screen, stage actor, and singer.

Appeared in: 1934 Transatlantic Merry-Go-Round. 1935 Sweet Surrender; a Vitaphone short.

PARKER, MARY
Born: 1915, Fort Worth, Tex. Died: June 1, 1966, Beverly Hills, Calif. Screen and stage actress.

Appeared in: 1938 Artists and Models. 1939 St. Louis Blues. 1944 Lady in the Dark; Music for Millions. 1952 Lure of the Wilderness. 1954 Deadly Game.

PARKER, MURRAY
Born: 1896. Died: Oct. 18, 1965, Hollywood, Calif.(heart attack). Screen, television, and vaudeville actor. He performed usually under name of "Uncle Murray."

PARKHURST, FRANCES
Died: Dec. 31, 1969, Caldwell, N.J. Screen actress.

Appeared in: 1926 Men of Steel.

PARKINGTON, BEULAH
Died: Nov. 7, 1958, Hollywood, Calif.(heart condition). Screen actress. Entered films approx. 1928. One of the founders of Screen Extra's Guild.

Appeared in: 1950 My Blue Heaven.

"PARKYAKARKUS" (Harry Einstein, aka HARRY PARKE)
Born: 1904, Boston, Mass. Died: Nov. 24, 1958, Los Angeles, Calif.(heart attack). Screen, stage, television, and radio actor.

Appeared in: 1936 Strike Me Pink. 1937 New Faces of 1937; The Life of the Party. 1938 Night Spot; She's Got Everything. 1940 Glamour Boy. 1942 A Yank in Libya; The Yanks Are Coming. 1944 Sweethearts of the U.S.A.; Earl Carroll's Vanities; Out of This World; Movie Pests (short); Badminton (short).

PARNELL, JAMES
Born: 1923. Died: Dec. 27, 1961, Hollywood, Calif. Screen, stage, and television actor. Son of screen actor Emory Parnell.

Appeared in: 1951 G.I. Jane. 1952 Yankee Buccaneer; No Room for the Groom. 1953 War Paint. 1954 White Christmas; The Looters. 1955 Crime against Joe; You're Never Too Young. 1956 The Birds and the Bees; Running Target. 1957 War Drums; Outlaw's Son. 1960 Walking Target. 1961 Gun Fight. 1962 The Clown and the Kid; Incident in an Alley.

PARRAVICINI, FLORENCIO
Born: 1874, South America. Died: Mar. 25, 1941, Buenos Aires, Argentina (suicide following long illness). Screen, stage actor, stage producer, and screenwriter.

Appeared in: 1937 Melgarejo. 1938 Que Tiempos Aquellos (Those Were the Days). 1939 La Vida es un Tango (Life Is a Tango).

PARRISH, HELEN
Born: Mar. 12, 1924, Columbus, Ga. Died: Feb. 22, 1959, Hollywood, Calif. Screen and television actress. Appeared in "Our Gang" series and "Smithy" comedies from 1927-1929.

Appeared in: 1927 Babe Comes Home (film debut). 1929 Words and Music. 1930 His First Command; The Big Trail. 1931 Cimarron; Seed; X Marks the Spot. 1932 When a Feller Needs a Friend. 1934 There's Always Tomorrow. 1935 A Dog of Flanders; Straight from the Heart. 1936 Make Way for a Lady; Three Smart Girls. 1938 Mad about Music; Little Tough Guy; Little Tough Guy in Society. 1939 Three Smart Girls Grow Up; First Love; Winter Carnival. 1940 I'm Nobody's Sweetheart Now; You'll Find Out. 1941 Where Did You Get That Girl?; Six Lessons from Madame La Zonga; Too Many Blondes. 1942 They All Kissed the Bride; In Old California; X Marks the Spot (and 1931 version); Tough as They Come. 1943 Cinderella Swings It; The Mystery of the 13th Guest. 1944 They Live in Fear; Meet Miss Bobby-Socks. 1945 Let's Go Steady; A Thousand and One Nights. 1948 Trouble Makers. 1949 The Wolf Hunters; Quick on the Trigger.

PARROTT, CHARLES. See Charley Chase

PARROTT, JAMES (aka POLL PARROTT)
Born: 1892, Baltimore; Md. Died: May 10, 1939, Hollywood, Calif.(heart attack). Screen actor, film director, producer, and screenwriter. Entered films for Pathe under name of Poll Parrott in 1918. Brother of screen actor Charlie Chase (dec. 1940).

Appeared in: 1921 Big Town Ideas.

PARSON, CAROL
Died: Dec. 18, 1958, New York, N.Y. Screen and stage actress.

PASHA, KALLA
Born: 1877, New York, N.Y. Died: June 10, 1933, Talmage, Calif. Screen and stage actor. Entered films with Mack Sennett.

Appeared in: 1921 Home Talent; A Small Town Idol. 1922 The

Dictator; Thirty Days. 1923 Breaking into Society; Hollywood; A Million to Burn; Racing Hearts; Scaramouche; Ruggles of Red Gap. 1924 Yukon Jake. 1925 Heads Up. 1926 Don Juan's Three Nights; Rose of the Tenements; Silken Shackles. 1927 Wolf's Clothing; The Devil Dancer; The Dove. 1928 Tillie's Punctured Romance; West of Zanzibar. 1929 Seven Footprints to Satan; The Show of Shows.

PASQUIER, CHARLES "BACH"
Born: 1881, France. Died: Nov. 19, 1953, Paris, France (heart attack). Screen, stage, radio, and circus actor.

PATCH, WALLY (Walter Vinicombe)
Born: Sept. 26, 1888, London, England. Died: Oct. 27, 1970, London, England. Screen actor.

Appeared in: 1930 Balaclava. 1931 Sport of Kings, Shadows, Jaws of Hell, The Battle of Gallipoli. 1933 Don Quixote; Trouble; Sorrel and Son; The Good Companions. 1934 Marooned; The Man I Want; Passing Shadows; The Scotland Yard Mystery; Those Were the Days; Say It with Song. 1935 Get Off My Foot. 1936 Not So Dusty; The Interrupted Honeymoon; The Man Who Could Work Miracles. 1937 Farewell Again; Doctor Syn; Men Are Not Gods. 1938 Bank Holiday; Alf's Button Afloat; Break the News; Pygmalion; The Ware Case; Troopship. 1939 Inspector Hornleigh. 1940 Quiet Wedding; Gasbags. 1941 Neutral Port; Inspector Hornleigh Goes to It; The Common Touch. 1942 In Which We Serve. 1943 Jeannie; Women in Bondage. 1944 Up in Mabel's Room. 1945 Old Mother Riley at Home. 1947 The Ghosts of Berkeley Square. 1949 The Guinea Pig. 1950 Appointment with Crime. 1953 Will Any Gentleman?. 1955 Private's Progress. 1957 Suspended Alibi; Morning Call. 1958 Your Past Is Showing (aka The Naked Truth). 1959 I'm All Right, Jack. 1960 It Takes a Thief (aka The Challenge-U.S. 1962). 1961 The Millionairess. 1963 Sparrows Can't Sing. Other British film: George in Civvy Street.

PATON, STUART
Born: 1885, Glasgow, Scotland. Died: Dec. 16, 1944, Woodland Hills, Calif. Screen and stage actor, film director, producer, and screenwriter. Married to screen actress Ethel Patrick (dec. 1944).

PATRICK, ETHEL
Born: 1887. Died: Sept. 18, 1944, Woodland Hills, Calif. Screen and stage actress. Married to screen actor/director Stuart Paton (dec. 1944)

PATRICK, JEROME
Born: 1883, New Zealand. Died: Sept. 26, 1923, N.Y.(heart disease). Screen and stage actor.

Appeared in: 1919 Three Men and a Girl. 1920 The Furnace; Officer 666. 1921 Don't Call Me Little Girl; School Days; The Other Woman; Forever; The Heart Line. 1924 Sinners in Silk.

PATRICOLA, TOM
Born: Jan. 27, 1894, New Orleans, La. Died: Jan. 1, 1950, Pasadena, Calif.(following brain surgery). Screen, stage, and vaudeville actor. Entered films in 1929.

Appeared in: 1929 Happy Days; Words and Music; Frozen Justice; Married in Hollywood; Si-Si Senor (short); South Sea Rose. 1930 The Three Sisters; One Mad Kiss; Anybody's Woman. 1931 Children of Dreams. 1932 Moonlight and Cactus (short). 1933 El Precio de un Beso; La Melodia Prohibida; No Dejes la Puerta Abierta. 1935 the following shorts: Moonlight and Melody; Dame Shy, Kiss the Bride. 1936 Fresh from the Fleet (short). 1945 Rhapsody in Blue.

PATSTON, DORIS
Born: 1904, London, England. Died: June 12, 1957, Darien, Conn. Screen and stage actress.

Appeared in: 1932 Smiling Faces.

PATTERSON, ELIZABETH
Born: 1876, Savannah, Tenn. Died: Jan. 31, 1966, Los Angeles, Calif. Screen, stage, television, and radio actress.

Appeared in: 1926 The Boy Friend; The Return of Peter Grimm. 1929 Words and Music; South Sea Rose. 1930 The Lone Star Ranger; Harmony at Home; The Big Party; The Cat Creeps. 1931 Tarnished Lady; The Smiling Lieutenant; Daddy Long Legs; Penrod and Sam; Heaven on Earth. 1932 Love Me Tonight; Miss Pinkerton; Husband's Holiday; A Bill of Divorcement; Dangerous Brunette; The Way of Life; Two against the World; The Expert; Play Girl; So Big; New Morals for Old; Life Begins; Guilty as Hell; They Call It Sin; Breach of Promise; No Man of Her Own; The Conquerors. 1933 They Just Had to Get Married; The In-

fernal Machine; Story of Temple Drake; Golden Harvest; Dinner at Eight; Hold Your Man; The Secret of the Blue Room; Doctor Bull. 1934 Hideout. 1935 Chasing Yesterday; Men without Names; So Red the Rose. 1936 The Return of Sophie Lang; Timothy's Quest; Her Master's Voice; Three Cheers for Love; Go West, Young Man; Small Town Girl; Old Hutch. 1937 A Night of Mystery; High, Wide and Handsome; Hold 'Em Navy; Night Club Scandal. 1938 Scandal Sheet; Bulldog Drummond's Peril; Bluebeard's Eighth Wife; Sing, You Sinners; The Adventures of Tom Sawyer; Sons of the Legion. 1939 The Story of Alexander Graham Bell; Bulldog Drummond's Bride; The Cat and the Canary; Our Leading Citizen; Bad Little Angel; Bulldog Drummond's Secret Police. 1940 Remember the Night; Adventure in Diamonds; Anne of Windy Poplars; Earthbound; Who Killed Aunt Maggie?; Michael Shayne, Private Detective. 1941 Kiss the Boys Goodbye; Tobacco Road; Belle Starr; The Vanishing Virginian. 1942 Almost Married; Beyond the Blue Horizon; Her Cardboard Lover; My Sister Eileen; I Married a Witch; Lucky Legs. 1943 The Sky's the Limit. 1944 Follow the Boys; Hail the Conquering Hero; Together Again. 1945 Colonel Effingham's Raid; Lady on a Train. 1946 I've Always Loved You; The Secret Heart. 1947 Welcome Stranger; The Shocking Miss Pilgrim; Out of the Blue. 1948 Miss Tatlock's Millions. 1949 Little Women; Intruder in the Dust; Song of Surrender. 1950 Bright Leaf. 1951 Katie Did It. 1952 Washington Story. 1955 Las Vegas Shakedown. 1957 Pal Joey. 1959 The Oregon Trail. 1960 Tall Story.

PATTERSON, JOY W.
Born: 1906. Died: Mar. 23, 1959, Santa Ana, Calif. Screen actress and dancer.

Appeared in: 1926-29 many of the "Collegians" series of shorts.

PAULIG, ALBERT
Born: Germany. Died: Mar. 1933 (heart trouble). Screen and stage actor.

Appeared in: 1929 Dancing Vienna; It's Easy to Become a Father. 1931 Ein Burschenlied aus Heidelberg; Susanne Macht Ordnung. 1932 Ein Ausgekochter Junge; Der Schrecken der Garnison; Girsekorn Greift Ein; Schoen 1st die Manoeverzeit; Drunter und Drueber. 1933 Der Tanzhusar. 1934 Zu Befehl, Herr Unteroffizier; Es War Einmal ein Walzer; Annemarie, Die Braut der Kompanie. 1935 Drei von der Kavallerie.

PAULL, TOWNSEND D.
Born: 1898. Died: Oct. 8, 1933, Los Angeles, Calif.(murdered). Screen and stage actor.

PAULSEN, ARNO
Born: 1900, Stettin, Germany. Died: Sept. 17, 1969, Baden-Baden, West Germany. Screen and stage actor.

Appeared in: 1948 Razzia; Murderers among Us. 1949 The Affair Blum. 1962 Wozzeck.

PAULSEN, HARALD
Born: 1895, Elmshorn, Hollstein, Germany. Died: Aug. 5, 1954, Hamburg, Germany (heart attack). Screen, stage, opera actor, and stage director.

Appeared in: 1932 Mein Leopold; Die Blumenfrau von Lindenau. 1934 Tausend Fuer Eine Nacht; Alraune. 1935 Ich Sing Mich in Dein Herz Hinein; Frischer Wind aus Kanada. 1936 Oberwachtmeister Schwenke; Traumulus; Der Mutige Seefahrer. 1937 Besuch am Abend; If We All Were Angels; For Her Country's Sake. 1938 Der Lachende Dritte; Krach und Blueckum Kuennemann (Row and Joy about Kuennemann); Sie und die Drei (She and the Three). 1939 1A in Oberbayern (1A in Upper Bavaria). 1940 The Living Dead. Other German films: Die Ledige Witwe; Stradivari; Kunstlerliebe.

PAUNCEFORT, GEORGE
Born: 1870. Died: Mar. 25, 1942, Los Angeles, Calif. Screen and stage actor. Entered films approx. 1932.

PAVLOVA, ANNA
Born: Jan. 3, 1885, St. Petersburg, Russia. Died: Jan. 23, 1931, The Hague, Netherlands. Ballerina and screen actress. Entered films in 1915.

Appeared in: 1916 The Dumb Girl of Portici.

PAVON, BLANCA ESTELA
Born: 1926, Mexico. Died: Sept. 26, 1949, near Mexico City, Mexico (plane crash). Screen and radio actress. Dubbed in Spanish voice of Vivien Leigh in 1939 Gone with the Wind and Ingrid Bergman in 1944 Gaslight (aka Angel Street).

PAWLE, LENNOX
Born: 1872, London, England. Died: Feb. 22, 1936, Los Angeles, Calif.(cerebral hemorrhage). Screen and stage actress.

Appeared in: 1918 The Admirable Crichton. 1922 The Glorious Adventure. 1929 Married in Hollywood; Hot for Paris; The Sky Hawk. 1931 The Sin of Madelon Claudet. 1935 David Copperfield; Sylvia Scarlet; The Gay Deception.

PAWLEY, WILLIAM
Born: 1905, Kansas City, Mo. Died: June 15, 1952, New York, N.Y. Screen and stage actor.

Appeared in: 1931 Bad Girl; The Spider; Over the Hill. 1932 Cheaters at Play; After Tomorrow; Careless Lady; Amateur Daddy; The Trial of Vivienne Ware; Letty Lynton; Speak Easily; Central Park. 1933 Robbers' Roost; Gabriel over the White House. 1935 The Daring Young Man; Stolen Harmony; Mary Burns, Fugitive; Kentucky Kernels. 1936 Boulder Dam; The Big Noise; Bullets or Ballots; Public Enemy's Wife. 1937 San Quentin; Born Reckless; The River of Missing Men; Trapped by G-Men. 1938 International Crime; Crime Takes a Holiday; White Banners. 1939 Boy Slaves; Panama Lady; Rough Riders Round-Up; Union Pacific; Disputed Passage. 1940 Grapes of Wrath; Johnny Apollo; The Great Profile; Double Alibi; Yukon Flight; West of Abilene; Mercy Plane; The Return of Frank James. 1941 The Great American Broadcast. 1942 Time to Kill.

PAXTON, SIDNEY
Born: 1861. Died: Oct. 13, 1930, Montauk, N.Y. Screen and stage actor.

Appeared in: 1925 The Midnight Girl; Old Home Week. 1928 Mark of the Frog (serial).

PAYNE, DOUGLAS
Born: 1875. Died: Aug. 1965, England. Screen and stage actor.
Appeared in: 1929 The Scarlet Devil; The Triumph of the Scarlet Pimpernel.

PAYNE, LOUIS "LOU" (Louis William Payne)
Born: Jan. 13, 1876, New York, N.Y. Died: Aug. 14, 1953, Woodland Hills, Calif. Screen and stage actor. Married to screen actress Mrs. Leslie Carter (dec. prior to 1953). Entered films approx. 1923.

Appeared in: 1924 True as Steel; For Sale; In Hollywood with Potash and Perlmutter. 1925 Alias Mary Flynn; The Last Edition; The Fate of a Flirt; We Moderns; As Man Desires; The Only Thing; The Lady Who Lied. 1926 The Blind Goddess; The Shamrock Handicap; The Outsider; A Woman's Heart. 1927 King of Kings; Broadway Madness; Vanity; The Yankee Clipper. 1928 The Whip. 1929 Evangeline; Big News; Interference; Lawful Larceny; Part Time Wife; The Dude Wrangler. 1945 Saratoga Trunk.

PAYSON, BLANCHE
Born: 1881. Died: July 3, 1964, Hollywood, Calif. Screen actress. Entered films with Mack Sennett.

Appeared in: 1916 Wife and Auto Trouble; A Bath House Blunder; A la Cabaret; Dollars and Sense. 1917 Oriental Love. 1925 Oh, Doctor!; We Moderns. 1926 La Boheme. 1927 Figures Don't Lie; The Bachelor's Baby. 1931 Wicked; Helpmates (short). 1932 The Impatient Maiden; Red Noses (short). 1935 Hoi Polloi (short). 1937 All over Town.

PAYTON, BARBARA
Born: Nov. 16, 1927, Cloquet, Minn. Died: May 8, 1967, San Diego, Calif.(natural causes). Screen actress. Divorced from screen actor Franchot Tone (dec. 1968).

Appeared in many westerns during the 1940s and the following: 1940 Once More, My Darling; Trapped. 1950 Dallas; Kiss Tomorrow Goodbye. 1951 Only the Valiant; Drums in the Deep South; Bride of the Gorilla. 1953 Run for the Hills; The Bad Blonde (aka This Woman is Trouble); The Great Jesse James Raid; Four-Sided Triangle. 1955 Murder Is My Beat; The Flanagan Boy.

PEABODY, EDDY
Born: Feb. 19, 1912, Reading, Mass. Died: Nov. 7, 1970, Covington, Ky.(stroke). Screen, television, radio actor, and banjo player. Known as "King of the Banjo."

Appeared in: 1927 Banjomania (short). 1928 In a Music Shop (short); Banjoland (short). 1934 The Lemon Drop Kid. 1935 Shoestring Follies (short). 1936-1938 Vitaphone and Paramount shorts.

PEACOCK, KEITH
Born: 1931. Died: Nov. 1, 1966, Perivale, England (accident while filming a stunt for television). Screen and television stuntman.

Appeared in: 1967 Casino Royale.

PEACOCK, KIM
Born: 1901, Watford, Herts, England. Died: Dec. 26, 1966, Emsworth, England (heart attack). Screen, stage, radio, and television actor.

Appeared in: 1930 The Manxman. 1934 Waltz Time. 1938 Captain's Orders; Climbing High; Night Alone; Alerte en Mediteranee (S.O.S. Mediterranean - U.S. 1940). 1940 Hell's Cargo. Other British films: Crooked Billet; Waltz Time; White Ensign; Warm Corner; Expert's Opinion; Mad Hatters; Things to Come; Grand Finale; Midnight at Mme. Tussaud's; Sunset in Vienna.

PEARCE, ALICE
Born: 1919. Died: Mar. 3, 1966, Los Angeles, Calif.(cancer). Screen, stage, and television actress.

Appeared in: 1949 On the Town. 1952 The Belle of New York. 1955 How to Be Very, Very Popular. 1956 The Opposite Sex. 1962 Lad: A Dog. 1963 The Thrill of It All; Tammy and the Doctor; Beach Party; My Six Loves. 1964 The Disorderly Orderly; Dear Heart; Kiss Me, Stupid. 1965 Dear Brigitte; Darn That Cat; Bus Riley's Back in Town. 1966 The Glass Bottom Boat.

PEARCE, GEORGE C.
Born: 1865, New York, N.Y. Died: Aug. 12, 1940, Los Angeles, Calif. Screen, stage, opera actor, and film director.

Appeared in: 1921 Black Beauty; The Traveling Salesman; Three Word Brand. 1922 The Primitive Lover; Watch Your Step. 1923 The Midnight Alarm; The Printer's Devil; The Country Kid. 1924 Cornered; Daring Youth; The Narrow Street; Wandering Husbands; Hold Your Breath. 1925 The Wife Who Wasn't Wanted. 1926 The Social Highwayman; Hold That Lion. 1927 The Irresistible Lover; Quarantined Rivals. 1928 Do Your Duty; Masquerade; Home James; Wild West Romance. 1929 The Valiant. 1930 The Lone Rider; Personality; Vengeance; The Right of Way. 1931 Men in Her Life; The Right to Love. 1932 This Reckless Age. 1933 Story of Temple Drake; Lone Cowboy. 1934 British Agent; Six of a Kind. 1936 The Singing Cowboy. 1937 When You're in Love.

PEARCE, VERA
Born: 1896, Australia. Died: Jan. 21, 1966, London, England. Screen, stage actress, and singer.

Appeared in: 1932 Yes, Mr. Brown; Just My Luck. 1933 That's a Good Girl. 1935 So You Won't Talk. 1938 Yes, Madam?. 1939 What's a Man. 1947 Nicholas Nickleby. 1951 Men of Sherwood Forest; One Wild Cat. 1961 Make Mine a Double.

PEARSON, LLOYD
Born; Dec. 13, 1897, Bradford, Yorkshire, England. Died: June 2, 1966, London, England. Screen, stage, and television actor.

Appeared in: 1938 The Challenge (film debut). 1940 Tilly of Bloomsbury. 1941 Kipps. 1942 When We Are Married. 1943 Schweig's New Adventure. 1944 Uncensored; My Learned Friend. 1949 Mr. Perrin and Mr. Trail; Under Capricorn. 1950 Dear Mr. Prohack; Bond Street. 1951 Portrait of Clare. 1952 Hindle Wakes. 1957 Good Companions. 1959 The Angry Silence. Other British films: Banana Ridge; Time Flies; Three Weird Sisters; Private Information; Robin Hood.

PEARSON, VIRGINIA
Born: 1888, Louisville, Ky. Died: June 6, 1958, Los Angeles, Calif.(uremic poisoning). Married to screen actor Sheldon Lewis (dec. 1958). Screen and stage actress.

Appeared in: 1916 The Vital Question; The Kiss of a Vampire; Blazing Love. 1917 A Royal Romance. 1919 The Bishop's Emeralds. 1923 Sister against Sister; A Prince of a King. 1925 The Phantom of the Opera; The Wizard of Oz; Red Kimona. 1926 Lightning Hutch (serial); Atta Boy; Silence; The Taxi Mystery. 1927 Driven from Home. 1928 What Price Beauty; The Big City; The Actress; The Power of Films. 1929 Smilin' Guns. 1930 Danger Man. 1931 Primrose Path. 1932 Back Street.

PECKHAM, FRANCES MILES
Born: 1893. Died: June 7, 1959, New York, N.Y. Screen and stage actress.

PEER, HELEN
Born: 1898. Died: May 6, 1942, New Rochelle, N.Y. Screen, stage actress, and singer.

Appeared on screen for the Thomas A. Edison Co.

"PEERLESS ANNABELLE" (Annabelle Whitford Buchan)
Born: 1878. Died: Nov. 30, 1961, Chicago, Ill. Screen and stage actress. She was the original "Gibson Girl" as created by Charles Dana Gibson.

Appeared in: 1897 Annabelle's Butterfly Dance.

PEIL, EDWARD, SR. (Charles Edward Peil)
Born: 1888. Died: Dec. 29, 1958, Hollywood, Calif. Screen actor. Father of actor Edward Peil, Jr.(dec. 1962). Entered films in 1908.

Appeared in: 1919 Broken Blossoms. 1920 Isobel. 1921 Dream Street; That Girl Montana; The Killer; The Servant in the House. 1922 Arabia; Don't Doubt Your Wife; Broken Chains; The Dust Flower; The Song of Life. 1923 Purple Dawn; The Lone Star Ranger; Stepping Fast; Three Jumps Ahead. 1924 The Iron Horse; $50,000 Reward; The Man Who Came Back; Teeth. 1925 The Hunted Woman; Double Action Daniels; The Man without a Country; The Pleasure Buyers; The Wife Who Wasn't Wanted; The Fighting Heart. 1926 The Girl from Montmartre; Midnight Faces; Black Paradise; Yellow Fingers; The Great K & A Train Robbery. 1927 King of Kings; Framed; Tumbling River. 1929 Masked Emotions; In Old Arizona. 1930 Cock O' the Walk. 1931 Clearing the Range; The Texas Ranger; Wild Horse; Cracked Nuts. 1932 The Gay Buckaroo; Charlie Chan's Chance; Local Bad Man; The Hatchet Man. 1933 Tombstone Canyon; The Big Cage. 1934 Blue Steel; The Man from Utah; Pursuit of Happiness. 1935 Million Dollar Baby; Mysterious Mr. Wong; Ladies Crave Excitement. 1936 Texas Rangers. 1937 Come on, Cowboys!; Two-Fisted Sheriff; Heroes of the Alamo. 1938 Colorado Trail. 1939 The Night Riders; Spoilers of the Range. 1940 One Man's Law. 1941 Billy the Kid's Fighting Pals; The Lone Rider in Ghost Town; Texas Marshal. 1942 Black Dragons; Pride of the Yankees; Foreign Agent. 1943 Robin Hood of the Range; Billy the Kid in the Kid Rides Again.

PEIL, EDWARD, JR. (Charles Edward Peil)
Born: 1908. Died: Nov. 7, 1962. Screen actor. Appeared as a child actor during silents as Johnny Jones and later as Edward Peil, Jr. See Johnny Jones for early films. Son of screen actor Edward Peil (dec. 1958).

Appeared in: 1925 The Goose Hangs High; Rose of the World. 1926 The Family Upstairs. 1928 The Little Yellow House. 1929 The College Coquette.

PEIRCE, EVELYN. See Evelyn Pierce

PELLICER, PINA (Josefina Pellicer Lopez Llergo)
Born: 1940, Mexico. Died: Dec. 10, 1964, Mexico City, Mexico (suicide). Screen, stage, and television actress.

Appeared in: 1960 Macario; 1961 One Eyed Jacks. 1963 Dias de Otoro (Autumn Days)—received the PECIME (Mexican Film Writers) award for Best Actress. 1967 Los Bandidos. 1968 Days of the Evil Gun.

PELLY, FARRELL
Born: 1891. Died: Apr. 23, 1963, New York, N.Y. Screen, stage, and television actor.

Appeared in: 1959 Darby O'Gill and the Little People.

PEMBERTON, HENRY W.
Born: 1875. Died: July 26, 1952, Orlando, Fla. Screen, stage, and vaudeville actor.

Appeared in: 1921 Luxury.

PENA, RALPH
Born: 1927. Died: May 20, 1969, Mexico City, Mexico (car accident injuries). Screen actor, screenwriter, and musician.

PENBROOK, HARRY
Born: 1887. Died: Sept. 14, 1960, Hollywood, Calif. Screen actor and extra. Entered films approx. 1908.

PENDLETON, NAT
Born: Aug. 9, 1899, Davenport, Iowa. Died: Oct. 11, 1967, San Diego, Calif.(heart attack). Screen, stage actor, and professional wrestler. Entered films as a juvenile with Lubin.

Appeared in: 1924 The Hoosier Schoolmaster. 1926 Let's Get Married; 1929 The Laughing Lady. 1930 Fair Warning; The Sea Wolf; Last of the Duanes; The Big Pond; Liliom. 1931 Secret Witness; Larceny Lane; Vigor of Youth; The Seas Beneath; The Star Witness; Mr. Lemon of Orange; Blonde Crazy; Spirit of Notre Dame; Pottsville Paluka; Cauliflower Alley. 1932 Play Girl; The Sign of the Cross; Cardigan's Last Case; Taxi; Attorney

for the Defense; Hell Fire Austin; Exposure; You Said a Mouthful; Night Club Lady; Horse Feathers; Manhattan Parade; Beast of the City; A Fool's Advice; By Whose Hands?. 1933 Deception; Whistling in the Dark; Baby Face; College Coach; Goldie Gets Along; Lady for a Day; Penthouse; The Chief; I'm No Angel. 1934 Fugitive Lovers; The Defense Rests; The Cat's Paw; Girl from Missouri; Straight Is the Way; Lazy River; Manhattan Melodrama; Death on the Diamond; The Thin Man; The Gay Bride; Sing and Like It. 1935 Times Square Lady; Baby Face Harrington; Reckless; Murder in the Fleet; Calm Yourself; Here Comes the Band; It's in the Air. 1936 The Garden Murder Case; The Great Ziegfeld; Sworn Enemy; Trapped by Television; Two in a Crowd; The Luckiest Girl in the World; Sing Me a Love Song. 1937 Under Cover of Night; Song of the City; Gangway; Life Begins in College. 1938 Meet the Mayor; Young Dr. Kildare; Swing Your Lady; Arsene Lupin Returns; Fast Company; Shopworn Angel; The Chaser; The Crowd Roars. 1939 Burn 'em up, O'Connor; Calling Dr. Kildare; It's a Wonderful World; 6,000 Enemies; On Borrowed Time; At the Circus; Another Thin Man; The Secret of Dr. Kildare; Young Dr. Kildare. 1940 The Ghost Comes Home; Dr. Kildare's Strange Case; Phantom Raiders; The Golden Fleecing; Flight Command; Dr. Kildare's Crisis; Dr. Kildare's Wedding Day; Dr. Kildare Goes Home; Northwest Passage. 1941 Death Valley; Buck Privates; Top Sergeant Mulligan; The Mad Doctor of Market Street. 1942 Jail House Blues; Calling Dr. Gillespie; Dr. Gillespie's New Assistant. 1943 Dr. Gillespie's Criminal Case. 1944 The Sign of the Cross (revised version of 1932 film); Swing Fever. 1945 Rookies Come Home. 1947 Buck Privates Come Home; Scared to Death. 1949 Death Valley. 1964 Big Parade of Comedy (documentary).

PENMAN, LEA
Born: 1895. Died: Oct. 12, 1962, Hollywood, Calif. Screen and stage actress.

Appeared in: 1926 The Romance of a Million Dollars. 1950 Stella; Fancy Pants. 1955 We're No Angels. 1957 Portland Expose.

PENNELL, RICHARD O.
Born: 1861, Chester, England. Died: Mar. 22, 1934, Hollywood, Calif. Screen actor. Entered films in 1914.

Appeared in: 1927 The Masked Woman. 1928 The Olympic Hero; Dressed to Kill; Clothes Make the Woman. 1930 On the Level.

PENNER, JOE (Joseph Pinter)
Born: Nov. 11, 1905, Budapest, Hungary. Died: Jan. 10, 1941, Philadelphia, Pa.(heart attack). Screen, stage, radio, vaudeville, and burlesque actor.

Appeared in: 1930 the following shorts: Seeing-Off-Service; Stepping Out; A Stuttering Romance; Surface Stripes. 1931 Making Good (short); Sax Appeal (short). 1932 the following shorts: Gangway; Moving In; Where Men Are Men. 1932-33 Big Star Comedies and Big "V" Comedies. 1934 College Rhythm. 1936 Collegiate. 1937 New Faces of 1937. 1938 I'm from the City; Mr. Doodle Kicks Off; Go Chase Yourself. 1939 The Day The Bookies Wept. 1940 Millionaire Playboy; Glamour Boy; The Boys from Syracuse.

PENNICK, JACK
Born: 1895, Portland, Oreg. Died: Aug. 16, 1964, Hollywood, Calif. Screen and stage actor.

Appeared in: 1927 The Broncho Twister; The Lone Eagle. 1928 Plastered in Paris; The Four Sons; Why Sailors Go Wrong. 1929 Strong Boy. 1930 The City Girl; Paramount on Parade; Way Out West; Born Reckless. 1931 Hell Divers. 1932 Strangers of the Evening; Phantom Express; Air Mail; If I Had a Million; Sky Bride. 1933 Strange People; Tugboat Annie; Renegades of the West; Hello Everybody!; Skyway, Man of Sentiment. 1934 Come on Marines!; The World Moves On. 1935 West Point of the Air; Steamboat 'Round the Bend; Waterfront Lady. 1936 Prisoner of Shark Island; The Music Goes 'Round; Under Two Flags; Private Number; Drift Fence. 1937 Wee Willie Winkie; The Big City; Live, Love and Learn; Navy Blue and Gold; Great Guy; Devil's Playground; Submarine. 1938 You and Me; The Buccaneer; Banjo on My Knee; Alexander's Ragtime Band; King of the Newsboys; Submarine Patrol; Cocoanut Grove. 1939 Union Pacific; Star Maker; Tail Spin; Young Mr. Lincoln; Stagecoach; Mountain Rhythm; Drums along the Mohawk. 1940 The Grapes of Wrath; The Long Voyage Home; The Westerner; Northwest Mounted Police. 1941 Tobacco Road; Sergeant York; Wild Geese Calling; Lady from Louisiana. 1945 They Were Expendable. 1946 My Darling Clementine. 1947 The Fugitive; Unconquered. 1948 Fort Apache; Three Godfathers. 1949 She Wore a Yellow Ribbon; Mighty Joe Young; The Fighting Kentuckian. 1950 When Willie Comes Marching Home; Rio Grande; Tripoli. 1951 Operation Pacific; The Fighting Coast Guard; The Sea Hornet. 1952 What

Price Glory?. 1953 The Sun Shines Bright; The Beast from 20,000 Fathoms. 1955 Mr. Roberts; The Long Gray Line. 1956 Searchers. 1957 The Wings of Eagles. 1958 The Last Hurrah; The Buccaneer (and 1938 version). 1959 The Horse Soldiers. 1960 The Alamo; Sergeant Rutledge. 1961 Two Rode Together. 1962 The Man Who Shot Liberty Valance.

PENNINGTON, ANN
Born: 1894, Camden, N.J. Died: Nov. 4, 1971, N.Y. Screen, stage actress, and dancer. Credited with having popularized the dance craze "The Black Bottom."

Appeared in: 1916 Susie Snowflakes; The Rainbow Princess. 1917 The Antics of Ann; Sunshine Nan; Little Boy Scout. 1924 Manhandled. 1925 The Mad Dancer; The Lucky Horseshoe; A Kiss in the Dark; The Golden Strain; Madame Behave; Pretty Ladies. 1929 Tanned Legs; The Gold Diggers of Broadway; Is Everybody Happy?; Night Parade; Night Club. 1930 Happy Days; Hello Baby (short). 1943 China Girl.

PENNY, FRANK
Born: 1895. Died: Apr. 20, 1946, New York. Screen, radio, vaudeville, and burlesque actor. Was in vaudeville in an act billed as "Penny, Reed and Gold."

Appeared in: 1941 Hold That Ghost, Keep 'Em Flying. 1942 Pardon My Sarong; Eagle Squadron; Who Done It?. 1943 It Ain't Hay. 1944 Lost in a Harem. 1945 Abbott and Costello in Hollywood; Dolly Sisters; Diamond Horseshoe.

PEPPER, BARBARA
Born: May 31, 1916, New York, N.Y. Died: July 18, 1969, Panorama City, Calif.(coronary). Screen, stage, and television actress.

Appeared in: 1933 Roman Scandals. 1934 Our Daily Bread. 1935 The Singing Vagabond; Let 'Em Have It; Waterfront Lady; Frisco Waterfront; Forced Landing; Sagebrush Troubadour. 1936 Showboat; Rogues' Tavern; Wanted: Jane Turner; M'Liss; Mummy's Boys; The Big Game; Winterset. 1937 Sea Devils; Too Many Wives; You Can't Buy Luck; You Can't Beat Love; The Big Shot; Forty Naughty Girls; The Westland Case; Portia on Trial; Music for Madame. 1938 Hollywood Stadium Mystery; Army Girl; Outside the Law; The Lady in the Morgue; Wide Open Faces. 1939 They Made Me a Criminal; The Magnificent Fraud; Colorado Sunset; Flight at Midnight; The Women; Three Sons. 1940 Forgotten Girls; Foreign Correspondent; The Castle on the Hudson; The Return of Frank James; Women in War. 1941 Manpower; Man at Large; Three Sons O'Guns; Birth of the Blues. 1942 One Thrilling Night. 1943 So This is Washington; Girls in Chains; Let's Face It; Star Spangled Rhythm. 1944 Since You Went Away; Henry Aldrich Plays Cupid; Cover Girl; Once upon a Time. 1945 The Hidden Eye; Brewster's Millions; Murder, He Says; Trouble Chasers; The Naughty Nineties. 1946 Prison Ship. 1947 Terror Trail; The Millerson Case. 1950 Unmasked. 1952 Thunderbirds. 1953 Inferno. 1957 The D.I. 1963 A Child Is Waiting. 1964 Kiss Me, Stupid.

PEPPER, ROBERT C.
Born: 1916. Died: Oct. 27, 1964, Hollywood, Calif. Screen actor and stuntman. Stand-in for Broderick Crawford and Lon Chaney, Jr.

PERCIVAL, WALTER C. (Charles David Lingenfelter)
Born: 1887, Chicago, Ill. Died: Jan. 28, 1934, Hollywood, Calif. Screen, stage, and vaudeville actor. Was partner in vaudeville with his wife, Rennie Noel.

Appeared in: 1924 The Moral Sinner. 1926 The Flying Horseman. 1928 The Big City; Lights of New York. 1930 Twixt Love and Duty (short); The Leather Pushers (serial); Shooting Straight; Lightnin'. 1931 Blonde Crazy; The Avenger; Smart Money; Sweepstakes; Pagan Lady; Homicide Squad; Larceny Lane; The Champ. 1932 Carnival Boat; Cabin in the Cotton.

PERCY, ESME (Saville Esme Percy)
Born: Aug. 8, 1887, London, England. Died: June 17, 1957, Brighton, England. Screen, stage actor, and stage producer.

Appeared in: 1930 Murder. 1932 The Lucky Number. 1933 On Secret Service; Summer Lightning, Bitter Sweet. 1934 Nell Gwyn; Unfinished Symphony. 1935 Abdul the Damned; Invitation to the Waltz; An Old Spanish Custom (aka The Invaders). 1936 The Amateur Gentleman; Accused; Land without Music; Spy 77; A Woman Alone; The Song of Freedom. 1937 Our Fighting Navy; When Thief Meets Thief; The Return of the Scarlet Pimpernel; Two Who Dared. 1938 Pygmalion. 1940 21 Days Together. 1945 Caesar

and Cleopatra. 1946 Dead of Night; The Ghosts of Berkeley Square. 1948 Death in the Hand. Other British film: Lisbon Story.

PERIOLAT, GEORGE
Born: 1876, Chicago, Ill. Died: Feb. 20, 1940, Los Angeles, Calif. (suicide-arsenic). Screen and stage actor. Entered films with Essanay in 1911.

Appeared in: 1915 The Adventures of Terence O'Rourke; The Diamond from the Sky (serial). 1916 Landon's Legacy. 1917 The Mate of the Sally Ann. 1920 The Mark of Zorro. 1921 Her Face Value; The Kiss; A Parisian Scandal; They Shall Pay; Wealth; Who Am I?. 1922 Blood and Sand; The Dust Flower; Gay and Devilish; Shattered Idols; The Young Rajah. 1923 Rosita; The Barefoot Boy; Slave of Desire; The Tiger's Claw. 1924 The Red Lily; The Girl on the Stairs; Lover's Lane; The Yankee Consul. 1925 Any Woman; Fighting Youth; The Phantom Express. 1926 Butterflies in the Rain; Atta Boy; The Nut-Cracker; The Mile-a-Minute Man. 1927 Fangs of Destiny; The Prairie King; Through Thick and Thin; Speedy Smith. 1928 The Secret Hour; The Night Watch; Black Butterflies. 1929 When Dreams Come True; One Splendid Hour; The Fatal Warning (serial).

PERIOT, ARTHUR
Born: 1899. Died: Feb. 24, 1929, Monterey, Calif.(auto accident). Screen actor and stuntman.

PERIQUIN (Armando Espinosa de los Monteros)
Born: 1912, Mexico. Died: Nov. 6, 1957, Mexico City, Mexico (cancer). Screen and stage actor.

PERKINS, JEAN EDWARD
Born: 1899. Died: 1923 (while filming The Eagle's Talons serial). Screen actor and stuntman.

Appeared in: 1921 Do or Die (serial). 1923 The Eagle's Talons (serial).

PERKINS, OSGOOD
Born: 1892, West Newton, Mass. Died: Sept. 23, 1937, Washington, D.C.(heart attack). Screen and stage actor. Father of screen actor Anthony Perkins.

Appeared in: 1922 The Cradle Buster. 1923 Puritan Passions; Second Fiddle. 1924 Grit. 1925 Wild, Wild Susan. 1926 Love 'Em and Leave 'Em. 1927 High Hat, Knockout Reilly. 1929 Mother's Boy; Syncopation. 1931 The Front Page (stage and film versions); Tarnished Lady; Loose Ankles. 1932 Scarface. 1934 Kansas City Princess; Madame Du Barry; The President Vanishes. 1935 I Dream Too Much; Secret of the Chateau. 1936 Golddiggers of 1937.

PERKINS, WALTER
Born: 1870, Biddleford, Maine. Died: June 3, 1925, Brooklyn, N.Y. Screen, stage, and vaudeville actor.

Appeared in: 1919 Bill Henry. 1920 Peaceful Valley. 1921 The New Disciple. 1922 Golden Dreams; When Romance Rides.

PERLEY, MRS. ANNA
Born: 1849. Died: Jan. 20, 1937, Los Angeles, Calif. Screen and stage actress.

PERLEY, CHARLES
Born: 1886. Died: Feb. 10, 1933, Santa Ana, Calif.(heart attack). Screen and stage actor.

Appeared in early Biograph films.

PERREDOM, LUIS
Born: 1882, Spain. Died: Apr. 7, 1958, Madrid, Spain. Screen and stage actor.

PERRIN, JACK
Born: 1896, Three Rivers, Mich. Died: Dec. 17, 1967, Hollywood, Calif.(heart attack). Screen and stage actor.

Appeared in: 1919 The Lion Man (serial); Blind Husbands. 1920 Pink Tights. 1921 The Match-Breaker; Partners of the Tide; The Rage of Paris; The Torrent. 1922 The Dangerous Little Demon; The Trouper; The Guttersnipe. 1923 The Santa Fe Trail (serial); Golden Silence; The Lone Horseman; The Fighting Shippers (serial); Mary of the Movies. 1924 Coyote Fangs; Riders of the Plains (serial); Crashin' Through; Lightnin' Jack; Travelin' Fast; Virginian Outcast; Shootin' Square; Ridin' West; Those Who Dance. 1925 Border Vengeance; Winning a Woman; Double Fisted; Cactus Trails; Canyon Rustlers; Desert Madness; The Knockout Kid; Starlight; The Untamed; Dangerous Fists; Silent Sheldon. 1926 A

Ridin' Gent; Mistaken Orders; Midnight Faces; Dangerous Traffic; The Grey Devil; Hi-Jacking Rustlers; The Thunderbolt Strikes; West of the Rainbow's End; Starlight's Revenge; The Man from Oklahoma. 1927 Code of the Range; Fire and Steel; The Laffin' Fool; Where the North Holds Sway; Thunderbolt's Tracks. 1928 Guardians of the Wild; The Vanishing West (serial); The Two Outlaws; The Water Hole. 1929 Wild Blood; The Harvest of Hate; Hoofbeats of Vengeance; Plunging Hoofs; 1930 The Apache Kid's Escape; Phantom of the Desert; Beyond the Rio Grande; Ridin' Law; Trails of Peril; Overland Bound; Romance of the West; The Jade Box (serial). 1931 Wild West Whoopee; The Kid from Arizona; The Sheriff's Secret; Lariats and Six-Shooters. 1932 Hell Fire Austin; .45 Calibre Echo; Dynamite Ranch. 1934 Rawhide Mail; Girl Trouble (short). 1936 Hair Trigger Casey; Desert Justice. 1937 The Painted Stallion (serial). 1938 The Purple Vigilantes. 1940 West of Pinto Basin. 1942 Broadway Big Shot. 1943-1949 numerous westerns. 1950 Bandit Queen.

PERRINS, LESLIE
Born: 1902, Moseley, England. Died: Dec. 13, 1962, Esher, England. Screen, stage, and radio actor.

Appeared in: 1931 The Sleeping Cardinal; Sherlock Holmes Fatal Hour; Betrayal; The Calendar. 1932 Whiteface; The Lost Chord. 1933 Just Smith. 1934 The Lash; Lily of Killarney; The Roof; The Pointing Finger; The Man Who Changed His Name; Lord Edgeware Dies; Open All Night; The Rocks of Valpre; D'ye Ken John Peel; The Triumph of Sherlock Holmes; Gay Love; Song at Lion; The Squire; White Lilac; Lucky Days; Experts Opinion; Line Engaged. 1936 The Scotland Yard Mystery; Nine Days a Queen; Tudor Rose. 1937 Sensation; Rhythm in the Air; Southern Roses; Double Error; Limping Man; No Exit; The General Goes Too Far; Bulldog Drummond at Bay; High Treason. 1939 Old Iron. 1943 The Woman's Angle. 1949 A Run for Your Money. 1956 Guilty. 1957 Haunted Strangler. Other British films: The Gang's All Here; Lucky of the Navy; I Killed the Count; All at Sea; Old Ironsides; No Parking; Dangerous Fingers; Gables Mystery; Calling All Crooks; Captain Moonlight.

PERRY, ANTOINETTE (aka ANNETTE PERRY)
Born: 1888. Died: June 28, 1946, New York, N.Y.(heart attack). Screen, stage actress, and stage director.

Appeared in: 1924 Yankee Madness. 1925 After Marriage.

PERRY, MARY
Born: 1888, Gainesville, Ga. Died: Mar. 6, 1971, N.Y. Screen, stage, and television actress.

Appeared in: 1958 Uncle Vanya (film and stage versions). 1960 The Fugitive Kind. 1963 All the Way Home.

PERRY, ROBERT E. "BOB"
Born: 1879, New York, N.Y. Died: Jan. 8, 1962, Hollywood, Calif. Screen and television actor.

Appeared in: 1921 The Devil Within. 1922 Oath-Bound; Iron to Gold. 1925 The Light of Western Stars; The Thundering Herd. 1926 Volcano; Gigolo. 1927 The Fortune Hunter; Finger Prints; Jaws of Steel; White Gold; Brass Knuckles. 1928 Beggars of Life; Dressed to Kill; The River Pirate; Me, Gangster. 1929 The Man I Love; Noisy Neighbors; Sin Town; Skin Deep. 1930 Those Who Dance; Trailin' Trouble; The Sea God. 1932 Carnival Boat; Hell's Highway. 1933 The Chief. 1936 Riffraff; My Man Godfrey. 1937 Manhattan Merry-Go-Round. 1941 The Big Store.

PERRY, SARA
Born: 1872. Died: Jan. 18, 1959, White Plains, N.Y. Screen and stage actress.

Appeared in: 1950 The Damned Don't Cry.

PERSSE, THOMAS
Died: Apr. 1920, Venice, Calif. Screen actor and opera singer.

Appeared in: 1920 It's a Great Life.

PERSSON, EDVARD
Born: 1887, Sweden. Died: Sept. 26, 1957, Halsinborg, Sweden. Screen actor.

Appeared in: 1934 Flickorna Fran Gamla Stan. 1935 Tjocka Slaekten (Near Relatives); Larsson I Andra Giftet. 1936 Loerdagskvaellar; Vaaran Pojke; Soederkaakar. 1937 The Old Gods Still Live. 1938 Baldvins Brollop (Baldwin's Wedding). 1939 Skanor-Falsterbo. 1940 Kalle Paa Spaangen; Kvinnorna Kring Larsson (The Women around Larsson). 1944 Sun over Klara. 1953 Pimpernel Sversson; Each Heart Has It's Own Story.

PETERS, FRED
Born: June 30, 1884, Waltham, Mass. Died: Apr. 23, 1963, Hollywood, Calif. Screen actor. Entered films in 1916.

Appeared in: 1921 Miracles of the Jungle (serial). 1923 Salome. 1924 The Millionaire Cowboy. 1927 "12" Miles Out; Tarzan and the Golden Lion. 1929 Spieler. 1936 I Conquer the Sea.

PETERS, HOUSE, SR. Born: 1880 or 1888, Bristol, England. Died: Dec. 1967, Woodland Hills, Calif. Screen actor. Father of screen actor House Peters, Jr.

Appeared in: 1913 Leah-Kleshna; Lady of Quality. 1914 The Pride of Jennico; Salomy Jane. 1915 The Girl of the Golden West; The Great Divide; Mignon. 1920 The Great Redeemer; Isobel. 1921 The Invisible Power; Lying Lips. 1922 The Man from Lost River; Human Hearts; The Storm; Rich Men's Wives. 1923 Held to Answer; Counsel for the Defense; Lost and Found; Don't Marry for Money. 1924 The Tornado. 1925 Raffles; Head Winds; The Storm Breaker. 1926 The Combat; Prisoners of the Storm. 1928 Rose Marie. 1952 O.Henry's Full House; The Old West.

PETERS, CAPT. JOHN
Born: Germany. Died: Oct. 21, 1940, Santa Rosa, Calif. Screen actor and circus performer.

Appeared in: 1926 Ranson's Folly.

PETERS, PETER
Born: 1926, Germany. Died: Oct. 1, 1955, Berlin, Germany (suicide-jump from building). Screen and stage actor.

PETERS, SUSAN (Suzanne Carnahan)
Born: July 3, 1921, Spokane, Wash. Died: Oct. 23, 1952, Visalia, Calif.(chronic kidney infection, pneumonia and starvation). Screen, stage, and television actress. Appeared in films originally as Suzanne Carnahan.

Appeared in: 1940 Money and the Woman; The Man Who Talked Too Much; Susan and God; Santa Fe Trail. 1941 Strawberry Blonde; Here Comes Happiness; Three Sons O'Guns; Scattergood Pulls the Strings. 1942 Escape from Crime; Dr. Gillespie's New Assistant; Random Harvest; The Big Shot; Tish; Andy Hardy's Double Life. 1943 Assignment in Brittany; Young Ideas. 1944 Song of Russia. 1945 Keep Your Powder Dry. 1948 The Sign of the Ram.

PETERS, WERNER
Born: 1919, Germany. Died: Mar. 31, 1971, Wiesbaden, West Germany. Screen, stage actor, and film producer.

Appeared in: 1951 The Subject. 1958 Nachts Wenn der Teufel Kam (Nights When the Devil Came aka The Devil Strikes at Night-U.S. 1959). 1959 Kriegsgericht (Court Martial-U.S. 1962). 1960 Liebe Kann Wie Gift Sein (Love Can Be Like Poison aka Magdalena); Rosemary. 1961 Rosen fur den Staarsanwalt (Roses for the Prosecutor). 1962 The Counterfeit Traitor. 1963 Das Feuerschiff (The Lightship). 1964 The Restless Night. 1965 36 Hours; Battle of the Bulge. 1966 A Fine Madness; I Deal in Danger. 1967 The Corrupt Ones. 1968 The Secret War of Harry Frigg.

PETERSEN, PETER
Born: 1876, Hamburg, Germany. Died: Apr. 1, 1956, Vienna, Austria. Screen, stage, burlesque actor, and stage director.

Appeared in: 1934 Masquerade. 1937 The Eternal Mask; Masquerade in Vienna, The Kreutzer Sonata. 1940 Der Spiegel des Lebens (Life's Mirror).

PETERSON, WILBUR "PETE"
Born: 1915, Hawaii. Died: Oct. 24, 1960, Miami, Fla. Screen, television, and vaudeville actor.

PETRIE, HAY (David Hay Petrie)
Born: July 16, 1895, Dundee, Scotland. Died: July 30, 1948. Screen and stage actor.

Appeared in: 1930 Suspense; Night Birds. 1932 The Private Life of Henry VIII. 1934 Nell Gwyn; The Old Curiosity Shop. 1935 I Give My Heart; Moscow Nights. 1936 The Ghost Goes West; Here We Are Again; The House of the Spaniard; Koenigsmark; Invitation to the Waltz; Hearts of Humanity; No Escape; Rembrandt; Knight without Armour; Not Wanted on Voyage; Peg of Old Drury; I Stand Condemned. 1937 Forever Yours. 1938 Keep Smiling; Loves of Madame Du Barry. 1939 Clouds over Europe; The Spy in Black; Q Planes; Jamaica Inn; Smiling Along; Four Feathers; U-Boat 29. 1940 Crimes at the Dark House; Contraband; Twenty-One Days Together; Conquest of the Air; The Thief of Bagdad; Pastor Hall; Blackout. 1941 Spellbound; Convoy. 1942 This Was Paris; One of Our Aircraft Is Missing; Wings and the Woman. 1943 The Great Mr. Handel. 1944 A Canterbury Tale. 1945 On Approval; Battle for Music. 1946 Great Expectations (U.S. 1947); Waltz Time. 1948 The Red Shoes; Queen of Spades. 1949 The Guinea Pig; The Fallen Idol. 1950 The Laughing Lady; Silk Noose.

PETRIE, HOWARD A.
Born: 1907, Beverly, Mass. Died: Mar. 26, 1968, Keene, N.H. Screen, radio, and television actor.

Appeared in: 1950 Walk Softly, Stranger; Rocky Mountain. 1951 No Questions Asked; Cattle Drive; The Golden Horde. 1952 The Wild North; Red Ball Express; Bend of the River; Carbine Williams; Woman in the North Country; Pony Soldier. 1953 Fort Ti; Fair Wind to Java; The Veils of Bagdad. 1954 Sign of the Pagan; The Bob Mathias Story; The Bounty Hunter; Seven Brides for Seven Brothers; Border River; Both Sides of the Law. 1955 Rage at Dawn; How to Be Very, Very Popular; The Return of Jack Slade; Timberjack. 1956 Johnny Concho; The Maverick Queen; A Kiss Before Dying. 1957 The Tin Star.

PETTINGELL, FRANK
Born: Jan. 1, 1891, Liverpool, England. Died: Feb. 17, 1966, London, England. Screen, stage, and television actor.

Appeared in: 1931 Hobson's Choice; Once Bitten; Double Dealing; Jealousy. 1932 A Cuckoo in the Nest. 1933 The Good Companions; This Week of Grace; The Medicine Man; Excess Baggage; Red Wagon. 1934 Say It with Diamonds; Sing as We Go; Yes Madam, That's My Wife; The Big Splash; Keep it Quiet; My Old Dutch. 1935 In a Monastery Garden; The Last Journey; Fame; On Top of the World; The Right to Marry; The Hope of His Side. 1936 The Amateur Gentleman; Millions. 1937 Take My Tip; Spring Handicap. 1938 Sailing Along; Once a Crook; Seventh Survivor; This England. 1942 Ships with Wings; The Young Mr. Pitt; When We Are Married. 1944 Get Cracking. 1946 Gaiety George. 1948 Showtime; Escape. 1949 No Room at the Inn. 1951 The Magic Box. 1952 Crimson Pirate; The Promoter. 1953 Tonight at 8:30. 1957 Value for Money. 1958 Up the Creek. 1962 Term of Trial; Trial and Error. 1963 Corridors of Blood. 1964 Becket. Other British films: Frail Women; The Crooked Lady; Lottery Ticket; Return to Yesterday; The Goose Steps Out.

PEUKERT-IMPEKOVEN, SABINE
Born: 1890, Germany. Died: May 5, 1970, Frankfurt, Germany. Screen and stage actress. Pioneer actress of German silent films.

PHELPS, LEE
Born: 1894. Died: Mar. 19, 1953, Culver City, Calif. Screen, stage, and vaudeville actor.

Appeared in: 1921 The Road Demon. 1922 The Freshie. 1927 Putting Pants on Philip (short). 1930 Annie Christie; The Criminal Code. 1932 Cross Examination; The Night Club Lady; Hold 'Em Jail. 1933 Parole Girl; The Woman I Stole. 1934 Six of a Kind; Beggars in Ermine. 1935 $1,000 a Minute; Wings in the Dark; Hot Money. 1936 Palm Springs; Crash Donovan; Boss Rider of Gun Creek; The Bohemian Girl; Our Relations. 1937 Tough to Handle; Under Suspicion; A Nation Aflame; Boss of Lonely Valley; Sandflow; Lefthanded Law. 1938 Long Shot; Trade Winds; Female Fugitive; The Gladiator. 1939 The Flying Irishman; Kid Nightingale; Gone with the Wind. 1940 Hidden Gold. 1941 Andy Hardy's Private Secretary; A Shot in the Dark; The Big Store. 1942 Scattergood Rides High; Two Yanks in Trinidad; Life Begins at 8:30; War Dogs. 1943 Air Raid Wardens. 1944 Nothing but Trouble. 1945 Don Juan Quilligan; The Hidden Eye. 1949 Angels in Disguise; Sky Dragon; The Lone Wolf and His Lady; Shadows of the West; Gun Law Justice. 1950 The Girl from San Lorenzo; Hills of Oklahoma; Square Dance Katy; Timber Fury; Western Pacific Agent. 1953 Man of Conflict; The Marshal's Daughter.

PHILIPE, GERARD
Born: France. Died: Nov. 27, 1959, Paris, France (heart attack). Screen, stage actor, and film director.

Appeared in: 1943 The Land without Stars (film debut). 1946 Le Diable au Corps (The Devil in the Flesh-U.S. 1949). 1947 L'Idiot (The Idiot). 1948 Une Si Folie Petite Plage. 1949 La Beautie du Diable (The Beauty of the Devil-U.S. 1952). 1950 La Ronde (U.S. 1954). 1951 Rip Tide. 1952 Fanfan La Tulipe (U.S. 1954); Belles de Nuit (Beauties of the Night). 1953 Seven Deadly Sins; Les Orgeuilleux; Knave of Hearts. 1954 Le Rouge et le Noir (The Red and the Black-U.S. 1958). 1955 Les Granes Manoeuvres (The Grand Maneuver-U.S. 1956); Lovers Happy Lovers. 1956 The Proud and the Beautiful; Till Eulenspiegel. 1957 It Happened in the Park; Royal Affairs in Versailles. 1958 Pot-Bouville; Lover's

of Paris. 1959 Les Liasons Dangereuses (U.S. 1961). 1961 Modigliani of Montparnasse. Other French films: The Fever Rises in El Pao; All Roads Lead to Rome.

PHILLIBER, JOHN
Born: 1872, Elkhart, Ind. Died: Nov. 6, 1944, Elkhart, Ind. Screen and stage actor.

Appeared in: 1943 A Lady Takes a Chance. 1944 The Imposter; It Happened Tomorrow; Ladies of Washington; Summer Storm; Double Indemnity. 1945 Gentle Annie.

PHILLIPS, CHARLES
Born: 1904. Died: May 25, 1958, Hollywood, Calif. Screen actor and stuntman. Doubled for Charles Laughton and Oliver Hardy.

PHILLIPS, CLEMENT K.
Died: Oct., 1928, Hayward, Calif. (airplane crash). Screen actor and stunt flier.

PHILLIPS, EDNA
Born: 1878. Died: Feb. 26, 1952, Los Angeles, Calif. Screen actress. Wife of screen actor Taylor Holmes (dec. 1959) and mother of screen actors Phillips (dec. 1942) and Ralph Holmes (dec. 1945).

PHILLIPS, EDWARD N.
Born: 1899. Died: Feb. 22, 1965, North Hollywood, Calif. (struck by auto). Screen actor and film editor.

Appeared in "The Collegians" series of shorts which began in 1926 with Benson at Calford and continued until 1929. The following are all "Collegians'" series of shorts: 1926 Benson at Calford; Fighting to Win; Making Good; The Last Lap; Around the Bases; Fighting Spirit; The Relay. 1927 Cinder Path; Flashing Oars; Breaking Records; Crimson Colors; Winning Five; The Dazzling Coeds; A Fighting Finish; Samson at Calford; The Winning Punch; Running Wild; Splashing Through; The Winning Goal; Sliding Home. 1928 The Junior Year; Calford vs. Redskins; Kicking Through; Calford in the Movies; Radding Co-eds; Fighting for Victory; Dear Old Calford; Calford on Horseback; The Bookworm Hero; Speeding Youth; Farewell; The Winning Point. 1929 King of the Campus; The Rivals; On Guard; Junior Luck; The Cross Country Run; Sporting Courage; Flying High; The Varsity Drag; On the Side Lines; Use Your Feet; Splash Mates; Graduation Daze.

PHILLIPS, FESTUS "DAD"
Born: 1872. Died: Sept. 5, 1955, Hollywood, Calif. Screen actor and makeup artist.

PHILLIPS, HELENA. See Helena Phillips Evans

PHILLIPS, MINNA
Born: June 1, 1885, Sydney, Australia. Died: Jan. 29, 1963, New Orleans, La. (heart ailment). Screen and stage actress.

Appeared in: 1942 The Male Animal; A Yank at Eaton; My Sister Eileen. 1943 Sherlock Holmes Faces Death; Girls, Inc. 1950 Bandit Queen. 1951 Queen for a Day.

PHILLIPS, NORMA
Born: 1893, Baltimore, Md. Died: Nov. 12, 1931, New York (cancer). Screen and stage actress. Known as "Our Mutual Girl" in series of silents in 1914.

Appeared in: 1915 Runaway June.

PHILLIPS, NORMAN, SR.
Born: 1892. Died: Feb. 11, 1931, Culver City, Calif. (heart attack). Screen and vaudeville actor. Father of screen actor Norman Phillips, Jr.

PHILLIPS, RICHARD
Born: 1826. Died: May 4, 1941, Los Angeles, Calif. Screen actor. Claimed to be 115 years old—oldest actor in the world!

PHILLIPS, WILLIAM "BILL"
Born: Washington, D.C. Died: June 27, 1957. Screen and stage actor.

Appeared in: 1940 City for Conquest. 1941 Sergeant York. 1942 Larceny, Inc; The Lady Gangster. 1943 Johnny Come Lately; Action in the North Atlantic; Swingtime Johnny. 1944 See Here Private Hargrove; Music for Millions; Thirty Seconds over Tokyo. 1945 Abbott and Costello in Hollywood. 1946 The Harvey Girls; Holiday in Mexico; 'Til the Clouds Roll By; What Next Corporal Hargrove?; The Hoodlum Saint. 1947 Sea of Grass; Living in a Big Way. 1949 Johnny Allegro; Easy Living; Big Jack; Prison

Warden; Man from Colorado. 1950 Customs Agent; Chain Gang; Mary Ryan, Detective; He's a Cockeyed Wonder; The Vanishing Westerner. 1951 Detective Story; Al Jennings of Oklahoma; Cavalry Scout; A Yank in Korea. 1952 High Noon; Bugles in the Afternoon. 1953 Devil's Canyon; Gun Belt; Private Eyes. 1954 Wicked Woman; The Law vs. Billy the Kid. 1955 New York Confidential; Fort Yuma; Ghost Town; Top Gun. 1956 The Broken Star; The Man in the Gray Flannel Suit; Stagecoach to Fury; The Fastest Gun Alive. 1957 Revolt at Fort Laramie; Hellcats of the Navy.

PIAF, EDITH (Edith Gassion)
Born: 1916, Paris, France. Died: Oct. 11, 1963, Paris, France (internal hemorrhage). Screen, stage actress, and singer.

Appeared in: 1947 Etoile Sans Lumiere (Star without Light). 1956 French-Cancan. 1957 Royal Affairs in Versailles. 1962 I Love, You Love.

PICA, TINA
Born: 1888, Italy. Died: Aug. 16, 1968, Naples, Italy. Screen and stage actress.

Appeared in: 1949 Guaglio. 1954 Bread, Love and Dreams. 1955 Frisky. 1957 Scandal in Sorrento. 1959 The Virtuous Bigamist. 1964 Leri, Oggi, Domani (Yesterday, Today and Tomorrow).

PICHEL, IRVING
Born: 1891, Pittsburgh, Pa. Died: July 13, 1954, Hollywood, Calif. (heart attack). Screen, stage actor, film director, and screenwriter.

Appeared in: 1930 The Right to Love. 1931 Murder by the Clock; The Road to Reno; An American Tragedy; The Cheat. 1932 Westward Passage; The Painted Woman; Strange Justice; Wild Girl; The Miracle Man; Two Kinds of Women; Forgotten Commandments; Island of Lost Souls; Most Dangerous Game; Madame Butterfly. 1933 Mysterious Rider; The Woman Accused; King of the Jungle; Oliver Twist; The Story of Temple Drake; I'm No Angel; The Right to Romance; The Billion Dollar Scandal. 1934 British Agent; Return of the Terror; Silver Streak; She Was a Lady; Such Women Are Dangerous; Cleopatra; Fog over Frisco. 1935 I Am a Thief; Three Kids and a Queen; Special Agent. 1936 Hearts in Bondage; Down to the Sea; The House of a Thousand Candles; Don't Gamble with Love; General Spanky; Dracula's Daughter. 1937 High, Wide and Handsome; There Goes My Heart; Jezebel; Gambling Ship. 1939 Newsboys' Home; Torture Ship; Rio; Topper Takes a Trip; Dick Tracy's G-Men (serial); Juarez. 1943 The Moon is Down. 1951 Santa Fe. 1953 Martin Luther.

PICK, LUPE
Born: 1886, Germany. Died: Mar. 1931 (poison). Screen actor and film director.

Appeared in: 1928 Spione (Spies).

PICKARD, HELENA
Born: 1900. Died: Sept. 27, 1959, Oxfordshire, England. Screen and television actress. Divorced from screen actor Sir Cedric Hardwicke (dec. 1964).

Appeared in: 1934 Nell Gwyn. 1935 Limelight. 1940 Let George Do It. 1944 The Lodger.

PICKETT, INGRAM B.
Born: 1899. Died: Feb. 14, 1963, Santa Fe, N.M. Screen actor. Was early member of Mack Sennett's Keystone Kops.

PICKFORD, JACK (Jack Smith)
Born: Aug. 18, 1896, Toronto, Canada. Died: Jan. 3, 1933, Paris, France (multiple neuritis). Screen and stage actor. Brother of screen actresses Mary Pickford and Lottie Pickford (dec. 1936). Married to screen actress Olive Thomas (dec. 1920) and divorced from screen actress Marilyn Miller (dec. 1936).

Appeared in: 1910 The Modern Prodigal; The Iconoclast; Examination Day at School; A Child's Strategem. 1912 Heredity; The Unwelcome Guest; The New York Hat. 1914 Wildflower; Home Sweet Home. 1915 The Pretty Sister of Jose. 1916 Seventeen; The Dummy; Great Expectations; Tom Sawyer. 1918 Huck and Tom; Sandy; His Majesty Bunker Bean; Mile-a-Minute Kendall. 1920 The Little Shepherd of Kingdom Come. 1921 Little Lord Fauntleroy; Just out of College; Man Who Had Everything; Through the Back Door. 1922 Valley of the Wolf. 1923 Hollywood; Garrison's Finish. 1924 The Hillbilly; The End of the World. 1925 Waking up the Town; My Son; The Goose Woman. 1926 The Bat; Brown of Harvard; Exit Smiling. 1928 Gang War.

PICKFORD, LOTTIE (Lottie Smith)
Died: Dec. 9, 1936, Brentwood, Calif. (heart attack). Screen actress. Sister of screen actress Mary Pickford and screen actor Jack Pickford (dec. 1933). Entered films with Imp Company in 1910.

Appeared in: 1915 The Diamond from the Sky (serial), 1918 Mile-a-Minute Kendall. 1924 Dorothy Vernon of Haddon Hall. 1925 Don Q.

PIDAL, JOSE
Born: 1896, Spain. Died: Oct. 26, 1956, Mexico City, Mexico (cancer). Screen and stage actor.

PIEL, EDWARD, SR. and also PIEL, EDWARD, JR. See "PEIL"

PIERCE, EVELYN
Born: Feb. 5, 1908, Del Rio, Tex. Died: Aug. 9, 1960, Oyster, Bay, N.Y. Screen actress. Married to stage actor Theodore Baehr. Entered films in 1925.

Appeared in: 1925 Don't. 1927 The Border Cavalier. 1928 Sonia; Tenderloin. 1929 The Million Dollar Collar. 1930 Once a Gentleman. 1931 An American Tragedy; Monkey Business.

PIERCE, GEORGE. See George C. Pearce

PIERLOT, FRANCIS
Born: 1876. Died: May 11, 1955, Hollywood, Calif. (heart ailment). Screen, stage, and television actor.

Appeared in: 1931 Night Angel. 1940 The Captain Is a Lady; Strike up the Band; Escape to Glory; Always a Bride. 1941 The Trial of Mary Dugan; International Lady; Rise and Shine; Remember the Day; A-Haunting We Will Go. 1942 Just Off Broadway; Henry Aldrich, Editor; Night Monster; Yankee Doodle Dandy; My Heart Belongs to Daddy; A Gentleman at Heart. 1943 Mission to Moscow; Mystery Broadcast. 1944 The Doughgirls; Uncertain Glory; Adventures of Mark Twain; Bathing Beauty; The Very Thought of You. 1945 Hit the Hay; Affairs of Susan; Fear; Grissly's Millions; The Hidden Eye; How Do You Do?; Life with Blondie; Our Vines Have Tender Grapes; Roughly Speaking; Yolanda and the Thief; A Tree Grows in Brooklyn; Bewitched. 1946 Dragonwyck; The Catman of Paris; The Crime Doctor's Manhunt; G.I. War Brides; Two Guys from Milwaukee; The Walls Came Tumbling Down. 1947 Cigarette Girl; The Late George Apley; Philo Vance's Gamble; Second Chance; The Senator Was Indiscreet; The Trespasser. 1948 The Dude Goes West; Chicken Every Sunday; The Accused; That Wonderful Urge; I, Jane Doe. 1949 Bad Boy; Take One False Step; My Friend Irma. 1950 Copper Canyon; Cyrano de Bergerac; The Flame and the Arrow. 1951 Anne of the Indies; The Lemon Drop Kid; Savage Drums; That's My Boy. 1952 Hold That Line; The Prisoner of Zenda. 1953 The Robe.

PIERRE, ANATOLE
Died: Feb. 1926, New Orleans, La. Negro screen and minstrel actor.

PIGOTT, TEMPE
Born: 1884. Died: Oct. 13, 1962, Hollywood, Calif. Screen and stage actress.

Appeared in: 1921 The Great Impersonation. 1922 The Masked Avenger. 1923 The Rustle of Silk; Vanity Fair. 1924 The Dawn of a Tomorrow; The Narrow Street. 1925 Without Mercy; Greed. 1926 The Midnight Kiss; The Black Pirate. 1927 Silk Stockings. 1928 Road House; Wallflowers. 1930 Night Work; America or Bust; Seven Days Leave. 1931 Devotion. 1932 Dr. Jekyll and Mr. Hyde. 1933 A Study in Scarlet; Doctor Bull; If I Were Free; Cavalcade; Oliver Twist; Man of the Forest. 1934 Long Lost Father; One More River; Of Human Bondage; The Lemon Drop Kid; Limehouse Blues. 1935 The Devil Is a Woman; Becky Sharp; Calm Yourself; Bride of Frankenstein. 1936 Little Lord Fauntleroy; The White Angel. 1938 Fools for Scandal. 1939 Boys Reformatory.

PIKE, NITA
Born: 1913. Died: May 10, 1954, Los Angeles, Calif. (suicide). Screen actress. Married to screen actor Alan Edwards (dec. 1954).

Appeared in: 1940 The Great Dictator.

PILA, MAXIMO
Born: 1886. Died: Aug. 2, 1939, Hollywood, Calif. Screen and stage actor.

PINE, ED
Born: 1904. Died: May 9, 1950, Woodland Hills, Calif. Screen actor.

PINERO, ANTHONY
Born: 1887. Died: Jan. 5, 1958, Bridgeport, Conn. Screen actor and circus performer.

PINZA, EZIO (Fortunato Pinza)
Born: May 8, 1892, Rome, Italy. Died: May 9, 1957, Stamford, Conn.(stroke). Opera star, screen, stage, and television actor.

Appeared in: 1947 Carnegie Hall. 1951 Mr. Imperium; Strictly Dishonorable. 1953 Tonight We Sing.

PIPO (Gustave Sofman)
Born: 1902, France. Died: Aug. 6, 1970, Paris, France. Screen actor and circus clown.

PITT, ARCHIE
Born: 1895, England. Died: Nov. 12, 1940, London, England. Screen, stage actor, and screenwriter. Divorced from screen actress Gracie Fields.

Appeared in: 1934 Danny Boy. 1935 Barnacle Bill. 1936 Excuse My Glove.

PITTMAN, MONTE
Born: 1918. Died: June 26, 1962, Hollywood, Calif.(cancer). Screen, stage actor, film director, and screenwriter. Entered films as an actor in early 1950s.

PITTMAN, TOM
Born: 1933. Died: Oct. 31, 1958, Hollywood, Calif.(auto accident). Screen and stage actor.

Appeared in: 1957 Blackpatch; Bernardine; No Time to Be Young; The True Story of Jesse James; The Way to Gold; The Young Stranger. 1958 Apache Territory; Proud Rebels. 1959 The High School Big Shot; Verboten!

PITTS, ZASU
Born: Jan. 3, 1898, Parsons, Kan. Died: June 7, 1963, Hollywood, Calif.(cancer). Screen and television actress. She appeared as part of the comedy film team of "Todd and Pitts" with Thelma Todd.

Appeared in: 1917 The Little Princess (film debut). 1918 A Society Sensation. 1919 Better Times. 1922 A Daughter of Luxury; For the Defense; Is Matrimony a Failure?; Youth to Youth. 1923 Patsy; The Girl Who Came Back; Three Wise Fools; Mary of the Movies; Poor Men's Wives; Souls for Sale; Tea with a Kick. 1924 Changing Husbands; Daughters of Today; The Goldfish; Greed; The Fast Set; The Legend of Hollywood; West of the Water Tower; Triumph; Wine of Youth. 1925 What Happened to Jones?; The Business of Love; The Great Divide; The Great Love; Pretty Ladies; Lazybones; Old Shoes; The Recreation of Brian Kent; A Woman's Faith; Wages for Wives; Thunder Mountain; Secrets of the Night. 1926 Early to Wed; Her Big Night; Risky Business; Mannequin; Monte Carlo; Sunny Side Up. 1927 Casey at the Bat. 1928 Wife Savers; Sins of the Father; The Wedding March; Buck Privates; 13 Washington Square. 1929 The Dummy; The Squall; Twin Beds; The Argyle Case; This Thing Called Love; The Locked Door; Her Private Life; Paris. 1930 The Squealer; Monte Carlo (and 1926 version); The Little Accident; The Lottery Bride; No, No, Nanette; Oh, Yeah!; Honey; The Devil's Holiday; War Nurse; Passion Flower; Sin Takes a Holiday; Free Love; All Quiet on the Western Front (She was only in original European version and was replaced in cast by Beryl Mercer). 1931 Terror by Night; Finn and Hattie; Bad Sister; Beyond Victory; Seed; Woman of Experience; The Guardsman; Their Mad Moment; Big Gamble; Penrod and Sam; Secret Witness; River's End; plus the following shorts made with Thelma Todd: Let's Do Things; Catch As Catch Can; The Pajama Party; War Mamas. 1932 Unexpected Father; Strangers of the Evening; Walking down Broadway; Broken Lullaby; Destry Rides Again; Steady Company; Shopworn; The Trial of Vivienne Ware; Westward Passage; Is My Face Red?; Blondie of the Follies; Roar of the Dragon; Make Me a Star; Vanishing Frontier; The Crooked Circle; Madison Square Garden; Back Street; Once in a Lifetime; Eternally Yours; The Man I Killed; plus the following shorts with Thelma Todd: Seal Skins; On the Loose; Red Noses; Strictly Unreliable; The Old Bull; Show Business; Alum and Eve; The Soilers. 1933 Out All Night; They Just Had to Get Married; Hello Sister!; Mr. Skitch; Her First Mate; Love, Honor and Oh, Baby; Professional Sweethearts; Aggie Appleby; Maker of Men; Meet the Baron, plus the following shorts with Thelma Todd: Sneak Easily; Asleep in the Feet; Maids a la Mode; Bargain of the Century; One Track Minds.

1934 Two Alone; Their Big Moment; The Meanest Gal in Town; Sing and Like It; Dames; Private Scandal; Mrs. Wiggs of the Cabbage Patch; The Gay Bride; Love Birds; Three on a Honeymoon. 1935 Ruggles of Red Gap; Spring Tonic; She Gets Her Man; Hot Tip; Going Highbrow; The Affairs of Susan. 1936 13 Hours by Air; Sing Me a Love Song; Mad Holiday; The Plot Thickens. 1937 Merry Comes to Town; Forty Naughty Girls; 52nd Street; Wanted. 1939 The Lady's from Kentucky; Mickey the Kid; Naughty but Nice; Nurse Edith Cavell; Eternally Yours. 1940 No, No, Nanette (and 1930 version); It All Came True. 1941 The Mexican Spitfire's Baby; Broadway Limited; Niagara Falls; Miss Polly; Weekend for Three. 1942 Meet the Mob; Mexican Spitfire at Sea; The Bashful Bachelor; So's Your Aunt Emma; Tish. 1943 Let's Face It. 1946 Breakfast in Hollywood; The Perfect Marriage. 1947 Life with Father. 1949 Francis. 1952 The Denver and the Rio Grande. 1954 Francis Joins the WACS. 1957 This Could Be the Night. 1959 The Gazebo. 1961 Teen-Age Millionaire. 1963 The Thrill of It All; It's a Mad, Mad, Mad, Mad World. 1964 Big Parade of Comedy (documentary).

PITTSCHAU, WERNER
Born: 1903, Germany. Died: Oct. 1928, Spandau, Germany (auto accident). Screen actor.

Appeared in: 1928 Women without Men.

PLOWDEN, ROGER S.
Born: 1902. Died: Sept. 26, 1960, N.Y. Screen and stage actor.

Appeared in: 1952 Five Fingers.

PLUES, GEORGE L.
Born: 1895. Died: Aug. 16, 1953, Woodland Hills, Calif. Screen actor.

Appeared in: 1937 Come on, Cowboys.

PLUMMER, LINCOLN
Born: 1876. Died: Feb. 14, 1928, Hollywood, Calif.(heart disease). Screen and stage actor.

Appeared in: 1921 The Girl in the Taxi; Her Face Value; See My Lawyer; The Ten Dollar Raise. 1922 The Barnstormer; The Glory of Clementina; The Deuce of Spades; Confidence. 1923 The Dangerous Maid; Within the Law. 1924 Hold Your Breath; Reckless Romance; Fool's Highway. 1925 A Regular Fellow. 1926 Atta Boy; When the Wife's Away. 1927 Backstage; The Tired Business Man; Down the Stretch. 1928 The Bullet Mark; Masked Angel; Alias the Deacon.

PLUMMER, ROSE LINCOLN
Died: Mar. 3, 1955, Hollywood, Calif. Screen, stage, and television actress.

Appeared in: 1934 Opened by Mistake (short). 1942 Pacific Blackout (aka Midnight Angel). 1943 Jack London. 1944 The Girl in the Case. 1949 Knock on Any Door. 1950 Ma and Pa Kettle Go to Town.

POGUE, TOM
Born: 1876. Died: Mar. 21, 1941, Hollywood, Calif. Screen, stage, and television actor.

Appeared in: 1936 I Married a Doctor; Stage Struck. 1937 Once a Doctor; It's Love I'm After; Lloyds of London. 1940 Foreign Correspondent; The Letter. 1941 Citizen Kane; Back Street; Meet John Doe.

POL, TALITHA
Born: 1940, Holland. Died: July 1971, Rome, Italy (heroin overdose). Screen actress. Married to oil scion Paul Getty, Jr.

Appeared in: 1961 Village of Daughters. 1965 Return from the Ashes.

POLK, GORDON
Born: 1924. Died: June 9, 1960, Hollywood, Calif.(during heart surgery). Screen, stage, and television actor.

Appeared in: 1960 Inherit the Wind.

POLLA, PAULINE M.
Born: 1868. Died: Apr. 19, 1940, Albany, N.Y. Screen actress and opera performer. Appeared in silents.

POLLACK, BEN
Born: 1904. Died: June 7, 1971, Palm Springs, Calif.(suicide-hanged). Bandleader, jazz drummer, screen actor, and song writer.

Appeared in: 1929 Ben Pollack and His Park Central Orchestra (short). 1934 Universal short. 1954 The Glenn Miller Story. 1955 The Benny Goodman Story.

POLLARD, BUD
Born: 1887. Died: Dec. 16, 1952, Hollywood, Calif.(heart attack). Screen actor, film director, and screenwriter.

Appeared in: 1933 Victims of Persecution.

POLLARD, HARRY "SNUB" (Harold Frazer)
Born: 1886, Melbourne, Australia. Died: Jan. 19, 1962, Burbank, Calif. Screen, stage, vaudeville, television actor, and film producer. Not to be confused with Harry Pollard, film actor and director (dec. 1934). Entered films as a bit player with Broncho Billy Anderson at Essanay Studios. He was one of the original Keystone Kops.

Appeared in: 1915 Great While It Lasted. 1919 Start Something; All at Sea; Call for Mr. Cave Man; Giving the Bride Away; Order in Court; It's a Hard Life; How Dry I Am; Looking for Trouble; Tough Luck; The Floor Below; His Royal Slyness. 1920 the following shorts: Red Hot Hottentots; Why Go Home?; Slippery Slickers; The Dippy Dentist; All Lit Up; Getting His Goat; Waltz Me Around; Raise the Rent; Find the Girl; Fresh Paint; Flat Broke; Cut the Cards; The Dinner Hour; Cracked Wedding Bells; Speed to Spare; Shoot on Sight; Don't Weaken; Drink Hearty; Trotting through Turkey; All Dressed Up; Grab the Ghost; All in a Day; Any Old Port; Don't Rock the Boat; The Home Stretch; Call a Taxi; Live and Learn; Run 'Em Ragged; A London Bobby; Money to Burn; Go As You Please; Rock-a-by-Baby; Doing Time; Fellow Citizens; When the Wind Blows; Insulting the Sultan; The Dearly Departed; Cash Customers; Park Your Car. 1921 the following shorts: The Morning After; Whirl O' the West; Open another Bottle; His Best Girl; Make it Snappy; Fellow Romans; Rush Orders; Bubbling Over; No Children; Own Your Own Home; Big Game; Save Your Money; Blue Sunday; Where's the Fire; The High Rollers; You're Next; The Bike Bug; At the Ringside; No Stopover; What a Whopper; Teaching the Teacher; Spot Cash; Name the Day; The Jail Bird; Late Lodgers; Gone to the Country; Law and Order; Fifteen Minutes; On Location; Hocus-Pocus; Penny-in-the-Slot; The Joy Rider; The Hustler; Sink or Swim; Shake 'Em Up; Corner Pocket. 1922 the following shorts. Lose No Time: Call the Witness; Years to Come; Blow 'Em Up; Stage Struck; Down and Out; Pardon Me; The Bow Wows; Hot off the Press; The Anvil Chorus; Jump Your Job; Full o'Pep; Kill the Nerve; Days of Old; Light Showers; Do Me a Favor; In the Movies; Punch the Clock; Strictly Modern; Hale and Hearty; Some Baby; The Dumb Bell; Bed of Roses; The Stone Age; 365 Days; The Old Sea Dog; Hook, Line and Sinker; Nearly Rich; Our Gang. 1923 the following shorts: Dig Up; A Tough Winter; Before the Public; Where Am I?; California or Bust; Sold at Auction; The Courtship of Miles Sandwich; Jack Frost; The Mystery Man; The Walkout; It's a Gift; Dear Ol' Pal; Join the Circus; Fully Insured; It's a Boy. 1924 the following shorts: The Big Idea, Why Marry?; Get Busy. 1925 Are Husbands Human? (short). 1926 the following shorts: Do Your Duty; The Old Warhorse; The Doughboy; The Yokel; The Fire; All Wet. 1927 The Bum's Rush. 1931 Ex-Flame; One Good Turn (short). 1932 Midnight Patrol; Make Me a Star; The Purchase Price. 1934 Stingaree; Cockeyed Cavaliers. 1936 Just My Luck; The Crime Patrol; The White Legion; The Gentleman from Louisiana; Headin' for the Rio Grande. 1937 Riders of the Rockies; Hittin' the Trail; Nation Aflame; Arizona Days; Tex Rides with the Boy Scouts. 1938 Frontier Town; Starlight over Texas; Where the Buffalo Roam. 1939 Song of the Buckaroo. 1940 Murder on the Yukon. 1943 Phony Express (short). 1947 Perils of Pauline. 1948 Blackmail. 1949 The Crooked Way. 1957 A Man of a Thousand Faces. 1958 Rock-a-bye Baby. 1960 Who Was That Lady?; Studs Lonigan; When Comedy Was King (documentary). 1962 Pocketful of Miracles; Days of Thrills and Laughter (documentary). 1963 Thirty Years of Fun (documentary). 1968 The Further Perils of Laurel and Hardy (documentary).

POLLARD, HARRY
Born: 1883. Died: July 6, 1934, Pasadena, Calif. Screen, stage, vaudeville actor, and film director. Married to screen actress Margarita Fisher. Entered films as an actor with Selig.

Appeared in: 1913 Uncle Tom's Cabin. 1915 The Peacock Feather Fan. 1916 Susie's New Shoes.

POLO, EDDIE (Edward P. Polo)
Born: 1875, Los Angeles, Calif. Died: June 14, 1961, Hollywood, Calif.(heart attack). Screen actor, film stuntman and circus performer. Not to be confused with Swedish circus performer Eddie Polo—Edward Kristensson—(dec. 1956).

Appeared in: 1915 Yellow Streak; The Broken Coin (serial). 1916

Heritage of Hate; The Adventures of Peg O'the Ring (serial); Liberty, a Daughter of the U.S.A.(serial). 1917 The Wolf and His Mate; The Gray Ghost (serial). 1918 Bull's Eye (serial); Lure of the Circus (serial). 1919 "Cyclone Smith" series including: Cyclone Smith Plays Trumps; Cyclone Smith's Partner; Cyclone Smith's Comeback. 1920 The Vanishing Dagger (serial); King of the Circus (serial). 1921 The Secret Four (serial); Do or Die (serial); The White Horseman (serial). 1922 Captain Kidd (serial). With Stanley in Africa (serial). 1923 Knock on the Door; Dangerous Hour; Prepared to Die. 1940 Son of Roaring Dan. 1942 Between Us Girls. 1943 Hers to Hold. Other "Cyclone Smith" series films he appeared in are: Square Deal Cyclone, Cyclone Smith's Vow.

POLO, ROBERT
Died: May 4, 1968, Hollywood, Calif.(brain tumor). Screen actor, extra, and stand-in for Gilbert Roland.

PONTO, ERICH
Born: Luebeck, Germany. Died: Feb. 4, 1957, Stuttgart, Germany. Screen, stage, and radio actor.

Appeared in: 1935 Das Maedchen Johanna. 1949 Palace Scandal. 1950 The Third Man. 1958 Das Fliegende Klassen-Zimmer (The Flying Classroom); Rosen Fuer Bettina (Roses for Bettina-aka Ballerina). 1959 Himmel ohne Sterne (Sky without Stars). Other German films: Tailor Wibbel; Film without Title; Love 47; If All of Us Were Angels; Robinson Shall Not Die.

POPE, UNOLA B.
Born: 1884. Died: Feb. 1, 1938, Fremont, Ohio. Screen and stage actress. Said to be a member of cast of first motion pictures made in Corning, N.Y.

PORCASI, PAUL
Born: 1880, Palermo, Italy. Died: Aug. 8, 1946, Hollywood, Calif. Screen, stage actor, and opera singer.

Appeared in: 1920 The Fall of the Romanoffs. 1926 Say It Again. 1929 Broadway. 1930 A Lady's Morals; Three Sisters; Murder on the Roof; Morocco; Born Reckless; Derelict. 1931 Children of Dreams; I Like Your Nerve; Doctor's Wives; Bought; Good Bad Girl; Svengali; Gentleman's Fate; Party Husbands; Under Eighteen; A Woman Commands; While Paris Sleeps; The Man Who Played God; Smart Money. 1932 The Devil and the Deep; Cynara. 1933 When Strangers Marry; Devil's Mate; I Loved a Woman; Footlight Parade; Flying Down to Rio; He Couldn't Take It; Grand Slam. 1934 British Agent; The Great Flirtation; Wake up and Dream; Imitation of Life. 1935 Rumba; Enter Madame; The Florentine Dagger; A Night at the Ritz; Stars over Broadway; Under the Pampas Moon; Charlie Chan in Egypt; Waterfront Lady; I Dream Too Much; Million Dollar Baby. 1936 Muss 'Em Up; Down to the Sea; Crash Donovan; The Leathernecks Have Landed. 1937 Maytime; The Emperor's Candlesticks; The Bride Wore Red; Seventh Heaven; Cafe Metropole. 1938 Crime School. 1939 Everything Happens at Night; Lady of the Tropics. 1940 Dr. Kildare's Strange Case; I Was an Adventuress; Torrid Zone; The Border Region; Argentine Nights. 1942 Star Spangled Rhythm; Road to Happiness; Quiet Please Murder. 1943 Hi Diddle Diddle. 1944 Hail the Conquering Hero; Swing Hostess; Nothing but Trouble. 1945 I'll Remember April.

PORTEN, HENNY
Born: 1890, Germany. Died: Oct. 15, 1960, Berlin, Germany. Screen actress. One of Germany's first silent film stars.

Appeared in: 1921 Deception. 1926 Backstairs. 1930 Skandal Um Eva (Scandal about Eva). 1931 Gretel and Liesel (aka Kohlhiesel's Daughters); Mother Love. 1934 Crown of Thorns; Mutter und Kind (Mother and Child). 1937 Krach im Hinterhaus (Trouble Back Stairs). Other German films: The Marriage of Luis Rohrbach; Rohrbach; Anne Boleyn; Rose Bernd; Queen Luis; Family Buchholz.

PORTER, EDWARD D.
Born: 1881. Died: July 29, 1939, Hollywood, Calif.(stroke). Screen and stage actor.

Appeared in: 1925 Friendly Enemies.

PORTER, HAROLD B.
Born: 1896. Died: July 30, 1939, Hollywood, Calif.(suicide). Screen actor, radio performer, and cameraman.

PORTER, VIOLA ADELE
Born: 1879. Died: Dec. 29, 1942, Hollywood, Calif. Screen actress.

PORTERFIELD, ROBERT H.
Born: 1905, Austinville, Va. Died: Oct. 28, 1971, Abingdon, Va. (heart attack). Screen, stage actor, and stage director.

Appeared in: 1941 Sergeant York. 1946 The Yearling. 1958 Thunder Road.

PORTMAN, ERIC
Born: July 13, 1903, Yorkshire, England. Died: Dec. 7, 1969, St. Veep, England. Screen, stage, and television actor.

Appeared in: 1934 The Murder in the Red Barn (film debut). 1935 Abul The Damned; Old Roses; Hyde Park Corner (U.S. 1940). 1937 The Prince and the Pauper. 1938 Crimes of Stephen Hawke; Moonlight Sonata. 1941 49th Parallel (aka The Invaders - U.S. 1942). 1942 One of Our Aircraft Is Missing, Uncensored (U.S. 1944). 1943 Squadron Leader X; We Dive at Dawn; Millions Like Us. 1944 A Canterbury Tale (U.S. 1949); Escape to Danger. 1945 The Cardinal. 1946 Great Day; Men of Two Worlds; Wanted for Murder. 1947 Dear Murderer (U.S. 1948). 1948 The Blind Goddess; The Mark of Cain. 1949 Daybreak; Corridor of Mirrors. 1950 Cairo Road (U.S. 1952). 1951 His Excellency (U.S. 1956). 1952 The Magic Box; The Spider and the Fly; Kisenga, Man of Africa. 1953 Colditz Story (U.S. 1957). 1954 The Golden Mask. 1955 The Deep Blue Sea. 1956 Child in the House. 1957 The Good Companions. 1961 The Naked Edge. 1962 Freud. 1963 West Eleven. 1965 The Bedford Incident. 1966 The Spy with a Cold Nose. 1967 The Whisperers. 1968 Deadfall; Assignment to Kill. 1969 The Man Who Finally Died.

POST, GUY BATES
Born: 1875, Seattle, Wash. Died: Jan. 16, 1968, Los Angeles, Calif. Screen and stage actor.

Appeared in: 1922 The Masquerader; Omar the Tentmaker. 1923 Gold Madness. 1932 Prestige. 1936 Camille; Till We Meet Again; The Case against Mrs. Ames; Fatal Lady; Trouble for Two; Ace Drummond (serial). 1937 Champagne Waltz; Daughter of Shanghai; Maid of Salem; Maytime; Blazing Barriers; The Mysterious Pilot. 1940 The Mad Empress. 1942 Crossroads. 1947 A Double Life.

POST, WILEY
Born: Grand Plain, Tex. Died: Aug. 15, 1935, near Barrow, Alaska (airplane crash). Aviator, screen actor, and stunt flyer. Died in crash with Will Rogers.

Appeared in: 1935 Air Hawks.

POST, WILMARTH H.
Died: Aug. 25, 1930, Rutherford, N.J.(heart failure). Screen, stage actor, film director, and author.

POTEL, VICTOR
Born: 1889, Lafayette, Ind. Died: Mar. 8, 1947, Los Angeles, Calif. Screen actor. Entered films in 1910. Was one of the original Keystone Kops.

Appeared in: 1910 Joyriding. 1911 "Snakeville" comedy series. 1916 His Last Scent. 1919 The Outcasts of Poker Flat; Captain Kidd, Jr. 1920 Mary's Ankle. 1921 Lavender and Old Lace; Bob Hampton of Placer. 1922 Step on It!. At the Sign of the Jack O'Lantern; Quincy Adams Sawyer; Don't Write Letters; A Tailor Made Man; The Loaded Door; I Can Explain. 1923 Anna Christie; Penrod and Sam; Itching Palms; The Meanest Man in the World; Refuge; Reno; Modern Matrimony; Tea with a Kick. 1924 Along Came Jones; The Law Forbids; A Self-Made Failure; Women Who Give; A Lost Lady. 1925 Below the Line; Ten Days; Contraband. 1926 The Bar-C Mystery (serial); The Carnival Girl; The Lodge in the Wilderness; Racing Romance; Morganson's Finish. 1927 Uneasy Payments; Special Delivery; The Craver. 1928 What Price Beauty; Little Shepherd of Kingdom Come; Lingerie; Melody of Love; Captain Swagger. 1929 Marianne; The Virginian. 1930 The Bad One; The Big Shot; Paradise Island; Virtuous Sin; Call of the West; Border Romance; Dough Boys. 1931 10¢ a Dance; The Squaw Man. 1932 Partners; Make Me a Star; The Purchase Price. 1933 Hallelujah, I'm a Bum. 1934 Thunder over Texas; Inside Information; Frontier Days. 1935 Mississippi; The Trail's End; Last of the Clintons; Lady Tubbs; Hard Rock Harrigan; Waterfront Lady; Whispering Smith Speaks. 1936 Three Godfathers; O'Malley of the Mounted; Yellow Dust; Song of the Saddle; The Captain's Kid; God's Country and the Woman; Down to the Sea. 1937 Two-Gun Law; White Bondage; Western Gold; Small Town Boy. 1938 Outside the Law. 1939 Rovin' Tumbleweeds. 1940 Girl from God's Country; Christmas in July. 1941 Birth of the Blues; Sullivan's Travels; The Big Store. 1944 The Miracle of Morgan's Creek; The Great Moment; Going to Town; Hail the Conquering Hero. 1945 Strange Illusion; Captain Tugboat Annie;

Medal for Benny; Rhythm Round-Up. 1946 The Glass Alibi. 1947 The Millerson Case; Mad Wednesday (aka The Sin of Harold Diddlebock); Ramrod; The Egg and I.

POWELL, DAVID
Born: Wales. Died: Apr. 16, 1925, N.Y.(pneumonia). Screen actor.

Appeared in: 1916 Less Than the Dust; Gloria's Romance (serial). 1917 The Beautiful Adventure. 1918 A Romance of the Underworld; The Unforseen. 1919 The Firing Line; His Parisian Wife. 1920 The Right to Love; Idols of Clay; On with the Dance; Lady Rose's Daughter. 1921 Appearances; The Princess of New York; Dangerous Lies; The Mystery Road. 1922 Outcast; The Siren Call; Anna Ascends; Her Gilded Cage; Missing Millions; Love's Boomerang; The Spanish Jade. 1923 The Glimpses of the Moon; Fog Bound; The Green Goddess. 1924 The Average Woman; Lend Me Your Husband; The Truth about Women; The Man without a Heart; Virtuous Liars. 1925 Back to Life; The Lost Chord.

POWELL, DICK
Died: Sept. 26, 1948, Hales Corners, Wisc.(accidental fall from plane). Screen actor and stunt flier. Not to be confused with actor dec. 1963.

Appeared in: 1920 The Great Air Robbery. 1925 The Cloud Rider; Air Hawks. 1930 Hell's Angels; Dawn Patrol. 1947 Blaze of Noon.

POWELL, DICK
Born: Nov. 24, 1904, Mt. View, Ark. Died: Jan. 2, 1963, Hollywood, Calif.(cancer). Screen, stage, radio, television actor, film director and producer, stage director, and singer. Married to screen actress June Allyson. Divorced from actress Joan Blondell.

Appeared in: 1931 Street Scene; Gold Diggers of 1933; Footlight Parade; College Coach; Convention City; The King's Vacation. 1934 Wonder Bar; Twenty Million Sweethearts; Happiness Ahead; Flirtation Walk; Dames. 1935 Gold Diggers of 1935; If You Could Only Cook; A Midsummer Night's Dream; Page Miss Glory; Broadway Gondolier; Shipmates Forever; Thanks a Million; Ginger. 1936 Colleen; Hearts Divided; Stage Struck; Gold Diggers of 1937, For Auld Lang Syne (documentary). 1937 On the Avenue; The Singing Marine; Varsity Show; Hollywood Hotel; The College Coed. 1938 The Cowboy from Brooklyn; Hard to Get; Going Places. 1939 Naughty but Nice. 1940 Christmas in July; I Want a Divorce. 1941 Model Wife; In the Navy. 1942 Star Spangled Rhythm. 1943 Happy Go Lucky; True to Life; Riding High. 1944 Meet the People; It Happened Tomorrow; Farewell, My Lovely. 1945 Cornered. 1947 Johnny O'Clock. 1948 To the Ends of the Earth; Pitfall; Station West; Rogue's Regiment. 1949 Mrs. Mike. 1950 The Reformer and the Redhead; Right Cross. 1951 Cry Danger; Callaway Went Thataway; Tall Target; You Never Can Tell. 1952 The Bad and the Beautiful. 1954 Susan Slept Here.

POWELL, LEE (Alfred E. Lee)
Born: 1896. Died: Feb. 3, 1954, Hollywood, Calif. Screen and stage actor.

POWELL, LEE B.
Born: May 15, 1908, Long Beach, Calif. Died: Aug. 1944 (killed in action in Marines in the South Pacific). Screen and stage actor. The original "Lone Ranger" of the films.

Appeared in: 1938 The Lone Ranger (serial); The Fighting Devil Dogs (serial); Come on, Rangers. 1939 Trigger Pals.

POWELL, RICHARD
Born: 1897. Died: Jan. 1, 1937, Hollywood, Calif.(fractured skull, from auto accident). Screen actor and opera performer. Not to be confused with actors Dick Powell (dec. 1948 and 1963).

Appeared in: 1935 The Wedding Night; Woman Wanted; Every Night at Eight. 1936 Yours for the Asking; Hollywood Boulevard. 1937 Another Dawn.

POWER, HARTLEY
Born: Mar. 14, 1894, New York, N.Y. Died: Jan. 29, 1966, London, England. Screen and stage actor.

Appeared in: 1932 Yes, Mrs. Brown; No More Orchids; Just Smith (U.S. 1934). 1933 Aunt Sally; Friday the Thirteenth; This Is the Life. 1934 Evergreen; The Camels Are Coming; Road-House; Along Came Sally. 1935 Jury's Evidence. 1936 Living Dangerously; Where There's a Will; Just Like a Woman. 1938 The Return of the Frog. 1939 Murder Will Out; A Window in London; Return to Yesterday; Atlantic Ferry (U.S. 1941). 1942 Lady in Distress. 1943 Alibi. 1945 Man from Morocco; Dead of Night. 1950

A Girl in a Million. 1953 Roman Holiday. 1954 Man with a Million; Cash on Delivery (U.S. 1956). 1957 Island in the Sun.

POWER, JOHN
Born: 1874. Died: Sept. 25, 1951, Culver City, Calif. Screen and stage actor.

POWER, PAUL (Luther Vestergard)
Born: 1902, Chicago, Ill. Died: Apr. 5, 1968, Hollywood, Calif. Screen, stage, and television actor. Entered films in 1925.

Appeared in: 1927 False Values. 1928 Trial Marriage; Hot Heels. 1929 Words and Music. 1938 Adventures of Robin Hood. 1955 The Girl in the Red Velvet Swing. 1958 Jet Attack. 1960 Ma Barker's Killer Brood. 1962 The Underwater City.

POWER, TYRONE F., SR.
Born: 1869, London, England. Died: Dec. 30, 1931, Hollywood, Calif.(heart attack). Screen and stage actor. Father of screen actor Tyrone Power, Jr.(dec. 1958). Married to stage actress Patia Power.

Appeared in: 1915 A Texas Steer. 1916 John Needham's Double; Where Are My Children?. 1919 The Miracle Man. 1921 The Black Panther's Cub; Dream Street; Footfalls. 1923 Bright Lights of Broadway; The Daring Years; Fury; The Truth about Wives; The Day of Faith; Wife in Name Only. 1924 Damaged Hearts; Janice Meredith; For Another Woman; The Law and the Lady; Trouping with Ellen; The Story without a Name; The Lone Wolf. 1925 Braveheart; Red Kimono; A Regular Fellow; Where Was I?. 1926 Bride of the Storm; Hands across the Border; The Wanderer; Out of the Storm; The Test of Donald Norton. 1930 The Big Trail.

POWER, TYRONE F, JR.
Born: May 5, 1914, Cincinnati, Ohio. Died: Nov. 15, 1958, Madrid, Spain (heart attack). Screen and stage actor. Son of screen actor Tyrone Power, Sr.(dec. 1931) and stage actress Patia Power. Divorced from screen actresses Annabella and Linda Christian. Married to screen actress Debbie Ann Minardos Power.

Appeared in: 1932 Tom Brown of Culver. 1934 Flirtation Walk. 1936 Girl's Dormitory; Ladies in Love; Lloyds of London. 1937 Love Is News; Cafe Metropole; Thin Ice; Second Honeymoon. 1938 In Old Chicago; Alexander's Ragtime Band; Marie Antoinette; Suez. 1939 Jesse James; Rose of Washington Square; Second Fiddle; The Rains Came; Daytime Wife. 1940 Johnny Apollo, Brigham Young—Frontiersman; The Mark of Zorro; The Return of Frank James. 1941 Blood and Sand; A Yank in the R.A.F. 1942 Son of Fury; This above All; The Black Swan. 1943 Crash Dive. 1946 The Razor's Edge. 1947 Nightmare Alley; Captain from Castile. 1948 Luck of the Irish; That Wonderful Urge. 1949 Prince of Foxes. 1950 The Black Rose; American Guerilla in the Philippines. 1951 Rawhide; I'll Never Forget You (aka Man of Two Worlds and The House in the Square). 1952 Diplomatic Courier; Pony Soldier. 1953 Mississippi Gambler; King of the Khyber Rifles. 1955 The Long Gray Line; Untamed. 1956 The Eddy Duchin Story. 1957 Abandon Ship!. Seven Waves Away; The Rising of the Moon (narr.); The Sun Also Rises; Witness for the Prosecution.

POWERS, JOHN H.
Born: 1885. Died: Jan. 17, 1941, New York, N.Y. Screen, stage, vaudeville actor, and circus performer. Was partner in vaudeville in an act billed as "McAvoy and Powers."

Appeared in: 1923 Adam and Eva. 1937 Hills of Old Wyoming. 1939 Zaza.

POWERS, JULE
Died: Feb. 1932, Hollywood, Calif. Screen and stage actress.

POWERS, RICHARD. See Tom Keene

POWERS, TOM
Born: 1890, Owensboro, Ky. Died: Nov. 9, 1955, Hollywood, Calif. (heart ailment). Screen, stage actor, and author. Entered films in 1910.

Appeared in: 1911 Saving an Audience. 1917 The Auction Block. 1944 Practically Yours; Double Indemnity. 1945 The Phantom Speaks; The Chicago Kid. 1946 Two Years before the Mast; The Blue Dahlia; The Last Crooked Mile; Her Adventurous Night. 1947 Son of Rusty; Angel and the Badman; The Farmer's Daughter; They Won't Believe Me. 1948 Angel in Exile; I Love Trouble; The Time of Your Life; Up in Central Park; Mexican Hayride; Station West. 1949 Special Agent; Scene of the Crime; Chicago Deadline; East Side, West Side. 1950 Destination Moon; Chinatown at Midnight; The Nevadan; Right Cross. 1951 Fighting Coast Guard; The Strip; The Tall Target; The Well. 1952 Denver and Rio Grande;

Diplomatic Courier; We're Not Married; Steel Trap; Deadline — U.S.A.; Jet Job; Phone Call from a Stranger; Bal Tabarin; The Fabulous Senorita; Horizons West. 1953 The Last Posse; The Marksman; Hannah Lee; Julius Caesar; Scared Stiff; Donovan's Brain; Sea of Lost Ships. 1955 The Americano; New York Confidential; Ten Wanted Men. 1956 UFO.

PRAGER, WILLY
Born: 1877, Germany. Died: Mar. 4, 1956, West Germany. Screen and stage actor.

Appeared in: 1931 Der Grosse Tenor. 1948 Marriage in Shadows.

PRATA, JOAQUIM
Born: 1882. Died: Nov. 18, 1953, Lisbon, Portugal. Screen, stage actor, and playwright.

PRATHER, LEE (Oscar Lee Prather)
Born: 1890. Died: Jan. 3, 1958, Los Angeles, Calif.(during surgery). Screen and stage actor.

Appeared in: 1935 Hot Money (short). 1938 The Buccaneer; Women in Prison. 1939 Homicide Bureau.

PRATT, LYNN
Born: 1863, Sylvan Center, Mich. Died: Jan. 1930, New York. Screen, stage, and vaudeville actor.

Appeared in: 1921 A Virgin Paradise.

PRATT, NEIL
Born: 1890, San Diego, Calif. Died: Jan. 3, 1934, Hollywood, Calif. (heart attack). Screen and stage actor. Entered films approx. 1933.

PRATT, PURNELL B.
Born: Oct. 20, 1886, Bethel, Ill. Died: July 25, 1941, Hollywood, Calif. Screen and stage actor.

Appeared in: 1925 The Lady Who Lied. 1926 Midnight Lovers. 1929 The Trespasser; Through Different Eyes; Fast Life; Is Everybody Happy?; Alibi; On with the Show. 1930 Painted Faces; The Furies; Road to Paradise; Common Clay; Sinner's Holiday; Lawful Larceny; The Silver Horde; The Locked Door; Puttin' on the Ritz. 1931 The Gorilla; The Road to Romance; Fires of Youth; Five Star Final; Woman Pursued; The Secret Witness; The Public Defender; The Spider; Terror by Night; The Gay Diplomat; Beyond Victory; Paid; The Prodigal; Dance, Fools, Dance; Up for Murder; Bachelor Apartments; Traveling Husbands. 1932 Hat Check Girl; Red Haired Alibi; False Faces; Unwritten Law; The Famous Ferguson Case; Roadhouse Murder; Grand Hotel; Scarface; Ladies of the Big House; Emma. 1933 The Billion Dollar Scandal; Pick Up; A Shriek in the Night; Headline Shooter; I Cover the Waterfront; Midshipman Jack; The Sweetheart of Sigma Chi; Love, Honor and Oh, Baby; The Chief; Son of a Sailor. 1934 Name the Woman; The Crimson Romance; School for Girls; The Witching Hour; Midnight Alibi; The Hell Cat. 1935 Death Flies East; Black Fury; The Winning Ticket; The Casino Murder Case; It's In the Air; Behind the Green Lights; Ladies Crave Excitement; Waterfront Lady; Diamond Jim; Red Salute; $1,000 a Minute; Frisco Waterfront; Rendezvous at Midnight; A Night at the Opera; Magnificent Obsession. 1936 Dancing Feet; The Return of Sophie Lang; Hollywood Boulevard; Straight from the Shoulder; Lady Be Careful; Murder with Pictures; Wives Never Know; Wedding Present; The Plainsman. 1937 Join the Marines; Let's Make a Million; Murder Goes to College; King of Gamblers; A Night of Mystery; Under Suspicion; High, Wide and Handsome. 1938 Come On, Rangers!. 1939 My Wife's Relatives; Grand Ole Opry; Colorado Sunset. 1941 Doctor's Don't Tell; Ringside Maisie.

PRAY, ANNA M.
Born: 1891. Died: June 30, 1971, N.Y. Screen and stage actress. Married to stage actor Fleming Ward (dec.)

PREER, EVELYN
Born: July 26, 1896, Chicago, Ill. or Vicksburg, Miss. Died: Nov. 18, 1932, Los Angeles, Calif.(pneumonia). Negro screen and stage actress.

Appeared in: 1921 The Gunsaulus Mystery. 1922 The Homesteader. 1923 Deceit. 1924 Birthright. 1925 The Brute. 1926 The Conjure Woman; The Devil's Disciple. 1927 The Spider's Web. 1929 Melancholy Dame. 1930 Georgia Rose. 1932 Blonde Venus.

PRENTIS, LEWIS R.
Born: 1905. Died: June 26, 1967, Chicago, Ill. Screen and stage actor.

PRESTON, EDNA
    Born: 1892. Died: Aug. 18, 1960, New York. Screen, stage, radio, and television actress.

PREVOST, FRANK G.
    Born: 1894. Died: Apr. 17, 1946, Hollywood, Calif. Screen actor.

PREVOST, MARIE (Marie Bickford Gunn)
    Born: Nov. 8, 1898, Sarnia, Canada. Died: Jan. 21, 1937, Los Angeles, Calif. Screen actress. Was an early Sennett bathing beauty.

    Appeared in: 1917 Her Nature Dance; Secrets of a Beauty Parlor; Two Crooks (aka A Noble Crook - working title). 1919 Uncle Tom's Cabin. 1920 East Lynn with Variations; Divorce Made Easy. 1921 Old Swimmin' Hole; Nobody's Fool; A Parisian Scandal; A Small Town Idol; Moonlight Follies. 1922 The Beautiful and the Damned; Don't Get Personal; Dangerous Little Demon; Her Night of Nights; Kissed; Married Flapper; Red Lights; Heroes of the Street. 1923 Brass; The Wanters. 1924 Conquered; Tarnish; The Marriage Circle; The Dark Swan; Being Respectable; Daughters of Pleasure; How to Educate a Wife; The Marriage Circle; Three Women; The Loves of Camille. 1925 Bobbed Hair; Kiss Me Again; Recompense; Seven Sinners. 1926 Up in Mabel's Room; Almost a Lady; The Caveman; His Jazz Bride; Other Women's Husbands. 1927 For Wives Only; Man Bait; Getting Gertie's Garter; The Night Bride; The Girl in the Pullman. 1928 The Rush Hour; On to Reno; A Blonde for a Night; The Racket. 1929 The Godless Girl; The Flying Fool; Side Show; Divorce Made Easy. 1930 Ladies of Leisure; Party Girl; War Nurse; Sweethearts on Parade. 1931 The Easiest Way; The Good Bad Girl; Reckless Living; Sporting Blood; Paid; A Gentleman's Fate; It's a Wise Child; The Runaround; Hell Divers; The Sin of Madelon Claudet. 1932 Three Wise Girls; Carnival Boat; Slightly Married. 1933 Parole Girl; Only Yesterday; The 11th Commandment; a Universal short. 1935 Hands across the Table; a Vitaphone short. 1936 Tango; Cain and Mabel; 13 Hours by Air.

PRICE, GEORGIE (George E. Price)
    Born: 1900. Died: May 10, 1964, New York, N.Y.(heart attack). Screen, vaudeville actor, and singer.

    Appeared in: 1929 Don't Get Nervous (short). 1930 Metro Movietone short.

PRICE, KATE (Kate Duffy)
    Born: Feb. 13, 1872, Cork, Ireland. Died: Jan. 4, 1943, Woodland Hills, Calif. Screen, stage, and vaudeville actress.

    Appeared in: 1912 Stenographers Wanted. 1916 The Waiter's Ball. 1919 The Perils of Thunder Mountain (serial). 1920 Dinty. 1921 God's Crucible; The Girl Montana; Little Lord Fauntleroy; The Other Woman. 1922 My Wife's Relations (short); Come on Over; Flesh and Blood; A Dangerous Game; Paid Back; The New Teacher; The Guttersnipe. 1923 Broken Hearts of Broadway; Good-By Girls!; The Spoilers; Crossed Wires; The Dangerous Maid; Enemies of Children; Her Fatal Millions; The Near Lady. 1924 Fool's Highway; Riders Up; The Tornado; Wife of the Centaur; Passion's Pathway; The Sea Hawk. 1925 The Desert Flower; The Man without a Conscience; The Way of a Girl; The Sporting Venus; His People; The Perfect Clown; Sally, Irene and Mary; Proud Heart. 1926 Irene; The Cohens and the Kellys; The Arizona Sweepstakes; Faithful Wives; Paradise; Love's Blindness; Memory Lane. 1927 Frisco Sally Levy; The Third Degree; Casey Jones; Mountains of Manhattan; Orchids and Ermine; The Sea Tiger; Quality Street.

PRICE, NANCY (Lillian Nancy Maude)
    Born: Feb. 3, 1880, Kinver, Staffs, England. Died: Mar. 31, 1970, Worthing, England. Screen, stage actress, and author. Not to be confused with actress Nancy Price born in 1918.

    Appeared in: 1939 The Stars Look Down. 1944 Madonna of the Seven Moons. 1945 I Live in Grosvenor Square. 1948 The Three Weird Sisters. 1952 Mandy (aka The Story of Mandy and aka Crash of Silence).

PRICE, STANLEY L.
    Born: 1900. Died: July 13, 1955, Hollywood, Calif.(heart attack). Screen, stage actor, and screenwriter.

    Appeared in: 1922 Your Best Friend. 1938 Hunted Men; Tom Sawyer, Detective. 1939 Sudden Money; Undercover Doctor. 1940 Seventeen; The Way of All Flesh; Moon over Burma; The Golden Trail. 1942 Outlaws of Pine Ridge; The Great Commandments. 1943 Lone Rider in Wild Horse Rustlers. 1944 Bride by Mistake; Zorro's Black Whip (serial); Range Law. 1945 Phantom of 42nd

Street; Lost Weekend; Crime, Inc.; Power of the Whistler. 1950 The Sundowners; Dopey Dicks (short). 1956 The Ten Commandments.

PRIETO, ANTONIO
    Born: 1915, Portugal. Died: Mar. 1965, Madrid, Spain (heart attack). Screen, stage, and television actor.

    Appeared in: 1964 Los Tarantos; 1967 A Fistful of Dollars.

PRINCE, JOHN T.
    Born: Sept. 11, 1871, Boston, Mass. Died: Dec. 24, 1937, Los Angeles, Calif. Screen and stage actor.

    Appeared in: 1913 Mission Bells. 1916 Phantom Island. 1917 Over There. 1922 Doctor Jack; Little Eva Ascends. 1923 East Side, West Side. 1924 The Battling Orioles; Defying the Law. 1925 Capital Punishment; Heartless Husbands; The Call of Courage; Women and Gold; The Gold Hunters. 1926 Jack O'Hearts; Money to Burn; The Phantom Bullet; Dame Chance; Prowlers of the Night; The Radio Detective (serial). 1927 King of Kings; Hawk of the Hills (serial). 1928 Ramona; Haunted Island (serial). 1929 Hawk of the Hills (feature of 1927 serial). 1936 The Country Beyond.

PRINCESS KANZA OMAR
    Born: 1912. Died: Mar. 6, 1958, Los Angeles, Calif.(cancer). Screen actress and dancer.

    Appeared in: 1938 The Buccaneer.

PRINGLE, JOHN
    Died: 1929. Screen and stage actor. Father of screen actor John Gilbert (dec. 1936).

    Appeared in: 1924 Black Lightning. Travelin' Fast. 1925 His Greatest Battle.

PROMIS, FLO
    Born: 1884. Died: Apr. 23, 1956, Hollywood, Calif. Screen actress.

    Appeared in: 1936 Ants in the Pantry (short).

PROSSER, HUGH
    Born: 1906. Died: Nov. 8, 1952, near Gallup, N.Mex.(auto accident). Screen actor.

    Appeared in: 1938 Blockade. 1942 The Boss of Hangtown Mesa; Sabotage Squad. 1943 Border Patrol; Lost Canyon. 1945 Flame of the Barbary Coast; Dillinger. 1946 People Are Funny. 1949 Western Renegades. 1950 Outlaw Gold; Across the Badlands. 1951 Montana Incident. 1952 Guns along the Border; The Greatest Show on Earth; Treasure of Lost Canyon; Bend of the River.

PROUTY, JED
    Born: Apr. 6, 1879, Boston, Mass. Died: May 10, 1956, New York. Screen, stage, radio, television, and vaudeville actor. At age sixteen he formed a vaudeville act known as "Maddux and Prouty."

    Appeared in: 1921 The Conquest of Canaan; Experience; Room and Board; The Great Adventure. 1922 Kick In. 1923 The Girl of the Golden West; Souls for Sale; The Gold Diggers. 1925 The Coast of Folly; Scarlet Saint; The Knockout; The Unguarded Hour. 1926 Bred in Old Kentucky; Don Juan's Three Nights; Miss Nobody; Unknown Treasures; Ella Cinders; Everybody's Acting; Her Second Chance; The Mystery Club. 1927 Smile, Brother, Smile; Orchids and Ermine; The Gingham Girl; No Place to Go. 1928 Domestic Meddlers; Name the Woman; The Siren. 1929 Imperfect Ladies; The Fall of Eve; His Captive Woman; Two Weeks Off; It's a Great Life; Why Leave Home?; Sonny Boy; The Broadway Melody. 1930 True to the Navy; No Questions Asked (short); The Floradora Girl; Girl in the Show; The Devil's Holiday. 1931 Strangers May Kiss; Annabelle's Affairs; The Secret Call; Age for Love. 1932 Business and Pleasure; Manhattan Tower; Hold 'Em Jail. 1933 Skyway; The Big Bluff; Jimmy and Sally. 1934 I Believed in You; Music in the Air; Private Scandal; One Hour Late; Hollywood Party. 1935 George White's 1935 Scandals; Black Sheep; Navy Wife; One Hour Late; A Trip to Paris. 1936 Every Saturday Night; Little Miss Nobody; Educating Father; Back to Nature; Can This Be Dixie?; Under Your Spell; Special Investigator; His Brother's Wife; The Texas Rangers; College Holiday; Happy Go Lucky. 1937 Borrowing Trouble; Off to the Races; Big Business; Hot Water; Life Begins in College; The Crime Nobody Saw; Sophie Lang Goes West; Dangerous Holiday; One Hundred Men and a Girl; Small Town Boy; You Can't Have Everything. 1938 Love on a Budget; Walking down Broadway; A Trip to Paris; Keep Smiling; Safety in Numbers; Duke of West Point; Goodbye Broadway; Danger on the Air; Down on the Farm. 1939 Everybody's Baby; The Jones Family in Hollywood; Too Busy to Work; The Gracie Allen Murder Case; Second Fiddle; The Jones Family in Grand Canyon; The Jones Family in Quick Millions; Hollywood Cavalcade; Exile Express. 1940 Young as You Feel; On Their Own; Barnyard Follies; Remedy for Riches. 1941 The Lone Wolf Keeps a Date; Pot 'O Gold; Father Steps Out; Bachelor Daddy; Unexpected Uncle; City Limits; Look Who's Laughing; Go West Young Lady; Roar of the Press. 1942 The Affairs of Jimmy Valentine; Scattergood Rides High; It Happened in Flatbush; Moonlight Masquerade; The Old Homestead; Mud Town. 1950 Guilty Bystander.

PRUD'HOMME, CAMERON
Born: 1892. Died: Nov. 27, 1967, Pompton Plains, N.J. Screen, stage, and radio actor.

Appeared in: 1930 Abraham Lincoln; Doorway to Hell; Half Shot at Sunrise. 1931 Soldiers' Plaything; Honor of the Family; I Like Your Nerve. 1956 The Power and the Prize; Back from Eternity; The Rainmaker. 1963 The Cardinal.

PRYOR, AINSLIE
Born: 1921, Memphis, Tenn. Died: May 27, 1958, Hollywood, Calif.(brain cancer). Screen, stage, and television actor.

Appeared in: 1955 The Girl in the Red Velvet Swing. 1956 Ransom!; The Last Hunt; Four Girls in Town; Walk the Proud Land. 1957 Guns at Fort Petticoat; The Shadow on the Window. 1958 Kathy-O; Cole Younger, Gunfighter; The Left Handed Gun; Onionhead.

PUDOVKIN, VSEVOLOD
Born: 1893, Russia. Died: 1953, Russia. Screen actor, film producer, film director, and author.

Appeared in: 1931 The Living Corpse. 1942 Ivan the Terrible—Part I (U.S. 1947). 1948 Admiral Nakhimov.

PURCELL, RICHARD "DICK"
Born: Aug. 6, 1908, Greenwich, Conn. Died: Aug. 10, 1944, Los Angeles, Calif.(heart attack). Screen and stage actor.

Appeared in: 1935 Ceiling Zero. 1936 Brides Are Like That; Times Square Playboy; Law in Her Hands; Bullets or Ballots; Jail Break; The Captain's Kid; Men in Exile; King of Hockey; Melody for Two; The Case of the Velvet Claws; Public Enemy's Wife; Man Hunt; Broadway Playboy; Bengal Tiger. 1937 Public Wedding; Navy Blues; Slim; Wine, Women and Horses; The Missing Witness; Reported Missing. 1938 Mystery House; The Daredevil Drivers; Alcatraz Island; Accidents Will Happen; Over the Wall; Penrod's Double Trouble; Garden of the Moon; Valley of the Giants; Flight into Nowhere; Air Devils; Broadway Musketeers; Nancy Drew, Detective. 1939 Blackwell's Island; Irish Luck; Tough Kid; Heroes in Blue; Streets of New York. 1940 Private Affairs; Outside the Three-Mile Limit; New Moon; The Bank Dick; Flight Command; Arise My Love. 1941 The Pittsburgh Kid; Flying Blind; Two in a Taxi; No Hands on the Clock; Bullets for O'Hara; King of the Zombies. 1942 Torpedo Boat; In Old California; The Old Homestead; I Live on Danger; X Marks the Spot; Phantom Killer. 1943 Aerial Gunner; Idaho; High Explosives; Reveille with Beverly; The Mystery of the Thirteenth Guest. 1944 Trocadero; Leave It to the Irish; Farewell My Lovely; Captain America (serial); Timber Queen.

PURDELL, REGINALD (Reginald Grasdorf)
Born: 1896. Died: Apr. 22, 1953, London, England. Screen, stage, television actor, and screenwriter.

Appeared in: 1930 The Middle Watch. 1931 Congress Dances. 1935 The Old Curiosity Shop. 1938 Q Planes. 1940 Many Tanks Mr. Atkins; Pack up Your Troubles; Haunted Honeymoon. 1943 Variety Jubilee; We Dive at Dawn. 1944 2,000 Women. 1947 Holiday Camp. 1948 Captain Boycott. Other British films: Up to the Neck; Key to Harmony; What's in a Name; Hail and Farewell; Quiet Please.

PURVIANCE, EDNA
Born: 1894, Reno, Nev. Died: Jan. 13, 1958, Woodland Hills, Calif. Screen actress. She was Charlie Chaplin's leading lady for nine years in his early films.

Appeared in: 1915 A Night Out; The Champion; Work. 1916 The Vagabond; Carmen; The Count; The Bank. 1917 The Cure; The Adventurer; Easy Street. 1918 A Dog's Life; Shoulder Arms. 1919 Sunnyside. 1921 The Kid; The Idle Class. 1923 The Pilgrim; A Woman of Paris. 1926 The Seagull; A Woman of the Sea. 1952 Limelight. 1963 30 Years of Fun (documentary)

PYNE, JOE
Born: 1925, Chester, Pa. Died: Mar. 23, 1970, Los Angeles, Calif. (lung cancer). Screen, television, and radio actor.

Appeared in: 1967 The Love-Ins.

QUARTERMAINE, LEON
Born: 1876. Died: June 28, 1967, Salisbury, England. Screen and stage actor.

Appeared in: 1935 Escape Me Never. 1936 As You Like It.

QUILLIAN, JOSEPH F.
Born: July 27, 1884, Glasgow, Scotland. Died: Nov. 16, 1952, Hollywood, Calif.(cancer). Screen and vaudeville actor.

Appeared in: 1928 A Little Bit of Everything (short). 1929 Noisy Neighbors.

QUINCE, LOUIS VEDA
Born: 1900. Died: Sept. 24, 1954, Dallas, Tex.(heart attack). Screen, stage, and radio actor.

Appeared in: 1945 Mildred Pierce.

QUINN, ALAN J.
Born: 1889. Died: Jan. 1944, Philadelphia, Pa. Screen actor.

Appeared in: 1915 The Sporting Duchess.

QUINN, JAMES "JIMMIE"
Born: 1885, New Orleans, La. Died: Aug. 22, 1940, Hollywood, Calif. Screen and stage actor. Entered films in 1919. Was featured with Billie Sullivan in a series of racetrack shorts.

Appeared in: 1922 Afraid to Fight; Rags to Riches. 1923 Mile-a-Minute Romeo; Second Hand Love. 1924 Broadway after Dark. 1925 Red Hot Tires; The Dixie Handicap; Pretty Ladies; Speed Madness; The Wife Who Wasn't Wanted; On Thin Ice; Soft Shoes. 1926 The Imposter. 1927 Two Flaming Youths. 1928 The Spieler; Ginsberg the Great; Women Who Dare. 1929 Come and Get It; The Dance of Life; The Argyle Case. 1930 Hold Everything. 1934 I Hate Women. 1935 The Gilded Lily.

QUINN, JOE
Born: 1917. Died: Feb. 2, 1971, Hollywood, Calif.(heart attack). Screen, stage, and television actor.

QUINN, PAUL
Born: 1870. Died: Apr. 20, 1936, Los Angeles, Calif. Screen, stage, vaudeville, and minstrel actor.

QUINN, TONY
Born: Ireland. Died: June 1, 1967, London, England. Screen, stage, and television actor. Not to be confused with actor Anthony Quinn.

Appeared in: 1937 Non-Stop, New York.

QUIRK, WILLIAM "BILLY"
Born: 1881. Died: Apr. 20, 1926, Hollywood, Calif. Screen actor.

Appeared in: 1909 The Son's Return; The Renunciation; Sweet and Twenty; His Wife's Visitor; Oh, Uncle; Getting Even; The Little Teacher; A Midnight Adventure; A Corner in Wheat; The Mended Lute; They Would Elope; 1776, or The Hessian Renegades; The Gibson Goddess. 1910 The Woman from Mellon's; A Rich Revenge; The Two Brothers; Muggsy's First Sweetheart. 1912 Fra Diavolo; The Blood Stain; Hubby Does the Washing. 1913 Billy's Troubles. 1914 Bridal Attire. 1915 Billy, the Bear Tamer. 1921 At the Stage Door; The Man Worth While. 1922 My Old Kentucky Home. 1923 A Bride for a Knight; Broadway Broke; Success. 1925 The Dixie Handicap.

QUIROZ, SALVADOR
Born: 1881, Mexico. Died: Nov. 23, 1956, Mexico City, Mexico. Screen actor.

RADCLIFF, JACK (Charles Smith)
Born: Sept. 18, 1900, Cleland, Scotland. Died: Apr. 26, 1967, Glasgow, Scotland (cancer). Screen, stage, vaudeville, and television actor.

Appeared in: 1956 Wee Geordie.

RADFORD, BASIL
Born: June 25, 1897, Chester, England. Died: Oct. 20, 1952, London, England (heart attack). Screen and stage actor.

Appeared in: 1929 Barnum Was Right (film debut). 1933 There Goes the Bride. 1936 Broken Blossoms. 1937 When Thief Meets

Thief; Young and Innocent. 1938 Convict 99; The Lady Vanishes; Climbing High; Just William. 1940 Spies of the Air; Crook's Tour; Among Human Wolves. 1941 The Girl in the News. 1942 Next of Kin; Flying Fortress. 1943 Millions Like Us. 1945 Dead of Night; The Way to the Stars; Johnny in the Clouds; The Randolph Family. 1946 A Girl in a Million (U.S. 1950); The Captive Heart. 1948 Quartet; It's Not Cricket; Passport to Pimlico. 1949 Whiskey Galore (aka Tight Little Island-U.S. & aka Mad Little Island). 1950 Chance of a Lifetime; The Winslow Boy. 1951 The Galloping Major. 1952 White Corridors. Other British films: The Flying Squad; Stop Press Girl.

RAE, CLAIRE
Born: 1889. Died: July 7, 1938, Canton, Ohio (leukemia). Screen and stage actress. Appeared in silents.

RAE, JACK (Alton Sampley)
Born: 1899. Died: May 3, 1957, Hollywood, Calif.(heart attack). Screen and stage actor.

RAE, MELBA
Born: 1922. Died: Dec. 29, 1971, N.Y.(cerebral hemorrhage). Screen, stage, radio, and television actress. Did film short subject narration and foreign film dubbing.

RAFFERTY, CHIPS (John Goffage)
Born: 1909, Australia. Died: May 27, 1971, Sydney, Australia (heart attack). Screen, stage, and television actor.

Appeared in: 1930 Ants in His Pants (film debut). 1939 Dan Rudd, M.P. 1940 Forty Thousand Horsemen. 1945 The Rats of Tobruk (aka The Fighting Rats of Tobruk-U.S. 1951). 1946 The Overlanders; The Loves of Joanna Godden. 1947 Eureka Stockade; Bush Country Adventure; Bush Christmas. 1951 Bitter Springs; Massacre Hill. 1952 Kangaroo. 1953 The Desert Rats. 1956 King of the Coral Sea; Walk into Paradise. 1957 Walk into Hell; Smiley. 1959 Smiley Gets a Gun. 1960 The Sundowners. 1961 The Wackiest Ship in the Army. 1962 Mutiny on the Bounty. 1966 They're a Weird Mob. 1968 Kona Coast. 1969 Return of the Boomerang; Skullduggery.

"RAFFLES BILL" (Andreas Aglassinger)
Born: 1895, Braunau-on-the-Inn, Austria. Died: Feb. 21, 1940, Berlin, Germany (stomach ailment). Screen, vaudeville, and circus actor. Appeared in German and U.S. films.

RAGAN, RUTH
Died: Sept. 15, 1962, Hollywood, Calif.(auto accident). Screen actress and dancer.

RAGLAN, JAMES
Born: 1901. Died: Nov. 15, 1961, London, England. Screen, stage, and television actor.

Appeared in: 1952 Whispering Smith vs. Scotland Yard.

RAGLAND, ESTHER
Born: 1912. Died: July 6, 1939, Los Angeles, Calif. Screen and vaudeville whistling actress. She did whistling numbers in 1937 Snow White and the Seven Dwarfs.

RAGLAND, RAGS (John Lee Morgan Beauregard Ragland)
Born: Aug. 23, 1905, Louisville, Ky. Died: Aug. 20, 1946, Los Angeles, Calif.(uremia). Screen, stage, and burlesque actor.

Appeared in: 1941 Whistling in the Dark; Ringside Masie. 1942 Masie Gets Her Man; Somewhere I'll Find You; Panama Hattie; Whistling in Dixie; The War against Mrs. Hadley; Sunday Punch; Born to Sing. 1943 Whistling in Brooklyn; Du Barry Was a Lady; Girl Crazy. 1944 The Centerville Ghost; Meet the People; Three Men in White. 1945 Anchors Aweigh; Her Highness and the Bellboy; Abbott and Costello in Hollywood. 1946 The Hoodlum Saint; Ziegfeld Follies.

RAIMU, JULES (Jules Muraire)
Born: 1883, France. Died: Sept. 20, 1946, Paris, France (heart attack). Screen and stage actor.

Appeared in: 1931 Marius (U.S. 1933). 1932 Fanny. 1933 Theodore et Cie (Theodore and Co.); Mam'zelle Nitouche. 1934 Caesar. 1935 Charlemagne. 1937 Un Carnet de Bal (U.S. 1938); Les Perles de le Couronne. 1939 Le Famille Lefrancois (Heroes of the Marne); Le Femme du Boulanger; Heart of Paris; Last Desire. 1940 The Baker's Wife; Le Fille du Puisatier (The Well-Digger's Daughter - U.S. 1946); Heart of a Nation (U.S. 1943). 1941 The Man Who Seeks the Truth; The King. 1942 Les Inconnus dans la Maison (Strangers in the House - U.S. 1949). 1944 Colonel

Chabert (U.S. 1947). 1945 Dawn Over France; L'Homme au Chapeau Rond. 1947 Midnight in Paris; Fanny (and 1932 version); The Eternal Husband (U.S. 1949); Hoboes in Paradise (U.S. 1950).

RAINS, CLAUDE
Born: Nov. 10, 1889, London, England. Died: May 30, 1967, Laconia, N.H.(intestinal hemorrhage). Screen, stage, and television actor.

Appeared in: 1933 The Invisible Man (film debut). 1934 Crime without Passion. 1935 The Man Who Reclaimed His Head; The Mystery of Edwin Drood; The Clairvoyant; The Last Outpost. 1936 Anthony Adverse; Hearts Divided; Stolen Holiday. 1937 The Prince and the Pauper; They Won't Forget. 1938 White Banners; The Adventures of Robin Hood; Four Daughters; Gold Is Where You Find It. 1939 They Made Me a Criminal; Juarez; Mr. Smith Goes to Washington; Four Wives; Sons of Liberty (short). 1940 Saturday's Children; The Sea Hawk; Lady with Red Hair. 1941 Four Mothers; Here Comes Mr. Jordan; Kings Row; The Wolf Man; Riot Squad. 1942 Moontide; Now, Voyager; Eyes of the Underworld; Casablanca. 1943 Forever and a Day; Phantom of the Opera. 1944 Passage to Marseilles; Mr. Skeffington. 1945 This Love of Ours. 1946 Caesar and Cleopatra; Angel on My Shoulder; Deception; Notorious; Strange Holiday. 1947 The Unsuspected. 1948 The Passionate Spring. 1949 Song of Surrender; Rope of Sand; One Woman's Story. 1950 The White Tower; Where Danger Lives. 1951 Sealed Cargo. 1952 The Man Who Watched Trains Go By. 1953 The Paris Express.

RALLI, PAUL
Born: Dec. 29, 1905, Cyprus. Died: Sept. 4, 1953, Van Nuys, Calif. Screen, stage actor, attorney, and author.

Appeared in: 1928 The Waterhole; Show People. 1929 Montmartre Rose; Married in Hollywood.

RALPH, JESSIE (Jessie Ralph Chambers)
Born: Nov. 5, 1876, Gloucester, Mass. Died: May 30, 1944, Gloucester, Mass. Screen and stage actress. Married to stage actor William Patton (dec.).

Appeared in: 1921 Such a Little Queen. 1933 Cocktail Hour; Child of Manhattan; Elmer the Great; Ann Carver's Profession. 1934 One Night of Love; Evelyn Prentice; Nana; We Live Again; Murder at the Vanities; The Affairs of Cellini; The Coming Out Party. 1935 David Copperfield; Les Miserables; Paris in Spring; Captain Blood; Enchanted April; Vanessa, Her Love Story; Mark of the Vampire; I Live My Life; Jalna; Metropolitan; I Found Stella Parish. 1936 Bunker Bean; San Francisco; Walking on Air; The Garden Murder Case; The Unguarded Hour; After the Thin Man; Camille; Little Lord Fauntleroy; Yellow Dust. 1937 The Good Earth; The Last of Mrs. Cheyney; Double Wedding. 1938 Love Is a Headache; Port of Seven Seas; Hold That Kiss. 1939 St. Louis Blues; Cafe Society; The Kid from Texas; Mickey the Kid; Drums along the Mohawk; Four Girls in White. 1940 Star Dust; Girl from Avenue A; I Can't Give You Anything but Love, Baby; I Want a Divorce; The Bank Dick; The Bluebird. 1941 The Lady from Cheyenne; They Met in Bombay.

RALSTON, JOBYNA
Born: Nov. 21, 1904, South Pittsburg, Tenn. Died: Jan. 22, 1967, Woodland Hills, Calif. Screen and stage actress. Divorced from screen actor Richard Arlen.

Appeared in: 1922 Grandma's Boy; The Call of Home; Three Must-Get-There's. 1923 Why Worry? 1924 Girl Shy; Hot Water. 1925 The Freshman. 1926 For Heaven's Sake; Gigolo; Sweet Daddies. 1927 A Racing Romeo; Special Delivery; Wings; The Kid Brother; Lightning; Pretty Clothes. 1928 The Power of the Press; Little Mickey Grogan; The Count of Ten; The Toilers; The Night Flyer; The Big Hop; Black Butterflies. 1929 Some Mother's Boy; The College Coquette. 1930 Rough Waters.

RAMBAL, ENRIQUE
Born: 1924, Mexico. Died: Dec. 15, 1971, Mexico City, Mexico (heart attack). Screen, stage, and television actor.

Appeared in: 1962 La Estrella Vacia (The Empty Star).

RAMBEAU, MARJORIE
Born: July 15, 1889, San Francisco, Calif. Died: July 7, 1970, Palm Springs, Calif. Screen and stage actress. Nominated for Academy Award in 1940 for Best Supporting Actress in Primrose Path.

Appeared in: 1916 The Dazzling Miss Davison (film debut). 1917 Mary Moreland; The Greater Woman. 1920 The Fortune Teller. 1926 Syncopating Sue. 1930 Her Man; Dark Star; Min and Bill. 1931 Leftover Ladies; Son of India; Inspiration; The Easiest Way;

Silence; Hell Divers; Laughing Sinners; This Modern Age; The Secret Six; Strangers May Kiss; A Tailor-Made Man. 1933 Strictly Personal; The Warrior's Husband; A Man's Castle. 1934 Palooka; A Modern Hero; Grand Canary; Ready for Love. 1935 Under Pressure; Dizzy Dames. 1937 First Lady. 1938 Merrily We Live; Woman against Woman. 1939 Sudden Money; The Rains Came; Laugh It Off. 1940 20 Mule Team; Tugboat Annie Sails Again; East of the River; Heaven with a Barbed Wire Fence; Santa Fe Marshal. 1941 Tobacco Road; Three Sons O'Guns; So Ends Our Night. 1942 Broadway. 1943 In Old Oklahoma. 1944 Oh What a Night; Army Wives. 1945 Salome, Where She Danced. 1948 The Walls of Jericho. 1949 Any Number Can Play; The Lucky Stiff; Abandoned. 1953 Torch Song; Forever Female; Bad for Each Other. 1955 A Man Called Peter; The View from Pompey's Head. 1956 Slander. 1957 Man of a Thousand Faces.

RAMBOVA, NATACHA (Winifred Shaunessy—aka WINIFRED HUDNUT-adopted name)
Born: Jan. 19, 1897, Salt Lake City, Utah. Died: June 5, 1966, Pasadena, Calif.(dietary complications). Screen, stage actress, dancer, and screenwriter. Divorced from screen actor Rudolph Valentino (dec. 1926).

Appeared in: 1925 When Love Grows Cold.

RAMIREZ, PEPITA
Born: 1902. Died Dec. 1927, Hollywood, Calif.(auto crash). Screen, stage actress, and dancer.

RAMOS, JESUS MAZA
Born: 1911. Died: Apr. 1955, Mexico. Screen, stage, and radio actor. Appeared in an act known as "Los Fikaros."

RAMSEY, JOHN NELSON
Died: Apr. 5, 1929, London, England (heart disease). Screen and stage actor.

Appeared in: 1929 A Romance of Seville.

RANALDI, FRANK
Born: 1905. Died: May 2, 1933, Hollywood, Calif.(complications from operation). Screen child actor and later a film casting director.

RAND, JOHN F.
Born: 1872. Died: Jan. 25, 1940, Hollywood, Calif. Screen, vaudeville, and circus actor.

Appeared in: 1928 The Circus.

RAND, LIONEL (Lionel Van Clouser)
Born: 1909, Shamokin, Pa. Died: Oct. 15, 1942, Queens, N.Y. Screen actor, song writer, and orchestra leader.

RANDALL, ADDISON "JACK" (Addison Owen Randall)
Born: 1907. Died: July 16, 1945, Canoga Park, Calif.(fall from horse while filming). Screen actor. Brother of screen actor Robert Livingston. Married to screen actress Barbara Bennett (dec. 1958).

Appeared in: 1935 His Family Tree; Another Face. 1936 Two in the Dark; Love on a Bet; Follow the Fleet; Don't Turn 'Em Loose; Navy Born; Flying Hostess. 1937 Red Lights Ahead; Riders of the Dawn; Stars over Arizona; Blazing Barriers. 1938 The Mexicali Kid. 1939 Driftin' Westward. 1940 Wild Horse Range.

RANDALL, BERNARD "BARNEY"
Born: 1884. Died: Dec. 17, 1954, New York, N.Y. Screen, stage, radio, and television actor.

Appeared in: 1920 The Master Mind; The Evil Eye (serial); The $1,000,000 Reward (serial). 1921 Closed Doors. 1922 Determination; Polly of the Follies. 1923 The French Doll; Ponjola. 1924 Sundown; Unmarried Wives. 1925 Classified; Counsel for the Defense; Pretty Ladies; Share and Share Alike; Shattered Lives. 1926 Say It Again; The Skyrocket; Subway Sadie. 1928 Show Girl.

RANDALL, LARRY
Born: 1920. Died: Oct. 17, 1951, near Port Hueneme, Calif. (auto accident). Screen actor.

RANDALL, RAE (Sigrum Salvason)
Born: 1909. Died: May 7, 1934, Hollywood, Calif.(suicide). Screen actress who doubled for Greta Garbo.

Appeared in: 1927 King of Kings. 1929 The Godless Girl.

RANDALL, WILLIAM
Born: 1877. Died: Apr. 22, 1939, Elizabeth, N.J. Screen, stage, and radio actor, author, and writer for radio. Appeared in silents.

RANDLE, FRANK (Arthur McEvoy)
Born: 1901, Wigan, England. Died: July 7, 1957, Blackpool, England. Screen, stage, vaudeville, and radio actor.

Appeared in: 1940 Somewhere in England. 1942 Somewhere in Camp. 1943 Somewhere in Civvies. 1947 School for Randle. 1948 Holidays with Pay. 1953 It's a Great Life.

RANDOLPH, AMANDA
Born: 1902. Died: Aug. 24, 1967, Duarte, Calif.(stroke). Negro screen, stage, radio, and television actress.

Appeared in: 1939 At the Circus. 1950 No Way Out. 1952 She's Working Her Way through College. 1953 Mr. Scoutmaster. 1955 A Man Called Peter.

RANDOLPH, ANDERS (aka ANDERS RANDOLF)
Born: Dec. 18, 1876, Den. Died: July 3, 1930, Hollywood, Calif. (relapse after operation). Screen and stage actor. Entered films with Vitagraph.

Appeared in: 1916 Hero of Submarine D-2. 1917 Within the Law. 1918 The Splendid Sinner. 1919 The Lion and the Mouse; Erstwhile Susan. 1920 The Love Flower. 1921 Buried Treasure; Jim the Penman. 1922 Notoriety; The Referee; Sherlock Holmes; Peacock Alley; Slim Shoulders; The Streets of New York. 1923 The Bright Shawl; The Eternal Struggle; Mighty Lak' a Rose; None So Blind; The Man from Glengarry. 1924 Behold This Woman; In Hollywood with Potash and Perlmutter; By Divine Right; Madonna of the Streets; Dorothy Vernon of Haddon Hall. 1925 The Happy Warrior; Her Market Value; Seven Keys to Baldpate; Souls for Sables. 1926 The Black Pirate; Broken Hearts of Hollywood; The Johnstown Flood; Miss Nobody; Ranson's Folly; Womanpower. 1927 The Climbers; The College Widow; Dearie; The Jazz Singer; The Love of Sunya; Old San Francisco; A Reno Divorce; Sinews of Steel; Slightly Used; The Tender Hour. 1928 The Crimson City; The Gateway of the Moon; Powder My Back; The Power of Silence; The Big Killing; Three Sinners; Women They Talk About; Me, Gangster. 1929 Four Devils; The Kiss; Shanghai Lady; The Show of Shows; The Sin Sister; Young Nowheres; The Viking; Dangerous Curves; Noah's Ark; Last Performance. 1930 Maybe It's Love; Son of the Gods; The Way of All Men. 1931 Going Wild. 1965 Laurel and Hardy's Laughing 20's (documentary).

RANDOLPH, MAY
Born: 1873. Died: Apr. 13, 1956, Hollywood, Calif. Screen actress.

RANGEL, ARTURO SOTO
Born: 1882, Mexico. Died: May 25, 1965, Mexico City, Mexico. Screen actor.

Appeared in: 1943 Silk, Blood and Sun; The Virgin of Guadalupe. 1944 Maria Candelaria. 1947 St. Francis of Assisi. 1948 The Treasure of Sierra Madre. 1953 Sombrero. 1954 Garden of Eden; Other Mexican films: La Intrusa; La Mentira; La Plegaria a Dios; Los Orgullosas; El Cristo de mi Cabacera.

RANIN, HELGE
Born: 1897. Died: Apr. 15, 1952, Stockholm, Sweden. Screen and stage actor. Appeared in Finnish films.

RANKIN, ARTHUR (Arthur Rankin Davenport)
Born: Aug. 30, 1900, New York, N.Y. Died: Mar. 23, 1947, Hollywood, Calif.(cerebral hemorrhage). Screen actor. Son of actor Harry Davenport (dec. 1949). See Harry Davenport regarding family information.

Appeared in: 1921 Enchantment; The Great Adventure; Jim the Penman; The Lure of Jade. 1922 Enter Madame; The Five Dollar Baby; Little Miss Smiles; To Have and to Hold. 1923 The Call of the Canyon. 1924 Broken Laws; The Dark Swan; Discontented Husbands; Vanity's Price. 1925 Fearless Lover; The Love Gamble; Pursued; Speed; Sun-Up; Tearing Through. 1926 The Hidden Way; The Man in the Shadow; The Millionaire Policeman; Old Loves and New; The Sporting Lover; Volga Boatman. 1927 The Adventurous Soul; Dearie; The Love Wager; Riding to Fame; Slightly Used; The Woman Who Did Not Care; The Blood Ship. 1928 Broken Laws; Say It with Sables; Walking Back; Making the Varsity; Finders Keepers; Companionate Marriage; Submarine; Code of the Air; Domestic Troubles; Runaway Girls; The Wife's Relations. 1929 Glad Rag Doll; The Fall of Eve; Below the Deadline; The Wild Party; Mexicali Rose;

Ships of the Night; The Wolf of Wall Street. 1930 Brothers. 1933 Thrill Hunter; Terror Trail. 1934 Search for Beauty; Carnival; Men in Black (short). 1935 Death Flies East; Hoi Polloi (short); Eight Bells; Case of the Missing Man. 1936 Roaming Lady.

RANKIN, HERBERT
Born: 1876. Died: July 16, 1946, Hollywood, Calif. Screen actor.

RAPHAEL, ENID
Died: Mar. 5, 1964, New York, N.Y. Screen and stage actress.

RAPPE, VIRGINIA
Died: Sept. 5, 1921, San Francisco, Calif.(ruptured bladder). Screen actress. Appeared in two-reel comedies.

RASUMNY, MIKHAIL
Born: 1890, Odessa, Russia. Died: Feb. 17, 1956, Los Angeles, Calif. Screen, stage, and television actor.

Appeared in: 1940 Comrade X. 1941 Hold Back the Dawn; The Shanghai Gesture; Forced Landing. 1942 Wake Island; This Gun for Hire; Road to Morocco; Yokel Boy. 1943 Her Heart in Her Throat; Hostages; For Whom the Bell Tolls. 1944 And the Angels Sing; Practically Yours; Henry Aldrich Plays Cupid. 1945 A Royal Scandal; The Unseen; A Medal for Benny; The Stork Club; Bring on the Girls; Masquerade in Mexico. 1946 Kitty; Holiday in Mexico; Anna and the King of Siam; Heart Beat; Our Hearts Were Growing Up. 1947 Her Husband's Affairs; Song of My Heart; Pirates of Monterey. 1948 Saigon. 1949 The Kissing Bandit; Free for All; The Pirates of Capri. 1950 Hit Parade of 1951. 1952 Anything Can Happen. 1953 The Stars Are Singing; Tonight We Sing. 1956 Hot Blood.

RATHBONE, BASIL (Philip St. John Basil Rathbone)
Born: June 13, 1892, Johannesburg, South Africa. Died: July 21, 1967, New York, N.Y.(heart attack). Screen, stage, radio, and television actor. Star of films Sherlock Holmes series.

Appeared in: 1921 Innocent; The Fruitful Vine. 1924 Trouping with Ellen; The School of Scandal. 1925 The Masked Bride. 1926 The Great Deception. 1929 The Last of Mrs. Cheyney; Barnum Was Right. 1930 The High Road; This Mad World; The Flirting Widow; A Notorious Affair; Sin Takes a Holiday; A Lady Surrenders; The Bishop Murder Case; The Lady of Scandal. 1931 Once a Lady. 1932 A Woman Commands. 1933 One Precious Year. After the Ball. 1934 Loyalties. 1935 David Copperfield; Anna Karenina; The Last Days of Pompeii; Captain Blood; Kind Lady; A Feather in Her Hat; A Tale of Two Cities. 1936 Romeo and Juliet; Private Number; The Garden of Allah. 1937 Love from a Stranger; Make a Wish; Confession; Tovarich. 1938 The Adventures of Robin Hood; The Adventures of Marco Polo; If I Were King; Dawn Patrol. 1939 Adventures of Sherlock Holmes (16 in series); The Sun Never Sets; The Hound of the Baskervilles; Son of Frankenstein; Tower of London; Rio. 1940 Rhythm on the River; The Mark of Zorro; A Date with Destiny. 1941 Paris Calling; International Lady; The Mad Doctor; The Black Cat. 1942 Crossroads; Sherlock Holmes and the Voice of Terror; Fingers at the Window; Sherlock Holmes and the Secret Weapon. 1943 Sherlock Holmes in Washington; Above Suspicion; Sherlock Holmes Faces Death; Crazy House. 1944 The Scarlet Claw; Pearl of Death; Frenchman's Creek; Spider Woman; Bathing Beauty. 1945 The House of Fear; Pursuit to Algiers; The Woman in Green. 1946 Terror by Night; Dress to Kill; Heartbeat. 1949 The Adventures of Ichabod and Mr. Toad (narrator). 1954 Casanova's Big Night. 1955 We're No Angels. 1956 The Black Sheep; The Court Jester. 1958 The Last Hurrah. 1962 The Magic Sword (voice only); Tales of Terror; Two before Zero. 1963 The Comedy of Terrors. 1965 The Adventures of Marco Polo (and 1938 version); Queen of Blood. 1966 Ghost in the Invisible Bikini; Prehistoric Planet Woman. 1967 Dr. Rock and Mr. Roll; Gill Women; Hillbillies in the Haunted House.

RATNER, ANNA
Born: 1892. Died: July 2, 1967, Chicago, Ill. Screen, stage actress, and dancer. Appeared in films between 1912 and 1916 at Essanay Studio.

RATOFF, GREGORY
Born: Apr. 20, 1897, Petrograd, Russia. Died: Dec. 14, 1960, Solothurn, Switzerland. Screen, stage actor, screenwriter; film director, film and stage producer.

Appeared in: 1929 For Sale (short). 1932 Melody of Life; Roar of the Dragon; Deported; Skyscraper Souls; Once in a Lifetime; Secrets of the French Police; Undercover Man; Symphony of Six Million; What Price Hollywood; Thirteen Women. 1933 Sweepings; Professional Sweetheart; Headline Shooters; I'm No Angel; Sitting

Pretty; Girl without a Room; Broadway Thru a Keyhole. 1934 The Great Flirtation; Let's Fall in Love; Forbidden Territory (U.S. 1938); George White's Scandals. 1935 King of Burlesque; Remember Last Night. 1936 Here Comes Trouble; Sins of Man; Under Two Flags; The Road to Glory; Sing, Baby, Sing; Under Your Spell; Trouble Ahead; Falling in Love. 1937 Top of the Town; Cafe Metropole; Seventh Heaven. 1938 Sally, Irene and Mary; Gateway. 1939 Rose of Washington Square; Barricade; Hotel for Women; Daytime Wife; Intermezzo. 1940 I Was an Adventuress; The Great Profile; Public Deb No. 1. 1941 Adam Had Four Sons; The Corsican Brothers. 1942 Two Yanks in Trinidad; Footlight Serenade. 1944 Irish Eyes Are Smiling. 1945 Where Do We Go from Here?; Paris Underground. 1946 Do You Love Me? 1947 Carnival in Costa Rica. 1950 If This Be Sin; All about Eve. 1951 Operation X. 1952 O. Henry's Full House. 1956 Abdullah's Harem. 1957 The Sun Also Rises. 1960 Once More, with Feeling; Exodus. 1961 The Big Gamble.

RATTENBERRY, HARRY (aka HARRY RATTENBURY)
Born: 1860. Died: Dec. 10, 1925, Hollywood, Calif. Screen and opera actor.

Appeared in: 1914 Lucille Love; Girl of Mystery (serial). 1921 The Broken Spur; His Pajama Girl; A Motion to Adjourn. 1922 Watch Your Step. 1923 The Printer's Devil; Soul of the Beast. 1924 Abraham Lincoln. 1925 Daring Days.

RAVEL, SANDRA
Died: Aug. 13, 1954, Milan, Italy. Screen actress.

Appeared in: 1930 L 'Enigmatique Monsieur Parkes; Those Three French Girls. 1931 The Single Sin. 1935 Une Etoile Disparait (A Star Disappears). 1937 Tre Anni Senza Donne; Al Buio Insieme. 1940 A Wife in Peril. Other Italian films: Two Million for a Smile; Ho Visto Brillare Una Stella.

RAVELLE, RAY. See Otto F. Wess

RAVENEL, JOHN (Donald M. Upshur)
Born: 1912. Died: Sept. 14, 1950, Chicago, Ill.(heart attack). Screen actor, and radio and television producer.

RAWLINS, HERBERT
Died: 1947. Screen actor. Married to screen actress Josephine Norman (dec. 1951).

RAWLINSON, HERBERT
Born: 1885, Brighton, England. Died: July 12, 1953, Woodland Hills, Calif.(lung cancer). Screen, stage, radio, and vaudeville actor.

Appeared in: 1912 The God of Gold; The Count of Monte Cristo. 1913 The Sea Wolf. 1914 Kid Regan's Hands; Flirting with Death. 1915 The Black Box; Damon and Pythias. 1917 Come Through. 1918 Back to the Woods; Turn of the Wheel. 1919 The Carter Case (serial); Good Gracious Annabelle. 1920 Passers By. 1921 Charge It; The Wakefield Case; The Conflict; Playthings of Destiny; Wealth; You Find It Everywhere; Cheated Hearts; The Millionaire. 1922 The Black Bag; The Man under Cover; The Scrapper; Another Man's Shoes; Confidence; Don't Shoot; One Wonderful Night. 1923 The Clean-Up; Fools and Riches; Nobody's Bride; The Prisoner; Railroaded; The Scarlet Car; Victor; His Mystery Girl; Million to Burn; Mary of the Movies. 1924 High Speed; Stolen Secrets; The Dancing Cheat; Dark Stairways; Jack O'Clubs; The Tomboy. 1925 The Man in Blue; My Neighbor's Wife; The Flame Fighter (serial); The Adventurous Sex; Every Man's Wife; The Great Jewel Robbery; The Prairie Wife; The Unnamed Woman. 1926 Phantom Police (serial); Trooper 77 (serial); The Belle of Broadway; The Gilded Butterfly; Her Big Adventure; Her Sacrifice; Men of the Night; Midnight Thieves; The Millionaire Policeman. 1927 The Bugle Call; The Hour of Reckoning; Wages of Conscience; Slipping Wives (short); Burning Gold. 1928 The Monologist of the Screen (short). 1933 Moonlight and Pretzels; Enlighten Thy Daughter. 1935 The People's Enemy; Show Them No Mercy; Men without Names; Confidential; Convention Girl. 1936 Hitchhike to Heaven; Ticket to Paradise; Dancing Feet; Bullets or Ballots; A Son Comes Home; Hollywood Boulevard; Mad Holiday; God's Country and the Woman. 1937 Don't Pull Your Punches; The Go Getter; That Certain Woman; Over the Goal; Love Is on the Air; Nobody's Baby; Mysterious Crossing; Back in Circulation; Make a Wish; Blake of Scotland Yard. 1938 Hawaii Calls; Orphans of the Street; Women Are Like That; Under the Big Top; The Kid Comes Back; Torchy Gets Her Man; Secrets of an Actress. 1939 You Can't Get Away with Murder; Dark Victory; Sudden Money. 1940 Money to Burn; The Five Little Peppers at Home; Free, Blonde and 21; Framed; Seven Sinners; Swiss Family Robinson. 1941

Scattergood Meets Broadway; A Gentleman from Dixie; Bad Man at Deadwood; I Killed That Man; Riot Squad; Flying Wild; I Wanted Wings; Arizona Cyclone. 1942 Smart Alecks; I Live on Danger; Tramp, Tramp, Tramp; Lady Gangster; The Broadway Big Shot; The Panther's Claw; SOS Coast Guard; The Yukon Patrol; Stagecoach Buckaroo; Hello, Annapolis; Foreign Agent; War Dogs. 1943 Colt Comrades; Where Are Your Children?; Border Patrol; Lost Canyon; Cosmo Jones in the Crime Smasher; Two Weeks to Live; The Woman of the Town. 1944 Riders of the Deadline; Sailor's Holiday; Shake Hands with Murder; Oklahoma Raiders; Marshal of Reno; Marshal of Gunsmoke; Nabonga; Goin' To Town; Sheriff of Sundown; Forty Thieves; Lumberjack. 1946 Accomplice. 1948 The Argyle Secrets; The Gallant Legion; The Counterfeiters; Silent Conflict; Sinister Journey; The Strange Gamble. 1949 Brimstone; Fighting Man of the Plains. 1951 Gene Autry and the Mounties.

RAY, BARBARA
Born: 1914. Died: May 19, 1955, Los Angeles, Calif.(leukemia). Screen actress. Married to screen actor Roscoe Ates (dec. 1962).

RAY, CHARLES
Born: May 15, 1891, Jacksonville, Ill. Died: Nov. 23, 1943, Los Angeles, Calif.(throat and jaw infection). Screen, stage, vaudeville actor, film producer, and film director.

Appeared in: 1915 The Lure of Woman; The Coward. 1916 Honor Thy Name; Home; Plain Jane; The Deserter. 1917 Clod Hopper; The Pinch Hitter. 1918 The Law of the North; The Claws of the Hun; Nine O'Clock Town; String Beans. 1919 Crooked Straight; Hayfoot, Strawfoot; The Sheriff's Son; Greased Lightning; The Girl Dodger; Bill Henry; The Busher; The Egg-Crate Wallop. 1920 Red Hot Dollars; Paris Green; Alarm Clock Andy; Homer Comes Home; Forty-five Minutes from Broadway; Village Sleuth; Old-Fashioned Boy; Peaceful Valley. 1921 Nineteen and Phyllis; The Old Swimmin' Hole; Scrap Iron; A Midnight Bell; R.S.V.P.; Two Minutes to Go. 1922 Gas, Oil or Water; The Deuce of Spades; Alias Julius Caesar; The Barnstormer; Smudge; Tailor-Made Man. 1923 The Girl I Love; The Courtship of Miles Standish; Ponjola. 1924 Dynamite Smith. 1925 Some Pun'kins; Vanity; Percy; Bright Lights. 1926 Sweet Adeline; Paris; The Auction Block; The Fire Brigade. 1927 Getting Gertie's Garter; Nobody's Widow; Vanity. 1928 The Garden of Eden; The Count of Ten. 1932 The Bride's Bereavement. 1934 Ladies Should Listen; Ticket to a Crime; School for Girls. 1935 By Your Leave; Welcome Home. 1936 Hollywood Boulevard; Just My Luck. 1940 A Little Bit of Heaven.

RAY, EMMA (Emma Sherwood)
Born: 1871. Died: Jan. 3, 1935, Los Angeles, Calif. Screen, stage, and vaudeville actress. Married to screen actor Johnny Ray (dec. 1927). They appeared in vaudeville together.

Appeared in: 1934 The Old Fashioned Way (short).

RAY, ESTELLE GOULDING
Born: 1888. Died: Aug. 1, 1970, Hollywood, Calif.(due to fall). Screen and stage actress. Appeared in early silents.

RAY, HELEN
Born: 1879, Fort Stockton, Tex. Died: Oct. 2, 1965, Wolfboro, N.H. Screen, stage, vaudeville, and television actress. Married to vaudeville actor Homer Miles (dec.) and they appeared in an act billed as "Homer and Helen Miles."

Appeared in: 1921 Experience; Sheltered Daughters.

RAY, JOHNNY (John Matthews)
Born: 1859, Wales England. Died: Sept. 4, 1927, Los Angeles, Calif.(paralytic stroke). Screen, stage, and vaudeville actor. Married to screen actress Emma Sherwood Ray (dec. 1935). They appeared in vaudeville together.

Appeared in: 1928 Bringing up Father.

RAY, MARJORIE
Born: 1900. Died: July 21, 1924, San Diego, Calif.(tetanus). Screen and stage actress.

RAY, NAOMI
Born: 1893. Died: Mar. 13, 1966, New York, N.Y. Screen, stage, and vaudeville actress. Appeared in vaudeville with her husband, Eddie Harrison, in an act billed as "Ray and Harrison."

Appeared in: 1932 The Riding Master (short), plus other early shorts.

RAYMOND, FORD
Born: 1900. Died: Apr. 25, 1960, Hollywood, Calif. Screen, stage, and vaudeville actor.

Appeared in: 1960 One Foot in Hell.

RAYMOND, FRANCES "FRANKIE"
Born: 1869. Died: June 18, 1961, Hollywood, Calif. Screen and stage actress. Entered films in 1915.

Appeared in: 1921 Garments of Truth; The March Hare; One a Minute; One Wild Week; Smiling All the Way; Two Weeks with Pay. 1922 The Ghost Breaker; Hurricane's Gal; Shadows; Young America. 1923 A Chapter in Her Life; The Grail; The Meanest Man in the World; Money, Money, Money. 1924 Abraham Lincoln; Excitement; Flirting with Love; The Girl on the Stairs; Girls Men Forget. 1925 Seven Chances. 1926 Behind the Front; What Happened to Jones. 1927 The Cruel Truth; The Gay Defender; The Gay Old Bird; Get Your Man; Stage Kisses; Three's a Crowd; Wandering Girls; Web of Fate; The Wreck. 1928 Rich Men's Sons. 1929 The Illusion. 1935 Love in Bloom. 1943 Happy Go Lucky.

RAYMOND, HELEN
Born: approx. 1885, Philadelphia, Pa. Died: Nov. 26, 1965, New York, N.Y. Screen and stage actress.

Appeared in: 1920 Twin Beds. 1921 Her Mad Bargain; My Lady Friends; Her Social Value; Through the Back Door. 1922 Very Truly Yours; Wild Honey; The Ableminded Lady. 1923 The Huntress.

RAYMOND, JACK (George Feder)
Born: Dec. 14, 1901, Minneapolis, Minn. Died: Dec. 5, 1951, Santa Monica, Calif.(heart attack). Screen, stage, vaudeville, television actor, cameraman, and film director.

Appeared in: 1921 The Miracle of Manhattan. 1924 Roulette. 1925 Lover's Island; Scarlet Saint. 1927 The Lunatic at Large; Pleasure before Business. 1928 Sally of the Scandals; The Butter and Egg Man; Lonesome; Melody of Love; Three Week Ends; The Last Command; The Price of Fear; Riley of the Rainbow Division; Thanks for the Buggy Ride. 1929 The Wild Party; Synthetic Sin; The Younger Generation; Points West. 1935 Headline Woman; Paris in Spring. 1936 Preview Murder Mystery; Night Club Scandal. 1949 Omoo Omoo. 1950 Abbott and Costello in the Foreign Legion.

REA, MABEL LILLIAN
Born: 1932. Died: Dec. 24, 1968, Charlotte, N.C.(auto accident). Screen and television actress.

Appeared in: 1956 Bundle of Joy. 1957 Pal Joey; The Devil's Hairpin. 1958 I Married a Woman. 1959 Submarine Seahawk.

REAL, BETTY
Died: Sept. 9, 1969, Miami, Calif. Screen and stage actress.

Appeared in: 1934 Crime without Passion.

REDWING, RODD (Rederick Redwing; aka ROD REDWING, RODRIC REDWING, ROD RED WING, and RODERIC REDWING)
Born: 1905, N.Y. Died: May 30, 1971, Los Angeles, Calif.(heart attack). Screen, stage, television actor, and gun coach. Full-blooded Chickasaw Indian.

Appeared in: 1931 The Squaw Man. 1939 Gunga Din!; Lives of a Bengal Lancer. 1945 Objective Burma! 1946 Out of the Depths. 1949 Apache Chief; Song of India. 1951 Little Big Horn. 1952 Buffalo Bill in Tomahawk Territory; Rancho Notorious; The Pathfinder; Hellgate. 1953 Winning of the West; Conquest of Cochise; Saginaw Trail; Flight to Tangier. 1954 Creature from the Black Lagoon; Cattle Queen of Montana; The Naked Jungle; Elephant Walk; The Cowboy. 1956 Jaguar; The Mole People. 1957 Copper Sky. 1958 The Flame Barrier. 1960 Flaming Star. 1962 Sergeants Three. 1968 Shalako. 1969 Charro!; The McMasters. 1972 The Red Sun.

REECE, BRIAN
Born: 1914. Died: Apr. 12, 1962, London, England (bone disease). Screen, stage, radio, and television actor.

Appeared in: 1954 Orders Are Orders. 1955 A Case for P.C. 49; Wee Geordie. 1957 Carry on Admiral (aka The Ship Was Loaded-U.S. 1959).

REED, DAVE
Born: 1872, New York, N.Y. Died: Apr. 11, 1946, N.Y. Screen, stage, vaudeville, radio actor, and song writer. Appeared in silents.

REED, FLORENCE
Born: Jan. 10, 1883, Philadelphia, Pa. Died: Nov. 21, 1967, East Islip, N.Y. Screen, stage, vaudeville, and television actress.

Appeared in: 1915 The Dancing Girl. 1916 New York. 1917 Today; The Eternal Sin. 1918 Wives of Men. 1921 The Eternal Mother; Black Panther's Cub; Indiscretion. 1930 The Code of Honor. 1934 Great Expectations. 1936 Frankie and Johnnie. 1941 Shanghai Gesture.

REED, GEORGE E.
Died: June 11, 1952, Camden, N.J. Screen and stage actor. Married to actress Alice Lucey. They appeared as a song and dance team billed as "Reed and Lucey."

Appeared in: 1920 The Veiled Mystery (serial). 1923 The Bishop of the Ozarks; Red Lights; Scars of Jealousy. 1924 Helen's Babies; The Vagabond Trail. 1925 The Golden Strain; The Isle of Hope. 1926 Danger Quest; Pals First. 1928 Absent; The Clean-Up Man; Three-Ring Marriage.

REED, GUS (Harold Nelson)
Born: 1880. Died: July 17, 1965, Cherry Valley, Calif. Screen, vaudeville, minstrel actor, and singer.

Appeared in: 1930 The Woman Tamer (short). 1934 Order in the Court (short).

REESE, W. JAMES
Born: 1898. Died: Feb. 17, 1960, N.Y. Screen, stage, and television actor.

Appeared in: 1957 The Young Don't Cry.

REEVE, ADA
Born: 1874, England. Died: Sept. 25, 1966, London, England. Screen and stage actress.

Appeared in: 1944 They Came to a City. 1947 When the Bough Breaks. 1948 Meet Me at Dawn. 1949 Dear Mr. Prohack. 1950 Night and the City. 1953 I Believe in You. 1956 Eye Witness. 1957 A Novel Affair (aka Passionate Stranger).

REEVES, BILLY
Born: 1864, England. Died: Dec. 29, 1943, Suffolk, England. Screen, stage, vaudeville actor, and pantomimist.

Appeared in: 1915 The New Butler.

REEVES, GEORGE (George Basselo)
Born: 1914, Ashland, Ky. Died: June 16, 1959, Beverly Hills, Calif.(suicide-gun). Screen, stage, and television actor.

Appeared in: 1939 Gone with the Wind. 1940 Torrid Zone; Tear Gas Squad; Calling All Husbands; Always a Bride; Argentine Nights; Gambling on the High Seas; Father Is a Prince; Knute Rockne—All American; The Fighting 69th; 'Til We Meet Again; Ladies Must Live. 1941 Blue, White and Perfect; Strawberry Blonde; Dead Men Tell; Man at Large; Blood and Sand; Lydia. 1942 The Mad Martindales. 1943 So Proudly We Hail; Border Patrol; Hoppy Serves a Writ; The Leather Burners; The Last Will and Testament of Tom Smith (documentary); Colt Comrades; Bar-20; Buckskin Frontier. 1944 Winged Victory. 1947 Variety Girl. 1948 Jungle Goddess; The Sainted Sisters; Thunder in the Pines. 1949 The Great Lover; Adventures of Sir Galahad (serial); The Mutineers; Special Agent; Pirate Ship; Jungle Jim. 1950 The Good Humor Man; Adventures of Sir Galahad (serial). 1951 Samson and Delilah; Superman and the Mole Men. 1952 Bugles in the Afternoon; Rancho Notorious. 1953 From Here to Eternity; The Blue Gardenia; Forever Female. 1956 Westward Ho the Wagons.

REEVES, JIM
Born: 1924. Died: July 31, 1964, near Nashville, Tenn.(airplane crash). Screen actor and country music singer.

Appeared in: 1964 Kimberly Jim.

REEVES, KYNASTON P.
Born: May 29, 1893, London, England. Died: Dec. 10, 1971, London, England. Screen, stage, and television actor. Entered films in 1919.

Appeared in: 1932 The Lodger; The Sign of the Four. 1933 Jew Seuss. 1934 The Broken Melody. 1935 The Phantom Fiend. 1938 The Citadel; Sixty Glorious Years. 1939 The Housemaster. 1940 The Prime Minister; The Outsider; Two for Danger. 1941 The Stars Look Down. 1942 The Young Mr. Pitt. 1945 Rake's Progress (U.S. 1946). 1946 Murder in Reverse; Dead of Night. 1947 Bedelia; Mrs. Fitzherbert (U.S. 1950). 1948 The Straw-

berry Roan; Vice Versa. 1949 The Guinea Pig; The Weaker Sex; This Was a Woman. 1950 The Mudlark; The Winslow Boy; Madness of the Heart; The Outsiders; Madeleine; Trio; Black Out. 1951 Tony Draws a Horse; Smart Alec; Captain Horatio Hornblower; The Undefeated. 1953 Top of the Form; Bachelor of Paris; Top Secret (aka Mr. Potts Goes to Moscow-U.S. 1954); Penny Princess. 1954 Scotch on the Rocks; Burnt Evidence. 1955 Fun at St. Fanny's; Eight O'Clock Walk. 1957 Brothers-in-Law; Light Fingers. 1958 High Flight; Fiend without a Face; A Question of Adultry (U.S. 1959); Prescription for Murder (aka Rx Murder; Family Doctor, and Prescription Murder); Carlton Browne of the F.O. 1960 School for Scoundrels; Man in a Cocked Hat. 1961 The Shadow of the Cat. 1963 Carry on Regardless. 1964 Hide and Seek. 1970 Anne of the Thousand Days. Other British films: Badgers Green; Moving House; Twenty Questions Murder Mystery; Flying Squad; In the Nick; Night We Got the Bird; Top Millions; The Millstone; Sherlock Holmes.

REEVES, ROBERT JASPER
Born: Jan. 28, 1892, Marlin, Tex. Died: Apr. 2, 1960, Hollywood, Calif.(heart attack). Screen and stage actor.

Appeared in: 1919 The Great Radium Mystery (serial). 1923 The Thrill Chaser. 1924 The Mask of Lopez; No Gun Man; The Silent Stranger. 1926 Ambushed; Cyclone Bob; Desperate Chance; Fighting Luck; Iron Fist; Ridin' Straight; Riding for Life. 1927 The Cherokee Kid. 1930 Canyon Hawks.

REEVES-SMITH, H.
Born: 1863. Died: Jan. 29, 1938, Elwell, Surrey, England (heart trouble). Screen and stage actor.

Appeared in: 1924 Three Weeks; No More Women. 1929 The Return of Sherlock Holmes (English version).

REGAN, BERRY
Born: 1914. Died: Jan. 16, 1956, Hollywood, Calif.(surgery for brain tumor). Screen actor.

Appeared in: 1955 A Bullet for Joey.

REGAN, EDGAR J.
Died: June 21, 1938, San Francisco, Calif.(heart attack). Screen and stage actor.

REGAN, JOSEPH
Born: 1896, Boston, Mass. Died: Nov. 9, 1931, New York, N.Y. (cerebral hemorrhage). Screen, stage, vaudeville, concert, and radio actor. Married to actress Alberta Curlis and appeared with her in vaudeville.

Appeared in: 1928 America's Foremost Irish Tenor (short).

REGAS, GEORGE (aka GEORGE RIGAS)
Born: Nov. 9, 1890, Sparta, Greece. Died: Dec. 13, 1940, Los Angeles, Calif. Screen and stage actor. Brother of screen actor Pedro Regas.

Appeared in: 1921 The Dangerous Moment; The Love Light. 1922 Omar the Tentmaker. 1923 Fashionable Fakers; The Rip Tide. 1925 Wanderer. 1926 That Royal Girl; Beau Geste; Desert Gold. 1929 Redskin; Wolf Song; The Rescue; Acquitted; Sea Fury; Hearts and Hoofs (short). 1930 The Lonesome Trail. 1931 Beau Ideal; Newly Rich. 1933 Destiny Unknown; The Way to Love; Blood Money. 1934 Kid Millions; Viva Villa; Sixteen Fathoms Deep; Bulldog Drummond Strikes Back; Grand Canary. 1935 Bordertown; Lives of a Bengal Lancer; The Marines Are Coming. 1936 Rose Marie; Hell-Ship Morgan; Under Two Flags; Isle of Fury; Daniel Boone; Robin Hood of El Dorado; The Charge of the Light Brigade. 1937 Waikiki Wedding; Another Dawn; Lefthanded Law; Love under Fire; Mr. Moto Takes a Chance; The Californian. 1938 Torchy Blane in Panama. 1939 Arrest Bulldog Drummond; The Adventures of Sherlock Holmes; The Light That Failed. 1940 Torrid Zone; The Mask of Zorro.

REHAN, MARY
Born: 1887. Died: Aug. 28, 1963, Rochester, Minn. Screen and stage actress.

Appeared in: 1922 Flesh and Spirit.

REICHER, FRANK
Born: Dec. 2, 1875, Munich, Germany. Died: Jan. 19, 1965, Playa del Rey, Calif. Screen, stage actor, film and stage director, and screenwriter. Entered films in 1915.

Appeared in: 1921 Behind Masks; Idle Hands; Out of the Depths; Wise Husbands. 1926 Her Man O'War. 1928 Beau Sabreur; The Blue Danube; The Masks of the Devil; Four Sons; Sins of the

Fathers; Someone to Love; Napoleon's Barber. 1929 His Captive Woman; Mister Antonio; Black Waters; Her Private Affair; The Changeling; Strange Cargo; Big News; Paris Bound. 1930 Girl of the Port; The Grand Parade; Die Sehnsucht Jeder Frau. 1931 Gentleman's Fate; Beyond Victory; Suicide Fleet. 1932 A Woman Commands; The Crooked Circle; Scarlet Dawn; Mata Hari. 1933 Topaze; Employees' Entrance; Jennie Gerhardt; Captured; Ever in My Heart; Before Dawn; Son of Kong; King Kong. 1934 I Am a Thief; Return of the Terror; The Case of the Howling Dog; The Fountain; Hi, Nellie; Journal of a Crime; Countess of Monte Cristo; Little Man, What Now?; Let's Talk It Over; No Greater Glory. 1935 The Great Impersonation; Star of Midnight; The Florentine Dagger. 1936 A Dog of Flanders; Mills of the Gods; The Man Who Broke the Bank at Monte Carlo; Remember Last Night; Rendezvous; Kind Lady; The Story of Louis Pasteur; The Murder of Dr. Harrigan; Magnificent Obsession; The Invisible Ray; Sutter's Gold; The Country Doctor; Under Two Flags; Girl's Dormitory; Star for a Night; 'Til We Meet Again; Murder on the Bridle Path; The Ex-Mrs. Bradford; Second Wife; Anthony Adverse; Stolen Holiday. 1937 Laughing at Trouble; Night Key; On Such a Night; The Great O'Malley; Under Cover of Night; Lancer Spy; Espionage; The Emperor's Candlesticks; The Road Back; Prescription for Romance; Fit for a King; Stage Door. 1938 City Streets; Torchy Gets Her Man; Prison Nurse; Rascals; I'll Give a Million; Suez. 1939 Unexpected Father; Mystery of the White Room; Woman Doctor; Juarez; The Magnificent Fraud; Our Neighbors, the Carters; The Escape; South of the Border; Everything Happens at Night. 1940 Dr. Cyclops; The Man I Married; Devil's Island; Typhoon; The Lady in Question; South to Karanga; Sky Murder. 1941 Flight from Destiny; They Dare Not Love; Shining Victory; The Nurse's Secret; Underground; Dangerously They Live. 1942 Nazi Agent; Salute to Courage; To Be or Not to Be; The Mystery of Marie Roget; Beyond the Blue Horizon; The Gay Sisters; Secret Enemies; Scattergood Survives a Murder; The Mummy's Tomb; Night Monster. 1943 Mission to Moscow; Yanks Ahoy; Tornado; The Song of Bernadette; The Canterville Ghost. 1944 Adventures of Mark Twain; The Hitler Gang; The Conspirators; The Mummy's Ghost; Address Unknown. Gildersleeve's Ghost. 1945 The Big Bonanza; Jade Mask; Hotel Berlin; The Tiger Woman; House of Frankenstein; Blonde Ransom; A Medal for Benny. 1946 The Strange Mr. Gregory; Home of the Whistler; The Shadow Returns; My Pal Trigger; Home in Oklahoma. 1947 Escape Me Never; The Secret Life of Walter Mitty; Violence; Yankee Faker; Mr. District Attorney. 1948 Carson City Raiders; Fighting Mad. 1949 Samson and Delilah; Barbary Pirate. 1950 Cargo to Capetown; Kiss Tomorrow Goodbye. 1951 The Lady and the Bandit.

REID, TREVOR
Born: 1909. Died: Apr. 19, 1965, London, England. Screen, stage, and television actor.

Appeared in: 1956 Satellite in the Sky; Murder Reported. 1957 How to Murder a Rich Uncle. 1958 A Question of Adultery. 1961 Mary Had a Little. 1963 The Fast Lady. 1964 Walk a Tightrope.

REID, WALLACE
Born: Apr. 15, 1891, St. Louis, Mo. Died: Jan. 18, 1923, Los Angeles, Calif.(dope addiction). Screen actor and film producer. Married to screen actress Dorothy Davenport (who also appeared under her married name "Reid") and father of screen actor Wallace Reid, Jr.

Appeared in: 1911 The Deerslayer; Leather Stocking Tales; The Leading Lady. 1912 Chumps. 1913 The Heart of a Cracksman; His Mother's Influence. 1914 The Test; At Dawn. 1915 The Chorus Lady; Birth of a Nation; Carmen; Enoch Arden; Old Heidelberg; The Cracksman's Christmas. 1916 Maria Rosa; Joan, the Woman; To Have and to Hold; The Love Mask; The Yellow Pawn; House of Silence; Intolerance. 1917 The Woman God Forgot; Big Timber; Nan of Music Mountain. 1918 The Firefly of France; The Source; Too Many Millions; Believe Me, Zantippe; Rimrock Jones; Less Than Kin; Ruggles of Red Gap. 1919 Valley of the Giants; The Roaring Road; You're Fired; The Love Burglar; The Lottery Man. 1920 What's Your Hurry?; Double Speed; Sick Bed; The Dancin' Fool; Excuse My Dust. 1921 The Affairs of Anatol; Too Much Speed; Don't Tell Everything; Forever; The Call of the North; The Love Special; The Hell Diggers; The Charm School. 1922 Across the Continent; Night Life in Hollywood; Rent Free; Nice People; The World's Champion; The Ghost Breaker; Clarence; The Dictator; Thirty Days.

REILLY, MICHAEL
Born: 1933. Died: Jan. 10, 1962, Newhaven, England (parachute jump). Parachutist and double for Robert Wagner.

Appeared in: 1962 The War Lover.

REINHARDT, JOHN
Born: 1901. Died: Aug. 6, 1953, Berlin, Germany (heart attack). Screen actor, film director, author, and screenwriter.

Appeared in: 1929 The Prince of Hearts; Love, Live and Laugh; The Climax. 1931 Der Tanz Geht Weiter. 1936 The Rest Cure.

REIS, ALBERTO
Born: 1902, Portugal. Died: Feb. 1953 (tropical disease). Screen and stage actor. Married to screen actress Branca Saldanha.

REISNER, CHARLES F. "CHUCK" (aka CHARLES F. RIESNER)
Born: Mar. 14, 1887, Minneapolis, Minn. Died: Sept. 24, 1962, La Jolla, Calif. Screen, stage, vaudeville actor, film director and film producer, screenwriter, and television writer.

Appeared in: 1916 His First False Step; His Lying Heart. 1918 A Dog's Life. 1921 The Kid. 1922 The Pilgrim. 1923 Her Temporary Husband; Breaking into Society; Hollywood. 1924 A Self-Made Failure; and Universal comedies. 1925 Man on the Box; Justice of the Far North. 1936 Everybody Dance.

REITHE, ALOISE D.
Born: 1890, Los Angeles, Calif. Died: Sept. 5, 1943, Los Angeles, Calif. Screen actor and film director. Appeared in and directed silent films.

REJANE, GABRIELLA
Born: 1857, Paris, France. Died: June 14, 1920, Paris, France. Screen and stage actress.

Appeared in: 1912 Madame Sans-Gene; Miarka, the Daughter of the Bear. 1922 Gypsy Passion.

RELPH, GEORGE
Born: 1888, England. Died: Apr. 24, 1960, London, England. Screen and stage actor.

Appeared in: 1947 Nicholas Nickleby. 1953 The Titfield Thunderbolt; I Believe in You. 1954 The Final Test. 1957 Doctor at Large; Davy. 1960 Ben Hur.

REMLEY, FRANK
Born: 1902. Died: Jan. 28, 1967, Newport Beach, Calif. Radio, screen guitarist, and actor. Appeared in films as Elliott Lewis.

Appeared in: 1949 The Story of Molly X. 1950 Ma and Pa Kettle Go to Town. 1951 Saturday's Hero. 1953 Let's Do It Again.

REMLEY, RALPH McHUGH
Born: 1885. Died: May 26, 1939, Los Angeles, Calif. Screen and stage actor.

Appeared in: 1934 Keep 'Em Rolling; Double Door; Behold My Wife; One Is Guilty; Home on the Range. 1935 Princess O'Hara; Dr. Socrates. 1936 Poppy; Yours for the Asking; Bullets or Ballots; Robin Hood of El Dorado. 1937 Let Them Live; Make Way for Tomorrow. 1938 Outside of Paradise. 1939 King of the Underworld; The Story of Alexander Graham Bell.

REMY, ALBERT
Born: 1912, France. Died: Jan. 26, 1967, Paris, France. Screen actor.

Appeared in: 1944 Les Enfants du Paradis (Children of Paradise-U.S. 1946). 1945 Groupi Mains Rouge (It Happened at the Inn). 1949 Devil's Daughter. 1950 Francois Villon. 1956 French Can-Can (aka Only the French Can). 1957 Razzle. 1958 Crime et Chatinaut (Crime and Punishment; aka The Most Dangerous Sin). 1959 Les Quartre Cents Coups (The 400 Blows). 1961 La Vache et le Prisonnier (The Cow and the Prisoner (aka The Cow and I). 1962 Gigot; Shoot the Piano Player; Four Horsemen of the Apocalypse. 1963 Lafayette; Mandrin. 1964 The Seventh Juror. 1965 The Train; How Not to Rob a Department Store. 1967 The 25th Hour.

REMY, DICK, SR.
Born: 1873. Died: June 1, 1947, Hollywood, Calif.(heart attack). Screen actor and film director. Appeared in and directed silent films.

RENAVENT, GEORGE (Georges de Cheux)
Born: Apr. 23, 1894, Paris, France. Died: Jan. 2, 1969, Gudala-jara, Mexico. Screen, stage actor, and film and stage director. Married to screen actress Selena Royle.

Appeared in: 1919 Erstwhile Susan. 1929 Rio Rita. 1930 Scotland Yard; Le Spectre Vert. 1931 East of Borneo. 1933 Moulin Rouge; Queen Christina. 1934 The Bombay Mail; House of Rothschild. 1935 Follies Bergere; Whipsaw; The White Cockatoo; Front Page Woman; The Last Outpost. 1936 The Invisible Ray; The Sky Parade; Lloyds of London. 1937 History Is Made at Night; Seventh Heaven; Cafe Metropole; Love under Fire; Wife, Doctor and Nurse; Charlie Chan at Monte Carlo; Love and Hisses; The Sheik Steps Out; Fight for Your Lady; Artists and Models Abroad; The King and the Chorus Girl. 1938 Jezebel; Gold Diggers in Paris; I'll Give a Million; Suez. 1939 Topper Takes a Trip; The Three Musketeers; Pack up Your Troubles. 1940 The House Across the Bay; Son of Monte Cristo; Comrade X; Turn-about. 1941 Sullivan's Travels; That Night in Rio; Road to Zanzi-bar; The Night of January 16th. 1943 Mission to Moscow; Winter-time; The Desert Song. 1944 Our Hearts Were Young and Gay. 1945 Captain Eddie. 1946 Tarzan and the Leopard Woman; The Catman of Paris. 1947 Ladies' Man; The Foxes of Harrow. 1951 Secrets of Monte Carlo. 1952 Mara Maru.

RENFRO, RENNIE
Born: 1893. Died: Mar. 2, 1962, Redding, Calif.(heart attack). Screen actor, dog trainer, and stuntman. Appeared in early Sennett comedies and trained "Daisy" for the "Blondie" series.

RENNIE, JAMES
Born: 1889, Toronto, Canada. Died: July 31, 1965, New York, N.Y. Screen and stage actor. Divorced from screen actress Dorothy Gish (dec. 1968).

Appeared in: 1920 Remodeling Her Husband. 1921 Stardust. 1922 The Dust Follower. 1923 Mighty Lak' a Rose; His Children's Children. 1924 Argentine Love; The Moral Sinner; Restless Wives. 1925 Clothes Make the Pirate; Share and Share Alike. 1930 The Bad Man; Girl of the Golden West; Two Rounds of Love (short). 1931 Illicit; Lash; Party Husband. 1932 The Little Damozel. 1941 Skylark. 1942 Crossroads; Tales of Manhattan; Now Voyager. 1945 Wilson; A Bell for Adano.

RENNIE, MICHAEL
Born: Aug. 29, 1909, Bradford, Yorkshire, England. Died: June 10, 1971, Harrogate, Yorkshire, England. Screen, stage, and television actor. Entered British films doing bit parts prior to W.W. II.

Appeared in: 1937 Gang Way. 1938 The Divorce of Lady X; This Man in Paris. 1940 Dangerous Moonlight. 1941 Ships with Wings. 1942 Tower of Terror. 1945 I'll Be Your Sweetheart. 1946 The Wicked Lady; White Cradle Inn; Caesar and Cleopatra. 1947 The Root of All Evil. 1948 Idol of Paris; Uneasy Terms. 1949 The Golden Madonna. 1950 Trio; The Black Rose; The Body Said No. 1951 The 13th Letter; The Day the Earth Stood Still; I'll Never Forget You (aka Man of Two Worlds; House in the Square). 1952 Phone Call from a Stranger; Five Fingers; Les Miserables. 1953 Sailor of the King; Dangerous Crossing; The Robe; King of the Khyber Rifles. 1954 Demetrius and the Gladiators; Princess of the Nile; Desiree. 1955 Mambo; Seven Cities of Gold; Soldier of Fortune; The Rains of Ranchipur. 1956 Teenage Rebel. 1957 Island in the Sun; Omar Khayyam. 1959 Third Man on the Mountain. 1960 The Lost World; Missile from Hell (aka Unseen Heroes; Battle of the V. One). 1963 Mary, Mary. 1965 Night of the Tiger. 1966 Ride Beyond Vengeance. 1967 Cyborg 2087; Hotel. 1968 The Power; The Devil's Brigade; Death on the Run; Subterfuge; The Young, the Evil and the Savage. 1969 Operation Terror; Krakatoa—East of Java.

RENOIR, PIERRE
Born: 1885, France. Died: Mar. 11, 1952, Paris, France. Screen actor. Son of artist Pierre August Renoir.

Appeared in: 1911 La Digue (Ou Pour Sauver la Hollande). 1932 Nuit du carrefour (The Night at the Crossroads). 1934 L'Agonie des Aigles; La Bandera; Madame Bovary. 1938 La Marseillaise; L'Affaire Lafarge; The Patriot; Sacrifice d'Honneur. 1939 Kreutzer Sonata; Le Recif de Corail; Escape from Yesterday; Marseillaise; Citadel of Silence. 1941 Hatred; The Mad Emperor; Personal Column. 1944 Les Enfants du Paradis (Children of Paradise-U.S. 1946). 1946 Peleton d'Execution (Resistance); Sirocco. 1948 Foolish Husbands. 1951 Dr. Knock (U.S. 1955).

RESTA, COL. FRANCIS E.
Born: 1894. Died: Aug. 16, 1968, Bronx, N.Y. Screen actor and leader of U.S. Military band.

REYES, EVA (Adaljina Ardura)
Born: 1915. Died: Mar. 20, 1970, Miami, Fla.(interstitial fibrosis of the lungs). Screen, stage actress, and dancer. Was part of dance team of "Paul and Eva Reyes." Also toured with Xavier Cugat's band at one time.

Appeared in: 1947 Copacabana.

REYNOLDS, ABE
Born: 1884. Died: Dec. 25, 1955, Hollywood, Calif. Screen, stage, burlesque, vaudeville, and radio actor.

Appeared in: 1930 Love at First Sight. 1936 Swing Time. 1949 My Dear Secretary.

REYNOLDS, ADELINE DeWALT
Born: Sept. 19, 1862, Benton County, Iowa. Died: Aug. 13, 1961, Los Angeles, Calif. Screen and stage actress.

Appeared in: 1941 Come Live with Me (film debut); Shadow of the Thin Man. 1942 Tales of Manhattan; Tuttles of Tahiti; Street of Chance. 1943 Behind the Rising Sun; The Human Comedy; Iceland; Happy Land; Son of Dracula. 1944 Going My Way; Old Lady; Since You Went Away. 1945 The Corn Is Green; Counterattack; A Tree Grows in Brooklyn. 1948 The Girl from Manhattan. 1949 Sickle or Cross. 1951 Here Comes the Groom. 1952 Lydia Bailey; Pony Soldier. 1954 Witness to Murder.

REYNOLDS, CRAIG (Hugh Enfield)
Born: July 15, 1907, Anaheim, Calif. Died: Oct. 22, 1949, Los Angeles, Calif.(result of motorcycle crash). Screen, stage, and vaudeville actor. Married to screen actress Barbara Pepper (dec. 1969).

Appeared in: 1930 Coquette. 1934 Cross Country Cruise; I'll Tell the World; Love Birds. 1935 Four Hours to Kill; Paris in Spring; The Case of the Lucky Legs; Man of Iron; Ceiling Zero. 1936 Broadway Playboy; Brides Are Like That; Times Square Playboy; Jailbreak; Smart Blonde; Here Comes Carter!; The Case of the Black Cat; Treachery Rides the Range; The Golden Arrow; Sons O'Guns; Stage Struck. 1937 The Case of the Stuttering Bishop; Footloose Heiress; Slim; The Great O'Malley; The Great Garrick; Back in Circulation; Under Suspicion; Penrod and Sam; Melody for Two. 1938 House of Mystery; Slander House; Romance on the Run; Gold Mine in the Sky; Making Headlines; Female Fugitive; I Am a Criminal. 1939 The Mystery of Mr. Wong; Navy Secrets; Bad Little Angel; The Gentleman from Arizona; Wall Street Cowboy. 1940 The Fatal Hour; Son of the Navy; I Take This Oath. 1944 Nevada. 1945 Divorce; The Strange Affair of Uncle Harry. 1946 Just before Dawn; Queen of Burlesque. 1948 My Dog Shep; The Man from Colorado.

REYNOLDS, LAKE
Born: 1889. Died: Feb. 9, 1952, Hollywood, Calif. Screen, stage, minstrel, vaudeville, and radio actor.

REYNOLDS, NOAH
Died: Sept. 19, 1948: No. Philadelphia, Pa. Screen and stage actor. Appeared in early Lubin Co. and McCurdy Film Co. films.

REYNOLDS, VERA
Born: Nov. 25, 1905, Richmond, Va. Died: Apr. 22, 1962, Woodland Hills, Calif. Screen actress. Married to screen actor Robert Ellis (dec. 1935).

Appeared in: 1923 Prodigal Daughters; Woman-Proof. 1924 Feet of Clay; Broken Barriers; Cheap Kisses; Flapper Wives; For Sale; Icebound; Shadows of Paris. 1925 Road to Yesterday; The Golden Bed; The Limited Mail; The Million Dollar Handicap; The Night Club; Without Mercy. 1926 Silence; Corporal Kate; Risky Business; Steel Preferred; Sunny Side Up. 1927 Almost Human; The Little Adventuress; The Main Event. 1928 Divine Sinner; Golf Widows; Jazzland. 1929 Tonight at Twelve. 1930 Back from Shanghai; The Last Dance; Lone Rider; Borrowed Wives. 1931 Hell Bent for Frisco; Lawless Woman; Neck and Neck. 1932 The Gorilla Ship; Dragnet Patrol; The Monster Walks; Tangled Destinies.

RHINE, JACK
Born: 1911. Died: Aug. 21, 1951, San Francisco, Calif.(poliomyelitis). Screen, stage, and radio actor.

RHUDIN, FRIDOLF
Born: 1895, Sweden. Died: Mar. 6, 1935 (brain fever). Screen and stage actor. Appeared in Scandinavian films.

RIANO, RENIE (aka RENIE)
Died: July 3, 1971, Woodland Hills, Calif. Screen, stage, and television actress. Daughter of stage actress Irene Riano (dec. 1940).

Appeared in: 1937 Tovarich; You're a Sweetheart. 1938 Outside of Paradise; Spring Madness; Thanks for Everything; Men Are Such Fools; Four's a Crowd; Nancy Drew, Detective; The Road to Reno. 1939 Wife, Husband and Friend; The Honeymoon's Over; Disputed Passage; Nancy Drew and the Hidden Staircase; Day Time Wife; Nancy Drew, Trouble Shooter. 1940 The Man Who Wouldn't Talk; The Ghost Comes Home; Kit Carson; Remedy for Riches. 1941 You're the One; Adam Had Four Sons; Affectionately Yours; Ice-Capades; You Belong to Me. 1942 Whispering Ghosts; Blondie for Victory. 1943 The Man from Music Mountain; None but the Lonely Heart. 1944 Jam Session; Take It or Leave It; Three Is a Family. 1945 Club Havana; A Song for Miss Julie. 1946 Bringing up Father; So Goes My Love; Bad Bascomb. 1947 Winter Wonderland. 1948 Jiggs and Maggie in Society; Jiggs and Maggie in Court; The Time of Your Life. 1949 Jackpot Jitters. 1950 Jiggs and Maggie Out West. 1951 As Young as You Feel; The Barefoot Mailman. 1953 Clipped Wings. 1964 Pajama Party. 1965 The Family Jewels. 1966 Three on a Couch; Fireball 500.

RICE, GRANTLAND
Born: 1881. Died: July 13, 1954, N.Y.(heart attack). Sports writer and screen actor. Appeared as narrator in his sports shorts. Won Academy Award for best one-reel picture, Amphibious Fighters (1943). Married to screen actress Florence Rice.

Appeared in: 1925 Grantland Rice "Sportlights" which included the following shorts: Rough and Tumbling; Brains and Brawn; By Hook or Crook; Sporting Armor; Neptune's Nieces; Traps and Troubles; Action; Beauty Spots; Sporting Judgment; All under One Flag; Dude Ranch Days; Twinkle-Twinkle; Animal Celebrities; Learning How; Why Kids Leave Home; Sons of Swat; Seven Ages of Sport; Barrier Busters; Starting an Argument; Outing for All; Clever Feet; Shooting Time; Walloping Wonders; Then and Now; Fins and Feathers. 1934-35 Grantland Rice "Sportlights." 1935 Nineteen "Sportlights" shorts. 1943 Amphibious Fighters (short).

RICE, NORMAN
Born: 1910. Died: Nov. 12, 1957, Hollywood, Calif.(heart attack). Screen, television actor, stage director, and writer.

Appeared in: 1952 The Miracle of Our Lady of Fatima.

RICE, SAM (George Samuel O'Hanlon)
Born: 1874. Died: Mar. 12, 1946, Burbank, Calif. Screen, stage, vaudeville, and burlesque actor. Known as "The King of Burlesque" in earlier days.

RICH, FREDDIE
Born: 1898, New York, N.Y. Died: Sept. 8, 1956, Beverly Hills, Calif. Bandleader, song writer, and screen actor.

Appeared in: 1933 Rambling 'Round Radio Row. 1944 A Wave, a Wac and a Marine.

RICH, LILLIAN
Born: 1900, Herne Hill, London, England. Died: Jan. 5, 1954, Woodland Hills, Calif. Screen actress.

Appeared in: 1921 Beyond; The Blazing Trail; Go Straight; Her Social Value; The Millionaire; The Ruse of the Rattler; The Sage Hen. 1922 The Bearcat; Afraid to Fight; Catch My Smoke; The Kentucky Derby; Man to Man; One Wonderful Night. 1924 Cheap Kisses; Empty Hearts; The Love Master; The Man from Wyoming; The Phantom Horseman; Never Say Die. 1925 Braveheart; A Kiss in the Dark; The Love Gamble; Seven Days; Ship of Souls; Simon the Jester; Soft Shoes. 1926 Dancing Days; Exclusive Rights; The Golden Web; The Isle of Retribution; Whispering Smith. 1927 God's Great Wilderness; Snowbound; Wanted a Coward; Web of Fate; Woman's Law. 1928 The Old Code; That's My Daddy. 1930 The Eternal Triangle (short). 1931 Once a Lady; Grief Street; The Devil Plays. 1932 Mark of the Spur.

RICH, PHIL
Born: 1896. Died: Feb. 22, 1956, Woodland Hills, Calif. Screen, vaudeville, and television actor. Teamed with his wife in vaudeville as "Rich and Adair."

RICHARD, FRIEDA
Born: 1873, Vienna, Austria. Died: Sept. 13, 1946, Salzburg, Austria. Screen and stage actress. Appeared in British and German films.

Appeared in: 1925 Peak of Fate. 1926 Manon Lescaut; Faust. 1928 The Two Brothers. 1930 The Burning Heart; Liebe im Ring. 1932 Liebe 1st Liebe. 1935 Unfinished Symphony. 1938 The Affairs of Maupassant.

RICHARDS, ADDISON W.
Born: 1887, Zanesville, Ohio. Died: Mar. 22, 1964, Los Angeles, Calif.(heart attack). Screen, stage, and television actor. Entered films in 1933.

Appeared in: 1933 Riot Squad. 1934 Lone Cowboy; Let's Be Ritzy; The Love Captive; The Case of the Howling Dog; Beyond the Law; Our Daily Bread; Gentlemen Are Born; Babbitt; St. Louis Kid; British Agent. 1935 Only Eight Hours; Home on the Range; The Eagle's Brood; The Frisco Kid; A Dog of Flanders; Sweet Music; Society Doctor; Here Comes the Band; The White Cockatoo; Front Page Woman; Little Big Shot; Dinky; Alias Mary Down; The Crusades; Freckles; G-Men. 1936 Sutter's Gold; Public Enemy's Wife; Trailin' West; Ceiling Zero; Road Gang; Song of the Saddle; The Law in Her Hands; Jail Break; Anthony Adverse; The Case of the Velvet Claws; Hot Money; China Clipper; Smart Blonde; God's Country and the Woman; Man Hunt; Colleen; The Walking Dead. 1937 Draegerman Courage; The Black Legion; Ready, Willing and Able; Her Husband's Secretary; White Bondage; Dance, Charlie, Dance; The Singing Marine; Love Is on the Air; The Barrier. 1938 Flight to Fame; Alcatraz Island; The Black Doll; The Last Express; Accidents Will Happen; Valley of the Giants; Boys Town; Prison Nurse. 1939 Whispering Enemies; They Made Her a Spy; Twelve Crowded Hours; Off the Record; Inside Information; Burn 'Em up O'Connor; Andy Hardy Gets Spring Fever; They All Come Out; Thunder Afloat; Geronimo; Espionage Agent; Nick Carter, Master Detective; Bad Lands; Exile Express; The Gracie Allen Murder Case. 1940 Andy Hardy Meets a Debutante; Boom Town; Northwest Passage; The Man from Dakota; The Man from Montreal; The Lone Wolf Strikes; Edison, the Man; Charlie Chan in Panama; South to Karanga; Wyoming; Gangs of Chicago; Girls from Havana; My Little Chickadee; Arizona; Flight Command; Moon over Burma; Black Diamonds; Cherokee Strip; Slightly Honorable. 1941 Western Pacific; Tall, Dark and Handsome; Back in the Saddle; Sheriff of Tombstone; The Great Lie; Men of Boys Town; Mutiny in the Arctic; International Squadron; Texas; Her First Beau; Badlands of Dakota; Andy Hardy's Private Secretary; I Wanted Wings; Strawberry Blonde; The Trial of Mary Dugan. 1942 My Favorite Blonde; The Lady Has Plans; Cowboy Serenade; Pacific Rendezvous; A-Haunting We Will Go; Secrets of a Co-ed; Man with Two Lives; Secret Agent for Japan; The Pride of the Yankees; Seven Day's Leave; Men of Texas; Top Sergeant; Secret Enemies; Flying Tigers; War Dogs. 1943 Headin' for God's Country; Corvette K-225; Where Are Your Children?; The Mystery of the 13th Guest; Mystery Broadcast; The Deerslayer; Air Force; Underground Agent; A Guy Named Joe. 1944 Smart Guy; The Fighting Seabees; Follow the Boys; Three Men in White; Moon over Las Vegas; Roger Touhy, Gangster; A Night of Adventure; Marriage Is a Private Affair; Since You Went Away; The Mummy's Curse; The Sullivans; Are These Our Parents?; Barbary Coast Gent; Three Little Sisters; Border Town Trail. 1945 Lady on a Train; The Chicago Kid; God Is My Co-Pilot; Betrayal from the East; Rough, Tough and Ready; Bells of Rosarita; Grissly's Millions; Come Out Fighting; I'll Remember April; Black Market Babies; Danger Signal; The Shanghai Cobra; Men in Her Diary; Strange Confession; The Adventures of Rusty; Spellbound; Bewitched; Leave Her to Heaven. 1946 Secrets of a Sorority Girl; Angel on My Shoulder; The Criminal Court; The Hoodlum Saint; Step by Step; Renegades; Don't Gamble with Strangers; The Tiger Woman; The Mummy's Curse; Anna and the King of Siam; Love Laughs at Andy Hardy; Dragonwyck. 1947 The Millerson Case. 1948 Lulu Belle. 1949 The Rustlers; Henry the Rainmaker; Call Northside 777. 1950 Davy Crockett, Indian Scout. 1955 Illegal; High Society; Fort Yuma. 1956 Walk the Proud Land; Reprisal!; Everything but the Truth; When Gangland Strikes; Fury at Gunsight Pass; The Broken Star. 1957 Last of the Badmen; Gunsight Ridge. 1958 The Saga of Hemp Brown. 1959 The Oregon Trail. 1961 Frontier Uprising; The Gambler Wore a Gun; The Flight That Disappeared. 1962 Saintly Sinners. 1963 The Raiders. 1964 For Those Who Think Young.

RICHARDS, CHARLES
Born: Dec. 16, 1899, Indianapolis, Ind. Died: July 29, 1948, Hollywood, Calif. Screen actor and casting director. Appeared in films from 1916-1923.

Appeared in: 1923 The Call of the Canyon.

RICHARDS, GORDON

Born: Oct. 27, 1893, Gillingham, Kent, England. Died: Jan. 13, 1964, Hollywood, Calif. Screen, stage, and television actor.

Appeared in: 1942 The Wife Takes a Flyer. 1943 Slightly Dangerous. 1944 The Canterville Ghost; The Story of Dr. Wassell; Mrs. Parkington; National Velvet. 1945 Molly and Me; Kitty; White Pongo; Weekend at the Waldorf. 1946 Larceny in Her Heart. 1947 Linda Be Good; The Imperfect Lady; Flight to Nowhere. 1948 Woman in the Night; Thirteen Lead Soldiers. 1950 The Man Who Cheated Himself; The Big Hangover. 1955 High Society.

RICHARDS, GRANT

Born: 1916, New York, N.Y. Died: July 4, 1963, Hollywood, Calif. (leukemia). Screen, stage, radio, and television actor.

Appeared in: 1936 Hopalong Cassidy Returns. 1937 A Night of Mystery; On Such a Night. 1938 My Old Kentucky Home; Under the Big Top. 1939 Risky Business; Inside Information. 1940 Isle of Destiny. 1942 Just Off Broadway. 1944 Winged Victory. 1959 Guns, Girls and Gangsters; The Four Skulls of Jonathan Drake; Inside the Mafia. 1960 Oklahoma Territory; Twelve Hours to Kill; The Music Box Kid. 1961 You Have to Run Fast; Secret of Deep Harbor.

RICHARDSON, FRANKIE

Born: Sept. 6, 1898, Philadelphia, Pa. Died: Jan. 30, 1962, Philadelphia, Pa.(heart attack). Screen, minstrel, and vaudeville actor.

Appeared in: 1925 Don Q.; Seven Sinners. 1926 King of the Pack; Racing Blood. 1928 The Joy Boy of Song (short); Chasing the Blues (short). 1929 Fox Movietone Follies of 1929; Happy Days; Masquerade; Sunny Side Up. 1930 Let's Go Places; New Movietone Follies of 1930.

RICHMAN, AL

Born: 1885. Died: Apr. 20, 1936, Hollywood, Calif.(heart attack). Screen actor.

RICHMAN, CHARLES

Born: 1870, Chicago, Ill. Died: Dec. 1, 1940, Bronx, N.Y. Screen and stage actor.

Appeared in: 1915 The Battle Cry of Peace. 1917 The Secret Kingdom (serial). 1923 Has the World Gone Mad? 1929 The Ninety-Ninth Amendment. 1931 The Struggle. 1933 Take a Chance. 1934 His Double Life; The President Vanishes; Woman Haters (short). 1935 In Old Kentucky; George White's 1935 Scandals; The Case of the Curious Bride; The Glass Key; Becky Sharp; Thanks a Million; My Marriage; After Office Hours; Biography of a Bachelor Girl. 1936 The Ex-Mrs. Bradford; Parole; In His Steps; Sing Me a Love Song; Under Your Spell; I'd Give My Life. 1937 The Life of Emile Zola; Make a Wish; Lady Behave; Nothing Sacred. 1938 The Adventures of Tom Sawyer; The Cowboy and the Lady; Blondes at Work. 1939 Torchy Runs for Mayor; Exile Express; Dark Victory. 1940 Devil's Island. 1921 The Sign on the Door; Stranger Than Fiction; Trust Your Wife. 1922 My Friend the Devil.

RICHMOND, WARNER

Born: Jan. 11, 1895, Culpepper County, Va. Died: June 19, 1948, Los Angeles, Calif.(coronary thrombosis). Screen and stage actor.

Appeared in: 1916 Betty of Graystone. 1918 Sporting Life. 1920 My Lady's Garter. 1921 Tol'able David; Heart of Maryland; The Mountain Woman. 1922 The Challenge; Isle of Doubt; Jan of the Big Snows. 1923 Luck; Mark of the Beast; The Man from Glengarry. 1924 Daughters of the Night; The Speed Spook. 1925 The Crowded Hour; Fear-Bound; The Making of O'Malley; The Pace That Thrills. 1926 Good and Naughty; The Wives of the Prophet. 1927 Slide, Kelly, Slide; The Fire Brigade; Finger Prints; Irish Hearts; White Flannels; Heart of Maryland (and 1921 version). 1928 Hearts of Men; Shadows of the Night; Chicago; Stop That Man; You Can't Beat the Law. 1929 Strange Cargo; Voice of the Storm; The Redeeming Sin; Stark Mad; Fifty-Fifty; Manhattan Madness; Big Brother; The Apache; Big News. 1930 Men without Women; Billy the Kid; Strictly Modern; Remote Control; Vengeance (short). 1931 Quick Millions; Huckleberry Finn. 1932 Hell's Highway; The Woman from Monte Carlo; Beast of the City; Strangers of the Evening; Night Court. 1933 Fast Workers; King of the Jungle; Corruption; Mama Loves Papa; This Day and Age; Police Call; Life in the Raw. 1934 Happy Landing; The Lost Jungle (serial); Gift of Gab. 1935 Mississippi; Rainbow's End; Smoky Smith; New Frontier; The Courageous Avenger; Under Pressure; Headline Woman; So Red the Rose; The Singing Vagabond. 1936 Below the Deadline;

Hearts in Bondage; The White Legion; Song of the Gringo; Headin' for the Rio Grande; In His Steps. 1937 A Lawman Is Born; Wallaby Jim of the Islands; Where Trails Divide; The Gold Racket; Riders of the Dawn; Stars over Arizona; Federal Bullets. 1938 Wolves of the Sea; Six-Shootin' Sheriff; Prairie Moon. 1939 Wild Horse Canyon. 1940 Rainbow over the Range; Rhythm of the Rio Grande; Pals of the Silver Sage; The Golden Trail; Men with Steel Faces. 1946 Colorado Serenade.

RICHTER, PAUL

Born: 1896, Germany. Died: Dec. 30, 1961, Vienna, Austria. Screen, stage, and television actor.

Appeared in: 1923 Siegfried (U.S. 1925). 1927 Peter the Pirate. 1928 Kriemhild's Revenge. 1929 Forbidden Love. 1931 Die Foresterchirstl. 1935 Jungfrau Gegen Moench (Maiden vs. Monk); Drei Kaiserjaeger; Ehestreik. 1936 Der Klosterjaeger; Die Frauen vom Tannhof; Der Wackere Schustermeister; Ein Liebesroman im Hause Habsburg. 1937 Das Schweigen im Walde (The Silence of the Forest). 1939 Der Edelweisskoenig; Starker als die Liebe (Stronger Than Love); Frau Sylvelin. 1940 Waldrausch (Forest Fever). Other German film: The Nibelungen (silent).

RICKETTS, THOMAS "TOM"

Born: 1853, London, England. Died: Jan. 20, 1939, Hollywood, Calif.(pneumonia). Screen, stage actor, film director, and stage manager.

Appeared in: 1921 The Parish Priest; Puppets of Fate; Sham; Beating the Game; The Killer; The Spenders. 1922 The Eternal Flame; Fools of Fortune; Putting It Over; Shattered Idols; A Tailor-Made Man; The Lavender Bath Lady. 1923 Alice Adams; The Dangerous Maid; Strangers of the Night; Within the Law. 1924 Black Oxen; The Gaiety Girl; Cheap Kisses; Circe, the Enchantress. 1925 The Fate of a Flirt; The Girl Who Wouldn't Work; Never the Twain Shall Meet; Was It Bigamy?; The Business of Love; A Fight to the Finish; My Wife and I; Oh, Doctor; Sealed Lips; Secrets of the Night; Steppin' Out; Wages for Wives; When Husbands Flirt; Bobbed Hair. 1926 Dancing Days; Ladies of Leisure; The Lily; The Nutcracker; The Belle of Broadway; The Cat's Pajamas; Going the Limit; Ladies at Play; Love's Blindness; The Old Soak; Poker Faces; Stranded in Paris; When the Wife's Away. 1927 Sailor's Sweetheart; Broadway Madness; Children of Divorce; In a Moment of Temptation; Too Many Crooks; Venus of Venice. 1928 My Friend from India; Doomsday; Just Married; Dry Martini; Interference; Freedom of the Press; Five and Ten Cent Annie; Law and the Man. 1929 The Glad Rag Doll; Beware of Bachelors; Light Fingers; Red Hot Speed. 1930 Prince of Diamonds; The Vagabond King; Broken Dishes; Sea Legs. 1931 Man of the World; Side Show; Ambassador Bill; Surrender. 1932 A Farewell to Arms; Forbidden; Thrill of Youth. 1933 He Learned about Women; Women Won't Tell; Mama Loves Papa; Forgotten. 1934 Stolen Sweets; The Curtain Falls; In Love with Life; Little Man, What Now?; No Greater Glory; The Count of Monte Cristo. 1935 Forsaking All Others; Sons of Steel; Now or Never; Cardinal Richelieu; A Tale of Two Cities. 1936 Hi, Gaucho; We Went to College; Pennies from Heaven. 1937 Maid of Salem; The Lady Escapes. 1938 Bluebeard's Eighth Wife; The Young in Heart; Young Fugitives.

RICKSON, LUCILLE (aka LUCILLE RICKSEN)

Born: Sept. 2, 1907. Died: Mar. 13, 1925. Screen actress.

Appeared in: 1921 The Old Nest. 1922 Forsaking All Others; The Married Flapper; The Girl Who Ran Wild; Remembrance; The Stranger's Banquet. 1923 Human Wreckage; The Rendezvous; Trimmed in Scarlet; The Social Buccaneer (serial). 1924 Vanity's Price; Behind the Curtain; Galloping Fish; The Hill Billy; Idle Tongues; Judgment of the Storm; The Painted Lady; Those Who Dance; Young Ideas. 1925 The Denial.

RIDDLE, RICHARD. See Richard Ainley. Occasionally he used "Riddle" on stage.

RIDGE, WALTER J.

Born: 1900. Died: Sept. 22, 1968, Los Angeles, Calif. Screen actor, extra, and vaudeville actor. Appeared in vaudeville in an act billed as "Mulroy, McNeece and Ridge."

RIDGELY, CLEO

Born: 1894. Died: Aug. 18, 1962, Glendale, Calif. Screen and stage actress.

Appeared in: 1914 The Spoilers. 1915 The Chorus Lady. 1916 The Yellow Mask; The Yellow Pawn. 1921 Dangerous Pastime. 1922 The Forgotten Law; The Law and the Woman; The Sleepwalker. 1923 The Beautiful and Damned.

RIDGELY, JOHN (John Huntington Rea)
Born: Sept. 6, 1909, Chicago, Ill. Died: Jan. 18, 1968, New York, N.Y.(heart ailment). Screen actor.

Appeared in: 1937 Larger Than Life; They Won't Forget; Submarine D-1. 1938 Forbidden Valley; The Invisible Menace; Torchy Gets Her Man; Secrets of an Actress; Patient in Room 18; He Couldn't Say No; Blondes at Work; Torchy Blane in Panama; Little Miss Thoroughbred; White Banners; Cowboy from Brooklyn; My Bill; Going Places; Hard to Get. 1939 The Cowboy Quarterback; Nancy Drew and the Hidden Staircase; Kid Nightingale; Dark Victory; Secret Service of the Air; Everybody's Hobby; Indianapolis Speedway; Torchy Plays with Dynamite; They Made Me a Criminal; You Can't Get Away with Murder; King of the Underworld; Private Detective; Wings of the Navy; The Return of Dr. X; The Kid from Kokomo. 1940 River's End; Father Is a Prince; The Man Who Talked Too Much; Saturday's Children; Flight Angels; Torrid Zone; Brother Orchid; They Drive by Night. 1941 The Wagons Roll at Night; Million Dollar Baby; International Squadron; The Great Mr. Nobody; The Man Who Came to Dinner; Here Comes Happiness; Strange Alibi; Navy Blues; Highway West. 1942 Bullet Scars; Wings for the Eagle; The Big Shot; Secret Enemies. 1943 Air Force; Northern Pursuit. 1944 Hollywood Canteen; The Doughgirls; Destination Tokyo; Arsenic and Old Lace. 1945 Pride of the Marines; God Is My Co-Pilot; Danger Signal. 1946 My Reputation; Two Guys from Milwaukee; The Big Sleep. 1947 High Wall; The Man I Love; Nora Prentiss; That Way with Women; That's My Man; Cheyenne; Cry Wolf; Possessed. 1948 Night Winds; Luxury Liner; Sealed Verdict; Trouble Makers; The Iron Curtain. 1949 Command Decision; Once More, My Darling; Border Incident; Task Force; Tucson. 1950 Backfire; Beauty on Parade; The Lost Volcano; South Sea Sinner; Petty Girl; Rookie Fireman; Saddle Tramp; Edge of Doom. 1951 The Last Outpost; When the Redskins Rode; Thunder in God's Country; Al Jennings of Oklahoma; Half Angel; A Place in the Sun; The Blue Veil; As You Were. 1952 Fort Osage; The Greatest Show on Earth; Room for One More; The Outcasts of Poker Flat. 1953 Off Limits.

RIDGES, STANLEY
Born: 1892, Southampton, England. Died: Apr. 22, 1951, Westbrook, Conn. Screen, stage, and television actor.

Appeared in: 1923 Success. 1930 For Two Cents (short); Let's Merge (short). 1932 The Sign of the Cross. 1934 Crime without Passion. 1935 The Scoundrel. 1936 Winterset; Sinner Take All. 1937 Interns Can't Take Money. 1938 Yellow Jack; If I Were King; There's That Woman Again; The Mad Miss Manton. 1939 Silver on the Sage; Confessions of a Nazi Spy; Each Dawn I Die; Let Us Live; Union Pacific; I Stole a Million; Dust Be My Destiny; Espionage Agent; Nick Carter, Master Detective. 1940 Black Friday. 1941 The Sea Wolf; Sergeant York; They Died with Their Boots On; Mr. District Attorney. 1942 The Lady Is Willing; Eagle Squadron; To Be or Not to Be; The Big Shot; Eyes in the Night. 1943 Tarzan Triumphs; Air Force; This Is the Army. 1944 Wilson; The Sign of the Cross (revised version of 1932 film); The Story of Dr. Wassell; The Master Race. 1945 The Suspect; God Is My Co-Pilot; Captain Eddie; The Phantom Speaks. 1946 Because of Him; Canyon Passage; Mr. Ace. 1947 Possessed. 1949 Streets of Laredo; Task Force; You're My Everything; An Act of Murder. 1950 No Way Out; Paid in Full; Thelma Jordon; There's a Girl in My Heart. 1951 The Groom Wore Spurs.

RIDGEWAY, FRITZI
Born: 1898, Missoula, Mont. Died: Mar. 29, 1961, Lancaster, Calif.(heart attack). Screen and stage actress. Entered films in 1917.

Appeared in: 1920 Judy of Rogues Harbor. 1921 Bring Him In; The Fatal 30. 1922 Boomerang Justice; Branded Man; The Hate Trail; The Menacing Past; The Old Homestead. 1923 Ruggles of Red Gap; The Cricket on the Hearth; Hollywood; Trifling with Honor. 1927 Man Bait; Face Value; Getting Gertie's Garter; Lonesome Ladies; Nobody's Widow. 1928 The Enemy; Flying Romeos; Son of the Golden West. 1929 Red Hot Speed; This Is Heaven; Hell's Heroes. 1930 Prince of Diamonds. 1931 The Mad Parade. 1932 Ladies of the Big House. 1934 We Will Live Again. 1935 No Ransom.

RIDLEY, ROBERT
Born: 1901. Died: Nov. 19, 1958, Hollywood, Calif. Screen actor. One of founders of Screen Extras Guild.

RIECHERS, HELENE
Born: 1869, Germany. Died: July 24, 1957, Berlin, Germany. Screen and stage actress.

RIEMANN, JOHANNES
Born: 1887, Berlin, Germany. Died: Oct. 8, 1959, Constance, West Germany. Screen actor, film director, and screenwriter.

Appeared in: 1932 Sein Scheldungsgrund; Der Falsche Ehemann; Drunter und Drueber. 1933 Heute Nacht-Eventuell; Der Hellscher; Kadetten. 1934 Fraeulein-Falsch Verbunden! 1940 Der Tag Nach der Scheidung (The Day after the Divorce); Ihr Erstes Erlebnis (Her First Experience). Other German films: Bel Ami; Liebeskomoedie (silent films).

RIES, WILLIAM J.
Born: 1895. Died: Nov. 16, 1955, Hollywood, Calif. Screen actor.

RIETTI, VICTOR
Born: Mar. 1, 1888, Ferrara, Italy. Died: Dec. 4, 1963, London, England (heart ailment). Screen, stage, television actor, stage director, and stage producer.

Appeared in: 1933 Jew Suess. 1935 Heads We Go; Two Hearts in Harmony; Oh, Daddy!; Escape Me Never. 1936 The Ghost Goes West; Dusty Ermine; Juggernaut; London Melody. 1938 First and Last; The Divorce of Lady X; The Viper; Transatlantic Trouble; Secretary in Trouble. 1944 Room for Two; Give Us the Moon; Yellow Canary; Hotel Reserve (U.S. 1946). 1949 A Man about the House. 1950 The Glass Mountain. 1957 The Story of Esther Costello. 1958 Your Past Is Showing (aka The Naked Truth). Other foreign films: Man of the Moment; Jack of All Trades; Show Flat; Shipmate O'Mine; Jimmy Boy; Twenty-One Days; Epitaph for a Spy; Prix of Rome.

RIGA, NADINE
Born: 1909. Died: Dec. 11, 1968, Hollywood, Calif.(cerebral hemorrhage). Screen actress.

Appeared in: 1928 Ramona. 1936 Anthony Adverse. 1943 For Whom the Bell Tolls.

RIGBY, ARTHUR (Arthur Turner)
Born: 1901. Died: Apr. 25, 1971, Worthing, England (stroke). Screen, stage, and television actor.

Appeared in: 1927 Q Ships (film debut). 1957 The Third Key.

RIBGY, EDWARD
Born: 1879, Ashford, Kent, England. Died: Apr. 5, 1951, London, England. Screen and stage actor.

Appeared in: 1935 Lorna Doone. 1936 Accused; Land without Music. 1937 When Thief Meets Thief; Young and Innocent; Mr. Smith Carries On. 1938 A Yank at Oxford; Yellow Sands; Keep Smiling; The Ware Case. 1939 Proud Valley. 1941 The Stars Look Down; Convoy; Kipps; The Common Touch. 1942 Let the People Sing; Salute John Citizen; Flying Fortress. 1943 Get Cracking; Penn of Pennsylvania (aka Courageous Mr. Penn). 1944 Canterbury Tale; Don't Take It to Heart (U.S. 1948). 1945 They Met in the Dark. 1947 The Years Between; Quiet Weekend. 1948 Piccadilly Incident (aka They Met at Midnight). 1949 Easy Money; Daybreak; Temptation Harbour; Christopher Columbus; The Happiest Days of Your Life; It's Hard to Be Good. 1950 Silknoose; The Mudlark; Perfect Strangers. 1951 Into the Blue; Circle of Danger; Double Confession; Tony Draws a Horse. Other British films: I Live in Grosvenor Square; What the Butler Saw; Don't Ever Leave Me; Loves of Joanne Godden.

RIGGS, TOMMY
Born: Oct. 21, 1908, Pittsburgh, Pa. Died: May 23, 1967, Pittsburgh, Pa. Screen, radio, and television actor.

Appeared in: 1938 Goodbye Broadway.

RIGHTMIRE, WILLIAM H.
Born: 1857. Died: Jan. 14, 1933, Long Beach, Calif.(heart disease). Screen, stage actor, and novelist.

RIHANI, NEGUIB
Born: 1891. Died: June 8, 1949, Cairo, Egypt. Screen and stage actor.

RILEY, JACK "SLIM"
Born: 1895. Died: July 9, 1933, Newhall, Calif. Screen actor.

Appeared in: 1921 A Broken Doll.

RIN TIN TIN, SR.
Born: 1916. Died: 1932. Dog screen actor. Father of Rin Tin Tin, Jr.(dec.). Entered films with Warner Bros. approx. 1922.

Appeared in: 1922 The Man from Hell's River; My Dad. 1923 Where the North Begins; Shadows of the North. 1924 Find Your Man; The Lighthouse by the Sea. 1925 Clash of the Wolves; Below the Line; Tracked in the Snow Country. 1926 The Night Cry; Hero of the Big Snows; While London Sleeps. 1927 Jaws of Steel; A Dog of the Regiment; Tracked by the Police; Hills of Kentucky. 1928 Rinty of the Desert; Race for Life; Land of the Silver Fox; The Famous Warner Brothers Dog Star (short). 1929 Show of Shows; Frozen River; Million Dollar Collar; Tiger Rose. 1930 Rough Waters; The Man Hunter; On the Border. 1931 Lightning Warrior (serial).

RIN TIN TIN, JR.
Died. Dog screen actor. Son of Rin Tin Tin, Sr.(dec. 1932).

Appeared in: 1927 Hills of Kentucky. 1933 The Wolf Dog (serial); The Big Pay-Off. 1934 Law of the Wild (serial). 1935 Adventures of Rex and Rinty (serial). 1936 Tough Guy.

RING, BLANCHE
Born: 1876, Boston, Mass. Died: Jan. 13, 1961, Santa Monica, Calif. Screen and stage actress. Divorced from screen actor Charles Winninger (dec. 1969). Sister of screen actress Frances (dec. 1951) and Julie Ring and screen actor Cyril Ring (dec. 1967).

Appeared in: 1915 The Yankee Girl. 1926 It's the Old Army Game. 1940 If I Had My Way.

RING, CYRIL
Born: 1893. Died: July 17, 1967, Hollywood, Calif. Screen and stage actor. For family information, see Blanche Ring.

Appeared in: 1921 The Conquest of Canaan. 1922 Back Home and Broke; Divorce Coupons. 1923 The Exciters; Homeward Bound; The Ne'er-Do-Well. 1924 The Breaking Point; The Guilty One; Hit and Run; Pied Piper Malone; Tongues of Flame; In Hollywood with Potash and Perlmutter. 1926 Mismates. 1928 The News Parade. 1929 The Cocoanuts. 1930 Top Speed; The Social Lion. 1932 Business and Pleasure. 1933 Emergency Call; Too Much Harmony; Neighbors Wives. 1934 Hollywood Hoodlums. 1936 Border Patrolman; Wedding Present. 1940 One Night in the Tropics. 1941 Hot Spot; Great Guns. 1942 The Navy Comes Through; Army Surgeon; Over My Dead Body. 1943 Dixie; Melody Parade. 1944 In Society; Hot Rhythm; Follow the Boys; Secret Command; The Bullfighters. 1945 Hollywood and Vine; The Naughty Nineties. 1947 Hollywood Barn Dance; Body and Soul.

RING, FRANCES
Born: 1882, N.Y. Died: Jan. 15, 1951, Hollywood, Calif. Screen and stage actress. Married to screen actor Thomas Meighan (dec. 1936). For family information, see Blanche Ring.

RIORDAN, ROBERT J.
Born: 1913. Died: Jan. 1, 1968, Hollywood, Calif.(heart attack). Screen actor.

Appeared in: 1959 Arson for Hire.

RIPLEY, RAYMOND "RAY"
Born: 1891. Died: Oct. 7, 1938, Los Angeles, Calif. Screen actor.

Appeared in: 1920 The Vanishing Dagger (serial). 1921 The Blazing Trail; Why Trust Your Husband? 1922 Turn to the Right. 1925 Heads Up; Smilin' at Trouble. 1926 The Speeding Venus; The Traffic Cop; Western Pluck. 1927 Stolen Pleasures.

RIPLEY, ROBERT L.
Born: Dec. 25, 1893. Died: May 27, 1949, New York, N.Y.(heart attack). Screen and radio actor, author, cartoonist, and creator of "Believe It or Not" series that appeared on film, radio, and in newspapers.

Appeared in: 1932-33 Vitaphone shorts of his "Believe It or Not" series.

RISCOE, ARTHUR
Born: Nov. 19, 1896, Yorkshire, England. Died: Aug. 6, 1954, London, England. Screen and stage actor.

Appeared in: 1932 For Love of Mike. 1933 For Love of You; Going Gay. 1935 Kiss Me Goodbye. 1936 Public Nusiance No. 1. 1937 Paradise for Two; Street Singer. 1938 The Gaiety Girls. 1941 Kipps.

RISDON, ELIZABETH
Born: 1887, London, England. Died: Dec. 20, 1958, Santa Monica, Calif.(brain hemorrhage). Screen, stage, and television actress. Married to screen actor Brandon Evans (dec. 1958).

Appeared in: 1919 A Star Overnight. 1935 Guard That Girl; Crime and Punishment. 1936 Don't Gamble with Love; Lady of Secrets; The King Steps Out; Craig's Wife; Theodora Goes Wild; The Final Hour. 1937 The Woman I Love; Make Way for Tomorrow; Mountain Justice; They Won't Forget; Mannequin; Dead End. 1938 Mad about Music; Tom Sawyer, Detective; Cowboy from Brooklyn; My Bill; Girls on Probation; The Affairs of Annabel. 1939 Sorority House; The Girl from Mexico; Full Confession; The Man Who Dared; The Mexican Spitfire; Huckleberry Finn; I Am Not Afraid; The Roaring Twenties; The Forgotten Woman; Disputed Passage; The Great Man Votes; Five Came Back. 1940 The Man Who Wouldn't Talk; Abe Lincoln in Illinois; Honeymoon Deferred; Ma, He's Making Eyes at Me; Saturday's Children; Sing, Dance, Plenty Hot; The Howards of Virginia; The Mexican Spitfire; Out West; Slightly Tempered; Let's Make Music. 1941 Nice Girl?; The Mexican Spitfire's Baby; High Sierra; Mr. Dynamite; Footlight Fever. 1942 The Lady Is Willing; Mexican Spitfire at Sea; Mexican Spitfire Sees a Ghost; Jail House Blues; The Man Who Returned to Life; Reap the Wild Wind; I Live on Danger; Are Husbands Necessary?; Mexican Spitfire's Elephant; Journey for Margaret; Random Harvest; Paris Calling. 1943 Never a Dull Moment; The Amazing Mrs. Holiday; Higher and Higher. 1944 The Canterville Ghost; Tall in the Saddle; Lost Angel; The Cobra Woman; Weird Woman; In the Meantime, Darling. 1945 Blonde Fever; Grissly's Millions; The Unseen; Song for Miss Julie; The Fighting Guardsman; Mama Loves Papa. 1946 Lover Come Back; Roll on Texas Moon; The Walls Came Tumbling Down; They Made Me a Killer. 1947 Life with Father; The Shocking Miss Pilgrim; Romance of Rosy Ridge; Mourning Becomes Electra; The Egg and I. 1948 The Bride Goes Wild; Sealed Verdict; Bodyguard; High Wall; Every Girl Should Be Married. 1949 Guilty of Treason; Down Dakota Way. 1950 Bunco Squad; The Milkman; Hills of Oklahoma; The Secret Fury; Sierra. 1951 Bannerline; My True Story; In Old Amarillo. 1952 Scaramouche.

RISING, WILLIAM S.
Born: 1851. Died: Oct. 5, 1930, New York, N.Y.(heart trouble). Screen, stage actor, and film director.

Appeared in: 1924 America.

RISS, DAN
Born: 1910. Died: Aug. 28, 1970, Hollywood, Calif.(heart attack). Screen and radio actor.

Appeared in: 1949 Pinky. 1950 Kiss Tom Goodbye; Love That Brute; Panic in the Streets; When Willie Comes Marching Home; Wyoming Mail. 1951 Appointment with Danger; Go for Broke; Little Egypt; Only the Valiant. 1952 Carbine Williams; Confidence Girl; Operation Secret; Scarlet Angel; Washington Story. 1953 Man in the Dark; The Miami Story; Vice Squad. 1954 Human Desire; Riders to the Stars; The Three Young Texans; The Yellow Tomahawk. 1957 Man on Fire; Kelly and Me. 1958 Badman's Country. 1960 Ma Barker's Killer Brood; The Story on Page One.

RISSMILLER, LAWSON J.
Born: 1914. Died: Apr. 2, 1953, Oley, Pa. Screen actor and orchestra leader.

Appeared in: 1939 Broadway Buckaroo.

RISSO, ATTILIO
Born: 1913. Died: Oct. 14, 1967, San Francisco, Calif.(liver disease). Screen and television actor. Appeared in films during the 1930s and 1940s with a group called the "Vagabonds."

Appeared in: 1943 It Ain't Hay.

RITCHIE, BILLIE
Born: 1879, Glasgow, Scotland. Died: July 6, 1921, Los Angeles, Calif. Screen and vaudeville actor. Appeared in Universal films in 1914.

RITTER, ESTHER
Born: 1902. Died: Dec. 30, 1925, Los Angeles, Calif.(appendicitis). Screen actress. Married to screen actor Cuyler Supplee.

RITTER, PAUL J.
Died: Apr. 27, 1962, Dacca, Pakistan. Screen actor and film producer.

RITTER, THELMA
Born: Feb. 14, 1905, Brooklyn, N.Y. Died: Feb. 5, 1969, New York, N.Y.(heart attack). Screen, stage, radio, and television actress.

Appeared in: 1947 Miracle on 34th Street (film debut). 1949 City across the River; Father Was a Fullback; A Letter to Three Wives. 1950 Perfect Strangers; All about Eve; I'll Get By. 1951 The Mating Season; The Model and the Marriage Broker; As Young as You Feel. 1952 With a Song in My Heart. 1953 The Farmer Takes a Wife; Pickup on South Street; Titanic. 1954 Rear Window. 1955 Lucy Gallant; Daddy Long Legs. 1956 The Proud and Profane. 1959 A Hole in the Head; Pillow Talk. 1961 The Misfits; The Second Time Around. 1962 Birdman of Alcatraz; How the West Was Won. 1963 A New Kind of Love; Move over, Darling; For Love or Money. 1965 Boeing Boeing. 1967 The Incident. 1968 What's So Bad about Feeling Good?

RITTERBAND, GERHARD
Born: 1905, Germany. Died: Oct. 1959, Berlin, Germany (jaundice). Screen actor. Appeared in early Ernst Lubitsch films and other silents.

RITZ, AL (Al Joachim)
Born: Aug. 27, 1901, Newark, N.J. Died: Dec. 22, 1965, New Orleans, La.(heart attack). Screen, stage, vaudeville, and television actor. Brother of actors Harry and Jimmy Ritz. Was member of "Ritz Bros." screen and vaudeville comedy team. All films beginning in 1934 include the three brothers.

Appeared in: 1918 The Avenging Trail (was an extra in this film). 1934 Hotel Anchovy (team film debut—short). 1936 Sing, Baby, Sing. 1937 One in a Million; On the Avenue; You Can't Have Everything; Life Begins in College. 1938 The Goldwyn Follies; Kentucky Moonshine; Straight, Place and Show. 1939 The Three Musketeers; Pack up Your Troubles. 1940 Argentine Nights. 1942 Behind the Eight Ball. 1943 Hi 'Ya, Chum; Screen Snapshots No. 5 (short); Screen Snapshots No. 8 (short); Never a Dull Moment. 1944 Take It or Leave It (scenes from On the Avenue (1937) in this film). 1945 Everything Happens to Us. 1963 The Sound of Laughter (documentary).

RIVAS, JOSE M. L. (Jose Maria Linares Rivas)
Born: 1901, Mexico. Died: Apr. 13, 1955, Mexico City, Mexico. Screen and stage actor.

Appeared in: 1939 El Romance del Palmar. 1962 The Criminal Life of Archibaldo de la Cruz.

RIVIERE, FRED "CURLY"
Born: 1875. Died: Nov. 6, 1935, Hollywood, Calif.(heart attack). Screen actor.

Appeared in: 1926 The Dangerous Dub.

ROACH, MARGARET
Born: Mar. 15, 1921, Los Angeles, Calif. Died: Nov. 22, 1964, Hollywood, Calif. Screen and stage actress. Daughter of producer Hal Roach.

Appeared in: 1939 Captain Fury; Fast and Furious. 1940 Turnabout. 1941 Road Show; Niagara Falls.

ROACHE, VIOLA
Born: 1886. Died: May 17, 1961, Hollywood, Calif.(heart attack). Screen and stage actress.

Appeared in: 1950 Harriet Craig. 1951 Royal Wedding; Goodbye, My Fancy.

ROBARDS, JASON, SR.
Born: Dec. 31, 1892, Hillsdale, Mich. Died: Apr. 4, 1963, Sherman Oaks, Calif.(heart attack). Screen and stage actor. Father of screen actor Jason Robards, Jr.

Appeared in: 1921 The Gilded Lily; The Land of Hope. 1925 Stella Maris. 1926 Footloose Widows; The Cohens and the Kellys; The Third Degree. 1927 Casey Jones; Wild Geese; Jaws of Steel; The Heart of Maryland; Hills of Kentucky; Irish Hearts; Polly of the Movies; Tracked by the Police; White Flannels. 1928 Streets of Shanghai; On Trial; The Death Ship (short); Polly of the Movies; Casey Jones; A Bird in the Hand (short). 1929 Paris; The Flying Marine; Trial Marriage; The Isle of Lost Ships; Some Mother's Boy; The Gamblers. 1930 The Last Dance; Jazz Cinderella; Lightnin'; Sisters; Crazy That Way; Peacock Alley; Abraham Lincoln; Trifles (short). 1931 Charlie Chan Carries On; Subway Express; Salvation Nell; Full of Notions; Caught Plastered; Law of the Tongs; Ex-Bad Boy. 1932 Discarded Lovers; Unholy Love; White Eagle; Klondike; Docks of San Francisco; Pride of the Legion; Slightly Married. 1933 Strange Alibi; Corruption; Devil's Mate; Dance Hall Hostess; Ship of Wanted Men; Public Stenographer; Carnival Lady; The Way to Love. 1934 Broadway Bill; One Exciting Adventure;

The President Vanishes; The Crimson Romance; Take the Stand; Woman Unafraid; All of Me; Woman Condemned; Burn 'Em up Barnes (serial and feature). 1935 Ladies Crave Excitement; The Crusades. 1936 The White Legion. 1937 Sweetheart of the Navy; Damaged Lives. 1938 The Clipped Wings; Flight to Fame; Mystery Plane; Cipher Bureau. 1939 Sky Pirate; Stunt Pilot; The Mad Empress; Range War; Danger Flight; I Stole a Million. 1940 The Fatal Hour. 1944 Mlle. Fifi; Bermuda Mystery; The Master Race. 1945 Betrayal from the East; What a Blonde; A Game of Death; Wanderer of the Wasteland; Isle of the Dead; Man Alive. 1946 Bedlam; Ding Dong Williams; The Falcon's Adventure; The Falcon's Alibi; Vacation in Reno; Step by Step. 1947 Seven Keys to Baldpate; Under the Tonto Rim; Wild Horse Mesa; Trail Street; Desperate; Thunder Mountain; Riffraff. 1948 Fighting Father Dunne; Guns of Hate; Mr. Blandings Builds His Dream House; Western Heritage; Son of God's Country; Return of the Bad Men. 1949 Rimfire; Post Office Investigator; Alaska Patrol; Impact; Feudin' Rhythm; Horseman of the Sierras; Riders of the Whistling Pines; South of Death Valley. 1951 The Second Woman. 1961 Wild in the Country.

ROBBINS, MARCUS B.
Born: 1868. Died: Apr. 7, 1931, Hollywood, Calif. Screen actor and screenwriter.

Appeared in: 1920 Alias Jimmy Valentine. 1922 The Gray Dawn; The Girl Who Ran Wild. 1923 The Marriage Market; The Scarlet Car.

ROBBINS, RICHARD
Born: 1919, Boston, Mass. Died: Oct. 23, 1969, New York, N.Y. (heart attack). Screen, stage, and television actor.

Appeared in: 1956 The Wrong Man.

ROBER, RICHARD
Born: May 14, 1906, Rochester, N.Y. Died: May 26, 1952, Santa Monica, Calif.(auto accident). Screen, stage, and television actor.

Appeared in: 1947 Call Northside 777 (film dubut). 1948 April Showers; Smart Girls Don't Talk; Embraceable You; Larceny. 1949 Illegal Entry; Any Number Can Play; Backfire; I Married a Communist; Port of New York; Task Force. 1950 Thelma Jordan; Deported; Dial 1119; Sierra; The Woman on Pier 13; There's a Girl in My Heart. 1951 The Well; Father's Little Dividend; Passage West; The Tall Target; Watch the Birdie; Man in the Saddle. 1952 The Devil Makes Three; O. Henry's Full House; Outlaw Woman; The Rose Bowl Story; The Savage; Kid Monk Baroni. 1957 Jet Pilot.

ROBERSON, LOU
Born: 1921. Died: Nov. 21, 1966, Hollywood, Calif. Screen actor and stuntman.

ROBERTI, LYDA
Born: 1909, Warsaw, Poland. Died: Mar. 12, 1938, Los Angeles, Calif.(heart ailment). Screen and stage actress.

Appeared in: 1932 Dancers in the Dark; The Kid from Spain; Million Dollar Legs. 1933 Torch Singer; Three-Cornered Moon. 1934 College Rhythm. 1935 George White's 1935 Scandals; The Big Broadcast of 1936. 1937 Nobody's Baby; Pick a Star; Wide Open Faces.

ROBERTS, A. CLEDGE
Born: 1905. Died: June 14, 1957, New York, N.Y. Screen, stage, radio, television actor, film and stage director, and film and stage producer.

ROBERTS, ALBERT G.
Born: 1902. Died: May 30, 1941, North Hollywood, Calif.(suicide-gun). Screen actor and cameraman. Married to screen actress Peggy Shannon (dec. 1941).

ROBERTS, DICK
Born: 1897. Died: Nov. 1, 1966, North Hollywood, Calif. Screen, radio actor, and banjoist.

Appeared in: 1936 Banjo on My Knee.

ROBERTS, EDITH (Edith Josephine Roberts)
Born: 1899, New York, N.Y. Died: Aug. 20, 1935, Los Angeles, Calif. Screen, stage, and vaudeville actress.

Appeared in: 1919 Bill Henry. 1920 The Adorable Savage. 1921 The Fire Cat; The Unknown Wife; White Youth; Thunder Island; Opened Shutters; Luring Lips; In Society. 1922 Saturday Night; Flesh and Blood; A Front Page Story; Pawned; The Son of the

Wolf; Thorns and Orange Blossoms. 1923 The Sunshine Trail; Big Brother; Backbone; The Dangerous Age. 1924 An Age of Innocence; The Bowery Bishop; Roaring Rails; Roulette; Thy Name Is Woman; $20 a Week. 1925 Heir-Loons; New Champion; Shattered Lives; Speed Mad; Three Keys; Wasted Lives; Seven Keys to Baldpate; On Thin Ice. 1926 There You Are; The Mystery Club; The Jazz Girl; The Road to Broadway; Shameful Behavior?; The Taxi Mystery. 1928 Man from Headquarters. 1929 The Phantom of the North; The Wagon Master.

ROBERTS, FLORENCE
Born: 1871. Died: July 17, 1927, Hollywood, Calif. Screen actress. Married to screen actor Frederick Vogeding (dec. 1942).

ROBERTS, FLORENCE
Born: Mar. 16, 1861, Frederick, Md. Died: June 6, 1940, Hollywood, Calif. Screen and stage actress. Married to stage actor Walter Gale (dec.). Appeared in "Jones Family" series, 1936-40.

Appeared in: 1912 Sapho. 1925 The Best People. 1930 Eyes of the World; Soup to Nuts. 1931 Bachelor Apartment; Fanny Foley Herself; Too Many Cooks; Kept Husband; Everything's Rosie. 1932 Make Me a Star; All American; Westward Passage. 1933 Officer 13; Daring Daughters; Dangerously Yours; Melody Cruise; Torch Singer; Hoopla; Ever in My Heart. 1934 Babes in Toyland; Miss Fane's Baby Is Stolen. 1935 Sons of Steel; Les Miserables; The Nut Farm; Rocky Mountain Mystery; Accent on Youth; Harmony Lane; Public Opinion; Your Uncle Dudley. 1936 The Next Time We Love; Nobody's Fool; Every Saturday Night; Educating Father; Back to Nature. 1937 Borrowing Trouble; Nobody's Baby; The Life of Emile Zola; Off to the Races; Big Business; Hot Water. 1938 Love on a Budget; The Storm; A Trip to Paris; Safety in Numbers; Down on the Farm; Personal Secretary. 1939 Everybody's Baby; Jones Family in the Grand Canyon; Jones Family in Hollywood; Too Busy to Work; Quick Millions. 1940 On Their Own; Young as You Feel.

ROBERTS, LEONA
Born: 1880. Died: Jan. 30, 1954, Santa Monica, Calif. Screen actress.

Appeared in: 1937 Border Cafe; There Goes the Groom. 1938 Of Human Hearts; Bringing up Baby; Condemned Women; This Marriage Business; Having a Wonderful Time; The Affair of Annabel; Crime Ring; Kentucky; I Stand Accused. 1939 Persons in Hiding; They Made Her a Spy; Bachelor Mother; The Escape; Swanee River; Gone with the Wind. 1940 Sued for Libel; Thou Shalt Not Kill; Queen of the Mob; The Blue Bird; Abe Lincoln in Illinois; Flight Angels; Ski Patrol; Gangs of Chicago; Golden Gloves; Comin' 'Round the Mountain; Wildcat Bus; Blondie Plays Cupid. 1946 The Madonna's Secret. 1947 Boomerang.

ROBERTS, MERRILL
Born: 1885. Died: Dec. 2, 1940, Hollywood, Calif. Screen actor.

ROBERTS, SARA JANE
Born: 1924. Died: Aug. 19, 1968, Hollywood, Calif. Screen actress. Appeared in "Our Gang" comedies.

ROBERTS, STEPHEN
Born: Nov. 23, 1895, Summerville, Va. Died: July 17, 1936, Beverly Hills, Calif.(heart attack). Screen, radio actor, stuntman, and film director. Entered films as a stuntman after W.W.I; was in early air films and later became an actor, then a director.

ROBERTS, THAYER
Born: 1903. Died: May 1968, Hollywood, Calif. Screen, stage, and vaudeville actor.

Appeared in: 1951 Sky High.

ROBERTS, THEODORE
Born: 1861, San Francisco, Calif. Died: Dec. 14, 1928, Los Angeles, Calif.(uremic poisoning). Screen and stage actor.

Appeared in: 1914 Where the Trail Divides. 1915 The Girl of the Golden West; The Wild Goose Chase. 1916 The Sowers; Pudd'n Head Wilson; The Trail of the Lonesome Pine; Honor Thy Name. 1918 M'Liss; We Can't Have Everything; The Source; Such a Little Pirate; The Squaw Man; War Relief (informational services film). 1919 Don't Change Your Husband; Male and Female; Fire of Faith; The Woman Thou Gavest Me; You're Fired; Secret Service; The Lottery Man; Hawthorne of the U.S.A.; The Roaring Road; Everywoman. 1920 Something to Think About; Judy of Rogue's Harbor; Double Speed. 1921 The Affairs of Anatol; Exit the Vamp; Forbidden Fruit; The Love Special; Miss

Lulu Bett; Too Much Speed; Sham. 1922 Across the Continent; If You Believe It, It's So; The Man Who Saw Tomorrow; Night Life in Hollywood; The Old Homestead; Our Leading Citizen; Saturday Night; Hail the Woman. 1923 Racing Hearts; Stephen Steps Out; To the Ladies; Prodigal Daughters; The Ten Commandments; Grumpy. 1925 Forty Winks; Locked Doors. 1926 Cat's Pajamas. 1928 The Masks of the Devil. 1929 Noisy Neighbors; Ned McCobb's Daughter.

ROBERTSHAW, JERROLD
Born: 1866, England. Died: 1941. Screen and stage actor.

Appeared in: 1918 Dombey and Son. 1921 The Bonnie Brier Bush. 1924 The Arab. 1925 She. 1928 Downhill. 1929 Kitty. 1933 Don Quixote.

ROBERTSON, IMOGENE. See Mary Nolan

ROBERTSON, JAMES "SCOTTY"
Born: 1859. Died: Nov. 13, 1936, Los Angeles, Calif. Screen actor.

ROBERTSON, JEAN
Born: 1894, Australia. Died: Aug. 1967, Sydney, Australia. Screen and stage actress.

Appeared in: 1922 Flesh and Spirit.

ROBERTSON, JOHN S.
Born: June 14, 1878, Ontario, Canada. Died: Nov. 7, 1964, Escondido, Calif. Screen, stage actor, and film director.

Appeared in one film: 1916 An Enemy to the King.

ROBERTSON, MARY. See Mary Nolan

ROBERTSON, ORIE O.
Born: 1881. Died: Apr. 14, 1964, Hollywood, Calif.(cancer). Screen actor and stuntman.

Appeared in: 1926 Bucking the Truth.

ROBERTSON, STUART
Born: Mar. 5, 1901, London, England. Died: Dec. 25, 1958, Elstree, Herts, England. Screen, stage, radio actor, and singer.

Appeared in: 1933 Bitter Sweet. 1935 Peg of Old Drury. 1936 As You Like It; Millions; Splinters in the Air; The Gang Show. 1938 Sixty Glorious Years. 1940 Irene; Queen of Destiny; Rivers End; No, No, Nanette. 1941 A Yank in the R.A.F.; Confirm or Deny; On the Sunny Side. 1942 This above All; The Black Swan. 1943 Forever and a Day. 1945 Meet the Navy (Canadian Naval film).

ROBEY, SIR GEORGE (George Edward Wade)
Born: Sept. 20, 1869, London, England. Died: Nov. 29, 1954, Saltdean, Sussex, England. Screen, stage, radio, television actor, and author.

Appeared in: 1923 The Rest Cure; Don Quixote. 1924 Her Prehistoric Man. 1932 Bindle; The Temperance Fete. 1933 Marry Me; Don Quixote (and 1923 version). 1934 Chu Chin Chow. 1935 Birds of a Feather. 1936 Men of Yesterday; Southern Roses. 1939 A Girl Must Live (U.S. 1941). 1940 Variety Jubilee. 1944 Henry V (U.S. 1946). 1945 The Trojan Bros. 1946 Waltz Time. 1952 The Pickwick Papers (U.S. 1953). 1953 Ali Baba Nights. 1958 Henry V (re-release of 1944 film). Other British films: The Bunting Family; Salute John Citizen.

ROBINSON, BILL "BOJANGLES"
Born: May 25, 1878, Richmond, Va. Died: Nov. 25, 1949, N.Y. (heart ailment). Screen, stage, vaudeville actor, and dancer.

Appeared in: 1930 Dixiana. 1935 The Little Colonel; In Old Kentucky; Hooray for Love; The Big Broadcast of 1936; The Littlest Rebel; Curly Top. 1936 Dimples. 1937 One Mile from Heaven. 1938 Rebecca of Sunnybrook Farm; Road Demon; Just around the Corner; Up the River; Hot Mikado; Cotton Club Revue. 1943 Stormy Weather.

ROBINSON, DEWEY
Born: 1898, New Haven, Conn. Died: Dec. 11, 1950, Las Vegas, Nev.(heart attack). Screen and stage actor.

Appeared in: 1931 Enemies of the Law. 1932 The Woman from Monte Carlo; Cheaters at Play; Law and Order; The Painted Woman; The Big Broadcast; Hat Check Girl; Blonde Venus; Six Hours to Live; Scarlet Dawn; Women Won't Tell; When Paris Sleeps; Captain's Wife. 1933 She Done Him Wrong; A Lady's Profession; Her Forgotten Past; Diplomaniacs; Soldiers of the

Storm; Laughing at Life; Notorious but Nice; Murder on the Campus. 1934 Shadows of Sing Sing; The Big Shakedown; Countess of Monte Cristo; Behold My Wife. 1955 Goin' to Town (short); Pursuit; A Midsummer Night's Dream; His Night Out; Too Young to Kill. 1936 Dangerous Waters; The Return of Jimmy Valentine; All American Chump; Missing Girls; Florida Special; Poppy; Mummy's Boys. 1937 On the Avenue; The Slave Ship; Super Sleuth; Marry the Girl; The Toast of New York, New Faces of 1937; Mama Runs Wild. 1938 Broadway Musketeers; Ride a Crooked Mile; Army Girl. 1939 Forged Passport; Navy Secrets. 1940 The Blue Bird; Diamond Frontier; The Great McGinty; I Can't Give You Anything but Love, Baby; Tin Pan Alley. 1941 The Big Store; Two Yanks in Trinidad; You're the One; Sing for Your Supper. 1942 Rubber Racketeers; The Palm Beach Story; The Big Street; Blondie for Victory; Jail House Blues; Isle of Missing Men; 'Neath Brooklyn Bridge. 1943 Casablanca; The Ghost Ship; The Woman of the Town. 1944 Wilson; Mrs. Parkington; Alaska; When Strangers Marry; Timber Queen; The Chinese Cat; Trocadero. 1945 Hollywood and Vine; There Goes Kelly; Fashion Model; Dillinger; The Lady Confesses; Black Market Babies; Pardon My Past. 1946 Behind the Mask; The Missing Lady. 1947 Mr. Hex; I Wonder Who's Kissing Her Now; The Wistful Widow of Wagon Gap; The Gangster. 1948 Angels' Alley; Fighting Mad; Let's Live Again; The Checkered Coat. 1949 The Beautiful Blonde from Bashful Bend; Hellfire; Tough Assignment; My Friend Irma. 1950 Buccaneer's Girl; At War with the Army.

ROBINSON, FORREST
Born: 1859. Died: Jan. 1924, Los Angeles, Calif. Screen and stage actor.

Appeared in: 1921 Tol'able David. 1922 Tess of the Storm Country. 1923 Adam's Rib; Ashes of Vengeance; The Meanest Man in the World; Souls for Sale. 1924 Good Bad Boy; When a Man's a Man.

ROBINSON, FRANCES (Marion Frances Ladd)
Born: Apr. 26, 1916, Ft. Wadsworth, N.Y. Died: Aug. 15, 1971, Hollywood, Calif.(heart attack). Screen actress.

Appeared in: 1937 Forbidden Valley; Tim Tyler's Luck (serial). 1938 A Letter of Introduction; Secrets of a Nurse; Exposed; The Last Warning; His Exciting Night; Service de Luxe. 1939 Risky Business; Tower of London; The Family Next Door. 1940 Riders of Pasco Basin; So You Won't Talk; Glamour for Sale; The Lone Wolf Keeps a Date; The Invisible Man Returns. 1941 Outlaws of the Panhandle; Smilin' Through; Dr. Jekyll and Mr. Hyde. 1946 The Missing Lady. 1947 Suddenly It's Spring. 1949 Backfire (U.S. 1950—aka Somewhere in the City). 1964 Bedtime Story; Kitten with a Whip; The Lively Set. 1967 The Happiest Millionaire.

ROBINSON, GERTRUDE R.
Born: 1891. Died: Mar. 19, 1962, Hollywood, Calif. Screen actress. Entered films with Biograph approx. 1909. Divorced from screen actor James Kirkwood (dec. 1963).

Appeared in: 1909 Pippa Passes; The Open Gate; The Death Disc. 1910 Gold Is Not All; The Purgation; What the Daisy Said; A Summer Idyll; Examination Day at School. 1913 Judith of Bethulia. 1922 Welcome to Our City. 1925 On Thin Ice.

ROBINSON, "SPIKE"
Born: 1884. Died: July 13, 1942, Maywood, Calif.(heart attack). Screen actor.

Appeared in: 1920 Daredevil Jack (serial). 1921 The Foolish Age. 1923 Boston Blackie. 1925 The Fear Fighter.

ROBLES, RICHARD
Born: 1902. Died: Apr. 20, 1940, Los Angeles, Calif. Screen actor.

Appeared in: 1939 Union Pacific.

ROBLES, RUDY
Born: Apr. 28, 1910, Manila, Philippine Islands. Died: Aug. 1970, Manila, Philippine Islands. Screen and stage actor.

Appeared in: 1939 The Real Glory. 1940 South of Pago Pago. 1941 Song of the Islands; Blue, White and Perfect; Blonde from Singapore; The Adventures of Martin Eden. 1942 Submarine Raider; Across the Pacific; Wake Island. 1946 Nocturne. 1947 Singapore; The Son of Rusty. 1949 Rusty Saves a Life; Omoo, Omoo; Flaxy Martin. 1952 Okinawa. 1953 White Goddess.

ROBSON, ANDREW
Born: 1867, Hamilton, Ontario, Canada. Died: Apr. 26, 1921, Los Angeles, Calif.(heart affliction). Screen and stage actor.

Appeared in: 1919 Upstairs and Down. 1920 Alarm Clock Andy; Scratch My Back; Cupid, the Cowpuncher. 1921 All's Fair in Love; Black Roses; Mother O'Mine; One a Minute.

ROBSON, MAY
Born: Apr. 19, 1858, Melbourne, Australia. Miss Robson had her date of birth recorded on casting director's records as being born in 1864. However, at time of her death, birth certificate was found showing she was born in 1858. Died: Oct. 20, 1942, Beverly Hills, Calif. Screen, stage, and radio actress.

Appeared in: 1915 How Molly Made Good. 1926 Pals in Paradise. 1927 The Angel of Broadway; A Harp in Hock; The Rejuvenation of Aunt Mary (film and stage versions); Rubber Tires; King of Kings. 1928 Chicago; The Blue Danube; Turkish Delight. 1931 Mother's Millions; She Wolf. 1932 If I Had a Million; Letty Lynton; Two against the World; The Engineer's Daughter; Little Orphan Annie; Red Headed Woman; Strange Interlude. 1933 Men Must Fight; The White Sister; Reunion in Vienna; Dinner at Eight; Beauty for Sale; Broadway to Hollywood; The Solitaire Man; Dancing Lady; Lady for a Day; One Man's Journey; Alice in Wonderland. 1934 You Can't Buy Everything; Straight Is the Way; Lady by Choice. 1935 Vanessa, Her Love Story; Reckless; Age of Indiscretion; Anna Karenina; Grand Old Girl; Strangers All; Mills of the Gods; Three Kids and a Queen. 1936 Wife vs. Secretary; The Baxter Millions; The Captain's Kid; Rainbow on the River. 1937 Woman in Distress; A Star Is Born; Rhythm of the River; The Perfect Specimen; Top of the Town. 1938 The Adventures of Tom Sawyer; Bringing up Baby; The Texans; Four Daughters. 1939 They Made Me a Criminal; Yes, My Darling Daughter; That's Right—You're Wrong; Daughters Courageous; Four Wives; The Kid from Kokomo; Nurse Edith Cavell. 1940 Irene; Granny Get Your Gun; Texas Rangers Ride Again. 1941 Four Mothers; Million Dollar Baby; Playmates. 1942 Joan of Paris.

ROBYN, GAY
Born: 1912. Died: July 25, 1942, Hollywood, Calif. Screen actress and dancer.

ROBYNS, WILLIAM
Born: 1855. Died: Jan. 22, 1936, Verdugo Hills, Calif. Screen and stage actor.

Appeared in: 1921 Get-Rich-Quick Wallingford. 1923 The Fair Cheat. 1932 The Expert; Hell Fire Austin. 1934 Elmer and Elsie.

ROCHA, MIGUEL F.
Born: Argentina. Died: Mar. 6, 1961, Buenos Aires, Argentine. Screen and stage actor.

ROCHE, FRANKLYN D. "FRANK"
Born: 1904. Died: Nov. 20, 1963, Burbank, Calif. Screen and stage actor. Entered films approx. 1930.

Appeared in: 1960 The Prime Time.

ROCHE, JOHN
Born: Feb. 6, 1896, Penn Yan, N.Y. Died: Nov. 10, 1952, Los Angeles, Calif.(stroke). Screen and stage actor.

Appeared in: 1922 The Good Provider. 1923 Bag and Baggage; Lucretia Lombard. 1924 Cornered; Flowing Gold; Her Marriage Vow; K—The Unknown; A Lost Lady; The Tenth Woman. 1925 Bobbed Hair; The Love Hour; A Broadway Butterfly; Kiss Me Again; Marry Me; My Wife and I; Recompense; Scandal Proof. 1926 The Return of Peter Grimm; Don Juan; Her Big Night; The Man Upstairs; Midnight Lovers. 1927 The Truthful Sex; Uncle Tom's Cabin. 1928 Their Hour; Diamond Handcuffs. 1929 Unholy Night; The Dream Melody; The Donovan Affair; The Awful Truth; This Thing Called Love. 1930 Sin Takes a Holiday; Monte Carlo. 1932 Winner Take All; Prosperity; The Cohens and the Kellys in Hollywood. 1933 Beauty for Sale. 1935 Just My Luck. 1959 Uncle Tom's Cabin (re-release of 1927 film).

ROCHIN, PAUL
Born: 1889. Died: May 5, 1964, Hollywood, Calif. Screen actor.

ROCKWELL, MARY. See Mary Rockwell Hummell

RODERICK, LESLIE
Born: 1907. Died: Aug. 16, 1927, Hollywood, Calif.(pneumonia). Screen actress and dancer.

RODGERS, WALTER
Born: 1887. Died: Apr. 24, 1951, Los Angeles, Calif.(following stroke). Screen actor.

Appeared in: 1917 The Fighting Trail (serial); Vengeance and the Woman (serial). 1918 A Fight for Millions (serial). 1919 Smashing Barriers (serial). 1921 Flower of the North; The Secret of the Hills; The Silver Car; The Son of Wallingford; Steelheart. 1922 They Like 'Em Rough. 1925 Rugged Water. 1926 The Flaming Frontier. 1927 The Heart of Maryland; Irish Hearts; Wolf's Clothing.

RODNEY, EARLE
Born: 1891. Died: Dec. 16, 1932, Los Angeles, Calif.(pneumonia). Screen, stage, vaudeville actor, screenwriter, and film director. Played screen parts with Sennett and Griffith and was a comedy director of Keystone Kop series.

Appeared in: 1915 Crooked to the End. 1916 The Village Vampire (working title The Great Leap); An Oily Scandal. 1917 The Nick of Time Baby; Secrets of a Beauty Parlor. 1920 A Roman Scandal. 1923 Winter Has Came.

RODNEY, JACK
Born: 1916. Died: Feb. 20, 1967, England (rheumatic fever). Screen, stage, and television actor.

Appeared in: 1960 The Concrete Jungle (aka The Criminal-U.S. 1962). 1964 The Devilship; Pirates. Other British films: The Horse without a Head; The Cracksman.

RODRIGUEZ, ESTELITA
Born: July 2, 1915, Guanajay, Cuba. Died: May 12, 1966. Screen, stage, radio actress, and night club performer.

Appeared in: 1945 Along the Navajo Trail; Mexicana. 1947 On the Spanish Trail. 1948 The Gay Ranchero; Old Los Angeles. 1949 Susanna Pass; The Golden Stallion. 1950 Belle of Old Mexico; Federal Agent at Large; Sunset in the West; Hit Parade of 1951; California Passage; Twilight in the Sierras. 1951 Cuban Fireball; In Old Amarillo; Havana Rose; Pals of the Golden West. 1952 The Fabulous Senorita; Tropical Heat Wave; South Pacific Trail. 1953 Tropic Zone; Sweethearts on Parade. 1959 Rio Bravo. 1966 Jesse James Meets Frankenstein's Daughter.

ROGERS, CARL D.
Born: 1900. Died: Mar. 1965, Humble, Tex. Child screen actor. Appeared in early "Our Gang" comedies and Keystone comedies.

ROGERS, JOSEPH
Born: 1871. Died: Dec. 29, 1942, Hollywood, Calif. Screen actor.

ROGERS, RENA
Born: 1901. Died: Feb. 19, 1966, Santa Monica, Calif. Screen and vaudeville actress.

Appeared in: 1916 Where Are My Children?

ROGERS, WILL
Born: Nov. 4, 1879, Colagah, U.S. Cherokee Indian Territory. Died: Aug. 15, 1935, near Barrow, Alaska (airplane crash). Screen, vaudeville actor, screenwriter, author, and journalist. Father of screen actor Will Rogers, Jr.

Appeared in: 1918 Laughing Bill Hyde (film debut). 1919 Almost a Husband; Jubilo. 1920 Jes' Call Me Jim; Cupid, the Cowpuncher. 1921 Honest Hutch; Guile of Women; Boys Will Be Boys; An Unwilling Hero; Doubling for Romeo. 1922 A Poor Relation; The Headless Horseman; One Glorious Day. 1923 Hollywood; Fruits of Faith. 1927 A Texas Steer. 1929 They Had to See Paris. 1930 Happy Days; So This Is London; Lightnin'. 1931 Young as You Feel; A Connecticut Yankee; Ambassador Bill; The Plutocrat. 1932 Business and Pleasure; Down to Earth; Too Busy to Work. 1933 State Fair; Doctor Bull; Mr. Skitch. 1934 Judge Priest; David Harum; Handy Andy; Hollywood on Parade (short). 1935 Life Begins at Forty; The County Chairman; Steamboat 'Round the Bend; In Old Kentucky; Doubting Thomas. 1957 Golden Age of Comedy (documentary).

ROLAND, FREDERICK
Born: 1886. Died: June 2, 1936, Los Angeles, Calif. Screen and stage actor.

Appeared in: 1935 The Rainmakers.

ROLAND, MARION. See Marion Ross

ROLAND, RUTH
Born: Aug. 26, 1892, San Francisco, Calif. Died: Sept. 22, 1937, Los Angeles, Calif.(cancer). Screen, vaudeville, and radio actress. Entered films in 1911. Appeared in "Ruth Roland" series. Married to actor Ben Bard.

Appeared in: 1911 A Chance Shot. 1912 Ruth Roland, the Kalem Girl; Hypnotic Nell; Ranch Girls on a Rampage. 1913 While Father Telephoned. 1914 Ham, the Piano Mover. 1915 The Red Circle (serial); Comrade John. 1917 The Neglected Wife (serial). 1918 Hands Up; Who Wins? (made in 1916, but released in 1918 retitled Price of Folly). 1919 The Tiger's Trail (serial); The Adventures of Ruth (serial); Love and the Law. 1920 Ruth of the Rockies (serial); What Would You Do? 1921 The Avenging Arrow (serial). 1922 White Eagle (serial); Timber Queen (serial). 1923 Haunted Valley (serial); Ruth of the Range (serial). 1925 Dollar Down; Where the Worst Begins. 1926 The Masked Woman. 1930 Reno. 1936 From Nine to Nine. 1961 Days of Thrills and Laughter (documentary).

ROLDAN, ENRIQUE (Andres Garcia)
Born: 1901, Argentina. Died: Feb. 4, 1954, Buenos Aires, Argentina (accidentally slipped under wheels of train). Screen and stage actor.

Appeared in: 1940 Oro Entre Barro (Gold in Clay).

ROLLAND, JEAN-CLAUDE
Born: 1933. Died: Apr. 1967 (suicide-hanging). Screen, stage, and television actor.

ROLLETT, RAYMOND
Born: 1907, England. Died: Dec. 19, 1961, London, England. Screen and stage actor.

Appeared in: 1949 Master of Bankdam. 1956 The Angel Who Pawned Her Harp. 1957 The Curse of Frankenstein; Men of Sherwood Forest. 1958 Blue Murder at St. Trinian's.

ROLLINS, DAVID
Born: Sept. 2, 1908, Kansas City, Mo. Died: Nov. 10, 1952. Screen actor.

Appeared in: 1927 Win That Girl; High School Hero. 1928 Thanks for the Buggy Ride; The Air Circus; Prep and Pep; Riley the Cop. 1929 Fox Movietone Follies of 1929; Love, Live and Laugh; The Black Watch; Why Leave Home? 1930 Happy Days; The Big Trail. 1931 Young Sinners; Girls Demand Excitement; Morals for Women. 1932 The Phantom Express; prior to 1933 the following Roach shorts: Papa Loves Mama; The Kickoff; Rogers and Hall; Personality Kid.

ROLLOW, PRESTON, J.
Born: 1871. Died: May 1947, N.Y. Screen and stage actor. Appeared in silents.

ROMA, CLARICE (Roma Hann)
Born: 1902. Died: May 3, 1947, Hollywood, Calif. Screen and stage actress.

ROMANO, JOHN
Born: 1896. Died: July 24, 1957, Hollywood, Calif. Screen and stage actor.

ROMANOFF, MICHAEL (aka PRINCE DIMITRI ROMANOFF OBOLENSKI, GRAND DUKE MICHAEL ROMANOFF and HARRY GERGUSON)
Born: 1890? or 1893?, Russia?; Brooklyn, N.Y. Died: Sept. 1, 1971, Los Angeles, Calif.(heart attack). Restaurateur and screen actor.

Appeared in: 1948 Arch of Triumph; An Innocent Affair. 1953 Paris Model. 1964 Goodbye, Charlie. 1965 Do Not Disturb. 1967 A Guide for the Married Man; Caprice.

ROME, STEWART (Septimus Wernham Ryott)
Born: Jan. 30, 1886, Newbury, Berkshire, England. Died: Feb. 26, 1965, Newbury, England. Screen and stage actor. Was a pioneer silent star in Britain.

Appeared in: 1906 Justice (film debut). 1924 The Desert Sheik. 1925 The Prodigal Son. 1926 The Silver Treasure; Sweet Lavender. 1927 Gentleman Rider. 1928 Thou Fool. 1929 The Ware Case; The Crimson Circle; Dark Red Roses. 1930 The Man Who Changed His Name. 1933 Designing Woman. 1934 The Girl in the Flat; Men of Yesterday. 1937 Murder on Diamond Row; Wings of the Morning; Dinner at the Ritz; The Squeaker. 1941 Banana Ridge. 1942 One of Our Aircraft Is Missing. 1947 The White Unicorn. 1949 Woman Hater. Other British films: Confidential Lady; Jassy; High Pavement; The Last Hour; Kissing-Cup's Race; Deadlock; Rynox; The Great Gay Road; The Marriage Bond; Other People's Sins; House of Dreams; Song of the Plough; Lest We Forget; Reunion; Temptation; Comin' Thru the Rye; The White Hope; Betrayal.

ROMEA, ALBERTO
Born: 1883, Spain. Died: Apr. 24, 1960, Madrid, Spain. Screen, stage, radio, television actor, and manager.

ROMER, LEILA
Born: 1878. Died: Feb. 10, 1944, Hollywood, Calif.(heart attack). Screen, stage, and vaudeville actress.

Appeared in: 1919 Anne of Green Gables.

ROMER, TOMI
Born: 1924. Died: July 21, 1969, New York, N.Y. Screen actress and stage, and television actress.

ROMERO, FLORITA
Born: 1931. Died: Feb. 6, 1961, Hollywood, Calif. Screen dancer.

ROMEYN, JANE
Born: 1901. Died: May 5, 1963, Hollywood, Calif. Screen, stage, and television actress.

ROONER, CHARLES
Born: 1901, Vienna, Austria. Died: Nov. 22, 1954, Mexico City, Mexico (heart attack). Screen, stage actor, and film director. Entered films in 1934.

Appeared in: 1944 La Dama de las Camelias. 1948 The Pear; Sofia. 1953 Plunder of the Sun.

ROONEY, PAT
Born: July 4, 1880, New York, N.Y. Died: Sept. 9, 1962, New York, N.Y. Screen and vaudeville actor. Married to stage actress Marian Bent.

Appeared in: 1924 Show Business. 1933 Universal short products. 1948 Variety Time.

ROONEY, PAT (Fred E. Ratsch)
Born: 1891. Died: Jan. 15, 1933, Hollywood, Calif.(lung abscess). Screen, stage, and vaudeville actor. Entered films with Essanay Co. in Chicago. Divorced from screen actress Grace Darling.

ROOPE, FAY
Born: 1893. Died: Sept. 13, 1961, Port Jefferson, N.Y. Screen, stage, and television actress.

Appeared in: 1951 You're in the Navy Now (aka U.S.S. Teakettle); The Day the Earth Stood Still; The Frogmen; Callaway Went Thataway. 1952 Young Man with Ideas; Washington Story; Viva Zapata!; The Brigand; Carbine Williams; Deadline U.S.A.; My Six Convicts. 1953 Down among the Sheltering Palms; All Ashore; The Charge at Feather River; The System; Clipped Wings; The Clown. 1954 Alaska Seas; The Atomic Kid; The Black Dakotas; The Lone Gun; Naked Alibi. 1955 Ma and Pa Kettle at Waikiki. 1956 The Proud Ones; The Rack. 1959 The F.B.I. Story.

ROQUEMORE, HENRY
Born: Mar. 13, 1888, Marshall, Tex. Died: June 30, 1943, Beverly Hills, Calif. Screen and stage actor.

Appeared in: 1927 The Fighting Three; For Ladies Only; Is Your Daughter Safe?; Ladies at Ease. 1928 Law and the Man; Branded Man; Gypsy of the North; City of Purple Dreams; The Oklahoma Kid; The Wagon Show. 1929 Sinners in Love; Stocks and Blondes; Anne against the World. 1930 The Last Dance; Beyond the Rio Grande; Second Honeymoon; The Social Lion; Romance of the West; The Parting of the Trails. 1931 Sporting Chance. 1933 Breed of the Border. 1934 City Limits. 1935 Without Regret; The Misses Stooge (short); Nevada; Powder Smoke Range; Racing Luck; The Singing Vagabond. 1936 The Milky Way; Too Many Parents; Hearts in Bondage. 1937 Battle of Greed; Love Takes Flight. 1938 The Arkansas Traveler; Goodbye Broadway; Young Fugitives; Barefoot Boy. 1939 Exile Express; Babes in Arms. 1941 Pot O'Gold; No Greater Sin. 1942 The Postman Didn't Ring; Broadway; That Other Woman.

RORKE, MARGARET HAYDEN
Born: 1884. Died: Mar. 2, 1969, Hollywood, Calif. Screen and stage actress. Mother of screen actor Hayden Rorke.

ROSAR, ANNIE
Born: 1888. Died: Aug. 1, 1963, Vienna, Austria (heart ailment). Screen and stage actress.

Appeared in: 1922 Ein Hirsekorn Greift. 1937 The World's in Love. 1938 Liebe im Dreiviertel Takt (Love in Waltz Time); Ihr Leibhusar. 1948 The Mozart Story. 1952 The Devil Makes Three. 1953 Marika. 1958 Corinna Darling (aka Beloved Corinna). 1959 Embezzled Heaven; The Life and Loves of Mozart (aka Give Me Your Hand, My Love). 1962 Am Galgen Hangt die Liebe (Love of the Gallows).

ROSAS, FERNANDO
Born: 1915, Mexico. Died: Mar. 1959, Mexico City, Mexico. Screen, stage actor, and singer.

ROSCOE, ALAN
Born: Aug. 23, 1888, Memphis, Tenn. Died: Mar. 8, 1933, Hollywood, Calif. Screen actor.

Appeared in: 1921 The Last of the Mohicans. 1923 The Spoilers. 1924 The Mirage; The Chorus Lady; Flirting with Love. 1925 Before Midnight; The Lure of the Wild; The Girl of Gold; Why Women Love; That Devil Quemado. 1926 The Texas Streak; The Wolf Hunters. 1927 Long Pants; Duty's Reward. 1928 Driftwood; The Sawdust Paradise; Marry the Girl; The Mating Call; Modern Mothers. 1929 The Sideshow; Flight; The Vagabond Lover; Seven Keys to Baldpate; Hurricane; Love in the Desert; The Red Sword. 1930 Call of the West; Rain or Shine; Half Shot at Sunrise; The Fall Guy; Danger Lights; The Pay Off. 1931 The Royal Bed; Dirigible; Subway Express; The Public Defender; Hell Divers. 1932 Ladies of the Jury; Strangers of the Evening; The Last Mile; The Last Man. 1933 The Death Kiss.

ROSE, BLANCHE
Born: 1878, Detroit, Mich. Died: Jan. 5, 1953, Hollywood, Calif. Screen and stage actress. Played in a number of Charlie Chaplin films.

Appeared in: 1921 The Old Swimming Hole. 1922 Smudge; The Barnstormer. 1923 Money, Money, Money. 1928 Satan and the Woman. 1930 Call of the West. 1948 The Paradine Case.

ROSE, HARRY
Born: approx. 1888. Died: Dec. 10, 1962, Hollywood, Calif. Screen, burlesque, vaudeville, and television actor.

ROSE, ZELMA
Born: 1873. Died: Nov. 21, 1933, Los Angeles, Calif.(heart attack). Screen and stage actress. Married to screen actor Col. Reginald Barlow (dec. 1943).

ROSELEIGH, JACK
Born: approx. 1887, Tenn. Died: Jan. 5, 1940 (heart attack). Screen, stage, and radio actor.

Appeared in: 1921 Bare Knuckles; The Light in the Clearing; That Girl Montana; Singing River.

ROSELLE, WILLIAM
Born: 1878. Died: June 1, 1945, N.Y. Screen and stage actor.

Appeared in: 1916 Gloria's Romance (serial). 1919 The Avalanche. 1921 The Black Panther's Cub; The Man Who; Wedding Bells.

ROSEMOND, CLINTON C.
Born: 1883. Died: Mar. 10, 1966, Los Angeles, Calif.(pneumonia-stroke). Negro screen actor.

Appeared in: 1936 Green Pastures. 1937 They Won't Forget; Hollywood Hotel. 1938 The Toy Wife; Young Dr. Kildare. 1939 Stand up and Fight; Golden Boy. 1940 Safari; George Washington Carver. 1941 Blossoms in the Dust. 1942 Yankee Doodle Dandy; Syncopation.

ROSEN, JAMES "JIMMY"
Born: 1885, Russia. Died: June 1, 1940, New York, N.Y. Midget screen and stage actor.

Appeared in: 1931 Alice in Wonderland. 1939 The Wizard of Oz.

ROSENBERG, SARAH
Born: 1874. Died: June 16, 1964, Hollywood, Calif. Screen actress. Entered films in 1913.

ROSENTHAL, HARRY
Born: May 15, 1900, New York or Ireland? Died: May 10, 1953, Hollywood, Calif.(heart attack). Screen, stage, radio actor, pianist, orchestra leader, and composer.

Appeared in: 1930 The Collegiate Model (short). 1939 Wife, Husband and Friend. 1940 Johnny Apollo; Christmas in July; The Great McGinty. 1941 Unfinished Business; Birth of the Blues. 1944 The Miracle of Morgan's Creek; The Great Moment. 1945 The Horn Blows at Midnight.

ROSING, BODIL (Bodil Hammerich)
Born: 1878, Copenhagen, Denmark. Died: Jan. 1, 1942, Hollywood, Calif.(heart attack). Screen and stage actress.

Appeared in: 1925 Pretty Ladies (film debut); Lights of Old Broadway. 1926 The Sporting Lover; It Must Be Love; The City; The Midnight Kiss; The Return of Peter Grimm. 1927 Sunrise; Wild Geese; Blondes by Choice; Stage Madness. 1928 The Big Noise; Out of the Ruins; Wheel of Chance; The Fleet's In; Ladies of the Mob; The Law of the Range; The Port of Missing Girls; The Woman from Moscow. 1929 Eternal Love; Why Be Good?; Betrayal; Broadway Babies; King of the Rodeo. 1930 The Bishop Murder Case; Hello Sister; A Lady's Morals; Oh, What a Man; Soul Kiss; Part Time Wife; All Quiet on the Western Front. 1931 An American Tragedy; Three Who Loved; Surrender. 1932 Downstairs; The Match King. 1933 The Crime of the Century; Ex-Lady; Hallelujah, I'm a Bum; Reunion in Vienna. 1934 King Kelly of the U.S.A.; The Crimson Romance; Mandalay; Little Man, What Now?; The Painted Veil; Such Women Are Dangerous. 1935 Roberta; Four Hours to Kill; A Night at the Ritz; Let 'Em Have It; Thunder in the Night. 1936 Hearts in Bondage. 1937 Michael O'Halloran; Conquest. 1938 The First Hundred Years; You Can't Take It with You. 1939 Confessions of a Nazi Spy; Beasts of Berlin; The Star Maker; Nurse Edith Cavell. 1941 Reaching for the Sun; Marry the Boss's Daughter; No Greater Sin; Man at Large.

ROSLEY, ADRIAN
Born: 1890, Marseilles, France. Died: Mar. 5, 1937, Hollywood, Calif.(heart attack). Screen, stage, and opera actor.

Appeared in: 1933 My Weakness; Girl without a Room. 1934 Bum Voyage (short); Handy Andy; Flying Down to Rio; Viva Villa; Of Human Bondage; The Great Flirtation; Notorious Sophie Lang. 1935 Enter Madame; Death Flies East; Roberta; The Girl from Tenth Avenue; Alibi Ike; Here's to Romance; Metropolitan. 1936 Sins of Man; The Magnificent Brute; The Gay Desperado; The Garden of Allah; Sing Me a Love Song. 1937 Ready, Willing and Able; The King and the Chorus Girl; A Star Is Born.

ROSMER, MILTON (Arthur Milton Lunt)
Born: Nov. 4, 1881, Southport, Lancashire, England. Died: Dec. 7, 1971, Chesham, England. Screen, stage, radio, television actor, and film and stage director. Entered British films in 1912. Married to stage actress Irene Rooke (dec. 1958).

Appeared in: 1921 General John Regan. 1922 The Passionate Friends. 1931 The "W" Plan. 1935 The Phantom Light. 1938 South Riding. 1939 Goodbye, Mr. Chips. 1940 The Lion Has Wings; The Stars Look Down; Ministry of Information. 1941 Atlantic Ferry. 1947 Frieda (U.S. 1949). 1948 The Monkey's Paw. 1949 Fame Is the Spur (U.S. 1952). 1952 The Small Back Room.

ROSS, ANTHONY
Born: 1906, N.Y. Died: Oct. 26, 1955, New York, N.Y. Screen, stage, and television actor.

Appeared in: 1947 Kiss of Death. 1950 The Gunfighter; Between Midnight and Dawn; Perfect Strangers; The Skipper Surprised His Wife; The Flying Missile; The Vicious Years. 1952 On Dangerous Ground. 1953 Girls in the Night; Taxi. 1954 Rogue Cop. 1955 The Country Girl.

ROSS, BARNEY (Barnet David Rosofsky)
Born: 1907, New York, N.Y. Died: Jan. 18, 1967, Chicago, Ill. (cancer of throat). Screen and vaudeville actor, and boxer.

Appeared in: 1962 Requiem for a Heavyweight.

ROSS, BETTY
Born: 1880. Died: Feb. 1, 1947, Hollywood, Calif. Screen actress. Appeared in a number of Tom Mix westerns.

ROSS, CHRIS
Born: 1946. Died: May 5, 1970, Hollywood, Calif. Screen, stage, radio, and television actor.

Appeared in: 1968 How Sweet It Is; Petulia. 1969 Viva Max.

ROSS, CORINNE H.S.
Born: 1879. Died: June 22, 1965, Hollywood, Calif. Screen actress.

Appeared in: 1964 My Fair Lady.

ROSS, MARION (aka MARION ROLAND)
Born: 1898. Died: July 23, 1966, Seattle, Wash.(cancer). Screen, stage, and vaudeville actress.

Appeared in: 1920 Over the Hill. 1954 Forever Female; Secret of the Incas; The Glenn Miller Story. 1956 The Proud and the Profane. 1957 God Is My Partner; Lizzie. 1958 Teacher's Pet. 1960 Operation Petticoat. 1961 Blueprint for Robbery.

ROSS, THOMAS W.
Born: 1875, Boston, Mass. Died: Nov. 14, 1959, Torrington, Conn. Screen and stage actor.

Appeared in: 1921 Fine Feather's; Without Limit. 1926 The Only Son. 1940 Seventeen; Remember the Night; The Saint's Double Trouble; The Mortal Storm; Phantom Raiders. 1942 King's Row; The Remarkable Andrew.

ROSS, WILLIAM
Born: 1925. Died: Feb. 25, 1963, Pittsburgh, Pa.(heart attack). Screen, stage, and radio actor.

ROSSON, ARTHUR H.
Born: Aug. 24, 1889, London, England. Died: June 17, 1960, Los Angeles, Calif. Screen actor, film and stage director, screenwriter, and stuntman. Entered films as actor and stuntman.

ROTH, "SANDY" (Sanford L. Roth)
Born: 1889. Died: Nov. 4, 1943, Beverly Hills, Calif.(heart attack). Screen, vaudeville actor, and assistant film director. Entered films as an actor with Mack Sennett in 1916.

Appeared in: 1932 The Beast of the City; Hell's Highways. 1933 Midnight Mary.

ROTMUND, ERNST
Born: 1887, Germany. Died: Mar. 2, 1955, Munich, Germany. Screen, stage, and radio actor.

Appeared in: 1935 Aufforderung zum Tanz (Invitation to the Dance).

ROUSE, HALLOCK
Born: 1897. Died: Jan. 2, 1930, over Pacific Ocean (airplane accident). Screen actor and film aviator.

Appeared in: 1929 Behind That Curtain.

ROWAN, DONALD W.
Born: 1906. Died: Feb. 17, 1966, Rocky Hill, Conn.(cerebral hemorrhage). Screen and television actor.

Appeared in: 1935 Whipsaw. 1936 And Sudden Death; The Arizona Raiders; The Return of Sophie Lang; Murder with Pictures; Wives Never Know. 1937 When's Your Birthday?; The Devil's Playground; The Affairs of Cappy Ricks; Sea Racketeers. 1938 Racket Busters; Wanted by the Police. 1939 Tough Kid. 1940 Brother Orchid.

ROWAN, ERNEST
Born: 1886. Died: Sept. 30, 1960, Hampton, Va. Screen and stage actor. Entered films approx. 1925.

ROWLAND, JAMES G.
Died: Nov. 27, 1951, Philadelphia, Pa. Screen, stage, vaudeville, and radio actor. Married to actress Ethel Ellet, with whom he appeared in vaudeville.

ROWLANDS, ART
Born: 1898. Died: May 25, 1944, Hollywood, Calif. Screen stunt actor.

Appeared in: 1928 The Black Pearl; Devil's Tower; Mystery Valley; Lightnin' Shot. 1929 Synthetic Sin. 1934 The Live Ghost (short). 1936 Ants in the Pantry (short).

ROY, DAN. See Ernie Lotinga

ROY, HARRY
Born: 1904. Died: Jan. 30, 1971, London, England. Bandleader, screen actor, and song writer.

Appeared in: 1940 Everything Is Rhythm.

ROYCE, FORREST "FROSTY"
Born: 1911. Died: May 15, 1965, Hollywood, Calif.(heart attack). Screen stuntman and double for Bill Boyd in "Hopalong Cassidy" films.

ROYCE, LIONEL
Born: Mar. 30, 1891, Dolina, Poland. Died: Apr. 1, 1946, Manila, Philippine Islands (touring with U.S.O.). Screen and stage actor.

Appeared in: 1937 Marie Antoinette (film debut). 1939 Six Thousand Enemies; Confessions of a Nazi Spy; Pack up Your Troubles; Nurse Edith Cavell; Conspiracy. 1940 The Son of Monte Cristo; The Man I Married; Four Sons; Victory. 1941 So Ends Our Night. 1942 The Lady Has Plans; My Favorite Spy; My Favorite Blonde. 1943 Mission to Moscow; Secret Service in Darkest Africa (serial); Let's Face It; Cross of Lorraine; Bomber's Moon. 1944 Seventh Cross; The Hitler Gang. 1945 Tarzan and the Amazons; White Pongo. 1946 Gilda.

ROYCE, ROSITA
Born: 1918, Lincoln, Neb. Died: Sept. 24, 1954, Miami, Fla. Screen, vaudeville, and burlesque actress.

ROYCE, VIRGINIA
Born: 1932. Died: July 8, 1962, Hollywood, Calif.(cerebral hemorrhage). Screen actress.

Appeared in: 1963 The Caretakers.

ROYER, HARRY "MISSOURI"
Born: 1889. Died: Aug. 1, 1951, Hollywood, Calif.(heart attack). Screen and stage actor.

Appeared in: 1926 The Block Signal; Sky High Corral.

ROYSTON, JULIUS
Died: July 1, 1935, Johannesburg, South Africa (bronchial pneumonia). Screen and stage actor. Appeared in films made in South Africa.

RUB, CHRISTIAN
Born: Apr. 13, 1887, Austria. Died: 1956. Screen actor.

Appeared in: 1932 Silver Dollar, Secrets of the French Police; The Trial of Vivienne Ware; The Man from Yesterday. 1933 Humanity; Mary Stevens, M.D.; The Kiss behind the Mirror. 1934 The Fountain; Music in the Air; Romance in the Rain; No Ransom; No More Women; No Greater Glory; Man of Two Worlds; Little Man, What Now? 1935 Metropolitan; A Dog of Flanders; We're Only Human; Stolen Harmony; Peter Ibbetson; Oil for the Lamps of China; Hitchhike Lady. 1936 Murder on the Bridal Path; Parole; Sins of Man; Mr. Deeds Goes to Town; Girl's Dormitory; Suzy; Next Time We Love; Dracula's Daughter; Murder with Pictures. 1937 One Hundred Men and a Girl; Cafe Metropole; Outcast; When Love Is Young; Tovarich; Heidi. 1938 You Can't Take It with You; Mad about Music; The Great Waltz; Professor Beware; I'll Give a Million. 1939 Never Say Die; Forged Passport; Everything Happens at Night. 1940 The Swiss Family Robinson; Pinocchio (voice of Gepetto); Four Sons; Earthbound. 1941 Father's Son; The Big Store. 1942 Berlin Correspondent; Tales of Manhattan; Dangerously They Live. 1944 The Adventures of Mark Twain; Three Is a Family. 1945 Strange Confession. 1948 Fall Guy. 1952 Something for the Birds.

RUBEN, JOSE
Born: 1889, Paris, France. Died: Apr. 28, 1969, N.Y. Screen, stage actor, stage director, and playwright.

Appeared in: 1922 The Man from Home. 1923 Dark Secrets. 1925 Salome of the Tenements.

RUBENS, ALMA (Alma Smith)
Born: 1897, San Francisco, Calif. Died: Jan. 23, 1931, Los Angeles, Calif.(pneumonia). Screen and stage actress. Divorced from screen actor Ricardo Cortez.

Appeared in: 1916 Intolerance. 1917 Firefly of Tough Luck. 1918 Madame Sphinx. 1919 Restless Souls. 1920 The World and His Wife; Humoresque. 1921 Thoughtless Women. 1922 Find the Woman; Valley of Silent Men. 1923 Under the Red Robe; The Enemies of Women. 1924 Cytherea; The Price She Paid; Gerald Cranston's Lady; Is Love Everything?; The Rejected Woman; Week-End Husbands. 1925 Fine Clothes; The Dangers; East Lynne; She Wolves; The Winding Stair; A Woman's Faith. 1926 The Gilded Butterfly; Marriage License; Siberia. 1927 The Heart of Salome. 1928 Masks of the Devil. 1929 Showboat; She Goes to War.

RUBIN, PEDRO
Born: Mexico. Died: Apr. 17, 1938, Mexico City, Mexico. Star of Mexican stage and screen and also appeared in several Florenz Ziegfeld productions.

RUBIOLA, JOE
Born: 1906, San Antonio, Tex. Died: Sept. 6, 1939, Mexico City, Mexico. Screen actor.

RUDAMI, ROSA
Born: 1899. Died: Feb. 2, 1966, Albany, N.Y. Screen actress.

Appeared in: 1925 The Wedding Song. 1926 A Poor Girl's Romance; The Lily.

RUFART, CARLOS
Born: 1887, Spain. Died: Apr. 1957, Madrid, Spain. Screen, stage actor, and singer.

RUFFO, TITTA (Ruffo Capero Titta)
Born: 1877, Pisa, Italy. Died: July 6, 1953, Florence, Italy (heart attack). Screen and opera actor. Appeared in Metro Movietone shorts.

RUGGLES, CHARLES (Charles Sherman Ruggles)
Born: Feb. 8, 1890, Los Angeles, Calif. Died: Dec. 23, 1970, Santa Monica, Calif.(cancer). Screen, stage, vaudeville, radio, and television actor.

Appeared in: 1915 Peer Gynt. 1923 The Heart Raider. 1928 Wives; Etc.(short). 1929 Gentlemen of the Press; The Lady Lies; The Battle of Paris. 1930 Young Man of Manhattan; Roadhouse Nights; Queen High; Charley's Aunt; Her Wedding Night. 1931 The Girl Habit; The Beloved Bachelor; Honor among Lovers; The Smiling Lieutenant; The Lawyer's Secret. 1932 One Hour with You; This Is the Night; The Night of June 13th; Trouble in Paradise; Evenings for Sale; Love Me Tonight; 70,000 Witnesses; Husband's Holiday; This Reckless Age; Make Me a Star; Madame Butterfly; If I Had a Million. 1933 Murders in the Zoo; Terror Aboard; Mama Loves Papa; Girl without a Room; Alice in Wonderland; Melody Cruise. 1934 Melody in Spring; Murder in the Private Car; Friends of Mr. Sweeney; Six of a Kind; Pursuit of Happiness; Goodbye Love. 1935 Ruggles of Red Gap; People Will Talk; The Big Broadcast of 1936; No More Ladies. 1936 Anything Goes; Early to Bed; Wives Never Know; Mind Your Own Business; Hearts Divided; The Preview Murder Mystery. 1937 Turn off the Moon; Exclusive. 1938 Bringing up Baby; Service de Luxe; His Exciting Night; Breaking the Ice. 1939 Yes, My Darling Daughter; Invitation to Happiness; Boy Trouble; Sudden Money; Night Work; Balalaika. 1940 The Farmer's Daughter; Opened by Mistake; Maryland; Public Deb No. 1; No Time for Comedy. 1941 The Invisible Woman; Model Wife; Honeymoon for Three; The Perfect Snob; Go West, Young Lady; The Parson of Panamint. 1942 Friendly Enemies. 1943 Dixie Dugan. 1944 Our Hearts Were Young and Gay; The Doughgirls; Three Is a Family. 1945 Bedside Manner; Incendiary Blonde. 1946 The Perfect Marriage; Gallant Journey; A Stolen Life; My Brother Talks to Horses. 1947 It Happened on Fifth Avenue; Ramrod. 1948 Give My Regards to Broadway. 1949 The Loveable Cheat; Look for the Silver Lining. 1961 The Pleasure of His Company; The Parent Trap; All in a Night's Work. 1963 Son of Flubber; Papa's Delicate Condition. 1964 I'd Rather Be Rich. 1966 The Ugly Dachshund; Follow Me, Boys!

RUIZ, JOSE RIVERO
Born: 1896. Died: Dec. 27, 1948, Madrid, Spain. Screen and stage actor. Appeared in first talkie in Spain in 1936.

RUMAN, SIEGFRIED (Siegfried Albon Rumann)
Born: 1885, Hamburg, Germany. Died: Feb. 14, 1967, Julian, Calif.(heart attack). Screen, stage, and television actor.

Appeared in: 1929 The Royal Box. 1934 Marie Galante; The World Moves On; Servants' Entrance. 1935 The Wedding Night; Under Pressure; Spring Tonic; The Farmer Takes a Wife; A Night at the Opera; Ease of Java. 1936 The Princess Comes Across; The Bold Caballero; I Loved a Soldier. 1937 On the Avenue; Dead Yesterday; Seventh Heaven; Midnight Taxi; Think Fast, Mr. Moto; This Is My Affair; Love under Fire; Thin Ice; Lancer Spy; Heidi; Thank You, Mr. Moto; Maytime A Day at the Races; The Great Hospital Mystery; Nothing Sacred. 1938 Paradise for Three; The Great Waltz; The Saint in New York; I'll Give a Million; Girls on Probation; Suez. 1939 Never Say Die; Honolulu; Remember?; Confessions of a Nazi Spy; Only Angels Have Wings; Ninotchka. 1940 Dr. Ehrlich's Magic Bullet; Outside the Three-Mile Limit; I Was an Adventuress; Four Sons; Victory; So Ends Our Night; That Bitter Sweet; Comrade X. 1941 That Uncertain Feeling; The Man Who Lost Himself; The Wagons Roll at Night; Shining Victory; Love Crazy; World Premiere; This Woman Is Mine. 1942 Remember Pearl Harbor; Crossroads; Enemy Agents Meet Ellery Queen; Berlin Correspondent; China Girl; Desperate Journey; To Be or Not to Be. 1943 Tarzan Triumphs; They Came to Blow up America; Sweet Rosie O'Grady; Government Girl. 1944 Summer Storm; The Devil's Brood; Goodbye My Love; The Hitler Gang; It Happened Tomorrow; The Song of Bernadette. 1945 She Went to the Races; A Royal Scandal; House of Frankenstein; The Dolly Sisters; The Men in Her Diary. 1946 Faithful in My Fashion; Night and Day; A Night in Casablanca. 1947 Mother Wore Tights. 1948 If You Knew Susie; Give My Regards to Broadway; The Emperor Waltz. 1949 Border Incident. 1950 Father Is a Bachelor. 1951 On the Riviera. 1952 O. Henry's Full House; The World in His Arms. 1953 Ma and Pa Kettle on Vacation; Houdini; Stalag 17. 1954 The Glenn Miller Story; White Christmas; Living It Up; Three-Ring Circus. 1955 Many Rivers to Cross; The Spy Chasers; Carolina Cannonball. 1957 The Wings of Eagles. 1962 The Errand Boy. 1964 Robin and the Seven Hoods; 36 Hours. 1966 The Fortune Cookie; The Last of the Secret Agents.

RUSS, PAULA (Pauline Ignatiev)
Born: 1893. Died: Mar. 14, 1966, Los Angeles, Calif. Screen actress.

RUSSELL, ANN (Audrey Ann Dosch)
Died: July 31, 1955, Burbank, Calif.(plane crash, which also killed actor Robert Francis). Screen actress and bit player.

RUSSELL, BILLY
Born: England. Died: Dec. 1956, Ealing, London, England. Screen, stage, and vaudeville actor. Resembled Adolph Hitler.

RUSSELL, BYRON
Born: 1884, Ireland. Died: Sept. 1963, New York, N.Y. Screen, stage, and television actor.

Appeared in: 1920 The World and His Wife. 1921 The Family Closet. 1922 Determination. 1924 It Is the Law; Janice Meredith. 1935 Mutiny on the Bounty. 1937 Parnell. 1938 a Vitaphone short. 1939 One Third of a Nation.

RUSSELL, EDD X.
Born: 1878. Died: Nov. 17, 1966, Los Angeles, Calif. Screen, stage, and vaudeville actor. Stand-in for Robert Benchley.

RUSSELL, GAIL
Born: Sept. 23, 1924, Chicago, Ill. Died: Aug. 26, 1961, Los Angeles, Calif. Screen and television actress. Divorced from screen actor Guy Madison.

Appeared in: 1943 Henry Aldrich Gets Glamour (film debut). 1944 Lady in the Dark; The Uninvited; Our Hearts Were Young and Gay. 1945 Salty O'Rourke; The Unseen; Duffy's Tavern. 1946 The Bachelor's Daughters; The Virginian; Our Hearts Were Growing Up. 1947 The Angel and the Badman; Variety Girl; Calcutta. 1948 Moonrise; The Night Has a Thousand Eyes; Song of Adventure; Wake of the Red Witch. 1949 El Paso; Song of India; The Great Dan Patch; Captain China. 1950 The Lawless. 1951 Air Cadet. 1953 Devil's Canyon. 1956 Seven Men from Now. 1957 The Tattered Dress. 1958 No Place to Land. 1961 The Silent Call.

RUSSELL, J. GORDON
Born: 1883. Died: Apr. 21, 1935, Los Angeles, Calif.(heart attack). Screen actor.

Appeared in: 1921 The Sea Lion; Three Word Brand. 1922 His Back against the Wall; Colleen of the Pines; The Kingdom Within; Trail of Hate. 1923 Kindled Courage; The Spoilers; The Scarlet Lily. 1924 Chastity; Hard Hittin' Hamilton; Singer Jim McKee; The Western Wallop; The No-Gun Man. 1925 Easy Going Gordon; Flying Hoofs; Parisian Love; Galloping Jinx; Quicker'n Lightnin'; Hearts and Spurs; A Roaring Adventure; Tumbleweeds; The Sign of the Cactus. 1926 Looking for Trouble. 1927 The Claw; Spurs and Saddles; Uncle Tom's Cabin; Wild Beauty. 1928 Beyond the Sierras; Saddle Mates. 1959 Uncle Tom's Cabin (re-release of 1927 film).

RUSSELL, JEAN
Died: July 8, 1922, New York, N.Y.(suicide). Screen actress.

RUSSELL, LEWIS
Born: 1885. Died: Nov. 12, 1961, Los Angeles, Calif. Screen and stage actor.

Appeared in: 1945 Molly and Me; Hold That Blonde; The Lost Weekend; She Wouldn't Say Yes. 1946 A Night in Casablanca; She Wrote the Book; If I'm Lucky; Cross My Heart. 1947 Jewels of Brandenburg; Ladies' Man; The Trouble with Women; Backlash. 1948 Kiss the Blood off My Hands. 1950 The Underworld Story. 1951 Corky of Gasoline Alley. 1956 The Naked Hills.

RUSSELL, LILLIAN (Helen Louise Leonard)
Born: 1860, Clinton, Iowa. Died: June 5, 1922, Pittsburgh, Pa. Screen, stage, burlesque, and vaudeville actress.

Appeared in: 1915 Wildfire (stage and film versions).

RUSSELL, WILLIAM
Born: Apr. 12, 1886. Died: Feb. 18, 1929, Beverly Hills, Calif. (pneumonia). Screen, stage, vaudeville actor, and film producer.

Appeared in: 1912 The Star of Bethlehem; Lucille. 1913 Robin Hood. 1914 The Straight Road. 1915 The Garden of Lies; The Diamond from the Sky (serial). 1916 The Sequel to the Diamond from the Sky (serial). 1917 The Pride and the Man. 1919 Brass Buttons; Six Feet Four. 1921 High Gear Jeffrey; Bare Knuckles; Challenge of the Law; The Cheater Reformed; Colorado Pluck; Quick Action; The Iron Rider; Children of Night; Singing River; The Roof Tree; Desert Blossoms. 1922 Strength of the Pines; A Self-Made Man; Money to Burn; The Men of Zanzibar; Lady from Longacre; The Great Night; Mixed Faces. 1923 Cursader; Alias the Nightwind; Boston Blackie; Goodbye Girls; Man's Size; Times Have Changed; When Odds Are Even; Anna Christie. 1924 The Beloved Brute. 1925 Before Midnight; Big Pal; My Neighbor's Wife; On Thin Ice; The Way of a Girl. 1926 The Blue Eagle; The Still Alarm; Wings of the Storm. 1927 Brass Knuckles; A Rough Shod Fighter; The Desired Woman; The Girl from Chicago. 1928 Danger Patrol; The Escape; The Head of the Family; The Midnight Taxi; State Street Sadie; Woman Wise. 1929 Girls Gone Wild.

RUTH, BABE (George Herman Ruth)
Born: Feb. 6, 1895, Baltimore, Md. Died: Aug. 16, 1948. Baseball player and screen actor.

Appeared in: 1920 Headin' Home. 1927 Babe Come Home. 1928 Speedy. 1937 a Vitaphone short. 1942 Pride of the Yankees; The Ninth Inning.

RUTH, MARSHALL
Born: Dec. 24, 1898, Marshalltown, Iowa. Died: Jan. 19, 1953, Hollywood, Calif. Screen, stage, and radio actor. Entered films in 1922.

Appeared in: 1926 Her Sacrifice. 1927 Ridin' Luck; Wild Born. 1928 Red Wine; Virgin Lips. 1929 Joy Street; Nix on Dames; The Broadway Melody; Wall Street. 1930 Navy Blues. 1935 False Pretenses. 1936 Wedding Present.

RUYSDAEL, BASIL
Born: 1888. Died: Oct. 10, 1960, Hollywood, Calif. Screen, stage, radio actor, and narrator.

Appeared in: 1929 The Cocoanuts. 1934 Dealers in Death (narr.). 1936 an Educational short. 1937 Vitaphone short. 1949 Colorado Territory; Come to the Stable; Thelma Jordan; The Doctor and the Girl; Pinky. 1950 Broken Arrow; Gambling House; High Lonesome; There's a Girl in My Heart; One Way Street. 1951 Half Angel; My Forbidden Past; People Will Talk; Raton Pass; The Scarf. 1952 Boots Malone; Carrie. 1954 Prince Valiant; The Shanghai Story. 1955 The Blackboard Jungle; Davy Crockett, King of the Wild Frontier; Diane; Pearl of the South Pacific; The Violent Men. 1956 Jubal; These Wilder Years. 1958 The Last Hurrah. 1959 The Horse Soldiers. 1960 The Story of Ruth.

RYAN, ANNIE
Born: 1865. Died: Feb. 14, 1943, Hollywood, Calif. Screen and stage actress.

Appeared in: 1927 The Claw.

RYAN, DICK
Born: 1897. Died: Aug. 12, 1969, Burbank, Calif.(protracted illness). Screen, vaudeville, radio, and television actor. He and his wife Mary teamed in vaudeville act billed as "Dick and Mary."

Appeared in: 1943 The Constant Nymph. 1948 Mr. Peabody and the Mermaid. 1949 Abandoned; Chicken Every Sunday; Jiggs and

Maggie in Jackpot Jitters; Top of the Morning. 1950 Born to Be Bad; For Heaven's Sake. 1951 Guy Who Came Back. 1956 The Search for Bridey Murphy. 1957 The Buster Keaton Story; Wild Is the Wind. 1958 Once upon a Horse.

RYAN, TIM
Born: 1899. Died: Oct. 22, 1956, Hollywood, Calif.(heart attack). Screen, radio, vaudeville, television actor, and screenwriter. Married to screen actress Irene Ryan (dec. 1973) with whom he appeared in vaudeville and radio in an act billed as "Tim and Irene."

Appeared in: 1940 Brother Orchid; I'm Nobody's Sweetheart Now; Private Affairs. 1941 Where Did You Get That Girl?; Lucky Devils; A Man Betrayed; Ice Capades; Public Enemies; Harmon of Michigan; Bedtime Story; Mr. and Mrs. North. 1942 The Man in the Trunk; Stand by for Action; Crazy Legs; Sweetheart of the Fleet; Get Hep to Love. 1943 Hit Parade of 1943; Sarong Girl; The Mystery of the 13th Guest; Riding High; The Sultan's Daughter; Two Weeks to Live; True to Life; Melody Parade; Reveille with Beverly. 1944 Hot Rhythm; Hi, Beautiful; Detective Kitty O'Day; Kansas City Kitty; Shadow of Suspicion; Swingtime Johnny; Crazy Knights. 1945 Swingin' on a Rainbow; Adventures of Kitty O'Day; Fashion Model; Rockin' in the Rockies. 1946 Bringing up Father; Dark Alibi; Wife Wanted. 1947 News Hounds; Blondie's Holiday; Body and Soul. 1948 Jiggs and Maggie in Court; Luck of the Irish; The Golden Eye; Force of Evil; The Shanghai Chest; Jiggs and Maggie in Society; Angels Alley. 1949 Ringside; Joe Palooka in the Counterpunch; Jiggs and Maggie in Jackpot Jitters; Shamrock Hill; Stampede; Sky Dragon; Forgotten Women. 1950 Military Academy with That 10th Avenue Gang; The Petty Girl; Maggie and Jiggs Out West; Humphrey Takes a Chance; Military Academy. 1951 The Cuban Fireball; All That I Have; Win, Place and Show; Crazy over Horses. 1952 Here Come the Marines; Fargo; No Holds Barred. 1953 From Here to Eternity; The Marksman; Private Eyes. 1956 Fighting Trouble. 1957 The Buster Keaton Story.

SABATINI, ERNESTO
Born: 1878, Italy. Died: Oct. 6, 1954, Milan, Italy (heart attack). Screen, stage, radio, and television actor.

Appeared in: 1938 Come le Foglie (Like the Leaves). 1940 Between Two Worlds.

SABEL, JOSEPHINE
Born: 1866, Lawrence, Mass. Died: Dec. 24, 1945, Patchogue, N.Y. Screen and vaudeville actress.

Appeared in: 1932 The March of Time (short).

SABIN, MRS. CATHERINE JEROME
Born: 1879. Died: May 19, 1943, New York, N.Y. Screen and stage actress.

Appeared in: 1925 New Toys.

SABOURET, MARIE
Born: France. Died: July 23, 1960, St. Jean de Luz, France. Screen actress.

Appeared in: 1956 Rififi. 1960 The Would-Be Gentleman.

SABU (Sabu Dastagir)
Born: Mar. 15, 1924, Karapur, Mysore, India. Died: Dec. 2, 1963, Chatsworth, Calif.(heart attack). Screen actor.

Appeared in: 1937 Elephant Boy. 1938 The Drum. 1940 The Thief of Bagdad. 1942 Arabian Nights; The Jungle Book. 1943 White Savage; Screen Snapshot No. 5 (short). 1944 Cobra Woman. 1946 Tangier. 1947 Black Narcissus. 1948 The End of the River; Man-Eater of Kumaon. 1949 Song of India. 1951 Savage Drums. 1954 Hello, Elephant. 1955 Black Panther. 1956 Jungle Hell; Jaguar. 1957 Sabu and the Magic Ring. 1963 Rampage. 1964 A Tiger Walks.

SACK, NATHANIEL
Born: 1882. Died: July 2, 1966, New York, N.Y. Screen, stage, and television actor.

SACKVILLE, GORDON
Died: Aug. 6, 1926, Los Angeles, Calif.(stroke of apoplexy). Screen actor.

Appeared in: 1911 The Best Man Wins. 1915 The Red Circle (serial). 1921 Dr. Jim; The Fighting Lover. 1922 With Stanley in Africa (serial); Any Night. 1923 Slow as Lightning. 1924 The Snob. 1925 Cowboy Courage.

SADLER, CHARLES R.
Born: 1875. Died: Mar. 23, 1950, Los Angeles, Calif. Screen stuntman.

SADLER, DUDLEY, JR.
Died: Sept. 25, 1951, Santa Monica, Calif. Screen actor.

Appeared in: 1947 Boomerang. 1951 Behave Yourself; Lone Star.

SADLER, IAN
Born: 1902, Glasgow, Scotland. Died: July, 1971, London, England. Screen, stage, and radio actor.

ST. CLAIR, MAURICE
Born: 1903. Died: May 9, 1970, Los Angeles, Calif. Screen, vaudeville, and television actor. Billed in vaudeville as half of "St. Clair and Day" team.

Appeared in: 1946 Black Angel.

ST. CLAIR, ROBERT
Born: 1910. Died: June 17, 1967, South Pasadena, Calif. Screen, stage, radio, television actor, screenwriter, and playwright.

ST. CLAIR, YVONNE
Born: 1914. Died: Sept. 22, 1971, Seattle, Wash. Screen, vaudeville actress, and night club dancer.

Appeared in: 1935 Anna Karenina; A Night at the Opera; A Midsummer Night's Dream. 1936 The Great Ziegfeld.

ST. CLAIRE, ADAH
Born: 1854, N.Y. Died: Aug. 16, 1928, Amityville, New York. Screen and stage actress.

ST. DENIS, JOE
Born: 1928. Died: May 15, 1968, Hollywood, Calif.(heart attack). Screen actor.

ST. DENIS, RUTH (Ruth Dennis)
Born: Jan. 20, 1878, Newark, N.J. Died: July 21, 1968, Hollywood, Calif.(heart attack). Dancer, screen, and vaudeville actress.

Appeared in: 1893 Dance. 1916 Intolerance. 1945 Kitty.

ST. HELIER, IVY (Ivy Aitchison)
Born: England. Died: Nov. 8, 1971, London, England. Screen, stage actress, and composer.

Appeared in: 1933 Bitter Sweet. 1948 Dulcimer Street. 1944 Henry the Fifth (U.S. 1946). 1958 Henry the Fifth (reissue of 1944 version).

ST. JOHN, AL "FUZZY" (aka FUZZY Q. JONES)
Born: Sept. 10, 1893, Santa Ana, Calif. Died: Jan. 21, 1963, Vidalia, Ga.(heart attack). Screen and vaudeville actor. Nephew of screen actor Roscoe "Fatty" Arbuckle (dec. 1933).

Appeared in: 1914 All at Sea; Bombs and Bangs; Lover's Luck; He Loved the Ladies; In the Clutches of a Gang; Mabel's Strange Predicament; The Knock-Out (reissued The Pugilist); Our Country Cousin; The Rounders; The New Janitor (reissued The New Porter); Tillie's Punctured Romance. 1915 Our Daredevil Chief; Crossed Love and Swords; Dirty Work in a Laundry (reissued A Desperate Scoundrel); Fickle Fatty's Fall; The Village Scandal; Fatty and the Broadway Stars. 1916 Fatty and Mabel Adrift; He Did and He Didn't (working title Love and Lobsters); His Wife's Mistakes; The Other Man; The Moonshiners; The Stone Age (working title Her Cave Man); The Waiters Ball. 1917 The Butcher Boy; Rough House; His Wedding Night; Fatty at Coney Island; Oh Doctor!; Out West (aka The Sheriff). 1918 The Bell Boy; Goodnight Nurse; Moonshine; The Cook. 1919 A Desert Hero; Backstage; A Country Hero; The Garage. 1920 The Scarecrow (short). 1921 The High Sign (short). 1922 All Wet (short). 1924 Stupid, but Brave (short); The Garden of Weeds. 1925 The Iron Mule (short). 1927 Casey Jones; American Beauty. 1928 Hello Cheyenne; Painted Post. 1929 The Dance of Life; She Goes to War. 1930 Land of Missing Men; The Oklahoma Cyclone; Hell Harbor; Western Knights; Two Fresh Eggs. 1931 Aloha; Son of the Plains; The Painted Desert. 1932 Police Court; Law of the North; Riders of the Desert; Fame Street. 1933 His Private Secretary. 1934 Public Stenographer. 1935 Wanderer of the Wasteland; Bar 20 Rides Again; Law of the 45's. 1936 The Millionaire Kid; West of Nevada; Hopalong Cassidy Returns; Trail Dust. 1937 A Lawman is Born; Outcasts of Poker Flat; Saturday's Heroes; Melody of the Plains; Sing, Cowboy, Sing. 1938 Song and Bullets; The Rangers Roundup; Knight of the Plains; Call of the Yukon; Frontier Scout. 1939 Trigger Pals; She Goes to War. 1940 Friendly

Neighbors; Texas Terrors; Murder on the Yukon; Marked Man.
1941 Billy the Kid's Fighting Pals; The Lone Rider in Ghost
Town; Apache Kid; Lone Rider Ambushed; A Missouri Outlaw;
Billy the Kid Wanted; Billy the Kid's Roundup; The Lone Rider
Fights Back. 1942 Law and Order; Billy the Kid Trapped; Billy
the Kid's Smoking Guns; Jesse James, Jr.; Stagecoach Express;
Arizona Terrors. 1943 My Son, the Hero; Mysterious Rider;
Fugitive of the Plains; The Renegade. 1944 Thundering Gun-
slingers; The Drifter; Law of the Saddle; Wolves of the Range;
Wild Horse Phantom; Oath of Vengeance; Rustler's Hideout;
Fuzzy Settles Down; I'm from Arkansas; Frontier Outlaws. 1945
Lightning Raiders; Stagecoach Outlaws; Gangster's Den; Devil
Riders; Prairie Rustlers; Fighting Bill Carson; Border Bad-
men. 1946 His Brother's Ghost; Gentlemen with Guns; Terrors
on Horseback; Overland Riders; Ghosts of Hidden Valley; Out-
laws of the Plains; Shadows of Death; Prairie Badmen; Blazing
Frontiers; Colorado Serenade. 1947 Ghost Town Renegades;
Fighting Vigilantes; Return of the Lash; Border Feud; Law of the
Lash; Pioneer Justice; Cheyenne Takes Over. 1948 Panhandle
Trail; Code of the Plains; My Dog Shep; Mark of the Lash;
Raiders of Red Rock; Stage to Mesa City; Frontier Fighters. 1949
Dead Man's Gold; Outlaw Country; Son of a Badman; Son of Billy
the Kid; Frontier Revenge. 1960 When Comedy Was King (docu-
mentary). 1961 Days of Thrills and Laughter (documentary).

ST. JOHN, JANE LEE
Born: 1912. Died: Mar. 17, 1957, New York, N.Y. Screen, stage,
and vaudeville actress. Appeared in vaudeville with her sister
Katherine as "Katherine and Jane Lee," a moppet sister team.

Appeared in: 1914 Neptune's Daughter (film debut). 1948 The
Troublemakers.

ST. MAUR, ADELE
Born: 1888. Died: Apr. 20, 1959, Sunnydale, Calif.(leukemia).
Screen and stage actress.

Appeared in: 1933 The Worst Woman in Paris; Broken Dreams.
1935 The Gay Deception; The Melody Lingers On. 1936 The Invisible Ray. 1937 History Is Made at Night. 1952 The Pathfinder. 1953 Little Boy Lost. 1955 Crashout.

ST. PIERRE, CLARA
Born: 1866, Canada. Died: Jan. 30, 1942, Santa Monica, Calif.
Screen and stage actress. Entered films approx. 1922.

SAKALL, S. Z. "CUDDLES" (Szdke Szadall and Eugene Gero
Szakall)
Born: Feb. 2, 1884, Budapest, Hungary. Died: Feb. 12, 1955, Los
Angeles, Calif.(heart attack). Screen, stage, vaudeville actor,
and author. Appeared in films in Germany, Vienna, and Budapest
from 1916 to 1936.

Appeared in: 1916 Suszterherceg; Ujszulott Apa. 1929 Cross-
tadt Schmetterling. 1930 Zwei Herzen im 3/4 Takt (Two Hearts
in Waltz Time); Kopfuber ins. Gluk; Why Cry at Parting?. 1931
Die Faschingsfee; Der Zinker; Die Frau von der man Spricht; Der
Unbekannte Gast; Ihr Junge; Die Schwebende Jungfrau; Ich Heirate
Meinan Mann (aka Her Wedding Night); Meine Cousine aus War-
schau. 1932 Ich will Nicht Wissen; Wer du Bist; Gluk uber Nacht;
Melodie der Liebe; Eine Staht Steht Kopf; Muss Man Sich Gluch
Scheiden Lassen?. 1933 Eine Frau Wie; Scandal in Budapest;
Grossfurstin Alexandra; Mindent a Noert; Az Ellopot Szerda.
1934 Helyet az Oregeknek; Fruhlingsstimmen; Romance in Buda-
pest. 1935 Harom es fel Musketas; Baratsagos Arcot Kerek;
Tagebuch der Geliebten; 4-1/2 Musketiere; Smile, Please. 1936
Mircha. 1938 The Affairs of Maupassant. 1940 It's a Date;
Spring Parade; The Lilac Domino; Florian; My Love Came Back.
1941 Ball of Fire; The Devil and Miss Jones; The Man Who Lost
Himself; That Night in Rio. 1942 Casablanca; Yankee Doodle
Dandy; Seven Sweethearts; Broadway. 1943 Wintertime; Thank
Your Lucky Stars; The Human Comedy. 1944 Hollywood Canteen;
Shine on, Harvest Moon. 1945 The Dolly Sisters; Christmas in
Connecticut; Wonder Man; San Antonio. 1946 Two Guys from
Milwaukee; Never Say Goodbye; The Time, the Place and the Girl;
Cinderella Jones. 1947 Cynthia. 1948 Whiplash; April Showers;
Romance on the High Seas; Embraceable You. 1949 Look for the
Silver Lining; In the Good Old Summertime; My Dream Is Yours;
Oh, You Beautiful Doll; It's a Great Feeling. 1950 Tea for Two;
Daughter of Rosie O'Grady; Montana; A Swing of Glory. 1951 Lul-
laby of Broadway; Sugarfoot; Painting the Clouds with Sunshine;
It's a Big Country. 1953 Small Town Girl. 1954 The Student
Prince. Other German film: Der Stumme von Portici.

SALAS, PACO (Francisco Lago Severino)
Born: 1875. Died: Dec. 24, 1964, Havana, Cuba. Screen, stage,
radio, and television actor.

SALE, CHARLES "CHIC"
Born: 1885, Huron, South Dakota. Died: Nov. 7, 1936, Los Angeles, Calif.(pneumonia). Screen, stage, and vaudeville actor.

Appeared in: 1922 His Nibs. 1924 The New School Teacher. 1929
Marching On. 1931 The Star Witness. 1932 Stranger in Town;
When a Feller Needs a Friend; The Expert; The Hurry Call. 1933
The Chief; Men of America; Lucky Day; Lucky Dog; Dangerous
Crossroads. 1934 an MGM short; Treasure Island. 1935 an MGM
short; Rocky Mountain Mystery. 1936 an MGM short; It's a Great
Life; Man Hunt; The Gentleman from Louisiana; The Man I Marry.
1937 You Only Live Once.

SALE, FRANCES
Born: 1892. Died: Aug. 6, 1969, Hollywood, Calif. Screen and
opera actress. Appeared in silents.

SALISBURY, MONROE
Born: 1876, Angola, N.Y. Died: Aug. 7, 1935, San Bernardino,
Calif.(skull fracture from fall). Screen and stage actor.

Appeared in: 1914 Rose of the Rancho; The Squaw Man. 1915 The
Goose Girl. 1916 Ramona. 1921 The Barbarian. 1922 The Great
Alone. 1930 The Jade Box (serial).

SALTER, HAROLD "HAL"
Died: May 1928, Los Angeles, Calif.(influenza). Screen, stage,
and vaudeville actor.

Appeared in: 1927 The Red Raiders; The Royal American. 1928
The Canyon of Adventure; The Code of the Scarlet.

SALTER, THELMA
Died: Nov. 17, 1953, Hollywood, Calif. Screen actress. Entered
films as a child actress in silents. Married to producer Edward
Kaufman.

Appeared in: 1920 Huckleberry Finn.

SAMBERG, ARNOLD
Born: 1899. Died: May 3, 1936, Alpine, Calif. Screen actor. Appeared in silents. Was stand-in for Joel McCrea.

SAMSON, IVAN
Born: 1895, London, England. Died: May 1, 1963, London, England.
Screen, stage, radio, and television actor.

Appeared in: 1921 March Hare. 1923 Single Handed. 1935 Blos-
som Time; The Student's Romance; Honours Easy; Music Hath
Charms; Experts Opinion; A Woman Alone. 1936 Hail and Fare-
well. 1937 April Romance. 1938 The Rhythm of My Heart. 1942
The Life of Handel. 1943 Flemish Farm. 1945 Waltz Time. 1950
Mrs. Fitzherbert. 1951 The Browning Version; That Winslow
Boy. 1953 Landfall; Three Men and a Girl; Paul Temple Tri-
umphs. 1954 Crest of the Wave (aka Seagulls over Sorrento).
1955 Innocents in Paris. 1959 Libel. Other British film: You Pay
Your Money.

SANBORN, FRED C.
Born: 1899, Mass. Died: Mar. 9, 1961, Cupertino, Calif. Screen,
stage, and vaudeville actor. Billed in vaudeville with Ted Healy
as "Ted Healy and His Racketeers."

Appeared in: 1930 Soup to Nuts. 1943 Crazy House.

SANDS, GEORGE
Born: 1900. Died: Dec. 7, 1933, Hollywood, Calif. Screen actor
and screenwriter.

SANFORD, AGNES
Died: Nov. 27, 1955, Staten Island, N.Y. Screen, stage, and vaudeville actress.

SANFORD, ALBERT, JR. "BERT"
Born: 1893, New York, N.Y. Died: Feb. 10, 1953, New York, N.Y.
Screen actor and film sales executive. Entered films as an actor
with D. W. Griffith at Biograph Studios.

SANFORD, RALPH
Born: May 21, 1899, Springfield, Mass. Died: June 20, 1963, Van
Nuys, Calif.(heart ailment). Screen actor.

Appeared in: 1937 Sea Racketeers; Escape by Night. 1938 If I
Were King; Angels with Dirty Faces; The Great Waltz; The Pa-
tient in Room 18; Give Me a Sailor. 1939 Little Accident; The
Star Maker; They Asked for It; Kid Nightingale. 1940 Alias the
Deacon; Carolina Moon; Three Cheers for the Irish. 1941 High
Sierra. 1942 I Live on Danger; My Favorite Spy; Torpedo Boat.
1943 High Explosive; Ladies' Day; Aerial Gunner. 1944 Lost in a

Harem. 1945 Thunderhead, Son of Flicka; The Bullfighters; High Powered. 1946 They Made Me a Killer; Girl on the Spot; It Shouldn't Happen to a Dog; Sioux City Sue; My Pal Trigger. 1947 Linda, Be Good; Hit Parade of 1947; Copacabana. 1948 Let's Live Again; French Leave; Shaggy; Winner Take All. 1949 Champion. 1950 Cowtown; Father's Wild Game; The Glass Menagerie; Hi-Jacked; Rogue River; Union Station. 1951 Danger Zone; Behave Yourself; My Favorite Spy; Bright Victory; Fort Defiance; Kentucky Jubilee; Let's Make It Legal. 1952 A Girl in Every Port; Somebody Loves Me; Sea Tiger. 1953 Count the Hours. 1954 The Forty Niners. 1955 The Lieutenant Wore Skirts; Night Freight; Shotgun. 1956 Blackjack Ketchum Desperado; Uranium Boom. 1957 All Mine to Give. 1958 Alaska Passage. 1959 The Purple Gang; The Remarkable Mr. Pennypacker. 1960 Cage of Evil.

SANGER, BERT
Born: 1894. Died: Sept. 1969, Blackpool, England. Screen and vaudeville actor. Appeared in "Keystone Kop" comedies.

SANTAMARIE, MANUEL
Born: Spain. Died: Mar. 1960, Mexico City, Mexico. Screen and television actor.

SANTANA, VASCO
Born: 1890, Portugal. Died: Aug. 1958, Lisbon, Portugal. Screen, stage, radio, and television actor.

SANTLEY, FREDERIC
Born: Nov. 20, 1888, Salt Lake City, Utah. Died: May 14, 1953, Hollywood, Calif. Screen, stage, and vaudeville actor. Entered films with Kalem in 1911.

Appeared in: 1930 Leathernecking. 1931 If I Had a Million. 1933 Double Harness; Morning Glory; Walls of Gold. 1934 Such Women Are Dangerous. 1935 George White's 1935 Scandals. 1936 Walking on Air. 1937 This Is My Affair; She's Got Everything. 1938 Topa Topa. 1953 The Farmer Takes a Wife.

SANTLEY, JOSEPH (Joseph Mansfield)
Born: Jan. 10, 1889, Salt Lake City, Utah. Died: Aug. 8, 1971, Los Angeles, Calif. Screen, stage, vaudeville child actor, film director, and film producer. Married stage actress Ivy Sawyer.

SANTSCHI, TOM
Born: 1879. Died: Apr. 9, 1931, Hollywood, Calif.(high blood pressure). Screen and stage actor.

Appeared in: 1909 The Power of the Sultan. 1913 The Adventures of Kathlyn (serial). 1914 The Spoilers. 1917 The Garden of Allah. 1918 The Hell Cat. 1919 Shadows; Little Orphan Annie; The Stronger Vow. 1920 The Cradle of Courage; The North Wind's Malice. 1922 Found Guilty; Two Kinds of Women. 1923 Are You a Failure?; Brass Commandments; Tipped Off; Is Divorce a Failure?; Thundering Dawn. 1924 The Street of Tears; The Plunderer; The Storm Daughter; Life's Greatest Game; Little Robinson Crusoe; The Right of the Strongest. 1925 Barriers Burned Away; Paths to Paradise; The Pride of the Force; The Primrose Path; Beyond the Border; My Neighbor's Wife; Frivolous Sal; The Night Ship; Flaming Love. 1926 The Desert's Toll; Hands across the Border; Three Bad Men; Forlorn River; The Hidden Way; Her Honor, the Governor; My Own Pal; Siberia; No Man's Gold; The Third Degree. 1927 The Adventurous Soul; Eyes of the Totem; When a Man Loves; The Cruise of the Hellion; The Haunted Ship; Hills of Kentucky; Jim the Conqueror; The Land beyond the Law; The Overland Stage; Tracked by the Police; Land of the Lawless. 1928 Into No Man's Land; Vultures of the Sea (serial); Crashing Through; Honor Bound; Law and the Man; Land of the Silver Fox; Isle of Lost Men. 1929 The Yellowback; The Shannons of Broadway; The Wagon Master; In Old Arizona. 1930 The Utah Kid; Paradise Island; The Fourth Alarm. 1931 Ten Nights in a Barroom; River's End. 1932 The Last Ride.

SARGENT, ALFRED MAXWELL
Born: 1881. Died: Jan. 1949, Kalamazoo, Mich. Screen and stage actor.

SARNO, HECTOR V.
Born: 1880, Naples, Italy. Died: Dec. 16, 1953, Pasadena, Calif. Screen and stage actor. Entered films in 1909.

Appeared in: 1921 Cheated Hearts; Diamonds Adrift; The Conflict; The Rough Diamond. 1922 Do and Dare; Arabia; The Wise Kid; While Justice Waits. 1923 Stepping Fast; Girl of the Golden West; Ashes of Vengeance. 1924 The Sea Hawk; The Song of Love; Great Diamond Mystery; Honor among Men. 1925 As Man Desires; Cobra. 1926 Her Sacrifice; The Temptress. 1927 King

of Kings; The Climbers. 1928 Sonia. 1929 Lucky Star; Hearts and Hoofs (short); Laughing at Death; Red Hot Speed. 1930 Oklahoma Cyclone.

SATZ, LUDWIG
Born: 1891, Poland. Died: Aug. 31, 1944, New York, N.Y. Screen, stage actor, and film director. Appeared in the first Yiddish musical talking film His Wife's Lover.

SAUM, CLIFFORD
Born: 1883. Died: Mar. 1943, Glendale, Calif. Screen and stage actor.

Appeared in: 1923 Wandering Daughters. 1925 The Bridge of Sighs. 1927 By Whose Hand?; Stage Kisses; The Tigress; The Siren. 1928 Fashion Madness. 1930 Three Sisters. 1937 He Couldn't Say No. 1938 Torchy Gets Her Man. 1940 Ladies Must Live. 1941 The Case of the Black Parrot.

SAUNDERS, JACKIE
Born: 1898. Died: July 14, 1954, Palm Springs, Calif. Screen and stage actress.

Appeared in: 1916 The Grip of Evil (serial). 1920 Drag Harlan. 1921 The Infamous Miss Ravell; Puppets of Fate. 1923 Shattered Reputations; Defying Destiny. 1924 Broken Laws; Alimony; Flames of Desire; The Great Diamond Mystery; The Courageous Coward. 1925 The People vs. Nancy Preston; Faint Perfume.

SAUNDERS, NELLIE PECK
Born: 1869, Saginaw, Mich. Died: Mar. 3, 1942, Greenwood, S.C. Screen and stage actress.

Appeared in: 1922 Tailor Made Man. 1925 A Little Girl in a Big City; The Mad Dancer. 1926 The Sorrows of Satan. 1927 The Broadway Drifter. 1929 The Hole in the Wall.

SAVILLE, GUS
Born: 1857. Died: Mar. 25, 1934, Hollywood, Calif. Screen and stage actor.

Appeared in: 1921 The Wolverine. 1922 Tess of the Storm Country. 1923 The Face on the Barroom Floor. 1925 Idaho (serial); Wild West (serial); Fighting Courage. 1926 The High Hand. 1930 The Light of Western Stars.

SAVO, JIMMY
Born: 1896, Bronx, N.Y. Died: Sept. 6, 1960, Teni, Italy (heart attack). Screen, stage actor, pantomimist, and juggler.

Appeared in: 1926 Exclusive Rights; prior to 1935 The House Dick (short). 1935 Once in a Blue Moon. 1937 Merry-Go-Round of 1938. 1938 Reckless Living.

SAWYER, LAURA
Born: 1885. Died: Sept. 7, 1970, Matawan, N.J. Screen and stage actress. Entered films with Edison Company.

Appeared in: 1912 The Lighthouse Keeper's Daughter.

SAXON, HUGH A.
Born: Jan. 14, 1869, New Orleans, La. Died: May 14, 1945, Beverly Hills, Calif. Screen actor. Entered films in 1916.

Appeared in: 1920 Sand. 1921 High Heels; Seven Years Bad Luck. 1922 The Guttersnipe; Watch Him Step. 1924 Cytherea. 1925 Fightin' Odds. 1926 Hair Trigger Baxter; The Fighting Boob. 1927 Is Your Daughter Safe?; Bulldog Pluck; King of the Herd. 1928 Tracked; Phantom of the Turf; Gypsy of the North. 1929 One Splendid Hour.

SAYLES, FRANCIS H.
Born: 1892, Buffalo, N.Y. Died: Mar. 19, 1944, Hollywood, Calif. Screen and stage actor. Entered films approx. 1930.

Appeared in: 1932 Strangers of the Evening; Blonde Venus. 1934 Home on the Range; Bum Voyage (short). 1937 The Black Legion. 1938 The Purple Vigilantes.

SAYLOR, SYD (Leo Sailor)
Born: Mar. 24, 1895, Chicago, Ill. Died: Dec. 21, 1962, Hollywood, Calif.(heart attack). Screen and stage actor. Entered films in 1925.

Appeared in: 1926-1927 54 "Syd Saylor" comedies. 1926 Red Hot Leather. 1928 The Mystery Rider (serial). 1929 Just off Broadway; Shanghai Rose. 1930 Border Legion; Men without Law; The Light of Western Stars. 1931 Unfaithful; Fighting Caravans; Playthings of Hollywood; The Lawyer's Secret; I Take This Woman; Caught; Sidewalks of New York. 1932 Law of the Seas;

Million Dollar Legs; Lady and Gent; The Crusader; Tangled Destinies; Horse Feathers. 1933 Justice Takes a Holiday; Man of Sentiment; The Nuisance; Gambling Ship. 1934 Young and Beautiful; The Dude Ranger; The Lost Jungle (serial); When a Man Sees Red; Mystery Mountain (serial). 1935 Headline Woman; Code of the Mounted; Men of Action; Ladies Crave Excitement; Wilderness Mail; Here Comes Cookie. 1936 Hitchhike to Heaven; The Last Assignment; Prison Shadows; The Sky Parade; Nevada; The Three Mesquiteers; Kelly the Second; Headin' for the Rio Grande; Secret Valley. 1937 Guns in the Dark; Wallaby Jim of the Islands; Wild and Woolly; Arizona Days; Forlorn River; Meet the Boy Friend; Sea Racketeers; The Wrong Road; Exiled to Shanghai; House of Secrets. 1938 Born to the West; There Goes My Heart; Crashin' through Danger; The Black Doll; Little Miss Broadway. 1939 $1,000 a Touchdown; Union Pacific; Geronimo. 1940 Arizona; Abe Lincoln in Illinois. 1941 Wyoming Wildcat; The Great American Broadcast; Miss Polly; Borrowed Hero. 1942 A Gentleman at Heart; The Man in the Trunk; That Other Woman; Time to Kill; Gentleman Jim; Lady in a Jam; It Happened in Flatbush. 1943 He Hired the Boss; Harvest Melody. 1944 Hey, Rookie!; Swingtime Johnny; Three of a Kind. 1945 The Navajo Kid; Bedside Manner; Frisco Sal; See My Lawyer. 1946 Six Guns for Hire; Thunder Town; Six Gun Man; Avalanche; Deadline for Murder; The Virginian. 1947 Fun on a Weekend. 1948 Prince of Thieves; Triple Threat; Snake Pit; Racing Luck; Sitting Pretty. 1949 Big Jack; Dancing in the Dark; That Wonderful Urge. 1950 Mule Train; Cheaper by the Dozen; The Jackpot. 1951 The Las Vegas Story. 1952 Abbott and Costello Meet Captain Kidd; The Hawk of Wild River; Belles on Their Toes. 1953 The Tall Texan; Abbott and Costello Go To Mars. 1955 Toughest Man Alive. 1956 Crime in the Streets; A Cry in the Night. 1957 Shoot-Out at Medicine Bend; The Spirit of St. Louis. 1959 Escort West.

SAZARINA, MARIA
Born: 1914, Germany. Died: Oct. 20, 1959, Hamburg, Germany. Screen actress.

SCADUTO, JOSEPH
Born: 1898. Died: Oct. 19, 1943, Hollywood, Calif. Screen actor.

Appeared in: 1924 Racing Luck.

SCANNELL, WILLIAM J.
Born: 1912, Boston, Mass. Died: July 8, 1963, Hollywood, Calif. (heart attack). Screen, vaudeville, and television actor.

Appeared in: 1963 The Greatest Story Ever Told.

SCARDON, PAUL
Born: May 6, 1878, Melbourne, Australia. Died: Jan. 17, 1954, Fontana, Calif.(heart attack). Screen, stage actor, film producer, and film director. Entered films as an actor with Majestic in 1911. Married to film actress Betty Blythe (dec. 1972).

Appeared in: 1915 The Goddess (serial). 1941 The Son of Davy Crockett; Lady from Louisiana. 1942 Mrs. Miniver; My Favorite Blonde; A Yank at Eton; Tish. 1944 Today I Hang; The Adventures of Mark Twain. 1946 Down Missouri Way. 1947 Magic Town. 1948 Sign of the Ram; Fighting Mad; The Shanghai Chest.

SCHABLE, ROBERT
Born: 1873, Hamilton, Ohio. Died: July 7, 1947, Hollywood, Calif. Screen and stage actor.

Appeared in: 1919 The Test of Honor. 1920 On with the Dance. 1921 Experience; Without Limit; Paying the Piper. 1922 Sherlock Holmes; Sisters; A Daughter of Luxury; The Cowboy and the Lady; The Woman Who Fooled Herself; Love's Masquerade. 1923 Bella Donna; Nobody's Money; The Cheat; In Search of a Thrill; Slander the Woman; The Silent Partner. 1924 The Stranger. 1926 Partners Again; Silken Shackles. 1927 Love of Sunya. 1928 Sailors' Wives. 1929 Careers; Man and the Moment.

SCHAEFER, ALBERT
Born: 1916. Died: Oct. 26, 1942, Hollywood, Calif. Screen actor. An original member of "Our Gang" comedies.

Appeared in: 1926 The Set-Up.

SCHAEFER, CHARLES N.
Born: 1864. Died: Feb. 5, 1939, Hollywood, Calif. Screen and stage actor.

Appeared in: 1927 Ridin' Luck; Wild Born; Gun-Hand Garrison; Man Power. 1929 The Winged Horseman.

SCHARF, HERMAN "BOO-BOO" (aka HERMAN SCHARFF)
Born: 1901. Died: Apr. 8, 1963, Hollywood, Calif.(heart attack). Screen actor and stuntman.

Appeared in: 1955 The Far Horizons.

SCHEFF, FRITZI
Born: 1879, Vienna, Austria. Died: Apr. 8, 1954, New York, N.Y. (natural causes). Screen, stage, vaudeville, and opera actress.

Appeared in: 1915 The Pretty Mrs. Smith.

SCHEINPFLUGOVA, OLGA
Born: 1902, Czechoslovakia. Died: Apr. 14, 1968, Prague, Czechoslovakia. Screen actress.

Appeared in: 1968 The Fifth Horseman Is Fear.

SCHENCK, JOSEPH T.
Born: 1891, Brooklyn, N.Y. Died: June 28, 1930, Detroit, Mich. (heart disease). Screen, stage, and vaudeville actor. Was part of vaudeville team with Gus Van (dec. 1968) billed as "Van and Schenck."

Together they appeared in: 1927 The Pennant Winning Battery of Songland (short). 1929 Metro Movietone (feature with their lives as a background entitled Take It Big); plus several song short subjects. 1930 They Learned about Women.

SCHERMAN, BARBARA
Died, Jan. 29, 1935, Cliffside Park, N.J.(gas poisoning). Screen actress.

SCHEU, JUST
Born: 1903, Germany. Died: Aug. 9, 1956, Bad Mergentheim, West Germany (appendicitis). Screen, radio actor, playwright, and composer.

SCHEUER, CONSTANCE
Born: 1910. Died: Nov. 27, 1962, Los Angeles, Calif.(heart attack). Screen actress and dancer.

SCHIESKE, ALFRED
Born: 1909, Stuttgart, Germany. Died: July 14, 1970, West Berlin, Germany. Screen, stage, and television actor.

Appeared in: 1949 The Affair Blum. 1951 Odette. 1960 A Day Will Come. 1961 Tomorrow Is My Turn.

SCHILDKRAUT, JOSEPH
Born: Mar. 22, 1896, Vienna, Austria. Died: Jan. 21, 1964, New York, N.Y.(heart attack). Screen, stage, and television actor. Son of screen actor Rudolph Schildkraut (dec. 1930). Won Academy Award in 1937 for Best Supporting Actor in The Life of Emile Zola.

Appeared in: 1922 Orphans of the Storm (film debut). 1923 Dust of Desire. 1924 The Song of Love. 1925 The Road to Yesterday. 1926 Meet the Prince; Young April; Shipwrecked. 1927 The Forbidden Woman; His Dog; King of Kings; The Heart Thief. 1928 The Blue Danube; Tenth Avenue. 1929 The Mississippi Gambler; Show Boat. 1930 Die Sehnsucht jeder Frau; Night Ride; Cock of the Walk. 1931 Carnival. 1932 Blue Danube (U.S. 1934 plus 1928 version). 1934 Viva Villa; Sisters under the Skin; Cleopatra. 1935 The Crusades. 1936 The Garden of Allah. 1937 Slave Ship; Lancer Spy; The Life of Emile Zola; Souls at Sea; A Star Is Born; Lady Behave. 1938 The Baroness and the Butler; Suez; Marie Antoinette. 1939 Lady of the Tropics; The Rains Came; Pack up Your Troubles; Mr. Moto Takes a Vacation; Idiot's Delight; The Three Musketeers; The Man in the Iron Mask. 1940 The Shop around the Corner; Rangers of Fortune; Meet the Wildcat; Phantom Raiders. 1941 The Parson of Panamint. 1945 The Cheaters; Flame of the Barbary Coast. 1946 Monsieur Beaucaire; The Plainsman and the Lady. 1947 Northwest Outpost; End of the Rainbow. 1948 Gallant Legion; Old Los Angeles. 1959 The Diary of Anne Frank. 1961 King of the Roaring Twenties. 1964 Dust of Desire; Song of Love. 1965 The Greatest Story Ever Told.

SCHILDKRAUT, RUDOLPH
Born: 1865, Constantinople, Turkey. Died: July 15, 1930, Los Angeles, Calif.(heart disease). Screen and stage actor. Father of screen actor Joseph Schildkraut (dec. 1964).

Appeared in: 1925 His People; Proud Heart. 1926 Pals in Paradise; Young April. 1927 A Harp in Hock; King of Kings; Turkish Delight; The Main Event; The Country Doctor. 1928 A Ship Comes In. 1929 Christina.

SCHILLING, AUGUST E. "GUS"
Born: June 20, 1908, New York, N.Y. Died: June 16, 1957, Hollywood, Calif.(heart attack). Screen, stage, burlesque, and radio actor. Divorced from burlesque actress Betty Rowland.

Appeared in: 1940 Mexican Spitfire Out West. 1941 Citizen Kane; Lucky Devils; It Started with Eve; Appointment for Love; Dr. Kildare's Victory; Ice Capades. 1942 The Magnificent Ambersons; Broadway; You Were Never Lovlier; Moonlight in Havana. 1943 Lady Bodyguard; Hi, Buddy; Hers to Hold; Larceny with Music; The Amazing Mrs. Holliday; Chatterbox. 1944 Sing a Jingle. 1945 See My Lawyer; River Gang; A Thousand and One Nights; It's a Pleasure. 1946 Dangerous Business. 1947 Calendar Girl; Stork Bites Man. 1948 Return of October; Macbeth; The Lady from Shanghai; Angel on the Amazon. 1949 Bride for Sale. 1950 Our Very Own; Hit Parade of 1951. 1951 Honeychile; On Dangerous Ground; Gasoline Alley. 1952 One Big Affair. 1954 She Couldn't Say No. 1955 Run for Cover. 1956 Glory; Bigger Than Life.

SCHINDEL, SEYMORE
Born: 1907. Died: Aug. 24, 1948, Hollywood, Calif. Screen and stage actor.

SCHIPA, TITO
Born: 1889, Lecee, Italy. Died: Dec. 16, 1965, New York, N.Y. (heart attack). Screen actor and opera singer.

Appeared in: 1929 Tito Schipa. 1930 Tito Schipa Concert No. 2. 1932 Tre Womane en Frak. 1937 Vivere (To Live—U.S. 1938); Terre de Feu; Chi e'piu Felice de Me? (Who Is Happier Than I— U.S. 1940). 1943 In Cerca de Felicita. 1944 Rosalba; Vivere an Cora. 1946 Il' Cavaliere del Sogna. 1947 Follie per l' Opera (Mad about Opera—U.S. 1950). 1951 Soho Conspiracy; I Misteri di Venezia. 1952 The Life of Donizetti.

SCHMITT, JOSEPH
Born: 1871. Died: Mar. 25, 1935, Los Angeles, Calif. Screen actor. Entered films in 1912.

SCHMITZ, LUDWIG
Born: 1884, Germany. Died: July 1954, Munich, Germany (heart attack). Screen and stage actor.

Appeared in: 1938 Der Maulkorb. Other German films: Bruen Ist Die Heide; Am Brunnen vor dem Tore; Pension Schoeller; Der Keusche Josef; Land of Smiles.

SCHMITZ, SYBILLE
Born: 1912, Germany. Died: Apr. 13, 1955, Munich, Germany (suicide—pills). Screen actress. Entered films in early 1930s.

Appeared in: 1935 Der Herr Der Welt. 1936 Oberwachtmeister Schwenke. 1937 Ein Idealer Gatte; Punks Kommt aus Amerika. 1938 Fahrmann Maria (Ferryman Maria). 1939 Hotel Sacher. 1954 The House on the Coast. Other German films: George Sand; Stradivari; FBI Does Not Answer; Farewell Waltz.

SCHNEIDER, JAMES
Born: 1882, New York, N.Y. Died: Feb. 14, 1967, Los Angeles, Calif. Screen actor and film director. One of the original Keystone Kops.

SCHONBERG, ALEXANDER
Born: 1886. Died: Oct. 1, 1945, Hollywood, Calif. Screen and stage actor. Entered films approx. 1930.

Appeared in: 1937 Nothing Sacred. 1938 Romance in the Dark. 1939 They Shall Have Music.

SCHONBERG, IB
Born: 1902, Denmark. Died: Sept. 26, 1955, Copenhagen, Denmark. Screen actor.

Appeared in: 1954 We Want a Child.

SCHROFF, WILLIAM
Born: 1889, Stuttgart, Germany. Died: Dec. 5, 1964, Hollywood, Calif. Screen, stage, circus actor, and stuntman.

SCHUKIN, BORIS
Born: 1894, Russia. Died: Oct. 7, 1939, Moscow, Russia (heart attack). Screen actor. He was holder of the title "People's Artist of the U.S.S.R."

Appeared in: 1938 Lenin in October.

SCHULTZ, MRS. CECIL E.
Born: 1905. Died: Sept. 2, 1953, New York, N.Y. Screen actress.

SCHULTZ, HARRY (Alexander Heinberg)
Born: 1883, Germany. Died: July 5, 1935, Hollywood, Calif. Screen actor.

Appeared in: 1926 Spangles. 1928 Riley the Cop. 1929 One Stolen Night. 1930 The Big House. 1931 Beau Hunks (short); War Mamas (short). 1933 Hypnotized; One Sunday Afternoon; I'm No Angel. 1934 The Pursuit of Happiness; Little Man, What Now?

SCHUMACHER, CAPT. MAX
Born: 1927. Died: Aug. 30, 1966, Los Angeles, Calif.(mid-air helicopter collision). KMPC radio traffic helicopter pilot and screen actor.

Appeared in: 1964 The Lively Set.

SCHUMANN-HEINK, ERNESTINE (Ernestine Rossler)
Born: 1861, Prague, Hungary. Died: Nov. 17, 1936, Los Angeles, Calif.(leukemia). Screen and opera actress. Mother of screen actor Ferdinand Schumann (dec. 1958) and screen technician Henry Schumann.

Appeared in: 1927 the following shorts: Danny Boy; By the Waters of Minnetonka; Der Erlkonig. 1935 Here's to Romance.

SCHUMANN-HEINK, FERDINAND
Born: Aug. 9, 1893, Hamburg, Germany. Died: Sept. 15, 1958, Los Angeles, Calif.(heart attack). Screen and stage actor. Entered films in 1924. Son of screen actress and opera star Ernestine Schumann-Heink (dec. 1936).

Appeared in: 1925 The Fighting Romeo. 1926 The Gallant Fool. 1928 Four Sons; The Awakening; Riley the Cop. 1930 Hell's Angels; Blaze O'Glory; Worldly Goods; Mamba. 1931 The Seas Beneath; My Pal, the King. 1933 Gigolettes of Paris; The Mad Game. 1934 The World Moves On; Fugitive Road; Orient Express. 1935 Symphony of Living. 1936 Two against the World. 1937 The King and the Chorus Girl. 1939 Thunder Afloat; Nurse Edith Cavell; Confessions of a Nazi Spy. 1940 Enemy Agent. 1943 Mission to Moscow.

SCHUMM, HARRY W.
Born: 1878. Died: Apr. 4, 1953, Hollywood, Calif. Screen and stage actor.

Appeared in: 1915 The Broken Coin (serial).

SCHUNZEL, REINHOLD
Born: 1886, Germany. Died: Sept. 11, 1954, Munich, Germany (heart ailment). Screen, stage actor, screenwriter, and film director.

Appeared in: 1922 The Last Payment. 1928 Fortune's Fool. 1931 Die Dreigroschenoper (The Beggar's Opera); Ihre Hoheit Befiehlt. 1932 1914: The Last Days before the War. 1943 First Comes Courage; Hangmen Also Die; Hostages. 1944 The Hitler Gang; The Man in Half Moon Street. 1946 Notorious; Dragonwyck; The Plainsman and the Lady. 1947 Golden Earrings. 1948 Berlin Express; The Vicious Circle; The Woman in Brown. 1952 Washington Story.

SCHWAMM, GEORGE S. "TONY"
Born: 1903. Died: Feb. 15, 1966, Elmendorf, Alaska. Screen stuntman.

SCHWARTZ, MAURICE
Born: 1891, Russia. Died: May 10, 1960, near Tel Aviv, Israel (heart attack). Screen and stage actor. Appeared in Yiddish stage productions, etc.

Appeared in: 1926 Broken Hearts. 1932 Uncle Moses. 1939 Tevya the Milkman (filmed for limited circulation). 1951 Bird of Paradise. 1953 Slaves of Babylon; Salome.

SCHWARTZ, WENDIE LEE
Born: 1923. Died: Aug. 23, 1968, Hollywood, Calif. Screen actress.

SCHWEISTHAL, HELEN. See Helen Allerton

SCOTT, CYRIL
Born: 1866, Ireland. Died: Aug. 16, 1945, Flushing, N.Y. Screen and stage actor.

Appeared in: 1915 How Molly Made Good.

SCOTT, DICK
Born: 1903. Died: Sept. 2, 1961, Hollywood, Calif. Screen, stage, and radio actor.

SCOTT, FREDERICK T.
Died: Feb. 22, 1942, Staten Island, N.Y. Screen actor and wild-west showman.

Appeared in: 1905 The Great Train Robbery. 1919 Over There. 1936 Romance Rides the Range.

SCOTT, HAROLD
Born: 1891. Died: Apr. 15, 1964, London, England. Screen, stage, radio, and television actor.

Appeared in: 1945 The Man in Grey. 1949 The Gay Lady (aka Trotti True—U.S. 1950). 1957 The Spanish Gardener. 1960 The Brides of Dracula. 1961 Hand. 1962 Wonderful to Be Young (aka The Young Ones). 1965 The Yellow Rolls Royce.

SCOTT, JAMES D.
Born: 1939. Died: Dec. 8, 1964, Pasadena, Calif.(leukemia). Screen and radio actor. Was Alexander on Blondie and Dagwood radio program.

SCOTT, KAY
Born: 1928. Died: Jan. 1, 1971, Los Angeles, Calif. Screen actress and composer.

Appeared in: 1947 Fear in the Night.

SCOTT, LESLIE (Zakariya Abullah)
Born: 1921. Died: Aug. 20, 1969, New York, N.Y.(cancer). Screen and stage actor, and singer.

Appeared in: 1958 Island Women. 1959 Porgy and Bess (screen and European stage versions).

SCOTT, MARK
Born: 1915. Died: July 13, 1960, Burbank, Calif.(heart attack). Screen, radio, and television actor.

Appeared in: 1955 Hell's Horizon. 1957 Chicago Confidential.

SCOTT, MARKLE
Born: 1873. Died: July 4, 1958, Hollywood, Calif. Cowboy screen actor. Appeared in silents.

SCOTT, PAUL
Born: 1894. Died: Nov. 24, 1944, Los Angeles, Calif.(heart attack). Screen and stage actor.

SCOTT, ZACHARY
Born: Feb. 24, 1914, Austin, Tex. Died: Oct. 3, 1965, Austin, Tex. (brain tumor). Screen and stage actor.

Appeared in: 1944 The Mask of Dimitrios (film debut); Hollywood Canteen. 1945 Mildred Pierce; The Southerner; San Antonio; Danger Signal. 1946 Her Kind of Man. 1947 Stallion Road; Cass Timberlane; The Unfaithful. 1948 Whiplash; Ruthless. 1949 Flamingo Road; Flaxy Martin; South of Saint Louis; Death in a Doll's House; Bed of Roses; One Last Fling. 1950 Born to Be Bad; Thundercloud; Colt .45; Shadow on the Wall; Pretty Baby; Guilty Bystander. 1951 Lightning Strikes Twice; The Secret of Convict Lake; Let's Make It Legal. 1952 Stronghold; Wings of Danger. 1953 Appointment in Honduras. 1955 Shotgun; Flame of the Islands; Treasure of Ruby Hills. 1956 Bandido. 1957 The Counterfeit Plan; Man in the Shadow; Flight into Danger. 1960 Natchez Trace. 1961 The Young One. 1962 It's Only Money.

SEARLES, CORA
Born: 1859. Died: Mar. 5, 1935, Los Angeles, Calif. Screen actress.

SEARS, ALLAN
Born: 1887. Died: Aug. 18, 1942, Los Angeles, Calif. Screen actor.

Appeared in: 1920 Rio Grande; Judy of Rogue's Harbor. 1923 Long Live the King. 1924 In Love with Love. 1925 The Scarlet Honeymoon. 1926 Into Her Kingdom. 1928 Into the Night; A Midnight Adventure. 1933 Secrets; 1935 The Singing Vagabond. 1937 Two-Fisted Sheriff.

SEARS, MRS. BLANCHE
Born: 1870. Died: Aug. 7, 1939, Los Angeles, Calif. Screen and radio actress.

SEARS, ZELDA
Born: 1873, Brockway, Mich. Died: Feb. 19, 1935, Hollywood, Calif. Screen, stage actress, author, playwright, and screenwriter.

Appeared in: 1921 The Highest Bidder. 1930 The Bishop Murder Case; The Divorcee. 1931 Inspiration. 1935 A Wicked Woman.

SEASTROM, VICTOR (aka VICTOR SJOSTROM)
Born: Sept. 21, 1879, Varmland, Sweden. Died: Jan. 3, 1960, Stockholm, Sweden. Screen, stage actor, film director, and stage director. Entered films as an actor with Swedish Biograp Co. in 1912. Known in Sweden as Victor Sjostrom.

Appeared in: 1913 Ingeborg Holm. 1916 Terje Vigen. 1920 A Man There Was. 1921 You and I; Ordet (The Word). 1922 The Stroke of Midnight. 1938 John Ericsson Victor of Hampton Roads. 1949 I Am with you. 1957 Wild Strawberries.

SEATON, SCOTT
Born: Mar. 11, 1878, Sacramento, Calif. Died: June 3, 1968, Hollywood, Calif. Screen, stage, and television actor.

Appeared in: 1927 Wild Beauty; Rich Men's Sons; Thumbs Down. 1929 The Greyhound Limited; Leathernecks. 1930 The Other Tomorrow. 1950 Father of the Bride. 1963 Twilight of Honor; Donovan's Reef.

SEBASTIAN, DOROTHY
Born: Apr. 1903, Birmingham, Ala. Died: Apr. 8, 1957, Hollywood, Calif. Screen and stage actress. Divorced from screen actor William "Hopalong Cassidy" Boyd (dec. 1972).

Appeared in: 1925 Sackcloth and Scarlet (film debut); Winds of Chance. 1926 Bluebeard's Seven Wives; You'd Be Surprised. 1927 The Demi-Bride; The Arizona Wildcat; California; The Haunted Ship; Isle of Forgotten Women; On Ze Boulevard; Tea for Three; Twelve Miles Out; The Show. 1928 Our Dancing Daughters; Show People; Their Hour; Wyoming; House of Scandal; The Adventurer. 1929 The Single Standard; Spite Marriage; A Woman of Affairs; The Rainbow; The Spirit of Youth; The Devil's Apple-tree; The Unholy Night; Morgan's Last Raid. 1930 His First Command; Our Blushing Brides; Free and Easy; Hell's Island; Ladies Must Play; Brothers; The Utah Kid; Montana Moon; Officer O'Brien. 1931 The Deceiver; Lightning Flyer; Ships of Hate; The Big Gamble. 1932 They Never Came Back. 1933 Contraband; Ship of Wanted Men. 1934 The Gold Ghost. 1937 The Mysterious Pilot (serial). 1939 Rough Riders' Round-Up; The Arizona Kid. 1941 Among the Living; Kansas Cyclone. 1942 True to the Army; Reap the Wild Wind.

SEDGWICK, EDIE (Edith Sedgwick)
Born: 1943. Died: Nov. 16, 1971, Santa Barbara, Calif.(acute barbitural intoxication).

Appeared in following Andy Warhol films: Restaurant; Kitchen; Afternoon; Beauty II; Vinyl; Face; Prison; Poor Little Rich Girl; Chow Manhattan.

SEEL, JEANNE N.
Born: 1898. Died: Sept. 9, 1964, Hollywood, Calif.(cancer). Screen and stage actress. Married to screen actor Charles Seel.

SEGAL, BERNARD
Born: 1868. Died: July 9, 1940, Hollywood, Calif. Screen actor.

Appeared in: 1937 Wells Fargo.

SEGAR, LUCIA (aka LUCIA SEGER)
Born: 1874. Died: Jan. 17, 1962, New York, N.Y. Screen, stage, and television actress.

Appeared in: 1921 The Wild Goose. 1922 The Bond Boy; The Bootleggers. 1923 Fury. 1927 Knockout Reilly. 1929 East Side Sadie. 1947 Boomerang.

SEGURA, LETICIA ESPINOSA
Born: Mexico. Died: Dec. 26, 1956, Mexico City, Mexico (auto accident). Screen and television actress.

SEIDEWITZ, MARIE
Died: Dec. 27, 1929, Baltimore, Md. Screen, stage, and vaudeville actress.

SEITER, WILLIAM A.
Born: June 10, 1892, New York, N.Y. Died: July 26, 1964, Beverly Hills, Calif.(heart attack). Screen actor, film director, television director, and film producer. Entered films as an actor with Sennett as a Keystone Kop.

SEITZ, GEORGE B.
Born: Jan. 3, 1888, Boston, Mass. Died: July 8, 1944, Hollywood, Calif. Screen, stage actor, film producer, film director, screenwriter, and playwright. Entered films with Pathe in 1914. Wrote the scenarios, produced, directed, and acted in the "Pearl White" Pathe serials.

Appeared in the following serials: 1919 The Black Secret; Bound and Gagged. 1920 Pirate Gold; Velvet Fingers. 1921 The Sky Ranger; Rogues and Romance (feature).

SEKELY, IRENE AGAY
Born: 1914, Hungary. Died: Sept. 2, 1950, Hollywood, Calif. Screen and stage actress.

Appeared in: 1946 The Fabulous Suzanne.

SELBIE, EVELYN
Born: July 6, 1882, Louisville, Ky. Died: Dec. 7, 1950, Hollywood, Calif.(heart ailment). Screen, stage, and radio actress. Entered films as G. M. Anderson's (Bronco Billy) leading lady in 1912; was known as the original "Bronco Billy Girl."

Appeared in: 1914 The Squaw Man. 1919 The Red Glove (serial). 1921 Devil Dog Dawson; The Devil Within; Without Benefit of Clergy. 1922 Omar the Tentmaker; Thorns and Orange Blossoms; The Half Breed. 1923 The Broken Wing; Snowdrift; The Tiger's Claw. 1924 A Cafe in Cairo; Flapper Wives; Name the Man; Mademoiselle Midnight; Romance Ranch; Poisoned Paradise. 1925 The Prairie Pirate. 1926 The Country Beyond; Hell-Bent for Heaven; Into Her Kingdom; Flame of the Argentine; The Test of Donald Norton; The Silver Treasure; Silken Shackles; Rose of the Tenements; Prisoners of the Storm. 1927 Camille; Wild Geese; King of Kings; Eager Lips. 1928 Freedom of the Press. 1929 Eternal Love; The Mysterious Dr. Fu Manchu. 1930 The Return of Dr. Fu Manchu; Love Comes Along; Dangerous Paradise. 1932 The Hatchet Man. 1935 A Notorious Gentleman.

SELBY, "KID McCOY" NORMAN
Born: 1874. Died: Apr. 18, 1940, Detroit, Mich.(suicide). Screen actor.

Appeared in: 1921 Bucking the Line; To a Finish; Straight from the Shoulder. 1922 Arabia; Oathbound. 1926 April Showers. 1929 The Painted Angel. 1931 Loose Ankles.

SELLON, CHARLES
Born: Aug. 24, 1878, Boston, Mass. Died: June 26, 1937, La Crescenta, Calif. Screen and stage actor. Entered films in 1923.

Appeared in: 1923 The Bad Man (stage and screen versions); Woman Proof; South Sea Love. 1924 Lover's Lane; The Roughneck; Flowing Gold; Merton of the Movies; Sundown. 1925 The Monster; The Night Ship; Tracked in the Snow Country; Private Affairs; The Calgary Stampede; Lucky Devil; Old Home Week; On the Threshold. 1926 High Steppers; The Speeding Venus; Racing Blood; Whispering Wires. 1927 Painted Ponies; Mysterious Rider; The Prairie King; Easy Pickings; King of Kings; The Valley of the Giants. 1928 Easy Come, Easy Go; Happiness Ahead; Something Always Happens; What a Night!; Feel My Pulse; The Count of Ten; Love Me and the World Is Mine. 1929 The Gamblers; Bulldog Drummond; Hot Stuff; Girl in the Glass Cage; Man and the Moment; The Mighty; The Saturday Night Kid; Big News; Men Are Like That; The Vagabond Lover; Sweetie. 1930 Under a Texas Moon; The Social Lion; Love among the Millionaires; Borrowed Wives; Big Money; For the Love of Lil; Sea Legs; Tom Sawyer; Let's Go Native; Burning Up; Honey. 1931 Man to Man; The Painted Desert; Behind Office Doors; Laugh and Get Rich; Dude Ranch; Age for Love; Penrod and Sam; The Tip-Off. 1932 The Drifter; Carnival Boat; The Dark Horse; Make Me a Star; Speed Madness; Ride Him, Cowboy!; Central Park. 1933 Employees' Entrance; Strictly Personal; As the Devil Commands; Central Airport; Golden Harvest. 1934 Ready for Love; Private Scandal; Elmer and Elsie; It's a Gift; Bright Eyes. 1935 One Hour Late; Alias Mary Dow; The Devil Is a Woman; Life Begins at 40; It's a Small World; In Old Kentucky; Welcome Home; The Casino Murder Case; Diamond Jim.

SELTEN, MORTON (Morton Stubbs)
Born: Jan. 6, 1860. Died: July 27, 1939, London, England. Screen and stage actor.

Appeared in: 1931 Reserved for Ladies. 1932 Wedding Rehearsal; Service for Ladies. 1933 Falling for You; The Love Wager. 1934 How's Chances!. 1935 Ten Minute Alibi; Moscow Nights. 1936 The Ghost Goes West; His Majesty and Company; Annie Leave the Room; The Dark World; Two's Company; In the Soup; I Stand Condemned. 1937 Juggernaut; Fire over England; Action for Slander. 1938 The Divorce of Lady X; A Yank at Oxford. 1940 Over the Moon; The Thief of Bagdad; Shipyard Sally.

SELWYN, RUTH
Born: 1905, Tazwell, Va. Died: Dec. 14, 1954, Hollywood, Calif. Screen, stage actress, stage producer, and writer.

Appeared in: 1931 Five and Ten. 1932 Speak Easily; Polly of the Circus; The Trial of Vivienne Ware; New Morals for Old. 1933 Men Must Fight. 1934 Fugitive Lovers. 1935 Baby Face Harrington.

SEMON, LARRY
Born: July 16, 1889, West Point, Miss. Died: Oct. 8, 1928, Garcelon Ranch, near Victorville, Calif.(pneumonia). Screen, vaudeville actor, film producer, film director, screenwriter, and newspaperman. Married to screen actress Dorothy Dawn.

Appeared in: 1917 Boasts and Boldness; Worries and Wobbles; Shells and Shivers; Chumps and Chances; Gall and Golf; Slips and Slackers; Risks and Roughnecks; Plans and Pajamas; Plagues and Puppy Love; Sports and Splashes; Toughluck and Tin Lizzies; Rough Toughs and Rooftops; Spooks and Spasms; Noisy Naggers and Nosey Neighbors. 1918 Guns and Greasers; Babes and Boobs; Rooms and Rumors; Meddlers and Moonshine; Stripes and Stumbles; Rummies and Razors; Whistles and Windows; Spies and Spills; Romans and Rascals; Skids and Scalawags; Boodle and Bandits; Hindoos and Hazards; Bathing Beauties and Big Boobs; Dunces and Danger; Mutts and Motors; Huns and Hyphens; Bears and Bad Men; Frauds and Frenzies; Humbus and Husbands; Pluck and Plotters. 1919 The Simple Life; Traps and Tangles; Scamps and Scandals; Soapsuds and Sapheads; Well, I'll Be...; Passing the Buck; The Star Boarder; His Home Sweet Home; Between the Acts; Dull Care; Dew Drop Inn; The Headwaiter. 1920 the following shorts: The Grocery Clerk; The Fly Cop; School Days; Solid Concrete; The Stagehand; The Suitor. 1921 the following shorts: The Sportsman; The Hick; The Rent Collector; The Bakery; The Fall Guy; The Bell Hop. 1922 the following shorts: The Sawmill; The Show; A Pair of Kings; Golf; The Sleuth; The Counter Jumper. 1923 the following shorts: No Wedding Bells; The Barnyard; Midnight Cabaret; The Gown Shop; Lightning Love; Horseshoes. 1924 The Girl in the Limousine, plus the following shorts: Her Boy Friend; Kid Speed. 1925 The Perfect Clown; The Wizard of Oz; Go Straight, plus the following shorts: The Dome Doctor; The Cloudhopper. 1926 Stop, Look and Listen. 1927 Spuds; Underworld, plus the following shorts: The Stuntman; Oh What a Man. 1928 Dummies (short); A Simple Sap (short).

SENNETT, MACK (Michael Sinnott)
Born: Jan. 17, 1880, Richmond, Quebec, Canada. Died: Nov. 5, 1960, Hollywood, Calif. Screen, stage, burlesque actor, film producer, and film director. Entered films as an extra with Griffith. Introduced the Keystone Kops.

Appeared in: 1908 Balked at the Altar; Father Gets in the Game; Mr. Jones Had a Card Party; The Curtain Pole; Mr. Jones at the Ball; An Awful Moment; A Wreath in Time; The Salvation Army Lass. 1909 The Slave; The Gibson Goddess; The Song of the Shirt; Politician's Love Story; The Lure of the Gown; Lucky Jim; The Jilt; The Seventh Day; A Convict's Sacrifice; The Better Way; Getting Even; The Awakening; In the Watches of the Night; The Trick That Failed; A Midnight Adventure; In a Hempen Bag; The Dancing Girl of Butte; A Corner in Wheat. 1910 The Newlyweds; A Midnight Cupid; A Mohawk's Way; Examination Day at School; An Arcadian Maid. 1911 The $500 Reward. 1912 Pedro's Dilemma; Stolen Glory; Ambitious Butler; Cohen at Coney Island; At It Again; The Rivals; Mr. Fix-It; A Bear Escape; Pat's Day Off; A Family Mix-Up; The Duel; Cohen Collects a Debt; The Water Nymph; Man's Genesis; The New York Hat. 1913 The Mistaken Masher; The Battle of Who Run; The Jealous Waiter; The Stolen Purse; Mabel's Heroes; The Sleuth's Last Stand; The Sleuths at the Floral Parade; A Strong Revenge; The Rube and the Baron; At Twelve O'Clock; Her New Beau; Mabel's Awful Mistake (retitled and reissued Her Deceitful Lover); Their First Execution; Barney Oldfield's Race for a Life; The Hansom Driver; His Crooked Career; Mabel's Dramatic Career (retitled and reissued Her Dramatic Debut); Love Sickness at Sea; For Lizzie's Sake; The Chief's Predicament; The Bangville Police. 1914 A False Beauty (retitled and reissued A Faded Vampire); Mack at It Again; Mabel at the Wheel (retitled and reissued His Daredevil Queen); The Fatal Mallet; The Knock-Out (retitled and reissued The Pugilist); In the Clutches of a Gang; Our Country Cousin; The Property Man (retitled and reissued The Roustabout); His Talented Wife; Tillie's Punctured Romance. 1915 Hearts and Planets; The Little Teacher (retitled and reissued A Small Town Bully); My Valet; Stolen Magic; Fatty and the Broadway Stars. 1921 Molly O. 1922 Oh, Mabel Behave. 1939 Hollywood Cavalcade. 1955 Abbott and Costello Meet the Keystone Kops. 1961 Days of Thrills and Laughter (documentary).

SERRANO, VINCENT
Born: 1867. Died: Jan. 10, 1935, New York, N.Y.(heart attack). Screen and stage actor.

Appeared in: 1919 Eyes of Youth. 1920 The Branded Woman. 1927 Convoy.

SERTEL, NEELA
Born: 1901, Turkey. Died: Dec. 1969, Istanbul, Turkey. Screen, stage, and radio actress.

SERVOSS, MARY
Born: 1908. Died: Nov. 20, 1968, Los Angeles, Calif.(heart ailment). Screen and stage actress.

Appeared in: 1941 The Lone Wolf Keeps a Date. 1942 The Postman Didn't Ring; In This Our Life. 1943 So Proudly We Hail. 1944 Four Jills in a Jeep; Youth Runs Wild; Mrs. Parkington; Summer Storm; Experiment Perilous; Danger Signal. 1945 Conflict. 1948 Live Today for Tomorrow. 1949 Beyond the Forest.

SETON, SIR BRUCE
Born: May 29, 1909, Simla, India. Died: Sept. 17, 1969, London, England. Screen, stage, and television actor.

Appeared in: 1934 Blue Smoke. 1936 Sweeney Tod. 1938 Love from a Stranger. 1940 Song of the Road. 1946 The Curse of the Wraydons. 1947 The Green Cockatoo. 1948 Bonnie Prince Charlie. 1949 Whiskey Galore (aka Tight Little Island-U.S. aka Mad Little Island). Scott of the Antarctic. 1950 The Blue Lamp. 1951 Paul Temple's Triumph; Take Me to Paris. 1952 The Cruel Sea; High Treason. 1955 Eight O'Clock Walk. 1957 The Fighting Wildcats; Morning Call; There's Always a Thursday; West of Suez. 1958 The Strange Case of Mr. Manning. 1959 John Paul Jones; The Crooked Sky. 1960 Hidden Homicide. 1961 The Frightened City; Gorgo. 1964 Life in Danger. Other British films: Wedding Group; Vandergilt Mystery; Melody of My Heart.

SEVAL, NEVIN
Born: 1920. Died: Nov., 1958, Adana, Turkey. Turkish screen and stage actress.

SEVER, ALFRED
Born: 1891. Died: Mar. 26, 1953, New York, N.Y. Silent screen actor.

SEVERIN-MARS
Born: France. Died: Sept. 1921 (pneumonia). Screen and stage actor.

Appeared in: 1918 La Dixiem Symphonie. 1921 La Roue.

SEWELL, ALLEN D.
Born: 1883. Died: Jan. 20, 1954, Hollywood, Calif. Screen actor.

Appeared in: 1914 The Squaw Man; The Spoilers. 1927 Between Dangers.

SEYFERTH, WILFRIED
Born: 1908, Germany. Died: Oct. 9, 1954, near Wiesbaden, West Germany (auto accident). Screen and stage actor.

Appeared in: 1933 Schleppzug 17 (film debut). 1951 Decision before Dawn. 1952 The Devil Makes Three. 1953 The Grapes Are Ripe. 1958 Zero Eight One Five (08/15—U.S. 1958). 1959 Das Tanzende Herz (The Dancing Heart). Other German films: Der Froehliche Weimberg; Toxi; Helmweh Nach Dir.

SEYMOUR, CLARINE
Died: Apr. 25, 1920, New York, N.Y. Screen actress.

Appeared in: 1919 True Heart Susie; The Girl Who Stayed at Home. 1920 The Idol Dancer.

SEYMOUR, HARRY
Born: 1890. Died: Nov. 11, 1967, Hollywood, Calif.(heart attack). Screen, stage, vaudeville actor, and composer.

Appeared in: 1925 East Lynne. 1932 The Tenderfoot; You Said a Mouthful; Man against Woman. 1934 The Crosby Case; The Case of the Howling Dog; Six Day Bike Rider. 1935 Shipmates Forever; Broadway Hostess; Behind Green Lights. 1938 A Slight Case of Murder; Boy Meets Girl. 1939 Kid Nightingale. 1940 A Fugitive from Justice. 1947 I Wonder Who's Kissing Her Now. 1948 Give My Regards to Broadway. 1949 It Happens Every Spring. 1950 A Ticket to Tomahawk. 1953 Vicki; Mr. Scoutmaster. 1955 The Girl in the Red Velvet Swing; Daddy Long Legs; How to Be Very, Very Popular; Violent Saturday.

SEYMOUR, JANE
Born: 1899. Died: Jan. 30, 1956, New York, N.Y. Screen, stage, radio, and television actress.

Appeared in: 1939 Back Door to Heaven. 1941 Tom, Dick and Harry; Remember the Day.

SHACKLETON, ROBERT W.
Born: 1914, Lawrence, Mass. Died: June 21, 1956, Jacksonville, Fla.(leukemia). Screen and stage actor.

Appeared in: 1951 The Wonder Kid. 1952 Where's Charley? (stage and film versions).

SHADE, JAMESSON
Born: 1895. Died: Apr. 18, 1956, Hollywood, Calif.(heart attack). Screen, stage, and television actor.

Appeared in: 1943 Santa Fe Scouts; The Woman of the Town. 1944 The Utah Kid. 1945 Wilson. 1949 Treasure of Monte Cristo; Cover-Up. 1955 Ain't Misbehavin'.

SHADOW, BERT
Born: 1890. Died: Nov., 1936, Hollywood, Calif.(heart ailment). Screen and vaudeville actor. Was partner in "Shadow and McNeill" vaudeville team with his wife Lillian McNeill.

SHAFER, MOLLIE B.
Born: 1872. Died: Nov. 19, 1940, Hollywood, Calif. Screen actress.

Appeared in: 1921 The Big Adventure; While the Devil Laughs.

SHAIFFER, "TINY" (Howard Charles Shaiffer)
Born: 1918. Died: Jan. 24, 1967, Burbank, Calif. Screen actor. Member of "Our Gang" comedies.

SHANKLAND, RICHARD
Born: 1904. Died: Jan. 18, 1953, New York, N.Y. Screen, stage, and television actor.

Appeared in: 1958 Love Island.

SHANLEY, ROBERT
Died: June 30, 1968, Los Angeles, Calif. Screen, stage, radio, and television actor, and singer.

Appeared in: 1943 This Is the Army (stage and film versions).

SHANNON, MRS. DALE
Died: June 1, 1923, New York, N.Y. Screen and stage actress. Appeared in early Lubin films.

SHANNON, EFFIE
Born: 1867, Cambridge, Mass. Died: July 24, 1954, Bay Shore, N.Y. Screen and stage actress.

Appeared in: 1914 After the Ball. 1921 Mama's Affair. 1922 The Man Who Played God; The Secrets of Paris; Sure-Fire Flint. 1923 The Tie That Binds; Bright Lights of Broadway; Jacqueline of the Blazing Barriers. 1924 Damaged Hearts; Roulette; Sinners in Heaven; Greater Than Marriage; The Side Show of Life. 1925 Sally of the Sawdust; Soul of Fire; The New Commandment; The Pearl of Love; Wandering Fires. 1932 The Wiser Sex.

SHANNON, ELIZABETH S. (aka BETTY SUNDMARK)
Born: 1914. Died: Aug. 18, 1959, N.Y. Screen actress. Divorced from screen actor Alan Curtis (dec. 1953).

SHANNON, ETHEL (Ethel Shannon Jackson)
Born: 1898. Died: July 14, 1951, Hollywood, Calif. Screen actress.

Appeared in: 1920 An Old Fashioned Boy. 1922 Man's Law and God's; The Top O' the Morning; Watch Him Step. 1923 The Hero; Daughters of the Rich; The Girl Who Came Back; Maytime. 1924 Lightning Romance; Riders Up. 1925 Charley's Aunt; High and Handsome; The Phantom Express; Stop Flirting; The Texas Trail; Speed Wild. 1926 Oh, Baby!; The Speed Limit; The Sign of the Cross; The Silent Power; The High Flyer; The Buckaroo Kid; Danger Quest. 1927 Babe Comes Home; Through Thick and Thin.

SHANNON, FRANK CONNOLLY
Born: 1875. Died: Feb. 1, 1959, Hollywood, Calif. Screen, stage, and radio actor.

Appeared in: 1921 The Bride's Play; Perjury. 1922 Boomerang Bill. 1924 Icebound; Monsieur Beaucaire. 1935 Men without Names; The Eagle's Brood. 1936 The Prisoner of Shark Island; Flash Gordon (serial); The Texas Rangers. 1937 The Affairs of Cappy Ricks; The Adventurous Blonde. 1938 Flash Gordon's Trip to Mars (serial); Mars Attacks the World; Torchy Blane in Panama; Torchy Gets Her Man. 1939 Torchy Runs for Mayor;

The Night of Nights. 1940 Flash Gordon Conquers the Universe (serial); The Return of Frank James; Wildcat Bus; Dancing on a Dime.

SHANNON, HARRY
Born: June 13, 1890, Saginaw, Mich. Died: July 27, 1964, Hollywood, Calif. Screen and stage actor.

Appeared in: 1930 Heads Up. 1940 Young as You Feel; Parole Fixer; One Crowded Night; Too Many Girls; Gambling on the High Seas; The Girl from Avenue A; Young Tom Edison; City of Chance; Tear Gas Squad; Tugboat Annie Sails Again; Sailor's Lady. 1941 Citizen Kane; The Saint in Palm Springs; Hold Back the Dawn. 1942 The Lady Is Willing; The Big Street; Mrs. Wiggs of the Cabbage Patch; Once upon a Honeymoon; This Gun for Hire; The Falcon Takes Over; In Old California; Random Harvest. 1943 Alaska Highway; Headin' for God's Country; True to Life; Idaho; Someone to Remember; Song of Texas; Gold Town; The Powers Girl. 1944 The Sullivans; The Mummy's Ghost; When the Lights Go on Again; Yellow Rose of Texas; Eve of St. Mark; Ladies of Washington. 1945 Captain Eddie; Crime, Inc.; Nob Hill; Within These Walls. 1946 Night Editor; San Quentin; I Ring Doorbells; Ziegfeld Follies; The Last Crooked Mile. 1947 The Devil Thumbs a Ride; The Farmer's Daughter; Nora Prentiss; The Red House; Time out of Mind; The Invisible Wall; Exposed; Dangerous Years. 1948 The Lady from Shanghai; Mr. Blanding Builds His Dream House; Fighting Father Dunne; Feudin', Fussin' and A-Fightin'. 1949 Tulsa; Rustlers; Champion; Mr. Soft Touch; The Devil's Henchmen. 1950 Mary Ryan, Detective; Tarnished; Cow Town; The Underworld Story; Singing Guns; Where Danger Lives; Three Little Words; Curtain Call at Cactus Creek; Hunt the Man Down; The Flying Missile; The Killer That Stalked New York; The Gunfighter. 1951 Pride of Maryland; The Scarf; Al Jennings of Oklahoma; Blue Blood; The Lemon Drop Kid. 1952 High Noon; Boots Malone; Flesh and Fury; The Outcasts of Poker Flat; Lure of the Wilderness. 1953 Cry of the Hunted; Kansas Pacific; Jack Slade; Phantom Stallion; Roar of the Crowd. 1954 Executive Suite; Witness to Murder; Rails into Laramie. 1955 The Tall Men; Violent Men; At Gunpoint; The Marauders. 1956 Come Next Spring; Written on the Wind; The Peacemaker. 1957 The Lonely Man; Duel at Apache Wells; Hell's Crossroads. 1958 The Buccaneer; Man or Gun. 1961 Wild in the Country. 1962 Gypsy.

SHANNON, JACK
Born: 1892. Died: Dec. 1968, Los Angeles, Calif. Screen actor and stuntman. Married to screen actress Grace Cunard (dec. 1967).

Appeared in: 1935 Stormy.

SHANNON, PEGGY
Born: Jan. 10, 1909, Pine Bluff, Ark. Died: May 11, 1941, North Hollywood, Calif.(natural causes). Screen and stage actress. Married to screen actor/cameraman Albert Roberts (dec.1941).

Appeared in: 1931 Silence; The Road to Reno; The Secret Call; Touchdown. 1932 False Faces; This Reckless Age; Hotel Continental; The Painted Woman; Society Girl. 1933 Girl Missing; Devil's Mate; The Deluge; Turn Back the Clock. 1934 Fury of the Jungle; Back Page. 1935 The Fighting Lady; Night Life of the Gods; The Case of the Lucky Legs. 1936 The Man I Marry. 1937 Youth on Parole. 1938 Girls on Probation. 1939 Blackwell's Island; The Adventures of Jane Arden; Fixer Dugan. 1940 The House across the Bay; Triple Justice; Cafe Hostess; Street of Missing Women.

SHANNON, RAY
Born: 1895. Died: Jan. 1, 1971, Cincinnati, Ohio. Screen, stage, vaudeville, and radio actor.

SHANOR, PEGGY
Died: May 30, 1935, New York, N.Y. Screen, stage, and vaudeville actress. Featured in vaudeville with Vera Gordon and Sam Selbert.

Appeared in: 1918 The House of Hate (serial). 1919 The Lurking Peril (serial). 1920 The Mystery Mind (serial). 1921 The Sky Ranger (serial). 1922 The Prodigal Judge.

SHARLAND, REGINALD
Born: 1887, Southend-on-Sea, Essex, England. Died: Aug. 21, 1944, Loma Linda, Calif. Screen, stage, and radio actor.

Appeared in: 1929 Show of Shows; Woman to Woman. 1930 Girl of the Port; Scotland Yard; What a Widow; Inside the Lines. 1931 Born to Love. 1934 Long Lost Father.

SHARP, HENRY (Henry Schacht)
Born: 1887. Died: Jan. 10, 1964, Brooklyn, N.Y. Screen, stage actor, and educator. Entered films with D. W. Griffith.

Appeared in: 1945 A Song to Remember. 1956 Singing in the Dark. 1957 A Face in the Crowd; The Violators.

SHARP, LEN
Born: 1890. Died: Oct. 24, 1958, Waterford, England. Screen, stage, and television actor.

Appeared in: 1955 Cocktails in the Kitchen. 1956 The Ladykillers; The Mudlark. 1958 At the Stroke of Nine.

SHARPLIN, JOHN
Born: 1916. Died: Apr. 1961, Harrogate, England. Screen, stage, and television actor.

SHATTUCK, EDWARD F.
Born: 1890. Died: Jan. 31, 1948, Hollywood, Calif. Screen and vaudeville actor.

SHATTUCK, TRULY
Born: 1876. Died: Dec. 6, 1954, Hollywood, Calif. Screen and stage actress.

Appeared in: 1921 A Wise Fool; The Great Impersonation; The Speed Girl. 1922 The Glory of Clementina; The Hottentot; Beauty's Worth. 1923 Daughters of the Rich. 1927 Rubber Heels. 1935 The Perfect Clue.

SHAW, C. MONTAGUE
Born: Mar. 23, 1884, Adelaide, South Australia. Died: Feb. 6, 1968, Woodland Hills, Calif. Screen and stage actor.

Appeared in: 1926 The Set-Up. 1928 The Water Hole. 1929 Behind That Curtain; Morgan's Last Raid; Square Shoulders. 1932 The Silent Witness; Pack up Your Troubles; Sherlock Holmes; Cynara; Letty Lynton; Rasputin and the Empress. 1933 The Big Brain; The Masquerader; Today We Live; Cavalcade; Gabriel over the White House; Queen Christina. 1934 Shock; Sisters under the Skin; Fog; Riptide; House of Rothschild. 1935 Vanessa, Her Love Story; David Copperfield; Becky Sharp; Two Sinners; I Live for Love. 1936 The Leathernecks Have Landed; Undersea Kingdom (serial); My American Wife; King of Burlesque. 1937 Riders of the Whistling Skull; The Frame Up; Parole Racket; The Sheik Steps Out; A Nation Aflame; Ready, Willing and Able; The King and the Chorus Girl. 1938 Mars Attacks the World; Four Men and a Prayer; Little Miss Broadway; Suez. 1939 The Three Musketeers; The Rains Came; Stanley and Livingstone. 1940 My Son, My Son; The Gay Caballero; Charlie Chan's Murder Cruise. 1941 Hard Guy; Burma Convoy; Charley's Aunt. 1942 Thunder Birds; Random Harvest; Pride of the Yankees. 1944 Faces in the Fog. 1945 An Angel Comes to Brooklyn; Tonight and Every Night. 1946 Road to the Big House. 1947 Thunder in the Valley.

SHAW, DENNIS
Born: 1921. Died: Feb. 28, 1971, London, England.(heart attack). Screen and television actor.

SHAW, FRANK M.
Born: 1894. Died: May 7, 1937, Kansas City, Mo. Screen, stage, and radio actor.

SHAW, OSCAR (Oscar Schwartz)
Born: 1891. Died: Mar. 6, 1967, Little Neck, N.Y. Screen, stage, and radio actor.

Appeared in: 1924 The Great White Way. 1925 King on Main Street. 1926 Going Crooked; Upstage. 1929 The Cocoanuts; Marianne. 1940 Rhythm on the River.

SHEA, BIRD
Died: Nov. 23, 1924, Los Angeles, Calif. Screen actress.

Appeared in: 1925 The Lady.

SHEA, JOHN "JACK"
Born: 1900, Charleston, W.Va. Died: Oct. 13, 1970, Huntington, W. Va. Screen, stage, and vaudeville actor.

Appeared in: 1951 Million Dollar Pursuit. 1955 Lucy Gallant. 1958 Satan's Satellites.

SHEAN, AL (Alfred Schoenberg)
Born: 1868, Dornum, Germany. Died: Aug. 12, 1949, New York, N.Y. Screen, stage, vaudeville actor, and song writer. Was partner in vaudeville act "Mr. Gallagher and Mr. Shean."

Appeared in: 1923 Around the Town. 1930 Chills and Fever

(short). 1934 Music in the Air. 1935 Sweet Music; Page Miss Glory; The Traveling Saleslady; Symphony of Living; It's in the Air. 1936 The Law in Her Hands; San Francisco; Hitchhike to Heaven; At Sea Ashore (short). 1937 The Road Back; It Could Happen to You; 52nd Street; Live, Love and Learn; The Prisoner of Zenda. 1938 Too Hot to Handle; The Great Waltz. 1939 Joe and Ethel Turp Call on the President; Broadway Serenade. 1940 The Blue Bird; Friendly Neighbors. 1941 Ziegfeld Girl. 1942 Tish. 1943 Hitler's Madmen; Crime Doctor. 1944 Atlantic City. 1946 People Are Funny.

SHEARN, EDITH
Born: 1870. Died: May 14, 1968, Hollywood, Calif. Screen actress. Married to actor Warner Oland (dec. 1938).

SHEEHAN, JOHN J.
Born: Oct. 22, 1890, Oakland, Calif. Died: Feb. 15, 1952, Hollywood, Calif. Screen, stage, and vaudeville actor. Entered films with American Film Co. in 1917.

Appeared in: 1930 Swing High; Broken Dishes; Kismet. 1931 Fair Warning; The Criminal Code. 1932 Hold 'Em Jail. 1933 Hard to Handle; The Warrior's Husband; The Past of Mary Holmes; King for a Night; The Gay Nighties (short). 1934 The Countess of Monte Cristo; Little Miss Marker; The Circus Clown; Such Women Are Dangerous. 1935 The Murder Man; The Goose and the Gander. 1936 It Had to Happen; Three Godfathers; Laughing Irish Eyes; Ticket to Paradise; The Ex-Mrs. Bradford; The Case of the Black Cat; Smart Blonde; Here Comes Carter. 1937 Join the Marines; All over Town; Mama Runs Wild; On the Avenue; Wake up and Live; Marked Woman; Midnight Court; Love Takes Flight; Night Club Scandal. 1940 Slightly Honorable; Margie; Young as You Feel. 1941 Broadway Limited. 1942 Wake Island. 1943 Swingtime Johnny. 1948 I Wouldn't Be in Your Shoes. 1949 The Doolins of Oklahoma. 1951 Stage to Tucson.

SHEFFIELD, REGINALD (Reginald Sheffield Cassan)
Born: Feb. 18, 1901, London, England. Died: Dec. 8, 1957, Pacific Palisades, Calif. Screen and stage actor. Entered films in 1913.

Appeared in: 1923 David Copperfield. 1924 Classmates. 1925 The Pinch Hitter. 1926 White Mice. 1927 The Nest; College Widow. 1928 Sweet Sixteen; The Adorable Cheat. 1930 Old English; The Green Goddess. 1931 Partners of the Trail. 1934 The House of Rothschild; Of Human Bondage. 1935 Black Sheep; Cardinal Richelieu; Society Fever; Splendor. 1937 Another Dawn. 1938 Female Fugitive; The Buccaneer. 1939 Gunga Din. 1940 Earthbound. 1941 Suspicion. 1942 Eyes in the Night; Eagle Squadron. 1943 Appointment in Berlin; The Man from Down Under; Tonight We Raid Calais; Bomber's Moon. 1944 Our Hearts Were Young and Gay; The Man in Half Moon Street; Wilson; The Great Moment. 1945 Captain Kidd; Devotion. 1946 Three Strangers; Centennial Summer. 1948 Kiss the Blood off My Hands. 1949 Mr. Belvedere Goes to College; Prison Warden. 1953 Second Chance. 1956 23 Paces to Baker Street; The Secret of Treasure Mountain. 1957 The Story of Mankind. 1958 The Buccaneer (and 1938 version).

SHELDON, CONNIE
Born: 1921. Died: Jan. 10, 1947, N.Y.(leukemia). Screen and stage actress.

SHELDON, JEROME
Born: 1891. Died: Apr. 15, 1962, Hollywood, Calif. Screen actor. Appeared in silents.

SHELDON, JERRY (Charles H. Patton)
Born: 1901. Died: Apr. 11, 1962, Hollywood, Calif. Screen and television actor.

Appeared in: 1952 Monkey Business. 1956 Love Me Tender.

SHELDON, MRS. MARION W.
Born: 1886. Died: Feb. 28, 1944, Hollywood, Calif. Screen and stage actress. Entered films in 1917.

SHELTON, GEORGE
Born: 1884. Died: Feb. 12, 1971, N.Y.(burns). Screen, stage, vaudeville, burlesque, radio, and television actor. Partner in vaudeville and radio with Tom Howard.

Appeared in: 1932 The Babbling Book (short). 1934-35 Educational shorts. 1945 The House on Ninety-Second Street. 1947 Kiss of Death.

SHEPLEY, MICHAEL (Michael Shepley-Smith)
Born: Sept. 29, 1907, Plymouth, England. Died: Sept. 28, 1961, London, England. Screen and stage actor.

Appeared in: 1930 Black Coffee. 1934 Bella Donna; Squibs; The Green Pack; Are You a Mason?; Triumph of Sherlock Holmes. 1935 The Lad; Vintage Wine; The Private Secretary; In the Soup. 1937 High Treason. 1938 Man with 100 Faces. 1939 Goodbye, Mr. Chips; Housemaster. 1940 It's in the Air; Quiet Wedding. 1943 The Great Mr. Handel. 1944 Henry V (U.S. 1946). 1949 Maytime in Mayfair; Mine Own Executioner; A Place of One's Own. 1952 Secret People. 1953 Murder on Monday. 1954 Tonight's the Night; Adventure for Two (aka Demi-Paradise). 1956 Doctor at Sea. 1957 An Alligator Named Daisy; Wanted on Voyage; A Novel Affair (aka Passionate Stranger). 1958 Henry V (reissue of 1944 film). 1959 Gideon of Scotland Yard (aka Gideon's Day); Teenage Bad Girl (aka My Teenage Daughter). 1961 Don't Bother to Knock; Double Bunk. Other British films: Crackerjack; I Lived in Grosvenor Square; Women Aren't Angels.

SHEPLEY, RUTH
Born: 1889, N.Y. Died: Oct. 5, 1951, New York, N.Y. Screen and stage actress.

Appeared in: 1922 When Knighthood Was in Flower.

SHERIDAN, ANN (Clara Lou Sheridan)
Born: Feb. 21, 1915, Denton, Tex. Died: Jan. 21, 1967, Hollywood, Calif.(cancer). Screen, stage, radio, and television actress. Divorced from screen actors Edward Norris and George Brent. Married to screen actor Scott McKay.

Appeared in: 1927 The Bandit's Son; Casey at the Bat; Casey Jones; Galloping Thunder; The Way of All Flesh; Wedding Bill$. 1933 Search; Bolero. 1934 Ladies Should Listen Come on, Marines; Notorious Sophie Lang; Limehouse Blues; Kiss and Make Up; Mrs. Wiggs of the Cabbage Patch; Wagon Wheels; Shoot the Works; College Rhythm; You Belong to Me. 1935 Enter Madame; Home on the Range; Behold My Wife; Car No. 99; Rocky Mountain Mystery; The Glass Key; The Crusades; Fighting Youth; Red Blood of Courage; Mississippi; Rumba. 1936 Sing Me a Love Song. 1937 The Great O'Malley; Black Legion; Footloose Heiress; San Quentin; Wine, Women and Horses. 1938 Alcatraz Island; Little Miss Thoroughbred; The Patient in Room 18; She Loved a Fireman; Mystery House; Cowboy from Brooklyn; Angels with Dirty Faces; Letter of Introduction; Broadway Musketeers. 1939 They Made Me a Criminal; Dodge City; Naughty but Nice; Indianapolis Speedway; Winter Carnival; Angels Wash Their Faces. 1940 It All Came True; Castle on the Hudson; Torrid Zone; They Drive by Night; City for Conquest. 1941 Honeymoon for Three; Navy Blues; The Man Who Came to Dinner; King's Row. 1942 Juke Girl; George Washington Slept Here; The Animal Kingdom; Wings for the Eagle. 1943 Edge of Darkness; Thank Your Lucky Stars. 1944 Shine on Harvest Moon; The Doughgirls. 1946 One More Tomorrow. 1947 Nora Prentiss; The Unfaithful. 1948 Good Sam; Treasure of the Sierra Madre; Silver River. 1949 I Was a Male War Bride. 1950 Woman on the Run; Stella. 1952 Steel Town; Just across the Street. 1953 Take Me to Town; Appointment in Honduras. 1956 Come Next Spring; The Opposite Sex. 1957 Woman and the Hunter.

SHERIDAN, FRANK
Born: June 11, 1869, Boston, Mass. Died: Nov. 24, 1943, Hollywood, Calif. Screen and stage actor.

Appeared in: 1921 Anne of Little Smoky; The Rider of the King Log; Her Lord and Master. 1922 One Exciting Night. 1923 The Man Next Door. 1924 Two Shall Be Born. 1925 Lena Rivers. 1929 Fast Life. 1930 Side Street; The Other Tomorrow; Danger Lights. 1931 The Public Defender; A Free Soul; Murder by the Clock; Silence; Donovan's Kid; The Ladies of the Big House; The Man I Killed; The Flood. 1932 The Last Mile; Okay America; Afraid to Talk; Washington Merry-Go-Round. 1933 The Man Who Dared; Mama Loves Papa; Deception; The Woman Accused. 1934 Wharf Angel; Upperworld; The Witching Hour; The Cat's Paw. 1935 Whispering Smith Speaks; Nevada; The Payoff. 1936 The Leavenworth Case; The Country Gentleman; Murder with Pictures; Conflict. 1937 The Life of Emile Zola; The Great O'Malley; Woman in Distress; A Fight to the Finish. 1938 City Streets.

SHERMAN, FRED E.
Born: 1905. Died: May 20, 1969, Woodland Hills, Calif. Screen, stage, and television actor.

Appeared in: 1946 Behind Green Lights; Lady in the Lake. 1950 Chain Lightning. 1957 The Tall T. 1959 Some Like It Hot.

SHERMAN, LOWELL
Born: Oct. 11, 1885, San Francisco, Calif. Died: Dec. 28, 1934, Hollywood, Calif.(pneumonia). Screen, stage, vaudeville, burlesque actor, and film director.

Appeared in: 1920 Way Down East; Yes or No. 1921 The Gilded Lily; What No Man Knows; Molly O. 1922 Grand Larceny; The Face in the Fog. 1923 Bright Lights of Broadway. 1924 Monsieur Beaucaire; The Masked Danger; The Truth about Women; The Spitfire. 1925 Satan in Sables. 1926 You Never Know Women; Lost at Sea; The Wilderness Woman; The Reckless Lady; The Love Toy. 1927 The Girl from Gay Paree; Convoy. 1928 The Whip Woman; The Ship; Mad Hour; The Divine Woman; The Garden of Eden; The Scarlet Dove; The Heart of a Follies Girl. 1929 Evidence; General Crack; Nearly Divorced (short); A Lady of Chance. 1930 Ladies of Leisure; He Knew Women; Midnight Mystery; Lawful Larceny; Oh Sailor, Behave!; The Pay Off; Losing Game; Mammy. 1931 High Stakes; Bachelor Apartment; The Royal Bed; Way Down East (reissue of 1920 version). 1932 What Price Hollywood?; False Faces; The Greeks Had a Word for Them; The Slippery Pearls (short). 1933 Broadway through a Keyhole; Morning Glory.

SHERRY, J. BARNEY (J. Barney Sherry Reeves)
Born: 1872, Germantown, Pa. Died: Feb. 22, 1944, Philadelphia, Pa. Screen, stage, vaudeville, and radio actor.

Appeared in: 1905 Raffles; The Amateur Cracksman. 1909-1912 western series; 1917 Flying Colors; Fuel of Life; Fanatics. 1918 Recording Day; The Secret Code; Evidence; Real Folks; Who Killed Walton?; Her Decision; High Stakes. 1919 The Lion Man (serial); May of Filbert. 1920 Go and Get It; Dinty. 1921 Burn 'Em up Barnes; The Barbarian; Just outside the Door; Man—Woman—Marriage; Thunderclap; The Lotus Eater. 1922 Sure-Fire Flint; Back Pay; The Inner Man; Island Wives; A Woman's Woman; When the Desert Calls; 'Til We Meet Again; Shadows of the Sea; Notoriety; John Smith; What Fools Men Are; The Secrets of Paris; The Broken Silence. 1923 The White Sister; Jacqueline of Blazing Barriers. 1924 Born Rich; Galloping Hoofs (serial); The Warrens of Virginia; Lend Me Your Husband; Miami. 1925 Daughters Who Pay; Play Ball (serial); Crackerjack; Lying Wives; The Live Wire; A Little Girl in a Big City; Enemies of Youth. 1926 The Brown Derby; The Prince of Tempters; Broken Homes; Casey of the Coast Guard (serial). 1927 Spider Webs; The Crimson Flash (serial). 1928 Alex the Great; The Wright Idea; Forgotten Faces. 1929 Jazz Heaven; Broadway Scandals; The Voice Within.

SHERWOOD, MILLIGE G.
Born: 1876. Died: Nov. 12, 1958, Hollywood, Calif. Screen and stage actor.

SHERWOOD, YORKE
Born: 1873. Died: Sept. 27, 1958, Hollywood, Calif. Screen actor.

Appeared in: 1926 The Man in the Saddle. 1928 The Cossacks; A Thief in the Dark; Gentlemen Prefer Blondes. 1930 The Man from Blankley's; Temple Tower. 1931 The Man in Possession. 1933 Eagle and the Hawk. 1936 Lloyds of London. 1944 Jane Eyre. 1956 23 Paces to Baker Street.

SHIELDS, ARTHUR
Born: 1896, Dublin, Ireland. Died: Apr. 27, 1970, Santa Barbara, Calif.(emphysema). Screen, stage, and television actor. Brother of screen actor Barry Fitzgerald (dec. 1961).

Appeared in: 1932 Sign of the Cross. 1936 The Plough and the Stars. 1939 Drums along the Mohawk. 1940 The Long Voyage Home; Little Nellie Kelly. 1941 Lady Scarface; The Gay Falcon; How Green Was My Valley; Confirm or Deny. 1942 Broadway; This above All; Pacific Rendezvous; Gentleman Jim; Nightmare; The Black Swan. 1943 Lassie Come Home; The Man from Down Under. 1944 Keys of the Kingdom; Youth Runs Wild; National Velvet; The White Cliffs of Dover; The Sign of the Cross (revised version of 1932 film). 1945 Roughly Speaking; The Corn Is Green; Too Young to Know; The Valley of Decision. 1946 Three Strangers; The Verdict; Gallant Journey. 1947 The Shocking Miss Pilgrim; Easy Come, Easy Go; The Fabulous Dorseys; Seven Keys to Baldpate. 1948 Fighting Father Dunne; Tap Roots; My Own True Love. 1949 She Wore a Yellow Ribbon; The Fighting O'Flynn; Challenge to Lassie; Red Light. 1950 Tarzan and the Slave Girl. 1951 The River; People against O'Hara; Apache Drums; Sealed Cargo; Blue Blood; A Wonderful Life; The Barefoot Mailman. 1952 The Quiet Man. 1953 Scandal at Scourie; South Sea Woman; Main Street to Broadway. 1954 Pride of the Blue Grass; World for Ransom. 1956 The King and Four Queens. 1957 Daughter of Dr. Jekyll. 1958 Enchanted Island. 1959 Night of the Quarter Moon. 1960 For the Love of Mike. 1962 The Pigeon That Took Rome.

SHIELDS, HELEN
Died: Aug. 7, 1963, New York, N.Y. Screen, stage, and television actress.

Appeared in: 1951 The Whistle at Eaton Falls. 1956 The Wrong Man.

SHIELDS, SANDY
Born: 1873. Died: Aug. 3, 1923, New York, N.Y. Screen and stage actor.

SHIELDS, SYDNEY
Born: 1888. Died: Sept. 19, 1960, Queens, N.Y. Screen and stage actress. Appeared in silents.

SHINE, WILFRED
Born: 1863, Manchester, England. Died: Mar. 14, 1939, Kingston, England. Screen, stage, burlesque, television actor, and radio writer. Father of screen actor Billy Shine.

SHINER, RONALD
Born: June 8, 1903, London, England. Died: June 30, 1966, London, England. Screen, stage, and radio actor. His enormous nose was insured for $30,000.

Appeared in: 1934 My Old Dutch (film debut). 1937 Dreaming Lips; Dinner at the Ritz. 1938 A Yank at Oxford; The Gang's All Here; They Ride by Night; Prison without Bars. 1941 Frightened Lady. 1942 King Arthur Was a Gentleman; Wings and the Woman. 1945 The Way to the Stars. 1948 The Smugglers. 1950 Worm's Eye View. 1951 Reluctant Heroes. 1953 Laughing Anne. 1954 Top of the Form. 1955 Up to His Neck; Innocents in Paris. 1956 Keep It Clean; Dry Rot. 1957 Not Wanted on Voyage; Carry on Admiral (aka The Ship Was Loaded—U.S. 1959). 1958 Girls at Sea (U.S. 1962). 1959 Operation Bullshine (U.S. 1959). 1960 The Night We Got the Bird. Other British films: Come on, George; I Killed the Count; Old Bill and Son; South American George; The Big Blockade; Unpublished Story; The Butler's Dilemma; Squadron Leader; Gentle Sex; Get Cracking; Thursday's Child; Bees in Paradise; Caesar and Cleopatra; I Remember the Unicorn; I Lived in Grosvenor Square; The Man Within; No Nightingales; Brighton Rock; George in Civvy Street; Forbidden; Rise and Shine; The Magic Box; Little Big Shot; Aunt Clara; See How They Run; My Wife's Family; The Navy Lark.

SHIRART, GEORGIA
Born: 1862. Died: Feb., 1929, Los Angeles, Calif. Screen actress. Entered films with Lubin Co. in 1913.

Appeared in: 1923 The Girl Who Came Back.

SHIRLEY, FLORENCE
Born: 1893. Died: May 12, 1967, Hollywood, Calif. Screen and stage actress.

Appeared in: 1940 Private Affairs. 1942 A Yank at Eton; Secret Agent of Japan; Her Cardboard Lover; We Were Dancing. 1952 Deadline U. S. A.; Stars and Stripes Forever.

SHIRLEY, TOM (Thomas P. Shirley)
Born: 1900. Died: Jan. 24, 1962, New York, N.Y. Screen, stage, radio, and television actor. Entered films as a child with Essenay Films in Chicago.

Appeared in: 1926 Lightning Bill; Red Hot Leather. 1927 King of Kings.

SHOOTING STAR
Born: 1890. Died: June 4, 1966, Hollywood, Calif.(stroke). Sioux Indian screen actor. Entered films approx. 1935.

Appeared in: 1949 Laramie.

SHORES, BYRON L.
Born: 1907. Died: Nov. 13, 1957, Kansas City, Mo.(multiple sclerosis). Screen and stage actor.

Appeared in: 1940 Too Many Girls. 1941 Johnny Eager; Blossoms in the Dust. 1943 This Is the Army; The Major and the Minor; The Mad Doctor of Market Street. 1943 Air Raid Wardens.

SHORT, FLORENCE
Born: 1889. Died: July 10, 1946, Hollywood, Calif. Screen and stage actress. Sister of screen actress Gertrude Short (dec. 1968) and daughter of screen actor Lewis Short (dec. 1958).

Appeared in: 1918 The Eagle's Eye (serial). 1921 Lessons in Love; Woman's Place. 1922 Cardigan; The Lights of New York; Silver Wings. 1923 Does It Pay?. 1924 The Enchanted Cottage. 1931 Way Down East.

SHORT, GERTRUDE
Born: Apr. 6, 1902, Cincinnati, Ohio. Died: July 31, 1968, Hollywood, Calif. Screen, stage, and vaudeville actress. Sister of screen actress Florence Short (dec. 1946) and daughter of screen actor Lewis Short (dec. 1958).

Appeared in: 1913 Uncle Tom's Cabin. 1920 You Never Can Tell. 1922 Rent Free; Boy Crazy; Headin' West; Youth to Youth. 1923 The Gold Diggers; Breaking into Society; Crinoline and Romance; The Prisoner; The Man Life Passed By. 1924 Barbara Frietchie; and "The Telephone Girl" series of shorts which included: Julius Sees Her; When Knighthood Was in Power; Money to Burn; Sherlock's Home; King Leary; William Tells; For the Love of Mike; The Square Sex; Bee's Knees; Love and Learn; Faster Foster; Hello and Good Bye. 1925 The Narrow Street; Beggar on Horseback; My Lady's Lips; The Other Woman's Story; Code of the West; Her Market Value; The People vs. Nancy Preston; The Talker; Tessie. 1926 Dangerous Friends; Ladies of Leisure; A Poor Girl's Romance; Sweet Adeline; The Lily. 1927 Ladies at Ease; Tillie the Toiler; Adam and Evil; The Show; The Masked Woman; Polly of the Movies; Women's Wares. 1928 None but The Brave. 1929 Trial Marriage; Gold Diggers of Broadway; The Broadway Hoofer; In Old California; The Three Outcasts. 1930 The Last Dance; Once a Gentleman; The Little Accident. 1931 Laughing Sinners. 1933 The Girl in 419; Son of Kong. 1934 Love Birds; The Key; St. Louis Kid. 1935 Helldorado; Woman Wanted; Affairs of Susan. 1937 Park Avenue Logger; Stella Dallas. 1938 Tip-Off Girls.

SHORT, HASSARD
Born: 1878, England. Died: Oct. 9, 1956, Nice, France. Screen actor, stage director, and stage producer.

Appeared in: 1918 The Turn of the Wheel. 1919 The Way of a Woman; The Stronger Vow. 1921 Woman's Place.

SHORT, LEWIS W. "LEW"
Born: Feb. 14, 1875, Dayton, Ohio. Died: Apr. 26, 1958, Hollywood, Calif. Screen and stage actor. Entered films with D. W. Griffith at Biograph in 1908. Father of screen actresses Gertrude (dec. 1968) and Florence Short (dec. 1946).

Appeared in: 1922 The Black Bag; The Heart of Lincoln. 1926 The Blue Eagle. 1927 The Heart of Maryland. 1928 Black Pearl; Big City; 1929 The Three Outcasts; Is Everybody Happy?. 1930 A Girl in the Show.

SHRINER, HERB (Herbert Arthur Schiner)
Born: May 29, 1918, Toledo, Ohio. Died: Apr. 23, 1970, Delray Beach, Fla.(auto accident). Screen, radio, and television actor.

Appeared in: 1953 Main Street to Broadway.

SHUBERT, EDDIE
Born: July 11, 1898, Milwaukee, Wisc. Died: Jan. 23, 1937, Los Angeles, Calif. Screen, stage, burlesque, and vaudeville actor.

Appeared in: 1934 6 Day Bike Rider; Murder in the Clouds; St. Louis Kid; The Case of the Howling Dog. 1935 The Goose and the Gander; Alibi Ike; Black Fury; While the Patient Slept; The Pay-Off; Don't Bet on Blondes. 1936 Song of the Saddle; Road Gang; Man Hunt; The Law in Her Hands; The Case of the Velvet Claws. 1937 Time Out for Romance.

SHUTTA, JACK
Born: 1899. Died: June 28, 1957, Houston, Tex.(cancer). Screen, stage, vaudeville, and burlesque actor.

Appeared in: 1930 Whoopee. 1935 False Pretenses. 1947 The Wistful Widow of Wagon Gap. 1948 The Burning Cross. 1950 Abbott and Costello Go to Mars.

SHY, GUS
Born: 1894, Buffalo, N.Y. Died: June 15, 1945, Hollywood, Calif. Screen, stage, vaudeville actor, and film dialog director.

Appeared in: 1930 Good News; New Moon; A Lady's Morals. 1933 a Vitaphone short; 1934 I Sell Anything. 1936 The Captain's Kid. 1937 Once a Doctor.

SIDNEY, GEORGE (Sammy Greenfield)
Born: Mar. 18, 1876, New York, N.Y. Died: Apr. 29, 1945, Los Angeles, Calif. Screen, stage, and vaudeville actor. He was Cohen in "The Cohens and the Kellys" series and Potash in the "Potash and Perlmutter" series.

Appeared in: 1923 Potash and Perlmutter. 1924 In Hollywood with Potash and Perlmutter. 1925 Classified. 1926 Millionaires; The Cohens and the Kellys; Partners Again; The Prince of Pilsen; Sweet Daddies. 1927 Clancy's Kosher Wedding; The Auctioneer; For the Love of Mike; The Life of Riley; Lost at the Front. 1928 The Flying Romeos; Give and Take; The Cohens and the Kellys in Paris; The Latest from Paris; We Americans. 1929 The Cohens and the Kellys in Atlantic City. 1930 Around the Corner; King of Jazz; The Cohens and the Kellys in Scotland; The Cohens and the Kellys in Africa. 1931 Caught Cheating. 1932 High Pressure; The Cohens and the Kellys in Hollywood. 1933 The Cohens and the Kellys in Trouble. 1934 Rafter Romance; Manhattan Melodrama. 1935 Diamond Jim. 1937 The Good Old Soak.

SIDNEY, MABEL
Born: 1884. Died: Oct. 18, 1969, New York, N.Y. Screen, vaudeville, and television actress.

SIDNEY, SCOTT (Scott Siggins)
Born: 1872. Died: July 20, 1928, London, England (heart trouble). Screen, stage actor, and film director. Entered films as an actor with Thomas Ince Productions.

SIEBEL, PETER
Born: 1884. Died: Mar. 4, 1949, Long Beach, Calif. Screen actor and circus performer.

SIEGMANN, GEORGE
Born: 1883. Died: June 22, 1928, Hollywood, Calif.(pernicious anemia). Screen, stage actor, and assistant film director.

Appeared in: 1909 The Sealed Room. 1915 Birth of a Nation. 1916 Intolerance. 1918 Hearts of the World; The Great Love. 1919 The Fall of Babylon. 1920 The Hawk's Trail (serial); Little Miss Rebellion. 1921 The Big Punch; A Connecticut Yankee at King Arthur's Court; Partners of Fate; Desperate Trails; The Three Musketeers; Silent Years; The Queen of Sheba; Shame. 1922 Fools First; Hungry Hearts; Monte Cristo; The Truthful Liar. 1923 Merry-Go-Round; Lost and Found; Anna Christie; The Eagle's Feather; Hell's Hole; Jealous Husbands; Enemies of Children; The Man Life Passed By; Stepping Fast; Scaramouche; Slander the Woman. 1924 Singer Jim McKee; The Guilty One; Manhattan; On Time; Janice Meredith; Revelation; The Right of the Strongest; A Sainted Devil; The Shooting of Dan McGrew; Stolen Secrets; When a Girl Loves. 1925 Sporting Life; Zander the Great; Manhattan Madness; Pursued; Never the Twain Shall Meet; The Phantom Express; Recompense. 1926 The Old Soak; Born to the West; The Carnival Girl; My Old Dutch; The Midnight Sun; Poker Faces; The Palaces of Pleasure. 1927 King of Kings; The Cat and the Canary; The Red Mill; Uncle Tom's Cabin; The Thirteenth Juror; Hotel Imperial. 1928 Stop That Man; Love Me and the World Is Mine; Man Who Laughs. 1959 Uncle Tom's Cabin (re-release of 1927 film).

SIELANSKI, STANLEY (aka STANLEY STANISLAW)
Born: Poland. Died: Apr. 28, 1955, New York, N.Y. Screen and stage actor.

Appeared in: 1934 Parade Rezerwistow; Maryika. 1936 Manewry Milosne. 1937 Cabman No. 13; Ksiazatko (The Lottery Prince); Krolowa Przedmiescia (Queen of the Market Place). 1938 Pan Redaktor Szaleje (Mr. Editor Is Crazy).

SIGGINS, JULIA WILLIAMS. See Julia Williams

SIGNORET, GABRIEL
Born: 1873. Died: Apr. 1937, France (appendicitis). Screen actor.

Appeared in: Bouclette (film debut); Le Reve (both silents) and later Veille d'Arme; 27 Rue de la Paix, and Les Hommes Noveaux.

SILBERT, LISA
Born: 1880, Rumania. Died: Nov. 29, 1965, Miami, Fla. Screen, stage, and television actress. Appeared in numerous Yiddish theatre productions.

Appeared in: 1926 Broken Hearts.

SILETTI, MARIO G.
Born: 1904. Died: Apr. 19, 1964, Los Angeles, Calif.(auto accident). Screen and television actor.

Appeared in: 1949 Thieves' Highway. 1950 Under My Skin; The Man Who Cheated Himself; Black Hand. 1951 The Enforcer; Ann of the Indies; Strictly Dishonorable; Force of Arms; The Great Caruso; House on Telegraph Hill; Stop That Cab. 1952 When in Rome; My Cousin Rachel; Captain Pirate. 1953 Big Leaguer; Wings of the Hawk; Hot News; Kansas City Confidential; So This Is Love; Taxi; Thunder Bay; The Caddy. 1954 Theodora;

Slave Empress; Three Coins in the Fountain. 1955 Hell's Island; The Naked Street; Bring Your Serenade. 1958 Man in the Shadow. 1960 Pay or Die.

SILLS, MILTON
Born: Jan. 10, 1882, Chicago, Ill. Died: Sept. 15, 1930, Santa Monica, Calif.(heart attack). Screen and stage actor.

Appeared in: 1915 The Rack; The Deep Purple. 1917 Patria (serial). 1918 The Hell Cat. 1919 Eyes on Youth; Shadows; The Stronger Vow. 1920 The Week-End; Behold My Wife. 1921 The Marriage Gamble; At the End of the World; The Great Moment; The Faith Healer; Savage; Miss Lulu Bett. 1922 Burning Sands; Borderland; Environment; One Clear Call; The Woman Who Walked Alone; Skin Deep; The Forgotten Law; The Marriage Chance. 1923 Why Women Re-Marry; The Last Hour; Adam's Rib; A Lady of Quality; The Spoilers; Flaming Youth; The Isle of Lost Ships; Legally Dead; Souls for Sale; What a Wife Learned. 1924 Madonna of the Streets; The Sea Hawk; Single Wives; Flowing Gold; The Heart Bandit. 1925 The Unguarded Hour; The Knockout; As Man Desires; I Want My Man; A Lover's Oath; The Making of O'Malley. 1926 Paradise; Men of Steel; Puppets; The Silent Lover. 1927 The Sea Tiger; The Valley of the Giants; Framed; Hard-Boiled Haggerty. 1928 The Barker; Burning Daylight; The Crash; The Hawk's Nest. 1929 His Captive Woman; Love and the Devil. 1930 Man Trouble; The Sea Wolf.

SILVA, ANTONIO JOAO
Born: 1870, Portugal. Died: Jan. 31, 1954, Lisbon, Portugal (result of fall). Screen and stage actor. Entered films in 1930.

SILVA, SIMONE
Born: 1928. Died: Nov. 30, 1957, London, England. Screen actress.

Appeared in: 1953 Shadow Man; Desperate Moment. 1954 Deadly Game; Duel in the Jungle; The Golden Mask; The Weak and the Wicked. 1956 The Dynamiters.

SILVANI, ALDO
Born: 1891, Italy. Died: Nov. 1964, Milan, Italy. Screen and television actor.

Appeared in: 1947 La Vita Ricomincia (Life Begins Anew); Anything for a Song; To Live in Peace. 1948 Four Steps in the Clouds. 1949 The Golden Madonna; Carmela. 1950 Difficult Years; Mad about Opera. 1951 Teresa; Measure for Measure. 1952 When in Rome; The Thief of Venice. 1953 Stranger on the Prowl; Paolo and Francesca. 1954 La Strada; Beat the Devil; Valley of the Kings. 1959 The Tempest. 1960 Cartagine in Fiamme (Carthage in Flames); Ben Hur. 1962 Damon and Pythias. 1963 Sodom and Gomorrah.

SILVER, CHRISTINE
Born: 1885. Died: Nov. 23, 1960, London, England. Screen, stage, and television actress.

Appeared in: 1939 Dead Men Tell No Tales. 1951 Mystery Junction.

SILVER, PAULINE
Born: 1888. Died: Jan. 1, 1969, West Hollywood, Calif.(murdered). Screen actress. Appeared in silents.

SILVERA, FRANK
Born: 1914, Kingston, Jamaica, West Indies. Died: June 11, 1970, Pasadena, Calif.(accidentally electrocuted). Negro screen, stage, television actor, stage producer, and stage director.

Appeared in: 1951 The Cimarron Kid. 1952 The Fighter; The Miracle of Our Lady of Fatima; Viva Zapata!. 1953 Fear and Desire. 1955 Killer's Kiss. 1956 Crowded Paradise; The Mountain; The Lonely Night. 1957 Hateful of Rain. 1958 The Bravados. 1959 Crime and Punishment, U.S.A. 1960 The Mountain Road; Key Witness. 1962 Mutiny on the Bounty. 1963 Toys in the Attic. 1965 The Greatest Story Ever Told. 1966 The Appaloosa. 1967 Hombre; The St. Valentine's Day Massacre. 1968 The Stalking Moon; Betrayal; Up Tight. 1969 Che!; Guns of the Magnificent Seven.

SIMANEK, OTTO
Born: 1901. Died: Oct. 15, 1967, New York, N.Y. Screen, stage, and television actor.

Appeared in: 1956 The Wrong Man.

SIMMONDS, ANNETTE (Viscountess Dangan)
Born: 1918, England. Died: Oct. 28, 1959, near London, England (auto accident). Screen and stage actress.

Appeared in: 1951 Blackout; No Orchids for Miss Blandish. 1955 The Wicked Lady.

SIMON, SOL S.
Born: 1864. Died: Apr. 24, 1940, Hollywood, Calif. Screen and stage actor. Credited with discovering oil in the Kern County (Calif.), in 1910.

Appeared in: 1925 Greed. 1928 The Barker; Desperate Courage. 1930 Headin' North; The Land of Missing Men.

SIMPSON, GRANT
Born: 1884, Sioux Falls, S.D. Died: Jan. 8, 1932, Asheville, N.C. Screen, stage, and vaudeville actor. Married to screen actress Lulu McConnell (dec. 1962), with whom he teamed in vaudeville.

SIMPSON, IVAN
Born: 1875, Glasgow, Scotland. Died: Oct. 12, 1951, New York, N.Y. Screen and stage actor.

Appeared in: 1915 The Dictator (film debut). 1916 Out of the Drifts. 1922 The Man Who Played God. 1923 Twenty-One; The Green Goddess. 1924 $20 a Week. 1925 Lovers in Quarantine; Miss Bluebeard; Wild, Wild Susan; Womanhandled. 1926 A Kiss for Cinderella. 1929 Disraeli; Evidence. 1930 The Green Goddess (and 1923 version); Old English; The Way of All Men; Manslaughter; The Sea God; Inside the Lines; Isle of Escape. 1931 The Millionaire; The Lady Who Dared; The Reckless Hour; I Like Your Nerve; Safe in Hell. 1932 The Man Who Played God (and 1922 version); A Passport to Hell; The Crash; The Phantom of Crestwood. 1933 The Monkey's Paw; The Past of Mary Holmes; Midnight Mary; Voltaire; Charlie Chan's Greatest Case; The Silk Express; Blind Adventure. 1934 Man of Two Worlds; The Mystery of Mr. X; The House of Rothschild; The World Moves On; British Agent; Among the Missing. 1935 David Copperfield; Shadow of Doubt; Mark of the Vampire; The Bishop Misbehaves; Captain Blood; The Perfect Gentleman; East of Java; Splendor. 1936 Little Lord Fauntleroy; Trouble for Two; Mary of Scotland; Lloyds of London. 1937 Maid of Salem; A Night of Mystery; The Prince and the Pauper; London by Night. 1938 The Baroness and the Butler; Invisible Enemy; Booloo; The Adventures of Robin Hood. 1939 The Hound of the Baskervilles; Made for Each Other; Never Say Die; Adventures of Sherlock Holmes; Ruler of the Seas; The Sun Never Sets. 1940 The Invisible Man Returns; New Moon. 1942 Nazi Agent; The Male Animal; They All Kissed the Bride; Youth on Parade; Nightmare; Random Harvest; The Body Disappears. 1943 My Kingdom for a Cook; Two Weeks to Live; Forever and a Day; This Land Is Mine. 1944 Jane Eyre; The Hour before the Dawn.

SIMPSON, RUSSELL
Born: June 17, 1880, San Francisco, Calif. Died: Dec. 12, 1959, Hollywood, Calif. Screen, stage, radio, and television actor. Entered films in 1910.

Appeared in: 1914 The Virginian. 1917 The Barrier. 1918 Blue Jeans. 1919 The Brand. 1920 The Branding Iron. 1921 Godless Men; Shadows of Conscience; Bunty Pulls the Strings; Snowblind; Under the Lash. 1922 Across the Dead Line; Fools of Fortune; The Kingdom Within; Rags to Riches; When Love Is Young; Human Hearts. 1923 Peg O' My Heart; The Girl of the Golden West; The Virginian (and 1914 version); Circus Days; Defying Destiny; Hearts Aflame; The Huntress; Rip Tide. 1924 The Narrow Street; Painted People. 1925 Beauty and the Bad Man; Paint and Powder; Faint Perfume; Old Shoes; Recreation of Brian Kent; Ship of Souls; The Splendid Road; Thunder Mountain; Why Women Love. 1926 The Earth Woman; The Social Highwayman; Lovely Mary; Rustling for Cupid. 1927 Wild Geese; Annie Laurie; The First Auto; The Frontiersman; God's Great Wilderness; Now We're in the Air; The Heart of the Yukon. 1928 Trail of '98; The Bushranger; Life's Mockery; Tropical Nights. 1929 Innocents of Paris; Noisy Neighbors; My Lady's Past; The Kid's Clever; The Sap; After the Fog. 1930 Billy the Kid; Lone Star Ranger; Abraham Lincoln. 1931 Man to Man; The Great Meadow; Susan Lennox, Her Rise and Fall. 1932 Law and Order; Ridin' for Justice; Lean Rivers; Honor of the Press; Riding Tornado; Flames; Cabin in the Cotton; Hello Trouble; Silver Dollar; Call Her Savage. 1933 Face in the Sky; Hello, Everybody!. 1934 Three on a Honeymoon; Carolina; The Frontier Marshal; Ever since Eve; Sixteen Fathoms Deep; The World Moves On. 1935 West of the Pecos; Motive for Revenge; The Hoosier Schoolmaster; Way Down East; Paddy O'Day; The County Chairman. 1936 Man Hunt; The Harvester; Girl of the Ozarks; The Crime of Dr. Forbes; Ramona; San Francisco. 1937 Green Light; That I May Live; Mountain Justice; Wild West Days (serial); Yodelin' Kid from Pine Ridge; Paradise Isle; Maid of Salem. 1938 Gold Is Where You Find It; Valley of the Giants; Hearts of the North. 1939 Western Caravans; Desperate Trails;

Drums along the Mohawk; Dodge City; Mr. Smith Goes to Washington; Young Mr. Lincoln; Geronimo. 1940 Girl of the Golden West (and 1923 version); Brigham Young—Frontiersman; Santa Fe Trail; Virginia City; Three Faces West; The Grapes of Wrath. 1941 The Last of the Duanes; Bad Men of Missouri; Wild Bill Hickok Rides; Tobacco Road; Wild Geese Calling; Citadel of Crime; Swamp Water; Outside the Law; Meet John Doe. 1942 Shut My Big Mouth; The Lone Ranger; The Spoilers; Tennessee Johnson. 1943 Woman of the Town; Border Patrol; Moonlight in Vermont. 1944 Texas Masquerade; Man from Frisco. 1945 Along Came Jones; The Big Bonanza; They Were Expendable; Incendiary Blonde. 1946 Bad Bascomb; California Gold Rush; My Darling Clementine. 1947 The Millerson Case; Bowery Buckaroos; The Fabulous Texan; Death Valley; Romance of Rosy Ridge. 1948 Albuquerque; My Dog Shep; Tap Roots; Caroner Creek; Sundown in Santa Fe. 1949 Tuna Clipper; The Beautiful Blonde from Bashful Bend; Free for All; The Gal Who Took the West. 1950 Call of the Klondike; Saddle Tramp; Wagon Master. 1951 Across the Wide Missouri; Comin' 'Round the Mountain. 1952 Feudin' Fools; Lone Star; Ma and Pa Kettle at the Fair; Meet Me at the Fair. 1953 The Sun Shines Bright. 1954 Broken Lance; Seven Brides for Seven Brothers. 1955 The Last Command; The Tall Men. 1956 The Brass Legend; Friendly Persuasion. 1957 The Lonely Man. 1959 The Horse Soldiers.

SINCLAIR, ARTHUR
Born: Aug. 3, 1883, Dublin, Ireland. Died: Dec. 14, 1951, Belfast, Northern Ireland. Screen and stage actor.

Appeared in: 1934 Wild Boy; Evensong. 1935 Peg of Old Drury. 1937 King Solomon's Mines. 1947 Hungry Hill.

SINCLAIR, DAISY
Born: 1878, N.Y. Died: Jan. 14, 1929, New York, N.Y. Screen and stage actress.

SINCLAIR, HORACE
Born: 1884, Sheffield, England. Died: Feb. 19, 1949, New York, N.Y. Screen, stage, vaudeville actor, stage director, and playwright.

Appeared in: 1939 One Third of a Nation.

SINCLAIR, HUGH
Born: May 19, 1903, London, England. Died: Dec. 29, 1962, Slapton, England. Screen and stage actor.

Appeared in: 1935 Escape Me Never. 1936 The Marriage of Corbal. 1937 Strangers on a Honeymoon. 1940 The Secret Four. 1941 The Saint's Vacation. 1942 A Girl Must Live; Tomorrow We Live; Alibi. 1943 At Dawn We Die; The Saint Meets the Tiger. 1945 They Were Sisters. 1949 Corridor of Mirrors; The Gay Lady (aka Trotti True—U.S. 1950). 1950 The Rocking Horse Winner. 1951 Circle of Danger. 1952 The Second Mrs. Tanqueray. 1953 Our Betters; Man in Hiding. 1958 Never Look Back. Other British films: The Four Just Men; Flight from Folly; Don't Ever Leave Me; Murder by the Book; Judgment Deferred.

SINGH, SARAIN
Born: 1888. Died: Apr. 14, 1952, Hollywood, Calif. Screen actor.

SINGLETON, CATHERINE
Born: 1904. Died: Sept. 9, 1969, Ft. Worth, Tex. Screen and stage actress. Miss Universe of 1926.

SINI'LETTA, VIC (Victor A. Smith)
Died: May 4, 1921, Chicago, Ill.("dropsy" and heart ailment). Screen and circus actor.

SIN-NUL, HUNG
Born: 1920, China. Died: Oct. 1966, Canton, China (suicide). Screen and opera actress. Jumped to her death after Red Guards (teenage militants) had cut off her hair and paraded her through the streets.

SINOEL (Jen Vies)
Born: 1868, France. Died: Aug. 31, 1949, Paris, France. Screen actor.

Appeared in: 1935 Le Dernier Milliardaire. 1947 Francis the First; Vie de Boheme. 1948 Voyage Surprise.

SKELLY, HAL (Joseph Harold Skelly)
Born: 1891, Allegheny, Pa. Died: June 16, 1934, West Cornwall, Conn.(auto accident). Screen, stage, circus, minstrel, opera actor, and stage producer.

Appeared in: 1929 The Dance of Life; Woman Trap. 1930 Behind the Makeup; Men Are Like That. 1931 The Struggle. 1933 Hotel Variety; Shadow Laughs.

SKELLY, JAMES
Born: 1936. Died: Apr. 19, 1969, Palm Springs, Calif.(pneumonia). Screen actor. Entered films approx. 1957.

SKINNER, OTIS
Born: June 28, 1857, Cambridge, Mass. Died: Jan. 5, 1942, New York, N.Y.(uremic poisoning). Screen, stage actor, stage producer, and stage director.

Appeared in: 1920 Romance; Kismet. 1922 Mister Antonio. 1930 Kismet (and 1920 version).

SKIPWORTH, ALISON
Born: July 25, 1865, 1870 or 1875?, London, England. Died: July 5, 1952, New York, N.Y. Screen, stage, and television actress.

Appeared in: 1921 Handcuffs or Kisses. 1930 Strictly Unconventional; Raffles; Outward Bound; Oh, For a Man!; Du Barry, Woman of Passion. 1931 Tonight or Never; Night Angel; Virtuous Husband; The Road to Singapore; Devotion. 1932 Sinners in the Sun; Madame Racketeer; Night after Night; High Pressure; If I Had a Million; Unexpected Father. 1933 Tonight Is Ours; He Learned about Women; A Lady's Profession; Song of Songs; Midnight Club; Tillie and Gus; Alice in Wonderland. 1934 Six of a Kind; Wharf Angel; The Notorious Sophie Lang; Here Is My Heart; Shoot the Works; The Captain Hates the Sea; Coming Out Party. 1935 The Devil Is a Woman; Shanghai; Becky Sharp; Doubting Thomas; The Casino Murder Case; The Girl from Tenth Avenue; Dangerous; Hitch Hike Lady. 1936 Satan Met a Lady; The Princess Comes Across; The Gorgeous Hussy; Two in a Crowd; White Hunter; Stolen Holiday. 1937 Two Wise Maids. 1938 King of the Newsboys; Ladies in Distress; Wide Open Faces.

SLACK, FREDDIE
Born: Aug. 7, 1910, La Crosse, Wisc. Died: Aug. 10, 1965, Hollywood, Calif.(natural causes). Bandleader and screen actor.

Appeared in: 1943 Reveille with Beverly; The Sky's the Limit. 1944 Hat Check Honey; Follow the Boys; Seven Days Ashore. 1946 High School Hero.

SLAUGHTER, TOD (N. Carter Slaughter)
Born: Mar. 19, 1885, Newcastle-on-Tyne, England. Died: Feb. 19, 1956. Screen and stage actor.

Appeared in: 1935 Maria Marten. 1936 Murder in the Red Barn; Sweeney Todd. 1938 The Crimes of Steven Hawke. 1939 The Demon Barber of Fleet Street. 1940 Crimes at the Dark House; The Face at the Window. 1943 The Curse of the Wraydons. 1948 The Greed of William Hart. 1951 Never Too Late to Mend. 1953 The Hooded Terror.

SLEZAK, LEO
Born: 1875. Died: June 6, 1946, Bavaria, Germany. Screen and opera actor. Father of screen actor Walter Slezak and screen actress Margarete Slezak (dec. 1953).

Appeared in: 1932 Ein Toller Einfall (A Mad Idea—U.S. 1934). 1934 Freut Euch des Lebens. 1935 Tanzmusik; Die Fahrt in Die Jugend; Mein Liebster 1st ein Jaegersmann; La Paloma. 1937 Freuhling im Wien; The World's in Love; The Postillion of Lonjumeau. 1938 Rendezvous in Wien; Gasparone; Husaren Heraus; Eine Nact an der Conau (A Night on the Danube); Unsterbliche Melodien (Immortal Melodies); Magda; Liebe im Driviertel Takt (Love in Waltz Time); Die Gluecklichste Ehe von Wien (The Happiest Married Couple in Vienna). 1939 Ihr Groesster Erfolg (Her Greatest Success); Die Pompadour; Herbst-Monoever (Fall Manoeuvres); Fasching in Wien; Die Blonde Carmen. Other Viennese films: Women's Paradise; Music in the Blood.

SLEZAK, MARGARETE
Born: 1901, Germany. Died: Aug. 30, 1953, Rottach-Egern, Bavaria, Germany (heart attack). Screen and opera actress. Daughter of screen actor Leo Slezak (dec. 1946) and sister of screen actor Walter Slezak.

Appeared in: 1953 Man on a Tightrope. Other German films: Derby; The Veiled Maja.

SLOANE, EVERETT
Born: Oct. 1, 1909, New York, N.Y. Died: Aug. 6, 1965, Brentwood, Calif.(suicide—sleeping pills). Screen, stage, radio, and television actor.

Appeared in: 1941 Citizen Kane. 1942 The Magnificent Ambersons; Journey into Fear. 1945 We Accuse (narr.). 1948 The Lady from Shanghai. 1949 Prince of Foxes. 1950 The Men. 1951 Bird of Paradise; The Enforcer; Sirocco; The Desert Fox; The Blue Veil; The Prince Who Was a Thief; Murder, Inc. 1952 The Sellout; Way of a Gaucho. 1955 The Big Knife. 1956 Massacre at Sand Creek; Patterson; Somebody up There Likes Me; Lust for Life. 1958 Marjorie Morningstar; The Gun Runners. 1960 Home from the Hill. 1961 By Love Possessed. 1962 Brushfire!. 1963 The Man from the Diner's Club. 1964 The Patsy; The Disorderly Orderly; Ready for the People.

SLOANE, OLIVE
Born: 1896. Died: June 28, 1963, London, England. Screen, stage, and vaudeville actress.

Appeared in: 1933 Soldiers of the King (film debut). 1937 Dreaming Lips. 1949 The Guinea Pig; Under Capricorn. 1950 Seven Days to Noon. 1952 Curtain Up; Franchise Affair; Waterfront Women. 1954 The Weak and the Wicked; A Prize of Gold. 1956 Brothers in Law; The Last Man to Hang. 1957 The Man in the Road. 1960 The Price of Silence. 1962 Immoral Change (aka A Touch of Hell).

SLOCUM, TEX
Born: 1902. Died: Jan. 18, 1963, Concord, Calif.(heart attack). Screen actor and stuntman who doubled for Tom Mix and Hoot Gibson.

SMALLEY, PHILLIPS (Phillips Wendell Smalley)
Born: Aug. 7, 1875, Brooklyn, N.Y. Died: May 2, 1939, Hollywood, Calif. Screen, stage actor, film director, and film producer. Appeared in early Rex pictures in 1909.

Appeared in: 1914 The Merchant of Venice; False Colors. 1915 A Cigarette—That's All. 1921 Two Wise Wives. 1922 The Power of a Lie. 1923 The Self-Made Wife; Temptation; Trimmed in Scarlet; Cameo Kirby; Flaming Youth; Nobody's Bride. 1924 Cheap Kisses; For Sale; Single Wives; Daughters of Today. 1925 The Awful Truth; Charley's Aunt; Soul Mates; Wandering Footsteps; Stella Maris; The Fate of a Flirt. 1926 Money Talks; There You Are!; Queen of Diamonds; The Taxi Mystery. 1927 The Broken Gate; Man Crazy; Sensation Seekers; Tea for Three; The Dice Woman; The Irresistible Lover; Stage Kisses. 1928 Blindfold; The Border Patrol; Sinners in Love; Honeymoon Flats; Broadway Daddies. 1929 The Aviator; True Heaven; High Voltage; The Fatal Warning (serial). 1930 Charley's Aunt (and 1925 version); Peacock Alley; The Midnight Special; Drumming It In (short); Liliom. 1931 Lawless Woman; Lady from Nowhere; High Stakes; Get-Rich-Quick Wallingford; A Free Soul. 1932 Murder at Dawn; Hell's Headquarters; Escapade; Sinister Hands; Widow in Scarlet; Face on the Barroom Floor; The Greeks Had a Word for Them. 1933 Midnight Warning; The Cocktail Hour. 1934 The Big Race; Stolen Sweets; Madame Du Barry; Bolero. 1935 All the King's Horses; Night Life of the Gods; It's in the Air; A Night at the Opera. 1937 Hotel Haywire. 1938 Booloo.

SMART, J. SCOTT
Born: 1903. Died: Jan. 15, 1960, Springfield, Ill. Screen and radio actor.

Appeared in: 1947 Kiss of Death. 1951 Fat Man (film and radio).

SMELKER, MARY
Born: 1909. Died: June 2, 1933, Tucson, Ariz.(auto accident). Screen actress.

SMILEY, JOSEPH W.
Born: 1881. Died: Dec. 2, 1945, N.Y. Screen, stage, vaudeville actor, and film director. Entered films as actor/director with the Original Imp Co. in 1910.

Appeared in: 1921 Experience; The Old Oaken Bucket; The Woman God Changed; The Rich Slave; The Scarab Ring; The Wild Goose. 1922 The Blonde Vampire; The Face in the Fog. 1925 Old Home Week; Wild, Wild Susan; The Police Patrol. 1926 Aloma of the South Seas; The Show Off; The Untamed Lady. 1927 The Potters.

SMITH, ALBERT J.
Born: 1894, New York, N.Y. Died: Apr. 12, 1939, Hollywood, Calif. Screen actor.

Appeared in: 1921 Terror Trail (serial). 1923 In the Days of Daniel Boone (serial). 1924 Big Timber; The Measure of a Man; The Sunset Trail; The Fast Express (serial). 1925 The Middler; Straight Through; The Taming of the West; Ace of Spades (serial); Barriers of the Law; Blood and Steel; The Burning Trail; The Circus Cyclone. 1926 The Scarlet Streak (serial); Strings of Steel (serial); Speed Crazed. 1927 Perils of the Jungle (serial);

Hills of Peril; Whispering Sage; The Swift Shadow; Hard Fists; Red Clay; Where Trails Begin. 1928 The Law of Fear; The Bullet Mark; Hold 'Em Yale. 1929 The Drifter; Fury of the Wild; "Half Pint Polly" comedies. 1932 The Last Mile.

SMITH, BEATRICE LIEB
Born: 1862. Died: Aug. 6, 1942, Los Angeles, Calif. Screen and stage actress.

SMITH, C. AUBREY
Born: July 21, 1863, London, England. Died: Dec. 20, 1948, Beverly Hills, Calif.(pneumonia). Screen and stage actor.

Appeared in: 1915 Builder of Bridges (film debut). 1916 The Witching Hour. 1920 The Face at the Window; The Shuttle of Life; Castles in Spain. 1922 The Bohemian Girl; Flames of Passion. 1924 The Unwanted; The Rejected Woman. 1931 Trader Horn; Never the Twain Shall Meet; The Bachelor Father; Daybreak; Son of India; Just a Gigolo; Man in Possession; The Phantom of Paris; Guilty Hands; Surrender; The Perfect Alibi; Dancing Partners. 1932 Polly of the Circus; Tarzan, the Ape Man; But the Flesh Is Weak; Love Me Tonight; Trouble in Paradise; No More Orchids. 1933 They Just Had to Get Married; Luxury Liner; Bombshell; The Barbarian; Secrets; Morning Glory; Adorable; Monkey's Paw; Queen Christina. 1934 The House of Rothschild; Gambling Lady; Riptide; We Live Again; Curtain at Eight; Bulldog Drummond Strikes Back; Cleopatra; Madame Du Barry; One More River; Caravan; The Firebird; The Scarlet Empress. 1935 Trans-Atlantic Tunnel; The Right to Live; Lives of a Bengal Lancer; The Florentine Dagger; The Gilded Lily; Clive of India; China Seas; Jalna; The Crusades. 1936 Little Lord Fauntleroy; Romeo and Juliet; The Garden of Allah; Lloyds of London. 1937 Wee Willie Winkie; The Prisoner of Zenda; Thoroughbreds Don't Cry; The Hurricane. 1938 Four Men and a Prayer; Kidnapped; Sixty Glorious Years. 1939 East Side of Heaven; The Four Feathers; Five Came Back; The Sun Never Sets; Eternally Yours; Another Thin Man; The Under-Pup; Balalaika. 1940 Rebecca; City of Chance; A Bill of Divorcement; Waterloo Bridge; Beyond Tomorrow; A Little Bit of Heaven; Queen of Destiny. 1941 Free and Easy; Maisie Was a Lady; Dr. Jekyll and Mr. Hyde. 1943 Forever and a Day; Two Tickets to London; Flesh and Fantasy; Madame Curie. 1944 The White Cliffs of Dover; The Adventures of Mark Twain; Secrets of Scotland Yard; Sensations of 1945. 1945 They Shall Have Faith; And Then There Were None; Scotland Yard Investigator. 1946 Cluny Brown; Rendezvous with Annie. 1947 High Conquest; Unconquered. 1948 An Ideal Husband. 1949 Little Women.

SMITH, CHARLES H.
Born: 1866. Died: July 11, 1942, Hollywood, Calif. Screen and vaudeville actor. Was member of "Smith and Campbell" vaudeville team.

Appeared in: 1921 Nobody; The Silver Lining. 1927 Naughty Nanette. 1929 Clear the Decks; Girl Overboard; The Girl on the Barge. 1930 The Bat Whispers.

SMITH, CYRIL
Born: Apr. 4, 1892, Peterhead, Scotland. Died: Mar. 5, 1963, London, England. Screen and stage actor.

Appeared in: 1924 The Desert Sheik. British films prior to 1932: The Milky Way; The Maid of the Mountains; Old Spanish Costumes; Waltzes from Vienna; Case for the Crown; I Was a Spy; The Camels Are Coming; Oh! Daddy; My Old Dutch; The Iron Duke; Me and Marlborough; Hullo, Sweetheart; Forever England; Black Abbott; Last Journey. 1932 The Good Companions. 1933 Channel Crossing; Friday the 13th. 1934 Evergreen; Wild Boy; The Fortunate Fool. 1935 Born for Glory; Alias Bulldog Drummond; Brown on Resolution. 1936 Bulldog Jack; O.H.M.S. (aka You're in the Army Now—U.S. 1937). 1937 Dark Journey; Storm in a Teacup; The Frog. 1938 The Challenge; No Parking; The Return of the Frog; St. Martin's Lane; Sword of Honour. 1940 Sidewalks of London. 1943 Squadron Leader. 1944 Fanny by Gaslight; The Shipbuilders. 1945 The Agitator. 1946 You Can't Do without Love; School for Secrets. 1947 So Well Remembered. 1948 It's Hard to Be Good. 1950 Appointment with Crime; The Rocking Horse Winner; Conspirator. 1951 Green Grow the Rushes. 1952 Stolen Face; Mother Riley Meets the Vampire. 1954 John and Julie; Svengali. 1956 The Angel Who Pawned Her Harp; Sailor, Beware. 1957 Panic in the Parlor; Value for Money. 1964 Operation Snafu. Other British films: Traitor Spy; The Flying Squad; Amy Johnson; Theatre Royal; When We Are Married; Music in the Night; Meet Sexton Blake; One Exciting Night; This Man Is Mine; Deep End; Vice Versa.

SMITH, DWIGHT
Born: 1857, Vevay, Ind. Died: May 30, 1949, Monsey, N.Y. Screen and stage actor. Appeared in silents.

SMITH, G. ALBERT
Born: 1898. Died: Sept. 3, 1959, New York, N.Y. Screen, stage, and television actor.

Appeared in: 1931 Stolen Heaven.

SMITH, GEORGE W.
Born: 1899. Died: Nov. 18, 1947, Chicago, Ill.(coronary thrombosis). Screen and stage actor.

Appeared in: 1946 Snafu.

SMITH, HOWARD I.
Born: 1893, Attleboro, Mass. Died: Jan. 10, 1968, Hollywood, Calif.(heart attack). Screen, stage, vaudeville, radio, and television actor.

Appeared in: 1922 Young America. 1946 Her Kind of Man. 1947 Kiss of Death. 1948 Call Northside 777; State of the Union; Street with No Name. 1950 Cry Murder. 1951 Death of a Salesman. 1952 Never Wave at a WAC. 1953 The Caddy. 1957 Don't Go Near the Water; A Face in the Crowd. 1958 Wind across the Everglades; No Time for Sergeants; I Bury the Living. 1959 Face of Fire. 1960 Murder, Inc. 1962 Bon Voyage!. 1963 The Brass Bottle.

SMITH, JACK
Born: 1896. Died: Jan. 14, 1944, Los Angeles, Calif. Screen actor and song writer.

Appeared in: 1928 Man in the Rough. 1929 Laughing at Death. 1937 Heroes of the Alamo. 1938 Paroled to Die; Frontier Scout. 1939 The Phantom Creeps (serial).

SMITH, JOE
Born: 1900. Died: May 5, 1952, Yuma, Ariz.(heart attack). Screen actor and stuntman.

Appeared in: 1952 Desert Song.

SMITH, COL. LEONARD R.
Born: 1889. Died: July 9, 1958, San Antonio, Tex. Screen actor and film director. Did trick riding in silent films for William S. Hart and also worked in Mack Sennett comedies.

SMITH, MARGARET M.
Born: 1881. Died: Dec. 9, 1960, Hollywood, Calif. Screen actress.

Appeared in: 1925 A Roaring Adventure.

SMITH, MATTHEW
Born: 1905. Died: Mar. 16, 1953, New York, N.Y. Screen and stage actor.

Appeared in: 1934 The Barretts of Wimpole Street.

SMITH, PLEASANT (aka TOMMY LEE PLEASANT, and JIMMY DEE SMITH)
Born: 1886. Died: Mar. 12, 1969, Las Vegas, Nev. Screen actor and wrestler. Appeared in films between 1913 and 1919.

SMITH, SIDNEY
Born: 1892. Died: July 4, 1928, Hollywood, Calif.(possibly effects of bad liquor). Screen actor and comedian.

Appeared in: 1921-1922 The "Hallroom Boys" series. 1917 Oriental Love; His Uncle Dudley. 1923 The Ne'er-Do-Well. 1928 Dugan of the Dugouts; Top Sergeant Mulligan.

SMITH, THOMAS C.
Born: 1892. Died: Dec. 3, 1950, Hollywood, Calif. Screen actor.

Appeared in: 1929 The Invaders.

SMOLLER, DOROTHY
Born: 1901, Memphis, Tenn. Died: Dec. 10, 1926, New York, N.Y. (suicide). Screen actress and dancer.

SMYTHE, FLORENCE
Born: 1878. Died: Aug. 29, 1925, Hollywood, Calif.(heart failure). Screen and stage actress.

SNELLING, MINNETTE
Born: 1878. Died: Dec. 19, 1945, Hollywood, Calif. Screen actress. Entered films in 1917. Appeared in Mack Sennett comedies.

SNOOKUMS. See Lawrence D. McKeen, Jr.

SNOW, MARGUERITE
Born: 1889. Died: Feb. 17, 1958, Hollywood, Calif.(kidney complications). Screen actress.

Appeared in: 1912 Lucille. 1913 Carmen. 1914 Zudora—The Twenty Million Dollar Mystery (serial); Joseph in the Land of Egypt. 1915 The Silent Voice. 1917 Broadway Jones. 1918 The Eagle's Eye (serial). 1921 Lavender and Old Lace. 1922 The Veiled Woman. 1924 Chalk Marks. 1925 Kit Carson over the Great Divide; Savages of the Sea.

SNOW, MORTIMER
Born: 1869. Died: June 20, 1935. Screen and stage actor.

Appeared in: 1922 The Mohican's Daughter; When Knighthood Was in Flower.

SODDERS, CARL
Died: Dec. 18, 1958, Dayton, Ohio. Screen actor. Appeared in silents.

SOKOLOFF, VLADIMIR
Born: Dec. 26, 1889, Moscow, Russia. Died: Feb. 14, 1962, Hollywood, Calif.(stroke). Screen, stage actor, and stage director.

Appeared in: 1927 Loves of Jeanne Ney. 1930 West Front 1918. 1931 Die Dreigroschenoper (The Beggar's Opera); Der Grosse Tenor. 1932 Niemandsland (No Man's Land); Teilnehmer Antworted Nicht; L' Atalantide. 1934 Hell on Earth. 1937 The Prisoner of Zenda; The Life of Emile Zola; West of Shanghai; Expensive Husbands; Tovarich; Conquest; Beg, Borrow or Steal; The Lower Depths; Mayerling. 1938 Alcatraz Island; Arsene Lupin Returns; Blockade; The Amazing Dr. Clitterhouse; Spawn of the North; Ride a Crooked Mile. 1939 Juarez; The Real Glory; Song of the Street. 1940 Comrade X. 1941 Compliments of Mr.Iflow; Love Crazy. 1942 Crossroads; The Road to Morocco. 1943 Mission to Moscow; Song of Russia; For Whom the Bell Tolls; Mr. Lucky. 1944 Passage to Marseille; The Conspirators; 'Til We Meet Again. 1945 The Blonde from Brooklyn; Paris Underground; Scarlet Street; A Royal Scandal; Back to Bataan. 1946 Two Smart People; Cloak and Dagger; A Scandal in Paris. 1948 To the Ends of the Earth. 1950 The Baron of Arizona. 1952 Macao. 1956 While the City Sleeps. 1957 Istanbul; I Was a Teenage Werewolf; Sabu and the Magic Ring. 1958 The Monster from Green Hill; Twilight for the Gods. 1960 Man on a String; Beyond the Time Barrier; The Magnificent Seven; Cimarron; Confessions of a Counterspy; Die Dreigroschenoper (The Three Penny Opera))and 1931 version). 1961 Mr. Sardonicus. 1962 Taras Bulba.

SOLIS, JAVIER
Born: 1931, Nogales, Sonora, Mexico. Died: Apr. 19, 1966, Mexico City, Mexico (following surgery). Screen actor and singer.

Appeared in Spanish films: Los 2 Juanes; Juan Pistola.

SOREL, CECILE (Cecile Emilie Seure)
Born: 1874, France. Died: Sept. 3, 1966, Deauville, France (heart attack). Screen and stage actress.

Appeared in: 1937 Les Perles de la Couronne (Pearls of the Crown).

SOREL, GEORGE S.
Born: 1899. Died: Jan. 19, 1948, Hollywood, Calif. Screen actor.

Appeared in: 1936 Sing Me a Love Song. 1937 The Sheik Steps Out. 1938 Swiss Miss. 1939 Three Musketeers. 1942 Ship Ahoy; Once upon a Honeymoon; Casablanca. 1943 The Desert Song; Hitler—Dead or Alive. 1944 Strange Affair; To Have and Have Not; The Conspirators. 1947 Northwest Outpost.

SORIN, LOUIS
Born: 1894. Died: Dec. 14, 1961, New York, N.Y.(pulmonary edema). Screen, stage, radio, and television actor.

Appeared in: 1929 Lucky in Love; Mother's Boy. 1930 Animal Crackers. 1937 an Educational short. 1950 With These Hands.

SOTHERN, EDWARD H.
Born: Dec. 6, 1859, New Orleans, La. Died: Oct. 28, 1933, New York, N.Y.(pneumonia). Screen and stage actor. Entered films with Vitagraph in 1916. Divorced from stage actress Virginia Harned and married to screen actress Julia Marlowe (dec. 1950).

Appeared in: 1916 An Enemy to the King; The Chattel.

SOTHERN, MRS. ETHEL
Born: 1882. Died: Feb. 20, 1957, Hollywood, Calif. Screen and stage actress.

SOTHERN, HARRY
Born: 1884. Died: Feb. 22, 1957, N.Y. Screen and stage actor. Nephew of Shakespearean actor E. H. Sothern (dec. 1933).

Appeared in: 1920 A Tragedy of the East Side. 1922 How Women Love; The Secrets of Paris.

SOTHERN, HUGH (aka ROY SUTHERLAND)
Born: July 20, 1881, Anderson County, Kan. Died: Apr. 13, 1947, Hollywood, Calif. Screen and stage actor. Known as Roy Sutherland on stage.

Appeared in: 1938 The Buccaneer; Dangerous to Know; Border G-Man. 1939 The Oklahoma Kid; Juarez. 1940 Northwest Passage; Dispatch from Reuters. 1941 The Mad Doctor; Bad Men of Missouri.

SOTHERN, JEAN
Born: 1895, Richmond, Va. Died: Jan. 8, 1924, Chicago, Ill.(cancer). Screen and vaudeville actress.

Appeared in: 1915 The Two Orphans. 1916 The Mysteries of Myra.

SOTO, LUCHY
Born: 1920, Spain. Died: Oct. 1970, Madrid, Spain. Screen and stage actress.

Appeared in: 1938 Morena Clara. Other Spanish film: Garden of Delights.

SOTO, ROBERTO (aka "EL PANZON" [THE BELLY])
Born: 1888, Mexico. Died: July 18, 1960, Mexico City, Mexico (heart attack). Screen and stage actor.

Appeared in: 1938 Tropic Holiday.

SOTOMAYOR, JOSE
Born: 1905, Mexico. Died: Jan. 24, 1967, Mexico City, Mexico (heart attack). Screen and stage actor.

Appeared in: 1919 Juan Soldado. 1941 Carnaval en el Tropico 1943 Palillo Vargas Heredia.

SOUTHARD, HARRY D.
Born: 1881. Died: Apr. 27, 1939, N.Y. Screen, stage, and radio actor.

Appeared in: 1922 The Broadway Peacock; Wildness of Youth. 1927 The Winning Oar. 1929 The House of Secrets.

SOUTHERN, SAM
Born: England. Died: Mar. 21, 1920, Los Angeles, Calif. Screen actor.

Appeared in: 1919 The Eyes of Youth.

SOUTHGATE, HOWARD S.
Born: 1895. Died: May 14, 1971, Orlando, Fla. Screen, stage actor, stage director, and playwright.

SOUTHWICK, DALE
Born: 1913, Long Beach, Calif. Died: Apr. 29, 1968, Compton, Calif. Screen actor. Appeared in "Our Gang" comedies.

SOVERN, CLARENCE
Born: 1900. Died: Mar. 14, 1929, Burbank, Calif. Screen cowboy actor and stuntman.

SOWARDS, LEN
Born: 1893. Died: Aug. 20, 1962, Los Angeles, Calif. Screen, television actor, and stuntman.

SPACEY, CAPT. JOHN G.
Born: 1895. Died: Jan. 2, 1940, Hollywood, Calif. Screen and stage actor.

Appeared in: 1936 The Moon's Our Home; Thank You, Jeeves. 1937 Women of Glamour; Parole Racket. 1938 Four Men and a Prayer; Who Killed Gail Preston?. 1939 I'm from Missouri; The Story of Alexander Graham Bell. 1940 British Agent.

SPANDARO, ODOARDO
Born: 1894. Died: 1965, Florence, Italy. Screen, stage, television actor, and singer.

SPANIER, MUGGSY (Francis Joseph Spanier)
Born: 1903. Died: Feb. 12, 1967, Sausalito, Calif. Dixieland Cornetist and screen actor.

Appeared in: 1929 Is Everybody Happy. 1935 Here Comes the Band.

SPARKS, NED (Edward A. Sparkman)
Born: 1883, Ontario, Canada. Died: Apr. 3, 1957, Apple Valley, Calif.(intestinal block). Screen and stage actor.

Appeared in: 1922 The Bond Boy; A Wide-Open Town. 1925 Bright Lights; The Only Thing; Seven Keys to Baldpate; Soul Mates; The Boomerang; Faint Perfume; His Supreme Moment. 1926 The Auction Block; Mike; Money Talks; Oh, What a Night!; The Hidden Way; Love's Blindness; When the Wife's Away. 1927 Alias the Lone Wolf; The Secret Studio; The Small Bachelor; Alias the Deacon. 1928 The Magnificent Flirt; The Big Noise; On to Reno. 1929 Nothing but the Truth; The Canary Murder Case; Strange Cargo; Street Girl. 1930 Love Comes Along; The Devil's Holiday; The Fall Guy; Double Cross Roads; Leathernecking; Conspiracy. 1931 The Iron Man; The Secret Call; Corsair; Kept Husbands. 1932 The Miracle Man; Big City Blues; Blessed Event; The Crusader. 1933 42nd Street; Lady for a Day; Too Much Harmony; Alice in Wonderland; Going Hollywood; Secrets; Gold Digger of 1933. 1934 Hi, Nellie; Private Scandal; Marie Galante; Sing and Like It; Imitation of Life; Down to Their Last Yacht; Servants' Entrance. 1935 Sweet Adeline; Sweet Music; George White's 1935 Scandals. 1936 Collegiate; The Bride Walks Out; One in a Million. 1937 Wake up and Live; This Way Please; Two's Company. 1938 Hawaii Calls. 1939 The Star Maker. 1941 For Beauty's Sake. 1943 Stage Door Canteen. 1947 Magic Town.

SPAULDING, GEORGE
Born: 1881. Died: Aug. 23, 1959, Hollywood, Calif. Screen, stage, radio, television actor, stage producer, and playwright.

Appeared in: 1950 When Willie Comes Marching Home. 1952 Lure of the Wilderness. 1953 The President's Lady.

SPEAR, HARRY
Born: Dec. 16, 1921, Los Angeles, Calif. Died: Feb. 10, 1969, Hollywood, Calif. Screen, stage, and vaudeville actor. Entered films at age of three with Big Boy at Educational Studios. Appeared in "Smith Family" and "Our Gang" series and Mack Sennett comedies.

SPELLMAN, LEORA (aka LEORA SPELLMEYER)
Born: 1891. Died: Sept. 4, 1945, Los Angeles, Calif.(heart attack). Screen, stage, and vaudeville actress. Married to screen actor Charles B. Middleton (dec. 1949) with whom she appeared in vaudeville as "Middleton and Spellmeyer."

Appeared in: 1929 Wise Girls. 1932 Kongo.

SPENCE, RALPH
Born: Nov. 4, 1889, Key West, Fla. or Houston, Tex. Screenwriter, playwright, and screen actor. Appeared in Mack Sennett and "Sunshine" comedies.

Appeared in: 1925 Ralph Spence Comedies (shorts), among them being Egged On. 1935 Millions in the Air.

SPENCER, DOUGLAS
Born: 1910. Died: Oct. 10, 1960, Hollywood, Calif.(diabetic condition). Screen and television actor.

Appeared in: 1948 The Big Clock. 1949 My Friend Irma; Bride of Vengeance; Follow Me Quietly. 1951 Come Fill the Cup; A Place in the Sun; The Thing; The Redhead and the Cowboy. 1952 Monkey Business; Untamed Frontier. 1953 The Glass Wall; Houdini; Shane; She's Back on Broadway; Trouble along the Way. 1954 The Raid; River of No Return. 1955 The Kentuckian; A Man Alone; Smoke Signal; This Island Earth. 1956 Man from Del Rio; Pardners. 1957 Saddle the Wind; Short Cut to Hell; The Three Faces of Eve; The Unholy Wife. 1958 Cole Younger, Gunfighter. 1959 The Diary of Anne Frank. 1961 The Sins of Rachel Cade.

SPENCER, FRED (Fred Spencer Bretherton)
Died: Oct. 13, 1952, Hollywood, Calif. Screen actor. Appeared in silents for Mack Sennett and others.

SPENCER, KENNETH
Born: 1913, Los Angeles, Calif. Died: Feb. 25, 1964, near New Orleans, La.(airline crash). Negro screen, stage, television actor, and singer. Appeared in U.S. and German films.

Appeared in: 1943 Cabin in the Sky; Bataan.

SPENCER, TERRY
Born: 1895. Died: Oct. 3, 1954, Hollywood, Calif. Screen actor.

SPIKER, RAY
Born: 1902. Died: Feb. 23, 1964, Hollywood, Calif. Screen actor and stuntman.

Appeared in: 1934 Our Daily Bread. 1947 The Brasher Doubloon. 1953 Shane. 1954 Demetrius and the Gladiators; Prince Valiant.

SPINGLER, HARRY
Born: 1890. Died: Apr. 22, 1953, Woodland Hills, Calif. Screen actor.

Appeared in: 1918 A Perfect Lady.

SPIRA, FRANCOISE
Died: Jan. 1965, Paris, France (suicide). French screen and stage actress, and stage producer.

SPITALNY, PHIL
Born: 1890. Died: Oct. 11, 1970, Miami Beach, Fla.(cancer). Bandleader, conductor, and radio and screen actor. Married to concert master Evelyn Kaye, known professionally as "Evelyn and Her Magic Violin."

Appeared in: prior to 1933 Metro Movietone Act. No. 82. 1934 a Vitaphone short. 1935 a Vitaphone short; a Paramount short. 1936 a Vitaphone short. 1945 Here Come the Co-eds.

SPIVY (Spivy Le Voe)
Born: 1907, Brooklyn, N.Y. Died: Jan. 8, 1971, Woodland Hills, Calif. Screen actor, nightclub entertainer, and singer.

Appeared in: 1958 Auntie Mame. 1960 The Fugitive Kind. 1962 Requiem for a Heavyweight.

SPLANE, ELZA K. (Elza Temary)
Born: 1905. Died: Feb. 16, 1968, Tucson, Ariz. Screen actress.

SPONG, HILDA
Born: 1875, London, England. Died: May 16, 1955, Norwalk, Conn. Screen and stage actress.

Appeared in: 1919 A Star Overnight.

SPOTTSWOOD, JAMES
Born: Wash. Died: Oct. 11, 1940, New York, N.Y.(heart attack). Screen, stage, and radio actor.

Appeared in: 1929 Thunderbolt. 1938 Hollywood Stadium Mystery.

SQUIRE, RONALD (Ronald Squirl)
Born: Mar. 1886, Tiverton, Devonshire, England. Died: Nov. 16, 1958, London, England. Screen, stage actor, stage producer, and stage director.

Appeared in: 1934 Wild Boy. 1935 Come Out of the Pantry; Unfinished Symphony. 1936 Love in Exile; Dusty Ermine. 1937 Action for Slander. 1944 Don't Take It to Heart. 1949 The Affairs of a Rogue; Woman Hater. 1950 While the Sun Shines; The Rocking Horse Winner. 1951 No Highway in the Sky. 1952 Encore. 1953 My Cousin Rachel; It Started in Paradise. 1954 Man with a Million; Always a Bride; Scotch on the Rocks. 1955 Now and Forever; Footsteps in the Fog. 1956 Around the World in 80 Days. 1957 The Silken Affair; Island in the Sun; Sea Wife; Raising a Riot. 1958 Law and Disorder. 1959 Count Your Blessings; The Inn of the Sixth Happiness; The Sheriff of Fractured Jaw. Other British films: First Gentleman; Laxdale Hall.

STAFFORD, HANLEY (John Austin)
Born: Sept. 22, 1898, Staffordshire, England. Died: Sept. 9, 1968, Los Angeles, Calif.(heart attack). Screen, stage, radio, and television actor. He was "Daddy" in the Fanny Brice Baby Snooks radio show and "Mr. Dithers" on the Blondie radio show.

Appeared in: 1936 The Great Ziegfeld. 1951 Lullaby of Broadway. 1952 Just This Once; A Girl in Every Port; Here Come the Marines. 1953 The Affairs of Dobie Gillis; Francis Covers the Big Town. 1955 The Go-Getter.

STAHL, WALTER O.
Born: 1884. Died: Aug. 6, 1943, Hollywood, Calif.(heart attack). Screen actor and stage producer.

Appeared in: 1937 I'll Take Romance. 1939 Beasts of Berlin. 1942 Once upon a Honeymoon; Woman of the Year. 1943 Watch on the Rhine.

STAHL-NACHBAUR, ERNEST (Ernest Guggenheimer)
Born: 1886, Germany. Died: May 13, 1960, Berlin, Germany. Screen and stage actor.

Appeared in: 1931 Mother Love; Danton; Ein Burschenlied aus Heidelberg. 1933 M.

STAMP-TAYLOR, ENID
Born: June 12, 1904, Monkseaton, England. Died: Jan. 13, 1946, London, England (injuries from fall). Screen and stage actress.

Appeared in: 1937 Feather Your Nest; Action for Slander; other British films prior to 1937: Virginia's Husband; Feathered Serpent; Mr. What's His Name; So You Won't Talk; While Parents Sleep; Jimmy Boy; Two Hearts in Harmony; Queen of Hearts; Blind Man's Bluff; House Broken; Keep Your Seats; Underneath the Arches; Take a Chance; OK for Sound. 1938 Climbing High; The Lambeth Walk. 1941 Hatter's Castle. 1944 Candlelight in Algeria. 1945 The Wicked Lady. 1946 Caravan.

STANDING, CHARLENE
Born: 1921. Died: Jan. 8, 1957, Dundas, Ontario, Canada. Screen and stage actress. Appeared in U.S. and British films.

STANDING, GORDON
Died: May 22, 1927. Screen actor.

Appeared in: 1921 Man and Woman. 1922 Are Children to Blame?. 1923 Outlaws of the Sea. 1925 The Substitute Wife. 1927 Skedaddle Gold; King of the Jungle (serial).

STANDING, SIR GUY, SR.
Born: Sept. 1, 1873, London, England. Died: Feb. 24, 1937, Los Angeles, Calif.(heart attack). Screen and stage actor. Father of screen actor Guy Standing, Jr.(dec. 1954) and brother of screen actor Herbert Standing (dec. 1955).

Appeared in: 1933 The Cradle Song; A Bedtime Story; The Story of Temple Drake; The Eagle and the Hawk; Midnight Club; Hell and High Water. 1934 Imitation of Life; Death Takes a Holiday; The Witching Hour; Double Door; Now and Forever. 1935 Lives of a Bengal Lancer; Car 99; Annapolis Farewell; The Big Broadcast of 1936. 1936 The Return of Sophie Lang; I'd Give My Life; Palm Springs. 1937 Lloyds of London; Bulldog Drummond Escapes.

STANDING, GUY, JR.
Died: Nov. 14, 1954, Reseda, Calif. Screen and stage actor. Son of screen actor Sir Guy Standing (dec. 1937).

Appeared in: 1953 Titanic.

STANDING, HERBERT
Born: 1884, London, England. Died: Sept. 23, 1955, New York, N.Y. Screen and stage actor. Brother of screen actor Sir Guy Standing (dec. 1937).

Appeared in: 1919 Through the Wrong Door; Strictly Confidential; Almost a Husband. 1920 Judy of Rogue's Harbor. 1921 Man and Woman; The Infamous Miss Revell; One Wild Week; The Man Worth While. 1922 The Trap; The Masquerader; While Satan Sleeps; The Crossroads of New York; The Impossible Mrs. Bellew. 1923 Jazzmania; Sawdust. 1926 The Brown Derby; Rainbow Riley.

STANDING, HERBERT
Died: Dec. 5, 1928, Los Angeles, Calif. Screen actor.

STANLEY, EDWIN
Born: 1880. Died: Dec. 24, 1944, Hollywood, Calif. Screen and stage actor.

Appeared in: 1932 Amateur Daddy. 1933 International House; My Woman; No Other Woman. 1934 The Life of Vergie Winters; You Belong to Me. 1936 Hot Money; The Mandarin Mystery. 1937 Alcatraz Island; Marked Woman; Some Blondes Are Dangerous. 1938 Born to Be Wild; Billy the Kid Returns; The Missing Guest. Wives under Suspicion. 1939 Unexpected Father; Eternally Yours; Espionage Agent; Ninotchka; 20,000 Men a Year. 1940 Charlie Chan in Panama; Youth Will Be Served. 1941 Meet John Doe; The Night of January 16th; A Man Betrayed; Arkansas Judge; Scattergood Baines. 1942 The Man Who Came to Dinner; Who Is Hope Schuyler?; Drums of the Congo; The Loves of Edgar Allan Poe; Gentleman Jim. 1944 Buffalo Bill. 1945 Youth on Trial; Conflict.

STANLEY, S. VICTOR
Born: 1892. Died: Jan. 29, 1939, London, England. Screen and stage actor.

STANTON, FREDERICK "FRED" R.
Born: 1881. Died: May 27, 1925, Hollywood, Calif.(cancer).
Screen and stage actor.

Appeared in: 1917 The Great Secret (serial). 1921 Her Sturdy Oak. 1922 Perils of the Yukon (serial); The Fire Bride; The Son of the Wolf. 1923 Canyon of the Fools; Danger Ahead; Little Church Around the Corner; A Million to Burn; Trifling with Honor. 1924 Find Your Man; When a Man's a Man.

STANTON, LARRY T.
Died: May 9, 1955, Hollywood, Calif.(heart attack). Screen actor.
Entered films approx. 1920.

STARK, MABEL
Born: 1889. Died: Apr. 29, 1968, Thousand Oaks, Calif.(heart attack). Wild animal trainer, and screen actress.

Appeared in: 1922 A Dangerous Adventure.

STARKEY, BERT
Born: 1880, England. Died: June 9, 1939, Los Angeles, Calif.
Screen and stage actor.

Appeared in: 1921 The Iron Trail. 1927 Wild Geese; Woman's Law. 1928 Put 'Em Up; You Can't Beat the Law. 1932 Scarface; Hell's Highway.

STARR, FREDERICK
Born: 1878, San Francisco, Calif. Died: Aug. 20, 1921, Los Angeles, Calif. Screen and stage actor.

Appeared in: 1919 Elmo, the Mighty (serial). 1920 Daredevil Jack (serial). 1921 The Man of the Forest; Mysterious Rider.

STARR, RANDY (Joseph Randall)
Born: 1931, Ill. Died: Aug. 5, 1970, Los Angeles, Calif.(undetermined illness). Screen stuntman. One-armed rodeo star who would have been a prosecution witness in 1970-71 Charles Manson (Tate-La Bianca murder) trial.

STEADMAN, VERA
Born: June 23, 1900, Monterey, Calif. Died: Dec. 14, 1966, Long Beach, Calif. Screen actress. Entered films as a Mack Sennett bathing beauty. Divorced from screen actor Jack Taylor (dec. 1932).

Appeared in: 1917 Hula Hula Land. 1921 Scrap Iron. 1925 Stop Flirting. 1926 Meet the Prince; The Nervous Wreck. 1934 Elmer and Elsie. 1936 Ring around the Moon.

STEDMAN, LINCOLN
Born: 1907, Denver, Colo. Died: Mar. 22, 1948, Los Angeles, Calif. Screen actor and film director. Entered films in 1918. Son of screen actress Myrtle Stedman (dec. 1938) and screen actor Marshall Stedman (dec. 1943).

Appeared in: 1920 Nineteen and Phyllis. 1921 Old Swimmin' Hole; Be My Wife; The Charm School; My Lady Friends; Two Minutes to Go; Under the Lash. 1922 The Dangerous Age; A Homespun Vamp; Youth to Youth; The Freshie; White Shoulders. 1923 The Man Life Passed By; The Meanest Man in the World; The Scarlet Lily; The Wanters; The Prisoner; Soul of the Beast. 1924 Captain January; Black Oxen; Cheap Kisses; On Probation; Wife of the Centaur. 1925 The Danger Signal; Sealed Lips; Red Hot Tires. 1926 Dame Chance; Made for Love; Remember; The Warning Signal; One Minute to Play. 1927 The Student Prince in Old Heidelberg; Let It Rain; The Prince of Headwaiters; Rookies; The Little Firebrand; Perch of the Devil. 1928 Farmer's Daughter; Devil's Cage; Green Grass Widows; Harold Teen. 1929 Why Be Good?; The Wild Party; Tanned Legs. 1931 The Woman Between. 1933 Sailor Be Good.

STEDMAN, MARSHALL
Born: 1874. Died: Dec. 16, 1943, Laguna Beach, Calif. Screen and stage actor. Married to screen actress Myrtle Stedman (dec. 1938) and father of screen actor Lincoln Stedman (dec. 1948).

STEDMAN, MYRTLE
Born: Mar. 3, 1889, Chicago, Ill. Died: Jan. 8, 1938, Los Angeles, Calif.(heart attack). Screen and stage actress. Entered films in 1913. Married to screen actor Marshall Stedman (dec. 1943). Mother of screen actor Lincoln Stedman (dec. 1948).

Appeared in: 1913 Valley of the Moon. 1915 Peer Gynt. 1920 The Silver Horde; The Tiger's Coat. 1921 Black Roses; The Whistle; Sowing the Wind; The Concert. 1922 Ashes; The Hands of Nara; Nancy from Nowhere; Rich Men's Wives; Reckless Youth. 1923 The Famous Mrs. Fair; Flaming Youth; Dangerous Age; The Age of Desire; Six Days; Crashin' Thru; Temporary Marriage. 1924

Wine; Lilies of the Field; Bread; The Breath of Scandal; The Woman on the Jury. 1925 Chickie; Sally; Tessie; The Mad Whirl; If I Marry Again; The Goose Hangs High. 1926 Don Juan's Three Nights; The Man in the Shadow; The Prince of Pilsen; The Far Cry. 1927 The Black Diamond Express; No Place to Go; Women's Wares; The Life of Riley; The Irresistible Lover; Alias the Deacon. 1928 Sporting Goods; Their Hour. 1929 The Wheel of Life; The Sin Sister; The Jazz Age. 1930 The Truth about Youth; The Love Racket; The Lummox; The Little Accident. 1932 Widow in Scarlet; Alias Mary Smith; Forbidden Company. 1933 One Year Later. 1934 Beggars in Ermine; School for Girls. 1936 Song of the Saddle; Gambling with Souls; Hollywood Hotel; Confession. 1937 Green Light; Hollywood Hotel; Confession.

STEELE, BILL (William A. Gittinger)
Born: 1889, Tex. Died: Feb. 13, 1966, Los Angeles, Calif. Screen actor and stuntman.

Appeared in: 1921 Riding with Death. 1922 The Fast Mail; Pardon My Nerve!; Bells of San Juan. 1923 Dead Game; Single Handed; Shootin' for Love; Don Quickshot of the Rio Grande. 1924 The Last Man on Earth; Hit and Run; The Ridin' Kid from Powder River; The Sunset Trail. 1925 The Saddle Hawk; Let 'Er Buck; Don Dare Devil; Two-Fisted Jones; The Sagebrush Lady; The Hurricane Kid. 1926 The Flaming Frontier; The Runaway Express; The Wild Horse Stampede; Six Shootin' Romance; Under Western Skies; The Fighting Peacemaker. 1927 Hoof Marks; Rough and Ready; Whispering Sage; The Valley of Hell; Loco Luck; Range Courage. 1928 The Black Ace; Thunder Riders; Call of the Heart; The Fearless Rider. 1930 Doughboys; The Lone Star Ranger. 1935 When a Man Sees Red. 1950 The Showdown.

STEELE, CLIFFORD
Born: 1878. Died: Mar. 5, 1940, Hollywood, Calif. Screen actor.
Entered films approx. 1915.

STEELE, MINNIE
Born: 1881, Australia. Died: Jan. 5, 1949, Hollywood, Calif.(stroke). Screen and vaudeville actress. Entered films in 1922.

Appeared in: 1924 "Christie" comedies and "Baby Peggy" pictures; The Darling of New York.

STEELE, VERNON
Born: 1883. Died: July 23, 1955, Los Angeles, Calif.(heart attack). Screen and stage actor.

Appeared in: 1915 Hearts in Exile. 1916 For the Defense. 1921 Beyond Price; Out of the Chorus; The Highest Bidder. 1922 The Danger Point; For the Defense (and 1916 version); A Wonderful Wife; Thelma; When the Devil Drives; The Girl Who Ran Wild; The Hands of Nara. 1923 Alice Adams; The Wanters; What Wives Want; Temptation; Forgive and Forget. 1924 Discontented Husbands; The House of Youth. 1933 Design for Living; The Silk Express. 1934 Where Sinners Meet; The Great Flirtation. 1935 Bonnie Scotland. 1936 Dracula's Daughter. 1937 Time out for Romance. 1945 They Were Expendable. 1949 Madam Bovary.

STEERS, LARRY (Lawrence Steers)
Born: 1881, Chicago, Ill. Died: Feb. 15, 1951, Woodland Hills, Calif. Screen and stage actor.

Appeared in: 1921 Wealth. 1922 Elope if You Must; South of Suva. 1923 Haunted Valley (serial); Mind over Motor; Soul of the Beast; The Huntress. 1924 Ten Scars Make a Man (serial); A Cafe in Cairo; The Girl in the Limousine. 1925 The Best People; Flattery; New Brooms; The Love Gamble. 1926 Bride of the Storm; The Lodge in the Wilderness; Hearts and Spangles. 1927 The Claw; No Control. 1928 The Terrible People (serial); The Phantom Flyer. 1929 The Fire Detective (serial); In Old California; Dark Skies; Just Off Broadway; Redskin; The Wheel of Life. 1930 The Thoroughbreds; Let's Go Places. 1931 The Secret Call; Grief Street. 1932 If I Had a Million. 1933 The Cocktail Hour. 1936 Navy Born; Pan Handlers (short). 1938 an RKO-Radio short. 1941 Riding the Wind. 1943 Hands across the Border. 1944 Atlantic City; The Mojave Firebrand. 1945 White Pongo. 1947 The Gangster. 1948 Fighting Mad.

STEFAN, VIRGINIA
Born: 1926. Died: May 5, 1964, New York, N.Y. Screen and television actress.

STEIN, CAROL EDEN
Born: 1927. Died: Oct. 18, 1958, San Francisco, Calif. Screen actress.

STEINER, ELIO

Born: Mar. 9, 1905, Venice, Italy. Died: Dec. 6, 1965, Rome, Italy. Screen actor. Appeared in Italian, French and German films.

Appeared in: 1928 Vena D'Oro. 1930 La Canzone Dell 'Amore; Corte D'Assisi; Stella Del Cinema. 1931 L'Uomo Dell 'Artiglio; Der Klown. 1932 Pergoleri. 1933 Acqua Cheta; Giallo. 1937 Amore e Dolore. 1942 Giarabub. 1944 Senza Famiglia. 1947 Tombolo. 1952 La Signora senza Camelie.

STEINKE, HANS

Born: 1893, Germany. Died: June 26, 1971, Chicago, Ill.(lung cancer). Screen actor and wrestler.

Appeared in: 1933 Deception; Island of Lost Souls. 1935 People Will Talk. 1936 Once in a Blue Moon. 1938 The Buccaneer.

STEINMETZ, EARL

Born: 1915. Died: May 22, 1942, Los Angeles, Calif.(neck broken by an airplane wing). Screen actor.

STEPHENS, JUD

Born: 1888. Died: Apr. 18, 1935, Los Angeles, Calif. Screen actor.

STEPHENSON, HENRY (H. S. Garroway)

Born: Apr. 16, 1871, Granada, British West Indies. Died: Apr. 24, 1956, San Francisco, Calif. Screen and stage actor.

Appeared in: 1917 The Spreading Dawn. 1921 The Black Panther's Cub. 1925 Men and Women; Wild, Wild Susan. 1932 Cynara; Red Headed Woman; Guilty as Hell; Animal Kingdom; Bill of Divorcement. 1933 Queen Christina; Blind Adventure; Tomorrow at Seven; Double Harness; My Lips Betray; Little Women; If I Were Free. 1934 One More River; Outcast Lady; She Loves Me Not; All Men Are Enemies; Man of Two Worlds; The Richest Girl in the World; Stingaree; The Mystery of Mr. X; What Every Woman Knows; Thirty Day Princess. 1935 The Night Is Young; Vanessa, Her Love Story; Reckless; The Flame Within; O'Shaughnessey's Boy; Mutiny on the Bounty; Rendezvous; The Perfect Gentleman; Captain Blood. 1936 Little Lord Fauntleroy; Beloved Enemy; Half Angel; Hearts Divided; Give Me Your Heart; Charge of the Light Brigade; Walking on Air. 1937 When You're in Love; The Prince and the Pauper; The Emperor's Candlesticks; Conquest; Wise Girl. 1938 Marie Walewska; The Baroness and the Butler; Suez; Marie Antoinette; Dramatic School; The Young in Heart. 1939 Tarzan Finds a Son; Private Lives of Elizabeth and Essex; Adventures of Sherlock Holmes. 1940 It's a Date; Spring Parade; Little Old New York; Down Argentine Way. 1941 The Man Who Lost Himself; The Lady from Louisiana. 1942 This above All; Rings on Her Fingers; Half Way to Shanghai. 1943 Mr. Lucky; The Man Trap. 1944 Two Girls and a Sailor; Secrets of Scotland Yard; The Hour before the Dawn; The Reckless Age. 1945 Tarzan and the Amazons. 1946 Heartbeat; The Return of Monte Cristo; The Locket; Night and Day; The Green Years; Of Human Bondage; Her Sister's Secret. 1947 The Homestretch; Ivy; Time out of Mind; Song of Love; Dark Delusion. 1948 Julia Misbehaves. 1949 Challenge to Lassie; Enchantment. 1951 Oliver Twist.

STEPHENSON, JAMES

Born: 1888, Yorkshire, England. Died: July 29, 1941, Pacific Palisades, Calif.(heart attack). Screen and stage actor.

Appeared in: 1937 The Perfect Crime; The Man Who Made Diamonds; Dark Stairway; It's in the Blood; Mr. Satan. 1938 Cowboy from Brooklyn; White Banners; Heart of the North; When Were You Born?; Boy Meets Girl; Nancy Drew, Detective. 1939 On Trial; Secret Service of the Air; Adventures of Jane Arden; Torchy Blane in Chinatown; The Old Maid; Private Lives of Elizabeth and Essex; Espionage Agent; We Are Not Alone; Confessions of a Nazi Spy; King of the Underworld; Beau Geste. 1940 Devil's Island; Murder in the Air; Wolf of New York; A Dispatch from Reuters; Calling Philo Vance; The Sea Hawk; The Letter; South of Suez; River's End. 1941 Shining Victory; Flight from Destiny; International Squadron.

STEPHENSON, ROBERT ROBINSON

Born: 1901. Died: Sept. 8, 1970, Hollywood, Calif.(cancer). Screen actor.

Appeared in: 1945 The Brighton Strangler; Hotel Berlin. 1951 David and Bathsheba.

STEPPAT, ILSE

Born: 1917, Wuppertal, West Germany. Died: Dec. 22, 1969, West Berlin, Germany. Screen and stage actress.

Appeared in: 1948 Marriage in the Shadows. 1958 The Confes-

sions of Felix Krull. 1959 The Eighth Day of the Week. 1960 The Bridge. 1961 Naked in the Night (aka Madeleine-TE 136211). 1969 On Her Majesty's Secret Service. Other German films: The Man Who Wanted to Live Twice; The Rabanser Case; Captain Wronski; The Guilt of Dr. Homma.

STEPPLING, JOHN C.

Born: 1869, Germany. Died: Apr. 5, 1932, Hollywood, Calif. Screen and stage actor.

Appeared in: 1920 Madame Peacock. 1921 Nobody's Kid; The Silver Car; The Hunch; Black Beauty; Garments of Truth. 1922 Confidence; Extra! Extra!; Too Much Business; The Sin Flood. 1923 Bell Boy 13; Going Up; A Man's Man; What a Wife Learned; The Man Next Door; Let's Go. 1924 Abraham Lincoln; The Fast Worker; The Reckless Age; The Breathless Moment; A Cafe in Cairo; Galloping Fish; Fools in the Dark. 1925 California Straight Ahead; Soft Shoes; Eve's Lover. 1926 The Better Man; Memory Lane; Collegiate; High Steppers. 1927 California or Bust; God's Great Wilderness; The Gay Old Bird; Her Father Said No; Wedding Bill$; By Whose Hands. 1928 Their Hour. 1932 Broken Lullaby.

STERLING, EDYTHE

Born: 1887. Died: June 4, 1962, Hollywood, Calif. Screen and vaudeville actress.

Appeared in: 1921 Vanishing Maid; The Stranger in Canyon Valley. 1923 Crimson Gold; Danger.

STERLING, FORD (George F. Stitch)

Born: Nov. 3, 1880, La Crosse, Wisc. Died: Oct. 13, 1939, Los Angeles, Calif.(thrombosis of veins—heart attack). Screen, stage, vaudeville, and circus actor. Married to screen actress Teddy Sampson. Was "Chief" of the original Keystone Kops.

Appeared in: 1912 Cohen Collects a Debt; The Water Nymph; Riley and Schultz; The Beating He Needed; Pedro's Dilemma; Stolen Glory; Ambitious Butler; The Flirting Husband; The Grocery Clerk's Romance; At Coney Island; At It Again; The Deacon's Trouble; A Temperamental Husband; The Rivals; Mr. Fix-It; The New Neighbor; A Bear Escape; Pat's Day Off; A Midnight Elopement; Mabel's Adventures; Hoffmeyer's Legacy. 1913 The Bangville Police; The Walter's Picnic; Out and In; Peeping Pete; His Crooked Career; Rastus and the Game Cock; Safe in Jail; Love and Rubbish; The Peddler; Professor Bean's Removal; Cohen's Outing; A Game of Pool; The Riot; The Firebugs; Baby Day; Mabel's Dramatic Career (reissued Her Dramatic Debut); The Faithful Taxicab; When Dreams Come True; The Bowling Match; A Double Wedding; The Cure That Failed; How Hiram Won Out; For Lizzie's Sake; The Mistaken Masher; The Deacon Outwitted; The Elite Ball; The Battle of Who Run; Just Brown's Luck; The Jealous Waiter; The Stolen Purse; Heinze's Resurrection; A Landlord's Troubles; The Professor's Daughter; A Red Hot Romance; The Man Next Door; Love and Pain; The Rube and the Baron; On His Wedding Day; The Sleuths at the Floral Parade; A Strong Revenge; The Two Widows; The Land Salesman; A Game of Poker; Father's Choice; A Life in the Balance; Murphy's IOU; A Fishy Affair; The New Conductor; The Ragtime Band (reissued The Jazz Band); His Ups and Downs; Toplitsky and Company; Barney Oldfield's Race for a Life; Schnitz the Tailor; A Healthy Neighborhood; Teddy Telzlaff and Earl Cooper; Speed Kings; Their Husbands; Love Sickness at Sea; A Small Time Act; A Muddy Romance (reissued Muddled in Mud); Cohen Saves the Flag; The Gusher; A Bad Game; Zuzu, the Band Leader; Some Nerve; The Speed Queen; The Hansom Driver. 1914 A Dramatic Mistake; Love and Dynamite; In the Clutches of a Gang; Too Many Brides (reissued The Love Chase); Double Crossed; A Robust Romeo; Baffles; Gentleman Burglar; Between Showers; A False Beauty (reissued A Faded Vampire); Tango Tangles; The Minstrel Man. 1915 That Little Band of Gold (reissued For Better or Worse); Our Daredevil Chief; He Wouldn't Stay Down; Court House Crooks; Dirty Work in a Laundry (reissued A Desperate Scoundrel); Only a Messenger Boy; His Father's Footsteps; Fatty and the Broadway Stars; The Hunt. 1916 His Pride and Shame; The Now Cure; His Wild Oats; His Lying Heart. 1917 Stars and Bars; Pinched in the Finish; A Maiden's Trust; His Torpedoes Love. 1922 Oh, Mabel Behave. 1923 The Stranger's Banquet; The Brass Bottle; Hollywood; The Spoilers; The Day of Faith; The Destroying Angel. 1924 Wild Oranges; The Woman on the Jury; Love and Glory; He Who Gets Slapped; Galloping Fish. 1925 So Big; Daddy's Gone A-Hunting; The Trouble with Wives; Stage Struck; My Lady's Lips; Steppin' Out. 1926 The Road to Glory; Stranded in Paris; Good and Naughty; Mike; The Show-Off; The American Venus; Miss Brewster's Millions; Everybody's Acting. 1927 For the Love of Mike; Casey at the Bat; Drums of the Desert; The Trunk Mystery. 1928 Sporting Goods; Gentlemen Prefer Blondes;

Wife Savers; Figures Don't Lie; Chicken a la King; Oh, Kay!. 1929 The Fall of Eve. 1930 Sally; Bride of Regiment; Spring Is Here; Kismit; The Girl in the Show; Showgirl in Hollywood. 1931 Stout Hearts and Willing Hands; Her Majesty, Love. 1932-1933 Paramount shorts; 1933 Alice in Wonderland. 1935 a Vitaphone short. Behind the Green Lights; Black Sheep; Headline Woman. 1936 an RKO short. 1961 Days of Thrills and Laughter (documentary).

STERLING, LARRY
Born: 1935. Died: Aug. 25, 1958, Clear Lake, Calif.(water skiing accident). Screen actor.

Appeared in: 1958 The Naked and the Dead.

STERLING, LEE
Born: 1904. Died: Mar. 4, 1951, Santa Monica, Calif.(heart attack). Screen actor.

STERLING, MERTA
Born: 1883. Died: Mar. 14, 1944, Hollywood, Calif. Screen actress.

Appeared in: 1924 The Star Dust Trail; Women First. 1927 Paid to Love.

STERN, BILL
Born: July 1, 1907, Rochester, N.Y. Died: Nov. 19, 1971, Rye, N.Y.(heart attack). Sportscaster on radio and television and screen actor.

Appeared in: 1942 The Pride of the Yankees. 1943 Stage Door Canteen. 1945 Here Come the Co-Eds. 1947 Spirit of West Point. 1954 Go, Man, Go.

STERN, LOUIS
Born: Jan. 10, 1860, New York, N.Y. Died: Feb. 15, 1941, Hollywood, Calif. Screen, stage, and vaudeville actor.

Appeared in: 1920 Humoresque. 1925 I Want My Man. 1927 Wedding Bills. 1929 The Little Wild Cat; Where East Is East; In Old California; The Diamond Master (serial).

STEVEN, BOYD
Born: 1875, Scotland. Died: Dec. 1967, Glasgow, Scotland. Singer and screen actress.

Appeared in: 1947 I Know Where I'm Going.

STEVENS, BYRON E.
Born: 1904. Died: Dec. 15, 1964, Encino, Calif.(heart attack). Screen actor. Entered films approx. 1939. Brother of screen actress Barbara Stanwyck.

STEVENS, CHARLES
Born: May 26, 1893, Solomansville, Ariz. Died: Aug. 22, 1964, Hollywood, Calif. Screen and vaudeville actor. Entered films in 1915. Appeared in all but one of Douglas Fairbanks' pictures. Was grandson of Apache chief Geronimo.

Appeared in: 1915 Birth of a Nation (film debut). 1921 The Three Musketeers. 1922 Robin Hood; Captain Fly-by-Night. 1923 Where the North Begins. 1924 Empty Hands; The Thief of Bagdad (played 6 roles). 1925 The Vanishing American; Don Q; Recompense; A Son of His Father. 1926 The Black Pirate; Man Trap; Across the Pacific. 1927 The Gaucho; King of Kings; Woman's Law. 1928 Diamond Handcuffs; Stand and Deliver. 1929 The Virginian; The Mysterious Dr. Fu Manchu; The Iron Mask. 1930 The Big Trail; Tom Sawyer. 1931 The Conquering Horde; The Cisco Kid. 1932 South of Rio Grande; The Stoker; Mystery Ranch. 1933 Drum Taps; When Strangers Marry; California Trail; Police Call. 1934 Fury of the Jungle. 1935 Lives of a Bengal Lancer; Call of the Wild. 1936 Here Comes Trouble; The Bold Caballero. 1937 Wild West Days (serial); Ebb Tide. 1938 The Crime of Dr. Hallett; Flaming Frontiers (serial). 1939 The Renegade Ranger; Desperate Trails; Frontier Marshal; The Girl and the Gambler. 1940 Kit Carson; Wagons Westward. 1941 The Bad Man; Blood and Sand. 1942 Beyond the Blue Horizon; Tombstone, the Town Too Tough to Die; Pierre of the Plains. 1944 Marked Trails. 1945 The Mummy's Curse; South of the Rio Grande; San Antonio. 1946 Border Bandits; My Darling Clementine. 1947 Buffalo Bill Rides Again. 1948 Fury at Furnace Creek; Belle Starr's Daughter. 1949 The Feathered Serpent; Ambush; The Walking Hills; Roll, Thunder, Roll; The Cowboy and the Indians. 1950 The Showdown; California Passage; Indian Territory; The Savage Horde; A Ticket to Tomahawk. 1951 Oh, Susanna!; Warpath. 1952 Smoky Canyon; The Lion and the Horse. 1953 Savage Mutiny; Ride, Vaquero; Eyes of the Jungle; Jeop-

ardy. 1954 Jubilee Trail; Killer Leopard. 1955 The Vanishing American (and 1925 version). 1956 Partners. 1962 The Outsider.

STEVENS, EMILY
Born: 1882, N.Y. Died: Jan. 2, 1928, New York, N.Y.(overdose of sedatives). Screen and stage actress. Sister of actor Robert Stevens (dec. 1963).

Appeared in: 1915 The Soul of a Woman. 1917 The Slacker.

STEVENS, EVELYN
Born: 1891. Died: Aug. 28, 1938, New York, N.Y. Screen and stage actress. Appeared in early Griffith films.

STEVENS, GEORGIA COOPER. See Georgia Cooper

STEVENS, INGER (Inger Stensland)
Born: Oct. 18, 1935, Stockholm, Sweden. Died: Apr. 30, 1970, Hollywood, Calif.(barbiturate overdose). Screen, stage, and television actress.

Appeared in: 1957 Man on Fire. 1958 Cry Terror; The Buccaneer. 1959 The World, the Flesh and the Devil. 1964 The New Interns. 1967 A Time for Killing; A Guide for the Married Man. 1968 Hang 'Em High; House of Cards; Firecreek; Madigan; 5 Card Stud. 1969 A Dream of Kings.

STEVENS, LANDERS (John Landers Stevens)
Born: Feb. 17, 1877, San Francisco, Calif. Died: Dec. 19, 1940, Hollywood, Calif.(heart attack following appendectomy). Screen, stage actor, and film producer. Entered films in 1920.

Appeared in: 1921 Keeping up with Lizzie; Shadows of Conscience. 1922 The Veiled Woman; A Wonderful Wife; Youth Must Have Love; Wild Honey; Handle with Care. 1925 Battling Bunyon. 1929 Frozen Justice; The Trial of Mary Dugan. 1930 The Gorilla. 1931 Hell Divers; The Rainbow Trail. 1936 We Who Are about to Die; Swing Time. 1937 Join the Marines; Bill Cracks Down. 1938 an RKO-Radio short.

STEVENS, LYNN (Franklin Feeney)
Born: 1898. Died: Mar. 28, 1950, Worcester, Mass. Screen and stage actor.

Appeared in: 1926 Men of Steel. 1928 Clothes Make the Woman.

STEVENS, MORTON L.
Born: 1890, Marlboro, Mass. Died: Aug. 5, 1959, Marlboro, Mass. Screen, stage, and television actor.

Appeared in: 1914 Perils of Pauline (serial). 1949 Lost Boundaries.

STEVENS, ROBERT
Born: approx. 1880. Died: Dec. 19, 1963, Lauderdale-by-the-Sea, Fla. Screen, stage actor, and stage director. Brother of screen actress Emily Stevens (dec. 1928).

STEVENS, VIOLET "VI"
Born: 1892, England. Died: Mar. 22, 1967, London, England. Screen, stage, and television actress. Entered films in 1946.

Appeared in: 1951 The Mudlark. 1959 A Cry from the Streets. 1962 Lisa.

STEVENSON, CHARLES A.
Born: 1851, Dublin, Ireland. Died: July 2, 1929, New York, N.Y. Screen and stage actor. Entered films in 1918.

Appeared in: 1921 Experience. 1922 Her Gilded Cage. 1923 The Bolted Door; The Spanish Dancer; The Woman with Four Faces; Legally Dead; Garrison's Finish. 1924 The Wise Virgin; The Breaking Point. 1927 Aflame in the Sky. 1928 Doomsday.

STEVENSON, CHARLES E.
Born: 1888, Sacramento, Calif. Died: July 4, 1943, Palo Alto, Calif. Screen actor. Entered films with Vitagraph.

Appeared in: 1928 Wallflower. 1929 The Mysterious Dr. Fu Manchu.

STEVENSON, HOUSELEY
Born: July 30, 1879, Liverpool or London, England. Died: Aug. 6, 1953, Los Angeles, Calif. Screen and stage actor. Father of screen actors Onslow Stevens and Houseley Stevenson, Jr.

Appeared in: 1936 Law in Her Hands (film debut); Isle of Fury. 1937 Once a Doctor. 1942 Native Land. 1943 Happy Land. 1946 Somewhere in the Night; Little Miss Big. 1947 Dark Passage;

The Brasher Doubloon; Time out of Mind; Ramrod; Thunder in the Valley. 1948 Four Faces West; The Challenge; Casbah; Kidnapped; Moonrise; Apartment for Peggy. 1949 Calamity Jane and Sam Bass; Bride of Vengeance; Colorado Territory; Knock on Any Door; The Lady Gambles; Leave It to Henry; Masked Raiders; Sorrowful Jones; Take One False Step; The Walking Hills; You Gotta Stay Happy; The Gal Who Took the West. 1950 All the King's Men; Edge of Doom; Sierra; Gunfighter; Joan of Arc; The Sun Sets at Dawn. 1951 Cave of Outlaws; Hollywood Story; The Secret of Convict Lake; All That I Have. 1952 The Atomic City; Oklahoma Annie; The Wild North.

STEVENSON, JOHN
Born: N.Y. Died: 1922, New York, N.Y.(results of a fall while filming Plunder). Screen actor and stuntman.

Appeared in: 1923 Plunder (serial).

STEWART, ANITA
Born: Feb. 17, 1895, Brooklyn, N.Y. Died: May 4, 1961, Beverly Hills, Calif. Screen, stage actress, and film producer. Sister of screen actor George Stewart (dec. 1945).

Appeared in: 1912 The Wood Violet (film debut). 1913 A Million Bid. 1914 Two Women. 1915 My Lady's Slipper; The Goddess. 1916 The Combat. 1917 Clovers Rebellion; The Girl Philippa. 1919 In Old Kentucky; The Mind-the-Paint Girl; Virtuous Weves; A Midnight Romance; Mary Regan; Her Kingdom of Dream. 1920 The Yellow Typhoon; The Fighting Shepherdess; Harriet and the Piper. 1921 Sowing the Wind; Playthings of Destiny. 1922 Her Mad Bargain; The Invisible Fear; A Question of Honor; The Woman He Married; Rose O' the Sea. 1923 Hollywood; The Love Piker; Mary of the Movies; Souls for Sale. 1924 The Great White Way. 1925 Baree, Son of Kazan; Never the Twain Shall Meet; The Boomerang; Go Straight. 1926 The Lodge in the Wilderness; Morganson's Finish; Whispering Wires; The Prince of Pilsen; Rustling for Cupid. 1927 Wild Geese. 1928 Name the Woman; The Romance of a Rogue; Sisters of Eve.

STEWART, ATHOLE
Born: June 25, 1879, Ealing, London, England. Died: Oct. 22, 1940, Buckinghamshire, England. Screen, stage actor, and stage director.

Appeared in: 1931 The Speckled Band; Canaries Sometimes Sing. 1932 The Little Damozel. 1933 Frail Women; The Constant Nymph. 1934 Loyalties; The Four Masked Men; The Path of Glory. 1935 The Clairvoyant. 1936 Accused; The Amateur Gentleman; While Parents Sleep; Jack of All Trades; Where's Sally. 1937 Hideout in the Alps; Dr. Syn; Action for Slander; Man with Two Faces; Jane Eyre; Wise Tomorrow; The Singing Cop; Thistledown; The Tenth Man. 1938 Break the New; Climbing High; His Lordship Regrets; U-Boat 29. 1939 Goodbye, Mr. Chips. 1940 The Secret Four; Tilly of Bloomsbury. 1941 Poison Pen; It Happened to One Man.

STEWART, BETTY
Born: 1912. Died: Sept. 29, 1944, Hollywood, Calif. Screen actress.

STEWART, CRAY
Born: 1924. Died: May 30, 1961, Salton Sea, Calif.(heart attack). Screen and stage actor.

STEWART, DANNY (Danny Kalauawa Stewart)
Born: 1907. Died: Apr. 15, 1962, Honolulu, Hawaii. Screen actor and steel guitarist. Appeared in 60 "South Seas" movies.

STEWART, DAVID J. (Abe J. Siegel)
Born: 1914, Omaha, Neb. Died: Dec. 23, 1966, Cleveland, Ohio (following surgery). Screen, stage, and television actor.

Appeared in: 1955 The Silver Chalice. 1960 Murder, Inc. 1961 The Young Savages.

STEWART, DONA JEAN
Born: 1939. Died: July 31, 1961, near Oceanside, Calif.(auto accident). Screen actress.

STEWART, DONALD
Born: 1911, Pa. Died: Mar. 1, 1966, Chertsey, England. Screen, stage, and television actor.

Appeared in: 1942 Eagle Squadron; Flying Fortress. 1943 Wild Horse Stampede. 1944 Arizona Whirlwind. 1946 You Can't Do without Love. 1955 Cross Up (aka Tiger by the Tail). 1957 Two Grooms for a Bride. 1959 The Sheriff of Fractured Jaw.

STEWART, FRED
Born: 1907, Ga. Died: Dec. 5, 1970, New York, N.Y. Screen, stage, and television actor. Entered films in 1931.

Appeared in: 1932 The Misleading Lady. 1961 Splendor in the Grass. 1964 The World of Henry Orient.

STEWART, GEORGE
Born: 1888. Died: Dec. 25, 1945, Beverly Hills, Calif. Screen actor. Brother of screen actress Anita Stewart (dec. 1961).

Appeared in: 1921 The Fighter; Gilded Lies; Over the Wire. 1922 The Seventh Day. 1923 Crossed Wires; Hollywood; The Abysmal Brute. 1925 Back to Life; Wings of Youth.

STEWART, JACK
Born: 1914, Larkhall, Scotland. Died: Jan. 2, 1966, London, England. Screen, stage, radio, and television actor.

Appeared in: 1951 Operation Disaster. 1952 The Stranger in Between; The Brave Don't Cry. 1954 High and Dry; The Little Kidnappers. 1957 The Heart Within. 1958 Steel Bayonet. 1961 The Frightened City. 1962 The Pirates of Blood River; Strongroom. 1963 The Three Lives of Thomasina.

STEWART, RICHARD
Died: 1938 or 1939? Screen actor. Son of opera performer William G. Stewart (dec. 1941).

Appeared in: 1922 Face to Face.

STEWART, ROY
Born: Oct. 17, 1889, San Diego, Calif. Died: Apr. 26, 1933, Los Angeles, Calif.(heart attack). Screen and stage actor. Entered films in 1913.

Appeared in: 1915 Just Nuts (short). 1916 Liberty, a Daughter of the U.S.A. 1917 Come Through; The Devil Dodger. 1918 Keith of the Border; The Law's Outlaw; Faith Endurin'. 1919 The Westerners. 1920 Riders of the Dawn; Just a Wife. 1921 Prisoners of Love; The Devil to Pay; The Heart of the North; Her Social Value; The Mistress of Shenstone. 1922 Back to the Yellow Jacket; The Innocent Cheat; Life's Greatest Question; A Motion to Adjourn; One Eighth Apache; The Radio King (serial); The Sagebrush Trail; The Snowshoe Trail. 1923 Burning Words; The Love Brand; Pure Grit; Trimmed in Scarlet. 1924 Sundown; The Woman on the Jury. 1925 Kit Carson over the Great Divide; Time, the Comedian; Where the Worst Begins. 1926 General Custer at Little Big Horn; Sparrows; Buffalo Bill on the U. P. Trail; Daniel Boone Thru the Wilderness; The Lady from Hell; You Never Know Women. 1927 The Midnight Watch; One Woman to Another; Roaring Fires. 1928 The Viking; The Candy Kid; Stormy Waters. 1929 Protection; In Old Arizona. 1930 Men without Women; The Great Divide; Born Reckless; Lone Star Ranger; Rough Romance. 1931 Fighting Caravans. 1932 Mystery Ranch; Exposed. 1933 Fargo Express; Come on, Tarzan!; Zoo in Budapest; Rustler's Roundup.

STIEBNER, HANS
Born: 1899, Germany. Died: Mar. 27, 1958, Baden-Baden, West Germany. Screen, stage, television actor, and film director.

Appeared in: 1937 Weisse Sklaven. 1938 Mit Versiegelter Order (Under Sealed Orders).

STOCKFIELD, BETTY (aka BETTY STOCKFELD)
Born: Jan. 15, 1905, Sydney, Australia. Died: Jan. 27, 1966, London, England (cancer). Screen and stage actress.

Appeared in: 1926 What Price Glory (film debut). 1930 City of Song. 1931 Captivation; Money for Nothing; Life Goes On. 1932 Woman in Chains; The Impassive Footman; King of the Ritz; The Maid of the Mountains. 1933 Farewell to Love. 1934 The Battle; The Man Who Changed His Name. 1936 The Beloved Vagabond. 1937 Club Des Femmes (Girls' Club). 1938 I See Ice; The Slipper Episode. 1940 Derriere La Facade (Behind the Facade). 1941 Hard Steel. 1942 Nine Bachelors. 1950 Edouard et Caroline (Edward and Caroline—U.S. 1952). 1955 The Lovers of Lisbon. 1957 True as a Turtle; Lover's Net.

STODDARD, BELLE
Born: 1869, Remington, Ohio. Died: Dec. 13, 1950, Hollywood, Calif. Screen and stage actress.

Appeared in: 1925 Kentucky Pride. 1928 Hangman's House. 1929 Anne against the World.

STODDARD, BETSY (Elizabeth S. Zimmerman)
Born: 1884. Died: Sept. 7, 1959, Hollywood, Calif. Screen actress.

STOECKEL, JOE
Born: 1894, Munich, Germany. Died: June 14, 1959, Munich, Germany (circulatory ailment). Screen, stage actor, and film director. Entered films in 1916.

Appeared in: 1920 Strong Man. 1934 Der Meisterdetektiv; Die Blonde Cristl; S A Mann Brand; Mit dir Durch Dick und Duenn; Bie der Blonden Kathrein. 1935 Zwischen Himmel und Erde (Between Heaven and Earth); Johannisnact. 1936 Ein Ganzer Kerl. 1937 Die Grobe Adele. 1939 Der Dampf mit dem Drachen (The Fight with the Dragon); 1A in Oberbayern (1A in Upper Bavaria).

STOKER, H. G.
Born: 1885, England. Died: Feb. 2, 1966, England. Screen, stage actor, and playwright.

Appeared in: 1934 Channel Crossing. 1935 Brown on Resolution; First Offense; Born for Glory. 1936 It's You I Want; Rhodes; Pot Luck. 1937 Moonlight Sonata; Non-Stop New York. 1938 The Man with 100 Faces; Crackerjack; Full Speed Ahead. 1940 Torpedo Raider. 1952 Where's Charley?.

STOKES, ERNEST L.
Born: 1907. Died: May 26, 1964, Wilson, N. C. Screen and radio actor. Appeared on radio with Frank Rice in a radio team billed "Mustard and Gravy."

STONE, ARTHUR
Born: 1884, St. Louis, Mo. Died: Sept. 4, 1940, Hollywood, Calif. Screen, stage, and vaudeville actor. Entered films in 1924.

Appeared in: 1925 Sherlock Sleuth (short); Change the Needle (short). 1926 It Must Be Love; Miss Nobody; The Silent Lover. 1927 The Patent Leather Kid; The Sea Tiger; An Affair of the Follies; Babe Comes Home; The Valley of the Giants; Hard-Boiled Haggerty. 1928 Chicken a la King; The Farmer's Daughter; Me, Gangster; Burning Daylight. 1929 Through Different Eyes; Captain Lash; The Far Call; Fugitives; New Year's Eve; Red Wine; Frozen Justice; Fox Movietone Follies of 1929. 1930 The Vagabond King; The Bad Man; Arizona Kid; On the Level; Mamba; Girl of the Golden West. 1931 The Lash; The Conquering Horde; Bad Company; The Secret Menace. 1932 The Big Shot; The Broken Wing; So Big; Roar of the Dragon; That's My Boy; plus the following shorts: The Girl in the Tonneau; Lady Please!; The Flirty Sleepwalker; The Line's Busy; Neighbor Trouble. 1934 She Had to Choose; I'll Tell the World; Love Birds. 1935 Bordertown; Charlie Chan in Egypt; Hot Tip. 1936 Fury. 1938 Go Chase Yourself.

STONE, FRED
Born: Aug. 19, 1873, Denver, Colo. Died: Mar. 6, 1959, North Hollywood, Calif. Screen, stage, vaudeville, and circus actor. Appeared in vaudeville as part of "Montgomery and Stone" team. Made a few western films for Lasky in 1917.

Appeared in: 1918 The Goat. 1919 Under the Top; Johnny Get Your Gun. 1921 The Duke of Chimney Butte. 1922 Billy Jim. 1924 Broadway after Dark. 1932 Smiling Faces. 1935 Alice Adams. 1936 The Trail of the Lonesome Pine; My American Wife; The Farmer in the Dell; Jury. 1937 Hideaway; Life Begins in College. 1938 Quick Money. 1939 No Place to Go. 1940 Konga, the Wild Stallion; The Westerner.

STONE, GEORGE E. (George Stein)
Born: May, 1903, Lodz, Poland. Died: May 26, 1967, Woodland Hills, Calif.(stroke). Screen, stage, vaudeville, and television actor. Known for gangster parts in "Boston Blackie" series and other films.

Appeared in: 1918 'Til I Come Back to You. 1921 Jackie; Penny of Top Hill Trail; The Whistle; White and Unmarried. 1923 The Fourth Musketeer. 1927 Seventh Heaven; Brass Knuckles. 1928 State Street Sadie; Tenderloin; The Racket; Walking Back; Beautiful but Dumb; Clothes Make the Woman; San Francisco Nights; Turn Back the Hours. 1929 Weary River; Skin Deep; Naughty Baby; The Girl in the Glass Cage; Two Men and a Maid; Melody Lane; Redeeming Sin. 1930 Under a Texas Moon; The Medicine Man; The Stronger Sex; So This Is Paris Green; Little Caesar. 1931 Cimarron; Five-Star Final; The Spider; Sob Sister; The Front Page. 1932 The Last Mile; Taxi!; File No. 113; The Woman from Monte Carlo; The World and the Flesh; The Phantom of Crestwood; Slippery Pearls (short). 1933 King for a Night; Vampire Bat; Sailor Be Good!; Song of the Eagle; The Big Brain; Emergency Call; The Wrecker; Sing, Sinner, Sing; Ladies Must Love; Penthouse; He Couldn't Take It; 42nd Street. 1934 Return of the Terror; The Dragon Murder Case; Embarrassing Moments; Frontier Marshal; Viva Villa!. 1935 Hold 'Em Yale; Public Hero No. 1; Make a Million; Moonlight on the Prairie; The Frisco Kid;

One Hour Late; Secret of the Chateau; Million Dollar Baby. 1936 Man Hunt; Freshman Love; Jailbreak; Anthony Adverse; Bullets or Ballots. The Captain's Kid; Polo Joe; King of Hockey; Here Comes Carter!; Rhythm on the Range. 1937 Back in Circulation; The Adventurous Blonde. 1938 Alcatraz Island; A Slight Case of Murder; Over the Wall; Mr. Moto's Gamble; Submarine Patrol; The Long Shot; You and Me. 1939 You Can't Get Away with Murder; The Housekeeper's Daughter. 1940 The Night of Nights; I Take This Woman; Island of Doomed Men; Northwest Mounted Police; Slightly Tempted; Cherokee Strip. 1941 Broadway Limited; Last of the Duanes; His Girl Friday; Road Show; The Face behind the Mask; Confessions of Boston Blackie. 1942 Lone Star Ranger; The Affairs of Jimmy Valentine; Little Tokyo, U.S.A.; The Devil with Hitler; Boston Blackie Goes to Hollywood. 1943 The Chance of a Lifetime; After Midnight with Boston Blackie. 1944 Roger Touhy—Gangster; Timber Queen; One Mysterious Night; Strangers in the Night; My Buddy. 1945 One Exciting Night; Boston Blackie's Rendezvous; Scared Stiff; Boston Blackie Booked on Suspicion; Doll Face. 1946 Boston Blackie and the Law; A Close Call for Boston Blackie; The Phantom Thief; Sentimental Journey; Suspense; Abie's Irish Rose. 1948 Trapped by Boston Blackie; Untamed Breed. 1950 Dancing in the Dark. 1952 A Girl in Every Port; Bloodhounds of Broadway. 1953 The Robe; Pickup on South Street; Combat Squad. 1954 Three Ring Circus; The Steel Cage; Broken Lance; The Miami Story. 1955 The Man with the Golden Arm; Guys and Dolls. 1956 Slightly Scarlet. 1957 Sierra Stranger; The Story of Mankind; The Tijuana Story; Baby Face Nelson; Calypso Heat Wave. 1959 Some Like It Hot. 1961 Pocketful of Miracles.

STONE, LEWIS
Born: Nov. 15, 1879, Worcester, Mass. Died: Sept. 11, 1953, Los Angeles, Calif.(heart attack). Screen and stage actor. Best known for role in "Andy Hardy" film series.

Appeared in: 1916 Honor Altar (film debut); The Havoc. 1918 Inside the Lines. 1920 Nomads of the North; The Concert; The River's End; Held by the Enemy; Milestones. 1921 The Northern Trail; The Golden Snare; Beau Revel; Pilgrims of the Night; The Child Thou Gavest Me; Don't Neglect Your Wife. 1922 The Prisoner of Zenda; Trifling Women; A Fool There Was; The Rosary. 1932 Scaramouche; The Dangerous Age; You Can't Fool Your Wife. 1924 The Stranger; Why Men Leave Home; Husbands and Lovers; Inez from Hollywood; Cytherea; The Lost World. 1925 The Lady Who Lied; The Talker; Cheaper to Marry; Confessions of a Queen; What Fools Men; Fine Clothes. 1926 Don Juan's Three Nights; Too Much Money; Old Loves and New; Girl from Montmarte; Midnight Lover; The Blonde Saint. 1927 An Affair of the Follies; Lonesome Ladies; The Prince of Head Waiters; The Notorious Ladies; The Private Life of Helen of Troy. 1928 The Foreign Legion; Freedom of the Press; The Patriot; Inspiration. 1929 The Trial of Mary Dugan; A Woman of Affairs; Wild Orchids; The Circle; Wonder of Women; Madame X. 1930 Their Own Desire; Strictly Unconventional; The Big House; Romance; The Office Wife; Passion Flower; Father's Son. 1931 The Sin of Madelon Claudet; My Past; Inspiration; Always Goodbye; Phantom of Paris; The Bargain; Stolen Heaven; The Secret Six. 1932 Mata Hari; Grand Hotel; The Divorce in the Family; Unashamed; Wet Parade; Night Court; Letty Lynton; New Morals for Old; Red Headed Woman; The Son-Daughter; The Mask of Fu Manchu; Strange Interlude. 1933 The White Sister; Service; Looking Forward; Queen Christina; Bureau of Missing Persons; Men Must Fight. 1934 You Can't Buy Everything; The Girl from Missouri; Treasure Island; The Mystery of Mr. X. 1935 David Copperfield; Vanessa, Her Love Story; West Point of the Air; Public Hero No. 1; Woman Wanted; China Seas; Shipmates Forever. 1936 Three Godfathers; The Unguarded Hour; Small Town Girl; Sworn Enemy; Suzy; Don't Turn 'Em Loose. 1937 Outcast; The Thirteenth Chair; The Man Who Cried Wolf. 1938 You're Only Young Once; Bad Man of Brimstone; Judge Hardy's Children; Stolen Heaven; Love Finds Andy Hardy; Yellow Jack; The Chaser; Out West with the Hardys. 1939 Ice Follies of 1939; The Hardy's Ride High; Andy Hardy Gets Spring Fever; The Andy Hardy Family; Judge Hardy and Son; Joe and Ethel Turp Call on the President. 1940 Andy Hardy Meets Debutante; Sporting Blood. 1941 The Bugle Sounds; Andy Hardy's Private Secretary; Life Begins for Andy Hardy. 1942 The Courtship of Andy Hardy; Andy Hardy's Double Life. 1944 Andy Hardy's Blonde Trouble. 1946 Love Laughs at Andy Hardy; The Hoodlum Saint; Three Wise Fools. 1948 State of the Union. 1949 The Sun Comes Up; Any Number Can Play. 1950 Stars in My Crown; Key to the City. 1951 Grounds for Marriage; Night into Morning; Angels in the Outfield; Bannerline; It's a Big Country; The Unknown Man. 1952 Just This Once; Talk About a Stranger; Scaramouche; The Prisoner of Zenda (and 1922 version). 1953 All the Brothers Were Valiant; One Came Home. 1964 Big Parade of Comedy (documentary).

STONE, MAXINE
Born: 1910. Died: Nov. 20, 1964, Hollywood, Calif. Screen, stage, and vaudeville actress. Appeared in vaudeville with her husband Benny Ross in act called "Ross and Stone."

Appeared in early Vitaphone shorts and: 1958 South Seas Adventure.

STONEHOUSE, RUTH
Born: 1893. Died: May 12, 1941, Hollywood, Calif. Screen and stage actress. Was part owner with Billy Anderson of the Essanay studios in Chicago.

Appeared in: 1911 The Papered Door. 1913 The Spy's Defeat. 1914 The Romance of an American Duchess; Blood Will Tell. 1916 The Adventures of Peg O' the Ring (serial). 1919 The Masked Rider (serial); The Master Mystery (serial). 1920 Parlor, Bedroom and Bath. 1921 I Am Guilty; Don't Call Me Little Girl. 1923 Lights Out; The Flash; Flames of Passion; The Way of the Transgressor. 1924 A Girl of the Limberlost; Broken Barriers. 1925 Blood and Steel; The Fugitive; Rough Going; Ermine and Rhinestones; Fifth Avenue Model; The Scarlet West; Straight Through; A Two-Fisted Sheriff. 1926 Broken Homes; The Wives of the Prophet. 1927 Poor Girls; The Ladybird; The Satin Woman. 1928 The Ape; The Devil's Cage.

STOWELL, CLARENCE W.
Born: 1878. Died: Nov. 26, 1940, Paterson, N.J. Screen actor.

Appeared in: 1940 The Ramparts We Watch (March of Time's first full-length feature).

STRADNER, ROSE
Born: July 31, 1913, Vienna, Austria. Died: Sept. 27, 1958, Bedford Village, N.Y. Screen and stage actress. Married to director Joseph L. Mankiewicz.

Appeared in: 1934 Ein Gewisser Herr Gran; Hochzeit am Wolfgangsee. 1936 One Hundred Days of Napoleon. 1937 The Postillion of Lonjumeau. 1938 The Last Gangster. 1939 Blind Alley. 1944 The Keys of the Kingdom.

STRANGE, ROBERT
Born: 1882. Died: Feb. 22, 1952, Hollywood, Calif. Screen and stage actor.

Appeared in: 1931 The Smiling Lieutenant; The Cheat. 1932 The Misleading Lady. 1934 These Thirty Years; Gambling. 1935 Special Agent; I Found Stella Parish; Frisco Kid. 1936 The Murder of Dr. Harrigan; The Walking Dead; Stolen Holiday; Trapped by Television; Beloved Enemy. 1937 Beware of Ladies; John Meade's Woman; Marked Woman. 1938 Sky Giant; I Stand Accused. 1939 In Name Only; They Made Me a Criminal; Hell's Kitchen; The Saint Strikes Back; The Story of Vernon and Irene Castle; The Spellbinder; Angels Wash Their Faces. 1940 The Castle on the Hudson; The Adventures of Captain Marvel (serial); King of the Royal Mounted. 1941 Robin Hood of the Pecos; High Sierra; All That Money Can Buy. 1942 Arizona Cyclone; The Yukon Patrol. 1952 The Devil and Daniel Webster (reissue and retitle of All That Money Can Buy—1941).

STRANGIS, JANE
Born: 1932. Died: Jan. 25, 1966, Hollywood, Calif.(leukemia). Screen and television actress.

STRATTON, CHESTER "CHET"
Born: 1913. Died: July 7, 1970, Los Angeles, Calif. Screen, stage, and radio actor.

Appeared in: 1937 a Vitaphone Short. 1953 Julius Caesar. 1961 Go Naked in the World. 1962 Lover Come Back; Advise and Consent. 1965 In Harm's Way; Bus Riley's Back in Town; The Greatest Story Ever Told. 1968 Track of Thunder; Journey to Shiloh.

STRATTON, HARRY
Born: 1898. Died: Aug. 19, 1955, Hollywood, Calif.(heart attack). Screen and burlesque actor. Stand-in for Bud Abbott.

STRAUB, MARY E.
Born: 1884. Died: Nov. 7, 1951, Hollywood, Calif. Screen actress.

STRAUSS, WILLIAM H.
Born: June 13, 1885, New York, N.Y. Died: Aug. 5, 1943, Hollywood, Calif.(heart attack). Screen, stage, vaudeville actor, and stage director.

Appeared in: 1920 North Wind's Malice. 1921 Magic Cup; The Barricade. 1922 Other Women's Clothes. 1923 Solomon in Society. 1925 Skinner's Dress Suit. 1926 Private Izzy Murphy; Law of the Snow Country; Millionaires. 1927 Ankles Preferred; For Ladies Only; Sally in Our Alley; The Shamrock and the Rose; The Rawhide Kid; Ladies at Ease; Ragtime; King of Kings; The Show Girl. 1928 So This Is Love; Abie's Irish Rose. 1929 Smiling Irish Eyes; Lucky Boy. 1930 Jazz Cinderella. 1934 Beloved; The House of Rothschild. 1938 Golden Boy.

STREET, DAVID
Born: 1917, Los Angeles, Calif. Died: Sept. 3, 1971, Los Angeles, Calif. Screen, radio, television actor, orchestra leader, and singer. Divorced from screen actress Debra Paget.

Appeared in: 1949 Moonrise. 1950 Holiday Rhythm.

STREET, GEORGE A.
Born: 1869, Montreal, Canada. Died: May 30, 1956, Weston-Super-Mare, England. Screen actor and wild west showman.

STRONG, CARL E.
Born: 1907. Died: Jan. 14, 1965, Minneapolis, Minn. Screen, circus, television actor, and rodeo rider.

STRONG, JAY
Born: 1896. Died: Dec. 1, 1953, New York, N.Y. Screen, vaudeville actor, stage producer/director, and television writer, director, and producer.

Appeared in: 1919 The Moonshine Trail.

STRYKER, GUSTAVE
Born: 1866, Chicago, Ill. Died: June 3, 1943, New York, N.Y. Screen, stage, and radio actor.

STUART, DONALD
Born: 1898, England. Died: Feb. 22, 1944, Hollywood, Calif. (heart attack). Screen and radio actor.

Appeared in: 1926 Beau Geste; Bride of the Storm. 1927 The Lone Eagle; Marriage. 1928 The Cheer Leader; The Girl-Shy Cowboy; The Olympic Hero; Interference. 1929 The Silver King. 1930 Derelict. 1931 Devotion. 1932 In a Monastery Garden; The Man from Yesterday; Cynara. 1933 The Invisible Man; The Woman Accused. 1934 Dancing Man. 1936 First a Girl. 1941 A Yank in the R.A.F. 1942 Eagle Squadron; Flying Fortress; Destination Unknown. 1943 Immortal Sergeant. 1944 The Hour Before the Dawn; The Canterville Ghost.

STUART, JEAN (Margaret Leisenring)
Born: 1904. Died: Nov. 23, 1926, Hollywood, Calif.(injuries from a fall from a horse). Screen actress.

Appeared in: 1926 The Campus Flirt.

STUART, RALPH R.
Born: 1890. Died: Nov. 4, 1952, New York, N.Y. Screen, stage actor, and stage director.

Appeared in: 1917 The Mystery of the Double Cross (serial).

SUDLOW, JOAN
Born: 1892. Died: Feb. 1, 1970, Hollywood, Calif.(died from fall). Screen, stage, and television actress.

Appeared in: 1951 Queen for a Day. 1952 Pride of St. Louis. 1966 A Fine Madness.

SUES, LEONARD
Born: 1921. Died: Oct. 24, 1971, Los Angeles, Calif.(cancer). Screen actor and musical director. Entered films in 1940.

Appeared in: 1949 Manhattan Angel.

SULLAVAN, MARGARET (Margaret Brooke Sullavan)
Born: May 16, 1911, Norfolk, Va. Died: Jan. 1, 1960, New Haven, Conn.(suicide—sleeping pills). Screen, stage, and television actress. Mother of screen actress Brooke Hayward.

Appeared in: 1933 Only Yesterday. 1934 Little Man, What Now?. 1935 The Good Fairy; So Red the Rose. 1936 Next Time We Love; The Moon's Our Home; I Love a Soldier. 1938 Three Comrades; The Shopworn Angel; The Shining Hour. 1939 When Tomorrow Comes. 1940 The Shop Around the Corner; The Mortal Storm. 1941 So Ends Our Night; Back Street; Appointment for Love. 1944 Cry Havoc. 1950 No Sad Songs for Me.

SULLIVAN, BRIAN (Harry Joseph Sullivan)
Born: Aug. 9, 1919, Oakland, Calif. Died: June 17, 1969, Lake Geneva, Switzerland. Screen, stage, and opera actor.

Appeared in: 1945 This Man's Navy. 1946 Courage of Lassie.

SULLIVAN, FRANCIS LOFTUS
Born: Jan. 6, 1903, London, England. Died: Nov. 19, 1956, New York, N.Y. Screen, stage, and television actor.

Appeared in: 1931 The Missing Rembrandt. 1932 F.P. No. 1. 1933 Red Wagon; The Stickpin; The Fire Raisers; The Right to Live. 1934 Jew Suess; Chu Chin Chow; The Return of Bulldog Drummond; Great Expectations; Cheating Cheaters; What Happened Then?; The Warren Case; Princess Charming. 1935 Mystery of Edwin Drood; Her Last Affair; Strange Wives; The Wandering Jew. 1936 Interrupted Honeymoon; Spy of Napoleon; Fine Feathers; A Woman Alone (aka Sabotage); The Limping Man. 1937 Non-Stop New York; Action for Slander; Dinner at the Ritz; The First and the Last; The Gables Mystery; Kate Plus Ten; Two Who Dared. 1938 Drums; The Citadel; The Vanishing Train. 1939 The Ware Case; Climbing High; The Four Just Men; Young Man's Fancy (U.S. 1943); Spy of Napoleon. 1940 21 Days Together; The Secret Four. 1941 Pimpernel Smith; The Foreman Went to France; The Day Will Dawn; Queen of Crime. 1942 The Avengers; Mister V. 1943 The Butler's Dilemma; Fiddlers Three. 1945 The Lady from Lisbon. 1946 Caesar and Cleopatra. 1947 Great Expectations (and 1934 version); The Smugglers. 1948 Joan of Arc. 1949 The Red Danube; Broken Journey; Christopher Columbus; Take My Life. 1950 The Winslow Boy; Night and the City; The Laughing Lady. 1951 My Favorite Spy; Behave Yourself; Oliver Twist. 1952 Caribbean. 1953 Sangaree; Plunder of the Sun. 1954 Drums of Tahiti. 1955 Hell's Island; The Prodigal.

SULLIVAN, FREDERICK R. "FRED"
Born: 1872, London, England. Died: July 24, 1937, Los Angeles, Calif.(heart trouble). Screen and stage actor.

Appeared in: 1922 Tailor-Made Man. 1923 The Courtship of Miles Standish; Face on the Barroom Floor. 1925 Winds of Chance; Beggar on Horseback. 1929 The Black Watch. 1930 Around the Corner; Prince of Diamonds. 1931 Murder by the Clock. 1932 If I Had a Million. 1933 Blind Adventure; Duck Soup. 1934 You're Telling Me. 1935 All the King's Horses.

SULLIVAN, JAMES E.
Born: 1864. Died: June 1, 1931. Screen and stage actor.

Appeared in: 1925 The Pinch Hitter.

SULLIVAN, JOE
Born: 1910. Died: Oct. 13, 1971, San Francisco, Calif. Pianist, and screen and radio actor. Appeared with Red Nichols' band and others.

SULLIVAN, JOHN MAURICE
Born: 1876. Died: Mar. 8, 1949, Hollywood, Calif. Screen and stage actor. Entered films in 1930.

Appeared in: 1930 Today. 1931 Silence. 1932 Strangers in Love; The Trial of Vivienne Ware; Down to Earth. 1933 Big Executive. 1934 You're Telling Me; Mystery Liner. 1936 Walking on Air. 1938 The Buccaneer. 1946 Blue Skies.

SUMMERVILLE, SLIM (George J. Summerville)
Born: 1896, Albuquerque, N.M. Died: Jan. 6, 1946, Laguna Beach, Calif.(stroke). Screen actor and film director.

Appeared in: 1914 The Knock-Out; Mabel's Busy Day; A Rowboat Romance; Laughing Gas; Gentlemen of Nerve (reissued Some Nerve); Cursed by His Beauty; Tillie's Punctured Romance. 1915 Her Winning Punch; The Home Breakers (reissued Other People's Wives); Caught in the Act; Gussle's Day of Rest; Their Social Splash; Those College Girls (reissued His Bitter Half); The Great Vacuum Robbery; Her Painted Hero; A Game Old Knight. 1916 Cinders of Love; The Winning Punch; Bucking Society (short); Her Busted Trust; The Three Slims; His Bread and Butter. 1917 Villa of the Movies; Her Fame and Shame; A Dog Catcher's Love; His Precious Life; A Pullman Bride. 1918 The Beloved Rogue. 1921 Skirts. 1926 The Texas Streak; The Beloved Rogue (and 1918 version). 1927 The Denver Dude; Painted Ponies; Hey, Hey, Cowboy; The Wreck of the Hesperus. 1928 The Chinese Parrot; Riding for Fame. 1929 King of the Rodeo; Strong Boy; Shannons of Broadway; Tiger Rose; The Last Warning. 1930 See America Thirst; Free Love; Her Man; The Spoilers; One Hysterical Night; Troopers Three; Under Montana Skies; All Quiet on the Western Front; King of Jazz; Little Accident; Hello Russia; We! We! Marie!; Parlez Vous. 1931 Bad Sisters; The

Front Page; Arabian Knights; Bless the Ladies; First to Fight; Hotter Than Haiti; Let's Play; Parisian Gaieties; Royal Bluff; Sargie's Playmates; Here's Luck; Reckless Living; Heaven on Earth. 1932 Racing Youth; Unexpected Father; Eyes Have It; In the Bag; Kid Glove Kisses; Meet the Princess; Sea Soldier's Sweeties; Tom Brown of Culver; Air Mail. 1932-33 Universal shorts. 1933 Out All Night; They Just Had to Get Married; Early to Bed; Her First Mate; Love, Honor and Oh, Baby!. 1934 Horse Play; The Love Birds; Their Big Moment. 1935 Life Begins at 40; The Farmer Takes a Wife; Way down East. 1936 Captain January; The Country Doctor; Pepper; White Fang; Reunion; Can This Be Dixie?. 1937 Off to the Races; Love Is News; Fifty Roads to Town; The Road Back; Five of a Kind. 1939 Charlie Chan in Reno. 1940 Anne of Windy Poplars; Gold Rush Maisie. 1941 Miss Polly; Western Union; Highway West; Tobacco Road. 1942 Niagara Falls; Jesse James; The Spoilers. 1944 I'm from Arkansas; Bride by Mistake. 1946 The Hoodlum Saint.

SUMNER, CORINNE HEATH. See Corine Heath Sumner Ross

SUNDMARK, BETTY. See Elizabeth S. Shannon

SUNSHINE, MARION
Born: 1897. Died: Jan. 25, 1963, New York, N.Y. Screen, stage, vaudeville actress, and song writer.

Appeared in: 1908 The Tavern Keeper's Daughter; The Red Girl. 1909 Her First Biscuits. 1910 In the Season of Buds; Sunshine Sue; Three Sisters; A Decree of Destiny. 1911 The Rose of Kentucky; The Stuff Heroes Are Made Of; Dan the Dandy. 1912 Heredity. 1944 I'm from Arkansas.

SUPPLEE, ESTHER RITTER. See Esther Ritter

SUSSENGUTH, WALTHER
Born: 1900, Germany. Died: May 1964, Berlin, Germany. Screen and stage actor.

Appeared in: 1935 Der Schimmelreiter (The Rider of the White Horse).

SUTHERLAND, DICK
Born: 1882, Benton, Ky. Died: Feb. 3, 1934, Hollywood, Calif. Screen, stage, and vaudeville actor.

Appeared in: 1921 The Magnificent Brute; God's Gold; Sailor-Made Man. 1922 Gas, Oil and Water; The Deuce of Spades; Rags to Riches; Grandma's Boy. 1923 Hell's Hole; The Rip-Tide; Quicksands; The Shriek of Araby; His Last Race; Masters of Men. 1924 The Dangerous Blonde; The Red Lily; The Tornado; The Mask of Lopez; Battling Mason; Defying the Law; Fighter's Paradise. 1925 The Fighting Demon; Flying Fool; With This Ring; Jimmie's Millions; The Road to Yesterday. 1926 The Beloved Rogue; Lloyd Hamilton Comedies; Broken Hearts of Hollywood; Don Juan; The Jazz Girl. 1927 The Claw; Uncle Tom's Cabin. 1928 Riders of the Dark. 1929 China Slaver; The Hoosegow (short). 1959 Uncle Tom's Cabin (re-release of 1927 film).

SUTHERLAND, VICTOR
Born: 1889. Died: Aug. 29, 1968, Los Angeles, Calif. Screen, stage, and television actor. Divorced from screen actress Pearl White (dec. 1938). Married to actress Linda Barrett.

Appeared in: 1923 The Valley of Lost Souls. 1924 The Love Bandit. 1950 The Sleeping City. 1951 The Whistle at Eaton Falls. 1952 Lone Star; The Pride of St. Louis; The Captive City. 1953 Powder River; Donovan's Brain.

SUTTON, JOHN
Born: Oct. 22, 1908, Rawalpindi, India. Died: 1963. Screen and stage actor.

Appeared in: 1937 Bulldog Drummond's Revenge; Bulldog Drummond Comes Back. 1938 Adventures of Robin Hood; The Blonde Cheat; Booloo; Four Men and a Prayer. 1939 Tower of London; Arrest Bulldog Drummond; Susannah of the Mounties; Bulldog Drummond's Bride; Charlie McCarthy, Detective; Zaza; The Private Lives of Elizabeth and Essex. 1940 Christable Caine; Sandy Is a Lady; I Can't Give You Anything but Love, Baby; South of Karanga; Murder over New York; Hudson Bay; The Invisible Man Returns. 1941 A Very Young Lady; Moon over Her Shoulder; A Yank in the RAF. 1942 Ten Gentlemen from West Point; My Gal Sal; Thunder Birds. 1943 Tonight We Raid Calais. 1944 Jane Eyre; The Hour before the Dawn. 1946 Claudia and David. 1947 Captain from Castile. 1948 The Three Musketeers; The Counterfeiters; Mickey. 1949 The Bride of Vengeance; Bagdad; The Fan. 1950 The Second Face. 1951 The Second Woman; Payment on Demand. 1952 David and Bathsheba; Thief of Damascus; Captain

Pirate; The Golden Hawk; My Cousin Rachel; The Lady in the Iron Mask. 1953 Sangaree; East of Sumatra. 1956 The Amazon Trader; Death of a Scoundrel. 1959 The Bat; The Return of the Fly; Beloved Infidel. 1961 The Canadians. 1964 Of Human Bondage.

SUTTON, PAUL
Born: 1912. Died: Jan. 31, 1970, Ferndale, Mich.(muscular dystrophy). Screen, radio, and television actor.

Appeared in: 1938 The Spy Ring; Air Devils; Bar 20 Justice; In Old Mexico; Shadows over Shanghai. 1939 Balalaika; The Girl and the Gambler. 1940 Little Old New York. 1941 Ride On Vaquero; Wild Geese Calling. 1942 Sundown Jim; In Old California; Riders of the Northland.

SUTTON, WILLIAM
Born: 1877. Died: Sept. 10, 1955, West Los Angeles, Calif. Screen, stage actor, and magician. Known as the "Great Fontonelle." Appeared in silents.

SVERDLIN, LEV N.
Born: 1902, Russia. Died: Aug. 30, 1969, Moscow, Russia. Screen actor.

Appeared in: 1938 The Defense of Volotchayevsk. 1942 Guerrilla Brigade. 1944 Adventures in Bokhara. 1945 Marriage; Wait for Me. 1946 Great Days; Days and Nights. 1951 Far from Moscow.

SWAIN, MACK
Born: Feb. 16, 1876, Salt Lake City, Utah. Died: Aug. 25, 1935, Tacoma, Wash. Screen and stage actor.

Appeared in: 1914 Caught in a Cabaret (reissued The Jazz Waiter); Caught in the Rain; A Busy Day; The Fatal Mallet; The Knock-Out (reissued The Pugilist); A Gambling Rube; A Missing Bride; Mabel's Married Life (reissued The Squarehead); A Rowboat Romance; Laughing Gas; Gentlemen of Nerve (reissued Some Nerve); His Musical Career; His Trysting Place; The Sea Nymphs (reissued His Diving Beauty); Among the Mourners; Leading Lizzie Astray; Getting Acquainted; Other People's Business; His Prehistoric Past; Tillie's Punctured Romance; Ambrose's First Falsehood; A Dark Lover's Play. 1915 Love, Speed and Thrills; The Home Breakers (reissued Other People's Wives); Ye Olden Grafter; Ambrose's Sour Grapes; Willful Ambrose; From Patches to Plenty; Ambrose's Little Hatchet; Ambrose's Fury; Ambrose's Lofty Perch; Ambrose's Nasty Temper; A Human Hound's Triumph; Our Daredevil Chief; Mabel Lost and Won; When Ambrose Dared Walrus; The Battle of Ambrose and Walrus. 1915 Saved by Wireless; The Best of Enemies. 1916 A Movie Star; Love Will Conquer; His Auto Ruination; By Stork Delivery; His Bitter Pill; His Wild Oats; Madcap Ambrose; Vampire Ambrose; Ambrose's Cup of Woe; Ambrose's Rapid Rise; Safety First Ambrose (working title Sheriff Ambrose); A Modern Enoch Arden. 1917 His Naughty Thought; Thirst (re-released 1923); Lost—A Cook; A Pullman Bride. 1918 "Poppy" series. 1919 Ambrose's Day Off. 1923 The Pilgrim. 1925 The Gold Rush. 1926 Hands Up; Sea Horses; Kiki; Footloose Widows; The Nervous Wreck; Her Big Night; Honesty—the Best Policy; The Torrent; Whispering Wires. 1927 Becky; Finnegan's Ball; The Shamrock and the Rose; The Tired Business Man; The Beloved Rogue; See You in Jail; Mockery; My Best Girl. 1928 Caught in the Fog; Gentlemen Prefer Blondes; A Texas Steer; The Last Warning; Tillie's Punctured Romance; The Cohens and the Kellys. 1929 Marianne; The Cohens and the Kellys in Atlantic City. 1930 Redemption; The Sea Bat; The Locked Door. 1931 Stout Hearts and Willing Hands; Finn and Hattie. 1932 Midnight Patrol. 1932-33 Paramount shorts. 1960 When Comedy Was King (documentary).

SWARTHOUT, GLADYS
Born: Dec. 25, 1904, Deepwater, Mo. Died: July 7, 1969, Florence, Italy. Opera, screen, stage, and radio actress.

Appeared in: 1936 Rose of the Rancho; Give Us This Night. 1937 Champagne Waltz. 1938 Romance in the Dark. 1939 Ambush.

SWARTS, SARA
Born: 1899. Died: Mar. 31, 1949, Woodland Hills, Calif. Screen actress. Entered films approx. 1918.

SWEENEY, EDWARD C.
Born: 1906. Died: Aug. 14, 1967, Miami, Fla. Film producer, lecturer, photographer, and founder of the "Explorers Club". He produced and appeared in eleven travel-lecture films.

SWEENEY, FRED C.
Born: 1894. Died: Dec. 10, 1954, Sylmar, Calif.(pulmonary tuberculosis). Screen, stage, and vaudeville actor. Appeared in vaudeville team of "Daffy and Sweeney."

SWEENEY, JACK
Born: 1889. Died: Apr. 12, 1950, Hollywood, Calif. Screen actor. Appeared in Sennett films in 1916.

SWEET, TOM
Born: 1933. Died: Nov. 19, 1967, High Sierras, Calif.(plane crash). Screen, television actor, and stuntman. Was the "Galloping White Knight" on television commercials.

Appeared in: 1961 Sniper's Ridge.

SWENSON, ALFRED G.
Born: 1883, Salt Lake City, Utah. Died: Mar. 28, 1941, Staten Island, N.Y.(heart attack). Screen, stage, and radio actor.

Appeared in: 1929 The Great Power.

SWICKARD, CHARLES F.
Born: 1861. Died: May 12, 1929, Fresno, Calif. Screen actor and film director. Brother of screen actor Joseph Swickard (dec. 1940).

SWICKARD, JOSEPH
Born: 1866, Coblenz, Germany. Died: Feb. 29, 1940, Hollywood, Calif. Screen and stage actor. Entered films in 1912. Brother of screen actor Charles Swickard (dec. 1929).

Appeared in: 1914 A Rowboat Romance; Laughing Gas; The Plumber. 1915 Love, Loot and Crash; A Home Breaking Hound; The Best of Enemies. 1916 Love Will Conquer; The Village Vampire (working title The Great Leap); His Wild Oats; Haystacks and Steeples; Ambrose's Cup of Woe. 1917 Tale of Two Cities. 1921 Beach of Dreams; No Woman Knows; Opened Shutters; Sowing the Wind. 1921 Serenade; Four Horsemen of the Apocalypse; Cheated Hearts; Who Am I?. 1922 The Adventures of Robinson Crusoe (serial); Across the Dead Line; Another Man's Shoes; My American Wife; The Golden Gift; Pawned; The Storm; The Young Rajah. 1923 The Age of Desire; Mr. Billings Spends His Dime; A Prince of a King; Bavu; Maytime; The Cricket on the Hearth; Daughters of the Rich; The Eternal Struggle; Forgive and Forget; Mothers-in-Law. 1924 Dante's Inferno; Men; Pal O'Mine; The Shadow of the East; A Boy of Flanders; Defying the Law; Poisoned Paradise; Untamed Youth; North of Nevada. 1925 Off the Highway; The Verdict; She Wolves; The Wizard of Oz; Easy Money; The Mysterious Stranger; Playing with Souls; Northern Code; Fifth Avenue Models; The Keeper of the Bees; The Sign of the Cactus. 1926 Officer Jim; The Unknown Cavalier; The Border Whirlwind; Three Pals; Senor Daredevil; Stop, Look and Listen; Desert Gold; Devil's Dice; Don Juan; The High Flyer; The Night Patrol; Kentucky Handicap; Whispering Canyon. 1927 One Increasing Purpose; Old San Francisco; Senorita; Time to Love; Get Your Man; The Golden Stallion (serial); Compassion; False Morals; King of Kings. 1928 Eagle of the Night (serial); Comrades; Sharp Shooters; Turn Back the Hours. 1929 Bachelor's Club; Dark Skies; Phantoms of the North; Devil's Chaplain; The Eternal Woman; The Veiled Woman; Frozen River; Times Square; Street Corners. 1930 Song of the Caballero; Mamba; Phantom of the Desert. 1934 Beloved; Return of Chandu; Cross Streets. 1935 A Dog of Flanders; The Lost City (serial); The Crusades; Custer's Last Stand (serial). 1936 The Millionaire Kid; Caryl of the Mountains; Boss Rider of Gun Creek. 1937 The Girl Said No; Sandflow. 1938 You Can't Take It with You.

SWITZER, CARL "ALFALFA"
Born: 1926. Died: Jan. 21, 1959, Sepulveda, Calif.(shot). Screen and television actor.

Appeared in: "Our Gang" comedies during the 1930s. 1936 Easy To Take; Right in Your Lap; Kelly the Second; Pick a Star; Too Many Parents; General Spanky. 1937 Wild and Woolly. 1938 an MGM short; Scandal Street. 1940 The New Pupil; I Love You Again; Barnyard Follies. 1941 Reg'lar Fellers. 1942 Johnny Doughboy; Henry and Dizzy; The War against Mrs. Hadley; Mrs. Wiggs of the Cabbage Patch; My Favorite Blonde. 1943 Shantytown. 1944 Rosie the Riveter; The Great Mike; Going My Way. 1946 The Gas House Kids; Courage of Lassie. 1947 The Gas House Kids Go West; The Gas House Kids in Hollywood. 1948 On Our Merry Way; State of the Union; Big Town Scandal; A Letter to Three Wives. 1950 Redwood Forest Trail. 1951 Two Dollar Bettor. 1952 I Dream of Jeanie; Pat and Mike. 1953 Island in the Sky. 1954 The High and the Mighty; Track of the Cat; This Is My Love. 1956 Between Heaven and Hell; Dig That Uranium. 1957 Motorcycle Game. 1958 The Defiant Ones.

SWOR, BERT
Born: 1878, Paris, Tenn. Died: Nov. 30, 1943, Tulsa,Okla. Screen, stage, vaudeville, and minstrel actor. Appeared in vaudeville and films for a short time as Moran in "Moran and Mack" comedy team, usually referred to as the "Two Black Crows." Brother of screen actor John Swor (dec. 1965).

Appeared in: 1928 Ducks and Deducts (short); A Colorful Sermon (short). 1929 Why Bring That Up. 1930 Anybody's War (with Mack).

SWOR, JOHN
Born: Apr. 7, 1883, Paris, Tenn. Died: July 15, 1965, Dallas, Tex. Screen, vaudeville, television, and minstrel actor. Appeared for a time in vaudeville team "Moran and Mack" as Moran, usually referred to as the "Two Black Crows." Did not appear in films as part of team. Brother of screen actor Bert Swor (dec. 1943).

Appeared in: 1930 Up the River. 1931 Charlie Chan Carries on; Quick Millions.

SYDNEY, BASIL
Born: Apr. 23, 1894, St. Osyth, Essex, England. Died: Jan. 10, 1968, London, England. Screen and stage actor. Divorced from screen actresses Joyce Howard and Doris Keane (dec. 1945).

Appeared in: 1920 Romance. 1922 Red Hot Romance. 1932 The Midshipmaid. 1935 Dirty Work; Transatlantic Tunnel. 1936 Rhodes; The Amateur Gentleman; Accused. 1937 Talk of the Devil; Riverside Murder. 1938 Traitor's Gate; The Four Just Men; Crime over London. 1940 The Secret Four. 1942 Ships with Wings; Big Blockade (war documentary); Next of Kin; They Came in Khaki; Went the Day Well?. 1944 48 Hours. 1946 Caesar and Cleopatra. 1947 The Man Within. 1948 Hamlet; Jassy; The Smugglers; Meet Me at Dawn. 1950 Angel with the Trumpet; Treasure Island. 1952 Ivanhoe; The Magic Box. 1953 Salome. 1954 Hell below Zero. 1955 Simba; Dam Busters. 1956 Around the World in 80 Days; Star of India. 1957 Sea Wife; Island in the Sun. 1959 A Question of Adultery; John Paul Jones; The Devil's Disciple. 1960 The Three Worlds of Gulliver.

SYDNEY, BRUCE
Born: 1889. Died: Oct. 18, 1942, Hollywood, Calif. Screen actor.

Appeared in: 1938 Kidnapped.

SYLVANI, GLADYS
Born: 1885, England. Died: Apr. 20, 1953, Alexandria, Va. Screen actress. One of the first silent film stars in England. Came to U.S. in 1939.

SYLVESTER, FRANK L.
Born: 1868. Died: Dec., 1931, Hollywood, Calif.(heart attack). Screen, stage, and vaudeville actor.

SYLVIE, (Louise Sylvain)
Born: 1882. Died: Jan. 1970, Paris, France. Screen and stage actress.

Appeared in: 1935 Crime et Chatiment (Crime and Punishment). 1939 The End of a Day. 1942 The Pasha's Wives. 1948 Le Corbeau (The Raven); Passionnelle. 1950 Angels of the Streets. 1952 Isle of Sinners (aka God Needs Men—Dieu a Besom des Hommes); Forbidden Fruit (U.S. 1959); The Little World of Don Camillo (U.S. 1953); Under the Paris Sky. 1955 Ulysses. 1957 The Adulteress (U.S. 1958). 1959 The Mirror Has Two Faces; Anatomy of Love. 1960 Michael Strogoff. 1963 Cronaca Familiare (Family Diary). 1964 Chateau en Swed (Castle in Sweden); Nutty, Naughty Chateau. 1966 La Viele Dame Indigne (The Worthless Old Lady aka The Shameless Old Lady). Other French film: Therese Raquin.

SZOLD, BERNARD
Born: 1894. Died: Nov. 15, 1960, Victoria, Tex.(heart attack). Screen actor and dramatic coach.

Appeared in: 1951 The Lemon Drop Kid; Flying Leathernecks; The Tanks Are Coming; M; Queen for a Day.

TABER, RICHARD
Born: 1885. Died: Nov. 16, 1957, New York, N.Y. Screen, stage, and television actor.

Appeared in: 1929 Lucky in Love. 1935 Two Fisted. 1948 The Naked City. 1950 The Sleeping City. 1951 Under the Gun.

TABOADA, JULIO, JR.
Born: 1926, Mexico. Died: Sept. 15, 1962, Mexico City, Mexico (heart attack). Screen, stage, television actor, and stage director.

TABOR, JOAN
Born: 1933. Died: Dec. 18, 1968, Culver City, Calif. Screen, stage, and television actress. Divorced from screen actor Borderick Crawford.

Appeared in: 1960 The Bellboy. 1961 Teenage Millionaire.

TAGGART, HAL
Born: 1892. Died: Dec. 12; 1971, Screen and vaudeville actor. Billed in vaudeville with Tommy Mann as a song and dance act.

Appeared in: 1957 The Monster That Challenged the World.

TAILLON, ANGUS D.
Born: 1888, Ontario, Canada. Died: May 8, 1953, Hollywood, Calif. Screen actor and stand-in for Barry Fitzgerald.

Appeared in: 1949 Top O' the Morning.

TALBOT, MAE
Born: 1869. Died: Aug. 4, 1942, Glendale, Calif.(heart attack). Screen and stage actress.

TALIAFERRO, EDITH
Born: 1894. Died: Mar. 2, 1958, Newtown, Conn. Sister of screen actress Mabel Taliaferro. Screen, stage, radio, and vaudeville actress. Entered films with Lasky Co. in 1915.

TALMADGE, NATALIE
Born: 1899, Brooklyn, N.Y. Died: June 19, 1969, Santa Monica, Calif. Screen actress. Divorced from screen actor Buster Keaton (dec. 1966) and mother of screen actor Robert Talmadge. Sister of screen actresses Norma (dec. 1957) and Constance Talmadge (dec. 1973).

Appeared in: 1919 The Isle of Conquest. 1921 The Passion Flower. 1923 Our Hospitality.

TALMADGE, NORMA
Born: May 26, 1897, Niagara Falls, N.Y. Died: Dec. 24, 1957, Las Vegas, Nev.(cerebral stroke—pneumonia). Screen, stage, radio, and vaudeville actress. Divorced from producer Joseph Schenck (dec. 1961) and comedian/producer George Jessel. Sister of screen actresses Natalie (dec. 1969) and Constance Talmadge (dec. 1973).

Appeared in: 1910 A Dixie Mother. 1911 A Tale of Two Cities; In Neighboring Kingdom. 1912 The Troublesome Stepdaughter; The First Violin. 1913 Mrs. 'Enry 'Awkins; Under the Daisies; He Fell in Love with His Mother-in-Law; The Doctor's Secret; Father's Hat Band; An Elopement at Home; Fanny's Conspiracy; The Sacrifice of Kathleen; His Little Page; Officer John Donovan; The Vavasour Ball. 1914 The Hero; Old Reliable; Sawdust and Salome; The Helpful Sisterhood; Cupid versus Money; Mister Murray's Wedding Present; The Right of Way; John Rance, Gentleman; Politics and the Press; The Loan Shark King; A Question of Clothes; Under False Colors; Goodby, Summer; Sunshine and Shadows; Memories in Men's Souls; The Hidden Letters; The Peacemaker; A Daughter of Israel. 1915 The Barrier of Faith; A Daughter's Strange Inheritance; Elsa's Brother; The Pilar of Flame; The Battle Cry of Peace; The Captivating Mary Carstairs; The Missing Links. 1916 The Crown Prince's Double; Martha's Vindication; The Children in the House; The Honorable Algy; The Criminal; The Devil's Needle; Going Straight. 1917 Panthea; Poppy; The Secret of Storm Country; The Law of Compensation; The Moth; The Lone Wolf; Under False Colors. 1918 The Forbidden City; The Safety Curtain; The Ghost of Yesterday; By Right of Purchase; De Luxe Annie; Her Only Way; The Heart of Wetona; Salome. 1919 The Probation Wife; The Way of a Woman; The New Moon; The Isle of Conquest. 1920 The Right of Way; The Loves and Lies; A Daughter of Two Worlds; The Woman Gives; Yes or No; The Branded Woman. 1921 The Passion Flower; The Sign on the Door; The Wonderful Thing. 1922 Foolish Wives; The Eternal Flame; Smilin' Through; Love's Redemption; Branded. 1923 Ashes of Vengeance; Dust of Desire; Within the Law; The Voice from the Minaret; Sawdust. 1924 Secrets; The Only Woman; The Song of Love; In Hollywood with Potash and Perlmutter. 1925 The Lady; Graustark. 1926 Kiki. 1927 The Dove; Camille. 1928 Show People; The Woman Disputed. 1930 New York Nights; Du Barry, Woman of Passion.

TALMAN, WILLIAM
Born: Feb. 4, 1915, Detroit, Mich. Died: Aug. 30, 1968, Encino, Calif.(cancer). Screen, stage, television actor, and screenwriter.

Appeared in: 1949 Red, Hot and Blue (film debut); I Married a Communist. 1950 The Woman on Pier Thirteen; The Armored Car Robbery; The Kid from Texas. 1951 The Racket. 1952 One Minute to Zero. 1953 The Hitch-Hiker; City that Never Sleeps. 1955 Smoke Signal; Big House, USA; Crashout. 1956 The Man is Armed; Two Gun Lady; Uranium Boom. 1957 The Persuader; Hell on Devil's Island. 1967 The Ballad of Josie.

TAMBLYN, EDWARD
Born: 1907, Yonkers, N.Y. Died: June 22, 1957, Hollywood, Calif. Screen and stage actor. Father of screen actor Russ Tamblyn.

Appeared in: 1931 The Flood. 1933 The Sweetheart of Sigma Chi. 1934 Harold Teen; Money Means Nothing. 1935 A Shot in the Dark. 1936 Palm Springs.

TANDY, VALERIE
Born: 1923, England. Died: Apr. 27, 1965, London, England. Screen and stage actress.

TANGUAY, EVA
Born: 1878, Marbleton, Canada. Died: Jan. 11, 1947, Los Angeles, Calif.(heart attack and cerebral hemorrhage). Screen, stage, and vaudeville actress. Referred to as the "I Don't Care Girl." Appeared in films for Selznick in 1917.

TANNEN, JULIUS
Born: 1881. Died: Jan. 3, 1965, Hollywood, Calif. Screen and vaudeville actor.

Appeared in: 1935 Collegiate. 1936 Half Angel; The Road to Glory; 36 Hours to Kill; Dimples; Pigskin Parade; Reunion; One in a Million; Stowaway. 1937 Fair Warning; Love Is News; Mama Runs Wild. 1938 Love Is a Headache. 1939 Danger Flight; The Magnificent Fraud. 1940 The Mortal Storm; Christmas in July. 1942 Harvard Here I Come. 1944 The Great Moment. 1945 House of Frankenstein. 1948 Unfaithfully Yours.

TANNER, JAMES J.
Born: 1873. Died: Apr. 3, 1934, Hollywood, Calif. Screen actor and artist.

TANO, GUY (Gaetano Rocco)
Born: 1914. Died: Aug. 19, 1952, New York, N.Y. Screen and stage actor.

TANSEY, MRS. EMMA
Born: 1884. Died: Mar. 23, 1942, Los Angeles, Calif. Screen and stage actress. Entered films approx. 1921.

Appeared in: 1922 Are Children to Blame?. 1925 Fast Fightin'. 1930 Beyond the Rio Grande. 1938 Knight of the Plains. 1941 Meet John Doe.

TAPLEY, ROSE
Born: June 30, 1883, Petersburg, Va. Died: Feb. 23, 1956, Woodland Hills, Calif. Screen and stage actress. Entered films with Thomas Edison Productions.

Appeared in: 1905 Wanted a Wife (film debut). 1911 Vanity Fair. 1912 As You Like It. 1914 The Christian. 1915 The "Jarr Family" Series. 1922 Her Majesty. 1923 Java Head. 1924 The Man Who Fights Alone. 1925 The Pony Express; The Scarlet Honeymoon; The Redeeming Sin. 1926 The Prince of Pilsen; Morganson's Finish. 1927 It; God's Great Wilderness; Out of the Past. 1929 The Charlatan. 1930 His First Command. 1931 Resurrection.

TARBAT, LORNA
Born: 1916, England. Died: Apr. 1961, Harrow, Middlesex, England. Screen, stage, and television actress.

TASHMAN, LILYAN
Born: Oct. 23, 1900, Brooklyn, N.Y. Died: Mar. 21, 1934, New York, N.Y.(advanced tumorous condition and/or cancer). Screen and stage actress. Married to screen actor Edmund Lowe (dec. 1971).

Appeared in: 1921 Experience. 1922 Head over Heels. 1924 The Garden of Weeds; Manhandled; The Dark Swan; Is Love Everything?; Nellie, the Beautiful Cloak Model; Winner Take All. 1925 Declasse; The Parasite; Ports of Call; Pretty Ladies; Bright Lights; Seven Days; The Girl Who Wouldn't Work; A Broadway Butterfly; I'll Show You the Town. 1926 Rocking Moon; The Skyrocket; Siberia; Whispering Smith; For Alimony Only;

Love's Blindness; So This Is Paris. 1927 Don't Tell the Wife; French Dressing; The Prince of Headwaiters; The Texas Steer; Camille; The Stolen Bride; The Woman Who Did Not Care. 1928 Phyllis of the Follies; Craig's Wife; Happiness Ahead; Lady Raffles; Manhattan Cocktail; Take Me Home. 1929 The Lone Wolf's Daughter; The Marriage Playground; Gold Diggers of Broadway; New York Nights; Bulldog Drummond; The Trial of Mary Dugan; Hardboiled. 1930 One Heavenly Night; On the Level; The Cat Creeps; Queen of Scandal; Puttin' on the Ritz; The Matrimonial Bed; Leathernecking; No, No, Nanette; Playing Around. 1931 Girls about Town; Up Pops the Devil; Finn and Hattie; Millie; The Mad Parade; The Road to Reno; Murder by the Clock. 1932 The Wiser Sex; Revolt; Scarlet Dawn; Those We Love. 1933 Mama Loves Papa; Too Much Harmony; Wine, Women and Song; Frankie and Johnny; Style. 1934 Riptide.

TATA, PAUL M., SR.
Born: 1883. Died: Mar. 30, 1962, Memphis, Tenn. Screen actor and fencing instructor.

Appeared in: 1908 The Three Musketeers.

TATE, HARRY (Ronald Macdonald Hutchinson)
Born: July 4, 1872, England. Died: Feb. 14, 1940, London, England (air raid). Screen, stage, vaudeville, and radio actor.

Appeared in: 1929 the following shorts: The Patent Office; Motoring; Selling a Car. 1932 Counsel's Opinion; Her First Affair. 1933 Happy; I Spy; My Lucky Star. 1935 Look up and Laugh. 1937 Keep Your Seats Please; Wings of the Morning.

TATE, REGINALD
Born: Dec. 13, 1896, Garforth, England. Died: Aug. 23, 1955, London, England. Screen, stage, television, and radio actor.

Appeared in: 1934 The Phantom Light (film debut). 1935 Riverside Murder. 1936 The Man behind the Mask. 1937 Dark Journey; For Valour. 1938 The Nursemaid Who Disappeared. 1939 Too Dangerous to Live; Poisen Pen. 1941 It Happened to One Man. 1942 Next of Kin. 1943 The Life and Death of Colonel Blimp. 1944 The Way Ahead. 1945 Man from Morocco. 1946 Madonna of the Seven Moons; Journey Together. 1947 So Well Remembered; Uncle Silas. 1950 Silk Noose; 1951 The Inheritance; Midnight Episode. 1952 The Story of Robin Hood; Secret People. 1953 I'll Get You. 1954 The Malta Story. 1955 King's Rhapsody. Other British films: Diamond City; Escape Route.

TATE, SHARON
Born: 1943, Dallas, Tex. Died: Aug. 9, 1969, Bel Air, Calif. (murdered). Screen and television actress. Married to screen actor/director Roman Polanski.

Appeared in: 1963 The Wheeler Dealers. 1964 The Americanization of Emily. 1965 Vampire Killers; "13," The Sandpiper. 1967 Don't Make Waves; Eye of the Devil; Valley of the Dolls. 1968 The Fearless Vampire Killers, or, Pardon Me but Your Teeth Are in My Neck. 1969 Thirteen Chairs; The Wrecking Crew; House of Seven Joys.

TATUM, BUCK
Born: 1897. Died: Oct. 2, 1941, Santa Monica, Calif. Screen actor and cowboy.

TAUBER, RICHARD
Born: May 16, 1892, Linz, Austria. Died: Jan. 8, 1948, London, England. Screen actor, Opera singer, songwriter, and composer.

Appeared in: 1930 Die Grosse Attraktion (The Big Attraction—U.S. 1933); Ich Glaut Nie Mehran Eine Frau (U.S. 1933). 1931 Melodie Der Liebe (The Melody of Love, aka The Right to Happiness). 1933 Das Lockende Ziel. 1934 Blossom Time. 1936 Land without Music. 1937 Heart's Desire; Pagliacci; April Romance. 1938 Forbidden Music; A Clown Must Laugh. 1945 The Lisbon Story. 1948 Waltz Time. Other German films: End of the Rainbow; The Land of Smiles; The Golden Goal.

TAYLOR, ALBERT
Born: Apr. 8, 1871, Montgomery, Ala. Died: Apr. 10, 1940, Hollywood, Calif. Screen and stage actor.

Appeared in: 1934 The Good Fairy; Little Man, What Now?; 1935 Reckless; Vanessa, Her Love Story; Times Square Lady; Woman Wanted; College Scandal; The Crusades; The Man on the Flying Trapeze; Accent on Youth. 1936 Nevada; Fury.

TAYLOR, BETH
Born: 1889. Died: Mar. 1, 1951, Hollywood, Calif. Screen and stage actress.

TAYLOR, ESTELLE
Born: May 20, 1899, Wilmington, Del. Died: Apr. 15, 1958, Los Angeles, Calif.(cancer). Screen, stage, and vaudeville actress. Divorced from exboxer Jack Dempsey.

Appeared in: 1920 While New York Sleeps; The Adventurer. 1921 Blind Wives; Footfalls. 1922 Monte Cristo; A Fool There Was; The Lights of New York; Only a Shop Girl; Thorns and Orange Blossoms. 1923 The Ten Commandments; Bavu; Desire; Forgive and Forget; Hollywood; Mary of the Movies. 1924 The Alaskan; Dorothy Vernon of Haddon Hall; Playthings of Desire; Passion's Pathway; Phantom Justice; Tiger Love. 1925 Manhattan Madness; Wandering Footsteps. 1926 Don Juan. 1927 New York. 1928 The Whip Woman; The Singapore Mutiny; Lady Raffles; Honor Bound. 1929 Where East Is East. 1930 Liliom. 1931 Cimarron; Street Scene; The Unholy Garden. 1932 Call Her Savage; The Western Limited. 1938 various shorts. 1945 The Southerner.

TAYLOR, FERRIS
Born: 1893. Died: Mar. 6, 1961, Hollywood, Calif.(heart attack). Screen actor.

Appeared in: 1937 Mr. Dodd Takes the Air. 1938 He Couldn't Say No; Santa Fe Stampede; The Daredevil Drivers; The Jury's Secret. 1939 You Can't Cheat an Honest Man; SOS Tidal Wave; Man of Conquest; The Zero Hour; Mountain Rhythm; Main Street Lawyer. 1940 Chip of the Flying U; Rancho Grande; Flight Angels; One Crowded Night; Grand Ole Opry; Ladies Must Live; Always a Bride; Diamond Frontier; Mexican Spitfire Out West. 1941 She Couldn't Say No; Ridin' on a Rainbow; The Saint in Palm Springs; A Man Betrayed; County Fair. 1942 Hello, Annapolis!. 1943 Henry Aldrich Haunts a House; Gold Town; Hoosier Holiday; Happy Land. 1944 Wilson; The Town Went Wild; Beautiful but Broke; End of the Road. 1945 Col. Effingham's Raid. 1946 Decoy; Rendezvous 24; Centennial Summer; The Man from Rainbow Valley; Bringing up Father. 1948 My Dog Rusty. 1950 The Gunfighter; Two Flags West. 1951 The Prince of Peace. 1954 The Siege of Red River.

TAYLOR, GEORGE
Born: 1889. Died: Nov. 2, 1939, Fillmore, Utah (injuries from auto crash). Screen actor. Not to be confused with stage actor George R. Taylor (dec. 1944).

Appeared in: 1937 Nancy Steele Is Missing; Angel's Holiday.

TAYLOR, JACK
Born: 1896. Died: Oct. 21, 1932, Long Beach, Calif.(stomach disorder). Screen actor and orchestra leader. Divorced from screen actress Vera Steadman (dec. 1966). Appeared in Warner shorts.

TAYLOR, JOSEPHINE (Josephine Motz)
Born: 1891. Died: Nov. 26, 1964, Calumet City, Ill. Screen actress. Appeared in early Essanay productions.

TAYLOR, LAURETTE (Laurette Cooney)
Born: 1884, New York, N.Y. Died: Dec. 7, 1946, New York, N.Y. (coronary thrombosis). Screen, stage, vaudeville actress, and playwright.

Appeared in: 1923 Peg O' My Heart. 1924 Happiness; One Night in Rome.

TAYLOR, LOUISE
Born: 1908. Died: Mar. 18, 1965, New York, N.Y. Screen, television actress, and dancer.

TAYLOR, ROBERT
Born: 1873. Died: Dec. 9, 1936, New York, N.Y.(gas explosion). Screen and stage actor. Not to be confused with actor with same name (dec. 1969).

TAYLOR, ROBERT (Arlington Spangler Brugh)
Born: Aug. 5, 1911, Filley, Nebr. Died: June 8, 1969, Santa Monica, Calif.(lung cancer). Screen, television, and radio actor. Divorced from screen actress Barbara Stanwyck. Married to screen actress Ursula Thiess.

Appeared in: 1934 Handy Andy (film debut); Only Eight Hours; There's Always Tomorrow; A Wicked Woman; Crime Does Not Pay. 1935 Lest We Forget (documentary); West Point of the Air; Society Doctor; Times Square Lady; Murder in the Fleet; Broadway Melody of 1936; appeared in "Crime Does Not Pay" series which included Buried Loot. 1936 The Magnificent Obsession; Small Town Girl; The Gorgeous Hussy; His Brother's Wife; Camille; Private Number; La Fiesta de Santa Barbara (short). 1937 Personal Property; Broadway Melody of 1938; This Is My Affair. 1938 A Yank at Oxford; Three Comrades; The Crowd

Roars. 1939 Stand up and Fight; Lucky Night; Lady of the Tropics; Remember?. 1940 Waterloo Bridge; Escape; Flight Command. 1941 Billy the Kid; When Ladies Meet; Johnny Eager. 1942 Her Cardboard Lover; Stand by for Action; Cargo of Innocents. 1943 Song of Russia; Bataan; The Youngest Profession. 1944 The Fighting Lady (narr. documentary). 1946 Undercurrent. 1947 High Wall. 1948 The Secret Land (narr.). 1949 Ambush; The Bribe. 1950 Conspirator; Devil's Doorway; Big Apple; Quo Vadis. 1951 Westward the Women. 1952 Ivanhoe; Above and Beyond. 1953 Ride, Vaquero; All the Brothers Were Valiant; Knights of the Round Table; I Love Melvin. 1954 Valley of the Kings; Rogue Cop. 1955 Many Rivers to Cross; Quentin Durward. 1956 D-Day, the Sixth of June; The Power and the Prize; The Last Hunt. 1957 Tip on a Dead Jockey. 1958 Saddle the Wind; The Law and Jake Wade; Party Girl. 1959 The Hangman; The House of Seven Hawks. 1960 The Killers of Kilimanjaro. 1963 Guns of Wyoming; The Miracle of the White Stallions. 1964 Big Parade of Comedy (documentary); A House Is Not a Home. 1964 The Night Walker. 1966 Johnny Tiger; Return of the Gunfighter. 1967 Hondo and the Apaches; Savage Pampas; As I Rode down to Laredo; The Glass Sphinx. 1968 Where Angels Go... Trouble Follows; The Day the Hot Line Got Hot; Devil May Care.

TAYLOR, WILLIAM DESMOND (William Cunningham Deanne Tanner)
Born: 1877, Carlow, Ireland. Died: Feb. 1, 1922, Los Angeles, Calif.(murdered—shot). Screen actor and film director.

Appeared in: 1917 Captain Alvarez.

TEACHOUT, H. ARTHUR
Born: 1888. Died: Mar. 5, 1939, Cedar Rapids, Iowa. Screen and stage actor.

TEAGARDEN, JACK
Born: 1906. Died: Jan. 15, 1964, New Orleans, La.(pneumonia). Bandleader, screen actor, and trombonist. He played with Pete Kelly, Red Nichols, collaborated with Glenn Miller on lyrics for "Basin Street Blues," joined Ben Pollack and Paul Whiteman's band.

Appeared in: 1941 Birth of the Blues. 1952 Glory Alley. 1953 The Glass Wall. 1960 Jazz on a Summer's Day.

TEAGUE, BRIAN
Born: 1937. Died: May 30, 1970, near Lake Isabella, Calif. (auto accident). Screen and television actor. Son of screen actor Guy Teague (dec. 1970).

TEAGUE, GUY
Died: Jan. 24, 1970, Tex. Screen actor. Father of screen actor Brian Teague (dec. 1970).

Appeared in: 1950 The Showdown; Vigilante Hideout. 1952 Cattle Town. 1953 The Outlaw Stallion. 1955 Wyoming Renegades. 1956 Fury at Gunsight Pass; The White Squaw.

TEARE, ETHEL
Born: 1894. Died: Mar. 4, 1959, San Mateo, Calif. Screen actress.

Appeared in: 1915 "Ham and Bud" series. 1917 Thirst; Lost—A Cook. 1921 Skirts; The Tomboy. 1923 Thirst (reissue of 1917 film). 1924 A Woman Who Sinned.

TEARLE, CONWAY (Frederick Levy)
Born: May 17, 1878, New York, N.Y. Died: Oct. 1, 1938, Los Angeles, Calif.(heart attack). Married to stage actress Adele Rowland. Half brother of screen actors Godfrey Tearle (dec. 1953) and Malcolm Tearle (dec. 1935). Screen and stage actor.

Appeared in: 1914 The Nightingale. 1915 Seven Sisters. 1916 The Common Law. 1917 The Fall of Romanoff. 1918 Stella Maris. 1919 Virtuous Wives; The Way of a Woman; The Mind-the-Paint Girl. 1920 A Virtuous Vamp; Two Weeks; The Forbidden Woman. 1921 Bucking the Tiger; Marooned Hearts; The Road of Ambition; Society Snobs; Whispering Devils; The Man of Stone; The Fighter; After Midnight; The Oath. 1922 The Eternal Flame; Love's Masquerade; The Referee; Shadows of the Sea; A Wide Open Town; One Week of Love. 1923 Bella Donna; Ashes of Vengeance; The Dangerous Maid; Woman of Bronze; The Common Law (and 1916 version); The Rustle of Silk. 1924 The White Moth; Black Oxen; Flirting with Love; Lilies of the Field; The Next Corner. 1925 The Mystic; The Great Divide; The Viennese Medley; Bad Company; The Heart of a Siren; Morals for Men; Just a Woman; School for Wives. 1926 Dancing Mothers; My Official Wife; The Dancer of Paris; The Greater Glory; The Sporting Lover. 1927 Altars of Desire; Isle of Forgotten Women; Moulders of Men. 1929 Smoke Bellew; Evidence; Gold Diggers of Broadway. 1930 The Lost Zeppelin; Truth about Youth. 1931 The Lady Who Dared; Morals for Women; Captivation. 1932 Vanity Fair; Pleasure; Her Mad Night; The Man about Town. 1933 Day of Reckoning; Should Ladies Behave?. 1934 Fifteen Wives; Stingaree; Sing Sing Nights. 1935 Headline Woman; The Trail's End; Judgement Book. 1936 The Preview Murder Mystery; Desert Guns; Klondike Annie; Romeo and Juliet.

TEARLE, SIR GODFREY
Born: Oct. 12, 1884, New York, N.Y. Died: June 8, 1953, London, England. Screen and stage actor. Entered films in 1906. Was half brother of screen actor Conway Tearle (dec. 1938) and brother of Malcolm Tearle (dec. 1935).

Appeared in: 1906 Romeo and Juliet. 1925 Salome of the Tenements. 1930 If Youth but Knew. 1935 The Thirty-Nine Steps. 1936 The Last Journey; East Meets West. 1942 One of Our Aircraft Is Missing. 1943 At Dawn We Die. 1945 The Rake's Progress. 1946 The Gay Intruders; Notorious Gentleman. 1947 The Beginning of the End. 1948 Private Angelo. 1952 Decameron Nights; White Corridors. 1953 I Believe in You; The Story of Mandy (aka Crash of Silence); The Titfield Thunderbolt. Other British films: Tomorrow We Live; Under Cover; The Lamp Still Burns; Medal for the General.

TEARLE, MALCOLM
Born: 1888. Died: Dec. 8, 1935, London, England (suicide). Brother of screen actor Godfrey Tearle (dec. 1953) and half brother of Conway Tearle (dec. 1938).

TEATHER, IDA
Died: Apr. 20, 1954, Ebbw Vale, Wales. Screen, stage, and radio actress.

TEEGE, JOACHIM
Born: 1925, Spremberg, Silesia. Died: Nov. 23, 1969, Munich, Germany. Screen, stage, and television actor.

TELL, ALMA
Born: 1892. Died: Dec. 30, 1937, San Fernando, Calif. Screen and stage actress. Sister of screen actress Olive Tell (dec. 1951).

Appeared in: 1916 The Smugglers. 1920 On with the Dance; The Right to Love. 1921 The Iron Trail; Paying the Piper. 1922 Broadway Rose. 1923 The Silent Command. 1928 San Francisco Nights. 1929 Saturday's Children. 1930 Love Comes Along.

TELL, OLIVE
Born: 1894, New York, N.Y. Died: June 8, 1951, New York, N.Y. Screen and stage actress. Sister of screen actress Alma Tell (dec. 1937). Entered films with Mutual in 1917.

Appeared in: 1918 The Unforseen. 1921 Clothes; Wings of Pride; The Wrong Woman; Worlds Apart. 1925 Chickie. 1926 The Prince of Tempters; Woman-Handled; Summer Bachelors. 1927 Slaves of Beauty. 1928 Sailors' Wives; Soft Living. 1929 Hearts in Exile; The Trial of Mary Dugan; The Very Idea. 1930 Lawful Larceny; Love Comes Along; The Right of Way; Woman Hungry; Devotion; Delicious. 1933 Strictly Personal. 1934 The Scarlet Empress; The Witching Hour; Private Scandal; Baby, Take a Bow. 1935 Four Hours to Kill; Shanghai. 1936 In His Steps; Polo Joe; Yours for the Asking; Brilliant Marriage. 1939 Zaza.

TELLEGEN, LOU
Born: 1884. Died: Nov. 1, 1934, Los Angeles, Calif. (suicide). Screen and stage actor.

Appeared in: 1911 Queen Elizabeth. 1915 The Explorer; The Unknown. 1916 The Victoria Cross; Maria Rosa; The Victory of Conscience. 1917 The Long Trail. 1919 Flame of the Desert; The World and Its Women. 1920 The Woman and the Puppet. 1924 Single Wives; Those Who Judge; Between Friends; The Breath of Scandal; Let Not Man Put Asunder; Greater Than Marriage. 1925 The Redeeming Sin; After Business Hours; East Lynne; The Sporting Chance; Borrowed Finery; Fair Play; Parisian Love; Parisian Nights; The Verdict; With This Ring. 1926 The Outsider; Siberia; The Silver Treasure; Womanpower; Three Bad Men. 1927 The Princess from Hoboken; The Little Firebrand; Married Alive; Stage Madness. 1928 No Other Woman. 1931 Enemies of the Law.

TEMARY, ELZA. See Elza K. Splane

TEMPEST, DAME MARIE (Marie Susan Etherington)
Born: 1864, London, England. Died: Oct. 15, 1942, London, England. Screen, stage actress, and opera singer.

Appeared in: 1915 Mrs. Plum's Pudding. 1937 Moonlight Sonata. 1938 Yellow Sands.

TEMPLETON, FAY
Born: Dec. 25, 1866, Little Rock, Ark. Died: Oct. 3, 1939, San Francisco, Calif. Screen, stage, and vaudeville actress. Entered films in 1929.

Appeared in: 1932 The March of Time (short). 1933 Broadway to Hollywood.

TERRANOVA, DINO (Corrado Vacirca)
Born: 1904, Italy. Died: Apr. 27, 1969, Miami, Fla. Screen and stage actor.

Appeared in: 1956 The Wrong Man (stage and film versions). 1963 Flipper. 1968 The Brotherhood.

TERRISS, ELLALINE
Born: 1871, England. Died: June 16, 1971, London, England. Married to screen actor Sir Seymour Hicks (dec. 1949). Screen and stage actress.

Appeared in: 1927 Blighty. 1930 Atlantic. 1931 Glamour. 1935 The Iron Duke. 1939 The Four Just Men. 1940 The Secret Four.

TERRY, DAME ELLEN
Born: 1848, Coventry, England. Died: July 21, 1928, Kent, England (heart trouble). Screen and stage actress. Entered films with Triangle in 1919. Married to screen actor James Carew (dec. 1938).

Appeared in: 1923 The Bohemian Girl.

TERRY, ETHEL GREY
Born: Oakland, Calif. Died: Jan. 6, 1931, Hollywood, Calif. Screen and stage actress. Entered films approx. 1917. Married to screen actor Carl Gerard.

Appeared in: 1917 Arsene Lupin. 1919 Hardboiled; The Carter Case (the "Craig Kennedy" serial). 1921 The Breaking Point; Suspicious Wives. 1922 The Crossroads of New York; The Kick Back; Oath-Bound; Shattered Idols; Too Much Business; Travelin' On; Under Two Flags. 1923 Brass; The Self-Made Wife; Garrison's Finish; Wild Bill Hickok; Why Women Remarry; What Wives Want; The Unknown Purple; Peg O' My Heart. 1924 The Fast Worker. 1925 Old Shoes; What Fools Men. 1926 Hard Boiled; The Love Toy. 1927 Cancelled Debts. 1928 Skinner's Big Idea; Modern Mothers; Confessions of a Wife; Sharp Tools (short). 1929 Object Alimony.

TERRY, FRED
Born: England. Died: Apr. 1933, London, England. Screen and stage actor. Married to stage actress Julia Nielson and father of screen actor Dennis Nielson-Terry (dec. 1932).

Appeared in: 1922 With Wings Outspread.

THATCHER, EVELYN "EVA"
Born: 1862, Omaha, Nebr. Died: Sept. 28, 1942, Los Angeles, Calif. Screen, stage, and vaudeville actress. Appeared in Mack Sennett comedies. Appeared in vaudeville as "The Irish Lady."

Appeared in: 1916 Haystacks and Steeples. 1917 Her Nature Dance; His Naughty Thought; She Needed a Doctor; Thirst; A Bedroom Blunder. 1923 Thirst (reissue of 1917 film). 1924 Not Built for Runnin'. 1925 Flash O'Lightning; Ranchers and Rascals; The Trouble Buster. 1926 Blind Trail; The Outlaw Express.

THAW, EVELYN NESBIT
Born: 1885. Died: Jan. 18, 1967, Santa Monica, Calif. Screen and vaudeville actress. Known as the "Girl in the Red Swing."

Appeared in: 1914 Threads of Destiny. 1917 Redemption. 1922 The Hidden Woman.

THAWL, EVELYN
Born: 1915. Died: Nov. 1945, Brooklyn, N.Y. Screen and stage actress.

THEIS, ALFRED
Born: 1899. Died: Sept. 16, 1951, Newfoundland, enroute from Germany (heart attack). Screen and vaudeville actor. Appeared in vaudeville in the "Alfred Theis Tiny Town Revue."

THESIGER, ERNEST
Born: Jan. 15, 1879, London, England. Died: Jan. 14, 1961, London, England. Screen and stage actor.

Appeared in: 1929 West End Wives. 1932 The Old Dark House.

1933 The Only Girl; The Ghoul; Night of the Party. 1934 My Heart Is Calling; Heart Song. 1935 The Bride of Frankenstein. 1936 The Man Who Could Work Miracles. 1938 They Drive by Night. 1942 Who Done It?. 1944 Henry V (U.S. 1946). 1946 Caesar and Cleopatra. 1947 Beware of Pity; The Ghosts of Berkeley Square. 1948 Jassy; The Smugglers. 1949 A Man Within; A Place of One's Own; Quartet. 1950 Last Holiday; The Winslow Boy. 1951 The Lucky Mascot; Laughter in Paradise; Scrooge. 1952 Bad Lord Byron; The Colonel's Lady; Portrait of Hildegarde; The Man in the White Suit; The Magic Box. 1953 The Robe; Meet Mr. Lucifer. 1954 The Detective (aka Father Brown); Man with a Million; A Woman's Angle. 1955 Quentin Durward; Midnight Episode. 1956 Make Me an Offer. 1957 An Alligator Named Daisy; Doctor at Large; Value for Money. 1958 The Horse's Mouth; Three Men in a Boat; The Truth about Women; Henry V (reissue of 1944 film). 1960 The Battle of the Sexes; Sons and Lovers. 1961 The Roman Spring of Mrs. Stone. Other British films: The Lamp Still Burns; The Murder Party.

THOMAS, GRETCHEN
Born: 1897. Died: Nov. 1, 1964, Hollywood, Calif. Screen, stage, and television actress.

Appeared in: 1930 Spring Is Here; Young Desire. 1937 Damaged Goods. 1938 Marriage Forbidden. 1957 I Was a Teenage Frankenstein.

THOMAS, GUS
Born: 1865, Toronto, Canada. Died: May 3, 1926, Everett, Wash. Screen, stage, and vaudeville actor.

Appeared in: 1922 Alias Julius Caesar.

THOMAS, JAMESON
Born: Mar. 24, 1889. Died: Jan. 10, 1939, Sierra Madre, Calif. (tuberculosis). Screen, stage actor, and film director.

Appeared in: 1925 Chu Chin Chow. 1927 Blighty. 1928 A Daughter of Love; Roses of Picardy; Tesha. 1929 Piccadilly; A Woman in the Night; The White Sheik. 1930 Elstree Calling; High Treason; The Hate Ship; The Farmer's Wife; Extravagance. 1931 Lover Come Back; Night Birds. 1932 Three Wise Girls; Trial of Vivienne Ware; Escapade; No More Orchids; The Phantom President. 1933 Brief Moment; Self Defense. 1934 Stolen Sweets; Now and Forever; The Moonstone; A Successful Failure; A Lost Lady; The Curtain Falls; It Happened One Night; Bombay Mail; The Scarlet Empress; A Woman's Man; Beggars in Ermine; Sing Sing Nights; Jane Eyre. 1935 Lives of a Bengal Lancer; Charlie Chan in Egypt; The Last Outpost; The World Accuses; Mr. Dynamite; Coronado; The Lady in Scarlet. 1936 Mr. Deeds Goes to Town; Lady Luck. 1937 The Man Who Cried Wolf; One Hundred Men and a Girl; The League of Frightened Men; House of Secrets. 1938 Death Goes North.

THOMAS, JOHN CHARLES
Born: 1887, Baltimore, Md. Died: Dec. 1960, Apple Valley, Calif. (intestinal cancer). Screen, stage, radio actor, and singer.

Appeared in: 1923 Under the Red Robe. 1927 the following shorts: Prologue to I Pagliacci; Danny Deever; Will You Remember Me?.

THOMAS, OLIVE
Born: Oct. 29, 1884, Charleroi, Pa. Died: Sept. 10, 1920, Paris, France (suicide). Screen and stage actress. Married to screen actor Jack Pickford (dec. 1933).

Appeared in: 1916 Beatrice Follies. 1917 Betty Takes a Hand. 1918 Limousine Life. 1919 The Glorious Lady; Upstairs and Down; The Follies Girl. 1920 The Flapper; Footlights and Shadows.

THOMAS, RUTH
Born: 1911. Died: Mar. 23, 1970, Columbus, Ohio. Screen, stage, and television actress.

THOMAS, WILLIAM "BUCKWHEAT"
Died: 1968, Biafra. Screen actor. Appeared in "Our Gang" comedies.

THOMASHEFSKY, MAX
Born: 1872. Died: July 24, 1932, New York, N.Y. Screen and stage actor.

THOMPSON, DAVID H.
Born: May 4, 1886, New York, N.Y. Died: May 20, 1957, Hollywood, Calif. Screen, stage actor, and film director. Appeared in Edison Film Co. productions in 1910 and in Thanhouser Film Co. productions 1911-14.

THOMPSON, FREDERICK A.
Born: 1870, Montreal, Canada. Died: Jan. 23, 1925, Hollywood, Calif. (heart disease). Screen and stage actor. Entered films in 1910.

Appeared in: 1921 The Heart Line. 1922 A Tailor Made Man.

THOMPSON, GEORGE
Born: 1868. Died: May 29, 1929, Los Angeles, Calif. (following surgery for stomach trouble caused by poisonous facial make-up which started infection). Screen and stage actor.

Appeared in: 1929 Why Bring That Up?

THOMPSON, MOLLY
Born: 1879. Died: Feb. 14, 1928, Culver City, Calif. (brain hemorrhage). Screen actress and casting director. Was an actress on the Roach lot and appeared in nearly all of Harold Lloyd's early comedies.

THOMPSON, THERESE
Born: 1876. Died: Sept. 17, 1936, Hollywood, Calif. Screen and stage actress. Sister of screen actress Trixie Friganza (dec. 1955).

THOMPSON, ULU M.
Born: 1873. Died: Apr. 13, 1957, Hollywood, Calif. (heart ailment). Screen actress.

THOMPSON, WILLIAM "BILL"
Born: 1913. Died: July 15, 1971, Los Angeles, Calif. Screen, radio, and television actor.

Appeared in: 1955 Lady and the Tramp (voice).

THOMSON, FRED
Born: Apr. 28, 1890, Pasadena, Calif. Died: Dec. 25, 1928, Los Angeles, Calif. (following surgery for gallstones). Screen actor, double, and stuntman.

Appeared in: 1921 The Love Light; Just around the Corner. 1922 Oath-Bound; Penrod. 1923 The Eagle's Talons (serial); The Mask of Lopez; A Chapter in Her Life. 1924 The Silent Stranger; The Dangerous Coward; The Fighting Sap; Galloping Gallagher; North of Nevada; Thundering Hoofs; Queniado. 1925 The Wild Bull's Lair; The Bandit's Baby; That Devil Quemado; All around Frying Pan; Ridin' the Wind. 1926 A Regular Scout; Hands across the Border; The Two-Gun Man; The Tough Guy; Lone Hand Saunders. 1927 Silver Comes Through; Jesse James; Arizona Nights; Don Mike. 1928 Kit Carson; The Sunset Legion; The Pioneer Scout.

THOMSON, KENNETH
Born: Jan. 7, 1899, Pittsburgh, Pa. Died: Jan. 27, 1967, Los Angeles, Calif. (emphysema and fibrosis). Screen and stage actor. One of the founders of the Screen Actors Guild.

Appeared in: 1926 Corporal Kate; Man Bait; Risky Business. 1927 White Gold; Almost Human; King of Kings; Turkish Delight. 1928 The Secret Hour; The Street of Illusion. 1929 The Letter; The Bellamy Trial; The Broadway Melody; Say It with Songs; The Careless Age; The Girl from Havana; The Veiled Woman; Song Writer. 1930 Children of Pleasure; Lawful Larceny; Sweethearts on Parade; Doorway to Hell; Just Imagine; Faithful; The Other Tomorrow; A Notorious Affair; Sweet Mama; Wild Company; Reno. 1931 Woman Hungry; Murder at Midnight; Bad Company; Oh! Oh! Cleopatra (short). 1932 By Whose Hands?; Man Wanted; The Famous Ferguson Case; Movie Crazy; 70,000 Witnesses; 13 Women; Her Mad Night; Lawyer Man; Fast Life. 1933 The Little Giant; Female; Son of a Sailor; Daring Daughters; Hold Me Tight; Sitting Pretty; From Headquarters; Jungle Bride. 1934 Change of Heart; Many Happy Returns; Cross Streets; In Old Santa Fe. 1935 Behold My Wife; Behind the Green Lights; Whispering Smith Speaks; Hopalong Cassidy; Manhattan Butterfly. 1936 With Love and Kisses; The Blackmailer. 1937 Jim Hanvey—Detective.

THORBURN, JUNE
Born: 1931, Kashmir, India. Died: Nov. 4, 1967, Fernhurst, Sussex, England (air crash). Screen and television actress.

Appeared in: 1951 The Pickwick Papers (U.S. 1953, film debut). 1953 The Cruel Sea. 1954 Orders Are Orders. 1956 True As a Turtle. 1958 Rooney; Tom Thumb. 1959 Broth of a Boy. 1960 The Price of Silence; Three Worlds of Gulliver. 1964 Master Spy; The Crimson Blade (aka The Scarlet Blade). 1965 Why Bother to Knock. Other British films: Fast and Loose; Children Galore; Fury at Smuggler's Creek; Transatlantic.

THORNDIKE, OLIVER
Born: Sept. 12, 1918, Boston, Mass. Died: Apr. 14, 1954, St. Thomas, Virgin Islands. Screen, stage, and television actor.

Appeared in: 1932 The Sign of the Cross. 1944 The Sign of the Cross (revised version of 1932 film); The Story of Dr. Wassell.

THORNDYKE, LUCYLE
Born: 1885, Seattle, Wash. Died: Dec. 17, 1935, Los Angeles, Calif. Screen and stage actress.

Appeared in: 1924 The Garden of Weeds. 1926 The Speed Limit.

THORNE, DICK
Born: 1905. Died: Jan. 31, 1957, Hollywood, Calif.(heart attack). Screen actor and stuntman. Entered films approx. 1925.

THORNE, ROBERT
Born: 1881. Died: July 3, 1965, New York, N.Y.(heart attack). Screen and stage actor.

Appeared in: 1924 Janice Meredith.

THORNHILL, CLAUDE
Born: 1908, Terre Haute, Ind. Died: July 1, 1965, Caldwell, N.J. (heart attack). Bandleader and screen actor.

THORNTON, GLADYS
Born: 1899. Died: Sept. 2, 1964, Hollywood, Calif. Screen, stage, and radio actress. Played "Aunt Jemima" on radio.

Appeared in: 1962 If a Man Answers.

THORPE, JIM
Born: 1888, North Canadian River, U.S. Died: Mar. 28, 1953, Los Angeles, Calif.(heart attack). Screen actor and sports figure. Rated as one of the greatest athletes of all time. Entered films as an extra.

Appeared in: 1932 White Eagle; My Pal, the King; Airmail; Hold 'Em Jail. 1933 Wild Horse Mesa. 1935 Code of the Mounted; Behold My Wife; The Red Rider; Wanderer of the Wasteland; Rustlers of Red Gap (serial); She; Fighting Youth. 1936 Sutter's Gold; Wildcat Trooper; Treachery Rides the Range; Hill Tillies (short). 1937 Big City. 1940 Henry Goes to Arizona; Arizona Frontier; Prairie Schooners. 1944 Outlaw Trail. 1950 Wagonmaster.

THURBER, J. KENT
Born: 1892. Died: May 26, 1957, St. Petersburg, Fla. Screen, stage actor, and stage director. Cousin of humorist James Thurber.

THURMAN, MARY
Born: 1894, Richmond, Utah. Died: Dec. 23, 1925 (effects of tropical fever). Screen actress.

Appeared in: 1916 Sunshine Dad; His Last Laugh; His First False Step; Bombs; The Scoundrel's Tale; The Stone Age (aka Her Cave Man). 1917 Maggie's First False Step; Pinched in the Finish. 1918 Watch Your Neighbor. 1921 Bare Knuckles; The Sin of Martha Queed; The Lady from Longacre; A Broken Doll; The Primal Law. 1922 The Bond Boy; The Green Temptation. 1923 A Bride for a Knight; Does It Pay?; Wife in Name Only; Zaza; The Tents of Allah. 1924 For another Woman; The Law and the Lady; The Truth about Women; Greater Than Marriage; Love of Woman; Playthings of Desire; Trouping with Ellen; Those Who Judge. 1925 Down upon the Swanee River; The Mad Marriage; The Necessary Evil; Back to Life; The Fool; A Little Girl in a Big City; Wildfire. 1926 The Wives of the Prophet.

THURSTON, CHARLES E.
Born: 1869, Oconto, Wisc. Died: Mar. 5, 1940, Hollywood, Calif. Screen, stage, and vaudeville actor. Entered films approx. 1917.

Appeared in: 1921 Boys Will Be Boys; Black Sheep. 1922 Doubling for Romeo; The Gray Dawn. 1924 Ridgeway of Montana. 1926 Rolling Home; Is That Nice? 1927 Between Dangers; The Fightin' Comeback; The Broken Gate; Spoilers of the West. 1928 When the Law Rides; The Chaser. 1932 The Big Shot. 1933 Unknown Valley.

THURSTON, MURIEL
Born: 1875, France. Died: May 1, 1943, Hollywood, Calif. Screen actress.

TIBBETT, LAWRENCE
Born: Nov. 16, 1896, Bakersfield, Calif. Died: July 15, 1960, New York, N.Y. Screen, radio actor, and opera singer.

Appeared in: 1930 The Rogue Song; New Moon. 1931 The Prodigal. 1932 Cuban Love Song. 1935 Metropolitan. 1936 Under Your Spell.

TIEDTKE, JAKOB
Born: June 23, 1875, Berlin, Germany. Died: June 30, 1960, Berlin, Germany. Screen and stage actor.

Appeared in: 1926 The Waltz Dream. 1929 Luther. 1932 Drunter und Drueber; Saison in Kairo. 1934 Fraeulein-Falsch Verbunden!; Tausend Fuer Eine Nacht; Strich Durch die Rechnung; Eines Prinzen Junge Liebe; Ja, Treu Ist die Soldatenliebe; Ein Toller Einfall; Das Blaue Vom Himmel; Heimat am Rhein. 1935 Lockvogel; Die Kalte Mansell; Gretl Zieht das Grosse Los; Die Liebe und die Erste Eisenbahn (Love and the First Railroad); Die Sonne Geht Auf; Der Deppelbraeutigam (The Double Fiancee); Die Grosse Chance; Freuhlingsmaerchen; Der Schuechterne Felix; Frischer Wind aus Kanada; Das Lied vom Gluech (The Song of Happiness); Wenn am Sonntagabend die Dorfmusik Spielt. 1936 Der Vetter aus Dengsda; Der Junge Graf. 1937 Besuch am Abend. 1939 Nanu, Sie Kennen Korff noch Nicht? (So, You Don't Know Korff Yet?); Verwehte Spuren (Covered Tracks). 1940 Peter, Paul und Nanette. 1955 Leave on Parole.

TIGHE, HARRY
Born: approx. 1885. Died: Feb. 10, 1935, Old Lyme, Conn. Screen, stage, vaudeville, radio actor, and film director.

Appeared in: 1922 A Wide-Open Town. 1930 Bright Sayings (short).

TILBURY, ZEFFIE
Born: 1863. Died: July 24, 1950, Los Angeles, Calif. Screen and stage actress.

Appeared in: 1919 The Avalanche. 1921 Camille; The Marriage of William Ashe; Big Game. 1924 Another Scandal. 1929 The Single Standard. 1930 The Ship from Shanghai. 1931 Charlie Chan Carries On. 1934 Mystery Liner. 1935 Women Must Dress; The Mystery of Edwin Drood; The Werewolf of London; Alice Adams; The Last Days of Pompeii. 1936 Desire; Give Me Your Heart; The Gorgeous Hussy; The Bohemian Girl. 1937 It Happened in Hollywood; Under Cover of Night; Bulldog Drummond Comes Back; Rhythm in the Clouds; Federal Bullets; Maid of Salem. 1938 Bulldog Drummond's Peril; Hunted Men; Woman against Woman; Josette. 1939 Arrest Bulldog Drummond; Boy Trouble; The Story of Alexander Graham Bell; Tell No Tales; Balalaika. 1940 The Grapes of Wrath; Comin' 'Round the Mountain. 1941 She Couldn't Say No; Tobacco Road; Sheriff of Tombstone.

TILDEN, BILL (William Tatem Tilden, II)
Died: June 5, 1953, Hollywood, Calif.(heart attack). Screen, stage actor, playwright, and former tennis champion.

Appeared in: 1932-33 Universal's Sport shorts. 1935 Commentator for British Lion shorts.

TILTON, EDWIN BOOTH
Born: 1860. Died: Jan. 16, 1926, Hollywood, Calif. Screen, stage actor, film director, and screenwriter.

Appeared in: 1921 Bare Knuckles; What Love Will Do; Children of the Night; Bucking the Line; Lovetime; The Mother Heart; While the Devil Laughs; The Primal Law; The Lamplighter. 1922 The Cub Reporter; Winning with Wits; Gleam O'Dawn; The Man under Cover; Hungry Hearts. 1923 Times Have Changed. 1924 The House of Youth; Thundergate; Racing for Life; The Lone Chance; The Midnight Express. 1925 The Taming of the West.

TIMBERG, HERMAN
Born: 1892. Died: Apr. 16, 1952, New York, N.Y. Screen, stage, vaudeville actor, stage producer, songwriter, radio writer, and screenwriter.

Appeared in: 1930 The Love Boat (short). 1936-38 Educational shorts.

TIMMONS, JOSEPH
Born: 1897. Died: Mar. 29, 1933, Los Angeles, Calif.(auto accident). Screen actor and stuntman.

TINDALE, FRANKLIN M.
Born: 1871. Died: Feb. 14, 1947, Los Angeles, Calif. Screen actor and film director.

TISSOT, ALICE
Born: 1890, France. Died: May 5, 1971, Paris, France (throat cancer). Screen and stage actress.

Appeared in: 1928 La Cousine Bette. 1930 Le Secret du Docteur. 1933 Mirages de Paris. 1935 La Maternelle. 1937 Les Petits. 1938 The Glory of the Faith. 1939 Last Desire. 1945 Les Dames aux Chapeaux Verts (The Women in Green Hats). 1947 Francis the First. 1950 Ignace. 1958 Gates of Paris.

TITHERADGE, DION
Born: 1879, England. Died: Nov. 16, 1934, London, England. Screen, stage actor, author, and playwright.

TITHERADGE, MADGE
Born: 1887, England. Died: Nov. 13, 1961, Fetcham, Surrey, England. Screen and stage actress.

Appeared in: 1922 David and Jonathan; Her Story.

TITUS, LYDIA YEAMANS
Born: 1866, Australia. Died: Dec. 30, 1929, Glendale, Calif. (paralytic stroke). Screen, stage, and vaudeville actress.

Appeared in: 1918 All Night. 1919 The Peace of Roaring River; Strictly Confidential. 1920 Nurse Marjorie. 1921 Queenie; The Invisible Power; The Mad Marriage; Nobody's Fool; All Dolled Up; Smiling All the Way; The Mistress of Shenstone; Beating the Game; Beau Revel; The Concert; The Freeze Out; The Marriage of William Ashe; His Nibs. 1922 The Glory of Clementina; The Married Flapper; Beauty's Worth; A Girl's Desire; The Lavender Bath Lady; Two Kinds of Women. 1923 Big Dan; The Famous Mrs. Fair; The Footlight Ranger; The Wanters; Winter Has Come; Scaramouche. 1924 Big Timber; In Fast Company; Tarnish; Young Ideas; A Boy of Flanders; Cytherea; The Lullaby 1925 The Rag Man; Up the Ladder; Head Winds; The Limited Mail; The Talker; The Arizona Romeo. 1926 Irene; The Lily; Sunshine of Paradise Alley. 1927 The Lure of the Night Club; Upstream; Heroes in Blue; Night Life. 1928 The Water Hole; Two Lovers; Sweet Sixteen; While the City Sleeps. 1929 Shanghai Lady; The Voice in the Storm. 1930 Lummox.

TODD, HARRY
Born: 1865, Allegheny, Pa. Died: Feb. 16, 1935, Glendale, Calif. (heart attack). Screen actor. Entered films with Essanay.

Appeared in: 1915 "Snakeville" comedies. 1927 The Third Degree; The Riding Rowdy; Skedaddle Gold; The Obligin' Buckaroo; The Bugle Call; Rawhide Kid. 1928 Under the Tonto Rim; The River Woman. 1929 Linda; One Stolen Night. 1930 Under Montana Skies; The Fighting Legion; Lucky Larkin; Sons of the Saddle. 1933 Sucker Money; Gun Law; Her Splendid Folly; Thrill Hunter. 1934 It Happened One Night; One Is Guilty.

TODD, THELMA
Born: July 29, 1905, Lawrence, Mass. Died: Dec. 18, 1935, Santa Monica, Calif. (carbon monoxide—murder—suicide—accident?). Screen actress. She appeared as part of the comedy film team of "Todd and Pitts" (Zasu) and "Todd and Kelly" (Patsy).

Appeared in: 1926 God Gave Me Twenty Cents; Fascinating Youth. 1927 Nevada; The Gay Defender; Rubber Heels; The Shield of Honor. 1928 Vamping Venus; The Crash; The Haunted House; Heart to Heart; The Noose. 1929 Naughty Baby; The King (short); The Fighting Parson (short); Unaccustomed as We Are (short); The Bachelor Girl; Trial Marriage; Careers; Her Private Life; The House of Horror; Look Out Below; Seven Footprints to Satan; The Real McCoy (short); Dollar Dizzy (short); Jack White Talking Comedies (shorts). 1930 Hell's Angels; Follow Through; Her Man; Another Fine Mess (short). 1931 Command Performance; The Maltese Falcon; Broad-Minded; The Hot Heiress; No Limit; Monkey Business; Beyond Victory; Aloha; Swanee River; Corsair; and the following shorts with Z. Pitts: Let's Do Things; Catch as Catch Can; The Pajama Party; War Mamas; Chicken Come Home. 1932 Call Her Savage; Klondike; Horse Feathers; Speak Easily; Big Timer; This Is the Night; No Greater Love; Cauliflower Alley; and the following shorts with Z. Pitts: Seal Skins; On the Loose; Red Noses; Strictly Unreliable; The Old Bull; Show Business; Alum and Eve; The Soilers. 1933 Air Hostess; Counsellor at Law; Son of a Sailor; Deception; Fra Diablo (The Devil's Brother); Sitting Pretty; Mary Stevens, M.D.; Cheating Blondes; and the following shorts with Z. Pitts: Sneak Easily; Asleep in the Feet; Maids a la Mode; Bargain of the Century; One Track Minds; and the following shorts with P. Kelly: Beauty and the Bus; Backs to Nature; Air Freight. 1934 You Made Me Love You; Hips, Hips, Horray!; The Cockeyed Cavaliers; Palooka; Bottoms Up; The Poor Rich; Take the Stand; and the following shorts with P. Kelly: Maid in Hollywood; Babes in the Goods; Soup and Fish; I'll Be Suing You; Three Chumps Ahead; One Horse Farmers; Opened by Mistake; Done in Oil; Bum Voyage. 1935 Lightning Strikes Twice; After the Dance; Two for Tonight; and the following shorts with P. Kelly: Treasure Blues; Sing, Sister, Sing; The

Tin Man; The Misses Stooge; Slightly Static; Twin Triplets; Hot Money; Top Flat; All American Toothache. 1936 The Bohemian Girl.

TOLER, HOOPER
Born: 1891, Wichita, Kan. Died: June 2, 1922, Los Angeles, Calif. (heart attack). Screen actor.

TOLER, SIDNEY
Born: Apr. 28, 1874, Warrensburg, Mo. Died: Feb. 12, 1947, Beverly Hills, Calif. Screen, stage actor, and playwright. He took over role of Charlie Chan in "Charlie Chan" film series after Warner Oland died in 1938.

Appeared in: 1929 Madame X (film debut); In the Nick of Time (short). 1931 Devil's Parade (short); White Shoulders; Strictly Dishonorable. 1932 Strangers in Love; Blonde Venus; The Phantom President; Is My Face Red?; Radio Patrol; Speak Easily; Blondie of the Follies; Tom Brown of Culver. 1933 He Learned about Women; King of the Jungle; The Way to Love; The World Changes; The Billion Dollar Scandal; The Narrow Corner. 1934 Dark Hazard; Massacre; Registered Nurse; Spitfire; The Trumpet Blows; Here Comes the Groom; Upperworld; Operator 13; Romance in Manhattan. 1935 This Is the Life; Call of the Wild; The Daring Young Man; Orchids to You; Champagne for Breakfast. 1936 Three Godfathers; The Gorgeous Hussy; The Longest Night; Our Relations; Give Us This Night. 1937 That Certain Woman; Double Wedding; Quality Street. 1938 Wide Open Faces; Gold Is Where You Find It; One Wild Night; Up the River; Charlie Chan in Honolulu; If I Were King; The Mysterious Rider; Three Comrades. 1939 Broadway Cavalier; King of Chinatown; Disbarred; Heritage of the Desert; The Kid from Kokomo; Charlie Chan in Reno; Charlie Chan at Treasure Island; Law of the Pampas; Charlie Chan in City in Darkness. 1940 Charlie Chan in Panama; Charlie Chan's Murder Cruise; Charlie Chan at the Wax Museum; Murder Over New York. 1941 Charlie Chan in Rio; Dead Men Tell. 1942 Castle in the Desert. 1943 A Night to Remember; White Savage; Isle of Forgotten Sins. 1944 Black Magic; Charlie Chan in the Secret Service; The Chinese Cat. 1945 Scarlet Clue; Jade Mask; It's in the Bag; The Shanghai Cobra; The Red Dragon. 1946 Dark Alibi; Dangerous Money. 1947 The Trap.

TOMACK, SID
Born: 1907, Brooklyn, N.Y. Died: Nov. 12, 1962, Palm Springs, Calif. (heart ailment). Screen, television, and vaudeville actor. Appeared in vaudeville as part of team of "Sid Tomack and the Reis Bros."

Appeared in: 1944 A Wave, a Wac and a Marine. 1946 The Thrill of Brazil. 1947 Blind Spot; For the Love of Rusty; Blondie's Holiday; Framed. 1948 A Double Life; My Girl Tisa; Hollow Triumph; Homicide for Three. 1949 House of Strangers; Boston Blackie's Chinese Venture; The Crime Doctor's Diary; Make-Believe Ballroom; Abandoned; Force of Evil. 1950 Love That Brute; The Fuller Brush Girl. 1951 Never Trust a Gambler; Joe Palooka in Triple Cross. 1952 Hans Christian Andersen; Somebody Loves Me. 1954 Living It Up. 1955 The Girl Rush. 1956 That Certain Feeling; The Kettles in the Ozarks. 1957 Spring Reunion. 1961 Sail a Crooked Ship.

TOMAMOTO, THOMAS (Tsunetaro Sugimoto)
Born: 1879, Japan. Died: Sept. 28, 1924, New York, N.Y. Screen and stage actor.

TOMEI, LUIGI
Born: 1910. Died: May 15, 1955 (injuries making movie). Screen actor, stuntman, and former Indianapolis Speedway contender.

Appeared in: 1956 Hell on Frisco Bay (died during filming).

TONE, FRANCHOT (Stanislas Pascal Franchot Tone)
Born: Feb. 27, 1905, Niagara Falls, N.Y. Died: Sept. 18, 1968, New York, N.Y. Screen, stage, television actor, film producer and film director. Divorced from four screen actresses: Joan Crawford; Jean Wallace; Dolores Dorn-Heft and Barbara Payton (dec. 1967).

Appeared in: 1932 The Wiser Sex (film debut). 1933 Dinner at Eight; Gabriel over the White House; Today We Live; Midnight Mary; The Stranger's Return; Stage Mother; Bombshell; Dancing Lady; Lady of the Night. 1934 Four Walls; Gentlemen Are Born; Moulin Rouge; The World Moves On; Sadie McKee; Straight Is the Way; The Girl from Missouri. 1935 The Lives of a Bengal Lancer; Reckless; One New York Night; No More Ladies; Mutiny on the Bounty; Dangerous. 1936 Exclusive Story; The Unguarded Hour; Suzy; The Gorgeous Hussy; Love on the Run; The King Steps Out; Girl's Dormitory. 1937 Quality Street; They Gave Him a Gun; Between Two Women; The Bride Wore Red. 1938 Man-

Proof; Love Is a Headache; Three Comrades; Three Loves Has Nancy. 1939 Fast and Furious; Thunder Afloat; The Girl Downstairs; The Gentle People. 1940 Trail of the Vigilantes. 1941 Virginia; Highly Irregular; Nice Girl?; This Woman Is Mine; She Knew All the Answers. 1942 The Wife Takes a Flyer. 1943 Five Graves to Cairo; Star Spangled Rhythm; Pilot No. 5; His Butler's Sister; True to Life. 1944 Phantom Lady; The Hour before the Dawn; Dark Waters. 1945 That Night with You. 1946 Because of Him. 1947 Her Husband's Affair; Two Men and a Girl; Honeymoon; Army Comes Across; Lost Honeymoon. 1948 I Love Trouble; Every Girl Should Be Married. 1949 Jigsaw; Without Honor; The Man on the Eiffel Tower. 1950 Gun Moll. 1951 Here Comes the Groom. 1958 Uncle Vanya. 1962 Advise and Consent. 1964 La Bonne Soupe (The Good Soup); Big Parade of Comedy (documentary). 1965 In Harm's Way; Mickey One. 1968 The High Comissioner.

TONG, KAM
Born: 1907. Died: Nov. 8, 1969, Costa Mesa, Calif. Screen and television actor.

Appeared in: 1942 Joan of Ozark; Rubber Racketeers; China Girl; The Hidden Hand; Across the Pacific. 1953 Target Hong Kong. 1954 This Is My Love. 1955 Love Is a Many Splendored Thing. 1960 Who Was That Lady?. 1961 Flower Drum Song. 1963 It Happened at the World's Fair. 1966 Mister Buddwing. 1967 Kill a Dragon.

TONG, SAMMEE
Born: 1901, San Francisco, Calif. Died: Oct. 27, 1964, Palms, Calif.(suicide). Screen and television actor.

Appeared in: 1934 Happiness Ahead (film debut); The Captain Hates the Sea. 1935 Oil for the Lights of China; Shanghai. 1937 The Good Earth. 1939 Only Angels Have Wings. 1957 Hell Bound. 1958 Suicide Battalion. 1963 It's a Mad, Mad, Mad, Mad World. 1964 For Those Who Think Young.

TONGE, PHILIP
Born: 1898. Died: Jan. 28, 1959, Hollywood, Calif. Screen and television actor.

Appeared in: 1933 His Double Life. 1947 Love from a Stranger; Miracle on 34th Street. 1952 Hans Christian Anderson. 1953 House of Wax; Scandal at Scourie; Small Town Girl. 1954 Elephant Walk; Khyber Patrol; Ricochet Romance; Track of the Cat. 1955 Desert Sands; The Prodigal; The Silver Chalice. 1956 Pardners; The Peacemaker. 1957 Les Girls; Witness for the Prosecution. 1958 Darby's Rangers; Macabre. 1959 Invisible Invaders.

TOOKER, WILLIAM H.
Born: 1864, New York, N.Y. Died: Oct. 12, 1936, Hollywood, Calif. Screen and stage actor.

Appeared in: 1921 God's Country and the Law; Worlds Apart; Proxies. 1922 The Power Within; Beyond the Rainbow; My Friend, the Devil; Peacock Alley; The Cradle Buster. 1923 The Woman in Chains; Sinner or Saint; A Bride for a Knight; The Purple Highway; The Net. 1924 Who's Cheating?; The Average Woman; The Lone Wolf. 1925 The Phantom Express. 1926 The Scarlet Letter; The Merry Cavalier; The White Black Sheep. 1927 Two Girls Wanted; Birds of Prey; Ladies Must Dress; The Devil Dancer; Tell It to Sweeney; Jake the Plumber. 1928 Good Morning, Judge; The Look Out Girl; The Night Watch; Sweet Sixteen; Virgin Lips; A Woman against the World. 1929 No Defense; Romance of the Under World; The Bellamy Trial; Protection; Love in the Desert. 1930 Soup to Nuts. 1931 A Woman of Experience. 1935 It's a Gift.

TOPART, LISE
Born: 1930, France. Died: Mar. 3, 1952, Nice, France (plane crash). Screen actress.

TOREN, MARTA
Born: May 21, 1926, Stockholm, Sweden. Died: Feb. 19, 1957, Stockholm, Sweden (rare brain disease). Screen and stage actress. Appeared in Swedish, U.S., Italian, and Spanish films.

Appeared in: 1948 Casbah (film debut); Rogues Regiment. 1949 Illegal Entry; Sword in the Desert. 1950 Deported; Mystery Submarine; Spy Hunt; One-Way Street. 1951 Panther's Moon; Sirocco. 1952 Assignment—Paris; The Man Who Watched the Trains Go By. 1953 The Paris Express. 1954 The House of Ricordi (U.S. 1956). 1955 Maddelena.

TORRENCE, ERNEST
Born: June 26, 1878, Edinburgh, Scotland. Died: May 15, 1933, New York, N.Y. Screen, stage actor, and opera performer.

Appeared in: 1921 Tol'able David (film debut). 1922 Broken Chains; The Kingdom Within; The Prodigal Judge; Singed Wings. 1923 The Trail of the Lonesome Pine; Ruggles of Red Gap; The Covered Wagon; The Hunchback of Notre Dame; The Brass Bottle. 1924 Fighting Coward; The Side Show of Life; West of the Water Tower; The Heritage of the Desert; North of 36. 1925 Peter Pan; The Pony Express; The Dressmaker from Paris; Night Life of New York; Mantrap; The American Venus; The Blood Goddess; The Lady of the Harem; The Rainmaker; The Wanderer. 1927 King of Kings; Captain Salvation; Twelve Miles Out. 1928 Steamboat Bill, Jr.; The Cossacks; Across to Singapore. 1929 Silks and Saddles; The Unholy Night; The Bridge of San Luis Rey; Desert Nights; Speedway; Untamed; Twelve Nights Out. 1930 Sweet Kitty Bellaire; Strictly Unconventional; Officer O'Brien; Call of the Flesh. 1931 Shipmates; The Great Lover; Sporting Blood; The New Adventures of Get-Rich-Quick Wallingford; Fighting Caravans. 1932 Hypnotized; Cuban Love Song; Sherlock Holmes. 1933 The Masquerader; I Cover the Waterfront.

TORRIANI, AIMEE
Born: 1890, New York, N.Y. Died: July 18, 1963, New York, N.Y. Screen, stage, and radio actress.

Appeared in: 1955 To Catch a Thief.

TORRUCO, MIGUEL
Born: 1920, Mexico. Died: Apr. 22, 1956, Orizaba, Vera Cruz, Mexico. Screen actor. Entered films in 1949. Married to Mexican screen actress Maria Elena Marques.

Appeared in: 1955 Massacre. Other Mexican film: Horas de Agonia (Agonized Hours).

TOSO, OTELLO
Born: Italy. Died: Mar. 15, 1966, Padua, Italy (auto accident). Screen and television actor.

Appeared in: 1950 Le Due Orfanelle (The Two Orphans). 1952 The Cliff of Sin. 1953 What Price Innocence?. 1958 Age of Infidelity (aka: Muerte de un Circlista—Death of a Cyclist). Other Italian films: Casanova; Ridi Pagliaccio; 1860.

TOTO (Antonio Furst de Curtis-Gagliardi)
Born: 1897, Italy. Died: Apr. 1967, Rome, Italy. Screen, television actor, author, song writer, playwright, and stage producer. Not to be confused with U.S. actor "Toto the Clown."

Appeared in: 1936 Fermo con le Mani. 1949 Toto Le Moko. 1953 Cops and Robbers. 1954 Side Street Story; The Gold of Naples (aka The Racketeer—U.S. 1957). 1955 Racconti Romani. 1958 Persons Unknown. 1959 The Law Is the Law; The Anatomy of Love. 1961 The Big Deal on Madonna Street. 1963 I Due Colonelli (The Two Colonels). 1964 South of Tana River. 1966 Mandragola; Uccellacci e Ucellini (The Hawks and the Sparrows). 1967 The Commander. 1968 Treasure of San Gennaro.

TOVER, MAY
Born: 1911. Died: Dec. 20, 1949, Thousand Oaks, Calif.(clawed to death by lion). Screen actress and lion tamer.

Appeared in: 1950 The Reformer and the Redhead.

TOWNSEND, ANNA
Died: Sept. 1923, Los Angeles, Calif. Screen and stage actress.

Appeared in: 1922 Grandma's Boy; Doctor Jack. 1923 Daddy; Safety Last.

TRACY, LEE (William Lee Tracy)
Born: Apr. 14, 1898, Atlanta, Ga. Died: Oct. 18, 1968, Santa Monica, Calif.(liver cancer). Screen, stage, television, and vaudeville actor. Nominated in 1964 for Academy Award as Best Actor in The Best Man.

Appeared in: 1929 Big Time (film debut). 1930 She Got What She Wanted; Born Reckless; Liliom; On the Level. 1932 Blessed Event; The Half-Naked Truth; Washington Merry-Go-Round; The Night Mayor; Strange Love of Molly Louvain; Doctor X; Love Is a Racket. 1933 Phantom Fame; The Nuisance; Advice to the Lovelorn; Turn Back the Clock; Dinner at Eight; Private Jones; Bombshell; Clear All Wires. 1934 You Belong to Me; The Lemon Drop Kid; I'll Tell the World. 1935 Carnival; Two Fisted. 1936 Wanted: Jane Turner; Sutter's Gold. 1937 Criminal Lawyer; Behind the Headlines. 1938 Crashing Hollywood. 1939 Fixer Dugan; The Spellbinder. 1940 Millionaires in Prison. 1942 The Payoff. 1943 Power of the Press. 1945 Betrayal from the East; I'll Tell the World (and 1934 version). 1947 High Tide. 1962 Advice and Consent. 1964 Big Parade of Comedy (documentary); The Best Man.

TRACY, SPENCER
Born: Apr. 5, 1900, Milwaukee, Wisc. Died: June 10, 1967, Beverly Hills, Calif.(heart attack). Screen and stage actor. Received Academy Award for Best Actor in 1937 for Captains Courageous and in 1938 for Boys Town. Was nominated for Academy Award as Best Actor in 1936 for San Francisco; in 1950 for Father of the Bride; in 1954 for Bad Day at Black Rock; in 1958 for The Old Man and the Sea; in 1960 for Inherit the Wind; in 1961 for Judgement at Nuremberg; and in 1967 for Guess Who's Coming to Dinner.

Appeared in: 1930 Taxi Talks (short—film debut); The Tough Guy (aka The Hard Guy—short); Up the River. 1931 Quick Millions; Six Cylinder Love; Goldie. 1932 She Wanted a Millionaire; Sky Devils; Disorderly Conduct; Young America; Society Girl; The Painted Woman; Me and My Gal. 1933 20,000 Years in Sing Sing; Face in the Sky; Shanghai Madness; The Power and the Glory; The Mad Game; A Man's Castle; State Fair. 1934 Looking for Trouble; The Show-Off; Bottoms Up; Now I'll Tell; Marie Galante. 1935 It's a Small World; The Murder Man; Dante's Inferno; Riffraff. 1936 Whipsaw; Fury; Libeled Lady; San Francisco. 1937 They Gave Him a Gun; Captains Courageous; Big City; Mannequin. 1938 Boys Town; Test Pilot. 1939 Stanley and Livingstone. 1940 I Take This Woman; Northwest Passage; Edison, the Man; Boom Town. 1941 Men of Boys Town; Dr. Jekyll and Mr. Hyde. 1942 Tortilla Flat; Keeper of the Flame; Woman of the Year; Ring of Steel (narr.). 1943 A Guy Named Joe. 1944 The Seventh Cross; Battle Stations (short); Thirty Seconds over Tokyo. 1945 Without Love. 1947 The Sea of Grass; Cass Timberlane. 1948 State of the Union. 1949 Edward, My Son; Adam's Rib. 1950 Malaya; Father of the Bride. 1951 Father's Little Dividend; The People against O'Hara. 1952 Pat and Mike; Plymouth Adventure. 1953 The Actress. 1954 Broken Lance; Bad Day at Black Rock. 1956 The Mountain. 1957 Desk Set. 1958 The Old Man and the Sea; The Last Hurrah. 1960 Inherit the Wind. 1961 The Devil at Four O'Clock; Judgement at Nuremberg. 1962 How the West Was Won (narr.). 1963 It's a Mad, Mad, Mad, Mad World. 1964 Big Parade of Comedy (documentary). 1967 Guess Who's Coming to Dinner.

TRACY, WILLIAM
Born: Dec. 1, 1917, Pittsburgh, Pa. Died: June 18, 1967, Hollywood, Calif. Screen and stage actor.

Appeared in: 1938 Brother Rat; Angels with Dirty Faces. 1939 Jones Family in Hollywood; Million Dollar Legs. 1940 The Amazing Mr. Williams; Terry and the Pirates (serial); The Shop around the Corner; Strike up the Band; Gallant Sons. 1941 Mr. and Mrs. Smith; Tobacco Road; Tillie the Toiler; She Knew All the Answers; Her First Beau; Tanks a Million; Cadet Girl. 1942 Young America; Hayfoot; To the Shores of Tripoli; About Face; Fall In; George Washington Slept Here. 1943 Yanks Ahoy. 1948 Here Comes Trouble; The Walls of Jericho. 1949 Henry, the Rainmaker. 1950 One Too Many. 1951 On the Sunny Side of the Street; As You Were. 1952 Mr. Walkie-Talkie. 1957 The Wings of Eagles.

TRAIN, JACK
Born: 1902. Died: Dec. 19, 1966, London, England. Screen, stage, and radio actor.

Appeared in: 1948 Showtime.

TRAINOR, LEONARD
Born: 1879. Died: July 28, 1940, Los Angeles, Calif.(heart attack). Screen actor. Will Rogers' double and stand-in.

Appeared in: 1922 You Never Know. 1925 Galloping Jinx; Fast Lightnin'. 1926 The Border Sheriff; Hi-Jacking Rustlers. 1928 Headin' for Danger. 1933 Terror Trail.

TRAUTMAN, LUDWIG
Born: 1886, Germany. Died: Jan. 24, 1957, Berlin, Germany. Screen actor. Entered films with Bioscop-Filmgesellshaft in 1912.

TRAVERS, ANTHONY
Born: 1920. Died: Jan. 16, 1959, Hollywood, Calif. Screen actor.

TRAVERS, HENRY (Travers Heagerty)
Born: 1874, Ireland. Died: 1965. Screen and stage actor.

Appeared in: 1933 Reunion in Vienna (stage and screen versions); Another Language; My Weakness; The Invisible Man. 1934 Born to Be Bad; Ready for Love; The Party's Over; Death Takes a Holiday. 1935 Maybe It's Love; Escapade; Pursuit; After Office Hours; Captain Hurricane; Seven Keys to Baldpate; Four Hours to Kill. 1936 Too Many Parents. 1938 The Sisters. 1939 Dark Victory; You Can't Get Away with Murder; On Borrowed Time; Remember?; Dodge City; Stanley and Livingstone; The Rains Came. 1940 The Primrose Path; Anne of Windy Poplars; Edison, the Man; Wyoming. 1941 High Sierra; The Bad Man; Ball of Fire; A Girl, a Guy, and a Gob; I'll Wait for You. 1942 Mrs. Miniver; Pierre of the Plains; Random Harvest. 1943 Shadow of a Doubt; Madame Curie; The Moon Is Down. 1944 Dragon Seed; None Shall Escape; The Very Thought of You. 1945 Thrill of Romance; The Bells of St. Mary's; The Naughty '90's. 1946 Gallant Journey; It's a Wonderful Life; The Yearling. 1947 The Flame. 1948 Beyond Glory. 1949 The Girl from Jones Beach.

TRAVERS, RICHARD C. (Richard Libb)
Born: Apr. 15, 1890, Hudson Bay Post, Northwest Territory, Canada. Died: Apr. 20, 1935, San Diego, Calif.(pneumonia). Screen and stage actor. Was in Essanay pictures in 1914.

Appeared in: 1915 The White Sister; In the Palace of the King; The Man Trail. 1916 Captain Jinks of the Horse Marines. 1921 The Mountain Woman; The Single Track; The Rider of the King Long. 1922 White Hell; The Love Nest; Dawn of Revenge; Notoriety. 1923 The Broad Road; The Acquittal; Mary of the Movies; The Rendezvous. 1924 The House of Youth. 1925 Head Winds; Lightnin'. 1926 The Still Alarm; The Dangerous Dude; The Truthful Sex. 1927 Melting Millions (serial). 1929 The Unholy Night; The Black Watch. 1930 The Woman Racket. 1936 Freshman's Love.

TRAVERSE, MADLAINE (Madlaine Businsky)
Born: 1876, Cleveland, Ohio. Died: Jan. 7, 1964, Cleveland, Ohio. Screen actress.

Appeared in: 1913 Leah Kleschna. 1914 Three Weeks. 1916 The Shielding Shadow (serial).

TREACY, EMERSON
Born: Sept. 7, 1905, Philadelphia, Pa. Died: Jan. 10, 1967, Woodland Hills, Calif. Screen, stage, television, and radio actor.

Appeared in: 1930 Once a Gentleman. 1931 The Sky Raiders. 1932 O.K. America. 1933 Wild Poses (short). 1934 Two Alone. 1937 California Straight Ahead. 1938 Long Shot; Give Me a Sailor. 1939 Gone with the Wind; Invitation to Happiness; They All Come Out. 1949 Adam's Rib. 1950 Wyoming Mail. 1951 Fort Worth; The Prowler. 1955 Prince of Players; Run for Cover. 1960 Dark at the Top of the Stairs. 1961 Return to Peyton Place. 1962 Lover Come Back.

TREADWAY, CHARLOTTE
Born: 1895. Died: Feb. 26, 1963, Hollywood, Calif. Screen and stage actress.

Appeared in: 1937 The Sheik Steps Out. 1938 Female Fugitive. 1939 The Women; a Jed Prouty short; a Leon Errol short.

TREADWELL, LAURA B.
Born: 1879. Died: Nov. 22, 1960, Hollywood, Calif. Screen and stage actress.

Appeared in: 1935 Accent on Youth. 1937 Nobody's Baby. 1939 The Night of Nights; Mr. Smith Goes to Washington. 1946 Bringing up Father. 1951 Strangers on a Train.

TREE, LADY (Helen Maude Holt)
Born: Oct. 5, 1863, London, England. Died: Aug. 7, 1937, London, England (following surgery). Screen and stage actress.

Appeared in: 1932 Wedding Rehearsal. 1933 The Girl from Maxim's; The Private Life of Henry VIII; Early to Bed. 1936 The Man Who Could Work Miracles. Other British films: Still Waters Run Deep; Such Is the Law.

TREE, VIOLA
Born: 1884. Died: Nov. 15, 1938, London, England (pleurisy). British screen, stage actress, author, and playwright.

Appeared in: 1935 Heart's Desire.

TRESKOFF, OLGA
Born: 1902. Died: Apr. 23, 1938, New York, N.Y. Screen and stage actress. Appeared in silent films.

TREVI, CHRISTINA (Christina Benitez Trevino)
Born: 1930, Mexico. Died: July 1, 1956, Mexico City, Mexico (following surgery). Screen, television actress, and opera soprano.

TREVOR, HUGH
Born: Oct. 28, 1903, Yonkers, N.Y. Died: Nov. 10, 1933, Los Angeles, Calif.(complications following appendectomy). Screen actor. Entered films in 1927.

Appeared in: 1927 Rangers of the North. 1928 Skinner's Big Idea; Wallflowers; Beau Broadway; Red Lips; Her Summer Hero; The Pinto Kid. 1929 Dry Martini; Hey, Rube; Taxi 13; Love in the Desert; Night Parade; The Very Idea. 1930 Cuckoos; Midnight Mystery; The Pay-Off; Conspiracy; Half Shot at Sunrise. 1931 The Royal Bed.

TREVOR, NORMAN
Born: 1877, Calcutta, India. Died: Oct. 31, 1929 Norwalk, Calif. Screen and stage actor.

Appeared in: 1917 The Runaway. 1920 Romance. 1921 The Black Panther's Cub; Jane Eyre. 1924 The Wages of Virtue; Roulette. 1925 Dancing Mothers; The Man Who Found Himself. 1926 Beau Geste; The Song and Dance Man; The Ace of Cads. 1927 Afraid to Love; Children of Divorce; The Siren; Sorrell and Son; The Music Master; New York; The Wizard; The Warning. 1928 Mad Hour.

TRIGGER
Born: 1932. Died: July 3, 1965. Roy Roger's Palomino horse. Screen and television performer. Appeared in 87 feature films and 101 half-hour television shows.

Appeared in: 1944 Hollywood Canteen. 1945 Utah. 1946 My Pal Trigger. 1947 Apache Rose. 1949 The Golden Stallion. 1950 Sunset in the West; Trigger, Jr. 1951 Heart of the Rockies.

TROUNCER, CECIL
Born: Apr. 5, 1898, Southport Lanes, England. Died: Dec. 15, 1953. Screen and stage actor.

Appeared in: 1938 Pygmalion. 1946 While the Sun Shines (U.S. 1950). 1948 London Belongs to Me. 1949 Saraband; The Guinea Pig. 1951 The Lady with a Lamp. 1952 Pickwick Papers (U.S. 1953); The Magic Box. 1954 The Weak and the Wicked.

TROUT, FRANCIS "DINK"
Born: June 18, 1898, Beardstown, Ill. Died: Mar. 26, 1950, Hollywood, Calif. Screen, stage, radio, vaudeville actor, and musician. Played with Ben Bernie's band.

Appeared in: 1941 Scattergood Baines. 1943 Gildersleeve's Bad Day. 1944 Up in Arms. 1945 Sudan.

TROWBRIDGE, CHARLES
Born: Jan. 10, 1882, Vera Cruz, Mexico. Died: Oct. 30, 1967. Screen and stage actor.

Appeared in: 1918 Thais. 1922 Island Wives. 1931 I Take This Woman; Damaged Love; A Secret Call; Silence. 1935 Calm Yourself; Mad Love; It's in the Air; Rendezvous. 1936 Exclusive Story; The Garden Murder Case; We Went to College; Born to Dance; Mother Steps Out; Man of the People; The Gorgeous Hussy; Libeled Lady; The Devil Is a Sissy; Robin Hood of El Dorado; Moonlight Murder; Love on the Run. 1937 Dangerous Number; Espionage; A Day at the Races; A Servant of the People; Fit for a King; Captains Courageous; They Gave Him a Gun; Sea Racketeers; Exiled to Shanghai; That Certain Woman; Without Warning; Saturday's Heroes; The 13th Chair. 1938 Crime School; Nancy Drew, Detective; Alcatraz Island; The Buccaneer; Kentucky; Thanks for Everything; Submarine Patrol; Gang Bullets; The Last Express; The Invisible Menace; The Patient in Room 18; College Swing; Gangs of New York; Crime Ring. 1939 Risky Business; King of Chinatown; Tropic Fury; King of the Underworld; Boy Trouble; The Story of Alexander Graham Bell; On Trial; Hotel for Women; Swanee River; Each Dawn I Die; Confessions of a Nazi Spy; The Man They Could Not Hang; Mutiny on the Blackhawk; Joe and Ethel Turp Call on the President; Pride of the Navy; Lady of the Tropics; Cafe Society; Sergeant Madden. 1940 My Love Came Back; House of Seven Gables; The Fighting 69th; Johnny Apollo; The Man with Nine Lives; Knute Rockne—All American; Cherokee Strip; The Mummy's Hand; Trail of the Vigilantes; The Fatal Hour. 1941 The Great Lie; The Tell-Tale Heart; Strange Alibi; Dressed to Kill; Blue, White and Perfect; The Nurse's Secret; Rags to Riches; Sergeant York; Hurricane Smith; Great Guns; We Go Fast; The Great Mr. Nobody; Belle Starr; Cadet Girl. 1942 Who Is Hope Schuyler?; Sweetheart of the Fleet; Over My Dead Body; That Other Woman; Ten Gentlemen from West Point; Wake Island. 1943 Action in the North Atlantic; Wintertime; The Story of Dr. Wassell; Salute to the Marines; Sweet Rosie O'Grady; Mission to Moscow; Adventures of the Flying Cadets (serial). 1944 Faces in the Fog; Summer Storm; Hey Rookie!; Wing and a Prayer;

Heavenly Days. 1945 Col. Effingham's Raid; Mildred Pierce; They Were Expendable; The Red Wagon. 1946 Don't Gamble with Strangers; Shock; Undercurrent; Secret of the Whistler; The Hoodlum Saint; Smooth as Silk; Valley of the Zombies. 1947 Key Witness; Buck Privates Come Home; Her Husband's Affairs; The Sea of Grass; The Beginning or the End?; Mr. District Attorney; The Private Affairs of Bel Ami; Tarzan and the Huntress; Song of My Heart; Tycoon; Black Gold; Shoot to Kill. 1948 Stage Struck; Hollow Triumph; The Paleface. 1949 Mr. Solf Touch; Bad Boy. 1950 Unmasked; Peggy. 1952 Bushwackers. 1957 The Wings of Eagles.

TROY, HELEN
Born: 1905. Died: Nov. 1, 1942, Santa Monica, Calif. Screen and radio actress.

Appeared in: 1936 Born to Dance; Song and Dance Man; Human Cargo. 1937 Thoroughbreds Don't Cry; Between Two Women; Broadway Melody of 1938; Big City; Everybody Sing. 1939 Kid Nightingale.

TRUJILLO, LORENZO L.
Born: 1906, Mexico. Died: Mar. 1962, Mexico City, Mexico (heart attack). Screen, stage, and television actor. Appeared in 200 Mexican films including The Exterminating Angel.

TSIANG, H. T.
Born: 1899. Died: July 16, 1971, Hollywood, Calif. Chinese screen, stage, television actor, poet, and author. Entered films in 1928.

Appeared in: 1944 The Purple Heart; Keys of the Kingdom. 1948 Chicken Every Sunday. 1949 State Department File 649. 1950 Panic in the Streets. 1951 Smuggler's Island. 1960 Ocean's 11. 1965 Winter A-Go-Go.

TUALA, MARIO (Eckard Schulz-Ewerth)
Born: 1924, Samoa, South Sea Islands. Died: July 10, 1961, Berlin, Germany (drowned in boating accident). Screen, radio actor, and singer.

TUBBS, WILLIAM
Born: 1908. Died: Jan. 25, 1953, London, England. Screen and stage actor.

Appeared in: 1948 Paisan. 1949 The Pirates of Capri. 1951 Quo Vadis; Three Steps North. 1952 Edward and Caroline. 1953 Singing Taxi Driver. 1954 The Greatest Love; The Golden Coach. 1955 The Wages of Fear.

TUCKER, CY
Born: 1889. Died: July 4, 1952, Hollywood, Calif. Screen actor.

TUCKER, RICHARD
Born: 1884, Brooklyn, N.Y. Died: Dec. 5, 1942, Woodland Hills, Calif.(heart attack). Screen and stage actor. Entered films with Edison in 1914.

Appeared in: 1915 While the Tide Was Rising; Vanity Fair. 1920 Branding Iron. 1921 Roads of Destiny; Don't Neglect Your Wife; The Old Nest; Everything for Sale; What Love Will Do; A Voice in the Dark; A Virginia Courtship; The Night Rose. 1922 Hearts Aflame; The Dangerous Age; A Self-Made Man; Strange Idols; Remembrance; Rags to Riches; Grand Larceny; When the Devil Drives; The Worldly Madonna; Yellow Men and Gold. 1923 Cameo Kirby; The Eleventh Hour; Her Accidental Husband; Poor Men's Wives; Is Divorce a Failure?; Lovebound; The Broken Wing. 1924 Beau Brummell; 40-Horse Hawkins; Helen's Babies; The Fast Worker; The Star Dust Trail; The Tornado. 1925 The Air Mail; The Lure of the Wild; The Man without a Country; The Bridge of Sighs. 1926 The Blind Goddess; The Golden Cocoon; Shameful Behavior?; The Lily; That's My Baby; Devil's Island. 1927 Dearie; Wings; Dress from Rio; The Lash (short); The Bush Leaguer; The Desired Woman; The Jazz Singer; A Kiss in a Taxi; The World at Her Feet; Matinee Ladies; Women's Wares. 1928 Thanks for the Buggy Ride; Loves of an Actress; On Trial; Captain Swagger; Love over Night; My Man; The Border Patrol; Daughters of Desire; Beware of Married Men; A Bit of Heaven; Show Girl; The Crimson City; The Grain of Dust. 1929 The Dummy; Half Marriage; King of the Kongo (serial); This Is Heaven; Lucky Boy; Synthetic Sin; The Unholy Night; The Squall. 1930 Madonna of the Streets; Brothers; Puttin' on the Ritz; Shadow of the Law; Broken Dishes; Recaptured Love; Safety in Numbers; The Bat Whispers; The Benson Murder Case; Painted Faces; Peacock Alley; Courage; The Man from Blankley's; College Lovers; Manslaughter. 1931 Too Young to Marry; A Holy Terror; Convicted; Devil Plays; Inspiration; Seed; X Marks the Spot; Stepping Out; Hellbound; Maker of Men; The Deceiver;

Graft; Up for Murder; The Black Camel. 1932 Careless Lady; A Successful Calamity; The Stoker; Guilty as Hell; The Crash; Pack up Your Troubles; Flames; Week-End Marriage. 1933 The Iron Master; Her Resale Value; Daring Daughters; The World Gone Mad; Saturday's Millions; Only Yesterday. 1934 Show-Off; Back Page; Take the Stand; Successful Failure; Public Stenographer; The Road to Ruin; Countess of Monte Cristo; A Modern Hero; Handy Andy; Baby Take a Bow; Money Means Nothing; Paris Interlude; Sing Sing Nights. 1935 Diamond Jim; Shadow of Doubt; Murder in the Fleet; Calm Yourself; Here Comes the Band; Sympathy of Living. 1936 In Paris A.W.O.L.; The Great Ziegfeld; Ring around the Moon; Flying Hostess; The Plot Thickens; I Loved a Woman; Shall We Dance?. 1937 She's Dangerous; Headline Crasher; I Cover the War; The Girl Who Said No; Armored Car; Something to Sing About; Make a Wish; The River of Missing Men; Trapped by G-Men. 1938 The Texans; She's Got Everything; The Higgins Family; Sons of the Legion. 1939 Risky Business; The Girl from Rio; The Covered Trailer; The Great Victor Herbert.

TUCKER, SOPHIE (Sophie Abuza)
Born: Jan. 13, 1884, Boston, Mass, or Russia. Died: Feb. 9, 1966, New York, N.Y. (lung & kidney ailment). Screen, stage, burlesque, vaudeville actress, and nightclub entertainer.

Appeared in: 1929 Honky Tonk. 1934 Gay Love (U.S. 1936). 1937 Broadway Melody of 1938; Thoroughbreds Don't Cry. 1944 Follow the Boys; Sensations of 1945; Atlantic City.

TUFTS, SONNY (Bowen Charleston Tufts, III)
Born: 1912, Boston, Mass. Died: June 5, 1970, Santa Monica, Calif. (pneumonia). Screen, stage, television actor, and film producer.

Appeared in: 1939 Ambush. 1943 So Proudly We Hail; Government Girl. 1944 In the Meantime, Darling; I Love a Soldier; Here Comes the Waves. 1945 Bring on the Girls; Duffy's Tavern. 1946 Miss Susie Slagle's; The Virginian; The Well-Groomed Bride. 1947 Swell Guy; Cross My Heart; Easy Come, Easy Go; Blaze of Noon; Variety Girl. 1948 Untamed Breed. 1949 Easy Living; The Crooked Way. 1952 The Gift Horse (aka Glory at Sea—U.S. 1953). 1953 Cat-Women of the Moon; No Escape; Run for the Hills. 1955 The Seven Year Itch. 1956 Come Next Spring. 1957 The Parson and the Outlaw. 1962 All the Way. 1965 The Town Tamer. 1967 Cottonpickin' Chickenpickers.

TULLEY, ETHEL
Born: 1898. Died: Oct. 1, 1968, San Antonio, Tex. Screen actress. Entered films with Vitagraph in 1916.

TUNIS, FAY
Born: 1890. Died: Dec. 4, 1967, Atlantic City, N.J. Screen and stage actress. Appeared in silent films.

TURNER, EMANUEL
Born: 1884. Died: Dec. 13, 1941, Hollywood, Calif. Screen and stage actor.

TURNER, FLORENCE
Born: 1885, New York, N.Y. Died: Aug. 28, 1946, Woodland Hills, Calif. Screen, stage, and vaudeville actress. She began her career on May 17, 1907, at Vitagraph Studios and was known only as "The Vitagraph Girl" and received no billing in early films.

Appeared in: 1910 The New Stenographer; St. Elmo; A Dixie Mother; A Tale of Two Cities. 1911 The Deerslayer. 1912 Francesca da Rimini. 1913 The Welch Singer. 1914 My Old Dutch. 1921 All Dolled Up; Passion Fruit. 1925 The Dark Angel; Never the Twain Shall Meet; The Mad Marriage; The Price of Success. 1926 Flame of the Argentine; The Last Alarm; Padlocked; The Gilded Highway. 1927 The Broken Gate; The Chinese Parrot; The Overland Stage; Stranded; College; The Cancelled Debts; Sally in Our Alley. 1928 Marry the Girl; The Law and the Man; Walking Back; Jazzland; The Pace That Kills; The Road to Ruin. 1929 The Kid's Clever. 1930 The Rampant Age.

TURNER, MAIDEL
Born: May 12, 1888, Sherman, Tex. Died: Apr, 12, 1953, Ocean Springs, Miss. Screen and stage actress.

Appeared in: 1926 The Boy Friend. 1933 Another Language; The Worst Woman in Paris; Olsen's Big Moment. 1934 It Happened One Night; The Life of Vergie Winters; Unknown Blonde; Money Means Nothing; Whom the Gods Destroy; A Modern Hero; Transcontinental Bus; The Perfect Clue; The Merry Frinks. 1935 Dante's Inferno; Mutiny Ahead; The Raven; Diamond Jim. 1936 Magnificent Obsession; Palm Springs; And Sudden Death; Make Way for a Lady. 1937 Slim.

TURNER, COL. ROSCOE
Born: 1896. Died: June 23, 1970, Indianapolis, Ind. Screen actor, aviation pioneer, and flying ace.

Appeared in: 1930 Hell's Angels. 1939 Flight at Midnight.

TURNER, WILLIAM H.
Born: 1861, Ireland. Died: Sept. 27, 1942, Philadelphia, Pa. Screen and stage actor.

Appeared in: 1916 Perils of Our Girl Reporters (serial). 1923 Blow Your Own Horn; Other Men's Daughters; The Satin Girl; The Darling of New York. 1924 The Enemy Sex; American Manners; The Garden of Weeds; Fast and Fearless; The Measure of a Man; The Gaiety Girl. 1925 The Phantom Bullet; The Pony Express; Gold and Grit; Heir-Loons; Where Was I?; White Thunder; A Woman's Faith. 1926 The Texas Streak; Three Pals; Her Big Adventure; Red Hot Leather; The Warning Signal. 1927 Broadway after Midnight. 1928 Driftin' Sands. 1929 The Trespasser; The Last Performance. 1932 Love Me Tonight.

TURPIN, BEN
Born: Sept. 17, 1874, New Orleans, La. Died: July 1, 1940, Santa Monica, Calif. (heart disease). Screen, stage, burlesque, and vaudeville actor. Appeared in early Vogue and Keystone comedies, having joined Keystone in 1917, and later in Sennett films and shorts, plus several Pathe shorts.

Appeared in: 1909 Midnight Disturbance. 1915 His New Job; A Night Out; The Champion. 1916 Carmen; When Papa Died; His Blowout (aka The Plumber); The Delinquent Bridegroom; The Iron Mitt; Hired and Fired (aka The Leading Man); A Deep Sea Liar (aka The Landlubber); For Ten Thousand Bucks; Some Liars; The Stolen Booking; Doctoring a Lead (aka A Total Loss); Poultry a la Mode (aka The Harem); Ducking a Discord; He Did and He Didn't; Picture Pirates; Shot in the Fracas; Jealous Jolts; The Wicked City. 1917 Roping Her Romeo; Are Waitresses Safe?; Taming Target Center; A Circus Cyclone; The Musical Marvels; The Butcher's Nightmare; His Bogus Boast (aka A Cheerful Liar); A Studio Stampede; Frightened Flirts; When Ben Bolted (aka He Looked Crooked); Masked Mirth; Bucking the Tiger; Caught in the End; A Clever Dummy; Lost—a Cook; The Pawnbroker's Heart. 1918 She Loved Him Plenty; Sheriff Nell's Tussle; Saucy Madeline; The Battle Royal; Two Tough Tenderfeet; Hide and Seek, Detectives. 1919 Yankee Doodle in Berlin; East Lynne with Variations; Uncle Tom without a Cabin; Salome vs. Shenendoah; Cupid's Day Off; When Love Is Blind; No Mother to Guide Him; Sleuths; Whose Little Wife Are You?. 1920 The Daredevil; Down on the Farm; Married Life; The Star Boarder (short), plus the following "Bloggie" series: Countless Bloggie; Bloggie's Vacation; and the following "Snakeville" series: Snakeville's Hen Medic; Snakeville's Champion, Snakeville's Debutantes. 1921 A Small Town Idol; Home Talent; Love's Outcast (short); Love and Doughnuts (short). 1922 Foolish Wives, plus the three following shorts: Bright Eyes; Step Forward; Home-Made Movies. 1923 The Shriek of Araby, plus the following shorts: Where's My Wandering Boy Tonight?; Pitfalls of a Big City; Asleep at the Switch. 1924 the following shorts: Romeo and Juliet; Yukon Jake; Ten Dollars or Ten Days; The Hollywood Kid; Three Foolish Weeks; The Reel Virginian. 1925 Hogan's Alley, plus the following shorts: Wild Goose Chaser; Rasberry Romance; The Marriage Circus. 1926 Steele Preferred, plus the following shorts: A Harem Knight; A Blonde's Revenge; When a Man's a Prince; A Prodigal Bridegroom. 1927 The College Hero; A Woman's Way, plus the following shorts: The Pride of Pickeville; Broke in China; A Hollywood Hero; The Jolly Jilter; Love's Languid Lure; Daddy Boy. 1928 The Wife's Relations. 1929 Show of Shows; The Love Parade. 1930 Swing High. 1931 Cracked Nuts; Our Wife (short). 1932 Make Me a Star; Million Dollar Legs. 1932-33 Paramount shorts; 1935 Educational shorts; Vitaphone shorts; 1939 Hollywood Cavalcade. 1940 Saps at Sea. 1960 When Comedy Was King (documentary). 1961 Days of Thrills and Laughter (documentary).

TWEDDELL, FRANK
Born: 1895, India. Died: Dec. 20, 1971, New Haven, Conn. Screen and stage actor.

Appeared in: 1943 Claudia (film and stage versions). 1946 Claudia and David. 1949 The Undercover Man. 1950 The Tattooed Stranger. 1951 I'd Climb the Highest Mountain. 1956 Carousel.

TWELVETREES, HELEN (Helen Jurgens)
Born: Dec. 25, 1908, Brooklyn, N.Y. Died: Feb. 14, 1958, Harrisburg, Pa. (overdose of drugs re kidney ailment). Screen and stage actress.

Appeared in: 1929 The Ghost Talks (film debut); True Heart; Blue

Skies; Paris to Bagdad; Words and Music. 1930 Her Man; The Grand Parade; Swing High; The Cat Creeps. 1931 Beyond Victory; The Painted Desert; A Woman of Experience; Bad Company; Millie; Cardigan's Last Case. 1932 Panama Flo; Young Bride; Is My Face Red?; State's Attorney; Unashamed. 1933 A Bedtime Story; Disgraced; My Woman; King for a Night. 1934 All Men Are Enemies; Now I'll Tell; She Was a Lady. 1935 One Hour Late; Times Square Lady; She Gets Her Man; 'Frisco Waterfront; Spanish Cape Mystery. 1937 Hollywood Round Up. 1939 Persons in Hiding.

TWITCHELL, A.R. "ARCHIE"
Born: Nov. 28, 1906, Pendleton, Oreg. Died: Jan. 31, 1957, Pacoima, Calif.(mid-air collision). Screen actor.

Appeared in: 1937 Daughters of Shanghai; Souls at Sea; Partners in Crime; Hold 'Em, Navy; Sophie Lang Goes West. 1938 You and Me; Her Jungle Love; Tip-Off Girls; Cocoanut Grove; Spawn of the North; The Texans; Illegal Traffic; Give Me a Sailor. 1939 Ambush; King of Chinatown; Mickey the Kid; Geronimo. 1940 Granny Get Your Gun; Charlie Chan at the Wax Museum; Young Bill Hickok; Behind the News. 1941 I Wanted Wings; West Point Widow; Among the Living; Prairie Stranger; Thundering Hoofs. 1942 A Tragedy at Midnight. 1945 The Missing Corpse. 1946 Affairs of Geraldine; The French Key; Accomplice. 1947 The Arnelo Affair; Second Chance; Web of Danger. 1949 Follow Me Quietly. 1950 Revenue Agent. 1951 Kentucky Jubilee; Yes Sir, Mr. Bones. 1954 The Bounty Hunter.

TYLER, HARRY
Born: 1888. Died: Sept. 15, 1961, Hollywood, Calif.(cancer). Screen, stage, and television actor.

Appeared in: 1929 The Shannons of Broadway; Oh, Yeah!. 1930 Big Money. 1934 Midnight Alibi; Friends of Mr. Sweeney; Housewife; The Case of the Howling Dog; Babbitt. 1935 The Glass Key; Lady Tubbs; Men without Names; A Night at the Opera. 1936 Two-Fisted Gentlemen; The Man I Marry; Pennies from Heaven; Three Wise Guys; a Vitaphone short. 1937 The Girl Said No; Don't Tell the Wife; Love Takes Flight; Mr. Boggs Steps Out; Jim Hanvey—Detective; Youth on Parole; Midnight Madonna 1939 The Story of Alexander Graham Bell; Jesse James; The Lady's from Kentucky; 20,000 Men a Year; Young Mr. Lincoln; The Gracie Allen Murder Case. 1940 Little Old New York; Johnny Apollo; Young People; Meet the Missus; Behind the News; The Grapes of Wrath; Go West. 1941 The Bride Wore Crutches; The Richest Man in Town; Tillie the Toiler; Remember the Day; Tobacco Road. 1942 The Mexican Spitfire Sees a Ghost. 1943 True to Life; The Dancing Masters. 1944 Casanova in Burlesque; The Adventures of Mark Twain; Atlantic City; Wilson. 1945 Identity Unknown; The Woman Who Came Back; Abbott and Costello in Hollywood. 1946 Behind Green Lights; The Fabulous Suzanne; I Ring Doorbells; Johnny Comes Flying Home; Somewhere in the Night. 1947 Fun on a Weekend; Sarge Goes to College; Winter Wonderland; Heading for Heaven. 1948 Smart Politics; Deep Waters; Strike It Rich; The Untamed Breed; That Wonderful Urge. 1949 Air Hostess; Beautiful Blonde from Bashful Bend; Hellfire. 1950 Lucky Losers; Rider from Tucson; The Traveling Saleswoman; A Woman of Distinction. 1951 Bedtime for Bonzo; Corky of Gasoline Alley; Santa Fe. 1952 Deadline, U.S.A.; The Quiet Man; This Woman Is Dangerous; Wagons West; Lost in Alaska. 1953 The Glass Web. 1954 Witness to Murder. 1955 Jail Busters; A Lawless Street; The Naked Street; Texas Lady; Abbott and Costello Meet the Keystone Kops. 1956 A Day of Fury; Glory. 1957 Plunder Road. 1958 Last Hurrah.

TYLER, TOM (Vincent Marko, or Markoski)
Born: Aug. 8, 1903, New York, N.Y. Died: May 1, 1954, Hamtramck, Mich. Screen actor. One of the "Three Mesquiteers." Voted top money-making western star in pictures in Herald—Fame Poll, 1942.

Appeared in: 1925 The Cowboy Musketeer; Let's Go Gallagher; The Wyoming Wildcat. 1926 The Cowboy Cop; Red Hot Hoofs; The Arizona Streak; Born to Battle; The Masquerade Bandit; Out of the West; Tom and His Pals; Wild to Go. 1927 The Sonora Kid; Cyclone of the Range; The Cherokee Kid; The Flying U Ranch; The Desert Pirate; Lightning Lariats; Splitting the Breeze; Tom's Gang. 1928 Phantom of the Range; Terror Mountain; The Avenging Rider; Terror; The Texas Tornado; Tyrant of Red Gulch; When the Law Rides. 1929 The Sorcerer; Trail of the Horse Thieves; Gun Law; Idaho Red; Pride of Pawnee; The Lone Horseman; The Man from Nevada; The Phantom Rider; 'Neath Western Skies; Law of the Plains. 1930 Phantom of the West (serial); Call of the Desert; The Canyon of Missing Men; Pioneers of the West. 1931 A Man from Death Valley; Rider of the Plains; Galloping Through; West of Cheyenne; Rose of the Rio Grande;

God's Country and the Man; Battling with Buffalo Bill (serial); Partners of the Trail. 1932 Jungle Mystery (serial); The Tenderfoot; Man from New Mexico; Single-Handed Sanders; Two-Fisted Justice; Honor of the Mounted; Vanishing Men; The Forty-Niners; prior to 1933: Half Pint Polly (short). 1933 War of the Range; When a Man Rides Alone; Deadwood Pass; Clancy of the Mounted (serial); The Phantom of the Air. 1934 Riding Through; Tracy Rides; Riding the Lonesome Trail; Mystery Ranch; Fighting Hero; Terror of the Plains. 1935 The Silent Code; Unconquered Bandit; Powder Smoke Range. 1936 Fast Bullets; Roamin' Wild; The Last Outlaw. 1937 Lost Ranch. 1938 Pinto Rustlers; Orphan of the Pecos; King of Alcatraz. 1939 The Night Riders; Frontier Marshal; The Westerner; Stagecoach; Gone with the Wind. 1940 The Lights of the Western Stars; Brother Orchid; Cherokee Strip; The Mummy's Hand. 1941 Buck Privates; Texas Rangers Ride Again; Border Vigilantes; West of Cimarron; Outlaws of Cherokee Trail; Riders of the Timberline; Gauchos of Eldorado; The Adventures of Captain Marvel (serial). 1942 Code of the Outlaw; Raiders of the Range; Westward Ho; The Talk of the Town; The Phantom Plainsmen; Valley of the Sun. 1943 The Phantom (serial); Wagon Tracks West; Shadows on Sage; Thundering Trails; Valley of Hunted Men; Blocked Trail; Riders of the Rio Grande; Santa Fe Scouts; Sylvester the Great. 1944 Boss of Boomtown; Ladies of Washington. 1945 San Antonio; Sing Me a Song of Texas. 1946 Badmen's Territory. 1947 Cheyenne. 1948 The Dude Goes West; Return of the Bad Men; Blood on the Moon; The Golden Eye. 1949 The Younger Brothers; For Those Who Date; Hellfire; Beautiful Blonde from Bashful Bend; I Shot Jesse James; Lust for Gold; Masked Raiders; Square Dance Jubilee; She Wore a Yellow Ribbon. 1950 Colorado Ranger; Crooked River; Fast on the Draw; Hostile Country; Marshal of Heldorado; Rio Grande Patrol; West of the Brazos. 1951 The Great Missouri Raid; Best of the Badmen. 1952 What Price Glory; Road Agent. 1953 Cow Country.

TYNAN, BRANDON
Born: 1879, Dublin, Ireland. Died: Mar. 19, 1967, New York, N.Y. Screen, stage actor, and playwright. Married to screen actress Lily Cahill (dec. 1955).

Appeared in: 1923 Loyal Lives; Success. 1924 Unrestrained Youth. 1937 Parnell; Sh! The Octopus; Wells Fargo. 1938 The Girl of the Golden West; Youth Takes a Fling; Nancy Drew, Detective. 1939 The Great Man Votes; Lady and the Mob; The Lone Wolf Spy Hunt. 1940 It All Came True; Lucky Partners; Rangers of Fortune. 1941 Marry the Boss's Daughter.

UHLIG, MAX E.
Born: 1896. Died: May 1958, North Tarrytown, N.Y. Screen actor. Appeared in silents.

ULRIC, LENORE
Born: 1894, New Ulm, Minn. Died: Dec. 30, 1970, Orangeburg, N.Y. Screen and stage actress. Divorced from screen actor Sidney Blackmer (dec. 1973).

Appeared in: 1915 Kilmeny; The Better Woman. 1916 Intrigue; The Heart of Paula. 1923 Tiger Rose. 1925 Capital Punishment. 1929 Frozen Justice. South Sea Rose. 1936 Camille. 1940 The Fifth Column. 1946 Temptation; Two Smart People; Notorious. 1947 Northwest Outpost; Anthony and Cleopatra.

UNCLE MURRAY. See Murray Parker

UNDERWOOD, LAWRENCE
Born: 1871, Albion, Iowa. Died: Feb. 2, 1939, Los Angeles, Calif. Screen, stage actor, film, stage director, and screenwriter.

Appeared in: 1920 Old Lady 31. 1925 Passionate Youth; Thundering Through. 1926 Twisted Triggers. 1927 The Phantom Buster.

UPDEGRAFF, HENRY
Born: 1889. Died: July 29, 1936, Hollywood, Calif.(heart attack). Screen and stage actor.

URBAN, DOROTHY K.
Born: 1869. Died: Oct. 29, 1961, Hollywood, Calif. Screen, stage, and vaudeville actress.

Appeared in: 1940 The Fight for Life.

URBANSKY, YEVGENY (aka EVGENY URBANSKY)
Born: 1931, Russia. Died: Nov. 5, 1965, Kyzyl-Kum Desert, Central Asia (auto accident). Screen and stage actor.

Appeared in: 1960 Ballad of a Soldier. 1961 The Letter That Was Never Sent. 1963 Cristoe Nebo (Clear Skies). Other Russian film: Kommunist.

URCELAY, NICOLAS
Born: 1920, Yucatan, Mexico. Died: July 3, 1959, Tampico, Mexico. Screen, stage, television, vaudeville actor, and singer.

URECAL, MINERVA
Born: 1894. Died: Feb. 1966, Glendale, Calif.(heart attack). Screen, radio, and television actress.

Appeared in: 1935 Bonnie Scotland. 1937 Her Husband's Secretary; Love in a Bungalow; Life Begins with Love; The Go Getter; Oh, Doctor; Exiled to Shanghai. 1938 Start Cheering; Prison Nurse; Frontier Scout; Air Devils. 1940 You Can't Fool Your Wife; Boys of the City. 1941 Man at Large; Arkansas Judge; The Cowboy and the Blonde; Accent on Love; Murder by Invitation; Never Give a Sucker an Even Break. 1942 Henry and Dizzy; Sweater Girl; Quiet Please, Murder; The Corpse Vanishes; That Other Woman; The Living Ghost; Sons of the Pioneers; My Favorite Blonde; Man in the Trunk. 1943 Riding through Nevada; The Ape Man; Kid Dynamite; Ghosts on the Loose; So This Is Washington; Hit the Ice. 1944 Louisiana Hayride; Moonlight and Cactus; County Fair; Crazy Knights; The Bridge of San Luis Rey. 1945 A Medal for Benny; Wanderer of the Wasteland; The Men in Her Diary; Who's Guilty (serial); State Fair. 1946 The Virginian; Wake up and Dream; Rainbow over Texas; Dark Corner; Sensation Hunters; The Trap. 1947 The Lost Moment; Apache Rose. 1948 Sitting Pretty; Secret Service Investigator; Variety Time; Good Sam; The Snake Pit; Marshal of Amarillo; Sundown at Santa Fe; The Noose Hangs High. 1949 The Lovable Cheat; Master Minds; Holiday in Havana; Outcasts of the Trail. 1950 Arizona Cowboy; Quicksand; Traveling Saleswoman; My Blue Heaven; The Jackpot. 1951 Stop That Cab. 1952 Aaron Slick from Punkin' Crick; Oklahoma Annie; Gobs and Gals; Anything Can Happen; Lost in Alaska; Harem Girl. 1953 The Woman They Almost Lynched; Niagara; Two Gun Marshal. 1955 Sudden Danger. 1956 Miracle in the Rain; Tugboat Annie; Crashing Las Vegas. 1960 The Adventures of Huckleberry Finn. 1962 Mr. Hobbs Takes a Vacation. 1964 Seven Faces of Dr. Lao.

URQUHART, ALASDAIR
Born: 1914, Scotland. Died: Aug. 25, 1954, Glasgow, Scotland. Screen and stage actor.

Appeared in: 1953 Rob Roy; The Highland Rogue.

USHER, GUY
Born: 1875. Died: June 16, 1944, San Diego, Calif. Screen and stage actor.

Appeared in: 1933 This Day and Age (film debut); Fast Worker; The Mystery Man; Face in the Sky. 1934 All of Me; Good Dame; The Witching Hour; The Hell Cat; Kid Millions. 1935 Grand Exit; Mills of the Gods; Hold 'Em Yale; The Crusades; Make a Million; Little Big Shot; The Goose and the Gander; It's a Gift. 1936 Dangerous Waters; Postal Inspector; The President's Mystery; The Case of the Black Cat; King of Hockey; Charlie Chan at the Opera. 1937 Marked Woman; Once a Doctor; White Bondage; Nancy Steele Is Missing; Boots and Saddles; The Mighty Treve; Sophie Lang Goes West; Boy of the Streets. 1938 State Police; Under Western Stars; Romance of the Limberlost; Spawn of the North. 1939 Timber Stampede; Invitation to Happiness; The Renegade Ranger; Mister Wong in Chinatown. 1940 Passport to Alcatraz; Doomed to Die. 1941 Lady for a Night; No Greater Sin. 1942 Mummy's Tomb; Shepherd of the Ozarks; I Was Framed; Bad Men of the Hills. 1943 Lost Canyon.

USHER, HARRY
Born: 1887. Died: Oct. 28, 1950, Hollywood, Calif.(heart attack). Screen and vaudeville actor.

Appeared in vaudeville with his wife, Frances Usher.

VACKOVA, JARMILA
Born: 1908. Died: Sept. 26, 1971, Santa Monica, Calif. Screen actress. Appeared in U.S. and European films.

VAIL, OLIVE
Born: 1904. Died: June 14, 1951, Cincinnati, Ohio. Screen, stage, and vaudeville actress.

Appeared in: 1947 The Spirit of Notre Dame.

VALDEMAR, TANIA
Born: 1904. Died: Nov. 12, 1955, New York, N.Y. Screen, stage actress, and ballet dancer.

VALEDON, LORA
Born: 1884. Died: Sept. 15, 1946, Providence, R.I. Screen, vaudeville, circus actress, and film stuntwoman.

VALENTINO, RUDOLPH (Rudolph Guglielimo)
Born: May 6, 1895, Castellaneta, Italy. Died: Aug. 23, 1926, New York, N.Y.(complications following operation—peritonitis). Screen actor and dancer. Divorced from screen actresses Jean Acker and Natacha Rambova (aka Winifred Hudnut—dec. 1966).

Appeared in: 1914 My Official Wife. 1916 Patria. 1918 Alimony; A Society Sensation; All Night. 1919 The Delicious Little Devil; A Rogue's Romance; The Homebreaker; Virtuous Sinners; The Big Little Person; Out of Luck; Eyes of Youth. 1920 The Married Virgin; An Adventuress; The Cheater; Once to Every Woman; Passion's Playground; Stolen Moments; The Wonderful Chance. 1921 The Four Horsemen of the Apocalypse; Unchained Seas; Camille; The Conquering Power; The Sheik. 1922 Moran of the Lady Letty; Beyond the Rocks; The Young Rajah; Blood and Sand; The Isle of Love. 1924 Monsieur Beaucaire; A Sainted Devil. 1925 The Eagle; Cobra. 1926 Son of the Sheik.

VALERIO, ALBANO
Born: 1889, San Jose, Calif. Died: Feb. 2, 1961, Los Angeles, Calif. Screen actor.

Appeared in: 1926 The Loves of Ricardo (and 1928 version). 1960 Can-Can.

VALK, FREDERICK
Born: 1901, Czechoslovakia. Died: July 23, 1956, London, England. Screen and stage actor.

Appeared in: 1940 Night Train; Gagbags. 1942 Thunder Rock (U.S. 1944); Suicide Squadron. 1945 Dead of Night. 1946 Frenzy; Latin Quarter. 1947 The Patient Vanishes. 1949 Saraband; Dear Mr. Prohack. 1950 Mrs. Fitzherbert. 1951 Outcast of the Islands. 1952 The Magic Box. 1953 The Colditz Story (U.S. 1957); Bad Blonde; Never Let Me Go. 1954 Mr. Potts Goes to Moscow (aka Top Secret—U.S. 1952). 1955 Break to Freedom; Secret Venture. 1956 Magic Fire. 1957 Wicked as They Come.

VALKYRIEN, VALDA
Born: 1894. Died: Oct. 22, 1953, Los Angeles, Calif. Screen actress and ballet dancer.

Appeared in: 1916 Hidden Valley.

VALLEE, FAY WEBB. See Fay Webb

VALLI, VIRGINIA (Virginia McSweeney)
Born: Jan. 19, 1900, Chicago, Ill. Died: Sept. 24, 1968, Palm Springs, Calif. Screen actress. Entered films in 1915. Married to screen actor Charles Farrell.

Appeared in: 1917 Efficiency Edgar's Courtship. 1921 The Devil Within; Man Who; The Idle Rich; Sentimental Tommy; A Trip to Paradise; The Silver Lining; Love's Penalty. 1922 The Village Blacksmith; The Black Bag; The Storm; His Back against the Wall; The Right That Failed; Tracked to Earth. 1923 A Lady of Quality; The Shock. 1924 The Signal Tower; K—the Unknown; Wild Oranges; The Confidence Man; In Every Woman's Life. 1925 Siege; The Price of Pleasure; Up the Ladder; The Lady Who Lied; Man Who Found Himself. 1926 The Family Upstairs; Flames; Watch Your Wife; Pleasure Garden. 1927 Ladies Must Dress; Paid to Love; East Side, West Side; Marriage; Judgement of the Hills; Evening Clothes; Stage Madness. 1928 Escape; Street of Illusion. 1929 Beyond Closed Doors; Mister Antonio; Isle of Lost Ships. 1930 Storm; The Lost Zeppelin; Guilty?. 1931 Night Life in Reno.

VALLIS, ROBERT
Born: England. Died: Dec. 19, 1932, Brighton, England. Screen and stage actor.

VALSTED, MYRTLE (Myrtle Christine Valsted)
Born: 1910. Died: Sept. 19, 1928, Hollywood, Calif.(following appendicitis operation). Screen actress. Entered films in 1928.

VAN, BILLY B.
Born: 1878, Pottstown, Pa. Died: Nov. 16, 1950, Newport, N.H. (heart attack). Screen, stage, and vaudeville actor. For a while did a vaudeville act with boxer/actor James J. Corbet (dec. 1933). Married to screen actress Grace Walsh.

Appeared in: 1922 The Beauty Shop.

VAN, CONNIE
Born: 1909. Died: July 16, 1961, Hollywood, Calif.(cerebral hemorrhage). Screen, stage, and radio actress.

Appeared in: 1955 The Far Country.

VAN, GUS
Born: 1888, Brooklyn, N.Y. Died: Mar. 13, 1968, Miami Beach, Fla.(injuries from being hit by auto). Screen, stage, vaudeville, radio, and television actor. Was part of vaudeville team with Joe Schenck (dec. 1930) billed as "Van and Schenck" and later did a single.

Together they appeared in: 1927 The Pennant; Wnning Battery of Songland (short). 1929 Metro Movietone Feature with their lives as a background entitled Take It Big, plus several song short subjects. 1930 They Learned about Women; without Schenck in the following: 1931-34 Universal and Columbia shorts. 1935 Gus Van's Music Shoppe (short). 1944 Atlantic City.

VAN AUKER, C. K. (Cecil Van Auker)
Died: Feb. 18, 1938, Prescott, Ariz.(tuberculosis). Screen, stage actor, and aviator for silent films.

Appeared in: 1921 Payment Guaranteed; Trailin'; The Girl from God's Country; Cinderella of the Hills; The Mother Heart. 1922 Up and Going; The Ragged Heiress; Youth Must Have Love. 1923 The Gunfighter; The Grub Stake. 1927 The Golden Yukon.

VAN BAILEY, POLLY
Died: Aug. 25, 1952, Hollywood, Calif. Screen and stage actress.

VAN BEERS, STANLEY
Born: 1911, England. Died: May 25, 1961, London, England (heart ailment). Screen, stage, and television actor.

Appeared in:1953 The Fake. 1954 The Dam Busters; Terror Ship. 1956 The Creeping Unknown; Shadow of Fear (aka Before I Wake). 1959 The Angry Hills.

VANBRUGH, DAME IRENE
Born: 1872. Died: Nov. 30, 1949, London, England. Screen, stage actress, and novelist.

Appeared in: 1927 The Gay Lord Quex. 1934 Catherine the Great. 1935 Escape Me Never. 1937 Moonlight Sonata; Wings of the Morning; Knight without Armor.

VAN BUREN, MABEL
Born: 1878, Chicago, Ill. Died: Nov. 4, 1947, Hollywood, Calif. Screen and stage actress. Entered films approx. 1914. Married to screen actor James Gordon (dec. 1941).

Appeared in: 1916 The Victoria Cross. 1920 Conrad in Quest of His Youth. 1921 The Four Horsemen of the Apocalypse; Miss Lulu Bett; Moonlight and Honeysuckle. 1922 The Man from Home; Beyond the Rocks; The Woman Who Walked Alone; For the Defense; Pawned; Youth to Youth; Manslaughter; While Satan Sleeps. 1923 In Search of a Thrill; Lights Out; Wandering Daughters; Light That Failed; The Girl of the Golden West. 1924 The Dawn of a Tomorrow. 1925 Smooth as Satin; The Top of the World; His Secretary. 1927 King of Kings; The Meddlin' Stranger. 1928 The Flying Buckaroo; Craig's Wife; Ramona. 1930 His First Command.

VANCE, VIRGINIA
Born: 1902. Died: Oct. 13, 1942, Hollywood, Calif.(heart attack). Screen actress.

Appeared in: 1925 Goat Getter. 1926 The Fighting Marine (serial). 1928 Undressed. 1929 New Year's Eve.

VANDERGRIFT, J. MONTE
Born: 1893. Died: July 29, 1939, North Hollywood, Calif.(heart attack). Screen, stage, and radio actor.

Appeared in: 1934 Shoot the Works. 1935 Private Worlds; Smart Girl; Seven Keys to Baldpate; Hot Money (short). 1936 The Moon's Our Home; Easy Money; The Mandarin Mystery. 1937 California Straight Ahead; Woman Chases Man. 1939 Miracles for Sale.

VAN DYK, JAMES
Born: 1895. Died: Dec. 17, 1951, Montclair, N.J.(heart attack). Screen, stage, radio, and television actor.

VANE, DENTON
Born: 1890. Died: Sept. 17, 1940, Union Hill, N.J.(heart attack). Screen and stage actor.

Appeared in: 1921 Women Men Love. 1922 Flesh and Spirit.

VAN EYCK, PETER
Born: July 16, 1913, Germany. Died: July 15, 1969, Zurich, Switzerland. Screen actor.

Appeared in: 1943 Five Graves to Cairo; The Moon Is Down. 1944 Address Unknown; The Imposter; The Hitler Gang. 1950 The Devil's Agent. 1951 The Desert Fox. 1953 Alerte au Said; Sailor of the King. 1954 Night People. 1955 Tarzan's Hidden Jungle; Jump Into Hell; Vengeance (aka The Brain—U.S. 1964); A Bullet for Joey; Wages of Fear. 1956 Attack!; The Rawhide Years; Run for the Sun. 1957 Mr. Arkadin (U.S. 1962). 1958 Flesh and the Woman; There's Always a Price Tag; The Snorkel; Sophie et le Crime (Sophie and the Crime, aka The Girl on the Third Floor); Le Chair et le Diable (The Flesh and the Devil, aka Flesh and Desire); Retour de Manivelle (Turn of the Handle, aka There's Always a Price Tag). 1959 Der Glaserne Turm (The Glass Tower). 1960 Rosemary; Der Rest 1st Schweigen (The Rest Is Silence). 1961 Foxhole in Cairo; Law of War. 1962 The Black Chapel; The Longest Day; Rebel Flight to Cuba; The World in My Pocket. 1963 The River Line; Verbrechen Nach Schulschluss (The Young go Wild). 1964 Station Six-Sahara; Das Grosse Liebesspiel (The Big Love Game). 1965 An Alibi for Death; The Spy Who Came In from the Cold; And So to Bed. 1966 The Dirty Game; The 1,000 Eyes of Dr. Mabuse; The Mystery of Thug Island. 1967 Million Dollar Man. 1968 Toviw and His Seven Daughters; Assignment to Kill; Shalako.

VAN HADEN, ANDERS
Born: 1876. Died: June 19, 1936, Hollywood, Calif.(heart attack). Screen actor, film producer, and film director.

Appeared in: 1932 Cheaters at Play; A Passport to Hell. 1933 Best of Enemies; The Secret of the Blue Room; Snug in the Jug (short). 1935 Barbary Coast.

VAN HORN, JAMES "JIMMY"
Born: 1917. Died: Apr. 20, 1966, Hollywood, Calif.(internal hemorrhage). Screen actor and stuntman.

Appeared in: 1927 The Cherokee Kid. 1950 Fast on the Draw; Hostile Country; Marshal of Heldorado. 1951 The Cave of the Outlaws. 1953 Gunsmoke.

VANNE, MARDA
Born: South Africa. Died: Apr. 27, 1970, London, England. Screen, stage, and television actress.

Appeared in: 1968 Joanna.

VAN SAHER, LILLA A.
Born: 1912, Hungary. Died: July 15, 1968, New York, N.Y. Screen actress and author.

Appeared in foreign film Grain au Vent.

VAN SLOAN, EDWARD
Born: 1882, San Francisco, Calif. Died: Mar. 6, 1964, San Francisco, Calif. Screen and stage actor.

Appeared in: 1931 Dracula; Frankenstein. 1932 Manhattan Parade; Play Girl; Man Wanted; Behind the Mask; Thunder Below; Forgotten Commandments; The Last Mile; Honeymoon in Bali; The Mummy. 1933 The Death Kiss; Silk Express; The Working Man; Infernal Machine; Trick for Trick; It's Great to Be Alive; The Man Who Reclaimed His Head; The Deluge; Murder on the Campus; Billion Dollar Scandal. 1934 Manhattan Melodrama; I'll Fix It; Death Takes a Holiday; The Scarlet Empress; The Crosby Case; The Life of Vergie Winters. 1935 Air Hawks; Mystery of the Black Room; The Story of Louis Pasteur; Grand Exit; Grand Old Girl; Mills of the Gods; The Woman in Red; A Shot in the Dark; The Last Days of Pompeii. 1936 Road Gang; Sins of Man; Dracula's Daughter. 1937 The Man Who Found Himself. 1938 Penitentiary; Storm over Bengal; Danger on the Air. 1939 The Phantom Creeps (serial). 1940 Abe Lincoln in Illinois; The Doctor Takes a Wife; The Secret Seven; Before I Hang. 1942 A Man's World. 1943 Mission to Moscow; Riders of the Rio Grande; Submarine Alert; The Masked Marvel (serial); Valley of the Hunted Men; End of the Road. 1944 Captain America (serial); The Conspirators; Wing and a Prayer. 1945 I'll Remember April. 1946 The Mask of Dijon. 1947 Betty Coed.

VAN TRUMP, JESSALYN
Born: 1885. Died: May 2, 1939, Hollywood, Calif. Screen and stage actress.

VAN TUYL, HELEN (Hellen Marr Van Tuyl)
Born: 1891. Died: Aug. 22, 1964, Hollywood, Calif.(heart attack). Screen and television actress.

Appeared in: 1952 Stars and Stripes Forever; Confidence Girl. 1953 Titanic. 1955 Daddy Long Legs; The Girl in the Red Velvet Swing.

VAN UPP, VIRGINIA
Born: 1902, Chicago, Ill. Died: Mar. 25, 1970, Hollywood, Calif. (results of a broken hip). Screen actress, film producer, and screenwriter. Appeared on screen in features with William Desmond, John Gilbert, and others when five years old.

VAN ZANDT, PHILIP
Born: Oct. 3, 1904, Amsterdam, Holland. Died: Feb. 16, 1958, Hollywood, Calif.(overdose of sleeping pills). Screen, stage, and television actor.

Appeared in: 1939 Those High Grey Walls. 1940 Boobs in Arms (short). 1941 City of Missing Girls; So Ends Our Night; Ride on Vaquero; Citizen Kane. 1942 Wake Island; The Hard Way; Desperate Journey. 1943 Tarzan Triumphs; Murder on the Waterfront; Tarzan's Desert Mystery; Hostages; Deerslayer; Air Raid Wardens; Sherlock Holmes and the Secret Weapon. 1944 Call of the Jungle; The Big Noise; Swing Hostess; The Unwritten Code. 1945 Outlaws of the Rockies; House of Frankenstein; Sudan; Counter-Attack; A Thousand and One Nights; I Love a Bandleader. 1946 The Avalanche; Below the Deadline; Joe Palooka, Champ; Decoy; Don't Gamble with Strangers; Somewhere in the Night. 1947 Slave Girl; The Last Frontier Uprising. 1948 The Vicious Circle; The Shanghai Chest; Embraceable You; Walk a Crooked Mile; The Loves of Carmen; Street with No Name; Big Clock; April Showers; Mummy's Dummies (short); Squareheads of the Round Table (short). 1949 The Lady Gambles; Red, Hot and Blue; The Blonde Bandit; Lone Wolf and His Lady. 1950 Between Midnight and Dawn; Indian Territory; The Petty Girl; Where Danger Lives; Copper Canyon; Dopey Dicks (short); The Jackpot. 1951 Submarine Command; The Ghost Chasers; His Kind of Woman; Ten Tall Men; Two Dollar Bettor; Cyrano de Bergerac; Three Arabian Nuts (short). 1952 Viva Zapata; Son of Ali Baba; Thief of Damascus; Yukon Gold. 1953 Prisoners of the Casbah; Capt. John Smith and Pocahontas; Spooks (short); Clipped Wings. 1954 Yankee Pasha; Knock on Wood; Playgirl; Gog; Knutzy Knights (short); Scotched in Scotland (short); Three Ring Circus. 1955 Untamed; The Big Combo; I Cover the Underworld; Bedlam in Paradise (short). 1956 Our Miss Brooks; Uranium Boom; Around the World in 80 Days; Hot Stuff (short). 1957 Man of a Thousand Faces; The Pride and the Passion; The Crooked Circle; The Lonely Man; Outer Space Jitters (short). 1958 Fifi Blows Her Top (short).

VARDEN, EVELYN
Born: 1895. Died: July 11, 1958. New York, N.Y. Screen, stage, radio, and television actress.

Appeared in: 1949 Pinky. 1950 Cheaper by the Dozen; Stella; When Willie Comes Marching Home. 1951 Elopement. 1952 Finders Keepers; Phone Call from a Stranger. 1954 Athena; Desiree; The Student Prince. 1955 The Night of the Hunter. 1956 Hilda Crane; The Bad Seed. 1957 Ten Thousand Bedrooms.

VASS, LULU
Born: 1877. Died: May 6, 1952, Haverstraw, N.Y. Screen, stage, and radio actress. Appeared in films from 1941 to 1946.

VASSAR, QUEENIE
Born: Oct. 28, 1870, Glasgow, Scotland. Died: Sept. 11, 1960, Hollywood, Calif.(following surgery). Screen and stage actress. Married to screen actor Joseph Cawthorne (dec. 1949).

Appeared in: 1940 The Primrose Path. 1942 Lady in a Jam. 1944 None but the Lonely Heart.

VAUGHAN, DOROTHY
Born: Nov. 5, 1889, St. Louis, Mo. Died: Mar. 15, 1955, Hollywood, Calif.(cerebral hemorrhage). Screen, stage, radio, and vaudeville actress.

Appeared in: 1935 Annapolis Farewell (film debut). 1936 Love Begins at 20; Times Square Playboy. 1937 The Hoosier Schoolboy; Here's Flash Casey; That Man's Here Again; The Black Legion; Michael O'Halloran. 1938 Little Miss Thoroughbred; Telephone Operator; Little Orphan Annie; Gambling Ship; Slander House; Quick Money. 1939 Unexpected Father; The Man in the Iron Mask; First Love; The Star Maker. 1940 Diamond Frontier; The Old Swimmin' Hole; The Ape. 1941 Secret Evidence; Bad Men of Missouri; Three Girls about Town. 1942 The Magnificent Ambersons; Lady Gangster; Gentleman Jim. 1943 The Iron Major; Sweet Rosie O'Grady; Doughboys in Ireland; Hit the Ice. 1944 The Adventures of Mark Twain; Sweet and Low Down; The Town Went Wild; Henry Aldrich's Little Secret. 1945 Dancing in Manhattan; What a Blonde; Those Endearing Young Charms; Ten Cents a Dance. 1946 That Brennan Girl. 1947 Trail to San Antone; The Egg and I; The Bishop's Wife; The Bamboo Blonde; Robin Hood in Texas. 1948 I Wouldn't Be in Your Shoes; Song of

Idaho. 1949 Fighting Fools; Home in San Antone; Manhattan Angel. 1950 Chain Gang; Rider from Tucson; Square Dance Katy. 1951 A Wonderful Life.

VAUGHN, ADAMAE
Born: 1906. Died: Sept. 1, 1943, Hollywood, Calif. Screen actress. She was a "Wampus Baby Star" in 1927.

Appeared in: 1920 The Show of Shows. 1923 The Courtship of Myles Standish. 1925 The Last Edition. 1926 The Arizona Streak; Flashing Fangs. 1930 Dancing Sweeties. 1936 Love before Breakfast.

VAUGHN, HILDA
Born: Dec. 27, 1898, Baltimore, Md. Died: Dec. 28, 1957, Baltimore, Md. Screen and stage actress.

Appeared in: 1929 Three Live Ghosts. 1930 Manslaughter. 1931 It's a Wise Child; A Tailor Made Man; Susan Lennox, Her Rise and Fall. 1932 Ladies of the Big House; The Phantom of Crestwood. 1933 Today We Live; Dinner at Eight; No Marriage Ties; No Other Woman. 1934 Anne of Green Gables. 1935 The Wedding Night; Straight from the Heart; Chasing Yesterday; Men without Names; I Live My Life. 1936 The Trail of the Lonesome Pine; Everybody's Old Man; Half Angel; Banjo on My Knee; The Accusing Finger; The Witness Chair. 1937 Nothing Sacred; Danger—Love at Work. 1938 Maid's Night Out. 1940 Charlie Chan at the Wax Museum.

VAUGHN, VIVIAN
Born: 1902. Died: Feb. 1, 1966, Hollywood, Calif. Screen, stage actress, and singer. Also known as "Gypsy Gould."

VAUGHN, WILLIAM. See Wilhelm Von Brincken

VAULTHIER, GEORGES
Born: France. Died: Apr. 1926, Paris, France. Screen actor.

VAVERKA, ANTON
Born: Czechoslovakia. Died: July 2, 1937, Prague, Czechoslovakia. Screen actor.

Appeared in: 1923 Merry Go Round. 1925 The Phantom of the Opera; Secrets of the Night. 1926 The Love Thief; Rolling Home. 1927 On Ze Boulevard. 1928 The Wedding March; Three Sinners. 1929 The Love Parade. 1930 The Melody Man.

VEDDER, WILLIAM H.
Born: 1872. Died: Mar. 3, 1961, Hollywood, Calif.(lung cancer). Screen and stage actor.

Appeared in: 1949 Leave It to Henry; Undercover Man. 1950 The Gunfighter. 1951 You Never Can Tell. 1952 O. Henry's Full House; Paula; Stars and Stripes Forever; Boots Malone. 1954 The Wild One. 1955 World without End.

VEIDT, CONRAD
Born: Jan. 22, 1893, Berlin, Germany. Died: Apr. 3, 1943, Los Angeles, Calif.(heart attack). Screen and stage actor.

Appeared in: 1921 The Cabinet of Dr. Caligari. 1924 Waxworks. 1925 Lucrezia Borgia (U.S. 1928). 1926 The Student of Prague; The Three Way Works. 1927 The Magic Flame; The Beloved Rogue; A Man's Past; The Last Performance; The Man Who Laughs; Impetuous Youth; Husbands or Lovers. 1928 Love Makes Us Blind; The Hands of Orlac; Unwelcome Children; Life's Mockery; Two Brothers; L'Homme qui Ric (The Man Who Laughs). 1929 The Man Who Cheated Life; The Black Huzzar; Three Wax Men (reissue of Waxworks, 1924); Erik the Great; Jerusalem. 1930 Bride 68; Great Power; Rasputin. 1931 The Last Company; Thirteen Men and a Girl; Der Mann der den Mord Beging (The Man Who Committed the Murder). 1932 The Congress Dances; Cape Forlorn; Die Letzke Kompagnie (The Last Company); Der Schwarze Husar; Rome Express. 1933 F.P.I.; Jew Suess; Ich and die Kaiserin (U.S. 1935). 1934 Bella Donna; I Was a Spy. 1935 The Wandering Jew; The Passing of the Third Floor Back; The Legend of William Tell. 1936 King of the Damned. 1937 Under the Red Robe; Dark Journey. 1938 Storm over Asia; The Chessplayer; The Spy in Black. 1939 Alex; U-Boat 29; The Devil Is an Empress. 1940 Escape; Blackout; Contraband; The Thief of Bagdad. 1941 A Woman's Face; Whistling in the Dark; The Men in Her Life. 1942 Nazi Agent; Casablanca; All through the Night. 1943 Above Suspicion.

VEJAR, HARRY J.
Born: Apr. 24, 1890, Los Angeles, Calif. Died: Mar. 1, 1968, Los Angeles, Calif. Screen and stage actor.

Appeared in: 1921 The Sheik. 1926 Mademoiselle Modiste. 1929

Mexicali Rose. 1930 Wings of Adventure. 1932 Scarface. 1935 Mutiny on the Bounty. 1948 The Treasure of Sierra Madre.

VEKROFF, PERRY
Born: 1881, Alexandria, Egypt. Died: Jan. 3, 1937, Hollywood, Calif.(heart disease). Screen, stage actor, film director, and screenwriter. Entered films as an actor with Lubin Co.

VELEZ, LUPE (Giadelupe Velez de Villalobos)
Born: July 18, 1908, San Luis Potosi, Mexico. Died: Dec. 14, 1944, Beverly Hills, Calif.(suicide). Screen actress. Divorced from screen actor and Olympic swimming star Johnny Weissmuller. Star of "Mexican Spitfire" series.

Appeared in: 1927 Sailor Beware! (short); The Gaucho. 1928 Stand and Deliver. 1929 Masquerade; Wolf Song; Lady of the Pavements; Where East Is East; Tiger Rose. 1930 Hell Harbor; The Storm; East Is West. 1931 Resurrection; The Squaw Man; Cuban Love Song; Men in Her Life. 1932 The Broken Wing; Kongo; The Half-Naked Truth. 1933 Mr. Broadway; Hot Pepper. 1934 Palooka; Laughing Boy; Hollywood Party; Strictly Dynamite. 1935 The Morals of Marcus. 1936 Gypsy Melody; Under Your Spell. 1937 High Flyers; Wings. 1938 La Zandunga; He Loved an Actress. 1939 Girl from Mexico; Mexican Spitfire. 1940 Mexican Spitfire Out West. 1941 Six Lessons from Madame La Zonga; Mexican Spitfire's Baby; Playmates; Honolulu Lu. 1942 Mexican Spitfire at Sea; Mexican Spitfire Sees a Ghost; Mexican Spitfire's Elephant. 1943 Ladies' Day; Redhead from Manhattan; Mexican Spitfire's Blessed Event; Nana. 1964 Big Parade of Comedy (documentary).

VENESS, AMY
Born: 1876, England. Died: Sept. 22, 1960, Saltdean, England. Screen and stage actress.

Appeared in: 1919 The Brat. 1931 My Wife's Family; Hobson's Choice. 1932 Let Me Explain, Dear. 1933 Their Night Out; Hawleys of High Street; The Love Nest. 1935 Lorna Doone; Brewster's Millions; The Old Curiosity Shop; Elizabeth of England. 1936 The Red Wagon. 1937 The Mill on the Floss (U.S. 1939); Aren't Men Beasts?; The Beloved Vagabond. 1938 Yellow Sands. 1941 This England. 1943 The Man in Grey. 1944 This Happy Breed. 1946 Madonna of the Seven Moons; They Were Sisters. 1947 This Happy Breed. 1948 Man of Evil; Blanche Fury. 1949 The Woman in the Hall; Here Come the Huggetts; My Brother's Keeper. 1950 Good Time Girl; Madeleine. 1951 Tom Brown's School Days; The Woman with No Name; Oliver Twist. 1954 Angels One Five. 1955 Doctor in the House. Other British films: Heartbreak House; Carnival; The Turners of Prospect Road.

VERDI, JOSEPH
Born: 1885. Died: Dec. 27, 1957, New York, N.Y. Screen, stage, vaudeville, and television actor. Billed in vaudeville as part of "Clark and Verdi" team.

Appeared in: 1936 The Crime of Dr. Crespi. 1957 The Vintage.

VERMILYEA, HAROLD
Born: Oct. 10, 1889, New York, N.Y. Died: Jan. 8, 1958, New York, N.Y. Screen, stage, radio, and television actor.

Appeared in: 1946 O.S.S. 1948 The Emperor Waltz; The Big Clock; The Miracle of the Bells; Gentleman's Agreement; The Sainted Sisters; Beyond Glory; Sorry, Wrong Number. 1949 Chicago Deadline; Manhandled. 1950 Born to Be Bad; Edge of Doom. 1951 Katie Did It. 1952 Finders Keepers.

VERNE, KAREN (aka KAAREN—aka CATHERINE YOUNG and INGABOR KATRINE KLINCKERFUSS)
Born: 1915 or 1918?, Berlin, Germany or Norway. Died: Dec. 23, 1967, Hollywood, Calif. Screen, stage, and television actress.

Appeared in: 1939 Ten Days in Paris. 1940 Sky Murder. 1941 King's Row; Underground; Missing Ten Days. 1942 All through the Night; The Great Impersonation. 1943 Sherlock Holmes and the Secret Weapon. 1944 The Seventh Cross. 1955 A Bullett for Joey. 1965 Ship of Fools. 1966 The Torn Curtain; Madam X.

VERNEY, GUY
Born: England. Died: Sept. 19, 1970, London, England. Screen, stage actor, and television producer and director.

Appeared in: 1947 This Happy Breed. 1948 Anna Karenina. 1949 Fame Is the Spur. 1951 Cage of Gold. 1953 Martin Luther.

VERNON, BOBBY
Born: Mar. 9, 1897, Chicago, Ill. Died: June 28, 1939, Hollywood, Calif.(heart attack). Screen, stage actor, and screenwriter. Entered films at age 16.

Appeared in: 1913 Mike and Jake at the Beach. 1914 Joker Comedies (shorts). 1915 Fickle Fatty's Fall; The Hunt. 1916 His Pride and Shame; A Dash of Courage; Hearts and Sparks; The Social Club; The Danger Girl (working title Love on Skates). 1917 The Nick of Time Baby; Teddy at the Throttle; Dangers of a Bride; Whose Baby?; The Sultan's Wife. 1920 Educational shorts. 1925 the following shorts: French Pastry; Great Guns; Don't Pinch; Air Tight; Watch Out; Slippery Feet; Oo-La-La. 1926 Footloose Widows. 1927-28 Christie Comedies (shorts). 1930 Cry Baby (short). 1931 Stout Hearts and Willing Hands. 1932 Ship A Hooey (short). 1960 When Comedy Was King (documentary).

VERNON, WALLY
Born: 1904, New York, N.Y. Died: Mar. 7, 1970, Van Nuys, Calif. (hit and run auto accident). Screen, stage, vaudeville, burlesque, and minstrel actor.

Appeared in: 1937 Mountain Music; This Way Please; You Can't Have Everything. 1938 Happy Landing; Kentucky Moonshine; Alexander's Ragtime Band; Sharpshooters; Meet the Girls. 1939 Chasing Danger; Tailspin; The Gorilla; Charlie Chan at Treasure Island; Broadway Serenade. 1940 Sailor's Lady; Margie; Sandy Gets Her Man. 1943 Tahiti Honey; Reveille with Beverly; Get Going; Fugitive from Sonora; Here Comes Elmer; Pistol Packin' Mama. 1944 Call of the South Seas; Outlaws of Santa Fe; Silent Partner; Silver City Kid; Stagecoach to Monterey; California Joe. 1948 King of Gamblers, Winner Take All; Fighting Mad. 1949 Always Leave Them Laughing; Square Dance Jubilee. 1950 Beauty on Parade; Border Rangers; Holiday Rhythm; Gunfire; Train to Tombstone; Everybody's Dancing. 1952 What Price Glory; Bloodhounds of Broadway. 1953 Affair with a Stranger. 1956 Fury at Gunsight Pass; The White Squaw. 1964 What a Way to Go.

VESPERMANN, KURT
Born: 1887, Kulmsee, West Prussia. Died: July 13, 1957, Berlin, Germany (heart disease). Screen and stage actor.

Appeared in: 1916 The Bear from Baskerville (film debut). 1930 Bride 58. 1932 Der Schrecken der Garnison; Pension Schoeller; Keine Feier Ohn Meyer. 1934 Schuss im Morgengrauen. 1935 Die Kalte Mansell; Konjunkturritter; Die Unschuld vom Lande; Der Unbekannte Gast (The Unknown Guest). 1936 Das Erbe in Pretoria; Die Stimme der Liebe; 1st Mein Mann Nicht Fabelhaft. 1937 Zwei im Sonnenschein. 1938 Wenn Du eine Schwiegermutter Hast (When You Have a Mother-in-Law); Sie and die Drei (She and the Three). 1939 Der Lustige Witwenball (The Merry Widow's Ball); Der Verkannte Lebemann (The Unrecognized Man of the World).

VICKERS, MARTHA (Martha MacVicar)
Born: 1925. Died: Nov. 2, 1971, Van Nuys, Calif. Screen actress. Divorced from screen actor Mickey Rooney.

Appeared in: 1941 The Wolf Man (film debut). 1944 The Falcon in Mexico. 1946 The Big Sleep; The Time, the Place and the Girl. 1947 The Man I Love; That Way with Women; Love and Learn. 1948 Ruthless. 1949 Bad Boy; Alimony; Daughter of the West. 1955 The Big Bluff. 1957 The Burglar. 1960 Four Fast Guns.

VICTOR, CHARLES
Born: 1896, England. Died: Dec. 23, 1965, London, England. Screen and stage actor.

Appeared in: 1940 Dr. O'Dowd; Contraband; Blackout; Hell's Cargo. 1941 You Will Remember; This England. 1942 The Invaders; Those Kids from Town; The Strangler; Seven Days' Leave; Ships with Wings; Wings and the Woman. 1945 The Silver Fleet. 1946 The Man from Morocco. 1948 Meet Me at Dawn; Showtime; The Calendar. 1949 The Cure for Love; Temptation Harbor; Broken Journey. 1950 The Man Who Cheated Himself; Motor Patrol; While the Sun Shines; Woman in Question (aka Five Angles on Murder—U.S. 1953). 1951 Calling Bulldog Drummond; The Galloping Major. 1952 The Ringer; Encore; Waterfront Women. 1953 Those People Next Door; Appointment in London; Meet Mr. Lucifer; The Steel Lady; Landfall. 1954 Man Crazy; The Saint's Girl Friday; Both Sides of the Law. 1955 The Embezzler; Cocktails in the Kitchen (aka For Better, For Worse). 1956 The Best Things In Life Are Free. 1957 Now and Forever; The Prince and the Showgirl; Value for Money; There's Always a Thursday. 1958 Tiger in the Smoke; Twelve Desperate Hours. 1961 The Pit and the Pendulum.

VICTOR, HENRY
Born: Oct. 2, 1898, London, England. Died: May 15, 1945, Hollywood, Calif.(brain tumor). Screen actor. Entered films in 1923.

Appeared in: 1923 Prodigal Son. 1925 She; Braveheart; The White Monkey. 1926 Crossed Signals; The Fourth Commandment; Muhall's Great Catch. 1927 The Beloved Rogue; Topsy and Eva. 1928 The Guns of Loos. 1929 Tommy Atkins. 1930 Are You There?; The Hate Ship; One Heavenly Night. 1931 Seas Beneath; Suicide Fleet. 1932 Freaks. 1933 The Mummy; Tiger Bay; I Spy; Handle with Care; Luxury Liner; Conquest of the Air. 1934 The Scotland Yard Mystery. 1936 The Silent Barrier. 1937 Our Fighting Navy. 1939 The Confessions of a Nazi Spy; Hotel Imperial; Thunder Afloat; Pack up Your Troubles; Nick Carter, Master Detective; Nurse Edith Cavell. 1940 Mystery Sea Raider; Zanzibar. 1941 King of the Zombies; Blue, White and Perfect. 1942 To Be or Not to Be; Desperate Journey. 1943 That Nazty Nuisance.

VIDACOVICH, IRVING J. "PINKY"
Born: 1905. Died: July 5, 1966, New Orleans, La. Screen actor, musician, radio writer, and composer. Known as "Cajun Pete" of radio.

Appeared in: 1950 Panic in the Streets.

VIDAL, HENRI
Born: 1919, France. Died: Dec. 10, 1959, Paris, France (heart attack). Screen actor. Married to screen actress Michele Morgan.

Appeared in: 1946 Les Maudits (The Damned). 1950 Quai de Grenelle. 1951 Fabiola. 1952 The Seven Capital Sins; The Strollers. 1953 Naughty Martine. 1954 Port du Desir; Desperate Decision. 1955 The Wicked Go to Hell. 1956 Porte Les Lilas. 1958 Gates of Paris; Attila; The House on the Waterfront; La Parisienne; What Price Murder. 1960 Voulez-Vous Danser Avec Moi (Come Dance with Me).

VIGNOLA, ROBERT G.
Born: 1882, Italy. Died: Oct. 25, 1953, Hollywood, Calif. Screen actor and film director. Entered films as an actor with Kalem in 1907.

VIKING, VONCEIL
Died: Dec. 2, 1929, Banning, Calif.(auto accident injuries). Screen and vaudeville actress. "Obtained a picture engagement by riding horseback from New York to Los Angeles in 120 days on a wager of $25,000."

VILAR, JEAN
Born: 1913, France. Died: May 28, 1971, Sete, France (heart attack). Screen, stage actor, and stage director.

Appeared in: 1950 Gates of the Night. 1952 The Thirst of Man.

VILCHES, ERNESTO
Born: Spain. Died: Dec. 8, 1954, Barcelona, Spain (auto accident). Screen and stage actor.

Appeared in: 1933 Cascarrabias; La Noche del Pecado. 1936 El Desaparecido. 1938 El 113.

VILLARET, JOAO
Born: 1914, Portugal. Died: Jan. 23, 1961, Lisbon, Portugal (cancer). Screen, stage, radio, and television actor.

VILLARREAL, JULIO
Born: 1885, Mexico. Died: Aug. 4, 1958, Mexico City, Mexico. Screen actor. One of first Spanish speaking actors to make talking pictures in Hollywood.

Appeared in: 1933 Una Vida Por Otra; El Rey de los Gitanos; La Ley Del Haren; La Noche del Pecado. 1934 Sagrario; Profanacion; Tiburon; La Sangre Manda; Oro y Plata; Tu Hijo; Quien Mato a Eva. 1935 Corazon Bandolero; Chucho el Roto; El Vuelo de la Muerte; Tribu. 1938 El Pasado Acusa (The Accusing Past). 1940 Odio (Hate); Mi Madrecita (My Little Mother). 1943 The Life of Simon Bolivar; El Conde de Monte Cristo. 1947 Honeymoon. 1950 The Torch. 1953 Plunder of the Sun; Eugene Grandet. 1955 Seven Cities of Gold. 1956 The Beast of Hollow Mountain.

VINCENT, GENE
Born: 1935. Died: Oct. 12, 1971, Saugus, Calif. Screen actor, rock-and-roll singer, song writer, and musical group leader.

Appeared in: 1956 The Girl Can't Help It (with "His Blue Caps"). 1958 Hot Rod Gang. 1962 It's Trad, Dad!; Ring-a-Ding Rhythm!. 1964 Sing and Swing.

VINE, BILLY
Born: 1915. Died: Feb. 10, 1958, New York, N.Y.(heart ailment). Screen, stage, vaudeville, and television actor.

Appeared in only two films: 1945 The Lucky Stiff. 1956 Vagabond King.

VINTON, ARTHUR ROLFE
Born: Brooklyn, N.Y. Died: Feb. 26, 1963, Guadalajara, Mexico. Screen, stage, and radio actor. Best known for portrayal of radio's "The Shadow."

Appeared in: 1931 The Viking. 1932 Washington Merry-Go-Round; Man against Woman; Laughter in Hell. 1933 Gambling Ship; Blondie Johnson; Picture Snatcher; Lilly Turner; Heroes for Sale; Son of a Sailor; When Strangers Marry; This Day and Age; The Avenger; Central Airport. 1934 Gambling Lady; Cross Country Cruise; A Very Honorable Guy; The Personality Kid; Dames; The Man Trailer; Jealousy. 1935 Society Doctor; Unknown Woman; Little Big Shot; Circumstantial Evidence; King Solomon of Broadway; Red Salute; Rendezvous at Midnight.

VISAROFF, MICHAEL
Born: Nov. 18, 1892, Russia. Died: Feb. 27, 1951, Hollywood, Calif.(pneumonia). Screen and stage actor.

Appeared in: 1925 The Swan (film debut). 1926 Paris; Valencia. 1927 The Sunset Derby; Camille; Two Arabian Knights. 1928 The Last Command; The Adventurer; The Night Bird; Plastered in Paris; Tempest; We Americans. 1929 Marquis Preferred; The House of Horror; Illusion; Disraeli; Hungarian Rhapsody; The Exalted Flapper; Four Devils. 1930 Dracula; Morocco. 1931 Arizona Terror; Mata Hari; Freaks; Chinatown after Dark. 1932 The Man Who Played God. 1933 Strange People; The Barbarian; The King of the Arena. 1934 Picture Brides; Fugitive Road; The Marines Are Coming!; The Merry Frinks; The Cat's Paw; Wagon Wheels; We Live Again. 1935 One More Spring; The Mark of the Vampire; The Break of Hearts; Anna Karenina; Paddy O'Day. 1936 The Gay Desperado. 1937 Champagne Waltz; Soldier and the Lady; Angel. 1938 Air Devils; Tropic Holiday; I'll Give a Million. 1939 Paris Honeymoon; Everything Happens at Night; On Your Toes; Juarez and Maximillian. 1940 Charlie Chan at the Wax Museum; The Son of Monte Cristo; Four Sons; Second Chorus. 1943 For Whom the Bell Tolls; Mission to Moscow; Hostages; Paris after Dark. 1945 Song to Remember; Yolanda and the Thief; Her Highness and the Bellboy. 1947 Flight to Nowhere; Intrigue.

VITERBO, PATRICIA
Born: 1943, France. Died: Nov. 10, 1966, Paris, France (drowned in car accident). Screen actress.

VOGEDING, FREDRIK
Born: Mar. 28, 1890, Nymegen, Netherland. Died: Apr. 18, 1942, Los Angeles, Calif.(heart attack). Screen, stage, and vaudeville actor. Married to screen actress Florence Roberts (dec. 1927).

Appeared in: 1921 Behind Masks; High Heels. 1933 Below the Sea; My Lips Betray. 1934 Orient Express; Murder on the Blackboard; Fury of the Jungle. 1935 Mills of the Gods; The Woman in Red; Charlie Chan in Shanghai; Barbary Coast. 1936 The House of a Thousand Candles; A Message to Garcia. 1937 Think Fast, Mr. Moto; Mr. Moto Takes a Chance; Charlie Chan at the Olympics; Cafe Metropole. 1938 Mysterious Mr. Moto; The Cowboy and the Lady; 6,000 Enemies. 1939 Confessions of a Nazi Spy; Charlie Chan in City in Darkness; The Three Musketeers. 1940 Enemy Agent; British Intelligence; Four Sons; The Man I Married; Man Hunt. 1942 The Great Impersonation.

VOGEL, HENRY
Born: 1865. Died: June 17, 1925, New York, N.Y. Screen and stage actor.

VOGEL, PATRICIA
Born: 1909. Died: June 25, 1941, Beverly Hills, Calif.(suicide—hanging). Screen actress.

VOGLER, WALTER A.
Born: 1897. Died: Aug. 26, 1955, Los Angeles, Calif.(heart attack). Screen actor and film technical adviser.

Appeared in: 1930 All Quiet on the Western Front.

VOINOFF, ANATOLE
Born: 1896, Russia. Died: Feb. 9, 1965, New York, N.Y. Screen actor. Appeared in silents.

VOLOTSKOY, VLADIMIR
Born: 1853, Russia. Died: Nov. 7, 1927, Hollywood, Calif. Screen and stage actor.

VON ALTEN, FERDINAND (Baron von Lamezan auf Altenhofen)
Born: 1885. Died: Mar. 17, 1933, Dessau, Germany (flu). Screen and stage actor.

Appeared in: 1928 Small Town Sinners. 1929 Sajenko, the Soviet; The Man Who Cheated Life.

VON BLOCK, BELA
Born: 1889. Died: Mar. 22, 1962, Hollywood, Calif. Screen actor. Appeared in films from 1924 to 1929.

VON BOLVARY, GEZA
Born: 1898, Hungary. Died: Aug. 11, 1961, Munich, West Germany (heart ailment). Screen actor, screenwriter, and film director. Appeared in German films shortly after W.W. I; then became director and screenwriter.

VON BRINCKEN, WILHELM (aka ROGER BECKWITH and WILLIAM VAUGHN)
Born: May 27, 1891, Flensburg, Germany. Died: Jan. 18, 1946, Los Angeles, Calif.(ruptured artery). Screen actor and film technical director. Entered films in 1921.

Appeared in: 1930 Mamba; Inside the Lines; Royal Flush; Leathernecking; This Mad World; Hell's Angels. 1932 The Night Club Lady; A Passport to Hell; prior to 1933 Manhattan Comedies (record series). 1933 Private Jones; Shanghai Madness. 1934 I'll Tell the World. 1936 Dracula's Daughter. 1937 The Prisoner of Zenda; Thank You, Mr. Moto; The Life of Emile Zola; Crack Up; Espionage; They Gave Him a Gun. 1938 International Crime; Bulldog Drummond in Africa. 1939 Confessions of a Nazi Spy; Pack up Your Troubles; Conspiracy. 1940 Four Sons.

VON COLLANDE, GISELA
Born: 1915, Dresden, Germany. Died: Oct. 23, 1960, Pforzheim, West Germany (auto accident). Screen, stage, and radio actress.

VON ELTZ, THEODORE
Born: 1894, New Haven, Conn. Died: Oct. 6, 1964, Woodland Hills, Calif. Screen, stage, radio, and television actor. Entered films in 1920.

Appeared in: 1923 Tiger Rose. 1924 Being Respectable. 1925 Paint and Powder; On Thin Ice; The Sporting Chance. 1926 The Red Kimono; Sea Wolf; Fools of Fashion. 1927 One Woman to Another; No Man's Law; The Great Mail Robbery. 1928 Way of the Strong; Life's Mockery; Nothing to Wear. 1929 Four Feathers; The Awful Truth; The Voice of the Storm; The Very Idea; The Rescue. 1930 Love among Millionaires; The Furies; The Arizona Kid; The Divorcee; Kismet; The Cat Creeps. 1931 Susan Lennox, Her Rise and Fall; Private Scandal; Heartbreak; The Prodigal; The Secret Six; Up Pops the Devil; Beyond Victory; Wicked; Once a Lady. 1932 Ladies of the Big House; Hotel Continental; The Midnight Lady; Drifting Souls; Strangers of the Evening; The Unwritten Law; Red-Haired Alibi; Breach of Promise; Scarlet Week-End. 1933 Eleventh Commandment; Pleasure Cruise; Arizona to Broadway; High Gear; Jennie Gerhardt; Her Splendid Folly; Dance, Girl, Dance; Master of Men; Luxury Liner. 1934 The Silver Streak; Change of Heart; Call It Luck; Bright Eyes. 1935 Elinore Norton; Streamline Express; Trails of the Wild; Private Worlds; Smart Girl; Behind the Green Lights; Headline Woman; Confidential; His Night Out; The Magnificent Obsession. 1936 Below the Deadline; I Cover Chinatown; Beloved Enemy; The Road to Glory; High Tension; Susy; Sinner Take All; Mind Your Own Business; Ticket to Paradise. 1937 Clarence; A Man Betrayed; Under Cover of Night; Jim Hanvey, Detective; Youth on Parole; California Straight Ahead; The Westland Case; Topper. 1938 Inside Story; Pardon Our Nerves; Blondes at Work; Smashing the Rackets. 1939 They Made Her a Spy; 5th Avenue Girl; The Sun Never Sets; Legion of Lost Flyers. 1940 The Old Swimmin' Hole; The Great Plane Robbery; The Son of Monte Cristo; Little Old New York; Dr. Ehrlich's Magic Bullet. 1941 Ellery Queen's Penthouse Mystery; A Shot in the Dark; I'll Wait for You. 1942 The Man in the Trunk; Quiet Please, Murder!; Lady in a Jam. 1944 Follow the Boys; Bermuda Mystery; Hollywood Canteen; Since You Went Away. 1945 Rhapsody in Blue. 1946 The Big Sleep. 1948 The Devil's Cargo. 1950 Trial without Jury. 1956 The Animal World (narr.).

VON LEDEBUR, LEOPOLD
Born: 1876, Germany. Died: Sept. 17, 1955, Wankendorf, Germany. Screen and stage actor.

VON MEYERINCK, HUBERT
Born: 1897, Germany. Died: May 13, 1971, Hamburg, Germany. Screen and stage actor. Entered films in 1924.

Appeared in: 1960 Holiday Island. 1961 One, Two, Three; The Secret Ways; Das Wirtshaus in Spessart (The Spessart Inn). 1964 The Man Who Walked through the Wall.

VON REMPERT, ALBERT
Born: Germany. Died: Oct. 1958 (injuries sustained filming fight scene in Slave Caravan). Screen actor.

VON SEYFFERTITZ, GUSTAV
Born: 1863, Vienna, Austria. Died: Dec. 25, 1943, Woodland Hills, Calif. Screen, stage actor, and film director. During W.W. I he was known as G. Butler Clonblough.

Appeared in: 1918 Old Wives for New. 1922 Sherlock Holmes; When Knighthood Was in Flower. 1924 The Bandolero; The Lone Wolf; Yolanda. 1925 Goose Woman. 1926 Don Juan; Diplomacy; Sparrows; The Bells; Red Dice. 1927 Barbed Wire; The Gaucho; The Magic Flame; The Wizard; Rose of the Golden West; Birds of Prey; The Student Prince. 1928 Yellow Lily; The Woman Disputed; Vamping Venus; Mysterious Lady; Me, Gangster; Docks of New York; The Red Mark. 1929 Chasing through Europe; His Glorious Night; The Canary Murder Case; The Case of Lena Smith; Come Across; Seven Faces. 1930 The Case of Sgt. Grischa; Dangerous Paradise; Are You There?. 1931 The Bat Whispers; Dishonored; Ambassador Bill. 1932 Shanghai Express; Roadhouse Murder; The Penguin Pool Murder; Rasputin and the Empress; Afraid to Talk; Doomed Battalion. 1933 When Strangers Marry; Queen Christina. 1934 Mystery Liner; The Moonstone; Change of Heart; Little Men. 1935 She; Remember Last Night. 1936 Little Lord Fauntleroy; Murder on the Bridle Path; Mad Holiday. 1938 In Old Chicago; King of Alcatraz; Cipher Bureau. 1939 Nurse Edith Cavell; Juarez and Maximilian.

VON STERNBERG, JOSEF (aka JO STERNBERG and JOE STERN)
Born: 1894, Vienna, Austria. Died: Dec. 22, 1969, Hollywood, Calif.(heart attack). Screen, stage actor, film director, photographer, and film narrator.

Narrated: 1954 Ana-Ta-Han (The Devil's Pitchfork).

VON STROHEIM, ERICH, SR. (Erich Oswald Hans Carl Maris Von Nordenwall)
Born: Sept. 22, 1885, Vienna, Austria. Died: May 12, 1957, Paris, France (spinal ailment). Screen actor, film director, film producer, and screenwriter. Awarded Legion of Honor by the French government for his contributions to the film industry. Father of screen actor Erich Von Stroheim, Jr. (dec. 1968).

Appeared in: 1914 Captain McLean. 1915 The Failure; Ghosts; A Bold Impersonation; Old Heidelberg. 1916 Birth of a Nation; Intolerance; The Social Secretary; His Picture in the Papers; Macbeth; Less Than the Dust. 1917 Panthea; In Again—Out Again; Sylvia of the Secret Service; For France. 1918 The Unbeliever; Hearts of the World; Hearts of Humanity; The Hun Within. 1919 Blind Husbands. 1921 Foolish Wives. 1928 Wedding March. 1929 The Great Gabbo. 1930 Three Faces East. 1931 Friends and Lovers. 1932 Lost Squadron; As You Desire Me; Hello Sister. 1934 Crimson Romance; House of Strangers; Fugitive Road. 1935 The Crime of Dr. Crespi. 1936 Marthe Richard au Service de la France; The Devil's Doll. 1937 Les Pirates du Rail; Between Two Women; Madamoiselle Docteur; La Grande Illusion. 1937 The Alibi. 1938 Les Desparus de St. Agil; Gibraltar; L'Affaire La Farge. 1939 Boys' School; Tempete sur Paris (Thunder over Paris—U.S. 1940); Macao l'enfer du jeu; Paris-New York; Derriere la Facade; Rappel Immediat; Pieges; Le Monde Tremblera. 1940 Ultimatum; I Was an Adventuress. 1941 So Ends Our Night; Personal Column. 1943 Five Graves to Cairo; North Star; Storm over Lisbon; It Happened in Gibraltar; Armored Attack. 1944 The Lady and the Monster; 32 Rue de Montmarte. 1945 The Great Flamarion; Scotland Investigator. 1946 The Mask of Dijon; La Foire aux Chimeres; One Ne Meurt Pas Comme Ca. 1947 La Danse de Mort. 1948 Le Signal Rouge. 1949 Portrait d'un Assassin; The Devil and the Angel. 1950 Sunset Boulevard. 1952 La Maison du Crime; Alraune. 1953 Minuit—Quai de Bercy; Alerte au Sud; L'Envers du Paradis. 1954 Napoleon; Serie Noire. 1955 La Madonna du Sleepings. 1958 L'homme aux Cent Visages.

VON STROHEIM, ERICH, JR.
Born: 1916, Los Angeles, Calif. Died: Oct. 26, 1968, Woodland Hills, Calif.(cancer). Screen actor and assistant film director. Entered films as a child actor. Son of screen actor/director Erich Von Stroheim, Sr.(dec. 1957).

Appeared in: 1962 Two Weeks in Another Town. 1968 Skidoo.

VON TWARDOWSKI, HANS (Hans Heinrich von Twardowski)
Born: Germany. Died: Nov. 19, 1958, New York, N.Y. Screen, stage, radio, television actor, and stage director.

Appeared in: 1932 Scandal for Sale. 1933 Private Jones; Adorable. 1934 The Scarlet Empress. 1935 The Crusades; Storm over the

Andes. 1939 Beasts of Berlin; Confessions of a Nazi Spy; Espionage Agent. 1942 Casablanca; Joan of Ozark. 1943 Hangmen Also Die.

VON WINTERSTEIN, EDUARD
Born: 1872, Vienna, Austria. Died: July 22, 1961, East Berlin, Germany. Screen and stage actor.

Appeared in: 1930 Three Faces East. 1931 Friends and Lovers. 1932 Lost Squadron.

VOSPER, JOHN
Born: Died: Apr. 6, 1954, Hollywood, Calif.(heart attack). Screen, stage, radio, and television actor.

Appeared in: 1942 The Wife Takes a Flyer; Undercover Man. 1945 Weekend at the Waldorf; Counter-Attack. 1947 A Stolen Life; The Perfect Marriage. 1949 Bride of Vengeance. 1951 The Desert Fox. 1952 Black Hills Ambush. 1953 The Magnetic Monster. 1956 Edge of Hell.

VROOM, FREDERIC WILLIAM
Born: 1858. Died: June 24, 1942, Hollywood, Calif.(heart attack). Screen and stage actor.

Appeared in: 1921 The Millionaire; The Faith Healer; The Great Impersonation; The Heart Line; White and Unmarried. 1922 The Lane That Had No Turning; The Fourteenth Lover; The Woman Who Walked Alone; The Glorious Fool; Tailor-Made Man. 1923 The Acquittal; The Day of Faith; The Tiger's Claw. 1924 The Navigator; His Hour; Hutch of the U.S.A.; Sporting Youth; The Reckless Age; Phantom Justice. 1926 Eyes Right. 1927 The General. 1928 The Terrible People. 1930 The Poor Millionaire.

WADE, JOHN W.
Born: 1876. Died: July 14, 1949, Hollywood, Calif. Screen, stage, and vaudeville actor. Entered films approx. 1924. Toured in "Marse Shelby's Chicken Dinner," vaudeville sketch.

Appeared in: 1938 Heroes of the Hills.

WADHAMS, GOLDEN
Born: 1869. Died: June 26, 1929, Hollywood, Calif.(heart illness). Screen and stage actor.

Appeared in: 1927 Hotel Imperial. 1929 Laughing at Death

WADKAR, HANSA "SWAN"
Born: 1924, India. Died: Aug. 23, 1971, Bombay, India (cancer). Screen and stage actress.

WADSWORTH, WILLIAM
Born: 1873. Died: June 6, 1950, N.Y. Screen and stage actor.

Appeared in: 1912 What Happened to Mary? (serial). 1913-1914 Mr. Wood B. Wedd's Sentimental Experiences Series including the following: Her Face Was Her Fortune; The Love Senorita; The Beautiful Leading Lady; The Vision in the Window; High Life; A Lady of Spirits; The Revengeful Servant Girl; A Canine Rival; The Busom Country Lass; Love by the Pound; Wood B. Wedd and the Microbes; Wood B. Wedd Goes Snipe Hunting; A Superfluous Baby. 1922 Young America. 1926 White Mice.

WAGENSELLER, WILLIAM H.
Born: 1880. Died: Apr. 25, 1951, North Hollywood, Calif. Screen and stage actor.

WAGNER, JACK
Born: 1897. Died: Feb. 6, 1965, Hollywood, Calif. Screen and stage actor.

Appeared in: 1935 Paris in the Spring.

WAGNER, WILLIAM
Born: 1885. Died: Mar. 11, 1964, Hollywood, Calif. Screen and stage actor. Entered films approx. 1930.

Appeared in: 1934 Jane Eyre; I'll Be Suing You (short); Done in Oil (short). 1936 Lloyd's of London. 1938 Rebecca of Sunnybrook Farm.

WAINWRIGHT, GODFREY
Born: 1879. Died: May 19, 1956, Woodland Hills, Calif. Screen actor.

WAINWRIGHT, MARIE
Born: 1856, Philadelphia, Pa. Died: Aug. 17, 1923, Scranton, Pa. Screen and stage actress.

Appeared in: 1921 Polly with a Past.

WAKEFIELD, DOUGLAS "DUGGIE"
Born: 1900, Hull, England. Died: Apr. 14, 1951, London, England. Screen, stage, and vaudeville actor.

Appeared in: 1933 This Week of Grace. 1934 I'll Be Suing You (short). 1935 Look up and Laugh. 1937 The Penny Pool. 1938 Calling All Crooks. 1939 Spy for a Day.

WAKEFIELD, FRANCES. See Frances Wakefield Mandel

WAKEFIELD, HUGH
Born: Nov. 10, 1888, Wanstead, England. Died: Dec. 1971, London, England. Screen and stage actor.

Appeared in: 1930 The City of Song. 1931 The Sport of Kings. 1932 The Crime at Blossoms. 1933 The Fortunate Fool. 1934 Farewell to Love; The Luck of a Sailor; My Heart Is Calling; The Man Who Knew Too Much. 1936 The Interrupted Honeymoon; It's You I Want; The Crimson Circle. 1937 Forever Yours; The Street Singer. 1945 Blithe Spirit. 1948 One Night with You. 1952 Love's a Luxury. 1954 The Million Pound Note.

WAKEFIELD, OLIVER
Born: 1909, England. Died: June 30, 1956, Rye, N.Y. Screen, stage, radio, and television actor.

Appeared in: 1933 a Universal Short. 1937 Let's Make a Deal of It. 1940 Shipyard Sally.

WALBROOK, ANTON (Adolph Anton Wilhelm Wohlbruck)
Born: Nov. 19, 1900, Vienna, Austria. Died: Aug. 9, 1967, Munich, West Germany (heart attack). Screen and stage actor.

Appeared in: 1931 Salto Mortale. 1933 Regine; Mond Uber Marvokko; The Waltz War. 1934 Masquerade in Vienna (U.S. 1937); Die Englishe Heirat; Eine Frau die Weisse Was Sie Will. 1935 Zigeunerbaron (Gypsy Baron); The Student of Prague. 1936 Allitria. 1937 Victoria the Great; The Soldier and the Lady. 1938 Sixty Glorious Years; The Rat. 1940 Gaslight; Dangerous Moonlight. 1941 I Give My Life; The 49th Parallel (aka The Invaders—U.S. 1942). 1942 Orders from Tokyo; Suicide Squadron. 1943 The Life and Death of Colonel Blimp (U.S. 1945). 1944 The Man from Morocco (U.S. 1946). 1948 The Red Shoes; The Queen of Spades. 1950 La Ronde. 1951 Vienna Waltzes. 1952 Angel Street. 1955 Oh, Rosalinda!; Lola Montez. 1957 Saint Joan. 1958 I Accuse. Other foreign films (French). L'Affaire Mauricuis; L'Affaire Menrizim.

WALBURN, RAYMOND
Born: Sept. 9, 1887, Plymouth, Ind. Died: July 26, 1969, New York, N.Y. Screen and stage actor.

Appeared in: 1916 The Scarlet Runner (serial). 1930 The Laughing Lady. 1934 The Defense Rests; Jealousy; The Great Flirtation; The Count of Monte Cristo; Broadway Bill; Lady by Choice. 1935 Only Eight Hours; She Married Her Boss; Death Flies East; Mills of the Gods; I'll Love You Always; Redheads on Parade; Society Doctor; It's a Small World; Welcome Home; Thanks a Million. 1936 Mr. Cinderella; Mr. Deeds Goes to Town; The Lone Wolf Returns; The King Steps Out; They Met in a Taxi; Craig's Wife; The Great Ziegfeld; Absolute Quiet; Three Wise Guys; Born to Dance. 1937 Let's Get Married; It Can't Last Forever; Murder in Greenwich Village; Thin Ice; Breezing Home; High, Wide and Handsome; Broadway Melody of 1938. 1938 Start Cheering; Sweethearts; Battle of Broadway; Gateway; Professor Beware. 1939 Let Freedom Ring; It Could Happen to You; The Under-Pup; Eternally Yours. 1940 Heaven with a Barbed-Wire Fence; The Dark Command; Millionaires in Prison; Flowing Gold; Third Finger, Left Hand; Christmas in July. 1941 San Francisco Docks; Kiss the Boys Goodbye; Puddin' Head; Bachelor Party; Confirm or Deny; Rise and Shine; Louisiana Purchase. 1942 The Man in the Trunk. 1943 Let's Face It; Dixie Dugan; Lady Bodyguard; Desperadoes; Dixie. 1944 Music in Manhattan; And the Angels Sing; Hail the Conquering Hero; Heavenly Days. 1945 The Cheaters; Honeymoon Ahead; I'll Tell the World. 1946 Affairs of Geraldine; Breakfast in Hollywood; Lover Come Back; The Plainsman and the Lady; Rendezvous with Annie. 1947 Mad Wednesday (aka Sin of Harold Diddlebock). 1948 State of the Union; The World and His Wife. 1949 Henry, the Rainmaker; Leave It to Henry; Red, Hot and Blue. 1950 Riding High; Key to the City; Father's Wild Game; Father Makes Good; Short Grass. 1951 Father Takes the Air; Golden Girl; Excuse My Dust. 1953 Beautiful but Dangerous. 1954 She Couldn't Say No. 1955 The Spoilers.

WALDAU, GUSTAV
Born: 1871, Germany. Died: May 25, 1958, Munich, Germany. Screen actor.

Appeared in: 1932 Der Falsche Ehemann. 1933 Saison in Kairo (Cairo Season). 1934 Eines Prinzen Junge Liebe (A Prince's Young Love). 1935 Klein Dorrit (Little Dorrit). 1937 Das Einmaleins der Liebe (Love's Arithmetic); Drei Maederl um Schubert (Three Girls around Schubert). 1938 Sie und die Drei (She and the Three); Der Schimmelkrieg von Holledau; Eine Nacht an der Donau (A Night on the Danube). 1940 Eine Kleine Nachtmusik. 1951 Eroica (aka The Beethoven Story). 1952 Singing Angels.

WALDOW, ERNST
Born: 1894, Germany. Died: June 5, 1964, Hamburg, Germany (heart attack). Screen and stage actor.

Appeared in: 1936 Wenn der Hahn Kraeht. 1938 Das Meadehen von Gestern Nacht (The Girl of Last Night); Die Kleine Suenderin (The Little Sinner); Streitum den Knaben Jo (Strife over the Boy Jo). 1939 Die Kluge Schwiegermutter (The Wise Mother-in-Law). 1949 The Affair Blum. 1963 Schneewittchen und die Sieben Gangler (Snow White and the Seven Jugglers).

WALDRIGE, HAROLD
Born: 1905, New Orleans, La. Died: June 26, 1957, New York, N.Y. Screen and stage actor.

Appeared in: 1922 The Ruling Passion. 1931 Five Star Final; June Moon; Sob Sister. 1932 The Heart of New York; Strangers of the Evening; High Pressure; Alias the Doctor; Play Girl; The Strange Love of Molly Louvain; The All American; False Faces. 1933 She Had to Say Yes; Devil's Mate; The Death Kiss; In the Money. 1934 Manhattan Love Song; Private Scandal; Easy to Love. 1935 Hitch Hike Lady; Slightly Static (short); Gigolette. 1936 Dancing Pirate; Three Men on a Horse. 1937 an Educational short.

WALDRON, CHARLES D.
Born: Dec. 23, 1874, Waterford, N.Y. Died: Mar. 4, 1946, Hollywood, Calif. Screen and stage actor. Father of screen actor Charles K. Waldron (dec. 1952).

Appeared in: 1921 Everyman's Price. 1935 Mary Burns, Fugitive; Wanderer of the Wasteland; The Great Impersonation; Crime and Punishment. 1936 The Garden of Allah; Career Woman; Ramona. 1937 A Doctor's Diary; My Dear Miss Aldrich; Navy Blue and Gold; It's All Yours; Escape by Night; The Emperor's Candlesticks. 1938 Kentucky; The Little Adventuress; Marie Antoinette. 1939 On Borrowed Time; The Real Glory. 1940 Three Faces West; Thou Shalt Not Kill; Remember the Night; Dr. Kildare's Strange Case; The Refugee; Streets of Memories; The Stranger on the Third Floor; Untamed. 1941 The Devil and Miss Jones; The Case of the Black Parrot; The Nurse's Secret; Three Sons O'Guns; Rise and Shine. 1942 Random Harvest; Through Different Eyes; The Gay Sisters. 1943 The Song of Bernadette; The Adventures of Mark Twain; Mlle. Fifi. 1944 Black Parachute. 1946 The Fighting Guardsman; The Big Sleep; Dragonwyck.

WALDRON, CHARLES K.
Born: 1915. Died: Apr. 18, 1952, Los Angeles, Calif. (airplane crash). Screen actor. Son of screen actor Charles D. Waldron (dec. 1946).

WALDRON, EDNA
Born: 1913. Died: Aug. 24, 1940, Hollywood, Calif. (burns sustained in an attempt to save the life of a child whose clothing was afire.). Screen actress.

WALDRON, ISABEL
Born: 1871. Died: Jan. 9, 1950, Mamaroneck, N.Y. Screen and stage actress. Married to stage actor Edward Emery (dec. 1938) and mother of screen actor John Emery (dec. 1964).

WALES, ETHEL
Born: 1881, New York, N.Y. Died: Feb. 15, 1952, Hollywood, Calif. Screen and stage actress. Entered films in 1920.

Appeared in: 1921 Miss Lulu Bett; After the Show. 1922 Nice People; The Old Homestead; Bobbed Hair; Is Matrimony a Failure?; The Bonded Woman; Bought and Paid For; Manslaughter; Our Leading Citizen. 1923 The Covered Wagon; The Marriage Maker; The Fog; Stepping Fast. 1924 The Bedroom Window; Revelation; The White Sin; Icebound; Lovers' Lane; Loving Lies; Merton of the Movies; Which Shall It Be? 1925 Go Straight; Shattered Lives; Steppin' Out; Beggar on Horseback; Don't Let Women Alone; The Overland Limited; When Husbands Flirt; The Wedding Song; Wandering Footsteps; The Monster. 1926 Bertha, the Sewing Machine Girl; Take It from Me; Made for Love; Ladies at Play. 1927 The Cradle Snatchers; The Country Doctor; Almost

Human; The Wreck of the Hesperus; Stage Kisses; The Satin Woman; The Girl in the Pullman; My Friend from India. 1928 Tenth Avenue; Craig's Wife; The Masks of the Devil; The Perfect Crime; Ladies' Night in a Turkish Bath; On to Reno; Taxi 13. 1929 Blue Skies; The Saturday Night Kid; The Doctor's Secret; The Donovan Affair. 1930 Loose Ankles; Tom Sawyer; Girl in the Show; The Dude Wrangler; Under Montana Skies. 1931 Subway Express; The Flood; Criminal Code; Honeymoon Lane; Maker of Men. 1932 The Fighting Fool; Love in High Gear; The 13th Guest; Love Me Tonight; Klondike; Tangled Destinies; The Racing Strain; A Man's Land. 1933 The 11th Commandment; The Fighting Parson. 1934 The Crime Doctor. 1935 Another Face; Bar 20 Rides Again. 1936 Collegiate. 1938 The Gladiator. 1939 In Old Caliente; Days of Jesse James. 1940 Knights of the Range; Hidden Gold; Young Bill Hickok. 1941 Border Vigilantes. 1944 The Lumberjack. 1950 Tarnished.

WALKER, CHARLOTTE
Born: 1878, Galveston, Tex. Died: Mar. 24, 1958, Kerville, Tex. Screen and stage actress.

Appeared in: 1915 Kindling. 1916 The Trail of the Lonesome Pine. 1917 Seven Deadly Sins (in one of the seven sequences). 1919 Eve in Exile. 1924 Classmates; The Lone Wolf; The Sixth Commandment. 1925 The Manicure Girl; The Midnight Girl. 1926 The Great Deception; The Savage. 1927 The Clown. 1928 Annapolis. 1929 South Sea Rose; Paris Bound. 1930 Scarlet Pages; Double Crossroads; Three Faces East; Lightnin'; 1931 Millie; Salvation Nell. 1933 Hotel Variety. 1941 Scattergood Meets Broadway.

WALKER, HELEN
Born: 1921, Worcester, Mass. Died: Mar. 10, 1968, North Hollywood, Calif. (cancer). Screen and stage actress.

Appeared in: 1942 Lucky Jordan. 1943 The Good Fellows. 1944 Abroad with Two Yanks; Man in Half-Moon Street. 1945 Duffy's Tavern; Murder, He Says. 1946 Brewster's Millions; Cluny Brown; Her Adventurous Night; Murder in the Music Hall; People Are Funny. 1947 Nightmare Alley; The Homestretch. 1948 Call Northside 777; My Dear Secretary; Nancy Goes to Rio. 1949 Impact. 1951 My True Story. 1952 Heaven Only Knows. 1953 Problem Girls. 1955 The Big Combo.

WALKER, JOHNNIE
Born: 1896, New York, N.Y. Died: Dec. 5, 1949, New York, N.Y. Screen, stage actor, film director, and stage and film producer.

Appeared in: 1920 Over the Hill to the Poor House. 1921 Live Wires; The Jolt; Play Square; What Love Will Do. 1922 In the Name of the Law; The Sagebrush Trail; Captain Fly-by-Night; Extra! Extra!; The Third Alarm; My Dad. 1923 Fashionable Fakers; Broken Hearts of Broadway; Children of Dust; Shattered Reputations; Red Lights; The Fourth Musketeer; Mary of the Movies; The Mailman; Souls for Sale. 1924 The Spirit of the U.S.A.; Soiled; The Slanderers; Girls Men Forget; Life's Greatest Game; Wine of Youth. 1925 The Scarlet West; Reckless Sex; Lilies of the Streets; Children of the Whirlwind; Lena Rivers; The Mad Dancer. 1926 Old Ironsides; So This Is Paris; Honesty—the Best Policy; The Earth Woman; Transcontinental Limited; Fangs of Justice; The Lightning Reporter; Morganson's Finish. 1927 Swell Head; A Boy of the Streets; Cross Breed; Pretty Clothes; The Princess on Broadway; Wolves of the Air; Rose of the Bowery; The Clown; Held by the Law; Snarl of Hate; Where the Trails Begin. 1928 Matinee Idol; So This Is Love; Bare Knees. 1930 The Melody Man; Ladies in Love; Up the River; Girl of the Golden West; Ladies of Leisure; Swellhead. 1931 Enemies of the Law. 1932 Speaking out of Turn (short). 1934 Fantomas.

WALKER, JUNE
Born: 1904, New York, N.Y. Died: Feb. 3, 1966, Sherman Oaks, Calif. Screen, stage, radio, and television actress.

Appeared in: 1921 Coincidence. 1930 War Nurse. 1942 Through Different Eyes. 1960 The Unforgiven. 1963 A Child Is Waiting.

WALKER, ROBERT (Robert Hudson Walker)
Born: Oct. 13, 1914, Utah. Died: Aug. 28, 1951, Santa Monica, Calif. (respiratory failure). Screen, stage, and radio actor. Divorced from screen actress Jennifer Jones and father of screen actor Robert Walker, Jr.

Appeared in: 1939 Winter Carnival. 1940 Pioneer Days. 1941 I'll Sell My Life. 1943 Bataan; Madame Curie. 1944 See Here, Private Hargrove; Since You Went Away; Thirty Seconds over Tokyo. 1945 The Clock; What Next, Corporal Hargrove?; Her

Highness and the Bellboy; The Sailor Takes a Wife. 1946 Blue
Skies; 'Til the Clouds Roll By. 1947 Song of Love; The Sea of
Grass; The Beginning or the End. 1948 One Touch of Venus.
1950 Please Believe Me; The Skipper Surprised His Wife. 1951
Strangers on a Train; Vengeance Valley. 1952 My Son John.

WALKER, ROSE (Rose Walker Dowsey)
Born: 1907. Died: July 29, 1951, Manhasset, N.Y.(injuries from
fall from building). Screen actress.

WALKER, SYD
Born: England. Died: Jan. 13, 1945, London, England. Screen,
stage, and radio actor.

Appeared in: 1934 Gift of Gab. 1936 a Universal short. 1937
Over She Goes; Let's Make a Night of It. 1938 Oh Boy. 1939 Hold
My Hand; What Would You Do, Chums?

WALKER, TEX (Charles Herbert Walker)
Born: 1867. Died: Aug. 22, 1947, Los Angeles, Calif.(pneumonia).
Screen and stage actor.

WALKER, VIRGINIA
Born: 1916. Died: Dec. 22, 1946, Hollywood, Calif. Screen
actress. Divorced from film producer Howard Hawks.

Appeared in: 1938 Bringing up Baby.

WALL, DAVID V.
Born: 1870. Died: June 1, 1938, New York, N.Y. Screen and
stage actor.

Appeared in: 1922 When the Desert Calls. 1924 Pied Piper
Malone.

WALL, GERALDINE
Born: 1913. Died: June 22, 1970, Woodland Hills, Calif.(pneumonia). Screen, stage, and television actress.

Appeared in: 1944 Winged Victory. 1945 Valley of Decision.
1946 Boys' Ranch. 1947 Love Laughs at Andy Hardy; Dark
Delusion; 1948 Scudda Hoo!, Scudda Hay!; Green Grass of
Wyoming; Beyond Glory. 1949 Alias Nick Beal; Everybody
Does It; The Green Promise. 1950 Mister 880; Thelma Jordon;
There's a Girl in My Heart. 1951 Appointment with Danger.
1953 By the Light of the Silvery Moon. 1956 The Man in the
Gray Flannel Suit. 1957 An Affair to Remember. 1958 This
Earth Is Mine; Mardi Gras. 1964 One Man's Way.

WALLACE, BERYL
Born: 1910. Died: June 17, 1948, near Mt. Carmel, Pa.(plane
crash). Screen actress. Divorced from screen actor Milton
Berle.

Appeared in: 1934 Murder at the Vanities. 1938 Air Devils.
1942 Sunset on the Desert. 1943 The Kansan. 1944 Enemy of
Women; The Woman of the Town.

WALLACE, BILL (William Lally)
Born: 1908. Died: Aug. 20, 1956, Hollywood, Calif.(heart attack).
Screen actor and film editor.

WALLACE, EDNA. See Edna Wallace Hopper

WALLACE, ETHEL LEE
Born: 1888, Springfield, Mo. Died: Sept. 7, 1956, Springfield,
Mo. Screen and stage actress. Appeared in silents.

WALLACE, GEORGE
Born: 1894, Aberdeen, New South Wales. Died: Nov. 1960,
Sydney, Australia. Screen, stage, vaudeville, television actor,
song writer, screenwriter, and playwright. Billed with Dinks
Paterson in a vaudeville act known as "Dinks and Onkus."

Appeared in: 1932 His Royal Highness. 1933 Harmony Row. 1934
A Ticket in Tatts. 1938 Let George Do It. 1939 Gone to the Dogs.
1952 Japanese War Bride; Radar Men from the Moon. 1953 Vigilante Terror; The Homesteaders; Kansas City Confidential; The
Star of Texas; Wherever She Goes. 1954 Border River; Drums
across the River; The Human Jungle. 1955 Destry; Soldier of
Fortune. 1956 Forbidden Planet. 1962 Six Black Horses.

WALLACE, INEZ
Died: June 28, 1966, Cleveland, Ohio. Screen, stage actress, and
screenwriter. Appeared in silents.

WALLACE, MAUDE
Born: 1894. Died: Apr. 23, 1952, Hollywood, Calif. Screen,
vaudeville, and television actress. Entered films approx. 1947.

Billed in vaudeville with her sister, Myrtle, as the "Hollingsworth Twins" and later billed as part of the "Towers and Wallace" vaudeville team.

Appeared in: 1951 Elopement; Love Nest; People Will Talk. 1952
Scarlet Angel; We're Not Married; Stars and Stripes Forever.

WALLACE, MAY (May Maddox)
Born: 1877. Died: Dec. 11, 1938, Los Angeles, Calif.(heart
disease). Screen and vaudeville actress.

Appeared in: 1921 The Cup of Life; My Lady Friends. 1923 Dol-
lar Devils; Gimme. 1924 The Reckless Age; Oh, You Tony! 1929
Painted Faces. 1932 County Hospital (short). 1933 What's Your
Racket? 1936 The Sky Parade. 1937 Midnight Madonna.

WALLACE, MILTON
Born: 1888. Died: Feb. 16, 1956, Hollywood, Calif. Screen,
stage, and vaudeville actor.

Appeared in: 1934 Kiss and Make Up. 1944 None but the Lonely
Heart; Seven Doors to Death. 1945 The Lost Weekend. 1947 Kiss
of Death.

WALLACE, MORGAN
Born: July 26, 1888, Lompoc, Calif. Died: Dec. 12, 1953,
Tarzana, Calif. Screen, stage actor, film, stage producer, and
playwright.

Appeared in: 1921 Dream Street (film debut). 1922 Orphans of
the Storm; One Exciting Night. 1923 The Dangerous Maid; The
Fighting Blade. 1924 Daring Love; Reckless Romance; Sandra;
Torment; A Woman Who Sinned. 1930 Sisters; Up the River;
Big Money. 1931 It Pays to Advertise; Safe in Hell; Alexander
Hamilton; Women Go on Forever; Smart Money; The Unholy
Garden; Expensive Women. 1932 Hell's House; Grand Hotel;
Lady and Gent; Blonde Venus; Wild Girl; Steady Company; Fast
Companions; The Final Edition; The Mouthpiece. 1933 Smoke
Lightning; Song of Songs; Terror Abroad; Jennie Gerhardt;
Mama Loves Papa; Above the Clouds. 1934 The Trumpet Blows;
It's a Gift; Cheating Cheaters; Many Happy Returns; The Merry
Widow; We Live Again; I Believed in You. 1935 Murder on a
Honeymoon; The Devil Is a Woman; Dante's Inferno; Headline
Woman; Confidential; Thunder Mountain; $1,000 a Minute. 1936
Mister Cinderella; Love on a Bet; Sutter's Gold; Human Cargo;
Fury. 1937 Charlie Chan at the Olympics; The Californian; Under
Suspicion; House of Secrets. 1938 Numbered Woman; Gang Bul-
lets; The Lady in the Morgue; Mr. Moto Takes a Vacation;
Woman against Woman; Billy the Kid Returns. 1939 The Mystery
of Mr. Wong; The Star Maker. 1940 I Love You Again; Three
Men from Texas; Ellery Queen, Master Detective. 1941 Scatter-
good Meets Broadway. 1945 I'll Remember April; Song of the
Sarong; Dick Tracy. 1946 The Falcon's Alibi.

WALLEN, SIGURD
Born: 1884, Sweden. Died: Mar. 20, 1947, Stockholm, Sweden.
Screen, stage actor, and film director.

Appeared in: 1931 Brokiga Blad. 1932 Roeda Dagen. 1934 Pat-
tersson and Bendel. 1938 Karl Fredrik Reigns; John Ericsson
Victor of Hampton Roads. 1939 Familjen Andersson (The Anderson Family); Med Folket Foer Fosterlandet; Du Gamla, Du
Fria (Thou Old, Thou Free). 1945 Crime and Punishment (U.S.
1948).

WALLER, THOMAS "FATS"
Born: 1904, New York, N.Y. Died: Dec. 15, 1943, Kansas City,
Mo.(pneumonia). Negro pianist, screen, radio, vaudeville actor,
bandleader, and song writer.

Appeared in: 1935 Hooray for Love. 1936 King of Burlesque.
1943 Stormy Weather.

WALLING, EFFIE B.
Born: 1879. Died: June 9, 1961, Berkeley, Calif. Screen and
stage actress. Entered films with DeMille in 1919.

WALLS, TOM
Born: Feb. 18, 1883, Northampton, England. Died: Nov. 27, 1949,
Edwell, England. Screen, stage actor, stage producer, and film
director.

Appeared in: 1929 Rookery Nook (U.S. 1931). 1930 A Night Like
This; On Approval; Plunder. 1931 Canaries Sometimes Sing.
1932 Leap Year; Thark. 1933 The Blarney Stone. 1934 Turkey
Time; Just Smith; A Cuckoo in the Nest. 1935 Fighting Stock;
Me and Marlborough; Stormy Weather; Foreign Affairs. 1937
Dishonour Bright. 1938 The Man with 100 Faces; Strange
Boarders; Second Best Man (aka Second Best Bed); Crackerjack;

Old Iron. 1943 The Halfway House (U.S. 1945). 1945 They Met in the Dark; Johnny Frenchman. 1947 A Lady Surrenders. 1948 Master of Bankdam. 1949 Spring in Park Lane; The Interrupted Journey. 1952 Maytime in Mayfair.

WALLY, GUS (Gustav Wallenberg)
Born: 1904, Stockholm, Sweden. Died: Mar. 3, 1966, Goquete, Panama. Screen, stage actor, and stage producer. Entered films with Paramount in 1936.

WALPOLE, HUGH
Born: 1884, Auckland, New Zealand. Died: June 1, 1941, Brackenburn, England (heart attack). Novelist, screen actor, and screenwriter.

Appeared in: 1935 David Copperfield.

WALSH, BILLY
Died: June 16, 1952, Brooklyn, N.Y. Screen, vaudeville, and radio actor. Signed with Sennett in 1915 and made Keystone comedies. Appeared in vaudeville as part of acts known as "Walsh, Reed and Walsh," "Walsh, Daly and Walsh," and "Walsh Bros."

WALSH, THOMAS H.
Born: 1863. Died: Apr. 25, 1925, N.Y. Screen, stage, and circus actor.

Appeared in: 1914 The Trey O'Hearts (serial).

WALTERS, JACK
Born: 1885, Kan. Died: Jan. 1944, Hollywood, Calif. Screen actor. Entered films in 1913.

Appeared in: 1919 Roped; Ace of the Saddle. 1920 Hitchin' Posts. 1921 A Daughter of the Law; Sure Fire. 1922 Headin' North; The Better Man Wins; Caught Bluffing; The Galloping Kid. 1923 McGuire of the Mounted. 1924 Hoodman Blind. 1928 Wild West Romance.

WALTERS, LAURA
Born: 1894. Died: Apr. 10, 1934, Toledo, Ohio. Screen and stage actress.

WALTERS, PATRICIA W.
Died: Dec. 31, 1967, Long Beach, Calif. Screen and stage actress. Daughter of actor Bert Wheeler (dec. 1968).

Appeared in: 1951 The River.

WALTHALL, HENRY B.
Born: Mar. 16, 1878, Shelby City, Ala. Died: June 17, 1936, near Monrovia, Calif.(chronic illness). Screen and stage actor. Married to stage actress Mary Charleston Walthall.

Appeared in: 1909 In Old Kentucky; A Convict's Sacrifice; The Sealed Room; 1776, or the Hessian Renegades; Pippa Passes; Leather Stocking; Fools of Fate; A Corner in Wheat; In Little Italy; The Call; The Honor of His Family; On the Reef; The Cloister's Touch. 1910 In Old California; The House with Closed Shutters; Ramona; His Last Burglary; The Converts; Gold Is Not All; The Gold Seekers; Thou Shalt Not; The Face at the Window; The Usurer; The Sorrows of the Unfaithful; In Life's Cycle; A Summer Idyll. 1912 The Inner Circle; Oil and Water; A Change of Spirit; Friends; A Feud in the Kentucky Hills; In the Aisles of the Wild; The One She Loved; My Baby; The Informer; The Burglar's Dilemma; The God Within. 1913 Judith of Bethulia; Love in an Apartment Hotel; Broken Ways; Her Mother's Oath; The Sheriff's Baby; The Little Tease; The Wanderer; Death's Marathon; The Battle of Elderberry Gulch; During the Round-Up. 1914 The Avenging Conscience; Home Sweet Home. 1915 Birth of a Nation; The Raven; Ghosts; Great Divide. 1916 The Sting of Victory; The Strange Case of Mary Page. 1918 Robe of Honor; Great Love. 1919 The False Faces. 1921 Splendid Hazard; Parted Curtains. 1922 The Able Minded Lady; One Clear Call; The Kick Back; The Long Chance; The Marriage Chance; Flowers of the North. 1923 Gimme; Boy of Mine; Face on the Barroom Floor; The Unknown Purple. 1924 Single Wives; The Bowery Bishop; The Woman on the Jury. 1925 The Scarlet Letter; The Golden Bed; Simon the Jester. 1926 Road to Mandalay; The Barrier; Everybody's Acting; The Ice Flood; Three Faces East; The Unknown Soldier; The Plastic Age. 1927 Wings; Fighting Love; London after Midnight. 1928 Love Me and the World Is Mine; Freedom of the Press; Man From Headquarters; Retribution (short). 1929 In Old California (and 1910 version); Speakeasy; The Bridge of San Luis Rey; Blaze O'Glory; Stark Mad; Phantom in the House; Black Magic; The River of Romance; The Jazz Age; Street Corners; The

Trespasser. 1930 Abraham Lincoln; The Payoff (short); Temple Tower; Love Trader; Tol'able David. 1931 Is There Justice?; Anybody's Blonde. 1932 Hotel Continental; Police Court; Strange Interlude; Alias Mary Smith; Chandu the Magician; Klondike; Cabin in the Cotton; Central Park; Me and My Gal; Fame Street; Ride Him, Cowboy. 1933 The Sin of Nora Moran; 42nd Street; Laughing at Life; Whispering Shadow (serial); Self Defense; Flaming Signal; Somewhere in Sonora; Headline Shooter; Her Forgotten Past. 1934 Men in White; Judge Priest; Viva, Villa!; Change of Heart; Dark Hazard; Beggars in Ermine; Operator 13; Murder in the Museum; A Girl of the Limberlost; The Lemon Drop Kid; Love Time; City Park; Bachelor of Arts. 1935 A Tale of Two Cities; Dante's Inferno; Helldorado. 1936 China Clipper; The Mine with the Iron Door; Hearts in Bondage; The Last Out-Law; The Devil-Doll; The Garden Murder Case.

WALTON, DOUGLAS (J. Douglas Duder)
Born: Woodstock, Toronto, Canada. Died: Nov. 15, 1961, N.Y. Screen and stage actor.

Appeared in: 1931 Over the Hill; Body and Soul. 1933 The Secret of Madame Blanche; Looking Forward; Cavalcade. 1934 The Lost Patrol; Madame Spy; Murder in Trinidad; Shock; The Count of Monte Cristo; Charlie Chan in London. 1935 Captain Hurricane; The Dark Angel; Hitchhike Lady; The Bride of Frankenstein. 1936 The Garden Murder Case; I Conquer the Sea; Mary of Scotland; Thank You, Jeeves; Camille. 1937 Damaged Goods; Wallaby Jim of the Islands; Flight from Glory; A Nation Aflame. 1938 Storm over Bengal. 1939 The Story of Vernon and Irene Castle; The Sun Never Sets; Bad Lands. 1940 Raffles; Northwest Passage; The Long Voyage Home; Too Many Girls. 1941 Singapore Woman; Hurry, Charlie, Hurry! 1942 Jesse James, Jr. 1944 Murder My Sweet. 1945 Bring on the Girls; The Picture of Dorian Gray. 1946 Kitty; Dick Tracy vs. Cueball. 1947 High Conquest; High Tide. 1949 Secret of St. Ives.

WALTON, FRED (Frederick Heming)
Born: 1865, England. Died: Dec. 28, 1936, Los Angeles, Calif. (pneumonia). Screen and stage actor. Entered films in 1924.

Appeared in: 1924 The Fast Set. 1925 New Brooms; She Wolves; Marriage in Transit. 1926 The City; 30 Below Zero; The Splendid Crime. 1927 The Wise Wife; Almost Human; His Dog; The Little Adventuress. 1928 The House of Shame. 1929 Below the Deadline; South of Panama; Circumstantial Evidence; Dynamite. 1930 The Last Dance; Sin Takes a Holiday. 1931 Kiki; The Big Gamble. 1935 Two Sinners. 1936 Little Lord Fauntleroy; The House of a Thousand Candles; Dracula's Daughter.

WALTON, VERA
Born: 1891. Died: Sept. 1, 1965, New York, N.Y.(auto accident). Screen, stage, vaudeville, and television actress. Appeared in a song and dance act in vaudeville billed as "Now and Then."

Appeared in: 1957 A Face in the Crowd. 1960 Butterfield 8.

WAN, MME. SUL TE (Nellie Conley)
Born: 1873. Died: Feb. 1, 1959, Hollywood, Calif. Negro screen actress. Entered films in 1914 with Griffith.

Appeared in: 1958 The Buccaneer.

WANGEL, HEDWIG
Born: 1875, Berlin, Germany. Died: Mar. 12, 1961, Rendsburg, West Germany. Screen and stage actress.

Appeared in: 1929 Rasputin. 1932 Pension Schoeller.

WANZER, ARTHUR
Died: Jan. 1949, Hollywood, Calif. Screen and vaudeville actor. Appeared in vaudeville as part of "Arthur Wanzer and Maybelle Palmer" team.

Appeared in: 1930 Dance with Me. 1933 Soldiers of the Storm; Unknown Valley. 1934 Tomorrow's Children. 1936 The Gentleman from Louisiana.

WARAM, PERCY, C.
Born: 1881, Kent, England. Died: Oct. 5, 1961, Huntington, N.Y. Screen, stage, and vaudeville actor.

Appeared in: 1939 One Third of a Nation. 1944 Ministry of Fear. 1947 It Had to Be You; The Late George Apley. 1950 The Big Hangover. 1957 A Face in the Crowd.

WARD, BEATRICE
Born: 1890. Died: Dec. 11, 1964, Hollywood, Calif. Screen actress. Entered films during silents.

WARD, CARRIE (Carrie Clarke-Ward)
Born: 1862, Virginia City, Nev. Died: Feb. 6, 1926, Hollywood,
Calif. Screen and stage actress.

Appeared in: 1919 Why Smith Left Home. 1920 Old Lady 31.
1921 One Wild Week; Sham; Black Roses; Her Winning Way;
Bob Hampton of Placer; The Love Charm. 1922 Ashes; The
Top of New York; Penrod; Through a Glass Window. 1923
Breaking into Society; Soul of the Beast; Scaramouche. 1924
Girls Men Forget; Thundering Hoofs; His Hour. 1925 The Awful
Truth; The Eagle; A Fool and His Money; The Man in Blue; Who
Cares; Rose of the World; The Only Thing. 1926 The Golden
Cocoon.

WARD, FANNIE
Born: 1872, St. Louis, Mo. Died: Jan. 27, 1952, New York,
N.Y.(cerebral hemorrhage). Screen, stage, and vaudeville ac-
tress. Appeared in Lasky Co. productions in 1915.

Appeared in: 1915 The Cheat. 1916 Each Hour a Pearl; Ten-
nessee's Pardner. 1917 The School for Husbands. 1918 The
Yellow Ticket. 1919 Our Better Selves; Common Clay. 1921
She Played and Paid. 1922 The Hardest Way. 1929 The Miracle
Woman (short).

WARD, "HAP", SR. (John Thomas O'Donnell)
Born: 1868. Died: Jan. 3, 1944, N.Y. Screen, stage, and vaudeville
actor. Father of screen actor Hap Ward, Jr.(dec. 1940). Was
half of vaudeville act billed as "Earl and Ward" (even though
his name was O'Donnell, he took name of the original team
partner, Ward, whom he replaced in the act). He later teamed
with Harry Vokes in a blackface act billed as "Harold and
Percy."

Appeared in: 1929 Fugitives.

WARD, "HAP", JR. (John Thomas O'Donnell)
Born: 1899. Died: July 9, 1940. Screen actor. Son of screen
actor "Hap" Ward, Sr.(dec. 1944).

WARD, HARRY (Angelo De Michele)
Born: 1890. Died: Apr. 16, 1952, Los Angeles, Calif. Screen actor.
Appeared in vaudeville with brother Anthony in an act known
as "Ward and Van."

WARD, KATHERINE CLARE
Born: 1871. Died: Oct. 14, 1938, Hollywood, Calif. Screen,
stage, and vaudeville actress. Entered films approx. 1923.

Appeared in: 1927 The Magic Garden. 1928 Beyond London
Lights. 1929 Drag; The Isle of Lost Ships; Midnight Daddies.
1930 Call of the West; Strictly Modern. 1931 The Conquering
Horde; Three Girls Lost. 1932 Three Wise Girls; Make Me a
Star; Vanity Street. 1933 Lilly Turner; Son of Kong. 1934
Once to Every Woman; White Lies; an RKO short; an MGM
short.

WARD, LUCILLE
Born: 1880. Died: Aug. 8, 1952, Dayton, Ohio. Screen and stage
actress.

Appeared in: 1921 High Gear Jeffrey; The Traveling Salesman.
1922 The Woman He Loved. 1923 East Side, West Side; Sixty
Cents an Hour. 1924 The Girl in the Limousine; Sporting Youth.
1925 Oh, Doctor!; His Majesty, Bunker Bean; California Straight
Ahead; A Woman of the World. 1926 Skinner's Dress Suit. 1930
What a Man. 1932 The Purchase Price; Rebecca of Sunnybrook
Farm. 1933 Zoo in Budapest; Marriage on Approval; Lilly Turner.
1934 Little Miss Marker. 1936 The Leavenworth Case; The Return
of Jimmy Valentine; The Harvester. 1938 Mother Carey's Chickens; Sons of the Legion. 1939 First Love. 1940 Christmas in July.

WARD, PEGGY
Born: 1878. Died: Mar. 8, 1960, Hollywood, Calif. Screen,
stage, and television actress.

WARD, SAM (George Herman Jacobs)
Born: 1889. Died: May 1, 1952, Los Angeles, Calif. Screen,
stage, burlesque, and vaudeville actor. Appeared in Hal Roach
comedies.

WARD, SOLLY
Born: 1891. Died: May 17, 1942, Hollywood, Calif. Screen,
stage, burlesque, and radio actor.

Appeared in: 1927 At the Party (short). 1932-33 Paramount
shorts. 1937 Flight from Glory; Living on Love; Danger Patrol;
She's Got Everything. 1938 Everybody's Doing It; Maid's Night
Out; Blind Alibi. 1939 Conspiracy.

WARD, VICTORIA
Born: 1914, Canada. Died: Nov. 6, 1957, Hollywood, Calif.
Screen, stage, and television actress.

Appeared in: 1956 D Day, the Sixth of June.

WARDE, ERNEST C.
Born: 1874, Liverpool, England. Died: Sept. 9, 1923, Los Angeles, Calif. Screen, stage actor, and stage director.

Appeared in: 1923 Ruth of the Range (serial); Blow Your Own
Horn.

WARDE, FREDERICK B.
Born: 1872, England. Died: Feb. 7, 1935, Brooklyn, N.Y.(heart
trouble). Screen and stage actor.

Appeared in: 1913 Richard III. 1916 King Lear. 1917 Vicar of
Wakefield; Under False Colors. 1921 Silas Marner. 1925 A Lover's Oath.

WARDELL, HARRY
Born: 1879. Died: Sept. 17, 1948, Hollywood, Calif.(heart attack).
Screen, vaudeville actor, and screenwriter. Originated phrases
like: "Life is just a bowl of cherries" and "I'm the matzo ball
in the soup of life."

WARE, HELEN
Born: 1877, San Francisco, Calif. Died: Jan. 25, 1939, Carmel,
Calif.(throat infection). Screen and stage actress. Married to
screen actor/writer/artist Frederic Burt (dec. 1943).

Appeared in: 1917 The Garden of Allah. 1920 The Deep Purple.
1921 Colorado Pluck. 1922 Fascination. 1923 Mark of the Beast.
1925 Soul Fire. 1928 Napoleon's Barber. 1929 Half Way to
Heaven; The Virginian; New Year's Eve; Speakeasy. 1930
Slightly Scarlet; One Night at Susie's; Abraham Lincoln; She's
My Weakness; Tol'able David. 1931 I Take This Woman; The
Reckless Hour. 1932 Night of June 13th. 1933 Ladies They
Talk About; Girl Missing; The Keyhole; She Had to Say Yes;
Warrior's Husband. 1934 Sadie McKee; That's Gratitude;
Flaming Gold; Romance in Manhattan. 1935 The Raven; Secret
of the Chateau.

WARE, WALTER
Born: 1880, Boston, Mass. Died: Jan. 3, 1936, Hollywood, Calif.
Screen and stage actor.

Appeared in: 1921 The Family Closet. 1935 Captain Blood;
Kind Lady.

WARING, MARY
Born: 1892. Died: Jan. 10, 1964, Washington, D.C. Screen and
radio actress. Appeared in films from 1920-24.

WARNER, GLORIA (Gloria Kelly)
Born: 1915, N.Y. Died: June 8, 1934, Los Angeles, Calif.(anemia).
Screen, stage actress, and dancer.

Appeared in: School for Romance (short).

WARNER, H. B. (Henry Byran W. Lickford)
Born: Oct. 26, 1876, St. John's Woods, London, England.
Died: Dec. 24, 1958, Los Angeles, Calif. Screen and stage actor.

Appeared in: 1916 The Beggar of Cawnpore; The Vagabond
Prince; The Raiders; The Market of Vain Desire. 1917 The
Danger Trail. 1919 The Man Who Turned White. 1920 One Hour
before Dawn. 1921 Below the Deadline; Dice of Destiny; Felix
O'Day; When We Were Twenty-One. 1923 Zaza. 1924 Is Love
Everything? 1926 The Temptress; Silence; Whispering Smith.
1927 French Dressing; King of Kings; Sorrell and Son. 1928
The Naughty Duchess; Man-Made Women; Romance of a Rogue.
1929 The Divine Lady; Conquest; The Argyle Case; The Doctor's
Secret; The Gamblers; Stark Mad; The Trial of Mary Dugan;
The Show of Shows; Tiger Rose. 1930 The Furies; Wild Company;
The Green Goddess; The Second Floor Mystery; On Your Back;
Wedding Rings; The Princess and the Plumber; Liliom. 1931
Five Star Final; A Woman of Experience; The Reckless Hour;
Expensive Women. 1932 Tom Brown of Culver; The Son-Daugh-
ter; The Menace; The Crusader; Cross Examination; Charlie
Chan's Chance; Unholy Love; A Woman Commands; The Phantom
of Crestwood. 1933 Christopher Bean; Jennie Gerhardt; Super-
natural; Justice Takes a Holiday. 1934 Grand Canary; In Old
Santa Fe; Sorrell and Son (and 1927 version). 1935 Behold My
Wife; Born to Gamble; A Tale of Two Cities. 1936 The Garden
Murder Case; Mr. Deeds Goes to Town; Moonlight Murder; Rose
of the Rancho; The Blackmailer; Along Came Love. 1937 The
Lost Horizon; Our Fighting Navy; Victoria the Great. 1938

Army Girl; Bulldog Drummond in Africa; The Adventures of Marco Polo; The Girl of the Golden West; The Toy Wife; You Can't Take It with You; Kidnapped. 1939 The Rains Came; Arrest Bulldog Drummond; Let Freedom Ring; Bulldog Drummond's Secret Police; Bulldog Drummond's Bride; The Gracie Allen Murder Case; Nurse Edith Cavell; Mr. Smith Goes to Washington. 1940 New Moon. 1941 The Corsican Brothers; Topper Returns; City of Missing Girls; Here Is a Man; Ellery Queen and the Perfect Crime; South of Tahiti; All That Money Can Buy. 1942 A Yank in Libya; Boss of Big Town; Crossroads. 1943 Hitler's Children; Women in Bondage; Queen Victoria. 1944 Action in Arabia; Enemy of Women; Faces in the Fog. 1945 Captain Tugboat Annie; Rogues' Gallery. 1946 Gentleman Joe Palooka; It's a Wonderful Life; Strange Impersonation. 1947 Driftwood; Bulldog Drummond Strikes Back. 1948 High Wall; Prince of Thieves. 1949 El Paso; Hellfire; The Judge Steps Out. 1950 Sunset Boulevard. 1951 The First Legion; Journey into Light; Here Comes the Groom; Savage Drums. 1952 The Devil and Daniel Webster (reissue and retitle of All That Money Can Buy-1941). 1956 The Ten Commandments. 1958 Darby's Rangers.

WARNOW, HELEN
Born: 1926. Died: Dec. 25, 1970, New York, N.Y. Screen and television actress.

WARREN, E. ALYN
Born: 1875. Died: Jan. 22, 1940, Los Angeles, Calif. Screen and stage actor.

Appeared in: 1921 The Millionaire; No Woman Knows; A Tale of Two Worlds; Outside the Law. 1922 East is West; The Truthful Liar; Hungry Hearts. 1923 The Courtship of Myles Standish. 1926 Sweet Rosie O'Grady; Born to the West. 1927 The Opening Night. 1928 The Trail of '98. 1929 Chasing through Europe; Red Wine. 1930 Prince of Diamonds; The Medicine Man; Abraham Lincoln; Son of the Gods; Du Barry, Woman of Passion. 1931 Fighting Caravans; Shipmates; A Free Soul; Daughter of the Dragon; Secret Service; The Hatchet Man. 1933 Tarzan the Fearless. 1934 Limehouse Blues. 1935 Chinatown Squad. 1936 The Devil Doll. 1937 They Won't Forget. 1938 Port of Seven Seas.

WARREN, C. DENIER
Born: July 29, 1889, Chicago, Ill. Died: Aug. 27, 1971, Torquay, England. Screen, stage, vaudeville, radio actor, and screenwriter.

Appeared in: 1933 Counsel's Opinion. 1934 The Great Defender; Kentucky Minstrels. 1935 The Clairvoyant; Heart's Desire; A Fire Has Been Arranged. 1936 A Star Fell from Heaven; Spy of Napoleon; Everybody Dance. 1937 Cotton Queen. 1938 Break the News; Strange Boarders; It's in the Air. 1939 Trouble Brewing. 1940 Lost on the Western Front. 1944 Kiss the Bride Goodbye. 1951 Old Mother Riley, Headmistress. 1952 Old Mother Riley. 1960 Bluebeard's Ten Honeymoons. 1961 The Secret of Monte Cristo. 1962 Lolita.

WARREN, EDWARD
Died: Apr.3, 1930, Los Angeles, Calif. Screen and stage actor.

Appeared in: 1916 The Little Orphan. 1926 The Belle of Broadway.

WARREN, ELIZA (Eliza Warren Sutton)
Born: 1865. Died: Jan. 20, 1935, Cleveland, Ohio. Screen and stage actress. Entered films with Griffith in 1906.

WARRENDER, HAROLD
Born: Nov. 15, 1903, London, England. Died: May 6, 1953, Gerrands Cross, England. Screen, stage, and radio actor.

Appeared in: 1928 Day Dreams (U.S. 1930-film debut). 1933 I Spy; Catherine the Great; Friday the 13th. 1935 Mimi; Invitation to the Waltz. 1940 Contraband; Convoy; Sailors Three. 1942 Jig Saw. 1949 A Warning to Wantons; Scott of the Antarctic (U.S. 1951). 1950 Conspirator. 1951 Pandora and the Flying Dutchman; The Six Men. 1952 The Ivory Hunter. 1953 Ivanhoe; Terror on a Train. 1954 Intimate Relations (aka Les Parents Terrible). Other British film: Under the Frozen Falls.

WARRENTON, LULE
Born: 1863. Died: May 14, 1932, Laguna Beach, Calif.(operation complications). Screen, stage actress, and film director.

Appeared in: 1920 The Sin That Was His. 1921 Blind Hearts; The Dangerous Moment; Ladies Must Live; The Jolt. 1922 Calvert's Valley; Strength of the Pines; Shirley of the Circus.

WARWICK, ROBERT (Robert Taylor Bien)
Born: Oct. 9, 1878, Sacramento, Calif. Died: June 4, 1964, Los Angeles, Calif. Screen, stage, and television actor. Married to screen actress Stella Lattimore (dec. 1960) and divorced from screen actress Josephine Whittell (dec. 1961).

Appeared in: 1915 The Face in the Moonlight. 1916 Human Driftwood. 1917 The Mad Lover. 1918 The Slient Master. 1919 In Mizzoura; Told in the Hills; Secret Service. 1920 Hunting Trouble; Thou Art the Man; Fourteenth Man. 1924 The Spitfire. 1929 Unmasked. 1931 A Holy Terror; The Royal Bed; Not Exactly Gentlemen; Three Rogues. 1932 So Big; The Dark Horse; The Woman from Monte Carlo; Dr. X.; The Rich Are Always with Us; Unashamed; I Am a Fugitive from a Chain Gang; Silver Dollar; The Girl from Calgary; Afraid to Talk; Secrets of Wu Sin. 1933 Pilgrimage; Charlie Chan's Greatest Case; Frisco Jenny; Ladies They Talk About; Female. 1934 The Dragon Murder Case; Jimmy the Gent; Cleopatra; School for Girls. 1935 Night Life of the Gods; A Shot in the Dark; The Murder Man; A Tale of Two Cities; Whipsaw; Hopalong Cassidy. 1936 Tough Guy; The Return of Jimmy Valentine; Bulldog Edition; The Bold Caballero; Sutter's Gold; The Bride Walks Out; Mary of Scotland; Romeo and Juliet; In His Steps; The White Legion; Adventure in Manhattan; Can This Be Dixie; an MGM short; Timber War. 1937 The Prince and the Pauper; The Life of Emile Zola; Let Them Live; The Road Back; The Awful Truth; Counsel for Crime; Conquest; Trigger Trio. 1938 The Spy Ring; Going Places; The Adventures of Robin Hood; Gangster's Boy; Blockade; Army Girl; Law of the Plains; Come on Leathernecks!; Squadron of Honor. 1939 Devil's Island; Almost a Gentleman; Juarez; The Private Lives of Elizabeth and Essex; The Magnificent Fraud; In Old Monterey. 1940 On the Spot; New Moon; Konga, the Wild Stallion; The Sea Hawk; Murder in the Air. 1941 A Woman's Face; I Was a Prisoner on Devil's Island; Louisiana Purchase; Sullivan's Travels; Spare a Copper. 1942 The Palm Beach Story; Tennessee Johnson; Secret Enemies; Cadets on Parade; Eagle Squadron; I Married a Witch. 1943 Two Tickets to London; Petticoat Larceny; Deerslayer; Dixie. 1944 Man from Frisco; The Princess and the Pirate; Bowery to Broadway; Kismit; Secret Command. 1945 Sudan. 1946 Criminal Court; The Falcon's Adventure. 1947 Gentleman's Agreement; Pirates of Monterey. 1948 Adventures of Don Juan; Fury at Furnace Creek; Million Dollar Weekend; Gun Smugglers. 1949 A Woman's Secret; Impact; Francis. 1950 In a Lonely Place; Tarzan and the Slave Girl; Vendetta. 1951 Sugarfoot; Mark of the Renegade; The Sword of Monte Cristo. 1953 Salome; Mississippi Gambler; Jamaica Run. 1954 Silver Lode; Passion. 1955 Chief Crazy Horse; Lady Godiva; Escape to Burma. 1956 Walk the Proud Land; While the City Sleeps. 1957 Shoot-Out at Medicine Bend. 1958 The Buccaneer. 1959 It Started with a Kiss; Night of the Quarter Moon.

WARWICK, STELLA LATTIMORE
Born: 1905. Died: Dec. 1, 1960, Hollywood, Calif. Screen actress. Married to screen actor Robert Warwick (dec. 1964).

WASHBURN, ALICE
Born: 1861. Died: Nov. 29, 1929, Ohskosh, Wisc. Screen actress. Appeared in Edison Co. films in 1912 and made one-reel comedies from 1912 to 1914. Among these was: 1914 On the Lazy Line.

WASHBURN, BRYANT
Born: Apr. 28, 1889, Chicago, Ill. Died: Apr. 30, 1963, Hollywood, Calif.(heart attack). Screen, stage actor, and film producer. Father of screen actor Bryant Washburn, Jr.

Appeared in: 1914 The Promised Land. 1915 The Blindness of Virtue. 1916 The Havoc; The Price of Graustark; Marriage a la Carte. 1917 The Fibbers; Skinner's Dress Suit; Skinner's Baby; Skinner's Bubble; The Golden Idiot. 1918 'Til I Come Back to You; Twenty-One; Kidder and Ko; Ghost of the Rancho; The Gypsy Trail; Venus in the East. 1919 It Pays to Advertise; Way of a Man with a Maid; Why Smith Left Home; Putting It Over; Poor Boob; Very Good Young Man; Something to Do; All Wrong; Love Insurance. 1920 The Six Best Cellars; Too Much Johnson; What Happened to Jones?; Mrs. Temple's Telegram; Sins of St. Anthony; Full House. 1921 An Amateur Devil; Burglar Proof; The Road to London. 1922 Night Life in Hollywood; Hungry Hearts; June Madness; The Woman Conquers; White Shoulders. 1923 Mine to Keep; Rupert of Hentzau; The Common Law; Hollywood; The Love Trap; The Meanest Man in the World; Mary of the Movies; Other Men's Daughters; Temptation. 1924 My Husband's Wives; Try and Get It; The Star Dust Trail. 1925 The Parasite; Passionate Youth; The Wizard of Oz; Wandering Footsteps. 1926 Flames; The Sky Pirate; Young April; Meet the Prince; That Girl Oklahoma; Wet Paint; Sitting Bull at Spirit Lake Massacre. 1927

Her Sacrifice; Breakfast at Sunrise; Beware of Widows; The Love Thrill; Black Tears; In the First Degree; King of Kings; Modern Daughters; Sky Pirates. 1928 Honeymoon Flats; Nothing to Wear; Skinner's Big Idea; A Bit of Heaven; The Chorus Kid; Jazzland; Undressed. 1930 Christmas Knight (short); Niagara Falls (short); Swing High. 1931 Liberty; Kept Husbands; Mystery Train. 1932 The Reckoning; Arm of the Law; Drifting Souls; Exposure; Forbidden Company; Parisian Romance; Thrill of Youth; What Price Hollywood? 1933 What Price Innocence?; Night of Terror; Devil's Mate. 1934 The Curtain Falls; Back Page; The Woman Who Dared; When Strangers Meet; Public Stenographer; The Return of Chandu. 1935 $20 a Week; Swell Head; Danger Ahead; The Throwback; The World Accuses. 1936 The Millionaire Kid; Bridge of Sighs; Gambling with Souls; Preview Murder Mystery; Hollywood Boulevard; Sutter's Gold; Conflict; Three of a Kind; It Couldn't Have Happened; We Who Are about to Die; Jungle Jim (serial). 1937 Sea Racketeers; The Westland Case; Million Dollar Racket. 1938 I Demand Payment. 1939 Stagecoach; Ambush; Sky Patrol. 1941 Paper Bullets; Gangs, Incorporated. 1942 The Yukon Patrol; Sin Town; War Dogs. 1943 Shadows on the Sage; You Can't Beat the Law; The Law Rides Again; Carson City Cyclone; The Girl from Monterey. 1944 The Falcon in Mexico; Nabonga. 1945 Two O'Clock Courage; West of the Pecos. 1947 Sweet Genevieve. 1968 The Further Perils of Laurel and Hardy (documentary).

WATERMAN, IDA (Ida Shaw Francoeur)
Born: 1852. Died: May 22, 1941, Cincinnati, Ohio. Screen and stage actress.

Appeared in: 1920 Lady Rose's Daughter. 1921 Her Lord and Master; Love's Redemption; The Inner Chamber; The Lotus Eater. 1922 Notoriety. 1924 A Society Scandal; The Enchanted Cottage. 1925 The Swan; That Royle Girl. 1926 Say It Again; A Social Celebrity.

WATKIN, PIERRE
Died: Feb. 3, 1960, Hollywood, Calif. Screen actor.

Appeared in: 1935 Dangerous. 1936 Bunker Bean; Love Letters of a Star; Forgotten Faces; It Had to Happen; The Gentleman from Louisiana; Sitting on the Moon; Country Gentlemen; Nobody's Fool; Counterfeit; Swing Time. 1937 Michael O'Halloran; Interns Can't Take Money; The Californian; The Green Light; The Go-Getter; Ever since Eve; The Singing Marine; The Devil's Playground; Larceny on the Air; Bill Cracks Down; The Hit Parade; Sea Devils; Stage Door; Breakfast for Two; Paradise Isle; Daughters of Shanghai. 1938 Young Dr. Kildare; The Lady Objects; Midnight Intruder; State Police; Mr. Moto's Gamble; Dangerous to Know; Tip-Off Girls; Illegal Traffic; There's Always a Woman; Girls' School; There's That Woman Again; The Chaser; Mr. Doodle Kicks Off. 1939 Risky Business; The Spirit of Culver; King of the Underworld; Wings of the Navy; Off the Record; Adventures of Jane Arden; The Mysterious Miss X; Wall Street Cowboy; Covered Trailer; They Made Her a Spy; Society Lawyer; Mr. Smith Goes to Washington; Geronimo; Death of a Champion; The Great Victor Herbert. 1940 The Road to Singapore; The Saint Takes Over; Street of Memories; Captain Caution; I Love You Again; Golden Gloves; Out West with the Peppers; Five Little Peppers in Trouble; The Bank Dick; Yesterday's Heroes; Father Is a Prince; Rhythm on the River. 1941 Nevada City; Buy Me That Town; Ellery Queen and the Murder Ring; Ice Capades Revue; Jesse James at Bay; Petticoat Politics; Cheers for Miss Bishop; A Man Betrayed; Meet John Doe; She Knew All the Answers; Adventures in Washington; Life with Henry; The Trial of Mary Dugan; Naval Academy; Great Guns. 1942 Pride of the Yankees; Whistling in Dixie; The Adventures of Martin Eden; Heart of the Rio Grande; Yokel Boy; The Magnificent Dope. 1943 Cinderella Swings It; Mission to Moscow; Old Acquaintance; Jack London; Riding High; Swing Shift Maisie; It Ain't Hay. 1944 Weekend Pass; Bermuda Mystery; Ladies of Washington; South of Dixie; Jubilee Woman; Oh, What a Night!; Atlantic City; The Great Mike; Dead Man's Eyes; Shadow of Suspicion; End of the Road; Song of the Range; Meet Miss Bobby-Socks. 1945 Here Come the Co-Eds; Strange Illusion; The Phantom Speaks; Docks of New York; I'll Remember April; Mr. Muggs Rides Again; Follow That Woman; Keep Your Powder Dry; Three's a Crowd; Allotment Wives; I'll Tell the World; Captain Tugboat Annie; Dakota; Over 21; I Love a Bandleader; Apology for Murder. 1946 Little Giant; So Goes My Love; The Shadow Returns; Murder Is My Business; Swamp Fire; Behind the Mask; High School Hero; The Missing Lady; Claudia and David; Secrets of a Sorority Girl; Sioux City Sue; G.I. War Brides; Her Sister's Secret; I Ring Doorbells; The Madonna's Secret; Shock. 1947 Violence; Hard-Boiled Mahoney; The Red Stallion; Her Husband's Affair; Wild Frontier; The Shocking Miss Pilgrim; Beyond Our Own; Jack Armstrong (serial). 1948 Fight-

ing Back; The Hunted; The Gentleman from Nowhere; Mary Lou; Glamour Girl; State of the Union; Trapped by Boston Blackie; An Innocent Affair; Daredevils of the Clouds; The Counterfeiters; The Shanghai Chest. 1949 Knock on Any Door; Frontier Outpost; Alaska Patrol; Hold That Baby; Zamba; Incident; The Story of Seabiscuit. 1950 The Big Hangover; Frontier Outpost; Last of the Buccaneers; Over the Border; Radar Secret Service; Redwood Forest Trail; Rock Island Trail; The Second Face; Sunset in the West; Blue Grass of Kentucky. 1951 Two Lost Worlds; The Dark Page; In Old Amarillo. 1952 Hold That Line; Scandal Sheet; Thundering Caravans; A Yank in Indo-China. 1953 The Stranger Wore a Gun. 1954 Johnny Dark; About Mrs. Leslie. 1955 The Big Bluff; Sudden Danger; Creature with the Atom Brain. 1956 The Maverick Queen; Shake, Rattle and Rock. 1957 Beginning of the End; Don't Knock the Rock; Pal Joey; Spook Chasers. 1959 The Flying Fontaines.

WATSON, ADELE
Born: 1890, Minn. Died: Mar. 27, 1933, Los Angeles, Calif. (double pneumonia). Screen, stage, and vaudeville actress. Entered films in 1918.

Appeared in: 1922 The Lying Truth. 1923 Reno. 1924 Don't Doubt Your Husband. 1925 Welcome Home; Tower of Lies. 1926 Rolling Home. 1927 Good as Gold; A Harp in Hock; Once and Forever; The Broken Gate. 1928 The Black Pearl. 1929 Blue Skies; The Very Idea; Jazz Heaven; This Thing Called Love. 1931 Street Scene; Compromised; Expensive Women; Arrowsmith. 1932 The Purchase Price; Pack up Your Troubles.

WATSON, "BOBBY" (Robert Watson Knucher)
Born: 1888, Springfield, Ill. Died: May 22, 1965, Hollywood, Calif. Screen, stage, and vaudeville actor. Best known for his portrayals of Hitler.

Appeared in: 1926 That Royle Girl; The Romance of a Million Dollars; The Song and Dance Man. 1929 Syncopation; Maid's Night Out (short); Follow the Leader, plus the following shorts: The Baby Bandit; Contrary Mary; The Stand Up; Nay, Nay, Nero. 1931 Manhattan Parade. 1932 High Pressure. 1933 Moonlight and Pretzels; Going Hollywood; Wine, Women and Song. 1934 Countess of Monte Cristo; I Hate Women. 1935 Society Doctor; The Murder Man. 1936 Mary of Scotland. 1937 The Adventurous Blonde; You're a Sweetheart. 1938 In Old Chicago; Boys Town; Kentucky; The Story of Alexander Graham Bell. 1939 Everything's on Ice; Dodge City; On Borrowed Time; Blackmail. 1940 Wyoming; Dr. Kildare's Crisis. 1941 Men of Boys Town; Hit the Road. 1942 The Devil with Hitler. 1943 Hitler-Dead or Alive; That Nazty Nuisance; It Ain't Hay. 1944 The Hitler Gang; The Miracle of Morgan's Creek; Practically Yours. 1945 Duffy's Tavern; Hold That Blonde. 1948 The Big Clock; The Paleface. 1949 Red Hot and Blue. 1950 Copper Canyon. 1951 G.I Jane. 1952 Singing in the Rain. 1957 The Story of Mankind.

WATSON, CAVEN
Born: 1904, Scotland. Died: 1953, Norholt, England. Screen and stage actor. Appeared in Scottish film The Net.

WATSON, FANNY
Born: 1886, Rochester, N.Y. Died: May 17, 1970, Albany, N.Y. Screen, vaudeville, burlesque, and radio actress. Appeared with her sister, Kitty, (dec. 1967) in vaudeville as the "Watson Sisters."

They appeared in 1929: Bigger and Better (short).

WATSON, GEORGE A.
Born: 1911. Died: Dec. 5, 1937, Hollywood, Calif. Screen actor.

WATSON, JOSEPH K (Joseph Koff)
Born: Feb. 12, 1887, Philadelphia, Pa. Died: May 17, 1942, Hollywood, Calif. Screen, stage, vaudeville actor, and screenwriter.

Appeared in: 1936 Melody for Two; Cherokee Strip; Bad Man's Territory; Echo Mountain; Champagne Hour.

WATSON, JUSTICE
Born: 1908. Died: July 6, 1962, Hollywood, Calif. Screen, stage, and television actor. Entered films approx. 1955.

Appeared in: 1956 Death of a Scoundrel.

WATSON, KITTY (Katherine Watson)
Born: 1887. Died: Mar. 1967, Buffalo, N.Y. Screen, vaudeville, and burlesque actress. Appeared with her sister, Fanny, (dec. 1970) in vaudeville as the "Watson Sisters."

They appeared in 1929: Bigger and Better (short).

WATSON, LUCILE

Born: May 27, 1879, Quebec, Canada. Died: June 24, 1962, New York, N.Y. Screen and stage actress.

Appeared in: 1916 The Girl with the Green Eyes. 1934 What Every Woman Knows; Men in Black (short). 1935 The Bishop Misbehaves. 1936 A Woman Rebels; The Garden of Allah. 1937 Three Smart Girls. 1938 The Young in Heart; Sweethearts. 1939 Made for Each Other; The Women. 1940 Waterloo Bridge; Florian. 1941 Rage in Heaven; Mr. and Mrs. Smith; Footsteps in the Dark; The Great Lie; Model Wife. 1943 Watch on the Rhine. 1944 'Til We Meet Again; Uncertain Glory; The Thin Man Goes Home. 1946 Song of the South; Tomorrow Is Forever; Never Say Goodbye; The Razor's Edge; My Reputation. 1947 Ivy. 1948 The Emperor Waltz; Julia Misbehaves; That Wonderful Urge. 1949 Everybody Does It; Little Women. 1950 Harriet Craig; Let's Dance. 1951 My Forbidden Past.

WATSON, MINOR

Born: Dec. 22, 1889, Marianna, Ark. Died: July 28, 1965, Alton, Ill. Screen, stage, and television actor.

Appeared in: 1931 24 Hours. 1933 Another Language; Our Betters. 1934 The Pursuit of Happiness; Babbitt. 1935 Charlie Chan in Paris; Mr. Dynamite; Lady Tubbs; Mary Jane's Pa; Age of Indiscretion; Pursuit; Annapolis Farewell. 1936 Rose of the Rancho; The Longest Night. 1937 When's Your Birthday?; The Woman I Love; Saturday's Heroes; Dead End; That Certain Woman; Navy Blue and Gold; Checkers. 1938 Of Human Hearts; Boys Town; Stablemates; While New York Sleeps; Touchdown Army; Love, Honor and Behave; Fast Company. 1939 The Hardys Ride High; Maisie; The Boy Friend; News Is Made at Night; Here I Am a Stranger; Angels Wash Their Faces; The Flying Irishman; Television Spy; Stand up and Fight; Huckleberry Finn. 1940 The Llamo Kid; 20 Mule Team; Hidden Gold; Young People; Rangers of Fortune; Viva, Cisco Kid!; Gallant Sons; Abe Lincoln in Illinois. 1941 The Monster and the Girl; Western Union; The Parson of Panamint; Kiss the Boys Goodbye; Birth of the Blues; They Died with Their Boots On; Moon over Miami; Mr. District Attorney. 1942 The Remarkable Andrew; Yankee Doodle Dandy; Woman of the Year; Frisco Lil; To the Shores of Tripoli; The Big Shot; Gentleman Jim; Flight Lieutenant; Enemy Agent Meets Ellery Queen. 1943 Action in the North Atlantic; Yanks Ahoy!; Secrets in the Dark; The Crime Doctor's Rendezvous; Crash Dive; Mission to Moscow; Princess O'Rourke; Happy Land; Guadalcanal Diary. 1944 Henry Aldrich, Boy Scout; That's My Baby; The Story of Dr. Wassell; Here Come the Waves; The Thin Man Goes Home; The Falcon Out West; Shadows in the Night. 1945 God Is My Co-Pilot; A Bell for Adano; You Came Along; Bewitched. 1946 Boys' Ranch; Courage of Lassie; The Virginian. 1948 A Southern Yankee. 1949 Beyond the Forest. 1950 Mister 880; The Jackie Robinson Story; There's a Girl in My Heart; Thelma Jordan. 1951 As Young as You Feel; Bright Victory; Little Egypt. 1952 My Son John; Untamed Frontier; Face to Face. 1953 The Star; Roar of the Crowd. 1955 Ten Wanted Men. 1956 Rawhide Years; Trapeze; The Ambassador's Daughter.

WATSON, ROY

Born: 1876. Died: June 7, 1937, Hollywood, Calif. Screen actor. Entered films with Selig.

Appeared in: 1914 The Hazards of Helen (serial). 1920 The Flaming Disc (serial); Elmo, the Fearless (serial). 1921 The Ranger and the Law. 1922 Blue Blazes. 1924 The Loser's End. 1925 Luck and Sand; Win, Lose or Draw; Wolf Blood. 1926 Chasing Trouble. 1927 Cactus Trails; Wanderer of the West. 1928 Restless Youth. 1934 Carolina.

WATSON, WYLIE (John Wylie Robertson)

Born: 1889, Scotland. Died: 1966. Screen and stage actor. Was member of "The Watson Family" on stage. Appeared in U.S. silent films from 1928 to 1931.

Appeared in: 1935 The 39 Steps. 1937 Paradise for Two; Radio Lover; Why Pick on Me? 1938 Yes, Madam; The Gaiety Girls. 1939 Jamaica Inn. 1946 Waltz Time; Murder in Reverse. 1947 Tawney Pipit; Years Between. 1948 London Belongs to Me; Dulcimer Street. 1949 My Brother Jonathan; Fame Is the Spur; Waterloo Road; Don't Take it to Heart; History of Mr. Polly; Whiskey Galore (aka Tight Little Island-U.S. & aka Mad Little Island; No Room at the Inn. 1950 A Girl in a Million; Eye Witness (aka Your Witness). 1951 Things Happen at Night; Happy go Lovely; The Magnet; Operation Disaster; Brighton Rock (aka Young Scarface). 1960 The Sundowners. Other British films: Saint Meets the Tiger; The Lamp Still Burns; Flemish Farm; Kiss the Bride Goodbye.

WATTS, CHARLES

Died: Dec. 13, 1966, Nashville, Tenn.(cancer). Screen, stage, and television actor.

Appeared in: 1952 Wait Till the Sun Shines Nellie; Just This Once; Million Dollar Mermaid; Something for the Birds. 1953 Silver Whip. 1954 Boy from Oklahoma; Ricochet Romance. 1955 Tall Man Riding; The View from Pompey's Head (aka Secret Interlude). 1956 Giant. 1957 An Affair to Remember; Don't Go Near the Water; The Lone Ranger and the Lost City of Gold; The Spirit of St. Louis; The Big Land. 1959 The Big Circus; No Name on the Bullet. 1961 Ada; Something Wild. 1962 Days of Wine and Roses; Jumbo; Lover, Come Back. 1963 The Wheeler Dealers. 1964 Dead Ringer. 1965 Baby, the Rain Must Fall.

WATTS, CHARLES H. "COTTON"

Born: 1902. Died: Mar. 5, 1968, Atlanta, Ga. Screen and minstrel actor.

Appeared in: 1951 Yes Sir, Mr. Bones.

WATTS, GEORGE

Born: 1877. Died: July 1, 1942, Hollywood, Calif.(heart attack). Screen, stage, and vaudeville actor. Appeared in vaudeville as part of "Watts and Hawley" team.

Appeared in: 1936 Soak the Rich. 1940 One Crowded Night; Sky Murder; Angels over Broadway. 1941 Mr. District Attorney; Wild Geese Calling; Hurry, Charlie, Hurry; No Hands on the Clock. 1942 The Remarkable Andrew; The Talk of the Town.

WAYNE, JUSTINA

Died: Dec. 2, 1951, Freeport, N.Y. Screen, stage, and radio actress.

WAYNE, NAUNTON

Born: June 22, 1901, Llanwonno; South Wales. Died: Nov. 17, 1970, Subiton, England. Screen, stage, vaudeville, and television actor.

Appeared in: 1931 The First Mrs. Fraser. 1933 Going Gay. 1934 For Love of You. 1935 Kiss Me Goodbye. 1938 A Girl Must Live; The Lady Vanishes. 1940 Night Train. 1941 Crooks Tour. 1941 Next of Kin. 1945 Dead of Night. 1947 The Calendar. 1948 It's Not Cricket; Quartet; Passport to Pimlico. 1949 The Hidden Room (aka Obsession-U.S. 1950). 1950 Mr. Lord Says No; Highly Dangerous; Trio. 1951 Circle of Danger. 1953 The Titfield Thunderbolt; You Know What Sailors Are; Double Confession. 1959 Operation Bullshine (U.S. 1962). 1961 Nothing Barred. Other British films: A Girl in a Million; Tall Headlines.

WAYNE, RICHARD

Died: Mar. 15, 1958, Hollywood, Calif. Screen actor.

Appeared in: 1921 Whatever She Wants; Wealth; The Snob; The Traveling Salesman. 1922 The Impossible Mrs. Bellew; Minnie; Her Husband's Trademark. 1923 Reno; The Unknown Purple; Broadway Gold; The Cheat; Truxton King; Wasted Lives. 1924 Good Bad Boy. 1925 Cheaper to Marry.

WEBB, CLIFTON (Webb Parmelee Hollenbeck)

Born: Nov. 19, 1889 or 1896?, Indianapolis, Ind. Died: Oct. 13, 1966, Beverly Hills, Calif.(heart attack). Screen and stage actor. Nominated for Academy Award in 1944 for Best Supporting Actor in Laura and in 1946 for The Razor's Edge and in 1948 nominated for Academy Award for Best Actor in Sitting Pretty.

Appeared in: 1920 Polly with a Past. 1924 New Toys. 1925 The Heart of a Siren. 1930 Still Alarm (short). 1944 Laura. 1946 The Razor's Edge; Dark Corner. 1948 Sitting Pretty; Julie. 1949 Mr. Belvedere Goes to College. 1950 Cheaper by the Dozen; For Heaven's Sake. 1951 Mr. Belvedere Rings the Bell; Elopement. 1952 Dreamboat; Stars and Stripes Forever. 1953 Titanic; Mr. Scoutmaster. 1954 Woman's World; Three Coins in the Fountain. 1956 The Man Who Never Was. 1957 Boy on a Dolphin. 1959 The Remarkable Mr. Pennypacker; Holiday for Lovers. 1962 Satan Never Sleeps.

WEBB, FAY

Born: 1906. Died: Nov. 18, 1936, Santa Monica, Calif.(following abdominal operation). Screen actress. Divorced from screen actor Rudy Vallee.

WEBB, MILLARD
Born: Dec. 6, 1893, Clay City, Ky. Died: Apr. 21, 1935, Los Angeles, Calif.(intestinal ailment). Screen, stage actor, film director, and screenwriter. Entered films as an extra with D.W. Griffith in 1915.

WEBER, JOE (Morris Weber)
Born: 1867, N.Y. Died: May 10, 1942, Los Angeles, Calif. Screen, stage, vaudeville, burlesque, and minstrel actor. Was partner in comedy team of "Weber and Fields" and appeared as such in the following films: 1915 Two of the Finest; Two of the Bravest; Fatty and the Broadway Stars; The Best of Enemies; Old Dutch. 1916 The Worst of Friends. 1918 The Corner Grocer. 1925 Friendly Enemies. 1927 Mike and Meyer (short). 1936 March of Time. 1937 Blossoms on Broadway. 1939 The Story of Vernon and Irene Castle. 1940 Lillian Russell.

WEBER, JOSEPH W.
Born: 1861. Died: Apr. 4, 1943. Screen and stage actor.

WEBER, LOIS
Born: 1883, Allegheny, Pa. Died: Nov. 13, 1939, Los Angeles, Calif. (stomach ailment). Screen actress, film producer, film director, and screenwriter. Entered films with Rex Pictures approx. 1906.

Appeared in: 1914 The Merchant of Venice; False Colors. 1919 A Midnight Romance.

WEBSTER, BEN
Born: June 2, 1864, London, England. Died: Feb. 26, 1947, Hollywood, Calif.(after operation). Screen and stage actor. Married to screen actress Dame May Whitty (dec. 1948). Father of screen actress Margaret Webster (dec. 1973).

Appeared in: 1910 The Hour of Temperley (film debut). 1914 Enoch Arden. 1919 Twelve:Ten. 1921 The Call of Youth. 1935 Old Curiosity Shop. 1937 The Prisoner of Zenda; Between Two Women. 1943 Lassie Come Home. Other British films: Elizabeth of England; Eliza Comes to Stay.

WEEKS, MARION
Born: 1887. Died: Apr. 20, 1968, New York, N.Y. Screen, stage, and vaudeville actress. Entered films with Edison in 1912.

Appeared in: 1912-13 The Office Boy's Birthday.

WEEMS, TED.
Born: 1901, Pitcairn, Pa. Died: May 6, 1963, Tulsa, Okla.(emphysema). Bandleader and screen actor.

Appeared in: 1938 Swing, Sister, Swing.

WEGENER, PAUL
Born: 1874, Germany. Died: Sept. 13, 1948, Berlin, Germany. Screen, stage actor, film director, and film producer.

Appeared in: 1913 The Student of Prague. 1914 The Golem. 1921 One Arabian Night; The Golem (and 1914 version). 1922 The Loves of Pharoah. 1923 Monna Vanna. 1927 Svengali; Lucrezia Borgia. 1926 The Magician. 1928 The Lost Shadow; Vanina; Alraune; The Strange Case of Captain Ramper. 1929 The Weavers. 1930 Survival. 1934 Inge und die Millionen. 1936 Ein Liebestroman im Hause Habsburg. 1939 Horst Wessel; Starker als die Liebe (Stronger Than Love). 1940 Das Recht auf Liebe (The Right to Love); The Living Dead. 1941 Der Grosse Konig. 1948 Der Grosse Mandarin.

WEIL, HARRY
Born: 1878. Died: Jan. 23, 1943, Los Angeles, Calif. Screen and stage actor.

WEILER, CONSTANCE
Born: 1918. Died: Dec. 10, 1965, San Francisco, Calif.(result of fall). Screen and stage actress. Entered films in 1938.

WEINBERG, GUS
Born: 1866. Died: Aug. 11, 1952, Portland, Maine. Screen, stage actor, playwright, and song writer.

Appeared in: 1921 The Frontier of the Stars. 1923 The Ne'er-Do-Well; Homeward Bound; Jacqueline of Blazing Barriers. 1925 Coming Through; Soul Fire.

WEIR, JANE
Born: 1916, Davenport, Iowa. Died: Aug. 21, 1937, Los Angeles, Calif.(appendectomy). Screen actress.

WEISER, GRETHE
Born: 1903, Germany. Died: Oct. 2, 1970, near Bad Toeiz, Bavaria, Germany (auto accident). Screen, stage, and television actress. Married to film producer/lawyer Hermann Schwerin (died in same accident).

Appeared in: 1935 Frischer Wind aus Kanada. 1936 Einer zu viel an Bord; Lotzte Rose. 1937 The Divine Jetta; Liebe auf Umwegen (Love by Indirection). 1938 Meine Fuer Veronika; Familie Schimek. 1939 Der Verkannte Lebemann (The Unrecognized Man of the World). 1940 Our Little Wife. 1952 Tromba, the Tiger Man. 1963 City of Secrets.

WEISSBURG, EDWARD
Born: 1876. Died: Aug. 30, 1950, Hollywood, Calif.(heart attack). Screen actor.

WEISSE, HANNI
Born: 1892, Germany. Died: Dec. 1967, Liebenzell, Black Forest, Germany. Screen actress. Appeared in films from 1909 to 1939.

Appeared in: 1913 The Golden Bed. 1929 Berlin after Dark.

WEITZ, EMILE
Born: 1883. Died: May 12, 1951, Hollywood, Calif. Screen actor.

WELCH, EDDIE
Born: 1900. Died: Jan. 15, 1963, Miami, Fla.(diabetes). Screen actor and stuntman. Doubled for Tom Mix and Buck Jones.

WELCH, JAMES T.
Born: 1869. Died: Apr. 6, 1949, Hollywood, Calif. Screen, stage, and minstrel actor.

Appeared in: 1921 The Broken Spur. 1922 Two-Fisted Jefferson; The Sheriff of Sun-Dog; The Marshal of Moneymint. 1924 Abraham Lincoln; The Iron Horse; Behind Two Guns; The Tornado. 1925 Tonio, Son of the Sierras; Warrior Gap. 1926 Speedy Spurs; West of the Rainbow's End. 1927 The Heart of Maryland. 1928 Rough Ridin' Red; Wizard of the Saddle; The Little Buckaroo. 1936 The Trail of the Lonesome Pine.

WELCH, JOSEPH N.
Born: Oct. 22, 1891. Died: Oct. 6, 1960, Hyannis, Mass. Attorney, screen, and television actor. Received Academy Award nomination for Best Supporting Actor in 1959 for Anatomy of a Murder.

WELCH, MARY
Born: 1923. Died: May 31, 1958, New York, N.Y. Screen, stage, and television actress.

Appeared in: 1952 Park Row.

WELCHMAN, HARRY
Born: Feb. 24, 1886, Barnstable, Devon, England. Died: Jan. 3, 1966, Penzance; England (coronary thrombosis). Screen, stage, radio, and television actor.

Appeared in: 1932 The Maid of the Mountains. 1933 A Southern Maid. 1934 Last Waltz By Strauss. 1946 Waltz Time. 1955 Eight O'Clock Walk.

WELDON, LILLIAN (Elizabeth Martin)
Born: 1869. Died: Aug. 22, 1941, Los Angeles, Calif. Screen, vaudeville, and burlesque actress. Appeared in vaudeville as part of "Murray and Martin" team.

WELFORD, DALLAS
Born: 1872, England. Died: Sept. 28, 1946, Santa Monica, Calif. Screen and stage actress.

Appeared in: 1921 Wedding Bells.

WELLESLEY, CHARLES
Born: 1875, London, England. Died: July 24, 1946, Amityville, N.Y. Screen and stage actor.

Appeared in: 1921 The Silver Lining; Stardust; His Greatest Sacrifice; It Isn't Being Done This Season; Nobody. 1922 Just a Song at Twilight; Outcast. 1923 Don't Marry for Money; The Acquittal; Does It Pay?; Enemies of Children; Legally Dead; Alias the Night Wind. 1924 The Wolf Man; Cytherea; Traffic in Hearts; The Perfect Flapper. 1925 The Half-Way Girl; The Lost World; The Unholy Three. 1926 College Days. 1927 The Stolen Bride; Sinews of Steel. 1928 Skinner's Big Idea.

WELLINGTON, BABE
Born: 1897. Died: Dec. 28, 1954, New York, N.Y. Screen, stage, vaudeville, and burlesque actress. Appeared in silents as a child actress and later was in vaudeville as part of dancing team billed as "The Dancing Kellers."

WELLS, "BOMBARDIER" BILLY
Born: 1888. Died: June 11, 1967, London, England. Screen actor and prizefighter. Heavyweight champ for seven years. He used to sound the gong in Rank films as their trademark.

Appeared in: 1937 Make Up.

WELLS, DEERING
Born: 1896. Died: Sept. 29, 1961, London, England. Screen and stage actor.

Appeared in: 1955 Richard III. 1959 The Two-Headed Spy.

WELLS, H. G.
Born: 1866, England. Died: Aug. 13, 1946, London, England. Author, screenwriter, and screen actor.

Appeared in: 1922 The Jungle Goddess (serial).

WELLS, MAI
Born: 1862. Died: Aug. 1, 1941, Los Angeles, Calif. Screen and stage actress.

Appeared in: 1921 Opened Shutters. 1923 The Pilgrim. 1925 Excuse Me. 1927 Blondes by Choice.

WELLS, MARIE
Born: 1894. Died: July 2, 1949, Hollywood, Calif.(overdose of sleeping pills-suicide). Screen and stage actress.

Appeared in: 1923 The Love Brand; The Man from New York. 1929 The Desert Song. 1930 The Song of the West. 1934 The Scarlet Empress; Elmer and Elsie.

WENCK, EDUARD
Born: 1894. Died: May 17, 1954, Berlin, Germany (suicide because of heart ailment). Screen and stage actor.

Appeared in: 1939 Der Lustige Witwenball (The Merry Widow's Ball); Der Biberpelz (The Beaver Coat).

WERBESIK, GISELA
Born: 1875. Died: Apr. 15, 1956, Hollywood, Calif. Screen and stage actress. Appeared in U.S., British, and German films.

Appeared in: 1944 The Hairy Ape. 1945 Wonder Man. 1946 A Scandal in Paris.

WERKMEISTER, LOTTE
Born: 1886, Germany. Died: July 1970, Bergholz-Rehbruecke, East Germany. Screen and stage actress.

Appeared in: 1931 Der Hampelmann. 1934 Zu Befehl Herr Unteroffizier. 1935 Die Toerichte Jungfrau.

WERNER, WALTER
Born: 1884, Germany. Died: Jan. 8, 1956, Berlin, Germany (pneumonia). Screen and stage actor.

Appeared in: 1938 The Kreutzer Sonata. 1948 Marriage in the Shadows.

WERNER-KAHLE, HUGO
Born: 1883, Germany. Died: May 1, 1961, Berlin, Germany. Screen and stage actor.

Appeared in: 1931 Mother Love. 1935 Gruen ist die Heide. Other German films: Der Maulkorb; Traummusik; Affair Roedern.

WERTZ, CLARENCE
Died: Dec. 2, 1935, Hollywood, Calif.(following operation). Film actor and stuntman.

Appeared in: 1922 The Three Must-Get-There's. 1926 Spangles.

WESS, OTTO FRANCIS
Born: 1914. Died: Mar. 18, 1969, Youngstown, Ohio. Screen, vaudeville, radio actor, and dancer. Appeared on stage as Ray Ravelle.

WESSEL, DICK (Richard Wessel)
Born: 1913. Died: Apr. 20, 1965, Studio City, Calif.(heart attack). Screen, stage, radio, and television actor.

Appeared in: 1935 In Spite of Danger. 1937 Round-up Time in Texas; The Game That Kills; Slim; Borrowing Trouble. 1938 Arson Gang Busters. 1939 Beasts of Berlin; Dust Be My Destiny; Missing Daughters; They Made Me a Criminal. 1940 Cafe Hostess; Brother Orchid; So You Won't Talk; The Border Legion. 1941 The Great Train Robbery; Desert Bandit; Tanks a Million. 1942 X Marks the Spot; Dudes Are Pretty People; The Traitor Within; You Can't Escape Forever; Gentleman Jim; Highways by Night. 1943 Silver Spurs; Action in the North Atlantic. 1946 In Old Sacramento; Dick Tracy vs. Cueball; In Fast Company. 1947 Merton of the Movies; Fright Night (short). 1948 Pitfall; Unknown Island; When My Baby Smiles at Me; Badmen of Tombstone. 1949 Thieves' Highway; Blondie Hits the Jackpot; Slattery's Hurricane; Frontier Outpost; Canadian Pacific. 1950 Beware of Blondie; Watch the Birdie; Punchy Cowpunchers (short). 1951 The Scarf; Reunion in Reno; Texas Carnival; Corky of Gasoline Alley; Honeychile. 1952 Love Is Better Than Ever; The Belle of New York; Blackbeard the Pirate; Wac from Walla Walla; Young Man with Ideas. 1953 Gentlemen Prefer Blondes; Champ for a Day; Let's Do It Again; The Caddy. 1955 Bowery to Bagdad; Fling in the Ring (short). 1956 Around the World in 80 Days. 1960 The Gazebo. 1963 Wives and Lovers; Pocketful of Miracles; Who's Minding the Store? 1966 The Ugly Dachshund.

WESSELHOEFT, ELEANOR (Elinor Wesselhoeft)
Born: 1873, Cambridge, Mass. Died: Dec. 9, 1945, Hollywood, Calif. Screen and stage actress.

Appeared in: 1931 Street Scene (film debut). 1932 Madame Racketeer. 1933 The Great Jasper; Cradle Song. 1934 All Men Are Enemies; Thirty Day Princess; Black Moon. 1935 Country Chairman; The Wedding Night; The Woman in Red. 1936 Boulder Dam; A Son Comes Home; Ladies in Love. 1938 The Baroness and the Butler. 1939 Intermezzo; Everything Happens at Night. 1940 Four Sons.

WEST, "BUSTER" JAMES
Born: 1902, Philadelphia, Pa. Died: Mar. 19, 1966, Encino, Calif. (brain tumor). Screen, stage, and vaudeville actor. Appeared in vaudeville with his parents in an act billed as "Wells, Virginia and West."

Appeared in the following Christie shorts prior to 1933: The Dancing Gob (film debut); Marching to Georgie; Don't Give Up. 1934-38 Educational shorts. 1938 Radio City Revels. 1949 Make Mine Laughs.

WEST, EDNA RHYS
Born: 1887. Died: Feb. 7, 1963, Middletown, N.Y. Screen and stage actress.

Appeared in: 1929 Half Way to Heaven.

WEST, KATHERINE
Born: 1883. Died: Sept. 26, 1936, Los Angeles, Calif.(heart attack). Screen and stage actress. Appeared as Katherine West, Lillian Westner, and Maxine Morton.

WEST, PAT (Arthur Pat West)
Born: 1889. Died: Apr. 1944, Hollywood, Calif. Screen, stage, and vaudeville actor. Appeared in vaudeville with his wife Lucille in an act billed as "Arthur and Lucille West."

Appeared in: 1929 Ship Ahoy (short). 1930 Russian Around (short); Gates of Happiness (short). 1935 Red Morning. 1936 Ceiling Zero; Song of the Saddle; Three of a Kind; On the Wrong Trek (short). 1937 Turn Off the Moon. 1938 Thanks for the Memory. 1939 Geronimo; Only Angels Have Wings; Some Like It Hot. 1940 His Girl Friday. 1942 Madame Spy; Invisible Agent. 1944 To Have and to Have Not.

WEST, THOMAS
Born: 1859. Died: July 28, 1932, Philadelphia, Pa.(liver ailment). Screen, stage, and vaudeville actor. Entered films with Lubin. Was known as "Chinese Tommy" for his interpretations of oriental characters.

WESTCOTT, GORDON
Born: 1903, near St. George, Utah. Died: Oct. 31, 1935, Hollywood, Calif.(injuries suffered in polo-playing fall). Screen and stage actor.

Appeared in: 1931 Enemies of the Law. 1932 Guilty as Hell; Devil and the Deep; Hot Saturday; Love Me Tonight. 1933 The Crime of the Century; He Learned about Women; Heritage of the Desert; The Working Man; Lilly Turner; Heroes for Sale; Convention City; Private Detective 62; Footlight Parade; Voltaire; The World Changes. 1934 Fashions of 1934; Fog over Frisco; I've Got Your Number; Call It Luck; The Circus Clown;

Registered Nurse; Six Day Bike Rider; The Case of the Howling Dog; Kansas City Princess; Murder in the Clouds; Dark Hazard; We're in the Money. 1935 The White Cuckatoo; A Night at the Ritz; Go into Your Dance; Going Highbrow; Bright Lights; Front Page Woman; This Is the Life; Two-Fisted; Ceiling Zero.

WESTERFIELD, JAMES "JIM"
Born: 1913. Died: Sept. 20, 1971, Woodland Hills, Calif.(heart attack). Screen, stage, and television actor. Married to stage actress Fay Tracy.

Appeared in: 1941 Highway West. 1946 Undercurrent; The Chase. 1951 The Whistle at Eaton Falls; The Human Jungle. 1954 Three Hours to Kill; On the Waterfront. 1955 Chief Crazy Horse; The Violent Men; The Cobweb; The Scarlet Coat; Lady Gallant; Man with the Gun. 1957 Three Brave Men; Jungle Heat; Decision at Sundown. 1958 Cowboy; The Proud Rebel. 1959 The Shaggy Dog; The Gunfight at Dodge City. 1960 Wild River; The Plunderers. 1961 The Absent-Minded Professor; Homicidal. 1962 Birdman of Alcatraz; The Scarface Mob. 1963 Son of Flubber. 1964 Man's Favorite Sport?; Bikini Beach. 1965 The Sons of Katie Elder; That Funny Feeling. 1966 Dead Heat on a Merry-Go-Round. 1968 Blue; Hang 'Em High. 1969 Smith!; A Man Called Gannon; The Love God; True Grit; Recent Mexican film: Arde (Burn).

WESTLEY, HELEN (Henrietta Remson Meserole Maney Conroy)
Born: 1879, Brooklyn, N.Y. Died: Dec. 12, 1942, Franklin Township, N.J. Screen and stage actress. Divorced from screen actor John Westley (dec. 1948).

Appeared in: 1934 Death Takes a Holiday; The House of Rothschild; Moulin Rouge; The Age of Innocence; Anne of Green Gables. 1935 Splendor; Roberta; Captain Hurricane; Chasing Yesterday; The Melody Lingers On. 1936 Showboat; Half Angel; Dimples; Banjo on My Knee; Stowaway. 1937 Sing and Be Happy; Cafe Metropole; Heidi; I'll Take Romance. 1938 Keep Smiling; Rebecca of Sunny Brook Farm; The Baroness and the Butler; Alexander's Ragtime Band; She Married an Artist; Wife, Husband and Friend. 1939 Zaza. 1940 All This and Heaven Too; The Captain Is a Lady; Lady with Red Hair; Lillian Russell. 1941 Henry Aldrich for President; Adam Had Four Sons; The Smiling Ghost; Bedtime Story; Million Dollar Baby; Sunny; Lady from Louisiana. 1942 My Favorite Spy.

WESTLEY, JOHN (John Conroy)
Died: Dec. 26, 1948, Hollywood, Calif. Screen and stage actor. Divorced from screen actress Helen Westley (dec. 1942).

WESTMAN, NYDIA
Born: 1902. Died: May 23, 1970, Burbank, Calif.(cancer). Screen, stage, and television actress.

Appeared in: 1932 Strange Justice; Manhattan Tower. 1933 Bondage; The Way to Love; The Cradle Song; Little Women; King of the Jungle; From Hell to Heaven. 1934 Two Alone; Success at Any Price; Ladies Should Listen; The Trumpet Blows; One Night of Love; Manhattan Love Song. 1935 Captain Hurricane; Dressed to Thrill; Sweet Adeline; A Feather in Her Hat. 1936 The Georgeous Hussy; Craig's Wife; The Rose Bowl; The Invisible Ray; Pennies from Heaven; Three Live Ghosts. 1937 When Love Is Young; Bulldog Drummond's Revenge. 1938 The Goldwyn Follies; The First Hundred Years; Bulldog Drummond's Peril. 1939 The Cat and the Canary; When Tomorrow Comes. 1940 Forty Little Mothers; Hullabaloo. 1941 The Bad Man; The Chocolate Soldier. 1942 They All Kissed the Bride; The Remarkable Andrew. 1943 Princess O'Rourke; Hers to Hold. 1944 Her Primitive Man. 1947 The Late George Apley. 1948 The Velvet Touch. 1962 For Love or Money; Don't Know the Twist. 1966 The Chase; The Ghost of Mr. Chicken; The Swinger. 1967 The Reluctant Astronaut. 1969 Nobody Loves Flapping Eagle; Run Rabbit Run.

WESTMORELAND, PAULINE
Born: 1910. Died: Jan. 28, 1947, Los Angeles, Calif. Screen actress.

WESTNER, LILLIAN. See Katherine West

WESTON, DORIS (Doris Wester)
Born: Sept. 9, 1917, Chicago, Ill. Died: July 27, 1960, N.Y. (cancer). Screen and radio actress.

Appeared in: 1937 Submarine D-1; The Singing Marine. 1938 Born to Be Wild. 1940 Chip of the Flying U.

WESTON, GEORGE
Died: Apr. 7, 1923, N.Y. Screen and stage actor.

WESTON, MAGGIE
Died: Nov. 3, 1926, New York, N.Y. Screen and stage actress.

WESTON, RUTH
Born: Aug. 31, 1906, Boston, Mass. Died: Nov. 5, 1955, East Orange, N.J. Screen and stage actress.

Appeared in: 1931 The Public Defender; Devotion; Smart Woman; The Woman Between. 1932 This Sporting Age. 1935 Splendor. 1938 That Certain Age. 1939 Made for Each Other.

WESTON, SAMMY
Born: 1889. Died: Feb. 1, 1951, Hollywood, Calif. Screen and stage actor.

WESTWOOD, MARTIN F.
Born: 1883. Died: Dec. 19, 1928, Glendale, Calif.(pneumonia). Screen actor.

WETHERELL, M.A.
Born: 1887. Died: Feb. 25, 1939, Johannesburg, South Africa. Screen actor and film producer.

Appeared in: 1929 Livingstone in Africa.

WHEELER, BERT (Albert Jerome Wheeler)
Born: 1895, Paterson, N.J. Died: Jan. 18, 1968, New York, N.Y. (emphysema). Screen, stage, vaudeville, television actor, and screenwriter. Father of screen actress Patricia Walters (dec. 1967). Was partner in vaudeville and film comedy team of "Wheeler and Woolsey." Unless otherwise noted, the films listed are for the team. See Robert Woolsey for films he appeared in without Wheeler.

Appeared in: 1922 Captain Fly-by-Night. 1929 The Voice of Hollywood (Wheeler only-short); Rio Rita (stage and film versions); Small Timers (Wheeler only-short). 1930 The Cuckoos; Dixiana; Half Shot at Sunrise; Hook, Line and Sinker. 1931 Cracked Nuts; Caught Plastered; Oh! Oh! Cleopatra (short); Peach O'Reno; Too Many Cooks (Wheeler only). 1932 Girl Crazy; The Slippery Pearls (short); Hold 'Em Jail; Hollywood Handicap (Wheeler only-short). 1933 So This Is Africa; Diplomaniacs. 1934 Hips, Hips, Hooray; Cockeyed Cavaliers; Kentucky Kernels. 1935 The Nitwits; The Rainmakers; A Night at the Biltmore Bowl (Wheeler only-short). 1936 Silly Billies; Mummy's Boys. 1937 On Again, Off Again; High Flyers. 1939 Cowboy Quarterback (Wheeler only). 1941 Las Vegas Nights (Wheeler only). 1951 The Awful Sleuth (Wheeler only-short).

WHELAN, LEO M.
Born: 1876, Bridgeport, Conn. Died: Oct. 15, 1952, Arlington, N.J. Silent screen and vaudeville actor. Appeared in vaudeville with members of his family in an act billed as "Four Happy Whelans."

WHELAN, RON
Born: 1905, England. Died: Dec. 8, 1965, Los Angeles, Calif. (leukemia). Screen, stage actor, and film director.

Appeared in: 1937 Wild Innocence. 1950 Massacre Hill. 1953 Kangaroo. 1963 Gun Hawk; The Three Stooges Go around the World in a Daze. 1965 Greatest Story Every Told.

WHELAN, TIM
Born: Nov. 2, 1893, Ind. Died: Aug. 12, 1957, Beverly Hills, Calif. Screen, stage actor, film director, film producer, and screenwriter. Entered films as an actor in 1922.

WHIFFEN, MRS. THOMAS
Born: 1845, London, England. Died: Nov. 26, 1936, Montvale, Va. Screen, stage, and opera actress.

Appeared in: 1915 Barbara Frietchie.

WHISTLER, MARGARET
Born: 1892. Died: Aug. 23, 1939, Hollywood, Calif. Screen actress.

WHITE, BILL (William A. Rattenberry)
Born: 1857. Died: Apr. 21, 1933, Los Angeles, Calif.(heart attack). Screen and stage actor.

Appeared in: 1921 A Motion to Adjourn. 1922 Two-Fisted Jefferson; The Sheriff of Sun-Dog. 1923 The Fighting Skipper (serial); At Devil's Gorge; The Devil's Dooryard. 1924 Western Yesterdays; Western Feuds.

WHITE, FRANCES
Born: 1898. Died: Feb. 24, 1969, Los Angeles, Calif. Singer and screen actress. Was a Ziegfeld Follies girl. Divorced from screen actor Frank Fay (dec. 1961).

Appeared in: 1922 Face to Face. 1936 The Great Ziegfeld.

WHITE, GEORGE
Born: 1890, Toronto, Ontario, Canada. Died: Oct. 11, 1968, Los Angeles, Calif.(leukemia). Stage, film producer, stage, film director, and screen and stage actor.

Appeared in: 1920 Scandals. 1930 Scandals. 1934 George White's Scandals of 1934. 1935 George White's 1935 Scandals. 1946 Rhapsody in Blue.

WHITE, HUGH "HUEY"
Born: 1896. Died: June 23, 1938, Hollywood, Calif.(injuries from auto accident). Screen and stage actor.

Appeared in: 1931 Hush Money. 1933 Female; Convention City. 1934 Gambling Lady; The Hell Cat; The Million Dollar Ransom. 1936 Crash Donovan. 1938 When G-Men Step In.

WHITE, J. IRVING
Born: 1865. Died: Apr. 17, 1944, Los Angeles, Calif. Screen and stage actor.

Appeared in: 1930 The Spoilers; Girl of the Golden West. 1932 Sign of the Cross (and revised version made in 1944).

WHITE, LEE ROY "LASSES"
Born: Aug. 28, 1888, Wills Point, Tex. Died: Dec. 16, 1949, Hollywood, Calif. Screen, stage, vaudeville, minstrel, and radio actor. Entered films in 1938.

Appeared in: 1939 Rovin' Tumbleweeds. 1940 Oklahoma Renegades; Grandpa Goes to Town. 1941 Scattergood Pulls the Strings; Dude Cowboy; Riding the Wind; The Bandit Trail; Come On, Danger!; Sergeant York; Scattergood Baines; Thundering Hoofs; The Roundup; Cyclone on Horseback. 1942 Talk of the Town. 1943 Cinderella Swings It!; The Unknown Guest. 1943 Something to Shout About; The Outlaw. 1944 The Minstrel Man; The Adventures of Mark Twain; Alaska; When Strangers Marry; Song of the Range. 1945 Red Rock Outlaws; In Old Mexico; The Lonesome Trail; Saddle Serenade; Springtime in Texas; Three's a Crowd; Dillinger. 1946 Moon over Montana; Trail to Mexico; West of the Alamo. 1947 Rainbow over the Rockies; Six Gun Serenade; Song of the Sierras; Louisiana; The Wistful Widow of Wagon Gap. 1948 The Dude Goes West; The Golden Eye; Indian Agent; The Valiant Hombre. 1949 Mississippi Rhythm. 1950 The Texan Meets Calamity Jane.

WHITE, LEO
Born: 1880, Manchester, England. Died: Sept. 21, 1948, Hollywood, Calif. Screen and stage actor. Entered films with Essanay Co. in 1914. Appeared in early Charlie Chaplin comedies.

Appeared in: 1914 "Swedie" series. 1921 Keeping up with Lizzie; The Rookie's Return; Her Sturdy Oak; The Rage of Paris. 1922 Blood and Sand; Headin' West; Fools First. 1923 Breaking into Society; The Rustle of Silk; Why Worry?; In Search of a Thrill; Vanity Fair. 1924 The Brass Bowl; When a Girl Loves; The Woman on the Jury; Wine; A Lady of Quality; Sporting Youth; The Goldfish. 1925 Ben-Hur; The Masked Bride; One Year to Live; American Pluck; The Lady Who Lied. 1926 Devil's Island; The Lady of the Harem; The Blonde Saint; The Truthful Sex; A Desperate Moment; The Far Cry. 1927 See You in Jail; Beauty Shoppers; The Girl from Gay Paree; The Slaver; A Bowery Cinderella; McFadden's Flats; The Ladybird. 1928 Breed of the Sunsets; What Price Beauty; Thunder Riders; How to Handle Women; Manhattan Knights. 1929 Campus Knights; Smilin' Guns; Born to the Saddle. 1930 Roaring Ranch. 1931 Along Came Youth; Monkey Business. 1933 Only Yesterday. 1934 Madame Du Barry; Done in Oil (short). 1935 All the King's Horses; A Night at the Opera. 1937 Tovarich. 1940 The Great Dictator. 1947 My Wild Irish Rose. 1949 The Fountainhead.

WHITE, MARJORIE (aka MARJORIE TIERNEY)
Born: July 22, 1908, Winnipeg, Canada. Died: Aug. 20, 1935, Los Angeles, Calif.(auto accident). Screen, stage, and vaudeville actress. Married to screen actor Eddie Tierney with whom she appeared in vaudeville. Entered films in 1929.

Appeared in: 1929 Happy Days; Sunny Side Up. 1930 Oh, for a Man!; The Golden Calf; Fox Movietone Follies of 1930; Just Imagine. 1931-32 "Voice of Hollywood" series. 1931 Women of All Nations; Charlie Chan Carries On; The Black Camel; Possessed. 1933 Diplomaniacs; Her Bodyguard. 1934 Woman Haters (short).

WHITE, PEARL
Born: Mar. 4, 1889 or '93 or '97?, Green Ridge, Mo. Died: Aug. 4, 1938, Paris, France (liver ailment). Screen and stage actress.

Appeared in: 1912 Mayblossom; The Girl in the Next Room. 1913 Where Charity Begins. 1914 The Exploits of Elaine (serial); The Perils of Pauline (serial). 1915 The New Exploits of Elaine (serial); The Romance of Elaine (serial). 1916 Hazel Kirke; The Iron Claw (serial); Pearl of the Army (serial). 1917 The Fatal Ring (serial). 1919 The Black Secret (serial); The Lightning Raider (serial). 1920 The White Moll. 1921 Know Your Men; A Virgin Paradise; Tiger's Cub; The Thief; The Mountain Women; Beyond Price. 1922 Without Fear; The Breadway Peacock; Any Wife. 1923 Plunder (serial). 1924 Parisian Nights. 1925 Perils of Paris. 1961 Days of Thrills and Laughter (documentary).

WHITE, RUTH
Born: 1914, Perth Amboy, N.J. Died: Dec. 3, 1969, Perth Amboy, N.J.(cancer). Screen, stage, and television actress.

Appeared in: 1956 Rumpus in the Harem (short). 1957 Muscle up a Little Closer (short); A Merry Mix-Up (short); Edge of the City. 1959 The Nun's Story. 1962 A Rage to Live; To Kill a Mockingbird. 1965 Baby, the Rain Must Fall. 1966 Cast a Giant Shadow. 1967 The Tiger Makes Out; Up the Down Staircase; Hang 'Em High; No Way to Treat a Lady; Charley. 1969 Midnight Cowboy; The Reivers. 1971 The Pursuit of Happiness.

WHITE, SAMMY
Born: May 28, 1896, Providence, R.I. Died: Mar. 3, 1960, Beverly Hills, Calif. Screen, stage, vaudeville, and television actor. First teamed in vaudeville with Lou Clayton and later with his wife Eva Puck (later divorced).

Appeared in: 1936 Show Boat; Cain and Mabel. 1937 The Hit Parade. 1938 Swing Your Lady. 1950 711 Ocean Drive. 1951 Half Breed. 1952 Pat and Mike. 1953 Remains to Be Seen; The Bad and the Beautiful. 1954 About Mrs. Leslie; Living It Up. 1956 Somebody up There Likes Me. 1957 The Helen Morgan Story.

WHITEHEAD, JOHN
Born: 1873. Died: Mar. 21, 1962, Hollywood, Calif. Screen actor and extra.

Appeared in: 1903 The Great Train Robbery. 1926 Ben Hur. 1962 Escape from Zahrain.

WHITELAW, BARRETT
Born: approx. 1897. Died: Oct. 3, 1947, Los Angeles, Calif. (cerebral hemorrhage). Screen actor and extra.

WHITEMAN, PAUL
Born: 1890, Denver, Colo. Died: Dec. 29, 1967, Doylestown, Pa. (heart attack). Bandleader, screen, stage, radio actor, and composer.

Appeared in: 1924 Broadway after Dark. 1930 King of Jazz. 1935 Thanks a Million. 1940 Strike up the Band. 1944 Atlantic City. 1945 Rhapsody in Blue. 1947 The Fabulous Dorseys.

WHITESIDE, WALKER
Born: 1869, Logansport, Ind. Died: Aug. 18, 1942, Hastings-on-Hudson, N.Y. Screen, stage actor, stage producer, and playwright.

Appeared in: 1915 The Melting Pot.

WHITFIELD, JORDAN
Born: 1917, Pittsburgh, Pa. Died: Nov. 11, 1967, Hollywood, Calif.(heart attack). Negro screen and television actor.

Appeared in: 1938 You Can't Take It with You. 1946 Swamp Fire; Three Little Girls in Blue. 1948 Another Part of the Forest. 1950 Right Cross. 1954 Carmen Jones. 1958 The Cry Baby Killer.

WHITFIELD, DR. WALTER W.
Born: 1888. Died: Jan. 13, 1966, Cleveland, Ohio. Negro screen, stage actor, singer, and dentist. Sang background music for films.

Appeared in: 1936 Green Pastures (stage and film versions).

WHITING, JACK
Born: June 22, 1901, Philadelphia, Pa. Died: Feb. 15, 1961, N.Y. Screen, stage, and vaudeville actor.

Appeared in: 1930 Top Speed (film debut); College Lovers; The Life of the Party. 1933 Take a Chance. 1935 Broadway Brevities (short). 1938 Sailing Along; Give Me a Sailor.

WHITMAN, ERNEST
Born: 1893. Died: Aug. 1954, Hollywood, Calif.(heart attack). Negro screen, radio, and television actor. Known as Bill Jackson on radio and television "Beulah" shows.

Appeared in: 1936 The Prisoner of Shark Island; White Hunter; The Green Pastures. 1937 Daughter of Shanghai. 1939 Jesse James. 1940 Congo Maisie; Maryland; The Return of Frank James; Third Finger, Left Hand. 1941 The Get-Away; The Pittsburgh Kid; Among the Living. 1942 The Bugle Sounds; Drums of the Congo. 1943 Cabin in the Sky; Stormy Weather. 1947 My Brother Talks to Horses; Blonde Savage.

WHITMAN, ESTELLE
Died: July 14, 1970, Los Angeles, Calif. Screen actress. Entered films with Triangle Films during silents.

WHITMAN, GAYNE
Born: 1890. Died: Aug. 31, 1958, Hollywood, Calif.(heart attack). Screen, stage, radio, television actor, and screenwriter. Was radio's original "Chandu, the Magician."

Appeared in: 1925 Three Weeks in Paris; The Wife Who Wasn't Wanted; His Majesty, Bunker Bean; The Love Hour; The Pleasure Buyers. 1926 Exclusive Rights; Oh, What a Nurse!; Hell Bent for Heaven; The Love Toy; The Night Cry; Sunshine of Paradise Alley; A Woman's Heart; A Woman of the Sea; His Jazz Bride. 1927 Backstage; Wolves of the Air; The Woman on Trial; Stolen Pleasures; Too Many Crooks; In the First Degree. 1928 The Adventurer; Sailors' Wives. 1929 Lucky Boy. 1930 Reno. 1935 Little America (narr.); Wings over Ethiopia (narr.). 1940 Misbehaving Husbands. 1941 Parachute Battalion. 1942 Phantom Killer. 1944 My Gal Loves Music. 1949 The Sickle or the Cross. 1952 Strange Facination; Big Jim McLain. 1953 Dangerous Crossing; One Girl's Confession.

WHITMAN, WALT
Born: 1868. Died: Mar. 27, 1928, Santa Monica, Calif. Screen and stage actor.

Appeared in: 1918 The Heart of Humanity. 1920 Mark of Zorro. 1921 The Three Musketeers; His Nibs; The Home Stretch; The New Disciple; Mysterious Rider; The Girl from God's Country. 1922 The Fire Bride; A Question of Honor; The Girl from Rocky Point. 1923 Hearts Aflame; Long Live the King; The Grub Stake; The Love Letter; Wasted Lives. 1924 Missing Daughters.

WHITNEY, CLAIRE
Born: 1890. Died: Aug. 27, 1969, Sylmar, Calif. Screen actress. Married to screen actor Robert Emmett Keane.

Appeared in: 1914 Life's Shop Window. 1915 The Nigger. 1919 The Isle of Conquest. 1921 Fine Feathers; The Leech; The Passionate Pilgrim. 1926 The Great Gatsby. 1928 Innocent Love. 1929 Gossip (short); Room 909 (short). 1931 A Free Soul. 1934 Enlighten Thy Daughter. 1939 Three Smart Girls Grow Up; When Tomorrow Comes. 1940 Chip of the Flying U. 1941 In the Navy. 1942 The Silver Bullet; Silver Queen; Frisco Lil. 1944 The Mummy's Ghost. 1945 She Gets Her Man; A Guy, a Gal and a Pal. 1949 Frontier Investigator; An Old Fashioned Girl; Roaring Westward.

WHITNEY, RALPH
Born: 1874. Died: June 14, 1928, Los Angeles, Calif.(injuries from fall). Screen actor and stuntman.

WHITNEY, ROBERT II
Born: 1945, Los Angeles, Calif. Died: Jan. 6, 1969, Los Angeles, Calif. Screen actor. Entered films approx. 1963.

WHITTELL, JOSEPHINE
Born: San Francisco, Calif. Died: June 1, 1961, Hollywood, Calif. Screen and stage actress. Divorced from screen actor Robert Warwick (dec. 1964).

Appeared in: 1921 The Inner Chamber. 1931 False Roomers (short); Caught Plastered (short); Peach O'Reno. 1932 Symphony of Six Million; What Price Hollywood. 1933 Infernal Machine; Zoo in Budapest; Baby Face. 1934 The Life of Vergie Winters; Servants' Entrance; Love Time. 1935 It's a Gift; Shanghai. 1936 Follow Your Heart. 1937 Hotel Haywire; Larceny on the Air; Beware of Ladies. 1938 Women Are Like That. 1942 The Magnificent Dope. 1944 Standing Room Only.

1945 State Fair; The Enchanted Cottage. 1946 The Virginian; Easy to Wed. 1948 An Act of Murder. 1949 Adventure in Baltimore. 1951 Molly. 1954 Forever Female.

WHITTY, DAME MAY
Born: June 19, 1865, Liverpool, England. Died: May 29, 1948, Beverly Hills, Calif. Screen and stage actress. Entered films at age 72. Married to screen actor Ben Webster (dec. 1947). Mother of screen actress Margaret Webster (dec. 1973).

Appeared in: 1937 Night Must Fall (film debut); Thirteenth Chair; Conquest (aka Marie Walewska). 1938 The Lady Vanishes; I Met My Love Again. 1939 Raffles. 1940 A Bill of Divorcement. 1941 Suspicion; One Night in Lisbon. 1942 Mrs. Miniver; Thunder Birds. 1943 Madame Curie; Slightly Dangerous; Crash Dive; Flesh and Fantasy; Stage Door Canteen. 1944 The White Cliffs of Dover; Gaslight. 1945 My Name Is Julia Ross. 1946 Devotion. 1947 This Time for Keeps; If Winter Comes; Green Dolphin Street. 1948 The Return of October; The Sign of the Ram.

WHORF, RICHARD
Born: 1906, Winthrop, Mass. Died: Dec. 14, 1966, Santa Monica, Calif.(heart attack). Screen, stage actor, film and television director, and television producer.

Appeared in: 1934 Midnight. 1941 Blues in the Night. 1942 Juke Girl; Yankee Doodle Dandy. 1943 Keeper of the Flame; Assignment in Brittany; The Cross of Lorraine. 1944 The Imposter; Christmas Holiday; Strange Confession. 1945 Champion of Champions; The Hidden Eye. 1947 Love from a Stranger; Call It Murder (reissue and retitle of Midnight-1934). 1948 Luxury Liner. 1950 Champagne for Caesar; Chain Lightning. 1951 The Groom Wore Spurs. 1954 Autumn Fever.

WICHART, LITA BELLE
Born: 1907. Died: Jan. 24, 1929 near Newhall, Calif.(attempting parachute jump from plane). Screen stunt double. Married to stuntman Floyd Bowman.

Appeared in: 1929 Winged Horseman (died while filming).

WICKLAND, LARRY
Born: June 28, 1898, Kansas City, Mo. Died: Apr. 18, 1938, Los Angeles, Calif. Screen actor, film director, and screenwriter. Appeared in early Universal Jesse Lasky Feature Play Company and DeMille productions.

Appeared in: 1916 Trail of the Lonesome Pine.

WIECK, DOROTHEA
Born: Jan. 3, 1908, Davos, Switzerland. Died: Mar. 1945, Dresden, Germany (during Allied air raid). Screen and stage actress.

Appeared in: 1932 Maedchen in Uniform; Teilnehmer Antwortet Nicht. 1933 Theodor Koerner; Cradle Song; Anna and Elizabeth (Anna and Elizabeth-U.S. 1936). 1934 Trenck; Miss Fane's Baby Is Stolen; Ein Toller Einfall. 1935 Graefin Mariza. 1936 The Private Life of Louis XIV.

WIEMAN, MATHIAS
Born: 1902, Germany. Died: Dec. 3, 1969, Zurich, Switzerland. Screen and stage actor. Entered films during the silents.

Appeared in: 1929 The Jolly Peasant. 1930 Bride 68. 1931 Rosenmontag (Monday's Roses—U.S. 1932). 1932 Avalanche; Mensch Ohne Namen; Die Graeffin von Monte Christo (The Countess of Monte Christo). 1933 Anna Und Elizabeth (Anna and Elizabeth-U.S. 1936). 1935 Klein Dorrit. 1936 Das Verlorene Tal. 1937 Togger; Patriots; The Eternal Mask. 1938 Winter Stuerme (Winter Storms); Wir Sind vom K u K Infantrie-Regiment. 1939 Die Hochzeitsreise (The Wedding Journey). 1956 As Long as You're Near Me; Fear. 1957 If All the Guys in the World. 1958 Eine Liebesgeschichte (A Love Story).

WIERE, SYLVESTER
Born: 1910, Prague, Germany. Died: July 7, 1970, Hidden Hills, Calif.(kidney ailment). Screen, stage, vaudeville, and television actor. Was member of comedy team "The Wiere Bros." with his brothers, Herbert and Harry.

They appeared in: 1941 The Great American Broadcast. 1943 Swing Shift Maisie; Hands across the Border. 1947 Road to Rio. 1967 Double Trouble.

WIGGINS, MARY L.
Born: 1910. Died: Dec. 1945, North Hollywood, Calif.(shot herself). Screen stunt woman.

WILCOX, ROBERT
Born: May 19, 1910, Rochester, N.Y. Died: June 11, 1955, near Rochester, N.Y.(heart attack on train). Screen and stage actor.

Appeared in: 1936 The Cop; The Stones Cry Out. 1937 Let Them Live; The Man in Blue; Armored Car; Carnival Queen; Wild and Woolly. 1938 City Girl; Reckless Living; Rascals; Young Fugitives; Little Tough Guy; Swing That Cheer; Gambling Ship. 1939 Undercover Doctor; Blondie Takes a Vacation; The Man They Could Not Hang; The Kid from Texas. 1940 Island of Doomed Men; Dreaming Out Loud; The Lone Wolf Strikes; Buried Alive; Gambling on the High Seas; Father Is a Prince; Mysterious Dr. Satan (serial). 1946 The Unknown; Wild Beauty. 1947 The Vigilantes Return. 1954 Day of Triumph.

WILCOX, VIVIAN
Born: 1912. Died: Jan. 5, 1945, Hollywood, Calif. Screen actress.

WILDHACK, ROBERT
Born: 1882. Died: June 19, 1940, Montrose, Calif.(pulmonary ailment). Screen and radio actor. Known on radio as the man of "Sneezes and Snores."

Appeared in: 1935 Broadway Melody of 1936. 1937 Broadway Melody of 1938. 1939 Back Door to Heaven.

WILEY, JOHN A.
Born: 1884. Died: Sept. 30, 1962, San Antonio, Tex. Screen actor.

Appeared in: 1923 The Covered Wagon. 1926 The Winning of Barbara Worth; Chasing Trouble.

WILHELM, THEODORE
Born: 1909, Germany. Died: Nov. 30, 1971, London, England. Screen, stage, and television actor.

Appeared in: 1955 Assignment Redhead. 1958 The Crawling Eye. 1961 Circle of Deception.

WILKERSON, GUY
Born: 1898. Died: July 15, 1971, Hollywood, Calif.(cancer). Screen, stage, and television actor.

Appeared in: 1937 Paradise Express; Mountain Justice; The Yodelin' Kid from Pine Ridge; Our Neighbors, the Carters; Untamed. 1941 Spooks Run Wild. 1942 Swamp Woman. 1943 The Rangers Take Over; Border Buckaroos. 1944 Boss of Rawhide; Brand of the Devil; Gangsters of the Frontier; Guns of the Law; Gunsmoke Mesa; The Pinto Bandit; Trail of Terror; Return of the Rangers; Spooktown; Outlaw Roundup; The Whispering Skull; Dead or Alive. 1945 Captain Tugboat Annie; Enemy of the Law; Three in the Saddle. 1946 Frontier Fugitives. 1947 The Michigan Kid; Thundergap Outlaws. 1948 Fury at Furnace Creek. 1949 Texas, Brooklyn and Heaven. 1950 The Great Missouri Raid; Ticket to Tomahawk. 1951 Comin' 'Round the Mountain. 1952 The Big Sky. 1953 The Last Posse; The Stranger Wore a Gun. 1955 Foxfire. 1956 Jubal. 1957 The Buster Keaton Story; Decision at Sundown. 1958 Cowboy; Wild Heritage; Man of the West. 1960 The Walking Target. 1961 Susan Slade. 1963 The Haunted Palace. 1965 War Party. 1969 True Grit.

WILKERSON, HERBERT
Born: 1881. Died: Aug. 19, 1943, Hollywood, Calif. Screen and stage actor.

WILKERSON, WILLIAM (William Penn Wilkerson)
Born: 1903, Okla. Died: Mar. 3, 1966, Hollywood, Calif. Indian screen actor.

Appeared in: 1939 Juarez. 1940 Dr. Cyclops. 1950 Davy Crockett, Indian Scout; The Rock Island Trail; Broken Arrow. 1951 Jungle Manhunt. 1952 Brave Warrior.

WILLENZ, MAX
Born: 1888. Died: Nov. 10, 1954, Hollywood, Calif.(heart attack). Screen and stage actor.

Appeared in: 1942 Pride of the Yankees; Pierre of the Plains; I Married an Angel. 1945 Yolanda and the Thief. 1953 Gentlemen Prefer Blondes.

WILLIAM, WARREN (William Krech)
Born: Dec. 2, 1895, Aitkens, Minn. Died: Sept. 24, 1948, Encino, Calif.(multiple myeloma, blood disease). Screen, stage, and radio actor. Star of films "Lone Wolf" series.

Appeared in: 1920 The Town that Forgot God. 1923 Plunder (serial). 1927 Twelve Miles Out. 1930 Let Us Be Gay. 1931 Expensive Women; Honor of the Family; Those Who Love. 1932 Woman from Monte Carlo; Beauty and the Boss; Dark Horse; Under Eighteen; Skyscraper Souls; The Mouthpiece; Three on a Match. 1933 The Mind Reader; The Match King; Employees' Entrance; The Great Jasper; Gold Diggers of 1933; Goodbye Again; Lady for a Day. 1934 Smarty; Upper World; The Case of the Howling Dog; The Secret Bride; Bedside; Dr. Monica; The Dragon Murder Case; Imitation of Life; Cleopatra. 1935 Living on Velvet; The Case of the Curious Bride; The Case of the Lucky Legs; Don't Bet on Blondes. 1936 The Widow from Monte Carlo; The Case of the Velvet Claws; Stage Struck; Satan Met a Lady; Times Square Playboy; Go West, Young Man. 1937 Outcast; Midnight Madonna; The Firefly; Madame X. 1938 Arsene Lupin Returns; The First Hundred Years; Wives under Suspicion. 1939 The Lone Wolf Spy Hunt; Gracie Allen Murder Case; The Man in the Iron Mask; Daytime Wife. 1940 Lillian Russell; The Lone Wolf Strikes; The Lone Wolf Meets a Lady; Arizona; Trail of the Vigilantes. 1941 The Lone Wolf Takes a Chance; The Wolf Man; Wild Geese Calling; The Lone Wolf Keeps a Date. 1942 Counter Espionage; Eyes of the Underworld; Wild Bill Hickok Rides. 1943 One Dangerous Night; Passport to Suez. 1945 Strange Illusion. 1946 Fear. 1947 The Private Affairs of Bel Ami.

WILLIAMS, BERESFORD
Born: 1904, England. Died: Apr. 22, 1966, England. Screen, stage, and television actor.

WILLIAMS, BERT (Egbert Austins Williams)
Born: 1877, New Providence, Nassau, British West Indies. Died: Mar. 4, 1922, New York, N.Y.(pneumonia). Negro screen, stage, minstrel, and vaudeville actor. Appeared in vaudeville and minstrel shows in team of "Williams and Walker."

Appeared in: 1916 A Natural Born Gambler.

WILLIAMS, BILL
Born: 1921. Died: Nov. 14, 1964, Gallup, N.M. Screen and television stuntman.

Appeared in: 1922 The Blue Mountain Mystery. 1932 The Lost Man. 1961 The Comancheros; Two Rode Together. 1964 Cheyenne Autumn. 1965 The Hallelujah Trail (killed while filming).

WILLIAMS, BRANSBY
Born: 1870, London, England. Died: Dec. 3, 1961, London, England. Screen, stage, vaudeville, and television actor.

Appeared in: 1925 The Gold Cure. 1926 Jungle Woman. 1928 Troublesome Wives. 1932 Hearts of Humanity. 1934 The Woman in Command. 1937 Song of the Road. 1942 Tomorrow We Live. 1943 At Dawn We Die. Other British films: Common Touch; Those Kids from Town; The Agitator; Trojan Brothers.

WILLIAMS, CHARLES B.
Born: Sept. 27, 1898, Albany, N.Y. Died: Jan. 3, 1958, Hollywood, Calif. Screen, stage actor, playwright, screenwriter, and television writer. Entered films as an actor with Paramount in N.Y.

Appeared in: 1922 The Old Homestead. 1925 Action Galore. 1932 Dance Team; Strangers of the Evening; The Devil Is Driving. 1933 Gambling Ship; The Gay Nighties (short). 1934 Search for Beauty; Woman in the Dark. 1936 Rhythm on the Range; Wedding Present. 1937 Four Days' Wonder; Love Is News; Wake up and Live; Charlie Chan on Broadway; Love and Hisses; Turn off the Moon; Jim Hanvey, Detective; Merry-Go-Round of 1938. 1938 Born to Be Wild; Hollywood Stadium Mystery; Mr. Moto's Gamble; Alexander's Ragtime Band; Little Miss Broadway; Just around the Corner. 1939 Wife, Husband and Friend; The Flying Irishman; Undercover Doctor. 1941 Convoy; Flying Cadets. 1942 Isle of Missing Men; Time to Kill. 1943 Sarong Girl; The Girl from Monterrey. 1944 End of the Road; Where Are Your Children? 1945 Guest Wife; Identity Unknown; Love on the Dole. 1946 Our Hearts Were Growing Up; Doll Face; Passkey to Danger; Heldorado; It's a Wonderful Life. 1948 Marshal of Amarillo; The Dude Goes West. 1949 Grand Canyon. 1950 The Missourians. 1951 According to Mrs. Hoyle; Corky of Gasoline Alley; Kentucky Jubilee. 1955 A Lawless Street. 1956 Fighting Trouble.

WILLIAMS, CLARA
Died: May 8, 1928, Los Angeles, Calif. Screen actress. Entered films with Selig in 1910.

Appeared in: 1916 Hell's Hinges. 1917 Paws of the Bear. 1918 Carmen of the Klondike.

WILLIAMS, CORA
Born: 1871. Died: Dec. 1, 1927, Los Angeles, Calif.(heart trouble). Screen and stage actress.

Appeared in: 1919 His Parisian Wife. 1925 His Buddy's Wife; Womanhandled. 1926 The Adorable Deceiver. 1927 Temptations of a Shop Girl; The Great Mail Robbery; Sensation Seekers.

WILLIAMS, CRAIG
Born: 1877, Germany. Died: July 5, 1941, New York, N.Y. Screen and stage actor.

WILLIAMS, EARLE
Born: Feb. 28, 1895, Sacramento, Calif. Died: Apr. 25, 1927, Los Angeles, Calif.(bronchial pneumonia). Screen, stage actor, and film producer. Entered films with Vitagraph approx. 1910.

Appeared in: 1911 Saving an Audience. 1912 Happy Go Lucky. 1913 The Artist's Madonna. 1914 Two Women; The Christian; My Official Wife. 1915 The Goddess (serial); My Lady's Slipper. 1916 The Scarlet Runner (serial). 1917 Arsene Lupin. 1918 The Seal of Silence. 1919 A Rogue's Romance. 1920 The Fortune Hunter. 1921 The Silver Car; A Master Stroke; The Purple Cipher; The Romance Promoters; Diamonds Adrift; It Can Be Done; Lucky Carson. 1922 The Man from Downing Street; Bring Him In; Restless Souls; Fortune's Mask; You Never Know. 1923 The Eternal Struggle; Masters of Men; Jealous Husbands. 1924 Borrowed Husbands. 1925 Lena Rivers; Was It Bigamy?; The Adventurous Sex; The Ancient Mariner. 1926 Diplomacy; You'd Be Surprised; The Skyrocket. 1927 Red Signals; Say It with Diamonds; She's My Baby.

WILLIAMS, FRED J.
Born: 1875. Died: May 29, 1942, Los Angeles, Calif. Screen actor and film producer. Entered films approx. 1917.

Appeared in: 1925 A Modern Cain.

WILLIAMS, GEORGE
Born: 1854. Died: Feb. 21, 1936, Los Angeles, Calif. Screen actor.

Appeared in: 1922 Foolish Wives; Little Miss Smiles. 1924 Geared to Go; The Fighting Sap; The Silent Stranger. 1925 Super Speed; The Rattler. 1926 The Winner.

WILLIAMS, GEORGE B.
Born: 1866. Died: Nov. 17, 1931, Santa Monica, Calif.(auto accident). Screen actor.

Appeared in: 1921 Cheated Love; A Poor Relation; Danger Ahead; Her Mad Bargain; One Man in a Million. 1922 Second Hand Rose; The Golden Gallows; Her Night of Nights; The Siren Call. 1923 The Ghost Patrol. 1924 The Gaiety Girl; A Lady of Quality; Captain Blood. 1925 Fifth Avenue Models; The Phantom of the Opera. 1926 The Midnight Sun.

WILLIAMS, GUINN "BIG BOY"
Born: Apr. 26, 1899, Decatur, Tex. Died: June 6, 1962, Hollywood, Calif.(uremic poisoning). Screen and television actor. For a time was U.S. Congressman from Texas. Father of screen actor Malcolm (aka "Big Boy") Williams.

Appeared in: 1919 Almost a Husband (as an extra). 1921 The Jack Rider; The Vengeance Trail; Western Firebrands. 1922 Trail of Hate; Across the Border; Blaze Away; Rounding up the Law; The Cowboy King. 1923 Freshie; End of the Rope; Cyclone Jones; $1,000 Reward; Riders at Night. 1924 The Avenger; The Eagle's Claw. 1925 Red Blood and Blue; Whistling Jim; Black Cyclone; Bad Man from Bodie; Big Stunt; Courages of Wolfheart; Fangs of Wolfheart; Riders of the Sand Storm; Rose of the Desert; Wolfheart's Revenge; Sporting West. 1926 Brown of Harvard; The Desert's Toll. 1927 Quarantined Rivals; Slide, Kelly, Slide; The College Widow; The Down Grade; Backstage; Lightning; Snowbound; The Woman Who Did Not Care. 1928 My Man; Burning Daylight; Vamping Venus; Ladies' Night in a Turkish Bath. 1929 Noah's Ark; Lucky Star; From Headquarters; The Forward Pass. 1930 The Big Fight; The Bad Man; College Lovers; Liliom; City Girl. 1931 The Great Meadow; The Bachelor Fathers; Catch as Catch Can (short); War Mamas (short). 1932 Polly of the Circus; Drifting Souls; 70,000 Witnesses; You Said a Mouthful; Ladies of the Jury; The Devil Is Driving. 1933 Heritage of the Desert; Man of the Forest; College Coach; Laughing at Life. 1934 Romance in the Rain; Palooka; The Mystery Squadron (serial); Half a Sinner; Flirtation Walk; One in a Million; Here Comes the Navy; The Silver Streak; The Cheaters; Rafter Romance. 1935 Society Fever; Cowboy Holiday; Private Worlds; Gun Play; The Glass Key; Village Tale; Powdersmoke Range; The Littlest Rebel; Miss Pacific Fleet; Society Fever; Law of

the 45's; Here Comes Cookie. 1936 The Vigilantes Are Coming (serial); Muss 'Em Up; Grand Jury; The Big Game; Kelly the Second; End of the Trail; North of Nome; Career Woman. 1937 You Only Live Once; A Star Is Born; Don't Tell the Wife; The Singing Marine; Dangerous Holiday; She's No Lady; Big City; My Dear Miss Aldrich; Wise Girl. 1938 I Demand Payment; Flying Fists; The Marines Are Here; Crashing Through; Hold That Co-ed; Everybody's Doing It; The Bad Men of Brimstone; Army Girl; Down in "Arkansaw"; You and Me; Professor Beware! 1939 6,000 Enemies; Blackmail; Fugitive at Large; Street of Missing Men; Mutiny on the Blackhawk; Legion of Lost Flyers; Badlands; Dodge City; Pardon Our Nerve. 1940 The Fighting 69th; Castle on the Hudson; Virginia City; Money and the Woman; Santa Fe Trail; Alias the Deacon; Dulcy; Wagons Westward. 1941 Six Lessons from Madame La Zonga; Country Fair; Billy the Kid; You'll Never Get Rich; Swamp Water; The Bugle Sounds; Riders of Death Valley (serial). 1942 Between Us Girls; Mr. Wise Guy; Lure of the Islands; American Empire; Silver Queen. 1943 Hands across the Border; Buckskin Frontier; Minesweeper; The Desperadoes. 1944 The Cowboy and the Senorita; The Cowboy Canteen; Thirty Seconds over Tokyo; Belle of the Yukon; Swing in the Saddle; Song of the Prairie. 1945 The Man Who Walked Alone; Rhythm Roundup; Sing Me a Song of Texas. 1946 Cowboy Blues; Singing on the Trail; Throw a Saddle on a Star; That Texas Jubilee. 1947 King of the Wild Horses; Singin' in the Corn; Road to the Big House. 1948 Bad Men of Tombstone; Station West. 1949 Brimstone. 1950 Hoedown; Rocky Mountain. 1951 Al Jennings of Oklahoma; Man in the Saddle. 1952 Springfield Rifle; Hangman's Knot. 1954 Massacre Canyon; Southwest Passage; The Outlaws' Daughter. 1956 Hidden Guns; Man from Del Rio. 1957 The Hired Gun. 1960 The Alamo; Five Bold Women. 1962 The Comancheros.

WILLIAMS, HANK
Born: 1924. Died: Jan.1, 1953, near Oak Hill, W. Va.(heart attack). Country singer/composer/instrumentalist and screen, radio, and television actor.

WILLIAMS, HARCOURT
Born: Mar. 30, 1880, Croyden Surrey, England. Died: 1957. Screen and stage actor.

Appeared in: 1944 Henry V (U.S. 1946). 1947 Brighton Rock (aka Young Scarface). 1948 Hamlet; Third Time Lucky. 1949 The Lost People; Under Capricorn; No Room at the Inn. 1950 Eye Witness (aka Your Witness). 1951 Cage of Gold; The Late Edwina Black; The Gay Lady; Young Scarface. 1952 The Magic Box; Obsessed. 1953 Terror on a Train; Roman Holiday. 1955 Quentin Durward. 1956 Around the World in 80 Days. 1958 Henry V (reissue of 1944 film).

WILLIAMS, HERB (Herbert Schussler Billerbeck)
Born: 1874, Philadelphia, Pa. Died: Oct. 1, 1936, Freeport, N.Y. (internal hemorrhages). Screen, stage, and vaudeville actor. Appeared in vaudeville with his wife Hulda in an act billed "Williams and Wolfus."

Appeared in: 1936 Rose of the Rancho.

WILLIAMS, HUGH
Born: Mar. 6, 1904, Boxhill-on-Sea, England. Died: Dec. 7, 1969, London, England. Screen, stage actor, screenwriter, and playwright.

Appeared in: 1930 Charley's Aunt. 1931 In a Monastery Garden (U.S. 1935). 1932 Down Our Street. 1933 Rome Express; Bitter Sweet; White Face. 1934 Sorrell and Son; All Men Are Enemies; Elinor Norton; David Copperfield (U.S. 1935); Outcast Lady. 1935 Let's Live Tonight; The Amateur Gentleman; The Last Journey. 1937 Gypsy; Man Behind the Mask; Windmill; Perfect Crime; Dark Stairway; Side Street Angel; Brief Ecstasy; Bank Holiday; Norwich Victims. 1938 Dark Eyes of London. 1939 Wuthering Heights; Inspector Hornleigh; Dead Men Tell No Tales. 1940 The Human Monster. 1942 Ship with Wings; One of Our Aircraft Is Missing; The Avengers. 1946 A Girl in a Million (U.S. 1950). 1947 Take My Life (U.S. 1948). 1948 An Ideal Husband; The Blind Goddess. 1949 Elizabeth of Ladymead. 1951 Naughty Arlette. 1952 Glory at Sea (aka Gift Horse-U.S. 1953). 1953 The Fake; The Intruder (U.S. 1955); Twice upon a Time. 1954 The Holly and the Ivy. 1966 Khartoum. Other British films: No Ladies Please; Paper Orchid; Romantic Age.

WILLIAMS, JEFFREY
Born: 1860. Died: Dec. 27, 1938, Los Angeles, Calif. Screen and stage actor.

Appeared in: 1921 The Saphead. 1934 Old Fashioned Way.

WILLIAMS, JULIA

Born: 1879. Died: Feb. 7, 1936, New York, N.Y. Screen, stage, opera, and vaudeville actress. Entered films during silents, appearing in early Pathe and Biograph films.

WILLIAMS, KATHLYN

Born: 1872 or 1888, Butte, Mont. Died: Sept. 23, 1960, Hollywood, Calif. Screen actress.

Appeared in: 1908 Harbor Island. 1910 The Fire Chief's Daughter. 1911 The Two Orphans; Back to the Primitive. 1913 A Mansion of Misery; The Adventures of Kathlyn (serial). 1914 The Spoilers; Chip of the Flying U. 1916 Sweet Lady Peggy; The Ne'er-Do-Well. 1917 Redeeming Love; Big Timber. 1918 The Highway of Hope; We Can't Have Everything. 1920 Just a Wife; Conrad in Quest of His Youth. 1921 Everything for Sale; Hush; A Man's Home; Morals; Forbidden Fruit; A Private Scandal; A Virginia Courtship. 1922 Clarence. 1923 The Spanish Dancer; Broadway Gold; Souls for Sale; Trimmed in Scarlet; The World's Applause. 1924 Single Wives; The City That Never Sleeps; The Enemy Sex; The Painted Flapper; Wanderer of the Wasteland; When a Girl Lives. 1925 The Best People; Locked Doors. 1926 The Wanderer. 1927 Sally in Our Alley. 1928 Our Dancing Daughters; We Americans; Honeymoon Flats. 1929 A Single Man; The Single Standard. 1930 Road to Paradise; Wedding Rings. 1931 Daddy Long Legs. 1932 Unholy Love. 1933 Blood Money. 1935 Rendezvous at Midnight. 1947 The Other Love.

WILLIAMS, LAWRENCE

Born: 1890. Died: Mar. 30, 1956, Hollywood, Calif.(heart attack). Screen actor. Entered films approx. 1931. Married to screen actress Helen Dickson.

Appeared in: 1938 Torchy Blane in Panama; Garden of the Moon; Girls on Probation; Brother Rat. 1939 Going Places; Wings of the Navy; Secret Service of the Air; On Trial; Waterfront. 1940 Brother Rat and a Baby. 1942 Flight Lieutenant; Hello Annapolis.

WILLIAMS, MACK

Born: 1907. Died: July 29, 1965, Hollywood, Calif.(heart attack). Screen and stage actor.

Appeared in: 1949 Trapped; Command Decision. 1950 Destination Big House; No Way Out; Where the Sidewalk Ends; Whirlpool. 1951 The Blue Veil; Force of Arms; Flying Leathernecks; Try and Get Me; Call Me Mister. 1953 The Bigamist. 1955 Unchained; Violent Saturday. 1956 The Monster That Challenged the World. 1958 Ten North Frederick; As Young as We Are. 1960 Chartroose Caboose. 1962 Cape Fear; A Public Affair.

WILLIAMS, MALCOLM

Born: 1870. Died: June 10, 1937, New York, N.Y.(heart attack). Screen and stage actor.

Appeared in: 1928 The First Kiss.

WILLIAMS, MARIE

Born: 1921. Died: July 5, 1967, Encino, Calif.(heart attack). Screen actress.

WILLIAMS, MARJORIE ROSE

Born: 1913. Died: July 18, 1933, Los Angeles, Calif.(suicide-gun). Screen actress.

WILLIAMS, MOLLY

Born: England. Died: Nov. 1, 1967, Halifax; Nova Scotia, Canada. Screen, stage, vaudeville, radio, and television actress.

WILLIAMS, RHYS

Born: 1892, England. Died: May 28, 1969, Santa Monica, Calif. Screen, stage, and television actor.

Appeared in: 1941 How Green Was My Valley. 1942 This above All; Eagle Squadron; Remember Pearl Harbor; Cairo; Random Harvest; Gentleman Jim; Mrs. Miniver. 1943 No Time for Love. 1945 The Corn Is Green; You Came Along; Blood on the Sun; The Bells of St. Mary's. 1946 So Goes My Love; The Strange Woman; The Spiral Staircase; Voice of the Whistler. 1947 Cross My Heart; Easy Come, Easy Go; The Trouble with Women; If Winter Comes; Moss Rose; The Farmer's Daughter; The Imperfect Lady. 1948 Black Arrow; Tenth Avenue Angel; Hills of Home. 1949 Fighting Man of the Plains; Bad Boy; The Crooked Way; The Inspector General; Tokyo Joe. 1950 The Showdown; Tyrant of the Sea; One Too Many; California Passage; Devil's Doorway; Kiss Tomorrow Goodbye. 1951 Sword of Monte Cristo; Million Dollar Pursuit; The Law and the Lady; The Light Touch; The Son of Dr. Jekyll; Never Trust a Gambler; Lightning Strikes Twice. 1952 Okinawa; Mutiny; The World in His Arms;

Carbine Williams; Les Miserables; Meet Me at the Fair; Plymouth Adventure. 1953 Scandal at Scourie; Julius Caesar; Bad for Each Other. 1954 Man in the Attic; The Black Shield of Falworth; Johnny Guitar; There's No Business Like Show Business; Battle Cry. 1955 The Scarlet Coat; How to Be Very, Very Popular; The King's Thief; The Kentuckian; Battle Cry; Many Rivers to Cross. 1956 The Desperadoes Are in Town; Nightmare; The Boss; Mohawk; The Fastest Gun Alive. 1957 The Restless Breed; Raintree County; Lure of the Swamp. 1958 Merry Andrew. 1960 Midnight Lace. 1965 The Sons of Katie Elder. 1966 Our Man Flint.

WILLIAMS, ROBERT

Born: Sept. 15, 1899, Morganton, N.C. Died: Nov. 3, 1931, Hollywood, Calif.(peritonitis following appendectomy). Screen and stage actor.

Appeared in: 1931 Rebound (stage and film versions); The Common Law; Platinum Blonde; Devotion.

WILLIAMS, SCOTT T. See Chief Thundercloud

WILLIAMS, SPENCER

Born: 1893, British West Indies. Died: Dec. 13, 1969, Los Angeles, Calif.(kidney ailment). Negro radio, television, and screen actor. The Andy of television's Amos 'n Andy program during the 1950s.

Appeared in: 1928 Tenderfeet. 1930 Georgia Rose. 1935 The Virginia Judge. 1937 Harlem on the Prairie.

WILLIAMS, WILLIAM A. (William Albert Williams)

Born: 1870. Died: May 4, 1942, Hollywood, Calif. Screen actor.

Appeared in: 1930 La Grande Mare.

WILLIAMSON, MELVIN E.

Born: 1900, Memphis, Tenn. Died: Feb. 15, 1959, Scott Air Force Base, Ill. Screen, radio actor, film director, television producer, and director.

Appeared in: 1929 Wings.

WILLINGHAM, HARRY G.

Born: 1881. Died: Nov. 17, 1943, North Hollywood, Calif.(suicide-gun). Screen actor. Entered films during silents.

WILLIS, LOUISE

Born: 1880. Died: Jan. 2, 1929, Chicago, Ill. Screen and stage actress.

WILLS, BEVERLY

Born: 1934. Died: Oct. 24, 1963, Palm Springs, Calif.(fire). Screen, radio, and television actress. Daughter of screen actress Joan Davis (dec. 1961).

Appeared in: 1945 George White's Scandals. 1948 Mickey. 1952 Skirts Ahoy. 1953 Small Town Girl. 1959 Some Like It Hot. 1961 The Ladies' Man. 1963 Son of Flubber.

WILLS, DRUSILLA

Born: Nov. 14, 1884, London, England. Died: Aug. 11, 1951, London, England. Screen and stage actress.

Appeared in: 1931 Old Spanish Customers. 1932 The Lodger; Little Miss Nobody. 1933 The Medicine Man; Britiannia of Billingsgate. 1935 Night Club Queen; The Black Abbot; Squibs; Broken Blossoms; The Big Splash; The Phantom Fiend. 1936 The Duchess; High Command; Non-Stop New York; All Quiet Please. 1938 Yellow Sands; The Outsider; Luck of the Navy; A Girl Must Live; A Spot of Bother; Sixty Glorious Years. 1939 Inspector Hornleigh on Holiday. 1942 A Girl Must Live. 1948 Champagne Charlie. 1949 The Queen of Spades.

WILLS, WALTER

Born: 1881. Died: Jan. 18, 1967, Hollywood, Calif. Screen and stage actor/dancer.

Appeared in: 1923 In Search of a Thrill. 1938 Santa Fe Stampede.

WILLSON, RINI. See Rini Zarova

WILMOT, LEE

Born: 1899. Died: Mar. 9, 1938, Hollywood, Calif.(suicide-fall from building). Screen and radio actor.

WILSON, BENJAMIN F.

Born: 1876, Clinton, Iowa. Died: Aug. 25, 1930, Glendale, Calif. (heart ailment). Screen actor, film director, and producer.

Entered films as an actor with Edison and Nestor film companies, approx. 1912.

Appeared in: 1912 What Happened to Mary (serial). 1914 Edison series. 1917 The Mystery Ship (serial); The Voice on the Wire. 1919 Trail of the Octopus (serial). 1920 Screaming Shadow (serial); The Branded Four (serial). 1921 The Mysterious Pearl (serial); Dangerous Paths. 1924 The Desert Hawk; His Majesty the Outlaw; Notch Number One. 1925 The Power God (serial); The Fugitive; A Daughter of the Sioux; The Man from Lone Mountain; Renegade Holmes, M.D.; Sand Blind; Tonio, Son of the Sierras; Fort Frayne; Warrior Gap; The Mystery Box (serial); Vic Dyson Pays. 1926 Officer 444 (serial); Baited Trap; Rainbow Riley; West of the Law; Wolves of the Desert; Sheriff's Girl. 1927 The Mystery Brand; A Yellow Streak; Riders of the West; The Range Riders. 1929 Bye, Bye Buddy; China Slaver; Girls Who Dare. 1930 Shadow Ranch.

WILSON, CLARENCE H. (Clarence Hummel Wilson)
Born: 1877, Cincinnati, Ohio. Died: Oct. 5, 1941, Hollywood, Calif. Screen and stage actor. Entered films approx. 1920.

Appeared in: 1927 Mountains of Manhattan; The Silent Avenger. 1928 Phantom of the Turf. 1930 Dangerous Paradise; Love in the Rough. 1931 Front Page; Night Life in Reno; Sea Ghost; Her Majesty, Love. 1932 Amateur Daddy; Winner Take All; Purchase Price; Down to Earth; The Phantom of Crestwood; The Penguin Pool Murder; The All American; The Jewel Robbery. 1933 Smoke Lightning; Pick-Up Girl; A Shriek in the Night; Flaming Guns; The Mysterious Rider; The Girl in 419; Terror Abroad; Tillie and Gus; King for a Night; Son of Kong. 1934 Count of Monte Cristo; Successful Failure; The Lemon Drop Kid; Wake up and Dream; I'll Fix It; Love Birds; I Like It That Way; Now I'll Tell; Unknown Blonde; Bachelor Bait; The Old-Fashioned Way. 1935 Ruggles of Red Gap; Let 'Em Have It!; Champagne for Breakfast; Waterfront Lady; Great Hotel Murder; When a Man's a Man; One Frightened Night. 1936 Little Miss Nobody; Love Begins at Twenty; The Case of the Black Cat; Rainbow on the River; Hats Off. 1937 Two Wise Maids; Damaged Goods; Small Town Boy; Westland Case. 1938 Rebecca of Sunnybrook Farm; Kentucky Moonshine; Little Miss Broadway; Having a Wonderful Time; You Can't Take It with You. 1939 Drums along the Mohawk; East Side of Heaven; Desperate Trails. 1940 Little Old New York. 1941 Angels with Broken Wings; Road Show; You're the One.

WILSON, DOOLEY
Born: Apr. 3, 1894, Tyler, Tex. Died: May 30, 1953, Los Angeles, Calif. Negro screen, stage, vaudeville, radio actor, and band leader. Toured Europe with his own band from 1919 to 1930.

Appeared in: 1942 Casablanca (film debut); Night in New Orleans; Take a Letter, Darling; Cairo; My Favorite Blonde. 1943 Two Tickets to London; Stormy Weather; Higher and Higher. 1944 Seven Days Ashore. 1948 Racing Luck. 1949 Come to the Stable; Free for All. 1951 Passage West.

WILSON, EDNA
Born: 1880. Died: July 23, 1960, N.Y. Screen and stage actress. One of the original "Gibson Girls" in early films.

WILSON, FRANCIS
Born: Feb. 1854, Philadelphia, Pa. Died: Oct. 7, 1935, N.Y. Screen, stage, minstrel actor, and author. Appeared in Sennett's comedies in 1915.

WILSON, FRANK H.
Born: 1886, N.Y. or Jacksonville, Fla. Died: Feb. 16, 1956, Queens, N.Y. Negro screen, stage, vaudeville, radio, and television actor.

Appeared in: 1933 Emperor Jones. 1936 Green Pastures (stage and film versions). 1937 The Devil Is Driving; All American Sweetheart; A Dangerous Adventure; Life Begins with Love. 1938 Extortion. 1943 Watch on the Rhine.

WILSON, GEORGE (Alfred Ensom)
Born: 1854, England. Died: July 30, 1954, London, England. Screen actor, "England's oldest."

Appeared in: 1944 Henry V (U.S. 1946). 1945 Colonel Blimp. 1946 Caesar and Cleopatra. 1958 Henry V (reissue of 1944 film).

WILSON, HAL
Born: Oct. 2, 1887, New York, N.Y. Died: May 22, 1933, Los Angeles, Calif.(paralytic stroke). Screen and stage actor. Entered films with Vitagraph in 1907.

Appeared in: 1908 The Clown's Adventures. 1921 The Secret

Four (serial); Charge It; The Unknown Wife. 1922 Lady Godiva; Nan of the North (serial); Blaze Away; According to Hoyle; Forget-Me-Not. 1923 Main Street. 1924 Sundown; The Love Master. 1925 Don Q; Smilin' at Trouble. 1929 Iron Mask; Divorce Made Easy. 1930 Big House. 1931 Guilty Hands.

WILSON, IMOGENE "BUBBLES". See Mary Nolan

WILSON, JACK
Born: 1917. Died: Dec. 18, 1966, Los Angeles, Calif.(cerebral hemorrhage). Screen and stage actor.

Appeared in: 1951 Francis Goes to the Races. 1953 Son of the Renegade.

WILSON, M. K.
Born: 1890. Died: Oct. 9, 1933, Long Beach, Calif.(auto accident injuries). Screen and stage actor.

Appeared in: 1930 The Costello Case.

WILSON, WARD (Harry Warden Wilson)
Born: 1904, Trenton, N.J. Died: Mar. 21, 1966, West Palm Beach, Fla. Screen, stage, radio, and television actor. He narrated numerous shorts for Paramount, Columbia, etc.

Appeared in: 1957 The Golden Age of Comedy (narr.).

WILSON, WAYNE
Born: 1899. Died: Jan. 1970, San Antonio, Tex. Screen, stage, radio, and television actor.

WILSON, WENDELL C.
Born: 1889. Died: Jan. 9, 1927, Vancouver, B.C., Canada (pneumonia). Screen, stage actor, stage manager, and stage director.

WILSON, WHIP
Born: 1915. Died: Oct. 23, 1964, Hollywood, Calif.(heart attack). Screen western actor and rodeo performer.

Appeared in: 1948 Silver Trails (film debut). 1949 Crashing Thru; Haunted Trails; Range Land; Riders of the Dusk; Shadows of the West. 1950 Arizona Territory; Canyon Raiders; Cherokee Uprising; Fence Riders; Gunslingers; Outlaw of Texas; Silver Raiders. 1951 Abilene Trail; Lawless Cowboys; Montana Incident; Nevada Badmen; Stagecoach Driver. 1952 Gunman; Hired Gun; Night Raiders; Wyoming Roundup.

WILSON, WILLIAM F.
Born: 1894. Died: May 10, 1956, Woodland Hills, Calif. Screen and stage actor.

Appeared in: 1927 The Bush Leaguer.

WINCHESTER, BARBARA
Born: approx. 1895. Died: Apr. 20, 1968, New York, N.Y. Screen, stage, radio, and television actress.

Appeared in: 1962 The Connection.

WINCOTT, ROSALIE AVOLO
Born: 1873. Died: Nov. 1951, Los Angeles, Calif. Screen and stage actress.

WINDHEIM, MAREK
Born: 1895, Poland. Died: Dec. 1, 1960. Screen, opera actor, and television producer.

Appeared in:1937 Something to Sing About;I'll Take Romance. 1938 She Married an Artist; Say It in French; Dramatic School. 1939 Ninotchka; On Your Toes; Hotel Imperial. 1941 Marry the Boss's Daughter. 1942 Holiday Inn; I Married an Angel; Mrs. Miniver; Crossroads. 1943 Mission to Moscow; Hi Diddle Diddle. 1944 In Our Time; Allergic to Love; Kismet; Mrs. Parkington; Our Hearts Were Young and Gay. 1945 Yolanda and the Thief; Weekend at the Waldorf. 1946 Tarzan and the Leopard Woman.

WING, DAN
Born: 1923. Died: June 14, 1969, Fresno, Calif.(heart attack). Screen, stage, and television actor.

WINN, GODFREY
Born: 1909, England. Died: June 19, 1971, England.(heart attack). Screen, stage, radio actor, and journalist.

Appeared in: 1962 A Coming-Out Party. 1963 Billy Liar. 1964 The Bargee.

WINNINGER, CHARLES
Born: May 26, 1884, Athens, Wisc. Died: Jan. 1969, Palm Springs, Calif. Screen, stage, vaudeville, radio, and television actor. Appeared in vaudeville with his parents, brothers and sisters. Entered films with Elko Comedy Co. in Hollywood under Henry Lehrman in 1916. Married to stage actress Gertrude Walker and divorced from screen actress Blance Ring (dec. 1931).

Appeared in: 1924 Pied Piper Malone. 1926 The Canadian; Summer Bachelors. 1930 Soup to Nuts. 1931 God's Gift to Women; Fighting Caravans; Gun Smoke; Children of Dreams; The Sin of Madelon Claudet; Bad Sister; Gambling Daughters; The Devil Was Sick; Night Nurse; Flying High. 1932 Husband's Holiday. 1934 Social Register. 1936 White Fang; Show Boat (stage and film versions). 1937 Dancing for Love; Three Smart Girls; You're a Sweetheart; Woman Chases Man; Nothing Sacred; Cafe Metropole; You Can't Have Everything; The Go-Getter; Every Day's a Holiday. 1938 Goodbye Broadway; Hard to Get. 1939 Barricade; Three Smart Girls Grow Up; Babes in Arms; Destry Rides Again; First Love; Fifth Avenue Girl. 1940 If I Had My Way; My Love Came Back; When Lovers Meet; Beyond Tomorrow; Little Nellie Kelly. 1941 The Get-Away; My Life with Caroline; Pot O'Gold; Ziegfeld Girl. 1942 Friendly Enemies. 1943 Coney Island; A Lady Takes a Chance; Flesh and Fantasy; Hers to Hold. 1944 Broadway Rhythm; Belle of the Yukon; Sunday Dinner for a Soldier. 1945 She Wouldn't Say Yes; State Fair. 1946 Lover Come Back. 1947 Living in a Big Way; Something in the Wind. 1948 Inside Story; Give My Regards to Broadway. 1950 Father Is a Bachelor. 1953 The Sun Shines Bright; Torpedo Alley; Perilous Journey; Champ for a Day. 1955 Las Vegas Shakedown. 1960 Raymie.

WINSCOTT, EDWIN C. See Teddy V. Armand

WINSTON, CHARLES BRUCE (aka BRUCE WINSTON)
Born: Mar. 4, 1879, Liverpool, England. Died: Sept. 27, 1946, at sea enroute to N.Y.(heart attack). Screen, stage actor, and stage producer. Entered films in silents in 1919.

Appeared in: 1931 Children of Dreams. 1933 Private Life of Henry VIII. 1934 Private Life of Don Juan; Blossom Time. 1936 The Man Who Worked Miracles; My Song for You; Everybody Dance. 1938 Alf's Button Afloat; Thief of Baghdad; Murder at the Arsenal; Leave It to George. 1940 The Thief of Bagdad (and 1938 version). Other British films: Lottie Dundass; Flight from Folly; Carnival.

WINSTON, IRENE
Born: 1920. Died: Sept. 1, 1964, Hollywood, Calif.(pneumonia complications). Screen, stage actress, and television writer.

Appeared in: 1951 Dear Brat. 1952 My Son, John. 1954 Rear Window. 1957 The Delicate Delinquent.

WINSTON, JACKIE
Born: 1915. Died: Nov. 9, 1971, N.Y. Screen, stage, television actor, and comedian. Entered show business when nine years old, winning a singing stint with Will Osborne's band.

Appeared in: 1967 The Happening.

WINTER, CHARLES R.
Born: 1876. Died: June 29, 1952, Redondo Beach, Fla. Screen, vaudeville, and radio actor. Appeared in vaudeville as part of "Williams and Charles" team (formerly entitled "Deltorelli and Glissandos"; then "Del and Gliss," and finally as "Williams and Charles").

WINTER, WINONA
Born: 1891. Died: Apr. 27, 1940, Hollywood, Calif. Screen, stage, and vaudeville actress.

WINTHROP, JOY (Josephine Williams)
Born: 1864. Died: Apr. 1, 1950, Hollywood, Calif. Screen and stage actress.

Appeared in: 1921 The Blazing Trail. 1922 Man's Law and God's. 1923 Her Fatal Millions. 1928 Stolen Love.

WINTON, JANE
Born: Oct. 10, 1905, Philadelphia, Pa. Died: Sept. 22, 1959, New York, N.Y. Screen, stage, and opera actress. Entered films in 1925.

Appeared in: 1925 Tomorrow's Love. 1926 Why Girls Go Back Home; Don Juan; The Beloved Rogue; Across the Pacific; Footloose Widows; The Honeymoon Express; The Love Toy; Millionaires; My Old Dutch; My Official Wife; The Passionate Quest. 1927 Sunrise; The Gay Old Bird; The Crystal Cup; The Fair Co-Ed; Upstream; Lonesome Ladies; The Monkey Talks; The Poor Nut; Perch of the Devil. 1928 Burning Daylight; The Yellow Lily; The Patsy; Melody of Love; Nothing to Wear; Bare Knees; Honeymoon Flats. 1929 Scandal; Captain Lash; The Bridge of San Luis Rey. 1930 In the Next Room; The Furies; Hell's Angels. 1934 The Hired Wife.

WISE, JACK
Born: 1893. Died: Mar. 6, 1954, Hollywood, Calif.(heart attack). Screen and vaudeville actor.

Appeared in: 1929 Smilin' Guns; In the Headlines. 1935 Bright Lights. 1936 The Captain's Kid. 1938 Comet over Broadway.

WISE, TOM (Thomas A. Wise)
Born: 1865, England. Died: Mar. 21, 1928, New York, N.Y. (heart and asthma complications). Screen and stage actor.

Appeared in: 1922 Father Tom. 1924 The Great White Way.

WITHERS, GRANT
Born: June 17, 1904, Pueblo, Colo. Died: Mar. 27, 1959, Hollywood, Calif.(suicide). Screen and television actor. Entered films as an extra for Douglas McLean. Divorced from screen actress Loretta Young and singer Estelita Rodriguez.

Appeared in: 1926 The Gentle Cyclone. 1927 College; The Final Extra; In a Moment of Temptation; Upstream. 1928 Bringing up Father; Tillie's Punctured Romance; Golden Shackles; The Road to Ruin. 1929 Tiger Rose; The Madonna of Avenue A; The Time, the Place and the Girl; In the Headlines; Hearts in Exile; Show of Shows; Saturday's Children; The Greyhound Limited; So Long Letty. 1930 Broken Dishes; Scarlet Pages; Soldiers and Women; Back Pay; The Other Tomorrow; Dancing Sweeties; The Second Floor Mystery; Sinners' Holiday; The Steel Highway. 1931 Other Men's Women; Too Young to Marry; Swanee River; In Strange Company; First Aid. 1932 Gambling Sex; Red Haired Alibi. 1933 Secrets of Wu Sin. 1934 The Red Rider (serial); Tailspin Tommy (serial). 1935 Rip Roaring Riley; The Fighting Marines (serial); Valley of Wanted Men; Skybound; Hold 'Em Yale; Goin' to Town; Ship Cafe; Storm over the Andes; Waterfront Lady; Society Fever. 1936 The Sky Parade; Border Flight; Lady Be Careful; The Arizona Raiders; Let's Sing Again; Jungle Jim (serial). 1937 Paradise Express; Bill Cracks Down; Radio Patrol (serial); Hollywood Round-Up. 1938 Telephone Operator; Held for Ransom; The Secret of a Treasure Island (serial); Three Loves Has Nancy; Touchdown Army; Mr. Wong, Detective. 1939 Irish Luck; Navy Secrets; Boys' Dormitory; Mr. Wong in Chinatown; Mutiny in the Big House; Mystery of Mr. Wong; Daughter of the Tong. 1940 The Fatal Hour; Son of the Navy; On the Spot; Tomboy; Doomed to Died; Phantom of Chinatown; Men against the Sky; The Mexican Spitfire Out West. 1941 Let's Make Music; Country Fair; Billy the Kid; You'll Never Get Rich; Swamp River; The Bugle Sounds; The Get-Away; Parachute Battalion; The Masked Rider. 1942 Between Us Girls; Woman of the Year; Lure of the Islands; Butch Minds the Baby; Northwest Rangers; Tennessee Johnson; Captive Wild Woman. 1943 In Old Oklahoma; Gildersleeve's Bad Day; Petticoat Larceny; No Time for Love; The Apache Trail; A Lady Takes a Chance. 1944 The Cowboy and the Senorita; Cowboy Canteen; The Fighting Seabees; The Girl Who Dared; Goodnight, Sweetheart; Silent Partners; The Yellow Rose of Texas. 1945 Utah; Bring on the Girls; Dangerous Partners; Road to Alcatraz; Dakota; Bells of Rosarita; The Vampire's Ghost. 1946 In Old Sacramento; Affairs of Geraldine; Throw a Saddle on a Star; That Texas Jamboree; Singing on the Trail; Cowboy Blues; Singin' in the Corn; My Darling Clementine. 1947 Gunfighters; King of the Wild Horses; Over the Santa Fe Trail; The Ghost Goes Wild; The Trespasser; Wyoming; Blackmail; Tycoon. 1948 Bad Men of Tombstone; Station West; Old Los Angeles; Gallant Legion; Daredevils of the Clouds; Sons of Adventure; Angel in Exile; The Plunderers; Homicide for Three; Night Time in Nevada; Wake of the Red Witch; Fort Apache. 1949 Brimstone; Hellfire; The Fighting Kentuckian; The Last Bandit; Duke of Chicago. 1950 Rocky Mountain; Hoedown; Bells of Coronado; Rio Grande; Rock Island Trail; The Savage Horde; Trigger, Jr.; Tripoli; Hit Parade of 1951. 1951 Man in the Saddle; Al Jennings of Oklahoma; Million Dollar Pursuit; The Sea Hornet; Spoilers of the Plains; Utah Wagon Train. 1952 Captive of Billy the Kid; Tropical Heatwave; Springfield Rifle; Hangman's Knot; Hoodlum Empire; Leadville Gunslinger; Oklahoma Annie; Women in the North Country. 1953 Champ for a Day; Fair Wind to Java; Iron Mountain Trail; The Sun Shines Bright; Tropic Zone. 1954 Massacre Canyon; Southwest Passage; Outlaw's Daughter. 1955 Lady Godiva; Run for Cover. 1956 Hidden Guns; The Man from Del Rio; The White Squaw. 1957 The Hired Gun; Hell's Crossroads; The Last Stagecoach West. 1958 I, Mobster.

WITHERSPOON, CORA
Born: Jan. 5, 1890, New Orleans, La. Died: Nov. 17, 1957, Las Cruces, N. M. Screen and stage actress. Entered films in 1931.

Appeared in: 1931 Night Angel; Peach O'Reno. 1932 Ladies of the Jury. 1934 Midnight; Gambling. 1935 an Educational short; Frankie and Johnnie. 1936 Picadilly Jim; Libeled Lady. 1937 Dangerous Number; Personal Property; Madame X; Beg, Borrow or Steal; On the Avenue; The Lady Escapes; Quality Street; Big Shot. 1938 He Couldn't Say No; Port of Seven Seas; Marie Antoinette; Three Loves Has Nancy; Professor, Beware!; Just around the Corner. 1939 Woman Doctor; Dodge City; For Love or Money; The Women; Dark Victory; The Flying Irishman. 1940 Charlie Chan's Murder Cruise; I Was an Adventuress; The Bank Dick. 1943 Follies Girl. 1945 Over 21; Colonel Effingham's Raid; This Love of Ours. 1946 I've Always Loved You; Dangerous Business; Young Widow. 1951 The Mating Season. 1952 The First Time; Just for You.

WITT, WASTL
Born: 1890. Died: Dec. 21, 1955, Harlachinger, West Germany. Screen and stage actor.

WIX, FLORENCE E.
Born: 1883, England. Died: Nov. 23, 1956, Woodland Hills, Calif. (cancer). Screen and stage actress.

Appeared in: 1924 The Female; Secrets. 1925 Enticement. 1927 Ladies Beware; The Return of Boston Blackie; Naughty Nanette. 1928 Beyond London Lights. 1929 She Goes to War. 1938 The Missing Guest.

WOEGERER, OTTO
Born: 1907. Died: July 1966, Schwanenstadt, Austria. Screen and stage actor.

Appeared in: 1937 Die Nacht mit dem Kaiser. 1956 The Last Ten Days.

WOLBERT, DOROTHEA
Born: 1874, Philadelphia, Pa. Died: Sept. 16, 1958, Hollywood, Calif. (arteriosclerosis). Screen actress.

Appeared in: 1921 Action; The Ruse of the Rattler. 1922 The Flirt; The Ninety and Nine; The Little Minister. 1923 The Abysmal Brute. 1924 The Galloping Ace; A Lady of Quality; The Guilty One. 1925 A Woman of the World; Duped. 1926 The College Boob; Pleasures of the Rich. 1927 Sailor's Sweetheart; Snowbound. 1928 Anybody Here Seen Kelly?; Love and Learn. 1929 Universal shorts. 1930 The Medicine Man; Dangerous Paradise; Borrowed Wives. 1931 Friends and Lovers. 1932 The Expert; Two Seconds. 1933 Hallelujah, I'm a Bum. 1934 The Scarlet Letter. 1935 Paris in Spring. 1950 Three Husbands. 1951 Little Egypt.

WOLD, DAVID
Born: 1890. Died: June 3, 1953, Hollywood, Calif. (heart attack). Screen actor.

WOLFF, FRANK (Frank Hermann)
Born: 1928, San Francisco, Calif. Died: Dec. 12, 1971, Rome, Italy (suicide). Screen actor.

Appeared in: 1959 Beast from a Haunted Cave; The Wild and Innocent. 1960 Ski Troop Attack. 1961 Atlas. 1963 The Four Days of Naples; The Demon; America, America. 1964 Salvatore Giuliano. 1965 Situation Hopeless—but Not Serious. 1966 Judith. 1968 Villa Rides; A Stranger in Town.

WOLFIT, SIR DONALD
Born: Apr. 20, 1902, England. Died: Feb. 17, 1968, London, England (heart attack). Screen, stage, and television actor.

Appeared in: 1935 Death at Broadcasting House (film debut); Elizabeth of England; Drake of England. 1936 Calling the Tune; Late Extra; The Silent Passenger; Mr. Hobo; Checkmate. 1937 Knight without Armor. 1940 Hyde Park Corner. 1947 Guilty. 1951 Two of a Kind. 1953 The Ringer; Pickwick Papers (U.S. 1954). 1954 Svengali (U.S. 1955); Isn't Life Wonderful. 1955 Prize of Gold. 1956 Satellite in the Sky; Guilty? 1957 The Traitor (aka The Accursed); Man in the Road. 1958 Blood of the Vampire; I Accuse! 1959 The Angry Hills; Room at the Top; The House of the Seven Hawks; The Rough and the Smooth (aka Portrait of a Sinner) (U.S. 1961). 1961 The Mark. 1962 Lawrence of Arabia. 1963 Dr. Crippen. 1964 Becket. 1965 Life at the Top; The Hands of Orlac. 1966 Ninety Degrees in the Shade. 1968 The Sandwich Man; Charge of the Light Brigade; Decline and Fall (aka Decline and Fall of a Birdwatcher). Other British film: Black Judge.

WOLHEIM, LOUIS
Born: Mar. 23, 1880, New York, N.Y. Died: Feb. 18, 1931, Los Angeles, Calif. (cancer). Screen and stage actor.

Appeared in: 1917 The Carter Case (serial). 1920 Dr. Jekyll and Mr. Hyde. 1921 Orphans of the Storm; Experience. 1922 Sherlock Holmes; Determination; The Face in the Fog. 1923 Little Old New York; The Go-Getter; The Last Moment; Love's Old Sweet Song; Unseeing Eyes. 1924 America; The Story Without a Name; The Uninvited Guest. 1925 Lover's Island. 1927 Two Arabian Knights; Sorrell and Son. 1928 Tempest; The Awakening; The Racket. 1929 Wolf Song; Square Shoulders; Condemned; Frozen Justice; The Shady Lady. 1930 Danger Lights; The Silver Horde; The Ship from Shanghai; All Quiet on the Western Front. 1931 Gentlemen's Fate; Sin Ship.

WONG, ANNA MAY (Lu Tsong Wong)
Born: Jan. 3, 1907, Los Angeles, Calif. Died: Feb. 3, 1961, Santa Monica, Calif. (heart attack). Screen actress.

Appeared in: 1919 Red Lantern. 1921 Bits of Life; Shame. 1922 The Toll of the Sea. 1923 Drifting; Thundering Dawn. 1924 The Thief of Bagdad; Alaskan; Peter Pan; The Fortieth Door. 1925 Forty Winks. 1926 The Desert's Toll; Fifth Avenue; The Silk Bouquet; A Trip to Chinatown. 1927 The Chinese Parrot; Old San Francisco; Mr. Wu; Driven from Home; Streets of Shanghai; The Devil Dancer. 1928 Across to Singapore; Chinatown Charlie; The Crimson City; Song. 1929 Picadilly. 1930 On the Spot; Wasted Love; The Flame of Love; L'Amour Maitre des Choses. 1931 Daughter of the Dragon. 1932 Shanghai Express. 1933 A Study in Scarlet; Tiger Bay. 1934 Chu Chin Chow; Limehouse Blues. 1935 Java Head. 1937 Daughter of Shanghai. 1938 Dangerous to Know; When Were You Born? 1939 King of Chinatown; Island of Lost Men. 1941 Ellery Queen's Penhouse Mystery. 1942 Bombs over Burma; Lady from Chungking. 1949 Impact. 1953 Ali Baba Nights. 1960 Portrait in Black; The Savage Innocents.

WONG, BRUCE
Born: 1906. Died: Nov. 1, 1953, Hollywood, Calif. (heart attack). Screen actor.

Appeared in: 1942 Time to Kill.

WONTNER, ARTHUR
Born: Jan. 21, 1875, London, England. Died: July 10, 1960, London, England. Screen, stage, and television actor. Entered films in 1915.

Appeared in: 1915 The Bigamist. 1930 The Message. 1931 The Missing Rembrandt; Condemned to Death; A Gentleman of Paris; Sherlock Holmes' Fatal Hour. 1932 The Sign of the Four; The Sleeping Cardinal. 1934 The Triumph of Sherlock Holmes. 1935 Jubilee Film. 1937 Thunder in the City; Storm in a Teacup; Silver Blaze. 1938 Kate Plus Ten. 1941 Queen of Crime. 1948 Blanche Fury. 1952 Brandy for the Parson. 1953 Sea Devils. 1954 Genevieve. 1955 Three Cases of Murder (aka Lord Mountdrago). Other British films: Lady Windermere's Fan; Bonnie Prince Charlie; Eugene Aram; The Elusive Pimpernel.

WOOD, BRITT
Born: 1885. Died: Apr. 13, 1965, Hollywood, Calif. Screen and vaudeville actor.

Appeared in: 1927 The Boob and His Harmonica (short). 1936 Trail Dust. 1937 Adventure's End. 1947 Riders of the Whistling Pines; Square Dance Jubilee. 1950 Return of the Frontiersman. 1962 The Choppers.

WOOD, CARL "BUDDY"
Born: 1905. Died: Apr. 17, 1948, Los Angeles, Calif. Screen and stage actor.

WOOD, DONNA
Born: 1918. Died: Apr. 9, 1947, Hollywood, Calif. (heart ailment). Singer and screen actress. Vocalist with Kay Kyser orchestra.

Appeared in: 1941 Pot O'Gold.

WOOD, DOUGLAS
Born: 1880, New York, N.Y. Died: Jan. 13, 1966, Woodland Hills, Calif. Screen and stage actor. Son of stage actress Ida Jeffreys.

Appeared in: 1934 The President Vanishes; Bottoms Up; The Trumpet Blows; The Fountain. 1935 The Wedding Night; Love in Bloom; College Scandal; Dangerous. 1936 Two in a Crowd; Hearts in Bondage; The Prisoner of Shark Island; Dracula's Daughter; Parole; Navy Born; Wedding Present; Two against the World. 1937 Great Guy; On the Avenue; This Is My Affair; Over the Goal; Dangerously Yours; West of Shanghai; Ali Baba Goes to Town. 1938 I Am the Law. 1939 Off the Record; East Side of Heaven; Eternally Yours; 20,000 Men a Year. 1940 The Man Who Wouldn't Talk; Dr. Ehrlich's Magic Bullet; Private Affair. 1941 Honky Tonk; H.M. Pullman, Esq.; Buck Privates; In the Navy. 1942 Murder in the Big House; Parachute Nurse. 1943 What a Woman; Never a Dull Moment. 1944 I'm from Arkansas; Meet Miss Bobby Socks; The Adventures of Mark Twain. 1945 Big Show-Off; Eadie Was a Lady; Come Out Fighting; Boston Blackie Booked on Suspicion. 1946 Because of Him; Voice of the Whistler; Tomorrow is Forever. 1947 My Wild Irish Rose; It Had to Be You; Two Blondes and a Redhead. 1948 An Old Fashioned Girl; Shamrock Hill. 1950 The Petty Girl; Harriet Craig; Border Outlaws. 1955 No Man's Woman. 1956 That Certain Feeling.

WOOD, ERNEST
Born: Apr. 17, 1892, Atchison, Kan. Died: July 13, 1942, Hollywood, Calif.(heart attack). Screen, stage, and vaudeville actor. Entered films in 1923.

Appeared in: 1925 Passionate Youth. 1926 Atta Boy. 1927 Horse Shoes; Out of the Past; Woman's Law; The Princess on Broadway. 1928 A Perfect Gentleman; A Certain Young Man; Take Me Home. 1929 Red Wine. 1930 Not Damaged; Sweethearts on Parade; Dining Out (short). 1931 June Moon; Annabelle's Affairs; Sob Sister; Ambassador Bill. 1933 Parole Girl; A Bedtime Story; International House; Jennie Gerhardt. 1934 Call It Luck; For Love or Money. 1935 Fugitive Lady; False Pretenses. 1937 Roaring Timber.

WOOD, EUGENE
Born: 1904. Died: Jan. 22, 1971, West Palm Beach, Fla.(heart attack). Screen, stage, and television actor.

Appeared in: 1970 Diary of a Mad Housewife. Other film: The Way We Live Now (not released).

WOOD, FRANKER
Born: 1883, Stromsburg, Neb. Died: Nov. 13, 1931, Farmingdale, N.Y. Screen, stage, and vaudeville actor. Appeared with his wife Bunnee Wyde in an act billed "Wood and Wyde."

Appeared in: 1930 Hit the Deck.

WOOD, FREEMAN N.
Born: 1897, Denver, Colo. Died: Feb. 19, 1956, Hollywood, Calif. Screen and stage actor.

Appeared in: 1921 Made in Heaven; Diane of Star Hollow; High Heels; The Rage of Paris. 1922 White Hands; Electric House. 1923 Gossip; Innocence; Broken Hearts of Broadway; Divorce; The Man Alone; The Wild Party; Out of Luck; Fashion Row. 1924 Butterfly; The Female; The Price She Paid; One Glorious Night; The Girl on the Stairs; The Gaiety Girl. 1925 The Dancers; Raffles, The Amateur Cracksman; Hearts and Spurs; The Part Time Wife; Scandal Proof; Wings of Youth. 1926 Josselyn's Wife; Mannequin; The Lone Wolf Returns; A Social Celebrity; The Prince of Broadway. 1927 McFadden's Flats; Taxi, Taxi; The Coward. 1928 Little Yellow House; Half a Bride; Scarlet Youth; The Legion of the Condemned; The Garden of Eden. 1929 Chinatown Nights; Why Bring That Up? 1930 Only the Brave; Young Eagles; Ladies in Love; Lilies of the Field; The Swellhead; 1931 Kept Husbands. 1932 Lady with a Past. 1936 Hollywood Boulevard.

WOOD, MARJORIE
Born: 1888. Died: Nov. 8, 1955, Hollywood, Calif. Screen and stage actress.

Appeared in: 1939 The Women; They Shall Have Music. 1940 Pride and Prejudice. 1941 Look Who's Laughing. 1942 Saboteur; Klondike Fury. 1951 The Company She Keeps; Excuse My Dust; Texas Carnival. 1953 Sweethearts on Parade. 1954 Seven Brides for Seven Brothers.

WOOD, MICKEY
Born: 1898. Died: Nov. 20, 1963, London, England. Screen actor and stuntman.

Appeared in: 1961 Circle of Deception.

WOOD, PHILIP
Born: 1896. Died: Mar. 3, 1940, Hollywood, Calif.(heart attack). Screen, stage actor, playwright, and author.

Appeared in: 1938 Room Service. 1940 Our Town.

WOOD, ROLAND
Born: 1897. Died: Feb. 3, 1967, New York, N.Y.(heart attack). Screen and stage actor.

Appeared in: 1967 The Tiger Makes Out.

WOOD, SAM
Born: July 10, 1883, Philadelphia, Pa. Died: Sept. 22, 1949, Hollywood, Calif.(heart attack). Screen, stage actor, and film director. Entered films as an actor with DeMille in 1910.

WOOD, SUZANNE
Died: Sept. 12, 1934, Hollywood, Calif. Screen, stage actress, and author.

WOOD, VICTOR
Born: 1914. Died: Oct. 1958, London, England. Screen, stage, and television actor.

Appeared in: 1947 Moss Rose. 1948 If Winter Comes; The Iron Curtain; Hills of Home. 1950 Joan of Arc. 1951 The Desert Fox; Kind Lady. 1952 My Cousin Rachel. 1953 Scandal at Scourie; The Snows of Kilimanjaro. 1959 The Lock.

WOODBURY, DOREEN
Born: 1927, Australia. Died: Feb. 6, 1957, New York, N.Y. (suicide-pills). Screen and television actress.

Appeared in: 1957 Space Ship Sappy (short); The Shadow on the Window.

WOODFORD, JOHN
Born: 1862, Tex. Died: Apr. 17, 1927, Saranac Lake, N.Y. Screen and stage actor.

Appeared in: 1921 Get-Rich-Quick-Wallingford; The Rider of the King Log. 1922 Ten Nights in a Bar Room. 1923 Success. 1925 The Mad Dancer.

WOODHOUSE, TODD
Born: 1902. Died: June 19, 1958, Hollywood, Calif. Screen actor and stuntman.

WOODRUFF, EDNA
Born: 1874. Died: Oct. 16, 1947, Los Angeles, Calif. Screen actress and novelist. Known as Edna Woodruff Montague at the time of death.

WOODRUFF, WILLIAM H. "BURT"
Born: 1856. Died: June 14, 1934, Los Angeles, Calif. Screen and stage actor. Appeared in Charles Ray films.

WOODS, AL (Frederick Ludwig Dreeke)
Born: 1895. Died: June 3, 1946, Pasadena, Calif.(heart attack). Screen and stage actor.

Appeared in: 1936 Easy Money.

WOODS, ERCELL
Born: 1916. Died: Apr. 23, 1948, Los Angeles, Calif.(auto crash). Screen actress.

WOODS, HARRY LEWIS, SR.
Born: 1889. Died: Dec. 28, 1968, Los Angeles, Calif.(uremia). Screen actor.

Appeared in: 1921 "Ruth Roland" serials. 1923 The Steel Trail (serial); Don Quickshot of the Rio Grande. 1924 The Fast Express (serial); Ten Scars Make a Man (serial); Wolves of the North (serial); Dynamite Dan. 1925 The Bandit's Baby; A Cafe in Cairo. 1926 A Regular Scout; A Trip to Chinatown; Man Four Square. 1927 Cyclone of the Range; Jesse James; Tom's Gang; Splitting the Breeze; Silver Comes Thru. 1928 The Candy Kid; When the Law Rides; Red Riders of Canada; Tyrant of Red Gulch; The Sunset Legion. 1929 China Bound; The Desert Rider; The Viking; Gun Law; The Phantom Rider; 'Neath Western Skies. 1930 The Lone Rider; Men without Law; Ranch House Blues; Pardon My Gun. 1931 West of Cheyenne; Texas Ranger; In Old Cheyenne; Palmy Days; Range Feud; Monkey Business; Pardon Us. 1932 Night World; I Am a Fugitive from a Chain Gang; Radio Patrol; Haunted Gold; Law and Order. 1933 Shadows of Sing Sing. 1934 St. Louis Kid; The President Vanishes; Belle of the Nineties; School for Girls; Devil Tiger; The Crosby Case; The Scarlet Empress; The Circus Clown. 1935 Let 'Em Have It; Robin Hood of El Dorado; Heir to Trouble; When a Man's a Man; Rustlers of Red Gap; The Call of the Savage (serial); Gallant Defender; Ship Cafe. 1936 The Lawless Nineties; Silly Billies; Human Cargo; The Unknown Ranger; Conflict; Rose of the Rancho; The Plainsman; Ticket to Paradise; Heroes of the Range. 1937

Courage of the West; Land Beyond the Law; Outcast; I Promise to Pay; Range Defenders. 1938 Hawaiian Buckaroo; The Arizona Wildcat; Come on, Rangers; Penamint's Bad Man; Blockheads; The Buccaneer; The Spy Ring; Crime Takes a Holiday. 1939 Frontier Marshal; Union Pacific; Days of Jesse James; Mr. Moto in Danger Island; The Man in the Iron Mask; In Old California; Blue Montana Skies; Beau Geste. 1940 South of Pago Pago; Isle of Destiny; Bullet Code; West of Carson City; The Ranger and the Lady; Triple Justice; Meet the Missus; Winners of the West (serial). 1941 Petticoat Politics; Sheriff of Tombstone; Last of the Duanes. 1942 Today I Hang; Romance on the Range; Down Texas Way; Riders of the West; Deep in the Heart of Texas; West of the Law; Forest Rangers; Reap the Wild Wind; Jackass Mail; Dawn on the Great Divide. 1943 Outlaws of Stampede Pass; Cheyenne Roundup; The Ghost Rider; Bordertown Gunfighters; Beyond the Last Frontier. 1944 Call of the Rockies; Marshal of Gunsmoke; Nevada; Westward Bound; The Adventures of Mark Twain; Tall in the Saddle. 1945 Wanderer of the Wasteland; West of the Pecos; Radio Stars on Parade. 1946 South of Monterey; My Darling Clementine. 1947 Wild Rose Mesa; Wyoming; Tycoon; Trail Street; Thunder Mountain; Code of the West. 1948 Western Heritage; The Gallant Legion; Indian Agent. 1949 Colorado Territory; The Fountainhead; Hellfire; Masked Raiders; She Wore a Yellow Ribbon. 1950 Traveling Saleswoman; Short Grass; Law of the Badlands. 1952 Lone Star; Rancho Notorious. 1954 Hell's Outpost. 1956 Ten Commandments.

WOODS, JOSEPH A.
Born: 1860, N.Y. Died: Feb. 13, 1926, New York, N.Y.(heart disease). Screen and stage actor. He often impersonated President Woodrow Wilson because of the marked resemblance.

WOODS, NICK (Nicholas Schaber)
Born: 1858. Died: Mar. 21, 1936, New Rochelle, N.Y. Screen and stage actor. Was billed on stage as "N. S. Woods, the Boy Actor."

WOODTHROPE, GEORGIA
Born: 1859. Died: Aug. 25, 1927, Glendale, Calif. Screen and stage actress.

Appeared in: 1919 The Midnight Man (serial). 1921 Four Horsemen of the Apocalypse; Bunty Pulls the Strings. 1922 The Song of Life. 1923 Gimme; Thundering Dawn; Rouged Lips. 1924 Daddies.

WOOLDRIDGE, DORIS
Born: 1890. Died: July 17, 1921, Los Angeles, Calif.(appendix operation). Screen and stage actress.

WOOLF, MRS. YETTI
Born: 1882. Died: Nov. 27, 1965, Hollywood, Calif. Screen actress.

WOOLLCOTT, ALEXANDER
Born: Jan. 19, 1887, Phalanx, N.J. Died: Jan. 23, 1943, New York, N.Y. Screen, stage, radio actor, drama critic, and playwright.

Appeared in: 1934 Gift of Gab. 1935 The Scoundrel. 1937 RKO shorts. 1942 Babes on Broadway.

WOOLLEY, MONTY (Edgar Montillion Wooley)
Born: Aug. 17, 1888, New York, N.Y. Died: May 6, 1963, Albany, N.Y.(kidney and heart ailment). Screen and stage actor. Entered films in 1931.

Appeared in: 1937 Live, Love and Learn; Nothing Sacred. 1938 Everybody Sing; Arsene Lupin Returns; The Girl of the Golden West; Three Comrades; Lord Jeff; Artists and Models Abroad; Young Dr. Kildare; Vacation from Love. 1939 Zaza; Dancing Co-ed; Man about Town; Midnight; Never Say Die. 1941 The Man Who Came to Dinner. 1942 The Pied Piper; Life Begins at 8:30. 1943 The Light of Heart; Holy Matrimony. 1944 Since You Went Away; Irish Eyes Are Smiling. 1945 Molly and Me. 1946 Night and Day. 1947 The Bishop's Wife. 1948 Miss Tatlock's Millions; Will You Love Me in December? 1950 Paris 1950 (narr.). 1951 As Young as You Feel. 1955 Kismet.

WOOLSEY, ROBERT
Born: Aug. 14, 1889, Oakland, Calif. Died: Oct. 1938, Malibu Beach, Calif.(kidney ailment). Screen, stage, and vaudeville actor. Was partner in vaudeville and film comedy team of "Wheeler and Woolsey." See Bert Wheeler for films they made together.

Appeared without Wheeler in: 1930 The Voice of Hollywood (short). 1931 Everything's Rosie. 1933 Hollywood on Parade (short).

WORTH, BILL
Born: 1884. Died: May 2, 1951, Westwood, Calif.(heart attack). Screen actor.

WORTH, PEGGY
Born: 1891. Died: Mar. 23, 1956, New York, N.Y. Screen and stage actress.

Appeared in: 1921 You Find It Everywhere.

WORTHING, HELEN LEE
Born: 1905. Died: Aug. 25, 1948, Los Angeles, Calif. Screen and stage actress.

Appeared in: 1924 Janice Meredith. 1925 The Crowded Hour; Flower of the Night; Night Life of New York; The Swan; The Other Woman's Story. 1926 Don Juan; The County of Luxembourg; Lew Tyler's Wives; Watch Your Wife. 1927 Vanity; Thumbs Down.

WORTHINGTON, WILLIAM J.
Born: 1872, Troy, N.Y. Died: Apr. 9, 1941, Beverly Hills, Calif. Screen, stage, vaudeville, opera actor, film director, and film producer. Entered films as an actor in 1915. Former president and treasurer of Multicolor Films.

Appeared in: 1915 Damon and Pythias; The Black Box (serial). 1921 High Heels. 1923 Red Lights; The Green Goddess. 1926 Her Honor, the Governor; Return of Boston Blackie; Kid Boots. 1928 Good Morning Judge; Half a Bride. 1930 The Climax; Shipmates; Laughing Sinners; Susan Lenox, Her Rise and Fall; Possessed; The Man Who Came Back. 1933 Duck Soup; No More Orchids. 1934 One Exciting Adventure. 1935 $20 a Week; Cardinal Richelieu; The Keeper of the Bees. 1936 Can This Be Dixie? 1937 Battle of Greed.

WRAY, ALOHA
Born: 1928. Died: Apr. 28, 1968, Hollywood, Calif. Screen actress and dancer. Divorced from screen actor Frankie Darro.

Appeared in: 1935 George White's 1935 Scandals.

WRAY, JOHN GRIFFITH (John Griffith Malloy)
Born: Feb. 13, 1888, Philadelphia, Pa. Died: Apr. 5, 1940, Los Angeles, Calif. Screen, stage actor, playwright, and film director. Entered films in 1929.

Appeared in: 1930 New York Nights; All Quiet on the Western Front; The Czar of Broadway. 1931 Quick Millions; Silence; Safe in Hell. 1932 High Pressure; The Woman from Monte Carlo; The Miracle Man; The Mouthpiece; The Rich Are Always with Us; Miss Pinkerton; Doctor X; Central Park; The Match King; I Am a Fugitive from a Chain Gang. 1933 The Death Kiss; After Tonight. 1934 I'll Fix It; Lone Cowboy; Bombay Mail; The Crosby Case; The Love Captive; Embarrassing Moments; The Big Shakedown; The Most Precious Thing in Life; The Defense Rests; Green Eyes; Fifteen Wives; The Captain Hates the Sea. 1935 I Am a Thief; Ladies Love Danger; Atlantic Adventure; Bad Boy; The Great Hotel Murder; The Whole Town's Talking; Stranded; Frisco Kid; Men without Names. 1936 Mr. Deeds Goes to Town; The Poor Little Rich Girl; Sworn Enemy; A Son Comes Home; Valiant Is the Word for Carrie; The President's Mystery; We Who Are about to Die. 1937 A Man Betrayed; You Only Live Once; Outcast; On Such a Night; The Devil Is Driving; The Women Men Marry; Circus Girl. 1938 House of Mystery; Making the Headlines; The Black Doll; Crime Takes a Holiday; Gangs of New York; A Man to Remember; Pacific Lines; Spawn of the North; Tenth Avenue Kid; Golden Boy. 1939 Risky Business; Pacific Liner; The Amazing Mr. Williams; Smuggled Cargo; Each Dawn I Die; Blackmail; The Cat and the Canary. 1940 The Man from Dakota; Remember the Night; Swiss Family Robinson.

WRAY, TED
Born: 1909. Died: Jan. 26, 1950, near Big Bear, Calif.(heart attack). Screen actor.

WREN, SAM
Born: 1897, Brooklyn, N.Y. Died: Mar. 15, 1962, Hollywood, Calif. Screen, stage, television actor, and stage director. Married to screen actress Virginia Sale.

Appeared in: 1935 Dr. Socrates. 1936 I Married a Doctor. 1937 Marked Woman. 1942 Over My Dead Body. 1943 Dixie Dugan.

WRIGHT, FRED
Died: Dec. 12, 1928, New York, N.Y. Screen actor.

Appeared in: 1922 The Glorious Adventure.

WRIGHT, HAIDEE
Born: 1898, London, England. Died: Jan. 29, 1943, London, England. Screen and stage actress.

Appeared in: 1933 The Blarney Kiss; Jew Suess. 1942 Tomorrow We Live. Other British film: Strange Evidence.

WRIGHT, HARRY WENDELL "WEN"
Born: 1916. Died: June 17, 1954, Humboldt, Nev.(auto accident). Screen actor and stuntman.

WRIGHT, HENRY OTHO
Born: 1892. Died: June 7, 1940, San Bernardino, Calif. Screen actor.

WRIGHT, HUGH E.
Born: Apr. 13, 1879, Cannes, France. Died: Feb. 13, 1940, Windsor, England. Screen, stage actor, playwright, and lyricist.

Appeared in: 1919 The Better 'Ole. 1929 The Silver King. 1932 The Good Companions. 1933 Cash; The Love Wager; You Made Me Love You. 1935 Adventures Ltd.; On the Air; Radio Parade of 1935; Scrooge. Other British film: Royal Eagle.

WRIGHT, HUNTLEY
Born: 1870, England. Died: July 10, 1941, Bangor, Wales (heart attack). Screen, stage, and radio actor.

Appeared in: 1934 Heart Song. Other British film: Look up and Laugh.

WRIGHT, WILL
Born: Mar. 26, 1891, San Francisco, Calif. Died: June 19, 1962, Hollywood, Calif.(cancer). Screen, stage, vaudeville, radio, and television actor.

Appeared in: 1936 China Clipper. 1939 Silver on the Sage. 1940 Blondie Plays Cupid. 1941 The Richest Man in Town. 1942 Shut My Big Mouth; True to the Army; Night in New Orleans; Wildcat; A Parachute Nurse; Sweetheart of the Fleet; Tennessee Johnson; The Daring Young Man; A Man's World; The Postman Didn't Ring. 1943 A Night to Remember; In Old Oklahoma; Reveille with Beverly; Lucky Legs; Murder in Times Square; Cowboy in Manhattan; Practically Yours. 1945 Eve Knew Her Apples; Road to Utopia; Rhapsody in Blue; Gun Smoke; Sleepy Lagoon; Blonde Fever; Grissly's Millions; Bewitched; Eadie Was a Lady; The Strange Affair of Uncle Harry; You Came Along; Salome, Where She Danced. 1946 Hot Cargo; The Inner Circle; Johnny Comes Flying Home; The Madonna's Secret; Rendezvous with Annie; One Exciting Week; The Blue Dahlia. 1947 Along the Oregon Trail; Keeper of the Bees; Wild Harvest; Mother Wore Tights; Blaze of Noon; Cynthia. 1948 Relentless; The Inside Story; Green Grass of Wyoming; The Twisted Road; The Walls of Jericho; Disaster; Whispering Smith; California's Golden Beginning; Black Eagle; Act of Violence; Act of Murder. 1949 Big Jack; Brimstone; For Those Who Dare; Mrs. Mike; All the King's Men; Adam's Rib; Lust for Gold; Miss Grant Takes Richmond. 1950 House by the River; The Savage Horde; Sunset in the West; A Ticket to Tomahawk; No Way Out; Dallas. 1951 My Forbidden Past; Vengeance Valley; Excuse My Dust; The Tall Target; People Will Talk. 1952 Lydia Bailey; The Las Vegas Story; Paula; Lure of the Wilderness; O'Henry's Full House; Happy Time; Holiday for Sinners. 1953 Niagara; The Last Posse. 1954 Johnny Guitar; The Wild One; River of No Return; The Raid. 1955 The Man with the Golden Arm; The Tall Men; The Court Martial of Billy Mitchell. 1956 These Wilder Years. 1957 The Iron Sheriff; Johnny Tremain; The Wayward Bus. 1958 The Missouri Traveler; Quantrille's Raiders; Gunman's Walk. 1959 Alias Jesse James; The Thirty Foot Bride of Candy Rock. 1961 The Deadly Companions; Twenty Plus Two. 1962 Cape Fear. 1964 Fail Safe.

WRIGHT, WILLIAM
Born: 1912, Ogden, Utah. Died: Jan. 19, 1949, Ensenada, Mexico (cancer). Screen and stage actor.

Appeared in: 1941 Rookies on Parade; Nothing but the Truth; World Premiere; Glamour Boy; The Devil Pays Off. 1942 Parachute Nurse; True to the Army; Night in New Orleans; Sweetheart of the Fleet. 1943 A Night to Remember; Here Comes Elmer. 1944 Dancing in Manhattan; One Mysterious Night. 1945 Eadie Was a Lady; State Fair; Escape in the Fog. 1946 Down Missouri Way; Lover Come Back; The Mask of Dijon. 1947

Philo Vance Returns; The Gas House Kids Go West. 1948 King of Gamblers. 1949 Daughter of the Jungle; Impact; Air Hostess; Rose of the Yukon.

WU, HONORABLE
Born: 1903, San Francisco, Calif. Died: Mar. 1, 1945, Hollywood, Calif. Screen, stage, vaudeville, and radio actor.

Appeared in: 1936 Stowaway. 1938 Mr. Moto; The Crime of Dr. Hallett; Mr. Moto Takes a Vacation. 1939 North of Shanghai. 1941 Ellery Queen and the Perfect Crime.

WUEST, IDA
Born: 1884, Wiesbaden, Germany. Died: Nov. 2, 1958, Berlin, Germany. Screen and stage actress.

Appeared in: 1929 The Last Waltz. 1930 The Burning Heart. 1931 Bockbierfest; Das Alte Lied; Ein Burschenlied aus Heidelberg; Die Lindenwirtin vom Rhein; Bomben auf Monte Carlo (The Bombardment of Monte Carlo). 1932 Die Csikos Baroness; Mein Leopold; Hurra! Ein Junge!; Schoen ist die Manoeverzeit (Beautiful Maneuver Time); Wenn die Soldaten; Man Braucht Kein Geld; Der Walzerkoenig; Das Schoene Abenteuer. 1933 Namensheirat; Friederike; Drei Tage Mittelarrest; Lachende Erben. 1934 Wie Sag' Ich's Meinem Mann?; Eines Prinzen Junge Liebe; Ja, Treu ist die Soldatenliebe; Zu Befehl; Herr Unteroffizier; Melodie der Liebe; Es War Einmal ein Walzer; Fleuchtlinge; Einmal Eine Grosse Dame Sein; Freut Euch des Lebesn. 1935 Die Liebe und die Erste Eisenbahn (Love and the First Railroad); Jungfrau Gegen Moench (Maiden vs. Monk); Csardasfuerstin (The Czardas Duchess); Fruehlingsmaerchen; So ein Maedel Vergisst Man Nicht. 1936 The Private Life of Louis XIV; Die Marquise von Pompadour; Annette in Paradise; Der Bettelstudent. 1937 The World's in Love. 1938 Wenn Du eine Schwiegermutter Hast (When You Have a Mother-in-Law); Husaren Heraus; Kater Lampe; Eine Seefahrt die ist Lustig (A Merry Sea Trip); Eine Nacht an der Donau (A Night on the Danube). 1939 Kleines Bezirksgericht (Little Country Court); Diskretion-Ehrensache (Discretion with Honor); Herbst-Monoever (Fall Manoeuvres); Der Lustige Witwenball (The Merry Widow's Ball); Die Blonde Carmen; Die Kluge Schwiegermutter (The Wise Mother-in-Law).

WUNDERLEE, FRANK
Born: 1875, St. Louis, Mo. Died: Dec. 11, 1925 (apoplexy). Screen and stage actor.

Appeared in: 1919 The Carter Case (serial); The Fatal Fortune (serial). 1921 A Divorce of Convenience. 1922 One Exciting Night; Reported Missing. 1923 No Mother to Guide Her. 1924 The Great White Way.

WYCHERLY, MARGARET
Born: 1881, London, England. Died: June 6, 1956, New York, N.Y. Screen, stage, vaudeville, and television actress.

Appeared in: 1929 Thirteenth Chair (film debut). 1934 Midnight. 1938 Wanderlust (short). 1940 Victory. 1941 Sergeant York. 1942 Crossroads; Random Harvest; Keeper of the Flame. 1943 The Moon Is Down; Assignment in Brittany; Hangmen also Die. 1944 Experiment Perilous. 1945 Johnny Angel. 1946 Enchanted Cottage. 1947 Something in the Wind; The Yearling; Forever Amber. 1948 The Loves of Carmen. 1949 White Heat. 1951 The Man with a Cloak. 1953 The President's Lady; That Man from Tangier. 1956 Richard III.

WYMAN, ELEANORE
Born: 1914. Died: Sept. 1, 1940, Lancaster, Calif.(auto accident). Screen actress.

WYMARK, PATRICK (Patrick Cheeseman)
Born: 1926, Grimsby, England. Died: Oct. 20, 1970, Melbourne, Australia (heart attack). Screen, stage, and television actor.

Appeared in: 1960 The Criminal (aka The Concrete Jungle-U.S. 1962); The Finest Hours (voice of Churchill-U.S. 1964). 1961 The League of Gentlemen. 1964 A King's Story (voice of Churchill). 1965 Operation Crossbow; The Secret of Blood Island; The Skull; Repulsion. 1966 The Psychopath. 1967 Woman Times Seven. 1968 Where Eagles Dare. 1969 Cromwell.

WYNN, DORIS (Doris Rink)
Born: 1910. Died: July 14, 1925, Los Angeles, Calif.(pneumonia). Fifteen-year-old screen actress. Appeared in Christie films.

WYNN, ED (Edward Leopold)
Born: Nov. 9, 1886, Philadelphia, Pa. Died: June 19, 1966, Los Angeles, Calif.(cancer). Screen, stage, vaudeville, radio, and

television actor. Received Academy Award nomination in 1959 for Best Supporting Actor in The Diary of Anne Frank. Father of screen actor Keenan Wynn.

Appeared in: 1927 Rubber Heels. 1930 Follow the Leader; Manhattan Mary. 1933 The Chief. 1943 Stage Door Canteen. 1951 Alice in Wonderland (voice only). 1956 The Great Man. 1958 Marjorie Morningstar. 1959 The Diary of Anne Frank. 1960 The Absent-Minded Professor; Cinderfella. 1961 Babes in Toyland. 1963 Son of Flubber. 1964 Those Calloways; Mary Poppins; The Sound of Laughter (documentary); Patsy; Erasmus with Freckles. 1965 That Darn Cat; Dear Brigitte; The Greatest Story Ever Told. 1966 The Daydreamer (voice only). 1967 Warning Shot; The Gnome Mobile.

WYNN, NAN
Born: 1916. Died: Mar. 21, 1971, Santa Monica, Calif.(cancer). Screen, stage actress, and singer. Her voice was dubbed for Rita Hayworth in several singing films.

Appeared in: 1941 A Shot in the Dark; Million Dollar Baby. 1942 Pardon My Sarong. 1943 Princess O'Rourke. 1944 Jam Session.

WYNARD, DIANA (Dorothy Cox)
Born: Jan. 16, 1906, London, England. Died: May 13, 1964, London, England (kidney ailment). Screen and stage actress.

Appeared in: 1932 Rasputin and the Empress (film debut). 1933 Cavalcade; Men Must Fight; Reunion in Vienna. 1934 Where Sinners Meet; Let's Try Again; One More River; Hollywood on Parade (short). 1939 Freedom Radio. 1940 Gaslight (British version); On the Night of the Fire. 1941 Kipps; The Voice in the Night; The Prime Minister. 1947 The Fugitive. 1948 An Ideal Husband. 1951 Tom Brown's School Days. 1955 The Feminine Touch. 1957 Island in the Sun; The Gentle Touch.

YAKOVLEV, YASHA
Born: 1912, Russia. Died: May 17, 1970, New York, N.Y.(heart attack). Screen actor and dancer.

Appeared in: 1960 L'Idiot (The Idiot).

YARBOROUGH, BARTON
Born: 1900. Died: Dec. 19, 1951, Hollywood, Calif. Screen, radio, and television actor.

Appeared in: 1941 Let's Go Collegiate. 1942 The Ghost of Frankenstein; Saboteur. 1945 Captain Tugboat Annie; I Love a Mystery. 1946 The Devil's Mask; Red Dragon; Wife Wanted; The Unknown. 1947 Kilroy Was Here. 1949 Henry, the Rainmaker.

YARDE, MARGARET
Born: Apr. 2, 1878, Dartmouth, England. Died: Mar. 11, 1944, London, England. Screen, stage, and opera actress.

Appeared in: 1932 Michael and Mary; The Man from Toronto; The Good Companions. 1933 Matinee Idol; A Shot in the Dark; Tiger Bay. 1934 Nine Forty Five. 1935 Scrooge; Broken Rosary; Widows Might; Faithful; Who's Your Uncle; Crouching Beast; Deputy Drummer. 1936 Fame; Gypsy Melody. 1939 Prison without Bars. 1940 French without Tears.

YBARRA, ROCKY
Born: 1900. Died: Dec. 12, 1965, Hollywood, Calif.(heart attack). Screen cowboy actor.

Appeared in: 1960 The Third Voice.

YEARSLEY, RALPH
Born: 1897. Died: Dec. 4, 1928, Hollywood, Calif.(suicide). Screen actor.

Appeared in: 1921 Tol'able David; Pardon My French. 1922 Arabia; Why Not Marry?; The Village Blacksmith. 1923 The Call of the Canyon; A Chapter in Her Life; Anna Christie. 1924 The Fighting Sap; One Night in Rome; The Valley of Hate; The Hill Billy. 1925 The Gambling Fool. 1926 Desert Gold. 1927 The Kid Brother. 1928 The Big Killing; Rose Marie; The Little Shepherd of Kingdom Come. 1929 Show Boat.

YENSEN, ULA
Born: 1940, Denmark. Died: Aug. 26, 1959, Mexico City, Mexico (suicide—pills). Screen and television actress.

Appeared in: Senoritas; Shube y Baja (Up and Down).

YEOMAN, GEORGE
Born: 1869. Died: Nov. 2, 1936, Hollywood, Calif. Screen, stage, and vaudeville actor. Appeared in vaudeville in an act billed as "George Yeoman and Lizzie."

YORK, DUKE
Born: 1902. Died: Jan. 24, 1952, Hollywood, Calif.(suicide—gun). Screen actor.

Appeared in: 1934 Elmer and Elsie; Pursuit of Happiness. 1935 Here Comes Cookie; All American Toothache (short). 1936 Strike Me Pink; Ticket to Paradise; The Three Mesquiteers; Mind Your Own Business; Flash Gordon (serial). 1937 Midnight Madonna. 1938 A Slight Case of Murder; Topper Takes a Trip. 1942 Who Done It?. 1943 Three Little Twerps (short). 1944 Idle Roomers (short). 1949 Stampede; Mississippi Rhythm. 1950 Call of the Klondike; Fortunes of Captain Blood; Rogue River; Snow Dog; Hit Parade of 1951. 1953 Trail Blazers. 1956 For Crimin' Out Loud (short).

YORKE, CAROL (Carol Bjorkman)
Born: 1929. Died: July 5, 1967, New York, N.Y.(leukemia). Screen actress.

Appeared in: 1948 Letter from an Unknown Woman (film debut).

YORKNEY, JOHN C.
Born: 1871, Argentina. Died: Aug. 20, 1941, Fort Lee, N.Y.(heart attack). Screen and stage actor. Entered films during silents.

YOST, HERBERT A.
Born: 1880, Harrison, Ohio. Died: Oct. 23, 1945, New York, N.Y. Screen and stage actor. Entered films with Biograph Studios in 1908 and later appeared in Edison series films in 1914. Herbert A. Yost was his stage name, but he appeared in some films as Barry O'Moore.

Appeared in: 1909 The Deception; Edgar Allan Poe. 1912 What Happened to Mary (serial); Every Rose Has Its Stem. 1914 The Man Who Disappeared (serial). 1929 Love, Honor and Oh, Baby (short). 1930 Fast and Loose. 1934 Age of Innocence.

YOUNG, ARTHUR
Born: 1898. Died: 1959. Screen and stage actor.

Appeared in: 1935 Radio Parade of 1935; No Limit. 1937 Victoria the Great. 1940 21 Days Together. 1941 Murder by Invitation. 1948 My Brother Jonathan. 1951 The Lady with a Lamp. 1954 An Inspector Calls; Paid to Kill. 1956 Dynamiters; The Gelignite Gang.

YOUNG, CARLETON G.
Born: 1907. Died: July 11, 1971, Hollywood, Calif.(cancer). Screen, radio, and television actor. Father of screen actor Tony Young.

Appeared in: 1936 Happy Go Lucky; A Man Betrayed. 1937 Join the Marines; Git Along Little Dogies; Navy Blues; Dangerous Holiday; Dick Tracy (serial). 1938 The Old Barn Dance; Heroes of the Hills; Cassidy of Bar 20; Gang Bullets. 1939 Convict's Code. 1941 Buck Privates; Keep 'Em Flying; Pride of the Bowery. 1942 Code of the Outlaw; SOS Coastguard. 1944 Ladies of Washington; Take It or Leave It; In the Meantime, Darling. 1945 Thunderhead, Son of Flicka; Thrill of a Romance; Abbott and Costello in Hollywood. 1947 Smash-Up, the Story of a Woman. 1948 The Kissing Bandit. 1950 American Guerilla in the Philippines; Double Deal. 1951 The Mob; People Will Talk; Red Mountain; Flying Leathernecks; Hard, Fast and Beautiful; Anne of the Indies; Chain of Circumstance; Best of the Bad Men; The Day the Earth Stood Still; His Kind of Woman. 1952 The Brigand; Diplomatic Courier; Deadline U.S.A.; Last of the Comanches; My Six Convicts; Battle Zone. 1953 The Glory Brigade; A Blueprint for Murder; Goldtown Ghost Riders; Mexican Manhunt; Niagara; Torpedo Alley. 1954 Arrow in the Dust; Prince Valiant; Bitter Creek; Riot in Cell Block 11; 20,000 Leagues under the Sea. 1955 The Court Martial of Billy Mitchell; Artists and Models; Battle Cry; Phantom of the Jungle; The Racers. 1956 Battle Hymn; The Bottom of the Bottle; Julie; Beyond a Reasonable Doubt; Flight to Hong Kong. 1957 The Spirit of St. Louis. 1958 Cry Terror; The Last Hurrah. 1959 The Horse Soldiers; Here Come the Jets. 1960 Sergeant Rutledge; Gallant Hours; The Music Box Kid. 1961 Armored Command; The Big Show. 1962 The Man Who Shot Liberty Valance.

YOUNG, CLARA KIMBALL
Born: 1890, Chicago, Ill. Died: Oct. 15, 1960, Woodland Hills, Calif. Screen, stage, vaudeville, television actress, and film producer.

Appeared in: 1912 Cardinal Wolsey (film debut); Happy-Go-Lucky; The Violin of Monsieur; Ann Boleyn. 1913 Beau Brummell; The Little Minister; Love's Sunset. 1915 Lola; Hearts in Exile; Trilby; Camille; The Fates and Flora Fourflush (The Ten Billion Dollar Vitagraph Mystery Serial). 1916 My Official Wife; Yellow Passport; Goodness Gracious; The Feast of Life; The Common Law. 1917 Magda; The Price She Paid; Shirley Kay; The Easiest Way. 1918 The Claw; House of Glass; The Reason Why; The Savage Woman. 1919 Cheating Cheaters; Eyes of Youth. 1920 Mid-Channel; The Forbidden Woman; Deep Purple. 1921 Charge It; Hush; Straight from Paris. 1922 Enter Madame; What No Man Knows; The Hands of Nara; The Worldly Madonna. 1923 Wandering Daughters; A Wife's Romance; The Woman of Bronze; Cordelia the Magnificent. 1925 Lying Wives. 1930 Mother and Son. 1931 Kept Husbands; Women Go on Forever. 1932 File No. 113; Probation; Love Bound. 1933 Souls for Sables. 1934 Return of Chandu (serial); I Can't Escape. 1935 Fighting Youth; She Married Her Boss; His Night Out. 1936 Three on a Trail; The Last Assignment; The Rogues Tavern; Love in September (short). 1937 Hills of Old Wyoming; The Mysterious Pilot (serial). 1938 The Frontiersman. 1941 Mr. Celebrity; The Roundup.

YOUNG, CLIFTON
Born: 1917. Died: Sept. 10, 1951, Los Angeles, Calif.(smoke asphyxiation). Screen, vaudeville, and radio actor.

Appeared in 1924 "Our Gang" comedies. 1947 Pursued; Possessed; My Wild Irish Rose; Dark Passage. 1948 Blood on the Moon. 1949 Abandoned Woman; Calamity Jane and Sam Bass; Illegal Entry. 1950 The Return of Jesse James; Salt Lake Raiders; Trail of Robin Hood; A Woman of Distinction; Bells of Coronado.

YOUNG, LUCILLE
Born: 1892. Died: Aug. 2, 1934, Hollywood, Calif.(following surgery). Screen actress. Entered films approx. 1914.

Appeared in: 1926 Quicker'n Lightnin'. 1930 Lightnin'.

YOUNG, MARY
Born: 1857. Died: Nov. 13, 1934, Los Angeles, Calif. Screen actress.

Appeared in: 1922 The Angel of Crooked Street; Ninety and Nine. 1925 After Marriage.

YOUNG, MARY MARSDEN
Born: 1879. Died: June 23, 1971, La Jolla, Calif. Screen, stage, and television actress.

YOUNG, NEDRICK "NED"
Born: Mar. 23, 1914, Philadelphia, Pa. Died: Sept. 16, 1968, Los Angeles, Calif.(heart attack). Screen actor and screenwriter.

Appeared in: 1942 Bombs over Burma. 1943 Ladies Day 1947 The Swordsman. 1948 Gallant Blade. 1949 Deadly Is the Female. 1950 A Lady without a Passport; Gun Crazy. 1952 The Iron Mistress; Retreat, Hell!; Springfield Rifle. 1953 Captain Scarlet. 1958 Terror in a Texas Town. 1966 Seconds.

YOUNG, OLIVE
Born: June 21, 1907, St. Joseph, Mo. Died: Oct. 4, 1940, Bayonne, N.J.(internal hemorrhages). Screen, stage, and vaudeville actress.

Appeared in: 1930 Trailing Trouble; Ridin' Law. 1931 The Man Who Came Back.

YOUNG, ROLAND
Born: Nov. 11, 1887 (or 1903), London, England. Died: June 5, 1953, New York, N.Y. Screen, stage, radio, television actor, and author. Married to stage actress Dorothy Patience.

Appeared in: 1922 Sherlock Holmes (film debut); Moriarty. 1923 Fog Bound. 1924 Grit. 1929 The Unholy Night; Her Private Life. 1930 The Bishop Murder Case; Wise Girls; Madam Satan; New Moon. 1931 Sin of Madelon Claudet; Don't Bet on Women; The Prodigal; Annabelle's Affairs; The Squaw Man; The Guardsman; Pagan Lady; He Met a French Girl. 1932 This Is the Night; One Hour with You; A Woman Commands; William and Mary; Wedding Rehearsal; Lovers Courageous; Street of Women. 1933 His Double Life; Pleasure Cruise; A Lady's Profession; Blind Adventure; They Just Had to Get Married. 1934 Here Is My Heart. 1935 David Copperfield; Ruggles of Red Gap. 1936 The Unguarded Hour; One Rainy Afternoon; Give Me Your Heart. 1937 The Man Who Could Work Miracles; Gypsy; Call It a Day; King Solomon's Mines; Ali Baba Goes to Town; Topper. 1938 Sailing Along; The Young in Heart. 1939 Topper Takes a Trip; Yes, My Darling Daughter; The Night of Nights; Here I Am a Stranger. 1940 He Married His Wife; Irene; Star Dust; Private Affairs; Dulcy; No, No, Nanette; Philadelphia Story. 1941 Topper Returns; Two-Faced Woman; Flame of New Orleans. 1942 The Lady Has Plans;

They All Kissed the Bride; Tales of Manhattan. 1943 Forever and a Day. 1944 Standing Room Only. 1945 And Then There Were None. 1948 You Gotta Stay Happy. 1949 The Great Lover. 1950 Let's Dance; Bond Street. 1951 St. Benny the Dip. 1953 That Man from Tangier.

YOUNG, TAMMANY
Born: 1887. Died: Apr. 26, 1936, Hollywood, Calif.(heart attack). Screen and stage actor. Was W. C. Fields' stooge in some of his films.

Appeared in: 1917 The Great Secret (serial). 1919 Checkers; A Regular Girl. 1921 Bits of Life; The Man Who; Rainbow; The Right Way; The Man Worth While. 1922 John Smith; The Seventh Day; 'Til We Meet Again; Women Men Marry; When the Desert Calls. 1923 A Bride for a Knight. 1924 The Great White Way. 1925 Camille of the Barbary Coast; The Wrongdoers; The White Monkey; New Toys; The Unguarded Hour; The Police Patrol. 1927 The Perfect Sap; Blind Alleys. 1930 Roadhouse Nights. 1933 She Done Him Wrong; Tugboat Annie; Heroes for Sale; The Bowery; Hallelujah, I'm a Bum; Gold Diggers of 1933. 1934 Search for Beauty; Little Miss Marker; The Lemon Drop Kid; The Mighty Barnum; Six of a Kind; You're Telling Me; Old Fashioned Way; It's a Gift; Gift of Gab. 1935 The Glass Key; Champagne for Breakfast; Little Big Shot; Wanderer of the Wasteland; The Man on the Flying Trapeze. 1936 Poppy.

YOUNG, WALTER
Born: 1878. Died: Apr. 18, 1957, New York, N.Y. Screen, stage actor, and stage and film director.

Appeared in: 1937 The Adventurous Blonde; Alcatraz Island.

YULE, JOE
Born: Apr. 30, 1894, Scotland. Died: Mar. 30, 1950, Hollywood, Calif.(heart attack). Screen, stage, and burlesque actor. Father of screen actor Mickey Rooney.

Appeared in: 1939 Sudden Money; Idiot's Delight; Fast and Furious; Judge Hardy and Son; They All Come Out; The Secret of Dr. Kildare. 1940 Broadway Melody of 1940; Go West; New Moon; Boom Town. 1941 The Big Store; I'll Wait for You; Billy the Kid; Kathleen. 1942 Born to Sing; Jackass Mail. 1943 Air Raid Wardens. 1944 Two Girls and a Sailor; Nothing but Trouble. 1946 Bringing up Father. 1949 Jiggs and Maggie in Jackpot Jitters. 1950 Jiggs and Maggie Out West.

ZABELLE, FLORA
Born: 1880. Died: Oct. 7, 1968, Manhattan, N.Y. Screen and stage actress. Married to screen actor Raymond Hitchcock (dec. 1929).

Appeared in: 1916 The Red Widow.

ZANETTE, GUY
Born: 1907. Died: July 11, 1962, Hollywood, Calif.(cancer). Screen actor and dancer.

Appeared in: 1950 Snow Dog; Under My Skin. 1951 Yellow Fin.

ZANY, KING
Died: Feb. 19, 1939, Mojave, Calif. Screen actor and poet.

Appeared in: 1923 Hollywood. 1924 Broadway or Bust; The Garden of Weeds. 1927 The City Gone Wild. 1928 The Danger Rider. 1929 The Rainbow.

ZAROVA, RINI
Born: 1912, Russia. Died: Dec. 6, 1966, Santa Monica, Calif. Screen, stage, opera, radio, and television actress. Married to conductor/composer Meredith Willson.

ZAYAS, ALFONSO
Born: 1910, Mexico. Died: Feb. 1961, Mexico City, Mexico (heart attack). Screen actor. Entered films approx. 1945.

Appeared in: I, Too, Was a Champion.

ZEARS, MARJORIE
Born: 1911. Died: Mar. 9, Hollywood, Calif.(murdered). Screen actress. Was once a Mack Sennett bathing beauty.

Appeared in silents.

ZEERS, FRED C.
Born: 1895. Died: Aug. 1946, Hollywood, Calif.(injuries following assault by bandits). Screen actor.

ZELAYA, DON ALFONSO

Born: 1894, Nicaragua. Died: Dec. 14, 1951, Hollywood, Calif. (heart attack). Screen actor and pianist.

Appeared in: 1940 Girl from God's Country. 1944 The Hairy Ape. 1949 Amazon Quest. 1952 Macao.

ZELLMAN, TOLLIE

Born: 1887. Died: Oct. 9, 1964, Stockholm, Sweden. Screen and stage actress.

Appeared in: 1911 The Judgment of the Society. 1932 Roeda Dagen. 1933 Vi Som Gar Koksvagen. 1936 Ungdom Av I Dag; Vaaran Pojke. 1939 Rena Rama Sanningen (Nothing but the Truth). 1947 While the Doors Are Closed.

ZIMINA, VALENTINA

Born: 1899, Russia. Died: Dec. 3, 1928, Hollywood, Calif.(influenza). Screen actress.

Appeared in: 1925 A Son of His Father. 1926 La Boheme; Rose of the Tenements. 1927 The Woman on Trial. 1928 The Scarlet Lady.

ZUCCO, GEORGE

Born: Jan. 11, 1886, Manchester, England. Died: May 28, 1960, Hollywood, Calif. Screen, stage, and vaudeville actor. Appeared in vaudeville in an act billed ''The Suffragette'' in 1913.

Appeared in: 1931 The Dreyfus Case (film debut). 1932 The Good Companions. 1934 Autumn Crocus (film and stage versions). 1936 After the Thin Man; Sinner Take All. 1937 The Man Who Could Work Miracles; Parnell; The Firefly; Saratoga; London by Night; Madame X; The Bride Wore Red; Conquest; Rosalie; Souls at Sea. 1938 Arsene Lupin Returns; Marie Antoinette; Lord Jeff; Fast Company; Vacation from Love; Suez; Charlie Chan in Honolulu. 1939 Arrest Bulldog Drummond; The Magnificent Fraud; Captain Fury; Here I Am a Stranger; The Cat and the Canary; The Hunchback of Notre Dame; The Adventures of Sherlock Holmes. 1940 Green Hell; Arise My Love; The Mummy's Hand; New Moon; Dark Streets of Cairo. 1941 The Monster and the Girl; Topper Returns; Ellery Queen and the Murder Ring; A Woman's Face; International Lady. 1942 Dr. Renault's Secret; The Mad Monster; The Mummy's Tomb; My Favorite Blonde; The Black Swan; Halfway to Shanghai. 1943 Holy Matrimony; Never a Dull Moment; Sherlock Holmes in Washington; The Mad Ghoul; The Black Raven; Dead Men Walk. 1944 The Devil's Brood; The Seventh Cross; The Mummy's Ghost; Return of the Ape Man; The Voodoo Man; One Body Too Many; Shadows in the Night. 1945 Hold That Blonde; The Woman in Green; One Exciting Night; Weekend at the Waldorf; House of Frankenstein; Having Wonderful Crime; Sudan; Confidential Agent; Midnight Manhunt. 1946 Flying Serpent. 1947 The Imperfect Lady; Lured; Desire Me; Moss Rose; Where There's Life; Captain from Castile. 1948 The Pirate; Tarzan and the Mermaids; Who Killed ''Doc'' Robbin?; Secret Service Investigator. 1949 Madame Bovary; The Secret Garden; The Barkleys of Broadway. 1950 Joan of Arc; Let's Dance; Harbor of Missing Men. 1951 The First Legion; Flame of Stamboul; David and Bathsheba.

BIBLIOGRAPHY

Aaronson, Charles S., ed. International Motion Picture Almanac. New York: Quigley Publications, 1933-1971.

Alicoate, Chas. A., ed. The Film Daily Year Book of Motion Pictures. New York: Wid's Films and Film Folk, Inc., 1926-1971.

Arno Press. The New York Times Directory of the Film. New York: Grosset & Dunlap, 1953.

Barbour, Alan G. Days of Thrills and Adventure. London: Collier-Macmillan Limited, 1971.

Barbour, Alan G. The Thrill of It All. London: Collier-Macmillan Limited, 1971.

Barbour, Alan G., Marill, Alvin H., and Parish, James Robert. Karloff. New York: Cinefax, 1969.

Blesh, Rudi. Keaton. New York: Macmillan, 1966.

Blum, Daniel. A New Pictorial History of the Talkies. New York: Grosset & Dunlap, 1970.

Blum, Daniel. A Pictorial History of the Silent Screen. New York: Grosset & Dunlap, 1953.

Blum, Daniel. A Pictorial History of the Talkies. New York: Grosset & Dunlap, 1958.

Brownlow, Kevin. The Parade's Gone By. New York: Alfred A. Knopf. Inc., 1968.

Catalog of Copyright Entries: 1912-1960. Washington, D.C.: Copyright Office of the Library of Congress.

Christopher, Milbourne. Houdini: The Untold Story, New York: Pocketbooks, 1970.

Dannenberg, Joseph. Film Year Book: 1922-1927. New York City, Hollywood: Joseph Dannenberg.

Deschner, Donald. The Films of W. C. Fields. New York: The Citadel Press, 1964.

Dimmitt, Richard Bertrand. Actor Guide to the Talkies, vols. 1, 2. Metuchen: The Scarecrow Press, Inc., 1968.

Everson, William K. The Bad Guys. New York: The Citadel Press, 1964.

Fenin, George N., and Everson, William K. The Western. New York: Bonanza Books, 1962.

Filmlexicon Degli Autori E Delle Opere. Italy: Edizioni di Bianco e Nero, 1958.

Franklin, Joe. Classics of the Silent Screen. New York: The Citadel Press, 1959.

Funk, R. D., ed. Evening Outlook (published daily in Santa Monica, California). Various issues 1965-1971.

Green, Abel, ed. Variety (published weekly). New York: Variety, Inc., Jan. 1920-Dec. 1971.

Griffith, Richard, and Mayer, Arthur. The Movies. New York: Simon and Schuster, 1957.

Halliwell, Leslie. The Filmgoer's Companion. New York: Hill and Wang, 1965.

Halliwell, Leslie. The Filmgoer's Companion, rev. & expanded ed. New York: Hill and Wang, 1967.

Halliwell, Leslie. The Filmgoer's Companion, 3rd ed. New York: Hill and Wang, 1970.

Henderson, Robert M. D. W. Griffith The Years at Biograph. New York: Farrar, Straus and Giroux, 1970.

Lahue, Kalton C. Continued Next Week. Norman: University of Oklahoma Press, 1964.

Lahue, Kalton C. Kops and Custards. Norman: University of Oklahoma Press, 1967.

Lahue, Kalton C. World of Laughter. Norman: University of Oklahoma Press, 1966.

Lebel, Jean. Buster Keaton. London: Zwemmer, 1967.

Limbacher, James L., ed. Remakes, Series and Sequels on Film and Television, 3rd ed. Dearborn: Audio-Visual Division, Henry Ford Centennial Library, 1970.

Maltin, Leonard. Movie Comedy Teams. New York: The New American Library, Inc., 1970.

Michael, Paul, ed. The American Movies Reference Book: The Sound Era. Englewood Cliffs: Prentice-Hall, Inc., 1969.

Michael, Paul. Humphrey Bogart: The Man and His Films. Indianapolis: The Bobbs-Merrill Company, Inc., 1965.

Motion Picture Studio Directory & Trade Annual: 1920-1921. New York. Motion Picture News, Inc.

Munden, Kenneth W., ed. The American Film Institute Catalog, vol. 2. New York & London: R. R. Bowker Company, 1971.

Parker, John. Who's Who in the Theatre, vol. 8-14. London: Sir Isaac Pitman & Sons Ltd., 1936-1967.

Springer, John. All Talking! All Singing! All Dancing! New York: The Citadel Press, 1966.

Stuart, Ray, ed. Immortals of the Screen. New York: Bonanza Books, 1965.

Thomas, William F., ed. Los Angeles' Times. Various issues 1930-1971.

Twomey, Alfred E., and McClure, Arthur F. The Versatiles. Cranbury: A. S. Barnes and Co., Inc., 1969.

Weaver, John T. Forty Years of Screen Credits: 1929-1969 vol. 1, 2. Metuchen: The Scarecrow Press, Inc., 1970.

BIBLIOGRAPHY